ALABAMA

Abbeville
Abbeville Memorial Library • 301 Kirkland St • Abbeville, AL 36310 • (334) 585-2818

Henry County Historical Society • c/o Abbevile Memorial Library, 301 Kirkland St, P.O. Box 222 • Abbeville, AL 35310 • (334) 585-3020

Alabaster
Albert L Scott Library • 100 9th St NW • Alabaster, AL 35007-9172 • (205) 664-6822 • http://www.cityofalabaster.com

Albertville
Albertville Public Library • 200 Jackson St, P.O. Box 430 • Albertville, AL 35950-0008 • (256) 891-8290 • http://www.albertvillelibrary.org

Aldrich
Aldrich Coal Mining Museum • 137 Hwy 203 • Aldrich, AL 35115 • (205) 665-2886 • http://www.cityofmontevallo.com/Default.asp?ID=126

Alexander City
Blankenship Indian Association • 12647 HWY 22 E, P.O. Box 1522 • Alexander City, AL 35011 • (256) 329-8718

Tallapoosa County Historical Society and Genealogical Committee • 1426 Cherokee Rd • Alexander City, AL 35010 • http://www.rootsweb.com/~altallap/

Thomas D Russell Library • Central Alabama Community College, 1675 Cherokee Rd, P.O. Box 699 • Alexander City, AL 35010-0699 • (256) 215-4290 • http://cacclibrary.cacc.cc.al.us/alexcitylibrar/

Aliceville
Aliceville Historical Preservation • 103 4th Ave NE • Aliceville, AL 35442 • (205) 373-6364

Aliceville Historical Society • Historical Museum, 104 Broad St • Aliceville, AL 35442 • (205) 373-2363 • http://www.cityofaliceville.com/MuseumMain.htm

Aliceville POW Museum and Cultural Center • 104 Broad St • Aliceville, AL 35442 • (205) 373-2363 • http://www.cityofaliceville.com/MuseumMain.htm

Aliceville Public Library • 416 3rd Ave NE • Aliceville, AL 35442 • (205) 373-6691 • http://home.nctv.com/apl/

Andalusia
Andalusia Public Library • 212 S Three Notch St • Andalusia, AL 36420 • (334) 222-6612 • http://www.andylibrary.com

Coastal Heritage Preservation Foundation • 203 Sanford Rd • Andalusia, AL 36420-4113

Covington Historical Society • P.O. Box 1582 • Andalusia, AL 36420 • http://www.rootsweb.com/~alcoving/

Lurleen B Wallace State Junior College Library • 1735 E Bypass, P.O. Box 1418 • Andalusia, AL 36420 • (334) 222-6591 • http://www.lbw.edu/library.html

Anniston
Ala-Benton Genealogical Society • c/o Public Library of Anniston and Calhoun County, 108 E 10th St, P.O. Box 308 • Anniston, AL 36201 • (256) 237-8501 • http://www.anniston.lib.al.us/alabenton.htm

Anniston Historical Society • 800 Museum Dr • Anniston, AL 36202

Berman Museum of World History • 840 Museum Dr, P.O. Box 2245 • Anniston, AL 36206 • (256) 237-6261 • http://www.bermanmuseum.org

Calhoun County Historical Society • P.O. Box 1771 • Anniston, AL 36202

Public Library of Anniston and Calhoun County • 108 E 10th St, P.O. Box 308 • Anniston, AL 36202-0308 • (256) 237-8501 • http://www.anniston.lib.al.us

Arab
Arab Historical Society • Route 4, Box 418C • Arab, AL 35016

Arab Public Library • 325 2nd St NW • Arab, AL 35016-1999 • (256) 586-3366

Ashland
Clay County Historical Society • P.O. Box 997 • Ashland, AL 36251

Ashville
Ashville Museum and Archives • Saint Clair Cty Courthouse, P.O. Box 1470 • Ashville, AL 35953 • (205) 594-2128 • http://www.stclairco.com

Looney House Pioneer Museum • 779 Greensport Rd • Ashville, AL 35953 • (205) 594-7849 • http://www.thecountrybulletin.com/looney_house.htm

Saint Clair County Library • 139 5th Ave, P.O. Box 308 • Ashville, AL 35953-0308 • (205) 594-3694

Saint Clair Historical Society • c/o Ashville Museum and Archives, Saint Clair City Courthouse, P.O. Box 1570 • Ashville, AL 35953 • (205) 594-2128 • http://www.stclairhistoricalsociety.org

Athens
Athens State University Library • 407 E Pryor St • Athens, AL 35611 • (256) 233-8218 • http://www.athens.edu/library/

Athens-Limestone Public Library • 405 E South St • Athens, AL 35611 • (256) 232-1233 • http://www.athenslimestone.lib.al.us

Civil War Descendants Society • P.O. Box 233 • Athens, AL 35611

Confederate Descendants Society • P.O. Box 233 • Athens, AL 35611

Limestone County Archives • 102 W Washington St, P.O. Box 658 • Athens, AL 35612 • (205) 233-6404 • http://friendsofthearchives.com

Limestone County Genealogical Society • Donnell House, 601 S Clinton St, P.O. Box 82 • Athens, AL 35611 • (256) 232-0743

Limestone County Historical Society • Donnell House, 601 S Clinton, P.O. Box 82 • Athens, AL 35611 • (205) 232-0743

Atmore
Atmore Public Library • 700 E Church St, P.O. Box 1026 • Atmore, AL 36504 • (251) 368-5234 • http://www.atmorelibrary.com

Poarch Band of Creek Indians • 5811 Jack Springs Rd • Atmore, AL 36502 • (251) 368-9136 • http://www.poarchcreekindians-nsn.gov

Poarch Creek Museum • 5811 Jack Springs Rd • Atmore, AL 36502 • (334) 368-0815

Auburn
Auburn Heritage Association • 159 N College St, P.O. Box 2248 • Auburn, AL 36830

Genealogical Society of East Alabama • P.O. Drawer 1351 • Auburn, AL 36830

Jule Collins Smith Museum • 901 S College St • Auburn, AL 36830 • (334) 844-1484 • http://jcsm.auburn.edu/index.php

Lovelace Athletic Museum • Auburn Univ, P.O. Box 351 • Auburn, AL 36831 • (334) 844-4750 • http://www.auburn.edu

Ralph Brown Draughon Library • Auburn Univ, 231 Mell St • Auburn, AL 36849-5606 • (334) 844-1737 • http://www.lib.auburn.edu/special/

Society of Alabama Archivists • Auburn Univ Archives • Auburn, AL 35849-5637 • (334) 826-4465

Bay Minette
Bay Minette Public Library • 205 W 2nd St • Bay Minette, AL 36507 • (251) 580-1648 • http://www.bayminettepubliclibrary.org

Bessemer
Bessemer Hall of History • 1905 Alabama Ave • Bessemer, AL 35020 • (205) 426-1633 • http://www.bessemerhallofhistory.com/

Owen House Museum • 740 Eastern Valley Rd • Bessemer, AL 35021 • (205) 491-5543

3

Alabama

Bessemer, cont.
West Jefferson County Historical Society • 1740 Eastern Valley Rd, P.O. Box 184 • Bessemer, AL 35021-0184 • (205) 426-1633 • http://www.sharehistory.com/westjefferson/

Birmingham
A M Brown House Museum • 319 4th Terr N • Birmingham, AL 35204-4207 • (205) 323-3010

Alabama Baptist Historical Society • Samford Univ Library, 800 Lakeshore Dr • Birmingham, AL 35229-0001 • (205) 870-2749

Alabama Genealogical Society & Archives • AGS Depository, Samford Univ, 800 Lakeshore Dr, P.O. Box 2296 • Birmingham, AL 35229-0001 • (205) 726-4009 • http://www.samford.edu/schools/ighr/ighr.html

Alabama Historical Radio Museum • 600 N 18th St, P.O. Box 130307 • Birmingham, AL 35213 • http://www.alabamahistoricalradiosociety.org

Alabama Jazz Hall of Fame • Carver Theater, 1631 4th Ave N • Birmingham, AL 35203 • (205) 254-2731 • http://www.jazzhall.com

Alabama Museum of the Health Sciences • 1700 University Blvd • Birmingham, AL 35294-1003 • (205) 934-4475 • http://www.uab.edu/historical/museum

Alabama National Guard Historical Society • 6900 43rd Ave N • Birmingham, AL 35206 • (205) 833-0135

Alabama Sports Hall of Fame • 2150 Richard Arrington Jr Blvd N • Birmingham, AL 2150 Richard Arrington Jr Blvd N • (205) 323-6665 • http://www.ashof.org

American Genealogical Society & Depository • Samford Univ, Box 2296, 800 Lakeshore Dr • Birmingham, AL 35229 • (205) 870-2749

Arlington Antebellum Home and Gardens Museum • 331 Cotton Ave SW • Birmingham, AL 35211 • (205) 780-5656 • http://www.informationbirmingham.com/arlington/index.htm

Birmingham Civil Rights Museum • 520 16th St N • Birmingham, AL 35203 • (866) 328-9696 • http://www.bcri.org

Birmingham Genealogical Society • P.O. Box 2432 • Birmingham, AL 35201 • http://www.birminghamgenealogy.org

Birmingham Historical Society & Library • 1 Sloss Quarters • Birmingham, AL 35222 • (205) 251-1880 • http://www.bhistorical.org

Birmingham Public Library • 2100 Park Pl • Birmingham, AL 35203 • (205) 226-3665 • http://www.bplonline.org

Birmingham-Jefferson Historical Society • P.O. Box 130285 • Birmingham, AL 35213-0285 • (205) 323-2442

Birmingham-Jefferson History Museum • 1731 1st Ave N, Ste 120 • Birmingham, AL 35203 • (205) 202-4146 • http://www.bjhm.org

Cahaba River Society • Historical Museum, 2717 7th Ave S, Ste 205 • Birmingham, AL 35233 • (205) 322-5326 • http://www.cahabariversociety.org

Charles Andrew Rush Library • Birmingham-Southern College, 900 Arkadelphia Rd, P.O. Box 549020 • Birmingham, AL 35254-0001 • (205) 226-4740 • http://www.bsc.edu

Discovery Place of Birmingham • 1320 22nd St S • Birmingham, AL 35205

Forney Historical Society • Stamford Univ, 3084 Sterling Rd, S-215 • Birmingham, AL 35229 • (205) 870-2784

Historic Fourth Avenue Museum • 319 17th St N • Birmingham, AL 35203 • (205) 328-1850 • http://www.soulofamerica.com/birmingham-fourth-avenue.phtml

Hoover Historical Society • 569 Park Ave • Birmingham, AL 35226 • (205) 822-9392

Institute of Genealogy and Historical Research • Samford Univ Library, 800 Lakeshore Dr • Birmingham, AL 35229 • (205) 870-2780 • http://davisweb.samford.edu

Jefferson County Historical Commission • 571 Landmark Center, 2027 1st Ave N, Ste 801 • Birmingham, AL 35203 • (205) 324-0988 • http://jeffersonhistorical.org

Lawson State Community College Library • 3060 Wilson Rd SW • Birmingham, AL 35221 • (205) 929-6333 • http://www.lawsonstate.edu

Mervyn H Sterne Library • Univ of Alabama at Birmingham, 917 13th St S • Birmingham, AL 35294-0014 • (205) 934-6364 • http://www.mhsl.uab.edu

Miles College Library • 5500 Myron Massey Blvd, P.O. Box 3800 • Birmingham, AL 35208 • (205) 929-1000 • http://www.miles.edu/lrc.htm

Piqua Shawnee Tribe • 3412 Wellford Cr • Birmingham, AL 35226

Reynolds Historical Library • Univ of Alabama-Birmingham, 1700 University Blvd • Birmingham, AL 35294 • (205) 934-4475

Rickwood Field Museum • 1137 2nd Ave • Birmingham, AL 35222 • (800) RICKWOOD • http://www.rickwood.com

Roebuck Springs Historic Preservation Society • 504 Valley Rd • Birmingham, AL 35206 • http://www.roebucksprings.org

Samford University Library • Special Collections Library, 800 Lakeshore Dr • Birmingham, AL 35229 • (205) 870-2749 • http://www.stamford.edu/library

Samuel Ullman-Morris Newfield House Museum • 2150 15th Ave S • Birmingham, AL 35205-3920 • (205) 934-5634

Sixteenth Street Baptist Church Museum • 1530 6th Ave N • Birmingham, AL 35203-1806 • (205) 251-9402

Sloss Furnaces National Historic Landmark • 20 32nd St N • Birmingham, AL 35222 • (205) 324-1911 • http://slossfurnaces.com/

Southern Museum of Flight • 4343 73rd St N • Birmingham, AL 35206-3642 • (205) 833-8226 • http://www.southernmuseumofflight.org

University of Alabama Birmingham Museum • 1825 University Blvd • Birmingham, AL 35294 • (205) 934-1896 • http://www.uab.edu/home/

University of Alabama-Birmingham Historical Collection • 1700 University Blvd • Birmingham, AL 35294 • (205) 934-4475 • http://www.uab.edu/historical

Vulcan Park Foundation • 1701 Valley View Dr • Birmingham, AL 35209 • (205) 933-1409 • http://www.vulcanpark.org

West Jefferson Historical Society • 2324 Teton Rd • Birmingham, AL 35216

Blountsville
Blountsville Historical Society • Freeman Cabin Museum, P.O. Box 399 • Blountsville, AL 35031 • (205) 429-2535 • http://www.rootsweb.com/~algenweb/

Blountsville Public Library • 65 Chestnut St, P.O. Box 219 • Blountsville, AL 35031-0219 • (205) 429-3156 • http://www.blountsvillepubliclibrary.com

Blue Mountain
AfriGeneas-African Ancestored Genealogy • P.O. Box 4906 • Blue Mountain, AL 36204 • (256) 820-8794 • http://www.afrigeneas.com

Boaz
Boaz Public Library • 404 Thomas Ave • Boaz, AL 35957 • (256) 593-8056 • http://www.cityofboaz.org

Virgil B McCain Jr Learning Resource Center • Snead State Community College, 220 N Walnut, P.O. Box 734 • Boaz, AL 35957-0734 • (256) 840-4173 • http://www.snead.edu/library/homepage/htm

Brewton
Brewton Public Library • 206 W Jackson St • Brewton, AL 36426 • (251) 867-4626 • http://www.cityofbrewton.org

Escambia County Genealogy Society • P.O. Box 161 • Brewton, AL 36427-0161 • (251) 867-3155 • http://www.up.to/genealogy

Escambia County Historical Society • P.O. Box 276 • Brewton, AL 36427 • (334) 867-7332 • http://www.rootsweb.com/~alescamb/

Leigh Library • Jefferson Davis Community College, 200 Alco Dr, P.O. Box 958 • Brewton, AL 36427-0958 • (251) 809-1584 • http://www.jdcc.edu/library.htm

Thomas E McMillan Museum • Jefferson Davis College, 220 Alco Dr, P.O. Box 958 • Brewton, AL 36426 • (251) 809-1584 • http://www.jdcc.net/library.htm

Brierfield
Bibb County Heritage Association • 240 Furnace Parkway • Brierfield, AL 35035 • (205) 665-1856 • http://www.rootsweb.com/~albibb

Brierfield Ironworks Historical State Park Museum • 240 Furnace Pkwy • Brierfield, AL 35035 • (205) 665-1856 • http://www.brierfieldironworks.com

Butler
Choctaw County Genealogical Society • 41133 Highway 17 • Butler, AL 36904 • http://www.rootsweb.com/~alccgs/

Choctaw County Historical Museum • P.O. Box 758 • Butler, AL 36904-0758 • (205) 459-3383

Choctaw County Historical Society • 210 W Smith St • Butler, AL 36904 • (205) 459-2428

Choctaw County Public Library • 124 N Academy Ave • Butler, AL 36904 • (205) 459-2542 • http://www.pinebelt.net/~ccpl

Calera
Heart of Dixie Railroad Museum • 1919 9th St, P.O. Box 727 • Calera, AL 35040 • (205) 668-3435 • http://www.heartofdixiemuseum.org

Camden
Wilcox County Library • 100 Broad St • Camden, AL 36726-1702 • (334) 682-4355

Wilcox Historical Society • P.O. Box 464 • Camden, AL 36726 • http://www.wilcoxwebworks.com/history

Carrollton
Carrollton Public Library • 225 Commerce Ave, PO Box 92 • Carrollton, AL 35447-0092 • (205) 367-2142 • www.tusc.net/~cpl/info.html

Pickens County Cooperative Library Headquarters • Hwy 17 S, P.O. Box 489 • Carrollton, AL 35447-0489 • (205) 367-8407 • http://www.pickens.net/~cpl

Centre
Cherokee County Historical Museum • 101 E Main St • Centre, AL 35960 • (256) 927-7835 • http://www.museumatcentre.com

Cherokee Historical Society • Main St • Centre, AL 35960

Coosa River Valley Historical and Genealogical Society • P.O. Box 295 • Centre, AL 35960 • (256) 447-2939

Coosa River Valley Historical and Genealogical Society • P.O. Box 295 • Centre, AL 35960 • (256) 447-2939

Southern Society of Genealogists • Stewart Univ, P.O. Box 295 • Centre, AL 35960 • (256) 447-2939

Centreville
Brent-Centreville Public Library • 20 Library St • Centreville, AL 35042 • (205) 926-4736

Chatom
Genealogical Society of Washington County • P.O. Box 399 • Chatom, AL 36518 • (334) 847-3156

Washington County Historical Society • P.O. Box 456 • Chatom, AL 36518 • http://members.aol.com/JORDANJM2/WCHS.htm

Washington County Museum • Washington County Courthouse, P.O. Box 52 • Chatom, AL 36518 • (334) 847-3156

Washington County Public Library • 14102 Saint Stephens Ave, P.O. Box 1057 • Chatom, AL 36518-1057 • (251) 847-2097 • http://www.wcpls.org

Citronelle
Citronelle Historical Preservation Society • 18990-19000 S Center St, P.O. Box 384 • Citronelle, AL 36522 • (251) 866-7730

Clanton
Chilton County Historical Society • c/o Chilton-Clanton Public Library, 100 1st Ave, P.O. Box 644 • Clanton, AL 35045-0644 • (205) 755-1768 • http://www.rootsweb.com/~alchilto/

Chilton County Museum • P.O. Box 644 • Clanton, AL 35045 • (205) 755-0750

Clanton Public Library • 100 1st Ave • Clanton, AL 35045 • (205) 755-1768 • http://ccpl.lib.al.us

Clayton
Clayton Historical Preservation Authority • P.O. Box 385 • Clayton, AL 36016 • (334) 775-3542

Clayton Town & County Library • 45 N Midway St, PO Box 518 • Clayton, AL 36016-0518 • (334) 775-3506 • http://www.towncounty.lib.al.us

Octagon House Museum • 205 Lowe Ave, P.O. Box 385 • Clayton, AL 36016 • (334) 775-3542

Collinsville
Collinsville Historical Association • P.O. Box 849 • Collinsville, AL 35961

Columbiana
Columbiana Library • 50 Lester St, P.O. Box 1459 • Columbiana, AL 35051-1459 • (205) 669-5812 • http://www.shelbycounty-al.org

Karl C Harrison Museum of George Washington • c/o Mildred B Harrison Regional Library, 50 Lester St • Columbiana, AL 33051 • (205) 669-4545 • http://www.washingtonmuseum.com

Shelby County Historical Society • 1854 Courthouse Museum, 1854 Main St, P.O. Box 457 • Columbiana, AL 35051-0457 • (205) 669-3912 • http://www.rootsweb.com/~alshelby/schs.html

Cottondale
American College of Heraldry • P.O. Box 710 • Cottondale, AL 35453 • http://www.americancollegeofheraldry.org/acheraldry.html

Crossville
Sons of the American Revolution, Alabama Society • 458 Cty Rd 482 • Crossville, AL 35962 • http://www.alssar.org

Cullman
Ava Maria Grotto Museum • 1600 St Bernard Dr SE • Cullman, AL 35055 • (256) 734-4110

Cullman County Historical Society • 1346 9th Street SE, P.O. Box 804 • Cullman, AL 35055 • (256) 734-4699 • http://www.co.cullman.al.us/cullco_historic_soc.htm

Cullman County Historical Society • Cullman Historical Museum, 211 2nd Ave NE, P.O. Box 804 • Cullman, AL 35055 • (256) 739-1258

Cullman County Museum • 211 2nd Ave NE • Cullman, AL 35055 • (256) 739-1258 • www.cullman.com/museum

Cullman County Public Library • 200 Clarke St NE • Cullman, AL 35055 • (256) 734-1068 • http://www.ccpls.com

Daughters of the American Revolution, Cullman County Chapter • c/o Mrs Richard Buettner • Cullman, AL 35055 • (256) 734-7324

Evelyn Burrow Museum • Wallace State Comm College, 1315 Cty Rd 222 • Cullman, AL 35057 • http://www.wallacestate.edu/museum

North Central Alabama Genealogical Society • P.O. Box 13 • Cullman, AL 35056-0013 • http://home.hiwaay.net/~lthurman/society.htm

Alabama

Dadeville
Horseshoe Bend Regional Library • 207 N West St • Dadeville, AL 36853 • (256) 825-9232 • http://horseshoebendlibrary.org/

Danville
Jesse Owens Memorial Park & Museum • 7010 County Rd 203 • Danville, AL 35619 • (256) 974-3636 • http://www.jesseowensmuseum. org

Daphne
American Sport Art Museum and Archives • 1 Academy Dr • Daphne, AL 36526 • (251) 626-3303 • http://www.asama.org

Daphne Public Library • 2607 US Hwy 98, P.O. Box 1225 • Daphne, AL 36526-1225 • (251) 621-2818 • http://www.daphnelibrary.org

Dauphin Island
Fort Gaines Historic Site Museum • 109 Bienville Blvd • Dauphin Island, AL 36528 • (334) 861-3607 • http://www.dauphinisland.org

Daviston
Horseshoe Bend National Military Park • 11288 Horseshoe Bend Rd • Daviston, AL 36256 • (256) 234-7111 • http://www.nps.gov/hobe/

Decatur
Albert P Brewer Library • Calhoun Community College, Hwy 31 N, P.O. Box 2216 • Decatur, AL 35609-2216 • (256) 306-2777 • http://www. libcalhoun.edu/lib

Decatur Public Library • 504 Cherry St NE, P.O. Box 1766 • Decatur, AL 35602-1766 • (256) 353-2993 • http://www.decatur.lib.al.us

Morgan County Archives • 624 Bank St • Decatur, AL 35601 • (256) 351-4726 • http://www.archives.alabama.gov/counties/morgan.html

Morgan County Genealogical Society • 624 Bank St • Decatur, AL 35601 • http://www.genealogyshoppe.com/almorgan/

Morgan County Historical Society • Historical Museum, 3216 Darlington Dr SW • Decatur, AL 35603 • (256) 350-3285

North Alabama Genealogical Society • 3327 Danville Rd SW • Decatur, AL 35603-9027

Old State Bank Museum • 952 Bank St NE, P.O. Box 582 • Decatur, AL 35602 • (256) 350-5060

Demopolis
Demopolis Public Library • 211 E Washington • Demopolis, AL 36732 • (334) 289-1595 • http://www.westal.net/dpl/

Gaineswood Historic Home Museum • 805 S Cedar Ave • Demopolis, AL 36732 • (334) 289-4846 • http://www.preserveala.org/gaineswood. aspx

Laird Cottage Museum • 311 N Walnut Ave, P.O. Box 159 • Demopolis, AL 36732 • (334) 289-0282

Lyon House Museum • P.O. Box 159 • Demopolis, AL 36732 • (334) 289-9644

Marengo County Genealogical Society • c/o Demopolis Public Library, 211 E Washington St • Demopolis, AL 36732 • (334) 289-1595 • http:// www.rootsweb.com/~almareng/

Marengo County Historical Society • Bluff Hall Antebellum Home, 405 N Commissioner's Ave, P.O. Box 159 • Demopolis, AL 36732 • (334) 289-1666 • http://www.rootsweb.com/~almareng/

Marengo County History & Archives Museum • 101 N Walnut Ave, P.O. Box 1144 • Demopolis, AL 36732 • (334) 627-3894

Dora
Alabama Mining Museum • 120 East St • Dora, AL 35062 • (205) 648-2442

Dothan
Alabama Agricultural Museum • Landmark Park, Hwy 431, P.O. Box 6362 • Dothan, AL 36302 • (334) 678-0171

Archives of Wiregrass History and Culture • Troy State Univ Library, 502 University Dr • Dothan, AL 36304 • (334) 983-6556 • http://www. tsud.edu/archives/

G W Carver Interpretive Museum • 305 N Foster St • Dothan, AL 36303 • (334) 712-0933 • http://www.gwcarvermuseum.org

Houston-Love Memorial Library • 212 W Burdeshaw St, P.O. Box 1369 • Dothan, AL 36302 • (334) 793-9767 • http://www.houstonlovelibrary. org

Lesker Waddel House Museum • 4925 Reeves St, P.O. Box 6362 • Dothan, AL 36302 • (334) 794-3452

Phillip G Hamm Library • George C Wallace State Community College, 1141 Wallace Dr • Dothan, AL 36303 • (334) 983-3521 • http://www. wallace.edu

Southeast Alabama Genealogical and Historical Society • P.O. Box 246 • Dothan, AL 36302-0246 • (334) 794-8378 • http://www.rootsweb. com/~algenweb/

Double Springs
Free State of Winston Historical Society • P.O. Box 26 • Double Springs, AL 35553-0026

Winston County Genealogical Society • P.O. Box 112 • Double Springs, AL 35553 • http://wcgs.ala.nu/

Douglas
Cherokee Tribe of Northeast Alabama • P.O. Box 252 • Douglas, AL 35964-0252 • (256) 593-8102

Elberta
Baldwin County Heritage Museum • 25521 Hwy 98, P.O. Box 356 • Elberta, AL 36530 • (251) 986-8375 • http://www. baldwincountyheritagemuseum.com

Enterprise
Enterprise Public Library • 101 E Grubbs St • Enterprise, AL 36330 • (334) 347-2636 • http://www.enterprise-pub-library.net

Learning Resource Center • Enterprise State Junior College, 600 Plaza Dr, P.O. Box 1300 • Enterprise, AL 36331-1300 • (334) 347-2623 • http://www.esjc.cc.al.us/lrc_hp.htm

Pea River Historical and Genealogical Society • Historical Museum, 108 S Main, P.O. Box 310628 • Enterprise, AL 36331-0628 • (334) 393-2901 • http://www.rootsweb.com/~alprhgs/

Pea River Historical Society • 749 Boll Weevil Cr • Enterprise, AL 36330-2036 • (334) 393-3977

Eufaula
Barbour County Genealogical and Local Historical Society • c/o Eufaula Carnegie Library, 217 N Eufaula Ave • Eufaula, AL 36027 • (334) 687-2337 • http://www.rootsweb.com/~albarbou/

Chattahoochee Indian Heritage Center • Hwy 165, P.O. Box 33 • Eufaula, AL 36072 • (334) 687-9755

Eufaula Carnegie Library • 217 N Eufaula Ave • Eufaula, AL 36027 • (334) 687-2337 • http://www.ecl.lib.al.us

Eufaula Heritage Association • Historical Museum, 340 N Eufaula Ave, P.O. Box 486 • Eufaula, AL 36027-0846 • (334) 687-3793 • http://www. eufaulapilgrimage.com

Fendall Hall Museum • 917 W Barbour St • Eufaula, AL 36027 • (334) 687-8469

Historic Chattahoochee Commission • 211 N Eufala Ave, P.O. Box 33 • Eufaula, AL 35072-0033 • (334) 687-9755 • http://www.hcc-al-ga.org

Shorter Mansion Museum • 340 N Eufaula Ave, P.O. Box 486 • Eufaula, AL 36027 • (334) 687-3793 • http://www.eufalapilgrimage.com

Eutaw

Greene County Historical Society & Friends of Historic Northport • P.O. Box 746 • Eutaw, AL 35462 • http://magnolia.cyriv.com/GreeneAlGenWeb/

Kirkwood Mansion Museum • 111 Kirkwood Dr • Eutaw, AL 35462 • (205) 372-2694

Evergreen

Evergreen-Conecuh Public Library • 201 Park St • Evergreen, AL 36401 • (251) 578-2670 • http://www.evergreenal.com

Fairhope

Fairhope Museum of History • 24 N Section St, P.O. Box 1751 • Fairhope, AL 36533 • (251) 929-1474 • http://www.cofairhope.com/history.html

Fairhope Public Library • 161 N Section St • Fairhope, AL 36532-2490 • (251) 928-7483 • http://www.fairhopelibrary.org

Falkville

Echota Cherokee Tribe of Alabama • 630 County Rd 1281 • Falkville, AL 35622 • (256) 734-7337 • http://www.echotacherokeetribe.com

Fayette

Fayette County Historical Society • P.O. Box 309 • Fayette, AL 35555-0309 • (205) 932-3255 • http://www.rootsweb.com/~alfayett/

Fayette County Memorial Library • 326 Temple Ave N • Fayette, AL 35555 • (205) 932-6625

Robertson Historical Museum • 530 N Temple Ave • Fayette, AL 3555 • (205) 932-8727

Florala

Florala Public Library • 1214 4th St • Florala, AL 36442 • (334) 858-3525

Florence

Collier Library • Univ of North Alabama, 1 Harrison Plaza, P.O. Box 5028 • Florence, AL 35632-0001 • (205) 765-4241 • http://www2.una.edu/library

Florence Historical Board • 2207 Berry Ave, P.O. Box 8 • Florence, AL 35630 • (256) 760-6300 • http://www.florenceal.org/Administration/City_Boards/Historical_Board/

Florence-Lauderdale Public Library • 350 N Wood Ave • Florence, AL 35630 • (256) 764-6564 • http://www.library-florence.org

Natchez Trace Genealogical Society • P.O. Box 420 • Florence, AL 35631-0420 • (256) 764-4749 • http://www.tvgs.org/general.htm

Pope's Tavern Museum • 203 Hermitage Dr • Florence, AL 35630 • (256) 760-6439 • http://www.florenceal.org

Rosenbaum House Museum • 601 Riverview Dr • Florence, AL 65903 • (256) 760-6379 • http://www.wrightinalabama.com

Tennessee Valley Historical Society & Archives • Dept of History, Univ of Northern Alabama, P.O. Box 5216 • Florence, AL 35630-0001 • (256) 760-4306 • http://home.HiWAAY.net/~krjohn/

W C Handy Home Museum and Library • 620 W College St • Florence, AL 35630 • (256) 760-6434 • http://www.florenceal.org

Foley

Baldwin County Genealogical Society • c/o Foley Public Library, 319 E Laurel Ave, P.O. Box 108 • Foley, AL 36536 • (251) 943-7665 • http://www.rootsweb.com/~albcgs/

Baldwin Heritage Museum Association • Historical Museum, P O. Box 1117 • Foley, AL 36536

Foley Public Library • 319 E Laurel Ave • Foley, AL 36535 • (251) 943-7665 • http://www.foleylibrary.org

Holmes Medical Museum • 509 East Section Ave • Foley, AL 36535 • (334) 943-4954

Fort Deposit

Lowndes County Historical Society • Route 1, Box 408 • Fort Deposit, AL 36032

Fort McClellan

US Army Chemical Corps Museum • Ft McClellan, Bldg 2299 • Fort McClellan, AL 36205-5020 • (256) 238-4449

US Army Military Police Corps Regimental Museum • Ft McClellan, Bldg 3182 • Fort McClellan, AL 36205 • (256) 848-3522

Women's Army Corps Museum • Ft McClellan Bldg 1077 • Fort McClellan, AL 36205 • (256) 848-4611 • http://www.tradoc.army.mi./mcclellan/wac.htm

Fort Payne

Alabama Fan Club and Museum • 101 Glenn Blvd SW • Fort Payne, AL 35967 • (256) 845-1646 • http://www.thealabamaband.com

DeKalb County Genealogical Society • P. O. Box 681087 • Fort Payne, AL 35968-1612 • http://www.webspawner.com/users/dekalbsociety/

Dekalb County Historical Society • 504 Grand Ave • Fort Payne, AL 35967

DeKalb County Public Library • 504 Grand Ave NW • Fort Payne, AL 35967 • (256) 845-2671 • http://web2.lmn.lib.al.us

Fort Payne Depot Museum • 105 5th St NE, P.O. Box 681420 • Fort Payne, AL 35968 • (256) 845-5714 • www.fortpaynedepotmuseum.org

Landmarks of DeKalb County • Historical Museum, 500 Gault Ave N, P.O. Box 680518 • Fort Payne, AL 35968-0518 • (256) 845-0419

Fort Rucker

US Army Aviation Museum • Ft Rucker, Bldg 6000 • Fort Rucker, AL 35362 • (334) 266-3169 • http://www.aviationmuseum.org

Gadsden

Etowah Historical Society • P.O. Box 8131 • Gadsden, AL 35901

Gadsden-Etowah County Library • 254 College St • Gadsden, AL 35999-3101 • (256) 549-4699 • http://www.librarycat.gadsden.com

Gunn-Bellinger House Museum • 872 Chestnut St, P.O. Box 267 • Gadsden, AL 35999 • (256) 549-4719

Meadows Library • Gadsden State Community College, 1001 George Wallace Dr, P.O. Box 227 • Gadsden, AL 35902-0227 • (256) 549-8411 • http://www.gadsdenstate.edu/library

Northeast Alabama Genealogical Society • 1 Dwight Ave, P.O. Box 8268 • Gadsden, AL 35902 • http://www.rootsweb.com/~alneags/

Gainesville

Sumter County Historical and Preservation Society • 10400 McKee St • Gainesville, AL 35464 • (205) 652-4822

Garden City

Garden City Public Library • Municipal Bldg, Hwy 31 • Garden City, AL 35070 • (205) 352-5408

Geneva

Emma Knox Kenan Public Library • 312 S Commerce St, P.O. Box 550 • Geneva, AL 36340-0550 • (334) 684-2459

Geneva County Historical Society • 406 S Commerce St, P.O. Box 27 • Geneva, AL 36340 • (334) 684-2100 • http://www.historyofgeneva.com

Georgiana

Hank Williams Boyhood Home Museum • 127 Rose St, P.O. Box 310 • Georgiana, AL 36033 • (334) 376-2396 • http://www.hankmuseum.com

Gilbertown

Choctaw County Historical Society • Historical Museum, AL Hwy 17 & Cty Rd 14, P.O. Box 162 • Gilbertown, AL 36908 • (334) 843-2501 • http://www.choctaw.net/museum/

Alabama

Glen Allen
Heritage of Marion County • P.O. Box 167 • Glen Allen, AL 35559

Gordo
Gordo Public Library • 287 Main St, P.O. Box 336 • Gordo, AL 35466-0336 • (205) 364-7148

Pickens County Genealogical Society • Old Jail Museum, 350 Springfield Rd, P.O. Box 336 • Gordo, AL 35466 • (205) 364-7830 • http://www.rootsweb.com/~alpicken/pcpage.htm

Goshen
Pike County Historical and Genealogical Society • Route 2, Box 272 • Goshen, AL 36035 • (205) 484-3314 • http://www.rootsweb.com/~alpike/

Greensboro
Hale County Historical Society • 1110 Main St • Greensboro, AL 36744 • http://www.halecoal.org

Hale County Public Library • 1105 Main St, P.O. Box 339 • Greensboro, AL 36744-0399 • (334) 624-3409

Magnolia Grove Historic House Museum • 1002 Hobston St • Greensboro, AL 36744 • (334) 624-8618 • http://www.preserveala.org/magnoliagrove.html

Greenville
Butler County Historical and Genealogical Society • c/o Greenville Public Library, 309 Fort Dale St, P.O. Box 561 • Greenville, AL 36037 • (334) 383-9564 • http://www.rootsweb.com/~albutler/

Butler County Historical Society • P.O. Box 561 • Greenville, AL 36037

Greenville-Butler County Public Library • 309 Ft Dale St • Greenville, AL 36037 • (334) 382-3216

Grove Hill
Alston House Museum • 116 Cobb St • Grove Hill, AL 36451 • (251) 275-8684

Clarke County Historical Society • Historical Museum, 116 W Cobb St • Grove Hill, AL 36451-3012 • (251) 275-2014 • http://www.clarkemuseum.com

Grove Hill Public Library • 108 Dubose Ave • Grove Hill, AL 36451-9502 • (334) 275-8157

Gulf Shores
Fort Morgan Museum • 51 Hwy 180 W • Gulf Shores, AL 36542 • (334) 540-7125

Gulf Shores Museum • 244 W 19th Ave, P.O. Box 299 • Gulf Shores, AL 36542 • http://www.gulfshoresal.gov

Thomas B Norton Public Library • 221 S 19th Ave • Gulf Shores, AL 36542 • (251) 968-1176 • http://www.ci.gulf-shores.al.us

Guntersville
Guntersville Historical Society • 3600 Colonial Dr • Guntersville, AL 35976

Guntersville Museum • 1215 Rayburn Ave • Guntersville, AL 35976 • (256) 571-7597 • http://www.guntersvillemuseum.org

Guntersville Public Library • 1240 O'Brig Ave • Guntersville, AL 35976 • (256) 571-7595 • http://www.guntersvillelibrary.org

United Cherokee Ani-Yum-Wiya Nation • 6407 Jarmon Rd • Guntersville, AL 35976 • (256) 582-2333 • http://www.ucan-online.org

Hanceville
Hanceville Library • Wallace State College, 801 Main St NW, 801 Main St NW, P.O. Box 2000 • Hanceville, AL 35077-2000 • (256) 352-8260 • http://www.wallacestatehanceville.edu/library.html

Tom Bevill Public Library • 151 Byars Rd • Hanceville, AL 35077 • (256) 287-1573

Hartselle
Hartselle Historical Society • P.O. Box 852 • Hartselle, AL 35640

Harvest
Rutherford County Genealogical Society • 14291 Hunter Rd • Harvest, AL 35749 • (256) 233-3176

Hayneville
Lowndes County Historical and Genealogical Society • P.O. Box 266 • Hayneville, AL 36040

Heflin
Cleburne County Historical Society • 120 Vickery St, Rm 105 • Heflin, AL 36264 • http://www.rootsweb.com/~alclebur/

Helena
InfoCenter Alabama Museum • 1123 Dearing Downs Dr • Helena, AL 35080 • (205) 620-5740 • http://www.infocenteralabama.com

Hillsboro
Pond Spring-General Joe Wheeler Home Museum • 12280 Al Hwy 20 • Hillsboro, AL 35643 • (256) 637-8513 • http://www.wheelerplantation.org

Wheeler Planation House Museum • 12280 AL Hwy 20 • Hillsboro, AL 35643 • (256) 637-8513

Hoover
Hoover Historical Society • 569 Park Ave • Hoover, AL 35226 • (205) 822-9392

Hope Hull
Pintlala Historical Association • c/o Pintlala Public Library, 255 Federal Rd • Hope Hull, AL 36043

Hueytown
Hueytown Historical Society • 310 South Pkwy, P.O. Box 3313 • Hueytown, AL 35023 • http://www.hueytown.org/historical/

Hueytown Public Library • 1372 Hueytown Rd • Hueytown, AL 35023 • (205) 491-1443 • http://www.hueytown.com/htnlib.html

Huntsville
Alabama Constitution Village Museum • 109 Gates Ave • Huntsville, AL 35801 • (205) 535-6565 • http://www.ci.hsv.al.us

Dr William H Burritt Museum and Park • 3101 Burritt Dr • Huntsville, AL 35801 • (256) 536-2882 • http://www.burrittmuseum.com

EarlyWorks Museum • 404 Madison St • Huntsville, AL 35801 • (256) 564-8100 • http://www.earlyworks.com

Eva B Dykes Library • Oakwood College, 7000 Adventist Blvd • Huntsville, AL 35896 • (256) 726-7246

Historic Huntsville Foundation • 128 Southside Sq, P.O. Box 786 • Huntsville, AL 35804 • (256) 539-0097

Huntsville-Madison County Historical Society • P.O. Box 666 • Huntsville, AL 35804 • (256) 534-7863

Huntsville-Madison County Public Library • 915 Monroe St SW, P.O. Box 443 • Huntsville, AL 35804 • (256) 532-5969 • http://hpl.lib.al.us

North Alabama Railroad Museum • 694 Chase Rd, P.O. Box 4163 • Huntsville, AL 35815-4163 • (256) 851-6276 • http://www.northalabamarailroadmuseum.com

Society of the Descendants of Washington's Army at Valley Forge, Alabama Brigade • 7905 Ensley Dr SW • Huntsville, AL 35802-2959

Tennessee Valley Genealogical Society • P.O. Box 1568 • Huntsville, AL 35807 • (256) 728-2788 • http://www.tvgs.org

US Space & Rocket Center Museum • 1 Tranquility Base • Huntsville, AL 35805 • (256) 837-3400 • http://www.spacecamp.com

Veterans Memorial Museum • 2060A Airport Rd • Huntsville, AL 35801 • (256) 883-3737 • http://www.memorialmuseum.org

Weeden House Museum • 300 Gates Ave • Huntsville, AL 35801 • (205) 536-7718

Jackson

Clarke County Historical Society • P.O. Box 131 • Jackson, AL 36545 • (334) 275-8684

Kimbell House Museum • Mayton Dr, P.O. Box 131 • Jackson, AL 36545 • (334) 246-3278

Jacksonville

Jacksonville Public Library • 200 Pelham Rd S • Jacksonville, AL 36265 • (256) 435-6332 • http://www.jacksonville-al.org

Jacksonville State University Library • 700 Pelham Rd N • Jacksonville, AL 36265 • (256) 782-5255 • http://jsucc.jsu.edu/depart/library

Jasper

Carl Elliot House Museum • Jasper Heritage Center, 1411 Indiana Ave • Jasper, AL 35501 • (205) 387-0511

Jasper Public Library • 98 E 18th St • Jasper, AL 35501 • (205) 221-8512

Walker County Genealogical Society • P.O. Box 3408 • Jasper, AL 35502-3408 • http://www.rootsweb.com/~alwalker/

Killen

Pettus Museum • 72 E Killen • Killen, AL 35645 • (256) 757-9229

Lanett

Ancestor Files Library • P.O. Box 249 • Lanett, AL 36863-0249 • (205) 576-2797

Leeds

Barber Vintage Motorsports Museum • 6030 Barber Motorsports • Leeds, AL 35094 • (205) 699-7275 • http://www.barbermuseum.com

Leeds Jane Culbreth Public Library • 802 Parkway Dr SE • Leeds, AL 35094 • (205) 699-5962 • http://www.leedsalabama.com/library.htm

Rowan Oaks Historic House • 1900 Montevallo Rd • Leeds, AL 35094 • (205) 699-1760

Lillian

Baldwin County Genealogical Society • P.O. Box 501 • Lillian, AL 36549

Livingston

Julie Tutwiler Learning Resources Center • Univ of West Alabama Sta 12, Box 2099 • Livingston, AL 35470 • (205) 652-3400 • http://www.lib.uwa.edu

Sumter County Historical and Preservation Society • 318 Washington St, P.O. Box 213 • Livingston, AL 35470 • (205) 652-4015 • http://www.rootsweb.com/~alsumter/

Loachapoka

Lee County Historical Society • Historical Museum, 6500 Stage Rd, P.O. Box 206 • Loachapoka, AL 36865 • (334) 887-3007 • http://www.leecountyhistoricalsociety.org

Lowndesboro

Calhoun School Museum • 17 Cesar Ln • Lowndesboro, AL 36752 • (334) 281-0513

Luverne

Crenshaw County Historical Society • P.O. Box 633 • Luverne, AL 36049-0633 • http://www.rootsweb.com/~alcrensh/

Madison

Madison African-American Alliance Group • P.O. Box 445 • Madison, AL 35758 • (256) 430-5790 • http://www.madisonaag.org

Madison Station Historical Preservation Society • 18 Arnett St • Madison, AL 35758 • (256) 461-8938 • http://www.knology.net/~madisonhistoricalsociety/

Marbury

Confederate Memorial Park • 437 County Rd 63 • Marbury, AL 36051 • (205) 744-1990 • http://www.preserveala.org/confederatepark.aspx

Marion

Baer Memorial Library • Marion Military Institute, 1101 Washington St • Marion, AL 36756 • (334) 683-2371 • http://www.marionmilitary.org

Marion-Perry County Library • 202 Washington St • Marion, AL 36756 • (334) 683-6411

Perry County Historical and Preservation Society • P.O. Box 257 • Marion, AL 36756

Maxwell AFB

Air Force Enlisted Heritage Museum • 550 McDonald St, Bldg 1210 • Maxwell AFB, AL 36114 • http://afehri.maxwell.af.mil

Air University Library • 600 Chennault Circle • Maxwell AFB, AL 36112-6424 • (334) 953-2888 • http://www.au.af.mil/au/aul/aul.htm

US Air Force-Historical Research Agency • AFHRA, 600 Chennault Circle, Bldg 1405 • Maxwell AFB, AL 36112-6424 • (334) 953-2395 • http://afhra.maxwell.af.mil

McCalla

Iron and Steel Museum, Tannehill Historical State Park • 12632 Confederate Pkwy • McCalla, AL 35111 • (205) 477-5711 • www.tannehill.org

Midfield

Midfield Public Library • 400 Breland Dr • Midfield, AL 35228-2732 • (205) 923-1027 • http://www.midfield.org

Midland City

Howell House Museum • Hilton Waters Ave, P.O. Box 69 • Midland City, AL 36350 • (334) 983-3511

Millbrook

Masonic Grand Lodge of Alabama • 341 Monument Dr • Millbrook, AL 36054 • http://www.alafreemasonry.org

Millbrook Public Library • 3650 Grandview Rd, P.O. Box 525 • Millbrook, AL 36054 • (334) 285-6688 • http://www.home.earthlink.net/~millbrookpl/

West Elmore County Historical Society • 2881 Gibson St • Millbrook, AL 36054 • http://www.rootsweb.com/~alelmore/

Minter

Lowndes County Historical and Genealogical Society • 5935 Cty Rd 4 • Minter, AL 36761 • http://www.rootsweb.com/~allownde/

Mobile

Bernstein-Bush House Museum • 355 Government St, P.O. Box 2068 • Mobile, AL 36652 • (334) 208-7569

Bragg-Mitchell Mansion Museum • 1906 Springhill Ave • Mobile, AL 36605 • (334) 471-6365 • http://www.braggmitchellmansion.com

Carlen House Museum • 54 S Carlen St • Mobile, AL 36606 • (334) 434-1565

City of Mobile Archives • 457 Church St • Mobile, AL 36602 • (334) 208-7740

Conde-Charlotte House Museum • 104 Theater St • Mobile, AL 36602 • (334) 432-4722 • http://www.condecharlottemuseum.com

Cox-Deasy Cottage Museum • 1115 Palmetto St • Mobile, AL 36604 • (334) 433-3265

Fort Conde Museum • 150 S Royal St, P.O. Box 2068 • Mobile, AL 36652 • (334) 208-7304 • http://www.forttours.com/pages/fortconde.asp

Historic Mobile Preservation Society • 300 Oakleigh Pl • Mobile, AL 36604 • (334) 432-6161 • http://www.historicmobile.org

Alabama

Mobile, cont.

J L Bedsole Library • University of Mobile, 5735 College Pkwy, P.O. Box 13220 • Mobile, AL 36663 • (251) 442-2242 • http://library.umobile.edu

Mobile Area Museum Association • Historical Museum, P.O. Box 334 • Mobile, AL 36601 • (251) 861-7550 • http://www.mobileareamuseums.org

Mobile Genealogical Society • 1400 Joyce Rd, P.O. Box 6224 • Mobile, AL 36660-6224 • (251) 414-1995 • http://www.mobileroots.org

Mobile Medical Museum • 1664 Spring Hill Ave • Mobile, AL 36604-1405 • (251) 415-1109 • http://www.mobilemedicalmuseum.com

Mobile Public Library • 701 Government St • Mobile, AL 36602-1499 • (251) 208-7076 • http://www.mplonline.org

Museum of Mobile • 111 S Royal St, P.O. Box 2068 • Mobile, AL 36602-3101 • (251) 438-7569 • http://www.museumofmobile.com

Museums of the City of Mobile • 355 Government St, P.O. Box 2068 • Mobile, AL 36652 • (334) 434-7569

National African-American Museum • 564 Martin Luther King Jr Ave • Mobile, AL 36603 • (251) 433-8511

National Maritime Museum of the Gulf of Mexico • 250 N Water St, Ste 131, P.O. Box 3005 • Mobile, AL 36602 • (251) 436-8901 • http://www.nationalmaritime.us

Oakleigh House Museum • 350 Oakleigh Pl • Mobile, AL 36604 • (334) 432-1281

Phoenix Fire Museum • 203 S Claiborne St, P.O. Box 2068 • Mobile, AL 36652 • (334) 434-7569 • http://www.museumofmobile.com

Richards-DAR House Museum • 256 N Joachim St • Mobile, AL 36603 • (251) 208-7320

Saint Ignatius Archives, Museum and Library • 3704 Springhill Ave • Mobile, AL 36608 • (251) 342-9716

Thomas Burne Memorial Library • Spring Hill College, 4000 Dauphin St • Mobile, AL 36608 • (251) 380-3871 • http://www.shc.edu

University Library • University of South Alabama, 307 University Blvd N, Rm 145 • Mobile, AL 36688 • (251) 460-7025 • http://library.southalabama.edu

University of South Alabama Archives • USA Springhill, Rm 0722 • Mobile, AL 36688 • (251) 434-3800 • http://www.southalabama.edu/archives

USS Alabama Battleship Memorial Park • 2703 Battleship Pkwy, P.O. Box 65 • Mobile, AL 36601 • (251) 433-2703 • http://www.ussalabama.com

William and Emily Hearin Carnival Museum • 355 Government St, P.O. Box 2121 • Mobile, AL 36601 • (251) 432-3324 • http://www.mobilecarnivalmuseum.com

Monroeville

Alabama River Museum • Claiborne Lock & Dam, P.O. Box 1637 • Monroeville, AL 6461 • (251) 575- 7433 • www.tokillamockingbird.com

Bethany Church Museum • P.O. Box 1637 • Monroeville, AL 36461 • (334) 575-7433

John Dennis Forte Library • Alabama Southern Community College, 2800 S Alabama Ave, P.O. Box 2000 • Monroeville, AL 36461-2000 • (251) 575-3156 • http://www.ascc.edu

Monroe County Heritage Museum • Old Monroe Cty Courthouse, P.O. Box 1637 • Monroeville, AL 36461-1637 • (251) 575-7433 • http://www.tokillamockingbird.com

Monroe County Heritage Society • Heritage Museum, Courthouse Square, P.O. Box 1637 • Monroeville, AL 36461-1637 • (251) 575-7433 • http://www.tokillamockingbird.com

Monroe County Public Library • 226 Pineville Rd • Monroeville, AL 36460 • (334) 743-3818

Rikard's Mill Historical Park Museum • c/o MCHM, P.O. Box 1637 • Monroeville, AL 36461 • (251) 575-7433

Montevallo

American Village Museum • 3727 AL Hwy 119, P.O. Box 6 • Montevallo, AL 35115 • (205) 665-3535 • http://www.americanvillage.org

King House Museum • Univ of Montevallo • Montevallo, AL 35115 • (205) 665-6292

Oliver Cromwell Carmichael Library • Univ of Montevallo, Sta 6100 • Montevallo, AL 35115-6100 • (205) 665-6100 • http://www.montevallo.edu/library

Parnell Memorial Library • 845 Valley St • Montevallo, AL 35115 • (205) 665-9207

Montgomery

Alabama Archives and History Department Library • World War Memorial Bldg, 624 Washington Ave, P.O. Box 300100 • Montgomery, AL 36104 • (334) 242-4435 • http://www.archives.state.al.us

Alabama Cattleman's Association Museum • 201 S Bainbridge • Montgomery, AL 36104 • (334) 265-1867 • http://www.bamabeef.org/NewMOOseum.htm

Alabama Department of Archives and History • 624 Washington Ave, P.O. Box 300100 • Montgomery, AL 36130-0100 • (334) 242-4435 • http://www.archives.state.al.us

Alabama Historical Association • 624 Washington Ave • Montgomery, AL 36130 • (334) 240-3433 • http://www.archives.state.al.us/aha/aha.html

Alabama Historical Commission • 468 South Perry St, P.O. Box 300900 • Montgomery, AL 36130-0900 • (334) 230-2690 • http://www.preserveala.org

Alabama Preservation Alliance • P.O. Box 2228 • Montgomery, AL 36102

Alabama State Library • 6030 Monticello Dr • Montgomery, AL 36130 • (334) 213-3950 • http://www.apls.state.al.us

Dexter Avenue Baptist Church Museum • 454 Dexter Ave • Montgomery, AL 36104 • (334) 263-3970

Dexter Parsonage Museum • 303 S Jackson St • Montgomery, AL 36104 • (334) 261-3270 • http://www.dexterkindmemorial.org

First White House of the Confederacy Museum • 644 Washington Ave, P.O. Box 1861 • Montgomery, AL 36103 • (334) 261-4624

Holt Street Baptist Church Historical Society • 903 S Holt St • Montgomery, AL 36108 • (334) 263-0554

Houghton Memorial Library • Huntingdon College, 1500 E Fairview Ave • Montgomery, AL 36106-2148 • (334) 833-4421 • http://www.huntingdon.edu/library/homepage.html

Landmarks Foundation-Old Alabama Town • 301 Columbus St • Montgomery, AL 36104 • (334) 240-4500 • http://www.mindspring.com/~olaltown

Lowndes County Historical Society • 300 Cantelou Rd • Montgomery, AL 36108-6000

Montgomery City-County Library • 245 High St, P.O. Box 1950 • Montgomery, AL 36102-1950 • (334) 240-4300 • http://www.mccpl.lib.al.us

Montgomery County Archives • Couthouse Annex, 100 S Lawrence St, P.O. Box 223 • Montgomery, AL 36101-0223 • (334) 832-7173 • http://www.mc-ala.org/probate/archive.htm

Montgomery County Historical Society • Figh-Pickett-Barnes School House, 512 S Court St, P.O. Box 1829 • Montgomery, AL 36104-4104 • (334) 834-9292 • http://montgomeryhistorical.com/

Montgomery Genealogical Society • 3110 Highfield Dr, P.O. Box 230194 • Montgomery, AL 36123-0194 • (334) 272-0481 • http://www.rootsweb.com/~almgs/

MOOseum • 201 S Bainbridge St, P.O. Box 2499 • Montgomery, AL 36102 • (334) 265-1867 • http://www.bamabeef.org

National Center for the Study of Civil Rights and African-American Culture • Alabama State Univ, 1345 Carter Hill Rd, P.O. Box 271 • Motngomery, AL 36101-0271 • (334) 229-4824 • http://www.lib.alasu.edu/natctr/

Old Alabama Town Museum • 301 Columbus St • Montgomery, AL 36104 • http://www.oldalabamatown.com

Ollie L Brown Afro-Amer Heritage Collection • Alabama State Univ, 915 S Jackson St, P.O. Box 271 • Montgomery, AL 36101 • (334) 262-3581 • http://www.lib.alasu.edu

Scott & Zelda Fitzgerald Museum • 919 Felder Ave, P.O. Box 64 • Montgomery, AL 36101 • (334) 264-4222

Society of Pioneers of Montgomery • P.O. Box 413 • Montgomery, AL 36101

Supreme Court Museum and State Law Library • 300 Dexter Ave • Montgomery, AL 36104 • (334) 242-4347 • http://www.judicial.state.al.us

Troy University Rosa Parks Museum • 252 Montgomery St, P.O. Drawer 4419 • Montgomery, AL 36104 • (334) 242-8615 • http://montgomery.troy.edu/museum/

University of Auburn-Montgomery Library • 7440 East Dr, P.O. Box 244023 • Montgomery, AL 36124-4023 • (334) 244-3200 • http://aumnicat.aum.edu/archives

Wallace Museum Foundation • 631 S Perry St • Montgomery, AL 36104 • (334) 834-1972 • http://www.wallacefoundation.org

William Cook House Museum • 929 Parkwood Dr • Montgomery, AL 36109 • (334) 272-1972

World Heritage Museum • 119 W Jeff Davis • Montgomery, AL 36109

Montrose
Baldwin County Historic Development Commission • P.O. Box 86 • Montrose, AL 36559 • (251) 928-3002

Moulton
Lawrence County Historical Commission • Lawrence County Archives, 698 Main St, P.O. Box 728 • Moulton, AL 35650-0728 • (256) 974-1757 • http://lawrencecoarchives.com/

Moundville
Moundville Public Library • 411 Market St, P.O. Box 336 • Moundville, AL 35474 • (205) 371-2283

Mount Vernon
Mowa Band of Choctaw Indians • 1080 Red Fox Rd • Mount Vernon, AL 36560 • (251) 829-5500 • http://www.mowachoctaw.com

Nauvoo
Camp McDowell Military Museum • 105 DeLong Rd • Nauvoo, AL 35578 • (205) 387-1806 • http://www.campmcdowell.com

Old Harbin Hotel Museum • 131 3rd Ave, P.O. Box 157 • Nauvoo, AL 35578

Newville
Henry County Historical Group • P.O. Box 125 • Newville, AL 36345 • (334) 693-2788 • http://www.rootsweb.com/~alhenry/

Normal
Afro-American Historical and Genealogical Society of North Alabama • P.O. Box 89 • Normal, AL 35762-0089 • http://www.aahgs.org/chapters

J F Drake Memorial Library • Alabama A&M Univ, P.O. Box 489 • Normal, AL 35762 • (205) 851-5764 • http://www.aamu.edu/lrc/departments.htm

State Black Archives Research Center and Museum • James Hembray Wilson Bldg, Alabama A&M Univ, P.O. Box 595 • Normal, AL 35762 • (256) 372-5846 • http://www.aamu.edu

Northport
Friends of Historic Northport • general delivery • Northport, AL 35473

Historic Shirley Place Museum and Gardens • 512 Main Ave • Northport, AL 35476 • (205) 349-1617

Oakman
Corry House Museum • Old York Heritage Park, Hwy 69 • Oakman, AL 35115

Old York Museum • 111 School St, P.O. Box 459 • Oakman, AL 35579

Odenville
Saint Clair County Historical Society • 11975 US Hwy 411, P.O. Box 125 • Odenville, AL 35120 • http://stclaircherish.org/

Oneonta
Blount County Archives • P.O. Box 45 • Oneonta, AL 35121 • (205) 625-4180

Blount County Historical Society • Historical Museum, 204 2nd St N, P.O. Box 45 • Oneonta, AL 35121 • (256) 625-6905 • http://www.coveredbridge.org

Oneonta Public Library • 221 2nd St S • Oneonta, AL 35121 • (205) 274-7641

Opelika
East Alabama Genealogical Society • 909 Avenue A, P.O. Box 2892 • Opelika, AL 36803-2892

Lewis Cooper Jr. Memorial Library • 200 S 6th St, P.O. Box 125 • Opelika, AL 36803-0125 • (334) 705-5380

Museum of East Alabama • 121 S 9th St, P.O. Box 3085 • Opelika, AL 36803-3085 • (334) 749-2751

Opp
Opp Historical Society • 208 N Whaley St • Opp, AL 36467 • (334) 493-1125

Orange Beach
Orange Beach Indian and Sea Museum • 25850 John M Snook Dr, P.O. Box 458 • Orange Beach, AL 36561 • (251) 981-2766

Orange Beach Public Library • 26267 Canal Rd, P.O. Box 1649 • Orange Beach, AL 36561-1649 • (251) 981-2923 • http://www.orangebeachlibrary.org

Orrville
Old Cahawba Historic Site • Historical Museum, 9518 Canaba Rd • Orrville, AL 36767 • (334) 872-8058 • http://www.cahawba.org

Ozark
Dale County Genealogical and Historical Society • 416 James St • Ozark, AL 36360

Dale County Historical Society • P.O. Box 1231 • Ozark, AL 36361

Mizell Mansion Museum • 409 E Broad St • Ozark, AL 36360 • (334) 774-9323

Ozark-Dale County Public Library • 416 James St • Ozark, AL 36360 • (334) 774-2399 • http://www.snowhill.com/~library/; http://www.odcpl.com

Alabama

Pell City
Pell City Library • 1921 1st Ave N • Pell City, AL 35125 • (205) 884-1015

Phenix City
Chattahoochee Valley Community College Library • 2602 College Dr • Phenix City, AL 36869-7960 • (334) 291-4978 • http://www.cv.edu/library

Russell County Historical Commission • 1003 Broad St • Phenix City, AL 36867 • (334) 298-9735 • http://www.rootsweb.com/~alrussel/

Russell County Historical Society • 1040 Broad St • Phenix City, AL 36867-5920 • (334) 297-8225

Phil Campbell
James A Glasgow Library • Northwest-Shoals Community College, 2080 College Rd • Phil Campbell, AL 35581 • (256) 331-6271 • http://www.nwscc.cc.al.us/library.html

Piedmont
Piedmont Museum • N Center Ave, P.O. Box 112 • Piedmont, AL 36272

Steward University System Library • RFD 5, Box 109 • Piedmont, AL 36272 • (256) 447-2939

Pleasant Grove
Pleasant Grove Historical Commission • 501 Park Rd • Pleasant Grove, AL 35127

Prattville
Autauga County Heritage Association • 102 E Main St, P.O. Box 178 • Prattville, AL 36067 • (334) 361-0961 • http://www.autaugaheritage.com

Autauga Genealogical Society • P.O. Box 680668 • Prattville, AL 36067-0668 • http://www.rootsweb.com/~alags/

Autauga-Prattville Public Library • 254 Doster St • Prattville, AL 36067-3933 • (334) 365-3396 • http://prattvillelibrary.compumise.com

Buena Vista Mansion Museum • 641 County Rd 4 • Prattville, AL 36067 • (334) 365-3690

People's Historical Museum • 130 W 4th St • Prattville, AL 36067

Reform
Reform Public Library • 216 1st St S, PO Box 819 • Reform, AL 35481-0819 • (205) 375-6240

Robertsdale
Robertsdale Public Library • 18301 Pennsylvania St • Robertsdale, AL 36567 • (251) 947-8960 • http://www.robertsdale.com/pl.htm

Rockford
Coosa County Historical Society • P.O. Box 5 • Rockford, AL 35136 • http://www.rootsweb.com/~alcoosa/coosa.html

Old Jail Museum • P.O. Box 388 • Rockford, AL 35136

Russellville
Northwest Regional Library-Russellville Branch • 110 E Lawrence St • Russellville, AL 35653 • (256) 332-1535

Russellville Heritage Preservation Society • P.O. 1095 • Russellville, AL 35653

Saint Stephens
Old Saint Stephens Museum • Old Saint Stephens Rd, P.O. Box 108 • Saint Stephens, AL 36569

Saraland
Saraland Historical and Museum Society • Historical Museum, P.O. Box 34 • Saraland, AL 36571

Scottsboro
Jackson County Genealogical Society • P.O. Box 1494 • Scottsboro, AL 35768

Scottsboro
Jackson County Historical Association • 435 Barbee Ln, P.O. Box 1494 • Scottsboro, AL 35768 • (205) 259-5286 • http://www.jacksoncountyal.com/historical/

Scottsboro Public Library • 1002 S Broad St • Scottsboro, AL 35768 • (256) 574-4335 • http://www.scottsborolibrary.com

Scottsboro-Jackson Historical Association • Heritage Center, 208 S Houston St, P.O. Box 53 • Scottsboro, AL 35768 • (205) 259-2122 • http://www.jacksoncountyal.com

Seale
Russell County Historical Commission • 801 Dillingham St • Seale, AL 36875

Selma
Central Alabama Genealogical Society • P.O. Box 125 • Selma, AL 36701 • http://www.prairiebluff.com/algenweb/dallas

Joe T Smitherman Historic Building • 109 Union St • Selma, AL 36701 • (334) 874-2174

National Voting Rights Museum • 1012 Water Ave, P.O. Box 1366 • Selma, AL 36702 • (334) 418-0800 • www.viterights.org

Old Cahawba State Historic Site Museum • 719 Tremont St • Selma, AL 36701

Old Depot Museum • 4 Martin Luther King St • Selma, AL 36703 • (334) 874-2197

Pilgrimage Council • P.O. Box 2542 • Selma, AL 36702

Selma and Dallas County Public Library • 1103 Selma Ave • Selma, AL 36703-4445 • (334) 874-1725 • http://www.selmalibrary.org

Selma-Dallas County Friends of the Trail • 816 Selma Ave • Selma, AL 36701 • (334) 875-3359

Selma-Dallas County Historic and Preservation Society • 719 Tremont St, P.O. Box 586 • Selma, AL 36702-0586 • (205) 872-8265 • http://pilgrimage.selmaalabama.com/SDCHPSinfo.htm

Sturdivant Hall Museum • 713 Mabry St, P.O. Box 1205 • Selma, AL 36701 • (334) 872-5626 • http://www.sturdivanthall.com

Sheffield
Sheffield Public Library • 316 N Montgomery Ave • Sheffield, AL 35660 • (256) 386-5633 • http://www.lmn.lib.al.us

Tennessee Valley Historical Society • P.O. Box 149 • Sheffield, AL 35660 • (205) 381-2298 • http://home.hiwaay.net/~krjohn/

Shelby
Shelby Iron Works Park • 10268 Hwy 42 • Shelby, AL 35143 • (205) 669-5385

Slocomb
First Baptist Church Library • P.O. Box 248 • Slocomb, AL 36375 • (334) 886-2200

Spanish Fort
Blakeley State Park • 34745 State Hwy 225 • Spanish Fort, AL 36527 • (251) 625-2773

Spring Garden
Cherokee County Genealogy Society • P.O. Box 90 • Spring Garden, AL 36275

Piedmont Historical and Genealogical Society • P.O. Box 47 • Spring Garden, AL 36275

Stevenson
Stevenson Railroad Depot Museum • P.O. Box 894 • Stevenson, AL 35772 • (256) 427-3012 • http://www.stevensondepotmuseum.com

Stockton
Baldwin County Historic Society • P.O. Box 69 • Stockton, AL 36579 • (251) 937-9464

Fort Mims Museum • Cty Rd 80 • Stockton, AL 46579 • (251) 937-4254 • http://www.preserveala.org/fortmims.aspx

Summerdale

Baldwin County Express Traveling Museums • 19432 Rada Rd • Summerdale, AL 36580 • (251) 989-6110 • http://www.baldwinexpress.org

Sylacauga

B B Comer Memorial Library • 314 N Broadway • Sylacauga, AL 35150-2528 • (256) 249-0961 • http://www.sylacauga.net/library/

Isabel Anderson Comer Museum • 711 N Broadway, P.O. Box 245 • Sylacauga, AL 35150 • (256) 245-4016 • http://comermuseum.freeservers.com

Talladega

Alabama Institute for the Deaf & Blind Museum • 205 E South St • Talladega, AL 35161

Hacksma House Genealogy Library • Heritage Hall, P.O. Box 1118 • Talladega, AL 35160

Jemison Carnegie Heritage Hall • 200 South St E, P.O. Box 118 • Talladega, AL 35160 • (256) 761-1364

Savery Library • Talladega College, 627 W Battle St • Talladega, AL 35160 • (256) 761-6279 • http://www.talladega.edu

Talladega County Historical Association • 106 Broome St, P.O. Box 1042 • Talladega, AL 35161 • (205) 362-2219

Talledega Public Library • 202 South St E • Talladega, AL 35160 • (256) 362-4211

Tallassee

Peterson Log Cabin Museum • Sims Ave • Tallassee, AL 36708 • (334) 283-5151

Talisi Historical Preservation Society • P.O. Box 780022 • Tallassee, AL 36078-0001

Talisi Historical Society • 104 N Johnson St • Tallassee, AL 36078 • (334) 252-0513

Tarrant

Tarrant Public Library • 1143 Ford Ave • Tarrant, AL 35217-2437 • (205) 849-2825 • http://www.tarrant.lib.al.us

Theodore

Bellingrath Museum and Gardens • 12401 Bellingrath Gardens Rd • Theodore, AL 36582 • (334) 973-2217 • http://www.bellingrath.org

Troy

Pike County Historical and Genealogical Society • c/o Mrs. Karen C. Bullard, 4041 Country Road 59 • Troy, AL 36079

Pike Pioneer Museum • 248 US Hwy 231 N • Troy, AL 36081 • (334) 566-3597 • www.pioneer-museum.org

Star Clan of Muscogee Creeks • 242 County Rd 2254 • Troy, AL 36079 • (334) 285-2491

Troy Public Library • 300 N Three Notch Rd • Troy, AL 36081 • (334) 566-1314

Troy State University Library • Wallace Hall • Troy, AL 36082 • (334) 670-3255

Trussville

Trussville Public Library • 201 Parkway Dr • Trussville, AL 35173 • (205) 665-2022 • http://www.trussvillelibrary.com

Tuscaloosa

Alabama Historical Association • P.O. Box 870380 • Tuscaloosa, AL 35487-0380 • (205) 348-5180 • http://www.uapress.ua.edu/journal.html

American College of Heraldry • P.O. Box 11084 • Tuscaloosa, AL 35486-0025 • (801) 298-5358 • http://www.heritagequest.com

Battle-Friedman House Museum • 1010 Greensboro Ave, P.O. Box 1665 • Tuscaloosa, AL 36503 • (205) 758-2238 • http://www.historictuscaloosa.org/tours5.html

Black Heritage Museum of West Alabama • Stillman College, P.O. Box 1430 • Tuscaloosa, AL 35403 • (205) 349-4240

Center for the Study of Tobacco and Society Museum • Univ of Alabama, 174 Nott Hall, Box 870327 • Tuscaloosa, AL 35487 • (205) 348-2162

Edgar's Closet Museum • 2000 1st Ave • Tuscaloosa, AL 35401 • (205) 887-3202 • http://www.edgarscloset.com

Ermine Society • P.O. Box 71839 • Tuscaloosa, AL 35407 • http://www.erminesociety.org

Gorgas House Museum • Capstone & McCorvy Dr, Univ of AL, P.O. Box 870340 • Tuscaloosa, AL 35487-0340 • (205) 348-5906 • www.ua.edu/gorgasmain.html

Mildred Warner House Museum • 1925 8th St • Tuscaloosa, AL 35404 • (205) 553 6200

Murphy African American Museum • 2601 Bryant Dr • Tuscaloosa, AL 35401 • (205) 758-2861

Niadh Nask: Military Order of the Golden Chain • P.O. Box 11084 • Tuscaloosa, AL 35486-0025

Old Tavern Museum • 500 28th Ave-Capitol Park, P.O. Box 1665 • Tuscaloosa, AL 35401 • (205) 758-2238 • http://www.historictuscaloosa.org

Paul W Bryant Museum • Univ of Alabama, 300 Paul W Bryant Dr, P.O. Box 870385 • Tuscaloosa, AL 35487 • http://www.bryantmuseum.ua.edu

Tuscaloosa County Preservation Society • 500 28th Ave, P.O. Box 1665 • Tuscaloosa, AL 35403 • (205) 758-2238

Tuscaloosa Genealogical Society • 2022 11th St, P.O. Box 020802 • Tuscaloosa, AL 35402-0802 • http://www.rootsweb.com/~altuscal/

Tuscaloosa Genealogical Society, Morning Group • 29 DuBois Terr • Tuscaloosa, AL 35401 • http://www.alabamagenealogy.org/ahgp/TuscaloosaGenSoc.html

Tuscaloosa Genealogical Society, Night Group • P.O. Box 020802 • Tuscaloosa, AL 35406 • (205) 349-4665 • http://web.dbtech.net/~hwood/

Tuscaloosa Heritage Commission • P.O. Box 1776 • Tuscaloosa, AL 35401 • (205) 752-2575

Tuscaloosa Public Library • 1801 Jack Warner Pkwy • Tuscaloosa, AL 35401-1027 • (205) 345-5820 • http://www.tuscaloosa-library.org

William H Sheppard Library • Stillman College, 3601 Stillman Blvd, P.O. Box 1430 • Tuscaloosa, AL 35403-1430 • (205) 366-8851 • http://www.stillman.edu

William Stanley Hoole Special Collections Library • University of Alabama, P.O. Box 870266 • Tuscaloosa, AL 35487-0266 • (205) 348-0500 • http://www.ua.edu/libraries/hoole

Tuscumbia

Alabama Music Hall of Fame • 617 Hwy 72 W, P.O. Box 740405 • Tuscumbia, AL 35674 • (256) 381-4417 • http://www.alamhof.org

Belle Mont Mansion Museum • 1569 Cook Ln • Tuscumbia, AL 35674 • http://www.preserveala.org/bellemont.aspx

Ivy Green - Birthplace of Helen Keller • 300 W North Commons • Tuscumbia, AL 35674 • (205) 383-4066 • http://www.helenkellerbirthplace.org

Sumter County Historical and Preservation Society • 207 N Washington St • Tuscumbia, AL 35674

Alabama

Tuskegee

Hollis Burke Frissell Library • Tuskegee Institute • Tuskegee, AL 36088 • (334) 727-8896 • http://www.tusk.edu

Macon County Genealogical Society • c/o Tuskegee Public Library, 302 S Main St • Tuskegee, AL 36083 • http://www.rootsweb.com/~almacon/

Oaks House Museum • 950 Old Montgomery Rd • Tuskegee, AL 36088 • (334) 727-3200

Tuskegee Human and Civil Rights Multicultural Center • 104 S Elm St, P.O. Box 830768 • Tuskegee, AL 36083 • (334) 724-0800 • http://www.tuskegeecenter.org

Tuskegee Institute National Historic Site Museum • 1212 Old Montgomery Rd, P.O. Drawer 10 • Tuskegee, AL 36087 • (334) 727-6390 • www.nps.gov

Union Springs

Bullock County Historical Society • P.O. Box 563 • Union Springs, AL 36089 • http://www.rootsweb.com/~albulloc/

Log Cabin Museum • 114 W Blackmon, P.O. Box 5236 • Union Springs, AL 36089 • (334) 738-5411

Union Springs Public Library • 103 N Prairie • Union Springs, AL 36089 • (334) 738-2760

Uniontown

Perry County Genealogical Society • P.O. Box 310 • Uniontown, AL 36786 • http://www.rootsweb.com/~alperry/

Valley

Chattahoochee Valley Historical Society • c/o Chambers County Library, 3419 20th Ave • Valley, AL 35854 • (334) 768-2050 • http://www.rootsweb.com/~alchambe

Cher-O-Creek Intra Tribal Indians • 2212 50th St • Valley, AL 36854 • (334) 756-2889

Cobb Memorial Archives • 3419 20th Ave • Valley, AL 36854

H Grady Bradshaw-Chambers County Library • 3419 20th Ave • Valley, AL 36854 • (334) 768-2161 • http://www.chamberscountylibrary.org

Vernon

Lamar County Genealogical and Historical Society • P.O. Box 357 • Vernon, AL 35592 • (205) 695-6123 • http://www.fayette.net/carruth/genealogysociety.htm

Northwest Regional Library-Mary Wallace Cobb Memorial Library • 110 1st Ave, P.O. Box 357 • Vernon, AL 35592-0357 • (205) 695-6123

Vernon City Museum • P.O. Box 357 • Vernon, AL 35592

Vinemont

Crooked Creek Civil War Museum • 516 Cty Rd 1127 • Vinemont, AL 35179 • (256) 739-2741

Wadley

McClintock-Ensminger Library • Southern Union State Community College, Robert St, P.O. Box 1000 • Wadley, AL 36276 • (256) 395-2211

Waterloo

Edith Newman Culver Museum • 501 Main St, P.O. Box 38 • Waterloo, AL 35677 • (205) 767-6081

Wetumpka

Elmore County Historical Society • Historical Museum, 1384 Jug Factory Rd, P.O. Box 912 • Wetumpka, AL 36092

Elmore County Museum of Black History • 1006 Lancaster, P.O. Box 310 • Wetumpka, AL 36092

Fort Toulouse-Fort Jackson Museum • 2521 W Fort Toulouse Rd • Wetumpka, AL 36093 • (334) 567-3002 • http://www.preserveala.org/forttoulousejackson.aspx

Winfield

Marion County Genealogical Society • P.O. Box 1527 • Winfield, AL 35594 • (205) 487-2484 • http://www.rootsweb.com/~almarion/mcgs.htm

Northwest Regional Library • 185 Ashwood Dr, P.O. Box 1527 • Winfield, AL 35594-1527 • (205) 487-2330

Woodville

Woodville Public Library • 26 Venson St, P.O. Box 116 • Woodville, AL 35776-0116 • (256) 776-2796 • http://www.home.highway.net/~woodplb

Adak
Adak Community Museum • PSC 486, Box 1313 • Adak, AK 96506-1271 • (907) 592-8064

Akhoik
Akhoik Native Village • P.O. Box 5030 • Akhoik, AK 99615 • (907) 836-2229

Akiachak
Akiachak Native Community • P.O. Box 70 • Akiachak, AK 99551-0070 • (907) 825-4626

Akiak
Akiak Native Community • P.O. Box 185 • Akiak, AK 99552 • (907) 765-7112

Akutan
Akutan Native Village • P.O. Box 89 • Akutan, AK 99553 • (907) 698-2300

Alakanuk
Alakanuk Native Village • P.O. Box 149 • Alakanuk, AK 99554-0149 • (907) 238-3419

Aleknagik
Aleknagik Native Village • P.O. Box 115 • Aleknagik, AK 99555 • (907) 842-5623

Allakaket
Alatna Village • P.O. Box 70 • Allakaket, AK 99720 • (907) 968-2304

Allakaket Village • P.O. Box 50 • Allakaket, AK 99720 • (907) 968-2237

Ambler
Ambler Native Village • P.O. Box 47 • Ambler, AK 99786 • (907) 445-2180

Anaktuvuk Pass
Anaktuvuk Pass Native Village • P.O. Box 21065 • Anaktuvuk Pass, AK 99721 • (907) 661-2535

Simon Paneak Memorial Museum • 341 Mekiana Rd, P.O. Box 21085 • Anaktuvuk Pass, AK 99721 • (907) 661-3413 • http://www.co.north-slope.ak.us/nsb/55.htm

Anchorage
Alaska Association for Historic Preservation • 1689 C Street, Ste 207 • Anchorage, AK 99501 • (907) 929-9870

Alaska Aviation Heritage Museum • 4721 Aircraft Dr, Lake Hood • Anchorage, AK 99502 • (907) 248-6391 • http://www.alaskaairmuseum.org

Alaska Federation of Natives • 1577 C Street, Ste 201 • Anchorage, AK 99501-5164 • (907) 274-3611

Alaska Genealogical Society • 7030 Dickerson Dr, P.O. Box 212265 • Anchorage, AK 99521-2265 • (907) 337-6377

Alaska Heritage Library and Museum • 301 W Northern Lights, P.O. Box 100600 • Anchorage, AK 99510-0600 • (907) 265-2834 • http://www.wellsfargohistory.com/museums/alaska.html

Alaska Historical Commission • 550 W 7th Ave., Suite 1310 • Anchorage, AK 99501-3565 • (907) 269-8721 • http://www.dnr.state.ak.us/parks/oha_web/ahc.htm

Alaska Historical Society • 524 W 4th St, Suite 208, P.O. Box 100299 • Anchorage, AK 99510-0299 • (907) 276-1596 • http://www.alaskahistoricalsociety.org/

Alaska Native Heritage Center Museum • 8800 Heritage Center Dr • Anchorage, AK 99506 • (907) 330-8000 • http://www.alaskanative.net

Alaska Office of History and Archaeology • 550 W 7th Ave, Ste 1310 • Anchorage, AK 99501-3565 • (907) 269-8721 • http://www.dnr.state.ak.us/parks/ohaweb/

Alaska State Library • 344 W 3rd Ave, Suite 125 • Anchorage, AK 99501 • (907) 269-6570 • http://www.library.state.ak.us

Alaska State Trooper Museum • 5th Ave Mall, P.O. Box 100280 • Anchorage, AK 88510 • (907) 279-5050 • http://www.alaskatroopermuseum.com

Anchorage Genealogical Society • 7805 Linda Ln, P.O. Box 242294 • Anchorage, AK 99524-2294 • (907) 337-6377 • http://www.rootsweb.com/~akags/

Anchorage Municipal Libraries • 3600 Denali St • Anchorage, AK 99503-6093 • (907) 261-2975 • http://lexicon.ci.anchorage.ak.us

Anchorage Museum of History and Art • 121 W 7th Ave, P.O. Box 196650 • Anchorage, AK 99519-6650 • (907) 343-4326 • http://www.anchoragemuseum.org

Cook Inlet Historical Society • Anchorage Museum of History & Art, 121 W 7th Ave • Anchorage, AK 99504 • (907) 343-6189 • http://www.anchoragemuseum.org

Georgetown Native Village • 1400 Virginia Ct • Anchorage, AK 99501 • (907) 274-2195

Historic Sites Advisory Committee • Office of History and Archaeology, P.O. Box 107011 • Anchorage, AK 99510 • (907) 762-2626

Historical Research Center • 3801 Old Seward Hwy, Ste 6 • Anchorage, AK 99503 • (907) 278-5427

Kaguyak Indian Village • 1400 W Benson Blvd, Ste 350 • Anchorage, AK 99503 • (907) 561-2668

Kanatak Tribal Council • 702 W 32nd Ac, Ste 100 • Anchorage, AK 99503 • (907) 336-7271

Masonic Grand Lodge of Alaska • 544 E 14th St, P.O. Box 190668 • Anchorage, AK 99519 • (907) 561-1477 • http://www.alaska-mason.org/

Museums Alaska • P.O. Box 242323 • Anchorage, AK 99524 • (907) 243-4714 • http://www.museumsalaska.org

National Archives Alaska Branch • Federal Office Bldg, 654 W 3rd Ave, Rm 012 • Anchorage, AK 99501-2145 • (907) 271-2441 • http://www.archives.gov/facilities/ak/anchorage.html

Oscar Anderson House Museum • 420 M St, Elderberry Park • Anchorage, AK 99501 • (907) 274-2336

Russian Orthodox Museum • 605 A Street, P.O. Box 210569 • Anchorage, AK 99521 • (907) 258-7257 • http://www.russianorthodoxmuseum.org

Sons of the American Revolution, Alaska Society • 6552 Lakeway Dr • Anchorage, AK 95502 • (907) 243-4768 • http://www.sar.org/akssar/

Ugashik Traditional Village • 206 E Fireweed Ln, Ste 204 • Anchorage, AK 99503 • (907) 338-7611

University of Alaska Library • 3211 Providence Dr • Anchorage, AK 99508-8176 • (907) 786-1848 • http://www.lib.uaa.alaska.edu

Angoon
Angoon Community Association • P.O. Box 188 • Angoon, AK 99820 • (907) 788-3411

Aniak
Aniak Native Village • P.O. Box 176 • Aniak, AK 99557 • (907) 675-4349

Napaimute Native Village • P.O. Box 96 • Aniak, AK 99557 • (907) 543-2726

Anvik
Anvik Historical Society • Historical Museum, P.O. Box 110 • Anvik, AK 99558 • (907) 663-6366 • http://www.anvik.org

Anvik Village • P.O. Box 10 • Anvik, AK 99558 • (907) 663-6322

Arctic Village
Arctic Village Native Village • P.O. Box 22069 • Arctic Village, AK 99722 • (907) 587-5328

Atka
Atka Native Village • P.O. Box 47030 • Atka, AK 99547 • (907) 839-2229

Atmautluak
Atmautlauk Traditional Council • P.O. Box 6568 • Atmautluak, AK 99559 • (907) 553-5610

Atqasuk
Atqasuk Native Village • P.O. Box 91008 • Atqasuk, AK 99791 • (907) 633-2575

Barrow
Barrow Inupiat Traditional Government • Native Village, 6970 Almaogak St, P.O. Box 1130 • Barrow, AK 99723 • (907) 852-4411

Inupiat Community of Arctic Slope • P.O. Box 934 • Barrow, AK 99723 • (907) 852-6907

Inupiat Heritage Center • 5421 North Star St, P.O. Box 749 • Barrow, AK 99723 • (907) 852-4594 • http://www.echonsb.org

Tuzzy Consortium Library • Ilisagvik College, 5421 N Star St, P.O. Box 2130 • Barrow, AK 99723-0749 • (907) 852-1720 • http://ilisagvik.co.north-slope.ak.us/tuzzy/library/

Beaver
Beaver Village • P.O. Box 24029 • Beaver, AK 99724 • (907) 628-6126

Bethel
Kuskokwim Consortium Library • 420 State Hwy, P.O. Box 368 • Bethel, AK 99559-0368 • (907) 543-4516

Orutsaramuit Native Council • 835 Ridgecrest Dr, P.O. Box 927 • Bethel, AK 99559 • (907) 543-2608

Yugtarvik Regional Museum • 3rd Ave, P.O. Box 338 • Bethel, AK 99559 • (907) 543-2911

Yupiit Piciryarait Cultural Center and Museum • 420 Chief Eddie Hoffman State Highway, P.O. Box 219 • Bethel, AK 99559 • (907) 543-1819 • http://www.avcp.org

Bettles Field
Evansville Native Village • 101 Hickle Hwy, P.O. Box 26087 • Bettles Field, AK 99726 • (907) 692-5005

Big Lake
Big Lake Public Library • Mile 4, S Big Lake Rd, P.O. Box 520829 • Big Lake, AK 99652 • (907) 892-6475 • http://www.biglake-ak.com/library/library.htm

Brevig Mission
Brevig Mission Native Village • P.O. Box 85063 • Brevig Mission, AK 99785 • (907) 642-4301

Buckland
Buckland Native Village • P.O. Box 67 • Buckland, AK 99727 • (907) 494-2171

Central
Circle District Historical Society • Historical Museum, 127 S Mile-Steese Hwy, P.O. Box 30189 • Central, AK 99730 • (907) 520-1893

Chalkyitsik
Chalkyitsik Village • P.O. Box 57 • Chalkyitsik, AK 99788 • (907) 848-8117

Cheformak
Cheformak Native Village • P.O. Box 110 • Cheformak, AK 99561-0110 • (907) 867-8850

Chenega Bay
Chenega Native Village • 824 Cata St, P.O. Box 8079 • Chenega Bay, AK 99574 • (907) 573-5132

Chevak
Chevak Native Village • P.O. Box 140 • Chevak, AK 99563 • (907) 858-7428

Chickaloon
Chickaloon Village Traditional Council • P.O. Box 1105 • Chickaloon, AK 99675-1105 • (907) 745-0707

Chignik
Chignik Native Village • P.O. Box 50 • Chignik, AK 99564 • (907) 749-2445

Chignik Lagoon
Chignik Lagoon Native Village • P.O. Box 9 • Chignik Lagoon, AK 99565 • (907) 840-2281

Chignik Lake
Chignik Lake Traditional Village Council • P.O. Box 33 • Chignik Lake, AK 99548 • (907) 845-2122

Chitina
Chitina Traditional Village • P.O. Box 31 • Chitina, AK 99566 • (907) 823-2215

Chuathbaluk
Chuathbaluk Native Village • P.O. Box CHU • Chuathbaluk, AK 99557-8999 • (907) 467-4313

Chugiak
Chugiak-Eagle River Historical Society • P.O. Box 670573 • Chugiak, AK 99567 • (907) 688-2548

Eklutna Native Village • 26339 Ekutna Native Village Rd • Chugiak, AK 99567 • (907) 688-6020

Chuloonawick
Chuloonawick Native Village • general delivery • Chuloonawick, AK 99581 • (907) 949-1147

Circle
Circle Native Community • P.O. Box 89 • Circle, AK 99733 • (907) 733-2822

Clark's Point
Clark's Point Native Village • P.O. Box 90 • Clark's Point, AK 99569-0090 • (907) 236-1427

Cooper Landing
Cooper Landing Community Library • Bean Creek Rd, P.O. Box 517 • Cooper Landing, AK 99572-0517 • (907) 595-1241

Copper Center
Copper Valley Historical Society • George Ashby Memorial Museum, Mile 101 Richardson Hwy, P.O. Box 84 • Copper Center, AK 99573 • (907) 822-5285 • http://www.coppercenterlodge.com/museum.html

Gakona Native Village • P.O. Box 303 • Copper Center, AK 99573 • (907) 822-4086

Kluti-kaah Native Village • P.O. Box 68 • Copper Center, AK 99573 • (907) 822-5541

Cordova
Cordova Historical Society • Historical Museum, 622 1st St, P.O. Box 391 • Cordova, AK 99574 • (907) 424-6665 • http://www.cordovamuseum.org

Cordova Public Library • 622 1st St, P.O. Box 391 • Cordova, AK 99574-0391 • (907) 424-6667 • http://www.cityofcordova.net

Eyak Native Village • 509 1st St, P.O. Box 1388 • Cordova, AK 99574-1388 • (907) 424-7738 • http://www.nveyak.com

Ilanka Cultural Center Museum • 110 Nicholoff Wy, P.O. Box 322 • Cordova, AK 99574 • (907) 424-7903 • http://www.nveyak.com

Valdez Museum & Historical Archives • P.O. Box 8 • Cordova, AK 99574 • (907) 835-2764

Craig
Craig Community Association • P.O. Box 828 • Craig, AK 99921 • (907) 826-3996

Craig Public Library • 504 3rd St, P.O. Box 769 • Craig, AK 99921-0769 • (907) 826-3281

Crooked Creek
Crooked Creek Native Village • P.O. Box 69 • Crooked Creek, AK 99575 • (907) 432-2201

Deering
Deering Native Village • P.O. Box 36089 • Deering, AK 99736 • (907) 363-2138

Ipnatchiaq Public Library • 59 Main St, P.O. Box 70 • Deering, AK 99736-9999 • (907) 363-2136

Delta Junction
Alaska Homestead and Historical Museum • Mile 1415.4 Alaska Hwy & Darshorst Rd, P.O. Box 389 • Delta Junction, AK 99737 • (907) 785-4431

Delta Historical Society • Big Delta State Historical Park, Mile 275 Richardson Hwy, P.O. Box 1089 • Delta Junction, AK 99737 • (907) 895-4201 • http://www.rikas.com

Rika's Roadhouse and Landing Museum • Mile 275 Richardson Hwy, P.O. Box 1229 • Delta Junction, AK 99737 • http://www.rikas.com

Ruth Riggs Library Association • 8.5 Mile Jack Warren Rd, HC 60 Box 3780 • Delta Junction, AK 99737-9455 • (907) 895-4408 • http://www.akpub.com/aktt/riggs.html

Sullivan Roadhouse Historical Museum • Mile 267 Richardson Hwy, P.O. Box 987 • Delta Junction, AK 99737 • http://www.alaskan.com/sullivanroadhouse

Denali National Park
Denali National Park & Preserve Library • Milepost 237, George Parks Hwy, P.O. Box 9 • Denali National Park, AK 99755-0009 • (907) 683-9536 • www.nps.gov/dena

Dillingham
Curyung Tribal Council • 134 1st Ave W, P.O. Box 216 • Dillingham, AK 99576 • (907) 842-2384

Dillingham Native Village • P.O. Box 216 • Dillingham, AK 99576 • (907) 842-2384

Dillingham Public Library • 361 D St W, P.O. Box 870 • Dillingham, AK 99576-0870 • (907) 842-5610 • http://www.ci.dillingham.ak.us/library.html

Samuel K Fox Museum • 306 D Street W, P.O. Box 870 • Dillingham, AK 99576 • (907) 842-5610 • http://www.nushtel.com/~dlgchmbr

Diomede
Diomede-Inalik Native Village • P.O. Box 7079 • Diomede, AK 99762 • (907) 686-2175

Dot Lake
Dot Lake Village Council • P.O. Box 2279 • Dot Lake, AK 99737-2279 • (907) 882-2695

Eagle
Eagle Native Village • P.O. Box 19 • Eagle, AK 99738 • (907) 547-2271

Eagle City
Eagle Historical Society • Historical Museum, 3rd & Chamberlain, P.O. Box 23 • Eagle City, AK 99738 • (907) 547-2325 • http://www.eagleak.org

Eek
Eek Native Village • P.O. Box 87 • Eek, AK 99578 • (907) 536-5128

Egelik
Egegik Village • P.O. Box 29 • Egelik, AK 99579 • (907) 233-2211

Ekuk
Ekuk Native Village • general delivery • Ekuk, AK 99576 • (907) 842-5937

Ekwok
Ekwok Village Council • 100 Main St, P.O. Box 70 • Ekwok, AK 99580 • (907) 464-3336

Elfin Cove
Elfin Cove Museum • P.O. Box 36 • Elfin Cove, AK 99825 • (907) 239-2222

Elim
Elim Native Village • P.O. Box 70 • Elim, AK 99739-0070 • (907) 890-3737

Elmendorf AFB
Elmendorf Air Force Base Library • 10480 22nd St • Elmendorf AFB, AK 99506-2530 • (907) 552-3787 • http://www.elmendorfservices.com/pages/library/library1.html

Emmonak
Emmonak Village • P.O. box 126 • Emmonak, AK 99581 • (907) 949-1720

Fairbanks
Alaskaland Pioneer Air Museum • P.O. Box 70437 • Fairbanks, AK 99707-0437 • (907) 451-0037

Catholic Diocese of Fairbanks Archives • Chancery Bldg, 1316 Peger Rd • Fairbanks, AK 99709 • (907) 474-0753 • http://www.cbna.org

Elmer E Rasmuson Library • Univ of Alaska Fairbanks, 310 Tanana Dr, P.O. Box 756800 • Fairbanks, AK 99775-6800 • (907) 474-7482 • http://www.uaf.edu/library/

Fairbanks Community Museum • Old City Hall, 410 Cushman • Fairbanks, AK 99701 • (907) 457-3669 • http://www.fairbankscommunitymuseum.com

Fairbanks Genealogical Society • P.O. Box 60534 • Fairbanks, AK 99706-0534 • (907) 479-2895 • http://www.ptialaska.net/~fgs/

Fairbanks Historical Preservation Foundation • 2400 Airport Way • Fairbanks, AK 99701 • (907) 456-8848

Fairbanks Native Association • Historical Museum, 605 Hughes Ave • Fairbanks, AK 99701 • (907) 452-1658 • http://www.fairbanksnative.org

Fairbanks North Star Borough Public Library • 1215 Cowles St • Fairbanks, AK 99701 • (907) 459-1020 • http://www.library.fnsb.lib.ak.us

Healy Lake Traditional Council • P.O. Box 60300 • Fairbanks, AK 99706 • (907) 876-5018

Museum of the North • Univ of Alaska Fairbanks, 907 Yukon Dr, P.O. Box 756960 • Fairbanks, AK 99775-6960 • (907) 474-7505 • http://www.uaf.alaska.edu/museum

Pioneer Museum & Big Stampede Show • Pioneer Park, 2300 Airport Wy, P.O. Box 70176 • Fairbanks, AK 99707 • (907) 459-1087 • http://co.fairbanks.ak.us/pioneerpark/attractions/museums/pioneer_museum.htm

Tanana-Yukon Historical Society • Wickersham House Museum, Airport Wy & Peger Rd, P.O. Box 71336 • Fairbanks, AK 99707 • (907) 455-8947 • http://www.fairbankshistory.org/

Wickersham House Museum • Pioneer Park, 2400 Airport Wy, P.O. Box 71336 • Fairbanks, AK 99707 • (907) 455-8947 • http://www.fairbankshistory.org

Alaska

False Pass
False Pass Native Village • P.O. Box 29 • False Pass, AK 99583 • (907) 548-2227

Fort Richardson
Fort Richardson Post Library • Bldg 5, Chilkoot Ave • Fort Richardson, AK 99505-0005 • (907) 384-1640

Fort Wainwright
Fort Wainwright Post Library • 1060 Gaffney Rd • Fort Wainwright, AK 99703-7130 • (907) 353-2642

Fort Yukon
Birch Creek Village • P.O. Box KBC • Fort Yukon, AK 99740 • (907) 221-2211

Fort Yukon Native Village • 3rd & Alder, P.O. Box 126 • Fort Yukon, AK 99740 • (907) 662-2581

Fortuna Ledge
Marshall Native Village • P.O. Box 110 • Fortuna Ledge, AK 99585 • (907) 679-6302

Ohogamiut Native Village • general delivery • Fortuna Ledge, AK 99585 • (907) 679-6740

Gakona
Cheesh-Na Tribal Council • P.O. Box 241 • Gakona, AK 99586 • (907) 822-3503

Gulkana Indian Village • P.O. Box 254 • Gakona, AK 99586 • (907) 822-5213

Galena
Charles Evans Community Library • 299 Atoski Dr, P.O. Box 149 • Galena, AK 99741-0149 • (907) 656-2105

Galena Indian Village • P.O. Box 38 • Galena, AK 99741 • (907) 656-1609

Louden Tribal Council • P.O. Box 244 • Galena, AK 99741 • (907) 656-1711

Gambell
Gambell Native Village • P.O. Box 90 • Gambell, AK 99742 • (907) 985-5346

Girdwood
Crow Creek Mine Museum • Mile 3.2 Crow Creek Rd, P.O. Box 113 • Girdwood, AK 99587

Glennallen
Ahtna Heritage Foundation • Historical Museum, Mile 106.8 Richardson Hwy, P.O. Box 231 • Glennallen, AK 99588 • http://www.ahtna-inc.com/heritage_foundation.html

Tazlina Native Village • P.O. Box 87 • Glenallen, AK 99588 • (907) 822-4375

Golovin
Chinik Eskimo Community - Golovin • P.O. Box 62020 • Golovin, AK 99762 • (907) 779-2214

Goodnews Bay
Goodnews Bay Native Village • P.O. Box 3 • Goodnews Bay, AK 99589 • (907) 967-8929

Grayling
Grayling Native Village • general delivery • Grayling, AK 99590 • (907) 453-5116

Haines
Chilkat Indian Village - Klukwan • P.O. Box 210 • Haines, AK 99827-0210 • (907) 767-5505

Chilkat Valley Historical Society • Sheldon Museum, 11 Main St, P.O. Box 269 • Haines, AK 99827 • (907) 877-2366 • http://www.sheldonmuseum.org

Chilkoot Indian Association • 207 Main St, St 2, P.O. Box 490 • Haines, AK 99827-0490 • (907) 766-2323

Haines Borough Public Library • P.O. Box 1089 • Haines, AK 99827-1089 • (907) 766-2545

Sheldon Museum and Cultural Center • 11 Main St, P.O. Box 269 • Haines, AK 99827-0269 • (907) 766-2366 • http://www.sheldonmuseum.org

Holy Cross
Holy Cross Indian Village • P.O. Box 89 • Holy Cross, AK 99602 • (907) 476-7124

Homer
Pratt Museum • 3779 Bartlett St • Homer, AK 99603 • (907) 235-2764 • http://www.prattmuseum.org

Hoonah
Hoonah Indian Association • P.O. Box 602 • Hoonah, AK 99829-0602 • (907) 945-3545

Hooper Bay
Hooper Bay Native Village • P.O. Box 41 • Hooper Bay, AK 99604 • (907) 758-4915

Piamuit Native Village • general delivery • Hooper Bay, AK 99604 • (907) 758-4420

Hope
Hope-Sunrise Historical and Mining Museum • 2nd Ave, P.O. Box 88 • Hope, AK 99605 • (907) 782-3740 • http://www.advenalaska.com/hope

Hughes
Hughes Indian Village • P.O. Box 45029 • Hughes, AK 99745 • (907) 889-2239

Huslia
Huslia Cultural Center • P.O. Box 70 • Huslia, AK 99746 • (907) 829-2294

Hydaburg
Hydaburg Cooperative Association • P.O. Box 349 • Hydaburg, AK 99922 • (907) 285-3666

Iguigig
Iguigig Indian Village • P.O. Box 4008 • Iguigig, AK 99613 • (907) 533-3211

Iliamna
Iliamna Native Village • P.O. Box 286 • Iliamna, AK 99606 • (907) 571-1246

Juneau
Alaska Department of Health and Social Services, Bureau of Vital Statistics • 5441 Commercial Blvd, P.O. Box 110675 • Juneau, AK 99811-0675 • (907) 465-3391 • http://vitalrecords.alaska.gov/dph/bvs/

Alaska State Archives & Records Management Services • 141 Willoughby Ave • Juneau, AK 99801-1720 • (907) 465-2275 • http://www.archives.state.ak.us

Alaska State Library • Alaska Historical Library, 333 Willoughby Ave, 8th Fl, P.O. Box 110571 • Juneau, AK 99811 • (907) 465-2910 • http://www.library.state.ak.us

Alaska State Museum • 395 Whittier St, P.O. Box 110571 • Juneau, AK 99801-1718 • (907) 465-2910 • http://www.museums.state.ak.us

Aukquan Traditional Council • 9296 Stephen Richards Memorial Dr • Juneau, AK 99801 • (907) 790-2550

Central Council of Tlingit and Haida Tribes of Alaska • 320 W Willoughby Ave, Ste 300 • Juneau, AK 99801 • (907) 586-1432 • http://www.ccthita.org

Douglas Indian Association • P.O. Box 240541 • Juneau, AK 99824 • (907) 364-2916

Gastineau Channel Historical Society • P.O. Box 21264 • Juneau, AK 99802 • (907) 586-5235

Gastineau Genealogical Society • 3270 Nowell Ave • Juneau, AK 99801 • (907) 586-3695

House of Wickersham Museum • 213 7th St • Juneau, AK 99801 • (907) 465-4563

Juneau Public Libraries • 292 Marine Way • Juneau, AK 99801 • (907) 586-5324 • http://www.juneau.lib.ak.us

Juneau-Douglas City Museum • 155 S Seward St • Juneau, AK 99801 • (907) 586-3572 • http://www.juneau.lib.ak.us/parksrec/museum/

Kake Tribal Heritage Foundation • 3017 Clinton Dr, Ste 100, P.O. Box 263 • Juneau, AK 99801 • (907) 790-2214

Last Chance Mining Museum • 1001 Basin Rd • Juneau, AK 99801 • (907) 586-5338

Sealaska Heritage Foundation • 1 Sealaska Plaza, Ste 201 • Juneau, AK 99801 • (907) 463-4844 • http://www.shfonline.org

Sentinel Island Lighthouse Museum • Lynn Canal, P.O. Box 21264 • Juneau, AK 99802 • (907) 586-5338

Kake
Kake Native Village • 541 Keku Rd, P.O. Box 316 • Kake, AK 99830 • (907) 785-6471

Kaktovik
Kaktovik Indian Village • P.O. Box 8 • Kaktovik, AK 99607 • (907) 640-6120

Kalskag
Kalskag Native Village • P.O. Box 50 • Kalskag, AK 99607 • (907) 471-2248

Kaltag
Kaltag Native Village • P.O. Box 129 • Kaltag, AK 99748 • (907) 534-2224

Karluk
Karluk Native Village • P.O. Box 22 • Karluk, AK 99608 • (907) 241-2218

Kasigluk
Kasigluk Native Village • P.O. Box 19 • Kasigluk, AK 99609 • (907) 477-6405

Kasilof
Kasilof Public Library • Mile 110 Sterling Hwy, P.O. Box 176 • Kasilof, AK 99610-0176 • (907) 262-4844

Kenai
K'beq: Kenaitze Indian Tribe • Historical Museum, 255 Ames St, P.O. Box 988 • Kenai, AK 99611-0988 • (907) 283-3633 • http://www.kenaitze.org

Kenai Community Library • 163 Main St Loop • Kenai, AK 99611 • (907) 283-4378 • http://www.kenalibrary.org

Kenai Historical Society • P.O. Box 1348 • Kenai, AK 99611 • (907) 283-7618

Kenai Totem Tracers • c/o Kenai Community Library, 163 Main St Loop, P.O. Box 4380 • Kenai, AK 99611-7723 • (907) 283-4378

Kenai Visitors & Cultural Center • 11471 Kenai Spur Hwy • Kenai, AK 99611 • (907) 283-1991

Kenitzee Indian Tribe • K'Beq' Museum, Mile 52.6 Kenai Spur Hwy, P.O. Box 988 • Kenai, AK 99611 • (907) 283-3633 • http://www.kenaitze.org

Salamatof Native Village • P.O. Box 2682 • Kenai, AK 99611 • (907) 283-6764

Ketchikan
Genealogical Society of Southeast Alaska • P.O. Box 6313 • Ketchikan, AK 99901-1313

Historic Ketchikan • 305 Main St #232 • Ketchikan, AK 99901-6445 • (907) 225-5515

Kassaan Native Village • P.O. Box KXA • Ketchikan, AK 99950-0340 • (907) 542-2230

Ketchikan Indian Corporation • 2960 Tongass Ave • Ketchikan, AK 99901 • (907) 225-5158

Kuiu Kwaan Tlingit Nation • P.O. Box 5531 • Ketchikan, AK 99901 • (425) 483-9251

Saxman Native Village • Route 2, Box 2 • Ketchikan, AK 99901 • (907) 247-2502

Southeast Alaska Visitor Center • 50 Main St • Ketchikan, AK 99901 • http://www.nps.gov/aplic/

Tongass Historical Museum • Totem Heritage Center, 629 Dock St • Ketchikan, AK 99901 • (907) 225-5600 • http://www.city.ketchikan.ak.us/ds/tonghist/

Totem Heritage Center • 629 Dock St • Ketchikan, AK 99901 • (907) 225-5900 • http://www.city.ketchikan.ak.us/ds/tonghert/

Kiana
Kiana Native Village • P.O. Box 69 • Kiana, AK 99749 • (907) 475-2109

King Cove
Agdaagux Tribe of King Cove • P.O. Box 249 • King Cove, AK 99612 • (907) 497-2648

Belkofski Native Village • P.O. Box 57 • King Cove, AK 99612 • (907) 497-3122

King Salmon
King Salmon Village Council • 1/2 Mile Marker, King Salmon Creek Rd, P.O. Box 68 • King Salmon, AK 99613-0068 • (907) 246-3553

Kipnuk
Kipnuk Native Village • P.O. Box 57 • Kipnuk, AK 99614 • (907) 896-5515

Kivalina
Kivalina Native Village • P.O. Box 50051 • Kivalina, AK 99750 • (907) 645-2153

Klawock
Klawock Cooperative Association • 403 Bayview Blvd, P.O. Box 430 • Klawock, AK 99925-0430 • (907) 755-2265

Kobuk
Kobuk Traditional Council • P.O. Box 39 • Kobuk, AK 99751 • (907) 948-2203

Kodiak
Afognak Native Village • 212 Mission Rd, Ste 014, P.O. Box 968 • Kodiak, AK 99615 • (907) 486-6357

Alutiiq Museum and Archaelogical Repository • 215 Mission Rd, Ste 101 • Kodiak, AK 99615 • (907) 486-7004 • http://www.alutiigmuseum.com

Carolyn Floyd Library • Kodiak College, 117 Benny Benson Dr • Kodiak, AK 99615-6643 • (907) 486-1241 • http://www.koc.alaska.edu/library/

Kodiac Public Library • 319 Lower Mill Bay Rd • Kodiak, AK 99615 • (907) 486-8686

Kodiak Historical Society • Baranov Museum, 101 Marine Way, P.O. Box 61 • Kodiak, AK 99615 • (907) 486-5920 • http://www.baranov.us

Kodiak Military History Museum • Ft Abercrombie State Historical Park, 1623 Mill Bay Rd • Kodiak, AK 99615 • (907) 486-7015 • http://www.kodiak.org

Kodiak, cont.

Kodiak Museum of the History of the Orthodox Church in Alaska • St Herman's Theological Seminary, 414 Mission Rd • Kodiak, AK 99615 • (907) 486-3524

Lesnoi Indian Village • P.O. Box 9009 • Kodiak, AK 99615 • (907) 486-2821

Shoonaq' Tribe of Kodiak • 713 E Rezanof Dr, #B • Kodiak, AK 99615 • (907) 486-4449

Kokhanok

Kokhanok Indian Village • P.O. Box 1007 • Kokhanok, AK 99606 • (907) 282-2202

Koliganek

New Koliganek Indian Village Council • P.O. Box 5057 • Koliganek, AK 99576 • (907) 596-3434

Kotlik

Hamilton Native Village • P.O. Box 20248 • Kotlik, AK 99620 • (907) 899-4252

Kotlik Native Village • P.O. Box 20210 • Kotlik, AK 99620 • (907) 899-4326

Native Village of Bill Moore's Slough • P.O. Box 20288 • Kotlik, AK 99620 • (907) 899-4232

Kotzebue

Kotzebue Museum • P.O. Box 46 • Kotzebue, AK 99752 • (907) 442-3747

Kotzebue Native Village • P.O. Box 296 • Kotzebue, AK 99752 • (907) 442-3467

NANA Museum of the Arctic • 100 Shore Ave, P.O. Box 49 • Kotzebue, AK 99752 • (907) 442-3304

Koyuk

Koyuk Native Village • P.O. Box 53030 • Koyuk, AK 99753 • (907) 963-3651

Koyukuk

Koyukuk Native Village • P.O. Box 109 • Koyukuk, AK 99754 • (907) 927-2253

Kwethluk

Kwethluk Native Village • P.O. Box 129 • Kwethluk, AK 99621-0129 • (907) 757-6714

Kwigillingok

Kwigillingok Native Village • P.O. Box 49 • Kwigillingok, AK 99622 • (907) 588-8114

Lake Arrowhead

Rim of the World Historical Society • P.O. Box 1550 • Lake Arrowhead, AK 92352 • (909) 336-6666 • http://www.rimoftheworldhistory.com

Larsen Bay

Larsen Bay Native Village • P.O. Box 35 • Larsen Bay, AK 99624 • (907) 847-2207

Levelock

Levelock Indian Village • P.O. Box 70 • Levelock, AK 99625 • (907) 287-3030

Lower Kalsag

Lower Kalskag Native Village • P.O. Box 27 • Lower Kalsag, AK 99626 • (907) 471-2307

Manley Hot Springs

Manley Hot Springs Indian Village • P.O. Box 23 • Manley Hot Springs, AK 99756 • (907) 672-3178

Manokotak

Manokotak Indian Village • P.O. Box 169 • Manokotak, AK 99628 • (907) 289-2067

McGrath

McGrath Community Library • 12 Chinana Ave, P.O. Box 249 • McGrath, AK 99627-0249 • (907) 524-3843

McGrath Native Village • P.O. Box 134 • McGrath, AK 99627 • (907) 524-3024

Telida Native Village • P.O. Box 32 • McGrath, AK 99627 • (907) 524-3550

Mekoryuk

Mekoryuk Native Village • P.O. Box 66 • Mekoryuk, AK 99630 • (907) 827-8828

Mentaska Lake

Mentasta Traditional Tribal Council • P.O. Box 6019 • Mentaska Lake, AK 99780-6019 • (907) 291-2319

Metlakatla

Duncan Cottage Museum • 501 Tait St, P.O. Box 8 • Metlakatla, AK 99926 • (907) 886-7363 • http://tours.metlakatla.net

Metlakatla Indian Community • Historical Museum, Tait St, P.O. Box 8 • Metlakatla, AK 99926 • (907) 886-4441 • http://www.ezec.gov/Communit/metlakatla.html

Minto

Minto Native Village • P.O. Box 58026 • Minto, AK 99758-0026 • (907) 798-7112

Mountain Village

Asa' Carsarmuit Tribe of Mountain Village • P.O. Box 32249 • Mountain Village, AK 99632 • (907) 591-2814

Naknek

Bristol Bay Historical Society • P.O. Box 36 • Naknek, AK 99633 • (907) 246-4406

Naknek Native Village • P.O. Box 106 • Naknek, AK 99633 • (907) 246-4210

Nanwalek

Nanwalek Native Village • P.O. Box 8028 • Nanwalek, AK 99603 • (907) 281-2274

Napakiak

Napakiak Native Village • P.O. Box 34069 • Napakiak, AK 99634 • (907) 589-2135

Napaskiak

Napaskiak Native Village • P.O. Box 6009 • Napaskiak, AK 99559 • (907) 737-7364

Oscarville Traditional Council • P.O. Box 6129 • Napaskiak, AK 99559 • (907) 737-7099

Nelson Lagoon

Nelson Lagoon Native Village • P.O. Box 13 • Nelson Lagoon, AK 99571 • (907) 989-2204

Nenana

Alfred Starr Nenana Cultural Center • 415 Riverfront, P.O. Box 1 • Nenana, AK 99760 • (907) 832-5532

Nenana Native Association • 307.8 Mile Parks Hwy, P.O. Box 356 • Nenana, AK 99760 • (907) 832-5461

Nenana Public Library • 202 E 2nd & Market, P.O. Box 40 • Nenana, AK 99760-0040 • (907) 832-5812

New Stuyahok

New Stuyahok Village • P.O. Box 49 • New Stuyahok, AK 99636 • (907) 693-3173

Newhalen

Newhalen Village • P.O. Box 206 TLF • Newhalen, AK 99606 • (907) 571-1410

Newtok
Newtok Native Village • P.O. Box 5545 • Newtok, AK 99559 • (907) 237-2314

Nightmute
Nightmute Native Village • P.O. Box 90021 • Nightmute, AK 99690 • (907) 647-6215

Umkumiute Native Village • general delivery • Nightmute, AK 99690 • (907) 647-6213

Nikolai
Nikolai Native Village • P.O. Box 9105 • Nikolai, AK 99691 • (907) 293-2311

Nikolski
Nikolski Native Village • P.O. Box 109 • Nikolski, AK 99638 • (907) 576-2225

Ninilchik
Ninilchik Traditional Tribal Council • 15910 Sterling Hwy, P.O. Box 39070 • Ninilchik, AK 99639 • (907) 567-3313

Noatak
Noatak Native Village • P.O. Box 89 • Noatak, AK 99761 • (907) 485-2173

Nome
Carrie M McLain Memorial Museum • 200 E Front St, P.O. Box 53 • Nome, AK 99762 • (907) 443-6630 • http://www.nomealaska.org

Kegoayah Kozga Public Library • 223 Front St, P.O. Box 1168 • Nome, AK 99762-1168 • (907) 443-6628

King Island Native Community • P.O. Box 992 • Nome, AK 99762 • (907) 443-5494

Nome Eskimo Community • P.O. Box 1090 • Nome, AK 99762 • (907) 443-2246

Nome Native Village Council • P.O. Box 2050 • Nome, AK 99762 • (907) 443-7649

Solomon Native Village • P.O. Box 2053 • Nome, AK 99762 • (907) 443-4985

Nondalton
Nondalton Native Village • P.O. Box 49 • Nondalton, AK 99640 • (907) 294-2257

Noorvik
Noorvik Native Communities • P.O. Box 71 • Noorvik, AK 99763 • (907) 636-2144

Northway
Northway Native Village • P.O. Box 516 • Northway, AK 99764 • (907) 778-2231

Nuiqsut
Nuiqsut Native Village • P.O. Box 112 • Nuiqsut, AK 99723 • (907) 480-3250

Nulato
Nulato Native Village • P.O. Box 65049 • Nulato, AK 99765 • (907) 898-2339

Nunapitchuk
Nunapitchuk Native Village • P.O. Box 130 • Nunapitchuk, AK 99641 • (907) 527-5705

Old Harbor
Old Harbor Native Village • P.O. Box 62 • Old Harbor, AK 99643 • (907) 286-2215

Ouzinkie
Ouzinkie Native Village • P.O. Box 130 • Ouzinkie, AK 99644 • (907) 680-2259

Palmer
Alpine Historical Park • P.O. Box 266 • Palmer, AK 99645 • (907) 745-7000

Alvin S Okeson Library • Univ of Alaska Anchorage, Matanuska-Susitna College, Mile Two Trunk Rd, P.O. Box 5001 • Palmer, AK 99645-5001 • (907) 745-9740 • http://www.matsu.alaska.edu

Historical Society of Palmer • HC 4, Box 7043 • Palmer, AK 99645 • (907) 746-0609

Palmer Historical Society • Colony House Museum, 316 E Elmwood Ave, P.O. Box 1925 • Palmer, AK 99645-1925 • (907) 745-3703 • http://www.palmerhistoricalsociety.org

Palmer Museum of History and Art • Palmer Visitors Center, 723 S Valley Way • Palmer, AK 99654 • (907) 746-7668 • http://www.palmermuseum.org

Palmer Public Library • 655 S Valley Wy • Palmer, AK 99645 • (907) 745-4690 • http://www.matsulibraries.org/palmer

Pedro Bay
Pedro Bay Native Village • P.O. Box 47020 • Pedro Bay, AK 99647 • (907) 850-2225

Perryville
Ivanoff Bay Indian Village • P.O. Box 500 • Perryville, AK 99648 • (907) 669-2200

Perryville Native Village • P.O. Box 101 • Perryville, AK 99648-0101 • (907) 853-2203

Petersburg
Clausen Memorial Museum • 203 Fram St, P.O. Box 708 • Petersburg, AK 99833 • (907) 772-3598 • http://www.clausenmuseum.alaska.net

Petersburg Indian Association • P.O. Box 1418 • Petersburg, AK 99833 • (907) 772-3636

Petersburg Public Library • 12 Nordic Ave, P.O. Box 549 • Petersburg, AK 99833 • (907) 772-3349 • http://ci.petersburg.ak.us/library/lib.html

Pilot Point
Pilot Point Native Village • P.O. Box 449 • Pilot Point, AK 99649 • (907) 797-2208

Pilot Station
Pilot Station Traditional Council • P.O. box 5119 • Pilot Station, AK 99650 • (907) 549-3373

Platinum
Platinum Traditional Village • P.O. Box 8 • Platinum, AK 99651 • (907) 979-8220

Point Hope
Point Hope Native Village • 910 Ippiq St, P.O. Box 109 • Point Hope, AK 99766 • (907) 368-2330

Point Lay
Point Lay Native Village • P.O. Box 101 • Point Lay, AK 99759 • (907) 833-2428

Port Graham
Port Graham Native Village • P.O. Box 5510 • Port Graham, AK 99603 • (907) 284-2227

Port Heiden
Port Heiden Native Village • P.O. Box 49007 • Port Heiden, AK 99549 • (907) 837-2296

Port Lions
Port Lions Native Village • 2006 Airport Rd, P.O. Box 69 • Port Lions, AK 99550 • (907) 454-2234

Portage Creek
Portage Creek Native Village • P.O. Box 330 • Portage Creek, AK 99576 • (907) 842-5218

Alaska

Quinhagak
Kwinhagak Native Village • P.O. Box 149 • Quinhagak, AK 99655 • (907) 556-8165

Rampart
Rampart Native Village • P.O. Box 67029 • Rampart, AK 99767 • (907) 358-3312

Red Devil
Red Devil Native Village • P.O. Box 61 • Red Devil, AK 99656 • (907) 447-3225

Ruby
Ruby Native Village • P.O. Box 210 • Ruby, AK 99768 • (907) 468-4479

Russian Mission
Iqurmuit Tribe • P.O. Box 9 • Russian Mission, AK 99657 • (907) 584-5511

Saint George
Aleut Community of Saint George • P.O. Box 940 • Saint George, AK 99591 • (907) 859-2205

Saint Mary's
Algaaciq Native Village • 200 Paukan Ave, P.O. Box 48 • Saint Mary's, AK 99658 • (907) 438-2932

Andreafski Tribal Council • P.O. Box 88 • Saint Mary's, AK 99658-0088 • (907) 438-2312

Pitka's Point Native Village • P.O. Box 127 • Saint Mary's, AK 99658 • (9070 438-2833

Yuplit of Andreafski Tribe • P.O. Box 368 • Saint Mary's, AK 99658 • (907) 438-2312

Saint Michael
Saint Michael Native Village • P.O. Box 59050 • Saint Michael, AK 99659 • (907) 923-2304

Saint Paul Island
Aleut Community of Saint Paul Island • P.O. Box 86 • Saint Paul Island, AK 99660 • (907) 546-2211

Sand Point
Pauloff Harbor Native Village • P.O. Box 194 • Sand Point, AK 99661

Qagun Tayagungin Tribe of Sand Point • P.O. Box 447 • Sand Point, AK 99661 • (907) 383-5616

Unga Native Village • P.O. Box 508 • Sand Point, AK 99661 • (907) 383-5215

Savoonga
Savoonga Native Village • P.O. Box 120 • Savoonga, AK 99769 • (907) 985-6414

Scammon Bay
Scammon Bay Native Village • 100 Front St, P.O. Box 126 • Scammon Bay, AK 99662 • (907) 558-5425

Selawik
Selawik Native Village • P.O. Box 59 • Selawik, AK 99770 • (907) 484-2225

Seldovia
Seldovia Village Tribe • 328 Main St, P.O. Box L • Seldovia, AK 99663 • (907) 234-7898

Seward
Chugach Heritage Center • 501 Railway Ave, P.O. Box 2388 • Seward, AK 99664 • (907) 563-8866 • http://www.chugachmuseum.org

Resurrection Bay Historical Society • Seward Museum, 336 3rd Ave, P.O. Box 55 • Seward, AK 99664 • (907) 224-3902

Seward Community Library • 238 5th Ave, P.O. Box 2389 • Seward, AK 99664-2389 • (907) 224-4082 • http://library.cityofseward.net

Shageluk
Shageluk Native Village • P.O. Box 35 • Shageluk, AK 96665 • (907) 473-8239

Shaktoolik
Shaktoolik Native Village • P.O. Box 100 • Shaktoolik, AK 99771-0100 • (907) 955-3701

Sheldon's Point
Sheldon's Point Native Village - Nunam Iqua Tribal Council • P.O. Box 27 • Sheldon's Point, AK 99666-0027 • (907) 498-4184

Shishmaref
Shishmaref Native Village • P.O. Box 72110 • Shishmaref, AK 99772 • (907) 649-3821

Shishmaref Tannery & Melvin Olanna Carving Center • P.O. Box 72067 • Shishmaref, AK 99772

Shungnak
Shungnak Native Village • P.O. Box 64 • Shungnak, AK 99773 • (907) 437-2163

Sitka
Kettleson Memorial Library • 320 Harbor Dr • Sitka, AK 99835-7553 • (907) 747-8708

Russian Bishop's House Museum • Lincoln St, P.O. Box 738 • Sitka, AK 99835 • (907) 747-6281

Sheldon Jackson Museum • 104 College Dr, P.O. Box 479 • Sitka, AK 99835 • (907) 747-8981 • http://www.museums.state.ak.us

Sitka Historical Society • Isabel Miller Museum, 330 Harbor Dr, P.O. Box 6181 • Sitka, AK 99835 • (907) 747-6455 • http://www.sitkahistory.org

Sitka National Historical Park • 106 Metlakatla St, P.O. Box 738 • Sitka, AK 99835 • (907) 747-0110 • http://www.nps.gov/sitk

Sitka Tribe of Alaska • 456 Katlia St • Sitka, AK 99835-7505 • (907) 747-3207

Southeast Alaska Indian Cultural Center • 106 Metlakatla St, Ste C • Sitka, AK 99835 • (907) 747-8061

Stratton Library • Sheldon Jackson College, 801 Lincoln St, SJC Box 120 • Sitka, AK 99835 • (907) 747-5259 • http://http://www.sheldonjackson.edu/661.cfm

Skagway
Klondike Gold Rush International Historical Park • 2nd Ave & Broadway, P.O. Box 517 • Skagway, AK 99840-0517 • (907) 983-2921 • http://www.nps.gov/klgo

Skagway Historical Museum • 700 Spring St, P.O. Box 521 • Skagway, AK 99840 • (907) 983-2420 • http://www.skagwaymuseum.org

Skagway Traditional Council • P.O. Box 1157 • Skaway, AK 99840 • (907) 983-4068

Trail of `98 City Museum • 7th & Spring Sts, P.O. Box 415 • Skagway, AK 99840 • (907) 983-2420

Sleetmute
Sleetmute Native Village • P.O. Box 34 • Sleetmute, AK 99668 • (907) 449-4205

Soldotna
Kenai Peninsula College Library • 34820 College Dr • Soldotna, AK 99669-8245 • (907) 262-0385 • http://www.kpc.alaska.edu

Soldotna Historical Society • Historical Museum, Centennial Park Rd, P.O. Box 1986 • Soldotna, AK 99669 • (907) 262-3756

South Naknek
South Naknek Village • P.O. Box 70029 • South Naknek, AK 99670 • (907) 246-8614

Stebbins
Stebbins Native Community Association • P.O. Box 71002 • Stebbins, AK 99671 • (907) 934-2653

Stevens Village
Stevens Native Village • P.O. Box 74016 • Stevens Village, AK 99774 • (907) 478-7228

Sutton
Alpine Historical Park • Mile 61.5 Glenn Highway, P.O. Box 266 • Sutton, AK 99674 • (907) 745-7000

Takutat
Yakutat Tlingit Tribe • P.O. Box 418 • Takutat, AK 99689 • (907) 784-3238

Talkeetna
Talkeetna Historical Society • Historical Museum, P.O. Box 76 • Talkeetna, AK 99676 • (907) 733-2487 • http://www.talkeetnahistoricalsociety.org

Tanacross
Heritage Resources • Tanacross, AK 99776 • (907) 883-5444

Tanacross Native Village • P.O. Box 76009 • Tanacross, AK 99776 • (907) 883-5024

Tanana
Tanana Native Village • P.O. Box 130 • Tanana, AK 99777 • (907) 366-7160

Tatitlek
Tatitlek Native Village • P.O. Box 171 • Tatitlek, AK 99677 • (907) 325-2311

Teller
Mary's Igloo Native Village • P.O. Box 630 • Teller, AK 99778 • (907) 642-3731

Teller Native Village • P.O. Box 567 • Teller, AK 99778 • (907) 642-3381

Tetlin
Tetlin Native Village • P.O. Box TTL • Tetlin, AK 99779 • (907) 324-2130

Thorne Bay
Thorne Bay Community Library • 1218 B Shoreline Dr, P.O. Box 19109 • Thorne Bay, AK 99919-0109 • (907) 828-3321

Togiak
Traditional Village of Togiak • P.O. Box 310 • Togiak, AK 99678 • (907) 493-5004

Toksook
Nunakauyak Traditional Council • P.O. Box 37048 • Toksook, AK 99637-7048 • (907) 427-7114

Trapper Creek
Trapper Creek Museum • Petersville Rd & Parks Hwy, P.O. Box 13011 • Trapper Creek, AK 99683 • (907) 733-2557 • http://www.trappercreekmuseum.com

Trapper Creek Public Library • Mile 115 Parks Hwy, P.O. Box 13388 • Trapper Creek, AK 99683-0388 • (907) 733-1546

Tuluksak
Tuluksak Native Community • P.O Box 95 • Tuluksak, AK 99679-0095 • (907) 695-6420

Tuntutuliak
Tuntutuliak Native Village • general delivery • Tuntutuliak, AK 99680 • (907) 256-2441

Twin Hills
Twin Hills Native Village • P.O. Box TWA • Twin Hills, AK 99576-8996 • (907) 525-4821

Tyonek
Tyonek Native Village • P.O. Box 82009 • Tyonek, AK 99682-0009 • (907) 583-2271

Unalakleet
Ticasuk Library • 28 Softball Field, P.O. Box 28 • Unalakleet, AK 99684-0028 • (907) 624-3053

Unalakleet Native Village • P.O. Box 270 • Unalakleet, AK 99684 • (907) 624-3622

Unalaska
Museum of the Aleutians • P.O. Box 648 • Unalaska, AK 99685 • (907) 581-5150 • http://www.aleutians.org

Qawalangin Tribe of Unalaska • 205 W Broadway, P.O. Box 334 • Unalaska, AK 99685 • (907) 581-2920

Unalaska Public Library • 64 Eleanor Dr, P.O. Box 1370 • Unalaska, AK 99685-1370 • (907) 581-5060 • http://www.ci.unalaska.ak.us

Upper Lake
Habematolel Upper Lake Pomo Tribe • P.O. Box 516 • Upper Lake, AK 95485 • (907) 275-0737

Valdez
Forget-Me-Not Genealogical Society • 705 N Glacier Dr, P.O. Box 6 • Valdez, AK 99686 • (907) 835-4367

Maxine and Jesse Whitney Museum • 300 Airport Rd, P.O. Box 97 • Valdez, AK 99686 • (907) 834-1690

Valdez Consortium Library • 212 Fairbanks St, P.O. Box 609 • Valdez, AK 99686-0609 • (907) 835-4632 • http://www.ci.valdez.ak.us/library/

Valdez Historical Society • Historical Museum, 217 Egan Dr, P.O. Box 8 • Valdez, AK 99686-0008 • (907) 835-2764 • http://www.valdezmuseum.org

Venetie
Venetie Native Village • P.O. Box 81080 • Venetie, AK 99781-0080 • (907) 849-8165

Wainwright
Wainwright Native Village • P.O. Box 184 • Wainwright, AK 99782 • (907) 763-2726

Wales
Wales Native Village • P.O. Box 549 • Wales, AK 99783 • (907) 664-3062

Wasilla
Herning-Teeland-Mead House Museum • Swanson & Boundary Sts • Wasilla, AK 99654 • (907) 373-9071

Knik Tribal Council • P.O. Box 871565 • Wasilla, AK 99654 • (907) 373-7991

Museum of Alaska Transportation and Industry • Mile 47, Parks Hwy, P.O. Box 870646 • Wasilla, AK 99687 • http://www.alaska.net/~rmorris/mati1.htm

Wasilla Public Library • 391 N Main St • Wasilla, AK 99654-7085 • (907) 376-5913

Wasilla-Knik-Willow-Creek Historical Society • Dorothy Page Museum & Old Wasilla Townsite Park, 323 Main St • Wasilla, AK 99654 • (907) 373-9071 • http://www.cityofwasilla.com/museum/

White Mountain
White Mountain Native Village • P.O. Box 84082 • White Mountain, AK 99784 • (907) 638-3651

Willow
Willow Public Library • 23557 W Willow Community Center Circle, Mile 69-5 Parks Hwy, P.O. Box 129 • Willow, AK 99688-0129 • (907) 495-6424 • http://msnlibraries.com

Alaska

Wrangell

Irene Ingle Public Library • 124 2nd Ave, P.O. Box 679 • Wrangell, AK 99929-0679 • (907) 874-3335 • http://www.wrangell.com/community/library.htm

Tribal House of the Bear Museum • Front St, P.O. Box 868 • Wrangell, AK 99929 • (907) 874-3747

Wrangell Genealogical Society • Wrangell Museum, 296 Outer Dr, P.O. Box 1050 • Wrangell, AK 99929 • (907) 874-3770 • http://www.wrangell.com

Wrangell Native Cooperative Association • P.O. Box 1198 • Wrangell, AK 99929 • (907) 874-3482

Ajo
Ajo Historical Society • Historical Museum, 160 S Mission Rd, P.O. Box 778 • Ajo, AZ 85321-2601 • (520) 387-7105 • http://www.ajochamber.com/historical.htm

Apache Junction
American Historical Society of Germans from Russia, Arizona Sun Chapter • 1384 S Main Dr • Apache Junction, AZ 85220 • (480) 982-6407

Apache Junction Public Library • 1177 N Idaho Rd • Apache Junction, AZ 85219 • (480) 474-8556 • http://www.aipl.org

Goldfield Historical Society • 4650 E Mammoth Mine Rd • Apache Junction, AZ 85219 • (480) 677-6463

High Plains Heritage Genealogical Society • 5775 E El Camino Quinto • Apache Junction, AZ 85219-8808

Superstition Mountain Historical Society • Historical Museum, 408 W Apache Trl, P.O. Box 3845 • Apache Junction, AZ 85217-3845 • (480) 983-4888 • http://www.superstitionmountainmuseum.com

Superstition Mountain Lost Dutchman Museum • 4087 N Apache Tr, P.O. Box 3845 • Apache Junction, AZ 85217-3845 • (480) 983-4888 • www.superstitionmountainmuseum.org

Arizona City
Arizona City Community Library • 13254 S Sunland Grin Rd, P.O. Box 118 • Arizona City, AZ 85223-0118 • (520) 466-5565 • http://www.co.pinal.az.us/library/azcity/

Bagdad
Bagdad Museum • N Lindahl • Bagdad, AZ 86321 • (928) 633-2642

Benson
Benson Public Library • 300 S Huachuca, P.O Drawer 1480 • Benson, AZ 85602-1480 • (520) 586-9535 • http://www.cochise.lib.az.us

San Pedro Valley Arts and Historical Society • Benson Museum, 180 S San Pedro St, P.O. Box 1090 • Benson, AZ 85602 • (520) 586-2844

Bisbee
Bisbee Historical Society • 37 Main St • Bisbee, AZ 85603

Bisbee Mining and Historical Museum • 5 Copper Queen Plaza, P.O. Box 14 • Bisbee, AZ 85603-0014 • (520) 432-7071 • http://www.bisbeemuseum.org

Copper Queen Library • 6 Main St, P.O. Box 1857 • Bisbee, AZ 85603-2857 • (520) 432-4232 • http://cochise.lib.az.us/bisbee/bisbee.htm

Muheim Heritage House Museum • 207 Youngblood, P.O. Box 14 • Bisbee, AZ 85603 • (520) 432-7698

Black Canyon
Old Canon School Museum • 18800 School House Rd, P.O. Box 502 • Black Canyon, AZ 85324

Bowie
Fort Bowie National Historic Site Museum • Apache Pass Rd, P.O. Box 158 • Bowie, AZ 85605 • (520) 847-2500 • http://www.nps.gov/fobo

Buckeye
Buckeye Historical Society • Historical Museum, 116 E US Hwy 85, P.O. Box 292 • Buckeye, AZ 85326-2625 • (623) 386-4333

Buckeye Public Library • 310 N 6th St • Buckeye, AZ 85326-2439 • (623) 386-2778 • http://www.buckeyeaz.org

Buckeye Valley Museum • 10th St & Monroe, P.O. Box 292 • Buckeye, AZ 85326 • (623) 386-4333 • http://www.buckeyeaz.gov

Bullhead City
Colorado River Historical Society • Historical Museum, Hwy 95 & Camp Davis, P.O. Box 1599 • Bullhead City, AZ 86430 • (928) 754-3399 • http://www.summittsriverrealty.com/museum.html

Colorado River Museum • Hwy 95 • Bullhead City, AZ 86442

Mohave Valley Campus Library • Mohave Community College, 3400 Hwy 95 • Bullhead City, AZ 86442-8204 • (928) 758-2420 • http://www.mohave.edu

Tri-State Genealogical Society • 1653 Bluebonnet Blvd • Bullhead City, AZ 86442 • http://www.rootsweb.com/~azcanvtsgs

Camp Verde
Camp Verde Historical Society • Historical Museum, 435 S Main St, P.O. Box 1184 • Camp Verde, AZ 86322 • (928) 567-9560

Fort Verde State Historic Park Library • 125 E Hollamon, P.O. Box 397 • Camp Verde, AZ 86322-0397 • (928) 567-3275 • http://www.azstateparks.com

Casa Grande
BeDillon's Museum and Cactus Garden • 800 N Park Ave, P.O. Box 10678 • Casa Grande, AZ 85230 • (520) 836-2045

Casa Grande Public Library • 449 E Dry Lake • Casa Grande, AZ 85222 • (520) 421-8710

Casa Grande Valley Historical Society • Historical Museum, 110 W Florence Blvd • Casa Grande, AZ 85222-4033 • (520) 836-2223 • http://www.cgvhs.org

Genealogy Society of Pinal County • 1128 N Kadota Ave • Casa Grande, AZ 85222

Pinal County Arizona Genealogy Society • 1107 E 10th St • Casa Grande, AZ 85222

Cave Creek
Arizona Council of Professional Genealogists • P.O. Box 1634 • Cave Creek, AZ 85327 • http://www.apgen.org/localchapters/

Cave Creek Historical Society • Cave Creek Historical Museum, 6140 E Skyline Dr, P.O .Box 1 • Cave Creek, AZ 85327 • (480) 488-2764 • http://www.cavecreekmuseum.org

Society of Mayflower Descendants in the State of Arizona • P.O. Box 7767 • Cave Creek, AZ 85327-7767 • (623-465-0075)

Chandler
Arizona Railway Museum • 330 E Ryan Rd, P.O. Box 842 • Chandler, AZ 85244 • (480) 821-1108 • www.azrymuseum.org

Chandler Historical Society • Historical Museum, 178 E Commonwealth, P.O. Box 926 • Chandler, AZ 85224 • (480) 786-2842 • http://www.chandlermuseum.org

Chandler Public Library • 22 S Delaware • Chandler, AZ 85226 • (480) 782-2803 • http://www.chandlerlibrary.org

Huhugam Heritage Center • 4759 N Maricopa Rd, P.O. Box 5041 • Chandler, AZ 85226 • (520) 796-3500

National Society, Children of the American Revolution • 2000 W Flint • Chandler, AZ 85224 • (602) 814-9281

Chloride
Chloride Historical Society • Historical Museum, 2nd & Elkhart Sts, P.O. Box 294 • Chloride, AZ 86431 • (928) 565-3619 • http://chloridearizona.com

Clarkdale
Clarkdale Heritage Center • 900 1st North St, P.O. Box 806 • Clarkdale, AZ 86324 • (928) 634-5857

Claypool
Arizona Cornish Society • P.O. Box 1 • Claypool, AZ 85532

Clifton
Clifton Public Library • 101 School St, P.O. Box 1226 • Clifton, AZ 85533-1226 • (928) 865-2461

Greenlee County Historical Society • 317 Chase Creek, P.O. Box 787 • Clifton, AZ 85533 • (928) 865-3115

Arizona

Coolidge

Coolidge Historical Society • Historical Museum, 161 W Harding Ave, P.O. Box 1186 • Coolidge, AZ 85228-4407 • (520) 723-7186

Pinal County Historical Society • Historical Museum, 715 S Main St • Coolidge, AZ 85228 • (520) 868-4382

Cottonwood

Cottonwood Public Library • 100 S 6th St • Cottonwood, AZ 86326 • (928) 634-7559

Jerome Historical Society • general delivery • Cottonwood, AZ 86326 • (928) 634-1066

Verde Historical Society Archives • Clemenceau Heritage Museum, 1 N Willard, P.O. Box 511 • Cottonwood, AZ 86326 • (928) 634-2868 • http://www.sedona-verdevalley-museum.org

Douglas

Border Air Museum • 3200 E 10th St • Douglas, AZ 85607 • (520) 805-0753

Charles Di Peso Library • Cochise College, 4190 W Hwy 80 • Douglas, AZ 85607 • (520) 417-4082 • http://www.cochise.edu/library

Cochise County Historical and Archaeological Society • 1001 D Avenue, P.O. Box 818 • Douglas, AZ 85608-0818 • (520) 364-5266 • http://www.mycochise.com/history.php

Douglas Public Library • 560 10th St • Douglas, AZ 85607 • (520) 364-3851 • http://cochise.lib.az.us/douglas

Slaughter Ranch Museum • 6153 Geronimo Tr, P.O. Box 438 • Douglas, AZ 85608 • (520) 558-2474 • http://www.vtc.net/~sranch

Dragoon

Amerind Foundation • Historical Museum, 2100 N Amerind Rd, P.O. Box 400 • Dragoon, AZ 85609 • (928) 596-3666 • http://www.amerind.org

Eloy

Eloy Public Library • 100 E 7th St • Eloy, AZ 85231 • (520) 466-3814 • http://www.co.pinal.az.us/library

Flagstaff

Arizona Historical Society • Pioneer Museum, 2340 N Fort Valley Rd • Flagstaff, AZ 86001 • (928) 774-6272 • http://www.arizonahistoricalsociety.org

Cline Library • Northern Arizona University, Bldg 028, Knoles Dr, P.O. Box 6022 • Flagstaff, AZ 86011-6022 • (928) 523-6805 • http://www.nau.edu/library

Flagstaff City-Coconino County Public Library System • 300 W Aspen Ave • Flagstaff, AZ 86001 • (928) 779-7670 • http://www.flagstaffpubliclibrary.org

Grand Canyon Historical Society • P.O. Box 31405 • Flagstaff, AZ 86003 • http://grandcanyonhistory.org/

Harold S Colton Memorial Research Library • Museum of Northern Arizona, 3101 N Fort Valley Rd • Flagstaff, AZ 86001 • (928) 774-5213 • http://www.musnaz.org

Museum of Northern Arizona • 3101 N Fort Valley Rd • Flagstaff, AZ 86001-8348 • http://www.musnaz.org

Navajo Nation Historic Preservation Department • 13 N San Francisco St • Flagstaff, AZ 86001 • (928) 773-1349

Riordan Mansion State Historic Park • 409 W Riordan Rd • Flagstaff, AZ 86001 • (928) 779-4395 • http://www.pr.state.az.us

Rocky Mountain Medieval and Renaissance Association • Northern Arizona Univ, Box 6032 • Flagstaff, AZ 86011-0001

US Geological Survey Library • 2255 N Gemini Dr • Flagstaff, AZ 86001 • (928) 556-7272 • http://library.usgs.gov/flaglib.html

Florence

McFarland Historical State Park • 24 W Ruggles Ave, P.O. Box 109 • Florence, AZ 85232 • (520) 868-5216 • http://www.co.pinal.az.us/mcfarland/

Pinal County Historical Society • Historical Museum, 715 S Main St, P.O. Box 851 • Florence, AZ 85232 • (520) 868-4382

Fort Apache

Apache Cultural Center Museum • P.O. Box 507 • Fort Apache, AZ 85926 • (928) 338-4625 • www.wmat.nsn.us

Fort Huachuca

Fort Huachuca Museum • Boyd & Frierson Sts • Fort Huachuca, AZ 85613 • (520) 533-3898 • http://www.huachaca.army.mil

Fort Mohave

Tri-States Genealogical Society • P.O. Box 9689 • Fort Mohave, AZ 86427

Fountain Hills

Family History Society of Arizona, Fountain Hills Chapter • New Community Center, 13001 N La Montana Dr • Fountain Hills, AZ 85268-8306

Fort McDowell Mohave-Apache Indian Community • P.O. Box 17779 • Fountain Hills, AZ 85269-7779 • (480) 837-5121 • http://www.ftmcdowell.org

Fountain Hills and Lower Verde River Valley Historical Society • River of Time Museum, P-Bar Ranch, P.O. Box 17445 • Fountain Hills, AZ 85269-7445 • (480) 837-2612 • http://www.riveroftimemuseum.org

Society of Mayflower Descendants in the State of Arizona • 15038 E Palomino Blvd • Fountain Hills, AZ 85268-4813 • (480-837-8632)

Fredonia

Kaibab-Paiute Tribe • HC 65, Box 2 • Fredonia, AZ 86022 • (520) 643-7245

Pipe Spring National Monument • 406 N Pipe Spring Rd • Fredonia, AZ 86022 • (928) 643-7105 • http://www.nps.gov/pisp

Ganado

Hubbell Trading Post National Historic Site Museum • Hwy 264, P.O. Box 150 • Ganado, AZ 86505 • (928) 755-3475 • http://www.nps.gov

Gilbert

Arizona Chapter, Ohio Genealogical Society • P.O. Box 677 • Gilbert, AZ 85234-0677

Black Family History Society of Arizona • P.O. Box 1515 • Gilbert, AZ 85299-1515

Gilbert Historical Society • Gilbert Historical Museum, 10 S Gilbert Rd, P.O. Box 1484 • Gilbert, AZ 85296-1045 • (480) 926-1577 • http://www.gilbertmuseum.com

National Society, Daughters of Founders-Patriots of America • 16330 E Villa Park Ct • Gilbert, AZ 85297

Glendale

Arizona Welsh Society • 4901 W Sandra Terr • Glendale, AZ 85306 • (623) 547-1107

Bead Museum • 5754 W Glenn Dr • Glendale, AZ 85301-2559 • http://www.beadmuseumaz.org

Czech & Slovak Genealogical Society of Arizona • c/o Glendale Public Library, 5959 W Brown • Glendale, AZ 85302 • http://www.rootsweb.com/~azcsgsa/

Family History Society of Arizona, Glendale Chapter • P.O. Box 310 • Glendale, AZ 85311 • (602) 841-4628

Glendale Arizona Historical Society • Sahuaro Ranch Park, 5127 W Northern Ave, P.O. Box 5606 • Glendale, AZ 85312-5606 • (623) 435-0072 • http://www.sahuaroranch.org

Glendale Historical Society • 9802 N 59th Ave • Glendale, AZ 85302-1203 • (623) 435-0072

Glendale Public Library • 5959 W Brown St • Glendale, AZ 85302 • (623) 930-3530 • http://www.glendaleaz.com/library

Historic Sahuaro Ranch • 9802 N 59th Ave, P.O. Box 1824 • Glendale, AZ 85311 • (623) 930-4200 • http://www.sahuaroranch.org

Library Media Center & Museum • Glendale Community College, 6000 W Olive Ave • Glendale, AZ 85302 • (623) 845-3112 • http://www.gc.maricopa.edu/lmc/

Manistee Ranch Museum • 5127 W Northern Ave, P.O. Box 5606 • Glendale, AZ 85312 • (602) 931-8848

National Society, Sons and Daughters of the Pilgrims • 6341 Prickly Pear Trl • Glendale, AZ 85310

National Society, United Daughters of 1812 • 6341 W Prickly Pear Tr • Glendale, AZ 85310-1002

Globe
Gila County Historical Society • Historical Museum, 1330 N Broad St, P.O. Box 2891 • Globe, AZ 85501-2712 • (928) 425-7385

Grand Canyon
Grand Canyon National Park Museum • Grand Canyon Village, South Rim, P.O. Box 129 • Grand Canyon, AZ 85023 • (928) 638-7769 • http://www.nps.gov

Green Valley
Green Valley Genealogical Society • P.O. Box 1009 • Green Valley, AZ 85622-1009 • (520) 648-0506 • http://www.rootsweb.com/~azgvgs/

Greer
Butterfly Lodge Museum • State Rte 373 & Cty Rd 1126, P.O. Box 76 • Greer, AZ 85927-0076 • (520) 735-7514

Holbrook
Navajo County Historical Society • Historical Museum, 100 E Arizona St, P.O. Box 563 • Holbrook, AZ 86025 • (928) 524-6558 • http://www.ci.holbrook.az.us

Huachuca City
Huachuca City Public Library • 506 N Gonzales Blvd • Huachuca City, AZ 85616-9610 • (520) 456-1063 • http://www.cochise.lib.az.us/hcl

Jerome
Jerome Historical Society • Historical Museum, 200 Main St, P.O. Box 156 • Jerome, AZ 86331 • (928) 634-5477 • http://www.jeromehistoricalsociety.org

Jerome State Historic Park • Douglas Mansion, 100 Douglas Rd, P.O. Box D • Jerome, AZ 86331 • (928) 634-5381 • http://www.azstateparks.com

Kearny
Arthur E Pomeroy Public Library • 912A Tilbury Rd, P.O. Box 220 • Kearny, AZ 85237-0220 • (520) 363-5861

Kingman
Kingman Army Airfield Historical Society • Historical Museum, 4540 Flightline Dr • Kingman, AZ 86401 • (928) 757-1892

Mohave County Historical and Genealogical Society • Historical Museum, 400 W Beale St, P.O. Box 928 • Kingman, AZ 86401 • (928) 757-2019 • http://www.ctaz.com/~mocohist/museum/geneal.htm

Mohave County Library District • 3269 N Burbank St, P.O. Box 7000 • Kingman, AZ 86402-7000 • (928) 692-2665 • http://www.co.mohave.az.us/library

Kykotsmovi
Hopi Tribal Council • P.O. Box 123 • Kykotsmovi, AZ 86309 • (520) 734-2441 • http://www.hopi.nsn.us

Lake Havasu City
Lake Havasu Genealogical Society • 2283 Holly Dr, P.O. Box 953 • Lake Havasu City, AZ 86405-0953 • (928) 855-7105

Lake Havasu Genealogical Society • 2126 McCulloch Blvd N, Ste 17, P.O. Box 953 • Lake Havasu City, AZ 86405-0953 • (928) 855-7105 • http://www.rootsweb.com/~azlhgs/

Lake Havasu Historical Society • Lake Havasu Museum of History, 320 London Bridge Rd • Lake Havasu City, AZ 86403 • (928) 854-4938 • http://www.havasumuseum.org

Lakeside
Pinetop-Lakeside Historical Museum • 1360 N Niels Hansen Ln • Lakeside, AZ 85929 • (928) 368-5008

Pinetop-Lakeside Historical Society • 1360 N Niels Hansen Ln # 1313 • Lakeside, AZ 85929 • (928) 368-8123

Luke AFB
Luke Air Force Base Library • Bldg 219, 7424 N Homer Dr, 56 SVS/SVMG FL 4887 • Luke AFB, AZ 85309-1220 • (623) 856-7191

Maricopa
Ak-Chin Him-Dak Eco Museum • 47685 N Eco Museum Rd • Maricopa, AZ 85239 • (520) 568-9480

Ak-Chin Indian Community • Route 2, Box 27 • Maricopa, AZ 85239 • (520) 568-2227

McNeal
MHE Heritage Library • 433 S Hobson • McNeal, AZ 85204-2513

Mesa
Arizona Genealogical Advisory Board • P.O. Box 5641 • Mesa, AZ 85211-5641 • (602) 542-5841 • http://www.azgab.org

Arizona Jewish Historical and Genealogical Society • 720 W Edgewood Ave • Mesa, AZ 85202 • (480) 969-1201

Arizona Wing Commemorative Air Force Museum • 2017 N Greenfield Rd • Mesa, AZ 85215 • http://www.arizonawingcaf.com

Black Family Genealogy and History Society • 3842 N Lomond Cr • Mesa, AZ 85215 • (480) 854-2504 • http://www.bfghs.net

Champlin Fighter Aircraft Museum • 4636 E Fighter Aces Dr • Mesa, AZ 85203 • (480) 830-4540

Cherokee Family Ties • 516 N 38th St • Mesa, AZ 85208

City of Mesa Library • 64 E 1st St • Mesa, AZ 86401 • (480) 644-2700 • http://www.ci.mesa.az.us/library/

Daughters of Union Veterans of the Civil War 1861-1865, Tent #1 Arizona • 1040 E Greenway St • Mesa, AZ 85203-4302

Family History Society of Arizona, East Valley Chapter • Fellowship Square, Bldg 4, 6945 E Main • Mesa, AZ 85207-8206 • (480) 649-6060 • http://www.fhsa.org

Genealogical Workshop of Mesa • 1948 E 2nd Ave, P.O. Box 6052 • Mesa, AZ 85206-6052 • (480) 461-3757 • http://members.cox.net/gwom/

Germans to America • 5735 E McDowell #234 • Mesa, AZ 85208 • (602) 396-4816

Jewish Genealogical Society of Arizona • 720 W Edgewood Ave • Mesa, AZ 85210 • (480) 969-1201

Mesa Genealogical Society • P.O. Box 6052 • Mesa, AZ 85216

Mesa Historical Society • Historical Museum, 2345 N Horne, P.O. Box 582 • Mesa, AZ 85211 • (480) 835-8358 • http://www.mesahistoricalmuseum.org

Mesa Public Library - Local History & Special Collections • 86 E 1st St • Mesa, AZ 85201 • (480) 644-5421 • http://www.mesalibrary.org

Mesa, cont.
Mesa Regional Family History Center • Church of Jesus Christ of Latter-Day Saints, 41 S Hobson • Mesa, AZ 85204 • (480) 964-1200 • http://www.mesarfhs.org

Mesa Southwest Museum • 53 N MacDonald St • Mesa, AZ 85201 • (480) 834-2230 • http://www.mesasouthwestmuseum.com

Monte Vista Genies • Monte Vista Village Resort, Hopi Room, 8865 E Baseline Rd • Mesa, AZ 85208-5309

National Society of the British Empire in the USA, Agin Court Chapter • 4046 E Melita Avenue • Mesa, AZ 85206

National Society, Daughters of the American Revolution • 1255 W Kilarea • Mesa, AZ 85203-6623

Sirrine House Museum • 160 N Center St • Mesa, AZ 85201 • (602) 644-2760

Miami
Gila County Historical Museum • Globe Miami Hwy • Miami, AZ 85539 • (928) 425-7385

Mohave Valley
Mohave Valley Genealogical Society • P.O. Box 6045 • Mohave Valley, AZ 86440

Tri-State Genealogical Society • P.O. Box 6045 • Mohave Valley, AZ 86440

Morenci
Morenci Community Library • Morenci Plaza, P.O. Box 1060 • Morenci, AZ 85540-1060 • (928) 865-2775

Nogales
Nogales-Santa Cruz County Public Library • 518 N Grand Ave • Nogales, AZ 85621 • (520) 287-3343 • http://nogales-santacruz.lib.az.us

Pimeria Alta Historical Society • Historical Museum, 136 N Grand Ave, P.O. Box 2281 • Nogales, AZ 85628-2281 • (520) 287-4621 • http://www.dakotacom.net/~museum.about.htm

Oracle
Oracle Historical Society • Acadia Ranch Museum, P.O. Box 10 • Oracle, AZ 85623 • (520) 896-9609 • http://www.oraclehistoricalsociety.org

Oro Valley
Sun City Vistoso Genealogical Society • Social Hall, Papago Room, 1565 E Rancho Vistoso • Oro Valley, AZ 85737 • (520) 825-8743 • http://www.rootsweb.com/~azscvgs

Page
Dine Bi Keyah Museum • Big Lake Trading Post, 1501 Hwy 98, P.O. Box 1925 • Page, AZ 86040

John Wesley Powell Memorial Museum • 6 Lake Powell Blvd, P.O. Box 547 • Page, AZ 86040 • (928) 645-2741 • http://www.powellmuseum.org

Page Public Library • 479 S Lake Powell Blvd, P.O. Box 1776 • Page, AZ 86040 • (928) 645-4270 • http://www.cityofpage.org/library/library.html

Paradise Valley
Linde Museum • 3300 E Stanford Dr • Paradise Valley, AZ 85253-7527

Parker
Colorado River Indian Tribes • Museum & Library, Route 1, Box 23B • Parker, AZ 85344 • (928) 669-9211 • http://www.crittourism.rraz.net

Parker Area Historical Society • 1214 California Ave, P.O. Box 1500 • Parker, AZ 85344-1500 • (928) 669-8077

Parker Public Library • 1001 Navajo Ave • Parker, AZ 85344 • (928) 669-2622 • http://www.parkerpublib.org

Patagonia
Patagonia Public Library • 346 Duquesne St, P.O. Box 415 • Patagonia, AZ 85624 • (520) 394-2010 • http://www.patagoniapubliclibrary.org

Payson
Museum of the Forest • 700 Green Valley Pkwy, P.O. Box 25 • Payson, AZ 85547 • (928) 474-3483

Northern Gila County Genealogical Society • 302 E Bonita St • Payson, AZ 85547-0952 • (928) 474-2139 • http://www.rootsweb.com/~azngcgs

Northern Gila County Historical Society • Rim Country Museum, 700 Green Valley Pkwy, P.O. Box 2532 • Payson, AZ 85547 • (928) 474-3483 • http://www.rimcountrymuseums.com

Payson Public Library • 328 N. McLane Rd • Payson, AZ 85541 • (928) 474-9260

Tonto Apache Tribe • 30 Tonto Apache Reservation • Payson, AZ 85541 • (520) 474-5000

Peach Springs
Hualaapai Tribal Council • P.O. Box 179 • Peach Springs, AZ 86434 • (520) 769-2216

Peoria
Associated Daughters of Early American Witches • 8601 N 103rd Ave #239 • Peoria, AZ 85345-7491

Peoria Arizona Historical Society • Historical Museum, 10304 N 83rd Ave, P.O. Box 186 • Peoria, AZ 85380 • (623) 487-8030 • http://www.historic-glendale.net/pahs.htm

Peoria Public Library • 8463 W Monroe • Peoria, AZ 85345 • (623) 773-7556 • http://ibrary.peoriaaz.com

Peridot
San Carlos Apache Cultural Center • Mile marker 272, Hwy 70, P.O. Box 760 • Peridot, AZ 85542 • (928) 475-2394 • http://www.apacheculture.com

Phoenix
Alwun House Museum • 1204 E Roosevelt • Phoenix, AZ 85006 • (602) 253-7887

Arizona Chapter, Ohio Genealogical Society • P.O. Box 50938 • Phoenix, AZ 85076-0938

Arizona Computer Interest Group • P.O. Box 51498 • Phoenix, AZ 85076-1498 • (480) 759-5171 • http://www.agcig.org

Arizona Department of Health Services Office of Vital Records • 1818 W Adams, P.O. Box 3887 • Phoenix, AZ 85030-3887 • (602) 364-1300 • http://www.hs.state.az.us/vitalrcd/

Arizona First Families • 4813 E Flower St • Phoenix, AZ 85018 • (602) 840-4538

Arizona Hall of Fame Museum • 1101 W Washington • Phoenix, AZ 85007 • (602) 542-4581 • http://www.azcama.com/museums/hofame.html

Arizona Humanities Council • Historical Museum, 1242 N Central Ave • Phoenix, AZ 85004 • (602) 257-0335

Arizona Jewish Historical Society • Historical Museum, 4710 N 16th St, Ste 201 • Phoenix, AZ 85013 • (602) 241-7870 • http://www.azjhs.org

Arizona Military Museum • 5636 E McDowell Rd • Phoenix, AZ 85008 • (602) 267-2676

Arizona Mining and Mineral Museum • 1502 N Washington • Phoenix, AZ 85007 • (602) 255-3795 • http://www.admmr.slate.az.us

Arizona State Capitol Museum • 1700 W Washington • Phoenix, AZ 85007 • (602) 542-4675 • http://www.lib.az.us/museum/capitol.htm

Arizona State Library, Archives and Public Records • State Capitol, 1700 W Washington, Rm 200 • Phoenix, AZ 85007 • (602) 542-4159 • http://www.lib.az.us

Arizona Street Railway Museum • 1218 N Central Ave • Phoenix, AZ 85004 • (602) 254-0307 • http://www.phoenixtrolley.com

Barbara Anderson Girl Scout Museum • 3806 N 3rd St, Ste 200 • Phoenix, AZ 85012 • (602) 452-7134 • http://www.girlscoutsaz.org

Black Family Genealogy and History Society • P.O. Box 90683 • Phoenix, AZ 85066-0683 • (480) 854-2504

Carver African American Historical and Genealogical Society • 415 E Grant St • Phoenix, AZ 85023 • (602) 276- 7931

Czech and Slovak Genealogical Society of Arizona • 4921 E Exeter Blvd • Phoenix, AZ 85018-2942 • (602) 840-0926 • http://www.rootsweb.com/~azcsgsa

Daughters of the American Revolution, Arizona Society • 4651 E Earll Dr • Phoenix, AZ 85018 • (602) 231-6264

Family History Society of Arizona • P.O. Box 63094 • Phoenix, AZ 85082-3094 • (480) 892-1778 • http://www.fhsa.org

Family History Society of Arizona, Scottsdale Chapter • c/o Shepherd of the Hills Congregational Church, 5524 E Lafayette Blvd • Phoenix, AZ 85018-4524

Fannin Library • Phoenix College, 1202 W Thomas Rd • Phoenix, AZ 85013 • (602) 285-7470 • http://www.pc.maricopa.edu/departments/library

Friends of Arizona Archives • P.O. Box 64532 • Phoenix, AZ 85082-4532 • http://faza.net

Greater Phoenix Jewish Genealogical Society • 4710 N 16th St • Phoenix, AZ 85013 • http://www.azjhs.org

Hall of Flame Museum of Firefighting • 6101 E Van Buren • Phoenix, AZ 85008-3421 • (602) 275-3473 • http://www.hallofflame.org

Heard Museum & Billie Jane Baguley Archives • 2301 N Central Ave • Phoenix, AZ 85004 • (602) 252-8848 • http://www.heard.org/researeh/

Heredity Order of the First Families of Massachusetts • 11424 N 40th St • Phoenix, AZ 85028

Maricopa County Library District • 2700 N Central Ave, Ste 700 • Phoenix, AZ 85004 • (602) 652-3000 • http://mcld.maricopa.gov

Masonic Grand Lodge of Arizona • 2723 W Northern Ave • Phoenix, AZ 85021-6624 • (602) 252-1924 • http://www.azmasons.org/

Musical Instrument Museum • 4725 E Mayo Blvd • Phoenix, AZ 85050 • (480) 481-2460 • http://www.themim.org

Mystery House Museum • 800 E Mineral Rd, P.O. Box 8265 • Phoenix, AZ 85066 • (602) 268-1581

National Colonial Dames of the 17th Century, Palo Verde Chapter • 11424 N 40th St • Phoenix, AZ 85028

National Huguenot Society • 16820 N 2nd Dr • Phoenix, AZ 85023-3630 • (602) 863-0821

National Society Colonial Dames of the 17th Century • 6131 N 8th Ave • Phoenix, AZ 85013-1405 • (602) 246-9340

National Society of New England Women • 6133 N 8th Ave • Phoenix, AZ 85013

National Society, Dames of the Court of Honor • 212 W Country Gables Dr • Phoenix, AZ 85023-5250

National Society, Daughters of American Colonists • P.O. Box 83061 • Phoenix, AZ 85013-3061 • (602) 938-6067

National Society, Daughters of American Colonists • 6131 N 6th Ave • Phoenix, AZ 85013-0879

National Society, Women Descendants of the Ancient and Honorable Artillery Company • 3139 N 47th Pl • Phoenix, AZ 85018-6511

Order of Founders and Patriots of America • 4264 W Morten Ave • Phoenix, AZ 85051 • (602) 939-6413

Phoenix Airport Museum • 3400 E Sky Harbor Blvd. Terminal 3 • Phoenix, AZ 85034 • http://phoenix.gov/skyharborairport/about/historymuseum.html

Phoenix Genealogical Society • 6220 N 35th Dr, P.O. Box 38703 • Phoenix, AZ 85069 • (602) 843-9392 • http://www.phxgensoc.com

Phoenix Museum of History • 105 N 5th St • Phoenix, AZ 85004 • (602) 253-2734 • http://www.pmoh.org

Phoenix Police Museum • 101 S Central Ave, Ste 100 • Phoenix, AZ 85004 • (602) 534-7278

Phoenix Public Library • 1221 N Central Ave • Phoenix, AZ 85004 • (602) 262-4636 • http://www.phoenixpubliclibrary.org

Pioneer Arizona Living History Museum • 3901 W Pioneer Rd • Phoenix, AZ 85027-7020 • (623) 465-1052 • http://www.pioneer-arizona.com

Pioneer's Cemetery Association • Smurtwaite House, 14th Ave & Jefferson, P.O. Box 63342 • Phoenix, AZ 85082-3342 • (602) 534-1262 • http://www.azhistcemeteries.org

Pueblo Grande Museum & Research Library • 4619 E Washington St • Phoenix, AZ 85034 • (602) 495-0901 • http://www.pueblogrande.com

Rosson House Museum • 113 N 6th St • Phoenix, AZ 85004 • (602) 261-8063 • http://www.rossonhousemuseum.org

State Historic Preservation Office • 1300 W Washington • Phoenix, AZ 85007 • (602) 542-4009 • http://www.pr.state.az.us/partnerships/shpo/shpo.html

Sunnyslope Historical Society • Historical Museum, 737 E Hatcher Rd • Phoenix, AZ 85020 • (602) 331-3150 • http://sunnyslopehistoricalsociety.org

Telephone Pioneer Museum • 20 E Thomas Rd #101 • Phoenix, AZ 85012 • (602) 630-2060

Wells Fargo History Museum • 100 W Washington • Phoenix, AZ 85003 • (602) 378-1578 • http://www.wellsfargohistory.com

Pima
Eastern Arizona Historical Society • Andrew Kimball Home Museum, 2 N Main St, P.O. Box 274 • Pima, AZ 85543 • (928) 485-9400 • http://www.visitgrahamcounty.com

Pima Public Library-Graham County • 50 S 200 W, P.O. Box 489 • Pima, AZ 85543-0489 • (928) 485-2822 • http://www.pimalibrary.org

Pine
Isabelle Hunt Memorial Public Library • 6124 N Randall Pl, P.O. Box 229 • Pine, AZ 85544-0229 • (928) 476-3678

Pine-Strawberry Archeological and Historical Society • Pine-Strawberry Museum, Route 87, P.O. Box 564 • Pine, AZ 85544 • (928) 476-3547 • http://www.pinestrahs.org

Pirtleville
Cochise Genealogical Society • Douglas Williams House, 1001 D Avenue, P.O. Box 68 • Pirtleville, AZ 85626 • (520) 364-3372 • http://www.mycochise.com

Prescott
Northern Arizona Genealogical Society • 945 Country Club Dr, P.O. Box 695 • Prescott, AZ 86302-0695 • (928) 445-3572 • http://www.rootsweb.com/~aznags/

Phippen Museum • 4701 N US Hwy 89 • Prescott, AZ 86301 • (520) 778-1385

Prescott Historical Society • Sharlot Hall Museum, 415 W Gurley St • Prescott, AZ 86301 • (928) 445-3122 • http://www.sharlot.org

Arizona

Prescott, cont.

Prescott Public Library • 215 E Goodwin St • Prescott, AZ 86303 • (928) 777-1500 • http://www.prescottlib.lib.az.us

Smoki Museumof American Indian Culture Library • 147 N Arizona St, P.O. Box 10224 • Prescott, AZ 86304-0224 • (928) 445-1230 • http://www.smoki.com

Yavapai College Library • 1100 Sheldon St • Prescott, AZ 86303 • (928) 776-2265 • http://www.yc.edu/lirary.nsf

Yavapai-Apache Tribe • P.O. Box 348 • Prescott, AZ 86322 • (520) 445-8790 • http://www.yavapai-apache-nation.com

Yavapai-Prescott Tribe • 530 E Merritt St • Prescott, AZ 86301-2038 • (520) 445-8790

Prescott Valley

Irish American Genealogical Society • P.O. Box 26507 • Prescott Valley, AZ 86312

Prescott Valley Historical Society • P.O. Box 26341 • Prescott Valley, AZ 86302 • (520) 775-5847 • http://www.pvaz.net/Index.aspx?page=205

Quartzsite

Quartzsite Historical Society • Historical Museum, 161 W Main St, P.O. Box 331 • Quartzsite, AZ 85346 • (928) 927-5229 • http://www.quartzsitemuseum.com

Quartzsite Public Library • 465 N Plymouth Ave, P.O. Box 2812 • Quartzsite, AZ 85346-2812 • (928) 927-6593 • http://www.ci.quartzsite.az.us/community/public_library1.htm

Queen Creek

San Tan Historical Society • 20435 S Ellsworth Rd • Queen Creek, AZ 85242 • (480) 987-9380 • http://www.queencreek.org

Rimrock

Camp Verde Historical Society • 435 S Main, P.O. Box 182 • Rimrock, AZ 86335 • (928) 567-7331 • http://www.sharlot.org/roundup/archives/CVHS.shtml

Sacaton

Gila River Cultural Center • P.O. Box 457 • Sacaton, AZ 85247 • (520) 963-3981

Gila River Pima-Maricopa Indian Community • P.O. Box 97 • Sacaton, AZ 85247 • (602) 562-3311 • http://gric.nsn.us

Safford

Family History Library • Church of Jesus Christ of Latter-Day Saints, 515 11th St, 822 16th St • Safford, AZ 85546-3520 • (928) 428-7927

Graham County Historical Society • Historical Museum, 808 8th Ave, P.O. Box 127 • Safford, AZ 85548 • (520) 348-3212 • http://www.rootsweb.com/~azgraham/histsoc.html

Safford City-Graham County Library • 808 7th Ave • Safford, AZ 85546 • (928) 428-1531 • http://www.saffordcitylibrary.org

Saint David

Holy Trinity Monastery Library • Hwy 80, Milepost 302, P.O. Box 298 • Saint David, AZ 85630-0298 • (520) 720-4754 • http://www.holytrinitymonatery.org

Saint Johns

Apache County Historical Society • Historical Museum, 180 W Cleveland, P.O. Box 146 • Saint Johns, AZ 85936 • (928) 337-4737

Apache County Library District • 205 W 1st S, P.O. Box 2760 • Saint Johns, AZ 85936-2760 • (928) 337-4923

Saint Michaels

Saint Michaels Mission Museum and Provincial Archives • Navajo Reservation, 24 Mission Rd, P.O. Box 680 • Saint Michaels, AZ 86511 • (928) 871-4171

San Carlos

San Carlos Apache Tribe • P.O. Box O • San Carlos, AZ 85550 • (520) 475-2331

Scottsdale

Bison Western Museum • 16641 N 91st St, Ste 101 • Scottsdale, AZ 85260 • (480) 837-8700

Caledonian Society of Arizona • P.O. Box 5853 • Scottsdale, AZ 85261 • (480) 839-9432 • http://www.arizonascots.com

Daughters of the American Revolution, Arizona State Chapter • 17239 N 59th Pl • Scottsdale, AZ 85254

Family History Society of Arizona, Paradise Valley Chapter • c/o Chaparral Christian Church, 6451 E Shea Blvd • Scottsdale, AZ 85254-5062

Greater Phoenix Jewish Genealogical Society • P.O. Box 4063 • Scottsdale, AZ 85261-4063 • (480) 905-3645

National Society of the British Empire in the USA, Plantagenet Chapter • P.O. Box 4156 • Scottsdale, AZ 85261

National Society, Daughters of Colonial Wars • 25150 Windy Walk Dr, Villa #16 • Scottsdale, AZ 85266-9274

Order of Founders and Patriots of America • 6801 Camelback Road, Apt S114 • Scottsdale, AZ 85251 • (480) 945-9816

Order of the Three Crusades, 1096-1192 • 17239 N 59th Pl • Scottsdale, AZ 85254 • (602) 867-4895

Salt River Pima-Maricopa Indian Community • Route 1, Box 216 • Scottsdale, AZ 86256 • (602) 941-7277 • http://www.saltriver.pima-maricopa.nsn.us

Scottsdale Historical Society • Historical Museum, 7333 Scottsdale Mall, P.O. Box 143 • Scottsdale, AZ 85252 • (480) 945-4499 • http://www.scottsdalemuseum.com

Scottsdale Public Library • 3839 Drinkwater Blvd • Scottsdale, AZ 85251-4434 • (480) 994-2476 • http://library.ci.scottsdale.az.us

Society of the Cincinnati • 17239 N 59th Pl • Scottsdale, AZ 85254 • (602) 867-4895

Sons of Confederate Veterans • 8787 E Mountain View Rd, Apt #1085 • Scottsdale, AZ 85258 • (480) 990-7914

Sylvia Plotkin Judaica Museum • 10460 N 56th St • Scottsdale, AZ 85253 • (480) 951-0323 • http://www.templebethisrael.org

Second Mesa

Hopi Cultural Center Museum • Route 264 • Second Mesa, AZ 86043 • (928) 734-6650

Sedona

Gordon Wheeler's Trading Post and Museum • 201 Hwy 179, P.O. Box 2937 • Sedona, AZ 86336 • (928) 282-4255

Sedona Genealogy Club • 260 Panorama, P.O. Box 4258 • Sedona, AZ 86340 • http://www.rootsweb.com/~azsgc

Sedona Historical Society • Sedona Heritage Museum, 735 Jordan Rd, P.O. Box 10216 • Sedona, AZ 96339-8216 • (928) 282-7038 • http://www.sedonamuseum.org

Sedona Public Library • 3250 White Bear Rd • Sedona, AZ 86336 • (928) 282-7714 • http://www.sedonalibrary.org

Sells

Tohono O'Odham Nation • P.O. Box 837 • Sells, AZ 85634 • (520) 383-2221

Show Low

Grace Lutheran Church Library • 700 S 19th Ave, P.O. Box 174 • Show Low, AZ 85902-0174 • (928) 537-4817

Show Low Historical Society • Historical Museum, 541 E Deuce of Clubs, P.O. Box 3468 • Show Low, AZ 85901-4803 • (928) 532-7115 • http://www.showlowmuseum.com

Show Low Public Library • 180 N 9th St • Show Low, AZ 85901 • (928) 532-4070 • http://www.ci.show-low.az.us/departments/library/

Sierra Vista
Apache Genealogy Society of Cochise County • c/o Sierra Vista Public Library, 2600 E Tacoma, P.O. Box 1084 • Sierra Vista, AZ 85636-1084 • (520) 458-4225

Daughters of the American Revolution, Arizona State • 2622 Papago Tr • Sierra Vista, AZ 85635

Henry Hauser Museum • 2950 E Tacoma • Sierra Vista, AZ 85635

Sierra Vista Genealogical Society • 2600 E Tacoma St, P.O. Box 1084 • Sierra Vista, AZ 85636-1084 • (520) 458-7770 • http://www.rootsweb.com/~azsvgs/

Sierra Vista Public Library • 2600 E Tacoma • Sierra Vista, AZ 85635-1399 • (520) 458-4225 • http://www.ci.sierra-vista.az.us/svlibrary

Snowflake
Snowflake-Taylor Public Library • 418 S 4th W • Snowflake, AZ 85937 • (928) 536-7103 • http://www.ci.snowflake.lib.az.us

Stinson Pioneer Museum • 100 E 1st St S • Snowflake, AZ 85937 • (928) 536-4881 • http://www.ci.snowflake.az.us

Somerton
Cocopah Indian Tribe • 15th & Ave G, P.O. Box G • Somerton, AZ 85350 • (520) 627-2102 • http://www.cocopah.com

Springerville
Casa Malpais Museum • 318 E Main St, P.O. Box 807 • Springerville, AZ 85938 • (520) 333-5375

White Mountain Historical Society • 504 E Mohave St, P.O. Box 12 • Springerville, AZ 85938 • (928) 333-2552

Sun City
Arizona Mayflower Society • 16401 N 99th Dr • Sun City, AZ 85351

National Society of New England Women • 11033 Sun City Blvd • Sun City, AZ 85351

National Society of the British Empire in the USA, Stonehenge Chapter • 10247 W Pineaire Dr • Sun City, AZ 85351-1120

National Society, Magna Carta Dames • 9510 Briarwood Cr • Sun City, AZ 85351-1431

Sun Cities Area Historical Society • 10801 W Oakmont Dr • Sun City, AZ 85351-3317 • (623) 974-2568 • http://www.scazhistory.org

Sun Cities Genealogical Society • 13801 Meeker Blvd, P.O. Box 1448 • Sun City, AZ 85372-1448 • (623) 933-4945

Sun City Library • 16828 N 99th Ave • Sun City, AZ 85351 • (623) 974-2569 • http://www.sclib.com

West Valley Genealogical Society • P.O. Box 1448 • Sun City, AZ 85372-1448 • (623) 933-4945 • http://www.rootsweb.com/~azwvgs/

Sun City West
Continental Society, Daughters of Indian Wars • 14630 Futura Dr • Sun City West, AZ 85375

R H Johnson Library • 13801 Meeker Blvd • Sun City West, AZ 85375 • (623) 544-6130

Supai
Hawasupai Tribal Museum • P.O. Box 10 • Supai, AZ 86435 • (928) 448-2961

Superior
Superior Historical Society • Historical Museum, 300 W Main St, P.O. Box 613 • Superior, AZ 85273 • (520) 689-1969

World's Smallest Museum • 111 W US 60 • Superior, AZ 85273 • www.worldssmallestmuseum.com

Taylor
Taylor-Shumway Historical Foundation • 400 E Center St, P.O. Box 566 • Taylor, AZ 95939 • (928) 536-7294

Tempe
American Museum of Nursing • ASU Comm Svcs Bldg, 200 E Curry Rd, 2nd Fl, P.O. Box 873008 • Tempe, AZ 85287 • (480) 965-2195 • http://nursing.asu.edu

Arizona Genealogical Computer Interest Group • 2105 S McClintock • Tempe, AZ 85282

Arizona Historical Foundation • c/o Hayden Library, Arizona State Univ, P.O. Box 871006 • Tempe, AZ 85287-1006 • (480) 965-3283 • http://www.ahfweb.org/

Arizona Historical Society, Central Arizona Division • Papago Park Museum, 1300 N College Ave • Tempe, AZ 85281 • (480) 929-0292 • http://www.arizonahistoricalsociety.org

Arizona State University Libraries • Univ of Arizona, Dept of Archives and Manuscripts, Box 871006 • Tempe, AZ 85287-1006 • (480) 965-6164 • http://www.asu.edu/lib/archives

Family History Society of Arizona, Tempe Chapter • P.O. Box 63094 • Tempe, AZ 85280 • http://www.fhsa.org.

Genealogical Society of Arizona • P.O. Box 27237 • Tempe, AZ 85282

Hacket House Museum • 95 W 4th St • Tempe, AZ 85281 • (602) 350-8181

Hayden Library • Arizona State Univ, P.O. Box 871006 • Tempe, AZ 85287-1006 • (480) 965-6164 • http://www.asu.edu/lib/hayden/

Hispanic Family History Society • 3607 S Kenneth Pl • Tempe, AZ 85282

National Council on Public History • Arizona State Univ, Dept of History • Tempe, AZ 85287 • (617) 437-2627

Polish Genealogical Interest Group of Arizona • 2015 E Redmon Dr • Tempe, AZ 85283 • (480) 839-8215 • http://www.azneighbors.com/212/

Sons of Sherman's March to the Sea • 1725 S Farmer Ave • Tempe, AZ 85281 • (480) 967-5405

Tempe Historical Society • Peterson House Museum, 809 E Southern Ave • Tempe, AZ 85282-5205 • (480) 350-5100 • http://www.tempe.gov/museum

Tempe Public Library • 3500 S Rural Rd • Tempe, AZ 85282 • (480) 350-5511 • http://www.tempe.gov/library

Thatcher
Alumni Library • Eastern Arizona College, 615 N Stadium Ave • Thatcher, AZ 85552 • (928) 428-8304 • http://www.eac.edu/library

Graham County Historical Society • Historical Museum, 3430 W Main St, P.O. Box 290 • Thatcher, AZ 85552 • (928) 348-0470

Tolleson
Tolleson Public Library • 9555 W Van Buren St • Tolleson, AZ 85353 • (623) 936-2746

Tombstone
Tombstone City Library • 4th & Toughnut Sts, P.O. Box 218 • Tombstone, AZ 85638-0218 • (520) 457-3612 • http://www.cochise.lib.az.us

Tombstone Courthouse State Historic Park • 219 Toughnut St, P.O. Box 216 • Tombstone, AZ 85638 • (520) 457-3311 • http://www.azstateparks.com

Tsaile
Ned A Hatathli Museum • Navajo Community College • Tsaile, AZ 86556 • (928) 724-3311

Arizona

Tsaile, cont.
Tsaile Campus Library • Dineh College, P.O. Box 1000 • Tsaile, AZ 86556 • (928) 724-6757 • http://crystal.ncc.cc.nm.us

Tuba City
San Juan Southern Paiute Council • P.O. Box 2656 • Tuba City, AZ 86045 • (520) 283-4583

Tuba City Public Library • Main St, P.O. Box 190 • Tuba City, AZ 86045-0190 • (928) 283-5856

Tubac
Tubac Historical Society • P.O. Box 3261 • Tubac, AZ 85646 • (520) 398-2020 • http://www.tubacaz.com/historical_society.asp

Tubac Presidio State Historic Park • 1 Burruel St, P.O. Box 1296 • Tubac, AZ 85646 • (520) 398-2252 • http://www.prstate.az.us

Tucson
390th Memorial Museum • 6000 E Valencia Rd • Tucson, AZ 85756 • www.390th.org

Afro-American Historical and Genealogical Society, Tucson Chapter • 2501 N Goyette, P.O. Box 58272 • Tucson, AZ 87554 • http://aztucson.com/nonprofit/aahgs-tucson

Arizona and the West Library • 318 University • Tucson, AZ 85721

Arizona Archaeological and Historical Society • Arizona State Museum, Univ of Arizona, P.O. Box 210026 • Tucson, AZ 85721 • (520) 621-3656 • http://www.statemuseum.arizona.edu/aahs/aahs.shtml

Arizona Historical Society Downtown Museum • 140 N Stone Ave • Tucson, AZ 85701 • (520) 770-1473 • http://www.arizonahistoricalsociety.org

Arizona Historical Society, Southern Arizona Division • Historical Museum, 949 E 2nd St • Tucson, AZ 85701 • (520) 628-5774 • http://www.arizonahistoricalsociety.org

Arizona Pioneer's Historical Society • 949 E 2nd St • Tucson, AZ 85719 • (520) 628-5774

Arizona Society of Genealogists • 6565 E Grant Rd • Tucson, AZ 85715

Arizona State Genealogical Society • P.O. Box 42075 • Tucson, AZ 85733-2075 • (520) 275-2747 • http://www.rootsweb.com/~asgs/

Arizona State Museum • Univ of Arizona, 1013 E University Blvd, P.O. Box 210026 • Tucson, AZ 85721-0026 • (602) 621-4695 • http://www.statemuseum.arizona.edu

B-26 Maruauder Historical Society • 3900 E Timrod St • Tucson, AZ 85711 • (520) 322-6226

Bloom Southwest Jewish Archives • Univ of Arizona, 1052 N Highland Ave, P.O. Box 2100055 • Tucson, AZ 85721-0555 • (520) 621-5774 • http://parentseyes.arizona.edu/bloom/

Finnish-American Club of Tucson • 2800 W Mesa Verde Pl • Tucson, AZ 85742-9616 • (520) 742-0266 • http://community.azstamet.com/finnclub

Fort Lowell Museum • 2900 N Craycroft Rd • Tucson, AZ 85710 • (520) 885-3832 • http://www.arizonahistoricalsociety.org

Historic Stone Avenue Temple Museum • 564 S Stone Ave • Tucson, AZ 85702 • (520) 670-9073

History of Pharmacy Museum • Univ of AZ College of Pharmacy, 1703 E Mabel, P.O. Box 210207 • Tucson, AZ 85721 • (520) 626-1427

Jewish Historical Society of Southern Arizona • 4181 E Pontatoc Canyon Dr; P.O. Box 57482 • Tucson, AZ 85732-7482 • (520) 882-6648

Jewish Historical Society of Southern Arizona, Genealogy Group • 4181 E Pontatoc Canyon Dr • Tucson, AZ 85718 • (520) 299-4486

La Pilita Museum • 420 S Main • Tucson, AZ 85701 • (520) 882-7454

Los Descendientes del Presidio de Tucson • 1711 N Painted Hills Rd, P.O. Box 50871 • Tucson, AZ 85703 • (520) 743-8233

Otis Chidester Scout Museum of Southern Arizona • 1937 E Blacklidge Dr • Tucson, AZ 85719 • (520) 326-7669 • http://www.azscoutmuseum.com

Pima Air and Space Museum & Titan Missile Museum • 6000 E Valencia Rd • Tucson, AZ 95706 • (520) 575-0462 • http://www.pimaair.org

Pima County Public Library • 101 N Stone Ave, P.O. Box 27470 • Tucson, AZ 85726-7470 • (520) 791-4391 • http://www.lib.ci.tucson.az.us

Pioneer Auto Trails Historical Society • Historical Museum, 11755 E Calle Aurora • Tucson, AZ 85748 • (520) 722-9363

Postal History Foundation • Historical Museum, P.O. Box 40725 • Tucson, AZ 85717 • (520) 623-6652

Rincon County West RV Resort Genealogy Club • 4555 S Mission Rd • Tucson, AZ 85746 • (520) 294-5899

SaddleBrooke Genealogy Club • 38418 S Golf Course Dr • Tucson, AZ 85739-1113 • (520) 818-0177

Society of Mayflower Descendants in the State of Arizona • 8101 N Wanda Rd • Tucson, AZ 85704-3447

Sons of the American Revolution, Arizona Society • Back House, 3110 E Lester St • Tucson, AZ 85716-3128 • (520) 834-5784 • http://www.azssar.org

Sosa-Carillo-Fremont House Museum • 151 S Granada, P.O. Box 2588 • Tucson, AZ 85702 • (520) 628-5774 • http://www.arizonahistoricalsociety.org

Southwest Center Museum • Univ of Arizona, 1052 N Highland Ave • Tucson, AZ 85721 • (520) 621-2484 • http://swctr.web.arizona.edu/

Temple Emanuel Library • 225 N Country Club Rd • Tucson, AZ 85716 • (520) 327-4501 • http://www.templeemanueltucson.org

Tucson Presidio Trust for Historic Preservation • Presidio San Agustin del Tucson, 133 W Washington, P.O. Box 1334 • Tucson, AZ 85702-1334 • (520) 884-4214 • http://www.tucsonpresidiotrust.org

Tucson Rodeo Parade Museum • 5823 S 6th Ave, P.O. Box 1788 • Tucson, AZ 85702 • (520) 294-1280 • http://www.tucsonrodeoparade.com

United Daughters of the Confederacy, John R. Baylor Chapter • 6341 E Calle Dened • Tucson, AZ 85710 • (520) 747-3769

United Daughters of the Confederacy, Thunderbird Chapter • 6501 N Camino Libby • Tucson, AZ 85718 • (520) 297-2983

University of Arizona Library • 1510 E University Blvd, P.O. Box 210055 • Tucson, AZ 85721-0055 • (520) 621-6423 • http://www.library.arizona.edu

Tumacacori
Tumacacori National Historical Park • I-19 at Exit 29, P.O. Box 67 • Tumacacori, AZ 85640 • (520) 398-2341 • http://www.nps.gov/tuma

Vail
Colossal Cave Mountain Park • 16721 E Old Spanish Tr • Vail, AZ 85641 • (520) 647-7121 • http://www.colossalcave.com

Whiteriver
White Mountain Apache Tribe • P.O. Box 700 • Whiteriver, AZ 85941 • (520) 338-4346

Whiteriver Public Library • Chief Ave N, P.O. Box 370 • Whiteriver, AZ 85941 • (928) 338-4884

Wickenburg
Desert Caballeros Western Museum • 21 N Frontier St • Wickenburg, AZ 85390 • (928) 684-2272 • http://www.westernmuseum.org

Maricopa County Historical Society • Desert Cabelleros Western Museum, 21 N Frontier St • Wickenburg, AZ 85390-1417 • (928) 684-8702 • http://www.westernmuseum.org

Wickenburg Public Library • 164 E Apache St • Wickenburg, AZ 85390 • (928) 684-2665

Willcox

Chiricahua National Monument Library • Dos Cabezas Rt, P.O. Box 6500 • Willcox, AZ 85643 • (520) 824-3560

Museum of the Southwest • 1500 N Circle I Road • Willcox, AZ 85643 • (520) 384-2272 • http://www.willcoxchamber.com

Rex Allen Arizona Cowboy Museum-Cowboy Hall of Fame • 150 Railroad Ave • Wilcox, AZ 85643 • (520) 384-4583 • http://www.rexallenmuseum.org

Sulphur Springs Valley Historical Society • 124 E Maley St • Willcox, AZ 85643 • (520) 384-3971

Williams

Arizona State Railroad Museum • 204 W Railroad Ave • Williams, AZ 86046-2556 • http://www.azstaterrmuseum.org

Coconino County Genealogical Society • 649 E Edison • Williams, AZ 86046

Planes of Fame Air Museum • 755 Mustang Wy • Williams, AZ 86046 • (628) 635-1000

Williams Historic Preservation Commission • 113 S 1st St • Williams, AZ 86046 • (928) 635-4451 • http://www.williamsarizona.gov

Williams Public Library • 113 S 1st St • Williams, AZ 86046 • (928) 635-2263

Window Rock

Navajo Museum • Hwy 264 & Post Ofice Loop Rd, P.O. Box 1840 • Window Rock, AZ 86515 • (928) 871-7941 • http://www.navajomuseum.org

Navajo Nation • P.O. Box 9000 • Window Rock, AZ 86515 • (928) 871-6352 • http://www.navajo.org

Navajo Nation Historic Preservation Department • P.O. Box 4950 • Window Rock, AZ 86515 • (928) 871-7198

Navajo Nation Museum • Hwy 264 & Post Office Loop Rd, P.O. Box 1840 • Window Rock, AZ 86515 • (928) 810-8537

Winslow

Navajo County Genealogical Society • P.O. Box 1403 • Winslow, AZ 86047

Winslow Public Library • 420 W Gilmore • Winslow, AZ 86047 • (928) 289-4982 • http://www.winslowarizona.com

Yarnell

Yarnell Public Library • 22278 N Hwy 89, P.O. Box 808 • Yarnell, AZ 85362 • (928) 427-3191 • http://www.yavapailibrary.org/yarnell.htm

Young

Young Public Library • 150 Community Ctr Rd, P.O. Box 150 • Young, AZ 85554 • (928) 462-3588

Youngtown

Sun Cities Genealogy Society Library • 12600 N 113th Ave #6G • Youngtown, AZ 85363

West Valley Genealogical Society • 12222 N 111th • Youngtown, AZ 85363 • (623) 933-4945

Youngtown Public Library • 12035 Clubhouse Sq • Youngtown, AZ 85363 • (623) 974-3401

Yuma

Arizona Historical Society, Rio Colorado Branch • Sarguinetti House Museum, 240 S Madison Ave • Yuma, AZ 85364 • (928) 782-1841 • http://www.arizonahistoricalsociety.org

Arizona Society Children of the American Revolution • 3000 S Arizona Ave • Yuma, AZ 85364 • (928) 344-8179

Arizona Western College Library • 2020 S Ave 8E, P.O. Box 929 • Yuma, AZ 85366-0929 • (928) 344-7777 • http://www.azwestern.edu/library

Fort Yuma Quechan Tribe • P.O. Box 11352 • Yuma, AZ 85364 • (619) 572-0213

Genealogical Society of Yuma, Arizona • 3117 W 17th St, P.O. Box 2905 • Yuma, AZ 85364-2905 • (602) 542-4102 • http://www.gsya.org

Quechan Indian Museum • Fort Yuma Indian Hill, P.O. Box 1899 • Yuma, AZ 85366 • (928) 572-0661

US Army Post Library • Bldg 530, 301 C St • Yuma, AZ 85365-9123 • (928) 328-2558 • http://www2.yuma.army.mil/newmwr.library.asp

Yuma County Library District • 350 3rd Ave • Yuma, AZ 85364 • (928) 782-1871 • http://www.yumalibrary.org

Yuma Crossing State Historical Park • 201 N 4th Ave • Yuma, AZ 85364 • (928) 329-0471 • http://www.azstateparks.com

Yuma Territorial Prison State Historic Park • 1 Prison Hill Rd • Yuma, AZ 85364-8792 • (928) 783-4771 • http://www.azstateparks.com

Arizona

Aileene
Will Reed Log Home Museum • P.O. Box 4 • Aileene, AR 71820 • (870) 542-6360

Alexander
Saline County Historical and Heritage Society • P.O. Box 221 • Alexander, AR 72022-0221

Alma
Crawford County Genealogical Society • 314 Fayetteville St, P.O. Box 276 • Alma, AR 72921

Almyra
United Daughters of the Confederacy, James Jackson Gillcoatt Chapter • 1836 Hwy 165 N • Almyra, AR 72003 • (870) 946-1889

Altus
Altus Heritage House Museum • 106 N Franklin, P.O. Box 197 • Altus, AR 97821

Arkadelphia
Clark County Genealogical and Historical Society • Ouachita Baptist Univ, P.O. Box 516 • Arkadelphia, AR 71923 • (870) 245-5332

Clark County Historical Association & Archives • Ouachita Baptist Univ, Special Collections, P.O. Box 3729 • Arkadelphia, AR 71923 • (870) 245-5332

Clark County Library • 609 Caddo St • Arkadelphia, AR 71923 • (870) 246-2271

Riley-Hickingbotham Library • Ouachita Baptist Univ, 410 Ouachita, P.O. Box 516 • Arkadelphia, AR 71923 • (870) 245-5119 • http://www.obu.edu

Ash Flat
Sharp County Historical Society • P.O. Box 185 • Ash Flat, AR 72513 • (870) 257-2323

Ashdown
Ashdown Community Library • 160 E Commerce St • Ashdown, AR 71822 • (870) 898-3233

Dallas County Genealogical and Historical Society • Hunter Coulter Museum, 310 N 2nd St • Ashdown, AR 71822

Little River Historical Society • Hunter Coulter Museum, 310 N 2nd St • Ashdown, AR 71822

Atkins
Pope County Library System-Atkins Centennial Library • 216 NE 1st St • Atkins, AR 72823 • (479) 641-7904

Augusta
East Central Arkansas Regional Library-Woodruff County Library • 201 Mulberry St • Augusta, AR 72006 • (870) 347-5331

Batesville
Batesville Genealogical Society • P.O. Box 3883 • Batesville, AR 72503-3883 • (870) 793-7725

Independence County Historical Society • P.O. Box 2722 • Batesville, AR 72503 • (870) 793-2383 • http://www.knology.net/~lizglenn/ichs.htm

Maybee-Simpson Library • Lyon College, Regional Studies Ctr, 2300 Highland Rd • Batesville, AR 72501 • (870) 698-4330 • http://www.lyon.edu/library

Old Independence Regional Museum • 380 S 9th St, P.O. Box 4506 • Batesville, AR 72503 • (870) 793-2121 • http://www.oirm.org

White River Regional Library • 368 E Main St • Batesville, AR 72501 • (870) 793-8814

Beebe
Abington Memorial Library • Arkansas State University-Beebe, 1000 W Iowa St • Beebe, AR 72012 • (501) 882-8207 • http://www.asub.edu

Bella Vista
Bella Vista Historical Society • Historical Museum, 1885 Bella Vista Wy • Bella Vista, AR 72714 • (479) 855-2335

Bella Vista Public Library • 11 Dickens Pl • Bella Vista, AR 72714-4603 • (479) 855-1753 • http://www.bvpl.org

Benton
Saline County Historical Commission • Gunn Museum of Saline County, 218 S Market St • Benton, AR 72015 • (501) 778-5513

Saline County History and Heritage Society • 410 River St, P.O. Box 1712 • Benton, AR 72018-1712 • (501) 778-3770 • http://www.rrootsweb.com/~arschhs

Saline County Public Library • 1800 Smithers Rd • Benton, AR 72015 • (501) 778-4766 • http://www.saline.lib.ar.us

Sons of the American Revolution, Arkansas Society • 1119 Scenic Wy • Benton, AR 72015 • http://www.rootsweb.ancestry.com/~arssar/

Bentonville
Benton County Historical Society • Peel Mansion Museum, 400 S Walton Blvd, P.O. Box 1034 • Bentonville, AR 72712 • (479) 273-9664 • http://www.peelmansion.org

Benton County Preservation Society • 400 S Walton Blvd • Bentonville, AR 72712-5705 • (501) 273-3890

Bentonville Public Library • 405 S Main • Bentonville, AR 72712 • (479) 271-3192 • http://www.bentonvillear.com

Northwest Arkansas Genealogical Society • Peel Mansion Museum, 400 S Walton Blvd • Bentonville, AR 72712 • (501) 273-9664 • http://biz/ipa.net/peel

Berryville
Carroll County Historical and Genealogical Society • Heritage Center Museum, 1880 Court House on the Square, P.O. Box 249 • Berryville, AR 72616-0249 • (870) 423-6312 • http://www.rootsweb.com/~arcchs

Saunders Memorial Museum • 113-15 E Madison St • Berryville, AR 72616 • (870) 423-2563

Blytheville
Blytheville Heritage Museum • 107 C Main St, P.O. Box 234 • Blytheville, AR 72316

Booneville
Booneville Public Library • 419 N Kennedy • Booneville, AR 72927 • (501) 675-2735

Bradley
Lafayette County Historical Society • P.O. Box 180 • Bradley, AR 71826

Brinkley
Central Delta Depot Museum • 100 W Cypress • Brinkley, AR 72021 • (870) 589-2124 • http://www.deltadepotmuseum.org

Central Delta Historical Society • c/o Folsom Memorial Library, 234 W Cedar • Brinkley, AR 72021 • (870) 734-3333

Folsom Memorial Library • 234 W Cedar • Brinkley, AR 72021 • (870) 734-3333

Bryant
Saline County History and Heritage Society • 410 S River St, P.O. Box 221 • Bryant, AR 72022-0221 • (501) 847-0402

Cabot
Arlene Cherry Memorial Library • 506 N Grant • Cabot, AR 72023 • (501) 843-7661

Cabot High School Museum • 504 E Locust • Cabot, AR 72023

Cabot Historical Society • P.O. Box 39 • Cabot, AR 72023

Calico Rock
Izard County Library-Calico Rock Branch • 1214 Pirate St, P.O. Box HC 61, Box 280 • Calico Rock, AR 72519 • (870) 297-3785

Camden
Camden-Ouachita County Public Library • 120 Harrison Ave SW • Camden, AR 71711 • (870) 836-5083

Cleveland County Historical Society • 926 Washington St NW • Camden, AR 71701

Ouachita County Historical Society • McCollum-Chidester House Museum, 926 Washington St NW • Camden, AR 71701 • (870) 836-9243

Ouachita-Calhoun Genealogical Society • P.O. Box 2092 • Camden, AR 71701-2092 • (870) 836-6575

Charleston
Charleston Public Library • 510 Main St, P.O. Box 338 • Charleston, AR 72949 • (501) 965-2605

Clarendon
Monroe County Historical and Cemetery Association • 804 Walker Str • Clarendon, AR 72029-2438

Monroe County Library • 270 Madison St • Clarendon, AR 72029 • (870) 747-5593

Clarksville
Johnson County Historical Society • P.O. Box 505 • Clarksville, AR 72830 • (501) 754-2824

Johnson County Library • 2 Taylor Cr • Clarksville, AR 72830 • (479) 754-3135

Clinton
Faulkner County Library-Van Buren County • 110 Paige St • Clinton, AR 72031 • (501) 745-2100

Van Buren County Historical Society • Historical Museum, 1123 3rd St, P.O. Box 1023 • Clinton, AR 72031 • (501) 745-4066 • http://www.ntanet.net/nta/historical.html

Clover Bend
Clover Bend Historic Preservation • 4679 Hwy 63 • Clover Bend, AR 72415

Conway
Ancestors Unknown • 404 Angus, P.O. Box 164 • Conway, AR 72033-0164 • (501) 329-2868

Arkansas Research • P.O. Box 303 • Conway, AR 72033 • (501) 470-1120 • http://www.arkansasresearch.com

Faulkner County Historical Society • Historical Museum, Courthouse Sq, 805 Locust St, P.O. Box 2442 • Conway, AR 72032 • (501) 329-6918 • http://www.faulknerhistory.com

Faulkner County Library • 1900 Tyler St • Conway, AR 72032 • (501) 327-7482 • http://www.fcl.org

Faulkner County Museum • Courthouse Sq, 805 Locust St, P.O. Box 2442 • Conway, AR 72032 • (501) 329-6918

J E Cobb Library • Central Baptist College, 1501 College Ave • Conway, AR 72034 • (501) 329-6872 • http://www.cbc.edu/library.htm

Olin C Bailey Library • Hendrix College, 1600 Washington Ave • Conway, AR 72032-3080 • (501) 450-1303 • http://www.hendrix.edu/baileylibrary

Professional Genealogists of Arkansas • P.O. Box 1807 • Conway, AR 72033-1807 • (501) 470-1120 • http://biz.ipa.net/arkresearch/

Torreyson Library • Univ of Central Arkansas, Special Collections, 201 Donaghey Ave • Conway, AR 72032 • (501) 450-5224 • http://www.uca.edu

Corning
Corning Library • 613 Pine St • Corning, AR 72422 • (870) 857-3453 • http://www.corninglibrary.com

Crossett
Ashley County Genealogical Society • P.O. Drawer R • Crossett, AR 71635-1819 • (870) 364-2885 • http://www.rootsweb.com/~arashley/

Crossett Company House & Wiggins Cabin Museum • Hwy 133T • Crossett, AR 71635 • (870) 364-6591

Crossett Historical Society • Wiggins Cabin, 1100 Oak • Crossett, AR 71635

Crossett Public Library • 1700 Main St • Crossett, AR 71635 • (870) 364-2230 • http://www.crossett.lib.ar.us

Danville
Yell County Library • 904 Atlanta St, P.O. Box 850 • Danville, AR 72833-0850 • (501) 495-2911

Dardanelle
Arkansas River Valley Regional Library System • 501 N Front St • Dardanelle, AR 72834-3507 • (501) 229-4418 • http://www.arvrls.com

Yell County Historical and Genealogical Society • P.O. Box 622 • Dardanelle, AR 72834

De Queen
Sevier County Genealogical Society • Historical Museum, 717 N Maple, P.O. Box 288 • De Queen, AR 71832 • (501) 642-6642 • http://www.dequeen.com/links.museum.html

Sevier County Historical Society • Historical Museum, 717 N Maple Ave, P.O. Box 892 • De Queen, AR 71832 • (870) 642-6642 • http://www.dequeen.com/links.museum.html

Sevier County Library, DeQueen Branch • 200 W Stillwell • De Queen, AR 72832 • (870) 584-4364

De Valls Bluff
Lonoke Prairie County Regional Library-Devalls Bluff Public Library • P.O. Box 504 • De Valls Bluff, AR 72041-0504 • (870) 998-7010

De Witt
Daughters of the American Revolution, Grand Prairie Chapter • 1120 S Tyler • De Witt, AR 72042 • (870) 946-1511

DeWitt Public Library • 205 W Maxwell • De Witt, AR 72042 • (870) 946-1151

Grand Prairie Historical Society • 203 S Monroe St • De Witt, AR 72042 • (870) 946-1336

Delight
Pike County Archives • 1684 Hwy 26E • Delight, AR 71940

Dermott
Southeast Arkansas Regional Library-Dermott Branch • 117 S Freeman St • Dermott, AR 71638 • (870) 538-3514

Des Arc
Lonoke Prairie County Regional Library-Des Arc • 408 Curran St, P.O. Box 542 • Des Arc, AR 72040-0542 • (870) 256-3003

Lower White River Museum • 2009 Main St • Des Arc, AR 72040 • (875) 256-3711 • http://www.arkansasstateparks.com

Prairie County Historical Society • W Main St • Des Arc, AR 72040

Dolph
Izard County Historical Society • P.O. Box 84 • Dolph, AR 72528 • (870) 297-3751

Dover
Pope County Library System-Dover Public Library • 81 Library Rd • Dover, AR 72837-0326 • (479) 331-2173

Dumas

Desha County Historical Society • 506 Henry Dr • Dumas, AR 76139

Desha County Museum Society • Desha County Museum, Hwy 165 E, P.O. Box 141 • Dumas, AR 72639 • (870) 382-4222

Southeast Arkansas Regional Library-Dumas Branch • 120 E Choctow • Dumas, AR 71639 • (870) 382-5763

Earle

Crittenden County Historical Society • Crittenden County Museum • 1112 Main St, P.O. Box 644 • Earle, AR 72331 • (870) 792-7374

El Dorado

Barton Library • 200 E 5th St • El Dorado, AR 71730 • (870) 863-5447 • http://www.bartonlibrary.org

South Arkansas Historical Foundation • 510 N Jackson Ave • El Dorado, AR 71730 • (870) 862-9890

South Arkansas Historical Society • P.O. Box 10201 • El Dorado, AR 71730-0201

Union County Genealogical Society • c/o Barton Library, 200 E 5th St • El Dorado, AR 71730-3897 • (870) 863-5447

England

Wagon Yard Museum • 2000 S Allis • England, AR 72046 • (501) 842-2222

Eureka Springs

Carnegie Public Library • 194 Spring St • Eureka Springs, AR 72632 • (870) 253-8754

Eureka Springs Historical Society • Historical Museum, 95 S Main St • Eureka Springs, AR 72632 • (479) 253-9417 • http://www.eshm.org

Gables House Museum • 44 Prospect Ave • Eureka Springs, AR 72632 • (501) 253-2428

Rosalie House Museum • 282 Spring St • Eureka Springs, AR 72632 • (479) 253-7377 • http://www.rosalietours-weddings.com

Fairfield Bay

Faulkner County Library-Fairfield Bay Branch • Lakewood Village Mall, Bldg 4, P.O. Box 1183 • Fairfield Bay, AR 72088-1183 • (501) 884-3287

Fayetteville

Arkansas Air Museum • 4290 S School Ave • Fayetteville, AR 72701 • (479) 521-4947 • http://www.arkairmuseum.org

Arkansas Historical Association • Old Main 416, Univ of Arkansas • Fayetteville, AR 72701 • (479) 575-5884 • http://www.uark.edu

Fayetteville Public Library • Grace Keith Genealogy Collection, 401 W Mountain St • Fayetteville, AR 72701 • (479) 571-2222 • http://www.faylib.org

Headquarters House Museum • 118 E Dickson St • Fayetteville, AR 72701 • (479) 521-2970

Mullins Library • Univ of Arkansas • Fayetteville, AR 72701-1201 • (479) 575-6645 • http://www.libinfo.uark.edu

University of Arkansas Libraries • Special Collections Dept, 365 N McIlroy Ave • Fayetteville, AR 72701 • (501) 575-8444 • http://cavern.uark.edu/libinfo/speccoll/

Washington County Historical Society • Historical Museum, 118 E Dickson St • Fayetteville, AR 72701-5612 • (479) 521-2970

Flippin

Arkansas Band of Western Cherokee • P.O. Box 142 • Flippin, AR 72634 • http://www.arkansascherokees.com

Marion County Historical Commission • P.O. Box 263 • Flippin, AR 72634

Fordyce

Dallas County Genealogical and Historical Society • c/o Dallas County Library, 501 E 4th St, P.O. Box 28 • Fordyce, AR 71742 • (870) 352-3592

Dallas County Historical Society • 210 N Main St • Fordyce, AR 71742-3236

Dallas County Library • 501 E 4th St, P.O. Box 584 • Fordyce, AR 71742 • (870) 352-3592

Foreman

Rocky Comfort Museum • 407 3rd Ave E, P.O. Box 268 • Foreman, AR 71836 • (870) 542-7887

Forrest City

East Arkansas Community College Library • 1700 Newcastle Rd • Forrest City, AR 72335-9598 • (870) 633-4480

Forrest City Public Library • 421 S Washington • Forrest City, AR 72335 • (870) 633-5646

Saint Frances County Museum • 603 Front St, P.O. Box 928 • Forrest City, AR 72336 • (870) 261-1744 • http://www.stfranciscounty.net/museum.html

Saint Francis County Historical Association • 112 S Izard • Forrest City, AR 72335

Fort Smith

Bonneville House Museum • 318 N 7th St • Fort Smith, AR 72901 • (501) 782-7854

Boreham Library • Univ of Arkansas Fort Smith, 5210 Grand Ave, P.O. Box 3649 • Fort Smith, AR 72913-3649 • (479) 788-7208 • http://www.uafortsmith.edu

Clayton House • 514 N 6th St • Fort Smith, AR 72901 • (479) 783-3000

Darby House Museum • 311 General Darby St, P.O. Box 1625 • Fort Smith, AR 72902-1625 • (479) 782-3388

Fort Smith Historical Society • 61 S 8th St, P.O. Box 3676 • Fort Smith, AR 72901 • (479) 783-1237 • http://www.fortsmithhistory.org

Fort Smith Museum of History • 320 Rogers Ave, P.O. Box 1406 • Fort Smith, AR 72902 • (479) 783-7841 • http://www.fortsmithmuseum.com

Fort Smith National Historic Site Museum • 301 Parker Ave, P.O. Box 1406 • Fort Smith, AR 72902 • (479) 783-3961 • http://www.nps.gov/fosm/

Fort Smith Public Library • 3201 Rogers Ave • Fort Smith, AR 72903 • (479) 783-0229 • http://www.fspl.lib.ar.us

Fort Smith Trolley Museum • 100 S 4th St • Fort Smith, AR 72901 • (479) 783-0205 • http://www.fstm.org

Frontier Researchers Genealogical Society • P.O. Box 2123 • Fort Smith, AR 72902

South Sebastian County Historical Society • Historical Museum, 8502 Bonanza Rd • Fort Smith, AR 72916

US Marshals Museum • 100 Garrison Ave • Fort Smith, AR 72901 • http://www.usmarshals.gov/history/museum.htm

Fouke

Miller County Historical Society • general delivery • Fouke, AR 71837 • (870) 653-4550

Garfield

Pea Ridge National Military Park • 15930 Hwy 62, P.O. Box 700 • Garfield, AR 72751-0700 • (479) 451-8122 • http://www.nps.gov/peri/

Gassville

Baxter County Historical and Genealogical Society • Historical Museum, 107 E Main St, P.O. Box 675 • Gassville, AR 72635 • (870) 425-4502 • http://www.baxtercountyhistory.org/

Arkansas

Gillett

Arkansas Post Museum • 5530 Hwy 165 S • Gillett, AR 72055 • (870) 548-2634 • http://www.arkansas.com

Grand Prairie Historical Society • P.O. Box 122 • Gillett, AR 72055 • (501) 548-2458

Refeld-Hinman House Museum • 5530 Hwy 1655 • Gillett, AR 72055 • (870) 548-2634 • http://www.arkansas.com

Gravette

Gravette Historical Museum • 503 Charlotte • Gravette, AR 72736 • (479) 787-7334 • http://www.gravette.com

Green Forest

Chickamauga Cherokee Nation • Route 2, Box 647 • Green Forest, AR 72638 • (510) 423-6464

Greenwood

Scott-Sebastian Regional Library • 18 N Adair, P.O. Box 400 • Greenwood, AR 72936-0400 • (479) 996-2856

South Sebastian County Historical Society • P.O. Box 523 • Greenwood, AR 72936 • (501) 996-2843

Gurdon

Hoo-Hoo International Forestry Museum • 207 Main St, P.O. Box 118 • Gurdon, AR 71743 • (870) 353-4997 • http://www.hoo-hoo.org

Hackett

Old Jail Museum • 2408 Reeves Rd • Hackett, AR 72937

Hamburg

Ashley County Historical Society • 300 N Cherry St • Hamburg, AR 71646 • (870) 853-5796

Ashley County Library • 211 E Lincoln • Hamburg, AR 71646 • (870) 853-2078

Hampton

Calhoun County Historical Society • P.O. Box 97 • Hampton, AR 71744

Columbia County Library-Calhoun County Library • 113 2nd St, P.O. Box 1162 • Hampton, AR 71744-1162 • (870) 798-4492

Hardy

Good Old Days Vintage Motorcar Museum • 301 W Main St, P.O. Box 311 • Hardy, AR 72542 • (870) 856-4884

Sharp County Library • 201 Church St • Hardy, AR 72542 • (870) 856-3934

Veteran's Museum of Hardy • 738 Main St, P.O. Box 1051 • Hardy, AR 72542 • (870) 856-4133

Harrisburg

Poinsett County Historical Society • P.O. Box 424 • Harrisburg, AR 72432

Harrison

Boone County Heritage Group • 110 S Cherry St • Harrison, AR 72601-5024

Boone County Historical and Genealogical Society • Boone County Heritage Museum, Central & Cherry Sts, P.O. Box 1094 • Harrison, AR 72601 • (870) 741-3312

Boone County Historical and Railroad Society • Heritage Museum, 110 S Cherry St, P.O. Box 1094 • Harrison, AR 72601 • (870) 741-3312

Boone County Public Library • 221 W Stephenson Ave • Harrison, AR 72601-4225 • (870) 741-5913 • http://bcl.state.ar.us

Buffalo National River Museum • US Fed Blvd, 402 N Walnut St, Ste 136 • Harrison, AR 72601 • (870) 741-5443 • http://www.nps.gov/buff/

North Arkansas College Library • 1515 Pioneer Dr • Harrison, AR 72601 • (870) 391-3358 • http://www.northark.net

Hatfield

Polk County Genealogical Society • 8th & Port Arthur, P.O. Box 317 • Hatfield, AR 71945 • (501) 394-6355

Hazen

Hazen Historical Society • 311 N Hazen Ave, P.O. Box 451 • Hazen, AR 72064 • (870) 255-4547

Lonoke Prairie County Regional Library-Hazen • Hwy 70 E, P.O. Box 428 • Hazen, AR 72064-0428 • (870) 255-3576

Prairie County Historical Society • P.O. Box 451 • Hazen, AR 72064 • (870) 255-4522

Heber Springs

Cleburne County Historical Society • 210 N Broadway, P.O. Box 794 • Heber Springs, AR 72543 • (501) 362-5225

Cleburne County Library • 1010 W Searcy St • Heber Springs, AR 72543 • (501) 362-2477

Olmstead Historical Society • Olmdstead Funeral & Historical Museum • 108 S 4th St • Heber Springs, AR 72543 • (501) 362-2422 • http://www.olmstead.ccom/museum.htm

Helena

Arkansas Institute For Historical Building Trades • 1000 Campus Dr • Helena, AR 72342 • (870) 338-3276

Delta Cultural Center • 114 Cherry St, P.O. Box 509 • Helena, AR 72342 • (870) 338-4350 • http://www.deltaculturalcenter.com

Phillips County Historical Society • c/o Phillips County Library, 623 Pecan St • Helena, AR 72342 • (870) 338-3537

Phillips County Library • 623 Pecan St • Helena, AR 72342 • (870) 338-3537 • http://www.geocities.com/athens/ithaca/4022

Phillips County Museum • 625 Pecan St, P.O. Box 38 • Helena, AR 72342 • (870) 338-7790

Hope

Hempstead County Genealogical Society • P.O. Box 1158 • Hope, AR 71801

Hempstead County Historical Society • 149 Highway 32E, P.O. Box 1257 • Hope, AR 71802-1257 • (870) 777-2491

Hempstead County Library • 500 S Elm St • Hope, AR 71801 • (870) 777-4564

Southwest Arkansas Regional Library • 500 S Elm St • Hope, AR 71801 • (870) 777-4564

Hot Springs

Arkansas Ancestors • 222 McMahan Dr • Hot Springs, AR 71913-6243 • (501) 623-6766 • http://home.cablelynx.com/~bjmclane

Arkansas Genealogical Society • 1411 Shady Grove Rd, P.O. Box 908 • Hot Springs, AR 71902-0908 • (870) 863-5447 • http://www.rootsweb.com/~args/

Garland County Historical Society • 210 W Woodbine, P.O. Box 21335 • Hot Springs, AR 71903 • (501) 623-6766

Garland County Library • 1427 Malvern Ave • Hot Springs, AR 71901 • (501) 623-4161

Hot Springs National Park • 369 Central Ave, P.O. Box 1860 • Hot Springs, AR 71902 • (501) 624-3383 • http://www.nps.gov/hosp

Melting Pot Genealogical Society • 223A Hazel St, P.O. Box 936 • Hot Springs, AR 71902-0936 • (501) 624-0229

National Park Community College Library • 101 College Dr • Hot Springs, AR 71913 • (501) 760-4101 • http://www.gccc.cc.ar.us/library/

United Daughters of the Confederacy, Hot Springs Chapter • general delivery • Hot Springs, AR 71902

Hot Springs National Park

Garland County Historical Society • 328 Quapaw Ave • Hot Springs National Park, AR 71901 • (501) 321-2159

Melting Pot Genealogical Society • 649 Ouachita Ave • Hot Springs National Park, AR 71901 • (501) 624-0229

Hot Springs Village

Village Genealogical Society • 5 Murcia Place • Hot Springs Village, AR 71909-4403 • (501) 922-4560 • http://pages.suddenlink.net/hsvgs/

Houston

Perry County Historical and Genealogical Society • RR2, Box 143 • Houston, AR 72070

Huntsville

Madison County Genealogical and Historical Society • Hwy 74 W & Mitchusson Park Rd, P.O. Box 427 • Huntsville, AR 72740 • (501) 738-6408 • http://www.theaurorareview.com/madcounty/mcindex.htm

Jacksonport

Jacksonport State Park Courthouse Museum • 205 Avenue St • Jacksonport, AR 72112 • (870) 523-2145 • http://www.arkanstateparks.com

Jasper

Newton County Historical and Genealogical Society • Bradley House Museum, 403 Clark St, P.O. Box 360 • Jasper, AR 72641 • (870) 446-6247 • http://www.newtoncountyar.com

Newton County Library • Hwy 7 S, HC31, Box 8 • Jasper, AR 72641 • (870) 446-2983

Jonesboro

Arkansas State University Museum • Museum Bldg, P.O. Box 490 • Jonesboro, AR 72467-0490 • (870) 972-2074

Arkansas State University Museum • 110 Cooley Dr, P.O. Box 490 • Jonesboro, AR 72467 • (870) 972-2074 • http://www.museum.astate.edu

Craighead County Historical Society • P.O. Box 1011 • Jonesboro, AR 72401 • (870) 935-6838 • http://www.craigheadhistorical.org

Craighead County Jonesboro Public Library • 315 W Oak Ave • Jonesboro, AR 72401-3513 • (870) 935-5133 • http://www.libraryinjonesboro.org

Dean B Ellis Library • Arkansas State University, 108 Cooley Dr • Jonesboro, AR 72401 • (870) 972-3208 • http://www.library.astate.edu

Genealogy Society of Craighead County, Arkansas • 1811 S Culberhouse, P.O. Box 844 • Jonesboro, AR 72403 • http://www.gscca.net

Lake Village

Museum of Chicot County Arkansas • 614 Cokley St, P.O. Box 762 • Lake Village, AR 71653 • (870) 265-2868

Lepanto

Museum Lepanto • 310 Greenwood Ave, P.O. Box 670 • Lepanto, AR 72354 • (870) 475-6166

Leslie

Ozark Heritage Museum • P.O. Box 217 • Leslie, AR 72645 • (870) 447-2500

Lewisville

Lafayette County Historical Society • P.O. Box 91 • Lewisville, AR 71845 • (870) 921-4785

Lincoln

Arkansas Country Doctor Museum • 13547 Lincoln-Canehill Rd, P.O. Box 1004 • Lincoln, AR 72744 • http://www.drmuseum.net

Little Rock

Afro-American Historical and Genealogical Society, Arkansas Chapter • 14617 Sara Drive, P.O. Box 4294 • Little Rock, AR 72214-4294 • http://www.rootsweb.com/araahgs

Arkansas Department of Health, Division of Vital Records • 4815 W Markham St • Little Rock, AR 72205-3867 • (501) 661-2336 • http://health.state.ar.us/htm/vr_faq.htm

Arkansas Department of Heritage Services • 1500 Tower Bldg, 323 Center St, Suite 1500 • Little Rock, AR 72201 • (501) 324-9150 • http://www.arkansasheritage.com

Arkansas Genealogical Society • 4200 A Street, P.O. Box 17653 • Little Rock, AR 72205 • (501) 262-4513 • http://www.agsgenealogy.org

Arkansas History Commission • 1 Capitol Mall • Little Rock, AR 72201 • (501) 682-6900 • http://www.ark-ives.com

Arkansas Museum of Science and History • 500 E Markham, Suite 500 • Little Rock, AR 72201 • (501) 396-7050 • http://www.amod.org

Arkansas State Library • 1 Capitol Mall, 5th Flr • Little Rock, AR 72201 • (501) 682-1527 • http://www.asl.lib.ar.us

Arkansas Territorial Restoration Museum • 200 E 3rd St • Little Rock, AR 72201-1608 • (501) 324-9351 • http://www.arkansashistory.com

Brownlee-Noland House Museum • 214 E 3rd St • Little Rock, AR 72201 • (501) 324-9351 • http://www.mscda.org/museums/arkansas.htm

Central Arkansas Library System • 100 Rock St • Little Rock, AR 72201 • (501) 370-5952 • http://www.cals.lib.ar.us

Central High School National Historic Site Museum • 2125 Daisy L Gaston Bates Dr • Little Rock, AR 72202 • (501) 374-1957 • http://www.nps.gov/chsc/

Civil War Round Table Associates • 9 Lefever Lane, P.O. Box 7388 • Little Rock, AR 72217-7388 • (501) 225-3996

Cleveland County Museum • 1919 Biscayne Dr • Little Rock, AR 72227

Confederate Historical Institute • 9 Lefever Lane, P.O. Box 7388 • Little Rock, AR 72217-7388 • (501) 225-3996

Heritage Seekers Genealogy Club • c/o Laman Public Library, 2801 Orange St • Little Rock, AR 72114-2296 • (501) 758-1720

HERITAGEPAC: Dedicated to the Preservation of American Battlefields • P.O. Box 7281 • Little Rock, AR 72217

Historic Arkansas Museum • 200 E 3rd St • Little Rock, AR 72201 • (501) 324-9351 • http://www.historicarkansas.org

Historic Preservation Alliance of Arkansas • 105 Main St, P.O. Box 305 • Little Rock, AR 72203-0305 • (501) 372-4757

Little Rock Central High School National Historic Site • 2120 Daisy L Gatson Bates Dr • Little Rock, AR 72202 • (501) 374-1957 • http://www.nps.gov/chsc/

M L Harris Library • Philander Smith College, 812 W 13th St • Little Rock, AR 72202 • (501) 370-5262

MacArthur Museum of Arkansas Military History • Tower Bldg, 503 E 9th St • Little Rock, AR 72214 • (501) 376-4602 • http://www.arkmilitaryheritage.com

Mosaic Templars Cultural Center • 1500 Tower Bldg, 323 Center St • Little Rock, AR 72201 • http://www.mosaictemplarscenter.com

Museum of Discovery • 500 E Markham • Little Rock, AR 72201 • (501) 396-7050

Old State House Museum • 300 W Markham St • Little Rock, AR 72201 • (501) 324-9685 • http://www.oldstatehouse.com

Order of the Indian Wars • 100 Rock St, P.O. Box 7401 • Little Rock, AR 72201 • (501) 225-3996 • http://lbha.org/oiw.html

Little Rock, cont.
Ottenheimer Library • Univ of Arkansas at Little Rock, 2801 S University • Little Rock, AR 72204 • (501) 569-3120 • http://libraryl.ualr.edu

Pike-Fletcher-Terry House Museum of Decorative Arts • 7th & Rock Sts, P.O. Box 2137 • Little Rock, AR 72203 • (501) 396-0357

Pope County Historical Association • 4200 A Street • Little Rock, AR 72205-4046 • (501) 663-3301

Pulaski County Historical Society • P.O. Box 251903 • Little Rock, AR 72225 • (501) 663-7161

Quapaw Quarter Association • 1206 S Main St, P.O. Box 165023 • Little Rock, AR 72216-5023 • (501) 371-0075

Villa Marre House Museum • 1321 S Scott St, P.O. Box 165023 • Little Rock, AR 72216 • (501) 374-9979

William J Clinton Presidential Library & Museum • 1200 President Clinton Ave • Little Rock, AR 72201 • (501) 244-2857 • http://www.clintonlibrary.gov

Lonoke
Lonoke County Historical Society • P.O. Box 14 • Lonoke, AR 72086 • (501) 676-6988

Lonoke Prairie County Regional Library • 204 E 2nd St • Lonoke, AR 72086-2858 • (501) 676-6635

Lowell
Lowell Museum and Historical Society • Historical Museum, 304 Jackson Pl, P.O. Box 979 • Lowell, AR 72745 • (479) 601-3713

Magazine
Logan County Historical Society • P.O. Box 40 • Magazine, AR 72943-0040 • (501) 675-4680

Magnolia
Columbia County Library • 220 E Main, P.O. Box 668 • Magnolia, AR 71753 • (870) 234-1991 • http://www.colcnty.lib.ar.us

Magale Library • Southern Arkansas Univ, 100 E University, SAU Box 9218 • Magnolia, AR 71754-9218 • (870) 235-5083 • http://www.saumag.edu/library

Southwest Arkansas Genealogical Society • 523 E Union • Magnolia, AR 71753 • (870) 234-1991

Malvern
Boyle House-Hot Spring County Museum • 310 E 3rd St • Malvern, AR 72104 • (501) 337-4775

Hot Spring County Library • 202 E 3rd St • Malvern, AR 72104 • (501) 332-5441 • http://www.hsc.lib.ar.us

Hot Springs County Historical and Genealogical Society • 2705 Southgate Dr, P.O. Box 674 • Malvern, AR 72104 • (501) 337-7488

Hot Springs County Historical Society • 302 E 3rd St • Malvern, AR 72104-3912

Mammoth Spring
Mammoth Spring State Park Depot Museum • P.O. Box 36 • Mammoth Spring, AR 72554 • (870) 625-7364 • http://www.arkansasstateparks.com

Marianna
Marianna Lee County Historical Society • Marianna-Lee County Museum • 67 W Main St, P.O. Box 584 • Marianna, AR 72360 • (870) 295-2469

Phillips-Lee-Monroe Regional Library-Lee County Library • 77 W Main St • Marianna, AR 72360-2297 • (870) 295-2688

Marion
Crittenden County Historical Society • P.O. Box 685 • Marion, AR 72364

Margaret Woolfolk Library • 110 Currie St • Marion, AR 72364 • (870) 739-3238

Marked Tree
Marked Tree Historical Society • P.O. Box 72 • Marked Tree, AR 72365

Marshall
North Arkansas Regional Library-Searcy County • HC80, Box 11 • Marshall, AR 72650 • (870) 448-2420

Search County Museum • Hwy 27 S, P.O. Box 819 • Marshall, AR 72650 • (870) 448-4786

Searcy County Historical Society • Hwy 27 S • Marshall, AR 72650

Marvell
Tri-County Genealogical Society • 406 S Midway St, P.O. Box 580 • Marvell, AR 72366-0580 • (870) 829-2772 • http://www.rootsweb.com/~armonroe

McCrory
Woodruff County Historical Society • P.O. Box Q • McCrory, AR 72101

McGehee
Desha County Historical Society • P.O. Box 432 • McGehee, AR 71654

Southeast Arkansas Regional Library-McGehee Branch Library • 211 N 4th St • McGehee, AR 71654-2296 • (870) 222-4097

Melbourne
Izard County Library • 915 E Main St, P.O. Box 343 • Melbourne, AR 72556-0343 • (870) 368-7467

Mena
Polk County Genealogical Society, Polk County Pioneers • P.O. Box 1525 • Mena, AR 71953

Southwest Arkansas Regional Library-Polk County • 410 8th St • Mena, AR 71953 • (479) 394-2314

Monticello
Drew County Historical Society • Historical Museum, 404 S Main St • Monticello, AR 71655 • (501) 367-7446

Southeast Arkansas Genealogical Society • Historical Museum, 404 S Main • Monticello, AR 71655 • (870) 367-7446

Southeast Arkansas Regional Library • 107 E Jackson St • Monticello, AR 71655 • (870) 367-8584

Univ of Arkansas-Monticello Library • 514 University Dr, P.O. Box 3599 • Monticello, AR 71656 • (870) 460-1080 • http://www.uamont.edu/library

Morrilton
Conway County Genealogical Association • 20 Rocky Point Rd, P.O. Box 865 • Morrilton, AR 72110 • (501) 354-4428

Conway County Historical Museum • 101 E Railroad Ave, P.O. Box 417 • Morrilton, AR 72110 • (501) 354-8578

Conway County Library • 101 W Church St • Morrilton, AR 72110 • (501) 354-5204

Museum of Automobiles • Petit Jean Mountain, 8 Jones Ln • Morrilton, AR 72110 • (501) 727-5427 • http://www.museumofautos.com

Mount Ida
Heritage House Museum of Montgomery County • 809 Luzerne St, P.O. Box 1362 • Mount Ida, AR 71957 • (870) 867-4422 • http://www.hhmmc.org

Montgomery County Historical Society • Hwy 270, P.O. Box 578 • Mount Ida, AR 71957-0520 • (870) 867-3121

Montgomery County Library • 145A Whittington St, P.O. Box 189 • Mount Ida, AR 71957-0189 • (870) 867-3812

Mountain Home

Baxter County Historical and Genealogical Society • 1505 Mistletoe, P.O. Box 1508 • Mountain Home, AR 72653 • (870) 425-4269 • http://www.geocities.com/Athens/2101/bchgs.htm

Baxter County Library • 424 W 7th St • Mountain Home, AR 72653 • (870) 425-3598 • http://www.baxtercountylibrary.org

Mountain View

Bessie Boehm Moore Stone County Library • 326 W Washington, P.O. Box 1105 • Mountain View, AR 72560-1105 • (870) 269-3100

Mid-America Folklore Society • P.O. Box 500 • Mountain View, AR 72560 • (870) 269-3280

Ozark Folk Center • 1032 Park Ave, P.O. Box 500 • Mountain View, AR 72560 • (870) 269-3851 • http://www.ozarkfolkcenter.com

Stone County Genealogical Society • P.O. Box 1477 • Mountain View, AR 72560 • http://members.nbci.com/stonecoargen/

Stone County Historical Society • Historical Museum, P.O. Box 210 • Mountain View, AR 72560-0210 • (870) 585-2256 • http://www.rootsweb.com/~arscgs

Mulberry

Mulberry Public Library • 207 N Main, P.O. Box 589 • Mulberry, AR 72947 • (501) 997-1226 • http://www.crawfordcounty.lib.org

Murfreesboro

Ka-Do-Ha Indian Village Museum • 1010 Caddo Dr, P.O. Box 669 • Murphreesboro, AR 71958 • (870) 285-3736 • http://www.caddotc.com

Pike County Archives and History Society • 112 Washington St, Ste B, P.O. Box 328 • Murfreesboro, AR 71958 • (870) 285-3528

Southwest Arkansas Regional Library • 204 Main St, P.O. Box 153 • Murfreesboro, AR 71958 • (870) 285-3732

Nashville

Howard County Heritage Club • 218 W Howard St • Nashville, AR 71852

Southwest Arkansas Regional Library-Howard County • 426 N Main St, Suite 5 • Nashville, AR 71852 • (870) 845-2566

Newport

Arkansas Records Association • 314 Vine St • Newport, AR 72112 • (870) 523-3736

Arkansas Records Center • 314 Vine St • Newport, AR 72112

Jackson County Historical Society • 7 Pickens St • Newport, AR 72112 • (870) 523-5150

Jackson County Library • 213 Walnut St, P.O. Box 748 • Newport, AR 72112-0748 • (870) 523-2952

Northeast Arkansas Genealogical Association • 314 Vine St • Newport, AR 72112

Norfolk

Jacob Wolf House Museum • Hwy 5, P.O. Box 118 • Norfolk, AR 72658 • (970) 499-WOLF

North Little Rock

Arkansas Municipal League • P.O. Box 38 • North Little Rock, AR 72115 • (501) 374-3484

Arkansas National Guard Museum • Lloyd England Hall, Camp Robinson • North Little Rock, AR 72199 • (501) 212-5215 • http://www.arngmuseum.com

Heritage Seekers Genealogy Club • c/o Laman Public Library, 2800 Orange St, P.O. Box 532 • North Little Rock, AR 72115-0532 • (501) 758-1720

Pulaski County Heritage Seekers • c/o William F Laman Public Library, 2800 Orange St • North Little Rock, AR 72114-2296 • (501) 758-1720

William F Laman Public Library • 2801 Orange St • North Little Rock, AR 72114-2296 • (501) 758-1720 • http://www.laman.lib.ar.us

Osceola

Mississippi County Historical and Genealogical Society • Historical Center, 209 W Hale Ave, P.O. Box 483 • Osceola, AR 72370 • (870) 563-6161

Mississippi County Library System-Osceola Branch • 320 W Hale • Osceola, AR 72370-2530 • (870) 563-2721

Ozark

Franklin County Historical Association • 1102 W School St • Ozark, AR 72949

Franklin County Library • 407 W Market, P.O. Box 222 • Ozark, AR 72949-2727 • (501) 667-2724

Paragould

Greene County Historical and Genealogical Society • c/o Greene County Library, 120 N 12th St • Paragould, AR 72450 • (870) 236-8711 • http://www.grnco.net/~michael/greene.htm

Greene County Library • 120 N 12th St • Paragould, AR 72450-4155 • (870) 236-8711 • http://www.paragouldlibrary.com

Greene County Museum of Paragould • 130 S 14th St, P.O. Box 991 • Paragould, AR 72450 • (870) 215-0788

Paris

Arkansas Historic Wine Museum • 101 N Carbon City Rd • Paris, AR 72855

Boyd T and Mollis Gattis Library • 100 E Academy • Paris, AR 72855-4432 • (501) 963-2371

Corbin Genealogical Society • RR 3, Box 86 • Paris, AR 72855-9517

Historic Preservation Center • 23 W Main St • Paris, AR 72855

Logan County Museum • 204 N Vine St, P.O. Box 129 • Paris, AR 72855 • (479) 963-3936

Pea Ridge

Pea Ridge Military Park Library • US National Park Service, P.O. Box 700 • Pea Ridge, AR 72751-0700 • (479) 451-8122

Perry

Tri-county Family History Association • P.O. Box 127 • Perry, AR 72125

Perryville

Max Milam Library • Hwy 60 & Cedar, P.O. Box 117 • Perryville, AR 72126 • (501) 889-2554

Perry County Historical and Genealogical Society • P.O. Box 156 • Perryville, AR 72126

Piggott

Clay County Genealogical and Historical Society • c/o Piggott Public Library, 361 W Main St • Piggott, AR 72454 • (870) 598-3666

Piggott Public Library • 361 W Main St • Piggott, AR 72454 • (870) 598-3666 • http://www.piggottlibrary.com

Pine Bluff

Arkansas Railroad Museum • 1700 Port Rd, P.O. Box 2044 • Pine Bluff, AR 71613 • (870) 535-8819

Band Museum • 423-425 Main St • Pine Bluff, AR 71601 • (870) 534-4676 • http://www.bandmuseum.tripod.com

Jefferson County Genealogical Society • P.O. Box 2215 • Pine Bluff, AR 71613 • (870) 535-2182

Jefferson County Historical Society • 1600 W 27th St • Pine Bluff, AR 71603 • (501) 534-8596

Masonic Grand Lodge of Arkansas • 2906 E Harding Ave • Pine Bluff, AR 71601 • (870) 534-5467 • http://arkphagrandlodge.com/

Arkansas

Pine Bluff, cont.

Pine Bluff and Jefferson Counties Public Library • 200 E 8th Ave, Civic Center Complex • Pine Bluff, AR 72601 • (870) 534-4802 • http://www.pbjclibrary.org

Pine Bluff-Jefferson County Historical Museum • 201 E 4th Ave • Pine Bluff, AR 71601 • (870) 541-5402 • http://www.pdjcmuseum.org

Lum and Abner Museum • 4652 Hwy 88 W, P.O. Box 38 • Pine Ridge, AR 71966 • (870) 326-4442 • http://www.lum-abner.com

Pineville

Izard County Historical and Genealogical Society • P.O. Box 306 • Pineville, AR 72566

Pocahontas

Randolph County Historical and Genealogical Society • c/o Randolph County Library, 111 W Everett St • Pocahontas, AR 72455-3316 • (870) 892-5617

Randolph County Library • 111 W Everett St • Pocahontas, AR 72455-3316 • (870) 892-5617 • http://www.randolphcountylibrary.com

Pottsville

Potts Inn Museum • Town Square • Pottsville, AR 72801 • (501) 968-1877

Powhatan

Ficklin-Imboden House Museum • Main St, P.O. Box 93 • Powhatan, AR 72458 • (870) 878-6794

Lawrence County Historical Society • Powhatan Courthouse, P.O. Box 93 • Powhatan, AR 72458 • (870) 878-6794

Powhatan Historic State Park • P.O. Box 93 • Powhatan, AR 72458 • (870) 878-6765 • http://www.arkansasstateparks.com/powhatancourthouse/

Prairie Grove

Latta House - Morrow House Museums • Hwy 62, P.O. Box 306 • Prairie Grove, AR 72753 • (501) 846-2990

Prairie Grove Battlefield State Park • 506 E Douglas St, P.O. Box 306 • Prairie Grove, AR 72753 • (479) 846-2990 • http://www.arkansasstateparks/prairiegrove

Prescott

Nevada County Depot Museum • 403 W 1st St S, P.O. Box 592 • Prescott, AR 71857 • (870) 887-5821 • http://www.depotmuseum.org

Nevada County Historical Society • 401 W 1st St S, P.O. Box 599 • Prescott, AR 71857-0599 • (870) 887-5821

Southwest Arkansas Regional Library-Nevada County • 129 W 2nd St, P.O. Box 613 • Prescott, AR 71857-0613 • (870) 887-5846

Rector

Rector Public Library • 121 W 4th St • Rector, AR 72461 • (870) 595-2410 • http://www.rectorlibrary.com

Rison

Cleveland County Historical Society • 100 Rusty W Ln, P.O. Box 342 • Rison, AR 71665 • (870) 325-7243

Pioneer Village • Mocking Bird Ln, P.O. Box 134 • Rison, AR 71665 • (501) 325-7289

Roy and Christine Sturgis Library of Cleveland Library • 203 W Magnolia, P.O. Box 388 • Rison, AR 71665 • (870) 325-7270

Rogers

Daughters of the American Revolution, Enoch Ashley Chapter • 2613 Dauphine Dr • Rogers, AR 72756

Hawkins House Museum • 322 S 2nd St • Rogers, AR 72756 • (501) 621-1154 • http://www.rogersarkansas.com/museum

Northwest Arkansas Genealogical Society • Peel Mansion Carriage House, 400 S Walton Blvd, P.O. Box 796 • Rogers, AR 72756 • (479) 273-3890

Rogers Historical Society • Rogers Historical Museum • 322 S 2nd St • Rogers, AR 72756 • (479) 621-1154 • http://www.rogersarkansas.com/museum/

Russellville

Arkansas Genealogical Research • 805 E 5th St, P.O. Box 1889 • Russellville, AR 72801 • (501) 967-7792

Arkansas Tech University Museum of History • P.O.Box 8526 • Russellville, AR 72801 • (501) 964-0826

Pope County Historical Association • 1120 N Detroit • Russellville, AR 72801

Pope County Historical Foundation • c/o Pope County Library, 116 E 3rd St • Russellville, AR 72801 • (501) 968-1147

Pope County Library • 116 E 3rd St • Russellville, AR 72801 • (479) 968-4368 • http://www.gorussellville.com

Yell County Historical and Genealogical Society • 108 West 18th, P.O. Box 356 • Russellville, AR 72801-7119

Salem

Fulton County Historical Society • P.O. Box 391 • Salem, AR 72576 • (870) 895-3472

Fulton County Library • 131 Pickren St, P.O. Box 277 • Salem, AR 72576-0277 • (870) 895-2014

Scott

Plantation Agriculture Museum • 4815 Hwy 161, P.O. Box 87 • Scott, AR 72142 • (501) 961-1409 • http://www.arkansasstateparks.com

Searcy

Brackett Library • Harding Univ, 915 E Market St • Searcy, AR 72149 • (501) 279-4354 • http://www.harding.edu

White County Historical Museum • White County Fair Grounds, P.O. Box 1605 • Searcy, AR 72143 • (501) 742-3808

White County Historical Society • P.O. Box 537 • Searcy, AR 72145 • (501) 268-8726 • http://www.rootsweb.com/~arwhite

White County Public Library • 113 E Pleasure Ave • Searcy, AR 72143-7798 • (501) 268-2449 • http://wcls.state.ar.us

Sheridan

Grant County Library • 216 N Oak St • Sheridan, AR 72150-2495 • (870) 942-4436

Grant County Museum • 521 Shackleford Rd, P.O. Box 25 • Sheridan, AR 72150 • (870) 942-4496

Sherwood

Arkansas Family History Association • 609 Colynwood • Sherwood, AR 72120 • (501) 835-7502

Siloam Springs

Siloam Springs Museum • 112 N Maxwell St, P.O. Box 1164 • Siloam Springs, AR 72761 • (479) 524-4011 • http://www.siloamspringsmuseum.com

Smackover

Arkansas Museum of Natural Resources • 3853 Smackover Hwy, P.O. Box 7 • Smackover, AR 91762 • http://www.amnr.org

Barton Library-Smackover Branch • 700 N Broadway • Smackover, AR 71762 • (870) 725-3741

Smackover Genealogical and Historical Society • 700 N Broadway • Smackover, AR 71762

Springdale

Orphan Train Heritage Society of America • Historical Museum, 614 E Emma Ave #115 • Springdale, AR 72764-4634 • (501) 756-2780 • http://pda.republic.net/othsa

Shiloh Museum of Arkansas History • 118 W Johnson St • Springdale, AR 72764 • (479) 750-8165 • http://www.springdaleark.org/shiloh

Stamps
Lafayette County Historical Society • 719 Hope Rd • Stamps, AR 71860

Star City
Lincoln County Genealogy and Historical Society • 300 S Drew St • Star City, AR 71667

Southeast Arkansas Regional Library-Star City Branch • 206 S Lincoln • Star City, AR 71667 • (870) 628-4711

State University
Crowley's Ridge Genealogical Society • P.O. Box 2091 • State University, AR 72467

Strong
Barton Library-Strong Branch • 246 W 2nd Ave, P.O. Box 157 • Strong, AR 71765-0157 • (870) 797-2165

Stuttgart
Daughters of the American Revolution, Arkansas Post Chapter • 808 W 18th St • Stuttgart, AR 72160 • (870) 673-8323

Grand Prairie Genealogical Society • c/o Stuttgart Public Library, 2002 S Buerkle • Stuttgart, AR 72160 • (870) 673-7124 • http://www.rootsweb.com/~ararkans/grandpra.htm

Grand Prairie Historical Society • c/o Stuttgart Public Library, 2002 S Buerkle St • Stuttgart, AR 72160 • (870) 673-7124

Museum of the Arkansas Grand Prairie • 921 E 4th St • Stuttgart, AR 72160 • (870) 673-7001 • http://www.stuttgartmuseum.org

Stuttgart Public Library • 2002 S Buerkle St • Stuttgart, AR 72160-6508 • (870) 673-1966 • http://www.rootsweb.com/~ararkans/grandpra.htm

Texarkana
Tex Ark Antique Auto Museum • 218 Laurel St • Texarkana, AR 71854 • (870) 772-2886

Texarkana Genealogical Society • 1605 E 29th St, P.O. Box 2323 • Texarkana, AR 75504-2323 • (903) 832-7419

Van Buren
Arkansas Historical Society • 422 S 6th St • Van Buren, AR 72956

Bob Burns Museum and River Valley Museum of Van Buren • Old Frisco Depot, 813 Main St, , P.O. Box 1518 • Van Buren, AR 72957 • (479) 474- 6164 • http://www.vanburen.org

Crawford County Historical Society • 929 E Main St, P.O. Box 1317 • Van Buren, AR 72956 • (501) 474-2218

Van Buren Public Library • 111 N 12th St • Van Buren, AR 72956 • (479) 474-6045 • http://www.crawfordcountylib.org

Waldron
Chickamauga Cherokee Nation - White River Band • HCR 67, Box 41B • Waldron, AR 72958 • (501) 637-2383

Scott County Historical and Genealogical Society • 125 W 2nd St, P.O. Box 1560 • Waldron, AR 72958 • (501) 637-2466

Scott County Museum • 635 N Main St • Waldron, AR 72858 • (501) 637-3730

Scott-Sebastian Regional Library-Scott County • 115 W 2nd, P.O. Box 957 • Waldron, AR 72958-0957 • (501) 637-3516

Walnut Ridge
Lawrence County Historical Society • 415 Eastwood Cr • Walnut Ridge, AR 72476

Lawrence County Library • 1315 W Main • Walnut Ridge, AR 72476-1430 • (870) 886-3222

Warren
Bradley County Genealogical Society • P.O. Box 837 • Warren, AR 71671-0837

Bradley County Historical Museum • Dr John Wilson Martin House, 200 Ash St • Warren, AR 71671 • (870) 226-7166

Southeast Arkansas Regional Library-Warren Branch • 115 W Cypress • Warren, AR 71671 • (870) 226-8420

Washington
Old Washington Historic State Park • Hempstead County Courthouse, 4954 Hwy 278, P.O. Box 129 • Washington, AR 71862 • (870) 983-2684 • http://www.arkansasstateparks.com

Southwest Arkansas Regional Archives • 201 Highway 195 S, P.O. Box 134 • Washington, AR 71862 • (870) 983-2633 • http://www.southwestarchives.com

Southwest Arkansas Regional Historical Society • Hwy 195 S • Washington, AR 71862 • (870) 983-2633

West Helena
Phillips-Lee-Monroe Regional Library-West Helena Library • 721 Plaza St • West Helena, AR 72390-2698 • (870) 572-2861

West Memphis
Crittenden County Historical Society • 401 Gibson St, P.O. Box 811 • West Memphis, AR 72301 • (870) 735-1659

West Memphis Public Library • 213 N Avalon • West Memphis, AR 72301 • (870) 732-7590

Williford
Hardy Historical Society • Route 1, Box 329 • Williford, AR 72482

Wynne
Cross County Historical Society • Cross County Courthouse, 705 E Union St, P.O. Box 943 • Wynne, AR 72396-0943 • (870) 238-4100 • http://www.cchs1862.org

East Central Arkansas Regional Library • 410 E Merriman • Wynne, AR 72396 • (870) 238-3850

Yellville
Marion County Historical and Genealogical Society • c/o Marion County Library, 308 Old Main, P.O. Box 761 • Yellville, AR 72687 • (870) 449-6015 • http://argenweb.net/marion/

Marion County Library • 308 Old Main, P.O. Box 554 • Yellville, AR 72687 • (870) 449-6015

North Arkansas Regional Library • 319 Hwy 14 S, P.O. Box 510 • Yellville, AR 72687-0510 • (870) 449-5808

Arkansas

Agoura

Las Virgenes Historical Society • 30473-50 Mulholland Hwy, P.O. Box 124 • Agoura, CA 91301 • (818) 889-0836

Agoura Hills

County of Los Angeles Public Library-Agoura Hills Library • 29901 Ladyface Ct • Agoura Hills, CA 91301 • (819) 889-2278 • http://colapublib.org/libs/agourahills/

International Association of Jewish Genealogical Societies • P.O. Box 1094 • Agoura Hills, CA 91376 • (818) 991-5864 • http://www.iajgs.org

Jewish Genealogical Society of the Conejo Valley and Ventura County • 6052 Hackers Ln • Agoura Hills, CA 91301 • (818) 889-6616 • http://www.iajgs.org/jgscv/

Russian Heritage Society • P.O. Box 364 • Agoura Hills, CA 91376-0364 • (818) 991-0242 • http://feefhs.org/ftg-rhs.html

Tree Tracers • 5453 Softwind Wy • Agoura Hills, CA 91301-1541 • (818) 991-0242

Alameda

Alameda Architectural Preservation Society • P.O. Box 1677 • Alameda, CA 94501 • (510) 523-AVPS • http://www.alameda-preservation.org

Alameda Free Library • 2200 A Central Ave • Alameda, CA 94501-4506 • (510) 747-7710 • http://www.alamedafree.org

Alameda Historical Society • 2264 Santa Clara Ave • Alameda, CA 94501

Alameda Museum • 2324 Alameda Ave • Alameda, CA 94501 • (510) 521-1233 • http://www.alamedamuseum.org

USS Hornet Museum • Pier 3, Alameda Point, P.O. Box 460 • Alameda, CA 94501 • (510) 521-8448 • http://www.uss-hornet.org

Albany

City of Albany Archives • 1000 San Pablo Ave • Albany, CA 94706 • (510) 528-5720 • http://www.albanyca.org

Alhambra

Alhambra Historical Society • Historical Museum, 1550 W Alhambra Rd , P.O. Box 6687 • Alhambra, CA 91802 • (626) 300-8845

Alhambra Public Library • 101 S 1st St • Alhambra, CA 91807 • (626) 570-5008 • http://www.alhambralibrary.org

Los Angeles Fire Museum • 1320 N Eastern Ave, P.O. Box 3325 • Alhambra, CA 91803 • (626) 881-2411

Alleghany

Underground Gold Miners Museum • 356 Main St, P.O. Box 907 • Alleghany, CA 95910 • (530) 287-3330 • http://www.undergroundgold.com

Allensworth

Colonel Allensworth State Historic Park • 4011 Grant Ave • Allensworth, CA 93219 • (661) 849-3433

Alpine

Alpine Historical Society • Historical Museum, 2116 Tavern Rd • Alpine, CA 91901-3130 • (619) 659-8740

Cuyapaipe Band of Mission Indians • 4054 Willows Rd, P.O. Box 2550 • Alpine, CA 91903-2250 • (619) 455-6315 • http://kumeyaay.com/reservations/tribal_home.html

Viejas Band of Mission Indians - Kumeyaay Diegueno • P.O. Box 908 • Alpine, CA 91903 • (619) 445-3810 • http://www.viejas.com

Altadena

Altadena Heritage • 730 E Altadena Dr, P.O. Box 218 • Altadena, CA 91003 • (626) 797-0054 • http://www.restorationcentral.com/orgs/altadenah/

Altadena Historical Society • 730 E Altadena Dr, P.O. Box 144 • Altadena, CA 91003 • (626) 797-8016

Altadena Library District • 600 E Mariposa St • Altadena, CA 91001 • (626) 798-0833 • http://library.altadena.ca.us

Alturas

Alturas Rancheria • P.O. Box 340 • Alturas, CA 96101 • (530) 233-5571

Cedarville Rancheria of Northern Paiute Indians • 200 S Howard St • Alturus, CA 96101 • (530) 233-3969

Modoc County Historical Society • Historical Museum, 600 S Main St • Alturas, CA 96101 • (530) 233-6328

Modoc County Library • 212 W 3rd St • Alturas, CA 96101 • (530) 233-6340 • http://www.infopeople.org/modoc

Niles Hotel and Saloon Museum • 304 S Main St • Alturas, CA 96101 • (530) 233-3261 • http://www.nileshotel.com

Anaheim

Anaheim Historical Society • Anaheim Blvd & Broadway, P.O. Box 927 • Anaheim, CA 92815 • (714) 778-3301

Anaheim Museum • 241 S Anaheim Blvd • Anaheim, CA 92805 • (714) 778-3301 • http://www.anaheimmuseum.net

Anaheim Public Library • 500 W Broadway • Anaheim, CA 92805-3699 • (714) 765-1880 • http://www.anaheim.net/library.html

California State Genealogical Alliance • 4808 E Garland St • Anaheim, CA 92807 • (714) 993-1168

Historic Ramon Peralta Adobe Museum • Fairmont & Santa Ana Canyon Rd • Anaheim, CA 92870 • (714) 528-4260

Mother Colony House Museum • 414 N West St • Anaheim, CA 92805 • (714) 765-1850

Mother Colony Household Association • Historical Museum, 685 N Helena, P.O. Box 3246 • Anaheim, CA 92803 • (949) 854-1115

Queen Mary Foundation • 217 S Knott Ave #7 • Anaheim, CA 92804 • (714) 821-3844 • http://www.queenmary.com/QMweb/html/rms.html

Angels Camp

Angels Camp Museum & Carriage House Museum • 753 S Main St • Angels Camp, CA 95222 • (209) 736-2963

Calaveras County Library-Angels Camp Branch • 426 N Main St, P.O. Box 456 • Angels Camp, CA 95222-0456 • (209) 736-2198

Calaveras Genealogical Society • 753 S Main St, P.O. Box 184 • Angels Camp, CA 95222-0184

Antioch

Antioch Historical Society • 1500 W 4th St, P.O. Box 12 • Antioch, CA 95409

Anza

Cahuilla Band of Mission Indians • P.O. Box 391760 • Anza, CA 92539-1760 • (909) 763-5549

De Anza Heritage Society • P.O. Box 390861 • Anza, CA 92539

Hamilton Museum and Ranch Foundation • Historical Museum, 39991 Contreras Rd, P.O. Box 391141 • Anza, CA 92539 • (951) 763-1350

Ramond Band of Mission Indians - Cahuilla • P.O. Box 391372 • Anza, CA 92539 • (909) 763-4105

Santa Rosa Band of Mission Indians - Cahuilla • P.O. Box 390611 • Anza, CA 92539 • (909) 763-5140

Apple Valley

San Bernardino County Library-Apple Valley Branch • 15001 Wakita Rd • Apple Valley, CA 92307 • (760) 247-2022

Victor Valley Museum • 11873 Apple Valley Rd • Apple Valley, CA 92308 • (619) 240-2111 • http://www.caohwy.com/v/vivamuag.htm

California

Arcadia
Arcadia Historical Society • Historical Museum, 380 W Huntington Dr, P.O. Box 60021 • Arcadia, CA 91007 • (626) 574-5468 • http://www.cgazette.com/towns/Newark/standing/organizations/arcadiahistorical.htm

Arcadia Public Library • 20 W Duarte St • Arcadia, CA 91007 • (626) 821-5567 • http://library.ci.arcadia.ca.us

Chilao Visitor Center Museum • 701 N Santa Anita Ave • Arcadia, CA 91006 • (818) 574-5200 • http://www.r5.pswfs.gov/heritage/001.HTM

Croatian Information Service • P.O. Box 660546 • Arcadia, CA 91066-0546

Arcata
Arcata Historical Museum • Phillips House, 7th & Union Sts, P.O. Box 4521 • Arcata, CA 95521 • (707) 822-4722

Historical Sites Society of Arcata • P.O. Box 4521 • Arcata, CA 95518 • (707) 822-4722

Humboldt State University Library • 1 Harpst St • Arcata, CA 95521-8299 • (707) 826-3418 • http://library.humboldt.edu

Arroyo Grande
Paulding House Museum • 551 Crown Hill St • Arroyo Grande, CA 93420 • (805) 473-3231

San Luis Obispo County Genealogical Society Library • 800 W Branch • Arroyo Grande, CA 93420

South County Historical Society • Heritage House, 126 S Mason St, P.O. Box 633 • Arroyo Grande, CA 93421 • (805) 481-4126

Arvin
Arvin Historical Society • P.O. Box 96 • Arvin, CA 93203

Atascadero
Atascadero Historical Society • 6500 Palma Ave, P.O. Box 1047 • Atascadero, CA 93423 • (805) 466-8341 • http://www.atascaderochamber.org

San Luis Obispo County Genealogical Society • 6500 Palma Ave, P.O. Box 4 • Atascadero, CA 93423-0004 • (805) 927-8172 • http://www.slonet.org/vv/slocgs/genweb.html

Atherton
Atherton Heritage Association • Atherton Town Hall, 91 Ashfield Rd • Atherton, CA 94027 • (650) 688-6540 • http://www.ci.atherton.ca.us/heritage.html

Atwater
Atwater Historical Society • 1020 Cedar Ave, P.O. Box 111 • Atwater, CA 95301 • (209) 358-6955

Castle Air Museum • 5050 Santa Fe Dr • Atwater, CA 95301 • (209) 723-2178 • http://www.elite.net/castle-air/

Auberry
Big Sandy Rancheria • Western Monache, P.O. Box 337 • Auberry, CA 93602 • (559) 855-2103

Eastern Fresno County Historical Society • general delivery • Auberry, CA 93602 • (559) 855-4478

Auburn
Auburn Joss House Museum • P.O. Box 9126 • Auburn, CA 95604 • (916) 888-6483 • http://www.museumsusa.org/data/museums/CA/14076.htm

Auburn-Placer County Library • 350 Nevada St • Auburn, CA 95603-3789 • (530) 886-4510 • http://www.placer.ca.gov/library

Bernhard Museum • 291 Auburn-Folsom Rd • Auburn, CA 95603 • (916) 889-7198 • http://www.placer.ca.gov/museum/local-museums/bernhard.htm

North American Indian Annex Museum • 1225 Lincoln Way • Auburn, CA 95603 • (530) 889-6500 • http://auburn-ca.com/historical/courthse.htm

Placer County Archives • 11437 D Avenue West, DeWitt Center • Auburn, CA 95603 • (530) 889-7994 • http://www.placer.ca.gov/museum/archives.htm

Placer County Genealogical Society • P.O. Box 7385 • Auburn, CA 95604 • (530) 887-2646 • http://www.webcom.com/gunruh/pogs.html

Placer County Museum • 101 Maple St • Auburn, CA 95603 • (530) 889-6500 • http://www.placer.ca.gov/museum/

Avalon
Catalina Island Museum Society • Casino Bldg, P.O. Box 366 • Avalon, CA 90704 • (310) 510-2414 • http://www.catalinamuseum.org

Catalina Island Museum Society • Historical Museum, 1 Casino Wy, P.O. Box 366 • Avalon, CA 90704 • (310) 510-2414 • http://www.catalinamuseum.org

County of Los Angeles Public Library-Avalon Library • 215 Sumner Ave • Avalon, CA 90704-0535 • (310) 510-1050 • http://colapublib.org/libs/avalon/

Azusa
Azusa Historical Society • City Hall Complex, 213 E Foothill Blvd • Azusa, CA 91702

Azuza City Library • 729 N Dalton Ave • Azuza, CA 91702-2586 • (626) 812-5232 • http://ci.azusa.ca.us

Bakersfield
Adobe Krow Archives • 430 18th St • Bakersfield, CA 93301 • (661) 633-2736

California Living Museum • 10500 Alfred Harold Hwy • Bakersfield, CA 93306 • (661) 872-2256 • http://www.calmzoo.org

California Mission Studies Association • P.O. Box 3357 • Bakersfield, CA 93385-3357

Chumash Council of Bakersfield • 1317 S Chester Ave • Bakersfield, CA 93304 • (805) 837-2133

Grace Van Dyke Bird Library • Bakersfield College, 1801 Panorama Dr • Bakersfield, CA 93305-1298 • (661) 395-4461 • http://www.bc.cc.ca.us/library

Kawaiisu Tribe • P.O. Box 20849 • Bakersfield, CA 93390

Kern County Genealogical Society • P.O. Box 2214 • Bakersfield, CA 93303 • (661) 832-7790

Kern County Historical Society • P.O. Box 141 • Bakersfield, CA 93302 • (805) 322-4962 • http://www.kchistoricalsociety.org

Kern County Library • 701 Truxtun Ave • Bakersfield, CA 93301-4816 • (661) 868-0700 • http://www.kerncountylibrary.org

Kern County Museum • 3801 Chester Ave • Bakersfield, CA 93301-1395 • (661) 852-5000 • http://www.kcmuseum.org

Walter W Stiern Library • California State Univ, 9001 Stockdale Hwy • Bakersfield, CA 93311-1099 • (661) 664-3231 • http://www.lib.csub.edu

Baldwin Park
Baldwin Park Historical Society • 4061 Sterling Wy • Baldwin Park, CA 91706 • (626) 338-7130

Banning
Banning Public Library • 21 W Nicolet St • Banning, CA 92220-4699 • (909) 849-3192

Gilman Historic Ranch and Wagon Museum • P.O. Box 733 • Banning, CA 92220 • (909) 922-9200

Malki Museum • 11-795 Fields Rd, Morongo Indian Reservation, P.O. Box 578 • Banning, CA 92220-0017 • (951) 849-7289 • http://www.malkimuseum.org

Morongo Band of Mission Indians - Cahuilla, Serano and Cupeno • 11581 Potrero Rd • Banning, CA 92220-2965 • (909) 849-4697 • http://www.naein.com/NativeAmerican/morongo.html

San Gorgonio Pass Genealogical Society • 1050 Brinton Ave • Banning, CA 92220

Sun Lakes Genealogical Society • 5104 W Hilton Head Dr • Banning, CA 92220-6429

Barstow
Barstow California Stake Branch Genealogical Library • 2571 Barstow Rd • Barstow, CA 92311 • (760) 252-4117

Barstow Route 66 Mother Road Museum • Historic Harvey House, 681 N 1st Ave • Barstow, CA 92311 • (760) 255-1890

Mojave Desert Genealogical Society • P.O. Box 1320 • Barstow, CA 92311

Mojave River Valley Museum Association • Historical Museum, 270 E Virginia Wy, P.O. Box 1282 • Barstow, CA 92312-1282 • (760) 252-4681 • http://mvm.4t.com

Newberry Springs Genealogy Club • 701 Montara Rd #27 • Barstow, CA 92311-5742

Beale AFB
Beale Air Force Base Library FL4686 • 9 SVS/SVMG, 17849 16th St, Bldg 25219 • Beale AFB, CA 95903-1612 • (530) 634-2314

Beaumont
Beaumont Library District • 125 E 8th St • Beaumont, CA 92223-2194 • (909) 845-1357 • http://www.bld.lib.ca.us

San Gorgonio Pass Historical Society • P.O. Box 753 • Beaumont, CA 92223 • (951) 845-1348 • http://www.sgphs.org

Beiber
Big Valley Historical Museum • P.O. Box 355 • Beiber, CA 96009 • (530) 284-5368

Bellflower
Bellflower Heritage Society • 16601 Civic Center Dr • Bellflower, CA 90706

Universal Genealogical Society of Bellflower • 9251 Cedar St • Bellflower, CA 90706

Belmont
Belmont Historical Society • Historical Museum, 1219 Ralston Ave • Belmont, CA 94002 • (650) 593-4213 • http://www.belmont.gov/hist/

Notre Dame de Namur Library • 1500 Ralston Ave • Belmont, CA 94002-9974 • (650) 508-3748 • http://www.library.ndnu.edu

Belvedere-Tiburon
Belvedere-Tiburon Landmarks Society • 1550 Tiburon Blvd, P.O. Box 134 • Belvedere-Tiburon, CA 94920 • (415) 435-5490 • http://www.landmarks-society.org

Old St Hilary's Landmark Museum • 201 Esperanza • Belvedere-Tiburon, CA 94920 • (415) 435-2567

Benecia
National Society, Descendants of Early Quakers • 495 Panorama Dr • Benecia, CA 94510-3901 • (707) 745-3085 • http://www.terraworld.net/mlwinton

Benicia Capitol State Historic Park • 115 West G Street, P.O. Box 5 • Benicia, CA 94510 • (707) 745-3385 • http://parks.ca.gov

Benicia Fire Museum • 900 E 2nd St • Benicia, CA 94510 • (707) 745-1688

Benicia Historical Museum at the Camel Barns • 2060 Camel Rd • Benicia, CA 94510 • (707) 745-5435 • http://www.beneciahistoricalmuseum.org

Benicia Historical Society • P.O. Box 773 • Benicia, CA 94510 • (707) 745-1822 • http://www.benicianews.com

Benicia Public Library • 150 East L Street • Benicia, CA 94510-3281 • (707) 746-4343 • http://www.ci.benicia.ca.us/library.html

Fischer-Hanlon House Museum • 135 West G Street • Benicia, CA 94510 • (707) 745-3385

Benton
Utu Utu Gwaitu Paiute Tribe of the Benton Paiute Reservation • Star Route 4, Box 56A • Benton, CA 93512 • (619) 933-2321

Berkeley
Bancroft Library • Univ of California • Berkeley, CA 94720 • (510) 642-3781 • http://bancroft.berkeley.edu

Berkeley Architectural Heritage Association • P.O. Box 1137 • Berkeley, CA 94701 • (510) 841-2242 • http://www.dnai.com/~baha/

Berkeley Historical Society • Historical Museum, 1931 Center St, P.O. Box 1190 • Berkeley, CA 94701-1190 • (510) 848-0181 • http://www.ci.berkeley.ca.us/histsoc/

Berkeley Public Library • 2090 Kittridge St • Berkeley, CA 94704 • (510) 981-6148 • http://www.infopeople.org/bpl/

California-Nevada United Methodist Archives • 2400 Ridge Rd • Berkeley, CA 94709 • (650) 952-6219

Chicano Studies Library • Univ of California, 3408 Dwinelle Hall • Berkeley, CA 94720 • (510) 642-3859

Commission for the Preservation of Pioneer Jewish Cemeteries and Landmarks • Judah L Magnes Memorial Museum, 2911 Russell St • Berkeley, CA 94710 • (510) 549-6932 • http://www.magnesmuseum.org/cemecom.htm

Judah L Magnes Museum • Blumenthal Library, 2911 Russell St • Berkeley, CA 94710 • (510) 549-6950 • http://www.magnesmuseum.org

Society of California Archivists • Bancroft Library, P.O. Box 605 • Berkeley, CA 94720 • (714) 643-4241 • http://www.calarchivists.org

Western Jewish History Center Archives • Blumenthal Library, 2911 Russell St • Berkeley, CA 94705 • (510) 549-6939 • http://www.magnesmuseum.org

William R Thorsen Residence Museum • 2307 Piedmont Ave • Berkeley, CA 94704 • (510) 929-3713

Beverly Hills
Beverly Hills Historical Society • 241 S Moreno Dr, P.O. Box 1919 • Beverly Hills, CA 90213 • (310) 246-1914

Big Bear City
Big Bear Valley Historical Society • Historical Museum, City Park, P.O. Box 513 • Big Bear City, CA 92314 • (909) 585-8100 • http://www.bigbear-goldmine-lodge.com/museum.htm

Big Pine
Big Pine Band of Owens Valley • Paiute-Shoshone, P.O. Box 700 • Big Pine, CA 93513 • (760) 938-2003

Big Sur
Big Sur Historical Society • Jwy 1, P.O. Box 176 • Big Sur, CA 93920 • (831) 620-0541

Bishop
Bishop Museum and Historical Society • Historical Museum, P.O. Box 363 • Bishop, CA 93514 • (760) 873-5950

Bishop Reservation • Paiute-Shoshone, 50 Tu Su Lane, P.O. Box 548 • Bishop, CA 93515 • (760) 873-3584 • http://www.paiute.com

Laws Railroad Museum & Historical Site Library • Libr & Arts Bldg, Silver Canyon Rd, P.O. Box 363 • Bishop, CA 93515-0363 • (760) 873-5950 • http://thesierraweb.com/bishop/laws/

California

Bishop, cont.
Timbisha Shoshone Tribe of the Western Shoshone Nation • 136 Edwards St • Bishop, CA 93514 • (760) 873-9004 • http://timbisha.org

Blairsden
Pluams-Eureka State Park • 310 Johnsville Rd • Blairsden, CA 96103 • (530) 836-2380

Blythe
Colorado River-Blythe Quartzite Genealogical Society • 411 S 5th St, P.O. Box 404 • Blythe, CA 92226

Palo Verde Historical Society • Historical Museum, 150 N Broadway • Blythe, CA 92225 • (760) 922-8770

Palo Verde Valley District Library • 125 W Chanslorway • Blythe, CA 92225-1293 • (760) 922-5371 • http://www.paloverdevalleylibrary.com

Palo Verde Valley Genealogy Society • P.O. Box 179 • Blythe, CA 92226 • http://www.rootsweb.com/~capvvgs

Bodega Bay
Bodega Bay Historical Society • 1580 Eastshore Rd • Bodega Bay, CA 94923 • (707) 875-9255

Bolinas
Bolinas Museum • 48 Wharf Rd, P.O. Box 450 • Bolinas, CA 94924 • (415) 868-0330 • http://www.bolinasmuseum.org

Bonita
Bonita Historical Museum • 4035 Bonita Rd • Bonita, CA 91902 • (619) 267-5141

Boonville
Anderson Valley Historical Society • Historical Museum, 12340 Highway 128, P.O. Box 676 • Boonville, CA 95415 • (707) 895-3207

Boron
Kern County Library-Boron Branch • 26967 Twenty Mule Team Rd • Boron, CA 93516-1550 • (760) 762-5606

Twenty Mule Team Museum • 26962 Twenty Mule Team Rd • Boron, CA 93516 • (760) 762-5810 • http://www.rnrs.com/20MuleTeam/

Borrego Springs
Campo Depot Museum • 200 Palm Canyon • Borrego Springs, CA 92004 • (760) 767-5311

Boulder Creek
Boulder Creek Historical Society • 12547 Highway 9, P.O. Box 139 • Boulder Creek, CA 95006 • (831) 338-6617

San Lorenzo Valley Museum • 12547 Hwy 9, P.O. Box 576 • Boulder Creek, CA 96006 • (831) 338-8382 • http://www.slvmuseum.com

Boulevard
La Posta Band of Mission Indians - Kumeyaay Diegueno • P.O. Box 1048 • Boulevard, CA 92905 • (619) 478-2113 • http://kumeyaay.com

Manzanita Band of Mission Indians - Kumeyaay Diegueno • P.O. Box 1302 • Boulevard, CA 91905 • (619) 766-4930 • http://kumeyaay.com

Brea
Association of Professional Genealogists, Southern California Chapter • P.O. Box 9486 • Brea, CA 92822-9486 • http://www.cagenweb.com/socapg/

Brea Historical Society • Historical Museum, P.O. Box 9764 • Brea, CA 92622 • (714) 529-2993 • http://breamuseum.org

Brentwood
East Contra Costa Historical Society • East Contra Costa Museum, 3890 Sellers Ave, P.O. Box 202 • Brentwood, CA 94513 • (925) 634-3553 • http://www.theschoolbell.com/history/

Bridgeport
Bodie State Historic Park • Hwy 395, P.O. Box 515 • Bridgeport, CA 93517 • (760) 657-6445 • http://www.ceres.ca.gov/sierradsp/

Mono County Free Library System-Northern Region • 94 N School St, P.O. Box 398 • Bridgeport, CA 93517-0398 • (760) 932-7482

Brooks
Rumsey Rancheria - Wintun • P.O. Box 18 • Brooks, CA 95606 • (530) 796-3400

Brownsville
Yuba Feather Historical Association • Forbestown Museum, P.O. Box 54 • Brownsville, CA 95919 • (530) 589-0218 • http://www.caohwy.com/f/forbestm.htm

Buelton
Coastal Band of Chumash • P.O. Box 579 • Buelton, CA 93422 • (805) 686-7942

Buena Park
Buena Park Historical Society • Historical Museum, 6631 Beach Blvd • Buena Park, CA 90621 • (714) 562-3570 • http://www.historicalsociety.org

United States Internet Genealogical Society • 8313 Los Altos Dr • Buena Park, CA 90620

Burbank
Burbank Historical Society • 1015 W Olive Ave • Burbank, CA 91506-2211 • (818) 841-6333 • http://www.cwire.com/pub/orgs/Burbank.Historical.Society/

French-Canadian Heritage Society of Southern California • 417 Irving Dr, P.O. Box 4377 • Burbank, CA 91503 • (818) 843-7247 • http://www.scgsgenealogy.com

Genealogical Society of Hispanic America, Southern California Chapter • 417 Irving Dr, P.O. Box 4377 • Burbank, CA 91503 • (818) 843-7247 • http://www.scgsgenealogy.com

Immigrant Genealogical Society and Library • 1310-B Magnolia Blvd #B, P.O. Box 7369 • Burbank, CA 91510 • (818) 848-3122 • http://feefhs.org/igs/frg-igs.html

Southern California Genealogical Society • 417 Irving Dr • Burbank, CA 91504-2408 • (818) 843-7247 • http://www.scgsgenealogy.com

Southern California Genealogical Society, Family Tree Maker Computer User's Group • 417 Irving Dr, P.O. Box 4377 • Burbank, CA 91503 • (818) 843-7247 • http://www.scgsgenealogy.com

Southern California Genealogical Society, Irish Interest Group • 417 Irving Dr, P.O. Box 4377 • Burbank, CA 91503 • (818) 843-7247 • http://www.scgsgenealogy.com

Southern California Genealogical Society, Personal Ancestral File Computer User's Group • 417 Irving Dr, P.O. Box 4377 • Burbank, CA 91503 • (818) 843-7247 • http://www.scgsgenealogy.com

Southern California Genealogical Society, Ultimate Family Tree Computer User's Group • 417 Irving Dr, P.O. Box 4377 • Burbank, CA 91503 • (818) 843-7247 • http://www.scgsgenealogy.com

Burlingame
Burlingame Classic Toy Museum • 214 California Dr • Burlingame, CA 94010 • (650) 347-2301 • http://www.pezmuseum.org

Burlingame Historical Society • 900 Burlingame Ave, P.O. Box 144 • Burlingame, CA 94011 • (650) 340-9960 • http://www.burlingamehistorical.org

Westerners International, San Francisco Corral • 751 Winchester Drive • Burlingame, CA 94108 • (415) 342-0291

Burney
Big Bend Rancheria - Pit River Tribe • P.O. Box 1570 • Burney, CA 96013 • (916) 335-5421

Intermountain Genealogical Society • P.O. Box 399 • Burney, CA 96013

Likely Rancheria - Pit River Tribe • P.O. Drawer 1570 • Burney, CA 96013 • (916) 335-5421

Lookout Rancheria - Pit River Tribe • P.O. Drawer 1570 • Burney, CA 96013 • (916) 335-5421

Montgomery Creek Rancheria - Pit River Tribe • P.O. Box 1570 • Burney, CA 96013 • (916) 335-5421

Roaring Creek Rancheria - Pit River Tribal Council • 37014 Main St, P.O. Drawer 1570 • Burney, CA 96013 • (916) 335-5421

Calabasas
Calabasas Historical Society • P.O. Box 8067 • Calabasas, CA 91372 • (818) 347-0470 • http://www.ci.calabasas.ca.us/history.html

Calabasas Public Library • 23975 Park Sorrento St • Calabasas, CA 91302 • (818) 225-7616 • http://www.ci.calabasas.ca.us/departments/library.html

Leonis Adobe Museum • 23537 Calabasas Rd • Calabasas, CA 91302 • (818) 222-6511

Calexico
Camarena Memorial Library • 850 Encinas Ave • Calexico, CA 92231 • (760) 768-2170 • http://bordernet3.calexico.k12.ca.us/cml

California City
East Kern Genealogical Society • 9716 Irene Ave • California City, CA 93505-1329 • (619) 373-4728

East Kern Historical Society • P.O. Box 2305 • California City, CA 93505

Calistoga
Bale Grist Mill State Historic Park • 3801 St Helena Hwy N • Calistoga, CA 94515 • (707) 942-4575 • http://www.parks.ca.gov

Napa City-County Library-Calistoga Branch • 1108 Myrtle • Calistoga, CA 94515-1730 • (707) 942-4833

Sharpsteen Museum • 1311 Washington, P.O. Box 573 • Calistoga, CA 94515 • (707) 942-5911 • http://www.sharpsteen-museum.org

Camarillo
CAF Southern California Wing - WWII Aviation Museum • 455 Aviation Dr • Camarillo, CA 93010 • (805) 482-0064 • http://www.orgsites.com/ca/caf-socal/

Cambria
Cambria Historical Society • general delivery • Cambria, CA 93428 • (805) 927-2891

Old Santa Rosa Chapel Museum • 2353 Main St • Cambria, CA 93428 • (805) 927-5212

Camp Roberts
Camp Roberts Historical Museum • Bldg 114 • Camp Roberts, CA 93451-5000 • (805) 238-8288 • http://www.militarymuseum.org/CampRobertsMuseum.html

Campbell
Campbell Historic Preservation Board • 70 N 1st St • Campbell, CA 95008 • (408) 866-2140

Campbell Historical Museum • Ainsley House, 51 N Central Ave • Campbell, CA 95008 • (408) 866-2119 • http://www.campbellmuseumfoundation.org

Campo
Campo Band of Kumeyaay Indians • 36190 Church Rd, Ste 1 • Campo, CA 91906 • (619) 478-9046

Mountain Empire Historical Society • Stone Store Museum, 31130 Highway 94, P.O. Box 394 • Campo, CA 92006 • (619) 478-5707

Canoga Park
Canoga-Owensmouth Historical Museum • 7248 Owensmouth Ave • Canoga Park, CA 91303-1529 • (818) 346-5252

Canoga-Owensmouth Historical Society • 7248 Owensmouth Ave • Canoga Park, CA 91303 • (818) 340-3696

Orcutt Ranch Museum • 23600 Roscoe Blvd • Canoga Park, CA 91304 • (818) 883-6641

San Fernando Valley Genealogical Society • 20387 Londeliuss • Canoga Park, CA 91306

Capitola
Capitola Historical Museum • 410 Capitola Ave • Capitola, CA 95010 • (831) 464-0322 • http://www.capitolamuseum.org

Carlotta
Grizzly Creek Redwoods State Park • 16949 Hwy 36 • Carlotta, CA 95528 • (707) 777-3683 • http://www.parks.ca.gov

Carlsbad
Carlsbad City Library • 1775 Dove Lane • Carlsbad, CA 92009-4048 • (760) 602-2011 • http://www.ci.carlsbad.ca.us

Carlsbad City Library-Georgina Cole Library • 1250 Carlsbad Village Dr • Carlsbad, CA 92008 • (760) 434-2931 • http://www.ci.carlsbad.ca.us/cserv/library.html

Carlsbad Historical Society • 258 Beech Ave • Carlsbad, CA 92008 • (760) 434-9189

Friends of Carrillo Ranch • 2622 El Aguila Lane • Carlsbad, CA 92009 • (760) 438-1666 • http://www.carrillo-ranch.org

Museum of Making Music • 5790 Armada Dr • Carlsbad, CA 92008 • (877) 551-9976 • http://www.museumofmakingmusic.org

North San Diego County Genealogical Society • c/o Carlsbad City Library, 1250 Carlsbad Village Dr, P.O. Box 581 • Carlsbad, CA 92008 • (858) 485-7684 • http://www.cagenweb.com/nsdcgs/

Ponto Historic Society • 7290 Ponto Dr • Carlsbad, CA 92009-4601 • (760) 438-2140

Carmel
Big Sur Historical Society • Hwy 1 • Carmel, CA 93923 • (831) 620-0541

Carmel Heritage • 6th & Lincoln Sts • Carmel, CA 93923 • (831) 624-4447

Carmel Mission Basilica Archives • P.O. Box 2235 • Carmel, CA 93921 • (831) 624-1271 • http://www.dioceseofmonterey.org/parishes/carmel.htm

Carmel Preservation Foundation • Ocean Ave • Carmel, CA 93923 • (408) 624-6025

Carmel Valley Historical Society • P.O. Box 1612 • Carmel, CA 93924 • (831) 659-5715

Harrison Memorial Library • Ocean Ave & Lincoln St, P.O. Box 800 • Carmel, CA 93921-0800 • (831) 624-4629 • http://www.hm-lib.org

Harrison Memorial Library-Park • Mission St & 6th Ave, P.O. Box 800 • Carmel, CA 93921 • (831) 624-1615 • http://www.hm-lib.org/7a.htm

Mission San Carlos Borromeo del Rio Carmelo Museum • 3100 Rio Rd • Carmel, CA 93923 • (831) 624-3600 • http://www.carmelmission.org

Tor House Museum • 26304 Ocean View, P.O. Box 2713 • Carmel, CA 93921 • (831) 624-1813 • http://www.torhouse.org

Carmel Valley
Carmel Valley Historical Society • 20 Carmel Valley Village Ctr • Carmel Valley, CA 93924 • (831) 659-5715

Carmel-by-the-Sea
Carmel Heritage Society • Murphy House Museum, Lincoln & 6th, P.O. Box 701 • Carmel-by-the-Sea, CA 93921 • (831) 624-4447 • http://www.carmelheritage.org

California

Carmichael
Carmichael Regional Library • 5605 Marconi Ave • Carmichael, CA 95608 • (916) 483-6055

LDS Sacramento Branch Genealogical Library • 5343 Halsted Ave • Carmichael, CA 95608 • http://ftp.cac.psu.edu/pub/genealogy/roots-l/genealog/genealog.gensrch1

Mission Oaks Genealogy Club • Mission Oaks Community Center, 4701 Gibbons Dr, P.O. Box 216 • Carmichael, CA 95609-0216 • (916) 482-8531

Sacramento-Carmichael Regional Library • 5605 Marconi Ave • Carmichael, CA 95608 • (916) 264-2700 • http://www.saclib.org

Carpenteria
Carpinteria Valley Historical Society • 956 Maple Ave • Carpenteria, CA 93013 • (805) 684-3112

Carpinteria Valley Historical Society • Historical Museum, 956 Maple Ave • Carpinteria, CA 93013 • (805) 684-3112 • http://www.carpinteriahistoricalmuseum.org

Carson
County of Los Angeles Public Library-Carson Library • 151 E Carson St • Carson, CA 90745-2797 • (310) 830-0901 • http://colapublib.org/libs/carson/

International Printing Museum • 315 Torrance Blvd • Carson, CA 90745 • (310) 515-7166 • http://www.printmuseum.org

Castro Valley
California Czech and Slovak Club • P.O. Box 20542 • Castro Valley, CA 94546-8542 • (510) 581-9986 • http://www.rahul.net/njs/ccsc/

San Francisco Bay Area Jewish Genealogical Society • 4430 School Wy • Castro Valley, CA 94546-1331

Cedar Ridge
Nevada County Genealogical Society • P.O. Box 176 • Cedar Ridge, CA 95924 • (530) 272-2119 • http://www.rootsweb.com/~cancgs

Cerritos
Cerritos Public Library • 18025 Bloomfield Ave • Cerritos, CA 90701 • (562) 916-1350 • http://library.ci.cerritos.ca.us

Chatsworth
Chatsworth Historical Society • Frank H Schepler Jr Memorial Library, 10385 Shadow Oak Dr • Chatsworth, CA 91311 • (818) 882-5614 • http://www.historicalsocieties.net

Homestead Acre and Hill-Palmer House Museum • 10385 Shadow Oak Dr • Chatsworth, CA 91311 • (818) 882-5614 • http://www.historicalsocieties.net

Cherokee
Cherokee Heritage and Museum Association • Historical Museum, Route 7, Box 297 • Cherokee, CA 95965 • (530) 533-1849

Cherry Valley
Edward-Dean Museum and Gardens • 9401 Oak Glen Rd • Cherry Valley, CA 92223 • (909) 845-2626 • http://www.edward-deanmuseum.org

Chester
Chester Genealogy Club • P.O. Box 107 • Chester, CA 96020

Chester-Lake Almanor Museum • P.O. Box 877 • Chester, CA 96020 • (530) 258-2742 • http://www.caohwy.com/c/chestlam.htm

Chicao
Glenn Genealogy Group • 745 Santiago Ct • Chicao, CA 95973

Chico
Association for Northern California Records and Research • 1st & Hazel Sts, P.O. Box 3024 • Chico, CA 95927 • (530) 895-5710 • http://www.csuchico.edu/ancrr/

Bidwell Mansion Association • Historical Museum, 525 Esplanade • Chico, CA 95926 • (530) 895-6144 • http://www.norcal.parks.state.ca.us/bidwell_mansion_association.htm

Chico Museum • 141 Salem St • Chico, CA 95928 • (530) 891-4336 • http://www.chicomuseum.org

Mechoopda Maidu Indian Tribe of the Chico Rancheria • 1907F Mangrove Ave • Chico, CA 95926 • (530) 899-8922

Meriam Library • California State Univ-Chico, 400 W 1st St • Chico, CA 95929 • (530) 898-5834 • http://www.csuchico.edu

Stansbury Home Preservation Association • The Stansbury Home, 307 W 5th St • Chico, CA 95928 • (530) 895-3848

Stansbury Home Victorian Museum • 307 W 5th St • Chico, CA 95928 • (530) 895-3848 • http://www.chicochamber.com/attractions.htm

China Lake
Maturango Museum of Indian Wells Valley • Halsey Ave, P.O. Box 1776 • China Lake, CA 93555

Chino
Chino Valley Historical Society • Old Schoolhouse Museum, 5493 B Street, P.O. Box 972 • Chino, CA 91708 • (909) 627-6464

Chino's Old Schoolhouse Museum • 5493 B Street • Chino, CA 91710 • (909) 627-6464

Costanoan Rumsen Carmel Tribe • 3929 Riverside Dr • Chino, CA 91710 • (909) 591-3117 • http://www.costanoanrumsen.org

Planes of Fame Museum • 7000 Merrill Ave #17 • Chino, CA 91710 • (909) 597-3722

Slovak Genealogy Research Center • 6962 Palmer Ct • Chino, CA 91710 • (909) 627-2897 • http://feefhs.org/SLOVAK/frg-sgrc.html

Yorba-Slaughter Adobe Museum • 17127 Pomona Rincos Rd • Chino, CA 91710 • (909) 597-8332 • http://www.sbcountymuseum.org

Chiriaco Summit
General Patton Memorial Museum • 62-510 Chiriaco Rd • Chiriaco Summit, CA 92201 • (760) 227-3483 • http://www.generalpattonmuseum.com

Chula Vista
Chula Vista Genealogy Society • c/o Chula Vista Public Library, 365 F Street • Chula Vista, CA 92010-2697 • (935) 691-5168

Chula Vista Historical Society • P.O. Box 1222 • Chula Vista, CA 92012

Chula Vista Public Library • 365 F Street • Chula Vista, CA 92010-2697 • (935) 691-5168 • http://www.chulavista.lib.ca.us

Native Cultures Institute of Baja California • P.O. Box 122229 • Chula Vista, CA 91912

Citrus Heights
Sacramento Genealogical Society • c/o California State Archives, 1020 'O' Street, P.O. Box 265 • Citrus Heights, CA 95611-0265 • (916) 481-4930 • http://www.rootcellar.org

City of Industry
John Rowland House Museum • 16021 E Gale Ave • City of Industry, CA 91745 • (626) 369-7220

Workman and Temple Family Homestead Museum • 15415 E Don Julian Rd • City of Industry, CA 91745-1029 • (626) 968-8492 • http://www.homesteadmuseum.org

Claremont
Asian American Resource Center • Pomona College, Smith Campus Ctr, 170 E 6th St • Claremont, CA 91711 • (909) 621-8639 • http://www.pomona.edu

California Folklore Society • 421 Baughman Ave • Claremont, CA 91711 • (213) 825-3962 • http://ls.berkeley.edu/dept/folklore/cfs.html

Claremont Heritage • 590 W Bonita Ave, P.O. Box 742 • Claremont, CA 91711-0742 • (909) 621-0848 • http://www.claremontheritage.org

County of Los Angeles Public Library-Claremont Library • 208 N Harvard Ave • Claremont, CA 91711 • (909) 621-4902 • http://colapublib.org/libs/claremont/

Fiske Musical Instrument Museum • Claremont University, 450 N College Wy • Claremont, CA 91711 • (909) 621-8307 • http://www.cuc.claremont.edu/fiske/welcome.htm

Honnold-Mudd Library • Claremont College, 800 N Dartmouth Ave • Claremont, CA 91711-3991 • (909) 621-8045 • http://voxlibris.claremont.edu

Medieval Association of the Pacific • Scripps College • Claremont, CA 91711 • (909) 607-3538

Clayton
Clayton Historical Society • 6101 Main St, P.O. Box 94 • Clayton, CA 94517-0094 • (925) 672-0240 • http://www.claytonhs.com

Clearlake Oaks
Elem Indian Colony of Pomo Indians - Sulphur Bank Rancheria • P.O. Box 1968 • Clearlake Oaks, CA 95423 • (707) 998-4551

Cloverdale
Cloverdale Historical Society • 215 N Cloverdale Blvd • Cloverdale, CA 95425-3131 • (707) 894-2067

Cloverdale Rancheria of Pomo Indians • 555 S Cloverdale Blvd #1 • Cloverdale, CA 95425 • (707) 894-5775

Clovis
California Memorial and Museum • 3500 Pelco Wy • Clovis, CA 93612 • (559) 292-1981

Clovis Big Dry Creek Historical Museum • 401 Pollasky Ave • Clovis, CA 93612 • (559) 297-8033

Coachella
Augustine Band of Mission Indians • P.O. Box 846 • Coachella, CA 92236 • (760) 398-4722 • http://www.naein.com/NativeAmerican/augustine.html

Twenty-Nine Palms Band of Mission Indians - Chemehuevi • 46-200 Harrison Pl • Coachella, CA 92236 • (760) 775-5566

Coalinga
Coalinga-Huron Library District • 305 N 4th St • Coalinga, CA 93210 • (559) 935-1676

Coarsegold
Coarsegold Historical Society • Historical Museum, 31899 Hwy 41, P.O. Box 117 • Coarsegold, CA 93614 • (559) 642-4448 • http://www.coarsegoldhistoricmuseum.com

Picayune Rancheria of Chukchansi Indians • 46575 Road 417 • Coarsegold, CA 93614 • (559) 683-6633 • http://www.chukchansi.net

Coleville
Antelope Valley Paiute Tribe • P.O. Box 119 • Coleville, CA 96107 • (760) 495-2801

Washoe-Paiute of Antelope Valley • P.O. Box 52 • Coleville, CA 96107 • (760) 495-2824

Colfax
Colfax Area Historical Society • P.O. Box 185 • Colfax, CA 95713-0185 • (530) 346-2267 • http://www.foothill.net/colfax/history/

Colma
Colma Historical Association • Historical Museum, 1500 Hillside Blvd • Colma, CA 94014 • (650) 757-1676 • http://www.colmahistory.org

Coloma
Marshall Gold Discovery State Historic Park Library • 310 Back St, P.O. Box 265 • Coloma, CA 95613 • (916) 622-3470 • http://www.jsgnet.com/coloma

Colton
Agua Mansa Pioneer Cemetery Museum • 2001 W Agua Mansa Rd • Colton, CA 92324 • (909) 778-1079 • http://www.co.san-bernardino.ca.us/ccr/museum/museums.html

Colton Area Museum • 380 N LaCadena Dr, P.O. Box 1648 • Colton, CA 92324 • (909) 824-8814

Columbia
Columbia State Historic Park • 11255 Jackson St • Columbia, CA 95310 • (209) 532-0150 • http://www.parks.state.ca.us

Colusa
Cachil Dehe Band of Wintun Indians • 3730 Hwy 45 • Colusa, CA 95932 • (530) 458-8231

Colusa County Free Library • 738 Market St • Colusa, CA 95932 • (530) 458-7671 • http://www.colusanet.com/ccl

Colusa County Historical Records Commission • c/o Colusa County Free Library 738 Market St • Colusa, CA 95932 • (530) 458-7671 • http://www.caohwy.com/s/sactovmu.htm

Compton
Compton Public Library • 240 W Compton Blvd • Compton, CA 90220 • (310) 637-0202

Concord
Concord Historical Society • 1601 Sutter St, P.O. Box 404 • Concord, CA 94522 • (925) 827-3380 • http://www.conhistsoc.org

Contra Costa County Genealogical Society • 3727 N Ranchford Ct, P.O. Box 910 • Concord, CA 94522-0910 • (925) 685-7244 • http://www.rootsweb.ancestry.com/~cacccgs

Contra Costa County Genealogical Society, Irish Roses Plus a Thorn • P.O. Box 910 • Concord, CA 94522-0910 • (925) 754-1885 • http://www.rootsweb.com/~cacccgs

Contra Costa County Genealogical Society, Using Computers in Genealogy • P.O. Box 910 • Concord, CA 94522-0910 • (925) 672-6996

Family Tree Searchers • 3564 Kimball Wy • Concord, CA 94518-1249 • (925) 676-2221

Salinan Tribe of Monterey County • P.O. Box 2166 • Concord, CA 93930 • (916) 458-4551

Corona
Corona Public Library • 650 S Main St • Corona, CA 92882 • (909) 736-2381 • http://www.coronapubliclibrary.org

Corona Del Mar
Coronado Historical Association • P.O. Box 393 • Corona Del Mar, CA 92625

Newport Beach Historical Society • c/o Sherman Library, 2647 E Pacific Coast Hwy • Corona del Mar, CA 92625 • (949) 673-1880 • http://www.slgardens.org

Coronado
Coronado Historical Association • Historical Museum, 1100 Orange Ave • Coronado, CA 92118 • (619) 435-7242 • http://www.coronadohistory.org

Coronado Public Library • 640 Orange Ave • Coronado, CA 92118-1526 • (935) 522-7390 • http://coronado.lib.ca.us

Corte Madera
Corte Madera Public Library • 707 Meadowsweet Dr • Corte Madera, CA 94948-1511

Costa Mesa
Costa Mesa Historical Society, SAAAB Wing • 1870 Anaheim Ave, P.O. Box 1764 • Costa Mesa, CA 92628 • (949) 631-5918 • http://www.goodtime.net/cme/locme036.htm

California

Costa Mesa, cont.
Diego Sepulveda Adobe Estancia Museum • 1900 Adams, P.O. Box 1764 • Costa Mesa, CA 92628 • (949) 631-5918 • http://www.costamesahistory.org

Coulterville
Northern Mariposa County History Center • 10301 Hwy 49, P.O. Box 149 • Coulterville, CA 95311 • (209) 878-3015 • http://www.home.inreach.com/nmchc

Covelo
Round Valley Reservation - Achomawi, Concow, Nomelaki, Wailaki, Wintun, Yuko and Pomo Tribes • P.O. Box 448 • Covelo, CA 95428 • (707) 983-6126 • http://covelo.net/tribes/pages/tribes.shtml

Covina
Covina Valley Historical Society • Firehouse Jail Museum, 125 E College St, P.O. Box 1862 • Covina, CA 91723-1824 • (626) 966-9871 • http://firehousejailmuseum.tripod.com/covinamuseum/

Daughters of the American Revolution, Covina California Chapter • 2441 SN Cameron Ave • Covina, CA 91724 • http://members.home.net/swelch/cssdar/

Gabrielino-Tongva Tribal Council • 727 S Calvados • Covina, CA 91723 • (818) 966-3417

Crescent City
Del Norte County Historical Society • Historical Museum, 577 H Street • Crescent City, CA 95531 • (707) 464-3922 • http://www.delnortehistory.org

Del Norte County Library District • 190 Price Mall • Crescent City, CA 95531 • (707) 464-9793

Elk Valley Rancheria - Tolowa • 375 Wyentae St, P.O. Box 1042 • Crescent City, CA 95531 • (707) 464-4680

Redwood National and State Parks Archives • 1111 2nd St • Crescent City, CA 95531 • (707) 464-6101 • http://www.nps.gov/redw/

Redwood National Park Museum • 111 2nd St • Crescent City, CA 95531 • (707) 464-6101 • http://www.nps.gov/redw

Crockett
Crockett Museum and Historical Society • Historical Museum, P.O. Box 194 • Crockett, CA 94525 • (510) 787-2178 • http://pages.zdnet.com:8083/keithglenn/crockettmuseum/

Culver City
Culver City Historical Society • P.O. Box 3428 • Culver City, CA 90231-3428

Genealogical Society of Hispanic America, Southern California Branch • 10736 Jefferson Blvd #690 • Culver City, CA 92030 • (310) 839-3140 • http://www.scgsgenealogy.com/GSHA.htm

Cupertino
California Council for the Promotion of History • California History Center, DeAnza College, 21250 Stevens Creek Blvd • Cupertino, CA 95014 • (408) 996-8712 • http://www.calhistory.org/chc.html

Cupertino Historical Society • Historical Museum, 10185 N Stelling Rd • Cupertino, CA 95014 • (408) 973-1495 • http://www.cupertino.org

De Anza Trek Lancers Society • 20739 Sunrise Dr • Cupertino, CA 95014 • (408) 252-6065

Cypress
Cypress Heritage Committee • 5700 Orange Ave • Cypress, CA 90630 • (714) 229-6794

Orange County Public Library-Cypress Branch • 5331 Orange Ave • Cypress, CA 90630-2985 • (714) 826-0350 • http://www.ocpl.org/cypress/Cypres.htm

Daggett
Augustan Society • P.O. Box 75 • Daggett, CA 92327-0075 • (760) 762-9138 • http://www.augustansociety.org

Daly City
Daly City Public Library • 40 Wembley Dr • Daly City, CA 94015-4399 • (650) 991-8025 • http://www.dalycitylibrary.org

Filipino American National Historical Society, San Francisco Chapter • 483 Green Ridge Dr #7 • Daly City, CA 94014 • (408) 927-2039 • http://www.fanhs-national.org

History Guild of Daly City-Colma • Historical Museum, 40 Wembley Dr • Daly City, CA 94015 • (650) 991-8025 • http://www.dalycityhistory.org/guild.htm

Dana Point
Dana Point Historical Society • 24642 San Juan Ave • Dana Point, CA 92629 • (949) 248-8121 • http://www.ocnow.com/community/groups/dpcbhs/

Danville
Blackhawk Museum • 3700 Blackhawk Plaza Cr • Danville, CA 94526 • (925) 736-2280 • http://www.blackhawkmuseum.org

California State Genealogical Alliance • P.O. Box 3113 • Danville, CA 94526-0311 • (858) 485-7684 • http://www.csga.com

Eugene O'Neill National Historic Site Museum • 1000 Kuss Rd, P.O. Box 280 • Danville, CA 94526 • (925) 838-0249 • http://www.nps.gov/euon

San Ramon Valley Historical Society • P.O. Box 521 • Danville, CA 94526 • (925) 837-0369

Davis
Croatian Genealogy Network • P.O. Box 4327 • Davis, CA 95617-4327 • http://feefhs.org/cro/frg-hr.html

Davis Genealogy Club • 646 A Street • Davis, CA 95616 • (530) 753-2672 • http://www.davisgenealogy.org

Federation of Eastern European Family History Societies • P.O. Box 4327 • Davis, CA 95617-4327 • (530) 753-3206 • http://feefhs.org

Hattie Weber Museum of Davis • 445 C Street • Davis, CA 95686 • (530) 758-5637

Shields Library • Univ of California, 100 N W Quad • Davis, CA 95616 • (530) 752-1126 • http://www.lib.ucdavis.edu/speccoll/

Western Australia Genealogical Society • P.O. Box 4327 • Davis, CA 95617-4327 • http://feefhs.org/msc/frg/wags.html

Death Valley
Death Valley National Monument Library • P.O. Box 57 • Death Valley, CA 92328 • (760) 786-2331 • http://www.nps.gov/deva/

Death Valley National Park • P.O. Box 579 • Death Valley, CA 92328 • (760) 786-3200 • http://www.nps.gov/deva

Scotty's Castle Museum • Death Valley National Park, P.O. Box 579 • Death Valley, CA 92328 • (760) 786-3200 • http://www.nps.gov/deva

Del Mar
Del Mar Historical Society • 1442 Canine del Mar • Del Mar, CA 92014 • (619) 259-0421 • http://www.ucsd-civic-collaborative.org

Delano
Delano Historical Society • Heritage Park Museum, 330 Lexington • Delano, CA 93215 • (661) 725-6730

Desert Hot Springs
Cabot's Old Indian Pueblo Museum • 67-616 E Desert View Ave, P.O. Box 1267 • Desert Hot Springs, CA 92240 • (760) 329-7610 • http://www.cabotsmuseum.org

Desert Hot Springs Historical Society • 67616 E Desert View Ave, P.O. Box 1267 • Desert Hot Springs, CA 92240 • (760) 329-7610

Diablo
San Ramon Valley Genealogical Society • P.O. Box 305 • Diablo, CA 94528 • (925) 820-9738

Dinuba
Alta District Historical Society • 289 South K Street, P.O. Box 254 • Dinuba, CA 93618 • (559) 591-2144 • http://www.altadistricthistoricalsociety.org

Dixon
Dixon Public Library • 230 N 1st St • Dixon, CA 95620-3028 • (707) 678-5447 • http://www.dixon.library.com

Downey
County of Los Angeles Public Library • 7400 E Imperial Hwy, P.O. Box 7011 • Downey, CA 90241-7011 • (562) 940-8462 • http://www.colapublib.org

Downey City Library • 11121 Brookshire Ave, P.O. Box 7015 • Downey, CA 90241-7015 • (562) 904-7360 • http://www.downeylibrary.org

Downey Historical Society • 12540 Rives Ave, P.O. Box 554 • Downey, CA 90241 • (562) 862-2777 • http://www.downeyca.org/visitor/hiscenter.htm

Downieville
Downieville Museum • 330 Main St, P.O. Box 484 • Downieville, CA 95936 • (530) 289-3423 • http://www.caohwy.com/d/downimus.htm

Duarte
Duarte Historical Society • Duarte Historical Museum, 777 Encanto Pkwy, P.O. Box 263 • Duarte, CA 91010 • (818) 357-9419 • http://www.duartehistory.org

Dublin
Dublin Historical Preservation Association • Dublin House Museum, P.O. Box 2245 • Dublin, CA 94568 • (510) 828-3377

Surveyor's Historical Society • P.O. Box 2820 • Dublin, CA 94086 • http://www.surveyhistory.org

Dunlap
Dunlap Band of Mono Indians • P.O. Box 344 • Dunlap, CA 93621 • (209) 228-5895

Eagle Rock
Eagle Rock Valley Historical Society • Eagle Rock Cultural Center, 2225 Colorado Blvd • Eagle Rock, CA 90041 • (323) 226-1617

Earlimart
Colonel Allensworth State Historic Park • Star Route 1, Box 148 • Earlimart, CA 93219 • (805) 849-3433 • http://parks.ca.gov

East Palo Alto
East Palo Also Historical and Agricultural Society • 1955 University Ave • East Palo Alto, CA 94303-2224 • (650) 329-0294

Echo Park
Echo Park Historical Society • 1471 Fairbanks Pl, P.O. Box 261022 • Echo Park, CA 90026 • (213) 250-0573 • http://www.echopark.net/org/ephs.htm

Edwards AFB
Air Force Flight Test Center Museum • 95 ABW.MU, 405 S Rosamond Blvd • Edwards AFB, CA 93524 • (661) 277-8050 • http://www.edwards.af.mil/museum/

El Cajon
El Cajon Historical Society • 280 N Magnolia Ave, P.O. Box 1973 • El Cajon, CA 92022-1973 • (619) 444-3800 • http://www.elcajonhistory.org/ec/

Heritage of the Americas Museum • 12110 Cuyamaca College Dr • El Cajon, CA 92019 • (619) 670-5194 • http://www.cuyamaca.net/museum/

Knox House Museum • 280 N Magnolia, P.O. Box 1973 • El Cajon, CA 92022 • (619) 444-3800 • http://www.elcajonhistory.org

San Diego Genealogical Society • 1050 Pioneer Way, Ste E • El Cajon, CA 92020-1943 • (619) 588-0065 • http://www.rootsweb.com/~casdgs/

Sycuan Band of Mission Indians - Kumeyaay, Diegueno • 5459 Dehesa Rd • El Cajon, CA 92019 • (619) 445-2613 • http://www.sycuan.com

Warbirds West Air Museum • 1942 Joe Crosson Dr • El Cajon, CA 92020 • (858) 414-6258 • http://www.wwam.org

El Centro
El Centro Public Library • 539 State St • El Centro, CA 92243-2973 • (760) 337-4565 • http://www.eclib.org

Imperial County Free Library • 1125 Main St • El Centro, CA 92243-2814 • (760) 482-4791 • http://www.imperialcounty.net/library

Imperial County Genealogical Society • 1573 Elm St, P.O. Box 2643 • El Centro, CA 92243-3133

El Dorado
El Dorado Research Society • Laarveld House Museum, P.O. Box 56 • El Dorado, CA 95623 • (530) 622-9434

El Monte
El Monte Historical Society • Historical Museum, 3150 N Tyler Ave, P.O. Box 6307 • El Monte, CA 91734 • (626) 444-3813

El Segundo
El Segundo Public Library • 111 W Mariposa Ave • El Segundo, CA 90245-2299 • (310) 524-2728 • http://www.elsegundo.org

El Toro
Saddleback Area Historical Society • 25151 Seranno Rd, P.O. Box 156 • El Toro, CA 92630 • (949) 586-8485

Elk Creek
Grindstone Indian Rancherie of Wintun-Wailaki • P.O. Box 63 • Elk Creek, CA 95939 • (530) 968-5365

Elk Grove
Elk Grove Historical Society • P.O. Box 562 • Elk Grove, CA 95759-0562 • (916) 687-7713

Encinitas
Encinitas Historical Society • 650 3rd St • Encinitas, CA 92024-3512 • (760) 942-9066

San Dieguito Heritage Museum • 561 Vulcan Ave, Pl.O. Box 230851 • Encinitas, CA 92023 • (760) 632-9711 • http://www.encinitas101.com/sdmuseum.htm

Encino
Encino Historical Society • 16756 Moorpark St • Encino, CA 91436

Jewish Genealogical Society of Los Angeles • 4530 Woodley Ave • Encino, CA 91436

Los Encinos State Park • 16756 Moorpark St • Encino, CA 91436 • (818) 706-1310 • http://parks.ca.gov

Escalon
Escalon Historical Society • Historical Museum, 1630 Main St • Escalon, CA 95320 • (209) 838-8070

Escondido
Deer Park Escondido Winery & Auto Museum • 29013 Champagne Blvd • Escondido, CA 92026 • (760) 749-1666 • http://www.deerparkwinery.com

Escondido Genealogial Society • P.O. Box 2190 • Escondido, CA 92033-2190 • (760) 480-7369 • http://www.rootsweb.com/~caegs

Escondido, cont.

Escondido Historical Society • Heritage Walk Museum Complex, 321 N Broadway, P.O. Box 263 • Escondido, CA 92025 • (760) 743-8207 • http://www.escondidohistoricalsociety.org

Escondido Public Library • 239 S Kalmia St • Escondido, CA 92025 • (760) 839-4315 • http://www.ci.escondido.ca.us/library/

Hoffman House Museum • 321 N Broadway, P.O. Box 263 • Escondido, CA 92033 • (760) 743-8207

Inaja and Cosmit Band of Mission Indians • 1040 East Valley Pkwy, Unit A • Escondido, CA 92025 • (760) 747-8581

San Pasqual Battlefield State Historic Park • 15808 San Pasqual Valley Rd • Escondido, CA 92030 • (619) 238-3380 • http://parks.ca.gov

Essex

Mojave Desert Heritage and Cultural Association • P.O. Box 66 • Essex, CA 92332-0066 • http://www.mdhca.org

Etiwanda

Etiwanda Historical Society • 7150 Etiwanda Ave, P.O. Box 363 • Etiwanda, CA 91739-9758 • (909) 899-8432

Eureka

Blue Ox Millworks Historic Park • 1 X Street • Eureka, CA 95501 • (800) 248-4259

Chilula Tribe • P.O. Box 724 • Eureka, CA 95502

Clarke Memorial Museum • 240 E Street • Eureka, CA 95501 • (707) 443-1947 • http://www.clarkemuseum.org

Eureka California Senior Center Genealogy Group • 1910 California St • Eureka, CA 95501

Fort Humboldt State Historic Park • 3431 Fort Ave • Eureka, CA 95501 • (707) 445-6567 • http://www.humboldtredwoods.org/forthumboldt.htm

Humboldt County Genealogical Society • 2336 G Street, P.O. Box 882 • Eureka, CA 95502

Humboldt County Historical Society • 703 8th St, P.O. Box 8000 • Eureka, CA 95501 • (707) 445-4342 • http://www.humboldthistory.org

Humboldt County Library • 1313 3rd St • Eureka, CA 95501-0533 • (707) 269-1918 • http://www.humlib.org

Samoa Cookhouse & Logging Museum • 79 Cookhouse Ln • Eureka, CA 95564 • (707) 442-1659 • http://www.humboldtdining.com/cookhouse

Yurok Tribe • 1034 6th St • Eureka, CA 95501 • (707) 444-0433

Fair Oaks

Fair Oaks Historical Society • P.O. Box 2044 • Fair Oaks, CA 95628 • (916) 961-0637

Fairfax

Fairfax Historical Society • P.O. Box 662 • Fairfax, CA 94978-0662 • (415) 454-3615 • http://www.marindirect.com/fxhistory/

Fairfield

Solano County Genealogical Society • P.O. Box 2494 • Fairfield, CA 94533-0249 • (707) 446-6869 • http://www.scgsinc.org

Solano County Historic Records Commission • County Archives, 1745 Enterprise Dr, Bldg 2, Ste A • Fairfield, CA 94533

Solano County Library • 1150 Kentucky St • Fairfield, CA 94533 • (707) 421-6510 • http://www.solanolibrary.com

Fall River Mills

Fort Crook Historical Society • Fort Crook Historical Museum • Fort Crook Ave & Hwy 299, P.O. Box 397 • Fall River Mills, CA 96028 • (530) 336-5110 • http://www.ftcrook.org

Fallbrook

Fallbrook Historical Society • 260 Rocky Crest Rd, P.O. Box 1375 • Fallbrook, CA 92088-1375 • (760) 723-4125 • http://sd.znet.com/~schester/fallbrook/history/society/

Ferndale

Fern Cottage Museum • 2099 Centerville Rd • Ferndale, CA 95536 • (707) 786-4735

Ferndale Museum • 515 Shaw Ave, P.O. Box 431 • Ferndale, CA 95536 • (707) 786-4466 • http://www.ferndale-museum.org/

Fiddletown

Chinese Museum • P.O. Box 12 • Fiddletown, CA 95629 • (209) 296-4519 • http://www.fiddletown.org

Fillmore

Fillmore Historical Society • Fillmore Historical Museum • 350 Main St, P.O. Box 314 • Fillmore, CA 93016 • (805) 524-0948

Santa Clara River Valley Railroad Historical Society • 455 Main St • Fillmore, CA 93015 • (805) 524-2254 • http://www.scrvhs.org

Folsom

Folsom Historical Society • Historical Museum, 823 Sutter St • Folsom, CA 95630 • (916) 985-2707 • http://www.folsomhistorymuseum.org

Fontana

Fontana Historical Society • 8459 Wheeler Ave, P.O. Box 426 • Fontana, CA 92335 • (909) 823-1733

Forbestown

Yuba-Feather Museum • 19096 New York Flat Rd • Forbestown, CA 95941 • (530) 675-1025 • http://www.yfhmuseum.org

Foresthill

Foresthill Divide Historical Society • Historical Museum, P.O. Box 646 • Foresthill, CA 95631 • http://mmoffet.mystarband.net

Foresthill Divide Museum • 24601 Harrison St • Foresthill, CA 95631 • (530) 367-3988 • http://mmoffet.mystarband.net/museum.htm

Fort Bidwell

Fort Bidwell Indian Community of Paiute Indians • P.O. Box 129 • Fort Bidwell, CA 96112 • (530) 279-6310

Fort Bragg

Fort Bragg Building Museum • 430 N Frnaklin St • Fort Bragg, CA 95437 • (707) 961-2825

Fort Bragg-Mendocino Coast Historical Society • 416 N Franklin St • Fort Bragg, CA 95437 • (707) 961-2840

Guest House Museum • 343 N Main St, P.O. Box 71 • Fort Bragg, CA 95437 • (707) 964-4251

Mendocino Coast Genealogical Society • P.O. Box 762 • Fort Bragg, CA 95437 • (707) 937-5482

Fort Dick

Tolowa Nation • P.O. Box 213 • Fort Dick, CA 95538 • (707) 464-7332

Fort Irwin

Fort Irwin Post Library • National Training Ctr, Bldg 331, Box 105091 • Fort Irwin, CA 92310-5091 • (760) 380-3462

National Training Center & 11th Armored Cavalry Regiment Museum • Bldg 222, C Avenue, P.O. Box 105029 • Fort Irwin, CA 92310 • (760) 380-6607

Fort Jones

Fort Jones Museum • 11913 Main St, P.O. Box 428 • Fort Jones, CA 96032 • (916) 468-5568 • http://www.sisqtel.net/~norm/fortjone.html

Shasta and Upper Klamath Tribes • Quartz Valley Reservation, P.O. Box 24 • Fort Jones, CA 96032 • (530) 468-5970

Shasta Nation • 10736 Quartz Valley Rd • Fort Jones, CA 96032 • (916) 739-0931

Fortuna

Fortuna Depot Museum • 1 Park St • Fortuna, CA 95540 • (707) 725-7645 • http://www.sunnyfortuna.com/departments/museum/

Fortuna Historical Commission • 621 11th St • Fortuna, CA 95540 • http://www.chamber.sunnyfortuna.com/memberspages/fortuna_historical_commission/

Redwood Genealogical Society • Rohner Park, 5 Park Wy, P.O. Box 645 • Fortuna, CA 95540-0645 • (707) 725-3791 • http://www.qworld.net/humboldt.rgs.html

Foster City

Foster City Historical Society • P.O. Box 4592 • Foster City, CA 94404 • http://www.fchistorysocy.homestead.com

Fountain Valley

Fountain Valley Historical Society • P.O. Box 8592 • Fountain Valley, CA 92708 • (714) 964-0814

Shroud Center of Southern California • 8840 Warner Ave, Ste 200 • Fountain Valley, CA 92708 • (714) 375-5723 • http://www.shroudcentersocal.com

Frazier Park

Ridge Route Communities Historical Society • Historical Museum, 3515 Park Dr, P.O. Box 684 • Frazier Park, CA 93225 • (661) 245-7747 • http://www.frazmtn.com/~rrchs/mainie.html

Freedom

Pajaro Valley Genealogical Society • 53 North Dr • Freedom, CA 95019

Santa Cruz County Railroad Historical Society • P.O. Box 612 • Freedom, CA 95019 • (831) 768-8211 • http://www.trainweb.org/sccrhs/

Fremont

Alameda County Library • 2400 Stevenson Blvd • Fremont, CA 94538 • (510) 745-1400 • http://www.aclibrary.org

Ardenwood Historic Farm Museum • 34600 Ardenwood Blvd • Fremont, CA 94555 • (510) 796-0199 • http://www.ebparks.org/parks/arden.htm

Fremont Museum of Local History • 190 Anza St, P.O. Box 3087 • Fremont, CA 94539 • (510) 623-7907 • http://www.museumoflocalhistory.org

Niles Depot Museum • 36997 Mission Blvd, P.O. Box 2716 • Fremont, CA 94536 • (510) 797-4449 • http://www.nilesdepot.railfan.net/ndhfhome.html

Old Mission San Jose Museum • 43300 Mission Blvd, P.O. Box 3159 • Fremont, CA 94539 • (510) 657-1797 • http://www.saintjosephmsj.org

Shinn House Museum • 40000 Paseo Padre Blvd, P.O. Box 3078 • Fremont, CA 94539 • (510) 791-4340 • http://www.ci.fremont.ca.us

Washington Township Historical Society • 43263 Mission Blvd, P.O. Box 3045 • Fremont, CA 94539 • (510) 656-3761

Fresno

African American Historical & Cultural Museum • 1857 Fulton St • Fresno, CA 93721 • (559) 268-7102

Afro-American Historical and Genealogical Society, Central California Chapter • P.O. Box 9161 • Fresno, CA 93790-9161 • http://www.aahgs.org/chapters

American Historical Society of Germans from Russia, Central California Chapter • 3233 N West Ave • Fresno, CA 94705 • (559) 229-8287 • http://www.ahsgr.org/Chapters/fresno/cacentra.html

California Christian College Library • 4881 E University Ave • Fresno, CA 93703 • (559) 251-4215 • http://calchristiancollege.org

California Mennonite Historical Society • 4824 E Butler • Fresno, CA 93727-5097 • (559) 453-2225 • http://www.fresno.edu/affiliation/cmhs/

Center for Mennonite Brethren Studies • 4824 E Butler St • Fresno, CA 93727 • (559) 453-2225 • http://www.fresno.edu/cmbs

Choinumni Tribe • 4233 W Sierra Madre • Fresno, CA 93722 • (559) 274-1580

Danish-American Historical Society of California • 905 R Street • Fresno, CA 93721-1311 • (559) 485-4005

Fresno City and County Historical Society • Kearney Mansion Museum, 7160 W Kearney Blvd, P.O. Box 2029 • Fresno, CA 93706 • (559) 441-0862 • http://www.valleyhistory.org

Fresno County Free Library • 2420 Mariposa St • Fresno, CA 93721 • (559) 488-6735 • http://www.fresnolibrary.org

Fresno Genealogical Society • c/o Fresno County Free Library, 2420 Mariposa St, P.O. Box 1429 • Fresno, CA 93716 • (559) 488-3185

Henry Madden Library • California State Univ at Fresno, 5200 N Barton Ave, Mail Stop ML-34 • Fresno, CA 93740-8014 • (559) 278-2174 • http://www.lib.csufresno.edu

Hiebert Library • Fresno Pacific Univ, 1717 S Chestnut Ave • Fresno, CA 93702 • (559) 453-2090 • http://www.fresno.edu/dept/library

Kearney Mansion Museum • 7160 W Kearney Blvd, P.O. Box 2029 • Fresno, CA 93718 • (209) 441-0862

Legion of Valor Veterans Museum • 2425 Fresno St • Fresno, CA 93721 • (559) 498-0510

Meux Home Museum • 1007 R Street, P.O. Box 70 • Fresno, CA 93707 • (559) 233-8007 • http://www.meux.mus.ca.us

Simonian Farms Museum • 2629 S Clovis Ave • Fresno, CA 93725 • (559) 237-2294 • http://www.simonianfarms.com

Temple Beth Israel Library • 6622 N Maroa Ave • Fresno, CA 93704 • (209) 432-3600

Friant

Millerton Courthouse Museum • 5290 Millerton Rd, P.O. Box 205 • Friant, CA 93626 • (559) 822-2225

Table Mountain Rancheria - Mono Indians • 23736 Sky Harbor Rd, P.O. Box 140 • Friant, CA 93626 • (559) 822-2587

Fullerton

Beckman Coulter Heritage Museum • 4300 N Harbor Blvd • Fullerton, CA 92835 • (714) 733-6924 • http://www.beckman/com

CalState-Fullerton Oral History Program • California State University • Fullerton, CA 92834 • (714) 278-3580 • http://ohp.fullerton.edu

Fullerton Historic Theater Foundation • 131 W Commonwealth Ave • Fullerton, CA 92832 • (714) 870-0069

Fullerton Museum Center • 301 N Pomona Ave • Fullerton, CA 92832 • (714) 738-6545 • http://www.ci.fullerton.ca.us/museum/

Fullerton Museum Center Association • Historical Museum, 301 N Pomona Ave • Fullerton, CA 92832 • (714) 738-6545 • http://www.ci.fullerton.ca.us/museum

Fullerton Public Library • 353 W Commonwealth Ave • Fullerton, CA 92832-1796 • (714) 738-6327 • http://www.ci.fullerton.ca.us/library

HEFA Kinseekers • P.O. Box 3310 • Fullerton, CA 92634

Heritage Coordinating Council • c/o Fullerton Public Library, 353 W Commonwealth Ave • Fullerton, CA 92832-1796 • (714) 738-6396 • http://ohp.fullerton.edu/HeritageCoordinatingCouncil.htm

Heritage House Library • California State Univ, 800 N State College Blvd • Fullerton, CA 92634 • (714) 773-3579

Heritage House Museum • 1900 Associated Rd • Fullerton, CA 92831 • (714) 278-3579

Hispanic Historical and Ancestral Research Society • P.O. Box 5294 • Fullerton, CA 92635 • http://members.aol.com/shhar/

Fullerton, cont.
Muckenthaler Cultural Center Museum • 1201 W Malvern Ave • Fullerton, CA 92833 • (714) 738-6595 • http://www.muckenthaler.org

William T Boyce Library • Fullerton College, 321 E Chapman Ave • Fullerton, CA 92832-2095 • (714) 992-7061 • http://www.fullcoll.edu

Galt
Galt Area Historical Society • P.O. Box 782 • Galt, CA 95632 • (209) 745-0951

Hungarian-American Friendship Society • 1035 Starbrook Dr • Galt, CA 95632 • (209) 744-8099 • http://www.dholmes.com/hafs.html

Portuguese Historical and Cultural Society • 1035 Starbrook Dr • Galt, CA 95632 • (209) 744-8099 • http://www.dholmes.com

Garberville
South Humboldt Historical and Genealogical Society • P.O. Box 656 • Garberville, CA 95440

Garden Grove
Garden Grove Historical Society • Stanley Ranch Museum, 12174 Euclid St, P.O. Box 4297 • Garden Grove, CA 92640 • (714) 530-8871 • http://www.gardengrovecity.com

Orange County-Garden Grove Regional Library • 11200 Stanford Ave • Garden Grove, CA 92640-5398 • (714) 530-0711 • http://www.ocpl.org/ggregnal/ggreg.htm

Southern California Indian Center • 12755 Brookhurst St, P.O. Box 2550 • Garden Grove, CA 92642-2550 • (714) 530-0221 • http://www.indiancenter.org

Ware-Stanley House Museum • 12174 Euclid Ave, P.O. Box 4297 • Garden Grove, CA 92842

Gardena
County of Los Angeles Public Library-Gardena Mayme Dear Library • 1731 W Gardena Blvd • Gardena, CA 90247-4726 • (310) 323-6363 • http://colapublib.org/libs/gardena/

Geserville
Dry Creek Rancheria • P.O. Box 607 • Geserville, CA 95441 • (707) 431-2388

Gilroy
Gilroy Historical Society • Historical Museum, 195 5th St, P.O. Box 1621 • Gilroy, CA 95021 • (408) 848-0470 • http://www.ci.gilroy.ca.us

Glen Ellen
Jack London State Historic Park • House of Happy Walls, 2400 London Ranch Rd • Glen Ellen, CA 95442 • (707) 938-5216 • http://www.parks.sonoma.net

Glendale
Casa Adobe de San Rafael Museum • 1330 Dorothy Dr • Glendale, CA 91202 • (818) 956-2000 • http://www.ci.glendale.ca.us/Historic/casa_adobe.html

Doctors' House Museum • Brand Park, 1601 W Montain Ave • Glendale, CA 91201 • (818) 548-2147

Forest Lawn Museum • 1712 S Glendale Ave • Glendale, CA 91205 • (323) 340-4707 • http://www.forestlawn.com

Glendale Historical Society • P.O. Box 4173 • Glendale, CA 91202 • (818) 242-7447 • http://www.glendalehistorical.org

Glendale Public Library • 222 E Harvard St • Glendale, CA 92105-1075 • (818) 548-2027 • http://www.glendalepubliclibrary.org

Sons of the American Revolution • 600 S Central Ave • Glendale, CA 91204 • (818) 240-1775 • http://www.srcalifornia.com

Southern California Genealogical Society • 600 S Central Ave • Glendale, CA 91204

Glendora
Glendora Genealogy Group • 1025 E Foothill Blvd, P.O. Box 1141 • Glendora, CA 91740 • (818) 963-6481 • http://www.cagenweb.com/kr/GlendoraGG/

Glendora Historical Society • Historical Museum, 314 N Glendora Ave, P.O. Box 532 • Glendora, CA 91740 • (626) 963-0419 • http://glendorahistoricalsociety.org/

Glendora Public Library • 140 S Glendora Ave • Glendora, CA 91741 • (626) 852-4891 • http://www.ci.glendora.ca.us/library/

Glenn
Colusa County Historical Society • P.O. Box 510 • Glenn, CA 95943

Goleta
Goleta Valley Historical Society • Stow House Museum, 304 N Los Carneros Rd • Goleta, CA 93117 • (805) 964-4407 • http://www.goletahistory.org, www.stowhouse.com

Historical Diving Society • 340 S Kellogg Ave #1182 • Goleta, CA 93117 • (805) 692-0072

Santa Barbara County Genealogical Society • 316 Castillo St, P.O. Box 1303 • Goleta, CA 93116-1303 • (805) 884-9909 • http://www.cagenweb.com/santabarbara/sbcgs/

South Coast Railroad Museum at Goleta Depot • 300 N Los Carneros Rd • Goleta, CA 93118-1507 • (805) 964-3540 • http://www.goletadepot.org

Granada Hills
Latvian Jewish Genealogy Special Interest Group • P.O. Box 3581 • Granada Hills, CA 91394-3581 • http://www1.jewishgen.org/latvia

Grass Valley
Grass Roots Genealogical Group • 11350 McCourtney Rd, P.O. Box 98 • Grass Valley, CA 95945 • http://www.nccn.net/leisure/crafthby/genealog.htm

Grass Valley Museum • 410 S Church St • Grass Valley, CA 95945 • (530) 273-6949

Lola Montez Home Museum • 248 Mill St • Grass Valley, CA 95945 • (916) 273-4667

Nevada County Library • 11130 Magnolia Rd • Grass Valley, CA 95949 • (530) 271-4147 • http://www.mynevadacounty.com/library

Greenville
Greenville Rancheria of Maidu Indians • P.O. Box 279 • Greenville, CA 95947 • (530) 284-7990

Gridley
Gridley Historical and Wildlife Museum • Kentucky & Hazel Sts • Gridley, CA 95948 • (530) 846-3142

Groveland
Southern Tuolumne County Historical Society • 18990 State Hwy 120 • Groveland, CA 95321 • (209) 962-0300

Yosemite Gateway Museum • 18990 Main St • Groveland, CA 95321 • (209) 962-0300 • http://www.grovelandmuseum.org

Guadalupe
Rancho de Quadalupe Historical Society • 1005 Guadalupe St • Guadalupe, CA 93434 • (805) 343-5901

Guerneville
Generations of Our Past! • 15170 Drake Rd • Guerneville, CA 95446

Miwok Tribe • P.O. Box 1433 • Guerneville, CA 95546

Gustine
Gustine Museum • 397 4th St • Gustine, CA 95322 • (209) 854-2344 • http://www.artcom.com/museums/nv/gl/95322-11.htm

Hacienda Heights

County of Los Angeles Public Library-Hacienda Heights Library • 16010 La Monde St • Hacienda Heights, CA 91745-4299 • (626) 968-9356 • http://colapublib.org/libs/haciendahts/

La Puente Valley Historical Society • 16021 Gale Ave • Hacienda Heights, CA 91745 • (626) 336-7644

Half Moon Bay

Spanishtown Historical Society • 505 Johnston St, P.O. Box 62 • Half Moon Bay, CA 94019 • (650) 726-7084 • http://www.spanishtownhs.org

Hanford

Hanford Carnegie Museum • 109 E 8th St • Hanford, CA 93230 • (559) 584-1367 • http://www.irwinsfreeinn.com/carnegie-museum.html

Kings County Library • 401 N Douty St • Hanford, CA 93230 • (559) 582-0261 • http://www.kingscountylibrary.org

Renegade Root Diggers • 9171 Fargo Ave • Hanford, CA 93230

Taoist Temple and Museum • 12 China Alley • Hanford, CA 93230 • (559) 582-4508 • http://www.visithanford.com

Happy Camp

Karuk Tribe of California • P.O. Box 1016 • Happy Camp, CA 96039 • (530) 493-1600 • http://www.karuk.us

Havasu Lake

Chemehuevi Tribal Council • P.O. Box 1976 • Havasu Lake, CA 92363 • (760) 858-4219

Hawthorne

Southern California Historical Aviation Foundation • Western Museum of Flight, 12016 South Prairie Ave • Hawthorne, CA 90250 • (310) 332-6228 • http://www.wmof.com

Hayfork

Nor-Rel-Muk - Wintun Indians • P.O. Box 673 • Hayfork, CA 96041 • (530) 628-4226

Hayward

Chabot College Library • 25555 Hesperian Blvd • Hayward, CA 94545 • (510) 723-7006 • http://www.chabotcollege.edu/library/

Hayward Area Genealogical Society • P.O. Box 754 • Hayward, CA 94543

Hayward Area Historical Society • Historical Museum, 22701 Main St • Hayward, CA 94541-5113 • (510) 581-0223 • http://www.haywardareahistory.org

Hayward Public Library • 835 C Street • Hayward, CA 94541-5120 • (510) 881-7954 • http://library.ci.hayward.ca.us

McConaghy House Museum • 18701 Hesperian Blvd • Hayward, CA 94541 • (510) 581-0223 • http://www.haywardareahistory.org

Surveyors' Historical Society • 31457 Hugh Wy • Hayward, CA 94544 • (510) 471-3905

Healdsburg

Healdsburg Historical Society • Historical Museum, 221 Matheson St, P.O. Box 952 • Healdsburg, CA 95448-0952 • (707) 431-3325 • http://www.gdmarch.com/healdsburg.html

Lower Lake Rancheria • 131 Lincoln St • Healdsburg, CA 95448

Hemet

Hemet Area Museum Association • Historical Museum, 100 W Florida, P.O. Box 2521 • Hemet, CA 92546 • (909) 929-4409 • http://www.hemetmuseum.org

Hemet Public Library • 300 E Latham • Hemet, CA 92543 • (909) 765-2440 • http://www.cityofhemet.org

Hemet-San Jacinto Genealogical Society • 1779 E Florida Ave #C4, P.O. Box 2516 • Hemet, CA 92346-2516 • (909) 925-1130

Hermosa Beach

Hermosa Beach Historical Society • 710 Pier Ave • Hermosa Beach, CA 90254 • (310) 318-9421 • http://www.ci.manhattan-beach.ca.us/commres/HermosaBeachHistoricalSociety.htm

Hollister

Costanoan-Mutsun Indians of California • P.O. Box 28 • Hollister, CA 95024-0028 • (408) 637-4238 • http://www.indiancanyon.org

San Benito County Free Library • 470 5th St • Hollister, CA 95023-3885 • (831) 636-4107 • http://www.sbclib.com

San Benito County Genealogical Society • 1021 Peach Ct • Hollister, CA 95023 • (831) 636-8229

San Benito County Historical Society • Historical Museum, 498 5th St, P.O. Box 357 • Hollister, CA 95023 • (831) 635-0335 • http://www.sbchistoricalsociety.org

Hollywood

Hollywood Entertainment Museum • 7021 Hollywood Blvd • Hollywood, CA 90028 • (323) 465-7900 • http://www.hollywoodmuseum.com

Hollywood Guinness World of Records Museum • 6767 Hollywood Blvd • Hollywood, CA 90028 • (323) 463-6433

Hollywood Heritage • Historical Museum, 2100 Highland Ave, P.O. Box 2586 • Hollywood, CA 90078 • (323) 874-2276 • http://www.hollywoodheritage.org

Hollywood History Museum • 1666 N Highland Ave • Hollywood, CA 90028 • (323) 464-7776

Hollywood Wax Museum • 6767 Hollywood Blvd • Hollywood, CA 90028 • (323) 462-5991 • http://www.hollywoodwax.com

Holtville

Imperial County Free Library-Holtville Branch • 101 E 6th St, P.O. Box 755 • Holtville, CA 92250-0755 • (760) 356-2385

Hoopa

Hoopa Tribal Museum • Highway 96 • Hoopa, CA 95546 • (530) 625-4110 • http://bss.sfsu.edu/calstudies/hupa/hoopa.htm

Hoopa Valley Indian Reservation - Hupa • P.O. Box 1348 • Hoopa, CA 95546 • (530) 625-4211

Hopland

Hopland Band of Pomo Indians • P.O. Box 610 • Hopland, CA 95449 • (707) 744-1647 • http://www.hoplandtribe.com

Humboldt

Humboldt Historical Society • 703 8th St • Humboldt, CA 95501 • (707) 445-4342 • http://www.humboldthistory.org

Huntington Beach

Hispanic History and Ancestry Research • 9511 Rockpoint Dr • Huntington Beach, CA 92646

Huntington Beach Central Library • 7111 Talbert Ave • Huntington Beach, CA 92648 • (714) 742-4481 • http://www.hbpl.org

Huntington Beach Historical Society • Newland House Museum, 19820 Beach Blvd • Huntington Beach, CA 92648 • (714) 962-5777 • http://www.stockteam.com/newland.html

Huntington Beach International Surfing Museum • 411 Olive Ave, P.O. Box 782 • Huntington Beach, CA 92648 • (714) 960-3483

Orange County Genealogical Society • c/o Huntington Beach Central Library, 7111 Talbert Ave • Huntington Beach, CA 92648 • (714) 742-4481

Orange County Genealogical Society, Computer Assisted Genealogy Group • c/o Huntington Beach Central Library, 7111 Talbert Ave • Huntington Beach, CA 92648-1296 • (714) 742-4481

Orange County Genealogical Society, Family Tree Maker Group • c/o Huntington Beach Central Library, 7111 Talbert Ave • Huntington Beach, CA 92648-1296 • (714) 742-4481

California

Huntington Beach, cont.
Orange County Genealogical Society, Irish-Scottish Group • c/o Huntington Beach Central Library, 7111 Talbert Ave • Huntington Beach, CA 92648-1296 • (714) 742-4481

Idyllwild
Idyllwild Area Historical Society • 54470 N Circle Dr, P.O. Box 3320 • Idyllwild, CA 92549 • (951) 659-2717 • http://www.idyllwildareahistoricalsociety.org

Imperial
Imperial County Historical Society • 373 W Aten Rd • Imperial, CA 92251-9653 • (760) 352-1165

Spencer Library • Imperial Valley College, 380 E Ira Aten Rd, P.O. Box 158 • Imperial, CA 92251 • (760) 355-6378 • http://www.imperial.cc.ca.us

Independence
Eastern California Museum • 155 N Grant St, P.O. Box 206 • Independence, CA 93526 • (760) 878-0364 • http://www.countyofinyo.org/ecmuseum/

Fort Independence Paiute Reservation • P.O. Box 67 • Independence, CA 93526 • (760) 787-2126

Inyo County Free Library • 168 N Edwards St, P.O. Drawer K • Independence, CA 93526 • (760) 873-5122

Indio
Cabazon Band of Mission Indians Cahuilla • 84-245 Indio Springs Pkwy • Indio, CA 92203 • (760) 342-2593 • http://www.cabazonindians-ns.gov

Coachella Valley Genealogical Society • P.O. Box 124 • Indio, CA 92202 • (760) 342-3725

Coachella Valley Historical Society • Historical Museum, 82616 Miles Ave, P.O. Box 595 • Indio, CA 92202-0505 • (760) 342-6651 • http://www.coachellavalleymuseum.org

Middletown First Settlers Descendants [1650-1700] Society • 81641 Ave 48 #89 • Indio, CA 92201-6723

Inglewood
City of Inglewood Public Library • 101 W Manchester Blvd • Inglewood, CA 90301-1771 • (310) 412-5397 • http://www.inglewoodlibrary.org

Ione
Ione Band of Miwok Indians • P.O. Box 1190 • Ione, CA 95640 • (209) 274-6753

Irvine
Irvine Historical Society • Historical Museum, 5 Rancho San Joaquin • Irvine, CA 92717 • (949) 786-4112

University of California Library • P.O. Box 19557 • Irvine, CA 92623-9557 • (949) 824-6836 • http://www.lib.uci.edu

Irwindale
Irwindale Public Library • 5050 N Irwindale Ave • Irwindale, CA 91706 • (626) 430-2229 • http://www.ci.irwindale.ca.us

Jackson
Amador County Archives • 12200-A Airport Rd • Jackson, CA 95642 • (209) 223-6389 • http://www.co.amador.ca.us/depts/archives/

Amador County Genealogical Society • 10193 Buena Vista Dr • Jackson, CA 95642

Amador County Historical Society • 18708 Clinton Rd, P.O. Box 761 • Jackson, CA 95642 • (209) 223-6386 • http://www.amadorarchives.org/achs.html

Amador County Library • 530 Sutter St • Jackson, CA 95642-2379 • (209) 223-6400 • http://www.co.amador.ca.us

Friends of the Amador County Museum • Historical Museum, 225 Church St, P.O. Box 913 • Jackson, CA 95642 • (209) 223-6386 • http://www.amadorarchives.org/museum.html

Jackson Rancheria Band of Miwuk Indians • P.O. Box 1090 • Jackson, CA 95642 • (209) 223-1935

Jamestown
Chicken Ranch Rancheria - Miwok Band • P.O. Box 1159 • Jamestown, CA 95327 • (209) 984-4806

Railtown 1897 State Historic Park • P.O. Box 1250 • Jamestown, CA 95327 • (209) 984-3953 • http://www.parks.ca.gov

Jamul
Jamul Band of Mission Indians - Kumeyaay Diegueno • P.O. Box 612 • Jamul, CA 91935 • (619) 669-4785 • http://kumeyaay.com

Jolon
Old Mission San Antonio de Padua Museum • Mission Creek Rd, P.O. Box 803 • Jolon, CA 93928 • (831) 385-4478 • http://www.sanantonio.mission.org

Julian
Julian Black Historical Society • 2024 3rd St • Julian, CA 92036 • (760) 765-1120

Julian Historical Society • P.O. Box 513 • Julian, CA 92036 • (760) 765-0436 • http://www.sandiegohistory.org/links/societies.htm

Julian Pioneer Museum • 2811 Washington St • Julian, CA 92036 • (760) 765-0227 • http://www.caohwy.com/j/julipimu.htm

Kelseyville
Anderson Marsh State Historic Park • 5300 Soda Bay Rd • Kelseyville, CA 95451 • (707) 994-0688

Clearlake State Park • 5300 Soda Bay Rd • Kelseyville, CA 95451 • (707) 279-2267 • http://www.parks.ca.gov

Kernville
Kern River Valley Historical Society • Kern Valley Museum, 49 Big Blue Rd, P.O. Box 651 • Kernville, CA 93238 • (760) 376-6683 • http://www.krvhistoricalsociety.org

Kern Valley Indian Community • P.O. Box 168 • Kernville, CA 93238 • (619) 376-4240

King City
Monterey County Agricultural and Rural Life Museum • 1160 Broadway • King City, CA 93930 • (408) 385-1484 • http://www.co.monterey.ca.us/parks/park_003.htm

San Antonio Valley Historical Association • 216 Grove Pl • King City, CA 93930 • (832) 385-3587

Kingsburg
Kingsburg Historical Park • Sierra St • Kingsburg, CA 93631 • (559) 897-5795

Klamath
Coast Indian Community of the Resighini Rancheria - Yurok • P.O. Box 529 • Klamath, CA 95548 • (707) 482-2431

Knightsen
Delta Genealogical Interest Group • P.O. Box 157 • Knightsen, CA 94548

La Canada-Flintridge
County of Los Angeles Public Library-La Canada Flintridge Library • 4545 N Oakwood Ave • La Canada-Flintridge, CA 91011-3358 • (818) 790-3330 • http://colapublib.org/libs/lacanada/

Lanterman House Museum • 4420 Encinas Dr • La Canada-Flintridge, CA 91011-3313 • (818) 790-1421

La Habra
La Habra Old Settlers Historical Society • 600 Linden Ln • La Habra, CA 90631 • (562) 697-1271

La Jolla
James S Copley Newspaper Museum • 1134 Kline St, P.O. Box 1530 • La Jolla, CA 92037 • (858) 454-0411

La Jolla Historical Society • 7846 Eads Ave, P.O. Box 2085 • La Jolla, CA 92038 • (619) 459-5335 • http://www.llajollahistory.org

Mingei International Museum of World Folk Art • P.O. Box 553 • La Jolla, CA 92038 • (619) 239-0003 • http://www.mingei.org

La Mesa
Horseless Carriage Foundation and Automotive Research Library • 8186 Center St, Ste F, P.O. Box 4119 • La Mesa, CA 91944-4119 • (619) 464-0301 • http://www.hcfi.org

La Mesa Depot Museum • 4695 Nebo Dr • La Mesa, CA 92041 • (619) 697-7762 • http://www.sdrm.org/la-mesa/

La Mesa Historical Society • 8369 University Ave, P.O. Box 882 • La Mesa, CA 92041 • (619) 466-0197 • http://www.grossmont.kl2.ca.us/lmhs/

La Porte
Estom Yukema Maidu Tribe • general delivery • La Porte, CA 95981 • (916) 532-9214

La Puente
La Puente Valley Historical Society • City Hall Museum, 13906 E Main, P.O. Box 522 • La Puente, CA 91747 • (626) 855-1500

La Quinta
La Quinta Historical Society • Historical Museum, 77885 Avenida Montezuma • La Quinta, CA 92247 • (760) 564-1283 • http://www.la-quinta.org

La Verne
German Genealogical Society of America • P.O. Box 291818 • La Verne, CA 90029 • (909) 593-0509 • http://feefhs.org

Historical Society of La Verne • 9462 Lemon Ave, P.O. Box 7761 • La Verne, CA 91750 • (909) 593-2242

La Verne Heritage Foundation • 5001 Via de Mansion • La Verne, CA 91750-1602 • (909) 593-2862

Wilson Library • Univ of LaVerne, 2040 3rd St • La Verne, CA 91750 • (909) 593-3511 • http://www.ulaverne.edu

Lafayette
Lafayette Historical Society • c/o Lafayette Public Library, 952 Moraga Rd, P.O. Box 133 • Lafayette, CA 94549 • (925) 283-6822 • http://lhs.lafayette.ca.us

Laguna Beach
Laguna Beach Historical Society • 278 Ocean Ave • Laguna Beach, CA 92651

Laguna Hills
Jewish Genealogical Society of Orange County • 2370-1D Via Mariposa W • Laguna Hills, CA 92653 • (949) 855-4692

Leisure World Historical Society of Laguna Hills • 23522 Paseo de Valencia, P.O. Box 2220 • Laguna Hills, CA 92653 • (949) 951-2330

Laguna Niguel
National Archives & Records Administration-Pacific Region • 24000 Avila Rd, 1st Flr E • Laguna Niguel, CA 92677-3497 • (949) 360-2641 • http://www.archives.gov/facilities/ca/laguna_niguel.html

Lake Elsinore
California State Genealogical Alliance • 19765 Grand Ave • Lake Elsinore, CA 93240

Lake Elsinore Genealogical Society • P.O. Box 807 • Lake Elsinore, CA 92330-0807 • (909) 674-5776 • http://www.bakerfamily.org/legs

Lake Elsinore Historical Society • Historical Museum, 106 S Main St, P.O. Box 84 • Lake Elsinore, CA 92530-4109 • (951) 245-4986 • http://www.lakeelsinorehistoricalsociety.org

Lake Forest
Amigos de la Colina Heritage Hill Historical Park • 25151 Serrano Rd • Lake Forest, CA 92630 • (949) 855-2028

Heritage Hill Historical Park Museum • 25151 Serrano Rd • Lake Forest, CA 92930 • (949) 855-2028

Orange County Public Library-El Toro Branch • 24672 Raymond Way • Lake Forest, CA 92630-4489 • (949) 855-8173 • http://www.ocpl.org/eltoro/Eltoro.htm

Saddleback Area Historical Society • P.O. Box 156 • Lake Forest, CA 92630 • (949) 951-6292

Lake Isabella
Clan Diggers Genealogical Society of the Kern River Valley • P.O. Box 531 • Lake Isabella, CA 93240 • (760) 376-6210

Lakeport
Big Valley Rancheria • Pomo & Pit River, 2726 Mission Rancheria Rd • Lakeport, CA 95453 • (707) 263-3924

Lake County Genealogical Society • Historical Museum, 255 N Main St, P.O. Box 1323 • Lakeport, CA 95453 • (707) 263-4555 • http://www.museum.lake.kiz.ca.us

Lake County Historical Society • Historic Courthouse Museum, 255 N. Main St, P.O. Box 1011 • Lakeport, CA 94543 • (707) 279-4466 • http://www.museum.lake.kl2.ca.us

Lake County Library • 1425 N High St • Lakeport, CA 95453-3800 • (707) 263-8816 • http://www.co.lake.ca.us/library/library.html

Pocahontas Trails Genealogical Society • 6015 Robin Hill Dr • Lakeport, CA 95453 • (707) 263-5829

Scotts Valley Band of Pomo Indians • 301 Industrial Ave • Lakeport, CA 95453 • (707) 263-4220

Lakeside
Barona Rancheria • Kumeyaay Diegueno, 1095 Barona Rd • Lakeside, CA 92040 • (619) 443-6612 • http://www.baronatribe.com

Lakeside Historical Society • 9906 Maine Ave, P.O. Box 1423 • Lakeside, CA 92040 • (619) 561-1886 • http://www.lakesidehistory.org

Lakewood
County of Los Angeles Public Library-Angelo M Iacoboni Library • 4990 Clark Ave • Lakewood, CA 90712-2676 • (562) 866-1777 • http://colapublib.org/libs/iacoboni/

Lamont
Dust Bowl Historical Foundation • P.O. Box 31 • Lamont, CA 93241 • (661) 832-1299 • http://www.weedpatchcamp.com

Lancaster
Antelope Valley African American Museum • 416 Lumber St • Lancaster, CA 93534 • (661) 723-0811 • http://www.antelopevalleyguide.com

Antelope Valley Genealogical Society • 44845 Cedar Ave, P.O. Box 1049 • Lancaster, CA 93534-1049 • (661) 947-4558 • http://www.rootsweb.com/~caavgs

Antelope Valley Indian Museum • 15701 East Avenue M • Lancaster, CA 93535 • (661) 946-3055 • http://www.avin.parks.ca.gov

County of Los Angeles Public Library-Lancaster Library • 601 W Lancaster Blvd • Lancaster, CA 93534 • (661) 948-5029 • http://colapublib.org/libs/lancaster/

Lancaster Museum • 44801 W Sierra Hwy • Lancaster, CA 92535 • (661) 723-6250 • http://www.coflancaster.org

Western Hotel Museum • 557 W Lancaster Blvd • Lancaster, CA 93534 • (661) 723-6250 • http://www.coflancasterca.org

Laytonville
Laytonville Rancheria - Cahto Indian Tribe • P.O. Box 1239 • Laytonville, CA 95454 • (707) 984-6197

Le Grand
Bright's Pioneer Museum • 5246 S Palinsburg Rd • Le Grand, CA 95333 • (209) 389-4511

Lebec
Fort Tejon Historical Association • P.O. Box 895 • Lebec, CA 93243

Fort Tejon State Historic Park • 4201 Fort Tejon Rd, P.O. Box 895 • Lebec, CA 93243 • (661) 248-6692 • http://www.parks.ca.gov

Lee Vining
Mono Basin Historical Society • Old Mono Basin Lake Schoolhouse Museum, Hwy 395 & 1st St, P.O. Box 31 • Lee Vining, CA 93541 • (619) 647-6461

Mono Lake Indian Community • P.O. Box 237 • Lee Vining, CA 93541 • (619) 647-6471

Lemon Grove
Lemon Grove Historical Society • Historical Museum, 3185 Oliver St, P.O. Box 624 • Lemon Grove, CA 91946 • (619) 460-4353 • http://www.lemongrovehistoricalsociety.com

Lemoore
Santa Rosa Rancheria - Tache, Rachi and Yokuts • P.O. Box 8 • Lemoore, CA 93245 • (559) 924-1278 • http://www.tachi-yokut.com

Sarah A Mooney Housel Museum • 542 West D Street, P.O. Box 413 • Lemore, CA 93245 • (559) 925-0321 • http://www.lemoore.com/sammm.htm

Leucadia
Encinitas Historical Society • P.O. Box 2293 • Leucadia, CA 92024 • (619) 753-5726

Livermore
Livermore Heritage Guild • 2155 3rd St, P.O. Box 961 • Livermore, CA 94551-0961 • (925) 443-3272 • http://www.livermorehistory.com

Livermore Public Library • 1000 S Livermore Ave • Livermore, CA 94550 • (925) 373-5500 • http://www.livermore.lib.ca.us

Livermore-Amador Genealogical Society • P.O. Box 901 • Livermore, CA 94556 • (925) 447-9386 • http://www.l-ags.org

Ravenswood Historic Site Museum • 2647 Arroyo Rd • Livermore, CA 94550 • (510) 373-5708

Lockwood
San Antonio Valley Historical Association • 216 Grove Pl, P.O. Box 184 • Lockwood, CA 93932 • (831) 385-3587

Lodi
Lodi Public Library • 201 W Locust • Lodi, CA 95240 • (209) 333-5503 • http://www.lodi.gov/library

San Antonio Valley Historical Society • Historical Museum, P.O. Box 21 • Lodi, CA 95241

San Joaquin County Historical Society • Historical Museum, 11793 N Micke Grove Rd, P.O. Box 30 • Lodi, CA 95241-0030 • (209) 331-2055 • http://www.sanjoaquinhistory.org

Loleta
Bear River Band of the Rohnerville Rancheria • 32 Bear River Rd, P.O. Box 108 • Loleta, CA 95551 • (707) 443-1900

Table Bluff Rancheria - Wiyot Indians • 1000 Wiyot Dr • Loleta, CA 95551 • (707) 733-5055 • http://www.wiyot.com

Loma Linda
Del E Webb Memorial Library • Loma Linda University, 11072 Anderson St • Loma Linda, CA 92350-0001 • (909) 558-4581 • http://www.library.llu.edu

Lomita
Lomita Historical Society • 24016 Benhill Ave, P.O. Box 549 • Lomita, CA 90717 • (310) 325-6884 • http://www.restorationcentral.com/orgs/lomita/

Lomita Railroad Museum • 2137 W 250th St • Lomita, CA 90717 • (310) 326-6255 • http://www.lomita-rr.org

Lompoc
La Purisima Mission State Historic Park • 2296 Purisima Rd • Lompoc, CA 93436 • (805) 733-3713 • http://www.lapurisimamission.org

Lompoc Museum • 200 South H Street • Lompoc, CA 93436 • (805) 736-3888

Lompoc Public Library • 501 E North Ave • Lompoc, CA 93436-3498 • (805) 736-3477 • http://www.blackgold.org

Lompoc Valley Genealogical Society • P.O. Box 81 • Lompoc, CA 93438-0081 • (805) 736-9637 • http://www.rootsweb.com/~calvgs

Lompoc Valley Historical Society • Historical Museum, 207 North L Street, P.O. Box 88 • Lompoc, CA 93436 • (805) 735-4626 • http://www.lompochistory.org

Vandenberg Genealogical Society • 1312 W Prune, P.O. Box 814 • Lompoc, CA 93438 • (805) 737-1170

Lone Pine
Lone Pine Community of Paiute-Shoshone Indians • P.O. Box 757 • Lone Pine, CA 93545 • (760) 876-1034

Museum of Lone Pine Film History • S US 395, P.O. Box 111 • Lone Pine, CA 93543 • (760) 937-1189 • http://www.lonepinefilmhistorymuseum.org

Long Beach
American Historical Society of Germans from Russia Southern California Chapter • 4350 Linden Ave • Long Beach, CA 90807-2725 • http://feefhs.org/frgahssc.html

California State University, Long Beach Library • 1250 Bellflower Blvd • Long Beach, CA 90840-1901 • (562) 985-4047 • http://www.csulb.edu/library

Electronic Railway Historical Association of Southern California • 1 World Trade Center • Long Beach, CA 90832 • (213) 452-0914 • http://www.erha.org

Historical Society of Long Beach • 210 E Ocean Blvd, P.O. Box 1869 • Long Beach, CA 90801-1869 • (562) 495-1210 • http://www.historicalsocietylb.org

Long Beach Heritage Coalition • 6232 E Vista St, P.O. Box 92521 • Long Beach, CA 90809 • (562) 493-7019

Long Beach Public Library • 101 Pacific Ave • Long Beach, CA 90822-1097 • (562) 570-7500 • http://www.lbpl.org

Los Pobladores 200 • 2830 E 56th Wy • Long Beach, CA 90805 • (213) 633-6179

Queen Mary Museum • 1126 Queens Hwy, Pier J • Long Beach, CA 90802 • (562) 435-3511 • http://www.queenmary.com

Questing Heirs Genealogical Society • P.O. Box 15102 • Long Beach, CA 90815-0102 • (562) 434-0101 • http://www.cagenweb.com/questing/

Questing Heirs Genealogical Society, Computer Interest Group • P.O. Box 15102 • Long Beach, CA 90815-0102 • (562) 434-0101

Rancho Los Alamitos • 6400 Bixby Hill Rd • Long Beach, CA 90815 • (562) 431-3541

Rancho Los Cerritos Historic Site Museum • 4600 Virginia Rd • Long Beach, CA 90807 • (562) 570-1755 • http://www.rancholoscerritos.org

Willmore City Heritage Association • 910 Daisy Ave • Long Beach, CA 90813 • (562) 436-8611

Willmore County Heritage Association • 525 E Seaside Wy, Unit 1807 • Long Beach, CA 90802 • (562) 436-8611

Los Alamitos

Los Alamitos Museum Association • Historical Museum, 11062 Los Alamitos Blvd • Los Alamitos, CA 90720 • (213) 431-8836 • http://www. goodtime.net/sflama.htm

Southern California Chapter, Ohio Genealogical Society • P.O. Box 5057 • Los Alamitos, CA 90721-5057

Los Altos

Chinese Cultural Association • 827 Mora Dr • Los Altos, CA 94024-6617 • (415) 948-2251

Los Altos History Museum • 51 S San Antonio Rd • Los Altos, CA 94022 • (650) 948-9427 • http://www.losaltoshistory.org

Los Altos Hills

Los Altos Hills Historical Society • History House, 1 N San Antonio Rd • Los Altos Hills, CA 94022 • (650) 948-1491 • http://losaltoshillshistory. org/

Los Altos Historical Commission • History House, 1 N San Antonio Rd • Los Altos Hills, CA 94022 • (650) 948-1491 • http://www.ci.los-altos. ca.us/committees-commissions/historical/index.html

Los Angeles

African American Fire Fighters Museum • 1401 Central Ave • Los Angeles, CA 90008 • (323) 294-0857 • http://www.cityofla.org/lafd/museum2.htm

Afro-American Genealogical Society of California • Afro-American Museum, Exposition Park, 600 State Dr • Los Angeles, CA 90037 • (213) 744-7432 • http://www.caam.ca.gov/

American Film Institute Museum • 2021 N Western Ave • Los Angeles, CA 90027 • (323) 856-7600

American Historical Association-Pacific Coast Branch • Loyola Marymount Univ, Dept of History • Los Angeles, CA 90045 • (310) 338-2805

American Indian Studies Center • 3220 Campbell Hall, UCLA Box 951548 • Los Angeles, CA 90024-1548 • (310) 825-7315 • http://www. sscnet.ucla-edu/indian/

American Society of Cinematographers Museum • 1782 N Orange Dr • Los Angeles, CA 90078 • (323) 969-4333

Association of German Nobility in North America • 3571 E 8th St • Los Angeles, CA 90023

Automobile Driving Museum • 2134 S Pontius Ave • Los Angeles, CA 90025 • (310) 909-9050

Avila Adobe Historic House Museum • 10 Olvera St • Los Angeles, CA 90012 • (213) 628-1274

Azusa Historical Society • P.O. Box 972 • Los Angeles, CA 90078

Beit Hashoah Museum • 9760 W Pico Blvd • Los Angeles, CA 90035 • (310) 553-8403 • http://motlc.wiesenthal.com

Braun Research Library • Southwest Museum, 234 Museum Dr, P.O. Box 41558 • Los Angeles, CA 90041-0558 • (323) 221-2164 • http://www.southwestmuseum.org

British Isles Family History Society of Los Angeles • 2531 Sawtelle Blvd #134 • Los Angeles, CA 90064-3163 • (310) 398-3924 • http://www.rootsweb.com/~bifhsusa/

California African-American Genealogical Society • P.O. Box 8442 • Los Angeles, CA 90008-0442

California African-American Museum • 600 State Dr, Exposition Park • Los Angeles, CA 90037 • (213) 744-7432 • http://www.caam.ca.gov

Chinese American Museum • 125 Paseo de la Plaza, Ste 400 • Los Angeles, CA 90012 • (213) 485-8567 • http://www.camla.org

Chinese Historical Society of Southern California • 978 North Broadway, Ste 206, P.O. Box 862647 • Los Angeles, CA 90086-2647 • (213) 617-0396 • http://www.chssc.org

Church of Jesus Christ of Latter-day Saints Visitors Center • 10777 Santa Monica Blvd • Los Angeles, CA 90025 • (310) 474-1549

Circulo Guinerode Los Angeles • 434 S Alvarado St • Los Angeles, CA 90057 • (213) 483-9126

County of Los Angeles Public Library-A C Bilbrew Library • 150 E El Segundo Blvd • Los Angeles, CA 90061-2356 • (310) 538-3350 • http://colapublib.org/libs/bilbrew/

County of Los Angeles Public Library-East Los Angeles Library • 4801 E 3rd St • Los Angeles, CA 90022-1601 • (323) 264-0155 • http://colapublib.org/libs/eastla/

Craft and Folk Art Museum • 5800 Wilshire Blvd • Los Angeles, CA 90024 • (213) 937-5544 • http://www.artcom.com/museums/nv/af/90036.htm

Cultural Heritage Foundation of Southern California • Heritage Square, 3800 Homer St • Los Angeles, CA 90031 • (323) 225-2700 • http://www.heritagesquare.org

Edward L Doheny Memorial Library • University of Southern California, University Park • Los Angeles, CA 90089-0182 • (213) 740-2543 • http://www.usc.edu/isd/elecresources/catalogs.html

El Pueblo de los Angeles Historical Monument • 845 North Alameda • Los Angeles, CA 90012 • (213) 680-2381 • http://cityofla.org/elp/

Ennis-Brown House Museum • 2655 Glendower Ave • Los Angeles, CA 90027 • (323) 668-0234 • http://www.ennisbrownhouse.org

Fowler Museum of Cultural History • UCLA, P.O. Box 951549 • Los Angeles, CA 90095 • (310) 825-4361 • http://www.fmch.ucla.edu

Frances-Henry Library • Hebrew Union College, 3077 University Ave • Los Angeles, CA 90007 • (213) 749-3432 • http://www.huc.edu/libraries/losangeles

Gene Autry Western Heritage Museum • 4700 Western Heritage Wy • Los Angeles, CA 90027-1462 • (323) 667-2000 • http://www.autry-museum.org

Grier Musser Antiques Museum • 403 S Bonnie Brae St • Los Angeles, CA 90057 • (213) 413-1814 • http://www.griermussermuseum.com

Hancock Mansion Museum • Univ Ave & Childs Wy • Los Angeles, CA 90089 • (213) 740-5141 • http://www.usc.edu

Hebrew Union College Skirball Museum & Cultural Center • 2701 N Sepulveda Blvd • Los Angeles, CA 90049 • (310) 440-4500 • http://www.skirball.org

Heritage Square Museum • 3800 Homer St • Los Angeles, CA 90031 • (626) 796-2898 • http://www.heritage.square.museum.org

Historical Society of Centinela Valley • 7634 Midfield Ave • Los Angeles, CA 90045 • (213) 649-6272

Historical Society of Southern California • Lummis Historic Home, 200 E Avenue 43 • Los Angeles, CA 90031-1304 • (323) 222-0546 • http://www.socalhistory.org

Hollyhock House Museum • Barnsdall Park, 2800 Hollywood Blvd • Los Angeles, CA 90027 • (323) 662-8139 • http://www.hollyhockhouse.net

Hollywood Bowl Museum • 2301 N Highland Ave • Los Angeles, CA 90068 • (323) 850-2058 • http://www.hollywoodbowl.com

International Association of Sri Lanka Genealogical Societies • 753 N Kings Rd, Ste 101 • Los Angeles, CA 90069 • (323) 651-5839

Japanese American National Museum • 369 E 1st St • Los Angeles, CA 90012 • (213) 625-0414 • http://www.janm.org

Jewish Community Library of Los Angeles • 6505 Wilshire Blvd #300 • Los Angeles, CA 90048 • (323) 761-8644 • http://www.jclla.org

Los Angeles, cont.

John F Kennedy Library • California State Univ, 5151 State University Dr • Los Angeles, CA 90032-8300 • (323) 343-4927 • http://web. calstatela.edu/library

Korean American Museum • P.O. Box 741879 • Los Angeles, CA 90004 • (213) 388-4229 • http://www.kamuseum.org

Los Angeles City Historical Society • 10801 La Grange Ave, P.O. Box 41046 • Los Angeles, CA 90041 • (213) 936-2912 • http://www. lacityhistory.org

Los Angeles Conservancy • 523 W 6th St, Ste 1216 • Los Angeles, CA 90014 • (213) 623-2489 • http://www.laconservancy.org

Los Angeles Fire Department Historical Society • Los Angeles Fire Department, 2900 W Temple St • Los Angeles, CA 90026 • (323) 464-2727 • http://www.lafd.org/society.htm

Los Angeles Police Historical Society • Historical Museum, 6045 York Blvd • Los Angeles, CA 90042 • (323) 344-9445 • http://www.laphs. com

Los Angeles Public Library System • 630 W 5th St • Los Angeles, CA 90071-2097 • (310) 228-7400 • http://www.lapl.org

Los Angeles Public Library-Vermont Square • 1201 W 48th St • Los Angeles, CA 90037-3787 • (323) 290-7406

Los Pobladores 200 • 7440 W 91st St • Los Angeles, CA 90045-3431 • (310) 670-0636 • http://www.lospobladores.org

Martyrs Memorial and Museum of the Holocaust • 6006 Wilshire Blvd • Los Angeles, CA 90036 • (323) 761-8170 • http://www. remembertoteach.com/museum.htm

Mary Norton Clapp Library • Occidental College, 1600 Campus Rd • Los Angeles, CA 90041 • (323) 259-2818 • http://www.oxy.edu/ departments/library

Mole-Richardson Moletown Museum • 900 N La Brea Ave • Los Angeles, CA 90038 • (323) 851-0111

Museum of the American West • 4700 Western Heritage Wy • Los Angeles, CA 90027 • (323) 667-2000 • http://www.autrynationalcenter. org

Museum of Tolerance • 9786 West Pico Blvd • Los Angeles, CA 90035 • (310) 553-8403 • http://www.museumoftolerance.com

Occidental College History Society • 1600 Campus Rd • Los Angeles, CA 90041

Oral History Association • 1093 Braxton Ave #720 • Los Angeles, CA 90024 • (818) 755-3437

Peter M Khan Memorial Library • Jewish Federation Council of Greater Los Angeles, 6505 Wilshire Blvd • Los Angeles, CA 90048 • (323) 761-8648 • http://www.jclla.org

Petersen Automotive Museum • 6060 Wilshire Blvd • Los Angeles, CA 90036 • (323) 964-6356 • http://www.petersen.org

Ramona Museum of California History • 4580 N Figueroa St • Los Angeles, CA 90065 • (310) 222-0012

Seaver Center for Western History Research • Natural History Museum of Los Angeles County, 900 Exposition Blvd • Los Angeles, CA 90007 • (213) 763-3359 • http://www.nhm.org/research/history/ seaver_center.html

Sepulveda Historic House Museum • 12 Olvera St • Los Angeles, CA 90012-2921 • (213) 680-2525

Simon Wiesenthal Center Library and Archives • 1399 S Roxbury Dr • Los Angeles, CA 90035-4709 • (310) 772-7605 • http://www. weisenthal.com

Southern California Jewish Historical Society • 6006 Wilshire Blvd • Los Angeles, CA 90048-4906 • (323) 761-8950 • http://www.cwire.com/ pub/orgs/Jewish.Historical.Society/

Southwest Museum • P.O. Box 41558 • Los Angeles, CA 90041-0558 • (213) 221-2164 • http://www.southwestmuseum.org

Travel Town Museum • 5200 Zoo Dr • Los Angeles, CA 90039 • (323) 662-5874 • http://www.laparks/grifmet/tt/

Wells Fargo History Museum • 333 S Grand Ave • Los Angeles, CA 90071 • (213) 253-7166

Westerners, Los Angeles Corral • 1506 Linda Rosa Ave • Los Angeles, CA 90041

Westwood Holmby Historical Society • 10956 Weyburn Ave • Los Angeles, CA 90024 • (310) 208-4652

Windsor Square-Hancock Park Historical Society • 137 N Larchmont Blvd #135 • Los Angeles, CA 90004 • (213) 243-8182 • http://www. wshphs.org

Young Research Library • Univ of California at Los Angeles, 11334 University, P.O. Box 951575 • Los Angeles, CA 90095-1575 • (310) 825-1201 • http://www.library.ucla.edu

Los Banos

Los Banos Genealogical Society • 16778 South Pl, P.O. Box 2525 • Los Banos, CA 93635 • (209) 826-4882

Ralph L Milliken Museum • Hwy 152, P.O. Box 2294 • Los Banos, CA 93635 • (209) 826-5505 • http://www.museumsusa.org/data/museums/ CA/16146.htm

Los Gatos

Forbes Mill Museum • 75 Church St • Los Gatos, CA 95032 • (408) 395-7375

Japanese American Resource Center Museum • 236 N Santa Cruz Ave #215 • Los Gatos, CA 95030

Los Gatos Historic Preservation Commission • P.O. Box 940 • Los Gatos, CA 95031 • (408) 354-6872 • http://www.town.los-gatos.ca.us/ services/7f.html

Los Gatos Public Library • 110 E Main St • Los Gatos, CA 95030-6981 • (408) 354-6891 • http://ibrary.town.los-gatos.ca.us

Museum of Los Gatos • 75 Church St • Los Gatos, CA 95031 • (408) 395-7375 • http://www.losgatosmuseum.org

Lucerne Valley

Lucerne Valley Library • 33103 Old Woman Springs Rd, P.O. Box 408 • Lucerne Valley, CA 92356 • (760) 248-7521

Root Diggers, Lucerne Valley Genealogy Association • c/o Lucerne Valley Library, 33103 Old Woman Springs Rd, P.O. Box 408 • Lucerne Valley, CA 92356 • (760) 248-7521

Macdoel

Shasta Nation • P.O. Box 40 • Macdoel, CA 96058

Madera

Genealogical Society of Madera • P.O. Box 495 • Madera, CA 93639-0495 • (559) 661-1219 • http://www.cagenweb.com/madera/

Madera County Historical Society • Historical Museum, 210 W Yosemite, P.O. Box 478 • Madera, CA 93639 • (559) 673-0291 • http:// www.maderahistory.org

Madera County Library • 121 North G Street • Madera, CA 93637-3592 • (209) 675-7871 • http://www.sjvls.org/madera

Malibu

American Historical Association, Pacific Coast Branch • Pepperdine University, Office of the Dean • Malibu, CA 90263 • (213) 642-2805 • http://arachnid.pepperdine.edu/amerhistassocp/

Malibu Lagoon Museum • Adamson House, 23200 Pacific Coast Hwy, P.O. Box 291 • Malibu, CA 90265 • (310) 456-8432 • http://www. adamsonhouse.org

Payson Library • Pepperdine University, 24255 Pacific Coast Hwy • Malibu, CA 90263 • (310) 506-4238 • http://library.pepperdine.edu

Mammoth Lakes
Southern Mono Historical Society • 5489 Sherwin Creek Rd, P.O. Box 65 • Mammoth Lakes, CA 93546 • (760) 934-6918

Manhattan Beach
Manhattan Beach Historical Society • Historical Museum, 1601 Manhattan Beach Blvd, P.O. Box 3355 • Manhattan Beach, CA 90266 • (310) 374-7575 • http://www.manhattanbeachhistorical.org

Manteca
Manteca Historical Society • Historical Museum, 600 W Yosemite Ave, P.O. Box 907 • Manteca, CA 95337 • (209) 825-3021 • http://www.artcom.com/museums/nv/mr/95336.htm

March AFB
March Field Air Museum • 22550 Van Buren Blvd, P.O. Box 6463 • March AFB, CA 92518 • (909) 697-6600 • http://www.marchfield.org

Marina
Monterey County Library • 188 Seaside Cr • Marina, CA 93933 • (831) 899-2055 • http://www.montereycountyfreelibraries.org

Marina del Rey
Los Angeles Westside Genealogical Society • P.O. Box 10447 • Marina del Rey, CA 90295-6447 • (310) 477-1501 • http://www.genealogy-la.com/lawgs.shtml

Society of Crypto Judaic Studies • 333 Washington Blvd #336 • Marina Del Rey, CA 90292 • http://cryptojews.com/

Mariposa
American Indian Council of Mariposa • P.O. Box 1200 • Mariposa, CA 95358 • (209) 966-4296

California State Mining and Mineral Museum • 5005 Fairgrounds, P.O. Box 1192 • Mariposa, CA 95338 • (209) 742-7625 • http://www.parks.ca.gov

Mariposa County Historical Society • Historical Museum, 5119 Jesse St, P.O. Box 606 • Mariposa, CA 95338 • (209) 966-2924

Mariposa County Library • 4978 10th St, P.O. Box 106 • Mariposa, CA 95338-0106 • (209) 966-2140 • http://www.mariposalibrary.org

Markleeville
Alpine County Free Library & Archives • 270 Laramie St, P.O. Box 187 • Markleeville, CA 96120-0187 • (530) 694-2120 • http://www.co.alpine.ca.us/dept/library/library.html

Alpine County Historical Society • Historical Museum, 1 School St, P.O. Box 517 • Markleeville, CA 96120-0517 • (530) 694-2317 • http://www.co.alpine.ca.us/dept/museum/museum.htm

Washoe Tribe • Route 1, Box 102 • Markleeville, CA 96120 • (916) 694-2174

Woodsfords Colony • 96 Washoe Blvd • Markleeville, CA 96120 • (916) 694-2170

Woodsfords Nation - Washoe • 2111 Carson River Rd • Markleeville, CA 96120 • (916) 694-2170

Martinez
Contra Costa County Historical Society • 610 Main St • Martinez, CA 94553 • (925) 229-1042 • http://www.cocohistory.com

John Muir National Historic Site Museum • 4202 Alhambra Ave • Martinez, CA 94553 • (925) 228-8860 • http://www.nps.gov

Martinez Historical Society • Historical Museum, 1005 Escobar St • Martinez, CA 94553 • (925) 228-8160 • http://www.martinezhistory.org

Marysville
Mary M Arron Memorial Museum • 704 D Street • Marysville, CA 95901 • (530) 743-1004 • http://www.museumsusa.org/data/museums/CA/13446.htm

Museum of the Forgotten Warriors • 5865 A Road • Marysville, CA 95901 • (530) 742-3090 • http://www.museumoftheforgottenwarriors.org

Yuba County Library • 303 2nd St • Marysville, CA 95901-6099 • (530) 741-6241 • http://www.co.yuba.ca.us/library/library

Yuba Historical Society • 330 9th St • Marysville, CA 95901 • (530) 741-0509

McClellan AFB
McClellan Aviation Museum • 3204 Palm Ave • McClellan AFB, CA 95660 • (916) 643-3192 • http://www.mcclellanaviationmuseum.org

Mendocino
Ford House Museum • Main St • Mendocino, CA 95460 • (707) 937-5397

Kelley House Museum • 45007 Albion St, P.O. Box 922 • Mendocino, CA 95460 • (707) 937-5791 • http://www.mendocinohistory.org

Mendocino Historical Research • Kelley House Museum, 45007 Albion St, P.O. Box 922 • Mendocino, CA 95460 • (707) 937-5791 • http://www.mendocinohistory.org

Mendocino Historical Research Library • 45007 Albion St, P.O. Box 922 • Mendocino, CA 95460 • (707) 937-5791 • http://www.mcn.org/ed/CUR/liv/ind/mark/kell.htm

Russian Gulch State Park • Highway 1 • Mendocino, CA 95460 • (707) 937-5804 • http://www.mcn.org/1/mendoparks/russian.htm

Menifee
Hadley Genealogical Society of Southern California • 33210 Baily Park Dr • Menifee, CA 92584

Menlo Park
Menlo Park Historical Association • c/o Menlo Park Library, 800 Alma St, P.O. Box 1002 • Menlo Park, CA 94026-1002 • (650) 858-3368 • http://www.pls.lib.ca.us/pls/mpl/HistAssoc.html

Menlo Park Public Library • 800 Alma St • Menlo Park, CA 94025-3460 • (650) 330-2500 • http://www.menloparklibrary.org

US Geological Survey Library • 345 Middlefield Rd, MS 955 • Menlo Park, CA 94025 • (650) 329-5027 • http://library.usgs.gov/menlib.html

Merced
Agricultural Museum • 4498 E Hwy 140 • Merced, CA 95340 • (209) 383-1912 • http://www.agmuseum.us

Merced County Genealogical Society • c/o Merced County Library, 2100 O Street, P.O. Box 3061 • Merced, CA 95344 • (209) 723-9019 • http://www.rootsweb.com/~camegs/

Merced County Historical Society • Old County Courthouse Museum, 21st & N Sts • Merced, CA 95340 • (209) 723-2401 • http://www.mercedmuseum.org

Merced County Library • 2100 O Street • Merced, CA 95340-3637 • (209) 385-7597 • http://www.co.merced.ca.us/library/

Middletown
Middletown Rancheria of Pomo Indians • 22223 Hwy 29, P.O. Box 1035 • Middletown, CA 95461 • (707) 987-3670

Midway City
Polish Genealogical Society of California • P.O. Box 713 • Midway City, CA 92655-0713 • http://www.pgsa.org

Society of Hispanic Historical and Ancestral Research • P.O. Box 490 • Midway City, CA 92655-0490 • (714) 894-8161 • http://www.somosprimos.com

Mill Valley
Golden Gate Baptist Theological Seminary Library • 201 Seminary Dr, Box 37 • Mill Valley, CA 94941-3197 • (415) 380-1660 • http://www.ggbts.edu

Mill Valley, cont.

Mill Valley Historical Society • c/o Mill Valley Public Library, 375 Throckmorton Ave • Mill Valley, CA 94941 • (415) 388-2190 • http://www.millvalleyhistoricalsociety.org

Mill Valley Public Library • 375 Throckmorton Ave • Mill Valley, CA 94941-2698 • (415) 389-4292 • http://www.millvalleylibrary.org

Mount Tamalpais State Park • 801 Panoramic Hwy • Mill Valley, CA 94941 • (415) 388-2070 • http://www.parks.ca.gov

Millbrae

Millbrae Historical Society • Millbrae Museum, 450 Poplar Ave, P.O. Box 511 • Millbrae, CA 94030 • (650) 697-5786

Milpitas

Milpitas Cultural Resources Preservation Board • 455 Calaveras Blvd • Milpitas, CA 95035 • (408) 942-2379

Milpitas Historical Society • P O Box 360975 • Milpitas, CA 95036 • (408) 262-1171 • http://www.milpitashistory.org

Society for Creative Anachronism • 93 W Montague Expy, P.O. Box 360789 • Milpitas, CA 95036-0789 • (408) 263-9305

Mira Loma

Mira Loma Genealogy Library • P.O. Box 527 • Mira Loma, CA 91752

Mission Hills

Mission San Fernando Historical Museum & Archival Center • 15151 San Fernando Mission Blvd • Mission Hills, CA 91345 • (818) 361-0186 • http://www.rootsweb.com/~casfvgs/mission.html

Saint Francis Historical Society • 15151 San Fernando Mission • Mission Hills, CA 91345 • (818) 365-1501 • http://www.miliserv.net/mkuspa/

San Fernando Valley Historical Society • Historical Museum, 10940 Sepulveda Blvd, P.O. Box 7039 • Mission Hills, CA 91346-7039 • (818) 365-7810 • http://sfvhs.com

Mission Viejo

South Orange County, California Genealogical Society • P.O. Box 4513 • Mission Viejo, CA 92690-4513 • (949) 470-8498 • http://www.rootsweb.com/~casoccgs/

Modesto

Book Nook • 2401 Silvaire Ct • Modesto, CA 95350 • (209) 523-1295

Genealogical Society of Stanislaus County • 1600 Carver Rd, P.O. Box A • Modesto, CA 95352-3660 • (209) 572-3227 • http://www.cagenweb/lr/stanislaus/gssc.html

McHenry Museum and Historical Society • McHenry Mansion Museum, 1402 I Street • Modesto, CA 95354 • (209) 577-5366 • http://www.mchenrymuseum.org

Pocahontas Trails Genealogical Society • 3628 Cherokee Ln • Modesto, CA 95356

Stanislaus County Free Library • 1500 I Street • Modesto, CA 95354 • (209) 558-7814 • http://www.stanislauslibrary.org

Stanislaus County Genealogical Society • 5216 Parker Rd, P.O. Box 4735 • Modesto, CA 95355

Modjeska Canyon

Helena Modjeska Historic House Museum • 29042 Modjeska Canyon Rd • Modjeska Canyon, CA 92676 • (949) 923-2230 • http://www.ocparks.com/modjeskahouse/

Mokelumne Hill

Mokelumne Hill Historical Society • 8367 Center St • Mokelumne Hill, CA 95245 • (209) 286-1770

Mokelumne Hill History Society • P.O. Box 267 • Mokelumne Hill, CA 95245 • (209) 286-1770 • http://www.visitcalaveras.org/ccmuseums.html

Monroe

Monroe Historical Society • Wheeler & Old Tannery Rds, P O. Box 212 • Monroe, CA 06468 • (203) 261-1383 • http://www.monroehistoricsociety.org

Monrovia

Costanoan Band of Carmel Mission Indians • P.O. Box 1657 • Monrovia, CA 91016

Monrovia Historical Society • 215 E Lime Ave • Monrovia, CA 91016 • (626) 358-0803

Monrovia Old House Preservation Group • P.O. Box 734 • Monrovia, CA 91017 • (408) 741-3421 • http://www.urly.com/monrovia/cc/mohpg1.html

Monrovia Public Library • 321 S Myrtle Ave • Monrovia, CA 91016-2888 • (626) 358-0174 • http://www.acityline.com/monrovia/

Montclair

San Bernardino County Library-Montclair Branch • Civic Center, 9955 Fremont Ave • Montclair, CA 91763 • (909) 624-4671 • http://www.sbcounty.gov/library

Monte Rio

Monte Rio Area Historical Society • P.O. Box 484 • Monte Rio, CA 95462 • (707) 865-2690 • http://www.russianriverhistory.org

Monte Sereno

City of Monte Sereno Historical Committee • 18041 Saratoga-Los Gatos Rd • Monte Sereno, CA 95030 • (408) 354-7635

Montebello

County of Los Angeles-Central Regional Office • 1550 W Beverly Blvd • Montebello, CA 90640-3993 • (323) 722-5621

Juan Matias Sanchez Adobe Museum • 946 Adobe Ave • Montebello, CA 90640 • (323) 887-4592

Montecito

Montecito History Committee • 1469 E Valley Rd • Montecito, CA 93108 • (805) 969-1597

Monterey

California Views Historical Photo Collection • 469 Pacific St • Monterey, CA 93940-2702 • (831) 373-3811 • http://www.caviews.com

Casa Amesti Museum • 516 Polk St • Monterey, CA 93940 • (831) 372-8173

Colton Hall Museum • Pacific & Jefferson Sts • Monterey, CA 93940 • (831) 646-5640 • http://www.monterey.org/museum/

Cooper-Molera Adobe Museum • 525 Polk St • Monterey, CA 93940 • (408) 649-7109

Dudley Knox Library • Naval Postgraduate School, 411 Dyer Rd • Monterey, CA 93943 • (831) 656-2485 • http://library.nps.navy.mil/home/

Maritime Museum of Monterey • 5 Custom House Plaza • Monterey, CA 93940 • (831) 372-2608 • http://www.montereyhistory.org/maritime_museum.org

Monterey History and Art Association • 5 Custom House Plaza • Monterey, CA 93942 • (831) 372-2608 • http://www.montereyhistory.org

Monterey Public Library & Local History Room • 625 Pacific St • Monterey, CA 93940-2866 • (831) 646-3933 • http://www.monterey.org/library/

Monterey State Historic Park • 20 Custom House Plaza • Monterey, CA 93940 • (831) 649-7118 • http://parks.ca.gov

Ohlone-Costanoan Esselen Nation • P.O. Box 1301 • Monterey, CA 93942 • (408) 924-1572 • http://www.esselennation.net

Old Monterey Jail Museum • City Hall, Pacific St • Monterey, CA 93940 • (831) 646-5640

Old Monterey Preservation Society • 525 Polk St • Monterey, CA 93940 • (408) 649-7111 • http://users.dedot.com/mchs/adobecoopermolera.html

Pat Hathaway Collection of Historical Photos • 469 Pacific St • Monterey, CA 93940-2702 • (831) 373-3811 • http://www.caviews.com

Paul Masson Museum of California Wine History • 700 Cannery Row • Monterey, CA 93940 • (831) 646-5446

Presidio of Monterey Museum • Corporal Ewing Rd, Bldg 113 • Monterey, CA 93940 • (831) 649-8547 • http://www.monterey.org/museum/pom/

Robert Louis Stevenson House Museum • 530 Houston St • Monterey, CA 93940 • (831) 649-7118 • http://www.mbay.net/~mshp/

Monterey Park
Bruggmeyer Memorial Library • 318 S Ramona Ave • Monterey Park, CA 91754-3399 • (626) 307-1368 • http://ci.monterey-park.ca.us/library

Historical Society of Monterey Park • 781 S Orange Ave, P.O. Box 272 • Monterey Park, CA 91754 • (626) 307-1267

Moorpark
Moorpark Historical Society • P.O. Box 662 • Moorpark, CA 93020 • (805) 529-1495 • http://www.vcnet.com/pumas/mpkhist.html

Moraga
American Historical Society of Germans from Russia, Mt Diablo Chapter • 849 Camino Ricardo • Moraga, CA 94556-1242 • (925) 376-6374

Moraga Historical Society • 1500 Saint Mary's Rd, P.O. Box 103 • Moraga, CA 94556 • (925) 377-8734 • http://www.moragahistory.org

Saint Albert Hall Library • Saint Mary's College of California, 1928 Saint Mary's Rd, P.O. Box 4290 • Moraga, CA 94575-4290 • (925) 631-4229 • http://library.stmarys-ca.edu

Moreno Valley
Moreno Valley Genealogical Society • 24177 Rothbury Dr • Moreno Valley, CA 92553 • (951) 653-5467

Moreno Valley Historical Society • P.O. Box 66 • Moreno Valley, CA 92556

Morgan Hill
Morgan Hill Architectural Cultural Resources Board • 17555 Peak Ave • Morgan Hill, CA 95037 • (408) 779-7247

Morgan Hill Historical Society • Morgan Hill House Museum, 17860 Monterey Rd, P.O. Box 1258 • Morgan Hill, CA 95037 • (408) 782-7191 • http://mhhistoricalsociety.org

Mount Shasta
Sisson Museum • 1 N Old Stage Rd • Mount Shasta, CA 96067 • (530) 926-3324

Mountain View
Computer History Museum • 1401 N Shoreline Blvd • Mountain View, CA 94043 • (650) 810-1010 • http://www.computerhistory.org

Lace Museum • P.O. Box 4420 • Mountain View, CA 94040 • (415) 327-4013 • http://www.thelacemuseum.org

Mountain View Pioneer and Historical Association • c/o Mountain View Library, 585 Franklin St, P.O. Box 252 • Mountain View, CA 94041 • (650) 968-6595

Mountain View Public Library • 585 Franklin St • Mountain View, CA 94041-1998 • (650) 903-6337 • http://www.library.ci.mtnview.ca.us

Rengstorff House Museum • 3070 N Shoreline Blvd • Mountain View, CA 94025 • (650) 903-6073

Murrieta
Colony Cousins Genealogical Society • 40492 Corte Lucia • Murrieta, CA 92562

National Society of the British Empire in USA • 40575 California Oaks Rd • Murrieta, CA 92562 • http://www.dbesociety.org

National Society, Daughters of the British Empire in the USA • 40575 California Oaks Rd, Ste D2 #269 • Murrieta, CA 92562 • http://www.dbesociety.org

Napa
Mumm Napa Valley Museum • 8445 Silverado Tr • Napa, CA 94558 • (707) 942-3434 • http://www.mumm.com

Napa City-County Library • 580 Coombs St • Napa, CA 94559-3396 • (707) 253-4235 • http://www.co.napa.ca.us/library

Napa County Historical Society • Goodman Library, 1219 1st St • Napa, CA 94559 • (707) 224-1739 • http://www.napahistory.org

Napa County Landmarks Society • 1026 1st St • Napa, CA 94559-2934 • (707) 255-1836

Napa Valley Genealogical and Biographical Society • 1701 Menlo Ave, P.O. Box 385 • Napa, CA 94558-4725 • (707) 252-2252 • http://www.napanet.net/~nvgbs

Napa Valley Model Railroad Historical Society • Fairgrounds • Napa, CA 94559 • (707) 253-8428

National City
Museum of American Treasures • 1315 E 4th St • National City, CA 92050 • (619) 477-7489

National City Historical Society • 1615 E 4th St, P.O. Box 1251 • National City, CA 91951 • (619) 477-3451

National City-Kile Morgan Local History Room • 1243 National City Blvd • National City, CA 92050 • (619) 336-4241 • http://www.cl.national-city.ca.us

South Bay Historical Society • 1615 E 4th St • National City, CA 91950 • (619) 477-3451

Needles
Fort Mohave Tribal Council • 500 Merriman Ave • Needles, CA 92363 • (619) 326-4591 • http://www.itcaonline.com/tribes_mojave.html

Needles Regional Museum • 923 Front St • Needles, CA 92363 • (760) 369-5678 • http://www.wemweb.com/traveler/towns/01needle/01_toc.html

Nevada City
American Victorian Museum • 203 S Pine St, P.O. Box 328 • Nevada City, CA 95959 • (530) 265-5804

Miners Foundry Cultural Center Museum • 325 Apring St, P.O. Box 1991 • Nevada City, CA 95959 • (530) 265-5040

Nevada County Historical Society • Searls Historical Library, 214 Church St, P.O. Box 1300 • Nevada City, CA 95959 • (530) 265-5190 • http://www.nevadacountyhistory.org

Nevada County Library • 980 Helling Wy • Nevada City, CA 95959 • (530) 265-4606

Nevada County Library-Doris Foley Branch • 211 N Pine St • Nevada City, CA 95959-2592 • (530) 265-4606 • http://www.mynevadacounty.com/library

New Almaden
New Almaden Quicksilver County Park Association • P.O. Box 124 • New Almaden, CA 95042 • http://www.newalmaden.org

Newbury Park
Conejo Valley Historical Society • Stagecoach Inn Museum, 51 S Ventu Park Rd • Newbury Park, CA 91320 • (805) 498-9441 • http://www.stagecoachmuseum.org

Newbury Park, cont.
Newbury Park Library, Thousand Oaks Branch • 2331 Bouchard Rd • Newbury Park, CA 91320 • (805) 498-2139 • http://www.toaks.org/library/

Satwiwa Native American Indian Culture Center • 41126 Potrero Rd • Newbury Park, CA 91320 • (805) 499-2837 • http://www.nps.gov/samo/fos/main.html

Stagecoach Inn Museum • 51 S Ventu Park Rd • Newbury Park, CA 91320 • (805) 498-9441 • http://www.stagecoachmuseum.org

Newcastle
United Auburn Indian Community • 661 Newcastle Rd, Ste 1 • Newcastle, CA 95658 • (916) 663-3720 • http://auburnindians.com

Newhall
Santa Clarita Valley Historical Society • Saugus Train Station, 24107 San Fernando Rd, P.O. Box 221925 • Newhall, CA 91322-1925 • (661) 254-1275 • http://www.scvhs.org

William S Hart Museum • 24151 San Fernando Rd • Newhall, CA 91321 • (661) 254-4584 • http://www.hartmuseum.org

Newport Beach
Balboa Island Historical Society • Historical Museum, 502 S Bay Front • Newport Beach, CA 92662 • (949) 675-3952

Institute for Historical Review • P.O. Box 2739 • Newport Beach, CA 92659-1339 • (949) 631-1490

Newport Beach Public Library • 1000 Avocado Ave • Newport Beach, CA 92660-6301 • (949) 717-3800 • http://www.newportbeachlibrary.org

Newport Harbor Nautical Museum • 151 East Coast Hwy • Newport Beach, CA 92660 • (714) 675-8915 • http://www.newportnautical.com

Orange County Jewish Genealogical Society • c/o Temple Bat Yahm, 1011 Camelback St, P.O. Box 7141 • Newport Beach, CA 92658 • (949) 423-3746 • http://www.ocjgs.org

Orange County Railway Historical Society • 1048 Irvine Ave, Box 272 • Newport Beach, CA 92660 • (714) 222-7014

Nice
Robinson Rancheria of Pomo Indians • 1545 E Hwy 20, P.O. Box 4015 • Nice, CA 95464 • (707) 257-0527

Nipomo
Dana Adobe Museum • Oak Glen • Nipomo, CA 93444 • (805) 929-5679 • http://www.danaadobe.org

Norco
Norco Historical Society • 3954 Old Hamner Rd, P.O. Box 159 • Norco, CA 91760 • (951) 734-9739 • http://www.norcohistoricalsociety.org

North Edwards
East Kern Genealogical Society • P.O. Box 961 • North Edwards, CA 93523-0961 • (619) 373-4728

North Fork
North Fork Rancheria - Mono Indians • P.O. Box 929 • North Fork, CA 93643-0929 • (559) 877-2461

Sierra Mono Indian Museum • 33103 Road 228, P.O. Box 426 • North Fork, CA 93643 • (559) 877-2115 • http://www.sierramonomuseum.org

North Hollywood
Campo de Cahuenga Museum • 3919 Lankershim Blvd • North Hollywood, CA 91604 • (818) 763-7651 • http://www.laparks.org

Portal of the Folded Wings Shrine to Aviation Museum • 10621 Victory Blvd • North Hollywood, CA 91606 • (818) 763-9121

Northridge
Delmar T Oviatt Library, Center for Southern California Studies • California State Univ - Northridge, 18111 Nordhoff St • Northridge, CA 91330-8326 • (818) 677-2285 • http://www.library.csun.edu

Norwalk
Hargitt House Museum • 12426 Mapledale • Norwalk, CA 90650 • (562) 864-9663

Novato
Federated Indians of Graton Rancheria - Coast Miwok • P.O. Box 481 • Novato, CA 94948 • (707) 566-2288 • http://www.coastmiwok.com

Marin County Genealogical Society • P.O. Box 1511 • Novato, CA 94948-1511 • (415) 435-2310 • http://www.maringensoc.org

Marin Museum of the American Indian • Miwok Park, 2200 Novato Blvd, P.O. Box 864 • Novato, CA 94948-0864 • (415) 897-4064 • http://www.marinindian.com

Novato History Museum • 815 De Long Ave • Novato, CA 94945 • (415) 897-4320 • http://www.ci.novato.ca.us/pres/museum

Old Timers Museum • 11 Knolltop Ct • Novato, CA 94945 • (209) 728-1160

Olompali State Historical Park • P.O. Box 1016 • Novato, CA 94948 • (415) 892-3383 • http://parks.ca.gov

Oakdale
Oakdale Museum • 355 East F Street, P.O. Box 1155 • Oakdale, CA 95361 • (209) 847-5163 • http://www.oakdalecowboymuseum.org

Oakhurst
Fresno Flats Historical Park • 49777 Rd 427, P.O. Box 451 • Oakhurst, CA 93644 • (559) 683-6570 • http://www.fresnoflatsmuseum.org

Sierra Historic Sites Association • P.O. Box 451 • Oakhurst, CA 93644 • (209) 683-6570 • http://www.fresnoflatsmuseum.org

Wild Wonderful King Vintage Clothing Museum • 49269 Golden Oak Loop, P.O. Box 303 • Oakhurst, CA 93644 • (559) 683-3370 • http://www.wildwonderfulwomen.org

Oakland
African American Museum and Library • 659 14th St, P.O. Box 71043 • Oakland, CA 94608 • (510) 658-3158 • http://www.oaklandlibrary.org/AAMLO/

African-American Historical and Genealogical Society of Northern California • P.O. Box 27485 • Oakland, CA 4602-0985 • (510) 496-2740 • http://www.aagsnc.org

Alameda County Historical Society • 484 Lake Park Ave • Oakland, CA 94610-2730 • (510) 531-7532 • http://www.alamedacountyhistory.org

Armstrong University Library • 1608 Webster St • Oakland, CA 94612 • (510) 865-1336 • http://www.armstrong-u.edu/library/

Ascension Historical Committee • 4700 Lincoln Ave • Oakland, CA 94602 • (510) 336-1913

California Genealogical Society • 1611 Telegraph Ave, Ste 100 • Oakland, CA 94612-2154 • (510) 663-1358 • http://www.calgensoc.org

California Preservation Foundation • 1611 Telegraph, Suite 820 • Oakland, CA 94612 • (510) 763-0972 • http://www.californiapreservation.org

Camron-Stanford House Museum • 1418 Lakeside Dr • Oakland, CA 94612 • (510) 444-1876 • http://www.cshouse.org

Cohen-Bray House Museum • 1440 29th Ave • Oakland, CA 94601 • (510) 532-0704 • http://www.cohen-brayhouse.info

Dunsmuir Historic Estate Museum • 2960 Peralta Oaks Ct • Oakland, CA 94615 • (510) 615-5555 • http://www.dunsmuir.org

East Bay Genealogical Society • 405 14th, Terrace Level, P.O. Box 20417 • Oakland, CA 94620-0417 • (510) 451-9599 • http://www.rootsweb.ancestry.com/~caebaygs/

Mayflower Descendants Society of California • 405 14th St, Terr Level • Oakland, CA 94612 • (916) 771-5094 • http://www.mayflowersociety.com

Oakland Museum of California • 1000 Oak St • Oakland, CA 94607 • (510) 238-2200 • http://www.museumca.org

Oakland Public Library • 125 14th St • Oakland, CA 94612 • (510) 238-3134 • http://www.oaklandlibrary.org

Pardee Home Museum • 672 11th St • Oakland, CA 94607 • (415) 444-2187 • http://www.pardeehome.org

Sociedade Portuguesa Raintta Santa Isabel • 3031 Telegraph Ave • Oakland, CA 94609 • (510) 658-0983

Society of Mayflower Descendants in the State of California • 405 14th St, Terr Level • Oakland, CA 94612 • (415) 451-9599

United Indian Nations • 1320 Webster St • Oakland, CA 94612 • (510) 763-3410 • http://www.uin.net

Western Aerospace Museum • P.O. Box 14264 • Oakland, CA 94614 • (510) 638-7100 • http://www.aerospace.org

Wixarika Research Center • 863 Leo Way • Oakland, CA 94611 • (510) 420-1116

Oceanside
Miracosta College Library • 1 Barnard Dr • Oceanside, CA 92056-3899 • (760) 795-6715

Mission San Luis Rey Museum • 4050 Mission Ave • Oceanside, CA 92049 • (760) 757-3651 • http://www.sanluisrey.org

Oceanside Historical Society • 305 N Nevada St • Oceanside, CA 92054 • (760) 722-4786 • http://www.ci.oceanside.ca.us/library/Associations/history.html

Oceanside Public Library • 330 North Coast Hwy • Oceanside, CA 92054-2824 • (760) 435-5580 • http://www.library.ci.oceanside.ca.us

Ocotillo
IVC Desert Museum & Southeastern Information Center • 11 W Frontage Rd • Ocotillo, CA 92259 • (760) 358-7016 • http://www.imperial.cc.ca.us/ivc-dm/

Imperial Valley College Museum and Society • Historical Museum, 11 Frontage Rd, P.O. Box 430 • Ocotillo, CA 92259 • (760) 358-7016 • http://www.imperial.cc.ca.us/ivc-dm/

Ojai
Ojai Valley Historical Society • Historical Museum, 130 W Ojai Ave, P.O. Box 204 • Ojai, CA 93024 • (805) 640-1390 • http://www.ojaivalleymuseum.org

Ontario
Costanoan Rumsen Carmel Tribe • 3025 E Brookside Ct • Ontario, CA 91761 • (909) 947-7331

Graber Oliver House Museum • 315 E 4th St, P.O. Box 511 • Ontario, CA 91764 • (909) 983-1761 • http://www.graberolives.com

Museum of History and Art • 225 S Euclid Ave • Ontario, CA 91761 • (909) 983-3198 • http://www.ci.ontario.ca.us/neighborhood/museum/museum.html

Ontario City Library • 215 East C Street • Ontario, CA 91764-4111 • (909) 395.2004 • http://www.ci.ontario.ca.us/library

Ontario Heritage • P.O. Box 1 • Ontario, CA 91762 • (909) 391-6252

Orange
Old Towne Preservation Association • P.O. Box 828 • Orange, CA 92856-6828 • (714) 639-6840

Orange Community Historical Society • 101 N Center, P.O. Box 5484 • Orange, CA 92613-5484 • (714) 998-0330

Orange County California Genealocial Society • 7111 Talbert Ave, P.O. Box 1587 • Orange, CA 92856-1587 • (714) 846-2205 • http://www.occgs.com

Orange Public Library • 101 N Center St • Orange, CA 92866-1594 • (714) 288-2410 • http://www.cityoforange.org/library

Thurmond Clarke Memorial Library • Chapman University, 1 University Dr • Orange, CA 92866-1099 • (714) 997-6806 • http://www.chapman.edu/libraries.html

Orangevale
American Historical Society of Germans from Russia, Sacramento Valley Chapter • 9491 Lake Natoma Dr • Orangevale, CA 95662 • (916) 967-2562

Orinda
Orinda Historical Society • 24 Orinda Way • Orinda, CA 94563 • (925) 254-1353

Orland
Glenn Genealogy Group • 1121 Marin • Orland, CA 95963

Orland Free Library • 333 Mill St • Orland, CA 95963 • (530) 865-1640 • http://www.orlandfreelibrary.net

Orland Historical and Cultural Society • P.O. Box 183 • Orland, CA 95963 • (530) 865-1444 • http://www.sierraii.com/orland/ohes.htm

Paskenta Band of Nomlaki Indians • 1012 South St, P.O. Box 398 • Orland, CA 95963 • (530) 865-3119

Oroville
Butte County Archives • 2335 Baldwin Avenue • Oroville, CA 95965 • (530) 533-9418 • http://www.buttecountyhistoricalsociety.org

Butte County Historical Society • 1749 Spencer Ave • Oroville, CA 95966 • (530) 533-9418 • http://www.buttecountyhistoricalsociety.org

Butte County Historical Society • Ehmann Home, 1480 Lincoln, P.O. Box 2195 • Oroville, CA 95965-2195 • (916) 533-5316 • http://www.buttecountyhistoricalsociety.org

Butte County Library • 1820 Mitchell Ave • Oroville, CA 95966-5387 • (530) 538-7642 • http://www.buttecounty.net/bclibrary/

Butte County Pioneer Memorial Museum • 2332 Montgomery St • Oroville, CA 95965 • (530) 538-2415 • http://www.oroville-city.com

Charles F Lott Historic Home Museum • 1007 Montgomery St • Oroville, CA 95965 • (530) 538-2417 • http://www.oroville-city.org

Cherokee Museum • 1084 Montgomery St • Oroville, CA 95965 • (530) 533-1849 • http://www.pe.net/~rksnow/cacountyoroville.htm#history

Cherokee Museum Association • Historical Museum, 4227 Cherokee Rd • Oroville, CA 95965 • (530) 533-1849 • http://www.alvaok.net/csm/assoc.htm

Enterprise Rancheria • 1940 Feather River Blvd, Ste B • Oroville, CA 95965 • (530) 532-9214

KonKow Valley Band of the Concow Maidu • 1185 18th St • Oroville, CA 95965 • http://www.maidu.com/maidu/

Lake Oroville State Historic Site Museum • 400 Glen Dr • Oroville, CA 95965 • (530) 538-2200 • http://www.parks.ca.gov

Mooretown Rancheria of Maidu Indians • 1 Alverda Dr, P.O. Box 1842 • Oroville, CA 95966 • (530) 533-3625 • http://www.featherfallscasino.com/tribal.htm

Oroville Chinese Temple Museum • 1500 Broderick St • Oroville, CA 95965 • (930) 538-2415 • http://www.oroville-city.com

Tyme Maidu Tribe - Berry Creek Reservation • 5 Tyme Wy • Oroville, CA 95966 • (503) 534-3859

Oxnard
Carnegie History and Cultural Arts Center • 424 South C Street • Oxnard, CA 93030 • (805) 385-8157 • http://www.vcnet.com/carnart/history.html

Murphy Auto Museum • 2230 Stratham Blvd • Oxnard, CA 93033 • (805) 487-4333 • http://www.murphyautomuseum.org

Oxnard Public Library • 251 South A Street • Oxnard, CA 93030 • (805) 385-7532 • http://www.oxnard.org

California

Oxnard, cont.
Ventura County Maritime Museum • 2731 S Victoria Ave • Oxnard, CA 93035 • (805) 984-6260

Pacific Grove
Pacific Grove Heritage Society • 605 Laurel Ave, P.O. Box 1007 • Pacific Grove, CA 93950 • (831) 372-2898 • http://www.mbay.net/~heritage

Stowitts Museum • 591 Lighthouse Ave • Pacific Grove, CA 93950 • (831) 655-4488 • http://www.stowitts.org

Pacific Palisades
Friends of Villa Aurora • 520 Paseo Miramar • Pacific Palisades, CA 90272-3019 • (310) 454-4231

Pacific Palisades Historical Society • P.O. Box 1299 • Pacific Palisades, CA 90272 • (213) 454-1974 • http://www.pp90272.com/pphs/

Will Rogers State Historic Park • 1501 Will Rogers State Park Rd • Pacific Palisades, CA 90272 • (310 454-8212 • http://www.cal-parks.ca.gov

Pacifica
Sanchez Adobe Historic Site Museum • 1000 Linda Mar Blvd • Pacifica, CA 94044 • (650) 359-1462 • http://www.sanmateocountyhistory.com

Pala
Pala Band of Mission Indians - Luiseno Cupeno • P.O. Box 50 • Pala, CA 92059 • (760) 742-3784 • http://www.palaindians.com

San Antonio de Pala Asistencia Museum • Pala Mission Rd • Pala, CA 92059 • (760) 742-3317

Palm Desert
Jewish Genealogical Society of Palm Springs • 40111 Portulaca Ct • Palm Desert, CA 92260-2332 • (760) 340-6554

Palm Desert Historical Society • 72861 El Paseo • Palm Desert, CA 92260 • (760) 346-6588

Palm Springs
Agua Caliente Band of Cahuilla Indians • 600 E Tahquitz Canyon Wy • Palm Springs, CA 92262 • (760) 325-3400 • http://www.aguacaliente.org

Agua Caliente Cultural Museum • 219 S Palm Canyon Dr • Palm Springs, CA 92262 • (760) 778-1079 • http://www.accmuseum.org

McCallum Adobe Museum • 221 S Palm Canyon Dr, P.O. Box 1498 • Palm Springs, CA 92263 • (760) 323-8297

Palm Springs Air Museum • 745 N Gene Autry Trail • Palm Springs, CA 92262 • (760) 778-6262 • http://www.palmsprings.com/airmuseum/

Palm Springs Desert Museum • 101 Museum Dr • Palm Springs, CA 92262 • (760) 325-7186 • http://www.psmuseum.org

Palm Springs Genealogical Society • c/o Palm Springs Public Library, 300 S Sunrise Wy, P.O. Box 2093 • Palm Springs, CA 92263-2093 • (760) 321-2768 • http://www.ci.palm-springs.ca.us/Library/lgen.html

Palm Springs Historical Society • Village Green Heritage Center, 221 S Palm Canyon Dr, P.O. Box 1498 • Palm Springs, CA 92263 • (760) 323-8297 • http://palmsprings.com/history/

Palm Springs Public Library • 300 S Sunrise Way • Palm Springs, CA 92262-7699 • (760) 323-8294 • http://www.ci.palm-springs.ca.us/library.html

Palmdale
Antelope Valley Genealogical Society • 39450 3rd St E • Palmdale, CA 93550 • (661) 947-4558

Palmdale City Library • 700 E Palmdale Blvd • Palmdale, CA 93550 • (661) 267-5647 • http://www.palmdalelibrary.org

Palo Alto
Association of Jewish Genealogical Societies • P.O. Box 50245 • Palo Alto, CA 94303 • (415) 424-1622 • http://www.jewishgen.org

Dalton Genealogical Society • 880 Ames Ct • Palo Alto, CA 94303

Museum of American Heritage • 351 Homer Ave • Palo Alto, CA 94301-2727 • (415) 321-1004 • http://www.moah.org

Palo Alto City Library • 1213 Newell Rd, P.O. Box 10250 • Palo Alto, CA 94303-0250 • (650) 329-2436 • http://www.cityofpaloalto.org/depts/lib/default.asp

Palo Alto Historic Resources Board • 250 Hamilton Ave • Palo Alto, CA 94301 • (415) 321-9875 • http://www.city.palo-alto.ca.us/clerk/hrb.html

Palo Alto Historical Association • c/o Palo Alto City Library, 1213 Newell Rd, P.O. Box 10250 • Palo Alto, CA 94302 • (650) 326-3555 • http://www.city.palo-alto.ca.us/library

Past Heritage • P.O. Box 308 • Palo Alto, CA 94302 • (650) 299-8878 • http://www.pastheritage.org

San Francisco Bay Area Jewish Historical Society • 3916 Louis Rd • Palo Alto, CA 94303-4541 • (650) 424-1622

Westerners International, San Francisco Corral • 201 Homer Ave • Palo Alto, CA 94301 • (650) 327-2717

Palos Verdes Estates
Palos Verdes Library District-Malaga Cove Plaza • 2400 Via Campesina • Palos Verdes Estates, CA 90274-3662 • (310) 377-9584 • http://www.palos-verdes.lib.ca.us

Palos Verdes Peninsula
POINT (Pursuing Our Italian Names Together) • P.O. Box 2977 • Palos Verdes Peninsula, CA 90274 • (310) 832-4041 • http://members.aol.com/pointhompg/home.htm

Paradise
Gold Nugget Museum • 502 Pearson Rd, P.O. Box 949 • Paradise, CA 95969 • (530) 872-8722

Paradise Genealogical Society • 5587 Scottwood Rd, P.O. Box 460 • Paradise, CA 95967-0460 • (530) 877-2330 • http://pweb.jps.net/~pargenso/

Paradise Historical Society • P.O. Box 1696 • Paradise, CA 95967 • (530) 873-0769

Pasadena
Association of Historical Societies of Los Angeles County • 1298 S El Molino Ave • Pasadena, CA 91006

Gamble House Museum • 4 Westmoreland Pl • Pasadena, CA 91103 • (626) 793-3334 • http://www.gamblehouse.org

Genealogical Friends of the Pasadena Public Library • c/o Pasadena Public Library, 285 E Walnut St • Pasadena, CA 91801 • (626) 744-4066 • http://www.cityofpasadena.net

Jet Propulsion Laboratory Museum • 4800 Oak Grove Dr • Pasadena, CA 91109 • (818) 354-9314

Ninth Circuit Historical Society • 125 S Grand Ave • Pasadena, CA 91105-1621 • (626) 795-0266

Pacific Asia Museum • 46 N Los Robles Ave • Pasadena, CA 91101 • (626) 449-2742 • http://www.pacasiamuseum.org

Pasadena City College Library • 1570 E Colorado Blvd • Pasadena, CA 91106-2003 • (626) 585-7360 • http://www.paccd.cc.ca.us/library

Pasadena Genealogy Society • 1080 N Holliston Ave, P.O. Box 94774 • Pasadena, CA 91109-4774 • (818) 794-7973 • http://bassett.net/genealogy/pasadenagenealogyresearch.htm

Pasadena Heritage • 651 S St John Ave • Pasadena, CA 91105 • (626) 441-6333 • http://www.pasadenaheritage.org

Pasadena Historical Society • Feynes Mansion Museum, 470 W Walnut St • Pasadena, CA 91103-3594 • (626) 795-3002 • http://www.pasadenahistory.org

Pasadena Public Library • 285 E Walnut St • Pasadena, CA 91101 • (626) 744-4066 • http://www.ci.pasadena.ca.us/library

Pasadena Public Library-La Pintoresca • 1355 N Raymond Ave • Pasadena, CA 91103 • (626) 744-7268 • http://www.ci.pasadena.ca.us/library/lapintoresca.asp

Society of Architectural Historians, Southern California Chapter • P. O. Box 92224 • Pasadena, CA 91109 • (800) 972-4722 • http://www.sahscc.org

Tournament House and Wrigley Gardens Museum • 391 S Orange Grove Blvd • Pasadena, CA 91184 • (626) 449-4100 • http://www.tournamentofroses.com

Tournament House Museum • 391 S Orange Grove Blvd • Pasadena, CA 91105 • (626) 449-4100

Paso Robles
Call-Booth House Museum • 1315 Vine St, P.O. Box 1636 • Paso Robles, CA 93446 • (805) 238-5473

El Paso De Robles Area Historical Society • c/o Carnegie Library, 2010 Riverside Ave, P.O. Box 2875 • Paso Robles, CA 93447 • (805) 238-4996

El Paso de Robles Area Pioneer Museum • P.O. Box 461 • Paso Robles, CA 93446 • (805) 239-4556

Estrella Warbird Museum • 4251 Drycreek Rd, Bldg A • Paso Robles, CA 93446 • (805) 227-0440 • http://www.ewarbirds.org

Paso Robles Public Library • 1000 Spring St • Paso Robles, CA 93446-2207 • (805) 237-3870 • http://www.prcity.com

Patterson
Patterson Genies • 525 Clover Ave • Patterson, CA 95363

Patterson Township Historical Society • 100 E Las Palmas Ave, P.O. Box 15 • Patterson, CA 95363 • (209) 892-2821 • http://www.patterson-ca.com/histsoc/

Patton
San Manuel Band of Mission Indians - Serrano • P.O. Box 266 • Patton, CA 92369 • (909) 864-8933 • http://www.sanmanuel-nsn.gov

Pauma Valley
La Jolla Band of Luiseno Indians • 22000 Hwy 76 • Pauma Valley, CA 92061 • (760) 742-3371

Pauma-Yuima Band of Mission Indians • P.O. Box 369 • Pauma Valley, CA 92061 • (760) 742-1289

Penn Valley
Sons of the American Revolution, California Society, • 19070 Hummingbird Dr • Penn Valley, CA 95946 • (530_ 205-9581 • http://www.californiasar.org

Perris
Lake Perrid Regional Indian Museum • 17801 Lake Perris Dr • Perris, CA 92571 • (951) 940-4500

Orange Empire Railway Museum • 2201 South A Street, P.O. Box 548 • Perris, CA 92370 • (951) 943-3020 • http://www.oerm.org

Perris Valley Historical and Museum Association • Historical Museum, P.O. Box 343 • Perris, CA 92572 • (951) 657-0274 • http://www.perrisvalleymuseum.com

Pescadero
Ano Nuevo State Reserve Museum • New Years Creek Rd • Pescadero, CA 94060 • (650) 879-2025 • http://www.anonuevo.org

Petaluma
Petaluma Adobe State Historic Park • 3325 Adobe Rd • Petaluma, CA 94952 • (707) 762-4871 • http://www.parks.sonoma.net/adobe.html

Petaluma Museum Association • Historical Museum, 20 4th St • Petaluma, CA 94952 • (707) 776-4308 • http://www.petalumamuseum.com

Petaluma Regional Library • 100 Fairgrounds Dr • Petaluma, CA 94952-3369 • (707) 763-9801 • http://www.sonomalibrary.org

Petrolia
Mattole Valley Historical Society • 34492 Mattole Rd • Petrolia, CA 95558 • (707) 629-3684

Pico Rivera
County of Los Angeles Public Library-Pico Rivera Library • 9001 Mines Ave • Pico Rivera, CA 90660-3098 • (562) 942-7394 • http://www.colapublib.org/libs/picorivera/

Pico Rivera Historical and Heritage Society • 9122 Washington Blvd, P.O. Box 313 • Pico Rivera, CA 90660-3836 • (562) 949-7100 • http://www.colapublib.org/history/picorivera/

Pine Grove
Amador County Historical Society • P.O. Box 147 • Pine Grove, CA 95665

Indian Grinding Rock State Historic Park Archives • 14881 Pine Grove-Volcano Rd • Pine Grove, CA 95665 • (209) 296-7488 • http://www.sierra.parks.state.ca.us/igr/igr_main.htm

Piru
Lechler Museum • 3886 E Market St • Piru, CA 93040 • (805) 521-1595

Rancho Camulos Museum • Highway 126 • Piru, CA 93040 • (805) 521-1561 • http://www.heritagevalley.net/Camulos.htm

Pittsburg
Pittsburg Historical Society • Historical Museum, 515 Railroad Ave • Pittsburg, CA 94565 • (925) 439-7501

Placentia
Bradford House Museum • 136 Palm Cr • Placentia, CA 92870 • (714) 993-2470

Historic George Key Ranch Museum • 625 W Bastanchury Rd • Placentia, CA 92670 • (714) 528-4260 • http://www.ocparks.com/keyranch/

Placentia Founders Society • Bradford House, 136 Palm Dr • Placentia, CA 92670 • (714) 993-2740 • http://www.bradfordhouse.com

Placentia Historical Committee • City Hall, 401 E Chapman Ave • Placentia, CA 92670 • (714) 993-8117 • http://www.placentia.org

Placentia Library District • 411 E Chapman Ave • Placentia, CA 92670-6198 • (714) 528-1906

Placerville
El Dorado County Historical Society • Historical Museum, 524 Main St • Placerville, CA 95667 • (530) 626-0773 • http://www.co.eldorado.ca.us/generalservices/museum.html

El Dorado County Library • 345 Fair Lane • Placerville, CA 95667-4196 • (530) 621-5540 • http://www.eldoradolibrary.org

El Dorado County Museum • 104 Placerville Dr • Placerville, CA 95667 • (530) 621-5865 • http://www.co.el-dorado.ca.us/generalservices/museum.html

Heritage Association of El Dorado County • P.O. Box 62 • Placerville, CA 95667 • (530) 622-8388 • http://www.geocities.com/RainForest/7589/

California

Pleasant Hill
Contra Costa County Historical Society • 1700 Oak Park Blvd C5, P.O. Box 821 • Pleasant Hill, CA 94522 • (925) 939-9180

Contra Costa County Library • 1750 Oak Park Blvd • Pleasant Hill, CA 94523-4497 • (925) 646-6423 • http://www.ccclib.org

Diablo Valley College Library & Museum • 321 Golf Club Rd • Pleasant Hill, CA 94523-1576 • (925) 685-1230 • http://www.dvc.edu/library

Pleasanton
Amador-Livermore Valley Historical Society • Historical Museum, 603 Main St, P.O. Box 573 • Pleasanton, CA 94566 • (925) 462-2766 • http://www.museumonmain.org

Pleasanton Public Library • 400 Old Bernal Ave • Pleasanton, CA 94566 • (925) 931-3400 • http://www.ci.pleasanton.ca.us/library.html

Point Arena
Manchester-Point Arena Rancheria - Pomo Indians • P.O. Box 623 • Point Arena, CA 95468 • (707) 882-2788

Point Arena Lighthouse Museum • 45500 Lighthouse Rd, P.O. Box 11 • Point Arena, CA 95468 • (877) 725-4448 • http://www.mcn.org/1palight

Point Mugu
Naval Base Ventura County Library • Point Mugu Sta, Bldg 221, Code N92V1 • Point Mugu, CA 93042-5000 • (805) 989-7771

Point Richmond
Point Richmond History Association • 139 1/2 Washington Ave • Point Richmond, CA 94801 • (510) 234-5334 • http://www.alkos.com/prha

Pomona
Adobe de Palomares Museum • 491 E Arrow Hwy • Pomona, CA 91767 • (909) 620-0264 • http://www.laokay.com/adobedepalomares.htm

Historical Society of Pomona Valley • 585 E Holt Ave • Pomona, CA 91767 • (909) 623-2198 • http://www.pomonahistorical.org

La Casa Primera de Rancho San Jose Museum • 1569 N Park Ave • Pomona, CA 91767 • (909) 623-2198 • http://www.laokay.com/lacasaprimera.htm

Pomona Public Library • 625 S Garey Ave, P.O. Box 2271 • Pomona, CA 91769-2271 • (909) 620-2043 • http://www.youseemore.com/pomona

Pomona Valley Genealogical Society • P.O. Box 286 • Pomona, CA 91769-0286 • (909) 599-2166 • http://www.pvgs.us

Pomona Valley Historical Society • 1569 N Park • Pomona, CA 91768 • (909) 620-0264 • http://www.osb.net/Pomona/

Railway Locomotive Historical Society • Historical Museum, 1101 W McKinley Ave, P.O. Box 2250 • Pomona, CA 91768 • (909) 623-0190 • http://www.trainweb.org/rlhs

Wally Parks Motorsports Museum • 1101 W McKinley Ave • Pomona, CA 91768 • http://museum.nhra.com

Port Huememe
Seabee Museum • Naval Construction Battalion Center, 1000 23rd Ave, Bldg 99, Code 10H • Port Huememe, CA 93043 • (805) 928-5163 • http://www.navfac.navy.mil

Porterville
Porterville Historical Museum • 257 North D Street • Porterville, CA 93257 • (559) 784-2053

Porterville Public Library • 41 W Thurman Ave • Porterville, CA 93257-3652 • (209) 784-0177 • http://www.sjvls.org

Tule River Tribe - Yokuts • P.O. Box 589 • Porterville, CA 93258 • (559) 781-4271

Tule Tree Tracers • c/o Porterville Public Library, 41 W Thurman Ave • Porterville, CA 93257 • (559) 784-0177

Zalud House Museum • 393 N Hockett St • Porterville, CA 93257 • (559) 782-7548

Portola
Jim Beckworth Museum • P.O. Box 2367 • Portola, CA 96122 • (530) 832-4888

Portola Railroad Museum • 700 Western Pacific Wy, P.O. Box 608 • Portola, CA 96122 • (530) 832-4131 • http://www.wplives.org

Potrero
Potrero-East County Museum Society • Historical Museum, P.O. Box 70 • Potrero, CA 92063 • (935) 478-5306

Poway
Poway Historical and Memorial Society • Old Poway Park, 14114 Midland Rd, P.O. Box 19 • Poway, CA 92074 • (858) 679-8587

San Luis Rey Band • 2064 Old Pomuno Rd • Poway, CA 92064 • (619) 748-1586

Presidio of Monterey
Defense Language Institute Historical Holding Museum • Presidio of Monterey, Area Studies Dept, DLIFLC • Presidio of Monterey, CA 93944 • (831) 647-5565

Project City
Wintu Tribe of Northern California • P.O. Box 71036 • Project City, CA 96079 • (530) 243-1766

Quincy
Plumas County Historical Society • Historical Museum, 500 Jackson St, P.O. Box 695 • Quincy, CA 95971 • (530) 283-6320 • http://www.countyofplumas.com/museum/

Plumas County Library • 445 Jackson St • Quincy, CA 95971-9410 • (530) 283-6310 • http://www.psln.com/pclibq

Plumas County Museum Association • 500 Jackson St, P.O. Box 695 • Quincy, CA 95971 • (530) 283-4379 • http://www.plumas.ca.us

Ramona
Ramona Pioneer Historical Society • Guy B. Woodward Museum, 645 Main St, P.O. Box 625 • Ramona, CA 92065 • (760) 789-7644 • http://www.ucsd-civic-collaborative.org

San Diego County Genealogical Association • P.O. Box 422 • Ramona, CA 92065 • (760) 789-2534

Rancho Cucamonga
Casa de Rancho Cucamonga Museum • 8810 Hemlock St • Rancho Cucamonga, CA 91730 • (714) 989-4970 • http://www.citivu.com/rc/hist1.html

City of Rancho Cucamonga Historical Program • 10500 Civic Center Dr, P.O. Box 807 • Rancho Cucamonga, CA 91729 • (909) 477-2750 • http://www.ci.rancho-cucamonga.ca.us/planning/histprog.htm

Rancho Cucamonga Public Library • 7368 Archibald Ave • Rancho Cucamonga, CA 91730 • (909) 477-2720 • http://www.rcpl.lib.ca.us

Wignall Museum • 5885 N Haven Ave • Rancho Cucamonga, CA 91737 • (909) 941-2703 • http://www.culturalcenter.org/orgs/wignall.htm

Rancho Murietta
Sloughhouse Area Genealogical Society • general delivery • Rancho Murietta, CA 95683 • (916) 354-2807

Rancho Palos Verdes
Salvation Army Western Territorial Museum • 30840 Hawthorne Blvd • Rancho Palos Verdes, CA 90274 • (310) 541-4721

Rancho Santa Fe
Rancho Santa Fe Historical Society • 6036 La Flecha, P.O. Box 2414 • Rancho Santa Fe, CA 92067 • (858) 756-9291

Randsburg
Desert Museum • 161 Butte St • Randsburg, CA 93554 • (619) 374-2111

Rand District Historical Corporation • P.O. Box 307 • Randsburg, CA 93554

Raymond
Chukchansi Yokotch Tribe • P.O. Box 329 • Raymond, CA 93653 • (209) 689-3318

Red Bluff
Kelly-Griggs House Association • Historical Museum, 311 Washington St • Red Bluff, CA 96080 • (916) 527-1129 • http://www.caohwy.com/k/kellyghm.htm

Tehama County Library • 645 Madison St • Red Bluff, CA 96080-3383 • (530) 527-0607 • http://www.tehamacountylibrary.org

Tehama Genealogical and Historical Society • P.O. Box 415 • Red Bluff, CA 96080 • (530) 527-6363 • http://tco1.tco.net/tehama/museum/tcmgene.html

William B Ide Adobe Museum • 21659 Adobe Road • Red Bluff, CA 96080 • (916) 527-5927 • http://www.parks.ca.gov

Redding
Redding Museum of Art & History • 56 Quartz Hill Rd, Caldwell Park, P.O. Box 992360 • Redding, CA 96099-2360 • (530) 243-8801 • http://www.artresources.com/guide/

Redding Rancheria - Wintun, Pit River and Yana Tribes • 2000 Redding Rancheria Rd • Redding, CA 96001 • (530) 225-8979

Shasta College Library • 11555 Old Oregon Trail, P.O. Box 496006 • Redding, CA 96003-7692 • (530) 225-4975 • http://library.shastacollege.edu

Shasta College Museum and Research Center • 1065 N Old Oregon Tr, P.O. Box 496006 • Redding, CA 96049 • (530) 225-4754 • http://www.shastacollege.edu

Shasta County Genealogical Society • P.O. Box 994562 • Redding, CA 96099-4652 • http://www.rootsweb.com/~cascogs/

Shasta Historical Society • 1449 Market St • Redding, CA 96001 • (530) 243-3720 • http://www.shastahistorical.org

Wintu Indian Cultural Organization • 2104 Waldon St • Redding, CA 96001 • http://www.winnememwintu.us

Redlands
Arkansas Smiley Public Library and Museum • 125 W Vine St • Redlands, CA 92373-4761 • (909) 798-7675 • http://www.akspl.org/heritage.html

Asistencia San Gabriel Mission Outpost Museum • 26930 Barton Rd • Redlands, CA 92373 • (909) 793-5402 • http://www.sbcountymuseum.org

Historical Glass Museum • 1157 N Orange St • Redlands, CA 92373 • (909) 793-3333 • http://www.historicalGLASSmuseum.com

Kimberly Crest House and Garden Museum • 1325 Prospect Dr, P.O. Box 206 • Redlands, CA 92373 • (909) 792-2111 • http://www.kimberlycrest.org

Lincoln Memorial Shrine • 125 W Vine St • Redlands, CA 92373 • (909) 798-7632 • http://www.lincolnshrine.org

Redlands Area Historical Society • P.O. Box 1024 • Redlands, CA 92373 • (909) 307-6060 • http://www.rahs.org

San Bernardino County Museum • 2024 Orange Tree Ln • Redlands, CA 92374 • (909) 307-2669 • http://www.sbcountymuseum.org

Redondo Beach
Gluckstal Colony Research Association • 611 Esplanade • Redondo Beach, CA 90277-4130 • (310) 540-1872 • http://www.raile.com/gluckstal

Redondo Beach Historical Society • P.O. Box 978 • Redondo Beach, CA 90277 • (310) 372-0197 • http://www.redondobeachhistorical.org

TRW Genealogical Society • One Space Park, R7-2214 • Redondo Beach, CA 90278 • (310) 813-6171

Redwood City
Golden Gate Railroad Museum • 1702 Cordilleras Rd • Redwood City, CA 94062 • (415) 822-8728 • http://www.ggrm.org

Lathrop House Museum • 627 Hamilton St • Redwood City, CA 94063 • (650) 365-5564

Redwood City Heritage Association • Lathrop House, 627 Hamilton St, P.O. Box 1273 • Redwood City, CA 95063-1617 • (650) 365-5564

Redwood City Public Library • Local History Collection, 1044 Middlefield Rd • Redwood City, CA 94063-1868 • (650) 780-7018 • http://www.redwoodcity.org/library/

San Mateo County Historical Association • 777 Hamilton St • Redwood City, CA 94063 • (650) 299-0104 • http://www.sanmateocountyhistory.com

Redwood Valley
Coyote Valley Band of Pomo Indians • P.O. Box 39 • Redwood Valley, CA 95470-0039 • (707) 485-8723

Redwood Valley Rancheria - Little River Band of Pomo Indians • 3250 Road I • Redwood Valley, CA 95470-9526 • (707) 485-0361

Reedley
Mennonite Quilting Center Museum • 1012 G Street • Reedley, CA 93654 • (559) 638-3560

Reedley Historical Society • Historical Museum, 1752 10th St, P.O. Box 877 • Reedley, CA 93654 • (559) 638-1913 • http://www.reedley.com/Lori/Community-Tourism/lo-reedley_museum.htm

Represa
Folsom Prison Museum • 300 Prison Rd, P.O. Box 71 • Represa, CA 95671 • (916) 985-2561

Rialto
Rialto Historical Society • 205 N Riverside Ave, P.O. Box 413 • Rialto, CA 92376 • (909) 875-1750 • http://www.wemweb.com/traveler/towns/20rialto/hstsoc.html

Richmond
Richmond Museum Association • Historical Museum, 400 Nevin Ave, P.O. Box 1267 • Richmond, CA 94802-0267 • (510) 235-7387 • http://richmond.museumofhistory.org

Richmond Public Library • 325 Civic Center Plaza • Richmond, CA 94804-9991 • (510) 620-6555 • http://www.richmondlibrary.org

Ridgecrest
Historical Society of the Upper Mojave Desert • Maturango Museum , 100 E Las Flores, P.O. Box 2001 • Ridgecrest, CA 93556-2001 • (760) 375-6900 • http://www.maturango.org

Indian Wells Valley Genealogical Society • 131 Los Flores, P.O. Box 2047 • Ridgecrest, CA 93555

Ridgecrest Historical Society • 302 Station Ave • Ridgecrest, CA 93555 • (760) 375-8456

Ringgold
Catoosa County Historian • P.O. Box 8 • Ringgold, CA 30736 • (706) 965-7438

Rio Linda
Rio Linda-Eiverta Historical Society • P.O. Box 478 • Rio Linda, CA 95673-0478 • (916) 332-0355

Rio Vista
Rio Vista Museum Association • Historical Museum, 16 N Front St • Rio Vista, CA 94571 • (707) 374-5169

California

Riverside

California Museum of Photography • Univ of California, 3824 Main St • Riverside, CA 92501 • (951) 827-4787 • http://www.cmp.ucr.edu

California Newspaper Project • Univ of California, P.O. Box 5900 • Riverside, CA 92517-5900 • (909) 787-2388 • http://www.cbsr.ucr.edu/cnp/

Genealogical Society of Riverside • c/o Riverside Public Library, 3581 Mission Inn Ave, P.O. Box 2557 • Riverside, CA 92516-2557 • (909) 782-5273 • http://www.gsor.org

Historic Resources Management Program • Univ of CA-Riverside, History Dept • Riverside, CA 92511 • (714) 787-5401 • http://history.ucr.edu

Jensen-Alvarado Ranch Historic Park Library • 4307 Briggs St, P.O. Box 3507 • Riverside, CA 92509 • (909) 369-6055

Jurnpa Mountains Cultural Center Library • 7621 Granite Hill Dr • Riverside, CA 92509 • (951) 685-5818 • http://www.the-jmcc.org

La Sierra University Library • 4700 Pierce St • Riverside, CA 92515 • (909) 785-2396 • http://www.lasierra.edu/library/

March Field Air Museum • 22550 Van Buren Ave, P.O. Box 6463 • Riverside, CA 92518 • (951) 697-6602 • http://www.MarchField.org

Mission Inn Museum • 3696 Main St • Riverside, CA 92501 • (951) 781-8241 • http://www.missioninnmuseum.com

Pioneer Historical Society of Riverside • P.O. Box 246 • Riverside, CA 92502 • (909) 684-4074

Riverside County Historical Commission • 4600 Crestmore Dr, P.O. Box 3507 • Riverside, CA 92519 • (909) 787-2551 • http://www.riversidecountyparks.org

Riverside Heritage House Museum • 8193 Magnolia Ave • Riverside, CA 92504 • (909) 826-5273 • http://www.riversideca.gov

Riverside Metropolitan Museum • 3580 Mission Inn Ave • Riverside, CA 92501 • (951) 826-5273 • http://www.riversideca.gov/museum

Riverside Museum Associates • Historical Museum, 3580 Mission Inn Avenue • Riverside, CA 92501 • (909) 782-5273 • http://www.riversideca.gov/museum/

Riverside Public Library • 3581 Mission Inn Ave • Riverside, CA 92501 • (909) 826-5213 • http://www.riversideca.gov/library/

Riviera Library - Special Collections • Univ of California Riverside, 3401 Watkins Dr, P.O. Box 5900 • Riverside, CA 92521 • (909) 787-3221 • http://www.library.ucr.edu

Sherman Indian Museum • 9010 Magnolia Ave • Riverside, CA 92503 • (909) 276-6719 • http://www.shermanindianmuseum.org

Southern California Medical Museum • 3993 Jurupa Ave • Riverside, CA 92506 • (951) 787-7700 • http://www.socalmedicalmuseum.org

Tongva Nation • 3462 Avocado • Riverside, CA 92507 • (909) 276-1161

Rocklin

Sierra Joint Community College Library • 5000 Rocklin Rd • Rocklin, CA 95677 • (916) 781-0566 • http://lrc.sierra.cc.ca.us

Rohnert Park

Jean & Charles Schulz Information Center • Sonoma State University, Finley McFarling Genealogy Collection, 1801 E Cotati Ave • Rohnert Park, CA 94928-3609 • (707) 664-2398 • http://libweb.sonoma.edu

Ruben Salazar Library • Sonoma State Univ, 1801 E Cotati Ave • Rohnert Park, CA 94928-3609 • (707) 664-2861 • http://www.sonoma.edu/library/special/finley.html

Sonoma County Wine Museum • 5000 Roberts Lake Rd • Rohnert Park, CA 94928 • (707) 586-3795

Rolling Hills Estates

Palos Verdes Library District • 701 Silver Spur Rd • Rolling Hills Estates, CA 90274 • (310) 377-9584 • http://www.pvld.org

Rosamond

Kern-Antelope Historical Society • P.O. Box 1255 • Rosamond, CA 93560 • (805) 943-3221

Rosemead

Rosemead Library • 8800 Valley Blvd • Rosemead, CA 91770 • (626) 573-5220 • http://www.colapublib.org/libs/rosemead/

Roseville

Maidu Interpretative Center • 1960 Johnson Ranch Dr • Roseville, CA 95661 • (916) 774-5934 • http://www.roseville.ca.us/indianmuseum

Roseville Genealogical Society • P.O. Box 459 • Roseville, CA 95678 • http://www.rootsweb.com/~carvgs/rgs.html

Roseville Historical Society • Carnegie Historical Museum, 557 Lincoln St • Roseville, CA 95678-1523 • (916) 773-3003 • http://www.rosevillehistorical.org

Roseville Public Library • 225 Taylor St • Roseville, CA 95678-2681 • (916) 774-5221 • http://www.roseville.ca.us/library

Sacramento

Anderson Marsh State Historic Park Archives • 1416 9th St • Sacramento, CA 94296 • (707) 994-0688 • http://parks.ca.gov

Blue Diamond Almond Growers Museum • 1701 C Street • Sacramento, CA 95814 • (916) 446-8409

California Committee for the Promotion of History • 6000 J Street , P.O. Box 221476 • Sacramento, CA 95822 • (916) 331-4349 • http://www.venet.com/sbra/ceph/

California Department of Health Services Office of the State Registrar of Vital Statistics • 1501 Capitol Ave, Suite 71, P.O. Box 997410 • Sacramento, CA 95899-7410 • (916) 445-2684 • http://www.dhs.ca.gov/org/hisp/chs/vorder.htm

California Historical Resources Commission, Office of Historic Preservation • 1416 9th St, P.O. Box 942896 • Sacramento, CA 91296 • (916) 445-8006 • http://ohp.parks.ca.gov

California Military Museum • 1119 2nd St • Sacramento, CA 95814 • (916) 442-2883 • http://www.militarymuseum.org

California State Archives • 1020 O Street, Rm 200 • Sacramento, CA 95814 • (916) 653-2246 • http://www.ss.ca.gov/archives/archives_home.htm

California State Capitol Museum • 10th & L Streets, State Capitol Room B-27 • Sacramento, CA 95814 • (916) 324-0312 • http://www.statecapitolmuseum.ca.gov

California State History Museum • 1020 O Street • Sacramento, CA 95814 • (916) 653-3476 • http://www.castatehistory.org

California State Indian Museum • 2618 K Street • Sacramento, CA 95816 • (916) 324-0971 • http://www.parks.ca.gov

California State Library • 914 Capitol Mall, P.O. Box 924837 • Sacramento, CA 94237-0001 • (916) 654-0261 • http://www.library.ca.gov/html/genealogy.html

California State Library California History Room • 900 N Street, Room 200 • Sacramento, CA 95814 • (916) 654-0176 • http://www.library.ca.gov/

California State Military Museum • 1119 2nd St • Sacramento, CA 95814 • (916) 442-2883 • http://www.militarymuseum.org

California State Museum Resource Center • 2505 Port St • Sacramento, CA 95691 • (916) 323-1950 • http://archaeology.parks.ca.gov/mc/

California State Railroad Museum • 113 I Street • Sacramento, CA 95814 • (916) 445-6645 • http://www.californiastaterailroadmuseum.org

California Vietnam Veterans Memorial • 1227 O Street • Sacramento, CA 95814 • (916) 327-5258

Center for California Studies • CalState-Sacramento, 6000 J Street • Sacramento, CA 95819 • (916) 278-6906 • http://www.csus.edu/calst/

Citizen Soldier's Museum Guard Historical Society • Historical Museum, 1119 2nd St • Sacramento, CA 95814 • (916) 442-2883

ComputerRooters • P.O. Box 161693 • Sacramento, CA 95816

Cosumnes River College Library • 8401 Center Pkwy • Sacramento, CA 95823-5799 • (916) 691-7265 • http://www.crc.losrios.edu

Donner Memorial State Park Archives • 1416 9th St • Sacramento, CA 95814 • (530) 582-7892 • http://parks.ca.gov

E Clampus Vitus, Sacramento Chapter • 1615 Markham Way • Sacramento, CA 95818 • (916) 448-0584

Emigrant Trail Museum • 1416 9th St • Sacramento, CA 95814 • (530) 582-7892 • http://ceres.ca.gov/sierradsp/donner.html

Genealogical and Historical Council of Sacramento Valley • P.O. Box 214749 • Sacramento, CA 95821-0749 • (916) 331-4349 • http://www.rootsweb.com/caghcsv

Genealogical Association of Sacramento • c/o Belle Coolege Library, 5600 S Land Park Dr, P.O. Box 292145 • Sacramento, CA 95829-2145 • (916) 446-5715

Golden State Museum • 1020 O Street • Sacramento, CA 95814 • (916) 653-7524 • http://www.californiamuseum.org

Governor's Mansion State Historical Park • 1526 H Street • Sacramento, CA 95814 • (916) 323-3047 • http://www.parks.ca.gov

Hungarian-American Friendship Society of Sacramento • 2811 Elvyria Wy #236 • Sacramento, CA 95821-5865 • (916) 489-9599 • http://www.dholmes.com/hafs.html

Jewish Genealogical Society of Sacramento • 5631 Wyda Wy • Sacramento, CA 95841 • (916) 486-0906 • http://www.jewishgen.org/ajgs/jgs-sacramento/

Leland Stanford Mansion State Historic Park • 802 N Street • Sacramento, CA 95814 • (916) 324-0575 • http://parks.ca.gov

Native American Heritage Commission • 915 Capitol Mall, Rm 288 • Sacramento, CA 95814 • (916) 445-7370 • http://www.ceres.ca.gov/nahc/

Northern California Chapter, Ohio Genealogical Society • P.O. Box 60191 • Sacramento, CA 95860-0101 • (916) 966-6558

Office of Historic Preservation, Planning Services • 1231 I Street, Suite 300 • Sacramento, CA 95814-3699 • (916) 264-5381 • http://www.cityofsacramento.org/planning/

Old Sacramento Schoolhouse Museum • 1200 Front St • Sacramento, CA 95608 • (916) 483-8818 • http://www.scoe.net/oldsacschoolhouse/

Old Sacramento State Historic Park • 111 I Street • Sacramento, CA 95814 • (916) 445-7387 • http://www.csrmf.org

Portuguese Historical and Cultural Society • P.O. Box 161990 • Sacramento, CA 95816 • (916) 392-1048 • http://www.dholmes.com/o-prog.html

Professional Genealogists of California • 5048 J Pkwy • Sacramento, CA 95823 • (916) 421-8332

Riverboat Museum • 1000 Front St • Sacramento, CA 95814 • (916) 444-5464

Sacramento Archives and Museum Center • 551 Sequoia Pacific Blvd • Sacramento, CA 95814-0229 • (916) 264-7072 • http://www.sacramentoarchives.org/

Sacramento City Cemetery Archives • 1000 Broadway, P.O. Box 255345 • Sacramento, CA 95865-5345 • (916) 448-5665

Sacramento County Historical Society • Historical Museum, 101 I Street, P.O. Box 160065 • Sacramento, CA 95816 • (916) 443-6265

Sacramento Genealogical Association • P.O. Box 28297 • Sacramento, CA 95828

Sacramento German Genealogy Society • P.O. Box 660061 • Sacramento, CA 95866-0061 • (530) 753-3206 • http://www.sacgergensoc.org

Sacramento Italian Cultural Society • 2791 24th St, P.O. Box 189427 • Sacramento, CA 95818 • (916) 482-5900 • http://italiancenter.net

Sacramento Museum and History Commission • Historical Museum, 1930 J Street • Sacramento, CA 95814

Sacramento Old City Cemetery Archives • 1000 Broadway • Sacramento, CA 95818-2105 • (916) 448-0811 • http://www.oldcitycemetery.com

Sacramento Public Library • 828 I Street • Sacramento, CA 95814-2589 • (916) 264-2920 • http://www.saclib.org

Sacramento Public Library-Belle Cooledge Community Library • 5600 S Land Park Dr • Sacramento, CA 95822 • (916) 264-2700

Sacramento Public Library-Rancho Cordova Community Library • 9845 Folsom Blvd • Sacramento, CA 95827 • (916) 264-2700 • http://www.saclib.org

Sierra Sacramento Valley Medical Society Museum • 5380 Elvas Ave • Sacramento, CA 95819 • (916) 452-2671 • http://www.ssvms.org

Stanford House State Historic Park Archives • 802 N Street • Sacramento, CA 95814 • (916) 324-0575

Surveyors' Historical Society • P.O. Box 160502 • Sacramento, CA 95816

Sutter's Fort State Historic Park • 2701 L Street • Sacramento, CA 95814 • (916) 445-4422 • http://parks.ca.gov

Towe Auto Museum • 2200 Front St • Sacramento, CA 95818 • (916) 442-6802 • http://www.toweautomuseum.org

Wells Fargo History Museum • 400 Capitol Mall • Sacramento, CA 95814 • (916) 440-4161

Wells Fargo Museum • BF Hastings Building, 1000 2nd St • Sacramento, CA 95814 • (916) 440-4263 • http://www.xphomestation.com/bfhastings.html

Saint Helena
Elmshaven-E G White Home Museum • 125 Glass Mountain Rd • Saint Helena, CA 94574 • (707) 963-9039

Robert Louis Stevenson Silverado Museum • 1490 Library Ln, P.O. Box 409 • Saint Helena, CA 94574 • (707) 963-3757 • http://www.caohwy.com/s/silvemus.htm

Vintage Hall Museum • 473 Main St • Saint Helena, CA 94574 • (707) 963-7411

Salida
Modern Ancestors • P.O. Box 1217 • Salida, CA 95368 • (209) 521-9830

Salinas
California Rodeo Heritage Collection Museum • California Rodeo Grounds, 1034 N Main St • Salinas, CA 93902 • (213) 244-7400

Harvey-Baker House Museum • 238 E Romie Ln • Salinas, CA 93901 • (831) 424-7155

Jose Eusibio Boronda Adobe Museum • 333 Baronda Dr, P.O. Box 3576 • Salinas, CA 93912 • (408) 757-8085

Monterey County Genealogical Society • P.O. Box 8144 • Salinas, CA 93912-8144 • (408) 484-1339 • http://www.mocogenso.org

California

Salinas, cont.

Monterey County Historical Society • 333 Boronda Rd, P.O. Box 3576 • Salinas, CA 93912 • (831) 757-8085 • http://www.mchmuseum.com

Monterey Hay Family History Center • 23040 Guidotti Dr • Salinas, CA 93908 • (408) 394-1124

National Steinbeck Center • 1 Main St • Salinas, CA 93901 • (831) 796-3833 • http://www.steinbeck.org

Steinbeck House Museum • 132 Central Ave • Salinas, CA 93901 • (408) 424-2735

Salyer

Tsnungwe Tribal Council - Hupa • P.O. Box 373 • Salyer, CA 95563 • (916) 629-3356

Samoa

Humboldt Bay Maritime Museum • 77 Cookhouse Rd, P.O. Box 282 • Samoa, CA 95564 • (707) 444-9440 • http://www.humboldtbaymaritimemuseum.com

San Andreas

Calaveras County Archives • 46 N Main St, P.O. Box 1281 • San Andreas, CA 95249 • (209) 754-3918

Calaveras County Historical Society • Historical Museum, 30 N Main St, P.O. Box 721 • San Andreas, CA 95249-0721 • (209) 754-4658 • http://www.visitcalaveras.org/ccmuseums.html

Calaveras County Library • 891 Mountain Ranch Rd, P.O. Box 338 • San Andreas, CA 95249-0338 • (209) 754-6510 • http://www.co.calaveras.ca.us

Calaveras County Museum and Archives • 30 N Main St, P.O. Box 1281 • San Andreas, CA 95249 • (209) 754-6513

San Anselmo

San Anselmo Public Library • 110 Tunstead Ave • San Anselmo, CA 94960 • (415) 258-4656 • http://www.sananselmotownhall.org/library

San Barnardino

City of San Bernardino Historical and Pioneer Society • 796 N D St, P.O. Box 875 • San Barnardino, CA 92402 • (714) 887-0587

International Blacksheep Society of Genealogists • 2505 W Foothill Blvd #41 • San Bernardino, CA 92410-1358

Law Library for San Bernardino County • 402 North D Street • San Bernardino, CA 92401 • (909) 885-3020

Railroad Historical Society • Historical Museum, P.O. Box 2878 • San Bernardino, CA 92406-2878 • (323) 277-7700 • http://www.sbrhs.org

San Bernardino County Archives • 777 E Rialto Ave • San Bernardino, CA 92415-0795 • (909) 387-2030

San Bernardino County Library & Historical Archives • 104 W 4th St • San Bernardino, CA 92415-0035 • (909) 387-5728

San Bernardino Historical and Pioneer Society • 796 North D Street, P.O. Box 875 • San Bernardino, CA 92402 • (909) 885-2204 • http://ci.san-bernardino.ca.us/about/history/historical_n_pioneer_society.asp

San Bernardino Public Library • 555 W 6th St • San Bernardino, CA 92410-3001 • (909) 381-8226 • http://www.sbpl.org

San Bernardino Public Library-Inghram • 1505 W Highland Ave • San Bernardino, CA 92411 • (909) 887-4494

San Bernardino Valley Genealogical Society • c/o San Bernardino Public Library, P.O. Box 2220 • San Bernardino, CA 92405 • (909) 883-7468 • http://www.sbpl.org/genealogy.html

San Bruno

National Archives & Records Administration-Pacific Region • 1000 Commodore Dr • San Bruno, CA 94066-2350 • (650) 238-3501 • http://www.archives.gov/facilities/ca/san_francisco.html

San Bernardino County Museum • 701 W Angus Ave • San Bruno, CA 94066

San Bruno Public Libr & Local History Room • 701 Angus Ave W • San Bruno, CA 94066-3490 • (650) 616-7078 • http://www.ci.sanbruno.ca.us/library

San Carlos

Croatian Genealogical and Heraldic Society • 2527 San Carlos Ave • San Carlos, CA 94070 • (650) 592-1190 • http://www.croatians.com

Croatian-Serbian-Slovenian Genealogical Society • 2527 San Carlos Ave • San Carlos, CA 94070 • (650) 592-1190

Hiller Aviation Museum • 601 Skyway Rd • San Carlos, CA 94070 • (650) 654-0200 ext. 203 • http://www.hiller.org

San Carlos Historical Museum • 533 Laurel St • San Carlos, CA 94070 • (650) 802-4354 • http://www.sancarloshistorymuseum.org

San Mateo County Library-San Carlos Branch • 610 Elm St • San Carlos, CA 94070 • (650) 591-0341 • http://www.sancarloslibrary.org

San Clemente

Nautical Heritage Society • Historical Museum, 1064 Calle Negocio, Unit B • San Clemente, CA 92673 • (949) 369-6773 • http://www.Californian.org

San Clemente Historical Society • 101 S El Camino Real, P.O. Box 283 • San Clemente, CA 92672 • (949) 492-9684

San Diego

British Isles Genealogical Research Association • P.O. Box 19775 • San Diego, CA 92159-0775 • (858) 679-6756

Cabrillo Historical Association • Cabrillo National Monument, 1800 Cabrillo Memorial, P.O. Box 6670 • San Diego, CA 92106 • (619) 293-5450 • http://www.nps.gov/cabr/

California State Genealogical Alliance - San Diego/Imperial Region • P.O. Box 500407 • San Diego, CA 92150-0407 • (619) 454-7046

Center for San Diego Studies • 2900 Lomaland Dr • San Diego, CA 92106 • (619) 221-2200

Centro de Studios Chicanos Research Center • San Diego State Univ • San Diego, CA 92182 • (619) 286-5145

Computer Genealogy Society of San Diego • P.O. Box 370357 • San Diego, CA 92137-0357 • (935) 656-8525 • http://www.cgssd.org

Distinguished Flying Cross Society • 4442 Vandever Ave • San Diego, CA 92120 • (619) 269-6377

Firehouse Museum • 1572 Columbia St • San Diego, CA 92101 • (619) 232-FIRE

First San Diego Courthouse Museum • 4346 Witherby Street • San Diego, CA 92103 • http://www.sandiegohistory.org/societies/firstcourthouse/

Fort Guijarros Museum • P.O. Box 23130 • San Diego, CA 92194 • (619) 229-0648

George S Patton Jr Historical Society • 3116 Thorn St • San Diego, CA 92104-4618 • (619) 282-4201 • http://www.pattonhq.com

German Research Association • P.O. Box 711600 • San Diego, CA 92111 • (858) 454-7046 • http://feefhs.org/gra/frg-gra.html

Heritage Genealogical Society • 12056 Lomica Dr • San Diego, CA 92128 • (619) 485-6009

Historical Shrine of San Diego County Museum • 2482 San Diego Ave • San Diego, CA 92110 • (619) 297-9327

House of Pacific Relations • Balboa Park • San Diego, CA 92101 • (619) 239-0592

Immigration Museum of New Americans Post WWII Museum • 3232 Dove St • San Diego, CA 92103 • (619) 515-0403 • http://www.immigrationmuseumofnewamericans.org

Jewish Genealogical Society of San Diego • P.O. Box 927089 • San Diego, CA 92192-7089 • (858) 453-8164 • http://www.homestead.com/sdjgs/

Jewish Historical Society of San Diego • Lipinsky Institute for Judaic Studies, San Diego State Univ, 5500 Campanile Dr • San Diego, CA 92182-8148 • (619) 232-5888 • http://www.rohan.sdsu.edu/lipinsky/jhssd_archives.html

Junipero Serra Museum • 2727 Presidio Dr • San Diego, CA 92103 • (619) 297-3258 • http://www.sandiegohistory.org

Los Californianos, Hispanic Ancestors of Alta California • 4530 LaCrosse Ave, P.O. Box 600522 • San Diego, CA 92160-0522 • (805) 525-5958 • http://www.loscalifornianos.org

Machado-Stewart Adobe Museum • Old Town, San Diego State Historic Park • San Diego, CA 92110 • (619) 220-5423 • http://www.mscda.org/museums/california.htm

Marine Corps Recruit Depot Command Museum • MCRD, Building 26 • San Diego, CA 92140 • (619) 524-6038 • http://www.usmchistory.com

Maritime Museum of San Diego • 1492 N Harbor Dr • San Diego, CA 92101 • (619) 234-9153 • http://www.sdmaritime.org

Marston House Museum • 3525 7th Ave • San Diego, CA 92138 • (619) 298-3142 • http://www.sandiegohistory.org

Mission San Diego Historical Society • Diocese of San Diego Mission, 10818 Mission San Diego Rd • San Diego, CA 92108 • (619) 283-6338 • http://www.sandiegohistory.org

Museum of San Diego History and Research • 1649 El Prado, P.O. Box 81825 • San Diego, CA 92138-1825 • (619) 232-6203 • http://www.sandiegohistory.org

National Association Civilian Conservation Corps Alumni, Chapter #55 • 5118 San Aquario Dr • San Diego, CA 92109 • (619) 270-5417

Naval Base Coronado Library • MWR Base Library, 2478 Munda Rd • San Diego, CA 92155-5396 • (619) 437-3026

Old Town San Diego State Historic Park • 9609 Waples St, Ste 200 • San Diego, CA 92110 • (619) 220-5422 • http://parks.ca.gov

Pacific Beach Historical Society • P.O. Box 9200 • San Diego, CA 92169 • (858) 272-6655

Rancho Bernardo Genealogy Group • c/o San Diego Public Library, Rancho Bernardo Branch, 16840 Bernardo Center • San Diego, CA 92128 • (619) 485-6977

Robinson-Rose House Museum • 4002 Wallace St • San Diego, CA 92110 • (619) 220-5422

San Diego Aerospace Museum • 2001 Pan American Plaza • San Diego, CA 92101 • (619) 234-8291 • http://www.aerospacemuseum.org

San Diego African-American Genealogy Research Group • P.O. Box 740240 • San Diego, CA 92174-0240 • (858) 566-7566

San Diego Automotive Museum • 2080 Pan American Plaza • San Diego, CA 92101 • (619) 231-2886 • http://www.sdautomuseum.org

San Diego Civil War Roundtable • P.O. Box 22369 • San Diego, CA 92192 • (619) 672-2593

San Diego County Historical Days Association • 3966 Mason St • San Diego, CA 92110 • (619) 283-1197

San Diego County Library • 5555 Overland Ave • San Diego, CA 92123-1296 • (858) 694-2414 • http://www.sdcl.org

San Diego Electric Railway Association • P.O. Box 89068 • San Diego, CA 92138 • (619) 262-8532 • http://www.sdera.org

San Diego Family History Center • 4195 Camino Del Rio S • San Diego, CA 92108 • (619) 584-7668

San Diego Genealogical Society • 2925 Kalmia St • San Diego, CA 92104 • (619) 284-7017

San Diego Historical Society • Marston House, 1649 El Prado, Balboa Park, P.O. Box 81825 • San Diego, CA 92138-1825 • (619) 232-6203 • http://www.sandiegohistory.org

San Diego Maritime Museum • 1492 North Harbor Dr • San Diego, CA 92101 • (619) 234-9153 • http://www.sdmaritime.com

San Diego Military Heritage Society • P.O. Box 33672 • San Diego, CA 92163

San Diego Model Railroad Museum • 1649 El Prado • San Diego, CA 92101 • (619) 696-0199

San Diego Public Library • 820 E Street • San Diego, CA 92101-6478 • (619) 236-5800 • http://www.sandiego.gov/public-library/

San Diego State University Library • 5500 Campanile Dr • San Diego, CA 92182-8050 • (619) 594-6724 • http://infodome.sdsu.edu

Save Our Heritage Organization • 2476 San Diego Ave • San Diego, CA 92110-2838 • (619) 297-9327 • http://www.sohosandiego.org

Scottish Rite Masonic Library • 1895 Camino del Rios S • San Diego, CA 92108 • (619) 293-4888

Shrine Foundation Historical Society • 2482 San Diego Ave • San Diego, CA 92110

Sierra Museum • 2727 Presidio Dr • San Diego, CA 92103 • (619) 297-3258 • http://www.sandiegohistory.org

Sikes Adobe Farmstead Museum • 12655 Sunset Dr • San Diego, CA 92138 • (760) 737-8620

Society of Acadian Descendants • 2568 Albatross St, Ste 6E • San Diego, CA 92101-1457 • (619) 232-1217

Thomas Whaley House Museum • 2482 San Diego Ave • San Diego, CA 92110 • (619) 298-2482 • http://www.whaleyhouse.org

US Mormon Battalion, California South Division • 2510 Juan St • San Diego, CA 92110 • (619) 298-3317 • http://www.ldssocal.org/ve/mbve.htm

Villa Montezuma Museum • 1925 K Street • San Diego, CA 92102 • (619) 232-6203 • http://www.sandiegohistory.org

Wells Fargo History Museum • 2733 San Diego Ave • San Diego, CA 92110 • (619) 238-3929

William Heath Davis House Museum • 410 Island Ave • San Diego, CA 92101 • (619) 233-4692 • http://www.gaslampquarter.org

San Dimas

County of Los Angeles Public Library-San Dimas Library • 145 N Walnut Ave • San Dimas, CA 91773-2603 • (909) 599-6738 • www.colapublib.org/libs/sandimas/

Life Pacific College Alumni Library • 1100 W Covina Blvd • San Dimas, CA 91773 • (909) 706-3009 • http://www.lifepacific.edu/library.html

San Dimas Historical Society • Historical Museum, 210 E Bonita Ave • San Dimas, CA 91773 • (909) 592-1190

San Fernando

County of Los Angeles Public Library-San Fernando Library • 217 N Maclay Ave • San Fernando, CA 91340-2433 • (818) 365-6928 • www.colapublib.org/libs/sanfernando/

Lopez Adobe Museum • 1100 Pico St • San Fernando, CA 91340 • (818) 365-7810

San Francisco

Alcatraz Island Museum • Pier 41 • San Francisco, CA 94123 • (415) 556-0560 • http://www.nps.gov/alcatraz

American Russian History Society • 1272 47th Ave • San Francisco, CA 94107

California

Balkan and Eastern European American Genealogical and Historical Society • 4843 Mission St • San Francisco, CA 94112

California Genealogical Society • 300 Brannan St #409, P.O. Box 77105 • San Francisco, CA 94107-0105 • (415) 777-9936 • http://members.aol.com/calgensoc/home/home.htm

California Heritage Council • 41 Sutter St, Ste 422, P.O. Box 475046 • San Francisco, CA 94147 • (415) 981-4860

California Historical Society • Historical Museum, 678 Mission St • San Francisco, CA 94105 • (415) 567-1848 • http://www.californiahistoricalsociety.org

California Society of Colonial Pioneers • 456 McAlister St • San Francisco, CA 94102

California State Library, Sutro Branch • Genealogical Collection, 480 Winston Dr • San Francisco, CA 94132-1777 • (415) 731-4477 • http://www.library.ca.gov

Chinese Cultural Center of San Francisco • 750 Kearny St, 3rd Fl • San Francisco, CA 94108 • (415) 986-1822 • http://www.c-c-c.org

Chinese Historical Society of America • 965 Clay St • San Francisco, CA 94111 • (415) 391-1188 • http://www.chsa.org

Fort Point and Army Museum Association • Presidio, P.O. Box 29333 • San Francisco, CA 94129-0333 • (415) 556-1693 • http://www.nps.gov/fopo/

Fort Point and Presidio Historical Association • Presidio Bldg T3, Funston Ave P.O. Box 29163 • San Francisco, CA 94129 • (415) 921-8193 • http://www.nps.gov/fopo

Golden Gate Genealogy Society • 236 W Portal Ave #210 • San Francisco, CA 94127-1423 • (650) 997-3311

Golden Gate Railroad Museum • Hunters Point Shipyard, P.O. Box 881686 • San Francisco, CA 94188 • (415) 822-8728 • http://www.ggrm.org

Grand Lodge of California, Sons of Italy • 5051 Mission St • San Francisco, CA 94112-3473 • (415) 586-1316 • http://www.sonsofitalyca.org

Haas-Lilienthal House Museum • 2007 Franklin St • San Francisco, CA 94109 • (415) 441-3000 • http://www.sfheritage.org

Henry Wilson Coil Library & Museum • Grand Lodge Free & Accepted Masons of California, 1111 California St • San Francisco, CA 94108 • (415) 776-7000 • http://www.freemason.org

Holocaust Center of Northern California Library • 601 14th Ave • San Francisco, CA 94118 • (415) 751-6040 • http://www.holocaust.sf.org

Institute for Historical Studies • 1791-A Pine St • San Francisco, CA 94109 • (415) 441-3759

Institute for Masonic Studies Library and Museum • 1111 California St • San Francisco, CA 94108 • (415) 776-7000

International Museum of Women • 101 Howard St #480, P.O. Box 642370 • San Francisco, CA 94164 • (415) 543-4669 • http://www.imow.org

Irish Cultural Center Library • 2700 45th St • San Francisco, CA 94116-2696 • (415) 661-2700 • http://www.irishcentersf.org

Japanese American History Museum • 1840 Sutter St • San Francisco, CA 94115 • (415) 776-0661 • http://www.amacord.com/fillmore/museum/jt/jaha/jaha.html

Jewish Community Library • 1835 Ellis St • San Francisco, CA 94115 • (415) 567-3327 • http://www.bjesf.org

Jewish Museum San Francisco • 166 Geary St, Suite 1500 • San Francisco, CA 94108 • (415) 591-8800 • http://www.jewishmuseumsf.org

Kalmanovitz Library • Univ of California, San Francisco, 530 Parnassus Ave • San Francisco, CA 94143 • (415) 476-2334 • http://www.library.ucsf.edu/collres/archives

Legion of Honor • 100 34th Ave • San Francisco, CA 94121 • (415) 750-3502 • http://www.famsf.org/legion/

Levi Strauss & Co Museum • 250 Valencia St • San Francisco, CA 94103 • (415) 565-9159

Los Californianos • P.O. Box 5155 • San Francisco, CA 94101

Masonic Grand Lodge of California • Henry Wilson Coil Library & Museum, 1111 California St • San Francisco, CA 94108 • (415) 776-7000 • http://www.freemason.org

Mechanics' Institute • 57 Post St • San Francisco, CA 94104 • (415) 393-0101 • http://www.milibrary.org

Mission Dolores Museum • 3321 16th St • San Francisco, CA 94114 • (415) 621-8203 • http://www.graphicmode.com/missiondolores/

Musee Mechanique • 1090 Point Lobos Ave • San Francisco, CA 94121 • (415) 386-1170

Museo ItaloAmericano • Fort Mason Center, Bldg C • San Francisco, CA 94123 • (415) 673-2200 • http://www.museoitalamericano.org

Museum of Russian Culture • 2450 Sutter St • San Francisco, CA 94115 • (415) 921-4082 • http://www.russiancentersf.com

Museum of the City of San Francisco • 945 Taraval St • San Francisco, CA 94116 • (415) 928-0289 • http://www.sfmuseum.org

Museum of Vision • 655 Beach St • San Francisco, CA 94109 • (415) 561-8500 • http://www.museumofvision.org

National Japanese American Historical Society • 1684 Post St • San Francisco, CA 94115 • (415) 921-5007 • http://www.nikkeiheritage.org

National Liberty Ship Memorial • SS Jeremiah O'Brien, Pier 45 • San Francisco, CA 94111 • (415) 544-0100 • http://www.ssjeremiahobrien.org

National Trust for Historic Preservation, Western Regional Office • 1 Sutter St • San Francisco, CA 94111-4803 • (415) 956-0610 • http://www.nthp.org

Native Daughters of the Golden West Society • 543 Baker St • San Francisco, CA 94117-1405 • (415) 563-9091 • http://www.ndgw.org

Native Sons of the Golden West, Grand Parlor • 414 Mason St, Ste 300 • San Francisco, CA 94102 • (415) 392-1223 • http://www.nsgw.org

North Beach Museum • 1429 Stockton St • San Francisco, CA 94133 • (415) 626-7070 • http://www.sfnorthbeach.com/nbmus.html

Octagon House Museum • 2645 Gough St • San Francisco, CA 94123 • (415) 441-7512

Pacific Heritage Museum • 608 Commercial St • San Francisco, CA 94111 • (415) 399-1124 • http://www.sfstation.com/museums/pacific.htm

Presidio Army Museum • William Penn Mott Jr. Visitor Center, Bldg 102, Montgomery St • San Francisco, CA 94129 • (415) 556-0560 • http://www.nps.gov/prsf/

San Francisco African-American Historical and Cultural Society • Fort Mason Center, 1857 Fulton St • San Francisco, CA 94102 • (415) 292-6172 • http://fortmason.org/museums/

San Francisco Bay Area Jewish Genealogical Society • P.O. Box 318214 • San Francisco, CA 94131 • (415) 921-6761 • http://www.jewishgen.org/sfbajgs/

San Francisco Cable Car Museum • 1201 Mason St • San Francisco, CA 94108 • (415) 474-1887 • http://www.cablecarmuseum.com

San Francisco Fire Department Museum • 67 Cityview Wy • San Francisco, CA 94131 • (415) 861-8000 • http://www.sffiremuseum.org

San Francisco Historical Society • Historical Museum, 88 5th St, P.O. Box 420569 • San Francisco, CA 94142 • (415) 775-1111 • http://www.sfhistory.org

San Francisco History Association • 2269 Chestnut #209 • San Francisco, CA 94123 • (415) 750-9986 • http://www.sanfranciscohistory.org

San Francisco Maritime National Historical Park • Fort Mason Center, Bldg E 900, Beach St, P.O. Box 470310 • San Francisco, CA 94147-0310 • (415) 556-9870 • http://www.maritime.org

San Francisco Public Library • 100 Larkin St • San Francisco, CA 94102-4733 • (415) 557-4596 • http://www.sfpl.org

San Francisco State University Library • 480 Winston Dr • San Francisco, CA 94132 • (415) 564-4010 • http://www.sfsu.edu

San Francisco's Gold Rush Trail Foundation • 57 Post St • San Francisco, CA 94104 • (415) 981-4849 • http://www.goldrushtrail.org

San Francisco's Architectural Heritage • 2007 Franklin St • San Francisco, CA 94109 • (415) 441-3000 • http://www.sfheritage.org

Society of California Pioneers • Historical Museum, 300 4th St • San Francisco, CA 94107-1272 • (415) 957-1849 • http://www.californiapioneers.org

Telephone Pioneer Communications Museum • 1515 19th Ave • San Francisco, CA 94122 • (415) 542-1570

Treasure Island Museum • 410 Palm Ave, Treasure Island • San Francisco, CA 94130 • (415) 928-6245 • http://www.dictyon.com/treasure

United States Lighthouse Society • 244 Kearny St, Flr 5 • San Francisco, CA 94108-4507 • (415) 362-7255

US District Court for the Northern District of California Historical Society • P.O. Box 36112 • San Francisco, CA 94102 • (415) 555-3488

Victorian Alliance • 824 Grove St • San Francisco, CA 94117 • (415) 826-1437 • http://www.victorianalliance.org

Wells Fargo History Museum • 420 Montgomery, 2nd flr • San Francisco, CA 94163 • (415) 396-2619 • http://www.wellsfargohistory.com/home/

San Gabriel

County of Los Angeles Public Library-San Gabriel Library • 500 S Del Mar Ave • San Gabriel, CA 91776-2408 • (626) 287-0761 • www.colapublib.org/libs/sangabriel/

Gabrielino-Tongva Tribal Council • P.O. Box 693 • San Gabriel, CA 91776 • (626) 286-1632 • http://www.tongva.com

Mount Lowe Preservation Society • P. O. Box 431 • San Gabriel, CA 91778-0431 • (626) 319-7224 • http://www.mountlowe.org

San Gabriel Historical Association • 546 W Broadway • San Gabriel, CA 91776 • (626) 309-3223

San Gabriel Mission Museum • 428 S Mission Dr • San Gabriel, CA 91776 • (626) 457-3035 • http://www.sangabrielmission.org

San Jacinto

San Jacinto Museum • 150 1/2 Dillon Dr • San Jacinto, CA 92581 • (909) 654-4952 • http://www.ci.san-jacinto.ca.us

San Jacinto Valley Museum Association • Historical Museum, 181 E Main St, P.O. Box 922 • San Jacinto, CA 92581 • (909) 654-4952 • http://www.ci.san-jacinto.ca.us/Museum.htm

Soboba Band of Mission Indians - Luiseno • 43750 Castile Cnyn Rd, P.O. Box 487 • San Jacinto, CA 92583 • (951) 654-8762

San Jose

Ancient Mystic Order Rosae Crucis • North American-English Grand Lodge, 1342 Naglee Ave • San Jose, CA 95191 • (408) 947-3600 • http://www.rusicrucian.org

Argonauts Historical Society • 612 Morse St • San Jose, CA 95126

Black Historical Society of Santa Clara • 468 N 11th St • San Jose, CA 95112 • (408) 295-9183

California Pioneers of Santa Clara County • 661 Empey Way, P.O. Box 8208 • San Jose, CA 95155 • (408) 998-1174

East Santa Clara Street Revitalization Committee • 72 N 5th St • San Jose, CA 95112 • (408) 993-0430

Evergreen Heritage Association • 4520 Cadwallader • San Jose, CA 95121 • (408) 238-8912

Finnish-American Society of Santa Clara County • 876 Hummingbird Dr • San Jose, CA 95125-2918 • (408) 558-9493

Hispanic Genealogical Society • 2175 The Alameda • San Jose, CA 95126-1151 • (408) 243-5287

History San Jose • Historical Museum & Archives, 1650 Senter Rd • San Jose, CA 95112 • (408) 287-2290 • http://www.historysanjose.org

Japanese American Resource Center • 565 N 5th St • San Jose, CA 95112 • (213) 830-5605 • http://www.jarc-m.org

King Library • San Jose State University, 1 Washington Sq • San Jose, CA 95192-0028 • (408) 808-2100 • http://www.sjlibrary.org

Los Fundadores-Founders and Friends of Santa Clara County • 1053 S White Rd • San Jose, CA 95127 • (408) 926-1165

Military Medal Museum and Research Center • 448 N San Pedro St • San Jose, CA 95110 • (408) 298-1100

Mount Diablo Surveyors Historical Society • 5042 Amethyst Ct • San Jose, CA 95136 • (408) 265-9869 • http://www.mdshs.org

Muwekma Ohlone Tribe • 226 Airport Pkwy, Ste 630 • San Jose, CA 95110-1029 • (408) 441-6473 • http://www.muwekma.org

New Almaden Quicksilver Mining Museum • 21350 Almaden Rd • San Jose, CA 95120 • (408) 323-1107 • http://www.parkhere.org/historical/history_almaden.html

Peralta Adobe & Fallon House Museum • 175 W Saint John St • San Jose, CA 95110 • (408) 993-8182 • http://www.historysanjose.org

Portuguese Heritage Society of California • Portuguese Historical Museum, P.O. Box 18277 • San Jose, CA 95158 • (650) 964-0406 • http://www.portuguesemuseum.org

Portuguese Historical Museum • 1650 Senter Rd • San Jose, CA 95112

Preservation Action Council of San Jose • P.O. Box 2287 • San Jose, CA 95109 • http://www.preservation.org

Salinan Nation • P.O. Box 610546 • San Jose, CA 94521 • (916) 458-4551

San Jose Historical Landmarks Commission • 400 City Hall Annex, 801 N 1st St • San Jose, CA 95110 • (408) 277-4576 • http://www.ci.san-jose.ca.us/planning/sjplan/histpro.htm

San Jose Historical Museum Association • Chinese Historical & Cultural Project Museum, Kelley Park, 1600 Senter Rd • San Jose, CA 95112 • (408) 287-2290 • http://www.historysanjose.org

San Jose Museum of Quilts and Textiles • 110 Paseo de San Antonio • San Jose, CA 95112 • (408) 971-0323 • http://www.sjquiltmuseum.org

Santa Clara County Archives • 1874 Senter Rd • San Jose, CA 95112 • (408) 792-1895 • http://www.sccgov.org

Santa Clara County Historical Heritage Commission • County Government Center, 70 W Hedding St, 10th Fl • San Jose, CA 95110 • (408) 299-2566

Santa Clara County Historical Pharmacy Association • 5080 Edenview Dr • San Jose, CA 95111

California

San Jose, cont.

Silicon Valley PAF Users Group • P.O. Box 23670 • San Jose, CA 95153-3670 • (650) 948-0477 • http://www.svpafug.org

Sourisseau Academy for State & Local History Archives • San Jose State University, Wahlquist Library North 606 • San Jose, CA 95192 • (408) 924-6510 • http://www.sjsu.edu/depts/history/resource/sourisseau.htm

Victorian Preservation Society of Santa Clara Valley • 792 S 3rd St • San Jose, CA 95112 • (415) 274-2864 • http://www.vpa.org

Winchester Mystery House Museum • 525 S Winchester Blvd • San Jose, CA 95128 • (408) 247-2000

San Juan

City of San Juan Capistrano Cultural Heritage Commission • 32400 Paseo Adelanto • San Juan, CA 92675 • (714) 493-1171 ext.222 • http://www.sanjuancapistrano.org/planning_dept.html

San Juan Bautista

Mission San Juan Bautista Museum • 2nd & Mariposa Sts, P.O. Box 400 • San Juan Bautista, CA 95045 • (408) 623-2127 • http://www.oldmission-sjb.org

San Juan Bautista Historical Society • 308 3rd St, P.O. Box 1 • San Juan Bautista, CA 95045 • (831) 623-4542 • http://archaeology.csumb.edu/sjbhs/

San Juan State Historic Park • Castro-Breen Adobe, 19 Franklin St • San Juan Bautista, CA 95045 • (408) 623-4881 • http://www.parks.ca.gov

San Juan Capistrano

Capistrano Indian Council • P.O. Box 304 • San Juan Capistrano, CA 92693 • (714) 443-4775 • http://www.santaanahistory.com/articles/ochistorgs.html

Juaneno Band of Mission Indians • 31411A La Matanza St • San Juan Capistrano, CA 92675 • (949) 488-3484 • http://www.juanano.com

Mission San Juan Capistrano Museum • 31522 Camino Capistrano, P.O. Box 697 • San Juan Capistrano, CA 92693 • (949) 234-1300 • http://www.missionsjc.com

Orange County-San Juan Capistrano Regional Library • 31495 El Camino Real • San Juan Capistrano, CA 92675-2600 • (949) 493-1752

San Juan Capistrano Historical Society • O'Neill Museum, 31831 Los Rios St, P.O. Box 81 • San Juan Capistrano, CA 92675 • (949) 493-8444 • http://www.sjchistoricalsociety.com

San Leandro

Basin Research Associates, Inc. • 1933 Davis St • San Leandro, CA 94577 • (510) 430-8441

Portuguese Library • 1120 E 14th St • San Leandro, CA 94577

San Leandro Historical Commission • 300 Estudillo Ave • San Leandro, CA 94577 • (510) 577-3971 • http://www.ci.san-leandro.ca.us/sllibrarylocations.html

San Leandro Historical Railway Society • 1302 Orchard Ave • San Leandro, CA 94577 • (510) 569-2490

San Leandro Historical Society • 1322 E 14th St, P.O. Box 1046 • San Leandro, CA 94577 • (510) 351-0904

San Leandro Public Library • 300 Estudillo Ave • San Leandro, CA 94577 • (510) 577-3970 • http://www.sanleandrolibrary.org

San Lorenzo

Alameda County Library-San Lorenzo Branch • 395 Paseo Grande • San Lorenzo, CA 94580-2491 • (510) 670-6283

Hayward Area Genealogical Society • c/o Alameda County Library, 395 Paseo Grande • San Lorenzo, CA 94538

San Luis Obispo

Camp San Luis Obispo Museum • 10 Sonoma Ave, Bldg 885 • San Luis Obispo, CA 93405 • (805) 594-6517 • http://www.militarymuseum.org

Dallidet Adobe and Gardens Museum • 1185 Pacific St • San Luis Obispo, CA 93401 • (805) 543-6762 • http://www.slochs.org/dallidet/main.html

Hollister Adobe Museum • Cuesta College • San Luis Obispo, CA 93406 • (805) 543-7831 • http://www.cuesta.cc.ca.us/maps/map76.htm

Old Mission San Luis Obispo de Tolosa Museum • 751 Palm St, P.O. Box 1483 • San Luis Obispo, CA 93406 • (805) 543-6850 • http://www.thegrid.net/slomission

Paulding History House Museum • 551 Crown Hill Rd, P.O. Box 1391 • San Luis Obispo, CA 93401 • (805) 473-3231 • http://www.southcountyhistory.org/pauldinghouse.html

Robert E Kennedy Library • California Polytechnic State University, 1 Grand Ave • San Luis Obispo, CA 93407 • (805) 756-2345 • http://www.lib.calpoly.edu

San Luis Obispo City-County Library • 995 Palm St, P.O. Box 8107 • San Luis Obispo, CA 93403-8107 • (805) 781-5784 • http://www.slolibrary.org

San Luis Obispo County Genealogical Society • 1288 Morro St • San Luis Obispo, CA 93401 • (805) 785-0383

San Luis Obispo County Historical Museum • 696 Monterey St, P.O. Box 1391 • San Luis Obispo, CA 93406 • (805) 543-0638 • http://www.caohwy.com/y/ysanlcom.htm

San Luis Obispo County Historical Society • 696 Monterey St, P.O. Box 1391 • San Luis Obispo, CA 93406-1391 • (805) 543-0638 • http://www.slochs.org

San Marcos

Palomar College Library • 1140 W Mission Rd • San Marcos, CA 92069-1487 • (760) 744-1150 • http://www.palomar.edu/library

San Marcos Historical Society • Historical Museum, 270 W San Marcos Blvd • San Marcos, CA 92069 • (760) 744-9025

San Marino

El Molino Viejo Museum • 1120 Old Mill Rd • San Marino, CA 91108 • (626) 449-5450 • http://www.oldmill.info

Huntington Library • 1151 Oxford Rd • San Marino, CA 91108 • (626) 405-2191 • http://www.huntington.org

Old Mill Museum • 1120 Old Mill Rd • San Marino, CA 91108 • (626) 449-5458 • http://www.old-mill.org

Pacific Railroad Society • P.O. Box 80726 • San Marino, CA 91118 • (818) 793-5290 • http://www.wprrhs.org

San Marino Historical Society • 2701 Huntington Dr, P.O. Box 80222 • San Marino, CA 91118-8222 • (626) 796-6023 • http://www.smnet.org/comm_group/historical/

San Marino Public Library • 1890 Huntington Dr • San Marino, CA 91108-2595 • (626) 300-0777

Westerners International, Huntington Corral • P.O. Box 80241 • San Marino, CA 91108 • (626) 284-2130

San Martin

Wings of History Air Museum • 12777 Murphy Ave, P.O. Box 495 • San Martin, CA 95046 • (408) 683-2290 • http://www.wingsofhistory.org

San Mateo

Coyote Point Museum • 1651 Coyote Point Dr • San Mateo, CA 94401 • (650) 342-7755 • http://www.coyoteptmuseum.org

San Mateo County Genealogical Society • 25 Tower Rd, P.O. Box 5083 • San Mateo, CA 94402 • (650) 572-2929 • http://www.smcgs.org

San Mateo County Historical Association • San Mateo Junior College Historical Museum, 1700 W Hillsdale Blvd • San Mateo, CA 94402 • (650) 574-6441 • http://www.sanmateocountyhistory.com

San Mateo County Library • 25 Tower Rd • San Mateo, CA 94402-4000 • (650) 312-5258 • http://www.smcl.org

San Mateo Public Library • 55 W 3rd Ave • San Mateo, CA 94402 • (650) 522-7818 • http://www.smplibrary.org

San Miguel
Camp Roberts History Museum • Camp Roberts • San Miguel, CA 93451 • (805) 238-8212 • http://www.militarymuseum.org/others.html

Friends of the Adobes • Rios Caladonia Adobe, P.O. Box 326 • San Miguel, CA 93451 • (805) 467-3357

Mission San Miguel • Historical Museum, 775 Mission St, P.O. Box 69 • San Miguel, CA 93451 • (805) 467-3256 • http://www.missionsanmiguel.org

Rios-Caledonia Adobe Museum • 700 S Mission St • San Miguel, CA 93451 • (805) 467-3537

San Pablo
Blume House Museum • San Pablo Ave & Church Ln • San Pablo, CA 94806 • (510) 215-3092 • http://www.ci-san-pablo.ca.us/main/museum.htm

San Pablo Historical and Museum Society • Alvarado Adobe Museum, 1 Alvarado Sq • San Pablo, CA 94806 • (510) 215-3046 • http://www.ci.san-pablo.ca.us/history/

San Pedro
Fort MacArthur Museum • 3601 S Gaffey St, P.O. Box 268 • San Pedro, CA 90731 • (310) 548-2631 • http://www.ftmac.org

Los Angeles Maritime Museum • Berth 84, end of 6th St • San Pedro, CA 90731 • (310) 658-7618 • http://www.lamaritimemuseum.org

Muller House Museum • 1542 S Beacon St • San Pedro, CA 90731 • (310) 831-1788 • http://www.sanpedrochamber.com

Point Fermin Lighthouse Museum • 807 W Paseo del Mar • San Pedro, CA 90731 • (310) 241-0684 • http://www.pointferminlighthouse.org

San Pedro Bay Historical Society • Muller House, 1542 S Beacon St, P.O. Box 1568 • San Pedro, CA 90731 • (310) 831-1788

SS Lane Victory Memorial Museum • Berth 94 • San Pedro, CA 90733 • (310) 519-9545 • http://www.LaneVictory.org

San Rafael
Blitz Information Center • 907 Mission Ave • San Rafael, CA 94901 • (415) 453-3579 • http://feefhs.org/blitz/frgblitz.html

China Camp State Park • Route 1, Box 244 • San Rafael, CA 94901 • (415) 456-0766 • http://parks.ca.gov

Falkirk Community Cultural Center • Robert Dollar Estate, 1408 Mission St, P.O. Box 60 • San Rafael, CA 94915 • (415) 485-3328 • http://www.falkirkculturalcenter.org

Marin County Free Library • 3501 Civic Center Dr • San Rafael, CA 94903-4177 • (415) 499-3220 • http://www.marinlibrary.org

Marin County Historical Society • Historical Museum, 1125 B Street • San Rafael, CA 94901 • (415) 454-8538 • http://www.marinhistory.org

Marin Heritage • P.O. Box 1432 • San Rafael, CA 94902 • (415) 454-2168

Mission San Rafael Arcangel Museum • 1104 5th Ave • San Rafael, CA 94901 • (415) 454-8141 • http://www.missiontour.org

Russian-Baltic Information Center • 907 Mission Ave • San Rafael, CA 94901 • (415) 453-3579 • http://feefhs.org/blitz/frgblitz.html

San Rafael Public Library • 1100 E Street • San Rafael, CA 94901-1900 • (415) 485-3321 • http://www.cityofsanrafael.org/Government/Library.htm

San Simeon
Friends of Hearst Castle • P.O. Box 32 • San Simeon, CA 93452 • (805) 543-6206 • http://www.friendsofhearstcastle.org

Hearst San Simeon State Historical Monument Staff Library • 750 Hearst Castle Rd • San Simeon, CA 93452-9741 • (800) 444-4445 • http://www.hearstcastle.org

Sanger
Traditional Choinumni Tribe • 2787 N Piedra Rd • Sanger, CA 93657 • (209) 787-2434

Santa Ana
American Aviation Historical Society • 2333 Otis St • Santa Ana, CA 92704 • (714) 549-4818 • http://aahs-online.org

California Association of Museums • Bowers Museum of Cultural Art, 2002 N Main St • Santa Ana, CA 92706 • (714) 567-3645 • http://www.calmuseums.net

Charles W Bowers Museum • 2002 N Main • Santa Ana, CA 92706 • (714) 567-3600 • http://www.bowers.org

Dr Howe Medical Museum • 120 Civic Center Dr • Santa Ana, CA 92701 • (714) 547-9645 • http://www.santaanahistory.com/house.html

First American Title Insurance Historical Photographic Library • 1 First American Wy • Santa Ana, CA 92707 • (714) 250-3298 • http://www.museumsusa.org/data/museums/CA/10224.htm

Heritage Orange County • 515 N Main St • Santa Ana, CA 92701 • (714) 835-7287

Juaneno Band of Mission Indians • P.O. Box 25628 • Santa Ana, CA 92799 • (714) 639-9164 • http://www.juanenoindians.com

Lyon Air Museum • 19300 Ike Jones Rd • Santa Ana, CA 92707 • (714) 210-4585 • http://www.lyonairmuseum.org

Old Courthouse Museum • 211 W Santa Ana Blvd, P.O. Box 4048 • Santa Ana, CA 92702 • (714) 834-3703 • http://www.ocparks.com

Old Courthouse Museum Society • Old Orange County Courthouse Museum, 211 W Santa Anna Blvd • Santa Ana, CA 92701 • (714) 834-3703

Orange County Historical Commission • 211 W Santa Ana Blvd, P.O. Box 4048 • Santa Ana, CA 91702-4048 • (714) 834-5560 • http://ohp.fullerton.edu/OChistoricalagencie.html

Orange County Historical Society • Dr Howe-Waffle Victorian House, 120 Civic Center Dr W, P.O. Box 10984 • Santa Ana, CA 92711 • (714) 547-9645 • http://www.orangecountyhistory.org

Orange County Pioneer Council • 2320 N Towner St • Santa Ana, CA 92706 • (714) 543-8282 • http://www.santaanahistory.com/articles/ochs.html

Orange County Public Library • 1501 E Saint Andrew Pl • Santa Ana, CA 92705-4048 • (714) 566-3000 • http://www.ocpl.org

Santa Ana Historical Preservation Society • 120 Civic Center Dr W • Santa Ana, CA 92701 • (714) 547-9645 • http://www.santaanahistory.com

Santa Ana Historical Society • 120 Civic Center Dr W • Santa Ana, CA 92701-7505 • (714) 547-9645

Santa Ana Public Library • 26 Civic Center Plaza • Santa Ana, CA 92701-4010 • (714) 647-5280 • http://www.ci.santa-ana.ca.us/library/

Santa Barbara
Carriage and Western Arts Museum • 129 Castillo St • Santa Barbara, CA 93101 • (805) 962-2353 • http://www.carriagemuseum.org

Casa del Herrero Foundation • 1387 E Valley Rd • Santa Barbara, CA 93108 • (805) 565-5653 • http://www.casadelherrero.com

California

Santa Barbara, cont.

Casa Del Herrero Museum • 1387 E Valley Rd • Santa Barbara, CA 93108 • (805) 565-5653

Donald C Davidson Library • Special Collections, Univ of California-Santa Barbara • Santa Barbara, CA 93106 • (805) 893-3062 • http://www.library.ucsb.edu/speccoll/index.html

La Casa de la Guerra Museum • 15 E de la Guerra St, P.O. Box 388 • Santa Barbara, CA 93102 • (805) 966-9179

Legion of Valor of the United States of America • 4706 Calle Reina • Santa Barbara, CA 93110-2018 • (919) 933-0989 • http://www.legionofvalor.com

Presidio State Historic Park • 123 E Canon Perdido St • Santa Barbara, CA 93101 • (805) 966-9719

Santa Barbara County Genealogical Society • Sahyun Library, 316 Castillo St, P.O. Box 1303 • Santa Barbara, CA 93116-1303 • (805) 884-9909 • http://www.sbgen.org

Santa Barbara Courthouse Museum • 1100 Anacapa St • Santa Barbara, CA 93101 • (805) 962-6464

Santa Barbara Historical Society • Historical Museum, 136 E De la Guerra St, P.O. Box 578 • Santa Barbara, CA 93102 • (805) 966-1601 • http://www.santabarbaramuseum.com

Santa Barbara Maritime Museum • 113 Harbor Wy, Ste 190 • Santa Barbara, CA 93109 • (805) 962-8404 • http://www.sbmm.org

Santa Barbara Mission Museum • Old Mission, 2201 Laguna St • Santa Barbara, CA 93105 • (805) 682-4713 • http://www.sbmission.org

Santa Barbara Orchid Estate Museum • 1250 Orchid Dr • Santa Barbara, CA 93111 • (805) 967-1284

Santa Barbara Public Library • 40 E Anapamu Dr, P.O. Box 1019 • Santa Barbara, CA 93102-1019 • (805) 564-5630 • http://www.sbplibrary.org

Santa Barbara Trust for Historic Preservation • 123 E Canon Perdido St, P.O. Box 388 • Santa Barbara, CA 93102 • (805) 965-0093 • http://www.sbthp.org

Susan Quinlan Doll and Teddy Bear Museum • 122 W Canon Perdido St, P.O. Box 3218 • Santa Barbara, CA 93130 • (805) 730-1705 • http://www.quinlanmuseum.com

University of California-Santa Barbara Library • Public History Information Unit • Santa Barbara, CA 93106 • (805) 893-3133 • http://www.library.ucsb.edu

Santa Clara

De Saisset Museum • Santa Clara University, 500 El Camino Real • Santa Clara, CA 95053 • (408) 554-4528 • http://www.scu.edu/deSaisset/

Harris-Lass House Museum • 1889 Market St, P.O. Box 3311 • Santa Clara, CA 95055 • (408) 249-7905

Mission Santa Clara de Asis Museum • Santa Clara Univ • Santa Clara, CA 95053 • (408) 554-4023 • http://www.missiontour.org

Santa Clara Arts and Historical Consortium • Headen-Inman House, 1509 Warburton Ave • Santa Clara, CA 95050 • (408) 248-ARTS • http://santaclaraca.gov/index.aspx?page=1159

Santa Clara County Historical and Genealogical Society • c/o Santa Clara Public Library, 2635 Homestead Rd • Santa Clara, CA 95051-5387 • (408) 248-8205 • http://www.katpher.com/sclarcty/sclarcty.htm

Santa Clara County Historical and Genealogical Society • c/o Santa Clara Central Library, 2635 Homestead Rd • Santa Clara, CA 95051-5387 • (408) 615-2900 • http://www.library.ci.santa-clara.ca.us

Santa Clara Historical Landmarks Commission • 473 Fulton Ct • Santa Clara, CA 95051 • (408) 984-3140 • http://cho.ci.santa-clara.ca.us/3074.html

Santa Clara Public Library • 2635 Homestead Rd • Santa Clara, CA 95051 • (408) 615-2900 • http://www.library.ci.santa-clara.ca.us

South Bay Historical Railroad Society • 1005 Railroad Ave • Santa Clara, CA 95050 • (408) 243-3969 • http://www.sbhrs.org

Triton Museum • 1505 Warburton Ave • Santa Clara, CA 95050 • (408) 247-3754 • http://www.tritonmuseum.org

Santa Clarita

French-Canadian Heritage Society of California • 22023 W Sunrise View Pl • Santa Clarita, CA 91310 • (661) 296-8740 • http://www.scgsgenealogy.com/FC-meetings.htm

International Society of Genetic Genealogy • 22023 W Sunrise View Pl • Santa Clarita, CA 91390 • (661) 296-8740 • http://www.isogg.org

Santa Cruz

Genealogical Library of Santa Cruz • 809 Center St • Santa Cruz, CA 95060 • (831) 420-5000

Genealogical Society of Santa Cruz County • c/o Santa Cruz Public Library, 224 Church St, P.O. Box 72 • Santa Cruz, CA 95063 • (831) 420-5000 • http://www.cagenweb.com/santacruz/

Lighthouse Surfing Museum • 1305 E Cliff Dr • Santa Cruz, CA 95062 • (831) 429-3429

McHenry Library • Univ of California at Santa Cruz • Santa Cruz, CA 95064 • (831) 459-2076 • http://library.ucsc.edu

Mission Santa Cruz Museum • Mission Plaza, 126 High St • Santa Cruz, CA 95060 • (831) 426-5686 • http://www.missiontour.org

Museum of Art and History • 705 Front St • Santa Cruz, CA 95060 • (831) 429-1964 • http://www.santacruzmah.org

National Civil War Association • P.O. Box 2201 • Santa Cruz, CA 95063-1862 • (831) 425-7041

Santa Cruz City-County Library System • 1543 Pacific Ave • Santa Cruz, CA 95060-3873 • (831) 429-3526

Santa Cruz City-County Library-Central • 224 Church St • Santa Cruz, CA 95060-3873 • (831) 420-5700 • http://www.santacruzpl.org/history

Santa Cruz County Historical Museum • 118 Cooper St • Santa Cruz, CA 95060 • (831) 425-2540

Santa Cruz Historical Society • McPherson Center, 705 Front St, P.O. Box 246 • Santa Cruz, CA 95061 • (831) 429-1964 • http://www.santacruzmah.org

Santa Cruz Mission State Historic Park • 144 School St • Santa Cruz, CA 95060-3726 • (831) 425-5849 • http://cal-parks.ca.gov

Shadows of the Past • P.O. Box 2201 • Santa Cruz, CA 95063

Santa Fe Springs

Genealogical Society of Hispanic America, Southern California • P.O. Box 2472 • Santa Fe Springs, CA 90670-0472 • (310) 214-8592 • http://www.gsha.net/sc/

Hathaway Ranch Museum • 11901 E Florence Ave • Santa Fe Springs, CA 90670 • (562) 777-3444

Heritage Park Museum • 12100 Mora Dr • Santa Fe Springs, CA 90670 • (562) 946-6476 • http://www.santafesprings.org/hpark.htm

Santa Fe Springs City Library • 11700 E Telegraph Rd • Santa Fe Springs, CA 90670-3600 • (562) 868-7738 • http://www.santafesprings.org/library.htm

Santa Fe Springs Historical Committee • c/o Santa Springs Public Library, 11710 Telegraph Rd • Santa Fe Springs, CA 90670 • (562) 864-4538 • http://www.santafesprings.org/library.htm

Santa Maria

Santa Maria Museum of Flight • 3015 Airpark Dr • Santa Maria, CA 93455 • (805) 922-8758 • http://www.smmof.org

Santa Maria Public Library • 420 S Broadway • Santa Maria, CA 93454 • (805) 925-0951 • http://www.ci.santa-maria.ca.us/library

Santa Maria Valley Genealogical Society • P.O. Box 1215 • Santa Maria, CA 93456-1215 • (805) 925-4093

Santa Maria Valley Historical Society • Historical Museum, 616 S Broadway, P.O. Box 584 • Santa Maria, CA 93454 • (805) 922-3130

Santa Monica
Angels Attic Museum • 516 Colorado Ave • Santa Monica, CA 90401 • (310) 394-8331 • http://www.angelsattic.com

California Heritage Museum • 2612 Main St • Santa Monica, CA 90405 • (310) 392-8537 • http://www.californiaheritagemuseum.org

La Senora Research Institute • Historical Museum, 560 E Channel Rd • Santa Monica, CA 90402 • (310) 454-0706 • http://www.lasenora.org

Museum of Flying • 2772 Donald Douglas Loop N • Santa Monica, CA 90405 • (310) 392-8822 • http://www..museumofflying.com

Santa Monica Heritage Museum • 2612 Main St • Santa Monica, CA 90405 • (310) 392-8537 • http://www.artcom.com/museums/nv/sz/90405-40.htm

Santa Monica Historical Society • Historical Museum, 1539 Euclid, P.O. Box 3059, Will Rogers Sta • Santa Monica, CA 90403 • (310) 395-2290 • http://www.santamonicahistory.org

Santa Monica Public Library • 1324 5th St, P.O. Box 1610 • Santa Monica, CA 90406-1610 • (310) 458-8600 • http://www.smpl.org

Santa Paula
Blancahard-Santa Paula Public Library Dist • 119 N 8th St • Santa Paula, CA 93060-2784 • (805) 525-3615 • http://www.rain.org/~stapaula

Santa Paula Historical Society • P.O. Box 842 • Santa Paula, CA 93060 • (805) 525-1297

Santa Rosa
Alexander Valley Mishewal Wappo • 1037 Kings St #D • Santa Rosa, CA 95404 • (707) 527-8168 • http://www.couey-finks.com/wappo.html

California Indian Museum and Cultural Center • 5250 Aero Drive • Santa Rosa, CA 95403 • (707) 561-3992 • http://www.cimcc.org

Charles M Schulz Museum • 2301 Hardies Ln • Santa Rosa, CA 95403 • (707) 579-4452 • http://www.schulzmuseum.org

Descendants of the Illegitimate Sons and Daughters of the Kings of Britain • 2153 Meadowbrook Ct #9 • Santa Rosa, CA 95403

Friends of the Carrillo Adobe • P.O. Box 2843 • Santa Rosa, CA 95405 • http://www.carrilloadobe.org

Luther Burbank Home Museum • Santa Rose Ave & Sonoma Ave • Santa Rosa, CA 95402 • (707) 524-5445 • http://www.lutherburbank.org

Lytton Band of Pomo Indians • 1250 Coddingtown Center, Ste 1 • Santa Rosa, CA 95401 • (707) 575-5917

Northwestern Pacific Railroad Historical Society • P.O. Box 667 • Santa Rosa, CA 95402 • (415) 892-5558

Pacific Beach Historical Society • 2330 Airport Blvd • Santa Rosa, CA 95403 • (707) 575-7900 • http://pacificcoastairmuseum.org

Pacific Coast Air Museum • 2230 Becker Blvd • Santa Rosa, CA 95403 • (707) 575-7900 • http://www.pacificcoastairmuseum.org

Santa Rosa Local History and Genealogy Annex • 211 E Street • Santa Rosa, CA 95404 • (707) 545-0831 • http://www.sonomalibrary.org

Santa Rosa-Sonoma County Library • 3rd & E Sts • Santa Rosa, CA 95404 • (707) 545-0831 • http://www.sonomalibrary.org

Sonoma County Genealogical Society • P.O. Box 2273 • Santa Rosa, CA 95405-0273 • (707) 838-1311 • http://www.scgs.org

Sonoma County Historical Society • 509 4th St, P.O. Box 1373 • Santa Rosa, CA 95402 • (707) 539-1786 • http://www.sonomacountyhistory.org

Sonoma County Museum • 425 7th St • Santa Rosa, CA 95401 • (707) 579-1500 • http://www.sonomacountymuseum.org

Stewart's Point Rancheria - Kashaya Pomo • 1420D Guerneville Rd, Ste 3, P.O. Box 6525 • Santa Rosa, CA 95403 • (707) 591-0580 • http://www.kashaya.homestead.com

Santa Ynez
Santa Ynez Band of Chumash Indians • P.O. Box 517 • Santa Ynez, CA 93460 • (805) 688-7997 • http://www.santaynez.org

Santa Ynez Valley Historical Society • Janeway Carriage House, 3596 Sagunto St, P.O. Box 181 • Santa Ynez, CA 93460 • (805) 688-7889 • http://www.santaynezvalleyhistoricalmuseum.org

Santa Ysabel
Mesa Grande Band of Mission Indians - Kumeyaay Diegueno • P.O. Box 270 • Santa Ysabel, CA 92070 • (760) 782-3818 • http://kumeyaay.com

Santa Ysabel Asistencia Museum • 23013 Hwy 79 • Santa Ysabel, CA 92070 • (619) 765-0810

Santa Ysabel Band of Mission Indians - Kumeyaay, Diegueno • P.O. Box 130 • Santa Ysabel, CA 92070 • (760) 765-0845 • http://kumeyaay.com

Saratoga
Saratoga Heritage Preservation Commission • 13777 Fruitvale Ave • Saratoga, CA 95070 • (408) 867-3438 • http://www.saratoga.ca.us/heritage.htm

Saratoga Historical Foundation • Historical Museum, 20450 Saratoga-Los Gatos Rd, P.O. Box 172 • Saratoga, CA 95070 • (408) 867-4311

Sausalito
Sausalito Historical Society • 420 Litho St, P.O. Box 352 • Sausalito, CA 94966 • (415) 289-4117 • http://www.ci.sausalito.ca.us/shs/contents.htm

Sausalito Public Library • 420 Litho St • Sausalito, CA 94965-1933 • (415) 289-4121 • http://www.ci.sausalito.ca.us

Scotia
PALCO Logging Museum • 125 Main St, P.O. Box 37 • Scotia, CA 95565 • (707) 764-2222 • http://www.palco.com

Seal Beach
Leisure World Genealogical Workshop • Leisure World Library, 2300 Beverly Manor Rd, P.O. Box 2069 • Seal Beach, CA 90740

Leisure World Historical Society • 1880 Golden Rain Rd • Seal Beach, CA 90740 • (562) 596-7666

Seal Beach Historical & Cultural Society • Red Car Museum, Main & Electric, P.O. Box 152 • Seal Beach, CA 90740 • http://www.sealbeachhistoricalsociety.com

Seaside
Seaside Community Library • 550 Harcourt • Seaside, CA 93955 • (831) 899-2055 • http://bbs.ci.seaside.ca.us/sealib/

Sebastopol
Eyelusion Museum • P.O. Box 1922 • Sebastopol, CA 95473 • http://www.eyelusion.com

Western Sonoma County Historical Society • Historical Museum, 261 S Main St, P.O. Box 816 • Sebastopol, CA 95472 • (707) 829-6711 • http://www.wschs-grf.pon.net

Selma
Selma Museum Historical Society • Historical Museum, 1880 Art Gonzales Pkwy • Selma, CA 93662 • (209) 896-8871

Shafter

Minter Field Air Museum • 401 Vultree St, P.O. Box 445 • Shafter, CA 93263 • (661) 393-0291 • http://www.minterfieldairmuseum.com

Shafter Historical Society • 150 Central Valley Hwy, P.O. Box 1088 • Shafter, CA 93263 • (661) 746-1557

Shasta

Shasta State Historic Park • Hwy 299 W, P.O. Box 2430 • Shasta, CA 96087 • (530) 243-8194 • http://www.parks.ca.gov

Weaverville Joss House State Historic Park • Highway 299 & Oregon St, P.O. Box 2430 • Shasta, CA 96087-2430 • (530) 623-5284 • http://www.norcal.parks.state.ca.us/weaverville.htm

Shasta Lake

Shasta Dam Museum • 16349 Shasta Dam Blvd • Shasta Lake, CA 96003 • (530) 275-1554

Shaver Lake

Central Sierra Historical Society • 40667 Shaver Forest Rd • Shaver Lake, CA 93664 • (559) 841-4478

Sherman Oaks

Jewish Genealogical Society of Los Angeles • P.O. Box 55443 • Sherman Oaks, CA 91343 • (818) 991-5864 • http://www.jgsla.org

Shingle Springs

Shingle Springs Band of Miwok Indians • P.O. Box 1340 • Shingle Springs, CA 95682 • (530) 676-6281 • http://www.shinglespringsrancheria.com

Shingletown

Mount Lassen Historical Society • P.O. Box 291 • Shingletown, CA 96088 • (530) 474-3061

Sierra City

Sierra County Historical Society • Kentucky Mine Museum, 100 Kentucky Mine Rd, P.O. Box 260 • Sierra City, CA 96125 • (916) 862-1310 • http://www.sierracounty.org/schs_home.html

Sierra Madre

Sierra Madre Historical Preservation Society • 440 W Sierra Madre Blvd, P.O. Box 202 • Sierra Madre, CA 91025-0202 • (626) 355-8129 • http://www.sierramadre.lib.ca.us

Sierra Madre Historical Society • P.O. Box 202 • Sierra Madre, CA 91025-0202 • (626) 355-8129 • http://www.sierramadre.lib.ca.us/smarchives/sierra_madre_historical_preserva.htm

Signal Hill

Signal Hill Public Library • 1700 E Hill St • Signal Hill, CA 90806 • (562) 989-7323 • http://www.ci.signal-hill.ca.us

Silverado

Santa Ana Mountain Historical Society • 28192 Silverado Canyon Rd, P.O. Box 301 • Silverado, CA 92676 • (714) 649-2216

Simi Valley

R P Strathearn Historical Park • 137 Strathearn Pl, P.O. Box 351 • Simi Valley, CA 93062 • (805) 526-6453 • http://www.simihistory.com

Ronald Reagan Presidential Library • 40 Presidential Dr • Simi Valley, CA 93065 • (800) 410-8354 • http://www.reagan.utexas.edu

Santa Susanna Railroad Historical Society • Historical Museum, 6503 Katherine Rd • Simi Valley, CA 93062 • http://www.santasusannadepot.org

Simi Valley Historical Society • Historical Museum, 137 Strathearn Pl, P.O. Box 351 • Simi Valley, CA 93062 • (805) 526-6453 • http://www.cyber-pages.com/strathearn/

Smith River

Ship Ashore Resort Museum • 12370 Hwy 101 N • Smith River, CA 95567 • (800) 487-3141

Smith River Rancheria • 250 N Indian Rd • Smith River, CA 95567-9525 • (707) 487-9255

Soda Springs

Western America Skisport Museum • P.O. Box 729 • Soda Springs, CA 95728 • (530) 426-3313

Solana Beach

Jewish Genealogical Society of San Diego • 255 S Rios Ave • Solana Beach, CA 92075 • (858) 481-8511 • http://www.sdjgs.org

Solana Beach Civic Historical Society • 712 Stevens Ave • Solana Beach, CA 92075 • (858) 755-2937

Soledad

Mission Nuestra Senora de la Soledad Museum • 36641 Fort Romie Rd, P.O. Box 506 • Soledad, CA 93960 • (831) 678-2586 • http://www.missiontour.org

Solvang

Elverhoj Museum • 1624 Elverjoy Wy, P.O. Box 769 • Solvang, CA 93464 • (805) 686-1211 • http://www.elverjoj.org

Old Mission Santa Ines Museum • 1760 Mission Dr, P.O. Box 408 • Solvang, CA 93464 • (805) 688-4815 • http://www.missionsantaines.org

Sonoma

Sonoma League for Historic Preservation • 129 E Spain St, P.O. Box 766 • Sonoma, CA 95476 • (707) 938-0510

Sonoma State Historic Park • 363 3rd St W • Sonoma, CA 95476 • (707) 938-1519 • http://www.napanet.net/~sshpa/

Sonoma Valley Historical Society • Depot Park Museum, 270 1st St W, P.O. Box 861 • Sonoma, CA 95476 • (707) 938-1762 • http://www.vom.com/~depot/

Sonora

Columbia College Library • 11600 Columbia College Dr • Sonora, CA 95370-8581 • (209) 588-5119 • http://columbia.yosmite.cc.ca.us/library

Tuolumne County Free Library • 480 Greenley Rd • Sonora, CA 95370-5956 • (209) 533-5507

Tuolumne County Genealogical Society • 158 W Bradford Ave, P.O. Box 695 • Sonora, CA 95370-0695 • (209) 532-1317 • http://www.tchistory.org

Tuolumne County Historical Society • 158 W Bradford Ave, P.O. Box 695 • Sonora, CA 95370 • (209) 532-1317

Soquel

Soquel Pioneer and Historical Association • 5270 Pringle Ln • Soquel, CA 95073 • (831) 688-2412 • http://soquelpioneers.com/

South El Monte

American Society of Military History • Historical Museum, 1918 N Rosemeade Blvd • South El Monte, CA 91733 • (626) 442-1776 • http://www.tankland.com

South Gate

County of Los Angeles Public Library-Leland R Weaver Library • 4035 Tweedy Blvd • South Gate, CA 90280-6199 • (323) 567-8853 • http://www.colapublib.org/libs/weaver/

South Lake Tahoe

Lake Tahoe Historical Society • Historical Museum, 3058 Lake Tahoe Blvd, P.O. Box 404 • South Lake Tahoe, CA 95705 • (530) 541-5458 • http://www.tahoenevada.com/_things/82.html

Tallac Historic Site Museum • 870 Emerald Bay Rd • South Lake Tahoe, CA 96150 • (530) 541-5227

South Pasadena

South Pasadena Public Library • 1100 Oxley St • South Pasadena, CA 91030-3198 • (626) 403-7350 • http://library.ci.south-pasadena.ca.us

South San Francisco
South San Francisco Historical Society • Historical Museum, 601 Grand Ave • South San Francisco, CA 94080 • (650) 829-3825

South San Francisco Library, Grand Ave Branch • 306 Walnut Ave • South San Francisco, CA 94080 • (650) 877-8533 • http://www.ssflibrary.org

South San Francisco Public Library • 840 W Orange Ave • South San Francisco, CA 94080-3125 • (650) 829-3860 • http://www.ssflibrary.org

Spring Valley
Spring Valley Historical Society • Bancroft Ranch House Museum, 9065 Memory Ln • Spring Valley, CA 91977 • (619) 469-1480

Springville
Tule River Historical Society • Springville Museum, 34902 Highway 190, P.O. Box 374 • Springville, CA 93265 • (559) 539-6701 • http://www.cvbvisalia.com/entertainment.htm

Stanford
Cecil H Green Library • Stanford Univ, 557 Escondido Mall • Stanford, CA 94305-6004 • (650) 725-1064 • http://www.sul.stanford.edu

Chicano Reference Library • 590S The Nitery, Stanford Univ • Stanford, CA 94305 • (650) 497-2798

Stanford Historical Society • P.O. Box 2328 • Stanford, CA 94309-2328 • (415) 725-3332 • http://www-sul.stanford.edu/depts/shs/

Stanford Historical Society • P.O. Box 20028 • Stanford, CA 94309 • (650) 725-3332 • http://histsoc.stanford.edu

Stanford University Museum • Lomita Drive at Museum Way • Stanford, CA 94305 • (650) 723-4177 • http://www.stanford.edu/dept/SUMA/

Stinson Beach
Audubon Canyon Ranch Museum • 4900 Hwy 1 • Stinson Beach, CA 94970 • (415) 868-9244 • http://www.egret.org

Stockton
Alameda May Petzinger Library of California • Haggin Museum, Victory Park, 1201 N Pershing Ave • Stockton, CA 95203-1699 • (209) 940-6324 • http://www.hagginmuseum.org

California Valley Miwok Tribe • 10601 Escondido Pl • Stockton, CA 95212 • (209) 931-4567

Conference of California Historical Societies • John Muir Center, Univ of the Pacific, 301 Pacific Ave • Stockton, CA 95211-0001 • (209) 946-2169 • http://www.californiahistorian.com

Jedediah Strong Smith Society • Univ of the Pacific • Stockton, CA 95211 • (209) 946-2404 • http://www.cs.uop.edu/organizations/JSS96.html

San Joaquin Genealogical Society • P.O. Box 4817 • Stockton, CA 95104 • http://www.rootsweb.com/~sjgs/

San Joaquin Pioneer and Historical Society • Haggin Museum, 1201 N Pershing Ave • Stockton, CA 95203 • (209) 462-4116 • http://www.hagginmuseum.org

Stockton-San Joaquin County Public Library • 605 N El Dorado St • Stockton, CA 95202-1999 • (209) 937-8221 • http://www.stockton.lib.ca.us

Westerners, Stockton Corral • P.O. Box 1315 • Stockton, CA 95201 • (209) 478-9266 • http://www.westerners-intl.org

William Knox Holt Library • Univ of the Pacific, Holt-Atherton Special Collections, 3601 Pacific Ave • Stockton, CA 95211 • (209) 946-2945 • http://library.uop.edu

Stratford
Stratford Historical Society • general delivery • Stratford, CA 95072

Suisun City
Western Railway Museum • 5848 State Hwy 12 • Suisun City, CA 94585 • (707) 374-3978 • http://www.wrm.org

Sun City
Genealogy Club of Sun City • P.O. Box 175 • Sun City, CA 92586 • (951) 244-0229

Sunnyvale
American Historical Society of Germans from Russia, Golden Gate Chapter • 898 Grap Ave • Sunnyvale, CA 94087-1613

Chinese Historical and Cultural Project • P.O. Box 70746 • Sunnyvale, CA 94086-0746 • http://www.chcp.org

Lace Museum • 552 S Murphy Ave • Sunnyvale, CA 94086 • (408) 730-4695

Sunnyvale Heritage Preservation Commission • P.O. Box 3707 • Sunnyvale, CA 94088 • (408) 730-7444 • http://www.ci.sunnyvale.ca.us/community-dev/planning/hpc/heritagepres.htm

Sunnyvale Historical Society • Historical Society, 235 E California Ave, P.O. Box 61301 • Sunnyvale, CA 94086 • (408) 749-0220 • http://www.heritageparkmuseum.org

Sunnyvale Historical Society and Museum Association Guild • Historical Museum, 169 Florence St • Sunnyvale, CA 94086 • (408) 245-1184

Sunnyvale Public Library • 665 W Olive Ave • Sunnyvale, CA 94088-3714 • (408) 730-7300 • http://www.ci.sunnyvale.ca.us/library/

Susanville
Lassen Community College Library • 478-200 Hwy 139, P.O. Box 3000 • Susanville, CA 96130-3000 • (530) 251-8830 • http://www.lassencollege.edu/library/library.html

Lassen County Historical Society • William H Pratt Museum, 105 N Weatherlow St, P.O. Box 321 • Susanville, CA 96130 • (530) 257-4584 • http://www.cagenweb.com/tp/lassen/

Lassen Historical Museum • P.O. Box 321 • Susanville, CA 96130 • (916) 257-6551 • http://www.cagenweb.com/tp/lassen/

Susanville District Library • 1618 Main St • Susanville, CA 96130-4515 • (530) 251-8127 • http://www.susanvillelib.org

Susanville Rancheria - Paiute Maidu, Pit River and Washoe Indians • 745 Joaquin St, P.O. Drawer U • Susanville, CA 96130 • (530) 257-6264

United Maidu Nation • P.O. Box 204 • Susanville, CA 96130 • (530) 257-9691

Winnemucca Colony • 420 Pardde • Susanville, CA 96130 • (916) 257-7093 • http://itcn.org/tribes/winn.html

Sutter Creek
Amador County Genealogical Society • 322 Via Verde, Sutter Terrace, P.O. Box 1115 • Sutter Creek, CA 95685

Sylmar
All Cadillacs of the Forties Museum • 12811 Foothill Blvd • Sylmar, CA 91342 • (818) 361-1147

Taft
Taft Genealogical Society • P.O. Box 1411 • Taft, CA 93268 • http://www.rootsweb.com/~catgs/

Tahoe City
North Lake Tahoe Historical Society • Gatekeepers Museum, 130 W Lake Blvd, P.O. Box 6141 • Tahoe City, CA 96145-6141 • (916) 583-1762 • http://www.tahoecountry.com/nlths/

Watson Cabin Museum • 560 N Lake Blvd • Tahoe City, CA 96145 • (530) 583-8717 • http://www.northtahoemuseums.org/

Tahoma

Ehrman Mansion Museum • Sugarpine Point State Park, P.O. Box 266, Hwy 89 • Tahoma, CA 96142 • (530) 525-7232 • http://www.parks.ca.gov

Vikingsholm Museum • Emerald Bay State Park, Hwy 89, P.O. Box 266 • Tahoma, CA 96142 • (530) 525-7232 • http://www.parks.ca.gov

Talmage

Guidiville Rancheria Tribe • P.O. Box 339 • Talmage, CA 95481 • (707) 462-3682

Tehachapi

Tehachapi Heritage League • 310 S Green St, P.O. Box 54 • Tehachapi, CA 93561 • (805) 822-6589 • http://tehachapi.cc/museum/

Tehama

Tehama County Museum • 275 C Street, P.O. Box 273 • Tehama, CA 96090 • (530) 384-2420 • http://tco1.tco.net/tehama/museum/

Tehama County Museum Foundation • Historical Museum, 275 C Street, P.O. Box 275 • Tehama, CA 96090 • (530) 384-2420 • http://www.tco.net/tehama/museum/

Temecula

Pechanga Band of Mission Indians • P.O. Box 1477 • Temecula, CA 92392 • (909) 676-2768 • http://www.pechanga.com

Riverside County Library System-Temecula Branch • 41000 County Center Dr • Temecula, CA 92591 • (951) 600-6263

Temecula Library • 41000 County Center Dr • Temecula, CA 92591

Temecula Valley Genealogical Society • 27475 Ynez Rd., Ste 291 • Temecula, CA 92591

Temecula Valley Historical Society • Historical Museum, 28314 Mercedes St, P.O. Box 157 • Temecula, CA 92592 • (951) 694-6450 • http://www.temeculavalleyhistoricalsociety.org

Temecula Valley Museum • 28315 Mercedes St, P.O. Box 792 • Temecula, CA 92593 • (951) 694-6452 • http://www.ci.temecula.ca.us/cityhall/commserv/Museum/

Temple City

Historical Society of Temple City • 5954 Kauffman Ave • Temple City, CA 91780 • (626) 451-0833

Temple City Historical Museum • 10144 Bogue St • Temple City, CA 91780 • (626) 279-1784

Templeton

Templeton Historical Museum • 309 Main St • Templeton, CA 93465 • (805) 434-0807

Thermal

Torres-Martinez Band of Desert Cahuilla Indians • 66-725 Martinez Rd, P.O. Box 1160 • Thermal, CA 92274 • (760) 397-8144

Thousand Oaks

California Indian Council • P.O. Box 3374 • Thousand Oaks, CA 91359 • (805) 493-2663

Chumash Interpretive Center • Oakbrook Regional Park, 3290 Long Ranch Pkwy • Thousand Oaks, CA 91362 • (805) 492-8076 • http://www.designplace.com/chumash/

Conejo Valley Genealogical Society • c/o Thousand Oaks Library, 1401 E Janss Rd, P.O. Box 1228 • Thousand Oaks, CA 91358-1228 • (805) 497-8293 • http://www.rootsweb.ancestry.com/~cacvgs/

Conejo Valley Historical Society • P.O. Box 1692 • Thousand Oaks, CA 91360 • (805) 498-9441

Oak Brook Chumash Tribe • 3920 Lang Ranch Pkwy • Thousand Oaks, CA 91362 • (805) 492-8076

Santa Monica Mountains National Recreational Area Museum • 401 W Hillcrest Dr • Thousand Oaks, CA 91360 • (805) 370-2300 • http://www.nps.gov/samo/

Thousand Oaks Library • 1401 E Janss Rd • Thousand Oaks, CA 91362-2199 • (805) 449-2660 • http://www.toaks.org/library/

Three Rivers

Three Rivers Historical Society • 42268 Sierra Dr • Three Rivers, CA 93271 • (559) 561-2707

Tiburon

Belvidere-Tiburon Public Library • 1501 Tiburon Blvd • Tiburon, CA 94920 • (415) 789-2665 • http://thelibrary.info

Immigration Station Barracks Museum • 1 mi E of Ayala Cove, P.O. Box 318 • Tiburon, CA 94920 • (415) 435-3522 • http://www.angelisland.org

Schwartz Collection of Skiing Heritage Museum • 9 Stevens Ct • Tiburon, CA 94920 • (415) 435-1076 • http://www.picturesnow.com

Tollhouse

Civil War Society • 35756 Black Mountain Rd • Tollhouse, CA 93667 • (559) 855-8637

Cold Springs Rancherie • P.O. Box 209 • Tollhouse, CA 93667 • (559) 855-5043

Tomales

Tomales Regional Local History Center Library • 26701 Hwy 1, P.O. Box 262 • Tomales, CA 94971 • (707) 878-9443 • http://www.tomaleshistory.org

Topanga

Topanga Historical Society • 120 S Topanga Canyon Blvd, P.O. Box 1214 • Topanga, CA 90290 • (310) 455-1969 • http://www.topangaonline.com

Torrance

British Family Historical Society of Los Angeles • 22941 Felbar Ave • Torrance, CA 90505

Byelorussian-American Association • P.O. Box 10353 • Torrance, CA 90505-1253

Curtiss-Wright Historical Association • 2735 Airport Dr • Torrance, CA 90505 • (310) 325-6155

Save Historic Old Torrance • 2028 Gramercy Ave • Torrance, CA 90501 • (310) 320-0269

South Bay Cities Genealogical Society • P.O. Box 11069 • Torrance, CA 90510-1069 • (310) 533-7053 • http://www.rootsweb.com/~casbcgs/

Torrance Historical Society • Historical Museum, 1345 Post Ave • Torrance, CA 90501 • (213) 328-5392 • http://www.visittorrance.com/historical.htm

Torrance Public Library • 3301 Torrance Blvd • Torrance, CA 90503 • (310) 618-5950 • http://www.library.torrnet.com

Tracy

Tracy Area Genealogical Society • Historical Museum, 1141 Adam St, P.O. Box 632 • Tracy, CA 95376 • (209) 832-1106 • http://rootsweb.com/~catags/

Travis AFB

Travis Air Force Museum • P.O. Box 1565 • Travis AFB, CA 94535 • (707) 424-5605

Trinidad

Big Lagoon Rancheria • Yorok & Tolowa, P.O. Box 3060 • Trinidad, CA 95570 • (707) 826-2079

Stone Lagoon Red Schoolhouse Museum • 265 Idlewood Ln • Trinidad, CA 95570 • (707) 488-2061

Trinidad Rancheria - Yurok, Wiyot and Tolowa • P.O. Box 630 • Trinidad, CA 95570 • (707) 677-0211

Trona

Searles Valley Historical Society • Old Guest House Museum, 13193 Main St, P.O. Box 630 • Trona, CA 93592 • (760) 372-5222 • http://www1.iwvisp.com/svhs/

Truckee

Donner Memorial State Park and Emigrant Trail Museum • 12593 Donner Pass Rd, P.O. Box 9210 • Truckee, CA 96161 • http://www.parks.ca.gov

Truckee-Donner Historical Society • Jail Museum, P.O. Box 893 • Truckee, CA 95734 • (530) 582-0893 • http://truckeehistory.tripod.com/jailmuseum.htm

Tujunga

Little Landers Historical Society • Bolton Hall Museum, 10116 Commerce Ave, P.O. Box 203 • Tujunga, CA 91042 • (818) 352-3420 • http://www.rootsweb.com/~casfvgs/bolton.html

Tulare

Heritage Complex Farm Equipment Museum • 4450 S Laspina St • Tulare, CA 93274 • (559) 688-1030 • http://www.heritagecomplex.org/museum/

Sequoia Genealogical Society • c/o Tulare Public Library, 113 North F Street • Tulare, CA 93274-3803 • (559) 685-2342 • http://www.sjvls.org

Tulare City Historical Society • 444 W Tulare Ave • Tulare, CA 93274 • (559) 686-2074

Tulare Public Library • 113 North F Street • Tulare, CA 93274 • (559) 685-2341 • http://www.sjvls.lib.ca.us/tularepub/

Tulelake

Lava Beds National Monument Museum • 1 Indian Wells HQ • Tulelake, CA 96134 • (530) 667-2282 • http://www.nps.gov/labe/

Tuolumne

Tyolumne Rancheria - Miwok, Me Wuk and Yokuts • P.O. Box 699 • Tuolumne, CA 94379 • (209) 928-3475

Turlock

Stanislaus Library • California State Univ, 801 W Monte Vista Ave • Turlock, CA 95380 • (209) 667-3233 • http://www.library.csustan.edu

Turlock Historical Society • 108 S Center St • Turlock, CA 95380 • (209) 668-7386

Tustin

Orange County Public Library-Tustin Branch • 345 E Main St • Tustin, CA 92680 • (714) 544-7725 • http://www.ocpl.org/tustin/tustin.htm

Tustin Area Historical Society • Historical Museum, 395 El Camino Real, P.O. Box 185 • Tustin, CA 92681 • (714) 731-5701 • http://www.tustinhistory.org

Twenty-Nine Palms

Joshua Tree and Southern Railroad Museum • 74485 National Park Dr • Twenty-Nine Palms, CA 92277 • (760) 367-5500 • http://www.nps.gov/jotr/

Twenty-Nine Palms Historical Society • 6760 National Park Dr, P.O. Box 1926 • Twenty-Nine Palms, CA 92277 • (760) 367-2366 • http://www.msnusers.com/29palmshistoricalsociety

Ukiah

Grace Hudson Museum & Sun House Museum • 431 S Main St, P.O. Box 865 • Ukiah, CA 95482 • (707) 467-2836 • http://www.gracehudsonmuseum.org

Mendocino County Historical Society • Held-Poage Memorial Home, 603 W Perkins St • Ukiah, CA 95482-4726 • (707) 462-6969 • http://www.pacificsites.com/~mchs/heldpoage.htm

Mendocino County Library • 105 N Main St • Ukiah, CA 95402-4482 • (707) 463-4493 • http://www.mendolibrary.org

Pinoleville of Pomo Indians • 367 N State St, Ste 204 • Ukiah, CA 95482 • (707) 463-1454 • http://www.pinoleville.org

Potter Valley Rancheria - Little River Band of Pomo Indians • 112 N School St • Ukiah, CA 95482 • (707) 485-1213

Ukiah Tree Tracers Genealogical Society • P.O. Box 72 • Ukiah, CA 95482

Yokayo Tribe of Indians • 1114 Helen Ave • Ukiah, CA 95482 • (707) 462-4074

Union City

Union City Historical Museum • 3841 Smith St • Union City, CA 94587 • (510) 324-3298 • http://www.unioncitymuseum.com

Upland

Chaffey Communities Cultural Center and Museum • 525 W 18th St, P.O. Box 772 • Upland, CA 91786 • (909) 982-8010 • http://www.culturalcenter.org

Cooper Regional History Museum • 217 East A Street, P.O. Box 772 • Upland, CA 91785-0722 • (909) 982-8010 • http://www.culturalcenter.org; http://www.coopermuseum.org

Upland Public Library • 450 N Euclid Ave • Upland, CA 91786-4732 • (909) 931-4200 • http://uplandpl.lib.ca.us

Vacaville

Vacaville Museum • 213 Buck Ave • Vacaville, CA 95688 • (707) 447-4513 • http://www.vacavillemuseum.org

Vallejo

Genealogy Society of Vallejo • Historical Museum, 734 Marin St • Vallejo, CA 94590-5913 • (707) 748-1367 • http://www.rootsweb.com/~cagsv/

Mare Island Historic Park Foundation • 328 Seawind Dr • Vallejo, CA 94590 • (707) 562-1854

McCune Rare Book Museum • JFK Library, 505 Santa Clara St • Vallejo, CA 94590 • (707) 644-0764 • http://www.mccunecollection.org

Solano County Historical Society • P.O. Box 922 • Vallejo, CA 94590 • (707) 644-3803 • http://www.rootsweb.com/~cascgsi

Vallejo Naval and Historical Museum • 734 Marin St • Vallejo, CA 94590 • (707) 643-0077 • http://www.vallejomuseum.org

Valley Center

Rincon San Luiseno Band of Mission Indians • P.O. Box 68 • Valley Center, CA 92082 • (760) 749-1051

San Pasqual Band of Diegueno Indians - Kumeyaay • P.O. Box 365 • Valley Center, CA 92082 • (619) 749-3200 • http://www.sanpasqualindians.org

Van Nuys

California Supreme Court Historical Society • 6946 Van Nuys Blvd • Van Nuys, CA 91405 • (818) 781-6008

Vandenberg AFB

Vandenberg Air Force Base Library FL4610 • 30 SVS/SVMG, 100 Community Loop Bldg 10343-A • Vandenberg AFB, CA 93437-6111 • (805) 606-1110

Venice

Venice Historical Society • P.O. Box 12844 • Venice, CA 90295 • (310) 967-5170 • http://www.members.nbci.com/venicehist/

Ventura

Center for the Study of Eurasian Nomads • 2158 Palomar Ave • Ventura, CA 93001 • (805) 653-2607 • http://www.csen.org

E P Foster Library • 651 E Main • Ventura, CA 93001 • (805) 648-2715

Mishkanaka-Chumash Tribe • 2125 Channel Dr • Ventura, CA 93001 • (805) 652-1013

California

Ventura, cont.

Olivas Adobe Museum • 4200 Olivas Park Dr • Ventura, CA 93003 • (805) 644-4346 • http://www.olivasadobe.org

Ortega Adobe Museum • 215 W Main St • Ventura, CA 93001 • (805) 658-4736 • http://www.ventura.com

San Buena Ventura Mission Museum • 225 E Main St • Ventura, CA 93001 • (805) 643-4318 • http://www.sanbuenaventuramission.org

San Buenaventura Heritage • Dudley House Museum, P.O. Box 6803 • Ventura, CA 93006 • (805) 642-3345 • http://www.dudleyhouse.org

San Buenaventura Historic Preservation Commission • P.O. Box 9 • Ventura, CA 93002 • (805) 654-7849 • http://www.dudleyhouse.org

Ventura County Genealogical Society • c/o EP Foster Library, 651 E Main, P.O. Box 24608 • Ventura, CA 93002 • (805) 805-648-2715 • http://www.rootsweb.com/~cavcgs

Ventura County Historical Society • Historical Museum, 100 E Main St • Ventura, CA 93001 • (805) 653-0323 • http://www.venturamuseum.org

Ventura County Library Services Agency • 800 S Victoria Ave • Ventura, CA 93009-1950 • (805) 662-6756

Victorville

California Route 66 Museum • 16825 Route 66 D Street, P.O. Box 2151 • Victorville, CA 92393 • (760) 951-0436 • http://www.califrt66museum.org

Hi-Desert Genealogical Society • c/o Victorville Public Library, 15011 Circle Dr, P.O. Box 1271 • Victorville, CA 92392-1271 • (760) 247-6142 • http://www.cagenweb.com/hdgs

Mohave Historical Society • P.O. Box 21 • Victorville, CA 92392 • http://wo.com/comm/mhs.htm

Roy Rogers and Dale Evans Museum • 15650 Seneca Rd • Victorville, CA 92392 • (619) 243-4547 • http://www.royrogers.com/museum.html

Victorville Public Library • 15011 Circle Dr, P.O. Box 1271 • Victorville, CA 92393-1271 • (760) 247-6142 • http://www.ci.victorville.c.us/services/library.html

Villa Park

Villa Park Historical Society • City Hall of Villa Park • Villa Park, CA 92667

Visalia

Central Valley Chinese Cultural Center • 500 Akers Rd • Visalia, CA 93727 • (559) 625-4545

Moravian Heritage Society • 31910 Road 160 • Visalia, CA 93292-9044 • (559) 798-1490 • http://www.czechusa.com/moravian/

Tulare County Historical Society • Historical Museum, 27000 Mooney Blvd, P.O. Box 295 • Visalia, CA 93279 • (559) 752-3318 • http://www.tularecountyhistoricalsociety.org

Tulare County Library System • 200 W Oak St • Visalia, CA 93291-4993 • (559) 733-6954 • http://www.tularecountylibrary.org

Wukchumni Tribal Council • 1420 N Encina • Visalia, CA 93291 • (559) 741-0659

Vista

Antique Gas and Steam Engine Museum • 2040 N Santa Fe • Vista, CA 92084 • (760) 941-1791 • http://www.agsem.com

Norwegian Genealogy Group • Sons of Norway Lodge, 2006 E Vista Wy • Vista, CA 92084-3321 • (760) 729-0604

POINTers in Person, San Diego County Area Chapter No. 16 • P. O. Box 2544 • Vista, CA 92085-2544 • (760) 734-1920 • http://www.cgssd.org/events.php3

Rancho Buena Vista Adobe Museum • 640 Alta Vista Drive • Vista, CA 92083 • (619) 724-6121 • http://www.ci.vista.ca.us/adobe/

Vista Ranchos Historical Society • Historical Museum, 651 E Vista Wy, Ste A, P.O. Box 1032 • Vista, CA 92085-1032 • (760) 630-0444 • http://vhsm.org

Walnut

W R Rowland Adobe Ranch House Museum • 130 Avenida Alipaz, P.O. Box 682 • Walnut, CA 91789 • (909) 598-5605

Walnut Creek

Galizien German Descendants • 2035 Dorsch Rd • Walnut Creek, CA 94598-1126 • (925) 944-9875 • http://www.galiziengermandescendants.org

Mount Diablo Genealogical Society • 1938 Tice Blvd, P.O. Box 4654 • Walnut Creek, CA 94596 • (925) 932-4423

Shadelands Ranch Historical Museum • 2660 Ygnacio Valley Rd • Walnut Creek, CA 94598 • (925) 935-7871

Walnut Creek Historical Society • Shadelands Ranch Historical Museum, 2660 Ygnacio Valley Rd, P.O. Box 4562 • Walnut Creek, CA 94596 • (925) 935-7871 • http://www.ci.walnut-creek.ca.us/wchs.html

Walnut Grove

Sacramento River Delta Historical Society • P.O. Box 293 • Walnut Grove, CA 95690

Warner Springs

Los Coyotes Rancheria Band of Mission Indians - Cahuilla and Copeno • P.O. Box 249 • Warner Springs, CA 92086 • (760) 782-0711

Wasco

Wasco Historical Society • Historical Museum, 918 6th St, P.O. Box 186 • Wasco, CA 93280 • (661) 758-8948 • http://www.ci.wasco.ca/Public_Documents/WascoCA_WebDocs/Wasco_history/

Watsonville

Agricultural History Project • 2601 E Lake Ave, P.O. Box 1181 • Watsonville, CA 95077 • (831) 724-5898 • http://www.aghistoryproject.org

Costanoan, Ohlone, Mutsun-Rumsen Tribes • 110 Dick Phelps Rd • Watsonville, CA 95065 • (408) 728-8471

Pajaro Valley Historical Association • William H Volck Memorial Museum, 261 E Beach St • Watsonville, CA 95076 • (831) 722-0305 • http://www.pvha.org

Weaverville

Laags Place - Big Ben's Doll Museum • P.O. Box 783 • Weaverville, CA 96093 • (530) 623-6383

Trinity County Historical Society • Jackson Memorial Museum, 508 Main St, P.O. Box 333 • Weaverville, CA 96093 • (530) 623-5211 • http://www.trinitymuseum.org

Trinity County Library • 211 N Main St, P.O. Box 1226 • Weaverville, CA 96093-1226 • (530) 623-1373

Weaverville Joss House State Park • 401 Main St, P.O. Box 1217 • Weaverville, CA 96093 • (530) 623-5384 • http://www.parks.ca.gov

Weed

College of the Siskiyous Library • 800 College Ave • Weed, CA 96094 • (530) 938-5331 • http://www.siskiyous.edu/library

West Covina

Historical Society of West Covina • Heritage House Museum, 3510 E Cameron Ave, P.O. Box 4597 • West Covina, CA 91791 • (626) 339-4419

Hurst Ranch Historical Museum • 1227 S Orange Ave • West Covina, CA 91791 • (626) 919-1133 • http://www.hurstranch.com

West Hollywood

Schindler House Museum • 835 N Kings Rd • West Hollywood, CA 90069 • (323) 651-1510

West Lancaster
Antelope Valley Indian Museum • 43779 15th St • West Lancaster, CA 93534 • (661) 942-0662 • http://www.avim.av.org

West Sacramento
West Sacramento Historical Society • Historical Museum, 324 3rd St • West Sacramento, CA 95605 • (916) 374-1849

Westminster
Ancestor Seekers • 14272 Hoover St #65 • Westminster, CA 92683-4321 • (714) 891-3394

Familia Ancestral Research Association • P.O. Box 10359 • Westminster, CA 92685-0359 • (714) 687-0390

Westminster Historical Society • P.O. Box 182 • Westminster, CA 92683 • (714) 891-1126 • http://www.santaanahistory.com/articles/ochistorgs.html

Whittier
Bonnie Bell Wardman Library • Whittier College, 7031 Founders Hill Rd • Whittier, CA 90608 • (562) 907-4829 • http://library.whittier.edu

Jonathan Bailey Home Museum • 13421 E Camilla St • Whittier, CA 90601 • (562) 945-3871 • http://www.whittiermuseum.org

Pio Pico State Historic Park • 6003 Pioneer Blvd • Whittier, CA 90606 • (213) 695-1217 • http://www.cal-parks.ca.gov

Southern California Chapter, OGS • P.O. Box 5553 • Whittier, CA 90607-5553

Whittier Area Genealogical Society • 13502 Quad Shopping Ctr, Suite J, P.O. Box 4367 • Whittier, CA 90607-4367 • (562) 919-1713 • http://www.cagenweb.com/~kr/wags

Whittier Area Genealogical Society, Beginner's Group • P.O. Box 4367 • Whittier, CA 90607-4367 • (626) 919-1713 • http://www.cagenweb.com/~kr/wags

Whittier Area Genealogical Society, Computer Interest Group • P.O. Box 4367 • Whittier, CA 90607-4367 • (626) 919-1713 • http://www.cagenweb.com/~kr/wags

Whittier Area Genealogical Society, Writer's Group • P.O. Box 4367 • Whittier, CA 90607 • (626) 919-1713 • http://www.cagenweb.com/~kr/wags

Whittier Historical Society • 6755 Newlin Ave • Whittier, CA 90601 • (562) 945-3871 • http://www.whittiermuseum.org

Whittier Public Library • 7344 S Washington Ave • Whittier, CA 90602-1778 • (562) 464-3450 • http://www.whittierlibrary.org

Wildomar
Mission Trail Community Library • 34303 Mission Trail • Wildomar, CA 92595 • (951) 471-3855 • http://www.riverside.lib.ca.us

Wildomar Historical Society • general delivery • Wildomar, CA 92595 • (951) 678-1385

Williams
Colusa County Genealogical Society • P.O. Box 973 • Williams, CA 95987

Cortina Rancheria - Wintun • P.O. Box 1630 • Williams, CA 95987 • (530) 473-3274

Sacramento Valley Museum • 1491 E Street, P.O. Box 1437 • Williams, CA 95987 • (530) 473-2978 • http://www.caohwy.com/s/sactovmu.htm

Willits
Mendocino County Library-Willits Branch • 390 E Commercial St • Willits, CA 95490 • (707) 459-5908

Mendocino County Museum • 400 E Commercial St • Willits, CA 95490 • (707) 459-2736 • http://www.co.mendocino.ca.us/museum/

Sherwood Valley Rancheria of Pomo Indians • 190 Sherwood Hill Dr • Willits, CA 95490 • (707) 459-9690

Willow Creek
Willow Creek Historical Society • China Flat Museum, Rts 96 & 299, P.O. Box 102 • Willow Creek, CA 95573 • (530) 629-2653 • http://www.bfro.net/NEWS/wcmuseum.htm

Willows
Colusa County Historical Society • P.O. Box 643 • Willows, CA 95988

Willows Museum • 336 W Walnut St, P.O. Box 1242 • Willows, CA 95988 • (530) 934-5644

Willows Public Library • 201 N Lassen St • Willows, CA 95988-3010 • (530) 934-5156

Wilmington
Drum Barracks Civil War Museum and Research Library • 1052 Banning Blvd • Wilmington, CA 90744 • (310) 548-7509 • http://www.drumbarracks.org

General Phineas Banning Residence Museum • 401 East M Street, P.O. Box 397 • Wilmington, CA 90748 • (310) 548-7777 • http://www.banningmuseum.org

Los Angeles Harbor College Library • 1111 Figueroa Pl • Wilmington, CA 90744-2397 • (310) 522-8292 • http://www.lahc.cc.ca.us/library

Wilmington Historical Society • 309 W Opp, P.O. Box 1435 • Wilmington, CA 90748-1435 • (310) 835-8239

Winchester
Winchester Historical Society of Pleasant Valley • P.O. Box 69 • Winchester, CA 92596 • (909) 926-4039 • http://www.homestead.com/winchesterCAhistory/home.html

Windsor
Windsor Historical Society • P.O. Box 726 • Windsor, CA 95492

Winnetka
San Fernando Valley Genealogy Society • P.O. Box 3486 • Winnetka, CA 91396-3486 • (818) 883-7851 • http://www.rootsweb.com/~casfvgs

Woodland
Hays Antique Truck Museum • 2000 E Main St, P.O. Box 2347 • Woodland, CA 95776 • (530) 666-1044

Yolo County Archives and Record Center • 226 Buckeye St • Woodland, CA 95695 • (530) 666-8010 • http://www.yolocounty.org/org/library/archives.htm

Yolo County Historical Museum • Gibson House, 512 Gibson Rd • Woodland, CA 95695 • (530) 666-1045 • http://www.yolo.net/ychm/historyh.html

Yolo County Historical Society • 123 Midway Dr, P.O. Box 1447 • Woodland, CA 95695 • (530) 661-2212 • http://www.yolo.net/ychs/

Yolo County Library • 226 Buckeye St • Woodland, CA 95695-2600 • (530) 666-8005 • http://yolocounty.org/org/library/library.html

Woodland Hills
Los Angeles Pierce College Library • 6201 Winnetka Ave • Woodland Hills, CA 91371 • (819) 710-2833 • http://www.piercecollege.com/homel.html

West Valley Museum • 22200 Ventura Blvd • Woodland Hills, CA 91364 • (818) 992-6814 • http://members.aol.com/cfowler429/interest.htm

Western States Jewish History Association • 22711 Cass Ave • Woodland Hills, CA 91364-1306 • (818) 225-9631

Woodside
Amah Mutsun Band of Mission Indians • 789 Canada Rd • Woodside, CA 94062 • (415) 851-7747

Filoli Center Museum • 86 Canada Rd • Woodside, CA 94062 • (650) 364-8600 • http://www.filoli.org

Woodside, cont.
Mathiesen Farmhouse Museum • 2961 Woodside Rd • Woodside, CA 94062 • (415) 851-1294

Woodside Store Historic Site Museum • 3300 Tripp Rd • Woodside, CA 94062 • (650) 299-0104

Yermo
Calico Ghost Town and Lane House Museum • 36600 Ghost Town Rd, P.O. Box 638 • Yermo, CA 92398 • (760) 254-2122 • http://www. calicotown.com

Yorba Linda
Genealogical Society of North Orange County California • P.O. Box 706 • Yorba Linda, CA 92885-0706 • (714) 993-2448 • http://www. cagenweb.com/gsnocc

Richard Nixon Library and Birthplace Museum • 18001 Yorba Linda Blvd • Yorba Linda, CA 92886 • (714) 993-5075 • http://www. nixonfoundation.org

Yorba Linda Genealogical Society • 4751 Libra Pl • Yorba Linda, CA 92686 • (714) 777-2873

Yorba Linda Historical Society • Heritage Museum, 5700 Susanna Bryant Dr, P.O. Box 396 • Yorba Linda, CA 92885-0396 • (714) 694-0235 • http://www.ylpl.lib.ca.us/bryant.htm

Yorba Linda Public Library • 18181 Imperial Hwy • Yorba Linda, CA 92886-3437 • (714) 777-2873 • http://www.ylpl.lib.ca.us

Yosemite National Park
Yosemite National Park Research Library • P.O. Box 577 • Yosemite National Park, CA 95389 • (209) 372-0200 • http://www.nps.gov

Yountville
Napa Valley Museum • 55 Presidents Cr, P.O. Box 3567 • Yountville, CA 94599 • (707) 963-7411 • http://www.napavalleymuseum.org

Yreka
First Families of Pacific States Society • c/o Siskiyou County Public Library, 719 4th St, P.O. Box 225 • Yreka, CA 96097 • (530) 841-4175 • http://www.snowcrest.net/siskiyoulibrary/

Genealogical Society of Siskiyou County • c/o Siskiyou County Public Library, 719 4th St, P.O. Box 225 • Yreka, CA 96097 • (530) 841-4175 • http://www.snowcrest.net/siskiyoulibrary/

Klamath National Forest Historical Research Library • 1312 Fairland Rd • Yreka, CA 96097 • (530) 842-6131

Shasta Nation • P.O. Box 1054 • Yreka, CA 96097 • (916) 468-2314

Siskiyou County Courthouse Museum • 311 4th St • Yreka, CA 96097 • (530) 842-8340

Siskiyou County Historical Society • Siskihou County Museum, 910 S Main St • Yreka, CA 96097 • (530) 842-3836 • http://www. siskiyoucounty.com/museum/

Siskiyou County Public Library • 719 4th St • Yreka, CA 96097 • (530) 841-4175 • http://www.snowcrest.net/siskiyoulibrary/

Yuba City
Community Memorial Museum of Sutter County • 1333 Butte House Rd, P.O. Box 1555 • Yuba City, CA 95992 • (530) 822-7141 • http:// www.syix.com/museum/

Sutter County Free Library • 750 Forbes Ave • Yuba City, CA 95991-3891 • (530) 822-7137 • http://www.saclibrary.org

Sutter County Historical Society • Historical Museum, 1333 Butte House Rd, P.O. Box 1004 • Yuba City, CA 95992 • (530) 673-2721

Sutter-Yuba Genealogical Society • P.O. Box 1274 • Yuba City, CA 95991

Yucaipa
Los Rios Ranch Museum • 39610 Oak Glen Rd • Yucaipa, CA 92399 • (909) 797-1005

Oak Glen School House Museum • 11911 S Oak Glen Rd • Yucaipa, CA 92399 • (909) 797-1691

Yucaipa Adobe Museum • 32183 Kentucky St • Yucaipa, CA 92399 • (714) 798-8570 • http://www.co.san-bernardino.ca.us/ccr/museum/ museums.html

Yucaipa Valley Genealogical Society • P.O. Box 32 • Yucaipa, CA 92399

Yucipa Valley Historical Society • Historical Museum, 35308 Panorama Dr, P.O. Box 297 • Yucaipa, CA 92399 • (909) 790-4684

Yucca Valley
Genealogical Society of Morongo Basin • P.O. Box 234 • Yucca Valley, CA 92284-0234 • (760) 228-5455 • http://www.yuccavalley.com/ genealogy

Morongo Basin Historical Society • P.O. Box 2046 • Yucca Valley, CA 92286

Sutter County Historical Society • 57117 Twenty-Nine Palms Hwy • Yucca Valley, CA 92284

Yucca Valley Branch Library • 57098 29 Palms Hwy • Yucca Valley, CA 92284 • (760) 228-5455

Aguilar
Aguilar Public Library • 146 W Main St, P.O. Box 578 • Aguilar, CO 81020-0578 • (719) 941-4426

Akron
Akron Public Library • 302 Main • Akron, CO 80720-1437

Wasington County Museum • 34445 Hwy 63 • Akron, CO 80720 • (970) 345-6446

Alamosa
Alamosa Cultural Center and Museum • Hwy 285 & Airport Rd • Alamosa, CO 81101 • (719) 589-4624 • http://www.museumtrail.org/AlamosaCulturalCenter.asp

Luther Bean Museum • Adams State College, 208 Edgemont Blvd • Alamosa, CO 81102 • (719) 587-7011 • http://www.museumtrail.org/Luther.asp

Nielsen Library • Adams State College, 208 Edgemont Ave • Alamosa, CO 81102 • (719) 587-7781 • http://www.library.adams.edu

San Luis Valley Genealogical Society • P.O. Box 911 • Alamosa, CO 81101-0911 • (719) 589-6592

San Luis Valley Historical Society • P.O. Box 982 • Alamosa, CO 81101-0982 • (719) 589-9217

San Luis Valley History Museum • 401 Hunt Ave, P.O. Box 1593 • Alamosa, CO 81101 • (719) 587-0667 • http://www.museumtrail.org/SanLuisValleyHistoryMuseum.asp

Southern Peaks Public Library • 423 4th St • Alamosa, CO 81101 • (719) 589-6592 • http://www.alamosalibrary.org

Antonito
Conejos Museum • 5252 US Hwy 285, P.O. Box 86 • Antonito, CO 81120 • (719) 376-2355 • http://www.museumtrail.org/ConejosMuseum.asp

Arvada
American Historical Society of Germans from Russia, Denver Metro Chapter • 6733 Reed St • Arvada, CO 80033-4055 • (303) 933-3180 • http://ahsgr.org/Chapters/denver/codenver.html

Arvada Center for the Arts and Humanities Museum • 6901 Wadsworth Blvd • Arvada, CO 80003 • (303) 431-3080 • http://www.arvadacenter.org

Arvada Flour Mill Museum • 7307 Grandview Blvd • Arvada, CO 80002 • (303) 431-1261 • http://www.arvadahistory.org

Arvada Historical Society • McIlvoy House Museum, 7307 Grandview Ave, P.O. Box 419 • Arvada, CO 80001 • (303) 431-1261 • http://arvadahistory.org

Cussler Museum • 14959 W 69th Ave • Arvada, CO 80007 • (303) 420-2795 • http://www.cusslermuseum.com

Grand Lodge of Colorado, Sons of Italy • P.O. Box 1231 • Arvada, CO 80001 • (303) 385-7025 • http://www.osiacolorado.org

Jefferson County Public Library-Standley Lake • 8485 Kipling St • Arvada, CO 80005 • (303) 456-0806 • http://jefferson.lib.co.us

Westminster Historical Society • 3924 W 72nd Ave • Arvada, CO 80002 • (303) 430-7929

Aspen
Aspen Historical Society • Wheeler Stallard House Museum, 620 W Bleeker St • Aspen, CO 81611 • (970) 925-3721 • http://www.aspenhistory.org; http://www.aspenhistoricalsociety.com

Holden Marolt Mining & Ranching Museum • 40180 Hwy 82 • Aspen, CO 81611 • (970) 544-0280

Pitkin County Library • 120 N Mill St • Aspen, CO 81611 • (970) 925-4025 • http://www.pitcolib.org

Ault
Northern Plains Public Library • 216 2nd St, P.O. Box 147 • Ault, CO 80610-0147 • (970) 834-1259

Aurora
Aurora Genealogical Society of Colorado • P.O. Box 31732 • Aurora, CO 80041-0732 • http://www.freewebs.com/auroragenealogysociety/

Aurora Historical Society • Aurora History Museum, 15051 E Alameda Dr • Aurora, CO 80012-1546 • (303) 360-8545 • http://www.aurora-museum.org

Aurora Public Library • 14949 E Alameda Dr • Aurora, CO 80012 • (303) 739-6630 • http://www.auroralibrary.org

Centennial House Museum • 1671 Galena St • Aurora, CO 80010 • (303) 739-6666 • http://www.auroragov.org

Cherry Creek Valley Historical Society • Melvin Schoolhouse Museum, 4950 S Laredo St • Aurora, CO 80015 • (303) 699-5145 • http://www.cherrycreekvalleyhistoricalsociety.org

Coal Creek School Museum • 800 Telluride St • Aurora, CO 80011 • (303) 739-6666 • http://www.auroragov.org

Colorado Grange Museum • 21901 E Hampden Ave • Aurora, CO 80013 • (303) 693-3621

Delaney Farm Museum • 170 S Chambers Rd • Aurora, CO 80012 • (303) 739-6666 • http://www.auroragov.org

Fantasy of Flight Foundation Museum • 12579 E Cedar Ave • Aurora, CO 80012 • (303) 367-0670 • http://www.fantasyofflight.org

John Gully Homestead Museum • 200 S Chambers Rd • Aurora, CO 80017 • (303) 739-6666 • http://www.auroragov.org

Lutheran Church-Missouri Synod Rocky Mountain District Library • 14334 E Evans Ave • Aurora, CO 80014 • (303) 695-8001

Patrol Squadron Colorado Museum • 3657 S Uravan St • Aurora, CO 80013 • (303) 699-8611

Plains Conservation Center • 21901 E Hampden Ave • Aurora, CO 80013 • (303) 693-3621 • http://www.plainsconservationcenter.org

Bailey
Mountain Genealogists • 160 Hummingbird Ct • Bailey, CO 80401 • http://www.rootsweb.ancestry.com/~comgs/

Park County Historical Society • P.O. Box 43 • Bailey, CO 80421 • (303) 838-9511 • http://www.parkcountyhistory.com

Park County Public Library • 350 Bulldogger Rd, P.O. Box 282 • Bailey, CO 80421-0282 • (303) 838-5539

Basalt
Basalt Regional Library District • 14 Midland Ave • Basalt, CO 81621 • (970) 927-4311 • http://www.basaltrld.org

Bayfield
Gem Village Museum • Route 1 • Bayfield, CO 81122 • (970) 884-2811

Pine River Public Library • 15 E Mill St, P.O. Box 227 • Bayfield, CO 81122-0227 • (970) 884-2222

Beckenridge
Breckenridge Mining Camp Museum • 115 N Main St • Beckenridge, CO 80424 • (970) 453-2342

Berthoud
Berthoud Historical Society • P.O. Box 1020 • Berthoud, CO 80513

Berthoud Historical Society • Pioneer Museum, 228 Mountain Ave, P.O. Box 225 • Berthoud, CO 80513 • (970) 532-2149 • http://www.berthoudhistoricalsociety.org

Berthoud Public Library • 236 Welch Ave, P.O. Box 1259 • Berthoud, CO 80513-2259 • (970) 532-2757 • http://pyramid.cudenever.edu/berthoud

Colorado

Beulah

Beulah Historical Society • P.O. Box 76 • Beulah, CO 81023

Slovenian Genealogical Society, Colorado Chapter • 8950 3R Road • Beulah, CO 81023 • http://sloveniangenealogy.org/chapters/Colorado.htm

Black Hawk

Lace House Museum • 161 Main St • Black Hawk, CO 80422 • (303) 582-5382

Boulder

Boulder County Health Department • 3450 Broadway • Boulder, CO 80304 • (303) 441-1100 • http://www.co.boulder.co.us

Boulder Genealogical Society • c/o Carnegie Library, 1125 Pine St, P.O. Box 3246 • Boulder, CO 80303-3246 • (303) 441-3110 • http://www.bouldergenealogy.org

Boulder Historical Society • Historical Museum, 1206 Euclid Ave • Boulder, CO 80302-7224 • (303) 449-3464 • http://www.boulderhistorymuseum.org

Boulder Public Library • 1000 Canyon Blvd, P.O. Drawer H • Boulder, CO 80306 • (303) 441-3100 • http://www.boulder.lib.co.us

Carnegie Branch Library for Local History • 1125 Pine St, P.O. Drawer H • Boulder, CO 80306-1326 • (303) 441-3100 • http://www.boulderlibrary.org

Colorado Chautauqua Association • Archive and History Room, 900 Baseline Rd • Boulder, CO 80302 • (303) 442-3282 • http://www.chautauqua.com

CU Heritage Center Museum • Old Main, 3rd Fl, Campus Box 459 • Boulder, CO 80309 • (303) 492-6329 • http://www.cualum.org/heritage/

Eldorado Springs Historical Society • P.O. Drawer H • Boulder, CO 80302

Historic Boulder • 1123 Spruce St • Boulder, CO 80302 • (303) 444-5192 • http://www.historicboulder.org

Norlin Library • Univ of Colorado, 1720 Pleasant St, UCB 184 • Boulder, CO 80309-0184 • (303) 492-7521 • http://www-libraries.colorado.edu

University of Colorado Museum • 17th & Broadway, 218 UCB • Boulder, CO 80309 • (303) 492-6892 • http://www.cumuseum.colorado.edu

Women of the West Museum • 250 Bristlecone Wy • Boulder, CO 80304 • (303) 499-9110 • www.wowmuseum.org

Breckenridge

Barney Ford House Museum • 111 E Washington Ave • Breckenridge, CO 80424 • (970) 453-5761

Breckenridge Heritage Alliance • 309 N Main St, P.O. Box 2460 • Breckenridge, CO 80424 • (970) 453-9767 • http://www.breckheritage.com

Breckenridge Mining Camp Museum • 115 N Main St • Breckenridge, CO 80424 • (970) 453-2342

Edwin Carter Museum • 111 N Ridge St, P.O. Box 745 • Breckenridge, CO 80424 • (970) 453-9022 • http://www.summithistorical.org

Rotary Snowplow Park • 111 N Ridge • Breckenridge, CO 80424 • (970) 453-9022 • http://www.summithisotircal.org/RailwayRotary.html

Saddle Rock Society • 111 E Washington, P.O. Box 4195 • Breckenridge, CO 80424 • (970) 453-5761

Summit County Historical Society • Historical Museum, 309 N Main St, P.O. Box 745 • Breckenridge, CO 97045-9022 • (970) 453-9022 • http://www.summithistorical.org

Brighton

Adams County Historical Society • Historical Museum, 9601 Henderson Rd • Brighton, CO 80601 • (303) 659-7103 • http://www.co.adams.co.us

Brighton Genealogical Society • 343 S 21st Ave, P.O. Box 1005 • Brighton, CO 80601-2525

Pleasant Plains County School Museum • 630 S 8th Ave • Brighton, CO 80601 • (303) 659-4820

Broomfield

Anthem Ranch Genealogical Society • 16151 Lowell Blvd • Broomfield, CO 80023

Broomfield Department of Health and Human Services • 6 Garden Center • Broomfield, CO 80020 • (720) 887-2270 • http://www.ci.broomfield.co.us

Broomfield Genealogical Society • c/o Mamie Doud Eisenhower Public Library, 3 Community Park Rd • Broomfield, CO 80020 • http://www.rootsweb.com/~cobgs

Mamie Doud Eisenhower Public Library • 3 Community Park Rd • Broomfield, CO 80020-3781 • (720) 887-2300, Ext 2356 • http://www.ci.broomfield.co.us/library

Brush

Brush Area Museum and Cultural Center • 314 S Clayton, P.O. Box 341 • Brush, CO 80723 • (970) 842-9879 • http://www.brushareamuseum.org

East Morgan County Library District • 500 Clayton St • Brush, CO 80723-2016 • (970) 842-4596 • http://emcl.lib.co.us

Buena Vista

Buena Vista Heritage Association • Historical Museum, 512 E Main, P.O. Box 1414 • Buena Vista, CO 81211 • (719) 395-8458

Buena Vista Heritage Museum • 511 E Main St, P.O. Box 924 • Buena Vista, CO 81211 • (719) 395-8458 • http://www.buenavistaheritage.org

Buena Vista Public Library • 131 Linderman Ave, P.O. Box 2019 • Buena Vista, CO 81211-2019 • (719) 395-8700 • http://www.buenavistalibrary.org

Burlington

Colorado Welcome Center Museum • 48265 Interstate 70, P.O. Box 157 • Burlington, CO 80807 • (719) 346-5554

Old Town Museum • 420 S 14th St • Burlington, CO 80807 • (970) 346-7382 • http://www.burlingtoncolo.com/oldtown.html

Canon City

Canon City Heritage Association • Royal Gorge Regional Museum and History Center, 612 Royal Gorge Blvd, P.O. Box 1460 • Canon City, CO 81212-3751 • (719) 269-9018 • http://www.ccpl.lib.co.us/RGRM&HC.htm

Canon City Municipal Museum • 612 Royal Gorge Blvd, P.O. Box 1460 • Canon City, CO 80215 • (719) 269-9018

Canon City Public Library & Fremont County Local History Center • 516 Macon St • Canon City, CO 81212-3380 • (719) 269-9021 • http://ccpl.lib.co.us/lhc.html

Colorado Territorial Prison Museum • 201 N 1st St • Canon City, CO 81212 • (719) 269-3015 • http://www.prisonmuseum.org

Dinosaur Depot Museum • 330 Royal Gorge Blvd #1 • Canon City, CO 81212 • (719) 269-7150 • http://www.dinosaurdepot.com

Fremont County Genealogical Society • c/o Canon City Public Library, 516 Macon Ave • Canon City, CO 81218

Fremont-Custer Historical Society • P.O. Box 965 • Canon City, CO 81212

Carbondale

Mount Sopris Historical Society • Historical Museum, P.O. Box 373 • Carbondale, CO 81623

Vintage Ski World Museum • 1521 Panorama Dr • Carbondale, CO 81623 • (970) 963-9025 • http://www.vintageskiworld.com

Castle Rock

Castle Rock Genealogical Society • P.O. Box 1881 • Castle Rock, CO 80104 • http://crcgs.com

Castle Rock Historical Museum • Denver & Rio Grande RR Station, 420 Elbert St, P.O. Box 1572 • Castle Rock, CO 80104 • (303) 814-3164 • http://www.ccpl.lib.co.us/RGRM&HC.htm

Castle Rock Historical Society • Historical Museum, 420 Elbert St • Castle Rock, CO 80104 • (303) 814-3164 • http://castlerockmuseum.org

Douglas County Historical Society • Castle Rock Museum, 620 Lewis St • Castle Rock, CO 80104

Douglas County Library & History Research Center • 100 S Wilcox St • Castle Rock, CO 80104 • (303) 688-7730 • http://douglascountyhistory.org

Douglas County Public Library-Philip S Miller Branch • 961 S Plum Creek Blvd • Castle Rock, CO 80104-2599 • (303) 688-5157 • http://douglas.lib.co.us

Historic Douglas County • P.O. Box 2032 • Castle Rock, CO 80104 • http://www.historicdouglascounty.org

Cedaredge

Surface Creek Historical Society • Pioneer Town Museum, 315 SW 3rd Ave, P.O. Box 906 • Cedaredge, CO 81413 • (970) 856-7554 • http://www.cedaredgecolorado.com; http://www.pioneertown.org

Centennial

Columbine Genealogical and Historical Society • P.O. Box 2074 • Centennial, CO 80161 • (303) 795-1150 • http://www.columbinegenealogy.com

Columbine Genealogical and Historical Society • P.O. Box 2074 • Centennial, CO 80161-2074 • (303) 770-7164 • http://columbinegenealogy.com

Central City

Central City Opera House Association • Historical Museum, 124 Eureka St, P.O. Box 218 • Central City, CO 80427 • (303) 623-7167 • http://centralcityopera.org

Central Gold Mine Museum • P.O. Box 161 • Central City, CO 80427

Gilpin County Historical Society • Gilpin County Museum, 228 E High St, P.O. Box 247 • Central City, CO 80427-0247 • (303) 582-5283 • http://www.gilpinhistory.org

Cherry Hills Village

Swedish Genealogical Society of Colorado • c/o Bethany Lutheran Church, 4500 E Hampden Ave • Cherry Hills Village, CO 80113 • (303) 758-2820 • http://swedgensoc.org/

Cheyenne Wells

Cheyenne County Public Health Office • 615 N 5th W, P.O. Box 38 • Cheyenne Wells, CO 80810 • (719) 767-5616

Cheyenne Wells Museum • 91 E 1st St • Cheyenne Wells, CO 80810 • (719) 767-5773

Eastern Colorado Historical Society • 85 W 2nd St • Cheyenne Wells, CO 80810 • (719) 767-5907

Clark

Hahns Peak Area Historical Society • Hahns Peak Village Museum, RCR 129 & Main St, P.O. Box 403 • Clark, CO 80428 • (970) 879-6781 • http://www.hahnspeakhistoric.com

Colona

Ouray County Ranch History Museum • 206 Cty Rd 1 • Colona, CO 81403 • (970) 626-5075 • http://ourayranchhistory.org/

Colorado Springs

Albert B Simpson Historical Library • Christian & Missionary Alliance, 8595 Explorer Dr, P.O. Box 35000 • Colorado Springs, CO 80935-3500 • (719) 599-5999 • http://www.cmalliance.org

American Historical Society of Germans from Russia, Colorado Springs Chapter • 3330 Templeton Gap Rd • Colorado Springs, CO 80907-5457 • (719) 579-9711

American Nimismatic Association • Money Museum, 818 N Cascade Ave • Colorado Springs, CO 80903 • (719) 632-2646 • http://www.money.org

Carriage House Museum • The Broadmoor, 16 Lake Cr • Colorado Springs, CO 80906 • (719) 577-7065

Charles Leaming Tutt Library • Colorado College, 1021 N Cascade • Colorado Springs, CO 80903 • (719) 389-6668 • http://www.coloradocollege.edu/library/specialcollections/special.html

Colorado Springs Pioneer Museum • Starsmore Center for Local History, 215 S Tejon St • Colorado Springs, CO 80903 • (719) 385-5650 • http://www.cspm.org

El Paso County Health Department and Environment • 301 S Union Blvd • Colorado Springs, CO 80910 • (719) 575-8492 • http://www.elpasocountyhealth.org/vitalstats

Ghost Town Museum • 400 S 21st St • Colorado Springs, CO 80904 • (719) 634-0696 • http://www.ghosttownmuseum.com

Kraemer Family Library • University of Colorado at Colorado Springs, 1420 Austin Bluffs Pkwy, P.O. Box 7150 • Colorado Springs, CO 80933-7150 • (719) -262-3295 • http://web.uccs.edu/library

Masonic Grand Lodge of Colorado • 1130 Panorama Dr • Colorado Springs, CO 80904 • (719) 471-9587 • http://www.coloradofreemasons.org

Masonic Grand Lodge of Colorado • 1130 Panorama Dr • Colorado Springs, CO 80904 • (719) 471-9587 • http://www.coloradofreemasons.org/

McAllister House Museum • 423 N Cascade Ave • Colorado Springs, CO 80903 • (719) 635-7925 • http://oldcolo.com/hist/mcallister

Museum of Orthodoxy • 2501 W Colorado Ave • Colorado Springs, CO 80904 • (719) 635-1390 • http://www.museumororthodoxy.org

National Museum of World War II Aviation • 765 Aviation Wy • Colorado Springs, CO 80916 • (719) 637-7559

National Railway Historical Society, Colorado Midland • P.O. Box 824 • Colorado Springs, CO 80901 • (719) 533-1311 • http://www.nrhs.com/chapters/colorado-midland

National Society of the Colonial Dames of America in the State of Colorado • McAlister House Museum, 423 N Cascade Ave • Colorado Springs, CO 80903 • (970) 635-7925 • http://www.nscda.org/co/mcallisterhousemuseum.html

Negro Historical Association of Colorado Springs (NHACS) • 5180 Mountain Villa Grove • Colorado Springs, CO 80917 • (719) 574-8332

Old Colorado City Historical Society • Historical Museum, 1 S 24th St • Colorado Springs, CO 80904-3319 • (719) 636-1225 • http://www.history.oldcolo.com

Pikes Peak Genealogical Society • P.O. Box 1262 • Colorado Springs, CO 80901 • (719) 630-8407 FAX • http://www.ppgs.org

Pikes Peak Historic Street Railway Museum • 2333 Steel Dr • Colorado Springs, CO 80907 • (719) 475-9508 • http://www.coloradospringstrolleys.com

Colorado

Colorado Springs, cont.

Pikes Peak Library District • 20 N Cascade, P.O. Box 1579 • Colorado Springs, CO 80902 • (719) 531-6333 x2252 • http://library.ppld.org/SpecialCollections/

Pikes Peak Library District • 5550 N Union Blvd, P.O. Box 5550 • Colorado Springs, CO 80901 • (719) 531-6333 • http://library.ppld.org

Pikes Peak Radio & Electronics Museum • 6735 Earl Dr • Colorado Springs, CO 80918 • (719) 550-5810 • http://www.pikespeakradiomuseum.com

Pro Rodeo Hall of Fame Museum • 101 Pro Rodeo Dr • Colorado Springs, CO 80919 • (719) 528-4761 • http://www.prorodeo.com; http://www.prorodeohalloffame.com

Rock Ledge Ranch Historic Site Museum • 3105 Gateway Rd • Colorado Springs, CO 80804 • (719) 578-6777 • http://www.rockledgeranch.com

Rocky Mountain Motorcycle Museum • 5865 N Nevada Ave • Colorado Springs, CO 80918 • (719) 633-6329 • http://www.travelassist.com/mag/a20.html

South Park Railway History Museum • 12345 Lindsey Ln • Colorado Springs, CO 80908 • (719) 495-0348

Trimble Library • Nazarene Bible College, 1111 Academy • Colorado Springs, CO 80910 • (719) 884-5000, Ext 5071 • http://www.nbc.edu

Turin Shroud Center of Colorado • 5875 Lehman Dr, P.O. Box 25326 • Colorado Springs, CO 80918 • (719) 599-5755 • http://www.shroudofturin.com

United States Space Foundation Museum • 310 S 14th St • Colorado Springs, CO 80904 • (719) 576-8000 • http://www.spacefoundation.org

Western Museum of Mining & Industry • 225 Northgate Blvd • Colorado Springs, CO 80921 • (719) 488-0880 • http://www.wmmi.org

White House Ranch Historic Site Museum • 3202 Chambers Wy • Colorado Springs, CO 80908

Will Rogers Shrine • 4250 Cheyenne Mountain Zoo Rd • Colorado Springs, CO 80906 • (719) 633-9925 • http://www.cmzoo.org

World Figure Skating Museum • 20 1st St • Colorado Springs, CO 80906 • (719) 635-5200 • http://www.worldskatingmuseum.org

Conifer

Conifer Historical Society • P.O. Box 295 • Conifer, CO 80433 • (303) 697-8123

Cortez

Colorado Welcome Center • 928 E Main St • Cortez, CO 81321 • (970) 565-4048

Cortez Cultural Center • 25 N Market St • Cortez, CO 81321 • (970) 565-1151 • http://www.cortezculturalcenter.org

Cortez Public Library • 202 N Park • Cortez, CO 81321-3300 • (970) 565-8117 • http://www.cityofcortez.com

Crow Canyon Archaeological Center • 23390 Road K • Cortez, CO 81321 • (970) 565-8975 • http://www.crowcanyon.org

Notah Dineh Trading Company Museum • 345 W Main St • Cortez, CO 81321 • (800) 444-2024 • http://www.notahdineh.com

Craig

Moffat County Libraries • 570 Green St • Craig, CO 81625-3027 • (970) 824-5116 • http://www.marmot.org

Museum of Northwest Colorado • 590 Yampa Ave • Craig, CO 81625 • (970) 824-6360 • http://www.museumnwco.org

Wyman Living History Ranch and Museum • 94350 E Hwy 40, P.O. Box 339 • Craig, CO 81626 • (970) 824-6346 • http://www.wymanmuseum.com

Creede

Creede Historical Society • Historical Museum, 17 Main St, P.O. Box 609 • Creede, CO 81130 • (719) 658-2303 • http://www.museumtrail.org/creedehistoricmuseum.asp

Creede Museum Association • Historical Museum, P.O. Box 608 • Creede, CO 81130

Creede Underground Mining Museum • 503 Forest Service Rd 9, P.O. Box 432 • Creede, CO 81130 • (719) 658-0811 • http://www.museumtrail.org/CreedeUndergroundMiningMuseum.asp

Crested Butte

Crested Butte Historical Society • P.O. Box 324 • Crested Butte, CO 81224

Crested Butte Mountain Heritage Museum • 331 Elk Ave, P.O. Box 2480 • Crested Butte, CO 81224 • (970) 349-1880 • http://www.crestedbuttemuseum.com

Mountain Bike Hall of Fame Museum • 331 Elk Ave, P.O. Box 845 • Crested Butte, CO 81224 • (970) 349-7382 • http://www.mtnbikehalloffame.com

Cripple Creek

Ancient and Honorable Order of the Jersey Blues • P.O. Box 2 • Cripple Creek, CO 80813-0002 • (719) 689-3000 • http://www.rootsweb.com/~genepool.njblues.htm

Cripple Creek District Museum • 500 E Bennett Ave, P.O. Box 1210 • Cripple Creek, CO 80813 • (719) 689-2634 • http://www.cripple-creek.com

Franklin Ferguson Memorial Library • 410 N B St, P.O. Box 975 • Cripple Creek, CO 80813 • (719) 689-2800

Mollie Kathleen Mine Museum • 9388 Hwy 67, P.O. Box 339 • Cripple Creek, CO 80813 • (719) 689-2466 • http://www.goldminetours.com

Old Homestead Parlour House Museum • 353 Myers Ave, P.O. Box 540 • Cripple Creek, CO 80813 • (719) 689-3090

Outlaws & Law Men Jail Museum • 136 W Bennett Ave • Cripple Creek, CO 80813 • (719) 689-6556

Pikes Peak Heritage Center • 9283 S Hwy 67 • Cripple Creek, CO 80813 • (719) 689-3315 • http://www.pikes-peak.com/Attraction/81.aspx

Crook

Crook Historical Society • Historical Museum, 4th St & 4th Ave, P.O. Box 194 • Crook, CO 80726

Crowley

Crowley County Heritage Center • 300 Main St, P.O. Box 24 • Corwley, CO 81033 • (719) 267-3384 • http://www.crowleyheritagecenter.com

Deer Trail

Deer Trail Pioneer Historical Society • Deer Trail Pioneer Museum, P.O. Box 176 • Deer Trail, CO 80105 • (303) 769-4577 • http://www.deertrailcolorado.org/Museum.htm

Del Norte

Del Norte Public Library • 790 Grand Ave • Del Norte, CO 81132 • (719) 657-2633

Lookout Mountain Observatory Association • P.O. Box 472 • Del Norte, CO 81132

Rio Grande County Historical Society • Historical Museum, 580 Oak St • Del Norte, CO 81132-2210 • (719) 657-2847 • http://www.rgcm.org

Delta

Delta County Historical Society • Delta County Museum, 251 Meeker St, P.O. Box 681 • Delta, CO 81416-1914 • (970) 874-8721 • http://www.deltacountymuseum.com

Delta County Public Library • 211 W 6th St • Delta, CO 81416 • (970) 874-9630 • http://www.dcpld.org

Fort Uncompahgre Living History Museum • 530 Gunnison Giver Dr • Delta, CO 80416 • (970) 874-8349 • http://www.deltafort.org

High Country Genealogical Society • 601 Willow Wood Ln • Delta, CO 81416-3037

Denver

Association of Professional Genealogists, Colorado Chapter • P.O. Box 40393 • Denver, CO 80204-0393 • (303) 422-9371 • http://www.apgen.org

Auraria Library • 1100 Lawrence St • Denver, CO 80204-2095 • (303) 556-2805 • http://library.auraria.edu

Black American West Museum and Heritage Center • 3091 California St • Denver, CO 80205 • (303) 292-2566 • http://www.blackamericanwestmuseum.com

Black Genealogy Search Group of Colorado • P.O. Box 7276 • Denver, CO 80207 • (303) 445-2150 • http://bgsgden.com

Boettcher Mansion Museum • 400 E 8th Ave • Denver, CO 80203 • (303) 866-5344 • http://www.colorado.gov/governor/mansion

Buckhorn Exchange Restaurant and Museum • 1000 Osage St • Denver, CO 80204 • (303) 534-9505 • http://www.buckhorn.com

Byers-Evans House Museum • 1310 Bannock St • Denver, CO 80304 • (303) 620-4933 • http://www.coloradohistory.org

Cable Center Museum • 2000 Buchtel Blvd • Denver, CO 80210 • (303) 871-4885 • http://www.cablecenter.org

Central City Opera House Museum • 621 17th St, St 1601 • Denver, CO 80293 • (303) 292-6500

Church of God - Seventh Day Church Library • 330 W 152nd Ave, P.O. Box 33677 • Denver, CO 80233 • http://www.cog7.org

Colorado Council of Genealogical Societies • P.O. Box 40270 • Denver, CO 80224-0379 • (303) 688-9652 • http://cocouncil.org

Colorado Department of Health and Environment Vital Records Division • 4300 Cherry Creek Dr S • Denver, CO 80222-1530 • (303) 756-4464 • http://www.cdphe.state.co.us/hs/genealogy.html

Colorado Division of State Archives and Public Records • 1313 Sherman St, Rm 120 • Denver, CO 80203-3534 • (303) 866-2055 • http://www.archives.state.co.us

Colorado Genealogical Society • P.O. Box 9218 • Denver, CO 80209-0218 • (303) 571-1535 • http://www.cogensoc.us

Colorado Genealogical Society, Computer Interest Group • P.O. Box 9218 • Denver, CO 80209-0218 • http://www.cogensoc.us/cigmain.htm

Colorado Society of Hispanic Genealogy • 2300 S Patton Ct • Denver, CO 80219-5212 • http://www.hispanicgen.org

Colorado Sports Hall of Fame • 1701 Bryant St • Denver, CO 80204 • (720) 258-3888 • http://www.coloradosports.com

Colorado State Library • 201 E Colfax Ave, No 309 • Denver, CO 80203-1799 • (303) 866-6900 • http://www.cde.state.co.us/library_index.htm

Colorado Welsh Society • P.O. Box 103192 • Denver, CO 80250 • (303) 427-7188 • http://coloradowelshsociety.org

Czech and Slovak Search Group • 209 S Ogden • Denver, CO 80209-2321

Dayton Memorial Library • Regis University, 3333 Regis Blvd • Denver, CO 80221-1099 • (303) 458-4030 • http://www.regis.edu

Denver Community Museum • 1610 Little Raven St, Ste 120 • Denver, CO 80202 • (303) 458-7541 • http://www.denvercommunitymuseum.org

Denver Firefighters Museum • 1326 Tremont Pl • Denver, CO 80204 • (303) 892-1436 • http://www.denverfirefightersmuseum.org

Denver Museum of Miniatures, Dolls and Toys • Pearce-McAllister Cottage, 1880 Gaylord St • Denver, CO 80206 • (303) 322-1053 • http://www.dmmdt.org

Denver Museum of Nature & Science • 2001 Colorado Blvd • Denver, CO 80205 • (303) 322-7009 • http://www.dmns.org

Denver Public Library • 10 W 14th Ave Pkwy • Denver, CO 80204-2731 • (720) 865-1821 • http://www.denver.lib.co.us

Forney Museum of Transportation • 4303 Brighton Blvd • Denver, CO 80216 • (303) 297-1113 • http://www.forneymuseum.com

Four Mile Historic Park • 715 S Forest St • Denver, CO 80246 • (303) 399-1859 • http://www.fourmilepark.org

Germanic Genealogical Society • c/o Denver Public Library, 10 W 14th Ave Pkwy • Denver, CO 80204 • (720) 865-1821

Goodwill Antique Doll Museum • 6850 Federal Blvd • Denver, CO 80221 • (303) 650-7700 • http://www.goodwilldenver.org

Grant-Humphreys Mansion Museum • 770 Pennsylvania St • Denver, CO 80203 • (303) 894-2506 • http://coloradohistory.org/grant_humphreys

Historic Denver • 1420 Ogden St, Ste 202 • Denver, CO 80218 • (303) 534-5288 • http://www.historicdenver.org

Historic Fort Logan • 3742 W Princeton Cr, P.O. Box 36011 • Denver, CO 80236 • (303) 789-3568 • http://www.friendsofhistoricfortlogan.org

History Colorado • Colorado Heritage Center, 1200 Broadway • Denver, CO 80203 • (303) 447-8679 • http://www.historycolorado.org

Ira M Beck Memorial Collection of Rocky Mountain Jewish History • 2000 E Asbury Ave • Denver, CO 80208 • (303) 871-3020

Jewish Genealogical Society of Colorado • 6965 E Girard Ave • Denver, CO 80224 • (303) 756-6028 • http://jgsco.org

Mizel Museum • 400 S Kearney St • Denver, CO 80224 • (303) 394-9993 • http://www.mizelmuseum.org

Molly Brown House Museum • 1340 Pennsylvania St • Denver, CO 80203 • (303) 832-4092 • http://www.mollybrown.org

Molly Brown Summer House Museum • 2690 S Wadsworth Blvd • Denver, CO 80227 • (303) 989-6639 • http://www.mollybrownsummerhouse.com

Museo de las Americas • 861 Santa Fe Dr • Denver, CO 80204 • (303) 571-4401 • http://www.museo.org

National Archives & Records Administration-Rocky Mountain Region • 17101 Huron St, P.O. Box 25307 • Denver, CO 80225-0307 • (303) 236-0804 • http://www.archives.gov/denver/

National Railway Historical Society, Intermountain Chapter • 4303 Brighton Blvd • Denver, CO 80216 • (303) 298-0377 • http://www.cozx.com/nrhs/

Penrose Library • University of Denver, 2150 E Evans • Denver, CO 80208-2007 • (303) 871-2905 • http://www.penlib.du.edu

Rocky Mountain Jewish Historical Society • Ira M Beck Memorial Jewish Archives, Univ of Denver, 2199 S University Blvd • Denver, CO 80208-0001 • (303) 871-2959 • http://www.du.edu/cjs/rmjhs

Saint John's Cathedral Library • 1350 Washington St • Denver, CO 80203 • (303) 831-7115 • http://www.sjc.den.org

Society of Rocky Mountain Archivists • Colorado State Archives, 1313 Sherman St • Denver, CO 80203 • (307) 766-2553

Stagecoach Library for Genealogical Research • 1840 S Wolcott Ct • Denver, CO 80219 • (303) 922-8856

Stiles African American Heritage Center • 2607 Glenarm Pl • Denver, CO 80205 • (303) 294-0597 • http://www.stilesheritagecenter.org

Turner Museum • 773 Downing • Denver, CO 80218 • (303) 832-0924

Colorado

Denver, cont.

United States Mint Museum • 320 W Colfax Ave • Denver, CO 80204 • (303) 844-3332

US Geological Survey Photographic Library • Denver Federal Ctr, Bldg 20 Box 25046, MS 914 • Denver, CO 80225-0046 • (303) 236-1005; (303) 236-1010 • http://library.usgs.gov/denlib.html

Vintage Motor Museum • 2762 Walnut St • Denver, CO 80205 • (303) 993-7693

Wings Over the Rockies Air & Space Museum • 7711 N Academy Blvd, Hanger 1 • Denver, CO 80230 • (303) 860-5360 • http://www.wingsmuseum.org

WISE Family History Society (Wales, Ireland, Scotland, England) • P.O. Box 48226 • Denver, CO 80204--0658 • (303) 922-8856 • http://www.wise-fhs.org/

Dillon

Summit Historical Society • Dillon School House Museum, 403 La Bonte, P.O. Box 747 • Dillon, CO 80435 • (970) 468-6079 • http://www.townofdillon.com

Dinosaur

Colorado Welcome Center • 101 E Stegosaurus, P.O. Box 207 • Dinosaur, CO 81610 • (970) 374-2205

Dolores

Anasazi Heritage Center Museum • 27501 Hwy 184 • Dolores, CO 81323 • (970) 882-5600 • http://www.blm.gov

Canyons of the Ancients National Monument • 27501 Hwy 184 • Dolores, CO 81323 • (970) 882-5600 • http://www.friendsofthecanyons.org

Dolores Library District • 1002 Railroad Ave, P.O. Box 847 • Dolores, CO 81323-0847 • (970) 882-4127 • http://www.doloreslibrary.org

Galloping Goose Historical Railway Society of Dolores • Historical Museum, 421 Railroad Ave, P.O. Box 443 • Dolores, CO 81323 • (970) 882-7082 • http://www.gallopinggoose5.com

Dove Creek

Dolores County Historical Society • P.O. Box 453 • Dove Creek, CO 81324

Drake

Estes Park Genealogical Society • c/o Estes Park Public Library, 335 E Elkhorn Ave • Drake, CO 80517 • (970) 586-8116

Durango

Animas Museum • 3065 W 2nd Ave, P.O. Box 3384 • Durango, CO 81302 • (970) 259-2402 • http://www.animasmuseum.org

Durango & Silver Narrow Gauge Railroad Museum • 479 Main St • Durango, CO 81301 • (970) 247-2733

Durango Public Library • 1900 E 3rd Ave • Durango, CO 81301 • (970) 375-3380 • http://www.durangopubliclibrary.org

Four Corners Genealogy Society • P.O. Box 2636 • Durango, CO 81302

Genealogical Research Society of Durango • 2720 Delwood • Durango, CO 81301

Grand Motorcar Collection • 586 Animas View Dr • Durango, CO 81301 • (970) 247-1250

John F Reed Library - Center for Southwest Studies • Fort Lewis College, 1000 Rim Dr • Durango, CO 81301-3999 • (970) 247-7551 • http://www.library.fortlewis.edu

La Plata County Historical Society • Animas School Museum, 3065 W 2nd Ave, P.O. Box 3384 • Durango, CO 81302 • (970) 259-2402 • http://www.animasmuseum.org

San Juan Basin Health Department • 281 Sawyer Dr, P.O. Box 140 • Durango, CO 81302 • (970) 247-5702 • http://www.sjbhd.org

Strater Hotel Museum • 699 Main Ave • Durango, CO 81501 • (970) 247-3451 • http://www.strater.com

Eads

Kiowa County Historical Society • P.O. Box 17 • Eads, CO 81036

Kiowa County Museum • 1313 Maine St • Eads, CO 81036 • (719) 438-2250

Eagle

Eagle Valley Historical Society • P.O. Box 192 • Eagle, CO 81631 • (970) 845-7741

Eagle Valley Library District • 600 Broadway, P.O. Box 240 • Eagle, CO 81631-0240 • (970) 328-8800 • http://www.evld.org

Eaton

Eaton House Museum • 207 Elm Ave • Eaton, CO 80615 • (970) 454-3338 • http://www.eatonco.org

Edgewater

Edgewater Historical Commission • 2401 Sheridan Blvd • Edgewater, CO 80214 • (303) 238-7803

Englewood

Cherry Creek School House & Melvin School Museum • 9300 E Union Ave • Englewood, CO 80111 • (303) 693-1500

Englewood Public Library • 1000 Englewood Pkwy • Englewood, CO 80110 • (303) 762-2555 • http://www.englewoodgov.org

Erie

American Historical Society of Germans from Russia, Northern Colorado Chapter • 6728 Cty Rd 3 1/4 • Erie, CO 80516 • (970) 301-4473 • http://ahsgr.org/Chapters/NorthernColoradoChapter.htm

Erie Historical Society • Wise Homestead Museum, 11611 Jasper Rd, P.O. Box 156 • Erie, CO 80515 • (303) 828-4561 • http://www.eriehistoricalsociety.org

Spirit of Flight Center • Erie Municipal Airport, 2650 S Main St • Erie, CO 80516-8155 • (303) 460-1156 • http://www.spiritofflight.com

Estes Park

Baldpate Inn Museum • 4900 S St Vrain • Estes Park, CO 80517 • (970) 586-6151 • http://www.baldpateinn.com

Enos Mills Cabin Museum • 6760 Hwy 7 • Estes Park, CO 80517 • (970) 586-4706 • http://www.enosmills.com

Estes Park Area Historical Society • Historical Museum, 200 4th St, P.O. Box 1691 • Estes Park, CO 80517-6339 • (970) 586-6256

Estes Park Public Library • Bond Park, 335 E Elkhorn Ave, P.O. Box 1687 • Estes Park, CO 80517-1687 • (970) 586-8116 • http://www.estes.lib.co.us

Fall River Hydro Interpretive Center • 1746 Fish Hatchery Rd • Estes Park, CO 80517 • (970) 577-7683

Lula W Dorsey Museum • YMCA of the Rockies, 2515 Tunnel Rd, P.O. Box 20500 • Estes Park, CO 80511 • (970) 586-3341 x1137

MacGregor Ranch Museum • 180 MacGregor Ln, P.O. Box 4675 • Estes Park, CO 80517 • (970) 586-3749 • http://www.macgregorranch.org

Stanley Hotel Museum • 333 Wonderview Ave • Estes Park, CO 80517 • (970) 577-1903 • http://www.stanleymuseum.org

Stanley Museum of Estes Park • 517 Big Thompson Ave, P.O. Box 788 • Estes Park, CO 80517 • (970) 577-1903 • http://www.stanleymuseum.org

Evans

Evans Historical Museum • 3720 Golden St • Evans, CO 80620 • (970) 339-5344 • http://www.cityofevans.org

Evergreen

Humphrey Memorial Park & Museum • 620 S Soda Creek Rd, P.O. Box 2122 • Evergreen, CO 80437 • (303) 674-5429 • http://www.hmpm.org

Jefferson County Historical Society • Hiwan Homestead Museum, 4208 S Timbervale Dr, P.O. Box 703 • Evergreen, CO 80439 • (303) 670-0784 • http://jchscolorado.org

Jefferson County Historical Society • P.O. Box 703 • Evergreen, CO 80437 • (720) 497-7650

Mountain Genealogists Society • c/o Church of the Hills, 28628 Buffalo Park Rd • Evergreen, CO 80439 • http://rootsweb.ancestry.com/~comgs/

Fairplay

Park County Local History Archives • P.O. Box 99 • Fairplay, CO 80440 • http://www.parkcoarchives.org

South Park Historical Foundation • South Park City Museum, 100 4th St, P.O. Box 634 • Fairplay, CO 80440 • (719) 836-2387 • http://www.southparkcity.org/museum_info

Flagler

Flagler Community Library • 311 Main Ave, P.O. Box 367 • Flagler, CO 80815-0367 • (719) 765-4310

Flagler Historical Society • P.O. Box 263 • Flagler, CO 80815

Fleming

Fleming Historical Society • Heritage Museum Park, 313 W Hall St • Fleming, CO 90728 • (970) 265-3721

Fleming Museum • 400 W Weston • Fleming, CO 80728 • (970) 265-2591

Florence

Florence Historical Society • Price Pioneer Museum, 100 E Front St, P.O. Box 87 • Florence, CO 81226 • (719) 784-1904

Rockvale Historical Club • Rte 1, 1215 Churchill • Florence, CO 81244

Florissant

Pikes Peak Historical Society • Historical Museum, 18033 Teller Cty Rd 1, P.O. Box 823 • Florissant, CO 80816 • (719) 748-8259 • http://www.pikespeakhsmuseum.org

Fort Carson

3rd Cavalry Museum • 6797 Barkeley Ave, Bldg 2160, AFZC-DT-T-M • Fort Carson, CO 80913-5000 • (719) 425-1368 • http://www.3acr.com

Grant Library • Fort Carson, 1637 Flint St • Fort Carson, CO 80913-4105 • (719) 526-2350 • http://peregrine.usafa.af.mil/grant.html

Fort Collins

Avery House Museum • 328 W Mountain Ave • Fort Collins, CO 80524 • (970) 221-0533 • http://www.poudrelandmarks.com/plf_avery_house.shtml

Bee Family Centennial Farm • 4320 E Cty Rd 58 • Fort Collins, CO 80524 • (970) 482-9168 • http://www.beefamilyfarm.com

Cache la Poudre Chapter, DAR • 508 Villanova • Fort Collins, CO 80525 • (970) 482-2378

Fort Collins Historical Society • Historical Museum, 200 Mathews St • Fort Collins, CO 80524 • (970) 221-6738 • http://www.fcgov.com/museum

Fort Collins Museum of Discovery Local History Archive • 408 Mason Ct • Fort Collins, CO 80524 • (970) 221-6688 • http://history.fcgov.com/

Fort Collins Public Library • 201 Peterson St • Fort Collins, CO 80524-2990 • (970) 221-6380 • http://www.fcgov.com/library

Larimer County Dept of Health and Environment • 1525 Blue Spruce Dr • Fort Collins, CO 80524 • (970) 498-6710 • http://www.larimer.org/health/admin/vital.asp

Larimer County Genealogical Society • P.O. Box 270737 • Fort Collins, CO 80527-0737 • http://www.lcgsco.org

Larimer County Genealogical Society • P.O. Box 270737 • Fort Collins, CO 80527 • (970) 223-5874 • http://www.lcgsco.org

Larimer County Historic Alliance • 3711 N Taft Hill Rd • Fort Collins, CO 80524 • (970) 493-5608

Larimer County Pioneer Association • P.O. Box 1732 • Fort Collins, CO 80522-1732 • (970) 482-8590

Pioneer Association-Pioneer Women • Donath Lake Farm, 8420 S Cty Rd 13 • Fort Collins, CO 80525 • (970) 482-4079

Poudre Landmarks Foundation • Historical Museum, 108 N Meldrum St • Fort Collins, CO 80524 • (970) 221-0533 • http://www.poudrelandmarks.com

Scottish Society of Northern Colorado • 3200 Silverthorn Dr • Fort Collins, CO 80526 • (303) 223-7730

Sidney Heitman Germans from Russia Collection • Colorado State Univ, Morgan Library • Fort Collins, CO 80523-1019 • (970) 491-1844

Webster House Museum • 301 E Olive St • Fort Collins, CO 80524

William E Morgan Library • Colorado State Univ, Special Collections & Archives • Fort Collins, CO 80523-1019 • (970) 491-3977 • http://manta.library.colostate.edu

Fort Garland

Fort Garland Heritage Association • Old Fort Garland Museum, Hwy 159, P.O. Box 368 • Fort Garland, CO 81133-0368 • (719) 379-3512 • http://www.coloradohistory.org

Old Fort Garland Museum • 29447 Hwy 159, P.O. Box 368 • Fort Garland, CO 81133 • (719) 379-3512 • http://www.coloradohistory.org/hist_sites/ft_Garland/ft_garland.htm

Fort Lupton

Fort Lupton Museum • 453 1st St • Fort Lupton, CO 80621 • (303) 857-1634 • http://www.fortlupton.org/museum

South Platte Valley Historical Society • Fort Lupton Historic Park, 1875 Factory Dr, P.O. Box 633 • Fort Lupton, CO 80621 • (303) 847-1710 • http://www.spvhs.org

Vintage Aero Flying Museum • Platte Valley Airpark, 7125 Parks Ln • Fort Lupton, CO 80621-8530 • (303) 502-5347 • http://www.vafm.org

Fort Morgan

Fort Morgan Museum and Heritage Foundation • Bledorn Research Ctr & Museum, 414 Main St, P.O. Box 184 • Fort Morgan, CO 80701 • (970) 542-4010 • http://www.cityoffortmorgan.com/index.aspx?NID=244

Fort Morgan Public Library • 414 Main St • Fort Morgan, CO 80701-2209 • (970) 867-9456

Oasis on the Plains Museum • 18881 Morgan Cty Rd 1 • Fort Morgan, CO 80701 • (970) 867-3191

US Military Historical Museum • 404 State St • Fort Morgan, CO 80701 • (970) 867-5520

Fowler

Fowler Historical Society • Historical Museum, 114 S Main St • Fowler, CO 81039 • (719) 263-4046

Fraser

Cozens Ranch Museum • 77849 US Hwy 40 • Fraser, CO 80442 • (970) 726-5488

Frisco

Frisco Historical Society • Historical Museum, 120 Main St, P.O. Box 820 • Frisco, CO 80433 • (970) 668-3428 • http://www.townoffrisco.com

Colorado

Frisco, cont.
Summit County Public Library • 37 Summit County Rd 10005, P.O. Box 770 • Frisco, CO 80443-0770 • (970) 668-5555 • http://www.co.summit.co.us

Fruita
Colorado National Monument Museum • Hwy 340 • Fruita, CO 81521 • (970) 858-3617

Colorado Welcome Center • 340 Hwy 340 • Fruita, CO 81521 • (970) 858-9335

Gateway
Gateway Colorado Auto Museum • 43200 Hwy 141 • Gateway, CO 81522 • (970) 931-2458 • http://www.gatewaycanyons.com

Genoa
Tower Museum • 30121 Frontage Rd • Genoa, CO 80818 • (719) 763-2309

Georgetown
Bowman White House Museum • 901 Rose St • Georgetown, CO 80444 • (303)569-3489

Georgetown Energy Museum • 600 Griffith St, P.O. Box 398 • Georgetown, CO 80444 • (303) 569-3557 • http://www.georgetownenergymuseum.org

Georgetown Loop Historic Mining & Railroad Museum • 646 Loop Dr, P.O. Box 249 • Georgetown, CO 80444 • (888) 456-6777 • http://www.georgetownlooprr.com

Historic Georgetown • Hamill House Museum, 305 Argentine, P.O. Box 667 • Georgetown, CO 80444 • (303) 569-2840 • http://www.historicgeorgetown.org

Hotel de Paris Museum • 409 6th Ave, P.O. Box 746 • Georgetown, CO 80444 • (303) 569-2311 • http://www.hoteldeparismuseum.org

John Tomay Memorial Library-Georgetown Library • 605 6th St, P.O. Box 338 • Georgetown, CO 80444-0338 • (303) 569-2620 • http://www.georgetownlibrary.org

Glen Haven
Heard Museum • 315 W Creek Rd • Glen Haven, CO 80532 • (970) 586-4849 • http://www.80532.net

Glenwood Springs
Frontier Historical Society • Historical Museum, 1001 Colorado Ave • Glenwood Springs, CO 81601-3319 • (970) 945-4448 • http://www.glenwoodhistory.com

National Railway Historical Society, Western Colorado Chapter • Glenwood Railroad Museum, 413 7th St • Glenwood Springs, CO 81601 • (970) 945-7044 • http://www.glenwoodrailroadmuseum.org

Gold Hill
Gold Hill Museum • 661 Pine St, P.O. Box 2015 • Gold Hill, CO 80466

Golden
Astor House Museum • 822 12th St • Golden, CO 80401 • (303) 278-3557 • http://www.astorhousemuseum.org

Bradford Washburn - American Mountaineering Museum • 710 10th St • Golden, CO 80401 • (303) 996-2755 • http://www.bwamm.org

Buffalo Bill Memorial Museum • 987 1/2 Lookout Mountain Rd • Golden, CO 80401 • (303) 526-0744 • http://www.buffalobill.org

Clear Creek History Park • 1020 11th St • Golden, CO 80401 • (303) 278-3557 • http://www.clearcreekhistorypark.org

Colorado Railroad Museum • 17155 W 44th Ave, P.O. Box 10 • Golden, CO 80403 • (800) 365-6263 • http://www.crrm.org

Colorado Ranching Museum • 1020 11th St • Golden, CO 80401 • (303) 216-1243

Geology Museum • Colorado School of Mines, 1310 Maple St • Golden, CO 80401 • (303) 274-3815 • http://www.mines.edu/Geology_Museum

Gilpin County Public Library • 15131 Hwy 119 • Golden, CO 80403 • (303) 582-5777 • http://www.gilpinlibrary.org

Golden Landmarks Association • P.O. Box 1136 • Golden, CO 80402 • (303) 279-1236

Golden Pioneer Museum • 923 W 10th St • Golden, CO 80401 • (303) 278-7151

Jefferson County Archives and Records Mgt • 100 Jefferson County Pkwy, Ste 1500 • Golden, CO 80419 • (303) 271-8451 • http://www.co.jefferson.co.us/archives/

Jefferson County Health and Environment • 800 Jefferson County Pkwy, Ste 1300 • Golden, CO 80401 • (303) 271-6450 • http://jeffco.us

Jefferson County Historical Commission • 100 Jefferson County Pkwy, Ste 3550 • Golden, CO 80419 • (303) 271-8700 • http://jeffco.us/planning/planning_T59_R47.htm

Jefferson County Public Library-Golden Branch • 1019 10th St • Golden, CO 80401 • (303) 279-4585 • http://jefferson.lib.co.us

Revolution Pioneer Museum • 911 10th St • Golden, CO 80401

Robert W Richardson Railroad Library • Colorado Railroad Historical Foundation, 17155 W 44th Ave, P.O. Box 10 • Golden, CO 80402-0010 • (303) 279-4591 • http://www.crrm.org

Rocky Mountain Quilt Museum • 1111 Washington Ave • Golden, CO 80401 • (303) 277-0377 • http://www.rnqm.org

Granby
Grand County Library • 225 E Jasper Ave, P.O. Box 1050 • Granby, CO 80446-1050 • (970) 887-9411 • http://www.gcld.org

Grand County Library District-Granby Branch • 13 E Jasper Ave, P.O. Box 1049 • Granby, CO 80446-1049 • (970) 887-2149

Grand Junction
Cross Orchards Historic Farm Museum • 3073 F Road (Patterson Rd) • Grand Junction, CO 81506 • (970) 434-9814 • http://www.wcmuseum.org/crossorchards

Mesa County Genealogical Society • P.O. Box 1506 • Grand Junction, CO 81502-1506 • (970)242-0971 • http://www.gjmesa.com/mcgs/

Mesa County Health Department • 510 29 1/2 Rd • Grand Junction, CO 81504 • (970) 248-6900 • http://www.health.mesacounty.us/records.cfm

Mesa County Historical Society • P.O. Box 841 • Grand Junction, CO 81502

Mesa County Public Library • 443 N 6th St • Grand Junction, CO 81501-2731 • (970) 241-5251 • http://www.mcpld.org

Museum of Western Colorado • 462 Ute Ave, P.O. Box 20000 • Grand Junction, CO 81502-5020 • (970) 242-0971 • http://www.wcmuseum.org/museum.htm

National Railway Historical Society, Rio Grand Chapter • P.O. Box 3381 • Grand Junction, CO 81501-3381 • (970) 242-0784 • http://www.nrhs.com/chapters/rio-grande

Rocky Mountain Wing of the Commemorative Air Force • 780 Heritage Wy, P.O. Box 4125 • Grand Junction, CO 81506 • (970) 256-0693 • http://www.rockymountainwingcaf.org

Sons of the American Revolution, Colorado Society • 530 Foy Dr • Grand Junction, CO 81507 • (970) 245-0673 • http://www.cossar.us

Tomlinson Library • Mesa State College, 1200 College Pl • Grand Junction, CO 81501 • (970) 248-1860 • http://www.mesastate.edu/msclibrary

Grand Lake

Grand County Library District-Juniper Library at Grand Lake • 315 Pitkin, P.O. Box 506 • Grand Lake, CO 80447-0506 • (970) 627-8353

Grand Lake Area Historical Society • Kaufman House Museum, 407 Pitkin Ave, P.O. Box 656 • Grand Lake, CO 80447 • (970) 627-9277 • http://www.kauffmanhouse.org

Granite

Clear Creek Canyon Historical Society of Chaffee County • P.O. Box 2181 • Granite, CO 81228 • (719) 486-2942

Greeley

Greeley Freight Station Museum • 680 10th St • Greeley, CO 80631 • (970) 392-2934 • http://www.gfsm.org

Greeley Heritage Association • Historical Museum, 919 7th Ave • Greeley, CO 80631-4174 • (970) 350-9220 • http://www.ci.greeley.co.us

Greeley Municipal Archives • 919 7th St • Greeley, CO 80631 • (970) 350-9220

Hazel E Johnson Genealogical Research Center • Greeley Historical Museum, 714 8th St • Greeley, CO 80631 • (970) 350-9220 • http://www.ci.greeley.co.us; http://www.friendsmuseums.com

Historic Centennial Village Museum • 1475 A Street • Greeley, CO 80631 • (970) 350-9224 • http://www.greeleymuseums.com

James A Michener Library • Univ of Northern Colorado, 501 20th St • Greeley, CO 80639 • (970) 351-2562 • http://www.univnortlico.edu/library/archives.htm

Kiefer Library • Aims Community College, 5401 W 20th St, P.O. Box 69 • Greeley, CO 80632-0069 • (970) 330-8008, Ext 6237

Meeker Home Museum • 1324 9th Ave • Greeley, CO 80631 • (970) 350-9220 • http://www.greeleygov.com/museum/MeekerHome.aspx

Plumb Farm Learning Center • 955 39th Ave • Greeley, CO 80631 • (970) 350-9220 • http://www.greeleymuseums.com

Weld County Genealogical Society • P.O. Box 278 • Greeley, CO 80632-0278 • (970) 356-2568 • http://www.rootsweb.ancestry.com/~cowcgs/

Weld County Health Department • 1555 N 17th Ave • Greeley, CO 80631 • (970) 304-6410 • http://www.co.weld.co.us/departments/health/publichealth.html

Weld County Library District-Centennial Park • 2227 23rd Ave • Greeley, CO 80631 • (970) 506-8600 • http://www.weld.lib.co.us

Weld Library District • 1939 61st Ave • Greeley, CO 80634-7940 • (970) 506-8500 • http://www.weld.lib.co.us

Weld Library District, Lincoln Park Branch • 919 7th St • Greeley, CO 80631 • (970) 350-9212

Greenwood Village

Tri-County Health Department • 700 E Belleview, Ste 301 • Greenwood Village, CO 80111 • (303) 220-9208 • http://www.tchd.org

Grover

Grover Historical Society • P.O. Box 7 • Grover, CO 80729

Pawnee Natural Historic Site Museum • 130 Chatoga Ave • Grover, CO 80729 • (970) 895-2341

Gunnison

Gunnison County Pioneer and Historical Society • Historical Museum, S Adams St & Hwy 50, P.O. Box 418 • Gunnison, CO 81230 • (970) 641-4350

Gunnison County Public Health • 225 N Pine St, Ste E • Gunnison, CO 81230 • (970) 641-0209 • http://www.gunnisoncounty.org/dept/pubhealth

Gunnison County Public Library • 307 N Wisconsin • Gunnison, CO 81230-2627 • (970) 641-3845 • http://www.colosys.net/gunnison

Leslie J Savage Library • Western State College, 600 N Adams St • Gunnison, CO 81231 • (970) 943-2053 • http://www.western.edu/lib/Welcome.html

Pioneer Museum • 803 E Tomichi Ave • Gunnison, CO 81230 • (970) 641-4530 • http://www.gunnisoncrestedbutte.com/activity/pioneer-museum

Hayden

Hayden Heritage Center • 300 W Pearl St, P.O. Box 543 • Hayden, CO 81639 • (970) 276-4380 • http://www.yampavalley.info/history0085

West Routt Library District-Hayden Public Library • 201 E Jefferson, P.O. Box 1813 • Hayden, CO 81639-1813 • (970) 276-3777

Highlands Ranch

Highlands Ranch Genealogical Society • c/o Highlands Ranch Library, 9292 Ridgeline Blvd • Highlands Ranch, CO 80129 • http://hrgenealogy.wordpress.com/

Saint Andrew Society of Colorado • 344 Southpark Rd • Highlands Ranch, CO 80126-2232 • (303) 238-6524 • http://coloradoscots.com

Holyoke

Phillips County Historical Society • Phillips County Museum, 109 S Campbell Ave • Holyoke, CO 80734-1501 • (970) 854-2129 • http://www.rootsweb.com/~copchs/

Homelake

Veterans History Center Museum • 3749 Sherman Ave, P.O. Box 97 • Homelake, CO 81135

Hot Sulphur Springs

Grand County Historical Association • Grand County Museum & Pioneer Village, 110 E Byers Ave, P.O. Box 165 • Hot Sulphur Springs, CO 80451 • (970) 725-3939 • http://www.grandcountymuseum.com

Cozens Ranch & Stage Stop Museum • 110 E Byers Ave, P.O. Box 165 • Hot Sulphus Springs, CO 80452 • (970) 725-3939 • http://www.grandcountymuseum.com/CozensRanch.htm

Hotchkiss

Hotchkiss-Crawford Historical Society • Historical Museum, 2nd & Hotchkiss Ave, P.O. Box 727 • Hotchkiss, CO 81419 • (970) 872-3780

Hugo

Eastern Trails Museum and Cultural Arts Center • 635 4th St • Hugo, CO 80821 • (719) 743-2332

Lincoln County Hedlund House Museum • 617 3rd Ave, P.O. Box 353 • Hugo, CO 80821 • (719) 743-2233

Lincoln County Historical Society • Hedlund House Museum, 617 3rd Ave, P.O. Box 115 • Hugo, CO 80821 • (719) 743-2485

Idaho Springs

Argo Gold Mine & Mill Museum • 2350 Riverside Dr, P.O. Box 1990 • Idaho Springs, CO 80452 • (303) 567-2421 • http://www.historcargotours.com

Clear Creek Historic Mining and Milling Museum • 23rd Ave & Riverside, P.O. Box 1498 • Idaho Springs, CO 80452 • (303) 567-2421

George Rowe Museum • 905 Main • Idaho Springs, CO 80452 • (303) 569-2562

Historical Society of Idaho Springs • Historical Museum, 2060 Miner St, P.O. Box 1318 • Idaho Springs, CO 80452 • (303) 567-4382 • http://www.historicidahosprings.com

Idaho Springs Public Library • 219 14th Ave, P.O. Box 1509 • Idaho Springs, CO 80452 • (303) 567-2020 • http://www.purplemtn.com/library

Colorado

Idaho Springs, cont.
James Underhill Museum • 1416 Miner St, P.O. Box 1318 • Idaho Springs, CO 80452 • (303) 567-2020 • http://www.historicidahosprings.com

Ignacio
Southern Ute Community Library • 330 Burns Ave, P.O. Box 989 • Ignacio, CO 81137-0348 • (970) 563-0235

Southern Ute Indian Cultural Center • Hwy 172 N, P.O. Box 737 • Ignacio, CO 81137 • (970) 563-4531 • http://www.southernutemuseum.org

Jefferson
Slovenian Genealogical Society, Colorado Chapter • 837 Swiggler Rd • Jefferson, CO 80456-9732

Johnstown
Glenn A Jones Memorial Library • 1011 Jay Ave, P.O. Box 457 • Johnstown, CO 80534-0457 • (970) 587-2459

Johnstown Historical Society • Parish House Museum, 701 Charlotte St • Johnstown, CO 80534-8611 • (970) 587-0278 • http://johnstownhistoricalsociety.org

Julesburg
Colorado Welcome Center • 20934 Cty Rd 28 • Julesburg, CO 80737 • (970) 474-2054

Fort Sedgwick Historical Society • Fort Sedgwick Museum, 201 W 1st St, P.O. Box 69 • Julesburg, CO 80737 • (970) 474-2061 • http://www.users.kci.net/history

Museum Depot • 201 W 1st St • Julesburg, CO 80730 • (970) 474-2264

Sedgewick County Genealogical Society • c/o Julesburg Public Library, 320 Cedar St • Julesburg, CO 80737 • (970) 474-2608 • http://www.rootsweb.com/~cosedgwi/society.htm

Kiowa
Elbert County Historical Society • Historical Museum, 515 Comanche St, P.O. Box 43 • Kiowa, CO 80117 • http://www.elbertcountymuseum.org

Elbert County Library • 331 Comanche, P.O. Box 538 • Kiowa, CO 80117 • (303) 621-2111 • http://www.elbertcountylibrary.org

Kit Carson
Kit Carson Historical Society • Historical Museum, 202 W Hwy 287, P.O. Box 67 • Kit Carson, CO 80825 • (719) 962-3306 • http://www.kcdr1.org

Kremmling
Log Cabin Heritage Museum • 114 N 4th St, P.O. Box 204 • Kremmling, CO 80459 • (970) 724-9390

La Junta
Bent's Old Fort National Historic Site Museum • 35110 Hwy 194 E • La Junta, CO 81050 • (719) 383-5010 • http://www.nps.gov/beol

Koshare Indian Museum • 115 W 18th St, P.O. Box 580 • La Junta, CO 81050-0580 • (719) 384-4411 • http://www.koshare.org

Otero County Dept of Health • County Courthouse, 13 W 3rd St, Rm 111 • La Junta, CO 81050 • (719) 383-3040

Otero County Historical Society • 109 Gilpin • La Junta, CO 81050

Otero Museum • 706 W 3rd St, P.O. Box 22 • La Junta, CO 81056 • (719) 384-7500 • http://www.coloradoplains.com/otero/museum/

Woodruff Memorial Library • 522 Colorado Ave, P.O. Box 479 • La Junta, CO 81050-0479 • (719) 384-4612 • http://lajunta.colibraries.org

La Veta
Fort Francisco Museum • 306 S Main St, P.O. Box 428 • La Veta, CO 81055 • (719) 742-5501 • http://www.hchstsoc.org

Huerfano County Historical Society • P.O. Box 428 • La Veta, CO 81055 • (719) 742-5501 • http://www.huerfanocounty.org/heritage/

La Veta Public Library • 310 Main St, P.O. Box 28 • La Veta, CO 81055 • (719) 742-3572 • http://www.laveta.lib.co.us

Lafayette
Lafayette Historical Society • Miner's Museum, 108 E Simpson St, P.O. Box 186 • Lafayette, CO 80026 • (303) 665-7030 • http://www.cifyoflafayette.com

Lafayette Public Library • 775 W Baseline Rd • Lafayette, CO 80026 • (303) 665-5200 • http://www.cityoflafayette/library

Wise Homestead Museum • 11611 Jasper Rd • Lafayette, CO 80026 • (303) 828-4568

Lake City
Hinsdale County Historical Society • Lake City Museum, 130 N Silver St, P.O. Box 353 • Lake City, CO 81235 • (970) 944-2050 • http://www.lakecitymuseum.com

Lakewood
Foothills Genealogical Society • P.O. Box 150382 • Lakewood, CO 80215-0382 • (303) 642-7262 • http://www.foothillsgenealogy.org

Jefferson County Public Library • 10200 W 20th Ave • Lakewood, CO 80215 • (303) 232-9507 • http://www.jefferson.lib.co.us

Lakewood Historical Society • Lakewood Heritage Center, 801 S Yarrow St • Lakewood, CO 80226 • (303) 987-7850 • http://www.lakewood.org

Lakewood's Historical Belmar Museum • 797 S Wadsworth Blvd • Lakewood, CO 80226 • (303) 987-7850 • http://www.lakewood.org

Western Heraldry Organization • 10195 W 17th Pl • Lakewood, CO 80215-2805

Lamar
Lamar Community College Library • Bowman Bldg, 2401 S Main St • Lamar, CO 81052-3999 • (719) 336-1540 • http://www.lamarcc.edu

Lamar Public Library • 104 E Parmenter St • Lamar, CO 81052-3239 • (719) 336-4632 • http://www.lamar.lib.co.us

Prowers County Genealogical Society • Big Timbers Museum, 7515 US Hwy 50, P.O. Box 362 • Lamar, CO 81052-0928 • (719) 336-2472 • http://www.bigtimbersmuseum.org

Prowers County Historical Society • Big Timbers Museum, 7515 US Hwy 50, P.O. Box 362 • Lamar, CO 81052 • (719) 336-2472 • http://www.bigtimbersmuseum.org

Larkspur
Larkspur Historical Society • 5254 Grimes Ln • Larkspur, CO 80118 • http://www.larkspurhistoricalsociety.com

Las Animas
Bent County Historical Society • 305 St Vrain Ave • Las Animas, CO 81054 • (719) 456-2005

Bent County Nusing Service - Birth & Death Records • 701 Park Ave • Las Animas, CO 81054 • (719) 456-6042

Kit Carson Historical Society • Historical Museum, 9th St & Bent Ave, P.O. Box 68 • Las Animas, CO 81054 • (719) 456-2597 • http://www.bentcounty.org

Las Animas-Bent County Public Library • 306 5th St • Las Animas, CO 81054 • (719) 456-0111 • http://www.bentcounty.org

Pioneer Historical Society of Bent County • E 9th St, P.O. Box 68 • Las Animas, CO 81054 • (719) 456-2005

Pioneer Museum • 560 Bent Ave, P.O. Box 68 • Las Animas, CO 81054 • (719) 456-6066

LaVeta

Huerfano County Historical Society • Fort Francisco Museum, P.O. Box 428 • LaVeta, CO 81055 • (719) 742-3676

Leadville

Healy House-Dexter Cabin Museum • 912 Harrison • Leadville, CO 80461 • (719) 486-0487 • http://www.coloradohistory.org

Lake County Public Library • 1115 Harrison Ave • Leadville, CO 80461-3398 • (719) 486-0569

Leadville Heritage Association • National Mining Museum, 102 E 9th St, P.O. Box 981 • Leadville, CO 80461-3302 • (719) 486-1229 • http://www.leadville.com/MiningMuseum

Leadville Historical Association • House with the Eye Museum, 127 W 4th St, P.O. Box 911 • Leadville, CO 80461 • (719) 427-0895 • http://leadvillemuseums.com/housewiththeeye.html

Matchless Mine Museum • 414 W 7th St, P.O. Box 532 • Leadville, CO 80461 • (719) 486-0371 • http://leadvillemuseums.com/matchlessmine.html

National Mining Hall of Fame Museum • 120 W 9th St, P.O. Box 981 • Leadville, CO 80461 • (719) 486-1229 • http://www.mininghalloffame.org

Tabor Historic Home Museum • 116 E 5th St • Leadville, CO 80461 • (719) 427-0895

Tabor Opera House Museum • 815 Harrison Ave, P.O. Box 1004 • Leadville, CO 80461 • (719) 486-8409 • http://www.taboroperahouse.net

Temple Israel Synagogue and Museum • 201 W 4th St • Leadville, CO 80461 • (719) 486-3625 • http://www.jewishleadville.org

Limon

Limon Heritage Museum & Railroad Park • 899 1st St, P.O. Box 341 • Limon, CO 80828 • (719) 775-8605 • http://www.townoflimon.com/tourism

Limon Heritage Society • P.O. Box 341 • Limon, CO 80828 • (719) 775-2373

Limon Memorial Public Library • 205 E Ave • Limon, CO 80828 • (719) 775-2163

Pioneer School House Museum • 517 D Avenue • Limon, CO 80828 • (719) 755-2350

Littleton

Colorado Cornish Cousins • 7945 S Gaylord Wy • Littleton, CO 80122 • http://www.cousinjack.org/links.html

Edwin A Bemis Library • 6014 S Datura St • Littleton, CO 80161 • (303) 795-3961 • http://www.littletongov.org/bemis/

Jewish Genealogical Society of Colorado • P.O. Box 2856 • Littleton, CO 80161 • (303) 756-6028 • http://www.jgsco.org

Ken-Caryl Ranch Historical Society • 7676 S Continental Divide Rd • Littleton, CO 80127 • (303) 979-1876

Littleton Historical Society • Historical Museum, 6028 S Gallup St • Littleton, CO 80120-2703 • (303) 795-3950 • http://www.littletongov.org/museum

Palatines to America, Colorado Chapter • 7079 S Marshall St • Littleton, CO 80123-4607 • (303) 827-4700 • http://www.palam.org/colorado-palam-chapter.php

Longmont

Agricultural Heritage Center • 8348 Ute Hwy • Longmont, CO 80503 • (303) 776-8848 • http://www.boulder.co.us

Dougherty Museum • 8306 Hwy 287 • Longmont, CO 80504 • (303) 776-2520 • http://www.bouldercounty.org/openspace/dougherty

Historic Longmont • 960 5th Ave • Longmont, CO 80501 • (303) 587-0528 • http://www.historiclongmont.org

Longmont Genealogical Society • P.O. Box 6081 • Longmont, CO 80501-2077 • (303) 776-9931 • http://www.rootsweb.com/~colgs/

Longmont Heritage Association • 375 Kimbark St • Longmont, CO 80501-5524

Longmont Museum and Cultural Center • 400 Quail Rd • Longmont, CO 80501 • (303) 651-8374 • http://www.ci.longmont.co.us/museum

Longmont Public Library • 409 4th Ave • Longmont, CO 80501-6006 • (303) 651-8470 • http://www.ci.longmont.co.us/library.htm

Saint Vrain Historical Society • 470 N Main St, P.O. Box 705 • Longmont, CO 80502-0705 • (303) 776-1870 • http://www.stvrainhistoricalsociety.org

Society of Mayflower Descendants in the State of Colorado • 1601 Sherman Wy • Longmont, CO 80501 • (303) 940-1609

Louisville

Lafayette and Louisville Genealogical Society • c/o Louisville Public Library, 950 Spruce St • Louisville, CO 80027 • (303) 335-4849 • http://www.rootsweb.ancestry.com/~collgs/

Louisville Historical Commission • Historical Museum, 1001 Main St • Louisville, CO 80027 • (303) 665-9048 • http://www.ci.louisville.co.us/museum.htm

Louisville Public Library • 950 Spruce St • Louisville, CO 80027 • (303) 335-4849 • http://www.ci.louisville.co.us/library/

Loveland

Colorado Computer Museum • 1241 W 8th St • Loveland, CO 80537 • (970) 669-1258 • http://www.trailedge.org

Loveland Museum • 503 N Lincoln Ave • Loveland, CO 80537 • (970) 962-2410 • http://www.ci.loveland.co.us/museum.htm

Loveland Public Library • 300 N Adams Ave • Loveland, CO 80537 • (970) 962-2665 • http://www.ci.loveland.co.us/Library/libmain.htm

Timberlane Farm Museum • 2306 E 1st St • Loveland, CO 80537 • (970) 663-7348 • http://www.timberlandfarmmuseum.org

Lyons

Lyons Depot Library • 430 5th Ave, P.O. Box 49 • Lyons, CO 80540-0049 • (303) 823-5165

Lyons Historical Society • Lyons Redstone Museum, 340 High St, P.O. Box 9 • Lyons, CO 80540 • (303) 823-6692 • http://lyonsredstonemuseum.com

Manassa

Jack Dempsey Museum • 412 Main St, P.O. Box 130 • Manassa, CO 81141 • (719) 843-5207

Mancos

Galloping Goose Historical Society • 421 Railroad Ave • Mancos, CO 81328 • (970) 882-3243

Mancos Valley Historical Society • P.O. Box 124 • Mancos, CO 81328

Montezuma County Historical Society • 10453 County Rd 42 • Mancos, CO 81328

Manitou Springs

Manitou Cliff Dwellings Museum • Hwy 24, P.O. Box 272 • Manitou Springs, CO 80829 • (719) 685-5242 • http://www.cliffdwellingsmuseum.com

Manitou Springs Historical Society • Miramont Castle, 9 Capitol Hill Ave • Manitou Springs, CO 80829 • (719) 685-1011 • http://www.miramontcastle.org

Manitou Springs Public Library • 701 Manitou Ave • Manitou Springs, CO 80829 • (719) 685-5206 • http://www.ci.manitou-springs.co.us

Pikes Peak Auto Hill Climb Museum • 135 Manitou Ave • Manitou Springs, CO 80829 • (719) 685-5996 • http://www.ppihc.com

Colorado

Marble
Marble Historical Society • Historical Museum, 412 W Main St • Marble, CO 81623 • (970) 963-1710

Meeker
Rio Blanco County Historical Society • White River Museum, 565 Park St, P.O. Box 413 • Meeker, CO 81641 • (970) 878-9982 • http://www.meekercolorado.com/whiterivermuseum/

White River Trace Genealogical Society • 425 12th St • Meeker, CO 81641

Mesa Verde National Park
Mesa Verde National Park Museum • P.O. Box 38 • Mesa Verde National Park, CO 81330 • (970) 529-5073 • http://www.mps.gov/meve; http://mesaverde.org

Milliken
Milliken Historical Society • Historical Museum, 1101 Broad St, P.O. Box 92 • Milliken, CO 80543 • (970) 587-4251 • http://www.millikenhistoricalsociety.org

Monte Vista
Carnegie Public Library • 120 Jefferson St • Monte Vista, CO 81144-1797 • (719) 852-3931

Monte Vista Historical Society • 110 Jefferson St, P.O. Box 323 • Monte Vista, CO 81144 • (719) 852-4396 • http://www.museumtrail.org

Transportation of the West Museum • 916 1st Ave • Monte Vista, CO 81144 • (719) 852-4396

Montrose
Fore-Kin Trails Genealogical Society • P.O. Box 802 • Montrose, CO 81401-0802 • (970) 249-8140 • http://www.rootsweb.ancestry.com/~comgc/Home.html

Montrose County Historical Society • Depot Museum, 21 N Rio Grand Ave, P.O. Box 1882 • Montrose, CO 81401 • (970) 249-2085 • http://www.visitmontrose.net/museum.htm

Montrose Genealogy Center • 700 E Main St, Ste 10-3 • Montrose, CO 81401 • (970) 240-1755

Montrose Library District • 320 S 2nd Ave • Montrose, CO 81401-3909 • (970) 249-9656 • http://www.colosys.net/montrose/

Museum of the Mountain West • 68169 E Miami Rd • Montrose, CO 81401 • (970) 240-3400 • http://www.mountainwestmuseum.com

Ute Indian Museum • 17253 Chipeta Dr, P.O. Box 1736 • Montrose, CO 81402 • (970) 249-3098 • http://www.coloradohistory.org

Morrison
Friends of Dinosaur Ridge • 16831 W Alameda Pkwy • Morrison, CO 80465 • (303) 697-3466

Morrison Heritage Museum • 501 Hwy 8, P.O. Box 564 • Morrison, CO 80465 • (303) 697-1873 • http://www.historicmorrison.org

Morrison Historical Society • P.O. Box 208 • Morrison, CO 80465 • (303) 697-8526 • http://morrisonhistory.wordpress.com/

Naturita
Rimrock Historical Society of West Montrose County • Historical Museum, 411 W 2nd Ave • Naturita, CO 81424 • (970) 864-7837 • http://www.rimrocker.org

Rimrocker Historical Museum • W Main St • Naturita, CO 81422

Nederland
Nederland Area Historical Society • Historical Museum, 200 Bridge Rd, P.O. Box 1252 • Nederland, CO 80466 • (303) 258-0567 • http://www.nederlandmuseums.org

New Castle
Garfield County Public Library-New Castle Branch • 402 W Main, P.O. Box 320 • New Castle, CO 81647-0320 • (970) 984-2347 • http://www.garfieldlibraries.org

New Castle Historical Society • P.O. Box 883 • New Castle, CO 81647

Northglenn
Northglenn Historical Preservation Foundation • c/o City of Northglenn, 11701 Community Center Dr • Northglenn, CO 80233 • (720) 232-4402 • http://www.northglenn.org/nhpf

Nucla
Rimrocker Historical Museum • Naturita Town Park, P.O. Box 913 • Nucla, CO 81424 • (970) 865-2877

Rimrocker Historical Society • P.O. Box 913 • Nucla, CO 81424

Nunn
High Plains Historical Society • Northern Drylanders Museum, 775 3rd St, P.O. Box 122 • Nunn, CO 80648 • (970) 897-3125 • http://www.highplainshistory.homestead.com

Oak Creek
Historical Society of Oak Creek and Phippsburg • Old Town Hall Museum, 129 E Main St, P.O. Box 1 • Oak Creek, CO 80467 • (970) 736-8245 • http://yampavalley.info/centers/history_%2526_genealogy/organizations/tracks_and_trails_museum

Tracks & Trails Museum • 129 W Main St • Oak Creek, CO 80467 • (970) 736-8245

Olathe
Fore-Kin Trails Genealogical Society • 8508 High Mesa Rd • Olathe, CO 81425

Ouray
Ouray County Historical Society • Historical Museum, 420 6th Ave, P.O. Box 151 • Ouray, CO 81427 • (970) 325-4576 • http://www.ouraycountyhistoricalsociety.org

Pagosa Springs
Archuleta County Genealogical Society • P.O. Box 1611 • Pagosa Springs, CO 81147 • (970) 264-2645 • http://www.rootsweb.com/~cosjhs/aegs.htm

Chimney Rock Indian Ruins Museum • Hwy 151, P.O. Box 310 • Pagosa Springs, CO 81147 • (970) 264-2268

San Juan Historical Society • Historical Museum, 1 Trinity Ln • Pagosa Springs, CO 81147 • (970) 264-4424

Sisson Memorial Library • 811 San Juan, P.O. Box 849 • Pagosa Springs, CO 81147-0849 • (970) 264-2209 • http://www.frontier.net/~ruby/

Southern Ute Indian Museum • 14826 Hwy 172 • Pagosa Springs, CO 81147 • (970) 563-9583

Upper San Juan Historical Society • Historical Museum, 1 St & Hwy 160, P.O. Box 1711 • Pagosa Springs, CO 81147 • (970) 264-4424

Palmer Lake
Palmer Lake Historical Society • Lucretia Vaile Museum, 66 Lower Glenway, P.O. Box 662 • Palmer Lake, CO 80133 • (719) 559-0837 • http://www.ci.palmer-lake.co.us

Paonia
Delta County Public Library District-Paonia Branch • P.O. Box 969 • Paonia, CO 81428-0969 • (970) 527-3470

Parachute
Grand Valley Historical Society • Historical Museum, 7201 Cty Rd 300, P.O. Box 363 • Parachute, CO 81635 • (970) 285-9114

Parker
Parker Area Historical Society • P.O. Box 604 • Parker, CO 80134 • http://www.parkerhistory.org

Parker Genealogical Society • P.O. Box 2672 • Parker, CO 80134 • http://www.rootsweb.ancestry.com/~copgs/

Penrose
Friend Genealogy Library • 1448 Que St • Penrose, CO 81240

Peterson AFB
Peterson Air & Space Museum • 21st Space Wing/MU, 150 E Ent Ave • Peterson AFB, CO 80914 • (719) 556-4915 • http://www.petemuseum.org

Platteville
Fort Vasquez Museum • 13412 US Hwy 85 • Platteville, CO 80651 • (970) 785-2832 • http://www.coloradohistory.org

Platteville Historical Society • Pioneer Museum, 502 Marion, P.O. Box 567 • Platteville, CO 80651 • (970) 785-6285 • http://www.plattevillegov.org

Platteville Public Library • 504 Marion Ave, P.O. Box 567 • Platteville, CO 80651 • (970) 785-2231 • http://www.weld.lib.co.us/plattevil.html

Pueblo
Bessemer Historical Society • Steelworks Museum and CF&I Archives, 215 Canal St • Pueblo, CO 81004 • (719) 564-9086 • http://www.cfisteel.org

City of Pueblo Municipal Reference Library • 211 East D Street • Pueblo, CO 81003 • (719) 543-6006

Colorado Mental Health Institute at Pueblo Museum • 1600 W 24th St • Pueblo, CO 81005 • (719) 543-2012 • http://www.cmhipmuseum.org

Dr Martin Luther King Jr Cultural Center • 2713-15 N Grand Ave • Pueblo, CO 81005 • (719) 253-1015

El Pueblo History Museum • 301 N Union • Pueblo, CO 81003 • (719) 583-0453 • http://www.coloradohistory.org

Genealogical Society of Hispanic America • P.O. Box 3040 • Pueblo, CO 81005 • http://www.gsha.net

Hose Company No. 3 - Pueblo's Fire Museum • 116 Broadway Ave • Pueblo, CO 81004 • (719) 553-2830 • http://www.pueblofire.org/museum.htm

Infozone News Museum • 100 E Abriendo Ave • Pueblo, CO 81004 • (719) 562-5604 • http://www.infozonenewsmuseum.com

Pueblo City-County Health Dept • 151 Central Main St • Pueblo, CO 81003 • (719) 583-4300 • http://www.co.pueblo.co.us/pcchd/admin/vitalstats/vitalstats

Pueblo County Historical Society • Edward H Broadhead Library, 201 West B Street • Pueblo, CO 81003 • (719) 543-6772 • http://www.pueblohistory.org

Pueblo History Museum • 119 Central Plz • Pueblo, CO 81003 • (719) 583-0453

Pueblo Railway Museum • 132 West B Street • Pueblo, CO 81003 • (719) 251-5024 • http://www.pueblorailway.org

Pueblo Regional Library • 100 E Abriendo Ave • Pueblo, CO 81004-4290 • (719) 562-5601 • http://www.pueblolibrary.org

Pueblo Weisbrod Aircraft Museum • 31001 Magnuson Ave • Pueblo, CO 81001 • (719) 748-9219 • http://www.pwam.org

Rosemount Museum • 419 W 14th St, P.O. Box 5259 • Pueblo, CO 81002 • (719) 545-5290 • http://www.rosemount.org

Saint Marys Genealogy Center • 211 E Mesa Ave • Pueblo, CO 81006 • (719) 542-6323

Slovenian Genealogy Center • Saint Mary's Church, 211 E Mesa • Pueblo, CO 81006

Southeastern Colorado Genealogical Society • c/o Pueblo City County Library, 100 E Abriendo • Pueblo, CO 81004 • (719) 564-7815

Southeastern Colorado Heritage Center • 201 West B Street • Pueblo, CO 81003 • (719) 295-1517 • http://www.theheritagecenter.us

University of Southern Colorado Library • 2200 Bonforte Blvd • Pueblo, CO 81001-4901 • (719) 549-2361 • http://www.uscolo.edu/library

Rangely
Colorado Northwestern Community College Library • 500 Kennedy Dr • Rangely, CO 81648 • (970) 675-3334 • http://www.cncc.edu

Rangely Museum • 132 W Main, P.O. Box 131 • Rangely, CO 81648 • (970) 675-2612 • http://www.rangely.com/Museum.htm

Rangely Outdoor Museum • 150 Kennedy Dr, P.O. Box 740 • Rangely, CO 81648 • (970) 675-2612

Ridgway
Ridgway Railroad Museum • 150 Racecourse Rd • Ridgway, CO 81432 • (970) 626-5458 • http://www.ridgewayrailroadmuseum.org

Rifle
Rifle Creek Museum • 337 East Ave • Rifle, CO 81650 • (970) 625-4862

Rocky Ford
American Historical Society of Germans from Russia, Melon Valley Chapter • 18635 Hwy 202 • Rocky Ford, CO 81067

Rocky Ford Historical Museum • 1005 Sycamore Ave, P.O. Box 835 • Rocky Ford, CO 81067 • (719) 254-6737 • http://www.rockyfordmuseum.com

Rye
Robbers Roost Old West Museum • 5991 Boulder • Rye, CO 81069 • (719) 489-3559

Saguache
Hazard House Museum • 807 Pitkin Ave • Saguache, CO 81149 • (719) 655-2805

Saguache County Museum • 405 8th St, P.O. Box 569 • Saguache, CO 81149 • (719) 655-2557 • http://www.coloradotrails.com

Saguache County Public Library • 8th & Pitkin Aves, P.O. Box 448 • Saguache, CO 81149-0448 • (719) 655-2551 • http://www.slv.org/saguachelibrary

Salida
City of Salida Archives • 125 E Street, P.O. Box 147 • Salida, CO 81201 • (719) 539-2311 • http://www.cityofsalida.com

Salida Museum • 406 W Hwy 50 • Salida, CO 81201 • (719) 539-4602 • http://www.salidachamber.org/museum

Salida Museum Association • Historical Museum, 406 1/2 Rainbow Blvd • Salida, CO 81201 • (970) 539-7483 • http://salidamuseum.org

San Luis
Costilla County Library • 413 Gasper St, P.O. Box 351 • San Luis, CO 81152-0351 • (719) 672-3309

San Luis Museum Cultural Center • 401 Church Pl, P.O. Box 657 • San Luis, CO 81152 • (719) 672-3611 • http://www.museumtrail.org/SanLuisMuseum.asp

Security
Security Public Library • 715 Aspen Dr • Security, CO 80911 • (719) 391-3195 • http://www.wsd3.k12.co.us/spl/home.html

Sheridan
Sheridan Historical Society • 4101 S Federal Blvd • Sheridan, CO 80110-5399 • http://www.rootsweb.ancestry.com/~coshs/

Silt
Silt Historical Society • Historical Museum, 707 Orchard, P.O. Box 401 • Silt, CO 81652 • (970) 876-2668

Silver Cliff
Silver Cliff Museum • 606 Main St, P.O. Box 835 • Silver Cliff, CO 81252 • (719) 783-2615

Silver Plume
Silver Plume School House Museum • 905 Main, P.O. Box 935 • Silver Plume, CO 80476 • (303) 569-2145

Colorado

Silverton
San Juan County Historical Society • Historical Museum, 1567 Greene St, P.O. Box 154 • Silverton, CO 81433 • (970) 387-5838 • http://www.silvertonhistoricalsociety.org

Silverton Public Library • 1111 Reese, P.O. Box 68 • Silverton, CO 81433-0068 • (970) 387-5770

Steamboat Springs
Bud Werner Memorial Library • 1289 Lincoln Ave • Steamboat Springs, CO 80487 • (970) 879-0240 • http://www.steamboatlibrary.org

Bud Werner Memorial Library Genealogy Club • c/o Bud Werner Memorial Library, 1289 Lincoln Ave • Steamboat Springs, CO 80487 • (970) 879-0240 x331 • http://www.steamboatlibrary.org/genealogy-club

Historic Routt County • 141 9th St, P.O. Box 775717 • Steamboat Springs, CO 80477 • (970) 875-1305 • http://www.historicrouttcounty.org

Tread of Pioneers Museum • 800 Oak St, P.O. Box 772372 • Steamboat Springs, CO 80477 • (970) 879-2214 • http://www.treadofpioneers.org

Sterling
Logan County Genealogical Society • 15349 Hiway 14 • Sterling, CO 80751

Logan County Genealogical Society • Route 1, P.O. Box 294 • Sterling, CO 80751

Logan County Historical Society • P.O. Box 564 • Sterling, CO 80751 • (970) 522-3895

Monahan Library • Northeastern Junior College, 100 College Ave • Sterling, CO 80751-2399 • (970) 521-6663 • http://www.njc.edu/library/

Northeast Colorado Health Dept • 700 Columbine St, P.O. Box 3300 • Sterling, CO 80751 • (970) 522-3741 • http://www.nchd.org

Overland Trail Museum • 110 Overland Trail • Sterling, CO 80751 • (970) 522-3895 • http://www.sterlingcolo.com

Sterling Public Library • 420 N 5th St, P.O. Box 4000 • Sterling, CO 80751-4000 • (970) 522-2023 • http://www.sterlingcolo.com

Strasburg
Comanche Crossing Historical Society • Historical Museum, 56060 E Colfax Ave • Strasburg, CO 80136-0647 • (303) 622-4690

Telluride
Telluride Historical Society • Historical Museum, 201 W Gregory Ave, P.O. Box 1597 • Telluride, CO 81435 • (970) 728-3344 • http://www.telluridemuseum.com

Thornton
Adams County Library System • 8992 N Washington • Thornton, CO 80229-4537 • (303) 288-2001 • http://www.adams.lib.co.us

Toponas
Toponas Public Library • 33650 Hwy 134, P.O. Box C • Toponas, CO 80479-0249 • (970) 638-4436

Towaoc
Ute Mountain Tribal Library • Education Ctr, 450 Sunset, P.O. Box CC • Towaoc, CO 81334-0048 • (970) 564-5348 • http://www.utemountainute.com

Trinidad
Baca House, Trinidad History Museum • 312 E Main St, P.O. Box 377 • Trinidad, CO 81082 • (719) 846-7217 • http://www.trinidadco.com

Carnegie Public Library • 202 N Animas St • Trinidad, CO 81082 • (719) 846-6841

Colorado Welcome Center • 309 Nevada Ave • Trinidad, CO 81082 • (719) 846-9512

Genealogical Society of Hispanic America, Trinidad Chapter • 811 Linden Ave • Trinidad, CO 81081 • (719) 846-2734

Las Animas-Huerfano Counties District Health Dept • 412 Benedicta Ave • Trinidad, CO 81082 • (719) 846-2213

Samuel Freudenthal Memorial Library • Trinidad State Junior College, 600 Prospect St • Trinidad, CO 81082 • (719) 846-5593 • http://www.tsjc.cccoes.edu/library/

Santa Fe Trail Museum • 312 E Main St • Trinidad, CO 81082 • (719) 846-7217 • http://www.trinidadco.com

Trinidad Historical Society • Bloom House Museum, 300 E Main St, P.O. Box 176 • Trinidad, CO 81082 • (719) 846-7217 • http://www.trinidadco.com

USAF Academy
McDermott Library • United States Air Force Academy, 2354 Fairchild Dr, Suite 3A10 • USAF Academy, CO 80840-6214 • (719) 333-4749 • http://www.usafa.af.mil/dfsel

US Air Force Academy Visitor Center • 2346 Academy • USAF Academy, CO 80840 • (719) 333-2569

Vail
Colorado Ski Museum • 231 S Frontage Rd, Vail Village, P.O. Box 1976 • Vail, CO 81657 • (970) 476-1876 • http://www.skimuseum.net

Victor
Victor Lowell Thomas Museum • 298 Victor Ave, P.O. Box 238 • Victor, CO 80860 • (719) 689-5509 • http://www.victorcolorado.com

Victor Public Library • 124 S 3rd St, P.O. Box 5 • Victor, CO 80860-0005 • (719) 689-2011

Walden
Jackson County Public Library • 412 4th St, P.O. Box 398 • Walden, CO 80480-0398 • (970) 723-4602

North Park Pioneer Association • Historical Museum, 365 Logan St, P.O. Box 678 • Walden, CO 80480 • (970) 723-8371

Walsenburg
Huerfano County Historical Society • Historical Museum, 112 W 5th St, P.O. Box 134 • Walsenburg, CO 81089 • (719) 738-1992

Ward
Columbia City Historical Society • Historical Museum, P.O. Box 191 • Ward, CO 80481

Wellington
Baker Schneider Archives • 3740 Cleveland Ave • Wellington, CO 80459 • (970) 490-2137

Wellington Public Library • 3800 Wilson Ave, P.O. Box 416 • Wellington, CO 80549-0416 • (970) 568-3040 • http://www.wellington.ipac.epixasp.com

Westcliffe
Custer County Historical Society • 59000 Hwy 69 • Westcliffe, CO 81252 • (719) 783-9448

West Custer County Library District • 209 Main St, P.O. Box 689 • Westcliffe, CO 81252-0689 • (719) 783-9138

Westminster
Westminster Historical Society • P.O. Box 492 • Westminster, CO 80036 • (303) 426-1858

Westminster Historical Society • Bowles House Museum, 3924 W 72nd Ave, P.O. Box 472 • Westminster, CO 80030 • (303) 430-7929

Wheat Ridge
Wheat Ridge Historical Society • Historical Museum, 4610 Robb St, P.O. Box 1833 • Wheat Ridge, CO 80034-1833 • (303) 467-0023 • http://www.wheatridgehistoricalsociety.org

Windsor
Windsor Museum • 116 N 5th St • Windsor, CO 80550 • (970) 686-7476 • http://www.sindsorgov.com/townmuseum.html

Winter Park
Cozens Ranch Museum • 77849 US Hwy 40 • Winter Park, CO 80482 • (970) 726-5488 • http://www.grandcountymuseum.com

Woodland Park
Rampart Regional Library District • 218 E Midland, P.O. Box 336 • Woodland Park, CO 80866-0336 • (719) 687-9281

Ute Pass Historical Society • Historical Museum, 222 E Midland Ave, P.O. Box 6875 • Woodland Park, CO 80866-6875 • (719) 686-7512 • http://www.utepasshistoricalsociety.org

Wray
East Yuma County Historical Society • Wray Museum, 205 E 3rd St, P.O. Box 161 • Wray, CO 80758-0161 • (970) 332-5063

Wray Heritage Association • Historical Museum, 205 E 3rd St • Wray, CO 80758-1106 • (970) 332-5063

Yampa
Yampa Historical Museum • 100 Main • Yampa, CO 80483 • (970) 638-4480

Yampa Public Library • 310 Main St, P.O. Box 10 • Yampa, CO 80483-0010 • (970) 638-4654

Yuma
West Yuma Genealogical Society • 503 S Buffalo St • Yuma, CO 80759

Yuma Area Genealogical Society • P.O. Box 454 • Yuma, CO 80759

Yuma Museum • 3rd & Detroit, P.O. Box 192 • Yuma, CO 80759 • (970) 858-5162

Colorado

Abington
Abington Social Library • 536 Hampton Rd • Abington, CT 06230-0091 • (203) 974-0415

Andover
Andover Historical Society • Bunker Hill Rd • Andover, CT 06232 • (860) 742-6796 • http://www.andoverconnecticut.homestead.com/HistoricalSociety.html

Museum of Andover History • Old Town Hall, Monument Ln • Andover, CT 06232 • http://andoverconnecticut.homestead.com/Museum.html

Ansonia
Ansonia Library • 53 S Cliff St • Ansonia, CT 06401-1909 • (203) 734-6275 • http://www.biblio.org/ansonia

Derby Historical Society • Gen David Humphreys House, 37 Elm St • Ansonia, CT 06401-3312 • (203) 735-1908 • http://www.derbyhistorical.org/humphrey.htm

Ashford
Ashford Historical Society • 630 Westford Rd • Ashford, CT 06278 • (860) 429-4568 • http://ashfordtownhall.org

Babcock Library • 25 Pompey Hollow Rd, P.O. Box 360 • Ashford, CT 06278-0360 • (860) 429-0287 • http://www.babcocklibrary.com

Avon
Avon Free Public Library • 281 Country Club Rd • Avon, CT 06001 • (860) 673-9712 • http://www.avon.lib.ct.us

Avon Historical Society • Avon Living History Museum, 8 E Main St, P.O. Box 448 • Avon, CT 06001-3801 • (860) 678-7621 • http://www.avonhistoricalsociety.org

Avon Town Historian • 215 Cider Brook Rd • Avon, CT 06001 • (860) 678-1043 • http://www.town.avon.ct.us

Baltic
Sprague Historical Society • 1 Main St • Baltic, CT 06330

Bantam
Bantam Historical Society • Main St, P.O. Box 436 • Bantam, CT 06750 • (860) 567-5037

Barkhamsted
Barkhamsted Historical Society • 100 E River Rd • Barkhamsted, CT 06063 • (860) 738-2456

Beacon Falls
Beacon Falls Historical Commission • 10 Maple Ave • Beacon Falls, CT 06403 • (203) 729-4340

Berlin
Berlin Historical Society • Historical Museum, 305 Main St • Berlin, CT 06037 • (860) 828-5114 • http://berlincthistorical.org

Berlin-Peck Memorial Library • 234 Kensington Rd • Berlin, CT 06037 • (860) 828-7125 • http://www.berlinpeck.lib.ct.us

Bethany
Bethany Historical Society • 512 Amity Rd • Bethany, CT 06524 • (203) 393-1832

Bethel
Bethel Historical Society • Historical Museum, 40 Main St • Bethel, CT 06810 • (203) 794-1050

Bethel Public Library • 189 Greenwood Ave • Bethel, CT 06801-2598 • (203) 794-8756 • http://www.biblio.org/bethel

Bethlehem
Abbey of Regina Laudis Library • Flanders Rd • Bethlehem, CT 06751 • (203) 266-7727

Bellamy-Ferriday House Museum • 9 Main St N, P.O. Box 181 • Bethlehem, CT 06751 • (203) 266-7596 • http://www.ci.bethlehem.ct.us/Bellamy/bellamy.htm

Bethlehem Public Library • 32 Main St S, P.O. Box 99 • Bethlehem, CT 06751-0099 • (203) 266-7792 • http://ci.bethlehem.ct.us

Old Bethlehem Historical Society • 4 Main St N, P.O. Box 132 • Bethlehem, CT 06751 • (203) 266-5188 • http://www.ci.bethlehem.ct.us/OBHSI/old.htm

Bloomfield
Archbishop Henry J O'Brien Library • Saint Thomas Seminary-Hartford Archdiocese, 467 Bloomfield Ave • Bloomfield, CT 06002 • (860) 242-5573 • http://pages.cthome.net/obrienlibrary/library.htm

Prosser Public Library • 1 Tunxis Ave • Bloomfield, CT 06002-2476 • (860) 243-9721 • http://www.bloomfieldct.com/library

Wintonbury Historical Society • 151 School St, P.O Box 7454 • Bloomfield, CT 06002 • (860) 243-1531 • http://www.bloomfieldcthistory.org

Bolton
Bolton Historical Society • Historical Museum, 25 Hebron Rd • Bolton, CT 06043

Branford
Branford Historical Society • Harrison House, 124 Main St, P.O. Box 504 • Branford, CT 06405 • (203) 488-4828 • http://www.branfordhistory.org

James Blackstone Memorial Library • 785 Main St • Branford, CT 06405-3697 • (203) 488-1441 • http://www.blackstone.lioninc.org

Bridgeport
Barnum Museum • 820 Main St • Bridgeport, CT 06604 • (203) 331-1104 • http://www.barnum-museum.org

Bridgeport Public Library • Historical Collections, 925 Broad St • Bridgeport, CT 06603 • (203) 576-7417 • http://www.bridgeportpubliclibrary.org

Society Farsarotul • 593 Clinton Ave • Bridgeport, CT 06605 • (203) 375-0600

Bridgewater
Bridgewater Historical Society • Main St, P.O. Box 153 • Bridgewater, CT 06752 • (203) 354-6507 • http://www.newmilford-chamber.com/towns/ bridgewater.htm

Bridgewater Library Association-Burnham Library • 62 Main St S, P.O. Box 430 • Bridgewater, CT 06752-0430 • (860) 354-6937

Bristol
American Clock & Watch Museum • 100 Maple St • Bristol, CT 06010 • (860) 583-6070 • http://www.clockmuseum.org

Bristol Historical Society • 98 Summer St, P.O. Box 1393 • Bristol, CT 06010 • (860) 583-6309 • http://www.bristolhistoricalsociety.org

Bristol Public Library • 5 High St, P.O. Box 730 • Bristol, CT 06010 • (860) 584-7787 • http://www.ci.bristol.ct.us/Library/MainLibrary/LibraryMain.htm

Greater Bristol Historical Society • 54 Middle St, P.O. Box 1393 • Bristol, CT 06010 • (860) 583-6309 • http://www.bristolhistoricalsociety.org

New England Carousel Museum • 95 Riverside Ave • Bristol, CT 96010 • (860) 585-5411 • http://www.thecarouselmuseum.org

Brookfield
Brookfield Historical Society • 165 Whisconier Rd, P.O. Box 5231 • Brookfield, CT 06804 • (203) 740-8140 • http://www.brookfieldhistory.org

Brooklyn
Brooklyn Historical Society • 25 Canterbury Rd, P.O. Box 90 • Brooklyn, CT 06234 • (860) 774-7728 • http://www.brooklynct.org

Brooklyn Town Library Association • 10 Canterbury Rd, P.O. Box 357 • Brooklyn, CT 06234-0357 • (860) 774-0649

Connecticut

Burlington

Burlington Historical Society • 781 George Washington Tpk, P.O. Box 1215 • Burlington, CT 06013 • (860) 404-0152 • http://www.burlington-history.org

Burlington Public Library • 34 Library Ln, P.O. Box 1379 • Burlington, CT 06013-0379 • (860) 673-3331

Canaan

Connecticut Railroad Historical Association • 7 Main St • Canaan, CT 06018 • (860) 824-7288

Canterbury

Canterbury Historical Society • 11 N Canterbury Rd, P.O. Box 2 • Canterbury, CT 06331 • (203) 546-6482 • http://www.canterburyhistorical.org

Finnish American Heritage Society of Connecticut • 76 N Canterbury Rd, P.O. Box 252 • Canterbury, CT 06331 • (860) 546-6671

Prudence Crandall Museum • Routes 14 & 169, P.O. Box 58 • Canterbury, CT 06331-0058 • (860) 546-9916 • http://www.cultureandtourism.org

Canton

Canton Historical Society • Historical Museum, 11 Front St • Canton, CT 06019 • (860) 693-4593

Central Village

Association of Northeastern Connecticut Historical Societies • P.O. Box 104 • Central Village, CT 06332 • (203) 928-6128

Plainfield Historical Society • Town Hall, 8 Community Ave, P.O. Box 104 • Central Village, CT 06332 • http://www.plainfieldhistory.org

Chaplin

Chaplin Historical Society • Historical Museum, 1 Chaplin St • Chaplin, CT 06235

Chaplin Public Library • 130 Chaplin St • Chaplin, CT 06235-2302 • (860) 455-9424

Cheshire

Barker Character Comic and Cartoon Museum • 1188 Highland Ave • Cheshire, CT 06410 • (203) 699-3822 • http://www.barkermuseum.com

Cheshire Historical Society • Hitchcock-Phillips House, 43 Church Dr, P.O. Box 281 • Cheshire, CT 06410 • (203) 272-2574 • http://www.cheshirehistory.org

Cheshire Public Library • 104 Main St • Cheshire, CT 06410-2499 • (203) 272-2245 • http://www.cheshirelibrary.org

Chester

Chester Historical Society • Mill Museum, 9 W Main St, P.O. Box 204 • Chester, CT 06412 • (860) 526-2393 • http://www.chesterhistoricalsociety.org

Chester Public Library • 21 W Main St, P.O. Box 310 • Chester, CT 06412-0310 • (860) 526-0018

Nehantic Tribe and Nation • 231 W Main St • Chester, CT 06412

Clinton

Clinton Historical Society • Capt Elisha White House Museum, 103 E Main St • Clinton, CT 06413 • (860) 669-2148

Stanton House Museum • 63 E Main St • Clinton, CT 06413 • (860) 669-2132 • http://www.stantonhousect.com

Colchester

Colchester Historical Society • Historical Museum , 24 Linwood Ave, P.O. Box 13 • Colchester, CT 06415 • (860) 537-4230

Cragin Memorial Library • 8 Linwood Ave, P.O. Box 508 • Colchester, CT 06415 • (860) 537-5752 • http://www.colchester.net/library.html

Colebrook

Colebrook Historical Society • 558 Colebrook Rd, P.O. Box 85 • Colebrook, CT 06021 • (860) 738-3142

Collinsville

Canton Historic District Commission • Town Hall • Collinsville, CT 06022

Canton Historical Society • Historical Museum, 11 Front St • Collinsville, CT 06022 • (860) 693-2793 • http://www.cantonmuseum.org

Canton Public Library • 26 Center St • Collinsville, CT 06022 • (860) 693-8266

Columbia

Columbia Historical Society • 486 Route 66 • Columbia, CT 06237 • (860) 228-9385

Saxton B Little Free Library • 319 Route 87 • Columbia, CT 06237-1143 • (860) 228-0350 • http://www.columbiact.org/SBLinfo.htm

Cornwall

Cornwall Historical Society • 7 Pine St, P.O. Box 115 • Cornwall, CT 06753 • (860) 672-0505 • http://www.cornwallhistoricalsociety.org

Cos Cob

Historical Society of the Town of Greenwich • Bush-Holley House, 39 Strickland Rd • Cos Cob, CT 06807 • (203) 869-6899 • http://www.hstg.org

Coventry

Booth and Dimock Memorial Library • 1134 Main St, P.O. Box 129 • Coventry, CT 06238-0129 • (860) 742-7606 • http://www.coventrypl.org

Coventry Historical Society • Strong-Porter House Museum, 2382 South St, P.O. Box 534 • Coventry, CT 06238 • (860) 742-9025 • http://www.coventryhistoricalsociety.org

Joseph Huntington House Museum • Parsonage House, 1346 South St • Coventry, CT 06238 • http://www.connecticutsar.org

Nathan Hale Homestead Museum • 229 South St • Coventry, CT 06238 • (860) 742-6917 • http://www.ctlandmarks.org

Cromwell

Cromwell Belden Public Library • 39 West St • Cromwell, CT 06416 • (860) 632-3460 • http://cromwellct.com/library

Cromwell Historical Society • Stevens-Frisbie House Museum, 395 Main St, P.O. Box 146 • Cromwell, CT 06416 • (860) 635-0501 • http://www.hometown.aol.com/cromwellhistory/

Danbury

Danbury Historical Society • Scott-Fanton House Museum, 43 Main St • Danbury, CT 06810 • (860) 743-5200 • http://www.danburyhistorical.org

Danbury Public Library • 170 Main St, P.O. Box 1160 • Danbury, CT 06810 • (203) 797-4527 • http://www.danburylibrary.org

Danbury Railway Museum • 120 White St, P.O. Box 90 • Danbury, CT 06813 • (860) 778-8337 • http://www.danbury.org/drm/museum.htm

John and Mary Ridder House Museum • 43 Main St • Danbury, CT 06810 • (860) 743-5200 • http://www.danburyhistorical.org

Military Museum of Southern New England • 125 Park Ave • Danbury, CT 06810 • (203) 790-9277 • http://www.usmilitarymuseum.org

Ruth A Haas Library • Western Connecticut State College, 181 White St • Danbury, CT 06810 • (203) 837-9100 • http://www.wcsu.edu/libraries

Danielson

Killingly Historical Society • Historical Center, 196 Main St, P.O. Box 6000 • Danielson, CT 06239 • (860) 779-7250 • http://www.killinglyhistory.org

Killingly Public Library • 25 Westcott Rd • Danielson, CT 06239 • (860) 779-5383 • http://www.state.ct.us/munic/killingly/killingly.htm

Darien

Connecticut League of Historical Societies • P.O. Box 906 • Darien, CT 06820

Darien Historical Society • Bates-Scofield Homestead, 45 Old Kings Highway N • Darien, CT 06820 • (203) 655-9233 • http://historical. darien.org

Darien Library • 35 Leroy Ave • Darien, CT 06820-4497 • (203) 655-1234 • http://www.darien.lib.ct.us

Middlesex Genealogical Society • 45 Old Kings Highway N, P.O. Box 1111 • Darien, CT 06820-1111 • (203) 655-2734 • http://www.darien.lib. ct.us/mgs/

Deep River

Deep River Historical Society • Historical Museum, 278 S Main St • Deep River, CT 06417 • (860) 526-1449

Derby

Derby Historical Society • David Humphreys House, 37 Elm St, P.O. Box 331 • Derby, CT 06418 • (203) 735-1908 • http://derbyhistorical. org

Derby Neck Library • 307 Hawthorne Ave • Derby, CT 06418-1199 • (203) 734-1492 • http://www.derbynecklibrary.org

Derby Public Library-Harcourt Wood Memorial • 313 Elizabeth St • Derby, CT 06418 • (203) 736-1482 • http://www.derbypubliclibrary.org

Dr John Ireland Howe House Museum • 213 Caroline St • Derby, CT 06418 • (203) 735-1908 • http://www.invalley.org/derby

Osborne Homestead Museum • 500 Hawthorne Ave • Derby, CT 96418 • (203) 734-2513

Schaghticoke Tribal Nation • 33 Elizabeth St • Derby, CT 06418 • (203) 736-0782 • http://www.schaghticoke.com

Durham

Durham Fair Farm Museum • P.O. Box 225 • Durham, CT 06422 • http://www.durhamfair.com

Durham Historical Society • Main St, P.O. Box 345 • Durham, CT 06422 • (203) 349-9273 • http://www.townofdurhamct.org

Durham Public Library • 7 Maple Ave • Durham, CT 06422 • (860) 349-9544 • http://www.durhamlibrary.lioninc.org

East Granby

East Granby Historical Society • Historical Museum, P.O. Box 188 • East Granby, CT 06026 • (203) 653-7548 • http://www.eastgranby.com/ HistoricalSociety/

East Granby Public Library • Alice Newman Historical Rm, 24 Center St, P.O. Box G • East Granby, CT 06026-0470 • (860) 653-3002 • http://www.eastgranbylibrary.org/alicenewmanhistoricalroom.htm

Old New Gate Prison and Copper Mine Museum • 115 Newgate Rd • East Granby, CT 96026 • (860) 653-3563

East Haddam

East Haddam Historical Society • Historical Museum, 264 Town St, P.O. Box 27 • East Haddam, CT 06423 • (860) 873-3944 • http://www. easthaddam.net

Gillette Castle State Park Museum • 67 River Rd • East Haddam, CT 06423 • (860) 424-3200

Nathan Hale Schoolhouse Museum • 29 Main St • East Haddam, CT 06423 • (860) 873-3399 • http://www.connecticutsar.org

Rathbun Free Library • 36 Main St, P.O. Box G • East Haddam, CT 06423 • (860) 873-8210 • http://www.rathbunlibrary.org

Sons of the American Revolution, Connecticut Society • P.O. Box 440 • East Haddam, CT 06423 • (860) 916-1804 • http://www.connecticutsar. org

East Hampton

Chatham Historical Society of East Hampton, Connecticut • Bevin Blvd • East Hampton, CT 06424 • http://chathamhs.tripod.com

East Hampton Public Library • 105 Main St • East Hampton, CT 06424 • (860) 267-6621 • http://www.easthamptonct.org

East Hartford

Connecticut Society of Genealogists • 175 Maple St • East Hartford, CT 06118-2634 • (860) 569-0002 • http://www.csginc.org

East Hartford Historical Society • Historical Museum, 307 Burnside Ave, P.O. Box 380166 • East Hartford, CT 06118 • (860) 568-7645 • http://www.hseh.org

East Hartford Public Library • 840 Main St • East Hartford, CT 06108 • (860) 289-6429 • http://www.easthartford.lib.ct.us

East Hartland

Hartland Historical Society • Historical Museum, 141 Center St, P.O. Box 221 • East Hartland, CT 06027 • (860) 653-3055 • http://www. munic.state.et.us/hartland/historical.htm

East Haven

East Haven Historical Society • Historical Museum, 200 Tyler St, P.O. Box 120052 • East Haven, CT 06512 • (203) 467-1766

Shore Line Trolley Museum • 17 River St • East Haven, CT 96512` • (203) 457-6927 • http://www.bera.org

East Lyme

East Lyme Historical Society • Smith Harris House, 33 Society Rd • East Lyme, CT 06357 • (860) 739-0761 • http://www.smithharris.org

East Windsor

Connecticut Fire & Trolley Museum • 58 North Rd, P.O. Box 360 • East Windsor, CT 06088-0360 • (860) 627-6540 • http://www.ct-trolley.org/ Firemuseum/fm4.htm

East Windsor Historical Society • Scantic Academy Museum, 115 Scantic Rd, P.O. Box 363 • East Windsor, CT 06028 • (860) 623-5327 • http://eastwindsorhistory.tk

Eastford

Eastford Historical Society • 26 Pilfershire Rd • Eastford, CT 06242 • (203) 974-2733

Easton

Easton Historical Society • Historical Museum, 691 Morehouse Rd, P.O. Box 121 • Easton, CT 06612 • (203) 261-2090 • http:// www.tomorrowseaston.com/guestwebpages/historicalsociety/ historicalsociety.htm

Easton Public Library • 691 Morehouse Rd, PO Box 2 • Easton, CT 06612-0002 • (203) 261-0134 • http://www.eastonlibrary.org

Ellington

Ellington Historical Society • Nellie Mcknight House Museum, 70 Main St, P.O. Box 73 • Ellington, CT 06029 • http://www.ellingtonhistsoc.org

Hall Memorial Library • 93 Main St, P.O. Box 280 • Ellington, CT 06029 • (860) 870-3160 • http://www.biblio.org/ellington/hall.htm

Enfield

Enfield Historical Society • 1294 Enfield St, P.O. Box 586 • Enfield, CT 06082-4928 • (860) 745-1729 • http://home.att.net/~mkm-of-enfct/

Enfield Public Library • 104 Middle Rd • Enfield, CT 06082 • (860) 763-7510 • http://www.enfield.lib.ct.us

Learning Resource Center • Asnuntuck Community College, 170 Elm St • Enfield, CT 06082-0068 • (860) 253-3174 • http://www.acc. commnet.edu

Martha A Parsons House Museum • 1387 Enfield St • Enfield, CT 06082 • (860) 745-6064 • http://www.att.net.~mkm-of-enfct/EHS/ EHSMartha.htm

Connecticut

Essex
Connecticut River Foundation • Connecticut River Museum, 67 Main St • Essex, CT 06426 • (860) 767-8269 • http://www.ctrivermuseum.org

Essex Historical Society • Hill's Academy, 22 Prospect St, P.O. Box 123 • Essex, CT 06426 • (860) 767-0681 • http://www.essexhistory.org

Pratt House Museum • West Ave • Essex, CT 06426 • (860) 767-8601 • http://www.essexhistory.org

Fairfield
Fairfield Historical Society • Historical Museum, 636 Old Post Rd • Fairfield, CT 06430-6647 • (203) 259-1598 • http://www.fairfieldhistoricalsociety.org

Fairfield Public Library • 1080 Old Post Road • Fairfield, CT 06430 • (203) 256-3155 • http://www.fairfieldpubliclibrary.org

Jewish Historical Society of Greater Bridgeport • 3135 Park Ave • Fairfield, CT 06432 • (203) 335-3638

Ogden House and Gardens • 1520 Bronson Rd • Fairfield, CT 06430 • (203) 259-1598 • http://fairfieldhistoricalsociety.org

Fairhaven
Coggeshall Museum Memorial House • 6 Cherry St • Fairhaven, CT 02719 • (508) 993-4877

Falls Village
David M Hunt Library • 63 Main St, P.O. Box 217 • Falls Village, CT 06031-0217 • (860) 824-7424

Falls Village-Canaan Historical Society • Depot Museum, 44 Railroad St, P.O. Box 206 • Falls Village, CT 06031 • (860) 824-8226 • http://www.betweenthelakes.com

Farmington
Farmington Historical Society • Historical Museum, 71 Main St, P.O. Box 1645 • Farmington, CT 06034 • (860) 678-1645 • http://www.farmingtonhistoricalsociety-ct.org

Farmington Library • 6 Montieth Dr, P.O. Box 407 • Farmington, CT 06034-0407 • (860) 673-6791 • http://www.farmington.lib.ct.us

Hill-Stead Museum • 35 Mountain Rd • Farmington, CT 06032 • (860) 677-4787 • http://www.hillstead.org

Stanley-Whitman House Museum, 37 High St • Farmington, CT 06032 • (860) 677-9222 • http://www.stanleywhitman.org

Franklin
Blue Slope Country Museum • 138 Blue Hill Rd • Franklin, CT 06254 • (860) 642-6413 • http://www.blueslope.com

Gales Ferry
Ledyard Water-Powered Sawmill Museum • Iron St & Route 214 • Gales Ferry, CT 06335 • (860) 433-4050

Nathan Lester House Museum • 153 Vinegar Hill Rd • Gales Ferry, CT 06335 • (860) 464-8662

Gaylordsville
Gaylordsville Historical Society • Historical Museum, P.O. Box 25 • Gaylordsville, CT 06755 • (860) 350-0300 • http://www.gaylordsville.org

Glastonbury
Connecticut Society of Genealogists • 2906 Main St, P.O. Box 435 • Glastonbury, CT 06033-0435 • (860) 569-0002 • http://www.csginc.org

Historical Society of Glastonbury • Museum on the Green, 1944 Main St, P.O. Box 46 • Glastonbury, CT 06033 • (860) 633-6890 • http://www.glasct.org/hissoc/home.htm

Welles-Turner Memorial Library • 2407 Main St • Glastonbury, CT 06033 • (860) 652-7720 • http://www.wtmlib.com

Goshen
Goshen Historical Society • Historical Museum, 21 Old Middle Rd, P.O. Box 457 • Goshen, CT 06756-0457 • (860) 491-9610 • http://www.goshenhistoricalsociety.org

Granby
Company of Fifers and Drummers Museum • 27 Creamery Hill Rd • Granby, CT 06035 • (860) 760-6513 • http://www.fifeanddrum.com

Salmon Brook Historical Society • Abijah Rowe House Museum, 208 Salmon Brook St, P.O. Box 840 • Granby, CT 06035 • (860) 653-9713 • http://www.salmonbrookhistorical.org

Greenwich
Colonial Order of the Acorn • 20 MacKenzie Glen • Greenwich, CT 06830

Daughters of the American Revolution, Putnam Hill Chapter • Putnam Cottage Archives, 243 E Putnam Ave • Greenwich, CT 06830 • (203) 869-9697 • http://www.putnamcottage.org

Greenwich Library • 101 W Putnam Ave • Greenwich, CT 06830 • (203) 622-7900 • http://www.greenwich.lib.ct.us

Greenwich Library-Byram Shubert Branch • 21 Mead Rd • Greenwich, CT 06830-6812 • (203) 531-0426

Jewish Romanian Genealogy Special Interest Group • 27 Hawthorne St • Greenwich, CT 06831-4201

Groton
Bill Memorial Library • 240 Monument St • Groton, CT 06340 • (860) 445-0392 • http://www.billmemorial.org

Groton Bank Historical Association • 5 Meridian St • Groton, CT 06340 • http://www.newlondonhistory.org

Groton Public Library • 52 Newtown Rd • Groton, CT 06340 • (860) 441-6750 • http://www.seconnlib.org

Historic Ship Nautilus-Submarine Force Museum • 1 Crystal Lake Rd • Groton, CT 06340-2464 • (860) 694-4276 • http://www.ussnautilus.org

Jabez Smith House Museum • Route 117 • Groton, CT 06340 • (860) 445-6689

Kelsey House Museum • 1702 Main St, P.O. Box 7213 • Groton, CT 06340 • (860) 667-0545

Mystic Nautical Heritage Society • 120 School St • Groton, CT 06340 • (860) 536-4209

Noank Historical Society • Exhibition Hall, 108 Main St, P.O. Box 9454 • Groton, CT 06340 • (860) 536-3021

Submarine Force Museum • Naval Submarine Base • Groton, CT 06349-5771 • (860) 694-3174 • http://www.ussnautilus.org

Guilford
Dorothy Whitfield Historic Society • Hyland House, 84 Boston St, P.O. Box 229 • Guilford, CT 06437 • (203) 453-9477 • http://www.hylandhouse.com

Guilford Free Library • Historical Room, 67 Park St • Guilford, CT 06437 • (203) 453-8282 • http://www.guilford.lib.ct.us

Guilford Keeping Society • Thomas Griswold House Museum, 171 Boston St, P.O. Box 363 • Guilford, CT 06437 • (203) 453-3176 • http://www.guilfordkeepingsociety.com; www.thomasgriswoldhouse.com

Henry Whitfield State Historical Museum • 248 Old Whitfield St, P.O. Box 210 • Guilford, CT 06437-0210 • (203) 453-2457 • http://www.whitfieldmuseum.org

Hyland House Museum • 84 Boston St • Guilford, CT 06437 • (203) 453-9477 • http://www.hylandhouse.com

Haddam
Brainers Memorial Library • 920 Saybrook Rd, P.O. Box 8 • Haddam, CT 06438 • (860) 345-2204

Haddam Historical Society • Thankful Arnold House Museum, 14 Hayden Hill Rd, P.O. Box 97 • Haddam, CT 06438-0097 • (860) 345-2400 • http://www.haddamhistory.org

Hamden

Arnold Bernhard Library • Quinnipiac University, 275 Mount Carmel Ave • Hamden, CT 06518 • (203) 582-8633

Congregation Mishkan Israel Library • 785 Ridge Rd • Hamden, CT 06517 • (203) 288-3877

Connecticut League of History Organizations • 940 Whitney Ave • Hamden, CT 06517-4002 • (203) 624-9186 • http://www.clho.org

Eli Whitney Museum • 915 Whitney Ave • Hamden, CT 06517 • (203) 777-1833 • http://www.eliwhitney.org

Esther Swinkin Memorial Library • Temple Beth Sholom, 1809 Whitney Ave • Hamden, CT 06517 • (203) 288-7748

Hamden Historical Society • Historical Museum, 105 Mt Carmel Rd, P.O. Box 5512 • Hamden, CT 06518-0512 • (860) 548-8001 • http://www.hamdenhistoricalsociety.com

Hamden Library • 2901 Dixwell Ave • Hamden, CT 06518-3135 • (203) 287-2686 • http://www.hamdenlibrary.org

Hampton

Hampton Antiquarian and Historical Society • Main St, P.O. Box 12 • Hampton, CT 06247 • (203) 455-9650

Windham Historical Society • Jillson House, 627 Main St • Hampton, CT 06247 • (860) 456-2316

Hartford

Antiquarian and Landmarks Society • Butler-McCook Homestead Museum, 255 Main St • Hartford, CT 06103 • (860) 247-8996 • http://www.hartnet.org/als

Connecticut Conference Archives • United Church Of Christ, 125 Sherman St • Hartford, CT 06105 • (860) 233-5564

Connecticut Historical Commission • 59 S Prospect St • Hartford, CT 06106 • (860) 566-3005 • http://www.cthistorical.com

Connecticut Historical Society • 1 Elizabeth St • Hartford, CT 06105-2292 • (860) 236-5621 • http://www.chs.org

Connecticut Professional Genealogists Council • P.O. Box 4273 • Hartford, CT 06147-4273 • http://www.rootsweb.com/~ctpgc/

Connecticut State Library & Archives • Museum of Connecticut History, 231 Capitol Ave • Hartford, CT 06115 • (860) 757-6500 • http://www.cslib.org

Episcopal Diocese of Connecticut Diocesan Library • 1335 Asylum Ave • Hartford, CT 06105 • (860) 233-4481 • http://www.ctdiocese.org

Hartford Public Library • 500 Main St • Hartford, CT 06103 • (860) 543-8628 • http://www.hartfordpl.lib.ct.us

Hartford Public Library-Mark Twain Memorial Branch • 256 Farmington Ave • Hartford, CT 06105 • (860) 722-6877 • http://www.hartnet.org/twain

Isham-Terry House Museum • 211 High St • Hartford, CT 06105 • (860) 247-8996

Mark Twain House and Museum • 351 Farmington Ave • Hartford, CT 06105 • (860) 247-0998 • http://www.marktwainhouse.org

Menser Museum of Medicine and Dentistry • 230 Scarborough St • Hartford, CT 06105 • (860) 236-5613 • http://www.library.tcbc.edu/hms

Museum of Connecticut History • 231 Capitol Ave • Hartford, CT 06106 • (860) 757-6535 • http://www.museumofcthistory.org

Old State House Museum • 800 Main St • Hartford, CT 06103 • (860) 522-6755 • http://www.ctosh.org

Society of Mayflower Descendants in Connecticut • 36 Arundel Ave • Hartford, CT 06457

State Capitol Museum • 210 Capitol Ave • Hartford, CT 06106 • (860) 240-0222 • http://www.cga.ct.gov/capitoltours

Stowe-Day Foundation • Harriet Beecher Stowe Center, 77 Forest St • Hartford, CT 06105-3296 • (860) 522-9258 • http://www.hartnet.org/~stowe/

Trinity College Library • 300 Summit St • Hartford, CT 06106 • (860) 297-2252 • http://www.trincoll.edu/depts/library/

Wadsworth Atheneum • 600 Main St • Hartford, CT 06103 • (860) 278-2670 • http://www.wadsworthatheneum.org

Watkinson Library • Trinity College, 300 Summit St • Hartford, CT 06106 • (860) 297-2268 • http://www.trincoll.edu/depts/library/watkinson/watk_intro.html

Wethersfield Historical Society • 212 Main St • Hartford, CT 06106 • (860) 529-4757

Harwinton

Harwinton Historical Society • Historical Museum, 50 Burlington Rd, P.O. Box 84 • Harwinton, CT 06791 • (860) 485-1202

Harwinton Public Library • 80 Bentley Dr • Harwinton, CT 06791 • (860) 485-9113 • http://www.libct.org/harwintonpl

Hebron

Douglas Library of Hebron • 22 Main St • Hebron, CT 06248 • (860) 228-9312 • http://www.douglaslibrary.org

Hebron Historical Society • Historical Museum, Main St, P.O. Box 43 • Hebron, CT 06248 • (860) 228-0075 • http://www.hebronhistoricalsociety.org

Ivoryton

Museum of Fife and Drum • 62 N Main St, P.O. Box 277 • Ivoryton, CT 06442 • (860) 767-2237 • http://www.companyoffifeanddrum.org

Jewett City

Griswold Historical Society • c/o Slater Library, 26 Main St • Jewett City, CT 06351 • (860) 376-0024 • http://www.rootsweb.ancestry.com/~ctghs/

Griswold Historical Society • Historical Museum, 167 E Main St, P.O. Box 261 • Jewett City, CT 06351 • (860) 376-4577 • http://hometown.aol.com/caseywilkz/griswold/griswold.htm

Kensington

Berlin-Peck Memorial Library • 234 Kensington Rd • Kensington, CT 06037-2604 • (860) 828-7125

Kent

Connecticut Antique Machinery Association • Historical Museum, 31 Kent Cornwall Rd, P.O. Box 425 • Kent, CT 06757 • (860) 927-0050 • http://www.ctamachinery.com

Kent Historical Society • 10 Maple St, P.O. Box 651 • Kent, CT 06757 • (860) 927-4587 • http://www.kenthistoricalsociety.org

Sloane-Stanley Museum and Kent Furnace • 31 Kent Cornwall Rd, P.O. Box 917 • Kent, CT 06757 • (860) 927-3849

Killingworth

Killingworth Historical Society • Historical Museum, 3 Fire Tower Rd, P.O. Box 707 • Killingworth, CT 06417 • (860) 663-1357

Lakeville

Salisbury Association • Holley-Williams House, 15 Millerton Rd, P.O. Box 553 • Lakeville, CT 06039 • (203) 435-2878 • http://www.salisburyassociation.org

Lebanon

Governor Trumbull's War Office Museum • 149 W Town St • Lebanon, CT 06426 • (860) 873-3399 • http://www.connecticutsar.org

Lebanon Historical Society • Historical Museum, 856 Trumbull Hwy, P.O. Box 151 • Lebanon, CT 06249 • (860) 642-6579 • http://www.LebanonCtHistSoc.org

Lebanon, cont.

William Beaumont House Museum • 169 W Town St • Lebanon, CT 06249 • (860) 642-7247 • http://www.james.com/beaumont/dr_birthplace.htm

Ledyard

Ledyard Historical Society • Nathan Lester House, Vinegar Hill & Long Cove Rds, P.O. Box 411 • Ledyard, CT 06339 • (860) 464-8540 • http://www.town.ledyard.ct.us

Ledyard Public Library • 718 Colonel Ledyard Hwy, P.O. Box 225 • Ledyard, CT 06339-0225 • (860) 464-9912 • http://www.lioninc.org/ledyard

Mashantucket Pequot Tribal Nation • P.O. Box 3060 • Ledyard, CT 06339 • (860) 572-6100 • http://www.mashantucket.com

Paucatuck Eastern Pequot Tribe • 935 Lantern Hill Rd • Ledyard, CT 06339

Western Mashantucket-Pequot Indians • Indiantown Rd, P.O. Box 160 • Ledyard, CT 06339 • (203) 536-2681

Lisbon

John Bishop House Museum • Routes 169 & 138 • Lisbon, CT 06351 • (860) 376-2708

Lisbon Historical Society • Historical Museum, 56 Blissville Rd • Lisbon, CT 06351 • (860) 887-4393

Litchfield

Litchfield Historical Society • Historical Museum, 7 South St, P.O. Box 385 • Litchfield, CT 06759 • (860) 567-4501 • http://www.litchfieldhistoricalsociety.org

Oliver Wolcott Library • 160 South St, P.O. Box 187 • Litchfield, CT 06759-0187 • (860) 567-8030 • http://www.owlibrary.org

Lyme

Lyme Public Library • 482 Hamburg Rd • Lyme, CT 06731 • (860) 434-2272 • http://www.lymepl.org

Madison

Deacon John Grave House Museum • 581 Boston Post Rd, P.O. Box 651 • Madison, CT 06443 • (203) 245-4798 • http://www.madisonct.com

E C Scranton Memorial Library • 801 Boston Post Rd, P.O. Box 631 • Madison, CT 06443-0631 • (203) 245-7365 • http://www.scrantonlibrary.com

Madison Historical Society • Allis-Bushnell House, 853 Boston Post Rd, P.O. Box 17 • Madison, CT 06443 • (203) 245-4567 • http://www.MadisonCT.com

Manchester

Cheney Homestead Museum • 106 Hartford Rd • Manchester, CT 06040 • (860) 643-5588 • http://www.manchesterhistory.org

Connecticut Firemen's Historical Society • Historical Museum, 230 Pine St • Manchester, CT 06040 • (860) 649-9436

Manchester Community College Library • Institute of Local History, 60 Bidwell St, P.O. Box 1046 • Manchester, CT 06045-1046 • (860) 512-3423 • http://www.mcc.commnet.edu/library

Manchester Historical Society • Old Manchester Museum, 126 Cedar St • Manchester, CT 06040 • (860) 647-9983 • http://www.manchesterhistory.org

Manchester Public Library • 586 Main St • Manchester, CT 06040-0071 • (860) 643-2471 • http://library.ci.manchester.ct.us

Marlborough

Marlborough Historical Society • P.O. Box 281 • Marlborough, CT 06447 • (860) 295-8106

Mashantucket

Mashantucket Pequot Museum & Research Center • 110 Pequot Trail, P.O. Box 3180 • Mashantucket, CT 06339-3180 • (860) 396-7073 • http://www.pequotmuseum.org

Meriden

1711 Solomon Goffe House Museum • 677 N Colony St • Meriden, CT 06451 • (203) 634-9088

Meriden Historical Society • 424 W Main St, P.O. Box 3005 • Meriden, CT 06451 • (203) 237-5079 • http://www.rootsweb.com/~ctmhs

Meriden Public Library • 105 Miller St, P.O. Box 868 • Meriden, CT 06450-4285 • (203) 630-2346 • http://www.cityofmeriden.com/services/library

National Shaving and Barbershop Museum • 39 W Main St • Meriden, CT 06451 • (203) 639-9778

Rosa Ponselle Museum • 39 W Main St • Meriden, CT 06451 • (203) 639-9778

Middle Haddam

Middle Haddam Public Library • 2 Knowles Landing, P.O. Box 221 • Middle Haddam, CT 06456-0221 • (860) 267-9093

Middlebury

Golden Age of Trucking Museum • 1115 Christian Rd, P.O. Box 1314 • Middlebury, CT 06762 • (203) 577-2181 • http://www.goldenagetruckmuseum.com

Middlebury Historical Society • 26 Wheeler Rd, P.O. Box 104 • Middlebury, CT 06762 • (203) 264-6340 • http://www.middlebury-ct.org/historical.shtml

Middlefield

Levi E Coe Library • 414 Main St, P.O. Box 458 • Middlefield, CT 06455-0458 • (203) 349-3857 • http://www.leviecoe.com

Middlefield Historical Society • 405 Main St • Middlefield, CT 06455 • (860) 349-0665

Middletown

Godfrey Memorial Library • 134 Newfield St • Middletown, CT 06457-2534 • (860) 346-4375 • http://www.godfrey.org

Middlesex County Historical Society • General Mansfield House Museum, 151 Main St • Middletown, CT 06457 • (860) 346-0746 • http://www.middlesexhistory.org

Olin Memorial Library • Wesleyan University, 252 Church St • Middletown, CT 06459-0108 • (860) 685-3844 • http://www.wesleyan.edu/libr/olinhome/olinhome.htm

Order of Descendants of Pirates and Privateers • 113 Highland Ave • Middletown, CT 06457 • (860) 347-7035 • http://www.piratesprivateers.org

Russell Library • 123 Broad St • Middletown, CT 06457 • (860) 347-2528 • http://www.russelllibrary.org

Society of Middletown First Settlers Descendants 1650-1700 • c/o Godfrey Memorial Library, 134 Newfield St • Middletown, CT 06457 • (860) 346-4375 • http://www.godfrey.org

Milford

Jewish Genealogical Society of Connecticut • 17 Salem Walk • Milford, CT 06430 • (203) 874-4572 • http://www.geocities.com/jgsct

Milford Historical Society • Eells-Stow House, 34 High St, P.O. Box 337 • Milford, CT 06460 • (203) 874-2664 • http://mhsoc.hom.ml.org

Milford Public Library • 57 New Haven Ave • Milford, CT 06460 • (203) 783-3290

Monroe

Monroe Historical Society • Historical Museum, 31 Great Ring Rd, P.O. Box 212 • Monroe, CT 06468 • (203) 261-1383 • http://www.monroehistoricsociety.org

Monroe Public Library • 7 Fan Hill Rd • Monroe, CT 06468 • (203) 452-5458 • http://www.biblio.org/monroe

Schaghticoke Indian Tribe • 601 Main St • Monroe, CT 06468 • (203) 459-2531

Montville
Montville Historical Society • P.O. Box 1786 • Montville, CT 06353 • (860) 848-9318

Moodus
Amasa Day House Museum • 33 Plain Rd • Moodus, CT 06469 • (860) 873-8144

East Haddam Free Public Library • 18 Plains Rd, P.O. Box 372 • Moodus, CT 06469 • (860) 873-8248 • http://www.ehfp.lib.ct.us/ehfp/

Morris
Morris Historical Society • 12 South St, P.O. Box 234 • Morris, CT 06763 • (860) 567-1776

Mystic
Denison Homestead Museum • Pequotsepos Manor, 120 Pequotsepos Rd, P.O. Box 42 • Mystic, CT 06355 • (860) 536-9248

Mystic and Noank Library • 40 Library St • Mystic, CT 06355 • (860) 536-7721 • http://www.mysticnoanklibrary.com

Mystic River Historical Society • 74 High St, P.O. Box 245 • Mystic, CT 06355 • (860) 536-4779 • http://www.mystichistory.org

Mystic Seaport Museum and Library • 75 Greenmanville Ave, P.O. Box 6000 • Mystic, CT 06355-6000 • (860) 572-5367 • http://www.mysticseaport.org

Naugatuck
Howard Whitemore Memorial Library • 243 Church St • Naugatuck, CT 06770-4198 • (203) 729-4591 • http://www.biblio.org/whittemore

Naugatuck Historical Society • Historical Museum, 195 Water St, P.O. Box 317 • Naugatuck, CT 06770 • (203) 729-9039 • http://www.naugatuckhistory.com

New Britain
Ellen Burritt Library • Central Connecticut State Univ, Connecticut Polish American Archive • New Britain, CT 06050 • (860) 832-2086 • http://library.ccsu.ctstateu.edu

New Britain Public Library • 20 High St, P.O. Box 1291 • New Britain, CT 06050 • (860) 224-3155 • http://www.nbpl.lib.ct

Polish Genealogical Society of Connecticut the Northeast • 8 Lyle Rd • New Britain, CT 06053 • (860) 223-5596 • http://www.pgsctne.org

Polish-American Archives • Elihu Burritt Library, Central Connecticut State Univ, Wells St • New Britain, CT 06050 • (860) 832-2055 • http://wilson.ctstateu.edu/lib/archives/polish/

New Canaan
New Canaan Historical Society • Hanford-Silliman House Museum, 13 Oenoke Ridge • New Canaan, CT 06480 • (203) 966-1776 • http://www.nchistory.org

New Canaan Library • 151 Main St • New Canaan, CT 06840 • (203) 594-5000 • http://newcanaanlibrary.org

New Fairfield
New Fairfield Free Public Library • 2 Brush Hill Rd, P.O. Drawer F • New Fairfield, CT 06812 • (203) 312-5679 • http://www.libct.org/newfairfieldpl/home.htm

New Fairfield Historical Society • Historical Museum, 2 Brush Hill Rd, P.O. Box 8156 • New Fairfield, CT 06810 • (203) 312-5679

New Hartford
Licia & Mason Beekley Community Library • 10 Central Ave, P.O. Box 247 • New Hartford, CT 06057 • (860) 379-7235 • http://www.newhartfordlibrary.org

New Hartford Historical Museum • P.O. Box 247 • New Hartford, CT 06057 • (860) 379-6626

New Hartford Historical Society • Greystone House, 367 Main St, P.O. Box 41 • New Hartford, CT 06057 • (860) 379-6894 • http://www.newhartfordhistory.org

New Haven
Beinecke Rare Book & Manuscript Library • Yale University Library, 121 Wall St, P.O. Box 208240 • New Haven, CT 06520-8240 • (203) 432-2972 • http://www.library.yale.edu/beinecke/

Cambodian Genocide Program • Yale Univ, P.O. Box 208206 • New Haven, CT 06520 • (203) 432-9346 • http://www.yale.edu/cgp

Connecticut Afro-American Historical Society • Historical Society, 444 Orchard St • New Haven, CT 06511 • (203) 776-4907

Connecticut Women's Hall of Fame • 320 Fitch St • New Haven, CT 06515 • (203) 392-9007 • http://www.cwhf.org

Ethnic History Archives Center • Wintergreen Ave • New Haven, CT 06512 • (203) 392-6126

Golden Hill Paugussett Tribe • 1440 Whalley Ave, Ste 236 • New Haven, CT 06515 • (203) 393-2227

Hilton C Buley Library • Southern Connecticut State University, 501 Crescent St • New Haven, CT 06515 • (203) 392-5732 • http://www.library.southernct.edu

Jewish Historical Society of New Haven • Historical Museum, 270 Fitch St, P.O. Box 3251 • New Haven, CT 06515-0351 • (203) 392-6125 • http://pages.cthome.net/hirsch/

John Hay Whitney Medical Museum • 333 Cedar St, P.O. Box 208014 • New Haven, CT 06520 • (203) 785-4354

Knights of Columbus • Historical Museum, 1 Columbus Plaza • New Haven, CT 06507 • (203) 772-2130 • http://www.kofc-supreme-council.org

New Haven City and Town Clerk • Hall of Records, 200 Orange St, Rm 204 • New Haven, CT 06510 • (203) 946-8346 • http://www.cityofnewhaven.com/TownClerk/

New Haven Colony Historical Society • Historical Museum, 114 Whitney Ave • New Haven, CT 06510 • (203) 562-4183 • http://www.nhchs.org

New Haven Free Public Library • 133 Elm St • New Haven, CT 06510 • (203) 946-8130 • http://www.cityofnewhaven.com/library

Pardee-Morris House Museum • 325 Lighthouse Rd • New Haven, CT 06512 • (203) 562-4183

Sterling Library • Yale University, 120 High St, P.O. Box 208240 • New Haven, CT 06520-8240 • (203) 432-1775 • http://www.library.yale.edu

Yale Divinity School Library • 409 Prospect St • New Haven, CT 06511 • (203) 432-6374 • http://www.library.yale.edu/div

New London
Charles E Shain Library • Connecticut College, 270 Monegan Ave • New London, CT 06320-4196 • (860) 439-2655 • http://www.conncoll.edu/is/info-resources/

Monte Cristo Cottage Museum • 325 Pequot Ave • New London, CT 06320 • (860) 443-0051 • http://www.eugeneoneill.org

Nathaniel Hempsted House Museum • 11 Hempstead • New London, CT 06320 • (860) 443-7949

New London County Historical Society • Shaw-Perkins Mansion Museum, 11 Blinman St • New London, CT 06320 • (860) 443-1209 • http://www.newlondonhistory.org

New London Maritime Society • Custom House Museum, 150 Bank St • New London, CT 06320 • (860) 447-2501 • http://www.nlmaritimesociety.org

Connecticut

New London, cont.

New London Public Library • 63 Huntington St • New London, CT 06320 • (860) 447-1411 • http://www.lioninc.org/newlondon/

US Coast Guard Academy Library • 35 Mohegan Ave • New London, CT 06320-8105 • (860) 444-8515 • http://www.uscg.mil

US Coast Guard Museum • US Coast Guard Academy, 15 Monhegan Ave • New London, CT 06320 • (860) 444-8511 • http://www.uscg.mil

New Milford

Gaylordsville Historical Society • 50 Gaylord Rd • New Milford, CT 06776 • (860) 350-0300

New Milford Historical Society • Historical Museum, 6 Aspetuck Ave, P.O. Box 566 • New Milford, CT 06776 • (860) 354-3069 • http://www.nmhistorical.org

New Milford Public Library • 24 Main St • New Milford, CT 06776 • (860) 355-1191 • http://www.biblio.org/newmilford/

Newington

Enoch Kelsey House • 1702 Main St • Newington, CT 06111 • (860) 666-7118 • http://www.newingtonhistoricalsociety.org

Lucy Robbins Welles Library • 95 Cedar St • Newington, CT 06111-2645 • (860) 665-8700 • http://www.newington.lib.ct.us

Museum of Amateur Radio • 225 Main St • Newington, CT 06111 • (860) 594-0200 • http://www.arrl.org

Newington Historical Society and Trust • Kellogg-Eddy House Museum, 679 Willard Ave • Newington, CT 06111 • (860) 666-7118 • http://www.newingtonhistoricalsociety.org

Newtown

Cyrenius H Booth Library • 25 Main St • Newtown, CT 06470 • (203) 426-4533 • http://www.biblio.org/chbooth/chbooth.htm

Fifth Connecticut Regiment Museum • 47 Hundred Acres Rd • Newtown, CT 06470 • http://www.5cr.org

Newtown Historical Society • Matthew Curtiss House, 44 Main St, P.O. Box 189 • Newtown, CT 06470 • (203) 426-5937 • http://www.newtownhistory.org

Niantic

East Lyme Historical Society • Thomas Lee House, 266 W Main St • Niantic, CT 06357 • (860) 739-6070

East Lyme Public Library • 39 Society Rd • Niantic, CT 06357 • (860) 739-6926 • http://www.lioninc.org/eastlyme

Smith-Harris House Museum • 33 Society Rd • Niantic, CT 06357 • (860) 739-0761

Noank

Noank Historical Society • Historical Museum, 14 Sylvan St, P.O. Box 9454 • Noank, CT 06340 • (860) 536-3021 • http://www.noankhistoricalsociety.org

Norfolk

Norfolk Historical Society • Historical Museum, 13 Village Green, P.O. Box 288 • Norfolk, CT 06058-1330 • (860) 542-5761 • http://www.norfolkhistoricalsociety.com

North Branford

North Branford Library Department • 1720 Foxon Rd, P.O. Box 258 • North Branford, CT 06471-0258 • (203) 315-6020 • http://www.townofnorthbranfordct.com

Totoket Historical Society • 1 Library Pl, P.O. Box 563 • North Branford, CT 06471 • (203) 488-0423

North Franklin

Franklin Historical Society • P.O. Box 73 • North Franklin, CT 06254

North Grosvenordale

Thompson Public Library • 934 Riverside Dr, P.O. Box 855 • North Grosvenordale, CT 06255 • (860) 923-9779 • http://www.thompsonpubliclibrary.org

North Haven

North Haven Historical Society • Historical Museum, 290 Quinnipiac Ave • North Haven, CT 06473 • (203) 239-7722 • http://www.northhavenhistoricalsociety.org

North Stonington

Eastern Pequot Indians of Connecticut • 391 Norwich Westerly Rd, P.O. Box 208 • North Stonington, CT 06359 • (860) 535-1868

North Stonington Historical Society • Historical Museum, 1 Wyassup Rd, P.O. Box 134 • North Stonington, CT 06359 • (860) 535-9448 • http://www.nostoningtonhistsoc.homestead.com

Paucatuck Eastern Pequot Indians of Connecticut • P.O. Box 370 • North Stonington, CT 06359 • (203) 572-9899

Wheeler Library • 101 Main St, P.O. Box 217 • North Stonington, CT 06359-0217 • (860) 535-0383 • http://www.wheelerlibrary.org

Northfield

Gilbert Library • 38 Main St • Northfield, CT 06778 • (860) 283-8176

Norwalk

Lockwood-Matthews Mansion Museum • 295 West Ave • Norwalk, CT 06850 • (203) 838-9799 • http://www.lockwoodmatthewsmansion.org

Norwalk Historical Commission • 141 East Ave • Norwalk, CT 06851 • (203) 866-0202

Norwalk Historical Society • Mill Hill Historic Museum, 2 E Wall St, P.O. Box 335 • Norwalk, CT 06852 • (203) 846-0525 • http://www.norwalkhistoricalsociety.org

Norwalk Museum Historical Reference Library • 141 N Main St • Norwalk, CT 06854-2702 • (203) 866-0202 • http://www.norwalkct.org/norwalkmuseum

Norwich

Christopher Leffingwell House Museum • 348 Washington St, P.O. Box 13 • Norwich, CT 06360 • (860) 889-9440 • http://www.leffingwellhousemuseum.org

Daughters of the American Revolution, Faith Trumbull Chapter • Historical Museum, 42 Rockwell St • Norwich, CT 06360 • (860) 887-8737

John Baldwin House Museum • 210 W Town St • Norwich, CT 06360

Mohegan & Thames Valley Learning Resource Centers • Three Rivers Community College, 574 New London Tpk • Norwich, CT 06360-6598 • (860) 383-5289 • http://www.trcc.commnet.edu/library

Mohegan Tribe and Nation • 232 Yantic St • Norwich, CT 06360 • (860) 889-8809 • http://www.mohegannation.org

Norwich Historical Society • 236 Haland Rd • Norwich, CT 06360 • (860) 886-1776 • http://www.norwichhistoricalsociety.org

Norwich Parks and Cemeteries Division • Mohegan Park • Norwich, CT 06360 • (860) 823-3798

Otis Library • 261 Main St • Norwich, CT 06360 • (860) 889-2365 • http://www.otislibrarynorwich.org

Perkins-Avery Private Collection • John Baldwin House, 210 W Town • Norwich, CT 06360 • (860) 889-5990

Rose City Genealogy Club • 160 Laurel Hill • Norwich, CT 06360 • (860) 886-4636 • http://www.rosecitygenealogy.org

Rose City Historical Society • 77 Scotland Rd • Norwich, CT 06360 • (860) 887-3081

Society of the Founders of Norwich Connecticut • Leffingwell House Museum, 348 Washington St, P.O. Box 13 • Norwich, CT 06360 • (860) 889-5990

Old Greenwich
Perrot Memorial Library • 90 Sound Beach Ave • Old Greenwich, CT 06870 • (203) 637-1066 • http://www.perrotlibrary.org

Old Lyme
Lyme Historical Society • Florence Griswold Museum, 96 Lyme St, P.O. Box 352 • Old Lyme, CT 06371-1426 • (860) 434-6259 • http://www.oldlymehistoricalsociety.org

Phoebe Griffin Noyes Library • 2 Library Lane • Old Lyme, CT 06371 • (860) 423-1684 • http://www.oldlyme.lioninc.org

Old Mystic
Indian and Colonial Research Center Library • 39 Main St, P.O. Box 525 • Old Mystic, CT 06372-0525 • (860) 536-9771 • http://www.theicrc.org

Old Saybrook
Acton Public Library • 60 Old Boston Post Rd • Old Saybrook, CT 06475-2200 • (860) 395-3184 • http://www.oldsaybrookct.com/library

Old Saybrook Historical Society • Gen William Hart House, 350 Main St, P.O. Box 4 • Old Saybrook, CT 06475 • (860) 388-2622 • http://www.oldsaybrook.com/History/society.htm

Saybrook Colony Founders Association • Historical Museum, P.O. Box 1635 • Old Saybrook, CT 06475-1000 • (860) 388-2234 • http://www.rootsweb.com/~ctscfa/

Orange
Academy Museum • 615 Orange Center Rd, P.O. Box 784 • Orange, CT 06477 • (203) 795-3106 • http://www.orangehistory.org

Case Memorial Library • 176 Tyler City Rd • Orange, CT 06477-2498 • (203) 891-2170 • http://www.leaplibraries.org/orange

Orange Historical Society • Stone-Otis House, 615 Orange Center Rd, P.O. Box 784 • Orange, CT 06447 • (203) 795-3106 • http://www.orangehistory.org

Orange Public Library • Orange Center Rd • Orange, CT 06477-2498 • (203) 891-2170

Oxford
Oxford Historical Society • 154 Bowers Hill Rd, P.O. Box 582 • Oxford, CT 06478 • (203) 888-0363 • http://www.oxford-historical-society.org

Oxford Public Library • 486 Oxford Rd • Oxford, CT 06478 • (203) 888-6944 • http://www.oxfordlib.org

Pine Meadow
New Hartford Historical Society • Historical Museum, 367 Main St • Pine Meadow, CT 06061 • (860) 379-6894 • http://www.town.new-hartford.ct.us/nhhs/

Plainville
Plainville Historical Society • Plainville History Center, 29 Pierce St • Plainville, CT 06062 • (860) 747-6577 • http://www.plainvillehistoricalsociety.org

Plainville Historical Society • Historical Center, 29 Pierce St, P.O. Box 464 • Plainville, CT 06062 • (860) 747-6577

Plantsville
Southington Genealogical Society • P.O. Box 698 • Plantsville, CT 06479-0698 • (860) 628-7831

Pleasant Valley
Barkhamsted Historical Society • Historical Museum, 100 E River Rd, P.O. Box 94 • Pleasant Valley, CT 06063 • (860) 379-1859 • http://www.barkhamstedhistory.org

Hitchcock Museum • 1 Robertsville Rd • Pleasant Valley, CT 06063 • (860) 738-4950

Stone Museum • Greenwoods Rd • Pleasant Valley, CT 06063 • (860) 379-1859

Plymouth
Plymouth Historical Society • 572 Main St, P.O. Box 176 • Plymouth, CT 06782 • (860) 585-7040

Plymouth Library Association • 692 E Main St • Plymouth, CT 06782 • (860) 283-5977

Pomfret
Pomfret Free Public Library • 449 Pomfret St • Pomfret, CT 06258-0091 • (860) 928-3475

Pomfret Center
Pomfret Historical Society • 11 Town House Rd, P.O. Box 152 • Pomfret Center, CT 06259

Portland
Portland Historical Society • 492 Main St, P.O. Box 98 • Portland, CT 06480 • (203) 342-1949 • http://www.portlandhistsoc.com

Portland Public Library • 20 Freestone Ave • Portland, CT 06480 • (860) 342-6770 • http://www.portland.lib.ct.us

Preston
Preston Historical Society • Town Hall, 389 Route 2 • Preston, CT 06360 • (860) 887-0662 • http://www.preston-ct.org/html/historical_soc.html

Preston Public Library • 389 Route 2 • Preston, CT 06365 • (860) 886-1010 • http://www.prestonlibrary.org

Prospect
Prospect Historical Society • Historical Museum, 6 Maria Hotchkiss Rd • Prospect, CT 06712 • (203) 758-4103

Putnam
Aspinock Historical Society of Putnam • Historical Museum, 208 School St, P.O. Box 465 • Putnam, CT 06260 • (860) 963-0092 • http://aspinockhs-putnam.org

Putnam Public Library • 225 Kennedy Dr • Putnam, CT 06260-1691 • (860) 963-6826

Redding
Mark Twain Library • Rte 53 & Diamond Hill Rd, P.O. Box 1009 • Redding, CT 06875-0009 • (203) 938-2545 • http://www.marktwainlibrary.org

Redding Historical Society • Daniel and Esther Bartlett House, 43 Lonetown Rd, P.O. Box 1023 • Redding, CT 06896-2004 • (203) 938-9095

Ridgefield
Keeler Tavern Museum • 132 Main St, P.O. Box 204 • Ridgefield, CT 06877 • (203) 438-5485 • http://www.keelertavernmuseum.org

Ridgefield Historical Association • Historical Collection, 472 Main St • Ridgefield, CT 06877-4585 • (203) 438-2282 • http://www.ridgefieldlibrary.org

Ridgefield Historical Society • Scott House, 4 Sunset Ln • Ridgefield, CT 06877 • (203) 438-5821 • http://www.ridgefieldct.org/history/history.htm

Rockville
New England Civil War Museum • 14 Park Pl, P.O. Box 153 • Rockville, CT 06066 • (860) 870-3563

Rocky Hill
Rocky Hill Historical Society • Academy Hall Museum, 785 Old Main St, P.O. Box 185 • Rocky Hill, CT 06067-0186 • (860) 379-6704 • http://www.rockyhillhistory.org

Rowayton
Rowayton Historical Society • Historical Museum, 177 Rowayton Ave, P.O. Box 106 • Rowayton, CT 06853 • (203) 838-8916 • http://www.rowaytonhistoricalsociety.org

Connecticut

Roxbury

Minor Memorial Library • 23 South St, P.O. Box 249 • Roxbury, CT 06783-0249 • (860) 350-2181 • http://www.biblio.org/roxbury

Order of Colonial Lords of Manors in America • P.O. Box 269 • Roxbury, CT 06783

Roxbury Historical Society • South St, P.O. Box 212 • Roxbury, CT 06783

Salem

Salem Historical Society • Historical Museum, 299 Old Colchester Rd • Salem, CT 06420 • (860) 537-8556 • http://www.salemct.gov/history.htm

Salisbury

Croatian Roots • P.O. Box 462 • Salisbury, CT 06068 • http://www.croatianroots.com

Salisbury Association • c/o Scoville Memorial Library, 38 Main St, P.O. Box 516 • Salisbury, CT 06068-0516 • (860) 435-2838 • http://www.biblio.org/scoville/

Scoville Memorial Library • 38 Main St, P.O. Box 567 • Salisbury, CT 06068-0567 • (860) 435-2838 • http://www.scovillelibrary.org

Scotland

Samuel Huntington Homestead Museum • 36 Huntington Rd, P.O. Box 231 • Scotland, CT 06264 • (860) 456-8381 • http://www.huntingtonhomestead.org

Scotland Historical Society • Waldo Rd, P.O. Box 1144 • Scotland, CT 06264 • (860) 456-0077

Seymour

Seymour Historical Society • Historical Museum, 69 Church St, P.O. Box 433 • Seymour, CT 06483 • (203) 888-7471

Seymour Public Library • 46 Church St • Seymour, CT 06483 • (203) 888-3903 • http://www.seymourpubliclibrary.org

Sharon

Hotchkiss Library of Sharon • 10 Upper Main St • Sharon, CT 06069 • (860) 364-5041

Sharon Historical Society • Gay-Hoyt House Museum, 18 Main St • Sharon, CT 06069-2052 • (860) 364-5688 • http://www.sharonhist.org

Shelton

Huntington Historical Society • 70 Ripton Rd, P.O. Box 2155 • Shelton, CT 06484 • (203) 925-1803

Plumb Memorial Library • 65 Wooster St • Shelton, CT 06468 • (203) 924-1580 • http://www.plumblibrary.org

Seeley Genealogical Society • 45 Windsor Rd • Shelton, CT 06484-5021 • (760) 329-0422 • http://www.seeley-society.net

Shelton Historical Society • Historical Museum, 70 Ripton Rd, P.O. Box 2155 • Shelton, CT 06484-2668 • (203) 925-1803 • http://www.sheltonhistoricalsociety.org

Tree Farm Historical Letters Archives • 272 Israel Hill Rd • Shelton, CT 06484 • (203) 929-0126

Sherman

Sherman Historical Society • Historical Museum, 10 Route 37 Center • Sherman, CT 06784 • (860) 354-3083 • http://www.shermanhistoricalsociety.org

Simsbury

Simsbury Genealogical and Historical Research Library • 749 Hopmeadow St • Simsbury, CT 06070 • (860) 658-5382

Simsbury Historical Society • Phelps Tavern Museum, 800 Hopmeadow St, P.O. Box 2 • Simsbury, CT 06070-0002 • (203) 658-2500 • http://www.simsburyhistory.org

Simsbury Public Library • 725 Hopmeadow St • Simsbury, CT 06070 • (860) 658-7663 • http://www.simsbury.lib.ct.us

Somers

Somers Historical Society • 11 Battle St, P.O. Box 652 • Somers, CT 06071 • (860) 749-3219 • http://www.somershistoricalsociety.org

Somers Mountain Indian Museum • 332 Turnpike Rd • Somers, CT 06071 • http://www.somersmountain.org

Somers Public Library • 51 9th District Rd • Somers, CT 06071-0368 • (860) 763-3501 • http://www.qwd.com/spl

South Glastonbury

Historical Society of Glastonbury • Welles Shipman Ward House Museum, 972 Main St • South Glastonbury, CT 06073-2103 • (860) 633-4572

South Meriden

Meriden Historical Society • Historical Museum, 1090 Hanover Ave, P.O. Box 3005 • South Meriden, CT 06451 • (203) 237-5079 • http://www.rootsweb.com/~ctmhs/MeridenHS.htm

South Norwalk

Norwalk Museum • 41 N Main St • South Norwalk, CT 96854 • (203) 866-0202

South Windsor

Jewish Genealogical Society of Connecticut • 22 Marilyn Rd • South Windsor, CT 06074 • http://www.jgsct-jewish-genealogy.org

South Windsor Historical Society • Historical Museum, 771 Ellington Rd, P.O. Box 216 • South Windsor, CT 06074 • http://www.southwindsorhistory.tk

South Windsor Public Library • 1550 Sullivan Ave • South Windsor, CT 06074 • (860) 644-1541 • http://www.ctconnect.com/swlibrary

Wood Memorial Library • 783 Main St, P.O. Box 131 • South Windsor, CT 06074 • (860) 289-1783 • http://pages.cthome.net/wood.memorial.lib

Southbury

Southbury Historical Society • Historical Museum, P.O. Box 124 • Southbury, CT 06488 • (203) 264-2993 • http://www.southburyhistorical.org

Southington

Barnes Museum • 85 N Main St • Southington, CT 06489 • (860) 628-5426 • http://www.southingtonlibrary.org

Southington Genealogical Society • Historical Center, 239 Main St • Southington, CT 06489 • (860) 628-7831

Southington Historical Society • Historical Center, 239 Main St • Southington, CT 06489 • (860) 621-4811 • http://southington.com/History

Southington Public Library • 255 Main St • Southington, CT 06489 • (860) 628-0947 • http://www.southingtonlibrary.org

Southington Public Library and Museum • 255 Main St • Southington, CT 06489-2509 • (860) 628-0947 • http://www.library.southington.org

Southport

Pequot Library • 720 Pequot Ave • Southport, CT 06490 • (203) 259-0346 • http://www.pequotlibrary.com

Stafford Springs

NE Civilian Conservation Corps Museum • 166 Chestnut Hill Rd • Stafford Springs, CT 06076

Stafford Historical Society • 5 Spring St, P.O. Box 56 • Stafford Springs, CT 06075 • (860) 684-7978

Stamford

Connecticut Ancestry Society • c/o Ferguson Library, 1 Public Library Plaza, P.O. Box 249 • Stamford, CT 06904-0249 • (203) 328-5173 • http://www.connecticutancestry.org

Ferguson Library • 1 Public Library Plaza • Stamford, CT 06904 • (203) 964-1000 • http://www.fergusonlibrary.org

Hoyt-Barnum House Museum • 733 Bedford St • Stamford, CT 06902 • (203) 329-1183 • http://www.stamfordhistory.org

Jewish Historical Society of Greater Stamford • 111 Prospect St • Stamford, CT 06905 • (203) 359-2196

Jewish Historical Society of Lower Fairfield County • P.O. Box 16918 • Stamford, CT 06905-8901 • (203) 359-2196

Saint Basil College Library • 39 Clovelly Rd • Stamford, CT 06902-3004 • (203) 964-8003

Stamford Historical Society • Historical Museum, 1508 High Ridge Road • Stamford, CT 06903-4107 • (203) 329-1183 • http://www.stamfordhistory.org

Stamford Museum • 39 Scofieldtown Rd • Stamford, CT 06903 • (203) 322-1646 • http://www.stamfordmuseum.org

Stonington
Old Lighthouse Museum • 7 Water St • Stonington, CT 06378 • (860) 535-1440 • http://www.stoningtonhistory.net

Stonington Free Library Association • 20 High St, P.O. Box 232 • Stonington, CT 06378-0232 • (860) 535-0658 • http://www.stoningtonfreelibrary.org

Stonington Historical Society • Captain Nathaniel B Palmer House Museum, 40 Palmer St, P.O. Box 103 • Stonington, CT 06378-0103 • (860) 535-1131 • http://www.stoningtonhistory.org

Storrs
Ballard Institute • Museum of Puppetry, 6 Bourn Pl, U212 • Storrs, CT 06269-5212 • (860) 486-4605 • http://www.bimp.uconn.edu

Mansfield Historical Society • Historical Museum, 954 Storrs Rd, P.O. Box 145 • Storrs, CT 06268 • (860) 429-6575 • http://www.mansfield.history.org

Thomas J Dodd Research Center • Univ of Connecticut, Archives and Special Collections, 405 Babbidge Rd • Storrs, CT 06269-1205 • (860) 486-4500 • http://www.lib.uconn.edu/DoddCenter/

University of Connecticut Library • 369 Fairfield Rd • Storrs, CT 06269-1005 • (860) 486-2219 • http://www.lib.uconn.edu

Stratford
Boothe Memorial Park Museum • 134 Main St, P.O. Box 902 • Stratford, CT 06497 • (203) 385-4080 • http://www.boothememorialpark.org

Stratford Historical Society • Catherine B Mitchell Museum, 967 Academy Hill, P.O. Box 382 • Stratford, CT 06615-0382 • (203) 378-0630 • http://www.stratfordhistoricalsociety.com

Stratford Library Association • 2203 Main St • Stratford, CT 06497 • (203) 385-4164 • http://www.stratford.lib.ct.us

Suffield
Hatheway House Museum • 55 S Main St • Suffield, CT 06078 • (860) 668-0055

Kent Memorial Library • 50 N Main St • Suffield, CT 06078-2117 • (860) 668-3896 • http://www.suffield-library.org

Suffield Historical Society • King House Museum, 232 S Main St, P.O. Box 893 • Suffield, CT 06093 • (860) 668-5256 • http://www.suffieldhistoricalsociety.org

Terryville
Lock Museum of America • 230 Main St • Terryville, CT 06786 • (860) 589-6359 • http://www.lockmuseum.com

Terryville Public Library • 238 Main St • Terryville, CT 06786 • (860) 582-3121 • http://www.terryvillepl.lib.ct.us

Thomaston
Railroad Museum of New England • P.O. Box 400 • Thomaston, CT 06787-0400 • (860) 283-7245 • http://www.rmne.org

Thomaston Historical Society • Town Hall, 158 Main St • Thomaston, CT 06787 • (860) 283-2159

Thomaston Public Library • 248 Main St • Thomaston, CT 06787 • (860) 283-4339 • http://www.biblio.org/thomaston

Thompson
Thompson Historical Society • 339 Thompson Rd, P.O. Box 47 • Thompson, CT 06277 • (860) 923-3200 • http://www.thompsonhistorical.org

Tolland
Daniel Benton Homestead Museum • Metcalf Rd, P.O. Box 107 • Tolland, CT 06804 • (860) 974-1875

French-Canadian Genealogical Society of Connecticut • 53 Tolland Green, P.O. Box 928 • Tolland, CT 06084-0928 • (860) 872-2597 • http://www.fcgsc.org

Hicks-Stearns Museum • 42 Tolland Green, P.O. Box 278 • Tolland, CT 06084 • (860) 875-7552

Tolland Genealogical Society • 52 Tolland Green • Tolland, CT 06084

Tolland Historical Society • Jail Museum, 52 Tolland Green, P.O. Box 107 • Tolland, CT 06084 • (860) 870-9599 • http://pages.cthome.net/tollandhistorical

Torrington
Municipal Historian of Torrington • City hall, 140 Main St, Rm 209 • Torrington, CT 06790

Torrington Historical Society • Hotchkiss-Fyler House Museum, 192 Main St • Torrington, CT 06790 • (860) 482-8260 • http://www.torringtonhistoricalsociety.org

Trumbull
Golden Hill Paugussett Indian Reservation • 95 Stanavage Rd • Trumbull, CT 06415 • (203) 377-4410 • http://pagussettitgo.com

Trumbull Historical Society • Town Hall, 1856 Huntington Tpke, P.O. Box 312 • Trumbull, CT 06611 • (203) 377-6620 • http://www.trumbullhistory.org

Uncasville
Mohegan Tribe • 5 Crow Hill Rd • Uncasville, CT 06382 • (860) 862-6100 • http://www.mohegan.nsn.us

Tantaquidgeon Indian Museum • 1819 Norwich New London Rd • Uncasville, CT 06382 • (860) 862-6144

Union
Union Historical Society • 1099 Buckley Hwy • Union, CT 06076 • (860) 684-7078

Vernon
Rockville Public Library • 52 Union St, P.O. Box 1320 • Vernon, CT 06066 • (860) 875-5892 • http://www.state.ct.us

Society of Mayflower Descendants in Connecticut • 39 Butternut Ln • Vernon, CT 06066 • http://www.ctmayflower.org

Vernon Historical Society • Historical Museum, 734 Hartford Tpk, P.O. Box 2055 • Vernon, CT 06066 • (860) 875-4326 • http://vhsvernonct.tripod.com

Vernon Rockville
Vernon Historical Society • Historical Museum, 734 Hartford Tpk • Vernon Rockville, CT 06066-5113 • (860) 875-4326

Voluntown
Voluntown Historical Society • Historical Museum, 448-H Tanglewood Ln, P.O. Box 130 • Voluntown, CT 06834 • (203) 376-9563

Voluntown Public Library • 107 Main St, P.O. Box 26 • Voluntown, CT 06384-0026 • (860) 376-0485

Connecticut

Wallingford
Masonic Grand Lodge of Connecticut • 69 Masonic Ave, P.O. Box 250 • Wallingford, CT 06492 • (203) 679-5903 • http://www.ctfreemasons.net/

Wallingford Historical Society • Samuel Parsons House Museum, 180 S Main St, P.O. Box 73 • Wallingford, CT 06492-0073 • (203) 294-1996

Wallingford Public Library • 200 N Main St • Wallingford, CT 06492-3791 • (203) 265-6754 • http://www.wallingford.lioninc.org

Warren
Warren Historical Society • 151 Melius Rd • Warren, CT 06754 • (860) 868-6724 • http://www.warrenct.com/historical-society

Washington
Gunn Memorial Library & Museum • 5 Wykeham Rd, P.O. Box 1273 • Washington, CT 06793-0273 • (860) 868-7586 • http://www.biblio.org/gunn/

Institute for American Indian Studies • 38 Curtis Rd, P.O. Box 1260 • Washington, CT 06783 • (860) 868-0518

Washington Green
Institute for American Indian Studies • 38 Cortis Rd • Washington Green, CT 06793 • (860) 868-0518 • http://www.birdstone.org

Waterbury
Jewish Historical Society of Waterbury • P.O. Box F • Waterbury, CT 06798

Mattatuck Historical Society • Historical Museum, 144 W Main St • Waterbury, CT 06702 • (203) 753-0381 • http://www.mattatuckmuseum.org

Silas Bronson Library • 267 Grand St • Waterbury, CT 06702 • (203) 574-8222 • http://www.biblio.org/bronson/silas.htm

Timexpo Museum • 175 Union St, Brass Mill Commons • Waterbury, CT 06706 • (203) 755-8463 • http://www.timexpo.com

Waterbury Republican & American Library • 389 Meadow St • Waterbury, CT 06702 • (203) 574-3636

Waterford
Harkness Memorial State Park Museum • 275 Great Neck Rd • Waterford, CT 06385 • (860) 443-5725

Southern Pequot Tribe • 97 Fog Plain Rd • Waterford, CT 06385

Waterford Historical Society • Jordan Green, Beebe-Phillips House Museum, 65 Rope Ferry Rd, P.O. Box 117 • Waterford, CT 06385-0117 • (860) 442-2707

Waterford Public Library • 49 Rope Ferry Rd • Waterford, CT 06385 • (860) 444-5805 • http://www.waterfordpubliclibrary.org

Watertown
Watertown Historical Society • Historical Museum, 22 De Forest St • Watertown, CT 06795 • (860) 274-1050 • http://www.watertownhistoricalsociety.org

West Hartford
Italian American Historical Society • Historical Museum, 3100 Albany Ave • West Hartford, CT 06117

Jewish Historical Society of Greater Hartford • 335 Bloomfield Ave • West Hartford, CT 06117-1542 • (860) 236-4571 • http://www.jhsgh.org

Museum of American Political Life • Univ of Hartford, 200 Bloomfield Ave • West Hartford, CT 06117 • (860) 768-4268 • http://www.hartford.edu/ao/

Noah Webster Foundation and Historical Society of West Hartford • Noah Webster House, 227 S Main St • West Hartford, CT 06107 • (860) 521-5362 • http://www.noahwebsterhouse.org

Sarah Whitman Hooker Homestead Museum • 1237 New Britain Ave • West Hartford, CT 06107 • (860) 523-5887

Society of the Descendants of the Founders of Hartford • P.O. Box 270215 • West Hartford, CT 06107 • http://www.societyct.org/hartford.htm

West Hartford Historical Society • 227 S Main St • West Hartford, CT 06107-3453 • (860) 521-5362 • http://www.ctstateu.edu/noahweb/

West Hartford Public Library • 20 S Main St • West Hartford, CT 06107-2432 • (860) 523-3277 • http://www.west-hartford.com/library/

West Haven
German Order of Harugari • 66 Highland St • West Haven, CT 06516 • (203) 933-9930 • http://www.harugari.org/who_we_are.htm

West Haven Historical Society • Historical Museum, 682 Main St • West Haven, CT 06516 • (203) 934-5852

West Haven Public Library • 300 Elm St • West Haven, CT 06516-4692 • (203) 937-4233 • http://www.westhavenpl.org

West Willington
Willington Historical Society • 48 Red Oak Hill • West Willington, CT 06279 • (860) 429-2656

Westbrook
Military Historians Headquarters Museum • N Main St • Westbrook, CT 06498 • (860) 399-9460

Westbrook Historical Society • Historical Museum, 1196 Boston Post Rd • Westbrook, CT 06498 • (860) 399-7473

Weston
Museum of Art & History • Weston Town Hall, N Field Rd • Weston, CT 06883 • (203) 227-3375 • http://www.weston-ct.com

Weston Historical Society • Coley Homstead Museum, 104 Weston Rd, P.O. Box 1092 • Weston, CT 06883 • (203) 226-1804 • http://www.westonhistoricalsociety.org

Westport
Westport Historical Society • Wheeler House, 25 Avery Pl • Westport, CT 06880-3215 • (203) 222-1424 • http://www.westporthistory.org

Westport Library Association • Arnold Bernhard Plaza, 20 Jesup Rd, P.O. Box 5020 • Westport, CT 06880 • (203) 227-8411 • http://www.westportlibrary.org

Wethersfield
Buttolph-Williams House Museum • 249 Broad St • Wethersfield, CT 06109 • (860) 247-8996

Hurlbut-Denham House Museum • 212 Main St • Wethersfield, CT 06109 • (860) 529-7656

Webb-Deane-Stevens Museum • 211 Main St • Wethersfield, CT 06109 • (203) 529-0612 • http://www.webb-deane-stevens.org

Wethersfield Historical Society • Historical Museum, 150 Main St • Wethersfield, CT 06109 • (860) 529-7656 • http://www.wethhist.org

Willimantic
Connecticut Eastern Railroad Museum • 55 Bridge St, P.O. Box 665 • Willimantic, CT 06226-0665 • (860) 456-9999 • http://www.cteastrrmuseum.org

J Eugene Smith Library • Eastern Connecticut State Univ, 83 Windham St • Willimantic, CT 06226 • (860) 465-4699 • http://library.easternct.edu

Windham Historical Society • Jillson House Museum, 627 Main St • Willimantic, CT 06226 • (860) 456-2316 • http://www.windhamhistory.org

Windham Textile and History Museum • 157 Union & Main St • Willimantic, CT 06226 • (203) 456-2178 • http://www.millmuseum.org

Willington

Mary D Edwards Public Library • 111 River Rd Route 32 • Willington, CT 06279 • (860) 429-3854 • http://www.willingtonct.org

Willington Historical Society • 48 Red Oak Hill • Willington, CT 06279 • (860) 429-2656 • http://www.willingtonct.org/whs.html

Wilton

Weir Farm National Historic Site Museum • 735 Nod Hill Rd • Wilton, CT 06897 • (203) 834-1896 • http://www.nps.gov/wefa/

Wilton Historical Society • Wilton Heritage Museum, 249 Danbury Rd • Wilton, CT 06897 • (203) 762-7257 • http://www.wiltonlhistorical.org

Wilton Library Association • 137 Old Ridgefield Rd • Wilton, CT 06897-3019 • (203) 762-3950 • http://www.wiltonlibrary.org

Windham

Windham Free Library Association • On the Green, P.O. Box 168 • Windham, CT 06280 • (860) 423-0636

Windsor

Descendants of the Founders of Ancient Windsor • 33 Hillcrest Rd, P.O. Box 39 • Windsor, CT 06095-0039 • (860) 688-6822 • http://www.societyct.org/windsor.htm

Dr Hezekiah Chaffee House Museum • 108 Palisado Ave • Windsor, CT 06095 • (860) 688-3813

Oliver Ellsworth Homestead Museum • 778 Palisado Ave, P.O. Box 791 • Windsor, CT 06095 • (860) 688-8717 • http://www.ctdar.org/homestead.htm

Windsor Historical Society • Historical Museum, 96 Palisado Ave • Windsor, CT 06095-2526 • (860) 688-3813 • http://www.windsorhistoricalsociety.org

Windsor Locks

Connecticut Aeronautical Historical Association • New England Air Museum, 36 Perimeter Rd • Windsor Locks, CT 06096 • (860) 623-3305 • http://www.neam.org

New England Air Museum • Bradley Intl Airport, 36 Perimeter Rd • Windsor Locks, CT 06096 • (860) 623-3305 • http://www.neam.org

Windsor Locks Historical Society • Noden-Reed Farm Museum, 58 West St, P.O. Box 733 • Windsor Locks, CT 06096 • (860) 627-9212 • http://www.cnctb.org

Winsted

Beardsley & Memorial Library • 40 Munro Pl • Winsted, CT 06098 • (860) 379-6043 • http://www.beardsleyandmemorial.org

Winchester Historical Society • Solomon Rockwell House Museum, 225 Prospect St, P.O. Box 206 • Winsted, CT 06090-0206 • (860) 379-8433

Wolcott

Wolcott Historical Society • Old Stone Schoolhouse, Nichols Rd, P.O. Box 6410 • Wolcott, CT 06716 • (203) 879-3013 • http://www.wolcotthistory.org

Woodbridge

Amity and Woodbridge Historical Society • Thomas Darling House, 1907 Litchfield Tpk • Woodbridge, CT 06525 • (203) 387-2823 • http://www.woodbridgehistory.org

Woodbury

Glebe House Museum • 49 Hollow Rd, P.O. Box 245 • Woodbury, CT 06798 • (203) 263-2855 • http://www.theglebehouse.org

Old Woodbury Historical Society • c/o Woodbury Public Library, 269 Main St S, P.O. Box 705 • Woodbury, CT 06798 • (203) 263-2695 • http://www.see-ct.com/?place=OldWoodburyHistoricalSociety

Woodbury Public Library • 269 Main St S • Woodbury, CT 06798-3408 • (203) 263-3502 • http://www.biblio.org/woodbury

Woodmont

Borough of Woodmont Archives • 59 Village Rd • Woodmont, CT 06460 • http://www.woodmontday.org

Woodstock

Photomobile Model Museum • 1728 Route 198 • Woodstock, CT 06281

Roseland Cottage Museum • 556 Route 169 • Woodstock, CT 06281 • (860) 928-4074 • http://www.historicnewengland.org

Rowen House Museum • 556 Route 169 • Woodstock, CT 06281 • (860) 928-4974

West Woodstock Library • 5 Bungay Hill Connector • Woodstock, CT 06281 • (860) 974-0376

Woodstock Historical Society • Bowen House Museum, 523 Route 169, P.O. Box 65 • Woodstock, CT 06281 • (860) 928-1035 • http://www.woodstockhistoricalsociety.org

Connecticut

DELAWARE

Bear
Bear Library • 101 Governors Pl • Bear, DE 19701 • (302) 838-3300 • http://www.lib.de.us

Bethel
Bethel Historical Society • Heritage Museum, N Main St, P.O. Box 55 • Bethel, DE 19931 • (302) 875-5425

Bridgeville
Bridgeville Historical Society • Bridgeville Fireshouse Museum, 102 S Williams St, P.O. Box 306 • Bridgeville, DE 19933 • (302) 337-7600

Bridgeville Public Library • 210 Market St • Bridgeville, DE 19933-1126 • (302) 337-7401

Centerville
Episcopal Church Diocese of Delaware Archives • 400 Burnt Mill Rd • Centerville, DE 19807 • (302) 254-2222 • http://www.dioceseofdelaware.net

Christiana
Christiana Historical Society • Historical Museum, 49 N Old Baltimore Pk • Christiana, DE 19702 • (302) 286-6223

Claymont
Brandywine Historical Society • 18 3rd Ave • Claymont, DE 19703 • (302) 792-2724

National Society of First Families of Delmarva • P.O. Box 304 • Claymont, DE 19703-0304 • (302) 798-7375 • http://www.delgensoc.org/ff-DMV.html

Robinson House Museum • Naamans Rd & Philadelphia Pk • Claymont, DE 19703 • (302) 792-0285

Delaware City
Fort Delaware Society • Historical Museum, 122 Washington St, P.O. Box 553 • Delaware City, DE 19706 • (302) 834-1630 • http://www.del.net/org/fort/

Fort Penn Museum • 45 Clinton St, P.O. Box 170 • Delaware City, DE 19706 • (302) 834-7941

Dover
Delaware Agricultural Museum & Village • 866 N Du Pont Hwy • Dover, DE 19901 • (302) 734-1618 • http://www.agriculturalmuseum.org

Delaware Public Archives • Hall of Records, 121 Duke of York Ave, P.O. Box 1401 • Dover, DE 19903 • (302) 739-5318 • http://www.archives.state.de.us

Delaware State Library • Dept of State, 43 S Dupont Hwy • Dover, DE 19901-7430 • (302) 739-4748 • http://www.state.lib.de.us

Delaware State Museum • Rose Cottage, 102 S State St • Dover, DE 19901 • (302) 739-5316 • http://www.destatemuseums.org

Delaware State Police Museum • 1425 N DuPont Hwy, P.O. Box 430 • Dover, DE 19903 • (302) 739-7700 • http://www.delawaretrooper.com/museum

Dover Public Library • 45 S State St • Dover, DE 19901-3526 • (302) 736-7094 • http://www.doverpubliclibrary.org

Downstate Delaware Genealogical Society • c/o Dover Public Library, 45 S State St, P.O. Box 1787 • Dover, DE 19901 • (302) 736-7030

First State Heritage Park • 121 Duke of York St • Dover, DE 19901 • (302) 739-9194 • http://www.destateparks.com/park/first-state-heritage/index.asp

John Dickinson Plantation Museum • 340 Kitts Hummock Rd • Dover, DE 19901 • (302) 739-3277 • http://www.dovermuseums.org/museums/dickinson.htm

Johnson Victrola Museum • Bank & New Sts • Dover, DE 19901 • (302) 739-5316 • http://www.dovermuseums.org/museums/victrola.htm

Meetinghouse Galleries Museum • 316 S Governors Ave • Dover, DE 19904-6706 • (302) 739-3260

Museum of Small Town Life • 316 S Governors Ave • Dover, DE 19901 • (302) 739-3261 • http://www.dovermuseums.org/museums/smalltown.htm

Office of Vital Statistics Division of Public Health • Federal & Wm Penn Sts, P.O. Box 637 • Dover, DE 19903-0637 • (302) 739-4721 • http://www.dhss.delaware.gov/dph/ss/vitalstats.html

PR Works Museum • 21 S Springview Dr • Dover, DE 19901 • (302) 698-9902

Robert H Parker Library • Wesley College, 120 N State St • Dover, DE 19901 • (302) 736-2413 • http://www.wesley.edu

State House Museum • On the Green, 406 Federal St • Dover, DE 19901 • (302) 739-4266 • http://www.dovermuseums.org/museums/statehouse.htm

William C Jason Library-Learning Center • Delaware State University, 1200 N Dupont Hwy • Dover, DE 19901-2277 • (302) 857-6176 • http://www.dsc.edu

Woodburn-the Governor's House Museum • 151 Kings Hwy, P.O. Box 1401 • Dover, DE 19903 • (302) 739-5656 • http://www.state.de.us

Dover AFB
Air Mobility Command Museum • 1301 Heritage Rd • Dover AFB, DE 19902-5301 • (302) 677-5938 • http://www.amcmuseum.org

Frankford
Frankford Public Library • 8 Main St, P.O. Box 610 • Frankford, DE 19945-0610 • (302) 732-9351 • http://www.hollipac.lib.de.us

Frederica
Barratt's Chapel and Museum • US Rte 113 • Frederica, DE 19946 • (302) 335-8844 • http://www.barrattschapel.org

Methodist Commission on Archives and History • Barratt's Chapel Museum, 6362 Bay Rd • Frederica, DE 19946 • (302) 335-5544 • http://users.aol.com/Barratts/home.html

Georgetown
Georgetown Historical Society • 510 S Bedford St • Georgetown, DE 19947 • (302) 855-9660 • http://www.marvelmuseum.org/2index2.html

Georgetown Public Library • 10 W Pine St • Georgetown, DE 19947 • (302) 856-7958 • http://www.lib.de.us

Nutter D Marvel Museum • 39 The Circle • Georgetown, DE 19947 • (302) 856-7391

Office of Vital Statistics, Division of Public Health • 546 S Bedford St • Georgetown, DE 19947 • (302) 856-5495 • http://www.dhss.delaware.gov

Redmen Nanticoke Tribe • Route 113 • Georgetown, DE 19947 • (302) 856-2405

Sussex County Department of Libraries • 9 S DuPont Hwy, P.O. Box 589 • Georgetown, DE 19947-0589 • (302) 855-7890

Treasures of the Sea Museum • 18 Seashore Hwy, P.O. Box 610 • Georgetown, DE 19947-0610 • (302) 856-5700 • http://www.treasuresofthesea.org

Grass Dale
Fort Delaware Society Archives • 108 Old Reedy Point Bridge Rd • Grass Dale, DE 19706 • (302) 834-1630

Greenville
Eleutherian Hills-Hagley Foundation • P.O. Box 3630 • Greenville, DE 19807 • (302) 658-2400

Harrington
Greater Harrington Historical Society • Historical Museum, 108 Fleming St, P.O. Box 64 • Harrington, DE 19952 • (302) 398-3698

Hockessin
Hockessin Public Library • 1023 Valley Rd • Hockessin, DE 19720-1648 • (302) 239-5160

Delaware

Laurel

Laurel Historical Society • 502 E 4th St, P.O. Box 102 • Laurel, DE 19956 • (302) 875-1344

Laurel Public Library • 101 E 4th St • Laurel, DE 19956-1547 • (302) 875-3184 • http://www.laurel.lib.de.us

Old Christ Church (Episcopal) League • P.O. Box 293 • Laurel, DE 19956 • (302) 875-3644

Old Christ Church Museum • Chipman's Pond, Route 24, P.O. Box 293 • Laurel, DE 19956 • (302) 875-3644

Lewes

Fisher Martin House Museum • 120 Kings Highway, P.O. Box 1 • Lewes, DE 19958 • (302) 645-8073 • http://www.leweschamber.com

Lewes Historical Society • Historical Museum, 110 Shipcarpenter St • Lewes, DE 19958 • (302) 645-7640 • http://www.historiclewes.org

Lewes Public Library • 111 Adams Ave • Lewes, DE 19958 • (302) 645-2733 • http://www.leweslibrary.org

Zwaanendael Museum • Savannah Rd & Kings Hwy • Lewes, DE 19958 • (302) 645-1148 • http://www.beach-net.com/Thingszwaanendael.html

Middletown

Middletown Historical Society • general delivery • Middletown, DE 19709 • (302) 378-7466

Milford

Milford Historical Society • Parson Thorne Mansion Museum, 501 NW Front St, P.O. Box 352 • Milford, DE 19963 • (302) 422-3702 • http://www.downtownmilford.org/mhs.html

Milford Museum • 121 S Walnut St • Milford, DE 19963 • (302) 424-1080

Milford Public Library • 11 SE Front St • Milford, DE 19963 • (302) 422-8996 • http://www.cityofmilford.com/library.cfm

Millsboro

Millsboro Public Library • 217 W State St, P.O. Box 458 • Millsboro, DE 19966-0458 • (302) 934-8743

Nanticoke Indian Association • Historical Museum, 27073 John J Williams Hw • Millsboro, DE 19966 • (302) 945-7022 • http://www.nanticokeindians.org

Milton

Friends of Coolspring Presbyterian Church • 201 Federal St • Milton, DE 19968 • (302) 684-4713

Lydia B Cannon Museum • 404 Chestnut St • Milton, DE 19968

Milton Historical Society • Historical Museum, 210-212 Union St • Milton, DE 19968 • (302) 684-8851 • http://www.historicmilton.org

New Castle

Immanuel Episcopal Church on the Green Archives • P.O. Box 47 • New Castle, DE 19720 • (302) 328-2413

New Castle Historical Society • Amstel House Museum, 2 E 4th St • New Castle, DE 19720 • (302) 322-2794 • http://www.newcastlehistory.org

New Castle Presbyterian Church Museum • 25 E 2nd St • New Castle, DE 19720

New Castle Public Library • 424 Delaware St • New Castle, DE 19720-5099 • (302) 328-1995 • http://www.newcastlepublic.lib.de.us

News-Journal Company Archives • 950 West Basin Rd • New Castle, DE 19720 • (302) 324-2500

Read House and Gardens Museum • 42 The Strand • New Castle, DE 19720 • (302) 322-8411 • http://www.hsd.org

Newark

Hale-Burnes House Museum • 606 Stanton-Christina Rd • Newark, DE 19713 • (302) 998-3792

Iron Hill Museum • 1355 Old Baltimore Pk • Newark, DE 19702 • (302) 368-5703 • http://www.ironhillmuseum.org

Morris Library • Univ of Delaware, 181 S College Ave • Newark, DE 19717-5267 • (302) 831-2231 • http://www.lib.udel.edu

Newark Historical Society • 951 Barksdale Rd, P.O. Box 711 • Newark, DE 19715 • (302) 731-0955

Odessa

Corbit-Calloway Memorial Library • 115 High St, P.O. Box 128 • Odessa, DE 19730 • (302) 378-8838 • http://www.corbitlibrary.org

Historic Houses of Odessa • 109 Main St, P.O. Box 507 • Odessa, DE 19730 • (302) 378-4020

Port Penn

Port Penn Area Historical Society • Historical Museum, P.O. Box 120 • Port Penn, DE 19731 • (302) 834-2464

Rehoboth Beach

Rehoboth Beach Historical Society • Anna Hazzard Museum, 17 Christian St, P.O. Box 42 • Rehoboth Beach, DE 19971 • (302) 227-6111 • http://www.cityofrehoboth.com/history.htm

Rehoboth Beach Public Library • 226 Rehoboth Ave • Rehoboth Beach, DE 19971-2141 • (302) 227-8044

Seaford

Seaford District Library • 402 N Porter St • Seaford, DE 19973 • (302) 629-2524 • http://www.seaford.lib.de.us

Seaford Historical Society • Governor Ross Plantation, 214 N Cornwell St • Seaford, DE 19973 • (302) 628-9500 • http://www.seafordhistoricalsociety.com

Seaford Museum • 203 High St • Seaford, DE 19973 • (302) 628-9828 • http://www.seafordhistoricalsociety.com

Selbyville

Friends of the Fenwick Island Lighthouse • 89 W Church St • Selbyville, DE 19940 • (302) 436-8410

Smyrna

Allee House Museum • Dutch Neck Rd • Smyrna, DE 19977 • (302) 736-4266

Duck Creek Historical Society • 227 E Mount Vernon St, P.O. Box 335 • Smyrna, DE 19977 • (302) 653-8844

Smyrna Heritage Association • Historical Museum, 11 S Main St • Smyrna, DE 19977-1430 • (302) 653-1320

Smyrna Museum and Colonial Plank House • 11 S Main St, P.O. Box 335 • Smyrna, DE 19977 • (302) 653-1320 • http://www.smyrnadelaware.com

Smyrna Public Library • 107 S Main St • Smyrna, DE 19977 • (302) 653-4579 • http://smyrnapubliclibrary.mybravenet.com

Wilmington

Afro-American Historical and Genealogical Society of Delaware • Historical Museum, 512 E 4th St • Wilmington, DE 19801 • (302) 571-1699 • http://www.discoverourtown.com

Brandywine Hundred Branch Library • 1300 Foulk Rd • Wilmington, DE 19803 • (302) 477-3150 • http://www.lib.de.us

Brandywine Valley Historical Collection • Weidener Univ School of Law, 4601 Concord Pk, P.O. Box 7475 • Wilmington, DE 19803 • (302) 477-2063 • http://www.widener.edu

Delaware Academy of Medicine Historical Archives • Lewis B Flinn Library, 1925 Lovering Ave • Wilmington, DE 19806 • (302) 656-6398

Delaware Genealogical Society • 505 Market Street Mall • Wilmington, DE 19801 • (302) 475-3616 • http://www.delgensoc.org

Delaware Swedish Colonial Society • Hendrickson House Museum, 606 Church St • Wilmington, DE 19801 • (302) 652-5629 • http://www.oldswedes.org/hendrick.htm

Greenbank Mills and Philips Farm Museum • 500 Greenbank Rd • Wilmington, DE 19808 • (302) 999-9001 • http://www.greenbankmill.com

Hagley Museum and Library • Eleutherian Mills Residence, 298 Buck Rd E, P.O. Box 3630 • Wilmington, DE 19807-0630 • (302) 658-2400 • http://www.hagley.org

Historic Red Clay Valley • P.O. Box 5787 • Wilmington, DE 19808 • (302) 998-1930

Historical Society of Delaware • Historical Museum, 505 Market Street Mall • Wilmington, DE 19801 • (302) 655-7161 • http://www.hsd.org

Holy Trinity Church Foundation Library • Old Swedes Church and Hendrickson House Museum, 606 Church St • Wilmington, DE 19801-4421 • (302) 652-5629 • http://www.oldswedes.org

Immanuel Baptist Church Library • 2414 Pennsylvania Ave • Wilmington, DE 19806 • (302) 652-3121 • http://www.immanuelchurch.us

Jewish Historical and Genealogical Society of Delaware • 505 Market St Mall • Wilmington, DE 19801 • (302) 655-6232 • http://www.hsd.org

Kalmar Nickel Foundation and Shipyard Museum • 1124 E 7th St • Wilmington, DE 19801 • (302) 429-7447 • http://www.kalnyc.org

Lombardy Hall Foundation • 1611 Concord Pike, P.O. Box 7036 • Wilmington, DE 19803 • (302) 655-5254

Masonic Grand Lodge of Delaware • 818 N Market St • Wilmington, DE 19801 • (302) 652-4614 • http://www.masonsindelaware.org/

Nemours Foundation • Nemours Mansion Museum , 1600 Rockland Rd, P.O. Box 109 • Wilmington, DE 19899 • (302) 651-6919 • http://www.nemoursmansion.org

Office of Vital Statistics, Division of Public Health • 2055 Limestone Rd • Wilmington, DE 19808 • (302) 995-8588 • http://www.dhss.delaware.gov

Old Swedes Foundation • Hendrickson House Museum and Old Swedes' Church, 606 N Church St • Wilmington, DE 19801-4421 • (302) 652-5629 • http://www.oldswedes.org

Preservation Delaware • 1405 Greenhill Ave • Wilmington, DE 19806-1124 • (302) 651-9617 • http://www.preservationde.org

Red Clay Creek Presbyterian Church Archives • 500 McKennan's Church Rd • Wilmington, DE 19808 • (302) 998-0434

Rockwood Museum • 610 Shipley Rd • Wilmington, DE 19809-3609 • (302) 761-4340 • http://www.rockwood.org

Shoenberg Memorial Chapel Cemetery Archives • 519 Philadelphia Pk • Wilmington, DE 19809-2185 • (302) 762-0334

Wilmington Family History Center • 143 Dickinson Ln • Wilmington, DE 19807 • (302) 654-1911

Wilmington Institute Free Library • 10 S Market St, P.O. Box 2303 • Wilmington, DE 19899-2303 • (302) 571-7416 • http://www.wilmlib.org

Wilmington Monthly Meeting of Friends • 4th & West Sts • Wilmington, DE 19801 • (302) 652-4491

Winterthur

Winterthur Heritage Association • Route 52 • Winterthur, DE 19735

Winterthur Museum and Gardens Library • Route 52 • Winterthur, DE 19735 • (302) 888-4681 • http://www.winterthur.org

Wyoming

Wyoming Historical Commission • Historical Museum, 105 Front St • Wyoming, DE 19934 • (302) 667-1025

Yorklyn

Auburn Heights Preserve Museum • 3000 Creek Rd, P.O. Box 61 • Yorklyn, DE 19736 • (302) 239-2385 • http://www.auburnheights.org

Delaware

Washington

Academy of American Franciscan History • Catholic Univ, 620 Michigan Ave NE, 240 Leahy Hall • Washington, DC 20064-0001 • (202) 319-5890

Advisory Council on Historic Preservation • 1100 Pennsylvania Ave NW, Ste 809 • Washington, DC 20004

African Methodist Episcopal Church Library • 1134 11th St NW • Washington, DC 20001 • http://www.amecnet.org

African-American Historical and Genealogical Society • P.O. Box 73086 • Washington, DC 20056-3086 • http://www.rootsweb.com/~mdaahgs/

African-American National Capital Area Historical Genealogical Society • P.O. Box 34683 • Washington, DC 20043

Afro-American Historical and Genealogical Society • P.O. Box 73086, T Street Sta • Washington, DC 20056-3086 • (202) 234-5356 • http://www.aahgs.org

Afro-American Historical and Genealogical Society, James Dent Walker Chapter • P.O. Box 60632 • Washington, DC 20039 • (202) 722-0408

American Association of Museums • 1575 Eye Street NW, Suite 400 • Washington, DC 20005 • (202) 289-1818 • http://www.aam-us.org

American Catholic Historical Association • Mullen Library, Catholic Univ • Washington, DC 20064 • (202) 635-5079

American Historical Association • 400 A Street SE • Washington, DC 20003-3807 • (202) 544-2422 • http://www.theaha.org

American Institute for the Conservation of Historic and Artistic Works • 1717 K St NW #301 • Washington, DC 20006-1501 • (202) 452-9545

American Jewish Committee • Founder's Library, Rm 314 • Washington, DC 20059 • (202) 806-7605

American Red Cross Museum • 1700 E Street NW • Washington, DC 20006 • (202) 639-3300 • http://www.redcross.org

Anacostia Museum for African American History & Culture • 1901 Fort Place SE, P.O. Box 37012 • Washington, DC 20013-7012 • (202) 633-4867 • http://www.sil.si.edu/libraries/anac-hp.htm

Archdiocese for the Military Services • 415 Michigan Ave NE, Ste 300 • Washington, DC 20017 • (202) 269-9100 • http://www.milarch.org

Armed Forces Medical Museum • 6825 16th St NW • Washington, DC 20306

Armenian Assembly of America • 1140 19th St NW, Ste 600 • Washington, DC 20036 • (202) 393-3434 • http://www.aaainc.org

Army & Navy Club Library • 901 17th St NW • Washington, DC 20006-2503 • (202) 721-2096 • http://www.armynavyclub.org

Association for the Study of Afro-American Life and History • 1407 14th St NW • Washington, DC 20005-3705 • (202) 667-2822

Association of Professional Genealogists • 3421 M St NW, Ste 236 • Washington, DC 20007-3552 • (202) 766-3018

Black Catholic History Project • Archdiocese of Washington, 5001 Eastern Ave, P.O. Box 29260 • Washington, DC 20017-0260 • (301) 853-4579

B'nai B'rith International • 2020 K Street NW • Washington, DC 20006 • (202) 857-6600

B'nai Brith Klutznick Museum • 1640 Rhode Island Ave NW • Washington, DC 20036 • (202) 857-6583 • http://www.bnaibrith.org

Board for Certification of Genealogists • P.O. Box 14291 • Washington, DC 20044-4291 • (540) 822-5282 • http://www.bcgcertification.org

Bolling Air Force Base Library • FL 4400 HQ 11 MSG/SVMG, 410 Tinker St Bolling AFB • Washington, DC 20032-0703 • (202) 767-5578

Bureau of Indian Affairs-Washington • 1849 C Street NW, MS-4542-MIB • Washington, DC 20240-0001 • (202) 208-3711 • http://www.doi.gov/bia/ancestry/

Bureau of Land Management • 1849 C Street, NW • Washington, DC 20240 • (202) 343-9435 • http://www.blm.gov

Cleveland Park Historical Society • 2938 Newark St NW • Washington, DC 20008 • (202) 363-6358

Congressional Cemetery Museum • 1801 E Street, SE • Washington, DC 20003 • (202) 543-0539 • http://www.congressionalcemetery.org

Decatur House Museum • 748 Jackson Pl NW • Washington, DC 20006 • (202) 842-0920 • http://www.decaturhouse.org

Department of State, Passport Correspondence Branch • 1111 19th St NW, Ste 510 • Washington, DC 20522 • (202) 955-0307

Department of the Treasury Museum A • 15th & Pennsylvania NW • Washington, DC 20220 • (202) 622-1250 • http://www.ustreas.gov/curator

Dept of Veterans Affairs, National Cemetery System • 810 Vermont Ave NW • Washington, DC 20420 • (800) 697-6957 • http://www.cem.va.gov

District of Columbia Archives • 1300 Naylor Ct NW • Washington, DC 20001-4225 • (202) 727-2054

District of Columbia Genealogical Society • P.O. Box 63467 • Washington, DC 20029-3467

District of Columbia Public Libr-Georgetown • 3260 R St NW • Washington, DC 20007 • (202) 282-0220 • http://www.dclibrary.org/branches/geo/

District of Columbia Public Libr-Southeast • 403 7th St SE • Washington, DC 20003 • (202) 698-3377

Dumbarton House Museum • 2715 Q Street NW • Washington, DC 20007-3071 • (202) 337-2288 • http://www.dumbartonhouse.org

Federal Bureau of Investigation Museum • E Street & 9th • Washington, DC 20535 • (202) 324-2080 • http://www.fbi.gov

Folger Shakespeare Library • 201 E Capitol St SE • Washington, DC 20003-1094 • (202) 544-4600 • http://www.folger.edu

Ford's Theatre National Historic Site Museum • 511 10th St NW • Washington, DC 20004 • (202) 426-6924 • http://www.nps.gov/foth/

Francis Scott Key Foundation • 3400 Prospect St NW • Washington, DC 20007-3218 • (202) 333-2041

Frederick Douglass National Historic Site Museum • 1411 W Street SE • Washington, DC 20020 • (202) 426-5961 • http://www.nps.gov

Gallaudet University Library • 800 Florida Ave NE • Washington, DC 20002 • (202) 651-5217 • http://library.gallaudet.edu

Genealogical Speaker's Guild • 3421 M St NW • Washington, DC 20007-3516 • (407) 892-9710 • http://www.genspeakguild.org

German Historical Institute • 1607 New Hampshire Ave NW, Ste 400 • Washington, DC 20009 • (202) 387-3355 • http://www.ghi-dc.org

Grange-Order of Patrons of Husbandry • 1616 H Street NY • Washington, DC 20006

Heritage Preservation Museum • 1012 14th St NW, Ste 1200 • Washington, DC 20005 • (202) 233-0800 • http://www.heritagepreservation.org

Hillwood Museum • 4155 Linncan Ave NW • Washington, DC 20008 • (202) 686-8500 • http://www.hillwoodmuseum.org

Historical Society of Washington DC • Heurich House Museum, 1307 New Hampshire Ave NW • Washington, DC 20036 • (202) 785-2068

Historical Society of Washington, DC • City Museum, 801 K Street NW • Washington, DC 20036 • (202) 383-1800 • http://www.hswdc.org

District of Columbia

House Where Lincoln Died Museum • 516 10th St, NW • Washington, DC 20004 • (202) 426-6924

Hurston Adult Library • Washington Hebrew Congregation, 35 Macomb St NW • Washington, DC 20016 • (202) 362-7100 • http://www.whctemple.org

Immigration and Naturalization Service • Historical Reference Librarym 425 I Street NW, Room 1100A • Washington, DC 20536 • (202) 514-3278 • http://www.uscis.gov

Institute of Museum and Library Services • 1100 Pennsylvania Ave, NW, Rm 609 • Washington, DC 20506 • (202) 606-8539 • http://www.imls.gov

International Spy Museum • 800 F Street NW • Washington, DC 20004 • (202) 393-7798 • http://www.spymuseum.org

Jewish Historical Society of Greater Washington • Lillian and Albert Small Jewish Museum, 701 3rd St NW • Washington, DC 20001 • (202) 789-0900 • http://www.jhsgw.org

Jewish Special Interest Group • 3701 Connecticut Ave NW #228 • Washington, DC 20008

John K Mullen of Denver Memorial Library • Catholic Univ, 620 Michigan Ave NE • Washington, DC 20064 • (202) 635-5055 • http://libraries.cua.edu

Joseph Mark Lauinger Library • Georgetown University, 37th & N Sts NW, P.O. Box 571174 • Washington, DC 20057-1174 • (202) 687-7444 • http://www.library.georgetown.edu

Knights of Columbus • 1275 Pennsylvania Ave NW • Washington, DC 20004-2404

Library of Congress - Local History & Genealogy • Thomas Jefferson Annex, 10 1st St SE • Washington, DC 20540 • (202) 707-5537 • http://lcweb.loc.gov/rr/genealogy/

Marine Corps Historical Center Library • 1254 Charles Morris St SE, Washington Navy Yard • Washington, DC 20374-5040 • (202) 433-3483 • http://www.usmc.mil/historical.nsf/

Martin Luther King Memorial Library • 901 G Street NW • Washington, DC 20001-4599 • (202) 727-1101 • http://www.dclibrary.org/washingtoniana/

Mary McLeod Bethune Museum • 1318 Vermont Ave NW • Washington, DC 20005 • (202) 673-2402 • http://www.mps.gov/memc

Masonic Grand Lodge of the District of Columbia • 5428 MacArthur Blvd NW • Washington, DC 20016-2524 • (202) 686-1811 • http://www.dcgrandlodge.org

Melvin Gelman Library • The George Washington University, 2130 H St NW, Suite 201 • Washington, DC 20052 • (202) 994-6455 • http://www.gwu.edu/gelman/

Metropolitan Memorial United Methodist Church Library • 3401 Nebraska Ave NW • Washington, DC 20016 • (202) 363-4900 • http://www.metro.church-dc.org

Military Order of the Carabao • Farragut Sq • Washington, DC 20006-2503 • http://www.carabao.org

Moorland-Spingarn Research Center • Howard University Museum, 500 Howard Pl NW • Washington, DC 20059 • (202) 806-7252 • http://www.founders.howard.edu

National Air and Space Museum • 6th & Independence Ave SW • Washington, DC 20560 • (202) 633-2370 • http://www.nasm.si.edu

National Archives and Records Administration • 700 Pennsylvania Ave NW • Washington, DC 20408 • (202) 523-3286 • http://www.archives.gov; http://www.nara.gov

National Building Museum • 401 F Street NW • Washington, DC 20001 • (202) 272-2448 • http://www.nbm.org

National Conference of State Historic Preservations Officers • 444 N Capitol St NW • Washington, DC 20001 • (202) 624-5465

National Defense University Library • Fort McNair, Marshall Hall • Washington, DC 20319-5066 • (202) 685-6100 • http://www.ndu.edu

National Geographic Museum • Explorer's Hall, 1145 17th St NW • Washington, DC 20036 • (202) 857-7588 • http://www.nationalgeographic.com

National Guard Memorial Library • 1 Massachusetts Ave NW • Washington, DC 20001 • (202) 408-5890 • http://www.ngaus.org

National Historical Publications and Records Commission • National Archives Bldg • Washington, DC 20408-0001 • (202) 501-5600 • http://www.nara.gov/nara/nhpro/

National Institute on Genealogical Research • P.O. Box 14274 • Washington, DC 20044-4274 • http://www.rootsweb.com/~natgenin/

National Italian American Foundation • 1860 19th St NW • Washington, DC 20009-5501 • (202) 387-0600 • http://www.niaf.org

National Museum of American History Library • Smithsonian Institution, NMAH 5016, MRC 630, 14th & Constitution Ave NW, P.O. Box 37012 • Washington, DC 20013-7012 • (202) 633-3865 • http://www.americanhistory.si.edu

National Museum of American Jewish Military History • 1811 R Street NW • Washington, DC 20009 • (202) 265-6280 • http://www.nmajmh.org

National Museum of Crime & Punishment • 575 7th St, NW • Washington, DC 20004 • (202) 393-1099 • http://www.crimemuseum.org

National Museum of Health and Medicine • Walter Reed Army Medical Center, 6900 Georgia Ave NW, Building 54 • Washington, DC 20307-5001 • (202) 576-2334 • http://www.natmedmuse.afip.org/collections/collections.html

National Museum of the American Indian • 4th & Independence SW • Washington, DC 20560 • (202) 633-1000 • http://www.nmai.si.edu

National Portrait Gallery • Smithsonian Institution, 8th & F Streets • Washington, DC 20560 • (202) 275-1738 • http://www.npg.si.edu

National Postal Museum • 2 Massachusetts Ave NE • Washington, DC 20002 • (202) 633-5555 • http://www.postalmuseum.si.edu

National Society of the Colonial Dames of America • Dumbarton House, 2715 Q Street, NW • Washington, DC 20007 • (202) 337-2288 • http://www.dumbartonhouse.org; http://www.nscda.org

National Society, Children of American Colonists • 2205 Massachusetts Ave NW • Washington, DC 20008-2813 • (202) 667-3076 • http://www.msdac.org; http://www.rootsweb.com/~flscac

National Society, Children of the American Revolution • 1776 D Street NW • Washington, DC 20006 • (202) 638-3153 • http://www.nscar.org

National Society, Colonial Dames of the XVII Century • 1300 New Hampshire Ave NW • Washington, DC 20036-1502 • (202) 293-1700 • http://www.colonialdames17c.net

National Society, Daughters of American Colonists • 2205 Massachusetts Ave, NW • Washington, DC 20008 • (202) 667-3076 • http://www.nsdac.org

National Society, Daughters of Founders and Patriots of America • Woodward Bldg, 733 15th St NW, #915 • Washington, DC 20005-2112

National Society, Daughters of the American Revolution • Historical Museum, 1776 D Street NW • Washington, DC 20006-5303 • (202) 879-3229 • http://www.dar.org

National Society, United States Daughters of 1812 • 1461 Rhode Island Ave, NW • Washington, DC 20005-5402 • (202) 332-3181 • http://www.usdaughters1812.org

National Trust for Historic Preservation • 1785 Massachusetts Ave NW • Washington, DC 20036-2189 • (202) 588-6000 • http://www.nationaltrust.org

Naval Historical Center • Washington Navy Yard, 805 Kidder Breese SE • Washington, DC 20374-5060 • (202) 433-4132 • http://www.history.navy.mil

Newseum: The Interactive Museum of News • Pennsylvania Ave & 6th St NW • Washington, DC 22209 • (703) 284-3544 • http://www.newseum.org

Octagon Museum • 1799 New York Ave • Washington, DC 20006-5292 • (202) 638-3221 • http://www.amerarchfoundation.com

Old Stone House Museum • 3051 M Street, NW • Washington, DC 2007 • (202) 426-6851

Order of AHEPA • 1909 Q St NW #500 • Washington, DC 20009-1007 • (202) 232-6300

Order of the Sons of Italy in America • 219 E Street, NE • Washington, DC 20002 • (202) 547-2900 • http://www.osia.org

Russian American Genealogical Archival Source • 1929 18th St NW, Ste 1112 • Washington, DC 20009-1710 • http://feefhs.org/ragas/frgragas.html

Saint Paul's College Library • 3015 4th St NE • Washington, DC 20017 • (202) 832-6262

Scottish Rite Supreme Council • House of the Temple Museum, 1733 16th Street, NW • Washington, DC 20009 • (202) 232-3579 • http://www.srmason-sj.org

SEC Historical Society • 1101 Pennsylvania Ave NW • Washington, DC 20004 • (202) 756-5015

Smithsonian Institute • 1000 Jefferson Dr • Washington, DC 20560 • (202) 357-2700 • http://www.si.edu

Society of the Cincinnati • Anderson House, 2118 Massachusetts Ave NW • Washington, DC 20008 • (202) 785-2040 • http://www.dkmuseums.com/cincin.html

Sons of the American Revolution, District of Columbia Society • 1801 E Street SE • Washington, DC 20003 • (202) 638-6444 • http://www.dcssar.org

Soviet-American Genealogical Archival Service • NARA, 7th & Pennsylvania Ave NW • Washington, DC 20408

Supreme Court Historical Society • 224 E Capitol St NE • Washington, DC 20003 • (202) 543-0614

Supreme Court of the United States Museum • 1 1st St NE • Washington, DC 20543 • (202) 479-3298 • http://www.supremecourtus.gov

Suwalk Lomza Interest Group for Jewish Genealogists • 3701 Connecticut Ave NW #228 • Washington, DC 20008-4556 • http://feefhs.org/jsig/frgslsig.html

Swedish Colonial Society • 3406 Macomb St NW • Washington, DC 20016 • http://www.colonialswedes.org

Tudor Place Museum • 1644 31st St NW • Washington, DC 20007 • (202) 965-0400 • http://www.tudorplace.org

US Customs and Border Protection • 1300 Pennsylvania Ave NW • Washington, DC 20229 • (202) 354-1000 • http://www.customs.ustreas.gov

US Army Center of Military History • 102 4th Ave, Building 35, Fort McNair • Washington, DC 20319-5058 • (202) 761-5413 • http://www.army.mil/cmh-pg/

US Army Center of Military History Museum • Fort McNair, 103 3rd Ave • Washington, DC 20319-5058 • (202) 685-2733 • http://www.army.mil/crnh-pg/

US Capitol Historical Society & Archives • 200 Maryland Ave NE • Washington, DC 20002 • (202) 543-8919 • http://www.uschs.org

US Coast Guard Historian's Office • 2100 2nd St SW • Washington, DC 20593 • (202) 267-0948 • http://www.uscg.mil/hq/g-cp/history/collect.html

US Holocaust Memorial Museum • 100 Raoul Wallenberg Pl SW • Washington, DC 20024 • (202) 488-0400 • http://www.ushmm.org

US Maritime Administration Museum • 400 7th St SW • Washington, DC 20590 • (800) 99-MARAD • http://marad.dot.gov

US Navy Memorial Foundation • Naval Heritage Center, 701 Pennsylvania Ave NW, Ste 123 • Washington, DC 20004-2608 • (202) 737-2300 • http://www.lonesailor.org

US Navy Museum • Washington Navy Yards 805 Kidder-Breese St SE • Washington, DC 20374-5060 • (202) 433-4132 • http://www.history.navy.mil/library

US Patent and Trademark Office Library • Crystal Park 3, Ste 481 • Washington, DC 20231 • (703) 308-5558 • http://www.uspto.gov

Vital Records Division - Department of Human Services Vital Records Branch • 825 N Capitol St NE • Washington, DC 20002 • (202) 442-9009 • http://dchealth.dc.gov/servicestvital_records/

White House Historical Association • 740 Jackson Pl NW • Washington, DC 20506 • (202) 737-8292 • http://www.whitehousehistory.org

White House Museum • 1600 Pennsylvania Ave NW • Washington, DC 20502 • (202) 456-2550 • http://www.whitehouse.gov

Woodrow Wilson House Museum • 2340 S Street NW • Washington, DC 20008 • (202) 387-4062 • http://www.woodrowwilsonhouse.org

Altamonte Springs
Altamonte Springs City Library • 281 N Maitland Ave • Altamonte Springs, FL 32701 • (407) 571-8830 • http://www.altamonteleisure.org

Anna Maria
Anna Maria Island Historical Society • 402 Pine Ave • Anna Maria, FL 34216 • (941) 778-0492 • http://www.annamariaislandchamber.org/history.cfm

Apalachicola
1838 Raney House Museum • 128 Market St, P.O. Box 75 • Apalachicola, FL 32320 • (850) 653-4321 • http://www.apalachicolahistory.org

Apalachicola Area Historical Society • George Chapel, 163 Avenue B, P.O. Box 75 • Apalachicola, FL 32320 • (850) 653-9524 • http://mailer.fsu.edu

John Gorrie Museum • 46 6th St & Avenue D, P.O. Box 267 • Apalachicola, FL 32329 • (850) 653-9347 • http://www.baynavigator.com

Apopka
Apopka Historical Society • Museum of Apopkans, 122 E 5th St • Apopka, FL 32703 • (407) 703-1707 • http://www.apopkamuseum.org

Arcadia
DeSoto County Historical Society • P.O. Box 1824 • Arcadia, FL 34265

Archer
Archer Historical Society • Magnolia & W Main, P.O. Box 1850 • Archer, FL 32618 • (352) 495-1044 • http://www.afn.org/~archer

Avon Park
Avon Park Historical Society • Historical Museum, 93 Museum Ave, P.O. Box 483 • Avon Park, FL 33825 • (863) 453-3938

Avon Park Library • 100 N Museum Ave • Avon Park, FL 33825 • (863) 452-3803 • http://www.heartlineweb.org/apl/

Highlands County Genealogical Society • 110 N Museum Ave • Avon Park, FL 33825 • (863) 382-4112 • http://www.heartlineweb.org/hcgs/

Babson Park
Grace & Roger Babson Learning Center • Webber International University, 1201 State Rd 17, P.O. Box 97 • Babson Park, FL 33827-0097 • (863) 638-2937 • http://www.webber.edu

Ridge Genealogical Society • P.O. Box 477 • Babson Park, FL 33827 • (863) 638-1616

Barberville
Pioneer Settlement Museum • 1776 Lightfoot Ln, P.O. Box 6 • Barberville, FL 32105 • (904) 749-2959 • http://www.barberville.net/pioneers_arts.htm

Bartow
Bartow Public Library • 2150 S Broadway • Bartow, FL 33830 • (863) 534-0131 • http://www.pclc.lib.fl.us/bartow/

Polk County Historical and Genealogical Association • Historic Courthouse Library, 100 E Main St, P.O. Box 2749 • Bartow, FL 33840-2749 • (863) 534-4380 • http://www.polk-county.net/library.html

Polk County Historical Association • 180 N Central Ave, P.O. Box 2749 • Bartow, FL 33831-2749 • (863) 533-3710

Belle Glade
Glades Historical Society • P.O. Box 1662 • Belle Glade, FL 33430-1662 • (561) 996-5198

Beverly Hills
Citrus County Library System • 425 W Roosevelt Blvd • Beverly Hills, FL 34465 • (352) 746-9077 • http://www.cclib.org

Big Coppitt Key
Monroe County Genealogical Society • 21 Ventana Ln • Big Coppitt Key, FL 33040

Blountstown
Calhoun County Library • 17731 NE Pear St • Blountstown, FL 32424 • (850) 674-8773

Boca Raton
Boca Raton Historical Society • 71 N Federal Hwy • Boca Raton, FL 33432-3919 • (561) 395-6766 • http://www.bocahistory.org

Boca Raton Public Library • 200 NW Boca Raton Blvd • Boca Raton, FL 33432-3706 • (561) 393-7906 • http://www.bocalibrary.org

LDS Family History Center • 1530 W Camino Real • Boca Raton, FL 33486 • (561) 395-6644

Wimberly Library • Florida Atlantic Univ, 777 Glades Rd, P.O. Box 3092 • Boca Raton, FL 33431-0992 • (561) 297-3785 • http://www.fau.edu/library

Bonita Springs
Bonita Spring Historical Society • 27142 S Riverside Dr • Bonita Springs, FL 34135 • (239) 992-6997

Bonita Springs Genealogical Club • 25311 Paradise Rd, P.O. Box 36647 • Bonita Springs, FL 34136

Bonita Springs Public Library • 26876 Pine Ave • Bonita Springs, FL 33923 • (239) 992-0101 • http://www.lee-county.com

Slovenian Genealogy Society • 12776 Maiden Cane Ln • Bonita Springs, FL 33923-3435

Bowling Green
Paynes Creek Historic State Park • 888 Lake Branch Rd • Bowling Green, FL 33834 • (863) 375-4717 • http://www.floridastateparks.org

Boynton Beach
Boynton Beach City Library • 208 S Seacrest Blvd • Boynton Beach, FL 33435 • (561) 742-6390 • http://www.coala.org/boynton

Bradenton
DeSoto National Memorial Museum • 75th St NW, P.O. Box 15390 • Bradenton, FL 34280 • (941) 792-0458 • http://www.nps.gov/deso

Hernando Desoto Historical Society • 910 3rd Ave W • Bradenton, FL 34205 • (941) 747-1998

Managee Village Historical Park • Settler's House, 1404 Manatee Ave E • Bradenton, FL 34208 • (941) 749-7165 • http://www.manateeclerk.com

Manasota Genealogical Society • 1405 4th Ave W, P.O. Box 9433 • Bradenton, FL 33506 • (941) 741-4070 • http://www.rootsweb.com/~flmgs/

Manatee County Historical Records Library • 1115 Manatee Ave W, P.O. Box 25400 • Bradenton, FL 34206 • (941) 749-1800 • http://www.clerkofcourts.com

Manatee County Historical Society • 604 15th St E, P.O. Box 1000 • Bradenton, FL 34206-1000 • (941) 741-4070

Manatee County Public Library System • 1301 Barcarrota Blvd W • Bradenton, FL 34205 • (941) 748-5555 • http://www.co.manatee.fl.us/library/master.html

Powel Crosley Museum of the Entrepreneur • 8374 N Tamiami Tr, P.O. Box 1000 • Bradenton, FL 34206 • (941) 729-9177 • http://www.crosleymuseum.com

Sara Scott Harllee Library • Manatee Community College, Family Heritage House Museum, 5840 26th St W, P.O. Box 1849 • Bradenton, FL 34206-7046 • (941) 752-5304 • http://www.mccfl.edu

South Florida Museum • 201 10th St W, P.O. Box 9265 • Bradenton, FL 34206 • (941) 746-4131 • http://www.southfloridamuseum.org

Tingley Memorial Library • 111 2nd St N • Bradenton Beach, FL 34217 • (941) 779-1208 • http://www.bythebeach.com/tingley

Florida

Brandon
Archives of J S G Boggs • 1208 Mitchell St • Brandon, FL 33511 •
(813) 689-8553

Bristol
Torreya State Park • HC2, Box 70 • Bristol, FL 32321 • (850) 643-2674
• http://www.dep.state.fl.us/parks/torreya

Brooksville
Genealogy Society of Hernando County • P.O. Box 1793 •
Brooksville, FL 34605-1793 • (352) 796-1623 • http://www.rootsweb.
com/~flhernan/#GSHC

Genealogy Society of Hernando County, Family Tree Maker Group •
P.O. Box 1793 • Brooksville, FL 34605-1793 • (352) 796-1623

Hernando County Library System • 238 Howell Ave • Brooksville, FL
34601 • (352) 754-4043 • http://www.hcpl.lib.fl.us

Hernando Heritage Museum • 601 Museum Ct, P.O. Box
12233 • Brooksville, FL 34603 • (352) 799-0129 • http://www.
hernandoheritagemuseum.com

Bruce
Muscogee Nation of Florida • P.O. Box 3028 • Bruce, FL 32455 • (850)
835-2078 • http://www.muscogeefl.com

Bunnell
Bulow Plantation Ruins Historic State Park • 3501 Kings Rd • Bunnell,
FL 32110 • (386) 517-2084 • http://www.floridastateparks.org/
bulowplantation/

Flagler County Historical Society • Historical Museum, 204 E Moody
Blvd • Bunnell, FL 32110 • (386) 437-0600

Bushnell
Dade Battlefield Historic State Park • 7200 County Rd 400 S,
Battlefield Dr • Bushnell, FL 33513 • (352) 793-4781 • http://www.
floridastateparks.org

Callahan
West Nassau Historical Society • 45383 Dixie Ave • Callahan, FL
32011 • (904) 879-3406

Cape Coral
Cape Coral Historical Society • Historical Museum, 544 Cultural Park
Blvd • Cape Coral, FL 33990 • (239) 772-7037

Lee County Genealogical Society • P.O. Box 150153 • Cape Coral, FL
33915-0153 • (941) 549-9625

Lee County Library-Cape Coral-Lee County • 921 SW 39th Terrace •
Cape Coral, FL 33914 • (239) 542-3953 • http://www.lee-county.com

Casselberry
Genealogical Group of Seminole County • P.O. Box 180993 •
Casselberry, FL 32707

Cedar Key
Cedar Key Historical Society • Historical Museum, 7070 D Street, P.O.
Box 222 • Cedar Key, FL 32625 • (352) 543-5071

Cedar Key Museum State Park • 12231 SW 166 Ct • Cedar Key, FL
32625 • (352) 543-5350 • http://www.dep.state.fl.us.parks

Century
Alger-Sullivan Historical Society • 610 4th St • Century, FL 32535 •
(850) 256-2447

Charlotte Harbor
Charlotte County Historical Center • 22959 Bayshore Rd • Charlotte
Harbor, FL 33980 • (941) 629-7278 • http://www.charlottecountyfl.com/
historical

Chokoloskee
Historic Smallwood Store and Museum • P.O. Box 367 • Chokoloskee,
FL 34138-0367 • (239) 695-2989 • http://www.florida-everglades.com/
chokol/smallw.htm

Ted Smallwood's Store Museum • 360 Marnie St, P.O. Box 310 •
Chokoloskee, FL 34138 • (239) 695-4454

Christmas
Orange County Historical Society • Historical Museum, 1300 N Fort
Christmas Rd • Christmas, FL 32709-9427 • (407) 568-4149

Citrus Springs
Citrus Springs Genealogical Society • 1826 W Country Club Blvd •
Citrus Springs, FL 34434 • (352) 489-4359 • http://www.rootsweb.
com/~flcsgc

Clearwater
Clearwater Historical Society • 1380 N Martin Luther King Jr Ave,
P.O. Box 175 • Clearwater, FL 34617 • (727) 446-4250 • http://www.
rootsweb.com/~flchs

Clearwater Public Library System • 100 N Osceola Ave • Clearwater,
FL 33755 • (727) 462-6800 • http://www.clearwater-fl.com/cpl/

Clearwater Public Library-North Greenwood • 905 N Martin Luther
King Jr Ave • Clearwater, FL 33755 • (727) 462-6895 • http://www.
clearwater-fl.com/cpl

Clearwater United Church Library • 411 Turner St • Clearwater, FL
33756 • (727) 446-5955 • http://www.fumc-clw.com

Jewish Genealogical Society of Tampa Bay • 14041 Icot Blvd •
Clearwater, FL 33760-3702 • (727) 842-5789 • http://www.rootsweb.
ancestry.com/~fljgstb/

Napoleonic Society of America • 1115 Ponce de Leon Blvd •
Clearwater, FL 34616 • (727) 586-1779 • http://www/napoleonic-
society.com

Clermont
Lake County Library System-Cooper Memorial Library • 2525 Oakley
Seaver Drive • Clermont, FL 34711 • (352) 536-2275 • http://www.
mylakelibrary.org

Pastfinders of South Lake County • 620 Montrose • Clermont, FL
34711

Clewiston
Ah-Tah-Thi-Ki Museum • County Rd 833 & W Boundary Rd, Big
Cypress Seminole Indian Reservation • Clewiston, FL 33440 • (863)
902-1113 • http://www.seminoletribe.com/museum

Clewiston Historical Society • 112 Commercio St • Clewiston, FL
33440

Clewiston Museum • 109 Central Ave • Clewiston, FL 33440 • (863)
983-2870 • http://www.clewiston.org/museum.htm

Cocoa
Alma Clyde Field Library of Florida History • 435 Brevard Ave • Cocoa,
FL 32922 • (321) 690-1971 • http://www.florida-historical-soc.org

Brevard Community College Library • 1519 Clearlake Rd • Cocoa, FL
32922-6597 • (321) 632-1111 x 62963 • http://www.brevard.cc.fl.us/lrc/
libc.htm

Brevard Genealogical Society • P.O. Box 1123 • Cocoa, FL 32922 •
(321) 632-6570 • http://www.rootsweb.com/~flbgs/

Brevard Museum of History and Science • 2201 Michigan Ave • Cocoa,
FL 32926 • (321) 632-1830 • http://www.brevardmuseum.com

Central Brevard Library and Reference Center • 308 Forrest Ave •
Cocoa, FL 32922-7781 • (321) 633-1792 • http://www.brev.lib.fl.us

Florida Historical Society • 435 Brevard Ave • Cocoa, FL 32922 • (321)
254-9855 • http://pegasus.cc.ucf.edu/~flhisqtr/quarterly.html

Sons of the American Revolution, Florida Society • 3403 Caraway St •
Cocoa, FL 32926 • (321) 632-5663 • http://www.flssar.org

Cocoa Beach
Cocoa Beach Public Library • 550 N Brevard Ave • Cocoa Beach, FL
32931 • (321) 868-1104 • http://www.brev.org

Coconut Grove
Barnacle Historic State Park • 3485 Main Hwy • Coconut Grove, FL 33133 • (305) 442-6866 • http://www.floridastateparks.org/thebarnacle

Coral Gables
Coral Gables Merrick House • 907 Coral Wy • Coral Gables, FL 33134 • (305) 460-5361

Mel Harrison Memorial Library • Temple Judea, 5500 Granada Blvd • Coral Gables, FL 33146 • (305) 667-5657 • http://www.judeagables.org

Otto G Richter Library • Univ of Miami, 1300 Memorial Dr, P.O. Box 248214 • Coral Gables, FL 33124-0320 • (305) 284-4722 • http://www.miami.edu/archives/intro.html

Cortez
Cortez Village Historical Society • P.O. Box 663 • Cortez, FL 34215 • (941) 795-7121

Florida Institute of Saltwater Heritage (FISH) • P.O. Box 606 • Cortez, FL 34215 • (941) 794-8275 • http://fishpreserve.org

Florida Maritime Museum at Cortez • 4415 119th St W, P.O. Box 100 • Cortez, FL 34215 • (941) 708-6120

Crawfordville
Wakulla County Historical Society • P.O. Box 151 • Crawfordville, FL 32326-0151

Wakulla County Public Library • 4330 Crawfordville Hwy, P.O. Box 1300 • Crawfordville, FL 32327-1300 • (850) 926-7415 • http://www.wakullalibrary.org

Cross City
Dixie County Historical Society • P.O. Box 928 • Cross City, FL 32628

Cross Creek
Marjorie Kinnan Rawlings Historic State Park • 18700 S County Rd 325 • Cross Creek, FL 32640 • (352) 466-3672 • http://www.floridastateparks.org

Crystal River
Citrus County Historical Society • Coastal Heritage Museum, 532 Citrus Ave • Crystal River, FL 34428 • (352) 795-1755 • http://www.cccourthouse.org

Dade City
Pasco County Genealogical Society • P.O. Box 2072 • Dade City, FL 33526-2072 • http://www.rootsweb.com/~flpcgs

Pioneer Florida Museum • 15602 Pioneer Museum Rd, P.O. Box 335 • Dade City, FL 33526 • (352) 567-0262 • http://www.pioneerfloridamuseum.org

Daytona Beach
Carl S Swisher Library & Learning Resource Center • Bethune-Cookman College, 640 Mary McLeod Bethune Blvd • Daytona Beach, FL 32114 • (386) 481-2180 • http://www.bethune.cookman.edu

Daytona Beach Community College Library • 1200 International Speedway Blvd, P.O. Box 2811 • Daytona Beach, FL 32120-2811 • (386) 254-3055 • http://www.dbcc.edu

Halifax Historical Society • Historical Museum, 252 S Beach St, P.O. Box 5051 • Daytona Beach, FL 32114 • (386) 255-6976 • http://www.halifaxhistorical.org

Howard Thurman Home Museum • 614 Whitehall St • Daytona Beach, FL 32114 • (386) 258-7514

Mary Mcleod Bethune Foundation • Historical Museum, 640 Mary Mcleod Bethune Blvd • Daytona Beach, FL 32115 • (904) 255-1401

Scottish-American Military Society • 631 S Ridgewood Ave • Daytona Beach, FL 32114-4931 • (386) 255-4564

Volusia County Archives • 252 S Beach St • Daytona Beach, FL 32014 • (386) 254-4647

Volusia County Genealogical and Historical Society • c/o Volusia County Library, 1290 Indian Lake Rd, P.O. Box 2039 • Daytona Beach, FL 32015 • (386) 255-3765

Volusia County Library Center • City Island • Daytona Beach, FL 32114 • (386) 257-6036 • http://merlin.vcpl.lib.fl.us

De Land
DeLand Naval Air Station Museum • 910 Biscayne Blvd • De Land, FL 32724 • (386) 738-4149 • http://www.delandnavalairstation.org

DeLand Public Library, Volusia County Branch • 130 E Howry Ave • De Land, FL 32724 • (386) 822-6430 • http://merlin.vcpl.lib.fl.us

DuPont-Ball Library • Stetson University, 421 N Woodland Blvd, Unit 8418 • De Land, FL 32723 • (386) 822-7188 • http://www.stetson.edu/departments/library

Florida Baptist Historical Society • Stetson Univ, P.O. Box 8353 • De Land, FL 32720-3757 • (904) 822-7175

Roots and Branches Genealogical Society of West Volusia County • c/o DeLand Public Library, 130 E Howry Ave, P.O. Box 612 • De Land, FL 32721-0612 • (386) 668-1071

West Volusia Historical Society • 137 W Michigan Ave, P.O. Box 733 • De Land, FL 32721-0733 • (386) 734-7029

Deerfield Beach
Deerfield Beach Historical Society • Butler House Museum, 380 E Hillsboro Blvd • Deerfield Beach, FL 33441 • (954) 429-0378 • http://www.deerfieldhistory.org

South Florida Railway Museum • 1300 W Hillsboro Blvd • Deerfield Beach, FL 33442 • (954) 698-6620

Delray Beach
Carson Cottage and Museum • 5 NW 1st St • Delray Beach, FL 33436 • (561) 243-0223

Delray Beach Historical Society • Cornell Museum, 51 N Swinton Ave • Delray Beach, FL 33444 • (561) 274-9578 • http://www.delraybeachhistoricalsociety.org

Delray Beach Library • 101 W Atlantic Ave • Delray Beach, FL 33444 • (561) 266-0194 • http://www.delraylibrary.org

Jewish Genealogical Society of Palm Beach County Florida • South County Civic Ctr, 16700 Jog Rd, P.O. Box 7796 • Delray Beach, FL 33482-7796 • (561) 495-9839 • http://www.jgspalmbeachcounty.org

Morikami Museum of Japanese Culture Library • 4000 Morikami Park Rd • Delray Beach, FL 33446 • (561) 495-0233 • http://www.morikami.org

Deltona
Afro-American Historical and Genealogical Society-Central Florida • P.O. Box 5742 • Deltona, FL 32728

Destin
Destin Library • 150 Sibert Ave • Destin, FL 32541-1523 • (850) 837-8572 • http://www.cityofdestin.com/library.html

Dunedin
Dunedin Historical Society • Historical Museum, 349 Main St, P.O. Box 2393 • Dunedin, FL 34697-2393 • (727) 736-1176 • http://www.dunedinmuseum.org

Dunedin Public Library • 223 Douglas Ave • Dunedin, FL 32698 • (727) 298-3080 • http://www.ci.dunedin.fl.us/dunedin/library/htm

East Naples
Collier County Museum • 3301 Tamiami Tr • East Naples, FL 34112 • (941) 774-8476 • http://www.colliermuseum.com

Edgewater
Genealogical Society of Southeast Volusia County • P.O. Box 895 • Edgewater, FL 32132 • http://www.rootsweb.com/~flgssvc

Eglin AFB
Air Force Armament Museum • 100 Museum Dr • Eglin AFB, FL 32542-1497 • (850) 882-4062 • http://www.eglin.af.mil/museum

Eglin Air Force Base Library • 305 W F St, Bldg 278 • Eglin AFB, FL 32542-6842 • (850) 882-5088

Ellenton
American Historical Society of Germans from Russia, Florida Suncoast Chapter • 83 Spoonbill Ln • Ellenton, FL 34222 • (941) 962-5095

Gamble Plantation Historic State Park • Juday P Benjamin Confederate Memorial, 3708 Patten Ave • Ellenton, FL 34222 • (941) 723) 4536 • http://www.dep.state.fl.us/parks

Englewood
Lemon Bay Historical and Genealogical Society • P.O. Box 1245 • Englewood, FL 34295-1245

Estero
Koreshan State Historic Site Museum • US 41 & Corkscrew Rd, P.O. Box 7 • Estero, FL 33928 • (239) 992-0311 • http://www.floridastateparks.org

US Catholic Historical Society • P.O. Box 321 • Estero, FL 33928-0321

Eustis
Eustis Historical Preservation Society • Clifford House Museum, 536 N Bay St • Eustis, FL 32726 • (352) 483-0046 • http://www.eustis.org

Eustis Memorial Library • 120 N Center St • Eustis, FL 32726-3512 • (352) 357-6110 • http://www.eustismemoriallibrary.org

Fernandina Beach
Amelia Island Genealogical Society • P.O. Box 6005 • Fernandina Beach, FL 32035 • (904) 261-2139 • http://library.nassau.lib.fl.us/aigs

Amelia Island Museum of History • 233 S 3rd St • Fernandina Beach, FL 32034 • (904) 261-7378 • http://www.ameliaislandmuseumofhistory.org

Fort Clinch State Park • 2601 Atlantic Ave • Fernandina Beach, FL 32034 • (904) 277-7274 • http://www.floridastateparks.org

Nassau County Public Library System • 25 N 4th St • Fernandina Beach, FL 32034-4123 • (904) 491-3620

Fort Lauderdale
African-American Research Library & Cultural Center • 2650 NW 6th St • Fort Lauderdale, FL 33311 • (954) 765-4269

Bonnet House Museum • 900 N Birch Rd • Fort Lauderdale, FL 33304 • (954) 563-5393 • http://www.bonnethouse.org

Broward County Division of Libraries • 100 S Andrews Ave • Fort Lauderdale, FL 33301 • (954) 357-7444 • http://www.broward.org/library/

Broward County Genealogical Society • P.O. Box 485 • Fort Lauderdale, FL 33302 • http://www.rootsweb.com/~flgsbc/

Broward County Historical Commission • Historical Museum, 151 SW 2nd St • Fort Lauderdale, FL 33301 • (954) 765-4670 • http://www.co.broward.fl.us/history.htm

Fort Lauderdale Historical Society • Historical Museum, 219 SW 2nd St • Fort Lauderdale, FL 33301 • (954) 463-4431 • http://www.oldfortlauderdale.org

Genealogical Society of Broward County • P.O. Box 485 • Fort Lauderdale, FL 33302 • (954) 584-2545 • http://www.rootsweb.com/~flgsbc

Jewish Genealogical Society of Broward County • P.O. Box 17251 • Fort Lauderdale, FL 33318 • (754) 223-9201 • http://www.jgsbc.org

King-Cromartie House • 231 SW 2nd Ave • Fort Lauderdale, FL 33301 • (954) 463-4431

Southeast Florida Regional Preservation Office • Florida Division of Historical Resources, 231 SW 2nd Ave • Fort Lauderdale, FL 33301 • (954) 467-4990

Stranahan House Museum • 335 SE 6th Ave • Fort Lauderdale, FL 33301 • (954) 524-4736 • http://www.stranahanhouse.com

University School Library • 7500 SW 36th St • Fort Lauderdale, FL 33066

Fort Meade
Fort Meade Public Library • 75 E Broadway • Fort Meade, FL 33841-2998 • (863) 285-8287 • http://www.pclc.lib.fl.us

Historical Society of Fort Meade • 1 N Tecumseh Ave • Fort Meade, FL 33841 • (863) 285-7474

Fort Myers
Edison & Ford Winter States Museum • 2350 McGregor Blvd, P.O. Box 2368 • Fort Myers, FL 33902 • (239) 334-7419 • http://www.edison-ford-estate.com

Fort Myers Historical Museum • 2300 Peck St, P.O. Drawer 2217 • Fort Myers, FL 33902 • (941) 332-5955 • http://www.tntonline.com/dtown/muse.htm

Fort Myers-Lee County Public Library • 2050 Central Ave • Fort Myers, FL 33901-3917 • (239) 479-4636 • http://www.lee-county.com/library/

Lee County Genealogical Society • 136 Pinebrook Dr • Fort Myers, FL 33907 • http://www.leecountygenealogy.org

Lee County Library-Fort Myers-Lee County • 2050 Central Ave • Fort Myers, FL 33901-3917 • (239) 479-4635

Lee Trust for Historic Preservation • general delivery • Fort Myers, FL 33901 • (239) 344-0100

Southwest Florida Historical Society • 10091 McGregor Blvd, P.O. Box 1381 • Fort Myers, FL 33902-1381 • (239) 939-4044

Southwest Florida Museum of History • 2300 Peck St • Fort Myers, FL 33901 • (239) 332-5955 • http://www.cityftmyers.com

Fort Myers Beach
Fort Myers Beach Public Library • 2755 Estero Blvd • Fort Myers Beach, FL 33931 • (239) 765-8163 • http://www.fmb.lib.fl.us

Mound House Museum • 289 Connecticut St • Fort Myers Beach, FL 33931 • (239) 765-0865 • http://www.moundhouse.org

Fort Pierce
Charles S Miley Learning Resources Center • Indian River Community College, 3209 Virginia Ave • Fort Pierce, FL 34981-5599 • (772) 462-4757 • http://www.ircc.edu

Okeechobee Historical Society • 1850 Hwy 98 N • Fort Pierce, FL 34950 • (863) 763-4344

Saint Lucie County Historical Museum • 414 Seaway Dr • Fort Pierce, FL 34949 • (772) 462-1795 • http://www.west-lucie.lib.fl.us/museum/

Saint Lucie County Library System • 124 N Indian River Dr • Fort Pierce, FL 34950-4331 • (772) 462-1615 • http://www.st-lucie.lib.fl.us

Saint Lucie County Library System-Fort Pierce Branch • 101 Melody Ln • Fort Pierce, FL 34950-4402 • (772) 462-2188 • http://www.st-lucie.lib.fl.us

Saint Lucie Historical Commission • Historical Museum, 414 Seaway Dr • Fort Pierce, FL 33449 • (772) 462-1795 • http://www.st-lucie.lib.fl.us/museum.htm

Treasure Coast Genealogical Society • P.O. Box 12582 • Fort Pierce, FL 34979-2582 • http://www.rootsweb.com/~fltcgs/

UDT-Seal Museum • 3300 N State Rd AIA • Fort Pierce, FL 34949-8520 • (772) 595-5845 • http://www.udt-sealmuseum.org

Fort Walton Beach

Indian Temple Mound Museum • 139 Miracle Strip Pkwy, P.O. Box 4009 • Fort Walton Beach, FL 32549 • (850) 833-9595

Okaloosa County Genealogical Society • P.O. Drawer 1175 • Fort Walton Beach, FL 32549-1175 • (850) 864-2270 • http://www.rootsweb.com/~flwalton/gsoc.txt

Frostproof

Latt Maxcy Memorial Library • 15 N Magnolia Ave • Frostproof, FL 33843 • (863) 635-7857 • http://www.pclc.lib.fl.us/frostproof.html

Gainesville

Alachua County Genealogical Society • 712 NW 95th Terr, P.O. Box 12078 • Gainesville, FL 32604-0078 • (352) 371-3097 • http://www.afn.org/~acgs/

Alachua County Historical Commission • 30 E University, P.O. Box 17 • Gainesville, FL 32602-0017 • (352) 374-5260

Alachua County Library District • 401 E University Ave • Gainesville, FL 32601-5453 • (352) 334-3900 • http://www.acld.lib.fl.us

Descendants of the Knights of the Bath • P.O. Box 357062 HSC • Gainesville, FL 32605-7062 • (352) 377-4164 • http://www.knights of the bath.com

George A Smathers Library • University of Florida Libraries, Library West, P.O. Box 117001 • Gainesville, FL 32611-7001 • (352) 392-0361 • http://www.uflib.ufl.edu

Historic Gainesville • P.O. Box 466 • Gainesville, FL 32602 • http://www.afn.org/~hgi/

Matheson Historical Center Library • 513 E University Ave • Gainesville, FL 32601 • (352) 378-2280 • http://www.mathesonmuseum.org

Order of the First World War • P.O. Box 357062 HSC • Gainesville, FL 32605-7062 • (352) 377-4164 • http://www.knightsofthebath.com

Order of the Second World War • P.O. Box 357062 HSC • Gainesville, FL 32605-7062 • (352) 377-4164 • http://www.knightsofthebath.com

P K Yonge Library of Florida History • Univ of Florida, 201 Smathers Library, P.O. Box 117007 • Gainesville, FL 32611-7001 • (352) 392-0319 • http://www.ufl.edu

Geneva

Geneva Historical and Genealogical Society • Geneva History Museum, 165 1st St, P.O. Box 91 • Geneva, FL 32732

Tuscola United Cherokee Tribe of Florida • 730 Harney Heights Rd • Geneva, FL 32732

Grant

Grant Historical House Museum • 4795 S US Hwy 1, P.O. Box 55 • Grant, FL 32949 • (407) 723-8543

Green Cove Springs

Clay County Genealogical Society • P.O. Box 1071 • Green Cove Springs, FL 32043

Clay County Historical Society • Walnut St • Green Cove Springs, FL 32043 • (904) 284-9644

Green Cove Springs Public Library • 403 Ferris St • Green Cove Springs, FL 32043 • (904) 284-6315

Historical Resource Center and Clay County Archives • 910 Ferris St • Green Cove Springs, FL 32043 • (904) 264-5576 • http://www.claycountygov.com

Greensboro

West Gadsden Historical Society • James A Dezell House • Greensboro, FL 32330 • (850) 442-6434

Gulfport

Gulfport Historical Society • 5301 28th Ave S, P.O. Box 5152 • Gulfport, FL 33737-5152

Haines City

Haines City Public Library • 303 Ledwith Ave, P.O. Box 1507 • Haines City, FL 33845-1507 • (863) 421-3633 • http://www.pclc.lib.fl.us

Hastings

Hastings Historical Society • 150 S Main St • Hastings, FL 32145

Hawthorne

Hawthorne Historical Museum • 7225 SE 221st St, P.O. Box 2099 • Hawthorne, FL 32640 • (352) 481-4491 • http://www.hawthorneflorida.org

Hialeah

Hialeah-John F Kennedy Library • 190 W 49th St • Hialeah, FL 33012-3798 • (305) 821-2700 • http://www.ci.hialeah.fl.us/library

Highland Beach

Highland Beach Library • 3614 S Ocean Blvd • Highland Beach, FL 33487 • (561) 278-5455 • http://www.highlandbch.com

Hollywood

Ah-Tah-Thi-Ki Museum at Okalee • 4710 Seminole Wy, Ste S2 • Hollywood, FL 33314 • (954) 797-5570

Hollywood Historical Society • 1520 Polk St • Hollywood, FL 33020 • (954) 923-5590

Holocaust Documentation and Education Center • 2031 Harrison St • Hollywood, FL 33020 • (954) 929-5690 • http://www.hdec.org

Seminole Tribe of Florida • 6073 Stirling Rd • Hollywood, FL 33024 • (305) 966-6300 • http://www.seminoletribe.com

Holmes Beach

Anna Maria Island Historical Society • 402 Pine Ave • Holmes Beach, FL 34218 • (941) 778-0492

Homestead

Miami-Dade Public Library-Homestead Branch • 700 N Homestead Blvd • Homestead, FL 33030 • (305) 246-0168 • http://www.largo.com/library/liby.htm

Hudson

Pasco County Library System • 8012 Library Rd • Hudson, FL 34667 • (727) 861-3020 • http://www.pasco.lib.fl.us

Hurlburt Field AFB

Hurlburt Field Base Library • 16 SVS/SVMG, 443 Cody Ave • Hurlburt Field AFB, FL 32544 • (850) 884-6947 • http://commandolibrary.com

Immokalee

Immokalee Pioneer Museum at Roberts Ranch • 1215 Roberts Ave • Immokalee, FL 34143 • (239) 658-2466 • http://www.colliermuseums.com

Indialantie

South Brevard Historical Society • 615 N Riverside • Indialantie, FL 32903 • (407) 723-6835

Inverness

Citrus County Genealogical Society • 1511 Druid Rd, P.O. Box 2211 • Inverness, FL 34451-2211 • (352) 344-8108 • http://www.rootsweb.com/~flccgs2

Citrus County Historical Society • Old Courthouse Heritage Museum, 1 Courthouse Sq • Inverness, FL 34450-4802 • (352) 341-6428 • http://www.citrushistorical.org

Jacksonville

Barnett Historic Preservation Society • 118 W Adams #510 • Jacksonville, FL 32202-3800 • (904) 353-6070

Carl S Swisher Library • Jacksonville University, 2800 University Blvd N • Jacksonville, FL 32211-3394 • (904) 256-7263 • http://www.ju.edu/library

Florida

Jacksonville, cont.

Durkeeville Historical Society • 3117 N Liberty St • Jacksonville, FL 32202 • (904) 353-1300

Eastside Historic Community Foundation • 112 W Adams St • Jacksonville, FL 32202 • (904) 720-3544

Fort Caroline National Memorial Museum • 12713 Fort Caroline Rd • Jacksonville, FL 32225 • (904) 641-7155

Jacksonville Fire Museum • 1408 Gator Bowel Blvd • Jacksonville, FL 32202 • (904) 630-0618

Jacksonville Genealogical Society • 1224 Knobb Hill Dr, P.O. Box 60756 • Jacksonville, FL 32205-0756 • (904) 781-9300 • http://users2.fdn.com/~jgs

Jacksonville Historical Society • 317-A Philip Randolph Blvd • Jacksonville, FL 32202 • (904) 665-0064 • http://www.jaxhistory.com

Jacksonville Maritime Museum • 1015 Museum Cr #2 • Jacksonville, FL 32207 • (904) 398-9011

Jacksonville Public Library • 122 N Ocean St • Jacksonville, FL 32203 • (904) 630-1994 • http://jpl.coj.net

Jean Miller Memorial Library • Riverside Presbyterian Church, 849 Park St • Jacksonville, FL 32204 • (904) 355-4585 • http://www.rpcjax.org

Kingsley Plantation Museum • 11676 Palmetto Ave • Jacksonville, FL 32225 • (904) 251-3537 • http://www.nps.gov/timu

Lavilla Museum • 829 N David St • Jacksonville, FL 32202 • (904) 632-5555 • http://www.ritzlevilla.org

Mandarin Historical Society • Historical Museum, 11964 Mandarin Rd, P.O. Box 23601 • Jacksonville, FL 32223 • (904) 268-0784 • http://www.mandarinmuseum.net

Masonic Grand Lodge of Florida • 220 N Ocean St • Jacksonville, FL 32202 • (800) 375-2339 • http://www.glflamason.org/

Museum of Science & History of Jacksonville • 1025 Museum Cr • Jacksonville, FL 32207 • (904) 396-7803 • http://www.themosh.org

Museum of Southern History • 4304 Herschel St • Jacksonville, FL 32210 • (904) 388-3574

Office of Vital Statistics, Dept of Health • 1217 Pearl St, P.O. Box 210 • Jacksonville, FL 32231 • (904) 359-6900 • http://www9.myflorida.com/planning_eval/vital_statistics/

Southern Genealogist's Exchange Society • 1580 Blanding Blvd, P.O. Box 2801 • Jacksonville, FL 32203-2801 • (904) 781-9809 • http://www.wgesjax.tripod.com

Thomas G Carpenter Library • University of North Florida, Bldg 12-Library, 4567 St John's Bluff Rd S, P.O. Box 17605 • Jacksonville, FL 32245-7605 • (904) 620-2616 • http://www.unf.edu/library

Jacksonville Beach

Beaches Area Historical Society • 380 Pablo Ave, P.O. Box 50646 • Jacksonville Beach, FL 32250 • (904) 242-9572

Jasper

Hamilton County Historical Museum • P.O. Box 929 • Jasper, FL 32052 • (386) 792-3850 • http://www.rootsweb.com/~flhchms

Hamilton County Historical Society • Historical Museum, P.O. Box 929 • Jasper, FL 32052 • (386) 792-2726

Jupiter

Loxahatchee Historical Society • Florida History Center & Museum, 805 N US Hwy 1 • Jupiter, FL 33477 • (561) 747-6639

Loxahatchee River Historical Society • Lighthouse Museum, 500 Captain Armour's Wy • Jupiter, FL 33469 • (561) 747-8380 • http://www.jupiterlighthouse.org

Jupiter Beach

Loxahatchee River Historical Society • Historical Museum, 805 N US Hwy 1 • Jupiter Beach, FL 33477 • (561) 747-6639 • http://www.jupiterlighthouse.org

Key Biscayne

Bill Baggs Cape Florida State Park • 1200 S Crandon Blvd • Key Biscayne, FL 33149-2713 • (305) 361-8779 • http://www.floridastateparks.org

Key West

Audubon House Museum • 205 Whitehead St • Key West, FL 33040 • (305) 294-2116 • http://www.audubonhouse.org

Donkey Milk House Museum • 613 Eaton St • Key West, FL 33040 • (305) 296-1866

Dry Tortugas National Park • P.O. Box 6208 • Key West, FL 33041 • (305) 242-7700 • http://www.nps.gov/drto

East Martello Museum • 3501 S Roosevelt Blvd • Key West, FL 33040 • (305) 296-3913 • http://www.kwahs.com

Ernest Hemingway House Museum • 907 Whitehead • Key West, FL 33040 • (305) 294-1136 • http://www.hemingwayhome.com

Fort Zachary Taylor State Historical Site Museum • Southard St, P.O. Box 6560 • Key West, FL 33041 • (305) 292-6713 • http://www.floridastateparks.org/forttaylor

Harry S Truman Little White House Museum • 111 Front St, P.O. Box 6443 • Key West, FL 33041 • (305) 294-9911 • http://wwwtrumanlittlewhitehouse.com

Heritage House Museum • Robert Frost Cottage, 410 Caroline St • Key West, FL 33040 • (305) 296-3573 • http://www.heritagehousemuseum.org

Historic Florida Keys Foundation • 510 Greene St • Key West, FL 33040 • (305) 292-6718

Historic Key West Preservation Board • 510 Greene St • Key West, FL 33040 • (305) 292-6718

Jessie Porter's Heritage House Museum • 410 Caroline St • Key West, FL 33040 • (305) 296-3573

Key West Art and Historical Society • East Martello Museum, 3501 S Roosevelt Blvd • Key West, FL 33040 • (305) 296-3913 • http://www.kwahs.org

Key West Lighthouse Museum • 938 Whitehead • Key West, FL 33041 • (305) 294-0012 • http://www.kwahs.com

Key West Maritime Historical Society • 631 Greene St • Key West, FL 33040-6624 • (305) 292-7903

Key West Museum of Art & History • 281 Front St • Key West, FL 33040 • (305) 295-6616 • http://www.kwahs.com

Mel Fisher Maritime Heritage Society • Historical Museum, 200 Greene St, P.O. Box 511 • Key West, FL 33041 • (305) 294-2633 • http://www.melfisher.org

Monroe County Public Library • 700 Fleming St • Key West, FL 33040 • (305) 292-3595 • http://www.keyslibraries.org

Oldest House Museum • Wrecker's Museum, 322 Duval St, P.O. Box 689 • Key West, FL 33040 • (305) 294-9502 • http://www.oirf.org

Pirate Soul Museum • 524 Front St • Key West, FL 33040 • (305) 292-1113 • http://www.piratesoul.com

Kissimmee

Flying Tigers Warbird Air Museum • 231 N Hoagland Blvd • Kissimmee, FL 34741 • (407) 933-1942 • http://www.warbirdmuseum.com

Osceola County Historical Society • Historical Museum, 750 N Bass Rd • Kissimmee, FL 34746 • (407) 396-8644

Osceola County Historical Society • 750 N Bass Rd • Kissimmee, FL 32743-8960 • (407) 396-8644

White 1 Foundation Military Museum • 822 N Hoagland Blvd • Kissimmee, FL 34741 • (727) 365-1713 • http://www.white1foundation. org

La Belle
Calusa Valley Historical Society • 439 Hickpochee, P.O. Box 818 • La Belle, FL 33935 • (863) 675-1616

Hendry County Historical Society • P.O. Box 1760 • La Belle, FL 33935-1760

LaBelle Heritage Museum • 150 S Lee St, P.O. Box 2846 • La Belle, FL 33935 • (863) 674-0034

Lady Lake
Lady Lake Public Library • 225 W Guava St • Lady Lake, FL 32159 • (352) 753-2957 • http://ladylakelibrary.com

Villages Genealogical Society • 1910 Del Norte Dr • Lady Lake, FL 32159-9220 • http://www.angelfire.com/fl3/genie3/new_index.html

Lake Alfred
Lake Alfred Public Library • 195 E Pomelo St • Lake Alfred, FL 33850 • (863) 291-5378 • http://www.pclc.lib.fl.us

Lake Butler
Union County Public Library • 175 W Main St • Lake Butler, FL 32055 • (386) 496-3432 • http://union.newriver.lib.fl.us

Lake City
Columbia County Historical Society • Historical Museum, 157 SE Hernando St, P.O. Box 3276 • Lake City, FL 32056 • (904) 755-9096

Lake Mary
Purcell-Cotter Finders • 120 Pine Circle Dr • Lake Mary, FL 32746 • (407) 444-6374

Lake Park
Lake Park Public Library • 529 Park Ave • Lake Park, FL 33403 • (561) 881-3330 • http://www.lakepark-fl.gov/

Lake Placid
Lake Placid Historical Society • Depot Museum, 19 W Park Ave • Lake Placid, FL 33852 • (863) 465-1771

Lake Placid Memorial Library • 47 Park Dr • Lake Placid, FL 33852 • (863) 699-3705 • http://www.heartlineweb.org

Lake Wales
Historic Lake Wales Society • Depot Museum, 325 S Scenic Hwy, P.O. Box 1320 • Lake Wales, FL 33859-1320 • (863) 678-9209 • http://www.cityoflakewales.com

Lake Wales Museum and Cultural Center • 325 S Scenic Hwy • Lake Wales, FL 33853 • (863) 678-4209 • http://www.cityoflakewales.com

Lake Wales Public Library • 200 Cypress Garden Ln • Lake Wales, FL 33853 • (863) 678-4004 • http://www.cityoflakewales.com/library

Lake Worth
Harold C Manor Library • Palm Beach Community College, 4200 Congress Ave • Lake Worth, FL 33461 • (561) 868-3800 • http://www.pbcc.cc.fl.us/llrc/

Lake Worth Public Library • 15 North M St • Lake Worth, FL 33460 • (561) 533-7356 • http://www.lwlibrary.org

Museum of the City of Lake Worth • 414 Lake Ave • Lake Worth, FL 33460 • (561) 586-1700

National Museum of Polo • 9011 Lake Worth Rd • Lake Worth, FL 33467 • (561) 969-3210 • http://www.polomuseum.com

Lakeland
E T Roux Library • Florida Southern College, 111 Lake Hollingsworth Dr • Lakeland, FL 33801-5698 • (863) 680-4164 • http://tblc.org/fsc/roux.html

Florida Air Museum • 4175 Medulla Rd, P.O. Box 7670 • Lakeland, FL 33807 • (863) 644-0741 • http://www.floridaairmuseum.org

Imperial Polk Genealogical Society • 120 Contractors Way • Lakeland, FL 33801 • (863) 667-2085

Lakeland Public Library • 100 Lake Morton Dr • Lakeland, FL 33801-5375 • (863) 834-4280 • http://www.lakelandgov.net/library

Largo
Armed Forces Military Museum • 2050 34th Wy N • Largo, FL 33771 • (727) 539-8371 • http://www.armedforcesmuseum.com

Heritage Village-Pinellas County Historical Museum • 11909 125th St N • Largo, FL 33544 • (727) 582-2123 • http://www.pinellascounty.org/heritage

Largo Area Historical Society • 805 S Palm Dr • Largo, FL 33541 • (727) 584-3480

Largo Library • 120 Central Park Dr • Largo, FL 33771-2110 • (727) 587-6715 • http://www.largo.com/departments/library/library.html

Pinellas County Historical Society • Heritage Village, 11909 125th St N • Largo, FL 34644 • (727) 462-3474 • http://www.pinellascounty.org/heritage

Pinellas Genealogy Society • c/o Largo Public Library, 351 East Bay Dr, P.O. Box 1614 • Largo, FL 33779-1614 • (727) 725-5045 • http://www.rootsweb.com/~flpgs/

Leesburg
Kinseekers Genealogical Society of Lake County • P.O. Box 492711 • Leesburg, FL 34749-2711 • http://members.aol.com/LakeCo1887

Leesburg Historical Museum • 111 S 6th St, P.O. Box 490630 • Leesburg, FL 34749 • (352) 435-9424

Leesburg Public Library • 100 E Main St • Leesburg, FL 34748 • (352) 728-9790 • http://www.ci.leesburg.fl.us/library

Lehigh Acres
Lee County Library-East County Regional • 881 Gunnery Rd N • Lehigh Acres, FL 33971 • (239) 461-7330

Lehigh Acres Genealogical Society • Homestead Rd, P.O. Box 965 • Lehigh Acres, FL 33970-0965 • (941) 369-1050

Lighthouse Point
Lighthouse Point Library • 2200 NE 38th St • Lighthouse Point, FL 33064-7497 • (954) 946-6398 • http://lighthousepointlibrary.com

Live Oak
Suwannee River Regional Library • 1848 Ohio Ave • Live Oak, FL 32064-4517 • (386) 362-2317 • http://www.neflin.org/srrl

Suwannee Valley Genealogical Society • Historical Museum, 208 N Ohio Ave, P.O. Box 967 • Live Oak, FL 32604 • (386) 330-0110 • http://www.rootsweb.com/~flsvgs/svgs.htm

Longboat Key
Longboat Key Historical Society • Historical Museum, 6960 Gulf of Mexico Dr, P.O. Box 96 • Longboat Key, FL 34228 • (941) 387-8323 • http://longboatkeyhistory.org

Longwood
Jewish Genealogical Society of Central Florida • P.O. Box 520583 • Longwood, FL 32752 • (407) 788-3898

Kielce-Radom Special Interest Group • P.O. Box 520583 • Longwood, FL 32752 • (407) 788-3898 • http://www1.jewishgen/krsig

Florida

Lutz

Florida Historical Research Foundation • 2301 E 148th Ave • Lutz, FL 33549 • (321) 254-9855 • http://www.florida-historical-soc.org

MacClenny

Baker County Historical Society • 42 W McIver Ave, P.O. Box 856 • MacClenny, FL 32063 • (904) 259-0587 • http://rootsweb.com/~flbaker/books.html

Madeira Beach

Gulf Beaches Public Library • 200 Municipal Dr • Madeira Beach, FL 33708 • (727) 391-2828 • http://www.tblc.org/gulfbeaches

Madison

Elmer's Genealogy Library • 203 S Range St • Madison, FL 32340-2437 • (850) 973-3282 • http://www.elmerslibrary.com

Florida Chapter, OGS • 220 E Rutledge St • Madison, FL 32340-2440 • (850) 973-3282 • http://www.elmerslibrary.com

Madison County Genealogy Society • 115-117 W Base St, P.O. Box 136 • Madison, FL 3234100136 • http://www.rootsweb.com/~flmadiso/

Marshall W Hamilton Library • North Florida Community College, 1000 Turner Davis Dr • Madison, FL 32340-1699 • (850) 973-1624 • http://www.nfcc.edu/library

Maitland

Holocaust Memorial and Resource Center of Central Florida • 851 N Maitland Ave • Maitland, FL 32751 • (407) 628-0555 • http://www.holocaustedu.org

Jewish Genealogical Society of Greater Orlando • Holocaust Memorial, P.O. Box 941332 • Maitland, FL 32794-1332 • (407) 644-4566 • http://www.jgsgo.blogspot.com

Maitland Historical Museum • 840 Lake Lily Dr, P.O. Box 841001 • Maitland, FL 32751 • (407) 644-2451 • http://www.maitlandhistory.org

Maitland Historical Society • Historical Museum, 820 Lake Lily Dr, P.O. Box 941001 • Maitland, FL 32794 • (407) 644-2451 • http://www.maitlandhistory.org

Mango

Greater Brandon Genealogical Society • P.O. Box 2297 • Mango, FL 33550-2297

Marianna

Chipola Historical Trust • 4448 Putnam St • Marianna, FL 32446-3457 • (850) 526-4168

Chipola Junior College Library • 3094 Indian Circle • Marianna, FL 32446 • (850) 718-2274 • http://www.chipola.cc.fl.us/library/library.htm

Jackson County Florida Library • 413 N Green St • Marianna, FL 32446

Jackson County Public Library System • 2929 Green St • Marianna, FL 32446 • (850) 482-9631 • http://www.jacksoncountyfl.com/library.htm

Melbourne

East Central Florida Genealogical Society • 1300 Airport Blvd #473 • Melbourne, FL 32901-2969 • (407) 351-9282 • http://www.rootsweb.com/~flecfgsc/

Florida Historical Society • 1320 Highland Ave • Melbourne, FL 32935-7005 • (321) 254-9855 • http://www.florida-historical-soc.org

French and Canadian Heritage Society, Florida Group • P.O. Box 786 • Melbourne, FL 32901-0786 • (321) 254-4819 • http://www.rootsweb.com/~flbreva/gssb1.html

Genealogical Society of South Brevard County • P.O. Box 786 • Melbourne, FL 32901-0786 • (321) 254-4819 • http://www.rootsweb.com/~flbreva/gssb1.html

Liberty Bell Memorial Museum • 1601 Oak St • Melbourne, FL 32901 • (321) 727-1776

Melbourne Campus Library • Brevard Community College, 3865 N Wickham Rd • Melbourne, FL 32935-2399 • (321) 632-1111 • http://www.brevard.cc.edu/library

Melbourne Public Library • 540 E Fee Ave • Melbourne, FL 32901 • (321) 952-4514 • http://www.brev.org

O'Mahoney Society • 303 Audobon Dr • Melbourne, FL 32901

South Brevard Historical Society • P.O. Box 1064 • Melbourne, FL 32902-1064 • (321) 723-6835

Melrose

Ohio Genealogical Society, Florida Chapter • P.O. Box 466 • Melrose, FL 32666-0466 • http://www.rootsweb.com/~flfcogs

Merritt Island

Brevard Heritage Council • 870 Indianola Dr • Merritt Island, FL 32953

Miami

Adler Shinensky Library • Center for the Advancement of Jewish Education, 4200 Biscayne Blvd • Miami, FL 33137 • (305) 576-4030

Bay of Pigs Museum • 1821 SW 9th St • Miami, FL 33135 • (305) 649-4719 • http://www.brigada2506.com/museum.htm

Black Archives History Foundation • 5400 NW 22nd Ave • Miami, FL 33142 • (305) 636-2390

Black Heritage Museum • 13801 SW 102nd Ave, P.O. Box 570327 • Miami, FL 33257-0327 • (305) 252-3535

Genealogical Society of Greater Miami • P.O. Box 162905 • Miami, FL 33116-2905 • (305) 385-0563 • http://www.rootsweb.com/~flgsgm/

Gold Coast Railroad Museum • 12450 SW 152nd St • Miami, FL 33177 • (305) 253-0063 • http://www.goldcoast-railroad.org

Greater Miami Genealogical Society • 6500 SW 46th St, P.O. Box 162905 • Miami, FL 33116-2905

Historical Association of Southern Florida • Historical Museum, 101 W Flagler St • Miami, FL 33130 • (305) 375-1492 • http://www.historical-museum.org

Jewish Genealogical Society of Greater Miami • 8340 SW 151st St, P.O. Box 560432 • Miami, FL 33156-0432 • (305) 266-3350 • http://www.jgs-miami.org

Jewish Historical Society of South Florida • 4200 Biscayne Blvd • Miami, FL 33137

Miami-Dade Public Library • 101 W Flagler St • Miami, FL 33130-1523 • (305) 375-5580 • http://www.historical-museum.org

Miccosukee Tribe • Tamiami Sta, P.O. Box 440021 • Miami, FL 33144 • (305) 233-8380 • http://www.miccosukeetribe.com

Nathan W Collier Library • Florida Memorial College, 15800 NW 42nd Ave • Miami, FL 33054 • (305) 626-3647 • http://www.fmc.edu

Niles Trammel Learning Resources Center • Miami Dade College, 11011 SW 104th St • Miami, FL 33176-3393 • (305) 237-2292 • http://www.mdcc.edu

Saint Thomas University Library • 16400 NW 32nd Ave • Miami, FL 33054 • (305) 628-6668 • http://www.stu.edu/library

Steven & Dorothea Green Library • Florida International University, 11200 SW 8th St • Miami, FL 33199 • (305) 348-2470 • http://library.fiu.edu

Vizcaya Museum and Gardens • 3251 S Miami Ave • Miami, FL 33129 • (305) 579-2708 • http://www.vizcayamuseum.org

William Anderson's National Historical General Store Museum • 15700 SW 232nd St • Miami, FL 33170 • (305) 248-0003

Wings Over Miami Museum • 14710 SW 128th St • Miami, FL 33196 • (305) 233-5197 • http://www.wingsovermiami.com

Miami Beach
Jewish Museum of Florida • 301 Washington Ave • Miami Beach, FL 33139 • (305) 672-5044 • http://www.jewishmuseum.com

Reed Institute Library • 1015 W 47th St • Miami Beach, FL 33140 • (305) 532-5456

Temple Beth Sholom Library • 4144 Chase Ave • Miami Beach, FL 33140 • (305) 538-7231 • http://www.tbsmb.org

Miami Lakes
Jay I Kislak Foundation Museum • 7900 Miami Lakes Dr W • Miami Lakes, FL 33016 • (305) 364-4208 • http://www.kislak.com

Society of Florida Archivists • 14220 Leaning Pine Dr • Miami Lakes, FL 33014 • http://mailer.fsu.edu/~baltman/sfa.html

Miami Shores
Ukranian Genealogical and Heraldic Society • 573 NE 102nd St • Miami Shores, FL 33138

Miami Springs
Miami Springs Historical Society • P.O. Box 660022 • Miami Springs, FL 33166 • (305) 805-3321

Micanopy
Micanopy Historical Society • Historical Museum, 607 NE 1st St, P.O. Box 462 • Micanopy, FL 32667 • (352) 466-3200 • http://www.afn.org/~micanopy/

Middleburg
Middleburg Historical Museum • 3912 Section St • Middleburg, FL 32068 • (904) 282-8691

Milton
First Americans and Early Settlers Foundation • 3171 Bernath Dr • Milton, FL 32583 • (850) 994-4688

Genealogical Society of Santa Rosa County • 805 Alabama St • Milton, FL 32570

Santa Rosa Historical Society • 6866 Caroline St • Milton, FL 32570 • (850) 626-9830

West Florida Railroad Museum • 206 Henry St • Milton, FL 32570 • (850) 623-3645

Molino
Barrineau Park Historical Society • P.O. Box 508 • Molino, FL 32577 • (850) 587-5389

Monticello
Jefferson County Genealogical Society • 695 E Washington St • Monticello, FL 32344-2546

Jefferson County Historical Association • P.O. Box 496 • Monticello, FL 32344 • (850) 997-2565

Jefferson County Public Library • 260 N Cherry St • Monticello, FL 32344 • (850) 342-0205 • http://www.jefferson.lib.fl.us

Keystone Genealogical Society • 695 E Washington St, P.O. Box 50 • Monticello, FL 32345 • (850) 997-3304

Keystone Genealogy Library • 695 E Washington, P.O. Box 911 • Monticello, FL 32345

Wilderness Coast Public Libraries • 1180 W Washington Street • Monticello, FL 32344 • (850) 997-7400 • http://www.wildernesscoast.org

Moore Haven
Charlotte Glades Library System-Glades County Public • Riverside Dr, P.O. Box 505 • Moore Haven, FL 33471 • (863) 946-0744

Glades County Historical Society • P.O. Box 10 • Moore Haven, FL 33471-0100 • (863) 946-9100

Mount Dora
Mount Dora Historical Society • Historical Museum, 450 Royellou Ln, P.O. Box 1166 • Mount Dora, FL 32756 • (352) 383-0006 • http://www.mountdorahistoricalsociety.com

Royellou Museum • 450 Royellou Ln, P.O. Box 1166 • Mount Dora, FL 32756

W T Bland Public Library • 1995 N Donnelly St • Mount Dora, FL 32757 • (352) 735-7180 • http://ci.mount-dora.fl.us/departments/library.htm

Myakka City
Myakka City Historical Society • 10060 Wauchula Rd, P.O. Box 500 • Myakka City, FL 34252 • (941) 322-6423

Naples
Collier County Genealogical Society • P.O. Box 7933 • Naples, FL 34101-7933 • (941) 348-3535 • http://aps.naples.net

Collier County Genealogical Society, British Special Interest Group • P.O. Box 7933 • Naples, FL 34101 • (941) 348-3535

Collier County Historical Society • 137 12th Ave S, P.O. Box 201 • Naples, FL 33939 • (941) 261-8164

Collier County Museum and Archives • Collier County Government Ctr, 3301 E Tamiami Tr E • Naples, FL 34112 • (941) 774-8476 • http://www.colliermuseum.com

Collier County Public Library • 2385 Orange Blossom Dr • Naples, FL 34109 • (941) 263-7768 • http://www.collier-lib.org

Collier County Public Library • 650 Central Ave • Naples, FL 33940 • (941) 263-7768

Golden Gate-Naples Genealogical Society • 1689 Bonita Ct • Naples, FL 33962

Holocaust Museum of Southwest Florida • 4760 Tamiami Tr N, Ste 7 • Naples, FL 34103 • (239) 263-9200 • http://www.hmswfl.org

Naples Depot Museum • 1051 5th Ave S • Naples, FL 34102 • (239) 262-6525 • http://www.colliermuseums.com

Naples Historical Society • Palm Cottage House Museum, 137 12th Ave S, P.O. Box 201 • Naples, FL 34102 • (239) 261-8164 • http://www.napleshistoricalsociety.org

New Port Richey
New Port Richey Public Library • 5939 Main St • New Port Richey, FL 34652 • (813) 841-4547 • http://www.tblc.org/newport

West Pasco Genealogical Society • 5636 Club House Dr • New Port Richey, FL 33653

West Pasco Historical Society • Historical Museum, 6431 Circle Blvd • New Port Richey, FL 34291 • (727) 847-0680 • http://www.westpascohistoricalsociety.org

New Smyrna Beach
Genealogical Society of Southeast Volusia County • c/o New Smyrna Beach Public Library, 1001 S Dixie Fwy • New Smyrna Beach, FL 32168 • (904) 424-2910

Southeast Volusia Historical Society • Historical Museum, 120 Sams Ave, P.O. Box 968 • New Smyrna Beach, FL 32170 • (386) 478-0052 • http://www.nsbhistory.org

Niceville
Okaloosa-Walton Community College Library • 100 College Blvd • Niceville, FL 32578 • (850) 729-5392 • http://www.owcc.cc.fl.us/lrc

North Miami
Biscayne Bay Campus Library • Florida International Univ, 3000 NE 151st St • North Miami, FL 33181-3600 • (305) 919-5726 • http://library.fiu.edu

North Miami Public Library • 835 NE 132nd St • North Miami, FL 33161 • (305) 891-5535 • http://www.ci.north-miami.fl.us

Florida

North Miami Beach
Ancient Spanish Monastery of St Bernard de Clairvaux Cloisters • 16711 W Dixie Hwy • North Miami Beach, FL 33160 • (305) 945-1462 • http://www.spanishmonastery.com

Holocaust Documentation and Education Center • 13899 Biscayne Blvd, Ste 404 • North Miami Beach, FL 33181 • (305) 919-5690 • http://www.firn.edu/doe/holocaust

North Miami Beach Public Library • 1601 NE 164th St • North Miami Beach, FL 33162 • (305) 948-2970 • http://www.citynmb.com

North Palm Beach
North Palm Beach Public Library • 303 Anchorage Dr • North Palm Beach, FL 33408 • (561) 841-3383

North Port
North Port Public Library • 13800 S Tamiami Tr • North Port, FL 34287-2030 • (941) 861-1300 • http://suncat.co.sarasota.fl.us

Oacala
Silver River Museum • 1445 NE 58th Ave • Oacala, FL 34470 • (352) 236-5401 • http://www.silverrivermuseum.com

Oakland Park
Oakland Park City Library • 1298 NE 37th St • Oakland Park, FL 33334 • (954) 561-6287 • http://oaklandparkfl.org/library.htm

Oakland Park Historical Society • 3876 NE 6th Ave • Oakland Park, FL 33334 • (954) 566-4284

Ocala
Historic Ocala-Marion County Genealogical Society • 18 SE 14th Ave, P.O. Box 1206 • Ocala, FL 34478-1206

Marion County Historical Society • 801 NE Sanchez Ave • Ocala, FL 34470-5821

Marion Public Library System • 2720 E Silver Springs Blvd • Ocala, FL 34471 • (352) 629-8551 • http://www.marion.lib.fl.us

Ocoee
Withers Maguire House Museum • 16 E Oakland Ave • Ocoee, FL 34761 • (407) 656-2051

Okeechobee
Big Lake Family History Society • P.O. Box 592 • Okeechobee, FL 34973-0592 • (863) 467-5678

Brighton Reservation • Route 6, Box 666 • Okeechobee, FL 33472 • (813) 763-4128

Genealogical Society of Okeechobee • P.O. Box 371 • Okeechobee, FL 33472-0371 • (863) 467-2482

Okeechobee County Historical Society • 55 S Parrott Ave • Okeechobee, FL 34974

Okeechobee County Public Library • 206 SW 16th St • Okeechobee, FL 34972 • (863) 763-3536 • http://www.heartlineweb.org/oke

Seminole Tribe of Florida Library • Route 6, Box 668 • Okeechobee, FL 34974-8912 • (863) 763-4236 • http://www.seminoletribe.com

Olustee
Olustree Battlefield Historic State Park • 3815 Battlefield Tr Rd, P.O. Box 40 • Olustee, FL 32072 • (386) 758-0400 • http://www.floridastateparks.org/olustee/

Orange Park
Mierfeldt Collection • Town of Orange Park, 2042 Park Ave • Orange Park, FL 32043 • (904) 264-9565

Seneca Indian Historical Society • P.O. Box 2313 • Orange Park, FL 32067-2313 • (904) 276-2735 • http://www.wolfclanteachinglodge.org

Orlando
Afro-American Historical and Genealogical Society, Central Florida Chapter • P.O. Box 780872 • Orlando, FL 32878-0872 • (407) 836-8332 • http://www.rootsweb.com/~flcfaahg/

Central Florida Genealogical and Historical Society • P.O. Box 536309 • Orlando, FL 32853-6309 • (407) 628-0584 • http://www.cfgs.org

Orange County Historical Society • Regional History Center, 65 E Central Blvd • Orlando, FL 32801-2401 • (407) 836-8500 • http://www.thehistorycenter.org

Orange County Library System • 101 E Central Blvd • Orlando, FL 32801 • (407) 835-7323 • http://www.ocls.lib.fl.us

Orlando Scottish Heritage Group • P.O. Box 2444 • Orlando, FL 32802 • (407) 977-1394

Scottish American Society of Central Florida • P.O. Box 2948 • Orlando, FL 32802 • (407) 426-7268 • http://www.flascot.com

University of Central Florida Library • 4000 Central Florida Blvd, P.O. Box 162666 • Orlando, FL 32816-2666 • (407) 823-5880 • http://library.ucf.edu/Special

Valencia Community College Library • 701 N Econlockhatchee Trail • Orlando, FL 32825 • (407) 582-2456 • http://eastlrc.valenciacc.edu

Ormond Beach
Halifax Genealogical Society • 30 Beach St, P.O. Box 5081 • Ormond Beach, FL 32175-5081

Ormond Beach Public Library • 30 S Beach St • Ormond Beach, FL 32174 • (386) 676-4191 • http://www.vcpl.lib.fl.us

Ospery
Gulf Coast Heritage Association • Historic Spanish Point, 500 N Tamiami Tr, P.O. Box 846 • Osprey, FL 34229 • (941) 966-5214 • http://www.historicspanishpoint.org

Historic Spanish Point Museum • 337 N Tamiami Tr • Osprey, FL 34229 • (941) 966-5214 • http://www.historicspanishpoint.org

Oviedo
Reformed Theological Seminary Library • 1231 Reformation Dr • Oviedo, FL 32765 • (407) 366-9493 • http://www.rts.edu

Palatka
B C Pearce Learning Resources Center • Saint John's River Community College, 5001 St Johns Ave • Palatka, FL 32177 • (386) 312-4154 • http://www.sjrcc.cc.fl.us/libraries/libhome.htm

David Browning Railroad Museum • 222 N 11th St • Palatka, FL 32177 • (386) 328-0305

Palatka Railroad Preservation Society • 222 N 11th St • Palatka, FL 32177 • (386) 328-0305

Putnam County Genealogical Society • c/o Putnam County Library, 601 College Rd, P.O. Box 2354 • Palatka, FL 32178-2354 • (386) 329-0126

Putnam County Library System • 601 College Rd • Palatka, FL 32177-3873 • (386) 329-0126 • http://www.putnam-fl.com/lib

Putnam County Museum • 110 Madison St • Palatka, FL 32177-3529 • (386) 325-9825

Palm Bay
Palm Bay Campus Library • Brevard Community College, 250 Community College Pkwy • Palm Bay, FL 32909 • (321) 433-5275 • http://www.brevardcc.edu/library

Palm Beach
Henry Morrison Flagler Museum • Whitehall Historic House, Cocoanut Row, P.O. Box 969 • Palm Beach, FL 33480 • (561) 655-2833 • http://www.flaglermuseum.us

Historical Society of Palm Beach County • 139 N County Rd, Ste 25 • Palm Beach, FL 33408 • (561) 832-4164 • http://www.historicalsocietypbc.org

Palm Coast
Flagler County Public Library • 2500 Palm Coast Pkwy NW • Palm Coast, FL 32137 • (904) 466-6763 • http://www.flaglercounty.org

Florida Agricultural Museum • 1850 Princess Place Rd • Palm Coast, FL 32137 • (386) 446-7630 • http://www.flaglerlibrary.org/history/agrimuseum/agri1.htm

Genealogical Society of Flagler County • P.O. Box 35-4671 • Palm Coast, FL 32135-4671 • http://www.flaglerlibrary.org/genealogy/genstart.htm

Palm Harbor
Palm Harbor Historical Society • Historical Museum, 2043 Curlew Rd • Palm Harbor, FL 34683 • (727) 724-3054

Palm Harbor Library • 2330 Nebraska Ave • Palm Harbor, FL 34683 • (727) 784-3332 • http://www.palmharborlibrary.org

Paul Hickey's Genealogy Corner • 68 Lakshore Dr • Palm Harbor, FL 34684 • (813) 934-7388

Suncoast Genealogy Society • P.O. Box 1294 • Palm Harbor, FL 34682-1294 • (813) 785-5167

Palmetto
Palmetto Historical Commission • 515 10th Ave W • Palmetto, FL 34221 • (941) 723-4991 • http://www.manateeclerk.com

South Hillsborough Genealogists • Route 1, Box 400 • Palmetto, FL 33561

Panama City
Bay County Genealogical Society • P.O. Box 662 • Panama City, FL 32401-0662 • (850) 872-9882 • http://www.rootsweb.com/~flbcgs/genealogical.htm

Northwest Regional Library System-Bay County Public Library • 25 W Government St, P.O. Box 59625 • Panama City, FL 32412-0625 • (850) 872-7500 • http://www.nwrls.com

Panama City Beach
Museum of Man in the Sea • 17314 Panama City Beach Pkwy • Panama City Beach, FL 32413-2020 • (850) 235-4101 • http://www.institute ofdiving.com

Parkland
City of Parkland Historical Society • 6500 Parkside Dr • Parkland, FL 33067 • (954) 757-5111

Genealogical Society of Broward County • 6500 Parkside Dr • Parkland, FL 33067 • http://www.rootsweb.com/~flgsbc/library.html

Parrish
Florida Gulf Coast Railroad Museum • US 301, 12210 83rd St E, P.O. Box 355 • Parrish, FL 34219-0355 • (941) 766-0906 • http://www.fgcrrm.org

Patrick AFB
Patrick Air Force Base Library • Bldg 722B, 842 Falcon Ave • Patrick AFB, FL 32925-3439 • (321) 494-6881

TROACC Family History Club • Military Officers Association of America, Cape Canaveral Chapter, P.O. Box 254186 • Patrick AFB, FL 32925-4186 • (321) 255-3561 • http://www.moaacc.org/history.htm

Pensacola
Civil War Soldiers Museum • 108 S Palafox Pl • Pensacola, FL 32501 • (850) 469-1900 • http://www.cwmuseum.org

Dorr House Museum • 311 S Adams St • Pensacola, FL 23051 • (850) 595-5985 • http://www.mscda.org/museums/florida.htm

Escambia County Historical Society • 223 S Palafox Pl • Pensacola, FL 32501-5845

Historic Pensacola Preservation Board of Trustees • Historic Pensacola Village, 120 E Church St • Pensacola, FL 32501 • (850) 595-5985 • http://www.historicpensacola.org

John C Pace Library • Univ of West Florida, 11000 University Dr • Pensacola, FL 32514 • (850) 474-2213 • http://library.uwf.edu/SpecialCollections/

Lelia Abercrombie Historical Resource Center • 110 E Church St • Pensacola, FL 32502 • (850) 434-5455 • http://www.pensacolahistory.org

National Museum of Naval Aviation • 1750 Radford Blvd, Ste C • Pensacola, FL 32508-5402 • (904) 452-3604 • http://www.naval.aviation.museum

Naval Air Station Library • Commanding Officer Sta Libr, Bldg 634, 250 Chambers Ave • Pensacola, FL 32508-5217 • (850) 452-4362

Pensacola Historical Society • Historical Museum, 115 E Zaragosa St • Pensacola, FL 32501 • (850) 433-1559 • http://www.pensacolahistory.org

Perdido Bay Tribe of Lower Muscogee Creeks • 12533 Polonious Pkwy • Pensacola, FL 32506 • http://www.perdidobaytribe.org

Slovenian Genealogical Society, Florida Chapter • 7605 Harvey St • Pensacola, FL 32506-5022 • http://sloveniangenealogy.org/chapters/Florida.htm

T T Wentworth Florida State Museum • 330 S Jefferson St • Pensacola, FL 32502 • (850) 595-5985 • http://www.historicpensacola.org

West Florida Genealogical Society • P.O. Box 947 • Pensacola, FL 32594-0947 • (850) 623-2928 • http://www.rootsweb.com/~flescamb/wfgs2.htm

West Florida Regional Library • 200 W Gregory St • Pensacola, FL 32501-4878 • (850) 436-5060 • http://www.wfrl.lib.fl.us

Pensacola Beach
Grand Lodge of Florida, Sons of Italy • 1201 Ariola Dr • Pensacola Beach, FL 32561 • (850) 932-8628 • http://www.osiafl.org

Perry
Forest Capital State Museum • S US Hwy 19 & 204 Forest Park Dr • Perry, FL 32348 • (850) 584-3227 • http://www.myflorida.com

Perry Historical Society • 118 E Main St • Perry, FL 32347 • (850) 584-4478

Pine Island Center
Museum of the Islands • 5728 Sesame • Pine Island Center, FL 33956 • (239) 283-1525 • http://www.museumoftheislands.com

Pinellas Park
American Council for Polish Culture • 6507 107th Terr • Pinellas Park, FL 34666-2432 • (703) 536-7085

Florida Society for Genealogical Research • 8461 54th St N • Pinellas Park, FL 33780 • (727) 391-2914

Pinellas Park Historical Society • 5851 Park Blvd • Pinellas Park, FL 33781 • (727) 546-7060

Pinellas Park Public Library • 7770 52nd St • Pinellas Park, FL 34665-3498 • (813) 541-0718 • http://pppl.tblc.lib.fl.us

Tampa Bay Automobile Museum • 3301 Gateway Centre Blvd • Pinellas Park, FL 33782 • (727) 579-8226 • http://www.tbauto.org

Placida
Boca Grande Historical Society • general delivery • Placida, FL 33946 • (941) 964-1600

Plant City
East Hillsborough Historical Society • Quintilla Geer Bruton Archives Center, 605 N Collins St, P.O. Box 1418 • Plant City, FL 33566-3321 • (813) 754-7031 • http://www.rootsweb.com/~flqgbac/ehhs.html

Florida

Plant City, cont.

Plant City Photo Archives • 119 N Collins St, P.O. Box 1118 • Plant City, FL 33564 • (813) 754-1578 • http://www.plantcityphotoarchives. org

Quintilla Geer Bruton Memorial Library • 302 McLendon St • Plant City, FL 33566 • (813) 757-9215 • http://www.hcplc.org/hcplc/bru/

Plantation

Helen B Hoffman-Plantation Library • 501 N Fig Tree Lane • Plantation, FL 33317 • (954) 797-2140

Plantation Historical Museum • 511 N Fig Tree Ln • Plantation, FL 33317 • (954) 797-2722

Pompano Beach

Pompano Beach Historical Society • 220 NE 3rd Ave • Pompano Beach, FL 33060 • (954) 782-3015

Ponce Inlet

Ponce De Leon Inlet Lighthouse Museum • 4931 S Peninsula Dr • Ponce Inlet, FL 32127 • (386) 761-1821 • http://www.ponceinlet.org

Ponte Vedra

Jacksonville Jewish Genealogical Society • 2710 Strasbourg Ct • Ponte Vedra, FL 32082 • (904) 285-4626

Ponte Vedra Beach

Ponte Vedra Historical Society • 101 Library Blvd • Ponte Vedra Beach, FL 32082

Port Charlotte

Alliance of Genealogical Society of Southwest Florida • P.O. Box 494707 • Port Charlotte, FL 33949-4707 • http://www.rootsweb. com/~flagsswf

Charlotte County Genealogical Society • P.O. Box 494707 • Port Charlotte, FL 33949-2682 • (941) 624-0098

Charlotte Glades Library System • 2050 Forrest Nelson Blvd • Port Charlotte, FL 33952-2128 • (941) 743-1460 • http://www. charlottecountyfl.com/library/library.htm

Charlotte Glades Library-Port Charlotte • 2280 Aaron St • Port Charlotte, FL 33952 • (941) 625-6470

Cornish American Heritage Society • 3438 Pennyroyal Rd • Port Charlotte, FL 33953

Port Charlotte Public Library • 2280 Aaron St • Port Charlotte, FL 33952 • (941) 625-6470

Port Richey

West Pasco County Genealogical Society • P.O. Box 1142 • Port Richey, FL 34673-1142 • (727) 848-0112 • http://homepages.rootsweb. com/~wpcgs/wpsgmember.htm

Port Saint Joe

Constitution Convention Museum State Park • 200 Allen Memorial Wy • Port Saint Joe, FL 32456 • (850) 229-8029 • http://www. floridastateparks.org/constitutionconvention/

Gulf County Genealogical Society • P.O. Box 541 • Port Saint Joe, FL 32457 • http://www.chigeechugee.com/gulfcounty/gcgsfl.html

Punta Gorda

Charlotte Glades Library System-Punta Gorda • 424 W Henry St • Punta Gorda, FL 33950 • (941) 639-2049

Florida Chapter, Ohio Genealogical Society • 15500 Burnt Store Rd #46 • Punta Gorda, FL 33955-9336 • (386) 755-7229 • http://www.ogs. org/chap.htm

Mayflower Society of Florida • general delivery • Punta Gorda, FL 33950 • http://www.flmayflower.com

Military Heritage Museum • 1200 W Retta Esplanade #48 • Punta Gorda, FL 33950 • (941) 575-9002 • http://www.freedomisntfree.org

Quincy

Gadsden County Historical Society • P.O. Box 231 • Quincy, FL 32351-0231

Riviera Beach

Riviera Beach Public Library • 600 W Blue Heron Blvd, P.O. Box 10682 • Riviera Beach, FL 33419-1329 • (561) 845-4195 • http://www. cityofrivierabeach.gov/

Safety Harbor

Safety Harbor Museum of Regional History • 329 Bayshore Blvd S • Safety Harbor, FL 35695 • (727) 726-1668 • http://www.safety-harbor-museum.org

Safety Harbor Public Library • 101 2nd St N • Safety Harbor, FL 34695 • (727) 724-1525 • http://www.tblc.org/shpl/

Saint Augustine

Castillo de San Marcos National Monument Museum • 1 S Castillo Dr • Saint Augustine, FL 32084 • (904) 829-6506 • http://www.nps.gov/casa

Colonial Spanish Quarter Museum • 29 St George St, P.O. Box 210 • Saint Augustine, FL 32085-1002 • (904) 825-6830 • http://www. historicstaugustine.com

Doctor Peck House Museum • 143 Saint George St • Saint Augustine, FL 32084 • (904) 829-5064

Florida Heritage Museum • 167 San Marco Ave • Saint Augustine, FL 32084 • (904) 829-3800

Fort Matanzas National Monument Museum • 8635 A1A South • Saint Augustine, FL 32080 • (904) 471-0116 • http://www.nps.gov

Historic Saint Augustine Preservation Board • Government House, P.O. Drawer 210 • Saint Augustine, FL 32085-0210 • (904) 824-5033

Lightner Museum • City Hall, 75 King St, P.O. Box 334 • Saint Augustine, FL 32084 • (904) 824-2874 • http://www.lightnermuseum. org

Los Floridanos Society • P.O. Box 4043 • Saint Augustine, FL 32085 • (904) 632-1811

Menorcan Cultural Society • P.O. Box 3565 • Saint Augustine, FL 32085-3565 • http://www.menorcansociety.net

Mission of Nombre De Dios and La Leche Shrine Museum • 27 Ocean Ave • Saint Augustine, FL 32084 • (904) 824-2809

Old Florida Museum • 254 D San Marco Ave • Saint Augustine, FL 32084 • (800) 813-3208

Oldest House Museum • 271 Charlotte St • Saint Augustine, FL 32084 • (904) 824-2872 • http://www.oldesthouse.org

Oldest Store Museum • 4 Artillery Ln • Saint Augustine, FL 32084 • (904) 829-9729

Pena-Peck House Museum • 143 St George St • Saint Augustine, FL 32084 • (904) 829-5064

Saint Augustine Genealogical Society • c/o Saint Johns County Public Library, 1960 N Ponce de Leon Blvd • Saint Augustine, FL 32084 • (904) 823-2650 • http://www.staugens.com

Saint Augustine Historical Society • Historical Museum, 271 Charlotte St • Saint Augustine, FL 32084-5033 • (904) 824-2872 • http://www. oldesthouse.com; www.staugustinehistoricalsociety.org

Saint Augustine Lighthouse Museum • 81 Lighthouse Ave • Saint Augustine, FL 32080 • (904) 829-0745 • http://www. staugustinelighthouse.com

Saint Johns County Public Library • 1960 N Ponce de Leon Blvd • Saint Augustine, FL 32084 • (904) 823-2650 • http://www.sjcpls.org

Saint Photios Greek Orthodox National Shrine Museum • 41 St George St, P.O. Box 1960 • Saint Augustine, FL 32085 • (904) 829-8205 • http://www.stphotios.com

Ximenez-Fatio House Museum • 20 Aviles St • Saint Augustine, FL 32084 • (904) 829-3575 • http://www.simenezfatiohouse.org

Saint Cloud
Genealogy Club of Osceola County • P. O. Box 701295 • Saint Cloud, FL 34771-1295 • (407) 957-4347 • http://www.rootsweb.com/~flosceol/oseeola.htm

Osceola County Department of Genealogical Research • 326 Eastern Ave • Saint Cloud, FL 32769

Saint Marks
San Marcos de Apalache Historic State Park • 148 Old Fort Rd • Saint Marks, FL 32355 • (850) 922-6007 • http://www.floridastateparks.org

Saint Petersburg
Florida Holocaust Museum • 55 5th St S • Saint Petersburg, FL 33701 • (727) 820-0100 • http://www.flholocaustmuseum.org

Saint Petersburg Historical Society • 335 2nd Ave NE • Saint Petersburg, FL 33701 • (727) 894-1052

Saint Petersburg Museum of History • 335 2nd Ave NE • Saint Petersburg, FL 33701-3501 • (727) 894-1052 • http://www.stpetemuseumofhistory.org

Saint Petersburg Public Library • 3745 9th Ave N • Saint Petersburg, FL 33713 • (727) 893-7724 • http://st-petersburg-library.org

Sanford
Museum of Seminole County History • 300 Bush Blvd • Sanford, FL 32773 • (407) 665-2489 • http://www.seminolecountyfl.gov

Sanford Museum • 520 E 1st St, P.O. Box 1788 • Sanford, FL 32772-1788 • (407) 302-1000 • http://ci.sanford.fl.us

Seminole County Historical Society • P.O. Box 409 • Sanford, FL 32772-0409

Seminole County Public Library System • 1101 E 1st St • Sanford, FL 32771 • (407) 330-3737

Sanibel
Sanibel Public Library • 770 Dunlop Rd • Sanibel, FL 33957 • (239) 472-2483 • http://www.sanlib.org

Sarasota
Crowley Museum • 16405 Myakka Rd • Sarasota, FL 34240 • (941) 322-1000 • http://www.crowleymuseumnaturectr.org

Genealogical Society of Sarasota • P.O. Box 1917 • Sarasota, FL 34230-1917 • (941) 923-7791 • http://www.rootsweb.com/~flgss/

Historical Society of Sarasota County • 900 S Euclid Ave • Sarasota, FL 33577 • (941) 364-9076

International Genealogy Fellowship of Rotarians • 5721 Antietam Dr • Sarasota, FL 34231-4903 • (941) 924-9170

Jewish Genealogical Society of Southwest Florida • 4462 Violet Ave • Sarasota, FL 34233-1825 • (941) 921-1433 • http://www.jgsswf.org

Sarasota County Archives • 701 Pl de San Dominic • Sarasota, FL 34236

Sarasota County Courthouse Archives • 2000 Main St • Sarasota, FL 34237

Sarasota County Department of Historical Resources Archives • History Center, 6062 Porter Wy • Sarasota, FL 34232 • (941) 861-1188 • http://www.scgov.net

Selby Public Library • 1331 1st St • Sarasota, FL 34236-4899 • (941) 861-1120 • http://suncat.co.sarasota.fl.us

Satellite Beach
Satellite Beach Public Library • 751 Jamaica Blvd • Satellite Beach, FL 32937 • (321) 779-4004 • http://www.brev.org

Sebastian
North Indian River County Library • 1001 Sebastian Blvd, CR 512 • Sebastian, FL 32958 • (772) 589-1355 • http://www.sebastianlibrary.com

Sebastian Area Historical Society • Historical Museum, 1235 Main St, P.O. Box 781348 • Sebastian, FL 32978-1348 • (772) 581-1380

Sebring
Highlands County Genealogial Society • c/o Sebring Public Library, 319 W Center Ave • Sebring, FL 33870 • http://www.heartlineweb.org/hcgs/

Highlands County Historical Society • 430 S Commerce Ave • Sebring, FL 33870

Highlands County Public Library System • 319 W Center Ave • Sebring, FL 33870 • (863) 386-6716 • http://www.heartlineweb.org

Sebring Historical Society • 321 W Center Ave, P.O. Box 3313 • Sebring, FL 33870 • (863) 471-2522 • http://www.sebringhistoricalsociety.org

Seminole
Florida Society of Genealogical Research • 8415 122nd St N • Seminole, FL 34642

Starke
Bradford County Historical Board of Trustees • W Call & Court Sts, P.O. Drawer A • Starke, FL 32091 • (904) 964-6305

Bradford County Public Library • 105 E Jackson St • Starke, FL 32091 • (904) 964-6400 • http://www.bradford-co-fla.org/departments/library

Camp Blanding Museum • Camp Blanding, 5629 SR 16 W Bld 3040 • Starke, FL 32091 • (904) 682-3196 • http://www.campblanding-museum.org

Stuart
Elliott Museum • 825 NE Ocean Blvd • Stuart, FL 34996 • (772) 225-1961 • http://www.elliottmuseumfl.org

Historical Society of Martin County • Elliott Museum, 825 NE Ocean Blvd • Stuart, FL 34996-1696 • (772) 225-1961 • http://www.elliottmuseumfl.org

House of Refuge Museum • 301 SE MacArthur Blvd • Stuart, FL 34996 • (772) 225-1875 • http://www.houseofrefugefl.org

Maritime and Yachting Museum of the Treasure Coast • 3250 SW Kanner Hwy • Stuart, FL 34994 • (772) 692-1234 • http://www.mymflorida.org

Martin County Genealogical Society • c/o Martin County Public Library, 701 E Ocean Blvd, P.O. Box 275 • Stuart, FL 34995 • (772) 221-1408 • http://www.rootsweb.com/~flmcgs

Martin County Library System • 2351 SE Monterey Rd • Stuart, FL 34996 • (772) 221-1413 • http://www.library.martin.fl.us

Martin County Public Library • 2351 SE Monterey Rd, Stuart, FL 34996 • Stuart, FL 34996 • (772) 288-5702

Stuart Heritage Museum • 161 SW Flagler Ave • Stuart, FL 34994 • (772) 220-4600

Sun City Center
South Bay Genealogy Club • P.O. Box 5202 • Sun City Center, FL 33571

Surfside
Surf-Bal-Bay Library • 9301 Collins Ave • Surfside, FL 33154 • (305) 865-2409 • http://town.surfside.fl.us

Surf-Bal-Bay Library • 9301 Collins Ave • Surfside, FL 33154 • (305) 865-2409

Florida

Tallahassee

Black Archives Research Center and Museum • Florida A&M Univ, 219 Apalachee Pkwy, P.O. Box 809 • Tallahassee, FL 32307 • (850) 599-3020 • http://www.famu.edu/acad/archives/

Black Resources Information Coordinating Services • 614 Howard Ave, Ste 125-9 • Tallahassee, FL 32301 • (850) 576-7522

Bureau of Historic Preservation • Museum of Florida History, 500 S Bronough St, State Capitol Bldg • Tallahassee, FL 32301 • (850) 245-6400 • http://www.dos.state.fl.us/dhr/museum/c_r.html

Carrie Meeks - James N Eaton Southeastern Regional Black Archives • Florida A&M Univ, 445 Gamble St • Tallahassee, FL 32307 • (850) 599-3020 • http://www.cis.famu.edu/BlackArchives/expventures.html

Florida Folklife Collection Museum • 500 S Bronough St • Tallahassee, FL 32399-0250 • http://www.floridamemory.com/Collections/folklife

Florida History Associates • Museum of Florida History, 500 S Bronough St • Tallahassee, FL 32399-0250 • (850) 245-6400 • http://www.dos.state.fl.us/dhr/museum/c_r.html

Florida State Archives • R A Gray Bldg, 500 S Bronough St • Tallahassee, FL 32399-0250 • (850) 245-6600 • http://www.dos.state.fl.us/dlis/barm/archives.html

Florida State Genealogical Society • P.O. Box 10249 • Tallahassee, FL 32302-2249 • (321) 733-5566 • http://www.rootsweb.com/~flsgs/

Florida State Library • Museum of History, 500 S Bronough St • Tallahassee, FL 32399-0250 • (850) 487-2651 • http://www.dos.state.fl.us/sos/divisions/dlis/dlis.html

Florida Supreme Court Historical Society • 500 S Duval St, P.O. Box 11344 • Tallahassee, FL 32302 • (850) 222-3703

Goodwood Plantation Museum • 1600 Miccosukee Rd • Tallahassee, FL 32308 • (850) 877-4202

Institute on World War II and the Human Experience • Florida State University, Department of History, Bellamy Bldg • Tallahassee, FL 32306-2200 • (850) 644-9033 • http://www.fsu.edu/~ww2

Jewish Genealogical Society of Tallahassee • 215 Hayden Rd #124 • Tallahassee, FL 32304 • (850) 385-3323 • http://www.jgst.org/

Knott House Museum • 301 E Park Ave • Tallahassee, FL 32301 • (850) 922-2459 • http://wwwflheritage.com/museum/sites/knotthouse

Leon County Public Library System • 200 W Park Ave • Tallahassee, FL 32301-7720 • (850) 487-2665 • http://www.co.leon.fl.us/library

Mission San Luis de Apalachee Museum • 2020 W Mission Rd • Tallahassee, FL 32304-1624 • (850) 487-3711 • http://www.missionsanluis.org

Museum of Florida History • 500 S Bronough St • Tallahassee, FL 32399 • (850) 245-6400 • http://dhr.dos.state.fl.us/museum

Museum of Florida History • R A Gray Bldg, 500 S Bronough St • Tallahassee, FL 32399-0250 • (850) 245-6400 • http://www.museumoffloridahistory.com

Riley House Museum of African American History • 419 E Jefferson St, P.O. Box 4261 • Tallahassee, FL 32301 • (850) 681-7881 • http://www.rileymuseum.org

Robert Manning Strozier Library • Florida State Univ, 105 Dogwood Way • Tallahassee, FL 32306-2047 • (850) 644-2706 • http://www.fsu.edu/~library/

Tallahassee Genealogical Society • P.O. Box 4371 • Tallahassee, FL 32315-4371 • (386) 878-2900 • http://www.rootsweb.com/~fltgs/

Tallahassee Genealogical Society, Computer Interest Group • P.O. Box 4371 • Tallahassee, FL 32315-4371 • (386) 878-2900 • http://www.freenet.tlh.fl.us/~tgs567

Tallahassee Historical Society • Florida State Univ, History Dep, 401 Bellamy Bldg, P.O. Box 3062200 • Tallahassee, FL 32306 • (850) 644-9524 • http://www.fsu.edu

Tallahassee Museum of History • 3945 Museum Dr • Tallahassee, FL 32310-6325 • (850) 575-8684 • http://www.tallahasseemuseum.org

Tampa

Cracker Country Archives • 4800 N Hwy 301, P.O. Box 11766 • Tampa, FL 33680 • (813) 627-4225 • http://www.crackercountry.org

Florida Genealogical Society • P.O. Box 18624 • Tampa, FL 33679-8624 • (305) 679-8624

Florida Genealogical Society of Tampa • P.O. Box 18624 • Tampa, FL 33679-8624 • http://www.rootsweb.com/~flfgs

Florida State Department of the Historic Preservation Board • 1802 E 9th Ave • Tampa, FL 33605 • (813) 272-3843

Henry B Plant Museum • 401 W Kennedy Blvd • Tampa, FL 33606 • (813) 258-7301 • http://www.plantmuseum.com

Hillsborough County Historical Museum • 3705 W San Rafael St • Tampa, FL 33629-5124

Noble Society of Celts • 1 Laurel Pl #709 • Tampa, FL 33602 • (859) 608-9288 • http://www.noblesocietyofcelts.org

Office of Vital Statistics, Hillsborough County Health Dept • P.O. Box 5735 • Tampa, FL 33675-5135 • (813) 272-6931

Order of Quetzalcoatl • International Shrine Headquarters, 2900 Rocky Point Dr • Tampa, FL 33607-1460 • (813) 281-0300 • http://www.shrinershq.org; http://quetzalcoatl.org

Order of the Daughters of the Nile • International Shrine Headquarters, 2900 Rocky Point Dr • Tampa, FL 33607-1460 • (813) 281-0300 • http://www.shringershq.org; http://www.daughtersofthenile.com

Providence Historical Society Library • 12712 DuPont Cr • Tampa, FL 33626 • (813) 855-4636

Tampa Bay History Center • 225 S Franklin St, P.O. Box 948 • Tampa, FL 33601 • (813) 228-0097 • http://www.tampabayhistorycenter.org

Tampa Bay Library Consortium • 1202 Tech Blvd, Ste 202 • Tampa, FL 33619-7864 • (813) 622-8252 • http://tblc.org

Tampa Campus Library - Special Collections • University of South Florida, 4202 E Fowler Ave • Tampa, FL 33620-5400 • (813) 974-2729 • http://www.lib.usf.edu/spccoll/genea.html

Tampa Historical Society • 245 S Hyde Park Ave • Tampa, FL 33606 • (813) 259-1111

Tampa Public Library - History and Genealogy Dept • 900 N Ashley St • Tampa, FL 33602-3704 • (813) 273-3628 • http://www.hcplc.org

Univ of South Florida Library • 4202 E Fowler Ave • Tampa, FL 33620-5400 • (813) 974-2731 • http://www.lib.usf.edu/spccoll/genea.html

Ybor City Museum • 2009 N 18th St, P.O. Box 5421 • Tampa, FL 33675 • (813) 247-6323 • http://www.ybormuseum.org

Tampa Bay

Hillsborough County Historical Commission • Tampa Bay History Center, 225 S Franklin St • Tampa Bay, FL 33602 • (813) 228-0097 • http://www.tampabayhistorycenter.org

Tarpon Springs

Safford Historic House Museum • 23 Parken Ct • Tarpon Springs, FL 34689 • (727) 937-1130

Tarpon Springs Area Historical Society • Depot Museum, 160 E Tarpon Ave • Tarpon Springs, FL 34689 • (727) 943-4624

Tarpon Springs Cultural Center • 101 S Pinellas Ave • Tarpon Springs, FL 34689 • (727) 942-5605

Tarpon Springs Heritage Museum • 100 Beekman Ln • Tarpon Springs, FL 34689 • (727) 937-0686 • http://www.ci.tarpon-springs.fl.us/tourtarpon

Tarpon Springs Public Library • 138 E Lemon St • Tarpon Springs, FL 34689 • (727) 943-4922 • http://www.tblc.org/tarpon/

Tavares
Lake County Historical Society • Historical Museum, 317 W Main, P.O. Box 7800 • Tavares, FL 32778 • (352) 343-9890

Lake County Library System • 312 W Main St, P.O. Box 7800 • Tavares, FL 32778 • (352) -253-6180 • http://www.lakeline.lib.fl.us

Tavares Public Library • 314 N New Hampshire Ave • Tavares, FL 32778 • (352) 742-6204 • http://www.tavares.org/library.html

Titusville
American Police Hall of Fame Museum • 6350 Horizon Dr • Titusville, FL 32780 • (321) 264-0911 • http://www.aphf.org

Genealogical Society of North Brevard • P.O. Box 897 • Titusville, FL 32781-0897 • (321) 752-7881 • http://www.nbbd.com/npr/gsnb/

Historical Society of North Brevard • Historical Museum, 301 S Washington Ave, P.O. Box 6199 • Titusville, FL 37282-6199 • (321) 269-5199 • http://www.nbbd.com

International Society of the Descendants of Charlemagne • 3960 Barcelona St, P.O. Box 5259 • Titusville, FL 32783 • (321) 267-0351

North Brevard Historical Society • Historical Museum, 301 S Washington Ave, P.O. Box 6199 • Titusville, FL 32782-6199 • (321) 269-3658 • http://www.nbbd.com/godo/history/

North Brevard Public Library • 2121 S Hopkins Ave • Titusville, FL 32780 • (321) 264-5026 • http://www.brev.org

Titusville Campus Library • Brevard Community College, Resource Ctr, 1311 N US 1 • Titusville, FL 32796-2192 • (321) 632-1111 • http://www.brevard.cc.edu/library

Valiant Air Command Warbird Air Museum • 6600 Tico Rd • Titusville, FL 32780 • (321) 268-1941 • http://www.vacwarbirds.org

Trenton
Gilchrist County Genealogical Society • 105 NE 11th Ave • Trenton, FL 32693

Tyndall AFB
Tyndall Air Force Base Library FL4819 • 325 SVS/SVMG/45, 640 Suwanee Rd, Bldg 916 • Tyndall AFB, FL 32403 • (850) 283-4287

Valparaiso
Heritage Museum of Northwest Florida • 115 Westview Ave, P.O. Box 488 • Valparaiso, FL 32580-0488 • (850) 678-2615 • http://heritage-museum.org

Historical Society of Okaloosa and Walton Counties • Historical Museum, 115 Westview Ave, P.O. Box 488 • Valparaiso, FL 32580-0488 • (850) 678-2615 • http://www.heritage-museum.org

Valparaiso Community Library • 459 Valparaiso Pkwy • Valparaiso, FL 32580 • (850) 729-5406 • http://vcl.valp.org

Valrico
Afro-American Historical and Genealogical Society • P.O. Box 1182 • Valrico, FL 33595 • http://www.aahgs.org

Brandon Area Genealogical and Historical Society • P.O. Box 2635 • Valrico, FL 33595 • http://www.rootsweb.com/~flbaghs

Venice
Genealogical Society of Sarasota • 944 Nokomis Ave S • Venice, FL 34285

Venice Archives and Area Historical Collection • 351 S Nassau St • Venice, FL 34285 • (941) 486-2487 • http://www.venice-florida.com/community/archive.htm

Venice Archives and Historical Society • 351 Nassau St S • Venice, FL 34285-2403 • (941) 486-2487

Vero Beach
Heritage Center and Citrus Museum • 2145 14th Ave • Vero Beach, FL 32960 • (772) 770-2263 • http://www.veroheritage.org

Indian River County Historical Society • Railroad Station, 2336 14th Ave, P.O. Box 6535 • Vero Beach, FL 32961 • (772) 778-3435

Indian River County Library • 1600 21st St • Vero Beach, FL 32960 • (561) 770-5060 • http://indian-river.lib.fl.us

Indian River Genealogical Society • c/o Indian River County Library, 1600 21st St, P.O. Box 1850 • Vero Beach, FL 32961-1850 • (561) 589-4290 • http://www.rootsweb.com/~flindigs/

Laura Riding Jackson Home Preservation Foundation • 1937 Old Dixie Hwy • Vero Beach, FL 32960 • (772) 569-6718

McLarty Treasure Museum • 13180 Hwy A1A • Vero Beach, FL 32962-9400 • (772) 589-2147 • http://www.myflorida.com

Weirsdale
Florida Carriage Museum • 3000 Marion County Rd • Weirsdale, FL 32195 • (352) 750-5500 • http://www.austincarriagemuseum.com

Welaka
Women's Club of Welaka Library • Hwy 309, P.O. Box 154 • Welaka, FL 32193-0154 • (386) 467-9706

West Palm Beach
Florida Historical Society • 514 Datura St • West Palm Beach, FL 33401 • (561) 802-3938

Historical Society of Palm Beach County • 400 N Dixie Hwy • West Palm Beach, FL 33401-4210 • (561) 832-4164 • http://www.gopbi.com/community/groups/pbehistory/

Palm Beach County Genealogical Society • c/o West Palm Beach Library, 100 Clematis St, P.O. Box 1746 • West Palm Beach, FL 33402-1746 • (561) 832-3279 • http://www.pbcgensoc.org

Palm Beach County Public Library System • 3650 Summit Blvd • West Palm Beach, FL 33406 • (561) 233-2600 • http://www.pbclibrary.org

Temple Israel Library of Judaica • 1901 N Flagler Dr • West Palm Beach, FL 33407 • (561) 833-8421 • http://www.temple-israel.com

West Palm Beach Public Library • 100 Clematis St • West Palm Beach, FL 33402 • (561) 868-7700 • http://www.wpbpl.com

Yesteryear Village Museum • 9067 Southern Blvd, P.O. Box 210367 • West Palm Beach, FL 33421 • (561) 793-0333 • http://www.southfloridafair.com/yesteryearvillage.html

White Springs
Stephen Foster Folk Center Museum • P.O. Drawer G • White Springs, FL 32096 • (386) 397-2733 • http://www.floridastateparks.org

Wilton Manors
Wilton Manors Public Library • 500 NE 26th St • Wilton Manors, FL 33305 • (954) 390-2195

Winter Garden
Central Florida Railroad Museum • 101 S Boyd St • Winter Garden, FL 34787 • (407) 656-0559

Winter Garden Heritage Museum • 1 N Main St • Winter Garden, FL 34787 • (407) 656-3244 • http://www.wghf.org

Winter Haven
James W Dowdy Memorial Library • Polk Community College, 999 Avenue H NE • Winter Haven, FL 33881-4299 • (863) 297-5326 • http://www.polk.edu

Winter Park
Hannibal Square Heritage Center • 642 W New England Ave • Winter Park, FL 32789 • (407) 539-2680 • http://www.crealde.org

Florida

Winter Park, cont.

Olin Library • Rollins College, 1000 Holt Ave, Campus Box 2744 • Winter Park, FL 32789 • (407) 646-2507 • http://www.rollins.edu/olin/

Winter Park Historical Association • Historical Museum, 200 W New England Ave, P.O. Box 51 • Winter Park, FL 32790 • (407) 547-8180 • http://www.winterparkhistorical.com

Winter Park Public Library • 460 E New England Ave • Winter Park, FL 32789-4493 • (407) 623-3300 • http://www.wppl.org

Winter Springs

Jewish Special Interest Group • 1601 Cougar Ct • Winter Springs, FL 32708-3855

Zellwood

Zellwood Historical Society • Historical Museum, 3160 Union St • Zellwood, FL 32798 • (407) 884-6222

Zephyrhills

Zephyrhills Depot Museum • 39110 South Ave • Zephyrhills, FL 33542 • (813) 780-0067 • http://www.ci.zephyrhills.fl.us

Zephyrhills Public Library • 5347 8th St • Zephyrhills, FL 34248 • (813) 780-0064 • http://www.ci.zephyrhills.fl.us

Zolfo Springs

Cracker Trail Museum • 2822 Museum Dr • Zolfo Springs, FL 33890 • (863) 735-0119

Abbeville

Ocmulgee Regional Library System-Wilcox County • Courthouse Sq, 104 N Broad St • Abbeville, GA 31001 • (229) 467-2075 • http://www.orls.org

Acworth

Acworth Society for Historic Preservation • P.O. Box 851 • Acworth, GA 30101 • (770) 975-1930

Adairsville

Bartow County Public Library System-Adairsville Branch • 202 N Main St • Adairsville, GA 30103 • (770) 769-9200

San Souci Club • P.O. Box 167 • Adairsville, GA 30103 • (770) 773-3281

Adel

Cook County Historical Society • P.O. Box 497 • Adel, GA 31620 • (229) 549-8241

Alamo

Ocmulgee Regional Library System-Wheeler County • 315 W Main St, P.O. Box 428 • Alamo, GA 30411 • (912) 568-7321 • http://www.orls.org

Albany

Albany Civil Rights Movement Museum • 326 Whitney Ave, P.O. Box 6036 • Albany, GA 31706 • (229) 432-1698 • http://www.albanycivilrights.org

American Cherokee Confederacy • 619 Pine Cone Rd • Albany, GA 31705 • (229) 787-5722

Dougherty County Public Library • 300 Pine Ave • Albany, GA 31701-2533 • (229) 420-3200 • http://www.docolib.org

Historic Albany • 100 W Roosevelt Ave • Albany, GA 31701 • (229) 432-6955 • http://www.heritagecenter.org

Southwest Georgia Genealogical Society • c/o Doughterty County Library, 300 Pine St, P.O. Box 4672 • Albany, GA 31706-4672 • (229) 435-9659 • http://www.swggs.org

Thronateeska Heritage Foundation • Heritage Museum, 100 Roosevelt Ave • Albany, GA 31701-2325 • (229) 432-6955 • http://www.heritagecenter.org

Alma

Historical Society of Alma-Bacon County • 406 Mercer St, P.O. Box 2026 • Alma, GA 31510 • (912) 632-8450

Alpharetta

Alpharetta Historical Society • Mansell House & Gardens, 1835 Old Milton Pkwy • Alpharetta, GA 30004 • (770) 475-4663 • http://www.ahsga.org

Sons of the American Revolution, Georgia Society • 12460 Crabapple Rd, Ste 202 • Alpharetta, GA 30004 • http://www.georgiasocietysar.org

Americus

Lake Blackshear Regional Library • 307 E Lamar St • Americus, GA 31709-3699 • (229) 924-8091 • http://www.lbrl.org

Sumter Historic Trust • 318 E Church St, P.O. Box 961 • Americus, GA 31709 • (229) 924-9051

Young Historians of Sumter County High School • 101 Industrial Blvd • Americus, GA 31709 • (229) 924-5914

Andersonville

Andersonville National Historic Site Museum • National POW Museum, 496 Cemetery Rd • Andersonville, GA 31711 • (229) 924-0343 • http://www.nps.gov/ande/

Andersonville

National Society of Andersonville • 305 Ellaville St, P.O. Box 65 • Andersonville, GA 31711 • (229) 924-2558

Appling

Columbia County Historical Society • P.O. Box 203 • Appling, GA 30802 • (770) 556-6629

Aragon

Aragon Historical Society • P.O. Box 333 • Aragon, GA 30104 • (770) 684-3771 • http://www.cityofaragon.com/historicalsociety.htm

Athens

Athens Historical Society • P.O. Box 7745 • Athens, GA 30604-7745 • (706) 548-6325 • http://www.rootsweb.com/~gaahs

Athens Regional Library • 2025 Baxter St • Athens, GA 30606 • (706) 613-3650 • http://www.clarke.public.lib.ga.us

Athens-Clarke Heritage Foundation • Fire Hall No. 2, 489 Prince Ave • Athens, GA 30601 • (706) 353-1801 • http://www.achfonline.org

Church-Waddel-Brumby House Museum • 280 E Dougherty St • Athens, GA 30601 • (706) 353-1820 • http://www.athenswelcomecenter.com

Clarke-Oconee Genealogical Society of Athens • P.O. Box 6403 • Athens, GA 30604 • (706) 543-6065 • http://www.rootsweb.com/~gacogs/

Hargrett Library - Rare Book and Manuscripts • Univ of Georgia • Athens, GA 30602 • (706) 542-8460 • http://www.libs.uga.edu/hargrett/speccoll.html

Old Athens Cemetery Foundation • 145 Pendleton Dr • Athens, GA 30606 • http://www.cviog.uga.edu

Richard B Russell Library • Univ of Georgia • Athens, GA 30602-1642 • (706) 542-5788 • http://www.libs.uga.edu/russell/

Society for Georgia Archaeology • P.O. Box 693 • Athens, GA 30603 • http://www.georgia-archaeology.org

Society of Georgia Archivists • Richard R Russell Library, P.O. Box 133085 • Athens, GA 30333 • (706) 542-5788 • http://www.soga.org

Southern Historical Association • Dept of History, Univ of Georgia, LeCone Hall, Rm 111A • Athens, GA 30602 • (706) 542-8848 • http://www.uga.edu/~sha

Taylor-Grady House Museum • 634 Prince Ave • Athens, GA 30601 • (706) 549-8688

US Navy Supply Corps School Station Museum • 1425 Prince Ave, Code 0333 • Athens, GA 30606-2205 • (706) 354-7349 • http://www.nscs.navy.mil

Atlanta

African-American Family History Association • C 2077 Bent Creek Wy SW, P.O. Box 115268 • Atlanta, GA 30310-8268 • (404) 730-1942

Afro-American Historical and Genealogical Society, Metro Atlanta Chapter • P.O. Box 54063 • Atlanta, GA 30308 • http://www.rootsweb.com/~gaahgs

Ansley Park Civic Association • P.O. Box 7775, Sta C • Atlanta, GA 30357 • http://www.ansleypark.org

Apex Museum • 135 Auburn Ave NE • Atlanta, GA 30303 • (404) 523-2739 • http://www.apexmuseum.org

Atlanta Cyclorama Museum • 800-C Cherokee Ave SE • Atlanta, GA 30315 • (404) 658-7625 • http://www.ci.atlanta.ga.us/ditydir/prca/cultural/cycl.htm

Atlanta Historical Society • History Center, 130 W Paces Ferry Rd N.W, P.O. Box 12423 • Atlanta, GA 30355 • (404) 814-4085 • http://www.atlantahistorycenter.com

Atlanta-Fulton Public Library • 1 Margaret Mitchell Square NW • Atlanta, GA 30303-1089 • (404) 730-1700 • http://www.af.public.lib.ga.us/central/gagen/

Georgia

Atlanta, cont.

Auburn Ave Library on African-American Culture • 101 Auburn Ave NE • Atlanta, GA 30303 • (404) 730-4001 • http://aarl.af.public.lib.ga.us

Catholic Archdiocese of Atlanta • 680 W Peachtree St NW • Atlanta, GA 30308 • (404) 885-7253 • http://www.archatl.com/archives/

CDC/Global Health Odyssey • 1600 Clifton Rd NE, MS A14 • Atlanta, GA 30333 • (404) 639-0830 • http://www.cdc.gov/global

Digging it Up African-American Research • 70 Fairlie St, Ste 330 • Atlanta, GA 30303 • (404) 688-6509

East Point Historical Society • 1685 Norman Berry Dr • Atlanta, GA 30344 • (404) 767-4656

Eleventh Circuit Historical Society • P.O. Box 1556 • Atlanta, GA 30301 • (404) 331-4605

Executive Mansion Museum • 391 W Paces Ferry Rd • Atlanta, GA 30305 • (404) 261-1776

First Families of Georgia, 1733-1797 • 1604 Executive Park Ln NE • Atlanta, GA 30329-3115 • (404) 634-9866

Georgia Capitol Museum • 431 State Capitol • Atlanta, GA 30334 • (404) 651-6996 • http://www.sos.state.ga.us/museum

Georgia Department of Archives and History • 330 Capitol Ave SE • Atlanta, GA 30334 • (404) 656-2350 • http://www.sos.state.ga.us/archives

Georgia Division of Public Library Services • 1800 Century Pl, Ste 150 • Atlanta, GA 30345-4304 • (404) 235-7200 • http://www.georgialibraries.org

Georgia Genealogical Society • P.O. Box 54575 • Atlanta, GA 30308-0575 • (770) 656-2350 • http://www.gagensociety.org

Georgia Historic Preservation Division • Dept of Natural Resources, 34 Peachtree St, NW, Ste 1600 • Atlanta, GA 30303-2316 • (404) 651-5568 • http://hpd.dnr.state.ga.us

Georgia Regional Library for the Blind and Physically Handicapped • 1150 Murphy Ave SW • Atlanta, GA 30310-3300 • (404) 756-4619

Georgia State Law Library • 40 Capitol Sq • Atlanta, GA 30334 • (404) 656-3468 • http://gsll.georgia.gov

Georgia State Library • 1800 Century Pl, Suite 150 • Atlanta, GA 30345-4304 • (404) 982-3560 • http://www.public.lib.ga.us

Georgia Trust for Historic Preservation • 1516 Peachtree NW • Atlanta, GA 30309 • (404) 881-9980 • http://www.georgiatrust.org

Hart County Historical Society • 31 E Howell St, P.O. Box 96 • Atlanta, GA 30643 • (706) 376-6330

Herndon House Museum • 587 University Pl • Atlanta, GA 30314 • (404) 581-9813

Historic Oakland Cemetery • 248 Oakland Ave SE • Atlanta, GA 30312 • (404) 688-2107 • http://www.oaklandcemetery.com

Jamestowne Society • 2310 Bohler Rd NW • Atlanta, GA 30327 • http://www.jamestowne.org

Jewish Genealogical Society of Georgia • 2492 Madison Commons • Atlanta, GA 30328 • (770) 458-6664 • http://www.jgsg.org

Jewish Genealogical Society of Georgia • Breman Jewish Heritage & Holocaust Museum, 1440 Spring St NW • Atlanta, GA 30309 • (678) 222-3700 • http://www.jewishgen.org/jgsg/

Jimmy Carter Library • 441 Freedom Pkwy • Atlanta, GA 30307-1498 • (404) 865-7100 • http://jimmycarterlibrary.org

Margaret Mitchell House and Museum • 990 Peachtree St • Atlanta, GA 30309-3964 • (404) 249-8015 • http://www.gwtw.org

Martin Luther King Birth Home Museum • 501 Auburn Ave NE • Atlanta, GA 30312 • (404) 331-5190

Martin Luther King Jr Center for Nonviolent Social Change • 449 Augurn Ave NE • Atlanta, GA 30312 • (404) 526-8900 • http://www.thekingcenter.org

Martin Luther King Jr National Historic Site Museum • 450 Auburn Ave NE • Atlanta, GA 30312 • (404) 331-5190 • http://www.nps.gov/malu

National Museum of Patiotism • 1405 Spring St NW • Atlanta, GA 30309 • (404) 875-0691 • http://www.museumofpatriotism.org

National Society, Sons and Daughters of Antebellum Planters 1607-1781 • 2799 Northside Dr • Atlanta, GA 30305

North Georgia Methodist Historical Society • Pitts Theology Library, Emory Univ, 505 Kilgo Cr • Atlanta, GA 30322 • (404) 727-4166 • http://www.gcah.org/Conference/umcdirectory.htm

Oglethorpe University Library • 4484 Peachtree Rd NE • Atlanta, GA 30319 • (404) 364-8511

Pitts Theology Library • Emory Univ, 505 Kilgo Cr • Atlanta, GA 30322 • (404) 727-4166 • http://www.pitts.emory.edu

Price Gilbert Memorial Library • Georgia Institute of Technology • Atlanta, GA 30332 • (404) 894-4501

Rhodes Hall Museum • 1516 Peachtree St NW • Atlanta, GA 30309 • (404) 885-7800 • http://www.georgiatrust.org

Robert W Woodruff Library • Emory University Libraries, 540 Asbury Circle • Atlanta, GA 30322-2870 • (404) 727-6887 • http://web.library.emory.edu

Robert W Woodruff Library • Atlanta Univ, 111 James P Brawley Dr SW • Atlanta, GA 30314 • (404) 522-8980 • http://www.auctr.edu

Salvation Army Southern Historical Center • 1032 Metropolitan Pkwy SW • Atlanta, GA 30310 • (404) 752-7578 • http://www.salvationarmysouth.org/museum.htm

Salvation Army Southern Historical Center • 1032 Metropolitan Pkwy SW • Atlanta, GA 30310 • (404) 752-7578

Society of the War of 1812 in the State of Georgia • 3065 River North Pkwy NW • Atlanta, GA 30328-1117 • (706) 396-7960

Southern Jewish Historical Society • P.O. Box 5024 • Atlanta, GA 30302-5024 • http://www.jewishsouth.org

Tullie Smith Farm Museum • 130 W Paces Ferry Rd NW • Atlanta, GA 30305-1366 • (404) 814-2041

United Creeks of Georgia • 565 Warwick St • Atlanta, GA 30316

Vinings Historic Preservation Society • 3010 Paces Mill Rd SE • Atlanta, GA 30339-3745 • (770) 432-3343

William Breman Jewish Heritage Museum • Ida Pearle & Joseph Cuba Center, 1440 Spring St • Atlanta, GA 30309 • (678) 222-3700 • http://www.thebreman.org

William Rusell Pullen Library • Georgia State Univ, 100 Decatur St SE • Atlanta, GA 30303-3202 • (404) 651-2185 • http://www.library.gsu.edu

Wren's Nest Historic Home Museum • 1050 RD Abernathy Blvd SW • Atlanta, GA 30310 • (404) 753-7735 • http://www.accessatlanta.com/community/groups/wrensnest/

Auburn

Piedmont Regional Genealogical Society • P.O. Box 65 • Auburn, GA 30203

Augusta

1797 Ezekiel Harris House Museum • 1822 Broad St, P.O. Box 37 • Augusta, GA 30903 • (706) 737-2800 • http://www.augustamuseum.org/harris.htm

Augusta Canal Authority • 20 8th St, P.O. Box 2367 • Augusta, GA 30903 • (706) 823-0440

Augusta Genealogical Society • 1109 Broad St, P.O. Box 3743 • Augusta, GA 30914-3743 • (706) 722-4073 • http://www.augustagensociety.org

Augusta Museum of History • 560 Reynolds St • Augusta, GA 30901 • (706) 722-8454 • http://www.augustamuseum.org

Augusta-Richmond County Historical Society • 2500 Walton Way • Augusta, GA 30904-2200 • (706) 737-1532 • http://www.thearchs.org

Augusta-Richmond County Museum • 540 Telfair St • Augusta, GA 30901-2396 • (706) 722-8454 • http://www.augustamuseum.org

Augusta-Richmond County Public Library • 902 Greene St • Augusta, GA 30901 • (706) 821-2600 • http://www.ecgrl.public.lib.ga.us

Boyhood Home of President Woodrow Wilson • 419 7th St • Augusta, GA 30901 • (706) 722-9828 • http://www.wilsonboyhoodhome.org

Collins-Callaway Library • Paine College, 1235 15th St • Augusta, GA 30901-2799 • (706) 821-8308 • http://www.painecollege.edu

Daughters of the American Revolution, Georgia State Society • Meadow Garden Historic House Museum, 1320 Independence Dr • Augusta, GA 30901-1038 • (706) 724-4174 • http://www.geocities.com/Heartland/Ridge/4935/

George Walton Home Museum • 1320 Independence Dr • Augusta, GA 30901 • (706) 724-4174

Historic Augusta • 111 10th St, P.O. Box 37 • Augusta, GA 30903-0037 • (706) 724-0436 • http://www.downtownaugusta.com/historicaugusta/

Lucy Craft Laney Museum of Black History • 1116 Phillips St • Augusta, GA 30901 • (706) 724-3576 • http://www.lucycraftmuseum.com

National Railway Historical Society, Atlanta Chapter • P.O. Box 5793 • Augusta, GA 30906-5793 • (770) 476-2013

Reese Library • Augusta State Univ, 2500 Walton Wy • Augusta, GA 30904-2200 • (706) 737-1744 • http://www.aug.edu/library/departments.html

Richmond County Historical Society • c/o Reese Library, Augusta State Univ, 2500 Walton Way • Augusta, GA 30904-4562 • (706) 737-1532 • http://www.downtownaugusta.com/heroes-overlook/ heroes-overlook.htm

Robert B Greenblatt Library - Special Collections • Medical College of Georgia, Laney-Waler Blvd • Augusta, GA 30912-0300 • (706) 721-3441 • http://www.mcg.edu

Saint Paul's Church Archives • 605 Reynolds St • Augusta, GA 30901 • (706) 724-2485

Spirit Creek Baptist Church Archives • 1783 Dixon Airline Rd • Augusta, GA 30906 • (706) 798-0765

Summerville Neighborhood Association • P.O. Box 12212 • Augusta, GA 30914-2212 • http://www.summervilleaugusta.org

Woodrow Wilson House Museum • 419 7th St, P.O. Box 37 • Augusta, GA 30901 • (706) 722-9828 • http://www.wilsonboyhoodhome.org

Austell
Austell City Museum • 2716 Broad St • Austell, GA 30001 • (770) 944-4309

Austell Historic Preservation Society • Austell City Hall, 2816 Broad St • Austell, GA 30001 • (770) 948-4909

Avondale Estates
Avondale Historical Society • 121 Berekely Rd • Avondale Estates, GA 30002

Bainbridge
Decatur County Genealogical Society • c/o Decatur County Library, 301 S Monroe St, P.O. Box 7492 • Bainbridge, GA 31718-7387 • (229) 246-6327

Decatur County Historian • 500 Cyrene Rd • Bainbridge, GA 31717 • (912) 246-4384

Decatur County Historical Society • Historical Museum, 119 W Water St, P.O. Box 682 • Bainbridge, GA 31717 • (229) 248-1719

Southwest Georgia Regional Library • 301 S Monroe St • Bainbridge, GA 31717 • (229) 248-2665 • http://www.swgrl.org

Barnesville
Barnesville-Lamar County Historical Society • Historic Museum, 888 Thomaston St, P.O. Box 805 • Barnesville, GA 30204 • (770) 358-0150 • http://www.rootsweb.com/galamar/society.html

Gordon College Library • 419 College Dr • Barnesville, GA 30204 • (770) 358-5078 • http://www.peachnet.edu/inst/gordon.html

Baxley
Appling County Heritage Center • Thomas & Harvey Sts, P.O. Box 87 • Baxley, GA 31513 • (912) 367-8133 • http://candlersonsofconfederacy.homestead.com

Appling County Historical Society • Community Education Center, P.O. Box 1063 • Baxley, GA 31513-7063 • (912) 367-2431

Blackshear
Pierce County Historian • P.O. Box 7 • Blackshear, GA 31516

Pierce County Historical and Genealogical Society • Historical Museum, S Central Ave, P.O. Box 443 • Blackshear, GA 31516 • (912) 449-7044 • http://www.piercecounty.com

Blairsville
Union County Historical Society • Historic Museum, Courthouse Square, P.O. Box 35 • Blairsville, GA 30514-0035 • (706) 745-5493 • http://www.unioncountyhistory.org

Blakely
Early County Historical Society • P.O. Box 564 • Blakely, GA 31723 • (229) 724-2150 • http://www.rootsweb.com/~gaearly/mist/early_historical_society.htm

Kolomoki Mounds State Park Museum • US Hwy 27, 205 Indian Mounds Rd • Blakely, GA 39823-9702 • (229) 724-2150 • http://www.gastateparks.org

Bogart
Order of the Scions of Colonial Cavaliers 1640-1660 • 1051 Forrest Hills Dr • Bogart, GA 30622-2442 • http://www.hereditary.us/societies/cavaliers

Bowdon
Bowdon Area Historical Society • Shelnutt-Wegginger House Museum, 105 Collegeview St, P.O. Box 112 • Bowdon, GA 30108 • (770) 258-8980 • http://www.bowdon.net

Bowersville
Hart County Historian • 237 Shirley Rd • Bowersville, GA 30516 • (706) 245-0395

Brunswick
Brunswick and Glynn County Regional Library • 208 Gloucester St • Brunswick, GA 31521-7007 • (912) 267-1212

Coastal Georgia Genealogical Society • 4106 Riverside Dr • Brunswick, GA 31520 • http://www.glynngen.com/cggs.htm

Gould Memorial Library • Coastal Georgia Community College, 3700 Altama Ave • Brunswick, GA 31520-3644 • (912) 264-7270 • http://www.cgcc.edu

Hofwyl-Broadfield Plantation Museum • 5536 US Hwy 17 N • Brunswick, GA 31525 • (912) 264-7333 • http://www.hofwylplantation.org

Old Town Brunswick Preservation Association • 1327 Union St • Brunswick, GA 31520-7226 • (912) 264-0442

Buchanan

Haralson County Historical Society • Old Haralson County Courthouse, 145 Van Wert St, P.O. Box 585 • Buchanan, GA 30113 • (770) 646-3369 • http://www.rootsweb.com/~gahchs/

Buckhead

Steffen Thomas Museum • 4200 Bethany Rd • Buckhead, GA 30625 • (706) 342-7557

Byron

Byron Area Historical Society • P.O. Box 755 • Byron, GA 31008 • (912) 956-5637

Cairo

Grady County Historical Society • c/o Roddenbery Memorial Library, 310 N Broad St, P.O. Box 586 • Cairo, GA 31728 • (229) 377-3632

Roddenbery Memorial Library • 320 N Broad St • Cairo, GA 39828-2109 • (912) 377-3632 • http://www.grady.public.lib.ga.us

Calhoun

Gordon County Historical Society • 335 S Wall St, P.O. Box 342 • Calhoun, GA 30701 • (706) 629-1515

New Echota State Historic Site Museum • 1211 Chatsworth Hwy NE • Calhoun, GA 30701 • (706) 624-132 • http://www.gastateparks.org

Camilla

De Soto Trail Regional Library • 145 E Broad St • Camilla, GA 31730-1842 • (229) 336-8372 • http://www.mitchell.public.lib.ga.us

Canton

Appalachian Heritage Guild • P.O. Box 303 • Canton, GA 30169 • http://www.ahguild.org

Cherokee County Historical Society • Crescent Farm Historical Center, 658 Marietta Hwy, P.O. Box 1287 • Canton, GA 30114 • (770) 345-3288 • http://www.rockbarn.org

Sequoyah Regional Library System-R T Jones Memorial • 116 Brown Industrial Pkwy • Canton, GA 30114-2899 • (770) 479-3090 • http://www.sequoyahregionallibrary.org

Carnesville

Franklin County Historical Society • Gainesville St, P.O. Box 482 • Carnesville, GA 30521 • (706) 384-4361

Carrollton

Carroll County Genealogical Society • P.O. Box 576 • Carrollton, GA 30117 • (770) 832-7746 • http://ccgs.westgeorgia.org

Carroll County Historical Society • West Ave, P.O. Box 1308 • Carrollton, GA 30117 • (770) 834-3081

Ingram Library - Special Collections • State Univ of West Georgia, 1601 Maple St • Carrollton, GA 30118 • (770) 836-6495 • http://www.westga.edu/~library/

Sons of Confederate Veterens, McDaniel-Curtis Camp #165 • P.O. Box 622 • Carrollton, GA 30112 • http://www.georgiascv.com

West Georgia Regional Library • 710 Rome St, P.O. Box 160 • Carrollton, GA 30117 • (770) 836-6711 • http://www.carroll.public.lib.ga.us/Branches/Carrollton/nlpl.html

Cartersville

Air Acres Museum • 255 Hwy 61 SE • Cartersville, GA 30120 • (770) 517-6090

Bartow County Genealogical Society & Family Research Library • 101 N Erwin St, P.O. Box 993 • Cartersville, GA 30120-0993 • (770) 606-0706 • http://www.barctygen.org

Bartow County Historical Society • 319 E Cherokee Ave, P.O. Box 1239 • Cartersville, GA 30120 • (404) 382-3818

Bartow County Library System • 429 W Main St • Cartersville, GA 30120 • (770) 382-4203 • http://www.bartowlibraryonline.org

Bartow History Center • 13 N Wall St, P.O. Box 1239 • Cartersville, GA 30120 • (770) 382-3818 • http://www.bartowhistorycenter.org

Etowah Valley Family Tree Climbers • Bartow County Courthouse, 115 W Cherokee Ave, P.O. Box 1886 • Cartersville, GA 30120 • (770) 606-8862 • http://www.evhsonline.org

Etowah Valley Historical Society • Bartow County Courthouse, 115 W Cherokee Ave, P.O. Box 1886 • Cartersville, GA 30120-3101 • (770) 606-8862 • http://www.evhsonline.org

Euharlee Creek Covered Bridge and Historic Museum • 116 Covered Bridge Rd • Cartersville, GA 30120 • (770) 607-2017

Historic Depot Museum • 1 Friendship Plaza • Cartersville, GA 30120 • (770) 387-1357

Roselawn Museum • 224 W Cherokee Ave • Cartersville, GA 30120 • (770) 387-5162 • http://www.roselawnmuseum.com

Cave Spring

Cave Spring Historical Society • 13 Cedartown Rd, P.O. Box 715 • Cave Spring, GA 30124 • (706) 777-8865

Cedartown

Polk County Historical Society • Historical Museum, 205 S College St, P.O. Box 203 • Cedartown, GA 30125-2603 • (770) 749-0073 • http://polkhist.home.mindspring.com

Centerville

Central Georgia Genealogical Society • 319 N Houston Lake Blvd • Centerville, GA 31028 • (478) 953-3114 • http://www.cggs.org

Chatsworth

Chief Vann House State Historical Park • 82 Highway 225 N • Chatsworth, GA 30705 • (706) 695-2598 • http://www.alltel.net/~vannhouse/

Chattanooga

Polk County Historical and Genealogical Society • 140 Commerce St • Chattanooga, GA 30751 • (423) 338-1005

Chickamauga

Cherokee Regional Library System-Chickamauga Public • 306 Cove Rd • Chickamauga, GA 30707-1410 • (706) 375-3004 • http://www.walker.public.lib.ga.us/branches/chick.html

Walker County Regional Heritage Museum • 100 Gordon St • Chickamauga, GA 30707 • (706) 375-6801

Clarkesville

Clarkesville-Habersham County Library • 178 E Green St, P.O. Box 2020 • Clarkesville, GA 30523-0034 • (706) 754-0416 • http://www.clarkesvillega.com/pages.library.html

Habersham County Historical Society • P.O. Box 1552 • Clarkesville, GA 30523

Claxton

Evans County Historical Society • P.O. Box 6 • Claxton, GA 30417 • (912) 739-4870

Clayton

Rabun County Historical Society • Historical Museum, 81 N Church St, P.O. Box 921 • Clayton, GA 30525 • (706) 746-2508 • http://www.rootsweb.com/~garchs/

Cleveland

White County Historical Society • Historical Museum, Cleveland Sq, P.O. Box 1139 • Cleveland, GA 30528 • (706) 865-3225 • http://www.georgiamagazine.com/counties/white/wchs/

Cochran

Bleckley County Historical Society • c/o Middle Georgia College Library, 1100 2nd St SE • Cochran, GA 31014 • (478) 934-3074

Ocmulgee Regional Library System-Tessie W Norris Public Library • 315 3rd St • Cochran, GA 31014 • (478) 934-2904 • http://www.orls.org

Roberts Memorial Library • Middle Georgia College, 1100 2nd St SE • Cochran, GA 31014-1599 • (478) 934-3074 • http://www.mgc.peachnet.edu

College Park
College Park Historical Society • City Hall, 3337 E Main St, P.O. Box 87137 • College Park, GA 30337 • (404) 761-8932 • http://collegeparkga.com

Georgia Military Academy Archives • Woodward Academy, P.O. Box 87190 • College Park, GA 30337 • (404) 765-1512 • http://www.archives.woodward.edu/archives.html

Colquitt
Southwest Georgia Regional Library-Miller County • 259 E Main St • Colquitt, GA 39837 • (229) 758-3131

Columbus
Columbus Heritage Association • Columbus Museum, 1251 Wynnton Rd • Columbus, GA 31906-2899 • (706) 748-2562 • http://www.columbusmuseum.com

Donovan Research Library • Bldg Four, Rm 101, Fort Benning Infantry School • Columbus, GA 31905-5452 • (706) 545-5661 • http://www.benning.army.mil/fbhome/library/donovan.htm

Genealogical Society of Original Muscogee County • c/o W C Bradley Memorial Library, 1120 Bradley Dr • Columbus, GA 31906 • (706) 649-0780

Historic Columbus Foundation • Historic Museum, 1440 2nd Ave, P.O. Box 5312 • Columbus, GA 31901 • (706) 322-0756 • http://www.historiccolumbus.com

Historic Linwood Foundation • 721 Linwood Blvd, P.O. Box 1057 • Columbus, GA 31909 • (706) 321-8285

Muscogee Genealogical Society • P.O. Box 761 • Columbus, GA 31902 • (706) 561-5831 • http://www.muscogeegenealogy.com

Port Columbus National Civil War Naval Museum • 1002 Victory Dr, P.O. Box 1022 • Columbus, GA 31902 • (706) 324-7334 • http://www.portcolumbus.org

Simon Schwob Memorial Library • Columbus College, 4225 University Ave • Columbus, GA 31907-5645 • (706) 568-2042 • http://library.colstate.edu

Springer Opera House Museum • 925 Blandford Ave • Columbus, GA 31906 • (706) 323-5249

Comer
Comer Historical Society • P.O. Box 100 • Comer, GA 30629 • (706) 783-3918

Commerce
Jackson County Historical Society • c/o Commerce Public Library, 1344 S Broad St, P.O. Box 1234 • Commerce, GA 30529 • (706) 355-5946

Piedmont Regional Library-Commerce Branch • Heritage Room, 1344 S Broad St • Commerce, GA 30529-1567 • (706) 335-5946 • http://www.arches.uga.edu

Conyers
Conyers-Rockdale Library System - Nancy Guinn Branch • 864 Green St SW • Conyers, GA 30012 • (770) 388-5040 • http://www.rockdale.public.lib.ga.us

Rockdale County Historical Society • 967 Milstead Ave, P.O. Box 351 • Conyers, GA 30207 • (770) 483-4398

Rockdale Genealogical Society • c/o Conyers-Rockdale Library System, 864 Green St • Conyers, GA 30012 • (770) 388-5040 • http://mtf.home.mindspring.com/newsltr.htm

Cordele
Cordele-Crisp County Historical Society • Route 2, Box 995 • Cordele, GA 31015

Georgia Veterans Memorial Museum • 2459-A Hwy 280 W • Cordele, GA 31015 • (912) 276-2371

Lake Blackshear Regional Library-Cordele-Crisp Carnegie • 115 E 11th Ave • Cordele, GA 31015-4296 • (229) 276-1300 • http://www.lbrl.org/cordele.html

Covington
Newton County Historical Society • Chamber of Commerce Bldg, 2100 Washington St, P.O. Box 2415 • Covington, GA 30210 • (770) 786-7510

Newton County Library System • 7116 Floyd St NE • Covington, GA 30014 • (770) 787-3231 • http://www.newton.public.lib.ga.us

Crawfordville
A H Stephens House Museum • 242 Alexander St, P.O. Box 283 • Crawfordville, GA 30631 • (706) 456-2221

Confederate Museum • 456 Alexander St, P.O. Box 310 • Crawfordville, GA 30631 • (706) 456-2221 • http://www.gastateparks.org

Taliaferro County Historical Society • Broad St, P.O. Box 32 • Crawfordville, GA 30631 • (706) 456-2339

Cumming
Forsyth County Heritage Foundation • Forsyth County Govt Bldg, P.O. Box 3121 • Cumming, GA 30028 • (770) 887-1626

Forsyth County Public Library • 585 Dahlonega Rd • Cumming, GA 30040-2109 • (770) 781-9840 • http://www.forsythpl.org

Georgia Tribe of Eastern Cherokee • P.O. Box 1915 • Cumming, GA 30040

Historical Society of Forsyth County • P.O. Box 1334 • Cumming, GA 30028 • (770) 887-8464 • http://www.rootsweb.com/~gafchs

Cuthbert
Kinchafoonee Regional Library-Randolph County • 200 E Pearl St • Cuthbert, GA 39840-1474 • (229) 732-2566

Pitts Library • Andrew College, 413 College St • Cuthbert, GA 31740 • (229) 732-5944 • http://www.andrewcollege.edu

Randolph Historical Society • P.O. Box 472 • Cuthbert, GA 31740 • (229) 732-6574

Dahlonega
Chestatee Regional Library System-Lumpkin County Library • 342 Courthouse Hill • Dahlonega, GA 30533 • (706) 864-3668 • http://www.dahlonega.org/library/library.html

Dahlonega Courthouse Gold Museum • 1 Public Square, P.O. Box 2042 • Dahlonega, GA 30533 • (706) 864-2257 • http://www.dahlonega.org/museum/goldmuseum.html

Dahlonega Historical Commission • City Hall, 465 Riley Rd • Dahlonega, GA 30533 • (706) 864-6133 • http://www.dahlonega-ga.gov

Lumpkin County Historical Society • The Old Jail, P.O. Box 894 • Dahlonega, GA 30533 • (706) 864-3668 • http://www.dahlonega.org/historicalsociety/historicalsociety.html

Stewart Library • North Georgia College, 238 Georgia Circle • Dahlonega, GA 30597-3001 • (706) 864-1520 • http://www.ngcsu.edu

Dallas
Paulding County Historical Society • Historical Museum, 295 Johnston St N, P.O. Box 333 • Dallas, GA 30132 • (770) 505-3485 • http://www.rootsweb.com/~gapauldi/historicalsociety/hsociety.html

Dalton

Blunt House Museum • 506 S Thornton Ave • Dalton, GA 30720 • (706) 278-0217

Derrell C Roberts Library • Dalton State College, 213 N College Dr • Dalton, GA 30720-3797 • (706) 272-4575 • http://www.daltonstate.edu/library.htm

Northwest Georgia Regional Library System • 310 Cappes St • Dalton, GA 30720 • (706) 876-1360 • http://www.ngrl.org

Prater's Mill Foundation • 848 Shugart Rd • Dalton, GA 30720-2429 • (706) 275-6455

Whitfield-Murray Historical Society • Crown Garden and Archives, 715 Chattanooga Ave, P.O. Box 6180 • Dalton, GA 30722 • (706) 278-0217 • http://www.southernmuse.com/whitfieldmurray.htm

Danielsville

Madison County Heritage Foundation • P.O. Box 74 • Danielsville, GA 30633 • (706) 795-2017

Darien

Ashantilly Center Archives • P.O. Box 1449 • Darien, GA 31305 • (912) 634-0303

Brunswick-Glynn County Regional Library-Ida Hilton Library • P.O. Box 1227 • Darien, GA 31305-1227 • (912) 437-2124

Fort King George Historic Site Museum • Ft King George Dr, P.O. Box 711 • Darien, GA 31305 • (912) 437-4770 • http://www.darientel.net/~ftkgeo/

Lower Altamaha Historical Society • P.O. Box 1405 • Darien, GA 31305 • (912) 280-9547

Dawson

Kinchafoonee Regional Library • 913 Forrester Dr SE • Dawson, GA 31742 • (229) 995-6331 • http://www.krl.public.lib.ga.us

Terrell County Historic Preservation Society • P.O. Box 63 • Dawson, GA 31742

Terrell County Restoration Society • P.O. Box 63 • Dawson, GA 31742 • (229) 995-2125

Dawsonville

Chestatee Regional Library System • 342 Allen St • Dawsonville, GA 30534 • (706) 344-3690 • http://www.chestateelibrary.org

Dawson County Historical and Genealogical Society • 1 Courthouse Sq, P.O. Box 1074 • Dawsonville, GA 30534 • (706) 265-3985 • http://www.dawsoncounty.org/dchshomepage.htm

Old Jail Museum • 54 Hwy 53 W, P.O. Box 299 • Dawsonville, GA 30534 • (706) 265-6278

Decatur

DeKalb County Public Library • 215 Sycamore St • Decatur, GA 30030 • (404) 370-3070 • http://www.dekalblibrary.org

DeKalb Historical Society • Historical Museum, 101 E Courthouse Sq • Decatur, GA 30030 • (404) 373-1088 • http://www.dekalbhistory.org

Family History Research • 2523 Fairoaks Rd • Decatur, GA 30033-1418 • (404) 325-1161

John Bulow Campbell Library • Columbia Theological Seminary, 701 Columbia Dr, P.O. Box 520 • Decatur, GA 30031 • (404) 687-4610 • http://www.ctsnet.edu

Sons of Confederate Veterans, Camp 1432 • Masonic Temple, 108 E Ponde de Leon Ave, Ste 201 • Decatur, GA 30030 • (706) 542-5788

Donalsonville

Seminole County Historical Society • P.O. Box 713 • Donalsonville, GA 31759 • (229) 524-2588

Southwest Georgia Regional Library-Seminole County Public Library • 103 W 4th St • Donalsonville, GA 39845 • (229) 524-2665

Douglas

Heritage Station Museum • 219 W Ward St • Douglas, GA 31533 • (912) 389-346

Satilla Regional Library • 200 S Madison Ave, Suite D • Douglas, GA 31533 • (912) 384-4667 • http://www.srlsys.org

Douglasville

Douglas County Genealogical Society • P.O. Box 5667 • Douglasville, GA 30154 • http://www.douglascountygenealogicalsociety.org

Historical Society of Douglas County • 8562 Campbellton St, P.O. Box 2018 • Douglasville, GA 30133 • (770) 942-0395

Dublin

Laurens County Historical Society • Dublin-Lauren Museum, 311 Academy Ave, P.O. Box 1461 • Dublin, GA 31021 • (478) 272-9242 • http://organizations.nlamerica.com/historical/

Oconee Regional Library • 801 Bellevue Ave, P.O. Box 100 • Dublin, GA 31040-0100 • (478) 272-5710 • http://www.laurens.public.lib.ga.us

Duluth

National Railway Historical Society, Atlanta Chapter • 3595 Peachtree Rd NW • Duluth, GA 30096 • (770) 476-2013

Southeastern Railway Museum • 3595 Peach Tree Rd, P.O. Box 1267 • Duluth, GA 30096-1267 • (770) 476-2013 • http://www.srmduluth.org

East Point

East Point Historical Society • 1685 Norman Berry Dr, P.O. Box 90675 • East Point, GA 30364-0675 • (404) 767-4656

East Point Public Library • 2757 Main St • East Point, GA 30344 • (404) 762-4842

National Archives-Southeast Region • 1557 St Joseph Ave • East Point, GA 30344-2593 • (404) 763-7477 • http://www.archives.gov/facilities/ga/atlanta.html

Eastman

Dodge Historical Society • 5315 Eastman St, P.O. Box 163 • Eastman, GA 31023

Murrell Memorial Library • 207 5th Ave NE, P.O. Box 606 • Eastman, GA 31203 • (478) 374-4711

Ocmulgee Regional Library System • 531 2nd Ave, P.O. Box 4369 • Eastman, GA 31023-4369 • (478) 374-4711 • http://www.orls.org

Orphans Cemetery Association • P.O. Box 4411 • Eastman, GA 31023 • (478) 374-2180

Wiregrass Genealogical Society • 366 Gum Swamp Rd • Eastman, GA 31023 • (478) 374-3758 • http://www.rootsweb.com/~gawgs

Eatonton

East Georgia Genealogical Society • 114 N Madison Ave • Eatonton, GA 31024-1095

Eatonton-Putnam County Historical Society • 104 Church St • Eatonton, GA 31024 • (706) 485-4532

Uncle Remus Museum • 360 Oak St, P.O. Box 3184 • Eatonton, GA 31024 • (706) 485-6856 • http://www.uncleremus.com/museum.html

Uncle Remus Regional Library System-Putnam County Library • 309 N Madison Ave • Eatonton, GA 31024 • (706) 485-6768 • http://www.uncleremus.org

Edison

Kinchafoonee Regional Library System-Calhoun County Library • 227 E Hartford St, P.O. Box 365 • Edison, GA 39846 • (229) 835-2012

Elberton

Elbert County Historical Society • Depot Museum, 1 Deadwyler St, P.O. Box 1033 • Elberton, GA 30635 • (706) 283-6977

Elbert County Public Library • 345 Heard St • Elberton, GA 30635 • (706) 283-5375 • http://www.sydney.georgialibraries.org

Elberton Granite Museum • 1 Granite Plaza, P.O. Box 640 • Elberton, GA 30635 • (706) 283-2551 • http://www.egaonline.com

Ellaville
Schley County Historical Society • Schley County Courthouse, P.O. Box 326 • Ellaville, GA 31806 • (229) 937-2689

Ellijay
Heritage Museum of Gilmer County • 207 Dalton St • Ellijay, GA 30540-9000 • (706) 635-4505

Evans
Georgia Civil War Heritage Trails • P.O. Box 1864 • Evans, GA 30809 • (706) 868-8403 • http://www.gcwht.org

Fairburn
Fulton County Historian • 592 Fayetteville Rd • Fairburn, GA 30213 • (770) 964-7585

Old Campbell County Historical Society • Courthouse Sq, 45 E Broad St, P.O. Box 342 • Fairburn, GA 30213-0342 • (770) 969-5618 • http://www.oldcampbellcountyhistoricalsociety.com

Fargo
Stephen C Foster State Park Museum • Route 1, Box 131, 17515 Georgia Hwy 177 • Fargo, GA 31631 • (912) 637-5325 • http://www.georgiastateparks.org

Fayetteville
Fayette County Historical Society • 195 Lee St, P.O. Box 421 • Fayetteville, GA 30214-0421 • (770) 716-6020 • http://www.historyfayettecoga.org

Flint River Regional Library-Fayette County • 1821 Heritage Park Way • Fayetteville, GA 30214 • (770) 461-8841 • http://www.admin.co.fayette.ga.us/faylib.htm

Fitzgerald
Blue and Gray Museum • 116 S Johnston St, P.O. Box 1285 • Fitzgerald, GA 31750 • (229) 426-5069 • http://www.fitzgeraldga.org

City of Fitzgerald History Museum • 119 Main St • Fitzgerald, GA 31750 • (912) 382-1792

Fitzgerald-Ben Hill County Library • 123 N Main St • Fitzgerald, GA 31750 • (229) 426-5080 • http://www.fitzgeraldga.org/comm6.mfr.html

Jefferson Davis Memorial Museum • 338 Jeff Davis Park Rd • Fitzgerald, GA 31750 • (229) 831-2335 • http://gastateparks.org/info/jeffd

Flovilla
Butts County Historical Society • 1835 S Hwy 42 • Flovilla, GA 30216 • (678) 752-9332

Indian Springs State Park Museum • 678 Lake Clark Rd • Flovilla, GA 30216 • (770) 504-2277 • http://www.georgiastateparks.org

Folkston
Brunswick-Glynn County Regional Library-Charlton County • 701 Indian Trail • Folkston, GA 31537 • (912) 496-2041

Charlton County Historical Society • 100 Cypress, P.O. Box 575 • Folkston, GA 31537-0575 • (912) 496-4578

Forsyth
Monroe County Historical Society • Historical Museum, 126 E Johnson St, P.O. Box 401 • Forsyth, GA 31029-2235 • (478) 994-5070 • http://www.rootsweb.com/~gamchs

Fort Benning
National Infantry Museum • US Army Infantry School, Bldg 396, Baltzell Ave • Fort Benning, GA 31905 • (706) 545-2958 • http://www.infantry.army.mil/museum

Fort Gaines
Fort Gaines Historical Society • 308 E Jefferson St, P.O. Box 825 • Fort Gaines, GA 39851

Kinchafoonee Regional Library-Clay County • 208 S Hancock St, P.O. Box 275 • Fort Gaines, GA 39851-0275 • (229) 768-2248 • http://www.krl.public.lib.ga.us

Fort Gordon
Fort Gordon Museum • Command Historian, U.S. Army Signal Center ATZH-MH, 36th St & 4th Ave, Bldg 36301 • Fort Gordon, GA 30905 • (706) 791-5212

US Army Signal Corps Museum • 504 Chamberlain Ave • Fort Gordon, GA 30905 • (706) 791-2818 • http://www.gordon.army.mil/museum/

Fort Oglethorpe
Chickamauga and Chattanooga National Military Park Library • Cravens House Museum, 3370 Lafayette Rd, P.O. Box 2128 • Fort Oglethorpe, GA 30742 • (706) 866-9241 • http://www.nps.gov/chch

Fort Oglethorpe Preservation Society • P.O. Box 5321 • Fort Oglethorpe, GA 30742

Sixth Cavalry Museum • 2 Barnhardt Cir • Fort Oglethorpe, GA 30742 • (706) 861-2860

Fort Stewart
Fort Stewart Main Post Library • Bldg 411, 316 Lindquist Rd • Fort Stewart, GA 31314-5126 • (912) 767-2260 • http://www.stewlib3.stewart.army.mil

Fort Stewart Museum • 2022 Frank Cochran Dr • Fort Stewart, GA 31314-4936 • (912) 767-7885

Fort Valley
Peach County Historical Society • P.O. Box 889 • Fort Valley, GA 31030 • http://www.rootsweb.com/~gapchs

Peach Public Library • 315 Martin Luther King Dr • Fort Valley, GA 31010-4196 • (478) 825-1640 • http://www.peach.public.lib.ga.us

Franklin
Heard County Historical Society • Heard County Museum, 161 Shady St, P.O. Box 990 • Franklin, GA 30217 • (706) 675-6507

Gainesville
Georgia Mountains Historical and Cultural Trust • 311 Green St SE • Gainesville, GA 30501 • (770) 536-0889 • http://www.lakelanier.com/ghcomm.htm

Hall County Historical Society • 380 Green St NE, P.O. Box 2999 • Gainesville, GA 30501 • (770) 503-1319 • http://www.hallcountyhistoricalsociety.org

Hall County Library System • 127 Main NW • Gainesville, GA 30501-3614 • (770) 532-3311 • http://www.hallcountylibrary.org

Northeast Georgia Historical and Genealogical Society • c/o Hall County Public Library, 127 Main St NW, P.O. Box 907085 • Gainesville, GA 30501-0902 • (404) 532-3311 • http://www.rootsweb.com/~gahall/nega/

Northeast Georgia History Center • Brenau Univ, 322 Academy St, P.O. Box 1451 • Gainesville, GA 30503 • (770) 536-0889 • http://www.gamtshistorymuseum.org

Glennville
Glennville Tattnall Museum • Old Glennville School, P.O. Box 607 • Glennville, GA 30427 • (912) 557-4010

Gordon
Wilkinson County Historical Society • P.O. Box 159 • Gordon, GA 31031 • (478) 528-5102

Gray
Old Clinton Historical Society • 154 Randolph St • Gray, GA 31032 • (478) 986-3394

Greensboro
Greene County Historian • 206 S Main St • Greensboro, GA 30642 • (706) 453-7409

Greene County Historical Society • Old Gaol Museum, 201 E Greene St, P.O. Box 238 • Greensboro, GA 30642 • (706) 453-7250

Uncle Remus Regional Library System-Greene County Library • 610 S Main St • Greensboro, GA 30642 • (706) 453-7276 • http://www. uncleremus.org

Greenville
Meriwether Historical Society • P.O. Box 741 • Greenville, GA 30222 • (706) 672-4121

Griffin
Bailey-Tebault House Museum • 633 Meriwether St • Griffin, GA 30223 • (770) 229-2432

Flint River Regional Library • 800 Memorial Dr • Griffin, GA 30233 • (770) 412-4770 • http://www.frrls.net

Griffin Historical and Preservation Society • 633 Meriwether St, P.O. Box 196 • Griffin, GA 30224 • (770) 229-2432

Griffin-Spalding Historical Society • 633 Meriwether St, P.O. Box 196 • Griffin, GA 30224 • (770) 229-2432

Guyton
Guyton Historical Society • 205 Lynn Bonds Ave, P.O. Box 15 • Guyton, GA 31312 • (912) 772-3344

Hahira
Hahira Historical Society • 102 S Church St • Hahira, GA 31632 • (912) 794-2330 • http://www.hahira.ga.us/historicalsociety.htm

Hapeville
Hapeville Historical Society • 620 S Central Ave, P.O. Box 82055 • Hapeville, GA 30354 • (404) 669-2175

Hartwell
Hart Company Historical Society • 31 E Howell St • Hartwell, GA 30643 • (706) 376-6330

Hart County Historical Society • Historical Museum, P.O. Box 96 • Hartwell, GA 30643 • (706) 245-039

Hart County Library • 150 Benson St • Hartwell, GA 30643 • (706) 376-4655 • http://www.hartwellga.com/hclibrary/

Savannah River Valley Genealogical Society • c/o Hart County Library, 150 Benson St, P.O. Box 895 • Hartwell, GA 30643 • (706) 376-4655 • http://www.srvgs.org

Hawkinsville
Ocmulgee Regional Library System-M E Roden Memorial • 400 Commerce St • Hawkinsville, GA 31036 • (478) 892-3155 • http://www. orls.org

Hiawassee
Towns County Historical and Genealogical Society • P.O. Box 932 • Hiawassee, GA 30546 • (706) 896-7369 • http://www.rootsweb. com/~gatowns/histsoc.txt

Hinesville
Liberty County Historical Society • P.O. Box 982 • Hinesville, GA 31313 • (912) 368-7002

Whisman Military Museum • 208 Dairy Rd • Hinesville, GA 31313 • (912) 368-3979 • http://www.whismanmilitarymuseum.com

Homer
Banks County Historical Society • P.O. Box 473 • Homer, GA 30547 • (706) 677-2108 • http://www.bankscountyhistoricalsociety.com

Homerville
Huxford Genealogical Society • 101 College Ave, P.O. Box 595 • Homerville, GA 31634 • (912) 487-2310 • http://www.huxford.com

Huxford Genealogical Society • 101 College Ave, P.O. Box 595 • Homerville, GA 31634 • (912) 487-2310 • http://www.huxford.com

Jackson
Butts County Genealogical Society • P.O. Box 1297 • Jackson, GA 30233 • http://www.lofthouse.com/USA/ga/butts/#society

Butts County Historical Society • Highway 42, Indian Spring, P.O. Box 215 • Jackson, GA 31233 • (770) 775-6734

Hawkes Library • 431 E College St • Jackson, GA 30233

Jasper
Marble Valley Historical Society • Main Street, P.O. Box 815 • Jasper, GA 30143 • (706) 268-3311 • http://www.marblevalley.org

Jefferson
Jackson County Historical Society • Crawford W Long Museum, 28 College St • Jefferson, GA 30549 • (706) 367-5307 • http://www. crawfordlong.org

Shields-Ethridge Heritage Farm • 2355 Ethridge Rd, P.O. Box 662 • Jefferson, GA 30549 • (706) 367-2949 • http://www. shieldsethridgefarm.org

Jekyll Island
Friends of Historic Jekyll Island • 375 Riverview Dr, P.O.Box 13031 • Jekyll Island, GA 31527 • (912) 635-2176

Jekyll Island Museum • 381 Riverview Dr • Jekyll Island, GA 31527 • (912) 635-2119 • http://www.jekyllisland.com

Jesup
Brunswick-Glynn County Regional Library-Wayne County • 759 Sunset Blvd • Jesup, GA 34545-4409 • (912) 427-2500

Wayne County Historical Society • 125 NE Broad St, P.O. Box 501 • Jesup, GA 31545 • (912) 427-3233 • http://www.georgiahistory.com/ affchapc.htm

Jonesboro
Ancestors Unlimited • P.O. Box 1507 • Jonesboro, GA 30237-1507 • (404) 366-3686

Ashley Oaks Mansion Museum • 144 College St • Jonesboro, GA 30236 • (770) 478-8986

Chattooga County Historian • 10617 Thrasher Rd • Jonesboro, GA 30236 • (770) 478-4387

Clayton County Library System • 865 Battlecreek Rd • Jonesboro, GA 30236-1919 • (770) 473-3850 • http://www.clayton.public.lib.ga.us

Historical Society of Jonesboro and Clayton County • 100 Carriage Ln, P.O. Box 922 • Jonesboro, GA 30237 • (770) 473-0197 • http://www. historicaljonesboro.org

Stately Oaks Plantation Museum • 100 Carriage Ln • Jonesboro, GA 30236-8114 • (770) 473-0197

Juliette
Jarrell Plantation State Historic Site • 711 Jarrell Plantation Rd • Juliette, GA 31046 • (478) 986-5172 • http://www.dnr.state.ga.us/dnr/ parks

Kennesaw
Horace W Sturgis Library • Kennesaw State University, 1000 Chastain Rd • Kennesaw, GA 30144 • (770) 423-6186 • http://www.kennesaw. edu/library/

Kennesaw Civil War and Locomotive Museum • 2829 Cherokee St • Kennesaw, GA 30144-2823 • (770) 427-2117 • http://www. southernmuseum.org

Kennesaw Historic Preservation Commission • 2529 J O Stephenson Ave • Kennesaw, GA 30144 • (770) 424-8274

Kennesaw Historical Society • Southern Museum of Civil War and Locomotive History, 2829 Cherokee St • Kennesaw, GA 30144 • (770) 975-0887 • http://www.southernmuseum.org

Kennesaw Mountain National Battlefield Park Library • 900 Kennesaw Mountain Dr • Kennesaw, GA 30152 • (770) 427-4686 • http://www.nps.gov/kemo

Museum of History and Holocaust Education • Kennesaw State Univ, 1000 Chastain Rd • Kennesaw, GA 30144 • (678) 797-2083 • http://www.kennesaw.edu/historymuseum

Kingston
Kingston Women's History Museum • 13 E Main St • Kingston, GA 30145 • (770) 336-5540

La Grange
Bellevue House Museum • 204 Ben Hill St • La Grange, GA 30240 • (706) 884-1832 • http://www.cityoflagrange.com/businesses/bellevue.html

Hills and Dales Historic House Museum • 1916 Hills and Dales Ln, P.O. Box 790 • LaGrange, GA 30240 • (706) 882-3242 • http://www.hillsanddalestate.org

Historic Chattahoochee Committee • 136 Main St • La Grange, GA 30240-3218 • (706) 845-8440

Troup County Archives • 136 Main St, P.O. Box 1051 • La Grange, GA 30241 • (706) 884-1828 • http://www.trouparchives.org

Troup County Historical Society • 136 Main St, P.O. Box 1051 • La Grange, GA 30241 • (706) 884-1828 • http://www.trouparchives.org

Troup-Harris-Coweta Regional Library • 115 Alford St • La Grange, GA 30240-3041 • (706) 882-7784 • http://www.thclibrary.net

West Central Georgia Genealogical Society • P.O. Box 2291 • La Grange, GA 30241

West Georgia Genealogical Society • c/o Troup County Historical Society Library, 136 Main St, P.O. Box 1051 • La Grange, GA 30241 • (706) 884-1828 • http://www.lgc.peachnet.edu/archives/tcarchiv.htm

William and Evelyn Banks Library • La Grange College, 601 Broad St • La Grange, GA 30240 • (706) 880-8312 • http://www.lgc.edu/library

Lafayette
Cherokee Regional Library System • 305 S Duke St, P.O. Box 707 • Lafayette, GA 30728-0707 • (706) 638-2992 • http://www.walker.public.lib.ga.us

Walker County Historical Society • 305 S Duke St, P.O. Box 707 • Lafayette, GA 30728-2936 • (706) 764-2132 • http://www.geocities.com/Heartland/Prairie/6370/walker/wchs.html

Lake Park
Echols County Historical Society • 814 Bethel Church Rd • Lake Park, GA 31636 • (229) 559-5230

Lake Park Area Historical Society • P.O. Box 803 • Lake Park, GA 31636-0803 • (229) 559-5771 • http://www.datasys.net/lakepark

Lakeland
Lanier County Historical Society • 103 E Main St • Lakeland, GA 31635

Lavonia
Hart County, Georgia Historical Society • 40 Bailey Pl Rd • Lavonia, GA 30553-9561 • (706) 377-5612

Lawrenceville
Gwinnett County Historical Society • Historical Museum, 185 Crogan St, P.O. Box 261 • Lawrenceville, GA 30046 • (770) 822-5174 • http://www.gwinnetths.org

Gwinnett County Public Library • 1001 Lawrenceville Hwy • Lawrenceville, GA 30045 • (770) 822-4522 • http://www.gwinnettpl.org

Gwinnett History Museum • Lawrenceville Female Seminary Bldg, 455 S Perry St • Lawrenceville, GA 30245 • (770) 822-5178 • http://www.gogwinnett.com/gwinnetthistorymuseum/

Leesburg
Lee County Historical Society • c/o Lee County Public Library 245 Walnut St, P.O. Box 393 • Leesburg, GA 31763-0393 • (229) 759-2369

Oakland Plantation Museum • 699 Oakland Rd • Leesburg, GA 31763 • (229) 432-5724

Leslie
Georgia Rural Telephone Museum • 135 Bailey Ave • Leslie, GA 31764 • (229) 874-4786

Lexington
Historic Oglethorpe County • P.O. Box 1793 • Lexington, GA 30648 • (706) 546-1850 • http://www.rootsweb.com/~gaogleth/hoci.htm

Lilburn
Wynne-Russell House Museum • 76 Main St • Lilburn, GA 30247

Lincolnton
Doctor's House-May House Museum • Lincoln Cty Historical Park, 147 Lumber St • Lincolnton, GA 30817 • (706) 359-7970

Elijah Clark Memorial Museum • 2959 McCormick Hwy • Lincolnton, GA 30817 • (706) 359-3458 • http://www.gastateparks.com

Lincoln County Historical Society • 2357 Hwy 220 E, P.O. Box 869 • Lincolnton, GA 30817

Lithia Springs
Cherokee Indian Museum • P.O. Box 713 • Lithia Springs, GA 30122 • (770) 944-3880 • http://www.lithaspringwater.com

Sweetwater Creek State Park • Mt Vernon Rd, P.O. Box 816 • Lithia Springs, GA 30122 • (770) 732-5871 • http://www.gastateparks.org

Sweetwater Historical Society • P.O. Box 713 • Lithia Springs, GA 30057

Loganville
Uncle Remus Regional Library System-O'Kelly Memorial Library • 363 Conyers Rd • Loganville, GA 30052 • (770) 466-2895 • http://www.uncleremus.org

Lookout Mountain
Battles for Chattanooga Museum • 1110 E Brow Rd • Lookout Mountain, GA 37350 • (423) 821-2812

Louisville
Jefferson County Historical Society • P.O. Box 491 • Louisville, GA 30434-0491 • (478) 625-7673

Jefferson County Library • 306 E Broad St • Louisville, GA 30434 • (478) 625-3751 • http://www.jefferson.public.lib.ga.us

Ludowici
Brunswick-Glynn County Regional Library-Long County • P.O. Box 640 • Ludowici, GA 31316-0640 • (912) 545-2521

Lumpkin
Bedingfield Inn Museum • Cotton State on the Square, P.O. Box 818 • Lumpkin, GA 31815 • (229) 838-6419 • http://www.bedingfieldinn.org

Stewart County Historical Commission • Broad & Cotton Sts, P.O. Box 817 • Lumpkin, GA 31815 • (229) 838-6769 • http://www.stewartcountyga.gov

Westville Historic Handicrafts • P.O. Box 1850 • Lumpkin, GA 31815

Westville Historic Museum • 1850 Martin Luther King Jr Dr, P.O. Box 1850 • Lumpkin, GA 31815-1850 • (229) 838-6310 • http://www.westville.org

Macon
Cannonball House and Confederate Museum • 856 Mulberry St • Macon, GA 31201 • (912) 745-5982

Georgia Baptist Historical Society • Jack Tarver Library, Mercer Univ, 1300 Edgewood Ave • Macon, GA 31207 • (478) 301-2055 • http://tarver.mercer.edu/special_collectionsidefault.htm

Georgia

Macon, cont.

Georgia Music Hall of Fame Museum • 200 Martin Luther King Jr Blvd, P.O. Box 870 • Macon, GA 31202-0870 • (478) 751-3334 • http://www.gamusichall.com

Hay House Museum • 934 Georgia Ave • Macon, GA 31201 • (478) 742-8155 • http://www.georgiatrust.org

Historic Vineville Neighborhood Association • P.O. Box 2704 • Macon, GA 31203 • http://www.vineville.org

Jack Tarver Library • Mercer University, 1300 Edgewood Ave • Macon, GA 31207 • (478) 301-2055 • http://tarver.mercer.edu

Macon Heritage Foundation • 652 Mulberry St, P.O. Box 6092 • Macon, GA 31201 • (478) 742-5084

Masonic Grand Lodge of Georgia • 811 Mulberry St • Macon, GA 32102-6779 • (478) 742-1475 • http://www.glofga.org

Mercer University Library • 1400 Coleman • Macon, GA 31207 • (478) 752-2968

Middle Georgia Archives • 1180 Washington Ave • Macon, GA 31201-1790 • (478) 744-0851 • http://www.co.bibb.ga.us/library/GH.htm

Middle Georgia Historical Society • Sidney Lanier Cottage Museum, 935 High St, P.O. Box 13358 • Macon, GA 31208-3358 • (478) 743-3851 • http://www.cityofmacon.net/Living/slcottage.htm

Middle Georgia Regional Library-Washington Memorial Branch • 1180 Washington Ave, P.O. Box 6334 • Macon, GA 31208-6334 • (478) 744-0851 • http://www.co.bibb.ga.us/library/

Ocmulgee National Monument Museum • 1207 Emery Hwy • Macon, GA 31201 • (912) 752-8257 • http://www.nps.gov/ocmu

Sidney Lanier Cottage House Museum • 935 High St, P.O. Box 13358 • Macon, GA 31208 • (478) 743-3851 • http://www.historicmacon.org

Tubman African-American Museum • 340 Walnut St, P.O. Box 6671 • Macon, GA 31208 • (478) 743-8544 • http://www.tubmanmuseum.com

Willett Memorial Library • Wesleyan College, 4760 Forsyth Rd • Macon, GA 31210-4462 • (478) 757-5200 • http://www.wesleyancollege.edu/academics/library

Woodruff House Museum • 988 Bond St • Macon, GA 31201 • (912) 744-2715 • http://www.maconga.com/woodruff.htm

Madison

Heritage Hall Museum • 277 S Main St • Madison, GA 30650 • (706) 342-9627

Madison-Morgan Cultural Center • 434 S Main St • Madison, GA 30650 • (706) 342-4743 • http://www.uncleremus.org/madmorg

Madison-Morgan Cultural Center Museum • 434 S Main St • Madison, GA 30650 • (706) 342-4743 • http://www.madisonmorgancultural.org

Morgan County African-American Historical Society • 156 Academy St • Madison, GA 30650-1202 • (706) 342-9191

Morgan County African-American Museum • 156 Academy St, P.O. Box 482 • Madison, GA 30650 • (706) 342-9191

Morgan County Historical Society • Heritage Hall, 277 S Main St • Madison, GA 30650 • (706) 342-9627

Morgan County Records Archives • Hancock St, P.O. Box 130 • Madison, GA 30650 • (706) 342-3605

Rogers House Museum • W Jefferson St • Madison, GA 30650 • (706) 343-0192

Uncle Remus Regional Library System • 1131 East Ave • Madison, GA 30650 • (706) 342-4974 • http://www.uncleremus.org

Manchester

Pine Mountain Regional Library • 218 Perry St NW, P.O. Box 709 • Manchester, GA 31816-0709 • (706) 846-3851 • http://www.pinemtnlibrary.info/

Marietta

Cobb County Genealogical Society • P.O. Box 1413 • Marietta, GA 30061-1413 • (770) 499-7356 • http://www.rootsweb.com/~gaccgs/

Cobb County Historic Preservation Commission • 191 Lawrence St, Ste 300 • Marietta, GA 30090 • (770) 528-2010

Cobb County Public Library System • 266 Roswell St • Marietta, GA 30060-2004 • (770) 528-2320 • http://www.cobbcat.org

Cobb Landmarks and Historical Society • Root House Museum, 145 Denmeade St • Marietta, GA 30060 • (770) 426-4982 • http://www.roothousemuseum.com

Jewish Genealogical Society of Georgia • P.O. Box 681022 • Marietta, GA 30068-0018 • (770) 980-6370 • http://www.jewishgen.org/jgsg/

Lawrence V Johnson Map Library • Southern Polytechnic State Univ, 1100 S Marietta Pkwy • Marietta, GA 30060-2896 • http://www.spsu.edu/library

Marietta Museum of History • 1 Depot St, Ste 200 • Marietta, GA 30060 • (770) 528-0430 • http://www.mariettahistory.org

Northeast Cobb County, Georgia Genealogical Society • P.O. Box 1413 • Marietta, GA 30060

McDonough

Genealogical Society of Henry and Clayton Counties • 71 Macon, P.O. Box 1296 • McDonough, GA 30253 • (770) 954-1456 • http://www.rootsweb.com/~gagshcc/

McRae

Ocmulgee Regional Library System-Telfair County • 815 College St • McRae, GA 31055 • (229) 868-2978 • http://www.orls.org

Pioneer Arts and Historic Society • 815 College St • McRae, GA 31055 • (229) 868-6365

Metter

Candler County Historical Society • Depot Museum, 346 College St, P.O. Box 325 • Metter, GA 30439 • (912) 685-6573 • http://www.railga.com/Depots/metter.html

Sons of Confederate Veterans for Metter and Candler County • P.O. Box 761 • Metter, GA 30439 • (912) 685-3347 • http://candlersonsofconfederacy.homestead.com

Midway

Fort Morris Historic Site Museum • 2559 Fort Morris Rd • Midway, GA 31320-6205 • (912) 884-5999 • http://www.gastateparks.org

Midway Heritage Association • Midway Museum , Hwy 17 & Martin Rd, P.O. Box 195 • Midway, GA 31320 • (912) 884-5837 • http://www.libertyconnection.com/midway/museum.html

Seabrook Village Museum • 660 Trade Hill Rd • Midway, GA 31320 • (912) 884-7008

Miledgeville

Andalusia Home Museum • 2628 N Columbia St, P.O. Box 947 • Miledgeville, GA 31061 • (478) 454-4029 • http://www.andalusiafarm.org

Center for Georgia Studies • Georgia College, Camput Box 047 • Milledgeville, GA 31061 • (478) 445-3520 • http://www.gcsu.edu

Friends of Baldwin County Cemeteries • 3690 Sussex Dr NE • Milledgeville, GA 31061

Georgia's Old Capital Museum • 201 E Greene St, P.O. Box 1177 • Milledgeville, GA 31059 • (478) 453-1803 • http://www.oldcapitalmuseum.org

Ina Dillard Russell Library • Georgia College, 231 W Hancock St, Campus Box 043 • Milledgeville, GA 31061-3397 • (478) 453-5573 • http://library.gcsu.edu

Museum and Archives of Georgia Education • Georgia College, P.O. Box 95 • Milledgeville, GA 31061 • (478) 445-4391 • http://www.library.gcsu.edu

Old Capital Historical Society • P.O. Box 4 • Milledgeville, GA 31061 • (478) 453-9049

Old Governor's Mansion Museum • 120 S Clarke St • Milledgeville, GA 31061 • (478) 445-4545 • http://www.gcsu.edu/mansion

Sibley-Cone Memorial Library • Georgia Military College, 201 E Greene St • Milledgeville, GA 31061 • (478) 445-1422 • http://www.gmc.cc.ga.us/academics/library/

Stetson-Sanford House Museum • Hancock & Jackson Sts • Milledgeville, GA 31061 • (800) 653-1804 • http://www.nscda.org/museums/georgia.htm

Twin Lakes Library System • 151 S Jefferson St SE • Milledgeville, GA 31061-3419 • (478) 452-0677 • http://www.twinlakeslibrarysystem.org

Millen
Jenkins County Historical Society • c/o Chamber of Commerce, 548 Cotton St • Millen, GA 30442 • (478) 982-5799

Mitchell
Hamburg State Park Museum • 60701 Hamburg State Park Rd • Mitchell, GA 30820 • (706) 552-2393 • http://www.accucomm.net/~hamburg

Monroe
Historical Society of Walton County • 238 N Broad St, P.O. Box 1733 • Monroe, GA 30655 • (770) 207-1229

McDaniel-Tichenor House Museum • 319 McDaniel St • Monroe, GA 30655 • (770) 267-9350

Uncle Remus Regional Library System-Monroe-Walton County Library • 217 W Spring St • Monroe, GA 30655 • (770) 267-4630 • http://www.uncleremus.org

Montezuma
Macon County Historical Society • N Dooly St, P.O. Box 571 • Montezuma, GA 31063 • (478) 472-5038

Monticello
Uncle Remus Regional Library System-Jasper County Library • 319 E Green St • Monticello, GA 31064 • (706) 468-6292 • http://www.uncleremus.org

Moody AFB
Moody Air Force Base Library FL4830 • 347 SVS/SVMG, 5107 Austin Ellipse Suite A Bldg 103 • Moody AFB, GA 31699-1594 • (229) 257-3539

Moreland
Erskine Caldwell Birthplace Museum • E Camp St, P.O. Box 207 • Moreland, GA 30259 • (770) 254-8657 • http://www.newnan.com

Moreland Community Historical Society • Historical Museum, P.O. Box 128 • Moreland, GA 30259 • (770) 253-1963

Old Mill Museum • On the Square, P.O. Box 128 • Moreland, GA 30259 • (770) 304-8859

Morrow
Church of God General Conference Library • P.O. Box 100 • Morrow, GA 30260 • http://abc-coggc.org

Clayton College & State University Library • 5900 N Lee St • Morrow, GA 30260 • (770) 961-3520 • http://www.clayton.edu/library/

Georgia Department of Archives & History Library • 5800 Jonesboro Rd • Morrow, GA 30260 • (678) 364-3710 • http://www.GeorgiaArchives.org

Moultrie
Colquitt County Historical Society • c/o Moultrie-Colquitt County Library, 204 5th St SE, P.O. Box 1110 • Moultrie, GA 31776 • (229) 890-3460

Council of Scottish Clans Association • P.O. Box 2828 • Moultrie, GA 31776-1110 • (229) 985-6540

Ellen Payne Odom Genealogy Library • 204 5th St SE, P.O. Box 1110 • Moultrie, GA 31776 • (912) 985-6540 • http://www.scottishtales.com/familytree

Moultrie-Colquitt County Reg Library • 204 5th St SE, P.O. Box 2828 • Moultrie, GA 31768-2828 • (229) 985-6540

Museum of Colquitt County History • 4th Ave & 5th St SE, P.O. Box 86 • Moultrie, GA 31776 • (229) 890-1626 • http://www.colquittmuseum.org

Mount Airy
Friends of Mountain Hall • P.O. Box 305 • Mount Airy, GA 30563 • (706) 435-0504 • http://www.mountainhall.org

Mount Berry
Oak Hill and the Martha Berry Museum • 24 Veterans Memorial Hwy, P.O. Box 490189 • Mount Berry, GA 31049-0189 • (706) 291-1883 • http://www.berry.edu/oakhill

Mount Vernon
Fountain-New Library • Brewton-Parker College, Hwy 280 • Mount Vernon, GA 30445 • (912) 583-3234 • http://www.bpc.edu/library/library.htm

Mountain City
Foxfire Fund • Historic Museum, P.O. Box 541 • Mountain City, GA 30562 • (706) 746-5828 • http://www.foxfire.org

Nahunta
Brantley County Historical and Preservation Society • Hwy 82, P.O. Box 1096 • Nahunta, GA 31553 • (912) 462-5961 • http://www.rootsweb.com/~gabrantl/branco-home.html

Brunswick-Glynn County Regional Library-Brantley County • P.O. Box 1090 • Nahunta, GA 31553-1090 • (912) 462-5454

Newnan
Coweta County Genealogical Research Center • P.O. Box 1014 • Newnan, GA 30264 • (770) 251-2877

Coweta County Genealogical Society • P.O. Box 1014 • Newnan, GA 30264 • (229) 549-8241 • http://members.tripod.com/~CowetaGS/

Male Academy Museum • 30 Temple Ave, P.O. Box 1001 • Newnan, GA 30264 • (770) 251-0207

Newnan-Coweta Historical Society • Male Academy Museum, 30 Temple Ave, P.O. Box 1001 • Newnan, GA 30264 • (770) 251-0207 • http://www.nchistoricalsociety.org

Oak Grove Plantation and Gardens Museum • 4537 N Hwy 29 • Newman, GA 30265 • (770) 463-3010

Newton
East Baker Historical Society • 139 Clear Lake Rd • Newton, GA 9870 • (229) 734-7075

Norcross
Asian American Resource Center • 6045 Atlantic Blvd #222 • Norcross, GA 30071 • http://www.aarc-atlanta.org

North Cornelia
Habersham County Historical Society • 228 Main St • North Cornelia, GA 30531 • (706) 776-2009

Ochlockee
Southeastern Cherokee Confederacy • P.O. Box 367 • Ochlockee, GA 31733 • (229) 547-5497

Ochlocknee
South Georgia Genealogical Society • P.O. Box 246 • Ochlocknee, GA 31773 • (229) 574-5349

Oxford
Hoke O'Kelley Memorial Library • Emory Univ, 100 Hammil St • Oxford, GA 30267 • (770) 784-8380 • http://www.oxford.emory.edu/oxford/library/

Oxford Historical Shrine Society • Historical Museum, Wesley & Fletcher Sts, P.O. Box 245 • Oxford, GA 30054 • (770) 786-2138

Perry
Houston County Public Library System • 1201 Washington Ave • Perry, GA 31069 • (478) 987-3050 • http://www.houpl.org

Perry Area Historical Society • 1138 Macon St, P.O. Drawer D • Perry, GA 31069 • (478) 987-2588

Perry United Methodist Church Library • 1001 Carrol St, P.O. Box 73 • Perry, GA 31069-0073 • (478) 987-1852

Pine Mountain
Chipley Historic Center of Pine Mountain • 146 N McDougal Ave, P.O. Box 1055 • Pine Mountain, GA 31822-2313 • (770) 663-4044

Plains
Jimmy Carter National Historic Site Museum • 300 N Bond St • Plains, GA 31780 • (229) 824-4104 • http://www.nps.gov/jica

Pooler
Mighty 8th Air Force Historical Society • Mighty 8th Air Force Museum, 175 Bourne Ave • Pooler, GA 31322 • (912) 748-8884 • http://www.mightyeighth.org

Powder Springs
Seven Springs Historical Society • Seven Springs Museum, 3901 Brownsville Rd, P.O. Box 4 • Powder Springs, GA 30073 • (678) 567-5611 • http://www.cityofpowdersprings.org/history.html

Quitman
Brooks County Historical Society • 404 Tallokas Rd, P.O. Box 676 • Quitman, GA 31643

Brooks County Public Library • 404 Barwick Rd • Quitman, GA 31643 • (229) 263-4412

Quitman-Brooks County Genealogical Society • 121 N Culpepper St • Quitman, GA 31643 • http://www.quitmangeorgia.org

Reidsville
Tattnall County Historical Society • P.O. Box 2012 • Reidsville, GA 30453 • (912) 557-4402

Richmond Hill
Fort McAllister Historic Park • 3894 Fort McAllister Rd • Richmond Hill, GA 31324 • (912) 727-2339 • http://www.fortmcallister.org

Richmond Hill Historical Society • Historical Museum, Hwy 144 & Timber Trail, P.O. Box 381 • Richmond Hill, GA 31324 • (912) 756-3697 • http://www.richmondhillga.com

Rincon
Georgia Salzburger Society • Historical Museum, 2980 Ebenezer Rd • Rincon, GA 31326-3716 • (912) 754-7001 • http://www.georgiasalzburgers.org

Ringgold
Catoosa County Historical Society • Old Stone Church, US 41 & GA Hwy 2, P.O. Box 113 • Ringgold, GA 30736 • (706) 935-4875

Old Stone Church Museum • 41 Old Cohutta Rd, P.O. Box 113 • Ringgold, GA 30736 • (706) 935-5232

Riverdale
Campbell County Historian • 1661 Lawrence Wy • Riverdale, GA 30296 • (770) 996-6796

Roberta
Crawford County Historical Society • Old Jail Museum, 100 Commerce Pl, P.O. Box 622 • Roberta, GA 31078 • (770) 836-5753 • http://crawfordcountyhistoricalsociety.org

Rome
Chieftains Museum • 501 Riverside Pkwy, P.O. Box 373 • Rome, GA 30162 • (706) 291-9494 • http://www.chieftainsmuseum.org

Livingston Library & Museum • Shorter College, 315 Shorter Ave • Rome, GA 30165 • (706) 291-2121 • http://www.shorter.edu

Northwest Georgia Historical and Genealogical Society • P.O. Box 5063 • Rome, GA 30161-5063 • (706) 236-4607 • http://www.rootsweb.com/~ganwhags/

Rome Area Heritage Foundation • 1092 Mount Alto Rd SW, P.O. Box 6181 • Rome, GA 30162-6181

Rome Area History Museum • 305 Broad St • Rome, GA 30161 • (706) 235-8051 • http://www.romehistorymuseum.com

Sara Hightower Regional Library • 205 Riverside Pkwy • Rome, GA 30161-2922 • (706) 236-4604 • http://www.floyd.public.lib.ga.us

Roopville
Roopville Historical Society • 165 S Hwy 27, P.O. Box 285 • Roopville, GA 30170 • (770) 854-4460

Rossville
Cherokee Regional Library System-Rossville Public • 504 McFarland Ave • Rossville, GA 30741-1253 • (706) 866-1368 • http://www.walker.public.lib.ga.us/branches/rossville.html

Chief John Ross House - Cherokee • 826 Chickamauga Ave • Rossville, GA 30741 • (706) 861-3954

Chief John Ross House Museum • 200 E Lake Ave • Rossville, GA 30741 • (404) 861-3954

Delta Genealogical Society • c/o Rossville Public Library, 504 McFarland Ave • Rossville, GA 30741 • (706) 866-1368 • http://www.rootsweb.com/~gadgs/

Roswell
Archibald Smith Plantation Home Museum • 935 Alpharetta St • Roswell, GA 30075 • (770) 641-3978 • http://www.archibaldsmithplantation.org

Atlanta-Fulton Public Library System-Roswell Regional Library • 115 Norcross St • Roswell, GA 30075 • (770) 640-3075 • http://www.af.public.lib.ga.us/roswell_regional.html

Barrington Hall Museum • 535 Barrington Dr • Roswell, GA 30075 • (770) 640-3855 • http://barringtonhall-roswell.com

Friends of Bulloch Hall • Bulloch Hall Museum, 180 Bulloch Ave • Roswell, GA 30077 • (770) 992-1731 • http://www.bullochhall.org

Historic Roswell Museum • 617 Atlanta St • Roswell, GA 30075 • (770) 640-3253

Roswell Historic Preservation Commission • 180 Bullock Ave, P.O. Box 1309 • Roswell, GA 30075 • (770) 992-1731

Roswell Historical Society • Roswell Research Library, 950 Forrest St, P.O. Box 274 • Roswell, GA 30075 • (770) 594-6405 • http://www.roswellhs.com

Smith Plantation Home Preservationists • 935 Alpharetta St • Roswell, GA 30075 • (770) 641-3978

Royston
Ty Cobb Museum • 461 Cook St • Royston, GA 30662

Rydal
Pine Log Historical Society • 3371 Pine Log Rd NE • Rydal, GA 30171 • (770) 382-7386

Saint Marys

Camden County Historical Commission • P.O. Box 398 • Saint Marys, GA 31558

Cumberland Island National Seashore Museum • 129 Osborne St, P.O. Box 806 • Saint Marys, GA 31558 • (912) 882-4336 • http://www.nps.gov

Guale Historical Society • P.O. Box 398 • Saint Marys, GA 31558 • (912) 882-4587

Plum Orchard Mansion Museum • Cumberland Island • Saint Marys, GA 31558 • (912) 880-4335

Saint Marys Historic Preservation Commission • 418 Osborne St • Saint Marys, GA 31558 • (912) 882-4667

Saint Marys Submarine Museum • 102 St Marys St W • Saint Marys, GA 31558 • (912) 882-2782 • http://www.stmaryssubmuseum.com

Saint Simons Island

Arthur J Moore Methodist Museum • Epworth-by-the-Sea, P.O. Box 24081 • Saint Simons Island, GA 31522-7081 • (912) 638-4050 • http://methmuse.darientel.net

Coastal Georgia Historical Society • 101 12th St, P.O. Box 21136 • Saint Simons Island, GA 31522-0636 • (912) 638-4666 • http://www.saintsimonslighthouse.org

Fort Frederica National Monument Museum • Route 9, Box 286C • Saint Simons Island, GA 31522 • (912) 638-3639 • http://www.nps.gov/fofr

Historical Society of the South Georgia Conference, United Methodist Church • P.O. Box 20407 • Saint Simons Island, GA 31522 • (912) 634-0105

Saint Simons Lighthouse Museum • 101 12th St, P.O. Box 21136 • Saint Simons Island, GA 31522 • (912) 638-4666 • http://www.saintsimonslighthouse.org

United Methodist Museum • Epworth by the Sea, P.O. Box 407 • Saint Simons Island, GA 31522 • (912) 638-4050 • http://www.epworthbythesea.org

Sandersville

Brown House Museum • 268 N Harris St, P.O. Box 6088 • Sandersville, GA 31082 • (478) 552-1965 • http://www.pollette.com/washington/washington.htm

T J Elder Community Center Museum • 316 Hall St • Sandersville, GA 31096 • (478) 553-9050

Washington County Historical Society • Genealogy Research Center and Museum, 129 Jones St, P.O. Box 6088 • Sandersville, GA 31082 • (478) 552-6965 • http://www.rootsweb.com/~gawashin/washingtoncounty002.htm

Sandy Springs

Heritage Sandy Springs • 135 Hilderbrand Dr NE • Sandy Springs, GA 30328 • (404) 851-9111

Sandy Springs Historic Site Museum • 6075 Sandy Springs Cr, P.O. Box 720213 • Sandy Springs, GA 30358 • (404) 851-9101

Sautee-Nacoochee

Sautee-Nacoochee Community Association • Historical Museum, 283 N 255 Hwy, P.O. Box 460 • Sautee-Nacoochee, GA 30571 • (706) 878-3300 • http://www.snca.org

Savannah

Andrew Low House Museum • 329 Abercorn St • Savannah, GA 31401 • (912) 233-6854 • http://www.andrewlowhouse.com

Bethesda Museum - Cunningham Historic Center • 9520 Ferguson Ave, P.O. Box 13039 • Savannah, GA 31416-0039 • (912) 351-2061 • http://www.bethesdahomeforboys.org

Bethesda-Union Society • P.O. Box 13039 • Savannah, GA 31416-0039 • (912) 351-2061 • http://www.bethesdahomeforboys.org

Bonaventure Historical Society • 1317 E 55th St, P.O. Box 5954 • Savannah, GA 31414-5954 • (912) 233-8121 • http://www.bonaventurehistorical.org

Catholic Diocese of Savannah • 601 E Liberty St • Savannah, GA 31401-5196 • (912) 201-4070 • http://www.dioceseofsavannah.org/Home/

Chatham County Historian • 1253 Little Neck Rd • Savannah, GA 31419 • (912) 920-2299

Coastal Heritage Society • 303 Martin Luther King Jr Blvd, P.O. Box 31093 • Savannah, GA 31401 • (912) 651-6840 • http://www.chsgeorgia.org

Coastal Scottish Heritage Society • P.O. Box 31093 • Savannah, GA 31410

Congregation Mickve Israel • 20 E Gordon St • Savannah, GA 31401 • http://www.mickveisrael.org

Davenport House Museum • 324 E State St • Savannah, GA 31402 • (912) 236-8097 • http://www.davenportsavga.com

Factor's Walk Military Museum • P.O. Box 10041 • Savannah, GA 31412 • (912) 232-8003

First African Baptist Church Museum • Franklin Sq, 23 Montgomery St • Savannah, GA 31401 • (912) 233-2244 • http://www.oldestblackchurch.org

First Presbyterian Church Library • 520 Washington Ave • Savannah, GA 31405 • (912) 354-7615 • http://www.fpc.presbychurch.net

Fort Pulaski National Monument Museum • US Hwy 80 E, P.O. Box 30757 • Savannah, GA 31410 • (912) 786-5787 • http://www.nps.gov/fopu

Georgia Historical Society • Historical Museum, 501 Whitaker St • Savannah, GA 31401-4889 • (912) 651-2128 • http://www.georgiahistory.com

Girl Scout First Headquarters Museum • 330 Drayton St • Savannah, GA 31401 • (912) 232-8200 • http://www.gshg.org

Green-Meldrim House Museum • 14 W Macon St • Savannah, GA 31401 • (912) 232-1251

Historic Savannah Foundation • 321 E York St, P.O. Box 1733 • Savannah, GA 31402 • (912) 233-7787 • http://www.historicsavannahfoundation.org

Independent Presbyterian Church Archives • P.O. Box 926 • Savannah, GA 31412 • (912) 236-3346

Juliette Gordon Low Birthplace Museum • 10 E Oglethorpe Ave • Savannah, GA 31401 • (912) 233-4501 • http://www.girlscouts.org/birthplace

King-Tisdell Cottage Museum • 514 E Huntingdon St • Savannah, GA 31401 • (912) 234-8000

Lane Library • Armstrong Atlantic State Univ, 11935 Abercorn St • Savannah, GA 31419-1997 • (912) 927-5332 • http://www.library.armstrong.edu

Live Oak Public Libraries • 2002 Bull St • Savannah, GA 31401 • (912) 652-3600 • http://www.liveoakpl.org

Massie Heritage Interpretation Center • 207 E Gordon St • Savannah, GA 31401 • (912) 651-7002 • http://www.massieschool.com

National Society of the Colonial Dames of America in the State of Georgia • Andrew Low House, 329 Abercorn St • Savannah, GA 31401 • (912) 233-6854 • http://www.andrewlow.com/location.html

Old Fort Jackson Museum • 1 Fort Jackson Rd • Savannah, GA 31404 • (912) 232-3945 • http://www.chsgeorgia.org

Savannah, cont.

Owens-Thomas House Museum • 124 Abercorn St • Savannah, GA 31401 • (912) 233-9743 • http://www.telfair.org

Ralph Mark Gilbert Civil Rights Museum • 460 Martin Luther King Jr Blvd • Savannah, GA 31401 • (912) 231-8900 • http://www.savannahcivilrightsmuseum.com

Savannah Area Genealogical Association • P.O. Box 15385 • Savannah, GA 31416 • (912) 354-2708 • http://www.rootsweb.com/~gasaga/

Savannah History Association • Historical Museum, 303 Martin Luther King Jr Blvd • Savannah, GA 31401-4217 • (912) 651-6825

Savannah Jewish Archives • Georgia Historical Society, 501 Whittaker St • Savannah, GA 31499 • (912) 651-2125 • http://www.georgiahistory.com/sja.htm

Savannah Ogeechee Canal Society • 681 Fort Argyle Rd • Savannah, GA 31419

SCAD Department of Architectural History • P.O. Box 3146 • Savannah, GA 31402

Screven County Historical and Genealogical Society • 384 Penrose Dr W • Savannah, GA 31410-1234

Ships of the Sea Maritime Museum • William Scarbrough House, 41 Martin Luther King Blvd • Savannah, GA 31401 • (912) 232-1511 • http://www.shipsofthesea.org

Society for the Preservation of Laurel Grove • P.O. Box 10315 • Savannah, GA 31412

Telfair Academy Historic House Museum • 121 Barnard St, P.O. Box 31412 • Savannah, GA 321412 • (912) 232-1177 • http://www.telfair.org

Temple Mickve Israel Museum • 20 E Gordon St, Monterey Square, P.O. Box 816 • Savannah, GA 31402 • (912) 233-1547 • http://www.mickveisrael.org

Thunderbolt Museum • 2702 Mechanics Ave • Savannah, GA 31401

Wormsloe State Historic Site Museum • 7601 Skidaway Rd • Savannah, GA 31406 • (912) 353-3023 • http://www.gastateparks.org

Senoia

Senoia Area Historical Society • P.O. Box 301 • Senoia, GA 30276 • (770) 599-6457

Sharpsburg

Coweta Chapter Genealogical and Historical Society • 8031 Hwy 54 • Sharpsburg, GA 30277

Smyrna

Smyrna Historical and Genealogical Society • Smyrna Museum, 2861 Atlanta St • Smyrna, GA 30082-3305 • (770) 435-7549 • http://www.smyrnahistory.org

Smyrna Public Library • 100 Village Green Cr • Smyrna, GA 30080-3478 • (770) 431-2860 • http://www.smyrna-library.com

Snellville

Snellville Historical Society • 2405 Springdale Dr • Snellville, GA 30078-3763 • (770) 736-3317 • http://www.snellville.org

Social Circle

Uncle Remus Regional Library System-W H Stanton Memorial Library • 1045 W Hightower Trail, P.O. Box 566 • Social Circle, GA 30025-0566 • (770) 464-2444 • http://www.uncleremus.org

Soperton

Treutlen County Historical Society • Treutlen County Museum of Local History, P.O. Box 235 • Soperton, GA 30457 • (912) 529-6711

Sparks

Cook County Historical Society • P.O. Box 497 • Sparks, GA 31647

Sparta

Sparta-Hancock County Historical Society • Old Jail Museum, 526 Court St • Sparta, GA 31087 • (843) 509-2584 • http://www.shchs.org

Uncle Remus Regional Library System-Hancock County Library • 403 E Broad St • Sparta, GA 31087 • (706) 444-5389 • http://www.uncleremus.org

Springfield

Historic Effingham Society • Old Jail Museum, 1002 Pine St, P.O. Box 999 • Springfield, GA 31329 • (912) 826-4770 • http://www.historiceffinghamsociety.org

Statenville

Echols County Historian • P.O. Box 210 • Statenville, GA 31648 • (912) 559-5798

Echols County Historical Society • 131 Tillman Ln • Statenville, GA 31648 • (229) 559-8310

South Georgia Regional Library System-Statenville Branch • US Hwy 129 & Jackson St • Statenville, GA 31648 • (229) 559-8182

Statesboro

Bulloch County Hill Dept - Vital Records • 1 W Altman St, P.O. Box 666 • Statesboro, GA 30459 • (912) 764-3800

Bulloch County Historian • 241 Donaldson St • Statesboro, GA 30458 • (912) 764-4093

Bulloch County Historical Society • P.O. Box 42 • Statesboro, GA 30459 • (912) 681-1956

Georgia Southern University Museum • Rosenwald Bldg, P.O. Box 8061 • Statesboro, GA 30460 • (912) 681-5444 • http://ceps.georgiasouthern.edu/museum

Statesboro Regional Library • 124 S Main St • Statesboro, GA 30458 • (912) 764-1337 • http://www.srls.public.lib.ga.us

Zach S Henderson Library • Georgia Southern College, P.O. Box 8074 • Statesboro, GA 30460-8074 • (912) 681-5115 • http://www2.gasou.edu/library

Stone Mountain

African American Cemeteries Archive • 5231-E Memorial Dr #353 • Stone Mountain, GA 30083 • http://www.prairiebluff.com/aacemetery

Jamestowne Society, First Georgia Company • 494 Hickory Hills Tr • Stone Mountain, GA 30083-4372 • (770) 469-5224 • http://www.jamestowne.org/company/gal.htm

Stone Mountain Park Museum • Memorial Hall Museum, Antebellum Plantation, P.O. Box 778 • Stone Mountain, GA 30086 • (770) 498-5690 • http://www.stonemountainpark.com

Summerville

Chattooga County Historical Society • 119 E Washington St, P.O. Box 626 • Summerville, GA 30747 • (404) 857-2553 • http://www.rootsweb.com/~gachatto/cchs.htm

Chattooga County Library • 360 Farrar Dr • Summerville, GA 30747-2016 • (706) 857-2553 • http://www.chattooga.public.lib.ga.us

Suwanee

Suwanee Historical Association • P.O. Box 815 • Suwanee, GA 30174

Swainsboro

East Georgia College Library • 131 College Circle • Swainsboro, GA 30401-2699 • (478) 289-2087 • http://www.ega.edu/library/

Emanuel County Historian • East Georgia College, 131 College Cr • Swainsboro, GA 30401 • (912) 289-2034

Emanuel County Historic Society • 161 Museum Rd • Swainsboro, GA 30401-3742 • (478) 237-6924

Emanuel Historic Preservation Society • 161 Museum Rd, P.O. Box 363 • Swainsboro, GA 30401 • (478) 289-0070

First Families of Georgia, 1733-1797 • P.O. Box 478 • Swainsboro, GA 30401-0478 • (478) 237-2635

Sylvania
Screven-Jenkins Regional Library • 106 S Community Dr • Sylvania, GA 30467 • (912) 564-7526 • http://www.tlc.library.net/screven

Sylvester
Worth County Historical Society • 1610 West St, P.O. Box 5073 • Sylvester, GA 31791 • (229) 776-4481

Tallapoosa
West Georgia Museum of Tallapoosa • 185 Mann St, P.O. Box 725 • Tallapoosa, GA 30176 • (770) 574-3125 • http://www.cyberspacemuseum.com/n7_8.html

Taylorsville
Euhaarlee History Museum • 1433 Old Alabama Rd • Taylorsville, GA 30178 • (770) 607) 2017

Thomaston
Pettigrew-White-Stamps House Museum • Andrews Dr • Thomaston, GA 30286 • (706) 647-9686

Thomaston-Upson Archives • 301 S Carter St, P.O. Box 1137 • Thomaston, GA 30286-0015 • (706) 646-2437 • http://www.tuarch.org

Upson County Historian • 105 Hill St • Thomaston, GA 30286 • (706) 647-7915

Upson Historical Society • 746 Andrews Dr, P.O. Box 363 • Thomaston, GA 30286 • (706) 647-6839 • http://www.rootsweb.com/~gauhs/

Thomasville
Lapham-Patterson House Museum • 626 N Dawson St • Thomasville, GA 31792 • (229) 225-4004 • http://www.gastateparks.org

Lapham-Patterson Society • 626 N Dawson St • Thomasville, GA 31792 • (229) 225-4004

Pebble Hill Plantation Museum • 1251 US 319 S, P.O. Box 830 • Thomasville, GA 31799 • (229) 226-2344 • http://www.pebblehill.com

South Georgia Genealogical Society • 706 Crabapple Dr • Thomasville, GA 31757

South Georgia Genealogical Society • P.O. Box 3307 • Thomasville, GA 31799-3307

Thomas College Library • 1501 Millpond Rd • Thomasville, GA 31792 • (229) 226-1621 • http://www.thomasu.edu

Thomas County Historical Society • Historical Museum, 725 N Dawson St, P.O. Box 1922 • Thomasville, GA 31799 • (229) 226-7664 • http://www.rose.net/~history/

Thomas County Public Library System • 201 N Madison St • Thomasville, GA 31792-5414 • (229) 225-5252 • http://www.tcpls.org

Thomas University Library • 1501 Millpond Rd • Thomasville, GA 31792 • (229) 226-1621 • http://www.thomascollege.edu

Thomasville Cultural Center Library • 600 E Washington, P.O. Box 2177 • Thomasville, GA 31799 • (229) 226-0588 • http://www.tccarts.org

Thomasville Genealogical and Historical Library • 135 N Broad St, P.O. Box 1597 • Thomasville, GA 31799 • (229) 226-9640 • http://www.rose.net/~glibrary/

Thomasville Genealogical History • 135 N Broad St • Thomasville, GA 31792 • (229) 226-9640

Thomasville Landmarks • 312 N Broad St, P.O. Box 1285 • Thomasville, GA 31799 • (229) 226-6016 • http://members.aol.com/shuknnjivn/CommPresProj.html

Thomson
Hickory Hill Historic House Museum • 502 Hickory Hill Dr • Thomson, GA 30824 • (706) 595-7777 • http://www.hickory-hill.org

McDuffie County Historical Society • 633 Hemlock Dr, P.O. Box 1816 • Thomson, GA 30824 • (706) 595-3548

Wrightsboro Quaker Community Foundation • 633 Hemlock Dr, P.O. Box 1816 • Thomson, GA 30824 • (706) 595-5335

Tifton
Agrirama Living History Museum • 1392 Whiddon Mill Rd, P.O. Box Q • Tifton, GA 31793 • (229) 386-3344 • http://www.agrirama.com

Coastal Plain Regional Library • 2014 Chestnut Ave, P.O. Box 7606 • Tifton, GA 31794 • (229) 386-3400 • http://www.tift.public.lib.ga.us

Toccoa
Stephens County Historical Society • 313 S Pond St, P.O. Box 125 • Toccoa, GA 30577 • (706) 282-5055 • http://www.toccoahistory.com

Toccoa Historical Group • 313 Pond St • Toccoa, GA 30577

Traveler's Rest State Historic Site Museum • 11 Stage Coach Dr • Toccoa, GA 30577 • (705) 886-2256 • http://www.travelersresthistorisite.com

Trenton
Cherokee Regional Library System-Dade County Public Library • 102 Court St, P.O. Box 340 • Trenton, GA 30752-0340 • (706) 657-7857 • http://www.mail.walker.public.lib.ga.us/branches/dade.html

Dade County Historical Society • New England Rd, P.O. Box 512 • Trenton, GA 30757 • (229) 386-3400

Tybee Island
Fort Pulaski National Monument Archives • US Hwy 80, P.O. Box 30757 • Tybee Island, GA 31410-0757 • (912) 786-5787 • http://www.nps.gov/fopu

Fort Screven Museum • P.O. Box 97 • Tybee Island, GA 31328 • (912) 786-4077

Tybee Island Historical Society • Lighthouse Museum, 30 Meddin Dr, P.O. Box 366 • Tybee Island, GA 31328-0366 • (912) 786-5801 • http://www.tybeelighthouse.org

Valdosta
Crescent Historic House Museum • 904 N Patterson St, P.O. Box 2423 • Valdosta, GA 31604 • (912) 244-6747

Genealogy Unlimited • 2511 Churchill Dr, P.O. Box 3013 • Valdosta, GA 31604-3013 • (229) 244-0464 • http://www.rootsweb.com/~gagus/

International Association of Tartan Studies • 4432 Huntington Pointe • Valdosta, GA 31602

Lowndes County Historical Society • Historical Museum, 305 W Central Ave, P.O. Box 56 • Valdosta, GA 31603-0056 • (229) 247-4780 • http://www.valdostamuseum.org

National Society of Colonial Dames of America in Georgia, Valdosta Town Committee • 821 Millpond Rd • Valdosta, GA 31602 • (912) 242-7997

Odum Library • Valdosta State College, 1500 N Patterson St • Valdosta, GA 31698 • (229) 333-5860 • http://www.libs.uga.edu/russell/books.valdosta.edu

South Georgia Regional Library • 300 Woodrow Wilson Dr • Valdosta, GA 31602 • (229) 333-0086 • http://www.sgrl.org

Varnell
Prater's Mill Foundation • Praters Mill Historic Site Museum • City Hall, 500 Praters Mill Rd, P.O. Drawer H • Varnell, GA 30756 • (706) 694-6455 • http://www.pratersmill.org

Vidalia

Altama Museum of History • 611 Jackson St, P.O. Box 33 • Vidalia, GA 30475 • (912) 537-1911

Ladson Genealogical and Historical Foundation • John E Ladson, Jr Genealogical Library, 119 Church St • Vidalia, GA 30474 • (912) 537-8186 • http://www.toombs.public.lib.ga.us/ladson.htm

Ohoopee Regional Library • 610 Jackson St • Vidalia, GA 30474-2835 • (912) 537-9283 • http://www.toombs.public.lib.ga.us

Toombs County Historical Society • 1906 Woodland Ct, P.O. Box 2825 • Vidalia, GA 30474 • (912) 537-2779

Vienna

George State Cotton Museum • 1321 E Union St, P.O. Box 309 • Vienna, GA 31092 • (229) 268-2045 • http://www.historicvienna.org

Vienna Historic Preservation Society • P.O. Box 309 • Vienna, GA 31092 • (229) 268-3663 • http://www.historicvienna.org

Vienna Historic Preservation Society • Historical Museum, 1321 E Union St • Vienna, GA 31092 • (912) 268-2045

Walter F George Law Office Museum • 106 N 4th St • Vienna, GA 31092 • (229) 268-3663 • http://www.historicvienna.org

Waleska

Funk Heritage Center • Reinhardt College, 7300 Reinhardt College Cr • Waleska, GA 30183 • (770) 720-9222 • http://www.reinhardt.edu/funkheritage

Warm Springs

Roosevelt Warm Springs Institute • P.O. Box 1000 • Warm Springs, GA 31830

Roosevelt's Little White House Historic Site Museum • 401 Little White House Rd • Warm Springs, GA 31830 • (706) 655-5870 • http://www.fdr-littlewhitehouse.org

Warner Robins

Central Georgia Genealogical Society • 1600 Elberta Rd, P.O. Box 2024 • Warner Robins, GA 31099-2024 • (478) 953-3114 • http://www.cggs.org

Houston County Public Library System • 721 Watson Blvd • Warner Robins, GA 31093 • (478) 923-0128 • http://www.houpl.org

Middle Georgia Railroad Association • 111 Blake Terr • Warner Robins, GA 31088

Museum of Aviation at Robins AFB • Hwy 247 & Russell Pkwy, P.O. Box 2469 • Warner Robins, GA 31099 • (478) 926-6870 • http://www.museumofaviation.org

Taylor County Historical-Genealogical Society • P.O. Box 5059 • Warner Robins, GA 31009 • (912) 923-1525

Warrenton

Warren County Genealogical Society • 103 Memorial Dr, P.O. Box 47 • Warrenton, GA 30828

Washington

Bartram Trail Regional Library • 204 E Liberty St • Washington, GA 30673 • (706) 678-7736 • http://ptquattlebaum.com/library/

Robert Toombs House Museum • 216 E Robert Toombs Ave, P.O. Box 605 • Washington, GA 30673 • (706) 678-2226 • http://www.gastateparks.org

Washington Township Historical Society • Historical Museum, 308 E Robert Toombs Ave • Washington, GA 30673-2038 • (706) 678-2105 • http://www.washingtonwilkes.org

Washington-Wilkes Historical Foundation • 308 E Robert Toombs Ave, P.O. Box 337 • Washington, GA 30673-2038 • (706) 678-2105

Watkinsville

Athens Regional Library System-Oconee County • 1080 Experiment Station Rd, P.O. Box 837 • Watkinsville, GA 30677-0019 • (706) 769-3950 • http://www.clarke.public.lib.ga.us/branches/oconee/oconee.html

Eagle Tavern Museum • 26 N Main St, P.O. Box 959 • Watkinsville, GA 30677 • (706) 769-5197 • http://www.visitoconee.com

Old Athens Cemetery Foundation • 1430 Broadlands • Watkinsville, GA 30677 • (706) 769-6698

Waycross

Hilliard House Museum • 1460 N Augusta Ave • Waycross, GA 31503 • (912) 285-4260

Okefenokee Heritage Center • 1460 N Augusta Ave • Waycross, GA 31503 • (912) 285-4260 • http://www.okeheritage.org

Okefenokee Historical and Genealogical Society • 1617 Ball St • Waycross, GA 31503

Okefenokee Regional Library • 401 Lee Ave, P.O. Box 1669 • Waycross, GA 31501 • (912) 287-4978 • http://www.ware.public.lib.ga.us

Waynesboro

Burke County Genealogical Society • Burke County Museum, 536 Liberty St • Waynesboro, GA 30830 • (706) 554-4889 • http://members.aol.com/J2525/gen.htm

Burke County Historical Association • Quaker Rd • Waynesboro, GA 30830

Burke County Historical Society • Burke County Museum, 536 Liberty St • Waynesboro, GA 30830 • (706) 554-4889

East Central Georgia Regional Library-Burke County Library • 412 4th St • Waynesboro, GA 30830 • (706) 554-3277 • http://www.ecgrl.public.lib.ga.us/burke.htm

West Point

Chattahoochee Valley Historical Society • 1213 5th Ave • West Point, GA 31833

Fort Tyler Association • P.O. Box 510 • West Point, GA 31833 • (706) 645-8162

Hawkes Library • W 8th St • West Point, GA 31833 • (706) 645-1549

Weston

Weston Woman's Club • P.O. Box 127 • Weston, GA 31832 • (229) 828-2555

Whigham

Lower Muskogee Creek Tribe • Tama Tribal Museum, 107 Long Pine Dr • Whigham, GA 31797 • (229) 762-3165

White

Clermont County (OH) Genealogical Society • 18 Black Water Dr • White, GA 30184-2880 • (770) 607-7682

Winder

Barrow County Historical Society • Barrow County Museum, 94 E Athens St, P.O. Box 277 • Winder, GA 30680 • (770) 307-1183 • http://www.cityofwinder.com/museum.asp

East Georgia Genealogical Society • P.O. Box 117 • Winder, GA 30680 • http://www.rootsweb com/~gaeggs/

Fort Yargo State Park • 210 S Broad St • Winder, GA 30680 • (770) 687-3489 • http://www.gastateparks.org

Piedmont Regional Genealogy Society • P.O. Box 368 • Winder, GA 30680

Piedmont Regional Library • 189 Bellvue St • Winder, GA 30680-9998 • (770) 867-2762 • http://library.barrow.public.lib.ga.us

Winterville
Athens Regional Library System-Winterville Branch • 115 Marigold Lane, P.O. Box 89 • Winterville, GA 30683-0089 • (706) 742-7735

Carter-Coile Country Doctors Museum • 111 Marigold Ln, P.O. Box 306 • Winterville, GA 30683 • (706) 742-8600 • http://www.cityofwinterville.com

Woodbine
Bryan Lang Historical Library • P.O. Box 715 • Woodbine, GA 31569 • (912) 576-5841

Bryan-Lang Historical Library • 4th St & Camden Ave, P.O. Box 715 • Woodbine, GA 31569-0715 • (912) 576-5841

Woodbine International Fire Museum • 110 Bedell Ave, P.O. Box 58 • Woodbine, GA 31569-0058 • (912) 476-5351

Woodstock
Cherokee County Historical Society • Haney Road • Woodstock, GA 30188

Wrightsville
Johnson County Historical Society • c/o Harlie Fulford Library, 301 Elm St, P.O. Box 87 • Wrightsville, GA 31096 • (478) 864-3940

Young Harris
Duckworth Library • Young Harris College, 1 College St, P.O. Box 39 • Young Harris, GA 30582-0039 • (706) 379-4313 • http://www.yhc.edu

Mountain Regional Library • 698 Miller St, P.O. Box 159 • Young Harris, GA 30582-0159 • (706) 379-3732 • http://pines.lib.ga.us

Georgia

Captain Cook
Kona Historical Society • Historical Museum, P.O. Box 398 • Captain Cook, HI 96704 • (808) 323-3222 • http://www.konahistorical.org

Ewa Station
Hawaiian Railway Society • Historical Museum, 91-1001 Renton Rd, P.O. Box 60369 • Ewa Station, HI 96706 • (808) 681-5461 • http://www.hawaiianrailway.com

Fort DeRussy
US Army Museum of Hawaii • Battery Randolph, Kaha Rd • Fort DeRussy, HI 96815 • (808) 438-2821 • http://www.2sidl.army.mil

Fort Shafter
Fort Shafter Library • United States Army, Bldg 650 • Fort Shafter, HI 96858-5005 • (808) 438-9521

US Army Museum of Hawaii • STOP 319, Directorate of Community Activities, CRD, USAG-HI • Fort Shafter, HI 96858-5000 • (808) 438-2822

Hana
Hana Cultural Center and Museum • 4974 Uakea Rd, P.O. Box 27 • Hana, HI 96713 • (808) 248-8622 • http://planet-hawaii.com/hana/

Hanalei
Hoopulapula Haraguchi Rice Mill Museum • 5-5070 Kuhio Hwy, P.O. Box 427 • Hanalei, HI 96714 • (808) 651-3399 • http://www.haraguchiricemill.org

Hickam AFB
Hickam Air Force Base Library FL5260 • 15 SVS/SVMG, 990 Mills Blvd, Bldg 595 • Hickam AFB, HI 96853-5316 • (808) 449-7163 • http://www.hickamservices.com/library1

Hilo
Association of Hawaiian Civic Clubs • 187 Hoomalu St • Hilo, HI 96720

Edwin H Mookini Library • University of Hawaii at Hilo, 200 W Kawili St • Hilo, HI 96720-4091 • (808) 974-7346 • http://library.uhh.hawaii.edu

Hawaii County Genealogical Society • Lyman House Museum, 276 Haili St • Hilo, HI 96720 • (808) 969-7685 • http://www.lymanmuseum.org

Pacific Tsunami Museum • 130 Kamehameha Ave, P.O. Box 806 • Hilo, HI 96721 • (808) 935-0926

Wailoa Center Museum • 200 Piopio St, P.O. Box 936 • Hilo, HI 96720 • (808) 933-4360

Honolulu
442nd Veterans Club Museum • 933 Wiliwili St • Honolulu, HI 96826 • (808) 945-0032

Ain Like-Native Hawaiian Library Project • 456 Keawe St • Honolulu, HI 96813-5125 • (808) 535-6750

Archives of the Episcopal Diocese of Honolulu • 229 Queen Emma Sq • Honolulu, HI 96813 • (808) 536-7776 • http://ecusa.anglican.org/hawaii/

Battleship Missouri Memorial Museum • 63 Cowpens St, P.O. Box 879 • Honolulu, HI 96818 • (808) 423-2263 • http://www.ussmissouri.com

Bernard Levinson Jewish Archives • Temple Emmanu-El, 2550 Pali Hwy • Honolulu, HI 96817 • (808) 595-7521

Bernice Pauahi Bishop Museum • 1525 Bernice St • Honolulu, HI 96817-2704 • (808) 848-4148 • http://www.bishopmuseum.org

Catholic Diocese of Honolulu • 1184 Bishop St • Honolulu, HI 96813 • (808) 533-1791

Center for Oral History Archives • Univ of Hawaii at Manoa, 2424 Maile Wy • Honolulu, HI 96822 • (808) 956-6259 • http://www.oralhistory.hawaii.edu

Central Union Church Archives • 1660 S Beretania St • Honolulu, HI 96826 • (808) 941-0957

Cooke Library • Punahou School Archives, 1601 Punahou St • Honolulu, HI 96822 • (808) 943-3225 • http://www.punahou.edu

DAR Memorial Library • 1914 Makiki Heights Dr • Honolulu, HI 96822 • (808) 949-7256 • http://www.geocities.com/darhawaii/

Daughters of Hawaii • Queen Emma's Summer Palace, 2913 Pali Hwy • Honolulu, HI 96817 • (808) 595-3167 • http://www.daughtersofhawaii.org

Daughters of the American Revolution, Aloha Chapter • 1914 Makiki Heights Dr • Honolulu, HI 96822

East-West Center Museum • 1601 East-West Rd • Honolulu, HI 96868 • (808) 944-7111 • http://www.eastwestcenter.org

Episcopal Church, Diocesan Archives • 229 Queen Emma Square • Honolulu, HI 96813 • (808) 536-7776

Gregg M Sinclair Library • University of Hawaii, 2425 Campus Rd • Honolulu, HI 96822 • (808) 956-8308 • http://www.sinclair.hawaii.edu

Hamilton Library • Univ of Hawaii, 2550 McCarthy Mall • Honolulu, HI 96822 • (808) 956-8264 • http://www2.hawaii.edu/~speccoll/arch/hours.htm

Hamilton Library, Special Collections • Univ of Hawaii at Manoa, 2550 The Mall • Honolulu, HI 96822 • (808) 956-8264 • http://www.hawaii.edu/speccoll/arch/

Hawaii Chinese History Center Library • 111 N King St, Rm 410 • Honolulu, HI 96817-4703 • (808) 521-5948

Hawaii Council on Portuguese Heritage • 810 N Vineyard Blvd, Rm 7 • Honolulu, HI 96817 • (808) 845-1616

Hawaii Maritime Center Library & Photo Archives • Pier 7 • Honolulu, HI 96813 • (808) 523-6151 • http://holoholo.org/maritime/

Hawaii State Archives • Iolani Palace Grounds, 478 S King St • Honolulu, HI 96813 • (808) 586-0329 • http://www.state.hi.us/dags/archives/

Hawaii State Dept of Health - Vital Records • 1250 Punchbowl St, Rm 103, P.O. Box 3378 • Honolulu, HI 96801 • (808) 808-586-4533 • http://www.hawaii.gov/health/records/

Hawaii State Library • 478 S King St • Honolulu, HI 96813 • (808) 586-3621 • http://www.hawaii.gov/hidocs

Hawaiian Historical Society • Historical Museum, 560 Kawaiahao St • Honolulu, HI 96813-5023 • (808) 537-6271 • http://www.hawaiianhistory.org

Hawaiian Mission Children's Society Library • 553 S King St • Honolulu, HI 96813-3002 • (808) 531-0481 • http://www.lava.net/~mhm/main.htm

Honolulu Community College Library • 874 Dillingham Blvd • Honolulu, HI 96817-4598 • (808) 845-9199 • http://www.honolulu.hawaii.edu

Honolulu County Genealogical Society • 1116 Kealaolou Ave, P.O. Box 235039 • Honolulu, HI 96816-5419 • (808) 262-8466 • http://www.rootsweb.com/~hihcgs

Honolulu Police Department Law Enforcement Museum • 801 S Beretania St • Honolulu, HI 96813 • (808) 529-3028 • http://www.honolulupd.org/irs/tours.htm

Iolani Palace Museum • 364 S King St, P.O. Box 2259 • Honolulu, HI 96804 • (808) 552-0822 • http://www.iolanipalace.org

Iolani School Museum • 563 Kamoku St • Honolulu, HI 96826 • (808) 943-2336

Japanese Cultural Center of Hawaii • 2454 S Beretania St • Honolulu, HI 96826 • (808) 945-7633 • http://www.jcch.com

Hawaii

Honolulu, cont.
Jewish Federation of Hawaii • 2550 Pali Hwy • Honolulu, HI 96817 • (808) 595-5218

Judiciary History Center Museum • 417 S King St • Honolulu, HI 96813 • (808) 539-4999 • http://www.jhchawaii.org

Kapiolani Community College Library • 4303 Diamond Head Rd • Honolulu, HI 96816 • (808) 734-9359 • http://library.kcc.hawaii.edu/main/

Kawaiahao Church Archives • 957 Punchbowl St • Honolulu, HI 96813 • (808) 522-1333

King Kamehameha History Center • S King St • Honolulu, HI 96813 • (808) 539-4999 • http://www.jhchawaii.org

Makiki Christian Church Archives • 829 Pensacola St • Honolulu, HI 96814 • (808) 594-6446

Mamiya Medical Heritage Museum • Hawaii Medical Library, 1221 Punchbowl St • Honolulu, HI 96813 • (808) 536-9302 • http://www.hml.org/mmhc/

Marianist Province of the Pacific Archives • 3140 Waialae Ave • Honolulu, HI 96816 • (808) 739-4738

Masonic Grand Lodge of Hawaii • 535 Ward Ave, Ste 212 • Honolulu, HI 96814 • (808) 596-9121 • http://hawaiifreemason.org

Masonic Public Library of Hawaii • 1611 Kewalo St • Honolulu, HI 96822 • (808) 521-2070

Mission Houses Museum • 553 S King St • Honolulu, HI 96813 • (808) 531-0481 • http://www.missionhouses.org

Municipal Reference and Records Center Archives • City Hall Annex, 558 S King St • Honolulu, HI 96813 • (808) 523-4044 • http://www.co.honolulu.hi.us/csd/lrmb/references.htm

Palama Settlement Museum • 810 N Vineyard Blvd • Honolulu, HI 96817 • (808) 845-3945

Polynesian Voyaging Society • Pier 7, 191 Ala Moana Blvd • Honolulu, HI 96813 • (808) 536-8405 • http://leahi.kcc.hawaii.edu/org/pvs/

Portuguese Genealogical Society of Hawaii • 810 N Vineyard Blvd, Rm 11 • Honolulu, HI 96817 • (808) 841-5044 • http://www.lusaweb.com/genealogy/html/phgs.cfm

Punahou School Archives • Cooke Library, 1601 Punahou St • Honolulu, HI 96822 • (808) 943-3225 • http://www.punahou.edu

Queen Emma Summer Palace Museum • 2913 Pali Hwy • Honolulu, HI 96817 • (808) 595-3167 • http://www.daughtersofhawaii.org

Royal Mausoleum State Monument • 2261 Nu'uanu Ave • Honolulu, HI 96817 • (808) 536-7602

Sisters of the Sacred Hearts Archives, Pacific Province • 1120 5th Ave • Honolulu, HI 96816 • (808) 737-5822 • http://www.glauco.it/sscc/

Society of the Descendants of the Alamo • P.O. Box 4641 • Honolulu, HI 96812

Sons of the American Revolution, Hawaii Society • P.O. box 240371 • Honolulu, HI 96824-0371 • (808) 780-3627 • http://www.hawaiisar.org

Thomas Hale Hamilton Library • University of Hawaii, 2550 McCarthy Mall • Honolulu, HI 96822 • (808) 956-7214 • http://www.libweb.hawaii.edu/uhmlib/

USS Arizona Memorial Library • 1 Arizona Memorial Pl • Honolulu, HI 96818-3145 • (808) 422-2771 • http://www.nps.gov

USS Bowfin Submarine Museum & Park • 11 Arizona Memorial Dr • Honolulu, HI 96818-3145 • (808) 423-1341 • http://www.bowfin.org

Kahului
Maui Community College Library • 310 Kaahumanu Ave • Kahului, HI 96732 • (808) 984-3298 • http://mauicc.hawaii.edu/unit/library/welcome.html

Paper Airplane Museum • 70 E Kaahumanu Ave • Kahului, HI 96768 • (808) 877-8916

Kailua
Jewish Genealogical Society of Hawaii • 237 Kuumele Pl • Kailua, HI 96734-2958 • (808) 262-0030

Kailua-Kona
Astronaut Ellison S Onizuka Space Center • Keahole Intl Airport, P.O. Box 833 • Kailua-Kona, HI 96745 • (808) 329-3441

Hulihee Palace Museum • 75-5718 Ali'i Dr • Kailua-Kona, HI 96740 • (808) 329-1877 • http://www.huliheepalace.org

Kalaupapa
Kalaupapa National Historical Park • 7 Puahi St, P.O. Box 2222 • Kalaupapa, HI 96742 • (808) 567-6802 • http://www.nps.gov/kala/gov

Kamuela
Historic Parker Ranch House Museum • 67-1435 Mamalahoa Hwy, P.O. Box 458 • Kamuela, HI 96743 • (808) 885-5433 • http://www.parkerranch.com/historichomes.php

Puukohola Heiau National Historic Site Museum • 62-3601 Kawaiihae Rd • Kamuela, HI 96743 • (808) 882-8718 • http://www.nps.gov/puhe

Kaneohe
Hawaiian Scottish Association • P.O. Box 636 • Kaneohe, HI 97644 • (808) 235-7605

He'eia Historical Society • 46 Kamehameha Hwy #205 • Kaneohe, HI 96744-3712 • (808) 247-3027

Windward Community College Library • 45-720 Keaahala Rd • Kaneohe, HI 96744 • (808) 235-7438 • http://www.library.wcc.hawaii.edu

Kaneohe Bay
MCCS Base Library • United State Marine Corps, P.O. Box 63073, MCBH • Kaneohe Bay, HI 96863-3073 • (808) 254-7624 • http://www.10.1.12.20/kaneohe/

Kapaa
Kaua'i Historical Society • 4-130 Kuhio Hwy • Kapaa, HI 96746 • (808) 821-1778

Kaumakani
Gay & Robinsons Sugar Plantation Museum • 2 Kaumakani Ave, P.O. Box 440 • Kaumakani, HI 96747 • (808) 335-2824 • http://www.gandrtours-kauai.com

Kawaihae
Puukohola Heiau National Historic Site • 62-3601 Kawaihae Rd, P.O. Box 44340 • Kawaihae, HI 96743 • (808) 882-7218 • http://www.hawaiimuseums.org

Keaau
Hawaii County Genealogical Society • P.O. Box 831 • Keaau, HI 96749-0831 • (808) 966-9206

Kealakekua
University of Hawaii Center • 81-964 Halekii St, P.O. Box 2059 • Kealakekua, HI 96750-2059 • (808) 322-4858

West Hawaii Center • Univ of Hawaii, P.O. Box 2059 • Kealakekua, HI 96750 • (808) 322-4858

Kihei
Maui Genealogical Society • 38A Alania Place • Kihei, HI 96753 • http://www.maui.net/~mauifun/mgs.htm

Koloa
Koloa Public & School Library • 3451 Poipu Rd, P.O. Box 9 • Koloa, HI 96756-0009 • (808) 742-8455

Lahaina
Friends of Mokuula • 505 Front St, Ste 234 • Lahaina, HI 96761 • (808) 661-3659

Lahaina Restoration Foundation • Historical Museum, 120 Dickenson • Lahaina, HI 96761 • (808) 661-3262 • http://www.lahainarestoration.org

Whalers Village Museum • 2435 Ka'anapali Pkwy • Lahaina, HI 96761 • (808) 661-5992 • http://www.whalersvillage.com

Laie
Joseph F Smith Library • Brigham Young Univ, 55-220 Kulanui St, BYU-H Box 1966 • Laie, HI 96762-1294 • (808) 293-3850 • http://www.library.byuh.edu

Mormon Pacific Historical Society • Brigham Young Univ, Hawaii Campus, P.O. Box 1887 • Laie, HI 96762 • (808) 393-3837

Polynesian Cultural Center Museum • 55-370 Kamehameha Hwy • Laie, HI 96762 • (808) 367-7060 • http://www.polynesia.com

Lanai City
Lanai Culture and Heritage Center • 730 Lanai Ave, P.O. Box 631500 • Lanai City, HI 96763 • http://www.lanaichc.org

Laupahoehoe
Laupahoehoe Train Museum • 36-2377 Mamalahoa Hwy, P.O. Box 358 • Laupahoehoe, HI 96764 • (808) 962-2221 • http://www.thetrainmuseum.com

Lihue
Grove Farm Homestead Museum • Hawiliwili Rd, P.O. Box 1631 • Lihue, HI 96766 • (808) 245-3202 • http://www.hawaiiweb.com/kauai/sites/grove_farm_homestead.html

Kaua'i Historical Society • Historical Museum 4428 Rice St, Ste 101, P.O. Box 1778 • Lihue, HI 96766 • (808) 245-3373 • http://www.kauaihistoricalsociety.org

Kauai Museum Association • Historical Museum, 4428 Rice St, P.O. Box 248 • Lihue, HI 96766 • (808) 245-6931 • http://www.kauaimuseum.org

Wai'oli Mission House Museum • Hanalei Historic Dist, P.O. Box 1631 • Lihue, HI 96766 • (808) 245-3202 • http://www.hawaiimuseums.org

Manoa Gardens
Manoa Gardens Community Center • 2790 Kahaloa Dr • Manoa Gardens, HI 96822 • http://www.hpcug.org/ancestors/sigs.html

Molokai
Moloka'i Museum and Cultural Center • Kala'e Hwy 470, MM4, P.O. Box 269, Kualapuu • Molokai, HI 96757 • (808) 567-6436 • http://www.hawaiimuseums.org

Pearl City
Leeward Community College Library • 96-056 Ala Ike • Pearl City, HI 96782 • (808) 455-0379 • http://www.lcc.hawaii.edu/lib/library.html

Pu'unene
Alexander & Baldwin Sugar Museum • 3957 Hansen Rd, P.O. Box 125 • Pu'unene, HI 96784 • (808) 871-8058 • http://www.sugarmuseum.com

Schofield Barracks
Sergeant Rodney J Yano Main Library • United States Army, Bldg 560 • Schofield Barracks, HI 96857-5000 • (808) 688-8001

Tropic Lightning Museum • Directorate of Community Activities, USAG-HI, Schofield Barracks • Schofield Barracks, HI 96857 • (808) 655-0438

US Army Garrison, Hawaii Library • 1336 Kolekole Ave, Bldg 560 • Schofield Barracks, HI 96857-5000 • (808) 655-9269

US Army Museum of Hawaii • Museum Div, DEPTMSEC, USASCH, Battery Randolph, Kalia Rd • Schofield Barracks, HI 96857 • (808) 438-2821

Waiehu
Maui Okinawa Cultural Center Museum • 688 Nukuwai Pl • Waiehu, HI 96793 • (808) 242-1560 • http://www.hawaiimuseums.org

Waikiki
Hawaii Army Museum • Kalia Rd, P.O. Box 96830 • Waikiki, HI 96815 • (808) 955-9552 • http://www.hiarmymuseumsoc.org

Wailuku
Maui Historical Society • Bailey House Museum, 2375-A Main St, P.O. Box 1018 • Wailuku, HI 96793 • (808) 244-3326 • http://www.mauimuseum.org

Waimea
Waimea Sugar Mill Camp Museum • Plantation Cottages, P.O. Box 1178 • Waimea, HI 96796 • (808) 335-2824 • http://www.hawaiimuseums.org

Waipahu
Hawaii Plantation Village Museum • 94-695 Waipahu St • Waipahu, HI 96797 • (808) 677-0110 • http://www.hawaiiplantationvillage.org

Aberdeen
Aberdeen District Library • 76 E Central, P.O. Box 207 • Aberdeen, ID 83210-0207 • (208) 397-4427 • http://www.lili.org/aberdeen

Albion
Albion Public Library • Market & Main, P.O. Box 534 • Albion, ID 83311-0534 • (208) 673-6233

American Falls
American Falls District Library • 308 Roosevelt St • American Falls, ID 83211-1219 • (208) 226-2335

Massacre Rocks State Park • 3592 N Park Ln • American Falls, ID 83211 • (208) 548-2672 • http://www.idahoparks.org/parks/massacre. html

Arimo
Genealogical Extraction Center • 286 Henderson Ave • Arimo, ID 83214 • (208) 254-3888

Bellevue
Idaho Heritage Trust • Old Town Hall • Bellevue, ID 83313 • (208) 788-7529

Blackfoot
Bingham County Historical Museum • 190 N Shilling Ave • Blackfoot, ID 83221 • (208) 785-8065

Blackfoot Public Library • 129 N Broadway, P.O. Box 610 • Blackfoot, ID 83221-0610 • (208) 785-8628 • http://www.blackfootidaho.org

Northwestern Band of Shoshoni Nation • P.O. Box 637 • Blackfoot, ID 83224 • (208) 785-7401

Boise
Ada Community Library • 10664 W Victory Rd • Boise, ID 83709 • (208) 362-0181 • http://www.adalib.org

Albertsons Library • Boise State University, 1910 University Dr • Boise, ID 83725 • (208) 426-3301 • http://library.boisestate.edu

Basque Museum and Cultural Center • 611 Grove St • Boise, ID 83702 • (208) 343-2671 • http://www.basquemuseum.com

Boise Basque Museum and Cultural Center • 611 Grove St • Boise, ID 83702 • (208) 343-2671 • http://www.basquemuseum.com

Boise Bible College Library • 8695 W Marigold St • Boise, ID 83714-1220 • (208) 376-7731 • http://www.boisebible.edu

Boise Public Library • 715 S Capitol Blvd • Boise, ID 83702-7195 • (208) 384-4026 • http://www.boisepubliclibrary.org

Catholic Diocese of Boise Archives • 303 Federal Wy • Boise, ID 83705 • (208) 342-1311 • http://www.cidaho.org

Dry Creek Historical Society • Schick-Otalasa Farmstead Historic Site, 5006 W Farm Ct • Boise, ID 83714 • (208) 229-2323 x 26

Idaho Black History Museum • 508 Julia Davis Dr • Boise, ID 83702 • (208) 433-0017 • http://www.ibhm.org

Idaho Center for Vital Statistics and Health Policy • 450 W State St, 1st Floor, P.O. Box 83720 • Boise, ID 83720-0036 • (208) 334-5988 • http://www.healthandwelfare.idaho.gov

Idaho Genealogical Library • 325 W State St • Boise, ID 83702 • (208) 334-2150 • http://www.state.id.us/isl/hp.htm

Idaho Genealogical Society • 2120 Cataldo Dr, P.O. Box 1854 • Boise, ID 83705-2816 • (208) 384-0542 • http://www.rmci.net/idaho/genidaho/

Idaho Military History Museum • 4748 Lindbergh St, Bldg 924 • Boise, ID 83705 • (208) 422-4841

Idaho Museum of Mining • 2455 Old Penitentiary Rd • Boise, ID 83712 • (208) 368-9876 • http://www.idahomuseum.org

Idaho State Historical Museum • 610 N Julia Davis Dr • Boise, ID 83702 • (208) 334-2120 • http://www.idahohistory.net/museum

Idaho State Historical Society • Old Idaho Penitentiary, 2445 Old Penitentiary Rd • Boise, ID 83712-8254 • (208) 334-2844 • http://www. idahohistory.net

Idaho State Library • 325 W State St • Boise, ID 83702-6072 • (208) 334-2150 • http://www.lili.org/isl/

Masonic Grand Lodge of Idaho • 219 N 17th St • Boise, ID 83702 • (208) 343-4562 • http://www.idahomasons.com

Oral History Center • 450 N 4th St • Boise, ID 83709 • (208) 334-3863 • http://www.idahohistory.net

Treasure Valley Chapter, Idaho Genealogical Society • 325 W State St • Boise, ID 83702

Bonners Ferry
Boundary County Historical Society • Historical Museum, 7229 Main St, P.O. Box 808 • Bonners Ferry, ID 83805 • (208) 267-7720

Boundary County Library • 6370 Kootenai, P.O. Box Y • Bonners Ferry, ID 83805-1276 • (208) 267-3750

Kootenai Tribal Council • County Rd 38A, P.O. Box 1269 • Bonners Ferry, ID 83805 • (208) 267-3519 • http://www.kootenai.org

Buhl
Buhl Public Library • 215 Broadway N • Buhl, ID 83316-1624 • (208) 543-6500

Burley
Burley Public Library • 1300 Miller Ave • Burley, ID 83318-1729 • (208) 678-7708 • http://www.bplibrary.org

Cassia County Historical Society • Historical Museum, E Main & Highland Ave, P.O. Box 331 • Burley, ID 83318-0331 • (208) 678-7172 • http://www.cassiacounty.org/historical-society/museum.htm

Seeley Lake Historical Society • Burley, ID 83318 • (208) 677-2990

Caldwell
Caldwell Genealogical Group • 3504 S Illinois St • Caldwell, ID 83605

Caldwell Public Library • 1010 Dearborn • Caldwell, ID 83605-4195 • (208) 459-3242 • http://www.lili.org/caldwell

Family Scanner Chapter, IGS • P.O. Box 581 • Caldwell, ID 83605

Kiwanis Van Slyke Museum • Caldwell Municipal Park • Caldwell, ID 83605 • (208) 459-1597

N L Terteling Library • Albertson College of Idaho, 2112 Cleveland Blvd • Caldwell, ID 83605 • (208) 459-5505 • http://www.albertson.edu/library/

Our Memories Museum • 1122 Main St • Caldwell, ID 83605 • (208) 459-1413

Cambridge
Idaho Heartland Genealogists • 2982 Hwy 71 • Cambridge, ID 83610-5004

Cascade
Cascade Public Library • 105 N Front St, P.O. Box 10 • Cascade, ID 83611-0010 • (208) 382-4757 • http://www.lili.org/cascade/

Valley County Genealogical Society • c/o Cascade Library, 105 Front St, P.O. Box 111 • Cascade, ID 83611-0111 • (208) 382-4757

Clayton
Custer Museum • Yankee Fork Ranger District • Clayton, ID 83227 • (208) 838-2201

Coeur d'Alene
Coeur d'Alene Public Library • 201 E Harrison Ave • Coeur d'Alene, ID 83814-2373 • (208) 769-2315 • http://www.cdalibrary.org

Molstead Library • North Idaho College History Center, 1000 W Garden Ave • Coeur d'Alene, ID 83814-2199 • (208) 769-3355 • http://www.nic.edu

Idaho

Coeur d'Alene, cont.
Museum of North Idaho • 115 Northwest Blvd, P.O. Box 812 • Coeur d'Alene, ID 83816-0812 • (208) 664-3448 • http://www.museumni.org

Cottonwood
College of Saint Gertrude Library • Keuterville Rd • Cottonwood, ID 83522 • (208) 962-7123 • http://www.rc/boise/stgertrude

Historical Museum at Saint Gertrude • HC3, Box 121 • Cottonwood, ID 83522-9408 • (208) 962-7123 • http://www.historicalmuseumatstgertrude.com

Prairie Community Library • 506 King St, P.O. Box 65 • Cottonwood, ID 83522-0065 • (208) 962-3714 • http://www.lili.org/directory

Craigmont
Ilo-Vollmer Historical Society • P.O. Box 61 • Craigmont, ID 83523 • (208) 924-5474

Prairie-River Library District-Craigmont Community • 112 W Main, PO Box 144 • Craigmont, ID 83523-0144 • (208) 924-5510

Donnelly
Valley County Historical Society • 13131 FM Rd • Donnelly, ID 83615

Dover
Bonner County Genealogical Society • P.O. Box 27 • Dover, ID 83825 • (208) 263-4949

Dubois
Heritage Hall Museum • HC 62, Box 41 • Dubois, ID 83446 • (208) 374-5359

Eagle
Eagle Public Library • 100 N Stierman Way • Eagle, ID 83616-5162 • (208) 939-6814 • http://www.eaglepubliclibrary.org

Emmett
Gem County Historical Society • Historical Museum, 501 E 1st, P.O. Box 312 • Emmett, ID 83617 • (208) 365-9530 • http://www.gemcohs.org

Fairfield
Camas County Historical Society • P.O. Box 125 • Fairfield, ID 83327

Filer
Filer Public Library • 219 Main St, P.O. Box 52 • Filer, ID 83328-0052 • (208) 326-4143

Twin Falls County Museum • 21337A Hwy 30 • Filer, ID 83341 • (208) 736-4675

Fort Hall
Shoshone-Bannock Indian Tribes • Tribal Museum, Simplot Rd, P.O. Box 306 • Fort Hall, ID 83203 • (208) 238-3700 • http://www.shoshonebannocktribes.com

Shoshone-Bannock Library • Pima & Bannock Dr, P.O. Box 306 • Fort Hall, ID 83203-0306 • (208) 478-3882

Garden City
Garden City Library • 9115 Chinden St, Suite 104 • Garden City, ID 83714-1429 • (208) 672-0433 • http://www.gardencitylibrary.org

Garden Valley
Garden Valley District Library • 342 Village Cr • Garden Valley, ID 83622 • (208) 462-3317 • http://www.lili.org/gardenvalley/

Glenns Ferry
Glenns Ferry Historical Society • Historical Museum, 211 W Cleveland Ave • Glenns Ferry, ID 83623 • (208) 366-2760

Three Island Crossing State Park • P.O. Box 609 • Glenns Ferry, ID 83623 • http://www.idahoparks.org/parks/threeisland.html

Gooding
Gooding County Genealogical Society • 1918 Whipkey Dr • Gooding, ID 83330

Gooding County Historical Society • Historical Museum, 210 N Main, P.O. Box 580 • Gooding, ID 83330

Gooding Public Library • 306 5th Ave W • Gooding, ID 83330-1205 • (208) 934-4089

Grace
DAV Veterans History Project • 105 W 2nd S • Grace, ID 83241 • (208) 425-3144

Grangeville
Bicentennial Historical Museum • 305 N College Street • Grangeville, ID 83530 • (208) 983-2573 • http://www.grangevilleidaho.com/historical_museum.htm

Grangeville Centennial Library • 215 W North St • Grangeville, ID 83530 • (208) 983-0951 • http://www.centennial-library.org

Idaho County Chapter, Idaho Genealogical Society • c/o Grangeville Centennial Library, 215 W North St • Grangeville, ID 83530 • (208) 983-0951

Hagerman
Hagerman Valley Historical Society • 100 S State St, P.O. Box 86 • Hagerman, ID 83322 • (208) 837-6288

Hailey
Blaine County Historical Society • Historcal Museum, 218 N Main St, P.O. Box 124 • Hailey, ID 83333 • (208) 788-1801 • http://www.gchistoricalmuseum.org

Hailey Public Library • 7 W Croy St • Hailey, ID 83333 • (208) 788-2036 • http://www.haileypubliclibrary.org

Hamer
Jefferson County District Library, Hamer Branch • P.O. Box 240 • Hamer, ID 83425-9999 • (208) 662-5275

Harrison
Crane Historical Society • Crane House, Main Street, P.O. Box 152 • Harrison, ID 83833 • (208) 689-3032

Hayden
Kootenai-Shoshone Library-Hayden Branch • 8385 N Government Wy • Hayden, ID 83835 • (208) 772-5612 • http://www.ksalibraries.org

Hayden Lake
Kootenai County Genealogical Society • c/o Hayden Lake Library, 8385 N Government Way • Hayden Lake, ID 83835 • (208) 772-5778 • http://www.rootsweb.com/~idkooten/kcgs.htm

Kootenai-Shoshone Area Libraries - Hayden Branch • 8385 N Government Wy • Hayden Lake, ID 83835 • (208) 772-5612 • http://hayden.ksalibraries.org

Heyburn
Magic Valley Chapter, Idaho Genealogical Society • Route 2, 770 S River Dr • Heyburn, ID 83336

Horseshoe Bend
Horseshoe Bend District Library • 392 Hwy 55 • Horseshoe Bend, ID 83629-9701 • (208) 793-2460

Idaho City
Boise Basin Library District • 404 Montgomery St, P.O. Box 228 • Idaho City, ID 83631-0228 • (208) 392-4558 • http://boisebasin.lib.id.us

Idaho City Historical Society • Historical Museum, 402 Montgomery St • Idaho City, ID 83631-4176

Idaho Falls
Bonneville County Historical Society • Northeastern & Elm, P.O. Box 1784 • Idaho Falls, ID 83401 • (208) 522-1400 • http://www.idahofallsmuseum.org

Eagle Rock Railroad Historical Society • P.O. Box 2685 • Idaho Falls, ID 83403-2685

Idaho Falls Public Library • 457 W Broadway • Idaho Falls, ID 83402 • (208) 529-1450 • http://www.ifpl.org

Museum of Idaho • 200 N Eastern Ave • Idaho Falls, ID 83402 • (208) 522-1400 • http://www.museumofidaho.org

Jerome
Jerome County Historical Society • Historical Museum, 220 N Lincoln Ave, P.O. Box 50 • Jerome, ID 83338-2325 • (208) 324-5641 • http://www.historicaljeromecounty.com

Jerome Public Library • 100 1st Ave E • Jerome, ID 83338 • (208) 324-5427 • http://www.ci.jerome.id.us

Kamiah
Kamiah Genealogical Society • P.O. Box 322 • Kamiah, ID 83536

Lewis County Historical Society • Route 2, Box 10 • Kamiah, ID 83536

Prairie-River Library District-Kamiah Community • 505 Main, P.O. Box 846 • Kamiah, ID 83536-0846 • (208) 935-0428

Kellogg
Shoshone County Genealogical Society • 904 S Division St, P.O. Box 182 • Kellogg, ID 83837 • http://www.rootsweb.com/~idshosho/scghs.htm

Ketchum
Community Library Association • 415 Spruce Ave N, P.O. Box 2168 • Ketchum, ID 83340-2168 • (208) 726-3493 • http://www.thecommunitylibrary.org

Ketchum-Sun Valley Historical Society • 180 1st Ave E • Ketchum, ID 83340 • (208) 726-8118

Wood River Historical Society • P.O. Box 552 • Ketchum, ID 83340

Kimberly
Kimberly Public Library • 120 Madison St W, P.O. Box 369 • Kimberly, ID 83341 • (208) 423-4556

Kootenai
Bonner County Genealogical Society • P.O. Box 221 • Kootenai, ID 83840 • http://www.rootsweb.com/~idbegs/

Kuna
Kuna School Community Library • 457 N Locust, P.O. Box 129 • Kuna, ID 83634-0129 • (208) 922-1025 • http://www.lili.org/kuna

Lapwai
Nez Perce Tribal Executive Committee • P.O. Box 305 • Lapwai, ID 83540 • (208) 843-2253 • http://www.nezperce.org

Prairie-River Library District • 103 N Main St, P.O. Box 1200 • Lapwai, ID 83540-1200 • (208) 843-7254

Lava Hot Springs
South Bannock County Historical Society • Historical Museum, 110 E Main St, P.O. Box 387 • Lava Hot Springs, ID 83246 • (208) 776-5254 • http://www.lavahotsprings.com/history.html

Lewiston
Lewis-Clark State College Library • 500 8th Ave • Lewiston, ID 83501 • (208) 799-2236 • http://www.lcsc.edu

Lewiston City Library • 428 Thain Road • Lewiston, ID 83501 • (208) 743-6519 • http://www.cityoflewiston.org/library/

Luna House Historical Society • 310 3rd St • Lewiston, ID 83501

Nez Perce County Historical Society • Luna House Museum, 306 3rd St • Lewiston, ID 83501 • (208) 743-2535 • http://www.npchistsoc.org

Twin Rivers Genealogical Society • P.O. Box 386 • Lewiston, ID 83501-2824

Mackay
South Custer County Historical Society • P.O. Box 355 • Mackay, ID 83251

Malad
Oneida County Pioneer Museum • 27 Bannock St • Malad, ID 83252 • (208) 766-4847

Malad City
Oneida County Free Library • 31 N 100 W, P.O. Box 185 • Malad City, ID 83252-0185 • (208) 766-2229 • http://www.maladidaho.org/library

Marsing
R-Lucky Star Ranch Museum • general delivery • Marsing, ID 83639

McCall
McCall City Library • 218 Park St • McCall, ID 83638 • (208) 634-5522 • http://www.mccall.id.us/library

Meridian
Meridian District Library • 1326 W Cherry Ln • Meridian, ID 83642 • (208) 888-4451 • http://www.mld.org

Sons of the American Revolution, Idaho Society • 2481 E Autumn Wy • Meridian, ID 83642 • (208) 888-4898

Middleton
Middleton Public Library • 307 E Main St, PO Box 519 • Middleton, ID 83644-0519 • (208) 585-3931

Midvale
Midvale District Library • 70 E Bridge St, P.O. Box 127 • Midvale, ID 83645-0127 • (208) 355-2213

Montpelier
Bear Lake County Historical Society • Rails and Trails Museum, 322 N 4th St • Montpelier, ID 83254 • (208) 847-3800 • http://www.railsandtrails.net

National Oregon/California Trail Center, 320 N 4th St, P.O. Box 323 • Montpelier, ID 83254 • (208) 847-3800 • http://www.oregontrailcenter.org

Moscow
Appaloosa Museum and Heritage Center • 2720 W Pullman Rd • Moscow, ID 83843 • (208) 882-5578 • http://www.appaloosamuseum.org

Latah County Genealogical Society • 327 E 2nd St • Moscow, ID 83843-2852 • (208) 882-1004

Latah County Historical Society • McConnell Mansion Museum, 110 S Adams • Moscow, ID 83843 • (208) 882-1004 • http://www.latahcountyhistoricalsociety.org/

Moscow-Latah County Library System • 110 S Jefferson • Moscow, ID 83843-2833 • (208) 882-3925 • http://norby.latah.lib.id.us

Pullman, Washington Branch Genealogical Library • 865 Bitterroot • Moscow, ID 83843

University of Idaho Library • Rayburn St, P.O. Box 442350 • Moscow, ID 83844-2350 • (208) 885-6584 • http://www.lib.uidaho.edu/specialcollections

Mountain Home
Elmore County Historical Foundation • Historical Museum, 180 S 3rd St E, P.O. Box 204 • Mountain Home, ID 83647 • (208) 587-9041

Mountain Home Public Library • 790 N 10th E • Mountain Home, ID 83647-2830 • (208) 587-4716 • http://www.mhlibrary.org

Mountain Home AFB
Mountain Home Air Force Base Library FL4897 • 366 SVS/SVMG, 520 Phantom Ave Bldg 2427 • Mountain Home AFB, ID 83648-5000 • (208) 828-2326 • http://http://library.mountainhome.accqolnet.org/library

Murphy
Owyhee County Historical Society • Historical Museum, 17085 Basey St, P.O. Box 62 • Murphy, ID 83650-0067 • (208) 495-2319 • http://www.owyheecountymuseum.org

Idaho

Nampa
Canyon County Historical Society • Historical Museum, 1200 Front St, P.O. Box 595 • Nampa, ID 83651 • (208) 467-7611

John E Riley Library • Northwest Nazarene College, 623 Holly St • Nampa, ID 83686 • (208) 467-8607 • http://www.nnu.edu/library

Nampa Public Library • 101 11th Ave S • Nampa, ID 83651 • (208) 465-2263 • http://www.lili.org/nampa

Warhawk Air Museum • 201 Municipal Dr • Nampa, ID 83687 • (208) 465-6446

New Meadows
Adams County Historical Society • P.O. Box 352 • New Meadows, ID 83654

Nez Perce
Nez Perce Historical Society • P.O. Box 86 • Nez Perce, ID 83542 • (208) 743-2535

Oakley
Oakley Library District • 185 E Main St • Oakley, ID 83346 • (208) 862-3434

Oakley Pioneer Museum • 108 W Main • Oakley, ID 83346 • (208) 862-3626

Orofino
Clearwater County Historical Society • Historical Museum, 315 College Ave, P.O. Box 1154 • Orofino, ID 83544 • (208) 476-5033 • http://www.clearwatermuseum.org

Osburn
Osburn Public Library • 921 E Mullan, P.O. Box 809 • Osburn, ID 83849-0809 • (208) 752-9711 • http://www.osburnlibrary.com

Parma
Old Fort Boise Historical Society • Old Fort Boise Park Museum, P.O. Box 942 • Parma, ID 83660 • (208) 722-5138

Patricia Romanko Public Library • 121 N 3rd St, P.O. Box 309 • Parma, ID 83660-0309 • (208) 722-6605

Payette
Payette County Historical Society • 90 S 9th St, P.O. Box 476 • Payette, ID 83661 • (208) 642-4883 • http://www.payettemuseum.qwestoffice.net/

Payette Public Library • 24 S 10th St • Payette, ID 83661-2861 • (208) 642-6029

Pierce
Pierce District Library • 208 S Main St, P.O. Box 386 • Pierce, ID 83546-0386 • (208) 464-2823

Plummer
Coeur D'Alene Tribe • general delivery • Plummer, ID 83851-9704 • (208) 274-3101 • http://www.cdatribe-nsn.gov

Pocatello
Bannock County Historical Society • Historical Museum, 3000 Alvord Loop, P.O. Box 253 • Pocatello, ID 83204-0253 • (208) 233-0434 • http://www.ohwy.com/id/b/bannochm.htm

E M Oboler Library • Idaho State University, 850 S 9th Ave, P.O. Box 8089 • Pocatello, ID 83209-8089 • (208) 282-3152 • http://www.isu.edu/library/

Marshall Public Library • 113 S Garfield • Pocatello, ID 83204-5722 • (208) 232-1263 • http://www.lili.org/marshall

Pocatello Branch Genealogical Society • 156 1/2 S 6th Ave, P.O. Box 4272 • Pocatello, ID 83201

Post Falls
Post Falls Public Library • 821 N Spokane St • Post Falls, ID 83855-9315 • (208) 773-1506 • http://postfallslibrary.kcl.org

Priest Lake
Priest Lake Public Library • 28769 N Highway 57 • Priest Lake, ID 83856 • (208) 443-2454

Rexburg
Arthur Porter Special Collections Library • BYU Idaho, 25 S Center St • Rexburg, ID 83460-0405 • (208) 356-2377 • http://www.lib.byui.edu

David O McKay Library • Brigham Young University-Idaho, 525 S Center St • Rexburg, ID 83460-0405 • (208) 496-2367 • http://www.lib.byui.edu

Madison Library District • 73 N Center • Rexburg, ID 83440-1539 • (208) 356-3461 • http://www.mad.eils.lib.id.us/madweb.htm

McKay Library • Ricks College, 525 S Center • Rexburg, ID 83440 • (208) 356-2390 • http://abish.byui.edu/SpecialCollections/

Upper Snake River Valley Historical Society • 51 N Center St, P.O. Box 244 • Rexburg, ID 83440-1539 • (208) 356-9101

Rigby
Jefferson County Historical Society • Pioneer Museum, 118 W 1st St, P.O. Box 284 • Rigby, ID 83442 • (208) 745-8423

Rupert
DeMary Memorial Library • 417 7th St • Rupert, ID 83350-1692 • (208) 436-3874

Minidoka County Historical Society • Historical Museum, 100 E Baseline, P.O. Box 21 • Rupert, ID 83350 • (208) 436-0336

Saint Anthony
Fremont County Historical Society • general delivery • Saint Anthony, ID 83445

Saint Maries
Hughes House Historical Society • 538 Main Ave • Saint Maries, ID 83861 • (208) 245-1501

Salmon
Lemhi County Historical Society • Lemhi County Historical Museum, 210 Main, P.O. Box 645 • Salmon, ID 83467 • (208) 756-3342 • http://www.sacajaweahome.com

Salmon Public Library • 204 Main St • Salmon, ID 83467-4111 • (208) 756-2311 • http://salmon.ipac.dynixasp.com

Sandpoint
Bonner County Historical Society • Historical Museum, 611 S Ella St • Sandpoint, ID 83864 • (208) 263-2344 • http://www.bonnercountyhistory.org

East Bonner County Free Public Library Dist • 1407 Cedar St • Sandpoint, ID 83864 • (208) 263-6930 • http://www.ebcl.lib.id.us/ebcl/

Shelley
North Bingham County District Library • 197 W Locust St • Shelley, ID 83274-1139 • (208) 357-7801 • http://www.lili.org

Utah Genealogical Association, Snake River Chapter • 410 N Park • Shelley, ID 83274 • (208) 357-5710

Shoshone
Shoshone Public Library • 250 S Rail St, P.O. Box 236 • Shoshone, ID 83352-0236 • (208) 886-2843

Soda Springs
Caribou County Historical Society • County Courthouse, 290 W 3rd St S • Soda Springs, ID 83276 • (208) 547-3506

Soda Springs Public Library • 149 S Main St • Soda Springs, ID 83276-1496 • (208) 547-2606 • http://www.lili.org/soda/

Spalding
Nez Perce National Historical Park Library • 39063 US Hwy 95 • Spalding, ID 83540 • (208) 843-2261 • http://www.nps.gov/nepc/

Spirit Lake
Spirit Lake Historical Society • 6042 W Maine St, P.O. Box 186 • Spirit Lake, ID 83869 • (208) 623-2110

Stanley
Land of the Yankee Fork Historic Association • Historical Museum, 350 Yankee Fork Rd, P.O. Box 524 • Stanley, ID 83226 • (208) 838-2201

Stanley Heritage Association • Hwy 75 • Stanley, ID 83278

Sugar City
Snake River Genealogical Society of Southeastern Idaho • 122 N Front St, P.O. Box 30 • Sugar City, ID 83448-0030 • (208) 356-7072

Twin Falls
College of Southern Idaho Library • Meyerhoeffer Bldg, 315 Falls Ave, P.O. Box 1238 • Twin Falls, ID 83303-1238 • (208) 732-6500 • http://www.library.csi.edu

Twin Falls Public Library • 201 4th Ave E • Twin Falls, ID 83301-6397 • (208) 773-2964 • http://www.lili.org/tfpl

Wallace
Wallace District Mining Museum • 509 Bank St, P.O. Box 469 • Wallace, ID 83873 • (208) 556-1592

Wallace Public Library • 415 River St • Wallace, ID 83873-2260 • (208) 752-4571

Weiser
Snake River Heritage Center • 2295 Paddock Ave, P.O. Box 307 • Weiser, ID 83672 • (208) 549-2390

Wilder
Wilder Public Library District • 207 A Ave, P.O. Box 128 • Wilder, ID 83676-0128 • (208) 482-7880

Winchester
Winchester Museum • Route 2, Box 28 • Winchester, ID 83524 • (208) 924-7772

Idaho

ILLINOIS

Abingdon
John Mosser Public Library • 106 W Meek St • Abingdon, IL 61410-1451 • (309) 462-3129

Addison
Addison Historical Museum • 135 Army Trail Rd • Addison, IL 60101 • (630) 638-1433 • http://www.addisonadvantage.org/History.htm

Addison Historical Society • 1 Friendship Plaza • Addison, IL 60101 • (630) 628-1433 • http://www.AddisonAdvantage.org/History.htm

Albany
Albany Mounds State Historic Site Museum • S Cherry St, P.O. Box 184 • Albany, IL 61230 • (309) 887-4335

Tri-County Heritage Society • 306 Lime St • Albany, IL 61230

Albion
Edwards County Genealogical Society • 212 W Main St • Albion, IL 62806 • (618) 445-2631

Edwards County Historical Museum • 25 N 5th St • Albion, IL 62806 • (618) 445-3072

Edwards County Historical Society • 212 W Main St, P.O. Box 205 • Albion, IL 62806 • (618) 445-3433 • http://www.rootsweb.com/~iledward/ehistsoc.html

Aledo
Mercer Carnegie Library • 200 N College Ave • Aledo, IL 61231 • (309) 582-2032

Mercer County Genealogical and Historical Society • Essley-Noble Museum, 1406 SE 2nd Ave • Aledo, IL 61231 • (309) 582-2280 • http://www.rootsweb.com/~ilmercer/mchs.htm

Algonquin
Algonquin Area Public Library District • 2600 Harnish Dr • Algonquin, IL 60102-3097 • (847) 458-6060 • http://www.aapld.org

Alton
Alton Area Historical Society • 239 W Elm St, P.O. Box 971 • Alton, IL 62002 • (618) 462-5853

Alton Museum of History and Art • 2809 College Ave • Alton, IL 62002 • (618) 462-2763 • http://www.altonweb.com/museum/

Hayner Public Library District • 326 Belle St • Alton, IL 62002 • (618) 462-0651 • http://www.haynerlibrary.org

Koenig House Museum • 820 E 4th St • Alton, IL 62002 • (618) 463-1795 • http://www.altonmuseum.com

Andover
Andover Historical Museum • 418 Locust St, P.O. Box 197 • Andover, IL 61233 • (309) 522-8378

Andover Historical Society • 340 4th St, P.O. Box 197 • Andover, IL 61233-0197 • (309) 476-8378

Anna
Union County Genealogical and Historical Research Committee • 101 E Spring St • Anna, IL 62906

Antioch
Antioch Township Library • 757 Main St • Antioch, IL 60002 • (847) 395-0874

Lakes Region Historical Society • 812 N Main St, P.O. Box 240 • Antioch, IL 60002-0240 • (847) 395-7337

Arlington Heights
American Historical Society of Germans from Russia, Northern Illinois Chapter • 1718 E Lilac Terr • Arlington Heights, IL 60004-3527 • (847) 253-4198 • http://www.ahsgr.org/ilnorthe.html

Arlington Heights Historical Society • Historical Museum, 110 W Fremont • Arlington Heights, IL 60004-5912 • (847) 255-1225 • http://www.ahmuseum.org

Arlington Heights Memorial Library • 500 N Dunston Ave • Arlington Heights, IL 60004-5966 • (847) 392-0100 • http://www.ahml.info/

Dunton Genealogical Society • c/o Arlington Heights Memorial Library, 500 N Dunston Ave • Arlington Heights, IL 60004 • (847) 392-0100 • http://www.ahmi.lib.il.us

Eastland Disaster Historical Society • P.O. Box 2013 • Arlington Heights, IL 60006-2013 • (877) 865-6295

Frederick W Muller House Museum • 500 N Vail Ave • Arlington Heights, IL 60004

Nathaniel Moore Banta House Museum • 514 N Vail Ave • Arlington Heights, IL 60004

Arthur
Arthur Public Library • 225 S Walnut • Arthur, IL 61911 • (217) 543-2037

Assumption
Assumption Public Library • 205 N Oak St • Assumption, IL 62510 • (217) 226-3915

Atkinson
Atkinson Public Library • 119 W Main St, P.O. Box 633 • Atkinson, IL 61235-0633 • (309) 936-7606

Atlanta
Atlanta Library and Museum • 100 Race St, P.O. Box 568 • Atlanta, IL 61723-0568 • (217) 648-2112 • http://npinil.circ.uiuc.edu/resource/logan/atlantapl.html

Atwood
Atwood-Hammond Public Library • 123 N Main St, P.O. Box 440 • Atwood, IL 61913-0440 • (217) 578-2727 • http://www.ahlibrary.com

Augusta
Greater West Center Public Library District-Augusta Branch • 202 Center St, P.O. Box 235 • Augusta, IL 62311-0235 • (217) 392-2211

Tri-County Genealogical Society • Historical Museum, P.O. Box 355 • Augusta, IL 62311 • (217) 392-2211

Aurora
Aurora Historical Society • Historical Museum, 20 E Downer Pl, P.O. Box 905 • Aurora, IL 60507 • (630) 906-0650 • http://www.aurorahistoricalsociety.org

Aurora Public Library • 1 E Benton St • Aurora, IL 60505-4299 • (630) 264-4106 • http://www.aurora.lib.il.us

Aurora Regional Fire Museum • 53 N Broadway, P.O. Box 1782 • Aurora, IL 60507 • (630) 892-1572 • http://www.auroraregionalfiremuseum.org

Blackberry Farm's Pioneer Village Museum • 100 S Barnes Rd • Aurora, IL 60506 • (630) 264-7408 • http://www.foxvalleyparkdistrict.org

Charles B Phillips Library of the Advent Christian Church • Aurora Univ, 347 S Gladstone • Aurora, IL 60506 • (630) 844-5437 • http://www.aurora.edu/library/

GAR Memorial and Veterans' Military Museum • 23 E Downer Pl, P.O. Box 1865 • Aurora, IL 60507-1865 • (630) 897-7221

Illinois Cornish Heritage Society • 450 W Galena • Aurora, IL 60506

Schingoethe Center for Native American Cultures • Dunham Hall, 1400 Marseillaise Pl • Aurora, IL 60506-4892 • (630) 844-5402 • http://www.aurora.edu/museum/

William Tanner House Museum • 305 Cedar St • Aurora, IL 60507 • (630) 897-9029

Avon
Avon Historical Society • Historical Museum, P.O. Box 483 • Avon, IL 61415-0483 • (309) 465-3189

Avon, cont.
Warren County Historical Society • RR2 • Avon, IL 61415 • (309) 465-3361

Barrington
Barrington Area Historical Society • Historical Museum, 212 W Main St • Barrington, IL 60010 • (847) 381-1730 • http://www.bahsil.org; http://www.barringtonareahistoricalsociety.org

Barrington Area Library • 505 N Northwest Hwy • Barrington, IL 60010 • (847) 382-1300 • http://www.barringtonarealibrary.org

Bartlett
Bartlett Historical Society • Bartlett History Museum, 228 S Main St, P.O. Box 8257 • Bartlett, IL 60103-8257 • (630) 837-0800 • http://www.village.bartlett.il.us/museum/museumhistory.html

Batavia
Batavia Historical Society • Batavia Depot Museum, 155 Houston, P.O. Box 14 • Batavia, IL 60510 • (630) 406-5274 • http://www.bataviahistoricalsociety.org

Batavia Public Library District • 10 S Batavia Ave • Batavia, IL 60510 • (630) 879-1393 • http://www.batavia.lib.il.us

Beardstown
Beardstown Public Library • 13 Boulevard Rd • Beardstown, IL 62618-8119 • (217) 323-4204

Bedford Park
Bedford Park Public Library District • 7816 W 65th Pl • Bedford Park, IL 60501 • (708) 458-6826 • http://www.bplib.net

Beecher
Beecher Community Historical Society • Washington Township Museum, 673 Penfield, P.O. Box 1469 • Beecher, IL 60401-1469 • (708) 946-2198

Beecher Community Library • 660 Penfield St, P.O. Box 818 • Beecher, IL 60401-0818 • (708) 946-9090

Belleville
Belleville Public Library • 121 E Washington St • Belleville, IL 62220 • (618) 234-0441 • http://www.compu-type.net/rengen/stclair/BPL.htm

Saint Clair County Genealogical Society • P.O. Box 431 • Belleville, IL 62222-0431 • (618) 277-0848 • http://www.computype.com/rengen/stclair/stchome.htm

Saint Clair County Historical Society • Emma Kunz House Museum, 602 Fulton St, P.O. Box 431 • Belleville, IL 62222-0431 • (618) 234-0600 • http://www.stcchs.org

Victorian Home Museum • 701 E Washington St • Belleville, IL 62220 • (618) 234-0600

Bellewood
Bellewood Public Library • 600 Bohland Ave • Bellewood, IL 60104-1896 • (708) 547-7393

Bellflower
Bellflower Genealogical and Historical Society • Historical Museum, 210 N Latcha St • Bellflower, IL 61724 • (309) 722-3757

Bellwood
Bellwood Public Library • 600 Bohland Ave • Bellwood, IL 60104-1896 • (708) 547-7393 • http://www.bellwoodlibrary.org

Belvidere
Boone County Historical Society • Log Cabin Museum, 311 Whitney Blvd • Belvidere, IL 61008-3609 • (815) 544-8391 • http://www.boonecountyhistoricalmuseum.org

Ida Public Library • 320 N State St • Belvidere, IL 61008-3299 • (815) 544-3838 • http://www.idapubliclibrary.org

Bement
Bement Public Library District • 349 S Macon • Bement, IL 61813 • (217) 678-7101 • http://www.bement.com/library.htm

Bryant Cottage Historic Home Museum • 146 E Wilson Ave, P.O. Box 41 • Bement, IL 61813 • (217) 678-8184

Bensenville
Bensenville Community Public Library • 200 S Church Rd • Bensenville, IL 60106 • (630) 766-4642 • http://www.bensenville.lib.il.us

Bensenville Historical Society • c/o Bensenville Community Library & Museum, 200 S Church Rd • Bensenville, IL 60106-2303 • (630) 595-3742

Benton
Benton Public Library District • 502 S Main St • Benton, IL 62812 • (618) 438-7511 • http://www.benton.lib.il.us

Franklin County Historical Society • 803 N McLeansboro St • Benton, IL 62812-2732 • (618) 435-6947

Berkeley
Berkeley Public Library • 1637 Taft Ave • Berkeley, IL 60163 • (708) 544-6017 • http://www.northstarnet.org/bkshome/berklib/

Berwyn
Berwyn Historical Society • 1241 Oak Park Ave, P.O. Box 479 • Berwyn, IL 60402 • (708) 484-0020 • http://www.berwyninformer.com/history.html

Bethalto
Bethalto Public Library District • 321 S Prairie St • Bethalto, IL 62010-1525 • (618) 377-8141 • http://www.bethaltolibrary.org

Ostfriesen Ancestral Research Association • 143 Virginia Ave • Bethalto, IL 62010

Biggsville
Henderson County District Library • 110 Hillcrest Dr • Biggsville, IL 61418-9736 • (309) 627-2450 • http://www.hendersoncounty.lib.il.us

Bishop Hill
Bishop Hill Heritage Association • Heritage Museum, 103 N Bishop Hill, P.O. Box 92 • Bishop Hill, IL 61419-0092 • (309) 927-3899 • http://www.bishophill.com

Bishop Hill Old Settlers Association • Descendants of the Bishop Hill Colonists, P.O. Box 68 • Bishop Hill, IL 61419

Bishop Hill State Historic Site • Bishop Hill Rd, P.O. Box 104 • Bishop Hill, IL 61419-0104 • (309) 927-3345

Henry County Historical Society • Historical Museum, 202 S Park St, P.O. Box 48 • Bishop Hill, IL 61419-9999 • (309) 927-3528

Society for the Historic Preservation of Franklin County • Bishop Hill State Historic Site, P.O. Box 104 • Bishop Hill, IL 61419-0104 • (309) 927-3345 • http://www.bishophill.com

Vasa Order of America • 109 S Main, P.O. Box 101 • Bishop Hill, IL 61419 • (309) 927-3898

Blandinsville
Blandin House Museum • 215 S Chestnut St, P.O. Box 253 • Blandinsville, IL 61420 • (309) 652-3673

Blandinsville-Hire Public Library • 130 S Main St, P.O. Box 50 • Blandinsville, IL 61420-0050 • (309) 652-3166

Bloomingdale
Bloomingdale Historical Society • c/o Bloomingdale Public Library & Museum, 101 Fairfield Way • Bloomingdale, IL 60108-1902 • (630) 529-3120

Bloomingdale Public Library • 101 Fairfield Way • Bloomingdale, IL 60108-1579 • (630) 529-3120 • http://www.bloomingdale.lib.il.us

Bloomington

Bloomington Public Library • 205 E Olive St, P.O. Box 3308 • Bloomington, IL 61701-3308 • (309) 828-6091 • http://www.bloomingtonlibrary.org

Commission on Archives and History, United Methodist Church • 1211 N Park St, P.O. Box 2050 • Bloomington, IL 61702 • (309) 828-5092

David Davis Mansion Museum • 1000 E Monroe Dr • Bloomington, IL 61701 • (309) 838-1084 • http://www.davismansion.org

Illinois Great Rivers Conference Historical Society • Historical Museum, 1211 N Park St, P.O. Box 515 • Bloomington, IL 61702 • (309) 828-5092

McLean County Genealogical Society • Old McLean County Courthouse Museum, 200 N Main St • Bloomington, IL 61701 • (309) 827-0428 • http://www.mchistory.org

McLean County Historical Society • Old McLean County Courthouse Museum, 200 N Main St • Bloomington, IL 61701 • (309) 827-0428 • http://www.mchistory.org

Blue Island

Blue Island Historical Society • c/o Blue Island Public Library & Museum, 2433 York St • Blue Island, IL 60406-2094 • (708) 388-1078 • http://www.blueisland.org/Historical.html

Blue Island Public Library • 2433 York St • Blue Island, IL 60406-2011 • (708) 388-1078 • http://www.blueislandlibrary.org

Bolingbrook

Bolingbrook Historical Society • 162 N Canyon Dr • Bolingbrook, IL 60440-1526 • (630) 759-4974

Northern Will County Genealogical Society • 603 Derbyshire Ln • Bolingbrook, IL 60439

Bourbonnais

Bourbonnais Grove Historical Society • Historical Museum, Stratford Dr & Route 102, P.O. Box 311 • Bourbonnais, IL 60914-0311 • (815) 933-2308 • http://www.bbhistory.us

Bourbonnais Public Library District • 250 W John Casey Rd • Bourbonnais, IL 60914 • (815) 933-1727 • http://www.bourbonnais.lib.il.us

Kankakee Valley Genealogical Society • P.O. Box 442 • Bourbonnais, IL 60914 • (815) 939-4564 • http://www.kvgs.org

Braidwood

Fossil Ridge Public Library • 386 W Kennedy Rd • Braidwood, IL 60408 • (815) 458-2187 • http://www.fossilridge.org

Bridgeport

Irene Black Genealogical Library • 125 E Olive St • Bridgeport, IL 62417 • (618) 945-7113

Lawrence County Genealogical Society • Route 1, Box 44 • Bridgeport, IL 62417 • (618) 945-7181 • http://www.rootsweb.com/~illawren/lcgs.htm

Bridgeview

Bridgeview Public Library • 7840 W 79th St • Bridgeview, IL 60455-1496 • (708) 458-2880 • http://www.bridgeviewlibrary.org

Brimfield

Brimfield Historical Society • c/o Brimfield Public Library, 111 S Galena, P.O. Box 55 • Brimfield, IL 61517 • (309) 446-3631

Brimfield Public Library • 111 S Galena St, P.O. Box 207 • Brimfield, IL 61517-0207 • (309) 446-9575 • http://www.brimfieldpubliclibrary.org

Brookfield

Brookfield Historical Society • 8820 1/2 Brookfield Ave • Brookfield, IL 60513-1670 • (708) 485-3420

Buda

Mason Memorial Public Library • Main St, P.O. Box 55 • Buda, IL 61314 • (309) 895-7701

Buffalo Grove

Raupp Memorial Museum • 901 Dunham Ln • Buffalo Grove, IL 60089 • (847) 459-2318 • http://www.bgparkdistrict.org

Burbank

Prairie Trails Public Library District • 8449 S Moody • Burbank, IL 60459-2525 • (708) 430-3688 • http://www.prairietrailslibrary.org

Burr Ridge

Flagg Creek Historical Society • Historical Museum, 7425 S Wolf Rd, P.O. Box 227 • Burr Ridge, IL 60525 • (708) 246-6169 • http://www.pleasantdaleparks.org/vial_house.htm

Bushnell

Bushnell Area Historical Society • Cultural Center, 300 Miller St • Bushnell, IL 61422 • (309) 772-3782

Byron

Byron Museum • 110 N Union, P.O. Box 186 • Byron, IL 61010-0186 • (815) 234-5031 • http://www.byronillinois.org

Cahokia

Cahokia Courthouse State Historic Site Museum • 107 Elm St • Cahokia, IL 62206 • (618) 332-1782

Jarrot Mansion Museum • 124 E 1st St • Cahokia, IL 62206 • (618) 332-1782

Cairo

Cairo Historical Association • 826 Charles St • Cairo, IL 62914-1458 • (618) 734-0201

Cairo Public Library • 1609 Washington Ave, P.O. Box 151 • Cairo, IL 62914-0151 • (618) 734-1840

Magnolia Manor Museum • 2700 Washington Ave, P.O. Box 286 • Cairo, IL 62914 • (618) 734-0201

Calumet City

Calumet City Historical Society • Historical Museum, 760 Wentworth Ave, P.O. Box 1917 • Calumet City, IL 60409-3515 • (708) 832-9390 • http://www.thetimesonline.com/org/cchs/

Calumet Park

Southeast Side Historical Museum • Calumet Park Fieldhouse, 9801 Avenue G • Calumet Park, IL 60617 • (773) 721-7948

Cambria

Mississippi Valley French Research Society • P.O. Box 502 • Cambria, IL 62915 • (618) 985-6857

Cambridge

Cambridge Historical Society • Historical Museum, RR2, Box 96 • Cambridge, IL 61238-9633 • (309) 937-2233

Cambridge Public Library District • 212 W Center St • Cambridge, IL 61238-1239 • (309) 937-2233

Canton

Fulton County Historical and Genealogical Society • Historical Museum, 45 N Park Dr, P.O. Box 583 • Canton, IL 61520 • (309) 647-0771 • http://www.outfitters.com/illinois/history/family/fulton/fulton.html

Parlin Ingersoll Public Library • 205 W Chestnut St • Canton, IL 61520 • (309) 647-0064 • http://www.parliningersoll.org

Carbondale

Afro-American Historical and Genealogical Society, Little Egypt Chapter • 207 Lendview Dr, P.O. Box 974 • Carbondale, IL 62901 • (618) 457-5537 • http://www.aahgs.org

Delyte W Morris Library - Special Collections • Southern Illinois Univ, 605 Agriculture Dr, Mailcode 6632 • Carbondale, IL 62901-6632 • (618) 453-2522 • http://www.lib.siu.edu/spcol/irad.shtml

Carbondale, cont.

University Museum • Southern IL Univ, MC 4508 • Carbondale, IL 62901 • (618) 453-5388 • http://www.museum.siu.edu

Carlinville

Carlinville Public Library • 510 N Broad St, P.O. Box 17 • Carlinville, IL 62626 • (217) 854-3505 • http://www.carlinvillelibrary.com

Macoupin County Historical Society • Historical Museum, 920 W Breckenridge St, P.O. Box 432 • Carlinville, IL 62626-0432 • (217) 854-2850 • http://www.macsociety.org

Carlyle

Case-Halstead Library • 571 Franklin St • Carlyle, IL 62231 • (618) 594-5210 • http://case-halstead.hypermart.net

Clinton County Historical Society • Historical Museum, 1091 Franklin St • Carlyle, IL 62231-1820 • http://www.carlyle.il.us/mus.htm

Carmi

L Haas Store Museum • 219 E Main St • Carmi, IL 62821

Matsel Cabin Museum • 304 E Robinson St • Carmi, IL 62821

Ratcliff Inn Museum • 218 E Main St, P.O. Box 121 • Carmi, IL 62821 • (618) 382-3334 • http://www.rootsweb.com/~ilwcohs/

Robinson-Stewart House Museum • 110 S Main Cross St • Carmi, IL 62821

White County Historical Society • Historical Museum, 203 N Church St, P.O. Box 121 • Carmi, IL 62821 • (618) 382-8425 • http://www.rootsweb.com/~ilwcohs/

Carol Stream

Carol Stream Historical Society • Historical Museum, 244 Tomahawk Ct • Carol Stream, IL 60188 • (630) 655-0686 • http://www.carolstreamhistorical.com

Gretna Station and Caboose Museum • 391 Illini Dr • Carol Stream, IL 60188 • (630) 260-7863

Historic Farmhouse Museum • 310 Lies Rd • Carol Stream, IL 60187 • (312) 655-2311 • http://www.carolstreamhistorical.com

Carrier Mills

Carrier Mills Public Library • 109 W Oak St, P.O. Box 338 • Carrier Mills, IL 62917-0338 • (618) 994-2011

Carrollton

Carrollton Public Library • 509 S Main St • Carrollton, IL 62016 • (217) 942-6715 • http://www.c-hawks.org/library/libabout.html

Green County Historical Museum • 532 N Main St, P.O. Box 137 • Carrollton, IL 62016 • (217) 942-6013 • http://www.c-hawks.org/greenehistoricalsociety/

Greene County Historical and Genealogical Society • 221 N 5th St, P.O. Box 137 • Carrollton, IL 62016 • (217) 942-6013 • http://www.rootsweb.com/~ilgreene/gcgs.htm

Carterville

Carterville Public Library • 117 S Division St • Carterville, IL 62918 • (618) 985-3298

Genealogy Society of Southern Illinois • John A Logan College, 700 Logan College Rd • Carterville, IL 62918-9599 • (618) 985-6213 • http://www.jal.cc.il.us/gssi.html

John A Logan College Museum • 700 Logan College Rd • Carterville, IL 62918 • (618) 985-3741 • http://www.jalc.edu/museum/

Shawnee Library System • 607 S Greenbriar Rd • Carterville, IL 62918-1602 • (618) 985-3711 • http://www.shawls.lib.il.us

Carthage

Carthage Public Library • 538 Wabash • Carthage, IL 62321-1360 • (217) 357-3232 • http://www.carthage.lib.il.us

Hancock County Genealogical and Historical Society • Hancock County Courthouse Museum, 306 Walnut St, P.O. Box 68 • Carthage, IL 62321-0068 • (217) 357-0043

Cary

Cary Grove Historical Society • 335 Wooded Knoll Dr • Cary, IL 60013 • (847) 639-9788

Cary-Fox River Grove Historical Society of Illinois • P.O. Box 483 • Cary, IL 60013

Catlin

Catlin Historical Society • Catlin Museum, 210 N Paris St, P.O. Box 658 • Catlin, IL 61817-0658 • (217) 427-5766 • http://www.rootsweb.com/~ilchs

Cedarville

Cedarville Area Historical Society • Cherry St, P.O. Box 46 • Cedarville, IL 61013-0046 • (815) 563-4523

Centralia

Centralia Public Library • 515 E Broadway St • Centralia, IL 62801 • (618) 532-5222 • http://www.centralialibrary.org

Kaskaskia College Library • 27210 College Rd • Centralia, IL 62801 • (618) 545-3130 • http://www.kc.cc.il.us/library/

Champaign

Champaign County Historical Museum • 102 E University Ave • Champaign, IL 61820-4111 • (217) 356-1010 • http://www.champaignmuseum.org

Champaign County Historical Society • Historical Museum, 102 E University • Champaign, IL 61820 • (217) 356-1010

Champaign Public Library • 505 S Randolf St • Champaign, IL 61820-5193 • (217) 403-2070 • http://www.champaign.org

Champaign-Urbana Jewish Genealogy Society • 808 La Sell Dr • Champaign, IL 61820-6820 • (217) 359-3102

Illinois Heritage Association • Historical Museum, 602 1/2 E Green St, P.O. Box C, Sta A • Champaign, IL 61820 • (217) 359-5600 • http://www.prairienet.org/iha/

John Philip Sousa Museum • Univ of IL, Harding Band Bldg, 1003 S 6th St • Champaign, IL 61829 • (217) 244-9309 • http://www.cucvb.org/museums/sousa.html

Channahon

Three Rivers Public Library • 25207 W Channahon Dr, P.O. Box 300 • Channahon, IL 60410-0300 • (815) 467-6200 • http://www.three-rivers-library.org

Chapin

Chapin Community Historical Society • Superior St • Chapin, IL 62628 • (217) 472-6216

Charleston

Booth Library - IL Regional Archives • Eastern Illinois University, 600 Lincoln Ave • Charleston, IL 61920 • (217) 581-6072 • http://www.eiu.edu/~booth/

Carnegie Public Library • 712 6th St • Charleston, IL 61920 • (217) 345-4913 • http://www.charlestonlibrary.org

Coles County Genealogical Society • P.O. Box 592 • Charleston, IL 61920-0592 • http://www.rootsweb.com/~ilcoles/ccgs.htm

Coles County Historical Society • Historical Museum, 800 Hayes Ave, P.O. Box 225 • Charleston, IL 61920 • (217) 345-6755

Greenwood School Museum • 895 7th St • Charleston, IL 61920 • (217) 345-2934

Chatsworth

Chatsworth Historical Society • 424 E Locust St, P.O. Box 755 • Chatsworth, IL 60921-0755 • (815) 635-3191

Chenoa
Matthew T Scott House Museum • 227 N 1st St • Chenoa, IL 61726-1019 • (815) 945-4555

Cherry Valley
Afro-American Historical and Genealogical Society, Northern Illinois-Southern Wisconsin Chapter • P.O. Box 478 • Cherry Valley, IL 61016 • http://www.aahgs.org

Cherry Valley Public District Library • 755 E State St • Cherry Valley, IL 61016-9699 • (815) 332-5161 • http://www.cherryvalley.lib.il.us

Chester
Chester Public Library • 733 State St • Chester, IL 62233-9998 • (618) 826-3711 • http://www.sirin.lib.il.us/docs/cht/docs/lib/

Randolph County Archives and Museum • 1 Taylor St • Chester, IL 62233-0332 • (618) 826-3743

Randolph County Genealogical Society • 600 State St, Rm 306 • Chester, IL 62233 • (618) 826-3807 • http://www.rootsweb.com/~ilrcgs/

Randolph County Historical Society • 104 Hillcrest Dr • Chester, IL 62233-2250 • (618) 826-2267

Chicago
A Philip Randolph Pullman Porter Museum • 10406 S Maryland Ave, P.O. Box 6276 • Chicago, IL 60680 • (773) 928-3935 • http://www.aphiliprandolphmuseum.com

AASR Valley of Chicago • 915 N Dearborn St • Chicago, IL 60610 • (312) 787-7605 ext. 9 • http://www.valleyofchicago.org

African-American Genealogical and Historical Society, Patricia Liddell Researchers • P.O. Box 438652 • Chicago, IL 60643 • http://www.aahgs.org

American Indian Center of Chicago • 1630 W Wilson Ave • Chicago, IL 60640 • (773) 275-5871 • http://www.aic-chicago.org

American Library Association, Genealogy Committee • 50 E Huron St • Chicago, IL 60611 • (800) 545-2433 • http://faculty.washington.edu/~mudrock/HIST/gen.html

American Police Center and Museum • 1717 S State St • Chicago, IL 60616 • (312) 939-1122

Archives of the Czechs and Slovaks Abroad • Regensburg Library, Univ of Chicago, 1100 E 57th St • Chicago, IL 60637 • (773) 702-4685 • http://www.lib.uchicago.edu

Archives of the Evangelical Lutheran Church in America • 8765 W Higgins Rd • Chicago, IL 60631-4198 • (773) 380-2818 • http://www.elea.org/os/archives/intro.html

Archives of the Lutheran Church in America • 1100 E 55th St • Chicago, IL 60615-5199 • (773) 667-3500

Arnold Damen Historical and Preservation Society • 1076 W Roosevelt Rd • Chicago, IL 60608-1519 • (312) 421-5900

Asian American Resource and Cultural Center • Univ of IL at Chicago, 826 S Halsted St, Rm 101 • Chicago, IL 60607-7029 • (312) 413-9569 • http://www.iuc.edu

Assyrian-American Federation • 1618 W Devon Ave • Chicago, IL 60660-1214 • (773) 743-9180

Balzekas Museum of Lithuanian Culture and Genealogical Archives • 6500 S Pulaski Rd • Chicago, IL 60632-5136 • (773) 582-6500 • http://www.lithuanianmuseum.org

Benevolent and Protective Order of Elks of the USA • 2750 N Lakeview Ave • Chicago, IL 60614-1889 • (773) 755-4708 • http://www.elks.org

Brandel Library - Special Collections • North Park University, 5114 N Christiana Ave • Chicago, IL 60625 • (773)244-5247 • http://www.northpark.edu

Brazilian Cultural Center • Chicago History Museum, 1436 W Jonquil Terr • Chicago, IL 60626 • (312) 404-7180 • http://www.brazilianculturalcenter.org

Bronzeville Historical Society • Historical Museum, 11431 S Forrestville Ave #1 • Chicago, IL 60628 • (773) 291-9114 • http://www.bronzevillehistoricalsociety.com

Bulgaria National Front • P.O. Box 59240 • Chicago, IL 60659

Cambodian Association of Illinois • Cambodian American Heritage Museum, 2831 W Lawrence • Chicago, IL 60625 • (773) 878-7090 • http://www.cambodian-association.org

Carter G Woodson Library • Malcolm X College, 1900 W Van Buren St • Chicago, IL 60612 • (312) 850-7250 • http://www.ccc.edu/malcolmx/

Charnley-Persky House Museum • 1365 N Astor St • Chicago, IL 60610-2144 • (312) 915-0105 • http://www.sah.org; http://www.charnleyhouse.org

Chicago Genealogical Society • 129 Berteau Ave, P.O. Box 1160 • Chicago, IL 60690-1160 • (773) 725-1306 • http://www.chgogs.org

Chicago Historical Society • Historical Museum, 1601 N Clark St • Chicago, IL 60614 • (312) 642-4600 • http://www.chicagohistory.org

Chicago Jewish Historical Society • Spertus Institute of Jewish Studies, 618 S Michigan Ave • Chicago, IL 60605 • (302) 322-1741 • http://www.spertus.edu; http://www.chicagojewishhistory.org

Chicago Lawn Historical Society • c/o Chicago Lawn Library, 6120 S Kedzie Ave • Chicago, IL 60629-4638 • (312) 747-0639

Chicago Municipal Reference Library • 400 S State St, 5th Fl S • Chicago, IL 60605 • (312) 747-4526

Chicago Public Library - Special Collections • 400 S State St • Chicago, IL 60605-1203 • (312) 747-4300 • http://www.chicagopubliclibrary.org

Chicago Public Library-Avalon • 8148 S Stony Island • Chicago, IL 60617 • (312) 747-5234

Chicago Public Library-Carter G Woodson Regional • 9525 S Halsted St • Chicago, IL 60628 • (312) 747-6900 • http://cpl.lib.uic.edu/002branches/woodson/woodson.html

Chicago Public Library-Chicago Lawn • 6120 S Kedzie Ave • Chicago, IL 60629 • (312) 747-0639 • http://www.chipublib.org

Chicago Public Library-Legler • 115 S Pulaski Rd • Chicago, IL 60624 • (312) 746-7730

Chicago Public Library-Mount Greenwood • 11010 S Kedzie Ave • Chicago, IL 60655-2222 • (312) 747-2805

Chicago Tribune Archives • Tribune Tower, 435 N Michigan Ave, Rm. 1231 • Chicago, IL 60611 • (312) 222-3026 • http://pgasb.pgarchiver.com/chicagotribune/

Clarke House Museum • 1827 S Indiana Ave • Chicago, IL 60616 • (312) 745-0040 • http://www.clarkehousemuseum.org

Conrad Sulzer Regional Library • 4455 N Lincoln Ave • Chicago, IL 60625-2192 • (312) 744-7616

Covenant Church Historical Archives • North Park Univ, 3225 W Foster Ave • Chicago, IL 60625 • (773) 244-6223 • http://www.campus.northpark.edu/library/archives

Croatian Ethnic Institute • 4851 S Drexel Blvd • Chicago, IL 60615 • (773) 373-2248 • http://www.croatian-institute.org

DePaul University Archives • 2323 N Seminary • Chicago, IL 60614 • (773) 341-8088

DePaul University Libraries • 2350 N Kenmore • Chicago, IL 60614 • (773) 325-7862 • http://www.lib.depaul.edu/speccoll/uarchive.htm

DuSable Museum of African-American History • 740 E 56th Pl • Chicago, IL 60637 • (773) 947-0600 • http://www.dusablemuseum.org

Illinois

Chicago, cont.

East Asian Library • Univ of Chicago, 1100 E 57th St • Chicago, IL 60637-1502 • (773) 702-8436

East Side Historical Society • Fitzgibbons Historical Museum, 3658 E 106th St • Chicago, IL 60617-6611 • (773) 721-7948

Edgebrook Historical Society • 6173 N McClellan • Chicago, IL 60646-4013 • (312) 631-2854

Edgewater Historical Society • 5358 N Ashland Ave • Chicago, IL 60660-4410 • (773) 506-4849 • http://www.edgewaterhistory.org

Episcopal Diocese of Chicago Archives • St James Cathedral, 65 E Huron • Chicago, IL 60611 • (312) 751-4200 • http://www.epischicago.org

Evangelical Covenant Church Archives • Archives and Special Collections, North Park Univ, 3225 W Foster Ave • Chicago, IL 60625-4895 • (773) 244-622 • http://www.campus.northpark.edu/library/archives/

Evangelical Covenant Church of America Archives • 5101 N Francisco Ave • Chicago, IL 60625 • (773) 784-3000 • http://www.covchurch.org/cov/

Filipino American Historical Society of Chicago • 5462 S Dorchester Ave • Chicago, IL 60615-5309 • (773) 752-2156

Frederick C Robie House Museum • 5757 S Woodlawn • Chicago, IL 60637 • (773) 834-1847 • http://www.wrightplus.org

Galewood-Mount Claire Historical Society • 1705 N Nashville Ave • Chicago, IL 60635-3904 • (312) 237-8960

German-American National Congress • 4740 N Western Ave • Chicago, IL 60625-2013 • (773) 275-1100

Glessner House Museum • 1800 S Prairie Ave • Chicago, IL 60616 • (312) 326-1480 • http://www.glessnerhouse.org

Grand Army of the Republic • GAR Memorial Museum, 78 E Washington St • Chicago, IL 60602 • (312) 269-2926 • http://suvcw.org/gar.htm

Hammond Library • Chicago Theological Seminary, 5757 S University Ave • Chicago, IL 60637 • (773) 752-5757 • http://www.chgosem.edu

Hellenic Museum and Cultural Center • 801 W Adams, 4th Fl • Chicago, IL 60607 • (312) 726-1234 • http://www.hellenicmuseum.org

Historic Pullman Foundation • Historical Museum, 11141 S Cottage Grove Ave • Chicago, IL 60628-4649 • (773) 785-8181 • http://www.pullmanil.org

Hyde Park Historical Society • Historical Museum, 5529 S Lake Park Ave • Chicago, IL 60637-1718 • (773) 493-1893 • http://www.HydeParkHistory.org

Illinois Labor History Society • 28 E Jackson Blvd • Chicago, IL 60604-2215 • (312) 663-4107 • http://www.kentlaw.edu/ilhs/

Independent Order of Svithiod • 5518 W Lawrence Ave • Chicago, IL 60630 • (773) 736-1191

International Museum of Surgical Science • 1526 Lake Shore Dr • Chicago, IL 60610 • (312) 642-6502 • http://www.imss.org

International Society of Sons and Daughters of Slave Ancestry • 2134 W 95th St, P.O. Box 436937 • Chicago, IL 60643-6937 • (773) 238-2686 • http://www.rootsweb.com/~ilissdsa

Irish American Heritage Center • 4626 N Knox Ave • Chicago, IL 60630-4030 • (773) 282-7035 • http://www.irishamhc.com

Irvin Park Museum • 3801 N Keeler Ave, P.O Box 34749 • Chicago, IL 60634 • (773) 777-2750

Irving Park Historical Society • 4122 N Kedvale, P.O. Box 34749 • Chicago, IL 60641-4749 • (773) 736-2143 • http://www.ihps.org

James P Fitzgibbons Historical Museum • Calumet Park Fieldhouse, 9800 Avenue G • Chicago, IL 60675

Jane Addams' Hull House Museum • Univ of Illinois-Chicago, 800 S Halsted St • Chicago, IL 60607-7017 • (312) 413-5353 • http://www.uic.edu/jaddams/hull/hull_house

Jesuit-Krauss-McCormick Library • Lutheran School of Theology, 1100 E 55th St • Chicago, IL 60615 • (773) 256-0739 • http://www.jkmlibrary.org

John Crerar Library • Univ of Chicago, 5730 South Ellis Ave • Chicago, IL 60637 • (312) 225-2526 • http://www.lib.uchicago.edu/e/crerar/

Joseph Regenstein Library • University of Chicago, 1100 E 57th St • Chicago, IL 60637 • http://www.lib.uchicago.edu/e/reg/

Kelly Memorial Library • Richard J Daley College, 7500 S Pulaski Rd • Chicago, IL 60652-1200 • (773) 838-7669 • http://www.ccc.edu

League of Americans of Ukranian Descent • 841 N Western Ave • Chicago, IL 60622

Lithuanian American Genealogy Society • Balzekas Museum of Lithuanian Culture, 6500 S Pulaski Rd • Chicago, IL 60629-5136 • (773) 582-6500 • http://www.feefhs.org/baltic/lt/frg-lags.html

Lithuanian Research and Studies Center • Historical Museum, 5600 S Claremont Ave • Chicago, IL 60636-1039 • (773) 434-4545 • http://www.lithuanianresearch.org

Lithuanian-American Council • Belzekas Museum, 6500 S Pulaski Rd • Chicago, IL 60629-5136 • (773) 582-6500

Moody Bible Institute Library • 820 N LaSalle • Chicago, IL 60610 • (312) 329-4000 • http://www.moody.edu

Morton B Weiss Museum of Judaica • 1100 Hyde Park Blvd • Chicago, IL 60615-2899 • (773) 924-1234 • http://www.kamii.org

Mount Greenwood Historical Society • c/o Mount Greenwood Public Library, 11010 S Kedzie Ave • Chicago, IL 60655 • (312) 239-2805

Mundelein College Archives-Chicago • 6363 Sheridan Rd • Chicago, IL 60660 • (773) 262-8100

National Archives & Records Administration-Great Lakes Region • 7358 S Pulaski Rd • Chicago, IL 60629-5898 • (773) 948-9000 • http://www.archives.gov/facilities/il/chicago.html

National Trust for Historic Preservation • 53 W Jackson Blvd • Chicago, IL 60604-3606 • (312) 939-5547

Newberry Library • 60 W Walton St • Chicago, IL 60610 • (312) 943-9090 • http://www.newberry.org

Newberry Library's Friends of Genealogy • c/o Newberry Library, 60 W Walton St • Chicago, IL 60610-7324 • (312) 943-9090 • http://www.newberry.org

Noble-Seymour-Crippen House Museum • 5624 N Newark Ave • Chicago, IL 60631 • (773) 631-4633

Norman & Helen Asher Library • Spertus Institute of Jewish Studies, 618 S Michigan Ave • Chicago, IL 60605 • (312) 322-1749 • http://www.spertus.edu

Norwood Park Historical Society • Historical Museum, 5624 N Newark Ave • Chicago, IL 60631 • (773) 631-4633 • http://www.norwoodparkhistoricalsociety.org

Old Edgebrook Historical Society • 6173 N McClellan Ave • Chicago, IL 60646-4013

Polish American Historical Association • Polish Museum of America, 984 N Milwaukee Ave • Chicago, IL 60622-4101 • (773) 229-1493 • http://www.prcua.org/pma

Polish Genealogical Society of America • Polish Museum of America, 984 N Milwaukee Ave • Chicago, IL 60622-4101 • (773) 384-3352 • http://pma.prcua.org

Polish Military Historical Society of America • Historical Museum, 984 N Milwaukee Ave • Chicago, IL 60622 • (312) 939-3737

Polish National Alliance • 6100 N Cicero • Chicago, IL 60646 • (773) 286-0500 • http://www.pna-znp.org

Ravenswood-Lake View Historical Association • c/o Conrad Sulzer Regional Library, 4455 N Lincoln Ave • Chicago, IL 60625-2192 • (312) 744-7616

Richard J Daley Library • University of Illinois at Chicago, 801 S Morgan St, M/C 234, P.O. Box 8198 • Chicago, IL 60680-8198 • (312) 996-2726 • http://www.uic.edu/depts/lib/

Ridge Historical Society • Historical Museum, 10621 S Seeley Ave • Chicago, IL 60643-2618 • (773) 881-1675

Rogers Park-West Ridge Historical Society • Historical Museum, 7344 N Western Ave • Chicago, IL 60645 • (773) 764-2824 • http://www.rpwrhs.org

Ronald Williams Library • Northeastern Illinois Univ, 5500 N St Louis Ave • Chicago, IL 60625-4699 • (773) 442-4410 • http://www.neiu.edu/~neiulib/

Society of American Archivists • 17 N State St, Ste 1425 • Chicago, IL 60602-3315 • (312) 606-0722 • http://www.archivists.org

Sons of the American Revolution, Illinois Society • 1360 North Lakeshore Dr • Chicago, IL 62610-2151 • (312) 327-0832 • http://www.illinois-sar.org

South Shore Historical Society • 7566 S Shore Dr • Chicago, IL 60649 • (773) 375-1699

Spertus Museum • 618 S Michigan Ave • Chicago, IL 60605-1901 • (312) 322-1747 • http://www.spertus.edu

Stephen A Douglas Tomb Museum • 636 E 35th St • Chicago, IL 60616 • (312) 225-2620

Swedish American Historical Society • Historical Museum, North Park Univ, 3225 W Foster Ave, Box 48 • Chicago, IL 60625 • (773) 583-5722 • http://www.swedishamericanhist.org

Swedish American Museum Association • Historical Museum, 5211 N Clark St • Chicago, IL 60640 • (773) 728-8111 • http://www.samac.org

Swedish Pioneer Historical Society • North Park College, 5125 N Spaulding Ave • Chicago, IL 60625 • (312) 583-5722

Swiss American Historical Society • 6440 N Bosworth Ave • Chicago, IL 60626-4921 • (773) 262-8336

Ukrainian National Museum & Archive • 2249 W Superior St • Chicago, IL 60612 • (312) 421-8020 • http://www.ukrntimuseum.com

University of Chicago Library • 1100 E 57th St • Chicago, IL 60637-1596 • (773) 702-4685 • http://www.lib.uchicago.edu

Uptown Historical Society • Historical Museum, 4531 N Dover St • Chicago, IL 60640 • (773) 561-5169

West Side Historical Society • c/o Chicago Public Library-Legler Branch, 115 S Pulaski Rd • Chicago, IL 60624 • (312) 746-7730

World Lithuanian Archives • 5620 S Claremont Ave • Chicago, IL 60636 • (773) 434-4545

Chicago Heights
American-Italian Historical Association • 169 County Club Rd • Chicago Heights, IL 60411 • (708) 756-5359 • http://www.mobilito.com/aiha

Chicago Heights Free Public Library • 25 W 15th St • Chicago Heights, IL 60411-3488 • (708) 754-0323 • http://www.chicagoheightslibrary.org

Chicago Heights Historical Society • c/o Chicago Heights Free Public Library, 25 W 15th St • Chicago Heights, IL 60411 • (708) 754-0323

Chillicothe
Chillicothe Historical Society • Old Rock Island Depot Museum, 723 N 4th St, P.O. Box 181 • Chillicothe, IL 61423-0181 • (309) 274-9076

Chillicothe Public Library District • 822 N 2nd St • Chillicothe, IL 61523-1822 • (309) 274-2719 • http://www.chillicothepubliclibrary.org

Chrisman
Chrisman Public Library • 112 S Illinois • Chrisman, IL 61924 • (217) 269-3011

Christopher
West Franklin Historical District and Genealogical Society • 2130 School House Rd • Christopher, IL 62822 • (618) 724-2445

Cicero
Czech and Slovak Genealogical Library • T G Masaryk School, 5701 22nd Pl • Cicero, IL 60804

Czechoslovak National Council of America • 2137 S Lombard Ave, Rm 202 • Cicero, IL 60650-2037 • (708) 656-1117

Historical Society of Cicero • Historical Museum, 2423 S Austin Blvd • Cicero, IL 60650-2695 • (708) 652-8305

Clarendon Hills
Clarendon Hills Public Library • 7 N Prospect Rd • Clarendon Hills, IL 60514 • (630) 323-8188

Clinton
C H Moore Homestead Museum • 219 E Woodlawn St • Clinton, IL 61727 • (217) 935-6066 • http://www.chmoorehomestead.org

DeWitt County Genealogical Society • c/o Warner Public Library, 310 N Quincy, P.O. Box 632 • Clinton, IL 61727 • (217) 935-3493

Vespasian Warner Public Library • 310 N Quincy • Clinton, IL 61727 • (217) 935-5174 • http://www.warner.lib.il.us

Coal City
Coal City Public Library District • 85 N Garfield St • Coal City, IL 60416 • (815) 634-4552 • http://www.coalcity.lib.il.us

Coal Valley
Robert R Jones Public Library • 2210 1st St, P.O. Box 190 • Coal Valley, IL 61240-0190 • (309) 799-3047

Cobden
Union County Historical and Genealogical Society • 104 Clemens • Cobden, IL 62920 • (618) 893-2067

Union County Museum • S Appleknocker St, P.O. Box 93 • Cobden, IL 62920 • (618) 893-2067

Colchester
Colchester Area Historical Society • 3975 E 650th St • Colchester, IL 62326

Colfax
Martin Township Public Library • 103 S Center St, P.O. Box 376 • Colfax, IL 61728-0376 • (309) 723-2541 • http://www.mtpl.lib.il.us

Collinsville
Cahokia Mounds Historic Site Museum • 30 Ramey Dr • Collinsville, IL 62234 • (618) 344-9221

Collinsville Memorial Public Library & Historical Museum • 408 W Main St • Collinsville, IL 62234 • (618) 344-1112 • http://www.collinsvillelibrary.org

Illinois Historical Preservation Agency • 30 Ramey St • Collinsville, IL 62234 • (618) 346-5160

Colona
Twin Rivers District Public Library • 911 1st St • Colona, IL 61241 • (309) 792-0548 • http://www.rbls.lib.il.us/cln/

Columbia

Columbia Historical Society • Historical Museum, 11562 Bluff Rd • Columbia, IL 62236 • (618) 281-5734

Columbia Public Library • 106 N Metter • Columbia, IL 62236-2299 • (618) 281-4237

Monroe County Genealogical Society • P.O. Box 381 • Columbia, IL 62236 • (618) 286-3449

Coulterville

Coulterville Public Library • 103 S 4th St, P.O. Box 373 • Coulterville, IL 62237-0373 • (618) 758-3013

Cowden

Family Tree Resource Network • 112 First Grand Ave, P.O. Box 107 • Cowden, IL 62422-0107 • (217) 783-2610

Crestwood

Chicago & East Illinois Railroad Historical Society • P.O. Box 606 • Crestwood, IL 60445-0606 • http://cei.justnet.com

Crystal Lake

Crystal Lake Historical Society • Col Gustavus Palmer House Museum, 660 E Terra Cotta, P.O. Box 1151 • Crystal Lake, IL 60039-1151 • (815) 455-1151 • http://www.cl-hs.org

Crystal Lake Public Library • 126 W Paddock St • Crystal Lake, IL 60014 • (815) 459-1687 • http://www.crystallakelibrary.org

McHenry County College Library • 8900 US Hwy 14 • Crystal Lake, IL 60012 • (815) 455-8533 • http://www.mchenry.edu/library/Library.asp

McHenry County Genealogical Society • c/o McHenry Public Library, 809 N Front St, P.O. Box 184 • Crystal Lake, IL 60039-0184 • (847) 639-1685 • http://www.mcigs.org

Cuba

Spoon River Public Library • 201 S 3rd St, P.O. Box 140 • Cuba, IL 61427-0140 • (309) 785-5496

Danvers

Danvers Historical Museum • 102 S West, P.O. Box 613 • Danvers, IL 61732

Danvers Historical Society • 118 W Park • Danvers, IL 61732 • (309) 392-2042

Danville

Danville Public Library • 307 N Vermilion St • Danville, IL 61832 • (217) 477-5228 • http://www.danville.lib.il.us

Illiana Genealogical and Historical Society • 307 N Vermillion St, P.O. Box 207 • Danville, IL 61834-0207 • (217) 431-8733 • http://www.tbox.com/www.danvillevirtual.com/vcclients/danville/IllianaGene/

Lamon House Museum • 1031 N Logan Ave • Danville, IL 61832 • (217) 442-2922

Vermilion County Museum Society • Historical Museum, 116 N Gilbert St • Danville, IL 61832-8506 • (217) 442-2922 • http://www.vermilioncountymuseum.org

Vermilion County War Museum • 307 N Vermilion St • Danville, IL 31832 • (217) 431-0034 • http://www.vcwn.org

Darien

Darien Historical Society • Historical Museum, 7422 Cass Ave, P.O. Box 2178 • Darien, IL 60561-2178 • (630) 969-5171

De Kalb

DeKalb Public Library • 309 Oak St • De Kalb, IL 60115 • (815) 756-9568 • http://www.dkpl.org

Ellwood House Museum • 509 N 1st St • De Kalb, IL 60115 • (815) 756-4609 • http://www.ellwoodhouse.org

Founders Memorial Library • Northern Illinois Univ, Illinois Regional Archives • De Kalb, IL 60115-2868 • (815) 753-9851 • http://www.niulib.niu.edu

Ilinois Association for the Advancement of History • Northern Illinois Univ, Dept of History • De Kalb, IL 60115-2302 • (815) 753-6818

Regional History Center Archives • Northern Illinois Univ, Swen Parson Hall, Rm 155 • De Kalb, IL 60115 • (815) 753-1779

De Pue

Selby Township Library District • 101 Depot, P.O. Box 49 • De Pue, IL 61322-0049 • (815) 447-2660

Decatur

African-American Cultural and Genealogical Society • 314 N Main, P.O. Box 25251 • Decatur, IL 62525 • (217) 429-7458 • http://www.decaturnet.org/afrigenes.html

Decatur Genealogical Society • 355 N Main St, P.O. Box 1548 • Decatur, IL 62521-1548 • (217) 429-0135 • http://www.rootsweb.com/~ildecgs

Decatur Public Library • 130 N Franklin St • Decatur, IL 62523-1327 • (217) 428-2900 • http://www.decatur.lib.il.us

Governor Oglesby Mansion Museum • 421 W William St • Decatur, IL 62521 • (217) 429-9422 • http://www.maconcountyconservation.org/historic.php

James Millikin Homestead Museum • 125 N Pine St • Decatur, IL 62526 • (217) 422-9003

Macon County Historical Society • Historical Museum, 5580 North Fork Rd • Decatur, IL 62521 • (217) 422-4919 • http://www.mchsdecatur.org

Deerfield

Deerfield Area Historical Society • Historical Museum, 450 Kipling Pl, P.O. Box 520 • Deerfield, IL 60015 • (847) 948-0680 • http://www.deerfield-il.org

Deerfield Public Library • 920 Waukegan Rd • Deerfield, IL 60015 • (708) 945-3311 • http://www.deerfieldlibrary.org

Delavan

Ayer Public Library District • 208 Locust St, P.O. Box 500 • Delavan, IL 61734-0500 • (309) 244-8236

Delavan Community Historical Society • Historical Museum, Locust St • Delavan, IL 61734-0512 • (309) 244-7321

Des Plaines

Des Plaines Genealogical Questers • Historical Museum, 789 Pearson St • Des Plaines, IL 60016 • (847) 391-5399

Des Plaines Historical Society • Historical Museum, 781 Pearson St • Des Plaines, IL 60016 • (847) 391-5399 • http://www.desplaineshistory.org

Des Plains Public Library • 1501 Ellinwood St • Des Plaines, IL 60016-4553 • (847) 827-5551 • http://www.dppl.org

Maine West Historical Society • c/o Main West High School, 1755 S Wolf Rd • Des Plaines, IL 60018-1994 • (847) 827-6176

McDonald's #1 Store Museum • 400 N Lee St • Des Plaines, IL 60016 • (847) 297-5022

Society of Colonial Wars in the State of Illinois • 2340 Des Plaines Ave, Ste 303 • Des Plaines, IL 60018-3224 • (847) 297-3700

Society of the Danube Swabians in Chicago • 625 Seegers Rd • Des Plaines, IL 60016-3041 • (847) 296-6172

Dixon

Dixon Public Library • 221 S Hennepin Ave • Dixon, IL 62021-3093 • (815) 284-7261 • http://www.dixonpubliclibrary.org

John Deere Historic Site Museum • 8393 S Main • Dixon, IL 61021 • (815) 652-4551 • http://www.johndeerehistoricsite.com

Lee County Genealogical Society • 213 S Peoria Ave, P.O. Box 63 • Dixon, IL 61021-0063 • (815) 288-6702 • http://www.rootsweb. com/~illee/lcgs.htm

Lee County Historical Society • Historical Museum, 113 Madison Ave, P.O. Box 58 • Dixon, IL 61021-0058 • (815) 284-1134 • http://www. leecountyhistory.com

Ronald Reagan Boyhood Home Museum • 816 S Hennepin Ave • Dixon, IL 60522 • (815) 288-3830

Sauk Valley Community College Library • 173 Illinois Route 2 • Dixon, IL 61021-9112 • (815) 288-5511 • http://www.svcc.edu/services/lrc/

Dolton
Dolton Public Library District • 14037 Lincoln St • Dolton, IL 60419-1091 • (708) 849-2385 • http://doltonpubliclibrary.org

Downers Grove
Downers Grove Historical Society • Downers Grove Park Museum, 831 Maple Ave • Downers Grove, IL 60515 • (630) 963-1309 • http:// www.dgparks.org/museum/mumain.html

Downers Grove Public Library • 1050 Curtiss St • Downers Grove, IL 60515 • (630) 960-1200 • http://www.downersgrovelibrary.org

Du Quoin
Du Quoin Public Library • 28 S Washington St • Du Quoin, IL 62832 • (618) 542-5045 • http://www.shawls.lib.il.us

Perry County Historical Society • P.O. Box 1013 • Du Quoin, IL 62832 • (618) 357-2225

Dundee
Dundee Township Public Library • 555 Burrington Ave • Dundee, IL 60118-1496 • (847) 428-3661 • http://www.dundeelibrary.info/

Dupo
Monroe County Genealogical Society • 508 N 4th St • Dupo, IL 62239

Dwight
Dwight Genealogical Society • P.O. Box 315 • Dwight, IL 60420

Dwight Historical Society • Historical Museum, 119 W Main St, P.O. Box 7 • Dwight, IL 60420-1302 • (815) 584-1865

Prairie Creek Public Library District • 501 Carriage House Ln • Dwight, IL 60420-1399 • (815) 584-3061

Earlville
Earl Township Public Library • 205 Winthrop St, P.O. Box 420 • Earlville, IL 60518 • (815) 246-9543 • http://www.earlvillelibrary.org

Earlville Community Historical Society • c/o Earl Township Public Library, 205 Winthrop St, P.O. Box 420 • Earlville, IL 60518-0420 • (815) 246-9543

East Alton
National Great Rivers Museum • 2 Lock & Dam Wy • East Alton, IL 62024 • (618) 462-6979 • http://www.mvs.usace.army.mil

East Carondelet
Martin-Boismenue House Museum • 2110 1st St • East Carondelet, IL 62240 • (618) 397-3990

East Moline
American Friends of the Swedish Emigrant Institute of Sweden • 3452 4th St • East Moline, IL 61244 • (309) 755-2858

East Peoria
Fondulac Public Library District • 140 E Washington St • East Peoria, IL 61611-2598 • (309) 699-3917 • http://www.fondulac.lib.il.us

East Saint Louis
East Saint Louis Public Library • 5300 State St • East Saint Louis, IL 62203 • (618) 397-0991

Edwardsville
Edwardsville Public Library • 112 S Kansas St • Edwardsville, IL 62025 • (618) 692-7556 • http://edwardsvillelibrary.org

Elijah P Lovejoy Library • Southern Illinois Univ at Edwardsville, P.O. Box 1063 SIUE • Edwardsville, IL 62026 • (618) 540-2711 • http://www. library.siue.edu

Madison County Genealogical Society • 112 S Kansas St, P.O. Box 631 • Edwardsville, IL 62025-0631 • (618) 692-7556 • http://www. rootsweb.com/~ilmadcgs

Madison County Historical Society • Weir House Museum, 715 N Main St • Edwardsville, IL 62025-1111 • (618) 656-7569 • http://www. plantnet.com/~museum

University Museum • 1150 Southern IL Univ • Edwardsville, IL 62026 • (618) 650-2996

Effingham
Effingham County Genealogical Society • c/o Helen Matthes Library, 100 Market St, P.O. Box 1166 • Effingham, IL 62401 • (217) 342-2210 • http://www.rootsweb.com/~ileffing/lookups.htm

Effingham Regional Historical Society • P.O. Box 1352 • Effingham, IL 62401-1352 • (217) 342-6280

Helen Mathes Library • 100 E Market Ave • Effingham, IL 62401-3499 • (217) 342-2464 • http://www.effinghamlibrary.org

El Paso
El Paso Public Library • 149 W 1st St • El Paso, IL 61738 • (309) 527-4360

Elburn
Elburn and Countryside Historical Society • 525 N Main, P.O. Box 1115 • Elburn, IL 60119-0115 • (630) 365-6655

Elgin
Benjamin P Browne Library • Judson College, 1151 N State St • Elgin, IL 60123 • (847) 628-2038

Elgin Area Historical Society • Historical Museum, 360 Park St • Elgin, IL 60120-4455 • (847) 742-4248 • http://www.elginhistory.org

Elgin Genealogical Society • P.O. Box 1418 • Elgin, IL 60121-1418 • (847) 697-5683 • http://nsn.nslsilus.org/elghome/egs/

Fellowship of Brethren Genealogists • Brethren Historical Library and Archives, 1451 Dundee Ave • Elgin, IL 60120 • (847) 742-5100 • http:// www.brethren.org/genbd/bhla/

Gail Borden Public Library • 270 N Grove Ave • Elgin, IL 60120-5596 • (847) 742-2411 • http://www.gailborden.info/

Kane County Historical Society • P.O. Box 503 • Elgin, IL 60121-0503

Elizabeth
Apple River Fort Museum • 311 E Myrtle St • Elizabeth, IL 61028 • (815) 858-2028 • http://www.appleriverfort.org

Elizabeth Historical Society • Historical Museum, 210 E Myrtle St, P.O. Box 115 • Elizabeth, IL 61028 • (815) 858-2212

Elizabethtown
Hardin County Historical and Genealogical Society • P.O. Box 72 • Elizabethtown, IL 62931 • (618) 287-2361

Elk Grove
Elk Grove Historical Society • 399 Biesterfield Rd • Elk Grove, IL 60007 • (847) 439-3994 • http://www.elkgrove.org/heritage/About.htm

Elk Grove Village
Archives of the Evangelical Lutheran Church In America • 321 Bonnie Ln • Elk Grove Village, IL 60007 • (847) 690-9410 • http://www.elca. org/os/archives/intro.html

Elk Grove Village Public Library • 1001 Wellington Ave • Elk Grove Village, IL 60007 • (847) 439-0447 • http://www.egvpl.org

Elk Grove, cont.

Schuette Bierman Farmhouse Museum • 399 Bierrman Rd • Elk Grove Village, IL 60007 • (847) 437-9494 • http://www.elkgrove.org/egpd

Elkhart

Elkhart Historical Society • Historical Museum, 116 N Latham, P.O. Box 225 • Elkhart, IL 62634-0225 • (217) 947-2238

Ellis Grove

Fort Kaskaskia Historic Site Museum • RR1, Box 63 • Ellis Grove, IL 62241 • (618) 859-3741

Pierre Menard Home State Historic Site Museum • 4230 Kashaska Rd • Ellis Grove, IL 62241 • (618) 859-3031 • http://www.state.il.us/hpa/hs/menard.htm

Elmhurst

Chicago and Northwestern Railroad Historical Society • P.O. Box 1436 • Elmhurst, IL 60126-9998 • http://www.cnwhs.org

Elmhurst Historical Museum • 120 E Park Ave • Elmhurst, IL 60126 • (630) 833-1457 • http://www.elmhurst.org

Elmhurst Historical Society • 455 N Larch Ave • Elmhurst, IL 60126-2315 • (630) 941-9310

Genealogical Forum of Elmhurst Illinois • Elmhurst Historical Museum, 120 E Park Ave • Elmhurst, IL 60126 • (630) 833-1457 • http://www.elmhurst.org/elmhurst/museum/

Theatre Historical Society of America • Historical Museum, 152 N York Rd • Elmhurst, IL 60126 • (630) 782-1800

Elmwood

Elmwood Historical Society • Lorado Taft Museum, 302 N Magnolia • Elmwood, IL 61529 • (309) 742-7791

Elmwood Park

Elmwood Park Historical Society • c/o Elmwood Park Public Library, 4 Conti Pkwy • Elmwood Park, IL 60707 • (708) 453-7645 • http://www.epcusd.w-cook.kl2.il.us/eppl/

Elmwood Park Public Library • 4 Conti Parkway • Elmwood Park, IL 60707 • (708) 453-7645 • http://www.epcusd.w-cook.k12.il.us/eppl

Historical Society of Elmwood Park • Historical Museum, 2823 N 77th Ave • Elmwood Park, IL 60635 • (708) 453-1133

Elsah

Historic Elsah Foundation • Village of Elsah Museum, 51 Mill St, P.O. Box 28 • Elsah, IL 62028-0117 • (618) 374-1059 • http://www.elsah.org

Eureka

Eureka Public Library District • 202 S Main St • Eureka, IL 61530 • (309) 467-222 • http://www.eureka.lib.il.us

Melick Library • Eureka College, 301 College Ave • Eureka, IL 61530-1563 • (309) 467-6892 • http://www.eureka.edu/melick

Woodford County Historical Society • 112 N Main St • Eureka, IL 61530 • (309) 467-4525 • http://www.eureka.lib.il.us/community/wchs/

Evanston

Evanston Public Library • 1703 Orrington • Evanston, IL 60201 • (847) 866-0300 • http://www.epl.org

Frances E Willard Memorial Library • National Woman's Christian Temperance Union, 1730 Chicago Ave • Evanston, IL 60201-4585 • (847) 864-1397 • http://www.wctu.org

Joseph W Walt Library • Sigma Alpha Epsilon Fraternity & Foundation, 1856 Sheridan Rd, P.O. Box 1856 • Evanston, IL 60204-1856 • (847) 475-1856 • http://www.saefraternity.net

Levere Memorial Temple Museum • 1856 Sheridan Rd, P.O. Box 1856 • Evanston, IL 60201-3837 • (847) 475-1856 • http://www.sae.net

Midwest Archives Conference • Northwestern Univ, 1935 Sheridan Road • Evanston, IL 60201 • (847) 491-3354 • http://www.library.northwestern.edu/archives/

Mitchell Museum of the American Indian • 3001 Central St • Evanston, IL 60201-2899 • (847) 475-1030 • http://www.mitchellmuseum.org

National Baha'i Archives • 1233 Central St • Evanston, IL 60201 • (847) 869-9039

Northern Illinois Conference of the United Methodist Church • Garrett-Evangelical Theological Seminary, 2121 Sheridan Rd • Evanston, IL 60201 • (847) 866-3911

Northwestern University Library, Special Collections • 633 Clark St • Evanston, IL 60201 • (847) 491-7658 • http://www.library.northwestern.edu

Public Works Historical Society • 1801 Maple Ave • Evanston, IL 60201-3135 • (847) 491-5829

Romanian Folk Art Museum • 2526 Ridgeway • Evanston, IL 60201-1160 • (847) 328-9099

Rotary International • 1 Rotary Center, 1560 Sherman Ave • Evanston, IL 60201 • (847) 866-3000 • http://www.rotary.org

Evergreen Park

Evergreen Park Historical Society • 3538 W 98th St • Evergreen Park, IL 60642

Fairfield

Wayne County Historical Society • Historical Museum, 300 SE 2nd St • Fairfield, IL 62837 • (618) 842-4701

Fairmount

Fairmount-Jamaica Historical Society • Historical Museum, 116 S Main St • Fairmount, IL 61841-9601 • (217) 288-8278

Vance Township Library • 107 S Main St, P.O. Box 230 • Fairmount, IL 61841-0230 • (217) 733-2164

Farmer City

Farmer City Genealogical and Historical Society • 226 S Main St, P.O. Box 173 • Farmer City, IL 61842 • (309) 928-9547

Farmer City Public Library • 105 E Green St, P.O. Box 201 • Farmer City, IL 61842-0201 • (309) 928-9532

Flossmoor

Illiana Jewish Genealogical Society • P.O. Box 384 • Flossmoor, IL 60422 • (708) 957-9457 • http://www.lincolnnet.net/ijgs

Illinois Association for the Preservation of Historic Arms and Armaments • 1800 Western Ave • Flossmoor, IL 60422-0339

Forest Park

Forest Park Historical Society • c/o Forest Park Library, 7555 Jackson Ave • Forest Park, IL 60130 • (708) 366-2865 • http://www.forestparkpubliclibrary.org

Forest Park Library • 7555 Jackson Ave • Forest Park, IL 60130 • (708) 366-7171 • http://www.forestparkpubliclibrary.org

German-American Heritage Institute • 7824 W Madison St • Forest Park, IL 60130-1485 • (708) 366-0017

Fort Sheridan

Fort Sheridan Museum • Bldg 33 • Fort Sheridan, IL 60037-5000 • (847) 926-5519

Fox Lake

Fox Lake Area Historical Society • P.O. Box 4 • Fox Lake, IL 60020 • http://www.rootsweb.com/~ilflahs/histsoc.html

Fox River Grove

Fox River Grove Public Library District • 306 Lincoln Ave • Fox River Grove, IL 60021-1406 • (847) 639-2274 • http://www.frgml.lib.il.us

Frankfort
Frankfort Area Historical Society of Will County • 132 Kansas St, P.O. Box 546 • Frankfort, IL 60423-0546 • (815) 469-4534

Franklin Park
Franklin Park Public Library & Historical Museum • 10311 Grand Ave • Franklin Park, IL 60131 • (847) 455-6016 • http://www.franklinparklibrary.org

Leyden Historical Society • P.O. Box 506 • Franklin Park, IL 60131 • (847) 678-1929

Freeburg
Freeburg Historical and Genealogical Society • c/o Freeburg Area Library, 407 S Belleville, P.O. Box 69 • Freeburg, IL 62243 • (618) 539-5771

Freeport
Freeport Public Library • 100 E Douglas St • Freeport, IL 61032 • (815) 223-3000 • http://www.freeportpubliclibrary.org

Silvercreek Museum • 2965 S Walnut Rd • Freeport, IL 61032 • (815) 232-2350 • http://www.thefreeportshow.com

Stephenson County Genealogical Society • P.O. Box 514 • Freeport, IL 61032 • (815) 232-4883 • http://www.rootsweb.com/~ilstephe/

Stephenson County Historical Society • Historical Museum, 1440 S Carroll Ave • Freeport, IL 61032-6530 • (815) 232-8419 • http://www.stephcohs.org

Galatia
Galatia Historical Society • P.O. Box 489 • Galatia, IL 62935

Galena
Belvedere Mansion Museum • 1008 Park • Galena, IL 61036 • (815) 777-0747

Dowling House Museum • 220 Diagonal • Galena, IL 61036 • (815) 777-1250

Eliju Benjamin Washburne House State Historic Site Museum • 908 3rd St, P.O. Box 333 • Galena, IL 61036 • (815) 777-9406

Galena Public Library • 601 S Bench St • Galena, IL 61036-2320 • (815) 777-0200

Galena-Jo Daviess County Historical Society • Galena Historical Museum, 211 S Bench St • Galena, IL 61036 • (815) 777-9129 • http://www.galenahistorymuseum.org

Illinois Historic Preservation Agency • 307 Decatur St, P.O. Box 333 • Galena, IL 61036 • (815) 777-3310 • http://www.granthome.com

Old Market House State Historic Site Museum • Market Sq, 307 Decatur St, P.O. Box 333 • Galena, IL 61036 • (815) 777-3310 • http://www.granthome.com

Ulysses S Grant Home State Historic Site Museum • 500 Bouthillier St • Galena, IL 61036 • (815) 777-0248

Galesburg
Browning Mansion Museum • 325 N Kellogg St • Galesburg, IL 61401 • (309) 344-2839

Carl Sandburg College Library • 2400 Tom L Wilson Blvd • Galesburg, IL 61401 • (309) 341-5290 • http://www.sandburg.edu

Carl Sandburg State Historic Site Museum • 331 E 3rd • Galesburg, IL 61401 • (309) 342-2361 • http://www.sandburg.org

Galesburg Historical Society • Historical Museum, 832 Bateman St • Galesburg, IL 61401 • (309) 344-9278 • http://www.galesburghistory.com

Galesburg Public Library • 40 E Simmons St • Galesburg, IL 61401-4591 • (309) 343-6118 • http://www.galesburglibrary.org

Galesburg Railroad Museum • 211 S Seminary • Galesburg, IL 61401 • (309) 342-9400 • http://www.galesburgrailroadmuseum.org

Henry W Seymour Library • Knox College, 2 E South St, P.O. Box 500X • Galesburg, IL 61402 • (309) 341-7228 • http://www.library.knox.edu

Illinois Citizen Soldier Museum • 1001 Michigan Ave • Galesburg, IL 61401 • (309) 342-1181

Knox County Genealogical Society • c/o Galesburg Public Library, 40 E Simmons St, P.O. Box 13 • Galesburg, IL 61402-0013 • (309) 343-6811 • http://www.rootsweb.com/lilknox/knindex.htm

Knox County Historical Society • P. O. Box 1757 • Galesburg, IL 61402-1747 • http://knoxchs.homestead.com

Galva
Galva Historical Society • Wiley House Museum, 906 W Division St, P.O. Box 24 • Galva, IL 61434-0024 • (309) 932-8992 • http://galva.com/historicalsociety.php

Galva Public Library District • 120 NW 3rd Ave • Galva, IL 61434 • (309) 932-2180 • http://www.galvalibrary.org

Garden Prairie
Garden Prairie Genealogical and Historical Society • P.O. Box 115 • Garden Prairie, IL 61038-0015 • (815) 597-1109

Geneseo
Geneseo Historical Association • Historical Museum, 212 N State St • Geneseo, IL 61254 • (309) 944-3043

Geneseo Public Library District • 218 S State St • Geneseo, IL 61254 • (309) 944-6452 • http://www.rbls.lib.il.us/gpl

Geneva
Fabyan Villa Museum • 1511 S Batavia Ave • Geneva, IL 60134 • (630) 232-4811

Geneva Historical Society • Historical Museum, 113 S 3rd St, P.O. Box 345 • Geneva, IL 60134-0345 • (630) 262-1086 • http://www.genevahistorycenter.org

Geneva Public Library District • 127 James St • Geneva, IL 60134 • (630) 232-0780

Kane County Genealogical Society • P.O. Box 504 • Geneva, IL 60134-0504 • http://www.rootsweb.com/~ilkcgs/

Genoa
Kishwaukee Valley Heritage Society • 700 W Park Ave, P.O. Box 59 • Genoa, IL 60135 • (815) 784-5498

Georgetown
Georgetown Historical Society • Historical Museum, 110 E 10th St • Georgetown, IL 61846 • (217) 662-8449

Gillespie
Gillespie Public Library • 201 W Chestnut • Gillespie, IL 62033 • (217) 839-3614

Gilman
Gilman Historical Society • Historical Museum, 217 N Central St • Gilman, IL 60938 • (815) 265-4381

Girard
Girard Township Library • 201 W Madison • Girard, IL 62640-1550 • (217) 627-2414

Glen Carbon
Glen Carbon Historical Museum • 124 School St • Glen Carbon, IL 62034 • (518) 288-1200

Glen Ellyn
Glen Ellyn Historical Society • Stacy's Tavern Museum, 557 Geneva Rd, P.O. Box 283 • Glen Ellyn, IL 60138 • (630) 858-8896 • http://www.gehs.org

Illinois

Glencoe
Glencoe Historical Society • 377 Park Ave • Glencoe, IL 60022 • (847) 835-0040

Glencoe Historical Society • Historical Museum, 999 Green Bay Rd • Glencoe, IL 60222 • (847) 835-4935 • http://www.glencoevillage.org/GCKHisS.html

Glenview
Chicago Japanese American Historical Society • 745 Beaver Rd • Glenview, IL 60025 • http://www.cjahs.org

Glenview Area Historical Society • Historical Museum, 1121 Waukegan Rd • Glenview, IL 60025-3036 • (847) 724-2235

Glenview Public Library • 1930 Glenview Road • Glenview, IL 60025-2899 • (847) 729-7500 • http://www.glenview.pl.org

Grove Heritage Association • P.O. Box 484 • Glenview, IL 60025-0484 • (847) 299-6096

Kennicott House Museum • 1421 Milwaukee Ave • Glenview, IL 60025 • (847) 299-6096

Northeastern Illinois Historical Council • 1720 Wildberry Dr • Glenview, IL 60025

Godfrey
Lewis and Clark Genealogical Society • P.O. Box 485 • Godfrey, IL 62035 • (618) 372-3997

Reid Memorial Library • Lewis & Clark Community College, 5800 Godfrey Rd • Godfrey, IL 62035 • (618) 468-4304 • http://www.lc.edu/libweb.nsf

Golconda
Golconda Public Library • Main St, P.O. Box 523 • Golconda, IL 62938-0523 • (618) 683-6531

Pope County Historical Society • Historical Museum, Main St, P.O. Box 387 • Golconda, IL 62938-0387 • (618) 683-3050

Golden
Golden Historical Society • Historical Museum, 902 Prairie Mills Rd, P.O. Box 148 • Golden, IL 62339-0148 • (217) 455-3151 • http://www.goldenwindmill.org

Granite City
Old Six Mile Historical Society • Emmert-Zippel House Museum, 3279 Maryville Rd, P.O. Box 483 • Granite City, IL 62040 • (618) 931-3023

Six Mile Regional Library • 2001 Delmar Ave • Granite City, IL 62040-4590 • (618) 452-6238 • http://www.lcls.lib.il.us/gce

Grayslake
Grayslake Historical Society • Historical Museum, 164 Hawley, P.O. Box 185 • Grayslake, IL 60030-0185 • (847) 223-7663

Grayville
Grayville Carnegie Public Library • 110 W Mill St • Grayville, IL 62844 • (618) 375-7121

Great Lakes
Great Lakes Naval Museum • Bldg 158, Camp Barry Naval Training Center, P.O. Box 886307 • Great Lakes, IL 60088 • (847) 688-3169 • http://www.nsgreatlakes.navy.mil/museum/

Naval Training Center Library • MWR Library, Bldg 160, 2601 E Paul Jones St, Bldg 3 • Great Lakes, IL 60088 • (847) 688-4617 • http://www.ntcmwr.com/library.html

Greenup
Cumberland County Historical and Genealogical Society • P.O. Box 393 • Greenup, IL 62428 • (217) 923-5425

Greenup Depot Museum • 213 E Cumberland St • Greenup, IL 62428 • (217) 923-9306

Greenup Township Carnegie Library • 101 N Franklin St, P.O. Box 275 • Greenup, IL 62428-0275 • (217) 923-3616

Illinois Military Museum • Route 1 • Greenup, IL 62428 • (217) 923-3235

Greenville
Bond County Genealogical Society • 911 Kilarney, P.O. Box 172 • Greenville, IL 62246 • (618) 664-3054 • http://www.GreenvilleUSA.org/bcgs

Bond County Historical Society • Hoiles-Davis Museum, 318 W Winter Ave, P.O. Box 376 • Greenville, IL 62246 • (618) 664-1590 • http://www.bondcountyhistorical.org

Greenville Public Library • 414 E Main St • Greenville, IL 62246-1615 • (618) 664-3115 • http://www.greenvilleusa.org/library.htm

Hoiles-Davis Museum • 318 W Winter St, P.O. Box 376 • Greenville, IL 62246

Ruby E Dare Library • Greenville College, 315 E College Ave • Greenville, IL 62246 • (618) 664-6603 • http://www.greenville.edu/learningresources/library

Gridley
Gridley District Library • 320 Center St, P.O. Box 370 • Gridley, IL 61744-0370 • (309) 747-2284

Griggsville
Griggsville Area Genealogical and Historical Society • P.O. Box 75 • Griggsville, IL 62340 • (217) 833-2308

Gurnee
Warren Township Historical Society • 4690 Old Grand Ave • Gurnee, IL 60031 • (847) 263-9540

Warren-Newport Public Library District • 224 N O'Plaine Rd • Gurnee, IL 60031 • (847) 244-5150 • http://www.wnpl.alibrary.com

Hampshire
Ella Johnson Memorial Public Library District • 109 S State St, P.O. Box 429 • Hampshire, IL 60140-0429 • (847) 683-4490 • http://www.ellajohnson.lib.il.us

Hampton
Hampton Historical Society • 107 5th St, P.O. Box 68 • Hampton, IL 61256 • (309) 755-0362

Hanover
Hanover Township Library • 204 Jefferson St, P.O. Box 475 • Hanover, IL 61041-0475 • (815) 591-3517

Hanover Park
Hanover Park Ontarioville Historical Commission • 2121 W Lake St • Hanover Park, IL 60103-4398 • (630) 372-4200

Hardin
Calhoun County Historical Society • Historical Museum, County Rd, P.O. Box 327 • Hardin, IL 62047-0327 • (618) 576-2660

Harrisburg
Harrisburg Public Library • 2 W Walnut St • Harrisburg, IL 62946 • (618) 253-7455 • http://www.harrisburg.lib.il.us

Saline County Genealogical Society • P.O. Box 4 • Harrisburg, IL 62946-0004 • (618) 994-2052

Saline County Historical Society • Historical Museum, 1600 S Feazel, P.O. Box 55 • Harrisburg, IL 62946-0055 • (618) 252-6665

Hartford
Hartford Public Library District • 143 W Hawthorne • Hartford, IL 62048 • (618) 254-9394

Harvard
Greater Harvard Area Historical Society • Historical Museum, 308 N Hart Blvd, P.O. Box 505 • Harvard, IL 60033 • (815) 943-6141

Harvey

Harvey Public Library • 15441 Turlington Ave • Harvey, IL 60426-3683 • (708) 331-0757 • http://www.harvey.lib.il.us

Park Forest Historical Museum • 154 E 154th St • Harvey, IL 60466 • (708) 596-2000

Thornton Township Historical Society • 154 E 154th St • Harvey, IL 60426 • (708) 331-4247

Harwood Heights

Eisenhower Public Library District • 4652 N Olcott Ave • Harwood Heights, IL 60706 • (708) 867-7828 • http://www.eisenhowerlibrary.org

Havana

Havana Public Library System • 201 W Adams St • Havana, IL 62644-1321 • (309) 543-4701 • http://www.havana.lib.il.us

Mason County Genealogical and Historical Society • c/o Havana Public Library, 201 W Adams St, P.O. Box 446 • Havana, IL 62644 • (309) 543-4701 • http://www.havana.lib.il.us/community/mcghs.html

Mason County History Project • 14454 N State Rt 78 • Havana, IL 62644

Mason County LDS Genealogical Project • Route 1, Box 193 • Havana, IL 62644

Hazel Crest

South Suburban Genealogical and Historical Society • 3000 W 170th Pl • Hazel Crest, IL 60429-1174 • (708) 335-3340

Hennepin

Pulsifer House Museum • Route 26 & Power Rd, P.O. Box 75 • Hennepin, IL 61327 • (815) 925-7560

Putnam County Historical Society • Historical Museum, Rt 26 & Power Rd, P.O. Box 74 • Hennepin, IL 61327 • (815) 825-7560 • http://www.rootsweb.com/~ilputnam/pchs.htm

Henry

Henry Historical and Genealogical Society • Historical Museum, 610 North St • Henry, IL 61537 • (309) 364-3272

Henry Public Library • 702 Front St, P.O. Box 183 • Henry, IL 61537-0183 • (309) 364-2516 • http://www.henry.lib.il.us

Herrick

Herrick Township Public Library • 303 N Broadway • Herrick, IL 62431 • (618) 428-5223 • http://207.63.58.66/

Herrin

Herrin City Library • 120 N 13th St • Herrin, IL 62948-3233 • (618) 942-6109

Herscher

Herscher Area Historical Society • Historical Museum, 3rd & Park Rd, P.O. Box 403 • Herscher, IL 60941

Highland

Highland Historical Society • 1739 Broadway, P.O. Box 51 • Highland, IL 62249-0051 • (618) 654-6781

Highland Park

Highland Park Historical Society • Historical Museum, 326 Central Ave, P.O. Box 56 • Highland Park, IL 60036 • (847) 432-7090 • http://www.highlandpark.org/histsoc

Highland Park Public Library • 494 Laurel Ave • Highland Park, IL 60035-2690 • (847) 432-0216 • http://www.hplibrary.org

Hillsboro

Hillsborough Public Library • 214 School St • Hillsboro, IL 62049-1547 • (217) 532-3055

Historical Society of Montgomery County • Solomon Harkey House Museum, 904 S Main St • Hillsboro, IL 62049-1738 • (217) 532-3329

Hinsdale

Hinsdale Historical Society • Historical Museum, 15 S Clay, P.O. Box 336 • Hinsdale, IL 60521 • (630) 789-2600 • http://www.hinsdalehistory.org

Holcomb

Vogel Genealogical Research Library • 305 N 1st St, P.O. Box 132 • Holcomb, IL 61043 • (815) 393-4110

Homer

Homer Historical Society • Historical Museum, 107 N Main St • Homer, IL 61849 • (217) 896-2549 • http://www.homerhistory.com

Hometown

Hometown Public Library • 4331 Southwest Hwy • Hometown, IL 60456 • (708) 636-0997

Homewood

Homewood Historical Society • Historical Museum, 2035 W 183rd St, P.O. Box 1144 • Homewood, IL 60430-1044 • (708) 799-1896 • http://home.nyc.rr.com/johnmiller/hmwd.html

Homewood Public Library District • 17900 Dixie Hwy • Homewood, IL 60430-1703 • (708) 798-0121 • http://homewoodlibrary.org

Hoopeston

Hoopeston Historical Society • Historical Museum, 617 E Washington • Hoopeston, IL 60942-1659 • (217) 283-7898

Huntley

Huntley Area Public Library District • 11000 Ruth Rd, P.O. Box 898 • Huntley, IL 60142 • (847) 669-5386 • http://www.huntleylibrary.org

Hutsonville

Hutsonville Historical and Genealogical Society • Memorial Village, 10953 E 1825th Ave • Hutsonville, IL 62443 • http://www.rootsweb.com/~ilcchs/hutson_historical.html

Ina

Rend Lake College Library • 468 N Ken Gray Pkwy • Ina, IL 62846 • (618) 437-5321 • http://www.rlc.edu

Itasca

Itasca Historical Society • Itasca Historical Depot Museum, 101 N Catalpa Ave, P.O. Box 101 • Itasca, IL 60143-2050 • (630) 773-3363

Jacksonville

Governor Duncan Mansion Museum • 4 Duncan Pl • Jacksonville, IL 62650 • (217) 243-5333

Henry Pfeiffer Library • MacMurray College, 447 E College Ave • Jacksonville, IL 62650-2510 • (217) 479-7110 • http://www.mac.edu/academ/lib.html

Heritage Cultural Center • 125 S Webster • Jacksonville, IL 62650-2012 • (217) 243-7488

Jacksonville Area Genealogical and Historical Society • 416 S Main St, P.O. Box 21 • Jacksonville, IL 62651-0021 • (217) 245-5911 • http://www.rootsweblcom/~iljaghs/

Jacksonville Public Library • 201 W College • Jacksonville, IL 62650-2497 • (217) 243-5435 • http://japl.lib.il.us/library

Morgan County Genealogical Association • P.O. Box 84 • Jacksonville, IL 62651-0084 • http://www.rootsweb.com/~ilmorgan/maga.html

Morgan County Historical Society • 1463 Gerkie Ln, P.O. Box 1033 • Jacksonville, IL 62651-1033 • (217) 243-3755

Schewe Library • Illinois College, 245 Park St • Jacksonville, IL 62650 • (217) 245-3022 • http://www.ic.edu/library.htm

Jerseyville

Col William H Fulkerson Mansion and Farm Museum • 25007 US Hwy 67 • Jerseyville, IL 62052 • (618) 498-5590 • http://www.greatriverroad.com

Jerseyville, cont.
Jersey County Genealogical Society • P.O. Box 12 • Jerseyville, IL 62052

Jersey County Historical Society • Cheney Mansion Museum, 601 N State St • Jerseyville, IL 62052-1612 • (618) 498-3514 • http://www.jvil. com/~jchs/

Joliet
Joliet Area Historical Museum • 204 N Ottawa St • Joliet, IL 60432 • (815) 723-5201 • http://www.jolietmuseum.org

Joliet Area Historical Society • 17 E Van Buren St, P.O. Box 477 • Joliet, IL 60431-1211 • (815) 722-7003

Joliet Public Library • 150 N Ottawa St • Joliet, IL 60431-4192 • (815) 740-2660 • http://www.joliet.lib.il.us

Slovenian Women's Union • Slovenian Heritage Museum, 431 N Chicago St • Joliet, IL 60432 • (815) 727-1926

Kampsville
Center For American Archeology • P.O. Box 366 • Kampsville, IL 62053 • (618) 653-4316 • http://www.caa-archeology.org

Kaneville
Kaneville Public Library • 2 S 101 Harter Rd, P.O. Box 29 • Kaneville, IL 60144-0029 • (630) 557-2441 • http://www.kaneville.lib.il.us

Kankakee
Kankakee County Historical Society • Historical Museum, 801 S 8th Ave • Kankakee, IL 60901-4744 • (815) 932-5279 • http://www. kankakeecountymuseum.com

Kankakee Public Library • 201 E Merchant St • Kankakee, IL 60901 • (815) 939-4564 • http://www.kankakee.lib.il.us/

Kankakee Valley Genealogical Society • 801 S 8th Ave • Kankakee, IL 60901 • http://www.kvgs.org

Keithsburg
Keithsburg Museum • 302 S 14th St, P.O. Box 79 • Keithsburg, IL 61442-0019 • (309) 371-3185

Kenilworth
Kenilworth Historical Society • Historical Museum, 415 Kenilworth Ave • Kenilworth, IL 60043-1134 • (847) 251-2565 • http://www. kenilworthhistory.org

Kewanee
Henry County Genealogical Society • c/o Kewanee Public Library, 102 S Tremont St, P.O. Box 346 • Kewanee, IL 61443-0346 • (309) 856-8475 • http://www.rootsweb.com/~ilhcgs/

Kewanee Historical Society • Historical Museum, 211 N Chestnut St • Kewanee, IL 61443 • (309) 894-9701 • http://www.kewaneehistory.com

Kewanee Public Library District • 102 S Tremont St • Kewanee, IL 61443-2190 • (309) 852-4505 • http://www.kewaneelibrary.org

Woodland Place Museum at Francis Park • US Route 34 • Kewanee, IL 61443 • (309) 852-0511

Knoxville
Knox County Historical Society • Historical Museum, City Hall, Public Sq • Knoxville, IL 61448 • (309) 289-2814 • http://www.webwinco. net/~tbould

La Fox
Garfield Farm and Tavern Museum • 3N016 Garfield Rd, P.O. Box 403 • La Fox, IL 60147 • (630) 584-8485 • http://www.garfieldfarm.org

Garfield Heritage Society • Garfield Farm and Tavern Museum, 3N016 Garfield Rd, P.O. Box 403 • La Fox, IL 60147 • (630) 584-8485 • http:// www.garfieldfarm.org

La Grange
Flagg Creek Heritage Society • Historical Museum, 7425 S Wolf Rd • La Grange, IL 60525 • (708) 246-1160 • http://www. flaggcreekheritagesociety.com

Garfield Heritage Society • 444 S LaGrange Rd • La Grange, IL 60525-2448 • (847) 584-8485

LaGrange Area Historical Society • Historical Museum, 444 S LaGrange Rd • La Grange, IL 60525-2448 • (708) 482-4248

LaGrange Public Library • 10 W Cossitt Ave • La Grange, IL 60525 • (708) 352-0576 • http://www.lagrangelibrary.org

Scottish Genealogy Group of the Illinois Saint Andrew Society • 321 S Madison Ave • La Grange, IL 60525 • (815) 886-1239

La Harpe
LaHarpe Carnegie Public Library • 209 E Main St, P.O. Box 506 • La Harpe, IL 61450-0506 • (217) 659-7729

LaHarpe Historical and Genealogical Society • E Main St, P.O. Box 289 • La Harpe, IL 61450 • http://www.outfitters.com/illinois/hancock/ laharpe/lhgs/

La Moille
La Moille-Clarion District Public Library • 81 Main St, P.O. Box 260 • La Moille, IL 61330-0260 • (815) 638-2356

Lacon
Lacon Public Library • 205 6th St • Lacon, IL 61540 • (309) 246-2855

Marshall County Historical Society • 314 5th St, P.O. Box 123 • Lacon, IL 61540-0123 • (309) 246-2349 • http://www.rootsweb.com/~ilmarsha/ mphs.htm; http://www.il-mchs.org

Lafayette
Ira C Reed Public Library • 302 Commercial St, P.O. Box 185 • Lafayette, IL 61449-0185 • (309) 995-3042

Lake Forest
Donnelly Library • Wake Forest College, 555 N Sheridan • Lake Forest, IL 60045-2396 • (847) 735-5056 • http://www.lib.lfc.edu

Lake County Historical Society • Historical Museum, 555 N Sheridan Rd • Lake Forest, IL 60045 • (847) 234-3100

Lake Forest Public Library • 360 E Deerpath Ave • Lake Forest, IL 60045 • (847) 234-0636 • http://lfkhome.northstarnet.org/library.html

Lake Forest-Lake Bluff Historical Society • Historical Museum, 361 E Westminster Rd, P.O. Box 82 • Lake Forest, IL 60045-0082 • (847) 234-5253 • http://www.lflbhistory.org

Urban History Association • Dept of History, Lake Forest College • Lake Forest, IL 60045

Lake in the Hills
Cornish American Heritage Society • 18 Indian Tr • Lake in the Hills, IL 60102

Lake in the Hills Historical Society • 183 Hilltop Dr • Lake in the Hills, IL 60102

Lake Villa
Lake Villa Historical Society • 113 Cedar Ave • Lake Villa, IL 60046 • (847) 265-8266

Lake Villa Public Library District • 1001 E Grand Ave • Lake Villa, IL 60046 • (847) 356-7711 • http://www.lvdl.org

Lake Zurich
Ela Historical Society • 95 E Main St • Lake Zurich, IL 60047 • (847) 438-2086

Long Grove Historical Society • 348 Old McHenry Rd • Lake Zurich, IL 60047 • (847) 634-6155

Lanark

Lanark Public Library • 110 W Carroll St • Lanark, IL 61046 • (815) 493-2166 • http://www.internetni.com/~lanarklib

North American Manx Association • P.O. Box 105 • Lanark, IL 60146-0105 • http://www.isle-of-man.com/interests/genealogy/nama

Lansing

Lansing Historical Society • Historical Museum, 2750 Indiana Ave, P.O. Box 1776 • Lansing, IL 60438 • (708) 474-6160

Lansing Veterans Memorial Museum • Lansing Municipal Airport, 194 4th, P.O. Box 321 • Lansing, IL 60438 • (708) 895-1321 • http://www.lansingmunicipal.com

La Salle

LaSalle Public Library • 305 Marquette St • LaSalle, IL 61301 • (815) 223-2341 • http://www.htls.lib.il.us/lsb

Lawrenceville

Lawrence County Historical Society • Historical Museum, 1012 9th St, P.O. Box 425 • Lawrenceville, IL 62439 • (618) 943-4203

Lawrenceville Public Library • 814 12th St • Lawrenceville, IL 62439 • (618) 943-3016

Le Roy

Crumbaugh Memorial Public Library • 405 E Center St, P.O. Box 129 • Le Roy, IL 61752-0129 • (309) 962-3911

LeRoy Historical Society • 301 E Cedar • Le Roy, IL 61752

Leaf River

Bertolet Memorial Library District • 705 Main St, P.O. Box 339 • Leaf River, IL 61047-0339 • (815) 738-2742

Lebanon

Holman Library • McKendree College, 701 College Rd • Lebanon, IL 62254-1299 • (618) 537-6952 • http://www.mckendree.edu/library

Lebanon Historical Society • Historical Museum, 309 W St Louis St • Lebanon, IL 62254 • (618) 537-4498

Lemont

Lemont Area Historical Society • Historical Museum, 306 Lemont St, P.O. Box 126 • Lemont, IL 60439-0126 • (630) 257-2972 • http://www.township.com/lemont/historical/

Lena

Lena Area Historical Society • Historical Museum, 427 W Grove St, P.O. Box 620 • Lena, IL 61048 • (815) 369-4555

Lena Community District Library • 300 W Mason St • Lena, IL 61048 • (815) 369-3180

Lerna

Lincoln Log Cabin State Historic Site Museum • 400 S Lincoln Hwy, P.O. Box 100 • Lerna, IL 62440 • (217) 345-1845 • http://www.lincolnlogcabin.org

Moore Home Museum • 400 S Lincoln Hwy Rd, P.O. Box 100 • Lerna, IL 62440 • (217) 345-1845 • http://www.lincolnlogcabin.org

Lewistown

Lewistown Carnegie Public Library District • 321 W Lincoln Ave • Lewistown, IL 61542 • (309) 547-2860

Lewistown Society For Historical Preservation • 396 S Main St • Lewistown, IL 61542 • (309) 547-1009

Lexington

Lexington Genealogical and Historical Society • 318 W Main St • Lexington, IL 61753-1328 • (309) 365-4591

Libertyville

Cook Memorial Library • 413 N Milwaukee Ave • Libertyville, IL 60048-2280 • (847) 362-2330 • http://www.cooklib.org

Lake County Genealogical Society • P.O. Box 721 • Libertyville, IL 60048-0721 • (847) 336-7151 • http://www.rootsweb.com/~illcgs/

Libertyville-Mundelein Historical Society • c/o Cook Memorial Library, 413 N Milwaukee Ave • Libertyville, IL 60048-2280 • (847) 362-2330 • http://www.cooklib.org

Lincoln

Jessie C Eury Library • Lincoln Christian College & Seminary, 100 Campus View Dr • Lincoln, IL 62656 • (217) 732-3168 • http://www.lccs.edu/library

Lincoln Public Library • 725 Pekin St • Lincoln, IL 62656 • (217) 732-8878 • http://www.lincolnpubliclibrary.org

Logan County Genealogical and Historical Society • 114 N Chicago St, P.O. Box 283 • Lincoln, IL 62656 • (217) 732-3988 • http://www.rootsweb.com/~illogan/logangh.htm

Postville Courthouse State Historic Site Museum • 914 5th St, P.O. Box 355 • Lincoln, IL 62656 • (217) 732-8930

Lincolnshire

Vernon Area Public Library District • 300 Olde Half Day Rd • Lincolnshire, IL 60069-2901 • (847) 634-3650 • http://www.vapld.info/

Lincolnwood

Lincolnwood Public Library District • 4000 W Pratt Ave • Lincolnwood, IL 60712 • (847) 677-5277 • http://www.lincolnwoodlibrary.org

Lisle

Center for Slavic Culture • Illinois Benedictine College • Lisle, IL 60532 • (630) 968-7270

Lisle Heritage Society • 921 School St • Lisle, IL 60532 • (630) 968-0499 • http://www.lisleparkdistrict.org

Lisle Library District • 777 Front St • Lisle, IL 60532-3599 • (630) 971-1675 • http://www.lislelibrary.org

Lisle Station Park Museum • 918-920 Burlington Ave • Lisle, IL 60532 • (630) 968-0499 • http://www.lisleparkdistrict.org/heritagesociety.htm

Netsley-Yender Farmhouse Museum • 920 Burlington • Lisle, IL 60532 • (630) 968-2747

Litchfield

Litchfield Carnegie Public Library • 400 N State St • Litchfield, IL 62056 • (217) 324-3866

Montgomery County Genealogical Society • c/o Litchfield Carnegie Public Library, 400 N State St, P.O. Box 212 • Litchfield, IL 62056 • (217) 324-4841 • http://www.rootsweb.com/~ilmontgo/gensoc.htm

Lockport

Council of Northeastern Illinois Genealogical Societies • 820 Lisdowney Dr • Lockport, IL 60441

Des Plaines Valley Public Library District • 121 E 8th St • Lockport, IL 60441 • (815) 838-0755 • http://www.dpv.lib.il.us

Gaylord Building Museum • 200 W 8th St • Lockport, IL 60441 • (815) 588-1100

Gladys Fox Museum • 1911 S Lawrence • Lockport, IL 60441-4498 • (815) 838-1183

Will County Historical Society • Illinois and Michigan Canal Museum, 803 S State St • Lockport, IL 60441 • (815) 838-5080 • http://www.willcountyhistory.org

Lombard

Brimson Grow Library • Northern Baptist Theological Seminary, 680 E Butterfield Rd • Lombard, IL 60148 • (630) 620-2104 • http://www.seminary.edu/library

DuPage County Genealogical Society • P.O. Box 133 • Lombard, IL 60148-0133 • (630) 983-6784 • http://www.dcgs.org

Illinois

Lombard, cont.
Lombard Historical Society • Historical Museum, 23 W Maple St • Lombard, IL 60148 • (630) 629-1885 • http://www.tccafe.com/apeck6/peck0.html

Sheldon Peck Homestead Museum • 355 E Parkside • Lombard, IL 60148 • (630) 629-1885 • http://www.villageoflonbard.org/lhsweb/

Long Grove
Long Grove Historical Society • Historical Museum, RFD, Box 3110 • Long Grove, IL 60047 • (847) 634-6155

Lostant
Lostant Community Library • 102 W 3rd St, P.O. Box 189 • Lostant, IL 61334 • (815) 368-3530

Louisville
Clay County Genealogical Society • Town Square, P.O. Box 94 • Louisville, IL 62858 • (618) 665-4544 • http://www.rootsweb.com/~ilclay/ccgs.htm

Loves Park
North Suburban Library-Loves Park • 6340 N 2nd St • Loves Park, IL 61111 • (815) 633-4247 • http://www.northsuburbanlibrary.org

Winnebago and Boone Counties Genealogical Society • P.O. Box 10166 • Loves Park, IL 61131-0166 • (815) 397-5885

Lyndon
Lyndon Historical Society • Historical Museum, 405 4th St W, P.O. Box 112 • Lyndon, IL 61261 • (815) 778-4511 • http://lyndonhs.whco.us

Lyons
Lyons Historical Commission • 7801 W Ogden Ave, P.O. Box 392 • Lyons, IL 60534-0392 • (708) 447-5815 • http://www.northstarnet.org/lyshome/hoffman/

Lyons Public Library • 4209 Joliet Ave • Lyons, IL 60534-1597 • (708) 447-3577 • http://www.lyons.lib.il.us

Mackinaw
Mackinaw Historical Society • RR1, Box 260 • Mackinaw, IL 61755-9637 • (309) 359-4001

Macomb
Center for Icarian Studies • Western Illinois Univ, 1 University Cr • Macomb, IL 61455-1391 • (309) 298-1575 • http://www.wiu.edu/library/

Macomb City Public Library • 235 S Lafayette St, P.O. Box 220 • Macomb, IL 61455 • (309) 833-2714 • http://www.macomb.lib.il.us

McDonough County Genealogical Society • c/o Macomb District Public Library, P.O. Box 202 • Macomb, IL 61455-0202 • (309) 837-4558 • http://www.macomb.com/mcgs/

McDonough County Historical Society • Historical Museum, 1200 E Grant St, P.O. Box 83 • Macomb, IL 61445 • (309) 254-3289

Western Illinois University Library - Special Collections • 1 University Cr • Macomb, IL 61455 • (309) 298-2762 • http://www.wlu.edu/library

Western Illinois University Museum • 900 W Adams St • Macomb, IL 61455-1396 • (309) 298-1808

Mahomet
Early American Museum • Route 47 N, Lake of the Woods Park, P.O. Drawer 1040 • Mahomet, IL 61853 • (217) 586-2612 • http://www.mah-online.com/early/

Manhattan
Manhattan Public Library District • 240 Whitson St, P.O. Box 53 • Manhattan, IL 60442 • (815) 478-3987 • http://www.manhattan.lib.il.us

Manhattan Township Historical Society • c/o Manhattan Public Library, 240 Whitson, P.O. Box 53 • Manhattan, IL 60442 • (815) 478-3374

Manito
Manito Historical Society • Historical Museum, 206 W State St, P.O. Box 304 • Manito, IL 61546-0304 • (309) 968-6985

Mansfield
Blue Ridge Township Public Library • 101 W Oliver, P.O. Box 459 • Mansfield, IL 61854-0459 • (217) 489-9033

Manteno
Manteno Historical Society • Historical Museum, 192 W 3rd • Manteno, IL 60950-1104 • (815) 458-3480

Maquon
Maquon Historical Association • West ST, P.O. Box 93 • Maquon, IL 61458-0093 • (309) 875-3481

Marion
Crab Orchard Public Library District • 19229 Bailey St • Marion, IL 62959 • (618) 982-2141

Marion Carnegie Library • 206 S Market St • Marion, IL 62959-2519 • (618) 993-5935 • http://www.sirin.lib.il.us/docs/mrn/docs/lib/

Williamson County Historical Society • Historical Museum, 105 S Van Buren St • Marion, IL 62959 • (618) 993-5758 • http://www.wchs.apexhosting.com/wchs.htm

Marissa
Marissa Historical and Genealogical Society • 610 S Main St, P.O. Box 47 • Marissa, IL 62257-0047 • (618) 295-2562 • http://www.bigtrief.net/marissa/

Marquette
Marquette Heights Public Library • 715 Lincoln Rd • Marquette, IL 61554-1313 • (309) 382-3778

Marseilles
Marseilles Public Library • 155 E Bluff St • Marseilles, IL 61341-1442 • (815) 795-4437

Marshall
Clark County Genealogical Society • 521 Locust St, P.O. Box 153 • Marshall, IL 62441 • (217) 826-2864

Clark County Historical Society • Historical Museum, 502 S 4th St • Marshall, IL 62441-0207 • (217) 826-6098

Mascoutah
Mascoutah Historical Society • Historical Museum, City Hall, 3 W Main St • Mascoutah, IL 62258-1421 • (618) 566-2567

Matteson
African-American Genealogical Research Institute • P.O. Box 637 • Matteson, IL 60443-6370

Matteson Historical Society • 813 School Ave • Matteson, IL 60443-1849 • (708) 748-3033

Mattoon
Coles County Historical Society • 1320 Lafayette Ave • Mattoon, IL 61938 • (217) 235-6744

Genealogical Society of Cumberland and Coles County • 1816 Walnut • Mattoon, IL 61938

Mattoon Public Library • 1600 Charleston Ave, P.O. Box 809 • Mattoon, IL 61938-0809 • (217) 234-2621 • http://www.mattoonlibrary.org

Maywood
Maywood Historical Society • Historical Museum, 202 S 2nd Ave • Maywood, IL 60153-2304 • (708) 865-4753

Maywood Public Library • 121 S 5th Ave • Maywood, IL 60153 • (708) 343-1847 • http://www.maywood.org

McConnell
McConnell Area Historical Society • general delivery • McConnell, IL 61050

McHenry

McHenry County Illinois Genealogical Society • c/o McHenry Library, 809 N Front St • McHenry, IL 60050 • (815) 385-6303

McHenry Library • 809 N Front St • McHenry, IL 60050 • (815) 385-0036 • http://www.mchenrylibrary.org

McLeansboro

Hamilton County Historical Society • c/o McCoy Memorial Library, 118 S Washington St • McLeansboro, IL 62859-1048 • (618) 643-4203

McCoy Memorial Library • 118 S Washington St • McLeansboro, IL 62859 • (618) 643-2125

Melrose Park

Melrose Park Historical Society • c/o Melrose Park Library, 801 N Broadway, P.O. Box 1453 • Melrose Park, IL 60160 • (708) 343-3391 • http://www.melrosepark.org/history/

Melrose Park Public Library • 801 N Broadway • Melrose Park, IL 60160 • (708) 343-3391 • http://www.melroseparklibrary.org

Mendota

Graves-Hume Public Library District • 1401 W Main St • Mendota, IL 61342 • (815) 538-5142

Mendota Historical Society • Historical Museum, 901 Washington St, P.O. Box 901 • Mendota, IL 61342 • (815) 539-3373

Meredosia

Meredosia Area Historical and Genealogical Society • Historical Museum, Main St, P.O. Box 304 • Meredosia, IL 62665-0304 • (217) 584-1356

Metamora

Illinois Mennonite Historical and Genealogical Society • Grossdawdy House Museum, 675 State Rte 116, P.O. Box 819 • Metamora, IL 61548 • (309) 367-2551 • http://www.imhgs.org

Illinois Prairie District Public Library • 208 E Partridge, P.O. Box 770 • Metamora, IL 61548-0770 • (309) 367-4594 • http://www.ipdpl.org

Metamora Courthouse Historic Site Museum • 113 E Partridge • Metamora, IL 61548 • (309) 367-4470

Metropolis

Fort Massac State Park and Historic Site • 1308 E 5th St • Metropolis, IL 62960 • (618) 524-4712 • http://www.dnr.state.il.us/parks/natlpage.html

Massac County Genealogical Society • P.O. Box 1043 • Metropolis, IL 62960 • http://www.rootsweb.com/~ilmcgs/

Massac County Historical Society • Elijah P Curtis Home Museum, 405 Market St • Metropolis, IL 62960-2467 • (618) 524-7203

Metropolis Public Library • 317 Metropolis St • Metropolis, IL 62960 • (618) 524-4312

Midlothian

Council of Northeastern Illinois Genealogical Society • 3629 W 14th Pl • Midlothian, IL 60445-3505

Midlothian Historical Society • Historical Museum, 14609 Springfield • Midlothian, IL 60445 • (708) 389-0200

Millburn

Historic Millburn Community Association • Historical Museum, 38757 N US Hwy 45 • Millburn, IL 60046 • (847) 265-1967 • http://www.hmca-il.org

Mineral

Mineral-Gold Public Library District • 120 E Main St, P.O Box 87 • Mineral, IL 61344 • (309) 288-3971 • http://www.mineralgold.com

Minooka

Three Rivers Public Library District, Minooka Branch Library • Local History Room, 109 North Wabena, P.O. Box 370 • Minooka, IL 60447-0370 • (815) 467-1600

Moline

Blackhawk Genealogical Society of Rock Island and Mercer County Illinois • 822 11th Ave • Moline, IL 61265 • (309) 786-3058 • http://www.rootsweb.com/~ilbgsrim

Butterworth Center Museum • 1105 8th St • Moline, IL 61265 • (309) 765-7970

Center for Belgian Culture of Western Illinois • 712 18th Ave • Moline, IL 61265 • (309) 762-0167

Deere & Company Museum • 1 John Deer Pl • Moline, IL 61265 • (309) 765-4207 • http://www.deere.com/en_us/attractions/dhq/

Deere-Wiman House Museum • 817 11th Ave • Moline, IL 61265 • (309) 765-7970

Rock Island County Historical Society • Rock Island Historical House, 822 11th Ave, P.O. Box 632 • Moline, IL 61265-1221 • (309) 764-8590 • http://www.netexpress.net/~richs/

Monmouth

Hewes Library • Monmouth College, 700 E Broadway • Monmouth, IL 61462-1963 • (309) 457-2301 • http://department.monm.edu/library

Stewart House Museum • 1015 E Euclid • Monmouth, IL 61462 • (309) 734-5154

Warren County Genealogical Society • P.O. Box 761 • Monmouth, IL 61462-0761 • (309) 734-2763 • http://www.maplecity.com/~wcpl/genhome.html

Warren County Public Library • 62 Public Square • Monmouth, IL 61462-1756 • (309) 734-3166 • http://www.wcpl.monmouth.net

Wyatt Earp Birthplace Museum • 406 S 3rd St • Monmouth, IL 61462-1435 • (309) 734-6419 • http://www.misslink.net/misslink/earp.htm

Monticello

Allerton Public Library • 201 N State St • Monticello, IL 61856 • (217) 762-4676 • http://www.monticellolibrary.org

Monticello Railway Museum • Market St at I-72, P.O. Box 401 • Monticello, IL 61856 • (217) 762-9011 • http://www.prairienet.org/mrm

Piatt County Historical and Genealogical Society • Courthouse Annex, 30 S Charter St, P.O. Box 111 • Monticello, IL 61856 • (217) 762-7570 • http://www.monticello.net/html/genealogy.html; http://www.rootsweb.com/~ilpiatt/pchs.htm

Piatt County Museum • 315 W Main St • Monticello, IL 61856 • (217) 762-4731 • http://www.piattmuseum.net

Mooseheart

Loyal Order of Moose • Headquarters, 155 S International Dr • Mooseheart, IL 60539 • (630) 859-2000

Morris

Grundy County Historical Society • Historical Museum, 102 Liberty St, P.O. Box 224 • Morris, IL 60450-2329 • (815) 942-4880

Morris Area Public Library District • 604 Liberty St • Morris, IL 60450 • (815) 942-6880 • http://www.morrislibrary.com

Morrison

Morrison Historical Society • Heritage Museum, 219 E Main St, P.O. Box 1 • Morrison, IL 61270-0001 • (815) 772-3287 • http://www.communitycourier.com/historical_society.htm

Odell Public Library • 307 S Madison St • Morrison, IL 61270 • (815) 772-7323

Morrisonville

Kitchell Memorial Library • 300 SE 5th, P.O. Box 49 • Morrisonville, IL 62546 • (217) 526-4553 • http://www.morrisonville.com

Morrisonville Historical Society • Historical Museum, 606 Carlin St, P.O. Box 227 • Morrisonville, IL 62546-0227 • (217) 526-3543

Morton Grove

Morton Grove Historical Society • Haupt-Yehl House, 6240 Dempster St, P.O. Box 542 • Morton Grove, IL 60053-2946 • (847) 965-7185 • http://www.mortongroveparks.com

Morton Grove Public Library • 6140 Lincoln Ave • Morton Grove, IL 60053-2989 • (847) 954-4220 • http://www.webrary.org

Mound City

Mound City Civic and Historical Association • 314 Main St • Mound City, IL 62963-1128

Mound City Public Library • 224 High St • Mound City, IL 62963 • (618) 748-9427

Mount Carmel

Mount Carmel Public Library • 727 Mulberry St • Mount Carmel, IL 62863-2047 • (618) 263-3531 • http://www.sirin.lib.il.us

Wabash County Historical Society • 119 W 3rd St, P.O. Box 911 • Mount Carmel, IL 62863

Mount Carroll

Carroll County Historical Society • 107 W Broadway, P.O. Box 65 • Mount Carroll, IL 61053 • (815) 244-3474

Mount Carroll Township Public Library • 208 N Main St • Mount Carroll, IL 61053-1022 • (815) 244-1751 • http://www.mtclib.org

Mount Morris

Franklin Grove Area Historical Society • 110 W Front • Mount Morris, IL 61054 • (815) 734-6905 • http://www.franklingroveil/histsoc.htm

Mount Morris Public Library • 105 S McKendrie Ave • Mount Morris, IL 61054 • (815) 734-4927 • http://www.mmmtmorris-il.org

Mount Olive

Mount Olive Public Library • 100 N Plum St • Mount Olive, IL 62069-1755 • (217) 999-7311

Mount Prospect

Mount Prospect Historical Society • Historical Museum, 1100 S Linneman Rd, P.O. Box 81 • Mount Prospect, IL 60056-0081 • (847) 392-9006 • http://www.mphist.org

Mount Prospect Public Library - Genealogy Room • 10 S Emerson St • Mount Prospect, IL 60056 • (847) 253-5675 • http://www.mtpospect.org/research/genealogy.html

Northwest Suburban Council of Genealogists • P.O. Box AC • Mount Prospect, IL 60056-9019 • (847) 394-3897 • http://www.mtprospect.org/nsgs/

Mount Pulaski

Mount Pulaski Courthouse State Historic Site Museum • 113 S Washington • Mount Pulaski, IL 62548 • (217) 792-3919

Mount Pulaski Public Library • 320 N Washington St • Mount Pulaski, IL 62548 • (217) 792-5919

Mount Pulaski Township Historical Society • Historical Museum, 102-104 Cooke St, P.O. Box 12 • Mount Pulaski, IL 62548-0012 • (217) 792-3436

Mount Vernon

C E Brehm Memorial Library • 101 S 7th St • Mount Vernon, IL 62864-4187 • (618) 242-6322 • http://www.sirin.lib.il.us/docs/bml/docs/lib/

Commission on Archives and History, Southern Illinois Conference of the United Methodist Church • 1919 W Broadway • Mount Vernon, IL 62864 • (618) 242-4070

Fulton County Genealogical Society • c/o Brehm Memorial Library, 101 S 7th St • Mount Vernon, IL 62864-4187 • (618) 242-6322

Jefferson County Genealogical Society • c/o Brehm Memorial Library, 101 S 7th St, P.O. Box 1131 • Mount Vernon, IL 62864-4187 • (618) 242-6322

Jefferson County Historical Society • Historical Village and Museum, P.O. Box 106 • Mount Vernon, IL 62864-0106 • (618) 242-5423

Mitchell Museum at Cedarhurst • Richview Rd, P.O. Box 923 • Mount Vernon, IL 62864 • (618) 242-1236 • http://www.cedarhurst.org

Mount Vernon Genealogical Society • c/o C E Brehm Memorial Library, 101 S 7th St • Mount Vernon, IL 62864 • (618) 242-6322

Moweaqua

Moweaqua Area Historical Society • 130 W Main St • Moweaqua, IL 62550 • (217) 768-3228

Moweaqua Public Library • 122 N Main St • Moweaqua, IL 62550 • (217) 768-4700

Mulkeytown

Mulkeytown Area Historical Society • 7570 Mulkeytown Rd, P.O. Box 485 • Mulkeytown, IL 62865 • (618) 724-1156

Mundelein

Fremont Public Library District • 1170 N Midlothian Rd • Mundelein, IL 60060 • (847) 566-8702 • http://www.fremontlibrary.org

Historical Society of the Fort Hill Country • Fort Hill Heritage Museum, 601 Noel Dr, P.O. Box 582 • Mundelein, IL 60060 • (847) 526-7566

Mundelein Park Cemetery Museum • 100 N Seymour • Mundelein, IL 60060 • (847) 566-0650

Northern Illinois Historical Society • 505 S Midlothian Rd • Mundelein, IL 60060-2633 • (847) 949-1776

Murphysboro

Jackson County Historical Society • Historical Museum, 1041 Walnut, P.O. Box 7 • Murphysboro, IL 62966-0007 • (618) 687-4388 • http://www.iltrails.org/jackson/jchs.htm

Naperville

American Historical Society of Germans from Russia • Historical Museum, 114 N Center St • Naperville, IL 60540 • (630) 357-2572

Community United Methodist Church Library • 20 N Center St • Naperville, IL 60540-4611 • (630) 355-1483 • http://www.communityunitedmethodist.org

Fox Valley Genealogical Society • 705 N Brainard St, P.O. Box 5435 • Naperville, IL 60566-5435 • (630) 369-0744 • http://www.rootsweb.com/~ilfvgs

Naper Settlement Museum • 523 S Webster St • Naperville, IL 60540 • (630) 420-6010 • http://www.napersettlement.museum

Naperville Heritage Society • Naper Settlement, 523 S Webster St • Naperville, IL 60540 • (630) 420-6010 • http://www.napersettlement.org

Naperville Public Libraries-Nichols Branch • 200 W Jefferson Ave • Naperville, IL 60540 • (630) 961-4100 • http://www.naperville-lib.org

Oesterle Library • North Central College, 320 E School St • Naperville, IL 60540 • (630) 637-5715 • http://www.noctrl.edu/library_ncc/

Sons of Union Veterans of the Civil War, Illinoir Department • P.O. Box 2314 • Naperville, IL 60567

Nashville

Nashville Public Library • 219 E Elm St • Nashville, IL 62263-1711 • (618) 327-3827

Washington County Genealogical Society • 14502 Cty Hwy 1 • Nashville, IL 62263

Washington County Historical Society • 326 S Kaskaskia St, P.O. Box 9 • Nashville, IL 62263-0009 • (618) 327-8953

Nauvoo

Joseph Smith Historic Center • 149 Water St, P.O. Box 338 • Nauvoo, IL 62354-0338 • (217) 453-2246 • http://www.joseph-smith.com

Nauvoo Historical Society • Historical Museum, 980 S Bluff St, P.O. Box 426 • Nauvoo, IL 62354 • (217) 453-6355

Nauvoo Public Library • 270 Mulholland St, P.O. Box 276 • Nauvoo, IL 62354-0276 • (217) 453-2707 • http://www.nauvoo.lib.il.us

Wilford Woodruff House Museum • SR 96 & Hotchkiss St • Nauvoo, IL 652365 • (217) 453-2716

Neponset
Neponset Public Library • 201 W Commercial St, P.O. Box 110 • Neponset, IL 61345-0110 • (309) 594-2204

Neponset Township Historical Society • Historical Museum • Neponset, IL 61345 • (309) 594-2197

New Boston
New Boston Historical Society • Historical Museum, 302 Main St, P.O. Box 284 • New Boston, IL 61272-0284 • (309) 587-8640

New Lenox
New Lenox Area Historical Society • Historical Museum, 205 W Maple St • New Lenox, IL 60451 • (815) 485-5576 • http://www.newlenoxhistory.org

New Lenox Public Library • 120 Veterans Pkwy • New Lenox, IL 60451-2390 • (815) 485-2605 • http://www.newlenoxlibrary.org

New Windsor
New Windsor Public Library • 412 Main St • New Windsor, IL 61465 • (309) 667-2515

Newark
Fern Dell Historic Association • Historical Museum, 9 E Front St, P.O. Box 254 • Newark, IL 60541-0254 • (815) 695-9525 • http://www.ferndell.org

Newton
Jasper County Genealogical and Historical Society • c/o Newton Public Library, 100 S Van Buren • Newton, IL 62448 • (618) 783-8141

Newton Public Library and Museum • 100 S Van Buren • Newton, IL 62448 • (618) 783-8141

Niles
Chicago and Northwestern Historical Society • 8703 N Olcott Ave • Niles, IL 60648-2023 • (847) 794-5633

Niles Historical Society • Historical Museum, 8970 Milwaukee Ave • Niles, IL 60714-1737 • (847) 390-0160

North Eastern Illinois Historical Council • 7007 Fargo Ave • Niles, IL 60714-3719 • (847) 390-0160

Nokomis
Nokomis Public Library • 22 S Cedar St • Nokomis, IL 62075 • (217) 563-2734

Normal
Bloomington-Normal Genealogical Society • P.O. Box 488 • Normal, IL 61761-0488

McLean County Genealogical Society • 201 E Grove St, P.O. Box 488 • Normal, IL 61761-0488 • (309) 454-4371 • http://www.fgi.net/~bsgreen

Milner Library • Illinois State University, 201 N School, Campus Box 8900 • Normal, IL 61791-8900 • (309) 438-3451 • http://www.mlb.ilstu.edu

University Museum • Illinois State Univ, 301 S Main St • Normal, IL 61761 • (309) 438-8800

Norris City
Norris City Memorial Public Library • 603 S Division St • Norris City, IL 62869 • (618) 378-3713

North Chicago
North Chicago Public Library • 2100 Argonne Dr • North Chicago, IL 60064 • (847) 689-0125 • http://www.ncpublib.org

Northbrook
Irving Rubenstein Memorial Library • Congregation Beth Shalom, 3433 Walters Ave • Northbrook, IL 60062-3298 • (847) 498-4100 • http://www.cbsnbk.org

Jewish Genealogical Society of Illinois • P.O. Box 515 • Northbrook, IL 60065-0515 • (312) 666-0100 • http://www.jgsi.org

Leica Historical Society of America • 60 Revere Dr • Northbrook, IL 60062 • (847) 564-2181

Northbrook Historical Society • Northfield Inn Museum, 1776 Walters Ave, P.O. Box 2021 • Northbrook, IL 60065-2021 • (847) 498-3404 • http://www.northstarnet.org/nbkhome/nbhsoc/

Oak Brook
Czechoslovak Heritage Museum • 122 W 22nd St • Oak Brook, IL 60523 • (630) 472-0500 • http://www.csafraternallife.org

Graue Mill and Museum • 3800 York Rd • Oak Brook, IL 60523 • (630) 655-2090 • http://www.grauemill.org

Lions Clubs International • 300 W 22nd St • Oak Brook, IL 60523-8842 • (630) 571-5466 • http://www.lionsclubs.org

Mayslake Peabody Estate Museum • 1717 W 31st St • Oak Brook, IL 60523 • (630) 850-2363 • http://www.mayslakepeabody.com

Oak Brook Historical Society • Historical Museum, 1112 Oak Brook Rd, P.O. Box 3821 • Oak Brook, IL 60521 • (630) 789-1734

Oak Forest
Oak Forest Historical Society • 15440 S Central Ave • Oak Forest, IL 60452-2104 • (708) 687-4050

Oak Lawn
Moraine Valley Oral History Association • c/o Oak Lawn Public Library, 9427 S Raymond Ave • Oak Lawn, IL 60453 • (312) 422-4990

Oak Lawn Historical Society • 4332 W 109th St • Oak Lawn, IL 60453 • (312) 425-3424

Oak Lawn Public Library • 9427 S Raymond Ave • Oak Lawn, IL 60453-2434 • (708) 422-4990 • http://www.lib.oak-lawn.il.us

Oak Park
Frank Lloyd Wright Home Museum • 951 Chicago Ave • Oak Park, IL 60302 • (708) 848-1976 • http://www.wrightplus.org

Frank Lloyd Wright Preservation Trust • 931 Chicago Ave • Oak Park, IL 60302 • (708) 848-1976

Hemingway Birthplace Museum • 200 N Oak Park Ave, P.O. Box 2222 • Oak Park, IL 60303 • (708) 848-2222 • http://www.ehfop.org

Historical Society of Oak Park and River Forest • Farson-Mills House Museum, 217 Home Ave, P.O. Box 771 • Oak Park, IL 60303-0771 • (708) 848-6755 • http://www.oprf.com/oprfhist/

National Railway Historical Society, Chicago Chapter • Historical Museum, 1104 S Oak Park Ave, P.O. Box 53 • Oak Park, IL 60303-0053 • (773) 836-9203 • http://www.chicagonrhs.com

Oak Park Public Library • 834 Lake St • Oak Park, IL 60301 • (708) 383-8200 • http://www.oppl.org

Oakland
Oakland Historical Foundation • Historical Museum, Washington & Walnut Sts, P.O. Box 431 • Oakland, IL 61943-0431 • (217) 346-3274

Oakwood
Illiana Civil War Historical Society • Historical Museum, P.O. Box 365 • Oakwood, IL 61868 • (217) 354-4519

Oakwood Public Library District • 110 E Finley, P.O. Box 99 • Oakwood, IL 61858-0099 • (217) 354-4777

Oblong
Illinois Oilfield Museum • 10570 N 150th St, P.O. Box 69 • Oblong, IL 62449

Odell
Odell Prairie Trails Historical and Genealogical Society • P.O. Box 82 • Odell, IL 60460-0082 • (815) 998-2324

O'Fallon
O'Fallon Historical Society • Historical Museum, 101 W State St, P.O. Box 344 • O'Fallon, IL 62269-0344 • (618) 632-3857 • http://www.ofallonhistory.org

O'Fallon Public Library • 120 Civic Plaza • O'Fallon, IL 62269-1197 • (618) 632-3783 • http://www.ofallonlibrary.org

Oglesby
Jacobs Memorial Library • Illinois Valley Community College, 815 Orlando Smith Ave • Oglesby, IL 61348-9692 • (815) 224-0306 • http://www.ivcc.edu/library

Oglesby Historical Society • 100 Oak St • Oglesby, IL 61348 • (815) 883-3619

Okawville
Dr Poos Home Museum • 202 N Front St • Okawville, IL 62271

Heritage House Museum • P.O. Box 305 • Okawville, IL 62271 • (618) 243-5535

Schlosser Home Museum • 109-114 W Walnut St • Okawville, IL 62271

Olmsted
Olmsted Historical Society • P.O. Box 64 • Olmsted, IL 62970-0064 • (618) 742-6238

Olney
Olney Public Library • 400 W Main St • Olney, IL 62450 • (618) 392-3711

Richland County Illinois Genealogical and Historical Society • c/o Anderson Library, Olney Central College, P.O. Box 202 • Olney, IL 62450-0202 • (618) 869-2425

Richland Heritage Museum • 401 E Main St, P.O. Box 153 • Olney, IL 62450-1548 • (618) 395-3893

Olympia Fields
Augustine Fathers, Province of Our Mother of Good Counsel • 20300 Governors Hwy • Olympia Fields, IL 60461

Jewish Genealogical Society, South Suburban Branch • 3416 Ithaca • Olympia Fields, IL 60461 • http://www.jewishgen.org/jgsi/

Oquawka
Henderson County Historical Society • Historical Museum, RR1, Box 130 • Oquawka, IL 61469-9711

Oregon
Ogle County Genealogical Society • c/o Oregon Township Library, 300 Jefferson St, P.O. Box 251 • Oregon, IL 61061 • (815) 734-6818

Ogle County Historical Society • Historical Museum, 111 N 6th St, P.O. Box 183 • Oregon, IL 61061 • (815) 732-7545

Oregon Public Library District • 300 Jefferson St • Oregon, IL 61061 • (815) 732-2724 • http://oregon.lib.il.us

Orion
Western District Library • 1111 4th St, P.O. Box 70 • Orion, IL 61273-0070 • (309) 526-8375

Orland Park
Humphrey House Museum • 9830 W 144th Pl, P.O. Box 324 • Orland Park, IL 60462 • (708) 349-0065

Orland Historical Society • 14228 Union Ave • Orland Park, IL 60462

Orland Historical Society • Jacob & Bernard Hostert Log Cabins Museums, 14228 Union Ave, P.O. Box 324 • Orland Park, IL 60462-0324 • (708) 349-0065

Oswego
Kendall County Genealogical Society • 83 Brockway, P.O. Box 1086 • Oswego, IL 60543 • (630) 554-8342

Oswego Public Library District • 32 W Jefferson St • Oswego, IL 60543 • (630) 554-3150 • http://www.oswego.lib.il.us

Oswegoland Heritage Association • 72 Polk St, P.O. Box 23 • Oswego, IL 60543 • (630) 554-2999

Ottawa
LaSalle County Historical Society and Genealogy Guild • 115 W Glover St, P.O. Box 534 • Ottawa, IL 61350 • (815) 433-5261 • http://genealogy.org/~dpc

LaSalle Genealogy Guild • 115 W Glover St • Ottawa, IL 61350-6734 • http://genealogy.org/~dpc

Ottawa Scouting Museum • 1100 Canal St, P.O. Box 2241 • Ottawa, IL 61350 • (815) 431-9253 • http://www.ottawascoutingmuseum.org

Reddick Library • 1010 Canal St • Ottawa, IL 61350 • (815) 434-0509 • http://www.reddicklibrary.org

Palatine
Palatine Historical Society • Clayson House Museum, 224 E Palatine Rd, P.O. Box 134 • Palatine, IL 60078-0134 • (847) 991-6460

Society of the War of 1812 in the State of Illinois • 419 N Plum Grove Rd • Palatine, IL 60067-3519 • (847) 358-3539

Palestine
Fort LaMotte Genealogical and Historical Society • c/o Palestine Public Library, 116 S Main • Palestine, IL 62451 • (618) 586-5317

Palestine Historical Society • 413 S Lincoln • Palestine, IL 62451

Palestine Public Library District • 116 S Main St • Palestine, IL 62451 • (618) 586-5317 • http://www.palestinelibrary.8m.com

Palos Heights
Jennie Huizenga Memorial Library • Trinity Christian College, 6601 W College Dr • Palos Heights, IL 60463 • (708) 597-3000 • http://www.trnty.edu/library

Palos Heights Historical Society • 7607 College Dr • Palos Heights, IL 60463

Palos Heights Public Library • 12501 S 71st Ave • Palos Heights, IL 60463 • (708) 371-6004 • http://www.palosheightslibrary.org

Woodlands Native American Indian Museum • 6384 W Willow Wood Dr • Palos Heights, IL 60463-1847 • (708) 614-0334

Palos Hills
Green Hills Genealogical Society • c/o Green Hills Public Library, 8611 W 103rd St • Palos Hills, IL 60465 • (708) 598-8446 • http://www.greenhills.lib.il.us

Green Hills Public Library District • 8611 W 103rd St • Palos Hills, IL 60465-1698 • (708) 598-8446 • http://www.greenhills.lib.il.us

Palos Park
Palos Historical Society • c/o Palos Park Library, 12330 Forest Glen Blvd • Palos Park, IL 60464-1707 • (708) 361-3118

Palos Park Public Library • 12330 Forest Glen Blvd • Palos Park, IL 60464 • (708) 448-1530 • http://www.palospark.org

Paris
Edgar County Genealogical Society • Historical Museum, 408 N Main, P.O. Box 304 • Paris, IL 61944-0304 • (217) 463-4209 • http://www.tigerpaw.com/ecgl/

Edgar County Historical Society • Historical Museum, 408 N Main • Paris, IL 61944-1549 • (217) 463-5305

Park Forest

1950s Park Forest House Museum • 141 Forest Blvd • Park Forest, IL 60466 • (708) 481-4252 • http://www.parkforesthistory.org

Illiana Jewish Genealogical Society • 404 Douglas • Park Forest, IL 60466 • (708) 748-5962

Park Forest Historical Society • c/o Park Forest Public Library, 400 Lakewood Blvd • Park Forest, IL 60466 • (708) 748-3731 • http://www.lincolnnet.net/users/lrpfhs/

Park Forest Public Library • 400 Lakewood Blvd • Park Forest, IL 60466 • (708) 748-3731 • http://www.pfpl.org

Thornton Township Historical Society • 66 Water St • Park Forest, IL 60466 • (708) 596-2000 x356

Park Ridge

National Society, Women Descendants of the Ancient and Honorable Artillery Company • 1234 S Cumberland Ave • Park Ridge, IL 60620 • (847) 823-0502 • http://my.execpc.com/~drg/wiwdah.html

Park Ridge Historical Society • Historical Museum, 41 W Prairie Ave • Park Ridge, IL 60068 • (847) 696-1973

Park Ridge Public Library • 20 S Prospect Ave • Park Ridge, IL 60068-4188 • (847) 825-3123 • http://www.parkridgelibrary.org

Polish Genealogical Society of America • 524 Parkwood • Park Ridge, IL 60068

Wood Library-Museum of Anesthesiology • 520 N Northwest Hwy • Park Ridge, IL 60068 • (847) 825-5586 • http://www.asahq.org/wlm

Paw Paw

Paw Paw Public Library District • 362 Chicago Rd, P.O. Box 60 • Paw Paw, IL 61363-0060 • (815) 627-9396

Pawnee

Pawnee Public Library • 613 Douglas St, P.O. Box 229 • Pawnee, IL 62558-0229 • (217) 625-7716

Paxton

Ford County Historical Society • Historical Museum, 200 W State St, P.O. Box 115 • Paxton, IL 60957 • (217) 379-4684 • http://www.rootsweb.com/~ilford

Pecatonica

Pecatonica Historical Society • Historical Museum, 314 Main St, P.O. Box 298 • Pecatonica, IL 61063-0599

Pekin

Pekin Public Library • 301 S 4th St • Pekin, IL 61554-4284 • (309) 347-7111 • http://www.pekin.net/library

Tazewell County Genealogical and Historical Society • Ehrlicher Research Center, 719 N 11th St, P.O. Box 312 • Pekin, IL 61555-0312 • (309) 477-3044 • http://www.tcghs.org

Peoria

African American Hall of Fame Museum • 309 S DuSable St • Peoria, IL 61605 • (309) 673-2206 • http://www.africanamericanhalloffame.org

Apostolic Christian Church of America • 3420 N Sheridan Rd • Peoria, IL 61604 • http://www.apostolicchristian.org

Central Illinois Landmarks Foundation-Architectural Archives • 107 NE Monroe St • Peoria, IL 61602-1070 • (309) 497-2158 • http://www.peoria.lib.il.us

Cullom-Davis Library • Bradley Univ, 1501 W Bradley Ave • Peoria, IL 61625 • (309) 677-2922 • http://www.bradley.edu/irt/lib/

Palatines to America, Illinois Chapter • P.O. Box 9638 • Peoria, IL 61612-9368 • (309) 691-0292

Peoria County Genealogical Society • P.O. Box 1489 • Peoria, IL 61602 • (309) 692-9758 • http://www.usgennet.org/~ilpeoria/pcgs.html

Peoria Historical Society • Flanagan House Museum, 942 NE Glen Oak Ave • Peoria, IL 61603 • (309) 674-0322

Peoria Historical Society • Historical Museum, 611 SW Washington St • Peoria, IL 61602 • (309) 674-4745 • http://www.peoriahistoricalsociety.org

Peoria Public Library • 107 NE Monroe St • Peoria, IL 61602-1070 • (309) 672-8663 • http://www.peorialib.il.us

Pettengill-Morron House Museum • 1212 W Moss Ave • Peoria, IL 61603 • (309) 674-1921 • http://www.peoriahistoricalsociety.org/House-Museums/Pettengill-Morron_House_Museum

Wheels O'Time Museum • 11923 N Knoxville Ave, P.O. Box 9636 • Peoria, IL 61612 • (309) 243-9020 • http://www.wheelsotime.org

Peoria Heights

Peoria Heights Public Library • 816 E Glen Ave • Peoria Heights, IL 61616 • (309) 682-5578 • http://www.peoriaheightslibrary.com

Peotone

H A Rathje Mill Museum • W Corning St • Peotone, IL 60468 • (708) 258-3436

Historical Society of Greater Peotone • 213 W North St, P.O. Box 87 • Peotone, IL 60468-0087 • (708) 258-3436

Peotone Public Library District • 213 W North St • Peotone, IL 60468 • (708) 258-3436 • http://www.peotone.lib.il.us

Peru

Peru Public Library • 1409 11th St • Peru, IL 61354 • (815) 223-0229 • http://www.htls.lib.il.us/pub

Petersburg

Edgar Lee Masters Memorial Museum • 7th & Jackson Sts • Petersburg, IL 62675 • (217) 632-2187

Lincoln's New Salem State Historic Site Museum • 15588 History Ln • Petersburg, IL 62675 • (217) 632-4000 • http://www.lincolnsnewsalem.com

Menard County Historical Society • Historical Museum, 125 S 7th St • Petersburg, IL 62675-1554 • (217) 632-7363

Petersburg Public Library • 220 S 6th St • Petersburg, IL 62675 • (217) 632-2807

Pinckneyville

Perry County Historical Society • Perry County Jail Museum, 108 W Jackson St • Pinckneyville, IL 62274 • (618) 357-2225 • http://www.fnbpville.com/perrycounty.html

Piper City

Piper City Community Historical Society • 39 W Main, P.O. Box 32 • Piper City, IL 60959 • (815) 686-2414

Piper City Public Library District • 39 W Main, P.O. Box 248 • Piper City, IL 60959-0248 • (815) 686-9234

Pittsfield

Pike County Historical Society • Historical Museum, 400 E Jefferson, P.O. Box 44 • Pittsfield, IL 62363 • (217) 285-4618

Pittsfield Public Library • 205 N Memorial • Pittsfield, IL 62363-1406 • (217) 285-2200

Plainfield

Plainfield Historical Society • Historical Museum, 217 E Main St, P.O. Box 291 • Plainfield, IL 60544 • (815) 436-4073

Plainfield Public Library District • 705 N Illinois St • Plainfield, IL 60544 • (815) 436-6639 • http://www.plainfield.lib.il.us

Plano

Farnsworth House Museum • 14520 River Rd, P.O. Box 194 • Plano, IL 60545 • (630) 552-0052 • http://www.farnsworthhouse.org

Plano, cont.

Little Rock Township Public Library Genealogy Group • c/o Little Rock Township Public Library, 15 N Center Ave • Plano, IL 60545 • (630) 552-8003

Plano Community Library District • 15 N Center Ave • Plano, IL 60545 • (630) 552-8003 • http://plano.lib.il.us

Pleasant Hill

Pike and Calhoun Counties Genealogical Society • 207 N Main St, P.O. Box 104 • Pleasant Hill, IL 62366 • (217) 734-2221

Pleasant Plains

Peter Cartwright United Methodist Church Museum • 205 W Church St, P.O. Box 108 • Pleasant Plains, IL 62677 • (217) 626-1087

Polo

Polo Historical Society • Historical Museum, 125 N Franklin St • Polo, IL 61064-1506 • (815) 946-4142

Pontiac

Catherine V Yost Museum • 298 Water St • Pontiac, IL 61764 • (815) 844-7401

Jones House Museum • 314 E Madison St, P.O. Box 680 • Pontiac, IL 61764 • (815) 842-3457

Livingston County Historical Society • Jones House, 314 E Madison St, P.O. Box 680 • Pontiac, IL 61764-0999 • (815) 844-3457

Pontiac Public Library • 211 E Madison St • Pontiac, IL 61764 • (815) 844-7229 • http://www.pontiac.lib.il.us

Port Byron

River Valley District Library • 214 S Main St, P.O. Box 10 • Port Byron, IL 61275-0010 • (309) 523-3440

Prairie du Rocher

Fort de Chartres State Historic Site Museum • 1350 State Route 155 • Prairie du Rocher, IL 62277 • (618) 284-7230

Henry-Lee-Brickey Creole House Museum • 220 Market St • Prairie du Rocher, IL 62278

Princeton

Bureau County Genealogical Society • c/o Matson Public Library, 15 Park Ave W, P.O. Box 402 • Princeton, IL 61356-0402 • (815) 875-2184 • http://www.rootsweb.com/~ilbcgs/

Bureau County Genealogical Society • Historical Museum, 629 S Main St, P.O. Box 402 • Princeton, IL 61356-0402 • (815) 875-8491 • http://www.rootsweb.com/~ilbcgs

Bureau County Historical Society • Historical Museum, 109 Park Ave W • Princeton, IL 61356-1927 • (815) 875-2184

Matson Public Library • 15 Park Ave W • Princeton, IL 61356 • (815) 875-1331 • http://www.matsonpubliclibrary.org

Owen Lovejoy Homestead Museum • E Peru St • Princeton, IL 61356 • (815) 879-9151

Princeville

Historical Association of Princeville • 130 N Walnut, P.O. Box 608 • Princeville, IL 61559-9635 • (309) 385-2394

Lillie M Evans Library District • 207 N Walnut Ave, P.O. Box 349 • Princeville, IL 61559-0349 • (309) 385-4540 • http://www.lmelibrary.org

Prophetstown

Henry C Adams Memorial Library • 209 W 3rd St • Prophetstown, IL 61277 • (815) 537-5462 • http://www.rbls.lib.il.us/ptn/

Prophetstown Area Historical Society • Historical Museum, 320 Washington St • Prophetstown, IL 61277 • (815) 537-2818

Putnam

Putnam County Historical Society • P.O. Box 95 • Putnam, IL 61560 • (815) 925-7560

Quincy

All Wars Museum • 1701 N 12th St • Quincy, IL 62301 • (217) 222-8641

Brenner Library - Local History Collection • Quincy College, 1800 College Ave • Quincy, IL 62301-2670 • (217) 228-5350

Dr Richard Eells House Museum • 415 Jersey St, P.O. Box 628 • Quincy, IL 62306 • (217) 223-1800

Great River Genealogical Society • c/o Quincy Public Library & Museum, 526 Jersey St • Quincy, IL 62301-3927 • (217) 222-0226 • http://www.outfittes.com/~grgs/

Historical Society of Quincy and Adams County • Gov John Wood Mansion Museum, 425 N 12th St • Quincy, IL 62301 • (217) 222-1835 • http://www.adamscohistory.org

Illinois Veterans' Home Library • 1707 N 12th St • Quincy, IL 62301 • (217) 222-8641 • http://www.quincynet.com/ivh/museum.htm

John Wood Community College Library • 1301 S 48th St • Quincy, IL 62305 • (217) 641-4537 • http://www.jwcc.edu/instruct/library/

Quincy Museum • 1601 Main St • Quincy, IL 62301-4264 • (217) 224-7669 • http://www.thequincymuseum.com

Quincy Public Library • 526 Jersey St • Quincy, IL 62301-3996 • (217) 223-1309 • http://www.quincylibrary.org

Villa Kathrine Museum • 532 Gardener Expwy • Quincy, IL 62306 • (217) 222-1835

Rantoul

Korean War Veterans National Museum • 1007 Pacesetter Dr, P.O. Box 20 • Rantoul, IL 61886 • (217) 893-4111 • http://www.kwvmuseum.com

Octave Chanute Aerospace Museum Foundation • 1011 Pacesetter Dr • Rantoul, IL 61866 • (217) 893-1613 • http://www.aeromuseum.org

Ostfriesian Heritage Society of East Central Illinois • 3154 CR 2000 E • Rantoul, IL 61866 • (217) 892-4776

Red Bud

Red Bud Public Library • 925 S Main St • Red Bud, IL 62278 • (618) 282-2255

Richmond

British Interest Group of Wisconsin and Illinois • P.O. Box 192 • Richmond, IL 60071-1092 • (815) 455-7150 • http://www.rootsweb.com/~wiilbig

River Forest

Forest Preserve District Museum • 536 N Harlem Ave • River Forest, IL 60305 • (708) 771-1330 • http://www.fpdcc.com

Trailside Museum • 738 Thatcher Ave • River Forest, IL 60305 • (708) 366-6530

River Grove

River Grove Historical Commission • 2561 N Budd St • River Grove, IL 60171-1736 • (708) 453-8000

River Grove Public Library • 8638 W Grand Ave • River Grove, IL 60171 • (708) 453-4484

Triton Community History Organization • Triton College, 2000 5th Ave • River Grove, IL 60171 • (708) 456-0300 • http://www.triton.edu

Riverdale

Riverdale Historical Society • c/o Riverdale Library, 208 W 144th St • Riverdale, IL 60627 • (708) 841-3311 • http://www.sls.lib.il.us/RDS/

Riverdale Library • 208 W 144th St • Riverdale, IL 60627-2788 • (708) 841-3311 • http://www2.sls.lib.il.us/RDS/

Riverside

Riverside Historical Museum • 10 Pine St • Riverside, IL 60546-2264 • (708) 447-2542 • http://www.riversidemuseum.net

Riverside Public Library • 1 Burling Rd • Riverside, IL 60546 • (708) 442-6366 • http://www.riversidelibrary.org

Riverside Village
Riverside Historical Commission • Historical Museum, 27 Riverside Rd • Riverside Village, IL 60546 • (708) 447-2542

Robbins
Robbins Historical Society • Historical Museum, 13822 S Central Park Ave, P.O. Box 1561 • Robbins, IL 60472-1561 • (708) 389-5393

Robinson
Crawford County Genealogical Society • 803 N Madison, P.O. Box 120 • Robinson, IL 62454

Crawford County Historical Society • Historical Museum, 408 S Cross St, P.O. Box 554 • Robinson, IL 62454-0554 • (618) 544-3087 • http://www.rootsweb.com/~ilcchs/county1.htm

Robinson Public Library District • 606 N Jefferson St • Robinson, IL 62454 • (618) 544-3273 • http://www.sirin.lib.il.us/docs/rob/docs/lib

Rochelle
Flagg Township Historical Society • Historical Museum, 600 N 10th St • Rochelle, IL 61068 • (815) 562-7423

Flagg-Rochelle Public Library District • 619 4th Ave • Rochelle, IL 61068 • (815) 562-3431

Rock Island
Augustana Historical Society • c/o Augustana College Library, 3435 9 1/2 Ave • Rock Island, IL 61201-2296 • (309) 794-7266

Blackhawk Genealogical Society of Rock Island and Mercer County Illinois • Historical Museum, 401 19th St, P.O. Box 3912 • Rock Island, IL 61204-3912 • (309) 786-3058 • http://www.rootsweb.com/~ilrockis/

Colonel Davenport Historical Foundation • Davenport Home Museum, Arsenal Island, P.O. Box 4603 • Rock Island, IL 61299 • (563) 324-8519 • http://www.davenporthouse.org

Corps of Engineers, Rock Island District Technical Library • Clock Tower Bldg, Rodman Ave, P.O. Box 2004 • Rock Island, IL 61204-2004 • (309) 794-5576 • http://www.mvr.usace.army.mil/library

Hauberg Indian Museum • Black Hawk State Park, 1510 46th Ave • Rock Island, IL 61201 • (309) 788-9536

Rock Island Arsenal Historical Society • SMCRI-ADW-B, Rock Island Arsenal • Rock Island, IL 61299 • (309) 794-5021

Rock Island Arsenal Museum • Bldg 60, Rock Island Arsenal, AMSTA-RI-CF-MUS • Rock Island, IL 61299 • (309) 782-5021 • http://www.ria.army.mil

Rock Island Historical Museum • 639 38th St • Rock Island, IL 61201 • (309) 794-7317

Rock Island Public Library • 401 19th St • Rock Island, IL 61201 • (309) 732-7341 • http://www.rbis.lib.il.us/rbls/

Swenson Swedish Immigration Research Center • Augustana College, 3520 7th Ave, P.O. Box 175 • Rock Island, IL 61201 • (309) 794-7204 • http://www.augustana.edu/administration/swenson/

Thomas Tredway Library • Augustana College, 3435 9 1/2 Ave • Rock Island, IL 61201-2296 • (309) 794-7266 • http://www.augustana.edu

Rockford
Camp Grant Museum • 1004 Samuelson Rd • Rockford, IL 61109 • (815) 395-0679

Ethnic Heritage Museum • 1129 S Main St, P.O. Box 382 • Rockford, IL 61005 • (815) 962-7402

Graham-Ginestra House Museum • 1115 S Main St • Rockford, IL 61101 • (815) 963-8111

Kishwaukee Genealogists • P.O. Box 5503 • Rockford, IL 61125-0503 • (815) 399-0220

National Railway Historical Society • Historical Museum, Mulford Rd, P.O. Box 5632 • Rockford, IL 61125 • (815) 226-8725

North Central Illinois Genealogical Society • Historical Museum, 8201 Cherry North Dr, P.O. Box 4635 • Rockford, IL 61110-4635 • (815) 397-3529 • http://www.rootsweb.com/~ilwinneb/ncengen.htm

Our Savior's Lutheran Church Library • 3300 Rural St • Rockford, IL 61107 • (815) 399-0531 • http://oursaviorslutheranchurch.org

Rockford Historical Society • Midway Village Museum, 6799 Guilford Rd • Rockford, IL 61107-2613 • (815) 397-9112 • http://www.midwayvillage.com

Rockford Public Library • 215 N Wyman St • Rockford, IL 61101-1061 • (815) 965-6735 • http://www.rpl.rockford.org

Swedish Historical Society of Rockford • Erlander Home Museum, 404 S 3rd St • Rockford, IL 61104 • (815) 963-5559 • http://www.swedishhistorical.org

Tinker Swiss Cottage Museum • 411 Kent St • Rockford, IL 61102 • (815) 964-2424 • http://www.tinkercottage.com

Winnebago and Boone Counties Genealogical Society • P.O. Box 10166 • Rockford, IL 61131-0166 • (815) 226-4884

Rockton
Macktown Living History Center • 2221 Freeport Rd • Rockton, IL 61072 • (815) 624-4200 • http://www.wcfpd.org

Rockton Township Historical Society • Historical Museum, 529 Green St, P.O. Box 37 • Rockton, IL 61072 • (815) 624-4541

Stephen Mack Home and Whitman Trading Post Museum • 316 N Black Hawk Blvd • Rockton, IL 61072 • (815) 624-7600

Rolling Meadows
Rolling Meadows Public Library • 3110 Martin Ln • Rolling Meadows, IL 60008 • (847) 259-6050 • http://www.rolling-meadows.lib.il.us

Romeoville
Canal and Regional History Collection • Lewis Univ, 1 University Pkwy • Romeoville, IL 60446 • (815) 838-0500

Fountaindale Public Library District-Romeoville Branch • 201 W Normantown Rd • Romeoville, IL 60446-1261 • (815) 886-2030

Lewis University Library • 1 University Pkwy • Romeoville, IL 60446-2298 • (815) 838-0500 • http://www.lewisu.edu/library/

Romeoville Historical Museum • Romeo Rd • Romeoville, IL 60441 • (708) 739-7951

Romeoville Historical Society • c/o Fountaindale Library, 201 W Normantown Rd, P.O. Box 504 • Romeoville, IL 60441 • (815) 886-2030

Roselle
DuPage County Historical Society • 617 White Oak Dr • Roselle, IL 60172

Law Enforcement Memorial Association Museum • P.O. Box 72835 • Roselle, IL 60172 • (847) 524-1369 • http://www.forgottenheroes-lema.org

Roselle Historical Foundation • 102 S Prospect St • Roselle, IL 60172 • (630) 351-5300

Rosemont
Archdiocese of the Evangelical Lutheran Church in America Archives • 5400 Milton Pkwy • Rosemont, IL 60018 • (773) 380-2818 • http://www.elea.org/os/archives/intro.html

Roseville
Warren County Historical Society • Route 116 E, P.O. Box 325 • Roseville, IL 61473 • (309) 426-2231

Illinois

Rosiclare
American Fluorite Museum • Main St, P.O. Box 755 • Rosiclare, IL 62982 • (618) 285-3513

Rossville
Rossville Historical Society • Historical Museum, 108 W Attica St, P.O. Box 263 • Rossville, IL 60963 • (217) 748-4080 • http://www. rossvilleshops.com/society.html

Rushville
Schuyler County Historical Museum and Genealogical Center • Schuyler Jail Museum, 200 S Congress, P.O. Box 96 • Rushville, IL 62681 • (217) 322-6975

Schuyler-Brown Historical and Genealogical Society • Schuyler Jail Museum, 200 S Congress, P.O. Box 96 • Rushville, IL 62681 • (217) 322-6975

Saint Charles
Beith House Museum • 10 W Indiana St, P.O. Box 903 • Saint Charles, IL 60174 • (630) 377-6424 • http://www.ppfv.org/beith.htm

Dunham Hunt Museum • Saint Charles Heritage Center, 304 Cedar Ave • Saint Charles, IL 60174 • (630) 584-6967

Durant House Museum • Bittersweet Rd & Dean St, P.O. Box 903 • Saint Charles, IL 60174 • (630) 377-6424 • http://www.ppfv.org/durant. htm

Saint Charles Historical Society • Saint Charles Heritage Center, 215 E Main St • Saint Charles, IL 60174 • (630) 584-6967 • http://www. stchistory.org

Saint Charles Public Library District • 1 S 6th Ave • Saint Charles, IL 60174-2195 • (630) 584-0076 • http://www.stcharleslibrary.org

Salem
Bryan-Bennett Library • 217 W Main St • Salem, IL 62881 • (618) 548-7784 • http://www.salembbl.lib.il.us

Marion County Genealogical and Historical Society • c/o Bryan-Bennett Library, 217 W Main, P.O. Box 342 • Salem, IL 62881 • (618) 548-7784

William Jennings Bryan Birthplace Museum • 408 S Broadway • Salem, IL 62881 • (618) 548-2222

Sandwich
Sandwich District Library • 107 E Center St • Sandwich, IL 60548-1603 • (815) 786-8308 • http://www.sandwich.lib.il.us

Sandwich Historical Society • Historical Museum, 315 E Railroad St, P.O. Box 82 • Sandwich, IL 60548 • (815) 786-7936

Savanna
Carroll County Genealogical Society • c/o Savanna Public Library, 326 3rd St, P.O. Box 354 • Savanna, IL 61074 • (815) 273-3707 • http:// homepages.rootsweb.com/~haliotis/

Savanna Public Library • 326 3rd St • Savanna, IL 61074 • (815) 273-3714

Schaumburg
Computer-Assisted Genealogy Group of Northern Illinois • P. O. Box 59567 • Schaumburg, IL 60695 • (847) 506-1830

Saint Peter Lutheran Church Museum • 208 E Schaumburg Rd • Schaumburg, IL 60194 • (847) 885-3350

Schaumburg Genealogical Society • c/o Schaumburg Public Library, 130 S Roselle Rd • Schaumburg, IL 60194-3421 • (847) 923-9044 • http://www.stdl.org

Schaumburg Township District Library • 130 S Roselle Rd • Schaumburg, IL 60193 • (847) 923-9044 • http://www.stdl.org

Schiller Park
Schiller Park Historical Society • 9526 Irving Park Rd • Schiller Park, IL 60176 • (847) 671-8513

Schiller Park Public Library • 4200 Old River Rd • Schiller Park, IL 60176-1699 • (847) 678-0433

Scott AFB
Scott Air Force Base Library FL4407 • 375 SVS/SVMG, 510 Ward Dr • Scott AFB, IL 62225-5360 • (618) 256-5100

Seneca
Seneca Public Library District • 210 N Main St • Seneca, IL 61360 • (815) 357-6566

Sesser
Goode-Barren Historical Genealogical Society • 201 E Callie St, P.O. Box 1024 • Sesser, IL 62884-0944 • (618) 625-2851

Shabbona
Shabbona-Lee-Rollo Historical Museum • 119 W Comanche, P.O. Box 334 • Shabbona, IL 60550 • (815) 824-2759

Shawneetown
Gallatin County Historical Society • Historical Museum, P.O. Box 693 • Shawneetown, IL 62984 • (618) 269-3716

Shawneetown Historic Site Museum • RR 1 • Shawneetown, IL 62984 • (618) 269-3303

Shawneetown Public Library • 320 N Lincoln Blvd E • Shawneetown, IL 62984-3262 • (618) 269-3761

Sheffield
Sheffield Historical Museum • Washington & Cook Sts • Sheffield, IL 61361 • (815) 454-2788

Sheffield Historical Society • Historical Museum, 235 Reed St • Sheffield, IL 61361-0103 • (815) 454-2788

Sheffield Public Library • 136 E Cook St • Sheffield, IL 61361-0608 • (815) 454-2628

Shelbyville
Shelby County Historical and Genealogical Society • 151 S Washington St, P.O. Box 286 • Shelbyville, IL 62565 • (217) 774-2260 • http://www.shelbycohistgen.org

Shelbyville Free Public Library • 154 N Broadway St • Shelbyville, IL 62565-1698 • (217) 774-4432

Shipman
Southwestern Farm and Home Museum • 203 Park St, P.O. Box 132 • Shipman, IL 62685 • (618) 729-4186

Shorewood
Shorewood-Troy Public Library District • 650 Deerwood Dr • Shorewood, IL 60431 • (815) 725-1715 • http://www.shorewood.lib.il.us

Sidell
Sidell Community Historical Society • Historical Museum, P.O. Box 42 • Sidell, IL 61876 • (217) 288-9030

Sidney
Sidney Historical Society • Historical Museum, 1985 CR 600 N, P.O. Box 87 • Sidney, IL 61877-0087 • (217) 688-2974

Skokie
Assyrain American League • 8324 Lincoln Ave • Skokie, IL 60077 • (847) 982-5800

Saul Silber Memorial Library • Hebrew Theological College, 7135 N Carpenter Rd • Skokie, IL 60077-3263 • (847) 982-2500 • http://www. htcnet.edu

Skokie Historical Society • 8031 Floral Ave • Skokie, IL 60077 • (847) 673-1888

Skokie Public Library • 5215 Oakton St • Skokie, IL 60077-3680 • (847) 673-7774 • http://www.skokielibrary.info/

South Beloit
South Beloit Historical Society • 440 Oak Grove Ave • South Beloit, IL 61080-1949 • (815) 389-2173

South Elgin
Fox River Trolley Museum • 361 S La Fox, P.O. Box 315 • South Elgin, IL 60177 • (630) 665-2581 • http://www.foxtrolley.org

South Holland
Paarlberg Farmstead Homestead Museum • 172nd Pl & Paxton Ave, P.O. Box 48 • South Holland, IL 60473-0048 • (708) 596-2722

South Holland Historical Society • c/o South Holland Public Library, 16250 Wausau Ave, P.O. Box 48 • South Holland, IL 60473 • (708) 596-2722 • http://www.southhollandlibrary.org

South Holland Public Library • 16250 Wausau Ave • South Holland, IL 60473 • (708) 331-5262 • http://www.southhollandlibrary.org

South Suburban College Library • 15800 S State • South Holland, IL 60473-9998 • (708) 596-2000 • http://www.southsuburbancollege.edu

South Suburban Genealogical and Historical Society • 320 E 161st Pl, P.O. Box 96 • South Holland, IL 60473-0096 • (708) 333-9474 • http://www.rootsweb.com/~ssghs/ssghs.htm

Sparta
Mr & Mrs Alfred A Brown Memorial Museum • P.O. Box 152 • Sparta, IL 62286 • (618) 443-2897

Randolph County Historical Society • RR1, Box 356 • Sparta, IL 62286

Sparta Public Library • 211 W Broadway • Sparta, IL 62286 • (618) 443-5014 • http://sirin.lib.il.us

Springfield
114th Regiment, Illinois Volunteer Infantry Museum • 1320 N Osburn • Springfield, IL 62702 • (217) 789-2340

Abraham Lincoln Association • Historical Museum, 1 Old State Capitol Pl • Springfield, IL 62701 • (217) 782-2118 • http://www.allincolnassoc.com

Abraham Lincoln Presidential Library and Museum • 112 N 6th St • Springfield, IL 62701 • (217) 558-8882 • http://www.alplm.org

Association of Illinois Museums • 1 Old State Capitol Pl • Springfield, IL 62701-1507 • (217) 524-6977 • http://www.illinoismuseums.org

Brinkerhoff Home Museum • 1500 N 5th St • Springfield, IL 62703 • http://www.sci.edu

Brunk-Morgan Horse Museum • 405 Clipper Rd • Springfield, IL 62563

Congress of Illinois Historical and Genealogical Societies • Old State Capitol • Springfield, IL 62701 • (217) 525-2781

Dana-Thomas House Museum • 301 E Lawrence Ave • Springfield, IL 62703 • (217) 782-6776 • http://www.dana-thomas.org

Daughters of the Union Veterans of the Civil War • DUV Registrar's Office, 503 S Walnut St • Springfield, IL 62704 • (217) 544-0616 • http://www.duvcw.org

Douglas County Genealogical Society • P.O. Box 1829 • Springfield, IL 62705-1829 • (217) 529-0542

Edwards Place Historic Home Museum • 700 N 4th St • Springfield, IL 62702 • (217) 523-2631 • http://www.springfieldart.org

Illinois Dept of Public Health, Division of Vital Records • 605 W Jefferson St • Springfield, IL 62702-5097 • (217) 782-6553 • http://www.idph.state.il.us/vitalrecords/

Illinois Historic Preservation Agency • 1 Old State Capital Plaza • Springfield, IL 62701 • (217) 524-6045 • http://www.illinois-history.gov

Illinois Historic Preservation Agency Library • 500 E Madison St • Springfield, IL 62701 • (217) 785-7934 • http://www.state.il.us/hpa

Illinois State Archives • Margaret Cross Norton Bldg, Capitol Complex • Springfield, IL 62756 • (217) 782-4682 • http://www.sos.state.il.us/depts/archives/arc_home.html

Illinois State Genealogical Society • Archives Bldg, 2nd & Edwards, P.O. Box 10195 • Springfield, IL 62705-0195 • (217) 789-1968 • http://www.tbox.com/isgs/

Illinois State Historical Library • 1 Old State Capitol • Springfield, IL 62701 • (217) 524-6358 • http://www.state.il.us/hpa/lib

Illinois State Historical Society • Old State Capitol, 210 1/2 S 6th St, Ste 200 • Springfield, IL 62701 • (217) 525-2781 • http://www.historyillinois.org

Illinois State Library • Gwendolyn Brooks Bldg, 300 S 2nd St • Springfield, IL 62701-1796 • (217) 782-7596 • http://www.libraty.sos.state.il.us

Illinois State Military Museum • 1301 N MacArthur Blvd • Springfield, IL 62702 • (217) 761-3910 • http://www.springfield-il.com/attract/military.html

Illinois State Museum • 502 S Spring St • Springfield, IL 62706-5000 • (217) 782-6623 • http://www.museum.state.il.us

Lincoln Herndon Law Offices State Historic Site Museum • 6th & Adams, Old Capitol Complex • Springfield, IL 62701 • (217) 785-7960 • http://www.illinois-history.gov

Lincoln Home National Historic Site Museum • 413 S 8th St • Springfield, IL 62701 • (217) 492-4241 • http://www.nps.gov/liho

Lincoln Library • 326 S 7th St • Springfield, IL 62701-1621 • (217) 753-4910 • http://lincolnlibrary.rpls.lib.il.us/llhome5.htm

Lincoln Tomb State Historic Site Museum • Oak Ridge Center, 1500 Monument Ave • Springfield, IL 62702 • (217) 782-2717

Masonic Grand Lodge of Illinois • 2866 Via Verde • Springfield, IL 62703 • (217) 529-8900 • http://www.ilmason.org

Museum of Funeral Customs • 1440 Monument Ave • Springfield, IL 62702 • (217) 544-3480 • http://www.funeralmuseum.org

Norris L Brookens Library • Univ of Illinois at Springfield, 1 University Plaza, MS BRK-140 • Springfield, IL 62703-5407 • (217) 206-6633 • http://library.uis.edu/archives

Pearson Museum • 801 N Rutledge, SLU School of Medicine • Springfield, IL 62794 • (217) 545-8017 • http://www.siumed.edu/medhum/pearson

Sangamon County Genealogical Society • 2856 S 11th St, P.O. Box 1829 • Springfield, IL 62705-1829 • (217) 529-0542 • http://www.rootsweb.com/~ilsangam/scgs.htm

Sangamon County Historical Society • Historical Museum, 308 E Adams • Springfield, IL 62701 • (217) 522-2500

Vachel Lindsay Home State Historic Site Museum • 603 S 5th St • Springfield, IL 62703 • (217) 524-0901 • http://www.illinois-history.gov

Women's Relief Corps National Headquarters • Grand Army of the Republic Museum, 629 S 7th St • Springfield, IL 62703-1636 • (217) 522-4373 • http://www.suvcw.org/wrc.htm

Staunton
Macoupin County Genealogical Society • c/o Staunton Public Library, 306 W Main St, P.O. Box 95 • Staunton, IL 62088-0095 • (618) 635-3852 • http://www.rootsweb.com/~ilmacoup/m_gensoc.htm

Staunton Public Library • 306 W Main St • Staunton, IL 62088 • (618) 635-3852

Sterling
Sterling Public Library • 102 W 3rd St • Sterling, IL 61081-3511 • (815) 625-1370 • http://www.sterlingpubliclibrary.org

Sterling-Rock Falls Historical Society • Dillon Home Museum, 1005 E 3rd St, P.O. Box 65 • Sterling, IL 61081 • (815) 622-6215

Sterling, cont.

Whiteside County Genealogists • c/o Sterling Public Library, 102 W 3rd St, P.O. Box 145 • Sterling, IL 61081 • (815) 625-8750 • http://www. serve.com/bmosher/WSCGen/ wscgen.htm

Stillman Valley

Julia Hull District Library • 100 Library Lane • Stillman Valley, IL 61084 • (815) 645-8611

Stockton

Heritage League of Northwest Illinois • c/o Stockton Public Library, 140 W Benton St • Stockton, IL 61085-1312 • (815) 947-2435

Stockton Township Public Library • 140 W Benton St • Stockton, IL 61085-1312 • (815) 947-2030

Stone Park

Italian Cultural Center Library • 1621 N 39th Ave • Stone Park, IL 60165-1105 • (708) 345-3842 • http://www.mobilito.com/ice/

Stone Park Historical Society • Village Hall, 1629 N Mannheim Rd • Stone Park, IL 60165-1118 • (708) 345-2272

Streamwood

Poplar Creek Genealogical Society • 200 Kosan Cr, P.O. Box 248 • Streamwood, IL 60103

Poplar Creek Public Library • 1405 S Park Ave • Streamwood, IL 60107-2997 • (630) 837-6800 • http://www.poplarcreek.lib.il.us

Streamwood Historical Society • Historical Museum, Hoosier Grove Park, 700 W Irving Park Rd • Streamwood, IL 60107 • (630) 372-7275

Streator

Streator Public Library • 130 S Park St • Streator, IL 61364 • (815) 672-2729

Stretorland Historical Society • Historical Museum, 306 S Vermillion St • Streator, IL 61364 • (815) 672-2443

Sugar Grove

Air Classic Museum of Aviation • 43 W 264 Rte 30 • Sugar Grove, IL 60554 • (630) 466-0888 • http://www.airclassicsmuseum.org

Czech and Slovak American Genealogy Society of Illinois • P.O. Box 313 • Sugar Grove, IL 60554-0313 • http://www.csagsi.org

Sugar Grove Historical Society • Historical Museum, 259 Main St, P.O. Box 102 • Sugar Grove, IL 60554-0102 • (630) 466-9726

Sullivan

Moultrie County Historical and Genealogical Society • Heritage Center, 117 E Harrison St, P.O. Box 588 • Sullivan, IL 61951-0588 • (217) 728-4085

Summit Argo

I & M Canal National Heritage Corridor Civic Center Museum • 7800 W 65th • Summit Argo, IL 60501 • (708) 496-0193

Sycamore

DeKalb County Historical and Genealogical Society • P.O. Box 295 • Sycamore, IL 60178-0295 • (815) 784-2015

Sycamore Historical Society • Historical Museum, 308 W State St, P.O. Box 502 • Sycamore, IL 60178 • (815) 895-5762 • http://www. sycamorehistory.org

Sycamore Public Library • Joiner History Room, 103 E State St • Sycamore, IL 60178-1440 • (815) 895-2500 • http://www. sycamorelibrary.org

Tampico

Reagan Birthplace Museum • 111 Main St, P.O. box 344 • Tampico, IL 61283 • (815) 438-7581 • http://www.tampicohistoricalsociety.org

Tampico Area Historical Society • Historical Museum, 119 S Main, P.O. Box 248 • Tampico, IL 61283-0248 • (815) 438-7581 • http://www. tampicohistoricalsociety.org

Taylorville

Christian County Genealogical Society • Historical Museum, Rts 29 & 48 E, P.O. Box 28 • Taylorville, IL 62568 • (217) 824-6922 • http:// homepage.macomb.com/~tkuntz/christianco.htm

Christian County Historical Society • Routes 29 & 48 E, P.O. Box 254 • Taylorville, IL 62568 • (773) 824-6922

Teutopolis

Teutopolis Monastery Museum • Route 40 & Garrott St • Teutopolis, IL 62467 • (217) 857-3586

Thebes

Thebes Historical Society • P.O. Box 14 • Thebes, IL 62990-0014 • (618) 764-2600

Thompsonville

Franklin County Historical Society • 17664 Ross Briley Rd • Thompsonville, IL 62890-2310

Thomson

Thomson Depot Museum • Main St, P.O. Box 392 • Thomson, IL 61285-0392 • (815) 259-2155

York Township Public Library • 1005 W Main St • Thomson, IL 61285 • (815) 259-2480

Thornton

Thornton Historical Society • Historical Museum, 114 N Hunter St, P.O. Box 34 • Thornton, IL 60476-0034 • (708) 877-6569 • http://www. thornton60476.com/historical%20society.htm

Village of Thornton Historical Society • 208 Schwab St, P.O. Box 34 • Thornton, IL 60476-0034 • (708) 877-9394

Tilton

Tilton Historical Society • Historical Museum, 201 W 5th St • Tilton, IL 61833-7427 • (217) 442-9309

Tinley Park

South Suburban Heritage Association • P.O. Box 917 • Tinley Park, IL 60430 • (708) 614-8713 • http://march14th.org

Tinley Moraine Genealogical Society • 17101 S 71st St, P.O. Box 521 • Tinley Park, IL 60477-0521

Tinley Park Historical Society • Historical Museum, 6727 W 174th St, P.O. Box 325 • Tinley Park, IL 60477-0325 • (708) 429-4210 • http:// www.lincolnnet.net/users/lrtphist

Tiskilwa

Tiskilwa Township Library • 119 E Main St, P.O. Box 150 • Tiskilwa, IL 61368-0150 • (815) 646-4511

Toledo

Cumberland and Coles County Genealogical Society • Route 1, Box 141 • Toledo, IL 62468

Tolono

Tolono Public Library • 111 Main St, P.O. Box 759 • Tolono, IL 61880-0759 • (217) 485-5558 • http://www.tolonolibrary.org

Toulon

Stark County Genealogical Society • 207 W Main, P.O. Box 83 • Toulon, IL 61483 • http://www.rootsweb.com/~ilscgs/

Stark County Historical Society • Historical Museum, 318 W Jefferson St, P.O. Box 524 • Toulon, IL 61483 • (309) 286-7139

Towanda

Towanda District Public Library • 301 S Taylor St • Towanda, IL 61776 • (309) 728-2176

Tremont

Tremont District Public Library • 215 S Sampson St, P.O. Box 123 • Tremont, IL 61568-0123 • (309) 925-5432 • http://www.tremont.lib.il.us

Tremont Historical Society • Historical Museum, Madison & S Sampson Sts, P.O. Box 738 • Tremont, IL 61568 • (309) 925-5262

Trenton
Trenton Public Library • 118 E Indiana St • Trenton, IL 62293 • (618) 224-7662

Troy
Tri-Township Public Library • 209 S Main St • Troy, IL 62294 • (618) 667-2133 • http://troylibrary.org

Tuscola
Douglas County Genealogical Society • P.O. Box 113 • Tuscola, IL 61953-0113 • (217) 253-4635

Douglas County Museum • 700 S Main St • Tuscola, IL 61953-1822 • (217) 253-2535 • http://www.dcmuseum-tuscola.org

Union
Illinois Railway Museum • 7000 Olson Rd, P.O. Box 427 • Union, IL 60180 • (815) 923-4391 • http://www.irm.org

McHenry County Historical Society • Historical Museum, 6422 Main St, P.O. Box 434 • Union, IL 60180 • (815) 923-2267 • http://www.mchsonline.org

Urbana
Champaign County Genealogical Society • c/o Urbana Free Library, 201 S Race St • Urbana, IL 61801-3283 • (217) 367-0270 • http://www.tbox.com/ccgs

Champaign County Historical Society • c/o Urbana Free Library, 201 S Race St • Urbana, IL 61801 • (217) 367-4025 • http://www.urbanafreelibrary.org

Illinois Historical Survey - University Archives • Univ of Illinois, 1408 W Gregory Dr • Urbana, IL 61801 • (217) 333-1777 • http://web.library.uiuc.edu/ahx/

Illinois Historical Survey • Univ of Illinois at Urbana-Champaign Archives, 1408 W Gregory Dr • Urbana, IL 61801 • (217) 333-0798 • http://web.library.uiuc.edu/ahx/

University of Illinois Library • 230 Main Library, 1408 W Gregory Dr • Urbana, IL 61801 • (217) 333-0790 • http://www.library.uiuc.edu

Urbana Free Library • 201 S Race St • Urbana, IL 61801 • (217) 367-4405 • http://www.urbanafreelibrary.org

Utica
LaSalle County Historical Society • Historical Museum, Mill & Canal Sts, P.O. Box 278 • Utica, IL 61373-0278 • (815) 667-4861 • http://www.lasallecountymuseum.org

Starved Rock State Park • P.O. Box 509 • Utica, IL 61373 • (815) 667-4906 • http://www.dnr.state.il.us

Utica Public Library District • Mill & Grove Sts, P.O. Box 367 • Utica, IL 61373-0367 • (815) 667-4509

Vandalia
Evans Public Library • 215 S 5th St • Vandalia, IL 62471-2792 • (618) 283-2824 • http://www.sirin.lib.il.us/docs/epl/docs/lib/

Fayette County Genealogical Society • c/o Evans Public Library, 215 S 5th St, P.O. Box 177 • Vandalia, IL 62471 • (618) 423-2625 • http://www.swetland.net/users/fcgs

Vandalia Historical Museum • 307 N 6th • Vandalia, IL 62471 • (618) 283-0024

Vandalia Historical Society • Little Brick House Museum, 621 St Clair St • Vandalia, IL 62471-2336 • (618) 283-0024

Vandalia State House Museum • 315 W Gallatin St • Vandalia, IL 62471 • (618) 283-1161

Vernon Hills
Cuneo Museum & Gardens • 1350 N Milwaukee • Vernon Hills, IL 60061 • (847) 362-3042 • http://www.cuneomuseum.org

Versailles
Versailles Area Genealogical and Historical Society • 113 W 1st St, P.O. Box 92 • Versailles, IL 62378 • (217) 225-9091 • http://vaghs.tripod.com

Vienna
Johnson County Genealogical and Historical Society • P.O. Box 1207 • Vienna, IL 62995 • http://www.angelfire.com/il/jcghs

Paul Powell Home Museum • 404 Vine St • Vienna, IL 62995 • (618) 658-4911

Villa Park
Villa Park Historical Society • 220 S Villa Ave • Villa Park, IL 60181 • (630) 941-0223

Villa Park Public Library • 305 S Ardmore Ave • Villa Park, IL 60181-2698 • (630) 834-1164 • http://www.villapark.lib.il.us

Virginia
Cass County Historical and Genealogical Society • 109 S Front St, P.O. Box 11 • Virginia, IL 62691 • (217) 452-7977 • http://www.rootsweb.com/~ilcchgs/

Virginia Memorial Public Library • 100 N Main St • Virginia, IL 62691-1364 • (217) 452-3846

Volo
Volo Antique Auto Museum and Village • 27582 Volo Village Rd • Volo, IL 60073 • (815) 385-3644 • http://www.volocars.com

Wadsworth
Newport Township Historical Society • Historical Museum, Wadsworth Rd, P.O. Box 98 • Wadsworth, IL 60083-0098 • (847) 623-0939

Walnut
Walnut Public Library • Heaton & Main Sts, P.O. Box 728 • Walnut, IL 61376 • (815) 379-2159 • http://www.villageofwalnut.com/library.htm

Waltonville
Prairie Historians • P.O. Box 301 • Waltonville, IL 62894

Warren
Warren Township Public Library • 210 Burnett Ave, P.O. Box 427 • Warren, IL 61087-0427 • (815) 745-2076

Warrenville
Warrenville Historical Society • 3 South 530 2nd St, P.O. Box 311 • Warrenville, IL 60555-0311 • (630) 393-3335

Warrenville Public Library District • 28 W 751 Stafford Pl • Warrenville, IL 60555 • (630) 393-1171 • http://www.warrenville.com

Warsaw
Warsaw Historical Society • Historical Museum, 401 Main St • Warsaw, IL 62379 • (217) 256-3382

Warsaw Public Library • 210 N 4th St • Warsaw, IL 62379-1050 • (217) 256-3417

Washington
Washington Historical Society • Zinser House Museum, 105 Zinser Pl, P.O. Box 54 • Washington, IL 61571 • (309) 444-4793

Waterloo
Monroe County Historical Society • Historical Museum, 709 S Church St, P.O. Box 48 • Waterloo, IL 62298-0048 • (618) 939-3088

Morrison-Talbott Library • 219 Park St • Waterloo, IL 62298-1305 • (618) 939-6232 • http://www.waterloolibrary.org

Peterstown Heritage Society • 275 N Main St • Waterloo, IL 62298-1245 • (618) 939-4222

Illinois

Waterman
Clinton Township Public Library • 110 S Elm St, P.O. Box 299 • Waterman, IL 60556-0299 • (815) 264-3339

Watseka
Iroquois County Genealogical Society • Old Courthouse Museum, 103 W Cherry St • Watseka, IL 60970-1524 • (815) 432-2215 • http://www.rootsweb.com/~ilicgs/

Iroquois County Historical Society • Old Courthouse Museum, 103 W Cherry St • Watseka, IL 60970-1524 • (815) 432-2215 • http://www.oldcourthousemuseum.org

Wauconda
Lake County Museum • 27277 N Forest Preserve Dr • Wauconda, IL 60084-2016 • (847) 968-3381 • http://www.lakecountydiscoverymuseum.org

Lake McHenry County Historical Alliance • 27277 N Forest Preserve Rd • Wauconda, IL 60084-2016

Slovak-American International Cultural Foundation • 1000 Brown St • Wauconda, IL 60084 • (847) 426-4396 • http://www.slovakculture.org

Wauconda Township Historical Society • Historical Museum, 711 N Main St, P.O. Box 256 • Wauconda, IL 60084 • (847) 526-9303 • http://www.waucondaarea.info/Wauconda_Township_Historical_Society.htm

Waukegan
Waukegan Historical Society • Haines Museum, 1917 N Sheridan Rd, P.O. Box 857 • Waukegan, IL 60079-0857 • (847) 336-1859 • http://www.waukeganparks.org

Waukegan Public Library • 128 N County St • Waukegan, IL 60085 • (847) 623-2041 • http://www.waukeganpl.org

Waverly
Waverly Genealogical and Historical Society • 157 E Tremont • Waverly, IL 62692-1026 • (217) 435-4961 • http://www.rootsweb.com/~ilmaga/

Wayne City
Wayne City Public Library • 103 E Mill St • Wayne City, IL 62895 • (618) 895-2661

Wenona
Bond Library • 208 S Chestnut St • Wenona, IL 61377 • (815) 853-4665

West Chicago
Kline Creek Farm Museum • 1N600 County Farm Rd • West Chicago, IL 60185 • (630) 876-5900 • http://www.dupageforest.com

West Chicago City Museum • 132 Main St • West Chicago, IL 60185-2835 • (630) 231-3376 • http://www.westchicago.org

West Chicago Historical Society • Kruse House Museum, 527 Main St, P.O. Box 246 • West Chicago, IL 60185 • (708) 231-0564

West Dundee
Dundee Township Historical Society • Historical Museum, 426 Highland Ave • West Dundee, IL 60118 • (847) 428-6996 • http://www.northstarnet.org/dukhome/DTHS

West Frankfort
Frankfort Area Genealogy Society • 1200 E St Louis St, P.O. Box 427 • West Frankfort, IL 62896-0427 • (618) 932-6159

Frankfort Area Historical Society • Historical Museum, 2000 E St Louis St • West Frankfort, IL 62896-1647 • (618) 932-6159

Franklin County Genealogical Society • P.O. Box 524 • West Frankfort, IL 62896

Veterans Depot Museum • 101 W Main St • West Frankfort, IL 62896-3710

West Frankfort Public Library • 402 E Poplar St • West Frankfort, IL 62896 • (618) 932-3313 • www.sirin.lib.il.us/docs/wft/lib/home.html

Westchester
American Historical Society of Germans from Russia, Northern Illinois Chapter • 704 Suffolk Ave • Westchester, IL 60154-2738 • http://www.ahsgr.org/ilnorthe.html

Slovenian Genealogical Society, Illinois Chapter • 1436 Gardner Rd • Westchester, IL 60154 • http://sloveniangenealogy.org/chapters/Illinois.htm

Westchester Historical Society • Historical Museum, 10332 Bond St • Westchester, IL 60154-4361 • (708) 865-1972

Western Springs
Federation of Genealogical Societies • P.O. Box 271 • Western Springs, IL 60558-0271

Flagg Creek Historical Society • P.O. Box 227 • Western Springs, IL 60558

Grand Avenue School Museum • 916 Hillgrove Ave, P.O. Box 139 • Western Springs, IL 60558 • (708) 246-9230

Western Springs Genealogical Society • 4211 Grand Ave, P.O. Box 139 • Western Springs, IL 60558 • (708) 246-9230

Western Springs Historical Society • 4211 Grand Ave, P.O. Box 139 • Western Springs, IL 60558-0139 • (708) 246-9230

Westmont
Westmont Historical Society • Gregg House Museum, 115 S Linden Ave • Westmont, IL 60559 • (630) 964-4174

Westville
Westville Public Library District • 233 S State St, P.O. Box 97 • Westville, IL 61883-0097 • (217) 267-3170

Wheaton
Billy Graham Center • Wheaton College, 500 E College Ave • Wheaton, IL 60187-5593 • (630) 752-5194 • http://www.billygrahamcenter.org/museum

Center for History Museum • 315 W Front St, P.O. Box 373 • Wheaton, IL 60189 • (630) 682-9472 • http://www.wheatonhistory.com

DuPage County Genealogical Society • 1477A Woodcutter, P.O. Box 3 • Wheaton, IL 60189-0003 • (630) 690-6402 • http://www.dcgs.org

DuPage County Historical Museum • 103 E Wesley St • Wheaton, IL 60187 • (630) 582-7343 • http://www.co.dupage.il/museum

DuPage County Historical Society • Historical Museum, 102 E Wesley St • Wheaton, IL 60187-5321 • (630) 682-7343 • http://www.dupageco.org/museum/

First Division Museum at Cantigny • 1s151 Winfield Rd • Wheaton, IL 60187-6097 • (630) 260-8186 • http://www.firstdivisionmuseum.org

Kline Creek Farm Museum • P.O. Box 5000 • Wheaton, IL 60189 • (630) 876-5900 • http://www.dupageforest.com

Robert R McCormick Museum at Cantigny • 1s151 Winfield Rd • Wheaton, IL 60187 • (630) 260-8159 • http://www.cantigny.org

Sons of Union Veterans of the Civil War, Illinois Department • 1271 Exeter Ct • Wheaton, IL 60187 • (630) 668-4887

Wheaton History Center • 606 N Main St, P.O. Box 373 • Wheaton, IL 60189-0373 • (630) 682-9472

Wheaton Public Library • 225 N Cross St • Wheaton, IL 60187-5376 • (630) 668-1374 • http://www.wheaton.lib.il.us

Wheeling
Wheeling Historical Society • Historical Museum, 251 N Wolf Rd, P.O. Box 3 • Wheeling, IL 60090-0003 • (847) 537-0327

White Hall
White Hall Township Library • 119 E Sherman St • White Hall, IL 62092 • (217) 374-6014

Wilmette

Illinois Postal History Society • P.O. Box 546 • Wilmette, IL 60091

Wilmette Historical Society • Historical Museum, 609 Ridge Rd • Wilmette, IL 60091 • (847) 853-7666 • http://www.wilmettehistory.org

Wilmette Public Library District • 1242 Wilmette Ave • Wilmette, IL 60091-2558 • (847) 256-5025 • http://www.wilmette.lib.il.us

Wilmington

Will-Grundy Counties Genealogical Society • c/o Wilmington Public Library, 201 S Kankakee, P.O. Box 24 • Wilmington, IL 60481-0024 • (815) 458-2187 • http://www.wggs.org

Wilmington Area Historical Society • Historical Museum, 104 N Water St, P.O. Box 1 • Wilmington, IL 60481-0001 • (815) 476-6330

Wilmington Public Library District • 201 S Kankakee St • Wilmington, IL 60481-1338 • (815) 476-2834 • http://www.wilmingtonlibrary.org

Winchester

Scott County Historical Society • Historical Museum, P.O. Box 85 • Winchester, IL 62694-0085 • (217) 742-5575

Winchester Public Library • 215 N Main St • Winchester, IL 62694 • (217) 742-3150

Winfield

Kline Creek Farm Museum • 1N600 County Farm Rd • Winfield, IL 60190

Winfield Historical Society • 555 Winfield Rd, P.O. Box 315 • Winfield, IL 60190 • (630) 653-1489

Winfield Public Library • 291 Winfield Rd • Winfield, IL 60190 • (630) 653-7599 • http://www.winfield.lib.il.us

Winnebago

Winnebago Public Library • 210 N Elida St, P.O. Box 536 • Winnebago, IL 61088-0536 • (815) 335-7050 • http://winnebagopubliclibrary.org

Winnetka

North Suburban Genealogical Society • c/o Winnetka Public Library, 768 Oak St • Winnetka, IL 60093-2515 • (847) 446-7220 • http://www.wpld.allibrary.com/nsgs.htm

Winnetka Historical Society • Historical Museum, 411 Linden, P.O. Box 365 • Winnetka, IL 60093 • (847) 501-6025 • http://www.winnetkahistory.org

Winnetka-Northfield Public Library • 768 Oak St • Winnetka, IL 60093 • (847) 446-7220 • http://www.wpld.alibrary.com

Witt

Witt Memorial Public Library • 18 N 2nd St, P.O. Box 442 • Witt, IL 62094-0442 • (217) 594-7333

Wood Dale

Wood Dale Historical Society • Historical Museum, 850 N Wood Dale Rd, P.O. Box 13 • Wood Dale, IL 60191-0013 • (630) 595-8777

Wood Dale Public Library District • 520 N Wood Dale Rd • Wood Dale, IL 60191 • (630) 766-6762 • http://www.wooddale.com

Woodhull

Clover Library District • 440 N Division St, P.O. Box 369 • Woodhull, IL 61490-0369 • (309) 334-2680 • http://www.woodhull.lib.il.us

Woodridge

Woodridge Area Historical Society • Historical Museum, 2628 Mitchell Dr • Woodridge, IL 60517-2929 • (630) 985-9423

Woodstock

Chester Gould-Dick Tracy Museum • 101 N Johnston St, P.O. Box 44 • Woodstock, IL 60098 • (815) 338-8281 • http://www.dicktracymuseum.org

Woodstock Public Library • 414 W Judd • Woodstock, IL 60098-3195 • (815) 338-0542 • http://www.woodstock-il.com

Worth

Worth Park Historical Museum • 11500 S Beloit • Worth, IL 60482 • (708) 448-7080 • http://www.worthparkdistrict.org

Wyanet

Raymond A Sapp Memorial Library • 103 E Main St, P.O. Box 23 • Wyanet, IL 61379-0023 • (815) 699-2342

Wyanet Historical Society • Historical Museum, 109 E Main St, P.O. Box 169 • Wyanet, IL 61379 • (815) 699-2531

Yorkville

Kendal County Historical Museum • N Bridge St, P.O. Box 123 • Yorkville, IL 60560 • (630) 553-6777

Kendall County Genealogical Society • P.O. Box 123 • Yorkville, IL 60560-0123

Kendall County Historical Society • 105 W Center, P.O. Box 123 • Yorkville, IL 60560-0123 • (630) 553-6777

Lyon Farm and Village Museum • Route 71 • Yorkville, IL 61021 • (630) 553-6777

Yorkville Public Library • 902 Game Farm Rd • Yorkville, IL 60560 • (630) 553-4354 • http://www.yorkville.lib.il.us

Zion

Zion Benton Public Library • 2400 Gabriel Ave • Zion, IL 60099-2296 • (847) 872-4680 • http://www.zblibrary.org

Zion Genealogical Society • c/o Zion Benton Public Library, 2400 Gabriel Ave • Zion, IL 60099 • (847) 360-0360 • http://wkkhome.northstarnet.org/zion/

Zion Historical Society • Shiloh House Museum, 1300 Shiloh Blvd, P.O. Box 333 • Zion, IL 60099 • (847) 746-2427

Illinois

Akron
Akron Carnegie Public Library • 204 E Rochester St, P.O. Box 428 • Akron, IN 46910-0428 • (219) 893-4113 • http://www.akron.lib.in.us

Albion
Noble County Genealogical Society • c/o Noble County Public Library, 813 E Main, P.O. Box 162 • Albion, IN 46701 • (219) 636-7197 • http://www.nobgensoc.org

Noble County Historian • P.O. Box 11 • Albion, IN 46701 • (260) 636-7871

Noble County Historical Society • Old Jail Museum, 210 E Main St, P.O. Box 152 • Albion, IN 46701 • (260) 636-3929 • http://www.noblehistoricalsociety.org

Noble County Library • 813 E Main St • Albion, IN 46701 • (260) 636-7197 • http://www.nobleco.lib.in.us

Alexandria
Alexandria-Monroe Public Library • 117 E Church St • Alexandria, IN 46001-2005 • (765) 724-2196 • http://www.alex.lib.in.us

Alexandria-Monroe Township Genealogy Society • 302 W Tyler St • Alexandria, IN 46001

Alexandria-Monroe Township Historical Society • Historical Museum, 313 N Harrison St • Alexandria, IN 46001-1624 • http://www.rootsweb.com/~inmadiso/alexandria.htm

Madison County Historian • 7117 North 100 West • Alexandria, IN 46001 • (765) 683-0052

Anderson
Anderson Public Library • 111 E 12th St • Anderson, IN 46016-2701 • (765) 641-2456 • http://www.andersonlibrary.net

Gruenewald Historic House Museum • 626 Main St • Anderson, IN 46016 • (765) 648-6875

Gustav Jeeninga Museum of Bible and Near Eastern Studies • 1100 E 5th St • Anderson, IN 46012 • (765) 641-4132 • http://www.anderson.edu/campus/museum/

Historical Military Armor Museum • 2330 Crystal St • Anderson, IN 46015 • (765) 649-8265

Indiana Genealogical Society • P.O. Box 618 • Anderson, IN 46015-0852

Madison County Historical Society • Historical Museum, 15 W 11th St, P.O. Box 523 • Anderson, IN 46015 • (765) 683-0052 • http://www.rootsweb.com/~inmadiso/mchs.htm#top

Robert A Nicholson Library • Anderson University, 1100 E 5th St • Anderson, IN 46012 • (765) 641-4280 • http://bones.anderson.edu

US Merchant Marine Museum • 2418 Poplar St • Anderson, IN 46012 • (765) 643-6305

Andrews
Andrews Dallas Township Public Library • 30 E Madison St, P.O. Box 367 • Andrews, IN 46702-0307 • (260) 786-3574

Angola
Angola-Carnegie Public Library • 322 S Wayne St • Angola, IN 46703 • (260) 665-3362 • http://www.steuben.lib.in.us

General Lewis B Hershey Museum • Hershey Hall, 1 University Ave • Angola, IN 46703 • (219) 665-4103 • http://www.tristate.edu

Hartman House Museum • 901 W Maumee St • Angola, IN 46703

Steuben County Genealogical Society • c/o Angola-Carnegie Public Library, 322 S Wayne St • Angola, IN 46703 • (219) 665-3362

Steuben County Historian • 127 Powers St • Angola, IN 46703 • (260) 665-2434

Steuben County Historical Society • Cline Memorial House Museum, 313 E Maumee St • Angola, IN 46703 • http://www.rootsweb.ancestry.com/~insteube/

Arcadia
Arcadia Heritage Center Museum • 107 W South St, P.O. Box 212 • Arcadia, IN 46030 • (317) 984-4888

Atlanta
Hamilton North Public Library-Atlanta Branch • 100 S Walnut St, P.O. Box 68 • Atlanta, IN 46031-0068 • (765) 292-2521

Tipton County Historical Society • 4161 S 200 E • Atlanta, IN 46031 • (765) 292-2451

Attica
Attica Public Library • 305 S Perry St • Attica, IN 47918-1494 • (765) 764-4194 • http://www.attica.lib.in.us

Auburn
Auburn Cord Duesenberg Museum • 1600 S Wayne St • Auburn, IN 46706 • (260) 925-1444 • http://www.acdmuseum.org

DeKalb County Genealogy Society • c/o Eckhart Public Library, 603 S Jackson St, P.O. Box 6085 • Auburn, IN 46706 • (260) 925-2414 • http://www.rootsweb.com/~indkigs/main_page.html

DeKalb County Historian • P.O. Box 686 • Auburn, IN 46706-0686 • (219) 925-4560

DeKalb County Historical Society • P.O. Box 686 • Auburn, IN 46706-0686 • (260) 925-4560

Eckhart Public Library • 603 S Jackson St • Auburn, IN 46706-2298 • (260) 925-2414 • http://www.epl.lib.in.us

National Military History Center • 5634 CR 11A, P.O. Box 1 • Auburn, IN 46706 • (260) 927-9144 • http://www.militaryhistorycenter.org

William H Willenar Genealogy Center • 700 S Jackson St • Auburn, IN 46706 • (219) 925-2414

Aurora
Aurora Public Library District • 414 2nd St • Aurora, IN 47001-1384 • (812) 926-0646 • http://www.eapld.org

Hillforest Historical Foundation • Hillforest House Museum, 213 5th St, P.O. Box 127 • Aurora, IN 47001 • (812) 926-0087 • http://www.hillforest.org

Avon
Avon-Washington Township Public Library • 498 N State Rd 267 • Avon, IN 46123 • (317) 272-4818 • http://www.avonlibrary.org

Bainbridge
Putnam County Genealogical Club • RR 1, Box 28 • Bainbridge, IN 46105

Putnam County Historian • 4565 E 650 N • Bainbridge, IN 46105 • (765) 522-6869

Bargersville
Indian Wars Museum • P.O. Box 635 • Bargersville, IN 46106

Batesville
Batesville Area Historical Society • c/o Batesville Memorial Public Library, 131 N Walnut St • Batesville, IN 47006 • (812) 934-4706

Batesville Memorial Public Library • 131 N Walnut St • Batesville, IN 47006 • (812) 934-4706 • http://www.bmpl.cnz.com

Tri-County Genealogical Society • 23184 Pocket Rd W, P.O. Box 118 • Batesville, IN 47006-0118 • (812) 934-2278

Battle Ground
Historic Prophetstown Museum • 3549 Prophetstown Tr, P.O. Box 331 • Battle Ground, IN 47902 • (765) 567-4700 • http://www.prophetstown.org

Indiana

Battle Ground, cont.
Tippecanoe Battlefield Museum • Tippecanoe & Railroad Sts, P.O. Box 225 • Battle Ground, IN 47920 • (765) 567-2147 • http://www.tcha.mus.in.us

Bedford
Bedford Public Library • 1323 K St • Bedford, IN 47421 • (812) 275-4471 • http://www.bedlib.org

Land of Limestone Museum • 405 I Street, P.O. Box 455 • Bedford, IN 47421 • (812) 279-8126

Lawrence County Historian • 1116 16th St, P.O. Box 1193 • Bedford, IN 47421 • (812) 275-7651

Lawrence County Historical and Genealogical Society • Historical Museum, 929 15th St • Bedford, IN 47421 • (812) 278-8575 • http://www.rootsweb.com/~Einlawren/lchgsbooks.html

Lawrence County Historical Museum • Courthouse Basement • Bedford, IN 47421 • (812) 275-4141

Lawrence County Historical Society, Jim Guthrie Chapter • 1617 M Street • Bedford, IN 47421 • (812) 279-6555

Beech Grove
Beech Grove Historical Society • 308 N 20th Ave • Beech Grove, IN 46107 • (317) 787-9918

Beech Grove Public Library • 1102 W Main St • Beech Grove, IN 46107 • (317) 788-4203 • http://www.bgpl.lib.in.us

Berne
Berne Public Library • 166 N Sprunger St • Berne, IN 46711 • (260) 589-2809 • http://www.bernepl.lib.in.us

Swiss Heritage Society • Heritage Village and Museum, 1200 Swiss Wy, P.O. Box 88 • Berne, IN 46711 • (219) 589-8007 • http://www.swissheritage.org

Beverly Shores
Beverly Shores Historical Society • P.O. Box 242 • Beverly Shores, IN 46301-0242

Heritage Society of Northwest Indiana • South Shore Line Passenger Depot Museum, 525 Broadway, P.O. Box 295 • Beverly Shores, IN 46301 • (219) 926-3669

Bicknell
Bicknell-Vigo Township Public Library • 201 W 2nd St • Bicknell, IN 47512-2109 • (812) 735-2317 • http://bicknell-vigo.lib.in.us

Bloomfield
Bloomfield Carnegie Public Library • 125 S Franklin St • Bloomfield, IN 47424-1406 • (812) 384-4125 • http://www.bloomfield.lib.in.us

Greene County Genealogical Society • P.O. Box 164 • Bloomfield, IN 47424-0164 • http://www.greencountyindiana.com

Greene County Historical Society • 27 S Washington St, P.O. Box 301 • Bloomfield, IN 47424-0301 • (812) 384-8155 • http://greenecountyindiana.com

Bloomington
African-American Historical and Genealogical Society • 502 Clover Terr • Bloomington, IN 47404-1809

American Historical Association • Indiana University, 914 Atwater St • Bloomington, IN 47405 • (812) 855-7609

Col William Jones House Museum • 1208 E Wylie St • Bloomington, IN 47401

Creole Institute • Indiana Univ, Ballentine 604 • Bloomington, IN 47405 • (812) 855-4988 • http://www.indiana.edu/~creole

Dolan Historical Society • c/o New Prospect Baptist Church, 6055 N Old State Rd 37 • Bloomington, IN 47401

Elizabeth Sage Historic Costume Collection Museum • Memorial Hall E 232, 1021 E 3rd St • Bloomington, IN 47405-7005 • (812) 855-4627

Indiana University Bloomington Library • 1320 E 10th St, Main Library 299D • Bloomington, IN 47405-1801 • (812) 855-8028 • http://www.libraries.iub.edu

Indiana University Folklore Institute • 504 N Fess • Bloomington, IN 47408-3890 • (812) 855-1027 • http://www.indiana.edu/~folklore

Indiana University Museum • Indiana Univ, 209 Student Bldg • Bloomington, IN 47405 • (812) 337-7224

Mathews Museum • 406 N Indiana Ave • Bloomington, IN 47405 • (812) 855-6873 • http://www.indiana.edu/~mathews/new/exhibits/

Monroe County Historian • 4791 Conti St • Bloomington, IN 47404 • (812) 876-1212

Monroe County Historical and Genealogical Society • Historical Museum, 202 E 6th St • Bloomington, IN 47408 • (812) 332-2517 • http://www.monroehistory.org

Monroe County Public Library • 303 E Kirkwood Ave • Bloomington, IN 47408 • (812) 349-3050 • http://www.monroe.lib.in.us

Organization of American Historians • 112 N Bryan St • Bloomington, IN 47408-4199 • (812) 855-2816 • http://www.indiana.edu/~oah/

William Hammond Mathers Museum • 416 N Indiana Ave • Bloomington, IN 47405 • (812) 855-6873 • http://www.indiana.edu/~mathers/

Wylie House Museum • 307 E 2nd St • Bloomington, IN 47401 • (812) 855-6224 • http://www.indiana.edu/~libwylie

Bluffton
Blackford-Wells Genealogy Society • P.O. Box 54 • Bluffton, IN 46714-0054 • http://www.rootsweb.com/~inwells/society.html

Twin Oaks Genealogy • 1371 East 400 North • Bluffton, IN 46714

Wells County Historian • 5211 SE State Rd 116 • Bluffton, IN 46714 • (260) 824-0214

Wells County Historical Society • Historical Museum, 420 W Market St, P.O. Box 143 • Bluffton, IN 46714-0143 • (219) 824-9956 • http://wchs-museum.org

Wells County Public Library • 200 W Washington St • Bluffton, IN 46714 • (260) 824-1612 • http://www.wellscolibrary.org

Boggstown
Joseph Boggs Society for Historic Preservation • P.O. Box 72 • Boggstown, IN 46110

Boonville
Boonville-Warrick County Public Library • 611 W Main St • Boonville, IN 47601-1544 • (812) 897-1500

Warrick County Historical Society • Historical Museum, 217 S 1st St, P.O. Box 581 • Boonville, IN 47601-0581 • (812) 897-3100

Warrick County Museum • 217 N 1st St, P.O. Box 581 • Boonville, IN 47601 • (812) 897-3100

Boswell
Boswell & Grant Township Public Library • 101 S Main St, P.O. Box 315 • Boswell, IN 47921-0315 • (765) 869-5428 • http://www.mwprairienet.lib.in.us/boswell-lib/

Bourbon
Bourbon Public Library • 307 N Main St • Bourbon, IN 46504 • (574) 342-5655 • http://www.bourbon.lib.in.us

Marshall County Genealogical Society • 3383 E Eights Rd • Bourbon, IN 46504

Brazil
Brazil Public Library • 204 N Walnut St • Brazil, IN 47834 • (812) 448-1981 • http://www.brazil.lib.in.us

Clay County Historical Society • Historical Museum, 100 E National Ave • Brazil, IN 47834 • (812) 446-4036

Bremen
Bremen Public Library • 304 N Jackson, P.O. Box 130 • Bremen, IN 46506-0130 • (574) 546-2849 • http://www.bremen.lib.in.us

Bristol
Bonneyville Mill Museum • 53373 Cty Rd 131 • Bristol, IN 46507 • (574) 825-9324 • http://www.elkhartcountyparks.org

Bristol-Washington Township Public Library • 505 W Vistula St • Bristol, IN 46507 • (574) 848-7458 • http://www.bristol.lib.in.us

Elkhart County Historical Society • Historical Museum, 304 W Vistula, P.O. Box 343 • Bristol, IN 46507 • (219) 848-4322 • http://www.elkhartcountyparks.org

Brook
Brook-Iroquois Township Carnegie Public Library • 100 W Main, P.O. Box 155 • Brook, IN 47922-0155 • (219) 275-2471 • http://www.brook.lib.in.us

George Ade House Museum • Hwy 16, P.O. Box 221 • Brook, IN 47922 • (219) 275-6161

Brookston
Brookston-Prairie Township Public Library • 111 W 2nd St • Brookston, IN 47923 • (765) 563-6511 • http://www.dcwi.com/~bptpl/welcome.html

Brookville
Brookville Town-Township Library • 919 Main St, P.O. Box 402 • Brookville, IN 47012-8217 • (765) 647-4031 • http://www.wvcl.org

Franklin County Historian • 11043 State Rd 1 • Brookville, IN 47012 • (765) 647-4763

Franklin County Historical Society • Franklin County Seminary Museum, 5th & Mill Sts, P.O. Box 342 • Brookville, IN 47012 • (765) 647-5413 • http://www.franklinchs.com

Brownsburg
Brownsburg Public Library • 450 S Jefferson St • Brownsburg, IN 46112-1310 • (317) 852-3167 • http://www.brownsburg.lib.in.us

Brownstown
Brownstown Public Library • 120 E Spring St • Brownstown, IN 47220-1546 • (812) 358-2853 • http://www.brownstown.lib.in.us

Jackson County Genealogical Society • 415 S Poplar St • Brownstown, IN 47220-1939 • (812) 358-2118 • http://www.rootsweb.com/~injackso/resources/gensoc.htm

Jackson County Historian • 439 East 100 South • Brownstown, IN 47220-9587 • (812) 522-3412

Jackson County Historical Museum • 3492 E Base Road • Brownstown, IN 47220

Jackson County Historical Society • 401 E Walnut St, P.O. Box 215 • Brownstown, IN 47220 • (812) 358-2182

Bryant
Balbec Historical Club • RR2, Box 65 • Bryant, IN 47326 • (219) 731-7786

Buckskin
Henager Memories and Nostalgia Museum • Hwy 57 • Buckskin, IN 47613 • (812) 795-2230

Butler
Butler Public Library • 340 S Broadway • Butler, IN 46721 • (260) 868-2351 • http://www.butler.lib.in.us

Dekalb County Historical Society • Historical Museum, 201 E Main St • Butler, IN 46721 • (260) 868-0979

Cambridge City
Cambridge City Public Library • 33 W Main St • Cambridge City, IN 47327 • (765) 478-3335 • http://www.cclib.lib.in.us

Historic Landmarks Foundation • Huddleston Farmhouse Inn Museum, 838 National Rd, P.O. Box 284 • Cambridge City, IN 47327-9776 • (765) 478-3172 • http://www.historiclandmarks.org

Upper Whitewater Historical Association • 302 E Main St • Cambridge City, IN 47327

Western Wayne Heritage • 800 National Rd, P.O. Box 254 • Cambridge City, IN 47327 • (765) 478-5993

Camby
Morgan County Historian • 5605 Donald Court E • Camby, IN 46113 • (317) 831-3319

Camden
Camden-Jackson Township Public Library • 183 W Main St, P.O. Box 24 • Camden, IN 46917-0024 • (574) 686-2120

Canaan
Jefferson County Genealogical Society • P.O. Box 4 • Canaan, IN 47224

Cannelton
Cannelton Public Library • 210 S 8th St • Cannelton, IN 47520 • (812) 547-6028

Historic Cannelton • P.O. Box 223 • Cannelton, IN 47520 • (812) 547-3190

Perry County Old Courthouse Museum • 7th St, P.O. Box 36 • Cannelton, IN 47520 • (812) 547-3190

Carbon
Mansfield Mill State Historic Site Museum • RR1, Box 146C • Carbon, IN 47837 • (765) 344-0741 • http://www.countyhistory.com/parke/mill.htm

Carmel
Carmel Clay Historical Society • Historical Museum, 211 1st St SW • Carmel, IN 46032 • (317) 846-7117 • http://www.carmelclayhistory.org

Carmel Clay Public Library • 55 4th Ave SE • Carmel, IN 46032 • (317) 844-3362 • http://www.carmel.lib.in.us

Museum of Miniature Houses • 111 E Main St • Carmel, IN 46032 • (317) 575-9465 • http://www.museumofminiatures.org

Carthage
Henry Henley Public Library • 102 N Main St, P.O. Box 35 • Carthage, IN 46115-0035 • (765) 565-6631

Cedar Lake
Cedar Lake Historical Association • Lake of the Red Cedars Museum, 7900 Constitution Ave, P.O. Box 421 • Cedar Lake, IN 46303 • (219) 374-6157

Center Point
Clay County Genealogical Society • 309 Main St, P.O. Box 56 • Center Point, IN 47840-0056 • (812) 835-5005 • http://www.ccgsilib.org

Clay County Historian • 2544 N County Rte 200 E • Center Point, IN 47840 • (812) 835-4891

Centerville
Centerville and Center Township Public Library • 115 W Main St • Centerville, IN 47330-1299 • (765) 855-5223 • http://www.cctpl.lib.in.us

Historic Centerville • 1811 Courthouse Museum, P.O. Box 73 • Centerville, IN 47330-0073 • (765) 855-5387

Charlestown
Charlestown-Clark County Public Library • 51 Clark Rd • Charlestown, IN 47111-1997 • (812) 256-3337 • http://www.clarkco.lib.in.us

Indiana

Charlestown, cont.
Clark County Historian • 4807 Stacy Rd • Charlestown, IN 47111 • (812) 256-4685

Grant Historical Society • Thomas Downs House Museum, 1045 Main St, P.O. Box 423 • Charlestown, IN 47111 • (812) 256-5777

Chesterfield
Museum of Wings and Things • P.O. Box 222 • Chesterfield, IN 46017-0222 • (765) 378-1055

Chesterton
Duneland Historical Society • Historical Museum, P.O. Box 809 • Chesterton, IN 46304 • (219) 921-0963

Heritage Society of Northwest Indiana • P.O. Box 508 • Chesterton, IN 46304-0508

Westchester Public Library • 200 W Indiana Ave • Chesterton, IN 46304-3122 • (219) 926-7696 • http://wpl.lib.in.us

Westchester Township History Museum • 700 W Porter Ave • Chesterton, IN 46304 • (219) 983-9715 • http://wpl.lib.in.us/museum

Churubusco
Churubusco Public Library • 116 N Mulberry St • Churubusco, IN 46723 • (260) 693-6466 • http://buscolibrary.whitleynet.org

Clarksville
Clarksville History Committee • Historical Museum, 2000 W Broadway • Clarksville, IN 47129 • (812) 288-7155

Clayton
Clayton-Liberty Township Public Library • 5199 Iowa St, P.O. Box E • Clayton, IN 46118-4905 • (317) 539-2991 • http://personalpages.tds.net/~cltpl/

Clinton
Clinton Public Library • 313 S 4th St • Clinton, IN 47842-2398 • (765) 832-8349 • http://www.clintonpl.lib.in.us

Wea Indian Tribe of Indiana • 643 Mulberry St • Clinton, IN 47842 • http://www.weaindiantribe.com

Coatesville
Coatesville Public Library • 4928 Milton St, P.O. Box 147 • Coatesville, IN 46121-0147 • (765) 386-2355

Colfax
Colfax Public Library • 207 S Clark St, P.O. Box 308 • Colfax, IN 46035-0308 • (765) 324-2915 • http://www.colfax.lib.in.us

Columbia City
Genealogical Society of Whitley County • P.O. Box 224 • Columbia City, IN 46725-0224 • http://home.whitleynet.org/genealogy/

Peabody Public Library • 1160 E Hwy 205, P.O. Box 406 • Columbia City, IN 46725-0406 • (260) 244-5541 • http://www.ppl.lib.in.us

Whitley County Historian • 403 Blue River Ct • Columbia City, IN 46725-1502 • (260) 244-6372

Whitley County Historical Society • Historical Museum, 108 W Jefferson St • Columbia City, IN 46725 • (219) 244-6372 • http://www.whitleynet.org/historical/

Columbus
Atterbury-Bakalar Air Museum • 4742 Ray Boll Blvd • Columbus, IN 47203 • (812) 372-4356 • http://www.atterburybakalarairmuseum.org

Bartholomew County Genealogical Society • 4432 Carya Square, P.O. Box 2455 • Columbus, IN 47202-2455 • (812) 342-4336

Bartholomew County Historian • 1130 Franklin • Columbus, IN 47201 • (812) 379-5620

Bartholomew County Historical Society • McEwen-Samuels-Marr House Museum, 524 3rd St • Columbus, IN 47201 • (812) 372-3541 • http://www.barthist.com

Bartholomew County Public Library • 536 5th St • Columbus, IN 47201-6225 • (812) 379-1255 • http://www.barth.lib.in.us

Connersville
Blommel Historic Auto Collection • 427 E County Rd 215 S • Connersville, IN 47331 • (317) 825-9259

Fayette County Historian • 660 S County Rd 450E • Connersville, IN 47331 • (765) 825-9262

Fayette County Historical Museum • 103 S Vine St • Connersville, IN 47331 • (765) 825-0946

Fayette County Public Library • 828 Grand Ave • Connersville, IN 47331 • (765) 827-0883 • http://www.fcplibrary.com

Heritage of Fayette County • P.O. Box 39 • Connersville, IN 47331

Historic Connersville • Canal House Museum, 111 E 4th St, P.O. Box 197 • Connersville, IN 47331 • (765) 825-1523

Whitewater Valley Genealogical Association • c/o Fayette County Public Library, 828 Grand Ave • Connersville, IN 47331 • (765) 827-0883 • http://www.rootsweb.com/~inwvga

Whitewater Valley Railroad Museum • P.O. Box 406 • Connersville, IN 47331 • (765) 925-2054 • http://www.whitewatervalleyrr.com

Corydon
Corydon Capitol Historic Site Museum • 126 E Walnut St • Corydon, IN 47112 • (812) 738-4890

Governor Hendricks Headquarters Museum • 202 E Walnut St • Corydon, IN 47112 • (812) 738-4890

Harrison County Historian • 161 Ponder Ln NE • Corydon, IN 47112 • (812) 738-3570

Harrison County Historical Society • 117 W Beaver St • Corydon, IN 47112

Harrison County Public Library • 105 N Capitol Ave • Corydon, IN 47112 • (812) 738-4110 • http://www.hcpl.lib.in.us

Posey House Museum • 225 Oak St • Corydon, IN 47112 • (812) 738-6921

Covington
Covington & Veedersburg Public Library • 622 5th St • Covington, IN 47932 • (765) 793-2572 • http://www.covingtonlibrary.org

Crawfordsville
Ben-Hur Museum-General Lew Wallace Study Museum • 501 W Pike St • Crawfordsville, IN 47933 • (765) 362-5769

Carnegie Museum of Montgomery County • 222 S Washington St • Crawfordsville, IN 47933 • (765) 362-4618 • http://www.dcpl.lib.in.us/carnegie

Crawfordsville District Public Library • 222 S Washington St • Crawfordsville, IN 47933 • (765) 362-2242 • http://www.cdpl.lib.in.us

Genealogical Society of Montgomery County • c/o Crawfordsville District Public Library, 222 S Washington St • Crawfordsville, IN 47933 • (765) 362-2242

General Lew Wallace Museum • 200 Wallace Ave, P.O. Box 662 • Crawfordsville, IN 47933 • (765) 362-5769 • http://www.ben-hur.com

Lane Place Historic Home Museum • 212 S Water St, P.O. Box 217 • Crawfordsville, IN 47933 • (765) 362-3416 • http://www.lane_mchs.org

Montgomery County Historical Society • Historical Museum, 212 S Water St, P.O. Box 127 • Crawfordsville, IN 47933 • (765) 362-3416 • http://www.lane-mchs.org

Montgomery County Historical Society, Genealogy Section • c/o Crawfordsville District Public Library, 222 S Washington St • Crawfordsville, IN 47933 • (765) 362-2242

Old Jail Museum • 225 N Washington • Crawfordsville, IN 47933 • (765) 362-5222 • http://www.crawfordsville.org/jail.html

Ropkey Armor Museum • 5649 E 150 N • Crawfordsville, IN 47933 • (317) 295-9295 • http://www.ropkeyarmormuseum.com

Who's Your Ancestor Genealogical Society • c/o Crawfordsville District Public Library, 222 S Washington St • Crawfordsville, IN 47933 • (317) 362-9493

Crown Point

Crown Point Community Library • 214 S Court St • Crown Point, IN 46307-3975 • (219) 663-0270 • http://www.icongrp.com/~refcpcl

Lake County Historical Museum • Courthouse Sq • Crown Point, IN 46307 • (219) 662-3975 • http://www.crownpoint.net

Lake County Historical Society • Historical Museum, Courthouse Sq, Ste 202 • Crown Point, IN 46410 • (219) 662-3975 • http://www.crownpoint.net/museum.htm

Lake Court House Foundation • Courthouse Square • Crown Point, IN 46307 • (219) 663-0660

Old Homestead Museum • 227 S Court St • Crown Point, IN 46307

Culver

Antiquarian and Historical Society of Culver Lake Maxinkuckee • 1275 E Shore Dr • Culver, IN 46511 • (219) 842-3940

Culver-Union Township Public Library • 107 N Main St • Culver, IN 46511 • (574) 842-2941 • http://www.culver.lib.in.us

Dale

Dr Ted's Musical Marvels Museum • 11896 South US 231 • Dale, IN 47523 • (812) 937-4250 • http://www.drteds.com

Lincoln Heritage Public Library • 105 N Wallace St, P.O. Box 784 • Dale, IN 47523 • (812) 937-7170 • http://www.lincolnheritage.lib.in.us

Daleville

Daleville Historical Society • P.O. Box 586 • Daleville, IN 47334

Dana

Ernie Pyle State Historic Site Museum • 120 W Briarwood Ave, P.O. Box 338 • Dana, IN 47847 • (765) 665-3633 • http://www.in.gov/ism/historicsites/erniepyle/historic.asp

Danville

County Seat Genealogy Society • 52 W Broadway • Danville, IN 46122

Danville Public Library • 101 S Indiana St • Danville, IN 46122-1809 • (317) 745-2604 • http://www.dpl.lib.in.us/genealogy.html

Hendricks County Genealogical Society • c/o Danville Public Library, 101 S Indiana St • Danville, IN 46122 • (317) 745-2604

Hendricks County Historical Society • Historical Museum, 170 S Washington St, P.O. Box 226 • Danville, IN 46122 • (317) 718-6158

Illiana Genealogical and Historical Society • 215 W North St, P.O. Box 207 • Danville, IN 61834-0207 • (217) 431-8733 • http://www.danvillevirtual.com/vcclients/danville/IllianaGene/

Darlington

Darlington Public Library • 203 Main St, P.O. Box 248 • Darlington, IN 47940-0248 • (765) 794-4813 • http://www.crawfordsville.org

De Motte

Jasper County Public Library-DeMotte Branch • 901 Birch St SW, P.O. Box 16 • De Motte, IN 46310-0016 • (219) 987-2221

Decatur

Adams County Historian • 6929 N Piqua Rd • Decatur, IN 46733 • (260) 724-1187

Adams County Historical Museum • 515 W Jefferson • Decatur, IN 46733 • (219) 724-2341

Adams County Historical Society • Historical Museum, 420 W Monroe St, P.O. Box 262 • Decatur, IN 46733 • (219) 724-2341

Decatur Public Library • 128 S 3rd St • Decatur, IN 46733-1691 • (260) 724-2605 • http://www2.decaturpl.lib.in.us

Delphi

Carroll County Historian • 1512 Old Camden Rd • Delphi, IN 46923 • (765) 564-3634

Carroll County Historical Society • Historical Museum, 101 W Main St, P.O. Box 277 • Delphi, IN 46923-0277 • (765) 564-3152 • http://www.carrollcountymuseum.org

Delphi Public Library • 222 E Main St • Delphi, IN 46923 • (765) 564-2929 • http://www.carlnet.org/dpl/

Wabash & Erie Canal Museum • 1030 N Washington St • Delphi, IN 46923 • (765) 564-6572

Demotte

Demotte Historical Society • P.O. Box 405 • Demotte, IN 46310

Dolan

Dolan Area Historical Society • New Prospect Baptist Church, 6055 N Old State Rd 37 • Dolan, IN 47401 • (812) 334-1886

Donaldson

Gerald J Ball Library • Ancilla College, 9601 S Union Rd, P.O. Box 1 • Donaldson, IN 46513 • (574)936-8898 • http://www.ancilla.edu/library

Dublin

Dublin Public Library • 2249 E Cumberland, P.O. Box 188 • Dublin, IN 47355-0188 • (765) 478-6206

Dugger

Dugger Coal Museum • 8178 E Main St, P.O. Box 501 • Dugger, IN 47848

Dyer

Dyer Historical Society • Historical Museum, Dyer Town Hall, 1 Town Sq • Dyer, IN 46311 • (219) 865-6108 • http://www.dyeronline.com/history/

Earl Park

Earl Park Public Library • 102 E 5th St, P.O. Box 97 • Earl Park, IN 47942-0097 • (219) 474-6932 • http://www.mwprairienet.lib.in.us/Social_Services/eplib.html

York Township Public Library • 8908 West 845 North • Earl Park, IN 47942-8701

East Chicago

East Chicago Historical Society • c/o East Chicago Public Library, 2401 E Columbus Dr • East Chicago, IN 46312 • (219) 397-2453

East Chicago Public Library & History Room • 2401 E Columbus Dr • East Chicago, IN 46312-2998 • (219) 397-2453 • http://www.ecpl.org

Marktown Preservation Society • 405 Prospect • East Chicago, IN 46312

Edinburg

Edinburg Wright-Hageman Public Library • 119 W Main Cross • Edinburg, IN 46124 • (812) 526-5487 • http://www.edinburgh.lib.in.us

Camp Atterbury Museum • Bldg 427 on Egglestone St, P.O. Box 5000 • Edinburgh, IN 46124 • (812) 526-1744 • http://www.campatterbury.org/post_museum.htm

Edinburgh Public Library • 119 W Main Cross St • Edinburgh, IN 46124-1499 • (812) 526-5487 • http://www.edinburgh.lib.in.us

Pow-Wow Museum • 109 E Main Cross • Edinburgh, IN 46124 • (812) 526-8454

Elberfield

Henager's Memories & Nostalgia Museum • 10001 Hwy 57 • Elberfield, IN 46313 • (812) 795-2230

Elkhart

CTS-Turner Museum • 905 N West Blvd • Elkhart, IN 46514-1875 • (219) 293-7511 • http://www.cts.com

Indiana

Elkhart, cont.

Elkhart County Genealogical Society • 1812 Jeanwood Dr, P.O. Box 1031 • Elkhart, IN 46515-1031 • (219) 522-4492 • http://www.rootsweb.com/~inelkhar/ecgs.htm

Elkhart Public Library • 300 S 2nd St • Elkhart, IN 46516-3184 • (574) 522-3333 • http://www.elkhart.lib.in.us

Jimtown Historical Museum • 59710 Cty Rd 3 South • Elkhart, IN 46517 • (219) 522-3362

Jimtown Historical Society • 59312 Hoover Ave • Elkhart, IN 46517-2446

National New York Central Railroad Museum • 721 S Main St, P.O. Box 1708 • Elkhart, IN 46515 • (574) 294-3001 • http://www.nyermuseum.org

Pennsylvania Deutch Society • 59549 CR 13 S • Elkhart, IN 46517-3501

Ruthmere Historic Home Museum • 302 E Beardsley Ave • Elkhart, IN 46514 • (574) 264-0330 • http://www.ruthmere.org

RV/MH Heritage Foundation • Historical Museum, 21565 Executive Pkwy • Elkhart, IN 46516-3369 • (219) 293-2344 • http://www.rv-mh-hall-of-fame.org

Elwood

Elwood Pipecreek Genealogical Society • c/o North Madison County Public Library, 1600 Main St • Elwood, IN 46036 • (765) 552-5001 • http://www.freewebs.com/genealogysocietyyelwoodindiana/

Elwood Pipecreek Historical Society • c/o Elwood Public Library, 1600 Main St • Elwood, IN 46036-2023 • (765) 552-5462

North Madison County Public Library System • 1600 Main St • Elwood, IN 46036-1598 • (765) 552-5001 • http://www.elwood.lib.in.us

English

Crawford County Public Library • 203 Indiana Ave, P.O. Box 159 • English, IN 47118-0159 • (812) 338-2606 • http://www.crawfordpublic.lib.in.us

Evansville

Angel Mounds State Historic Site Library • 8215 Pollack Ave • Evansville, IN 47715 • (812) 853-3956 • http://www.angelmounds.org

Canal Society of Indiana • P.O. Box 40087 • Evansville, IN 46804 • (219) 432-0279 • http://user.centralnet.net/zepp/Canal.html

David L Rice Library - Special Collections • Univ of Southern Indiana, 8600 University Blvd • Evansville, IN 47712-3596 • (812) 464-1907 • http://www.usi.edu/library/library.asp

Evansville African American Museum • 579 S Garvin St, P.O. Box 3124 • Evansville, IN 46804 • (812) 423-5188 • http://www.evansvillecvb.org

Evansville Museum of Arts and Science • 411 SE Riverside Dr • Evansville, IN 47713 • (812) 425-2406 • http://www.emuseum.org

Evansville-Vanderburgh County Public Library • 22 SE 5th St • Evansville, IN 47708-1604 • (812) 428-8218 • http://www.evpl.org

Museum of Brewery Families of Southern Indiana • 1302 SE 1st St • Evansville, IN 47713 • (812) 422-8596 • http://www.evansvillebrewerymuseum.org

Old Vanderburg County Courthouse Museum • 4th & Vine Sts • Evansville, IN 46804

Reitz Home Museum • 224 SE 1st St, P.O. Box 1322 • Evansville, IN 47706 • (812) 426-1871 • http://www.reitzhome.evansville.net

Southwestern Indiana Historical Society • 435 S Spring St • Evansville, IN 47714-1550 • (812) 477-6777

Tri-State Genealogical Society • c/o Willard Library, 21 1st Ave • Evansville, IN 47710-1212 • (812) 425-4309 • http://www.rootsweb.com/~intsgs/

Vanderburgh County Historical Society • Historical Museum, 201 NW 4th St, Rm 105, P.O. Box 2626 • Evansville, IN 47728-0626

Warrick County Historian • 6000 Lincoln Ave • Evansville, IN 47715 • (812) 476-2604

Willard Library - Regional Family History Center • 21 N 1st Ave • Evansville, IN 47710 • (812) 425-4309 • http://www.willard.lib.in.us

Fairmount

Fairmount Historical Museum • 203 E Washington St, P.O. Box 92 • Fairmount, IN 46928 • (765) 948-4555 • http://www.jamesdeanartifacts.com

Fairmount Public Library • 205 S Main St, P.O. Box 27 • Fairmount, IN 46928-0027 • (765) 948-3177 • http://www.fairmountlibrary.com

Farmland

Farmland Public Library • 116 S Main St, P.O. Box 189 • Farmland, IN 47340-0189 • (765) 468-7292

Randolph County Historian • 6094 W 300 N • Farmland, IN 47340 • (765) 468-9616

Ferdinand

Dubois County Genealogical Society • P.O. Box 84 • Ferdinand, IN 47532-0084

Ferdinand Historical Society • Historical Museum, P.O. Box 194 • Ferdinand, IN 47532 • (812) 367-1803 • http://www.ferdinandhistory.org

Fishers

Conner Prairie Library & Museum • Earlham College, 13400 Allisonville Rd • Fishers, IN 46038 • (317) 776-6000 • http://www.connerprairie.org

Flora

Flora-Monroe Public Library • 109 N Center St • Flora, IN 46929-1004 • (574) 967-3912 • http://www.carlnet.org/floralib/

Fort Branch

Fort Branch-Johnson Township Public Library • 107 E Locust St • Fort Branch, IN 47648 • (812) 753-4212 • http://www.library.gibsoncounty.net

Fort Ritner

Fort Ritner Heritage Museum • general delivery • Fort Ritner, IN 47430

Fort Wayne

Achduth Versholom Jewish Museum • 5200 Old Mill Rd • Fort Wayne, IN 46807 • (260) 744-4245

African-American Historical Society • Historical Museum, John Dixie Bldg, 436 E Douglas Ave • Fort Wayne, IN 46802 • (260) 420-0765 • http://www.african-americanfw.com

Allen County Genealogical Society • P.O. Box 12003 • Fort Wayne, IN 46862 • (219) 672-2585 • http://www.ipfw.edu/ipfwhist/historgs/acgsi.htm

Allen County Historian • 13707 Brook Hollow Ct • Fort Wayne, IN 46814 • (260) 625-5987

Allen County Public Library • 900 Library Plaza, P.O. Box 2270 • Fort Wayne, IN 46801-2270 • (260) 421-1235 • http://www.acpl.lib.in.us/genealogy/genealogy.html

Allen County-Fort Wayne Historical Society • History Center Museum, 302 E Berry St, P.O. Box 7003 • Fort Wayne, IN 46802 • (260) 426-2882 • http://www.fwhistorycenter.com

Cathedral Museum • 122 S Clinton St, P.O. Box 10898 • Fort Wayne, IN 46802 • (219) 424-1485

Fort Wayne Firefighters Museum • 226 W Washington Blvd, P.O. Box 10404 • Fort Wayne, IN 46802 • (260) 426-0051

Fort Wayne Railroad Historical Society • P.O. Box 11017 • Fort Wayne, IN 46855 • (219) 493-0765 • http://www.765.org

Greater Fort Wayne Aviation Museum • 3801 W Ferguson Rd, P.O. Box 9573 • Fort Wayne, IN 46899-9573 • (219) 478-7146

Historic Fort Wayne • Historical Museum, 107 S Clinton St • Fort Wayne, IN 46802 • (219) 424-3476

Indiana Genealogical Society • P.O. Box 10507 • Fort Wayne, IN 46852-0507 • (260) 421-5631 • http://www.indgensoc.org

Indiana Jewish Historical Society • 6301 Constitution Dr • Fort Wayne, IN 46804 • (260) 459-6862

Indiana Jewish Historical Society • 203 W Wayne St • Fort Wayne, IN 46802-3610 • (260) 459-6862 • http://www.ijhs.org

Lincoln Museum • 200 E Berry St • Fort Wayne, IN 46802 • (260) 455-3864 • http://www.thelincolnmuseum.org

Macedonian Tribune Museum • 124 W Wayne St • Fort Wayne, IN 46802 • (260) 422-5900 • http://www.macedonian.org

Swinney Homestead Museum • 1424 W Jefferson Blvd • Fort Wayne, IN 46802 • (260) 424-7212

University of Saint Francis Library & Museum • 2701 Spring St • Fort Wayne, IN 46808 • (260) 434-7455 • http://www.sf.edu/library

Veterans Memorial Shrine & Museum • 2122 O'Day Rd • Fort Wayne, IN 46818 • (260) 625-4944

Walter E Helmke Library • Indiana Univ, 2101 E Coliseum Blvd • Fort Wayne, IN 46805 • (219) 481-6514 • http://www.lib.ipfw.indiana.edu

Fountain City
Levi Coffin House Museum • 113 US 27 N, P.O. Box 77 • Fountain City, IN 47341 • (765) 847-2497 • http://www.waynenet.org

Fowler
Benton County Genealogical Society • 711 E 3rd St • Fowler, IN 47944-2343 • (765) 884-1764

Benton County Historian • 711 E 3rd St • Fowler, IN 47944-1343 • (765) 884-1764

Benton County Historical Society • Historical Museum, 404 E 6th St, P.O. Box 341 • Fowler, IN 47944-0341 • (765) 844-1848

Benton County Public Library • 102 N Van Buren Ave • Fowler, IN 47944 • (765) 884-1720 • http://www.bcpl.lib.in.us

Francesville
Francesville-Salem Township Public Library • 201 W Montgomery, P.O. Box 577 • Francesville, IN 47946-0577 • (219) 567-9433 • http://www.pulaski-libraries.lib.in.us

Frankfort
Clinton County Genealogical Society • c/o Frankfort Community Library, 208 W Clinton St • Frankfort, IN 46041 • (765) 654-8746

Clinton County Historian • 4641 E County Rd 250 N • Frankfort, IN 46041-8256 • (765) 659-2030

Clinton County Historical Society • Old Stoney Museum, 301 E Clinton St • Frankfort, IN 46041 • (765) 659-2030 • http://www.cchsm.org

Frankfort Community Public Library • 208 W Clinton St • Frankfort, IN 46401 • (765) 654-8746 • http://www.accs.net/fcpl/; http://genealogy.fcpl.accs.net

Franklin
B F Hamilton Library • Franklin College, 501 E Monroe St • Franklin, IN 46131 • (317) 738-8164 • http://www.franklincollege.edu

Brown County Historian • 525 Dove Dr E • Franklin, IN 46131 • (317) 736-1447

Johnson County Historical and Genealogical Society • Historical Museum, 135 N Main St • Franklin, IN 46131 • (317) 736-4655 • http://www.johnsoncountymuseum.com

Johnson County Public Library • 401 S State St • Franklin, IN 46131-2545 • (317) 738-2833 • http://www.jcplin.org

Masonic Library and Museum of Indiana • 690 State St • Franklin, IN 46131 • (812) 597-5536

Fremont
Fremont Public Library • 1004 W Toledo St, P.O. Box 7 • Fremont, IN 46737-0007 • (260) 495-7157 • http://www.fremont.lib.in.us

French Lick
Indiana Railway Museum • 8594 W SR 56, P.O. Box 56 • French Lick, IN 46432 • (800) 748-7426 • http://www.indianarailwaymuseum.org

Melton Public Library • 8496 W College St • French Lick, IN 47432-1026 • (812) 936-2177 • http://www.melton.lib.in.us

Garrett
Garrett Historical Society • Historical Museum, 300 N Randolph St, P.O. Box 225 • Garrett, IN 46738 • (219) 357-5575 • http://www.garretthistoricalsociety.org

Garrett Public Library • 107 W Houston St • Garrett, IN 46738 • (260) 357-5485 • http://www.gpl.lib.in.us

Gary
Calumet Regional Archives • Indiana Univ, 3400 Broadway • Gary, IN 46408 • (219) 980-6628

Gary Historical and Cultural Society • Historical Museum, 1 E Gateway Park, P.O. Box M603 • Gary, IN 46407 • (219) 882-6873 • http://members.tripod.com/~ghes/

Gary Public Library • 220 W 5th Ave • Gary, IN 46402-1215 • (219) 886-2484 • http://www.gary.lib.in.us

Langston Hugh Family Museum • 1911 Massachusetts St, P.O. Box 64221 • Gary, IN 46401 • (219) 886-2007 • http://www.langstonhughesfamily.com

Le Cercle de La Fleur de Lis • P.O. Box 2756 • Gary, IN 46403 • (219) 938-7403

Gas City
Gas City Historical Society • Historical Museum, 505 E South F Street, P.O. Box 192 • Gas City, IN 46933 • (765) 674-1892

Gas City-Mill Township Public Library • 135 E Main St • Gas City, IN 46933-1496 • (765) 674-4718 • http://www.gcmtpl.lib.in.us

Geneva
Adams County Genealogical Society • P.O. Box 33 • Geneva, IN 46740 • http://www.rootsweb.com/~inadams2/acigs.htm

Geneva Public Library • 307 E Line St, P.O. Box 189 • Geneva, IN 46740-0189 • (260) 368-7270 • http://www.genevapl.lib.in.us

Limberlost State Historic Site Museum • 200 E 6th St, P.O. Box 356 • Geneva, IN 46740 • (260) 368-7428 • http://www.genestrattonporter.net

Gentryville
Col William Jones State Historic Site Museum • Route 1, Box 60D • Gentryville, IN 47537 • (812) 937-2802

Goodland
Goodland & Grant Township Public Library • 111 S Newton St, P.O. Box 405 • Goodland, IN 47948-0405 • (219) 297-4431 • http://www.mwprairienet.lib.in.us/social_services/goodlib

Goshen
Bonneyville Mill Museum • 211 W Lincoln Ave • Goshen, IN 46526-3280 • (219) 825-9324 • http://www.elkhartcountyparks.org

Indiana

Goshen, cont.

Elkhart County Historian • 1402-1 Pembroke Cr • Goshen, IN 46526 • (574) 533-8163

Goshen Historical Society • Historical Museum, 124 S Main St, P.O. Box 701 • Goshen, IN 46526 • (574) 975-0033

Goshen Public Library • 601 S 5th St • Goshen, IN 46526 • (574) 533-9531 • http://www.goshenpl.lib.in.us

Harold and Wilma Good Library • Goshen College, 1700 S Main St • Goshen, IN 46526-4794 • (574) 535-7431 • http://www.goshen.edu/library

Historical Committee of the Mennonite Church • 1700 S Main St • Goshen, IN 46526 • (574) 535-7418 • http://www.goshen.edu/mcarchives

Mennonite Historical Society • Goshen College • Goshen, IN 46526-4794 • (219) 535-7111

Gosport

Gosport History Museum • 19 N 4th St, P.O. Box 56 • Gosport, IN 47433 • (812) 879-4450

Greencastle

Genealogy Club of Putnam County • c/o Putnam County Public Library, 103 E Poplar St, P.O. Box 116 • Greencastle, IN 46135-0116 • (765) 653-2755

Putnam County Historical Society • c/o Roy O West Library, DePauw Univ, P.O. Box 801 • Greencastle, IN 46135 • (765) 658-4406 • http://www.depauw.edu/library/archives/archiveshome.htm

Putnam County Museum • 209 W Liberty St • Greencastle, IN 46135 • (765) 653-8419

Putnam County Public Library • 103 E Poplar St, P.O. Box 116 • Greencastle, IN 46135-0116 • (765) 653-2755 • http://www.putnam.lib.in.us

Roy O West Library • DePauw Univ, 400 S College Ave, P.O. Box 37 • Greencastle, IN 46135 • (765) 658-4406 • http://www.depauw.edu/library/archives/

United Methodist Historical Society • P.O. Box 331 • Greencastle, IN 46135

Greenfield

Hancock County Auditor Archives • 111 S American Legion Pl, Ste 217 • Greenfield, IN 46140 • (317) 477-1105 • http://www.hancockcoingov.org/auditor

Hancock County Genealogical Society • c/o Greenfield Public Library, 900 W McKenzie Rd • Greenfield, IN 46140 • (317) 462-5141

Hancock County Historian • 523 N Swope St • Greenfield, IN 46140-1640 • (317) 298-6257

Hancock County Historical Society • Historical Museum, 28 N Apple St, P.O. Box 375 • Greenfield, IN 46140-0375 • (317) 462-7780

Hancock County Public Library • 900 W McKenzie Rd • Greenfield, IN 46140 • (317) 462-5141 • http://www.hancockpub.lib.in.us

James Whitcomb Riley Birthplace Museum • 250 W Main St • Greenfield, IN 46140 • (317) 462-4340 • http://www.hccn.org/parks/rileyhouse.htm

James Whitcomb Riley Home Museum • 246 W Main St • Greenfield, IN 46140 • (317) 462-8556

Old Log Jail and Chapel Museums • 203 N Wood St, P.O. Box 375 • Greenfield, IN 46140 • (317) 462-7780

Greensburg

Decatur County Auditor Archives • 150 Courthouse Sq, Ste 5 • Greensburg, IN 47240 • (812) 663-2570 • http://www.decaturcounty.in.gov

Decatur County Historian • 1024 E Lakeshore Dr • Greensburg, IN 47240 • (812) 663-8290

Decatur County Historical Society • Historical Museum, 222 N Franklin St, P.O. Box 143 • Greensburg, IN 47240 • (812) 663-2478

Greensburg-Decatur County Public Library • 1110 E Main St • Greensburg, IN 47240 • (812) 663-2826 • http://www.greensburglibrary.org

Indiana Rural Letter Carriers Museum • 825 W 8th St • Greensburg, IN 47240 • (812) 663-4877

Greentown

Greentown Historical Society • 103 E Main St, P.O. Box 313 • Greentown, IN 46936 • (765) 628-3800

Greentown Public Library • 421 S Harrison St • Greentown, IN 46936 • (765) 628-3534 • http://www.eastern.k12.in.us/gpl/grentown.htm

Howard-Miami Heritage Society • P.O. Box 156 • Greentown, IN 46936

Greenwood

Greenwood Public Library • 310 S Meridian St • Greenwood, IN 46143-3135 • (317) 883-4224 • http://www.greenwood.lib.in.us

Griffith

Griffith Historical Society • Historical Museum, 201 S Broad St, P.O. Box 678 • Griffith, IN 46319 • (219) 924-9701 • http://www.thetimesonline.com/org/griffithhistsoc/table.htm

Northwest Indiana Genealogical Society • P.O. Box 595 • Griffith, IN 46319 • http://www.rootsweb.com/~inlake/nwigs.htm

Hagerstown

Clay Township Historical Society • 19 S Pearl St • Hagerstown, IN 47346 • (765) 886-5166

Collectible Classics Car Museum • 403 E Main St • Hagerstown, IN 47346 • (765) 489-5598

Hagerstown-Jefferson Township Public Library • 10 W College St • Hagerstown, IN 47346-1295 • (765) 489-5632 • http://www.hagerstown.lib.in.us

Historic Hagerstown • Nettle Creek Valley Museum, 96 1/2 E Main St, P.O. Box 126 • Hagerstown, IN 47346 • (765) 489-4005 • http://www.waynet.org/nonprofit/nettlecreek_museum.htm

Wayne County Historian • 14030 W E Oler Rd • Hagerstown, IN 57346-9726 • (765) 489-5429

Wilbur Wright Birthplace Museum • 1525 N Cty Rd 750 E • Hagerstown, IN 47346 • (765) 332-2495 • http://www.wilburwrightbirthplace.com

Hammond

Hammond Historical Society • Historical Museum, 564 State St • Hammond, IN 46320 • (219) 931-5100 • http://www.hammondindiana.com/society_page.html

Hammond Public Library • 564 State St • Hammond, IN 46320-1532 • (219) 931-5100 • http://www.hammond.lib.in.us

Hessville Historical Society • Historical Museum, 7205 Kennedy Ave • Hammond, IN 46323 • (219) 844-5666

Little Red Schoolhouse Museum • 1250 150th St • Hammond, IN 46327 • (219) 931-7559

Hanover

Duggan Library • Hanover College, 121 Scenic Dr, P.O. Box 287 • Hanover, IN 47243-0287 • (812) 866-7171 • http://www.hanover.edu/library

Hanover Historical Association • P.O. Box 157 • Hanover, IN 47243 • (812) 866-2901

Hartford City

Blackford County Historian • 227 W 7th St • Hartford City, IN 47348 • (765) 348-2726

Blackford County Historical Society • Historical Museum, 321 N High St, P.O. Box 264 • Hartford City, IN 47348 • (317) 348-1905 • http://www.bchs-in.org

Hartford County Public Library • 314 N High St • Hartford City, IN 47348-2143 • (765) 348-1720 • http://www.hartfordcity.lib.in.us

Haubstadt

Haubstadt Area Historical Society • P.O. Box 161 • Haubstadt, IN 47639

Hayden

Hayden Historical Museum • 6715 W County Rd 20 S, P.O. Box 58 • Hayden, IN 47245 • (812) 346-8212 • http://www.seidata.com/~haydenmu/

Hayden Historical Society • P.O. Box 58 • Hayden, IN 47245

Hebron

Hebron Historical Society • P.O. Box 675 • Hebron, IN 46341

Porter County Public Library System-Hebron Public • 201 W Sigler St, P.O. Box 97 • Hebron, IN 46341 • (219) 996-3684 • http://www.pcpls.lib.in.us/brhebron.htm

Stagecoach Museum • P.O. Box 679 • Hebron, IN 46341 • (219) 966-2638

Highland

Highland Historical Society • Historical Museum, 2611 Highway Ave • Highland, IN 46322 • (219) 838-2962 • http://www.rootsweb.com/~inlake/highland.htm

Hobart

Hobart Historical Society • Historical Museum, 706 E 4th St, P.O. Box 24 • Hobart, IN 46342-0024 • (219) 942-0970

Wood's Historic Grist Mill Museum • 9410 Old Lincoln Hwy • Hobart, IN 46342 • (219) 947-1958

Hope

Yellow Trail Museum • SR 9 • Hope, IN 47246 • (812) 546-4084

Huntertown

Huntertown Historical Society • P.O. Box 662 • Huntertown, IN 46748 • (260) 637-8598 • http://www.huntertownhistoricalsoc.org

Huntingburg

Huntingburg Public Library • 419 N Jackson St • Huntingburg, IN 47542 • (812) 683-2052 • http://www.huntingburg.lib.in.us

Huntington

Day Quayle Museum • 815 Warren St • Huntington, IN 46750 • (260) 356-6356 • http://www.quaylemuseum.org

Historic Forks of the Wabash • Historical Museum, 3011 W Park Dr, P.O. Box 261 • Huntington, IN 46750 • (219) 356-1903 • http://www.historicforks.org

Huntington City-Township Public Library • 200 W Market St • Huntington, IN 46750 • (260) 356-0824 • http://www.huntingtonpub.lib.in.us

Huntington County Genealogical Society • c/o Huntington Township Public Library, 200 W Market St • Huntington, IN 46750 • (219) 356-0824

Huntington County Historical Society • Huntington County Courthouse Museum, 315 Court St, P.O. Box 1012 • Huntington, IN 46750-2862 • (219) 356-7264 • http://www.huntingtonhistoricalmuseum.org

Markle Area Historical Society • 1430 Oak • Huntington, IN 46750 • (219) 758-2642

United Brethren Archives • Huntington College, RichLyn Library, 2303 College Ave • Huntington, IN 46750 • (219) 356-6000 • http://www.huntington.edu/library

Wings of Freedom Museum • 1365 Warren Rd • Huntington, IN 46750 • (219) 356-1945

Idaville

Parrish Pioneer Farm Museum • RR1, Box 147 • Idaville, IN 47950 • (219) 826-4163

Indianapolis

American Evangelical Christian Churches • P.O. Box 47312 • Indianapolis, IN 46277 • http://www.aeccministries.com

American Legion National Headquarters Library • 700 N Pennsylvania St, P.O. Box 1055 • Indianapolis, IN 46206-1055 • (317) 630-1366 • http://www.legion.org/library.htm

Archives of the Kentucky-Indiana Synod, Lutheran Church of America • 3733 N Meridian St • Indianapolis, IN 46208

Benjamin Harrison Presidential Library • 1230 N Delaware St • Indianapolis, IN 46202-2531 • (317) 631-1898 • http://www.presidentbenjaminharrison.org

Center for Agricultural Herigage Museum • 1201 E 38th St • Indianapolis, IN 46206 • (317) 925-2410 • http://www.centerforag.com

Christian Theological Seminary Library • 1000 W 42nd St • Indianapolis, IN 46208 • (317) 924-1331 • http://www.cts.edu

Clay Township Library & Museum Society • Historical Museum, 10855 N College Ave • Indianapolis, IN 46280

Crispus Attucks Center Museum • 1140 Dr Martin Luther King St • Indianapolis, IN 46202 • (317) 226-2430

Crossroads Bible College Library • 601 N Shortridge Rd • Indianapolis, IN 46219-4912 • (317) 352-8736 • http://www.crossroads.edu

Crown Hill Cemetery Archives • 700 W 38th St • Indianapolis, IN 46208 • (317) 925-8231 • http://www.crownhill.org

Crown Hill Heritage Foundation • 700 W 38th St • Indianapolis, IN 46208 • (317) 920-2726 • http://www.crownhill.org/heritage/

Ed Taylor Radio Museum • 245 N Oakland Ave • Indianapolis, IN 46201-3360 • (317) 638-1641

Eiteljorg Museum of American Indians and Western Art • 500 W Washington St • Indianapolis, IN 46204 • (317) 636-9378 • http://www.eiteljorg.org

Emil A Blackmore Museum of the American Legion • 700 Pennsylvania St, P.O. Box 1055 • Indianapolis, IN 46280 • (317) 630-1366 • http://www.legion.org

Family Tree and Crests • 6233 Carollton Ave • Indianapolis, IN 46220

Fort Benjamin Harrison Historical Society • 5830 N Post Rd, P.O. Box 269597 • Indianapolis, IN 46226 • (317) 377-3403 • http://www.msnusers.com/FortBenjaminHarrisonHistoricalSociety/homepage.msnw

Franklin Township Historical Society • Historical Museum, P.O. Box 39015 • Indianapolis, IN 46239 • http://fths.org

Freetown Village Museum • P. O. Box 1041 • Indianapolis, IN 46206-1041 • (317) 631-1870 • http://www.freetown.org

Heritage Learning Center Museum • 830 Dr. Martin Luther King Jr St • Indianapolis, IN 46202 • (317) 632-2340

Historic Landmarks Foundation of Indiana • Historical Museum, 340 W Michigan St • Indianapolis, IN 46202-3204 • (317) 639-4534 • http://www.historiclandmarks.org

Hook's American Drug Store Museum • 1180 E 38th St • Indianapolis, IN 46205 • (317) 951-2222

Indiana

Indianapolis, cont.

Indiana Covered Bridge Society • 725 Sanders St • Indianapolis, IN 46302 • (317) 632-3081

Indiana German Heritage Society • Das Deutsche Haus, 401 E Michigan Ave • Indianapolis, IN 46204 • (317) 464-9004 • http://www.ulib.iupui.edu/kade/ighstran.html

Indiana Historical Bureau • 140 N Senate Ave, Rm 408 • Indianapolis, IN 46204 • (317) 232-2537 • http://www.statelib.lib.in.us/www.inh.inh.html

Indiana Historical Society • Historical Museum, 450 W Ohio St • Indianapolis, IN 46202-3269 • (317) 234-0321 • http://www.indianahistory.org

Indiana Junior Historical Society • 450 W Ohio St • Indianapolis, IN 46202-3269 • (317) 232-4549 • http://www.indianahistory.org

Indiana Medical History Museum • 3045 W Vermont St • Indianapolis, IN 46222 • (317) 635-7329 • http://www.imhm.org

Indiana Religious History Association • P.O. Box 88267 • Indianapolis, IN 46208

Indiana School for the Deaf Museum • 1200 E 42nd St • Indianapolis, IN 46205 • (317) 924-4374

Indiana State Archives • 6440 E 30th St • Indianapolis, IN 46219 • (317) 591-5222 • http://www.in.gov/icpr/webfile/archives/

Indiana State Department of Health, Vital Records • 6 W Washington St • Indianapolis, IN 46206-1964 • (317) 233-2700 • http://www.state.in.us/isdh/

Indiana State Library • 140 N Senate Ave • Indianapolis, IN 46204-2296 • (317) 232-3675 • http://www.statelib.lib.in.us

Indiana State Museum • 650 W Washington St • Indianapolis, IN 46204 • (317) 232-1637 • http://www.indianamuseum.org

Indiana University-Purdue Indianapolis Library • 755 W Michigan St • Indianapolis, IN 46202 • (317) 274-0464 • http://www-lib.iupui.edu

Indiana War Memorials Museum • 431 N Meridian St • Indianapolis, IN 46204 • (317) 232-7615 • http://www.state.in.us/iwm

Indianapolis Firefighters Historical Society • Historical Museum, 748 Massachusetts Ave • Indianapolis, IN 46204 • (317) 262-5161 • http://www.survivealive.org

Indianapolis Motor Speedway Hall of Fame Museum • 4790 W 16th St • Indianapolis, IN 46201 • (317) 448-6747

Indianapolis-Marion County Public Library • 202 N Alabama St, P.O. Box 211 • Indianapolis, IN 46206-0211 • (317) 269-1700 • http://www.imcpl.org

Irvington Historical Society • Benton House Museum, 312 S Downey Ave • Indianapolis, IN 46219 • (317) 357-0318

Irvington Historical Society • 5350 University Ave • Indianapolis, IN 46219 • (317) 353-2662

Irwin Library • Butler University, 4600 Sunset Ave • Indianapolis, IN 46208 • (317) 940-9235 • http://www.butler.edu/libraries

James Whitcomb Riley Home Museum • 528 Lockerbie St • Indianapolis, IN 46202 • (317) 631-5885

Jewish Family Name File • 238 S Meridian St #502 • Indianapolis, IN 46225-1024 • http://www.jewishpostopinion.com

Jewish Genealogical Society of Indiana • Congregation Beth-El Zedeck, 600 W 70th St, P.O. Box 68280 • Indianapolis, IN 46268-0280 • (317) 388-0632

Kelley Agricultural Museum • 36 S Pennsylvania St • Indianapolis, IN 46260 • (317) 963-2727

Kiwanis International • 3636 Woodview Trace • Indianapolis, IN 46268-3196 • (317) 875-8755 • http://www.kiwanis.org

Lyles Station Historic Preservation Society • 3537 N Gladstone • Indianapolis, IN 46218 • (317) 542-0453

Marion County Genealogical Society • P.O. Box 2292 • Indianapolis, IN 46206-2292 • (317) 635-7278 • http://www.rootsweb.com/~ingsmc/

Marion County Historian • 4415 Broadway • Indianapolis, IN 46205 • (317) 274-2718

Marion County Historical Society • P.O. Box 2223 • Indianapolis, IN 46206 • (317) 786-4561

Marion County-Indianapolis Historical Society • 735 Woodruff Pl E Dr, P.O. Box 2223 • Indianapolis, IN 46206 • (317) 635-7278

Marston Memorial Historical Center • Free Methodist Church of North America, 770 N High School Rd, P.O. Box 535002 • Indianapolis, IN 46253-5002 • (317) 244-3660 • http://freemethodistchurch.org

Masonic Grand Lodge of Indiana • 525 N Illinois St, P.O. Box 44210 • Indianapolis, IN 46244-0410 • (317) 634-7904 • https://www.indianafreemasons.com/

Morris-Butler House Museum • 1204 N Park Ave • Indianapolis, IN 46202 • (317) 636-5409 • http://www.historiclandmarks.org

National Council on Public History • 327 Cavanaugh Hall, 425 Univ Blvd • Indianapolis, IN 46202 • (317) 274-2716 • http://www.iupui.edu

Nimkii Band of the United Metis Tribe • 2254 Walnut Ridge Ln • Indianapolis, IN 46234

Order of Descendants of Colonial Physicians and Chirurgeons • 4245 Washington Blvd • Indianapolis, IN 46205-2618

Palatines to America, Indiana Chapter • 716 Wallbridge, P.O. Box 40435 • Indianapolis, IN 46202-0435 • (317) 875-7210

Phi Kappa Psi Fraternity Heritage Hall Museum • 510 Lockerbie St • Indianapolis, IN 46207 • (317) 632-6452 • http://www.phikappapsi.com

Pike Township Historical Society • P.O. Box 78645 • Indianapolis, IN 46278

Ruth Lilly Special Collections and Archives • IUPUI, Univ Library, 755 W Michigan St • Indianapolis, IN 46202-5195 • (317) 274-0464 • http://www.ulib.iupui.edu/special/home.html

Society of Indiana Archivists • 140 N Senate Ave • Indianapolis, IN 46204 • (317) 232-2537 • http://cawley.archives.nd.edu/sia/

Society of Indiana Pioneers • 450 W Ohio St, P.O. Box 88255 • Indianapolis, IN 46202 • (317) 233-6588 • http://www.indianapioneers.com

Sons of the American Legion • 700 N Pennsylvania, P.O. Box 1055 • Indianapolis, IN 46206 • (317) 630-1200 • http://www.sal.legion.org

Wayne Township Historical Society • 1220 S High School Rd • Indianapolis, IN 46241

Wishard Memorial Nursing Alumni Museum • 1001 W 10th St • Indianapolis, IN 46202-2859 • (317) 630-6233

Jamestown

Ladoga Historical Society • P.O. Box 228 • Jamestown, IN 46147-0163

Jasonville

Jasonville Public Library • 611 W Main St, P.O. Box 105 • Jasonville, IN 47438-0105 • (812) 665-2025

Jasper

Dubois County Genealogical Society • P.O. Box 343 • Jasper, IN 47547-0343 • http://www.rootsweb.com/!indubois/dubges.htm

Dubois County Historian • 737 W 8th St • Jasper, IN 47546-2605 • (812) 482-3074

Dubois County Historical Society • 737 W 8th St • Jasper, IN 47546 • (812) 482-3074

Dubois County Museum • 1103 Main St, P.O. Box 1086 • Jasper, IN 47547 • (812) 634-7733

Ireland Historical Society • 7154 W 150 N • Jasper, IN 47546 • http://www.irelandindiana.com/IrelandHistoricalSociety/

Jasper Public Library • 1116 Main St • Jasper, IN 47546 • (812) 482-2712

Jeffersonville

Bureau of the Census-Personal Search Unit • 1201 E 10th St, Bldg 48, P.O. Box 1545 • Jeffersonville, IN 47131-0001 • (812) 218-3046 • http://www.census.gov/genealogy/www/agesearch.html

Clark County Historical Society • Howard Steamboat Museum, 1101 E Market St, P.O. Box 606 • Jeffersonville, IN 47130 • (812) 283-3728 • http://www.steamboatmuseum.org

Howard Steamboat Museum and Mansion • 1101 E Market St, P.O. Box 606 • Jeffersonville, IN 47130 • (812) 283-3728 • http://www.steamboatmuseum.org

Jeffersonville Township Public Library • 211 E Court Ave, P.O. Box 1548 • Jeffersonville, IN 47131-1548 • (812) 285-5634 • http://jefferson.lib.in.us

Jonesboro

Jonesboro Historical Society • 407 E River St • Jonesboro, IN 46938

Jonesboro Public Library • 124 E 4th St • Jonesboro, IN 46938-1105 • (765) 677-9080

Kendallville

Kendallville Historical Society • Historical Museum, P.O. Box 5048 • Kendallville, IN 46755 • http://www.noblecan.org/~kpc/wind/

Kendallville Public Library • 126 W Rush St • Kendallville, IN 46755 • (260) 347-2768 • http://www.kendallvillelibrary.org

Mid-America Windmill Museum • P.O. Box 5048 • Kendallville, IN 46755 • (219) 347-2334

Kendallville Public Library • 126 W Rush St • Kendallville, IN 46755-1740 • (260) 347-2768 • http://www.kendallvillelibrary.org

Kennard

Kennard Historical Society • P.O. Box 227 • Kennard, IN 47351

Kentland

Kentland-Jefferson Township Public Library • 201 E Graham St • Kentland, IN 47951 • (219) 474-5044 • http://www.kentland.lib.in.us

Newton County Historical Society • Historical Museum, 224 N 3rd St, P.O. Box 303 • Kentland, IN 47951 • (219) 474-6944

Kewanna

Kewanna Public Library • 210 E Main St, P.O. Box 365 • Kewanna, IN 46939-0365 • (574) 653-2011

Kingman

Fountain County Genealogical Society • 2855 S Kingman Rd • Kingman, IN 47952 • (765) 294-4954 • http://glenmar.com/~emoyhbo/fcgs.html

Fountain County Historical Society • 724 S Layton, P.O. Box 148 • Kingman, IN 47952

Kingman Public Library • 123 State St, P.O. Box 116 • Kingman, IN 47952-0116 • (765) 397-3138

Kirklin

Kirklin Public Library • 115 N Main St, P.O. Box 8 • Kirklin, IN 46050-0008 • (765) 279-8308 • http://www.kirklinlibrary.com

Knightstown

Knightstown Public Library • 5 E Main St • Knightstown, IN 46148-1248 • (765) 345-5095

Trumps' Texaco Museum • 39 N Washington St • Knightstown, IN 46148 • (765) 345-7135

Knox

Henry F Schricker Library • 152 W Culver Rd • Knox, IN 46534-2220 • (574) 772-7323 • http://www.scpl.lib.in.us

Starke County Genealogical Society • c/o Henry F Schricker Library, 152 W Culver Rd • Knox, IN 46534 • (574) 772-7323 • http://www.rootsweb.com/~inscgs/

Starke County Historian • P.O. Box 448 • Knox, IN 46534-0448 • (574) 772-5936

Starke County Historical Society • Historical Museum, 401 S Main St • Knox, IN 46534 • (574) 772-5393

Kokomo

Automotive Heritage Museum • 1500 N Reed Rd • Kokomo, IN 46901 • (765) 454-9999 • http://www.automotiveheritagemuseum.com

Elwood Haynes Home Museum • 1815 S Webster St • Kokomo, IN 46901 • (765) 456-7500

Howard County Genealogical Society • c/o Kokomo Public Library, 220 N Union • Kokomo, IN 46901 • (317) 457-3242 • http://kokomo.lib.in.us/genealogy/

Howard County Historian • 2310 W King St • Kokomo, IN 46901-5080 • (765) 452-4314

Howard County Historical Society • Historical Museum, 1200 W Sycamore St • Kokomo, IN 46901 • (765) 452-4314 • http://www.howardcountymuseum.org

Howard-Miami Counties Heritage Society • 3976 East 1400 South • Kokomo, IN 46901 • (765) 395-3790

Kokomo Public Library • 222 N Union St • Kokomo, IN 46901 • (765) 457-3242 • http://kokomo.lib.in.us/genealogy/

North Central Indiana Genealogical Society • 1404 Zartman Rd • Kokomo, IN 46901

La Grange

LaGrange County Historical Society • Machan House Museum, 405 S Popular St, P.O. Box 134 • La Grange, IN 46761 • (260) 463-2632

LaGrange County Library • 203 W Spring St • La Grange, IN 46761 • (260) 463-2841 • http://www.lagrange.lib.in.us

La Porte

Hesston Steam Museum • 1201 E 100 N • La Porte, IN 46350 • (219) 872-5055 • http://www.hesston.org

Kesling Automobile Museum • 2405 Indiana Ave • La Porte, IN 46350 • (219) 324-6767 • http://www.laportecountyhistory.org

LaPorte County Genealogical Society • c/o LaPorte County Public Library, 904 Indiana Ave • La Porte, IN 46350 • (219) 362-6156 • http://www.rootsweb.com/~inleigs/

LaPorte County Historian • 5817 W Johnson Rd • La Porte, IN 46350-8586 • (219) 326-6458

LaPorte County Historical Society • Historical Museum, 2405 Indiana Ave • La Porte, IN 46350-3329 • (219) 324-6767 • http://www.laportscountyhistory.org

LaPorte County Public Library • 904 Indiana Ave • La Porte, IN 46350 • (219) 362-6156 • http://www.lapcat.org

Ladoga

Ladoga-Clark Township Public Library • 128 E Main St, P.O. Box 248 • Ladoga, IN 47954-0248 • (765) 942-2456 • http://www.ladoga.lib.in.us

Lafayette

Alameda McCollough Library • 909 South St • Lafayette, IN 47901 • (765) 476-8407 • http://www.tcha.mus.in.us

Shawnee Historical Association • 5501 E 200 N • Lafayette, IN 47905 • (765) 589-8049

Indiana

Lafayette, cont.
Tippecanoe County Area Genealogical Society • Historical Museum, 909 South St • Lafayette, IN 47901 • (765) 476-8420 • http://tcha.mus.in.us

Tippecanoe County Historian • 801 Hitt St • Lafayette, IN 47901

Tippecanoe County Historical Association • Historical Museum, 909 South St • Lafayette, IN 47901 • (765) 742-8411 • http://www.tcha.mus.in.us

Tippecanoe County Public Library • 627 South St • Lafayette, IN 47901-1157 • (765) 429-0100 • http://www.tcpl.lib.in.us

Tippecanoe County Public Library • 627 South St • Lafayette, IN 47901-1470 • (765) 429-0100 • http://www.tcpl.lib.in.us

Wabash Valley Trust for Historic Preservation • 325 N 5th St • Lafayette, IN 47901 • (765) 420-0268

Wea Indian Tribe • 715 Park Ave • Lafayette, IN 47904 • http://www.wea-indian-tribe.com

Lake Station
Lake Station Historical Society • Historical Museum, 3220 Grove Ave • Lake Station, IN 46405-2233 • (219) 962-2836

Lake Village
Newton County Public Library • 9458 N 315 W, P.O. Box 206 • Lake Village, IN 46349-0206 • (219) 992-3490

Lapel
Lapel Historical Society • P.O. Box 149 • Lapel, IN 46051

Laurel
Whitewater Valley Community Library - Laurel • 200 N Clay St, P.O. Box 402 • Laurel, IN 47024 • (765) 698-2626 • http://www.wvcl.org

Lawrenceburg
Dearborn County Historian • 14684 Wilson Creek • Lawrenceburg, IN 47025 • (812) 537-2775

Dearborn County Historical Society • Historical Museum, 508 W High St • Lawrenceburg, IN 47025 • (812) 537-4075 • http://www.dearborninhistorical.org

Lawrenceburg Public Library • 123 W High St • Lawrenceburg, IN 47025 • (812) 537-2775 • http://www.lpld.lib.in.us

Surveyors Historical Society • 300 W High St, Ste 2 • Lawrenceburg, IN 47025-1912 • (812) 537-2000

Leavenworth
Crawford County Historical and Genealogical Society • P.O. Box 133 • Leavenworth, IN 47137 • (812) 739-2358

Crawford County Indiana Museum • Route 1 • Leavenworth, IN 47137

Southern Indiana Genealogical Society • RR 1 • Leavenworth, IN 47137

Stephenson's General Store & Museum • P.O. Box 127 • Leavenworth, IN 47137 • (812) 739-4242

Lebanon
Boone County Health Department • 116 W Washington St, B201-2 • Lebanon, IN 46052 • (765) 482-3942 • http://www.bccn.boone.in.us/health/vital_records.html

Boone County Historical Society • Historical Museum, 404 W Main St, P.O. Box 141 • Lebanon, IN 46052 • (765) 483-9414 • http://www.bccn.boone.in.us/bchs/

Lebanon Public Library • 104 E Washington St • Lebanon, IN 46052 • (765) 482-3460 • http://www.bccn.boone.in.us/LPL

Lexington
Lexington Historical Society • Historical Museum, 5764 S State Rd 203, P.O. Box 238 • Lexington, IN 47138 • (812) 869-2044

Scott County Genealogical Society • 5764 S State Rd 203, P.O. Box 258 • Lexington, IN 47138-0258 • (812) 889-2044

Liberty
Union County Historian • 101 Maple Ct` • Liberty, IN 47353 • (765) 458-5294

Union County Historical Museum • 156 E County Rd 300 S • Liberty, IN 47353

Union County Historical Society • Railroad St, P.O. Box 143 • Liberty, IN 47353 • (765) 458-5500

Union County Public Library • 2 E Seminary St • Liberty, IN 47353 • (765) 458-5355 • http://www.union-county.lib.in.us

Ligonier
Indiana Historic Radio Museum • 800 Lincolnway S • Ligonier, IN 46767-0353 • (219) 894-9000 • http://home.att.net/~indianahistoricalradio/

Ligonier Historical Society • Historical Museum, 300 S Main St • Ligonier, IN 46767 • (260) 894-7580 • http://www.nccvb.org/attract/ilhm.htm

Ligonier Public Library • 300 S Main St • Ligonier, IN 46767-1812 • (260) 894-4511 • http://www.gonier.lib.in.us

Stone's Tavern Museum • State Rd 5 & US 33 • Ligonier, IN 46767 • (260) 856-2871 • http://www.stonestrace.com

Stone's Trace Historical Society • Historical Museum, 4946 N State Rd 5 • Ligonier, IN 46767 • (219) 856-2871

Lincoln City
Colonel William Jones Home Museum • Hwy 162, P.O. Box 216 • Lincoln City, IN 47552 • (812) 937-4710 • http://www.in.gov/dnr/parklake/parks/lincoln.html

Lincoln Boyhood National Memorial Library • 3027 E South St, P.O. Box 1816 • Lincoln City, IN 47552-1816 • (812) 937-4541 • http://www.nps.gov/libo

Linden
Linden Railroad Museum • 520 N Main St, P.O. Box 154 • Linden, IN 47955 • (765) 339-4895 • http://www.lindenrailroadmuseum.com

Linden-Carnegie Public Library • 102 S Main St, PO Box 10 • Linden, IN 47955-0010 • (765) 339-4239

Linden-Madison Township Historical Society • Historical Museum, P.O. Box 154 • Linden, IN 47955 • (765) 339-7245 • http://www.crawfordsville.org/depot.htm

Linton
Margaret Cooper Public Library & Museum • 110 E Vincenne St, PO Box 613 • Linton, IN 47441-0613 • (812) 847-7802 • www.margaret-cooper.lib.in.us

Logansport
Cass County Genealogical Society • P.O. Box 373 • Logansport, IN 46927 • http://www.rootsweb.com/~inccgs/

Cass County Historian • 723 Wheatland • Logansport, IN 46947 • (574) 732-1875

Cass County Historical Society • Historical Museum, 1004 E Market St • Logansport, IN 46947 • (574) 753-3866 • http://www.casshistory.com

Cole Clothing Museum • 900 E Broadway • Logansport, IN 46947 • (219) 753-4058

Indiana Chapter, OGS • Route 5 • Logansport, IN 46947

Iron Horse Museum • 300 E Broadway, Ste 103 • Logansport, IN 46947 • (219) 753-6388

Logansport Public Library • 616 E Broadway • Logansport, IN 46947-3187 • (574) 753-6383 • http://www.logan.lib.in.us

Loogootee

Frances L Folks Memorial Library • 408 N Line St • Loogootee, IN 47553-1263 • (812) 295-3713

Lowell

Lowell Public Library • 1505 E Commercial Ave • Lowell, IN 46356 • (219) 696-7704 • http://www.lowellpl.lib.in.us

Obadiah Taylor Historical Association • 15517 Barman • Lowell, IN 46356

Three Creeks Historical Association • c/o Lowell Public Library, 1505 E Commercial Ave • Lowell, IN 46356 • (219) 696-7704 • http://www.lowellpl.lib.in.us

Lynn

Randolf Southern Historical Society • P.O. Box 127 • Lynn, IN 47335 • (765) 874-2267

Washington Township Public Library & Museum • 107 N Main St, P.O. Box 127 • Lynn, IN 47355-0127 • (765) 874-1488

Lyons

Greene County Historian • P.O. Box 910 • Lyons, IN 47443 • (812) 659-2315

Madison

Early American Trades Museum • 313 E 1st St • Madison, IN 47250

Historic Madison • Historical Museum, 500 West St, P.O. Box 4004 • Madison, IN 47250 • (812) 265-2967 • http://www.historicmadisoninc.com

Jefferson County Genealogical Society • 735 W Main St • Madison, IN 47250 • (812) 265-4472

Jefferson County Historian • 131 Hillcrest Dr • Madison, IN 47250 • (812) 273-5368

Jefferson County Historical Society • Madison Railroad Station, 615 W 1st St • Madison, IN 47250 • (812) 265-2335 • http://www.jchs.org

Lanier Mansion State Historic Site Museum • 601 W 1st St • Madison, IN 47250 • (812) 265-3526 • http://www.state.in.us/sites/lanier

Madison-Jefferson County Public Library • 420 W Main St • Madison, IN 47250 • (812) 265-2744 • http://www.madison-jeffco.lib.in.us

Schofield House Museum • 217 W 2nd • Madison, IN 47250 • (812) 265-4759

Shrewsbury Windle House Museum • 301 W 1st St • Madison, IN 47250 • (812) 265-4481

Marion

Grant County Genealogical Society • County Courthouse, P.O. Box 1951 • Marion, IN 46952

Grant County Genealogy Club • 1419 W 11th St • Marion, IN 46952

Grant County Historian • 715 Berkley Dr • Marion, IN 46952 • (765) 664-2150

Grant County Historical Society • 1713 N Quarry Rd, PLO. Box 1951 • Marion, IN 46952 • (765) 662-9133

Jackson Library • Indiana Wesleyan University, 4201 S Washington St • Marion, IN 46953 • (765) 677-2184 • http://www.indwes.edu/library/

Marion Public Library & Museum • 600 S Washington St • Marion, IN 46952-1992 • (765) 668-2900 • http://www.marion.lib.in.us

Matthews Historical Society • 1628 W 2nd St • Marion, IN 46952

Mississinewa Battlefield Society • P.O. Box 1812 • Marion, IN 46952 • (765) 662-1809

Quilter's Hall of Fame • Webster Home, 926 S Washington St, P.O. Box 681 • Marion, IN 46952 • (765) 664-9333 • http://www.quiltershalloffame.org

Martinsville

Morgan County Historic Preservation Society • P.O. Box 1377 • Martinsville, IN 46151

Morgan County History and Genealogy Association • c/o Morgan County Public Library, 110 S Jefferson St, P.O. Box 1012 • Martinsville, IN 46151-1012 • (765) 349-1537 • http://www.rootsweb.com/~inmchaga/mchagai.html

Morgan County Public Library • 110 S Jefferson St • Martinsville, IN 46151 • (765) 342-3451 • http://www.scican.net/morglib/libweb.html

Matthews

Matthews Covered Bridge Historical Society • P.O. Box 153 • Matthews, IN 46957

Mauckport

Squire Boon Caverns & Village Museum • 100 Squire Boone Rd SW • Mauckport, IN 47142 • (812) 732-4381 • http://www.squireboonecaverns.com

McCordsville

World Wars Aircraft Museum • 5986 W 900 N • McCordsville, IN 46055-9739 • (317) 335-3310

Mentone

Bell Memorial Public Library • 101 W Main, P.O. Box 368 • Mentone, IN 46539-0368 • (219) 353-7234 • http://www.bell.lib.in.us

Lawrence D Bell Aircraft Museum • SR 25 W, P.O. Box 411 • Mentone, IN 46539 • (219) 223-2646

Merom

Sullivan County Historian • 8422 W Phillip St • Merom, IN 47861 • (812) 268-4957

Merrillville

Lake County Public Library • 1919 W 81st Ave • Merrillville, IN 46410-5382 • (219) 769-3541 • http://www.lakeco.lib.in.us

Merrillville-Ross Township Historical Society • 13 W 73rd Ave • Merrillville, IN 46410 • (219) 756-2042

Metamora

Whitewater Canal State Historic Site Museum • 19083 Clayborn St, P.O. Box 88 • Metamora, IN 47030 • (765) 647-6512

Michigan City

Barker Mansion Museum • 631 Washington St • Michigan City, IN 46360 • (219) 8730-520 • http://www.michigancity.org

Great Lakes Museum of Military History • 360 Dunes Plaza • Michigan City, IN 56360 • (219) 872-2702 • http://www.militaryhistorymuseum.org

Michigan City Historical Society • Old Lighthouse Museum, Heisman Harbor Rd, P.O. Box 512 • Michigan City, IN 46360 • (219) 872-6133 • http://www.michigancity.com/MCHistorical/

Michigan City Public Library • 100 E 4th St • Michigan City, IN 46360-3393 • (219) 873-3044 • http://www.mclib.org

Middletown

Middletown Public Library • 780 High St • Middletown, IN 47356 • (765) 354-4071 • http://www.mplib.org

Middletown-Fall Creek Township Historical Society • Historical Museum, 559 Locust St, P.O. Box 63 • Middletown, IN 47356 • (765) 354-2000

Vera's Little Red Dollhouse Museum • 4385 W CR 850 N • Middletown, IN 47356 • (765) 533-3453

Milford

Milford Public Library • 101 N Main St, P.O. Box 269 • Milford, IN 46542-0269 • (574) 658-4312 • http://www.milford.lib.in.us

Indiana

Mishawaka

Beiger Heritage Corporation • 317 Lincoln Way E • Mishawaka, IN 46544 • (219) 256-0365

Bowen Library & Museum • Bethel College, 1001 W McKinley Ave • Mishawaka, IN 46545 • (574) 257-3283 • http://www.bethel-in.edu

Mishawaka Sports-Michiana Sports Hall of Fame • 109 Lincoln Way E • Mishawaka, IN 46544 • (219) 257-0039 • http://www.sportsmuseum.8m.com

Mishawaka-Penn Public Library • 209 Lincoln Way E • Mishawaka, IN 46544-2084 • (574) 259-5277 • http://www.mppl.lib.in.us

Society for the Preservation of Old Mills • 1431 Folkstone Ct • Mishawaka, IN 46544 • (219) 259-4483

South Bend Area Genealocial Society • c/o Mishawaka-Penn Public Library, 209 Lincoln Way E • Mishawaka, IN 46644 • (219) 234-6747 • http://www.rootsweb.com/~insbags

Mitchell

Mitchell Community Public Library • 804 W Main St • Mitchell, IN 47446 • (812) 849-2412 • http://www.mitlib.org

Pioneer Village & Virgil Girssom Memorial Museum • 3333 State Rd 60 E, P.O. Box 376 • Mitchell, IN 47446 • (812) 849-4129 • http://www.in.gov/dnr/parklake/properties/park_springmill.html

Virgil I Grissom State Memorial • P.O. Box 376 • Mitchell, IN 47446

Monon

Monon Historical Society • P.O. Box 193 • Monon, IN 47959

Monon Town & Township Public Library • 427 N Market, PO Box 305 • Monon, IN 47959-0305 • (219) 253-6517 • http://www.dcwi.com/~nhartman/monon.htm

Monterey

Monterey-Tippecanoe Township Public Library • 6260 E Main St, P.O. Box 38 • Monterey, IN 46960-0038 • (574) 542-2171 • http://www.pulaski-libraries.lib.in.us

Monticello

Monticello-Union Township Public Library • 321 W Broadway • Monticello, IN 47960 • (574) 583-5643 • http://www.monticello.lib.in.us

White County Genealogy Society • Historical Museum, 101 S Bluff St, P.O. Box 149 • Monticello, IN 47960-2308 • (219) 583-3998 • http://www.buffaloindiana.org/whitecountyindiana/whgen.htm

White County Historian • 2202 N Norway Tr • Monticello, IN 47960 • (574) 583-5221

White County Historical Society • Historical Museum, 101 S Bluff St • Monticello, IN 47960-2308 • (574) 583-3998 • http://www.buffaloindiana.org/whitecountyindiana/hist.htm

Montpelier

Montpelier Historical Society • Historical Museum, 109 W Huntington St • Montpelier, IN 47359 • (765) 728-8642

Montpelier Public Library • 301 S Main St • Montpelier, IN 47359 • (765) 728-5969

Moores Hill

Carnegie Historic Landmarks • Carnegie Hall Museum, 14687 Main St • Moores Hill, IN 47032 • (812) 744-4015

Carnegie Historic Landmarks Preservation Society • 14687 Main St, P.O. Box 118 • Moores Hill, IN 47032 • (812) 744-4015

Mooresville

Mooresville Public Library • 220 W Harrison St • Mooresville, IN 46158 • (317) 831-7323 • http://www.mooresvillelib.org

Morocco

Newton County Historian • P.O. Box 86 • Morocco, IN 47963 • (219) 285-2861

Mount Vernon

Alexandrian Public Library • 115 W 5th St • Mount Vernon, IN 47620-1869 • (812) 838-3286 • http://www.apl.lib.in.us

Posey County Historian • 9016 Schroeder Ct • Mount Vernon, IN 47620-9695 • (812) 985-9346

Posey County Historical Society • P.O. Box 171 • Mount Vernon, IN 47620 • http://www.rootsweb.com/~inposey/society.htm

Muncie

Alexander M Bracken Library • Ball State University, 2000 University Ave • Muncie, IN 47306-1099 • (765) 285-5078 • http://www.library.bsu.edu

Delaware County Historical Alliance • Moore-Youse Historical Museum, 120 E Washington • Muncie, IN 47308 • (765) 282-1550 • http://www.dchsmunciein.org

Emily Kimbrough House Museum • 715 E Washington • Muncie, IN 47305 • (317) 282-1550

Minnetrista Cultural Center & Oakhurst Gardens • 1200 N Minnetrista Pkwy • Muncie, IN 47303 • (765) 282-4848 • http://www.minnetrista.net

Muncie Center Township Public Library • 2005 S High St • Muncie, IN 47302 • (765) 747-8204 • http://www.munpl.org

Muncie-Center Township Public Library • 301 E Jackson St • Muncie, IN 47305-1878 • (765) 757-8200 • http://www.munpl.org

National Model Aviation Museum • 515 E Memorial Dr • Muncie, IN 47302 • (765) 289-4236 • http://www.modelaircraft.org

Munster

Munster Historical Society • 1005 Ridge Rd, Town Hall • Munster, IN 46321 • (219) 838-3296 • http://members.aol.com/_hta/oldmunster/mhstree/Page_lx.html

Nappanee

Museum at Amish Acres • 1600 W Market St • Nappanee, IN 46550 • (219) 773-4188 • http://www.amishacres.com

Nappanee Public LIbrary • 157 N Main St • Nappanee, IN 46550 • (574) 773-7919 • http://www.nappanee.lib.in.us

Nashville

Brown County Genealogical Society • P.O. Box 1202 • Nashville, IN 47448 • (812) 988-4297 • http://www.rootsweb.com/~inbcgs/title.htm

Brown County Historical Society • Historical Museum, 1934 State Rd 135 N, P.O. Box 668 • Nashville, IN 47448 • (812) 988-6089 • http://www.browneountyhistory.info

Brown County Public Library • 205 Locust Lane, P.O. Box 8 • Nashville, IN 47448-0008 • (812) 988-2850 • http://www.browncounty.lib.in.us

T C Steele State Historic Site Museum • 4220 T C Steele Rd • Nashville, IN 47448 • (812) 988-4785 • http://www.state.in.us.ism

New Albany

Carnegie Center for History • 201 E Spring St • New Albany, IN 47150 • (812) 944-7336 • http://www.carnegiecenter.org

Culbertson Mansion State Historic Site • 914 E Main St • New Albany, IN 47150 • (812) 944-9600 • http://www.indianamuseum.com

Floyd County Historical Society • P.O. Box 455 • New Albany, IN 47151-0455 • (812) 948-0256

Floyd County Museum • 509 W Market St • New Albany, IN 47150 • (812) 949-2551

New Albany-Floyd County Public Library • 180 W Spring St • New Albany, IN 47150-3692 • (812) 944-8464 • http://www.nafcpl.lib.in.us

Schribner House Museum • P.O. Box 881 • New Albany, IN 47151 • (812) 949-1776

Southern Indiana Genealogical Society • P.O. Box 665 • New Albany, IN 47151-0665 • (812) 923-3492 • http://www.rootsweb.com/~insigs/

Vintage Fire Engines Museum • 402 Mount Tabor Rd • New Albany, IN 47151 • (812) 941-9901

New Carlisle
Historic New Carlisle • P.O. Box 107 • New Carlisle, IN 46552

New Carlisle and Olive Township Public Library • 408 S Bray St, P.O. Box Q • New Carlisle, IN 46552-0837 • (574) 654-3046 • http://www.ncpl.lib.in.us

Saint Joseph County Historian • 7982 E Potato Hole Ct • New Carlisle, IN 46552 • (574) 284-5282

Henry County Genealogical Society • c/o New Castle-Henry County Public Library, 376 S 15th St, P.O. Box J • New Castle, IN 47362 • (765) 529-0362 • http://www.nchcpl.lib.in.us

Henry County Historical Society • Historical Museum, 606 S 14th St • New Castle, IN 47362-3339 • (765) 529-7218 • http://www.kiva.net/~hchisoc/museum.htm

New Castle-Henry County Public Library • 376 S 15th St, P.O. Box J • New Castle, IN 47362-1050 • (765) 529-0362 • http://www.nchcpl.lib.in.us

New Harmony
Historic New Harmony • David Lenz House Museum, 506 1/2 Main St, P.O. Box 579 • New Harmony, IN 47631 • (812) 682-4488 • http://www.newharmony.org

New Harmony State Historic Site Museum • 410 N Main St, P.O. Box 607 • New Harmony, IN 47631 • (812) 682-3271

New Harmony Workingmen's Library & Museum • 407 W Tavern St, P.O. Box 368 • New Harmony, IN 47631 • (812) 682-4806 • http://www.newharmonywmi.lib.in.us

New Haven
Besancon Historical Society • 15535 Lincoln Hwy E • New Haven, IN 46774 • (219) 749-4525 • http://www.ipfw.edu/ipfwhist/historgs/besanco.htm

Fort Wayne Railroad Historical Society • 15808 Edgerton Rd • New Haven, IN 46774 • (260) 493-0765

Maumee Valley Antique Steam and Gas Engines Associates • 1702 S Webster Rd • New Haven, IN 46774 • (260) 748-4985

New Palestine
Order of the Indian Wars of the United States • 126 E Main St • New Palestine, IN 46163 • (317) 861-1875 • http://www.oiwus.org

New Paris
New Paris Historical Society • P.O. Box 101 • New Paris, IN 46553

New Pekin
Pekin Historical Society • 50 W Main St, P.O. Box 310 • New Pekin, IN 47165-7939

New Whiteland
West Indianapolis Historical Society • 48 Bradford Pl • New Whiteland, IN 46184

Newburgh
Historic Newburgh • Historical Museum, 200 State St, P.O. Box 543 • Newburgh, IN 47630 • (812) 853-2815 • http://www.newburgh.org

Ohio Township Public Library System • 23 W Jennings St • Newburgh, IN 47630-1408 • (812) 853-5468 • http://www.ohio.lib.in.us

Simpson Mortuary Museum • P.O. Box 367 • Newburgh, IN 47630

Newport
Newport-Vermillion County Library • 385 E Market St, P.O. Box 100 • Newport, IN 47966-0100 • (765) 492-3555 • http://www.rootsweb.com/~invermil/library.htm

Vermillion County Historical Society • 220 E Market St, P.O. Box 273 • Newport, IN 47966 • (765) 492-3570 • http://vcihs.homestead.com

Noblesville
Hamilton County Historian • 384 N 11th St • Noblesville, IN 46060-2146 • (317) 773-3454

Hamilton County Historical Society • Historical Museum, 810 Conner St, P.O. Box 397 • Noblesville, IN 46061 • (317) 770-0775 • http://www.noblesville.com/history.htm

Indiana Transportation Museum • 325 Cicero Rd, P.O. Box 83 • Noblesville, IN 46060 • (317) 773-6000 • http://www.itm.org

Noblesville Public Library • 1 Library Plaza • Noblesville, IN 46060-5639 • (317) 773-1384 • http://www.hepl.lib.in.us

North Judson
Hoosier Valley Railroad Museum • 507 Mulberry St, P.O. Box 75 • North Judson, IN 46366-0075 • (574) 896-3950 • http://hvrm.railfan.net

North Judson-Wayne Township Public Library • 208 Keller Ave • North Judson, IN 46366 • (574) 896-2841 • http://www.njwt.lib.in.us

North Manchester
Manchester College Museum • Manchester College • North Manchester, IN 46962 • (219) 982-5361

North Manchester Historical Society • Historical Museum, 120 E Main St, P.O. Box 361 • North Manchester, IN 46962 • (219) 982-4706 • http://mcs.kl2.in.us/histsoc/

North Manchester Public Library • 405 N Market St • North Manchester, IN 46962 • (260) 982-4773 • http://www.nman.lib.in.us

North Vernon
Jennings County Genealogical Society • P.O. Box 863 • North Vernon, IN 47265-0863

Jennings County Historian • 1090 East 50 North • North Vernon, IN 47265-1090 • (812) 346-8989

Jennings County Public Library • 2375 N State Hwy 3 • North Vernon, IN 47265-1596 • (812) 346-2091 • http://www.jenningscounty.lib.in.us

Vernon High Memorabilia Room • 2730 W County Rd 200 N • North Vernon, IN 47265 • (812) 346-2780

Notre Dame
Cushwa Center for the Study of American Catholicism • Hesburgh Library, Univ of Notre Dame • Notre Dame, IN 46556 • (219) 631-5441 • http://www.nd.edu

Indiana Province Archives Center, Congregation of Holy Cross • Douglas Rd & US 33, P.O. Box 568 • Notre Dame, IN 46556 • (219) 631-5371

University Libraries of Notre Dame • 221 Hesburgh Library • Notre Dame, IN 46556 • (574) 631-5252 • http://www.nd.edu/~ndlibs

Oakford
Howard County Genealogical Society • P.O. Box 2 • Oakford, IN 46965-0002 • (765) 457-3242 • http://www.rootsweb.com/~inhoward/gensoc.html

Oakland City
Oakland City-Columbia Township Public Library • 210 S Main • Oakland City, IN 47660 • (812) 749-3559

Odon
Odon Winkelpleck Memorial Library • 202 W Main St • Odon, IN 47562 • (812) 636-4949 • http://www.odon.lib.in.us

Ogden Dunes
Historical Society of Ogden Dunes • Hour Glass Museum, 115 Hillcrest Rd • Ogden Dunes, IN 46368-1001 • (219) 762-1268 • http://members.tripod.com/~Ogden_Dunes/

Orestes
Orestes Historical Society • P.O. Box 155 • Orestes, IN 46063 • (317) 754-8893

Orland
Fort Collins School Museum • 200 Mathews St, P.O. Box 93 • Orland, IN 46776 • (970) 416-2705

Orleans
Orleans Town & Township Public Library • 174 N Maple St, P.O. Box 142 • Orleans, IN 47452 • (812) 865-3270 • http://www.orleans.lib.in.us

Osceola
Osceola Historical Society • P.O. Box 14 • Osceola, IN 46561 • (219) 674-8956

Osgood
Osgood Public Library • 136 W Ripley St • Osgood, IN 47037-0235 • (812) 689-4011 • http://www.osgoodlibrary.org

Ripley County Historian • 643 Columbia Ave • Osgood, IN 47037-1124 • (812) 689-4755

Ossian
Twin Oaks Genealogy • P.O. Box 94 • Ossian, IN 46777-0094

Otterbein
Otterbein Public Library • 104 S Main St, P.O. Box 550 • Otterbein, IN 47970 • (765) 583-2107 • http://www.otterbein.lib.in.us

Owensville
Owensville Carnegie Library • 110 S Main St, P.O. Box 218 • Owensville, IN 47665-0218 • (812) 724-3335

Oxford
Heritage House Museum • 208 N Justus St • Oxford, IN 47971 • (765) 385-5380

Oxford Public Library • 201 E Smith St, P.O. Box 6 • Oxford, IN 47971-0006 • (765) 385-2177 • http://www.mwprairienet.lib.in.us/Social_Services/oxford.html

Palmyra
Palmyra Historical Society • Historical Museum, Commercial Bldg • Palmyra, IN 47164

Paoli
Orange County Genealogical Society • 301 W Main St, P.O. Box 344 • Paoli, IN 47454 • (812) 723-3437 • http://www.usgennet.org/usa/in/county/orange/gensoc.htm

Orange County Historian • 28 Library St • Paoli, IN 47454-1356 • (812) 723-4238

Orange County Historical Society • Thomas Elwood Lindley House Museum, P.O. Box 454 • Paoli, IN 47454 • (812) 723-4769 • http://www.rootsweb.com/~inochs/ocmuseum.htm

Paoli Public Library • 10 NE Court Square • Paoli, IN 47454 • (812) 723-3841 • http://www.sanroy.com/Pll/library

Pekin
Pekin Historical Society • general delivery • Pekin, IN 47165

Pendleton
Pendleton Community Library • 595 E Water St • Pendleton, IN 46064 • (765) 778-7527 • http://www.pendleton.lib.in.us

Pendleton Historical Museum • 299 Falls Park Dr, P.O. Box 345 • Pendleton, IN 46064 • (765) 778-4248

Pennville
Pennville Township Public Library • 195 N Union, P.O. Box 206 • Pennville, IN 47369-0206 • (260) 731-3333

Perrysville
Skinner Farm Museum & Village • 1850 W SR 32 • Perrysville, IN 47974 • (765) 793-4079 • http://skinnervillage.eshire.net

Vermillion County Historian • 1850 W State Rd 32 • Perrysville, IN 47974 • (765) 793-3022

Peru
Belgian Researchers • 495 E 5th St • Peru, IN 46970 • (765) 473-5667

Circus City Festival Museum • 154 N Broadway • Peru, IN 46970 • (765) 472-3918 • http://www.perucircus.com

Grissom Air Museum • 1000 W Hoosier Blvd • Peru, IN 46970 • (765) 689-8011 • http://www.grissomairmuseum.com

International Circus Hall of Fame • 3076 E Circus Ln, P.O. Box 700 • Peru, IN 46970 • (765) 472-7553 • http://www.circushalloffame.com

Miami County Genealogical Society • P.O. Box 542 • Peru, IN 46970 • (765) 985-3435 • http://www.rootsweb.com/~inmiami/gensoc.html

Miami County Historian • 14 W 6th St, P.O. Box 414 • Peru, IN 46970 • (765) 472-3987

Miami County Historical Society • Miami County Museum, 51 N Broadway, Rm 102 • Peru, IN 46970 • (765) 473-9183 • http://www.miamicountymuseum.com

Miami Nation of Indians in the State of Indiana • 80 W 6th St, P.O. Box 41 • Peru, IN 46970 • (765) 473-9631

Peru Public Library • 102 E Main St • Peru, IN 46970-2338 • (765) 473-3069 • http://www.peru.lib.in.us

Petersburg
Pike County Historian • 709 Locust St • Petersburg, IN 47567 • (812) 354-1043

Pike County Historical Society • c/o Pike County Public Library, 1104 Main St, P.O. Box 216 • Petersburg, IN 47567

Pike County Public Library • 1104 Main St • Petersburg, IN 47567 • (812) 354-6257 • http://www.pikeco.lib.in.us

Pierceton
Pierceton & Washington Township Library • 101 Catholic St, P.O. Box 328 • Pierceton, IN 46562-0328 • (574) 594-5474

Plainfield
Guilford Township Historical Society • c/o Plainfield Public Library, 1120 Stafford Rd • Plainfield, IN 46168 • (317) 839-6602

Plainfield Public Library • 1120 Stafford Rd • Plainfield, IN 46163 • (317) 839-6602 • http://www.plainfield.lib.in.us/history/history.html

Plymouth
Marshall County Genealogical Society • Historical Museum, 123 N Michigan St • Plymouth, IN 46563-2132 • (574) 936-2306 • http://www.mchistoricalsociety.org

Marshall County Historian • 430 Clark St • Plymouth, IN 46562 • (574) 936-2306 • http://www.mchistoricalsociety.org

Marshall County Historical Center • 317 W Monroe St • Plymouth, IN 46563

Marshall County Historical Society • Historical Museum, 123 N Michigan St • Plymouth, IN 46563-2132 • (574) 936-2306 • http://www.mchistoricalsociety.org

Plymouth Public Library • 201 N Center St • Plymouth, IN 46563 • (574) 936-2324 • http://www.plymouth.lib.in.us

Portage
Al Goin Historical Museum • Countryside Park, 5250 US Hwy 6 • Portage, IN 46368 • (219) 762-8349

Historical Society of Ogden Dunes • 101 Ogden Dunes • Portage, IN 46368-1268 • (219) 762-1268 • http://members.tripod.com/~Ogden_Dunes/

Lake County Historical Society • 5131 Canterbury Ave • Portage, IN 46368 • (219) 662-3975 • http://www.crownpoint.net/museum.htm

Portage Community Historical Society • Countryside Museum, 2100 Willowcreek Rd • Portage, IN 46368 • (219) 762-4218

Porter County Public Library-Portage Public • 2665 Irving St • Portage, IN 46368 • (219) 763-1508 • http://www.pcpls.lib.in.us

Porter
Bailly-Chellberg Historic Area Museum • 1100 N Mineral Springs Rd • Porter, IN 46304 • (219) 926-7561

Portland
Jay County Genealogy Society • 109 S Commerce St, Ste E, P.O. Box 1086 • Portland, IN 47371 • (260) 726-4323 • http://www.rootsweb.com/~injay/jaygene.htm

Jay County Historian • 1400 S Meridian St • Portland, IN 47371 • (260) 726-7111

Jay County Historical Society • Historical Museum, 903 E Main St, P.O. Box 1282 • Portland, IN 47371 • (260) 726-7168 • http://www.rootsweb.com/~injay/research/ jayhist.htm

Portland
Jay County Public Library • 15 N Ship St • Portland, IN 47371 • (260) 726-7890 • http://www.jaycpl.lib.in.us

Museum of the Soldier • 510 E Arch St, P.O. Box 518 • Portland, IN 47371 • (260) 726-2967 • http://www.museumofthesoldier.com

Poseyville
Poseyville Carnegie Public Library • 55 S Cale St, P.O. Box 220 • Poseyville, IN 47633-0220 • (812) 874-3418 • http://www.librarydirector.com

Princeton
Gibson County Historian • Route 2, Box 97 • Princeton, IN 47670 • (812) 386-1221

Gibson County Historical Society • Historical Museum, P.O. Box 516 • Princeton, IN 47670 • (812) 385-5834

Princeton Public Library • 124 S Hart St • Princeton, IN 47670 • (812) 385-4464 • http://www.princetonpl.lib.in.us

Raub
York Township Public Library • 8475 North 885th West • Raub, IN 47976 • (219) 474-5689

Remington
Remington-Carpenter Township Public Library • 105 Ohio St, P.O. Box 65 • Remington, IN 47977 • (219) 261-2543 • http://www.rctpl.com

Rensselaer
Jasper County Historian • 128 S Augusta St • Rensselaer, IN 47978 • (219) 866-5433

Jasper County Historical Museum • 605 Milroy • Rensselaer, IN 47978 • (219) 866-6227

Jasper County Historical Society • 475 N Van Rensselaer St • Rensselaer, IN 47978 • (219) 866-5433

Jasper County Public Library • 208 W Susan St • Rensselaer, IN 47978 • (219) 866-5881 • http://www.jasperco.lib.in.us

Richmond
Lilly Library-Friends Collection • Earlham College, 801 National Rd W • Richmond, IN 47374-4095 • (765) 983-1360 • http://www.earlham.edu/~libr/

Morrison-Reeves Library • 80 N 6th St • Richmond, IN 47374-3079 • (765) 966-8291 • http://www.mrl.lib.in.us

Wayne County Genealogical Society • Historical Museum, 1150 North A Street, P.O. Box 2599 • Richmond, IN 47375-2599 • (765) 935-0164 • http://www.waynet.org/nonprofit/wcgs.htm

Wayne County Historical Society • Historical Museum, 1150 North A Street • Richmond, IN 47374 • (765) 962-5756 • http://www.wchm.org; http://www.waynecountyhistoricalmuseum.com

Ridgeville
Ridgeville Public Library • 308 N Walnut St, P.O. Box 63 • Ridgeville, IN 47380-0063 • (765) 857-2025

Rising Sun
Ohio County Historian • 832 4th St • Rising Sun, IN 47040 • (812) 438-3264

Ohio County Historical Society • Historical Museum, 212 S Walnut St, P.O. Box 194 • Rising Sun, IN 47040 • (812) 438-4915 • http://www.ohiocountyinmusem.org

Ohio County Public Library • 100 N High St • Rising Sun, IN 47040-1022 • (812) 438-2257 • http://www.ohioco.lib.in.us

Roachdale
Roachdale-Franklin Township Public Library • 100 E Washington St, P.O. Box 399 • Roachdale, IN 46172-0399 • (765) 522-1491

Roann
Roann Paw Paw Township Public Library • 240 S Chippewa Rd, P.O. Box 248 • Roann, IN 46974-0248 • (765) 833-5231 • http://www.roannpubliclibrary.com

Roanoke
Roanoke Area Heritage Center • 102 W 1st St, P.O. Box 13 • Roanoke, IN 46783

Roanoke Public Library • 126 N Main St, P.O. Box 249 • Roanoke, IN 46783-0249 • (260) 672-2989 • http://www.roanoke.lib.in.us

Rochester
Fulton County Historical Society • Historical Museum, 37 East 375 North • Rochester, IN 46975 • (574) 223-4436 • http://www.icss.net/~fchs/

Fulton County Public Library • 320 W 7th St • Rochester, IN 46975-1332 • (574) 223-2713 • http://www.fulco.lib.in.us

Prill School Museum • 500 W 7th St • Rochester, IN 46975 • (219) 223-5108

Rockport
Lincoln Pioneer Village & Museum • 416 Main St • Rockport, IN 47635 • (812) 649-2615

Spencer County Historical Society • c/o Spencer County Public Library, 210 Walnut St • Rockport, IN 47635 • (812) 649-4866 • http://www.rockport-spco.lib.in.us

Spencer County Public Library • 210 Walnut St • Rockport, IN 47635-1398 • (812) 649-4866 • http://www.rockport-spco.lib.in.us

Rockville
Billie Creek Village Museum • Route 2, Box 27 • Rockville, IN 47872 • (765) 569-3430 • http://www.billiecreekvillage.org

Parke County Historian • 418 N College St • Rockville, IN 47872-1509 • (765) 569-5826

Parke County Historical Society • 503 W Ohio St, P.O. Box 332 • Rockville, IN 47872 • (765) 569-2223 • http://www.parkecountyhistoricalsociety.org

Rockville Public Library • 106 N Market St • Rockville, IN 47872 • (765) 569-5544 • http://rockvillepl.lib.in.us

Rome
Perry County Historical Society • P.O. Box 220 • Rome, IN 47574

Rome City
Gene Stratton-Porter State Historic Site Museum • 1205 Pleasant Point, P.O. Box 639 • Rome City, IN 46784 • (260) 854-3700 • http://www.genestratton-porter.com

Roselawn
Newton County Public Library-Roselawn Library • 4077 Kellar, P.O. Box 87 • Roselawn, IN 46372-0087 • (219) 345-2010

Royal Center
Royal Center-Boone Township Public Library • 203 N Chicago St, P.O. Box 459 • Royal Center, IN 46978-0459 • (574) 643-3185

Rushville
Gowdy House Museum • Route 1, Box 199 • Rushville, IN 46173 • (765) 932-4904

Rush County Historian • 1744 N 450 E • Rushville, IN 46173 • (765) 932-5204

Rush County Historical Society • Historical Museum, 619 N Perkins St, P.O. Box 302 • Rushville, IN 46173 • (765) 932-2492 • http://www.rushcounty.com/hstgen/society.html

Rushville Public Library • 130 W 3rd St • Rushville, IN 46173-1899 • (765) 932-3496 • http://www.rushcounty.com/library/

Saint John
Saint John Historical Society • 9490 Keilman St, P.O. Box 134 • Saint John, IN 46373 • (219) 365-8550

Saint Mary-of-the-Woods
Saint Mary-of-the-Woods College Library • 3301 Saint Mary's Rd • Saint Mary-of-the-Woods, IN 47876 • (812) 535-5255 • http://www.smwc.edu/current/library

Salem
Piper Aircraft Museum • 2593 W SR 56 • Salem, IN 47167 • (812) 883-9772

Salem Public Library • 212 N Main St • Salem, IN 47167 • (812) 883-5600 • http://www.salemlib.lib.in.us

Washington County Historian • 407 W Market St • Salem, IN 47167 • (812) 883-6495

Washington County Historical Society • Stevens Museum, 307 E Market St • Salem, IN 47167 • (812) 833-6495 • http://www.stevensmuseum.com

Santa Claus
Holiday World Museum • One Holiday Square, P.O. Box 179 • Santa Claus, IN 47579 • (812) 937-4401 • http://www.holidayworld.com

Schererville
Schererville Historical Society • Historical Museum, P.O. Box 333 • Schererville, IN 46375 • (219) 322-1699

Scipio
Jennings County Genealogical Society • RR1, Box 227 • Scipio, IN 47273

Scotland
Scotland Historical Society • Historical Museum, P.O. Box 173 • Scotland, IN 47457 • http://www.greenecountyin.org/scotland.htm

Scottsburg
Preservation Alliance Museum • P.O. Box 122 • Scottsburg, IN 47170 • (812) 752-7268

Scott County Genealogical Society • Heritage Center Museum, 1050 S Main St, P.O. Box 23 • Scottsburg, IN 47170-0023 • (812) 752-3388 • http://SCGSI.com

Scott County Historian • 4898 Wind Drift Farm • Scottsburg, IN 47170-8420 • (812) 794-4205

Scott County Historical Society • Scottsburg Heritage Station, 90 N Main St, P.O. Box 245 • Scottsburg, IN 47170-0245

Scott County Public Library • 108 S Main St • Scottsburg, IN 47170 • (812) 752-2751 • http://www.scott.lib.in.us

Sellersburg
Charlestown-Clark County Public Library • 430 N Indiana • Sellersburg, IN 47172 • (812) 246-4493 • http://www.clarkco.lib.in.us/sellersburg.htm

Seymour
Jackson County Genealogical Society • 415 Walnut St, P.O. Box 986 • Seymour, IN 47274

Jackson County Public Library • 303 W 2nd St • Seymour, IN 47274-2147 • (812) 522-3412 • http://www.japl.lib.in.us

Jennings County Historical Society • 134 E Brown St • Seymour, IN 47274 • (812) 346-8989

Shelbyville
Shelby County Genealogical Society • Grover Museum, 52 W Broadway, P.O. Box 434 • Shelbyville, IN 46176-0434 • (317) 392-4634 • http://www.rootsweb.com/~inshelby/

Shelby County Historian • 309 E Jackson St • Shelbyville, IN 46176 • (317) 392-3826

Shelby County Historical Society • Grover Museum, 52 W Broadway, P.O. Box 74 • Shelbyville, IN 46176 • (317) 392-4634 • http://www.grovermuseum.org

Shelbyville Public Library - Gen & History Rm • 57 W Broadway • Shelbyville, IN 46176 • (317) 398-7121 • http://www.sscpl.lib.in.us/library/

Sheridan
Marion-Adams Historical and Genealogical Society • 308 Main St • Sheridan, IN 46069 • (317) 758-5765

Sheridan Historical Society • 308 S Main St • Sheridan, IN 46069 • (317) 758-5054 • http://www.sheridannews.net/historicalsociety

Sheridan Public Library • 214 S Main St • Sheridan, IN 46069 • (317) 758-5201 • http://www.sheridan.lib.in.us

Shipshewana
Menno-Hof Museum • P.O. Box 701 • Shipshewana, IN 46565 • (219) 768-4117

Shipshewana Area Historical Society • 240 N Talmadge St • Shipshewana, IN 46565 • (260) 768-3030

Shirley
Shirley Centennial Historical Society • Historic Museum, 402 S Railroad St, P.O. Box 69 • Shirley, IN 47384-0069 • (765) 737-6119

Shoals
Martin County Genealogical Society • P.O. Box 45 • Shoals, IN 47581 • (812) 247-3297 • http://www.rootsweb.com/~inmartin/society.htm

Martin County Historian • P.O. Box 58 • Shoals, IN 47581 • (812) 247-2293

Martin County Historical Society • 220 Capitol Ave, P.O. Box 564 • Shoals, IN 47581 • (812) 247-1133

Martin County Museum • 505 High St • Shoals, IN 47581 • (812) 247-2293

Shoals Public Library • 402 N High St, P.O. Box 909 • Shoals, IN 47581-0909 • (812) 247-3838 • http://www.shoals.lib.in.us

South Bend
College Football Hall of Fame • 111 S Saint Joseph St • South Bend, IN 46601 • (219) 235-5605 • http://www.collegefootball.org

Fellowship of Brethren Genealogists • 828 Cavanaugh • South Bend, IN 46617-2205

Michiana Jewish Historical Society • P.O. Box 11074 • South Bend, IN 46634-0074 • (219) 233-9553

Northern Indiana Historical Society • Center For History, 808 W Washington • South Bend, IN 46601 • (574) 235-9664 • http://www.centerforhistory.org

Old Lakeville School Museum • P.O. Box 1558 • South Bend, IN 46634-1558 • (219) 784-2749

Saint Joseph County Public Library • 304 S Main St • South Bend, IN 46601 • (574) 282-4630 • http://www.sjcpl.lib.in.us

South Bend Archives and Records Center • 1140 S Lafayette Blvd • South Bend, IN 46601 • (574) 235-9091 • http://www.stjosephcountyindiana.com

South Bend Area Genealogical Society • P.O. Box 1222 • South Bend, IN 46624-1222

Studebaker National Museum • 201 S Chapin St • South Bend, IN 46601 • (574) 235-9714 • http://www.studebakermuseum.org

South Whitley
South Whitley-Cleveland Township Public Library • 201 E Front St, P.O. Box 536 • South Whitley, IN 46787-0536 • (260) 723-5321

Southport
Perry Township-Southport Historical Society • 6901 Derbyshire Rd • Southport, IN 46227

Speedway
Speedway Public Library • 5633 W 25th St • Speedway, IN 46224 • (317) 243-8959 • http://www.speedway.lib.in.us

Spencer
Owen County Historian • P.O. Box 654 • Spencer, IN 46460 • (812) 325-9007

Owen County Historical and Genealogical Society • 110 E Market St, P.O. Box 569 • Spencer, IN 47460-0569 • (812) 829-3392 • http://www.owen.in.us/owenhist/owen.htm

Owen County Public Library • 10 S Montgomery St • Spencer, IN 47460 • (812) 829-3392 • http://www.owenlib.org

Spiceland
Henry County Historian • 303 S Pearl St • Spiceland, IN 47385 • (765) 987-7182

Spiceland Town-Township Public Library • 106 W Main St • Spiceland, IN 47385 • (765) 987-7472

Springport
Genealogical Society of Henry County Indiana • 6884 N Prairie Rd • Springport, IN 47386 • http://www.rootsweb.com/~ingshc/

Sullivan
Sullivan County Genealogical Society • Historical Museum, 10 S Court, P.O. Box 3266 • Sullivan, IN 47882 • (812) 268-6253 • http://www.rootsweb.com/~inschs

Sullivan County Historical Society • Historical Museum, 10 S Court St, P.O. Box 326 • Sullivan, IN 47882-0326 • (812) 268-6253 • http://www.rootsweb.com/~inschs/

Sullivan County Public Library - Gen & Local History • 100 S Crowder St • Sullivan, IN 47882 • (812) 268-4957 • http://www.sullivan.lib.in.us

Summitville
Summitville Van Buren Township Historical Society • P.O. Box 242 • Summitville, IN 46070 • (765) 536-4222

Swayzee
Swayzee Public Library • 301 S Washington, P.O. Box 307 • Swayzee, IN 46986-0307 • (765) 922-7526

Syracuse
Kosciusko County Historian • 1010 N Huntington • Syracuse, IN 46567 • (574) 457-3891

Syracuse Turkey Creek Township Public Library • 115 E Main St • Syracuse, IN 46567 • (574) 457-3022 • http://www.syracuse.lib.in.us

Syracuse-Wawasee Historical Museum • 1013 N Long Dr • Syracuse, IN 46542 • (574) 457-3599 • http://www.syracusemuseum.org

Taswell
Crawford County Historian • 866 N Sycamore Rd • Taswell, IN 47175 • (812) 338-2057

Tell City
Perry County Historian • P.O. Box 92 • Tell City, IN 46586 • (812) 547-3441

Perry County Historical Society • 538 11th St • Tell City, IN 47586

Tell City Historical Society • Historical Museum, 948 9th St, P.O. Box 728 • Tell City, IN 47586 • (812) 547-9695

Tell City-Perry County Public Library • 2328 Tell St • Tell City, IN 47586 • (812) 547-2661 • http://www.psci.net/~tcpublib

Terre Haute
Candles Holocaust Museum and Education Center • 1532 S 3rd St • Terre Haute, IN 47802 • (812) 234-7881 • http://www.candles-museum.com

Central Presbyterian Church Library • 125 N 7th St • Terre Haute, IN 47807-3195 • (812) 232-5049 • http://home1.gte.net/cenpres/

Cunningham Memorial Library - Special Collections • Indiana State Univ, 650 Sycamore • Terre Haute, IN 47809 • (812) 237-2580 • http://library.indstate.edu

Emline Fairbanks Memorial Library • 222 N 7th • Terre Haute, IN 47807

Eugene V Debs Foundation • Debs Historic Home, 451 N 8th St, P.O. Box 843 • Terre Haute, IN 47808 • (812) 232-2163 • http://www.eugenevdebs.com

Lost Creek Lineage Company • 1408 N 30th St • Terre Haute, IN 47803 • (812) 466-7845

Native American Museum • 5170 E Poplar St • Terre Haute, IN 47803 • (812) 877-6007

Paul Dresser Memorial Birthplace • 1411 S 6th St • Terre Haute, IN 47802-1114 • (812) 235-9717 • http://www.indstate.edu/community/uchs/

Terre Haute Brewery Museum • P.O. Box 2027 • Terre Haute, IN 47802-0027 • (812) 234-2800

Vigo County Historian • 236 McKinley Blvd • Terre Haute, IN 47803-1914 • (812) 232-3800

Vigo County Historical Society • Historical Museum, 1411 S 6th St • Terre Haute, IN 47807 • (812) 235-9717 • http://vigohistory.com

Vigo County Public Library • 1 Library Square • Terre Haute, IN 47807 • (812) 232-1113 • http://www.vigo.lib.in.us

Wabash Valley Genealogical Society • 2906 E Morris Ave, P.O. Box 85 • Terre Haute, IN 47805 • (812) 466-1065 • http://www.inwvgs.org

Thorntown
Boone County Genealogical Society • P. O. Box 83 • Thorntown, IN 46071-0083 • http://www.bccn.boone.in.us/tpl/bcgs/

Society for Preservation of Indiana Heritage • P.O. Box 23 • Thorntown, IN 46071 • (765) 436-2202

Sugar Creek Historical Society • Heritage Museum, 124 W Main St, P.O. Box 23 • Thorntown, IN 46071 • (765) 436-2202 • http://www.countyhistory.com/thorntown/

Thorntown Public Library • 124 N Market St • Thorntown, IN 46071-1144 • (765) 436-7348 • http://www.bccn.boone.in.us/tpl/

Tipton

Palatines to America, Indiana Chapter • 234 W Jefferson St • Tipton, IN 46072-1850

Tipton County Historian and Genealogist • 124 N Conde • Tipton, IN 46072 • (765) 675-7781

Tipton County Historical Museum • 337 Sweetland Ave • Tipton, IN 46072 • (765) 675-4466

Tipton County Historical Society • Heritage Center, 323 W South St • Tipton, IN 46072 • (765) 675-5828 • http://tiptonhistorical.org

Tipton County Public Library • 127 E Madison St • Tipton, IN 46072 • (765) 675-8761 • http://www.tiptonpl.lib.in.us

Topeka

LaGrange County Historian • P.O. Box 555 • Topeka, IN 46571 • (260) 593-2593

Topeka Area Historical Society • 123 Indiana St, P.O. Box 33 • Topeka, IN 46571 • (219) 593-3613

Topeka Depot Museum • P.O. Box 33 • Topeka, IN 46571 • (219) 593-2531

Union City

Union City Public Library • 408 N Columbia St • Union City, IN 47390-1404 • (765) 964-4748 • http://www.unioncity.lib.in.us

Uniondale

Who When Where • 7077 N 100 W • Uniondale, IN 46791 • (219) 543-2423

Upland

Upland Area Historical Society • 101 N Main St, P.O. Box 577 • Upland, IN 46989

Vallonia

Fort Vallonia Museum • P.O. Box 104 • Vallonia, IN 47281 • (812) 358-3137

Valparaiso

Northwest Indiana Genealogical Society • c/o Valparaiso Public Library, 103 Jefferson St • Valparaiso, IN 46383 • (219) 462-0524

Porter County Historian • 107 E Jefferson St • Valparaiso, IN 46383 • (219) 462-0524

Porter County Historical Society • Old Jail Museum, 153 Franklin St • Valparaiso, IN 46383 • (219) 465-3595 • http://www.portercountymuseum.org

Porter County Public Library • 103 Jefferson St • Valparaiso, IN 46383-4820 • (219) 462-0524 • http://www.pcpls.lib.in.us

Porter County Public Library Genealogical Group • c/o Porter County Public Library, 103 Jefferson St • Valparaiso, IN 46383 • (219) 462-0524 • http://www.rootsweb.com/~inlake/nwigs.htm

Veedersburg

Fountain County Genealogical Society • 405 N Mill St, P.O. Box 273 • Veedersburg, IN 47987 • (765) 294-4954 • http://glenmar.com/~emoyhbo/fcgs.html

Fountain County Historical Society • Historical Museum, 3219 E New Richmond Rd • Veedersburg, IN 47994 • (765) 295-2604

Fountain County War Museum • 116 E 1st St • Veedersburg, IN 47987 • (765) 793-2321

Veedersburg Public Library • 408 N Main St • Veedersburg, IN 47987 • (765) 294-2808 • http://glenmar.com/~emoyhbo/vburglib.html

Vernon

Jennings County Historical Society • 134 E Brown St, P.O. Box 335 • Vernon, IN 47282 • (812) 377-7706 • http://jenningscohs.org

North American House Museum • 3375 N Linden Rd, P.O. Box 335 • Vernon, IN 47282 • (812) 346-8989

Versailles

Ripley County Historical Society • Historical Museum, 125 Washington St, P.O. Box 525 • Versailles, IN 47042 • (812) 689-3031 • http://www.seidata.com/~rchslib/

Tyson Library • 325 W Tyson St, P.O. Box 769 • Versailles, IN 47042-0769 • (812) 689-5894 • http://tysonlibrary.org

Vevay

Life on the Ohio River History Museum • 208 E Market St, P.O. Box 201 • Vevay, IN 47043

Switzerland County Historian • 59 Knox Ford Rd • Vevay, IN 47043 • (812) 427-2272

Switzerland County Historical Society • Historical Museum, Main & Market Sts, P.O. Box 201 • Vevay, IN 47043 • (812) 427-3560 • http://www.switzcpl.lib.in.us/historicalsociety.html

Switzerland County Public Library • 205 Ferry St, P.O. Box 133 • Vevay, IN 47043-0133 • (812) 427-3363 • http://www.switzcpl.lib.in.us

UP Schenk House Museum • 209 W Market • Vevay, IN 47043

Vincennes

Byron R Lewis Historical Collections Library • Vincennes Univ, 1002 N 1st St • Vincennes, IN 47591 • (812) 888-5810 • http://www.vinu.edu/lewis.htm

George Rogers Clark National Historical Park • 2nd St • Vincennes, IN 47591 • (812) 882-1776 • http://www.nps.gov/gero

Grouseland-Harrison Mansion Museum • 3 W Scott St • Vincennes, IN 47591 • (812) 882-2096

Indiana Military Museum • 4305 Bruceville Rd, P.O. Box 977 • Vincennes, IN 47591 • (812) 882-8668 • http://www.indianamilitarymuseum.org

Knox County Historian • 2742 S Hickory Corner Rd • Vincennes, IN 47591 • (812) 882-1776

Knox County Public Library • 502 N 7th St • Vincennes, IN 47591-2119 • (812) 886-4380 • http://www.kcpl.lib.in.us

Knox County Records Library • 819 Broadway • Vincennes, IN 47591 • (812) 885-2557 • http://Jbirch.palni.edu/~bspangle/reclib.htm

Michel Brouillet House & Museum • 509 N 1st St, P.O. Box 1979 • Vincennes, IN 47591 • (812) 882-7422

Northwest Territory Genealogical Society • c/o Knox County Public Library, 502 N 7th St • Vincennes, IN 47591 • (812) 888-4330 • http://www.vinu.edu/lewis.htm

Old Cathedral Library • 205 Church St • Vincennes, IN 47591-1191 • (812) 882-5638

Old State Bank Museum • 114 N 2nd St • Vincennes, IN 47591 • (812) 882-7422 • http://www.state.in.us/ism/sites/vincennes/

Vincennes Historical and Antiquarian Society • c/o Byron R Lewis Historical Collections Library, Vincennes Univ, 1002 N 1st St, P.O. Box 487 • Vincennes, IN 47591 • (812) 735-3800

Vincennes State Historic Site Museum • 1st & Harrison Sts, P.O. Box 81 • Vincennes, IN 47591 • (812) 882-7422 • http://www.state.in.us/ism/sites/vincennes/

Wabash

Dr James Ford Historic Home Museum • 177 W Hill St • Wabash, IN 46992 • (260) 563-8686 • http://www.jamesfordmuseum.org

Wabash Carnegie Public Library • 188 W Hill St • Wabash, IN 46992 • (260) 563-2972 • http://www.wabash.lib.in.us

Wabash County Genealogical Society • P.O. Box 825 • Wabash, IN 46992

Wabash County Historian • 574 Ferry St • Wabash, IN 46992 • (260) 563-2794

Wabash County Historical Museum • 36 E Market St • Wabash, IN 46992 • (219) 563-9070 • http://www.wabashmuseum.org

Wabash County Historical Society • Historical Museum, 89 W Hill St, P.O. Box 4 • Wabash, IN 46992 • (219) 563-0661 • http://www.ohwy.com/in/w/sabcohmu.htm

Wakarusa

Bird's Eye View Museum of Miniatures • 325 S Elkhart St • Wakarusa, IN 46573 • (574) 862-2367

Old Wakarusa Tractor Museum • 66402 SR 19, P.O. Box 591 • Wakarusa, IN 46573 • (219) 862-2714

Wakarusa Historical Society • Historical Museum, 208 S Elkhart St, P.O. Box 2 • Wakarusa, IN 46573 • (219) 862-4407

Wakarusa-Olive & Harrison Township Public Library • 124 N Elkhart, P.O. Box 485 • Wakarusa, IN 46573-0485 • (574) 862-2465 • http://www.wakarusa.lib.in.us

Walkerton

Walkerton Area Historical Society • Historical Museum, 300 Michigan St • Walkerton, IN 46574 • (574) 586-3868

Walkerton-Lincoln Township Historical Society • 607 Roosevelt Rd • Walkerton, IN 46574-1296

Walkerton-Lincoln Township Public Library • 300 N Michigan St • Walkerton, IN 46574 • (574) 586-2933

Walton

Walton-Tipton Township Public Library • 103 E Bishop, P.O. Box 406 • Walton, IN 46994-0406 • (574) 626-2234 • http://www.waltonllib.in.us

Wanatah

Wanatah Historical Society • P.O. Box 156 • Wanatah, IN 46390-0156

Wanatah Public Library • 104 N Main St, P.O. Box 299 • Wanatah, IN 46390-0299 • (219) 733-9303

Warren

Warren Public Library • 123 E 3rd St, P.O. Box 327 • Warren, IN 46792-0327 • (260) 375-3450 • http://www.warren.lib.in.us

Warsaw

Kosciusko Area Genealogy Researchers • 1134 S Ferguson • Warsaw, IN 46580

Kosciusko County Historical Society • County Jail Museum, 121 N Indiana St, P.O. Box 1071 • Warsaw, IN 46580-1071 • (574) 269-1078 • http://culture.kconline.com/kchs/

Pound Store Museum • P.O. Box 1071 • Warsaw, IN 46581 • (219) 269-1078

Warsaw Community Public Library • 310 E Main St • Warsaw, IN 46580-2882 • (574) 267-6011 • http://www.wcpl.lib.in.us

Washington

Daviess County Genealogical Society • 703 Front St • Washington, IN 47501

Daviess County Historian • 812 E National Hwy • Washington, IN 47501 • (812) 254-2627

Daviess County Historical Society • Masonic Temple Museum, 201-212 E Main St, P.O. Box 2341 • Washington, IN 47501 • (812) 257-0301 • http://www.daviesscountyhistory.org

Daviess County Museum • 2 Donaldson Rd, P.O. Box 2341 • Washington, IN 47501 • (812) 254-5122

Washington Carnegie Public Library • 300 W Main St • Washington, IN 47501-2698 • (812) 254-4586 • http://www.washingtonpubliclibrary.org

Waveland

Waveland-Brown Township Public Library • 115 E Green, P.O. Box 158 • Waveland, IN 47989-0158 • (765) 435-2700

Waynetown

Montgomery County Historian • 2205 S 830 W • Waynetown, IN 47990 • (765) 866-0154

West Baden Springs

West Baden Historical Society • P.O. Box 6 • West Baden Springs, IN 47469 • (812) 936-9630

West Lafayette

Historic Archaeological Research • 4338 Hadley Ct • West Lafayette, IN 47906

John Philip Sousa Museum • 345 Overlook Dr • West Lafayette, IN 47906 • (765) 463-1738

Shelby Township Historical Association • 7537 W US 52 • West Lafayette, IN 47906 • (765) 583-2165

Society of the History of the Early American Republic • Dept of History, Purdue Univ, 1358 University Hall • West Lafayette, IN 47907-1358 • (765) 494-4135

Tippecanoe County Area Genealogical Society • P.O. Box 2464 • West Lafayette, IN 47996 • (765) 476-8420 • http://www.rootsweb.com/~intcags

West Lafayette Public Library • 208 W Columbia St • West Lafayette, IN 47906-3096 • (765) 743-2261 • http://www.wlaf.lib.in.us

West Newton

Decatur Township Historical Society • P.O. Box 42 • West Newton, IN 46183 • (317) 856-6567

Westfield

Slovenian Genealogical Society, Indiana Chapter • P.O. Box 59 • Westfield, IN 46074-0059

Sons of the American Revolution, Indiana Society • 103 E Bloomfield Ln • Westfield, IN 46074 • (317) 727-8651 • http://www.inssar.org

Westfield Public Library • 333 W Hoover St • Westfield, IN 46074-9283 • (317) 896-9391 • http://www.westfieldlibrary.lib.in.us

Westfield-Washington Historical Society • 130 Penn St, P.O. Box 103 • Westfield, IN 46074 • (317) 896-5000 • http://www.wwhs.us

Westville-New Durham Township Public Library • 153 Main St, P.O. Box 789 • Westville, IN 46391-0789 • (219) 785-2015

Wheatfield

Jasper-Newton Counties Genealogical Society • Route 1, Box 307 • Wheatfield, IN 46392

Whiteland

Johnson County Historian • 6298 N Hurricane Rd • Whiteland, IN 46184-9315 • (317) 535-8649

West Indianapolis Historical Society • 48 Bradford Place • Whiteland, IN 46184

Whiting

Whiting Public Library • 1735 Oliver St • Whiting, IN 46394-1794 • (219) 659-0269 • http://www.whiting.lib.in.us

Whiting-Robertsdale Historical Society • Historical Museum, 1610 119th St • Whiting, IN 46394 • (219) 659-1432

Williamsport

Warren County Historian • 3404 W 575 S • Williamsport, IN 47993 • (765) 893-4605

Warren County Historical Society • Historical Museum, P.O. Box 176 • Williamsport, IN 47993 • (765) 893-4605 • http://www.warrencohistory.org

Williamsport-Washington Township Public Library • 28 E 2nd St • Williamsport, IN 47993 • (765) 762-6555 • http://www.wwtpl.lib.in.us

Winamac

Pulaski County Genealogical Society • c/o Pulaski County Public Library, 121 S Riverside Dr • Winamac, IN 46996 • (219) 946-3432

Pulaski County Historical Society • Historical Museum, 123 S Riverside, P.O. Box 135 • Winamac, IN 46996 • (219) 946-3712 • http://www.pulaskihistory.com

Pulaski County Public Library • 121 S Riverside Dr • Winamac, IN 46996-1596 • (574) 946-3432

Winchester

Randolph County Genealogical Society • Route 3, Box 60 • Winchester, IN 47394

Randolph County Historical and Genealogical Society • Historical Museum, 416 S Meridian St • Winchester, IN 47394 • (765) 584-1334

Winchester Community Library • 125 N East St • Winchester, IN 47394-1698 • (765) 584-4824

Winona Lake

Billy Sunday Historic Site Museum • 1101 Park Ave • Winona Lake, IN 46590 • (574) 268-0660

Morgan Library & Reneker Museum of History • Grace College & Grace Theological Seminary, 200 Seminary Dr • Winona Lake, IN 46590 • (574) 372-5100 • http://www.grace.edu

Winona Lake Historical Society • 101 4th St • Winona Lake, IN 46590

Wolcott

Anson Wolcott Historical Society • Historic Wolcott House Museum, 500 N Range St, P.O. Box 294 • Wolcott, IN 47995 • (219) 279-2123

Wolcott Community Public Library • 101 E North St, P.O. Box 376 • Wolcott, IN 47995-0376 • (219) 279-2695 • http://www.mwprairienet.lib.in.us/Social_Services/wollib.html

Worthington

Worthington Historical Society • 12 N Washington • Worthington, IN 47471 • (812) 875-2369

Worthington Public Library • 26 N Commercial St • Worthington, IN 47471-1415 • (812) 875-3815

Zionsville

Boone County Historian • 635 W Pine St • Zionsville, IN 46077 • (317) 873-4900

Hussey-Mayfield Memorial Public Library • 250 N 5th St, P.O. Box 840 • Zionsville, IN 46077 • (317) 873-3149 • http://www.zionsville.lib.in.us

Patrick Henry Sullivan Foundation • Museum and Genealogy Library, 225 W Hawthorne St, P.O. Box 182 • Zionsville, IN 46077 • (317) 783-4900 • http://www.sullivanmunce.org

Zionsville Historical Society • 714 Sugarbush Dr • Zionsville, IN 46077 • (317) 482-1848

 **IOWA**

Ackley
Ackley Heritage Center Museum • 737 Main St • Ackley, IA 50601

Adel
Adel Historical Society • 2160 312th St • Adel, IA 50003 • (515) 993-4124

Agency
Agency Public Library • 104 E Main St, P.O. Box 346 • Agency, IA 52530-0346 • (641) 937-6002

Albert City
Albert City Historical Association • Historical Museum, 212 N 2nd St • Albert City, IA 50510 • (712) 843-4584

Albia
Carnegie-Evans Public Library • 203 Benton Ave E • Albia, IA 52531 • (641) 932-2469

Monroe County Genealogical Society • c/o Carnegie-Evans Public Library, 203 Benton Ave E • Albia, IA 52531-2036 • (641) 932-2469 • http://www.iamonroe.org/monroeco.htm

Monroe County Historical Society • Historical Museum, 114-116A Avenue E • Albia, IA 52531 • (641) 932-7046

Algona
Algona Public Library • 210 N Phillips St • Algona, IA 50511 • (515) 295-5476 • http://www.algona.org

Allison
Butler County Genealogical Society • P.O. Box 177 • Allison, IA 50602-0177

Butler County Historical Society • Historical Museum, 219 1/2 S Main St, P.O. Box 14 • Allison, IA 50602 • (319) 278-4321

Alton
Alton Public Library • 905 3rd Ave, P.O. Box 379 • Alton, IA 51003-0379 • (712) 756-4516

Amana
Amana Heritage Society • Amana Heritage Museum, 4310 220th Tr, P.O. Box 81 • Amana, IA 52203-0081 • (319) 622-3567 • http://amanaheritage.org

Communal Agriculture Museum • 505 P Street, P.O. Box 81 • Amana, IA 52203 • (319) 622-3567 • http://www.AmanaColonies.com

Ames
Ames Public Library • 515 Douglas Ave • Ames, IA 50010 • (515) 239-5630 • http://www.amespubliclibrary.org

Danish American Heritage Society • 4105 Stone Brooke Rd • Ames, IA 50010 • (515) 232-7479

Farm House Museum • IA State Univ, 290 Scheman Bldg • Ames, IA 50011 • (515) 294-3342 • http://www.museums.iastate.edu

Parks Library • Iowa State Univ • Ames, IA 50011 • (515) 294-1442 • http://www.iastate.edu/spcl/spcl.html

Story County Genealogical Society • P.O. Box 692 • Ames, IA 50010 • (515) 292-3283 • http://www.rootsweb.com/~iastory/chapter.htm

Anamosa
Anamosa State Penitentiary Museum • 406 N High St, P.O. Box 144 • Anamosa, IA 52205 • (319) 462-2386 • http://www.asphistory.com/museum

Jones County Genealogical Society • 100 Park Ave, P.O. Box 174 • Anamosa, IA 52205 • (563) 462-3911 • http://www.rootsweb.com/~iajones/research/research.htm

Ankeny
Ankeny Area Historical Society • 301 SW 3rd St • Ankeny, IA 50023 • (515) 965-5795

Ankeny Genealogical Society • 1110 NW 2nd St, P.O. Box 136 • Ankeny, IA 50021

Arnolds Park
Abbie Gardner Cabin Museum • 34 Monument Dr, P.O. Box 74 • Arnolds Park, IA 51331 • (712) 332-7248 • http://www.state.ia.us/government/dca/shsi

Iowa Great Lakes Maritime Museum • 243 W Broadway, P.O. Box 609 • Arnolds Park, IA 51331 • (712) 332-2183 • http://www.okobojimuseum.org

Ashton
Ostfriesen Genealogical Society • 2185 Monroe • Ashton, IA 51232

Atlantic
Atlantic Public Library • 507 Poplar • Atlantic, IA 50022 • (712) 243-5466 • http://www.atlantic.lib.ia.us

Cass County Genealogical Society • c/o Atlantic Public Library, 507 Poplar St • Atlantic, IA 50022 • (712) 781-2227

Cass County, Iowa Genealogical Society • 706 Hazel St • Atlantic, IA 50022 • (712) 781-2227

Audubon
Audubon County Genealogical Society • 505 Brayton • Audubon, IA 50025

Audubon Public Library • 401 N Park Pl • Audubon, IA 50025-1258 • (712) 563-3301

Nathaniel Hamlin Museum • 1745 160th St • Audubon, IA 50025 • (712) 563-3984

Aurelia
Aurelia Public Library • 232 Main St, P.O. Box 188 • Aurelia, IA 51005-0188 • (712) 434-5330

Avoca
Avoca Historical Society • 701 W Elm St, P.O. Box 57 • Avoca, IA 51521 • (712) 343-2477

Bagley
Bagley Public Library • 117 Main St, P.O. Box 206 • Bagley, IA 50026-0206 • (641) 427-5214

Bancroft
Ostfriesland Society of Iowa • 518 E Ramsey St, P.O. Box 317 • Bancroft, IA 50517-0317 • (515) 885-2676

Beacon
Keomah Genealogical Society • 301 Sherman • Beacon, IA 52534

Beaman
Beaman Community Memorial Library • 223 Main St P.O. Box 135 • Beaman, IA 50609-0135 • (641) 366-2912

Bedford
Bedford Public Library • 507 Jefferson St • Bedford, IA 50833-1314 • (712) 523-2828

Taylor County Genealogical Society • RR3 • Bedford, IA 50833

Taylor County Museum • 1001 W Pollock Ave • Bedford, IA 50833 • (712) 523-2041

Belle Plaine
Belle Plaine Community Library • 904 12th St • Belle Plaine, IA 52208-1711 • (319) 444-2902

Belle Plaine Historical Society • 903 12th St • Belle Plaine, IA 52208 • (319) 434-6458

Benton County Genealogical Society • 1808 9th Ave • Belle Plaine, IA 52208 • http://www.rootsweb.com/~iabenton/bcgs.htm

Iowa

Bellevue
Young Museum • 406 N Riverview • Bellevue, IA 52031 • (319) 872-4456

Bettendorf
Bettendorf Public Library and Family Museum • 2950 Learning Center Dr, P.O. Box 1330 • Bettendorf, IA 52722-1330 • (563) 344-4175 • http://www.bettendorflibrary.com

Bloomfield
Bloomfield Public Library • 107 N Columbia St • Bloomfield, IA 52537-1431 • (641) 664-2209

Davis County Genealogical Society • c/o Bloomfield Public Library, 107 N Columbia St, P.O. Box 94 • Bloomfield, IA 52537 • (641) 664-2209

Davis County Historical Society • 201 S Dodge St • Bloomfield, IA 52537 • (641) 664-1855

Boone
Boone & Scenic Valley Railroad Museum • 225 10th St, P.O. Box 603 • Boone, IA 50036 • (800) 626-0319 • http://www.scenic-valleyrr.com

Boone County Genealogical Society • 423 Benton, P.O. Box 453 • Boone, IA 50036-0453 • (515) 432-1907 • http://www.rootsweb.com/~iabcgs/

Boone County Historical Society • Historical Center, 602 Story St, P.O. Box 1 • Boone, IA 50036 • (515) 432-1907 • http://homepages.opencominc.com/bchs/

Ericson Public Library • 702 Greene St • Boone, IA 50036 • (515) 432-3727 • http://www.booneiowa.homestead.com/ericsonlibrary.html

Iowa Railroad Historical Society • 225 10th St, P.O. Box 603 • Boone, IA 50036 • (515) 432-4249 • http://www.scenic-valleyrr.com

Kate Shelley Railroad Museum • 1198 232nd St • Boone, IA 50036 • (515) 432-1907 • http://www.homepages.opencominc.com/bchs

Mamie Doud Eisenhower Birthplace Museum and Library • 709 Carroll St, P.O. Box 55 • Boone, IA 50036-0055 • (515) 432-1896 • http://www.booneiowa.com

Brighton
Polishville Cemetery and Grotto Association • 1157 Raspberry Ave • Brighton, IA 52540-8553 • (319) 694-3495

Brooklyn
Brooklyn Historical Society • 304 Jackson St • Brooklyn, IA 52211 • (641) 522-7744

Burlington
Burlington Public Library • 501 N 4th St • Burlington, IA 52601 • (319) 753-1647 • http://www.burlington.lib.ia.us

Des Moines County Genealogical Society • P.O. Box 493 • Burlington, IA 52601-0493 • (319) 753-1576 • http://www.dmcgs.com

Des Moines County Historical Society • Apple Trees Museum, 1616 Dill St • Burlington, IA 52601 • (319) 753-2449

Hawkeye Log Cabin Museum • 2915 S Main St • Burlington, IA 52601 • (319) 753-2449

Phelps House Museum • 521 Columbia St • Burlington, IA 52601 • (319) 753-5880

Burr Oak
Laura Ingalls Wilder Museum • 3603 236th Ave • Burr Oak, IA 52101 • (563) 735-5916 • http://lauraingallswilder.us

Calmar
Wilder Library • Northeast Iowa Community College, 1625 Hwy 150, P.O. Box 400 • Calmar, IA 52132-0400 • (563) 562-3263 • http://www.nicc.edu

Camanche
Camanche Historical Society • 12th Ave & 2nd St • Camanche, IA 52730 • (563) 259-1268

Camanche Public Library • 102 12th Ave • Camanche, IA 52730 • (563) 259-1106

Clinton County Gateway Genealogical Society • 618 14th Ave • Camanche, IA 52730-1755

Gateway Genealogical Society • 618 14th Ave • Camanche, IA 52730-1755 • (563) 259-1285

Carlisle
Carlisle Public Library • 135 School St, P.O. Box S • Carlisle, IA 50047-0718 • (515) 989-0909

Carroll
Carroll County Genealogical Society • Genealogical Library at Lidderdale, P.O. Box 21 • Carroll, IA 51401-0021 • http://www.rootsweb.com/~iacarrol/CarGenie.html

Carroll County Historical Society • Historical Museum, 704 W 15th St • Carroll, IA 51401

Carroll Public Library • 118 E 5th St • Carroll, IA 51401 • (712) 792-3432 • http://www.carrolliowa.com/library.htm

Casey
Duncan Memorial Library • 610 Antique Country Dr, P.O. Box 178 • Casey, IA 50048-0178 • (641) 746-2670

Castalia
Bloomfield Historical Society • general delivery • Castalia, IA 52133 • (563) 567-8470

Cedar Falls
Cedar Falls Historical Society • Historical Museum, 308 W 3rd St • Cedar Falls, IA 50613 • (319) 266-5149 • http://www.cedarfallshistorical.org; http://www.cfhistory.org

Cedar Falls Public Library • 524 Main St • Cedar Falls, IA 50613-2830 • (319) 273-8643 • http://www.cedar-falls.lib.ia.us

Marshall Center School Museum • 3219 Hudson Rd • Cedar Falls, IA 50614 • (319) 273-2188 • http://www.uni.edu/museum/school.html

Rod Library - Special Collections • Univ of Northern Iowa, 1227 W 27th St • Cedar Falls, IA 50613-3675 • (319) 273-2838 • http://www.library.uni.edu

University of Northern Iowa Museum • 3219 Hudson Rd • Cedar Falls, IA 50614 • (319) 273-2188 • http://www.uni.edu/museum

Wyth House Museum • 303 Franklin St • Cedar Falls, IA 50613

Cedar Rapids
African American Heritage Foundation • Heritage Museum, 809 8th Ave SE, P.O. Box 2756 • Cedar Rapids, IA 52406 • (319) 298-9772

African American Historical Museum • 55 12th Ave SE, P.O. Box 1626 • Cedar Rapids, IA 52406 • (319) 862-2105

Brucemore Museum • 2160 Linden Dr SE • Cedar Rapids, IA 52406 • (319) 362-7375 • http://www.brucemore.org

Cedar Rapids Historical Archives • 1201 6th St SW • Cedar Rapids, IA 52404 • (319) 398-0419

Cedar Rapids Public Library • 221 3rd St SE • Cedar Rapids, IA 52401 • (319) 363-3286 • http://www.crlibrary.org

Czech Heritage Foundation • 48 16th Ave SW, P.O. Box 761 • Cedar Rapids, IA 52406 • (319) 286-6011

Genealogical Society of Linn County Iowa • 813 1st Ave SE, P.O. Box 175 • Cedar Rapids, IA 52406-0175 • (319) 369-0022 • http://www.usgennet.org/usa/ia/county/linn/gen_soc.htm

Linn County Heritage Society • Historical Museum, 101 8th Ave SE, P.O. Box 175 • Cedar Rapids, IA 52406-0175 • (319) 369-1501

Linn County Historical Society • History Center, 615 1st Ave SE • Cedar Rapids, IA 52401 • (319) 362-1501 • http://www.historycenter. org

Masonic Grand Lodge of Iowa • Library & Museum, 813 1st Ave SE • Cedar Rapids, IA 52401-50001 • (319) 365-1438 • http:// grandlodgeofiowa.org

National Czech and Slovak Museum and Library • 30 16th Ave SW • Cedar Rapids, IA 52404 • (319) 362-8500 • http://www.ncsml.org

Pioneer Village • City Hall • Cedar Rapids, IA 52401 • (319) 398-5104

Ushers Ferry Historic Village • 5925 Seminole Valley Tr • Cedar Rapids, IA 52411 • (319) 286-5763

Centerville
Appanoose County Genealogy Society • 1020 Shamrock Ln #107 • Centerville, IA 52544 • (641) 437-4077

Central City
John C Clegg Public Library • 137 4th St N • Central City, IA 52214 • (319) 438-6685 • http://www.centralcityia.org/library

Chapin
Franklin County Chapter, IGS • P.O. Box 335 • Chapin, IA 50427

Chariton
Chariton Free Public Library • 803 Braden Ave • Chariton, IA 50049 • (641) 774-5514 • http://www.lucasco.net/cityhall/Library.html

Lucas County Genealogical Society • c/o Chariton Free Public Library, 803 Braden Ave • Chariton, IA 50049-1742 • (641) 774-5514 • http:// www.lucasoo.net/cityhall/Library.html

Lucas County Museum • 17th & Braden Ave • Chariton, IA 50049 • (641) 774-4464

Lucus County Historical Society • 217 N 17th St • Chariton, IA 50049-1618 • (641) 774-4464

Charles City
Charles City Public Library • 106 Milwaukee Mall • Charles City, IA 50616 • (641) 257-6319

Floyd County Historical Society • Historical Museum, 500 Gilbert St • Charles City, IA 50616 • (641) 228-1099 • http://www. floydcountymuseum.org

Cherokee
Cherokee Area Archives • 215 S 2nd St • Cherokee, IA 51012 • (712) 225-3498

Cherokee Public Library • 215 S 2nd St • Cherokee, IA 51012 • (712) 225-3498

Joseph A Tallman Museum • 1205 W Cedar Loop • Cherokee, IA 51012 • (712) 225-2594

Clarinda
Glenn Miller Birthplace Museum • 107 E Main, P.O. Box 61 • Clarinda, IA 51632 • (712) 542-2461

Nodaway Valley Historical Museum • 420 S 16th St, P.O. Box 393 • Clarinda, IA 51632 • (712) 542-3073

Clarion
4-H Schoolhouse Museum • Central Ave W • Clarion, IA 50525 • (515) 532-2256 • http://www.clarion-iowa.com

Clarion Historical Society • 713 3rd St NE • Clarion, IA 50525

Wright County Genealogical Searchers • P.O. Box 225 • Clarion, IA 50525-0225

Wright County Historical Society • 615 5th Ave • Clarion, IA 50525 • (515) 532-3669

Clarksville
Butler County Genealogical Society • c/o Clarksville Public Library, 103 W Greene St • Clarksville, IA 50619

Butler County Historical Society • 420 W Jefferson St • Clarksville, IA 50619 • (319) 278-4479

Cleghorn
Cherokee County Historical Society • 105 E Front St, P.O. Box 247 • Cleghorn, IA 51014-0247 • (712) 436-2624

Cherokee County Tree Stumpers • 105 E Front St, P.O. Box 247 • Cleghorn, IA 51014-0247 • (712) 436-2624

Clermont
Clermont Historical Society • Montauk Museum, Hwy 18 E, P.O. Box 372 • Clermont, IA 52135 • (563) 423-7173 • http://www.state.ia.us/ government/dca/shsi

Clinton
Clinton County Gateway Genealogical Society • P.O. Box 2256 • Clinton, IA 52732-2256 • (563) 242-4712 • http://www. clintongatewaygensoc.homestead.com

Clinton County Genealogical Society • P.O. Box 2062 • Clinton, IA 52732-2062

Clinton County Historical Society • Historical Museum, 601 S 1st St, P.O. Box 2435 • Clinton, IA 52732 • (563) 242-1201

Clinton Public Library • 306 8th Ave S • Clinton, IA 52732 • (563) 242-8441 • http://www.cis.net/~clintonlibrary

George M Curtis House Museum • 420 5th Ave S • Clinton, IA 52732 • (319) 242-8556

Clive
Roots 'n' Branches • P.O. Box 23293 • Clive, IA 50325-9410 • (515) 830-1390

Colfax
Colfax Historical Society • general delivery • Colfax, IA 50054 • (515) 674-0215

Trainland USA Museum • 3135 Hwy 117 N • Colfax, IA 50054 • (515) 674-3813

Conrad
Conrad Public Library • 102 E Grundy, P.O. Box 189 • Conrad, IA 50621-0189 • (641) 366-2583

Coralville
Johnson County Historical Society • Heritage Museum, 310 5th St, P.O. Box 5081 • Coralville, IA 52241 • (319) 351-5738 • http://www. johnsiowa.org

Corning
Corning Public Library • 603 9th St • Corning, IA 50841-1304 • (641) 322-3866 • http://corningia.com/library.htm

House of History • 1000 Benton Ave • Corning, IA 50841 • (515) 322-3241

National Icarian Heritage Society • 503 8th St • Corning, IA 50848 • (641) 322-4717

Correctionville
Correctionville Museum • general delivery • Correctionville, IA 51016 • (712) 372-4341

Corydon
Karl Miles LeCompte Memorial Library • 110 S Franklin St • Corydon, IA 50060-1518 • (641) 872-1621 • http://www.corydon.swilsa.lib.ia.us

Wayne County Genealogical Society • c/o Karl Miles LeCompte Memorial Library, 110 S Franklin St • Corydon, IA 50060-1518 • (641) 872-1621

Iowa

Corydon, cont.

Wayne County Historical Society • Prairie Trails Museum, Hwy 2, 515 E Jefferson St, P.O. Box 104 • Corydon, IA 50060 • (641) 872-2211 • http://www.prairietrailsmuseum.org

Council Bluffs

Council Bluffs Free Public Library • 400 Willow Ave • Council Bluffs, IA 51503-4269 • (712) 323-7553 • http://www.cbpl.lib.ia.us

Frontier Heritage Library • 622 4th St, P.O. Box 394 • Council Bluffs, IA 51502-0394 • (712) 322-1171

Historic General Dodge House Museum • 605 3rd St • Council Bluffs, IA 51503 • (712) 322-2406 • http://www.councilbluffsiowa.com

Historical Society of Pottawattamie County • 226 Pearl St, P.O. Box 2 • Council Bluffs, IA 51503 • (712) 323-2509 • http://www.thehistoricalsociety.org

Pottawattamie County Genealogical Society • 622 S 4th St, P.O. Box 394 • Council Bluffs, IA 51502-0394 • (712) 325-9368 • http://www.rootsweb.com/~iapottaw/PCGS.htm

Union Pacific Railroad Museum • 200 Pearl St • Council Bluffs, IA 51503 • (712) 329-8307 • http://www.up.com

Western Historic Trails Center • 3434 Richard Downing Ave • Council Bluffs, IA 51501 • (712) 366-4900 • http://www.state.ia.us/government/dca/shsi

Cresco

Cresco Public Library • 320 N Elm St • Cresco, IA 52136 • (563) 547-2540 • http://www.crescoia.com/library/

Howard County Historical Society • Kellow House Museum, 324 4th Ave W • Cresco, IA 52136 • (563) 547-5593

Howard-Winneshieck Genealogy Society • c/o Cresco Public Library, 320 N Elm, P.O. Box 362 • Cresco, IA 52136 • http://www.rootsweb.com/~iawinnes/wcgs.htm

Creston

Matilda J Gibson Memorial Library • 200 W Howard • Creston, IA 50801 • (641) 782-2277 • http://www.swilsa.lib.ia.us/libs/creston/home.htm

Union County Genealogical Society • c/o Gibson Memorial Library, 200 W Howard • Creston, IA 50801-2339 • (641) 782-2277 • http://1server.aea14.k12.ia.us/SWP/jbriley/ucgen/ucgenhome.html

Union County Historical Complex • McKinley Park, 1101 N Vine • Creston, IA 50801 • (515) 782-4247

Union County Historical Society • 1101 N Vine St • Creston, IA 50801 • (641) 782-8159

Dakota City

Humboldt County Historical Association • Historical Museum, 905 1st Ave N, P.O. Box 162 • Dakota City, IA 50548 • (515) 332-5280

Dallas Center

Dallas County Genealogical Society • c/o Estle Memorial Library, 1308 Walnut, P.O. Box 264 • Dallas Center, IA 50063-0264 • (515) 992-3185 • http://www.rootsweb.com/~iadcgs

Roy R Estle Memorial Library • 1308 Walnut, P.O. Box 521 • Dallas Center, IA 50063-0521 • (515) 992-3185 • http://estlelibrary.org

Davenport

American-Schleswig-Holstein Heritage Society • P.O. Box 313 • Davenport, IA 52805-0313 • (563) 324-7326

Buffalo Bill Cody Homestead & Pioneer Village • 14910 110th Ave • Davenport, IA 52804 • (319) 328-3281

Cody-McCausland House Museum • Route 61 N • Davenport, IA 52758 • (319) 226-2981 • http://www.nscda.org/museums/iowa.htm

Davenport Public Library • 321 Main St, P.O. Box 3132 • Davenport, IA 52808-3132 • (563) 326-7844 • http://www.davenportlibrary.com

German American Heritage Center • 712 W 2nd St, P.O. Box 243 • Davenport, IA 52805-0243 • (563) 322-8844 • http://www.germanamerheritage.org

Mid-America Genealogical Society • P.O. Box 316 • Davenport, IA 52801

O'Keefe Library • Saint Ambrose University, 518 W Locust St • Davenport, IA 52803 • (563) 333-6245 • http://library.sau.edu

Putnam Museum • 1717 W 12th St • Davenport, IA 52804 • (563) 324-1933 • http://www.putnam.org

Richardson-Sloan Genealogical Society • 1019 Mound St, Suite 301 • Davenport, IA 52803 • (563) 383-0007

Scott County Genealogical Society • c/o Davenport Public Library, 321 Main St, P.O. Box 3132 • Davenport, IA 52808-3132 • (563) 326-7902 • http://www.rootsweb.com/~iascott/scigs.htm

Village of East Davenport Association • 2119 E 12th St • Davenport, IA 52803 • (563) 322-1860

De Witt

Central Community Historical Society • Historical Museum, 628 6th St • De Witt, IA 52742 • (563) 659-3686

Central Community Historical Society • RR2 ,Box 98 • De Witt, IA 52742 • (563) 659-3686

Decorah

Decorah Genealogy Association • c/o Decorah Public Library, 202 Winnebago St • Decorah, IA 52101 • (563) 382-8559 • http://www.rootsweb.com/~iawinnes/dga.htm

Decorah Public Library • 202 Winnebago St • Decorah, IA 52101 • (563) 382-3717 • http://www.decorah.lib.ia.us

Luther College Museum • 700 College Dr • Decorah, IA 52101 • (563) 387-1805 • http://archives.luther.edu

Norwegian American Museum Association • Vesterheim Norwegian-American Museum Museum, 523 W Water St, P.O. Box 379 • Decorah, IA 52101 • (563) 382-9681 • http://www.vesterheim.org

Porter House Museum • 401 W Broadway St • Decorah, IA 52101 • (319) 382-8465 • http://www.luther.edu.decorah.htm

Preus Library • Luther College, 700 College Dr • Decorah, IA 52101 • (563) 387-1163 • http://library.luther.edu

Winneshieck County Genealogical Society • P.O. Box 344 • Decorah, IA 52101-0344

Winneshieck County Historical Society • c/o Decorah Public Library, 202 Winnebago • Decorah, IA 52101 • (563) 382-8559

Delmar

Delmar Depot Museum • City Hall, P.O. Box 329 • Delmar, IA 52037 • (319) 674-4256

Denison

Crawford County Genealogical Society • c/o Norelius Community Library, 1403 1st Ave S • Denison, IA 51442 • (712) 263-9355

Crawford County Historical Society • 2134 Rocky Run • Denison, IA 51442

Norelius Community Library • 1403 1st Ave S • Denison, IA 51442-2014 • (712) 263-9355 • http://www.denisonlibrary.org

W A McHenry House Museum • 1428 1st Ave N • Denison, IA 51442 • (712) 263-3806

Denver

Bremer County Genealogical Society • 426 Washington St • Denver, IA 50622 • http://www.rootsweb.com/~iabremer/GenealogicalSociety.html

Des Moines

Charter-Pierce Memorial Internet Genealogical Society • 3221 Villa Vista Dr • Des Moines, IA 50316-1338 • (515) 264-9149 • http://home.sprynet.com/sprynet/duapie/

Cowles Library • Drake University, 2507 University Ave • Des Moines, IA 50311-4505 • (515) 271-2113 • http://www.lib.drake.edu

Danish Immigrant Archives • Grandview College Library, 1351 Grandview Ave • Des Moines, IA 50316 • (515) 263-3877

Danish-American Heritage Society • Grandview College Library, 1351 Grandview Ave • Des Moines, IA 50316 • (515) 263-3877

Flynn Mansion at Living History Farms • 2600 NW 111th St • Des Moines, IA 50322 • (515) 278-5286 • http://www.ilf.org

Grand View College Library • 1351 Grandview Ave • Des Moines, IA 50316-1494 • (515) 263-2949 • http://library.gvc.edu

Hoyt Sherman Place Museum • 501 Woodland • Des Moines, IA 50309 • (515) 244-0507

Iowa Dept of Public Health, Vital Records Bureau • Lucas State Office Bldg, 321 E 12th St • Des Moines, IA 50319-0075 • (515) 281-4944 • http://www.idph.state.ia.us/pa/vr.htm

Iowa Genealogical Society • 628 E Grand Ave, P.O. Box 7735 • Des Moines, IA 50309 • (515) 276-0287 • http://www.iowagenealogy.org

Iowa Jewish Historical Society • 910 Polk Blvd • Des Moines, IA 50312 • (515) 277-6321 • http://www.dmjfed.org/jewish_historical_soc.html; http://www.jewishdesmoines.org

Latvian Society of Iowa • 2653 Grandview Ave • Des Moines, IA 50317 • (515) 262-7707

P E O International • 3700 Grand Ave • Des Moines, IA 50312 • (515) 255-3153 • http://www.peointernational.org

Pioneer Sons and Daughters Chapter, IGS • P.O. Box 13133 • Des Moines, IA 50310-0133

Polk County Heritage Museum • 111 Court St • Des Moines, IA 50309 • (515) 286-2242 • http://www.heritagegallery.org

Polk County Historical Society • Historical Museum, 317 SW 42nd St • Des Moines, IA 50312 • (515) 255-6657

Public Library of Des Moines • 100 Locust St • Des Moines, IA 50309 • (515) 283-4152 • http://www.desmoineslibrary.com

Salisbury House Foundation Museum • 4025 Tonawanda Dr • Des Moines, IA 50312 • (515) 274-1777 • http://www.salisburyhouse.org

State Archives of Iowa • State of Iowa Historical Bldg, 600 E Locust • Des Moines, IA 50319 • (515) 281-3007 • http://www.iowahistory.org

State Historical Society of Iowa • Historical Museum, 600 E Locust • Des Moines, IA 50319 • (515) 281-6200 • http://www.iowahistory.org

State Library of Iowa • State Capitol Bldg, 1007 E Grand Ave • Des Moines, IA 50319 • (515) 281-4105 • http://www.silo.lib.ia.us

Terrace Hill Historic Site and Governor's Mansion • 2300 Grand Ave • Des Moines, IA 50312 • (515) 281-7205 • http://www.terracehill.org

Diagonal

Ringgold County Genealogical Society • 202 Adams St • Diagonal, IA 50845-1001

Donnellson

Donnellson Public Library - Family History Dept • 500 Park St, P.O. Box 290 • Donnellson, IA 52625-0290 • (319) 835-5545 • http://homepages.rootsweb.com/~donnlibr/

Dow City

Dow House Museum • S Prince St • Dow City, IA 51528 • (712) 674-3734

Dows

Dows Community Library • 114 Ellsworth, P.O. Box 427 • Dows, IA 50071-0427 • (515) 852-4326

Dows Depot Museum • 1896 Railroad St • Dows, IA 50071 • (515) 852-3595 • http://www.dowsiowa.com/welcomecenter.html

Dows Historical Society • 1896 Railroad St • Dows, IA 50071-0287

Dows Welcome Center Museum • 1896 Railroad St • Dows, IA 50071 • (515) 852-3595 • http://www.state.ia.us/tourism

Quasdorf Blacksmith and Wagon Museum • Train St & the Depot, P.O. Box 312 • Dows, IA 50071 • (515) 852-3595 • http://www.beautifuliron.com/dows.htm

Dubuque

Carnegie-Stout Public Library • 360 W 11th St • Dubuque, IA 52001 • (563) 589-4225 • http://www.dubuque.lib.ia.us

Center for Dubuque History • Loras College, P.O. Box 178 • Dubuque, IA 52004-0178 • (563) 588-7163

Dubuque County Historical Society • Mathias Ham House, 2241 Lincoln Ave, P.O. Box 266 • Dubuque, IA 52004-0266 • (563) 557-9545 • http://www.mississippirivermuseum.com

Dubuque County-Key City Genealogical Society • Masonic Temple, 1155 Locust St, P.O. Box 13 • Dubuque, IA 52004-0013 • http://www.rootsweb.com/~iadckcgs/

Mathias Ham House Historic Site Museum • 2241 Lincoln Ave, P.O. Box 266 • Dubuque, IA 52001 • (563) 557-9545 • http://www.mississippirivermuseum.com

Mississippi River Museum • 350 E 3rd St, P.O. Box 266 • Dubuque, IA 52004 • (563) 557-9545 • http://www.mississippirivermuseum.com

Reu Memorial Library • Wartburg Theological Seminary, 333 Wartburg Pl, P.O. Box 5004 • Dubuque, IA 52004-5004 • (563) 589-0267 • http://www.wartburgseminary.edu/campus/library.htm

University of Dubuque Library • 2000 University Ave • Dubuque, IA 52001 • (563) 589-3100 • http://www.dbq.edu

Wahlert Memorial Library • Loras College, 1450 Alta Vista St • Dubuque, IA 52004-0178 • (641) 588-7009 • http://www.loras.edu/~LIB/

Dyersville

Dyer-Botsford House Museum • 331 1st Ave E • Dyersville, IA 52040 • (319) 875-2414

Dyersville Area Historical Society • 120 3rd St SW • Dyersville, IA 52040 • (563) 875-2504

National Farm Toy Museum • 1110 16th Ave SE • Dyersville, IA 52040 • (563) 875-2727 • http://www.nationalfarmtoymuseum.com

Dysart

Dysart Historical Society • 612 Crisman St • Dysart, IA 52224 • (319) 476-4747

Eagle Grove

Wright County Historical Society, Eagle Grove Chapter • 917 W Broadway • Eagle Grove, IA 50533 • (515) 448-4220

Earlville

Ruth Suckow Memorial Library & Museum • 138 Northern Ave, PO Box 189 • Earlville, IA 52041-0189 • (563) 923-5235

Eldon

American Gothic House Museum • 301 American Gothic St • Eldon, IA 52554 • (319) 335-3927 • http://www.state.ia.us/government/dca/shsi

Eldon Public Library • 608 W Elm St, Box 430 • Eldon, IA 52225-8774 • (641) 652-7517

Eldora
Eldora Public Library • 1202 10th St • Eldora, IA 50627 • (641) 939-2173 • http://www.eldorapublib.org

Hardin County Genealogical Society • 1414 19th Ave, P.O. Box 252 • Eldora, IA 50627

Hardin County Historical Society • 1603 S Washington St, P.O. Box 187 • Eldora, IA 50627 • (641) 858-3616

Eldridge
Scott County Library System • 200 N 6th Ave • Eldridge, IA 52748-1284 • (563) 285-4794 • http://www.scottcountylibrary.org

Elgin
Elgin Public Library • 214 Main St, P.O. Box 36 • Elgin, IA 52141-0036 • (563) 426-5313 • http://www.elgin.lib.ia.us

Elk Horn
Bedstemor's (Grandmother's) House Museum • 2104 College, P.O. Box 470 • Elk Horn, IA 51531 • (712) 764-6082

Danish Immigrant Museum • 2212 Washington St, P.O. Box 470 • Elk Horn, IA 51531-0470 • (712) 764-7001 • http://www.danishmuseum.org/genealogy

Danish Windmill Museum • 4038 Main, P.O. Box 245 • Elk Horn, IA 51531 • (712) 764-7472 • http://www.danishwindmill.com

Elkader
Clayton County Genealogical Society • P.O. Box 846 • Elkader, IA 52043 • (563) 245-1418 • http://www.rootsweb.com/~iaccgs/

Elkader Historical Society • Carter House Museum, 101 High St • Elkader, IA 52043 • (563) 245-2622

Elkader Public Library • 130 N Main St, P.O. Box 310 • Elkader, IA 52043-0310 • (563) 245-1446

Elliott
Elliott Public Library • 401 Main St P.O. Box 306 • Elliott, IA 51532-0306 • (712) 767-2355

Ellston
Cornwall Pioneer Home Museum • Main St • Ellston, IA 50074 • (515) 772-4419

Ellsworth
Ellsworth Public Library • 1549 Dewitt St, P.O. Box 338 • Ellsworth, IA 50075-0338 • (515) 836-4852

Elma
Elma Public Library • 710 Busti Ave, P.O. Box 287 • Elma, IA 50628 • (641) 393-8100

Ely
Ely Public Library • 5 Dows St, P.O. Box 249 • Ely, IA 52227-0249 • (319) 848-7616 • http://www.elyiowa.com

Emerson
Emerson Public Library • 410 Manchester, P.O. Box 282 • Emerson, IA 51533-0282 • (712) 824-7866

Indian Creek Historical Society • Historical Museum, 59256 380th St • Emerson, IA 51533 • (712) 824-7730

Emmetsburg
Emmetsburg Public Library • 707 N Superior • Emmetsburg, IA 50536 • (712) 852-4009 • http://www.emmetsburglibrary.com

Iowa Lakes Genealogical Society • 601 Monroe St • Emmetsburg, IA 50536

Palo Alto County Genealogical Society • c/o Emmetsburg Public Library, 707 N Superior • Emmetsburg, IA 50536 • (712) 852-4009 • http://www.rootsweb.com/~iapaloal/pageone.htm

Victorian on Main Museum • 1703 Main • Emmetsburg, IA 50536 • (712) 852-2283

Estherville
Emmet County Genealogical Society • c/o Estherville Public Library, 613 Central Ave • Estherville, IA 51334-2294 • (712) 362-7731

Emmet County Historical Society • Albee Memorial Museum, 1720 3rd Ave S, P.O. Box 101 • Estherville, IA 51334 • (712) 362-2750

Estherville Public Library • 613 Central • Estherville, IA 51334-2294 • (712) 362-7731 • http://www.esthervillepubliclibrary.com

Exira
Audubon County Historical Society • Courthouse Museum • Exira, IA 50076 • (712) 563-3984

Courthouse Museum • E Washington & Kilworth St • Exira, IA 50076 • (712) 268-2831

Fairfax
Fairfax Public Library • 313 Vanderbilt St, P.O. Box 187 • Fairfax, IA 52228-0187 • (319) 846-2994 • http://www.fairfield.lib.ia.us

Fairfield
Carnegie Historical Museum • 114 S Court St • Fairfield, IA 52556

Fairfield Public Library • 104 W Adams Ave • Fairfield, IA 52556 • (641) 472-6551 • http://www.fairfield.lib.ia.us

Jefferson County Genealogical Society • 2791 240th St • Fairfield, IA 52556 • (641) 472-4667 • http://www.rootsweb.com/~iajeffer/jcgs.htm

Jefferson County Historical Society • 304 E Broadway • Fairfield, IA 52556 • (641) 472-8071

Farley
Dubuque County Library • 310 4th St SW, P.O. Box 10 • Farley, IA 52046-0010 • (563) 744-3577 • http://www.dubcolib.lib.ia.us

Farmersburg
Farmersburg Public Library • 208 S Main St, P.O. Box 167 • Farmersburg, IA 52047-0167 • (563) 536-2229

Farmington
Pioneer Historical Society • 203 S 4th St • Farmington, IA 52626

Forest City
Forest City Public Library • 115 East L St • Forest City, IA 50436 • (641) 585-4542

Lime Creek-Winnebago County Genealogical Society • c/o Forest City Public Library, 115 East L Street • Forest City, IA 50436 • (641) 585-4542 • http://www.pafways.org/genealogy/societies/winnebago.htm

Lunstrum Swedish Immigrant Log Cabin Museum • 36400 165th Ave • Forest City, IA 50436 • (515) 581-4196

Winnebago Historical Society • 336 N Clark St, P.O. Box 27 • Forest City, IA 50436

Fort Dodge
Fort Dodge & Frontier Village Museum • Museum Rd • Fort Dodge, IA 50501 • (515) 573-4231 • http://www.fortmuseum.com

Fort Dodge Center Library • Iowa Central Community College, 330 Avenue M • Fort Dodge, IA 50501 • (515) 576-7201 • http://www.iccc.cc.ia.us/libraries/

Fort Dodge Historical Foundation • Frontier Village, US Hwy 20 & Museum Rd, P.O. Box 1798 • Fort Dodge, IA 50501 • (515) 573-4231 • http://www.fortmuseum.com

Fort Dodge Public Library • 424 Central Ave • Fort Dodge, IA 50501 • (515) 573-8167 • http://www.fortdodge.lib.ia.us

Webster County Genealogical Library • P.O. Box 1584 • Fort Dodge, IA 50501

Webster County Genealogical Society • 424 Central Ave, P.O. Box 1584 • Fort Dodge, IA 50501-1584 • http://www.rootsweb.com/~iawebste/webgenso.htm

Fort Madison

Fort Madison Public Libraries • 614 7th St • Fort Madison, IA 52627 • (319) 372-5721 • http://www.fortmadisonlibrary.org

North Lee County Historical Society • Historic Museum, 922 Avenue H, P.O. Box 285 • Fort Madison, IA 52627-0285 • (319) 372-7661 • http://www.fortmadisonhistory.org

Old Fort Genealogical Society • P.O. Box 1 • Fort Madison, IA 52627-0001 • (319) 372-2987 • http://freepages.genealogy.rootsweb.com/~oldfort/

Rashid Memorial Library • 3421 Avenue L • Fort Madison, IA 52627 • (319) 372-2071 • http://www.fortmadisonlibrary.org

Garden Grove

J J McClung House Museum • Main & Vine Sts • Garden Grove, IA 50103 • (515) 443-2965

Garnavillo

Garnavillo Historical Society • Historical Museum, 205 N Washington, P.O. Box 371 • Garnavillo, IA 52049 • (563) 964-2341

Garner

Garner Public Library • 416 State St, P.O. Box 406 • Garner, IA 50438-0406 • (641) 923-2850

Gilmore City

Gilmore City Public Library • 308 S Gilmore St • Gilmore City, IA 50541 • (515) 373-6562

Glenwood

Glenwood Public Library • 109 N Vine St • Glenwood, IA 51534-1516 • (712) 527-5252 • http://www.glenwood.lib.ia.us

Mills County Genealogical Society • c/o Glenwood Public Library, 109 N Vine St • Glenwood, IA 51534-1516 • (712) 527-5252 • http://www.glenwood.lib.ia.us

Mills County Historical Society • Historical Museum, Glenwood Lake Park, P.O. Box 255 • Glenwood, IA 51534 • (712) 527-9221

Goldfield

Wright County Historical Society • P.O. Box 3 • Goldfield, IA 50542 • (515) 825-3641

Gowrie

Gowrie Historical Society • Beek St, P.O. Box 297 • Gowrie, IA 50543

Grafton

Grafton Heritage Depot Museum • Main St • Grafton, IA 50440 • (641) 748-2337

Gravity

Taylor County Genealogical Society • 102 Washington, P.O. Box 8 • Gravity, IA 50848-0008 • (712) 523-2041

Taylor County Historical Society • Historical Museum, P.O. Box 8 • Gravity, IA 50848 • (712) 539-2475 • http://www.rootsweb.com/~iataylor/tci93.htm

Greene

Greene Public Library • 231 W Tracer, P.O. Box 280 • Greene, IA 50636-0280 • (641) 816-5642

Greenfield

Adair County Anquestors Genealogy Society • c/o Greenfield Public Library, 215 S 1st St, P.O. Box 328 • Greenfield, IA 50849 • (515) 986-3551 • http://www.rootsweb.com/~iaaags

Adair County Chapter, IGS • c/o Greenfield Library, 215 S 1st St, P.O. Box 328 • Greenfield, IA 50849 • (515) 986-3551

Adair County Historical Society • Heritage Museum, Hwy 92 W, P.O. Box 214 • Greenfield, IA 50849 • (641) 743-2232

Greenfield Public Library • 202 S 1st St, P.O. Box 328 • Greenfield, IA 50849-0328 • (641) 743-6120

Iowa Aviation Museum • Greenfield Municipal Airport, 2251 Airport Rd, P.O. Box 31 • Greenfield, IA 50849 • (641) 343-7184 • http://www.flyingmuseum.com

Grinnell

Burling Library • Grinnell College, 1111 6th Ave • Grinnell, IA 50112-1690 • (641) 269-3353 • http://www.lib.grinnell.edu

Grinnell Historical Museum • 1125 Broad St • Grinnell, IA 50112 • (641) 236-5005

Stewart Library • 926 Broad St, P.O. Box 390 • Grinnell, IA 50112-0390 • (641) 236-2661 • http://www.grinnell.lib.ia.us

Griswold

Cass County Historical Society • Historical Museum, Main & Cass Sts, P.O. Box 254 • Griswold, IA 51535 • (712) 778-2695

Grundy Center

Grundy County Genealogical Society • 18419 205th St • Grundy Center, IA 50638-8733

Grundy County Historical Society • RFD 1 • Grundy Center, IA 50638 • (319) 824-3585

Kling Memorial Library • 708 7th St • Grundy Center, IA 50638-1430 • (319) 825-3607

Ostfriesian Heritage Society • Historical Musem, 905 E Avenue • Grundy Center, IA 50638 • (319) 824-6321

Guthrie County Historical Society • 901 Grand • Guthrie Center, IA 50115 • (641) 747-3403

Mary Barnett Memorial Library • 400 Grand St • Guthrie Center, IA 50115-1439 • (641) 747-8110 • http://www.guthriecenter.com/library

Hamburg

Hamburg Public Library • 1301 Main St • Hamburg, IA 51640 • (712) 382-1395

Hampton

Franklin County Genealogical Society • c/o Hampton Public Library, 4 Federal St S • Hampton, IA 50441-1934 • (641) 456-4451 • http://www.iowagenealogy.org/Counties/franklin.htm

Franklin County Historical Society • Historical Museum, P.O. Box 114 • Hampton, IA 50441 • (641) 456-5777

Hampton Public Library • 4 Federal St S • Hampton, IA 50441-1934 • (641) 456-4451

Hanlontown

Kinney Memorial Library • 214 Main St, P.O. Box 58 • Hanlontown, IA 50444-0058 • (641) 896-2888

Harlan

Harlan Community Library • 718 Court St • Harlan, IA 51537 • (712) 755-5934 • http://www.harlan.lib.ia.us

Nishnabotna Genealogical Society • 847 Road M56 • Harlan, IA 51537 • (712) 782-3400 • http://www.rootsweb.com/~iashelby/scgs.htm

Shelby County Historical Society • Historical Museum, 1805 Morse • Harlan, IA 51537 • (712) 755-2437

Haverhill

Matthew Edel Blacksmith Shop Museum • 1st St & 3rd Ave • Haverhill, IA 50120 • (515) 752-6664 • http://www.state.ia.us/iowahistory/sites/edel_blacksmith/edel_blacksmith.html

Hawarden

Big Sioux River Valley Historical Society • 1934 410th St • Hawarden, IA 51023 • (712) 552-2985

Hawarden Public Library • 803 10th St • Hawarden, IA 51023 • (712) 551-2244 • http://www.hawardenlibrary.org

Historical House and Photo Exhibit Museum • 803 Avenue H • Hawarden, IA 51023 • (712) 552-2233

Iowa

Hawkeye
Hawkeye Public Library • 104 S 2nd St • Hawkeye, IA 52147-0216 • (563) 427-5536

Holstein
Ida County Historical Society • 505 W 2nd St • Holstein, IA 51025

Homestead
Community Church Museum • 4210 V Street • Homestead, IA 52236 • (319) 622-3567 • http://www.AmanaColonies.com

Hopkinton
Delaware County Historical Society • Historical Museum, P.O. Box 70 • Hopkinton, IA 52237-0070 • (563) 926-2639

Hopkinton Public Library • 110 1st St SE, P.O. Box 220 • Hopkinton, IA 52237-0220 • (563) 926-2514

Hull
Hull Public Library • 1135 Main St, P.O. Box 822 • Hull, IA 51239 • (712) 439-1321

Humboldt
Humboldt County Genealogical Society • c/o Humboldt County Library, 30 6th St N • Humboldt, IA 50548-1799 • (515) 332-1439

Humboldt County Historical Association • 401 13th St SW, P.O. Box 162 • Humboldt, IA 50548 • (515) 332-1230

Humboldt County Library • 30 6th St N • Humboldt, IA 50548 • (515) 332-1925 • http://chiana.trunet.net/humboldt

Huxley
Huxley Public Library • 515 N Main Ave, P.O. Box 5 • Huxley, IA 50124-0005 • (515) 597-2552

Ida Grove
Ida County Genealogical Society • 506 Moorehead St • Ida Grove, IA 51445-1631

Moorehead House Museum • 410 Moorehead St • Ida Grove, IA 51445 • (712) 364-3816

Independence
Buchanan County Genealogical Society • 331 1st St E, P.O. Box 4 • Independence, IA 50644-0004 • (319) 334-9333 • http://www.rootsweb.com/~iabuchan/gen.htm

Independence Public Library • 210 2nd St NE • Independence, IA 50644 • (319) 334-2470 • http://www.indylibrary.org

Indianola
Indianola Public Library • 207 North B St • Indianola, IA 50125 • (515) 961-9418 • http://www.indianola.lib.ia.us

National Baloon Museum • 1601 N Jefferson Wy, P.O. Box 149 • Indianola, IA 50125 • (515) 961-8144 • http://www.nationalballoonmuseum.com

Warren County Genealogical Society • 306 W Salem St • Indianola, IA 50125-2438 • (515) 961-4409

Warren County Historical Society • 1400 W 2nd Ave, P.O. Box 256 • Indianola, IA 50125 • (515) 961-8085

Iowa City
Iowa City Public Library • 123 S Linn St • Iowa City, IA 52240 • (319) 356-5200 • http://www.icpl.org

Iowa City-Johnson County Genealogical Society • P.O. Box 822 • Iowa City, IA 52244-0822 • (319) 358-0466 • http://www.rootsweb.com/~iajohnso/icgensoc.htm

Old Capitol Library • 24 Old Capitol Museum • Iowa City, IA 52242-1420 • (319) 335-0548 • http://www.uiowa.edu/~oldcap/

Plum Grove Historic Home Museum • 1030 Carroll St • Iowa City, IA 52240 • (319) 337-6846 • http://www.uiowa.edu/~plumgrov/

State Historical Society of Iowa • Dept of Cultural Affairs, 402 Iowa Ave • Iowa City, IA 52240 • (319) 335-3916 • http://www.iowahistory.org

University of Iowa Libraries - Special Collections • 100 Main Library • Iowa City, IA 52242-1420 • (319) 335-5299 • http://www.lib.uiowa.edu/spec-coll

University of Iowa Medical Museum • 200 Hawkins Dr • Iowa City, IA 52242 • (319) 356-1616 • http://www.trihealthcare.com/medmuseum/

Iowa Falls
Iowa Falls Historical Society • 519 Stevens St • Iowa Falls, IA 50126-2213 • (641) 648-4603

Jamaica
Guthrie County Genealogical Society • P.O. Box 96 • Jamaica, IA 50128-0096 • (641) 429-3362 • http://www.rootsweb.com/~iaguthri/html/society.html

Jamaica Public Library • 316 Main St, P.O. Box 122 • Jamaica, IA 50128 • (641) 429-3362

Janesville
Janesville Public Library • 227 Main St, P.O. Box 328 • Janesville, IA 50647-0328 • (319) 987-2925 • http://www.cedarnet.org/library/janesvil.html

Jefferson
Greene County Genealogical Society • P.O. Box 133 • Jefferson, IA 50129 • http://www.rootsweb.com/~iagreene/gcgs.htm

Greene County Historical Society • Historical Museum, 219 E Lincolnway St • Jefferson, IA 50129 • (515) 386-8544

Jefferson Public Library • 200 W Lincolnway • Jefferson, IA 50129 • (515) 386-2835

Jewell
Montgomery Memorial Library • 711 Main St, P.O. Box 207 • Jewell, IA 50130-0207 • (515) 827-5112

Johnston
Iowa Gold Star Museum • 7700 NW Beaver Dr • Johnston, IA 50131 • (515) 252-4531 • http://www.iowanationalguard.com/Museum/Museum.html

Kalona
Kalona Historical Society • Historical Museum, P.O. Box 292 • Kalona, IA 52247 • (319) 646-5665

Kalona Public Library • 511 C Avenue, P.O. Box 1212 • Kalona, IA 52247-1212 • (319) 656-3501 • http://www.kctc.net/kaloplib

Mennonite Historical Society of Iowa • Historical Museum, 411 9th St, P.O. Box 576 • Kalona, IA 52247 • (319) 656-3271

Kellogg
Kellogg Historical Society • Historical Museum, 218 High St, P.O. Box 295 • Kellogg, IA 50135-0295 • (641) 526-3430

Keokuk
George M Verity Riverboat Museum • 415 Blondeau, P.O. Box 400 • Keokuk, IA 52632 • (319) 524-2943 • http://www.geomverity.org

Keokuk Public Library • 210 N 5th St • Keokuk, IA 52632 • (319) 524-1483 • http://www.keokukpl.org

Lee County Genealogical Society • P.O. Box 303 • Keokuk, IA 52632-0303 • (319) 524-1633 • http://www.rootsweb.com/~ialeecgs/

Lee County Historical Society • Miller House Museum, 318 N 5th St, P.O. Box 125 • Keokuk, IA 52632 • (319) 524-7283

Keosauqua
Keosauqua Public Library • 1st & Van Buren, P.O. Box 158 • Keosauqua, IA 52565-0158 • (319) 293-3766 • http://showcase.netins.net/web/keolibrary

Pearson House Museum • 718 Dodge St • Keosauqua, IA 52565 • (319) 293-3311

Selma Log Cabin Museum • P.O. Box 10 • Keosauqua, IA 52565

Van Buren County Genealogical Society • c/o Keosauqua Public Library, 1st & Van Buren, P.O. Box 158 • Keosauqua, IA 52565-0158 • (319) 293-3766 • http://www.rootsweb.com/~iavanbur/app.htm

Van Buren County Historical Society • Historical Museum, 801 1st St, P.O. Box 236 • Keosauqua, IA 52565 • (319) 293-3211 • http://www.villagesofvanburen.com

Kimballton
Kimballton Public Library • 118 Main St, P.O. Box 67 • Kimballton, IA 51543-0067 • (712) 773-3002

Kingsley
Kingsley Historical Society • general delivery • Kingsley, IA 51028 • (712) 378-2636

Klemme
Hancock County Genealogical Society • P.O. Box 81 • Klemme, IA 50449 • (641) 587-2324

Knoxville
Knoxville Public Library • 213 E Montgomery St • Knoxville, IA 50138-2296 • (641) 828-0585 • http://www.youseemore.com/knoxville/

Marion County Genealogical Society • c/o Knoxville Public Library, 213 E Montgomery St, P.O. Box 385 • Knoxville, IA 50138 • (641) 842-0585 • http://www.rootsweb.com/~iamcgs/

Marion County Historical Society • Marion County Park, RR 3 • Knoxville, IA 50138

La Porte City
Hawkins Memorial Library • 308 Main St • La Porte City, IA 50651 • (319) 342-3025 • http://www.cedarnet.org/library/laport.html

Ladora
Iowa County Historical Society • general delivery • Ladora, IA 52251

Lake View
Lake View Historical Society • 114 Crescent Park Dr • Lake View, IA 51450 • (712) 657-8010

Lake View Public Library • 202 Main St, P.O. Box 20 • Lake View, IA 51450 • (712) 657-2310

Lamoni
Decatur County Genealogical Society • c/o Lamoni Public Library, 133 E Main St • Lamoni, IA 50140 • (641) 784-6686

Frederick Madison Smith Library • Graceland College, 1 University Pl • Lamoni, IA 50140 • (641) 784-5301 • http://www.graceland.edu/library/

John Whitmer Historical Association • c/o Graceland College Library, 700 College Ave • Lamoni, IA 50140 • (641) 784-5350

Lamoni Public Library • 301 W Main St • Lamoni, IA 50140 • (641) 784-6686

Liberty Hall Historic Center • 1138 W Main St • Lamoni, IA 50140 • (641) 784-6133 • http://www.libhall.net

Laurens
Laurens Genies-Pocahontas County Chapter, IGS • 273 N 3rd St • Laurens, IA 50554-1215

Pocahontas County Iowa Historical Society • Historical Museum, 272 N 3rd, P.O. Box 148 • Laurens, IA 50554 • (712) 845-2577

Pocahontas County-Laurens Genealogical Society • c/o Laurens Public Library, 273 N 3rd St • Laurens, IA 50554-1215 • (712) 841-4612 • http://www.rootsweb.com/~iapcilgs

Le Claire
American-Schleswig-Holstein Heritage Society • P.O. Box 21 • Le Claire, IA 52753 • (563) 324-7326

Buffalo Bill Museum of LeClaire • 200 N River Dr, P.O. Box 284 • Le Claire, IA 52753 • (563) 289-5580 • http://www.buffalobillmuseumleclaire.com

Le Grand
Pioneer Heritage Library • 204 N Vine St, P.O. Box 188 • Le Grand, IA 50142-0188 • (641) 479-2122

Le Mars
LeMars Public Library • 46 1st St SW • Le Mars, IA 51031-3696 • (712) 546-7004

Northwest Iowa Genealogical Society • c/o LeMars Public Library, 46 1st St SW • Le Mars, IA 51031 • (712) 546-5004 • http://www.homestead.com/genealogynwia/gen.html

Plymouth County Historical Museum • 335 1st Ave SW • Le Mars, IA 51031 • (712) 546-7002

Lenox
Lenox Public Library • 101 N Main St • Lenox, IA 50851 • (641) 333-4411 • http://www.lenox.swilsa.lib.ia.us

Leon
Decatur County Historical Society • Main St • Leon, IA 50144 • (641) 446-4186

Lewis
Hitchcock House Museum • RR1, Box 5 • Lewis, IA 51544 • (712) 769-2323

Lisbon
Lisbon Public Library • 101 E Main St, P.O. Box 217 • Lisbon, IA 52253-0217 • (319) 455-2800

Livermore
Livermore Public Library • 402 5th St, P.O. Box 18 • Livermore, IA 50558-0018 • (515) 379-2078 • http://www.trvnet.net/~livplib

Logan
Harrison County Historical Society • 119 W 4th St • Logan, IA 51546 • (712) 644-2941

Long Grove
Dan Nagle Walnut Grove Pioneer Village Museum • 18817 290th St • Long Grove, IA 52756 • (563) 328-3283

Lost Nation
Lost Nation Public Library • 301 Pleasant St • Lost Nation, IA 52254-0397 • (563) 678-2114

Lowden
Lowden Historical Society • Next Door to City Hall • Lowden, IA 52255

Lucas
John L Lewis Mining and Labor Museum • 102 Division St, P.O. Box 3 • Lucas, IA 50151 • (641) 766-6831

Malvern
Malvern Public Library • 502 Main St, P.O. Box 180 • Malvern, IA 51551-0180 • (712) 624-8554

Manchester
Delaware County Genealogical Society • c/o Manchester Public Library, 300 N Franklin • Manchester, IA 52057 • (563) 927-3719

Manchester Public Library • 304 N Franklin St • Manchester, IA 52057 • (563) 927-3719 • http://www.manchester.lib.ia.us

Maquoketa
Jackson County Genealogical Chapter, IGS • Jackson County Historical Museum, P.O. Box 1065 • Maquoketa, IA 52060-1065 • (563) 652-5020 • http://www.rootsweb.com/~iajackso/JCGenie.html

Jackson County Historical Society • Pearson Memorial Ctr, 1212 E Quarry, P.O. Box 1245 • Maquoketa, IA 52060 • (563) 652-5020 • http://www.clintonengine.com

Maquoketa, cont.
Maquoketa Public Library • 126 S 2nd St • Maquoketa, IA 52060 • (563) 652-3874 • http://maquoketapubliclibrary.com

Marble Rock
Marble Rock Historical Society • Historical Museum, 313 Bradford St • Marble Rock, IA 50653 • (641) 397-2216

Marcus
Marcus Public Library • 106 N Locust St, P.O. Box 528 • Marcus, IA 51035 • (712) 376-2328

Marengo
Iowa County Historical Society • Pioneer Heritage Museum, 675 E South St, P.O. Box 288 • Marengo, IA 52301 • (319) 642-7018

Marengo Public Library • 1020 Marengo Ave • Marengo, IA 52301 • (319) 642-3825

Marion
Granger House Museum • 970 10th St, P.O. Box 753 • Marion, IA 52302 • (319) 377-6672 • http://www.community.marion.ia.us/granger/

Marion Heritage Center Museum • 590 10th St, P.O. Box 753 • Marion, IA 52302 • (319) 477-6377

Marshalltown
Central Iowa Genealogical Society • P.O. Box 945 • Marshalltown, IA 50158-0945 • http://www.marshallnet.com/~manor/genea/cigs.html

Historical Society of Marshall County • Historical Museum, 202 E Church St, P.O. Box 304 • Marshalltown, IA 50158 • (641) 752-6664 • http://www.marshallhistory.org

Marshalltown Public Library • 36 N Center St • Marshalltown, IA 50158 • (641) 754-5738 • http://www.marshallnet.com/library

Mason City
George and Elinor Stockman House Museum • 530 1st St NE • Mason City, IA 50401 • (515) 424-3444

Mason City Public Library • 225 2nd St SE • Mason City, IA 50401 • (641) 421-3668 • http://www.mcpl.org

Mason County Genealogical Society • c/o Mason City Public Library, 225 2nd St SE, P.O. Box 237 • Mason City, IA 50402-0237 • (641) 421-3668

North Central Iowa Genealogical Society • P.O. Box 237 • Mason City, IA 50402-0237 • http://www.pafways.org/genealogy/societies/northcentraliowa/

North Iowa Historical Society • Kinney Pioneer Museum, Hwy 18 W, P.O. Box 421 • Mason City, IA 50402-0421 • (641) 423-1258

River City Society for Historic Preservation • Historical Museum, P.O. Box 565 • Mason City, IA 50401

Maxwell
Maxwell Community Historical Museum • Main St • Maxwell, IA 50055 • (641) 385-2376

Maxwell Public Library • 107 Main St, P.O. Box 128 • Maxwell, IA 50161-0128 • (515) 387-8780

McGregor
McGregor Historical Society • Historical Museum, 254 Main St • McGregor, IA 52157 • (563) 873-3450

McGregor Public Library • 334 Main St, P.O. Box 398 • McGregor, IA 52157-0398 • (563) 873-3318

Menlo
Adair County Anquestors Genealogical Society • 2787 335th St • Menlo, IA 50164 • (641) 524-5110

Daughters of Union Veterans of the Civil War, Iowa Dept • Route 1, Box 23 • Menlo, IA 50164 • (641) 524-5110

Genie Bug Club Genealogical Society • 2787 335th St • Menlo, IA 50164 • (641) 524-5110

Menlo Public Library • 417 Sherman St, P.O. Box 39 • Menlo, IA 50164 • (641) 524-4201

Meriden
Tree Stumpers • Route 1, Box 65 • Meriden, IA 51037

Middle Amana
Communal Kitchen and Coopershop Museum • 1003 26th Ave • Middle Amana, IA 52203 • (319) 622-3567 • http://www.amanacolonies.com

Milford
Milford Memorial Library • 1009 9th St, Suite 5 • Milford, IA 51351 • (712) 338-4643

Milo
Milo Public Library • 123 Main St • Milo, IA 50166 • (641) 942-6557 • http://www.cityofmilo.org

Missouri Valley
Harrison County Historic Village • 2931 Monroe Ave • Missouri Valley, IA 51555 • (712) 642-2114

Steamboat Bertrand Museum • 1434 316th Ln • Missouri Valley, IA 51555 • (712) 642-2772 • http://www.refuges.fws.gov

Moingona
Kate Shelley Railroad Museum • 1198 232nd St • Moingona, IA 50036 • (515) 432-1907

Monona
Monona Historical Society • 302 S Egbert St, P.O. Box 434 • Monona, IA 52159 • (563) 539-8083

Murphy Memorial Library • 111 N Page, Box 430 • Monona, IA 52159-0430 • (563) 539-2356

Monroe
Monroe Public Library • 103 W Washington, P.O. Box 780 • Monroe, IA 50170-0780 • (641) 259-3065

Montezuma
Montezuma Public Library • 200 S 3rd St, P.O. Box 158 • Montezuma, IA 50171-0158 • (641) 623-3417

Poweshiek County Historical and Genealogical Society • 206 N Mill St, P.O. Box 280 • Montezuma, IA 50171-0280 • (641) 623-3322 • http://showcase.netins.net/web/powshk/

Monticello
Jones Company Historical Society • 13838 Edinburgh Rd • Monticello, IA 52310 • (563) 487-3711

Montrose
Montrose Public Library • 202 Main St, P.O. Box 100 • Montrose, IA 52639-0100 • (319) 463-5532

Moravia
Moravia Public Library • 00 E Chariton • Moravia, IA 52571-9530 • (641) 724-3440

Moulton
Garrett Memorial Library • 123 S Main St • Moulton, IA 52572-1327 • (641) 642-3664

Moulton Historical Society • 111 E 4th St • Moulton, IA 51572 • (641) 642-3770

Mount Ayr
Mount Ayr Public Library • 121 W Monroe St • Mount Ayr, IA 50854 • (641) 464-2159

Ringgold County Genealogical Society • c/o Mount Ayr Public Library, 121 W Monroe St • Mount Ayr, IA 50854 • (641) 464-3594

Ringgold County Historical Society • general delivery • Mount Ayr, IA 50584 • (641) 464-2140

Mount Pleasant
Harlan-Lincoln House Museum • 101 W Broad St • Mount Pleasant, IA 52641 • (319) 385-8021 • http://www.iwc.edu

Henry County Genealogical Society • P.O. Box 81 • Mount Pleasant, IA 52641-0081

Iowa City Genealogical Society • 403 S Walnut • Mount Pleasant, IA 52641

J Raymond Chadwick Library • Iowa Wesleyan College, 107 W Broad St • Mount Pleasant, IA 52641 • (319) 385-6316 • http://chadwick.iwc.edu

Midwest Old Settlers and Threshers Association • Historical Museum, 405 E Threshers Rd • Mount Pleasant, IA 52641 • (319) 385-8937 • http://www.oldthreshers.org

Mount Pleasant Public Library • 200 N Main St • Mount Pleasant, IA 52641 • (319) 385-1490 • http://www.mountpleasantiowa.org

Moville
Woodbury County Library • 309 Main St, P.O. Box AL • Moville, IA 51039-0830 • (712) 873-3322

Muscatine
Muscatine County Genealogical Society • 323 Main St • Muscatine, IA 52761-3867

Muscatine History Museum • 117 W 2nd St • Muscatine, IA 52761 • (563) 263-1052 • http://www.pearlbuttoncapital.com

Musser Public Library • 304 Iowa Ave • Muscatine, IA 52761-3875 • (563) 263-3472 • http://www.muscatinelibrary.us

Pine Creek Grist Mill Museum • 1884 Wildcat Den Rd • Muscatine, IA 52761 • (319) 263-4337 • http://www.pinecreekgristmill.com

Nashua
Chickasaw County Historical Society • Old Bradford Pioneer Village Museum, 2729 Cheyenne Ave • Nashua, IA 50658 • (641) 435-2567

Nashua Public Library • 220 Brasher, P.O. Box 619 • Nashua, IA 50658-0619 • (641) 435-4635

Nevada
Community Historical Society • 512 E Avenue • Nevada, IA 50201 • (515) 382-4085

Nevada Historical Society • Dyer-Dowell Victorian House Museum, 922 5th St • Nevada, IA 50201-2148 • (515) 382-6684

Nevada Public Library • 631 K Ave • Nevada, IA 50201 • (515) 382-2628

New Hampton
Chickasaw County Genealogical Society • c/o New Hampton Public Library, 20 W Spring, P.O. Box 434 • New Hampton, IA 50659-0434 • (641) 394-4343 • http://www.rootsweb.com/~iachicka/CK_CCGS.htm

New Hampton Public Library • 20 W Spring • New Hampton, IA 50659 • (641) 394-2184

New London
Dover Historical Society • Historical Museum, 213 W Main • New London, IA 52645 • (319) 367-2573

New Providence
Honey Creek Church Preservation Group • 30293 'O' Avenue • New Providence, IA 50206-8008 • (641) 497-5458

Honey Creek Church Preservation Library • 31031 PP Ave • New Providence, IA 50206-9707 • (641) 497-5458

Newton
Jasper County Genealogical Society • 113 W 2nd St S, P.O. Box 163 • Newton, IA 50208-0163 • (641) 792-1522 • http://www.rootsweb.comt/~iajasperco.htm

Jasper County Historical Society • Historical Museum, 1700 S 15th Ave W, P.O. Box 834 • Newton, IA 50208 • (641) 792-9118

Nora Springs
Nora Springs Historical Society • 20 W Congress St • Nora Springs, IA 50458 • (641) 749-5517

North English
Iowa County Genealogical Society • P.O. Box 207 • North English, IA 62316 • (319) 655-7733

North English Public Library • 123 S Main St, P.O. Box 427 • North English, IA 52316 • (319) 664-3725 • http://www.northenglish.com

Oakland
Botna Valley Genealogical Society of East Pottawattamie County • P.O. Box 693 • Oakland, IA 51560 • (712) 482-3209

Eckles Memorial Library • 207 South Highway, P.O. Box 519 • Oakland, IA 51560-0519 • (712) 482-6668

Oakland Historical Society • Nishna Heritage Museum, 117 N Main St • Oakland, IA 51560 • (712) 482-6802 • http://www.nishnaheritagemuseum.com

Odebolt
Peterson Pioneer House Museum • Walnut St • Odebolt, IA 51458

Oelwein
Oelwein Area Genealogical Society Chapter, IGS • c/o Oelwein Public Library, 1st Ave NW • Oelwein, IA 50662 • (319) 283-1515

Oelwein Area Historical Society • Historical Museum, 900 2nd Ave SE, P.O. Box 445 • Oelwein, IA 50662-0389 • (319) 283-5322 • http://www.rootsweb.com/~iaoahs

Oelwein Public Library • 22 1st Ave NW • Oelwein, IA 50662-1604 • (319) 283-1515 • http://www.oelwein.com

Ogden
Hickory Grove Rural School Museum • Don William Ln • Ogden, IA 50212 • (515) 432-1907 • http://www.homepages.opencominc.com/bchs

Okoboji
Higgins Banking Museum • 1507 Sanborn Ave, P.O. Box 258 • Okoboji, IA 51355 • (712) 332-5859

Onawa
Monona County Genealogical Society • 901 12th St, P.O. Box 16 • Onawa, IA 51040-0016

Monona County Historical Society • Historical Museum, 47 12th St • Onawa, IA 51040 • (712) 423-3452

Onawa Public Library - Genealogist • 707 Iowa Ave • Onawa, IA 51040 • (712) 423-1167

Oran
Bremer County Genealogical Society • P.O. Box 15 • Oran, IA 50664 • http://www.rootsweb.com/iabremer

Orange City
Orange City Public Library • 112 Albany St, P.O. Box 346 • Orange City, IA 51041-0346 • (712) 737-4302 • http://www.orangecity.lib.ia.us

Ramaker Library • Northwestern College, 101 7th St SW • Orange City, IA 51041-1996 • (712) 707-7234 • http://www.nwciowa.edu

Orient
Henry A Wallace Birthplace Museum • 2773 290th St • Orient, IA 50858 • (515) 337-5019

Osage

Cedar Valley Memories Museum • Hwy 9, P.O. Box 51 • Osage, IA 50461 • (641-732-1269

Mitchell County Historical Society • Historical Museum, 6th & Mechanic, P.O. Box 51 • Osage, IA 50461 • (641) 732-4047

Osage Public Library • 406 Main St • Osage, IA 50461-1125 • (641) 732-3323 • http://www.osage.net/~osagepl

Osceola

Clarke County Historical Society • Hwy 69 S • Osceola, IA 50213 • (641) 342-3550 • http://www.rootsweb.com/~iaclarke/hissoc.html

Clarke County Iowa Genealogical Society • c/o Osceola Public Library, 300 S Fillmore • Osceola, IA 50213-1414 • (641) 342-2237 • http://www.rootsweb.com/~iaclarke/ccgs.html

Osceola Public Library • 300 S Fillmore St • Osceola, IA 50213-2237 • (641) 342-2237 • http://www.osceola.lib.ia.us

Oskaloosa

Keo Mah Genealogical Society • 103 N 3rd St, P.O. Box 616 • Oskaloosa, IA 52577 • (641) 673-9373 • http://www.keo-mah.com

Mahasha County Historical Society • Irma Glatty Library, RR1, P.O. Box 578 • Oskaloosa, IA 52577 • (641) 672-2989

Nelson Pioneer Farm Museum • 2294 Oxford Ave, P.O. Box 578 • Oskaloosa, IA 52577 • (641) 672-2989 • http://www.nelsonpioneer.org

Oskaloosa Public Library • 301 S Market St • Oskaloosa, IA 52577 • (641) 673-0441 • http://www.opl.oskaloosa.org

Wilcox Library • William Penn College, 201 Trueblood Ave • Oskaloosa, IA 52577 • (641) 673-1096 • http://www.wmpen.edu/pennweb/library/library.html

Ottumwa

Airpower Museum • 22001 Bluegrass Rd • Ottumwa, IA 52501 • (641) 938-2773 • http://www.aaa-apm.org

Ottumwa Public Library • 102 W 4th St • Ottumwa, IA 52501 • (641) 682-7563 • http://www.ottumwalibrary.com

Wapello County Genealogical Society • Depot Museum & Genealogical Library, 210 W Main St, P.O. Box 163 • Ottumwa, IA 52501-0163 • (641) 682-8676 • http://www.rootsweb.com/~iawapegs/

Wapello County Historical Society • Depot Museum, 201 W Main St • Ottumwa, IA 52501 • (641) 682-8676

Oxford Junction

Wregie Memorial Library • 105 W Broadway, P.O. Box 345 • Oxford Junction, IA 52323-0345 • (563) 826-2450 • http://www.netins.net/showcase/wregiememlib

Palmer

Weigert Prairie Farm Museum • RR • Palmer, IA 50571 • (712) 359-7778

Parkersburg

Butler County Genealogical Society • P.O. Box 177 • Parkersburg, IA 50665

Parkersburg Historical Home Museum • 401 5th St • Parkersburg, IA 50665 • (319) 346-1849

Pella

Geisler Library • Central College, Box 6500, 812 University St • Pella, IA 50219-1999 • (641) 628-5219 • http://www.central.edu/library/libhome.htm

Pella Historical Society • Historical Village & Wyatt Earp House Museum, 507 Franklin St • Pella, IA 50219 • (641) 628-2409 • http://www.pellatuliprime.com

Pella Public Library • 603 Main St • Pella, IA 50219 • (641) 628-4268 • http://www.cityofpella.com/librarybody.htm

Scholte House Museum • 728 Washington • Pella, IA 50219 • (515) 628-3684

Peosta

Burton Payne Library • Northeast Iowa Community College, 10250 Sundown Rd • Peosta, IA 52068 • (563) 556-5110 • http://www.nicc.cc.ia.us

Perry

Forest Park Museum • 1477 K Ave • Perry, IA 50220 • (515) 465-3577 • http://www.dallascountyconservation.org

Peterson

Kirchner-French Memorial Library • 101 Main St, P.O. Box 203 • Peterson, IA 51047-0203 • (712) 295-6705

Peterson Heritage • P.O. Box 222 • Peterson, IA 51047 • (712) 295-6401

Plainfield

Bremer County Genealogical Society • 1378 Badger Ave • Plainfield, IA 50666-9743 • (319) 276-3234

Bremer County Historical Society • Historical Museum, 219 Main St, P.O. Box 218 • Plainfield, IA 50666-0218 • (319) 276-4674

Pleasantville

Webb Shadle Memorial Library • 301 W Dallas, P.O. Box 338 • Pleasantville, IA 50225 • (515) 848-5617

Plover

Plover Public Library • 301 Main St, P.O. Box 112 • Plover, IA 50573-0112 • (712) 857-3532

Pocahontas

Pocahontas County Genealogical Society • c/o Pocahontas Library, 14 2nd Ave NW • Pocahontas, IA 50574-1611 • (712) 335-4471

Pocahontas Library • 14 2nd Ave NW • Pocahontas, IA 50574-1611 • (712) 335-4471 • http://www.ncn.net/~pokypl/

Postville

Postville Historical Society • 205 W Williams St, P.O. Box 396 • Postville, IA 52162 • (563) 864-3818

Prairie City

Prairie City Historical Society • Historical Museum, P.O. Box 344 • Prairie City, IA 50228

Prescott

Adams County Genealogical Society • P.O. Box 117 • Prescott, IA 50859-0177 • (641) 335-2352

Primghar

O'Brien County Historical Society • 1st St NE & Heritage Park Rd, P.O. Box 385 • Primghar, IA 51245 • (712) 757-1511

Princeton

Buffalo Bill Cody Homestead Museum • 28050 230th Ave • Princeton, IA 52768 • (563) 225-2981 • http://www.scottcountyiowa.com

Quasqueton

Cedar Rock House Museum • 2611 Quasqueton Diagonal Blvd, P.O. Box 25 • Quasqueton, IA 52326 • (319) 934-3572

Randolph

Randolph Public Library • 106 S Main St, P.O. Box 112 • Randolph, IA 51649-0112 • (712) 625-3561

Red Oak

Montgomery County Genealogial Society • 320 A Coolbaugh • Red Oak, IA 51566-2416

Montgomery County Historical Society • Historical Museum, 2700 N 4th St, P.O. Box 289 • Red Oak, IA 51566 • (712) 623-2289

Red Oak Public Library • 400 W 2nd St • Red Oak, IA 51566-2251 • (712) 623-6516 • http://www.redoaklibrary.net

Reinbeck
Grundy County Genealogical Society • 708 West St, P.O. Box 2 • Reinbeck, IA 50669

Rock Rapids
Lyon County Historical Society • general delivery • Rock Rapids, IA 51246

Rock Valley
Rock Valley Public Library • 1531 Main St • Rock Valley, IA 51247-1127 • (712) 476-5651

Rockwell City
Calhoun County Genealogical Society • c/o Carnegie Public Library, 426 5th St • Rockwell City, IA 50579 • (712) 297-8422

Calhoun County Genies • Historical Museum, 150 E High St • Rockwell City, IA 50579 • (712) 297-7237

Calhoun County Historical Society • Calhoun County Museum, 150 E High St • Rockwell City, IA 50579 • (712) 297-8139

Rockwell City Public Library • 426 5th St • Rockwell City, IA 50579-1415 • (712) 297-8422 • http://www.iowatelecom.net

Rolfe
Pocahontas County Historical Society • RR 2, Box 12 • Rolfe, IA 50581 • (712) 848-3342

Rolfe Public Library • 401 Garfield St • Rolfe, IA 50581 • (712) 848-3143

Sac City
Sac City Public Library • 1001 Main St • Sac City, IA 50583 • (712) 662-7276

Sac County Genealogical Society • P.O. Box 54 • Sac City, IA 50583-0054 • (712) 662-4094 • http://www.rootsweb.com/~iasae/gensociety/gensoc.htm

Salem
Lewelling Quaker House Museum • 401 S Main, P.O. Box 28 • Salem, IA 52649 • (319) 258-4341

Schleswig
Schleswig Public Library • 202 Cedar St • Schleswig, IA 51461-0306 • (712) 676-3470

Scotch Grove
Jones County Historical Society • 13838 Edinburgh Rd • Scotch Grove, IA 52310 • (563) 487-3711

Sheldon
Sheldon Public Library • 925 4th Ave • Sheldon, IA 51201-1517 • (712) 324-2442

Shell Rock
Benny Gambaiani Public Library • 104 S Cherry St, P.O. Box 320 • Shell Rock, IA 50670-0811 • (319) 885-4345

Shenandoah
Greater Shenandoah Historical Society • Historical Museum, 800 W Sheridan Ave, P.O. Box 182 • Shenandoah, IA 51601 • (712) 246-1669

Page County Genealogical Society • RR2, Box 236 • Shenandoah, IA 51610

Sibley
Brunson Heritage Home Museum • 719 5th St • Sibley, IA 51249 • (712) 754-3882

Osceola County Historical Society • McCallum Museum, 719 5th St • Sibley, IA 51249 • (712) 754-4000 • http://www.osceolacountyia.com/info/museums.htm

Sidney
Fremont County Genealogical Society • P.O. Box 671 • Sidney, IA 51652-0337

Fremont County Historical Society • 801 Indiana, P.O. Box 671 • Sidney, IA 51652-0337 • (712) 374-3248

Sidney Public Library • 604 Clay St, P.O. Box 479 • Sidney, IA 51652-0479 • (712) 374-2223

Sigourney
Keokuk County Historical Society • 402 E Elm Sts, P.O. Box 324 • Sigourney, IA 52591 • (641) 622-3005

Sioux Center
Dordt College Library • 498 4th Ave NE • Sioux Center, IA 51250 • (712) 722-6340 • http://www.dordt.edu/academics/library/

Greater Sioux County Genealogical Society • c/o Sioux Center Public Library, 327 1st Ave NE, P.O. Box 624 • Sioux Center, IA 51250-1801 • (712) 722-2138 • http://www.rootsweb.com/~iasioux/gscgs/gscgs.htm

Sioux Center Public Library • 102 S Main Ave • Sioux Center, IA 51250-1801 • (712) 722-2138 • http://siouxcenter.lib.ia.us

Sioux City
Loren D Callendar Gallery Museum • City Hall, 6th & Douglas Sts • Sioux City, IA 51101 • (712) 279-6174 • http://www.sioux-city.org/museum

Sergeant Floyd Museum • 1000 Larsen Park Rd • Sioux City, IA 51103 • (712) 279-0198 • http://www.sioux-city.org/museum

Sioux City Public Library-Wilbur Aalfs Main Library • 529 Pierce St • Sioux City, IA 51001-1203 • (712) 255-2933 • http://www.siouxcitylibrary.org

Sioux City Public Museum and Historical Association • Historical Museum, 2901 Jackson St • Sioux City, IA 51104-3697 • (712) 279-6174 • http://www.sioux-city.org/museum/

Sons of the American Revolution, Iowa Society • 4908 Ravie Park Ln • Sioux City, IA 51006 • (712) 266-0378 • http://www.iassar.org

Woodbury County Genealogical Society • c/o Sioux City Public Library, 529 Pierce St, P.O. Box 624 • Sioux City, IA 51102-0624 • (712) 279-6972 • http://rootsweb.com/~iawoodbu/

Sioux Rapids
Sioux Rapids Memorial Library • 215 2nd St • Sioux Rapids, IA 50585 • (712) 283-2064

Slater
Slater Public Library • 105 N Tama St, P.O. Box 598 • Slater, IA 50244-0598 • (515) 685-3558

Sloan
Sloan Historical Society • general delivery • Sloan, IA 51055

Sloan Museum • 417-419 Evans St • Sloan, IA 51055

Sloan Public Library • 311 4th St, P.O. Box 8 • Sloan, IA 51055-0008 • (712) 428-4200

South Amana
Communal Agriculture Museum • 505 P Street • South Amana, IA 52334 • (319) 622-3567 • http://www.cr.nps.gov/nr/travel/agr.htm

Spencer
Iowa Lakes Genealogical Society • 600 W 11th St • Spencer, IA 51301 • (712) 262-1318 • http://www.pionet.net/~nwiowa/spencer/clubs/ilgs.htm

Parker Historical Society of Clay County • Historical Museum, 300 E 3rd St, P.O. Box 91 • Spencer, IA 51301 • (712) 262-3304 • http://www.parkermuseum.org

Spencer Public Library • 21 E 3rd St • Spencer, IA 51301-4188 • (712) 264-7290 • http://www.spencerlibrary.com

Spillville
Bily Clocks Museum • 323 Main St, P.O. Box 258 • Spillville, IA 52168 • (563) 562-3569 • http://www.bilyclocks.org

Spillville, cont.
Spillville Historic Action Group • P.O. Box 187 • Spillville, IA 51268-0187 • (563) 562-3186

Spirit Lake
Dickinson County Historical Society • Historical Museum, P.O. Box 532 • Spirit Lake, IA 51360 • (712) 338-2138

Spirit Lake Public Library • 702 16th St • Spirit Lake, IA 51360 • (712) 336-2667 • http://www.spiritlakepubliclibrary.org

Stacyville
Stacyville Public Library • 105 W Main St, P.O. Box 219 • Stacyville, IA 50476-0219 • (641) 737-2531

Stanhope
Country Relics Little Village Museum • 3290 Briggs Woods Rd • Stanhope, IA 50246 • (515) 826-4FUN

Stanton
Stanton Community Library • 310 Broad Ave, P.O. Box 130 • Stanton, IA 51573-0130 • (712) 829-2290

Swedish Heritage & Cultural Center • 410 Hilltop, P.O. Box 231 • Stanton, IA 51573 • (712) 829-2840 • http://www.stantoniowa.com/community/cultural_center.htm

Storm Lake
Buena Vista County Genealogical Library • 221 W Railroad St • Storm Lake, IA 50588

Buena Vista County Historical and Genealogical Society • 221 West Railroad St • Storm Lake, IA 50588 • (712) 732-7111

Buena Vista County Historical Society • 214 West 5th St, P.O. Box 882 • Storm Lake, IA 50588

Buena Vista University Library • 610 W 4th St • Storm Lake, IA 50588 • (712) 749-2203 • http://www.bvu.edu/library/

Storm Lake Public Library • 609 Cayuga St • Storm Lake, IA 50588 • (712) 732-8026 • http://www.stormlakepubliclibrary.org

Stratford
Stratford Public Library • 816 Shakespeare • Stratford, IA 50249 • (515) 838-2131

Strawberry Point
Strawberry Point Historical Society • Wilder Memorial Museum, 123 W Mission • Strawberry Point, IA 52076 • (563) 933-4615

Stuart
Stuart Public Library • 111 E Front St, P.O. Box 220 • Stuart, IA 50250-0220 • (515) 523-2152 • http://www.stuart.swilsa.lib.ia.us

Sutherland
Sutherland Public Library • 315 Ash St, P.O. Box 280 • Sutherland, IA 51058-0280 • (712) 446-3839

Swedesburg
Swedish Heritage Society Foundation • Historical Museum, 107 James Ave • Swedesburg, IA 52652 • (319) 254-2317

Tabor
Todd House Museum • 405 Park St, P.O. Box 417 • Tabor, IA 51653 • (712) 629-2675

Tama
Louise & Lucile Hink Library • 401 Siegel St, PO Box 308 • Tama, IA 52339-0308 • (641) 484-4484

Sac and Fox Tribe • 3137 F Avenue • Tama, IA 52339 • (515) 484-4678

Terril
Terril Community Library • 115 N State St, P.O. Box 38 • Terril, IA 51364-0038 • (712) 853-6224

Tipton
Cedar County Genealogical Society • P.O. Box 52 • Tipton, IA 52772-0052

Cedar County Historical Society • Historical Museum, 607 Orange St • Tipton, IA 52772 • (563) 886-2740

Tipton Public Library • 206 Cedar St • Tipton, IA 52772-1753 • (563) 886-6266 • http://www.tiptonpubliclibrary.us

Toledo
Tama County Historical Society • Historical Museum, 200 N Broadway, P.O. Box 84 • Toledo, IA 52342 • (641) 484-6767

Tama County Tracers Genealogical Society • 200 N Broadway, P.O. Box 84 • Toledo, IA 52342-0084 • (641) 484-6767

Toledo Public Library • 206 E High St • Toledo, IA 52342-1617 • (641) 484-3362

Tripoli
Tripoli Public Library • 101 4th Ave SW, P.O. Box 430 • Tripoli, IA 50676-0430 • (319) 882-4807

Urbandale
American Historical Society of Germans from Russia, Wild Rose Chapter • 9612 Tanglewood Dr • Urbandale, IA 50322 • (515) 253-0523 • http://www.ahsgr.org/Chapters/wild_rose_chapter_of_iowa.htm

Living History Farms Museum • 11121 Hickman Rd • Urbandale, IA 50322 • (515) 278-5286 • http://www.livinghistoryfarms.org

Urbandale Historical Society • 4010 70th St • Urbandale, IA 50322-2616 • (515) 270-2917

Urbandale Public Library • 3520 86th St • Urbandale, IA 50322 • (515) 278-3945 • http://www.urbandalelibrary.org

Vail
Crawford County Genealogical Society • P.O. Box 26 • Vail, IA 51465

Vinton
Benton County Historical Society • 612 1st Ave • Vinton, IA 52349-1705

Frank G Ray House Museum • 912 1st Ave • Vinton, IA 52349 • (319) 472-2991 • http://www.rootsweb.com/~iabenton/bchs/ray.htm

Horridge House Museum • 612 1st Ave • Vinton, IA 52349 • (319) 472-4573

Railway, Agricultural, Industrial Lineage Society • P.O. Box 186 • Vinton, IA 52349-0186

Vinton Depot Museum • 512 2nd Ave • Vinton, IA 52349 • (319) 472-5939

Wadena
Wadena Public Library • 136 S Mill St, P.O. Box 19 • Wadena, IA 52169-0019 • (563) 774-2039

Wapello
Louisa County Genealogical Society • Heritage Center, 607 Hwy 61 N, P.O. Box 202 • Wapello, IA 52653-1158 • (319) 523-8381 • http://www.rootsweb.com/~ialcgs/

Louisa County Historical Society • Heritage Center, 609 Hwy 61 N • Wapello, IA 52653 • (319) 523-8381

Louisa County Registrar - Vital Records • County Courthouse, 117 S Main St, P.O. Box 264 • Wapello, IA 52623-5364 • (319) 523-5361 • http://www.louisacountyiowa.org/louisa/recorder/recorder.html

Washington
Iowa Historic Preservation Alliance • 205 E Washington St • Washington, IA 52353 • (319) 863-7141

Washington County Genealogical Society • c/o Washington Public Library, 120 E Main St, P.O. Box 446 • Washington, IA 52353-0446 • (319) 653-2726 • http://www.rootsweb.com/~iawashin/wcgs.htm

Washington County Historical Society • Conger House Museum, 903 E Washington, P.O. Box 364 • Washington, IA 52353 • (319) 653-3125

Washington Public Library • 120 E Main St • Washington, IA 52353 • (319) 653-2726 • http://www.washlib.net/genealogy.html

Washta
Grand Meadow Heritage Center • Route 1, Box 45 • Washta, IA 51061 • (712) 375-5117

Waterloo
Grout Museum of History and Science • Hans J Chryst Archives, 503 South St • Waterloo, IA 50701-1517 • (319) 234-6357 • http://www.groutmuseumdistrict.org

Northeast Iowa Genealogical Society • c/o Grout Museum of History, 503 South St • Waterloo, IA 50701-1517 • (319) 234-6357 • http://www.iowa-counties.com/blackhawk/gene.htm

Rensselaer Russell House Museum • 520 W 3rd St • Waterloo, IA 50701 • (319) 233-0262

Waterloo Public Library • 415 Commercial St • Waterloo, IA 50701-1385 • (319) 291-4521 • http://www.wplwloo.lib.ia.us

Waukon
Allamakee County Historical Society • 121 N Allamakee St • Waukon, IA 52172 • (563) 568-2954

Robey Memorial Library • 401 1st Ave NW • Waukon, IA 52172-1803 • (563) 568-4424

Waverly
Vogel Library • Wartburg College, 100 Wartburg Blvd • Waverly, IA 50677-0903 • (319) 352-8506 • http://www.wartburg.edu/library/

Waverly Public Library • 1500 W Bremer Ave • Waverly, IA 50677-3299 • (319) 352-1223 • http://www.waverlyia.com

Webb
Webb Public Library • 124 Main St, P.O. Box 97 • Webb, IA 51366-0097 • (712) 838-7719

Webster City
Hamilton Heritage Hunters Genealogical Society • c/o Kendall Young Public Library, 1201 Wilson St, P.O. Box 364 • Webster City, IA 50595 • (515) 832-9100

Kendall Young Library • 1201 Wilson St • Webster City, IA 50595-2294 • (515) 832-9100 • http://www.kendall-young.lib.ia.us

Wellsburg
Wellsburg Public Library • 515 N Adams, P.O. Box 489 • Wellsburg, IA 50680-0489 • (641) 869-5234

West Bend
West Bend Historical Society • 4473 550th Ave • West Bend, IA 50597 • (515) 887-3241

West Branch
Herbert Hoover National Historic Site Museum • 110 Parkside Dr, P.O. Box 607 • West Branch, IA 52358 • (319) 643-2541 • http://www.nps.gov/heho

Herbert Hoover Presidential Library • 210 Parkside Dr, P.O. Box 498 • West Branch, IA 52358 • (319) 643-5301 • http://www.hoover.nara.gov

Herbert Hoover Presidential Library Association • 302 Parkside Dr, P.O. Box 696 • West Branch, IA 52358 • (319) 643-5327 • http://www.hooverassociation.org

West Des Moines
Bennett School Museum • Fuller Rd & 50th St • West Des Moines, IA 50061 • (515) 225-1286

Polk County-Tree Shakers Genealogical Society • 933 41st St W • West Des Moines, IA 50265-3023

West Des Moines Historical Society • Jordan House Museum, 2001 Fuller Rd • West Des Moines, IA 50265 • (515) 225-1286

West Liberty
West Liberty Historical Society • 600 E 4th St • West Liberty, IA 52776

West Union
Fayette County Genealogical Society • Historical Museum, 100 N Walnut St • West Union, IA 52175 • (563) 422-5797 • http://www.rootsweb.com/iafayet/

Fayette County Helpers & Historical Society • Historical Museum, 100 N Walnut St • West Union, IA 52175 • (563) 422-5797

Westside
Westside Public Library • 150 Main St, Box 163 • Westside, IA 51467-0163 • (712) 663-4493

Wheatland
Curtis Memorial Library • 116 S Main, P.O. Box 429 • Wheatland, IA 52777-0429 • (563) 374-1534

Wilton
Wilton Public Library • 106 E 4th St, P.O. Box 447 • Wilton, IA 52778-0008 • (563) 732-2583 • http://showcase.netins.net/web/wiltonpl

Winfield
Winfield Historical Society • Historical Museum, 114 S Locust St, P.O. Box 184 • Winfield, IA 52659 • (319) 257-6974 • http://www.winfieldhistoricalsociety.com

Winterset
Birthplace of John Wayne Museum • 216 S 2nd St • Winterset, IA 50273 • (515) 462-1044 • http://www.johnwaynebirthplace.org

Madison County Genealogy Society • c/o Winterset Public Library, 123 N 2nd St, P.O. Box 26 • Winterset, IA 50273-0026 • (515) 462-1731

Madison County Historical Complex • 815 Couth Ave, P.O. Box 15 • Winterset, IA 50273 • (515) 462-2134

Madison County Historical Society • Historical Museum, 812 S 2nd St, P.O. Box 15 • Winterset, IA 50273 • (515) 462-2134 • http://www.madisoncountyhistoricalsociety.com

Winterset Public Library • 123 N 2nd St • Winterset, IA 50273-1508 • (515) 462-1731

Woodbine
Harrison County Genealogical Society • Merry Brook School Museum, 212 Lincolnway St • Woodbine, IA 51579-1328 • (712) 647-2593 • http://www.rootsweb.com/~iaharris/hcgs/

Harrison County Genealogical Volunteers Chapter, IGS • Merry Brook School Museum, 210 Lincoln Wy • Woodbine, IA 51579 • (712) 647-2593 • http://www.rootsweb.com/iaharris

Zearing
Zearing Public Library • 101 E Main • Zearing, IA 50278-0197 • (641) 487-7888

Iowa

Abilene

Abilene Free Public Library • 209 NW 4th • Abilene, KS 67410-2690 • (785) 263-3082

Dickinson County Historical Society • Heritage Center, 412 S Campbell St, P.O. Box 506 • Abilene, KS 67410 • (785) 263-2681 • http://www. ku.edu/heritage/abilene/heretr.html

Dwight D Eisenhower Library • 200 SE 4th St • Abilene, KS 67410-2900 • (785) 263-4751 • http://www.eisenhower.archives.gov

Eisenhower Family Home Museum • 201 SE 4th St • Abilene, KS 67410 • (785) 263-4751 • http://eisenhower.nara.gov

Genealogical Researchers • Dickinson County Heritage Center, 412 S Campbell St, P.O. Box 506 • Abilene, KS 67410 • (785) 263-2681 • http://www.heritageenterdk.com

Seeley Genealogical Society • 1105 N Buckeye • Abilene, KS 67410-0337

Seelye Mansion Museum • 1105 N Buckeye Ave • Abilene, KS 67410 • (785) 263-1084

Western Museum • 201 SE 6th • Abilene, KS 67410 • (785) 263-4612

Alden

AT & SF Depot Museum • P.O. Box 158 • Alden, KS 67512 • (316) 534-2425

Allen

Lyon County Library District • 421 Main St, P.O. Box 447 • Allen, KS 66833-0447 • (620) 528-3451

Alma

Wabaunsee County Historical Society • Historical Museum, 227 Missouri St, P.O. Box 387 • Alma, KS 66401 • (785) 765-2200

Anthony

Anthony Public Library • 624 E Main • Anthony, KS 67003-2738 • (620) 842-5344 • http://skyways.lib.ks.us/town/Anthony/library.html

Argonia

Argonia and West Sumner County Historical Society • Salter Museum, 220 W Garfield, P.O. Box 126 • Argonia, KS 67004 • (620) 435-6376

Arkansas City

Arkansas City Genealogical Society • c/o Arkansas City Public Library, 120 E 5th Ave • Arkansas City, KS 67705-2695 • (620) 442-1280

Arkansas City Historical Society • 1400 N 3rd • Arkansas City, KS 67005 • (620) 442-0333

Arkansas City Public Library • 120 E 5th Ave • Arkansas City, KS 67705-2695 • (620) 442-1280 • http://www.acpl.org

Cherokee Strip Land Rush Museum & Genealogy Library • 31639 US 77, P.O. Box 778 • Arkansas City, KS 67005-0778 • (620) 442-6750 • http://www.arkansascityks.gov

Cowley County Genealogical Society • P.O. Box 102 • Arkansas City, KS 67005 • (620) 442-6750

Renn Memorial Library • Cowley County Community College, 125 S 2nd St • Arkansas City, KS 67005 • (620) 441-5257 • http://www. cowley.cc.ks.us/support_services/library.htm

Arma

Arma City Library • 501 N West St, P.O. Box 822 • Arma, KS 66712-0822 • (620) 347-4811

Arnold

Heritage of the Plains Historical Society • general delivery • Arnold, KS 67515 • (913) 731-2701

Ashland

Ashland Public Library • 604 Main St, P.O. Box 397 • Ashland, KS 67831-0397 • (620) 635-2589 • http://www.ashland.lib.oh.us

Clark County Historical Society • Pioneer-Krier Museum, 430 W 4th St, P.O. Box 862 • Ashland, KS 67831 • (620) 635-2227 • http://users. ucom.net/~pioneer/

Atchison

Amelia Earhart Birthplace Museum • 223 N Terrace St • Atchison, KS 66002 • (913) 367-4217 • http://www.ameliaearhartmuseum.org

Atchison County Genealogical Society • c/o Atchison Public Library, 401 Kansas Ave, P.O. Box 303 • Atchison, KS 66002-0303 • (913) 367-1902 • http://skyways.lib.ks.us/genweb/society/achison/ackgs.htm

Atchison County Historical Society • Santa Fe Depot Museum, 200 S 10th St, P.O. Box 201 • Atchison, KS 66002 • (913) 367-6238 • http://www.atchisonhistory.org

Atchison Public Library • 401 Kansas Ave • Atchison, KS 66002-2495 • (913) 367-1902 • http://www.atchisonlibrary.org

Evah C Gray Home Museum • 805 N 5th St • Atchison, KS 66002 • (913) 367-3046

Atwood

Atwood Public Library • 102 S 6th St • Atwood, KS 67730 • (785) 626-3805 • http://skyways.lib.ks.us/genweb/rawlins/library.html

Rawlins County Genealogical Society • c/o Atwood Public Library, 102 S 6th St, P.O. Box 203 • Atwood, KS 67730-0203 • (785) 626-3805 • http://skyways.lib.ks.us/genweb/rawlins/library.html

Rawlins County Historical Society • Historical Museum, 308 State St • Atwood, KS 67730 • (785) 626-3885

Augusta

Augusta Historical and Genealogical Society • Historical Museum, 303 State St, P.O. Box 545 • Augusta, KS 67010 • (316) 775-5655 • http://www.augusta-ks.org/Museum.htm

Red Nation of the Cherokee • 1509 Washington Ln • Augusta, KS 67010 • (316) 775-3549 • http://www.rednation.org

Baldwin City

Baker University Archives • P.O. Box 65 • Baldwin City, KS 66006 • (785) 594-6451 • http://www.bakeru.edu/library/archives/

Baldwin City Library • 800 7th St • Baldwin City, KS 66006 • (785) 594-3411

Collins Library & Archives • Baker University, 518 8th St, P.O. Box 65 • Baldwin City, KS 66006-0065 • (785) 594-8442 • http://www.bakeru. edu/library

Old Castle Museum • 515 5th St, Baker Univ, P.O. Box 65 • Baldwin City, KS 66006 • (785) 594-6809 • http://www.bakeru.edu

Santa Fe Trail Historical Society • 1314 8th St, P.O. Box 443 • Baldwin City, KS 66006 • (785) 594-5495

Basehor

Basehor Historical Society • 17271 Hollingsworth Rd • Basehor, KS 66007 • (913) 724-4022

Baxter Springs

Baxter Springs Historical Society • Heritage Center, 740 East Ave, P.O. Box 514 • Baxter Springs, KS 66713 • (620) 856-2385 • http:// home.4state.com/~heritagectr/

Johnston Public Library • 210 W 10th St • Baxter Springs, KS 66713-1611 • (620) 856-5591

Belleville

Belleville Public Library • 1327 19th St • Belleville, KS 66935-2296 • (785) 527-5305 • http://www.nckcn.com/bellevillelibrary/homepage.htm

Republic County Genealogical Society • Historical Museum, 2726 Hwy 36, P.O. Box 218 • Belleville, KS 66935 • (785) 527-5971

Republic County Historical Society • Historical Museum, 2726 Hwy 36, P.O. Box 218 • Belleville, KS 66935-0218 • (785) 527-5971 • http:// www.ncken.com/homepage/repuglic_co/repmus.htm

Kansas

Beloit
Little Red Schoolhouse-Living Library • Roadwide Park, P.O. Box 97 • Beloit, KS 67420 • (785) 738-5301

Mitchell County Historical Society • Historical Museum, 402 W 8th, P.O. Box 472 • Beloit, KS 67420 • (785) 738-5355 • http://members.nckcn.com/mchs/

Blue Mound
Linn County District Library • 316 Main St, P.O. Box 13 • Blue Mound, KS 66010-0013 • (913) 756-2628

Bogue
Nicodemus Historical Society • P.O. Box 131 • Bogue, KS 67625 • (785) 674-3311

Bonner Springs
National Agricultural Center & Hall of Fame Museum • 630 Hall of Fame Dr • Bonner Springs, KS 66012 • (913) 721-1075 • http://www.aghalloffame.com

Wyandotte County Historical Society • Historical Museum, 631 N 126th St, P.O. Box 12040 • Bonner Springs, KS 66012-0040 • (913) 721-1078 • http://www.kumc.edu/wcedc/museum/wcmuseum.html

Brewster
High Plains Historical Association • Northwest Kansas Heritage Center, 401 Kansas St, P.O. Box 284 • Brewster, KS 67732 • (785) 694-2891

Bucklin
Bucklin Public Library • 201 N Main, P.O. Box 596 • Bucklin, KS 67834-0596 • (620) 826-3223 • http://www.trails.net/swkls/bucklinlibrary.htm

Bunker Hill
Bunker Hill Historical Society • P.O. Box 112 • Bunker Hill, KS 67626 • (785) 483-3637

Burden
East CCC Historical Society • 512 N Main • Burden, KS 67019 • (620) 438-3526

Burlington
Coffey County Genealogical Society • 712 Saunders St • Burlington, KS 66839-2157 • (620) 364-8795

Coffey County Historical Society • Historical Museum, 1101 Neosho • Burlington, KS 66839 • (620) 364-2653 • http://www.coffeycountymuseum.org

Coffey County Library • 410 Juniatta • Burlington, KS 66839 • (620) 364-2010 • http://www.cclibraryks.org

Burns
Burns Community Historical Society • Main St • Burns, KS 66840 • (620) 726-5528

Bushton
Farmer Township Community Library • Main St • Bushton, KS 67427 • (620) 562-3352

Caney
Caney Valley Historical Society • Historical Museum, 310 W 4th St, P.O. Box 354 • Caney, KS 67333 • (620) 879-5131

Carbondale
Carbondale Historical Museum • 234 Main St, P.O. Box 272 • Carbondale, KS 66414 • (785) 272-8681

Cassoday
Cassoday Historical Museum • 133 S Washington • Cassoday, KS 66842 • (620) 735-7286

Cawker City
Cawker City Public Library • 802 Locust St • Cawker City, KS 67430 • (785) 781-4925 • http://skyways.lib.ks.us/kansas/towns/Cawker/library.html

North Central Kansas Genealogical Society • c/o Cawker City Public Library, 802 Locust St, P.O. Box 251 • Cawker City, KS 67430-0251 • (785) 781-4343 • http://skyways.lib.ks.us/kansas/towns/Cawker/library.html#society

Cedar Vale
Cedar Vale Historical Society • 600 Cedar St • Cedar Vale, KS 67024

Chanute
Chanute Genealogical Society • 607 S Ashby • Chanute, KS 66720 • (620) 429-2992 • http://www.rootsweb.com/~kscgs/

Chanute Public Library • 111 N Lincoln St • Chanute, KS 66720-1819 • (620) 431-3820

Chapman Library • Neosho County Community College, 800 W 14th St • Chanute, KS 66720 • (620) 431-2820

Martin and Osa Johnson Safari Museum • 111 N Lincoln Ave • Chanute, KS 66720 • (630) 431-2730 • http://www.sararimuseum.com

Cheney
Souders Historical Farm Museum • MacArthur Rd, P.O. Box 527 • Cheney, KS 67025 • (316) 542-3573

Chetopa
Chetopa Historical Society • Chetopa Historical Museum, 419 Maple St, P.O. Box 135 • Chetopa, KS 67336 • (620) 236-7195 • http://skyways.lib.ks.us/towns/Chetopa/ museum.html

Claflin
Independent Township Library • 108 Main St, P.O. Box 163 • Claflin, KS 67525-0163 • (316) 587-3488

Clay Center
Clay County Historical Society • Historical Museum, 2021 7th St • Clay Center, KS 67432 • (785) 632-3786

Clearwater
Clearwater Historical Society • Historical Museum, 149 N 4th, PO. Box 453 • Clearwater, KS 67026 • (620) 584-2444 • http://www.clearwaterhistoricalsociety.com

Clifton
Clifton Historical Society • Historical Museum, 108 Clifton St, P.O. Box 5 • Clifton, KS 66937 • (785) 455-3763

Coffeyville
Brown Mansion Museum • 2019 S Walnut, P.O. Box 843 • Coffeyville, KS 67337 • (620) 251-0431 • http://www.coffeyville.com

Coffeyville Historical Society • 113 E 8th, P.O. Box 843 • Coffeyville, KS 67337 • (620) 251-0550

Coffeyville Public Library • 311 W 10th St • Coffeyville, KS 67337-5816 • (620) 251-1370 • http://www.skyways.lib.ks.us/library/coffeyville

Dalton Defenders Museum • 113 E 8th, P.O. Box 843 • Coffeyville, KS 67337 • (620) 251-5448

Montgomery County Genealogical Society • c/o Coffeyville Public Library, 311 W 10th, P.O. Box 444 • Coffeyville, KS 67337-0444 • (620) 251-5265

Colby
H F Davis Memorial Library • Colby Community College, 1255 S Range • Colby, KS 67701 • (785) 462-4689 • http://www.colby.cc.ks.us:8000/www/library

Thomas County Genealogical Society • Prairie Museum of History, 1905 S Franklin • Colby, KS 67701-0465 • (785) 462-4590 • http://www.prairiemuseum.org

Thomas County Historical Society • Prairie Museum of History, 1905 S Franklin, P.O. Box 465 • Colby, KS 67701-0165 • (785) 462-4590

Thomas County Museum • 75 W 4th St • Colby, KS 67701 • (785) 462-6301

Coldwater
Comanche County Historical Society • 410 S Baltimore, P.O. Box 177 • Coldwater, KS 67029 • (620) 582-2679

Columbus
Cherokee County Genealogical and Historical Society • 100 S Tennessee, P.O. Box 33 • Columbus, KS 66725-0033 • (620) 429-2992 • http://www.skyways.lib.us/genweb/cherokee/society/cckghs.html

Columbus Public Library • 205 N Kansas Ave • Columbus, KS 66725-1221 • (620) 429-2086 • http://skyways.lib.ks.us/library/columbus/

Concordia
Cloud County Genealogical Society • c/o Frank Carlson Library, 702 Broadway, P.O. Box 202 • Concordia, KS 66901 • (785) 243-2250 • http://www.dustdevil.com/towns/concordia/history/cogs/

Cloud County Historical Society • Historical Museum, 635 Broadway • Concordia, KS 66901 • (785) 243-2866 • http://www.cloudcountyks.org

Frank Carlson Library • 702 Broadway • Concordia, KS 66901 • (785) 243-2250

Orphan Train Heritage Society of America • 201 W 6th St • Concordia, KS 66901 • (785) 243-4471

Cottonwood Falls
Chase County Historical Society • Historical Museum, 301 Broadway, P.O. Box 375 • Cottonwood Falls, KS 66845 • (620) 273-8500 • http://www.wkyways.lib.ks.us/genweb/society/cottonwd

Roniger Memorial Museum • 315 Union St, P.O. Box 70 • Cottonwood Falls, KS 66845 • (620) 273-6310

Council Grove
Council Grove Public Library • 829 W Main St • Council Grove, KS 66846 • (620) 767-5716 • http://www.skyways.lib.ks.us/norcen/cgrove

Morris County Historical Society • Kaw Mission State Historic Site, 500 N Mission • Council Grove, KS 66846 • (620) 767-5410 • http://www.kawmission.org

Seth Hays Home Museum • Wood & Hall Sts • Council Grove, KS 66848 • (620) 767-5413

Dighton
Lane County Historical Society • Historical Museum, 333 N Main St, P.O. Box 821 • Dighton, KS 67839 • (620) 397-5652

Lane County Library • 114 S Lane, P.O. Box 997 • Dighton, KS 67839-0997 • (620) 397-2808 • http://www.trails.net/laneco

Dodge City
Boot Hill Museum • 500 Front St • Dodge City, KS 67801 • (620) 227-8188 • http://www.boothill.org

Dodge City Public Library • 1001 N 2nd Ave • Dodge City, KS 67801-4484 • (620) 226-0248 • http://www.dcpl.info

Ford County Historical Society • 1881 Mueller-Schmidt House, 112 E Vine, P.O. Box 131 • Dodge City, KS 67801-0131 • (620) 227-6791 • http://www.ku.edu/kansas/ford/

Home of Stone & Ford County Museum • Avenue A & Elm St, P.O. Box 131 • Dodge City, KS 67801-0131 • (620) 227-6791

Kansas Genealogical Society • Village Square Mall, P.O. Box 103 • Dodge City, KS 67801 • (620) 225-1951 • http://www.dodgecity.net/kgs

Kansas Heritage Center • 1000 2nd Ave, P.O. Box 1207 • Dodge City, KS 67801-1207 • (620) 227-1616 • http://www.ksheritage.org

Kansas State DAR Library • 700 Ave G & Vine St • Dodge City, KS 67801

Douglass
Douglass Historical Museum • 318 S Forest, P.O. Box 95 • Douglass, KS 67039 • (316) 747-2319

Downs
Downs Carnegie Library • 504 S Morgan Ave • Downs, KS 67437-2019 • (785) 454-3821

Downs Genealogical Society • c/o Downs Carnegie Library, 504 S Morgan Ave • Downs, KS 67437-2019 • (785) 454-3821

Historical Society of Downs • c/o Downs Carnegie Library, 504 S Morgan Ave • Downs, KS 67437-2019 • (785) 454-3821

Edgerton
Lanesfield School Historical Society • Route 1 • Edgerton, KS 66021 • (913) 882-6645

Edna
Edna Historical Museum • 100 S Delaware • Edna, KS 67342

El Dorado
Bradford Memorial Library • 611 S Washington St • El Dorado, KS 67042 • (316) 321-3363 • http://skyways.lib.ks.us/library/bradford

Butler County Historical Society • Historical Museum, 383 E Central St, P.O. Box 696 • El Dorado, KS 67042 • (316) 321-9333 • http://www.skyways.org/museum/kom

Elkhart
Morton County Historical Society • Historical Museum, 370 Hwy 56, P.O. Box 1248 • Elkhart, KS 67950 • (620) 697-2833 • http://www.mtcoks.com/museum/museum.html

Ellinwood
Ellinwood Community Historical Society • P.O. Box 111 • Ellinwood, KS 67526

Ellis
Bukovina Society of the Americas • 722 Washington, P.O. Box 81 • Ellis, KS 67637 • (913) 625-9492 • http://www.bukovinasociety.org

Ellis Public Library • 907 Washington, P.O. Box 107 • Ellis, KS 67637-0107 • (785) 726-3464 • http://www.ellis.ks.us/library/library.html

Walter P Chrysler Boyhood Home and Museum • 102 W 10th, P.O. Box 299 • Ellis, KS 67637 • (785) 726-3636

Ellsworth
Ellsworth County Historical Society • Hodgden House Museum, 104 SW Main St, P.O. Box 144 • Ellsworth, KS 67439-0144 • (785) 472-3059 • http://www.cityofellsworth.org

J H Robbins Memorial Library • 219 N Lincoln St • Ellsworth, KS 67439-3313 • (785) 472-3969 • http://skyways.lib.ics.us

Emporia
Center for Great Plains Studies • Emporia State Univ, 1200 Commercial • Emporia, KS 66801-5087 • (620) 341-5574 • http://www.emporia.edu

Emporia Public Library • 110 E 6th Ave • Emporia, KS 66801-3960 • (620) 340-6450 • http://skyways.lib.ks.us/library/emporia/

Flint Hills Genealogical Society • P.O. Box 555 • Emporia, KS 66801-0555 • http://www.lyoncountyks.org

Flint Hills Genealogy Club • Historical Museum, 110 E 6th St, P.O. Box 555 • Emporia, KS 66801-0555 • (620) 343-2719 • http://www.rootsweb.com/~ksfhgslc/

Lyon County Historical Society • Historical Museum, 118 E 6th Ave • Emporia, KS 66801 • (620) 340-6310 • http://slim.emporia.edu/resource/lchs/LyonCo.htm

William Allen White House Museum • 927 Exchange St • Emporia, KS 66801 • (316) 342-4800

Kansas

Emporia, cont.
William Allen White Library • Emporia State Univ, 1200 Commercial St, P.O. Box 4051 • Emporia, KS 66801-5087 • (620) 341-5207 • http://library.emporia.edu

Erie
Erie City Public Library • 204 S Butler • Erie, KS 66733-1349 • (620) 244-5119

Erie Historical Museum • 225 S Main St, P.O. Box 107 • Erie, KS 66733 • (620) 244-3218

Eudora
Eudora Area Historical Society • c/o Eudora Public Library, 14 E 9th St, P.O. Box 370 • Eudora, KS 66025 • (785) 542-2496

Eudora Public Library • 14 E 9th St, P.O. Box 370 • Eudora, KS 66025-0370 • (785) 542-2496

Eureka
Bluestem Genealogical Society • Historical Museum, 120 W 4th St, P.O. Box 582 • Eureka, KS 67045-0582 • (620) 583-6682

Greenwood County Historical Society • Historical Museum, 120 W 4th St • Eureka, KS 67045-1445 • (620) 583-6682 • http://skyways.lib.ks.us/kansas/genweb/greenwoo/gchs.htm

Everest
Everest Community Historical Society • 7th & Chestnut Sts • Everest, KS 66424 • (785) 548-7792

Florence
Florence Historical Society • Harvey House Museum, 221 Marion • Florence, KS 66851 • (620) 878-4474 • http://www.members.tripod.com/harvey_house

Fort Leavenworth
Combined Arms Research Library • US Army Command & General Staff, College, Eisenhower Hall, 250 Gibbon Ave • Fort Leavenworth, KS 66027 • (913) 758-3053 • http://cgsc.leavenworth.army.mil/carl

Fort Leavenworth Historical Society • Frontier Army Museum, 20 Reynolds Ave • Fort Leavenworth, KS 66027 • (913) 684-3767 • http://garison.leavenworth.army.mil/sites/services.museum.asp

Leavenworth Afro-American Historical Society • P.O. Box 3151 • Fort Leavenworth, KS 66027 • (913) 651-4584

Fort Riley
Custer House Museum • Bldg 24A, Sheridan St, P.O. Box 2160 • Fort Riley, KS 66442 • (785) 239-6243

First Territorial Capitol of Kansas • Bldg 693, Huebner Rd, P.O. Box 2122 • Fort Riley, KS 66442 • (785) 784-5535 • http://www.kshs.org

United States Cavalry Association • Cavalry Museum, Cameron & Beeman Sts, P.O. Box 2160 • Fort Riley, KS 66442-0325 • (785) 784-5797 • http://www.riley.army.mil; http://www.uscavalry.org

US Cavalry Memorial Research Library • Bldg 247, Cameron Ave, P.O. Box 2325 • Fort Riley, KS 66442-0325 • (785) 784-5797 • http://www.cavalry.org

Fort Scott
Chenault Mansion Museum • 820 S National Ave • Fort Scott, KS 66701 • (316) 223-6800

Cheney-Witt Memorial Chapel - Death Records Archives • 201 S Main St, P.O. Box 347 • Fort Scott, KS 66701 • (620) 223-1186 • http://www.cheneywitt.com

Fort Scott Community College Library • 2108 S Horton • Fort Scott, KS 66701 • (620) 223-2700 • http://www.fortscott.edu

Fort Scott National Historic Site Museum • Old Fort Blvd, P.O. Box 918 • Fort Scott, KS 66701 • (620) 223-0310 • http://www.nps.gov/fosc

Fort Scott Public Library • 201 S National St • Fort Scott, KS 66701 • (620) 223-2882

Historic Preservation Association of Bourbon County • Historical Museum, 117 S Main • Fort Scott, KS 66701 • (620) 223-6423

Old Fort Genealogical Society of Southeast Kansas • 502 S National Ave, P.O. Box 786 • Fort Scott, KS 66701-0786 • (620) 223-3300 • http://skyways.lib.ks.us/genweb/society/ftscott/

Frankfort
Frankfort City Library • 104 E 2nd St • Frankfort, KS 66427-1403 • (785) 292-4320

Fredonia
Wilson County Historical Society and Genealogical Chapter • Historical Museum, 420 N 7th St • Fredonia, KS 66736-1315 • (620) 378-3965

Freeport
Harper County Genealogical Society • P.O. Box 224 • Freeport, KS 67049 • (620) 896-2959 • http://skyways.lib.ks.us/kansas/genweb/society/harper/

Galena
Four State Genealogy Club • 922 Galena Ave • Galena, KS 66739 • (620) 783-5132

Galena Mining and Historical Museum Association • Historical Museum, 319 W 7th St • Galena, KS 66739 • (620) 783-2192

Galena Public Library • 315 W 7th St • Galena, KS 66739-1293 • (620) 783-5132

Garden City
Finney County Genealogical Society • c/o Finney County Public Library, 605 E Walnut St, P.O. Box 592 • Garden City, KS 67846-0592 • (620) 272-3680

Finney County Historical Society • Historical Society, 403 S 4th St, P.O. Box 796 • Garden City, KS 67846-0796 • (620) 272-3664 • http://www.finneycounty.org

Finney County Public Library • 605 E Walnut St • Garden City, KS 67846 • (620) 272-3680 • http://www.fcpl.homestead.com

Finnup Home Museum • 405 N 9th St, P.O. Box 795 • Garden City, KS 67846 • (316) 276-2619

Garden City Public Library • 210 N 7th • Garden City, KS 67846

Garnett
Anderson County Genealogical Society • P.O. Box 194 • Garnett, KS 66032 • (785) 489-2395 • http://www.grapevine.net/~swguinn/acgs.html

Anderson County Historical Society • Historical Museum, 6th & Maple, P.O. Box 217 • Garnett, KS 66032 • (785) 448-5740

East Central Kansas Genealogical Society • P.O. Box 101 • Garnett, KS 66032

Geneseo
Geneseo City Museum • Silver Ave • Geneseo, KS 67444

Geneseo Public Library • 725 Main St, P.O. Box 166 • Geneseo, KS 67444-0166 • (620) 824-6140

Girard
Girard Public Library • 128 W Prairie Ave • Girard, KS 66743 • (620) 724-4317 • http://skyways.lib.ks.us/kansas.html

Goessel
Mennonite Immigrant Historical Foundation • Mennonite Heritage Museum, 200 N Poplar, P.O. Box 231 • Goessel, KS 67053 • (620) 367-8200 • http://www.skyway.lib.ks.us/towns/goessel/museum/

Goodland
High Plains Museum • 1717 Cherry • Goodland, KS 67735 • (785) 899-4595 • http://www.goodlandnet.com/museum/

Sherman County Historical and Genealogical Society • Ennis-Handy House Museum, 202 W 13th St, P.O. Box 684 • Goodland, KS 67735 • (785) 899-2983 • http://skyways.lib.ks.us/genweb/sherman/shchs.html

Great Bend
Barton County Genealogical Society • c/o Great Bend Public Library 1409 Williams St, P.O. Box 425 • Great Bend, KS 67530 • (620) 792-2409 • http://www.ckls.org/~gbpl/

Barton County Historical Society • Historical Museum, 315 Point Dr, P.O. Box 1091 • Great Bend, KS 67530 • (620) 793-5125 • http://www.bartoncountymuseum.org

Barton County Village Museum • 85 S Hwy 281 • Great Bend, KS 67530 • (620) 783-5125

Great Bend Public Library • 1409 Williams St • Great Bend, KS 67530-4090 • (620) 792-2409 • http://www.ckls.org/~gbpl

Greensburg
Kiowa County Library • 120 S Main St • Greensburg, KS 67054 • (620) 723-2683

Grenola
Elk County Historical Society • Caney Valley Ranch, Route 1 • Grenola, KS 67346 • (620) 358-2291

Grenola Historical Society • 109 E Railroad • Grenola, KS 67346 • (620) 358-2820

Halstead
Halstead Historical Society • Heritage Museum, 116 E 1st St, P.O. Box 88 • Halstead, KS 67056 • (316) 835-2267 • http://www.halsteadkansas.com/historical.html

Halstead Public Library • 264 Main St • Halstead, KS 67056-0285 • (316) 835-2170

Hanover
Friends of Hollenberg Station • Hollenberg Pony Express Station Museum, 2889 23rd Rd, Hwy 243 • Hanover, KS 66945 • (785) 337-2635 • http://www.history.cc.ukans.edu/heritage/kshs/places/howlenbg

Harper
Harper City Historical and Genealogical Society • Historical Museum, 804 E 12th St • Harper, KS 67058 • (620) 896-2959 • http://skyways.lib.ks.us/genweb/society/harper

Harper Public Library • 1002 Oak St • Harper, KS 67058-1233 • (620) 896-2959 • http://skyways.lib.ks.us/town/Harper/library.html

Haviland
Worden Memorial Library • Barclay College, 100 E Cherry St • Haviland, KS 67059 • (620) 852-5274 • http://www.barclaycollege.edu

Hays
Ellis County Historical Society • Volga-German House Museum, 100 W 7th St • Hays, KS 67601 • (785) 628-2624 • http://www.elliscountyhistoricalmuseum.org

Forsyth Library • Fort Hays State Univ, 600 Park St • Hays, KS 67601-4099 • (785) 628-4431 • http://www.fhsu.edu/forsyth_lib/

Fort Hays State Historic Site Museum • 1472 Hwy 183 Alt • Hays, KS 67601 • (785) 625-6812 • http://history.cc.ukans.edu/heritage/kshs/kshs1.html

Fort Hays, Kansas Genealogical Society • c/o Forsyth Library, Fort Hays State Univ, 600 Park St • Hays, KS 67601-4099 • (785) 628-4431 • http://www.fhsu.edu/forsyth_lib/specoll1.htm

Genealogical Society of Northwest Kansas • c/o Forsyth Library, Fort Hays State Univ, 600 Park St • Hays, KS 67601-4099 • (785) 628-4431

Hays Masonic Bodies (A F & A M) • 107 W 11th • Hays, KS 67601 • (785) 625-3127 • http://spidome.net/~masons/

Hays Public Library • 1205 Main St • Hays, KS 67601-3693 • (785) 625-9014 • http://www.hayspublib.org

Haysville
Haysville Community Library • 130 W Grand • Haysville, KS 67060 • (316) 524-5242 • http://www.haysville.lib.ks.us

Herington
Tri-County Historical Society • Railroad Baggage Car Annex Museum, 800 S Broadway, P.O. Box 9 • Herington, KS 67449 • (785) 258-2842

Hesston
Hesston Public Library • 110 E Smith, P.O. Box 640 • Hesston, KS 67062-0640 • (620) 327-4666 • http://skyways.lib.ks.us/library/hesston/homepage.htm

Hiawatha
Brown County Agricultural Museum • 302 E Iowa • Hiawatha, KS 66434 • (785) 742-3330

Brown County Genealogical Society • 116 S 7th St • Hiawatha, KS 66434 • (785) 742-7511 • http://skyways.lib.ks.us/genweb/society/hiawatha

Brown County Historical Society • Historical Museum, 611 Utah St • Hiawatha, KS 66434 • (785) 742-3330

Morrill Public Library • 431 Oregon • Hiawatha, KS 66434-2290 • (785) 742-3831 • http://skyways.lib.ks.us/towns/Hiawatha/library.html

Highland
Highland Community College Library • 606 W Main St • Highland, KS 66035-0398 • (785) 442-6054 • http://highlandcc.edu/hcc_library/library.html

Native American Heritage Museum • Highland Mission, 1727 Elgin Rd • Highland, KS 66035-9801 • (785) 442-3304 • http://www.kshs.org

Hill City
Graham County Historical Society • 103 E Cherry St • Hill City, KS 67642 • (785) 421-2854 • http://www.grahamhistorical.ruraltel.net/

Graham County Public Library • 414 N West St • Hill City, KS 67642-1646 • (785) 421-2722

Hillsboro
Center for Mennonite Brethren Studies • Tabor College Library, 400 S Jefferson • Hillsboro, KS 67063 • (620) 947-3121

Hillsboro Historical Society • Pioneer Adobe House Museum, 501 S Ash St • Hillsboro, KS 67063 • (620) 947-3775 • http://www.hillsboro-museums.com

Tabor College Library • 400 S Jefferson St • Hillsboro, KS 67063 • (620) 947-3121 • http://www.tabor.edu/library

William Schaeffler House Museum • 312 E Grand • Hillsboro, KS 67063 • (316) 947-3775

Holton
Beck Bookman Library • 420 W 4th St • Holton, KS 66436-1572 • (785) 364-3532 • http://www.holtonks.net/library/

Jackson County Historical Society • Historical Museum, 216 New York Ave, P.O. Box 104 • Holton, KS 66436 • (785) 364-2087 • http://www.holtonks.net/jchs

Hope
Hope Community Historical Association • 203 S Main St • Hope, KS 67451 • (785) 366-7262

Horton
Horton Free Public Library • 809 1st Ave E • Horton, KS 66439-1898 • (785) 486-3326

Kickapoo Tribe in Kansas • P.O. Box 271 • Horton, KS 66349-0271 • (913) 486-2131 • http://www.minisose.org

Howard
Elk County Historical Society • P.O. Box 1033 • Howard, KS 67349 • (620) 374-2266

Kansas

Howard, cont.
Howard City Library • 126 S Wabash, P.O. Box 785 • Howard, KS 67349-0785 • (620) 374-2890

Hoxie
Sheridan County Historical Society • 1224 Oak Ave, P.O. Box 274 • Hoxie, KS 67740 • (785) 675-3501

Sheridan County Library • 801 Royal Ave, P.O. Box 607 • Hoxie, KS 67740-0607 • (785) 675-3102

Hugoton
Stevens County Genealogical Society • HC 01, Box 12 • Hugoton, KS 67951

Stevens County Historical Museum • 905 S Adams, P.O. Box 87 • Hugoton, KS 67951 • (620) 544-8751

Stevens County History Association • 1601 S Monroe St • Hugoton, KS 67951

Stevens County Library • 500 Monroe • Hugoton, KS 67951-2639 • (620) 544-2301 • http://stevenscountylibrary.com

Humboldt
Humboldt Historical Society • Historical Museum, 416 N 2nd, P.O. Box 63 • Humboldt, KS 66748 • (620) 473-2886 • http://www.usd258.net/~humbmuseum

Humboldt Public Library • 916 Bridge St • Humboldt, KS 66758-1834 • (620) 473-2243

Hutchinson
Hutchinson Public Library • 901 N Main St • Hutchinson, KS 67501-4492 • (620) 663-5441 • http://www.hplsck.org

Reno County Genealogical Society • c/o Hutchinson Public Library, 901 N Main St, P.O. Box 5 • Hutchinson, KS 67504-0005 • (620) 663-5441 • http://www.hplsck.org/200.htm

Reno County Historical Society • Historical Museum, 100 S Walnut St, P.O. Box 664 • Hutchinson, KS 67504-0664 • (620) 662-1184 • http://www.renocomuseum.org

Independence
Independence Historical Museum • 8th & Myrtle, P.O. Box 294 • Independence, KS 67301 • (620) 331-3515 • http://www.comgen.com/museum

Independence Public Library • 220 E Maple St • Independence, KS 67301-3899 • (620) 331-3030 • http://www.iplks.org

Little House on the Prairie Museum • Hwy 75, P.O. Box 110 • Independence, KS 67301

Montgomery County Historical Society • P.O. Box 100 • Independence, KS 67301 • (620) 331-3770

Ingalls
Santa Fe Trail Museum • 204 S Main St, P.O. Box 143 • Ingalls, KS 67853 • (620) 335-5220

Inman
Inman Heritage Association • P.O. Box 217 • Inman, KS 67546 • (620) 585-6748

Iola
Allen County Genealogical Society • c/o Iola Public Library, 218 E Madison, P.O. Box 393 • Iola, KS 66749 • (620) 365-3562 • http://www.iola.lib.ks.us

Allen County Historical Society • Historical Museum, 20 S Washington Ave • Iola, KS 66749 • (620) 365-3051 • http://www.frederickfunston.org

Iola Public Library • 218 E Madison Ave • Iola, KS 66749 • (620) 365-3262 • http://www.iola.lib.ks.us

Kaweah Indian Nation • P.O. Box 264 • Iola, KS 66749-0264 • (316) 832-0554

Major General Frederick Funston Museum • 14 S Washington Ave • Iola, KS 66749 • (620) 365-6728 • http://www.frederickfunston.org

Southeast Kansas Genealogical Society • c/o Iola Public Library, 218 E Madison • Iola, KS 66749-0393 • (620) 365-3262 • http://skyways.lib.ks.us/kansas/Sekis/

Jennings
High Plains Preservation Projects • P.O. Box 19a • Jennings, KS 67643 • (785) 678-2475

Jennings City Library • Kansas Ave, P.O. Box 84 • Jennings, KS 67643-0084 • (785) 678-2666

Jetmore
Haun Museum • general delivery • Jetmore, KS 67854 • (620) 357-6181

Hodgeman County Genealogical Society • P.O. Box 441 • Jetmore, KS 67854-0441 • (620) 357-8568 • http://skyways.lib.ks.us/genweb/hodgeman/hgplaces.html

Hodgeman County Historical Society • P.O. Box 128 • Jetmore, KS 67854 • (620) 357-8794 • http://skyways.lib.ks.us/towns/Jetmore/museum.html

Jetmore Municipal Library • 308 Main St, P.O. Box 608 • Jetmore, KS 67854-0608 • (620) 357-8336

Jewell
Palmer Museum • P.O. Box 282 • Jewell, KS 66949

Johnson
Stanton County Historical Society • Historical Museum, 104 E Highland, P.O. Box 806 • Johnson, KS 67855 • (620) 492-1526

Junction City
Dorothy Bramlage Public Library • 230 W 7th St • Junction City, KS 66441-3097 • (785) 238-4311 • http://www.jclib.org

Geary County Historical Society • Historical Museum, 530 N Adams, P.O. Box 1161 • Junction City, KS 66441-1161 • (785) 238-1666

Kanopolis
Fort Harker Museum • 309 W Ohio St, P.O. Box 144 • Kanopolis, KS 67454 • (785) 572-3059

Kansas City
Clendening History of Medicine Library and Museum • 3901 Rainbow Blvd • Kansas City, KS 66160 • (913) 588-7244 • http://www.clendening.kumc.edu

Grinter Place State Historic Site Museum • 1420 S 78th St • Kansas City, KS 66111 • (913) 299-0373 • http://www.kshs.org

Kansas City Public Library • 625 Minnesota Ave • Kansas City, KS 66101-2872 • (913) 551-3280 • http://www.kckpl.lib.ks.us

Sons of the American Revolution, Kansas Society • 11315 Applewood Dr • Kansas City, KS 64134-3122 • (816) 76107453 • http://www.ksssar.org

Strawberry Hill Museum • 720 N 4th • Kansas City, KS 66101 • (913) 371-3264

Trant Memorial Library • Donnelly College, 608 N 18th St • Kansas City, KS 66102 • (913) 621-8735 • http://www.donnelly.cc.ks.us

Wyandotte County Genealogical Society • 150 N 38th St, P.O. Box 4228 • Kansas City, KS 66104-0228 • http://kcgenealogy.com/wyandotte_county_genealogical_so.htm

Kensington
Smith County Historical Society • P.O. Box 247 • Kensington, KS 66951 • (785) 476-3214

Kingman

Branches and Twigs Genealogical Society • c/o Kingman Carnegie Public Library, 455 N Main St • Kingman, KS 67068-1395 • (620) 532-3061 • http://skyways.lib.ks.us/library/kingman/

Kingman Carnegie Public Library • 455 N Main St • Kingman, KS 67068-1395 • (620) 532-3061 • http://skyways.lib.ks.us/kansas/library/kingman/about.html

Kingman County Historical Society • Historical Museum, 400 N Main, P.O. Box 281 • Kingman, KS 67068 • (620) 532-5274 • http://skyways.lib.ks.us/towns/Kingman/museum/

Kinsley

Edwards County Historical Society • Sod House Museum, Hwy 56, P.O. Box 64 • Kinsley, KS 67547 • (620) 659-2420

Kinsley Public Library • 208 E 8th St • Kinsley, KS 67547-1422 • (620) 659-3341 • http://www.trails.net/kinsley

Kiowa

Kiowa Historical Society • Historical Museum, 107 N 7th St • Kiowa, KS 67070 • (620) 825-4727

Kirwin

Kirwin City Library • 1st & Main, P.O. Box 445 • Kirwin, KS 67644-0445 • (785) 543-6652 • http://www.cityofkirwin.com

La Crosse

Barbed Wire Museum • W 1st St • La Crosse, KS 67548 • http://www.rushcounty.org/barbedwiremuseum

Barnard Library • 521 Elm, P.O. Box 727 • La Crosse, KS 67548-0727 • (785) 222-2826

Rush County Historical Society • 202 W 1st, P.O. Box 473 • La Crosse, KS 67548 • (785) 222-2719

La Cygne

La Cygne Genealogical Society • c/o Linn County Library, 2210 N Commercial, P.O. Box 127 • La Cygne, KS 66040 • (913) 757-2151

Linn County Library • 2210 N Commercial, P.O. Box 127 • La Cygne, KS 66040-0127 • (913) 757-2151

Lakin

Kearny County Historical Society • 101-111 S Buffalo St, P.O. Box 329 • Lakin, KS 67860 • (620) 355-7448 • http://skyways.lib.ks.us/towns/Lakin/museum.html

Kearny County Library • 101 E Prairie, P.O. Box 773 • Lakin, KS 67860-0773 • (620) 355-6674

Lansing

Lansing Historical Society • 115 E Kansas Ave, P.O. Box 32 • Lansing, KS 66043 • (913) 727-3731

Larned

Central States Scout Museum • 815 Broadway • Larned, KS 67550 • (620) 285-8938

Fort Larned Historical Society • Santa Fe Trail Center, 1349 Hwy 156 • Larned, KS 67550 • (620) 285-2054 • http://www.santafetrail.org; http://www.santefetrailcenter.org

Fort Larned National Historic Site Library • Rural Rte 3 • Larned, KS 67550-9803 • (620) 285-6911 • http://www.nps.gov/fols/

Jordaan Memorial Library • 724 Broadway • Larned, KS 67550-3051 • (620) 285-2876 • http://www.jordaanlibrary.com

Lawrence

Anschutz Library • University of Kansas, 1301 Hoch Auditoria Dr • Lawrence, KS 66045-2800 • (785) 864-4928 • http://kuhttp.cc.ukans.edu/cwis/units/kulib/maps/collect.html

Douglas County Genealogical Society • P.O. Box 3664 • Lawrence, KS 66046-0664 • (785) 842-3732 • http://skyways.lib.ks.us/genweb/douglas/dckgs.htm

Douglas County Historical Society • Watkins Community Museum, 1047 Massachusetts St • Lawrence, KS 66044 • (785) 841-4109 • http://www.dchsks.org

Haskell Indian Nations Museum • 155 Indian Ave • Lawrence, KS 66046 • (785) 749-8470

Kansas Heritage Center for Family and Local History • Univ of KS • Lawrence, KS 60045-2800 • http://history.cc.ukans.edu/heritage/heritage_main.html

Lawrence Public Library • 707 Vermont St • Lawrence, KS 66044 • (785) 843-1178 • http://www.lawrencepubliclibrary.org

Pelathe Indian Center • 1423 Haskell Ave • Lawrence, KS 66044 • (913) 841-7202 • http://www.pelathe.org

Spencer Research Library • Univ of Kansas, Genealogical Collection, 1450 Poplar Lane • Lawrence, KS 66045-7616 • (785) 864-4334 • http://history.cc.ukans.edu/heritage/heritage_main.html

Tommaney Library • Haskell Indian Nations University, 155 Indian Ave • Lawrence, KS 66046 • (785) 749-8470 • http://www.haskell.edu

University of Kansas Museum • 868 Hwy 40 • Lawrence, KS 66049 • (785) 865-1380

Watson Library • University of Kansas, 1425 Jayhawk Blvd • Lawrence, KS 66045-7544 • (785) 864-3956 • http://www.lib.ku.edu

Leavenworth

De Paul Library • University of Saint Mary, 4100 S 4th St • Leavenworth, KS 66048 • (913) 758-6163 • http://www.stmary.edu

Leavenworth County Genealogical Society • c/o Leavenworth Public Library, 417 Spruce St, P.O. Box 362 • Leavenworth, KS 66048-0362 • (913) 682-8181

Leavenworth County Historical Society • Edward Carroll Victorian Mansion Museum, 1128 5th Ave • Leavenworth, KS 66048-3213 • (913) 682-7759 • http://leavenworth-net.com/lchs/

Leavenworth Public Library • 417 Spruce St • Leavenworth, KS 66048 • (913) 682-5666 • http://skyways.lib.ks.us/library/leavenworth

Leawood

Civil War Round Table of Kansas City • P.O. Box 6924 • Leawood, KS 66206 • (816) 356-1113

Lebanon

Lebanon Community Library • 404 N Main St, P.O. Box 67 • Lebanon, KS 66952-0067 • (785) 389-5711

Lecompton

Lecompton Historical Society • 609 Woodson, P.O. Box 372 • Lecompton, KS 66050 • (785) 887-6285 • http://www.lecomptonkansas.com

Territorial Capital-Lane Museum • 393 N 1900 Rd • Lecompton, KS 66050 • (785) 887-6267 • http://www.lecomptonkansas.com

Lenexa

Lenexa Historical Society • Legler Barn Museum, 14907 W 87th St Pkwy • Lenexa, KS 66215-4135 • (913) 492-0038 • http://www.leglerbarn.org

Leoti

Wichita County Genealogical Society • Historical Museum, 201 N 4th St, P.O. Box 1561 • Leoti, KS 67861-1561 • (620) 375-2316 • http://wichitacountymuseum.org/gensociety.htm

Wichita County Historical Society • Historical Museum, 201 N 4th St, P.O. Box 1561 • Leoti, KS 67861-9769 • (620) 375-2316 • http://wichitacountymuseum.org

Wichita County Library • 208 S 4th St, P.O. Box 490 • Leoti, KS 67861-0490 • (620) 375-4322

Liberal

Liberal Area Genealogical Society • c/o Liberal Memorial Library, 519 N Kansas, P.O. Box 1094 • Liberal, KS 67905-1094 • (620) 626-0181

Liberal Memorial Library • 519 N Kansas St • Liberal, KS 67905-1399 • (620) 626-0180 • http://www.lmlibrary.org

Methodist Mexican American Affairs • 311 N Grand • Liberal, KS 67901 • (316) 624-6865

Mid-America Air Museum • 2000 W 2nd, P.O. Box 2199 • Liberal, KS 67905 • (316) 624-5454 • http://www.liberalairmuseum.com

Seward County Historical Society • Dorothy's House and Coronado Museum, 567 E Cedar St • Liberal, KS 67901 • (620) 624-7624

Lincoln

Lincoln Carnegie Library • 203 S 3rd St • Lincoln, KS 67455 • (785) 524-4034

Lincoln County Historical Society • Kyne House Museum, 214 W Lincoln Ave, P.O. Box 85 • Lincoln, KS 67455 • (785) 524-9997

Yohe House Museum • 316 S 2nd St, P.O. Box 85 • Lincoln, KS 67455 • (785) 524-4934

Lindsborg

Lindsborg Community Library • 111 S Main St • Lindsborg, KS 67456-2417 • (785) 227-2710

McPherson County Old Mill Museum • 120 Mill St, P.O. Box 94 • Lindsborg, KS 67456 • (785) 227-3595 • http://www.oldmillmuseum.org

Smoky Valley Historical Association • c/o Lindsborg Community Library, 111 S Main • Lindsborg, KS 67456 • (785) 227-2710

Linwood

Linwood Community Library • 302 Main St, P.O. Box 80 • Linwood, KS 66052-0080 • (913) 723-3686

Little River

Little River Community Library • 125 Main St, P.O. Box 98 • Little River, KS 67457-0098 • (620) 897-6610 • http://skyways.lib.ks.us/kansas/towns/littleriver/

Young Historical Library • 2770 Avenue I • Little River, KS 67457 • (620) 897-6236

Logan

Dane G Hansen Memorial Museum • 110 W Main St, P.O. Box 187 • Logan, KS 67646 • (785) 689-4846 • http://www.hansenmuseum.org

Logan Public Library • 109 W Main St, P.O. Box 356 • Logan, KS 67646-0356 • (785) 689-4333

Long Island

Long Island Community Library • Main St, P.O. Box 68 • Long Island, KS 67647-0068 • (785) 854-7474

Luray

Luray Historical Society • 505 N Fairview Ave, P.O. Box 134 • Luray, KS 67649 • (785) 698-2371

Lyndon

Lyndon Carnegie Library • 126 E 6th, P.O. Box 563 • Lyndon, KS 66451 • (785) 828-4520 • http://skyways.lib.ks.us/towns/Lyndon/library/

Osage County Genealogical Society • c/o Lyndon Carnegie Library, 126 E 6th St, P.O. Box 563 • Lyndon, KS 66451 • (785) 828-4520

Osage County Historical Society • Historical Museum, 631 Topeka Ave, P.O. Box 361 • Lyndon, KS 66451 • (785) 828-3477 • http://www.osagechs.org

Lyons

Lyons Public Library • 217 East Ave S • Lyons, KS 67554-2721 • (620) 257-2961

Rice County Historical Society • Coronado-Quivira Museum, 105 W Lyon St • Lyons, KS 67554-2703 • (620) 257-3941 • http://skyways.lib.ks.us/towns/Lyons/museum/

Madison

Madison Public Library • 112 S 1st St • Madison, KS 66860 • (620) 437-2634

Manhattan

B D Phillips Memorial Library • Manhattan Christian College, 1415 Anderson Ave • Manhattan, KS 66502-4081 • (785) 539-3571 • http://www.mccks.edu

Goodnow House Museum and Historical Site Museum • 2224 Stone Post Rd • Manhattan, KS 66502 • (785) 539-3731

Hale Library • Kansas State University, Manhattan & Anderson Aves • Manhattan, KS 66506-1200 • (785) 532-7421 • http://www.lib.ksu.edu

Manhattan Public Library • 629 Poyntz Ave • Manhattan, KS 66502-6086 • (785) 776-4741 • http://www.manhattan.lib.ks.us

Morse Department of Special Collections • Kansas State University, 323 Seaton Hall • Manhattan, KS 66506 • (785) 532-7456 • http://www.lib.ksu.edu/depts/spec/

Pioneer Log Cabin Museum • City Park, 11th & Poyntz • Manhattan, KS 66502 • (785) 565-6491 • http://www.rileycountyks.gov

Riley County Genealogical Society • 2005 Claflin Rd • Manhattan, KS 66502-3415 • (785) 565-6495 • http://www.rileycgs.com

Riley County Genealogical Society, Computer Coordinating Group • 2005 Claflin Rd • Manhattan, KS 66502-3415 • (785) 565-6495 • http://www.flinthills.com/~rcgs

Riley County Historical Society • Hartford-Goodenow House Museum, 2309 Claflin Rd • Manhattan, KS 66502-3421 • (785) 565-6490 • http://www.kshs.org

Wolf House Museum • 630 Fremont • Manhattan, KS 66502 • (785) 565-6490 • http://www.rileycountyks.gov

Mankato

Jewell County Historical Society • Historical Museum, 118 N Commercial St • Mankato, KS 66956 • (785) 378-3218 • http://skyways.lib.ks.us/towns/Mankato/museum.html

Marion

Marion City Library • 101 Library St • Marion, KS 66861 • (620) 382-2442

Marion County Genealogical Society • 401 S Cedar • Marion, KS 66861-1331

Marion Historical Museum • 625 E Main • Marion, KS 66861 • (620) 382-3432 • http://www.marionks.com/museum.html

Marquette

Marquette Historical Society • 202 N Washington • Marquette, KS 67464 • (785) 546-2252

Marysville

Blue Valley Genealogical Society • P.O. Box 53 • Marysville, KS 66508

Koester House Museum • 919 Broadway • Marysville, KS 66508 • (785) 562-2417

Marshall County Historical Society • 1207 Broadway • Marysville, KS 66508 • (785) 562-5012

Marysville Public Library • 1009 Broadway • Marysville, KS 66508-1814 • (785-562-2491 • http://www.skyways.lib.ks.us/library/marysville/

Mayetta

Prairie Band Potawatomi Tribe • Route 2, Box 50A • Mayetta, KS 66509 • (913) 966-2255 • http://www.pbpindiantribe.com

McConnell AFB
Air Mobility Command, McConnell Air Force Base Library • 53476 Wichita St, Suite 412 • McConnell AFB, KS 67221 • (316) 759-4207

McCracken
McCracken Public Library • 303 Main St, P.O. Box 125 • McCracken, KS 67556-0125 • (785) 394-2444

McPherson
Briner Library • Central Christian College of Kansas, 1200 S Main • McPherson, KS 67460 • (620) 241-0723 • http://www.centralchristian.edu/library.html

McPherson County Genealogical Society • P.O. Box 483 • McPherson, KS 67460-0483

McPherson County Historical Society • 540 E Hill St • McPherson, KS 67460 • (620) 241-2699

McPherson Genealogy Club • c/o McPherson College Library, 1600 E Euclid, P.O. Box 1402 • McPherson, KS 67460 • (620) 241-0731 x1213

McPherson Public Library • 214 W Marlin St • McPherson, KS 67460-4299 • (620) 245-2570 • http://www.mpks.net/library

McPherson-Vaniman House Museum • 1130 E Euclid • McPherson, KS 67460 • (620) 245-2574

Miller Library • McPherson College, 1600 E Euclid, P.O. Box 1402 • McPherson, KS 67460-1402 • (620) 241-0731 • http://www.mcpherson.edu/library/

Meade
Dalton Gang Hideout and Museum • 502 S Pearlette St • Meade, KS 67864 • (316) 873-2731

Meade County Historical Society • Historical Museum, 200 E Carthage, P.O. Box 893 • Meade, KS 67864-0893 • (620) 873-2359

Medicine Lodge
Carry A Nation Home Museum • 209 W Fowler Ave, P.O. Box 208 • Medicine Lodge, KS 67104 • (620) 886-3553

Lincoln Library • 201 N Main St • Medicine Lodge, KS 67104 • (620) 886-5746 • http://www.cyberlodg.com/lincoln/

Medicine Lodge Historical Society • Hwy 160 • Medicine Lodge, KS 67104 • (620) 886-3417

Milan
Milan Historical Association • Park House Museum, Monroe & Market Sts, P.O. Box 144 • Milan, KS 67105 • (620) 435-6423

Minneapolis
Ottawa County Historical Museum • 110 S Concord • Minneapolis, KS 67467 • (785) 392-3621 • http://www.cyberspacemuseum.com/n3_3.html

Ottawa County Museum • 403 N Ottawa • Minneapolis, KS 67467 • (785) 392-3496

Montezuma
Stauth Memorial Museum • 111 N Aztec, P.O. Box 396 • Montezuma, KS 67867 • (620) 846-2527 • http://www.stauthmemorialmuseum.org

Moundridge
Moundridge Historical Association • P.O. Box 69 • Moundridge, KS 67107 • (620) 345-8420

Swiss Mennonite Cultural and Historical Society • 109 E Hirschler • Moundridge, KS 67107 • (620) 345-2844 • http://www.swissmennonite.org

Mulvane
Mulvane Historical Society • Historical Museum, 300 W Main St, P.O. Box 117 • Mulvane, KS 67110 • (316) 777-0506

Sumner County Historical Society • P.O. Box 213 • Mulvane, KS 67110 • (316) 777-1434

Munjor
American Historical Society of Germans from Russia, Sunflower Chapter • Munjor Parish Hall • Munjor, KS 67601 • http://www.sunflowerchapterofahsgr.net/

Neodesha
Heritage Genealogical Society • c/o W A Rankin Memorial Library, 502 Indiana • Neodesha, KS 66757 • (620) 325-3275 • http://skyways.lib.ks.us/kansas/genweb/wilson/rankin.html

Norman #1 Oil Well and Museum Historical Society • Historical Museum, 109 Mill • Neodesha, KS 66757 • (620) 325-5316

W A Rankin Memorial Library • 502 Indiana St • Neodesha, KS 66757-1352 • (620) 325-3275 • http://www.telepath.com/sysjer/rankin.htm

Ness City
Ness City Public Library • 113 S Iowa • Ness City, KS 67560-1992 • (785) 798-3415 • http://skyways.lib.ks.us/kansas/towns/nesscity/library.html

Ness County Historical Society • Historical Museum, 123 S Pennsylvania Ave • Ness City, KS 67560 • (785) 798-3298 • http://skyways.lib.ks.us/towns/NessCity/museum.html

Newton
American Historical Society of Germans from Russia, Golden Wheat Chapter • 928 Spruce • Newton, KS 67114 • (316) 283-3129 • http://www.ahsgr.org/Chapters/Golden_Wheat_Chapter.htm

Harvey County Historical Society • Historical Museum, 203 Main St, P.O. Box 4 • Newton, KS 67114 • (316) 283-2221 • http://www.hchm.org

Newton Public Library • 720 N Oak St • Newton, KS 67114 • (316) 283-2890 • http://www.newtonplks.org

Warkentin House Museum • 211 E 1st St • Newton, KS 67114 • (316) 283-3113

North Newton
Kaufman Museum • Bethel College, 2801 N Main • North Newton, KS 67117 • (316) 283-7646 • http://www.bethelks.edu/kauffman

Mennonite Historical Library & Archives • Bethel College, 300 E 27th St • North Newton, KS 67117-0531 • (316) 284-5304 • http://www.bethelks.edu/services/Mla/

Norton
Adobe Home Museum • Prairie Dog State Park, P.O. Box 431 • Norton, KS 67654 • (785) 877-2953

Northwest Kansas Library System • 2 Washington Sq, P.O. Box 446 • Norton, KS 67654-0046 • (785) 877-5148 • http://skyways.lib.ks.us/nwkls/norwest.html

Norton County Genealogical Society • 101 East Lincoln, P.O. Box 446 • Norton, KS 67654 • (785) 877-2481

Norton County Historical Museum • 907 Hartford Dr • Norton, KS 67654 • (785) 877-5586

Norton County Historical Society • 105 East Lincoln, P.O. Box 303 • Norton, KS 67654 • (785) 877-5107 • http://www.nex-tech.com/clients/nchistory/

Norton Public Library • 1 Washington Sq, P.O. Box 446 • Norton, KS 67654-0446 • (785) 877-2481

Station 15 Museum • Hwy 36, P.O. Box 97 • Norton, KS 67654 • (785) 877-2501 • http://www.us36.net/nortonkansas

Oakley
Northwest Kansas Genealogical and Historical Society • c/o Oakley Public Library, 700 W 3rd St • Oakley, KS 67748-1256 • (785) 672-4776 • http://www.discoveryoakley.com

Oakley, cont.
Oakley Public Library • 700 W 3rd St • Oakley, KS 67748 • (785) 672-4776

Oberlin
Decatur County Genealogical Society • Last Indian Raid Museum, 238 S Penn Ave • Oberlin, KS 67749 • (785) 475-2712 • http://www.indianraidmuseum.org

Oberlin City Library • 104 E Oak • Oberlin, KS 67749-1997 • (785) 475-2412

Offerle
Edwards County Historical Society • Historical Museum, Hwy 56 • Offerle, KS 67563 • (620) 659-2420

Oketo
Oketo Community Museum • general delivery • Oketo, KS 66518 • (785) 744-3516

Olathe
Ensor Park Farmsite and Museum • 18995 W 183rd St • Olathe, KS 66062-9278 • (913) 592-4141 • http://www.ensorparkandmuseum.org

Johnson County Archives • 111 S Cherry St, Suite 500 • Olathe, KS 66061-3441 • (913) 764-8484 x6174 • http://www.jocogov.org/agencies

Mabee Library • Mid-America Nazarene University, 2030 College Way • Olathe, KS 66062 • (913) 782-3750 • http://www.mnu.edu/mabee/

Mahaffie Stagecoach Stop Museum • 1100 Kansas City Rd, P.O. Box 768 • Olathe, KS 66051 • (913) 782-6972 • http://www.mahaffie.com

Olathe Historical Society • 12466 Twilight • Olathe, KS 66062 • (913) 782-5918

Olathe Public Library • 201 E Park St • Olathe, KS 66061 • (913) 971-6888 • http://olathe.lib.ks.us

Onaga
Onaga Historical Society • 310 E 2nd St • Onaga, KS 66521 • (785) 889-4457

Osawatomie
Adair Cabin State Historic Site Museum • John Brown Park, 10th & Main, P.O. Box 37 • Osawatomie, KS 66064 • (913) 755-4384

Osawatomie Historical Society • 420 16th St • Osawatomie, KS 66064 • (913) 755-6961

Osawatomie Public Library • 527 Brown St • Osawatomie, KS 66064 • (913) 755-2136

John Brown State Historic Site Museum • 10th & Main Sts, P.O. Box 37 • Osawattomie, KS 66064 • (913) 755-4384

Osborne
Osborne County Genealogical and Historical Society • 202 S 9th St • Osborne, KS 67473-2215 • (785) 346-2418

Osborne County Historical Museum • 929 N 2nd St • Osborne, KS 67473 • (785) 346-2418

Osborne Public Library • 307 W Main St • Osborne, KS 67473-2425 • (785) 346-5486 • http://www.osbornepubliclibrary.org

Oskaloosa
Jefferson County Genealogical Society • Old Jefferson Town, Highway 59, P.O. Box 174 • Oskaloosa, KS 66066-0174 • (785) 863-2070 • http://skyways.lib.ks.us/kansas/genweb/jefferso/jfcogen.html

Jefferson County Historical Society • Old Jefferson Town, Highway 59, P.O. Box 146 • Oskaloosa, KS 66066 • (785) 863-2070 • http://www.ditigalhistory.com/schools/Oskaloosa/Old_Jeff_Town.html

Oskaloosa Public Library • 315 Jefferson St, P.O. Box 347 • Oskaloosa, KS 66066-0347 • (785) 863-2475 • http://skyways.lib.ks.us/kansas/towns/Oskaloosa/library.html

Oswatomie
Osawatomie Museum • 628 Main St • Oswatomie, KS 66064 • (913) 755-6781

Oswego
Oswego Historical Society • Historical Museum, 410 Commercial • Oswego, KS 67356 • (620) 795-4500

Otis
Otis Community Library • 121 S Main, P.O. Box 9 • Otis, KS 67565-0009 • (785) 387-2403

Ottawa
Dietrich Cabin Museum • 5th & Main, P.O. Box 145 • Ottawa, KS 66067 • (785) 242-1232

Franklin County Genealogical Society • P.O. Box 353 • Ottawa, KS 66067 • (785) 242-5383 • http://www.ukans.edu/~hisite/franklin/fcgs/

Franklin County Historical Society • Old Depot Museum, 135 W Tecumseh St, P.O. Box 145 • Ottawa, KS 66067 • (785) 242-1232 • http://www.ott.net

Lake Region Historical Society Association • 121 E 2nd St • Ottawa, KS 66067 • (785) 242-2073

Myers Library • Ottawa Univ, 1001 S Cedar St • Ottawa, KS 66067-3399 • (785) 242-5200 • http://www.ottawa.edu

Ottawa Public Library • 105 S Hickory St • Ottawa, KS 66067-2306 • (785) 242-3080 • http://www.ottawa.lib.ks.us

Overbrook
Clinton Lake Historical Society • 261 N 851 Diagonal Rd • Overbrook, KS 66524 • (785) 748-9836

Overland
Johnson County Library • 9875 W 87th St • Overland, KS 66212 • (913) 495-2400 • http://www.jocolibrary.org

Overland Park
Heart of America Jewish Historical Society • 9648 Walmer Ln • Overland Park, KS 66212

Johnson County Library • 9875 W 87th St • Overland Park, KS 66212 • (913) 495-2400 • http://www.jocolibrary.org

Overland Park Historical Society • 8045 Santa Fe Dr • Overland Park, KS 66204 • (913) 381-8867

Oxford
Oxford Public Library • 115 S Sumner, P.O. Box 266 • Oxford, KS 67119-0266 • (620) 455-2221

Paola
Miami County Genealogical Society • P.O. Box 123 • Paola, KS 66071-0123 • (913) 294-3529 • http://www.micoks.net/~mcsrm

Miami County Historical Society • Swan River Museum, 12 E Peoria St, P.O. Box 393 • Paola, KS 66071 • (913) 294-4940

Parker
Parker Community Historical Society • 207 W Main • Parker, KS 66072

Parsons
Iron Horse Historical Society • P.O. Box 8 • Parsons, KS 67357 • (620) 421-1959

Labette Community College Library • 200 S 14th St • Parsons, KS 67357 • (620) 820-1168 • http://www.labette.edu/library

LaBette Genealogical Society • P.O. Box 544 • Parsons, KS 67357 • http://skyways.lib.ks.us/kansas/genweb/society/parsons

Parsons Historical Commission • Historical Museum, 401 S 100th, P.O. Box 457 • Parsons, KS 67357 • (620) 421-7000

Parsons Historical Society • 401 S Corning • Parsons, KS 67357 • (620) 421-3382

Parsons Public Library • 311 S 17th St • Parsons, KS 67357 • (620) 421-5920 • http://skyways.lib.ks.us/kansas/library/parsons/

Partridge

Partridge Public Library • 23 S Main St, P.O. Box 96 • Partridge, KS 67566-0096 • (620) 567-2467

Peabody

Peabody Historical Society • RR 2 • Peabody, KS 66866 • (620) 983-2815

Phillipsburg

Phillips County Genealogical Society • c/o Phillipsburg City Library, 888 4th St, P.O. Box 114 • Phillipsburg, KS 67661-0114 • (785) 543-5325 • http://skyways.lib.ks.us/kansas/genweb/phillips/plgensoc.html

Phillips County Historical Society • Old Fort Bissell, City Park, Route 2, Box 18A • Phillipsburg, KS 67661 • (785) 543-6212 • http://www.phillipsburgks.us

Phillipsburg City Library • 888 4th St • Phillipsburg, KS 67661 • (785) 543-5325 • http://www.phillipsburgks.us/community/library/

Pittsburg

Crawford County Genealogical Society • c/o Pittsburg Public Library, 308 W Walnut • Pittsburg, KS 66762-4797 • (620) 231-8110 • http://skyways.lib.ks.us/library/pittsburg/

Crawford County Historical Society • Historical Museum, 651 S Hwy 69 • Pittsburg, KS 66762 • (620) 231-1440

Pittsburg Public Library • 308 W Walnut • Pittsburg, KS 66762-4732 • (620) 231-8110 • http://skyways.lib.ks.us/library/pittsburg/

Pleasanton

Linn County Historical and Genealogical Society • Historical Museum and Genealogy Library, P.O. Box 137 • Pleasanton, KS 66075-0137 • (913) 352-8739

Marais des Cygnes Memorial Historic Site Museum • Route 2, Box 157 • Pleasanton, KS 66075 • (913) 352-6174

Pleasanton-Lincoln Library • 201 W 9th, P.O. Box 101 • Pleasanton, KS 66075-0101 • (913) 352-8854

Trading Post Historical Society • Historical Museum, 15710 N 4th St • Pleasanton, KS 66075-9479 • (913) 352-6441

Prairie Village

Choteau Society • 56 Coventry Ct • Prairie Village, KS 66208 • (913) 341-7372

Pratt

Pratt County Historical Society • Historical Museum, 212 S Ninnescah • Pratt, KS 67124 • (620) 672-7874

Pratt Public Library • 4th & Jackson Sts, P.O. Box O • Pratt, KS 67124-1112 • (620) 672-3041

Prescott

Prescott City Public Library • 3rd & W Main Sts, P.O. Box 112 • Prescott, KS 66767-0112 • (913) 471-4837

Quinter

Jay Johnson Public Library • 411 Main St, P.O. Box 369 • Quinter, KS 67752 • (785) 754-2171 • http://skyways.lib.ks.us/towns/Quinter/library/

Republic

Pawnee Indian Village State Historic Park • 480 Pawnee Tr • Republic, KS 66964 • (785) 361-2255 • http://www.kshs.org

Reserve

Sac and Fox Tribe of Missouri • Route 1, Box 60 • Reserve, KS 66434-9723 • (913) 742-7471 • http://www.mnisose.org/profiles/sacfox.htm

Russell

American Historical Society of Germans from Russia, Post Rock Chapter • 18350 Homer Rd • Russell, KS 67665 • (785) 483-3976

Gernon House Museum • 808 N Kansas • Russell, KS 67665 • (913) 483-3637

Russell County Historical Society • Fossil Station Museum, 331 N Kansas St, P.O. Box 245 • Russell, KS 67665 • (785) 483-3637 • http://www.rchs.russellks.net

Russell Springs

Butterfield Trail Association and Logan County Historical Society • Hwy 25 & Museum Dr, P.O. Box 336 • Russell Springs, KS 67775 • (785) 751-4242 • http://www.windyplains.com/butterfield/

Sabetha

Albany Historical Society • Historical Museum, 415 Grant • Sabetha, KS 66534 • (785) 284-3446 • http://www.albanydays.org

Mary Cotton Public Library • 915 Virginia, P.O. Box 70 • Sabetha, KS 66534-0070 • (785) 284-3160 • http://www.skyways.org/towns/sabetha/library.htm

Saint Francis

Cheyenne County Historical Society • Cheyenne County Museum, West Hwy 36, P.O. Box 611 • Saint Francis, KS 67756 • (785) 332-2504

Saint John

Ida Long Goodman Memorial Library • 406 N Monroe St • Saint John, KS 67576-1836 • (620) 549-3227 • http://skyways.lib.ks.us/library/stjohn

Saint Marys

Pottawatomie-Wabaunsee Regional Library • 306 N 5th St • Saint Marys, KS 66536 • (785) 437-2278 • http://www.skyways.lib.ks.us/kansas/library/pottwablib

Saint Marys Historical Society • 710 Alma St • Saint Marys, KS 66536 • (913) 437-6387

Saint Paul

Graves Memorial Public Library • P.O. Box 354 • Saint Paul, KS 66771-0354 • (620) 449-2001

Osage Mission-Neosho County Historical Society • P.O. Box 113 • Saint Paul, KS 66771 • (620) 449-2320

Salina

American Historical Society of Germans from Russia, Heart of America Chapter • 117 E Minneapolis • Salina, KS 67401 • (785) 827-0782

Salina Public Library • 301 W Elm St • Salina, KS 67401 • (785) 825-4624 • http://www.salpublib.org

Saline County Historical Society • 216 W Bond St, P.O. Box 32 • Salina, KS 67401 • (785) 825-7573

Smoky Hill Museum • 211 W Iron Ave, P.O. Box 101 • Salina, KS 67402-0101 • (785) 826-7460 • http://www.smokyhillmuseum.org

Smoky Valley Genealogical Society • Smoky Hill Museum, 211 W Iron Ave, Ste 205 • Salina, KS 67401-2613 • (785) 825-7573 • http://skyways.lib.ks.us/kansas/genweb/ottawa/smoky.html

Satanta

Dudley Township Public Library • 105 N Sequoyah St, P.O. Box 189 • Satanta, KS 67870-0189 • (620) 649-2213

Scandia

Scandia Museum • Main St, P.O. Box 153 • Scandia, KS 66966 • (785) 335-2271 • http://www.nckcn.com/homepage/republic_co/museum1.htm

Scott City

Scott County Historical Society • 211 College St, P.O. Box 155 • Scott City, KS 67871-0155 • (620) 872-3708

Scranton
Scranton Historical Society • 631 S Topeka Ave • Scranton, KS 66537 • (785) 828-3477

Sedan
Chautauqua County Historical and Genealogical Society • 215 N Chautauqua, P.O. Box 227 • Sedan, KS 67361 • (620) 725-3101 • http://skyways.lib.ks.us/genweb/chautaq/cchgs.html

Emmett Kelly Historical Museum • 202 E Main St • Sedan, KS 67361 • (620) 725-3470 • http://www.emmettkellymuseum.com

Seneca
Nemaha County Genealogical Society • 113 N 6th St • Seneca, KS 66538 • (785) 336-2494 • http://www.ku.edu/kansas/seneca/gensoc/gensoc.html

Nemaha County Historical Society • 113 N 6th St • Seneca, KS 66538 • (785) 336-3645 • http://www.ukans.edu/kansas/seneca/histsoc/nemcohis.html

Seneca Free Library • 606 Main St • Seneca, KS 66538 • (785) 336-2377 • http://skyways.lib.ks.us/library/seneca/

Sharon Springs
Sharon Springs Public Library • 113 W 2nd, P.O. Box 640 • Sharon Springs, KS 67758-0640 • (785) 852-4685

Shawnee
Johnson County Museum of History • 1950s All-Electric Model House, 6305 Lackman Rd • Shawnee, KS 66217 • (913) 631-6709 • http://www.jocomuseum.org

Shawnee Historical Society • Old Shawnee Town, 11501 W 57th St, P.O. Box 3042 • Shawnee, KS 66203 • (913) 268-8772 • http://www.cityofshawnee.org

Shawnee Town Museum • 11501 W 57th St • Shawnee, KS 66203 • (913) 248-2360 • http://www.shawneetown.org

Shawnee Mission
Civil War Round Table of Kansas City • 23414 W 54th St • Shawnee Mission, KS 66226 • (913) 469-5040

Historic Old Mission Enthusiasts • 6029 Larsen Ln • Shawnee Mission, KS 66203 • (913) 631-8485

Johnson County Genealogical Society • c/o Johnson County Library, 9875 W 87th St, P.O. Box 12666 • Shawnee Mission, KS 66282-2666 • (913) 780-4764 • http://www.johnsoncountykansasgenealogy.org

Johnson County Library • 9875 W 87th St, P.O. Box 2933 • Shawnee Mission, KS 66201-1333 • (913) 495-2400 • http://www.jocolibrary.org

Johnson County Museum of History • 6305 Lackman Rd • Shawnee Mission, KS 66217 • (913) 631-6709

Kansas City Posse of the Westerners • 23414 W 54th St • Shawnee Mission, KS 66226

Shawnee Historical Society • Old Shawnee Town Museum, 11501 W 57th St, P.O. Box 3042 • Shawnee Mission, KS 66203 • (913) 268-8772

Shawnee Mission Indian Historical Society • 4833 Black Swan • Shawnee Mission, KS 66202 • (913) 631-9990

South Hutchinson
American Historical Society of Germans from Russia, Heritage Seekers Chapter • 411 Sunnydell Cr • South Hutchinson, KS 67505-1726 • http://www.ahsgr.org/Chapters/heritage_seekers_chapter.htm

Stafford
Nora E Larabee Memorial Library • 108 N Union St • Stafford, KS 67578-1339 • (620) 234-5762 • http://skyways.lib.ks.us/towns/stafford/library.html

Stafford County Historical and Genealogical Society • 100 N Main St, P.O. Box 249 • Stafford, KS 67578 • (620) 234-5664 • http://home.earthlink.net/~mjhathaway6l/

Stockton
Rooks County Historical Museum • S Walnut St • Stockton, KS 67660 • (785) 425-7217

Rooks County Historical Society • Historical Museum, 921 S Cedar, P.O. Box 43 • Stockton, KS 67669 • (785) 425-7217 • http://www.rookscounty.net/museum.htm

Stockton Public Library • 124 N Cedar St • Stockton, KS 67669-1636 • (785) 425-6372 • http://www.stocktonkansas.net

Studley
Cottonwood Ranch Site Museum • Hwy 24 • Studley, KS 67740 • (875) 627-5866 • http://wwwkshs.org/places/cottonwo.htm

Sublette
Haskell County Historical Society • Historical Museum at the Fairgrounds, P.O. Box 101 • Sublette, KS 67877 • (620) 675-8344

Summerfield
Summerfield Public Library • 300 Main, P.O. Box 146 • Summerfield, KS 66541-0146 • (785) 244-6531

Syracuse
Hamilton County Library • 102 W Avenue C, P.O. Box 1307 • Syracuse, KS 67878-1307 • (620) 384-5622 • http://skyways.lib.ks.us/library/hamilton/

Hamilton County Museum • Harvey House, 108 E Highway 50, P.O. Box 923 • Syracuse, KS 67878 • (620) 384-7496 • http://skyways.lib.ks.us/museums/

Santa Fe Trail Genealogical Society • P.O. Box 528 • Syracuse, KS 67878 • (620) 384-7614

Tescott
Tescott Historical Society • 109 Sunset Ln • Tescott, KS 67484-9725

Tonganoxie
Tonganoxie Community Historical Society • 201 W Washington St, P.O. Box 325 • Tonganoxie, KS 66086 • (913) 845-2960 • http://www.tongie.org/organizations.html

Tonganoxie Genealogical Society • c/o Tonganoxie Public Library, 305 S Bury St, P.O. Box 354 • Tonganoxie, KS 66086 • (913) 845-3281 • http://skyways.lib.ks.us/library/tongie/

Tonganoxie Public Library • 303 Bury St, P.O. Box 890 • Tonganoxie, KS 66086-0890 • (913) 845-3281 • http://www.tongie.org

Topeka
American Historical Society of Germans from Russia, Northeastern Kansas Chapter • 3121 SW Dorr St • Topeka, KS 66604 • (785) 271-2132 • http://www.ahsgr.org/Chapters/northeastern_kansas_chapter.htm

Cedar Crest House Museum • 1 SW Cedar Crest Rd • Topeka, KS 66606 • (785) 296-3636

Combat Air Museum • Forbes Field, J Street, P.O. Box 19142 • Topeka, KS 66619 • (785) 862-3303 • http://www.combatairmuseum.org

Great Overland Station Museum • 701 N Kansas Ave, P.O. Box 8792 • Topeka, KS 66608 • (785) 232-5533 • http://www.greatoverlandstation.com

Historic Ward-Meade Mansion Park • 121 NW Fillmore • Topeka, KS 66606 • (785) 368-3888 • http://www.topeka.org

Kansas Council of Genealogical Societies • P.O. Box 3858 • Topeka, KS 66604-6858 • (785) 272-7550 • http://skyways.lib.ks.us/genweb/kcgs/

Kansas Dept of Health - Vital Records • 1000 SW Jackson, Rm 120 • Topeka, KS 66612-2221 • (785) 296-1500 • http://www.kdhe.state. ks.us

Kansas Press Association • 5423 SW 7th • Topeka, KS 66606 • (785) 271-5304 • http://www.kspress.com

Kansas State Historical Society • Kansas History Center, 6425 SW 6th Ave • Topeka, KS 66615-1099 • (785) 272-8681 • http://www.kshs.org

Kansas State Library • State Capitol Bldg, 300 SW 10th St, Rm 343N • Topeka, KS 66612-1593 • (785) 296-3296 • http://skyways.lib.ks.us/ kansas/KSL/

Mabee Library • Washburn University, 1700 SW College Ave • Topeka, KS 66621 • (785) 231-1483 • www.washburn.edu/mabee

Masonic Grand Lodge of Kansas • 320 SW 8th Ave • Topeka, KS 66603-3912 • (785) 234-5518 • http://www.kansasmason.org

Ritchie House and Freedom's Pathway Museum • 1116 SE Madison St • Topeka, KS 66607 • (785) 234-6097

Shawnee County Historical Society • P.O. Box 2201 • Topeka, KS 66601

Topeka Genealogical Society • 2717 Indiana Ave, P.O. Box 4048 • Topeka, KS 66604-0048 • (785) 233-5762 • http://www.tgstopeka.org

Topeka High School Historical Society • 800 W 10th • Topeka, KS 66612 • (785) 232-0483

Topeka Public Library • 1515 SW 10th Ave • Topeka, KS 66604-1374 • (785) 580-4400 • http://www.tscpl.org

Towanda
Towanda Public Library • 620 Highland, P.O. Box 580 • Towanda, KS 67144-0580 • (316) 536-2464 • http://www.skyways.org/towns/ towanda/

Tribune
Greeley County Historical Society • Horace Greeley Museum, 214 E Harper, P.O. Box 231 • Tribune, KS 67879-0231 • (620) 376-2659

Troy
Doniphan County Historical Society • c/o Doniphan County Library, 105 N Main St, P.O. Box 220 • Troy, KS 66087 • (785) 985-2597

Doniphan County Library • 105 N Main St, P.O. Box 220 • Troy, KS 66087-0220 • (785) 985-2597 • http://skyways.lib.ks.us/library/ doniphan

Udall
Udall Historical Society • 109 E 1st St • Udall, KS 67146-9009 • (620) 782-3004

Ulysses
Grant County Historical Society • Historic Adobe Museum, 300 E Oklahoma, P.O. Box 906 • Ulysses, KS 67880-0906 • (620) 356-3009 • http://www.historicadobemuseum.org

Grant County Library • 215 E Grant St • Ulysses, KS 67880-2958 • (620) 356-1433 • http://ns.trails.net/grant

Valley Center
Slovenian Genealogical Society, Mid-Continent States Chapter • 200 E 5th St • Valley Center, KS 67147-2602 • http://sloveniangenealogy.org/ chapters/MidContinental.htm

Valley Center Historical and Cultural Society • 112 N Meridian, P.O. Box 173 • Valley Center, KS 67147 • (785) 755-7340

Valley Falls
Valley Falls Historical Society • 310 Broadway • Valley Falls, KS 66088 • (785) 945-6698

Wakeeney
Trego County Historical Society • Historical Museum, Hwy 283, P.O. Box 132 • Wakeeney, KS 67672 • (785) 743-6651 • http://skyways.lib. ks.us/towns/WaKeeney/museum.html

WaKeeney Public Library • 610 Russell Ave • WaKeeney, KS 67672-2135 • (785) 743-2960 • http://skyways.lib.ks.us/kansas/nwkls/trego/ wakeeney.htm

Wakefield
Wakefield Museum • 604 6th St, P.O. Box 36 • Wakefield, KS 67487-0101 • (785) 461-5516 • http://www.wakefieldmuseum.org/~online

Wakefield Public Library • 207 3rd St • Wakefield, KS 67487-0348 • (785) 461-5510 • http://www.starband.net

Wallace
Fort Wallace Memorial Association • Hwy 40 • Wallace, KS 67761 • (785) 891-3564

Wamego
Log Cabin Museum • 4th St, P.O. Box 84 • Wamego, KS 66547 • (785) 456-2040

Wamego Historical Society • Old Dutch Mill Museum Complex, P.O. Box 84 • Wamego, KS 66547 • (785) 456-2040

Wamego Public Library • 431 Lincoln • Wamego, KS 66547-1620 • (785) 456-9181

Washington
Washington County Historical and Genealogical Society • 206 Ballard, P.O. Box 31 • Washington, KS 66968 • (785) 325-2198

Washington County Historical Society • 208 Ballard, P.O. Box 31 • Washington, KS 66968 • (785) 325-2198

Waverly
Coffey County Library-Waverly Branch • 608 Pearson • Waverly, KS 66871-9688 • (785) 733-2400 • http://www.cclibraryks.org

Wellington
Chisholm Trail Museum • 502 N Washington St • Wellington, KS 67152 • (620) 326-3820 • http://skyways.lib.ks.us/towns/Wellington/museum. html

Sumner County Historical and Genealogical Society • Chisholm Trail History & Genealogy Center, 208 N Washington, P.O. Box 402 • Wellington, KS 67152 • (620) 326-3820 • http://www.rootsweb. com/~ksscgs

Wellsville
Black Jack Historical Society • 163 E 2000 Rd • Wellsville, KS 66092 • (785) 883-2584

Wellsville City Library • 115 W 6th, P.O. Box 517 • Wellsville, KS 66092-0517 • (785) 883-2870

Westmoreland
Rock Creek Valley Historical Society • 507 Burkman St, P.O. Box 13 • Westmoreland, KS 66549 • (785) 457-0100

White City
Morris County Genealogical Society • 210 W Grant St, P.O. Box 114 • White City, KS 66872 • (785) 349-2987

White Cloud
Iowa Tribe of Kansas and Nebraska • Route 1, Box 58A • White Cloud, KS 66094 • (913) 595-3258

Ma Hush Kah Historical Society • Route 2, Box 16 • White Cloud, KS 66094 • (785) 595-3320

Whitewater
Frederick Remington Area Historical Society • P.O. Box 133 • Whitewater, KS 67154 • (316) 799-2470 • http://skyways.lib.ks.us/ towns/Brainerd/

Kansas

Wichita

Ablah Library • Wichita State University, 1845 Fairmount • Wichita, KS 67260-0001 • (316) 978-3584 • http://specialcollections.wichita.edu

Allen-Lambe House Museum • 255 N Roosevelt • Wichita, KS 67208 • (316) 687-1027

American Overseas Schools Historical Society • 704 W Douglas Ave • Wichita, KS 67203 • (316) 265-6837

Black Historical Society • 4230 East 25th North • Wichita, KS 67220 • (316) 683-1247

Daughters of the American Revolution, Kansas Society • 100 W 55th St S • Wichita, KS 67217

Edmund Stanley Library • Friends Univ, 2100 W University Ave • Wichita, KS 67213 • (316) 261-5880 • http://www.friends.edu/library/SpecialCollections/

First National Black Historical Society of Kansas • 601 N Water, P.O. Box 2695 • Wichita, KS 67201 • (316) 262-7651

Great Plains Transportation Museum • 700 E Douglas • Wichita, KS 67202 • (316) 263-0944 • http://www.gptm.us

Kansas African American Museum • 601 N Water St • Wichita, KS 67203 • (316) 262-7651 • http://www.thekansasafricanamericanmuseum.org

Kansas Aviation Museum • 3350 S George Washington Blvd • Wichita, KS 67210 • (316) 683-9242 • http://www.kansasaviationmuseum.org

Kansas West Conference Archives of the United Methodist Church • 9440 E Boston, Suite 198 • Wichita, KS 67207-3600 • (316) 684-0266

Mid-America All Indian Center Museum • 650 N Seneca • Wichita, KS 67203 • (316) 262-5221 • http://www.theindiancenter.com

Midwest Historical and Genealogical Society • 1203 N Main St, P.O. Box 1121 • Wichita, KS 67201-1121 • (316) 264-3611 • http://skyways.lib.ks.us/genweb/mhgs/

Native Mid-America All-Indian Center • 650 N 2nd • Wichita, KS 67203 • (316) 262-5221 • http://www.theindiancenter.org

Old Cowtown Museum • 1865 Museum Blvd • Wichita, KS 67203-3203 • (316) 219-1871 • http://www.oldcowtown.org

Pioneer Historical Museum • Friends Univ, 2100 W University Ave • Wichita, KS 67213 • (316) 261-5800

Sons and Daughters of the Colonial and Antebellum Bench and Bar 1585-1861 • 7505 10th Street Cr N • Wichita, KS 67206-3844 • (316) 634-1774

Wichita Genealogical Society • P.O. Box 3705 • Wichita, KS 67201-3705 • (316) 262-0611 • http://skyways.lib.ks.us/orgs/wgs/

Wichita Public Library • 223 S Main St • Wichita, KS 67226-1026 • (316) 261-8510 • http://www.wichita.lib.ks.us

Wichita-Sedgwick County Historical Museum • 204 S Main St • Wichita, KS 67202 • (316) 265-9314 • http://www.wichitahistory.org

Wichita-Sedgwick County Historical Museum Association • Historical Museum, 204 S Main • Wichita, KS 67202 • (316) 265-9314 • http://www.wichitahistory.org

Wilson

Czech Opera House Museum • 415 27th St, Old Hwy 40, P.O. Box 271 • Wilson, KS 67490-0271 • (785) 658-3505

Winfield

Cowley County Genealogical Society • 1518 E 12th St • Winfield, KS 67156-3923 • (620) 221-4591

Cowley County Historical Society • Historical Museum, 1011 Mansfield St • Winfield, KS 67156 • (620) 221-4811 • http://www.cchsm.com

Memorial Library • Southwestern College, 100 College St • Winfield, KS 67156-2498 • (620) 229-6271 • http://www.sckans.edu/library

Winfield Public Library • 605 College St • Winfield, KS 67156-3199 • (620) 221-4470 • http://www.wpl.org

Yates Center

Woodson County Genealogical Society • 608 N Prairie • Yates Center, KS 66783 • (620) 625-2705

Woodson County Historical Society • Historical Museum, 208 W Mary • Yates Center, KS 66783 • (620) 625-2371

Adairville
Red River Meeting House and Cemetery Association • 2459 Trimble Rd • Adairville, KY 42202 • (270) 539-6528 • http://www.redriverrevival.com

Albany
Clinton County Historical Society • Historical Museum, 103 N Cross St, P.O. Box 177 • Albany, KY 42602 • (606) 387-5519

Clinton County Public Library • 302 King Dr • Albany, KY 42602 • (606) 387-5989

Alexandria
Campbell County Historical and Genealogical Society • 8352 E Main St • Alexandria, KY 41001 • (859) 635-6407 • http://www.rootsweb.com/~kycchgs

Campbell County Log Cabin Museum • 234 W Clayridge Rd • Alexandria, KY 41001 • (606) 635-5913

Historic Home Museum • 19 E Main St • Alexandria, KY 41001

Anchorage
Anchorage Civic Club Archives • City Hall, P.O. Box 23266 • Anchorage, KY 40223 • (502) 245-4654

Ashland
Boyd County Historical Society • c/o Boyd County Public Library, 1740 Central Ave • Ashland, KY 41101 • (606) 329-0090

Boyd County Public Library • 1740 Central Ave • Ashland, KY 41101 • (606) 329-0090 • http://www.thebookplace.org

Eastern Kentucky Genealogical Society • c/o Boyd County Public Library, 1740 Central Ave, P.O. Box 1544 • Ashland, KY 41105-1544 • (606) 329-0090

Kentucky Highlands Museum • 1620 Winchester Ave, P.O. Box 1494 • Ashland, KY 41005 • (606) 329-8888 • http://www.highlandsmuseum.com

Auburn
Auburn Historical Museum • 918 H Street SE • Auburn, KY 42206

Auburn Historical Society • Historical Museum, 433 W Main St, P.O. Box 114 • Auburn, KY 42206 • (270) 542-4677 • http://www.logantele.com/~aubhis

Shaker Museum • 860 Shaker Museum Rd, P.O. Box 177 • Auburn, KY 42206 • (502) 542-4167 • http://www.shakermuseum.com

Augusta
Bracken County Historical Society • 302 E 4th • Augusta, KY 41002 • (606) 756-2409

Knoedler Memorial Library • 315 Main St • Augusta, KY 41002 • (606) 756-3911

National Underground Railroad Museum • P.O. Box 8 • Augusta, KY 41002

Auxier
Floyd County Historical and Genealogical Society • P.O. Box 217 • Auxier, KY 41602 • http://www.rootsweb.ancestry.com/~kyfloyd/floyd.htm

Barboursville
Dr Thomas Walker Cabin Museum • HC 83, Box 868 • Barboursville, KY 40906 • (606) 546-4400

Knox County Historical Society • Historical Museum, 601 N Main St, P.O. Box 528 • Barbourville, KY 40906

Knox County Public Library • 206 Knox St • Barbourville, KY 40906 • (606) 546-5339

Knox Historical Museum • 196 Daniel Boone Dr, P.O. Box 1446 • Barbourville, KY 40906-5446 • (606) 546-4300

Weeks-Townsend Memorial Library • Union College, 310 College St, CPO 21 • Barbourville, KY 40906-1499 • (606) 546-1240 • http://www.unionky.edu

Bardstown
Bardstown Historical Museum • 114 N 5th St • Bardstown, KY 40004 • (502) 348-2999

My Old Kentucky Home State Park • 501 E Stephen Foster Ave, P.O. Box 323 • Bardstown, KY 40004 • (502) 348-3502 • http://www.kystateparks.com

Nelson County Genealogical Roundtable • c/o Nelson County Public Library, 201 Cathedral Manor, P.O. Box 409 • Bardstown, KY 40004-0409 • (502) 348-3714

Nelson County Old Records Archives • 311 E Stephen Foster, P.O. Box 312 • Bardstown, KY 40004-0312 • (502) 348-1832

Nelson County Public Library • 201 Cathedral Manor • Bardstown, KY 40004 • (502) 348-3714 • http://www.nelsoncopublib.org

Wickland House Museum • 107 E Stephen Foster Ave, P.O. Box 867 • Bardstown, KY 40004 • (502) 348-5428 • http://www.state.ky/tour/bluegras/bardstow.htm

Barlow
Barlow House Museum • 509 Broadway, P.O. Box 300 • Barlow, KY 42024 • (502) 334-3010

Beattyville
Lee County Historical and Genealogical Society • P.O. Box V • Beattyville, KY 41311

Bedford
Trimble County Public Library • 112 US Hwy 42 E, P.O. Box 249 • Bedford, KY 40006-0249 • (502) 255-7362

Belcher
Belcher History Center • US 460 E, P.O. Box 10 • Belcher, KY 41513 • (606) 754-8876

Benham
Kentucky Coal Mining Museum • 231 Main St, P.O. Box A • Benham, KY 40807 • (606) 848-1530

Benton
Marshall County Genealogical and Historical Society • County Courthouse, P.O. Box 373 • Benton, KY 42025 • (270) 527-4749

Marshall County Public Library • 1003 Poplar St • Benton, KY 42025 • (270) 527-9969 • http://www.marshallcolibrary.org

Berea
Bereal College Appalachian Museum • P.O. Box 2298 • Berea, KY 40404 • (859) 986-9341

Hutchins Library • Berea College, Campus Dr • Berea, KY 40404 • (859) 985-3109 • http://www.berea.edu/library/library.html

Booneville
Owsley Company Historical Society • Main St • Booneville, KY 41314 • (606) 593-6755

Owsley County Public Library • 2 Action Pl, P.O. Box 280 • Booneville, KY 41314-0280 • (606) 593-5700 • http://www.owsleycountykentucky.org/library.html

Bowling Green
Bowling Green Public Library • 1225 State St • Bowling Green, KY 42101 • (270) 781-4882 • http://www.bgpl.org

Felts Log House Museum • Western Kentucky Univ, 1 Big Red Wy • Bowling Green, KY 42104 • (502) 745-2592

Helm-Cravens Library • Western Kentucky Univ, 1 Big Red Way • Bowling Green, KY 42101-3576 • (270) 745-6125 • http://www.wku.edu/library/

Kentucky

Bowling Green, cont.
Kentucky Library & Museum • Western Kentucky Univ, 1906 College Heights Blvd #11092 • Bowling Green, KY 42101 • (270) 745-2592 • http://www.wku.edu/library/kylim

Pioneer America Society • Dept of Geography & Geology, Western Kentucky Univ, 1906 College Heights Blvd #31066 • Bowling Green, KY 42101-1066 • http://www.pioneeramerica.org

Riverview House at Hobson Grove Museum • 1100 W Main Ave, P.O. Box 10059 • Bowling Green, KY 42101 • (270) 843-5565 • http://www.bgky.org/riverview.htm

Southern Kentucky Genealogical Society • P.O. Box 1782 • Bowling Green, KY 42102-1782 • (270) 843-9452 • http://members.aol.com/kygen/skgs/gen-1.htm

Brandenburg
Meade County Public Library • 400 Library Pl • Brandenburg, KY 40108-1045 • (270) 422-2094 • http://www.meadereads.org

Brooksville
Bracken County Historical Society • 207 Madison St, P.O. Box 307 • Brooksville, KY 41004 • (606) 735-3337 • http://www.rootsweb.com/~kybchs/bracken.html

Brownsville
Edmonson County Public Library • 503 Washington St, P.O. Box 219 • Brownsville, KY 42210-0219 • (502) 597-2146

Burlington
Boone County Historic Preservation • 2950 Washington St • Burlington, KY 41005 • (859) 334-2111

Dinsmore Homestead Museum • 5656 Burlington Pk, P.O. Box 453 • Burlington, KY 41005 • (859) 586-6117 • http://www.dinsmorefarm.org

Cadiz
Cadiz Log Cabin Museum • 22 Main St, P.O. Box 735 • Cadiz, KY 42211 • (502) 522-3892

John L Street Memorial Library • 244 Main St • Cadiz, KY 42211-9153 • (270) 522-6301 • http://tclibrary.org

Trigg County Historical Society • Historical Museum, P.O Box 609 • Cadiz, KY 42211

Campbellsville
American Civil War Institute • Campbellsville Univ, 1 University Dr • Campbellsville, KY 42718-2799 • (270) 789-5000 • http://www.campbellsvil.edu/campbellsville/civilwar/

Hiestand House Museum • Hodgenville Rd • Campbellsville, KY 42718 • (270) 789-4343

Montgomery Library • Campbellsville University, 1 University Dr • Campbellsville, KY 42718-2799 • (270) 789-5272 • http://www.campbellsvil.edu~library/

Taylor County Historical Society • Historical Museum, 204 N Columbia, P.O. Box 14 • Campbellsville, KY 42719-0014 • (270) 465-3400

Taylor County Public Library • 205 N Columbia St • Campbellsville, KY 42718 • (270) 465-2562

Campton
Wolfe County Library • Main St, P.O. Box 10 • Campton, KY 41301-0010 • (606) 668-6571 • http://www.wolfecountypubliclibrary.org

Carlisle
Nicholas County Historical Society • Historical Museum, P.O. Box 222 • Carlisle, KY 40311 • (859) 289-9135

Nicholas County Public Library • 223 Broadway • Carlisle, KY 40311 • (859) 289-5595 • http://www.nicholascountylibrary.com

Carrollton
Butler-Turpin Historic House Museum • 1608 Hwy 227, P.O. Box 325 • Carrollton, KY 41008 • (502) 732-4384 • http://parks.ky.gov/findparks/resortparks/gb/

Carroll County Public Library • 136 Court St • Carrollton, KY 41008 • (502) 732-7020 • http://www.carrollcolibrary.org

Catlettsburg
Catlettsburg Historical Society • Historical Museum, 3420 Spring St • Catlettsburg, KY 41129

Central City
Muhlenberg County Genealogical Society • c/o Central City Public Library, Broad St • Central City, KY 42330 • (502) 338-3713

Muhlenberg County Libraries-Central City Branch • 108 E Broad St • Central City, KY 42330 • (270) 754-4630

Clay City
Red River Historical Society • Historical Museum, 4541 Main St, P.O. Box 195 • Clay City, KY 40312 • (606) 663-2555 • http://www.redriverky.com

Clinton
Hickman County Historical and Genealogical Society • 101 E Clay St • Clinton, KY 42031 • (270) 653-7346

Hickman County Memorial Library • 209 Mayfield Rd • Clinton, KY 42031-1427 • (270) 653-2225

Columbia
Adair County Genealogical Society • c/o Adair County Public Library, 307 Greensburg St, P.O. Box 613 • Columbia, KY 42728 • (270) 384-2472 • http://www.rootsweb.com/~kyacgs/

Adair County Historical Society & Heritage Association • 201 Jamestown St • Columbia, KY 42728-1323 • (270) 384-2501

Adair County Public Library • 307 Greensburg St • Columbia, KY 42728-1488 • (270) 384-2472 • http://www.youseemore.com/adair/

Katie Murrell Library • Lindsey Wilson College, 210 Lindsey Wilson St • Columbia, KY 42728 • (270) 384-8102 • http://www.lindsey.edu/library

Columbus
Columbus-Belmont Civil War Museum • 350 Park Rd, P.O. Box 9 • Columbus, KY 42032 • (270) 677-2327 • http://www.kystateparks.com/agencies/parks/columbus.htm

Corbin
Corbin Genealogy Society • 906 Barbourville St, P.O. Box 353 • Corbin, KY 40701 • (606) 878-8074

Corbin Public Library • 305 Roy Kidd Ave • Corbin, KY 40701 • (606) 528-6366

Covington
Acadian Genealogy Exchange • 863 Wayman Branch Rd • Covington, KY 41015-2201 • (859) 356-9825 • http://www.acadiangenexch.com

Behringer-Crawford Museum • 1600 Montague Rd, P.O. Box 67 • Covington, KY 41012 • (859) 491-4003 • http://www.bcmuseum.org

Kenton County Historical Society • Historical Museum, 501 E Southern Ave, P.O. Box 641 • Covington, KY 41012 • (859) 292-2188

Kenton County Public Library • 502 Scott Blvd • Covington, KY 41011 • (859) 962-4071 • http://www.kenton.lib.ky.us

Mimosa Mansion Museum • 412 E 2nd St • Covington, KY 41001 • (606) 261-9000

Office of Historic Properties • Berry Hill-Louisville Rd • Covington, KY 41001

Railway Exposition Company Museum • 315 W Southern Ave • Covington, KY 41015 • (513) 761-3500

Crab Orchard
Lincoln County Historical Society • 11475 Brodhead Rd • Crab Orchard, KY 40419 • (606) 355-2204

Cynthiana
Cynthiana-Harrison County Museum • 112 S Walnut St, P.O. Box 207 • Cynthiana, KY 41031 • (859) 234-3147

Cynthiana-Harrison County Public Library • 110 N Main St • Cynthiana, KY 41031 • (859) 234-4881 • http://www.harrisonlibrary.org

Danville
Boyle County Genealogical Association • 2825 Shakertown Rd • Danville, KY 40422 • (859) 332-7313

Boyle County Public Library-Danville Library • 307 W Broadway • Danville, KY 40422 • (859) 236-8466 • http://www.boylepublib.org

Constitution Square State Historic Site Museum • 134 S 2nd St • Danville, KY 40422 • (859) 239-7089 • http://www.kystateparks.com/agencies/parks/countsq2.htm

Danville and Boyle County Historical Society • 100 E Main St #3 • Danville, KY 40422 • (859) 236-9690

Grace Doherty Library - Special Collections • Centre College of Kentucky, 600 W Walnut St • Danville, KY 40422-1394 • (859) 238-5272 • http://www.centre.edu/web/library/homepage.html

McDowell House Museum • 125 S 2nd St • Danville, KY 40422 • (859) 236-2804 • http://www.mcdowellhouse.org

Dawson Springs
Dawson Springs Museum • 127 S Main St, P.O. Box 107 • Dawson Springs, KY 42408 • (502) 797-3503

Dixon
Webster County Historical and Genealogical Society • Webster County Courthouse, P.O. Box 215 • Dixon, KY 42409 • (270) 639-5170 • http://www.rootsweb.com/~kywebste/wch_gs.htm

Webster County Public Library • 101 State Route 132 E, P.O. Box 50 • Dixon, KY 42409-0050 • (270) 639-9171

Dry Ridge
Grant County Historical Society • Historical Museum, 117 Charles Givin Dr • Dry Ridge, KY 41035

Eddyville
Lyon County Historical Society • Lyon County Museum, 68 Hawk Nest Ln, P.O. Box 894 • Eddyville, KY 42038 • (270) 388-9986

Lyon County Public Library • 261 Commerce St, P.O. Box 546 • Eddyville, KY 42038-0546 • (270) 388-7720

Edmonton
Metcalfe County Historical Society • P.O. Box 910 • Edmonton, KY 42129 • http://www.rootsweb.com/~kymetea2/historicalsociety.htm

Metcalfe County Public Library • Main St, P.O. Box 626 • Edmonton, KY 42129 • (270) 432-4981

Elizabethtown
Caudill Store & History Center • 7822 Hwy 7, P.O. Box 274 • Elizabethtown, KY 42701 • (606) 633-3281

EHS Heritage Council • 201 W Dixie Ave • Elizabethtown, KY 42701 • (270) 737-4126

Elizabethtown Community College Library • 600 College Street Rd • Elizabethtown, KY 42701 • (270) 769-2371 • http://www.elizabethtowncc.com/ecdweb/Library/

Hardin County Historical Society • Brown-Pusey House Museum, 128 N Main St, P.O. Box 381 • Elizabethtown, KY 42701 • (270) 769-2301

Lincoln Heritage House • 704 Woodland Dr • Elizabethtown, KY 42701 • (800) 437-0092

Sarah Bush Johnston Lincoln Memorial • Freeman Lake Park, P.O. Box 291 • Elizabethtown, KY 42701 • (502) 737-8727

Schmidt Coca-Cola Museum • P.O. Box 848 • Elizabethtown, KY 42701

Elkhorn City
Elkhorn City Public Library • 150 Main St, P.O. Drawer L • Elkhorn City, KY 41522-0408 • (606) 754-5451

Elkton
Todd County Public Library • 302 E Main St • Elkton, KY 42220 • (270) 265-9071 • http://www.anglefire.com/ky/toddcopl

Erlanger
Erlanger Historical Society • Historical Museum, 3313 Crescent Ave, P.O. Box 18062 • Erlanger, KY 41018 • http://www.erlangerhistoricalsociety.org

Evansville
Tri-State Genealogical Society • c/o Willard Library, 21 1st Ave • Evansville, KY 47710 • (812) 425-4309

Falmouth
Pendleton County Historical and Genealogical Society • Historical Museum, Hwy 27, P.O. Box 130 • Falmouth, KY 41040 • (859) 442-7334 • http://www.rootsweb.com/~kypendle/

Pendleton County Public Library • 228 Main St • Falmouth, KY 41040-1223 • (859) 654-8535

Flatwoods
Greenup County Public Libraries-Flatwoods Public • 1705 Argillite Rd • Flatwoods, KY 41139 • (606) 836-3771

Flemingsburg
Fleming County Museum • 400 W Weston, P.O. Box 24 • Flemingsburg, KY 41041 • (970) 265-2591

Fleming County Public Library • 303 S Main Cross • Flemingsburg, KY 41041-1298 • (606) 845-7851 • http://members.tripod.com/~edneyj/index-2.html

Florence
Boone County Historical Society • Historical Museum, 8100 Ewing Blvd, P.O. Box 23 • Florence, KY 41042 • http://www.boonecountyky.org/bchs/

Boone County Public Library • 7425 US 42 • Florence, KY 41042 • (859) 371-6222 • http://www.bcpl.org

Fort Campbell
Don F Pratt Museum • 5702 Tennessee Ave • Fort Campbell, KY 42223 • (270) 798-4986 • http://www.campbell.army.mil/pratt/

Fort Campbell Historical Foundation • 2703 Michigan Ave • Fort Campbell, KY 42223 • (270) 439-9463

R F Sink Memorial Library • 38 Screaming Eagle Blvd • Fort Campbell, KY 42223-5342 • (270) 956-3344 • http://www.campbell.army.mil/library/library.htm

Fort Knox
Barr Memorial Library • 400 Quartermaster St • Fort Knox, KY 40121 • (502) 624-4636

Cavalry Armor Foundation • 133 Gold Vault Rd • Fort Knox, KY 40121 • (502) 943-8977

Patton Museum of Cavalry and Armor Library • 4554 Fayette Ave, P.O. Box 208 • Fort Knox, KY 40121-0208 • (502) 624-3812 • http://www.knox.army.mil/museum/

Fort Mitchell
Northern Kentucky Heritage League • P.O. Box 104 • Fort Mitchell, KY 41017 • (859) 441-7000

Kentucky

Fort Mitchell, cont.
Vent Haven Museum • 33 W Maple • Fort Mitchell, KY 41011 • (859) 341-0461 • http://www.venthavenmuseum.net

Frankfort
Brown County Genealogical Society • c/o Kentucky History Center, 100 W Broadway • Frankfort, KY 40601 • (877) 564-1792

Department of Military Affairs • Military Records & Research Branch, 1121 Louisville Rd • Frankfort, KY 40601 • (502) 564-4873 • http://www.state.ky.us/agencies/military/mrrb.htm

Friends of Fort Hill • Historical Museum, 201 Pin Oak Pl • Frankfort, KY 40601

Governor's Mansion Museum • 704 Capitol Ave • Frankfort, KY 40601 • (502) 564-8004 • http://www.governorsmansion.ky.gov

Historic Frankfort • P.O. Box 775 • Frankfort, KY 40602 • (502) 223-3923

Historical Confederation of Kentucky • KY History Center, 100 W Broadway • Frankfort, KY 40602-1792 • (502) 564-1792 • http://www.kentuckyhistory.org

Kentucky Department for Libraries and Archives • 300 Coffee Tree Rd, P.O. Box 537 • Frankfort, KY 40602-0537 • (502) 564-8300 • http://www.kdla.net

Kentucky Dept for Health - Vital Statistics Branch • 275 E Main St • Frankfort, KY 40621-0001 • (502) 564-4212 • http://publichealth.state.ky.us/vital.htm

Kentucky Genealogical Society • P.O. Box 153 • Frankfort, KY 40602-0153 • (502) 875-4452 • http://www.kygs.org

Kentucky Heritage Council • 300 Washington St • Frankfort, KY 40601 • (502) 564-7005 • http://www.kyheritage.org

Kentucky Historical Society • Historical Museum, 100 W Broadway, P.O. Box H • Frankfort, KY 40602-2108 • (502) 564-1792 • http://www.history.ky.gov

Kentucky Military History Museum • Old State Arsenal, 125 E Main St, P.O. Box 1792 • Frankfort, KY 40602-1792 • (502) 564-3265 • http://www.kyhistory.org

Kentucky Oral History Commission • KY History Center, 100 W Broadway • Frankfort, KY 40602-0537 • (502) 564-1792

Kentucky State Capitol Museum • Capital Ave • Frankfort, KY 40601 • (502) 564-3000 • http://www.state.ky.us/agencies/finance/attract/capitol.htm

Kentucky State Library and Archives • Public Records Division, 300 Coffee Tree Rd, P.O. Box 537 • Frankfort, KY 40602-0537 • (502) 875-7000 • http://www.kdla.ky.us

Liberty Hall-Orlando Brown House Museum • 218 Wilkinson St • Frankfort, KY 40601 • (502) 227-2560 • http://www.libertyhall.org

Old Governor's Mansion Museum • 420 High St • Frankfort, KY 40601 • (502) 564-5500

Oral History Association • Old Capitol Annex, P.O. Box H • Frankfort, KY 40601 • (502) 564-3016

Paul G Blazer Library • Kentucky State Univ, 400 E Main St • Frankfort, KY 40601 • (502) 597-6852 • http://www.kysu.edu/library

Vest-Lindsey House Museum • 700 Louisville • Frankfort, KY 40601 • (502) 564-3000

Franklin
Goodnight Memorial Library • 203 S Main St • Franklin, KY 42134 • (270) 586-8397 • http://www.goodnightlibrary.org

Simpson County Historical Society • Historical Museum, 206 N College St • Franklin, KY 42134 • (270) 586-4228 • http://www.rootsweb.com/~kyschs/

South Kentucky Genealogical Society • Route 1, Box 3332 • Franklin, KY 42134

Frenchburg
Menifee County Public Library • 1555 Walnut St, P.O. Box 49 • Frenchburg, KY 40322-0049 • (606) 768-2212

Menifee County Roots • P.O. Box 114 • Frenchburg, KY 40322 • (606) 768-3323

Fulton
Fulton County Genealogical and Historical Society • P.O. Box 1031 • Fulton, KY 42041

Fulton Public Library • 312 Main St • Fulton, KY 42050 • (270) 472-3439 • http://www.fultonlibrary.com

Gallatin County Historical Society • Historical Museum, Highland Dr, P.O. Box 165 • Fulton, KY 42021

Georgetown
Ensor Library • Georgetown College, 400 E College St • Georgetown, KY 40324-1695 • (502) 863-8401 • http://spider.georgetowncollege.edu/library

Georgetown and Scott County Museum • 229 E Main St • Georgetown, KY 40324 • (502) 863-6201 • http://www.scottcountymuseum.org

Scott County Genealogical Society • c/o Scott County Public Library, 104 S Bradford Ln • Georgetown, KY 40324 • (502) 863-3566 • http://www.rootsweb.com/~kyscott/scgs.htm

Scott County Historical Society • Historical Museum, 119 N Hamilton St • Georgetown, KY 40324

Scott County Public Library • 104 S Bradford Lane • Georgetown, KY 40324-2335 • (502) 863-3566 • http://www.scottpublib.org

Ward Hall Museum • 1782 Frankfrot Pk • Georgetown, KY 40324

Glasgow
Barren County Historical Foundation • 109 Robin Dr • Glasgow, KY 42141 • (270) 651-7425

Mary Wood Weldon Memorial Library • 107 W College St • Glasgow, KY 42141 • (270) 651-2824 • http://www.glasgowbarren.com/commun/library/library.htm

South Central Kentucky Cultural Center • P.O. Box 1714 • Glasgow, KY 42142

South Central Kentucky Historical and Genealogical Society • Historical Museum, P.O. Box 157 • Glasgow, KY 42142-0157 • (270) 651-5514 • http://www.rootsweb.com/~kybarren/society.html

Grayson
Carter County Historical and Genealogical Society • P.O. Box 1128 • Grayson, KY 41143

Young Library • Kentucky Christian College, 100 Academic Pkwy, KCC Box 900 • Grayson, KY 41143-2205 • (606) 474-3240

Greensburg
Green County Historical Society • P.O. Box 276 • Greensburg, KY 42743

Green County Public Library • 116 S Main St • Greensburg, KY 42743 • (270) 932-7081

Greenup
Greenup County Public Library • 614 Main St • Greenup, KY 41144-1036 • (606) 473-6514

Greenville
Duncan Cultural Center Museum • 122 S Cherry St, P.O. Box 289 • Greenville, KY 42345 • (270) 338-2605

Muhlenberg County Genealogical Society • c/o Muhlenberg County Library, 117 S Main St, P.O. Box 758 • Greenville, KY 42345 • (502) 338-3713

Muhlenberg County Library • 117 S Main St • Greenville, KY 42345 • (270) 338-4760 • http://www.mcplib.org

Otto Rothert Historical Society • 2727 State Route 189 S • Greenville, KY 42345-4646

Guthrie

Robert Penn Warren Birthplace Museum • 3rd & Cherry Sts, P.O. Box 296 • Guthrie, KY 42234 • (502) 483-2683

Hardinsburg

Breckinridge County Archives • P.O. Box 538 • Hardinsburg, KY 40143 • (502) 756-6166 • http://www.breckinridgecounty.net/government.html

Breckinridge County Historical Society • Courthouse Square, P.O. Box 498 • Hardinsburg, KY 40143-0498 • (270) 756-2246

Breckinridge County Public Library • 112 S Main St, P.O. Box 248 • Hardinsburg, KY 40143-0248 • (270) 756-2323

Harlan

Harlan County Genealogical Society • P.O. Box 1498 • Harlan, KY 40831

Harlan County Public Library • 107 N 3rd St • Harlan, KY 40831-2394 • (606) 573-5220

Harlan Heritage Seekers • P.O. Box 853 • Harlan, KY 40831-0853 • (606) 573-5220

Harrodsburg

Harrodsburg Historical Society • Morgan Row House Museum, 220 S Chiles St, P.O. Box 316 • Harrodsburg, KY 40330-1631 • (859) 734-5985 • http://www.harrodsburg.org

Harrodsburg Historical Society, Genealogy Committee • 220 S Chiles St, P.O. Box 316 • Harrodsburg, KY 40330 • (859) 734-5985 • http://www.rootsweb.com/~kymercer/hhs/

Mercer County Public Library • 109 W Lexington St • Harrodsburg, KY 40330-1542 • (859) 734-3680 • http://www.mcplib.info/

Old Fort Harrod State Park Mansion Museum • 123 S College St, P.O. Box 156 • Harrodsburg, KY 40330 • (859) 734-3314 • http://www.oldfortharrod.com

Shaker Village of Pleasant Hill • 3501 Lexington Rd • Harrodsburg, KY 40330 • (859) 734-5411 • http://www.shakervillageky.org

Hartford

Ohio County Historical Society • Historical Museum, 415 Mulberry St, P.O. Box 44 • Hartford, KY 42347 • (270) 298-3177

Ohio County Public Library • 413 Main St • Hartford, KY 42347 • (270) 298-3790

Hawesville

Genealogical Society of Hancock County • Old Courthouse, P.O. Box 667 • Hawesville, KY 42348-0146 • (270) 927-8095

Hancock County Archives • Old Court House, 3rd Floor, P.O. Box 667 • Hawesville, KY 42348 • (270) 927-8095

Hancock County Historical Society • Old Courthouse, 200 Court Sq • Hawesville, KY 42348 • (270) 927-8095

Hancock County Library • 240 Court Sq, P.O. Box 249 • Hawesville, KY 42348-0249 • (270) 927-6760

Hancock County Museum • 110 River St, P.O. Box 605 • Hawesville, KY 42348 • (270) 927-8672

Hazard

Bobby Davis Museum and Park • 234 Walnut St • Hazard, KY 41701 • (606) 439-4325 • http://www.bobbydavismuseum.com

Hazard Community College Library • 1 Community College Dr • Hazard, KY 41701 • (606) 436-5721 • http://www.uky.edu/libraries/dephazdet

Perry County Genealogical and Historical Society • c/o Perry County Public Library, 479 High St, P.O. Box 928 • Hazard, KY 41702 • (606) 436-3864

Perry County Public Library • 479 High St, P.O. Box 928 • Hazard, KY 41701-0928 • (606) 436-2475 • http://www.perrycountylibrary.org

Henderson

Henderson County Genealogical and Historical Society • 101 N Water St, P.O. Box 303 • Henderson, KY 42420 • (270) 830-7514 • http://www.rootsweb.com/~kyhender/Henderson/ HCHGS/HCHGSpg.htm

Henderson Public Library • 101 S Main St • Henderson, KY 42420-3599 • (270) 826-3712 • http://www.hcpl.org

Southern Cherokee Nation of Kentucky • 7919 Pleasant Hill Rd • Henderson, KY 42420 • http://www.southerncherokeenation.net

Highland Heights

Christopher Gist Historical Society Archives • Northern Kentucky Univ, University Dr • Highland Heights, KY 41099 • (859) 572-5456 • http://www.nku.edu/~refdept/gist.html

Hindman

East Kentucky Museum and History Center • P.O. Box 1323 • Hindman, KY 41822

Knott County Historical and Genealogical Society • 147 Carew Dr, P.O. Box 1023 • Hindman, KY 41822 • (606) 785-5751 • http://www.rootsweb.ancestry.com/~kyletch/letcher.htm

Knott County Public Library • 238 S Hwy 160, P.O. Box 667 • Hindman, KY 41822-0667 • (606) 785-5412

Hodgenville

Abraham Lincoln Birthplace National Historic Site Library • 2995 Lincoln Farm Rd • Hodgenville, KY 42748 • (270) 358-3137 • http://www.nps.gov/abli

Larue County Historical Society • Historical Museum, Route 210, P.O. Box 361 • Hodgenville, KY 42748

Larue County Public Library • 201 S Lincoln Blvd • Hodgenville, KY 42748 • (502) 358-3851 • http://laruelibrary.org

Lincoln Museum • 66 Lincoln Sq • Hodgenville, KY 42748 • (270) 358-3163 • http://www.lincolnmuseum-ky.org

Hopkinsville

Christian County Genealogical Society • 1101 Bethel St • Hopkinsville, KY 42240 • (270) 887-4262 • http://www.kyseeker.com/christian/ccgsbks.htm

Christian County Historical Society • Historical Museum, 1101 Bethel St, P.O. Box 306 • Hopkinsville, KY 42240 • (270) 886-3921

Hopkinsville Community College Library • 720 North Dr, P.O. Box 2100 • Hopkinsville, KY 42241-2100 • (270) 886-3921

Hopkinsville-Christian County Public Library • 1101 Bethel St • Hopkinsville, KY 42240 • (270) 887-4262

Jefferson Davis Monument State Park • Hwy 68 • Hopkinsville, KY 42240 • (270) 886-1765

Pennyroyal Area Museum • 217 E 9th St, P.O. Box 1093 • Hopkinsville, KY 42241 • (270) 887-4270 • http://www.hopkinsville.net/~museum

Horse Cave

Horse Cave Free Public Library • 111 Higbee St, P.O. Box 127 • Horse Cave, KY 42749-0127 • (270) 786-1130

Hyden

Leslie County Historical Society • c/o Leslie County Public Library, 22065 Main St, P.O. Box 498 • Hyden, KY 41749 • (606) 672-2460

Leslie County Public Library • 22065 Main St, P.O. Box 498 • Hyden, KY 41749-0498 • (606) 672-2460 • http://www.leslielibrary.com

Inez
Martin County Historical and Genealogical Society • P.O. Box 501 • Inez, KY 41224 • http://www.rootsweb.com/~Kymchgs/MCHGS

Martin County Public Library • Main St, P.O. Box 1318 • Inez, KY 41224-1318 • (606) 298-7766

Irvine
Estill County Public Library • 246 Main St • Irvine, KY 40336-1099 • (606) 723-3030 • http://estilcolib.state.ky.us

Jackson
Breathitt County Genealogical Society • c/o Breathitt County Public Library, 1024 College Ave • Jackson, KY 41339 • (606) 666-5541 • http://www.breathittcountylibrary.com/Community/History.html

Breathitt County Historical and Genealogical Society • 121 Turner Dr • Jackson, KY 41339

Breathitt County Museum • Broadway St, P.O. Box 228 • Jackson, KY 41339 • (606) 666-4159

Breathitt County Public Library & Museum • 1024 College Ave • Jackson, KY 41339 • (606) 666-5541 • http://www. breathittcountylibrary.com

Lees College Campus Library • Hazard Community College, 601 Jefferson Ave • Jackson, KY 41339 • (606) 666-7521

Jamestown
Russell County Historical Society • Historical Museum, N Main St, P.O. Box 544 • Jamestown, KY 42629 • (270) 866-7434 • http://www.duo-county.com/~rcplib/historicalsociety1.htm

Russell County Public Library • 94 N Main, P.O. Box 970 • Jamestown, KY 42629-0970 • (270) 343-3545 • http://www.russellcountylibrary.com

Jeffersontown
Jeffersontown and Southeast Jefferson County Historical Society • 2432 Merriwood Dr • Jeffersontown, KY 40299 • (502) 267-1715

Jeffersontown Museum • 10434 Watterson Tr • Jeffersontown, KY 40299

Jeffersonville
Red River Historical Society • Historical Museum, 11720 Main St • Jeffersonville, KY 40337

Jenkins
Zegeer Coal-Railroad Museum • P.O. Box 4 • Jenkins, KY 41537

La Grange
Icelandic National League of the USA • P.O. Box 265 • La Grange, KY 40031

Oldham County Historical Society • Oldham County History Center, 106 N 2nd St • La Grange, KY 40031-1102 • (502) 222-0826 • http://www.oldhamcountyhistoricalsociety.org

Oldham County Public Library • 106 E Jefferson St • La Grange, KY 40031 • (502) 222-1113 • http://www.oldhampl.org

Owen County Historical Society • Historical Museum, 10 S Montgomery St, P.O. Box 84 • La Grange, KY 40031

Lancaster
Garrard County Historical Society • Historical Museum, 208 Danville St • Lancaster, KY 40444 • (859) 792-3065

Garrard County Public Library • 101 Lexington St • Lancaster, KY 40444 • (859) 792-3424 • http://www.garrardpublib.state.ky.us

Pleasant Retreat Museum • 656 Stanford Rd • Lancaster, KY 40444

Latonia
Kenton Company Historical Society • 501 E Southern Ave • Latonia, KY 41015 • (859) 431-2666

Lawrenceburg
Anderson County Historical Society • P.O. Box 212 • Lawrenceburg, KY 40342 • (502) 839-3248

Lebanon
Marion County Historical Society • Historical Society, 342 W Main St • Lebanon, KY 40033

Marion County Public Library • 201 E Main St • Lebanon, KY 40033-1133 • (270) 692-4698

Lebanon Junction
National Muzzle Loading Association • Historical Museum, 1680 Optimist Rd • Lebanon Junction, KY 41050 • (270) 737-1163

Ledbetter
Ledbetter Historical Society • general delivery • Ledbetter, KY 42058 • (502) 564-1792

Leitchfield
Grayson County Historical Society • Historical Museum, 122 E Main St, P.O. Box 84 • Leitchfield, KY 42755 • (270) 230-8989

Grayson County Public Library • 130 E Market St • Leitchfield, KY 42754 • (270) 259-5455 • http://www.graysoncountylibrary.org

Lewisburg
Lewisburg-North Logan Historical Commission • P.O. Box 239 • Lewisburg, KY 42256 • (270) 755-4828

Lexington
American Saddle Horse Museum • 4093 Iron Works Pike • Lexington, KY 40511

Aviation Museum of Kentucky • 4316 Hangar Dr, Blue Grass Airport • Lexington, KY 40510 • (859) 231-1219 • http://www.aviationky.org

Blue Grass Trust for Historic Preservation • Hunt-Morgan House, 201 N Mill St • Lexington, KY 40508 • (859) 253-0362 • http://www.bluegrasstrust.org

Bluegrass African-American History Museum • 644 Georgetown St • Lexington, KY 40508

Bodley-Bullock House Museum • 200 Market St • Lexington, KY 40507 • (859) 259-1266

Boone Station State Historic Site Museum • 240 Gentry Rd • Lexington, KY 40509 • (859) 263-1073

Calvary Cemetery Archives • 874 W Main St • Lexington, KY 40507 • (859) 252-5415

Fayette County Genealogical Society • P.O. Box 8113 • Lexington, KY 40533-8113 • (859) 278-9966 • http://www.rootsweb.com/~kyfcgs/

Headley-Whitney Museum • 4435 Old Frankfort Pk • Lexington, KY 40510 • (859) 255-6653 • http://www.headley-whitney.org

Henry Clay-Ashland Mansion Museum • 120 Sycamore Blvd • Lexington, KY 40502 • (859) 266-8581 • http://www.henryclay.org

Kentucky Hemp Museum • 149 Lexington St, P.O. Box 8551 • Lexington, KY 40533 • (606) 873-8957

Kentucky Tree-Search • P.O. Box 22621 • Lexington, KY 40522-2621 • (859) 272-4380

Lexington Cemetery Museum • 833 W Main St • Lexington, KY 40508-2094 • (859) 255-5522 • http://www.lexcem.org

Lexington History Museum • 215 W Main St, P.O. Box 116 • Lexington, KY 40588 • (859) 254-0530 • http://www.lexingtonhistorymuseum.org

Lexington Public Library • 140 E Main St • Lexington, KY 40507-1376 • (859) 231-5520 • http://www.lexpublib.org

Lexington-Fayette Records Center and Archives • 1306 Versailles Rd, Ste 180 • Lexington, KY 40508 • (859) 425-2070 • http://www.lfucg.com/council_clerk/index.asp

Margaret I King Library • Univ of Kentucky, Special Collections, 500 S Limestone St • Lexington, KY 40506-0039 • (859) 257-8611 • http://www.uky.edu/Libraries/Special/

Mary Todd Lincoln House Museum • 578 W Main, P.O. Box 132 • Lexington, KY 40588 • (859) 233-9999 • http://www.mtlhouse.org

Morgan's Men Association • Historical Museum, 1691 Kilkenny Dr • Lexington, KY 40505

Photographic Archives • Univ of KY, Special Collections, King Library • Lexington, KY 40506 • (859) 257-2654 • http://www.uky.edu/libraries/special/av

Senator John Pope House Museum • 326 Grosvenor Ave • Lexington, KY 40508 • (606) 253-0352

Southern Historical Association • Univ of Kentucky • Lexington, KY 40506

Transylvania University Library & Museum • 300 N Broadway • Lexington, KY 40508 • (859) 233-8225 • http://www.transy.edu/library/library.htm

University of Kentucky Basketball Museum • P.O. Box 89 • Lexington, KY 40588

Waveland State Historic Site Museum • 225 Waveland Museum Ln • Lexington, KY 40514 • (859) 272-3611 • http://www.parks.ky.gov

William T Young Library • University of Kentucky, 1000 University Dr • Lexington, KY 40506-0456 • (859) 257-0500 • http://www.uky.edu/libraries

Liberty
Bicentennial Heritage Corporation of Casey County • 148 Wolford St • Liberty, KY 42539 • (606) 787-6194

Casey County Bicentennial Heritage Association • P.O. Box 356 • Liberty, KY 42539

Casey County Public Library & Genealogical Research Center • 238 Middleburg St • Liberty, KY 42529 • (606) 787-9381 • http://www.caseylibrary.org

London
Laurel County Historical Society • Old City Hall Bldg, 203 S Broad St, P.O. Box 816 • London, KY 40741 • (606) 864-0607 • http://www.laurelcountyhistoricalsociety.org

Laurel County Museum • 310 W 3rd St, P.O. Box 816 • London, KY 40743 • (606) 864-0607

Laurel County Public Library • 120 College Park Dr • London, KY 40741 • (606) 864-5759 • http://www.laurelllibrary.org

Mountain Life Museum • 998 Levi Jackson Park Rd • London, KY 40744 • (606) 878-8000 • http://www.kystateparks.com/agencies/parks/levijack.htm

Louisa
Big Sandy Valley Historical Society • Historical Museum, 125 S Jefferson St • Louisa, KY 41230 • (606) 638-4889

Lawrence County Public Library • 102 W Main, P.O. Box 600 • Louisa, KY 41230-0600 • (606) 638-4497 • http://www.lawrencecountypubliclibrary.org

Louisville
Beargrass-Saint Matthews Historical Society • 3940 Grandview Ave • Louisville, KY 40207 • (502) 899-2524

Brennan House Museum • 631 S 5th St • Louisville, KY 40202 • (502) 540-5145

City of Louisville Archives • 970 S 4th St • Louisville, KY 40203 • (502) 574-3508 • http://www.louisvilleky.gov

Conrad-Caldwell House Museum • 1402 St James Ct • Louisville, KY 40208 • (502) 636-5023 • http://www.conradcaldwell.org

Ernest Miller White Library • Louisville Presbyterian Theological Seminary, 1044 Alta Vista Rd • Louisville, KY 40205-1798 • (502) 895-3411 • http://www.lpts.edu/academic_resources/emwhite_library.asp

Farmington Historic Home Museum • 3033 Bardstown Rd • Louisville, KY 40205 • (502) 452-9920 • http://www.farmingtonhistorichome.org

Filson Historical Society • Historical Museum, 1310 S 3rd St • Louisville, KY 40208 • (502) 635-5083 • http://www.filsonhistorical.org

Frazier Historical Arms Museum • 829 W Main St • Louisville, KY 40202 • (502) 412-2280 • http://www.frazierarmsmuseum.org

Historic Homes Foundation • Historical Museum, 3110 Lexington Rd • Louisville, KY 40206 • (502) 899-5079 • http://www.historichomes.org

Israel T Naamani Library • Jewish Community Center, 3600 Dutchmans Ln • Louisville, KY 40205 • (502) 459-0660 • http://www.jccoflouisville.org

Jefferson County Archives • 514 W Liberty St, Rm 100 • Louisville, KY 40202 • (502) 595-3034 • http://courts.ky.gov/counties/Jefferson/archives

Jefferson County Office of Historic Preservation and Archives • 810 Barret Ave • Louisville, KY 40204 • (502) 574-5761

Jewish Genealogical Society of Louisville • c/o Israel T Naamani Library, 3600 Dutchmans Ln • Louisville, KY 40205 • (502) 459-0798

Kentucky Council on Archives • University Archives and Records Center, Univ of Louisville • Louisville, KY 40292-0001

Kentucky Derby Museum • 704 Central Ave, Gate 1 • Louisville, KY 40201 • (502) 637-1111 • http://www.derbymuseum.org

Knox County Genealogical Society • 2603 Aintree Wy • Louisville, KY 40220 • (502) 459-8718

Leica Historical Society • 125 Chenoweth Ln • Louisville, KY 40207 • (502) 895-7272

Little Loomhouse Museum • 328 Kenwood Hill Rd, P.O. Box 9124 • Louisville, KY 40214 • (502) 367-4792

Locust Grove Historic Home Museum • 561 Blankenbaker Ln • Louisville, KY 40207 • (502) 897-9845 • http://www.locustgrove.org

Louisville Free Public Library • 301 York St • Louisville, KY 40203-2257 • (502) 574-1616 • http://www.lfpl.org

Louisville Genealogical Society • 200 Cambridge Station Rd, P.O. Box 5164 • Louisville, KY 40255-0164 • (502) 425-6578 • http://www.rootsweb.com/~kylgs/

National Society of the Dames of the Court of Honor • 3535 Hanover Rd • Louisville, KY 40207

National Society, Daughters of the Union 1861-1865 • P.O. Box 7041 • Louisville, KY 40257-7041 • (502) 895-3146

National Society, Sons of the American Revolution • National Headquarters, 1000 S 4th St • Louisville, KY 40203 • (502) 589-1776 • http://www.sar.org

Photographic Archives • Ekstrom Library, Univ of Louisville • Louisville, KY 40292 • (502) 852-6752 • http://www.louisville.edu/library/ekstrom/special/pa_info.html

Portland Museum • 2308 Portland Ave • Louisville, KY 40212 • (502) 776-7678 • http://www.goportland.org

Riverside-Farnsley-Moremen Landing Museum • 7410 Moorman Rd • Louisville, KY 40272 • (502) 935-6809 • http://www.riverside-landing.org

Sons of the American Revolution, Kentucky Society • 3527 St Germaine Cr • Louisville, KY 40207 • (502) 893-0164 • http://www.kyssar.org

Spalding University Library • 853 Library Lane • Louisville, KY 40203-9986 • (502) 585-7130 • http://www.spalding.edu/library/home1

Kentucky

Louisville, cont.
Thomas Edison House Museum • 729-731 E Washington St • Louisville, KY 40202 • (502) 585-5247 • http://www.edisonhouse.org

Tompkins-Buchanan-Rankin Mansion Museum • 851 S 4th • Louisville, KY 40203 • (502) 585-9911 • http://www.spalding.edu

University Archives and Records Center • Univ of Louisville, Ekstrom Library • Louisville, KY 40292 • (502) 852-6745 • http://www.louisville.edu/library/uarc/

Whitehall State Historic Site • 3110 Lexington Rd • Louisville, KY 40206 • (502) 897-2944

William F Ekstrom Library • Univ of Louisville, Belknap Campus • Louisville, KY 40292 • (502) 852-6674 • http://www.louisville.edu/library

Lovely
Rufus M Reed Public Library • Rte 292, P.O. Box 359 • Lovely, KY 41232-0359 • (606) 395-5809

Madisonville
Historical Society of Hopkins County • Ruby Laffoon Log Cabin Museum, 107 S Union St • Madisonville, KY 42431 • (270) 821-3986

Hopkins County Genealogical Society • c/o Madisonville-Hopkins County Public Library, 31 S Main St, P.O. Box 51 • Madisonville, KY 42431 • (502) 821-3736 • http://www.rootsweb.com/~kyhopkin/hcgs/

Hopkins County-Madisonville Public Library • 31 S Main St • Madisonville, KY 42431 • (270) 825-2680 • http://www.publiclibrary.org

Manchester
Clay County Genealogical and Historical Society • Courthouse Museum, 115 Court St, P.O. Box 394 • Manchester, KY 40962-0394 • (606) 598-5507 • http://members.tripod.com/~Sue_1/clay.html

Clay County Public Library • 211 Bridge St • Manchester, KY 40962 • (606) 598-2617 • http://www.claycountypubliclibrary.org

Maple Mount
Ursuline Sisters Archives • Mount Saint Joseph • Maple Mount, KY 42356-9999 • (270) 299-4103 • http://www.catholic-chur.org/owensboro/archivist.html

Marion
B Clements Mineral Museum • 107 S Main • Marion, KY 42064

Crittenden County Genealogical Society • c/o Crittenden County Library, 204 W Carlisle, P.O. Box 61 • Marion, KY 42064 • (270) 965-3354

Crittenden County Historical Society • Historical Museum, 124 E Bellville St, P.O. Box 25 • Marion, KY 42064 • (270) 965-3354

Crittenden County Public Library • 204 W Carlisle St • Marion, KY 42064 • (270) 965-3354

Mason
Grant County Historical Society • P.O. Box 33 • Mason, KY 41054 • (859) 924-9202

Masonic Home
Masonic Grand Lodge of Kentucky • 300 Masonic Home Dr • Masonic Home, KY 40041 • (502) 893-0192 • http://grandlodgeofkentucky.org

Mayfield
Anne Parish Markham Library • Mid-Continent Baptist Bible College, 99 Powell Rd E • Mayfield, KY 42066-9007 • (270) 247-8521 • http://www.midcontinent.edu

Graves County Genealogical Society • P.O. Box 245 • Mayfield, KY 42006 • http://www.rootsweb.com/-kygraves/gravesghs.html

Graves County Library • 601 N 17th St • Mayfield, KY 42066 • (270) 247-2911 • http://www.gcpl.org

Maysville
Mason County Genealogical Society • 8031 Day Pike, P.O. Box 266 • Maysville, KY 41056 • (606) 759-7257

Mason County Historical Society • Historical Museum, 215 Sutton St, P.O. Box 13 • Maysville, KY 41056 • (606) 564-0900 • http://www.masoncountymuseum.org

Mason County Public Library • 218 E 3rd St • Maysville, KY 41056 • (606) 564-3286

Maysville and Mason County Historical and Scientific Society • c/o Mason County Public Library, 218 E 3rd St • Maysville, KY 41056 • (606) 564-3286

Maysville Community College Library • 1755 US 68 • Maysville, KY 41056 • (606) 759-7141 • http://www.maycc.kctcs.net/library/

National Underground Railroad Museum • Bierbower House, 38 W 4th St • Maysville, KY 41056 • (606) 564-3200

McKee
Jackson County Public Library • 2nd St, P.O. Box 160 • McKee, KY 404447-0160 • (606) 287-8113

Middlesboro
Bell County Historical Society • Historical Museum, 207 N 20th St, P.O. Box 1344 • Middlesboro, KY 40965 • (606) 242-0005 • http://www.bellcountymuseum.com/

Cumberland Gap National Historical Park • US 25 E, P.O. Box 1848 • Middlesboro, KY 40965 • (606) 248-2817 • http://www.nps.gov/cuga

Lost Squadron Museum • Bell County Airport, P.O. Box 776 • Middlesboro, KY 40965 • (606) 248-1149

Middlesboro-Bell County Public Library • 126 S 20th St, P.O. Box 1677 • Middlesboro, KY 40965-1677 • (606) 248-4812 • http://www.tcnet.net/~pinevillelib/

Middletown
Historic Middletown Museum • P.O. Box 43893 • Middletown, KY 40253

Montgomery
Montgomery County Historical Society • 30 E Main St, P.O. Box 861 • Montgomery, KY 40353 • (270) 598-1413

Monticello
Wayne County Historical and Genealogical Society • c/o Wayne County Public Library, 159 S Main St, P.O. Box 320 • Monticello, KY 42633 • (606) 348-8565 • http://www.rootsweb.com

Wayne County Public Library • 159 S Main St • Monticello, KY 42633 • (606) 348-8565 • http://www.waynepubliclibrary.net

Morehead
Camden-Carroll Library • Morehead State University, University Blvd • Morehead, KY 40351 • (606) 783-5491 • http://www.morehead-st.edu/units/library

Kentucky Folk Art Center Museum • 102 W 1st St • Morehead, KY 40351 • (606) 783-2204 • http://www.kyfolkart.org

Rowan County Historical Society • 236 Allen Ave, P.O. Box 60 • Morehead, KY 40351 • (606) 784-9145

Rowan County History Museum • 302 E 2nd St • Morehead, KY 40351

Rowan County Public Library • 185 E 1st St • Morehead, KY 40351 • (606) 784-7137 • http://rowancountypubliclibrary.state.ky.us

Morganfield
Union County District Library • 126 S Morgan St • Morganfield, KY 42437 • (270) 389-1696 • http://www.uclibrary.8m.com

Union County Historical Museum • 130 E Geiger • Morganfield, KY 42437

Union County Historical Society • 221 W McElroy • Morganfield, KY 42437 • http://www.comsource.net/~kyseeker/union/society.htm

Morgantown
Butler County Historical and Genealogical Society • P.O. Box 435 • Morgantown, KY 42261 • (270) 526-4408

Hammers House Museum • 205 S Main St • Morgantown, KY 42261 • (502) 526-2300

Mount Olivet
Blue Licks Battlefield Museum • Hwy 68 • Mount Olivet, KY 41064 • http://www.state.ky.us/agencies/parks/bluelick.htm

Robertson County Historical Society • Historical Museum, P.O. Box 282 • Mount Olivet, KY 41064

Robertson County Public Library • 148 N Main St, P.O. Box 282 • Mount Olivet, KY 41064-0282 • (606) 724-5746 • http://robertsonlibrary.com

Mount Sterling
Montgomery County Historical Society • Historical Museum, 607 Elmwood Dr • Mount Sterling, KY 40353 • (859) 498-1154

Mount Sterling Montgomery County Library • 241 W Locust St • Mount Sterling, KY 40353 • (859) 498-2404

Mount Vernon
Rockcastle County Historical Society • Historical Museum, P.O. Box 930 • Mount Vernon, KY 40456 • (606) 256-2397

Rockcastle County Library • 60 Ford Dr • Mount Vernon, KY 40456 • (606) 256-2388 • http://www.rockcastlelibrary.com

Mount Washington
Mount Washington Historical Society • P.O. Box 212 • Mount Washington, KY 40047-0212

Munfordville
Hart County Historical Society • Historical Museum, 940 S Dixie Hwy, P.O. Box 606 • Munfordville, KY 42765 • (270) 524-0101 • http://www.historichart.org/museum.htm

Hart County Public Library • 500 E Union St, P.O. Box 337 • Munfordville, KY 42765-0337 • (270) 524-1953

Murray
Calloway County Public Library • 710 Main St • Murray, KY 42071 • (270) 753-2288

Harry Lee Waterfield Library • Murray State Univ, 208 Waterfield Library • Murray, KY 42071-3307 • (270) 762-2053 • http://www.murraystate.edu/msml/msml.htm

Wrather West Kentucky Museum • Murray State Univ, P.O. Box 9 • Murray, KY 42071-3308 • (270) 762-4771 • http://www.murraystate.edu

Nazareth
Nazareth Archival Center • P.O. Box 3000 • Nazareth, KY 40048-3000 • (502) 348-1500

New Castle
Henry County Historical Society • P.O. Box 570 • New Castle, KY 40050

New Haven
Kentucky Railway Museum • 136 S Main St, P.O. Box 240 • New Haven, KY 40051 • (502) 549-5470 • http://www.kyrail.org

Newport
Campbell County Public Library District-Newport Branch • 4th & Monmouth Sts • Newport, KY 41071-1695 • (859) 572-5035

Nicholasville
Jessamine County Public Library • 600 S Main St • Nicholasville, KY 40356 • (859) 885-3523 • http://www.jesspublib.org

Jessamine Historical Society • 501 S 3rd St • Nicholasville, KY 40356-1811

Owensboro
Daviess County Historical Society • c/o Owensboro-Daviess County Public Library, 450 Griffith Ave • Owensboro, KY 42301 • (270) 684-0211 x24

Daviess County Public Library • 2020 Frederica St • Owensboro, KY 42301 • (270) 684-0211 • http://dcplibrary.org

Father Leonard Alvey Library • Brescia University, 717 Frederica St • Owensboro, KY 42301 • (270) 686-4212 • http://www.brescia.edu/bulibrary

Kentucky Wesleyan College Library • 3000 Frederica St, P.O. Box 1039 • Owensboro, KY 42302-1039 • (270) 852-3258 • http://www.kwc.edu/library

Owensboro Area Museum of History • 220 Daviess St • Owensboro, KY 42303 • (270) 687-2732 • http://www.owensboromuseum.com

West Central Kentucky Family Research Association • 3133 Commonwealth Ct, P.O. Box 1932 • Owensboro, KY 42302 • (270) 684-4150 • http://www.rootsweb.com/~kywckfra/

Owenton
Owen County Historical Society • Historical Museum, 106 N 2nd St • Owenton, KY 40359 • (502) 463-2633

Owen County Public Library • 118 N Main St • Owenton, KY 40359 • (502) 484-3450 • http://www.owentonky.com/LIBRARY/library.html

Owingsville
Bath County Memorial Library • 24 W Main St, P.O. Box 380 • Owingsville, KY 40360-0380 • (606) 674-2531 • http://bathcountylibrary.tripod.com

Paducah
Alben W Barkley Museum • 533 Madison St • Paducah, KY 42001 • (270) 443-0512

McCracken County Genealogical Society • 4640 Buckner Ln • Paducah, KY 42001

McCracken County Historical and Genealogical Society • c/o McCracken County Public Library, 555 Washington St, P.O. Box 7651 • Paducah, KY 42001 • (270) 442-2510

McCracken County Public Library • 555 Washington St • Paducah, KY 42003-1735 • (270) 442-2510 • http://www.mclib.net

Museum of the American Quilter's Society • 215 Jefferson, P.O. Box 1540 • Paducah, KY 42002 • (270) 442-8856 • http://www.quiltmuseum.org

River Heritage Museum • 117 S Water St • Paducah, KY 42001 • (270) 575-9958 • http://www.riverheritagemuseum.org

Tilghman Heritage Center • 1520 Monroe St • Paducah, KY 42001

Whitehaven Mansion Museum • Lone Oak Rd, P.O. Box 8265 • Paducah, KY 42002 • (270) 554-2077

William Clark Market House Museum • Market House Sq, 121 S 2nd St • Paducah, KY 42001 • (270) 443-7759

Paintsville
Big Sandy Valley Genealogical Society • 1215 Stafford Ave • Paintsville, KY 41240 • (606) 789-3416

Big Sandy Valley Historical Society • 319 FM Stafford Ave • Paintsville, KY 41240 • (606) 789-3416

Johnson County Historical and Genealogical Society • c/o Johnson County Public Library, 444 Main St, P.O. Box 788 • Paintsville, KY 41240 • (606) 789-4355 • http://www.rootsweb.com/~kyjchstjohnson.html

Paintsville, cont.

Johnson County Public Library & Museum • 444 Main St • Paintsville, KY 41240 • (606) 789-4355

Paintsville Historical Association • Historical Museum, P.O. Box 809 • Paintsville, KY 41240

Paris

Cane Ridge Meeting House Museum • 1655 Cane Ridge Rd • Paris, KY 40361 • (859) 987-5350 • http://www.ccinky.net/CaneRidge

Duncan Tavern Historic Center & Genealogical Library • 323 High St • Paris, KY 40361 • (859) 987-1788 • http://www.kentuckydar.org/johnfoxjrlibrary

Historic Paris-Bourbon • Historical Museum, 1181 Hill Rd • Paris, KY 40361

Hopewell Museum • 800 Pleasant St • Paris, KY 40361 • (859) 987-8107 • http://www.hopewellmuseum.org

John Fox Memorial Library • DAR Shrine, Duncan Tavern, 323 High St • Paris, KY 40361 • (859) 987-1788 • http://www.mindspring.com/~jogt/johnfoxjr.htm

Pembroke

Order of Americans of Armorial Ancestry • 426 S Main St, P.O. Box 339 • Pembroke, KY 42266-0339

Pendleton

Trimble County Historical Society • 2926 Patton's Creek • Pendleton, KY 40055 • http://www.ole.net/~maggie/trimble/histsoc.htm

Perryville

Perryville Battlefield Museum • 1825 Battlefield Rd, P.O. Box 296 • Perryville, KY 40468 • (859) 332-8631 • http://www.perryvillereenactment.org

Perryville Heritage Center • 216 S Buell St • Perryville, KY 40468-1024

Pikeville

Augusta Dils York House Museum • 209 Elm St, P.O. Box 2913 • Pikeville, KY 41502

Frank M Allara Library • Pikeville College, 214 Sycamore St • Pikeville, KY 41501-9042 • (606) 218-5605 • http://library.pc.edu

Pike County Public Library • 119 College St, Suite 3, P.O. Box 1197 • Pikeville, KY 41502-1197 • (606) 432-9977 • http://www.pikelibrary.org

Pike County Society for Historical and Genealogical Research • Historical Museum, P.O. Box 97 • Pikeville, KY 41502 • (606) 432-9371

Pineville-Bell County Public Library • Tennessee Ave & Walnut St, P.O. Box 1490 • Pineville, KY 40977-1490 • (606) 337-3422 • http://www.tcnet.net/~pinevillelib/

Pippa Passes

McGaw Library • Alice Lloyd College, 100 Purpose Rd • Pippa Passes, KY 41844 • (606) 368-6112 • http://www.alc.edu

Prestonsburg

Big Sandy Community & Technical College Library • 1 Bert T Combs Dr • Prestonsburg, KY 41653 • (606) 886-3863 • http://www.prestonsburgcc.edu

Floyd County Historical and Genealogical Society • P.O. Box 982 • Prestonsburg, KY 41653

Floyd County Public Library • 18 N Arnold Ave • Prestonsburg, KY 41653 • (606) 886-2981 • http://www.fclib.org

Princeton

Adsmore Musuem Museum • 304 N Jefferson St • Princeton, KY 42445 • (270) 365-3114 • http://www.adsmore.org

Caldwell County Historical Railroad Society • 116 Edwards St • Princeton, KY 42445 • (270) 365-0582

Caldwell County Historical Society • P.O. Box 1 • Princeton, KY 42445

Caldwell County Railroad Museum • 116 Edwards St • Princeton, KY 42445

George Coon Public Library • 114 S Harrison St, P.O. Box 230 • Princeton, KY 42445-0230 • (270) 365-2884

Prospect

Louisville Genealogical Society • Historical Museum, 3502 River Bluff Rd • Prospect, KY 40059

Quicksand

Breathitt County Historical Society • general delivery • Quicksand, KY 41363

Radcliff

Hardin County Library-North Branch • 800 S Logsdon Pkwy • Radcliff, KY 40160-1932 • (270) 351-9999 • http://www.hcpl.info

Ravenna

Estill County Historical and Genealogical Society • Historical Museum, 133 Broadway, P.O. Box 221 • Ravenna, KY 40472 • (606) 723-3806 • http://www.rootsweb.com/~kyestill/echgs.htm

Renfro Valley

Appalachian Pioneer Village Museum • Hummel Rd, P.O. Box 57 • Renfro Valley, KY 40473

Renfro Valley Museum • Hwy 25 • Renfro Valley, KY 40473

Richmond

Crabbe Library & University Archives • Eastern Kentucky Univ, 521 Lancaster Ave • Richmond, KY 40475-3102 • (859) 622-1792 • http://www.library.eku.edu

Fort Boonesborough Museum • 4375 Boonesboro Rd • Richmond, KY 40475 • (859) 527-3131 • http://www.kystateparks.com

Garrard County Historical Society • 128 Redwood • Richmond, KY 40475

Jonathan Truman Dorris Museum • Eastern Kentucky Univ • Richmond, KY 40475 • (859) 622-5585

Madison County Historical Society • Historical Museum, 126 Buckwood Dr, P.O. Box 5066 • Richmond, KY 40476-5066 • (859) 623-1398 • http://www.iclub.org/kentucky/madison/ history/

Madison County Public Library • 507 W Main St • Richmond, KY 40475 • (859) 623-6704 • http://madisonlibrary.org

Society of Boonesborough • P.O. Box 226 • Richmond, KY 40475 • (859) 623-3471 • http://www.rootsweb.ancestry.com/.../PioneersFtBoonesborough.htm

White Hall State Historic Site • 500 White Hall Shrine Rd • Richmond, KY 40475 • (859) 623-9178 • http://www.kystateparks.com/shthall.htm

Roark

Red Bird Missionary Conference, United Methodist Church • General Delivery • Roark, KY 40979 • (606) 374-6341

Russellville

Bibb House Museum • 183 W 8th St, P.O. Box 116 • Russellville, KY 42276 • (502) 726-2085

Hardy Memorial Museum • 296 S Main • Russellville, KY 42276

Historic Russellville • P.O. Box 116 • Russellville, KY 42276 • (270) 726-9501 • http://www.logantele.com/~loganhistory

Logan County Archives • Old County Jail, 278 W 4th St, P.O. Box 853 • Russellville, KY 42276 • (270) 726-8179

Logan County Genealogical Society • Old County Jail, 278 W 4th St, P.O. Box 853 • Russellville, KY 42276 • (270) 726-8179 • http://www.logancountygenealogicalsociety.org

Logan County Public Library • 201 W 6th St • Russellville, KY 42276 • (270) 726-6129 • http://www.loganlibrary.org

Southern Kentucky Past Finders • 1095 Sportsman Club Rd • Russellville, KY 42276 • (270) 726-6604

Salyersville
Magoffin County Genealogical Society • Pioneer Village, 191 S Church St, P.O. Box 222 • Salyersville, KY 41465 • (606) 349-2411 • http://www.rootsweb.ancestry.com/~kymhs/

Magoffin County Historical Society • 191 S Church St, P.O. Box 222 • Salyersville, KY 41465 • (606) 349-1607 • http://www.rootsweb.com/~kymhs/

Scottsville
Allen County History Society • Historical Museum, 301 N 4th St, P.O. Box 393 • Scottsville, KY 42164-1517 • (270) 237-3026 • http://www.rootsweb.com/~kyallen/Society.htm

Allen County Public Library • 106 W Main St • Scottsville, KY 42164 • (502) 237-3861

Shelbyville
Shelby County Historical Society • Historical Museum, P.O. Box 444 • Shelbyville, KY 40066-0444 • (502) 633-2767

Shelby County Library District • 309 8th St • Shelbyville, KY 40065 • (502) 633-3803 • http://www.scplibrary.net

Shepherdsville
Bullitt County Genealogical Society • c/o Bullitt County Public Library, 127 N Walnut St, P.O. Box 960 • Shepherdsville, KY 40165-0960 • (502) 538-6428 • http://www.bcplib.org/genealogy/

Bullitt County Public Library • 127 N Walnut St, P.O. Box 146 • Shepherdsville, KY 40165 • (502) 543-7675 • http://www.bcplib.org

Jefferson County Genealogical and Historical Society • P.O. Box 960 • Shepherdsville, KY 40165-0960

Slade
Gladdie Creek Cabin Museum • Red River Gorge Park • Slade, KY 40376 • (606) 663-2852

Smithland
Livingston County Historical and Genealogical Society • Historical Museum, 117 State St, P.O. Box 96 • Smithland, KY 42081 • (270) 928-4656

Somerset
Harold B Strunk Library • Somerset Community College, 808 Monticello St • Somerset, KY 42501 • (606) 679-8501 • http://www.somcc.kctcs.edu/library

Pulaski County Historical Society • Historical Museum, P.O. Box 36 • Somerset, KY 42502-0036 • (606) 679-8401 • http://www.rootsweb.com/~kypchs/

Pulaski County Public Library • 107 N Main St, P.O. Box 36 • Somerset, KY 42502-0036 • (606) 679-8401 • http://www.pcpl.lib.ky.us

South Shore
Greenup County Public Libraries-McKell Public • Rt 4, Box 330 • South Shore, KY 41175 • (606) 932-4478

South Union
Shaker Museum at South Union • 850 Shaker Museum Rd, P.O. Box 30 • South Union, KY 42283-0030 • (270) 542-4167 • http://www.logantele.com/~shakmus/

South Williamson
Hatfield-McCoy Historical Society • P.O. Box 2676 • South Williamson, KY 41503 • (606) 237-4646

Tug Valley Genealogical Society • P.O. Box 2676 • South Williamson, KY 41503 • (606) 237-4646

Springfield
Lincoln Homestead State Park • 5079 Lincoln Park Rd • Springfield, KY 40069 • (859) 336-7461 • http://www.state.ky.us/agencies/parks/linchome.htm

Washington County Genealogical Society • c/o Washington County Public Library, 210 E Main St • Springfield, KY 40069 • (859) 336-7655

Washington County Public Library • 210 E Main St • Springfield, KY 40069 • (859) 336-7655 • http://www.wcpl.ky.gov

Staffordsville
Mountain Homeplace Museum • 745 Ky Route 2275, P.O. Box 1850 • Staffordsville, KY 41256 • (606) 297-1850

Stanford
Harvey Helm Memorial Library • 301 3rd St • Stanford, KY 40484 • (606) 365-7513

Lincoln County Historical Society • Historical Museum, 315 W Main, P.O. Box 570 • Stanford, KY 40484 • (606) 365-2883

William Whitely House State Historic Site • 625 William Whitley Rd • Stanford, KY 40484 • (606) 355-2881 • http://www.parks.ky.gov/statehistoricsites/ww/

Stearns
Stearns Museum • P.O. Box 452 • Stearns, KY 42647

Summer Shade
Metcalfe County Historical Society • Route 1, Box 371 • Summer Shade, KY 42166 • (270) 428-3391

Taylorsville
Spencer County Historical and Genealogical Society • P.O. Box 266 • Taylorsville, KY 40071

Tompkinsville
Old Mulkey State Historic Site Museum • 1819 Old Mulkey Rd • Tompkinsville, KY 42167

Trappist
Abbey of Gethsemani Library • 3642 Monks Rd • Trappist, KY 40051 • (502) 549-3117 • http://www.monks.org

Union
Big Bone Lick State Park Museum • 3380 Beaver Rd • Union, KY 41091 • (859) 384-3522 • http://www.parks.ky.gov

Utica
Society of Kentucky Pioneers • 11129 Pleasant Ridge • Utica, KY 42376 • http://kinnexions.com/ancestries/pioneer/ky.htm

Valley Station
Southwest Jefferson County Historical Society • Historical Museum, 13700 Sandray Blvd • Valley Station, KY 40172

Van Lear
Van Lear Historical Society • Coal Museum, 78 Millers Creek Rd, P.O. Box 369 • Van Lear, KY 41265 • (606) 789-8540 • http://www.vanlear.org

Vanceburg
Lewis County Historical Society • Historical Museum, 318 Lexington Ave, P.O. Box 212 • Vanceburg, KY 41179-0212 • (606) 796-3778

Lewis County Public Library • 422 2nd St • Vanceburg, KY 41179 • (606) 796-2532

Versailles
Bluegrass Railway Museum • 175 Beasley Rd, P.O. Box 27 • Versailles, KY 40383 • (859) 873-2468 • http://www.bgrm.org

Jack Jouett House Museum • 255 Craigs Creek • Versailles, KY 40383 • (606) 873-7902

Logan-Helm Woodford County Public Library • 115 N Main St • Versailles, KY 40383-1289 • (859) 873-5191

Versailles, cont.
Woodford County Historical Society • Historical Museum, 121 Rose Hill • Versailles, KY 40383-1221 • (859) 873-6786 • http://www.woodfordkyhistory.org

Vine Grove
Ancestral Trails Genealogical Society • 127 W Main St, P.O. Box 573 • Vine Grove, KY 40175-0573 • (270) 877-2628 • http://www.aths.com

Ancestral Trails Historical Society • P.O. Box 573 • Vine Grove, KY 40175

Warfield
Martin County Historical Society • Historical Museum, P.O. Box 261 • Warfield, KY 41267

Warfield Historical Society • Historical Museum, P.O. Box 261 • Warfield, KY 41267

Warsaw
Fulton County Historical Society • Historical Museum, P.O. Box 1031 • Warsaw, KY 41095

Gallatin County Historical Society • Hawkins-Kirby House, P.O. Box 405 • Warsaw, KY 41095 • (859) 567-4591

Gallatin Public Library • 209 W Market St, P.O. Box 848 • Warsaw, KY 41095 • (859) 567-2786 • http://www.gallatincountypubliclibrary.org

Washington
Harriet Beecher Stowe Museum • Marshall Key House, P.O. Box 184 • Washington, KY 41096 • (606) 759-7411

Old Washington Museum • P.O. Box 227 • Washington, KY 41096

Wayland
Wayland Historical Society • 2662 KY Route 7 • Wayland, KY 41666 • (606) 358-9471

West Liberty
John F Kennedy Memorial Library • 408 Prestonburg St • West Liberty, KY 41472 • (606) 743-4151

Morgan Company Historical Society • 5973 Hwy 460 E • West Liberty, KY 41472 • (606) 743-2588

White Oak
Morgan County Historical Society • Historical Museum, HC 68, Box 154-22 • White Oak, KY 41472

Whitesburg
Harry Caudill Memorial Library • 220 Main St • Whitesburg, KY 41858 • (606) 633-7547 • http://www.users.kih.net/~hmclib/

Letcher County Historical and Genealogical Society • P.O. Box 312 • Whitesburg, KY 41858 • http://www.rootsweb.com/~kyletch/lchgs/lchgs.htm

Whitesburg Campus Library • Southeast Community College, 201 Long Ave • Whitesburg, KY 41858 • (606) 633-0279 • http://www.secc.kctcs.edu/library

Whitley City
McCreary County Public Library District • 6 N Main St, P.O. Box 8 • Whitley City, KY 42653-0008 • (606) 376-8738 • http://www.mccrearylibrary.org

Wickliffe
Ballard-Carlisle County Historical and Genealogical Society • c/o Ballard-Carlisle-Livingston Public Library, 410 Ohio St, P.O. Box 279 • Wickliffe, KY 42087 • (270) 335-5059 • http://www.ballardconet.com/bchgs/

Ballard-Carlisle-Livingston Public Library & Museum • 410 Ohio St • Wickliffe, KY 42087 • (270) 335-5039

Williamsburg
Whitley County Historical and Genealogical Society • 530 Main St • Williamsburg, KY 40769 • (606) 549-7089

Williamstown
Grant County Public Library • 201 Barnes Rd • Williamstown, KY 41097-9482 • (859) 824-2080

Wilmore
B L Fisher Library • Asbury Theological Seminary, 204 N Lexington Ave • Wilmore, KY 40390-1199 • (859) 858-2233 • http://www.asburyseminary.edu

Winchester
Bluegrass Heritage Museum • 217 S Main St, P.O. Box 147 • Winchester, KY 40391 • http://www.bgheritage.com

Clark County Historical Society • Historical Museum, 122 Belmont Ave • Winchester, KY 40391

Clark County Public Library • 370 S Burns Ave • Winchester, KY 40391 • (859) 744-5661

Holly Rood Clark Mansion Museum • 28 Beckner St • Winchester, KY 40391 • (606) 744-6616

Woodbury
Green River Museum • 108 N Church St • Woodbury, KY 42288 • (270) 526-6921 • http://www.woodburyky.com

LOUISIANA

Abbeville

Vermilion Parish Library-Cow Island • 19635 Columbus, P.O. Drawer 640 • Abbeville, LA 70511-0640 • (337) 642-5474

Vermillion Genealogical Society • 307 N Main St, P.O. Box 117 • Abbeville, LA 70511-0117 • (337) 893-1363

Vermillion Historical Society • P.O. Box 877 • Abbeville, LA 70510-0877 • (318) 893-7142

Vermillion Parish Library • 200 N Magdalen Sq, P.O. Drawer 640 • Abbeville, LA 70511 • (337) 893-2655 • http://www.vermilion.lib.la.us

Albany

Harrison County, Mississippi Historical Society • P.O. Box 1881 • Albany, LA 70711

Alexandria

Alexandria Historical and Genealogical Society • 503 Washington St • Alexandria, LA 71301 • (318) 487-8556

Ama Bontemps African-American Museum • 1327 3rd St • Alexandria, LA 71301 • (318) 473-4692

Central Louisiana Genealogical Society • P.O. Box 12206 • Alexandria, LA 71315-2006 • http://www.rootsweb.com/~laclgs/

Central Louisiana Historical Society • P.O. Box 841 • Alexandria, LA 71301-0841

James C Bolton Library • Louisiana State University at Alexandria, 8100 Hwy 71 S • Alexandria, LA 71302 • (318) 473-6442 • http://www.lsua.edu/academics/library/

Kent Plantation House • 3601 Bayou Rapides Rd • Alexandria, LA 71303 • (318) 487-5998 • http://www.kenthouse.org

Louisiana History Museum • 503 Washington St • Alexandria, LA 71301 • (318) 487-8556 • http://www.louisianahistorymuseum.org

Masonic Grand Lodge of Louisiana • 5746 Masonic Dr • Alexandria, LA 71315-2357 • (318) 443-5610 • http://new.la-mason.com

Rapides Parish Library • 411 Washington St • Alexandria, LA 71301 • (318) 445-2411 • http://www.rpl.org

Sons of the American Revolution, Louisiana Society • 3915 Maywood Dr • Alexandria, LA 71302-2626 • http://www.sar.org/lassar/

Amite

Amite City Museum • 101 SE Central Ave, P.O. Box 977 • Amite, LA 70422 • (504) 748-8615

Amite Genealogical Club • 200 E Mulberry St, P.O. Box 578 • Amite, LA 70422

Saint Helena Historical Society • Route 1, Box 131 • Amite, LA 70422-9415

Tangipahoa Parish Historical Society • 200 E Mulberry St • Amite, LA 70422-2524

Tangipahoa Parish Library • 200 E Mulberry St • Amite, LA 70422 • (985) 748-7559 • http://www.tangipahoa.lib.la.us

Anacoco

Vernon Historical and Genealogical Society • P.O. Box 159 • Anacoco, LA 71403-0159

Arcadia

Bienville Parish Library • 2768 Maple St • Arcadia, LA 71001-3699 • (318) 263-7410 • http://www.bienville.lib.la.us

Baker

Baker Heritage Center • 1606 Main St, P.O. Box 707 • Baker, LA 70704 • (225) 774-1776 • http://www.bakerheritagemuseum.org

Barksdale AFB

Barksdale Air Force Base Library • 744 Douhet Dr, Bldg 4244 • Barksdale AFB, LA 71110 • (318) 456-4182

Bastrop

Morehouse Parish Library • 524 E Madison, P.O. Box 232 • Bastrop, LA 71221-0232 • (318) 281-3683 • http://www.youseemore.com/morehouse

Snyder Museum • 1620 E Madison Ave • Bastrop, LA 71220 • (318) 281-8760

Baton Rouge

American Committee to Promote Studies of the History of the Habsburg Monarchy • Dept of History, Louisiana State Univ • Baton Rouge, LA 70803 • (225) 388-4471

Baton Rouge Genealogical and Historical Society • P.O. Box 80565, SE Sta • Baton Rouge, LA 70895-0565 • (985) 766-2609 • http://www.intersurf.com/~rcollins/brg.htm

Brec's Magnolia Mound Plantation • 2161 Nicholson Dr • Baton Rouge, LA 70802 • (225) 343-4955 • http://www.magnoliamound.org

Cajun Clickers Computer Club • 10120 Red Oak Dr • Baton Rouge, LA 70815 • (225) 273-7113 • http://www.clickers.org

Center for Political and Governmental History • Louisiana Secretary of State, 100 North Blvd • Baton Rouge, LA 70801 • (225) 342-0500

Daughters of the American Revolution, Louisiana Chapter • 2564 Donald Dr • Baton Rouge, LA 70809

Division of Historic Preservation • 666 N Foster Dr, P.O. Box 44247 • Baton Rouge, LA 70804-4247 • (225) 922-0358

East Baton Rouge Parish Library • 7711 Goodwood Blvd • Baton Rouge, LA 70806-7699 • (225) 231-3700 • http://www.ebr.lib.la.us

East Baton Rouge Parish Library-Bluebonnet Reg Branch • 9200 Bluebonnet Blvd • Baton Rouge, LA 70810 • (225) 763-2250

East Baton Rouge Parish Library-Centroplex • 120 St Louis St, P.O. Box 1471 • Baton Rouge, LA 70821-1471 • (225) 389-4967

Enchanted Mansion Museum • 190 Lee Dr • Baton Rouge, LA 70808 • (225) 769-0005 • http://www.enchantedmansion.org

Foundation for Historical Louisiana • 900 North Blvd • Baton Rouge, LA 70802-5728 • (985) 387-2464

Hill Memorial Library • Louisiana State Univ, Special Collections • Baton Rouge, LA 70803 • (225) 388-6568 • http://www.lib.lsu.edu/special/

Historic Textile & Costume College Museum • LSU, School of Human Ecology • Baton Rouge, LA 70803 • (225) 388-2403

John B Cade Library • Southern University, 167 Roosevelt Steptoe Ave • Baton Rouge, LA 70813 • (225) 771-4990 • http://www.lib.subr.edu

Le Comite des Archives de la Louisiane • 124 Main St, P.O. Box 44370, Capitol Sta • Baton Rouge, LA 70804-4730 • (225) 355-9906 • http://www.sos.louisiana.gov/archives/archives/archives-comite.htm

Los Islenos de Galvez Heritage and Cultural Society • 7437 Meadowbrook Ave • Baton Rouge, LA 70810-2014 • (225) 769-9456

Louisiana Dept of Culture, Recreation and Tourism • Office of State Parks, 1051 N 3rd St • Baton Rouge, LA 70802 • (225) 342-8111 • http://crt.g2ditigal.com/home.cfm

Louisiana Division of Historical Preservation • P.O. Box 44247 • Baton Rouge, LA 70804 • (225) 342-8160 • http://www.crt.state.la.us/crt/ocd/hp.lcdhp.htm

Louisiana Genealogical and Historical Society • P.O. Box 82060 • Baton Rouge, LA 70884-2060 • (225) 926-3929 • http://www.rootsweb.com/~la-lghs/lghs.htm

Louisiana Naval War Memorial • USS Kidd, 305 S River Rd • Baton Rouge, LA 70802 • (225) 342-1942 • http://www.premier.net/~uss_kidd/home.html

Louisiana

Baton Rouge, cont.

Louisiana State Archives and Records • 3851 Essen Ln, P.O. Box 94125 • Baton Rouge, LA 70804-9125 • (225) 922-1207 • http://www. sec.state.1a.us/archives/archives/archivesindex.htm

Louisiana State Library • 701 N 4th St, P.O. Box 131 • Baton Rouge, LA 70821-0131 • (225) 342-4913 • http://www.state.lib.la.us

Louisiana's Old State Capitol Museum • 100 North Blvd, P.O. Box 94125 • Baton Rouge, LA 70804 • (225) 342-0500 • http://www.sos. louisiana.gov

LSU Rural Life Museum • 4560 Essen Ln, P.O. Box 80498 • Baton Rouge, LA 70898 • (225) 765-2639 • http://appl027.lsu.edu/rlm/ rurallifeweb.nsf/index

Middleton Library - Archives and Manuscripts • Louisiana State Univ, 295 Middleton • Baton Rouge, LA 70803-3300 • (225) 578-8875 • http://www.lib.lsu.edu

Old Governor's Mansion Museum • 502 North Blvd • Baton Rouge, LA 70802 • (225) 344-5272

Robert A Bogan Fire Museum • 427 Laurel St • Baton Rouge, LA 70003 • (225) 344-8558 • http://www.383arts.org

Sons and Daughters of the Province and Republic of West Florida, 1763-1810 • P.O. Box 82672 • Baton Rouge, LA 70884-2672 • http:// homepages.xspedius.net/mmoore/lghs/sonsdau.htm

United States Civil War Center • Louisiana State Univ • Baton Rouge, LA 70803 • (225) 578-3151 • http://www.cwc.lsu.edu

University Baptist Church Library • 203 Leeward Dr • Baton Rouge, LA 70808 • (225) 766-9474 • http://www.ubc-br.org

USS Kidd & Nautical Center • 305 S River Rd • Baton Rouge, LA 70802 • (225) 342-1942

Benton

Bossier Restoration Foundation • 231 Merry Ln • Benton, LA 71006

Bermuda

Beau Fort Plantation Home Museum • 4078 Hwy 494 & Hwy 119 • Bermuda, LA 71456

Bernice

Bernice Historical Society • Depot Museum & Capt Henderson Caboose, 4th & Louisiana, P.O. Box 186 • Bernice, LA 71222 • (318) 285-9071 • http://www.bernicela.org

Bienville

Bienville Historical Society • Route 1, Box 9 • Bienville, LA 71008-9653

Blanchard

First Baptist Church Archives • 201 Attaway St, P.O. Box 65 • Blanchard, LA 71009-0065 • (318) 929-2346

Bogalusa

Washington Parish Library System, Bogalusa Branch • 304 Avenue F • Bogalusa, LA 70427 • (985) 735-1961

Bossier City

Bossier Parish Central Library & Historical Center • 2206 Becker St • Bossier City, LA 71111 • (318) 746-1693 • http://www.bossierlibrary.org

Bossier Parish Community College Library • 2719 Airline Dr • Bossier City, LA 71111 • (318) 746-9851 • http://www.bpcc.edu/library

Buras

Plaquemines Deep Delta Genealogical Society • c/o Plaquemines Parish Library, 35572 Hwy 11 • Buras, LA 70041 • (985) 657-7121

Plaquemines Parish Library • 35572 Hwy 11 • Buras, LA 70041 • (985) 657-7121 • http://www.plaquemines.lib.la.us

Cameron

Cameron Parish Historical and Genealogical Society • P.O. Box 1107 • Cameron, LA 70631

Cameron Parish Library • 498 Marshal St, P.O. Box 1130 • Cameron, LA 70631-1130 • (337) 775-5421 • http://www.cameron.lib.la.us

Carville

National Hansen's Disease Museum • 5445 Point Clair Rd • Carville, LA 70721 • (225) 642-1950 • http://www.hrsa.gov/hansens/museum

Chalmette

Chalmette Battlefield Library • Jean Lafitte National Historical Park & Preserve, 8606 W St Bernard Hwy • Chalmette, LA 70043 • (504) 281-0511 • http://www.nps.gov/jela

Nunez Community College Library • 3710 Paris Rd • Chalmette, LA 70043 • (504) 680-2602 • http://www.nunez.edu/library/ncclib.htm

Saint Bernard Parish Genealogical Society • P.O. Box 271 • Chalmette, LA 70044-0271 • (504) 271-0896 • http://www.ccugpc.org/ sbgs/sbgs.htm

Charenton

Chitimacha Tribe of Louisiana • Historical Museum, 343 Navarro St, P.O. Box 661 • Charenton, LA 70523

Church Point

Pointe de l'Eglise Historical and Genealogical Society • P.O. Box 160 • Church Point, LA 70525-0160

Clifton

Clifton Choctaw Tribe • 1312 Clifton Rd • Clifton, LA 71447 • (318) 793-4253

Clinton

Audubon Regional Library • Lawyers Row & Woodville St, P.O. Box 545A • Clinton, LA 70722-1565 • (225) 683-4290

Audubon Regional Library-East Feliciana • 12220 Woodville St, P.O. Box 8389 • Clinton, LA 70722 • (225) 634-7508

East Feliciana History Committee • P.O. Box 8341 • Clinton, LA 70722

Cloutierville

Kate Chopin House and Bayou Folk Museum • 243 Hwy 495 • Cloutierville, LA 71416 • (318) 379-2233

Colfax

Grant Genealogical Society • 300 Main St • Colfax, LA 71417-1830

Grant Parish Library • 300 Main St • Colfax, LA 71417-1830 • (318) 627-9920 • http://www.grant.lib.la.us

Columbia

Caldwell Parish Library • 211 Jackson, P.O. Box 1499 • Columbia, LA 71418-1499 • (318) 649-2259

Martin Homeplace Museum • 203 Martin Place Rd, P.O. Box 196 • Columbia, LA 71418 • (318) 649-2877

Schepis Museum • P.O. Box 743 • Columbia, LA 71418 • (318) 649-9931

Coushatta

Red River Heritage Association • Route 4, Box 363 • Coushatta, LA 71019-8730

Red River Parish Library • 2022 Alonzo, PO Box 1367 • Coushatta, LA 71019-1367 • (318) 932-1367

Covington

Saint Tammany Genealogical Society • c/o Saint Tammany Parish Library, 310 W 21st Ave, P.O. Box 1904 • Covington, LA 70433-3154 • (985) 893-6280 • http://www.stgsgenealogy.org

Saint Tammany Historical Society • c/o Saint Tammany Parish Library, 310 W 21st Ave • Covington, LA 70433 • (985) 893-6280

Saint Tammany Parish Library • 310 W 21st Ave • Covington, LA 70433 • (985) 871-1219 • http://www.sttammany.lib.la.us

Crowley

Acadia Parish Library • 1125 N Parkenson, P.O. Box 1509 • Crowley, LA 70526-1509 • (337) 788-1880 • http://www.acadia.lib.la.us

Crowley Historical Society • Rice Museum, W Hwy 90, P.O. Box 1176 • Crowley, LA 70527-1176 • (337) 783-6842

Crystal Rice Plantation Museum • 6428 Airport Rd, P.O. Box 1425 • Crowley, LA 70527 • (337) 783-6417 • http://www.crystalrice.com

Pointe d'Eglise: Acadia Genealogical and Historical Society • P.O. Box 497 • Crowley, LA 70527 • http://www.rootsweb.com/~lapehgs/

Cutoff

Les Memoirs du Bayou Lafourche • 121 W 111th St • Cutoff, LA 70345 • (504) 475-5757

Darrow

Tazcuco Plantation Museum • 3138 Hwy 44 • Darrow, LA 70725 • (225) 562-3929

De Ridder

Beauregard Historical Society • P.O. Box 658 • De Ridder, LA 70634-0658

Beauregard Parish Public Library • 205 S Washington Ave • De Ridder, LA 70634 • (337) 463-6217 • http://www.beau.lib.la.us

Delcambre

Vermilion Parish Library-Delcambre Branch • 206 W Main St • Delcambre, LA 70528-2918 • (337) 685-2388

Destrehan

German-Acadian Coast Historical and Genealogical Society • P.O. Box 517 • Destrehan, LA 70047-0517 • http://www.rootsweb.com/~lastjohn/geracadn.htm

River Road Historical Society • Historical Museum, 13034 River Rd, P.O. Box 5 • Destrehan, LA 70047-0005 • (985) 764-9345 • http://www.destrehanplantation.org

Saint Charles Historical Foundation • Historical Museum, P.O. Box 204 • Destrehan, LA 70047 • (504) 764-2698

Destrehen Plantation Museum • 13034 River Rd • Destrehen, LA 70047 • (504) 764-9315

Deville

Louisiana Czech Heritage Association • 14 Locker Rd • Deville, LA 71328-9318

Donaldsonville

Ascension Heritage Association • P.O. Box 1085 • Donaldsonville, LA 70346-1085

Ascension Parish Library-Donaldsonville Branch • 500 Mississippi St • Donaldsonville, LA 70346-2535 • (225) 473-8052 • www.ascension.lib.la.us/apl

Belle Alliance Plantation Museum • 7254 Hwy 308 • Donaldsonville, LA 70346 • (225) 474-3443

Historic Donaldsonville • Historical Museum, 318 Mississippi St, P.O. Box 1085 • Donaldsonville, LA 70346 • (225) 746-0004

Erath

Vermilion Parish Library-Erath Branch • 210 S Broadway • Erath, LA 70533-4004 • (337) 937-5628

Eunice

Arnold LeDoux Library • Louisiana State Univ at Eunice, P.O. Box 1129 • Eunice, LA 70535-1129 • (337) 550-1380 • http://www.lsue.edu

Eunice Depot Museum • 220 S CC Duson Dr • Eunice, LA 70535 • (318) 457-6540 • http://www.eunice-la.com/historic.html

Fort Polk

Allen Memorial Library • Bldg 400, 6880 Radio Rd • Fort Polk, LA 71459 • (337) 531-1987 • http://www.jrtc-polk.army.mil/library/

Fort Polk Military Museum • 917 S Carolina Ave, P.O. 3916 • Fort Polk, LA 71459-0916 • (337) 535-7905 • http://www.polk.army.mil

Franklin

Grevemberg House Museum • 407 Sterling Rd, P.O. Box 400 • Franklin, LA 70538 • (337) 828-2092 • http://www.grevemberghouse.com

Oaklawn Manor Museum • 3296 E Oaklawn Dr • Franklin, LA 70538 • (318) 838-0434

Saint Mary Parish Library • 206 Iberia St • Franklin, LA 70538-4906 • (337) 828-1624

Franklinton

Washington Parish Library System • 825 Free St • Franklinton, LA 70438 • (985) 839-7805

French Settlement

French Settlement Historical Society • P.O. Box 365 • French Settlement, LA 70733

Frogmore

Frogmore Plantation and Gins Museum • 11054 Hwy 84 • Frogmore, LA 71334 • (318) 757-2453

Galliano

Lafourche Parish Public Library-Cut Off Galliano Branch • Hwy 1 at W 154th St, P.O. Box 488 • Galliano, LA 70354-0488 • (985) 632-7140

Garyville

San Francisco Plantation Museum • River Rd • Garyville, LA 70051 • (504) 535-2341

Gibsland

Mount Lebanon Historical Society • Stage Coach Trail Museum, Route 2, Box 50 • Gibsland, LA 71028 • (318) 843-6455

Gilliam

Red River Crossroads Historical and Cultural Association • P.O. Box 322 • Gilliam, LA 71029 • (318) 296-4303

Red River Crossroads Museum • P.O. Box 159 • Gilliam, LA 71209 • (318) 296-4303

Golden Meadow

La Societie Des Cajuns • Les Memoirs du Bayou Lafourche, P.O. Box 581 • Golden Meadow, LA 70357-0581 • (504) 475-5757

Gonzales

Ascension Parish Library-Gonzales Branch • 708 S Irma Blvd • Gonzales, LA 70737 • (225) 647-3955 • http://www.ascension.lib.1a.us/apl

East Ascension Genealogical and Historical Society • P.O. Box 1006 • Gonzales, LA 70707-1006 • (225) 644-4547

River Road African American Museum • P.O. Box 1357 • Gonzales, LA 70707 • (225) 562-7703

Tee Joe Gonzales Museum • 1006 W Hwy 30 • Gonzales, LA 70737 • (225) 647-9566

Gramercy

Saint James Historical Society • P.O. Box 426 • Gramercy, LA 70052 • (504) 869-9752

Greenwell Springs

Christmas History of Louisiana • 7024 Morgan Rd • Greenwell Springs, LA 70739 • (985) 261-5515

Gretna

Gretna Historical Society • Historical Museum, 5 Lafayette St, P.O. Box 115 • Gretna, LA 70054-0115 • (504) 362-3854

Gueydan

Vermilion Parish Library-Gueydan Branch • 605 McMurtry St • Gueydan, LA 70542-4139 • (337) 536-6781

Louisiana

Hamburg
Commission des Avoyelles • P.O. Box 28 • Hamburg, LA 71339-0028 • (318) 964-2675

Hammond
Linus A Sims Memorial Library • Southeastern Louisiana Univ, 10896 SGA Dr • Hammond, LA 70402 • (985) 549-3860 • http://www.selu.edu/library/

Southeast Louisiana Historical Association • Southeastern Louisiana Univ, P.O. Box 789 • Hammond, LA 70401-0789 • (985) 549-3860

Harrisonburg
Catahoula Parish Library • Bushley St, P.O. Box 218 • Harrisonburg, LA 71340-0218 • (318) 744-5271 • http://www.catahoula.lib.la.us

Harvey
Jefferson Parish Library-West Bank Regional • 2751 Manhattan Blvd • Harvey, LA 70058 • (504) 364-3720

West Bank Genealogy Society • 2751 Manhattan Blvd, P.O. Box 872 • Harvey, LA 70058-0872 • (504) 364-3727 • http://groups.yahoo.com/group/WestBankGenealogySociety

Homer
Claiborne Historical Association • 931 N Main St • Homer, LA 71040

Claiborne Parish Library • 901 Edgewood Dr • Homer, LA 71040 • (318) 927-3845

Herbert S Ford Museum • 519 S Main St, P.O. Box 157 • Homer, LA 71040 • (318) 927-9190 • http://www.claiborneone.org/ford/

Houma
Terrebonne Genealogical Society • P.O. Box 20295 • Houma, LA 70360-0295 • (985) 876-2348 • http://www.rootsweb.com/laterreb/laterreb.htm

Terrebonne Historical and Cultural Society • Southdown Plantation Museum, 1208 Museum Dr, P.O. Box 2095 • Houma, LA 70360 • (985) 851-0154 • http://www.southdownmuseum.org

Terrebonne Parish Library • 151 Civic Center Blvd • Houma, LA 70361 • (985) 876-5861 • http://www.terrebonne.lib.la.us

Jackson
Jackson Assembly of the Felicianas • P.O. Box 494 • Jackson, LA 70748-0494 • (985) 634-7155

Rep of West Florida Historical Association • Historical Museum, P.O. Box 297 • Jackson, LA 70748

Jena
La Salle Museum • 1606 Front St, P.O. Box 2782 • Jena, LA 71342 • (318) 992-4475

LaSalle Parish Library • 221 N 1st St, P.O. Drawer 3199 • Jena, LA 71342-3199 • (318) 992-5675 • http://www.lasalle.lib.la.us

Jennings
Jefferson Davis Parish Library • 118 W Plaquemine St, P.O. Box 356 • Jennings, LA 70546 • (337) 824-1210 • http://www.beau.lib.la.us/jd.html

Jennings Carnegie Public Library • 303 Cary Ave • Jennings, LA 70546-5223 • (337) 821-5517

Jennings Genealogical Society • 136 Greenwood Dr • Jennings, LA 70546-4302

W H Tupper General Store Museum • 311 N Main St • Jennings, LA 70546 • (318) 821-5532

Jonesboro
Jackson Heritage Museum and Fine Arts Center • 515 Cooper Ave S • Jonesboro, LA 71251 • (318) 259-3119

Jackson Parish Library • 614 S Polk St • Jonesboro, LA 71251-3442 • (318) 259-5697 • http://www.jackson.lib.la.us

Kaplan
Le Musee de la Ville de Kaplan • general delivery • Kaplan, LA 70548 • (318) 643-1528

Vermilion Parish Library-Kaplan Branch • 815 N Cushing Ave • Kaplan, LA 70548-3315 • (337) 643-7209

Vermilion Parish Library-Vaugh-Copel Memorial Branch-Pecan Island • 28736 W LA Hwy 82 • Kaplan, LA 70548-9403 • (337) 737-2510

Kenner
Mardi Gras Museum • 415 Williams Blvd • Kenner, LA 70062 • (504) 468-7231 • http://www.rivertownkenner.com

Rivertown Museum • 405 Williams Blvd • Kenner, LA 70062 • (504) 468-7231

Kentwood
Tangipahoa Parish Historical Society • 77139 North River Rd • Kentwood, LA 70444-3841

Kinder
Allen Genealogical and Historical Society • P.O. Box 789 • Kinder, LA 70648

La Place
Saint John the Baptist Parish Library • 2920 Hwy 51 • La Place, LA 70068-3721 • (985) 652-6857 • http://www.stjohn.lib.la.us

Lacombe
Bayou Lacombe Rural Museum • P.O. Box 63 • Lacombe, LA 70445 • (504) 882-3043

Lafayette
Action Cadienne • P.O. Box 60104 • Lafayette, LA 70596-0104 • http://www.actioneadienne.org

Alexandre Mouton House Museum • 1122 Lafayette St • Lafayette, LA 70501 • (337) 234-2208

Attakpas Historical Association • c/o Edith Garland Dupre Library, Univ of Louisiana, 302 E Saint Mary Blvd, P.O. Box 43010 • Lafayette, LA 70504-3010 • (337) 482-6031 • http://www.usl.edu/departments/library

Edith Garland Dupre Library • Univ of Louisiana, 302 E Saint Mary Blvd, P.O. Box 40199 • Lafayette, LA 70504-0199 • (337) 482-6030 • http://www.louisiana.edu/InfoTech/Library/

Lafayette Genealogical Society • 1021 Rosedown Ln, P.O. Box 30293 • Lafayette, LA 70593-0293

Lafayette Historical Society • 324 N Sterling • Lafayette, LA 70501

Lafayette Public Library • 301 W Congress St, P.O. Box 3427 • Lafayette, LA 70501-6866 • (337) 261-5787 • http://www.lafayette.lib.la.us

Louisiana Folklore Society • Univ of Louisiana Lafayette, P.O. Box 44691 • Lafayette, LA 70504 • (337) 482-5493 • http://www.louisiana.edu

Louisiana Historical Association • Univ of Louisiana-Lafayette, P.O. Box 40831 USL • Lafayette, LA 70504-0831 • (337) 231-6029

Vermillion Historic Foundation • Vermillionville House Museum, 1600 Surrey St, P.O. Box 2266 • Lafayette, LA 70502-2266 • (337) 233-4077

Lafitte
Louisiana Marine Fisheries Museum • 580 Jean Lafitte Blvd • Lafitte, LA 70036

Lake Charles
Calcasieu Historical Preservation Society • 1635 Hodges St • Lake Charles, LA 70601-6016

Calcasieu Parish Public Library • 301 W Claude St • Lake Charles, LA 70605-3457 • (337) 475-8792 • http://www.calcasieu.lib.la.us

Imperial Calcasieu Museum • 204 W Sallier St • Lake Charles, LA 70601 • (337) 439-3797

Lether E Frazar Memorial Library • McNeese State University, 4205 Ryan St, P.O. Box 91445 • Lake Charles, LA 70609 • (337) 475-5725 • http://www.library.mcneese.edu

Southwest Louisiana Genealogical Society • P.O. Box 5652, Drew Sta • Lake Charles, LA 70606-5632 • (337) 447-3087 • http://homepages. xspedius.net/mmoore/caleasie/swlgs.htm

Southwest Louisiana Genealogy and History Library • 411 Pujo St • Lake Charles, LA 70601-4254 • (337) 437-3490 • http://www.calcasieu. lib.la.us/genealogy.htm

Southwest Louisiana Historical Association • 4201 Alma Ln • Lake Charles, LA 70605 • (318) 478-5753

Lake Providence
East Carroll Parish Library • 109 Sparrow St • Lake Providence, LA 71254-2645 • (318) 559-2615 • http://www.ecarroll.lib.la.us

Lake Providence Historical Society • 1002 S Lake St • Lake Providence, LA 71254-2428

Louisiana Cotton Museum • 7162 Hwy 65 N, P.O. Box 548 • Lake Providence, LA 71254 • (318) 559-2041

Lawtell
Matt's Museum • McClelland St & Hwy 190, P.O. Box 23 • Lawtell, LA 70550 • (337) 543-7223

Leesville
Museum of West Louisiana • 803 S 3rd St • Leesville, LA 71446-4703 • (337) 239-0927 • http://www.museumofwestla.org

Vernon Historical and Genealogical Society • 3713 Hwy 121 • Leesville, LA 71440-0310 • (318) 238-2963

Vernon Parish Library • 1401 Nolan Trace • Leesville, LA 71446-4331 • (337) 239-2027 • http://www.vernon.lib.la.us

Livingston
Edward Livingston Historical Association • P.O. Box 67 • Livingston, LA 70754-0067

Florida Parishes Genealogical Society • P.O. Box 520 • Livingston, LA 70754-0520

Livingston Parish Library • 13986 Florida Blvd, P.O. Drawer 397 • Livingston, LA 70754 • (225) 686-2436 • http://www.livingston.lib.la.us

Sumter County Tax Collector Archives • P.O. Box 277 • Livingston, LA 35470 • (205) 652-2424

Lockport
Bayou Lafourche Folklife and Heritage Museum • 110 Main St, P.O. Box 416 • Lockport, LA 70374 • (985) 532-5609

Logansport
Desoto Parish Library-Logansport Branch • 808 Main St, P.O. Box 970 • Logansport, LA 71049-0970 • (318) 697-2311

Long Leaf
Southern Forest Heritage Museum • Route 497, P.O. Box 101 • Long Leaf, LA 71448 • (318) 748-8404 • http://www.forestheritagemuseum. org

Luling
Saint Charles Parish Library • 105 Lakewood Dr, P.O. Box 949 • Luling, LA 70070-0949 • (985) 785-8471 • http://www.stcharles.lib.la.us

Lutcher
Saint James Parish Library • 1879 W Main St • Lutcher, LA 70071-9704 • (985) 869-3618 • http://www.stjames.lib.la.us

Madisonville
Lake Pontchartrain Basin Maritime Museum • 133 Mabel Dr • Madisonville, LA 70447 • (985) 845-9200 • http://www. lpbmaritimemuseum.org

Madisonville Heritage Center • 201 Cedar St • Madisonville, LA 70447

Mandeville
Saint Tammany Genealogical Society • P.O. Box 1001 • Mandeville, LA 70470-1001

Saint Tammany Historical Society • 129 Lamarque St, P.O. Box 1001 • Mandeville, LA 70470-1001

Mansfield
De Soto Historical Society and Genealogical Society • P.O. Box 447 • Mansfield, LA 71052-0447 • (318) 872-1591

De Soto Parish Library • 109 Crosby St • Mansfield, LA 71052 • (318) 872-6100

Mansfield State Historic Site Museum • 15149 Hwy 175 • Mansfield, LA 71052 • (318) 872-1474 • http://www.crt.state.la.us

Many
Sabine Parish Library • 750 Main St • Many, LA 71449-3199 • (318) 256-4150

Marksville
Avoyelles Parish Library • 101 N Washington St • Marksville, LA 71351-2496 • (318) 253-7559 • http://www.avoyelles.lib.la.us

Louisiana Roots • P.O. Box 383 • Marksville, LA 71351 • (318) 253-5413

Tunica-Biloxi Native American Museum • 150 Melancon Rd, P.O. Box 1589 • Marksville, LA 71351 • (318) 253-8174 • http://www.tunica.org

Marrero
Jefferson Parish Library-Belle Terre • 5550 Belle Terre Rd • Marrero, LA 70072 • (504) 349-5910

Marthaville
Rebel State Historic Site Museum • 1260 Hwy 1221 • Marthaville, LA 71450 • (318) 472-6255 • http://www.lastateparks.com

Maurice
Vermilion Parish Library-Maurice Branch • 100 E Joseph St, P.O. Box 127 • Maurice, LA 70555-0127 • (337) 893-5583

Melrose
Melrose Plantation Home Museum • Hwy 119 • Melrose, LA 71452 • (318) 379-0055

Saint Augustine Historical Society • P.O. Box 39 • Melrose, LA 71456 • (318) 357-0602 • http://members.tripod.com/creoles/

Merryville
Four Winds Tribe Louisiana Cherokee • P.O. Box 118 • Merryville, LA 70653 • (337) 825-8641

Metairie
Comite Lousiane Francaise • 2717 Massachusetts Ave • Metairie, LA 70003-5213 • (504) 469-2555

Jefferson Genealogical Society • P.O. Box 961 • Metairie, LA 70004-0961 • (504) 466-4711 • http://www.gnofn.org/~jgs/

Jefferson Parish Library • 4747 W Napoleon Ave • Metairie, LA 70010-7490 • (504) 838-1100 • http://www.jefferson.lib.la.us

Jewish Genealogical Society of New Orleans • 25 Waverly Pl, P.O. Box 7811 • Metairie, LA 70010-7811 • (504) 888-3817 • http://www. jewishgen.org/jgsno/

West Bank Regional Library • 2751 Manhattan Blvd • Metairie, LA 70058-6144 • (504) 364-2660

Minden
Dorcheat Historical Association of Webster Parish • P.O. Box 774 • Minden, LA 71055-0774

Germantown Commission Association • P.O. Box 389 • Minden, LA 71055-0389

Louisiana

Minden, cont.
Webster Parish Library • 521 East & West St • Minden, LA 71055 • (318) 371-3080 • http://www.webster.lib.la.us

Mobile
Immigration and Naturalization Office • P.O. Box 1526 • Mobile, LA 36633

Mongegut
Point au Chien Tribe • 793 Aragon Rd • Mongegut, LA 70377

Monroe
Aviation Historical Museum • 701 Kansas Ln, P.O. Box 13113 • Monroe, LA 71213 • (318) 361-9020

Joseph Biedenharn Home Museum • 2006 Riverside Dr • Monroe, LA 71201 • (318) 387-5281 • http://www.bmuseum.org

Monroe Genealogy Society • general delivery • Monroe, LA 71201

Northeast Louisiana Delta African American Heritage Museum • 503 Plum St, P.O. Box 168 • Monroe, LA 71210 • (318) 323-1167

Northeast Louisiana Genealogical Society • P. O. Box 7177 • Monroe, LA 71211-7177 • (318) 388-0619

Ouachita African-American Historical Society • Northeast Louisiana Delta African American Heritage Museum, P.O. Box 168 • Monroe, LA 71210 • (318) 323-1167

Ouachita Parish Public Library • 1800 Stubbs Ave • Monroe, LA 71201 • (318) 327-1490 • http://www.ouachita.lib.la.us

Sandel Library • Univ of Louisiana at Monroe, 700 University Ave • Monroe, LA 71209-0720 • (318) 342-1071 • http://www.ulm.edu/library

Montpelier
Saint Helena Historical Association • 6370 Hwy 43 • Montpelier, LA 70422-8227

Morgan City
Morgan City Public Library • 220 Everett St, P.O. Box 988 • Morgan City, LA 70380-0988 • (985) 380-4646

Saint Mary Genealogical and Historical Society • P.O. Box 662 • Morgan City, LA 70381-0662

Turn of the Century House Museum • P.O. Box 1218 • Morgan City, LA 70381 • (504) 380-4651

Young-Sanders Center Research Library & City Archives • Commercial St & Teche Dr, P.O. Box 595 • Morgan City, LA 70381 • (337) 413-1861 • http://www.youngsanders.org

Mount Lebanon
Mount Lebanon Historical Society • 2510 Hwy 517 • Mount Lebanon, LA 71028-4682 • (318) 843-1998

Napoleonville
Assumption Parish Library • 293 Mapoleon Ave • Napoleonville, LA 70390-2123 • (985) 369-7070 • http://www.assumption.lib.la.us

Natchez
Magnolia Plantation Home Museum • 5487 Hwy 119 • Natchez, LA 71421 • (318) 379-2221

Natchitoches
Bayou Folk Museum • P.O. Box 2248 • Natchitoches, LA 71457 • (318) 352-2994

Beau Fort Plantation Museum • P.O. Box 2300 • Natchitoches, LA 71457 • (318) 352-9580

Eugene P Watson Memorial Library • Northwestern State Univ, 913 College Ave • Natchitoches, LA 71497 • (318) 357-4574 • http://www.nsula.edu/watson_library/

Fort St Jean Baptiste State Historic Site Museum • 130 Monroe • Natchitoches, LA 71458 • (318) 357-3101 • http://www.crt.state.la.us

Founders of Natchitoches • 184 Moss Hill Terrace Rd, P.O. Box 3 • Natchitoches, LA 71457-0003 • (318) 357-1357

Immaculate Conception Catholic Church Museum • 145 Church St, P.O. Box 13 • Natchitoches, LA 71457 • (318) 352-3422

Lemee House Museum • 310 Jefferson St, P.O. Box 2248 • Natchitoches, LA 71457 • (318) 357-7907

Melrose Plantation Home Museum • P.O. Box 2248 • Natchitoches, LA 71457 • (318) 379-0055

Natchitoches Genealogical and Historical Association • 716 Callage Ave, P.O. Box 1349 • Natchitoches, LA 71458-1349 • (318) 357-2235 • http://www.rootsweb.com/~lanatchi.htm

Natchitoches Parish Library • 450 2nd St • Natchitoches, LA 71457-4699 • (318) 357-3280 • http://www.youseemore.com/Natchitoches/

Southern Studies Institute • Northwestern State Univ of Louisiana • Natchitoches, LA 71497-0001 • (318) 357-6195

New Brockton
Ma-Chis Lower Creek Indian Tribe • 708 S John St • New Brockton, LA 36351 • (334) 347-0373

New Iberia
Iberia Cultural Resources • 924 E Main St • New Iberia, LA 70560-3866

Iberia Parish Library • 445 E Main St • New Iberia, LA 70560-3710 • (337) 373-0075 • http://www.iberia.lib.la.us

Rip Van Winkle House Museum • 5505 Rip Van Winkle Rd • New Iberia, LA 70560 • (337) 359-8525 • http://www.ripvanwinklegardens.com

Shadows-on-the-Teche Plantation Museum • 317 E Main St • New Iberia, LA 70560 • (337) 369-6446 • http://www.shadowsontheteche.org

New Orleans
1850 House Museum • 523 Saint Anne St, P.O. Box 2448 • New Orleans, LA 70176 • (504) 568-6968

American-Italian Renaissance Foundation • 537 S Peters St, P.O. Box 2392 • New Orleans, LA 70176 • (504) 522-7294 • http://www.airf.org

Amistad Research Center • Tulane Univ, Tilton Hall, 6823 Saint Charles Ave • New Orleans, LA 70118-5698 • (504) 865-5535 • http://www.amistadresearchcenter.org

Beauregard-Keys House Museum • 1113 Chartres St • New Orleans, LA 70130 • (504) 523-7257

Blaine S Kern Library • Our Lady of Holy Cross College, 4123 Woodland Dr • New Orleans, LA 70131 • (504) 394-7744 • http://www.olhcc.edu

Confederate Museum • 929 Camp St • New Orleans, LA 70130 • (504) 523-4522 • http://www.confederatemuseum.com

Earl K Long Library • Univ of New Orleans - Lakefront Campus • New Orleans, LA 70148 • (504) 280-6556 • http://www.uno.edu

Fort Pike State Park Museum • Route 6, Box 194 • New Orleans, LA 70129 • (504) 662-5703 • http://www.crt.state.la.us

Friends of Cabildo • 701 Chartres St • New Orleans, LA 70115 • (504) 523-3939 • http://www.friendsofthecabildo.org

Gallier House Museum • 1118-32 Royal St • New Orleans, LA 70116 • (504) 525-5661 • http://www.hgghh.org

Genealogical Research Society of New Orleans • P.O. Box 51791 • New Orleans, LA 70151-1791 • (504) 488-1660 • http://www.rootsweb.com/~lagrsno/

Genealogy West • 5644 Abby Dr • New Orleans, LA 70131-3808 • (504) 393-8565

Genealogy West, West Bank of the Mississippi River • 5644 Abby Dr • New Orleans, LA 70131-3808 • (504) 393-8565

Greater New Orleans Archivists • c/o Amistad Research Center, Tulane Univ, 6823 Saint Charles Ave • New Orleans, LA 70118 • (504) 568-8577 • http://www.arc.tulane.edu

Hermann-Grima Historic House Museum • 820 St Louis St • New Orleans, LA 70112 • (504) 525-5661 • http://www.gnofn.org/~hggh; http://www.hgghh.org

Historic New Orleans Collection Library • William Research Center, 410 Chartres St • New Orleans, LA 70130-2102 • (504) 598-7171 • http://www.hnoc.org

Howard Tilton Library • Tulane University, 7001 Freret St • New Orleans, LA 70118-5682 • (504) 865-5131 • http://www.tulane.edu/~lmiller/

J Edgar & Louise S Monroe Library • Loyola University, 6363 Saint Charles Ave, P.O. Box 198 • New Orleans, LA 70118-0198 • (504) 864-7155 • http://library.loyno.edu

Jackson Barracks Military Library • Office of the Adjutant General, Bldg 53 • New Orleans, LA 70146 • (504) 278-8241 • http://www.army.mil

Jean Lafitte National Historic Park • 419 Decatur St • New Orleans, LA 70130-1142 • (504) 589-3882 • http://www.nps.gov/jela

Longue Vue House & Gardens Museum • 7 Bamboo Rd • New Orleans, LA 70124 • (504) 488-5488 • http://www.longuevue.com

Los Islenos Heritage and Cultural Society • Historical Museum, 206 Decatur St • New Orleans, LA 70130 • (504) 524-1659

Louisiana Archives and Manuscripts Association • P.O. Box 17203 • New Orleans, LA 70151-1213 • (225) 578-6529 • http://home.gnofn.org/~noplilinks/archives/lama.htm

Louisiana Colonials • 5 S Lark St • New Orleans, LA 70124 • (504) 282-3553

Louisiana Historical Society • Maritime Bldg, 5801 St Charles Ave • New Orleans, LA 70115-5053 • (504) 588-9044

Louisiana Jewish Historical Society • Temple Sinai, 6227 St Charles Ave • New Orleans, LA 70118

Louisiana State Museum and Historic Center Library • 751 Chartres St, P.O. Box 2448 • New Orleans, LA 70176-2448 • (504) 568-8214 • http://lsm.crt.state.la.us

Louisiana Vital Records Registry • 325 Loyola Ave, Rm 102, P.O. Box 60630 • New Orleans, LA 70160-0630 • (504) 568-5152 • http://oph.dhh.state.la.us/recordsstatistics/vitalrecords/

Moss Memorial Library • Delgado Community College, 615 City Park Ave • New Orleans, LA 70119 • (504) 483-4119 • http://www.dcc.edu/library

Multicutural Genealogical Society • 4310 St Anthony Ave • New Orleans, LA 70122-3104

National D-Day Museum • 945 Magazine St • New Orleans, LA 70130 • (504) 527-6012 • http://www.ddaymuseum.org

New Orleans Conservation Guild • Historical Museum, 4101 Burgundy St • New Orleans, LA 70117 • (504) 944-7900

New Orleans Fire Department Museum • 1135 Washington St • New Orleans, LA 70130 • (504) 896-4756 • http://www.nofd.com

New Orleans Pharmacy Museum • 514 rue Chartres • New Orleans, LA 70130-2110 • (504) 565-8027 • http://www.pharmacymuseum.org

New Orleans Public Library and City Archives • 219 Loyola Ave • New Orleans, LA 70112-2044 • (504) 596-2610 • http://www.nutrias.org

Pilot House Museum • 1440 Moss St • New Orleans, LA 70119 • (504) 482-1312 • http://www.pilothouse.org

Plantation Society in the Americas • Dept of History, Univ of New Orleans • New Orleans, LA 70148 • (504) 280-6886

Preservation Resource Center • 923 Tchoupitoulas St • New Orleans, LA 70130-3819 • (504) 581-7032 • http://www.prcno.org

Saint-Dominique Special Interest Group • 1514 Saint Roch Ave • New Orleans, LA 70117-8347 • (504) 944-4908

Save Our Cemeteries • 2520 Pyrtania St • New Orleans, LA 70130 • (504) 282-0125

Society of the Founders of the City of New Orleans • 2818 Palmer Ave • New Orleans, LA 70118 • (504) 866-5809

University of New Orleans Museum • 2000 Lakeshore Dr • New Orleans, LA 70148 • (504) 280-5544

Will W Alexander Library • Dillard University, 2601 Gentilly Blvd • New Orleans, LA 70122-3097 • (504) 816-7486 • http://www.dillard.edu

Xavier University of Louisiana Library • 1 Drexel Dr • New Orleans, LA 70125-1098 • (504) 520-7305 • http://www.xula.edu/Library_Services/library.html

New Roads
Le Circle Historique, Pointe Coupee Parish • 734 W Main St • New Roads, LA 70760-3522 • (225) 638-7733

Pointe Coupee Historical Society • 500 W Main St, P.O. Box 462 • New Roads, LA 70760

Pointe Coupee Museum • 8348 False River Rd • New Roads, LA 70760 • (225) 638-7788

Pointe Coupee Parish Library • 201 Claiborne St • New Roads, LA 70760-3403 • (225) 638-7593 • http://www.pointe-coupee.lib.la.us

Oak Grove
West Carroll Parish Library • 101 Marietta St, P.O. Box 703 • Oak Grove, LA 71263-0703 • (318) 428-4100

Oberlin
Allen Parish Library • 320 S 6th St, P.O. Box 400 • Oberlin, LA 70655-0400 • (337) 639-4315 • http://www.allen.lib.la.us

Oil City
Oil City Historical Society • Historical Museum, 207 S Land Ave, P.O. Box 897 • Oil City, LA 71061 • (318) 995-6845 • http://www.sos.louisiana.gov

Opelousas
Imperial-Saint Landry Genealogy and Historical Society • P.O. Box 108 • Opelousas, LA 70571-0108 • (337) 942-3332 • http://www.imperialstlandry.org

Louisiana Genealogical Seminar • Route 4, Box 478 • Opelousas, LA 70750

Opelousas Historical Society • Opelousas Museum, 329 N Main St, P.O. Box 712 • Opelousas, LA 70571-0712 • (318) 948-2589 • http://www.cityofopelousas.com

Opelousas-Eunice Public Library • 249 E Grolee St, P.O. Box 249 • Opelousas, LA 70570 • (337) 948-3693 • http://www.opelousas.lib.la.us

Patterson
Louisiana State Museum - Patterson • 394 Airport Cr, P.O. Box 38 • Patterson, LA 70392 • (504) 395-7067

Wedell-Williams Memorial Aviation Museum • 394 Airport Circle Rd • Patterson, LA 70392

Pineville
Richard W Norton Memorial Library • Louisiana College, 1140 College Blvd • Pineville, LA 71359 • (318) 487-7201 • http://norton.lacollege.edu/lacollege/

Plaquemine

Association for Preservation and Promotion of Iberville Parish • 602 Main St • Plaquemine, LA 70764 • (985) 687-8496

Iberville Museum • 57735 Main St, P.O. Box 701 • Plaquemine, LA 70764 • (225) 687-7197

Iberville Parish Library • 1501 J Gerald Berret Blvd, P.O. Box 736 • Plaquemine, LA 70765-0736 • (225) 687-4397 • http://www.iberville.lib.la.us

Plaquemine Lock State Historic Site • 57730 Main St • Plaquemine, LA 70764 • (225) 687-7158

Port Allen

West Baton Rouge Genealogical Society • Historical Museum, P.O. Box 1126 • Port Allen, LA 70767-1126 • (224) 343-8417 • http://www.westbatonrougemuseum.com

West Baton Rouge Historical Association • Historical Museum, 845 N Jefferson St • Port Allen, LA 70767-2417 • (985) 383-2422 • http://www.westbatonrougemuseum.com

West Baton Rouge Parish Library • 830 N Alexander St • Port Allen, LA 70767-2327 • (225) 342-7920 • http://www.wbr.lib.la.us

Rayne

Bernard-Bertrand House Museum • 1023 The Boulevard, P.O. Box 69 • Rayne, LA 70578 • (337) 334-8347

Rayne Historical Association • 110 W South 1st St • Rayne, LA 70578-5844

Rayville

Richland Parish Library • 1410 Louisa St • Rayville, LA 71269-3299 • (318) 728-4806 • http://www.richland.lib.la.us

Reserve

San Francisco Plantation Museum • P.O. Drawer AX • Reserve, LA 70084 • (504) 535-2341

Robeline

Adais Caddo • 4500 Hwy 85 • Robeline, LA 71469 • (318) 472-8680

Ruston

Lincoln Parish Library • 910 N Trenton St • Ruston, LA 71270 • (318) 251-5030 • http://www.lincoln.lib.la.us

Lincoln Parish Museum • 609 N Vienna St • Ruston, LA 71270 • (318) 251-0018

Lincoln Parish Museum and Historical Society • Historical Museum, 609 N Vienna St, P.O. Drawer F • Ruston, LA 71270 • (318) 251-0018

North Louisiana Genealogical Society • c/o Lincoln Parish Library, 509 W Alabama, P.O. Box 324 • Ruston, LA 71270-0324 • (318) 251-5030

North Louisiana Military Museum • 201 Memorial Dr • Ruston, LA 70170 • (318) 255-5999

Prescott Memorial Library • Louisiana Tech Univ, P.O. Box 10408 • Ruston, LA 71272 • (318) 257-3555 • http://www.latech.edu/tech/library

University Museum • Louisiana Tech • Ruston, LA 71272 • (318) 257-2264

Saint Francisville

Audubon State Historic Site Museum • Louisiana State Hwy 965, P.O. Box 546 • Saint Francisville, LA 70775 • (225) 635-3739 • http://www.crt.state.la.us

Oakley Plantation House Museum • Audubon State Commemorative Area, P.O. Box 546 • Saint Francisville, LA 70775 • (225) 635-3739

West Feliciana Historical Society • Historical Museum, Ferdinand St, P.O. Box 338 • Saint Francisville, LA 70775 • (985) 635-6330

West Feliciana Parish Public Library • 11865 Ferdinand St, P.O. Box 3120 • Saint Francisville, LA 70775-3120 • (225) 634-7508

Saint Joseph

Tensas Parish Library • 135 Plank Rd, P.O. Box 228 • Saint Joseph, LA 71366-0228 • (318) 766-3781

Saint Martinville

Longfellow Evangeline State Historic Site Museum • 1200 N Main St • Saint Martinville, LA 70582 • (337) 394-3754 • http://www.lastateparks.com

Maison Olivier Museum • 1200 N Main St • Saint Martinville, LA 70582 • (318) 394-3754

Saint Martin Parish Library • 201 Porter St, P.O. Box 79 • Saint Martinville, LA 70582 • (337) 394-2207 • http://www.stmartin.lib.la.us

Saint Rose

La Branche Plantation Museum • 11244 River Rd • Saint Rose, LA 70087 • (504) 468-8843 • http://www.labrancheplantation.com

Shreveport

Ark-La-Tex Antique and Classic Vehicle Museum • 601 Spring St, P.O. Box 5040 • Shreveport, LA 71101

Ark-La-Tex Genealogical Association • P.O. Box 4463 • Shreveport, LA 71134-0463 • (318) 868-0036 • http://www.rootsweb.com/~laaltga

Friends of Genealogy • P.O. Box 17835 • Shreveport, LA 71138-0835 • (318) 424-7648

GENCOM PC User Group of Shreveport • 9913 Dagger Point • Shreveport, LA 71115 • http://www.softdisk.com/comp/gencom

Grindstone Bluff Museum • 875 Cotton St • Shreveport, LA 71101 • (318) 222-3325

Historic Preservation of Shreveport • P.O. Box 857 • Shreveport, LA 71162 • (318) 221-3334

John F Magale Library • Centenary College of Louisiana, 2834 Woodlawn St, P.O. Box 41188 • Shreveport, LA 71134-1188 • (318) 869-5058 • http://www.centenary.edu/library

Louisiana State Exhibit Museum • 3015 Greenwood Rd, P.O. Box 38356 • Shreveport, LA 71109 • (318) 632-2020 • http://www.sos.louisiana.gov

Mississippi Memories Society • P.O. Box 18991 • Shreveport, LA 71138

Noel Memorial Library • Louisiana State University in Shreveport, 1 University Pl • Shreveport, LA 71115-2399 • (318) 798-5068 • http://www.lsus.edu/library/

North Louisiana Historical Association • P.O. Box 6701 • Shreveport, LA 71106-6701 • (318) 797-5337

Pioneer Heritage Center • LSU-Shreveport, 1 University Pl • Shreveport, LA 71115 • (318) 797-5332 • http://www.lsus.edu/comm/social.htm

R W Norton Art Gallery Library • 4747 Creswell Ave • Shreveport, LA 71106 • (318) 865-4201

Red River Regional Studies Center • 1 University Pl, Bronson Hall 106 • Shreveport, LA 71115-2399 • (318) 797-5332

Shreve Memorial Library • 424 Texas St, P.O. Box 21523 • Shreveport, LA 71120-1523 • (318) 226-5894 • http://www.shreve-lib.org

Shreve Memorial Library-Broadmoor • 1212 Captain Shreve Dr • Shreveport, LA 71105 • (318) 869-0120 • http://www.shreve-lib.org/images/genealogy.htm

Shreveport Campus Library • Southern University at Shreveport, 3050 Martin Luther King Jr Dr • Shreveport, LA 71107 • (318) 674-3400 • http://www.susla.edu

Shreveport Exhibit Museum • 3015 Greenwood Rd • Shreveport, LA 71109 • (318) 632-2020 • http://www.sec.state.la.us/museums/shreve/shreveindex.htm

Southern Genealogical Institute • 9418 Shartel Dr • Shreveport, LA 71118

Sports Museum of Champions • P.O. Box 1723 • Shreveport, LA 71166 • (318) 221-0712

Spring Street Historical Museum • 525 Spring St • Shreveport, LA 71101 • (318) 686-1388 • http://www.springstreetmuseum.com

Stephens African American Museum • 2810 Lindlohm • Shreveport, LA 71108 • (318) 635-2147

United Daughters of the Confederacy, Louisiana Chapter • 3413 Fernwood Ln • Shreveport, LA 71108-5113 • (318) 686-3112

Slidell

Slidell Cultural Center • 444 Erlanger St, P.O. Box 828 • Slidell, LA 70459 • (985) 646-4200 • http://www.slidell.la.us

Slidell Museum • 2020 1st St, P.O. Box 828 • Slidell, LA 70459 • (985) 646-4380 • http://www.slidell.la.ur

Sorrento

Cajun Village Museum • 6482 Hwy 22 • Sorrento, LA 70778 • (800) 460-6815

South Buras

Plaquemines Parish Genealogical Society • 203 Highway 11 • South Buras, LA 70041 • (985) 657-7121

Starks

Starks Historical Society • 308 Old River Rd • Starks, LA 70661

Sulphur

Brimstone Historical Society • Brimstone Museum, 800 Picard Rd, P.O. Box 242 • Sulphur, LA 70663-4362 • (337) 527-7142 • http://www.brimstonemuseum.org

Tallulah

Madison Parish Historical Society • Historical Museum, 400 N Mulberry St, P.O. Box 268 • Tallulah, LA 71282-4202 • (318) 574-3542

Madison Parish Library • 403 N Mulberry St • Tallulah, LA 71282 • (318) 574-4308 • http://www.madison.lib.la.us

Thibodaux

Allen J Ellender Memorial Library • Nicholls State University, Leighton Dr, P.O. Box 2028 • Thibodaux, LA 70310 • (985) 448-4646 • http://www.nicholls.edu/library

Edward Douglas White Historic Site Museum • 2295 LA Hwy 1, P.O. Box 5932 • Thibodaux, LA 70302 • (985) 447-0915

Lafourche Heritage Society • 412 Menard St, P.O. Box 913 • Thibodaux, LA 70392-0567

Lafourche Parish Library • 303 W 5th St • Thibodaux, LA 70301 • (985) 446-1163 • http://www.lafourche.lib.la.us

Lafourche Parish Public Library-Martha Sowell Utley Memorial • 314 St Mary St • Thibodaux, LA 70301 • (985) 447-4119 • http://www.lafourche.org/newsite/branches/thibodaux.html

Trout

Lasalle Art and Genealogical Association • Route 1, Box 234 • Trout, LA 71371 • (318) 992-6210

Vacherie

Laura: A Creole Plantation Museum • 2247 Hwy 18 • Vacherie, LA 70090 • (504) 265-6590 • http://www.lauraplantation.com

Oak Allen Plantation Museum • 3645 Hwy 18 • Vacherie, LA 70090 • (504) 265-2151

Ville Platte

Evangeline Genealogical and Historical Society • P.O. Box 664 • Ville Platte, LA 70586-0664 • (318) 599-2047

Evangeline Parish Library • 242 W Main St • Ville Platte, LA 70586 • (337) 363-1369 • http://www.eplibrary.org

Vivian

Historical Society of North Caddo • Historical Museum, 100 SW Front St, P.O. Box 31 • Vivian, LA 71082 • (318) 375-5300 • http://pages.prodigy.net/scollier/hsne/

Washington

Washington Museum • 402 N Main St, P.O. Box 597 • Washington, LA 70589 • (337) 826-3627

West Monroe

Ouachita Genealogical Society • 221 Riverbend • West Monroe, LA 71292-3627

White Castle

Nottoway Plantation Museum • 30970 Hwy 405, P.O. Box 160 • White Castle, LA 70788 • (504) 545-2730

Winnfield

Winn Parish Genealogical and Historical Society • P.O. Box 652 • Winnfield, LA 71483-0652 • (318) 628-6768 • http://www.rootsweb.com/~lawpgha/

Winn Parish Library • 204 W Main St • Winnfield, LA 71483-2718 • (318) 628-4478 • http://www.winn.lib.la.us

Winnfield Historical Society • P.O. Box 1039 • Winnfield, LA 71483

Winnsboro

Franklin Parish Genealogical and Historical Society • Route 4, Box 150 • Winnsboro, LA 71295

Franklin Parish Library • 705 Prairie St • Winnsboro, LA 71295 • (318) 435-4336 • http://www.franklin.lib.la.us

Zachary

Biloxi Chitimacha • P.O. Box 856 • Zachary, LA 70791 • (225) 658-0055

Zachary Historic Village Museum • 4524 Virginia St • Zachary, LA 70791 • (225) 933-3261

Zwolle

Chictaw-Apache Community of Ebarb • 35 Lonnie Rd, P.O. Box 1428 • Zwolle, LA 71486 • (318) 645-2588 • http://www.choctaw-apache.org

Louisiana

Abbot
Abbot Historical Society • Historical Museum, P.O. Box 65 • Abbot, ME 04406

Acton
Acton-Shapleigh Historical Society • P.O. Box 545 • Acton, ME 04001-0545 • (207) 636-2606 • http://www.actonmaine.com/histscty.htm

Albion
Albion Historical Society • P.O. Box 68 • Albion, ME 04910 • http://www.albionmaine.org

Alexander
Alexander-Crawford Historical Society • 216 Pokey Rd • Alexander, ME 04694 • (207) 454-7476 • http://www.mainething.com/achs.htm

Alna
Alna Historical Society • Old Alna Meeting House, Rte 218 • Alna, ME 04535 • (207) 586-6928

Wiscasset, Waterfille & Farmington Railway Museum • 97 Cross Rd, P.O. Box 242 • Alna, ME 04535 • (207) 563-2516 • http://www.wwfry.org

Andover
Andover Historical Society • general delivery • Andover, ME 04216

Anson
Anson Historical Society • Historical Museum, Main St, P.O. Box 572 • Anson, ME 04911 • (207) 635-2231 • http://www.rootsweb.com/~meahs/ahsindex.html

Appleton
Mildred Stevens Williams Memorial Library • 2957 Sennebec Rd • Appleton, ME 04862 • (207) 785-5656

Ashland
Ashland Community Library • 57 Exchange St, P.O. Box 639 • Ashland, ME 04732-0639 • (207) 435-6532

Ashland Logging Museum • Garfield Rd, P.O. Box 866 • Ashland, ME 04732 • (207) 435-6039

Town of Ashland • 17 Bridgham St, P.O. Box 910 • Ashland, ME 04732 • (207) 435-2311 • http://www.townofashland.com

Athens
Athens Historical Society • Academy St • Athens, ME 04912-4640

Auburn
Androscoggin Historical Society • Historical Museum, County Bldg, 2 Turner St • Auburn, ME 04210 • (207) 784-0586 • http://www.rootsweb.com/~meandrhs/

Auburn Public Library • 49 Spring St • Auburn, ME 04210 • (207) 782-3191 • http://www.auburnpubliclibrary.org

Augusta
Bennett D Katz Library • University of Maine at Augusta, 46 University Dr • Augusta, ME 04330-9410 • (207) 621-3348 • http://www.uma.maine.edu/libraries/indexa.html

Blaine House Museum • 192 State St • Augusta, ME 04330 • (207) 287-2121

Kennebec Historical Society • 61 Winthrop St, P.O. Box 5582 • Augusta, ME 04332-5582 • (207) 622-7718 • http://www.kennebechistorical.org

Le Club Calumet, Genealogical Section • P.O. Box 110 • Augusta, ME 04330-0110

Maine Dept of Human Services - Vital Statistics • 221 State St, 11 State House Station • Augusta, ME 04333-0111 • (207) 287-3181 • http://www.vitalrec.com/me.html

Maine Military Historical Society • Historical Museum, Camp Keyes, Upper Winthrop St • Augusta, ME 04330 • (207) 626-4338 • http://www.me.ngb.army.mil

Maine State Archives • 84 State House Station • Augusta, ME 04330-0084 • (207) 287-5795 • http://www.state.me.us/sos/arc/general/admin/mawww00l.htm

Maine State Library • 64 State House, Station • Augusta, ME 04333 • (207) 287-5620 • http://www.state.me.us/msl/

Maine State Museum • LMA Bldg, 83 State House Station • Augusta, ME 04333-0083 • (207) 287-2301 • http://www.mainestatemuseum.org

Old Fort Museum • 16 Cony Street • Augusta, ME 04330 • (207) 626-2385 • http://www.oldfortwestern.org

Baileyville
Woodland Public Library • 169 Main St, P.O. Box 549 • Baileyville, ME 04694-0549 • (207) 427-3235

Bancroft
Town of Bancroft • 18 School House Rd • Bancroft, ME 04497 • (207) 456-7542 • http://www.maine.gov/local/aroostook/bancroft

Bangor
Bangor Historical Society • Historical Museum, 159 Union St • Bangor, ME 04401 • (207) 942-5766 • http://www.bangormuseum.org

Bangor Public Library • 145 Harlow St • Bangor, ME 04401-1802 • (207) 947-8336 • http://www.bpl.lib.me.us

Cole Land Transportation Museum • 405 Perry Rd • Bangor, ME 04401 • (207) 990-3660 • http://www.colemuseum.org

Hose 5 Fire Museum • 247 State St • Bangor, ME 04401 • (207) 941-3229 • http://www.bgrme.org/bangorfire

Isaac Farrar Mansion Museum • 17 2nd St • Bangor, ME 04401 • (207) 941-2808

Maine Aviation Historical Society • 99 Maine Ave • Bangor, ME 04401 • (207) 941-6757

Bar Harbor
Abbe Museum • 26 Mount Desert St, P.O. Box 286 • Bar Harbor, ME 04609-0286 • (207) 288-3519 • http://www.abbemuseum.org

Acadia National Park Research Center • Route 233, Eagle Lake Rd, P.O. Box 177 • Bar Harbor, ME 04609 • (207) 288-5459 • http://www.nps.gov/htdocs2/acad/home.htm

Bar Harbor Historical Society • Historical Museum, 33 Ledgelawn Ave • Bar Harbor, ME 04609 • (207) 288-4245 • http://www.barharborhistorical.org

Jesup Memorial Library • 34 Mount Desert St • Bar Harbor, ME 04609 • (207) 288-4245

Sawtelle Research Center • Route 233, Eagle Lake Rd, P.O. Box 177 • Bar Harbor, ME 04609 • (207) 288-8729 • http://www.nps.gov/acad/home.html

Bar Mills
Berry Memorial Library • 4A Main St, P.O. Box 25 • Bar Mills, ME 04004-0025 • (207) 929-5484

Bass Harbor
Hancock County Genealogical Society • P.O. Box 243 • Bass Harbor, ME 04653 • http://ellsworthme.org/hcgs

Bath
Bath Historical Society • c/o Patten Free Library, 33 Summer St • Bath, ME 04530-2687 • (207) 443-5141 • http://www.biddeford.com/~pfl/shgr.htm

Maine Maritime Museum • 243 Washington St • Bath, ME 04530 • (207) 443-1316 • http://www.mainemaritimemuseum.org

Patten Free Library • 33 Summer St • Bath, ME 04530 • (207) 443-5141 • http://www.patten.lib.me.us

Sagadahoc Preservation Museum • 880 Washington St • Bath, ME 04530 • (207) 443-2174

Bath, cont.
Sagadahoc Preservation • 804 Washington St, P.O. Box 322 • Bath, ME 04530

Beals
Beals Historical Society • P.O. Box 280 • Beals, ME 04611

Belfast
Belfast Free Library • 106 High St • Belfast, ME 04915-1799 • (207) 338-3884 • http://www.belfastlibrary.org

Belfast Historical Society • Historical Museum, 10 Market St • Belfast, ME 04915 • (207) 338-9229 • http://www.belfastmuseum.org

Belfast Historical Society • Ivy House, 7 Park St • Belfast, ME 04915 • (207) 338-3403

Morrill Historical Society • Route 3, Box 585 • Belfast, ME 04915 • (207) 338-1405

Belmont
Greene Plantation Historical Society • Greer's Corner, 169 Howard Rd • Belmont, ME 04952 • (207) 342-5208 • http://www.lincolnvillehistory. org/green/green.html

Berwick
Berwick Historical Society • P.O. Box 904 • Berwick, ME 03901-0904

Berwick Public Library • 43B Rte 236, P.O. Box 838 • Berwick, ME 03901-0838 • (207) 698-5737

Bethel
Bethel Historical Society • Dr Moses Mason House Museum, 14 Broad St, P.O. Box 12 • Bethel, ME 04217-0012 • (207) 824-2908 • http:// www.bethelhistorical.org

Bethel Library Association • 5 Broad St, P.O. Box 130 • Bethel, ME 04217-0130 • (207) 824-2520

Biddeford
Biddeford Historical Society • c/o McArthur Library, 270 Main St, P.O. Box 200 • Biddeford, ME 04005-0200 • (207) 284-6841 • http://www. mcarthur.lib.me.us/bidhisso.htm

Franco-American Genealogical Society of York County • c/o McArthur Library, 270 Main St, P.O. Box 180 • Biddeford, ME 04005-0180 • (207) 284-4167

McArthur Public Library • 270 Main St, P.O. Box 346 • Biddeford, ME 04005-0346 • (207) 284-6841 • http://www.mcarthur.lib.me.us

Bingham
Old Canada Road Historical Society • P. O. Box 742 • Bingham, ME 04920 • http://www.rootsweb.com/~meocrhs

Old Carratunk Historical Society • P.O. Box 303 • Bingham, ME 04920

Blue Hill
Blue Hill Historical Society • 51 State St, P.O. Box 710 • Blue Hill, ME 04614 • http://www.bluehillhistory.org

Blue Hill Public Library • Parker Point Rd, P.O. Box 824 • Blue Hill, ME 04614-0824 • (207) 374-5515 • http://www.bluehill.lib.me.us

Holt House Museum • Water St • Blue Hill, ME 04614 • http://www. bluehillhistory.org

Parson Fisher House Museum • 44 Mines Rd, P.O. Box 537 • Blue Hill, ME 04614 • (207) 374-5082 • http://www.parsonfisherhouse.org; http:// www.jonathanfisherhouse.org

Boothbay
Boothbary Railway Village Museum • 586 Wiscasset Rd, P.O. Box 123 • Boothbay, ME 04537 • (207) 633-4727 • http://www.railwayvillage.org

Boothbay Harbor
Boothbay Harbor Memorial Library • 4 Oak St • Boothbay Harbor, ME 04538 • (207) 633-3112 • http://www.bmpl.lib.me.us

Boothbay Regional Historical Society • Historical Society, 72 Oak St, P.O. Box 272 • Boothbay Harbor, ME 04538-0272 • (207) 633-0820 • http://www.boothbayregister.maine.com

Bowdoinham
Bowdoinham Public Library • 13A School St • Bowdoinham, ME 04008 • (207) 666-8405 • http://www.bowdoinham.lib.me.us

Bradford
Bradford Historical Society • Heritage Museum, 1163 Main Rd • Bradford, ME 04110 • (207) 327-1246

John B Curtis Free Public Library • 187 Wilder Davis Rd • Bradford, ME 04410 • (207) 327-2923

Brewer
Brewer Historical Society • Clewly Museum, 199 Wilson St • Brewer, ME 04412 • (207) 989-7468 • http://www.brewerme.org/ HistoricalSociety/historical_society.htm

Bridgewater
Bridgewater Historical Society • Historical Museum, P.O. Box 341 • Bridgewater, ME 04735 • (207) 524-2120

Bridgton
Bridgton Historical Society • Historical Museum, 5 Gibbs Ave, P.O. Box 44 • Bridgton, ME 04009-0044 • (207) 647-3699 • http://www. bridgtonhistory.org

Bridgton Public Library • 65 Main St • Bridgton, ME 04009 • (207) 647-2472 • http://www.bridgton.lib.me.us

Rufus Porter Museum • 67 N High St, P.O. Box 544 • Bridgton, ME 04009 • (207) 647-2828 • http://www.rufusportermuseum.org

Sweden Historical Society • RR 1, Box 230 • Bridgton, ME 04009

Brooksville
Brooksville Free Public Library • 1 Townhouse Rd, P.O. Box 38 • Brooksville, ME 04617 • (207) 326-4560 • http://www.brooksvillelibrary. org

Brooksville Historical Society • Historical Museum, Route 176 • Brooksville, ME 04617 • (207) 326-8681

Brownfield
Brownfield Historical Society • Historical Museum, Main St, P.O. Box 264 • Brownfield, ME 04010 • (207) 935-4392

Brunswick
Captain John Curtis Memorial Library • 23 Pleasant St • Brunswick, ME 04011-2295 • (207) 725-5242 • http://www.curtislibrary.com

Hawthorne-Longfellow Library - Archives & Special Collections • Bowdoin College, 3000 College Sta • Brunswick, ME 04011-8421 • (207) 725-3288 • http://library.bowdoin.edu

Peary-MacMillan Arctic Museum • Bowdoin College, 9500 College Station • Brunswick, ME 04011 • (207) 725-3416 • http://www. academic.bowdoin.edu/arcticmuseum

Pejepscot Historical Society • Chamberlain House Museum, 159 Park Row • Brunswick, ME 04011 • (207) 729-6606 • http://www. curtislibrary.com/pejepscot.htm

Skolfield-Whittier House Museum • 161 Park Row • Brunswick, ME 04011

Bryant Pond
Woodstock Historical Society • Historical Museum, 70 S Main St • Bryant Pond, ME 04219 • (207) 665-2450

Buckfield
Buckfield Historical Society • 53 Young Ln • Buckfield, ME 04220

Bucksport
Bucksport Historical Society • Historical Museum, Main St, P.O. Box 798 • Bucksport, ME 04416 • (207) 469-2464

Burlington
Stewart M Lord Historical Society • Historical Museum, Town Sq • Burlington, ME 04448 • (207) 732-4121

Buxton
Buxton-Hollis Historical Society • P.O. Box 34 • Buxton, ME 04093 • (207) 929-8895 • http://www.hollismaine.org

Calais
Calais Free Library • 3 Union St • Calais, ME 04619 • (207) 454-2758 • http://www.calais.lib.me.us

Friends of the Florence Stockade • RFD 1, Box 93 • Calais, ME 04619 • http://members.aol.com/qmsgtboots/florenceto.html

Saint Croix Historical Society • Historical Museum, 245 Main St, P.O. Box 242 • Calais, ME 04619 • (207) 454-2521 • http://www.stcroixhistorical.org

Washington County Genealogical Society • 5C Apple Orchard Ln • Calais, ME 04619

Camden
Camden Historical Society • 80 Mechanic St • Camden, ME 04843

Camden Public Library • 55 Main St • Camden, ME 04843-1703 • (207) 236-3440 • http://www.camden.lib.me.us

Camden-Rockport Historical Society • Old Conway Homestead, Conway Rd, Route 1, P.O. Box 747 • Camden, ME 04843 • (207) 236-2257 • http://www.crmuseum.org

Cape Elizabeth
Cape Elizabeth Historical Preservation Society • Historical Museum, 6 Scott Dyer Rd • Cape Elizabeth, ME 04107

Thomas Memorial Library • 6 Scott Dyer Rd • Cape Elizabeth, ME 04107 • (207) 799-1720

Caribou
Caribou Historical Society • historical Museum, P.O. Box 1058 • Caribou, ME 04736 • (207) 498-2556

Caribou Public Library • 30 High St • Caribou, ME 04736 • (207) 493-4214 • http://www.caribou-public.lib.me.us

Nylander Museum • 657 Main St, P.O. Box 1062 • Caribou, ME 04736 • (207) 493-4209 • http://www.nylandermuseum.org

Carthage
Carthage Historical Society • Historical Museum, HC 67, Box 863 • Carthage, ME 04224

Casco
Raymond-Casco Historical Society • general delivery • Casco, ME 04015 • (207) 627-4220

Castine
Castine Historical Society • Abbot School Museum, P.O. Box 238 • Castine, ME 04421 • (207) 326-4118

Castine Scientific Society • Wilson Museum, 120 Perkins St, P.O. Box 196 • Castine, ME 04421-0196 • (207) 326-8545 • http://www.wilsonmuseum.org

Nutting Memorial Library • Maine Maritime Academy, Pleasant St, Box C-1 • Castine, ME 04420 • (207) 326-2263 • http://bell.mma.edu/~library/

Witherle Memorial Library • 41 School St, P.O. Box 202 • Castine, ME 04421-0202 • (207) 326-4375 • http://www.witherle.lib.me.us

Chebeague Island
Chebeague Island Historical Society • Schoolhouse Museum, P.O. Box 28 • Chebeague Island, ME 04017 • (207) 846-5237

Chebeague Island Library • 247 South Rd #3 • Chebeague Island, ME 04017 • (207) 846-4351 • http://web.nlis.net/~bjohnson/library.html

Cherryfield
Cherryfield-Narraguagus Historical Society • Historical Museum, Main St, P.O. Box 96 • Cherryfield, ME 04622 • (207) 546-7979

Clinton
Clinton Historical Society • Historical Museum, 1 Fountain St, P.O. Box 624 • Clinton, ME 04927 • (315) 859-1392

Columbia Falls
Ruggles House Museum • 146 Main St, P.O. Box 99 • Columbia Falls, ME 04623 • (207) 483-4637 • http://www.ruggleshouse.org

Corinna
Corinna Historical Society • 44 St Albans Rd • Corinna, ME 04928 • (207) 278-4650

Stewart Free Library • 8 Levi Stewart Dr • Corinna, ME 04928 • (207) 278-2454

Corinth
Corinth Historical Society • P.O. Box 541 • Corinth, ME 04427-0541 • http://www.angelfire.com/me2/corinthhistorical

Cornish
Cornish Historical Society • Historical Museum, HC 69, P.O. Box 242 • Cornish, ME 04020

Cumberland Center
Center North Yarmouth Historical Society • Old North Yarmouth Townhouse, Route 9, Box 391 • Cumberland Center, ME 04021

Cumberland Historical Society • Historical Museum, 6 Blanchard Rd, P.O. Box 82 • Cumberland Center, ME 04021 • (207) 827-5423

Prince Memorial Library • 266 Main • Cumberland Center, ME 04021-9754 • (207) 829-2215 • http://www.princememorial.lib.me.us

Cushing
Cushing Historical Society • Historical Museum, Hawtorne Point Rd, P.O. Box 110 • Cushing, ME 04563 • (207) 354-8262 • http://www.rootsweb.com/~usgenweb/me/knox/cushing.htm

Olson House Museum • Hawthorne Point Rd • Cushing, ME 04563 • (207) 596-6457

Damariscotta
Pemaquid Historical Association • Route 2, Box 4000-314 • Damariscotta, ME 04543-9766

Skidompha Library • 184 Main St, P.O. Box 70 • Damariscotta, ME 04543-0070 • (207) 563-5513 • http://www.skidompha.org

Danville
MeGenWeb • P.O. Box 152 • Danville, ME 04223 • (207) 786-2129 • http://www.rootsweb.com/~megenweb

New England Old Newspaper Index Project • P.O. Box 152 • Danville, ME 04223 • (207) 786-2129 • http://www.rootsweb.ancestry.com/~megenweb/newspaper/project

Deer Isle
Deer Isle-Stonington Historical Society • Historical Museum, 416 Sunset Rd, P.O. Box 652 • Deer Isle, ME 04627 • (207) 367-8978

Dennysville
Dennys River Historical Society • Historical Museum, 1 King St, P.O. Box 11 • Dennysville, ME 04628 • (207) 726-3905

Dexter
Abbott Memorial Library • 1 Church St • Dexter, ME 04930 • (207) 924-7292 • http://www.dextermaine.org/library.html

Dexter Historical Society • Historical Museum, 13 Water St, P.O. Box 481 • Dexter, ME 04930 • (207) 924-5721 • http://www.dexterhistoricalsociety.com

Dixfield

Dixfield Historical Society • Historical Museum, 63 Main St, P.O. Box 182 • Dixfield, ME 04224 • (207) 562-7595

Ludden Memorial Library • 40 Main St, P.O. Box 805 • Dixfield, ME 04224-0805 • (207) 562-8838 • http://www.dixfield.org/library.html

Dover-Foxcroft

Blacksmith Shop Museum • 103 Dawes Rd • Dover-Foxcroft, ME 04426 • (207) 564-8618

Dover-Foxcroft Historical Society • 128 Union Sq • Dover-Foxcroft, ME 04426 • (207) 564-8618

Thompson Free Library • 186 E Main St • Dover-Foxcroft, ME 04426 • (207) 564-3350 • http://www.dover-foxcroft.org/lib.htm

Dresden

Dresden Historical Society • Dresden Brick School House, Route 128 • Dresden, ME 04342 • (207) 737-8892

Lincoln County Historical Association • 1761 Pownalborough Courthouse, Courthouse Rd, Route 128 • Dresden, ME 04342 • (207) 737-2504 • http://www.lincolncountyhistory.org

Durham

Durham Historical Society • Historical Museum, 27 Cyr Rd • Durham, ME 04222 • (207) 353-8570

Durham Historical Society • 15 Cyr Rd • Durham, ME 04222

East Baldwin

Brown Memorial Library • School St, P.O. Box 24 • East Baldwin, ME 04024-0024 • (207) 787-3155

East Lebanon

Lebanon Area Library • New Rd, P.O. Box 339 • East Lebanon, ME 04027 • (207) 457-1171

East Machias

East Machias Historical Society • P.O. Box 658 • East Machias, ME 04654-0658

East Vassalboro

Vassalboro Historical Society • Historical Museum, Route 32, P.O. Box 62 • East Vassalboro, ME 04935-0062 • (207) 923-3533

Vassalboro Public Library • Bog Rd, P.O. Box 62 • East Vassalboro, ME 04935-0062 • (207) 923-3233

East Waterboro

Waterborough Historical Society • Route 5 • East Waterboro, ME 04030 • (207) 247-5878

East Winthrop

Winthrop Historical Society • P.O. Box 111 • East Winthrop, ME 04343

Easton

Easton Historical Society • Station Rd, P.O. Box 44 • Easton, ME 04740 • (207) 488-6652 • http://www.historiceaston.org

Eastport

Border Historical Society • Barracks Museum, 74 Washington St, P.O. Box 95 • Eastport, ME 04631 • (207) 853-2328 • http://www.borderhistoricalsociety.com

Peavey Memorial Library • 26 Water St • Eastport, ME 04631 • (207) 853-4021

Edgecomb

Friends of Fort Edgecomb • Historical Museum, P.O. Box 48 • Edgecomb, ME 04556

Eliot

Eliot Historical Society • John F Hill Grange Museum, P.O. Box 3 • Eliot, ME 03903

William Fogg Library • Old Rd, P.O. Box 359 • Eliot, ME 03903-0359 • (207) 439-9437 • http://www.william-fogg.lib.me.us

York County Genealogical Society • 42 Goodwin Rd, P.O. Box 431 • Eliot, ME 03903-0431 • (207) 439-4243

Ellsworth

Col Black Mansion Museum • 172 Ellsworth, P.O. Box 1478 • Ellsworth, ME 04605 • (207) 667-8671 • http://www.woodlawnmuseum.com

Ellsworth Historical Society • P.O. Box 355 • Ellsworth, ME 04605

Ellsworth Public Library • 20 State St • Ellsworth, ME 04605 • (207) 667-6363 • http://www.ellsworth.lib.me.us

New England Telephone Museum • 166 Winkampaugh Rd, P.O. Box 1377 • Ellsworth, ME 04605 • (207) 664-2463 • http://www.thetelephonemuseum.org

Stanwood Homestead Museum • High St, P.O. Box 485 • Ellsworth, ME 04605 • (207) 667-8460

Woodlawn Museum • Black House, 19 Black House Dr, P.O. Box 1478 • Ellsworth, ME 04605 • (207) 667-8671 • http://www.woodlawnmuseum.com

Enfield

Cole Memorial Library • 789 Hammett Rd • Enfield, ME 04493 • (207) 732-4270

Fairfield

Fairfield Historical Society • Historical Museum, 42 High St • Fairfield, ME 04937 • (207) 453-2998 • http://www.fairfieldmehistoricalsociety.net

Lawrence Public Library • 33 Lawrence Ave • Fairfield, ME 04937 • (207) 453-6867 • http://www.lawrence.lib.me.us

Falmouth

Bustins Island Historical Society • 2 Homestead Ln • Falmouth, ME 04105 • (207) 781-4727 • http://www.falmouthmehistory.org

Falmouth Historical Society • 2 Homestead Ln • Falmouth, ME 04105 • (207) 781-4727 • http://www.falmouthmehistory.org; http://www.falmouthhistoricalsociety.org

Falmouth Memorial Library • 5 Lunt Rd • Falmouth, ME 04105-1292 • (207) 781-2351 • http://www.falmouth.lib.me.us

Farmington

Farmington Historical Society • Historical Museum, 118 Academy St, P.O. Box 275 • Farmington, ME 04938 • (207) 667-2835

Farmington Public Library • 117 Academy St • Farmington, ME 04938 • (207) 778-4312 • http://www.farmington.lib.me.us

Maine Genealogical Society • P.O. Box 221 • Farmington, ME 04938 • (207) 623-9147 • http://www.rootsweb.com/~megs/MaineGS.htm

Mantor Library • Univ of Maine at Farmington, 116 South St • Farmington, ME 04938 • (207) 778-7210 • http://www.umf.maine.edu

Nordica Homestead Museum • Holley Rd, RFD3, P.O. Box 3062 • Farmington, ME 04938 • (207) 778-2042

Nordica Memorial Association • Historical Museum, 100 High St • Farmington, ME 04938 • (207) 778-2042

Sandy River & Rangeley Lakes Railroad Museum • 349 Voter Hill Rd • Farmington, ME 04938

Fayette

Underwood Memorial Library • RR 1, Box 1305 • Fayette, ME 04349 • (207) 685-3778

Fort Fairfield

Fort Fairfield Public Library • 339 Main St • Fort Fairfield, ME 04742-1199 • (207) 472-3880 • http://www.fortfairfield.org

Frontier Heritage Historical Society • Historical Museum, P.O. Box 9 • Fort Fairfield, ME 04742

Fort Kent

Acadian Archives • Univ of Maine at Fort Kent, 25 Pleasant St • Fort Kent, ME 04743 • (207) 834-7535 • http://www.umfk.maine.edu/archives/main.htm

Blake Library • University of Maine at Fort Kent, 23 University Dr • Fort Kent, ME 04743 • (207) 834-7527 • http://www.umfk.maine.edu/infoserv/library

Fort Kent Historical Society • 10 Market St, P.O. Box 181 • Fort Kent, ME 04743 • (207) 834-3933

Franklin

Franklin Historical Society • Historical Museum, Route 200, P.O. Box 317 • Franklin, ME 04634 • (207) 565-3635

Maine Civil War Reenactment Society • Hog Bay Rd • Franklin, ME 04634

Freeport

Freeport Historical Society • Enoch Harrington House, 45 Main St, P.O. Box 358 • Freeport, ME 04032 • (207) 865-0477 • http://www.freeporthistoricalsociety.org

Frenchboro

Frenchboro Historical Society • Historical Museum, Schoolhouse Hill • Frenchboro, ME 04635 • (207) 334-2929 • http://members.aol.com/frboro

Friendship

Friendship Museum • 1 Martin Point Rd, P.O. Box 226 • Friendship, ME 04547 • (207) 832-4221

Fryeburg

Fryeburg Fair Farm Museum • 203 Main St, P.O. Box 78 • Fryeburg, ME 04037 • (207) 935-3268 • http://www.fryefair.com

Fryeburg Historical Society • Historical Museum, 96 Main St • Fryeburg, ME 04037-1126 • (207) 935-4192 • http://www.fryeburghistorical.org

Gardiner

Commission on Archives and History, United Methodist Church • 35 Highland Ave • Gardiner, ME 04345 • (207) 933-0412

Friends of Gardiner Heritage • Historical Museum, P.O. Box 1055 • Gardiner, ME 04345

Gardiner Public Library • 152 Water St • Gardiner, ME 04345 • (207) 582-3312 • http://www.gpl.lib.me.us

Georgetown

Georgetown Historical Society • Historical Museum, 20 Bay Point Rd, P.O. Box 441 • Georgetown, ME 04548 • (207) 371-9200

Gorham

Baxter House Museum • 67 South St • Gorham, ME 04038 • (207) 839-5031

Gorham Historical Society • Historical Museum, 16 High Acre Ln • Gorham, ME 04038 • (207) 839-4313 • http://www.cascofcu.com/ghs/home.html

Gouldsboro

Gouldsboro Historical Society • Historical Museum, 418 Pond Rd • Gouldsboro, ME 04607 • (207) 963-5530

Gray

Gray Historical Society • Historical Museum, 22 Main St, P.O. Box 544 • Gray, ME 04039 • (207) 657-2235 • http://www.graymaine.org/history.htm

Gray Public Library • 5 Hancock St, P.O. Box 1319 • Gray, ME 04039-1319 • (207) 657-4110 • http://www.gray.lib.me.us

Windham Historical Society • 26 Dutton Hill Rd • Gray, ME 04039 • (207) 892-9667

Greene

Greene Historical Society • 1092 N River Rd • Greene, ME 04236

Greenville

Moosehead Historical Society • 444 Pritham Ave, P.O. Box 1116 • Greenville, ME 04441-1116 • (207) 695-2909 • http://www.mooseheadhistory.org

Moosehead Marine Museum • North Main, P.O. Box 1151 • Greenville, ME 04441 • (207) 695-2716

Guilford

Guilford Historical Society • N Main St • Guilford, ME 04443 • (207) 876-2787

Hallowell

Arnold Expedition Historical Society • Colburn House • Hallowell, ME 04347 • (207) 582-7080

Hubbard Free Library • 115 2nd St • Hallowell, ME 04347 • (207) 621-6582

Hampden

Edythe L Dyer Community Library • 269 Main Rd N • Hampden, ME 04444 • (207) 862-3550 • http://www.edl.lib.me.us

Hampden Historical Society • Kinsley House Museum, 83 Main Rd S, P.O. Box 456 • Hampden, ME 04444 • (207) 862-2027

Hancock

Hancock Historical Society • Historical Museum, Hancock Corner, P.O. Box 212 • Hancock, ME 04640 • (207) 422-3080

Harmony

Harmony Historical Society • Historical Museum, P.O. Box 83 • Harmony, ME 04942

Harrison

Harrison Historical Society • 121 Haskell Hill Rd • Harrison, ME 04040 • (207) 583-6225 • http://www.caswell.lib.me.us/histsoc.html

Sweden Historical Society • Blacksmith Shop Museum, RR2 • Harrison, ME 04040 • (207) 647-5397

Hartland

Hartland Public Library • 8 Mill St, P.O. Box 620 • Hartland, ME 04943 • (207) 938-4702

Hebron

Hebron Historical Society • Historical Museum, 24 Main St • Hebron, ME 04238

Hinckley

LC Bates Museum • Hinckley Home-School-Farm, Route 201 • Hinckley, ME 04944 • (207) 453-4894 • http://www.gwh.org/lcabates

Hiram

Hiram Historical Society • 158 Sebago Rd • Hiram, ME 04041 • (207) 625-4663 • http://www.rootsweb.som~mechiram/contacts.htm

Soldiers Memorial Library • 85 Main St, P.O. Box 281 • Hiram, ME 04041-0281 • (207) 625-4650

Holden

Masonic Grand Lodge of Maine • Library & Museum, 107 Main Rd, P.O. Box 430 • Holden, ME 04429-0430 • (207) 843-1086 • http://www.mainemason.org

Hope

Hope Historical Society • 374 Camden Rd • Hope, ME 04847 • http://www.hopehist.com

Houlton

Aroostook County Historical Society • Historical Museum, P.O. Box 761 • Houlton, ME 04730

Houlton, cont.

Cary Library • 107 Main St • Houlton, ME 04730 • (207) 532-1302 • http://www.cary.lib.me.us

Houlton Band of Maliset Indians • 88 Bell Rd • Houlton, ME 04730-9514 • (207) 532-4273 • http://www.maliseets.com

Southern Aroostook Historical Society • Aroostook Historical Museum, 109 Main St • Houlton, ME 04730 • (207) 532-6687

Howland

Stewart M Lord Memorial Historical Society • P.O. Box 367 • Howland, ME 04448-0367 • (207) 732-4121

Indian Island

Penobscot Nation Historical Society • Penobscot Nation Museum, 5 Downstreet St • Indian Island, ME 04468 • (207) 827-4513 • http://www.penobscotnation.org

Island Falls

Island Falls Historical Society • Burley St • Island Falls, ME 04747 • (207) 463-2264

John E and Walter D Webb Museum of Vintage Fashion • Sherman St, Route 2, P.O. Box 541 • Island Falls, ME 04747 • (207) 463-2404 • http://www.coffeenews.net/webbmuseum

Katahdin Public Library • 20 Library St, P.O. Box 148 • Island Falls, ME 04747-0148 • (207) 463-2282

Islesboro

Alice L Pendleton Memorial Library • 309 Main Rd, P.O. Box 77 • Islesboro, ME 04848-0077 • (207) 734-2218 • http://www.alpl.lib.me.us

Islesboro Historical Society • Old Town Hall, 388 Main Rd, P.O. Box 301 • Islesboro, ME 04848 • (207) 734-6733

Sailor's Memorial Museum • Grindle Point, P.O. Box 76 • Islesboro, ME 04848 • (207) 734-2253

Islesford

Islesford Historical Museum • Little Cranberry Island, P.O. Box 12 • Islesford, ME 04646 • (207) 288-8729 • http://www.nps.gov/acad/home.html

Islesford Historical Society • c/o Islesford Library, Moosewood Rd • Islesford, ME 04646 • http://www.cranberryisles.com/little/hist_soc/

Jackman

Jackman-Moose River Historical Society • 574 Main St, P.O. Box 875 • Jackman, ME 04945 • http://www.jackman.us/historic.html

Moose River Historical Museum • P.O. Box 875 • Jackman, ME 04945

Jay

Jay Historical Society • Historical Museum, P.O. Box 236 • Jay, ME 04239

Kennebunk

Brick Store Museum • 117 Main St • Kennebunk, ME 04043 • (207) 985-4802 • http://www.brickstoremuseum.org

Kennebunk Free Library • 112 Main St • Kennebunk, ME 04043 • (207) 985-2173 • http://www.kennebunk.lib.me.us

Sons of the American Revolution, Maine Society • 1 Thompson Rd • Kennebunk, ME 04043 • (207) 985-1223 • http://www.messar.org

Taylor-Barry House Museum • 24 Summer St, P.O. Box 177 • Kennebunk, ME 04043 • (207) 985-4296

Kennebunkport

Kennebunkport Historical Society • Nott House, 125 North St, P.O. Box 1173 • Kennebunkport, ME 04046-1173 • (207) 967-2751 • http://www.kporthistory.org

Seashore Trolley Museum • 195 Log Cabin Rd, P.O. Box A • Kennebunkport, ME 04046 • (207) 967-2712 • http://www.trolleymuseum.org

Kezar Falls

Parsonsfield-Porter Historical Society • Hickory House, Main St • Kezar Falls, ME 04047 • (207) 625-4667

Kingfield

Kingfield Historical Society • Historical Museum, Maple St, P.O. Box 238 • Kingfield, ME 04947 • (207) 265-4032

Stanley Museum • 40 School St, P.O. Box 77 • Kingfield, ME 04947 • (207) 265-2722 • http://www.stanleymuseum.org

Kittery

Kittery Historical Society • Historical and Naval Museum, Rogers Rd, P.O. Box 453 • Kittery, ME 03904 • (207) 439-3080

Rice Public Library • 8 Wentworth St • Kittery, ME 03904 • (207) 439-1553 • http://www.rice.lib.me.us

Kittery Point

Friends of Fort McClary • P.O. Box 82 • Kittery Point, ME 03905

Lebanon

Lebanon Area Library • Center Rd, P.O. Box 279 • Lebanon, ME 04027-0279 • (207) 457-1171

Lee

Lee Historical Society • Historical Museum, Route 6, P.O. Box 306 • Lee, ME 04455 • (207) 738-4125

Lewiston

American-Canadian Genealogical Society, Father Leo E Begin Chapter • 14 Tanglewood Dr, P.O. Box 2125 • Lewiston, ME 04240-2125

Edmund S Muskie Archives • Baker College, 70 Campus Ave • Lewiston, ME 04240-6018 • (207) 786-6354

George & Helen Ladd Library • Bates College, 48 Campus Ave • Lewiston, ME 04240 • (207) 786-6264 • http://www.bates.edu/library

Le Centre D'Heritage Franco American • 81 Ash St, P.O. Box 1251 • Lewiston, ME 04240 • (207) 783-9248

Lewiston Historical Commission • 36 Oak St • Lewiston, ME 04240

Lewiston Public Library • 200 Lisbon St • Lewiston, ME 04240 • (207) 784-0135 • http://www.lplonline.org

Lewiston-Auburn College Library • 51 Westminster St, P.O. Box 1937 • Lewiston, ME 04241 • (207) 753-6546 • http://ibrary.usm.maine.edu

Maine Franco-American Genealogical Society • P.O Box 2125 • Lewiston, ME 04240-2125

Society of Maine Archivists • Baker College, 70 Campus Ave • Lewiston, ME 04240-6018 • (207) 786-6354

Liberty

Davistown Museum • 58 Main St #4, P.O. Box 346 • Liberty, ME 04949 • (207) 288-5126 • http://www.davistownmuseum.org

Liberty Historical Society • Old Octagonal Post Office, Main St, Rte 173 • Liberty, ME 04949 • (207) 589-4393

Lille

Mount Carmel Museum and Cultural Center • US Route 1, P.O. Box 155 • Lille, ME 04749-0155 • (207) 895-3339 • http://www.mainehumanities.org/programs/barnagainevents.html

Limerick

Limerick Historical Society • Historical Museum, 55 Washington St, P.O. Box 208 • Limerick, ME 04048 • http://www.limerickhistory.org

Limestone

Robert A Frost Memorial Library • 42 Main St • Limestone, ME 04750-1399 • (207) 325-4706

Limington

Davis Memorial Library • 928 Cape Rd • Limington, ME 04049 • (207) 637-2422 • http://www.davis.lib.me.us

Limington Historical Society • 7 Joe Webster Rd, P.O. Box 84 • Limington, ME 04049 • http://www.limingtonhistory.org

Lincolnville Center

Lincolnville Historical Society • Historical Museum, 33 Beach Rd, P.O. Box 211 • Lincolnville Center, ME 04850 • (207) 789-5445 • http://www.lincolnvillehistory.org

Lisbon

Lisbon Historical Society • 14 High St • Lisbon, ME 04250

Lisbon Falls

Lisbon Falls Community Library • 28 Main St • Lisbon Falls, ME 04252-0028 • (207) 353-6564 • http://www.lisbon.lib.me.us

Maine Genealogical Society, Pejepscot Chapter • 35 Grove St • Lisbon Falls, ME 04252 • (207) 353-4680

Livermore

Livermore Historical Society • Historical Museum, 360 Sanders Rd • Livermore, ME 04253

Norlands Living History Center & Washburn Mansion • 290 Norlands Rd • Livermore, ME 04253 • (207) 897-4366 • http://norlands.org

Livermore Falls

Town of Livermore Falls • 2 Main St • Livermore Falls, ME 04254 • (207) 897-3321 • http://www.lfme.org

Long Island

Long Island Historical Society • Historical Museum, 77 Wharf St, P.O. Box 282 • Long Island, ME 04050

Lovell

Charlotte E Hobbs Memorial Library • 227 Main St, P.O. Box 105 • Lovell, ME 04051-0105 • (207) 925-3177

Lovell Historical Society • Historical Museum, Route 5, P.O. Box 166 • Lovell, ME 04051-0166 • (207) 925-3234 • http://www.lovellhistoricalsociety.org

Lubec

Lubec Historical Society • Historical Museum, P.O. Box 5 • Lubec, ME 04652 • (207) 733-4696

Lubec Memorial Library • 10 School St • Lubec, ME 04652-1122 • (207) 733-2491

Roosevelt Campobello International Park Commission • Historical Museum, P.O. Box 129 • Lubec, ME 04652 • (506) 752-2922 • http://www.fdr.net

Machias

Burnham Tavern Museum • Main St • Machias, ME 04654 • (207) 256-4432 • http://www.burnhamtavern.com

Hannah Weston Chapter, DAR • 2 Free St • Machias, ME 04654 • (207) 255-4432

Merrill Library • University of Maine at Machias, 9 O'Brien Ave • Machias, ME 04654-1397 • (207) 255-1254 • http://www.umm.maine.edu/library/welcome.html

Porter Memorial Library • 52 Court St • Machias, ME 04654 • (207) 255-3933 • http://www.porter.lib.me.us

Sunrise Research Institute • Historical Museum, P.O. Box 417 • Machias, ME 04654

Machiasport

Machiasport Historical Society • Gates House Museum, 344 Port Rd, P.O. Box 301 • Machiasport, ME 04655 • (207) 255-8461

Madawaska

Acadian Cultural Exchange of Northern Maine • 776 Main St • Madawaska, ME 04756 • (207) 738-4272

Madawaska Historical Society • Tante Blanche Museum, US 1, P.O. Box 258 • Madawaska, ME 04756 • (207) 728-4518

Madawaska Public Library • 411 E Main St • Madawaska, ME 04756 • (207) 728-3606

Madrid

Madrid Historical Society • Historical Museum, RR1, Box 868 • Madrid, ME 04966

Mapleton

Haystack Historical Society • Historical Museum, P.O. Box 306 • Mapleton, ME 04757

Mars Hill

Walter T A Hansen Memorial Library • 10 Hansen St, P.O. Box 1008 • Mars Hill, ME 04758 • (207) 429-9625 • http://www.wtahansen.com

Mechanic Falls

Town of Mechanic Falls • 108 Lewiston St, P.O. Box 130 • Mechanic Falls, ME 04256 • (207) 345-2871 • http://mechanicfalls.govoffice.com

Mexico

Mexico Free Public Library • 134 Main St • Mexico, ME 04257 • (207) 364-3281 • http://www.mexico.lib.me.us

Mexico Historical Society • 3 Oxford St • Mexico, ME 04257 • (207) 364-4496

Milbridge

Milbridge Historical Society • Historical Museum, Main St • Milbridge, ME 04658 • (207) 546-4471

Milbridge Historical Society • Historical Museum, Main St, P.O. Box 194 • Milbridge, ME 04658

Millinocket

Millinocket Memorial Library • 5 Maine Ave • Millinocket, ME 04462 • (207) 723-7020 • http://www.millinocket.lib.me.us

Milo

Milo Free Public Library • 4 Pleasant St • Milo, ME 04463 • (207) 943-2612 • http://www.milo.lib.me.us

Milo Historical Society • Historical Museum, 23 Park St • Milo, ME 04463 • (207) 943-2268

Monhegan

Monhegan Cultural and Historical Association • Historical Museum, 1 Lighthouse Hill • Monhegan, ME 04852 • (207) 596-7003 • http://www.monheganmuseum.org

Monmouth

Cumston Public Library • 796 Main St, P.O. Box 239 • Monmouth, ME 04259 • (207) 933-4788 • http://www.cumston.lib.me.us

Monmouth Historical Society • Historical Museum, 751 Main St, P.O. Box 352 • Monmouth, ME 04259-0352 • (207) 933-2287 • http://www.rootsweb.com/~mekenneb/monmouth/monhs.htm; http://www.monmouthmuseuminc.org

Morrill

Greene Plantation Historical Society • Route 1, Box 2040 • Morrill, ME 04952-9729 • (207) 342-5208

Morrill Historical Society • general delivery • Morrill, ME 04952 • (207) 338-1405

Mount Desert

Mount Desert Island Historical Society • Historical Museum, 373 Sound Dr, P.O. Box 653 • Mount Desert, ME 04660-0653 • (207) 276-9323 • http://mdihistory.org

Maine

Mount Desert, cont.
Mount Desert Island Historical Society • School House Museum, 373 Sound Dr, P.O. Box 653 • Mount Desert, ME 04660 • (207) 276-9323 • http://www.mdihistory.org

Naples
Naples Historical Society • Historical Museum, 137 12th Ave S, P.O. Box 1757 • Naples, ME 04055 • (207) 693-4297

Naples Public Library • Rte 302 • Naples, ME 04055 • (207) 693-6841 • http://www.naples.lib.me.us

Sweden Historical Society • Historical Museum, RR1, Box 405 • Naples, ME 04055

New Gloucester
New Gloucester Maine Historical Society • Meeting House Museum, 389 Intervale Rd, P.O. Box 531 • New Gloucester, ME 04260 • (207) 926-4126

Shaker Museum • 707 Shaker Rd • New Gloucester, ME 04260 • (207) 926-4597 • http://www.shaker.lib.me.us

United Society of Shakers • Shaker Library at Sabbathday Lake, 707 Shaker Rd • New Gloucester, ME 04260-2652 • (207) 926-4597 • http://www.shaker.lib.me.us

New Harbor
Colonial Pemaquid State Historical Site Museum • P.O. Box 304 • New Harbor, ME 04554 • (207) 677-2423 • http://www.friendsofcolonialpemaquid.org

Fishermen's Museum • Lighthouse Park, Route 30, 3007 Bristol Rd • New Harbor, ME 04554 • (207) 677-2494

New Portland
Nowetahs American Indian Museum • 2 Colegrove Rd • New Portland, ME 04954 • (207) 628-4981

New Sweden
Lars Noak Blacksmith Shop Museum • Larsson Log Home, Capitol School, Station Rd, P.O. Box 50 • New Sweden, ME 04762 • (207) 896-3199 • http://www.arroostook.me.us/newsweden/historical.html

Maine's Swedish Colony Museum • P.O. Box 50 • New Sweden, ME 04762 • (207) 896-5624 • http://www.maineswedishcolony.info

New Sweden Historical Society • Swedish Museum, Capitol Hill Rd, P.O. Box 33 • New Sweden, ME 04762 • (207) 896-3018

Newcastle
Newcastle Historical Society • 64 Main St • Newcastle, ME 04553 • (207) 563-5741

Newfield
19th Century Willowbrook Village • P.O. Box 28 • Newfield, ME 04056 • (207) 793-2784 • http://www.willowbrookmuseum.org

Newfield Historical Society • P.O. Box 82 • Newfield, ME 04056 • (207) 793-2343

Willowbrook Museum Village • Route 11 & Elm St, P.O. Box 28 • Newfield, ME 04056 • (207) 793-2784 • http://www.willowbrookmuseum.org

Nobleboro
Nobleboro Historical Society • Historical Museum, 198 Center St, P.O. Box 122 • Nobleboro, ME 04555-0122 • (207) 563-5874

Norridgewock
Norridgewock Historical Society • Historical Museum, 11 Mercer Rd, P.O. Box 903 • Norridgewock, ME 04957 • (207) 634-5032

North Amith
Town of Amity • HC 61, Box 3A • North Amith, ME 04465 • (207) 532-2485 • http://www.maine.gov/local/aroostook/amity

North Anson
Embden Historical Society • Historical Museum, P.O. Box 278 • North Anson, ME 04958 • http://www.rootsweb.ancestry.com/~meehs

North Berwick
D A Hurd Library • 41 High St, P.O. Box 399 • North Berwick, ME 03906-0399 • (207) 676-2215 • http://www.hurd.lib.me.us

North Haven
North Haven Historical Society • Historical Museum, 33 Iron Point Rd • North Haven, ME 04853 • (207) 867-2096

North Jay
Jay Historical Society • Holmes-Crafts Homestead, Rt 4, Jay Hill • North Jay, ME 04262 • (207) 645-2732

North Leeds
Leeds Historical Commision • P.O. Box 1 • North Leeds, ME 04263

North Waterford
Waterford Historical Society • Mary Gage Rice Museum, Waterford Village, P.O. Box 201 • North Waterford, ME 04267

North Yarmouth
North Yarmouth Historical Society • 10 Village Square Rd • North Yarmouth, ME 04097

Northeast Harbor
Great Harbor Maritime Museum • 124 Main St, P.O. Box 145 • Northeast Harbor, ME 04662 • (207) 276-5262

Northeast Harbor Library • Joy Rd, P.O. Box 279 • Northeast Harbor, ME 04662-0279 • (207) 276-3333 • http://www.acadia.net/nehlib/

Thuya Lodge Museum • general delivery • Northeast Harbor, ME 04662 • (207) 276-5130

Norway
Norway Historical Society • Historical Museum, 232 Main St, P.O. Box 167 • Norway, ME 04268 • (207) 743-7377

Norway Memorial Library • 258 Main St • Norway, ME 04268 • (207) 743-5309 • http://www.norway.lib.me.us

Oakfield
Oakfield Historical Museum • general delivery • Oakfield, ME 04763 • (207) 757-8575

Oakfield Historical Society • Oakfield Railroad Museum, Station St, P.O. Box 62 • Oakfield, ME 04763 • (207) 757-8575

Oakland
Macartney House Museum • 110 Main St, P.O. Box 59 • Oakland, ME 04963 • (207) 465-7549

Oakland Public Library • 18 Church St • Oakland, ME 04963 • (207) 465-9554

Ogunquit
York County Genealogical Society • P.O. Box 2242 • Ogunquit, ME 03907 • (207) 646-3753

Old Orchard Beach
Edith Belle Libby Memorial Library • 27 Staples St • Old Orchard Beach, ME 04064 • (207) 934-4351 • http://www.oldorchardbeach.org/library

Old Orchard Beach Historical Society • Harmon Museum, 4 Portland Ave, P.O. Box 464 • Old Orchard Beach, ME 04064 • (207) 934-9319

Old Town
Old Town Museum • 138 S Main St, P.O. Box 375 • Old Town, ME 04468 • (207) 827-7256

Old Town Public Library • 46 Middle St • Old Town, ME 04468 • (207) 827-3972 • http://www.old-town.lib.me.us

Penobscot Nation Museum • 5 Center St • Old Town, ME 04468 • (207) 827-4153

Penobscot National Historical Society • 6 River Rd, Indian Island Reservation, P.O. Box 313 • Old Town, ME 04468 • (207) 827-7776 • http://www.penobscotnation.org

Orland
Orland Historical Society • Historical Museum, Castine Rd, P.O. Box 242 • Orland, ME 04472 • (207) 469-2476

Orono
Orono Historical Society • Historical Museum, P.O. Box 324 • Orono, ME 04473

Orono Maine Folklife Center Museum • Univ of Maine, South Stevens 5773 • Orono, ME 04469-5773 • (207) 581-1891 • http://www.umaine.edu/folklife/

Orono Public Library • Goodridge Dr • Orono, ME 04473 • (207) 866-5060 • http://www.orono.lib.me.us

Raymont H Fogler Library - Special Collections • Univ of Maine, 5729 Fogler Library • Orono, ME 04469-5729 • (207) 581-1661 • http://www.library.umaine.edu/speccoll/

Orrington
Curran Homestead Living History Farm and Museum • 372 Fields Pond Rd • Orrington, ME 04474 • (207) 945-9311 • http://www.curranhomestead.org

Orr's Island
Harpswell Historical Society • Old Meeting House, 1334 Harpswell Islands Rd • Orr's Island, ME 04066 • (207) 721-8950 • http://www.curtislibrary.com/hhs/

Otisfield
Otisfield Historical Society • 877 State Rte 121 • Otisfield, ME 04270 • (207) 539-2664 • http://www.rootsweb.com/~mecotisf/otis8.htm

Owls Head
Owls Head Transportation Museum • Route 73, P.O. Box 277 • Owls Head, ME 04854 • (207) 594-4118 • http://www.ohtm.org

Oxford
Oxford Historical Society • 683 Main St • Oxford, ME 04270

Paris
Paris Hill Historical Society • Historical Museum, P.O. Box 51 • Paris, ME 04271

Paris Hill-Hamlin Memorial Library & Museum • Hannibal Hamlin Dr, P.O. Box 43 • Paris, ME 04271-0043 • (207) 743-2980 • http://www.hamlin.lib.me.us

Parsonsfield
Parsonsfield Public Library • 717 North Rd, P.O. Box 120 • Parsonsfield, ME 04047-0120 • (207) 625-4689

Patten
Patten Lumbermen's Museum • 25 Waters Rd, P.O. Box 300 • Patten, ME 04765 • (207) 528-2650 • http://www.lumbermensmuseum.org

Peaks Island
5th Maine Regiment Center Museum • 45 Seashore Ave, P.O. Box 41 • Peaks Island, ME 04108 • (207) 773-5514 • http://www.fifthmainemuseum.org

Pemaquid
Pemaquid Historical Association • Harrington Meeting House, 293 Old Harrington Rd • Pemaquid, ME 04558 • (207) 677-2193

Penobscot
Penobscot Historical Society • Historical Museum, P.O. Box 64 • Penobscot, ME 04476

Perry
Passamaquoddy - Pleasant Point Reservation • P.O. Box 343 • Perry, ME 04667-0343 • (207) 853-2600 • http://www.wabanaki.com

Waponahki Resource Center, Sipayik Museum • Rt 190, Pleasant Point • Perry, ME 04667 • (207) 853-4001

Washington County Genealogical Society • RR1, Box 28, Shore Rd • Perry, ME 04667

Phillips
Phillips Historical Society • Historical Museum, 8 Pleasant St, P.O. Box 216 • Phillips, ME 04966 • (207) 639-5013

Phillips Public Library • Main St, P.O. Box O • Phillips, ME 04966-1514 • (207) 639-2665 • http://www.phillips.lib.me.us

Phippsburg
Maine League of Historical Societies and Museums • Stone House Museum • Phippsburg, ME 04562

Phippsburg Historical Society • Phippsburg Center, 24 Parker Head Rd, P.O. Box 21 • Phippsburg, ME 04562 • (207) 389-2393

Pittsfield
Pittsfield Historical Society • Depot House Museum, 8 Central St, P.O. Box 181 • Pittsfield, ME 04967 • (207) 487-3447 • http://www.rootsweb.com/~mephs

Pittsfield Public Library • 89 S Main St • Pittsfield, ME 04967 • (207) 487-5880 • http://www.pittsfield.lib.me.us

Poland
Alvan Bolster Ricker Memorial Library • 1211 Maine St • Poland, ME 04274 • (207) 998-4390 • http://www.rickerlibrary.org

Historical Society of Poland, Maine • Old School House, 1229 Main St • Poland, ME 04015 • (207) 998-2403 • http://www.polandhistoricalsociety.org

Porter
Parsonfield-Porter Historical Society • Historical Museum, 27 Danfort Ln • Porter, ME 04068 • (207) 625-4667

Portland
Episcopal Diocese of Maine Museum • 143 State St • Portland, ME 04101 • (207) 772-1953 • http://www.episcopalmaine.org

Maine Historical Society • Historical Museum, 489 Congress St • Portland, ME 04101 • (207) 774-1822 • http://www.mainehistory.com

Maine Narrow Gauge Railroad Museum • 58 Forest St • Portland, ME 04101 • (207) 828-0814 • http://www.mngrr.org

McLellan House Museum • High St • Portland, ME 04101 • (207) 775-6148 • http://www.portlandmuseum.org

Portland Public Library • 5 Monument Square • Portland, ME 04101-4072 • (207) 871-1700 • http://www.portlandlibrary.com

Tate House Museum • 1270 Westbrook St, P.O. Box 8800 • Portland, ME 04104 • (207) 774-6177 • http://www.tatehouse.org

Victoria Mansion Museum • 109 Danforth St • Portland, ME 04101 • (207) 772-4841 • http://www.victoriamansion.org

Victoria Society of Maine • Victoria Mansion, 109 Danforth St • Portland, ME 04101 • (207) 772-4841 • http://www.portlandarts.com/victoriamansion

Wadsworth-Longfellow House Museum • 487 Congress St • Portland, ME 04101 • (207) 879-0427 • http://www.mainehistory.com

Pownal
Pownal Scenic and Historical Society • Historical Museum, 584 Poland Range Rd • Pownal, ME 04069

Presque Isle
Aroostook Band of Micmacs • 521D Mani St, P.O. Box 772 • Presque Isle, ME 04769 • (207) 764-1972 • http://www.micmac.org

Mark and Emily Turner Memorial Library • 39 2nd St • Presque Isle, ME 04769 • (207) 764-2571 • http://www.presqueisle.lib.me.us

Maine

Presque Isle, cont.
Presque Isle Historical Society • Vera Estey House Museum, 16 3rd St • Presque Isle, ME 04769-2416 • (207) 762-1151

University of Maine at Presque Isle Library • 181 Main St • Presque Isle, ME 04769-2888 • (207) 768-9594 • http://www.umpi.maine.edu/info/lib/specol.htm

Princeton
Passamaquoddy Tribe of Maine • Indian Township Reservation, P.O. Box 301 • Princeton, ME 04668 • (207) 796-2301

Prospect
Fort Knox State Historic Site Museum • 711 Fort Knox Rd • Prospect, ME 04981 • (207) 469-6906 • http://www.fortknox.maineguide.com

Rangeley
Rangeley Lakes Region Historical Society • Historical Museum, 2472 Main St, P.O. Box 521 • Rangeley, ME 04970 • (207) 864-5647

Rangeley Lakes Region Logging Museum • 2695 Main St, P.O. Box 154 • Rangeley, ME 04970 • (207) 864-5595 • http://www.mason.gmu.edu/~myocom

Raymond
Hawthorne Community Association • Hawthorne Rd • Raymond, ME 04077

Raymond Village Library • 3 Meadow Rd, P.O. Box 297 • Raymond, ME 04071-0297 • (207) 655-4283

Raymond-Casco Historical Society • 10 McDermott Rd • Raymond, ME 04071 • http://www.raymondmaine.org/historical_society/

Readfield
Readfield Historical Society • Route 17, P.O. Box 354 • Readfield, ME 04355-0354 • (207) 685-4424 • http://www.rootsweb.com/~mecreadf/rdfldrhs.htm

Richmond
Richmond Historical Society • 7 Gardiner St • Richmond, ME 04357 • (207) 737-4166

Southard House Museum • 75 Main St • Richmond, ME 04357 • (207) 737-8772

Rockland
Farnsworth Homestead Museum • 21 Elm St, P.O. Box 466 • Rockland, ME 04841 • (207) 596-6457 • http://www.farnsworthmuseum.org

Maine Lighthouse Museum • 1 Park Dr, P.O. Box F • Rockland, ME 04841 • (207) 594-3301 • http://www.mainlighthousemuseum.com

Rockland Historical Society • 80 Union Ln • Rockland, ME 04841 • (207) 594-6193

Rockland Public Library • 80 Union St • Rockland, ME 04841 • (207) 594-0310 • http://midcoast.com/rpl

Shore Village Museum • 104 Limerock St • Rockland, ME 04841 • (207) 594-0311 • http://www.lighthouse.c/shorevillage

William A Farnsworth Library • 352 Main St, P.O. Box 466 • Rockland, ME 04841 • (207) 596-6457

Rockport
American Society of Genealogists • P.O. Box 250 • Rockport, ME 04856-0250 • (207) 236-6565 • http://www.pictonpress.com

Camden-Rockport Historical Society • Historical Museum, P.O. Box 747 • Rockport, ME 04856 • (207) 236-2257 • http://www.crmuseum.org

Rockport Public Library • 1 Limerock St, P.O. Box 8 • Rockport, ME 04856-0008 • (207) 236-3642 • http://www.rockport.lib.me.us

Rumford
Acadian Heritage Society • 159 E Andover Rd • Rumford, ME 04276 • (207) 364-8651 • http://www.acadian.org

Rumford Area Historical Society • Historical Museum, 145 Congress St • Rumford, ME 04276 • (207) 364-2540 • http://www.rumfordmaine.net/history.htm

Rumford Public Library • 56 Runford Ave • Rumford, ME 04276-1919 • (207) 364-3661 • http://www.rumford.lib.me.us

Sabattus
Showme Museum • P.O. Box 637 • Sabattus, ME 04280

Saco
Dyer Library & Museum • 371 Main St • Saco, ME 04072 • (207) 283-3861

Saco Museum • 371 Main St • Saco, ME 04072 • http://www.sacomuseum.org

Saint Agatha
Saint Agatha Historical Society • Historical Museum, Main St, P.O. Box 237 • Saint Agatha, ME 04772-0237 • (207) 543-6364 • http://www.stagatha.com/society.html

Saint Albans
Saint Albans Historical Society • Historical Museum, P.O. Box 62 • Saint Albans, ME 04971

Saint Francis
Allagash Historical Society • Rte 161 • Saint Francis, ME 04774 • (207) 398-3335 • http://www.aroostook.me.us/allagash/historical.html

Saint George
Marshall Point Lighthouse Museum • Marshall Point Rd • Saint George, ME 04860 • http://www.marshallpoint.org

Sanford
Sanford Historical Committee • 919 Main St • Sanford, ME 04073 • http://www.sanfordhistory.org

Scarborough
Scarborough Historical Society • Historical Museum, 649-A US 1, P.O. Box 156 • Scarborough, ME 04070-0156 • (207) 883-3539 • http://www.scarboroughmaine.com/historical/

Seal Cove
Tremont Historical Society • Historical Museum, P.O. Box 66 • Seal Cove, ME 04674

Searsport
Carver Memorial Library • 12 Union St, P.O. Box 439 • Searsport, ME 04974-0439 • (207) 548-2303 • http://www.carver.lib.me.us

Penobscot Marine Museum • 5 Church St, P.O. Box 498 • Searsport, ME 04974 • (207) 548-2529 • http://www.penobscotmarinemuseum.org

Searsport Historical Society • Main Street, Rt 1 • Searsport, ME 04974 • (207) 548-0245

Sebago
Sebago Historical Society • Historical Museum, P.O. Box 59 • Sebago, ME 04029 • (207) 787-3330 • http://www.rootsweb.com/~mecsebag/HistSoc.html

Spaulding Memorial Library • 282 Sebago Rd, P.O. Box 300 • Sebago, ME 04029-0300 • (207) 787-2321 • http://www.spaulding.lib.me.us

Sedgwick
Sedgwick-Brooklin Historical Society • Historical Museum, Rte 172, P.O. Box 63 • Sedgwick, ME 04676 • (207) 359-8977 • http://www.mainemuseums.org

Shapleigh
Shapleigh Community Library • Route 11, P.O. Box 97 • Shapleigh, ME 04076-0097 • (207) 636-3630

Sherman
Sherman Public Library • Church St, P.O. Box 276 • Sherman, ME 0476-0276 • (207) 365-4882

Skowhegan
Skowhegan History House Museum • 66 Elm St, P.O. Box 832 • Skowhegan, ME 04976 • (207) 474-6632 • http://www.skowhegan. maine.usa.com/kb/historyh/

Solon
Solon Historical Society • P.O. Box 316 • Solon, ME 04979

Somesville
Mount Desert Island Historical Society • Main St • Somesville, ME 04660

Somesville Museum • 2 Oak Hill Rd • Somesville, ME 04661 • (207) 276-9323 • http://www.mdhistory.org

South Berwick
Dunnybrook Historical Foundation • Historical Museum, 24 Academy St, P.O. Box 17 • South Berwick, ME 03908 • (207) 384-2018 • http://www.dunnybrook.org

Hamilton House Museum • 40 Vaughan's Ln • South Berwick, ME 03908 • (207) 384-2454 • http://www.spnea.org

Old Berwick Historical Society • Counting House Museum, 2 Liberty St, P.O. Box 296 • South Berwick, ME 03908 • (207) 384-8041 • http://www.obhs.net

Sarah Orne Jewett House Museum • 5 Portland St • South Berwick, ME 03908 • (207) 384-2454 • http://www.historicnewengland.org

South Bristol
South Bristol Historical Society • 2124 State Route 129 • South Bristol, ME 04568 • (207) 644-1234

South China
China Historical Society • Maine St, P.O. Box 587 • South China, ME 04358 • (207) 445-3954

South China Library • Old Route 202, P.O. Box 417 • South China, ME 04358-0417 • (207) 445-3094 • http://www.southchina.lib.me.us

South Freeport
Bustins Island Historical Society • P.O. Box 118 • South Freeport, ME 04078

South Harpswell
Harpswell Historical Society • RFD 1 • South Harpswell, ME 04079 • (207) 883-7798

South Paris
Paris Cape Historical Society • Historical Museum, 19 Park St • South Paris, ME 04281 • (207) 743-2462 • http://www.rootsweb.com/~mecparis/pariscphs.html

Paris Public Library • 37 Market Sq • South Paris, ME 04281 • (207) 743-6994 • http://www.paris.lib.me.us

South Portland
Portland Harbor Museum • 2 Fort Rd • South Portland, ME 04106 • (207) 799-6337 • http://www.portlandharbormuseum.org

South Portland Public Library • 482 Broadway • South Portland, ME 04106 • (207) 767-7660 • http://home.maine.rr.com/southportlandlib

South Portland-Cape Elizabeth Historical Society • Historical Museum, 245 High St, P.O. Box 2623 • South Portland, ME 04106 • (207) 799-1977

Southport
Friends of Southport Historical Society • Historical Museum, 32 Blair Rd • Southport, ME 04576

Hendricks Hill Museum • 417 Hendricks Hill Rd, Route 27, P.O. Box 3 • Southport, ME 04576 • (207) 633-1102

Southwest Harbor
Southwest Harbor Public Library • 338 Main St, P.O. Box 157 • Southwest Harbor, ME 04679-0157 • (207) 244-7065 • http://www.swharbor.lib.me.us

Wendell Gilley Museum • Main St & Hendrick Rd, P.O. Box 254 • Southwest Harbor, ME 04679 • (207) 244-7555 • http://www.wendellgilleymuseum.org

Springvale
Nasson Heritage Center • 21 Bradeen St, P.O. Box 416 • Springvale, ME 04083 • (207) 324-0888

Standish
Marrett House Museum • Route 25 • Standish, ME 04084 • (207) 642-3032 • http://www.historicnewengland.org

Standish Historical Society • Old Red Church Museum, Oak Hill Rd, P.O. Box 228 • Standish, ME 04084 • (207) 642-5170

Steep Falls
Steep Falls Public Library • Pequawket Trail, P.O. Box 140 • Steep Falls, ME 04085 • (207) 675-3132 • http://www.steepfallslibrary.org

Steuben
Steuben Historical Society • Historical Museum, P.O. Box 153 • Steuben, ME 04680

Stockholm
Stockholm Historical Society • Historical Museum, 280 Main St • Stockholm, ME 04783 • (207) 896-5759 • http://www.aroostook.me.us

Stockton Springs
Stockton Springs Historical Society • P.O. Box 101 • Stockton Springs, ME 04981 • http://www.bairnet.org/organizations/sshs

Stonington
Stonington Museum • Moose Island • Stonington, ME 04681

Stratton
Dead River Area Historical Society • 172 Main St, P.O. Box 150 • Stratton, ME 04982 • (207) 246-2271

Ski Museum of Maine • P.O. Box 464 • Stratton, ME 04982

Strong
Strong Historical Society • Vance & Dorothy Hammond Museum, Upper Main St • Strong, ME 04983 • (207) 684-2975

Sweden
Sweden Historical Society • general delivery • Sweden, ME 04040

Temple
Temple Historical Society • Historical Museum, 346 Varnum Pond Rd • Temple, ME 04984

Thomaston
Knox Memorial Association • General Henry Knox Museum, 33 Knox St, P.O. Box 326 • Thomaston, ME 04861 • (207) 354-8062 • http://www.knoxmuseum.org

Thomaston Historical Society • Historical Museum, 80 Knox St, P.O. Box 384 • Thomaston, ME 04861 • (207) 354-2295 • http://www.thomastonhistoricalsociety.com

Thomaston Public Library • 60 Main St • Thomaston, ME 04861 • (207) 354-2453

Thorndike
Unity Historical Society • P.O. Box 133 • Thorndike, ME 04986 • (207) 948-2798

Topsham
Pejepscot Historical Society • 159 Main St • Topsham, ME 04086 • (207) 729-6606

Troy
Unity Historical Society • Historical Museum, RR1, Box 1570 • Troy, ME 04897

Turner
Buckfield Historical Society • RR 4, Box 780 • Turner, ME 04282-9604 • http://www.sad39.k12.me.us/zadoc/society.html

Union
Matthews Museum of Maine Heritage • Union Fairgrounds, 695 Middle Rd, P.O. Box 582 • Union, ME 04862 • (207) 785-3321

Union Historical Society • Historical Museum, 343 Common Rd, P.O. Box 154 • Union, ME 04862-4252 • (207) 785-5444

Unity
Unity Historical Society • Historical Museum, P.O. Box 4 • Unity, ME 04988 • (207) 948-2798 • http://unitymaine.org/orgs/uhs/

Van Buren
Abel J Morneault Memorial Library • 303 Main St • Van Buren, ME 04785 • (207) 868-5076

L'Heritage Vivant-Living Heritage Society • Acadian Village and Museum, Rte 1, P.O. Box 165 • Van Buren, ME 04765 • (207) 868-5042 • http://themainelink.com/acadianvillage/

Vanceboro
Vanceboro Historical Society • Water St, P.O. Box 200 • Vanceboro, ME 04491 • http://members.tripod.com/vanceborohs/

Vassalboro
Vassalboro Historical Society • US Route 32 • Vassalboro, ME 04989 • (207) 923-3505

Vinalhaven
Vinalhaven Historical Society • Historical Museum, 14 High St, P.O. Box 339 • Vinalhaven, ME 04863 • (207) 863-4410 • http://www.midcoast.com/~vhhissoc/

Waldoboro
Broad Bay Family History Project • P.O. Box 10 • Waldoboro, ME 04572

Waldoboro Historical Society • Historical Museum, 1164 Main St, P.O. Box 110 • Waldoboro, ME 04572 • (207) 832-7552

Wales
Town of Wales • 302 Centre Rd • Wales, ME 04280 • (207) 375-8881 • http://www.maine.gov

Warren
Warren Historical Society • Historical Museum, 225 Main St, P.O. Box 11 • Warren, ME 04864 • (207) 273-2726

Washburn
Salmon Brook Historical Society • Historical Museum, Main St, P.O. Box 68 • Washburn, ME 04786 • (207) 455-4339

Washburn Memorial Library • 2 Main St, P.O. Box 571 • Washburn, ME 04786-0571 • (207) 455-4814

Waterford
Waterford Historical Society • Historical Museum, P.O. Box 201 • Waterford, ME 04088

Waterville
Colby College Library • 5100 Mayflower Hill • Waterville, ME 04901 • (207) 872-3463 • http://www.colby.edu/library

Waterville Historical Society • Redington Museum, 64 Silver St • Waterville, ME 04901-6524 • (207) 872-9439 • http://www.redingtonmuseum.org

Waterville Public Library • 73 Elm St • Waterville, ME 04901-6078 • (207) 872-5433 • http://www.waterville.lib.me.us

Wayne
Wayne Historical Society • P.O. Box 243 • Wayne, ME 04284

Weld
Weld Historical Society • Historical Museum, Wilton Rd, P.O. Box 31 • Weld, ME 04285 • (207) 585-2340

Wells
Historical Society of Wells and Ogunquit • Meetinghouse Museum, Rte 1, 938 Post Rd, P.O. Box 801 • Wells, ME 04090 • (207) 646-4775 • http://www.historicalsocietyofwellsandogunquit.com

Order of the Founders and Patriots of America • 1285 Branch Rd • Wells, ME 04090 • (207) 985-9143 • http://www.founderspatriots.org

Wells Auto Museum • 1181 Post Rd, P.O. Box 496 • Wells, ME 04090 • (207) 646-9064

West Paris
Finnish American Heritage Society of Maine • P.O. Box 249 • West Paris, ME 04289 • (207) 674-3094

West Sullivan
Sullivan-Sorrento Historical Society • Historical Museum, Route 1, P.O. Box 44 • West Sullivan, ME 04689 • (207) 422-6816 • http://ellsworthme.org/sshs

Westbrook
Walker Memorial Library • 800 Main St • Westbrook, ME 04092-3423 • (207) 854-0630 • http://www.westbrookmaine.com/library

Warren Memorial Library • 479 Main St • Westbrook, ME 04092-4330 • (207) 854-5891 • http://www.javanet.com/~warren.html

Westbrook Maine Historical Society • Historical Museum, 17B Dunn St • Westbrook, ME 04092 • (207) 854-5588 • http://www.westbrookhistoricalsociety.org

Whitefield
Whitefield Historical Society • Historical Museum, 749 E River Rd, P.O. Box 176 • Whitefield, ME 04353 • (207) 549-5064

Whiting
Trescott Historical Society • P.O. Box 1 • Whiting, ME 04691 • (207) 733-5548 • http://www.trescotthistory.org

Whitneyville
Sunrise Research Institute • P.O. Box 156 • Whitneyville, ME 04692

Wilton
Wilton Free Public Library • 6 Goodspeed Rd, P.O. Box 454 • Wilton, ME 04294-0454 • (207) 645-4831

Wilton Historical Society • Kineowatha Park Farm Museum, P.O. Box 33 • Wilton, ME 04294 • (207) 645-2091

Windham
Windham Historical Society • 234 Windham Center Rd • Windham, ME 04062 • (207) 892-1433

Winslow
Winslow Historical Society • 16 Benton Ave • Winslow, ME 04902

Winter Harbor
Winter Harbor Historical Society • Main St, P.O. Box 400 • Winter Harbor, ME 04693 • (207) 963-7461

Winterport
Winterport Historical Association • 760 N Main, P.O. Box 342 • Winterport, ME 04496-0342 • (207) 223-5556

Wiscasset
Castle Tucker Museum • Lee & High Sts • Wiscasset, ME 04578 • (207) 882-7169 • http://www.historicnewengland.org

Lincoln County Cultural and Historical Association • Old Lincoln County Jail, 133 Federal St, P.O. Box 61 • Wiscasset, ME 04578 • (207) 882-6817 • http://www.lincolncountyhistory.org

Lincoln County Genealogical Society • P.O. Box 61 • Wiscasset, ME 04578 • http://www.rootsweb.com/~wvlincol/LCGS.html

Musical Wonder House Museum • 18 High St, P.O. Box 604 • Wiscasset, ME 04578 • (207) 882-7163 • http://www.musicalwonderhouse.com

Nickels-Sortwell House Museum • 121 Main St • Wiscasset, ME 04578 • (207) 882-0218 • http://www.historicnewengland.org

Wiscasset Historical Committee • c/o Wiscasset Public Library, 21 High St, P.O. Box 367 • Wiscasset, ME 04578 • (207) 882-7161 • http://www.wiscasset.lib.me.us

Wiscasset Public Library • 21 High St, P.O. Box 367 • Wiscasset, ME 04578-0367 • (207) 882-7161 • http://www.wiscasset.lib.me.us

Woolwich

Woolwich Historical Society • Historical Museum, Rte 1 & Nequasset Rd, P.O. Box 98 • Woolwich, ME 04579 • (207) 443-4833 • http://www.woolwichhistory.org

Yarmouth

Merrill Memorial Library • 215 Main St • Yarmouth, ME 04096 • (207) 846-4763 • http://www.yarmouth.me.us

Yarmouth Historical Society • Museum of Yarmouth History, 215 W Main St, P.O. Box 107 • Yarmouth, ME 04906 • (207) 846-6259 • http://www.yarmouth.me.us

York

Biddeford Historical Society • P.O. Box 346 • York, ME 04005

Old York Historical Society • Elizabeth Perkins House Museum, 207 York St, P.O. Box 312 • York, ME 03909-0312 • (207) 363-4974 • http://www.oldyork.org

York Public Library • 15 Long Sands Rd • York, ME 03909 • (207) 363-2818 • http://www.york.lib.me.us

York Harbor

Sayward-Wheeler House Museum • 9 Barrell Ln • York Harbor, ME 03911 • (207) 384-2454 • http://www.historicnewengland.org

Maine

Aberdeen

Harford County Genealogical Society • P.O. Box 15 • Aberdeen, MD 21001 • http://www.rtis.com/reg/md/org/hcgs/

Harford County Public Library-Aberdeen Branch • 21 Franklin St • Aberdeen, MD 21001-2495 • (410) 273-5608

Aberdeen Proving Ground

Aberdeen Proving Ground Post Library • Bldg 3320 • Aberdeen Proving Ground, MD 21005-5001 • (410) 278-3417

US Army Ordnance Center & Ordnance Museum • Bldg 2601, USAOC&S • Aberdeen Proving Ground, MD 21005-5201 • (410) 278-3602 • http://www.ordmusfound.org

Abingdon

National Society of Descendants of Early Quakers • P.O. Box 453 • Abingdon, MD 21009-0453 • http://www.terraworld.net/mlwinton/index.htm#quaker

Accokeek

Accokeek Foundation • Agricultural Museum, 3400 Bryan Point Rd • Accokeek, MD 20607 • (301) 283-2113 • http://www.accokeek.org

Adamstown

Descendants of the Signers of the Declaration of Independence • 3137 Periwinkle Ct • Adamstown, MD 21710 • http://www.dsdi1776.com

Allen

Allen Historical Society • P.O. Box 31 • Allen, MD 21810 • (410) 749-9064

Andrews AFB

Air Force Historical Foundation • 535 Command Dr, Ste A-122 • Andrews AFB, MD 20762-7002 • (301) 736-1959

Annapolis

Annapolis Maritime Museum • 133 Bay Shore Ave • Annapolis, MD 21403

Anne Arundel County Public Library • 5 Harry S Truman Pkwy • Annapolis, MD 21401 • (410) 222-7371 • http://www.aacpl.net

Anne Arundel County Public Library-Annapolis Area • 1410 West St • Annapolis, MD 21401 • (410) 222-1750 • http://www.aacpl.net

Banneker-Douglass Museum • Mount Moriah AME Church, 84 Franklin St • Annapolis, MD 21401 • (410) 974-2553 • http://www.hometownannapolis.com/tour_banneker.html

Charles Carroll House Museum • 107 Duke of Gloucester St • Annapolis, MD 21401 • (410) 269-1737

Chase-Lloyd House Museum • 22 Maryland Ave • Annapolis, MD 21401 • (410) 263-2723

Frederick Douglass Museum • 3200 Wayman Ave • Annapolis, MD 21403

Governor's Mansion Museum • State Circle & School St • Annapolis, MD 21401 • (410) 974-3531

Hammon-Harwood House Museum • 19 Maryland Ave • Annapolis, MD 21401 • (410) 263-4683 • http://www.hammondharwoodhouse.org

Historic Annapolis Foundation • Shiplap House Museum, 18 Pinkney St • Annapolis, MD 21401 • (410) 267-7619 • http://www.annapolis.org

James Brice House Museum • 42 East St • Annapolis, MD 21401 • (410) 280-1305

Jewish Historical Society of Annapolis, Maryland • 5 Sampson Pl • Annapolis, MD 21401 • (410) 268-4887

Maryland State Archives • 350 Rowe Blvd • Annapolis, MD 21401 • (410) 260-6400 • http://www.mdsa.net; http://mdarchives.state.md.us

Maryland State House Museum • State Cr • Annapolis, MD 21401

Maryland State Law Library • 361 Rowe Blvd • Annapolis, MD 21401 • (410) 974-3395

Maryland State Library • Court of Appeals Bldg, 361 Rowe Blvd • Annapolis, MD 21401

Naval Institute History, Reference & Preservation Dept Library • 291 Wood Rd • Annapolis, MD 21402 • (410) 295-1021 • http://www.usni.org

Nimitz Library • United States Naval Academy, 589 McNair Rd • Annapolis, MD 21402-5029 • (410) 293-2220 • http://www.usna.edu/library

US Naval Academy Museum • Preble Hall, 118 Maryland Ave • Annapolis, MD 21402 • (410) 293-2108 • http://www.usna.edu/museum

William Paca House and Garden • 186 Prince George St • Annapolis, MD 21401 • (410) 263-5553 • http://www.annapolis.org

Baltimore

Afro-American Historical and Genealogical Society, Baltimore Chapter • P.O. Box 9366 • Baltimore, MD 21229-3125

Albin O Kuhn Museum • Univ of MD, 1000 Hilltop Cr • Baltimore, MD 21250 • (410) 455-2270 • http://www.umbc.edu/library

Babe Ruth Birthplace Museum • 216 Emory Pl • Baltimore, MD 21230 • (410) 727-1539 • http://www.baberuthmuseum.com

Ballestone Manor Museum • 1935 Back River Neck Rd • Baltimore, MD 21221 • (410) 887-0218

Baltimore & Ohio Railroad Museum • 901 W Pratt St • Baltimore, MD 21223 • (410) 752-2490 • http://www.borail.org

Baltimore American Indian Center • 113 S Broadway • Baltimore, MD 21231

Baltimore City Archives • 2165 Druid Park Dr • Baltimore, MD 21211 • (410) 396-0306

Baltimore City Fire Museum • Old Town Mall, 414 N Gay St • Baltimore, MD 21202

Baltimore Civil War Museum • 601 President St • Baltimore, MD 21202 • (410) 385-5188 • http://www.mdhs.org

Baltimore Maritime Museum • Pier3, 5 Pratt St • Baltimore, MD 21231 • (410) 396-3453 • http://www.baltimomaritimemuseum.org

Baltimore Museum of Industry • 1415 Key Hwy, Inner Harbor South • Baltimore, MD 21230 • (410) 727-4808 • http://www.thebmi.org

Baltimore Streetcar Museum • 1901 Falls Rd P.O. Box 4881 • Baltimore, MD 21211 • (410) 547-0264 • http://www.baltimorestreetcar.org

Baltimore's Black American Museum • 1769 Carswell St • Baltimore, MD 21218

Bard Library • Baltimore City Community College, 2901 Liberty Heights Ave • Baltimore, MD 21215 • (410) 462-8400 • http://www.bccc.state.md.us

Benjamin Banneker Park Museum • 300 Oella Ave • Baltimore, MD 21228 • (410) 887-1081 • http://www.thefriendsofbanneker.org

Carroll Mansion Museum • 800 E Lombard St • Baltimore, MD 21202 • (410) 396-3523

Dr Samuel D Harris National Museum of Dentistry • 31 S Greene St • Baltimore, MD 21201 • (410) 706-0600 • http://www.dentalmuseum.org

Edgar Allan Poe House & Museum • 203 N Amity St • Baltimore, MD 21223 • (410) 396-7932 • http://www.ci.baltimore.md.us/government/historic/poehouse.html

Enoch Pratt Free Library • 400 Cathedral St • Baltimore, MD 21201 • (410) 396-5430 • http://www.epfl.net

Maryland

Baltimore, cont.

Evergreen House Museum • Johns Hopkins Univ, 4545 N Charles St • Baltimore, MD 21210 • (410) 516-0341 • http://www.jhu.edu/historichouses/

Faith Presbyterian Church Library • 5400 Loch Raven Blvd • Baltimore, MD 21239 • (410) 435-4330

Fells Point Maritime Museum • 1724 Thames St • Baltimore, MD 21231 • http://www.mdhs.org

Fort McHenry National Monument and Historic Shrine Museum • 2400 E Fort Ave • Baltimore, MD 21230-5393 • (410) 962-4290 • http://www.nps.gov/fomc

Genealogical Council of the Jewish Historical Society of Maryland • 3200 Pinkney Rd • Baltimore, MD 21215-3711 • (410) 732-6400 • http://www.jewishgen.org/jgsgw/

General Society of Colonial Wars • Langsdale Library, 1420 Maryland Ave • Baltimore, MD 21201 • http://www.gscw.org

George Peabody Library • John Hopkins Univ, 17 E Mt Vernon Pl • Baltimore, MD 21202-2397 • (410) 659-8179 • http://www.peabody.jhu.edu/lib/archives.html

Geppi's Entertainment Museum • 301 W Camden St • Baltimore, MD 21201 • (410) 625-7064 • http://www.geppismuseum.com

Glenn L Martin Maryland Aviation Museum • 701 Wilson Point Rd, P.O. Box 5024 • Baltimore, MD 21220 • (410) 682-6122 • http://www.marylandaviationmuseum.org

H L Mencken House Museum • 1524 Hollins St • Baltimore, MD 21202 • (410) 396-3523

Heritage Museum • 4509 Prospect Cr • Baltimore, MD 21216 • (410) 664-6711

Historical Society for 20th Century China • Loyola College, Dept of History, 4501 N Charles St • Baltimore, MD 21210-2699 • (410) 617-2893 • http://www.eou.edu

Homewood House Museum • Johns Hopkins Univ, 3400 N Charles St • Baltimore, MD 21210 • (410) 516-5589 • http://www.jhu.edu/historichouses/

Jewish Genealogical Society of Maryland • c/o Jewish Museum of Maryland, 15 Lloyd St • Baltimore, MD 21202 • http://www.jewishgen.org/JGS-Maryland/

Jewish Historical Society of Maryland • Jewish Museum of Maryland, 15 Lloyd St • Baltimore, MD 21209 • (410) 732-6400 • http://www1.jshm.org; http://www.jewishmuseummd.org

John Work Garrett Library • Johns Hopkins University, Evergreen House, 4545 N Charles St • Baltimore, MD 21210 • (410) 516-5571

Joseph Meyerhoff Library • Baltimore Hebrew Univ, 5800 Park Heights Ave • Baltimore, MD 21215 • (410) 578-6936 • http://www.bhu.edu/meyerhoff/

Julia Rogers Library • Goucher College, 1021 Dulaney Valley Rd • Baltimore, MD 21204 • (410) 337-6212 • http://www.goucher.edu/library

Knott Library • Saint Mary's Seminary & University, 5400 Roland Ave • Baltimore, MD 21210-1994 • (410) 864-3621 • http://www.stmarys.edu

Langsdale Library • Univ of Baltimore, 1420 Maryland Ave • Baltimore, MD 21201 • (410) 837-4274 • http://langsdale.ubalt.edu

Maryland Genealogical Society • 201 W Monument St • Baltimore, MD 21201-4674 • (410) 685-3750 • http://www.mdgensoc.org

Maryland Historical Society • Historical Museum, 201 W Monument St • Baltimore, MD 21201 • (410) 685-3750 • http://www.mdhs.org

Milton S Eisenhower Library • Johns Hopkins Univ, 3400 N Charles St • Baltimore, MD 21218 • (410) 516-8348 • http://archives.mse.jhu.edu:8000/

Mother Seton House Museum • 600 N Paca St • Baltimore, MD 21201

Mount Clare Museum House • 1500 Washington Blvd • Baltimore, MD 21230 • (410) 837-3262 • http://www.mountclare.org

Mount Vernon Place United Methodist Church Museum • 10 E Mount Vernon Pl • Baltimore, MD 21117 • (410) 685-5290 • http://www.mvp-umc.org

National Historic Seaport of Baltimore Museum • 802 S Caroline St • Baltimore, MD 21231

Old Otterbein United Methodist Church Museum • 112 W Conway St • Baltimore, MD 21201 • (410) 685-4703 • http://www.oldotterbeinumc.org

Old Saint Paul's Cemetery • 737 W Redwood • Baltimore, MD 21201 • (410) 539-3793 • http://www.oldstpauls.ang.md.org

Parlett Moore Library • Coppin State College, 2500 W North Ave • Baltimore, MD 21216-3698 • (410) 951-3400 • http://www.coppin.edu/library

Peabody Institute Archives & Museum • Johns Hopkins Univ, 1 E Mount Vernon Pl • Baltimore, MD 21202

Polish Nobility Association • Villa Anneslie, 529 Dunkirk Rd • Baltimore, MD 21212 • (703) 383-0594 • http://www.pgsa.org/pna.htm

Reginald E Lewis Museum of Maryland African American History • 19 E Fayette St, Ste 404 • Baltimore, MD 21202 • (443) 263-1800 • http://www.africanamericanculture.org

Society for the History of Germans in Maryland • 107 E Chase St, P.O. Box 22585 • Baltimore, MD 21203 • (410) 685-0450

Society for the Preservation of Federal Hill and Fells Point • Robert Long House Museum, 812 S Ann St • Baltimore, MD 21231 • (410) 675-6750

Society of the Ark and Dove • 201 W Monument St • Baltimore, MD 21201 • (410) 685-3750 • http://www.thearkandthedove.com

Star Spangled Banner Flag House & 1812 Museum • 844 E Pratt St • Baltimore, MD 21202 • (410) 837-1793 • http://www.flaghouse.org

Steamship Historical Society • Univ of Baltimore, Langsdale Library & Museum, 1420 Maryland Ave • Baltimore, MD 21201 • (410) 837-4334 • http://www.ubalt.edu/steamship/collect.htm

United Methodist Historical Society • Lovely Lane United Methodist Church Museum, 2200 Saint Paul St • Baltimore, MD 21218 • (410) 889-4458 • http://www.lovelylanemuseum.com

United Methodist Historical Society Library • Lovely Lane Museum, 2200 St Paul St • Baltimore, MD 21218 • (410) 889-4458 • http://www.bwconf.org/archivehistory/

University of Maryland Museum • 655 W Lombard St • Baltimore, MD 21201

US Army Publications Center • 2800 Eastern Blvd • Baltimore, MD 21220-2896 • (410) 671-2272

US Lacrosse Museum • 113 W University Pkwy • Baltimore, MD 21210 • http://www.lacrosse.org

USS Constellation Museum • Pier 1, 301 E Pratt St • Baltimore, MD 21202 • (410) 539-1797 • http://www.constellation.org

Walter P Carter Library • Sojourner-Douglass College, 500 N Caroline St • Baltimore, MD 21205 • (410) 276-0306 • http://www.sdc.edu

Bel Air

Harford Community College Library • 401 Thomas Run Rd • Bel Air, MD 21015 • (410) 836-4000 • http://www.harford.edu

Harford County Historical Society • Hayes House Museum, 324 Kenmore Ave, P.O. Box 366 • Bel Air, MD 21014-0366 • (410) 838-7691 • http://www.harfordhistory.net

Harford County Public Library-Bel Air Branch • 100 E Pennsylvania Ave • Bel Air, MD 21014 • (410) 638-3151 • http://www.harf.lib.md.us

Hereditary Order of the Signers of the Bush Declaration • 707 Bedford Rd • Bel Air, MD 21014 • (410) 836-3433 • http://www.bushdeclaration.org

Historical Society of Harford County • 143 N Main St, P.O. Box 366 • Bel Air, MD 21014-0366 • (410) 838-7691 • http://www.harfordhistory.net

MD and PA Railroad Preservation and Historical Society • Princeton Lane • Bel Air, MD 21014

Preservation Association for Tudor Hall • Tudor Hall Museum, 17 Tudor Ln • Bel Air, MD 21015 • (410) 838-0466

Belcamp
Hartford County Library • 1221 Brass Mill Rd • Belcamp, MD 21017-1209 • (410) 273-5600 • http://www.hcplonline.info/

Beltsville
Agricultural Research Hall of Fame Museum • USDA Visitors Center, Bldg 302, Loghodge & Powder Mill Rds • Beltsville, MD 20705

Berlin
Berlin Heritage Foundation • Calvin B Taylor House Museum, 208 N Main St, P.O. Box 351 • Berlin, MD 21811 • (410) 641-1019 • http://www.taylorhousemuseum.org

Bethesda
Bethesda United Methodist Church Library • 8300 Old Georgetown Rd • Bethesda, MD 20814 • (301) 652-2990

Dewitt Stetten Museum of Medical Research • NIH, Bldg 31, Rm 5B38, MSC 2092 • Bethesda, MD 20892 • (301) 496-6610 • http://www.history.nih.gov

Latvian Jewish Genealogy Special Interest Group • 5450 Whitley Park Terr #901 • Bethesda, MD 20814 • http://www.jewishgen.org/latvia

Big Pool
Fort Frederick State Park • 11100 Fort Frederick Rd • Big Pool, MD 21711 • (301) 842-2155 • http://www.dwr.state.md.us

Bladensburg
National Capital Buckeye Chapter, Ohio Genealogical Society • P.O. Box 105 • Bladensburg, MD 20710-0105 • (301) 927-7241

Boonsboro
Boonesboro Museum of History • 113 N Main St • Boonsboro, MD 21713 • (301) 432-6969

Boonsboro Historical Society • 323 N Main St • Boonsboro, MD 21713-1011 • (301) 432-5889

Gathland State Park • 21843 National Pk • Boonsboro, MD 21713 • (301) 791-4767 • http://www.dnr.state.md.us

Washington County Rural Heritage Museum • 7313 Sharpsburg Pk • Boonsboro, MD 21713 • (240) 313-2839 • http://www.ruralheritagemuseum.org

Bowie
Belair Mansion Museum • 12207 Tulip Grove Dr • Bowie, MD 20715 • (301) 809-3089 • http://www.cityofbowie.org/comserv/museums.htm

Belair Stable Museum • 2835 Balair Dr • Bowie, MD 20715 • (301) 809-3089 • http://www.cityofbowie.org/comserve/museums.htm

Bowie Railroad Station and Huntington Museum • 8614 Chestnut Ave • Bowie, MD 20715 • (301) 809-3089 • http://www.cityofbowie.org/comserv/museum.htm

Prince George's County Genealogical Society • 12219 Tulip Grove Dr, P.O. Box 819 • Bowie, MD 20718-0819 • (301) 345-8058 • http://www.pghistory.org

Radio & Television Museum • 2608 Mitchellville Rd • Bowie, MD 20716 • (301) 390-1020 • http://www.radiohistory.org

Thurgood Marshall Library • Bowie State Univ, 14000 Jericho Park Rd • Bowie, MD 20715 • (301) 860-3850 • http://www.bowiestate.edu

Boyds
Boyds-Clarksburg Historical Society • Boyds Negro Schoolhouse Museum, 19510 White Ground Rd, P.O. Box 161 • Boyds, MD 20841 • (301) 972-0578 • http://www.boydshistory.org

Brookeville
Oakley Cabin Museum • 3610 Brookeville Rd • Brookeville, MD 20833 • (301) 563-3405 • http://www.montgomeryparkfnd.org

Brunswick
Brunswick Historical Society • 1 W Potomac St • Brunswick, MD 21716-1111 • (301) 834-7500

Brunswick Railroad Museum • 40 W Potomac St • Brunswick, MD 21716 • (301) 834-7100 • http://www.brrm.net

Burkittsville
South Mountain Heritage Society • 3 E Main St, P.O. Box 509 • Burkittsville, MD 21718 • (301) 834-7851

Cambridge
Dorchester County Historical Society • Meredith House Museum, 904 LaGrange St • Cambridge, MD 21613 • (410) 228-7953 • http://www.bluecrab.org/dchs/

Dorchester County Public Library • 303 Gay St • Cambridge, MD 21613 • (410) 228-7331 • http://www.dorchesterlibrary.org

Heritage Resource Group • 305 Oakley St • Cambridge, MD 21613 • (410) 228-8934

Nathan of Dorchester Museum • Long Whart & High St, P.O. Box 1224 • Cambridge, MD 21613 • (410) 228-7141 • http://www.skipjack-nathan.org

Old Trinity Association • Historical Museum, 1716 Taylors Island Rd • Cambridge, MD 21613

Richardson Maritime Museum • 401 High St, P.O. Box 1198 • Cambridge, MD 21613 • (410) 221-1871 • http://www.richardsonmuseum.org

Catonsville
Afro-American Historical and Genealogical Society, Agnes Kane Callum-Baltimore Chapter • P.O. Box 9366 • Catonsville, MD 21228 • http://www.aahgs.org

Albin O Kuhn Library • Univ of Maryland, 5401 Wilkens Ave • Catonsville, MD 21228 • (410) 455-2346 • http://www.umbc.edu/library

Catonsville Branch Library • 1100 Frederick Rd • Catonsville, MD 21228-5092 • (410) 887-0951 • http://www.bcpl.lib.md.us/branchpgs/ca/cahome.html

Catonsville Historical Society and Genealogical Section • Townsend House Museum, 1824 Frederick Rd, P.O. Box 9311 • Catonsville, MD 21228 • (410) 744-3034 • http://www.catonsvillehistory.org

Spring Grove Hospital Museum • Garrett Blvd • Catonsville, MD 21228 • (410) 402-7786 • http://www.springgrove.com/history.html

Centreville
Circuit Court for Queen Anne's County • 100 Court House Sq • Centreville, MD 21617 • (410) 758-1773 • http://www.courts.state.md.us/clerks/queenannes

Queen Anne's County Free Library • 121 S Commerce St • Centreville, MD 21617 • (410) 758-0980 • http://www.quan.lib.md.us

Queen Anne's County Historical Society • Wright's Chance Museum, 121 S Commerce St, P.O. Box 62 • Centreville, MD 21617 • (410) 758-3010 • http://www.qachistory.org

Maryland

Charlestown
107 House-Tory House Museum • Market St, P.O. Box 33 • Charlestown, MD 21914 • (410) 287-8262

Colonial Charlestown Archives • 343 Market St, P.O. Box 11 • Charlestown, MD 21914 • (410) 287-8793

Genealogical Society of Cecil County • Colonial Charlestown, 343 Market St, P.O. Box 11 • Charlestown, MD 21914 • (410) 287-8793

Chesapeake Beach
Chesapeake Beach Railway Museum • 4155 Mears Ave, P.O. Box 1227 • Chesapeake Beach, MD 20732 • (410) 257-3892 • http://www.cbrm.org

Chesapeake City
Chesapeake & Delaware Canal Museum • 815 Bethel Rd, P.O. Box 77 • Chesapeake City, MD 21915 • http://www.nap.usace.army.mil

Chestertown
Clifton M Miller Library • Washington College, 300 Washington Ave • Chestertown, MD 21620-1192 • (410) 778-7292

Historical Society of Kent County • Geddes-Piper House Museum, 101 Church Alley, P.O. Box 665 • Chestertown, MD 21620 • (410) 778-3499 • http://www.hskcmd.com

Cheverly
Gypsy Lore Society • 5607 Greenleaf Rd • Cheverly, MD 20785 • (301) 341-1261

Chevy Chase
Chevy Chase Historical Society • Historical Museum, 8005 Connecticut Ave, P.O. Box 15145 • Chevy Chase, MD 20815 • (301) 986-4313

Jewish Special Interest Group, Gesher Galicia • 3128 Brooklawn Terr • Chevy Chase, MD 20815

Supreme Court Historical Society • 3615 Spring St • Chevy Chase, MD 20815 • (301) 654-2098

Clear Spring
Clear Spring District Historical Association • Historical Museum, 106 Cumberland Ct, P.O. Box 211 • Clear Spring, MD 21722 • (301) 842-1393

Rufus Wilson House Museum • 14921 Rufus Wilson Rd • Clear Spring, MD 21722

Clinton
His Lordship's Kindness Museum • 7606 Woodyard Rd • Clinton, MD 20735 • (310) 856-0358

Poplar Hill Historic House Museum • 7606 Woodyard Rd • Clinton, MD 20735 • (301) 856-0368 • http://www.poplarhillonhlk.com

Surratt House Museum • 9118 Brandywine Rd, P.O. Box 427 • Clinton, MD 20735 • (301) 868-1121 • http://www.surratt.org

Cockeysville
Baltimore County Historical Society • Historical Museum, 9811 Van Buren Ln • Cockeysville, MD 21030 • (410) 666-1878 • http://www.baltocohistsoc.org

Masonic Grand Lodge of Maryland • 304 International Cr • Cockeysville, MD 21010 • (410) 527-0600 • http://www.mdmasons.org/

Peter Goff Tenant House Museum • 13555 Beaver Dam Rd • Cockeysville, MD 21030

Sons of the American Revolution, Maryland Society • P.O. Box 1 • Cockeysville, MD 21030-0001 • http://www.marylandsar.org

College Park
College Park Aviation Museum • 1985 Cpl Frank Scott Dr • College Park, MD 20740 • (301) 864-6029 • http://www.collegeparkaviationmuseum.com

McKeldin Library • Univ of Maryland • College Park, MD 20742 • (301) 405-9128 • http://www.lib.umd.edu

National Archives - College Park Branch • 8601 Adelphi Rd, Room 6050 • College Park, MD 20740-6001 • (301) 837-0470 • http://www.archives.gov

Nixon Presidential Museum • 8601 Adelphi Rd, Rm 1320 • College Park, MD 20724 • (301) 837-3290 • http://www.nixon.archives.gov

R Lee Hornbake Undergraduate Library • University of Maryland • College Park, MD 20742-7011 • (301) 405-9257 • http://www.lib.umd.edu/mdrm

Coltons Point
Saint Clement's Island Heritage Group • Saint Clements Island-Potomac River Museum, 38370 Point Breeze Rd • Coltons Point, MD 20626 • (301) 769-2222 • http://www.stmarysmd.com/recreate/museums

Columbia
Afro-American Historical and Genealogical Society, Central Maryland Chapter • P.O. Box 648 • Columbia, MD 21045 • http://www.aahgs.org

Historic Oakland Museum • 5430 Vantage Point Rd • Columbia, MD 21044 • (410) 730-4801 • http://www.historic-oakland.com

Howard County Center of African American Culture • 5434 Vantage Point Rd • Columbia, MD 21044 • (410) 715-1921

Howard County Genealogical Society • 10545 Rivulet Row, P.O. Box 274 • Columbia, MD 21045-0274 • (410) 465-6696 • http://www.rootsweb.com/~mdhoward

Howard County Library-East Columbia • 6600 Cradlerock Way • Columbia, MD 21045-4912 • (410) 313-7700 • http://www.hclibrary.org

Order of the First Families of Maryland • 9409 Farewell Rd • Columbia, MD 21045-4413 • http://www.rootsweb.com/~mdoffmd/member.htm

Crisfield
Crisfield Heritage Foundation • 3 9th St • Crisfield, MD 21817-1028 • (410) 968-2501 • http://www.crisfield.org/Crisfieldheritage.htm

Crownsville
Commission on Indian Affairs • 100 Community Pl • Crownsville, MD 21032-2025 • http://www.dhcd.state.md.us/mcia/

Maryland Historical Trust • 100 Community Pl • Crownsville, MD 21032-2022 • (410) 514-7675 • http://www.MarylandHistoricalTrust.net

Rising Sun Inn Museum • 1090 Generals Hwy • Crownsville, MD 21032

Cumberland
Allegany College of Maryland Library - Appalachian Collection • 12401 Willowbrook Rd SE • Cumberland, MD 21502-2596 • (301) 784-5138 • http://www.allegany.edu/library

Allegany County Genealogical Society • 215 Bowen St • Cumberland, MD 21502 • (301) 777-8850 • http://www.rootsweb.com/~mdallegh/acgs.html

Allegany County Historical Society • Gordon-Roberts House Museum, 218 Washington St • Cumberland, MD 21502 • (301) 777-8678 • http://www.historyhouse.allconet.org

Allegany County Library • 31 Washington St • Cumberland, MD 21502-2981 • (301) 777-1220 • http://www.lib.allconet.org

Allegany Museum • 81 Baltimore St • Cumberland, MD 21502 • (301) 777-7200 • http://www.alleganymuseum.org

C&O Canal Boat Replica Museum • 13 Canal St • Cumberland, MD 21502 • (301) 724-3655

George Washington's Headquarters Museum • Greene St • Cumberland, MD 21502 • (301) 759-6636

Darlington

Harford County Public Library-Darlington Branch • 1134 Main St • Darlington, MD 21034-1418 • (410) 638-3750 • http://www.harf.lib.md.us

Darnestown

Darnestown Historical Society • 14101 Berryville Rd • Darnestown, MD 20874 • (301) 869-8969

John Brown Historical Foundation • 13701 Deakins Ln • Darnestown, MD 20874 • (301) 963-3300

Sons of Confederate Veterans • 14101 Berryville Rd • Darnestown, MD 20874-3517 • (800) MYSOUTH • http://www.scv.org

Davidsonville

Anne Arundel County Free School Museum • Lavall Dr • Davidsonville, MD 21401

Deale

Deale Area Historical Society • P.O. Box 650 • Deale, MD 20751 • (443) 321-8720 • http://www.dahs.us

Denton

Caroline County Historical Society • Courthouse Green, 16 N 2nd St, P.O. Box 514 • Denton, MD 21629 • (410) 482-8072

Caroline County Public Library • 100 Market St • Denton, MD 21629 • (410) 479-1343 • http://www.caro.lib.md.us/library/

Museum of Rural Life • 16 N 2nd St, P.O. Box 514 • Denton, MD 21629 • (410) 479-2055

Derwood

Maryland Agricultural History Farm Park • 18400 Muncaster Rd • Derwood, MD 20855-1421 • (301) 948-5053 • http://www.marylandagriculture.com

Dundalk

Dundalk Patapsco Neck Historical Society • Historical Museum, 4 Center Pl, P.O. Box 21781 • Dundalk, MD 21222 • (410) 284-2331

Dundalk-Patapsco Neck Historical Society • 43 Shipping Pl, P.O. Box 9235 • Dundalk, MD 21222 • (410) 284-2331

Earleville

Mount Harmon Plantation Museum • 600 Grove Neck Rd • Earleville, MD 21919 • (410) 275-8819 • http://www.mountharmon.org

Easton

Historical Society of Talbot County • Historical Museum, 25 S Washington St, P.O. Box 964 • Easton, MD 21601 • (410) 822-0773 • http://www.hstc.org

Talbot County Free Library & Museum • 100 W Dover St • Easton, MD 21601 • (410) 822-1626 • http://www.talb.lib.md.us

Talbot County Historical Society • 25 S Washington St • Easton, MD 21601

Upper Shore Genealogical Society of Maryland • P.O. Box 275 • Easton, MD 21301 • (410) 745-3050 • http://www.chronography.com/usgs/center.html

Edgewater

Historic London Town Museum and Gardens • 839 Londontown Rd • Edgewater, MD 21037 • (410) 222-1919 • http://www.historiclondontown.com

London Town Publik House and Gardens Library • 839 Londontown Rd • Edgewater, MD 21037 • (410) 222-1919 • http://www.historiclondontown.com

Edgewood

Harford County Public Library-Edgewood Branch • 629 Edgewood Rd • Edgewood, MD 21040-2607 • (410) 612-1600

Elkton

Cecil County Public Library • 301 Newark Ave • Elkton, MD 21921-5441 • (410) 996-5600 • http://www.ebranch.cecil.lib.md.us

Historical Society of Cecil County • Historical Museum, 135 E Main St • Elkton, MD 21921 • (410) 398-1790 • http://www.cchistory.org

Ellicott City

Bagpipe Music Museum • 840 Oella Ave • Ellicott City, MD 21043

Ellicott City B&O Railroad Station Museum • 2711 Maryland Ave • Ellicott City, MD 21043 • (410) 461-1945 • http://www.ecborail.org

Firehouse Museum • 3829 Church Rd, P.O. Box 292 • Ellicott City, MD 21041 • (410) 987-0232

Howard County Historical Society • Historical Museum, 8324 Court Ave, P.O. Box 109 • Ellicott City, MD 21043 • (410) 461-1050 • http://www.hchsmd.org

Emmitsburg

Emmitsburg Area Historical Society • 15339 Sixes Bridge Rd, P.O. Box 463 • Emmitsburg, MD 21727 • (301) 447-2220 • http://www.emmitsburg.net/history/

Hugh J Phillips Library • Mount Saint Mary's College & Seminary, 16300 Old Emmitsburg Rd • Emmitsburg, MD 21727-7799 • (301) 447-5244 • http://www.msmary.edu/studentsandstaff/library

National Shrine of Saint Elizabeth Ann Seton • 333 S Seton Ave • Emmitsburg, MD 21727 • (301) 447-6606 • http://www.setonshrine.org

Essex

Essex and Middle River Heritage Society • Historical Museum, 516 Eastern Blvd • Essex, MD 21221-6701 • (410) 574-6934 • http://www.heritsoc-esx-midriv.com

Fallston

Harford County Public Library-Fallston-Jarrettsville • 1461 Fallson Rd • Fallston, MD 21047-1699 • (410) 638-3003

Fort Meade

Family Historians • 9800 Savage Rd • Fort Meade, MD 20755-6000

Fort George G Meade Museum • 4674 Griffin Ave • Fort Meade, MD 20744 • (301) 677-6966 • http://www.ftmeade.army.mil/museum/

National Cryptologic Museum • 9900 Colony 7 Rd • Fort Meade, MD 20755 • (301) 688-5848 • http://www.nsa.gov/museum

Fort Washington

Afro-American Historical and Genealogial Society, Prince George's County Chapter • P.O. Box 44772 • Fort Washington, MD 20744-9998 • (301) 292-2751 • http://www.rootsweb.com/~mdaahgs/pgcm/

Fort Washington Park Museum • 13551 Fort Washington Rd • Fort Washington, MD 20744 • (301) 763-4600 • http://www.nps.gov/fowa

Frederick

Barbara Fritchie House Museum • 154 W Patrick St • Frederick, MD 21701 • (301) 698-0630

Beatty-Cramer House Museum • 9010 Liberty Rd • Frederick, MD 21701 • (301) 668-6088 • http://www.frederickcountylandmarksfoundation.org

Children's Museum of Rose Hill Manor Park • 1611 N Market St • Frederick, MD 21701 • (301) 600-1646 • http://www.co.frederick.md.us/rosehill

Frederick County Genealogical Society • P.O. Box 412 • Frederick, MD 21705-0415 • (301) 831-5781 • http://www.frecogs.com

Frederick County Public Libraries • 110 E Patrick St • Frederick, MD 21701 • (301) 694-1613 • http://www.fcpl.org

Historic Preservation Training Center • 4801 Urbana Pike • Frederick, MD 21704 • (301) 663-0856

Frederick, cont.
Historical Society of Frederick County • Historical Home Museum, 24 E Church St • Frederick, MD 21701 • (301) 663-1188 • http://www. hsfcinfo.org

Monocacy National Battlefield Museum • 4801 Urbana Pike • Frederick, MD 21704 • (301) 662-3515 • http://www.nps.gov.mono/ mo_visit.htm

Mount Olivet Cemetery & Francis Scott Key Monument • 515 S Market St • Frederick, MD 21701

National Museum of Civil War Medicine • 48 E Patrick St, P.O. Box 470 • Frederick, MD 21701 • (301) 695-1864 • http://www.civilwarmed. org

Prospect Hill Mansion Museum • 889 Butterfly Ln • Frederick, MD 21703

Roger Brooke Taney House and Museum • 121 S Bentz St • Frederick, MD 21701 • (301) 663-3540

Saint John's Cemetery Museum • 115 E 2nd St • Frederick, MD 21701

Schifferstadt Architectural Museum • 1110 Rosemont Ave • Frederick, MD 21701 • (301) 663-3885 • http://www. frederickcountylandmarksfoundation.org

Thurmont Historical Society • 11 N Church St, P.O. Box 251 • Frederick, MD 21788-0251 • (301) 271-1860

Fredericktown
Iron County Genealogical Society • 316 Sherlock Dr • Fredericktown, MD 63645 • (573) 783-5739

Friendsville
Friend Family Association • Historical Museum, 261 Maple Ave, P.O. Box 96 • Friendsville, MD 21531 • (301) 746-4690 • http://www. FriendFamilyAssociation.org

Frostburg
Frostburg Museum • Hill & Oak Sts, P.O. Box 92 • Frostburg, MD 21532 • (301) 689-1195 • http://www.frostmuseum.allconet.org

Thrasher Carriage Museum • 19 Depot St • Frostburg, MD 21532 • (301) 689-3380 • http://www.thrashercarriagemuseum.com

Funkstown
Historic Funkstown • Historical Museum, P.O. Box 235 • Funkstown, MD 21734

Gaithersburg
Cornish American Heritage Society • 13 Saint Ives Pl • Gaithersburg, MD 20877 • http://www.cousinjack.org

Gaithersburg Historical Association • Historical Museum, 9 S Summit Ave, P.O. Box 211 • Gaithersburg, MD 20884

Genealogical Council of Maryland Bible Records • P.O. Box 10096 • Gaithersburg, MD 20898-0096

Galesville
Galesville Heritage Society • Carrie Weedon House Museum, 988 Main St, P.O. Box 373 • Galesville, MD 20765-0373 • (410) 867-9499 • http://www.galesvilleheritagesociety.org

Germantown
Afro-American Historical and Genealogical Society, James Dent Walker Chapter • P.O. Box 1848 • Germantown, MD 20875-1848

Germantown Historical Society • Historical Museum, 19334 Mateny Hill Rd, P.O. Box 475 • Germantown, MD 20875 • (301) 492-6282

Gibson Island
Gibson Island Historical Society • Historical Museum, P.O. Box 667 • Gibson Island, MD 21056 • (410) 437-5270

Glen Arm
Society of Middletown First Settlers Descendants 1650-1700 • 10 Windy Hill Rd • Glen Arm, MD 21057 • http://www.rootsweb. com/~ctsmfsd/

Glen Burnie
Anne Arundel County Historical Society • Benson Hammond House, 5 Crain Hwy S • Glen Burnie, MD 21061-3525 • (410) 760-9679

Kuethe Library, Historical & Genealogical Research Center • 5 Crain Highway SE • Glen Burnie, MD 21061 • (410) 760-9679 • http://www. aagensoc.org/kuenthe.shtml

Glen Echo
Clara Barton National Historic Site Library • 5801 Oxford Rd • Glen Echo, MD 20812 • (301) 492-6245 • http://www.nps.gov/clba

Saint Andrew's Society of Washington DC • P.O. Box 372 • Glen Echo, MD 20812 • http://www.stas-dc.thecapitalscot.com

Glenn Dale
Marietta House Museum • 5626 Bell Station Rd • Glenn Dale, MD 20769 • (301) 464-5291 • http://www.pghistory.org/MariettaMansion. html

Prince George's County Historical Society • Historical Museum, 5626 Bell Station Rd • Glenn Dale, MD 20769 • (301) 220-0330 • http://www. pghistory.org

Grantsville
Grantsville Community Museum • 153 Main St • Grantsville, MD 21536 • (301) 895-5454

Greenbelt
Greenbelt Historical Society • 204 Lastner Ln • Greenbelt, MD 20770-1617 • (301) 474-5156

Greenbelt Museum • 15 Crescent Rd • Greenbelt, MD 20770 • (301) 474-1936 • http://www.greenbeltmuseum.org

National Institute on Genealogical Research • P.O. Box 118 • Greenbelt, MD 20768-0118 • http://www.rootsweb.com/~natgenin/

Hagerstown
Chesapeake & Ohio Canal National Historical Park Library • 1850 Dual Hwy, Suite 100 • Hagerstown, MD 21740 • (301) 739-4200 • http://www.nps.gov/choh

Genealogical Computer Society of Georgia • 1500 Pennsylvania Ave • Hagerstown, MD 21742 • (301) 766-9155 • http://www.mindspring. com/~noahsark/gcsga.html

Hagerstown Roundhouse Museum • 300 S Burhans Blvd, P.O. Box 2858 • Hagerstown, MD 21741 • (301) 739-4665

Jonathan Hager House Museum • 19 Key St • Hagerstown, MD 21740 • (301) 739-8393 • http://www.hagerhouse.org

Train Room Museum • 360 S Burhans Blvd • Hagerstown, MD 21740

Washington County Free Library • 101 Tandy Dr • Hagerstown, MD 21740 • (301) 739-3250 • http://www.wc-link.org/wcfl

Washington County Historical Society • Jamieson Memorial Library, 135 W Washington St, P.O. Box 1281 • Hagerstown, MD 21741-1281 • (301) 797-8782 • http://www.rootsweb.com/~mdwchs

Washington County Historical Society • Miller House Museum, 135 W Washington St, P.O. Box 1281 • Hagerstown, MD 21740 • (301) 797-8782 • http://www.rootsweb.com/~mdwchs

Halethorpe
Baltimore & Ohio Railroad Historical Society • 2905 Lakebrook Cr, Apt T3 • Halethorpe, MD 21227 • (410) 247-8165

Hancock
Hancock Historical Society • 126 W High St • Hancock, MD 21750 • (301) 678-7377 • http://www.hancockmd.com/org/historic/

Havre de Grace

Friends of Concord Point Lighthouse • Historical Museum, Concord & Lafayette Sts, P.O. Box 212 • Havre de Grace, MD 21078 • (410) 939-3213

Harford County Public Library-Havre de Grace Branch • 120 N Union Ave • Havre de Grace, MD 21078-3000 • (410) 939-6700

Havre de Grace Maritime Museum • 100 Lafayette St • Havre de Grace, MD 21078 • (410) 939-4800 • http://www.hdgmaritimemuseum. org

Rock Run House Museum • 801 Stafford Rd • Havre de Grace, MD 21078 • (410) 557-7994

Steppingstone Farm Museum • 461 Quaker Bottom Rd • Havre de Grace, MD 21078 • (410) 939-2299 • http://www. steppingstonemuseum.org

Susquehanna Museum of Havre de Grace • 817 Conesteo St, P.O Box 253 • Havre de Grace, MD 21078 • (410) 939-5780 • http://www.users. erols.com/susqmuseum/; http://www.lockhousemuseum.org

Hollywood

Sotterley Plantation Museum • 44300 Sotterley Ln, P.O. Box 57 • Hollywood, MD 20636 • (301) 373-2280 • http://www.sotterley.org

Hurlock

Sharptown Historical Society • 408 S Main St • Hurlock, MD 21643 • (410) 883-2269

Hyattsville

Prince George's County Memorial Library System • 6532 Adelphi Rd • Hyattsville, MD 20782-2098 • (301) 699-3500 • http://www.prge.lib. md.us

Prince George's County Memorial Library System -Hyattsville Branch • 6530 Adelphi Rd • Hyattsville, MD 20782-2098 • (301) 985-4690

Indian Head

Naval Surface Warfare Center Library • Strauss Ave, Bldg 620 • Indian Head, MD 20640 • (301) 744-4747 • http://www.ih.navy.mil

Star of the Sea Golden Hill Foundation • Historical Museum • Indian Head, MD 20640

Jessup

National Railway Historical Society • general delivery • Jessup, MD 20794 • (301) 490-7311

Joppa

Harford County Public Library-Joppa Branch • 655 Towne Center Dr • Joppa, MD 21085-4497 • (410) 612-1660

Keedysville

Washington County Genealogical Society • RR 1, Box 77-A • Keedysville, MD 21756

Kensington

Kensington Historical Society • Historical Museum, P.O. Box 453 • Kensington, MD 20895-0453 • (301) 942-8933

Mid-Atlantic Germanic Society • P.O. Box 2642 • Kensington, MD 20891-2642 • http://www.rootsweb.com/~usmags

Temple Branch Genealogical Library • 1000 Stoneybrook Dr, P.O. Box 49 • Kensington, MD 20895

La Plata

Charles County Historical Society • Historical Museum, Charles County Community College, Mitchell Rd • La Plata, MD 20646

Charles County Public Library-La Plata Branch • 2 Garrett Ave • La Plata, MD 20646-5959 • (301) 934-9001 • http://www.ccplonline.org

College of Southern Maryland Library • 8730 Mitchell Rd, P.O. Box 910 • La Plata, MD 20646-0910 • (301) 934-7626 • http://www.csmd. edu/library

Friendship House Museum • Charles County Community College • La Plata, MD 20646

Historical Society of Charles County • 101 Kent Ave, P.O. Box 2806 • La Plata, MD 20646 • (301) 934-2564

McConabie School and Farm Museum • 9162 Cedar St • La Plata, MD 20646

Piscataway Conoy Confederacy and Subtribes • P.O. Box 1484 • La Plata, MD 20646 • (301) 609-7625

La Vale

Allegany County Genealogical Society • P.O. Box 3103 • La Vale, MD 21504 • http://www.rootsweb.com/~mdallegh/acgs.html

Laurel

Laurel Heritage Association • Laurel Museum, 817 Main St • Laurel, MD 20707-3429 • (301) 725-7975 • http://www.laurelhistory.org

Laurel Historical Society • P.O. Box 774 • Laurel, MD 20707 • (301) 286-7031

Maryland TMG Users Group • 3535 Falling Run Rd • Laurel, MD 20724

Montpelier Mansion Museum • Route 197 & Muirkirk Rd • Laurel, MD 20708 • (301) 953-7572 • http://www.pgparks.com

Prince George's County Historical Society • Montpelier Mansion, Route 197 & Muirkirk Rd • Laurel, MD 20810 • (301) 953-1376 • http:// www.smart.net/~parksrec

Leonardtown

Saint Mary's County Genealogical Society • P.O. Box 1109 • Leonardtown, MD 20650 • (301) 373-8458 • http://www.smcgsi.org

Saint Mary's County Historical Society • Historical Museum, 11 Court House Dr, P.O. Box 212 • Leonardtown, MD 20650-0212 • (301) 475-2467 • http://www.somd.lib.md.us/smchs

Saint Mary's County Memorial Library • 23250 Hollywood Rd • Leonardtown, MD 20650 • (301) 475-2846 • http://www.stmalib.org

Lexington Park

Patuxent River Naval Air Museum • Route 235 & Shangri-La Dr • Lexington Park, MD 20635 • http://www.paxmuseum.com

Lineboro

Heritage Genealogical Society • P.O. Box 113 • Lineboro, MD 21088-0113

Linthicum

Anne Arundel Historical Society • Benson-Hammond House Museum, Aviation Blvd & Andover Rd, P.O. Box 385 • Linthicum, MD 21090 • (410) 768-9518 • http://www.aachs.org

Historical Electronics Museum • 1745 W Nursery Rd • Linthicum, MD 21090 • (410) 765-0230 • http://www.hem-usa.org

Lloyds

Spocott Windmill Foundation • Historical Museum, 1611 Hudson Rd • Lloyds, MD 21613

Lothian

Presidential Pet Museum • 1102 Wrighton Rd • Lothian, MD 20711 • (410) 741-0899 • http://www.presidentialpetmuseum.com

Prince Georges County Historic Historical and Cultural Trust • 193 Main St • Lothian, MD 20711 • (301) 627-4499

Lusby

One Room School Museum • 12741 Soundings Rd • Lusby, MD 20657

Lutherville

Fire Museum of Maryland • 1301 York Rd • Lutherville, MD 21093 • (410) 321-7500 • http://www.firemuseummd.org

General Society of the War of 1812 • 1219 Charmuth Rd • Lutherville, MD 21093-6404 • http://www.societyofthewarof1812.org

Maryland

Lutherville, cont.
Lutherville Historical Colored School Museum • 1426 School Ln • Lutherville, MD 21093 • (410) 825-6114 • http://www.luthervillecoloredschool.webs.com

Madison
Dorchester County Genealogical Society • 1058 Taylors Island Rd • Madison, MD 21648-1110 • (410) 228-5442

Marbury
Smallwood Retreat House Museum • 2750 Sweden Point Rd • Marbury, MD 20658 • (301) 743-7613 • http://www.dor.state.md.us

Mardela Springs
Adkins Museum and Historical Complex • 106 Brattan St, P.O. Box 160 • Mardela Springs, MD 21837 • (410) 677-4740

Westside Historical Society • Historical Museum, P.O. Box 194 • Mardela Springs, MD 21837 • (410) 543-6502

Marion
Accohannock Tribe • P.O. Box 404 • Marion, MD 21838 • (410) 623-2660 • http://skipjack.net/le_shore/accohannock/

Marriottsville
Society for the Preservation of Maryland Antiquities • 2335 Marriottsville Rd • Marriottsville, MD 21104 • (410) 442-1772

McHenry
Garrett College Library • 687 Mosser Rd • McHenry, MD 21541 • (301) 387-3009 • http://www.garrettcollege.edu/library

Middletown
Central Maryland Heritage League • Lamar Heritage and Cultural Center, 200 W Main St • Middletown, MD 21769

Dr Lamar's Sanitarium Museum • 200 W Main St • Middletown, MD 21769 • (301) 371-7090

Middletown Valley Historical Society • Historical Museum, 305 W Main St, P.O. Box 294 • Middletown, MD 21769-0294 • (301) 371-7582

Millersville
Kinder Farm Park Museum • 1001 Kinder Farm Park Rd • Millersville, MD 21108 • (410) 222-6115 • http://kinderfarmpark.org

Monrovia
Frederick County Genealogical Society • P.O. Box 234 • Monrovia, MD 21770-0234 • (301) 831-5781 • http://www.rootsweb.com/~mdgenweb/frecogs.htm

Mount Airy
Mount Airy Historical Society • Town Hall, 110 S Main St, P.O. Box 244 • Mount Airy, MD 21771-0244 • (301) 829-0489

New Windsor
New Windsor Heritage Committee • 136 Church St • New Windsor, MD 21776

Springdale School Museum • Springfield Rd • New Windsor, MD 21776 • (410) 848-8355

Newark
Queponco Railway Station Museum • 2378 Patey Woods Rd • Newark, MD 21841

Newburg
National Society of Descendants of Lords of Maryland Manors • 13070 Riverhaven Pl • Newburg, MD 20664-3235

North East
Upper Bay Museum • Walnut St at the River, P.O. Box 275 • North East, MD 21901

Veterans Memorial Library • Cecil Community College, 1 Seahawk Dr • North East, MD 21901-1904 • (410) 287-6060 • http://www.cec.lcc.edu/about/resources/library

Oakland
Garrett County Historical Society • Historical Museum, 107 S 2nd St, P.O. Box 28 • Oakland, MD 21550 • (301) 334-3226 • http://www.deepcreektimes.com/gchs.html

Ruth Enlow Library of Garrett County • 6 N 2nd St • Oakland, MD 21550-1393 • (301) 334-3996 • http://www.relib.net

Ocean City
Ocean City Museum Society • Ocean City Life Saving Museum, Boardwalk & Inlet Sts, P.O. Box 603 • Ocean City, MD 21842 • (410) 289-4991 • http://www.ocmuseum.org

Odenton
Odenton Heritage Society • P.O. Box 282 • Odenton, MD 21113 • http://www.odentonheritage.org

Olney
Menare Foundation • P.O. Box 1366 • Olney, MD 20830 • (301) 379-8898 • http://www.menare.org

Owings Mills
Jewish Genealogical Society of Maryland • Jewish Community Center, 3506 Gwynbrook Ave • Owings Mills, MD 21117 • (443) 255-8228

Oxford
Oxford Historical Society • Historical Museum, 100 S Morris St, P.O. Box 131 • Oxford, MD 21654 • (410) 226-0191 • http://www.oxfordmuseum.org

Oxon Hill
Oxon Cove Park Museum • 6411 Oxon Hill Rd • Oxon Hill, MD 20745 • (301) 763-1066 • http://www.nps.gov/nace/oxhi

Oxon Hill Manor Museum • 6901 Oxon Hill Rd • Oxon Hill, MD 20745 • (301) 839-7782

Prince George's County-Oxon Hill Branch • 6200 Oxon Hill Rd • Oxon Hill, MD 20745-3091 • (301) 839-2400

Parkville
Baltimore County Genealogical Society • 9601 Harford Rd • Parkville, MD 21234 • http://www.serve.com/bcgs/bcgs.html

Pasadena
Anne Arundel Genealogical Society • c/o Glen Burnie Library, 3 Crain Hwy SE, P.O. Box 221 • Pasadena, MD 21122 • (410) 760-9679 • http://www.aagensoc.org

Downs Park Historical Society • 8311 John Downs Loop • Pasadena, MD 21122 • (410) 222-6230

Historic Hancock Resolution Museum • 2795 Bayside Beach Rd • Pasadena, MD 21056 • (410) 255-4048 • http://www.historichancocksresolution.org

Jewish Genealogical Society of Maryland • 11 Slade Ave • Pasadena, MD 21122

Perry Hall
Grand Lodge of Maryland, Sons of Italy • P.O. Box 85 • Perry Hall, MD 21128 • (410) 668-6742 • http://www.osiamd.org

Perryville
Rodgers Tavern Museum • 259 Broad St, P.O. Box 773 • Perryville, MD 21903 • (410) 642-3703 • http://www.perryvillemd.org

Pocomoke City
Costen House Museum & Garden • 204 Market St • Pocomoke City, MD 21851 • (410) 957-4364

Delmarva Discovery Center • 2 Market St, P.O. Box 727 • Pocomoke City, MD 21851 • (410) 857-9933 • http://www.delmarvadiscoverycenter.org

Worcester County Historical Society • Historical Museum, 209 Willow St, P.O. Box 697 • Pocomoke City, MD 21851

Poolesville

Historic Medley District • Seneca Schoolhouse Museum, 16800 River Rd, P.O. Box 232 • Poolesville, MD 20837 • (301) 972-8588 • http://www.senecaschoolhouse.com

Port Deposit

Port Deposit Heritage Corporation • Paw Paw Museum, 98 N Main St, P.O. Box 101 • Port Deposit, MD 21904-1210 • (410) 378-3866

Port Tobacco

Society for the Restoration of Port Tobacco • Catslide House Museum, Chapel Point Rd, P.O. Box 302 • Port Tobacco, MD 20677 • (301) 934-4313

Thomas Stone National Historic Site Museum • 6655 Rose Hill Rd • Port Tobacco, MD 20677 • (301) 934-6027 • http://www.nps.gov/thst/

Preston

Caroline County Historical Society • 3395 Linchester Rd • Preston, MD 21655 • (410) 673-9204

Prince Frederick

Calvert County Historical Society • Historical Museum, 70 Church St, P.O. Box 358 • Prince Frederick, MD 20678 • (410) 535-2452 • http://www.calverthistory.org

Princess Anne

Frederick Douglass Library • University of Maryland-Eastern Shore, Backbone Rd • Princess Anne, MD 21853 • (410) 651-6621 • http://www.fdl.umes.edu

Lower Shore Genealogical Society • 1133 Somerset Ave • Princess Anne, MD 21853

Somerset County Historical Society • Treackle Mansion Museum, 11736 Mansion St, P.O. Box 181 • Princess Anne, MD 21853 • (410) 651-2238 • http://www.teackle.mansion.museum

Somerset County Historical Trust • 11380 Anderson Rd • Princess Anne, MD 21853 • (410) 651-0788

Somerset County Library System • 11767 Beachwood St • Princess Anne, MD 21853 • (410) 651-0852 • http://www.some.lib.md.us

Reisterstown

Baltimore County Public Library-Reisterstown Branch • 21 Cockeys Mill Rd • Reisterstown, MD 21136-1285 • (410) 887-1165 • http://www.bcpl.lib.md.us/branchpgs/re/rehome.html

Riverdale Park

Prince George's County Historical Society • Riverdale House Museum, 4811 Riverdale Rd, P.O. Box 14 • Riverdale Park, MD 20737 • (219) 886-2007 • http://www.pghistory.org; http://www.riverdalehousemuseum.com

Rockville

Czechoslovak Society of Arts and Sciences • 1703 Mark Ln • Rockville, MD 20852-4106 • (301) 881-7222 • http://www.svu2000.org/genealogy/

Genealogical Club of the Montgomery County Historical Society • 42 W Middle Ln • Rockville, MD 20850 • (301) 340-2974 • http://www.montgomeryhistory.org

Isaac Franck Jewish Archives • 4928 Wyaconda Rd • Rockville, MD 20852 • (301) 255-1970 • http://www.bjedc.org/bje/library/library.cfm

Jewish Genealogical Society of Greater Washington • P.O. Box 1614 • Rockville, MD 20849-1614 • (301) 299-8739 • http://www.jewishgen.org/jgsgw/

Kass Judaic Library • Weiner Judaic Museum, 6125 Montrose Rd • Rockville, MD 20852 • (301) 881-0100 • http://www.jccgw.org

Latvian Museum • 400 Hurley Ave • Rockville, MD 20850 • (301) 340-8732 • http://www.alausa.org

Lincoln Park Historical Society • Historical Museum, 111 W Montgomery Ave, P.O. Box 1884 • Rockville, MD 20849-1884 • (301) 340-2974 • http://www.montgomeryhistory.org

Montgomery County Archives • Red Brick Courthouse, 29 Courthouse Sq, Rm G09 • Rockville, MD 20850 • (301) 279-1218 • http://www.montgomeryarchives.org

Montgomery County Genealogical Society • Beall-Dawson House Museum, 103 W Montgomery Ave • Rockville, MD 20850 • (301) 340-2974 • http://www.montgomeryhistory.org/Genealogy.htm

Montgomery County Historical Society • Beall-Dawson House Museum, 111 W Montgomery Ave • Rockville, MD 20850 • (301) 340-2974 • http://www.montgomeryhistory.org

Montgomery County Public Libraries • 99 Maryland Ave • Rockville, MD 20850-2372 • (240) 777-0002 • http://www.montgomerycountymd.gov/libraries

Montgomery County-Rockville Library • 99 Maryland Ave • Rockville, MD 20850-2371 • (240) 777-0001

Needwood Mansion Museum • 6700 Needwood Rd • Rockville, MD 20855

Peerless Rockville Historic Preservation • Historical Museum, P.O. Box 4262 • Rockville, MD 20849 • (301) 762-0096 • http://www.peerlessrockville.org

Society for Historical Archaeology • 15245 Shady Grove Rd • Rockville, MD 20850 • (301) 990-2454

Saint Leonard

Jefferson Patterson Park Museum • 10515 Mackall Rd • Saint Leonard, MD 20685 • (410) 586-8510 • http://www.jefpat.org

Saint Mary's City

Historic Saint Mary's City • 18751 Hogaboom Ln, P.O. Box 39 • Saint Mary's City, MD 20686 • (240) 895-4990 • http://www.stmaryscity.org

Historic Saint Mary's City Library • 18401 Rosecroft Rd, P.O. Box 39 • Saint Mary's City, MD 20686-0039 • (240) 895-4974

Saint Mary's College of Maryland Library • general delivery • Saint Mary's City, MD 20686 • (301) 862-0264 • http://www.smcm.edu/library/

Saint Michaels

Cheasapeake Bay Maritime Museum • Navy Point, P.O. Box 636 • Saint Michaels, MD 21663 • (410) 745-2916 • http://www.cbmm.org

Salisbury

Blackwell Library • Salisbury State Univ, 1101 Camden Ave • Salisbury, MD 21801-6863 • (410) 543-6130 • http://www.salisbury.edu/library

City Hall Museum and Cultural Center • 110 W Church St, P.O. Box 884 • Salisbury, MD 21801 • (410) 546-9007

Edward H. Nabb Research Center for DelMarVa History & Culture • 1101 Camden Ave, Room 190 • Salisbury, MD 21801 • (410) 543-6312 • http://nabbhistory.salisbury.edu

Lower Del-Mar-Va Genealogical Society • 116 N Division St, P.O. Box 3602 • Salisbury, MD 21801-3602 • (410) 219-5250 • http://www.rootsweb.com/~ldgs

Newtown Association • P.O. Box 543 • Salisbury, MD 21801 • (410) 543-2111

Poplar Hill Mansion Museum • 117 Elizabeth St • Salisbury, MD 21801 • (410) 749-1776

Sons of the American Revolution, Delaware Society • 316 London Ave • Salisbury, MD 21801 • http://www.dessar.org

Wicomico County Free Library • 122 S Division St • Salisbury, MD 21801 • (410) 749-3612 • http://www.wicomicolibrary.org

Maryland

Salisbury, cont.

Wicomico County Historical Society • Pemberton House Museum, Plantation Ln, P.O. Box 573 • Salisbury, MD 21803-0573 • (410) 860-0447 • http://skipjack.net/le_shore/whs/

Sandy Spring

Sandy Spring Heritage Group • 2707 Olney Sandy Spring Rd • Sandy Spring, MD 20860

Sandy Spring Museum • 17901 Bentley Rd • Sandy Spring, MD 20860 • (301) 774-0022 • http://www.sandyspringmuseum.org

Sandy Spring Slave Museum • 18524 Brooke Rd, P.O. Box 13 • Sandy Spring, MD 20860 • http://www.SandySpringSlaveMuseum.org

Scotland

Point Lookout Civil War Museum • Point Lookout State Park, P.O. Box 48 • Scotland, MD 20867

Severna Park

Gesher Galicia • 549 Cypress Ln • Severna Park, MD 21146 • http://feefhs.org/jsig/frg-gsig.html

Shady Side

Shady Side Rural Heritage Society • Capt Salem Avery House Museum, 1418 E W Shadyside Rd, P.O. Box 89 • Shady Side, MD 20750 • (410) 867-4486 • http://www.averyhouse.org

Shady Side Rural Heritage Society • 1418 EW Shady Side Rd, P.O. Box 89 • Shady Side, MD 20764 • (410) 867-4486

Sharpsburg

Antietam National Battlefield Museum • 5831 Dunker Church Rd, P.O. Box 158 • Sharpsburg, MD 21782 • (301) 432-5124 • http://www.nps.gov/anti

Barron's Chesapeake & Ohio Canal Museum • 5632 Mose Cr, P.O. Box 356 • Sharpsburg, MD 21782 • (301) 583-5299 • http://www.nps.gov

Chesapeake & Ohio Canal Tavern Museum • 11710 MacArthur Blvd, P.O. Box 4 • Sharpsburg, MD 20854 • http://www.cr.nps.gov

Silver Spring

Abraham Lincoln Institute • 721 Dartmouth Ave • Silver Spring, MD 20910 • (301) 495-2850

Association for the Study of Afro-American Life and History • 7961 Eastern Ave, Ste 301 • Silver Spring, MD 20910 • (301) 587-5900 • http://www.artnoir.com/asalh/

Capital View Park Historical Society • 10023 Menlo Ave • Silver Spring, MD 20910-1055 • (301) 588-4420

East Europe Connection • 1711 Corwin Dr • Silver Spring, MD 20910-1533 • (301) 585-0117 • http://feefhs.org/frgeec.html

General Conference of Seventh Day Adventists • 12501 Old Columbia Pk • Silver Spring, MD 20904 • (301) 680-5022 • http://www.adventistarchives.org

George Meany Memorial Museum • 10000 New Hampshire Ave • Silver Spring, MD 20903 • (301) 431-5451 • http://www.georgemeany.org

Mid-Atlantic Germanic Society • 347 Scott Dr • Silver Spring, MD 20904

National Capital Trolley Museum • 1313 Bonifant Rd • Silver Spring, MD 20905 • (301) 384-6352 • http://www.dctrolley.org

National Railway Historical Society, Potomac Chapter • general delivery • Silver Spring, MD 20906 • (301) 946-9461

Silver Spring Historical Society • P.O. Box 1160 • Silver Spring, MD 20910-4504 • http://www.homestead.com/silverspringhistory

Association for the Study of African-American Life and History • CB Powell Bldg, 525 Bryant St NW, Ste C142 • Silver Springs, MD 20059 • (202) 865-0053

Smithsburg

Smithsburg Historical Society • 9 N Main St, P.O. Box 403 • Smithsburg, MD 21783 • (301) 824-7154 • http://pilot.wash.lib.md.us/smithsburg/HIST.htm

Smithsburg History Museum • 21 W Water St, P.O. Box 403` • Smithsburg, MD 21783

Snow Hill

Furnace Town Living Heritage Museum • 3816 Old Furnace Rd, P.O. Box 207 • Snow Hill, MD 21863 • (410) 632-2032 • http://www.furnacetown.cjb.net

Julia A Purnell Museum • 208 W Market St • Snow Hill, MD 21863 • (410) 632-0515 • http://www.purnellmuseum.com

Worcester County Historical Society • P.O. Box 111 • Snow Hill, MD 21863-0111

Worcester County Library • 307 N Washington St • Snow Hill, MD 21863 • (410) 632-2600 • http://www.worc.lib.md.us/library/home.html

Solomons

Calvert Marine Museum • 14200 Solomons Islands Rd, P.O. Box 97 • Solomons, MD 20688 • (410) 326-2042 • http://www.calvertmarinemuseum.com

Stevensville

Hero Library • Historical Evaluation & Research Organization, 1407 Love Point Rd • Stevensville, MD 21666 • (410) 643-8807 • http://www.herolibrary.org

Kent Island Heritage Society • Cray House Museum, Cockney's Ln, P.O. Box 321 • Stevensville, MD 21666 • (410) 643-5969 • http://www.historicqac.org/sites/STpo.htm

Old Stevensville Post Office Museum • 408 Love Point Rd, P.O. Box 321 • Stevensville, MD 21666 • (410) 643-5969 • http://www.historicqac.org/sites/STop.htm

Suitland

Airmen Memorial Museum • 5211 Auth Rd • Suitland, MD 20746 • (301) 899-8386 • http://www.afsahq.org

National Museum of the American Indian in Maryland • 4220 Silver Hill Rd • Suitland, MD 20746 • (301) 238-1435 • http://www.nmai.si.edu

Washington National Records Center • 4205 Suitland Rd • Suitland, MD 20746-8001 • (403) 788-1600 • http://www.archives.gov

Sunderland

Calvert County Genealogy Society • P.O. Box 9 • Sunderland, MD 20689-0009 • (410) 535-0839

Sykesville

Sykesville Gate House Museum of History • 7283 Cooper Dr • Sykesville, MD 21784

Takoma Park

Historic Takoma Carriage House Museum • 7333 Carroll Ave • Takoma Park, MD 20912

Historic Takoma Park • 6903 Laurel Ave • Takoma Park, MD 20912 • (301) 270-2831

Takoma Park Campus Library • Montgomery College, 7600 Takoma Ave • Takoma Park, MD 20912 • (301) 650-1536 • http://montgomerycollege.org/library

Takoma Park Historical Society • Municipal Bldg, 7500 Maple Ave • Takoma Park, MD 20912 • (301) 585-3542

Takoma Park Library • 101 Philadelphia Ave • Takoma Park, MD 20912 • (301) 891-7259 • http://www.cityoftakomapark.org/library

Weis Library • Columbia Union College, 7600 Flower Ave • Takoma Park, MD 20912-7796 • (301) 891-4217 • http://www.cuc.edu/library/

Thurmont

Catoctin Furnace Historical Society • Catoctin Furnace Museum, 12320 Auburn Rd • Thurmont, MD 21788 • (301) 271-2306

Thurmont Historical Society • Creeger House Museum, 11 N Church St • Thurmont, MD 21788 • (301) 271-1860

Tilghman

Tilghman Island Museum • P.O. Box 297 • Tilghman, MD 21671

Towson

Archives of the Maryland Synod, Lutheran Church of America • 7604 York Rd • Towson, MD 21204

Baltimore County Genealogical Society • P.O. Box 10085 • Towson, MD 21204 • (410) 750-9315 • http://www.serve.com/bcgs/bcgs.html

Baltimore County Public Library • 320 York Rd • Towson, MD 21204-5179 • (410) 887-6100 • http://www.bcpl.info/

Hampton National Historic Site Museum • 535 Hampton Ln • Towson, MD 21286 • (410) 823-1309 • http://www.mps.gov/hamp

Union Bridge

Hard Lodging Museum • 4625 Ladiesburg Rd • Union Bridge, MD 21791 • (410) 858-6494

Western Maryland Railway Historical Society • Historical Museum, 41 N Main St, P.O. Box 395 • Union Bridge, MD 21791 • (410) 775-0150 • http://www.moosevalley.org/smrhs/wmrhsindex.htm

Upper Malboro

Prince George's County Memorial Library System-Public Documents Reference • County Administration Bldg, Rm 2198 • Upper Malboro, MD 20772-3050 • (301) 952-3904

Billingsley Manor Museum • 6900 Green Landing Rd • Upper Marlboro, MD 20772 • (301) 627-0730

Darnall's Chance House Museum • 14800 Gov Oden Bowie Dr • Upper Marlboro, MD 20772 • (301) 952-8010 • http://www.pgparks.com

Patuxent Rural Life Museum • Patuxent River Park, 16000 Croom Airport Rd • Upper Marlboro, MD 20772 • (301) 627-0730 • http://www.pgparks.com

Upperco

Maryland Steam Historical Society • 541 Arcadia Ave • Upperco, MD 21155 • (410) 374-1332

Waldorf

Cedarville Band of Piscataway Indians • American Indian Cultural Ctr, 16816 Country Ln • Waldorf, MD 20601 • (301) 372-1932

Dr Samuel A Mudd Society • Historical Museum, 7325 Doctor Samuel Mudd Rd • Waldorf, MD 20601 • (301) 645-6870 • http://www.somd.lib.md.us/MUSEUMS/Mudd.htm

Maryland Indian Heritage Society • Historical Museum, 16816 Country Ln • Waldorf, MD 20601

Warwick

Old Bohemia Historical Society • Historical Museum, Bohemia Church Rd, P.O. Box 61 • Warwick, MD 21912 • (301) 378-5800 • http://www.stjosephmiddletown.com

Washington Grove

Washington Grove Heritage Committee • McCathran Hall Museum, P.O. Box 5 • Washington Grove, MD 20880 • (301) 926-4786

West Denton

Old Harford Town Maritime Center • 10215 River Landing Rd • West Denton, MD 21122 • http://www.riverheritage.org

Westminster

Association of One-Name Studies • 65 E Main St • Westminster, MD 21157 • (410) 876-6101 • http://www.WillowBend.net/aons.htm

Carroll County Farm Museum • 500 S Center St • Westminster, MD 21157 • (410) 848-7775 • http://www.ccgov.carr.org/farm

Carroll County Genealogical Society • c/o Carroll County Public Library, 50 E Main St, P.O. Box 1752 • Westminster, MD 21158 • (410) 876-6018 • http://www.carr.lib.md.us/ccgs/ccgs.html

Historical Society of Carroll County • Kimmey House Museum, 210 E Main St • Westminster, MD 21157 • (410) 848-6494 • http://www.carr.org/hscc/

Mason Dixon Historical Society • Carroll County Farm Museum, 500 S Center St • Westminster, MD 21157 • (410) 876-2667

Sherman-Fisher-Shellman House Museum • 206 E Main St • Westminster, MD 21157 • (410) 848-6494

Springdale School Museum • 6 N Court S • Westminster, MD 21776

Union Mills Homestead & Grist Mill Museum • 3311 Littlestown Pk • Westminster, MD 21158 • (410) 848-2288 • http://www.unionmills.org

Whiteford

Harford County Public Library-Whiteford Branch • 2407 Whiteford Rd • Whiteford, MD 21160-1218 • (410) 638-3608

Whitehaven

Whitehaven Heritage Association • 2689 Church St • Whitehaven, MD 21856

Woodsboro

Woodsboro Historical Society • P.O. Box 348 • Woodsboro, MD 21798

Wye Mills

Friends of Wye Mill • Wye Grist Mill Museum, Route 662, P.O. Box 277 • Wye Mills, MD 21679-0277 • (410) 827-6909

Maryland

Abington

Abington Historical Commission • Historical Museum, 600 R F Gliniewicz Wy • Abington, MA 02315 • (781) 982-0059 • http://www.abingtonhistory.org

Abington Public Library • 600 Gliniewicz Way • Abington, MA 02351 • (781) 982-2139

Dyer Memorial Library • 28 Centre Ave, P.O. Box 2245 • Abington, MA 02351 • (781) 878-8480 • http://www.dyerlibrary.org

Old Abington Historical Society • c/o Dyer Memorial Library, 28 Centre Ave, P.O. Box 2245 • Abington, MA 02351 • (781) 878-8480

Acton

Acton Historical Society • 300 Main St, P.O. Box 2389 • Acton, MA 01720 • (978) 264-0690

Acton Memorial Library • 486 Main St • Acton, MA 01720 • (978) 264-9641 • http://www.actonmemoriallibrary.org

Acushnet

Russell Memorial Library • 88 Main St • Acushnet, MA 02743 • (508) 998-0270

Adams

Adams Free Library • 92 Park St • Adams, MA 01220-2005 • (413) 743-8345 • http://town.adams.ma.us

Adams Historical Society • 5 Woods Dr • Adams, MA 01220 • (413) 743-1799

Agawam

Agawam Historical Commission • Historical Museum, 36 Main St • Agawam, MA 01001 • (413) 786-3236

Agawam Historical Society • Fire House Museum, 35 Elm St, P.O. Box 552 • Agawam, MA 01001 • (413) 789-4631 • http://www.agawam-history.org

Agawam Public Library • 750 Cooper St • Agawam, MA 01001 • (413) 789-1550

Air Station Cape Cod

US Coast Guard Base Library-Otis • Bldg 5205 • Air Station Cape Cod, MA 02542-5017 • (508) 968-6456

Amesbury

Amesbury Carriage Museum • 270 Main St, P.O. Box 252 • Amesbury, MA 01913 • (978) 834-9981

Amesbury History Committee • Lion's Mouth Rd • Amesbury, MA 01913 • (978) 388-1420

Amesbury Public Library • 149 Main St • Amesbury, MA 01913 • (978) 388-8148 • http://www.amesburylibrary.org

Bartlett Museum • 270 Main St, P.O. Box 692 • Amesbury, MA 01913-0016 • (978) 388-4528

Lowell's Boat Shop Museum • 459 Main St • Amesbury, MA 01913 • (978) 388-0162 • http://www.lowellsboatshop.com

Macy-Colby House Museum • 257 Main St • Amesbury, MA 01913 • (978) 388-7979

Mary Baker Eddy Historic House Museum • 227 Main St • Amesbury, MA 01913 • (617) 277-8943

Whittier Home Museum • 86 Friend St, P.O. Box 632 • Amesbury, MA 01913 • (978) 388-1337

Amherst

Amherst Historical Society • Strong House Museum, 67 Amity St, P.O. Box 739 • Amherst, MA 01002 • (413) 256-0678 • http://www.amhersthistory.org

Berkshire Conference of Women Historians • Dept of History, Univ of Mass • Amherst, MA 01003 • (413) 545-6778 • http://www.berksconference.org

Emily Dickinson Museum • The Evergreens, 280 Main St • Amherst, MA 01002 • (413) 542-8161 • http://www.emilydickinsonmuseum.org

Jones Library • 43 Amity St • Amherst, MA 01002-2285 • (413) 256-4090 • http://www.joneslibrary.org

National Yiddish Book Center Museum • Weinberg Bldg, 1021 West St • Amherst, MA 01002 • (413) 245-4900 • http://www.yiddishbookcenter.org

W E B Du Bois Library - Special Collections • Univ of Massachusetts Amherst, 154 Hicks Way • Amherst, MA 01003-9275 • (413) 545-0150 • http://www.library.umass.edu/spcoll/spec.html

Andover

Andover Historical Society • Historical Museum, 97 Main St • Andover, MA 01810 • (978) 475-2236 • http://www.andhist.org; http://www.andoverhistorical.org

Memorial Hall Library • Elm Square • Andover, MA 01810 • (978) 623-8401 • http://www.mhl.org

Northeast Document Conservation Center • 100 Brickstone Sq • Andover, MA 01810 • (617) 470-1010 • http://www.nedcc.org

Aquinnah

Wampanoag Tribe of Gay Head - Aquinnah • 20 Black Brook Rd • Aquinnah, MA 02535-9701 • (508) 645-9265 • http://www.wampanoagtribe.net

Arlington

Arlington Historical Society • Jason Russell Farmhouse Museum, 7 Jason St • Arlington, MA 02476-6410 • (781) 648-4300 • http://www.arlingtonhistorical.org

Armenian Cultural Foundation • 441 Mystic St • Arlington, MA 02174 • (781) 646-3090

Menotomy Minutemen Museum • 7 Jason St • Arlington, MA 02474 • (781) 648-4300 • http://www.menotomy.org

Old Schwamb Mill Museum • 17 Mill Ln • Arlington, MA 02476-4189 • (781) 643-0554 • http://www.oldschwambmill.org

Robbins Library • 700 Massachusetts Ave • Arlington, MA 02474 • (781) 316-3200 • http://www.mln.lib.ma.us

Ashburnham

Ashburnham Historical Society • Main St, P.O. Box 692 • Ashburnham, MA 01430

Ashby

Ashby Historical Society • Historical Museum, 471 Wheeler Rd, P.O. Box 90 • Ashby, MA 01431 • (978) 386-2319

Ashfield

Ashfield Historical Society • Historica Museum, 456 Main St, P.O. Box 277 • Ashfield, MA 01330 • (413) 628-4541

Ashland

Ashland Historical Society • Historical Museum, 2 Myrtle St, P.O. Box 145 • Ashland, MA 01721-0145 • (508) 881-8183

Massachusetts Society of Genealogists • P.O. Box 215 • Ashland, MA 01721 • (508) 792-5066 • http://www.rootsweb.com/~masgi/msog/

Ashley Falls

Col Ashley House Museum • Cooper Hill Rd • Ashley Falls, MA 01222 • (413) 229-5024 • http://www.thetrustees.org

Assonet

Assonet Bay Shores Association • Historical Museum, P.O. Box 201 • Assonet, MA 02702 • (401) 624-6259

Freetown Historical Society • Historical Museum, 1 Slab Bridge Rd, P.O. Box 253 • Assonet, MA 02717 • (508) 644-5310 • http://freetownhistory.8m.com

Assonet, cont.
James White Memorial Library-G H Hathaway Library • N Main St, No 6 • Assonet, MA 02702 • (508) 644-2385

Athol
Athol Historical Society • 1307 Main St, P.O. Box 21 • Athol, MA 01331 • (978) 249-4890

Athol Public Library • 568 Main St • Athol, MA 01331 • (978) 249-9515 • http://athollibrary.org

Attleboro
Attleboro Area Industrial Museum • 42 Union St • Attleboro, MA 02703 • (508) 222-3918 • http://www.industrialmuseum.com

Attleboro Museum • 86 Park St • Attleboro, MA 02703 • (508) 222-2644

Attleboro Public Library • 74 N Main St • Attleboro, MA 02703 • (508) 222-0157 • http://www.sailsinc.org/attleboro/apl.asp

Auburn
Auburn Historical Society • Historical Museum, 9B Homestead Ave • Auburn, MA 01501 • (508) 832-5665

Auburn Public Library • 369 Southbridge St • Auburn, MA 01501 • (508) 832-7790

Avon
New England Coastal Schaghticoke Indian Association and Tribal Council • P.O. Box 551 • Avon, MA 02322

Barnstable
Barnstable Historical Society • Donald G Trayser Museum, 3353 Main St • Barnstable, MA 02630 • (508) 362-2092 • http://www.barnstable-patriot.com/trayser

Olde Colonial Courthouse Museum • Rondezvous Ln & Route 6A, P.O. Box 41 • Barnstable, MA 02630 • (508) 362-9056 • http://www.talesofcapecod.org

Sturgis Library • 3090 Main St, P.O. Box 606 • Barnstable, MA 02630-0606 • (508) 362-6636 • http://www.sturgislibrary.org

Barre
Barre Historical Society • Historical Museum, 18 Common St, P.O. Box 755 • Barre, MA 01005 • (978) 355-4067

Woods Memorial Library • 19 Pleasant St, P.O. Box 489 • Barre, MA 01005-0489 • (978) 355-2533 • http://www.town.barre.ma.us/library

Bedford
Bedford Free Public Library • 7 Mudge Way • Bedford, MA 01730-2168 • (781) 275-9440 • http://www.bedfordlibrary.net

Jacob Lane House Museum • 295 North Rd, P.O. Box 720 • Bedford, MA 01730 • (781) 564-4761

Belchertown
Belchertown Historical Association • Stone House Museum, 20 Maple St, P.O. Box 1211 • Belchertown, MA 01007 • (413) 323-6573 • http://www.stonehousemuseum.org

Elbow Plantation Historical Society • 281 Chauncey Walker St, lot 53 • Belchertown, MA 01007-9134

Belmont
Belmont Historical Society • c/o Belmont Memorial Library, 336 Concord Ave, P.O. Box 125 • Belmont, MA 02178 • (617) 489-2000 • http://www.belmonthistoricalsociety.org

Belmont Memorial Library • 336 Concord Ave, P.O. Box 125 • Belmont, MA 02478-0125 • (617) 489-2000 • http://www.belmont.lib.ma.us

Grand Lodge of Massachusetts, Sons of Italy • 93 Concord Ave • Belmont, MA 02478-4061 • (617) 489-5234 • http://www.osiama.org

Berkley
Berkley Historical Society • 725 Berkley St • Berkley, MA 02779 • (508) 824-5367

Berkley Public Library & Museum • 1 N Main St • Berkley, MA 02779 • (508) 822-3329

Berlin
Berlin Art & Historical Society • Historical Museum, 51 South St, P.O. Box 87 • Berlin, MA 01503 • (978) 838-2502 • http://www.townofberlin.com/historical/

Berlin Art and Historical Collections • 4 Woodward Ave, P.O. Box 87 • Berlin, MA 01503 • (978) 838-2502 • http://www.townofberlin.com

Beverly
Beverly Historical Society • John Cabot House Museum, 117 Cabot St • Beverly, MA 01915-5196 • (978) 922-1186 • http://www.beverlyhistory.org

Essex County Historical Association • 23 Bancroft Ave • Beverly, MA 01915 • (978) 927-0138

John Balch House Museum • 448 Cabot St • Beverly, MA 01915

Reverend John Hale House Museum • 39 Hale St • Beverly, MA 01915

Billerica
Billeria Colonial Minutemen Museum • 1 Passaconaway Dr • Billerica, MA 01821 • (978) 470-0555

Billerica Historical Society • Historical Museum, 430 Boston Rd, P.O. Box 381 • Billerica, MA 01821 • (978) 262-0888 • http://www.billericahistory.org

Billerica Historical Society • Clara Sexton House Museum, 36 Concord Rd, P.O. Box 381 • Billerica, MA 01821 • (978) 663-8769

Billerica Public Library • 15 Concord St • Billerica, MA 01821 • (978) 671-0948 • http://www.billericalibrary.org

Blackstone
Barrett(e) Genealogy Association • 10 Ascension St • Blackstone, MA 01504

Blandford
Blandford Historical Society • 1 North St • Blandford, MA 01008 • (413) 848-0108

Porter Memorial Library • 87 Main St, P.O. Box 797 • Blandford, MA 01008-0797 • (413) 848-2853

Bolton
Bolton Historical Society • Sawyer House Museum, 676 Main St, P.O. Box 211 • Bolton, MA 01740 • (978) 779-6392

Bolton Public Library • 738 Main St, P.O. Box 188 • Bolton, MA 01740-0188 • (978) 779-2839 • http://www.townofbolton.com

Boston
African Meeting House Museum • 14 Beacon St, Ste 506 • Boston, MA 02108 • (617) 742-5415

American Congregational Library • 14 Beacon St • Boston, MA 02108-9999 • (617) 523-0470 • http://www.14beacon.org

Ancient and Honorable Artillery Company of Massachusetts • Historical Museum, Armory at Faneuil Hall • Boston, MA 02109 • (617) 227-1638 • http://www.ahac.us.com

Archives of the Episcopal Diocese of Massachusetts • 138 Tremont St • Boston, MA 02111 • (617) 482-4826 • http://www.diomass.org

Association for the Study of Connecticut History • Emerson College, 100 Beacon St • Boston, MA 02116-1501 • (617) 824-8762

Bay State Historical League • Vale Lyman Estate, 185 Lyman St • Boston, MA 02133 • (617) 899-3920

Beatley Library • Simmons College, 300 The Fenway • Boston, MA 02115 • (617) 521-2784 • http://www.simmons.edu

Boston Athenaeum & Museum • 10 1/2 Beacon St • Boston, MA 02108 • (617) 227-0270 • http://www.bostonathenaeum.org

Boston Fire Museum • 344 Congress St • Boston, MA 02210 • (617) 482-1344 • http://www.bostonfiremuseum.com

Boston National Historical Park • Charlestown Navy Yard • Boston, MA 02129 • (617) 242-5642 • http://www.nps.gov/bost/

Boston Public Library • 700 Boylston St, P.O. Box 286 • Boston, MA 02117-0286 • (617) 536-5400 • http://www.bpl.org

Boston Tea Party Ship & Museum • Congress St Bridge • Boston, MA 02127 • http://www.bostonteapartyship.com

Bostonian Society • Old State House Museum, 206 Washington St • Boston, MA 02109 • (617) 720-1713 • http://www.bostonhistory.org

Catholic Archdiocese of Boston Archives • 2121 Commonwealth Ave • Boston, MA 02135 • (617) 746-5797 • http://www.reab.org/archives/welcome.htm

Chinese Historical Society of New England • Historical Museum, 2 Boylston St • Boston, MA 02116-4704 • (617) 338-4339

Colonial Society of Massachusetts • 87 Mt Vernon St • Boston, MA 02108 • (617) 227-2782 • http://www.colonialsociety.org

Committee for a New England Bibliography • 233 Bay State Rd • Boston, MA 02215 • (617) 266-9706

Commonwealth of Massachusetts Museum & Archives • Columbia Point, 220 Morrissey Blvd • Boston, MA 02125 • (617) 727-9150 • http://www.sec.state.ma.us/mus/musidx.htm

Congregational Christian Historical Society • 14 Beacon St • Boston, MA 02108 • (617) 523-0470 • http://www.14beacon.org

Fall River Office of Historic Preservation • Historical Museum, 45 School St • Boston, MA 02108 • http://www.preservationmass.org/historic.shtml

First Church of Christ, Scientist, Church History Library • 175 Huntington Ave • Boston, MA 02115 • (617) 450-3503

French Library and Cultural Center • 53 Marlborough St • Boston, MA 02116 • (617) 266-4351 • http://www.frenchlib.org

Gibson Society • Gibson House Museum, 135 Beacon St • Boston, MA 02116 • (617) 267-6338 • http://www.thegibsonhouse.org

Goethe Institute • 170 Beacon St • Boston, MA 02116 • (617) 262-6050 • http://www.goethe.de/boston

Hichborn House Museum • 29 North Sq • Boston, MA 02113

Historic Massachusetts • Historical Museum, 45 School St • Boston, MA 02108 • (617) 723-3383

Historic New England • Harrison Gray Otis House Museum, 141 Cambridge St • Boston, MA 02114 • (617) 227-3956 • http://www.historicnewengland.com

John F Kennedy Presidential Library • Columbia Point • Boston, MA 02125 • (617) 514-1600 • http://www.jfklibrary.org

Joseph P Healey Library • University of Massachusetts at Boston, 100 Morrissey Blvd • Boston, MA 02125-3393 • (617) 287-5940 • http://www.lib.umb.edu

Marshall Street Historical Society • 156 Milk St, Ste 2 • Boston, MA 02109 • (617) 426-9375

Mary Baker Eddy Library Museum • 200 Massachusetts Ave • Boston, MA 02115 • (617) 450-7000 • http://www.mbelibrary.org

Masonic Grand Lodge of Massachusetts • 186 Tremont St • Boston, MA 02111 • (617) 426-6040 • http://www.massfreemasonry.org

Massachusetts Center for Native American Awareness • P.O. Box 5885 • Boston, MA 02114 • (617) 884-4227 • http://www.mcnaa.org

Massachusetts Historical Commission • 220 Morrissey Blvd • Boston, MA 02116 • (617) 727-8470 • http://www.state.ma.us/sec/mhc/

Massachusetts Historical Society • Historical Museum, 1154 Boylston St • Boston, MA 02215 • (617) 646-0524 • http://www.masshist.org

Massachusetts Society of Mayflower Descendants • 100 Boylston St. Suite #750 • Boston, MA 02116 • (617) 266-1624 • http://www.massmayflower.org

Massachusetts State Archives and Library • Archives of the Commonwealth, 220 Morrissey Blvd • Boston, MA 02125 • (617) 727-2816 • http://www.state.ma.us/see/are/arcidx.htm

Massachusetts State Library • 24 Beacon St • Boston, MA 02133 • (617) 727-2590 • http://www.state.ma.us/lib/homepage.htm

Mugar Memorial Library • Boston University, 771 Commonwealth Ave • Boston, MA 02215 • (617) 353-3710 • http://web.bu.edu/library/

Museum of Afro-American History • 14 Beacon St, Ste 719 • Boston, MA 02108 • (617) 725-0022 • http://www.afroammuseum.org

National Trust for Historic Preservation • 7 Faneuil Hall Marketplace, 5th Fl • Boston, MA 02109 • (617) 523-0885

New England Archivists • c/o Massachusetts Archives, 220 Morrissey Blvd • Boston, MA 02125 • (617) 727-2816

New England Historic Genealogical Society • 99 Newbury St • Boston, MA 02116-3007 • (617) 296-3447 • http://www.nehgs.org; www.newenglandancestors.org

New England Historic Genealogical Society Library • 101 Newbury St • Boston, MA 02116-3007 • (617) 536-5740 • http://www.nehgs.org; http://www.newenglandancestors.org

New England Museum Association • Boston National Historic Park, Charlestown Navy Yard • Boston, MA 02129 • (617) 242-5620 • http://www.nps.gov/bost

Nichols House Museum • 55 Mount Vernon St • Boston, MA 02108 • (617) 227-6993 • http://www.nicholshousemuseum.org

Old North Foundation of Boston • 193 Salem St • Boston, MA 02113 • (617) 523-6793 • http://www.oldnorth.com

Old South Association in Boston • Meeting House Museum, 310 Washington St • Boston, MA 02108 • (617) 482-6439 • http://www.oldsouthmeetinghouse.org

Oral History Center • 403 Richards Hall • Boston, MA 02115 • (617) 373-4814

Paul Revere Memorial Association • Paul Revere House Museum, 19 North Sq • Boston, MA 02113 • (617) 523-2338 • http://www.paulreverehouse.org

Photographic Resource Center • 832 Commonwealth Ave • Boston, MA 02215 • (617) 975-0600 • http://www.prcboston.org

Revolving Museum • 288-300 A Street • Boston, MA 02210 • (617) 439-8617 • http://www.revolvingmuseum.org

Roslindale Historical Society • P.O. Box 356 • Boston, MA 02131

Shirley-Eustis House Museum • 33 Shirley St • Boston, MA 02119 • (617) 442-2275 • http://www.shirleyeustishouse.org

Society for the Preservation of New England Antiquities • Historical Museum, 141 Cambridge St • Boston, MA 02114 • (617) 227-3956 • http://www.spnea.org

South End Historical Society • 532 Massachusetts Ave • Boston, MA 02118 • (617) 536-4445

Sports Museum of New England • 100 Legends Wy • Boston, MA 02114 • (617) 624-1234 • http://www.sportsmuseum.org

Massachusetts

Boston, cont.
Supreme Judicial Court Historical Society • 1200 Court House • Boston, MA 02108 • (617) 742-6090

Temple Israel Library • Longwood Ave & Plymouth St • Boston, MA 02215 • (617) 566-3960

Unitarian Universalist Association of Congregations Archives • 25 Beacon St • Boston, MA 02108 • (617) 742-2100 • http://www.uua.org

Unitarian Universalist Historical Society • 25 Beacon St • Boston, MA 02108 • (617) 495-9766

United Methodist Church, Southern New England Conference • Historical Society Library, 745 Commonwealth Ave • Boston, MA 02215 • (617) 353-1323 • http://www.bu.edu/sth/archives/cahhome.htm

USS Constitution Museum • Boston National Historical Park, Charlestown Navy Yard, P.O. Box 1812 • Boston, MA 02129 • (617) 426-1812 • http://www.ussconstitutionmuseum.org

Vilna Center for Jewish Heritage • 1 Financial Center, 40th Fl • Boston, MA 02111 • (617) 247-2141

Bourne
Bourne Historical Society • Aptucxet Trading Post Museum, 24 Aptucxet Rd, P.O. Box 3095 • Bourne, MA 02532 • (508) 759-8167 • http://www.bournehistoricalsoc.org

Cape and Islands Historical Association • P.O. Box 50 • Bourne, MA 02559-0050 • (508) 888-3300

Jonathan Bourne Historical Center • Bourne Archives, 30 Keene St • Bourne, MA 02532 • (508) 749-6928

Jonathan Bourne Public Library • 19 Sandwich Rd • Bourne, MA 02532-3699 • (508) 759-0644 • http://www.bournelibrary.org

Boylston
Boylston Historical Society • Historical Museum, 7 Central St, P.O. Box 459 • Boylston, MA 01505-459 • (508) 869-2720 • http://www.boylstonhistory.org

Braintree
Braintree Historical Society • Historical Museum, 31 Tenney Rd • Braintree, MA 02184-6512 • (781) 848-1640 • http://www.braintreehistorical.org

General Sylvanus Thayer Birthplace Museum • 786 Washington St • Braintree, MA 02184 • (617) 848-1640

Thayer Public Library • 798 Washington St • Braintree, MA 02184 • (781) 848-0405 • http://www.thayerpubliclibrary.org

Brewster
Brewster Historical Society • Historical Museum, Main St, P.O. Box 1146 • Brewster, MA 02631 • (508) 896-3058

Brewster Ladies' Library • 1822 Main St • Brewster, MA 02631 • (508) 896-3913 • http://www.gis.net/~brewllib

New England Fire and History Museum • 1439 Main St, Route 6A • Brewster, MA 02631 • (508) 896-5711

ROOTS Users Group of Cape Cod • P. O. Box 906 • Brewster, MA 02631 • (508) 896-3434

Bridgewater
Bridgewater Public Library • 15 South St • Bridgewater, MA 02324-2593 • (508) 697-3331 • http://www.bridgewaterpubliclibrary.org

Clement C Maxwell Library • Bridgewater State College, 10 Shaw Rd • Bridgewater, MA 02325 • (508) 531-1392 • http://www.bridgew.edu/library

Brighton
Brighton-Allston Historical Society • 30 Kenrick St • Brighton, MA 02135-3804 • (617) 562-6348

Brimfield
Brimfield Public Library • 25 Main St • Brimfield, MA 01010 • (413) 245-3518

Brockton
Brockton Historical Society • Historical Museum, 216 N Pearl St • Brockton, MA 02401 • (508) 583-1039 • http://www.brocktonma.com

Brockton Public Library • 304 Main St • Brockton, MA 02301 • (508) 580-7860 • http://www.brocktonpubliclibrary.org

Little Red Schoolhouse Association • Historical Museum, Concord Ave, P.O. Box 3036 • Brockton, MA 02403 • (508) 559-8871

Plymouth Colony Genealogists • 60 Sheridan St, P.O. Box 1766 • Brockton, MA 02301-1766 • (508) 583-6106 • http://www.rootsweb.com/~maplymou/pcgs/pcgsmain.htm

Brookfield
Merrick Public Library • 2 Lincoln St, P.O. Box 528 • Brookfield, MA 01506 • (508) 867-6339

Merrick Public Library • 2 Lincoln St, P.O. Box 528 • Brookfield, MA 01506-0528 • (508) 867-6339

Brookline
Brookline Historical Society • Edward Devotion House, 347 Harvard St • Brookline, MA 02146 • (617) 566-5747

Brookline Public Library • 361 Washington St • Brookline, MA 02445 • (617) 730-2370 • http://www.brooklinelibrary.com

Frederick Law Olmsted National Historic Site Museum • 99 Warren St • Brookline, MA 02445 • (617) 566-1689 • http://www.nps.gov/frla

John Fitzgerald Kennedy National Historic Site Museum • 83 Beals St • Brookline, MA 02446 • (617) 566-7937 • http://www.nps.gov/jofi

Larz Anderson Auto Museum • 15 Newton St • Brookline, MA 02445 • (617) 522-6547 • http://www.mot.org

Longyear Historical Society • Historical Museum, 120 Seaver St • Brookline, MA 02467-1811 • (617) 277-8943

Webster House Museum • 20 Webster Place • Brookline, MA 02445 • (617) 739-5461

Buckland
Buckland Historical Society • Historical Museum, 32 Upper St • Buckland, MA 01338 • (413) 625-6619

Burlington
Burlington Historical Commission • Historical Museum, Bedford & Cambridge Sts • Burlington, MA 01803 • (781) 272-0606 • http://www.burlington.org/archives

Burlington Historical Society • Town Hall, Center St • Burlington, MA 01803 • (781) 272-4840

Buzzards Bay
Bourne Historical Society • 30 Keene St • Buzzards Bay, MA 02532 • (508) 759-8167

Capt Charles H Hurley Museum • Massachusetts Maritime Academy, 101 Academy Dr • Buzzards Bay, MA 02532 • (508) 830-5035 • http://www.maritime.edu

Cambridge
Arthur and Elizabeth Schlesinger Library • Radcliffe College, 10 Garden St • Cambridge, MA 02138 • (617) 495-8647

Cambridge Historical Commission • 831 Massachusetts Ave • Cambridge, MA 02139 • (617) 349-4683 • http://www.ci.cambridge.ma.us/~Historic/

Cambridge Historical Society • Hooper-Lee-Nichols House Museum, 159 Brattle St • Cambridge, MA 02138 • (617) 547-4252 • http://www.cambridgehistory.org

Cambridge Public Library • 449 Broadway • Cambridge, MA 02138 • (617) 349-4044 • http://www.cambridgema.gov/~cpl

Harvard University Library • Wadsworth House • Cambridge, MA 02138 • (617) 495-3650 • http://www.hcl.harvard.edu

Longfellow National Historic Site Library • 105 Brattle St • Cambridge, MA 02138 • (617) 876-4491 • http://www.nps.gov/long

Medieval Academy of America • 104 Mount Auburn, 5th Floor • Cambridge, MA 02138-3810 • (617) 491-1622

Ukrainian Research Institute Reference Library • Harvard University, 1583 Massachusetts Ave • Cambridge, MA 02138 • (617) 496-5891 • http://www.huri.harvard.edu

Canton
Canton Historical Society • Historical Museum, 1400 Washington St • Canton, MA 02021 • (781) 828-8537 • http://www.canton.org

Corkery Genealogical Society • 4 Osage Rd • Canton, MA 02021-1225 • (781) 821-0387

Carlisle
Carlisle Historical Society • Red Brick Schoolhouse Museum, 698 Concord St, P.O. Box 703 • Carlisle, MA 01741 • (978) 371-5529

Gleason Public Library • 22 Bedford Rd, P.O. Box 813 • Carlisle, MA 01741-0905 • (978) 369-4898

Carver
Carver Public Library • 2 Meadowbrook Wy • Carver, MA 02330 • (508) 866-3415 • http://www.carverpl.org

Centerville
Centerville Historical Society • Historical Museum, 513 Main St, P.O. Box 491 • Centerville, MA 02632 • (978) 775-0331 • http://www.centervillehistoricalmuseum.org

Charlemont
Heath Historical Society • Brunelle Rd RFD • Charlemont, MA 01339

Tyler Memorial Library • 157 Main St, P.O. Box 618 • Charlemont, MA 01339-0618 • (413) 339-0301

Charlestown
Bunker Hill Museum • 43 Monument Sq, P.O. Box 1776 • Charlestown, MA 02129 • (617) 242-1843

Charlestown Historical Society • Bunker Hill Museum, 43 Monument Sq • Charlestown, MA 02129 • (617) 242-2724 • http://www.charlestownhistoricalsociety.org

New England Historic Seaport Museum • 197 8th St • Charlestown, MA 02129 • (617) 242-1414

USS Constitution Museum • Charlestown Navy Yard, Bldg 22, P.O. Box 1812 • Charlestown, MA 02129 • (617) 426-1812 • http://www.ussconstitutionmuseum.org

Charlton
Charlton Historical Society • Historical Museum, 255 Statford St, P.O. Box 252 • Charlton, MA 01507-0252 • (508) 248-3202

Chatham
Chatham Historical Society • Old Atwood House Museum, 347 Stage Harbor Rd, P.O. Box 381 • Chatham, MA 02633 • (508) 945-2493 • http://www.chathamhistoricalsociety.org

Chatham Railroad Museum • 153 Depot Rd • Chatham, MA 02633 • http://www.chathamrailroadmuseum.com

Eldredge Public Library • 564 Main St • Chatham, MA 02633-2296 • (508) 945-5170 • http://www.eldredgelibrary.org

Mayo House Museum • 540 Main St • Chatham, MA 02633 • (508) 945-4084

Chelmsford
Chelmsford Historical Society • Historical Museum, 40 Byam Rd • Chelmsford, MA 01824 • (978) 256-2311

Chelmsford Public Library • 25 Boston Rd • Chelmsford, MA 01824-3088 • (978) 256-5521 • http://www.chelmsfordlibrary.org

Garrison House Museum • 105 Garrison Rd • Chelmsford, MA 01824 • (978) 256-8832

Chelsea
Chelsea Public Library & Historical Archives • 569 Broadway • Chelsea, MA 02150-2991 • (617) 889-8399 • http://chelseama.gov

Chester
Chester Historical Society • 15 Middlefield St • Chester, MA 01011

Chesterfield
Chesterfield Historical Society • Edwards Museum, 3 North St • Chesterfield, MA 01012 • (413) 296-4054

Chesterfield Historical Society • Bisbee Mill Museum, 66 East St • Chesterfield, MA 01012 • (413) 296-4750 • http://www.bisbeemillmuseum.org/historical.html

Chesterfield Public Library • 408 Main Rd, P.O. Box 305 • Chesterfield, MA 01012-0305 • (413) 296-4735

Chestnut Hill
Institute for Boston Studies • c/o John J Burns Library, Boston College, 140 Commonwealth Ave • Chestnut Hill, MA 02467 • (617) 552-3282

John J Burns Library • Boston College, 140 Commonwealth Ave • Chestnut Hill, MA 02467 • (617) 552-4472 • http://www.bc.edu/libraries.html

Longyear Museum • 1125 Boylston St • Chestnut Hill, MA 02467 • (617) 278-9000 • http://www.longyear.org

Society for Italian American History • Boston College, 140 Commonwealth Ave • Chestnut Hill, MA 02167

Society for Italian Historical Studies • Boston College, Lower Campus Office Bldg, 140 Commonwealth Ave • Chestnut Hill, MA 02467 • (617) 552-3814

Society for Spanish and Portuguese History • Boston College, 140 Commonwealth Ave • Chestnut Hill, MA 02167

Chicopee
Chicopee Historical Society • Historical Museum, 93 Church St • Chicopee, MA 01020 • (413) 592-0126

Chicopee Public Library • 449 Front St • Chicopee, MA 01013 • (413) 594-1800 • http://www.chicopeepubliclibrary.org

Clinton
Clinton Historical Society • Historical Museum, 210 Church St, P.O. Box 286 • Clinton, MA 01510 • (978) 365-4208

Cochituate
Massachusetts Genealogical Council • P.O. Box 5393 • Cochituate, MA 01778-5393 • (617) 222-3197 • http://home.attbi.com/~sages/mgc/

Cohasset
Capt John Wilson House Museum • 4 Elm St • Cohasset, MA 02025 • (781) 383-1434 • http://www.cohassethistoricalsociety.org

Cohasset Historical Society • Caleb Lothrop House Museum, 14 Summer St • Cohasset, MA 02025 • (781) 383-1434 • http://www.cohassethistoricalsociety.org

Pratt Building Museum • 106 S Main St • Cohasset, MA 02025 • (781) 383-1434 • http://www.cohassethistoricalsociety.org

Colrain
Colrain Historical Society • G William Pitt House Museum, 91 E Catamount Hill Rd • Colrain, MA 01340-9514 • (413) 624-0106 • http://www.co.franklin.ma.us/colrain.htm

Concord

Concord Free Public Library • 129 Main St • Concord, MA 01742-0129 • (978) 318-3300 • http://www.concordnet.org/library/

Concord Genealogical Roundtable • P.O. Box 654 • Concord, MA 01742 • (978) 371-6242

Concord Museum • 200 Lexington Rd, P.O. Box 146 • Concord, MA 01742 • (978) 369-9763 • http://www.concordmuseum.org

Genealogical Roundtable • P.O. Box 654 • Concord, MA 01742-0654 • (508) 358-7444

Louisa May Alcott Memorial Association • Orchard House Museum, 399 Lexington Rd, P.O. Box 343 • Concord, MA 01742 • (978) 369-4118 • http://www.louisamayalcott.org

Minute Man National Historic Park Library • 174 Liberty St, P.O. Box 160 • Concord, MA 01742 • (978) 369-6993 • http://www.nps.gov/mima

Old Manse Museum • 269 Monument St, P.O. Box 572 • Concord, MA 01742 • (978) 287-6154 • http://www.oldmanse.org

Ralph Waldo Emerson House Museum • 28 Cambridge Tpk • Concord, MA 01742 • (978) 369-2236

Wayside Museum • 455 Lexington Rd • Concord, MA 01742 • (508) 369-6975

Conway

Conway Historical Society • Historical Museum, 50 Main St • Conway, MA 01341 • (413) 369-4224

Cotuit

Historical Society of Santuit and Cotuit • Samuel B Dottridge Homestead Museum, 1148 Main St, P.O. Box 1484 • Cotuit, MA 02635-1484 • (508) 428-0461

Cummington

Cummington Historical Commission • Kingman Tavern Historical Museum, 41 Main St • Cummington, MA 01026 • (413) 634-8828 • http://www.hiddenhills.com/kingmantavern/

William Cullen Bryant Homestead Museum • 207 Bryant Rd • Cummington, MA 01026 • (413) 634-2244 • http://www.thetrustees.org

Cuttyhunk

Cuttyhunk Historical Society • 23 Tower Hill Rd • Cuttyhunk, MA 02713 • (508) 984-4611

Dalton

Dalton Free Public Library • 426 Main St • Dalton, MA 01226 • (413) 684-6112 • http://www.vgernet.net/dfplib/

Dalton Historical Commission • 462 Main St • Dalton, MA 01226 • (413) 684-6111 • http://www.dalton-ma.gov

Danvers

Danvers Alarm List Company • Rebecca Nurse Homestead Museum, 149 Pine St • Danvers, MA 01923 • (798) 774-8799

Danvers Archival Center • 15 Sylvan St • Danvers, MA 01923 • (978) 774-0554 • http://www.etext.virginia.edu/salem/witchevafl

Danvers Historical Society • Glen Magna Farms Museum, 9 Page St, P.O. Box 381 • Danvers, MA 01923 • (978) 777-1666 • http://www.danvershistory.org

General Israel Putnam Chapter, DAR • Judge Samuel Holten House Museum, 171 Holten St • Danvers, MA 01923 • http://www.generalisraelputnamchapter.org

Peabody Institute Library • 15 Sylvan St • Danvers, MA 01923-2735 • (978) 774-0554 • http://www.noblenet.org/danvers

Rebecca Nurse Homestead Museum • 149 Pine St • Danvers, MA 01923 • (978) 774-8799 • http://www.rebeccanurse.org

Dedham

Dedham Historical Society • Historical Museum, 612 High St, P.O. Box 215 • Dedham, MA 02027-0215 • (781) 326-1385 • http://www.dedhamhistorical.org

Dedham Public Library • 43 Church St • Dedham, MA 02026 • (781) 751-9280 • http://www.dedhamlibrary.org

Fairbanks House Museum • 511 East St • Dedham, MA 02026 • (781) 326-1170 • http://www.fairbankshouse.org

Deerfield

Allen House Museum • 104 Old Main St • Deerfield, MA 01342

Ashley House Museum • 129A Old Main St • Deerfield, MA 01342

Dwight House Museum • 37A Old Main St • Deerfield, MA 01342

Frary House Museum • 60A Old Main St • Deerfield, MA 01342

Hinsdale and Anna Williams House Museum • 128 Old Main St • Deerfield, MA 01342

Historic Deerfield • Historical Museum, The Street, P.O. Box 321 • Deerfield, MA 01342-0321 • (413) 774-5581 • http://www.historic-deerfield.org

Historic Deerfield Library Museum • 84B Old Main St, P.O. Box 53 • Deerfield, MA 01342 • (413) 775-7125

Memorial Library & Museum • 6 Memorial St, P.O. Box 53 • Deerfield, MA 01342-0053 • (413) 775-7125 • http://www.historic-deerfield.org/libraries.html

Pocumtuck Valley Memorial Association • Memorial Hall Museum, 8 Memorial St, P.O. Box 428 • Deerfield, MA 01342 • (413) 774-7476 • http://www.old-deerfield.org; http://www.deerfield-ma.org

Reverend John Farwell Moors House Museum • 103 Old Main St • Deerfield, MA 01342

Sheldon-Hawks House Museum • 125 Old Main St • Deerfield, MA 01342

Stebbins House Museum • 88A Old Main St • Deerfield, MA 01342

Wells-Thorne House Museum • 52 Old Main St • Deerfield, MA 01342

Wright House Museum • 130 Old Main St • Deerfield, MA 01342

Dennis

Dennis Historical Society • 1736 Josiah Dennis Manse Museum, Nobscusset & Whig St, P.O. Box 963 • Dennis, MA 02638 • (508) 385-2255

Dennis Memorial Library • 1020 Old Bass River Rd • Dennis, MA 02638-2523 • (508) 385-2255

Dennisport

Cape Cod Genealogical Society • c/o Dennis Public Library, 673 Main St • Dennisport, MA 02638 • (508) 385-4574

Dennis Public Library • 673 Main St • Dennisport, MA 02638

Dighton

Dighton Historical Society • Historical Museum, 1217 Williams St, P.O. Box 655 • Dighton, MA 02715-0655 • (508) 669-5514

Dighton Public Library • 395 Main St • Dighton, MA 02715 • (508) 669-6421 • http://www.dighton.com

Dorchester

Dorchester Historical Society • William Clapp House Museum, 195 Boston St • Dorchester, MA 02125 • (617) 265-7802 • http://www.dorchesterhistoricalsociety.org

Massachusetts Department of Public Health • 150 Mount Vernon Street, 1st Floor • Dorchester, MA 02125-310 • (617) 740-2600 • http://www.state.ma.us/dph/bhsre/rvr/rvr.htm

Douglas

Douglas Historical Society • E Main St • Douglas, MA 01516 • (508) 476-3856

Dover

Caryl House and Fisher Barn Museum • 107 Dedham St, P.O. Box 534 • Dover, MA 02030 • (508) 785-1832 • http://www.doverhistoricalsociety.org

Dover Historical Society • Sawin Museum, 107 Dedham St, P.O. Box 534 • Dover, MA 02030 • (508) 785-1832 • http://www.doverhistoricalsociety.org

Dover Town Library • 56 Dedham St, P.O. Box 669 • Dover, MA 02030-0669 • (508) 785-8113 • http://www.doverma.org/library.html

Dracut

Dracut Historical Society • Historical Museum, 1600 Lakeview Ave • Dracut, MA 01826 • (978) 957-3100

Moses Greeley Parker Memorial Library • 28 Arlington St • Dracut, MA 01826 • (978) 957-8539 • http://www.dracutlibrary.org

Drury

Town of Florida Historical Committee • Town Hall, 367 Mohawk Tr • Drury, MA 01343 • http://www.townofflorida.org

Dudley

Black Tavern Historical Society • Historical Museum, Centre Rd, P.O. Box 1804 • Dudley, MA 01571 • (508) 943-8391

Chaubunagungamaug Nipmuck Indian Council • 265 W Main St • Dudley, MA 01571 • (508) 949-1651 • http://www.nipmuck.org

Conant Library • Nichols College, Center Rd • Dudley, MA 01571 • (508) 213-2222 • http://www.nichols.edu/library/

Dunstable

Dunstable Free Public Library • 511 Main St, P.O. Box 219 • Dunstable, MA 01827-0219 • (978) 649-7830

Duxbury

Capt Gershom Bradford House Museum • 931 Tremont St • Duxbury, MA 02332 • (617) 934-6106

Duxbury Free Library • 77 Alden St • Duxbury, MA 02332 • (781) 934-2721 • http://www.duxburyfreelibrary.org

Duxbury Rural and Historical Society • Historical Museum, 479 Washington St, P.O. Box 2865 • Duxbury, MA 02331 • (781) 934-6106 • http://www.duxburyhistory.org

John Alden House Museum • 105 Alden St, P.O. Box 2794 • Duxbury, MA 02361 • (781) 934-9092

King Caesar House Museum • King Caesar Rd • Duxbury, MA 02331 • (781) 934-6101

Marshfield Historical Society • 65 Webster St • Duxbury, MA 02332 • (781) 834-0100

East Bridgewater

East Bridgewater Historical Society • Historical Museum, 33 Plymouth St • East Bridgewater, MA 02333

East Bridgewater Public Library • 32 Union St • East Bridgewater, MA 02333 • (508) 378-1616 • http://www.sailsinc.org/ebpl

East Dennis

Jacob Sears Memorial Library • 23 Center St, P.O. Box 782 • East Dennis, MA 02641-0782 • (508) 385-8151 • http://www.vsy.cape.com/~jacobsrs

East Douglas

Douglas Historical Society • Jenckes Store Museum, 238 Main St, P.O. Box 176 • East Douglas, MA 01516 • (508) 476-3856

Simon Fairfield Public Library • 290 Main St, P.O. Box 607 • East Douglas, MA 01516-0607 • (508) 476-2695

East Freetown

James White Memorial Library • 5 Washburn Rd • East Freetown, MA 02717-1220 • (508) 763-5344

East Harwich

Cape Cod Genealogical Society • P.O. Box 1394 • East Harwich, MA 02645 • (508) 432-5769 • http://www.capecodgensoc.org

East Sandwich

Benjamin Nye Homestead Museum • 85 Old County Rd, P.O. Box 134 • East Sandwich, MA 02537 • (508) 888-4213 • http://www.nyefamily.org

Thornton W Burgess Society • Historical Museum, 6 Discovery Hill Rd • East Sandwich, MA 02537 • (508) 888-6870 • http://www.thorntonburgess.org

Wing Fort House Museum • 69 Spring Hill Rd • East Sandwich, MA 02537 • (508) 888-3591

Eastham

Capt Edward Penniman House Museum • Governor Prence Rd • Eastham, MA 02642 • (508) 255-3421

Eastham Historical Society • Historical Museum, Nauset Rd, P.O. Box 8 • Eastham, MA 02642 • (508) 255-0788 • http://www.easthamhistorical.org

Eastham Public Library • 190 Samoset Rd • Eastham, MA 02642 • (508) 240-5950 • http://www.easthamlibrary.org

Swift-Daley House Museum • Route 6, P.O. Box 167 • Eastham, MA 02642 • (508) 240-1247

Easthampton

Easthampton Historical Commission • Town Hall, Main St • Easthampton, MA 01027 • (413) 527-2211

Easthampton Historical Society • Historical Museum, 7 Holyoke St, P.O. Box 992 • Easthampton, MA 01027 • (413) 527-3108

Easton

Easton Historical Society • 80 Mechanics St, Box 3 • Easton, MA 02356

Edgartown

Dr Daniel Fisher House • 96 Main St • Edgartown, MA 02539 • (508) 627-4440

Dukes County Historical Society • Vineyard Museum, 59 School St, P.O. Box 827 • Edgartown, MA 02539-0827 • (508) 627-4441

Martha's Vineyard Historical Society • Vineyard Museum, 59 School St, P.O. Box 1310 • Edgartown, MA 02539-0827 • (508) 627-4441 • http://www.marthasvineyardhistory.org

Vincent House Museum • Church St • Edgartown, MA 02539 • (508) 627-4440

Egremont

Egremont Historical Commission • Archives Room, Academy Rm, P.O. Box 127 • Egremont, MA 01252 • (413) 528-5226

Erving

Erving Historical Society • Main St • Erving, MA 01344

Essex

Cogswell's Grant Museum • 60 Spring St • Essex, MA 01929 • (978) 768-3632

Essex Historical Society • Shipbuilding Museum, 66 Main St, P.O. Box 277 • Essex, MA 01929-0277 • (978) 768-7541 • http://www.essexshipbuildingmuseum.org

Everett

Everett Historical Society • Town Hall • Everett, MA 02149 • (617) 387-7059

Massachusetts

Everett, cont.
Frederick E Parlin Memorial Library • 410 Broadway • Everett, MA 02149 • (617) 394-2300 • http://www.noblenet.org/everett

Fairhaven
Fairhaven Historical Society • Historical Museum, 45 Center St • Fairhaven, MA 02719

Millicent Library • 45 Cente St, P.O. Box 30 • Fairhaven, MA 02719-0030 • (508) 992-5342 • http://www.millicentlibrary.org

Fall River
Battleship Massachusetts Museum • Battleship Cove, 5 Water St, P.O. Box 111 • Fall River, MA 02722 • (508) 678-1100 • http://www.battleshipcove.org

Fall River Firefighters Memorial Museum • P.O. Box 2888 • Fall River, MA 02722 • (508) 674-1810 • http://www.fallrivermassfirebuff.com

Fall River Historical Society • Historical Museum, 451 Rock St • Fall River, MA 02721 • (508) 679-1071 • http://www.lizzieborden.org

Fall River Public Library • 104 N Main St • Fall River, MA 02720 • (508) 324-2700 • http://sailsinc.org/fallriver/main.htm

Marine Museum at Fall River • 70 Water St, P.O. Box 1147 • Fall River, MA 02721 • (508) 674-3533 • http://www.marinemuseum.org

USS Massachusetts Museum • Battleship Cove, 5 Water St, P.O. Box 111 • Fall River, MA 02721 • (617) 878-1100 • http://www.battleshipcove.com

Falmouth
Falmouth Genealogical Society • general delivery • Falmouth, MA 02540

Falmouth Historical Society • Julia Wood House Museum, 55-65 Palmer Ave #65, P.O. Box 174 • Falmouth, MA 02541-0174 • (508) 548-4857 • http://www.falmouthhistoricalsociety.org

Falmouth Public Library • 123 Katherine Lee Bates Rd • Falmouth, MA 02540-2895 • (508) 457-2555 • http://www.falmouthpubliclibrary.org

Historic Highfield • Historical Musuem, 36 Highfield Dr, P.O. Box 494 • Falmouth, MA 02541 • (508) 548-9641

Woods Hole Historical Collection • 573 Woods Hole Rd, P.O. Box 185 • Falmouth, MA 02543 • (508) 548-7270

Fitchburg
Acadian Cultural Society • P.O. Box 2304 • Fitchburg, MA 01420-8804 • (978) 342-7173 • http://www.angelfire.com/ma/1755/

Amelia V Galucci-Cirio Library • Fitchburg State College, 160 Pearl St • Fitchburg, MA 01420 • (978) 665-3196 • http://www.fsc.edu/library

Finnish American Club of Saima • P.O. Box 30 • Fitchburg, MA 01420-0030 • (508) 745-9614

Fitchburg Historical Society • Historical Museum, 50 Grove St, P.O. Box 953 • Fitchburg, MA 01420 • (978) 345-1157 • http://www.fitchburghistory.fsc.edu

Fitchburg Public Library • 610 Main St • Fitchburg, MA 01420-3146 • (978) 345-9635 • http://www.net1plus.com/users/fpl

Florence
Hadley Historical Society • 50 Middle St • Florence, MA 01062 • (413) 587-2623

Western Massachusetts Jewish Genealogical Society • 26 Nutting Ave • Florence, MA 01062 • (413) 587-0801 • http://www.wmjgs.org

Foxborough
Boyden Library • 10 Bird St • Foxborough, MA 02035 • (508) 543-1245

Foxborough Historical Society • P.O. Box 437 • Foxborough, MA 02035 • (617) 543-8298

Framingham
Framingham Historical Society • Old Academy Museum, 16 Vernon St, P.O. Box 2032 • Framingham, MA 01703-2032 • (508) 872-3780 • http://www.framinghamhistory.com

Framingham Public Library • 49 Lexington St • Framingham, MA 01702-8278 • (508) 879-3570 • http://www.framinghamlibrary.org

Henry Whittemore Library • Framingham State College, 100 State St • Framingham, MA 01701 • (508) 626-4654

New England Historic Genealogical Society, Great Migration Study Project • 1 Watson Pl, P.O. Box 5089 • Framingham, MA 01701 • (888) 296-3447 • http://www.NewEnglandAncestors.org

Franklin
Cowasuck Band of the Pennacook-Abenaki People • 160 Dailey Dr • Franklin, MA 02038 • (508) 528-7629 • http://www.cowasuck.org

Franklin Historical Society • c/o Franklin Public Library, 21 School St • Franklin, MA 02038 • (508) 520-4940

Franklin Public Library • 118 Main St • Franklin, MA 02038 • (508) 520-4940 • http://www.franklin.ma.us/town/library/

GenealogyForum.com • 430 Franklin Village Dr • Franklin, MA 02038-4020 • (508) 528-2906 • http://www.genealogyforum.com

Gardner
Central Massachusetts Genealogical Society • American Legion Post 129, Elm St • Gardner, MA 01440 • http://cmgs-inc.org

Gardner Museum • 28 Pearl St, Route 101, P.O. Box 511 • Gardner, MA 01440 • (978) 632-3277 • http://www.thegardnermuseum.com

South Gardner Historical Society • 55 Union St • Gardner, MA 01440 • (978) 632-5118

South Gardner Historical Society • Historical Museum, 24 Lovewell St • Gardner, MA 01440 • (978) 632-4369

Georgetown
Brocklebank Museum • 108 E Main St • Georgetown, MA 01833 • (978) 352-8526 • http://www.georgetownhistoricalsociety.com

Georgetown Historical Society • Brocklebankd House Museum, 108 E Main St, P.O. Box 376 • Georgetown, MA 01833 • (978) 352-8372

Georgetown Peabody Library • Lincoln Park • Georgetown, MA 01833 • (508) 352-5728 • http://www.georgetownpl.org

Gloucester
Beauport Sleeper-McCann House Museum • 75 Eastern Point Blvd • Gloucester, MA 01930 • (978) 283-0800 • http://www.historicnewengland.org

Cape Ann Historical Association • Historical Museum, 27 Pleasant St • Gloucester, MA 01930 • (978) 283-0455 • http://www.capeannhistoricalmuseum.org

Hammond Castle Museum • 80 Hesperus Ave • Gloucester, MA 01930 • (978) 283-2080 • http://www.hammondcastle.org

Sargent House Museum • 49 Middle St • Gloucester, MA 01930 • (978) 281-2432 • http://www.sargenthouse.org

Sawyer Free Library • 2 Dale Ave • Gloucester, MA 01930 • (978) 281-9763 • http://www.sawyerfreelibrary.org

Grafton
Grafton Historical Society • Historical Museum, 1 Grafton Common • Grafton, MA 01519 • (508) 839-5453

Hassanamisco Nipmuc Council • Hassanamisco Reservation • Grafton, MA 01519 • (508) 839-7394 • http://www.fas.harvard.edu

MASSOG, Worcester Chapter • 27 Brigham Hill Rd • Grafton, MA 02519

Willard House Museum • 11 Willard St • Grafton, MA 01536 • (508) 839-3500 • http://www.willardhouse.org

Granby
Granby Free Public Library • Library Ln • Granby, MA 01033-9416 • (413) 467-3320 • http://www.granbylibrary.com

Great Barrington
Great Barrington Historical Society • Historical Museum, P.O. Box 1106 • Great Barrington, MA 01230 • (413) 292-1513

Mason Library • 231 Main St • Great Barrington, MA 01230 • (413) 528-2403 • http://www.gblibraries.net

Greenfield
Association for Gravestone Studies • 278 Main St, Ste 207 • Greenfield, MA 01301-3230 • (413) 772-0836 • http://www.gravestonestudies.org

Greenfield Community College Library • 1 College Dr • Greenfield, MA 01301-9739 • (413) 775-1834 • http://www.gcc.mass.edu

Greenfield Historical Commission • 14 Court Square • Greenfield, MA 01301 • (413) 774-5363

Greenfield Public Library • 402 Main St • Greenfield, MA 01301 • (413) 772-1544 • http://www.greenfieldpubliclibrary.org

Historical Society of Greenfield • Historical Museum, 43 Church St, P.O. Box 415 • Greenfield, MA 01301 • (413) 775-7203

Groton
Groton Historical Society • Gov Boutwell House Museum, 172 Main St, P.O. Box 202 • Groton, MA 01450 • (978) 448-0092

Groton Public Library • 99 Main St • Groton, MA 01450 • (978) 448-1167 • http://www.gpl.org

Groveland
Groveland Historical Society • Historical Museum, 423 Main St, P.O. Box 178 • Groveland, MA 01834 • (978) 373-5060

Hadley
Goodwin Memorial Library • 50 Middle St • Hadley, MA 01035-9544 • (413) 584-7451 • http://www.hadley-goodwin.org

Hadley Farm Museum • 208 Middle St, P.O. Box 323 • Hadley, MA 01035 • (413) 586-1812 • http://www.hadleyonline.com/farmmuseum

Hadley Historical Society • c/o Goodwin Memorial Library, 50 Middle St • Hadley, MA 01035 • (413) 584-7451

Porter-Phelps-Huntington Foundation • Porter-Phelps-Huntington House Museum, 130 River Dr • Hadley, MA 01035 • (413) 584-4699 • http://www.pphmuseum.org

Hamilton
Hamilton Historical Society • Town Hall Historical Museum, 577 Bay Rd, P.O. Box 108 • Hamilton, MA 01936 • (978) 468-4243

Hamilton Wenham Public Library • 14 Union St • Hamilton, MA 01982 • (978) 468-4477 • http://www.hwlibrary.org

Hampden
Historical Society of the Town of Hampden • 616 Main St, P.O. Box 363 • Hampden, MA 01036 • (413) 566-5803

Hanover
Hanover Historical Society • Stetson House, 514 Hanover St, P.O. Box 156 • Hanover, MA 02339 • (781) 826-9575

John Curtis Free Library • 534 Hanover St • Hanover, MA 02339-2228 • (781) 826-2972 • http://www.hanovermass/library

Hanscom AFB
Hanscom Air Force Base Library FL2835 • 66 SVS/SVMG, 98 Barksdale St, Bldg 1530 • Hanscom AFB, MA 01731-1807 • (781) 377-2177

Hanson
Hanson Public Library • 132 Maquan St • Hanson, MA 02341 • (781) 293-2151 • http://www.sailsinc.org/hansonpl/

Hardwick
Hardwick Historical Society • Historical Museum, On the Common, P.O. Box 492 • Hardwick, MA 01037 • (413) 477-6635

Harvard
Fruitlands Museum • 102 Prospect Hill Rd • Harvard, MA 01451 • (978) 456-3924 • http://www.fruitlands.org

Harvard Historical Society • 215 Still River Rd, P.O. Box 542 • Harvard, MA 01451 • (978) 456-3148 • http://www.harvard.ma.us/hhs.htm

Harvard Public Library • Harvard Common, P.O. Box 666 • Harvard, MA 01451-0666 • (508) 456-4114

Harwich
Brooks Free Library • 739 Main St • Harwich, MA 02645 • (508) 430-7562 • http://www.vsg.cape.com/~brooks

Cape Cod Genealogical Society • P.O. Box 1394 • Harwich, MA 02645 • http://www.capecodgensoc.org

Harwich Historical Society • Brooks Academy Museum, 80 Parallel St, P.O. Box 17 • Harwich, MA 02645 • (508) 432-8089 • http://www.harwichhistoricalsociety.org

Hatfield
Hatfield Historical Society • 35 Main St, P.O. Box 168 • Hatfield, MA 01038 • (413) 247-5545

Hatfield Public Library • 39 Main St • Hatfield, MA 01038 • (413) 247-9097

Haverhill
Haverhill Historical Society • Buttonwoods Museum, 240 Water St • Haverhill, MA 01830 • (978) 374-4626 • http://www.haverhillhistory.org

Haverhill Public Library • 99 Main St • Haverhill, MA 01830-5092 • (978) 373-1586 • http://www.haverhillpl.org

John Greenleaf Whittier Homestead Museum • 150 Whittier Rd • Haverhill, MA 01830 • (978) 373-3979

Hawley
Hawley Historical Commission • Middle Rd • Hawley, MA 01339 • (413) 339-5513

Hingham
Bare Cove Fire Museum • P.O. Box 262 • Hingham, MA 02043 • (781) 749-0028 • http://www.carecovefiremuseum.org

Hingham Historical Society • Old Ordinary Museum, 21 Lincoln St, P.O. Box 434 • Hingham, MA 02043 • (781) 749-0013 • http://www.hinghamhistorical.org

Hingham Public Library • 66 Leavitt St • Hingham, MA 02043 • (781) 741-1405 • http://www.hingham-ma.com/library

Hinsdale
Hinsdale Public Library • 58 Maple St, P.O. Box 397 • Hinsdale, MA 01235-0397 • (413) 655-2303 • http://www.hinsdalelibrary.org

Holbrook
Holbrook Historical Society • Historical Museum, 320 Union St • Holbrook, MA 02343 • (781) 767-5885 • http://www.holbrookhistoricalsociety.org

Holden
Gale Free Library • 23 Highland St • Holden, MA 01520-2599 • (508) 829-0228 • http://www.galefreelibrary.org

Holden Historical Society • Hendricks House Museum, 1157 Main St, P.O. Box 421 • Holden, MA 01520-0421 • (508) 829-5576

Holliston
Holliston Historical Society • 547 Washington St, P.O. Box 17 • Holliston, MA 01746 • (508) 429-5795

Holyoke
Holyoke Public Library & Museum • 335 Maple St • Holyoke, MA 01040-4999 • (413) 322-5640 • http://www.holyokelibrary.org

Wistariahurst Museum • 238 Cabot St, P.O. Box 349 • Holyoke, MA 01041 • (413) 322-5660 • http://www.wistiarhurst.org

Hopkinton
Hopkinton Historical Society • Historical Museum, 168 Hayden Rowe St • Hopkinton, MA 01748-2512 • (781) 642-0125

Hopkinton Public Library • 13 Main St • Hopkinton, MA 01748 • (508) 497-9777 • http://www.hopkintonma.org

Hubbardston
Hubbardston Historical Society • Jonas Clark Bldg, Main St, P.O. Box 119 • Hubbardston, MA 01452-0119 • (508) 928-4073

Hudson
Hudson Historical Society • 78 Main St • Hudson, MA 01749 • (978) 562-9963

Hudson Public Library • Washington St at Wood Sq • Hudson, MA 01749-2499 • (978) 568-9644 • http://users.rcn.com/hudslib

Hull
Hull Public Library • 9 Main St • Hull, MA 02045-1199 • (781) 925-2295 • http://www.ocln.org

Museum of Boston Harbor Heritage • 1117 Nantucket Ave, P.O. Box 221 • Hull, MA 02045 • (781) 925-5438 • http://www.lifesavingmuseum.org

Hyannis
Hyannis Public Library Association • 401 Main St • Hyannis, MA 02601 • (508) 775-2280 • http://www.hyannislibrary.org

John F Kennedy Hyannis Museum • 397 Main St • Hyannis, MA 02601 • (508) 790-3077 • http://www.jrkhyannismuseum.org

Hyde Park
54th Mass Glory Brigade Foundation • 1295 River St • Hyde Park, MA 02136 • (617) 333-9970

Boston Public Library-Hyde Park Branch • 35 Harvard Ave • Hyde Park, MA 02136-2862 • (617) 361-2524 • http://www.bpl.org

Hyde Park Historical Society • c/o Hyde Park Library, 35 Harvard Ave • Hyde Park, MA 02136 • (617) 361-2524 • http://www.bostonhistory.org/hphshome.html

National Society of Old Plymouth Colony Descendants • 189 Sherrin St • Hyde Park, MA 02136-1851

Indian Orchard
Titanic Historical Society • 207 Centre St • Indian Orchard, MA 01151 • (413) 543-4770

Ipswich
Ipswich Historical Society • John Heard House Museum, 54 S Main St • Ipswich, MA 01938 • (978) 356-2811 • http://www.ipswichmuseum.org

Ipswich Public Library • 25 N Main St • Ipswich, MA 01938-2287 • (978) 356-6648 • http://www.town.ipswich.ma.us/library

John Whipple House Museum • 1 S Village Green • Ipswich, MA 01938

Jamaica Plain
Jamaica Plain Historical Society • P.O. Box 2924 • Jamaica Plain, MA 02130

North American Indian Center of Boston • 105 S Huntington Ave • Jamaica Plain, MA 02130 • (617) 232-0343 • http://www.bostonindiancenter.org

Kingston
Jones Ridge Village Historical Society • Major John Bradford House Museum, Maple St & Landing Rd, P.O. Box 22 • Kingston, MA 02364 • (781) 585-6300 • http://www.jrvhs.org

Kingston Public Library • 6 Green St • Kingston, MA 02364 • (781) 585-0517 • http://www.kingstonpubliclibrary.org

Lancaster
Fifth Meeting House Museum • 725 Main St, P.O. Box 66 • Lancaster, MA 01523 • (978) 365-2427

Lancaster Historical Commission • Town Hall, 695 Main St, P.O. Box 351 • Lancaster, MA 01523-0351 • (978) 368-1162

Lancaster Historical Society • Historical Museum, 695 Main St, P.O. Box 266 • Lancaster, MA 01523 • (978) 368-1162

Lancaster Town Library • 717 Main St • Lancaster, MA 01523-0005 • (978) 368-8928

Thayer Memorial Library • 717 Main St, P.O. Box 5 • Lancaster, MA 01523-0005 • (978) 368-8928

Lawrence
Historical Society of Lawrence and Its People • Lawrence History Center, 6 Essex St • Lawrence, MA 01842 • (978) 686-9230 • http://www.lawrencehistorycenter.org

Lawrence Heritage State Park • 1 Jackson St • Lawrence, MA 01840 • (978) 794-1655 • http://www.mass.gov/dcu/parks/northeast/lwhp.htm

Lawrence Public Library • 51 Lawrence St • Lawrence, MA 01841 • (978) 682-1727 • http://www.lawrencefreelibrary.org

Lee
Lee Library Association • 100 Main St • Lee, MA 01238-1688 • (413) 243-0385 • http://www.leelibrary.org

Leicester
Leicester Historical Society • 1136 Main St • Leicester, MA 01524 • (508) 892-9900

Lenox
Berkshire Scenic Railway Museum • Willow Creek Rd, P.O. Box 2195 • Lenox, MA 01240 • (413) 637-2210 • http://www.berkshirescenicrailroad.org

Lenox Historical Society • Historical Museum, 75 Main St, P.O. Box 1856 • Lenox, MA 01240 • (413) 637-1824

Lenox Library Association • 18 Main St • Lenox, MA 01240 • (413) 637-0197

The Mount Museum • 2 Plunkett St, P.. Box 974 • Lenox, MA 01240 • (413) 637-1899

Leominster
Leominster Historical Society • Historical Museum, 17 School St • Leominster, MA 01453 • (978) 537-5424

Leominster Public Library • 30 West St • Leominster, MA 01453 • (978) 534-7522 • http://www.leominsterlibrary.org

Leverett
Leverett Historical Society • Historical Museum, N Leverett Rd, P.O. Box 354 • Leverett, MA 01054 • (413) 548-9092

Lexington
Cary Memorial Library • 1605 Massachuesetts Ave • Lexington, MA 02421 • (781) 862-6288 • http://www.carylibrary.org

Hancock-Clarke House Museum • 36 Hancock St • Lexington, MA 02420 • (617) 861-0928

Lexington Historical Society • Historical Museum, 1332 Massachusetts Ave, P.O. Box 514 • Lexington, MA 02420-0005 • (781) 862-1703 • http://www.lexingtonhistory.org

National Heritage Museum • Scottish Rite Masonic Library, 33 Marrett Rd, P.O. Box 519 • Lexington, MA 02421 • (781) 861-6559 • http://www.mohn.org; http://www.nationalheritagemuseum.org

Leyden
Leyden Historical Commission • 27 Eden Tr • Leyden, MA 01337 • (413) 773-7336

Lincoln
Drumlin Farm Education Center Museum • 208 S Great Rd • Lincoln, MA 01773 • (781) 259-2200 • http://www.massaudubon.org

Gropius House Museum • 68 Baker Bridge Rd • Lincoln, MA 01773 • (781) 259-8098 • http://www.historicnewengland.org

Lincoln Historical Commission • Town Offices • Lincoln, MA 01773 • (781) 259-2610

Lincoln Historical Society • Historical Museum, 64 Conant Rd, P.O. Box 6084 Lincoln Center • Lincoln, MA 01773 • (781) 259-8360 • http://www.walden.org

Lincoln Public Library • 3 Bedford Rd • Lincoln, MA 01773 • (781) 259-8465

Thoreau Institute at Walden Woods • Historical Museum, 44 Baker Farm • Lincoln, MA 01773 • (781) 259-4730 • http://www.walden.org/institute

Littleton
Littleton Historical Society • 4 Rogers St, P.O. Box 721 • Littleton, MA 01460 • (978) 486-8202 • http://www.littletonhistoricalsociety.org

Reuben Hoar Library • 41 Shattuck Rd, P.O. Box 1506 • Littleton, MA 01460-4506 • (978) 486-4046 • http://www.littletonlibrary.org

Longmeadow
Longmeadow Historical Society • Richard Salter Storrs House Museum, 697 Longmeadow St • Longmeadow, MA 01106 • (413) 567-3600 • http://www.longmeadow.org/hist_soc/histsoc_ main.html

Richard Salter Storrs Library • 693 Longmeadow St • Longmeadow, MA 01106 • (413) 565-4181 • http://www.longmeadow.org

Lowell
American Textile History Museum • 491 Dutton St • Lowell, MA 01854 • (978) 441-0400 • http://www.athm.org

Boston & Maine Railroad Historical Society • 25 Shattuck St • Lowell, MA 01852 • (978) 454-3600

Greater Lowell Genealogy Club • general delivery • Lowell, MA 01853

Lowell Heritage State Park Museum • 500 Pawtucket Blvd • Lowell, MA 01854 • (978) 369-6312 • http://www.mass.gov/dcr/parks/northeast/llhp.htm

Lowell Historical Society • Boott Cotton Mill Museum, 400 Foot of John St, P.O. Box 1826 • Lowell, MA 01853 • (978) 970-5180

Lowell National Historical Park Library • 67 Kirk St • Lowell, MA 01852 • (978) 970-5000 • http://www.nps.gov/lowe

Middlesex Canal Association • Center for Lowell History, 40 French St • Lowell, MA 01852 • (978) 934-4997 • http://www.library.unl.edu/clh

New England Quilt Museum • 18 Shattuck St • Lowell, MA 01852 • (978) 452-4207 • http://www.nequiltmuseum.org

Norwell Historical Society • 4 Jacobs Ln • Lowell, MA 02061-1149 • (781) 659-1888

Pollard Memorial Library • 401 Merrimack St • Lowell, MA 01852 • (978) 970-4120 • http://www.pollardml.org

Tsongas Industrial History Center • 400 Foot of John St • Lowell, MA 01852 • (978) 970-5080 • http://www.uml.edu/tsongas

Ludlow
Hubbard Memorial Library • 24 Center St • Ludlow, MA 01056 • (413) 583-3408 • http://www.hubbardlibrary.org

Lunenburg
Lunenburg Historical Society • 10 School St • Lunenburg, MA 01462 • (978) 582-0858

Lynn
Lynn Historical Society • Lynn Museum, 125 Green St • Lynn, MA 01902 • (781) 592-2465 • http://www.lynnmuseum.org

Lynn Public Library • 5 N Common St • Lynn, MA 01902 • (781) 595-0567 • http://www.noblenet.org/lynn/

Lynnfield
Essex Society of Genealogists • 18 Summer St, P.O. Box 313 • Lynnfield, MA 01940-0313 • (978) 664-9279 • http://www.esog.org

Lynnfield Historical Society • 617 Main St, P.O. Box 274 • Lynnfield, MA 01940-1777 • (781) 334-4899

Lynnfield Public Library • 18 Summer St • Lynnfield, MA 01940 • (781) 334-5411 • http://www.noblenet.org/lynnfield/

Saugus Historical Society • 21 Lovell Rd • Lynnfield, MA 01940 • (781) 233-1191

Malden
Malden Hebrew School Museum • 60 Willow St • Malden, MA 02148

Malden Historical Society • c/o Malden Public Library, 36 Salem St • Malden, MA 02148-5291 • (781) 324-0218

Malden Public Library & Museum • 36 Salem St • Malden, MA 02148 • (781) 324-0218 • http://www.maldenpubliclibrary.com

Manchester
Boxford Historical Society • Elm St • Manchester, MA 01944 • (978) 887-5078

Manchester Historical Society • Trask House Museum, 10 Union St • Manchester, MA 01944-1553 • (978) 526-7230 • http://www.manchesterhistorical.org

Mansfield
Mansfield Historical Society • 53 Rumford Ave • Mansfield, MA 02048 • (508) 339-8793

Mansfield Public Library • 255 Hope St • Mansfield, MA 02048 • (508) 261-7380 • http://www.sailsinc.org/mansfield

Marblehead
1768 Jeremiah Lee Mansion Museum • 161 Washington St • Marblehead, MA 01945 • (781) 631-1768 • http://www.marbleheadmuseum.org

Jewish Historical Society of the North Shore • Historical Museum, 1 Community Rd • Marblehead, MA 01945 • (781) 631-0831 • http://www.jshns.net

King Hooper Mansion Museum • 8 Hooper St • Marblehead, MA 01945 • (781) 631-2608 • http://www.marbleheadarts.org

Marblehead Historical Society • Historical Museum, 170 Washington St, P.O. Box 1048 • Marblehead, MA 01945 • (781) 631-1768 • http://www.marbleheadmuseum.org

Marion
Elizabeth Taber Library • 8 Spring St, P.O. Box 116 • Marion, MA 02738-0116 • (508) 748-1252 • http://www.sailsinc.org/marion

Sippican Historical Society • Historical Museum, 139 Front St, P.O. Box 541 • Marion, MA 02738 • (508) 748-1116

Marlborough
Marlborough Historical Society • Peter Rice Homestead Museum, 377 Elm St, P.O. Box 513 • Marlborough, MA 01752 • (508) 485-4763 • http://www.historicmarlborough.org

Marlborough Public Library • 35 W Main • Marlborough, MA 01752-5510 • (508) 624-6900 • http://www.marlborough.com/mpl.html

Marshfield

Isaac Winslow House Museum • 634 Careswell St • Marshfield, MA 02050 • (781) 837-5753 • http://www.winslowhouse.org

Marshfield Historical Society • Isaac Winslow House Museum, Webster & Careswell Sts, P.O. Box 1244 • Marshfield, MA 02050 • (781) 834-7236

Ventress Memorial Library • 15 Library Plaza • Marshfield, MA 02050 • (781) 834-5535 • http://www.ventresslibrary.org

Marstons Mills

Marstons Mills Public Library • 2160 Main St, P.O. Box 9 • Marstons Mills, MA 02648 • (508) 428-5175 • http://www.mmpl.org

Mashpee

Mashpee Historical Commission • Historical Museum, 16 Great Neck Rd • Mashpee, MA 02649 • (508) 539-1438

Mashpee Wampanoag Indian Tribal Council • Historical Museum, 483 Great Neck Rd S, P.O. Box 1048 • Mashpee, MA 02649 • (508) 477-0208 • http://www.mashpeewampanoagtribe.com

Mattapoisett

Descendants of Whaling Masters • P.O. Box 824 • Mattapoisett, MA 02739 • (508) 758-6090 • http://www.whalingmasters.org

Mattapoisett Free Public Library • 7 Barstow St, PO Box 475 • Mattapoisett, MA 02739-0475 • (508) 758-4171

Mattapoisett Historical Society • Historical Museum and Carriage House, 5 Church St, P.O. Box 535 • Mattapoisett, MA 02739 • (508) 758-2844 • http://www.mattapoisetthistoricalsociety.org

Ralph Eustis Museum • general delivery • Mattapoisett, MA 02739 • (508) 758-6427

Maynard

Maynard Historical Society • Town Bldg, Main St • Maynard, MA 01754 • (978) 897-9696

Maynard Public Library • 197 Main St • Maynard, MA 01754 • (978) 897-1010

Medfield

Dwight-Derby House Museum • 10 Copperwood Rd • Medfield, MA 02052 • (617) 969-1501

Medfield Historical Commission • Town Hall Museum, 459 Main St • Medfield, MA 02052 • (508) 359-6871

Medfield Historical Society • 6 Pleasant St, P.O. Box 233 • Medfield, MA 02052-0233 • (508) 359-4773

Society of Descendants of the Colonial Clergy • 17 Lowell Mason Rd • Medfield, MA 02052 • http://www.colonialclergy.org

Medford

Medford Historical Society • Historical Museum, 10 Governors Ave • Medford, MA 02155 • (781) 391-8739

Medford Public Library • 111 High St • Medford, MA 02155 • (781) 395-7950 • http://www.medfordlibrary.org

Medford-Brooks Estate Museum • P.O. Box 328 • Medford, MA 02155

Royall House Association • Royall House Museum, 15 George St • Medford, MA 02155 • (617) 396-9032 • http://www.royallhouse.org

Medway

Medway Historical Society • 223 Main St • Medway, MA 02053 • (508) 533-7222

Medway Public Library • 26 High St • Medway, MA 02053 • (508) 533-3217 • http://www.medway.lib.org

Melrose

Beebe Estate Museum • 235 W Foster St • Melrose, MA 02176 • (781) 727-8470

Hereditary Order of the First Families of Massachusetts • 253 Tremont St • Melrose, MA 02176-1835 • (781) 662-8034

Melrose Historical Society • 131 W Emerson St, P.O. Box 301 • Melrose, MA 02176 • (781) 665-5010

Melrose Public Library • 69 W Emerson St • Melrose, MA 02176 • (781) 665-2313 • http://www.noblenet.org/melrose/

Order of Descendants of the Ancient and Honorable Artillery Company • 253 Tremont St • Melrose, MA 02176-1835 • (781) 662-8034

Mendon

Mendon Historical Society • 3 Main St, P.O. Box 196 • Mendon, MA 01756 • (508) 473-7672

Sons of the American Revolution, Massachusetts Society • P.O. Box 17 • Mendon, MA 01756 • (508) 229-1776 • http://www.massar.org

Taft Public Library • 18 Main St, P.O. Box 35 • Mendon, MA 01756-0035 • (508) 473-3259 • http://www.lightband.com/~taft

Merrimac

Merrimac Historical Society • Historical Museum, 3 Locust Grove Ave • Merrimac, MA 01860 • (978) 346-9834

Merrimac Public Library • 34 W Main St • Merrimac, MA 01860 • (978) 346-9441 • http://www.merrimaclib.org

Methuen

Methuen Historical Society • Historical Museum, 1 Stevens St, P.O. Box 52 • Methuen, MA 01844-3123 • (978) 683-2252

Middleborough

Middleborough Historical Association • Historical Museum, 18 Jackson St, P.O. Box 304 • Middleborough, MA 02346 • (508) 947-1969

Soule Homestead Education Center • 46 Soule St • Middleborough, MA 02346 • (508) 947-6744

Middleton

Middleton Historical Society • Lura Woodside Watkins Museum, 9 Pleasant St, P.O. Box 456 • Middleton, MA 01949 • (978) 774-9301

Milford

Milford Town Library • 80 Spruce St • Milford, MA 01757 • (508) 473-2145 • http://www.infofind.com/library/

Millbury

Millbury Historical Society • Asa Waters Mansion Museum, 123 Elm St, P.O. Box 367 • Millbury, MA 01527 • (508) 865-4192 • http://www.millburyhistory.org

Millers Falls

Erving Historical Society • 9 Moore St • Millers Falls, MA 01349

Montague Public Libraries-Millers Falls Branch • 23 Bridge St • Millers Falls, MA 01349 • (413) 659-3801

Millis

Millis Historical Commission • 410 Exchange St • Millis, MA 02054 • (508) 376-8043

Millis Public Library • 25 Auburn Rd • Millis, MA 02054-1203 • (508) 376-8282 • http://www.millis.org/library

Millville

J G FitzGerald Historical Society • Historical Museum, 8 Central St • Millville, MA 01529

Millville Historical Society • 63 Central St • Millville, MA 01529 • (508) 883-8449 • http://www.millvillehistory.com

Milton

Capt Forbes House Museum • 215 Adams St • Milton, MA 02186 • (617) 696-1815 • http://www.forbeshousemuseum.org

Friends of the Blue Hills Trust • Blue Hills Trailside Museum, 1894 Canton Ave • Milton, MA 02186 • (617) 333-0690 • http://www.massaudubon.org

Milton Historical Society • Suffolk Resolves House, 1370 Canton Ave • Milton, MA 02186 • (617) 333-9700 • http://world.std.com/~ssn/Milton/mhs.html

Milton Public Library • 476 Canton Ave • Milton, MA 02186 • (617) 698-5757 • http://www.miltonlibrary.org

Monson
Keep Homestead Museum • 110 Main St • Monson, MA 01057 • (413) 267-9715

Monson Free Library • 2 High St • Monson, MA 01057-1095 • (413) 267-3866 • http://www.monsonlibrary.com

Monson Historical Society • Historical Museum, 1 Green St, P.O. Box 114 • Monson, MA 01057 • (413) 267-4292 • http://www.monsonhistoricalsociety.org

Montague
Montague Historical Society • 34 Central St • Montague, MA 01351 • (413) 367-2216

Montague Public Libraries-Montague Center Branch • 17 Center St, P.O. Box 157 • Montague, MA 01351-0157 • (413) 367-2852

Monterey
Bidwell House Museum • 100 Art School Rd, P.O. Box 537 • Monterey, MA 01245 • (413) 428-6888 • http://www.bidwellhousemuseum.org

Monterey Historical Society • Main St • Monterey, MA 01245 • (413) 528-3044

Monterey Library • 452 Main Rd, P.O. Box 172 • Monterey, MA 5-0172 • (413) 428-3795

Montgomery
Grace Hall Memorial Library • 161 Main Rd • Montgomery, MA 01085-9525 • (413) 862-3894 • http://www.community.masslive.com/cc/gracehall

Montgomery Historical Society • Historical Museum, 1689 Russell Rd • Montgomery, MA 01085 • (413) 862-4359

Nahant
Nahant Historical Society • Historical Museum, 41 Valley Rd, P.O. Box 42 • Nahant, MA 01908 • (781) 581-2727 • http://www.nahanthistory.org

Nahant Public Library • 15 Pleasant St, O Box 76 • Nahant, MA 01908-0076 • (781) 581-0306 • http://www.nahant.org

Nantucket
1800 House Museum • 8 Mill St • Nantucket, MA 02554

African Meeting House on Nantucket Museum • 29 York St, P.O. Box 1802 • Nantucket, MA 02554 • (508) 228-9833 • http://www.afroammuseum.org

Egan Institute of Maritime Studies Museum • Coffin School, 4 Winter St • Nantucket, MA 02554 • (508) 228-2505 • http://www.eganinstitute.com

Greater Light Museum • 8 Howard St • Nantucket, MA 02554

Hadwen House Museum • 96 Main St • Nantucket, MA 02554

Jethro Coffin House Museum • 16 Sunset Hill • Nantucket, MA 02554

Macy-Christian House Museum • 12 Liberty St • Nantucket, MA 02554

Maria Mitchell Birthplace House Museum • 1 Vestal St • Nantucket, MA 02554 • (508) 228-9198

Nantucket Atheneum Library • 1 India St, P.O. Box 808 • Nantucket, MA 02554-0808 • (508) 228-1110 • http://www.nantucketatheneum.org

Nantucket Historical Association • Historical Museum, 15 Broad St, P.O. Box 1016 • Nantucket, MA 02554-1016 • (508) 228-1655 • http://www.nha.org

Nantucket Life-Saving Museum • 158 Polpis Rd • Nantucket, MA 02554 • (508) 228-1885 • http://www.nantucketlifesavingmuseum.com

Nantucket Lightship Basket Museum • 49 Union St, P.O. Box 2517 • Nantucket, MA 02584 • (508) 228-1177 • http://www.nantucketlightshipbasketmuseum.org

Thomas Macy House Museum • 99 Main St • Nantucket, MA 02554

Natick
Morse Institute Library • 14 E Central St • Natick, MA 01760 • (508) 647-6521 • http://www.morseinstitute.org

Natick Historical Society • Historical Museum, 58 Eliot St • Natick, MA 01760 • (508) 647-4841 • http://www.natickhistoricalsociety.org

Needham
Needham Free Public Library • 1139 Highland Ave • Needham, MA 02494 • (781) 455-7559 • http://www.town.needham.ma.us/library

Needham Historical Society • Historical Museum, 1147 Central Ave • Needham, MA 02192 • (781) 455-8860 • http://www.needhamhistory.org

New Ashford
New Ashford Historical Commission • Historical Museum, Town Hall, Route 7 • New Ashford, MA 01237

New Bedford
Cuttyhunk Historical Society • 3 Broadway • New Bedford, MA 02740 • (508) 984-4611

Hetty Green Historical Society • 52 Union St • New Bedford, MA 02745

Institute of Family History and Genealogy • 99 Ash St • New Bedford, MA 02740

New Bedford Fire Museum • Old Station No. 4, 51 Bedford St • New Bedford, MA 02740 • (508) 992-2162

New Bedford Free Public Library • 613 Pleasant St • New Bedford, MA 02740 • (508) 991-6280 • http://www.ci.new-bedford.ma.us/nbfpl.htm

New Bedford Historical Society • Johnson House Museum, 21 7th St, P.O.Box 40084 • New Bedford, MA 02744 • (508) 979-8828 • http://www.newbedfordhistory.org

New Bedford Whaling Museum • 18 Johnny Cake Hill • New Bedford, MA 02740 • (617) 997-0046 • http://www.whalingmuseum.org

New Beford Whaling National Historic Park • 33 William St • New Bedford, MA 02740 • (508) 996-4095 • http://www.nps.gov/nebe/

New England Steamship Foundation • Historical Museum, 63 Union St • New Bedford, MA 02740 • (508) 999-1925

Old Dartmouth Historical Society • Whaling Museum, 18 Johnny Cake Hill • New Bedford, MA 02740-6398 • (508) 997-0046 • http://www.whalingmuseum.org

Rotch-Jones-Duff House Museum • 396 County St • New Bedford, MA 02740 • (508) 997-1401 • http://www.rjdmuseum.org

Schooner Ernestina Museum • 89 N Water St, P.O. Box 2010 • New Bedford, MA 02741-2010 • (508) 992-4900 • http://www.ernestina.org

New Braintree
New Braintree Historical Society • Historical Museum, 10 Utley Rd, P.O. Box 112 • New Braintree, MA 01531 • (508) 867-8608 • http://www.newbraintreehistoricalsociety.org

New Salem
Swift River Valley Historical Society • 40 Elm St N, P.O. Box 22 • New Salem, MA 01355 • (978) 544-6885

Massachusetts

Newbury
Coffin House Museum • 14 High Rd, Route 1A • Newbury, MA 01951 • (978) 462-2634 • http://www.historicnewengland.org

Spencer-Pierce-Little Farm Museum • 5 Little's Ln • Newbury, MA 01951 • (978) 462-2634 • http://www.historicnewengland.org

Newburyport
Custom House Maritime Museum • 25 Water St • Newburyport, MA 01950 • (978) 462-8681

Historical Society of Old Newbury • Cushing House Museum, 98 High St • Newburyport, MA 01950 • (978) 462-2681 • http://www.newburyhist.com

Newburyport Maritime Society • Custom House Maritime Museum, 25 Water St • Newburyport, MA 01950 • (978) 462-8681 • http://www.themaritimesociety.org

Newburyport Public Library • 94 State St • Newburyport, MA 01950-6619 • (978) 465-4428 • http://www.newburyportpl.org

Sons and Daughters of the First Settlers of Newbury, Massachusetts • 76 State St, P.O. Box 444 • Newburyport, MA 01950

Newton
Brennan Library • Lasell College, 1844 Commonwealth Ave • Newton, MA 02466 • (617) 243-2244 • http://student.lasell.edu/library.htm

Jackson Homestead Museum • 527 Washington St • Newton, MA 02458 • (617) 552-7228 • http://www.newtonhistorymuseum.org

Jewish Genealogical Society of Greater Boston • P.O. Box 610366 • Newton, MA 02161-0366 • (866) 611-5698 • http://www.jgsgb.org

Lowell House Museum • 23 Needham St • Newton, MA 02461

Newton Free Library • 330 Homer St • Newton, MA 02459-1429 • (617) 796-1360 • http://www.ci.newton.ma.us/library/

Newton Historical Society • Jackson Homestead Museum, 527 Washington St • Newton, MA 02158 • (617) 552-7238 • http://www.newtonhistorymuseum.org

Newton History Museum at the Jackson Homestead • 527 Washington St • Newton, MA 02458 • (617) 796-1450 • http://www.newtonhistorymuseum.org

Wadsworth Library • Mount Ida College, 777 Dedham St • Newton, MA 02459-0249 • (617) 928-4552

Newton Centre
American Jewish Historical Society • Newton Centre, 160 Herrick Rd • Newton Centre, MA 02459 • (617) 559-8880 • http://www.ajhs.org

Franklin Trask Library • Andover Newton Theological School, 169 Herrick Rd • Newton Centre, MA 02459 • (617) 964-1100 • http://library.ants.edu\lib

Jewish Cemetery Association of Massachusetts • 1320 Centre St, Ste 306 • Newton Centre, MA 02159 • (617) 244-6509 • http://www.jcam.org

Newton Historic Preservation Association • Historical Museum, 14 Kenwood Ave • Newton Centre, MA 02459 • (617) 527-5981

Rae and Joseph Gann Library • Hebrew College, 160 Herrick Rd • Newton Centre, MA 02459 • (617) 559-8750 • http://www.hebrewcollege.edu/library

North Adams
Freel Library - Special Collections • North Adams State College, P.O. Box 9250 • North Adams, MA 01247 • (413) 662-5321

North Adams Historical Society • Heritage State Park, P.O. Box 333 • North Adams, MA 01247-0333 • (413) 664-4700 • http://www.northadamshistory.org

North Andover
Barson Barnard House Museum • 179 Osgood St • North Andover, MA 01845

Museum of Printing • 800 Massachusetts Ave • North Andover, MA 01845 • (978) 686-0450 • http://www.museumofprinting.org

North Andover Historical Society • Ballard-Johnson Cottage Museum, 153 Academy Rd • North Andover, MA 01845 • (978) 686-4035 • http://www.essexheritage.org/north_andover_hist_soc.htm

Stevens Memorial Library • 345 Main St, P.O. Box 8 • North Andover, MA 01845-0008 • (978) 688-9505 • http://www.stevensmemlib.org

Stevens-Coolidge Place Museum • 137 Andover St • North Andover, MA 01845 • (978) 682-3580

North Attleboro
North Attleboro Historical Society • Historical Museum, 362 N Washington St, P.O. Box 1102 • North Attleboro, MA 02760 • (508) 695-3349

North Attleborough Historical Commission • Town Hall, 43 S Washington St • North Attleboro, MA 02760 • (508) 699-0100 • http://www.north-attleboro.ma.us/historical/

North Billerica
Middlesex Canal Museum • 71 Faulkner St • North Billerica, MA 01862 • (978) 670-2740 • http://www.middlesexcanal.org/museum

North Brookfield
North Brookfield Historical Society • Historical Museum, 50 Waite Corner Rd • North Brookfield, MA 01535 • (508) 885-8267

North Dartmouth
Center for Jewish Culture Archives • Univ of Massachusetts, Dartmouth Library, 285 Old Westport Rd • North Dartmouth, MA 02747-2300 • (508) 999-8678 • http://www.lib.umassd.edu

North Easton
Ames Free Library of Easton • 53 Main St • North Easton, MA 02356 • (508) 238-2000 • http://amesfreelibrary.org

Easton Historical Society • North Easton RR Station Museum, 80 Mechanic St, P.O. Box 3 • North Easton, MA 02356 • (508) 238-7774

North Grafton
Willard House and Clock Museum • 11 Willard St • North Grafton, MA 01536 • (508) 839-3500 • http://www.willardhouse.org

North Oxford
Clara Barton Birthplace Museum • 68 Clara Barton Rd, P.O. Box 356 • North Oxford, MA 01537 • (508) 987) 5375 • http://www.clarabartonbirthplace.org

North Reading
Flint Memorial Library • 147 Park St • North Reading, MA 01864 • (978) 664-4942 • http://www.flintmemoriallibrary.org

North Reading Historical and Antiquarian Society • 27 Bow St, P.O. Box 354 • North Reading, MA 01864 • (978) 664-1066 • http://www.nreadinghistory.org

North Reading Historical Commission • Historical Museum, 235 North St • North Reading, MA 01864 • (978) 664-6010 • http://www.nreadinghistory.org/histcom.html

North Weymouth
Abigail Adams Historical Society • Abigail Smith Adams Birthplace Museum, 180 Norton St, P.O. Box 147 • North Weymouth, MA 02191 • (781) 335-4205 • http://www.abigailadamsbirthplace.org

North Woburn
Rumford Historical Association • Historical Museum, 90 Elm St • North Woburn, MA 01801 • (617) 933-0781

Northampton

Calvin Coolidge Presidential Library & Museum • 20 West St • Northampton, MA 01060 • (413) 587-1014 • http://www.forbeslibrary.org

Forbes Library • 20 West St • Northampton, MA 01060-3798 • (413) 587-1012 • http://www.forbeslibrary.org

Northampton Historical Commission • Historical Museum, 210 Main St • Northampton, MA 01060 • (413) 586-0138

Northampton Historical Society • Damon House Museum, 46 Bridge St • Northampton, MA 01060 • (413) 584-6011 • http://www.historic-northampton.org

Parsons House Museum • 58 Bridge St • Northampton, MA 01060

Polish Genealogical Society of Massachusetts • P.O. Box 381 • Northampton, MA 01061-0381 • (413) 586-1827 • http://www.rootsweb.com/~mapgsm/

Shepherd House Museum • 66 Bridge St • Northampton, MA 01060

Northborough

Northborough Free Library • 34 Main St • Northborough, MA 01532 • (508) 393-5025 • http://www.town.northborough.ma.us/library

Northborough Historical Society • Historical Museum, 50 Main St, P.O. Box 661 • Northborough, MA 01532 • (508) 393-6298 • http://www.northboroughhistsoc.org

Northbridge

Northbridge Historical Society • 183 Cooper Rd • Northbridge, MA 01534 • (508) 234-5110

Northfield

Northfield Mass Historical Society • Historical Museum, Pine St, P.O. Box 159 • Northfield, MA 01360 • (413) 498-5565

Norton

Madeleine Clark Wallace Library • Wheaton College, 26 E Main St • Norton, MA 02766-2322 • (508) 286-3700

Norton Historical Society • 18 W Main, P.O. Box 1711 • Norton, MA 02766 • (508) 285-7070 • http://cs.wheatonma.edu/nhs

Norton Public Library • 68 E Main St • Norton, MA 02766 • (508) 285-0265 • http://www.sailsinc.org/norton/

Norwell

Jacob's Farmhouse Museum • Jacobs Lane • Norwell, MA 02061 • (781) 659-1888

James Library • 24 West St, P.O. Box 164 • Norwell, MA 02061 • (781) 659-7100

Norwell Historical Society • Historical Museum, 328 Main St, P.O. Box 693 • Norwell, MA 02061 • (781) 659-1888

Norwell Public Library • 64 South St • Norwell, MA 02061-2433 • (781) 659-2015 • http://www.ocln.org

South Shore Genealogical Society • West St, P.O. Box 396 • Norwell, MA 02061-0396 • (781) 837-8364

Norwood

Morrill Memorial Library • 33 Walpole St, P.O. Box 220 • Norwood, MA 02062-0220 • (781) 769-0200 • http://www.ci.norwood.ma.us/library/

Norwood Historical Society • 93 Day St • Norwood, MA 02062 • (781) 762-9197 • http://www.norwoodhistoricalsociety.org

Oak Bluffs

Cottage Museum • 1 Trinity Park, P.O. Box 1176 • Oak Bluffs, MA 02557 • (508) 693-7784

Soldiers' Memorial Fountain Restoration Committee • P.O. Box 1003 • Oak Bluffs, MA 02557

Oakham

Fobes Memorial Library • 4 Maple St • Oakham, MA 01068 • (508) 882-3372

Oakham Historical Museum • 1221 Old Turnpike Rd, P.O. Box 236 • Oakham, MA 01068 • (508) 882-3111 • http://www.oakhamhistory.com

Orange

Orange Historical Society • 41 N Main St • Orange, MA 01364 • (978) 544-3141

Wheeler Memorial Library • 49 E Main St • Orange, MA 01364-1267 • (978) 544-2495 • http://www.cwmorris.org

Orleans

French Cable Station Museum in Orleans • 41 S Orleans Rd, P.O. Box 85 • Orleans, MA 02653 • (508) 255-0343

Orleans Historical Society • Margaret Stranger House Museum, 3 River Rd, P.O. Box 353 • Orleans, MA 02653 • (508) 240-1329

Snow Library • 67 Main St, P.O. Box 246 • Orleans, MA 02653-0246 • (508) 240-3760 • http://www.clamsnet.org

Osterville

Cape Cod Genealogical Society • P.O. Box 127 • Osterville, MA 02644

Osterville Free Library • 43 Wianno Ave • Osterville, MA 02655 • (508) 428-5757

Osterville Historical Society • Cammett House Museum, 155 W Bay Rd, P.O. Box 3 • Osterville, MA 02655 • (508) 428-5861 • http://www.osterville.org

Oxford

Oxford Free Library & Museum • 339 Main St • Oxford, MA 01540 • (508) 987-6003

Oxford Historical Society • Historical Museum, 8A Pond St • Oxford, MA 01540 • (508) 987-5057

Palmer

Palmer Public Library • 1085 Park St • Palmer, MA 01069 • (413) 283-3330 • http://www.palmer.lib.ma.us

Paxton

Paxton Historical Commission • Historical Museum, 17 West St • Paxton, MA 01612 • (508) 755-6789

Peabody

George Peabody House Museum • 205 Washington St • Peabody, MA 01960 • (978) 531-0355 • http://www.georgepeabodyhousemuseum.org

Italian Genealogical Society of America • P.O. Bbox 3572 • Peabody, MA 01961-3572 • http://www.italianroots.org

Peabody Historical Society • Historical Museum, 35 Washington St • Peabody, MA 01960-5520 • (978) 531-0805 • http://www.peabodyhistorical.org

Pelham

Pelham Historical Society • Historical Museum, 373 Amherst Rd • Pelham, MA 01002 • (413) 253-7313

Pelham Historical Society • 2 South Valley Rd • Pelham, MA 01002

Pelham Public Library • 2 S Valley Rd • Pelham, MA 01002 • (413) 253-0657 • http://www.pelham-library.org

Pembroke

Pembroke Historical Society • Historical Museum, 116 Center St, P.O. Box 122 • Pembroke, MA 02359-2613 • (781) 293-9083

Pepperell

C F Lawrence Memorial Library • 15 Main St, P.O. Drawer 1440 • Pepperell, MA 01463-3440 • (978) 433-0330 • http://www.lawrencelibrary.org

Massachusetts

Petersham
Fisher Museum of Forestry • 326 N Main St, P.O. Box 68 • Petersham, MA 01366 • (978) 724-3302 • http://www.harvardforest.fas.harvard. edu/mus.html

Petersham Historical Society • Historical Museum, 10 N Main St, P.O. Box 364 • Petersham, MA 01366 • (978) 724-3380

Petersham Memorial Library • 22 Petersham Common • Petersham, MA 01366-0056 • (978) 724-3405

Phillipston
Historical Society of Phillipston • 50 State Rd • Phillipston, MA 01331 • (978) 939-4025 • http://www.historicalsocietyofphillipston.org

Pittsfield
Berkshire Athanaeum • 1 Wendell Ave • Pittsfield, MA 01201-6385 • (413) 499-9488 • http://www.berkshire.net

Berkshire County Historical Society • Herman Melville's Arrowhead Museum, 780 Holmes Rd • Pittsfield, MA 01201-7199 • (413) 442-1793 • http://www.berkshirehistory.org

Berkshire Family History Association • P.O. Box 1437 • Pittsfield, MA 01202-1437 • (413) 445-5521 • http://www.berkshire.net/~bfha/

Berkshire Jewish Archives Council • 75 Mountain Dr • Pittsfield, MA 01201

Berkshire Museum • 39 South St • Pittsfield, MA 01201 • (413) 443-7171 • http://www.berkshiremuseum.org

Hancock Shaker Village Museum • 1843 W Housatonic St, P.O. Box 927 • Pittsfield, MA 01202 • (413) 443-0188 • http://www. hancockshakervillage.org

National Archives & Records Administration-Northeast Region • 10 Conte Dr • Pittsfield, MA 01201-8230 • (413) 445-6885 • http://www. archives.gov/facilities/ma/pittsfield.html

Plainfield
Plainfield Historical Society • 344 Main St • Plainfield, MA 01070 • (413) 534-5417

Plainville Public Library • 198 South St • Plainville, MA 02762-1512 • (508) 695-1784 • http://www.sailsinc.org/plainville/

Plymouth
Harlow Old Fort House Museum • 119 Sandwich St • Plymouth, MA 02360 • (508) 746-3017

National Headquarters, General Society of Mayflower Descendants • Historical Museum, 4 Windslow St, P.O. Box 3297 • Plymouth, MA 02361 • (508) 746-3188 • http://www.mayflower.org

Pilgrim Hall Museum • 75 Court St • Plymouth, MA 02360 • (508) 746-1620 • http://www.pilgrimhall.org

Pilgrim John Howland Society • Jabez Howland House Museum, 33 Sandwich St • Plymouth, MA 02360 • (617) 746-9590

Pilgrim Society • Pilgrim Hall Museum, 75 Court St • Plymouth, MA 02360-3891 • (508) 746-1620 • http://www.pilgrimhall.org

Plimoth Plantation • Historical Museum, 137 Warren Ave, P.O. Box 1620 • Plymouth, MA 02362-1620 • (508) 746-1622 • http://www. plimoth.org

Plymouth Antiquarian Society • Hedge House Museum, 126 Water St, P.O. Box 3773 • Plymouth, MA 02361 • (508) 746-0012 • http://www. plymouthantiquariansociety.org

Plymouth Public Library • 132 South St • Plymouth, MA 02360-3309 • (508) 830-4250 • http://www2.pcix.com/users/ppl/public-html/

Plymouth Rock Foundation • 1120 Long Pond Rd • Plymouth, MA 02360 • (508) 833-1189

Richard Sparrow House • 42 Summer St • Plymouth, MA 02360 • (508) 747-1240 • http://www.sparrowhouse.com

Spooner House Museum • 27 North St, P.O. Box 3773 • Plymouth, MA 02361 • (508) 746-0012

Plympton
Plympton Historical Society • Historical Museum, 189 Main St, P.O. Box 21 • Plympton, MA 02367-1112 • (781) 585-2725

Pocasset
Chappiquiddic Band of Massachusetts • P.O. Box 3931 • Pocasset, MA 02559 • http://chappiquiddic.org

Princeton
Princeton Historical Society • P.O. Box 199 • Princeton, MA 01541-0199

Princeton Public Library • 2 Town Hall Dr • Princeton, MA 01541 • (978) 464-2115 • http://www.library.town.princeton.ma.us

Rhode Island Families Association • P.O. Box 585 • Princeton, MA 01541-0585 • (508) 464-5588 • http://www.erols.com/rigr

Provincetown
Cape Cod Pilgrim Memorial Association • Pilgrim Monument and Provincetown Museum, 1 High Pole Hill, P.O. Box 1125 • Provincetown, MA 02657 • (508) 487-1310 • http://www.pilgrim-monument.org

Provincetown Heritage Museum • 260 Commercial St • Provincetown, MA 02657 • (508) 487-7098

Provincetown Public Library • 330 Commercial St • Provincetown, MA 02657-2209 • (508) 487-7094 • http://www.ptownlib.com

Quincy
Adams National Historic Site Museum • 135 Adams St, P.O. Box 531 • Quincy, MA 02269 • (617) 773-1177 • http://www.nps.gov.adam

Birthplace of John Adams Museum • 133 Franklin St • Quincy, MA 02169

Birthplace of John Quincy Adams Museum • 141 Franklin St • Quincy, MA 02169

Josiah Quincy House Museum • 20 Muirhead St • Quincy, MA 02114 • (617) 227-3956 • http://www.historicnewengland.org

Order of Knights of Pythias • Supreme Lodge, 59 Coddington St, Ste 202 • Quincy, MA 02169 • (617) 472-8800 • http://www.pythias.org

Quincy Historical Society • Adams Academy Museum, 8 Adams St • Quincy, MA 02169 • (617) 773-1144 • http://www.quincyhistory.org

Quincy Homestead Museum • 1010 Hancock St • Quincy, MA 02169 • (617) 472-5117

Thomas Crane Public Library • 40 Washington St • Quincy, MA 02269-9164 • (617) 376-1300 • http://ci.quincy.ma.us/tcpl

United American Indians of New England • P.O. Box 7501 • Quincy, MA 02269 • (617) 773-0406 • http://home.earthlink.net/~uainendom

United States Naval Shipbuilding Museum • 739 Washington St • Quincy, MA 02169 • (617) 479-7900

Randolph
Randolph Historical Society • Historical Museum, 360 N Main St • Randolph, MA 02368 • (781) 963-9645

Raynham
Raynham Historical Commission • 54 Orchard St • Raynham, MA 02767

Raynham Center
Raynham Historical Society • Historical Museum, P.O. Box 136 • Raynham Center, MA 02768 • http://www.raynhamhistory.home. comcast.net

Reading
Reading Antiquarian Society • Parker Tavern Museum, 103 Washington St, P.O. Box 842 • Reading, MA 01867 • (781) 944-4030

Reading Public Library • 64 Middlesex Ave • Reading, MA 01867 • (781) 944-0840 • http://www.readingpl.org

Rehoboth
Annawan Historical Society of Rehoboth • P.O. Box 71 • Rehoboth, MA 02769 • (508) 669-6464

Blanding Public Library • 124 Bay State Rd • Rehoboth, MA 02769 • (508) 252-4236 • http://www.town.rehoboth.ma.us

Carpenter Museum • 4 Locust Ave, P.O. Box 2 • Rehoboth, MA 02769 • (508) 252-3031

Genealogy Central • 37 Martin St • Rehoboth, MA 02769 • (508) 252-6540

Rehoboth Antiquarian Society • Bay State Rd, P.O. Box 2 • Rehoboth, MA 02769

Revere
Revere Historical and Cultural Commission • 281 Broadway • Revere, MA 02151 • (781) 284-3600 x140

Revere Public Library • 179 Beach St • Revere, MA 02151 • (781) 286-8380 • http://www.noblenet.org/revere

Revere Society for Cultural and Historic Preservation • 108 Beach St, P.O. Box 44 • Revere, MA 02151 • (781) 284-9366

Richmond
Richmond Historical Society • Historical Museum, P.O. Box 428 • Richmond, MA 01254 • (413) 698-3247

Rochester
Joseph H Plumb Memorial Library • 17 Constitution Way, PO Box 69 • Rochester, MA 02770 • (508) 763-8600 • http://www.plumblibrary.com

Rockland
Rockland Historical Commission • Historical Museum, 242 Union St • Rockland, MA 02370 • (781) 871-6220

Rockland Memorial Library • 20 Belmont St • Rockland, MA 02370 • (781) 878-1236 • http://www.rocklandmemoriallibrary.org

Rockport
Paper House Museum • 52 Pigeon Hill St • Rockport, MA 01966 • (978) 546-2629

Rockport Public Library • 17 School St • Rockport, MA 01966 • (978) 546-6934 • http://www.mvlc.org

Sandy Bay Historical Society • Historical Museum, 40 King St, P.O. Box 63 • Rockport, MA 01966-0063 • (978) 546-9533 • http://www.sandybayhistorical.org

Rowe
Rowe Historical Society • Kemp-McCarthy Museum, 288 Zoar Rd, P.O. Box 456 • Rowe, MA 01367 • (413) 339-4238

Rowe Town Library • 318 Zoar Rd • Rowe, MA 01367 • (413) 339-4761

Rowley
Rowley Historical Society • Historical Museum, 233 Main St, P.O. Box 41 • Rowley, MA 01969 • (978) 948-7483

Rowley Public Library • 141 Main St • Rowley, MA 01969 • (978) 948-2850 • http://www.town.rowley.ma.us/library/lib_home.htm

Roxbury
Roxbury Historical Society • Heritage Park Museum, 183 Roxbury St, P.O. Box 5, Dudley Sta • Roxbury, MA 02119 • (617) 445-3399 • http://www.state.ma.us/dem/parks/rxhp.htm

Shirley-Eustis House Museum • 33 Shirley St • Roxbury, MA 02119 • (617) 442-2275

Royalston
Village Improvement and Historical Society of Royalston • Society Bldg • Royalston, MA 01368 • (978) 249-2598

Rutland
Rutland Historical Society • Historical Museum, 232 Main St, P.O. Box 69 • Rutland, MA 01543-1300 • (508) 886-4329

Salem
Crowninshield-Bentley House Museum • 126 Essex St • Salem, MA 01970 • (508) 745-1876

Essex County Historical Association • Peabody Essex Museum, East India Sq • Salem, MA 01970 • (978) 745-1876 • http://www.pem.org

Essex Heritage Commission • Historical Museum, 221 Essex St • Salem, MA 01970 • (978) 740-0444 • http://www.essexheritage.org

Essex Institute • John Ward House Museum, 132 Essex St • Salem, MA 01970 • (617) 744-3390

Gardner Pingree House Museum • 128 Essex St • Salem, MA 01970 • (508) 745-1876

Historic Salem • Old Town Hall, P.O. Box 865 • Salem, MA 01970 • (978) 745-6470

House of the Seven Gables Museum • 54 Turner St • Salem, MA 01970 • (978) 744-0991 • http://www.7gables.org

New England Pirate Museum • 274 Derby St • Salem, MA 01970 • (978) 741-2800 • http://www.piratemuseum.com/pirate.htm

North Shore Jewish Historical Society • 2 East India Sq, Ste 200 • Salem, MA 01970 • (978) 564-0741

Peabody Museum of Salem • 161 Essex St • Salem, MA 01970-3783 • (978) 745-9500 • http://www.pem.org/phillips.html

Ropes Mansion Museum • 318 Essex St • Salem, MA 01970 • (508) 744-0718

Salem 1630 Pioneer Village • Forest River Park • Salem, MA 01970 • (978) 744-0991 • http://www.essexheritage.org

Salem Maritime National Historic Site Museum • 174 Derby St • Salem, MA 01970 • (978) 740-1680 • http://www.nps.gov/sama/

Salem Public Library • 370 Essex St • Salem, MA 01970 • (978) 744-0860 • http://www.noblenet.org

Salem Witch Museum • 19 1/2 Washington Sq N • Salem, MA 01970 • (978) 744-1692 • http://www.salemwitchmuseum.com

Stephen Phillips Memorial Trust House Museum • 34 Chestnut St • Salem, MA 01970 • (978) 744-0440 • http://www.phillipsmuseum.org

Witch House Museum • 310 1/2 Essex St • Salem, MA 01970 • (508) 744-0180

Yin Yu Tang House Museum • Peabody Essex Museum, 161 Essex St • Salem, MA 01970 • (877) 736-8499 • http://www.pem.org

Salisbury
Salisbury Historical Commission • Historical Museum, Beach Rd, P.O. Box 5464 • Salisbury, MA 01950 • (978) 372-7744

Salisbury Public Library • 17 Elm St • Salisbury, MA 01952 • (978) 465-5071

Sandisfield
Sandisfield Historical Society • SR66, Box 96 • Sandisfield, MA 01255

Sandwich
Heritage Museum & Gardens • 67 Grove St • Sandwich, MA 02563 • (508) 888-3300 • http://www.heritagemuseumsandgardens.org

Old Hoxie House Museum • 16 Water St • Sandwich, MA 02563 • (508) 888-1173

Sandwich Archives and Historical Center • Sandwich Public Library, 145 Main St • Sandwich, MA 02563 • (617) 888-0340 • http://www.sandwichmass.org

Sandwich Historical Society • Glass Museum, 129 Main St, P.O. Box 103 • Sandwich, MA 02563 • (508) 888-0251 • http://www.sandwichglassmuseum.org

Massachusetts

Sandwich, cont.

Thornton W Burgess Museum • 4 Water St, P.O. Box 972 • Sandwich, MA 02563 • (508) 888-4668 • http://www.thorntonburgess.org

Yesteryears Museum Association • Historical Museum, Main & River Sts, P.O. Box 609 • Sandwich, MA 02563 • (508) 888-1711

Saugus

Saugus Historical Society • 59 Water St • Saugus, MA 01906 • (781) 233-7232

Saugus Iron Works National Historic Site Museum • 244 Central St • Saugus, MA 01906 • (781) 233-0050 • http://www.nps.gov/sair

Saugus Public Library • 295 Central St • Saugus, MA 01906-2191 • (781) 231-4168 • http://www.saugus.ma.us/Library

Swampscott Historical Commission • Historical Museum, 16 Richard St • Saugus, MA 01906

Savoy

Savoy Historic Commission • 720 Main Rd • Savoy, MA 01256 • (413) 743-4197

Scituate

Cudsworth House Museum • First Parish Rd • Scituate, MA 02066 • (781) 545-1083

Mann Farmhouse Museum • Stockbridge Rd & Greenfield Ln, P.O. Box 276 • Scituate, MA 02066 • (781) 545-1083

Scituate Historical Society • Laidlaw Historical Museum, 43 Cudworth Rd, P.O. Box 276 • Scituate, MA 02066-0276 • (781) 545-1083 • http://www.scituatehistoricalsociety.org

Scituate Maritime and Irish Mossing Museum • Driftway, P.O. Box 276 • Scituate, MA 02066 • (781) 545-1083 • http://www.scituatehistoricalsociety.org

Scituate Town Archives • Town Hall, 600 Chief Justice Cushing Hwy • Scituate, MA 02066 • (781) 545-8745 • http://town.scituate.ma.us/gov_archives.htm

Scituate Town Library • 85 Branch St • Scituate, MA 02066 • (781) 545-8727 • http://www.scituatetownlibrary.org

Sharon

Kendall Whaling Museum • 27 Everett St, P.O. Box 297 • Sharon, MA 02067 • (617) 784-5642 • http://www.kwm.org

Sharon Historical Society • Historical Museum, 15 High St, P.O. Box 175 • Sharon, MA 02067 • (781) 784-5834

Sharon Public Library • 11 N Main St • Sharon, MA 02067-1299 • (781) 784-1578 • http://www.sharonpubliclibrary.org

Sheffield

Sheffield Historical Society • Historical Museum, 159 Main St, P.O. Box 747 • Sheffield, MA 01257-0747 • (413) 229-2694 • http://www.sheffieldhistory.org

Shelburne

Shelburne Historical Society • 33 Severance, P.O. Box 86 • Shelburne, MA 01370 • (413) 625-6150

Shelburne Falls

Shelburne Falls Trolley Museum • 14 Depot St, P.O. Box 272 • Shelburne Falls, MA 01370 • (413) 625-9443

Sherborn

Sherborn Historical Society • Historical Museum, 19 Washington St, P.O. Box 186 • Sherborn, MA 01770-0186 • (508) 653-0560

Shirley

First Parish Meetinghouse Preservation Society • Shirley Meeting House Museum, 25 Whitney Rd, P.O. Box 1426 • Shirley, MA 01464 • (978 425-2600 • http://www.shirleymeetinghouse.org

Hazen Memorial Library • 3 Keady Way • Shirley, MA 01464 • (978) 425-2620 • http://www.shirleylibrary.org

Shirley Historical Society • Historical Museum, 182 Center Rd, P.O. Box 217 • Shirley, MA 01464 • (978) 425-9328 • http://www.shirleyhistory.org

Shrewsbury

Gen Artemus Ward Home Museum • 786 Main St • Shrewsbury, MA 01545 • (508) 842-8900

Shrewsbury Historical Society • 17 Church Rd • Shrewsbury, MA 01545 • (508) 842-5239

Shrewsbury Public Library • 609 Main St • Shrewsbury, MA 01545 • (508) 842-0081 • http://www.shrewsbury-ma.gov

Somerset

Somerset Historical Society • Historical Museum, 274 High St • Somerset, MA 02726 • (508) 675-9010

Somerset Public Library • 1464 County St • Somerset, MA 02726 • (508) 646-2829 • http://www.sailsinc.org/somerset/

Somerville

Somerville Historic Preservation Commission • Historical Museum, 93 Highland Ave • Somerville, MA 02143 • (617) 625-6600

Somerville Historical Museum • 1 Westwood Rd • Somerville, MA 02143 • (617) 666-9810

Somerville Historical Society • Historical Museum, 1 Westwood Rd • Somerville, MA 02143 • (617) 666-9810

Somerville Public Library • 79 Highland Ave • Somerville, MA 02143 • (617) 623-5000 • http://www.ultranet.com/~somlib/

South Boston

Free Albania Organization • 397-B N Broadway • South Boston, MA 02127

South Chelmsford

Chelmsford Historical Society • 40 Byam Rd • South Chelmsford, MA 01824 • (978) 256-2311 • http://www.chelmhist.org

South Dartmouth

Early American Industries Society • 167 Bakerville Road • South Dartmouth, MA 02748-1174 • (508) 993-4198

South Deerfield

Tilton Library • 75 N Main St • South Deerfield, MA 01373 • (413) 665-4683

South Dennis

Dennis Historical Society • Historical Museum, 77 Nobscussett Rd, P.O. Box 607 • South Dennis, MA 02660 • (508) 394-0017 • http://www.dennishistsoc.org

Jericho House and Barn Museum • Trotting Park Rd & Old Main St, P.O. Box 1419 • South Dennis, MA 02660

South Hadley

Skinner Museum of Mount Holyoke College • 35 Woodbridge St • South Hadley, MA 01075 • (413) 538-2245 • http://www.mtholyoke.edu/go/artmuarum

South Hadley Historical Society • 43 Woodbridge St • South Hadley, MA 01075 • (413) 538-2349

South Hadley Library System • 27 Bardwell St • South Hadley, MA 01075 • (413) 538-5045 • http://www.shadleylib.org

South Hamilton

Burton L Goddard Library • Gordon-Conwell Theological Seminary, 130 Essex St • South Hamilton, MA 01982-2361 • (978) 646-4076 • http://gcts.library.net

Hamilton-Wenham Public Library • 14 Union St • South Hamilton, MA 01982 • (978) 468-5527 • http://www.hwlibrary.org

South Natick

Bacon Free Library • 58 Eliot St • South Natick, MA 01760-596 • (508) 653-6730 • http://users.rcn.com/bfl

Natick Historical Society • Historical Museum, 58 Eliot St • South Natick, MA 01760 • (508) 647-4841 • http://www.natickhistory.com

South Royalston

Royalston Historical Society • Fernald Rd • South Royalston, MA 01331 • (978) 249-4964

South Weymouth

Ukelele Museum • P.O. Box 22 • South Weymouth, MA 02190

South Yarmouth

Yarmouth Historical Commission • 8 Old Cedar Ln • South Yarmouth, MA 02664 • (508) 398-2231

Yarmouth Town Libraries • 312 Old Main St • South Yarmouth, MA 02664 • (508) 760-4820 • http://www.yarmouthlibraries.org

Southampton

Edwards Public Library • 30 East St • Southampton, MA 01073-9324 • (413) 527-9480 • http://www.southamptonlibrary.org

Southampton Historical Commission • Historical Museum, P.O. Box 59 • Southampton, MA 01073-0059 • (413) 527-1520

Southborough

Southborough Historical Society • 25 Common St, P.O. Box 364 • Southborough, MA 01772 • (508) 229-8055

Southbridge

Jacob Edwards Library • 236 Main St • Southbridge, MA 01550-2598 • (508) 764-5426 • http://www.southridgelibrary.org

Southwick

Southwick Historical Society • Historical Museum, P.O. Box 323 • Southwick, MA 01077 • (413) 998-3018

Spencer

Richard Sudgen Library • 8 Pleasant St • Spencer, MA 01562 • (508) 885-7513

Springfield

Connecticut Valley Historical Museum • 220 State St • Springfield, MA 01103 • (413) 263-6800 • http://www.springfieldmuseum.org

Connecticut Valley Historical Museum • The Quadrangle, 220 State St • Springfield, MA 01103 • (413) 263-6800 • http://www.quadrangle.org/cvhm.htm

French Canadian-American Genealogy • c/o Springfield Public Library, 220 State St • Springfield, MA 01103 • (413) 263-6800

Mattoon Street Historical Preservation Association • P.O. Box 3274 • Springfield, MA 01101 • (413) 787-6527

Springfield Armory National Historic Site Library • 1 Armory Square • Springfield, MA 01105 • (413) 734-8551 • http://www.nps.gov/spar/

Springfield City Library • 220 State St • Springfield, MA 01103 • (413) 263-6800 • http://www.springfieldlibrary.org

Springfield Museums at the Quad • 220 State St • Springfield, MA 01103 • (413) 263-6800 • http://www.springfieldmuseums.org

Western Massachusetts Genealogical Society • P.O. Box 80206, Forest Park Sta • Springfield, MA 01108-0206 • http://www.rootsweb.com/mawmgs/

Sterling

Sterling Historical Society • Historical Museum, 7 Pine St, P.O. Box 356 • Sterling, MA 01564 • (978) 422-6139

Still River

Harvard Historical Society • Historical Museum, 215 Still River Rd • Still River, MA 01467 • (978) 456-8285 • http://www.harvardhistory.org

Stockbridge

Chesterwood Museum • 4 Williamsville Rd, Glendale Station, P.O. Box 827 • Stockbridge, MA 01262-0827 • (413) 298-3579 • http://www.chesterwood.org

Merwin House-Tranquility Museum • 14 Main St • Stockbridge, MA 01262 • (617) 227-3956 • http://www.historicnewengland.org

Mission House Museum • 19 Main St, P.O. Box 792 • Stockbridge, MA 01262 • (413) 298-3239 • http://www.thetrustees.org

Naumkeag Historic Home Museum • 5 Prospect Hill, P.O. Box 792 • Stockbridge, MA 01262 • (413) 298-3239 • http://www.thetrustees.org

Stockbridge Library & Museum • 46 Main St, P.O. Box 119 • Stockbridge, MA 01262 • (413) 298-5501 • http://www.masscat.org

Stoneham

Stoneham Historical Society • 36 William St • Stoneham, MA 02180 • (781) 438-4185

Stoneham Public Library • 431 Main St • Stoneham, MA 02180 • (781) 438-1324 • http://www.noblenet.org/stoneham

Stoughton

Afro-American Historical and Genealogical Society, New England Chapter • 42 Laurelwood Dr • Stoughton, MA 02072 • http://www.aahgs-ne.org

Capen Reynolds Farm Museum • 7 Glen Echo Blvd • Stoughton, MA 02072 • (781) 297-7500

Mary Baker Eddy Historic House Museum • 133 Central St • Stoughton, MA 02072 • (617) 277-8943

Stoughton Historical Society • Historical Museum, 6 Park St, P.O. Box 542 • Stoughton, MA 02072 • (781) 344-5456

Stoughton Public Library • 84 Park St, P.O. Box 209 • Stoughton, MA 02072 • (781) 344-2711 • http://www.stoughton.org/library/spl.html

Stow

Randall Library & Museum • 19 Crescent St • Stow, MA 01775-0263 • (978) 897-8572

Stow Historical Society • P.O. Box 261 • Stow, MA 01775 • (978) 897-5996

Stow West 1825 School Museum • Harvard Rd • Stow, MA 01775 • (978) 562-6843

Sturbridge

Joshua Hyde Public Library • 306 Main St • Sturbridge, MA 01566-1242 • (508) 347-2512 • http://www.sturbridgelibrary.org

Old Sturbridge Village • 1 Old Sturbridge Village Rd • Sturbridge, MA 01566 • (508) 347-3362 • http://www.osv.org

Sturbridge Historical Society • Historical Museum, 481 Leadmine Rd • Sturbridge, MA 01566 • (508) 347-3705

Sudbury

Friends of Sudbury's Historic Town Center • 11 Ford Rd • Sudbury, MA 01776 • (978) 443-4540

Goodnow Library & Town Archives • 21 Concord Rd • Sudbury, MA 01776-2383 • (978) 443-1035 • http://www.library.sudbury.ma.us

Irish Ancestral Research Association • P.O. Box 619 • Sudbury, MA 01776-0619 • (978) 894-0062 • http://www.tiara.ie/

Longfellow's Wayside Inn Museum • Wayside Inn Rd • Sudbury, MA 01776 • (978) 443-1776 • http://www.wayside.org

Sudbury Historical Commission • Town Hall Museum, 299 Old Sudbury Rd • Sudbury, MA 01776 • (978) 443-6722 • http://www.town.sudbury.ma.us

Sudbury Historical Society • Loring Parsonage Museum, 322 Concord Rd, P.O. Box 233 • Sudbury, MA 01776 • (978) 443-6672 • http://www.sudbury01776.org

Massachusetts

Sudbury, cont.

Sudbury Historical Society • 322 Concord Rd • Sudbury, MA 01776 • (978) 443-3747

Sunderland

Sunderland Historical Commission • Historical Museum, 12 School St • Sunderland, MA 01375 • (413) 665-8190

Sutton

Nipmuc Nation Tribal Office • 156 Worcester Providence Rd • Sutton, MA 01590 • (508) 865-9800 • http://www.nipmucnation.org

Sutton Historical Society • Historical Museum, 4 Uxbridge Rd • Sutton, MA 01590 • (508) 865-2010

Waters Farm Museum • 53 Waters Rd • Sutton, MA 01590 • (508) 865-0101

Swampscott

Atlantic 1 Fire-Fighting Museum • Burrill St • Swampscott, MA 01907 • (781) 581-5833

Lindsay Library • Marian Court College, 35 Littles Point Rd • Swampscott, MA 01907-2896 • (781) 595-6768 • http://www.mariancourt.edu

Mary Baker Eddy Historic House Museum • 23 Paradise Rd • Swampscott, MA 01907 • (781) 599-1853 • http://www.longyear.org

Swampscott Historical Commission • Administration Bldg • Swampscott, MA 01907 • (781) 596-8850

Swampscott Historical Society • John Humphrey House Museum, 99 Paradise Rd • Swampscott, MA 01907 • (781) 599-1297 • http://www.usgennet.org/usa/ma/town/swampscott/docs/histsoc.html

Swampscott Public Library • 61 Burrill St • Swampscott, MA 01907 • (781) 596-8867 • http://www.noblenet.org/swampscott

Swansea

Swansea Free Public Library • 69 Main St • Swansea, MA 02777 • (508) 674-9609

Swansea Historical Society • Historical Museum, 69 Main St, P.O. Box 723 • Swansea, MA 02777 • (508) 678-6432

Taunton

American-Portuguese Genealogical and Historical Society • P.O. Box 644 • Taunton, MA 02780-0644 • http://www.tauntonma.com/apghs/

Old Colony Historical Society • Historical Museum, 66 Church Green • Taunton, MA 02780 • (508) 822-1622 • http://www.oldcolonyhistoricalsociety.org

Taunton Public Library • 12 Pleasant St • Taunton, MA 02780 • (508) 821-1410 • http://www.tauntonlibrary.org

Teaticket

Falmouth Genealogical Society • P.O. Box 2107 • Teaticket, MA 02536 • (508) 540-2849 • http://www.rootsweb.com/~mafgs/; http://www.falgen.org

Templeton

Narragansett Historical Society • Historical Museum, 1 Boynton Rd, P.O. Box 354 • Templeton, MA 01468 • (978) 939-2303 • http://www.narragansetthistoricalsociety.org

Tewksbury

Tewksbury Historical Society • Historical Museum, 10 Lloyd Rd, P.O. Box 522 • Tewksbury, MA 01876 • (978) 640-7870

Topsfield

Topsfield Historical Society • Parson Capen House Museum, 1 Howlett St, P.O. Box 323 • Topsfield, MA 01983 • (978) 887-9724 • http://www.topsfieldhistory.org

Townsend

Harbor Church Historical Society • 80 Main St • Townsend, MA 01469 • (978) 597-5215

Townsend Historic Commission • 181 Fitchburg Rd • Townsend, MA 01469 • (978) 597-2668

Townsend Historical Society • Historical Society, 72 Main St, P.O. Box 95 • Townsend, MA 01469-1353 • (978) 597-2106

Townsend Public Library • 276 Main St, P.O. Box 526 • Townsend, MA 01469-0526 • (978) 597-1714 • http://www.townsendlibrary.org

Truro

Truro Historical Society • Historical Museum, Highland Rd, P.O. Box 486 • Truro, MA 02666 • (508) 487-0017

Turners Falls

Montague Public Libraries • 201 Avenue A • Turners Falls, MA 01376 • (413) 863-3214

Tyngsborough

Tynsboro-Dunstable Historical Society • Historical Museum, P.O. Box 57 • Tyngsborough, MA 01879 • (978) 649-3879

Tyringham

Santarella Museum • 75 Main Rd, P.O. Box 466 • Tyringham, MA 01264 • (413) 243-2819 • http://www.santarella.us

Tyringham Historical Commission • Historical Museum, Church Rd • Tyringham, MA 01264 • (413) 243-0416

Upton

Upton Historical Society • P.O. Box 171 • Upton, MA 01568 • (508) 529-6200

Uxbridge

Uxbridge Historical Commission • Historical Museum, 1 N Main • Uxbridge, MA 01569 • (508) 278-5544

Vineyard

Historical Records of Dukes County, MA • RR2, Box 247 • Vineyard, MA 02568 • http://www.vineyard.net/vineyard/history/

Vineyard Haven

Vineyard Haven Public Library • 200 Main St, RFD 139 A • Vineyard Haven, MA 02568-9710 • (508) 696-4211 • http://www.vhlibrary.org

Wakefield

Lucius Beebe Memorial Library • 345 Main St • Wakefield, MA 01880-5093 • (781) 246-6334 • http://www.wakefieldlibrary.org

Wakefield Historical Society • American Civic Center Museum, 467 Main St, P.O. Box 1092 • Wakefield, MA 01880 • (781) 245-0549 • http://www.wakefieldma.org

Wales

Wales Historical Society • Historical Museum, P.O. Box 208 • Wales, MA 01081 • (413) 744-2699

Walpole

Walpole Historical Society • 33 West St, P.O. Box 1724 • Walpole, MA 02081 • (508) 668-0449

Waltham

American Jewish Historical Society • Lee M Friedman Library & Museum, 2 Thornton Rd • Waltham, MA 02154 • (781) 891-8110 • http://www.ajhs.org

Bay State Historical League • The Vale-Lyman Estate Museum, 185 Lyman St • Waltham, MA 02254-9998 • (781) 899-3920 • http://www.masshistory.org

Boston States Migration • 48 Lake St • Waltham, MA 02451 • (781) 893-6142

Brandeis University Library • 415 South St, Mailstop 045 • Waltham, MA 02454-9110 • (781) 736-4670 • http://www.library.brandeis.edu

Charles River Museum of Industry • 154 Moody St • Waltham, MA 02453 • (781) 893-5410 • http://www.crmi.org

Gore Place Museum • 52 Gore St • Waltham, MA 02453 • (781) 894-2798 • http://www.goreplace.org

Lyman Estate Museum • The Vale, 185 Lyman St • Waltham, MA 02452 • (781) 891-1985 • http://www.historicnewengland.org

National Archives & Records Administration-Northeast Region • Frederick C Murphy Federal Ctr, 380 Trapelo Rd • Waltham, MA 02452-6399 • (781) 647-8104 • http://www.archives.gov/facilities/ma/boston.html

New England Heritage Center • 175 Forest St • Waltham, MA 02452 • (781) 891-2814

Solomon R Baker Library • Bentley College, 175 Forest St • Waltham, MA 02154-4705 • (781) 891-2168 • http://ecampus.bentley.edu/dept/li

Waltham Historical Society • Historical Museum, 190 Moody St • Waltham, MA 02154 • (781) 891-5815 • http://www.walthamhistoricalsociety.org

Waltham Museum • 196 Charles St • Waltham, MA 02154 • (781) 893-8017 • http://www.walthammuseum.com

Waltham Public Library • 735 Main St • Waltham, MA 02451 • (781) 314-3425 • http://www.waltham.library.ma.us

Ware
Ware Historical Society • Historical Museum, 42 Shoreline Dr • Ware, MA 01082 • (413) 967-6882 • http://www.warehistoricalsociety.wetpaint.com

Young Men's Library • 37 Main St • Ware, MA 01082-1317 • (413) 967-5491 • http://www.warelibrary.org

Wareham
Wareham Free Library • 59 Marion Rd • Wareham, MA 02571 • (508) 295-2343

Wareham Historical Society • Historical Museum, 8 Elm St, P.O. Box 211 • Wareham, MA 02571 • (508) 295-3227

Warren
Warren Public Library • 934 Main St • Warren, MA 01083-0937 • (413) 436-7690

Warwick
Warwick Historical Society • Historical Museum, 625 Winchester Rd • Warwick, MA 01378 • (978) 544-3461

Washington
Washington Historical Commission • 1338 Washington Mtn • Washington, MA 01223 • (413) 623-8348

Watertown
Armenian Library and Museum of America • 65 Main St • Watertown, MA 02472 • (617) 926-2562 • http://www.armenianlibraryandmuseum.org

Historical Society of Watertown • Edmund Fowle House Museum, 28 Marshall St • Watertown, MA 02172 • (617) 923-6067

New England Country Museum Historical Society • Historical Museum, 53 Summer St, P.O. Box 575 • Watertown, MA 02471 • (617) 924-6585

Perkins History Museum • Perkins School for the Blind, 175 N Beacon St • Watertown, MA 02472 • (617) 924-3064 • http://www.perkins.org

Watertown Free Public Library • 123 Main St • Watertown, MA 02472 • (617) 972-6431 • http://www.watertownlib.org

Wayland
Wayland Free Public Library • 5 Concord Rd • Wayland, MA 01778 • (508) 358-2311 • http://www.wayland.ma.us/library/

Wayland Historical Society • 12 Cochituate Rd, P.O. Box 56 • Wayland, MA 01778 • (508) 358-7959

Webster
Chester C Corbin Public Library • 2 Lake St • Webster, MA 01570-2699 • (508) 949-3880 • http://www.corbinlibrary.org

Webster Dudley Historical Society • 43 Union Count Rd • Webster, MA 01570 • (508) 943-1965

Wellesley
Wellesley Historical Society • Historical Museum, 229 Washington St, P.O. Box 81142 • Wellesley, MA 02481 • (781) 235-6690 • http://www.wellesleyhsoc.com

Wellesley Hills
Wellesley Free Library • 530 Washington St • Wellesley Hills, MA 02481-5989 • (781) 235-1610 • http://www.wellesleyfreelibrary.org

Wellesley Historical Society • 229 Washington St, P.O. Box 81142 • Wellesley Hills, MA 02181 • (781) 235-6690

Wellesley Historical Society • 229 Washington St, P.O. Box 81142 • Wellesley Hills, MA 02181 • (781) 235-6690 • http://www.wellesleyhsoc.com

Wellfleet
Wellfleet Historical Society • Historical Museum, 266 Main St, P.O. Box 58 • Wellfleet, MA 02667 • (508) 349-9157 • http://www.wellfleethistoricalsociety.com

Wellfleet Public Library • 55 W Main St • Wellfleet, MA 02667 • (508) 349-0310 • http://www.wellfleetlibrary.org

Wendell
Wendell Historic Commission • 45 Depot Rd, P.O. Box 112 • Wendell, MA 01379 • (978) 544-7502

Wenham
Wenham Historical Association • Col Timothy Pickering Museum, 132 Main St • Wenham, MA 01984 • (978) 468-2377 • http://www.wenhammuseum.org

Wenham Museum • 132 Main St • Wenham, MA 01984 • (978) 468-2377

Wenham Public Library • 138 Main St • Wenham, MA 01984 • (508) 468-5527

West Barnstable
Whelden Memorial Library • 2401 Meetinghouse Wy, P.O. Box 147 • West Barnstable, MA 02668-0147 • (508) 362-2262 • http://home.comcast.net/~whelden

William Brewster Nickerson Memorial Room • Cape Cod Community College, 2240 Iyanough Rd • West Barnstable, MA 02668-1599 • (508) 362-2131 • http://www.capecod.edu/library

West Boylston
West Boylston Historical Society • 65 Worcester St, P.O. Box 201 • West Boylston, MA 01583 • (508) 835-6971

West Bridgewater
Old Bridgewater Historical Society • Historical Museum, 162 Howard St, P.O. Box 17 • West Bridgewater, MA 02379 • (508) 559-1510 • http://www.oldbridgewater.org

West Bridgewater Public Library • 80 Howard St • West Bridgewater, MA 02379-1710 • (508) 894-1255 • http://www.sailsinc.org/westbridgewater

West Brookfield
Merriam-Gilbert Public Library • 3 W Main St, P.O. Box 364 • West Brookfield, MA 01585-0364 • (508) 867-1410 • http://www.brookfieldlibrary.org

Quaboag Historical Society • Historical Museum, 27 Front St, P.O. Box 635 • West Brookfield, MA 01585 • (413) 436-9212

Massachusetts

West Brookfield, cont.
West Brookfield Historical Commission • Town Hall, Main St, P.O. Box 372 • West Brookfield, MA 01585 • (508) 867-2006 • http://www. westbrookfield.org

West Dennis
Dennis Historical Society • 1801 Jericho-Totting Park & Main • West Dennis, MA 02670 • (508) 394-0017

West Newbury
West Newbury Historical Association • P.O. Box 332 • West Newbury, MA 01985 • (978) 465-8046

West Roxbury
West Roxbury Historical Society • 1961 Centre St • West Roxbury, MA 02132-2516 • (617) 327-6331

West Springfield
Ramapogue Historical Society • Joshua Day House Museum, 70 Park St, P.O. Box 826 • West Springfield, MA 01090 • (413) 734-8322 • http://www.west-springfield.ma.us

Storrowton Village Museum • 1305 Memorial Ave • West Springfield, MA 01089 • (413) 205-5051 • http://www.thebige.com

West Tisbury
African American Heritage Trail • P.O. Box 1513 • West Tisbury, MA 02575 • (508) 693-1033

Westborough
Westborough Historical Commission • c/o Westborough Public Library, 55 W Main St • Westborough, MA 01581 • (508) 366-3050

Westborough Historical Society • 13 Parkman St, P.O. Box 149 • Westborough, MA 01581 • (508) 898-0975

Westborough Public Library • 55 W Main St • Westborough, MA 01581 • (508) 366-3050 • http://www.westboroughlib.org

Westfield
Ely Library • Westfield State College, 577 Western Ave • Westfield, MA 01086 • (413) 572-5231 • http://www.lib.wsc.ma.edu

Institute for Massachusetts Studies • Ely Library, Westfield State College, P.O. Box 1630 • Westfield, MA 01086 • (413) 572-5208

Western Hampden Historical Society • Dewey House Museum, P.O. Box 256 • Westfield, MA 01086 • (413) 562-3657

Westfield Athanaeum & Historical Museum • 6 Elm St • Westfield, MA 01085 • (413) 568-7833 • http://www.westath.org

Westford
J V Fletcher Library • 50 Main St • Westford, MA 01886-2599 • (978) 692-5555 • http://www.westfordlibrary.org

Westford Historical Society • Historical Museum, 4 Boston Rd, P.O. Box 411 • Westford, MA 01886 • (978) 692-8513 • http://www.westford.com/museum

Westminster
Central Massachusetts Genealogical Society • P.O. Box 811 • Westminster, MA 01473-0811 • (978) 874-2505

Forbush Memorial Library • 118 Main St, P.O. Box 468 • Westminster, MA 01473 • (978) 874-7416 • http://www.westminster-ma.org/library

Westminster Historical Society • Historical Museum, 110 Main St, P.O. Box 177 • Westminster, MA 01473 • (978) 874-0544

Weston
Cardinal Spellman Philatelic Museum • 235 Wellesley St • Weston, MA 02493 • (781) 768-7343

Golden Ball Tavern Trust Library • 662 Boston Post Rd, P.O. Box 223 • Weston, MA 02493 • (617) 894-1751 • http://www.goldenhalltavern.org

Piscataqua Pioneers • 110 North Ave • Weston, MA 02193 • (617) 893-7581

Weston Historical Society • Historical Museum, 358 Boston Post Rd, P.O. Box 343 • Weston, MA 02193 • (781) 237-1447

Weston Public Library • 87 School St • Weston, MA 01760 • (781) 893-4090 • http://www.weston.org/library

Westport
Westport Historical Society • Historical Museum, 25 Drift Rd, P.O. Box 3031 • Westport, MA 02790-0700 • (508) 636-3532

Westwood
Blue Hill Adventure and Quarry Museum • 29 Westwood Terr • Westwood, MA 02090 • (781) 326-0079

Westwood Historical Society • Historical Museum, 830 High St, P.O. Box 2575 • Westwood, MA 02090 • (781) 326-5334 • http://www. westwoodhistoricalsociety.com

Weymouth
Abigail Adams Birthplace Museum • 180 Norton St, P.O. Box 350 • Weymouth, MA 02188 • (781) 335-4205

Tufts Library • 46 Broad St • Weymouth, MA 02188 • (781) 337-1402

Weymouth Historical Society • Historical Museum, 46 Broad St, P.O. Box 56 • Weymouth, MA 02190 • (781) 340-1022 • http://www. weymouthhistoricalsociety.org

Whately
S White Dickinson Memorial Library • 202 Chestnut Plain Rd • Whately, MA 01093 • (413) 665-2170

Whately Historical Society • Historical Museum, 218 Chestnut Plain Rd, P.O. Box 7 • Whately, MA 01093 • (413) 665-4400 • http://www. whatelyhistorical.org

Whitinsville
Whitinsville Social Library • 17 Church St • Whitinsville, MA 01588 • (508) 234-2151 • http://www.northbridgemass.org/wsl/wslhome.htm

Whitman
Whitman Public Library • 100 Webster St • Whitman, MA 02382 • (781) 447-7613 • http://whitmanpubliclibrary.org

Wilbraham
Atheneum Society of Wilbraham • 450 Main St, P.O. Box 294 • Wilbraham, MA 01095 • (413) 596-8754

MASSOG, Hampden Chapter • 6 Ridgewood Rd • Wilbraham, MA 01095

Wilbraham Public Library • 25 Crane Park Dr • Wilbraham, MA 01095-1799 • (413) 596-6141 • http://www.wilbrahamlibrary.org

Williamstown
African Methodist Episcopal Church Histiographer • P.O. Box 301 • Williamstown, MA 01267 • (413) 597-2484 • http://www.amecnet.org

Chapin Library of Rare Books • Williams College, 26 Hopkins Hall Dr, P.O. Box 426 • Williamstown, MA 01267-0426 • (413) 597-2462 • http://www.williams.edu/resources/chapin

David and Joyce Milne Public Library • 1095 Main St • Williamstown, MA 01267-2627 • (413) 458-5369 • http://www.milnelibrary.org

Williamstown House of Local History • 1095 Main St • Williamstown, MA 01267 • (413) 458-2160 • http://www.williamstown.net/house_of_local_history.htm

Wilmington
Col Joshua Harnden Tavern Museum • 430 Salem St • Wilmington, MA 01887 • (978) 658-5475

Winchendon
Beals Memorial Library & Museum • 50 Pleasant St • Winchendon, MA 01475 • (978) 297-0300

Winchendon Historical Society • Historical Museum, 151 Front St, P.O. Box 279 • Winchendon, MA 01475 • (978) 297-2142

Winchester

Griffin Museum of Photography • 67 Shore Rd • Winchester, MA 01890 • (781) 729-1158 • http://www.griffinmuseum.org

Winchester Historical Society • Historical Museum, 1 Copley St, P.O. Box 127 • Winchester, MA 01890 • (781) 721-7146 • http://www.winchesterhistoricalsociety.org

Winchester Public Library • 80 Washington St • Winchester, MA 01890 • (781) 721-7171 • http://mln.lib.ma.us

Winthrop

Winthrop Public Library • 2 Metcalf Sq • Winthrop, MA 52-3157 • (617) 846-1703

Woburn

Woburn Historical Association • 90 Elm St N • Woburn, MA 01801 • (781) 935-3561 • http://www.middlesexcanal.org/docs/rumford.htm

Woburn Public Library • 45 Pleasant St, P.O. Box 298 • Woburn, MA 01801-0298 • (781) 933-0148 • http://www.woburnpubliclibrary.org

Woods Hole

Woods Hole Library & Museum • 581 Woods Hole Rd, P.O. Box 185 • Woods Hole, MA 02453-0185 • (508) 548-8961 • http://www.woodsholepubliclibrary.org; http://www.woodsholemuseum.org

Worcester

American Antiquarian Society • Historical Museum, 185 Salisbury St • Worcester, MA 01609-1634 • (508) 755-5221 • http://www.americanantiquarian.org

Dinand Library • College of the Holy Cross, 1 College St • Worcester, MA 01610 • (508) 793-2259 • http://www.holycross.edu/departments/library/website

Higgins Armory Museum • 100 Barber Ave • Worcester, MA 01606-2444 • (508) 853-6015 • http://www.higgins.org

Massachusette National Guard Museum • 44 Salisbury St • Worcester, MA 01609

Massachusetts Society of Genealogists • 705 Southbridge St • Worcester, MA 01610 • (508) 792-5066

Preservation Worcester • Historical Museum, 10 Cedar St • Worcester, MA 01609-2520 • (508) 754-8760

Quinsigamond Band of the Nipmucs • 630 Pleasant St • Worcester, MA 01602 • (800) 584-6040

Salisbury Mansion Museum • 40 Highland St • Worcester, MA 01609 • (508) 753-8278

Strassler Family Center for Holocaust and Genocide Studies • Clark Univ, 950 Main St • Worcester, MA 01610 • (508) 793-8897 • http://www.clarku.edu/holocaust

Swedish Ancestry Research Association • P.O. Box 70603 • Worcester, MA 01607-0603 • http://sarassociation.tripod.com

Worcester Historical Museum • 30 Elm St • Worcester, MA 01609 • (508) 753-8278 • http://www.worcesterhistory.org

Worcester Public Library • 3 Salem Sq • Worcester, MA 01608-2074 • (508) 799-1655 • http://www.worcpublib.org

Worthington

Worthington Historical Society • Historical Museum, 6 Williamsburg Rd, P.O. Box 12 • Worthington, MA 01098 • (413) 238-5363

Wrentham

Wrentham Historical Commission • Historical Museum, 79 South St, P.O. Box 841 • Wrentham, MA 02093 • (508) 384-5400

Wrentham Historical Society • P.O. Box 300 • Wrentham, MA 02093 • (508) 384-7151

Yarmouth Port

Historical Society of Old Yarmouth • Capt Bangs Hallet House Museum, 11 Strawberry Ln, P.O. Box 11 • Yarmouth Port, MA 02675-0011 • (508) 362-3021 • http://www.hsoy.org

Winslow Crocker House Museum • 250 Route 6A • Yarmouth Port, MA 02675 • (617) 227-3956 • http://www.historicnewengland.org

Yarmouth Library • 297 Main St • Yarmouth Port, MA 02675 • (508) 362-3717 • http://www.yarmouthcapecod.org/libraries

Massachusetts

Acme

Music House Museum • 7377 US 31N, Box 297 • Acme, MI 49610 • (231) 938-9300

Ada

Ada Historical Society • Historical Museum, 7144 Headley, P.O. Box 741 • Ada, MI 49301 • (616) 676-9346 • http://www.adahistoricalsociety.org

Ada Township Historical Society • 7170 Rix • Ada, MI 49301

Adrian

Adrian Public Library • 143 E Maumee St • Adrian, MI 49221 • (517) 265-2265 • http://woodlands.lib.mi.us/adrian/adrian.htm

Detroit Conference United Methodist Archives • c/o Shipman Library, Adrian College, 110 S Madison • Adrian, MI 49221 • (517) 265-5161

Lanawee County Library • 4459 W US 223 • Adrian, MI 49221-1294 • (517) 263-1011 • http://lenawee.lib.wi.us

Lenawee County Historical and Genealogical Society • Historical Museum, 110 E Church St, P.O. Box 511 • Adrian, MI 49221 • (517) 265-6071

Shipman Library • Adrian College, 110 S Madison St • Adrian, MI 49221 • (517) 264-3828 • http://www.adrian.edu/library

Alba

Alba Historical Museum • Jordan River Rd • Alba, MI 49611

Albion

Albion Historical Society • Gardner House Museum, 509 S Superior St • Albion, MI 49224 • (517) 629-5100 • http://www.forks.org/history/albion.htm

Albion Public Library • 501 S Superior St • Albion, MI 49224 • (517) 629-3993 • http://www.albionlibrary.org

Brueckner Museum of Starr Commonwealth • 13725 Starr Commonwealth Rd • Albion, MI 49224 • (517) 629-5591 • http://www.starr.org

Calhoun County Genealogical Society • c/o Albion Public Library, 501 S Superior St • Albion, MI 49224 • (517) 629-3993

Gardner House Museum • 509 S Superior St • Albion, MI 49224 • (517) 629-5100

Stockwell-Mudd Libraries • Albion College, 602 E Cass St • Albion, MI 49224-1879 • (517) 629-0382 • http://www.albion.edu/fac/libr

Algonac

Algonac Clay Historical Society • 1240 Saint Clair River Dr • Algonac, MI 48001 • (810) 794-9015

Allegan

Allegan County Historical Society • Old Jail Museum, 113 N Walnut St • Allegan, MI 49010 • (269) 673-8292 • http://www.alleganmuseum.com

Allegan Public Library • 331 Hubbard • Allegan, MI 49010 • (269) 673-4625 • http://www.alleganlibrary.org

Allen

Southern Michigan Genealogical Society • 239 E Chicago Rd • Allen, MI 49227 • (517) 869-2505

Allen Park

Allen Park Library • 8100 Allen Rd • Allen Park, MI 48101 • (313) 381-2425 • http://www.allen-park.lib.mi.us

Allendale

Zumberge Library & Museum • Grand Valley State University, 1 Campus Dr • Allendale, MI 49401-9403 • (616) 331-3252 • http://www.gvsu.edu/library

Alma

Masonic Grand Lodge of Michigan • 1204 Wright Ave • Alma, MI 48801-1133 • (989) 968-4440 • http://www.gl-mi.org

Alpena

Alpena County Library • 211 N 1st Ave • Alpena, MI 49707 • (989) 356-6188 • http://www.alpenalib.org

Jesse Besser Museum • 491 Johnson St • Alpena, MI 49707 • (989) 356-2202 • http://www.bessermuseum.org

Northeast Michigan Genealogical Society • Jesse Besser Museum, 491 Johnson St • Alpena, MI 49707 • (989) 595-2384 • http://www.members.aol.com/alpenaco/migenweb

Alto

Bowne Township Historical Society • 1735 92nd St SE • Alto, MI 49302

Caledonia Township Historical Society • 8573 84th St SE • Alto, MI 49341

Los German Club of NW Ohio • 10748 100th St • Alto, MI 49302

Anchorville

Rootstalkers • P.O. Box 161 • Anchorville, MI 48004

Ann Arbor

AAUW Genealogy Colloquium • American Association of Univ Women, 1830 Washtenaw Ave • Ann Arbor, MI 48104 • http://www.aauwaa.org

African American Cultural and Historical Museum • 1100 N Main St, Ste 201C, P.O. Box 130-724 • Ann Arbor, MI 48113-0724 • http://www.anotherannarbor.org

Ann Arbor District Public Library • 343 S 5th Ave • Ann Arbor, MI 48104-2293 • (734) 327-4200 • http://www.aadl.org

Ann Arbor Hands-On Museum • 219 E Huron St • Ann Arbor, MI 48104 • (313) 995-5439

Ann Arbor Historical Foundation • 312 S Division St • Ann Arbor, MI 48104 • (734) 996-3008

Bentley Historical Library • Univ of Michigan, 1150 Beal Ave • Ann Arbor, MI 48109-2113 • (734) 764-3482 • http://www.umich.edu/~bhl/

Center for Afro-American and African Studies Library • Univ of Michigan, 550 E University St • Ann Arbor, MI 48109 • (734) 764-5518

Clements Library • Univ of Michigan, 909 S University Ave • Ann Arbor, MI 48109-1190 • (734) 764-2347 • http://clements.umich.edu/associates.html

Genealogical Society of Washtenaw County • P.O. Box 7155 • Ann Arbor, MI 48107 • (734) 483-2799 • http://www.hvcn.org/info/gswc

Gerald R Ford Library • 1000 Beal Ave • Ann Arbor, MI 48109-2114 • (734) 205-0555 • http://www.fordlibrarymuseum.gov/

Historical Society of Michigan • 2117 Washtenaw Ave • Ann Arbor, MI 48104-4599 • (734) 769-1828 • http://www.hsofmich.org

Kempf House Center for Local History Library • 312 S Division St • Ann Arbor, MI 48104 • (313) 996-3008

Political Graveyard • P.O. Box 2563 • Ann Arbor, MI 48106 • http://politicalgraveyard.com

Sindecuse Museum of Dentistry • Univ of MI, 1011 N University, G532 Dental Bldg • Ann Arbor, MI 48109 • (734) 763-0767 • http://www.dent.umich.edu/museum/

Washtenaw County Historical Society • 500 N Main, P.O. Box 3336 • Ann Arbor, MI 48106-3336 • (734) 662-9092 • http://www.washtenawhistory.org

Arcadia

Arcadia Area Historical Museum • 3202 Mill St • Arcadia, MI 49613

Arcadia Area Historical Society • 3340 Lake St • Arcadia, MI 49613 • (231) 889-4360

Michigan

Arcadia, cont.
Arcadia Township Historical Commission • Historical Museum, Lake St, P.O. Box 67 • Arcadia, MI 49613 • (616) 889-4830 • http://www.arcadiami.com

Armada
Armada Area Historical and Genealogical Society • c/o Armada Free Public Library, 73930 Church St • Armada, MI 48005-3331 • (586) 784-5921 • http://www.armadalib.org

Athens
Athens Area Historical Society • P.O. Box 22 • Athens, MI 49011

Au Gres
Arehac County Historical Society • 304 W Michigan Ave, P.O. Box 272 • Au Gres, MI 49703 • (989) 876-6399

Au Train
Paulson House Museum • USFS Rd 2278 • Au Train, MI 49806

Auburn Hills
Auburn Hills Genealogical and Historical Society • general delivery • Auburn Hills, MI 48321

Walter P Chrysler Museum • 1 Chrysler Dr • Auburn Hills, MI 48326 • (248) 944-0432 • http://www.chryslerheritage.com

Augusta
McKay Library • 105 S Webster St, P.O. Box 308 • Augusta, MI 49012-0308 • (616) 731-4000

Bad Axe
Bad Axe Historical Society • 147 W Hopson • Bad Axe, MI 48413 • (989) 269-8165

Bax Axe Public Library • 200 S Hanselman • Bad Axe, MI 48413 • (989) 269-8538 • http://www.badaxelibrary.org

Huron County Historical Society, Bad Axe Chapter • 223 Willis St • Bad Axe, MI 48413 • (989) 269-8165

Baraga
Keweenaw Bay Indian Community • 107 Beartown Rd • Baraga, MI 49908 • (906) 353-8160 • http://www.ojibwa.com

Battle Creek
Historical Society of Battle Creek • Kimball House Museum, 165 N Washington Ave • Battle Creek, MI 49017 • (616) 965-2613 • http://www.kimballhouse.org

Willard Library • 7 W Van Buren St • Battle Creek, MI 49017-3009 • (269) 968-8166 • http://www.willard.lib.mi.us

Bay City
Bay City Branch Library • 708 Center Ave • Bay City, MI 48706 • (989) 893-9566 • http://www.baycountylibrary.org

Bay County Genealogical Society • P.O. Box 1366 • Bay City, MI 48708 • (989) 684-6819 • http://community.mlive.com/cc/baygenealogy

Bay County Historical Society • Historical Museum, 321 Washington Ave • Bay City, MI 48708 • (989) 893-5733 • http://www.bchsmuseum.org

Bay County Library System-Sage Branch • 100 E Midland St • Bay City, MI 48706-4597 • (989) 892-8555 • http://www.baycountylibrary.org/bsa.htm

Bay County Library-South Side Branch • 311 Lafayette Ave • Bay City, MI 48708-7796 • (989) 893-1287 • http://www.baycountylibrary.org/bss.htm

Saginaw River Marine Historical Society • P.O. Box 2051 • Bay City, MI 48707 • http://www.boatnerd.com/museums/srmhs/

Trombley House Museum • 901 John F Kennedy Dr • Bay City, MI 48708 • (517) 892-9431 • http://www.saginawvalley.com

Bay View
Bay View Historical Museum • Bay View Association Encampment, P.O. Box 1628 • Bay View, MI 49770 • (616) 347-6225 • http://www.bayviewassoc.com

Beaver Island
Beaver Island Historical Society • Historical Museum, 26275 Main St, P.O. Box 263 • Beaver Island, MI 49782 • (231) 448-2479 • http://www.beaverisland.net/history

Beaver Island Preservation Association • 26215 Main St • Beaver Island, MI 49782 • (231) 448-2022

Belding
Alvah N Belding Library • 302 E Main St • Belding, MI 48809 • (616) 794-1450 • http://belding.llcoop.org

Belrockton Museum • 108 Hanover St, P.O. Box 45 • Belding, MI 48809 • (616) 794-5720

Bellaire
Bellaire Area Historical Society • 202 N Bridge St, P.O. Box 1016 • Bellaire, MI 49615 • (231) 533-8631

Belleville
Belleville Area Museum • 405 Main St • Belleville, MI 48111 • (734) 697-1944 • http://www.vanburen-mi.org

Belleville Historical Society • 8 Church St • Belleville, MI 48111 • (734) 697-0764

Bellevue
Bellevue Area Historical Society • 212 N Main St • Bellevue, MI 49021 • (616) 763-3369

Belmont
Hyser Rivers Museum • 6440 W River Rd NE • Belmont, MI 49306 • (616) 364-8466

Benton Harbor
Benton Harbor Public Library • 213 E Wall St • Benton Harbor, MI 49022-4499 • (269) 926-6139 • http://www.bentonharborlibrary.com

Berrien County Genealogical Society • P.O. Box 8808 • Benton Harbor, MI 49023-8808 • http://www.qtm.net/bcgensoc

Josphine Morton House Museum • 501 Territorial Rd • Benton Harbor, MI 49023 • (616) 925-7011 • http://www.parrett.net/~morton

Benzonia
Benzie Area Historical Society • Historical Museum, 6941 Traverse Ave, P.O. Box 185 • Benzonia, MI 49616 • (231) 882-5539 • http://www.bahmuseum.org

Benzonia Public Library • 891 Michigan Ave, P.O. Box 445 • Benzonia, MI 49616-0445 • (231) 882-4111

Genealogy Group of the Benzie Area Historical Society • Historical Museum, 6941 Traverse Ave, P.O. Box 185 • Benzonia, MI 49616 • (231) 882-5539

Berkley
Berkley Historical Committee • c/o Berkley Public Library, 3155 Coolidge Hwy • Berkley, MI 48072 • (248) 546-2440 • http://www.berkley.lib.mi.us

Bulgarian Heritage Society • 2706 Tyler • Berkley, MI 48072

Berrien Springs
Berrien County Historical Association • 1839 Courthouse Museum, 313 N Cass St, P.O. Box 261 • Berrien Springs, MI 49103-0261 • (269) 471-1202 • http://www.berrienhistory.org

Berrien Springs Community Library • 215 W Union St • Berrien Springs, MI 49103-1077 • (269) 471-7074 • http://bsclibrary.org

James White Library • Andrews University, 1400 Campus Dr • Berrien Springs, MI 49104 • (269) 471-3283 • http://www.andrews.edu/library

Big Rapids

Abigail S Timme Library • Ferris State College, 1201 S State St • Big Rapids, MI 49307 • (616) 582-3727

Jim Crow Museum • Ferris State Univ, 820 Campus Dr, ASC 2108 • Big Rapids, MI 49307 • (231) 591-5873 • http://www.ferris.edu/jimcrow

Mecosta County Genealogical Society • P.O. Box 1068 • Big Rapids, MI 49307-0968 • (231) 796-2504

Mecosta County Historical Society • Historical Museum, 129 S Stewart St, P.O. Box 613 • Big Rapids, MI 49307 • (616) 592-5091

Birmingham

Baldwin Public Library • 300 W Merrill St, P.O. Box 3002 • Birmingham, MI 48012-3002 • (248) 647-1700 • http://www.baldwinlib.org

Birmingham Historical Society • Historical Museum, 556 W Maple, P.O. Box 223 • Birmingham, MI 48012 • (248) 642-2817 • http://www.ci.birmingham.mi.us

Oakland County Genealogical Society • c/o Baldwin Public Library, 300 W Merrill St, P.O. Box 1094 • Birmingham, MI 48012-1094 • (248) 335-4061 • http://www.rhpl.org/OCGS

Black River

Alcona County Historical Society • 4028 Black River Rd • Black River, MI 48721 • (989) 471-2088

Blissfield

Blissfield Area Historical Society • Depot Museum, 7148 E Weston Rd • Blissfield, MI 49228 • (517) 486-2432

Bloomfield Hills

Cranbrook Archives and Historical Collections • 1221 N Woodward Ave, P.O. Box 801 • Bloomfield Hills, MI 48013 • (248) 645-3581 • http://www.cranbrook.edu

Cranbrook House Museum & Gardens • 380 Lone Pine Rd, P.O. Box 801 • Bloomfield Hills, MI 48303 • (248) 645-3110 • http://www.cranbrook.edu

Order of the Founders and Patriots of America, Michigan Society • 2961 Woodcreek Wy • Bloomfield Hills, MI 48304-1974

Prentis Memorial Library • Temple Beth El, 7400 Telegraph Rd • Bloomfield Hills, MI 48301-3876 • (248) 851-1100 • http://www.templebethel.org

Rabbi Leo M Franklin Archive • Temple Beth El, 7400 Telegraph Rd • Bloomfield Hills, MI 48301 • (248) 851-1100 • http://www.tbeonline.org/education/archives/

Sons of the American Revolution, Michigan Society • 1101 Timberlake Dr • Bloomfield Hills, MI 48302 • (248) 642-0973 • http://missar.org

Boyne City

Ace Genealogical Society • c/o Boyne City Public Library, 201 E Main St • Boyne City, MI 49712 • (616) 582-7861

Boyne City Public Library • 201 E Main St • Boyne City, MI 49712 • (231) 582-7861 • http://nlc.lib.mi.us/members/boyne_c.htm

Charlevoix County Genealogical Society • c/o Boyne City Public Library, 201 E Main St • Boyne City, MI 49712 • (616) 582-7861 • http://www.rootsweb.com/~micharle/charleux.htm

Charlevoix County Historical Society • 481 E Crozier, P.O. Box 7 • Boyne City, MI 49712

Bridgeport

Historical Society of Bridgeport • 6190 Dixie Hwy, P.O. Box 117 • Bridgeport, MI 48722 • (989) 777-5230

Bridgman

Bridgman Public Library • 4460 Lake St • Bridgman, MI 49106-9510 • (616) 465-3663

Brighton

Brighton Area Historical Society • P.O. Box 481 • Brighton, MI 48116-0481 • (810) 229-6402

Brighton District Library • 100 Library Dr • Brighton, MI 48116 • (810) 229-6571 • http://brightonlibrary.info/

Green Oak Township Historical Society • Gage Museum, 6440 Kensington Rd, P.O. Box 84 • Brighton, MI 48116 • (810) 437-1271

Brimley

Bay Mills Chippewa Indian Community • 12140 W Lakeshore Dr • Brimley, MI 49715 • (906) 248-3241 • http://www.baymills.org

Bay Mills-Brimley Historic Research Society • P.O. Box 274 • Brimley, MI 49715 • (906) 248-3665

Buchanan

Buchanan District Library • 128 E Front St • Buchanan, MI 49107 • (269) 695-3681

Burt

Taymouth Township Library • 2361 E Burt Rd, 2361 E Burt Rd • Burt, MI 48417-0158 • (989) 770-4651

Byron Center

Byron Center Historical Society • 2506 Prescott, P.O. Box 20 • Byron Center, MI 49315-0020

Cadillac

Cadillac Area Genealogical Society • 8499 South 27 1/2 Mile Rd • Cadillac, MI 49601

Cadillac-Wexford Public Library • 411 S Lake St, P.O. Box 700 • Cadillac, MI 49601-0700 • (231) 775-6541 • http://mmll.org

Wexford County Historical Society • Historical Museum, 127 Beech St, P.O. Box 124 • Cadillac, MI 49601 • (231) 775-1717

Caledonia

Caledonia Historical and Genealogical Society • 240 Emmonn • Caledonia, MI 49316 • (616) 891-1502

Kent District Library-Caledonia Branch • 240 Emmons St • Caledonia, MI 49316 • (616) 647-3840

Calumet

Coppertown USA Museum • 25815 Red Jacket Rd • Calumet, MI 49913 • (906) 337-4354 • http://www.uppermichigan.com/coppertown

Canton

Canton Historical Society • 1150 S Canton Center Rd, P.O. Box 87362 • Canton, MI 48187 • (734) 397-0088

Capac

Capac Community Historical Society • Historical Museum, 401 E Kempf Ct • Capac, MI 48014 • (810) 395-7701

Caro

Caro Area District Library • 840 W Frank St • Caro, MI 48723 • (989) 673-4329 • http://www.carolibrary.org/

Tuscola County Genealogical Society • 1658 W Gilford Rd • Caro, MI 48723

Carson City

Carson City Public Library • 102 W Main St • Carson City, MI 48811 • (989) 584-3680 • http://www.carsoncity.llcoop.org

Caseville

Historical Society of Caseville • 6727 Main St • Caseville, MI 48725 • (989) 856-9090

Caspian

Iron County Historical and Museum Society • Raymond Gustafson Archives, Museum Park, P.O. Box 272 • Caspian, MI 49915-0272 • (906) 265-2617 • http://www.ironcountymuseum.com

Caspian, cont.
Iron County Museum • 100 Brady, P.O. Box 272 • Caspian, MI 49915 • (906) 265-2617 • http://www.ironcountymuseum.com

Cass City
Cass City Area Historical Society • c/o Rawson Memorial Library, 6495 Pine • Cass City, MI 48726-4073 • (517) -872-2856 • http://www.rawson.lib.mi.us

Rawson Memorial Library • 6495 Pine • Cass City, MI 48726-4073 • (517) -872-2856 • http://www.rawson.lib.mi.us

Cassopolis
Cass County Historical Commission • 24010 Hospital St #105 • Cassopolis, MI 49031-9690 • (616) 445-9016

Cass County Library • 319 Michigan Rd 62 N • Cassopolis, MI 49031-1099 • (269) 445-3400 • http://www.cass.lib.mi.us

Cass District Library-Local History Room • 145 N Broadway St • Cassopolis, MI 49031 • (269) 445-0412 • http://cass.lib.mi.us/clh.html

Cedar Springs
Cedar Springs Historical Society • Historical Museum, 60 Cedar St, P.O. Box 296 • Cedar Springs, MI 49319 • (616) 696-3042

Cedarville
Les Cheneaux Historical Association • Les Cheneaux Historical & Maritime Museum, 105 W Meridian Rd, P.O. Box 301 • Cedarville, MI 49719 • (906) 484-2821

Central Lake
Central Lake District Library • 7900 Maple St, P.O. Box 397 • Central Lake, MI 49622-0397 • (231) 544-2517

Centreville
Nottawa Stone School Museum • 204 E Burr Oak St • Centreville, MI 49032 • (616) 467-5400

Saint Joseph County Historical Society • Historical Museum, P.O. Box 482 • Centreville, MI 49032 • (616) 651-5668

Charlevoix
Charlevoix Historical Society • Depot Museum, 307 Chicago Ave • Charlevoix, MI 49720 • (231) 547-1816

Charlevoix Historical Society • Harsha House Museum, 103 State St, P.O. Box 525 • Charlevoix, MI 49720 • (231) 547-0373

Charlevoix Public Library • 109 Clinton St • Charlevoix, MI 49720-1399 • (231) 547-2651 • http://www.charlevoix.lib.mi.us

Charlotte
Charlotte Community Library • 226 S Bostwick St • Charlotte, MI 48813-1801 • (517) 543-8859 • http://www.charlottelibrary.org

Courthouse Square Museum • 100 W Lawrence Ave, P.O. Box 411 • Charlotte, MI 48813 • (517) 543-6999 • http://www.visitcourthsquare.org

Eaton County Genealogical Society • 1885 Eaton County Courthouse, 100 W Lawrence Ave, P.O. Box 337 • Charlotte, MI 48813-0337 • (517) 543-8792 • http://www.rootsweb.com/~miecgs/

Eaton County Historical Commission • P.O. Box 25 • Charlotte, MI 48813

Chassell
Chassell Historical Organization • 202 Hancock, P.O. Box 479 • Chassell, MI 49916 • (906) 523-4612

Cheboygan
Cheboygan County Genealogical Society • P.O. Box 51 • Cheboygan, MI 49721 • (231) 238-7611 • http://www.rootsweb.com/~miccgs/CCGSmainx.html

Cheboygan Public Library • 107 S Ball St • Cheboygan, MI 49721-1661 • (231) 627-2381 • http://www.nlc.lib.mi.us

Historical Society of Cheboygan County • Historical Museum, 427 Court St P.O. Box 5005 • Cheboygan, MI 49721 • (231) 627-9597 • http://www.cheboyganmuseum.com

Chelsea
Chelsea Area Historical Society • 125 Jackson Rd • Chelsea, MI 48118 • (734) 475-9330

Chelsea District Library • 221 S Main St • Chelsea, MI 48118-1267 • (734) 475-8732 • http://chelsea.lib.mi.us

Chelsea Historical Society • P.O. Box 117 • Chelsea, MI 48118 • (734) 475-7047

Heritage Room Museum • Chelsea Retirement Community, 805 W Middle St • Chelsea, MI 48118

Chesaning
Chesaning Area Historical Society • Historical Museum , 602 W Broad St • Chesaning, MI 48616-1120 • (989) 845-3155

Chesaning Genealogical Society • 227 E Broad St • Chesaning, MI 48616

Chesaning Public Library • 227 E Broad St • Chesaning, MI 48616 • (989) 845-3211 • http://www.vlc.lib.mi.us/~chelib

Clare
Clare County Historical Society • Historical Museum, 109 1/2 W 5th St • Clare, MI 48617 • (517) 386-7242

Clarkston
Clarkston Community Historical Society • 6495 Clarkston Rd • Clarkston, MI 48346 • (248) 922-0270

Clarkston Historical Society • 6085 S Main St, P.O.Box 261 • Clarkston, MI 48347

French-Canadian Heritage Society of Michigan • 9513 Whipple Shores Drive • Clarkston, MI 48348 • http://habitant.org/fchsm/

Yesteryear House & Central Mine Museum • 7995 Perry Lake Rd • Clarkston, MI 48348 • (248) 625-2092

Clawson
Clawson Historical Commission • Historical Museum, 41 Fisher Ct • Clawson, MI 48017 • (248) 588-9169

Climax
Climax Historical Society • c/o Lawrence Memorial Public Library, 107 N Main St • Climax, MI 49034 • (616) 746-4125

Lawrence Memorial Public Library • 107 N Main St • Climax, MI 49034 • (269) 746-4125

Clinton Township
Clinton-Macomb County Library • 40900 Romeo Plank Rd • Clinton Township, MI 48038-2955 • (586) 226-5040 • http://www.cmpl.org

Coldwater
Branch County Genealogical Society • P.O. Box 443 • Coldwater, MI 49036 • (517) 278-2419 • http://www.rootsweb.ancestry.com/~mibranch/CountyResources/BCGenealogy.htm

Branch County Historical Society • Wint House Museum, 27 S Jefferson St, P.O. Box 443 • Coldwater, MI 49036 • (517) 278-2871

Branch County Library • 10 E Chicago St • Coldwater, MI 49036 • (517) 278-2341 • http://www.brnlibrary.org

Coloma
American Historical Society of Germans from Russia, Southwest Michigan Chapter • 3829 E Bundy Rd • Coloma, MI 49038 • (269) 849-2804 • http://www.ahsgr.org/Chapters/southwest_michigan_chapter.htm

Coloma Public Library • 262-264 N Paw Paw, P.O. Box 430 • Coloma, MI 49038-0430 • (269) 468-3431 • http://www.ameritech.net/users/cdickinson/

North Berrien Historical Society • 300 Coloma Ave, P.O. Box 207 • Coloma, MI 49038 • (616) 468-4228

Colon
Colon Historical Society • Colon Museum, 219 Blackstone Ave, P.O. Box 136 • Colon, MI 49040-0136 • (616) 432-3804

Comstock
Comstock Township Library • 6130 King Hwy, P.O. Box 25 • Comstock, MI 49041-0025 • (616) 345-0136 • http://www.comstocktownshiplib.org

Kalamazoo Valley Genealogical Society • Western Michigan Univ Archives, P.O. Box 405 • Comstock, MI 49041-0405 • (616) 323-9406 • http://www.rootsweb.com/~mikvgs/

Concord
Historic Mann House Museum • 205 Hanover St • Concord, MI 49237 • (517) 524-8943 • http://www.michiganhistory.org

Constantine
Governor Barry Historical Association • 340 Florence • Constantine, MI 49042 • (616) 435-7316

John S Barry Historical Society • Historical Museum, 300 N Washington, P.O. Box 68 • Constantine, MI 49042 • (616) 435-5825

Coopersville
Coopersville Area Historical Society • Historical Museum, 363 Main St • Coopersville, MI 49404 • (616) 997-7240 • http://www.coopersville.com

Northeast Ottawa District Library • 333 Ottawa St • Coopersville, MI 49404-1243 • (616) 837-6809 • http://www.coopersville.llcoop.org

Copper Harbor
Fort Wilkins Historic Complex Museum • Fort Wilkins State Park, P.O. Box 71 • Copper Harbor, MI 49918 • (906) 289-4215 • http://www.michiganhistory.org

Corunna
Corunna Public Library • 401 N Shiawassee St • Corunna, MI 48817 • (989) 743-4800 • http://www.shianet.org/community/orgs/cpl

Crystal Falls
Barbour House Museum • 17 N 4th St, P.O. Box 65 • Crystal Falls, MI 49920 • (906) 875-4341

Davisburg
Carpatho-Rusyn Knowledge Base • P.O. Box 339 • Davisburg, MI 48350-0339 • http://www.carpatho-rusyn.org

Springfield Township Historical Society • P.O. Box 203 • Davisburg, MI 48019 • (313) 673-9191

Davison
Davison Area Historical Museum • 263 E 4th St • Davison, MI 48423

Genesee District Library-Davison Area • 203 E 4th St • Davison, MI 48423 • (810) 653-2022

De Tour Village
DeTour Passage Historical Museum • P.O. Box 111 • De Tour Village, MI 49725

De Witt
De Witt Public Library • 13101 Schavey Rd • De Witt, MI 48820-9008 • (517) 669-3156 • http://www.dewittlibrary.com

Dearborn
Arab American National Museum • 13624 Michigan Ave • Dearborn, MI 48126 • (313) 582-2266 • http://www.theaanm.org

Armenian Research Center - Mardigian Library • Univ of Michigan - Dearborn, 4901 Evergreen Rd • Dearborn, MI 48128-1491 • http://www.umd.umich.edu/dept/armenian/

Automotive Hall of Fame • 21400 Oakwood Blvd • Dearborn, MI 48124 • (313) 240-4000 • http://www.automotivehalloffame.org

Dearborn Genealogical Society • McFadden-Ross House Museum, 915 S Brady St, P.O. Box 1112 • Dearborn, MI 48121-1112 • (313) 565-3000 • http://www.rootsweb.com/~midgs/

Dearborn Historical Commission • Dearborn Historical Museum, 915 S Brady St • Dearborn, MI 48124 • (313) 565-3000 • http://www.cityofdearborn.org

Dearborn Historical Society • Dearborn Historical Museum, 915 S Brady St • Dearborn, MI 48128 • (313) 565-3000

Dearborn Public Library • 16301 Michigan Ave • Dearborn, MI 48126 • (313) 943-2037 • http://dearborn.lib.mi.us

Fair Lane Estate Museum • Univ of MI-Dearborn, 4901 Evergreen Rd • Dearborn, MI 48128 • (313) 593-5590 • http://www.henryfordestate.org

Ford Genealogy Club • Ford Motor Credit Company Building, Room 1491, P.O. Box 1652 • Dearborn, MI 48121-1652 • http://www.wwnet.net/~krugmanl/fgc/

Henry Ford Museum • 20900 Oakwood Blvd, P.O. Box 1970 • Dearborn, MI 48121 • (313) 982-6070 • http://www.thehenryford.org

Mardigian Library & Museum • University of Michigan-Dearborn, 4901 Evergreen Rd • Dearborn, MI 48128-1491 • (313) 593-5445 • http://www.libraryweb.umd.umich.edu

Richard III Society • 16151 Longmeadow St • Dearborn, MI 48120

Spirit of Ford Museum • 1151 Village Rd • Dearborn, MI 48124 • (313) 248-2851

Dearborn Heights
Sokol Detroit • 23600 W Warren Ave • Dearborn Heights, MI 48127 • (313) 278-2558

Decatur
Historic Newton Home Museum • 20689 Marcellus Hwy • Decatur, MI 49045 • (616) 445-9016

Van Buren County Library • Webster Memorial Library Bldg, 200 N Phelps St • Decatur, MI 49045 • (269) 423-4771 • http://www.vbdl.org

Van Buren Regional Genealogical Society • c/o Van Buren County Library, 200 N Phelps St, P.O. Box 143 • Decatur, MI 49045 • (616) 423-4771 • http://woodlands.lib.mi.us/van/vbrgs.htm

Deckerville
Deckerville Historical Museum • 4028 Ruth Rd • Deckerville, MI 48427

Deckerville Public Library • 3542 N Main St • Deckerville, MI 48427-9638 • (810) 376-8015 • http://www.deckervillelibrary.com

Delton
Bernard Historical Society • Historical Museum, 7135 W Delton Rd • Delton, MI 49046 • (616) 623-5451 • http://www.delton-mi-com/bernard

Detroit
Americans of Italian Origin Society • 18336 Lister E • Detroit, MI 48021

Catholic Archdiocese of Detroit Archives • 1234 Washington Blvd • Detroit, MI 48226 • (313) 237-5846 • http://www.archdioceseofdetrolt.org

Charles H Wright Museum of African American History • 315 E Warren • Detroit, MI 48201 • (313) 494-5800 • http://www.maah-detroit.org

Commanding Officer's Residence Museum • Historic Fort Wayne National Historic Site • Detroit, MI 48209 • (313) 297-8376

Detroit Historical Society • Historical Museum, 5401 Woodward • Detroit, MI 48202 • (313) 833-1805 • http://www.detroithistorical.org

Detroit Public Library • Burton Historical Collection, 5201 Woodward Ave • Detroit, MI 48202 • (313) 833-1480 • http://www.detroit.lib.mi.us/special_collections.htm

Detroit Society for Genealogical Research • c/o Detroit Public Library, 5201 Woodward Ave • Detroit, MI 48202-4007 • (313) 833-1480 • http://www.dsgr.org

Detroit, cont.

Dossin Great Lakes Museum • 100 The Strand-on-Belle-Isle • Detroit, MI 48207 • (313) 852-4051 • http://www.glmi.org

Fisher Mansion Museum • 383 Lenox Ave • Detroit, MI 48215 • (313) 331-6740

Fred Hart Williams Genealogical Society • c/o Detroit Public Library, 5201 Woodward Ave • Detroit, MI 48202 • (313) 833-1480 • http://www.detroit.lib.mi.us/special_collections.htm

French-Canadian Heritage Society of Michigan, Detroit Chapter • c/o Detroit Public Library, 5201 Woodward Ave • Detroit, MI 48202 • (313) 833-1480 • http://www.detroit.lib.mi.us/special_collections.htm

Friends of the First Underground Railroad Museum • 33 E Forest Ave • Detroit, MI 48201 • http://www.the-ugrr.org

Indian Village Association • 3481 Seminole • Detroit, MI 48214 • (313) 922-1736

Irish Genealogical Society of Michigan • 2068 Michigan Ave • Detroit, MI 48216 • (313) 964-8700

Motown Historical Museum • 2648 W Grand Blvd • Detroit, MI 48208 • (313) 875-2264 • http://www.motownmuseum.org

Polish American Historic Site Association • 4231 Saint Aubin St • Detroit, MI 48207 • (313) 831-9727

Polish Genealogical Society of Michigan • c/o Detroit Public Library, 5201 Woodward Ave • Detroit, MI 48202-4007 • (313) 892-5445 • http://www.pgsm.org

Dexter

Dexter Area Historical Society • Dexter Museum, 3443 Inverness St • Dexter, MI 48130 • (734) 426-2519 • http://www.hvcn.org/info/dextermuseum/

Huron Valley Railroad Historical Society • 3487 Broad St • Dexter, MI 48130 • (734) 426-5100

Dorr

Match-e-be-nash-she-wish Band of Potawatomi Indians of Michigan • 1743 142nd Ave, P.O. Box 218 • Dorr, MI 49323 • (616) 681-8830

Douglas

Saugatuck-Douglas Historical Society • Historical Museum, P.O. Box 619 • Douglas, MI 49406 • (269) 857-7900 • http://www.accn.org/~sdhistory/Home.php

Steamship Keewatin Museum • Harbour Village, Union St & Blue Star Hwy, P.O. Box 638 • Douglas, MI 49406 • (616) 857-2464 • http://www.keewatinmaritimemuseum.org

Dowagiac

Dowagiac Public Library • 211 Commrcial St • Dowagiac, MI 49047-1728 • (269) 782-3826

Fred L Matthews Library & Museum • Southwest Michigan College, 58900 Cherry Grove Rd • Dowagiac, MI 49047 • (269) 782-1339 • http://www.smc.cc.mi.us/camplife/lib.htm

Heddon Museum • 414 West St • Dowagiac, MI 49047 • (269) 782-5698

Pokagon Band of Potawatomi Indians • 901 Spruce St, P.O. Box 180 • Dowagiac, MI 49047 • (616) 782-4141 • http://www.pokagon.com

Southwestern Michigan College Museum • 5880 Cherry Grove Rd • Dowagiac, MI 49047 • (269) 782-1374 • http://www.swmich.edu/museum

Drummond Island

Detour Reef Light Preservation Society • general delivery • Drummond Island, MI 49726 • (906) 493-6711

Drummond Island Historical Society • Historical Museum, Water St, P.O. Box 293 • Drummond Island, MI 49726 • (906) 493-5746

Dryden

Dryden Historical Society • 5488 Main St • Dryden, MI 48428 • (313) 796-3850

Dundee

Old Mill Museum • 242 Toledo St • Dundee, MI 48131 • (231) 264-5692 • http://www.elkrapidshistory.org

Durand

Shiawassee District Library-Durand Memorial Branch • 700 N Saginaw St • Durand, MI 48429-1245 • (989) 288-3743

Eagle Harbor

Keweenaw County Historical Society • Historical Museum, Lighthouse St, HC1, Box 265L • Eagle Harbor, MI 49950 • (906) 296-2561 • http://www.keweenawhistory.org

East Grand Rapids

Arnold's Archives Library • 1106 Eastwood SE • East Grand Rapids, MI 49506 • (616) 949-1398

East Jordan

East Jordan Portside Historical Museum • 1787 S M-66 Hwy • East Jordan, MI 49727 • (616) 536-2393

East Lansing

East Lansing Historical Society • P.O. Box 6146 • East Lansing, MI 48826

East Lansing Public Library • 950 Abbott Rd • East Lansing, MI 48823-3193 • (517) 351-2420 • http://www.elpl.org

Historical Society of Michigan • 1305 Abbott Rd • East Lansing, MI 48823 • (517) 324-1828 • http://www.hsofmich.org

Michigan State University Archives & Historical Collections • 100 Library • East Lansing, MI 48824-1048 • (517) 353-8700 • http://www.lib.msu.edu

Michigan State University Museum • W Circle Dr • East Lansing, MI 48824 • (517) 355-2370 • http://museum.msu.edu

East Tawas

Iosco County Historical Museum Association • Historical Museum, 405 W Bay, P.O. Box 135 • East Tawas, MI 48730 • (989) 362-8911 • http://www.ioscomuseum.org

Iosco-Arenac District Library • 120 W Westover St • East Tawas, MI 48730 • (989) 362-2651 • http://www.ioscoarenaclibrary.org

Tosco Bay Historical Society • 405 W Bay St, P.O. Box 144 • East Tawas, MI 48730 • (989) 362-8911

Eastpointe

East Detroit Historical Society • 15500 E 9 Mile Rd • Eastpointe, MI 48021 • (586) 775-1414

Eastpoint Memorial Library • 15875 Oak St • Eastpointe, MI 48021-2390 • (586) 445-5096 • http://www.ci.eastpointe.mi.us/library

Tri-County Genealogical Society • 21715 Brittany • Eastpointe, MI 48021-2503 • (586) 774-7953

Eau Claire

Eau Claire District Library • 6528 E Main St, P.O. Box 328 • Eau Claire, MI 49111-0328 • (269) 461-6241 • http://hometown.aol.com/ecdistlibrary/

Ecorse

Ecorse Public Library • 4184 W Jefferson Ave • Ecorse, MI 48229 • (313) 389-2030 • http://ecorse.lib.mi.us

Edwardsburg

Cass District Library-Edwardsburg Branch • 26745 Church St, P.O. Box 709 • Edwardsburg, MI 49112-0710 • (269) 663-5875

Edwardsburg Area Historical Collection • 28616 Main St, P.O. Box 694 • Edwardsburg, MI 49112 • (269) 663-8408

Genealogical Society of Cass County • c/o Edwardsburg Community Library, 26745 Church St, P.O. Box 709 • Edwardsburg, MI 49112 • (269) 663-5875

Elk Rapids
Elk Rapids Area Historical Society • Historical Museum, 401 River St, P.O. Box 2 • Elk Rapids, MI 49629 • (231) 264-5692 • http://www.elkrapidshistory.org

Elsie
Elsie Historical Society • 145 W Main St, P.O. Box 125 • Elsie, MI 48831-0125 • http://www.rootsweb.com/~migratio/elsiehiso/elsiehistsoc.html

Empire
Empire Area Heritage Group • Historical Museum, 11655 S La Core, P.O. Box 192 • Empire, MI 49630 • (616) 326-5568

Engadine
Engadine Historical Society • Route 1, Box 163 • Engadine, MI 49827

Luce-Mackinac Genealogical Society • P.O. Box 113 • Engadine, MI 49827-0013 • http://www.rootsweb.com/~miluce/luce-mac.htm

Escabana
Delta County Historical Society • 18 Water Plant Rd, P.O. Box 484 • Escabana, MI 49829 • (906) 786-3763

Escabana Public Library • 400 Ludington St • Escabana, MI 49829 • (906) 789-7323

Bay De Noc Community College Library • 2001 N Lincoln Rd • Escanaba, MI 49829-2511 • (906) 786-5802 • http://www.lrcweb.baydenoc.cc.mi.us

Delta County Genealogical Society • 314 N 20th St • Escanaba, MI 49829 • (906) 786-1893

Delta County Historical Society • Historical Museum, 18 Waterplant Rd, P.O. Box 1776 • Escanaba, MI 49829 • (906) 786-3763 • http://www.ohwy.com/mi/d/decohimu.htm

Escanaba Public Library • 400 Ludington St • Escanaba, MI 49829 • (906) 786-4463 • http://www.uproc.lib.mi.us/epl

Sandpoint Lighthouse Museum • Sandpoint, Luddington Park • Escanaba, MI 49829 • (906) 786-3763

Essexville
Bay County Genealogical Society • P.O. Box 27 • Essexville, MI 48732 • (989) 892-5951

Farmington
Farmington Community Library • 23500 Liberty St • Farmington, MI 48335-3570 • (248) 474-7770

Farmington Genealogical Society • c/o Farmington Community Library, 23500 Liberty • Farmington, MI 48335 • (248) 474-7770 • http://www.rootsweb.com/~mifarmgs/

Farmington Historical Commission • Historical Museum, 23600 Liberty St • Farmington, MI 48024 • (248) 476-4125

Farmington Historical Society • 33309 Shiawassee • Farmington, MI 48336 • (248) 476-4125

Farmington Hills
Farmington Community Library • 32737 W 12 Mile Rd • Farmington Hills, MI 48334-3302 • (248) 553-0300 • http://www.farmlib.org

Farmington Genealogical Society • c/o Farmington Community Library, 23500 Liberty St • Farmington Hills, MI 48024 • (248) 474-7770

Farmington Hills Historical Commission • City Hall, 31555 Eleven Mile Rd • Farmington Hills, MI 48018 • (248) 474-6115

Holocaust Memorial Center Museum • 28123 Orchard Lake Rd • Farmington Hills, MI 48334 • (248) 553-2400 • http://www.holocaustcenter.org

Fennville
Fennville District Library • 400 W Main St, P.O. Box 1130 • Fennville, MI 49408 • (616) 561-5050 • http://www.lakeland.lib.mi.us/fennville

Fenton
Fenton Historical Museum • 310 S Leroy St, P.O. Box 289 • Fenton, MI 48430

Fenton Historical Society • P.O. Box 451 • Fenton, MI 48430

Pioneer Memorial Association of Fenton-Mundy Townships • Historical Museum, 2436 N Long Lake Rd, P.O. Box 154 • Fenton, MI 48430 • (810) 629-7748

Ferndale
Ferndale Historical Society • 1651 Livernois • Ferndale, MI 48220

Fife Lake
Fife Lake Historical Museum • 10901 Marsh Rd • Fife Lake, MI 49633

Fife Lake Historical Society • Merritt St • Fife Lake, MI 49633

Flat Rock
Flat Rock Historical Society • 25486 Gibraltar Rd, P.O. Box 386 • Flat Rock, MI 48134 • (734) 782-5220

Flint
Alfred P Sloan Museum • 1221 E Kearsley St • Flint, MI 48503 • (810) 237-3450 • http://www.sloanmuseum.org

American Historical Society of Germans from Russia, Flint Michigan Chapter • 4426 Ashlawn Dr • Flint, MI 48507 • (810) 232-6949 • http://www.ahsgr.org/Chapters/flint_michigan_chapter.htm

Flint Genealogical Society • c/o Flint Public Library, 1026 E Kearsley St, P.O. Box 1217 • Flint, MI 48501-1217 • (810) 232-7111 x253 • http://www.rootsweb.com/~mifgs/

Flint Historic Commission • 1101 S Saginaw St • Flint, MI 48506 • (810) 766-7426

Flint Public Library • 1026 E Kearsley St • Flint, MI 48502-1994 • (810) 232-7111 • http://www.flint.lib.mi.us/fpl.html

Frances Willson Thompson Library • University of Michigan-Flint, 303 E Kearsley • Flint, MI 48502-1950 • (810) 762-3400 • http://www.flint.umich.edu/departments/library/

Genesee County Historical Society • Historical Museum, P.O. Box 13455 • Flint, MI 48501

Genesee District Library • G-4195 W Pasadena Ave • Flint, MI 48504 • (810) 732-0123 • http://gdl.falcon.edu

Genesee History Collection Center • Flint Library, Univ of Michigan-Flint • Flint, MI 48502 • (810) 762-3402

Genesee Valley Indian Association • 609 W Court St • Flint, MI 48503-5019 • (810) 239-6621

Historical Crossroads Village Archives • 5045 E Stanley Rd • Flint, MI 48506 • (810) 736-7100

Whaley Historical House Museum • 624 E Kearsley St • Flint, MI 48503 • (810) 235-6841 • http://www.whaleyhouse.com

Flushing
Cornish Connection of Lower Michigan • 8494 Wesley Dr • Flushing, MI 48433

Cornish-American Heritage Society • 8494 Wesley Dr • Flushing, MI 48433-1165 • (732) 776-5909

Flushing Area Historical Society • Historical Museum, 431 W Main St, P.O. Box 87 • Flushing, MI 48433 • (810) 732-1024 • http://www.flushinghistorical.org

Frankenmuth
Cass River Genealogy Society • 359 S Franklin St • Frankenmuth, MI 48734 • http://www.frankenmuthcity.com/library/genealogy.htm

Michigan

Frankenmuth, cont.

Frankenmuth Historical Association • Historical Museum, 613 S Main St • Frankenmuth, MI 48734 • (989) 652-9701 • http://frankenmuth.michigan.museum

James E Wickson Memorial Library • 359 S Franklin • Frankenmuth, MI 48734 • (989) 652-8323 • http://www.frankenmuthcity.com/library

Franklin Village

Franklin Historical Society • P.O. Box 7 • Franklin Village, MI 48025 • (313) 626-5160

Fraser

Fraser Historical Society • Fraser Historical Museum, 16330 Fourteen Mile Rd • Fraser, MI 48026 • (810) 293-4036 • http://www.ci.fraser.mi.us/library/part/historical.html

Fremont

Fremont Public Library • 104 E Main St • Fremont, MI 49412 • (231) 928-0256 • http://www.fadl.ncats.net

Newaygo County Society of History and Genealogy • 2305 S Warner Ave • Fremont, MI 49412

Fulton

Huron Potawatomi Tribe • 2221 1 1/2 Mile Rd • Fulton, MI 49052 • (616) 729-5151

Gagetown

Friends of The Thumb • 6948 Richie Rd • Gagetown, MI 48735 • (989) 665-9902

Galesburg

Galesburg Historical Museum • 1 E Battle Creek St, P.O. Box 398 • Galesburg, MI 49053

Galesburg Memorial Library • 188 E Michigan Ave • Galesburg, MI 49053 • (269) 665-7839

Galien

Galien Woods Historical Society • 708 Galien-Buchanan Rd • Galien, MI 49113 • (616) 545-8151

Garden

Fayette Historic State Park • 13700 13.25 Ln • Garden, MI 49835 • (906) 644-2603 • http://www.michigan/gov/dnr

Garden Peninsula Historical Society • 7344 00.25 Rd • Garden, MI 49835 • (906) 644-2695

Gaylord

Gaylord Fact-Finders Genealogical Society • P.O. Box 1524 • Gaylord, MI 49735 • (231) 584-2625 • http://www.otsego.org/factfinders/

Otsego County Historical Society • Historical Museum, 320 W Main St, P.O. Box 1223 • Gaylord, MI 49735

Otsego County Library • 700 S Otsego Ave • Gaylord, MI 49735-1723 • (989) 732-5841 • http://otsego.lib.mi.us

Gladstone

Gladstone Area School and Public Library • 300 S 10th St • Gladstone, MI 49837-1518 • (906) 428-4224

Gladwin

Gladwin County Historical Society • 515 E Cedar Ave • Gladwin, MI 48624 • (989) 426-7410

Gobles

Van Buren Historical Society • 36112 Cherry St • Gobles, MI 49055

Goodells

Saint Clair County Farm Museum • 8310 County Park Dr • Goodells, MI 48027-1400 • (810) 325-1737

Grand Blanc

Grand Blanc Heritage Association • Historical Museum, 203 E Grand Blanc Rd • Grand Blanc, MI 48439 • (810) 694-7274

National Society, Daughters of the Union 1861-1865 • 11396 Grand Oak Dr • Grand Blanc, MI 48439 • (313) 694-6879

Grand Haven

Grand Haven Area Historical Society • P.O. Box 234 • Grand Haven, MI 49417 • (616) 842-0700

Grand Haven Genealogical Society • c/o Loutit Library, 407 Columbus • Grand Haven, MI 49417 • (616) 842-5560 • http://grandhavengenealogy.blogspot.com

Loutit District Library • 407 Columbus St • Grand Haven, MI 49417 • (616) 842-5560 • http://www.loutitlibrary.org

Tri-Cities Historical Society • Historical Museum, 200 Washington Ave • Grand Haven, MI 49417 • (616) 842-0700 • http://www.tri-citiesmuseum.org

Grand Ledge

Grand Ledge Area Historical Society • Historical Museum, 118 W Lincoln St, P.O. Box 203 • Grand Ledge, MI 48837 • (517) 627-3149

Grand Ledge Public Library • 131 E Jefferson St • Grand Ledge, MI 48837-1534 • (517) 627-7014

Grand Rapids

Association for the Advancement of Dutch-American Studies • c/o Heckman Library, Calvin College and Seminary, 3207 Burton St SE • Grand Rapids, MI 49506 • (616) 957-6313 • http://www.aadas.net

Dutch International Society • 1742 Cambridge Dr SE • Grand Rapids, MI 49506-4424 • http://www.dismagazine.xodian.net

Gaines Township Historical Society • 421 68th St SE • Grand Rapids, MI 49508

Gerald R Ford Museum • 303 Pearl St NW • Grand Rapids, MI 49504 • (616) 451-9263 • http://www.fordlibrarymuseum.gov

Grand Rapids Historical Society • c/o Grand Rapids Public Library, 60 Library Plaza NE • Grand Rapids, MI 49503-3093 • (616) 456-4097

Grand Rapids Public Library • 111 Library St NE • Grand Rapids, MI 49503-3268 • (616) 988-5400 • http://www.grapids.lib.mi.us

Grand Rapids Public Museum • 272 Pearl St NW • Grand Rapids, MI 49504-5371 • (616) 456-3977 • http://www.grmuseum.org

Grand Rapids-Kent County Community Archives and Research Center • 223 Washington St SE • Grand Rapids, MI 49503 • http://www.communityarchive.org

Grand River Historical Society • c/o Grand Rapids Public Library, 60 Library Plaza NE • Grand Rapids, MI 49503 • (616) 456-3600

Heckman Library • Calvin College and Seminary, 1855 Knollcrest Circle SE • Grand Rapids, MI 49546-4301 • (616) 526-6307 • http://www.calvin.edu/library/

Heritage Hill Association • 126 College St SE • Grand Rapids, MI 49503 • (616) 459-8950

Kent County Council for Historic Preservation • Voigt House Victorian Museum, 115 College Ave SE • Grand Rapids, MI 49503 • (616) 456-4600 • http://www.grmuseum.org

Kent District Library-Cutlerville • 421 68th St SE • Grand Rapids, MI 49548 • (616) 455-1430

Kent District Library-Plainfield • 2650 Five Mile Rd NE • Grand Rapids, MI 49525 • (616) 361-0611

Meyer May House Museum • 450 Madison Ave SE • Grand Rapids, MI 49503 • (616) 246-4821

Michigan Masonic Museum • 233 E Fulton St • Grand Rapids, MI 49503-3270 • (616) 459-9336 • http://www.gl-mi.org/library

Palatines to America, Michigan Chapter • 868 Beechwood St NE • Grand Rapids, MI 49505

Polish Heritage Society • P.O. Box 1844 • Grand Rapids, MI 49501 • (616) 452-3363

Western Michigan Genealogical Society • c/o Grand Rapids Public Library, 60 Library Plaza NE • Grand Rapids, MI 49503 • (616) 456-3640 • http://www.wmgs.org

Western Michigan Genealogical Society, Computer Users Group • c/o Grand Rapids Public Library, 60 Library Plaza • Grand Rapids, MI 49503 • (616) 456-3640 • http://www.iserv.net/~wmgs

Grandville
Grandville Historical Association • 3195 Wilson SW, P.O. Box 124 • Grandville, MI 49418 • (616) 534-2687

Kent District Library-Grandville Branch • 4055 Maple St SW • Grandville, MI 49418 • (616) 530-4995

Grant
Grant Public Library • 51 Front St, P.O. Box 695 • Grant, MI 49327-0695 • (231) 834-5713 • http://grant.llcoop.org

Grass Lake
Grass Lake Area Historical Society • Coe House Museum, 371 W Michigan, P.O. Box 53 • Grass Lake, MI 49240 • (517) 522-5141

Waterloo Area Farm Museum • 9998 Waterloo-Munith Rd • Grass Lake, MI 49240 • (517) 596-2254 • http://www.waterloofarmmuseum.org

Grayling
Crawford County Library-Devereaux Memorial • 201 Plum St • Grayling, MI 49738 • (989) 348-9214 • http://www.nlc.lib.mi.us/members/crawford

Greenbush
Greenbush Historical Society • P.O. Box 222 • Greenbush, MI 48738 • (989) 739-4036

Greenville
Flat River Community Library • 200 W Judd St • Greenville, MI 48838 • (616) 754-6359 • http://www.flatriverlibrary.org

Flat River Historical and Genealogical Society • 524 W Grant St, P.O. Box 188 • Greenville, MI 48838 • (616) 754-5296

Flat River Historical Society • Historical Museum, 213 N Franklin St, P.O. Box 188 • Greenville, MI 48838 • (231) 754-5296 • http://www.flatriverhistoricalsociety.org

Grosse Ile
Grosse Ile Historical Society • Historical Museum, E River Rd & Grosse Ile Parkway, P.O. Box 131 • Grosse Ile, MI 48138 • (734) 675-1250

Grosse Point Shores
Edsel & Eleanor Ford House Museum • 1100 Lake Shore Rd • Grosse Point Shores, MI 48236 • (313) 884-4222 • http://www.fordhouse.org

Grosse Pointe
Grosse Pointe Historical Society • 376 Kercheval Ave • Grosse Pointe, MI 48236 • (313) 885-9241

Grosse Pointe Farms
Grosse Pointe Public Library • 10 Kercheval • Grosse Pointe Farms, MI 48236 • (313) 343-2074 • http://www.gp.lib.mi.us

Grosse Pointe Park
Detroit 300 Museum • 1174 Kensington • Grosse Pointe Park, MI 48230

Gulliver
Gulliver Historical Society • Route 1, Box 1 • Gulliver, MI 49840

Gwinn
Forsyth Township Historical Society • 114 N Pine St • Gwinn, MI 49841

Hamburg
Hamburg Township Library • 10411 Merrill Rd, P.O. Box 247 • Hamburg, MI 48139 • (810) 231-1771 • http://www.hamburg.lib.mi.us

Hamtramck
Albert J Zak Memorial Library • 2360 Caniff • Hamtramck, MI 48212 • (313) 365-7050

Hancock
Finnish-American Heritage Center • Suomi College, 601 Quincy St • Hancock, MI 49930 • (906) 487-7367 • http://www.suomi.edu/lnk/FHC.html

Finnish-American Historical Archives • Finlandia University, 435 Quincy St • Hancock, MI 49930-1845 • (906) 487-7347 • http://www.finlandia.edu.fahc.html/

Maki Library • Finlandia University, 601 Quincy St • Hancock, MI 49930-1882 • (906) 487-7252 • http://www.finlandia.edu

Hanover
Hanover-Horton Area Historical Society • Historical Museum, 101 Fairview St, P.O. Box 256 • Hanover, MI 49241 • (517) 563-8927 • http://www.conklinreedorganmuseum.org

Harbor Beach
Grice Museum and Historical Society • Historical Museum, 244 S 4th St • Harbor Beach, MI 48441 • (989) 479-6093

Huron County Historical Society • 223 3rd St • Harbor Beach, MI 48441

Harbor Springs
Chief Andrew J Blackbird Home Museum • 368 E Main St • Harbor Springs, MI 49740 • (231) 526-2104 • http://www.freeway.net/community/civic/blackbirdmuseum

Harbor Springs Area Historical Society • Josephine R Ford Park • Harbor Springs, MI 49740

Harrison
Charles A Amble Library • Mid Michigan Community College, 1375 S Clare Ave • Harrison, MI 48625 • (989) 386-6617 • http://www.midmich.edu/library

Harrison Area Genealogical Society • P.O. Box 796 • Harrison, MI 48625 • http://www.rootsweb.com/~miclare/harrison.htm

Harrison Community Library • 105 E Main St, P.O. Box 380 • Harrison, MI 48625-0380 • (989) 539-6711

Harrisville
Alcona County Library • 312 W Main St, P.O. Box 348 • Harrisville, MI 48740-0348 • (989) 724-6796

Hart
Hart Area Public Library • 407 S State St • Hart, MI 49420-1228 • (231) 873-4476

Oceana County Historical and Genealogical Society • 114 Dryden St, P.O. Box 53 • Hart, MI 49420-1105 • (231) 873-2600

Hartford
Hartford Public Library • 15 Franklin St, P.O. Box 8 • Hartford, MI 49057-0008 • (616) 621-3408

Van Buren County Historical Society • 6215 E Red Arrow Hwy E, P.O. Box 452 • Hartford, MI 49057 • (269) 621-2188

Hartland
Cromaine District Library • 3688 N Hartland Rd, P.O. Box 308 • Hartland, MI 48353-0308 • (810) 632-5200 • http://www.cromaine.org

Hastings
Barry County Historical Society • 912 E State St • Hastings, MI 49058 • (616) 945-3775

Michigan

Hastings, cont.

Charlton Park Historic Village and Museum • 2545 S Charlton Park Rd • Hastings, MI 49058 • (269) 945-3775 • http://www.charltonpark.org

Hastings Public Library • 121 S Church St • Hastings, MI 49058-1817 • (269) 945-4263 • http://hastings.llcoop.org

Hemlock

Rauchholz Memorial Library • 1140 N Hemlock Rd • Hemlock, MI 48626 • (989) 642-8621 • http://www.richlandtownship.com

Hickory Corners

Gilmore Car Museum • 6865 W Hickory Rd • Hickory Corners, MI 49060 • (269) 671-5089 • http://www.gilmorecarmuseum.org

Hillsdale

Friends of Mitchell Library Research Committee • c/o Michell Public Library, 22 N Manning St, P.O. Box 873 • Hillsdale, MI 49242-0873 • (517) 437-2581

Hillsdale County Historical Society • 22 N Manning St • Hillsdale, MI 49242 • (517) 437-2797

Mitchell Public Library • 22 N Manning St • Hillsdale, MI 49242 • (517) 437-2581

Holland

1st Michigan Museum of Military History • US 31 & New Holland St • Holland, MI 49424 • (616) 399-1955

Beardslee Library • Kolkman Archives, Western Theological Seminary, 101 E 13th St • Holland, MI 49423 • (616) 392-8555 • http://www.westernsem.edu/library

Cappon & Settlers House Museum • 228 W 9th St • Holland, MI 49423 • (616) 392-6740 • http://www.hollandmuseum.org

Herrick District Library • 300 S River Ave • Holland, MI 49423-3290 • (616) 355-1400 • http://www.herrickdl.org

Holland Area Historical Society • c/o Van Wylen Library, Hope College • Holland, MI 49423 • (616) 395-7790

Holland Genealogical Society • c/o Herrick Public Library, 300 S River Ave • Holland, MI 49423 • (616) 394-1400

Holland Museum • 31 W 10th St • Holland, MI 49423 • (616) 394-1362 • http://www.hollandmuseum.org

Joint Archives of Holland • Hope College, History Research Center, P.O. Box 9000 • Holland, MI 49422-9000 • (616) 395-7798 • http://www.jointarchives.org

Van Wylen Library • Hope College, 53 Graves Pl, P.O. Box 9012 • Holland, MI 49422-9012 • (616) 395-7790 • http://www.hope.edu/lib

Windmill Island Municipal Park Museum • 1 Lincoln Ave • Holland, MI 49423 • (616) 355-1030 • http://www.windmillisland.org

Holly

Holly Historical Society • 306 S Saginaw St • Holly, MI 48442 • (248) 634-9233

Holly Township Library • 1116 N Saginaw St • Holly, MI 48442 • (248) 634-1754

Homer

Homer Historical Society • 505 Grandview • Homer, MI 49245 • (517) 568-3116

Houghton

Isle Royale National Park Library • 800 E Lakeshore Dr • Houghton, MI 49931 • (906) 487-7153 • http://www.nps.gov/isro

J Robert Van Pelt Library - Copper County Historical Collections • Michigan Tech Univ, 1400 Townsend Dr • Houghton, MI 49931-1295 • (906) 487-2505 • http://www.lib.mtu.edu/jrvp/

Houghton Lake Heights

Houghton Lake Area Historical Society • 1701 E Houghton Lake Dr, P.O. Box 146 • Houghton Lake Heights, MI 48630 • (989) 366-9124

Howard City

Reynolds Township Library • 215 E Edgerton, P.O. Box 220 • Howard City, MI 49329-0220 • (231) 937-5575 • http://www.reynolds.llcoop.org

Howell

Howell Carnegie Library & Howell Archives • 314 W Grand River St • Howell, MI 48843 • (517) 546-0720 • http://www.howelllibrary.org

Livingston County Genealogical Society • P.O. Box 1073 • Howell, MI 48844-1073 • (517) 545-0903 • http://www.livgenmi.com/lcgslogo.htm

Livingston County Historical Society • P.O. Box 154 • Howell, MI 48844 • (517) 548-3692

Marine Historical Society of Detroit • 514 Aberdeen Wy • Howell, MI 48843

Hubbell

Keweenaw Kernewek • 101 Gregory St, Box 511 • Hubbell, MI 49934

Hudson

Bean Creek Valley Historical Society • 205 S Market Church • Hudson, MI 49247 • (517) 448-3801

Hudson Public Library • 205 S Market St • Hudson, MI 49247 • (517) 448-3801

Huntington Woods

Huntington Woods Public Library • 26415 Scotia Rd • Huntington Woods, MI 48070-1198 • (248) 543-9720 • http://www.huntingon-woods.lib.mi.us

Imlay City

Imlay City Historical Museum • 77 Main St • Imlay City, MI 48444

Lapeer County Library-Goodland • 2370 N Van Dyke Rd • Imlay City, MI 48444 • (810) 724-1970

Indian River

Tuscarora Historical Society • P.O. Box 807 • Indian River, MI 49749 • (616) 238-9072

Inkster

Inkster Historical Commission • c/o Inkster Public Library, 2005 Inkster Rd • Inkster, MI 48141 • (313) 563-2822

Inkster Public Library • 2005 Inkster Rd • Inkster, MI 48141 • (313) 563-2822 • http://www.inkster.lib.mi.us

Ionia

Hall-Fowler Memorial Library • 126 E Main St • Ionia, MI 48846 • (616) 527-3680 • http://ionia.llcoop.org

Ionia County Historical Society • John C Blanchard House, 59 E Main St, P.O. Box 1776 • Ionia, MI 48846 • (616) 527-3487 • http://www.ioniahistory.org/blanchard-house.html

Iron Mountain

Dickinson County Genealogical Society • c/o Dickinson County Library, 401 Iron Mountain St • Iron Mountain, MI 49801 • (906) 774-1218 • http://www.upclics.org/dcgs/

Dickinson County Library • 401 Iron Mountain St • Iron Mountain, MI 49801 • (906) 774-1218 • http://www.dcl-lib.org

Menominee Range Historical Society • Historical Museum, 3000 E Ludington St, P.O. Box 237 • Iron Mountain, MI 49801 • (906) 774-4276

Iron River

Iron County Historical and Museum Society • Historical Museum, 233 Bernhardt Rd • Iron River, MI 49935 • (906) 265-3942

Ironwood

Gogebic County Historical Society • P.O. Box 339 • Ironwood, MI 49938

Ironwood Area Historical Society • Historical Museum, 150 N Lowell St, P.O. Box 553 • Ironwood, MI 49938 • (906) 932-0287 • http://www.ironwood.org

Ironwood Carnegie Public Library • 235 E Aurora St • Ironwood, MI 49938-2178 • (906) 932-0203 • http://www.ironwoodlibrary.com

Ithaca

Gratiot County Historical and Genealogical Society • 228 W Center St, P.O. Box 73 • Ithaca, MI 48847 • (989) 875-6232 • http://www.rootsweb.com/-migratio/gchgs/

Thompson Home Public Library • 125 W Center St • Ithaca, MI 48847 • (989) 875-4184

Jackson

Ella Sharp Museum • 3225 4th St • Jackson, MI 49203 • (517) 787-2320 • http://www.ellasharp.org

Jackson County Genealogical Society • c/o Jackson District Library, 244 W Michigan Ave • Jackson, MI 49201 • (517) 788-4316 • http://www.rootsweb.com/~mijackso/jcgs.htm

Jackson County Historical Society • 244 W Michigan Ave • Jackson, MI 49201

Jackson District Library • 244 W Michigan Ave • Jackson, MI 49201 • (517) 788-4087 • http://www.jackson.lib.mi.us

Romanian American Heritage Center • 2540 Grey Tower Rd • Jackson, MI 49201-9120 • (517) 522-8260 • http://feefhs.org//ro/frg-rahc.html

Jonesville

Grosvenor House Museum • 211 Maumee St, P.O. Box 63 • Jonesville, MI 49250 • (517) 849-9596

Kalamazoo

Alamo Township Museum • 8119 N 6th St • Kalamazoo, MI 49009 • (616) 344-9479

Archives and Regional History Collection • Western Michigan Univ, 111 East Hall • Kalamazoo, MI 49008-5081 • (616) 387-8490 • http://www.wmich.edu/library/depts/archives

Dwight B Waldo Library • Western Michigan University, Arcadia at Vande Giessen St • Kalamazoo, MI 49008-5080 • (269) 387-5178 • http://www.wmich.edu/library

Kalamazoo Aviation History Museum • 6151 Portage Rd • Kalamazoo, MI 49002 • (269) 385-6555 • http://www.airzoo.org

Kalamazoo County Historical Society • 315 S Rose St, P.O. Box 1623 • Kalamazoo, MI 49005 • (616) 345-7092

Kalamazoo Model Railroad Historical Society • 9336 N Riverview Dr • Kalamazoo, MI 49004 • (269) 343-8269

Kalamazoo Public Library • 315 S Rose St • Kalamazoo, MI 49007 • (269) 342-9837 • http://www.kpl.gov/

Kalamazoo Valley Community College Library • 6767 W O Ave, P.O. Box 4070 • Kalamazoo, MI 49003-4070 • (269) 488-4380 • http://www.kvcc.edu

Kalamazoo Valley Genealogical Society • 6130 King Hwy, Comstock Township, P.O. Box 405 • Kalamazoo, MI 49041-0405 • (616) 665-9697 • http://www.rootsweb.com/~mikvgs/

Kalamazoo Valley Museum • 230 N Rose St, P.O. Box 4070 • Kalamazoo, MI 49003-4070 • (616) 373-7984 • http://www.kalamazoomuseum.org

Thomas F Reed Library • Davenport University, 4123 W Main St • Kalamazoo, MI 49006 • (269) 382-2835

Upjohn Library • Kalamazoo College, 1200 Academy St • Kalamazoo, MI 49006-3285 • (269) 337-7149 • http://kzoo.edu/library/

Kaleva

Kaleva Historical Society • 14551 Wuoski Ave • Kaleva, MI 49645 • (231) 362-2080

Kalkaska

Kalkaska County Historical Society • 4360 Spencer Rd SE • Kalkaska, MI 49646 • (231) 258-8285

Kalkaska County Library • 247 S Cedar St • Kalkaska, MI 49646 • (231) 258-9411

Kalkaska County Museum • 335 S Cedar St • Kalkaska, MI 49646 • (616) 258-5603

Kalkaska Genealogical Society • P.O. Box 353 • Kalkaska, MI 49646-0353 • (616) 258-9265 • http://hometown.aol.com/fiddlerben/kasgensoc.html

Kent City

Kent City Area Historical Society • 16652 Fruit Ridge • Kent City, MI 49330

Kentwood

Society for the Preservation of Old Mills • 5667 Leisure South Dr SE • Kentwood, MI 49548 • (616) 455-0609

Kingsford

Mid-Peninsula Library Cooperative • 1525 Pyle Dr • Kingsford, MI 49802 • (906) 774-3005

Kinross

Kinross Heritage Society • P.O. Box 39 • Kinross, MI 49752 • (906) 478-5267

Laingsburg

Laingsburg Public Library • 255 E Grand River, P.O. Box 280 • Laingsburg, MI 48848-0280 • (517) 651-6282

Victor Township Historical Society • 6843 Alword Rd • Laingsburg, MI 48848

Lake City

Missaukee District Library • 210 S Canal St, P.O. Box 340 • Lake City, MI 49651 • (231) 839-2166 • http://www.missaukeelibrary.org

Lake Linden

Houghton County Historical Society • Historical Museum, 5000 Hwy M26, P.O. Box 127 • Lake Linden, MI 49945 • (906) 296-4121 • http://www.houghtonhistory.org

Lake Odessa

First Families of Ionia County Society • 13051 Ainsworth Rd, Route 3 • Lake Odessa, MI 48849 • (616) 374-3141 • http://www.usgennet.org/~ahmiioni/icgshome.htm

Ionia County Genealogical Society • 1117 Emerson St • Lake Odessa, MI 48849 • (616) 374-8455 • http://www.rootsweb.com/~miionia/icgs.htm

Lake Odessa Area Historical Society • Depot Museum, 839 4th Ave • Lake Odessa, MI 48849 • (616) 374-8698

Lake Orion

North Oakland Genealogical Society • c/o Orion Township Public Library, 824 Joslyn Rd • Lake Orion, MI 48352-2124 • (248) 693-3001 • http://tln.lib.mi.us/~pont/genealog.htm

Orion Township Public Library • 824 Joslyn Rd • Lake Orion, MI 48362 • (248) 693-3000 • http://www.orion.lib.mi.us

Lakeview

Tamarack District Library • 407 S Lincoln Ave, P.O. Box 469 • Lakeview, MI 48850-0469 • (989) 352-6274 • http://lakeview.llcoop.org

Michigan

L'Anse
Alberta Village Museum • Courthouse Annex • L'Anse, MI 49946

Baraga County Historical Society • Historical Museum, 41 Baraga Ave • L'Anse, MI 49946 • (906) 353-8444

Lansing
Capitol Area District Library • 401 S Capitol Ave, P.O. Box 40719 • Lansing, MI 48909-7919 • (517) 367-6350 • http://www.cadl.org

Clinton County Historical Commission • 5580 W State Rd • Lansing, MI 48906 • (517) 321-1746

French-Canadian Heritage Society of Michigan • c/o Library of Michigan, 717 W Allegan, P.O. Box 10028 • Lansing, MI 48901-0028 • (517) 373-1300 • http://habitant.org/fchsm/

Friends of Michigan History • P.O. Box 17035 • Lansing, MI 48901 • (517) 373-2565

Genealogists of the Clinton County Historical Society • 16101 Brook Rd • Lansing, MI 48906-5627 • (517) 482-5117

Historical Society of Greater Lansing • P.O. Box 12095 • Lansing, MI 48901 • (517) 321-1746

Library of Michigan • 702 W Kalamazoo St, P.O. Box 30007 • Lansing, MI 48909 • (517) 373-1300 • http://www.michigan.gov/hal

Michigan Department of Public Health Office of the State Registrar • 3423 North Martin Luther King Blvd, P.O. Box 30721 • Lansing, MI 48909 • (517) 335-8656 • http://www.mdch.state.mi.us/pha/osr/

Michigan Genealogical Council • P.O. Box 80953 • Lansing, MI 48908 • http://www.rootsweb.com/~mimgc

Michigan Historical Commission • 505 State Office Bldg • Lansing, MI 48913

Michigan State Archives-Historical Center • 702 W Kalamazoo St • Lansing, MI 48909-8240 • (517) 373-1408 • http://www.michiganhistory.org

Mid-Michigan Genealogical Society • 201 Hillside Ct, P.O. Box 16033 • Lansing, MI 48901-6033 • (517) 629-2345 • http://userdata.acd.net/mmgs/mmgssoc.html

Museum of Surveying • 220 Museum Dr • Lansing, MI 48933 • (517) 484-6605 • http://www.surveyhistory.org

R E Olds Transportation Museum • 240 Museum Dr • Lansing, MI 48933 • (517) 372-0529 • http://www.reoldsmuseum.org

Sons of Union Veterans of the Civil War, Michigan Society • 411 Bartlett St • Lansing, MI 48915 • http://suvcw.org

Lapeer
Banat Genealogy • P.O. Box 262 • Lapeer, MI 48446-0262 • http://feeflis.org/banat/frgbanat.html

Lapeer County Genealogical Society • c/o Marguerite DiAngeli Branch Library, 921 W Nepressing St • Lapeer, MI 48446-1872 • (810) 664-6971 • http://www.library.lapeer.org/deAngeli/mdeangeli. Htm

Lapeer County Historical Society • Old Courthouse Museum, 518 W Nepressing St, P.O. Box 72 • Lapeer, MI 48446

Lapeer County Library • 201 Village West Dr S • Lapeer, MI 48446-1699 • (810) 664-9521 • http://www.library.lapeer.org

Lapeer County Library-Marguerite de Angeli Branch • 921 W Nepessing St • Lapeer, MI 48446 • (810) 664-6971 • http://www.library.lapeer.org/main/

Marguerite De Angeli Library • 921 W Nepressing St • Lapeer, MI 48446 • (810) 664-6971

Le Roy
Leroy Community Library • 104 W Gilbert, P.O. Box 110 • Le Roy, MI 49655-0110 • (231) 768-4493

Leland
Leelanau Historical Society • Historical Museum, 203 E Cedar St, P.O. Box 246 • Leland, MI 49654-0246 • (231) 256-7475 • http://www.leelanauhistory.org

Leland Township Public Library • 203 E Cedar St, P.O. Box 736 • Leland, MI 49654-0736 • (231) 256-9152

Lewiston
Lewiston Area Historical Society • 4384 Michelson Ave, P.O. Box 461 • Lewiston, MI 49756-8853 • (989) 786-2451

Lincoln Park
Downriver Genealogical Society • 1335 Southfield Rd, P.O. Box 476 • Lincoln Park, MI 48146 • (313) 382-3229 • http://www.rootsweb.com/~midrgs/drgs.htm

Lincoln Park Historical Society • Historical Museum, 1335 Southfield, P.O. Box 1776 • Lincoln Park, MI 48146 • (313) 386-3137 • http://www.lphistorical.org; http://www.rootsweb.com/~milphsm/lphsm.htm

Linden
Linden Mills Historical Society • P.O. Box 551 • Linden, MI 48451

Litchfield
Southern Michigan Genealogical Society • P.O. Box 371 • Litchfield, MI 49252

Livonia
Livonia Historical Society • Greenmead Historic Site Museum, 38125 Eight Mile Rd • Livonia, MI 48152 • (734) 477-7375

Livonia Public Library • 32777 5 Mile Rd • Livonia, MI 48154-3045 • (734) 466-2450

Western Wayne County Genealogical Society • P.O. Box 530063 • Livonia, MI 48153-0063 • (248) 349-4846

Lowell
Fallasburg Historical Society • Historical Museum, 13944 Covered Bridge Rd • Lowell, MI 49331 • (616) 897-7161 • http://www.fallasburg.org

Lowell Area Historical Museum • 325 W Main St, P.O. Box 81 • Lowell, MI 49331 • (616) 897-7688 • http://www.lowellmuseum.org

Ludington
Mason County District Library • 217 E Ludington Ave, P.O. Box 549 • Ludington, MI 49431-0549 • (231) 843-8465 • http://www.masoncounty.lib.mi.us

Mason County Genealogical Society • P.O. Box 352 • Ludington, MI 49431 • (616) 843-8465

Mason County Historical Society • White Pine Village Museum, 1687 S Lakeshore Dr • Ludington, MI 49431 • (231) 843-4808 • http://www.historicwhitepinevillage.org

Mackinac Island
Biddle House Museum • Market St • Mackinac Island, MI 49757

Fort Mackinack Museum • 7127 Huron Rd • Mackinac Island, MI 49757 • http://www.mackinacparks.com/fort-mackinac/

Mackinac Island Public Library • 903 Main St, P.O. Box 903 • Mackinac Island, MI 48757-0903 • (906) 847-3421

Mackinac Island State Park Museum • Huron Rd, P.O. Box 873 • Mackinac Island, MI 49701 • (906) 847-3328 • http://www.mackinacparks.com

McGulpin House Museum • Fort Hill Rd • Mackinac Island, MI 49757

Stuart House Museum • Market St, P.O. Box 906 • Mackinac Island, MI 49757 • (906) 847-8181

Mackinaw City
Colonial Michilimackinac Museum • 102 W Straits Ave • Mackinaw City, MI 49701 • http://www.mackinacparks.com/colonial-michilimackinac/

Historic Mill Creek Museum • 9001 US 23 S, P.O. Box 873 • Mackinaw City, MI 49701 • (231) 436-4100 • http://www.mackinacparks.com

Mackinaw Area Public Library • 428 W Central Ave, P.O. Box 67 • Mackinaw City, MI 49701-0067 • (231) 436-5451 • http://nlc.lib.mi.us/members/mackinaw.htm

Old Mackinac Point Lighthouse Museum • 102 W Straits Ave, P.O. Box 873 • Mackinaw City, MI 49701 • (231) 436-4100 • http://www.mackinacparks.com

Teysen's Woodland Indian Musuem • 415 W Huron Ave, P.O. Box 399 • Mackinaw City, MI 49701 • (616) 436-7011

Madison Heights
Madison Heights Historical Society • c/o Madison Heights Public Library, 240 W 13 Mile Rd • Madison Heights, MI 48071-1894 • (248) 588-7763 • http://www.madison-hgts.lib.mi.us

Madison Heights Public Library • 240 W 13 Mile Rd • Madison Heights, MI 48071-1894 • (248) 588-7763 • http://www.madison-hgts.lib.mi.us

Mancelona
Mancelona Area Genealogy Society • P.O. Box 517 • Mancelona, MI 49659

Mancelona Area Historical Society • 202 W State, P.O. Box 103 • Mancelona, MI 49659

Mancelona Township Library • 202 W State St, PO Box 499 • Mancelona, MI 49659-0499 • (231) 587-9451 • http://www.upnorthlife.com/mancelona/Library.asp

Manchester
Manchester District Library • 912 City Rd • Manchester, MI 48158 • (734) 428-8045 • http://manchester.lib.mi.us

Manistee
Little River Band of Odawa Indians • 1762 US 31 S • Manistee, MI 49660 • (231) 723-8288 • http://www.lrboi.com

Manistee County Historical Museum • 425 River St • Manistee, MI 49660 • (231) 723-5531

Manistee County Library • 95 Maple St • Manistee, MI 49660 • (231) 723-2519 • http://www.manisteelibrary.org

Manistee Genealogical Society • Manistee Museum • Manistee, MI 49660 • (616) 723-2519

Manistique
Log Cabin Genealogical Society • 103 N 3rd St • Manistique, MI 49854-1018

Schoolcraft Historical Society • Imogene Herbert Historical Museum, Deer St, Pioneer Park, P.O. Box 284 • Manistique, MI 49854 • (906) 341-8131

Manton
Manton Area Historical Society • P.O. Box 86 • Manton, MI 49663

Maple Rapids
Maple Rapids Public Library • 130 S Maple Ave, P.O. Box 410 • Maple Rapids, MI 48853-0410 • (989) 682-4464

Marlette
Marlette District Library • 3116 Main St • Marlette, MI 48453 • (989) 635-2838 • http://www.vlc.lib.mi.us

Marquette
Bishop Baraga Association and Archives • Diocese of Marquette, 347 Rock St, P.O. Box 550 • Marquette, MI 49855-0550 • (906) 227-9117 • http://www.dioceseofmarquette.org

John Burt House Museum • Little Island Point 25 • Marquette, MI 49855 • (906) 226-2413

Marquette County Genealogical Society • c/o Peter White Public Library, 217 N Front St • Marquette, MI 49855 • (906) 228-9510 • http://members.aol.com/MQTCGS/MCGS/mcgs.html

Marquette County Historical Society • Historical Museum, 213 N Front St • Marquette, MI 49855-4220 • (906) 226-3571 • http://www.marquettecohistory.org

Marquette Maritime Museum • 300 Lakeshore Blvd, P.O. Box 1096 • Marquette, MI 49855 • (906) 226-2006

Peter White Public Library • 217 N Front St • Marquette, MI 49855 • (906) 228-9510 • http://lib.up.net/pwpl/Pwplhome.htm

Slovenian Genealogical Society, Michigan Upper Peninsula Chapter • 347 Rock St, P.O. Box 550 • Marquette, MI 49855

Marshall
Calhoun County Genealogical Society • P.O. Box 879 • Marshall, MI 49068-0879 • (616) 729-5258 • http://www.rootsweb.com/~micalhou/cegs.htm

Marshall Historical Society • Honolulu House Museum, 107 N Kalamazoo Ave, P.O. Box 68 • Marshall, MI 49068 • (269) 781-8544 • http://www.marshallhistoricalsociety.org

Marysville
Marysville Historical Museum • 887 E Huron Blvd • Marysville, MI 48040 • http://www.cityofmarysvillemi.com

Mason
Ingham County Genealogical Society • 145 Ash St, P.O. Box 85 • Mason, MI 48854 • http://userdata.acd.net/mmgs/icgs.html

Ingham County Historical Commission • County Courthouse, P.O. Box 319 • Mason, MI 48854 • (517) 676-7213 • http://www.ingham.org

Mason Historical Society • 122 Walnut Ct • Mason, MI 48854 • (517) 676-2209

Mayville
Mayville Area Museum of History and Genealogical Library • 2124 Ohmer Rd, P.O. Box 242 • Mayville, MI 48744 • (989) 843-6712

Mayville Historical Society • 22 Turner, P.O. Box 242 • Mayville, MI 48744 • (989) 843-6429

Mendon
Mendon Township Library • 314 W Main St, P.O. Box 38 • Mendon, MI 49072-0038 • (616) 496-4865

Menominee
Menominee County Historical Society • Historical Museum, 904 11th Ave, P.O. Box 151 • Menominee, MI 49858 • (906) 863-9000

Spies Public Library • 940 1st St • Menominee, MI 49858-3296 • (906) 863-3911 • http://www.uproc.lib.mi.us/spies

West Shore Fishing Museum • N6634 Harbor Ln • Menominee, MI 49858 • (906) 863-3347

Merrill
Merrill District Library • 136 N Midland St • Merrill, MI 48637-0009 • (989) 643-7300

Metamora
Lapeer County Library-Metamora Branch • 4018 Oak St, P.O. Box 77 • Metamora, MI 48455-0077 • (810) 678-2991

Middleville
Historic Bowens Mills and Pioneer Park • 200 Old Mill Rd • Middleville, MI 49333 • (616) 795-7530 • http://www.bowensmills.com

Midland
Alden B Dow Home Museum • 315 Post St • Midland, MI 48640 • (989) 839-2744

Michigan

Midland, cont.

Grace A Dow Memorial Library • 1710 W St Andrews Ave • Midland, MI 48640-2698 • (989) 837-3430 • http://www.midland-mi.org/gracedowlibrary

Herbert H Dow Historical Museum • 3200 Cook Rd • Midland, MI 48640

Memorial Presbyterian Church Greenhoe Library • 1310 Ashman St • Midland, MI 48640 • (989) 835-6759

Midland County Historical Society • Bradley Home Museum, 3417 W Main St • Midland, MI 48640 • (989) 631-5930 • http://www.mcfta.org/historical_society

Midland Genealogical Society • c/o Grace A Dow Library, 1710 W St. Andrews Dr • Midland, MI 48640 • (989) 835-7151 • http://members.mdn.net/billword/mgs.htm

Milan

Milan Historical Society • 775 County St • Milan, MI 48160 • (734) 439-8693

Milan Public Library • 151 Wabash St • Milan, MI 48160 • (734) 439-1240 • http://woodlands.lib.mi.us/milan

Milford

Huron Valley Genealogical Society • c/o Milford Township Library, 330 Family Dr • Milford, MI 48381-2000 • (248) 684-0845 • http://www.milford.lib.mi.us

Milford Historical Society • Historical Museum, 124 E Commerce St • Milford, MI 48381 • (248) 685-7308 • http://www.milfordhistory.org

Milford Township Library • 330 Family Dr • Milford, MI 48381-2000 • (248) 684-0845 • http://www.milford.lib.mi.us

Mio

Oscoda County Library • 430 W 8th St • Mio, MI 48647 • (989) 826-3613 • http://www.oscoda.lib.mi.us

Monroe

Genealogical Society of Monroe County • Museum & Archives, 126 S Monroe St, P.O. Box 1428 • Monroe, MI 48161-1428 • (734) 243-7137 • http://www.tdi.net/havekost/gsmc.htm

Monroe County Historical Commission • Historical Museum, 126 S Monroe St • Monroe, MI 48161 • (734) 240-7787

Monroe County Library • 3700 S Custer Rd • Monroe, MI 48161 • (734) 241-5277 • http://www.monroe.lib.mi.us

Montague

Montague Museum and Historical Association • Historical Museum, Church & Meade Sts • Montague, MI 49437 • (231) 893-8603

White Lake Area Historical Society • 8679 Sheridan • Montague, MI 49437

Montrose

Montrose Historical Association • Pioneer Museum, 114 E Hickory St, P.O. Box 577 • Montrose, MI 48457 • (810) 639-6644 • http://www.gfn.org/telemusm

Mount Clemens

French-Canadian Heritage Society of Michigan • c/o Mount Clemens Public Library, 150 Cass Ave • Mount Clemens, MI 48403 • (586) 469-6200 • http://www.macomb.lib.mi.us/mountclemens/

Greater Clinton Township Historical Society • 115 S Main St • Mount Clemens, MI 48043 • (586) 463-8690

Macomb County Genealogy Group • c/o Mount Clemens Public Library, 150 Cass Ave • Mount Clemens, MI 48043-2222 • (586) 469-6200 • http://www.macomb.lib.mi.us/mountclemens/

Macomb County Historical Society • Crocker House Museum, 15 Union St • Mount Clemens, MI 48043 • (586) 465-2488 • http://www.macombonline.com

Michigan Transit Museum • 200 Grand Ave, P.O. Box 12 • Mount Clemens, MI 48046 • (586) 463-1863 • http://www.mtmrail.com

Mount Clemens Public Library • 150 Cass Ave • Mount Clemens, MI 48043-2222 • (586) 469-6200 • http://www.libcoop.net/mountclemens

Mount Pleasant

Clarke Historical Library • Central Michigan Univ, 409 Park Library • Mount Pleasant, MI 48859 • (989) 774-3864 • http://www.lib.cmich.edu/clarke/clarke.htm

Isabella County Genealogical Society • 523 N Fancher St • Mount Pleasant, MI 48858

Saginaw Chippewa Tribal Council • 7070 E Broadway • Mount Pleasant, MI 48858 • (517) 775-4000 • http://www.sagchip.org

Veterans Memorial Library • 305 S University Ave • Mount Pleasant, MI 48858 • (989) 773-6934

Ziibiwing Center of Anishinabe Culture • 6650 E Broadway • Mount Pleasant, MI 48858 • (989) 775-4750 • http://www.sagchip.org/ziibiwing/

Mulliken

Mulliken District Library • 135 Main St, P.O. Box 246 • Mulliken, MI 48861-0246 • (517) 649-8611

Munising

Alger County Heritage Center • 1496 Washington St, P.O. Box 201 • Munising, MI 49862 • (906) 387-4308

Alger County Historical Society • Historical Museum, 203 W Onota St • Munising, MI 49862 • (906) 387-4186

Muskegon

Great Lakes Clipper Preservation Association • Historical Museum, 2098 Lakeshore Dr, P.O. Box 1370 • Muskegon, MI 49443 • (231) 755-8066

Great Lakes Naval Memorial and Museum • 1346 Bluff St, P.O. Box 1692 • Muskegon, MI 49443 • (231) 755-1230 • http://www.silversides.org

Hackley Heritage Association • 484 W Webster Ave, P.O. Box 32 • Muskegon, MI 49443-0032 • (231) 722-7578

Hackley Public Library • 316 W Webster Ave • Muskegon, MI 49440 • (616) 772-7276 • http://www.hackleylibrary.org

Lakeshore Museum Center & Archives • 430 W Clay Ave • Muskegon, MI 49440-1040 • (231) 722-0278 • http://www.muskegonmuseum.org

Mackley & Hume Historic Site • 472 W Webster Ave & 6th St • Muskegon, MI 49440 • (231) 722-7578 • http://www.muskegonmuseum.org

Muskegon County Genealogical Society • c/o Hackley Library, 316 W Webster Ave • Muskegon, MI 49440-1209 • (616) 722-7276

Muskegon Railroad Historical Society • 561 W Western Ave • Muskegon, MI 49440 • (231) 726-3657

Muskegon Heights

Muskegon County Museum of African American History • 7 E Center St, P.O. Box 3965 • Muskegon Heights, MI 49444 • (231) 777-3688

Nashville

Putnam District Library • 327 N Main St, P.O. Box 920 • Nashville, MI 49073-9578 • (517) 852-9723

Negaunee

Michigan Iron Industry Museum • 73 Forge Rd • Negaunee, MI 49866 • (906) 475-7857

Negaunee Historical Society • Historical Museum, 303 E Main St, P.O. Box 221 • Negaunee, MI 49866 • (906) 475-4614

New Baltimore
New Baltimore Historical Society • Historical Museum, 51065 Washington • New Baltimore, MI 48047 • (810) 725-4755

New Buffalo
New Buffalo Township Public Library • 33 N Thompson • New Buffalo, MI 49117 • (269) 469-2933

New Haven
Lenox Township Library • 58976 Main St, P.O. Box 0367 • New Haven, MI 48048-2685 • (586) 749-3430

New Hudson
Lyon Township Genealogical Society • c/o Lyon Township Public Library, 27025 Milford Rd, P.O. Box 326 • New Hudson, MI 48165 • (248) 437-8800 • http://www.lyon.lib.mi.us

Lyon Township Public Library • 27025 S Milford Road, P.O. Box 326 • New Hudson, MI 48165 • (248) 437-8800 • http://www.lyon.lib.mi.us

Newaygo
Newaygo County Society of History and Genealogy • Newaygo County Museum, 85 Water St • Newaygo, MI 49337 • (231) 542-9281

Newberry
Luce County Historical Society • Historical Museum, 110 E McMillan • Newberry, MI 49868 • (906) 293-5946

Niles
Fort Saint Joseph Museum • 508 E Main St, P.O. Box 487 • Niles, MI 49120 • (616) 683-4702 • http://www.ci.niles.mi.us

Four Flags Area Genealogical Society • c/o Niles Community Library, 620 E Main St, P.O. Box 414 • Niles, MI 49120-0414 • (616) 463-4696

Niles Community Library • 620 E Main St • Niles, MI 49120 • (616) 683-8545 • http://www.nileslibrary.com

North Branch
North Branch Village Orr Museum • 6714 Jefferson St • North Branch, MI 48461

Northport
Leelanau Township Public Library • 119 E Nagonaba, P.O. Box 235 • Northport, MI 49670-0235 • (231) 386-5131

Northville
Northville District Library • 212 W Cady St • Northville, MI 48167-1560 • (248) 349-3020 • http://www.northville.lib.mi.us

Northville Genealogical Society • 42254 Sunnydale Ln, P.O. Box 932 • Northville, MI 48167-0932 • (248) 348-1857 • http://www.rootsweb.com/~mings/

Northville Historical Society • Mill Race Historical Village, 215 Griswold Rd, P.O. Box 71 • Northville, MI 48167 • (248) 348-1845 • http://www.history.northville.lib.mi.us

Novi
Novi Historical Society • 24541 Hampton Ct, P.O. Box 751 • Novi, MI 48050

Novi Public Library • 4545 W Ten Mile Rd • Novi, MI 48050 • (248) 349-0720 • http://www.novi.lib.mi.us

Oak Park
Jewish Historical Society of Michigan • 24680 Rensselaer • Oak Park, MI 48237 • (313) 548-9176

Okemos
Friends of Historic Meridian • 5151 Marsh Rd, P.O. Box 155 • Okemos, MI 48864-0155 • (517) 347-7300

Onaway
Presque Isle County Genealogical Society • c/o Onaway Library, 20774 State St, P.O. Box 742 • Onaway, MI 49765 • (989) 733-6621 • http://nlc.lib.mi.us/members/presque.htm

Presque Isle District Library-Onaway Branch • 20774 State St, PO Box 742 • Onaway, MI 49765-0742 • (989) 733-6621 • http://nlc.lib.mi.us/members/presque.htm

Onsted
Onsted Community Historical Society • 1145 Sand Lake • Onsted, MI 49265 • (517) 467-2378

Ontonagon
Ontonagon County Genealogical Society • 303 Tamarack Ln • Ontonagon, MI 49953 • (906) 884-2298 • http://www.ontonagonmi.com/ocgs

Ontonagon County Historical Lighthouse Museum • general delivery • Ontonagon, MI 49953 • (906) 884-6535

Ontonagon County Historical Society • Historical Museum, 422 River St, P.O. Box 92 • Ontonagon, MI 49953-0092 • (906) 884-6165 • http://www.ontonagon.com/mi/ochs.html

Ontonagon Township Library • 311 N Steel St • Ontonagon, MI 49953-1398 • (906) 884-4411 • http://www.uproc.lib.mi.us/Ontonagon

Orchard Lake
Central Archives of Polonia • St Mary's College, 3535 Indian Tr • Orchard Lake, MI 48324 • (248) 683-0524

Greater West Bloomfield Historical Society • Museum Library, 3951 Orchard Lake Rd, P.O. Box 240514 • Orchard Lake, MI 48033 • (248) 682-2279

Polish American Historical Association • Saint Mary's College, 3535 Indian Tr • Orchard Lake, MI 48324 • (248) 683-1743 • http://www.historians.org/affiliates/polish_am_hisl_assn.htm

Orleans
Belding Area Historical Society • 5143 Orleans Rd • Orleans, MI 48865

Ortonville
Brandon Township Public Library • 304 South St • Ortonville, MI 48462 • (248) 627-6449

Ortonville Community Historical Society • 366 Mill St • Ortonville, MI 48462

Oscoda
Au Sable-Oscoda Historical Society • 114 East River Rd, P.O. Box 679 • Oscoda, MI 48750 • (989) 739-2782

Huron Shores Genealogical Society • c/o Parks Public Library, 6010 N Skeel Ave • Oscoda, MI 48750 • (517) 362-5425 • http://www.rootsweb.com/~miiosco/huronpage.html

Iosco County Genealogical Society • 1909 Bobwhite St N • Oscoda, MI 48750

Otisville
Otisville Area Historical Association • Historical Museum, P.O. Box 93 • Otisville, MI 48463

Otisville Historical Society • 8064 Wilson Rd • Otisville, MI 48463

Otsego
Otsego District Public Library • 219 S Farmer St • Otsego, MI 49078-1313 • (269) 694-9690 • http://www.otsegolibrary.org

Ovid
Ovid Historical Society • 206 N Main St • Ovid, MI 48866 • (989) 834-5517

Owosso
Movie Museum • 318 E Oliver St • Owosso, MI 48867 • (989) 725-7621

Shiawassee County Archives • P.O. Box 526 • Owosso, MI 48867-0526 • (989) 725-8549

Michigan

Owosso, cont.

Shiawassee County Genealogical Society • Matthews Bldg, P.O. Box 841 • Owosso, MI 48867 • (989) 725-8549 • http://www.shianet.org/community/orgs/segs/

Shiawassee County Historical Society • Curwood Castle Museum, 224 Curwood Castle Dr • Owosso, MI 48867 • (989) 725-0511

Shiawassee District Library-Owosso Branch • 502 W Main St • Owosso, MI 48867-2607 • (989) 725-5134 • http://www.sdl.lib.mi.us

Steam Railroading Institute Museum • 405 S Washington St, P.O. Box 665 • Owosso, MI 48867 • (989) 725-9464 • http://www.mstrp.com

Oxford

Library and Museum of Slovak Heritage, Literature and Culture • 775 W Drahner Rd, P.O. Box 167 • Oxford, MI 48371 • (248) 628-2872

Northeast Oakland Historical Society • Historical Museum, 1 N Washington St • Oxford, MI 48371 • (800) 628-8413

Palmer

Richmond Township Historical Society • Richmond Township Bldg • Palmer, MI 49871

Richmond Township Public Library • Smith St, P.O. Box 35 • Palmer, MI 49871-0035 • (906) 475-5241

Paradise

Great Lakes Shipwreck Museum • 18335 N Whitefish Point Rd • Paradise, MI 49768 • (888) 492-3747

Parchment

Parchment Community Library • 401 S Riverview Dr • Parchment, MI 49004-1200 • (616) 343-7747 • http://www.mlc.lib.mi.us/~moeningk/

Paw Paw

Paw Paw District Library • 609 W Michigan Ave • Paw Paw, MI 49079 • (269) 657-3800 • http://www.pawpaw.lib.mi.us

Pelkie

Hanka Homestead Museum • P.O. Box 10 • Pelkie, MI 49958 • (906) 344-2601

Laird Township Historical Society • Route 1, Box 59A • Pelkie, MI 49958 • (906) 338-2680

Sturgeon Valley Historical Society • HCO1, Box 7 • Pelkie, MI 49958 • (906) 353-7529

Pentwater

Pentwater Township Library • 402 E Park, P.O. Box 946 • Pentwater, MI 49449-0946 • (231) 869-8581 • http://www.pentwaterlibrary.com

Peshawbestwon

Eyaawing Museum • 2605 NW Bayshore Dr • Peshawbestwon, MI 49682-9275 • (231) 534-7764

Petoskey

Emmet County Genealogical Society • 423 Beech St, P.O. Box 2476 • Petoskey, MI 49770

Little Traverse Bay Band of Odawa Indians • 1345 US 31 N, P.O. Box 246 • Petoskey, MI 49770 • (616) 439-3809 • http://www.ltbbodawa-nsn.gov

Little Traverse Historical Society • Historical Museum, 100 Depot Ct, P.O. Box 162 • Petoskey, MI 49770 • (231) 347-2620 • http://www.petoskeymuseum.org

Petosky Public Library • 451 E Mitchell St • Petoskey, MI 49770 • (231) 347-4211 • http://www.petoskeylibrary.org

Pickford

Pickford Historical Society • P.O. Box 81 • Pickford, MI 49774 • (906) 647-6488

Pigeon

Pigeon District Library • 7236 Nitz St, P.O. Box 357 • Pigeon, MI 48755-0357 • (989) 453-2341 • http://www.pigeondistrictlibrary.com

Pinckney

Pinckney Community Public Library • 350 Mower Rd • Pinckney, MI 48169 • (734) 878-3888 • http://www.pinckney.lib.mi.us

Plymouth

Plymouth District Library • 223 S Main St • Plymouth, MI 48170 • (734) 453-0750 • http://plymouthlibrary.org

Plymouth Historical Society • Historical Museum, 155 S Main St • Plymouth, MI 48170 • (734) 455-8940 • http://www.plymouthhistory.org

Pontiac

Oakland County Pioneer and Historical Society • Pine Grove Historical Museum, 405 Cesar F Chavez Ave • Pontiac, MI 48342-1068 • (248) 338-6732 • http://www.wwnet.net/~ocphs/

Oakland County Research Library • 1200 N Telegraph Rd • Pontiac, MI 48341-0453 • (248) 858-0738 • http://www.oakland.lib.mi.us

Pontiac Area Historical and Genealogical Society • c/o Pontiac Public Library, 60 East Pike, P.O. Box 430901 • Pontiac, MI 48343-0901 • (248) 334-9929 • http://members.tripod.com/ginblock/pahags.html

Pontiac Public Library • 60 E Pike St • Pontiac, MI 48058 • (248) 758-3942 • http://www.pontiac.lib.mi.us

Port Austin

House of Seven Gables Museum • 7930 Huron City Rd • Port Austin, MI 48467 • (517) 428-4123

Huron City Museum • 7995 Pioneer Dr • Port Austin, MI 48467-9400 • (989) 428-4123 • http://www.huroncitymuseums.org

Port Austin Area Historical Society • 335 Washington, P.O. Box 137 • Port Austin, MI 48467 • (517) 738-8623

Port Austin Township Library • 114 Railroad St, P.O. Box 325 • Port Austin, MI 48467-0325 • (989) 738-7212

Port Huron

Huron County Genealogical Society • 2843 Electric Ave • Port Huron, MI 48060

Knowlton's Ice Museum • 317 Grand River, P.O. Box 610234 • Port Huron, MI 48061 • (810) 987-5441

Port Huron Museum • 1115 6th St • Port Huron, MI 48060 • (810) 982-0891 • http://www.phmuseum.org

Saint Clair County Family History Group • 1115 6th St, P.O. Box 611483 • Port Huron, MI 48061-1483 • (810) 982-0441

Saint Clair County Library • 210 McMorran Blvd • Port Huron, MI 48060-4098 • (810) 987-7323 • http://www.sccl.lib.mi.us

Port Sanilac

Sanilac County Historical Society • Loop-Harrison Historic House Museum, 228 S Ridge St & State Hwy M-25, P.O. Box 158 • Port Sanilac, MI 48469 • (810) 622-9946 • http://www.sanilacmuseum.com

Sanilac District Library • 7130 Main St, P.O. Box 525 • Port Sanilac, MI 48469 • (810) 622-8623 • http://www.sanilacdistrictlibrary.lib.mi.us

Portage

Air Zoo Aviation Museum of Kalamazoo • 6151 Portage Rd • Portage, MI 49002 • (269) 382-6555 • http://www.airzoo.com

Portage District Library • 300 Library Ln • Portage, MI 49002 • (269) 329-4544 • http://www.portagelibrary.info/

Portland

Clinton County Historical Commission • 8565 Grange • Portland, MI 48875 • (989) 587-6839

Ionia County Genealogical Society • 3011 Knoll Rd • Portland, MI 48875 • http://www.rootsweb.com/~miionia/icgshome.htm

Portland Area Historical Society • 344 Kent St • Portland, MI 48875 • (517) 647-6305

Portland District Library • 334 Kent St • Portland, MI 48875-1735 • (517) 647-6981

Presque Isle
Presque Isle Township Museum • 4500 E Grand Lake Rd, P.O. Box 208 • Presque Isle, MI 49777

Prudenville
Roscommon County Genealogical Society • 2597 S Gladwin Rd • Prudenville, MI 48651 • (989) 366-1774

Redford
Redford Township Historical and Genealogical Society • c/o Redford Community Ctr, 12121 Hemingway • Redford, MI 48239-9998

Reed City
Old Rugged Cross Historical Society • 4918 Park St, P.O. Box 27 • Reed City, MI 49677 • (616) 832-5431

Read City Area Genealogical Society • 780 N Park St, P.O. Box 27 • Reed City, MI 49677-0027 • (231) 832-5431

Reed City Public Library • 410 W Upton Ave • Reed City, MI 49677-1152 • (231) 832-2131 • http://www.multimag.com/reedcity/library.html

Richland
Richland Community Library • 8951 Park St • Richland, MI 49083-9630 • (269) 629-9085 • http://www.richlandlibrary.org

Richmond
Lois Wagner Memorial Library • 35200 Division • Richmond, MI 48062 • (586) 727-2665 • http://www.libcoop.net/richmond/

Richmond Area Historical and Genealogical Society • P.O. Box 68 • Richmond, MI 48062

River Rouge
River Rouge Historical Museum • 10750 W Jefferson Ave • River Rouge, MI 48218

River Rouge Public Library • 221 Burke • River Rouge, MI 48218 • (313) 843-2040 • http://www.river-rouge.lib.mi.us

Rochester
Kresge Library • Oakland University, 2200 N Squirrel Rd • Rochester, MI 48309 • (248) 370-4426 • http://www.kl.oakland.edu

Meadow Brook Hall Museum • Oakland Univ • Rochester, MI 48309 • (248) 364-6200 • http://www.meadowbrookhall.org

Oakland Township Historical Society • 4075 Collins Rd • Rochester, MI 48064 • (248) 651-4440

Rochester Hills Public Library • 500 Olde Towne Rd • Rochester, MI 48307-2043 • (248) 650-7130 • http://www.rhpl.org

Rochester-Avon Historical Society • P.O. Box 783 • Rochester, MI 48307

Rochester Hills
Rochester Avon Historical Society • P.O. Box 783 • Rochester Hills, MI 48063 • (313) 651-2433

Rochester Hills Museum • Van Hoosen Farm, 1005 Van Hoosen Rd • Rochester Hills, MI 48309 • (248) 656-4663 • http://www.rochesterhills.org

Rockford
Grattan Township Historical Society • 7880 Ramsdell • Rockford, MI 49341

Kent District Library-Rockford Branch • 140 E Bridge St • Rockford, MI 49341 • (616) 647-3940

Oakfield Pioneer Heritage Society • 9751 15 Mile Rd • Rockford, MI 49341

Rockford Area Historical Society • P.O. Box 781 • Rockford, MI 49341-9112

Rockland
Old Victoria Restoration Site Museum • Victoria Dam Rd, P.O. Box 43 • Rockland, MI 49950 • (906) 886-2617

Rockland Historical Society • Historical Museum, Hwy 45 • Rockland, MI 49960

Rockwood
Rockwood Area Historical Society • P.O. Box 68 • Rockwood, MI 48173

Sons of the Spanish-American War Veterans • 32028 Mount Vernon • Rockwood, MI 48173-9650 • (734) 379-4996 • http://www.spanamwar.com/SSAWV.htm

Rogers City
Presque Isle County Historical Museum • 176 W Michigan Ave, P.O. Box 175 • Rogers City, MI 49779 • (989) 734-4121 • http://www.ohwy.com/mi/p/priscomu.htm

Presque Isle District Library • 181 E Erie St • Rogers City, MI 49779-1709 • (517) 734-2477

Romeo
Romeo Historical Society • Historical Museum, 290 N Main St, P.O. Box 412 • Romeo, MI 48065 • (586) 752-4111

Romeo Historical Society • 132 Church St, P.O. Box 412 • Romeo, MI 48065 • (586) 336-9201

Romulus
Romulus Historical Museum • P.O. Box 74386 • Romulus, MI 48174-0386

Romulus Historical Society • c/o Romulus Public Library, 11121 Wayne Rd • Romulus, MI 48174 • (734) 941-0775

Rose City
Ogemaw District Library • 107 W Main St, P.O. Box 427 • Rose City, MI 48654-0427 • (989) 685-3300 • http://www.wplc.org

Rose City Area Historical Society • c/o Ogemaw District Library, 107 W Main, P.O. Box 427 • Rose City, MI 48654 • (989) 685-3300

Roseville
Genealogical Society of Flemish Americans • 18740 13 Mile Rd • Roseville, MI 48066 • (586) 776-9579 • http://www.rootsweb.com/~gfsa/

Roseville Historical and Genealogical Society • c/o Roseville Public Library, 29777 Gratiot Ave • Roseville, MI 48066 • (586) 445-5407 • http://www.macomb.lib.mi.us/roseville/ historical_ genealogical_ society.htm

Roseville Public Library • 29777 Gratiot Ave • Roseville, MI 48066 • (586) 445-5407 • http://www.libcoop.net/roseville

Royal Oak
Royal Oak Historical Society • 3031 Maplewood • Royal Oak, MI 48073

Royal Oak Public Library • 211 E Eleven Mile Rd, P.O. Box 494 • Royal Oak, MI 48068 • (248) 246-3727 • http://www.ci.royal-oak.mi.us/library

Royal Oak Women's Historical Guild • Starr House, 3123 N Main • Royal Oak, MI 48073

Saginaw
American Historical Society of Germans from Russia, Saginaw Valley Chapter • 2876 N Michigan Ave • Saginaw, MI 48604 • (989) 752-0441 • http://www.ahsgr.org/Chapters/saginaw_valley_chapter.htm

Historical Society of Saginaw County • Castle Museum, 500 Federal Ave, P.O. Box 390 • Saginaw, MI 48606 • (989) 752-2861 • http://www.castlemuseum.org

Michigan

Saginaw, cont.
Public Libraries of Saginaw • 505 Janes Ave • Saginaw, MI 48607 • (989) 755-0904 • http://www.saginawlibrary.org

Saginaw Genealogical Society • c/o Saginaw Public Library, 505 Janes Ave • Saginaw, MI 48507 • (989) 755-0904

Saint Charles
Saint Charles District Library • 104 W Spruce St • Saint Charles, MI 48655-1238 • (989) 865-9451

Saint Charles Historical Society • Saginaw St • Saint Charles, MI 48655

Saint Clair Shores
Historical Society of Saint Clair Shores • c/o Saint Clair Shores Public Library & Museum, 22500 Eleven Mile Rd • Saint Clair Shores, MI 48081-1307 • (586) 771-9020

Saint Clair Shores Genealogy Group • c/o Saint Clair Shores Public Library & Museum, 22500 Eleven Mile Rd • Saint Clair Shores, MI 48081 • (586) 771-9020

Saint Clair Shores Historical Commission • c/o Saint Clair Shores Public Library & Museum, 22500 Eleven Mile Rd • Saint Clair Shores, MI 48081-1399 • (586) 771-9020

Saint Clair Shores Public Library • 22500 Eleven Mile Rd • Saint Clair Shores, MI 48081-1399 • (586) 771-9020 • http://www.libcoop.net/stclairshores/

Saint Ignace
Father Marquette National Memorial Museum • 720 Church St • Saint Ignace, MI 49781 • (906) 643-8620

Fort DeBuade Indian Museum • 334 N State St • Saint Ignace, MI 49781

Marquette Mission Park and Museum of Ojibwa Culture • 500-566 N State St • Saint Ignace, MI 49781 • (906) 643-9161 • http://www.stignace.com/attractions/ojibwa

Saint James
Beaver Island Historical Society • Main & Forest Sts • Saint James, MI 49782 • (616) 448-2254

Saint Johns
Briggs Public Library • 108 E Railroad St • Saint Johns, MI 48879-1526 • (989) 224-4702

Clinton County Genealogical Society • 110 Lewis St, P.O. Box 23 • Saint Johns, MI 48879

Clinton County Historical Society • Paine-Gillam-Scott Museum, 106 Maple Ave, P.O. Box 174 • Saint Johns, MI 48879 • (989) 224-2894

Genealogists of the Clinton County Historical Society • P.O. Box 23 • Saint Johns, MI 48879-0023 • (517) 482-1291 x147

Saint Joseph
Fort Miami Heritage Society • Priscilla U Byrns Heritage Center, 708 Market St • Saint Joseph, MI 49085 • (269) 983-1191 • http://www.fortmiami.org

Genealogical Association of Southwestern Michigan • P.O. Box 573 • Saint Joseph, MI 49085 • (616) 429-7914

Maud Preston Palenske Memorial Library • 500 Market St • Saint Joseph, MI 49085 • (269) 983-7167 • http://www.stjoseph.lib.mi.us

Saint Louis
Saint Louis Historical Society • Historical Museum, 110 E Crawford St • Saint Louis, MI 48880-1522 • (989) 681-4636 • http://www.rootsweb.com/~mislahs

Theodore Austin Cutler Memorial Library • 312 Michigan Ave • Saint Louis, MI 48880 • (989) 681-5141

Salem
Salem Area Historical Society • P.O. Box 75011 • Salem, MI 48175 • (810) 437-5007

Saline
Saline Area Historical Society • Historical Museum, 2515 Textile Rd, P.O. Box 302 • Saline, MI 48176 • (724) 429-9621

Saline District Library • 555 N Maple Rd • Saline, MI 48176 • (734) 429-5450 • http://www.saline.lib.mi.us

Sandusky
Sandusky Public Library • 55 E Sanilac Rd, P.O. Box 271 • Sandusky, MI 48471-0271 • (810) 648-2644 • http://www.sandusky.lib.mi.us

Sanford
Sanford Historical Society • N Saginaw & Smith Sts, P.O. Box 243 • Sanford, MI 48657 • (989) 687-2771

Saugatuck
Saugatuck-Douglas Historical Society • 735 Park St • Saugatuck, MI 49453 • (269) 857-7900

Saugatuck-Douglas Museum • 128 Van Dalson, P.O. Box 378 • Saugatuck, MI 49453 • (616) 857-5605

Sault Sainte Marie
Bayliss Public Library • 541 Library Dr • Sault Sainte Marie, MI 49783 • (906) 632-9331 • http://www.uproc.lib.mi.us/bpl

Chippewa County Genealogical Society • general delivery • Sault Sainte Marie, MI 49783-0324

Chippewa County Historical Society • 409 Ashmun St, P.O. Box 342 • Sault Sainte Marie, MI 49783-0324 • (906) 635-7082

Great Lakes Shipwreck Historical Society • Historical Museum, 400 W Portage Ave • Sault Sainte Marie, MI 49783 • (906) 635-1742 • http://www.shipwreckmuseum.com

Kenneth J Shouldice Library • Lake Superior State University, 906 Ryan St • Sault Sainte Marie, MI 49783 • (906) 635-2815 • http://www.lssu.edu/library

Sault de Sainte Marie Historical Sites • 501 E Water St, P.O. Box 1668 • Sault Sainte Marie, MI 49783 • (906) 632-3658 • http://www.thevalleycamp.com

Sault Sainte Marie Chippewa Tribal Council • 2864 Ashman St • Sault Sainte Marie, MI 49783 • (906) 635-6050 • http://www.sootribe.org

Sault Sainte Marie Foundation for Culture and History • 209 E Portage Ave, P.O. Box 627 • Sault Sainte Marie, MI 49783 • (906) 632-1999

Schoolcraft
Schoolcraft Historical Society • 16278 Prairie Rounde • Schoolcraft, MI 49087

Sebawaing
Luckhard Indian Museum • Indian Mission, 612 E Bay St • Sebawaing, MI 48759 • (989) 883-2539

Sebewaing Township Library • 41 North Center St • Sebewaing, MI 48759-1406 • (989) 883-3520

Shelfridge ANGB
Garrison-Selfridge Library • Shelfridge Air National Guard Base, Bldg 780 W • Shelfridge ANGB, MI 48045-5016 • (586) 307-5238

Shepherd
Shepherd Area Genealogical Society • 7859 E Walton Rd • Shepherd, MI 48883

Shepherd Area Historical Society • 3426 E Blanchard Rd, P.O. Box 505 • Shepherd, MI 48883 • (989) 828-5881

Skanee
Arvon Township Historical Society • RR1, Box 886 • Skanee, MI 49962 • (906) 524-6934

Arvon Township Historical Society • P.O. Box 151 • Skanee, MI 49962 • (906)524-6934

Sodus

Log Cabin Society of Michigan • 3503 Edwards Rd • Sodus, MI 49126 • (269) 925-3836

Sodus Township Library • 3776 Naomi Rd • Sodus, MI 49126-9714 • (269) 925-0903

South Haven

Dr Liberty Hyde Bailey Birthsite Museum • 903 S Bailey Ave • South Haven, MI 49090 • (616) 637-3251

Michigan Maritime Museum • 260 Dyckman Ave • South Haven, MI 49090 • (269) 637-8078 • http://www.michiganmaritimemusem.org

South Haven Memorial Library • 314 Broadway • South Haven, MI 49090 • (269) 637-2403

South Lyon

Salem-South Lyon District Library • 9800 Pontiac Trail • South Lyon, MI 48178-1307 • (248) 437-6431 • http://salemsouthlyonlibrary.info

South Lyon Area Historical Society • 300 Dorothy St, P.O. Box 263 • South Lyon, MI 48178 • (248) 437-9929

South Range

Copper Range Historical Museum • Champion St • South Range, MI 49963 • (906) 482-6125

Southfield

Finnish American Historical Society of Michigan • 19885 Melrose • Southfield, MI 48075 • (248) 354-1994

Jewish Historical Society of Michigan • 29699 Southfield Rd #217 • Southfield, MI 48076

Southfield Historical Society • Historical Museum, 26082 Berg Rd • Southfield, MI 48034 • (248) 354-4711

Southgate

Southgate Historical Society • Historical Museum, 14400 Dix-Toledo Rd • Southgate, MI 48195

Sparta

Algoma Township Historical Society • 11731 Pine Island Dr • Sparta, MI 49345

Sparta Township Library • 80 N Union St • Sparta, MI 49345 • (616) 887-9937 • http://www.lakeland.lib.mi.us/sparta

Stanton

White Pine Library • 106 E Walnut • Stanton, MI 48888-9294 • (989) 831-4327

Sterling Heights

Sterling Heights Genealogical and Historical Society • c/o Sterling Heights Public Library, 40255 Dodge Park Rd, P.O. Box 1154 • Sterling Heights, MI 48311-1154 • (586) 977-6267 • http://www.rootsweb.com/~mishghs/

Sterling Heights Public Library • 40255 Dodge Park Rd • Sterling Heights, MI 48313-4140 • (586) 446-2642 • http://www.shpl.net

United Romanian Society • 14512 Royal Dr • Sterling Heights, MI 48312-4368 • http://feefhs.org/ro/urs/frg-urs.html

Stevensville

Lincoln Township Public Library • 2099 W John Beers Rd • Stevensville, MI 49127 • (269) 429-9575 • http://www.lincolnpublic.lib.mi.us

Stockbridge

Stockbridge Area Genealogical and Historical Society • P.O. Box 966 • Stockbridge, MI 49285

Waterloo Area Historical Society • Historical Museum, P.O. Box 37 • Stockbridge, MI 49285 • (517) 596-2254

Sturgis

Sturgis Public Library • 255 North St • Sturgis, MI 49091 • (269) 659-7224

Tri-State Genealogical Society • c/o Sturgis Public Library, 255 North St • Sturgis, MI 49091 • (269) 659-7224

Suttons Bay

Grand Traverse Band of Ottawa and Chippewa Indians • 2300 Stallman Rd • Suttons Bay, MI 49682 • (231) 271-4906 • http://www.gtb.nsn.us

Tawas City

Iosco-Arenac Regional Library • 951 Turtle Rd • Tawas City, MI 48763 • (989) 362-2651

Tecumseh

Tecumseh Area Historical Society • 302 E Chicago Blvd, P.O Box 26 • Tecumseh, MI 49286 • (517) 423-2374 • http://www.HistoricTecumseh.com

Tecumseh Public Library • 215 N Ottawa St • Tecumseh, MI 49286-1564 • (517) 423-2238 • http://www.tecumseh.lib.mi.us

Temperance

Monroe County Library System-Bedford Branch • 8575 Jackman Rd • Temperance, MI 48182 • (734) 847-6747

Three Oaks

Three Oaks Township Library • 3 N Elm St • Three Oaks, MI 49128-1303 • (616) 756-5621

Three Rivers

Three Rivers Genealogy Club • 13724 Spence Rd • Three Rivers, MI 49093

Three Rivers Public Library • 920 W Michigan St • Three Rivers, MI 49093-2137 • (269) 273-8666 • http://threeriverslibrary.org

Traverse City

Con Foster Museum • 181 E Grandview Pkwy • Traverse City, MI 49684 • (231) 922-4905

Grand Traverse Genealogical Society • 430 S Airport Rd E, P.O. Box 2015 • Traverse City, MI 49685-2015 • (231) 995-9388 • http://www.rootsweb.com/~migtags/gtag.htm

Grand Traverse Pioneer and Historical Society • 232 Front St, P.O. Box 1108 • Traverse City, MI 49685

Maritime Heritage Alliance • 322 6th St • Traverse City, MI 49684-2414

Mark and Helen Osterlin Library • Northwestern Michigan College, 1701 E Front St • Traverse City, MI 49686-3061 • (231) 995-1540 • http://www.nmc.edu/library

Northwestern Michigan College Genealogy Group • c/o Mark & Helen Osterlin Library, Northwestern Michigan College, 1701 E Front St • Traverse City, MI 49684 • (616) 922-1060

Traverse Area District Library • 610 Woodmere Ave • Traverse City, MI 49686 • (231) 932-8500 • http://tadl.tcnet.org

Trenton

Estonian Educational Society of Detroit • P.O. Box 344 • Trenton, MI 48183 • (734) 676-8783

Trenton Historical Museum • 306 St Joseph • Trenton, MI 48183 • (313) 675-4340

Trenton Historical Society • 2309 Boxford • Trenton, MI 48183 • (734) 676-4038

Michigan

Troy
Troy Historical Society • Troy Museum & Historical Village, 60 W Wattles Rd • Troy, MI 48098 • (248) 524-3570 • http://www.ci.troy.mi.us

Troy Public Library • 510 W Big Beaver Rd • Troy, MI 48084-5289 • (248) 524-3538 • http://www.libcoop.net/troy

Union City
Branch District Library-Union Township Branch • 221 N Broadway • Union City, MI 49094-1153 • (517) 741-5061 • http://www.brnlibrary.org

Union City Genealogical Society • 510 Saint Joseph St • Union City, MI 49094 • (517) 741-3597

Union City Historical Society • 407 Broadway • Union City, MI 49094

Union City Society for Historic Preservation • 210 Charlotte St • Union City, MI 49094 • (517) 741-7347

Union Pier
Wilkinson Heritage Museum • 15300 Red Arrow Hwy • Union Pier, MI 49129 • (616) 469-2090

Utica
Utica Public Library • 7530 Auburn Rd • Utica, MI 48317-5216 • (586) 731-4141 • http://www.libcoop.net/utica

Vermontville
Kalamo Township Historical Society • 8889 Spore Hwy • Vermontville, MI 49096 • (517) 726-0408

Vermontville Historical Society • 101 N Main St • Vermontville, MI 49096

Vicksburg
Searchers • 14300 Vicksburg Ave • Vicksburg, MI 49097-9630 • (616) 778-3712

Vicksburg District Library • 215 S Michigan Ave • Vicksburg, MI 49097 • (269) 649-1648 • http://www.vicksburglibrary.org

Vicksburg Historical Society • 302 N Richardson • Vicksburg, MI 49097 • (616) 649-2876

Vulcan
Iron Mountain Iron Mine Museum • Hwy US 2 • Vulcan, MI 49801 • (906) 774-7914 • http://www.ironmountainironmine.com

Wakefield
Wakefield Historical Society • 306 Sunday Lake St • Wakefield, MI 49968 • (906) 224-1045

Walled Lake
Commerce Township Area Historical Society • 207 Liberty St, P.O. Box 264 • Walled Lake, MI 48088 • (248) 624-2554

Wixom Historical Society • Historical Museum, 2111 Park Place Dr • Walled Lake, MI 48390

Warren
British Heritage Society • 4177 Garrick Ave • Warren, MI 48091 • (810) 757-4177

Italian American Cultural Society • 28111 Imperial • Warren, MI 48063 • http://www.italianamerica.org

Ukranian-American Museum • 26601 Ryan Rd • Warren, MI 48091 • (248) 757-8130

Warren Historical Society • P.O. Box 1773 • Warren, MI 48090-1773 • (313) 754-4574

Warren Public Library-Walt Whitman Branch • 1 City Square, Ste 100 • Warren, MI 48093 • (586) 751-0771 • http://www.libcoop.net/warren/branches/www/html

Washington
Greater Washington Area Historical Society • 58230 Van Dyke • Washington, MI 48094 • (313) 652-2458

Washington Historical Museum • 58230 Van Dyke Rd • Washington, MI 48094

Waterford
Waterford Historical Society • 4490 Hatchery Rd • Waterford, MI 48329 • (248) 673-0342

Waterford Township Public Library • 5168 Civic Center Dr • Waterford, MI 48329 • (248) 674-4831 • http://www.waterford.lib.mi.us

Waterloo Township
Waterloo Area Farm Museum • 9998 Waterloo-Munith Rd • Waterloo Township, MI 49240 • (517) 596-2254

Watersmeet
Lac Vieux Desert Band of Lake Superior Chippewa Indians • 23950 Choate Rd, P.O. Box 249 • Watersmeet, MI 49969 • (906) 358-4940 • http://www.lvdtribal.com

Watervliet
Watervliet District Library • 333 N Main St, P.O. Box 217 • Watervliet, MI 49098-9793 • (269) 463-6382 • http://www.ameritech.net/users/hartmanlr/

Wayland
Henika Public Library • 149 S Main St • Wayland, MI 49348-1208 • (269) 792-2891 • http://wayland.llcoop.org

Then and Now Society of East Allegan County • 532 N Main • Wayland, MI 49348-1043

Wayland Area Tree Tracers Genealogical Society • 129 W Cedar St • Wayland, MI 49348 • (616) 792-2891

Wayne
Wayne Historical Society • Wayne Historical Museum, 1 Town Square • Wayne, MI 48184 • (734) 722-0113 • http://www.ci.wayne.mi.us/museum/php

West Bloomfield
Greater West Bloomfield Historical Society • 3951 Orchard Lake Rd • West Bloomfield, MI 48323 • (248) 682-2279

Holocaust Memorial Center Museum • Jewish Community Center of Metropolitan Detroit, 6600 W Maple Rd • West Bloomfield, MI 48322 • (248) 661-1000 • http://www.jccdet.org

Jewish Genealogical Society of Detroit • 3345 Buckingham Trail W • West Bloomfield, MI 48033

Jewish Genealogical Society of Michigan • 4275 Strathdale Ln, P.O. Box 251693 • West Bloomfield, MI 48325-1693 • (248) 661-0668 • http://www.jgsmi.org

Jewish Historical Society of Michigan • Historical Museum, 6600 W Maple Rd • West Bloomfield, MI 48033 • (248) 661-1000 • http://www.michjewishhistory.org

Temple Israel Library • 5725 Walnut Lake Rd • West Bloomfield, MI 48323 • (248) 661-5700 • http://www.temple-israel.org

West Branch
Ogemaw County Historical Museum • 123 S 5th St, P.O. Box 734 • West Branch, MI 48661-0734

Ogemaw Genealogical and Historical Society • c/o West Branch Public Library, 119 N 4th St • West Branch, MI 48661-0734 • (989) 345-2235

West Branch Public Library • 119 N 4th St • West Branch, MI 48661 • (989) 345-2235 • http://www.westbranchlibrary.com

Westland
Wayne County Irish Society • 31985 Cowan • Westland, MI 48185 • (313) 261-9267

White Cloud

Newaygo County Society of History and Genealogy • c/o White Cloud Library, 1038 Wilcox Ave, P.O. Box 68 • White Cloud, MI 49349-0068 • (616) 689-6631

White Cloud Community Library • 1038 Wilcox Ave, P.O. Box 995 • White Cloud, MI 49349-0995 • (231) 689-6631 • http://www.whitecloudlibrary.net

White Lake

White Lake Historical Society • 7525 Highland Rd • White Lake, MI 48383 • http://www.whitelaketwp.com

White Pigeon

Saint Joseph Genealogical Society • 71062 Roosevelt Rd, P.O. Box 486 • White Pigeon, MI 49099

Whitehall

White Lake Community Library • 3900 White Lake Dr • Whitehall, MI 49461-9257 • (231) 894-9531

Wilson

Hannahville Potawatomi Indian Community • N-15019 Hannaville B1 Road • Wilson, MI 49896-9717 • (906) 466-9230 • http://www.hannahville.com

Wixom

Wixom Historical Society • 49045 Pontiac Tr • Wixom, MI 48096

Wyandotte

Bacon Memorial Public Library • 45 Vinewood St • Wyandotte, MI 48192-5221 • (734) 246-8347 • http://www.baconlibrary.org

Wyandotte Historical Society • Ford-McNichol Home Museum, 2610 Biddle Ave • Wyandotte, MI 48192 • (734) 324-7297 • http://www.wyandotte.net

Wyoming

Kent District Library-Wyoming Branch & City Archives • 3350 Michael SW • Wyoming, MI 49509 • (616) 530-3183

Wyoming Historical and Cultural Commission • 1155 28th St SW, P.O. Box 905 • Wyoming, MI 49509 • (616) 534-7671

Ypsilanti

Michigan Antique Fire Equipment Museum • 110 W Cross St • Ypsilanti, MI 48197 • (734) 547-0663 • http://www.michiganfirehousemuseum.org

Yankee Air Force Museum • Hangar 2, Willow Run Airport • Ypsilanti, MI 48198 • (734) 483-4030 • http://www.yankeeairmuseum.org

Ypsilanti District Library • 5577 Whitaker Rd • Ypsilanti, MI 48197 • (734) 482-4110 • http://www.ypsilibrary.org

Ypsilanti Historical Society • Historical Museum, 220 N Huron St • Ypsilanti, MI 48197 • (734) 482-4990 • http://www.ypsilantihistoricalsociety.org

Zeeland

Dekker Huis and Zeeland Historical Museum • 37 E Main St, P.O. Box 165 • Zeeland, MI 49464 • (616) 772-4079 • http://www.zeelandmuseum.org

First Christian Reformed Church Library • 15 S Church St • Zeeland, MI 49464 • (616) 772-2866

Zeeland Historical Society • Historical Museum, 37 E Main Ave, P.O. Box 165 • Zeeland, MI 49464 • (616) 772-4079 • http://www.zeelandmuseum.org

Michigan

Ada

Memorial Museum • 12 1st St E • Ada, MN 56510 • (218) 784-4989

Norman County Historical Society • 409 E 1st Ave, P.O. Box 303 • Ada, MN 56510 • (218) 784-7311

Adolph

Saint Louis County Historical Society • general delivery • Adolph, MN 55701 • (218) 726-8526

Afton

Afton Historical Society • Historical Museum, 3165 Saint Croix Tr, P.O. Box 178 • Afton, MN 55001 • (612) 436-8895 • http://www.pressenter.com/~aftonhist

Aitkin

Aitkin County Historical Society • Depot Museum, 20 Pacific St SW, P.O. Box 215 • Aitkin, MN 56431 • (218) 927-3348

Akeley

Paul Bunyon Historical Society • Historical Museum, Main St • Akeley, MN 56433 • (218) 652-2725

Albany

Albany Heritage Society • P.O. Box 550 • Albany, MN 56307 • (320) 845-2344

Albany Historical Society • P.O. Box 25 • Albany, MN 56307 • (320) 845-2982

Albert Lea

Albert Lea Public Library • 211 E Clark St • Albert Lea, MN 56007 • (507) 377-4350 • http://www.city.albertlea.org

Freeborn County Genealogical Society • 1033 Bridge Ave • Albert Lea, MN 56007-2205 • (507) 256-4561 • http://www.fcgs.org

Freeborn County Historical Society • Historical Museum and Village, 1031 N Bridge Ave • Albert Lea, MN 56007 • (507) 373-8003 • http://www.smig.net/fchm

Alden

Alden Community Historical Society • Alden Museum, 115 N Broadway, P.O. Box 323 • Alden, MN 56009 • (507) 874-3462

Alexandria

Douglas County Genealogical Society • 1219 Nokomis St, P.O. Box 505 • Alexandria, MN 56308-0505 • (320) 763-3896 • http://www.rootsweb.com/~mndougla/dcgs.html

Douglas County Historical Society • Knute Nelson Home, 1219 S Nokomis • Alexandria, MN 56308 • (320) 762-0382 • http://www.rea-alp.com/~historic

Kensington Runestone Museum • 206 N Broadway, P.O. Box 517 • Alexandria, MN 56308 • (320) 763-3160 • http://www.runestonemuseum.org

Angle Inlet

North West Angle #33 First Nation (Ojibwe) • general delivery • Angle Inlet, MN 56711 • (807) 733-2200

Annandale

Minnesota Pioneer Park Library • 725 Pioneer Park Tr, P.O. Box 219 • Annandale, MN 55302 • (763) 274-8489 • http://www.pioneerpark.org

Anoka

Anoka County Genealogical Society • 2135 3rd Ave N • Anoka, MN 55303 • (763) 421-0600 • http://freepages.genealogy.rootsweb.ancestry.com/~relativememory/

Anoka County Historical Society • Historical Museum, 2135 3rd Ave N • Anoka, MN 55303-2421 • (763) 421-0600 • http://www.ac-hs.org

Anoka County History Center • 2135 3rd Ave N • Anoka, MN 55303 • (763) 421-0600 • http://www.ac-hs.org

Arden Hills

Bethel Seminary Library • 3949 Bethel Dr • Arden Hills, MN 55112 • (651) 638-6184 • http://www.bethel.edu/seminary_academics/semlibrary/home.htm

Askov

Pine County Historical Society • Depot Museum, 3851 Glacier Rd, P.O. Box 213 • Askov, MN 55704 • (320) 838-3792

Atwater

Atwater Area History Society • 108 N 3rd St • Atwater, MN 56209 • (320) 974-8284

Austin

Austin Public Library • 323 4th Ave NE • Austin, MN 55912-3370 • (507) 433-2391 • http://www.ci.austin.mn.us/Library/libhome.htm

Mower County Genealogical Society • P.O. Box 145 • Austin, MN 55912-0145 • (507) 433-7859

Mower County Historical Society • 1303 6th Ave SW, P.O. Box 804 • Austin, MN 55912 • (507) 437-6082 • http://www.mowercountyhistory.org

SPAM Museum • 1937 SPAM Blvd • Austin, MN 55912 • (800) 444-5713 • http://www.spammmuseum.com

Babbitt

Babbitt Public Library • 71 South Dr • Babbitt, MN 55706-1232 • (218) 827-3345 • http://arrowhead.library.mn.us

Bagley

Clearwater County Historical Society • 24 1st St, P.O. Box 241 • Bagley, MN 56621 • (218) 785-2000 • http://www.rrv.net/bagleyweb/histcult.htm

Barnesville

Barnesville Heritage Society • P.O. Box 126 • Barnesville, MN 56514 • (218) 354-2364

Baudette

Lake of the Woods Historical Society • Historical Museum, 119 8th Ave SE, P.O. Box 808 • Baudette, MN 56623 • (218) 534-1200

Bayport

Bayport Public Library • 582 N 4th St • Bayport, MN 55003-1111 • (651) 439-7454 • http://www.bayportlibrary.org

Becker

Sherburne County Historical Society • Historical Museum, 13122 1st St • Becker, MN 55308 • (763) 261-4433 • http://www.rootsweb.com/~mnschs/

Belle Plaine

Belle Plaine Historical Society • 410 N Cedar St, P.O. Box 73 • Belle Plaine, MN 56011 • (952) 873-6109

Belview

Belview Depot School Museum • general delivery • Belview, MN 56214

Bemidji

A C Clark Library • Bemidji State Univ, 1500 Birchmont Dr NE • Bemidji, MN 56601-2699 • (218) 755-3342 • http://www.bemidjistate.edu/library

Beltrami County Historical Society • History Center, 130 Minnesota Ave SW, P.O. Box 683 • Bemidji, MN 56619-0683 • (218) 444-3376 • http://www.paulbunyan.net/users/depot.html; http://www.beltramihistory.org

Bemidji Genealogical Society • c/o Bemidji Public Library, 509 America Ave NW • Bemidji, MN 56601 • (218) 751-3963

Bemidji Public Library • 509 America Ave NW • Bemidji, MN 56601 • (218) 751-3963

Bemidji State Univ Museum • 4111 Mill St NE • Bemidji, MN 56601

Minnesota

Benson
Swift County Historical Society • Historical Museum, 2135 Minnesota Ave, Bldg 2 • Benson, MN 56215 • (320) 843-4467

Bertha
Bertha Historical Society • Main & 2nd Ave, P.O. Box 307 • Bertha, MN 56437 • (218) 924-4095

Blaine
American Wings Air Museum • Airport Rd, P.O. Box 49322 • Blaine, MN 55449 • (763) 786-4146 • http://www.americanwings.org

Anoka County Library • 707 County Rd 10 NE • Blaine, MN 55434-2398 • (763) 785-3695 • http://www.anoka.lib.mn.us

Rusin Association of Minnesota • 1817 121st Ave NE • Blaine, MN 55449 • (763) 754-7463 • http://feefhs.org/rusyn/frg-ramn.html

Bloomington
Bloomington Historical Society • 2525 W Old Shakopee Rd • Bloomington, MN 55431 • (952) 948-8881 • http://www.bloomingtonhistoricalsociety.org

Bloomington Historical Society Museum • 10200 Penn Ave S • Bloomington, MN 55431 • (952) 881-4114 • http://www.bloomingtonhistoricalsociety.org

Continental Society Sons of Indian Wars • 3917 Heritage Hills Dr #104 • Bloomington, MN 55437-2633 • (952) 893-9747

Descendants of the First Families of Minnesota • 3917 Herritage Hills Dr #104 • Bloomington, MN 55437-2633 • (952) 893-9747

Masonic Grand Lodge of Minnesota • 11501 Masonic Home Dr • Bloomington, MN 55437-3699 • (952) 948-6700 • http://www.mn-masons.org

National Bydgelag Council • 10129 Goodrich Cr • Bloomington, MN 55437 • (952) 831-4409

National Huguenot Society • 9033 Lyndale Ave S, Ste 108 • Bloomington, MN 55420-3535 • (952) 885-9776 • http://www.huguenot.netnation.com/general/

National Society, Sons of American Colonists • 9033 Lyndale Ave S, Ste 108 • Bloomington, MN 55420-3535 • (952) 885-9776 • http://myt.execpc.com/~drg/wisac.html

Norwegian American Bygdelagenes Fellesraad do • 10129 Goodrich Cr • Bloomington, MN 55437 • (952) 831-4409 • http://www.hfaa.org/bygdelag/

Blue Earth
Blue Earth Community Library • 124 W 7th St • Blue Earth, MN 56013-1308 • (507) 526-5012 • http://libraries.tds.lib.mn.us/blueearth

Faribault County Historical Society • Wakefield House Museum, 405 E 6th St, P.O. Box 485 • Blue Earth, MN 56013 • (507) 526-5421

Bovey
Bovey Public Library • 402 2nd St, P.O. Box 130 • Bovey, MN 55709-0130 • (218) 245-3691

Heart O' Lakes Genealogical Society • P.O. Box 261 • Bovey, MN 55709-0261

Itasca County Genealogical Club • Bovey Village Hall, P.O. Box 261 • Bovey, MN 55709-0261 • (218) 326-1329

Brainerd
Crow Wing County Genealogical Society • 2103 Graydon Ave • Brainerd, MN 56401 • (314) 829-9738 • http://www.rootsweb.com/~mncwcghs

Crow Wing County Historical Society • Historical Museum, 1933 Graydon Ave, P.O. Box 722 • Brainerd, MN 56401-0722 • (218) 829-3268 • http://www.rootsweb.com/~mncwchgs/

Historic Heartland Association • P.O. Box 1 • Brainerd, MN 56401 • (218) 963-2218

Breckenridge
Wilkin County Historical Society • Historical Museum, 704 Nebraska Ave • Breckenridge, MN 56520 • (218) 643-1303

Wilkin-Richland Counties Genealogy Guild • RR1, Box 116 • Breckenridge, MN 56520 • (218) 643-3166

Brooklyn Center
Brooklyn Historical Society • 3824 58th Ave N, P.O. Box 29345 • Brooklyn Center, MN 55429-0345 • (763) 537-2118 • http://www.thebrooklyns.com

Browns Valley
Browns Valley Historical Society • Sam Brown Log House Museum, W Broadway, P.O. Box 165 • Browns Valley, MN 56219 • (612) 695-2110

Buffalo
Wright County Genealogical Society • 911 2nd Ave S • Buffalo, MN 55313

Wright County Historical Society • Historical Museum, 2001 N Hwy 25, P.O. Box 304 • Buffalo, MN 55313 • (763) 682-7323 • http://www.wrighthistory.org

Byron
Byron Historical Society • 933 Byron Ave N • Byron, MN 55920

Caledonia
Caledonia Public Library • 231 E Main St • Caledonia, MN 55921-1321 • (507) 724-2671

Houston County Historical Society • Historical Museum, 104 History Ln • Caledonia, MN 55921 • (507) 725-3884

Cambridge
East Central Regional Library • 244 S Birch St • Cambridge, MN 55008-1588 • (763) 689-7390 • http://ecrl.lib.mn.us

Isanti County Historical Society • Historical Museum, 33525 Flanders St NE, P.O. Box 525 • Cambridge, MN 55008-0525 • (763) 689-4229 • http://www.ichs.ws/

Cannon Falls
Cannon Falls Area Historical Society • Historical Museum, 208 W Mill St, P.O. Box 111 • Cannon Falls, MN 55009 • (507) 263-4080

Cannon Falls Library • 306 W Mill St • Cannon Falls, MN 55009-2045 • (507) 263-2804

Vasa Luthern Church Museum • P.O. Box 6582 • Cannon Falls, MN 55009

Carver
Carver-on-the-Minnesota • Broadway & Main Sts, P.O. Box 281 • Carver, MN 55315 • (952) 448-4580

Cass Lake
Leech Lake Tribal College Library • 023 2nd St & Elm Ave, P.O. Box 180 • Cass Lake, MN 56633 • (218) 335-4240 • http://www.lltc.org

Leech Lake Tribe of Ojibwe • Route 3, Box 100 • Cass Lake, MN 56633 • (218) 335-8200

Minnesota Chippewa Tribal Executive Committee • Box 217C • Cass Lake, MN 56633 • (218) 335-8581

Center City
Center City Historical Society • P.O. Box 366 • Center City, MN 55012 • (763) 257-6818

Chisago County Genealogical Group • P.O. Box 360 • Center City, MN 55012

Ceylon
Ceylon Area Historical Society • P.O. Box 276 • Ceylon, MN 56121

Chaska

Carver County Library • 4 City Hall Plaza • Chaska, MN 55318-1963 • (952) 448-9395 • http://www.carverlib.org

Chaska Historical Society • City Hall • Chaska, MN 55318 • (952) 448-4458

Chatfield

Chatfield Historical Society • 314 S Main St • Chatfield, MN 55923

Chatfield Public Library • 314 S Main St • Chatfield, MN 55923 • (507) 867-3480

Chisago City

Iron Horse Central Railroad Museum • 24880 Morgan Ave • Chisago City, MN 55013 • (651) 336-4531 • http://www.ironhorsecentral.com

Chisholm

Iron Range Research Center • 801 SW Hwy 169, Suite 1 • Chisholm, MN 55719 • (218) 254-7959 • http://www.ironrangeresearchcenter.org

Range Genealogical Society • P.O. Box 388 • Chisholm, MN 55719 • (218) 258-3676

Slovenian Genealogical Society, Minnesota Chapter • 417 NW 9th St • Chisholm, MN 55719-1542 • (218) 254-5891 • http://sloveniangenealogy.org/chapters/Minnesota.htm

Clarks Grove

Clarks Grove Area Heritage Society • P.O. Box 188 • Clarks Grove, MN 56016

Cleveland

Cleveland Historical Center • 303 Broadway • Cleveland, MN 56017 • (507) 931-20254

Cloquet

Carlton County Historical Society • History and Heritage Center, 406 Cloquet Ave • Cloquet, MN 55720-1750 • (218) 879-1938 • http://www.carltoncountyhs.org

Fond du Lac Chippewa Nation • 105 University Rd • Cloquet, MN 55720 • (218) 879-4593

Genealogical Society of Carlton County • History and Heritage Center, 406 Cloquet Ave, P.O. Box 204 • Cloquet, MN 55720 • (218) 389-6229 • http://www.carltoncountyhs.org

Cokato

Cokato Historical Society • Cokato Museum, 175 W 4th St, P.O. Box 686 • Cokato, MN 55321 • (320) 286-2427 • http://www.cokato.mn.us/cmhs/

Cokato-Finnish American Society • 10783 Cty Road 3 SW • Cokato, MN 55321 • (320) 286-2833

Coleraine

Coleraine Public Library • 203 Cole Ave, P.O. Box 225 • Coleraine, MN 55722-0225 • (218) 245-2315

Collegeville

Alcuin Library • Saint John's Univ • Collegeville, MN 56321 • (320) 363-2122 • http://ww.csbsju.edu/library/

Comfrey

Comfrey Area Historical Society • P.O. Box 218 • Comfrey, MN 56019

Coon Rapids

Coon Rapids Historical Commission • 1313 Coon Rapids Blvd • Coon Rapids, MN 55433 • (763) 755-2880

Coon Rapids Historical Society • 11155 Robinson Dr NW • Coon Rapids, MN 55433

Corcoran

North Hennepin Historical Society • 8905 Cty Rd 19 • Corcoran, MN 55357

Cottonwood

Cottonwood Area Historical Society • 61 Main St E, P.O. Box 106 • Cottonwood, MN 56229 • (507) 423-5373

Crookston

Polk County Historical Society • Historical Museum, 719 E Robert St, P.O. Box 214 • Crookston, MN 56716-0214 • (218) 281-1038 • http://www.crookston.com

Crosby

Cuyuna Country Heritage Preservation Society • 101 1st St SW • Crosby, MN 56441

Cuyuna Range Historical Society • Historical Museum, 101 1st St NW, P.O. Box 128 • Crosby, MN 56441 • (218) 546-6178

Crosslake

Crosslake Area Historical Society • Historical Museum, P.O. Box 369 • Crosslake, MN 56442 • (218) 692-3731 • http://www.crosslakehistoricalsociety.org

Currie

End-O-Line Railroad Park Museum • 440 N Mill St • Currie, MN 56123 • (507) 763-3708 • http://www.endoline.com

Darwin

Dassel Area Historical Society • P.O. Box D • Darwin, MN 55325

Dassel

Dassel Area Historical Society • Historical Museum, 901 1st St Nm P.O. Box D • Dassel, MN 55325 • (320) 275-3077 • http://www.dassel.com

Old Depot Railroad Museum • 651 W Hwy 12 • Dassel, MN 55325 • (320) 275-3876 • http://www.theolddepot.com

Detroit Lakes

Becker County Historical Society • Historical Museum, 714 Summit Ave, P.O. Box 622 • Detroit Lakes, MN 56502-0622 • (218) 847-2938 • http://www.beckercountyhistory.org

Heart O' Lakes Genealogical Society • Becker County Museum, 714 Summit Ave, P.O. Box 622 • Detroit Lakes, MN 56501-2824 • (218) 847-2938 • http://perham.eot.com/~bolerud/heart.html

Dillon

Beaverhead County Historical Society • 15 S Montana St • Dillon, MN 59725-2433

Dodge Center

Dodge County Genealogical Society • P.O. Box 683 • Dodge Center, MN 55927 • (507) 374-6401 • http://www.dodgecohistorical.addr.com

Duluth

Canosia Historical Society • 5762 N Pike Lake • Duluth, MN 55811 • (218) 729-8963

Duluth Public Library • 520 W Superior St • Duluth, MN 55802 • (218) 723-3802 • http://www.duluth.lib.mn.us

Glensheen Historic Estate Museum • 3300 London Rd • Duluth, MN 55804 • (218) 726-8910 • http://www.glensheen.org

Lake Superior Maritime Museum • 600 Lake Ave S • Duluth, MN 55802 • (218) 727-2497 • http://www.lsmma.com

Lake Superior Railroad Museum • 506 W Michigan St • Duluth, MN 55802 • (218) 733-7590 • http://www.lsrm.org

Northeast Minnesota Historical Center • Univ of Minnesota-Duluth, 416 Library Dr, Annex 202 • Duluth, MN 55812 • (218) 726-8526 • http://www.d.umn.edu/lib

Pilgrim Congregational Church Library • 2310 E 4th St • Duluth, MN 55812 • (218) 724-8503

Saint Louis County Historical Society • Historical Museum, 506 W Michigan St • Duluth, MN 55802-1505 • (218) 733-7586 • http://www.vets-hall.org

Minnesota

Duluth, cont.
Twin Ports Genealogical Society • P.O. Box 16895 • Duluth, MN 55816-0895

Eagan
Dakota County Library System • 1340 Wescott Rd • Eagan, MN 55123-1099 • (651) 688-1500 • http://www.co.dakota.mn.us/library

Eagle Bend
Eagle Bend Historical Society • 117 3rd Ave NE • Eagle Bend, MN 56446-9580

Eagle Lake
Saint Piran Society of Minnesota • 237 Ann Dr • Eagle Lake, MN 56024-0164

East Grand Forks
Heritage Foundation of East Grand Forks • 218 NW 4th St, P.O. Box 281 • East Grand Forks, MN 56721 • (218) 773-7481

MinnKota Genealogical Society • P.O. Box 126 • East Grand Forks, MN 56721

Eden Prairie
Eden Prairie Historical Society • 8950 Eden Prairie Rd • Eden Prairie, MN 55344 • (952) 944-2486

Edina
Edina Historical Society • Historical Museum, 4711 W 70th St • Edina, MN 55435 • (952) 920-8952

Hennepin County Library, Southdale • 7001 York Ave S • Edina, MN 55435 • (952) 830-4933 • http://www.hennepin.lib.mn.us

Eitzen
Eitzen Historical Society • general delivery • Eitzen, MN 55931

Elbow Lake
Grant County Historical Society • Historical Museum, 115 2nd St NE, P.O. Box 1002 • Elbow Lake, MN 56531 • (218) 685-4864 • http://www.rootsweb.com/mn/hist.htm

Elk River
Oliver Kelley Farm Museum • 15788 Kelley Farm Rd • Elk River, MN 55330 • (763) 441-5302 • http://www.mnhs.org/kelleyfarm

Ellendale
Ellendale Area Historical Society • P.O. Box 334 • Ellendale, MN 56026

Elmore
Elmore Area Historical Society • 108 N Henry St • Elmore, MN 56027 • (507) 943-3855

Ely
Dorothy Molter Museum • Hwy 169, P.O. Box 391 • Ely, MN 55731 • (218) 365-4155

Ely-Winton Historical Society • Vermillion College Interpretative Center, 1900 E Camp St • Ely, MN 55731 • (218) 354-3226

Vermillion Community College Library • 1900 E Camp St • Ely, MN 55731 • (218) 365-7225 • http://www.vcc.mnscu.edu/info_sru/library/libmain.htm

Elysian
LeSueur County Historical Society • Historical Museum and Genealogy Center, 301 2nd St NE, P.O. Box 240 • Elysian, MN 56028-0240 • (507) 267-4620 • http://www.lchs.mus.mn.us

Embarrass
Sisu Heritage • P.O. Box 127 • Embarrass, MN 55732 • (218) 984-3012

Esko
Esko Historical Society • 5 Elizabeth Ave, P.O. Box 83 • Esko, MN 55733 • (218) 879-4400

Evansville
Evansville Historical Foundation • 304 Grand St, P.O. Box 337 • Evansville, MN 56326 • (218) 948-2010 • http://www.evansvillemn.net

Eveleth
Range Genealogical Society • 4412 Maple Ln • Eveleth, MN 55734 • (218) 258-3676

Excelsior
Excelsior-Lake Minnetonka Historical Society • Village Hall Museum, 420 3rd Ave, P.O. Box 305 • Excelsior, MN 55331 • (952) 474-8956

Fairfax
Fairfax Depot Restoration Association • Route 2, Box 57 • Fairfax, MN 55332

Fort Ridgely History Site Museum • 72404 County Road 30 • Fairfax, MN 55332 • (507) 426-7888

Fairmont
Martin County Genealogical Society • 222 E Blue Earth Ave, P.O. Box 169 • Fairmont, MN 56031 • (507) 238-4579 • http://www.rootsweb.com/~mnmartin

Martin County Historical Society • Pioneer Museum, 304 Blue Earth Ave • Fairmont, MN 56831 • (507) 235-5178 • http://www.co.martin.mn.us/mchs/

Martin County Library • 110 N Park St • Fairmont, MN 56031-2822 • (507) 238-4207 • http://www.martincountylibrarysystem.org

South Central Genealogical Society • 110 N Park St • Fairmont, MN 56031

Falcon Heights
Gibbs Museum of Pioneer and Dakotah Life • 2097 W Larpenteur Ave • Falcon Heights, MN 55113 • (651) 646-8629 • http://www.rchs.com

Faribault
Alexander Faribault House Museum • 12 1st Ave • Faribault, MN 55021 • (507) 334-7913

Faribault Heritage Preservation Commision • 208 NW 1st Ave • Faribault, MN 55021 • (507) 334-2222

Rice County Historical Society • Historical Museum, 1814 2nd Ave NW • Faribault, MN 55021 • (507) 332-2121 • http://www.rchistory.org

Farmington
Dakota City Heritage Village • 2008 220th St W, P.O. Box 73 • Farmington, MN 55024 • (651) 460-8050 • http://www.dakotacity.org

Fergus Falls
Otter Tail County Genealogical Society • 1110 Lincoln Ave W • Fergus Falls, MN 56537 • (218) 736-6038 • http://jsenterprises.com/ottertail/genealogicalsociety.htm

Otter Tail County Historical Society • Historical Museum, 1110 Lincoln Ave W • Fergus Falls, MN 56537 • (218) 736-6038 • http://www.otchs.org

Finland
Finland Historical Society • 5653 Little Marais Rd, P.O. Box 583 • Finland, MN 55603 • (218) 353-7393

Forest Lake
Forest Lake Historical Society • 144 4th Ave NE • Forest Lake, MN 55025

Gammel Garden Museum • 9885 202nd St N • Forest Lake, MN 55025 • (612) 641-3419

Fosston
East Polk Heritage Center • general delivery • Fosston, MN 56542

Fountain
Fillmore County Historical Society • Historical Center, 202 County Rd 8 • Fountain, MN 55935 • (507) 258-4449

Fridley
Fridley Historical Society • 5273 NE Horizon Dr • Fridley, MN 55432 • (763) 571-5041

Fulda
Fulda Heritage Society • Front St & St Paul Ave, P.O. Box 275 • Fulda, MN 56131 • (507) 425-2583

Gilbert
Iron Range Historical Society • Old Gilbert City Hall, 19 S Broadway, P.O. Box 786 • Gilbert, MN 55741-0786 • (218) 749-3150

Glenwood
Pope County Historical Society • Historical Museum, 809 S Lake Shore Dr • Glenwood, MN 56334 • (320) 634-3293

Glyndon
Glyndon Area Historical Society • general delivery • Glyndon, MN 56547

Golden Valley
Golden Valley Historical Society • 7800 Golden Valley Rd • Golden Valley, MN 55427 • (763) 544-4547

Goodhue
Goodhue Area Historical Society • Historical Museum, P.O. Box 141 • Goodhue, MN 55027

Goodridge
Goodridge Area Historical Society • P.O. Box 171 • Goodridge, MN 56725 • (218) 378-4380

Granada
Granada Historical Society • P.O. Box 115 • Granada, MN 56039

Grand Marais
Cook County Historical Society • Historical Museum, 5 S Broadway, P.O. Box 1293 • Grand Marais, MN 55604-1293 • (218) 387-2883

Grand Marais Public Library • 104 2nd Ave W, P.O. Box 280 • Grand Marais, MN 55604-0280 • (218) 387-1140 • http://www.grandmaraislibrary.org

Grand Portage National Monument Museum • 315 S Broadway, P.O. Box 668 • Grand Marais, MN 55604 • (218) 387-2788 • http://www.nps.gov/grpo

Grand Portage
Grand Portage Chippewa Tribe • P.O. Box 428 • Grand Portage, MN 55604 • (218) 475-2277

Grand Rapids
Forest History Center • 2609 County Rd 76 • Grand Rapids, MN 55744 • (218) 327-4482

Grand Rapids Area Library • 140 NE 2nd St • Grand Rapids, MN 55744-2601 • (218) 326-7640 • http://www.grandrapids.lib.mn.us

Itasca County Historical Society • Central School Museum, 10 NW 5th St, P.O. Box 664 • Grand Rapids, MN 55744 • (218) 326-6431 • http://www.itascahistorical.com

Judy Garland Museum • 2727 US Hwy 169 S • Grand Rapids, MN 55744 • (800) 664-5839 • http://www.judygarlandmuseum.com

Granite Falls
Granite Falls Public Library • 155 7th Ave • Granite Falls, MN 56421 • (320) 564-3738

Upper Sioux Community • P.O. Box 147 • Granite Falls, MN 56241 • (612) 564-2360

Yellow Medicine County Historical Society • Historical Museum, 255 10th Ave, P.O. Box 145 • Granite Falls, MN 56241-9467 • (320) 564-4479 • http://www.kilowatt.net/ymchs .

Grove City
Grove City Area Historical Society • 200 South Ave W • Grove City, MN 56243 • (320) 857-9450

Harmony
Harmony Public Library • 225 3rd Ave SW, P.O. Box 426 • Harmony, MN 55939-0426 • (507) 886-8133 • http://www.selco.lib.mn.us/harmony/

Hastings
Hastings Historical Society • 109 1/2 2nd St E • Hastings, MN 55033

Hayfield
Saint Olaf Heritage Association • general delivery • Hayfield, MN 55940

Henderson
Henderson Public Library • 110 S 6th St, P.O. Box 404 • Henderson, MN 56044-0404 • (507) 248-3880

Sibley County Historical Society • Historical Museum, 700 Main St, P.O. Box 407 • Henderson, MN 56044 • (507) 248-3434 • http://www.history.sibley.mn.us

Hendricks
Lincoln County Historical Society • Pioneer Museum, 610 W Elm St • Hendricks, MN 56136 • (507) 275-3537

Hewitt
Hewitt Historical Society • Route 1, Box 90A • Hewitt, MN 56453

Hibbing
Hibbing Historical Society • Historical Museum, 400 E 23rd St • Hibbing, MN 55746-1923 • (218) 263-8522

Hinckley
Hinckley Fire Museum • 106 Old Highway 61, P.O. Box 40 • Hinckley, MN 55037 • (320) 384-7338 • http://www.hinckleyfire.com

Hinkley House
Rock County Historical Society • P.O. Box 741 • Hinkley House, MN 55037

Hollandale
Hollandale Area Historical Society • Heritage Huis Museum, P.O. Box 184 • Hollandale, MN 56045 • (507) 889-4491

Hopkins
Hopkins Historical Society • 1010 1st St S • Hopkins, MN 55343 • (952) 938-7315

Houston
Houston County Historical Society • 1212 E Main St, P.O. Box 173 • Houston, MN 55943 • (507) 724-3884

Hutchinson
Crow River Genealogical Society • 380 School Rd N • Hutchinson, MN 55350

McLeod County Historical Society • Heritage and Cultural Center, 380 School Rd N • Hutchinson, MN 55350 • (320) 587-2109 • http://www.mcleodhistory.org

International Falls
International Falls Public Library • 750 4th St • International Falls, MN 56649 • (218) 283-8051 • http://www.intlfallslibrary.org

Koochiching County Historical Society • Historical Museum, 216 6th Ave, P.O. Box 1147 • International Falls, MN 56649 • (218) 283-4316

Rainy River Valley Genealogical Society • P.O. Box 1032 • International Falls, MN 56649

Ironton
Cuyuna Country Heritage Preservation Society • P.O. Box 68 • Ironton, MN 56455

Minnesota

Isabella
Isabella Community Council • 9521 Kankinen Rd, P.O. Box 5 • Isabella, MN 55607 • (218) 323-7738

Isanti
Isanti County Historical Society • P.O. Box 525 • Isanti, MN 55008

Isle
Mille Lacs Lake Historical Society • Main St, P.O. Box 42 • Isle, MN 56342

Jackson
Jackson County Historical Society • 307 North Hwy # 86 • Jackson, MN 56143 • (507) 662-5505

Jasper
Jasper Historical Society • 217 2nd St SE • Jasper, MN 56144 • (507) 348-9841

Kasson
Olmsted County Historical Society • Historical Museum, 408 6th Ave NW • Kasson, MN 55944

Kenyon
Kenyon Area Historical Society • Gunderson House, 107 Gunderson Blvd • Kenyon, MN 55946 • (507) 789-5936

West Concord Historical Society • 600 1st St • Kenyon, MN 55946 • (507) 527-2628

La Crescent
La Crescent Area Historical Society • 171 Skunk Hollow Rd • La Crescent, MN 55947 • (507) 895-1857

La Crescent Public Library • 321 Main St • La Crescent, MN 55947 • (507) 895-4047 • http://www.selco.lib.mn.us/lacpl/

Lake Benton
Lake Benton Historical Society • 110 South St, P.O. Box 218 • Lake Benton, MN 56149-0218 • (507) 358-9480 • http://itctel.com/lbenton

Lake Bronson
Kittson County Historical Society • Historical Museum, 332 E Main St, P.O. Box 100 • Lake Bronson, MN 56734 • (218) 754-4100

Lake City
Lake City Historical Society • City Hall • Lake City, MN 55041

Wabasha County Historical Society • 503 W Center St, P.O. Box 255 • Lake City, MN 55041 • (507) 282-4027

Lake Crystal
Lake Crystal Historical Society • 132 N Grove • Lake Crystal, MN 56055

Lake Elmo
Oakdale-Lake Elmo Historical Society • 8281 N 15th St • Lake Elmo, MN 55042

Saint Croix Valley Farm Life Museum • 2315 Lake Elmo Ave • Lake Elmo, MN 55042

Lake Hubert
Niswaa Area Historical Society and Pioneer Park • 25611 Main St • Lake Hubert, MN 56459 • (218) 963-3570

Lake Park
Lake Park Area Historical Society • P.O. Box 45 • Lake Park, MN 56544-9731 • (218) 238-5896

Lakefield
Cottonwood-Jackson Genealogy Group • Historical Museum, 307 N Hwy 86, P.O. Box 238 • Lakefield, MN 56150 • (507) 662-5505

Jackson County Historical Society • Historical Museum, 307 N Hwy 86, P.O. Box 238 • Lakefield, MN 56150 • (507) 662-5505

Lakeville
Lakeville Area Historical Society • 20195 Holyoke Ave • Lakeville, MN 55044

Lamberton
Lamberton Area Historical Society • 110 2nd Ave W • Lamberton, MN 56152 • (507) 752-7063

Lanesboro
Lanesboro Historical Preservation Association • 105 Parkway S, P.O. Box 345 • Lanesboro, MN 55949 • (507) 467-2177

Lanesboro Historical Society • P.O. Box 354 • Lanesboro, MN 55949

Le Crescent
Le Crescent Area Historical Society • 171 Skunk Hollow Rd • Le Crescent, MN 55947

Le Sueur
LeSueur Historians • 709 N 2nd St • Le Sueur, MN 56058 • (507) 665-2050

LeSueur Museum • 709 N 2nd St • Le Sueur, MN 56058 • (507) 357-4488

Ottawa Church Historical Society • RR1, Box 102 • Le Sueur, MN 56058

W W Mayo House Museum • 118 N Main St • Le Sueur, MN 56058 • (507) 665-3250

Lindstrom
Chisago County Genealogical Society • P.O. Box 146 • Lindstrom, MN 55045-0146 • (651) 257-5310

Chisago County Historical Society • 13100 N 3rd Ave, P.O. Box 146 • Lindstrom, MN 55045-0146 • (651) 257-5310

Lindstrom Historical Society • P.O. Box 12 • Lindstrom, MN 55045 • (651) 257-2700

Litchfield
Litchfield Public Library • 216 N Marshall Ave, P.O. Box 817 • Litchfield, MN 55355 • (320) 693-2483 • http://www.litch.com/library

Litchfield
Meeker County Historical and Genealogical Society • Historical Museum, 308 Marshall Ave N • Litchfield, MN 55355 • (320) 693-6830 • http://www.garminnesota.org

Little Canada
Little Canada Historical Society • 515 E Little Canada Rd • Little Canada, MN 55117 • (651) 484-4783

Little Falls
Charles A Lindbergh Historic Site • 1620 Lindbergh Dr S • Little Falls, MN 56345 • (320) 616-6421 • http://www.mnhs.org

Dewey-Radke House Museum • 1200 W Broadway • Little Falls, MN 46345 • (320) 632-8902

Morrison County Historical Society • Weyerhaeuser Museum, 2151 S Lindbergh Dr, P.O. Box 239 • Little Falls, MN 56345-0239 • (320) 632-4007 • http://www.morrisoncountyhistory.org

Long Lake
West Hennepin County Pioneers Association • Historical Museum, 1953 W Wayzata Blvd, P.O. Box 332 • Long Lake, MN 55356-0332 • (952) 473-6557 • http://www.amatalon.co/pioneermuseum/

Long Prairie
Christie Home Historical Society • 110 2nd Ave N • Long Prairie, MN 56347

Todd County Historical Society • 33 Central Ave, P.O. Box 146 • Long Prairie, MN 56347 • (320) 732-4426

Lucan
Lucan Historical Society • general delivery • Lucan, MN 56255

Luverne
Rock County Historical Society • Hinkley House Museum, 123 N Freeman St, P.O. Box 741 • Luverne, MN 56156 • (507) 449-2115

Mabel
Hesper-Mabel Area Historical Society • P.O. Box 56 • Mabel, MN 55954 • (507) 493-5018

Madelia
Watonawan County Historical Society • Historical Center, 423 Dill Ave SW, P.O. Box 126 • Madelia, MN 56062 • (507) 642-3247

Madison
Lac Qui Parle County Historical Society • Historical Museum, 250 8th Ave S • Madison, MN 56256 • (320) 598-7678

Madison Lake
Madison Lake Area Historical Society • 525 Main St • Madison Lake, MN 56063

Mahnomen
Mahnomen County Historical Society • Courthouse, P.O. Box 123 • Mahnomen, MN 56557 • (218) 935-5490

Mankato
Blue Earth County Historical Society • Historical Museum, 415 E Cherry St • Mankato, MN 56001 • (507) 345-5566 • http://www.rootsweb.com/~mnbechs/welcome.html; http://www.bechshistory.com

Blue Earth County Library • 100 E Main St • Mankato, MN 56001 • (507) 387-1856 • http://www.beclibrary.org

Evangelical Lutheran Synod, Dept of Archives • 734 Marsh St • Mankato, MN 56001 • (507) 388-5969

Memorial Library • Bethany Lutheran College, 700 Luther Dr • Mankato, MN 56001 • (507) 344-7349 • http://www.blc.edu/library

Memorial Library - Southern Minnesota Historical Center • Mankato State Univ, ML3097, P.O. Box 8419 • Mankato, MN 56002-8419 • (507) 389-5952 • http://www.lib.mnsu.edu

R D Hubbard House Museum • 606 S Broad St • Mankato, MN 56601 • (507) 345-5566 • http://www.bechshistory.com

Traverse de Sioux Library System • 1400 East Madison Ave, Suite 622 • Mankato, MN 56001 • (507) 625-6169

Mantorville
Dodge County Historical Society • Historical Museum, 615 N Main St, P.O. Box 433 • Mantorville, MN 55955-0433 • (507) 635-5508 • http://www.dodgecohistorical.addr.com

Mantorville Restoration Association • P.O. Box 157 • Mantorville, MN 55955

Restoration House Museum • 540 Main St, P.O. Box 311 • Mantorville, MN 55955 • (507) 635-5141

Maple Grove
Maple Grove Historical Preservation Society • P.O. Box 1194 • Maple Grove, MN 55311

Maple Lake
Nisswa Area Historical Society • 1688 County Road 8 NW • Maple Lake, MN 55358 • (320) 963-3570

Maplewood
Maplewood Area Historical Society • 1890 Barclay St • Maplewood, MN 55109 • (651) 748-8645

Marine
Marine Preservation Commission • P.O. Box 225 • Marine, MN 55047

Marine on Saint Croix
Marine Historical Society • Stone House Museum, 5th & Oak Sts • Marine on Saint Croix, MN 55047

Marine Historical Society • Historical Museum, 14020 195th St N, P.O. Box 84 • Marine on Saint Croix, MN 55047 • (651) 433-4014

Marshall
Lyon County Historical Society • Historical Museum, 114 N 3rd St • Marshall, MN 56258 • (507) 537-6580

Prairieland Genealogical Society • c/o Southwest Minnesota Historical Center, Southwest State Univ, 703 N 6th St • Marshall, MN 56358 • (507) 537-7373 • http://freepages.genealogy.rootsweb.com/~cmolitor

Southwest Minnesota Historical Center • Southwest State Univ, 1501 State St • Marshall, MN 56358 • (507) 537-6176 • http://www.southweststate.edu/library/

McGregor
Sandy Lake Band of Ojibwe • HCR 3, Box 562-7 • McGregor, MN 55760 • (218) 839-3504 • http://www.sandylakeojibwe.org

Melrose
Melrose Area Historical Society • 518 E 2nd St S • Melrose, MN 56352 • (320) 256-4996

Menahga
Menahga Area Historical Society • Historical Museum, 320 Helsinki Blvd SE, P.O. Box 299 • Menahga, MN 56464 • (218) 564-5063

Mendota
Dakota County Historical Society, Mendota-West Saint Paul Chapter • 370 G St • Mendota, MN 55150

Daughters of the American Revolution, Sibley House Association of the Minnesota Branch • Fairbault-Sibley House Museum, 1357 Sibley Memorial Hwy • Mendota, MN 55150 • (952) 452-1596

Mendota Heights
Mendota-West Saint Paul Historical Society • 1160 Dodd Rd • Mendota Heights, MN 55118

Milaca
Milaca Area Historical Society • c/o Milaca Community Library and Museum, 145 Central Ave S • Milaca, MN 56353 • (320) 983-3677

Milaca Community Library • 145 S Central • Milaca, MN 56353-1122 • (320) 983-3677 • ecrl.lib.mn.us

Milaca Museum • 440 2nd Ave NW • Milaca, MN 56353 • (952) 983-6666

Minneapolis
American Swedish Institute • Historical Museum, 2600 Park Ave • Minneapolis, MN 55407 • (612) 871-4907 • http://www.americanswedishinst.org

Bakken Museum • 3537 Zenith Ave S • Minneapolis, MN 55416 • (612) 926-3878 • http://www.thebakken.org

Brooklyn Historical Society • 5637 Brooklyn Blvd, Ste 102 • Minneapolis, MN 55429 • (763) 536-0842

Center for Holocaust and Genocide Studies • Univ of Minnesota, 315 Pillsbury Dr • Minneapolis, MN 55455 • http://www.chgs.umn.edu

Commission on Archives and History, United Methodist Church Library • 122 W Franklin Ave, Rm 400 • Minneapolis, MN 55404 • (612) 230-6149

Danish American Fellowship • 3030 West River Parkway South • Minneapolis, MN 55406 • (612) 729-3800

Danish American Fellowship • 4200 Cedar Ave S • Minneapolis, MN 55407 • (612) 729-3800

Fridley Historical Society • Historical Museum, 611 Mississippi St NE • Minneapolis, MN 55432 • (763) 571-0120

Minnesota

Minneapolis, cont.

Grodno Genealogy Group • 2601 Princeton Ave S • Minneapolis, MN 55416 • (952) 920-4344 • http://www.jewishgen.org/Belarus/grodno1.htm

Hennepin County Historical Society • Hennepin History Museum, 2303 3rd Ave S • Minneapolis, MN 55404-3599 • (612) 870-1329 • http://www.hhmmuseum.org

Hennepin Overland Railway Historical Society • 2501 E 38th St • Minneapolis, MN 55406 • (612) 276-9034

Immigration History Society • Immigration History Research Center • Univ of Minnesota, 311 Andersen Library, 222 21st Avenue S • Minneapolis, MN 55455 • (612) 625-4800 • http://www.umn.edu/ihrd

Jewish Historical Society of the Upper Midwest • Kaplan Jewish History Ctr, 4330 Cedar Lake Rd S • Minneapolis, MN 55416 • (952) 381-3360 • http://www.tx.umn.edu/~schlo006

Kashubian Association of North America • P.O. Box 27732 • Minneapolis, MN 55427 • (763) 545-7107 • http://www.KA-NA.org

Minneapolis Public Library • 300 Nicholet Mall • Minneapolis, MN 55401-1992 • (612) 630-6000 • http://www.mplib.org

Minneapolis Public Library-Sumner • 611 Emerson Ave N • Minneapolis, MN 55411-4196

Minneapolis Regional Native American Center • 1530 E Franklin Ave • Minneapolis, MN 55404 • (612) 348-5600

Minnesota Dept of Health - Vital Statistics • 717 Delaware St SE, P.O. Box 9441 • Minneapolis, MN 55440-9441 • (612) 623-5121 • http://www.health.state.mn.us

National Danish-American Genealogical Society • Danish American Center, 3030 W River Pkwy S • Minneapolis, MN 55406-2361 • (763) 544-5315 • http://www.danishgenealogy.org

National Society, Sons and Daughters of the Pilgrims • 3917 Heritage Hills Dr #104 • Minneapolis, MN 55437-2633 • (952) 893-9747 • http://www.nssdp.com

Norsemen Federation • 3749 47th Ave S • Minneapolis, MN 55406

O Meredith Wilson Library • Univ of Minnesota, 309 19th Ave S • Minneapolis, MN 55455 • (612) 624-4520 • http://www.lib.umn.edu

OMII Genealogical Project • 3131 18th Ave S • Minneapolis, MN 55407-1824

Plymouth Historical Society • 2605 Fernbrook Ln N • Minneapolis, MN 55447 • (763) 559-9201

Polish American Cultural Institute of Minnesota • 4935 Abbott Ave N • Minneapolis, MN 55429

Rusin (Slovakian) Association • 1115 Pineview Ln N • Minneapolis, MN 55441

Sons of Norway • 1455 W Lake St • Minneapolis, MN 55408 • (612) 827-3611 • http://www.sonsofnorway.com

Sons of the American Revolution, Minnesota Society • 2700 E Minnehaha Pkwy • Minneapolis, MN 55406-3743 • (612) 721-4275 • http://www.minnesotasar.org

Stevens House Museum • P.O. Box 17241 • Minneapolis, MN 55417

Swedish Council of America • 2600 Park Ave • Minneapolis, MN 55407-1007 • (612) 871-0593 • http://www.swedishcouncil.org

Transcultural Tour Company Museum • 4029 14th Ave S #18 • Minneapolis, MN 55407 • (612) 822-3666

University of Minnesota - Minneapolis Law Library • 229 19th Ave S • Minneapolis, MN 55455 • (612) 625-4309 • http://www.umn.edu/law/library/welcome.htm

Wells Fargo History Museum • 90 S 7th St, Skyway Level • Minneapolis, MN 55479 • (612) 667-4210 • http://www.wellsfargohistory.com

Minnesota Lake

Minnesota Lake Area Historical Society • Kremer House Library and Museum, 317 Main, P.O. Box 225 • Minnesota Lake, MN 56068 • (507) 462-3420

Minnetonka

Charles H Burwell House Museum • 13209 McGinty Rd E • Minnetonka, MN 55305 • (952) 933-1611

Hennepin County Library • 12601 Ridgedale Dr • Minnetonka, MN 55343 • (952) 847-8500 • http://www.hclib.org

Minnetonka Historical Society • 14600 Minnetonka Blvd • Minnetonka, MN 55345 • (952) 933-1611 • http://www.minnetonka-history.org

Montevideo

Chippewa County Genealogical Society • Historical Museum, 151 Pioneer Dr, P.O. Box 303 • Montevideo, MN 56265 • (612) 269-7636 • http://www.montevideomn.com

Chippewa County Historical Society • Historical Museum, 151 Pioneer Dr, P.O. Box 303 • Montevideo, MN 56222 • (320) 269-7636 • http://www.montevideomn.com

Monticello

Monticello Historical Committee • P.O. Box 581 • Monticello, MN 55362

Moorhead

Carl B Ylvisaker Library • Concordia College, 901 S 8th St • Moorhead, MN 56562 • (218) 299-4640 • http://library.cord.edu

Clay County Historical Society • Heritage-Hjemkomst Museum, 202 1st Ave N, P.O. Box 501 • Moorhead, MN 56560 • (218) 299-5520 • http://www.hjemkomst-center.com

Comstock Historic House Society • Comstock Historic Home Museum, 506 8th St S • Moorhead, MN 56560 • (218) 233-0848

Livingston Lord Library - Northwest Minnesota Historical Center • Moorhead State Univ, 1104 7th Ave S • Moorhead, MN 56560 • (218) 477-2345 • http://www.mnstate.edu/library

Red River Valley Heritage Society • 202 1st Ave N, P.O. Box 157 • Moorhead, MN 56561-0157 • (218) 233-5604

Moose Lake

Moose Lake Historical Society • Historical Museum, 4252 N Birch Rd • Moose Lake, MN 55767 • (218) 485-4680

Village Hall Museum • 205 Elm • Moose Lake, MN 55767 • (218) 485-4680

Mora

Association for the Certification of Minnesota Genealogists • 330 S Park • Mora, MN 55051

Kanabec County Historical Society • History Center, 805 W Forest Ave, P.O. Box 113 • Mora, MN 55051-0113 • (320) 679-1665 • http://www.kanabechistory.org

Morris

Morris Public Library • 102 E 6th St • Morris, MN 56267-1211 • (320) 589-1634 • http://www.viking.lib.mn.us

Stevens County Genealogical Society • c/o Morris Public Library, 102 E 6th St • Morris, MN 56267 • (320) 589-1719

Stevens County Historical Society • Historical Museum, 116 W 6th St • Morris, MN 56267 • (320) 589-1719

West Central Minnesota Historical Center • Univ of Minnesota, 4th & College Sts • Morris, MN 56267 • (320) 689-6172 • http://www.mrs.umn.edu/library

Morristown
Morristown Historical Society • P.O. Box 113 • Morristown, MN 55052

Morton
Lower Sioux Mdewakanton Community • RR1, Box 308 • Morton, MN 56270-9801 • (507) 697-6185

Renville County Historical Society • Historical Museum, 441 N Park Dr, P.O. Box 266 • Morton, MN 56270 • (507) 697-6147

Mound
Westonka Historical Society • 3740 Enchanted Ln • Mound, MN 55364

Mountain Iron
Mountain Iron Public Library • 5742 Mountain Ave, P.O. Box 477 • Mountain Iron, MN 55768-0477 • (218) 735-8625

Mountain Lake
Heritage Village Museum • County Rd 1, P.O. Box 152 • Mountain Lake, MN 56159 • (507) 427-2709

Mountain Lake Public Library • 1054 4th Ave, P.O. Box 477 • Mountain Lake, MN 56159-0477 • (507) 427-2506

Nett Lake
Bois Forte Band of Chippewa • P.O. Box 16 • Nett Lake, MN 55772 • (218) 757-3261 • http://www.boisforte.com

New Brighton
New Brighton Area Historical Society • P.O. box 12062 • New Brighton, MN 55112 • (763) 633-6991

New Hope
Cultural Society of South Slavs • 3510 Xylon Ave N • New Hope, MN 55427 • (612) 544-6433 • http://feefhs.org/frg-csss.html

New Hope Preservation Committee • New Hope City Hall • New Hope, MN 55428

New London
Monongalia Historical Society • 18946 Hwy 9 NE, P.O. Box 41 • New London, MN 56273 • (320) 354-2990

New Prague
New Prague Historical Society • 28438 141st Ave • New Prague, MN 56071 • (952) 758-2201

New Ulm
Brown County Historical Society • Historical Museum, 2 N Broadway • New Ulm, MN 56073 • (507) 354-2016 • http://www.browncountyhistorymnusa.org

German-Bohemian Heritage Society • P.O. Box 822 • New Ulm, MN 56073-0822 • (507) 354-2763 • http://www.rootsweb.com/~gbhs/

John Lind House Museum • 622 Center St • New Ulm, MN 56073 • (507) 354-8802

New York Mills
New York Mills Finnish-American Historical Society • Finn Creek Museum, Rd 135, P.O. Box 314 • New York Mills, MN 56567 • (218) 385-2200

Nisswa
Nisswa Caboose Society • 2151 Cty Rd 29 • Nisswa, MN 56468

North Eagan
Valdres Samband Lag • 1522 N Greenwood Ct • North Eagan, MN 55112 • http://www.valdressamband.org

North Mankato
Traverse des Sioux Genealogical Society • 815 Nicollet Ave • North Mankato, MN 56001 • (507) 387-2290

North Oaks
Hill Farm Historical Society • 28 Meadowlark Ln • North Oaks, MN 55127 • (651) 484-1434

North Saint Paul
North Saint Paul Historical Society • Historical Museum, 2526 E 7th Ave • North Saint Paul, MN 55109 • (651) 779-6402

North Star Museum of Boy Scouting and Girl Scouting • 2640 E 7th Ave • North Saint Paul, MN 55109 • (651) 748-2880 • http://www.nssm.org

Ramsey County Library-North Saint Paul Branch • 2640 E 7th Ave • North Saint Paul, MN 55109-3199 • (651) 704-2040

Northfield
Laurence McKinley Gould Library • Carleton College, 1 N College St • Northfield, MN 55057-4097 • (507) 646-4264 • http://www.library.carleton.edu

Northfield Historical Society • Historical Museum, 408 Division St, P.O. Box 372 • Northfield, MN 55057 • (507) 645-9268 • http://www.northfieldhistory.org

Northfield Public Library • 210 Washington St • Northfield, MN 55057 • (507) 645-6606 • http://www.northfield.mn.info/

Norwegian-American Historical Association • Saint Olaf College Museum, 1510 St Olaf St • Northfield, MN 55057 • (507) 646-3221 • http://www.stolaf.edu/stolaf/other/naha/naha.html

Rice County Genealogical Society • 408 Division St • Northfield, MN 55057 • (507) 645-9268

Rolvaag Memorial Library • St Olaf College, 1510 St Olaf Ave • Northfield, MN 55057 • (507) 646-3452 • http://www.stolaf.edu/library

Society for German-American Studies • Saint Olaf College, German Dept • Northfield, MN 55057-1098 • (507) 645-8562 • http://feeths.org/frg-sgas.html

Olivia
Olivia Historic Preservation Corporation • 907 W Park St, P.O. Box 148 • Olivia, MN 56277 • (320) 523-1322

Olivia Public Library • 405 S 10th St • Olivia, MN 56277-1287 • (320) 523-1738 • http://www.olivia.mn.us/library

Onamia
Mille Lacs Band of Ojibwe • HRC 67, Box 194 • Onamia, MN 56359 • (612) 532-4181 • http://www.millelacsojibwe.org

Mille Lacs Indian Museum and Trading Post • P.O. Box 195 • Onamia, MN 56359 • (320) 532-3632

Ortonville
Big Stone County Historical Society • 985 US Hwy 12 • Ortonville, MN 56278 • (320) 839-3359

Osakis
Osakis Heritage Center • P.O. Box 327 • Osakis, MN 56360 • (320) 859-3777 • http://www.lakeOsakis.com

Owatonna
Owatonna Public Library • 105 N Elm, P.O. Box 387 • Owatonna, MN 55060-0387 • (507) 444-2460 • http://www.owatonna.info/

Steele County Historical Society • 1448 Austin Rd, P.O. Box 204 • Owatonna, MN 55060 • (507) 451-1420

Park Rapids
Hubbard County Genealogical Society • Hubbard County Museum, 301 Court Ave, P.O. Box 361 • Park Rapids, MN 56470 • http://www.rootsweb.com/~mnhgs

Hubbard County Historical Society • Hubbard County Museum, 301 Court Ave, P.O. Box 327 • Park Rapids, MN 56470 • (218) 732-5237

Ira Benham Resource Center • Hubbard County Museum, 301 Court Ave, P.O. Box 361 • Park Rapids, MN 56470 • (218) 732-5237

Paynesville
Paynesville Historical Society • 543 River St • Paynesville, MN 56362 • (320) 243-4433

Pequot Lakes
Pequot Lakes Historical Society • 4285 Tower Sq • Pequot Lakes, MN 56472 • (218) 568-5324

Perham
East Otter Tail Historical Society • 349 2nd Ave SE • Perham, MN 56573

History Museum of East Otter Tail County • 230 1st Ave N • Perham, MN 56573 • (218) 346-7676 • http://www.HistoryMuseumEOT.org

Peterson
1877 Peterson Station Museum • 228 Mill St, P.O. Box 233 • Peterson, MN 55962 • (507) 895-2551

Pine City
North West Company Fur Post Museum • general delivery • Pine City, MN 55063 • (320) 629-6356

Pine Island
Van Horn Public Library • 115 SE 3rd St, P.O. Box 38 • Pine Island, MN 55963-0038 • (507) 356-8558

Pine River
Kitchigami Regional Library • 310 2nd St N, P.O. Box 84 • Pine River, MN 56474-0084 • (218) 587-2171 • http://krls.org

Pipestone
Historic Pipestone • 704 4th St SE, P.O. Box 470 • Pipestone, MN 56164 • (507) 825-3333

Pipestone County Genealogical Society • Historical Museum, 113 S Hiawatha, P.O. Box 175 • Pipestone, MN 56164 • (507) 825-2510 • http://www.pipestone.mn.us/museum/homepa~ 1.htm

Pipestone County Historical Society • Historical Museum, 113 S Hiawatha, P.O. Box 175 • Pipestone, MN 56164 • (507) 825-2563 • http://www.pipestoneminnesota.com/museum

Pipestone National Monument Library & Archives • 36 Reservation Ave • Pipestone, MN 56164-1269 • (507) 825-5464 • http://www.nps.gov/pipe

Plainview
Millville Historical Association • 905 2nd Ave NW • Plainview, MN 55964

Plainview History Association • Route 1, Box 209 • Plainview, MN 55944

Plainview Public Library • 345 1st Ave NW • Plainview, MN 55964-1295 • (507) 534-3425

Plymouth
Order of the Crown of Charlemagne in the United States of America • 14115 41st Ave N • Plymouth, MN 55446 • http://www.charlemagne.org

Order of the Merovingian Dynasty • 14115 41st Ave N • Plymouth, MN 55446 • (763) 553-1122 • http://www.merovingiandynasty.com

Plymouth Historical Society • 3400 Plymouth Blvd • Plymouth, MN 55447 • (763) 559-9201

Preston
Preston Historical Society • Houston & Preston Sts, P.O. Box 63 • Preston, MN 55965 • (507) 765-4555

Princeton
Mille Lacs County Historical Society • Depot Museum, 101 10th Ave N, P.O. Box 42 • Princeton, MN 55371 • (763) 389-1296

Spencer Brook Historical Society • RR3 • Princeton, MN 55371

Prior Lake
Shakopee Mdewakanton Sioux (Dakota) • Historical Museum, 2330 Sioux Trail NW • Prior Lake, MN 55372 • (952) 496-6179 • http://www.ccsmdc.org; Shakopeedakota.org

Reads Landing
Wabasha County Historical Society • Historical Museum • Reads Landing, MN 55041 • (507) 282-4027

Red Lake
Red Lake Band of Chippewa Indians of Minnesota • P.O. Box 550 • Red Lake, MN 56671 • (218) 679-3341 • http://www.redlakenation.org

Red Lake Falls
Red Lake County Historical Society • Lake Pleasant School House, Route 1, Box 298 • Red Lake Falls, MN 56750 • (218) 253-2833

Red Wing
Goodhue County Family Tree Club • 1166 Oak St • Red Wing, MN 55066 • (651) 388-6024

Goodhue County Historical Society • Historical Museum, 1166 Oak St • Red Wing, MN 55066 • (651) 388-6024 • http://www.goodhuehistory.mus.mn.us

Red Wing Public Library • 225 East Ave • Red Wing, MN 55066-2298 • (651) 385-3673 • http://www.redwing.lib.mn.us

Redwood Falls
Redwood County Historical Society • Historical Museum, 915 W Bridge St • Redwood Falls, MN 56283 • (507) 637-3329

Redwood Falls Public Library • 509 S Lincoln St • Redwood Falls, MN 56283 • (507) 637-8650 • http://www.ci.redwood-falls.mn.us

Renville
Historic Renville Preservation Commission • Historical Museum, 813 N Main St, P.O. Box 681 • Renville, MN 56284 • (612) 329-3545

Renville County Genealogical Society • 211 N Main St, P.O. Box 331 • Renville, MN 56284 • (612) 329-8193

Richfield
American Historical Society of Germans from Russia, North Star Chapter • c/o Berea Lutheran Church, 7538 Emerson Ave S • Richfield, MN 55423 • (763) 784-8626 • http://www.northstarchapter.org/default.htm

Richfield Historical Society • Bartholomew House Museum, 6901 Lynndale Ave S, P.O. Box 23304 • Richfield, MN 55423 • (612) 798-6140 • http://www.richfieldhistory.org

Robbinsdale
Robbinsdale Historical Society • 4221 Lake Rd • Robbinsdale, MN 55422

Rochester
Historic Mayowood Mansion Museum • 3720 SW Mayowood Rd • Rochester, MN 55902 • (507) 282-9447

Mayo Foundation Archives and Historical Area • 200 1st St SW • Rochester, MN 55901 • (507) 282-2511

Olmstead County History Center Library • P.O. Box 6411 • Rochester, MN 55903

Olmsted County Genealogical Society • 1195 W Circle Dr SW, P.O. Box 6411 • Rochester, MN 55903-6411 • (507) 282-9447 • http://www.millcomm.com/~gzimmer/ochs.html

Olmsted County Historical Society • 1195 W Circle Dr SW • Rochester, MN 55901 • (507) 282-9447 • http://www.olmstedhistory.com

Rochester Public Library • 11 1st St SE • Rochester, MN 55904-3776 • (507) 285-8002 • http://www.rochesterpubliclibrary.org

Wabasha County Historical Society • 3243 60th Ave SW • Rochester, MN 55902

Rockford

Rockford Area Historical Society • Ames-Florida-Stork House Museum, 8136 Bridge St, P.O. Box 186 • Rockford, MN 55373 • (763) 477-5383 • http://www.cityofrockford.org/storkhouse/

Rogers

Ellingson Car Museum • 20950 Rogers Dr • Rogers, MN 55074 • (612) 428-7337 • http://www.ellinsoncarmuseum.com

Roseau

Pioneer Farm and Village • Hwy 11 • Roseau, MN 56751 • (218) 463-2187

Rosseau County Historical Society • Historical Museum, 110 2nd Ave NE • Roseau, MN 56751 • (218) 463-1918 • http://www.roseaucohistoricalsociety.org

Rosemount

Rosemount Area Historical Society • 3130 145th St W • Rosemount, MN 55068

Roseville

Ramsey County Public Library • 2180 N Hamline Ave • Roseville, MN 55113-4241 • (651) 628-6803 • http://library.usask.ca/hytelnet/us4/us479.html

Roseville Historical Society • 1787 Centennial Dr • Roseville, MN 55113 • (612) 490-2280 • http://mnrhs.tripod.com

Royalton

Royalton Historical Society • Center St, P.O. Box 196 • Royalton, MN 56373 • (320) 584-5641

Rush City

Chisago County Historical Society, North Chapter • 51245 Fairfield Ave • Rush City, MN 55609 • (320) 674-4122

Rushford

Rushford Area Historical Organization • 403 E North St, P.O. Box 98 • Rushford, MN 55971 • (507) 864-7223

Rushford Public Library • 101 N Mill St, P.O. Box 250 • Rushford, MN 55971-0250 • (507) 864-7600 • http://www.rushford.lib.mn.us

Sacred Heart

Sacred Heart Area Historical Society • 77407 145th St • Sacred Heart, MN 56285-9802 • (320) 765-2274

Saint Bonifacius

Peter Watne Memorial Library • Crown College, 6425 County Rd 30 • Saint Bonifacius, MN 55375-9001 • (952) 446-4239 • http://www.crown.edu/library/

Saint Charles

Saint Charles Public Library • 125 W 11th St • Saint Charles, MN 55972-1141 • (507) 932-3227 • http://www.selco.info/

Saint Cloud

Central Minnesota Historical Center Library • Saint Cloud State Univ, Miller Center, 3140 720 Fourth Ave S • Saint Cloud, MN 56301-4498 • (320) 255-3254 • http://lrts.saintcloudstate.edu

Great River Regional Library • 1300 W Saint Germain St • Saint Cloud, MN 56301 • (320) 650-2500 • http://www.griver.org

James W Miller Library • Saint Cloud State University, 720 Fourth Ave S • Saint Cloud, MN 56301-4498 • (320) 308-2022 • http://www.lrs.stcloudstate.edu

Minnesota Alliance of Local Historical Museums • c/o Stearns County Historical Society, 235 33rd Ave S, P.O. Box 702 • Saint Cloud, MN 56302-0702

Saint Cloud Area Genealogists • P.O. Box 213 • Saint Cloud, MN 56302 • (320) 632-3360 • http://www.rootsweb.com/~mnscag/SCAG

Stearns County Historical Society • Historical Museum, 235 33rd Ave S, P.O. Box 702 • Saint Cloud, MN 56301-3752 • (320) 253-8424 • http://www.stearns-museum.org

Saint Francis

Saint Francis Historical Society • 22731 Rum River Blvd NW • Saint Francis, MN 55070

Saint James

Saint James Depot Museum • 1021 Armstrong Blvd S • Saint James, MN 56081

Watonwan County Library • 511 2nd Ave S • Saint James, MN 56081-1736 • (507) 375-1278 • http://www.tds.lib.mn.us

Saint Joseph

Clemens Library & College of St Benedict Museum • Saint John's University, 37 S College Ave • Saint Joseph, MN 56374 • (320) 363-2119 • http://www.csbsju.edu/library

Saint Louis Park

Pavek Museum of Broadcasting • 3515 Raleigh Ave • Saint Louis Park, MN 55416 • (952) 926-8198 • http://www.pavekmuseum.org

Saint Louis Park Historical Society • 3700 Monterey Dr • Saint Louis Park, MN 55416 • (612) 929-9486

Saint Paul

3M Club Genealogy Club • 3M Center, Bldg 230-BS-39 • Saint Paul, MN 55144-1000 • (651) 733-8055

Alexander Ramsey House Museum • 265 S Exchange St • Saint Paul, MN 55102 • (651) 296-8760 • http://www.mnhs.org

Archbishop Ireland Memorial Library • Univ of Saint Thomas, 2260 Summit Ave • Saint Paul, MN 55105 • (651) 962-5453

Baptist General Conference History Center • 3949 Bethel Dr • Saint Paul, MN 55112-6940 • (651) 638-6282 • http://www.bethel.edu/bgcarchive

Buenger Memorial Library • Concordia College, 275 N Syndicate St • Saint Paul, MN 55104-5494 • (651) 641-8278 • http://www.csp.edu/virtuallibrary

Bush Memorial Library • Hamline Univ, 1536 Hewitt Ave • Saint Paul, MN 55104 • (651) 523-2375 • http://www.hamline.edu/bushlibrary/

Catholic Archdiocese of Saint Paul and Minneapolis Archives • 226 Summit Ave • Saint Paul, MN 55102 • (763) 291-4429

Czechoslovak Genealogical Society International • P.O. Box 16225 • Saint Paul, MN 55116-0225 • (651) 454-6247 • http://www.cgsi.org

DeWitt Wallace Library • Macalester College, 1600 Grand Ave • Saint Paul, MN 55105 • (651) 696-6346 • http://www.macalester.edu/library

Fort Snelling History Center • 200 Tower Ave • Saint Paul, MN 55111 • (612) 725-2413 • http://www.mnhs.org/fortsnelling

Genealogical Society of Minnesota • 2642 University Ave • Saint Paul, MN 55114 • (612) 724-2101

Germanic Genealogy Society • Concordia Univ Library, 1282 Concordia Ave • Saint Paul, MN 55104-5479 • http://www.ggsmn.org

Germanic Genealogy Society • c/o Buenger Memorial Library, Concordia College, 275 N Syndicate St, P.O. Box 16312 • Saint Paul, MN 55116-0312 • (651) 777-6463 • http://feefhs.org/ger/frg-ggs.html

Irish American Cultural Institute • Univ of Saint Thomas, 2115 Summit #5026 • Saint Paul, MN 55105-1048 • (651) 962-6040

Irish Genealogical Society International • P.O. Box 16585 • Saint Paul, MN 55116-0585 • (612) 595-9347 • http://www.rootsweb.com/~irish/

James J Hill House Museum • 240 Summit Ave • Saint Paul, MN 55102 • (651) 296-8205 • http://www.mnhs.org

Saint Paul, cont.

Jewish Historical Society of the Upper Midwest • Bush Library, Hamline Univ, 1536 Hewitt Ave • Saint Paul, MN 55104 • (952) 641-2407

Julian H Sleeper House Museum • 66 St Albans St S • Saint Paul, MN 55105 • (651) 225-1505

Masonic Historical Society • Historical Museum, 200 E Plato Blvd • Saint Paul, MN 55107 • (612) 222-6051

Minnesota Air National Guard Historical Foundation Museum • 670 General Miller Dr, P.O. Box 11598 • Saint Paul, MN 55111 • (612) 713-2524 • http://www.mnangmuseum.org

Minnesota Coalition of Scottish Clans • 1940 Inglehart Ave #31 • Saint Paul, MN 55104 • (952) 645-7413

Minnesota Historical Society • Mill City Museum, 345 Kellogg Blvd W • Saint Paul, MN 55102-1906 • (651) 297-4462 • http://www.mnhs.org

Minnesota State Archaeologist's Office - Cemetery Records • Fort Snelling History Center, 200 Tower Ave • Saint Paul, MN 55111

Minnesota State Capitol Historic Site Museum • 75 Rev Dr Martin Luther King Jr Blvd • Saint Paul, MN 55155 • (651) 296-2881 • http://www.mnhs.org/statecapitol

Minnesota State Law Library • 25 Rev Dr Martin Luther King Jr Blvd • Saint Paul, MN 55155 • (651) 296-2775 • http://www.lawlibrary.state.mn.us

Minnesota Territorial Pioneers • 176 Snelling Ave N, Ste 328 • Saint Paul, MN 55104 • (651) 379-1849 • http://www.mnterritorialpioneers.org

Minnesota Transportation Museum • 193 E Pennsylvania Ave • Saint Paul, MN 55101 • (651) 228-0263 • http://www.mtromuseum.org

Minnesota Vetrinary Historical Museum • College of Veterinary Medicina, 1365 Gortner Ave, Rm 143 • Saint Paul, MN 55108 • (612) 625-7770 • http://www.mvma.org/historical_museum.asp

Museum of Minnesota • 30 10th St E • Saint Paul, MN 55101

National Council of the Swedish Cultural Society in America • P.O. Box 8042 • Saint Paul, MN 55108-8042 • (952) 645-8578

O'Shaughnessy-Frey Library • Univ of Saint Thomas, 2115 Summit Ave, P.O. Box 5004 • Saint Paul, MN 55105 • (651) 962-5014 • http://www.stthomas.edu/libraries/

Ramsey County Historical Society • Historical Museum, 323 Landmark Center, 75 W 5th St • Saint Paul, MN 55102 • (651) 222-0701 • http://www.rchs.com

Saint Paul Central Library • Univ of Minnesota, 1984 Buford Ave • Saint Paul, MN 55108 • (612) 624-1212 • http://www.stplib.umn.edu/stp

Saint Paul Public Library • 90 W 4th St • Saint Paul, MN 55102-1668 • (651) 266-7000 • http://www.stpaul.lib.mn.us

Scandinavian American Genealogical Society • P.O. Box 16069 • Saint Paul, MN 55116-0069 • http://www.mtn.org/mgs/branches/sags.html

Schubert Club Museum • 75 W 5th St, Lower Level • Saint Paul, MN 55102

Twin City Model Railroad Museum • 1021 Bandana Blvd E • Saint Paul, MN 55108 • (651) 647-9628 • http://www.tcmrm.org

Warren E Burger Law Library • William Mitchell College of Law, 871 Summit Ave • Saint Paul, MN 55105 • (612) 290-6424 • http://www.wmitchell.edu/library/

West Side Historical Society • 625 Stryker Ave • Saint Paul, MN 55107

Saint Peter

E Saint Julien Cox House Museum • 500 W Washington Ave • Saint Peter, MN 56082 • (507) 934-2160 • http://www.mchsmn.org

Folke Bernadette Memorial Library • Gustavus Adolphus College, 800 W College Ave • Saint Peter, MN 56082 • (507) 933-7567 • http://www.gac.edu/oncampus/academics/library/

Nicollet County Historical Society • Treaty Site History Center, 1851 N Minnesota Ave • Saint Peter, MN 66082 • (507) 931-2160 • http://www.tourism.st-peter.mn.us/nicollet.php3

Soderlund Pharmacy Museum • 201 S 3rd St • Saint Peter, MN 56082 • (507) 931-4410 • http://www.drugstoremuseum.com

Sanborn

Sod House on the Prairie Museum • RR2, Box 75 • Sanborn, MN 56083 • (507) 723-5138

Sandstone

Pine County Historical Society • 305 Governors Wy • Sandstone, MN 55704

Sandstone History and Art Center • 4th & Main, P.O. Box 398 • Sandstone, MN 55072 • (320) 245-2271

Sauk Centre

Sauk Centre Area Historical Society • c/o Bryant Public Library, 430 Main St S, P.O. Box 211 • Sauk Centre, MN 56378 • (320) 351-8777

Sinclair Lewis Boyhood Home Museum • 810 Sinclair Lewis Ave, P.O. Box 222 • Sauk Centre, MN 56378 • (320) 352-5201

Sinclair Lewis Museum • I94 & US 71, P.O. Box 25 • Sauk Centre, MN 56378 • (320) 352-5201

Sauk Rapids

Benton County Historical Society • Historical Museum, 218 N 1st St, P.O. Box 426 • Sauk Rapids, MN 56379 • (320) 253-9614 • http://members.aol.com/bchsmus

Saum

First Consolidated School in Minnesota Museum • Saum Community Club, 41982 Pioneer Rd NE • Saum, MN 56650 • (218) 647-8531

Savage

Scott County Library System • 13090 Albabama Ave S • Savage, MN 55378-1479 • (952) 707-1760 • http://www.scott.lib.mn.us

Scandia

Hay Lake School Museums • CR3 & Old Marine Tr, P.O. Box 123 • Scandia, MN 55073

Schroeder

Schroeder Area Historical Society • 9248 W Hwy 61 • Schroeder, MN 55613-9702 • (218) 663-7706

Sebeka

Sebeka Finnish-American Historical Society, Chapter 38 • Route 1, Box 233 • Sebeka, MN 56477

Shakopee

Murphy's Landing Museum • 2187 E Hwy 101 • Shakopee, MN 55379 • (952) 445-6900

Scott County Historical Society • Stans Historical Center, 235 Fuller St S, P.O. Box 275 • Shakopee, MN 55379 • (952) 445-0378 • http://www.scottcountyhistory.org

Shakopee Heritage Society • 1708 6th Ave E • Shakopee, MN 55379

Sherburn

Sherburn Historical Society • 410 N Prairie • Sherburn, MN 56171

Shevlin

Clearwater County Historical Society • Historical Museum, 264 1st St W • Shevlin, MN 56676 • (218) 785-2000

Shoreview

Ramsey County Public Library • 4570 N Victoria St • Shoreview, MN 55126 • (763) 486-2200 • http://ramsey.lib.mn.us

Shoreview Historical Society • 4035 N Victoria St #110 • Shoreview, MN 55126-2912

Silver Bay
Bay Area Historical Society • 80 Outer Dr, P.O. Box 33 • Silver Bay, MN 55614 • (218) 226-3143

Silver Bay Public Library • 9 Davis Dr • Silver Bay, MN 55614-1318 • (218) 226-4331 • http://www.arrowhead.lib.mn.us

Slayton
Murray County Historical Society • Historical Museum, 2480 29th St, P.O. Box 61 • Slayton, MN 56172 • (507) 836-6533

Sleepy Eye
Dyckman Free Library • 345 W Main St • Sleepy Eye, MN 56085-1331 • (507) 794-7655

Sleepy Eye Historical Society • 316 Walnut SE • Sleepy Eye, MN 56085

South Saint Paul
Canadian Genealogical and Heritage Society • 1185 Concord St N, Ste 218 • South Saint Paul, MN 55075-1150 • (651) 455-9057 • http://www.cghsm.net

Dakota County Genealogical Society • Lawshe Museum, 130 3rd Ave N, P.O. Box 74 • South Saint Paul, MN 55075-0074 • (651) 455-7080

Dakota County Historical Society • Lawshe Museum, 130 3rd Ave N • South Saint Paul, MN 55075 • (651) 552-7548 • http://www.dakotahistory.org

Minnesota Genealogical Society • 1185 Concord St N, Ste 218 • South Saint Paul, MN 55075-1150 • (651) 455-9057 • http://www.mngs.org

Minnesota Genealogical Society, Computer Interest Group • 1185 Concord St N, Ste 218 • South Saint Paul, MN 55075-1150 • (651) 455-9057 • http://www.mngs.org

Minnesota Genealogical Society, Danish Genealogy Group • 1185 Concord St N, Ste 218 • South Saint Paul, MN 55075-1150 • (651) 455-9057 • http://www.wolfbors.com/~danish

Minnesota Genealogical Society, English Branch • 1185 Concord St N, Ste 218 • South Saint Paul, MN 55075-1150 • (651) 455-9057 • http://www.mngs.org

Minnesota Genealogical Society, Finnish Genealogy Group • 1185 Concord St N, Ste 218 • South Saint Paul, MN 55075-1150 • (651) 455-9057 • http://www.minnesotafinnish.org

Minnesota Genealogical Society, Irish Group • 1185 Concord St N, Ste 218 • South Saint Paul, MN 55075-1150 • (651) 455-9057 • http://www.irishgenealogical.org

Minnesota Genealogical Society, Northwest Territory French and Canadian Heritage Institute • 1185 Concord St N, Ste 218 • South Saint Paul, MN 55075-1150 • (651) 455-9057 • http://www.mngs.org

Minnesota Genealogical Society, Norwegian Branch • 1185 Concord St N, Ste 218 • South Saint Paul, MN 55075-1150 • (651) 455-9057 • http://www.mngs.org

Minnesota Genealogical Society, Pommern Group • 1185 Concord St N, Ste 218 • South Saint Paul, MN 55075-1150 • (651) 455-9057 • http://www.rootsweb.com/~mnprgm/

Norwegian-American Genealogical Association • 1185 Concord St N, Ste 218 • South Saint Paul, MN 55075-1150 • (651) 455-9057 • http://www.norwegianamerican.org

Ostfriesen Genealogical Society of America • 1185 Concord St N, Ste 218 • South Saint Paul, MN 55075-1150 • (651) 455-9057 • http://www.ogsa.us

Polish Genealogical Society of Minnesota • 1185 Concord St N, Ste 218 • South Saint Paul, MN 55075-1150 • (651) 455-9057 • http://www.rootsweb.com/~mnpolgs/

South Saint Paul Historical Society • 345 7th Ave S • South Saint Paul, MN 55075

South Saint Paul Public Library • 106 3rd Ave N • South Saint Paul, MN 55075-2098 • (651) 554-3240 • http://www.southstpaul.org/departments/library

Swedish Genealogy Society of Minnesota • 1185 Concord St N, Ste 218 • South Saint Paul, MN 55075-1150 • (651) 455-9057 • http://sgsmn.org

Yankee Genealogical Society • 1185 Concord St N, Ste 218 • South Saint Paul, MN 55075-1150 • (651) 455-9057 • http://www.mngs.org/yankee

Spring Valley
Spring Valley Community Historical Society • Historical Museum, 220 W Courtland St • Spring Valley, MN 55975 • (507) 346-7659 • http://www.ci.spring-valley.mn.us

Spring Valley Historical Society • 221 W Courtland St • Spring Valley, MN 55975 • (507) 346-7659

Springfield
Springfield Area Historical Society • P.O. Box 76 • Springfield, MN 56087-0076

Springfield Public Library • 202 N Cass St • Springfield, MN 56087-1506 • (507) 723-3510

Staples
Staples Historical Society • 418 2nd Ave NE • Staples, MN 56479 • (218) 895-5959

Starbuck
Starbuck Depot Society • P.O. Box 613 • Starbuck, MN 56381

Stephen
Old Home Town Museum • 608 5th St, P.O. Box 593 • Stephen, MN 56757 • (218) 478-3092

Stewartville
Stewartville Area Historical Society • 305 N Main St, P.O. Box 362 • Stewartville, MN 55976-0362 • (507) 533-6470

Stillwater
History Network of Washington County • 101 W Pine St • Stillwater, MN 55082

Stillwater Public Library - St Croix Collection • 223 N 4th St • Stillwater, MN 55082 • (651) 439-1675 • http://www.ci.stillwater.mn.us/library

Washington County Historical Society • Warden's House Museum, 602 N Main St, P.O. Box 167 • Stillwater, MN 55082 • (763) 439-5956 • http://www.wchsmn.org

Taylors Falls
Chisago County Historical Society, Taylors Falls Chapter • 505 Folsom St • Taylors Falls, MN 55084 • (651) 465-3125

Taylors Falls Historical Society • W H C Folsom House Museum, 272 W Government St, P.O. Box 333 • Taylors Falls, MN 55084 • (651) 465-3125 • http://www.folsomhouse150th.com

Taylors Falls Public Library • P.O. Box 195 • Taylors Falls, MN 55084-9998 • (651) 465-6905

Thief River Falls
Pennington County Historical Society • Peder Engelstad Pioneer Village Museum, 825 Oakland Park Rd, P.O. Box 127 • Thief River Falls, MN 56701 • (218) 681-5767

Tofte
Tofte Historical Society • North Shore Commercial Fishing Museum, P.O. Box 2312 • Tofte, MN 55615-2312 • (218) 663-7150 • http://www.boreal.org/nshistory

Minnesota

Tower
Tower Soudan Historical Society • P.O. Box 413 • Tower, MN 55790 • (218) 753-3039

Trimont
Trimont Area Historical Society • 701 W Main • Trimont, MN 56176

Two Harbors
Lake County Historical Society • Depot Museum, 520 South Ave, P.O. Box 313 • Two Harbors, MN 55616 • (218) 834-4898 • http://www.lakecountyhistoricalsociety.org

Split Rock Lighthouse Museum • 2010 Hwy 61 E • Two Harbors, MN 55616 • (218) 226-4372 • http://www.mnhs.org

Ulen
Ulen Historical Society • general delivery • Ulen, MN 56585

Upsala
Upsala Area Historical Society • Main St, P.O. Box 35 • Upsala, MN 56384 • (320) 573-4208 • http://www.upstel.net/~johns/History/History.html

Verndale
England Prairie Pioneer Club • Route 1, Box 36 • Verndale, MN 56481 • (218) 631-1770

Verndale Historical Society • 112 N Farwell • Verndale, MN 56481 • (218) 445-5745

Vesta
Vesta Legion Pioneer Society • P.O. Box 5 • Vesta, MN 56292

Virginia
Iron Range Historical Society • 300 2nd St S • Virginia, MN 55792 • (218) 749-3150

Virginia Area Historical Society • Heritage Center Museum, 800 Olcott Park, P.O. Box 736 • Virginia, MN 55792 • (218) 741-1136 • http://www.virginiamn.com/~historicalsociety

Wabasha
Wabasha Public Library • 168 Alleghany Ave • Wabasha, MN 55981-1286 • (651) 565-3927 • http://www.selco.lib.mn.us/wabasha

Wabasso
County Center Historical Society • Historical Museum, 564 South St • Wabasso, MN 56293 • (507) 342-5759

Waconia
Carver County Historical Society • Historical Museum, 555 W 1st St • Waconia, MN 55387 • (952) 442-4234 • http://www.carvercountyhistoricalsociety.org

Wadena
Wadena County Historical Society • 603 N Jefferson St • Wadena, MN 56482-2336 • (218) 631-9079

Walker
Cass County Historical Society • Pioneer School Museum, 201 Minnesota Ave, P.O. Box 505 • Walker, MN 56484 • (218) 547-7251

Walnut Grove
Laura Ingalls Wilder Museum • 330 8th St • Walnut Grove, MN 56180 • (507) 859-2358 • http://www.walnutgrove.org

Wanamingo
Wanamingo Historical Society • Historic Log House, Main St • Wanamingo, MN 55983 • (507) 824-2556

Warren
Marshall County Historical Society • Settlers Square Museum, 808 E Johnson Ave, P.O. Box 103 • Warren, MN 56762 • (218) 745-4803

Warroad
Warroad Area Historical Society • Historical Museum, 909 Lake St NE, P.O. Box 688 • Warroad, MN 56763 • (218) 386-2500

Warroad Heritage Center • 202 Main Ave NE, P.O. Box 688 • Warroad, MN 56763 • (218) 386-1283

Waseca
Farm America Museum • 7367 360th Ave • Waseca, MN 56093 • (507) 835-2052 • http://www.farmamerica.org

Waseca Area Genealogy Society • Historical Museum, P.O. Box 314 • Waseca, MN 56093-0314 • (507) 835-7700 • http://www.historical.waseca.mn.us

Waseca County Historical Society • 315 2nd Ave NE, P.O. Box 314 • Waseca, MN 56093 • (507) 835-7700 • http://www.historical.waseca.mn.us

Waseca-Le Sueur Regional Library • 408 N State St • Waseca, MN 56093 • (507) 835-2910 • http://www.tds.lib.mn.us

Wawina
Wawina Area Historical Society • P.O. Box 102 • Wawina, MN 55794

Wayzata
Wayzata Historical Society • Depot Museum, 402 E Lake St • Wayzata, MN 55391 • (952) 473-3631

Welch
Prairie Island Community Council - Minnesota Mdewakanton Sioux • 5636 Sturgeon Lake Rd • Welch, MN 55089 • (800) 554-5473 • http://www.prairiesland.org

Welcome
Welcome Historical Society • 109 Hulseman • Welcome, MN 56181 • (507) 728-8806

West Concord
West Concord Historical Society • 600 1st St, P.O. Box 346 • West Concord, MN 55985 • (507) 527-2628

Westbrook
Westbrook Heritage Society • P.O. Box 354 • Westbrook, MN 56183

Wheaton
Traverse County Historical Society • Historical Museum, 1201 Broadway, P.O. Box 868 • Wheaton, MN 56296 • (320) 563-4110 • http://www.cityofwheaton.com

White Bear Lake
White Bear Lake Area Historical Society • Depot Museum, P.O. Box 10543 • White Bear Lake, MN 55110 • (651) 426-0479 • http://www.wblareahistoricalsociety.org

White Bear Lake Genealogical Society • P.O. Box 10555 • White Bear Lake, MN 55110 • (952) 426-2705

White Earth
White Earth Chippewa Nation • P.O. Box 418 • White Earth, MN 56591 • (218) 983-3285

Willmar
Heritage Searchers of Kandiyohi County • Lawson Memorial Research Center, 610 NE Hwy 71, P.O. Box 175 • Willmar, MN 56201 • (320) 235-1881

Kandiyohi County Historical Society • Lawson Memorial Research Center, 610 NE Hwy 71 • Willmar, MN 56201 • (320) 235-1881 • http://freepages.genealogy.rootsweb.com/~kchs123/

Windom
Cottonwood County Historical Society • Historical Museum, 812 4th Ave • Windom, MN 56101 • (507) 831-1134 • http://www.mtn.org/mgs/othersoc/cottonwd.html

Winnebago
Winnebago Area Historical Society • Historical Museum, 18 1st Ave NE, P.O. Box 218 • Winnebago, MN 56098 • (507) 893-4660

Winona

Fitzgerald Library • St Mary's University, 700 Terrace Heights, No 26 • Winona, MN 55987-1399 • (507) 457-1561 • http://www.smumn.edu/deptpages/~library

Historic Pickwick Mill Museum • 26421 Cty Rd 1 • Winona, MN 55987 • (507) 457-3296 • http://www.pickwickmill.org

Maxwell Library • Winona State Univ, 175 W Mark St, P.O. Box 5838 • Winona, MN 55987-5838 • (507) 457-5146 • http://www.winona.msus.edu/library/

Willard B Bunnell House Museum • 160 Johnston St • Winona, MN 55987 • (507) 454-2723

Winona Area Genealogy Roundtable • Arches Museum of Pioneer Life, 160 Johnson St, P.O. Box 363 • Winona, MN 55987 • (507) 454-2723

Winona County Historical Society • Arches Museum of Pioneer Life, 160 Johnson St • Winona, MN 55987 • (507) 454-2723 • http://www.winonahistory.org

Winona Public Library • 151 W 5th St, P.O. Box 1247 • Winona, MN 55987-7247 • (507) 452-4582 • http://www.selco.lib.mn.us/winona/

Winthrop

Winthrop Historical Society • RR2 • Winthrop, MN 55396

Wolf Lake

Finnish-American Historical Society • R O. Box 34 • Wolf Lake, MN 56593

Woodbury

Washington County Library • 8595 Central Park Pl • Woodbury, MN 55125-9453 • (651) 275-8500 • http://www.washington.lib.mn.us

Woodbury Heritage Society • 2100 Radio Dr • Woodbury, MN 55125

Worthington

Nobles County Genealogical Society • Historical Museum, 407 12th St, Ste 2 • Worthington, MN 56187-2411 • (507) 376-4431 • http://www.frontiernet.net; http://www.wgtn.net/gp/genealogicalgroup.htm

Nobles County Historical Society • Historical Museum, 407 12th St Ste 2 • Worthington, MN 56187 • (507) 376-4431

Nobles County Library • 407 12th St • Worthington, MN 56187-2411 • (507) 372-2981 • http://www.plumcreeklibrary.org/Adrian/page11.html

Wykoff

Wykoff Area Historical Society • general delivery • Wykoff, MN 55994

Wyoming

Ostfriesen Genealogical Society of America • P.O. Box 474 • Wyoming, MN 55092 • http://www.rootsweb.com/~mnogsm

Aberdeen

Aberdeen Genealogical Society • general delivery • Aberdeen, MS 38851

Evans Memorial Library • 105 S Long St • Aberdeen, MS 39730 • (662) 369-4601 • http://www.tombigbee.lib.ms.us/

Monroe County Historical Society • 30062 Sand Hill Rd • Aberdeen, MS 39730 • (662) 369-8120 • http://www.rootsweb.com/~msmonroe/histoc.htm

Ackerman

Choctaw County Historical and Genealogical Society • P.O. Box 1382 • Ackerman, MS 39735

Amory

Amory Regional Museum • 715 S 3rd St • Amory, MS 38821 • (601) 256-2761 • http://www.amoryms.us

Ashland

Benton County Historical Society • 671 Ripley Ave • Ashland, MS 38603 • (662) 224-6254

Baldwyn

Brice's Crossroads Museum • Hwys 45 & 370, P.O. Box 100 • Baldwyn, MS 38824 • (662) 365-2383 • http://www.bricescrossroads.com

Batesville

First Regional Library-Batesville Public • 206 Hwy 51 N • Batesville, MS 38606 • (662) 563-1038 • http://www.first.lib.ms.us

Historical and Genealogical Society of Panola County • 210 Kyle St • Batesville, MS 38606

Bay Saint Louis

Hancock County Historical Society • 108 Cue St, P.O. Box 312 • Bay Saint Louis, MS 39520 • (228) 467-4090 • http://datasync.copm/~history

Hancock County Library System • 312 Hwy 90 • Bay Saint Louis, MS 39520-3595 • (228) 467-5282 • http://www.hancock.lib.ms.us

Belzoni

Humphreys County Library System • 105 S Hayden • Belzoni, MS 39038 • (601) 247-3606

Biloxi

Beauvoir - Jefferson Davis Home & Presidential Library • 2244 Beach Blvd • Biloxi, MS 39531 • (601) 388-9074 • http://www.beavoir.org

Harrison County Library-Local History & Genealogy • 135 Main St, Ste 301 • Biloxi, MS 39530-4298 • (228) 435-4613 • http://www.harrison.lib.ms.us

Mardi Gras Museum • 119 Rue Magnolia • Biloxi, MS 39530 • (228) 435-6245 • http://www.biloxi.ms.us

Mississippi Coast Genealogical and Historical Society • c/o Biloxi Public Library, 139 Lemeuse St, P.O. Box 513 • Biloxi, MS 39533 • (228) 374-0330

Old Brick House Museum • 622 Bayview Ave, P.O. Box 508 • Biloxi, MS 39533 • (228) 435-6121

Tullis-Toledano Manor Museum • 360 Beach Blvd, P.O. Box 508 • Biloxi, MS 39533 • (228) 435-6293

Booneville

Eula Dees Memorial Library • Northeast Mississippi Community College, 103 Veterans Loop • Booneville, MS 38829 • (662) 728-7751 • http://www.necc.cc.ms.us

Prentiss County Genealogical and Historical Society • P.O. Box 491 • Booneville, MS 38829 • http://www.rootsweb.com/~mspcgs/

Brandon

Brandon Public Library • 1475 W Government St, P.O. Box 1537 • Brandon, MS 39043-1537 • (601) 825-2672

Rankin County Historical Society • P.O. Box 841 • Brandon, MS 39042 • (601) 825-5937

Brookhaven

Lincoln-Lawrence-Franklin Regional Library • 100 S Jackson St, P.O. Box 541 • Brookhaven, MS 39601 • (601) 833-3369 • http://www.llf.lib.ms.us/Winnebago/

Camp Shelby

Mississippi Armed Forces Museum • Bldg 850 • Camp Shelby, MS 39407 • (601) 558-2757 • http://www.armedforcesmuseum.us

Canton

Madison County Historical Society • 234 E Fulton St • Canton, MS 39046-4510 • (601) 859-5552

Madison County-Canton Public Library • 102 Priestley St • Canton, MS 39046 • (601) 859-3202

Carrollton

Carroll County Genealogy Society • P.O. Box 282 • Carrollton, MS 38917

Merrill Museum • Route 1, Box 152B • Carrollton, MS 38917 • (601) 237-9254

Carthage

Carthage-Leake County Library • 114 E Franklin St • Carthage, MS 39051-3716 • (601) 267-7821 • http://www.mmrlsopac.lib.ms.us

Dancing Rabbit Genealogical Society • c/o Carthage-Leake County Library, 114 E Franklin St, P.O. Box 166 • Carthage, MS 39051 • (601) 267-7821 • http://www.drgs.org

Cary

Order of the First Families of Mississippi, 1699-1817 • W Cypress Dr • Cary, MS 39054 • (601) 873-2649

Centreville

Camp Van Dorn WWII Museum • 138 Main St, P.O. Box 1113 • Centreville, MS 39631-1113 • (601) 645-9000 • http://www.vandorn.org

Clarksdale

Carnegie Public Library of Clarksdale & Coahoma County • 114 Delta Ave, P.O. Box 280 • Clarksdale, MS 38614-0280 • (662) 624-4461 • http://www.cplclarksdale.lib.ms.us

Cleveland

Bolivar County Historical Society • 1615 Terrace Rd • Cleveland, MS 38732 • (662) 843-8204

Bolivar County Library • 104 S Leflore Ave • Cleveland, MS 38732 • (662) 843-2774 • http://www.bolivar.lib.ms.us

Roberts-LaForge Library • Delta State University, Laflore Circle at 5th Ave • Cleveland, MS 38733-2599 • (662) 846-4440 • http://library.deltastate.edu

Clinton

Leland Speed Library • Mississippi College, P.O. Box 51 • Clinton, MS 39056 • (601) 925-3434

Mississippi Baptist Historical Commission • Mississippi College Library, P.O. Box 4024 • Clinton, MS 39056 • (601) 925-3434 • http://www.mc.edu

Coffeeville

Yalobusha County Historical Society • P.O. Box 258 • Coffeeville, MS 38922

Columbia

Marion County Historical Society • John Ford Home, 200 2nd St, P.O. Box 430 • Columbia, MS 39429 • (601) 731-3999

Mississippi

Columbus

Amzi Love House • 305 7th St S • Columbus, MS 39701 • (601) 328-5413

Blewett-Harrison-Lee Home and Museum • 316 7th St N • Columbus, MS 39701 • (601) 327-8888

Columbus and Lowndes County Historical Society • Florence McLeod Hazard Museum, 316 7th St N • Columbus, MS 39701 • (662) 328-5437 • http://www.historic-columbus.org

Columbus-Lowndes Genealogical Society • c/o Columbus-Lowndes Public Library, 314 7th St N • Columbus, MS 39701 • (662) 329-5300

Columbus-Lowndes Public Library • 314 N 7th St • Columbus, MS 39701 • (662) 329-5300 • http://www.lowndes.lib.ms.us

John Clayton Fant Memorial Library • Mississippi Univ for Women, P.O. Box W-1625 • Columbus, MS 39701 • (662) 329-7332 • http://www.muw.edu

Mississippi University Archives and Museum • Fant Library, P.O. Box W 1625 • Columbus, MS 39701 • (662) 329-7332 • http://www.muw.edu

Corinth

Alcorn County Genealogy Society • P.O. Box 1808 • Corinth, MS 38835-1808 • http://www.avsia.com/acgs/

Corinth Interpretive Center • 501 W Linden St • Corinth, MS 38834 • (662) 287-9273

Curlee House Museum • 301 Childs St • Corinth, MS 38834 • (662) 287-9501

Jacinto Foundation • Historical Museum, P.O. Box 1174 • Corinth, MS 38835 • (662) 286-8662

Northeast Mississippi Museum • 204 E 4th St, P.O. Box 993 • Corinth, MS 38835 • (662) 287-3120

Northeast Regional Library • 1023 Fillmore St • Corinth, MS 38834-4199 • (662) 287-7311 • http://www.nereg.lib.ms.us

Verandah House Museum • 705 Jackson St • Corinth, MS 38834 • (662) 287-9501

De Kalb

De Kalb Public Library • P.O. Box 710 • De Kalb, MS 39328-0710 • (601) 743-5981 • http://www.rootsweb.com/~mskemper/library.html

Sciple's Water Mill Museum • Sciples Mill Rd • De Kalb, MS 39328-7940 • (601) 743-2295

Decatur

Newton County Historical Society • 15309 Hwy 15 • Decatur, MS 39327 • (601) 635-2350

Eupora

Webster County Historical Society • Route 3, Box 14 • Eupora, MS 39744 • (662) 258-6898

Webster County Museum • Route 3, Box 14 • Eupora, MS 39744

Fayette

Copiah-Jefferson Regional Library • 218 S Main St • Fayette, MS 39069 • (601) 786-3982

Springfield Plantation House Museum • Hwy 553 & Natchez Trace Pkwy • Fayette, MS 39069 • (601) 786-3802

Flora

Flora Area Historical Society • P.O. Box 348 • Flora, MS 39071

Forest

Forest Public Library • 210 S Raleigh St, P.O. Box 737 • Forest, MS 39074-0737 • (601) 469-1481 • http://www.cmrls.lib.ms.us

Scott County Genealogical and Historical Society • P.O. Box 128 • Forest, MS 39074 • http://msgw.org/scott/genrsrc.html

Scott County Genealogical Society • P.O. Box 737 • Forest, MS 39074 • (601) 469-4799 • http://www.msgen.net/co/scott/scgs

French Camp

Col James Drane Home Museum • MM 181, Natchez Trace Pkwy • French Camp, MS 39745 • (601) 547-6482

Friars Point

North Delta Museum • 2nd St, P.O. Box 22 • Friars Point, MS 38631 • (662) 645-9251

Gloster

Amite County Historical Society • 3112 Leslie Ln • Gloster, MS 39638

Greenville

Old Firehouse Museum • 340 Main St • Greenville, MS 38701 • (662) 378-1538

Washington County Library-Wm A Percy Memorial Library • 341 Main St • Greenville, MS 38701-4097 • (601) 335-2331 • http://www.washington.lib.ms.us

Wetherbee House Museum • 503 Washington Ave • Greenville, MS 38701 • (601) 332-2246

Greenwood

Cottonlandia Foundation • Historical Museum, 1608 Hwy 82 W • Greenwood, MS 38930 • (662) 453-0925 • http://www.cottonlandia.org

Florewood River Plantation Museum • Fort Loring Rd, P.O. Box 680 • Greenwood, MS 38930 • (601) 455-3821

Florewood State Park • 1999 County Rd 145 • Greenwood, MS 38930 • (662) 455-3821 • http://www.mdwfp.com

Greenwood-Leflore Public Library • 408 W Washington • Greenwood, MS 38930-4297 • (662) 453-3634 • http://www.mlc.lib.ms.us

Gulfport

Gulfport-Harrison County Public Library • 1300 21st Ave • Gulfport, MS 39501-2081 • (228) 868-1383 • http://www.harrison.lib.ms.us

Hamilton

Cedarwycke Plantation Museum • 40310 Hwy 373 • Hamilton, MS 39746 • (601) 343-8400

Hattiesburg

Center for Oral History and Cultural Heritage • Univ of Southern Mississippi, College Hall, Rm 112, P.O. Box 5175 • Hattiesburg, MS 39406-5175 • (601) 266-4575 • http://www.dept.usm.edu/~ocach; http://www.usm.edu/msoralhistory

Hattiesburg Area Historical Society • Historical Museum, 127 W Front St, P.O. Box 1573 • Hattiesburg, MS 39403 • (601) 545-4582

Hattiesburg Genealogical Society • c/o Hattiesburg Public Library, 329 Hardy St • Hattiesburg, MS 39401 • (601) 582-4461

Hattiesburg Public Library System • 329 Hardy St • Hattiesburg, MS 39401-3496 • (601) 582-4461 • http://www.hpfc.lib.ms.us

McCain Library • Univ of Southern Mississippi, P.O. Box 5148, Southern Station • Hattiesburg, MS 39401 • (601) 266-4345 • http://www.lib.usm.edu/~spcol

Mississippi Junior Historical Society • William Carrey College • Hattiesburg, MS 39401 • (601) 582-5051

South Mississippi Genealogical Society • 507 Louise St, P.O. Box 15271 • Hattiesburg, MS 39404-5271 • (601) 544-3202 • http://members.tripod.com/'smsghs

Turner House Museum • 500 Bay St • Hattiesburg, MS 39401 • (601) 582-4249

Univ of Southern Mississippi Museum • P.O. Box 5137 • Hattiesburg, MS 39406

Hazlehurst
Copiah-Jefferson Regional Library • 223 S Extension St • Hazlehurst, MS 39083 • (601) 894-1681 • http://www.copjef.lib.ms.us

Hernando
First Regional Library • 370 W Commerce St • Hernando, MS 38632 • (601) 429-4439 • http://www.first.lib.ms.us

Genealogical Society of DeSoto County • DeSoto County Courthouse, P.O. Box 607 • Hernando, MS 38632-0632 • (662) 429-1310 • http://www.rootsweb.com/~msdesoto/gsdcm.htm

Sons of the American Revolution, Mississippi Society • 9580 County Line Rd • Hernando, MS 38632 • (662) 233-2387 • http://www.msssar.org

Holly Springs
Kate Freeman Clark Museum • 300 E College Ave, P.O. Box 580 • Holly Springs, MS 38635

Marshall County Genealogical Society • 109 E Gholson Ave • Holly Springs, MS 38635

Marshall County Historical Society • Historical Museum, 111 Van Dorn Ave, P.O. Box 806 • Holly Springs, MS 38635 • (662) 252-3669

Montrose Museum • Salem Ave, P.O. Box 696 • Holly Springs, MS 38635 • (601) 252-2045

Houston
Chickasaw County Historical and Genealogical Society • 101 Tindall Dr, P.O. Box 42 • Houston, MS 38851 • (662) 456-4512 • http://www.rootsweb.com/~mschchgs

Indianola
Sunflower County Historical Society • c/o Sunflower County Library, 201 Cypress Dr • Indianola, MS 38751 • (662) 887-1672

Sunflower County Library System • 201 Cypress Dr • Indianola, MS 38751-2499 • (662) 887-1672 • http://www.sunflower.lib.ms.us

Itta Bena
James Herbert White Library • Mississippi Valley State University, 14000 Hwy 82 W, Box 5232 • Itta Bena, MS 38941 • (662) 254-3501 • http://www.mvsu.edu/library

Iuka
Iuka Public Library • 204 N Main St • Iuka, MS 38852 • (662) 423-6300 • http://www.nereg.lib.ms.us/iuka.html

Tishomingo County Historical and Genealogical Society • 203 E Quitman St, P.O. Box 273 • Iuka, MS 38852 • (601) 423-2543 • http://www.rootsweb.com/~mstchgs/

Jackson
Catholic Diocese of Jackson Archives • 237 E Amite St, P.O. Box 2248 • Jackson, MS 39225-2248 • (601) 969-1880

Dizzy Dean Museum • 1152 Lakeland Dr, P.O. Box 8719 • Jackson, MS 39204 • (601) 982-8264

Family Research Association of Central Mississippi • P.O. Box 13334 • Jackson, MS 39236-3334 • (601) 981-9220

Historical and Genealogical Association of Mississippi • 618 Avalon Rd • Jackson, MS 39206 • (601) 362-3079

Jackson-Hinds Library System • 300 N State St • Jackson, MS 39201 • (601) 968-5811

Manship House Museum • 420 E Fortification St • Jackson, MS 39202 • (601) 961-4724 • http://www.mdah.state.ms.us/museum/manship

Mississippi Agriculture, Forestry & Aviation Museum • 1150 Lakeland Dr • Jackson, MS 39216 • (601) 713-3365 • http://www.mdac.state.ms.us

Mississippi Dept of Archives and History • Records Mgt Div, 200 North St, P.O. Box 571 • Jackson, MS 39202 • (601) 359-6876 • http://www.mdah.state.ms.us

Mississippi Genealogical Society • P.O. Box 5301 • Jackson, MS 39216-5301

Mississippi Governor's Mansion Museum • 300 E Capitol St • Jackson, MS 39201 • (601) 359-3175 • http://www.mdah.state.ms.us

Mississippi Historical Society • 100 S State St, P.O. Box 571 • Jackson, MS 39205-0571 • (601) 359-6850

Mississippi State Dept of Health - Vital Statistics • 571 Stadium Dr, P.O. Box 1700 • Jackson, MS 39215-1700 • (601) 576-7960 • http://www.msdh.state.ms.us/phs

Mississippi State Historical Museum • Old Capitol, 100 S State St • Jackson, MS 39201 • (601) 354-6222

Museum of the Southern Jewish Experience • 4915 I-55 N, Suite 204B, P.O. Box 16528 • Jackson, MS 39236-6528 • (601) 362-6357 • http://www.msje.org

Oaks House Museum • 823 N Jefferson St • Jackson, MS 39202 • (601) 353-9339

Old Capitol Museum of Mississippi History • N State & Capitol Sts, P.O. Box 571 • Jackson, MS 39205 • (601) 359-6920 • http://www.mdah.state.ms.us

Reformed Theological Seminary Library • 5422 Clinton Blvd • Jackson, MS 39209-3099 • (601) 923-1623 • http://www.rts.edu/libraries

Smith Robertson Museum • 528 Bloom St • Jackson, MS 39202 • (601) 960-1457

Wilson Library • Milsaps College • Jackson, MS 39210 • (601) 974-1077 • http://www.millsaps.edu/www/library/archives/

Kosciusko
Attla Historical Society • Mary Ricks Thornton Cultural Center, 200 N Huntington St, P.O. Box 127 • Kosciusko, MS 39090 • (662) 289-5516 • http://www.rootsweb.com/~msahs

Mid-Mississippi Regional Library System • 201 S Huntington St • Kosciusko, MS 39090 • (601) 289-5151

Laurel
A R Reddin Memorial Library • Southeastern Baptist College, 4229 Hwy 15 N • Laurel, MS 39440 • (601) 426-6346

Jones County Genealogical Organization • P.O. Box 2644 • Laurel, MS 39442-2644

Laurel-Jones County Library • 530 Commerce St • Laurel, MS 39440 • (662) 423-4313 • http://www.laurel.lib.ms.us

Lauren Rogers Memorial Library and Museum • 5th at 7th St, P.O. Box 1108 • Laurel, MS 39440 • (601) 649-6374

Liberty
Amite County Historical and Genealogical Society • Little Red School House Museum, P.O. Box 2 • Liberty, MS 39645 • (925) 254-1679

Louisville
American Heritage Fire Museum • 332 N Church Ave • Louisville, MS 39339 • (662) 773-3421 • http://www.taylorbigred.com

Winston County Historical and Genealogical Society • P.O. Box 387 • Louisville, MS 39339

Macon
Noxubee County Historical Society • 411 S Jefferson St, P.O. Box 392 • Macon, MS 39341 • (662) 726-5218 • http://www.rootsweb.ancestry.com/~msnoxube/society.htm

Noxubee County Library System • 103 E Martin Luther King St • Macon, MS 39341 • (662) 726-5461 • http://www.noxubee.lib.ms.us

Mantachie
Itawamba County Historical Society • George Poteet History Center, N Church St & Museum Dr, P.O. Box 7G • Mantachie, MS 38855 • (662) 282-7664 • http://www.network-one.com/~ithissoc

Marks
Marks-Quitman County Library • 315 E Main St • Marks, MS 38646 • (601) 326-7141

McComb
Pike-Amite-Walthall Library System • 1022 Virginia Ave • McComb, MS 39648 • (601) 684-2661 • http://www.pawls.lib.ms.us

Meridian
Grand Opera House of Mississippi Museum • 2206 5th St, P.O. Box 5792 • Meridian, MS 39302 • (601) 485-3278

Jimmie Rodgers Museum • 1725 Jimmie Rogers Dr, P.O. Box 4153 West Sta • Meridian, MS 39301 • (601) 485-1808

Lauderdale County Dept of Archives and History • Courthouse Annex, 410 Constitution Ave, P.O. Box 5511 • Meridian, MS 39302 • (601) 482-9752 • http://lauderdalecounty.org/archives.html

Masonic Grand Lodge of Mississippi • 2400 23rd Ave, P.O. Box 1030 • Meridian, MS 39302 • (601) 482-2914 • http://www.msgrandlodge.org

Meridian Restorations Foundation • Merrehope & Williams House Museums, 905 Martin Luther King Jr Memorial Dr • Meridian, MS 39301 • (601) 483-8439

Meridian-Lauderdale County Public Library • 2517 7th St • Meridian, MS 39301 • (601) 693-6771 • http://www.meridian.lib.ms.us

Merrehope Archives • 905 Martin Luther King Dr • Meridian, MS 39301 • (601) 483-8439

Mississippi State
Mitchell Memorial Library • Mississippi State Univ, Hardy Rd, P.O. Box 5408 • Mississippi State, MS 39762-5408 • (662) 325-3061 • http://www.msstate.edu/library/spcoll

Monticello
Longino House Museum • 136 Caswell St, P.O. Box 100 • Monticello, MS 39654 • (601) 587-7732

Natchez
Auburn House Museum • Duncan & Auburn • Natchez, MS 39120 • (601) 446-6345

Daughters of the American Revolution, Rosalie Branch • Rosalie House Museum, 100 Orleans St • Natchez, MS 39120 • (601) 446-5676 • http://www.rosalie.net

Descendants of the Jersey Settlers of Adams County, Mississippi • 309 John Glenn Ave • Natchez, MS 39120-4311 • (601) 446-8677 • http://www.djs.org

Grand Village of the Natchez Indians • Historical Museum, 400 Jefferson Davis Blvd • Natchez, MS 39120 • (601) 446-6502 • http://www.mdah.state.ms.us

Historic Natchez Foundation • Historical Museum, P.O. Box 1761 • Natchez, MS 39120 • (601) 442-2500

House on Ellicott's Hill Museum • N Canal & Jefferson Sts • Natchez, MS 39120 • (601) 446-6345

Judge George W Armstrong Library • 220 S Commerce St • Natchez, MS 39120 • (601) 445-8862 • http://www.homochitto.lib.ms.us

Longwood House Museum • Lower Woodville Rd • Natchez, MS 39120 • (601) 446-6345

Lower Lodge Conservation Museum • 712 Franklin St • Natchez, MS 39120 • (601) 442-2617

Magnolia Hall Museum • Pearl & Wahsington Sts • Natchez, MS 39120 • (601) 542-0814

Melrose House Museum • 1 Melrose-Montebello Pkwy • Natchez, MS 39120

Natchez Historical Society • 307 S Wall St, P.O. Box 49 • Natchez, MS 39121

Natchez Museum of Afro-American History and Culture • 307-A Market St • Natchez, MS 39120

Natchez National Historic Park • 605 S Canal St • Natchez, MS 39120 • (601) 446-7047

Stanton Hall Museum • High & Pearl Sts • Natchez, MS 39120 • (601) 542-0814

William Johnson House Museum • 210 State St • Natchez, MS 39120

Nesbit
Jerry Lee Lewis Ranch • 1595 Malone Rd, P.O. Box 384 • Nesbit, MS 38651 • (601) 429-1290

New Albany
Union County Heritage Museum • 112 Cleveland St, P.O. Box 657 • New Albany, MS 38652 • (662) 538-0014

Union County Historical Society • Heritage Museum, 114 Cleveland St, P.O. Box 657 • New Albany, MS 38652-4050 • (662) 538-0014 • http://www.ucheritagemuseum.com

Union County-Jennie Stephens Smith Library • 219 King St, P.O. Box 846 • New Albany, MS 38652-0846 • (662) 534-1991 • http://www.newalbanymainstreet.com/library.htm

Oakland
Oakland Public Library • 324 Holly St, P.O. Box 69 • Oakland, MS 38948-0069 • (662) 623-8651

Ocean Springs
1699 Historical Committee • 810 Iberville, P.O. Box 713 • Ocean Springs, MS 39564 • (228) 875-0664

Ocean Springs Genealogy Society • P.O. Box 1765 • Ocean Springs, MS 39566-1765 • (601) 388-3071 • http://www.rootsweb.com/~msogs

William M Colmer Museum • 3500 Park Rd, Davis Bay • Ocean Springs, MS 39564

Oxford
First Regional Library-Lafayette County-Oxford Public • 401 Bramlett Blvd • Oxford, MS 38655 • (662) 234-5751 • http://www.first.lib.ms.us

Skipwith Historical and Genealogical Society • c/o Oxford-Lafayette County Public Library, 401 Bramlett Blvd, P.O. Box 1382 • Oxford, MS 37655 • (662) 234-7289 • http://www.rootsweb.com/~mslafaye/books.htm

William Faulkner-Rowan Oak Home Museum • 916 Old Taylor Ave • Oxford, MS 38655 • (662) 915-7073 • http://www.olemiss.edu

Pascagoula
Jackson County Genealogical Society • 815 Lake Ave, P.O. Box 984 • Pascagoula, MS 39568-0984 • (228) 762-7777

Jackson County Historical Society • Old Spanish Fort Museum, 4602 Fort Dr • Pascagoula, MS 39567 • (228) 769-1505

Jackson-George Regional Library System • 3214 Pascagoula St, P.O. Box 937 • Pascagoula, MS 39567 • (228) 769-3060 • http://www.jgrl.lib.ms.us

Pass Christian
Pass Christian Historical Society • 203 E Scenic Dr, P.O. Box 58 • Pass Christian, MS 39571

Philadelphia
Choctaw Museum of the Southern Indian • Route 7, Box 21 • Philadelphia, MS 39350

Mississippi Band of Choctaw Indians • P.O. Box 6010 Choctaw Branch • Philadelphia, MS 39350 • (601) 656-1521 • http://www.choctaw.org

Neshoba County Historical Society • 303 Water Ave • Philadelphia, MS 39350-2621

Neshoba County Public Library • 230 Beacon St • Philadelphia, MS 39350 • (601) 656-4911 • http://www.neshoba.lib.ms.us

Picayune

Pearl River County Library System • 900 Goodyear Blvd • Picayune, MS 39466 • (601) 798-5081 • http://www.pearlriver.lib.ms.us

Pearl River Historical Group • 120 Tate St • Picayune, MS 39466 • (601) 795-6773 • http://www.gulfcoastplus.com/histsoc/pearlriv.htm

Piney Woods

Laurence C Jones Museum • Piney Woods Country Life School • Piney Woods, MS 39148 • (601) 845-2214 • http://www.pineywoods.org

Pittsboro

Calhoun County Historical and Genealogical Society • P.O. Box 114 • Pittsboro, MS 38951 • (662) 412-2414 • http://personalpages.tds.net/~rosediamond/societymainpage.html

Pontotoc

Dixie Regional Library System • 111 N Main St • Pontotoc, MS 38863-2103 • (662) 489-3960 • http://www.dixie.lib.ms.us

Pontotoc County Pioneers • 207 N Main St • Pontotoc, MS 38863 • (662) 489-6748

Poplarville

Pearl River Community College Library • 101 Hwy 11 N, P.O. Box 5660 • Poplarville, MS 39470 • (601) 403-1330 • http://www.prcc.edu

Pearl River Historical Society • 134 Newman Rd • Poplarville, MS 39470

Port Gibson

Claiborne-Jefferson County Genealogical Society • c/o Harriet Person Memorial Library, 1005 College, St, P.O. Box 1017 • Port Gibson, MS 39150 • (601) 437-5202

Grand Gulf Military Park Museum • 12006 Grand Gulf Rd • Port Gibson, MS 39150 • (601) 437-5911 • http://www.grandgulfpark.state.ms.us

Harriette Person Memorial Library • 606 Main St, P.O. Box 1017 • Port Gibson, MS 39150-1017 • (601) 437-5202

Quitman

Eastern Mississippi Regional Library • 116 Water St • Quitman, MS 39355-2336 • (601) 776-3881 • http://www.emrl.lib.ms.us

Raleigh

Smith County Genealogical Society • P.O. Box 356 • Raleigh, MS 39153

Raymond

McLendon Library • Hinds Community College, Raymond Campus, P.O. Box 1100 • Raymond, MS 39154-1100 • (601) 857-3378 • http://www.lrc.hindscc.edu

Richton

Pine Forest Regional Library • 210 Front St, P.O. Box 1208 • Richton, MS 39746-1208 • (601) 788-6539 • http://www.pineforest.lib.ms.us

Ripley

Northeast Regional Library-Ripley Public Library • 308 N Commerce St • Ripley, MS 38663 • (662) 837-7773 • http://www.nereg.lib.ms.us

Tippah County Historical and Genealogical Society • c/o Ripley Public Library, 308 N Commerce St • Ripley, MS 38663 • (662) 837-7773

Saint Louis

Hancock County Historical Society • 108 Cue Street Bay • Saint Louis, MS 39520

Sandy Hook

Marion County Historical Society • John Ford Home Museum • Sandy Hook, MS xxxx • (601) 736-4328

Sardis

Heflin House Museum • 304 S Main St, P.O. Box 377 • Sardis, MS 38666 • (601) 487-3451

Scooba

Tubb-May Memorial Library • East Mississippi Community College, 1527 Kemper, P.O. Box 158 • Scooba, MS 39358-0158 • (662) 476-5054 • http://www.emcc.cc.ms.us

Senatobia

Heritage Museum Foundaiton of Tate County • 103 N Ward St, P.O. Box 375 • Senatobia, MS 38668 • (662) 562-8715

Tate County Genealogical and Historical Society • 105 Court St, P.O. Box 974 • Senatobia, MS 38668 • (662) 562-0390

Tate County Genealogical Library • 102-B Robinson St • Senatobia, MS 38668

Starkville

Historical Society of Oktibbeha County • Historical Museum, 206 Fellowship St • Starkville, MS 39759-3378 • (662) 323-0211

Oktibbeha County Heritage Museum • 203 Fellowship Rd • Starkville, MS 39759 • (662) 323-0211

Starkville-Oktibbeha County Library Sys • 326 University Dr, P.O. Box 1406 • Starkville, MS 39760-1406 • (662) 323-2766 • http://www.starkville.lib.ms.us

Summit

Southwest Mississippi Community College Library • College Dr • Summit, MS 39666 • (601) 276-2004 • http://www.smcc.edu

Taylorsville

Watkins Museum • Eureka St, P.O. Box 617 • Taylorsville, MS 39168 • (601) 785-9816

Tishomingo

Tishomingo Baptist Church Museum • 10 jackson St, P.O. Box 89 • Tishomingo, MS 38873 • (601) 925-3434

Tougaloo

L Zenobia Coleman Library • Tougaloo College, 500 W County Line Rd • Tougaloo, MS 39174 • (601) 977-7705 • http://www.tougaloo.edu

Tougaloo College Museum • Tougaloo College • Tougaloo, MS 39174 • (601) 977-7700 • http://www.tougaloo.edu/artcolony

Tunica

Tunica Museum • 1 Museum Blvd, P.O. Box 1914 • Tunica, MS 38676 • http://www.tunicamuseum.com

Tupelo

Elvis Presley Birthplace Museum • 306 Elvis Presley Dr, P.O. Box 1339 • Tupelo, MS 38802 • (601) 841-1245

Lee County Library • 219 Madison St • Tupelo, MS 38801 • (662) 841-9029 • http://www.li.lib.ms.us

Mount Locust Museum • MM 15.5 Natchez Trace Pkwy • Tupelo, MS 38801 • (601) 680-4024

Northeast Mississippi Historical and Genealogical Society • c/o Lee County Library, 219 Madison Ave, P.O. Box 434 • Tupelo, MS 38801 • (662) 841-9013

Tupelo Automobile Museum • 1 Otis Blvd • Tupelo, MS 38804 • (662) 842-4242 • http://www.tupeloautomuseum.com

Union

Kemper-Newton Regional Library System • 101 Peachtree St • Union, MS 39365 • (601) 774-5096 • http://www.mlc.lib.ms.us

University

John Davis Williams Library - Special Collections • University of Mississippi, P.O. Box 1848 • University, MS 38677-1848 • (662) 915-5855 • http://www.olemiss.edu

Mississippi

University, cont.
Walton-Young Historic House Museum • Univ of Mississippi, 5th & University Ave, P.O. Box 1848 • University, MS 38677 • (662) 915-7073 • http://www.olemiss.edu/depts/u_museum

Utica
William Holtzclaw Library • Hinds Community College, Hwy 18 W • Utica, MS 39175-9599 • (601) 354-2327

Vicksburg
Balfour House Museum • 1002 Crawford St, P.O. Box 781 • Vicksburg, MS 39181 • (601) 638-7113

Biedenharn Coca-Cola Museum • 2207 Washington St • Vicksburg, MS 39183 • (601) 638-6514 • http://www.biedenharmcoca-colamuseum.com

Cedar Grove Mansion Inn Museum • 2200 Oak St • Vicksburg, MS 39181 • (601) 634-6126 • http://www.cedargroveinn.com

Columns House Museum • 2002 Cherry St • Vicksburg, MS 39180 • (601) 634-4751

Martha Vick House Museum • 1300 Grove St • Vicksburg, MS 39180 • (601) 638-7036

McRaven Tour Home Museum • 1445 Harrison St • Vicksburg, MS 39180 • (601) 636-1663 • http://www.mcraven.com

Vicksburg and Warren County Historical Society • Old Courthouse Museum, 1008 Cherry St • Vicksburg, MS 39183 • (601) 636-0741 • http://www.oldcourthouse.org

Vicksburg Battlefield Museum • 4139 I-20 Frontage Rd • Vicksburg, MS 39183 • (601) 638-6500 • http://www.vicksburgbattlefieldmuseum.com

Vicksburg Genealogical Society • 104 Evelyn St, P.O. Box 1161 • Vicksburg, MS 39181-1161 • http://www.rootsweb.com/~msvgs/

Vicksburg National Military Park • 3201 Clay St • Vicksburg, MS 39183-3495 • (601) 619-2908 • http://www.nps.gov/vick

Warren County-Vicksburg Public Library • 700 Veto St • Vicksburg, MS 39180-3595 • (601) 636-6411 • http://www.warren.lib.ms.us

Yesterday's Children Antique Doll & Toy Museum • 1104 Washington St • Vicksburg, MS 39183 • (601) 638-0650

Washington
Genealogical Society of Adams County • P.O. Box 187 • Washington, MS 39130

Historic Jefferson College Library & Museum • Dept of Archives and History, US Hwy 61 N, P.O. Box 700 • Washington, MS 39190 • (601) 442-2901 • http://www.mdah.state.ms.us

Water Valley
Blackmur Memorial Library • 608 Blackmur Dr • Water Valley, MS 38965-6070 • (662) 473-2444

Waynesboro
East Mississippi Regional Library System-Waynesboro Memorial Library • 712 Wayne St • Waynesboro, MS 39367 • (601) 735-2268 • http://www.wwcls.lib.ms.us

Wayne County Genealogy Organization • c/o Waynesboro Memorial Library, 712 Wayne St • Waynesboro, MS 39367 • (601) 735-2268

West Point
Tombigbee Regional Library • 338 Commerce St, P.O. Box 675 • West Point, MS 39773 • (662) 494-4872 • http://www.tombigbee.lib.ms.us

Waverly Plantation Mansion Museum • Route 2, Box 234 • West Point, MS 39773 • (601) 494-1399

Woodville
Rosemont Plantation Museum • general delivery • Woodville, MS 39669

Wilkinson County Historical Society • Wilkinson County Museum, 203 Boston Row, P.O. Box 1055 • Woodville, MS 39669 • (601) 888-3998

Woodville Civic Club, Friends of the Museum • County Museum, Courthouse Sq, P.O. Box 1055 • Woodville, MS 39669 • (601) 888-3998

Yazoo City
South Delta Library Services • 310 N Main St • Yazoo City, MS 39194-4253 • (662) 746-5557 • http://www.southdelta.lib.ms.us

Yazoo Historical Society • Historical Museum, 332 N Main St, P.O. Box 575 • Yazoo City, MS 39194 • (662) 746-2273

Albany

Albany Public Library • 101 W Clay St • Albany, MO 64402 • (660) 726-5615 • http://carnegie.lib.mo.us

Gentry County Genealogical Society • c/o Albany Public Library, 101 W Clay St • Albany, MO 64402 • (660) 726-5615

Gentry County Historical Society • Historical Museum, 103 W Clay • Albany, MO 64402 • (660) 726-3315

Altenburg

Perry County Lutheran Historical Society • Historical Museum, 75 Church St, P.O. Box 53 • Altenburg, MO 63752 • (573) 824-5542 • http://www.altenburgmuseum.org

Alton

Oregon County Genealogical Society • County Courthouse, P.O. Box 324 • Alton, MO 65606 • (417) 778-6414 • http://www.rootsweb.com/~mooregon/

Appleton City

Appleton City Landmarks Restoration • 503 N Maple, P.O. Box 44 • Appleton City, MO 64724 • (660) 476-5579 • http://www.appletoncitymo.com

Arcadia

Iron County Genealogy Society • 202 Orchard, P.O. Box 343 • Arcadia, MO 63621 • (573) 546-7842 • http://www.rootsweb.com/~moicgs/icgs_home.html

Arnold

Arnold Missouri Historical Society • 1838 Big Bill Rd • Arnold, MO 63010 • (636) 282-2828 • http://www.arnoldhistoricalscociety.org

Arrow Rock

Arrow Rock State Historic Site Museum • Bingham House Museum, 4th & Van Buren, P.O. Box 1 • Arrow Rock, MO 65320 • (660) 837-3330 • http://www.mostateparks.com

Friends of Arrow Rock • Historical Museum, 309 Main St, P.O. Box 124 • Arrow Rock, MO 65320 • (660) 837-3231 • http://www.friendsar.org

Prairie Park Museum • Hwy TT • Arrow Rock, MO 65320

Ash Grove

Ash Grove Historical Society • 606 W Boone • Ash Grove, MO 65604 • (417) 672-2025

Augusta

Augusta Historical Society • Historical Museum, 119 Jackson St, P.O. Box 182 • Augusta, MO 63332 • (636) 228-4338

Friends of Historic Augusta • Historic Museum, 176 Jackson St • Augusta, MO 63332 • (314) 228-4303

Aurora

Aurora Historical Society • 121 E Olive • Aurora, MO 65060

Ava

Chickamauga Cherokee Nation - White River Band • P.O. Box 982 • Ava, MO 65609-0931 • (417) 751-3422

Douglas County Historical and Genealogical Society • Wilson House Museum, 401 E Washington Ave, P.O. Box 986 • Ava, MO 65608 • (417) 683-5779 • http://www.rootsweb.com/~modougla/HISTSOC.htm

Ballwin

Ballwin Historical Commission • 14811 Manchester Rd • Ballwin, MO 63011-4617 • (636) 227-8580 • http://www.ballwin.mo.us/history.html

Barnard

Barnard Community Historical Society • 633 2nd Street • Barnard, MO 64423 • http://www.barnardnews.com

Belton

Belton Historical Society • Belton Museum of History, 512-A Main St, P.O. Box 1144 • Belton, MO 64012-1144 • (816) 322-3977

Belton, Grandview and Kansas City Railroad Company • 502 E Walnut St • Belton, MO 65012-2516 • (816) 331-0630 • http://www.beltonrailroad.org

Benton

Riverside Regional Library-Benton Branch • 44 N Winchester, PO Box 108 • Benton, MO 63736-0108 • (573) 545-3581 • http://www.riversideregionallibrary.org

Scott County Historical and Genealogical Society • P.O. Box 151 • Benton, MO 63736-0151 • (573) 335-0989 • http://www.scottcountygenealogy.org

Bethany

Harrison County Genealogical Society • 2307 Central St, P.O. Box 65 • Bethany, MO 64424-1335 • (660) 425-2459 • http://www.rootsweb.com/~moharris/

Harrison County Historical Society • Edna Cuddy House Museum, 1218 W Main St, P.O. Box 65 • Bethany, MO 64424 • (660) 425-6811 • http://www.rootsweb.com/~moharris/hcgen.html

Bethel

Historic Bethel German Colony • Historical Museum, 127 N Main St, P.O. Box 127 • Bethel, MO 63434 • (660) 284-6493

Bismarck

Iron Mountain Historical Society • 324 Highway W • Bismarck, MO 63624 • (573) 734-1175

Blackburn

Blackburn Historical Society • R1, Box 129 • Blackburn, MO 65321 • (660) 538-4639

Bloomfield

Bloomfield Public Library • 200 Seneca St, P.O. Box 294 • Bloomfield, MO 63825-0294 • (573) 568-3626

Stars and Stripes Museum • 17377 Stars and Stripes Way, P.O. Box 1861 • Bloomfield, MO 63825 • (573) 568-2055 • http://starsandstripesmuseumlibrary.org

Stoddard County Historical Society • Historical Museum, 400 Center St • Bloomfield, MO 63825 • (573) 568-2163 • http://www.rootsweb.com/~moschs/

Blue Springs

Blue Springs Historical Society • Dillingham-Lewis Museum, 101 SW 15th St, P.O. Box 762 • Blue Springs, MO 64013-0762 • (816) 224-8979 • http://www.rootsweb.com/~mobshs

Friends of Missouri Town 1855 • Historical Museum, 22807 Woods Chapel Rd, P.O. Box 1907 • Blue Springs, MO 64063 • (816) 373-9734

Jackson County Heritage Museums and Programs • 22101 Woods Chapel Rd • Blue Springs, MO 64015 • (816) 795-8200 • http://www.jacksongov.org

Bolivar

Polk County Genealogical Society • 120 E Jackson St, P.O. Box 420 • Bolivar, MO 65613 • (417) 777-2820 • http://www.rootsweb.com/~mopolkgs/

Polk County Historical Society • 516 N Water Ave, P.O. Box 423 • Bolivar, MO 65613-0632 • (417) 326-7698 • http://www.rootsweb.com/~mopolkgs

Southwest Baptist University Library • 1600 University Ave • Bolivar, MO 65613 • (417) 328-1613 • http://www.sbuniv.edu/library/

Bonne Terre

Bonne Terre Memorial Library • 5 SW Main St • Bonne Terre, MO 63628 • (573) 358-2260

Boonesboro

Boone's Lick State Historic Site Museum • State Rd 187 • Boonesboro, MO 65233 • (660) 837-3330 • http://www.mostateparks.com/booneslick.htm

Boonville

Boonslick Historical Society of Cooper and Howard Counties • P.O. Box 324 • Boonville, MO 65233 • (660) 882-5938

Friends of Historic Boonville • Historical Museum, 614 E Morgan St, P.O. Box 1776 • Boonville, MO 65233 • (660) 882-7977 • http://www. friendsofhistoricboonville.org

Roslyn Heights • 821 Main St, P.O. Box 297 • Boonville, MO 65233-0297 • (816) 882-5320

Bowling Green

Champ Clark - Honey Shuck Restoration Museum • 207 E Champ Clark, P.O. Box 162 • Bowling Green, MO 63334 • (573) 324-3154

Pike County Genealogical Society • 14530 Pike 139, P.O. Box 313 • Bowling Green, MO 63334 • (573) 324-5224 • http://www.pcgenweb. com/pcgs/

Branson

America's Presidency Museum • 2849 Gretna Rd • Branson, MO 65616 • (417) 334-8583 • http://www.americaspresidency.com

Bonniebrook Historical Society • P.O. Box 263 • Branson, MO 65615-0263 • (800) 539-7437 • http://www.kewpie-museum.com

National Veterans Center Museum • 1984 State Hwy 165 • Branson, MO 65616 • (417) 335-3511

Old Matt's Cabin - Shepherd of the Hills Homestead Museum • 5586 W Hwy 76 • Branson, MO 65616 • (417) 334-4191

Roy Rogers-Dale Evans Museum • 3950 Green Mountain Dr • Branson, MO 65616 • (417) 339-1900

Taneyhills Community Library • 200 S 4th St • Branson, MO 6566-2738 • (417) 334-1418

World's Largest Toy Museum • 3609 W Hwy 76 • Branson, MO 65616 • (417) 332-1499 • http://www.worldslargesttoymuseum.com

Brazeau

Brazeau Historical Society • Historical Museum, P.O. Box 5 • Brazeau, MO 63737 • (573) 824-5865

Brentwood

Daughters of Union Veterans of the Civil War 1861-1865, Missouri Department • 2615 Porter Ave • Brentwood, MO 63144

Bridgeton

Payne-Gentry House Museum • 4211 Fee Fee Rd, P.O. Box 922 • Bridgeton, MO 63044

Brookfield

Brookfield Public Library • 102 E Boston • Brookfield, MO 64628 • (660) 258-7439 • http://www.brookfield.lib.mo.us

Genealogical Researchers of Linn County • 708 McGowan St • Brookfield, MO 64628 • http://www.rootsweb.com/~molinn/holdings. htm

Buffalo

Dallas County Genealogical Society • 224 Hemlock Dr, P.O. Box 594 • Buffalo, MO 65622-8649 • (417) 345-8694 • http://www.rootsweb. com/~modallaws/DCHS.html

Dallas County Historical Society • Historical Museum, S Hwy 65, P.O. Box 594 • Buffalo, MO 65622-0594 • (417) 345-8694 • http://www. rootsweb.com/~modallas/DCHS.html

Dallas County Library • 219 W Main St, P.O. Box 1008 • Buffalo, MO 65622-1008 • (417) 345-2647

Bunceton

Cooper County Historical Society • Historical Museum, 5236 Hwy A • Bunceton, MO 65237 • (660) 882-6362 • http://www.mo-river.net/ Community/social-services/cooper/historical-society.htm

Burfordville

Bollinger Mill State Historic Site Museum • 113 Bollinger Mill Rd, P.O. Box 248 • Burfordville, MO 63739 • (573) 243-4591 • http://www. mostateparks.com

Butler

Bates County Genealogical Society • c/o Heinlein Library, 100 W Atkinson, P.O. Box 501 • Butler, MO 64730 • (816) 679-4321 • http:// www.rootsweb.com/~mobates/bchs.htm

Bates County Historical Society • Museum of Pioneer History, 403 S Olive St • Butler, MO 64730 • (660) 679-4777

Cabool

Cabool History Society • City Hall, P.O. Box 710 • Cabool, MO 65689 • (417) 962-4775

Cadet

Old Mines Area Historical Society • RR1, Box 1466 • Cadet, MO 63630-9801 • (573) 586-5171 • http://www.rootsweb.com/~mowashin/ omahs.html

Caledonia

Bellevue Valley Historical Society • 10454 Robinson Rd • Caledonia, MO 63631 • (573) 766-5711

California

Moniteau County Historical Society • Historical Museum, 201 N High St, P.O. Box 263 • California, MO 65018 • (573) 796-3563 • http://www. rootsweb.com/~momonite/moniteauhomepage.htm

Wood Place Library • 501 S Oak St • California, MO 65018 • (573) 796-2642 • http://www.woodplacelibrary.org

Camdenton

Camden County Genealogical Association • P.O. Box 3316 • Camdenton, MO 65020-3316 • http://www.rootsweb.com/~moccga

Cameron

Cameron Historical Preservation Society • 116 W 4th St • Cameron, MO 64429-1713 • (816) 632-6063

Cameron Historical Society • Historical Museum, 508 S Walnut St, P.O. Box 189 • Cameron, MO 64429 • (816) 632-3877 • http://www. cameronhistory.com

Campbell

Campbell Area Genealogical and Historical Society • 104 S Ash St, P.O. Box 401 • Campbell, MO 63933-0401 • (573) 246-2112

Canton

Canton Public Library • 409 Lewis St • Canton, MO 63435 • (573) 288-5279

Carl Johann Memorial Library • Culver-Stockton College, 1 College Hill • Canton, MO 63435 • (217) 231-6369 • http://www.culver.edu/library

Center for Living History Preservation • Route 2, Box 226-A • Canton, MO 63435 • (573) 288-3995

Lewis County Historical Society • Historical Museum, 112 N 4th St • Canton, MO 63435-1313 • (573) 288-5713

Northeast Missouri Genealogical Society • 701 Madison, P.O. Box 1574 • Canton, MO 63435 • (217) 656-3853 • http://www.rootsweb. com/~monemgs/

Purvines Genealogical Library • 614 Clark St • Canton, MO 63435 • (573) 288-5713

Remember When Toy Museum and Historic Village of Cedar Falls • 19481 State Hwy B • Canton, MO 63435 • (573) 288-3995

Cape Girardeau

Cape Girardeau Public Library • 711 N Clark St • Cape Girardeau, MO 63701 • (573) 334-5279 • http://www.cgpl.clas.net

Cape River Heritage Museum • 538 Independence St • Cape Girardeau, MO 63703 • (573) 335-6333 • http://www.rosecity.net/museum.html

Historic Hotel Marquette • 338 Broadway • Cape Girardeau, MO 63701-7331 • http://www.pamsuella.com/marquette/index.html

Historical Association of Greater Cape Girardeau • Glenn House, 325 S Spanish St, P.O. Box 1982 • Cape Girardeau, MO 63701 • (573) 334-1177 • http://www.rosecity.net/glennhouse/

Kent Library • Southeast Missouri State Univ, 1 University Plaza • Cape Girardeau, MO 63701-4799 • (573) 651-2235 • http://www.library.semo.edu

Pioneer America Society • Dept of Earth Science, Southeast Missouri State Univ • Cape Girardeau, MO 63701 • (573) 651-2354

Red House Interpretive Center • 128 S Main • Cape Girardeau, MO 63701 • (573) 334-0757 • http://www.capegirardeaucvb.org/museums.html

Rocky Holler USA Museum • P.O. Box 686 • Cape Girardeau, MO 63701 • (314) 243-6440

Rosemary Berkel and Harry L Crisp II Museum • Southeast Missouri State Univ, 518 S Fountain St • Cape Girardeau, MO 63701 • (573) 651-2260 • http://www.semo.edu/museum/

Southeast Missouri Regional Museum • 1 University Plaza, Southeast Missouri State Univ • Cape Girardeau, MO 63701 • (573) 651-2260 • http://www5.semo.edu/museum

Carrollton

Austin Memorial Home Museum • 102 Smith St • Carrollton, MO 64633 • (660) 542-3242

Carroll County Genealogical Association • P.O. Box 354 • Carrollton, MO 64633 • (660) 542-0183 • http://www.carrollcountygen.com

Carroll County Historical Society • 510 N Mason • Carrollton, MO 64633 • (660) 542-1511 • http://www.carolnet.com/cchs/

Carrollton Public Library • 1 N Folger St • Carrollton, MO 64633 • (660) 542-0183 • http://www.carrolltonlibrary.com

Carthage

Carthage Genealogical Society • 611 Bellaire • Carthage, MO 64836 • (417) 358-6494

Carthage Historic Preservation • Phelps House Museum, 1146 Grand Ave, P.O. Box 375 • Carthage, MO 64836 • (417) 358-1776

Carthage Public Library - Genealogy Records • 612 S Garrison • Carthage, MO 64836 • (417) 237-7040 • http://carthage.lib.mo.us

Kendrick Place Museum • 130 E North Woods, P.O. Box 406 • Carthage, MO 63836 • (417) 358-0636

Powers Museum • 1617 W Oak St, P.O. Box 593 • Carthage, MO 63836 • (417) 358-2667 • http://www.powersmuseum.com

Southwest Missouri Genealogical Society • 5676 County Rd 120 • Carthage, MO 64836 • (417) 358-6494

Caruthersville

Caruthersville Public Library • 707 W 13th St • Caruthersville, MO 63830 • (573) 333-2480 • http://cville.lib.mo.us

Pemiscot County Historical Society • c/o Caruthersville Public Library, 707 W 13th St, P.O. Box 604 • Caruthersville, MO 63830-0604 • (573) 333-2480

Cassville

Barry County Genealogical Society • P.O. Box 291 • Cassville, MO 65625 • (417) 652-3577 • http://www.rootsweb.com/~mobarry/society.html

Barry-Lawrence Regional Library-Cassville Branch • 301 W 17th St • Cassville, MO 65625-1044 • (417) 847-2121 • http://tlc.library.net/barry-lawrence/

Center

Ralls County Historical Society • Historical Museum, 120 E Main St, P.O. Box 182 • Center, MO 63436 • (636) 565-1941 • http://www.rootsweb.com/~morchs/

Centralia

Centralia Historical Society • Historical Museum, 319 E Sneed St • Centralia, MO 65240 • (573) 682-5711

Centralia Public Library • 210 S Jefferson • Centralia, MO 65240 • (573) 682-2036 • http://www.centralia.missouri.org/library/

Chaffee

Chaffee Historical Society • Historical Museum, 109 S Main, P.O. Box 185 • Chaffee, MO 63740 • (573) 887-6962

Charleston

Mississippi County Genealogical Society • 403 N Main St, P.O. Box 5 • Charleston, MO 63834 • (573) 683-3837

Mississippi County Historical Society • Historical Museum, 403 N Main, P.O. Box 312 • Charleston, MO 63834 • (573) 683-4348

Mississippi County Library • 105 E Marshall St, P.O. Box 160 • Charleston, MO 63834-0160 • (573) 683-6748 • http://missco.lib.mo.us

Chesterfield

Faust Cultural Heritage Park • Thornhill House Museum, 15185 Olive Blvd • Chesterfield, MO 63017-1805 • (636) 532-7298 • http://www.stlouisecarousel.com

Chillicothe

Grand River Historical Society • Historical Museum, 1401 Forest Dr, P.O. Box 154 • Chillicothe, MO 64601 • (660) 646-1341

Livingston County Genealogical Society • c/o Livingston County Library, 450 Locust St • Chillicothe, MO 64601 • (660) 646-2168 • http://www.greenhills.net/~fwoods

Livingston County Library • 450 Locust St • Chillicothe, MO 64601-2597 • (660) 646-0547 • http://www.livcolibrary.org

Clarksville

Historic 1845 Elgin-Cottrell House Museum • 209 S 1st St, P.O. Box 443 • Clarksville, MO 63336 • http://www.clarksvillemo.ur

Clayton

Clayton Historical Society • Historical Museum, 2 Mark Twain Cr • Clayton, MO 63105 • (314) 746-0427

Hanley House Museum • 7600 Westmoreland Rd • Clayton, MO 63105 • (314) 290-8516

Historical Society of Saint Louis County • 7900 Carondelet Ave • Clayton, MO 63105

Clinton

Henry County Historical and Genealogical Society • Historical Museum, 203 W Franklin St, P.O. Box 65 • Clinton, MO 64735 • (660) 885-8414 • http://www.henrycountymomuseum.org

Henry County Public Library • 123 E Green St • Clinton, MO 64735 • (660) 885-2612 • http://www.tacnet.missouri.org/hcl

Cole Camp

Cole Camp Area Historical Society • c/o Cole Camp Branch, Boonslick Regional Library, P.O. Box 151 • Cole Camp, MO 65325 • (660) 668-3887

Columbia

Boone County Historical Society • Historical Museum, 3801 Ponderosa Dr • Columbia, MO 65203 • (573) 443-8936 • http://members.socket.net/~bchs/

Boone County Historical Society • c/o Wilson-Wulff History and Genealogy Library, 3801 Ponderosa Dr, P.O. Box 1544 • Columbia, MO 65203 • (573) 443-8936 • http://www.boonehistory.org

Columbia, cont.

Calvary Episcopal Church Library • 123 S 9th St • Columbia, MO 65201 • (573) 449-3194 • http://calvary-episcopal.missouri.org

Columbia Online Information Network • P.O. Box 1693 • Columbia, MO 65205-1693 • http://www.coin.org/community/genealogy/

Daniel Boone Regional Library • 100 W Broadway, P.O. Box 1267 • Columbia, MO 65201 • (573) 443-3161 • http://www.dbrl.org

Elmer Ellis Library - Western Historical Manuscript Collection • Univ of Missouri-Columbia • Columbia, MO 65201-5149 • (573) 882-6028 • http://www.system.missouri.edu/whmc

Genealogical Society of Central Missouri • c/o Wilson-Wulff History and Genealogy Library, 3801 Ponderosa Dr, P.O. Box 26 • Columbia, MO 65205-0026 • (573) 443-8936 • http://www.gscm.gen.mo.us

John G Neihardt Corral of the Westerners • 4013 Faurot Dr • Columbia, MO 65203

John William Boone Heritage Foundation • P.O. Box 562 • Columbia, MO 65211 • (573) 445-5032 • http://blindboone.missouri.org

Masonic Grand Lodge of Missouri • 6033 Masonic Dr, Ste B • Columbia, MO 65202 • (543) 474-8561 • http://www.momason.org

Mid-Missouri Civil War Round Table • P.O. Box 165 • Columbia, MO 65205-0165 • http://www.mmcwrt.org

Mid-Missouri Railfans Club • 1017 Lakeside Dr • Columbia, MO 65203 • (573) 446-0228

Missouri Alliance for Historic Preservation • 1008 Sunset Dr, P.O. Box 1715 • Columbia, MO 65203-1715 • (573) 443-5946 • http://www.preservemo.org

Missouri Folklore Society • P.O. Box 1757 • Columbia, MO 65205 • (573) 449-1757 • http://www2.truman.edu/~adavis/mfs.html

Missouri State Genealogical Association • P.O. Box 833 • Columbia, MO 65205-0833 • (573) 364-1275 • http://mosga.org

Northern Cherokee Nation of the Old Louisiana Territory • 5614 E Saint Charles Rd, Ste D • Columbia, MO 65202 • (573) 474-9277 • http://www.ncnolt.org

State Historical Society of Missouri • Historical Museum, 1020 Lowry St • Columbia, MO 65201-7298 • (573) 882-7083 • http://www.system.missouri.edu/shs

Walters-Boone County Historical Society • c/o Wilson-Wulff History and Genealogy Library, 3801 Ponderosa Dr • Columbia, MO 65201-5460 • (573) 443-8936 • http://members.sockets.net/~bchs

Wilson-Wulff History and Genealogy Library • Maplewood House Museum, 3801 Ponderosa Dr • Columbia, MO 65201 • (573) 443-8936

Commerce

Commerce Historical and Genealogical Society • 201 Missouri St, P.O. Box 93 • Commerce, MO 63742-0093 • (573) 264-0038 • http://www.rootsweb.com/~moscott/commerce.htm

Conception

Conception Abbey & Seminary Library • 37174 State Hwy, P.O. Box 501 • Conception, MO 64433-0501 • (660) 944-2803 • http://www.conception.edu

Concordia

Concordia Area Heritage Society • Historical Museum, 802 S Gordon St • Concordia, MO 64020 • (660) 463-2414

Saint Paul's College Historical Society • Saint Paul's College • Concordia, MO 64020 • (660) 463-2238

Craig

Holt County Historical Society • 115 Ada St • Craig, MO 64437 • (660) 442-5949

Crestwood

Sappington House Foundation • Thomas Sappington House Museum, 1015 S Sappington Rd • Crestwood, MO 63126 • (314) 822-8171

Creve Coeur

Creve Coeur-Chesterfield Historical Society • 11631 Olive Blvd • Creve Coeur, MO 63141 • (314) 434-5163 • http://www.creve-coeur.org/historic/

Jewish Genealogical Society of Saint Louis • United Hebrew Congregation, 13788 Conway Rd • Creve Coeur, MO 63141-07236 • (314) 469-0700 • http://www.jewishgen.org/jgs-StLouis

Crocker

Genealogy Society of Pulaski County • P.O. Box 226 • Crocker, MO 65452 • (573) 736-2391

Crystal City

Crystal City Historical Society • 130 Mississippi • Crystal City, MO 63019

Crystal City Public Library • 736 Mississippi Ave • Crystal City, MO 63019-1646 • (636) 937-7166 • http://www.jefcolib.lib.mo.us/joinn/libraries/crystalcity/crystalctylibrary.htm

Cuba

Crawford County Historical Society • Historical Museum, 308 N Smith St, P.O. Box 706 • Cuba, MO 65453 • (573) 885-6009 • http://www.rootsweb.com/~mocrawfo/cchs.htm

Davisville

Davisville Historical Society • 10 Davisville Rd • Davisville, MO 65456 • (573) 743-3663

De Soto

De Soto Historical Society • 604 S Main St, P.O. Box 513 • De Soto, MO 63020-2206 • (636) 586-9242 • http://www.rootsweb.com/~mojchs/

De Soto Public Library • 712 S Main St • De Soto, MO 63020-2199 • (314) 586-3858

Johnson County Historical Society • c/o De Soto Public Library, 712 S Main St • De Soto, MO 63020 • (314) 586-3858 • http://www.rootsweb.com/~mojchs/

Deepwater

Benton County Historical Society • 1115 SE Z Hwy • Deepwater, MO 64740 • (660) 438-7590

Defiance

Historic Daniel Boone Home and Boonesfield Village Museum • 1868 Highway F • Defiance, MO 63341 • (636) 798-2005 • http://www.lindenwood.edu

Dexter

Heritage House Museum • Cooper & Market Sts • Dexter, MO 63841 • (573) 624-7458

Keller Public Library • 402 W Grant • Dexter, MO 63841 • (573) 624-3764

Stoddard County Genealogical Society • 402 W Grant • Dexter, MO 63841 • http://www.rootsweb.com/~moscgs

Diamond

George Washington Carver National Monument Library • 5646 Carver Rd • Diamond, MO 64840 • (417) 325-4151 • http://www.nps.gov

Doniphan

Doniphan-Ripley County Public Library • 207 Locust St • Doniphan, MO 63935 • (573) 996-2616

Ripley County Historical and Genealogical Society • Current River Heritage Museum, 101 Washington St • Doniphan, MO 63935 • (573) 996-5298 • http://www.ripleycountymissouri.org

Ripley County Regional Historical and Genealogical Library • Current River Heritage Museum, 101 Washington St • Doniphan, MO 63935

Eagle Rock
Barry-Lawrence Regional Library-Eagle Rock Branch • Hwy 87, HCR01, Box 1210 • Eagle Rock, MO 65641-0147 • (417) 271-3186

Tree Trackers • HCR 1, Box 1210 • Eagle Rock, MO 65641 • (417) 271-3532

Edina
Knox County Historical Society • Historical Museum, 107 N 4th St, P.O. Box 75 • Edina, MO 63537-0075 • (660) 397-2349

El Dorado Springs
Preserve Our Past Society • P.O. Box 301 • El Dorado Springs, MO 64744

Ellington
Ellington Library • 110 S Main • Ellington, MO 63638 • (573) 663-7289

Reynolds County Genealogy and Historical Society • c/o Ellington Library, 110 S Main, P.O. Box 281 • Ellington, MO 63638 • (573) 663-7289 • http://www.rootsweb.com/~moreynol/

Ellsinore
Ellsinore Pioneer Museum • 11 Herren Ave, P.O. Box 74 • Ellsinore, MO 63937 • (573) 322-0102 • http://www.pioneermusem.com

Excelsior Springs
Clay County Historical Society • Historical Museum, 101 E Broadway, P.O. Box 144 • Excelsior Springs, MO 64024-2513 • (816) 630-0101 • http://www.exsmo.com/museum/

Excelsior Springs Genealogical Society • 1000 Magnolia W, P.O. Box 601 • Excelsior Springs, MO 64024 • (816) 637-3712

Excelsior Springs Historical Society • Historical Museum, 101 E Broadway • Excelsior Springs, MO 64024 • (816) 630-3712 • http://www.exsmo.com

Fair Grove
Fair Grove Historical and Preservation Society • Main St & Hwy 125, P.O. Box 93 • Fair Grove, MO 65648 • (417) 759-2807 • http://www.smsu.edu/rls/Fair%20Grove/fari_grove_historical_society.htm

Farmington
Farmington Public Library • 108 W Harrison St • Farmington, MO 63640 • (573) 756-5779

Saint Francis Historical and Genealogical Society • c/o Farmington Public Library, 108 W Harrison St • Farmington, MO 63640 • (573) 756-5779

Saint Francois Historical Society • P.O. Box 575 • Farmington, MO 63640 • http://freepages.genealogy.rootsweb.com/~mackley/St_Francois_Hist_Soc_page.htm

Fayette
Fayette Area Heritage Society • 120 N Church St, P.O. Box 124 • Fayette, MO 65248 • (660) 248-2200

Fayette Public Library • 201 S Main • Fayette, MO 65248 • (660) 248-3348 • http://www.hocopub.lib.mo.us

Howard County Genealogical Society • 201 S Main St • Fayette, MO 65248 • (660) 248-3348 • http://www.rootsweb.com/~mohoward

Smiley Memorial Library-Methodist Archives • Central Methodist College, 411 Central Methodist Sq • Fayette, MO 65248 • (660) 248-6271 • http://www.cmc.edu

Stephens Museum • Central Methodist Univ • Fayette, MO 65248 • (660) 248-3391 • http://www.cmu.edu

Fenton
Fenton Historical Society • 1 Church St • Fenton, MO 63026 • (636) 326-0808

Ferguson
Ferguson Historical Society • Historical Museum, 315 Darst Rd • Ferguson, MO 63135 • (314) 521-0977

Ferguson Municipal Public Library • 35 N Florissant Rd • Ferguson, MO 63135 • (314) 521-4820 • http://www.ferguson.lib.mo.us

Florida
Mark Twain Birthplace State Historic Site • 37352 Shrine Rd • Florida, MO 65283 • (573) 565-3449

Florissant
Civil War Round Table of Saint Louis • 3930 Marietta Dr • Florissant, MO 63033 • (314) 837-2458 • http://www.civilwarstlouis.org/intro.html

Eastern Slovakia, Slovak and Carpatho-Rusyn Genealogial Research • 2233 Keeven Ln • Florissant, MO 63031 • (314) 831-9482 • http://www.iarelative.com/slovakia.html

Florissant Valley Historical Society • Taille de Noyer House Museum, 1896 Florissant Rd, P.O. Box 298 • Florissant, MO 63032 • (314) 524-1100 • http://www.florissantoldtown.com

Friends of Old Saint Ferdinand Shrine • 1 Rue St Francois, P.O. Box 222 • Florissant, MO 63032 • (314) 839-3626 • http://www.florissantoldtown.com

Historic Florissant • Historical Museum, 1067 Dunn Rd • Florissant, MO 63031-8205 • (314) 921-7055 • http://www.florissantoldtown.com/historicflorissantinc.shtml

Museum of Western Jesuit Mission • 700 Howdershell Rd, P.O. Box 1095 • Florissant, MO 63031

Old Saint Ferdinand Shrine Museum • 1 Saint Francois St, P.O. Box 222 • Florissant, MO 63032 • (314) 837-2110

Saint Louis Christian College Library • 1360 Grandview Dr • Florissant, MO 63033 • (314) 837-6777 • http://www.slcc4ministry.edu

Saint Stanislaus Historical Museum • P.O. Box 1095 • Florissant, MO 63031 • (314) 838-2658

Forsyth
White River Valley Historical Society • 186 Forsyth Rd, P.O. Box 841 • Forsyth, MO 65653 • (573) 288-5713 • http://www.wrvhs.org

Fort Leonard Wood
Fort Leonard Wood Museum • Army Engineer Museum Building 1607, 427 Freedom Dr • Fort Leonard Wood, MO 65473 • (573) 596-8015 • http://www.wood.army.mil/museum/

Manscen Academic Library • Bldg 3202, 597 Manscen Loop, Suite 200 • Fort Leonard Wood, MO 65473-8928 • (573) 563-4109 • http://www.wood.army.mil/ttic

US Army Military Police Corps Museum • 495 S Dakota Ave • Fort Leonard Wood, MO 65473 • (573) 596-0604 • http://www.wood.army.mil/museum

Fortescue
Holt County Historical Society • 115 Ada St • Fortescue, MO 64470 • (660) 442-5949 • http://www.rootsweb.com/~mohchs/index2.htm

Franklin
Santa Fe Trail Researchers Genealogical Society • 3096 State Rd J • Franklin, MO 65250 • (660) 848-2962

Fredericktown
Madison County Historical Society • 122 N Main St • Fredericktown, MO 64673 • (573) 783-2722

Freeman
Freeman Historical Society • 29818 S State Route O, P.O. Box 13 • Freeman, MO 64746

Fulton
Daniel Boone Regional Library-Callaway County • 710 Court St • Fulton, MO 65251 • (573) 642-7261 • http://dbrl.org/branch/callaway/

Kingdom of Callaway Historical Society • Historical Museum, 513 Court St, P.O. Box 6073 • Fulton, MO 65251 • (573) 642-0570 • http://history.fulton.missouri.org; http://www.kchsoc.org

Winston Churchill Memorial Library • Westminster College, 501 Westminster Ave • Fulton, MO 65251-1299 • (573) 592-5369 • http://www.churchillmemorial.org

Gainesville
Ozark County Genealogical and Historical Society • P.O. Box 8 • Gainesville, MO 65655

Galena
Galena Historical Preservation Society • P.O. Box 22 • Galena, MO 65656

Stone County Historical and Genealogical Society • P.O. Box 63 • Galena, MO 65656 • http://www.rootsweb.com/~mostone/society/society.html#help

Stone County Library • 106 E 5th St, P.O. Box 225 • Galena, MO 65656-0225 • (417) 357-6410 • http://www.stonecountylibrary.org

Gallatin
Daviess County Historical Society • 310 E Jackson, P.O. Box 97 • Gallatin, MO 64640 • (660) 663-4098

Daviess County Library • 306 W Grand • Gallatin, MO 64640 • (660) 663-3222 • http://www.grm.net/~daviess

Glasgow
Glasgow Area Historical and Preservation Society • 100 Market • Glasgow, MO 65254 • (660) 338-2377

Lewis Library • 315 Market St • Glasgow, MO 65254-1537 • (660) 338-2395

Glencoe
Rockwoods Reservation Museum • 2751 Glencoe Ave • Glencoe, MO 63038

Wabash Frisco and Pacific Railroad Museum • 199 Grand Ave • Glencoe, MO 63038 • (636) 587-3538 • http://www.wfprr.com

Glendale
Glendale Historical Society • 816 N Sappington Rd • Glendale, MO 63122 • (314) 821-5911

Goldman
Sandy Creek Covered Bridge State Historic Site Museum • Old Lemay Ferry Rd • Goldman, MO 65658 • (636) 464-2976 • http://www.mostateparks.com

Grain Valley
Grain Valley Historical Society • 506 Main St, P.O. Box 414 • Grain Valley, MO 64029 • (816) 443-2616

Granby
Granby Historical Society • Historical Museum, P.O. Box 45 • Granby, MO 64844 • (417) 472-3171

Grandview
Grandview Historical Society • Depot Museum, 1205 Jones, P.O. Box 512 • Grandview, MO 64030 • (816) 761-0414

Truman Farm Home Museum • 12301 Blue Ridge Rd • Grandview, MO 64030 • (816) 254-2720 • http://www.nps.gov/hstr

Grant City
Worth County Historical Society • 206 S High St • Grant City, MO 64456 • (641) 324-1589

Greenfield
Dade County Genealogical Society • P.O. Box 155 • Greenfield, MO 65661-0155 • (417) 637-5334 • http://www.dadegenealogy.4T.com

Dade County Historical Society • Historical Museum, 207 McPherson, P.O. Box 344 • Greenfield, MO 65661 • (417) 637-2744 • http://www.rootsweb.com/~modad/dcgs.htm

Dade County Library • 209 S Main • Greenfield, MO 65661-1217 • (417) 637-5334

Hamilton
J C Penney Museum and Boyhood Home • 312 N Davis • Hamilton, MO 64644 • (816) 583-2168

Hannibal
Becky Thatcher House Museum • 211 Hill St • Hannibal, MO 63401 • (573) 221-0822

Friends of Historic Hannibal • P.O. Box 1548 • Hannibal, MO 63401 • (573) 221-0313 • http://www.hannibal.net/historicgroups

Hannibal Free Public Library • 200 S 5th St • Hannibal, MO 63401 • (573) 221-0222

Ilasco Area Historical Preservation Society • 62744 Brown Estates • Hannibal, MO 63401 • (573) 248-1216

L A Foster Library • Hannibal-LaGrange College, 2800 Palmyra Rd • Hannibal, MO 63401-1999 • (573) 221-3675 • http://www.hlg.edu

Marion County Historical Society • P.O. Box 1548 • Hannibal, MO 63401 • (573) 221-0313 • http://www.hannibal.net/historicgroups

Mark Twain Boyhood Home Museum • 208 Hill St • Hannibal, MO 63401-3316 • (573) 221-9010 • http://www.marktwainmuseum.org

Northeast Missouri Genealogical Society • P.O. Box 1574 • Hannibal, MO 63401-1574 • (573) 288-5713 • http://www.rootsweb.com/~monemgs/

Rockcliffe Mansion Museum • 1000 Bird St • Hannibal, MO 63401 • (573) 221-4140

Harrison
Cass County Genealogical Society • 400 E Mechanic St, P.O. Box 406 • Harrison, MO 64701-0406 • (816) 380-4396 • http://www.casscountyhistoricalsociety.org/gensoc.htm

Harrisonville
Cass County Family History Guild • 511 Sycamore St • Harrisonville, MO 64701 • (816) 380-3010 • http://www.orgsites.com/mo/casscountygenealogicalsocietyinc/

Cass County Historical Society • Sharp-Hopper Log Cabin Museum, 400 E Mechanic St, P.O. Box 406 • Harrisonville, MO 64701-0406 • (816) 380-4396 • http://www.casscountyhistoricalsociety.org

Cass County Public Library • 400 E Mechanic St • Harrisonville, MO 64701 • (816) 884-6223 • http://www.casscolibrary.org

Hartville
Wright County Historical and Genealogical Society • 101 E Rolla St, P.O. Box 66 • Hartville, MO 65667 • (417) 741-6265 • http://www.rootsweb.com/~mowright/wright.htm

Wright County Library • 125 Court Square, P.O. Box 70 • Hartville, MO 65667-0070 • (417) 741-7595

Hawk Point
Lincoln County Genealogical Society • P.O. Box 192 • Hawk Point, MO 63349 • (636) 338-4639

Hayti
Conran Memorial Library • 302 E Main St • Hayti, MO 63841 • (573) 359-0599

Hazelwood

City of Hazelwood Historic Preservation Commission • 415 Elm Grove Ln • Hazelwood, MO 63042 • (314) 731-3424

Wabash, Frisco & Pacific Museum • 1569 Villa Angela Ln • Hazelwood, MO 63042

Hermann

Brush and Palette Club • P.O. Box 145 • Hermann, MO 65041 • (573) 486-2633

Daniel Boone and Frontier Families Research Association • 1770 Little Bay Rd • Hermann, MO 65041 • (573) 943-6423

Deutschheim State Historic Site Library • 107 W 2nd St • Hermann, MO 65041 • (573) 486-2200 • http://www.mostateparks.com/deutschheim.htm

Deutschheim Verein • 109 W 2nd St • Hermann, MO 65041 • (573) 486-2200

Gasconade County Historical Society • 315 Schiller St, P.O. Box 131 • Hermann, MO 65041 • (573) 486-4028

Historic Hermann • Historical Museum, 312 Schiller St, P.O. Box 105 • Hermann, MO 65041 • (573) 486-2017 • http://www.hermannno.com

Scenic Regional Library-Hermann • 113 E 4th St • Hermann, MO 65041 • (573) 486-2024

Hermitage

Hickory County Historical Society • Museum St, P.O. Box 248 • Hermitage, MO 65668 • (573) 745-6716

Higbee

Higbee Area Historical Society • P.O. Box 38 • Higbee, MO 65257

Higginsville

Confederate Memorial State Historic Site Museum • 211 W 1st St • Higginsville, MO 64037 • (660) 584-2853 • http://www.mostateparks.com

Harvey J Higgins Historical Society • 2113 S Main St • Higginsville, MO 64037-1732 • (660) 584-6474

Lafayette County Historical Society • 1201 W 19th St, #326B, P.O. Box 514 • Higginsville, MO 64037 • (660) 584-4447

High Ridge

Jefferson County Genealogical Society • P.O. Box 1342 • High Ridge, MO 63049 • (636) 677-8186 • http://www.rootsweb.com/~mojcgs/

Jefferson County Library • 3021 High Ridge Blvd • High Ridge, MO 63049-2216 • (636) 677-8689 • http://www.jeffersoncountylibrary.org

Jefferson County Library-Northwest • 3033 High Ridge Blvd • High Ridge, MO 63049-2216 • (636) 677-8186

Hillsboro

Jefferson College Library • 1000 Viking Dr • Hillsboro, MO 63050 • (636) 789-3000 • http://www.jeffco.edu

Jefferson County History Center • Jefferson College, 1000 Viking Dr • Hillsboro, MO 63050 • (636) 789-3000

Holden

Holden Public Library • 101 W 3rd St • Holden, MO 64040 • (816) 732-4545 • http://www.go.holden.org/library.html

Hopkins

Hopkins Historical Society • 113 N 3rd St, P.O. Box 292 • Hopkins, MO 64461

Houston

Texas County Genealogical and Historical Society • 300 S Grand Ave, P.O. Box 12 • Houston, MO 65483 • (417) 967-3126

Texas County Library • 117 W Walnut St • Houston, MO 65483 • (417) 967-2258 • http://train.missouri.org

Huntsville

Huntsville Historical Society • Mayo Log Cabin Museum, 107 N Main • Huntsville, MO 65259 • (660) 277-3639

Independence

1859 Jail and Marshal's Home Museum • 217 N Main St • Independence, MO 64050 • (816) 252-1892 • http://www.jchs.org

Bingham-Waggoner Historical Society • Bingham-Waggoner Estate Museum, 313 W Pacific, P.O. Box 1163 • Independence, MO 64050 • (816) 461-3491 • http://www.bwestate.org

Blackburn Historical Society • 313 W Pacific, P.O. Box 1163 • Independence, MO 64050 • (660) 538-4639

Civil War Round Table of the Trans Mississippi • 2704 Glenwood • Independence, MO 64052 • (816) 461-4776

Community of Christ Library • 201 S River • Independence, MO 64050-3689 • (816) 833-1000 • http://www.cofchrist.org

Community of Christ Museum • 1001 W Walnut • Independence, MO 64050 • (816) 833-1000 • http://www.cofchrist.org

General Society, Sons of the Revolution • 201 W Lexington Ave, Ste 1776 • Independence, MO 64050-3718 • (816) 254-1776 • http://www.sr1776.org

Harry S Truman Independence 76 Fire Company Historical Society • P.O. Box 394 • Independence, MO 64051

Harry S Truman National Historic Site • 223 N Main St • Independence, MO 64050 • (816) 254-2720 • http://www.nps.gov/hstr/

Harry S Truman Office & Courtroom Museum • 1933 Jackson County Courthouse • Independence, MO 64050 • (816) 252-7454

Harry S Truman Presidential Library • 500 W US Hwy 24 • Independence, MO 64050-1798 • (816) 833-1400 • http://www.trumanlibrary.org

Jackson County Genealogical Society • Truman Depot Museum, 111 W Pacific, P.O. Box 2145 • Independence, MO 64152 • (816) 252-8128

Jackson County Historical Society • Historical Museum, 112 W Lexington Ave • Independence, MO 64050-3700 • (816) 461-1897 • http://www.jchs.org

Mid-Continent Public Library • 15616 E US Hwy 24 • Independence, MO 64050 • (816) 836-5200 • http://www.mcpl.lib.mo.us

Mid-Continent Public Libr-N Independence Branch • 317 W US Hwy 24 • Independence, MO 64050 • (816) 252-7228

Midwest Genealogy Center • 3440 S Lee's Summit Rd • Independence, MO 64055 • (816) 252-7228

Missouri Mormon Frontier Foundation • P.O. Box 3186 • Independence, MO 64055 • (816) 257-5588 • http://www.jwha.info/mmff/mmffhp.htm

Missouri Territorial Pioneers • 3929 Milton Dr • Independence, MO 64055-4043 • (816) 373-5809

Mormon Visitors Center Museum • 937 W Walnut St • Independence, MO 64050 • (816) 836-3466 • http://www.ldschurch.org

National Frontier Trails Center Museum • 318 W Pacific • Independence, MO 64050 • (816) 324-7575 • http://www.frontiertrailsmuseum.org

Oregon-California Trails Association • 524 S Osage St, P.O. Box 1019 • Independence, MO 64051 • (816) 252-2276 • http://www.octa-trails.org

Pioneer Spring Cabin Museum • Noland & Truman Rds • Independence, MO 64050 • (816) 325-7111

Reorganized Church of Jesus Christ of Latter Day Saints Museum • 201 River St, P.O. Box 1059 • Independence, MO 64051 • (816) 833-1000 • http://www.rlds.org

Missouri

Independence, cont.

Restoration Trail Foundation • 1235 W Lexington, P.O. Box 1059 • Independence, MO 64051-0559 • (816) 836-4671

Saint Mary's Pioneer Historical Society • 923 N Main St • Independence, MO 64050 • (816) 252-0121

Vaile Mansion & Dewitt Museum • 1500 N Liberty • Independence, MO 64050 • (816) 325-7111 • http://www.visitindependence.com

William Clarke Quantrill Society • P.O. Box 520123 • Independence, MO 64052 • http://www.wcqsociety.com

Iron Mountain

Iron Mountain Historical Society • P.O. Box 2 • Iron Mountain, MO 63650 • (573) 734-1175

Ironton

Iron County Historical Society • Historical Museum, 123 W Wayne St • Ironton, MO 63650-1327 • (573) 546-3513 • http://www.rootsweb.com/~moiron2/ironcohs.htm

Ozark Regional Library-Ironton Branch • 402 N Main St • Ironton, MO 63650 • (573) 546-2615

Jackson

Cape Girardeau County Archive Center • 112 E Washington • Jackson, MO 63755 • (573) 204-2331 • http://www.showme.net/CapeCounty/archive/

Cape Girardeau County Genealogical Society • c/o Riverside Regional Library, 204 S Union Ave, P.O. Box 389 • Jackson, MO 63755 • (573) 243-8141 • http://www.rosecity.net/genealog.html

Cape Girardeau County Historical Society • P.O. Box 251 • Jackson, MO 63755

Friends of Steam Railroading • Historical Museum, Jct Hwys 34 & 61 & 72 • Jackson, MO 63755

Jackson Heritage Association • Oliver House Museum, 224 E Adams St, P.O. Box 352 • Jackson, MO 63755 • (573) 243-0533 • http://www.jacksonmo.com/orgs/heritage.htm

Jackson Public Library • 100 N Missouri St • Jackson, MO 63755 • (573) 243-5150 • http://www.jackson.lib.mo.us

National Trail of Tears Association, Missouri Chapter • 429 Moccasin Springs Rd • Jackson, MO 63755 • (573) 334-1711

Oliver House Museum • 224 E Adams St • Jackson, MO 63755 • (573) 243-0533

Riverside Regional Library • 204 S Union, P.O. Box 389 • Jackson, MO 63755-0389 • (573) 243-8141 • http://www.riversideregionallibrary.org

Jamesport

Hook and Eye Amish Dutch House Museum • 509 N Elm St • Jamesport, MO 64648 • (660) 684-6179

Jefferson City

Cole County Historical Society • Historic House Museum, 109 Madison St • Jefferson City, MO 65101-3015 • (573) 635-1850 • http://www.colecohistsoc.org

Inman E Page Library • Lincoln University of Missouri, 712 Lee St • Jefferson City, MO 65101 • (573) 681-5504 • http://www.lincolnu.edu/~library

Jefferson Landing State Historic Site Museum • Rm B2, Capitol Bldg • Jefferson City, MO 65101 • (573) 751-2854 • http://www.mostateparks.com

Mid-Missouri Genealogical Society • c/o Missouri State Library, 600 W Main St, P.O. Box 715 • Jefferson City, MO 65102-0715 • (573) 751-3615 • http://mosl.sos.state.mo.us/lib-ser/libser.html

Missouri Dept of Health - Vital Statistics • 930 Wildwood, P.O. Box 570 • Jefferson City, MO 65102-0570 • (573) 751-6400 • http://www.health.state.mo.us/cgi-bin/uncgi/birthanddeathrecords

Missouri Forest Heritage Center • 611 E Capitol Ave, Ste 2 • Jefferson City, MO 65101 • (573) 634-6002 • http://www.moforest.org/mfhc.htm

Missouri Lewis and Clark Bicentennial Commission • P.O. Box 176 • Jefferson City, MO 65201 • (573) 522-9019 • http://lewisandclarkmo.state.mo.us

Missouri Mansion Preservation • 115 Jefferson St, P.O. Box 1133 • Jefferson City, MO 65102 • (573) 751-7929 • http://www.missourimansion.org

Missouri River Regional Library • 214 Adams St, P.O. Box 89 • Jefferson City, MO 65102-0089 • (573) 634-2464 • http://www.mrrl.org

Missouri Society for Military History • Historical Museum, 2302 Militia Drive • Jefferson City, MO 65101 • (573) 638-9603 • http://www.moguard.com/museum/mong.museum.htm

Missouri State Archives • 600 W Main St, P.O. Box 1747 • Jefferson City, MO 65102-1747 • (573) 751-3280 • http://www.sos.state.mo.us/archives

Missouri State Hiway Patrol Museum • P.O. Box 568 • Jefferson City, MO 65102

Missouri State Museum • 201 Capitol Ave • Jefferson City, MO 65101 • (573) 751-2854 • http://www.mostateparks.com/statecapcomplex/statemuseum/geninfo.htm

Osage Village State Historic Site Museum • P.O. Box 176 • Jefferson City, MO 65102

Sons of the American Revolution, Missouri Society • 3113 Hogan Dr • Jefferson City, MO 65109 • (573) 893-7030 • http://mossar.org

Supreme Court of Missouri Historical Society • P.O. Box 448 • Jefferson City, MO 65102 • (573) 751-2636

Jennings

Jennings Historical Society • 8743 Jennings Rd • Jennings, MO 63136 • (314) 381-6650

Joplin

Dorothea B Hoover Historical Society • Historical Museum, 504 Schifferdecker Ave, P.O. Box 555 • Joplin, MO 64802 • (417) 623-1180 • http://www.joplinmuseum.org

Joplin Genealogical Society • c/o Joplin Public Library, 300 S Main St, P.O. Box 152 • Joplin, MO 64802 • (417) 623-7953

Joplin Historical Society • Historical Museum, 504 Schifferdecker, P.O. Box 555 • Joplin, MO 64801 • (417) 623-1180 • http://www.joplinmuseum.org

Joplin Public Library • 300 S Main St • Joplin, MO 64801 • (417) 624-5465

Kahoka

Clark County Historical Society • Historical Museum, 152 N Morgan St, P.O. Box 202 • Kahoka, MO 63445 • (660) 727-1072

Northeast Missouri Library Service • 207 W Chestnut St • Kahoka, MO 63445-1489 • (660) 727-2327

Northeast Missouri Library Service-H E Sever Memorial • 207 W Chestnut • Kahoka, MO 63445 • (660) 727-3262

Kansas City

Afro-American Historical and Genealogical Society, MAGIC Chapter • 3700 Blue Pkwy, P.O. Box 300972 • Kansas City, MO 64139-0972 • (816) 921-5293 • http://www.magickc.org/id3.html

Airline History Museum • 201 NW Lou Holland Dr • Kansas City, MO 64116-4223 • (816) 421-3401 • http://www.airlinehistorymuseum.com

Alexander Majors Historical House and Park • 8201 State Line Rd • Kansas City, MO 64114 • (816) 333-5556

American Family Records Association • c/o Kansas City Public Library, 311 E 12th St, P.O. Box 15505 • Kansas City, MO 64106-0505 • (816) 252-0950

American Royal Museum • 1701 American Royal Ct • Kansas City, MO 64102 • (816) 221-9800 • http://www.americanroyal.com

American Truck Historical Society • Historical Museum, 10380 NW Ambassador Dr • Kansas City, MO 64153 • (816) 891-9900 • http://www.aths.org

Black Archives of Mid-America • 2033 Vine St • Kansas City, MO 64108 • (816) 483-1300 • http://www.blackarchives.org

Broadhurst Library • Nazarene Theological Seminary, 1700 E Meyer Blvd • Kansas City, MO 64131 • (816) 333-6254 • http://www.nts.edu

Church of the Nazarene Archives • 6401 The Paseo • Kansas City, MO 64131 • (816) 333-7000 • http://www.nazarene.org/hoo/archives.html

Daughters of Old Westport • 8124 Pennsylvania Ln • Kansas City, MO 64114 • (816) 931-5260

Friends of the Truman Farm Home • 5906 E 100th Terr • Kansas City, MO 64134-1258 • (816) 765-2252

Grace and Holy Trinity Cathedral Archives • 415 W 13th St, P.O. Box 23218 • Kansas City, MO 64141 • (816) 474-8260

Greater Kansas City Cornish Society • 209 W 74 Terr • Kansas City, MO 64114-5730

Heart of America Genealogical Society • c/o Kansas City Public Library, 311 E 12th St • Kansas City, MO 64106-2412 • (816) 221-2685

Heritage League of Greater Kansas City • c/o University of Missouri-Kansas City Library, 5100 Rockhill Rd, P.O. Box 10366 • Kansas City, MO 64110-2499 • (913) 663-9731 • http://www.heritageleaguekc.org

Historic Kansas City Foundation • 201 Westport Rd • Kansas City, MO 64141-4413 • (816) 931-8448

Irish Genealogical Foundation • P.O. Box 7575 • Kansas City, MO 64116 • (816) 454-2410 • http://www.irishroots.com

John Whitmer Historical Association • 427 W 70th St • Kansas City, MO 64133-2022

John Wornall House Museum • 6115 Wornall Rd • Kansas City, MO 64113 • (816) 444-1858 • http://www.wornallhouse.org

Kansas City Area Archivists • Univ of Missouri-Kansas City, 5100 Rockhill Rd • Kansas City, MO 64110 • http://www.umkc.edu/KCAA/

Kansas City Branch Genealogical Library • 8144 Holmes • Kansas City, MO 64131

Kansas City Fire Brigade Museum • 1019 Cherry St • Kansas City, MO 64106 • (816) 474-0200

Kansas City Landmarks Commission • City Hall, 414 E 12th St • Kansas City, MO 64106 • (816) 513-2902 • http://www.kcmo.org

Kansas City Museum • 3218 Gladstone Blvd • Kansas City, MO 64123 • (816) 483-8300 • http://www.kcmuseum.com

Kansas City Public Library • 14 W 10th St • Kansas City, MO 64105 • (816) 701-3541 • http://www.kclibrary.org

Liberty Memorial Association Museum • 100 W 26th St • Kansas City, MO 64108-4616 • (816) 221-1918 • http://www.libertymemorialmuseum.org

Liberty Memorial Museum of World War I • 100 W 26th St • Kansas City, MO 64108 • (816) 784-1918 • http://www.libertymemorialmuseum.org

Miller Nichols Library • University of Missouri-Kansas City, 5100 Rockhill Rd • Kansas City, MO 64110-2499 • (816) 235-1531 • http://www.umkc.edu/lib

NARA - Central Plains Region • 2312 E Bannister Rd • Kansas City, MO 64131-3011 • (816) 926-6272 • http://www.nara.gov/regional/kansas.html

National Office Equipment Historical Museum • 12411 Wornall Rd • Kansas City, MO 64145

Native Sons of Greater Kansas City • P.O. Box 10046 • Kansas City, MO 64113 • (816) 926-9397 • http://www.native-sons.org

Negro Leagues Baseball Museum • 1616 E 18th St • Kansas City, MO 64108-1610 • (816) 221-1920 • http://www.nlbm.com

New Santa Fe Historical Society • Historical Museum, 712 W 121st St • Kansas City, MO 64145-1009 • (816) 942-5033 • http://www.octa-trails.org/newsantafe/

Order of De Molay • De Molay Leadership Center, 10200 NW Ambassador Dr • Kansas City, MO 64153 • (800) DEMOLAY • http://www.demolay.org

Piper Memorial Medical Museum • 1000 Carondelet Dr • Kansas City, MO 64110 • (816) 943-2183

Shoal Creek Living History Museum • 7000 NE Barry Rd • Kansas City, MO 64156 • (816) 792-26555 • http://www.kemo.org

Steamboat Arabia Museum • 400 Grand Blvd • Kansas City, MO 64106 • (816) 471-1856 • http://www.1856.com

Thomas Hart Benton Home Museum • 3616 Belleview • Kansas City, MO 64111 • (816) 931-5722 • http://www.mostateparks.com/benton.htm

Toy & Miniature Museum of Kansas City • 5235 Oak St • Kansas City, MO 64112 • (816) 333-9328 • http://www.umkc.edu/tmm

Union Cemetery Historical Society • 227 E 28th Terr • Kansas City, MO 64108-3277 • (816) 472-4990

Union Station Kansas City Museum & Archives • 30 W Pershing Rd • Kansas City, MO 64108-2422 • (816) 460-2052 • http://www.unionstation.org

University of Missouri-Kansas City Library • 5100 Rockhill Rd, 302 Newcomb Hall • Kansas City, MO 64110-2499 • (816) 235-1543 • http://www.umkc.edu/whmckc/

Welsh-American Family History Association • 4202 Clark St • Kansas City, MO 64111

Westerners, Kansas City Posse • 1815 E 76th Terr • Kansas City, MO 64132-2148 • (816) 333-2560

Westport Historical Society • Harris-Kearney House Museum, 4000 Baltimore Ave, P.O. Box 10076, Westport Sta • Kansas City, MO 64111 • (816) 561-1821 • http://www.westporthistorical.org

Kearney
Civil War Round Table of Western Missouri • 17216 NE 134th Terr • Kearney, MO 64060-8909 • (816) 628-9910

Clay County Historic Sites • Jesse James Farm Museum, 21216 Jesse James Rd • Kearney, MO 64060 • (816) 628-6065 • http://www.jessejames.org

Claybrook House Museum • 21216 James Farm Rd • Kearney, MO 64060 • (816) 628-6065

Medal of Honor Historical Society • 17126 NE 134th Terr • Kearney, MO 64060-8909 • (816) 628-9910

Kennett
Dunklin County Genealogical Society • c/o Dunklin County Library, 226 N Main St • Kennett, MO 63857 • (573) 888-3561

Dunklin County Library • 209 N Main St • Kennett, MO 63857 • (573) 888-3561 • http://dunklin-co.lib.mo.us

Dunklin County Missouri Genealogical Society • 1101 N Ricky Rd • Kennett, MO 64469

Dunklin County Museum • 122 College Ave, P.O. Box 762 • Kennett, MO 63857 • (573) 888-6620 • http://www.kennettmo.com/history.html

Missouri

Keytesville
Friends of Keytesville • General Sterling Price Museum, 412 W Bridge St, P.O. Box 40 • Keytesville, MO 65261-0040 • (660) 288-3204 • http://www.kytesvillechamberofcommerce.org

Keytesville Public Library • 406 W Bridge St • Keytesville, MO 65261 • (660) 288-3204

Kimmswick
Kimmswick Historical Society • 6000 3rd St, P.O. Box 41 • Kimmswick, MO 63053 • (636) 464-8687

King City
Tri-County Historical Society of King City • Historical Museum, 508 N Grand Ave, P.O. Box 647 • King City, MO 64463 • (660) 535-4472 • http://www.nwmooline.com/museum /

Kingston
Caldwell County Historical Society • 76 N Franklin St, P.O. Box 32 • Kingston, MO 64650 • (816) 586-2750 • http://www.genealogybuff.com/mo/cchs

Kingsville
Powell Museum and Gardens • Route 1, Box 90 • Kingsville, MO 64061

Kirksville
Adair County Historical Society • Historical Museum, 211 SE Elson Rd, P.O. Box 342 • Kirksville, MO 63501-3466 • (636) 665-6502 • http://www.rootsweb.com/~moadair

Adair County Public Library • 1 Library Lane • Kirksville, MO 63501 • (660) 665-6038 • http://adair.lib.mo.us

E M Violette Museum • Truman State Univ • Kirksville, MO 63501 • (660) 785-4532 • http://www.library.truman.edu/weblinks/violette_museum/mainpage.htm

Phi Alpha Theta Museum • Truman State Univ, CAOC, Student Union • Kirksville, MO 63501 • (660) 785-7118

Pickler Memorial Library - Special Collections • Truman State Univ, 100 E Normal • Kirksville, MO 63501-4211 • (660) 785-4051 • http://library.truman.edu

Still National Osteopathic Museum • 800 W Jefferson • Kirksville, MO 63501 • (660) 626-2369 • http://www.atsu.edu/museum/

Kirkwood
Kirkwood Historical Society at Mudd's Grove • Historical Museum, 302 W Argonne, P.O. Box 220602 • Kirkwood, MO 63122 • (314) 965-5151 • http://www.kirkwoodarea.com/historic/events_main.htm

Kirkwood Public Library • 140 E Jefferson Ave • Kirkwood, MO 63122 • (314) 821-5770 • http://kpl.lib.mo.us

Koshkonong
Historical Society of Oregon County • 302 Diggins, Route 2, Box 3A • Koshkonong, MO 65692 • (417) 867-3285

Koshkonong Area Historical Society • 602 Lyster • Koshkonong, MO 65692 • (417) 264-3163

La Plata
La Plata Public Library • 103 E Moore • La Plata, MO 63549 • (660) 332-4945

Laclede
General John J Pershing Boyhood Home • 1000 General Pershing Dr, P.O. Box 141 • Laclede, MO 64651 • (660) 963-2525 • http://www.mostateparks.com/pershingsite

Locust Creek Covered Bridge State Historic Site Museum • US 36 & Dart Rd, P.O. Box 141 • Laclede, MO 64651 • (660) 963-2525 • http://www.missouristateparks.com

Lake Saint Louis
Lake Saint Louis Historical Society • 100 Cognac Ct • Lake Saint Louis, MO 6367 • (636) 561-6030

Lamar
Barton County Historical Society • Barton County Courthouse, 1004 Gulf St, P.O. Box 416 • Lamar, MO 64759 • (417) 682-4141 • http://www.rootsweb.com/~mobarton/bchs.htm

Harry S Truman Birthplace Museum • 1009 Truman Ave • Lamar, MO 64759 • (417) 682-2279 • http://www.mostateparks.com

Osage Village State Historic Site Museum • 1009 Truman Ave • Lamar, MO 64759 • (417) 682-2279 • http://www.mostateparks.com

Lancaster
Schuyler County Historical Society • Historical Museum, Washington & Lynn Sts, P.O. Box 215 • Lancaster, MO 63548-0006 • (660) 457-3473

Lawrence
Sons of Union Veterans of the Civil War • Historical Museum, P.O. Box 1196 • Lawrence, MO 01840 • (978) 681-6342

Lawson
Family Tree Climbers • D Hwy & Doniphan St, P.O. Box 422 • Lawson, MO 64062-0422 • (816) 776-2305

Watkins Mill Association • Watkins Woolen Mill State Historic Site, 26600 Park Rd N • Lawson, MO 64062 • (816) 296-3357 • http://www.watkinsmill.org

Leasburg
Leasburg Missouri Historical Society • Historical Museum, P.O. Box 127 • Leasburg, MO 65535 • (573) 245-6140 • http://leasburghistoricalsociety.org

Lebanon
Kinderhook Regional Library • 135 Harwood St • Lebanon, MO 65536 • (417) 532-2148

Laclede County Genealogical Society • 186 N Adams, P.O. Box 350 • Lebanon, MO 65536 • (417) 588-8588 • http://www.rootsweb.com/~molcgs2

Laclede County Historical Society • Historical Museum, 262 N Adams St, P.O. Box 1341 • Lebanon, MO 65536 • (417) 588-2441 • http://www.rootsweb.com/~molacled/

Lebanon-Laclede County Library • 915 S Jefferson • Lebanon, MO 65536 • (417) 532-2148 • http://lebanon.lacled.library.mo.org

Lee's Summit
1855 Missouri Town Museum • 8010 E Park Rd • Lee's Summit, MO 64064 • (816) 503-4860 • http://www.jacksongov.org/content/3279/3838/3863.aspx

Lee's Summit Historical Society • 625 NE Applewood • Lee's Summit, MO 64063 • (816) 524-3367

Longview Farm National Historic District Museum • 3361 SW Longview Rd • Lee's Summit, MO 64081 • (816) 761-6669

NARA - Central Plains Division • 200 Space Center Dr • Lee's Summit, MO 64064 • (816) 268-8150 • http://www.archives.gov/facilities/mo/lees_summit.html

Old Train Depot Museum • 220 SE Main St • Lee's Summit, MO 64063

Lexington
1830s Log House Museum • Main & Broadway, P.O. Box 132 • Lexington, MO 64067 • (660) 259-4960

Battle of Lexington State Historic Site • Anderson House Museum, John Stiles Dr, P.O. Box 6 • Lexington, MO 64067 • (660) 259-4654 • http://www.mostateparks.com

Lafayette County Historical Society • 101 W Phillips • Lexington, MO 64067 • (660) 259-6313

Lexington Library and Historical Association • Historical Museum, 112 E 13th St, P.O. Box 121 • Lexington, MO 64067 • (660) 259-6313

Liberty

Baptist Historical Society • c/o Charles F Curry Library, William Jewell College, 500 College Hill • Liberty, MO 64068-1896 • (816) 781-7700 • http://www.jewell.edu

Charles F Curry Library • William Jewell College, 500 College Hill • Liberty, MO 64068-1896 • (816) 781-7700 • http://www.jewell.edu/curry/library/

Clay County Archives and Historical Library • 210 W Franklin St, P.O. Box 99 • Liberty, MO 64069-0099 • (816) 781-3611 • http://claycountyarchives.org

Clay County Historical Society • Historical Museum, 14 N Main St, P.O. Box 99 • Liberty, MO 64086 • (816) 792-1849

Friends of Jesse James Farm • P.O. Box 404 • Liberty, MO 64068 • (816) 635-6065

Genealogical Society of Liberty • P.O. Box 99 • Liberty, MO 64068 • (816) 781-5443

Historic Liberty Jail Museum • 216 N Main • Liberty, MO 64068 • (816) 781-3188

Jesse James Bank Museum • 103 N Water • Liberty, MO 64068 • (816) 781-4458

Linn

Osage County Historical Society • Historical Museum, 402 E Main St, P.O. Box 402 • Linn, MO 65051 • (573) 897-2932 • http://www.osagecounty.org

Linn Creek

Camden County Genealogical Association • P.O. Box 1094 • Linn Creek, MO 65054-1094 • http://www.rootsweb.com/~moccga/

Camden County Historical Society • Camden County Museum, 206 S Locust St, P.O. Box 19 • Linn Creek, MO 65052 • (573) 346-7191 • http://www.camdencountymuseum.com

Lockwood

Lockwood Public Library • 721 Main St, P.O. Box 286 • Lockwood, MO 65682-0286 • (417) 232-4204

Lone Jack

Civil War Museum of Lone Jack • 301 S Bynum Rd, P.O. Box 34 • Lone Jack, MO 64070 • (816) 566-2272 • http://www.historiclonejack.org

Nancy Museum of Antiquity • P.O. Box 292 • Lone Jack, MO 64070 • (816) 697-2526

Louisiana

Louisiana Area Historical Museum • 304 Georgia St • Louisiana, MO 63353 • (573) 754-5550 • http://www.louisiana-mo.com

Pike County Historical Society • 304 W Georgia St • Louisiana, MO 63353 • (573) 754-5504 • http://www.pcgenweb.com/pchs/

Lowndesbor

Afro-American Historical and Genealogical Society, Freedom Trail Chapter • 220 Oak Dr • Lowndesbor, MO 36752

Macon

Macon County Historical Society • 120 Bennett Ave • Macon, MO 63552 • (660) 385-2826

Macon Public Library • 210 N Rutherford • Macon, MO 63552 • (660) 385-3314 • http://www.maconlibrary.org

Malden

Bootheel Youth Museum • 700 N Douglas St • Malden, MO 65863 • (573) 276-3600 • http://bootheelyouthmuseum.org

Malden Historical Museum • 201 N Beckwith St, P.O. Box 142 • Malden, MO 63863-1903 • (573) 276-5008 • http://www.maldenmuseum.com

Manchester

Old Trails Historical Society • Bacon Log Cabin, 687 Henry Ave, P.O. Box 852 • Manchester, MO 63011 • (636) 227-5772

Mansfield

Laura Ingalls Wilder Historic Home and Museum • 3068 Highway A • Mansfield, MO 65704 • (417) 924-3626 • http://www.lauraingallswilderhome.com

Mansfield Area Historical Society • Historical Museum, 111 W Park Sq, P.O. Box 374 • Mansfield, MO 65704 • (417) 924-4041 • http://www.mansfieldhistorical.org

Maplewood

Historical Society of Maplewood • 7844 Manchester Rd • Maplewood, MO 63143 • (314) 647-2952 • http://www.maplewood.lib.mo.us/maphisoc.htm

Maplewood Public Library • 7601 Manchester • Maplewood, MO 63143 • (314) 781-2174 • http://www.maplewood.lib.mo.us

Marble Hill

Bollinger County Historical Society • Massey House Museum, Mill St, P.O. Box 402 • Marble Hill, MO 63764 • (573) 238-4374 • http://www.rootsweb.com/~mobollin/society.htm

Bollinger County Library • 302 Conrad St, P.O. Box 919 • Marble Hill, MO 63764-0919 • (573) 238-2713

Will Mayfield Heritage Foundation • 206 Railroad St, P.O. Box 230 • Marble Hill, MO 63764 • (573) 238-1174 • http://www.willmayfield.org

Marceline

Linn County Historical Society • RR1, Box 247 • Marceline, MO 64658

Marshall

Marshall Public Library • 214 N Lafayette • Marshall, MO 65340 • (660) 886-3391 • http://www.marshallpubliclibrary.com

Saline County Historical Society • 101 N Lafayette, P.O. Box 4028 • Marshall, MO 65340 • (660) 886-7546

Marshfield

Webster County Historical Society • 219 S Clay St, P.O. Box 13 • Marshfield, MO 65706 • (417) 468-7407 • http://www.rootsweb.com/~mowebste/wchs.html

Webster County Library • 219 W Jackson St, P.O. Box 89 • Marshfield, MO 65706-0089 • (417) 468-3335 • http://webstercounty.lib.mo.us

Maryland Heights

Missouri Postal History Society • 12737 Glenage Dr • Maryland Heights, MO 63043 • http://www.mophil.org/mopohissoc.stm

Maryville

B D Owens Library • Northwest Missouri State Univ, 800 University Dr • Maryville, MO 64468-6001 • (660) 562-1192 • http://www.nwmissouri.edu/library/

Caleb Burns House Museum • 422 W 2nd, P.O. Box 324 • Maryville, MO 64468 • (660) 582-8176

Graham Historical Society • 417 S Walnut • Maryville, MO 64468 • (660) 939-2275

Maryville Public Library • 509 N Main St • Maryville, MO 64468 • (660) 582-5281

Nodaway County Genealogical Society • Historical Museum, 110 N Walnut St, P.O. Box 214 • Maryville, MO 64468 • (660) 582-8176 • http://www.rootsweb.com/~monodawa/ncgs.htm

Nodaway County Historical Society • Historical Museum, 110 N Walnut, P.O. Box 324 • Maryville, MO 64468-0324 • (660) 582-8176 • http://www.nodawayhistorical.org

Maryville, cont.
Sons and Daughters of the Blue and Gray Civil War Roundtable • P.O. Box 316 • Maryville, MO 64468 • (660) 582-2159

Maysville
DeKalb County Historical Society • 116 E Main St, P.O. Box 477 • Maysville, MO 64469-0477 • (816) 449-5451 • http://www.rootsweb. com/~modekalb/dchs.html

Memphis
Scotland County Genealogical Society • 115 W Madison, P.O. Box 232 • Memphis, MO 63555 • http://www.scotlandcounty.net

Scotland County Historical Society • Downing House Museum, 311 S Main, P.O. Box 232 • Memphis, MO 63555 • (660) 465-2275 • http:// www.rootsweb.com/moscotla/

Scotland County Memorial Library • 306 W Madison St • Memphis, MO 63555 • (660) 465-7042

Mexico
American Saddlebred Horse Museum • 501 S Muldrow • Mexico, MO 65265 • (573) 581-7155 • http://www.audrain.org

Audrain County Area Genealogical Society • c/o Mexico-Audrain Public Library, 305 W Jackson St • Mexico, MO 65265 • (573) 581-4939 • http://members.sockets.net/~macld/genealogy.htm

Audrain County Historical Society • Graceland Museum, 501 S Muldrow St, P.O. Box 398 • Mexico, MO 65265 • (573) 581-3910 • http://www.audrain.org

Mexico-Audrain County Library District • 305 W Jackson St • Mexico, MO 65265 • (573) 581-4939 • http://mexico-audrain.lib.mo.us/mexico-audrain/

Miami
Friends of Miami • P.O. Box 26 • Miami, MO 65344 • (660) 886-5987 • http://www.sullivanfarms.net/friendsofmiami/

Van Meter State Park • Route 1, Box 47, Hwy 122 • Miami, MO 65344 • (660) 886-7537 • http://www.dnr.state.mo.us/dsp/homedsp.htm

Milan
Sullivan County Historical Society • Genealogical Library, 117 N Water St • Milan, MO 63556-1023 • (660) 265-3476 • http://www.rootsweb. com/~mosulliv/schistoricalsociety.html

Sullivan County Public Library • 109 E 2nd St • Milan, MO 63556 • (660) 265-3911

Moberly
Little Dixie Regional Libraries • 111 N 4th St • Moberly, MO 65270-1577 • (660) 263-4426 • http://www.little-dixie.lib.mo.us

Randolph County Historical Society • Historical Center, 226 N Clark, P.O. Box 116 • Moberly, MO 65270 • (660) 263-9396 • http://www. randolphhistory.com

Monett
Barry-Lawrence Regional Library • 213 6th St • Monett, MO 65708 • (417) 235-6646 • http://tlc.library.net/bll/

Chickamauga Cherokee Nation • 501 Fron Rd 2030 • Monett, MO 65708 • (417) 654-4003

Root Diggers • 704 5th St • Monett, MO 65708-1732

Montgomery City
Montgomery City Historical Society • Historical Museum, 112 W 2nd St • Montgomery City, MO 63361 • (573) 564-2370

Montgomery County Genealogical Society • 112 W 2nd St • Montgomery City, MO 63361 • http://www.montgomery.mogenweb.org

Moscow Mills
Lincoln County Genealogical Society • Shapley Ross House Museum, 125 W 2nd St • Moscow Mills, MO 63362-1216 • (636) 528-8345 • http://www.rootsweb.com/~molincol/research/lcsociety.htm

Mound City
Holt County Historical Society • Historical Museum, 115 Ava St, P.O. Box 55 • Mound City, MO 64470 • (660) 442-5949 • http://www. rootsweb.com/~mohchs/

Mound City Museum • 104 E 7th • Mound City, MO 64470 • (660) 442-5635

Mount Vernon
Barry-Lawrence Library • 112 W Dallas • Mount Vernon, MO 65712

Lawrence County Historical Society • Historical Museum, P.O. Box 406 • Mount Vernon, MO 65712 • (417) 466-3446 • http://www.rootsweb. com/~molawre2/society.htm

Mountain View
Mountain View Public Library • 125 S Oak St, P.O. Box 1389 • Mountain View, MO 65548 • (417) 934-6154 • http://mvpl.lib.mo.us

Neelyville
Neelyville Historical Society • Route 1, Box 1C • Neelyville, MO 63954

Nelson
Sappington Cemetery State Historic Site Museum • Rds AA & TT • Nelson, MO 65347 • (660) 837-3300 • http://www.mostateparks.com/ sappingtoncem.htm

Neosho
Crowder College Library and Longwell Museum • 601 Laclede Ave • Neosho, MO 64850 • (417) 451-3223 • http://www.crowdercollege.edu

Genealogy Friends of the Library • c/o Neosho-Newton County Library, 201 W Spring, P.O. Box 314 • Neosho, MO 64850-0314 • (417) 451-4231 • http://www.rootsweb.com/~monewton/gf.html

Longwell Museum • Crowder College, 601 La Clede • Neosho, MO 64850 • http://www.crowder.edu

Neosho-Newton County Library • 201 W Spring • Neosho, MO 64850 • (417) 451-4231 • http://www.neosholibrary.org

Newton County Historical Society and Genealogical Study Group • Historical Museum, 121 N Washington St, P.O. Box 675 • Neosho, MO 64850 • (417) 451-4940 • http://www.newtoncountyhistoricalsociety.org

Newton County Museum • 121 N Washington, P.O. Box 675 • Neosho, MO 64850

Nevada
Nevada Public Library • 218 W Walnut, P.O. Box B • Nevada, MO 64772-0931 • (417) 448-2770

Tri-County Genealogical Society • 218 W Walnut St, P.O. Box B • Nevada, MO 64772 • (417) 922-3596 • http://www.rootsweb. com/~motcogs/

Vernon County Genealogical Society • 225 W Austin, P.O. Box B • Nevada, MO 64772 • (417) 667-2831

Vernon County Historical Society • Bushwhacker Museum, 212 W Walnut • Nevada, MO 64772 • (417) 667-9602 • http://www. bushwhacker.org

New Franklin
Franklin or Bust • P.O. Box 324 • New Franklin, MO 65274 • (660) 848-2451

South Howard County Historical Society • Historical Museum, 101 East Broadway, P.O. Box 234 • New Franklin, MO 65274 • (660) 848-2102

New Haven
Scenic Regional Library-New Haven Branch • 901 Maupin • New Haven, MO 63068 • (573) 237-2189

New Lebanon
New Lebanon Preservation Society • 5236 Hwy A • New Lebanon, MO 65237 • (660) 366-4482

New Madrid

Higgerson School Historic Site Museum • 300 Main St • New Madrid, MO 63869 • (573) 748-5716 • http://new-madrid.mo.us/higgersonschool.htm

Hunter-Dawson Home State Historic Site Museum • 1012 Dawson Rd, P.O. Box 308 • New Madrid, MO 63869 • (573) 748-5891 • http://www.mostateparks.com

New Madrid Historical Museum • 1 Main St • New Madrid, MO 63869 • (573) 748-5944 • http://www.newmadridmuseum.com

New Melle

Boone-Duden Historical Society • Kamphoefner House Museum, 3565 Mill St, P.O. Box 82 • New Melle, MO 63365-0082 • (636) 798-2136 • http://www.rootsweb.com/~moboonhs/

Norborne

Norborne Public Library • 109 E 2nd St • Norborne, MO 64668 • (660) 594-3514

Normandy

Normandy Area Historical Association • 7450 Natural Bridge R, P.O. Box 210208 • Normandy, MO 63121 • (417) 865-1318 • http://normandyhistorical.homestead.com

Sisters of Divine Providence Museum • 8351 Florissant Rd • Normandy, MO 63121 • (314) 524-3803

North Kansas City

Thrailkill Genealogical Society • 2018 Gentry St • North Kansas City, MO 64116

Novinger

Novinger Log Home Museum • Snyder & Coal Sts • Novinger, MO 63559 • (660) 488-5280

O'Fallon

O'Fallon Historical Society • Historical Museum, 308 Civic Park Dr, P.O. Box 424 • O'Fallon, MO 63366 • (636) 272-5152 • http://www.ofallonmohistory.org

Old Mines

Old Mines Area Historical Society • Route 1, Box 1466 • Old Mines, MO 63630 • (573) 438-2368 • http://www.rootsweb.com/~mowashin/omahs.html#meetings

Osceola

Saint Clair County Historical Society • 225 Market St, P.O. Box 376 • Osceola, MO 64776 • (417) 644-2913 • http://freepages.genealogy.rootsweb.com/~cbell/historical.htm

Saint Clair County Library • 115 Chestnut St, P.O. Box 575 • Osceola, MO 64776-0575 • (417) 646-2214 • http://mostclair.lib.mo.us

Overland

Overland Historical Society • Log House Museum, 2409 Sunnybrook Dr • Overland, MO 63114 • (314) 426-7027

Saint Louis Regional Historical Societies • 2315 Woodson Rd • Overland, MO 63114 • (314) 427-4810

Owensville

Gasconade County Historical Society • Historical Museum, 105 W McFadden Ave • Owensville, MO 65041 • (573) 437-5617 • http://www.rootsweb.com/~mogascon /

Ozark

Christian County Historical Society • Historical Museum, 202 E Church, P.O. Box 442 • Ozark, MO 65721 • (417) 587-7154

Christian County Library • 1005 N 4th Ave • Ozark, MO 65721 • (417) 581-2432 • http://christiancounty.lib.mo.us

Pacific

Meramec Valley Genealogical and Historical Society • c/o Scenic Regional Library, 140 W Saint Louis St • Pacific, MO 63069 • (636) 257-2712 • http://www.rootsweb.com/~mofrankl/hsmeramecvalgen.htm

Scenic Regional Library-Pacific • 140 W St Louis St • Pacific, MO 63069 • (636) 257-2712

Palmyra

Heritage Seekers • Gardner House Museum, 417 S Main St • Palmyra, MO 63461 • (573) 769-3076 • http://www.palmyraheritageseekers.org

Palmyra Bicentennial Public Library • 212 S Main St • Palmyra, MO 63461 • (573) 769-2830

Paris

Little Dixie Regional Libraries-Dulany Memorial • 101 N Main • Paris, MO 65275-1398 • (660) 327-4707

Monroe County Historical Society • Historical Museum, N Main, P.O. Box 131 • Paris, MO 65275 • (660) 327-5302 • http://www.rootsweb.com/~momchs2

Union Covered Bridge State Historic Site Museum • County Rd C & Hwy 24 • Paris, MO 65275 • (573) 565-3449 • http://www.mousestateparks.com/unionbridge.htm

Park Hills

Missouri Mines Museum Society • Historical Museum, 75 Highway 32, P.O. Box 492 • Park Hills, MO 63601 • (573) 431-6226

Park Hills Public Library • 8 Municipal Dr • Park Hills, MO 63601 • (573) 431-4842

Parkville

McAfee Library - Frances Fishburn Archives • Park College, 8700 NW River Park Dr, P.O. Box 61 • Parkville, MO 64152 • (816) 741-2000 • http://www.park.edu

Missouri River Frontier Museum • 128 S Main St, Ste 412 • Parkville, MO 64152 • (816) 741-1482

Northland Genealogical Society • P.O. Box 14121 • Parkville, MO 64152 • (816) 741-3981 • http://homepages.rootsweb.com/~kcngs/

Park University Historical Society • c/o McAfee Library, Park College, 8700 NW River Park Dr, P.O. Box 61 • Parkville, MO 64152 • (816) 741-2000

Park University Library • 8700 NW River Park Dr • Parkville, MO 64152-3795 • (816) 584-6840 • http://www.kepl.lib.mo.us

Perry

Ralls County Historical Museum • 120 Main St • Perry, MO 63462 • http://www.rootsweb.com/~morchs/

Ralls County Historical Society • 120 E Main St • Perry, MO 63462 • (573) 565-2025

Perryville

Friedenberg Lutheran Historical Society • 1142 PCR 302 • Perryville, MO 63775 • (573) 547-8607

Perry County Historical Society • Faherty House Museum, 11 S Spring St, P.O. Box 97 • Perryville, MO 63775 • (573) 547-2927 • http://www.perryvillemissouri.com/perrycountyhistoricalsociety.htm

Riverside Regional Library-Perryville Branch • 800 City Park Dr, Suite A • Perryville, MO 63775 • (573) 547-6508 • http://www.riversideregionallibrary.org

Vincentian Studies Institute • 1701 W Joseph St • Perryville, MO 63775 • (573) 547-6533

Piedmont

Wayne County Historical Society • Historical Museum, P.O. Box 222 • Piedmont, MO 63957 • (573) 223-7130

Missouri

Pierce City
Harold Bell Wright Museum • 404 N Walnut St • Pierce City, MO 65723 • (417) 476-2323 • http://hometown.aol.com/hbwmuseuminpcmo/myhomepage/

Pilot Grove
Cooper County Historical Society • P.O. Box 51 • Pilot Grove, MO 65276 • (660) 834-3582

Crestmead House Museum • 7400 A Hwy • Pilot Grove, MO 65276 • (816) 834-4140

Pleasant Green House Museum • 7045 Hwy 135 • Pilot Grove, MO 65276 • (660) 834-3945

Pilot Knob
Fort Davidson State Historic Site Museum • Hwy 21 & Hwy V, P.O. Box 509 • Pilot Knob, MO 63663 • (573) 546-3454 • http://www.mostateparks.com/ftdavidson.htm

Pineville
McDonald County Historical Museum • 302 Harmon St, P.O. Box 572 • Pineville, MO 64856 • http://www.mcdonaldcohistory.org/museum.htm

McDonald County Historical Society • 208 E 1st St, P.O. Box 572 • Pineville, MO 64856 • (417) 223-4127 • http://www.mcdonaldcohistory.org

McDonald County Library • 808 Bailey Rd • Pineville, MO 64856 • (417) 223-4489 • http://mcdonaldcountylibrary.org

Platte City
Platte County Historical and Genealogical Society • 1882 Home Museum, 220 Ferrel Dr, P.O. Box 103 • Platte City, MO 64079 • (816) 431-5121 • http://www.rootsweb.com/~mopchgs/

Plattsburg
Clinton County Historical and Genealogical Society • 608 W Maple • Plattsburg, MO 64477 • (816) 930-1909 • http://members.aol.com/ClintonCo

Clinton County Historical Society • Historical Museum, 509 Broadway • Plattsburg, MO 64477 • (816) 539-2992 • http://www.rootsweb.com/~moclinto/histsoc/

Riley-Carmack House Museum • 408 Birch Ave • Plattsburg, MO 64477

Pleasant Hill
Pleasant Hill Historical Society • 125 Wyoming St, P.O. Box 31 • Pleasant Hill, MO 64080 • (816) 540-4010 • http://www.orgsites.com/mo/pleasanthillhistoricalsociety/

Point Lookout
Brownell Research Center Library • College of the Ozarks, 1 Cultural Court, P.O. Box 17 • Point Lookout, MO 65726 • (417) 334-6411 • http://www.cofo.edu

Lyons Memorial Library • College of the Ozarks, 1 Opportunity Ave • Point Lookout, MO 65726 • (417) 334-6411 • http://www.cofo.edu

Point Lookout
Ralph Foster Museum • 100 Cultural Ct, P.O. Box 17 • Point Lookout, MO 65726 • (417) 334-6411 • http://www.rfostermuseum.com

White River Valley Historical Society • P.O. Box 555 • Point Lookout, MO 65726-0555 • (417) 369-2413 • http://http//thelibrary.springfield.missouri.org

Poplar Bluff
Butler County Historical Society • Historical Museum, 1016 N Main, P.O. Box 1526 • Poplar Bluff, MO 63901 • (573) 785-7558 • http://www.butlercountyhistory.org

Genealogical Society of Butler County • 316 N Main St, P.O. Box 426 • Poplar Bluff, MO 63901 • (314) 785-8330 • http://www.rootsweb.com/~mobcgs/

MO-ARK Regional Railroad Museum • 303 Moran St • Poplar Bluff, MO 63901 • (573) 785-4539 • http://www.pbrail.org

Rutland Library • Three Rivers Community College, 2080 Three Rivers Blvd • Poplar Bluff, MO 63901 • (573) 840-9654 • http://www.trcc.edu/library

Portage Des Sioux
Land Between the Rivers Society • P.O. Box 200 • Portage Des Sioux, MO 63307 • (636) 250-3812

Portageville
New Madrid County Library • 309 E Main St • Portageville, MO 63873 • (573) 379-3583

Potosi
Mine Au Breton Historical Society • 10205 Weber Ln • Potosi, MO 63664 • (573) 438-4973 • http://www.mogenweb.org/washington/mabhs.html

Washington County Library • 235 E High St • Potosi, MO 63664-1998 • (573) 438-4691 • http://www.rootsweb.com/~mowashin/wclib.html

Princeton
Casteel-Linn House and Museum • 902 E Oak St • Princeton, MO 64673 • (660) 748-3905

Mercer County Genealogical and Historical Society • c/o Mercer County Library, 601 Grant St, P.O. Box 97 • Princeton, MO 64673 • (660) 748-3725 • http://www.rootsweb.com/~momercer/mcghs.html

Mercer County Historical Society • 310 W Main St • Princeton, MO 64673 • (660) 748-3905

Mercer County Library • 601 Grant St • Princeton, MO 64673 • (660) 748-3725 • http://www.mcl.lib.mo.us

Qulin
Melville-Qulin Historical Society • Historical Museum, P.O. Box 295 • Qulin, MO 63961 • (573) 328-4868

Oller-Reynolds House Museum • 10 South St • Qulin, MO 63961 • (573) 328-4488

Raymore
Raymore Historical Society • Historical Museum, 612 W Foxwood Dr, P.O. Box 1483 • Raymore, MO 64083 • http://www.birch.net/~rudroff/raymore/

Raytown
Raytown Historical Society • Historical Museum, 9705 E 63rd St, P.O. Box 16652 • Raytown, MO 64133 • (816) 353-5033 • http://raytownhistoricalsociety.org

Republic
General Sweeny's Civil War Museum • 5228 S State Hwy ZZ • Republic, MO 65738 • (417) 732-1224 • http://www.civilwarmuseum.com

Republic Historical Society • 146 N Main St • Republic, MO 65738

Wilson's Creek National Battlefield Library • Civil War Library, 6424 W Farm Rd 182 • Republic, MO 65738-9514 • (417) 732-2662 • http://www.nps.gov/wicr

Revere
Thome-Benning Cannonball House Museum • Route 1, Box 26 • Revere, MO 63465 • (660) 887-3871

Richland
Pulaski County Library District • 111 Camden St, PO Box 304 • Richland, MO 65556-0304 • (573) 765-3642 • http://www.pulaskicounty.lib.mo.us

Richmond
Ray County Genealogical Association • 809 W Royle St, P.O. Box 2 • Richmond, MO 64085-1545 • (816) 776-2305 • http://www.rootsweb.com/~morcga/

Ray County Historical Society • Historical Museum, 901 W Royle St, P.O. Box 2 • Richmond, MO 64085-0002 • (816) 776-2305

Ray County Library • 219 S College St • Richmond, MO 64085 • (816) 470-3291 • http://www.raycountylibrary.homestead.com

Rocheport
Friends of Rocheport • Historical Museum, 101 Moniteau St • Rocheport, MO 65279 • (573) 698-3210

Rock Port
Atchison County Historical Society • 210 S Main St • Rock Port, MO 64482 • (660) 744-5800

Atchison County Library • 200 S Main St • Rock Port, MO 64482-1532 • (660) 744-5404

Brownville Historical Society • 117 S Main St • Rock Port, MO 64482 • (660) 825-6001

Chickamauga Cherokee Nation • P.O. Box 95 • Rock Port, MO 65279-0095 • (314) 698-2097

Rolla
Memoryville USA • P.O. Box 569 • Rolla, MO 65402 • (573) 364-1810 • http://www.memoryvilleusa.com

Phelps County Archives • Courthouse, 200 N Main, Rm 308 • Rolla, MO 65401 • (573) 364-1891

Phelps County Genealogical Society • 305 W 3rd St, P.O. Box 571 • Rolla, MO 65401 • (573) 364-9597 • http://www.rollanet.org/~pcgs/

Phelps County Historical Society • Dillon Log Cabin Museum, 305 W 3rd St, P.O. Box 1861 • Rolla, MO 65402-1861 • (573) 364-3877 • http://www.umr.edu/~whmcinfo/pchs/

Rolla Free Public Library • 900 Pine St • Rolla, MO 65401 • (573) 364-2604 • http://rollapubliclibrary.org

Western Historical Manuscript Collection • Univ of Missouri-Rolla, 1870 Miner Cr • Rolla, MO 65409 • (573) 341-4874 • http://www.umr.edu

Saint Charles
First Missouri State Capitol Museum • 200-216 S Main St • Saint Charles, MO 63301 • (636) 946-9282 • http://www.dot.state.mo.us

Frenchtown Museum • 1400 N 2nd St • Saint Charles, MO 63301 • (636) 946-2865 • http://home.stlnet.com/~tgodwin/vinson.html

Gateway Military Historical Society • 1008 Motherhead Rd • Saint Charles, MO 63304-7664 • (314) 521-1675 • http://www.gmhs.us

Katy Railroad Historical Society • 1364 Timothy Ridge • Saint Charles, MO 63304 • http://www.katyrailroad.org

Lewis & Clark Boat House Museum • 1050 Riverside Dr • Saint Charles, MO 63301 • (636) 947-3199 • http://www.lewisandclark.net

Saint Charles City County-Linnemann Library • 2323 Elm St • Saint Charles, MO 63301 • (636) 723-0232 • http://www.win.org/library/scccld.htm

Saint Charles County Genealogical Society • Old Courthouse, 100 N 3rd, Ste 106, P.O. Box 715 • Saint Charles, MO 63302-0715 • (636) 724-6668 • http://www.rootsweb.com/~mosccgs/

Saint Charles County German Heritage Club • 1450 Wall St • Saint Charles, MO 63303 • (636) 946-6860

Saint Charles County Historical Society • Historical Museum, 101 S Main St • Saint Charles, MO 63301-2802 • (636) 946-9828 • http://www.scchs.org

Saint Clair
Phoebe Apperson Hearst Historical Society • 2808 Sycamore Ln • Saint Clair, MO 63077 • (636) 629-2596

Phoebe Apperson Hearst Museum • 850 Walton • Saint Clair, MO 63077 • (636) 629-3186

Saint Clair Historical Museum • 38370 Point Breeze Rd, P.O. Box 137 • Saint Clair, MO 63077 • (636) 629-3199 • http://www.rootsweb.com/~mofrankl/hsstclair.htm

Saint James
James Foundation • 320 South Bourbeuse • Saint James, MO 65559 • (573) 265-7124 • http://members.socket.net/~tjf/

James Memorial Library • 300 W Scioto St • Saint James, MO 65559 • (573) 265-7211

Maramec Museum • Maramed Spring Park, 21180 Marmec Spring Dr • Saint James, MO 65559 • (573) 265-7124

Saint Joseph
Glore Psychiatric Museum • 3406 Frederick Ave, P.O. Box 8096 • Saint Joseph, MO 64508 • (816) 387-2300 • http://www.stjosephmuseum.org

Jesse James Home Museum • 12th & Penn Sts • Saint Joseph, MO 64502 • (816) 232-8206 • http://www.st.joseph.net/ponyexpress

Jesse James Home-Pony Express Historical Association • Patee House Museum, 1202 Penn St, P.O. Box 1022 • Saint Joseph, MO 64502-1022 • (816) 232-8206 • http://www.stjoseph.net/ponyexpress/

Knee-Von Black Archives and Museum • 118 S 8th St • Saint Joseph, MO 64501 • (816) 233-0231 • http://stjosephmuseum.org

Missouri Western State College Library • 4525 Downs Dr • Saint Joseph, MO 64507 • (816) 271-4573 • http://www.mwsc.edu/library

National Military Heritage Society • Historical Museum, 701 Messanie St • Saint Joseph, MO 64501-2219 • (816) 233-4321 • http://nationalmilitaryheritagemuseum.org

Northwest Missouri Genealogical Society • 719 Francis St, P.O. Box 382 • Saint Joseph, MO 64502 • (816) 233-0524 • http://www.rootsweb.com/~monwmgs/

Pony Express Museum • 914 Penn St, P.O. Box 244 • Saint Joseph, MO 64502-0244 • (816) 279-5059 • http://www.ponyexpress.org

River Bluffs Regional Library-Belt Branch • 1904 N Belt Hwy • Saint Joseph, MO 64506 • (816) 238-0526

Saint Joseph Black Archives • 3406 Frederick Ave, P.O. Box 8096 • Saint Joseph, MO 64508 • (816) 387-2300 • http://www.stjosephmuseum.org

Saint Joseph Historical Society • 217 E Poulin St, P.O. Box 246 • Saint Joseph, MO 64501 • (816) 232-5861

Saint Joseph Museum • 3406 Frederick Ave, P.O. Box 8096 • Saint Joseph, MO 64508 • (816) 232-8471 • http://www.stjosephmuseum.org

Saint Joseph Preservation • 122 S 8th St, P.O. Box 575 • Saint Joseph, MO 64502-0575 • (816) 232-8300

Saint Joseph Public Library • 927 Felix St • Saint Joseph, MO 64501-2799 • (816) 232-8151 • http://sjpl.lib.mo.us

Wyeth Tootle Mansion Museum • 1100 Charles St, P.O. Box 128 • Saint Joseph, MO 64502-0128 • (816) 232-8471 • http://www.st.josephmuseum.org

Saint Louis
Affton Historical Society • Oakland House, 7801 Genesta, P.O. Box 28855 • Saint Louis, MO 63123 • (314) 544-1006 • http://www.afftonoaklandhouse.com

Afro-American Historical and Genealogical Society, Landon Cheek Chapter • P.O. Box 32116 • Saint Louis, MO 63121-0804 • http://www.aahgs.org

Anheuser-Busch Companies Museum • 1 Busch Pl • Saint Louis, MO 63118

Archives of the Catholic Central Union of America • 3855 Westminster Pl • Saint Louis, MO 63108 • (314) 371-1653 • http://www.socialjusticereview.org

Saint Louis, cont.

Association of Saint Louis Area Archivists • 7800 Natural Bridge Rd, P.O. Box 11940 • Saint Louis, MO 63112-0040 • (314) 746-4518 • http://library.wustl.edu/units/spec/archives/aslaa/

Brentwood Historical Society • 8764 Rosalie • Saint Louis, MO 63144 • (314) 961-7948

Buswell Library • Covenant Theological Seminary, 12330 Conway Rd • Saint Louis, MO 63141 • (314) 434-4044 • http://library.covenantseminary.edu

Campbell House Museum • 1508 Locust St • Saint Louis, MO 63103 • (314) 421-0325 • http://stlouis.missouri.org/501c/chm/

Carondelet Historical Society • Historic Center, 6303 Michigan Ave • Saint Louis, MO 63111 • (314) 481-6303 • http://stlouis.missouri.org/carondelet/history/HisSoc.html

Centenary United Methodist Church-Missouri East Archives • 55 Plaza Square • Saint Louis, MO 63103 • (314) 421-3136

Center for Reformation Research • 6477 San Bonita Ave • Saint Louis, MO 63105-3117 • (314) 727-6655

Chatillon-Demenil Mansion Museum • 3352 DeMenil Pl • Saint Louis, MO 63118 • (314) 771-5828 • http://www.chatillondementilhouse.org

City Museum • 701 N 15th St • Saint Louis, MO 63103 • (314) 231-2089 • http://www.citymuseum.org

Concordia Historical Institute • Lutheran Church-Missouri Synod, 804 Seminary Pl • Saint Louis, MO 63105 • (314) 505-7901 • http://www.lutheranhistory.org

Creve Coeur-Chesterfield Historical Society • 1672 Redbluff Ct • Saint Louis, MO 63146-3915 • (314) 878-3142

Dogtown Historical Society • 6314 West Park • Saint Louis, MO 63139 • (314) 646-0364 • http://www.webster.edu/~corbetre/dogtown/dhs/dhs.html

Eden-Webster Library • Webster Univ, 475 E Lockwood Ave • Saint Louis, MO 63119 • (314) 961-3627 • http://library2.websteruniv.edu/webdata/libhome.html

Episcopal Diocese of Missouri Archives • 1210 Locust St • Saint Louis, MO 63103-2322 • (314) 231-1220

Eugene Field House and Toy Museum • 634 S Broadway • Saint Louis, MO 63102 • (314) 421-4689 • http://www.eugenefieldhouse.org

Fort Belle Fontaine Historical Society • Bissell House Museum, 10225 Bellefontaine Rd • Saint Louis, MO 63137 • (314) 868-0973

General Daniel Bissell House Museum • 10225 Bellefontaine Rd • Saint Louis, MO 63017 • (636) 532-7298 • http://www.stlouisco.com/parks

German American Heritage Society • 121 S Meramec Ave, Ste 1004 • Saint Louis, MO 63105 • (314) 862-1733 • http://www.gahs-stlouis.org

Greater Ville Historic Redevelopment • 4223 Martin Luther King Dr • Saint Louis, MO 63113 • (314) 534-8015

Historical Association of Greater Saint Louis • 3601 Lindell Blvd • Saint Louis, MO 63108 • (314) 658-2588

Holocaust Museum • 12 Millstone Campus Dr • Saint Louis, MO 63146 • (314) 432-0020

Jefferson Barracks Historic Site Museum • 533 Grant Rd • Saint Louis, MO 63125-4121 • (314) 544-5714 • http://www.stlouisco.com

Jefferson National Expansion Memorial Museum • 11 N 4th St • Saint Louis, MO 63102 • (314) 655-1700 • http://www.nps.gov/jeff/

Jewish Genealogical Society of Saint Louis • 13147 Strawberry Wy • Saint Louis, MO 63146-4321 • (314) 434-8392 • http://uahc.org/congs/mo/mo005/jgsstl

Jewish Special Interest Group of the Saint Louis Genealogical Society • 4 Sunnen Dr, Ste 140, P.O. Box 432010 • Saint Louis, MO 63143 • (314) 647-8547 • http://www.stlgs.org

Lafayette Square Restoration Committee • 2023 Lafayette Ave • Saint Louis, MO 63104 • (314) 772-5724

Landmarks Association of Saint Louis • 917 Locust St • Saint Louis, MO 63101-1413 • (314) 421-6474 • http://stlouis.missouri.org/501c/landmarks/

Mary Institute Museum • 425 Warson Rd • Saint Louis, MO 63124 • (314) 995-7385

Maryland Heights Historical Society • 12225 Prinster • Saint Louis, MO 63146

Mercantile Money Museum • 7th & Washington • Saint Louis, MO 63101

Missouri Historical Society • Historical Museum, 5700 Lindell Blvd, P.O. Box 11940 • Saint Louis, MO 63112-0040 • (314) 746-4558 • http://www.mohistory.org

Missouri Museums Association • 1508 Locust St • Saint Louis, MO 63103-1816 • (314) 746-4529 • http://www.missouri-museum.org

Monticello Association • 9530 Park Ln • Saint Louis, MO 63124 • (314) 961-0922 • http://www.monticello-assoc.org

Museum of Optometry • 243 N Lindbergh Blvd • Saint Louis, MO 63141 • (800) 365-2219 • http://www.aoa.org

Museum of Transportation • 3015 Barrett Station Rd • Saint Louis, MO 63122 • (314) 965-7998 • http://www.museumoftransport.org

National Archives-Civilian Personnel Records Facility • 111 Winnebago St • Saint Louis, MO 63118-4126 • (314) 801-9250 • http://www.archives.gov

National Archives-Military Personnel Records • 9700 Page Ave • Saint Louis, MO 63132-5100 • (314) 538-4261 (Army), (314) 538-4243 (Air Force), (314) 538-4141 (Navy/Coast Guard/Marine Corps) • http://www.archives.gov

National Society of New England Women • 7576 Clayton Rd • Saint Louis, MO 63117-1418 • (314) 647-7986 • http://www.newenglandwomen.org

Old Cathedral Museum • 209 Walnut • Saint Louis, MO 63102 • (314) 231-3251 • http://www.catholic-forum.com/stlouisking

Polish-American Cultural Society of Saint Louis • 10257 Halls Ferry Rd • Saint Louis, MO 63136-4315 • (314) 869-2399

Richmond Heights Historical Society • 1203 Claytonia Terr • Saint Louis, MO 63117

Saint Louis Area Historical Association • Saint Louis Univ, Pius XII Library and Archives, 3650 Lindell • Saint Louis, MO 63108-3302 • http://www.slu.edu/libraries/pius

Saint Louis Aviation Museum • 1571 Tryon • Saint Louis, MO 63146 • (314) 878-7032

Saint Louis Cardinals Hall of Fame • 100 Stadium Dr • Saint Louis, MO 63102 • (314) 982-7334

Saint Louis County Library • 1640 S Lindbergh St • Saint Louis, MO 63131-3501 • (314) 994-3300 • http://www.slcl.lib.mo.us

Saint Louis County Library-Tesson Ferry • 9920 Lin-Ferry Dr • Saint Louis, MO 63123-6914 • (314) 843-0560

Saint Louis Genealogical Society • 4 Sunnen Dr, Ste 140, P.O. Box 43010 • Saint Louis, MO 63144-2543 • (314) 647-8547 • http://www.rootsweb.com/~nostlogs/stindex.htm

Saint Louis Mercantile Library • 1 University Blvd • Saint Louis, MO 63121-4401 • (314) 516-7240 • http://www.umsl.edu/mercantile

Saint Louis Police Library and Museum • 315 S Tucker • Saint Louis, MO 63102

Saint Louis Public Library • 1301 Olive Blvd • Saint Louis, MO 63103-2389 • (314) 539-0353 • http://www.slpl.lib.mo.us

Samuel Cupples House Museum • John E Connelly Mall, Saint Louis Univ • Saint Louis, MO 63108 • (314) 977-3025

Sappington-Concord Historical Society • 9533 Spitz Ln • Saint Louis, MO 63126 • (314) 849-3130

Saul Brodsky Jewish Community Library • 12 Millstone Campus Dr • Saint Louis, MO 63146-5776 • (314) 432-0020 • http://www.brodskylibrary.org

Scott Joplin House State Historic Site Museum • 2658A Delmar Blvd • Saint Louis, MO 63103 • (314) 340-5790

Society of the Sacred Heart • 4537 W Pine Blvd • Saint Louis, MO 63108 • (314) 367-1704

Soldiers' Memorial Military Museum • 1315 Chestnut St • Saint Louis, MO 63103 • (314) 622-4550

South County Historical Society • 4935 Viento Dr • Saint Louis, MO 63129

Southwestern Bell Library • Harris-Stowe State College, 3026 Laclede Ave • Saint Louis, MO 63103 • (314) 340-3622 • http://www.hssc.edu

Spanish Lake Historical Society • 1064 Prigge Rd • Saint Louis, MO 63138

Thomas Jefferson Library and Museum • University of Missouri-Saint Louis, 8001 Natural Bridge Rd • Saint Louis, MO 63121-4499 • (314) 516-5060 • http://www.umsl.edu

Tower Grove House Museum • Missouri Botanical Garden, 2345 Tower Grove, P.O. Box 299 • Saint Louis, MO 63166 • (314) 577-5100

Town and Country Historical Society • 1011 Municipal Center Dr • Saint Louis, MO 63131

Vaugan Cultural Center Museum • 3701 Grandel Sq • Saint Louis, MO 63108

Washington University Library • 1 Brookings Dr, Campus Box 1061 • Saint Louis, MO 63130-4899 • (314) 935-5410

Saint Peters

National Railway Historical Society • 18 Mill Spring Ct • Saint Peters, MO 63376 • (636) 928-6634

Saint Charles City County Library District • 77 Boone Hills Dr, P.O. Box 529 • Saint Peters, MO 63376-0529 • (636) 441-2300 • http://www.win.org/library/scccld.htm

Sainte Genevieve

Amoureux House Museum • 339 St Mary's Rd • Sainte Genevieve, MO 63670

Bolduc House Museum • 123 S Main St • Sainte Genevieve, MO 63670 • (573) 883-3105 • http://ww.nscda.org/museums/missouri.htm

Felix Valle State Historic Site Museum • 198 Merchant St, P.O. Box 89 • Sainte Genevieve, MO 63670 • (573) 883-7102 • http://www.mostateparks.com

Foundation for Restoration of Sainte Genevieve • 70 S 3rd St • Sainte Genevieve, MO 63670 • (573) 883-2839

Guibourd Valle House Museum • N 4th & Merchant Sts, P.O. Box 88 • Sainte Genevieve, MO 63670 • (573) 883-9622

Sainte Genevieve Historical and Genealogical Society • Sainte Genevieve Museum, 225 Market St • Sainte Genevieve, MO 63670 • (573) 883-3461 • http://www.greatriverroad.com/stegen/sgattract/sgmuseum.htm

Salem

Dent County Historical Society • Historical Museum, 1202 Gertrude St • Salem, MO 65560 • (573) 729-5707

Salem Public Library • 102 N Jackson • Salem, MO 65560 • (573) 729-4331 • http://www.salempubliclibrary.lib.mo.us

Western Cherokee Nation • 409 N Main St • Salem, MO 65560 • (573) 729-2233 • http://www.westerncherokeenation.org

Salisbury

Chariton County Historical Society • Historical Museum, 115 E 2nd St, P.O. Box 114 • Salisbury, MO 65281-0114 • (816) 388-5941 • http://www.cvalley.net/~museum/

Dulany Library • 501 S Broadway • Salisbury, MO 65281 • (660) 388-5712

Savannah

Andrew County Historical Society • Historical Museum, 202 E Duncan Dr, P.O. Box 12 • Savannah, MO 64485-0012 • (816) 324-4720 • http://www.rootsweb.com/~moandrew/and-society.html

Sedalia

Boonslick Regional Library • 219 W 3rd St • Sedalia, MO 65301-4347 • (660) 827-7111 • http://brl.lib.mo.us

Bothwell Lodge State Historic Site Museum • 19349 Bothwell Park Rd • Sedalia, MO 65301 • (660) 827-0510

Pettis County Historical Society • Historical Museum, 228 Dundee Ave • Sedalia, MO 65301 • (816) 826-1314

Seneca

Eastern Shawnee Tribe of Oklahoma • P.O. Box 350 • Seneca, MO 64865 • (918) 666-2435

Little Country School Restoration Project • 14175 Bethel Rd • Seneca, MO 64865 • (417) 776-8232

Seneca Historical Committee • 14175 Bethel Rd • Seneca, MO 64865 • (417) 776-8232

Shelbina

Kathleen Wilham Genealogical Library • 2 Sharon Dr • Shelbina, MO 63468-1562 • (573) 588-440 • http://www.marktwain.net/~kwilham/

Shelbina Carnegie Public Library • 102 N Center St • Shelbina, MO 63468 • (573) 588-2271 • http://www.shelbinalibrary.org

Shelbina Genealogical Society • c/o Shelbina Carnegie Public Library, 102 N Center St, P.O. Box 247 • Shelbina, MO 63468 • (573) 588-2271

Shelby County Historical Museum • 215 S Center St • Shelbina, MO 63468

Shelby County Historical Society • 107 S Center St, P.O. Box 245 • Shelbina, MO 63468 • (573) 588-4480 • http://www.rootsweb.com/~moshelby/

Sheldon

South Vernon Genealogical Society • Route 2, Box 10 • Sheldon, MO 64784 • (417) 884-2619

Shrewsbury

Shrewsbury Historical Society • 5200 Shrewsbury Ave • Shrewsbury, MO 63119 • (314) 647-1003

Sibley

Fort Osage National Historic Landmark • 105 Osage St • Sibley, MO 64015 • (816) 795-8200

Friends of Historic Fort Osage • P.O. Box 195 • Sibley, MO 64088 • (816) 650-6370

Slater

Slater Public Library • 311 N Main • Slater, MO 65349 • (660) 529-3100

Missouri

Smithville
Smithville Historical Society • Historical Museum, 112 E Church St, P.O. Box 119 • Smithville, MO 64089 • http://www.smithvillehistoricalsociety.org

Springfield
Celtic Society of the Ozarks • 940 E Caravan • Springfield, MO 65803 • (417) 833-9792 • http://www.ozarkcelts.org

Civil War Round Table of the Ozarks • P.O. Box 3451 • Springfield, MO 65808 • (417) 887-7844 • http://history.smsu.edu/WGPiston/CWRT.htm

Duane G Meyer Library • Southwest Missouri State University, 901 S National • Springfield, MO 65804-0095 • (417) 836-4535 • http://www.library.smsu.edu

Flower Pentecostal Heritage Center • 1445 Boonville Ave • Springfield, MO 65802 • (417) 862-1447 • http://www.agheritage.org

French-Belgian-Franco-Swiss Historical and Heritage Society of the Ozarks • 2214 E Cherryvale • Springfield, MO 65804-4524 • (417) 883-8396

G B Vick Memorial Library • Baptist Bible College Library, 628 E Kearney St • Springfield, MO 65803 • (417) 268-6074 • http://www.library.bbcnet.edu

German-Austrian-Swiss Historical Society • 2214 E Cherryvale • Springfield, MO 65804-4524 • (417) 883-8396

Greene County Archives and Records Center • 1126 Boonville Ave • Springfield, MO 65802 • (417) 868-4021 • http://www.greenecountymo.org/web/Archives

Greene County Historical Society • P.O. Box 344 • Springfield, MO 65808 • (417) 881-6147 • http://www.rootsweb.com/~gcmohs

Klaude Kendrick Library & Museum • Evangel University, 1111 N Glenstone • Springfield, MO 65802 • (417) 865-2815 • http://www.evangel.edu/library/

Missouri Pacific Historical Society • 2226 W Walnut • Springfield, MO 65806-1518 • http://www.mopac.org

Ozarks Genealogical Society • 534 W Catalpa St, P.O. Box 3945 • Springfield, MO 65808-3945 • (417) 831-2773 • http://www.rootsweb.com/~ozarksgs

Ozarks Genealogical Society, Computer Workshop • 534 W Catalpa St, P.O. Box 3494, Glenston Sta • Springfield, MO 65808 • (417) 831-2773 • http://www.rootsweb.com/~osociety/

Ozarks Genealogical Society, Day Workshop • 534 W Catalpa St, P.O. Box 3494, Glenston Sta • Springfield, MO 65808 • (417) 831-2773 • http://www.rootsweb.com/~osociety/

Ozarks Genealogical Society, Night Workshop • 534 W Catalpa St, P.O. Box 3494, Glenston Sta • Springfield, MO 65808 • (417) 831-2773 • http://www.rootsweb.com/~osociety/

Railroad Historical Museum • 1300 N Grant St • Springfield, MO 65804 • (417) 883-5319 • http://www.rrhistoricalmuseum.zoomshare.com

Scottish Saint Andrew's Society of Springfield • 940 E Caravan • Springfield, MO 65803 • (417) 890-5653 • http://www.springfieldscots.org

Springfield Medical Museum • 1423 N Jefferson • Springfield, MO 65802

Springfield-Greene County Library • 4653 S Campbell, P.O. Box 760 • Springfield, MO 65801-0760 • (417) 874-8110 • http://thelibrary.springfield.missouri.org

Wilson's Creek National Battlefield Foundation • 1351 N Belcrest, P.O. Box 8163 • Springfield, MO 65801 • (417) 864-3041 • http://www.wilsonscreek.com

Stanberry
Gentry County Library • 304 N Park St • Stanberry, MO 64489 • (660) 783-2335 • http://www.gentrycountylibrary.org

Stella
Stella Historical Society • Historical Museum, Main St • Stella, MO 64867 • (417) 628-3417

Stockton
Cedar County Historical Society • Historical Museum, 115 W Jackson St, P.O. Box 111 • Stockton, MO 65785 • (417) 276-4974 • http://www.rootsweb.com/~mocchs/

Stoutsville
Friends of Florida • P.O. Box 132 • Stoutsville, MO 65283 • (573) 672-3330

Mark Twain Birthplace State Historic Site Library • Route 1, Box 54 • Stoutsville, MO 65283 • (573) 565-3449

Sweet Springs
Sweet Springs Historical Society • 102 W Ray St • Sweet Springs, MO 65251 • (660) 335-6862

Tarkio
Atchison County Historical Society • Tarkio College Alumni Historical Museum, 402 Main St • Tarkio, MO 64491 • (660) 739-4208 • http://www.footsweb.com/~moatchis/museum/tarkio/musum1.htm

Tipton
Maclay House Museum • 208 Howard St, P.O. Box 4 • Tipton, MO 65081 • (660) 433-2068

Trenton
Grundy County Genealogical Society • 1331 Main St, P.O. Box 223 • Trenton, MO 64683 • (660) 359-6512 • http://www.rootsweb.com/~mogrundy/gcgen.html

Grundy County Historical Society • Historical Museum, 1100 Mabel Dr, P.O. Box 292 • Trenton, MO 64683 • (660) 359-2411 • http://www.grundycountymuseum.org

Grundy County-Jewett Norris Library • 1331 Main St • Trenton, MO 64683 • (660) 359-3577 • http://grundycountylibrary.org

Troy
Lincoln County Historical and Archaeological Society • 211 W Collier St, P.O. Box 86 • Troy, MO 63379 • (636) 528-7562

Powell Memorial Library • 951 W College • Troy, MO 63379 • (636) 528-7853

Turney
Turney Historical Society • Historical Museum, 207 Sherman, P.O. Box 462 • Turney, MO 64493-9018 • (660) 664-2471

Tuscumbia
Miller County Historical Society • Historical Museum, Hwy 52 W, P.O. Box 57 • Tuscumbia, MO 65082 • (573) 793-6998 • http://www.millercountymuseum.org

Union
Franklin County Historical Society • P.O. Box 293 • Union, MO 63084 • (314) 239-5426 • http://www.rootsweb.com/~mofrankl/hsFCHS.htm

Scenic Regional Library • 308 Hawthorne Dr • Union, MO 63084 • (636) 583-3224 • http://catalog.scenic.lib.mo.us

Scenic Regional Library-Union • 308 Hawthorne Dr • Union, MO 63084 • (636) 583-3224

Unionville
Putnam County Historical Society • 201 S 16th St • Unionville, MO 63565 • (660) 947-2955

Putnam County Public Library • 115 S 16th St, P.O. Box 305 • Unionville, MO 63565-0305 • (660) 947-3192 • http://putnamcountylibrary.lib.mo.us

Unity Village
Unity Library • 1901 NW Blue Pkwy • Unity Village, MO 64065-0001 • (816) 524-3550 • http://www.unityonline.org

University City
Historical Society of University City • c/o University City Public Library, 6701 Delmar • University City, MO 63130 • (314) 727-3150

University City Public Library • 6701 Delmar Blvd • University City, MO 63130 • (314) 727-3150 • http://www.ucpl.lib.mo.us

Urich
Urich Community Historical Society • 323 Main St, P.O. Box 105 • Urich, MO 64788 • (816) 322-7246

Valley Park
Meramec Station Historical Society • 20 Fern Ridge Ave • Valley Park, MO 63088 • (314) 825-2711

Valley Park Community Library • 320 Benton St • Valley Park, MO 63088 • (636) 225-5608

Van Buren
Carter County Library District • 111 Sycamore St, P.O. Box 309 • Van Buren, MO 63965-0309 • (573) 323-4315

Hidden Log Cabin Museum • John & Ash Sts, P.O. Box 135 • Van Buren, MO 63965 • (573) 323-4563

West Carter County Genealogy Society • c/o Carter County Library, 111 Sycamore St, P.O. Box 309 • Van Buren, MO 63937 • (573) 323-4315 • http://www.rootsweb.com/~mocarter/

Versailles
Morgan County Historical Society • Historical Museum, 120 N Monroe St, P.O. Box 181 • Versailles, MO 65084 • (573) 378-5530

Morgan County Library • 102 N Fisher • Versailles, MO 65084-1297 • (573) 378-5319

Vienna
Historical Society of Maries County • Historical Museum, P.O. Box 289 • Vienna, MO 65582 • (573) 422-3932 • http://www.rootsweb.com/~momaries/marihiso.htm

Warrensburg
Central Missouri State University Archives and Museum • JCK Library 1470 • Warrensburg, MO 64093 • (660) 543-4649

James C Kirkpatrick Library • Central Missouri State University, 601 S Missouri • Warrensburg, MO 64093 • (660) 543-4140 • http://library.cmsu.edu

Johnson County Historical Society • Mary Miller Smiser Heritage Library, 302 N Main St • Warrensburg, MO 64093 • (660) 747-6480 • http://www.jchs64093.org

Trails Regional Library • 125 N Holden St • Warrensburg, MO 64093 • (660) 747-1699 • http://www.trailsregional.org

West Central Missouri Genealogical Society • c/o Trails Regional Library, 125 N Holden St, P.O. Box 4 • Warrensburg, MO 64093 • (660) 747-7912 • http://www.rootsweb.com/~mojohnso/library/Society.htm

Warrenton
Ernst Schowengerdt National Historic Site Museum • 308 E Boone's Lick Rd • Warrenton, MO 63383

Scenic Regional Library-Warrenton • 912 S Hwy 47, P.O. Box 308 • Warrenton, MO 63383-0308 • (636) 456-3321

Warren County Genealogical Society • P.O. Box 92 • Warrenton, MO 63383

Warren County Historical Society • Historical Museum, 102 W Walton St, P.O. Box 12 • Warrenton, MO 63383 • (636) 456-3820

Warsaw
Benton County Historical Society • Historical Museum, 212 W Kosciusko, P.O. Box 1082 • Warsaw, MO 65355 • (660) 438-6707

Washington
Four Rivers Genealogical Society • 314 W Main St, P.O. Box 146 • Washington, MO 63090 • http://www.rootsweb.com/~mofrankl/hsfourrivers.htm

Washington
Washington Historical Society • Historical Museum, 113 E 4th St, P.O. Box 146 • Washington, MO 63090-2616 • (636) 239-0280 • http://www.washmohistorical.org

Washington Public Library-Warrensburg Branch • 415 Jefferson St • Washington, MO 63090 • (636) 390-1070

Waynesville
Genealogy and Historical Society of Pulaski County • 415 Historic Route 66, P.O. Box 144 • Waynesville, MO 65583 • (573) 774-6883 • http://www.rootsweb.com/~mopulask/

Old Stagecoach Stop Foundation • Historical Museum, 106 Lynn St, P.O. Box 585 • Waynesville, MO 65583 • (573) 435-6766

Pulaski County Library District-Waynesville Branch • 306 Historic 66 W, P.O. Box 562 • Waynesville, MO 65583 • (573) 774-2965 • http://www.pulaskicountylib.org

Webb City
Webb City Area Genealogical Society • 101 S Liberty St • Webb City, MO 64870 • (417) 673-4326

Webb City Historical Society • 1 S Main #3 • Webb City, MO 64870 • (417) 673-5866

Webb City Preservation Committee • Historical Museum, 108 W Broadway • Webb City, MO 64870 • (417) 673-5154

Webb City Public Library • 101 S Liberty St • Webb City, MO 64870 • (417) 673-4326 • http://www.webbcitylibrary.com

Webster Groves
Webster Groves Archives • 475 E Lockwood Ave • Webster Groves, MO 63119 • (314) 961-3627

Webster Groves Historical Society • Hawken House Museum, 1155 S Rock Hill Rd • Webster Groves, MO 63119 • (314) 968-1776 • http://www.historicwebster.org/hawken_house.shtml

Webster Groves Public Library • 301 E Lockwood Ave • Webster Groves, MO 63119-3195 • (314) 961-3784 • http://www.wgpl.lib.mo.us

Wellsville
Prairie Life Historical Foundation • 300 N 2nd St, P.O. Box 52 • Wellsville, MO 63384 • (573) 648-2743

Wellsville Depot Museum • N Hudson St • Wellsville, MO 63384

Wentzville
Foristell Area Historical Society • 626 Ball St • Wentzville, MO 63385 • (636) 327-8234

Wentzville Community Historical Society • Historical Museum, 506 S Linn Ave, P.O. Box 202 • Wentzville, MO 63385 • (636) 332-0075

West Plains
Harlin House Museum • 606 Worcester St, P.O. Box 444 • West Plains, MO 65775 • (417) 256-7801

South-Central Missouri Genealogical Society • 9 Court Sq • West Plains, MO 65775-2147 • (417) 256-3769

West Plains Genealogical Society • P.O. Box 138 • West Plains, MO 65775

Weston
Price-Loyles House Museum • 718 Spring St • Weston, MO 64098 • (816) 891-6535

Weston, cont.

Walter Herbert Bonnell Museum • 20755 Lamar Rd • Weston, MO 64098 • (816) 386-5587

Weston Historical Museum • 601 Main St, P.O. Box 266 • Weston, MO 64098 • (816) 386-2977

Westphalia

Westphalia Historical Society • 119 E Main St, P.O. Box 244 • Westphalia, MO 65808 • (573) 445-9920 • http://www.whs65085.org

Westphalian Heritage Society • 130 E Main, P.O. Box 244 • Westphalia, MO 65085-0244 • (573) 455-2337

Wildwood

Missouri Civil War Museum • Jefferson Barracks Historic Site, P.O. Box 24 • Wildwood, MO 63040 • http://www.missouricivilwarmuseum. org

Wildwood Historical Society • P.O. Box 125 • Wildwood, MO 63040 • (636) 458-3306

Willow Springs

Fire Museum of Missouri • 908 E Business Rte 60-63 • Willow Springs, MO 65793 • (417) 469-4589

Windsor

Windsor Historical Society • 104 S Franklin St, P.O. Box 111 • Windsor, MO 65360 • (660) 647-2345

Winona

Shannon County Historical and Genealogical Society • 106 N Ash St, P.O. Box 335 • Winona, MO 65588 • (573) 325-4728

Winston

Winston Historical Society • Historical Museum, Hwys 69 & Y, P.O. Box 177 • Winston, MO 64689 • (660) 749-5725

Worthington

Worthington Historical Society • Route 1, Box A-5 • Worthington, MO 63567 • (660) 355-4804

MONTANA

Anaconda

Anaconda-Deer Lodge County Historical Society • Historical Museum, 401 E Commercial St • Anaconda, MT 59711-2327 • (406) 563-2220

Copper Village Museum • 401 E Commercial St • Anaconda, MT 59711 • (406) 846-2422 • http://www.mt-magda.org/cprvil.htm

Arlee

Arlee Historical Society • Historical Museum, 655 S Valley Creek Rd • Arlee, MT 59821

Jocko Valley Public Library • Hwy 93, P.O. Box 158 • Arlee, MT 59821-0158 • (406) 726-3572

Baker

Fallon County Library • 6 W Fallon Ave, PO Box 1037 • Baker, MT 59313-1037 • (406) 778-7160

Historic O'Fallon Museum • 723 S Main St, P.O. Box 285 • Baker, MT 59313 • (406) 778-3265 • http://www.falloncounty.net

O'Fallon Historical Society • Historical Museum, P.O. Box 43 • Baker, MT 59313

Belgrade

Belgrade Community Library • 106 N Broadway, P.O. Box 929 • Belgrade, MT 59714-0929 • (406) 388-4346

Big Timber

Carnegie Public Library • 314 McLeod St, P.O. Box 846 • Big Timber, MT 59011-0846 • (406) 932-5608

Crazy Mountain Museum • Cemetery Rd, P.O. Box 83 • Big Timber, MT 59011 • (406) 932-5126

Billings

Billings Preservation Society • Moss Mansion Museum, 914 Division St • Billings, MT 59101 • (406) 256-5100 • http://www.mossmansion.com

Friends of Chief Plenty Coups Museum • 2802 Patricia Ln • Billings, MT 59102

Montana State University-Billings Library • Mindworks Museum, 1500 N 30th St • Billings, MT 59101-0298 • (406) 657-1662 • http://www.msubillings.edu

MSU - Billings Museum • 226 Avenue C • Billings, MT 59101

Museum of Women's History • 2824 3rd Ave N • Billings, MT 59101

Oscar's Dreamland Yesteryear Museum • 3100 Harrow Dr • Billings, MT 59102

Parmly Billings Library • 510 N Broadway • Billings, MT 59101-1196 • (406) 657-8258 • http://www.billings.lib.mt.us

Paul M Adams Memorial Library • Rocky Mountain College, 1511 Poly Dr • Billings, MT 59102-1796 • (406)657-1087 • http://www.library.rocky.edu

Peter Yegen Yellowstone County Museum • 1950 Terminal Cr, P.O. Box 959 • Billings, MT 59103 • (406) 256-6811 • http://www.pyjrcm.org

Yellowstone Genealogy Forum • c/o Parmly Billings Library, 510 N Broadway • Billings, MT 59101-1156 • (406) 657-8258 • http://www.rootsweb.com/~mtygf

Boulder

Jefferson County Genealogy Society • P.O. Box 1094 • Boulder, MT 59632

Jefferson County Library System-Boulder Community Library • 202 S Main St, P.O. Box 589 • Boulder, MT 59632-0589 • (406) 225-3241

Montana State Genealogical Society • P.O. Box 989 • Boulder, MT 59632-0989 • http://www.rootsweb.com/~mtmsgs/

Box Elder

Chippewa-Cree Indian Business Committee • Rocky Boy Route, P.O. Box 544 • Box Elder, MT 59521 • (406) 395-4282 • http://tlc.wtp.net/chippewa.htm

Bozeman

Bozeman Public Library • 625 E Main St • Bozeman, MT 59715 • (406) 582-2400 • http://www.bozemanlibrary.org

Country Grain Elevator Historical Society • Historical Museum, 155 Prospector Tr, P.O. Box 338 • Bozeman, MT 59771 • (406) 388-9282

First Families of Montana • P.O. Box 913 • Bozeman, MT 59771 • (406) 961-3159 • http://www.rootsweb.com/~mtmsgs

Gallatin County Historical Society • Pioneer Museum, 317 W Main St • Bozeman, MT 59741 • (406) 522-8122

Gallatin County Pioneer Group • 317 W Main St • Bozeman, MT 59715-4576

Gallatin Genealogy Society • P.O. Box 1783 • Bozeman, MT 59771-1783 • http://www.rootsweb.com/~mtmsgs/soc_ggs.htm

Merrill C Burlingame Special Collections and Archives • Montana State Univ - Bozeman, P.O. Box 17332 • Bozeman, MT 59717-2851 • (406) 994-4242 • http://www.lib.montana.edu

Montana State Genealogical Society • P.O. Box 913 • Bozeman, MT 59771 • (406) 961-3159 • http://www.rootsweb.com/~mtmsgs

Museum of the Rockies • 600 W Kagy Blvd, Montana State Univ • Bozeman, MT 59717 • (406) 994-6342 • http://www.museumoftherockies.org

Roland R Renne Library • Montana State Univ, P.O. Box 173320 • Bozeman, MT 59717 • (406) 994-3119 • http://www.lib.montana.edu

Bridger

Bridger Public Library • 119 W Broadway Ave, P.O. Box 428 • Bridger, MT 59014 • (406) 662-3598

Broadus

Powder River Genealogical Society • P.O. Box 394 • Broadus, MT 59317 • http://www.rangeweb.com/~emmov/prgs/prgs.html

Powder River Historical Society • Historical Museum, 210 N Lincoln, P.O. Box 575 • Broadus, MT 59317 • (406) 436-2474

Browning

Blackfeet Community College Library • US Hwy 2 & 89, P.O. Box 819 • Browning, MT 59417-0819 • (406) 338-7755

Blackfeet Nation & Cultural Program • P.O. Box 850 • Browning, MT 59417 • (406) 338-7406 • http://www.blackfeetnation.com

Butte

Butte and Silver Bow Public Library • 226 W Broadway St • Butte, MT 59701-9297 • (406) 723-3361

Butte Genealogical Society • 1231 W Park St • Butte, MT 59701

Butte Historical Society • c/o Butte-Silver Bow Public Archives, 17 W Quartz, P.O. Box 3913 • Butte, MT 59702 • (406) 723-8262 x306

Butte-Silver Bow Public Archives • 17 W Quartz, P.O. Box 81 • Butte, MT 59701 • (406) 723-8262 x306 • http://www.buttearchives.org

Copper King Mansion Museum • 219 W Granite • Butte, MT 59701 • (406) 782-7580 • http://www.thecopperkingmansion.com

Mai Wah Society • Historical Museum, 17 W Mercury St, P.O. Box 404 • Butte, MT 59703 • (406) 723-3231 • http://www.maiwah.org

Montana Tech Library - Newspaper Collection • Mineral Museum, 1300 W Park St • Butte, MT 59701-8997 • (406) 496-4281 • http://www.mtech.edu/library

Piccadilly Museum of Transportation • 20 W Broadway St • Butte, MT 59701 • (406) 723-3034 • http://www.piccadillymuseum.com

Montana

Butte, cont.
World Museum of Mining • 155 Museum Wy • Butte, MT 59703 • (406) 723-7211 • http://www.miningmuseum.org

Cascade
Wedsworth Memorial Library • 13 Front St N, P.O. Box 526 • Cascade, MT 59421-0526 • (406) 468-2848 • http://www.mcn.net/~wedsworth

Charlo
Ninepipes Museum of Early Montana • 41000 Hwy 93 • Charlo, MT 59824

Chester
Broken Mountains Genealogical Society • c/o Liberty County Library, 100 E 1st St, P.O. Box 567 • Chester, MT 59522 • (406) 759-5445 • http://www.rootsweb.com/~mtmsgs/soc_bmgs.htm

Liberty County Historical Society • general delivery • Chester, MT 59522

Liberty County Library • 100 E 1st St, P.O. Box 458 • Chester, MT 59522-0458 • (406) 759-5445

Liberty County Museum • 230 2nd St E, P.O. Box 417 • Chester, MT 59522 • (406) 759-5256

Montana State Genealogical Society • P.O. Box 554 • Chester, MT 59522

Chinook
Blaine County Historical Society • Blaine County Museum, 501 Indiana, P.O. Box 927 • Chinook, MT 59523 • (406) 357-2590 • http://www.chinookmontana.com

Milk River Genealogical Society • P.O. Box 1000 • Chinook, MT 59523 • http://www.rootsweb.com/~mtmsgs/soc_mrgs.htm

Choteau
Choteau-Teton Public Library • 17 N Main, P.O. Box 876 • Choteau, MT 59422-0876 • (406) 466-2052

Old Trail Museum • Teton Trail Village, 823 N Main St, P.O. Box 919 • Choteau, MT 59422 • (406) 466-5332 • http://www.oldtrailmuseum.net

Circle
Circle Museum • 801 1st Ave S, P.O. Box 158 • Circle, MT 59215 • (406) 485-2414

George McCone Memorial County Library • 1101 C Ave, P.O. Box 49 • Circle, MT 59215-0049 • (406) 485-2350

McCone County Museum • 1507 Avenue B, P.O. Box 127 • Circle, MT 59215 • (406) 485-2414

Colstrip
Rosebud County Historical Society • Historical Museum, 400 Woodrose, P.O. Box 430 • Colstrip, MT 59323

Schoolhouse History Center Museum • 400 Woodrose St, P.O. Box 430 • Colstrip, MT 59323 • (406) 748-4822 • http://www.schoolhouseartcenter.com

Columbus
Stillwater County Library • 27 N 4th St, P.O. Box 266 • Columbus, MT 59019-0266 • (406) 322-5009

Stillwater Historical Society • Museum of the Beartooths, P.O. Box 1 • Columbus, MT 59019

Conrad
Conrad Public Library • 15 4th Ave SW • Conrad, MT 59425 • (406) 271-5751

Crow Agency
Crow Tribal Council • P.O. Box 159 • Crow Agency, MT 59022 • (406) 638-2601 • http://tlc.wtp.net/crow.htm

Custer Battlefield Historical and Museum • I-90 & Hwy 212, P.O. Box 39 • Crow Agency, MT 59022 • (406) 638-2382 • http://www.nps.gov/libi

Culbertson
Culbertson Museum • US Hwy 2 E, P.O. Box 95 • Culbertson, MT 59218

Northeastern Montana Threshers Museum • P.O. Box 12 • Culbertson, MT 59218 • (406) 787-5265

Cut Bank
Glacier County Historical Society • 107 Old Kevin Hwy, P.O. Box 576 • Cut Bank, MT 59427 • (406) 873-4904 • http://www.glaciercountymt.org/museum

Glacier County Library • 21 1st Ave SE • Cut Bank, MT 59427-2992 • (406) 873-4572

Tangled Roots Genealogical Society • P.O. Box 1992 • Cut Bank, MT 59427 • http://www.rootsweb.com/~mtmsgs/soc_trgs.htm

Darby
Pioneer Memorial Museum • Hwy 93, Council Park, RR • Darby, MT 59829

Deer Lodge
Grant-Kohrs Ranch National Historic Site Museum • 210 Missouri Ave, P.O. Box 790 • Deer Lodge, MT 59722-0790 • (406) 846-2070 • http://www.nps.gov/grko/

Old Prison Museum • 1106 Main St • Deer Lodge, MT 59722 • (406) 846-3111 • http://www.pcmaf.org

Powell County Genealogical Society • 912 Missouri Ave • Deer Lodge, MT 59722-8713 • http://www.rootsweb.com/~mtmsgs/soc_pcgs.htm

Powell County Museum • 1199 Main St • Deer Lodge, MT 59722 • (406) 846-3294

William K Kohrs Memorial Library • 501 Missouri Ave • Deer Lodge, MT 59722-1152 • (406) 846-2622

Derby
Pioneer Memorial Museum • 334 Bunkhouse Rd • Derby, MT 59875

Dillon
Beaverhead County Museum • 15 S Montana, P.O. Box 830 • Dillon, MT 59725 • (406) 683-5027

Beaverhead Hunters Genealogical Society • Historical Museum, 15 S Montana • Dillon, MT 59725-2433 • (406) 683-5027 • http://www.rootsweb.com/~mtbeaver

Lima Historical Society • general delivery • Dillon, MT 59725 • (406) 276-3394

Lucy Carson Memorial Library • University of Montana Western, 710 S Atlantic St • Dillon, MT 59725 • (406) 683-7492 • http://www.umwestern.edu/library

Drummond
Drummond Public Library • 152 W Edwards St, P.O. Box 378 • Drummond, MT 59832-0378 • (406) 745-3281

Lower Valley Historical Society • Historical Museum, P.O. Box 215 • Drummond, MT 59832

East Helena
Kleffner Ranch Museum • 305 Hwy 518, P.O. Box 427 • East Helena, MT 59635 • (406) 227-6645 • http://www.kleffnerranch.com

Ekalaka
Ekalaka Public Library • Main St, P.O. Box 482 • Ekalaka, MT 59324-0482 • (406) 775-6336

Elmo
Kootenai Cultural Center • P.O. Box 1452 • Elmo, MT 59917 • (406) 849-5541

Eureka
Lincoln County Public Libraries-Eureka Branch • 318 Dewey Ave, PO Box 401 • Eureka, MT 59917-0401 • (406) 296-2613 • http://www.lincolncountylibraries.com/eureka_library.html

Tobacco Valley Historical Village • P.O. Box 301 • Eureka, MT 59917

Forsyth
Rosebud County Library • 201 N Ninth Ave, P.O. Box 7 • Forsyth, MT 59327-0007 • (406) 346-7561

Rosebud County Pioneer Museum • 1335 Main St, P.O. Box 88 • Forsyth, MT 59327 • (406) 356-7547

Fort Benton
Chouteau County Free Library • 1418 Main St, P.O. Box 639 • Fort Benton, MT 59442-0639 • (406) 622-5222

Fort Benton Museum of the Upper Missouri • 1801 Front St, P.O. Box 262 • Fort Benton, MT 59442 • (406) 622-5316

Museum of the Northern Great Plains • 20th & Washington, P.O. Box 262 • Fort Benton, MT 59442 • (406) 622-5133

River and Plains Society • Fort Benton Heritage Complex, 1205 20th St, P.O. Box 262 • Fort Benton, MT 59442 • (406) 622-5316 • http://www.fortbenton.com/museums/

Fromberg
Clark's Fork Valley Museum • 101 E River St, P.O. Box 1054 • Fromberg, MT 59029 • (406) 668-7650

Little Cowboy Bar and Museum • 105 W River, P.O. Box 183 • Fromberg, MT 59029 • (406) 668-9502 • http://www.littlecowboy.com

Garryowen
Custer Battlefield Museum • Town Hall, P.O. Box 200 • Garryowen, MT 59031 • (406) 638-1876 • http://www.custermuseum.org

Glasgow
Glasgow City County Library • 408 3rd Ave S • Glasgow, MT 59230 • (406) 228-2731 • http://www.crystalpixels.com/town/library.html

Root Diggers Genealogical Society • 102 Bonnie St, P.O. Box 249 • Glasgow, MT 59230-0249 • (406) 228-8507 • http://www.rootsweb.com/~mtmsgs/soc_grd.htm

Valley County Historical Society • Pioneer Museum, 816 US Hwy 2 W, P.O. Box 44 • Glasgow, MT 59230 • (406) 228-8692 • http://www.valleycountymuseum.com

Glendive
Frontier Gateway Museum • Belle Prairie Frontage Rd, P.O. Box 1181 • Glendive, MT 59330 • (406) 377-8168

Glendive Public Library • 200 S Kendrick • Glendive, MT 59330 • (406) 365-3633

Tree Branches • P.O. Box 1275 • Glendive, MT 59330-1275 • (406) 365-4014 • http://www.cheyenneancestors.com/dawson/dwsgens.html

Great Falls
C M Russell Home Museum • 400 13th St N • Great Falls, MT 59401 • (406) 727-8787

Cascade County Historical Society • High Plains Heritage Center, 422 2nd St S • Great Falls, MT 59405-1816 • (406) 452-3462 • http://www.highplainsheritage.org

Great Falls Genealogical Society • High Plains Heritage Center, 422 2nd St S • Great Falls, MT 59405-1815 • (406) 727-3922 • http://www.mcn.net/~gfgs

Great Falls Public Library • 301 2nd Ave N • Great Falls, MT 59401-2593 • (406) 453-0349 • http://www.greatfallslibrary.org

Little Shell Tribe • 105 Smelter Ave, P.O. Box 1384 • Great Falls, MT 59403 • (406) 771-8722 • http://tlc.wtp.net/little.htm

Malmstrom Historical Foundation • Historical Museum, 2225 9th Ave S • Great Falls, MT 59405

Ursuline Centre Museum • 2300 Central Ave • Great Falls, MT 59401

Hamilton
Bitter Root Genealogical Society • Ravalli County Museum, 205 Bedford, P.O. Box 941 • Hamilton, MT 59840 • (406) 961-4879 • http://www.rootsweb.com/~mtbgs/bvgs_information.htm

Bitter Root Valley Historical Society • Ravalli County Museum, 205 Bedford • Hamilton, MT 59840 • (406) 363-3338 • http://www.cybernet1.com/rcmuseum

Bitterroot Public Library • 306 State St • Hamilton, MT 59840-2759 • (406) 363-1670

Daly Mansion Museum • 251 Eastside Hwy, P.O. Box 223 • Hamilton, MT 59840 • (406) 363-6004

Ravalli County Historical Society • 205 Bedford St • Hamilton, MT 59840-2853

Hardin
Big Horn County Genealogical Society • P.O. Box 51 • Hardin, MT 59034 • http://www.rootsweb.com/~mtmsgs/soc_bhcgs.htm

Big Horn County Historical Society • Historical Museum, Route 1, Box 1206A • Hardin, MT 59034 • (406) 665-1671 • http://www.bighorncountymuseum.org

Big Horn County Public Library • 419 N Custer Ave • Hardin, MT 59034-1892 • (406) 665-1808

Hardin Historical Museum • general delivery • Hardin, MT 59034 • (406) 665-1671

Historic Preservation of Big Horn County • general delivery • Hardin, MT 59034 • (406) 665-2137

Harlem
Fort Belknap College Library & Tribal Archives • Hwy 2 & 66, Box 159 • Harlem, MT 59526-0159 • (406) 353-2607 • http://www.fbcc.edu/library/

Fort Belknap Community Council - Gros Ventre and Assiniboine Tribes • P.O. Box 249 • Harlem, MT 59526 • (406) 353-2205 • http://tlc.wtp.net/fort.htm

Harlowton
Upper Musselshell Historical Society • Historical Museum, 11 S Central Ave, P.O. Box 364 • Harlowton, MT 59036 • (406) 632-5519 • http://www.harlowtonmuseum.org

Havre
Fort Assiniboine Genealogical Society • c/o Havre-Hill County Library, 402 3rd St, P.O. Box 321 • Havre, MT 59501 • (406) 265-4409 • http://www.rootsweb.com/~mtmsgs/soc_fags.htm

H Earl Clak Museum • Holiday Village Mall, 1753 US Hwy 2 NW • Havre, MT 59531 • http://www.co.hill.mt.us

Havre-Hill County Library • 402 3rd St • Havre, MT 59501 • (406) 265-2123 • http://www.mtha.mt.lib.org

Vande Bogart Library • Montana State Univ-Northern Campus, 300 11th St W, P.O. Box 7751 • Havre, MT 59501-7751 • (406) 265-3706 • http://www.msun.edu/infotech/library

Helena
Grand Lodge of Masons Museum • 425 N Park Ave, P.O. Box 1158 • Helena, MT 59624-1158 • (406) 442-7774 • http://www.grandlodgemontana.org

Historic Virginia and Nevada Cities • 1275 Rimini Rd • Helena, MT 59601

Jack & Sallie Corette Library • Carroll College, 1601 N Benton Ave • Helena, MT 59625 • (406) 447-4344 • http://www.carroll.edu/library

Montana

Helena, cont.
Lewis and Clark County Genealogical Society • c/o Lewis & Clark Library, 120 S Last Chance Gulch, P.O. Box 5313 • Helena, MT 59604 • (406) 442-2380 • http://www.rootsweb.com/~mtlcgs/

Lewis and Clark Library • 120 S Last Chance Gulch • Helena, MT 59601-4133 • (406) 447-1690 • http://www.lewisandclarklibrary.org

Masonic Grand Lodge of Montana • 524 N Park Ave • Helena, MT 59601 • (406) 442-7774 • http://www.grandlodgemontana.org

Montana Dept of Health - Vital Records • 111 N Sanders, P.O. Box 4210 • Helena, MT 59604 • (406) 444-4228 • http://www.dphhs.mt.gov/

Montana Heritage Commission • 101 Reeder's Alley • Helena, MT 56901 • (406) 449-6522 • http://www.montanaheritagecommission.com

Montana Historical Society • Historical Museum, 225 N Roberts St, P.O. Box 201201 • Helena, MT 59620-1201 • (406) 444-0974 • http://www.montnahistoricalsociety.org

Montana State Archives • 225 N Roberts St, P.O. Box 201201 • Helena, MT 59620 • (406) 444-4774

Montana State Library • 1515 E 6th Ave, P.O. Box 201800 • Helena, MT 59620-1800 • (406) 444-5351 • http://msl.state.mt.us

Montana's Original Governor's Mansion Museum • 304 N Ewing, P.O. Box 201201 • Helena, MT 59620 • (406) 444-4710

Pioneer Cabin Museum • 200 S Park • Helena, MT 59601 • (406) 443-7641

Records Management Section • 1320 Bozeman St, P.O. Box 202801 • Helena, MT 59601 • (406) 444-2716 • http://www.mt.gov/sos/sectst. htm#anchor360717

Helmville
Upper Blackfoot Historical Society • general delivery • Helmville, MT 59843 • (406) 362-4099

Heron
Cabinet Wilderness Historical Society • Historical Museum, P.O. Box 333 • Heron, MT 59844

Hinsdale
Valley County Historical Society • Pioneer Museum, P.O. Box 38 • Hinsdale, MT 59241

Hobson
Utica Historical Society • Utica Museum,100 Main St, P.O. Box 560 • Hobson, MT 59492 • (406) 423-5531

Hot Springs
Preston Town-County Library of Hot Springs • 203 E Main St, P.O. Box 850 • Hot Springs, MT 59845-0850 • (406) 741-3491 • http://www. hotsprgs.net/~hslibrar/

Hysham
Treasure County '89ers Museum • P.O. Box 324 • Hysham, MT 59038

Jordan
Garfield County Museum • P.O. Box 145 • Jordan, MT 59337 • (406) 557-2589 • http://www.paleoworld.org

Kalispell
Conrad Mansion Museum • 4th & Woodland Ave, P.O. Box 1041 • Kalispell, MT 59903-1041 • (406) 755-2166 • http://www. conradmansion.com

Flathead County Library • 247 1st Ave E • Kalispell, MT 59901 • (406) 758-5820 • http://www.flatheadcountylibrary.org

Flathead Valley Genealogical Society • 134 Lawrence Ln, P.O. Box 584 • Kalispell, MT 59903-0584

Northwest Montana Historical Society • Central School Museum, 124 2nd Ave E • Kalispell, MT 59901 • (406) 756-8381 • http://www. yourmuseum.org

Sons of the American Revolution, Montana Society • 4193 Foothill Rd • Kalispell, MT 59901 • (406) 250-0825 • http://montanasar.weebly.com

Lambert
Lambert Historical Society • Historical Museum, Main St, P.O. Box 108 • Lambert, MT 59243 • (406) 774-3439

Lame Deer
Dr John Woodenlegs Memorial Library • Dull Knife Memorial College, 1 College Dr, P.O. Box 98 • Lame Deer, MT 59043-0098 • (406) 477-8293 • http://www.cdkc.edu

Northern Cheyenne Cultural Center • Dull Knife Memorial College, 1 College Dr, P.O. Box 98 • Lame Deer, MT 59043 • (406) 477-6215

Northern Cheyenne Tribe • P.O. Box 128 • Lame Deer, MT 59043 • (406) 477-6284 • http://www.ncheyenne.net

Laurel
American Historical Society of Germans from Russia, Yellowstone Valley Chapter • 715 W 5th St • Laurel, MT 59044 • (406) 628-6795 • http://www.ahsgr.org/Chapters/yellowstone_valley_chapter.htm

Lewistown
Central Montana Historical Association • Historical Museum, 408 NE Main St, P.O. Box 818 • Lewistown, MT 59457 • (406) 538-5436

Lewistown Genealogy Society • c/o Lewistown Public Library, 701 W Main St • Lewistown, MT 59457-2501

Lewistown Public Library • 701 W Main St • Lewistown, MT 59457 • (406) 538-5212 • http://lewistownlibrary.org

Libby
Libby Heritage Museum • 1367 US Highway 2 S, P.O. Box 628 • Libby, MT 59923-9011 • (406) 293-7521 • http://www.folksways.org/Libby/museum.html

Lincoln County Public Library • 220 W 6th St • Libby, MT 59923-1898 • (406) 293-2778 • http://www.lincolncountylibraries.com

Lincoln
Upper Blackfoot Historical Society • P.O. Box 922 • Lincoln, MT 59639-0922 • (406) 362-4099 • http://shopsite.hicountry.com/page16.html

Livingston
Livingston Depot Center Museum • 200 W Park, P.O. Box 1319 • Livingston, MT 59047 • (406) 222-2300 • http://www.livingstondepot. org

Park County Genealogy Society • c/o Park County Public Library, 228 W Callender St • Livingston, MT 59047 • (406) 222-9369

Park County Historical Society • Park County Museum, 118 W Chinook St • Livingston, MT 59047-2011 • (406) 222-4184 • http://www. livingstonmuseums.org

Park County Public Library • 228 W Callender St • Livingston, MT 59047-2618 • (406) 222-0862 • http://library.ycsi.net

Yellowstone Gateway Museum of Park County • 118 W Chinook • Livingston, MT 59047 • (406) 222-4184

Lorna
House of a Thousand Dolls Museum • 106 1st St, P.O. Box 136 • Lorna, MT 59460 • (406) 739-4338

Malta
Phillips County Genealogical Society • P.O. Box 334 • Malta, MT 59538 • http://www.rootsweb.com/~mtmsgs/soc_phcgs.htm

Phillips County Historical Society • Historical Museum, 133 S 1st W, P.O. Box 913 • Malta, MT 59538 • http://icstech.com/~mteast/museum. html

Manhattan
Little Bear School House Museum • 2610 Yadon Rd • Manhattan, MT 59741

Martinsdale
Chalres M Bair Family Museum • 2759 Mt Hwy 294 • Martinsdale, MT 59053 • (406) 572-3314

Medicine Lake
Sheridan Daybreakers Genealogical Society • 60 E Lake Hwy • Medicine Lake, MT 59247 • http://www.rootsweb.com/~mtmsgs/soc_sdgs.htm

Melrose
Beaverhead Hunters • P.O. Box 8 • Melrose, MT 59743

Miles City
Miles City Genealogical Society • c/o Miles City Public Library, 1 S 10th St, P.O. Box 711 • Miles City, MT 59301 • (406) 232-1496

Miles City Historic Preservation Office • 907 Main St • Miles City, MT 59301 • (406) 234-3090

Miles City Public Library • 1 S 10th St • Miles City, MT 59301-3398 • (406) 232-1496 • http://milescitypubliclibrary.org

Range Riders Museum • Route 1, Box 2203 • Miles City, MT 59301

Missoula
Fort Missoula Historical Society • Historical Museum, Fort Missoula Bldg 322 • Missoula, MT 59804 • (406) 728-3476 • http://www.fortmissoulamuseum.org

K Ross Toole Archives • 2600 Mitten Mountain Rd • Missoula, MT 59803

Maureen and Mike Mansfield Library • Univ of Montana, 32 Campus Dr, No 9936 • Missoula, MT 59812-9936 • (406) 243-6866 • http://www.lib.umt.edu

Missoula Public Library • 301 E Main • Missoula, MT 59802-4799 • (406) 721-2665 • http://www.missoula.lib.mt.us

Montana Women's History Project • 315 S 4th St E • Missoula, MT 59801 • (406) 728-3041

Museum of Mountain Flying • Aviation Wy • Missoula, MT 59801 • (406) 549-8488

Northern Rockies Heritage Center • 3255 Fort Missoula Rd, P.O. Box 8382 • Missoula, MT 59806 • (406) 728-3662

Rocky Mountain Museum of Military History • P.O. Box 7263 • Missoula, MT 59807

Smokejumper Visitor Center • 5765 W Broadway St • Missoula, MT 59808 • (406) 329-4972 • http://www.fs.fed.us/fire/people/smokejumpers/missoula/

Western Montana Genealogical Society • P.O. Box 2714 • Missoula, MT 59806 • (406) 728-1628 • http://www/rootsweb.com/~mtwmgs

Pablo
Confederated Salish and Kootenai Tribal Council • Flathead Reservation, P.O. Box 278 • Pablo, MT 56855 • (406) 675-2700 • http://www.peoplescenter.org

D'arcy McNickle Library • Salish Kootenai College, 5200 Hwy 93, P.O. Box 117 • Pablo, MT 59855 • (406) 275-4874 • http://www.skc.edu

People's Center Museum • 63263 Hwy 93, P.O. Box 278 • Pablo, MT 59855

Philipsburg
Granite County Museum • 135 S Sansome, P.O. Box 502 • Philipsburg, MT 59858 • (406) 859-3020

Plains
Plains Public Library District • 108 W Railroad, P.O. Box 399 • Plains, MT 59859-0339 • (406) 826-3101

Plentywood
Sheridan County Library • 100 W Laurel Ave • Plentywood, MT 59254 • (406) 765-2317 • http://www.co.sheridan.mt.us/library.htm

Sheridan County Museum • P.O. Box 1153 • Plentywood, MT 59254

Polson
Miracle of America Museum • 58176 Hwy 93 • Polson, MT 59860 • (406) 883-6804 • http://www.cyperport.net/museum

Polson Flathead Historical Society • 708 Main St • Polson, MT 59860-3225

Poplar
Fort Peck Community College-Tribal Library • Hwy 2 E, P.O. Box 398 • Poplar, MT 59255-0398 • (406) 768-5551

Fort Peck Tribal Council - Assiniboine and Sioux Tribes • P.O. Box 1027 • Poplar, MT 59255 • (406) 768-5155 • http://tlc.wtp.net/fortpeck.htm

Poplar Museum • P.O. Box 157 • Poplar, MT 59255

Pryor
Chief Plenty Coups State Monument • Edgar Rd, P.O. Box 100 • Pryor, MT 59066 • (406) 252-1289 • http://www.plentycoups.org

Red Lodge
Carbon County Historical Society • Historical Museum, 206 N Broadway, P.O. Box 881 • Red Lodge, MT 59068 • (406) 446-1920

Richey
Richey Historical Society • Historical Museum, Main St, P.O. Box 194 • Richey, MT 59259 • (406) 773-5615

Ronan
Ronan City Library • 203 Main St SW • Ronan, MT 59864 • (406) 676-3682 • http://www.ronan.net/~ronanlib/

Roundup
Musselshell Valley Historical Museum • 524 1st W • Roundup, MT 59072 • (406) 323-1403 • http://www.mvhm.us

Rudyard
Rudyard Historical Society • Historical Museum, P.O. Box 44 • Rudyard, MT 59540

Saint Ignatius
Flathead Indian Museum • 1 Museum Ln, P.O. Box 460 • Saint Ignatius, MT 59865 • (406) 745-2951

Scobey
Daniels County Museum and Pioneer Town • 7 W County Rd, P.O. Box 133 • Scobey, MT 59263 • (406) 487-5965 • http://www.scobey.org

Seeley Lake
Seeley Lake Historical Society • Historical Museum, 2920 Hwy 83 N, P.O. Box 1261 • Seeley Lake, MT 59868 • (406) 677-2990

Swan Museum • P.O. Box 514 • Seeley Lake, MT 69868

Shelby
Marias Museum of History • 206 12th Ave N, P.O. Box 895 • Shelby, MT 59474 • (406) 434-5422

Toole County Free Library • 229 Maple Ave • Shelby, MT 59474 • (406) 424-8345

Sheridan
Madison County History Association • 207 Mill St • Sheridan, MT 59849 • (406) 842-5410

McFarland Curatorial Center • general delivery • Sheridan, MT 59749 • (406) 843-5441

Montana Heritage Commission at Virginia City • general delivery • Sheridan, MT 59749 • (406) 843-5457

Sidney
MonDak Historical and Arts Society • MonDak Heritage Center • 120 3rd Ave SE, P.O. Box 50 • Sidney, MT 59270-0050 • (406) 482-3500 • http://www.mondakheritagecenter.org

Stanford
Judith Basin County Museum • 19 3rd St S, P.O. Box 104 • Stanford, MT 59479 • (406) 566-2974

Judith Basin Historical Society • Historical Museum, P.O. Box 34 • Stanford, MT 59479

Sod Buster Museum • general delivery • Stanford, MT 59479 • (406) 423-5358

Stevensville
North Valley Public Library-Stevensville Library • 208 Main St • Stevensville, MT 59870 • (406) 777-5061

Stevensville Historical Museum • 517 Main St • Stevensville, MT 59870

Sun River
Sun River Valley Historical Society • 13847 Hwy 200 • Sun River, MT 59483 • (406) 264-5572

Superior
Mineral County Historical Society • Historical Museum, 301 2nd Ave, P.O. Box 533 • Superior, MT 59872-0533 • (406) 822-4626

Mineral County Public Library • 301 2nd Ave E, P.O. Box 430 • Superior, MT 59872-0430 • (406) 822-3563 • http://www.mineralcountylibrary.org

Terry
Prairie County Museum • P.O. Box 368 • Terry, MT 59349

Thompson Falls
Sanders County Historical Society • Old Jail Museum, P.O. Box 774 • Thompson Falls, MT 59873

Three Forks
Headwaters Heritage Museum • 202 S Main, P.O. Box 116 • Three Forks, MT 59752 • (406) 285-3644

Three Forks Area Historical Society • Historical Museum, P.O. Box 116 • Three Forks, MT 59752

Townsend
Broadwater County Museum • 133 N Walnut • Townsend, MT 59644 • (406) 266-5252 • http://www.onewest.net~inmontana/broadwater_county_museum/

Twin Bridges
Twin Bridges Historical Association • Historical Museum, P.O. Box 227 • Twin Bridges, MT 59754

Twin Bridges Public Library • 206 S Main St, P.O. Box 246 • Twin Bridges, MT 59754-0246 • (406) 684-5416

Utica
Utica Historical and Museum Society • Historical Museum, HC 81, Box 560 • Utica, MT 59452 • (406) 423-5208

Valier
Marmarth Historical Society • general delivery • Valier, MT 59486 • (406) 279-6782

Victor
Victor Heritage Association • Heritage Museum, 125 N Blake St, P.O. Box 610 • Victor, MT 59875-9470 • (406) 642-3997

Virginia City
McFarland Curatorial Center • P.O. Box 63 • Virginia City, MT 59755 • (406) 843-5447

Montana Heritage Commission • 300 W Wallace St • Virginia City, MT 59755 • (406) 843-5247 • http://www.montanaheritagecommission.com

Nevada City Living History Museum • 300 W Wallace St, P.O. Box 338 • Virginia City, MT 59795 • (406) 843-5247 • http://www.virginiacitymt.com/LivHistory.asp

Virginia City-J Spencer Watkins Historical Museum • W Wallace St, P.O. Box 215 • Virginia City, MT 59755 • (406) 843-5500

West Glacier
George C Ruhle Library • Glacier National Park • West Glacier, MT 59936 • (406) 888-5441

West Yellowstone
Museum of the Yellowstone • 146 Yellowstone Ave, P.O. Box 411 • West Yellowstone, MT 59758 • (406) 646-7814

White Sulphur Springs
Meagher County City Library • 15 1st Ave SE, P.O. Box S • White Sulphur Springs, MT 59645-0819 • (406) 547-2250

Meagher County Historical Association • Historical Museum, 310 2nd Ave SE, P.O. Box 389 • White Sulphur Springs, MT 59645 • (406) 547-3965

Whitefish
Stumptown Historical Society • Historical Museum, 500 Depot St #101 • Whitefish, MT 59937 • (406) 862-0067

Whitehall
Jefferson Valley Historical Society • Historical Museum, 303 S Division, P.O. Box 902 • Whitehall, MT 59759-0902

Wibaux
Pierre Wibaux Complex Museum • E Origin Ave, P.O. Box 74 • Wibaux, MT 59323

Winnett
Petroleum County Community Library • 205 S Broadway, P.O. Box 188 • Winnett, MT 59087-0188 • (406) 429-2451 • http://www.midrivers.com/~whsrams

Wisdom
Big Hole National Battlefield • 16425 Hwy 43 W, P.O. Box 237 • Wisdom, MT 59761 • (406) 689-3155 • http://www.nps.gov/biho

Wolf Point
Friends of the Assinboines Foundation • 623 Knapp St, P.O. Box 254 • Wolf Point, MT 59201-0254 • (406) 653-1804

Roosevelt County Library • 220 2nd Ave S • Wolf Point, MT 59201-1599 • (406) 653-2411

Wolf Point Area Historical Society • Historical Museum, 200 2nd Ave, P.O. Box 977 • Wolf Point, MT 59201-0977 • (406) 653-1912

Ainsworth

Ainsworth Public Library • 445 N Main St, P.O. Box 207 • Ainsworth, NE 69210-0207 • (402) 387-2032 • http://www.ainsworthlibrary.com

Brown County Historical Society • Coleman House Museum, 339 N Ash • Ainsworth, NE 69210 • (402) 387-2427 • http://www.rootsweb.com/~nebrown

Sellor's Log Cabin Museum • Hwy 20 • Ainsworth, NE 69210 • (402) 387-2429

Albion

Boone County Historical Society • Historical Museum, 1025 W Fairview • Albion, NE 68620 • (402) 395-2971 • http://www.albionne.org/community1.htm

Pawnee Genealogy Scouters • P.O. Box 112 • Albion, NE 68620

Allen

Dixon County Historical Society • Historical Museum, S Clark St, P.O. Box 95 • Allen, NE 68710 • (402) 287-2885

Alliance

Alliance Public Library • 1750 Sweetwater Ave • Alliance, NE 69301-4438 • (308) 762-1387 • http://www.cityofalliance.net

Dobby Lee's Frontier Town • 320 E 25th St • Alliance, NE 69301 • (308) 762-2270

Knight Museum of the High Plains Heritage • 908 Yellowstone, P.O. Box D • Alliance, NE 69301 • (308) 762-5400 • http://www.cityofalliance.net

Nebraska DAR • 202 W 4th St • Alliance, NE 69301

Northwest Nebraska Genealogical Society • P.O. Box 6 • Alliance, NE 69301-0006 • (308) 762-3677

Alma

Hoesch Memorial Public Library • City Park, W 2nd, P.O. Box 438 • Alma, NE 68920-0438 • (308) 928-2600 • http://www.almalibrary.com

Arapahoe

Furnas-Gosper County Historical Society • Historical Museum, 401 Nebraska Ave, P.O. Box 202 • Arapahoe, NE 68922-0303 • (308) 962-5236 • http://www.visitnebraska.org

Arthur

Arthur County Historical Society • Historical Museum, P.O. Box 134 • Arthur, NE 69121-0134 • (308) 764-2426

Ashland

Saline Ford Historical Preservation Society • Historical Museum, 1004 Oxbow • Ashland, NE 68003 • (402) 944-2944

Strategic Air and Space Museum • 28210 West Park Hwy • Ashland, NE 68003 • (402) 827-3100 • http://www.strategicairandspace.com

Atkinson

Atkinson Historical Society • P.O. Box 145 • Atkinson, NE 68713-0145

Sturdevant-McKee Foundation • Historical Museum, 308 S Main St, P.O. Box 225 • Atkinson, NE 68713 • (402) 925-2726

Auburn

Nemaha Valley Genealogical Society • P.O. Box 25 • Auburn, NE 68305-0025 • http://www.rootsweb.com/~nenemaha/nvgs.html

Nemaha Valley Museum • 1423 19th St, P.O. Box 25 • Auburn, NE 68305 • (402) 274-3203

Aurora

Alice M Farr Library • 1603 L St • Aurora, NE 68818-2132 • (402) 694-2272 • http://www.auroranebraska.com

Hamilton County Historical Society • Plainsman Museum, 210 16th St • Aurora, NE 68818 • (402) 694-6531 • http://www.plainsmanmuseum.org

Axtell

Axtell Public Library • P.O. Box 65 • Axtell, NE 68924-7245 • (308) 743-2592

Bancroft

Nebraska State Historical Society • John G Neihardt Center Museum, 306 W Elm St, P.O. Box 344 • Bancroft, NE 68004-0344 • (402) 648-3388 • http://www.nebraskahistory.org; http://www.neihardtcenter.org

Bassett

Rock County Historical Society • Historical Museum, W Hwy 20, P.O. Box 116 • Bassett, NE 68714-0116 • (402) 684-3774

Bayard

Bayard Public Library • 500 Avenue A, P.O. Box B • Bayard, NE 69334-0676 • (308) 586-1144

Bayard-Chimney Rock Historical Society • Historical Museum, 1339 Main St, P.O. Box 369 • Bayard, NE 69334-0369 • (308) 586-1259

Chimney Rock Historical Society • P.O. Box 626 • Bayard, NE 69334 • (308) 586-1005

Beatrice

Beatrice Public Library • 100 N 16th St • Beatrice, NE 68310-4152 • (402) 223-3584 • http://www.beatrice.lib.ne.us

Gage County Heritage Preservation Society • Historical Museum, 6795 W Scott Rd • Beatrice, NE 6310 • (402) 239-3127

Gage County Historical Society • Historical Museum, 102 N 2nd St, P.O. Box 793 • Beatrice, NE 68310-0783 • (402) 228-1679 • http://www.beatrice.com/gagecountymuseum

Homestead National Monument • 8523 W State Hwy 4 • Beatrice, NE 68310 • (402) 223-3514 • http://www.nps.gov

Nebraska State Genealogical Society • c/o Beatrice Public Library, 100 N 16th St • Beatrice, NE 68505 • (402) 266-8881 • http://www.rootsweb.com/~nesgs

Southeast Nebraska Genealogical Society • c/o Beatrice Public Library, 100 N 16th St, P.O. Box 562 • Beatrice, NE 68301 • (402) 228-0695

Wakpa Sica Historical Society • general delivery • Beatrice, NE 68310 • (402) 223-9099

Beaver City

Beaver City Public Library • 408 10th St, P.O. Box 431 • Beaver City, NE 68926-0431 • (308) 268-4115

Furnas County Genealogical Society • c/o Beaver City Public Library, 408 10th St, P.O. Box 166 • Beaver City, NE 68926 • (308) 268-4115

Furnas-Gosper Historical Society • Historical Museum, P.O. Box 315 • Beaver City, NE 68926 • (308) 268-2208

Belgrade

Boone-Nance County Genealogical Society • P.O. Box 231 • Belgrade, NE 68623 • (308) 358-0836 • http://www.rootsweb.com/~nenance/bngensoc.html

Bellevue

Bellevue Public Library • 1003 Lincoln Rd • Bellevue, NE 68005-3199 • (402) 293-3157

Sarpy County Historical and Genealogical Society • Historical Museum, 2402 Sac Pl • Bellevue, NE 68005-3932 • (402) 292-1880

Belvidere

Thayer County Genealogical Society • Thayer County Museum and Genealogical Library, P.O. Box 387 • Belvidere, NE 68315 • (402) 768-7313

Thayer County Historical Society • Thayer County Museum, P.O. Box 387 • Belvidere, NE 68315-0387 • (402) 768-2147

Nebraska

Benkelman
Dundy County Historical Society • Historical Museum, 522 Arapahoe, P.O. Box 634 • Benkelman, NE 69021 • (308) 423-5404

Big Springs
Big Springs Public Library • 400 Pine St, P.O. Box 192 • Big Springs, NE 69122-0192 • (308) 889-3482

Phelps Hotel Historic Preservation Society • Historical Museum, RR2, Box 133 • Big Springs, NE 69122

Blair
Blair Public Library • 210 S 17th St • Blair, NE 68008 • (402) 426-3617 • http://www.blairpubliclibrary.com

C A Dana-Life Library • Dana College, 2848 College Dr • Blair, NE 68008-1099 • (402) 426-7300 • http://www.dana.edu/Academics/library.htm

Washington County Genealogical Society • c/o Blair Public Library, 210 S 17th St • Blair, NE 68008 • (402) 426-3617

Boys Town
Boys Town Hall of History • 14057 Flanagan Blvd • Boys Town, NE 68010 • (402) 498-1185 • http://www.boystown.org

Brady
Fort Brady Museum • P.O. Box 11 • Brady, NE 69123 • (308) 584-3215

Brewster
Blaine County Historical Society • Historical Museum, P.O. Box 7 • Brewster, NE 68821 • (308) 547-2474 • http://www.blainecounty.ne.gov/history.html

Bridgeport
Bridgeport Public Library • 722 Main St, P.O. Box 940 • Bridgeport, NE 69336-0940 • (308) 262-0326

Macedonia Historical Preservation Society • Pioneer Trails Museum, Main St • Bridgeport, NE 69336 • (308) 262-0108

Broadwater
Broadwater Public Library • Route 2, Box 64 • Broadwater, NE 69125 • (308) 489-0119

Broken Bow
Broken Bow Public Library • 626 South D Street • Broken Bow, NE 68822 • (308) 872-2927

Custer County Genealogical Society • 445 S 9th Ave, P.O. Box 334 • Broken Bow, NE 68822

Custer County Historical Society • Historical Museum, 455 S 9th St, P.O. Box 334 • Broken Bow, NE 68822-0334 • (308) 872-2203 • http://www.rootsweb.com/~necuster

Brownville
Brownville Historical Society • Historical Museum, Main St, P.O. Box 1 • Brownville, NE 68321 • (402) 825-6001 • http://www.ci.brownville.ne.us

Meriwether Lewis Dredge Museum • Brownville State Recreation Area, RR1, Box 38 • Brownville, NE 68321 • (402) 825-3341

Burwell
Fort Hartsuff State Historical Park Museum • RR1, Box 37 • Burwell, NE 68823 • (308) 346-4715 • http://www.ngpe.state.ne.us

Garfield County Historical Society • Historical Museum, 737 H St, P.O. Box 545 • Burwell, NE 68823-0545 • (308) 346-5070

Butte
Butte Community Historical Center and Museum • 721 1st St • Butte, NE 68722 • (605) 384-3509 • http://www.buttenebraska.com

Butte Historical Society • Historical Museum, 410 Thayer St, P.O. box 286 • Butte, NE 68722 • (402) 775-2426

Cairo
Cairo Roots Historical and Genealogical Society • P.O. Box 308 • Cairo, NE 68804

Callaway
Seven Valleys Historical Society • Historical Museum, RR1, Box 45 • Callaway, NE 68825 • (308) 836-2728

Cambridge
Cambridge Museum • 612 Penn St, P.O. Box 129 • Cambridge, NE 69022 • (308) 697-4385

Central City
Central City Public Library • 1604 15th Ave • Central City, NE 68826 • (308) 946-2512 • http://www.cconline.net/library.htm

Merrick County Historical Museum • 211 E Street • Central City, NE 68826 • (308) 946-2867

Merrick County Historical Society • Historical Museum, 215 E Street • Central City, NE 68826 • (308) 946-3309

Chadron
Chadron Public Library • 507 Bordeaux St • Chadron, NE 69337 • (308) 432-0531 • http://www.members.panhandle.net/chadronpubliclibrary

Dawes County Historical Society • Historical Museum, 341 Country Club Rd, P.O. Box 1319 • Chadron, NE 69337-1319 • (308) 432-4999 • http://www.chadron.com/cdhm

Mari Sandoz Heritage Society • Chadron State College, High Plains Heritage Center, 300 E 12th St • Chadron, NE 69337 • (308) 432-6276

Museum Association of the Fur Trade • 6321 Hwy 20 • Chadron, NE 69337 • (308) 432-3843 • http://www.furtrade.org

Nebraska Historical Society • c/o Chadron State College Library • Chadron, NE 69337 • (308) 432-6271

Northwest Nebraska Genealogical Society • P.O. Box 666 • Chadron, NE 69337 • (308) 762-3677

Reta E King Library • Chadron State College, 300 E 12th St • Chadron, NE 69337 • (308) 432-6271 • http://www.csc.edu

Champion
Champion Mill State Historical Park • P.O. Box 117 • Champion, NE 69023 • (308) 862-5860 • http://www.ngpc.state.ne.us

Chapell
Deuel County Historical Society • Depot Museum, P.O. Box 324 • Chapell, NE 69129

Chappell Historical Society • Sudman-Neumann Heritage House Museum, 5th & Vincent Sts, P.O. Box 324 • Chappell, NE 69129-0324 • (308) 874-2866

Chappell Public Library • 289 Babcock Ave, P.O. Box 248 • Chappell, NE 69129-0248 • (308) 874-2626

Clarkson
Clarkson Historical Society • Historical Museum, 221 Pine St • Clarkson, NE 68629 • (402) 892-3629

Clay Center
Clay County Historical Society • Historical Museum, 320 W Glenville St, P.O. Box 201 • Clay Center, NE 68933-0201 • (402) 762-3563

Columbus
Columbus Public Library • 2504 14th St • Columbus, NE 68601-4988 • (402) 564-7116 • http://www.megavision.net/library

Platte County Historical Society • Historical Museum, 2916 16th St, P.O. Box 31 • Columbus, NE 68601 • (402) 564-1856

Platte Valley Kinseekers • Historical Museum, 2916 16th St, P.O. Box 153 • Columbus, NE 68601 • (402) 564-5829

Comstock
William R Dowsse Sod House Museum • general delivery • Comstock, NE 68828

Cook
Cook Community Historical Society • Historical Museum, 220 E Cherry St • Cook, NE 68329 • (402) 864-2441

Cozad
Cozad Genealogy Club • c/o Wilson Public Library, 910 Meridian Ave, P.O. Drawer C • Cozad, NE 69130 • (308) 784-2019

Cozad Historical Society • 100th Meridian Museum, 206 E 8th St, P.O. Box 325 • Cozad, NE 69130-0325 • (308) 784-1100

Dawson County Genealogical Society • 514 E 8th St • Cozad, NE 69130

Robert Henri Museum • 218 E 8th St, P.O. Box 355 • Cozad, NE 69130 • (308) 794-4154

Wilson Public Library • 910 Meridian Ave • Cozad, NE 69130-1755 • (308) 784-2019

Crawford
Crawford Historical Society • 337 2nd St, P.O. Box 165 • Crawford, NE 69339 • (308) 665-1732

Crawford Public Library • 601 2nd St • Crawford, NE 69339 • (308) 665-1780

Fort Robinson Museum • US Hwy 20, P.O. Box 304 • Crawford, NE 69339 • (308) 665-2919

Nebraska State Historical Society • Fort Robinson Museum, US Hwy 20, P.O. Box 304 • Crawford, NE 69339 • (308) 665-2919

Creighton
Creighton Historical Center • P.O. Box 535 • Creighton, NE 68729

Creighton Public Library • 701 State St, P.O. Box 158 • Creighton, NE 68729-0158 • (402) 358-5115

Crete
Crete Public Library • 305 E 13th St, P.O. Box 156 • Crete, NE 68333-0156 • (402) 826-3809 • http://www.crete-ne.com

Perkins Library • Doane College, 1014 Doane Dr • Crete, NE 68333-2495 • (402) 826-8565 • http://www.doane.edu

Saline County Genealogical Society • c/o Crete Public Library, 305 E 13th St, P.O. Box 24 • Crete, NE 68333-0024 • (402) 826-3809

Saline County Pastfinders • 730 E 13th St • Crete, NE 68333-2308 • (402) 826-3462

Culbertson
Culbertson Public Library • 507 New York Ave, P.O. Box 327 • Culbertson, NE 69024-0327 • (308) 278-2125

Curtis
Frontier County Genealogical Society • P.O. Box 242 • Curtis, NE 69025

Frontier County Historical Society • Historical Museum, P.O. Box 242 • Curtis, NE 69025-0242

Klyte Burt Memorial Public Library • 316 Center Ave, P.O. Box 29 • Curtis, NE 69025-0029 • (308) 367-4148

Dakota City
Dakota City Public Library • 1710 Broadway, P.O. Box 482 • Dakota City, NE 68731-0482 • (402) 987-3778

Dakota County Genealogical Society • 101 W Colonial Dr, Route 2 S, P.O. Box 482 • Dakota City, NE 68731

Dakota County Historical Society • Historical Museum, P.O. Box 971 • Dakota City, NE 68731 • (402) 987-3388

Dalton
Dalton Historical Society • Prairie Schooner Museum, Hwy 385, P.O. Box 314 • Dalton, NE 69131-0314 • (308) 377-2637

Dalton Public Library • 306 Main St, P.O. Box 206 • Dalton, NE 69131-0206 • (308) 377-2413

David City
Butler County Historical Society • Historical Museum, 2020 D Street • David City, NE 68632 • (402) 367-4734

Roman L & Victoria E Hruska Memorial Public Library • 399 5th St • David City, NE 68632 • (402) 367-3100

Saint Joseph Villa Museum • 927 7th St • David City, NE 68632 • (402) 367-3855

Dawson
Pennsylvania Colony Historical Society • Historical Museum, RR1, Box 127 • Dawson, NE 68337 • (402) 855-2485

Denton
Denton Community Historical Society • Historical Museum, 7115 Lancaster Ave, P.O. Box 405 • Denton, NE 68339 • (402) 797-5700

Dewitt
Dewitt Historical Society • Historical Museum, 15124 N Blue Ridge Rd • Dewitt, NE 68341 • (402) 683-5815

Diller
Diller Historical Society • Route 1, Box 2A • Diller, NE 68342

Dixon
Dixon County Historical Society • Route 1, Box 26 • Dixon, NE 68732

Dorchester
Saline County Historical Society • Historical Museum, Hwy 33 • Dorchester, NE 68343 • (402) 947-2911

Dunbar
Mellette County Historical Society • general delivery • Dunbar, NE 68346 • (402) 259-3494

Elgin
Elgin Historical Society • Historical Museum, 360 Park St, P.O. Box 161 • Elgin, NE 68636-0161 • (847) 742-4248

Elkhorn
Eastern Nebraska Genealogical Society • 8686 N 204th St • Elkhorn, NE 68022-0541 • (402) 721-9553

Elmwood
Bess Streeter Aldrich House Museum • 204 East F Street, P.O. Box 172 • Elmwood, NE 68349 • (402) 994-3855

Exeter
Fillmore Heritage Genealogical Society • 307 Road T • Exeter, NE 68351 • (402) 266-8881

Fairbury
Fairbury City Historical Society • Historical Museum, 910 2nd St, P.O. Box 83 • Fairbury, NE 68352 • (402) 729-3151

Fairbury City Museum • 1228 Elm St • Fairbury, NE 68352 • (402) 729-3707 • http://www.rootsweb.ancestry.com/~nejeffer/museum.htm

Jefferson County Genealogical Society • P.O. Box 163 • Fairbury, NE 68352-0163 • http://www.rootsweb.com~nejeffgs

Jefferson County Historical Society • 910 Bacon Rd, P.O. Box 154 • Fairbury, NE 68352-0154 • (402) 720-3191

Rock Creek Station State Historic Park Museum • 57426 710 Rd • Fairbury, NE 68352 • (402) 729-5777 • http://www.outdoornebraska.org

Fairmont
Fillmore County Historical Society • 600 6th Ave, P.O. Box 333 • Fairmont, NE 68354 • (402) 268-6081

Nebraska

Falls City
Lydia Bruun Woods Memorial Library • 120 E 18th St • Falls City, NE 68355 • (402) 245-2913 • http://www.scentco.net/subscribers/fclib

Richardson County Historical Society • Bell-Jenne House Museum, 312 W 17th St, P.O. Box 45 • Falls City, NE 68355 • (402) 245-3326

Tri-State Corners Genealogical Society • c/o Lydia Bruun Wood Memorial Library, 120 E 18th St • Falls City, NE 68355 • (402) 245-2913

Fort Calhoun
Fort Atkinson State Historical Park • 7th & Madison Sts, P.O. Box 240 • Fort Calhoun, NE 68023 • (402) 468-5611 • http://www.ngpc.state.ne.us

Washington County Historical Association • Historical Museum, 14th & Monroe Sts, P.O. Box 25 • Fort Calhoun, NE 68023-0025 • (402) 468-5740 • http://www.newashcohist.org

Franklin
Franklin County Historical Society • Historical Museum, Hwy 136 & Hwy 10, RR1, Box 156 • Franklin, NE 68939 • (308) 425-3603

Fremont
Dodge County Historical Society • Louis E May Museum, 1643 N Nye St, P.O. Box 766 • Fremont, NE 68025-0766 • (402) 721-4515 • http://www.connectfremont.org

Eastern Nebraska Genealogical Society • P.O. Box 541 • Fremont, NE 68026-0541 • (402) 721-9553 • http://www.connectfremont.org/club/engs.htm

Keene Memorial Library • 1030 N Broad St • Fremont, NE 68025-4199 • (402) 727-2694 • http://keene.lib.ne.us

Friend
Saline County Historical Society • Historical Museum, 1127 E 2nd St • Friend, NE 68359-1113 • (402) 947-2911

Fullerton
Nance County Historical Society • Historical Museum, 501 Broadway, P.O. Box 10 • Fullerton, NE 68638-0010 • (308) 536-2377

Geneva
Fillmore County Historical Society • 633 N 11th • Geneva, NE 68361

Geneva Public Library • 1043 G Street • Geneva, NE 68361 • (402) 759-3416 • http://www.ci.geneva.ne.us

Genoa
Genoa Historical Museum • 402 Willard Ave, P.O. Box 279 • Genoa, NE 68640 • (402) 993-6602

Genoa Historical Society • 302 Willard, P.O. Box 425 • Genoa, NE 68640

US Indian School Museum • 209 Webster Ave, P.O. Box 382 • Genoa, NE 68640 • (402) 993-6636

Gering
Farm and Ranch Museum • 2930 Old Oregon Tr, P.O. Box 398 • Gering, NE 69341 • (308) 436-7998 • http://www.farmandranchmuseum.com

Gering Public Library • 1055 P Street • Gering, NE 69341 • (308) 436-7433 • http://www.geringlibrary.org

North Platte Valley Historical Association • Historical Museum, 11th & J Sts, P.O. Box 435 • Gering, NE 69341-0435 • (308) 436-5411 • http://www.npvm.org

Scotts Bluff National Monument Library • Oregon Trail Museum, 190276 Hwy 92, P.O. Box 27 • Gering, NE 69341-0027 • (308) 436-4340 • http://www.nps.gov/scbl

Gibbon
Flatwater Genealogical Society • P.O. Box 373 • Gibbon, NE 68840 • (308) 468-5656

Gibbon Heritage Center • 2nd & Court Sts, P.O. Box 27 • Gibbon, NE 68840 • (308) 468-5531

Goehner
Seward County Historical Society • Historical Museum, I-80 exit 373 • Goehner, NE 68635 • (402) 523-4055

Gordon
Gordon City Library • 101 W 5th St • Gordon, NE 69343 • (308) 282-1198 • http://www.gordoncitylibrary.org

Scamahorn Church Museum • W 5th St • Gordon, NE 69343

Tri-State Old Time Cowboys' Museum • P.O. Box 202 • Gordon, NE 69343 • (308) 282-0887

Gothenburg
Cozad Historical Society • 503 Lake Ave • Gothenburg, NE 69138 • (308) 537-7217

Gothenburg Historical Museum • 1420 Avenue F, P.O. Box 263 • Gothenburg, NE 69138 • (308) 537-4293 • http://www.gothenburgdelivers.com

Gothenburg Historical Society • 520 9th St, P.O. Box 153 • Gothenburg, NE 69138

Gothenburg Public Library • 1104 Lake Ave • Gothenburg, NE 69138-1903 • (308) 537-2591

Pony Express Station Museum • 1500 Lake Ave, P.O. Box 263 • Gothenburg, NE 69138 • (308) 537-3505 • http://www.gothenburgdelivers.com

Sod House Museum • I-80 & Hwy 47 • Gothenburg, NE 69138 • (308) 537-2680

Grand Island
Daughters of the American Revolution, Lue R Spencer Chapter • c/o Edith Abbott Memorial Library, 211 N Washington St • Grand Island, NE 68801 • (308) 385-5333

Edith Abbott Memorial Library • 211 N Washington St • Grand Island, NE 68801-5855 • (308) 385-5333 • http://www.gi.lib.ne.us

Hall County Historical Society • Historical Museum, 522 W Charles St, P.O. Box 1683 • Grand Island, NE 68802 • (308) 385-1545

Nebraska Vintage Base Ball Association • 3133 Hwy 34 W • Grand Island, NE 68801 • (308) 382-3481

Prairie Pioneer Genealogical Society • P.O. Box 1122 • Grand Island, NE 68802 • (308) 384-3218

Stuhr Museum of the Prairie Pioneer • 3133 W Hwy 34 • Grand Island, NE 68801-7280 • (308) 385-5316 • http://www.stuhrmuseum.org

Grant
Perkins County Genealogical Society • P.O. Box 418 • Grant, NE 69140

Perkins County Historical Society • Historical Museum, 6th & Central Ave, P.O. Box 737 • Grant, NE 69140-0737 • (308) 326-4233

Greeley
Greeley County Historical Society • Historical Museum, P.O. Box 6 • Greeley, NE 68842

Greenwood
Greenwood Historical Society • Historical Museum, Broad St, P.O. Box 1 • Greenwood, NE 68366 • (402) 789-3175

Gretna
Gretna Heritage Society • 23702 Schramm Rd • Gretna, NE 68028

Harrisburg
Banner County Historical Society • Historical Museum, 200 N Pennsylvania, HC55, Box 6 • Harrisburg, NE 69345 • (308) 436-4514 • http://www.bannercountyhistoricalsociety.com

Harrison
Sioux County Historical Society • Historical Museum, P.O. Box 312 • Harrison, NE 69346-0312 • (308) 668-2379

Hartington
Cedar County Historical Museum • 304 W Franklin St • Hartington, NE 68739 • (402) 254-6597

Cedar County Historical Society • 405 Hoese St • Hartington, NE 68739

Hastings
Adams County Genealogical Society • P.O. Box 424 • Hastings, NE 68902-0424 • (402) 463-5838 • http://www.adamshistory.org/acgs.html

Adams County Historical Society • Hastings Museum, 1330 N Burlington Ave, P.O. Box 102 • Hastings, NE 68902-0102 • (402) 463-5358 • http://www.hastingsmuseum.org

Hastings Historical Society • P.O. Box 1286 • Hastings, NE 68901

Hastings Public Library • 517 W 4th St, P.O. Box 849 • Hastings, NE 68902-0849 • (402) 461-2346 • http://www.hastings.lib.ne.us

Nebraska Military Historical Society • 5272 East J Street • Hastings, NE 68901-8343

Perkins Library • Hastings College, 800 N Turner Ave • Hastings, NE 68901-7695 • (402) 461-7330 • http://www.hastings.edu/html/library/services1_library1.stm

Hay Springs
Cravath Memorial Library • 243 N Main St, P.O. Box 309 • Hay Springs, NE 69347 • (308) 638-4541

Hay Springs Heritage Center • P.O. Box 236 • Hay Springs, NE 69347

Hayes Center
Hayes County Historical Society • Historical Museum, HC 62, Box 47 • Hayes Center, NE 69032 • (308) 286-3452

Hebron
Hebron Secrest Library • 146 N 4th St, P.O. Box 125 • Hebron, NE 68370 • (402) 768-6701

Thayer Genealogical Society • 3454 9th St • Hebron, NE 68370

Hemingford
Hemingford Public Library • 812 Box Butte, P.O. Box 6 • Hemingford, NE 69348-0006 • (308) 487-3454 • http://angelfire.com/ne/hplibrary/

Holdrege
Holdrege Area Genealogy Club • Nebraska Prairie Museum, N Burlington St, P.O. Box 164 • Holdrege, NE 68949 • (308) 995-5015 • http://www.nebraskaprairie.org

Holdrege Public Library • 604 East Ave • Holdrege, NE 68949 • (308) 995-6556 • http://www.socentral.lib.ne.us/pls/

National Sod House Society • Nebraska Prairie Museum, N Hwy 183, P.O. Box 164 • Holdrege, NE 68949 • (308) 995-5015 • http://www.nebraskaprairie.org

Phelps County Historical Society • Historical Museum, N Burlington Hwy 183, P.O. Box 164 • Holdrege, NE 68949-0164 • (308) 995-5015 • http://www.nebraskaprairie.org

Howells
Howells Historical Society • Historical Museum, 417 E 7th St, P.O. Box 297 • Howells, NE 68641-0297 • (402) 986-1795

Hyannis
Grant County Historical Society • Grant County Courthouse Museum, Grant & Harrison, HC88, Box 32 • Hyannis, NE 69350-9706 • (308) 458-2277

Imperial
Chase County Genealogical Society • P.O. Box 303 • Imperial, NE 69033

Chase County Historical Society • Historical Museum, 73989 320 Ave, P.O. Box 577 • Imperial, NE 69033-0577 • (308) 882-5774 • http://www.genealogy.rootsweb.com/~chasecountyne

Indianola
Red Willow Historical Society • Historical Museum, P.O. Box 426 • Indianola, NE 69034-0426

Inland
Clay County Historical Society • general delivery • Inland, NE 68954-0218 • (402) 463-8198

Kearney
Buffalo County Historical Society • Trails and Rails Museum, 710 W 11th St, P.O. Box 523 • Kearney, NE 68848 • (308) 234-3041 • http://www.bchs.kearney.net

Calvin T Ryan Library • University of Nebraska at Kearney, 2508 11th Ave • Kearney, NE 68849-2240 • (308) 865-8586 • http://www.unk.edu/acad/library/home.html

Fort Kearney Genealogical Society • c/o Kearney Public Library, 2020 1st Ave, P.O. Box 22 • Kearney, NE 68847 • (308) 233-3282 • http://www.rootsweb.com/~nebuffal/fkgs.htm

Fort Kearney Museum • 131 S Central Ave • Kearney, NE 68847 • (308) 234-5200

Fort Kearney State Historical Park Museum • 1020 V Rd • Kearney, NE 68847 • (308) 865-5305 • http://www.outdoornebraska.org

Frank House Museum • 2010 W 24th St • Kearney, NE 6847 • (308) 865-8284

Kearney Public Library • 2020 1st Ave • Kearney, NE 68847-5397 • (308) 233-3282 • http://www.kearneylib.org

Nebraska Firefighters Museum • 2434 E 1st St • Kearney, NE 68847 • (308) 338-3473 • http://www.nebraskafirefightersmuseum.com

Keystone
Keystone Community Church Museum • 1891 N Hwy 61 • Keystone, NE 69144 • (308) 726-4463

Kimball
Kimball County Plains Historical Society • 200 S Myrtle • Kimball, NE 69145

Kimball Public Library • 208 S Walnut St • Kimball, NE 69145 • (308) 235-4523 • http://www.ci.kimball.ne.us

Plains Genealogical Society • c/o Kimball Public Library, 208 S Walnut St • Kimball, NE 69145 • (308) 235-2008

Plains Historical Museum • 2nd & Chestnut Stst • Kimball, NE 69145 • (308) 235-3782

Plains Historical Society • Historical Museum, 200 S Chestnut St • Kimball, NE 69145 • (308) 235-2205

Leigh
House of Yesteryear Museum • S Beech St, P.O. Box 341 • Leigh, NE 68643 • (402) 487-2283

Lewellen
Ash Hollow State Historical Park • Hwy 26, P.O. Box 70 • Lewellen, NE 69147 • (308) 778-5651

Historical Society of Garden County • Route 1, Box 16 • Lewellen, NE 69147 • (308) 772-3333

Lewellen Public Library • 208 Main St, P.O. Box 104 • Lewellen, NE 69147-0104 • (308) 778-5428

Lexington
Dawson County Historical Society • Historical Museum, 805 N Taft, P.O. Box 369 • Lexington, NE 68850-0369 • (308) 324-5340

Heartland Museum of Military Vehicles • 606 Heartland Rd • Lexington, NE 68850 • (308) 324-6329 • http://www.heartlandmuseum.com

Lexington, cont.

Lexington Genealogical Society • c/o Lexington Public Library, 103 E 10th St, P.O. Box 778 • Lexington, NE 68850 • (308) 324-2151 • http://www.rootsweb.com/~nedawson/lexsoc.html

Lexington Public Library • 103 E 10th St, P.O. Box 778 • Lexington, NE 68850-0778 • (308) 324-2151 • http://library.cityofflex.com

Lincoln

American Historical Society of Germans from Russia • Historical Museum, 631 D Street • Lincoln, NE 68502-1199 • (402) 474-3363 • http://www.ahsgr.org

American Historical Society of Germans from Russia, Lincoln Nebraska Chapter • 2221 Devonshire Dr • Lincoln, NE 68506 • (402) 489-2583

Capitol Museum • 521 S 14th St, Ste 500 • Lincoln, NE 68508 • (402) 471-3191

Center for Great Plains Studies • Univ of Nebraska, 1214 Oldfather Hall • Lincoln, NE 68585 • (402) 472-6058

Frank H Woods Telephone Historical Museum • 2047 M Street, P.O. Box 81309 • Lincoln, NE 68501 • (402) 436-4640

Historical Center of the Nebraska Conference of the United Methodist Church • Cochrane-Woods Library, 5000 St Paul, Nebraska Wesleyan Univ, P.O. Box 4553 • Lincoln, NE 68504-0553 • (402) 465-2175 • http://www.umcneb.org

International Quilt Study Center • 234 HE Bldg Univ of Nebraska-Lincoln • Lincoln, NE 6583-0838 • (402) 472-6301 • http://www.quiltstudy.org

Lincoln City Libraries • 136 S 14th St • Lincoln, NE 68508-1899 • (402) 441-8500 • http://www.lcl.lib.ne.us

Lincoln Fire & Rescue Department Museum • 1801 Q Street • Lincoln, NE 68508 • (402) 441-8360 • http://www.lincoln.ne.gov/city/fire/museum.htm

Lincoln Historic Preservation Commission • 555 S 10th St • Lincoln, NE 68508 • (402) 441-7491

Lincoln-Lancaster County Genealogy Society • P.O. Box 30055 • Lincoln, NE 68503-0055 • http://www.rootsweb.com/~nellcgs

Lincoln-Lancaster Historical Society • P.O. Box 30055 • Lincoln, NE 68503-0055

Love Library - Special Collections • Univ of Nebraska, P.O. Box 880410 • Lincoln, NE 68588-0410 • (402) 472-2526 • http://iris.unl.edu

Masonic Grand Lodge of Nebraska • 301 N Cotner Blvd • Lincoln, NE 68505-2315 • (402) 475-4640 • http://www.glne.org

Museum of Nebraska History • 131 Centennial Mall N, P.O. Box 82554 • Lincoln, NE 68501 • (402) 471-3270

Nebraska Health Records Mgt - Vital Records • 301 Centennial Mall S, P.O. Box 95065 • Lincoln, NE 68509-5066 • (402) 471-2872 • http://www.hhs.state.ne.us/ced/bicert.htm

Nebraska Library Commission • 1200 N Street • Lincoln, NE 68508 • (402) 471-2045 • http://www.nlc.state.ne.us

Nebraska National Guard Historical Society • Historical Museum, 1300 Military Rd • Lincoln, NE 68508 • (402) 471-4182

Nebraska State Capitol Library & Museum • 1445 K Street, P.O. Box 94926 • Lincoln, NE 68502 • (402) 471-3191 • http://www.capitol.org

Nebraska State Genealogical Society • P.O. Box 5608 • Lincoln, NE 68505-0608 • (402) 455-2111 • http://www.rootsweb.com/~nesgs

Nebraska State Historical Society • Historical Museum, 131 Centennial Mall N, P.O. Box 82554 • Lincoln, NE 68501-2554 • (402) 471-4747 • http://www.nebraskahistory.org

Nebraska State Historical Society Museum • 1500 R Street, P.O. Box 82554 • Lincoln, NE 68501 • (402) 471-3270 • http://www.nebraskahistory.org

Nebraskans of Irish and Scotch-Irish Ancestry • P.O. Box 5049 • Lincoln, NE 68505-5049 • (402) 489-7564

Preservation Association of Lincoln • 2145 B Street • Lincoln, NE 68502

Senator J J Exon Library and Museum • 985 S 27th St • Lincoln, NE 68510 • (402) 434-2474

Thomas P Kennard House Museum • 1627 H Street, P.O. Box 82554 • Lincoln, NE 68501 • (402) 471-4764 • http://www.nebraskahistory.org

Union College Library • 3800 S 48th St • Lincoln, NE 68506-4386 • (402) 486-2514 • http://www.ucollege.edu/library

University of Nebraska State Museum • 307 Morrill Hall, 14th & U Streets • Lincoln, NE 68588 • (402) 472-3779 • http://www.museum.unl.edu

University of Nebraska-Lincoln Library • 13th & R St, P.O. Box 884100 • Lincoln, NE 68588-4100 • (402) 472-2848 • http://iris.unl.edu

William Jennings Bryan House Museum • 4900 Sumner St • Lincoln, NE 68506 • (402) 438-8303

Lodgepole

Lodgepole Depot Museum • 722 McCall St • Lodgepole, NE 69149 • (308) 483-5339

Lodgepole Historical Society • general delivery • Lodgepole, NE 69149

Nancy Fawcett Memorial Library • 724 Oberfelder St, P.O. Box 318 • Lodgepole, NE 69149-0318 • (308) 483-5714

Long Pine

Long Pine Heritage Society • P.O. Box 333 • Long Pine, NE 69217

Loup City

Loup City Public Library • 880 N 8th St, P.O. Box 38 • Loup City, NE 68853-0505 • (308) 745-0548

Sherman County Historical Society • Historical Museum, 433 S 7th, P.O. Box 34 • Loup City, NE 68853

Lyman

Lyman Public Library • 313 Jeffers St, P.O. Box 384 • Lyman, NE 69352-0384 • (308) 787-1366

Lynch

Boyd County Historical Society • P.O. Box 317 • Lynch, NE 68746-0317

Lyons

Northeastern Nebraska Genealogical Society • P.O. Box 249 • Lyons, NE 68038

Macy

Omaha Nation Cultural Preservation Committee • P.O. Box 382 • Macy, NE 68039 • (402) 837-5078

Omaha Tribal Council • P.O. Box 368 • Macy, NE 60839 • (402) 837-5391 • http://www.mnisose.org

Madison

Madison County Historical Society • 208 W 3rd St, P.O. Box 708 • Madison, NE 68748-0708 • (402) 454-3733

Mason City

Muddy Creek Historical Society • Historical Museum, P.O. Box 62 • Mason City, NE 68855 • (308) 732-3269

Sunshine Township Library • Main St, P.O Box 12 • Mason City, NE 68855-0012 • (308) 732-3269

Maxwell
Fort McPherson National Cemetery Museum • HC01, Box 67 • Maxwell, NE 69151 • (308) 582-4433

McCook
High Plains Historical Society • High Plains Museum, 421 Norris Ave • McCook, NE 69001 • (308) 345-3661

McCook Army Air Base Historical Society • Historical Museum, P.O. Box B-29 • McCook, NE 69001 • (308) 334- 5372

Norris Home Museum • 706 Norris Ave • McCook, NE 69001 • (308) 345-8484

Ray's Surname Index File • 205 West M Street • McCook, NE 69001 • (308) 345-1443

Senator George Norris State Historic Site Museum • 706 Norris Ave • McCook, NE 69001 • (308) 345-8484 • http://www.nebraskahistory.org

Southwest Nebraska Genealogical Society • McCook Community College, 1205 E 3rd St, P.O. Box 156 • McCook, NE 69001 • (308) 345-1738 • http://www.rootsweb.com/~neswngs

Von Riesen Library • McCook Community College, 1205 E 3rd St • McCook, NE 69001 • (308) 345-6303

McCool Junction
Douglas County Historical Society • Historical Museum • McCool Junction, NE 68401 • (402) 724-2115

Iron Horse Station Museum • 5th & O Streets, P.O. Box 126 • McCool Junction, NE 68401 • (402) 724-2346

Minatare
Minatare Public Library • 309 Main St, P.O. Box 483 • Minatare, NE 69356-0483 • (308) 783-1414

Minden
Harold Warp Pioneer Village Museum • 138 E Hwy 6 • Minden, NE 68959 • (308) 832-1181 • http://www.pioneervillage.org

Jensen Memorial Library • 443 N Kearney, P.O. Box 264 • Minden, NE 68959-0264 • (308) 832-2648

Kearney County Historical Society • Historical Museum, 530 N Nebraska Ave • Minden, NE 68959 • (308) 832-1765

South Central Nebraska Genealogical Society • c/o Jensen Memorial Library, 443 N Kearney • Minden, NE 68959 • (308) 832-2648

Mitchell
Quivey Memorial Library • 1449 Center Ave • Mitchell, NE 69357 • (308) 623-2222

Morrill
Morrill Historical Society • 215 1/2 Adams Ave • Morrill, NE 69358

Morrill Public Library • 119 E Webster, PO Box 402 • Morrill, NE 69358-0402 • (308) 247-2611

Mullen
Hooker County Genealogical Society • c/o Hooker County Library, P.O. Box 280 • Mullen, NE 69152 • (308) 546-2458

Hooker County Historical Society • P.O. Box 185 • Mullen, NE 69152-0185

Hooker County Library • P.O. Box 479 • Mullen, NE 69152-0479 • (308) 546-2240

Murdock
Murdock Historical Society • Historical Museum, 9014 310th St • Murdock, NE 68407-2206 • (402) 867-3331

Naponee
Naponee Historical Society • Historical Museum, P.O. Box 128 • Naponee, NE 68960-0128 • (308) 269-2791

Nebraska City
Arbor Lodge State Historical Park • 2600 Arbor Ave, P.O. Box 15 • Nebraska City, NE 68410 • (402) 873-7222

Nebraska City Historical Society • Historical Museum, 711 3rd Corso, P.O. Box 175 • Nebraska City, NE 68410-0175

Old Freighter's Museum • 407 N 14th St, P.O. Box 175 • Nebraska City, NE 68410 • (402) 873-7198

Otoe County Historical Society • P.O. Box 175 • Nebraska City, NE 68410-0175 • (402) 873-7198

Wildwood Center and Period House Museum • 420 S Steinhart Park Rd • Nebraska City, NE 68410 • (402) 873-6340

Neligh
Antelope County Historical Society • Historical Museum, 305 K Street • Neligh, NE 68756 • (402) 887-4275

Antelope County Pioneers • Jail Museum, 506 L Street • Neligh, NE 68756 • (402) 887-4999 • http://www.jailmuseum.org

Neligh Mills State Historic Site • N Street & Wylie Dr, P.O. Box 271 • Neligh, NE 68756 • (402) 887-4303 • http://www.nebraskahistory.org/sites/mill

Neligh Public Library • 710 Main St • Neligh, NE 68756-1246 • (402) 887-5140

Nenzel
Sandhills Area Heritage Society • P.O. Box 100 • Nenzel, NE 69219 • (402) 823-4131

Newman Grove
Newman Grove Public Library • 615 Hale Ave, P.O. Box 430 • Newman Grove, NE 68758-0430 • (402) 447-2331

Niobrara
Niobrara Historical Society • Historical Museum, 89054 519 Ave • Niobrara, NE 68760 • (402) 857-3794

Niobrara Public Library • 254-14 Park Ave, P.O. Box 15 • Niobrara, NE 68760-0015 • (402) 857-3565 • http://www.niobrarane.com

Ponca Tribe of Nebraska • Historical Museum, P.O. Box 288 • Niobrara, NE 66760 • (402) 857-3391 • http://www.mnisose.org/profiles/ponca.htm

Santee Sioux • Route 2 • Niobrara, NE 68760 • (402) 857-3302 • http://www.santeedakota.org

Norfolk
American Historical Society of Germans from Russia, Northeast Nebraska Chapter • 314 S 13th Pl • Norfolk, NE 68701-1214 • (402) 371-0693 • http://www.ahsgr.org/Chapters/northeast_nebraska_chapter.htm

Elkhorn Valley Historical Society • Elkhorn Valley Museum and Research Center • 515 Queen City Blvd • Norfolk, NE 68701 • (402) 371-3886 • http://www.elkhornvalleymuseum.org

Madison County Genealogical Society • Elkhorn Valley Museum, 515 Queen City Blvd, P.O. Box 1031 • Norfolk, NE 68702-1031

Nebraska Veterans Hall of Honor • general delivery • Norfolk, NE 68702 • (402) 379-1011

Norfolk Public Library • 308 Prospect Ave • Norfolk, NE 68701-4138 • (402) 844-2100 • http://www.ci.norfolk.ne.us/library

North Loup
North Loup Public Library • 200 B Street, P.O. Box 157 • North Loup, NE 68859-0157 • (308) 496-4230

North Platte
Buffalo Bill Ranch State Historic Park • 2921 Rest Ranch Rd • North Platte, NE 69101 • (308) 535-8035 • http://www.outdoornebraska.com

Nebraska

North Platte, cont.
Lincoln County Historical Society • Historical Museum, 2403 N Buffalo Bill Ave • North Platte, NE 69101 • (308) 534-5640

North Platte Genealogical Society • P.O. Box 1452 • North Platte, NE 69103-1452 • (308) 534-4619

North Platte Public Library • 120 W 4th St • North Platte, NE 69101-3993 • (308) 535-8036 • http://www.ci.north-platte.ne.us/library

Oakdale
Oakdale Public Library • 406 5th St, P.O. Box 187 • Oakdale, NE 68761-0187 • (402) 776-2602

Oakland
Swedish Heritage Center • 301 N Chard Ave • Oakland, NE 68045

Ogallala
Front Street Museum • 519 E 1st • Ogallala, NE 69153 • (308) 284-6000 • http://www.megavision.net/frontstreet

Goodall City Library • 203 West A St • Ogallala, NE 69153 • (308) 284-4354 • http://www.goodallcitylibrary.com

Kearney County Historical Society • Mansion on the Hill Museum, 1004 N Spruce St • Ogallala, NE 69153 • (308) 284-3052

Keith County Historical Society • 315 W 4th St • Ogallala, NE 69153

Omaha
American Historical Society of Germans from Russia, Midlands Chapter • 9373 Maplewood Blvd • Omaha, NE 68134-4663 • (402) 572-8871 • http://www.ahsgr.org/Chapters/midlands_chapter.htm

Benson Historical Society • Historical Museum, 5831 Corby St, P.O. Box 4153 • Omaha, NE 68104

Carl M Reinert Library • Creighton Univ, 2500 California Plaza • Omaha, NE 68178 • (402) 280-2927 • http://www.creighton.edu

Cathedral Cultural Center Museum • 39th & Webster • Omaha, NE 68131 • (402) 551-4888 • http://www.cathedralartsproject.org

Czech Cultural Club • Sokol Auditorium, 2234 S 13th St • Omaha, NE 69103 • (402) 931-8669

Douglas County Historical Society • General Crook House Museum, 5730 N 30th St #11B, P.O. Box 11398 • Omaha, NE 68111 • (402) 455-9990 • http://www.omahahistory.org

Durham Western Heritage Museum • 801 S 10th St • Omaha, NE 68108 • (402) 444-5071 • http://www.dwhm.org

Florence Historical Foundation • Historical Museum, 5215 Jackson St, P.O. Box 12331 • Omaha, NE 68112

Grand Lodge of Nebraska, Sons of Italy • 1238 S 10th St • Omaha, NE 68108 • (402) 345-4639 • http://sonsofitalyne.com

Great Plains Black Museum • 2213 Lake St • Omaha, NE 68110 • (402) 345-2212 • http://members.aol.com/asmith8955/ahist.htm

Greater Omaha Genealogical Society • c/o W Dale Clark Library, 215 S15th St, P.O. Box 4011 • Omaha, NE 68104-0011 • (402) 444-4826 • http://hometown.aol.com/gromahagensoc/myhomepage/

Historic Florence Mill Museum • 9102 N 30th St • Omaha, NE 68112 • (402) 551-1233

Kripke Jewish Federation Library • 333 S 132nd St • Omaha, NE 68154 • (402) 334-6462 • http://www.jewishomaha.org

Mormon Pioneer Cemetery Museum • 3215 State St • Omaha, NE 68112 • (402) 453-9372

National Park Service-Midwest Regional Library • 1709 Jackson St • Omaha, NE 68102-2571 • (402) 221-3471

Nebraska Jewish Historical Society • Historical Museum, 333 S 132nd St • Omaha, NE 68154 • (402) 334-8200 • http://www.epodunk.com

Nebraska Military Historical Society • Freedom Park Museum, 2497 Freedom Park Rd • Omaha, NE 68110 • (402) 345-1959

Omaha Home for Boys Visitors Center History Museum • 4343 N 52nd St • Omaha, NE 68104 • (402) 457-7000

Omaha Public Library-Charles B Washington Branch • 2868 Ames • Omaha, NE 68111 • (402) 444-4849

Oran's Black Americana Historical Society • 1240 S 13th St • Omaha, NE 68108

Servants of Mary Museum • 7400 Military Ave • Omaha, NE 68134 • (402) 572-7935

Sokol South Omaha Czechoslovak Museum • 2021 U Street • Omaha, NE 68107 • (402) 291-2893

Trans-Mississippi Exposition Historical Association • P.O. Box 55063 • Omaha, NE 68155

Trinity Cathedral Historical Society • Historical Museum, 113 N 18th St • Omaha, NE 68102-4969 • (402) 342-7012

University Library & Museum • University of Nebraska-Omaha, 6001 Dodge St • Omaha, NE 68182-0237 • (402) 554-2640 • http://library.unomaha.edu

W Dale Clark Library • 215 S 15th St • Omaha, NE 68102 • (402) 444-4826 • http://www.omaha.lib.ne.us

Western Heritage Society • Durham Western Heritage Museum, 801 S 10th St • Omaha, NE 68108 • (402) 444-5071

O'Neill
Holt County Genealogical Society • P.O. Box 376 • O'Neill, NE 68763

Holt County Historical Society • Historical Museum, 401 E Douglas, P.O. Box 231 • O'Neill, NE 68763 • (402) 336-2344

North Central Nebraska Genealogical Society • P.O. Box 376 • O'Neill, NE 68763-0362

Northern Nebraska Genealogical Society • 401 E Douglas, P.O. Box 362 • O'Neill, NE 68763

Orchard
Northern Antelope County Genealogical Society • P.O. Box 56 • Orchard, NE 68764 • (402) 893-4565

Orchard Historical Society • Historical Museum, 225 Windom St, P.O. Box 56 • Orchard, NE 68764 • (402) 893-3816

Orchard Public Library • 232 Windom, P.O. Box 317 • Orchard, NE 68764-0317 • (402) 893-4606

Ord
Ord Township Library • 1718 M St, P.O. Box 206 • Ord, NE 68862-0206 • (308) 728-3012

Valley County Genealogical Society • 619 S 10th St • Ord, NE 68862 • (308) 728-3012

Valley County Historical Society • Historical Museum, 117 S 16th St, P.O. Box 101 • Ord, NE 68862 • (308) 728-5178

Orleans
Cordelia B Preston Memorial Library • 510 Orleans Ave, P.O. Box 430 • Orleans, NE 68966-0430 • (308) 473-3425

Harlan County Historical Society • P.O. Box 187 • Orleans, NE 68966-0187 • (308) 473-3725

Osceola
Polk County Historical Society • Historical Museum, 561 South St, P.O. Box 565 • Osceola, NE 68651 • (402) 747-7901

Oshkosh
Historical Society of Garden County • Historical Museum, W 1st & Avenue E, P.O. Box 90 • Oshkosh, NE 69154 • (308) 772-3115

Oshkosh Public Library • 307 W 1st St, P.O. Box 140 • Oshkosh, NE 69154-0140 • (308) 772-4554

Oxford
Oxford Municipal Library • 411 Ogden St, P.O. Box 156 • Oxford, NE 68967-0156 • (308) 824-3381

Papillion
Audubon County, Iowa Genealogical Research • 1019 Tekamah Ln • Papillion, NE 68128-6245 • (402) 339-7291

Lyman County Historical Museum • 9400 S 120th St • Papillion, NE 68046 • (402) 895-9446

Papillion Area Historical Society • Historical Museum, 242 N Jefferson St • Papillion, NE 68046 • (402) 339-6984

International Order of Job's Daughters • 233 W 6th St • Papillion, NE 68046-2210 • (402) 592-7987 • http://www.iojd.org

Pawnee City
Hyde Historical and Genealogical Society • general delivery • Pawnee City, NE 68420 • (402) 852-3148

Pawnee City Historical Society • Historical Museum, 1041 5th St, P.O. Box 33 • Pawnee City, NE 68420 • (402) 852-3131 • http://www.rootsweb.com/~nepawnee/county/resources/pehsm.html

Paxton
Paxton Public Library • 108 N Oak St, P.O. Box 278 • Paxton, NE 69155-0278 • (308) 239-4763

Pender
Thurston County Heritage Society • Heritage Museum, 500 Ivan St, P.O. Box 624 • Pender, NE 68047-0624 • (402) 385-3210

Peru
Peru Historical Society • Historical Museum, 5th & California Sts, P.O. Box 195 • Peru, NE 68421 • (402) 872-6875

Peru State College Library • 600 Hoyt St • Peru, NE 68421 • (402) 872-2218 • http://www.peru.edu

Petersburg
Rae Valley Heritage Association • 1249 State Hwy 14 • Petersburg, NE 68652 • (402) 386-5334 • http://www.raevalley.org

Pierce
Pierce County Historical Society • Historical Musuem, 120 N Brown, P.O. Box 122 • Pierce, NE 68767-0122 • (402) 329-4576

Pilger
Historical Society of Stanton County • Historical Museum, 345 N Main St, P.O. Box 213 • Pilger, NE 68768 • (402) 768-2147 • http://www.stanton.net

Plainview
Plainview Historical Society • Historical Museum, 302 S Main St, P.O. Box 495 • Plainview, NE 68769-0752 • (402) 582-4627

Plattsmouth
Cass County Genealogy Club • 1116 3rd Ave • Plattsmouth, NE 68048

Cass County Historical Society • Historical Museum, 646 Main St • Plattsmouth, NE 68048 • (402) 296-4770 • http://www.nebraskamuseums.org/casscountymuseum.htm

Plattsmouth Conservancy • Historical Museum, 437 Main St, P.O. Box 104 • Plattsmouth, NE 68048 • (402) 296-5002

Plattsmouth Public Library • 401 Avenue A • Plattsmouth, NE 68048 • (402) 296-4154

Polk
Polk Public Library • 180 N Main St, P.O. Box 49 • Polk, NE 68654-0049 • (402) 765-6471

Ponca
Ponca Historical Society • Adams House Museum, 100 E 3rd St, P.O. Box 403 • Ponca, NE 68770-0530 • (402) 755-2202

Ponca Public Library • 203 2nd St, P.O. Box 368 • Ponca, NE 68770-0368 • (402) 755-2739 • http://www.poncapubliclibrary.org

Potter
Potter Historical Society • P.O. Box 155 • Potter, NE 69156-0155

Potter Public Library • 333 Chestnut, P.O. Box 317 • Potter, NE 69156 • (308) 879-4345

Ralston
Hollis and Helen Baright Public Library • 5555 S 77th St • Ralston, NE 68127-2899 • (402) 331-7636 • http://www.omaha.lib.ne.us/ralstonlibrary

Northeast Scottish Society • c/o Hollis & Helen Baright Public Library, 7900 Park Ln • Ralston, NE 68051 • (402) 331-7636

Ralston Genealogical Society • c/o Hollis & Helen Baright Public Library, 7900 Park Ln • Ralston, NE 68051 • (402) 331-7636

Ravenna
Ravenna Genealogical and Historical Society • 210 Grand Ave, P.O. Box 84 • Ravenna, NE 68869 • http://www.rootsweb.com/~nebuffal/ravenna.htm

Red Cloud
Webster County Historical Society • Historical Museum, 721 W 4th Ave, P.O. Box 464 • Red Cloud, NE 68970-0464 • (402) 746-2444

Willa Cather Memorial and Educational Foundation • Willa Cather State Historic Site & Pioneer Museum, 326 N Webster • Red Cloud, NE 68970 • (402) 746-2653 • http://www.willacather.org

Rushville
Rushville Public Library • 207 Sprague St, P.O. Box 473 • Rushville, NE 69360-0389 • (308) 327-2740

Sheridan County Historical Society • Historical Museum, E Hwy 20 & Nelson Ave, P.O. Box 274 • Rushville, NE 69360 • (308) 327-2917

Ruskin
Ruskin Public Library • Main St, P.O. Box 87 • Ruskin, NE 68974 • (402) 226-2311

Saint Paul
Howard County Historical Society • Historical Museum, 6th St, P.O. Box 304 • Saint Paul, NE 68873-0304

Museum of Nebraska Major League Baseball • 619 Howard Ave • Saint Paul, NE 68873 • (308) 754-5558

Schuyler
Schuyler Historical Society • 202 E 20th St • Schuyler, NE 68661 • (402) 352-3781

Schuyler-Colfax County Museum • 309 E 11th St • Schuyler, NE 68661 • (402) 352-5145

Scottsbluff
American Historical Society of Germans from Russia, Nebraska Panhandle Chapter • 2430 Ave C • Scottsbluff, NE 69361 • (308) 632-2459 • http://www.ahsgr.org/Chapters/nebraska_panhandle_chapter.htm

Mexican-American Historical Museum • Broadway & 27th St, P.O. Box 1662 • Scottsbluff, NE 69361 • (308) 635-2988 • http://www.westnebraska.com

Panhandle Landmarks • 1517 Broadway, Ste 125 • Scottsbluff, NE 69361 • (308) 632-1311

Rebecca Winters Genealogical Society • 1121 Avenue L, P.O. Box 323 • Scottsbluff, NE 69361-0323 • http://www.rootsweb.com/~nerwgs

Nebraska

Scottsbluff, cont.
Scottsbluff Public Library • 1809 3rd Ave • Scottsbluff, NE 69361-2493 • (308) 630-6250 • http://scottsbluff.org

Scribner
Musbach Museum • 439 Main St, P.O. Box 136 • Scribner, NE 68057 • (402) 664-3085

Seward
Nebraska History Network • 1997 280th • Seward, NE 68434-7823

Seward County Genealogical Society • 616 Bradford, P.O. Box 72 • Seward, NE 68434-0072 • (402) 532-7635 • http://www.rootsweb.com/~neseward/scgs.html

Seward County Historical Society • Historical Museum, 508 N 6th St #5, P.O. Box 274 • Seward, NE 68434-0274 • (402) 761-3181

Seward Public Library • 233 S 5th St • Seward, NE 68434 • (402) 643-3318 • http://www.sewardpubliclibrary.org

Shelton
Wood River Valley Historical Society • Shelton History Center, Hwy 30 & C Street, P.O. Box 188 • Shelton, NE 68876 • (308) 647-5264

Sidney
Cheyenne County Genealogical Society • P.O. Box 802 • Sidney, NE 69162

Cheyenne County Historical Association • Fort Sidney Museum, 6th & Jackson Sts, P.O. Box 596 • Sidney, NE 69162 • (308) 254-2150

Cheyenne County Historical Society • P.O. Box 802 • Sidney, NE 69162

Sidney Public Library • 1112 12th Ave • Sidney, NE 69162 • (308) 254-3110 • http://www.sidneypubliclibrary.org

South Sioux City
South Sioux City Public Library • 2219 Dakota Ave • South Sioux City, NE 68776 • (402) 494-7545 • http://www.southsiouxcity.org/departments/library/intro.html

Spalding
Spalding Historical and Genealogical Society • Route 1, Box 13 • Spalding, NE 68665

Wheeler County Historical Society • Courthouse Museum, HC 61, Box 2 • Spalding, NE 68665 • (308) 497-2163

Springfield
Sons of the American Revolution, Nebraska Society • 16902 S Hwy 50 • Springfield, NE 68059-4827 • (402) 253-2577 • http://www.rootsweb.ancestry.com/~nesar/

Springview
Keya Paha County Historical Society • Historical Museum, 305 Courthouse Dr, P.O. Box 334 • Springview, NE 68778 • (402) 497-2526

Stanton
Historical Society of Stanton County • P.O. Box 934 • Stanton, NE 68779 • (402) 439-2952

Stapleton
Logan County Historical Society • Historical Museum, 248 Main St, P.O. Box 147 • Stapleton, NE 69163-0147 • (308) 636-2461

Steinauer
Steinauer Historical Society • Historical Museum, P.O. Box 114 • Steinauer, NE 68441-0114 • (402) 423-7170

Strang
Strang Museum • P.O. Box 62 • Strang, NE 68444 • (402) 627-2085

Stratton
Little House Museum • 908 Hartford St • Stratton, NE 69043 • (308) 276-2360

Stuart
North Central Nebraska Historical Society • general delivery • Stuart, NE 68780

White Horse Ranch Museum • RR1, Box 176 • Stuart, NE 68780 • (402) 924-3831

Superior
Nuckolls County Genealogical Society • 1218 Commercial, P.O. Box 324 • Superior, NE 68978-0441

Nuckolls County Historical Society • Historical Museum, 612 E 6th St, P.O. Box 441 • Superior, NE 68978-0441 • (402) 879-4144

Syracuse
Otoe County Historical Society • Otoe County Museum of Memories • 366 Poplar, P.O. Box 62 • Syracuse, NE 68446 • (402) 269-3482

Table Rock
Table Rock Historical Society • Historical Museum, 414-16 Houston St, P.O. Box 194 • Table Rock, NE 68447-0194 • (402) 839-4135 • http://www.pawneecountyhistory.com/trhsm

Tarnov
Saint Michael's Historical Society • Historical Museum, Route 1, Box 225 • Tarnov, NE 68642 • (402) 923-1275

Taylor
Loup County Historical Society • Historical Museum, 401 Murry St, P.O. Box 102 • Taylor, NE 68879-0102 • (308) 942-3403 • http://www.rootsweb.com/~nelchs

Tecumseh
Johnson County Historical Society • Historical Museum, 3rd & Lincoln Sts • Tecumseh, NE 68450 • (402) 335-3292

Tekamah
Burt County Historical Society • P.O. Box 125 • Tekamah, NE 68061

Burt County Museum & E C Houston House • 319 N 13th St, P.O. Box 125 • Tekamah, NE 68061-0125 • (402) 374-1505 • http://www.huntel.net/community/burtcomuseum

Fremont Historical Society • general delivery • Tekamah, NE 68061 • (402) 374-3248

Thedford
Thomas County Genealogical Society • P.O. Box 136 • Thedford, NE 69166

Thomas County Historical Society • Historical Museum, 503 Main St, P.O. Box 131 • Thedford, NE 69166 • (308) 645-2477

Thomas County Library • 503 Main St, P.O. Box 228 • Thedford, NE 69166-0228 • (308) 645-2237

Tobias
Tobias Community Historical Society • Historical Museum, Main St, P.O. box 45 • Tobias, NE 68453 • (402) 243-2356

Trenton
Hitchcock County Historical Society • Historical Museum, 311 E 1st St, P.O. Box 511 • Trenton, NE 69044-0511 • (308) 334-5748

Tryon
McPherson County Historical Society • Historical Museum, HC 71, Box 20 • Tryon, NE 69167 • (308) 587-2276

Valentine
Cherry County Genealogical Society • P.O. Box 380 • Valentine, NE 69201

Cherry County Historical Society • Historical Museum, 311 N Valentine St, P.O. Box 284 • Valentine, NE 69201-0284 • (402) 376-2015

Saint Johns Episcopal Church Library • 372 N Main, P.O. Box 261 • Valentine, NE 69201-0261 • (402) 376-1723

Nebraska

Sawyer's Sandhills Museum • 440 Valentine St • Valentine, NE 69201 • (402) 376-3293

Valley
Valley Historical Society • Historical Museum, 218 W Alexander St, P.O. Box 685 • Valley, NE 68064 • (402) 359-2678 • http://www.valleyne.org

Verdigre
Verdigre Heritage Museum • general delivery • Verdigre, NE 68783

Verdigre Heritage Society • Historical Museum, P.O. Box 241 • Verdigre, NE 68783-0241 • (402) 668-2248

Waco
Paradise Mills Historical Society • general delivery • Waco, NE 68460

Wahoo
Saunders County Genealogical Seekers • Historical Museum, 240 N Walnut • Wahoo, NE 68066-1858 • (402) 443-3090

Saunders County Historical Society • Historical Museum, 240 N Walnut, P.O. Box 25555 • Wahoo, NE 68066 • (402) 443-3090 • http://www.visitsaunderscounty.org

Wahoo Genealogical Seekers • 871 West 6th • Wahoo, NE 68066

Wayne
Wayne County Genealogical Society • 220 Sherman • Wayne, NE 68787

Wayne County Historical Society • Historical Museum, 908 Windom St, P.O. Box 408 • Wayne, NE 68787 • (402) 375-3885

Wayne Public Library • 410 N Pearl St • Wayne, NE 68787 • (402) 375-3135

Weeping Water
Weeping Water Valley Historical Society • Historical Museum, 215 W Eldora Ave, P.O. Box 43 • Weeping Water, NE 68463 • (402) 267-5306

West Point
Cuming County Historical Society • Historical Museum, 130 N River • West Point, NE 68788 • (402) 372-3690

Elkhorn Valley Genealogical Society • 341 E Walnut • West Point, NE 68788 • http://www.rootsweb.com/~necuming/evgs.html

John A Stahl Library • 330 N Colfax St, P.O. Box 258 • West Point, NE 68788-0258 • (402) 372-3831

Wilber
Wilber Czech Museum • 102 W 3rd, P.O. Box 253 • Wilber, NE 68465 • (402) 821-2183

Wilber Historical Society • Historical Museum, 102 W 3rd St, P.O. Box 253 • Wilber, NE 68465-0253 • (402) 821-2485

Winnebago
Ho-Chunk Historical Society • Historical Museum, Route 1, Box 21 • Winnebago, NE 68071-9802 • (402) 878-2976

Winnebago Tribe • P.O. Box 687 • Winnebago, NE 68071 • (402) 878-3100 • http://www.winnebagotribe.com

Winnetoon
Winnetoon Historical Society • Historical Museum, P.O. Box 94 • Winnetoon, NE 68789 • (402) 847-3368

Winside
Wayne County Historical Society • Historical Museum, 104 Whitten St, P.O. Box 7 • Winside, NE 68790 • (402) 286-4839

Wisner
Wisner Heritage Society • P.O. Box 520 • Wisner, NE 68791-0520

Wood River
Nebraska Military Historical Society • Historical Museum, 107 E 11th St • Wood River, NE 58883 • (308) 583-2133

York
Anna Bemis Palmer Museum • 211 E 7th St, P.O. Box 403 • York, NE 68467-0403 • (402) 363-2630

Genealogical Society of York County • Route 1, Box 5 • York, NE 68467

Greater York Area Genealogical Society • c/o Kilgore Memorial Library, 520 Nebraska Ave • York, NE 68467 • (402) 363-2620

Kilgore Memorial Library • 520 Nebraska Ave • York, NE 68467 • (402) 363-2620

Levitt Library • York College, 1125 E 8th • York, NE 68467-2699 • (402) 353-5704 • http://www.york.edu/library/

York County Historical Association • Historical Museum, York College, 2329 Nebraska Ave, P.O. Box 81 • York, NE 68467

Yutan
Yutan Historical Society • Historical Museum, 214 Rose Ave • Yutan, NE 68073 • (402) 652-2276

Nebraska

Amargosa Valley
Amargosa Valley Community Library • HCR 69, Box 401T • Amargosa Valley, NV 89020-9701 • (702) 372-5340

Austin
Austin Historical Society • Historical Museum, 180 Main St, P.O. Box 25 • Austin, NV 9310 • (775) 964-1202

Gridley Store Museum • 247 Main • Austin, NV 89310 • (775) 964-1202

Yomba Shoshone Tribe • HC 61, Box 6275 • Austin, NV 89310 • (702) 964-2448 • http://itch.org/tribes/yomba.html

Battle Mountain
Battle Mountain Band • 35 Mountain View Drive #138-13 • Battle Mountain, NV 89820 • (702) 635-2004 • http://itcn.org/tribes/batmount.html

Beatty
Beatty Library District • 400 N 4th St, P.O. Box 129 • Beatty, NV 89003-0129 • (775) 553-2257

Beatty Museum Historical Society • Historical Museum, 417 W Main St, P.O. Box 244 • Beatty, NV 89003 • (775) 553-2303 • http://www.beattymuseum.com

Pioneer Museum • State Route 374 • Beatty, NV 89003 • (775) 553-2424

Rhyolite Historic Site Museum • Gold Well Open Air Museum, P.O. Box 958 • Beatty, NV 89003 • (775) 553-2424

Boulder City
Boulder City Historical Society • Historical Museum, 444 Hotel Plaza, P.O. Box 60516 • Boulder City, NV 89006 • (702) 294-1988

Boulder City Library • 701 Adams Blvd • Boulder City, NV 89005-2697 • (702) 293-1281 • http://www.bclibrary.org

Hoover Dam Museum • 1305 Arizona St, P.O. Box 60516 • Boulder City, NV 89005 • (702) 294-1988 • http://www.bcmha.org; http://www.hooverdam.com

Caliente
Caliente Railroad Depot Museum • 100 Depot, P.O. Box 553 • Caliente, NV 89008 • (775) 726-3129

Carson City
Carson City Genealogical Society • 1509 Sharon Dr • Carson City, NV 89701

Carson City Library • 900 N Roop St • Carson City, NV 89701 • (775) 887-2244 • http://www.clan.lib.nv.uc/docs/nsla/clan/clan.htm

Carson Colony • 3311 Paiute St • Carson City, NV 89703 • (702) 883-6431

Nevada State Capitol Museum • Carson & Musser Sts • Carson City, NV 89710 • (775) 687-4810

Nevada State Dept of Health - Vital Statistics • 505 E King St #102 • Carson City, NV 89710-4761 • (775) 687-4480 • http://health2k.state.nv.us/vital

Nevada State Library and Archives • 100 N Stewart St • Carson City, NV 89710-4285 • (775) 684-3310 • http://www.dmla.clan.lib.nv.us/docs/nsla; http://www.NevadaCulture.org

Nevada State Museum • 600 N Carson St • Carson City, NV 89701 • (775) 687-4810 • http://www.nevadaculture.org

Nevada State Railroad Museum • 2180 S Carson St • Carson City, NV 89701 • (775) 687-6953 • http://www.msrm-friends.org

Stewart Indian School Museum • 5366 Snyder Ave • Carson City, NV 89701 • (775) 882-6929

Stewart Native Colony • 5258 Snyder Ave • Carson, NV 89701 • (702) 883-7767

Washoe Archive and Cultural Resource Center • 861 Crescent Dr • Carson City, NV 89701 • (702) 888-0936

Duckwater
Duckwater Shoshone Tribe of the Duckwater Reservation • P.O. Box 140068 • Duckwater, NV 89314 • (702) 863-0227 • http://itcn.org/tribes/duckwat.html

Dyer
Fish Lake Library • Hwy 264-Bluebird Lane, P.O. Box 250 • Dyer, NV 89010-0250 • (775) 572-3311

Elko
Elko Band of the Te-Moak Tribe of Western Shoshone Indians • 525 Sunset St, P.O. Box 748 • Elko, NV 89801 • (702) 738-8889 • http://itcn.org/tribes/elko.html

Elko Genealogical Society • 3001 N 5th St • Elko, NV 89801

Elko-Lander-Eureka County Library System • 720 Court St • Elko, NV 89801-3397 • (775) 738-3066

Great Basin College Library • 1500 College Pkwy • Elko, NV 89801 • (775) 753-2280 • http://www.gbcnv.edu/library/

Northeastern Nevada Genealogical Society • Historical Museum, 1515 Idaho St • Elko, NV 89801-4021 • (775) 738-3418 • http://www.rootsweb.com/~nvnengs/

Northeastern Nevada Historical Society • Historical Museum, 1515 Idaho St, P.O. Box 2550 • Elko, NV 89801 • (775) 738-3418 • http://www.museum-elko.us

Western Shoshone Historical Society • 1545 Silver Eagle • Elko, NV 89801-5021 • (775) 738-7070

Ely
East Ely Railroad Depot Museum • 110 Avenue A • Ely, NV 89301 • (775) 289-1663

Ely Shoshone Tribe • 16 Shoshone Cr • Ely, NV 89301 • (702) 289-3013 • http://itcn.org/tribes/ely.html

Nevada Native American Cultural Society • Historical Museum, 598 Aultman St • Ely, NV 89301 • (775) 289-4848

Nevada Northern Railway Museum • 1100 Avenue A, P.O. Box 150040 • Ely, NV 89315 • (775) 289-2085 • http://www.nnry.com

White Pine County Historical Society • Historical Museum, 2000 Aultman St • Ely, NV 89301 • http://www.wpmuseum.org

White Pine County Library • 950 Compton • Ely, NV 89301 • (775) 289-3737 • http://www.whitepinecountylibrary.com

Eureka
Eureka County Historical Society • Eureka Sentinel Museum, 10 N Monroe St, P.O. Box 178 • Eureka, NV 89316 • http://www.co.eureka.nv.us/tourism/museum01.htm

Eureka Opera House Museum • 31 S Main St, P.O. Box 284 • Eureka, NV 89316 • (775) 237-6006 • http://www.co.eureka.nv.us

Fallon
Churchill County Historical and Genealogical Society • Historical Museum, 533 S Main St, P.O. Box 1937 • Fallon, NV 89406 • (775) 423-3677 • http://www.ccmuseum.org

Churchill County Library • 553 S Maine St • Fallon, NV 89406-3387 • (775) 423-7581 • http://www.clan.lib.nv.us

Churchill County Museum and Archives • 1050 S Maine St, P.O. Box 1937 • Fallon, NV 89406 • (775) 423-3677 • http://www.ccmuseum.org

Fallon Paiute-Shoshone Tribe • 8955 Mission Rd • Fallon, NV 89406 • (702) 423-6075 • http://itcn.org/tribes/fallon.html

US Navy NAS Fallon Station Library • 4755 Pasture Rd • Fallon, NV 89496-5000 • (775) 426-2599

Nevada

Fernley
Wigwam Native American Museum • 225 W Main St, P.O. Box 97 • Fernley, NV 89408 • (775) 575-2573

Gardnerville
Carson Valley Historical Society • Historical Museum, 1477 US Hwy 395 • Gardnerville, NV 89410

Carson Valley Museum & Cultural Center • US Hwy 395 S • Gardnerville, NV 89410 • (775) 782-2555

Dresslerville Colony of the Washoe Tribe of Nevada and California • 1585 Watsheamu Dr • Gardnerville, NV 89410 • (702) 265-4191 • http://itcn.org/tribes/washoe/dville.html

Washoe Tribal Council • 919 Hwy 395 S • Gardnerville, NV 89410 • (702) 883-1446 • http://itcn.org/tribes/washoe/washo.html

Genoa
Carson Valley Historical Society • Genoa Courthouse Museum • 2304 Main St • Genoa, NV 89411 • http://www.historicnevada.org/html/genoa_courthouse_museum.html

Mormon Station State Historic Park Museum • 2295 Main St • Genoa, NV 89411 • (775) 782-2590 • http://www.parks.nv.gov

Goldfield
Goldfield Historical Society • P.O. Box 225 • Goldfield, NV 89013

Parsonage Museum • 427 Broad St, P.O. Box 219 • Goldfield, NV 89013 • (773) 485-3560

Hawthorne
Mineral County Historical Society • Historical Museum, 400 10th St, P.O. Box 1584 • Hawthorne, NV 89415 • (775) 945-5142

Mineral County Public Library • 110 1st St, P.O. Box 1390 • Hawthorne, NV 89415-1390 • (775) 945-2778

Henderson
Clark County Heritage Center • 1830 S Boulder Hwy • Henderson, NV 89015-8502 • (702) 455-7955 • http://www.co.clark.nv.us

Ethel M Chocolate Factory Museum and Cactus Garden • 2 Cactus Garden Dr • Henderson, NV 89014 • (702) 458-8864

Henderson District Public Library • 280 Water St • Henderson, NV 89015 • (702) 565-8402

Howard W Cannon Aviation Museum • 1830 S Boulder Hwy • Henderson, NV 89015 • (702) 455-7968 • http://www.co.clark.nv.us/parkrec/aviation.htm

MacDonald Center of Ancient History • 1700 Horizon Ridge #200 • Henderson, NV 89012 • (702) 458-0001

New Hope Historical Society • S Main St • Henderson, NV 89044 • (702) 862-5652

Incline Village
Washoe County Library System-Incline Village Library • 846 Tahoe Blvd • Incline Village, NV 89451 • (775) 832-4130

Las Vegas
African American Museum and Research Center • 705 W Van Buren Ave • Las Vegas, NV 89106 • (702) 647-2242

Atomic Testing Museum • 755 E Flamingo Rd • Las Vegas, NV 89119 • (702) 794-5151 • http://www.atomictestingmuseum.org

Clark County Genealogical Society • P.O. Box 1929 • Las Vegas, NV 89125-1929 • (702) 225-5838 • http://www.lvrj.com/communitylink/ccngs/

Clark County Regional Library • 1401 Flamingo Rd • Las Vegas, NV 89119-6160 • (702) 733-7810

James R Dickinson Library - Special Collections • Univ of Nevada, 4505 Maryland Pkwy, Box 457001 • Las Vegas, NV 89154-7001 • (702) 895-2100 • http://www.library.unlv.edu

Jewish Federation of Las Vegas-Holocaust Studies Library • 2317 Renaissance Dr • Las Vegas, NV 89119 • (702) 732-0556

Jewish Genealogical Society of Southern Nevada • P.O. Box 370522 • Las Vegas, NV 89127 • (702) 363-8230 • http://www.jewishgen.org/jgs/jgs-southernnevada/

Knights of Pythias • 2785 Desert Inn Rd, Ste 150 • Las Vegas, NV 89121

Las Vegas Genealogical Library • 509 S 9th St • Las Vegas, NV 89101 • (702) 382-9695

Las Vegas International Scouting Museum • 2915 W Charleston, Ste 2 • Las Vegas, NV 89102 • (702) 878-7268 • http://www.worldscoutmuseum.org

Las Vegas-Clark County Library District • 833 Las Vegas Blvd N • Las Vegas, NV 89101 • (702) 507-3500 • http://www.lvccld.org

Las Vegas-Clark County Library-Clark County • 1401 E Flamingo Rd • Las Vegas, NV 89119 • (702) 507-3400

Las Vegas-Clark County Library-West Las Vegas • 951 W Lake Mead Blvd • Las Vegas, NV 89106 • (702) 507-3980

Magic and Movie Hall of Fame • 3555 Las Vegas Blvd S • Las Vegas, NV 89109 • (702) 737-1343

Neon Museum • by private appointment only • Las Vegas, NV 89101 • (702) 387-6366 • http://www.neonmuseum.org

Nevada State Historical Society • Nevada State Museum, 700 Twin Lakes Dr • Las Vegas, NV 89107 • (702) 486-5205 • http://www.nevadaculture.net

POINT-Pursuing our Italian Names Together • P.O. Box 14966 • Las Vegas, NV 89114 • (702) 257-6628 • http://www.point-pointers.net

Red Rock Canyon Visitor Center • State Route 159 • Las Vegas, NV 89124 • (702) 363-1921 • http://www.redrockcanyon.blm.gov

Sons of the American Revolution, Nevada Society • 2730 Darby Falls Dr • Las Vegas, NV 89134-7499 • http://sar.annetta.com

US Air Force Thunderbirds Museum • general delivery • Las Vegas, NV 89191 • (702) 652-4019 • http://www.airforce.com/thunderbirds/

Walker African American Museum • 705 W Van Buren Ave • Las Vegas, NV 89106 • (702) 649-2238

Laughlin
Classic Auto Exhibition Hall • 1650 Casino Wy, P.O. Box 500 • Laughlin, NV 89029 • (702) 298-2535

Colorado River Museum • 355 Hwy 95 • Laughlin, NV 89029 • (928) 754-3399 • http://www.bullheadcity.com

Lee
South Fork Band of the Te-Moak Tribe of Western Shoshone Indians • P.O. Box B13 • Lee, NV 89829 • (702) 744-4223 • http://itcn.org/tribes/sfork.html

Logandale
Old Logandale School Historical Society • Historical Museum, 3011 Moapa Valley Blvd, P.O. Box 65 • Logandale, NV 89021 • (702) 398-7272 • http://www.rootsweb.com/~nvolshcs

Lovelock
Lovelock Paiute Tribe • P.O. Box 878 • Lovelock, NV 89419 • (702) 273-7861 • http://itcn.org/tribes/lovelock.html

Marzen House Museum • 25 Marzen Ln, P.O. Box 212 • Lovelock, NV 89419 • (775) 273-2115

Pershing County Courthouse Museum • 400 Main St, P.O. Box 986 • Lovelock, NV 89419 • (775) 273-7144

Pershing County Library • 1125 Central, P.O. Box 781 • Lovelock, NV 89419 • (775) 273-2216 • http://ahontan.clan.lib.nv.us/polpac/html_client/

Lund
Cherry Creek Museum • 200 N Main St • Lund, NV 89317 • (775) 591-0405

McDermitt
Fort McDermitt Paiute and Shoshone Tribe • P.O. Box 457 • McDermitt, NV 89421 • (702) 532-8259 • http://itcn.org/tribes/ftmcderm.html

Mina
Mineral County Public Library-Mina-Luning Community • P.O. Box 143 • Mina, NV 89422-0143 • (775) 573-2505

Minden
Douglas County Public Library • 1625 Library Ln, P.O. Box 337 • Minden, NV 89423 • (775) 782-9841 • http://www.douglas.lib.nv.us

Moapa
Moapa Paiute Band of the Moapa Indian Reservation • P.O. Box 56 • Moapa, NV 89025-0340 • (702) 865-2787 • http://itcn.org/tribes/moapa.html

Nellis AFB
Nellis Air Force Base Library FL4852 • 99 SVS/SVMG, 4311 N Washington Blvd, Bldg 312, Suite 101 • Nellis AFB, NV 89191-7064 • (702) 652-5072 • http://www.nellis.af.mil/facilities5.htm

Nixon
Pyramid Lake Paiute Tribe • P.O. Box 256 • Nixon, NV 89424-7401 • (702) 574-1000

North Las Vegas
North Las Vegas Municipal Library • 2300 Civic Center Dr • North Las Vegas, NV 89030 • (702) 633-1070

Omyhee
Shoshone Paiute Tribal Business Council • P.O. Box 219 • Omyhee, NV 89832

Overton
Lost City Museum • 721 S Moapa Valley Blvd, P.O. Box 807 • Overton, NV 89040 • (702) 397-2193 • http://www.comnett.net/~kolson/

Owyhee
Duck Valley Reservation - Shoshone-Piute Tribes • P.O. Box 219 • Owyhee, NV 89832 • (702) 757-3161 • http://itcn.org/tribes/dkvly.html

Pahrump
Pahrump Community Library • 701 E Street • Pahrump, NV 89048-2164 • (775) 727-5930 • http://www.pahrumplibrary.com

Pahrump Museum • 171 S Ford Pl • Pahrump, NV 89041 • (775) 727-5218

Pahrump Valley Genealogy Group • P.O. Box 66 • Pahrump, NV 89041-0066 • (775) 727-9297 • http://members.aol.com/pngs

Pioche
Lincoln County Historical Society • Historical Museum, P.O. Box 515 • Pioche, NV 89043 • (775) 962-5207

Million Dollar Courthouse Museum • Lacour St, P.O. Box 515 • Pioche, NV 89043 • (775) 962-5182

Reno
Church of Jesus Christ of Latter-Day Saints Reno Family History Center • 4751 Neil Rd • Reno, NV 89502 • (775) 826-1130

Masonic Grand Lodge of Nevada • 40 W 1st St, 3rd Fl • Reno, NV 89501-1417 • (775) 786-5261 • http://www.nvmasons.org

National Automobile Museum • 10 S Lake St • Reno, NV 89501 • (775) 333-9300 • http://www.automuseum.org

Nevada Historical Society • Historical Museum, 1650 N Virginia St • Reno, NV 89503 • (775) 688-1190 • http://www.nevadaculture.org

Nevada Rock Art Foundation • 305 S Arlington Ave • Reno, NV 89501 • (775) 315-5497

Nevada State Genealogical Society • P.O. Box 20666 • Reno, NV 89515 • http://www.rootsweb.com/~nvsgs

Noble H Getchell Library - Special Collections • University of Nevada-Reno, 1664 N Virginia St, Mailstop 322 • Reno, NV 89557-0044 • (702) 784-6500 • http://www.library.unr.edu

Reno Historic Preservation Society • P.O. Box 14003 • Reno, NV 89507 • (775) 747-4478 • http://www.historicreno.org

Reno-Sparks Indian Colony • 98 Colony Rd • Reno, NV 89502 • (702) 329-2936 • http://itcn.org/tribes/rsic.html

Washoe County Historical Society • 629 Jones St • Reno, NV 89503

Washoe County Library • 301 S Center St, P.O. Box 2151 • Reno, NV 89505-2151 • (775) 327-8312 • http://www.washoe.lib.nv.us

Washoe County Library System-NW Reno Library • 2325 Robb Dr, P.O. Box 2151 • Reno, NV 89505 • (775) 787-4100

Wilbur D May Museum • 1502 Washington St • Reno, NV 89503 • (775) 785-4707

Round Mountain
Town of Round Mountain Nevada Genealogical Group • P.O. Box 330 • Round Mountain, NV 89045

Schurz
Walker River Paiute Tribe • P.O. Box 220 • Schurz, NV 89427 • (702) 773-2306 • http://itcn.org/tribes/wrpt.html

Searchlight
Searchlight Historic Museum & Mining Park • 200 Michael Wendell Wy, P.O. Box 36 • Searchlight, NV 89046 • (702) 297-1642

Sparks
Inter-Tribal Council of Nevada • 680 Greenbrae Dr, Ste 280 • Sparks, NV 89431 • (702) 355-0600 • http://itcn.org

Sparks Heritage Society • Historical Museum, 814 Victorian Ave • Sparks, NV 89431 • (775) 355-1144

Tonopah
Central Nevada Historical Society • Central Nevada Museum, 1900 Logan Field Rd, P.O. Box 326 • Tonopah, NV 89049-0326 • (775) 482-9676 • http://www.tonopahnevada.com

Tonopah Mining Park Museum • 520 McCulloch Ave, P.O. Box 965 • Tonopah, NV 89049 • (775) 482-9274 • http://www.tonopahnevada.com/tonopahhistoricminingpark.htm

Virginia City
Historic Earth Ward School and Museum • P.O. Box 4 • Virginia City, NV 89440 • (775) 884-3538

Mackay Mansion Museum • 129 South D Street • Virginia City, NV 89440 • (775) 847-0336 • http://www.mackaymansion.com

Mark Twain Museum of Memories • 4753 South C Street • Virginia City, NV 89440 • (775) 847-0525

Marshall Mint Museum • 96 North C Street • Virginia City, NV 89440 • (775) 837-0777

Nevada State Fire Museum • 125 South C Street, P.O. Box 466 • Virginia City, NV 89440 • (775) 847-0954 • http://www.comstockfiremuseum.com

Piper's Opera House Museum • B & Union Sts • Virginia City, NV 89440 • (773) 847-0433

Washoe Valley
Bowers Mansion Museum • 4005 US 395 N • Washoe Valley, NV 89794 • (775) 849-0201

Wellington
Wellington Historical Society • P.O. Box 36 • Wellington, NV 89444

Wells
Wells Band of the Te-Moak Tribe of Western Shoshone Indians • P.O. Box 809 • Wells, NV 89835 • (702) 752-3045 • http://itcn.org/tribes/wells.html

Winnemucca
Buckaroo Hall of Fame • 30 W Winnemucca Blvd • Winnemucca, NV 89445 • (541) 573-2921 • http://www.buckaroohalloffame.com

Humboldt County Genealogical Society • c/o Humboldt County Library, 85 E 5th St • Winnemucca, NV 89445 • (775) 623-6388

Humboldt County Library • 85 E 5th St • Winnemucca, NV 89445 • (775) 623-6388

North Central Nevada Historical Society & Archvies • Historical Museum, Maple Ave & Jungo Ave, P.O. Box 819 • Winnemucca, NV 89446-0819 • (775) 623-2912 • http://www.humboldtmuseum.org

Summit Lake Paiute Tribe • 510 Melakey #11, Ste 207 • Winnemucca, NV 89445 • (702) 623-5151

Yerington
Lyon County Library • 20 Nevin Wy • Yerington, NV 89447 • (775) 463-6645 • http://www.lyon-county.org

Lyon County Museum • 215 S Main St • Yerington, NV 89447 • (775) 463-2245 • http://www.yerington.net/museum.html

Yerington Paiute Tribe • 171 Campbell Ln • Yerington, NV 89447 • (702) 463-3301 • http://itcn.org/tribes/ypt.html

Zephyr Cove
Douglas County Public Library-Lake Tahoe • 233 Warrior Way • Zephyr Cove, NV 89448 • (775) 588-6411

Acworth

Acworth Historical Society • c/o Acworth Silsby Library, 1 Cold Pond Rd • Acworth, NH 03601 • (603) 835-2150

Acworth Silsby Library • 1 Cold Pond Rd, P.O. Box 179 • Acworth, NH 03601-0179 • (603) 835-2150 • http://www.sover.net/~acworthl

Albany

Albany Historical Society • 1972 Route 16 • Albany, NH 03818 • http://www.conwayhistory.org

Alexandria

Haynes Memorial Library • 33 Washburn Rd • Alexandria, NH 03222-6532 • (603) 744-6529

Allenstown

Allenstown Public Library • 59 Main St • Allenstown, NH 03275-1716 • (603) 485-7651

New Hampshire Snowmobile Museum • Bear Brook State Park, Route 28 • Allenstown, NH 03275 • (603) 648-2304 • http://www.nhsnowmobilemuseum.com

Alstead

Alstead Historical Society • Historical Museum, P.O. Box 16 • Alstead, NH 03602 • (603) 835-2150

Alton

Alton Historical Society • Historical Museum, P.O. Box 536 • Alton, NH 03809 • (603) 875-3535

Harold S Gilman Historical Museum • Route 140 & Main St, P.O. Box 428 • Alton, NH 03809 • (603) 875-2161

Amherst

Historical Society of Amherst, New Hampshire • Chapel Museum, P.O. Box 717 • Amherst, NH 03031 • (603) 672-4616 • http://www.hsahn.org

Wigwam Museum • P.O. Box 717 • Amherst, NH 03031 • (603) 672-4616

Andover

Andover Historical Society • Historical Museum, 105 Depot St, P.O. Box 167 • Andover, NH 03216 • (603) 735-5690 • http://www.andoverhistory.org

Antrim

Antrim Historical Society • 63 Pleasant St, P.O. Box 172 • Antrim, NH 03440 • (603) 588-2894

Antrim Museum • 66 Main St, P.O. Box 297 • Antrim, NH 03440 • (603) 588-6785

Bennington Historical Society • general delivery • Antrim, NH 03440 • (603) 588-4871

James A Tuttle Library • 45 Main St, P.O. Box 235 • Antrim, NH 03440-0235 • (603) 588-6786

Ashland

Ashland Genealogy Society • P.O. Box 1163 • Ashland, NH 03217

Ashland Historical Society • Whipple House Museum, Pleasant St, P.O. Box 175 • Ashland, NH 03217 • (603) 967-7716 • http://www.ashlandnh.org

Ashland Railroad Station Museum • 69 Depot St, P.O. Box 175 • Ashland, NH 03217

Glidden Toy Museum • 4 Pleasant St, P.O. Box 175 • Ashland, NH 03217 • (603) 968-7716

Grafton County Historic and Genealogy Society • P.O. Box 1163 • Ashland, NH 03217

Whipple House Museum • P.O. Box 175 • Ashland, NH 03217 • (603) 968-7716

Atkinson

Atkinson Historical Society • Historical Musuem, 3 Academy Ave, P.O. Box 863 • Atkinson, NH 03811 • (603) 362-9317 • http://www.town-atkinsonnh.com/historical_society.htm

Kimball Public Library • 3 Academy Ave • Atkinson, NH 03811-2202 • (603) 362-5234

Auburn

Auburn Historical Society • 102 Hooksett Rd • Auburn, NH 03032 • (603) 483-5401

Barrington

Barrington Historical Society • 49 Mallego Rd • Barrington, NH 03825 • (603) 664-9551

Barrington Public Library • 39 Province Ln • Barrington, NH 03825 • (603) 664-9715 • http://www.barringtonlibrary.com

Green Hill Chapel Museum • P.O. Box 462 • Barrington, NH 03825 • (603) 664-2740

Bartlett

Bartlett Historical Society • P.O. Box 514 • Bartlett, NH 03812 • (603) 383-4110 • http://www.bartletthistory.org

Bath

Bath Historical Society • P.O. Box 44 • Bath, NH 03740 • (603) 747-2454

Bedford

Bedford Historical Society • Historical Museum, 24 N Amherst Rd • Bedford, NH 03110-5404 • (603) 471-6336 • http://www.bedfordhistoricalnh.org

US Marconi Museum • 18 N Amherst Rd • Bedford, NH 03110 • (603) 472-8312 • http://www.marconiusa.org

Belmont

Belmont Historical Society • 504 Province Rd • Belmont, NH 03220

Bennington

Bennington Historical Society • P.O. Box 50 • Bennington, NH 03442 • (603) 588-4871

Berlin

Berlin Fortier Library • New Hampshire Technical College, 2020 Riverside Dr • Berlin, NH 03570 • (603) 752-1113

Berlin-Coos County Historical Society • 119 High St, P.O. Box 52 • Berlin, NH 03570-2062 • (603) 752-4590 • http://www.conwayhistory.org/phl/berlin.html

Bethlehem

Bethlehem Heritage Society • 2182 Main, P.O. Box 148 • Bethlehem, NH 03574 • (603) 869-3409 • http://www.bethlehemwhitemtns.com/heritagesociety.html

Crossroads of America Museum • 6 Trudeau Rd • Bethlehem, NH 03574 • (603) 869-3919 • http://www.travel.to/cofa

Boscawen

Boscawen Historical Society • Historical Museum, 226 King St, P.O. Box 3067 • Boscawen, NH 03303 • (603) 796-2660

Boscawen Public Library • King St, P.O. Box 3099 • Boscawen, NH 03303-3099 • (603) 796-2442

Muchido Hose House Museum • 712 King St, P.O. Box 3067 • Boscawen, NH 03303 • (603) 796-2660

Bow

Bow Historical Society • 10 Grandview Rd • Bow, NH 03304 • (603) 224-3008

Sons of the American Revolution, New Hampshire Society • 31 Logging Hill Rd • Bow, NH 03304-3719 • (603) 224-4881 • http://www.nhssar.org

New Hampshire

Bradford
Bradford Historical Society • P.O. Box 551 • Bradford, NH 03221 • (603) 938-5386

Brentwood
Brentwood Historical Society & Archives • Historical Museum, 140 Crawley Falls Rd • Brentwood, NH 03833 • (603) 772-6997 • http://brentwood.town-center.org

Bridgewater
Old River Road School Museum • 773 River Rd • Bridgewater, NH 03264 • (603) 968-7000

Bristol
Alexandria Historical Society • 115 Worfield Cr • Bristol, NH 03222 • (603) 744-3762

Bristol Historical Society • P.O. Box 400 • Bristol, NH 03222

Brookfield
Wakefield-Brookfield Historical Society • P.O. Box 795 • Brookfield, NH 03872 • (603) 522-3739 • http://www.conwayhistory.org/phl/wakefield.html

Brookline
Brookline New Hampshire Historical Society & Archives • Meetinghouse Hall, 17 Meetinghouse Hill Rd, P.O. Box 595 • Brookline, NH 03033-0595 • (603) 672-2502

Campton
Barnet Historical Society • Historical Museum, 97 Old West Rd, P.O. box 380 • Campton, NH 03223 • (802) 633-2611

Campton Historical Society • Old Campton Town Hall Museum, Route 175, P.O. Box 160 • Campton, NH 03223 • (603) 726-3813 • http://www.camptonhistorical.org

Thornton Historical Society • P.O. Box 1176 • Campton, NH 3223 • (603) 726-4232

Canaan
Canaan Historical Society • Historical Museum, Canaan St. P.O. Box 402 • Canaan, NH 03741 • (603) 523-4202 • http://www.rootsweb.com/~nhchs

Candia
Candia Historical Society • Historical Museum, 29 High St, P.O. Box 300 • Candia, NH 03034 • (603) 483-2308

Fitts Museum • P.O. Box 91 • Candia, NH 03034

Smyth Public Library • 55 High St • Candia, NH 03034 • (603) 483-8245 • http://www.smythpl.org

Canterbury
Canterbury Historical Society • Elizabeth Houser Museum & Archives, Old Tilton Rd, P.O. Box 81 • Canterbury, NH 03224 • (603) 783-9831

Canterbury Shaker Village Museum • 288 Shaker Rd • Canterbury, NH 03224 • (603) 783-9511 • http://www.shakers.org

Elkins Public Library • 1 Baptist Rd, P.O. Box 300 • Canterbury, NH 03224-0300 • (603) 783-4386

Carroll
Twin Mountain Public Library • 92 School St, P.O. Box 163 • Carroll, NH 03595-0163 • (603) 846-5754

Center Barnstead
Barnstead Historical Society • Town Hall • Center Barnstead, NH 03255 • (603) 269-8991

Center Conway
Chatham Historical Society • Main Rd • Center Conway, NH 03813 • (603) 694-2099

Center Harbor
Center Harbor Historical Society • Historical Museum, Route 25B, P.O. Box 98 • Center Harbor, NH 03226 • (603) 253-6746 • http://www.centerharbornh.org/history.html

Center Ossipee
Ossipee Historical Museum • 52 Route 16B • Center Ossipee, NH 03814 • (603) 539-2404

Ossipee Public Library • 74 Main St, P.O. Box 638 • Center Ossipee, NH 03814 • (603) 539-6390 • http://communities.msn.com/publiclibrarytownofossipeenhusa

Center Sandwich
Samuel H Wentworth Library • 35 Main St • Center Sandwich, NH 03227 • (603) 284-6665

Sandwich Historical Society • Historical Museum, 4 Maple St, P.O. Box 106 • Center Sandwich, NH 03227-3440 • (603) 284-6269 • http://www.sandwichhistorical.org

Center Strafford
Strafford Historical Society • Austin Hall Museum, Route 126 & Route 202A, P.O. Box 33 • Center Strafford, NH 03815 • (603) 664-2244

Center Tuftonboro
Tuftonboro Free Library • 221 Middle Rd, P.O. Box 73 • Center Tuftonboro, NH 03816-0073 • (603) 569-4256 • http://www.worldpath.net/~tborolib

Tuftonboro Historical Society • Center Tuftonboro, NH 03816 • (603) 544-8131

Charlestown
Charlestown Historical Society • Town Hall, Summer St, P.O. Box 159 • Charlestown, NH 03603 • (603) 826-9726

Old Fort Number 4 Museum • 267 Springfield Rd, Route 11, P.O. Box 336 • Charlestown, NH 03603 • (603) 826-5700 • http://www.fortat4.org

Silsby Free Public Library • 226 Main St, P.O. Box 307 • Charlestown, NH 03603-0307 • (603) 826-7793

Unity Free Public Library • 13 Center Rd • Charlestown, NH 03603 • (603) 543-3253

Chatham
Chatham Historical Society • 1209 Main Rd • Chatham, NH 03813 • (603) 694-2099 • http://www.conwayhistory.org/phl/chatham.html

Chester
Chester Historical Society • 1 Chester St, P.O. Box 34 • Chester, NH 03036 • (603) 887-4545

Chesterfield
Chesterfield Historical Society • Main St, P.O. Box 204 • Chesterfield, NH 03443-0204 • (603) 363-8018

Chesterfield Public Library • 524 Rte 63 • Chesterfield, NH 03443-0158 • (603) 363-4621 • http://www.chesterfieldlibrary.org

Friends of Pisgah • P.O. Box 134 • Chesterfield, NH 03443 • (603) 336-5462

Chichester
Chichester Historical Society • Historical Museum, 53 Main St • Chichester, NH 03263 • (603) 798-5609 • http://www.chichesternh.org

Chichester Library • 161 Main St • Chichester, NH 03258 • (603) 798-5613

Claremont
Claremont Historical Society • Historical Museum, 26 Mulberry St • Claremont, NH 03743 • (603) 543-1400

Fiske Free Library • 108 Broad St • Claremont, NH 03743-2673 • (603) 542-7017 • http://www.claremontnewhampshire.com/fiskefree.htm

New Hampshire Community Technical College Library • 1 College Dr • Claremont, NH 03743 • (603) 542-7744 • http://www.claremont.tec. nh.us/libraryhome.html

Colebrook
Colebrook Area Historical Society • Town Hall Museum, 10 Bridge St, P.O. Box 32 • Colebrook, NH 03576 • (603) 237-4470

Concord
American Baptist Churches of New Hampshire Archives • 89 N State St • Concord, NH 03301

Association of Historical Societies of New Hampshire • 26 S Main St, PMB 101 • Concord, NH 03301-4848 • (603) 926-2543 • http://www. historicalsocietynh.org

Boscawen Historical Society • 226 King St • Concord, NH 03303 • (603) 796-2001

Concord Public Library • 45 Green St • Concord, NH 03301-4294 • (603) 225-8670 • http://www.ci.concord.nh.us/library

Kimball-Jenkins Estate Museum • 266 N Main St • Concord, NH 03301 • (603) 225-3932 • http://www.kimballjenkins.com

Merrimack Society of Genealogists • P.O. Box 1035 • Concord, NH 03302

Museum at Eagle Square • 30 Park St • Concord, NH 03301 • (603) 226-3189

Museum of New Hampshire History • 6 Eagle Sq • Concord, NH 03301-4923 • (603) 228-6308 • http://www.nhhistory.org/museum.html

New Boston Historical Society • 30 Park St • Concord, NH 03301-6384 • (603) 225-3381 • http://newww.com/org/nhhs

New Hampshire Bureau of Vital Records • 29 Hazen Dr • Concord, NH 03301-6527 • (603) 271-4650

New Hampshire Historical Society • Tuck Library & Museum, 30 Park St • Concord, NH 03301 • (603) 225-3381 • http://www.nhhistory.org

New Hampshire Records & Archives Library • 71 S Fruit St • Concord, NH 03301-2410 • (603) 271-2236 • http://www.state.nh.us/state/ archives.htm

New Hampshire Society of Genealogists • P.O. Box 2316 • Concord, NH 03302-2316 • (603) 269-4371 • http://www.nhsog.org

New Hampshire State Library • 20 Park St • Concord, NH 03301-6314 • (603) 271-2392 • http://www.state.nh.us/nhsl

New Hampshire Technical Institute Library • 31 College Dr • Concord, NH 03301 • (603) 271-7186 • http://www.nhti.net/library/farnum.htm

Pierce Brigade Museum • Penacook & N Main, P.O. Box 425 • Concord, NH 03301 • (603) 224-5954

Pierce Manse-New Hampshire Political Library • 14 Horseshoe Pond Ln, P.O. Box 425 • Concord, NH 03302 • (603) 225-4555 • http://www. politicallibrary.org

State of New Hampshire Historic Preservation Office • 19 Pillsbury St • Concord, NH 03301 • (603) 271-3483

Contoocook
International Churchill Society • P.O. Box 385 • Contoocook, NH 03229-0385 • (603) 746-4433

Merrimack Society of Genealogists • P.O. Box 173 • Contoocook, NH 03229-0173

United Methodist Church Archives • Fountain Sq, P.O. Box 505 • Contoocook, NH 03229

Conway
Conway Historical Society • Eastman Lord House Museum, 100 Main St, P.O. Box 1949 • Conway, NH 03818 • (603) 447-5551 • http://www. conwayhistory.org/eastman_lord_museum.html

Conway Public Library • 15 Main St, P.O. Box 2100 • Conway, NH 03818-2100 • (603) 447-5552 • http://www.conway.lib.nh.us

Cornish
Cornish Historical Society • Route 2, Box 416 • Cornish, NH 03745 • (603) 675-6003

Saint-Gaudens National Historic Site Museum • 139 Saint Gaudens Rd • Cornish, NH 03745 • (603) 675-2175 • http://www.nps.gov/saga/

Cornish Flat
George H Stowell Free Library • 24 School St, P.O. Box 360 • Cornish Flat, NH 03746-0360 • (603) 543-3644

Meetinghouse Museum • Stage Rd, Route 120 • Cornish Flat, NH 03746 • (603) 675-6003

Croydon
Croydon Historical Society • 879 NH Route 10 • Croydon, NH 03773

Dalton
Dalton Historical Society • 220 Union Rd • Dalton, NH 03598 • (603) 837-9120 • http://www.daltonhistoricalsociety.org

Danbury
George Gamble Library • P.O. Box 209 • Danbury, NH 03230-0209 • (603) 768-3765

Danville
Hawke Historical Society • Old Red School House Museum, P.O. Box 402 • Danville, NH 03819 • (603) 642-8366

Deerfield
Deerfield Heritage Commission • 60 South Rd • Deerfield, NH 03037-1709 • (603) 463-7151

Deerfield Historical Society • 141 Middle Rd, P.O. Box 41 • Deerfield, NH 03037 • (603) 463-7567

Derry
American Society of Genealogists • P.O. Box 1515 • Derry, NH 03038

Derry Historical Society • Historical Museum, 29 W Broadway • Derry, NH 03038 • (603) 432-3188

Derry Public Library • 64 E Broadway • Derry, NH 03038-2412 • (603) 432-6140 • http://www.derry.lib.nh.us

Robert Frost Farm Museum • NH Route 28, P.O. Box 1075 • Derry, NH 03038 • (603) 432-3091 • http://www.robertfrostfarm.com

Dorchester
Dorchester Historical Society • 2048 Route 118 • Dorchester, NH 03266 • (603) 523-7136

Dover
Annie E Woodman Institute • Historical Museum, 182 Central Ave, P.O. Box 146 • Dover, NH 03821-0146 • (603) 742-1038 • http://www. woodmaninstitutemuseum.org

Dover Public Library • 73 Locust St • Dover, NH 03820-3785 • (603) 743-6050 • http://www.dover.lib.nh.us

Lighthouse Preservation Society • 11 Seaborne Dr • Dover, NH 03820 • (603) 740-0055

Northam Colonists Historical Society • 55 Applevale Dr • Dover, NH 03820 • (603) 742-3786

Strafford County Society of Genealogists • 36 Park St, P.O. Box 322 • Dover, NH 03820 • (603) 742-6394

Dublin
Dublin Historical Society • Main Street Schoolhouse Museum, Main St, P.O. Box 415 • Dublin, NH 03444 • (603) 563-8545

Dummer
Dummer Historical Society • 1344 East Side River Rd • Dummer, NH 0358 • (603) 449-6628

Dunbarton

Dunbarton Historical Society • 1 Rangeway Rd • Dunbarton, NH 03045

Dunbarton Public Library • 10004 School St • Dunbarton, NH 03046-4816 • (603) 774-3546 • http://www.mv.com/org/dunlib

Durham

Dimond Library - Special Collections & Museum • Univ of New Hampshire, 18 Library Wy • Durham, NH 03824-3592 • (603) 862-2714 • http://www.sc.library.unh.edu/specoll/izaak.htm

Durham Historic Association • Historical Museum, Newmarket Rd & Main St, P.O. Box 305 • Durham, NH 03824 • (603) 858-5436 • http://www.ci.durham.nh.us/community/historic.dha.html

Lee Historical Society • Lee Town Hall, 7 Mast Rd • Durham, NH 03824

Piscataqua Pioneers • Dimond Library, Univ of New Hampshire, 18 Library Wy • Durham, NH 03824 • (603) 862-2714 • http://www.sc.library.unh.edu/specoll/izaak.htm

East Kingston

East Kingston Historical Society • 24 Depot Rd • East Kingston, NH 03827 • (603) 642-5405

East Wakefield

Wakefield Brookfield Historical Society • Mountain Laurel Rd • East Wakefield, NH 03830 • (603) 522-6011

Effingham

Effingham Historical Society • RR 153 • Effingham, NH 03882 • (603) 539-6715

Effingham Public Library • 30 Town House Rd, P.O. Box 25 • Effingham, NH 03882-0025 • (603) 539-1537 • http://groups.msn.com/EffinghamNHPublicLibrary

Enfield

Enfield Free Public Library • 23 Main St, P.O. Box 1030 • Enfield, NH 03748-1030 • (603) 632-7145

Enfield Historical Society • P.O. Box 612 • Enfield, NH 03748 • (603) 623-7740

Enfield Shaker Museum • 447 NH Route 4A • Enfield, NH 03748 • (603) 632-4346 • http://www.shakermuseum.org

Lockehaven Schoolhouse Museum • Lockehaven Rd, P.O. Box 612 • Enfield, NH 03748 • (603) 632-7740

Enfield Center

Enfield Historical Society • Historical Museum, Route 4A, P.O. Box 612 • Enfield Center, NH 03748 • (603) 632-7740

Epping

Epping Historical Society • Historical Museum, 2 Water St, P.O. Box 348 • Epping, NH 03042 • (603) 679-2944

Harvey-Mitchell Memorial Library • 151 Main St • Epping, NH 03042 • (603) 679-5944

Epsom

Epsom Historical Association • P.O. Box 814 • Epsom, NH 03234 • http://www.epsomhistory.com/epsom/ehapage.htm

Errol

Errol Historical Society • P.O. Box 225 • Errol, NH 03579 • (603) 482-7771

Errol Public Library • 69 Main St, P.O. Box 7 • Errol, NH 03579-0007 • (603) 482-7720

Umbagog Area Heritage Committee • P.O. Box 113 • Errol, NH 03579 • (603) 482-3884

Etna

Hanover Town Library • 130 Etna Rd, 130 Etna Rd • Etna, NH 03750-0207 • (603) 643-3116 • http://www.thehowe.org

Exeter

American Independence Museum • 1 Governor's Lane • Exeter, NH 03833-2420 • (603) 772-2622 • http://www.independencemuseum.org

Exeter Historical Society • Historical Museum, 47 Front St, P.O. Box 924 • Exeter, NH 03833 • (603) 778-2335 • http://www.exeternh.org

Exeter Public Library • 1 Founders Park • Exeter, NH 03833 • (603) 772-3101 • http://www.exeterpl.org

Gilman Garrison House Museum • 12 Water St • Exeter, NH 03833 • (603) 436-3205 • http://www.historicnewengland.org

New Hampshire Society of Genealogists • P.O. Box 633 • Exeter, NH 03833 • (603) 432-8137

Rockingham Society of Genealogists • 28 Prentiss Wy, P.O. Box 81 • Exeter, NH 03833-0081 • (603) 436-5824

Farmington

Farmington Historical Society • Historical Museum, 422 Main St • Farmington, NH 03835 • (603) 755-2944 • http://www.goodwinlibrary.com/historical.html

Fitzwilliam

Fitzwilliam Historical Society & Archives • Amos J Blake House, P.O. Box 87 • Fitzwilliam, NH 03447 • (603) 585-7742

Francestown

Francestown Improvement and Historical Society • Historical Museum, 15 Main St • Francestown, NH 03043 • (603) 547-3600

George Holmes Bixby Memorial Library • 52 Main St, P.O. Box 69 • Francestown, NH 03043-0069 • (603) 547-2730

Franconia

Abbie Greenleaf Library • Main St, P.O. Box 787 • Franconia, NH 03580-0787 • (603) 823-8424

Franconia Area Heritage Council • Town Hall Museum, 553 Main St, P.O. Box 169 • Franconia, NH 03580 • (603) 823-5000 • http://www.franconiaheritage.org

Frost Place Museum • P.O. Box 74 • Franconia, NH 03580 • (603) 823-5510 • http://www.frostplace.org

Iron Furnace Museum • Route 117 & Main St, P.O. Box 169 • Franconia, NH 03850

New England Ski Museum • Franconia Notch Pkwy, P.O. Box 267 • Franconia, NH 03580 • (603) 823-7177 • http://www.skimuseum.org

Franconia Notch

Old Man of the Mountains • Cannon Mountain • Franconia Notch, NH 03580 • (603) 823-5563 • http://mutha.com/oldmanmt.html

Franklin

Franklin Historical Society • P.O. Box 43 • Franklin, NH 03235

Franklin Public Library • 310 Central St • Franklin, NH 03235 • (603) 934-2911

Freedom

Carroll County Chapter, NHSOG • P.O. Box 250 • Freedom, NH 03836

Freedom Historical Society • Allard House and Works Barn Museum, Old Portland Rd, P.O. Box 481 • Freedom, NH 03836 • (603) 367-4626 • http://www.conwayhistory.org/phl/freedom.htm

Freedom Public Library • 38 Old Portland Rd, P.O. Box 159 • Freedom, NH 03836-0159 • (603) 539-5176

Fremont

Fremont Historical Society • Historical Museum, 225 South Rd • Fremont, NH 03044 • (603) 895-4032 • http://www.fremont.nh.gov/fnhghistoricalsociety1.shtml

New England Historical Research Associates • 225 South Rd • Fremont, NH 03044 • (603) 895-4032

Gilford
Gilford Public Library • 2 Belknap Mountain Rd • Gilford, NH 03249-6807 • (603) 524-6042 • http://www.gilfordlibrary.org

Meeting House Museum • 34 Belknap Mountain Rd, P.O. Box 7404 • Gilford, NH 03247 • (603) 524-0990

Thompson-Ames Historical Society • Grange Museum, 8 Belknap Mountain Rd, P.O. Box 7404 • Gilford, NH 03249 • (603) 524-0990

Gilmanton
Gilmanton Historical Society • Historical Museum, Route 107, P.O. Box 236 • Gilmanton, NH 03237 • (603) 267-6308 • http://www.gilmantonnh.org/historical_society.htm

Gilsum
Gilsum Historical Society • P.O. Box 205 • Gilsum, NH 03448 • (603) 352-8542

Gilsum Public Library • 650 Rte 10, P.O. Box 57 • Gilsum, NH 03448-7502 • (603) 357-0320

Goffstown
Goffstown Historical Society • Historical Museum, 18 Parker Station Rd, P.O. Box 284 • Goffstown, NH 03045 • (603) 497-4306 • http://www.rootsweb.com/~nhghs

Gorham
Gorham Historical Society • 25 Railroad St • Gorham, NH 03581 • (603) 466-5338 • http://www.conwayhistory.org/phl/gorham.html

Gorham Public Library • 35 Railroad St • Gorham, NH 03581 • (603) 466-2525

Goshen
Olive G Pettis Library • Mill Village Rd, P.O. Box 521 • Goshen, NH 03752-0251 • (603) 863-6921

Grafton
Township of Grafton Historical Society • P.O. Box 173 • Grafton, NH 03240 • (603) 523-7522

Greenfield
Greenfield Historical Society • 828 Forest Rd • Greenfield, NH 03047 • (603) 547-2759

Stephenson Memorial Library • 761 Forest Rd, P.O. Box 127 • Greenfield, NH 03047-0127 • (603) 547-2790

Greenland
Greenland Historical Society • 459 Portsmouth Ave • Greenland, NH 03840 • (603) 436-8232

Weeks Public Library • 36 Post Rd, P.O. Box 430 • Greenland, NH 03840-0430 • (603) 436-8548 • http://www.weekslibrary.org

Greenville
Greenville Historical Society • 240 Adams Hill Rd • Greenville, NH 03848 • (603) 878-4117

Groveton
Northumberland Historical Society • 2 State St • Groveton, NH 03582 • (603) 636-1450

Hampstead
Hampstead Historical Society • Historical Museum, 67 Main St, P.O. Box 654 • Hampstead, NH 03841-0654 • (603) 329-6670 • http://www.hampsteadhistoricalsociety.org

Hampstead Public Library • 9 Mary E Clark Dr, P.O. Box 190 • Hampstead, NH 03841-0190 • (603) 329-6411 • http://www.hampstead.lib.nh.us

Hampton
Association of Historical Societies of New Hampshire • 107 Locke Rd • Hampton, NH 03842 • (603) 926-2543 • http://www.historicalsocietiesnh.org

Hampton Historians • 3 Thomsen Rd • Hampton, NH 03842 • (603) 926-2111

Hampton Historical Association • Tuck Museum, 40 Park Ave, P.O. Box 1601 • Hampton, NH 03843 • (603) 929-0781 • http://www.hamptonhistoricalsociety.org

Lane Memorial Library • 2 Academy Ave • Hampton, NH 03842 • (603) 926-3368 • http://www.hampton.lib.nh.us

Hampton Falls
Hampton Falls Historical Society • P.O. Box 104 • Hampton Falls, NH 03844 • (603) 926-9081

Hancock
Hancock Historical Society • Historical Museum, 7 Main St, P.O. Box 138 • Hancock, NH 03449 • (603) 525-9379 • http://www.hancocknh.org/hhs/home.htm

Hancock Historical Society • Main St, P.O. Box 138 • Hancock, NH 03449 • (603) 525-9379

Hancock Town Library • 25 Main St, P.O. Box 130 • Hancock, NH 03449-0130 • (603) 525-4411

Hanover
Baker Memorial Library • Dartmouth College • Hanover, NH 03755 • (603) 646-2236 • http://www.dartmouth.edu/~library/

Hanover Historical Society • Webster Cottage Museum, 32 N Main St, P.O. Box 142 • Hanover, NH 03755 • (603) 643-6529

Harrisville
Historic Harrisville • 6 Mill Alley, P.O. Box 79 • Harrisville, NH 03450 • (603) 827-3722

Haverhill
Haverhill Historical Society • Haverhill Center, Court St • Haverhill, NH 03765 • (603) 989-3337

Hebron
Hebron Historical Society • P.O. Box 89 • Hebron, NH 03241 • (603) 744-3597 • http://www.hebronhistsoc.org

Henniker
H Raymond Danforth Library • New England College, 28 Bridge St • Henniker, NH 03242-3298 • (603) 428-2344

Henniker Historical Society & Archives • Academy Hall Museum, 5A Maple St, P.O. Box 674 • Henniker, NH 03242-0674 • (603) 428-6267 • http://www.hennikerhistory.org

Tucker Free Library • 11 Western Ave P.O. Box 688 • Henniker, NH 03242-0688 • (603) 428-3471 • http://henniker.org

Hill
Hill Historical Society • 265 Murray Hill Rd, P.O. Box 193 • Hill, NH 03243 • (603) 744-3138

Hillsboro
Derring Historical Society • Route 1, Box 69 • Hillsboro, NH 03244 • (603) 529-2441

Hillsborough Historical Society • Homestead Museum, E Washington Rd, P.O. Box 896 • Hillsboro, NH 03244 • (603) 478-3165 • http://www.conknet.com

Hillsborough
Hillsborough Historical Society • Franklin Pierce Homestead, P.O. Box 896 • Hillsborough, NH 03244 • (603) 478-3913 • http://www.conknet.com/~hillsboro/pierce/

Hinsdale
Hinsdale Historical Society • Town Hall, Main St, P.O. Box 122 • Hinsdale, NH 03451 • (603) 336-7408

New Hampshire

Holderness
Holderness Free Library • Main St, P.O. Box L • Holderness, NH 03245-0712 • (603) 968-7066

Holderness Historical Society • Curry Place Museum, P.O. Box 319 • Holderness, NH 03245 • (603) 968-7532

Hollis
Always Ready Engine House Museum • 26 Main St, P.O. Box 754 • Hollis, NH 03049 • (603) 465-2494 • http://www.hollis.nh.us

Hollis Historical Society & Archives • Ruth E Wheeler House Museum, 20 Main St, P.O. Box 138 • Hollis, NH 03049 • (603) 465-3935 • http://www.hollis-history.org

Hollis Social Library • 2 Monument Sq, P.O. Box 659 • Hollis, NH 03049-0659 • (603) 465-7721 • http://www.hollis.nh.us/library

Hooksett
Hooksett Historical Society • 16 Main St • Hooksett, NH 03106 • (603) 485-2318

Hopkinton
New Hampshire Antiquarian Society • Historical Museum, 300 Main St • Hopkinton, NH 03229 • (603) 746-3825 • http://www.nhantiquarian.org

Hudson
Hills Memorial Library • 18 Library St • Hudson, NH 03051-4244 • (603) 886-6030 • http://www.hillsml.lib.nh.us

Hudson Historical Society • Historical Museum, 211 Derry Rd, P.O. Box 475 • Hudson, NH 03051 • (603) 880-2020

Interval
Hartmann Model RR & Toy Museum • Route 16, 302 Town Hall Rd • Interval, NH 03845 • (603) 356-9922

Jackson
Jackson Historical Society • Route 16, P.O. Box 8 • Jackson, NH 03846 • (603) 383-4060 • http://www.conwayhistory.org/phl/jackson.html

Jaffrey
Jaffrey Historical Society • Jaffrey Civic Center Museum, 40 Main St • Jaffrey, NH 03452 • (603) 532-6527

Jafrey Public Library • 38 Main St • Jaffrey, NH 03452-1196 • (603) 532-7301 • http://town.jaffrey.nh.us

Jefferson
Jefferson Historical Society • 900 Presidential Hwy, P.O. Box 143 • Jefferson, NH 03583 • (603) 586-7004

Jefferson Public Library • 737 Presidential Hwy, P.O. Box 27 • Jefferson, NH 03583-0027 • (603) 586-7791

Keene
Cheshire County Historical Society • Archive Center & Museum, 246 Main St, P.O. Box 803 • Keene, NH 03431 • (603) 352-1895 • http://www.hscenh.org

Horatio Colony House Museum • 199 Main St • Keene, NH 03431 • (603) 352-0460 • http://www.horatiocolonymuseum.org

Keene Historical Society • 246 Main St • Keene, NH 03431-4143

Keene Public Library • 60 Winter St • Keene, NH 03431-3360 • (603) 352-0157 • http://www.ci.keene.nh.us/library/

Wallace E Mason Library • Keene State College, 229 Main St • Keene, NH 03435-3201 • (603) 358-2710 • http://www.keene.edu/library

Wyman Tavern Museum • 339 Main St, P.O. Box 803 • Keene, NH 03431 • (603) 352-1895 • http://www.hsccnh.org

Kensington
Kensington Historical Society • c/o Kensington Public Library, 126 Amesbury Rd • Kensington, NH 03833 • (603) 772-5022

Kensington Public Library & Museum • 126 Amesbury Rd • Kensington, NH 03833-5621 • (603) 772-5022 • http://www.town.kensington.nh.us/library/

Kingston
Church on the Plains Museum • Main St, P.O. Box 663 • Kingston, NH 03848 • (603) 642-5262

Kingston Improvement and Historical Society • Church on the Plains, Main St, P.O. Box 663 • Kingston, NH 03848 • (603) 642-5419

Kingston Town Museum • P.O. Box 710 • Kingston, NH 03842 • (603) 642-8838

New Hampshire Old Graveyard Association • 8 Great Pond Rd • Kingston, NH 03848-3747 • (603) 642-5419

Nichols Memorial Library • 169 Main St • Kingston, NH 03848-0128 • (603) 642-3521 • http://www.nichols.lib.nh.us

Laconia
Belknap Mill Society • Historical Museum, 25 Beacon St E • Laconia, NH 03246 • (603) 524-8813 • http://www.belknapmill.org

Laconia Historical Society • c/o Laconia Public Library, 695 Main St, P.O. Box 1126 • Laconia, NH 03247 • (603) 524-4775 • http://www.city.laconia.nh.us

Laconia Public Library & Historical Museum • 695 Main St • Laconia, NH 03246-2780 • (603) 524-4775 • http://www.laconialibrary.org

Lake Winnipesaukee Historical Society • Historical Museum, 503 Endicott St N • Laconia, NH 03246 • (603) 366-5950

Lancaster
Lancaster Historical Society • Wilder Holton House Museum, 226 Main St, P.O. Box 473 • Lancaster, NH 03584 • (603) 788-3004

William D Weeks Memorial Library • 128 Main St • Lancaster, NH 03584-3031 • (603) 788-3352

Lebanon
Lebanon Historical Society • 40 Mascoma St • Lebanon, NH 03766 • (603) 448-3118 • http://www.lebanonnhhistory.org

Lebanon Public Library • 9 E Park St • Lebanon, NH 03766 • (603) 448-2459 • http://www.library.lebcity.com

Lee
Lee Historical Society • Town Hall Museum, Mast Rd • Lee, NH 03824 • (603) 659-5925

Leighton Corner
Early Settlers Meeting House Museum • Granite & Foggs Ridge Rds • Leighton Corner, NH 03864 • (603) 539-2161

Lempster
Lempster Historical Society • HCR 66, Box 875 • Lempster, NH 03606

Lempster Meeting House Museum • 484 Dodge Hollow Rd • Lempster, NH 03605

Lincoln
Lincoln Public Library • Church St, P.O. Box 98 • Lincoln, NH 03251-0098 • (603) 745-8159 • http://www.lincoln.lib.nh.us

Lisbon
Lisbon Historical Society • 45 School St • Lisbon, NH 03585 • (603) 838-6615

Lisbon Public Library • 45 School St • Lisbon, NH 03585 • (603) 838-6615

Sugar Hill Historical Society • Route 117 Village Green • Lisbon, NH 03585

Litchfield
Aaron Cutler Memorial Library • 269 Charles Bancroft Hwy • Litchfield, NH 03051 • (603) 424-4044

Litchfield Historical Society • 255 Charles Bancroft Hwy • Litchfield, NH 03052 • (603) 424-6190

Littleton
Littleton Area Historical Society • Historical Museum, 1 Cottage St • Littleton, NH 03561 • (603) 444-6435

Littleton Public Library • 92 Main St • Littleton, NH 03561-1238 • (603) 444-5741 • http://www.ncia.net/library/littleton/

North County Genealogical Society • P.O. Box 618 • Littleton, NH 03561 • (603) 444-2001

Londonderry
Leach Library • 276 Mammouth Rd • Londonderry, NH 03053-3097 • (603) 432-1132 • http://www.londonderry.org

Londonderry Historical Society • Morrison House Museum, 140 Pillsbury Rd, P.O. Box 136 • Londonderry, NH 03053 • (603) 432-2005 • http://www.londerryhistory.org

Lyme
Academy Hall Museum • 84 Lyme St • Lyme, NH 03768 • (603) 795-2287

Lyme Historians • P.O. Box 41 • Lyme, NH 03768 • (603) 795-2287

Lyme Historical Society • general delivery • Lyme, NH 03678

Lyndeborough
Lyndeborough Historical Society • 1325 Center Rd • Lyndeborough, NH 03082

Madbury
Madbury Historical Society • 13 Town Hall Rd • Madbury, NH 03820 • (603) 742-7713

Madison
Madison Historical Society • Historical Museum, E Madison Rd, P.O. Box 505 • Madison, NH 03849 • http://ci.madison.nh.us/historical/

Manchester
Abenaki Indian Center • 381 Chestnut St • Manchester, NH 03101 • (603) 644-4555

Abenaki Nation of New Hampshire • 1001 Elm St • Manchester, NH 03101 • (603) 644-4555

Acadian Genealogical and Historical Association • Franco-American Centre Museum, 52 Concord St, P.O. Box 668 • Manchester, NH 03105 • (603) 669-4045 • http://www.francoamericancentrenh.com

American-Canadian Genealogical Society • 4 Elm St, P.O. Box 6478 • Manchester, NH 03108-6478 • (603) 622-1554 • http://www.acgs.org

Geisel Library • Saint Anselm College, 100 Saint Anselm Dr • Manchester, NH 03102 • (603) 641-7306 • http://www.anselm.edu

Institut Canado-Americain & Bibliotheque • 52 Concord St, P.O. Box 989 • Manchester, NH 03101-0989 • (603) 625-8577

Jewish Genealogical Society of New Hampshire • P.O. Box 1019 • Manchester, NH 03105-1019 • (603) 623-1212

Lawrence L Lee Scouting Museum • 40 Blondin Rd • Manchester, NH 03109 • (603) 669-8919 • http://www.scoutingmuseum.org

Manchester City Library • 405 Pine St • Manchester, NH 03104-6199 • (603) 624-6550 • http://www.manchester.lib.nh.us

Manchester Historic Association • Millyard Museum, 255 Commercial St • Manchester, NH 03101 • (603) 622-7531 • http://www.manchesterhistoric.org

New Hampshire Aviation Historical Society • 1 Garside Way • Manchester, NH 03103 • (603) 669-4820

Pennacook New Hampshire Tribe • 83 Hanover St • Manchester, NH 03101

Marlborough
Frost Free Library & Museum • 28 Jaffrey Rd, P.O. Box 416 • Marlborough, NH 03455-0416 • (603) 876-4479

Marlborough Historical Society • P.O. Box 202 • Marlborough, NH 03455 • (603) 876-3980

Marlow
Marlow New Hampshire Historical Society • P.O. Box 12 • Marlow, NH 03456 • (603) 446-6201 • http://www.marlow-nh.org

Mason
Mason Historical Society • 16 Darling Hill Rd • Mason, NH 03048 • (603) 878-2070

Melvin Village
Tuftonboro Historical Society • Historical Museum, 449 GWH, Route 109, P.O. Box 372 • Melvin Village, NH 03850 • (603) 544-2400

Meredith
Meredith Historical Society • Historical Museum, 45 Main St, P.O. Box 920 • Meredith, NH 03253 • (603) 279-1190

Meredith Public Library • 91 Main St, P.O. Box 808 • Meredith, NH 03253-0808 • (603) 279-4303

Meriden
Meriden Library • 22 Bean Rd, P.O. Box 128 • Meriden, NH 03770-0128 • (603) 469-3252

Merrimack
Merrimack Historical Society • Historical Museum, 520 Boston Post Rd, P.O. Box 1525 • Merrimack, NH 03054 • (603) 880-4343 • http://www.merrimackonline.com

Milan
Milan Public Library • 20 Bridge St, P.O. Box 263 • Milan, NH 03588-0263 • (603) 449-7307

Milford
Masonic Grand Lodge of New Hampshire • 30 Mont Vernon St, P.O. Box 486 • Milford, NH 03055-0486 • (603) 554-1723 • http://www.nhgrandlodge.org

Milford Historical Society • Historical Museum, 6 Union St, P.O. Box 609 • Milford, NH 03055 • (603) 673-3385 • http://www.milfordnh.com

Wadleigh Memorial Library • 21 Nashua • Milford, NH 03055 • (603) 673-2408

Wadleigh Memorial Library • 49 Nashua St • Milford, NH 03055-3753 • (603) 673-2408 • http://www.wadleigh.lib.nh.us

Milton
New Hampshire Farm Museum • 1305 White Mountain Hwy, P.O. Box 644 • Milton, NH 03851 • (603) 652-7840 • http://www.farmmuseum.org

Nute Library • 22 Elm St • Milton, NH 03851-4503 • (603) 652-7829 • http://www.milton.k12.nh.us/nute/nutelibrary.htm

Milton Mills
Milton Historical Society • Historical Museum, Main St, P.O. Box 284 • Milton Mills, NH 03852 • (603) 473-2347

Monroe
Monroe Historical Society • Historical Museum, 60 Fairfield Rd • Monroe, NH 03771 • (603) 638-4104

Mont Vernon
Mont Vernon Historical Society • Town Hall Museum, Main St, P.O. Box 1525 • Mont Vernon, NH 03057 • (603) 673-5886

Moultonborough
Moultonborough Public Library • 4 Holland St, P.O. Box 150 • Moultonborough, NH 03254-0150 • (603) 476-8895

New Hampshire

Moultonborough, cont.
Moultonborough Historical Society • Old Town House Museum, Route 25B, P.O. Box 659 • Moultonborough, NH 03254 • (603) 476-5631 • http://moultonboroughhistory.org

Nashua
Abbot-Spaulding House Museum • 1 Nashville St • Nashua, NH 03060 • (603) 883-0015

Nashua Historical Society • Florence Speare Museum, 5 Abbot St • Nashua, NH 03060 • (603) 883-0015

Nashua Public Library • 2 Court St • Nashua, NH 03060 • (603) 589-4611 • http://www.nashua.lib.nh.us

Nelson
Nelson Town Archives • HCR 33, Box 660 • Nelson, NH 03457 • (603) 847-9945

Olivia Rodham Memorial Library • HCR 33, Box 656 • Nelson, NH 03457-9703 • (603) 847-3214

New Castle
New Castle Historical Society • P.O. Box 89 • New Castle, NH 03854 • (603) 436-0509

New Castle Public Library • Wentworth Rd, P.O. Box 329 • New Castle, NH 03854-0329 • (603) 431-6773

New Durham
New Durham Archives and Historical Collections • Town Hall, Main St • New Durham, NH 03885 • (603) 859-6881

New Durham Public Library • 20 Old Bay Rd, P.O. Box 206 • New Durham, NH 03855 • (603) 859-2201 • http://www.worldpath.net/~ndpl

New Hampton
Gordon-Nash Library & Museum • 69 Main St, P.O. Box 549 • New Hampton, NH 03256 • (603) 744-8061 • http://www.gordon-nash.org

New Hampton Historical Society • P.O. Box 422 • New Hampton, NH 03256 • (603) 744-6334

New Ipswich
Barrett House Museum • Forrest Hall, Main St • New Ipswich, NH 03101 • (617) 227-3956 • http://www.historicnewengland.org

New Ipswich Historical Society • P.O. Box 422 • New Ipswich, NH 03071-0422 • (603) 878-4450

New London
New London Historical Society • Historical Museum, Little Sunapee Rd, P.O. Box 965 • New London, NH 03257 • (603) 526-6564 • http://www.nlhs.net

New London Historical Society • Little Sunapee Rd, P.O. Box 965 • New London, NH 03257 • (603) 526-6564

Newbury
Newbury Historical Society • Sherman Hall Museum, Village Rd S, P.O. Box 176 • Newbury, NH 03255 • (603) 938-2892

Newfields
Newfields Historical Society • P.O. Box 126 • Newfields, NH 03856 • (603) 772-5960

Newfields Public Library • 76 Main St, P.O. Box 200 • Newfields, NH 03856-0200 • (603) 778-8169

Newington
Langdon Public Library • 328 Nimble Hill Rd, Route 151 • Newington, NH 03801 • (603) 436-5154

Newington Historical Society • 133 Fox Point Rd • Newington, NH 03801

Old Parsonage & Old Town Hall Museums • Nimble Hill Rd • Newington, NH 03801 • http://www.newington.nh.us

Newmarket
New Market Historical Society • Stone School Museum, Granite St • Newmarket, NH 03857-1216 • (603) 659-7420

Newmarket Public Library • 1 Elm St • Newmarket, NH 03857-1201 • (603) 659-5311

Newport
Goshen Historical Society • RFD2, Box 177 • Newport, NH 03773 • (603) 863-1509

Newport Historic District Commission • 15 Sunapee St • Newport, NH 03773 • (603) 863-1877

Newport Historical Society • Historical Museum, 22 Main St, P.O. Box 413 • Newport, NH 03773 • (603) 863-1294

Richards Free Library • 58 N Main St • Newport, NH 03773-1597 • (603) 863-3430 • http://www.newport.lib.nh.us

Unity New Hampshire Historical Society • Historical Museum, HCR 66, Box 140 • Newport, NH 03773

Newton
Gale Library • 16 S Main St, P.O. Box 329 • Newton, NH 03858-0329 • (603) 382-4691 • http://members.ttlc.net/~gale

Marian Hatch Museum • 22 S Main St • Newton, NH 03858 • (603) 382-4279

Marshall House Museum • 73 N Main St • Newton, NH 03858 • (603) 382-4279

Newton Historical Society • P.O. Box 289 • Newton, NH 03858 • (603) 382-4279

North Conway
Conway Scenic Railroad Museum • 38 Norcross Cr, P.O. Box 1947 • North Conway, NH 03860 • (603) 356-5251 • http://www.conwayscenic.com

Jackson Historical Society • P.O. Box 16A • North Conway, NH 03860 • (603) 383-4060

Mount Washington Museum and Observatory • 2936 White Mountain Hwy, P.O. Box 2310 • North Conway, NH 03860 • (603) 356-8345 • http://www.mountwashington.org

North Hampton
North Hampton Historical Society • 120 Walnut Ave, P.O. Box 17 • North Hampton, NH 03862 • (603) 964-8829

North Hampton Public Library & Museum • 327A Atlantic Ave • North Hampton, NH 03862-0628 • (603) 964-6326 • http://www.nhplib.org

North Stratford
Cohos Historical Society • Marion Blodgett Museum, Hollow & Bog Rds, P.O. Box 262 • North Stratford, NH 03590 • (603) 922-8337 • http://www.cohoshistoricalsociety.org

North Woodstock
Moosilauke Public Library • Lost River Rd, P.O. Box 21 • North Woodstock, NH 03262 • (603) 745-9971

Northfield
Hall Memorial Library • 18 Park St • Northfield, NH 03276 • (603) 285-8971

Northfield Historical Society • Town Hall, 21 Summer St • Northfield, NH 03276 • (603) 286-3362

Northwood
Northwood Historical Society • Museum, School St, P.O. Box 114 • Northwood, NH 03261 • http://www.rootsweb.com/~nhnhs

Nottingham
Nottingham Historical Society • Van Dame Museum and Research Center, P.O. Box 241 • Nottingham, NH 03290 • (603) 868-2098

Orford
Orford Historical Society • P.O. Box 44 • Orford, NH 03777 • (603) 353-4656 • http://www.orfordnh.us

Orfordville
Orford Free Library • 311 Rte 25A, P.O. Box 186 • Orfordville, NH 03777-0186 • (603) 353-9166

Ossipee
Ossipee Historical Society • P.O. Box 245 • Ossipee, NH 03864 • (603) 539-2404

Pelham
Pelham Historical Society • Historical Museum, 5 Main St • Pelham, NH 03076 • (603) 635-6977 • http://www.pelhamnhhistory.org

Pelham Public Library • 24 Village Green • Pelham, NH 03076 • (603) 635-7581 • http://www.pelhamweb.com/library/

Pembroke
Pembroke Historical Society • Town Hall, 311 Pembroke St • Pembroke, NH 03275 • (603) 224-8790

Peterborough
Peterborough Historical Society • Historical Museum, 19 Grove St, P.O. Box 58 • Peterborough, NH 03458-0058 • (603) 924-3235 • http://www.peterboroughhistory.org

Peterborough Town Library • 2 Concord St • Peterborough, NH 03458 • (603) 924-8040 • http://www.townofpeterborough.com/library

Piermont
Piermont Historical Society • Historical Museum, High St, P.O. Box 273 • Piermont, NH 03779 • (603) 272-4359

Pittsburg
Pittsburg Historical Society • Historical Museum, Main St, P.O. Box 128 • Pittsburg, NH 03592 • (603) 246-7233

Pittsfield
Carpenter Memorial Library • 41 Main St • Pittsfield, NH 03263 • (603) 435-8406 • http://www.pittsfield-nh.com/library.htm

Pittsfield Historical Society • Historical Museum, 13 Elm St • Pittsfield, NH 03263 • (603) 435-8004

Plainfield
Philip Read Memorial Library • 1088 Route 12A • Plainfield, NH 03781 • (603) 675-6866 • http://homepage.fcgnetworks.net/plfdlib

Plainfield Historical Society • Historical Museum, Route 12A, P.O. Box 107 • Plainfield, NH 03781 • (603) 675-5265

Plaistow
Plaistow Historical Society • Town Hall, 127 Main St, P.O. Box 434 • Plaistow, NH 03865 • (603) 382-1675 • http://www.plaistowhistorical.org

Plymouth
Bridgewater Historical Society • RFD 2, Box 390 • Plymouth, NH 03264

Holderness Historical Society • RR 3 • Plymouth, NH 03264 • (603) 968-9898

Old Town Library Museum • Daniel Webster Courthouse, Court St • Plymouth, NH 03264 • (603) 362-6152

Pease Public Library • 1 Russell St • Plymouth, NH 03264-1414 • (603) 536-2616 • http://www.worldpath.net/~pease/home.htm

Plymouth Historical Society • Historical Museum, Court St • Plymouth, NH 03264 • (603) 536-2337

Portsmouth
Governor John Langdon House Museum • 143 Pleasant St • Portsmouth, NH 03801 • (603) 436-3205 • http://www.historicnewengland.org

Jackson House Museum • 76 Northwest St • Portsmouth, NH 03801 • (603) 436-3205

James E Whalley Museum • 351 Middle St • Portsmouth, NH 03801 • (603) 436-3712

Moffatt-Ladd House Museum • 154 Market St • Portsmouth, NH 03801 • (603) 436-8221 • http://www.moffattladd.org

Piscataqua Pioneers • P.O. Box 1511 • Portsmouth, NH 03802

Portsmouth Athenaeum • 9 Market Sq, P.O. Box 848 • Portsmouth, NH 03802-0848 • (603) 431-2538

Portsmouth Historical Society • John Paul Jones House, 43 Middle St, P.O. Box 728 • Portsmouth, NH 03802-0728 • (603) 436-8420 • http://www.portsmouthhistory.org

Portsmouth Public Library • 8 Islington St • Portsmouth, NH 03801-4261 • (603) 766-1720 • http://www.cityofportsmouth.com/library

Rundlet-May House Museum • 364 Middle St • Portsmouth, NH 03801 • (603) 436-3205 • http://www.historicnewengland.org

Strawbery Banke Museum • 14 Hancock St, P.O. Box 300 • Portsmouth, NH 03801-0300 • (603) 422-7502 • http://www.strawberybanke.org

Warner House Museum • 150 Daniel St, P.O. Box 895 • Portsmouth, NH 03802 • (603) 436-5909 • http://www.warnerhouse.org

Wentworth Gardner & Tobias Lear Houses Association • 50 Mechanic St, P.O. Box 563 • Portsmouth, NH 03802 • (603) 436-4406 • http://www.wentworthgardnerandlear.org

Wentworth-Coolidge Mansion Museum • 375 Little Harbor Rd • Portsmouth, NH 03801 • (603) 436-6607 • http://www.wentworthcoolidge.org

Raymond
Raymond Historical Society • Historical Museum, 1 Depot St, P.O. Box 94 • Raymond, NH 03077 • (603) 895-2866 • http://www.raymondhistoricalsociety.home.comcast.net

Richmond
Richmond Archives • c/o Richmond Public Library, Route 119 • Richmond, NH 03470 • (603) 239-4598

Richmond Historical Society • 105 Old Homestead Hwy • Richmond, NH 03470 • (604) 239-6486

Richmond Public Library • 19 Winchester Rd • Richmond, NH 03470 • (603) 239-6164

Rindge
Ingalls Memorial Library & Museum • 252 Main St, P.O. Box 224 • Rindge, NH 03461-0224 • (603) 899-3303

Rindge Historical Society • School St • Rindge, NH 03461 • (603) 899-2341

Rochester
Rochester Historical Society • Historical Museum, 58 Hanson St, P.O. Box 65 • Rochester, NH 03867 • (603) 330-3099

Rochester Public Library • 65 S Main St • Rochester, NH 03867-2707 • (603) 332-1428 • http://www.rpl.lib.nh.us

Rumney
Byron G Merrill Library • 10 Buffalo Rd • Rumney, NH 03266 • (603) 786-9520

Groton Massachusetts Historical Society • P.O. Box 50 • Rumney, NH 03266 • (603) 786-2335

Rumney Historical Society • P.O. Box 945 • Rumney, NH 03266 • (603) 786-9291

Rye
Rye Historical Society • Historical Museum, 10 Old Parish Rd, P.O. Box 483 • Rye, NH 03870 • (603) 964-7730 • http://ryhistoricalsociety. blogs.com; http://ryehistoricalsociety.org

Rye Public Library • 581 Washington Rd • Rye, NH 03870 • (603) 964-8401 • http://www.rye.lib.nh.us

Salem
Kelley Library • 234 Main St • Salem, NH 03079-3190 • (603) 898-7064 • http://www.salem.lib.nh.us

Salem Historical Society • Old Town Hall Museum, 310 Main St • Salem, NH 03079 • (603) 890-2280 • http://www.historialsocietiesnh. org/salem

Salisbury
Salisbury Historical Society • Historical Museum, Salisbury Heights, Route 4, P.O. Box 263 • Salisbury, NH 03268 • (603) 648-2774

Sanbornton
Sanbornton Historical Society • P.O. Box 2 • Sanbornton, NH 03269 • (603) 286-7227

Sanbornton Public Library • 27 Meeting House Hill, P.O. Box 88 • Sanbornton, NH 03269-0088 • (603) 286-8288

Sanbornton Square
Lane Tavern Museum • 510 Sanborn Rd • Sanbornton Square, NH 03269 • (603) 286-4526

Sanbornville
Wakefield Heritage Commission • 2 High St, P.O. Box 279 • Sanbornville, NH 03872 • (603) 522-3259

Wakefield-Brookfield Historical Society • P.O. Box 795 • Sanbornville, NH 03872 • (603) 522-6415

Sandown
Old Meetinghouse Historical Association • Historical Museum, Fremont Rd, P.O. Box 27 • Sandown, NH 03873 • http://www.firstperiodcolonial. com

Sandown Historical Society • Historical Museum, 1 Depot Rd, P.O. Box 373 • Sandown, NH 03873 • (603) 887-6100 • http://www.sandownnh. com/history

Seabrook
Historical Society of Seabrook • Historical Museum, 109 Washington St, P.O Box 500 • Seabrook, NH 03874 • (603) 474-3538

Shelburne
Shelburne Heritage Commission • 74 Village Rd • Shelburne, NH 03581 • (603) 466-2621

Shelburne Public Library • 397 North Rd • Shelburne, NH 03581-3106 • (603) 466-3465

Somersworth
Somersworth Historical Society • 6 Drew Rd • Somersworth, NH 03878

Somersworth Public Library • 25 Main St • Somersworth, NH 03878-3198 • (603) 692-4587 • http://www.somersworth.com

South Effingham
Effingham Historical Society • Historical Museum, P.O. Box 33 • South Effingham, NH 03882 • (603) 539-6715 • http://www.conwayhistory. org/phl/effingham.html

South Hampton
South Hampton Free Public Library • 3-1 Hilldale Ave • South Hampton, NH 03827 • (603) 394-7319

South Sutton
Old Store Museum • 12 Meeting House Hill Rd, P.O. Box 555 • South Sutton, NH 03273 • (603) 938-5843

Old Store Museum Society of South Sutton • Old Store Museum, 12 Meeting House Hill Rd, P.O. Box 462 • South Sutton, NH 03273 • (603) 927-4472

Sutton Historical Society • South Sutton Village Museum, P.O. Box 457 • South Sutton, NH 03273 • (603) 927-4925

Stoddard
Stoddard Historical Society • Historical Museum, Forrest Rd, P.O. Box 213 • Stoddard, NH 03464

Strafford
Strafford Historical Society • RR, Box 202a • Strafford, NH 03884 • (603) 664-7334

Stratham
Stratham Historical Society • Historical Museum, Portsmouth Ave, P.O. Box 39 • Stratham, NH 03885 • (603) 778-0434 • http://www. strathamhistoricalsociety.org

Wiggin Memorial Library • 10 Bunker Hill Ave • Stratham, NH 03885 • (603) 772-4346 • http://www.wigginml.org

Sugar Hill
Sugar Hill Historical Society • Historical Museum, Village Green, P.O. Box 591 • Sugar Hill, NH 03585 • (603) 823-5336 • http://franconianoteh.org

Sullivan
Sullivan Public Library • 436 Centre St, PO Box 92 • Sullivan, NH 03445-0092 • (603) 847-3458

Sunapee
Sunapee Historical Society • 74 Main St • Sunapee, NH 03782-2731 • (603) 763-9872

Suncook
Allenstown Historical Society • P.O. Box 94 • Suncook, NH 03275 • (603) 485-9720

Surry
Reed Free Library • 8 Village Rd • Surry, NH 03431-8314 • (603) 352-1761

Surry Historical Committee • c/o Reed Free Library, 8 Village Rd • Surry, NH 03431 • (603) 352-1743

Swanzey
Mount Caesar Union Library • 628 Old Homestead Hwy • Swanzey, NH 03446 • (603) 357-0456

Swanzey History Museum • P.O. Box 416W • Swanzey, NH 03469 • (603) 352-6639

Tamworth
Cook Memorial Library • 93 Main St • Tamworth, NH 03886 • (603) 323-8510 • http://www.tamworth.lib.nh.us

Remick Country Doctor Museum and Farm • 58 Cleveland Hill Rd, P.O. Box 250 • Tamworth, NH 03886 • (603) 323-7591 • http://www. remickmuseum.org

Tamworth Historical Society • Historical Museum, 25 Great Hill Rd, P.O. Box 13 • Tamworth, NH 03886 • (603) 323-8639 • http://www. conwayhistory.org/phl/tamworth.html

Temple
Mansfield Public Library • 5 Main St, P.O. Box 210 • Temple, NH 03084-0210 • (603) 878-3100

Temple Historical Society • P.O. Box 114 • Temple, NH 03084 • (603) 878-3100

Tilton
Sanbornton Historical Society • Sanbornton Sq • Tilton, NH 03276 • (603) 286-7227

Tilton Historical Society • 11 Grange Rd, P.O. Box 351 • Tilton, NH 03276 • (603) 524-1135

Troy
Gay-Kimball Public Library • 10 S Main St, P.O. Box 837 • Troy, NH 03465-0837 • (603) 242-7743

Troy Historical Society • Kimball Hall, P.O. Box 593 • Troy, NH 03465 • (603) 242-7731 • http://www.troy-nh-us/histsoc.html

Twin Mountain
Twin Mountain-Bretton Woods Historical Society • P.O. Box 464 • Twin Mountain, NH 03595 • (603) 864-5573 • http://www.twinmountain.com/historical.php

Wakefield
Wakefield-Brookfield Historical Society • Historical Museum, Wakefield Rd • Wakefield, NH 03872 • (603) 522-6415

Walpole
Academy Museum • 50 E Westminster St, P.O. Box 292 • Walpole, NH 03608 • (603) 756-3449

Walpole Historical Society • Historical Museum, Main St, P.O. Box 292 • Walpole, NH 03608 • (603) 756-3589

Walpole Town Library • 48 Main St, P.O. Box 487 • Walpole, NH 03608-0487 • (603) 756-3306

Warner
Mount Kearsarge Indian Museum • Kearsarge Mtn Rd, P.O. Box 142 • Warner, NH 03278 • (603) 456-3244 • http://www.indianmuseum.org

Pillsbury Free Library • 18 E Main St, P.O. Box 299 • Warner, NH 03278-0299 • (603) 456-2289 • http://warner.lib.nh.us

Warner Historical Society • Main Street House Museum, 15 W Main St, P.O. Box 189 • Warner, NH 03278 • (603) 456-2437

Warren
Warren Historical Society • Historical Museum, Water St, P.O. Box 114 • Warren, NH 03279 • (603) 764-5794

Washington
Washington Historical Society • Half Moon Pond Rd • Washington, NH 03280 • (603) 495-6009

Waterville Valley
Osceola Library • W Branch Rd, P.O. Box 367 • Waterville Valley, NH 03215-0367 • (603) 236-4730

Weare
Weare Historical Society • Historical Museum, Route 114, P.O. Box 33 • Weare, NH 03281 • (603) 529-2555

Webster
Old Meeting House Museum • 1220 Battle St • Webster, NH 03303

Weirs
Lake Winnipesaukee Historical Society • Historical Museum, 503 Endicott St N, P.O. Box 5386 • Weirs, NH 03246 • (603) 366-5950 • http://www.lwhs.us

Wentworth
Wentworth Historical Society • P.O. Box 13 • Wentworth, NH 03282-0013 • (603) 764-9404

West Springfield
Springfield Historical Society • Historical Museum, Route 114 & Four Corners Rd, P.O. Box 63 • West Springfield, NH 03284 • (603) 763-2282

West Swanzey
Stratton Free Library • 9 Main St, P.O. Box 578 • West Swanzey, NH 03469-0578 • (603) 352-9391

Westmoreland
Westmoreland Historical Society • Historical Museum, 118 Pierce Ln, P.O. Box 55 • Westmoreland, NH 03467 • (603) 399-7745

Westmoreland Public Library • 33 S Village Rd • Westmoreland, NH 03467 • (603) 399-7750

Whitefield
Whitefield Historical Society • Kings Library, P.O. Box 21 • Whitefield, NH 03598 • (603) 837-2386

Wilmot Flat
Wilmot Historical Society • Town Hall Museum, P.O. Box 2010 • Wilmot Flat, NH 03287 • (603) 927-4119

Wilton
Frye's Measure Mill Museum • 12 Frye Mill Rd • Wilton, NH 03086 • (603) 654-6581 • http://www.fryemueasuremill.com

Wilton Historical Society • 120 Marden Rd, P.O. Box 845 • Wilton, NH 03086 • (603) 654-2581

Winchester
Conant Public Library • 111 Main St, P.O. Box 6 • Winchester, NH 03470 • (603) 239-4331 • http://adam.cheshire.net/~conantlibrary/home.htm

Windham
Nesmith Library • 8 Fellows Rd, P.O. Box 60 • Windham, NH 03087 • (603) 432-7154 • http://www.nesmithlibrary.org

Windham Historical Society • P.O. Box 441 • Windham, NH 03087 • (603) 848-7433

Windham Museum • P.O. Box 120 • Windham, NH 03087 • (603) 432-7732 • http://www.windhamnewhampshire.com

Wolfeboro
Libby Museum • Route 109 N, P.O. Box 629 • Wolfeboro, NH 03894 • (603) 569-1035 • http://www.wolfeboroonline.com/libby

New Hampshire Boat Museum • 397 Centre St, P.O. Box 1195 • Wolfeboro, NH 03896 • (603) 569-4554 • http://www.nhbm.org

Society of the Descendants of the Founding Fathers of New England • P.O. Box 215 • Wolfeboro, NH 03894 • (603) 569-7902 • http://groups.msn.com/descendantsofthefoundingfathersofnewengland

Wentworth House Plantation Museum • Route 109 S, P.O. Box 2126 • Wolfeboro, NH 03894 • (603) 522-8567

Wolfeboro Historical Society • Historical Museum, 233 S Main St, P.O. Box 1066 • Wolfeboro, NH 03894-1066 • (603) 569-4997 • http://www.wolfeborohistoricalsociety.org

Wolfeboro Public Library • 259 S Main St, P.O. Box 710 • Wolfeboro, NH 03894 • (603) 569-2428 • http://www.worldpath.net

Wright Museum • 77 Center St, Route 28, P.O. Box 1212 • Wolfeboro, NH 03894 • (603) 569-1212 • http://www.wrightmuseum.org

Woodsville
Woodsville Free Public Library • 14 School Lane • Woodsville, NH 03785 • (603) 747-3483

Absecon

Absecon Historical Society • Howlett Hall Museum, 100 New Jersey Ave, P.O. Box 1422 • Absecon, NJ 08201 • (609) 677-5776

Galloway Township Historical Society • 366 Upland Ave • Absecon, NJ 08201 • (609) 652-3049

Allaire

Historic Allaire Village • Allaire State Park, Route 524, P.O. Box 220 • Allaire, NJ 07727-0220 • (732) 938-2253 • http://www.allairevillage.org

Allendale

Allendale Historical Society • P.O. Box 294 • Allendale, NJ 07401 • (201) 327-0605

Allentown

Allentown-Upper Freehold Historical Society • P.O. Box 328 • Allentown, NJ 08501 • (609) 259-3171

Lemko Association of the US and Canada • 555 Provinceline Rd, P.O. Box 156 • Allentown, NJ 08501 • (609) 758-1115

Alpine

Alpine Historical Society • P.O. Box 59 • Alpine, NJ 07620 • (201) 768-1360

Andover

Byram Township Historical Society • 3 Ghost Pony Rd • Andover, NJ 07821 • (973) 347-4585

Historical Society of Andover Boro • 189 Main St • Andover, NJ 07821 • (973) 786-6829

Asbury

Bethelehen Township Historical Society • P.O. Box 56 • Asbury, NJ 08802

West Portal Historical Society • P.O. Box 134 • Asbury, NJ 08802

Asbury Park

Asbury Park Free Public Library • 500 1st Ave • Asbury Park, NJ 07712 • (732) 774-4221 • http://www.asburypark.lib.nj.us

Asbury Park Historical Society • general delivery • Asbury Park, NJ 07712 • (732) 869-4478

Ashland

Pauline E Glidden Toy Museum • Pleasant St • Ashland, NJ 03217

Atlantic City

Atlantic City Free Public Library • 1 N Tennessee Ave • Atlantic City, NJ 08401 • (609) 345-2269 • http://www.acfpl.org

Atlantic City Historical Museum • New Jersey Ave & the Boardwalk, P.O. Box 7273 • Atlantic City, NJ 08404 • (609) 347-5839 • http://www.acmuseum.org

Chicken Bone Beach Historical Foundation • 1721 McKinley Ave • Atlantic City, NJ 08401 • (609) 441-9064 • http://www.chickenbonebeach.org

Historic Gardner's Basin Museum • 800 N New Hampshire Ave & the Bay • Atlantic City, NJ 08401 • (609) 348-2880 • http://www.oceanlifecenter.com

Atlantic Highlands

Atlantic Highlands Historical Society • 22 Prospect Ave, P.O. Box 108 • Atlantic Highlands, NJ 07716 • (732) 872-1957

Audubon

Audubon Historical Society • 238 Washington Terr • Audubon, NJ 08106 • (856) 547-0586

Batsto Citizens Committee • 355 Mansion Ave • Audubon, NJ 08106 • (856) 547-6006

Avalon

Avalon Historical Society • Historical Museum, 215 39th St • Avalon, NJ 08202 • (609) 967-0090

Baptistown

Kingwood Township Historical Society • Rte 519, P.O. Box 199 • Baptistown, NJ 08803-0199

Barnegat

Barnegat Historical Society • E Bay Ave, P.O. Box 381 • Barnegat, NJ 08005 • (609) 698-5284

Barnegat Light

Barnegat Light Historical Society • Historical Museum, 5th & Central Sts, P.O. Box 386 • Barnegat Light, NJ 08006 • (609) 494-8578

Barrington

Barrington Historical Society • 9 Beaver Dr • Barrington, NJ 08007

Basking Ridge

Basking Ridge Historical Society • 107 Dyckman Pl • Basking Ridge, NJ 07920 • (908) 766-3786

Bernards Township Library • 32 S Maple St • Basking Ridge, NJ 07920-1216 • (908) 204-3031 • http://www.bernards.org/library

Historical Society of the Somerset Hills • 15 W Oak St, P.O. Box 136 • Basking Ridge, NJ 07920 • (908) 221-1770

Batsto

Historic Batsto Village • Route 542 • Batsto, NJ 08037 • (609) 561-0024

Bay Head

Bay Head Historical Society • P.O. Box 127 • Bay Head, NJ 08742 • (732) 892-0223

Bayonne

Bayonne Free Public Library • 697 Avenue C • Bayonne, NJ 07002 • (201) 858-6970 • http://www.bayonnenj.org/library

Bayville

Berkeley Township Historical Society • 759 US Hwy 9 • Bayville, NJ 08721-2538 • (732) 269-9527

Beach Haven

Beach Haven Free Public Library • 247 Beach Ave • Beach Haven, NJ 08008-1865 • (609) 492-7081

Long Beach Island Historical Association • Engleside & Beach Ave, P.O. Box 1222 • Beach Haven, NJ 08008 • (609) 492-0700 • http://lbimuseum.org

Bedminster

Clarence Dillon Public Library • 2336 Lamington Rd • Bedminster, NJ 07921 • (908) 234-2325 • http://www.clarencedillonpl.org

Belle Mead

Van Harlingen Historical Society • Ludlow Ave, P.O. Box 23 • Belle Mead, NJ 08502 • (908) 359-3498

Belleville

Belleville Historical Society • c/o Belleville Public Library, 221 Washington Ave • Belleville, NJ 07109 • (973) 450-3434 • http://www.intac.com/~bplibn/hpfront.htm

Belleville Public Library • 30 Magnolia St • Belleville, NJ 07109 • (973) 450-3438

Belleville Township Free Public Library • 221 Washington Ave • Belleville, NJ 07109-3189 • (973) 450-3434 • http://www.bellepl.org

Belmar

Old Wall Historical Society • 1701 New Bedford Rd • Belmar, NJ 07719 • (732) 974-1430

Belvidere

Belvidere Historic Preservation Commission • 691 Water St • Belvidere, NJ 07823 • (908) 475-5331

New Jersey

Belvidere, cont.

Warren County Historical and Genealogical Society • Historical Museum, 313 Mansfield St, P.O. Box 313 • Belvidere, NJ 07823-0313 • (908) 475-4246 • http://www.bccls.org/westcaldwell

Warren County Library • 199 Hardwick St • Belvidere, NJ 07823 • (908) 475-6322 • http://www.warrenlib.com

Warren County Morris Canal Commission • Administration Bldg, Route 519 • Belvidere, NJ 07823 • (201) 475-8000 x631

Bergenfield

Association of Jewish Genealogical Societies • 155 N Washington Ave • Bergenfield, NJ 07621 • (201) 387-7200 • http://www.avotaynu.com

Bergenfield Free Public Library • 50 W Clinton Ave • Bergenfield, NJ 07621-2799 • (201) 387-4040 • http://www.bccls.org/bergenfield/

Bergenfield Museum Society • Historical Museum, P.O. Box 95 • Bergenfield, NJ 07621 • (201) 385-4599

Jewish Genealogical Society of Bergen County New Jersey • 56 Beucler Pl • Bergenfield, NJ 07621 • (201) 387-2892 • http://home.att.net/~erosenbaum/JGSBC.htm

New York Historical Society • 1 McDermott Pl • Bergenfield, NJ 07621 • (201) 244-0064

Berkeley Heights

Historical Society of Berkeley Heights • P.O. Box 237 • Berkeley Heights, NJ 07922 • (908) 464-0961

Berlin

Berlin Historical Society • 99 Washington Ave • Berlin, NJ 08009 • (856) 768-0946

Berlin Long-a-Coming Historical Society • 59 S White Horse Pike • Berlin, NJ 08009 • (856) 767-6221 • http://www.nexination.com/longacoming/

Bernardsville

Bernardsville Public Library • 1 Anderson Hill Rd • Bernardsville, NJ 07924 • (908) 766-0118 • http://www.bernardsville.org

Watchung Hills Historical Society • 102 Old Army Rd • Bernardsville, NJ 07924

Beverly

Beverly Free Library • 441 Cooper St • Beverly, NJ 08010 • (609) 387-1259

Riverfront Historical Society • 1029 Cooper St • Beverly, NJ 08010 • (609) 871-0592

Bloomfield

Bloomfield Public Library • 90 Broad St • Bloomfield, NJ 07003 • (973) 566-6200 • http://www.bloomfieldtwpnj.com/library.html

Historical Society of Bloomfield • Historical Museum, 90 Broad St • Bloomfield, NJ 07003 • (973) 743-8844

Bloomingdale

Bloomingdale Free Public Library • 101 Hamburg Tpk • Bloomingdale, NJ 07403-1297 • (973) 838-0077

Boonton

Boonton Historical Society • Historical Museum, 210 Main St • Boonton, NJ 07005 • (973) 627-6205

Boonton Holmes Public Library • 621 Main St • Boonton, NJ 07005 • (973) 334-2980 • http://www.boonton.org/library

Historical Society of Boonton Township • Route 2, Box 152 • Boonton, NJ 07005

Montville Historical Society • 415 Boyd St, P.O. Box 497 • Boonton, NJ 07005 • (973) 335-1970

Parsippany Historical Society • 93 Intervale Rd • Boonton, NJ 07005 • (973) 334-2116

Bordentown

Bordentown Historical Society • Gidder House, 211 Crosswicks Rd • Bordentown, NJ 08505 • (609) 298-2399 • http://bc.emanon.net/bhs

Burlington County Library-Bordentown Branch • 18 E Union St • Bordentown, NJ 08505 • (609) 298-0622

Chesterfield Township Historical Society • general delivery • Bordentown, NJ 08505 • (609) 291-5001

Bound Brook

Bound Brook Memorial Library • 402 E High St • Bound Brook, NJ 08805 • (732) 356-0043 • http://www.boundbrooklibrary.org

Bradley Beach

Bradley Beach Historical Society • c/o Bradley Beach Library, 511 4th Ave • Bradley Beach, NJ 07720 • (732) 776-2995

Bradley Beach Public Library • 511 4th Ave • Bradley Beach, NJ 07720 • (732) 776-2995 • http://www.bradleybeachlibrary.org

Branchville

Wallpack Historical Society • Wallpack Center • Branchville, NJ 07890

Brick

Brick Township Historical Society • Havens Homestead, 521 Herbertsville Rd, P.O. Box 160 • Brick, NJ 08723 • (732) 785-2500

Bridgeton

Bridgeton Antiquarian League • 353 Roadstown-Greenwich Rd • Bridgeton, NJ 08302 • (856) 455-4100

Bridgeton Free Public Library • 150 E Commerce St • Bridgeton, NJ 08302-2684 • (856) 451-2620 • http://www.clueslibs.org

Nanticoke Lenni-Lenape Indians of New Jersey • 18 E Commerce St, P.O. Box 544 • Bridgeton, NJ 08302 • (609) 455-6910 • http://www.nanticoke-lenape.org

New Sweden Farmstead Museum • City Park, 50 E Broad St • Bridgeton, NJ 08302 • (856) 451-4551

Woodruff Museum of Indian Artifacts • 150 E Commerce St • Bridgeton, NJ 08302 • (856) 451-2620

Bridgewater

Somerset County Historical Society • Van Veghten House, 9 Van Veghten Dr • Bridgewater, NJ 08807-3259 • (908) 218-1281

Somerset County Library • 1 Vogt Dr, P.O. Box 6700 • Bridgewater, NJ 08807-0700 • (908) 426-4016 • http://www.somerset.lib.nj.us

Brielle

Brielle Public Library • 610 South St • Brielle, NJ 08730-1494 • (732) 528-9381 • http://www.cybercomm.net/~tensen/brielle

Union Landing Historical Society • P.O. Box 473 • Brielle, NJ 08730 • (732) 528-5550

Brigantine

Brigantine Historical Society • Historical Museum, 3607 Atlantic Brigantine Blvd, P.O. Box 833 • Brigantine, NJ 08203 • (609) 266-3437 • http://www.brigantinebeachnj.com/history_museum.html

Brookside

Mendham Township Public Library • Cherry Ln, P.O. Box 500 • Brookside, NJ 07926 • (973) 543-4018

Buena

Buena Historical Society • P.O. Box 114 • Buena, NJ 08310 • (856) 692-5227

New Kuban Historical Museum • 228 Don Rd • Buena, NJ 08310 • (856) 697-2255

New Kuban Historical Society • 521 Weymoth Rd • Buena, NJ 08310 • (856) 697-2255

Burlington

Burlington County Historical Society • Historical Museum, 451 High St • Burlington, NJ 08016 • (609) 386-4773 • http://www.burlingtoncountyhistoricalsociety.org

Burlington Library Company • 23 W Union St • Burlington, NJ 08016 • (609) 386-1273

City of Burlington Historical Society • Historical Museum, 437 High St • Burlington, NJ 08016 • (609) 386-0200 • http://www.tourburlington.org

Colonial Burlington Foundation • Historical Museum, 213 Wood St, P.O. Box 1552 • Burlington, NJ 08016 • (609) 239-2266

Delia Biddle Pugh Library • 451 High St • Burlington, NJ 08016 • (609) 386-4773

Oliver Cromwell Black History Society • 348 High St • Burlington, NJ 08016 • (609) 387-8133

Butler

Butler Museum and Historical Committee • Historical Museum, 1 Ace Rd • Butler, NJ 07405 • (973) 838-7222

Caldwell

Caldwell Public Library • 268 Bloomfield Ave • Caldwell, NJ 07006-5198 • (973) 226-2837 • http://www.caldwellpl.org

Grover Cleveland Birthplace Museum • 207 Bloomfield Ave • Caldwell, NJ 07006 • (973) 226-0001 • http://www.westessexguide.com

Jennings Library • Caldwell College, 9 Ryerson Ave • Caldwell, NJ 07006-6195 • (973) 618-3312 • http://jenningslibrary.caldwell.edu

Califon

Califon Historical Society • Old Stone Railroad Station, 25 Academy St, P.O. Box 424 • Califon, NJ 07830 • (908) 832-2941

Camden

Battleship New Jersey Museum • 62 Battleship Pl • Camden, NJ 08103 • (856) 966-1652 • http://www.battleshipnewjersey.org

Camden County Historical Society • Pomona Hall Museum, 1900 Park Blvd, P.O. Box 378 • Camden, NJ 08108-0378 • (856) 964-3333 • http://www.cchsnj.com

Camden Free Public Library • 852 Ferry Ave • Camden, NJ 08104 • (856) 757-7640 • http://www.camdencountylibrary.org

Campbell Museum • Campbell Pl • Camden, NJ 08103 • (609) 342-6440

Fairview Historic Society • 3081 Fenwick Rd • Camden, NJ 08104-2706 • (856) 966-9899

Walt Whitman House Museum • 328 Mickle Blvd • Camden, NJ 08103 • (856) 964-5383 • http://www.ci.camden.nj.us

Cape May

Cape May Historic District Commission • 643 Washington St • Cape May, NJ 08204 • (609) 884-8411

Cape May Historical and Genealogical Society • John Holmes House, 504 Route 9 N, P.O. Box 495 • Cape May, NJ 08204 • (609) 465-3535 • http://www.cmcmuseum.org

Greater Cape May Historical Society • Colonial House Museum, 643 1/2 Washington Blvd, P.O. Box 495 • Cape May, NJ 08204 • (609) 884-9100 • http://www.capemayhistory.org

Historic Cold Spring Village Museum • 720 Rte 9 S • Cape May, NJ 08204 • (609) 898-2300 • http://www.hcsv.org

Mid-Atlantic Center for the Arts/Cape May Lighthouse Museum • 1048 Washington St, P.O. Box 340 • Cape May, NJ 08204-0340 • (609) 884-5404 • http://www.capemaymac.org

Cape May Court House

Cape May County Historical and Genealogical Society • Historical Museum, 504 Route 9 • Cape May Court House, NJ 08210 • (609) 465-3535 • http://www.cmcmuseum.org

Cape May County Public Library • 30 W Mechanic St • Cape May Court House, NJ 08210 • (609) 463-6352 • http://www.cape-may.county.lib.nj.us

Carlstadt

Carlstadt Historical Society • Firehouse Museum, 6th St • Carlstadt, NJ 07072 • (201) 933-1070 • http://www.carlstadtnj.us/historical.html

William E Dermody Free Public Library • 420 Hackensack St • Carlstadt, NJ 07072 • (201) 438-8866 • http://www.bccls.org

Cedar Grove

Cedar Grove Historical Society • Historical Museum, 903 Pompton Ave, P.O. Box 461 • Cedar Grove, NJ 07009 • (973) 239-5414 • http://www.cedargrvenj.org/historical.htm

Cedarville

Lawrence Township Historical Society • 177 Main St • Cedarville, NJ 08311 • (856) 447-1810

Chatham

Chatham Township Historical Society • 24 Southern Blvd, P.O. Box 682 • Chatham, NJ 07928 • (973) 635-4911

Joint Free Public Library of the Chathams • 214 Main St • Chatham, NJ 07928 • (973) 635-0603 • http://www.chatham-nj.org

Cherry Hill

Cherry Hill Public Library • 1100 Kings Hwy N • Cherry Hill, NJ 08034-1911 • (856) 667-0300 • http://www.cherryhill.lib.nj.us

Garden State Discovery Museum • 16 N Springdale Rd • Cherry Hill, NJ 08003 • (856) 424-1233 • http://www.discoverymuseum.com

Grand Lodge of New Jersey, Sons of Italy • 510 Marlboro Ave • Cherry Hill, NJ 08002 • http://www.njsonsofitaly.com

Holocaust Awareness Museum • 1301 Springdale Rd • Cherry Hill, NJ 08003 • (609) 751-9500

Chester

Chester Historical Society • 245 W Main St, P.O. Box 376 • Chester, NJ 07930 • (973) 879-2761

Clark

Clark Historical Society • Dr William Robinson Plantation, 593 Madison Hill Rd • Clark, NJ 07066 • (732) 340-1571

Clark Public Library • 303 Westfield Ave • Clark, NJ 07066 • (732) 388-5999 • http://www.clarklibrary.org

Clifton

Clifton Public Library • 292 Piaget Ave • Clifton, NJ 07011 • (973) 772-5500

Hamilton-Van Wagoner House Museum • 971 Valley Rd • Clifton, NJ 07013 • (973) 744-5707

Clinton

Grandin Library Association • 6 Leigh St • Clinton, NJ 08809 • (908) 735-4812

Red Mill Museum • 56 Main St, P.O. Box 5005 • Clinton, NJ 08809 • (908) 735-4101 • http://www.theredmill.org

Closter

Closter Free Public Library • 280 High St • Closter, NJ 07624-1898 • (201) 768-4197 • http://www.bccls.org/closter

Closter Historical Society • 68 Taylor Dr • Closter, NJ 07624 • (201) 767-7974 • http://www.closterboro.com/organizations/organizations.shtml

Collingswood
Collingswood Free Public Library • 771 Haddon Ave • Collingswood, NJ 08108-3714 • (856) 858-0649

Colts Neck
Colts Neck Historical Society • 16 Crusius Pl, P.O. Box 101 • Colts Neck, NJ 07722 • (732) 462-1378

Columbus
Mansfield Township Historical Society • Historical Museum, 4 Fitzgerald Lane • Columbus, NJ 08022 • (609) 298-4174

Convent Station
Morris Area Genealogy Society • P.O. Box 105, Convent Sta • Convent Station, NJ 07961

Cranbury
Cranbury Historical and Preservation Society • Historical Museum, 4 Park Place E, P.O. Box 77 • Cranbury, NJ 08512 • (609) 860-1889

Cranbury Public Library • 23 N Main St • Cranbury, NJ 08512 • (609) 655-0555 • http://www.cranburypubliclibrary.org

Cranford
Cranford Free Public Library • 224 Walnut Ave, P.O. Box 400 • Cranford, NJ 07016-0400 • (908) 709-7272 • http://cranford.com/library

Cranford Historical Society • Hanson House Museum, 38 Springfield Ave • Cranford, NJ 07016 • (908) 276-0082 • http://cranfordhistoricalsociety.org

Crosswicks
Chesterfield Township Historical Society • P.O. Box 86 • Crosswicks, NJ 08515

Crosswicks Public Library • 483 Main St • Crosswicks, NJ 08515 • (609) 298-6271 • http://www.burlingtoncounty.com

Denville
Denville Historical Society • Diamond Spring Rd, P.O. Box 466 • Denville, NJ 07834-0466 • (973) 625-1165

Deptford
James H Johnson Memorial Library • 670 Ward Dr • Deptford, NJ 08096 • (856) 848-9149

Dorothy
Weymouth Township Historical Museum • 45 S Jersey Ave • Dorothy, NJ 08317 • (609) 476-2633 • http://www.weymouthnj.org/weymouth_museum.htm

Dover
Dover Area Historical Society • Rockaway Boro Plaza, P.O. Box 609 • Dover, NJ 07801 • (973) 366-0786

Ferromonte Historical Society • 11 Hillside Ave, Mine Hill • Dover, NJ 07801 • (973) 361-8813

Historical Society of Rockaways • Faesch House, Mount Hope Rd • Dover, NJ 07801 • (973) 366-6730

Lake Hopatcong Historical Society • 211 Park Heights Ave • Dover, NJ 07801 • (973) 366-2103

Dumont
Old Schralenburgh Historical Society • 43 Overlook Rd • Dumont, NJ 07628

Dunellen
Dunellen Historical Society • 322 Whittier Ave • Dunellen, NJ 08812

East Brunswick
East Brunswick Historical Association • 43 Sullivan Wy • East Brunswick, NJ 08816 • (732) 249-3522

East Brunswick Museum • 16 Maple St, P.O. Box 875 • East Brunswick, NJ 08816 • (973) 257-1508

East Brunswick Public Library • 2 Jean Walling Civic Center • East Brunswick, NJ 08816-3599 • (732) 390-6767 • http://www.ebpl.org

New Jersey Graveyard Preservation Society • P.O. Box 5 • East Brunswick, NJ 08816

East Hanover
East Hanover Historical Society • 181 Mount Pleasant Ave • East Hanover, NJ 07936 • (973) 884-0038

East Orange
East Orange Public Library • 21 S Arlington Ave • East Orange, NJ 07018-3892 • (973) 266-7049 • http://www.eopl.org

Eatontown
Eatontown Historical Committee • 25 Cloverdale Ave, P.O. Box 109 • Eatontown, NJ 07724 • (732) 542-5445

Edison
Edison Township Free Public Library • 340 Plainfield Ave • Edison, NJ 08817 • (732) 287-2298 • http://www.lmxac.org/edisonlib

Edison Township Historical Society • 328 Plainfield Ave • Edison, NJ 08817 • (732) 248-7310

Metuchen-Edison Genealogy Club • 48 Elliot Pl • Edison, NJ 08817

Egg Harbor City
Egg Harbor City Historical Society • Roundhouse Museum, 533 London Ave • Egg Harbor City, NJ 08215-1565 • (609) 965-9073 • http://www.ehchs.org

Greater Egg Harbour Township Historical Society • 3515 Bargaintown Rd • Egg Harbor Township, NJ 08234 • http://www.eht.com/history/

Elizabeth
Boxwood Hall Museum • 1073 E Jersey St • Elizabeth, NJ 07201 • (908) 282-7617

Computer Center for Jewish Genealogy • 654 Westfield Ave • Elizabeth, NJ 07208 • (908) 353-5575

Elizabeth Public Library • 11 S Broad St • Elizabeth, NJ 07202 • (908) 354-6060 • http://www.njpublib.org

Elizabethtown Heritage Society • 500 N Broad St • Elizabeth, NJ 07207 • (973) 558-3044

Elizabethtown Historical Foundation • 24 52 Rahway Ave, P.O. Box 1 • Elizabeth, NJ 07201 • (908) 558-2550

Union County Division of Cultural and Heritage Affairs • 633 Pearl St • Elizabeth, NJ 07202 • (908) 558-2550

Union County Historical Society • 1045 E Jersey St • Elizabeth, NJ 07201 • (908) 353-1511

Elmwood Park
Elmwood Park Historical Society • 210 Lee St • Elmwood Park, NJ 07407 • (201) 797-2109

Emerson
Paramus Historical and Preservation Society • 27 Sullivan Dr • Emerson, NJ 07630 • (201) 262-8711 • http://maple.nis.net/~wardell/BCAssoc.htm

Englewood
Englewood Historical Society • 500 Liberty Rd • Englewood, NJ 07631 • (201) 568-0678

Englewood Public Library • 31 Engle St • Englewood, NJ 07631 • (201) 568-2215 • http://www.englewoodlibrary.org

Englishtown
Battleground Historical Society • Village Inn Museum, 2 Water St • Englishtown, NJ 07726 • (732) 462-4947

Monroe Area Historical Society • Dey Grove Rd, RD2, Box 60B • Englishtown, NJ 07726

Essex Fells

Essex Fells Historical Society • 96 Forest Wy • Essex Fells, NJ 07021

Roseland Historical Society • 36 Buttonwood Rd • Essex Fells, NJ 07021 • (973) 226-2708

Estell Manor

Estell Manor Historical Society • 134 Cape May Ave, P.O. Box 72 • Estell Manor, NJ 08319-0072 • (609) 476-1100

Ewing

Ewing Township Historical Preservation Society • 27 Federal City Rd • Ewing, NJ 08638 • (609) 883-2455 • http://www.ethps.org

Roscoe L West Library • The College of New Jersey, 2000 Pennington Rd, P.O. Box 7718 • Ewing, NJ 08628-0718 • (609) 771-2417 • http://www.tcnj.edu/~library

Fair Haven

Fair Haven Historical Society • 142 Lexington Ave, P.O. Box 72 • Fair Haven, NJ 07701 • (732) 842-4453

Fairfield

Fairfield Hitstoric Committee • Town Hall, 230 Fairfield Rd • Fairfield, NJ 07004 • (973) 882-8399

Fanwood

Fanwood Memorial Library • 14 Tillotson Rd • Fanwood, NJ 07023-1399 • (908) 332-6400 • http://www.lmxac.org/fanwood

Farmingdale

Farmingdale Historical Society • 2 Goodenough Rd • Farmingdale, NJ 07727 • (732) 938-2009

Flanders

Mount Olive Public Library • 202 Flanders-Drakestown Rd • Flanders, NJ 07836 • (973) 691-8686 • http://www.mopl.org

Flemington

Fleming Castle Museum • 5 Bonnell St • Flemington, NJ 08822 • (908) 872-4607 • http://www.flemingcastle.com

Hunterdon County Cultural and Heritage Commission • 3 Chorister Pl, P.O. Box 2900 • Flemington, NJ 08822-2900 • (908) 788-1256

Hunterdon County Historical Society • Doric House Museum, 114 Main St • Flemington, NJ 08822 • (908) 782-1091 • http://hunterdonhistory.org

Hunterdon County Library • 314 State Hwy 12 • Flemington, NJ 08822 • (908) 788-1444 • http://www.hunterdon.lib.nj.us

Florence

Florence Historical Society • 35 W 5th Str • Florence, NJ 08518

Florham Park

Historical Society of Florham Park • P.O. Box 193 • Florham Park, NJ 07932 • (973) 377-6291

Forked River

Lacey Township Historical Society • Historical Museum, 126 S Main St, Route 9, P.O. Box 412 • Forked River, NJ 08731 • (609) 971-0467

Fort Dix

Fort Dix Museum • AFZT-GCM • Fort Dix, NJ 08640 • (609) 562-6983

Fort Hancock

Fort Hancock Museum • Sandy Hook Unit, Gateway Natl Rec Area, P.O. Box 530 • Fort Hancock, NJ 07732 • (732) 872-5970

Fort Lee

Fort Lee Historic Park Museum • Hudson Terr • Fort Lee, NJ 07024 • (201) 461-1776 • http://www.njpalisades.org

Fort Lee Historical Society • Borough Hall, 309 Main St • Fort Lee, NJ 07024 • (201) 592-3580

Fortescue

Fortescue Historical Society • Pier 1 Bayside • Fortescue, NJ 08321

Franklin Park

Franklin Township Historical Society • 84 Hillview Ave • Franklin Park, NJ 08823 • (973) 297-2641

Freehold

Freehold Public Library • 28 1/2 E Main St • Freehold, NJ 07728-2202 • (732) 462-5135

Monmouth County Genealogical Club • 70 Court St • Freehold, NJ 07728 • (732) 462-1466 • http://nj5.injersey.com/kjshelly/mcgc.html

Monmouth County Historical Association • Historical Museum, 70 Court St • Freehold, NJ 07728 • (732) 462-1466 • http://www.monmouthhistory.org

Frenchtown

Alexandria Township Historical Society • 174 Warsaw Rd • Frenchtown, NJ 08825

Frenchtown Historical Association • Borough Hall, 2nd St • Frenchtown, NJ 08825

Oak Summit School Historical Society • 190 Oak Summit Rd • Frenchtown, NJ 08825 • (908) 996-4633

Galloway Township

Galloway Township Historical Society • Historical Museum, 300 E Jimmie Leeds Rd • Galloway Township, NJ 08201 • (609) 652-3049

Garfield

Garfield Free Public Library • 500 Midland Ave • Garfield, NJ 07026 • (973) 478-3800 • http://www.bccls.org/garfield

Garwood

Garwood Free Public Library • 223 Walnut St • Garwood, NJ 07027 • (908) 789-1670

Gibbstown

Gloucester County Cultural and Heritage Commission • 406 Swedesboro Rd • Gibbstown, NJ 08027 • (856) 423-0916

Glassboro

Glassboro Public Library • 2 Center St • Glassboro, NJ 08028-1995

Keith & Shirley Campbell Library • Rowan University, 201 Mullica Hill Rd • Glassboro, NJ 08028-0701 • (856) 256-4800 • http://www.rowan.edu/library

Savitz Library • Glassboro State College • Glassboro, NJ 08028 • (856) 863-6303

Glen Ridge

Glen Ridge Free Public Library • 240 Ridgewood Ave • Glen Ridge, NJ 07028 • (973) 748-5482 • http://www.glenridgenj.org/library.htm

Glen Ridge Historical Society • Glen Ridge Congregational Church, P.O. Box 164 • Glen Ridge, NJ 07028 • (973) 748-1784

Glen Rock

Glen Rock Historical and Preservation Society • Municipal Bldg, Borough Hall • Glen Rock, NJ 07452 • (201) 447-2414

Glen Rock Historical Society • 176 Rock Rd • Glen Rock, NJ 07452 • (201) 445-1322

Gloucester City

Gloucester City Historical Society • 34 N King St • Gloucester City, NJ 08030 • (856) 456-3487

Great Meadows

Allamuchy Township Historical Society • RD1, Box 111 • Great Meadows, NJ 07838

New Jersey

Greenwich
Cumberland County Historical Society • Pirate House Museum, 981 YeGreate St, P.O. Box 16 • Greenwich, NJ 08323 • (856) 455-8580 • http://www.cchistsoc.org

John Dubois Maritime Museum • 949 Ye Greate St • Greenwich, NJ 08323 • (856) 455-1774

Hackensack
Bergen County Office of Cultural and Historic Afffairs Library • 21 Main St • Hackensack, NJ 07601 • (201) 646-2786

Johnson Free Public Library • 274 Main St • Hackensack, NJ 07601-5797 • (201) 343-4169 • http://www.bccls.org/hackensack

New Jersey Naval Museum • 78 River St, P.O. Box 395 • Hackensack, NJ 07601 • (201) 342-3268 • http://www.njnm.com

Hackettstown
Hackettstown Free Public Library • 110 Church St • Hackettstown, NJ 07840 • (908) 852-4936 • http://www.goes.com/hfplinfo

Hackettstown Historical Society • Historical Museum, 106 Church St • Hackettstown, NJ 07840-2206 • (908) 852-8797

Taylor Memorial Library • Centenary College, 400 Jefferson St • Hackettstown, NJ 07840 • (908) 852-1400 • http://www.students.centenarycollege.edu

Haddon Heights
Haddon Heights Historical Society • c/o Haddon Heights Public Library, 608 Station Ave • Haddon Heights, NJ 08035 • (856) 547-7132

Haddon Heights Public Library • 608 Station Ave, P.O. Box 240 • Haddon Heights, NJ 08035-0240 • (856) 547-7132 • http://www.haddonheights.lib.nj.us

Haddon Township
Camden County Cultural and Heritage Commission • Hopkins House, 240 S Park Dr • Haddon Township, NJ 08057 • (856) 858-0040 • http://arts.camden.lib.nj.us

Haddonfield
Haddonfield Preservation Society • 120 Warwick Rd, P.O. Box 196 • Haddonfield, NJ 08033 • (856) 429-5486

Haddonfield Public Library • 60 Haddon Ave • Haddonfield, NJ 08033-2422 • (856) 429-1304 • http://www.haddonfield.camden.lib.nj.us

Historical Society of Haddonfield • Historical Museum, 343 King's Hwy E • Haddonfield, NJ 08033-1214 • (856) 429-7375 • http://www.historicalsocietyofhaddonfield.org

Indian King Tavern Museum • 233 Kings Hwy E • Haddonfield, NJ 08033 • (856) 429-6792 • http://www.indiankingtavern.com

Haledon
American Labor Museum • Botto House, 83 Norwood St • Haledon, NJ 07508 • (973) 595-7953 • http://www.labormuseum.net

Hamilton
Central Jersey Genealogical Club • P.O. Box 9903 • Hamilton, NJ 08650-1903 • (609) 587-6012 • http://www.rootsweb.com/~njcjgc/

Hamilton Township Historical Society • Historical Museum, 2200 Kuser Rd • Hamilton, NJ 08620 • (609) 585-1686

Hamilton Township Public Library • 1 Municipal Dr • Hamilton, NJ 08619-3895 • (609) 581-4060 • http://www.hamiltonpl.org

Kuser Farm Mansion Museum • 390 Newkirk Ave • Hamilton, NJ 08610 • (609) 890-3630 • http://www.hamiltonnj.com

Hammonton
Batsto Village Museum • 4110 Nesco Rd • Hammonton, NJ 08037 • (609) 561-0024 • http://www.batsovillage.org

Hammonton Historical Society • 230 Vine St • Hammonton, NJ 08037 • (609) 561-2830 • http://www.historicalsocietyofhammonton.org

Hampton
Lebanon Township Museum at New Hampton • 57 Musconetcong River Rd • Hampton, NJ 08827 • (908) 537-6464

Hancock's Bridge
Hancock House Museum • 3 Front St, P.O. Box 139 • Hancock's Bridge, NJ 08038 • (856) 935-4373 • http://www.nj.us/dep/forestry/histsite.htm

Harrington Park
Harrington Park Historical Society • 10 Herring St • Harrington Park, NJ 07640 • (201) 768-5675

Hasbrouck Heights
Hasbrouck Heights Free Public Library • 301 Division Ave • Hasbrouck Heights, NJ 07604 • (201) 288-0488 • http://www.bccls.org/hasbrouck

Haworth
Haworth Municipal Library • 300 Haworth Ave • Haworth, NJ 07641 • (201) 384-1020 • http://www.bccls.org/haworth

Hawthorne
Hawthorne Public Library • 345 Lafayette Ave • Hawthorne, NJ 07506-2599 • (973) 427-5745 • http://www.bccls.org/hawthorne

Hazlet
Hazlet Township Historical Society • Municipal Offices, 319 Middle Rd • Hazlet, NJ 07730

Helmetta
Helmetta Historical Society • 60 Main St • Helmetta, NJ 08828 • (732) 521-2402

Hibernia
Historical Society of the Rockaways • P.O. Box 100 • Hibernia, NJ 07842 • (973) 366-6730

High Bridge
Solitude House Museum • 7 River Rd • High Bridge, NJ 08829 • (908) 638-3200 • http://www.highbridge.org/heritage.html

Highland Lakes
Vernon Township Historical Society • Historical Museum, 173 Barrett Rd • Highland Lakes, NJ 07422 • (973) 764-8554

Highland Park
Highland Park Historical Commission • P.O. Box 1330 • Highland Park, NJ 08904 • (732) 572-3400

Highlands
Atlantic Highlands Historical Society • 27 Prospect St • Highlands, NJ 07732 • (732) 291-1861

Historical Society of Highlands • P.O. Box 13 • Highlands, NJ 07732 • (732) 291-4956

Sandy Hook Museum • Gateway NRA, P.O. Box 437 • Highlands, NJ 07732 • (732) 872-0115

Twin Lights Historical Site Museum • 2 Lighthouse Rd • Highlands, NJ 07732 • (732) 872-1814 • http://www.twin-lights.org

Hightstown
Hightstown-East Windsor Historical Society • 164 N Main St • Hightstown, NJ 08520 • (609) 371-9580

Hillsborough
Hillsborough Township Historic Commission • 379 S Branch Rd • Hillsborough, NJ 08853 • (908) 369-4313

Hillside
Hillside Historical Society • 111 Conant St • Hillside, NJ 07205 • (908) 353-8828

Hoboken

Hoboken Historical Museum • 1301 Hudson St, P.O. Box 3296 • Hoboken, NJ 07030 • (201) 656-2240 • http://www.hobokenmuseum.org

Hoboken Public Library • 500 Park Ave • Hoboken, NJ 07030 • (201) 420-2346 • http://www.bccls.org/hoboken

Ho-Ho-Kus

Friends of the Hermitage • Hermitage Museum, 335 N Franklin Tpk • Ho-Ho-Kus, NJ 07423 • (201) 445-8311 • http://www.thehermitage.org

Holmdel

Holmdel Historical Society • Stilwell Rd, P.O. Box 282 • Holmdel, NJ 07733 • (732) 946-8618

Longstreet Farm Museum • Holmdel Park • Holmdel, NJ 07733 • (732) 946-3758 • http://www.monmouthcountyparks.com

Monmouth County Library-Holmdel Branch • 4 Crawfords Corner Rd • Holmdel, NJ 07733 • (732) 946-4118

Vietnam Era Educational Center • 1 Memorial Ln, P.O. Box 648 • Holmdel, NJ 07733 • (800) 648-8387 • http://www.njvvmf.org

Hope

Hope Historical Society • Historical Museum, High St, Route 519, P.O. Box 52 • Hope, NJ 07844 • (908) 637-4120

Hopewell

Hopewell Museum • 28 E Broad St • Hopewell, NJ 08525 • (609) 466-0103

Hopewell Public Library • 13 E Broad St • Hopewell, NJ 08525 • (609) 466-1625

Swan Historical Foundation • 355 Washington Crossing Pennington Rd • Hopewell, NJ 08525 • (609) 737-0746

Howell

Howell Historical Society • Historical Museum, 427 Lakewood-Farmingdale Rd • Howell, NJ 07731 • (732) 938-2212 • http://www.howellnj.com/historic/

Kuban Cossacks Association • Library & Museum, 47-49 E 3rd St • Howell, NJ 07731 • (732) 367-0088 • http://www.kubancossackviosko.com

Monmouth County Library-Howell Branch • 318 Old Tavern Rd • Howell, NJ 07731 • (732) 938-2300

Hurffville

Margaret E Heggan Free Public Library • 208 E Holly Ave • Hurffville, NJ 08080 • (856) 589-3334 • http://www.hegganlibrary.org

Ironia

Historical Society of Old Randolph • P.O. Box 1776 • Ironia, NJ 07845 • (973) 989-7095

Irvington

Cherokee Nation of New Jersey • 1164 Stuyvesant Ave • Irvington, NJ 07111 • (973) 351-1210

Irvington Historical Society • 34 Clinton Terr • Irvington, NJ 07111-1417 • (973) 374-7500

Irvington Public Library • Civic Square • Irvington, NJ 07111-2498 • (973) 372-6400 • http://www.irvingtonpubliclibrary.org

Island Heights

Island Heights Cultural and Heritage Association • P.O. Box 670 • Island Heights, NJ 08732 • (732) 929-0695

Jamesburg

Jamesburg Historical Association • 203 Buckelew Ave • Jamesburg, NJ 08831 • (732) 521-2040

Monroe Township Public Library • 4 Municipal Plaza • Jamesburg, NJ 08831 • (732) 521-5000

Jersey City

Afro-American Historical and Genealogical Society of New Jersey • Historical Museum, 1841 Kennedy Blvd • Jersey City, NJ 07305-2106 • (201) 547-5262

Billie Holiday NYC Landmark Society • 620 Pavonia Ave • Jersey City, NJ 07306 • (201) 533-0014

Historic Paulus Hook Association • 66 Sussex St • Jersey City, NJ 07302 • (201) 333-6048

Jersey City Public Library • 472 Jersey Ave • Jersey City, NJ 07302-3499 • (201) 547-4500 • http://www.jclibrary.org

Theresa & Edward O'Toole Library • Saint Peter's College, 99 Glenwood Ave • Jersey City, NJ 07306 • (201) 915-9392 • http://library.spc.edu

Johnsonburg

Frelinghuysen Township Historical Society • P.O. Box 411 • Johnsonburg, NJ 07846 • (908) 852-7362

Kearny

Kearney Public Library • 318 Kearney Ave • Kearny, NJ 07032 • (201) 998-2666 • http://www.kearnylibrary.org

Kearny Museum • 318 Kearny Ave • Kearny, NJ 07032 • (201) 997-6911

Kenilworth

Kenilworth Historical Society • 567 Kenilworth Blvd • Kenilworth, NJ 07033 • (908) 276-8449

Keyport

Imperial German Military Collector's Association • 82 Atlantic St • Keyport, NJ 07735-1857 • (732) 739-1799

Keyport Free Public Library • 109 Broad St • Keyport, NJ 07735-1202 • (732) 264-0543

Keyport Historical Society • Steamboat Dock Museum, 2 Broad St, P.O. Box 312 • Keyport, NJ 07735 • (732) 739-6390

Kingston

Rockingham House Museum • P.O. Box 496 • Kingston, NJ 08528 • (609) 921-8835 • http://www.rockingham.net

Kinnelon

Kinnelon Historical Commission • 25 Kiel Ave • Kinnelon, NJ 07405 • (973) 838-0185

Kinnelon Public Library • 132 Kinnelon Rd • Kinnelon, NJ 07405-2393 • (973) 838-1321 • http://www.kinnelonlibrary.org

Lake Hopatcong

Lake Hopatcong Historical Museum • State Park, P.O. Box 668 • Lake Hopatcong, NJ 07850 • (973) 398-2616 • http://www.hopatcong.org/museum

Lakehurst

Boro of Lakehurst Historical Society • 505 Oak St • Lakehurst, NJ 08733 • (732) 657-8864

Lakewood

Descendants of Founders of New Jersey • 850-A Thornhill Ct • Lakewood, NJ 08701

Lambertville

Howell Living History Farm Museum • 70 Wooden's Ln • Lambertville, NJ 08560 • (609) 737-3299 • http://www.howellfarm.org

Lambertville Free Public Library • 6 Lilly St • Lambertville, NJ 08530-1805 • (609) 397-0275

Lambertville, cont.

Lambertville Historical Society • Historical Museum, 62 Bridge St, P.O. Box 2 • Lambertville, NJ 08530-2120 • (609) 397-0770 • http://www. lambertvillehistoricalsociety.org

My Italian Family • 59 S Main St • Lambertville, NJ 08530 • (888) 472-0171 • http://www.myitalianfamily.com

Landing

Lake Hopatcong Historical Society • Historical Museum, Hopatcong State Park • Landing, NJ 07850 • (973) 398-2616 • http://www. hopatcong.org/museum

Lawnside

Lawnside Historical Society • 26 Kings Ct, P.O. Box 608 • Lawnside, NJ 08045 • (856) 546-8850

Lawrenceville

Franklin F Moore Library • Rider University, 2083 Lawrenceville Rd • Lawrenceville, NJ 08648 • (609) 896-5115 • http://library.rider.edu

Koppelman Holocaust-Genocide Resource Center • Rider Univ, 2083 Lawrenceville Rd • Lawrenceville, NJ 08648-3099 • (609) 896-5345 • http://www.rider.edu/holctr

Lawrence Historical Society • P.O. Box 6025 • Lawrenceville, NJ 08648 • (609) 243-9108

Mercer County Library • 2751 Brunswick Pk • Lawrenceville, NJ 08648-4132 • (609) 989-6922 • http://www.mcl.org

Trenton Jewish Historical Society • 282 Glenn Ave • Lawrenceville, NJ 08648 • (609) 883-0251

Layton

Wallpack Historical Society • 4 Main St • Layton, NJ 07851 • (973) 948-6671

Lebanon

Tewksberry Historical Society • 6 Saw Mill Rd • Lebanon, NJ 08833 • (908) 832-2562

Leonardo

Middletown Township Historical Society • Macleod-Rice House Museum, Leonardville Rd • Leonardo, NJ 07737 • (732) 291-8739

Leonia

Leonia Historical Society • 199 Christie St • Leonia, NJ 07605 • (201) 947-5647

Leonia Public Library • 227 Fort Lee Rd • Leonia, NJ 07605 • (201) 592-5770 • http://www.leoniaboro.com/library

Lincoln Park

Beavertown Historical Society • 94 Beaver Brook Rd • Lincoln Park, NJ 07035 • (973) 694-0640

Lincoln Park Public Library • 12 Boonton Tpk • Lincoln Park, NJ 07035 • (973) 694-8283

Lincroft

Bankier Library • Brookdale Community College, 765 Newman Springs Rd • Lincroft, NJ 07738-1597 • (732) 224-2706 • http://library. brookdalecc.edu; http://holocaustbcc.org

Mid-Atlantic Association for Living Historical Farms • 805 Newman Springs Rd • Lincroft, NJ 07738

Monmouth County Genealogy Society • P.O. Box 5 • Lincroft, NJ 07738 • (732) 671-0593 • http://home.infi.net/~kjshelly/mcgs.html

Monmouth Museum • Brookdale Community College Campus, Newman Springs Rd, P.O. Box 359 • Lincroft, NJ 07738 • (732) 747-2266 • http://www.monmouthmuseum.org

Linden

Linden Free Public Library • 31 E Henry St • Linden, NJ 07036 • (908) 298-3830 • http://www.lindenpl.org

Linwood

Linwood Historical Society • 16 Poplar Ave • Linwood, NJ 08221 • (609) 927-8293 • http://www.linwoodnj.org

Linwood Public Library • 301 Davis Ave • Linwood, NJ 08221 • (609) 926-7991

Little Falls

Little Falls Free Public Library • 8 Warren St • Little Falls, NJ 07424 • (973) 256-2784 • http://www.palsplus.org/lfpl

Little Falls Historical Society • 19 Warren St, P.O. Box 1083 • Little Falls, NJ 07424 • (973) 256-3651

Little Silver

Little Silver Historical Society • Borough Hall, 480 Prospect Ave • Little Silver, NJ 07739 • (732) 842-2400

Livingston

Livingston Historical Society • S Livingston Ave, P.O. Box 220 • Livingston, NJ 07039

Ruth L Lockwood Memorial Library • 10 Robert H Harp Dr • Livingston, NJ 07039 • (973) 992-4600 • http://www.bccls.org/livingston

Lodi

Lodi Memorial Library • 1 Memorial Dr • Lodi, NJ 07644-1692 • (973) 365-4044 • http://www.bccls.org/lodi

Long Branch

Long Branch Free Public Library • 328 Broadway • Long Branch, NJ 07740 • (732) 222-3900 • http://www.lmxac.org/longbranch

Long Branch Historical Museum • c/o Saint James Episcopal Church, 1260 Ocean Ave • Long Branch, NJ 07740 • (732) 229-0600 • http://www.churchofthepresidents.org

Long Valley

Washington Township Historical Society • Historical Museum, 6 Fairview Ave, P.O. Box 189 • Long Valley, NJ 07853-0189 • (908) 876-4480

Longport

Longport Historical Society • Borough Hall, 2305 Atlantic Ave • Longport, NJ 08403-1103 • (609) 823-1115

Lumberton

Air Victory Museum • 68 Stacy Haines Rd • Lumberton, NJ 08048 • (609) 267-4488 • http://www.airvictorymuseum.org

Lumberton Historical Society • P.O. Box 22 • Lumberton, NJ 08048 • (609) 247-4067

Lyndhurst

Lyndhurst Free Public Library • 355 Valley Brook Ave • Lyndhurst, NJ 07071 • (201) 804-2478 • http://www.bccls.org/lyndhurst

Lyndhurst Historical Society • P.O. Box 135 • Lyndhurst, NJ 07071 • (201) 804-2513

Madison

Center for Holocaust Study • Drew Univ • Madison, NJ 07940 • (973) 408-3290 • http://www.depts.drew.edu/chs

Drew University Library • 36 Madison Ave • Madison, NJ 07940 • (973) 408-3661 • http://www.depts.drew.edu/lib/

Florham-Madison Campus Library • Fairleigh Dickinson Univ, 285 Madison Ave • Madison, NJ 07940 • (973) 443-8515 • http://alpha.fdu. edu/library/

Historical Society of the United Methodist Church • 36 Madison Ave, P.O. Box 127 • Madison, NJ 07940 • (973) 408-3189 • http://www. gcah.org

Madison Historical Society • c/o Madison Public Library, 39 Keep St, P.O. Box 148 • Madison, NJ 07940 • (973) 377-3924 • http://www. rosenet.org/nhs

Madison Public Library • 39 Keep St • Madison, NJ 07940 • (973) 377-0722 • http://www.rosenet.org/library/

Messler Library - New Jersey Room • Fairleigh Dickinson Univ • Madison, NJ 07940 • (973) 443-8515

Museum of Early Trades & Crafts • 9 Main St • Madison, NJ 07940 • (973) 377-2982 • http://www.metc.org

World Methodist Historical Society • 36 Madison Ave, P.O. Box 127 • Madison, NJ 07940-0127 • (973) 408-3189

Magnolia
Magnolia Historical Society • 208 Brooke Ave • Magnolia, NJ 08049 • (856) 783-8585

Mahwah
Mahwah Historical Society • 1871 Old Station Ln • Mahwah, NJ 07430 • (201) 891-9049

Ramapough Lenape Nation • 189 Stag Hill Rd • Mahwah, NJ 07430 • (201) 529-1171 • http://www.ramapoughlenapenation.org

Manahawkin
Ocean County Genealogical Society • 135 Nautilus Dr • Manahawkin, NJ 08058-2452

Stafford Township Historical Society • 87 Stafford Ave • Manahawkin, NJ 08050

Manalapan
Craig House Museum • Monmouth Battlefield State Park, 347 Freehold-Englishtown Rd • Manalapan, NJ 07726 • (732) 462-9616

Monmouth Battlefield State Park Museum • 347 Freehold-Englishtown Rd • Manalapan, NJ 07726 • (732) 462-9616

Monmouth County Archives • 125 Symmes Dr • Manalapan, NJ 07726 • (732) 308-3772 • http://www.visitmonmouth.com/archives

Monmouth County Library • 125 Symmes Dr • Manalapan, NJ 07726 • (732) 431-7220 • http://www.monmouth.lib.nj.us

Manasquan
Squan Village Historical Society • 105 South St, P.O. Box 262 • Manasquan, NJ 08736 • (732) 223-6770

Manhawkin
Ocean County Genealogical Society • 376B Lighthouse Dr • Manhawkin, NJ 08050-2327

Maple Shade
Maple Shade Historical Society • P.O. Box 368 • Maple Shade, NJ 08052 • (856) 779-7022

Maplewood
Judaica Society International • 16 Housman Ct • Maplewood, NJ 07040 • (973) 761-6642

Maplewood Memorial Library • 51 Baker St • Maplewood, NJ 07040-2618 • (973) 762-1622 • http://www.maplewoodlibrary.org

Morrow Memorial Church Library • 600 Ridgewood Rd • Maplewood, NJ 07040-1228 • (973) 763-7676 • http://www.morrowmem.org

Margate
Margate City Historical Society • 7 S Washington Ave • Margate, NJ 08402 • (609) 823-6546

Marlboro
Monmouth County Library-Marlboro Branch • 1 Library Ct • Marlboro, NJ 07746-1102 • (732) 536-9406

Marlton
Evesham Historical Society • 65 N Locust Ave, P.O. Box 199 • Marlton, NJ 08053 • (856) 988-0995

Marmora
Historical Preservation Society of Upper Township • 859 South Shore Rd, P.O. Box 659 • Marmora, NJ 08223 • (609) 628-3041

Matawan
Madison Township Historical Society • Thomas Warne Historical Museum, 4216 Route 516 • Matawan, NJ 07747 • (732) 566-2108 • http://www.thomas-warne-msueum.com

Matawan Historical Society • Burrowes Mansion Museum, 94 Main St, P.O. Box 41 • Matawan, NJ 07747-2630 • (732) 566-5605

Mauricetown
Maurice River Historical Society • P.O. Box 161 • Mauricetown, NJ 08329

Mauricetown Historical Society • 1229 Front St, P.O. Box 1 • Mauricetown, NJ 08329 • (856) 785-0457

Mays Landing
Atlantic County Cultural and Heritage Commission • 40 Farragut Ave • Mays Landing, NJ 08330 • (609) 625-2776

Atlantic County Library • 40 Farragut Ave • Mays Landing, NJ 08330-1750 • (609) 625-2776 • http://www.atlanticlibrary.org

Township of Hamilton Historical Society • 49 Mill St • Mays Landing, NJ 08330 • (609) 909-0272 • http://hamiltonhistorical.tripod.com

William Spangler Library • Atlantic Cape Community College, 5100 Blackhorse Pike • Mays Landing, NJ 08330 • (609) 343-4952 • http://www.atlantic.edu/library/library.html

Maywood
English Neighborhood Historical Society • 656 Elm St • Maywood, NJ 07607

Maywood Historical Committee • 652 Grant Ave • Maywood, NJ 07607 • (201) 843-1130

McGuire AFB
McGuire Air Force Base Library • 305 SVS/SVMG, 2603 Tuskegee Airmen Ave • McGuire AFB, NJ 08641-5016 • (609) 754-2346 • http://www.305services.com

Medford
Medford Historical Society • 275 Church Rd, P.O. Box 362 • Medford, NJ 08055 • (856) 835-2652

Mendham
John Ralston Historical Association • 313 Mendham Rd • Mendham, NJ 07945 • (973) 543-4347 • http://www.ralstonmuseum.org

Mendham Borough Library • 10 Hilltop Rd • Mendham, NJ 07945 • (973) 543-4152 • http://www.mbl.gti.net

Mendham Township
Mendham Township Library • Cherry Lane • Mendham Township, NJ 07926 • (973) 543-4018 • http://www.gti.net/main/ment/

Merchantville
Merchantville Historical Society • 1 W Maple Ave • Merchantville, NJ 08109 • (856) 665-1819

Merchantville School and Public Library • 130 S Centre St • Merchantville, NJ 08109-2201 • (856) 663-1091

Metuchen
Metuchen Public Library • 480 Middlesex Ave • Metuchen, NJ 08840 • (732) 632-8526 • http://www.lmxac.org

Metuchen-Edison Historical Society • P.O. Box 61 • Metuchen, NJ 08840 • (732) 906-0529

Middletown
Middletown Township Historical Society • P.O. Box 180 • Middletown, NJ 07748 • (732) 291-8739

New Jersey

Middletown, cont.
Middletown Township Public Library • 55 New Monmouth Rd • Middletown, NJ 07748 • (732) 671-3700 • http://www.middletown.lib.nj.us

Murray Farmhouse and Barn Museum • Oak Hill Rd, P.O. Box 36 • Middletown, NJ 07748 • (732) 842-5966

Sons of the American Revolution, New Jersey Society • 98 New Monmouth Rd • Middletown, NJ 07748 • (732) 671-1108 • http://www.njssar.org

Taylor Butler House Museum • 127 Kings Hwy • Middletown, NJ 07748 • (732) 671-0500

Midland Park
Bergen County Genealogical Society • P.O. Box 432 • Midland Park, NJ 07432 • (201) 444-4319

Midland Park Memorial Library • 250 Godwin Ave • Midland Park, NJ 07432 • (201) 444-2390 • http://www.bccls.org

Milford
Alexandria Township Historical Society • 110 Frenchtown Rd • Milford, NJ 08848 • (908) 996-4565

Volendam Windmill Museum • 231 Adamic Hill Rd • Milford, NJ 08848 • (908) 995-4365 • http://www.CharlieBrownsTreeFarm.com

Milltown
Eureka Fire Museum • 39 Washington Ave • Milltown, NJ 08850 • (732) 828-7207

Milltown Historical Society • 116 S Main St, P.O. Box 96 • Milltown, NJ 08850 • (908) 828-0458

Milltown Public Library • 20 W Church St • Milltown, NJ 08850 • (732) 247-2270 • http://www.lmxac.org/milltown

Millville
Millville Army Air Field Museum • 1 Leddon St, Millville Airport • Millville, NJ 08332 • (856) 327-2347 • http://www.p47millville.org

Millville Historical Society • 2nd & Main Sts • Millville, NJ 08332 • (856) 825-0789

Millville Public Library • 210 Buck St • Millville, NJ 08332 • (856) 825-7087 • http://www.cumberland.county.lib.nj.us

Milton
Jefferson Township Historical Society • Dover Milton Rd • Milton, NJ 07438

Monmouth Beach
Monmouth Beach Historical Society • 23 Navesink Dr • Monmouth Beach, NJ 07750 • (908) 222-2244

Monmouth Beach Library • 18 Willow Ave • Monmouth Beach, NJ 07750 • (732) 229-1187 • http://www.shore.co.monmouth.nj.us

Monmouth Junction
South Brunswick Public Library • 110 Kingston Ln • Monmouth Junction, NJ 08852 • (732) 329-4000 • http://www.lmxac.org/sobr

Monroe Township
Annuity Museum • 8 Talmadge Dr • Monroe Township, NJ 08831 • (800) 872-6684 • http://www.immediateannuities.com/museumofinsurance/

Montague
Montague Association for the Restoration of Community History • 320 River Rd, P.O. Box 1101 • Montague, NJ 07827 • (973) 293-3106

Montclair
Montclair Free Public Library • 50 S Fullerton Ave • Montclair, NJ 07042 • (973) 744-0500 • http://www.montlib.com

Montclair Historical Society • Historical Museum, 108 Orange Rd, P.O. Box 322 • Montclair, NJ 07042 • (973) 744-1796 • http://www.montclairhistorical.org

Montvale
Jewish Genealogical Society of Bergen County • 135 Chestnut Ridge Rd • Montvale, NJ 07645 • (201) 384-8851 • http://www.erosenbaum.netfirms.com/jgsbc

Montville
Montville Historical Society • Historical Museum, Taylor Town Rd, P.O. Box 510 • Montville, NJ 07045 • (973) 334-3665 • http://www.montville-township.org

Moorestown
Historical Society of Moorestown • Smith-Cadbury Mansion, 12 High St, P.O. Box 477 • Moorestown, NJ 08057 • (856) 253-0353 • http://www.moorestown.com/community/history/

Morris Plains
Stickley Museum at Craftsman Farms • 2352 Route 10 W • Morris Plains, NJ 07950 • (973) 540-0311 • http://www.stickleymuseum.org

Morristown
Canal Society of New Jersey • Waterloo Village Historical Museum, P.O. Box 737 • Morristown, NJ 07963-0737 • (973) 722-9556 • http://www.canalsocietynj.org

Fosterfields Living Historical Farm Museum • 73 Kaldena Rd • Morristown, NJ 07960 • (973) 326-7644 • http://www.morrisparks.net

Harding Township Historical Society • 1 Village Dr • Morristown, NJ 07960 • (973) 292-0161

Historic Speedwell • Historical Museum, 333 Speedwell Ave • Morristown, NJ 07960 • (973) 540-0211 • http://www.morrisparks.net

Historic Speedwell Museum • 333 Speedwell Ave • Morristown, NJ 07960 • (973) 285-6550 • http://www.speedwell.org

Irish-American Cultural Association • 1 Lackawanna Pl • Morristown, NJ 07960 • (973) 605-1991 • http://www.irishaci.org

Joint Free Public Library of Morristown and Morris Township • 1 Miller Rd • Morristown, NJ 07960 • (973) 538-6161 • http://www.jfpl.org

Macculloch Hall Historical Museum • 45 Macculloch Ave • Morristown, NJ 07960 • (973) 538-2404 • http://www.macullochhall.org

Mahoney Library • College of Saint Elizabeth, 2 Convent Rd • Morristown, NJ 07960-6989 • (973) 290-4237 • http://www.cse.edu

Morris Area New Jersey Jewish Genealogical Society • 21 Rolling Hill Dr • Morristown, NJ 07960 • (973) 829-0242

Morris County Heritage Commission • Morris County Courthouse, 300 Mendham Rd, P.O. Box 900 • Morristown, NJ 07960 • (973) 829-8117 • http://www.co.morris.nj.us/Heritage/

Morris County Historical Society • Acorn Hall House, 68 Morris Ave • Morristown, NJ 07960 • (973) 267-3465 • http://www.acornhall.org

Morris County Trust for Historic Preservation • Macculloch Hall Museum, 45-A Macculloch Ave • Morristown, NJ 07960 • (973) 538-2404 • http://www.machall.org

Morris Museum • 6 Normandy Heights Rd • Morristown, NJ 07960 • (973) 971-3700 • http://www.morrismuseum.org

Morristown National Historic Park Museum • 30 Washington Pl • Morristown, NJ 07960 • (973) 539-2016 • http://www.nps.gov/mon

Schuyler-Hamilton House Museum • 5 Olyphant Pl • Morristown, NJ 07928 • (973) 539-7502

Tri State Railway Historical Society • Maple Ave • Morristown, NJ 07960 • (973) 656-0707

Mount Holly

Burlington County Genealogy Club • Woodlane Rd, Route 2, Box 2449 • Mount Holly, NJ 08060-9765 • (609) 267-0881

Burlington County Library • 5 Pioneer Blvd • Mount Holly, NJ 08060 • (609) 267-9660

Historic Burlington County Prison Museum • 128 High St • Mount Holly, NJ 08060 • (609) 265-5068 • http://www.co.burlington.nj.us

John Woolman Memorial Museum • 99 Branch St • Mount Holly, NJ 08060 • (609) 267-3226 • http://www.woolmancentral.com

Mount Holly Historical Society • 23 Washington St, P.O. Box 4081 • Mount Holly, NJ 08060 • (609) 267-8844

Mount Holly Public Library • 307 High St • Mount Holly, NJ 08060 • (609) 267-7111

Old School House Museum • 35 Brainerd St • Mount Holly, NJ 08060 • (609) 267-6996 • http://colonialdamesnj.org

Westampton Historical Society • general delivery • Mount Holly, NJ 08060 • (609) 267-2641

Mount Laurel

Mount Laurel Historical Society • 314 Union Mill Rd • Mount Laurel, NJ 08054 • (609) 234-2108

Mount Tabor

Mount Tabor Historical Society • P.O. Box 137 • Mount Tabor, NJ 07878-0137 • (973) 625-8742

Mountainside

Mountainside Historical Society • c/o Mountainside Free Public Library, Constitution Plaza • Mountainside, NJ 07092 • (908) 233-0115

Mountainside Public Library • Constitution Plaza • Mountainside, NJ 07092 • (908) 233-0115 • http://www.mountainsidelibrary.org

Mountainville

Tewksbury Historical Society • Historical Museum, 60 Water St • Mountainville, NJ 08833 • (908) 832-6734 • http://www. tewksburyhistory.net

Mullica Hill

Harrison Township Historical Society • Main St, P.O. Box 4 • Mullica Hill, NJ 08062 • (856) 478-4949

Neptune

Cornish Heritage Society East • 5 Hampton Ct • Neptune, NJ 07753-5672 • (732) 776-5909

Neptune Public Library • 25 Neptune Rd • Neptune, NJ 07753-1125 • (732) 775-8241 • http://www.neptunepubliclibrary.org

Township of Neptune Historical Society • Historical Museum, 25 Neptune Blvd, P.O. Box 1125 • Neptune, NJ 07754-1125 • (732) 775-8241 • http://www.mon.edu/irs/library/melon/neptune/heptune.htm

Neshanic

Hillsborough Historical Society • P.O. Box 720 • Neshanic, NJ 08853 • (908) 369-3659

New Brunswick

American Hungarian Foundation • Historical Museum, 300 Sommerset, P.O. Box 1084 • New Brunswick, NJ 08903 • (732) 846-5777 • http://www.ahfoundation.org

Archibald Stevens Alexander Library • Rutgers University, 169 College Ave • New Brunswick, NJ 08901 • (732) 932-7006 • http://www.rutgers.edu

Buccleuch Mansion Museum • 200 College Ave • New Brunswick, NJ 08901 • (732) 745-5094

Dr Andrew T Udvardy Reference Library • 66 Plum St • New Brunswick, NJ 08902

Gardiner A Sage Theological Library • New Brunswick Theological Seminary, 21 Seminary Pl • New Brunswick, NJ 08901-1159 • (732) 247-5243 • http://www.nbts.edu

Genealogical Society of New Jersey • P.O. Box 1291 • New Brunswick, NJ 08903 • (732) 356-6920

Henry Guest House Museum • 58 Livingston Ave • New Brunswick, NJ 08901 • (732) 745-5108

Historical Society of the Reformed Church in America • c/o Gardiner A Sage Library, New Brunswick Theological Seminary, 21 Seminary Pl • New Brunswick, NJ 08901-1107 • (732) 246-1779

Jewish Historical Society of Central Jersey • 222 Livingston Ave • New Brunswick, NJ 08901 • (732) 249-4894 • http://www.jewishgen.org/jhscj/

Middlesex County Cultural & Heritage Commission • Historical Museum & Library, 703 Jersey Ave • New Brunswick, NJ 08901 • (732) 745-4489 • http://www.cultureheritage.org

Mongol-American Cultural Association • 50 Louis St • New Brunswick, NJ 08901 • (732) 297-1140

New Brunswick Free Public Library • 60 Livingston Ave • New Brunswick, NJ 08901 • (732) 745-5108 • http://www.lmxac.org/nbfpl

New Brunswick Historical Club • 278 George St • New Brunswick, NJ 08901 • (732) 247-1695

New Egypt

New Egypt Historical Society • 125 Evergreen Rd, P.O. Box 295 • New Egypt, NJ 08533 • (609) 758-8111

New Lisbon

Whitesbog Village Museum • P.O. Box 215 • New Lisbon, NJ 08064 • (609) 726-1191

New Milford

Campbell-Christie House Historical Society • Historical Museum, 530 James St • New Milford, NJ 07646

New Providence

New Providence Historical Society • Historical Museum, 1350 Springfield Ave • New Providence, NJ 07974 • (908) 665-1034

New Providence Memorial Library • 377 Elkwood Ave • New Providence, NJ 07974 • (908) 665-0311 • http://www.newprovidencelibrary.org

Saltbox House Museum • 1350 Springfield Ave • New Providence, NJ 07974 • (908) 665-1065

New Shrewsbury

New Shrewsbury Historical Society • Water St • New Shrewsbury, NJ 07724

New Vernon

Harding Township Historical Society • Historical Museum, Village & Millbrook Rds, P.O. Box 1776 • New Vernon, NJ 07976 • (973) 292-3661

Newark

George F Smith Library - Special Collections • Univ of Medicine and Dentistry of New Jersey Library, 30 12th St • Newark, NJ 07103-2754 • (973) 982-6293 • http://www3.umdnj.edu/~libcwis/univlibs.html

New Jersey Historical Society • Historical Museum, 52 Park Pl • Newark, NJ 07102 • (973) 596-8500 • http://www.jerseyhistory.org

Newark Landmark and Historic Preservation • general delivery • Newark, NJ 07101 • (973) 733-4828

Newark Museum • 49 Washington St, P.O. Box 540 • Newark, NJ 07101 • (973) 596-6625 • http://www.newarkmuseum.org

Newark Preservation and Landmarks Committee • 868 Broad St, P.O. Box 1066 • Newark, NJ 07102 • (201) 622-4910

Newark, cont.
Newark Public Library • 5 Washington St, P.O. Box 630 • Newark, NJ 07101-0630 • (973) 733-7793 • http://www.npl.org

Newfield
Matchbox Road Museum • 17 Pearl St • Newfield, NJ 08344 • (856) 697-6900 • http://www.mbroad.com

Newfield Historical Society • 107 North East Blvd • Newfield, NJ 08344 • (856) 697-3811

Newton
Newton Fire Department Museum • 150 Spring St • Newton, NJ 07860 • (973) 383-0396

Sussex County Historical Society • Historical Museum, 82 Main St, P.O. Box 913 • Newton, NJ 07860 • (973) 383-6010 • http://www.sussexcountyhistory.com

Sussex County Library System • 125 Morris Turnpike • Newton, NJ 07860-0076 • (973) 948-3660 • http://www.sussexcountylibrary.org

Sussex County Library System-Dennis Library • 101 Main St • Newton, NJ 07860 • (973) 383-4810 • http://www.sussexcountylibrary.org

North Arlington
North Arlington Free Public Library • 210 Ridge Rd • North Arlington, NJ 07031 • (201) 955-5641 • http://www.bccls.org/northarlington

North Arlington Historical Society • 89 Canterbury Ave • North Arlington, NJ 07032 • (201) 998-6290

North Bergen
North Bergen Free Public Library • 8411 Bergenline Ave • North Bergen, NJ 07047-5097 • (201) 869-4715 • http://www.northbergenpubliclibrary.org

North Brunswick
New Jersey Museum of Agriculture • College Rd & Route 1, P.O. Box 780 • North Brunswick, NJ 08902 • (732) 249-2077 • http://www.agriculturemuseum.org

North Brunswick Historical Society • 690 Cranbury Crossroad • North Brunswick, NJ 08902

North Caldwell
North Caldwell Historical Society • 120 Grandview Ave • North Caldwell, NJ 07006 • (973) 228-7257

North Plainfield
Blue Hills Historical Society • 311 West End Ave • North Plainfield, NJ 07060

North Plainfield Exempt Fireman's Association Museum • 300 Somerset St • North Plainfield, NJ 07060 • (908) 757-5720

North Wildwood
Hereford Inlet Lighthouse Museum • 111 N Central Ave • North Wildwood, NJ 08260 • (609) 522-4520 • http://www.herefordlighthouse.org

Northfield
Northfield Historical Society •Casto House and Northfield Museum • 1700 Burton Ave • Northfield, NJ 08225 • (609) 383-1505

Otto Bruyns Public Library of Northfield • 241 W Mill Rd • Northfield, NJ 08225 • (609) 646-4476

Nutley
Nutley Free Public Library • 93 Booth Dr • Nutley, NJ 07110-2782 • (973) 667-0405 • http://www.bccls.org/nutley

Nutley Historical Society • Alice J Bickers Library, 65 Church St • Nutley, NJ 07110 • (973) 667-1528

Oak Ridge
Jefferson Township Historical Society • Dover-Milton Rd, P.O. Box 1776 • Oak Ridge, NJ 07438 • (973) 697-0258

Oakhurst
Cornish Heritage Society East • 439 Brookside Ave • Oakhurst, NJ 07755

Monmouth County Library-Township of Ocean • Monmouth & Deal Rds • Oakhurst, NJ 07755 • (732) 531-5092

Township of Ocean Historical Society • Historical Museum, 163 Monmouth Rd • Oakhurst, NJ 07755 • (732) 531-2136

Oakland
Oakland Historical Society • 1 Franklin Ave, P.O. Box 296 • Oakland, NJ 07436 • (201) 337-0924

Oaklyn
Oaklyn Memorial Library • 602 Newton Ave • Oaklyn, NJ 08107 • (856) 858-8226 • http://www.oaklyn.camden.lib.nj.us

Ocean City
Ocean City Free Public Library • 1735 Simpson Ave • Ocean City, NJ 08226 • (609) 399-2434 • http://www.oceancitylibrary.org

Ocean City Historical Museum • 1735 Simpson Ave • Ocean City, NJ 08226 • (609) 399-1801 • http://www.ocnjmuseum.org

Ocean Gate
Ocean Gate Historical Society • Cape May & Asbury Aves, P.O. Box 342 • Ocean Gate, NJ 08753 • (732) 269-8040

Ocean Grove
Historical Society of Ocean Grove, New Jersey • Historical Museum, 50 Pittman Ave, P.O. Box 446 • Ocean Grove, NJ 07756-0446 • (732) 774-1869 • http://www.oceangrovehistory.org

Ocean View
Historical Preservation Society of Upper Township • 26 Tyler Rd • Ocean View, NJ 08230 • (609) 390-5656

Oceanport
Oceanport Historical Society • 20 Pemberton Ave • Oceanport, NJ 07757

Ogdensburg
Ogdensburg Historical Society • 15 Richards St • Ogdensburg, NJ 07439

Sterling Hill Mining Museum • 30 Plant St • Ogdensburg, NJ 07439 • (973) 209-7212 • http://www.sterlinghill.org

Old Bridge
Old Bridge Public Library • 1 Old Bridge Plaza • Old Bridge, NJ 08857-2498 • (732) 721-5600 • http://www.lmxac.org/obpl

Thomas Warne Historical Museum • 4216 Route 516 • Old Bridge, NJ 08857 • (732) 566-0348

Old Bridge Township
Madison Township Historical Society • Thomas Warne Historical Museum, Route 516 • Old Bridge Township, NJ 08857 • (732) 566-0348

Old Bridge Historical Commission • 1 Old Bridge Plaza • Old Bridge Township, NJ 08857 • (732) 721-5600

Oldwick
Tewksbury Historical Society • P.O. Box 457 • Oldwick, NJ 08858 • (908) 832-6734 • http://www.tewksburyhistory.net

Oradell
Oradell Free Public Library • 375 Kinderkamack Rd • Oradell, NJ 07649-2122 • (201) 262-2613 • http://www.bccls.org/oradell

Orange
Orange Public Library • 348 Main St • Orange, NJ 07050-2794 • (973) 673-0153

Oxford
Oxford Historical Society • 46 Kent Rd, P.O. Box 60 • Oxford, NJ 07863 • (908) 453-3142

Paramus
Paramus Public Library • E 116 Century Rd • Paramus, NJ 07652-4398 • (201) 599-1305 • http://www.bccls.org/paramus

Park Ridge
Park Ridge Public Library • 51 Park Ave • Park Ridge, NJ 07656 • (201) 391-5151 • http://www.bccls.org/members.html

Pascack Historical Society • Historical Museum, 19 Ridge Ave, P.O. Box 285 • Park Ridge, NJ 07656 • (201) 573-0307 • http://www.pasackhistoricalsociety.org

Parsippany
Stickley Museum at Craftsman Farms • 2352 Route 10, W Manor Ln • Parsippany, NJ 07950 • (973) 540-0311 • http://www.stickleymuseum.org

Ukranian National Association • 2200 Route 10, P.O. Box 280 • Parsippany, NJ 07054 • (973) 434-0237 • http://www.ukrweekly.com

Passaic
Passiac Public Library • 195 Gregory Ave • Passaic, NJ 07055 • (973) 779-0474 • http://www.bccls.org

Paterson
Passaic County Community College Library • Historical Museum, 1 College Blvd • Paterson, NJ 07505 • (973) 684-8007 • http://www.pccc.cc.nj.us/library

Passaic County Cultural and Heritage Council • 1 College Blvd • Paterson, NJ 07505 • (973) 684-6555

Passaic County Genealogy Club • Lambert Castle Museum, 3 Valley Rd • Paterson, NJ 07509 • (201) 881-2761

Passaic County Historical Society • Lambert Castle Museum, 3 Valley Rd • Paterson, NJ 07503-2932 • (973) 247-0085 • http://www.lambertcastle.org

Paterson Free Public Library • 250 Broadway • Paterson, NJ 07501 • (973) 357-3000

Paterson Free Public Library-Danforth Memorial Library • 250 Broadway • Paterson, NJ 07501 • (973) 321-1223 • http://www.palsplus.org/patersonpl

Paterson Historic Preservation Commission • 65 McBride Ave • Paterson, NJ 07501 • (973) 357-1911

Paterson Museum • 2 Market St • Paterson, NJ 07501 • (973) 881-3874 • http://www.thepatersonmuseum.org

Paulsboro
Gill Memorial Library • 145 E Broad St • Paulsboro, NJ 08066 • (856) 423-5155 • http://www.gillmemoriallibrary.org

Pedricktown
Oldman Township Historical Society • Railroad Ave, P.O. Box 158208 • Pedricktown, NJ 08067 • (856) 299-1743

Pemberton
Burlington County College Library • County Route 530 • Pemberton, NJ 08068 • (609) 894-9311 • http://www.bcc.edu

Pennington
Hopewell Valley Historical Society • 124 S Main St, P.O. Box 371 • Pennington, NJ 08534 • (609) 737-8726 • http://www.rootsweb.com/~njhvhs

Pennington Public Library • 30 N Main St • Pennington, NJ 08534 • (609) 737-0404

Penns Grove
Historical Society of Penns Grove and Carnes Point • 48 W Main St • Penns Grove, NJ 08069 • (856) 299-1556

Pennsauken
Pennsauken Historical Society • 2506 Denby Ave • Pennsauken, NJ 08110-1000 • (856) 663-1251

Pennsville
Fort Mott Museum • 454 Fort Mott Rd • Pennsville, NJ 08070 • (856) 935-3218

Pennsville Public Library • 190 S Broadway • Pennsville, NJ 08070 • (856) 678-5473

Pennsville Township Historical Society • 86 Church Landing Rd • Pennsville, NJ 08070 • (856) 678-4453 • http://www.pvhistorical.njcool.net

Perth Amboy
Kearny Cottage Historical Association • Kearny Cottage Museum, 63 Catalpa Ave • Perth Amboy, NJ 08861 • (732) 826-1826

Perth Amboy Free Public Library • 196 Jefferson St • Perth Amboy, NJ 08861 • (732) 826-2600 • http://www.lmxac.org

Perth Amboy Historical Society • 1 Lewis St • Perth Amboy, NJ 08861

Proprietary House-Royal Governor's Mansion Museum • 149 Kearny Ave • Perth Amboy, NJ 08861 • (732) 826-5527 • http://www.proprietaryhouse.org

Phillipsburg
Phillipsburg Area Historical Society • Municipal Bldg, 675 Corliss Ave • Phillipsburg, NJ 08865 • (908) 454-3478

Phillipsburg Free Public Library • 200 Frost Ave • Phillipsburg, NJ 08865 • (908) 454-3712 • http://www.pburglib.com

Piscataway
East Jersey Old Towne Museum • 1050 River Rd, P.O. Box 661 • Piscataway, NJ 08854 • (732) 463-9077 • http://www.culturalheritage.org

Middlesex County Museum • Cornelius Low House, 1225 River Rd • Piscataway, NJ 08854 • (732) 745-4177 • http://www.co.middlesex.nj.us/cultureheritage

Piscataway Historical and Heritage Society • 1001 Maple Ave • Piscataway, NJ 08854 • (732) 752-5252

Piscataway Township Free Public Library • 500 Hoes Ln • Piscataway, NJ 08854 • (732) 463-1633 • http://www.lmxac.org/piscataway

Plainfield
Historical Society of Plainfield and North Plainfield • Drake House Museum, 602 W Front St • Plainfield, NJ 07060-1004 • (908) 755-5831 • http://www.drakehousemuseum.org

Plainfield Free Public Library • 8th St & Park Ave • Plainfield, NJ 07060-2594 • (908) 757-1111 • http://www.plainfieldlibrary.info/

Plainsboro
Plainsboro Free Public Library • 641 Plainsboro Rd • Plainsboro, NJ 08536-0278 • (609) 275-2897 • http://www.lmxac.org/plainsboro

Plainsboro Historical Society • 641 Plainsboro Rd, P.O. Box 278 • Plainsboro, NJ 08536-0278 • (609) 799-9040

Pleasantville
Pleasantville Historical Society • 805 Oneita Ave • Pleasantville, NJ 08232 • (609) 646-4115

Point Pleasant Beach
Point Pleasant Historical Society • P.O. Box 1273 • Point Pleasant Beach, NJ 08742

Pomona
Richard Stockton College of New Jersey Library • Jim Leeds Rd, P.O. Box 195 • Pomona, NJ 08240-0195 • (609) 652-4343 • http://library. stockton.edu/~holocau/hrc.htm

Pompton Lakes
Free Public Library of the Borough of Pompton Lakes • 333 Wanaque Ave • Pompton Lakes, NJ 07442 • (973) 835-0482 • http://www. palsplus.org/pomptonlakes

Pompton Plains
Pequannock Township Public Library • 477 Newark Pompton Turnpike • Pompton Plains, NJ 07444 • (973) 835-7460 • http://www.gti.net/ peqlib

Port Republic
Port Republic Historical Society • 14 Saint Johns Ln, P.O. Box 215 • Port Republic, NJ 08241 • (609) 652-1352

Princeton
Clarke House Museum • Princeton Battlefield State Park, 500 Mercer Rd • Princeton, NJ 08540 • (609) 921-0074

Firestone Library • Princeton University, 1 Washington Rd • Princeton, NJ 08544-2098 • (609) 258-5964 • http://www.princeton.edu

Historic Morven House Museum • 55 Stockton St • Princeton, NJ 08540 • (609) 924-8144 • http://www.morven.org; http://www. historicmorven.org

Historical Society of Princeton • Bainbridge House Museum, 158 Nassau St • Princeton, NJ 08542-7006 • (609) 921-6748 • http://www. princetonhistory.org

Port Mercer Canal House • 4274 Quakerbridge Rd • Princeton, NJ 08540 • (609) 243-9108

Princeton Battlefield State Park • Thomas Clarke House, 500 Mercer Rd • Princeton, NJ 08540-4810 • (609) 921-0074

Princeton History Project • Bainbridge House, 158 Nassau St • Princeton, NJ 08542-7006 • (609) 921-6748

Princeton Public Library • 65 Witherspoon St • Princeton, NJ 08540 • (609) 924-9539 • http://www.princetonlibrary.org

Rockingham Association • 175 Hun Rd • Princeton, NJ 08540 • (609) 924-3625

Rockingham State Historic Site Museum • 108 CR 518 • Princeton, NJ 08540 • (609) 921-8835 • http://www.rockingham.net

Princeton Junction
Historical Society of West Windsor • P.O. Box 38 • Princeton Junction, NJ 08550 • (609) 452-8598

Rahway
Rahway Historical Society • 1632 Saint Georges Ave, P.O. Box 1842 • Rahway, NJ 07065 • (732) 381-0441

Rahway Public Library • 75 E Cherry St • Rahway, NJ 07065 • (732) 388-0761 • http://www.lmxac.org/rahway/

Ramsey
Ramsey Free Public Library • 30 Wyckoff Ave • Ramsey, NJ 07446 • (201) 327-1445 • http://www.bccls.org/ramsey

Ramsey Historical Association • 65 N Island Ave • Ramsey, NJ 07446-2528 • (201) 327-6467

Rancocas
Powhatan Renape Nation • Rankokus Indian Reservation, Indian Heritage Museum, P.O. Box 225 • Rancocas, NJ 08073 • (856) 261-4747

Westampton Township Historical Society • P.O. Box 132 • Rancocas, NJ 08073-0132

Randolph
Historic Society of Old Randolph • Historical Museum, 630 Millbrook Ave • Randolph, NJ 07869 • (973) 989-7060 • http://www.randolphnj. org

Raritan
Raritan Public Library • 54 E Somerset St • Raritan, NJ 08869 • (908) 725-0413 • http://www.raritanlibrary.org

Red Bank
Red Bank Public Library • 84 W Front St • Red Bank, NJ 07701 • (732) 842-0690 • http://www.lmxac.org/redbank

Ridgefield
Ridgefield Public Library • 725 Slocum Ave • Ridgefield, NJ 07657 • (201) 941-0192 • http://www.bccls.org/ridgefield

Ridgewood
Genealogical Society of Bergen County, New Jersey • c/o Ridgewood Public Library, 125 N Maple St • Ridgewood, NJ 07450-3288 • (201) 670-5600 • http://www.rootsweb.com/~njgsbc

Paramus Historical and Preservation Society • 650 E Glen Ave • Ridgewood, NJ 07450 • (201) 447-3242

Ridgewood Historical Society • Schoolhouse Museum, 650 E Glen Ave • Ridgewood, NJ 07450 • (201) 652-4584 • http://www. ridgewoodhistorical.org

Ridgewood Public Library • 125 N Maple St • Ridgewood, NJ 07450-3288 • (201) 670-5600 • http://www.lib.ridgewood.nj.us

Ringwood
Long Pont Ironworks Historic District Museum • 1304 Sloatsburg Rd • Ringwood, NJ 07456 • (973) 962-7031

Ringwood Manor House Museum • 1304 Sloatsburg Rd, P.O. Box 1304 • Ringwood, NJ 07456 • (973) 962-7031 • http://www. ringwoodmanor.com

Ringwood Public Library • 30 Cannici Dr • Ringwood, NJ 07456 • (973) 962-6256 • http://www.palsplus.org/rpl

Skylands Association • P.O. Box 302 • Ringwood, NJ 07456 • (973) 362-7527

Skylands Manor House Museum & Gardens • Ringwood State Park, P.O. Box 1304 • Ringwood, NJ 07456 • (973) 962-7031

River Edge
Bergen County Historical Society • Historical Museum, 120 Main St, P.O. Box 55 • River Edge, NJ 07661-0055 • (201) 343-9492 • http:// www.bergencountyhistory.org

Steuben House Museum • 1209 Main St • River Edge, NJ 07661 • (201) 487-1739 • http://www.bergencountyhistory.org

Riverside
Riverside Township Historical Society • 220 Heulings Ave • Riverside, NJ 08075 • (856) 461-7850

Riverton
Historical Society of Riverton • 405 Midway • Riverton, NJ 08077 • (856) 829-6315

Rockaway
Historical Society of Rockaway • Fraesch House, Mount Hope Rd • Rockaway, NJ 07866 • (973) 366-6730

Mount Hope Historical Conservancy • 32 Mountain Ave • Rockaway, NJ 07866 • (973) 625-2508

Rockaway Free Public Library • 82 E Main St • Rockaway, NJ 07866 • (973) 627-5709 • http://rockboro.gti.net

Rockaway Township Free Public Library • 61 Mt Hope Rd • Rockaway, NJ 07866 • (973) 627-2344 • http://www.gti.net/rocktwp

Roebling
Roebling Historical Society • 119 2nd St • Roebling, NJ 08554 • (609) 499-7632

Roseland
Roseland Free Public Library • 20 Roseland Ave • Roseland, NJ 07068 • (973) 226-8636 • http://www.roselandnj.org

Roseland Historical Society • 35 Livingston Ave • Roseland, NJ 07068 • (973) 226-3664

Roseland Historical Society • 126 Eagle Rock Ave • Roseland, NJ 07068-1320 • (973) 228-1812

Roselle
Roselle Free Public Library • 104 W 4th Ave • Roselle, NJ 07203 • (908) 245-5809

Roselle Historical Society • 116 E 4th Ave • Roselle, NJ 07203 • (908) 245-9010

Union County Historical Society • 116 E 4th Ave • Roselle, NJ 07203 • (908) 245-9010

Roselle Park
Roselle Park Historical Society • 9 W Grant Ave, P.O. Box 135 • Roselle Park, NJ 07204 • (908) 245-5422 • http://www.rosellepark.org/upclose/history/museuminfo.htm

Roselle Park Public Library • 404 Chestnut St • Roselle Park, NJ 07204-1506 • (908) 245-2456 • http://www.roselleparklibrary.org

Rumson
Rumson Historical Society • Wilson Cr • Rumson, NJ 07760 • (732) 842-0338

Rutherford
Meadowlands Museum • 91 Crane Ave, P.O. Box 3 • Rutherford, NJ 07070 • (201) 935-1175 • http://www.meadowlandsmuseum.org

Messier Library • Fairleigh Dickinson Univ, Montross Ave • Rutherford, NJ 07070 • (201) 460-5074

Saddle Brook
Armenian General Benevolent Union • 585 Saddle River Rd • Saddle Brook, NJ 07663-4535 • (201) 797-7600

Salem
Gouldtown Historical Society • 372 Magnolia St • Salem, NJ 08079

Pennsville Township Historical Society • 273 Fort Mott Rd • Salem, NJ 08079 • (856) 935-6538

Salem County Historical Society • Alexander Grant House, 79-83 Market St • Salem, NJ 08079 • (856) 935-5004 • http://www.salemcounty.com/schs/

Salem Free Public Library • 112 W Broadway • Salem, NJ 08079-1302 • (856) 935-0526

Sandy Hook
Fort Hancock Museum • Sandy Hook, Gateway National Recreational Area • Sandy Hook, NJ 07732 • (732) 872-5970 • http://www.nps.gov/gate

Sayreville
Sayreville Historical Society • Historical Museum, 425 Main St, P.O. Box 18 • Sayreville, NJ 08872 • (732) 257-0893 • http://www.sayhistory.com

Scotch Plains
Historical Society of Scotch Plains and Fanwood • 1840 Front St, P.O. Box 261 • Scotch Plains, NJ 07076 • (908) 232-1199

Scotch Plains Public Library • 1927 Bartle Ave • Scotch Plains, NJ 07076-1299 • (908) 322-5007 • http://www.scotlib.org

Sea Bright
Moss Archives • P.O. Box 3336 • Sea Bright, NJ 07760-3336 • (732) 842-0336

Sea Girt
National Guard Militia Museum of New Jersey • Sea Girt & Washington Aves, P.O. Box 277 • Sea Girt, NJ 07850 • (732) 794-5966 • http://www.state.nj.us/military/museum

Sea Isle City
Sea Isle City Historical Museum • 4416 Landis Ave • Sea Isle City, NJ 08243 • (609) 263-2992

Seaside Park
Double Trouble Village • Island Beach State Park • Seaside Park, NJ 08752 • (732) 793-0506

Secaucus
Routes to Roots • 136 Sandpiper Key • Secaucus, NJ 07094-2210 • (201) 866-4075 • http://www.routestoroots.com

Secaucus Free Public Library • 1379 Patterson Plank Rd • Secaucus, NJ 07094 • (201) 330-2083 • http://www.bccls.org/secaucus

Sewaren
Sewaren Historical Club • 434 Cliff St • Sewaren, NJ 07077

Sewell
Gloucester County College Library • 1400 Tanyard Rd • Sewell, NJ 08080-4222 • (856) 468-5000

Mantua Historical Society • 506 Buckingham Dr • Sewell, NJ 08080

Short Hills
Millburn-Short Hills Historical Society • 1 Station Plaza, P.O. Box 243 • Short Hills, NJ 07078 • (973) 564-9519 • http://community.nj.com/cc/millburn-shhistsoc

Shrewsbury
Irish Families Historical Society • 1050 Broad St • Shrewsbury, NJ 07702 • (732) 758-9860

Shrewsbury Historical Society • Historical Museum, 419 Sycamore Ave, P.O. Box 333 • Shrewsbury, NJ 07702 • (732) 530-7974

Somers Point
Atlantic County Historical Society • Historical Museum, 907 Shore Rd, P.O. Box 301 • Somers Point, NJ 08244-2335 • (609) 927-5218 • http://www.aclink.org/achs; http://www.atlanticheritagecenternj.org

Somers Mansion Museum • 1000 Shore Rd • Somers Point, NJ 08244 • (609) 927-2212

Somers Point Historical Society • 745 Shore Rd, P.O. Box 517 • Somers Point, NJ 08244 • (609) 927-8002 • http://somerspointhistory.org

Somerset
Blackwells Mills Canal Historical Association • 598 Elizabeth St • Somerset, NJ 08873 • (732) 873-2959

Blackwells Mills Canal House Museum • Delaware & Raritan Canal State Park, 625 Canal Rd • Somerset, NJ 08873 • (732) 873-3050

Franklin Township Free Public Library • 485 De Mott Ln • Somerset, NJ 08873 • (732) 873-8700 • http://www.franklintwp.org

Immigration and Ethnic History Society • 390 Campus Dr • Somerset, NJ 07830 • (888) 999-6778

Somerville
Canal Society of New Jersey • Historical Museum, 214 N Bridge St • Somerville, NJ 08876 • (908) 722-9556 • http://www.canalsocietynj.org

Old Dutch Parsonage Museum • 71 Somerset St • Somerville, NJ 08876 • (908) 725-1015

Somerville, cont.

Somerville Historical Society • 16 E Summit St • Somerville, NJ 08876

Somerville Public Library • 35 West End Ave • Somerville, NJ 08876 • (908) 725-1336 • http://www.lmxac.org/somervillelib/

Wallace House Museum • 71 Somerset St • Somerville, NJ 08876 • (908) 725-1015

South Amboy

Dowdell Library of South Amboy • 100 Harold G Hoffman Plaza • South Amboy, NJ 08879 • (732) 721-6060 • http://www.dowdell.org

South Amboy Historical Society • 109 Fletus St • South Amboy, NJ 08879 • (201) 721-6060

South Dennis

Dennis Township Historical Society • P.O. Box 109 • South Dennis, NJ 08245

South Orange

Afro-American Historical and Genealogical Society, New Jersey Chapter • 785 Sterling Dr E • South Orange, NJ 07079

Seton Hall University Museum • 400 S Orange Ave • South Orange, NJ 07079 • (973) 761-7966

South Orange Historical and Preservation Society • 162 Irving Ave • South Orange, NJ 07079 • (973) 761-5508

Walsh Library • Seton Hall Univ, 400 S Orange Ave • South Orange, NJ 07079 • (973) 761-9437 • http://www.shu.edu/library/speccoll.html

South Plainfield

South Plainfield Historical Society • P.O. Box 11 • South Plainfield, NJ 07080 • (908) 754-3503

South River

South River Historical and Preservation Society • 64 Main St, P.O. Box 545 • South River, NJ 08882 • (732) 257-2200 • http://www.rootsweb.com/~njsrhps

Sparta

Sparta Public Library • 22 Woodport Rd • Sparta, NJ 07871 • (973) 729-3101 • http://www.sparta.library.com

Spotswood

Spotswood Public Library • 548 Main St • Spotswood, NJ 08884 • (732) 251-1515 • http://www.spotswoodboro.com/library1.htm

Spring Lake

Spring Lake Historical Society • Historical Museum, 5th & Warren Aves, P.O. Box 703 • Spring Lake, NJ 07762 • (732) 449-0772

Springfield

Millburn Short Hills Historical Society • 67 Hillside Ave • Springfield, NJ 07081 • (973) 564-9519

Springfield Free Public Library • 66 Mountain Ave • Springfield, NJ 07081-1786 • (973) 376-4930 • http://www.springfieldpubliclibrary.com

Springfield Historical Society • Historical Museum, 126 Morris Ave • Springfield, NJ 07081-1306 • (973) 912-4464 • http://www.springfield.nj.com/history.htm

Stanhope

Waterloo Village Museum • Waterloo Rd • Stanhope, NJ 07874 • (973) 398-7010

Stanton

Bouman-Stickney Farmstead Museum • 114 Deahook Rd • Stanton, NJ 08885 • (908) 236-2327

Cold Brook School Museum • Potterstown Rd • Stanton, NJ 08885 • (908) 236-2327

Stillwater

Stillwater Township Historical Society • P.O. Box 23 • Stillwater, NJ 07855 • (973) 383-4822

Stirling

Long Hill Township Free Public Library • 91 Central Ave • Stirling, NJ 07980 • (908) 647-2088 • http://www.gti.net/lhtlib

Long Hill Township Historical Society • 1336 Valley Rd • Stirling, NJ 07087 • (908) 647-5762

Stockholm

Hardyston Heritage Society • N Woods Tr, P.O. Box 434 • Stockholm, NJ 07460 • (973) 697-8733

Stratford

Stratford Historical Society • 201 S Atlantic Ave • Stratford, NJ 08084 • (856) 435-5901

Succasunna

Roxbury Township Historical Society • P.O. Box 18 • Succasunna, NJ 07876

Roxbury Township Public Library • 103 Main St • Succasunna, NJ 07876 • (973) 584-2400 • http://www.roxburylibrary.org

Summit

Summit Historical Society • Carter House, 90 Butler Pkwy, P.O. Box 464 • Summit, NJ 07901 • (908) 277-1747

Sussex

Vernon Township Historical Society • 5 Sleepy Hollow Rd • Sussex, NJ 07461 • (973) 875-9562

Swainton

Leaming's Run Colonial Farm Museum • 1845 Route 9 N • Swainton, NJ 08210 • (609) 465-5871 • http://www.leamingsrungardens.com

Swedesboro

Gloucester County Library System-Swedesboro Public • 1442 Kings Hwy • Swedesboro, NJ 08085 • (856) 467-0111

Swedesboro Historical Society • Swedesboro-Paulsboro Rd, P.O. Box 219 • Swedesboro, NJ 08085

Teaneck

Teaneck Public Library • 840 Teaneck Rd • Teaneck, NJ 07666 • (201) 837-4171 • http://www.teaneck.org

Weiner Library • Fairleigh Dickinson University, 1000 River Rd • Teaneck, NJ 07666-1914 • (201) 692-2100

Tenafly

Tenafly Public Library • 100 River Edge Rd • Tenafly, NJ 07670-2087 • (201) 568-8680 • http://www.bccls.org/tenafly

Tennent

Battleground Historical Society • P.O. Box 61 • Tennent, NJ 07763 • (732) 466-2825

Teterboro

Aviation Hall of Fame and Museum • 400 Fred Wehram Dr • Teterboro, NJ 07608 • (201) 288-6344 • http://www.njahof.org

Titusville

Howell Living History Farm Museum • 70 Wooden's Ln • Titusville, NJ 08560 • (609) 737-3299 • http://howellfarm.org

Johnson Ferry House Museum • 355 Washington Crossing Penn Rd • Titusville, NJ 08560 • (609) 737-2515

Washington Crossing Museum • 355 Washington Crossing-Pennington Rd • Titusville, NJ 08560 • (609) 737-9303

Toms River

Col Charles Waterhouse Museum • 17 Washington St • Toms River, NJ 08753 • (732) 818-9040 • http://www.waterhousemuseum.com

Mid-Atlantic Germanic Society • 17 Swaine Ave • Toms River, NJ 08755-4034 • (732) 240-7349

Ocean County Historical Society • Strickler Research Library, 26 Hadley Ave, P.O. Box 2191 • Toms River, NJ 08754-2191 • (732) 341-1880 • http://www.oceancountyhistory.org

Ocean County Library • 101 Washington St • Toms River, NJ 08753 • (732) 349-6200 • http://www.oceancountylibrary.org

Toms River Seaport Society • Historical Museum, 78 Water St, P.O. box 1111 • Toms River, NJ 08753 • (732) 349-9209

Tranquility
Green Township Historical Society • P.O. Box 203 • Tranquility, NJ 07879 • (973) 383-5928

Trenton
1719 William Trent House Museum • 15 Market St • Trenton, NJ 08611 • (609) 989-3027 • http://www.williamtrenthouse.org

Brearley House Museum • Meadow Rd • Trenton, NJ 08648 • (609) 895-1728

Descendants of the Founders of New Jersey • 10 Buckingham Ave • Trenton, NJ 08618 • http://www.njfounders.org

Hamilton Township Public Library • 1 Municipal Dr • Trenton, NJ 08619 • (609) 890-3460

Masonic Grand Lodge of New Jersey • 100 Barrack St • Trenton, NJ 08608-2008 • (609) 239-3950 • http://www.newjerseygrandlodge.org

New Jersey Historic Trust • Historical Museum, 101 S Broad St, P.O. Box 457 • Trenton, NJ 08625 • (609) 984-0473 • http://www.njht.org

New Jersey Historical Commission • 225 W State St, P.O. Box 305 • Trenton, NJ 08625-0305 • (609) 292-6062 • http://www.state.nj.us/state/history.hisidx.html

New Jersey Office of Historic Sites • 501 E State St • Trenton, NJ 08625 • (609) 777-0238 • http://www.state.nj.us/dep/forestry/histsite.htm

New Jersey State Archives • 185 W State St, P.O. Box 307 • Trenton, NJ 08625-0307 • (609) 633-8334 • http://www.njarchives.org

New Jersey State Bureau of Vital Statistics • P.O. Box 370 • Trenton, NJ 08625-0370 • (609) 292-4087 • http://www.state.nj.us/health/vital/vital.shtml

New Jersey State House Museum • 125 W State St • Trenton, NJ 08625 • (609) 633-2709 • http://www.njleg.state.nj.us

New Jersey State Library • 185 W State St, P.O. Box 520 • Trenton, NJ 08625-0520 • (609) 292-6200 • http://www.njstatelib.org

New Jersey State Museum • 205 W State St, P.O. Box 530 • Trenton, NJ 08625 • (609) 292-5420 • http://www.newjerseystatemuseum.org

North American Vexillological Association • 1977 N Olden Ave, Ste 225 • Trenton, NJ 08618-2193 • (860) 354-0686 • http://www.nava.org

Office of Historic Sites • 501 E State St, P.O. Box 404 • Trenton, NJ 08625 • (609) 777-0238

Old Barracks Association • Historical Museum, Barrack St • Trenton, NJ 08608 • (609) 396-1776 • http://www.barracks.org

Old Mill Hill Society • P.O. Box 1263 • Trenton, NJ 08607-1263

Preservation New Jersey • 30 S Warren St • Trenton, NJ 08608 • (609) 392-6409 • http://www.preservationnj.org

Sixth Regiment United States Colored Troops • 685 Martin Luther King Jr Blvd • Trenton, NJ 08618 • (609) 396-3350

Trenton City Museum • Cadwalader Park, 319 E State St • Trenton, NJ 08618 • (609) 989-3632 • http://www.ellarslie.org

Trenton Historical Society • P.O. Box 1112 • Trenton, NJ 08606-1112 • (609) 396-4478 • http://trentonhistory.org

Trenton Public Library • 120 Academy St • Trenton, NJ 08608 • (609) 392-7188 • http://www.trenton.lib.nj.us

Trentonian Museum • Perry St • Trenton, NJ 08602 • (254) 287-8811

Tuckerton
Barnegat Bay Decoy and Bayman's Museum • 137 W Main St, P.O. Box 52 • Tuckerton, NJ 08087 • (609) 296-8868 • http://www.charlesjobesdecoys.com/barnegat/museum.htm

Tuckerton Historical Society • 35 Leitz Blvd, P.O. Box 43 • Tuckerton, NJ 08087 • (609) 294-1547

Tuckerton Seaport Museum • 120 W Main St, P.O. Box 52 • Tuckerton, NJ 08087 • (609) 296-8868 • http://www.tuckertonseaport.org

Union
Liberty Hall Museum • 1003 Morris Ave • Union, NJ 07083 • (908) 527-0400 • http://www.kean.edu/libertyhall/

Nancy Thompson Library • Kean University, 1000 Morris Ave • Union, NJ 07083 • (908) 737-4600 • http://www.library.kean.edu

Union County Historical Society • Caldwell Parsonage Museum, 909 Caldwell Ave • Union, NJ 07083 • (908) 964-9047

Upper Freehold Township
Historic Walnford Museum • 78 Walnford Rd • Upper Freehold Township, NJ 07738 • (609) 259-5275 • http://www.monmouthcountyparks.com

Upper Saddle River
Upper Saddle River Historical Society • 245 Lake St • Upper Saddle River, NJ 07458 • (201) 327-6470

Ventnor
Ventnor City Historical Society • 6500 Atlantic Ave, P.O. Box 2668 • Ventnor, NJ 08406 • (609) 822-4257

Vincentown
Sally Stretch Keen Memorial Library • 94 Main St • Vincentown, NJ 08088 • (609) 859-3598 • http://www.vincentown.lib.nj.us

Southampton Historical Society • 17 Mill St, P.O. Box 2086 • Vincentown, NJ 08088 • (609) 859-9237

Tabernacle Historical Society • 162 Carranza Rd • Vincentown, NJ 08008 • (609) 268-0473

Vineland
Beth Israel Synagogue Library • 1015 E Park Ave • Vineland, NJ 08360 • (856) 691-0852

Cumberland County College Library • 3322 College Dr • Vineland, NJ 08360 • (856) 691-8600 • http://www.cccnj.net

Taino Jatibonucu Tribe of Puerto Rico • 703 S 8th St • Vineland, NJ 08360 • http://www.hartford-hwp.com/Taino/jatibonuco.html

Vineland Historical and Antiquarian Society • Historical Museum, 108 S 7th St,P.O. Box 35 • Vineland, NJ 08362-0035 • (856) 691-1111 • http://www.vineland.org

Voorhees
Camden County Library • Echelon Urban Center, 203 Laurel Rd • Voorhees, NJ 08043 • (609) 772-1636 • http://www.camden.lib.nj.us

Voorhees Township Historical Society • 820 Berlin Rd • Voorhees, NJ 08043

Waldwick
Waldwick Public Library • 19-21 E Prospect St • Waldwick, NJ 07463-2099 • (201) 652-5104 • http://www.bccls.org/waldwick/

Wall
Allaire Village Museum • 4265 Atlantic Ave • Wall, NJ 07727 • (732) 938-3500 • http://www.allairevillage.org

Blansingburg Schoolhouse • 1701 New Bedford Rd • Wall, NJ 07719 • (732) 974-1393

Monmouth County Library-Wall • 2700 Allaire Rd • Wall, NJ 07719 • (732) 449-8877

Wall Township
Old Wall Historical Society • Allgor-Barkalow Homestead Museum, 1701 New Bedford Rd, P.O. Box 1203 • Wall Township, NJ 07719 • (732) 974-1430

Walpack Center
Walpack Historical Society • P.O. Box 3 • Walpack Center, NJ 07881

Warren Township
Warren Township Historical Society • 5 Wychwood Wy • Warren Township, NJ 07059 • (732) 469-2318

Washington
Washington Free Public Library • 20 W Carlton Ave • Washington, NJ 07882 • (908) 689-0201 • http://www.wpl.hublib.lib.nj.us

Watchung
Watchung Historical Society • 105 Turtle Rd • Watchung, NJ 07060

Wayne
David & Lorraine Cheng Library • William Paterson University, 300 Pompton Rd • Wayne, NJ 07470 • (973) 720-2116 • http://www.wpunj.edu/library

Jewish Genealogical Society of North Jersey • c/o Y of Wayne, 1 Pike Dr • Wayne, NJ 07470 • (973) 595-0100 • http://www.jgsnj.org

North Jersey Highlands Historical Society • 177 Valley Rd • Wayne, NJ 07470

Verona Historical Society • 31 Thomas St • Wayne, NJ 07470 • (973) 694-5835

Washington's Headquarters Museum • Dey Mansion, Totowa Rd • Wayne, NJ 07470 • (973) 696-1776

Wayne Public Library • 461 Valley Rd • Wayne, NJ 07470 • (973) 694-4272 • http://www.waynepubliclibrary.org

Wayne Township Historical Commission • Van Riper-Hopper House, 533 Berdan Ave • Wayne, NJ 07470 • (973) 694-7192 • http://www.waynetownship.com

Wenonah
Wenonah Historical Society • 206 S Princeton Ave • Wenonah, NJ 08090 • (856) 468-6594

West Caldwell
Historical Society of West Caldwell • 278 Westville Ave, P.O. Box 1701 • West Caldwell, NJ 07006 • (973) 226-8976

West Caldwell Public Library • 30 Clinton Rd • West Caldwell, NJ 07006 • (973) 226-5441 • http://www.bccls.org/westcaldwell

Yankee Air Force Museum • P.O. Box 1729 • West Caldwell, NJ 07007 • (973) 374-2400

West Creek
Eagleswood Historical Society • Route 9, Main St • West Creek, NJ 08092

West Long Branch
Guggenheim Memorial Library • Monmouth University, 400 Cedar Ave • West Long Branch, NJ 07764 • (732) 571-3450 • http://bluehawk.monmouth.edu/library/

West Long Branch Historical Society • P.O. Box 151 • West Long Branch, NJ 07764

West Long Branch Public Library • 95 Poplar Ave • West Long Branch, NJ 07764 • (732) 222-5993 • http://www.wlbpl.org

West Milford
North Jersey Highlands Historical Society • 8 Stoney Ln • West Milford, NJ 07480 • (973) 208-0034

West Milford Museum • 1480 Union Valley Rd • West Milford, NJ 07480 • (973) 728-1823 • http://www.westmilfordmuseum.org

West New York
West New York Public Library • 425 60th St • West New York, NJ 07093-2211 • (201) 295-5135

West Orange
Edison National Historic Site Museum • Main St & Lakeside Ave • West Orange, NJ 07052 • (973) 736-0550 • http://www.nps.gov/edis/

West Paterson
Jewish Historical Society of North Jersey • P.O. Box 708 • West Paterson, NJ 07424-0708 • (973) 785-9119

New Jersey Genealogy Club of Passaic County • 430 Mt Pleasant Ave • West Paterson, NJ 07424

West Paterson Historical Society • 556 McBride Ave • West Paterson, NJ 07424 • (973) 345-1876

West Trenton
New Jersey State Police Museum • River Rd, P.O. Box 7068 • West Trenton, NJ 08628 • (609) 882-2000 • http://www.njspmuseum.org

Westampton
Burlington County Library • 5 Pioneer Blvd • Westampton, NJ 08060 • (609) 267-9660 • http://www.burlco.lib.nj.us

National Society of the Colonial Dames of America in New Jersey • Peachfield Plantation, 180 Burrs Rd • Westampton, NJ 08060 • (609) 267-6996 • http://colonialdamesnj.org

Westfield
Genealogical Society of the West Fields • c/o Westfield Memorial Library, 425 E Broad St • Westfield, NJ 07090 • (908) 789-4090 • http://westfieldnj.com/gswf

Genealogical Society of Westfield • 550 E Broad St • Westfield, NJ 07090

Jersey Central Railway Historical Society • general delivery • Westfield, NJ 07090 • (908) 233-3603

Miller-Cory House Museum • 614 Mountain Ave, P.O. Box 455 • Westfield, NJ 07091 • (908) 232-1776 • http://www.westfieldnj.com

Westfield Historical Society • Town Hall, 425 E Broad St, P.O. Box 613 • Westfield, NJ 07091 • (908) 232-1776 • http://www.westfieldnj.com/history/

Westfield Memorial Library • 550 E Broad St • Westfield, NJ 07090 • (908) 789-4090 • http://www.wmlnj.org

Westmont
Haddon Township Historical Society • 224 Hazel Terr • Westmont, NJ 09108

Wharton
Wharton Historical Society • 10 N Main St, P.O. Box 424 • Wharton, NJ 07885

Whippany
Jewish Historical Society of Metro West • 901 Route 10 E • Whippany, NJ 07981-1156 • (973) 929-2995 • http://www.jhsmw.org

Morris County Free Library • 30 E Hanover Ave • Whippany, NJ 07981 • (973) 285-6969 • http://www.mclib.info/

Morris County Historical Society • 18 Jeffrie Tr • Whippany, NJ 07891 • (973) 672-7278

Whippany Railway Museum • 1 Railroad Plaza, Route 10 W & Whippany Rd • Whippany, NJ 07981 • (973) 887-8177 • http://www.whippanyrailwaymuseum.org

Yesteryear Museum • 20 Harriet Dr • Whippany, NJ 07981 • (973) 386-1920

Whitehouse Station
Eversole-Hall House Museum • 511 Route 253 • Whitehouse Station, NJ 08889 • (908) 236-2327

Readington Museums • 509 Route 523 • Whitehouse Station, NJ 08889 • (908) 236-2327

Readington Township Library • 255 Main St, P.O. Box 87 • Whitehouse Station, NJ 08889-0087 • (908) 534-4421

Whiting
Manchester Historical Society • 18 Bowie Dr • Whiting, NJ 08759

Wildwood
Wildwood Historical Society • George F Boyer Museum, 3907 Pacific Ave • Wildwood, NJ 08260 • (609) 523-0277 • http://www.beachcomber.com/Ocean/Chamber/ocmuse.html

Wildwood Crest
Wildwood Crest Historical Society • Crest Pier, 5800 Ocean Ave • Wildwood Crest, NJ 08260 • (609) 729-4515 • http://www.cresthistory.org

Williamstown
Monroe Township Historical Society • Main Sts, P.O. Box 474 • Williamstown, NJ 08094 • (856) 728-0458

Willingboro
Willingboro Historical Society • Municipal Complex • Willingboro, NJ 08046

Willingboro Public Library • 1 Salem Rd • Willingboro, NJ 08046-2896 • (609) 877-6668 • http://www.willingboro.org

Woodbine
Upper Township Historic Preservation Society • Route 2, Box 1056 • Woodbine, NJ 08270

Woodbridge
Historical Association of Woodbridge • 23 E Green St • Woodbridge, NJ 07095 • (732) 636-5874

Woodbridge Public Library • George Frederick Plaza • Woodbridge, NJ 07095 • (732) 634-4450 • http://www.woodbridge.lib.nj.us

Woodbury
Friendship Fire Company Museum • 29 Delaware St • Woodbury, NJ 08096 • (856) 845-0066

Gloucester County Cultural and Heritage Commission • Historical Museum, Route 45 & Budd Blvd, P.O. Box 337 • Woodbury, NJ 08096 • (856) 251-6725

Gloucester County Historical Society • Historical Museum, 58 N Broad St • Woodbury, NJ 08096 • (856) 848-8531 • http://www.rootsweb.com/~njglouce/gchs

Wood-Ridge
Wood-Ridge History Committee • c/o Wood-Ridge Memorial Library, George Frederick Plaza • Wood-Ridge, NJ 07075 • (201) 438-2455

Wood-Ridge Memorial Library • 231 Hackensack St • Wood-Ridge, NJ 07075 • (201) 438-2455

Wood-Ridge Memorial Library • 231 Hackensack St • Wood-Ridge, NJ 07075 • (201) 438-2455

Woodstown
Genealogical Society of Salem County • P.O. Box 231 • Woodstown, NJ 08098 • http://www.rootsweb.com/~njsalem/gsscnj.html

Pilesgrove-Woodstown Historical Society • Historical Museum, 42 N Main St • Woodstown, NJ 08098 • (856) 769-4588

Woodstown Historical Preservation Committee • 250 Howard Ave • Woodstown, NJ 08098

Woodstown-Pilesgrove Public Library • 14 School Ln • Woodstown, NJ 08098-1331 • (856) 769-0098

Wyckoff
Wyckoff Historical Society • P.O. Box 73 • Wyckoff, NJ 07481

Wyckoff Public Library • 200 Woodland Ave • Wyckoff, NJ 07481 • (201) 891-4866 • http://www.wyckoff-nj.com

New Jersey

Abiquiu
Ghost Ranch Living Museum • HC 77, Box 11 • Abiquiu, NM 87510-9601 • (505) 685-4333

Acoma Pueblo
Acoma Pueblo Historical Society • Historical Museum, Hwy 23, P.O. Box 309 • Acoma Pueblo, NM 87034 • (505) 252-1139

Acoma Tourist and Visitation Center Museum • I-38 & I-23, P.O. Box 309 • Acoma Pueblo, NM 87034 • (800) 747-0181

Sky City Cultural Center • I-40 W, SPA 30 & 32 • Acoma Pueblo, NM 87034 • (800) 747-0181 • http://www.puebloofacoma.org

Alamogordo
Alamogordo Genealogical Society • P.O. Box 734 • Alamogordo, NM 88311-0734

Alamogordo Museum of History • 1301 N White Sands Blvd • Alamogordo, NM 88310 • (505) 434-4438 • http://www.alamogordomuseum.org

Alamogordo Public Library • 920 Oregon Ave • Alamogordo, NM 88310 • (505) 439-4140 • http://www.ci.alamogordo.nm.us/library/coalibrary.html

David H Townsend Library • New Mexico State University at Alamogordo, 2400 N Scenic Dr • Alamogordo, NM 88310 • (505) 439-3650 • http://alamo.nmsu.edu/library

New Mexico Museum of Space History • Hwy 2001, P.O. Box 5430 • Alamogordo, NM 88311 • (505) 437-2840 • http://www.spacefame.org

Toy Train Depot Museum • 1991 N White Sands Blvd • Alamogordo, NM 88310 • (888) 207) 3564 • http://www.toytraindepot.homestead.com

Tularosa Basin Historical Society • Historical Museum, 1301 N White Sands Blvd, P.O. Box 518 • Alamogordo, NM 88311 • (505) 434-4438 • http://www.alamogordomuseum.org

Albuquerque
Albuquerque Historical Society • P.O. Box 4552 • Albuquerque, NM 87103 • (505) 255-4595

Albuquerque Museum • 2000 Mountain Rd NW • Albuquerque, NM 87103 • (505) 243-7255 • http://www.cabq.gov/museum

Albuquerque Public Library-Special Collections • 423 Central Ave NE • Albuquerque, NM 87102 • (505) 848-1376 • http://www.cabq.gov/rgvls/specol.html

Albuquerque-Bernadillo County Library System • 501 Copper Ave NW • Albuquerque, NM 87102 • (505) 768-5100 • http://www.cabq.gov/library

Anderson-Abruzzo International Balloon Museum Archives • 400 Marquette Ave NW • Albuquerque, NM 87102 • (505) 768-3555 • http://www.cabq.quu.balloon

Center for Southwest Research • Univ of New Mexico, Zimmerman Library • Albuquerque, NM 87131-1466 • (505) 277-6451 • http://www.unm.edu/~cswrref

Central United Methodist Church Library • 1615 Copper NE • Albuquerque, NM 87106-4596 • (505) 243-7834

Church of Jesus Christ of Latter-Day Saints Family History Center • 5709 Haines Ave NE • Albuquerque, NM 87110-5203 • (505) 266-4867 • http://www.lds.org/

Daughters of the American Revolution, New Mexico State Society • 3936 Garcia St NE • Albuquerque, NM 87111

Ernie Pyle Home • 900 Girard Blvd SE • Albuquerque, NM 87106 • (505) 265-2065

First Presbyterian Church Library • 215 Locust NE • Albuquerque, NM 87102 • (505) 764-2900

Genealogy Club of Albuquerque • 11605 Hughes Ave NE • Albuquerque, NM 87112-1813 • (505) 298-8018

Genealogy Club of the Albuquerque Public Library • c/o Albuquerque Public Library, 423 Central Ave NE • Albuquerque, NM 87102-3517 • (505) 848-1376 • http://www.cabq.gov/rgvls/specol.html

Hispanic Genealogical Research Center of New Mexico • Lourdes Hall, St. Pius X Campus, 4060 St Joseph Pl. NW; P.O. Box 27250 • Albuquerque, NM 87125 • (505) 833-4197 • http://www.hgrc-nm.org

Indian Pueblo Cultural Center • 2401 12th St NW • Albuquerque, NM 87104 • (505) 843-7270 • http://www.indianpueblo.org

Masonic Grand Lodge of New Mexico • 1638 University Blvd NE, P.O. Box 25004 • Albuquerque, NM 87125-0004 • (505) 243-4931 • http://nmmasons.org

Menaul Historical Library of the Southwest • 301 Menaul Blvd NE • Albuquerque, NM 87107 • (505) 343-7480

National Atomic Museum • 1905 Mountain Rd NW • Albuquerque, NM 87104 • (505) 245-2137 • http://www.atomicmuseum.com

National Museum of Nuclear Science & History • 601 Eubank Blvd SE • Albuquerque, NM 87123 • (505) 245-2137 • http://www.nuclearmuseum.org

New Mexico Genealogical Society • c/o Albuquerque Public Library, 423 Central Ave NE, P.O. Box 8283 • Albuquerque, NM 87198-8283 • (505) 848-1376 • http://www.nmgs.org

New Mexico Hispanic Cultural Center • 1701 4th St SW, P.O. Box 12317 • Albuquerque, NM 87195 • (505) 724-4720

New Mexico Jewish Historical Society • Jewish Community Ctr, 5520 Wyoming Blvd NE • Albuquerque, NM 87109 • (505) 348-4471 • http://www.nmjewishhistory.org

New Mexico Museum of Military History • 800 Rio Grande Blvd NW • Albuquerque, NM 87104 • (505) 243-2238

San Felipe de Neri Church Museum • 2005 N Plaza NW, P.O. Box 7007 • Albuquerque, NM 87194 • (505) 243-4628

Sons of the American Revolution, New Mexico Society • 905 Santa Ana SE • Albuquerque, NM 87123 • (505) 296-0446 • http://www.nmssar.org

Spanish History Museum • 2215 Lead SE, P.O. Box 25531 • Albuquerque, NM 87125-0531 • (505) 268-9981

Telephone Pioneer Museum of New Mexico • 110 4th St NW • Albuquerque, NM 87103 • (505) 842-2937 • http://www.nmculture.org

Tuquoise Museum • 2107 Central NW, P.O. Box 7598 • Albuquerque, NM 87194 • (505) 247-8650 • http://www.turqoisemuseum.com

Western History Association • Univ of New Mexico, Dept of History • Albuquerque, NM 87131-0001 • (435) 750-1301

Zimmerman Library • University of New Mexico, 1900 Roma NE, MSC 05-3020 • Albuquerque, NM 87131-0001 • (505) 277-5761 • http://www.unm.edu; elibrary.unm.edu

Algodones
Legends of New Mexico Museum • 601 Frontage Rd • Algodones, NM 87001 • (505) 867-8600

Angel Fire
Genealogy Club of Angel Fire • P.O. Box 503 • Angel Fire, NM 87710 • (505) 377-6969

Anthony
Valley Community Library • 735 Church St, P.O. Box 1297 • Anthony, NM 88021 • (505) 882-7982 • http://www.nmsu.edu/library/valley.html

Artesia
Artesia Historical and Genealogical Society • c/o Artesia Public Library, 306 W Richardson Ave, P.O. Box 803 • Artesia, NM 88210 • (505) 746-4252

Artesia, cont.
Artesia Historical Society • Historical Museum, 505 W Richardson Ave • Artesia, NM 88210 • (505) 748-2390 • http://www.vpa.org/museumsnm.html

Artesia Public Library • 306 W Richardson Ave • Artesia, NM 88210-2499 • (505) 746-4252 • http://www.pvtnetworks.net/~apublib

Aztec
Aztec Museum Association • Pioneer Village Museum, 125 N Main • Aztec, NM 87410 • (505) 334-9829 • http://www.aztecnm.com/museum/museum_index.htm

Belen
Belen Public Library • 333 Becker Ave • Belen, NM 87002 • (505) 864-7797 • http://golibrary.org

Valencia County Historical Society • Harvey House Museum, P.O. Box 166 • Belen, NM 87002 • (505) 861-0581

Bernalillo
Sandia Pueblo • P.O. Box 6008 • Bernalillo, NM 87004 • (505) 867-3317

Sandoval County Historical Society • 151 Edmund Rd, P.O. Box 692 • Bernalillo, NM 87004 • (505) 867-5872

Santa Ana Pueblo • 2 Dove Rd • Bernalillo, NM 87004 • (505) 867-3301

Town of Bernalillo Public Library • 134 Calle Malinche, P.O. Box 638 • Bernalillo, NM 87004-0638 • (505) 867-1440 • http://www.townofbernalillo.lib.nm.us

Bloomfield
Salmon Ruins Museum • 6131 US Hwy 64, P.O. Box 125 • Bloomfield, NM 87413-0125 • (505) 632-2013 • http://www.salmonruins.com

San Juan County Archaeological Research Center • 6131 US Hwy 64, P.O. Box 125 • Bloomfield, NM 87413 • (505) 632-2013

San Juan County Museum Association • Historical Museum, P.O. Box 125 • Bloomfield, NM 87413 • (505) 632-2013

Totah Tracers Genealogical Society • P.O. Box 125 • Bloomfield, NM 87413-0125 • (505) 632-3668

Capitan
Smokey Bear Museum • 104 W Smokey Bear Blvd • Capitan, NM 88316

Carlsbad
Carlsbad Historical Society • 418 W Fox St • Carlsbad, NM 88220 • (505) 628-0697

Carlsbad Historical Society Archives • 2004 Iona St • Carlsbad, NM 88220 • (505) 628-0697

Carlsbad Museum • 418 W Fox St • Carlsbad, NM 88220 • (505) 887-0276 • http://www.carlsbadmuseum.org

Carlsbad Public Library • 101 S Halagueno • Carlsbad, NM 88220 • (505) 885-0731

Eddy County Genealogical Society • c/o Carlsbad Public Library, 101 S Halagueno, P.O. Box 461 • Carlsbad, NM 88220 • (505) 885-0731

Southeastern New Mexico Historical Society • 101 S Halagueno • Carlsbad, NM 88220 • (505) 885-6776

Carrizozo
Lincoln County Historical Society • 11th St • Carrizozo, NM 88301 • (505) 648-2443

Cerrillos
Cerrillos Turqoise Mining Museum • 17 Waldo St, P.O. Box 131 • Cerrillos, NM 87010 • (505) 438-3008 • http://www.casagrandetradingpost.com

Chama
Eleanor Daggett Memorial Public Library • 299 W 4th St, P.O. Box 795 • Chama, NM 87520-0795 • (505) 756-2388

Chloride
Pioneer Store Museum • Wall St • Chloride, NM 87943 • (505) 743-2736 • http://www.pioneerstoremuseum.com

Church Rock
Red Rock Museum • P.O. Box 328 • Church Rock, NM 87311 • (505) 863-1337

Cimarron
Cimmaron Historical Society • Old Mill Museum, 220 W 17th St, P.O. Box 58 • Cimarron, NM 87714 • (505) 376-2417 • http://www.nmculture.org/HTML/northe.htm

Philmont Museum • Philmont Scout Ranch, 17 Deer Run Rd • Cimarron, NM 87714 • (505) 376-2281

Clayton
A W Thompson Public Library & Museum • 17 Chestnut St • Clayton, NM 88415 • (505) 374-9423

Union County Historical Society • Herzstein Memorial Museum, 22 S 2nd St, P.O. Box 75 • Clayton, NM 88415 • (505) 374-2977 • http://www.herzsteinmuseum.org

Cleveland
Cleveland Historical Society • Roller Mill Museum, NM 518, P.O. Box 287 • Cleveland, NM 87715 • (505) 387-2645

Cloudcroft
Sacramento Mountains Historical Society • Historical Museum, 1000 US Hwy 82, P.O. Box 435 • Cloudcroft, NM 88317 • (505) 682-2932

Clovis
Clovis Depot Model Train Museum • 221 W 1st St • Clovis, NM 88101 • (505) 762-0066 • http://www.clovisdepot.com

Clovis-Carver Public Library • 701 Main • Clovis, NM 88101 • (505) 769-7840 • http://www.cityofclovis.org/library

Curry County Genealogy Society • c/o Clovis-Carter Public Library, 701 Main St • Clovis, NM 88101 • (505) 769-7840

Eula Mae Edwards Memorial Museum • 417 Schepps Blvd • Clovis, NM 88101 • (505) 769-4115

High Plains Historical Foundation • 313 Prairieview • Clovis, NM 88101 • (505) 763-6361

Cochiti
Cochiti Pueblo • P.O. Box 70 • Cochiti, NM 87041 • (505) 867-3211

Pueblo de Cochiti Community Library • 255 Cochiti St, P.O. Box 70 • Cochiti, NM 87072-0070 • (505) 465-2885

Cochiti Lake
Cochiti Lake Public Library • 6515 Hoochaneetsa Blvd • Cochiti Lake, NM 87083 • (505) 465-2561

Columbus
Columbus Historical Society • 1902 Railroad Station, Hwys 9 & 11, P.O. Box 562 • Columbus, NM 88029 • (505) 531-2620 • http://www.nmculture.org

Corrales
Corrales Community Library • 84 W La Entrada, P.O. Box 1868 • Corrales, NM 87048-1868 • (505) 897-0733

Corrales Historical Society • Corrales Rd, P.O. Box 1051 • Corrales, NM 87048 • (505) 897-1513

Cuba
Cuba Public Library • 45 Hwy 126, P.O. Box 426 • Cuba, NM 87013-0426 • (505) 289-3100

Deming
Deming Historical Society • Deming Luna Membres Museum, 301 S Silver St, P.O. Box 1617 • Deming, NM 88030 • (505) 546-2382 • http://www.deminglunamembresmuseum.com

Luna County Historical Society • Deming Luna Membres Museum, 301 S Silver St, P.O. Box 1617 • Deming, NM 88030 • (505) 546-2382

Marshall Memorial Library • 301 S Tin Ave • Deming, NM 88030-3698 • (505) 546-9202 • http://www.zianet.com/demingpl/

Dulce
Jicarilla Apache Tribe • Chieftain Office Complex, P.O. Box 547 • Dulce, NM 87528-0547 • (505) 759-3242

Espanola
Bond House Museum • 710 Bond • Espanola, NM 87532 • (505) 747-8535

Espanola Public Library • 314-A Onate St • Espanola, NM 87532 • (505) 747-6087

Northern New Mexico Community College Library • 921 Paseo de Onate • Espanola, NM 87532 • (505) 747-2241 • http://nnmcc.edu/www/library

Santa Clara Pueblo • P.O. Box 580 • Espanola, NM 87532 • (505) 753-7326

Estancia
Estancia Public Library • 10th & Highland, P.O. Box 166 • Estancia, NM 87016-0167 • (505) 384-9655

Eunice
Eunice Public Library • 10th & N Sts, P.O. Box 1629 • Eunice, NM 88231-1629 • (505) 394-2336

Farmington
Farmington Museum • 3041 E Main St • Farmington, NM 87402 • (505) 599-1174

Farmington Pioneer History Society • 302 N Orchard • Farmington, NM 87401-6227

Farmington Public Library • 2101 Farmington Ave • Farmington, NM 87401 • (505) 599-1270 • http://www.infoway.lib.nm.us

Harvest Grove Farm and Orchards Museum • Animas Park, Browning Pkwy • Farmington, NM 87402 • (505) 599-1423

McKee/Carsons Collectors Memorial Museum • 309 W Main St • Farmington, NM 87401 • (505) 327-1347

Salmon Ruins Museum • 6131 US Hwy 64, • Farmington, NM 87401 • (505) 632-3668

San Juan College Library • 4601 College Blvd • Farmington, NM 87402 • (505) 566-3249 • http://www.sanjuancollege.edu/lib/

San Juan County Museum • 6131 US Hwy 64 • Farmington, NM 87401 • (505) 632-2013

Folsom
Folsom Historical Society • Main St • Folsom, NM 88419

Fort Sumner
Billy the Kid Museum • 1601 E Sumner Ave • Fort Sumner, NM 88119 • (505) 355-2380 • http://www.billythekidmuseumfortsumner.com

Fort Sumner State Monument • Billy the Kid Rd, P.O. Box 356 • Fort Sumner, NM 88119 • (505) 425-8025

Gallup
Navajo Colde Talker Museum • 103 Historic Route 66 • Gallup, NM 87301 • (505) 722-2228

Octavia Fellin Public Library & Museum • 115 W Hill Ave • Gallup, NM 87301 • (505) 863-1291 • http://www.ci.gallup.nm.us

Red Rock Historical Society • P.O. Box 328 • Gallup, NM 87311

Storyteller Museum • 100 E Hwy 66 • Gallup, NM 87301 • (505) 863-4131

Grants
Mother Whiteside Memorial Library • 525 W High St • Grants, NM 87020-2526 • (505) 287-4793

New Mexico Museum of Mining • 100 N Iron Ave, P.O. Box 297 • Grants, NM 87020 • (505) 287-4802

New Mexico State University-Grants Branch Library • 1500 3rd St • Grants, NM 87020 • (505) 287-6637 • http://www.grants.nmsu.edu

Hillsboro
Black Range Museum • NM 152, P.O. Box 454 • Hillsboro, NM 88042 • (505) 895-5233

Hobbs
Lea County Western Heritage Center • 5317 Lovington Hwy, NMJC Campus • Hobbs, NM 88240 • (505) 392-5118

Scarborough Memorial Library & Southwest Heritage Room • College of the Southwest, 6610 Lovington Hwy • Hobbs, NM 88240 • (505) 392-6565 • http://www.csw.edu

Southeastern New Mexico Genealogical Society • Will Rogers Community Center, 200 E Park St, P.O. Box 5725 • Hobbs, NM 88240 • (505) 393-3658

Isleta
Isleta Pueblo • P.O. Box 1270 • Isleta, NM 87022 • (505) 869-3111

Rio Grande Filipino American National Society • P.O. Box 953 • Isleta, NM 87022

Isleta Pueblo
Filipino American National Historical Society, Rio Grande Chapter • P.O. Box 953 • Isleta Pueblo, NM 87022

Jal
Woolworth Community Library • Utah & 3rd Sts, P.O. Box 1249 • Jal, NM 88252-1249 • (505) 395-3268 • http://www.woolworth.org

Jemez Pueblo
Jemez Pueblo • P.O. Box 100 • Jemez Pueblo, NM 87024 • (505) 834-7359

Jemez Springs
Jemez State Monument Museum • NM Hwy 4, P.O. Box 143 • Jemez Springs, NM 87025 • (505) 829-3530 • http://www.nmmonuments.org

Kingston
Percha Bank Museum • 119B Main St • Kingston, NM 88042 • (505) 895-5032 • http://www.perchabank.com

Kirtland AFB
Kirtland Air Force Base Library FL4469 • 377 SVS/SVMG, 2050-B Second St SE Bldg 20204 • Kirtland AFB, NM 87117-5525 • (505) 846-1071

La Luz
Alamogordo Genealogical Society • P.O. Box 246 • La Luz, NM 88337 • (505) 434-1675

Laguna
Laguna Pueblo • P.O. Box 194 • Laguna, NM 87026 • (505) 552-6654

Las Cruces
American Historical Society of Germans from Russia, New Mexico Chapter • 2217 Santo Domingo Ave • Las Cruces, NM 88011 • (575) 532-9284 • http://www.ahsgr.org/Chapters/new_mexico_chapter.htm

Bicentennial Log Cabin Museum • Main & Lucero Sts, P.O. Box 20000 • Las Cruces, NM 88001 • (505) 541-2155

Branigan Cultural Center • 490 Water St • Las Cruces, NM 88052 • (505) 541-2155

Las Cruces, cont.
Branson Library • New Mexico State Univ, 2911 McFie Circle, P.O. Box 30006, MSC 3475 • Las Cruces, NM 88003-8006 • (505) 646-5792 • http://www.lib.nmsu.edu

Institute of Historical Survey Foundation • 3035 S Main • Las Cruces, NM 88005-3756 • (505) 525-3035

Las Cruces Historical Museum • 500 N Water • Las Cruces, NM 88001 • (505) 541-2155 • http://www.lascruces-culture.org

New Mexico Farm & Ranch Heritage Museum • 4100 Dripping Springs Rd • Las Cruces, NM 88011 • (505) 272-4100 • http://www. nmfarmandranchmuseum.org

Southern New Mexico Genealogical Society • c/o Thomas Branigan Memorial Library, 200 E Picacho Ave, P.O. Box 2563 • Las Cruces, NM 88004 • (505) 526-1047 • http://www.zianet.com/wheelerwc/Gen/ SSNM

Thomas Branigan Memorial Library • 200 E Picacho Ave • Las Cruces, NM 88001-3499 • (505) 528-4004 • http://library.las-cruces.org

Las Vegas
Carnegie Public Library • 500 National Ave • Las Vegas, NM 87701 • (505) 454-1401

Citizens' Committee for Historic Preservation • 1823 N Gonzales St, P.O. Box 707 • Las Vegas, NM 87701 • (505) 425-8803

City of Las Vegas and Rough Riders Memorial Museum • 727 Grand Ave, P.O. Box 160 • Las Vegas, NM 87701 • (505) 454-1401 • http:// www.lasvegasmuseum.org

Las Vegas City Historical Society • 729 Grand Ave • Las Vegas, NM 87701

Las Vegas Genealogical Society • c/o Carnegie Public Library, 500 National Ave • Las Vegas, NM 87701-4399 • (505) 454-1401

Las Vegas Paiute Tribe • 1 Paiute Dr • Las Vegas, NM 89106 • (702) 386-3926 • http://itcn.org/tribes/lasvegas.html

Thomas C Donnelly Library • New Mexico Highlands Univ, National Ave • Las Vegas, NM 87701 • (505) 425-7511 • http://donelly.nmhu. edu

Lincoln
Historic Lincoln Museum • Hwy 380, P.O. Box 98 • Lincoln, NM 88388 • (505) 653-4025 • http://www.zianet.com/museum

Lincoln County Heritage Trust • P.O. Box 36 • Lincoln, NM 88338 • (505) 653-4025

Lincoln State Monument Museum • Hwy 380, P.O. Box 36 • Lincoln, NM 88338 • (505) 653-4372

Old Lincoln County Courthouse Museum • Hwy 380, P.O. Box 36 • Lincoln, NM 88338 • (505) 653-4372

Lordsburg
Shakespeare Ghost Town Museum • 2.5 mi S of Main St, P.O. Box 253 • Lordsburg, NM 88045 • (505) 542-9034

Los Alamos
Los Alamos County Historical Society • Historical Museum, 1921 Juniper, P.O. Box 43 • Los Alamos, NM 87544-0043 • (505) 662-6272 • http://www.losalamos.com/historicalsociety

Los Alamos Family History Society • c/o Mesa Public Library, 2400 Central Ave, P.O. Box 900 • Los Alamos, NM 87544-0900 • (505) 662-8240 • http://www.glenda.com/lafhs

Los Alamos Genealogical Association • P.O. Box 900 • Los Alamos, NM 87544 • (505) 662-3381

Los Alamos Historical Museum • 1050 Bathtub Row, P.O. Box 43 • Los Alamos, NM 87544 • (505) 662-6272 • http://www.losalamoshistory.org

Los Alamos Public Library System • 2400 Central Ave • Los Alamos, NM 87544 • (505) 662-8240 • http://library.lac-nm.us

University of New Mexico-Los Alamos Campus Library • 4000 University Dr • Los Alamos, NM 87544 • (505) 662-0343 • http://www. la.unm.edu/~lalib/lib-home.html

Los Ojos
Sociedad Historica de la Tierra Amarilla • P.O. Box 24 • Los Ojos, NM 87551 • (505) 345-5147

Lovington
Lea County Genealogical Society • McKibben Senior Center, 14 West Ave, P.O. Box 1044 • Lovington, NM 88260-1044 • (505) 396-2608

Lea County Historical Society • P.O. Box 1195 • Lovington, NM 88260

Lea County Museum • 103 S Love • Lovington, NM 88260 • (505) 396-4805 • http://www.leacountymuseum.org

Lovington Public Library • 115 S Main St • Lovington, NM 88260 • (505) 396-3144 • http://lovingtonpublib.leaco.net

Magdalena
Box Car Museum • 108 N Main St • Magdalena, NM 87825 • (505) 854-2261

Alamo Navajo Chapter • P.O. Box 383 • Magdelena, NM 87825 • (505) 854-2686

Mescalero
Mescalero Apache Cultural Center • P.O. Box 176 • Mescalero, NM 88340 • (505) 671-4494

Mesilla
Gadsden Historical Society • Gadsden Museum, 1875 Boutz Rd, P.O. Box 147 • Mesilla, NM 88046 • (575) 526-6293 • http://www. gadsdenmuseummesilla.com/

Moriarty
Moriarty Historical Society • Historical Museum, 202 Broadway St, P.O. Box 1366 • Moriarty, NM 87035 • (505) 832-0839

Mountainair
Salinas Pueblo Missions Research Library • 102 S Ripley St, P.O. Box 517 • Mountainair, NM 87036 • (505) 847-2585 • http://www.nps.gov

Old Mesilla
Casasola Museum • 2251 Calle de Santiago • Old Mesilla, NM 88046

Pecos
Pecos National Historical Park • State Rd 63, P.O. Box 418 • Pecos, NM 87552 • (505) 757-6414

Santa Fe County Genealogical Society • HC70, Box 18AA • Pecos, NM 87552 • (505) 757-2796

Penasco
Picuris Pueblo • P.O. Box 127 • Penasco, NM 87553 • (505) 587-2519

Picuris Pueblo Museum Center • P.O. Box 487 • Penasco, NM 87533 • (505) 587-2957

Pinos Altos
Fort Cobre Pioneers of the West Museum • 25 Main St • Pinos Altos, NM 88053 • (505) 388-2211

Portales
Bill Daley's Windmill Museum • 1506 S Kilgore • Portales, NM 88130 • (505) 356-6263

Golden Library & Museum • Eastern New Mexico Univ, 1300 S Ave K, Sta 32 • Portales, NM 88130-7402 • (505) 562-2624 • http://www. enmu.edu/golden.html

Portales Public Library • 218 S Avenue B • Portales, NM 88130 • (505) 356-3940 • http://www.portalesnm.org/library

Roosevelt County Museum • Eastern New Mexico Univ, Station 9, ENMU • Portales, NM 88130 • (505) 562-2592 • http://www.enmu.edu

Roosevelt County Searchers • P.O. Box 471 • Portales, NM 88130-0451 • (505) 359-0772 • http://www.rootsweb.com/~nmrcs/

Radium Springs
Fort Selden State Monument Library • I-25 & Hwy 185, P.O. Box 58 • Radium Springs, NM 88054 • (505) 526-8911 • http://www.nmmculture.org

Raidoso Downs
Hubbard Museum of the American West • 841 Hwy 70 W, P.O. Box 40 • Raidoso Downs, NM 88346 • (505) 378-4142 • http://www.hubbardmuseum.org

Ramah
El Morro National Monument Museum • Hwy 53, HC 61, Box 43 • Ramah, NM 87321 • (505) 783-4226 • http://www.nps.gov/elmo

Ramah Historical Society • general delivery • Ramah, NM 87321 • (505) 783-4150

Ramah Navajo Chapter • Route 2, Box 13 • Ramah, NM 87321 • (505) 775-3383

Raton
Arthur Johnson Memorial Library • 244 Cook Ave • Raton, NM 87740 • (505) 445-9711

Colfax County Historical Museum • 216 S 1st St • Raton, NM 87740 • (505) 445-8979

Dorsey Mansion Museum • LLP 50 S 6th St • Raton, NM 87740 • (505) 375-2222

Raton Historical Society • Raton Museum, 216 S 1st St • Raton, NM 87740 • (505) 445-8979

Rio Rancho
J & R Vintage Auto Museum • 3650 NM 528 NW #A • Rio Rancho, NM 87174 • (505) 867-2881

Rio Rancho Public Library • 950 Pinetree Rd SE, P.O. Box 15670 • Rio Rancho, NM 87174-0670 • (505) 891-5013 • http://www.ci.rio-rancho.nm.us/library.htm

Suomi Conference of the Lutheran Church in America Archives • 516 Villa Verde • Rio Rancho, NM 87124 • (505) 898-6673

Roswell
Chaves County Genealogical Society • P.O. Box 51 • Roswell, NM 88201

Chaves County Historical Society • Historical Center for Southeast New Mexico, 200 N Lea Ave • Roswell, NM 88201-4655 • (505) 622-8333

General Douglas L McBride Museum • 101 W College Blvd, P.O. Box J • Roswell, NM 88201 • (505) 624-8220 • http://www.nmmi.cc.nm.us

Historical Society of Southeast New Mexico • Historical Center for Southeast New Mexico, 200 N Lea Ave • Roswell, NM 88201-4655 • (505) 622-8333 • http://roswell-usa.com/historic/

Paul Horgan Library • New Mexico Military Institute, 101 W College • Roswell, NM 88201-5173 • (505) 624-8380 • http://www.nmmi.cc.nm.us/toles/learning.html

Roswell Genealogical Society • Roswell Adult Center, 807 N Missouri • Roswell, NM 88201 • (505) 622-6725

Roswell Historical Society • Historical Museum, 100 W 11th St • Roswell, NM 88201 • (505) 624-6744 • http://www.roswellmuseum.org

Roswell Public Library • 301 N Pennsylvania Ave • Roswell, NM 88201 • (505) 622-7101

Wilson-Cobb History and Genealogy Research Library • 1018 North Plains Park • Roswell, NM 88203-2516 • (505) 622-0967

Ruidoso Downs
Hubbard Museum of the American West • 841 Hwy 70 W, P.O. Box 40 • Ruidoso Downs, NM 88346 • (575) 378-4142

San Felipe Pueblo
San Felipe Pueblo • P.O. Box A • San Felipe Pueblo, NM 87001 • (505) 867-3381

San Juan
San Juan Pueblo • P.O. Box 1099 • San Juan, NM 87566 • (505) 852-4400

Sandia Park
Tinkertown Museum • 121 Sandia Crest Rd, P.O. Box 303 • Sandia Park, NM 87047 • (505) 281-5233 • http://www.tinkertown.com

Santa Cruz
San Gabriel Historical Society • P.O. Box 1528 • Santa Cruz, NM 87567 • (505) 852-2112

Santa Fe
Bataan Memorial Military Museum • 1050 Old Pecos Tr • Santa Fe, NM 87505 • (505) 474-1670

Bureau of Land Management-Western States • 1474 Rodeo Rd, P.O. Box 27115 • Santa Fe, NM 87502 • (505) 438-7400 • http://www.blm.gov

Colonial New Mexico Historical Foundation • 135 Camino Escondido • Santa Fe, NM 87501 • (505) 982-5644

El Rancho de las Golondrinas Museum • 334 Los Pinos Rd • Santa Fe, NM 87507 • (505) 471-2261 • http://www.golondrinas.org

Fogelson Library Center • College of Santa Fe, 1600 St Michael's Dr • Santa Fe, NM 87505 • (505) 473-6569 • http://www.library.csf.edu

Fray Angelico Chavez History Library and Photographic Archives • 110 Washington Ave, P.O. Box 2087 • Santa Fe, NM 87504 • (505) 827-6470 • http://www.palaceofthegovernors.org

Guadalupe Historic Foundation • 100 S Guadalupe St • Santa Fe, NM 87501-5503 • (505) 988-2027

Historical Society of New Mexico • P.O. Box 1912 • Santa Fe, NM 87504-1912

Museum of New Mexico • 725 Camino Lejo, P.O. Box 2087 • Santa Fe, NM 87504 • (505) 476-1125 • http://www.museumofnewmexico.org

Museum of the Catholic Church in New Mexico • 223 Cathedral Pl • Santa Fe, NM 87501 • (505) 983-3811

Nambe Pueblo • Route 1, Box 117BB • Santa Fe, NM 87501 • (505) 455-7692

New Mexico Dept of Health - Vital Records • Harold Runnels Bldg, 1190 St Francis Dr, P.O. Box 26110 • Santa Fe, NM 87504-6110 • (505) 827-2321 • http://dohewbs2.health.state.nm.us/VitalRec/

New Mexico Jewish Historical Society • 1428 Miracerros Loop S, P.O. Box 15598 • Santa Fe, NM 87506 • (505) 988-5751 • http://www.nmculture.org/HTML/northc.html

New Mexico Jewish Historical Society, Genealogy and Family History Committee • 1428 Miracerros Loop S, P.O. Box 15598 • Santa Fe, NM 87506 • (505) 988-5751

New Mexico Records Center and Archives • 1205 Camino Carlos Rey • Santa Fe, NM 87505 • (505) 476-7900 • http://www.nmcpr.state.ms.us

New Mexico State Library • 1209 Camino Carlos Rey • Santa Fe, NM 87507 • (505) 476-9700 • http://www.stlib.state.nm.us

Palace of the Governors • 228 E Palace Ave, P.O. Box 2087 • Santa Fe, NM 87504 • (505) 827-6320 • http://www.palaceofthegovernors.com

Poeh Museum and Cultural Center • 78 Cities of Gold Rd • Santa Fe, NM 87506 • (505) 455-3334 • http://www.poehmuseum.com

Pojoaque Pueblo • Route 11, Box 71 • Santa Fe, NM 87501 • (505) 455-2278

Santa Fe, cont.
San Ildefonso Historical Society • Route 5, Box 315-A • Santa Fe, NM 87501

San Ildefonso Pueblo • Route 5, Box 315A • Santa Fe, NM 87501 • (505) 455-2273

San Miguel Mission Museum • 401 Old Santa Fe Trail • Santa Fe, NM 87501 • (505) 983-3974

Santa Fe County Historical Society • P.O. Box 1985 • Santa Fe, NM 87504

Santa Fe Genealogical Society • 140 W Coronado Rd • Santa Fe, NM 87501

Santa Fe Public Library • 145 Washington Ave • Santa Fe, NM 87501 • (505) 955-6781 • http://www.ci.santa-fe.nm.us/sfpl/

Santuario de Nuestra Senora de Guadalupe Museum • 100 S Guadalupe St • Santa Fe, NM 87501 • (505) 988-2027

Site Santa Fe Museum • 1606 Paseo de Peralta • Santa Fe, NM 87501 • (505) 989-1199

Tesuque Pueblo • Route 11, Box 1 • Santa Fe, NM 87501 • (505) 983-2667

Wheelwright Museum of the American Indian • 704 Camino Lejo, P.O. Box 5153 • Santa Fe, NM 87502 • (505) 982-4636 • http://www.wheelwright.org

Santa Rosa
Moise Memorial Library • 208 5th St • Santa Rosa, NM 88435 • (505) 472-3101

Santa Teresa
War Eagle Air Museum • Dona Ana County Airport, 8012 Airport Rd, P.O. Box 1225 • Santa Teresa, NM 88088 • (505) 589-2000 • http://www.war-eagles-air.museum.com

Santo Domingo Pueblo
Santo Domingo Pueblo • P.O. Box 99 • Santo Domingo Pueblo, NM 87052 • (505) 465-2688

Silver City
ComGenes • P.O. Box 1581 • Silver City, NM 88062

Grant County Genealogical Society • P.O. Box 1581 • Silver City, NM 88062 • (505) 538-2329

Historical Society of Southwestern New Mexico • WNMU Museum • Silver City, NM 88061 • (505) 538-6386

J Cloyd Miller Library • Western New Mexico University, 1000 W College, P.O. Box 680 • Silver City, NM 88062-0680 • (505) 538-6350 • http://voyager.wnmu.edu

Silver City Historical Society • Silver City Museum, 312 W Broadway • Silver City, NM 88061 • (505) 538-5921 • http://www.silvercitymuseum.org

Silver City Public Library • 515 W College Ave • Silver City, NM 88061 • (505) 538-3672 • http://townofsilvercity.org/library/library_home.htm

Western New Mexico University Museum • 1000 W College Ave, P.O. Box 680 • Silver City, NM 88062 • (505) 538-6386 • http://www.wnmw.edu/univ/museum.htm

Socorro
Socorro County Historical Society • 600 6th St N, P.O. Box 923 • Socorro, NM 87801 • (505) 838-4141 • http://www.rootsweb.com/~nmschs

Socorro Public Library • 401 Park St • Socorro, NM 87801-4544 • (505) 835-1114 • http://www.sdc.org/~library

Springer
Santa Fe Historical Society • P.O. Box 323 • Springer, NM 87747

Santa Fe Trail Museum • 614 Maxwell Ave • Springer, NM 87747 • (505) 483-0477

Sumner
Fort Sumner State Monument Museum • 3647 Billy the Kid, P.O. Box 356 • Sumner, NM 88119 • (505) 355-2573 • http://www.nmmonuments.org

Taos
Fechin Institute • Fechin Home Museum, 277 Paseo del Pueblo Norte • Taos, NM 87571 • (505) 758-1710

Governor Bent Museum • 117 Bent St, P.O. Box 153 • Taos, NM 87571 • (505) 758-2376

Harwood Foundation • 25 Ledoux St, P.O. Box 766 • Taos, NM 87571 • (505) 748-9826

Kit Carson Historic Society • Kit Carson Historic Museum, 113 Kit Carson Rd • Taos, NM 87557 • (505) 758-4945 • http://www.laplaza.org; www.taosmuseums.org

Millicent Rogers Museum • 1504 Museum Rd, P.O. Box A • Taos, NM 87571-0546 • (505) 758-2462 • http://www.millicentrogers.org

Taos County Historical Society • 121C North Plaza, Old Courthouse, P.O. Box 2447 • Taos, NM 87571 • http://www.taos-history.org

Taos Pueblo • P.O. Box 1846 • Taos, NM 87571 • (505) 758-8626

Tierra Amarilla
Rio Arriba County Historical Society • P.O. Box 158 • Tierra Amarilla, NM 87575

Tijeras
Old Church of Santo Nino Museum • general delivery • Tijeras, NM 87059

Tome
Tome Parish Museum • 07 N Church Loop, P.O. Box 397 • Tome, NM 87060 • (505) 865-7497

Truth or Consequences
Callihan's Auto Museum • 410 Cedar St • Truth or Consequences, NM 87901 • (505) 894-6900

Sierra County Genealogical Society • c/o Truth or Consequences Public Library, 325 Library Ln, P.O. Box 311 • Truth or Consequences, NM 87901 • (505) 894-3027 • http://www.rootsweb.com/~nmscgs2

Sierra County Historical Society • Geronimo Springs Museum, 211 Main St • Truth or Consequences, NM 87901 • (505) 894-6600

Truth or Consequences Public Library • 325 Library Ln • Truth or Consequences, NM 87901-2375 • (505) 894-3027 • http://ci.truth-or-consequences.nm.us/library.htm

Tucumcari
Tucumcari Historical Research Institute • Historical Museum • 416 S Adams • Tucumcari, NM 88401 • (505) 461-4201 • http://www.cityoftucumcari.com

Tucumcari Public Library • 602 S 2nd St • Tucumcari, NM 88401-2899 • (505) 461-0295

Tularosa
Tularosa Village Historical Society • Historical Museum, 608 Central Ave • Tularosa, NM 88352 • (505) 585-2057

Watrous
Fort Union National Monument Library • I-25, exit 366, P.O. Box 127 • Watrous, NM 87753 • (505) 425-8025 • http://www.nps.gov/foun/

White Sands Missile Range
US Army Consolidated Library • Bldg 464 • White Sands Missile Range, NM 88002-5039 • (505) 678-5820

White Sands Missile Range Museum • Bldg 8T 304, P.O. Box 400 • White Sands Missile Range, NM 88002 • (505) 678-8824

White's City
Million Dollar Museum • Carlsbad Caverns Hwy • White's City, NM 88268 • (505) 785-2291 • http://www.caverns.com/~chamber/rec.htm

Zia Pueblo
Zia Pueblo • 123 Capital Square Dr • Zia Pueblo, NM 87053-6013 • (505) 867-3304

Zuni
A:Shiwi A:Wan Museum and Heritage Center • Caliente Rd, P.O. Box 1009 • Zuni, NM 87327 • (505) 782-4403

Zuni Heritage and Historic Preservation Society • P.O. Box 339 • Zuni, NM 87327 • (505) 782-4113

Zuni Pueblo • P.O. Box 339 • Zuni, NM 87327 • (505) 782-4481

Accord

Friends of Historic Rochester • 12 Main St, P.O. Box 229 • Accord, NY 12404 • (845) 626-7104

Adams

Adams Free Library • 2 N Main St • Adams, NY 13605 • (315) 232-2265 • http://www.nc3r.org/admfl

Historical Association of South Jefferson County • 29 E Church St, P.O. Box 55 • Adams, NY 13605 • (315) 232-2616 • http://hasjny.tripod.com

Adams Basin

Ogden Historical Society • Historical Museum, P.O. Box 777 • Adams Basin, NY 14410 • (585) 352-3672 • http://www.monroecounty.gov

Adams Center

Adams Center Free Library • 18267 State Route 177 • Adams Center, NY 13606 • (315) 583-5501 • http://www.nc3r.org/adc

Afton

Afton Free Library • 105A Main St • Afton, NY 13730-9504 • (607) 639-1212 • http://www.4cls.org/webpages/members/Afton/Afton.html

Afton Historical Society • Historical Museum, 116 Main St, P.O. Box 18 • Afton, NY 13730-0018 • (607) 639-1110 • http://tri-countryny.net/ahs

Akron

Newstead Historical Society • Knight-Sutton Museum, Main St & Parkview Dr, P.O. Box 222 • Akron, NY 14401 • (716) 542-4369 • http://www.newsteadhistoricalsociety.org

Albany

Albany County Historical Association • Ten Broeck Mansion Museum, 9 Ten Broeck Pl • Albany, NY 12210-2524 • (518) 436-9826 • http://www.timesunion.com/communities/tenbroeck

Albany Heritage Area Museum • 25 Quakenbush Sq • Albany, NY 12207 • (518) 434-1217

Albany Institute of History and Art • 125 Washington Ave • Albany, NY 12210 • (518) 463-4478 • http://www.albanyinstitute.org

Albany Institute of History and Art Library • 125 Washington Ave • Albany, NY 12210 • (518) 463-4478 • http://www.albanyinstitute.org

Albany Public Library • 161 Washington Ave • Albany, NY 12210 • (518) 449-3380 • http://www.albanypubliclibrary.org

Albany South End Historical Society • 20 2nd Ave • Albany, NY 12202 • (518) 463-0249

American Italian Heritage Association • P.O. Box 3136 • Albany, NY 12203-0136 • (518) 435-0591 • http://www.aiha-albany.org

American Italian Heritage Museum • 1227 Central Ave • Albany, NY 12205 • http://www.americanitalianmuseum.org

Capital District Genealogical Society • P.O. Box 2175, Empire State Plaza Sta • Albany, NY 12220-0175 • (518) 355-6640

Capital District Genealogical Society, Computer Interest Group • P.O. Box 2175, Empire State Plaza Sta • Albany, NY 12220-0175 • (518) 355-6640

Capital District Genealogical Society, German Interest Group • P.O. Box 2175, Empire State Plaza Sta • Albany, NY 12220-0175 • (518) 355-6640

Capital District Genealogical Society, Irish Interest Group • P.O. Box 2175, Empire State Plaza Sta • Albany, NY 12220-0175 • (518) 355-6640

Capital District Genealogical Society, Rensselaer Interest Group • P.O. Box 2175, Empire State Plaza Sta • Albany, NY 12220-0175 • (518) 355-6640

Capital District Genealogical Society, Schenectady Group • P.O. Box 2175, Empire State Plaza Sta • Albany, NY 12220 • (518) 355-6640

Daughters of Charity Archives Albany • 96 Menands Rd • Albany, NY 12204-1499 • (518) 462-5593

Dutch Settlers Society of Albany • 174 D&R Village • Albany, NY 12065-9813 • (518) 456-7202

Historic Albany Foundation • 472 Madison Ave • Albany, NY 12206 • (518) 465-0876 • http://www.historic-albany.org

Historic Cherry Hill • Historical Museum, 523 1/2 S Pearl St • Albany, NY 12202 • (518) 434-4791 • http://www.historiccherryhill.org

Historical Society for the Preservation of the Underground Railroad • 45 Forest Ave • Albany, NY 12208 • (518) 458-7888

Institute for New York State Studies • P.O. Box 2432 • Albany, NY 12220-0432

Irish American Heritage Museum & Research Library • 991 Broadway, Ste 101 • Albany, NY 12204 • (518) 432-6598 • http://irishamericanheritagemuseum.org

Jewish Genealogical Society of Capital District • 176 Hollywood Ave, P.O. Box 5002 • Albany, NY 12205-0002 • (518) 482-2898

M E Grenander Dept of Special Collections and Archives • SUNY at Albany, Science Library, LE-352, 1400 Washington Ave • Albany, NY 12222 • (518) 437-3935 • http://library.albany.edu/speccoll

Military Heritage Museum • 195 Washington Ave • Albany, NY 12205 • (518) 436-0103

Museum of Prints and Print Making • P.O. Box 6578, Fort Orange Sta • Albany, NY 12206 • (518) 432-9514

National Railway Historical Society • Historical Museum, P.O. Box 2131 • Albany, NY 12220 • (518) 449-8450

New Netherland Project • New York State Library, Empire State Plaza • Albany, NY 1223 • (518) 486-4815 • http://www.nnp.org

New York State Archives • Cultural Education Ctr, Rm 11D40 • Albany, NY 12230 • (518) 474-8955 • http://www.archives.nysed.gov

New York State Commission on the Capitol • Empire State Plaza, Corning Tower, 40th Fl • Albany, NY 12242 • (518) 473-0341

New York State Dept of Health - Vital Records Section • Corning Tower, Empire State Plaza, P.O. Box 2602 • Albany, NY 12220-2602 • (518) 474-3077

New York State Historian • 3097 Cultural Education Center, Empire State Plaza • Albany, NY 12230 • (518) 473-7091 • http://www.archives.nysed.gov/aindex.shtml

New York State Library & Newspaper Project • State Education Bldg Annex, Empire State Plaza • Albany, NY 12230 • (518) 474-5161 • http://www.nysl.nysed.gov/

New York State Museum • Cultural Education Ctr, Empire State Plaza, Rm 3099 • Albany, NY 12230 • (518) 474-2854 • http://www.nysm.nysed.gov

New York State Office of Parks, Recration and Historic Preservation Library • Agency Bldg 1, Rockefeller Empire State Plaza • Albany, NY 12238 • (518) 237-8643 • http://www.nysparks.state.ny.us

Preservation League of New York State • 44 Central Ave • Albany, NY 12206-3002 • (518) 462-5658 • http://www.preservenys.org/seven.htm

Saint Michael's Episcopal Church Museum & Botanic Gardens • 35 Culver Ave • Albany, NY 12205 • (518) 456-2958

Schuyler Mansion Museum • 32 Catherine St • Albany, NY 12202 • (519) 434-0834 • http://nysparks.state.ny.us

Shaker Heritage Society • 1848 Shaker Meeting House Museum, 25 Meeting House Rd • Albany, NY 12211 • (518) 456-7890 • http://www.shakerheritage.org

New York

Albion

Cobblestone Society • Historical Museum, 14393 Ridge Rd W, P.O. Box 363 • Albion, NY 14411 • (585) 589-9013 • http://www.cobblestonesocietymuseum.org

Orleans County Genealogical Society • Albion Town Hall, 3665 Clarendon Rd, P.O. Box 103 • Albion, NY 14411 • http://www.OrleansCountyGenealogicalSociety.org

Orleans County Historical Association • P.O. Box 181 • Albion, NY 14411 • http://www.orleanshistory.org

Swan Library • 4 N Main St • Albion, NY 14411 • (585) 589-4246

Alden

Alden Historical Society • Historical Museum, 13213 Broadway • Alden, NY 14404 • (716) 937-7606

Alexandria Bay

Alexandria Town Historian • P.O. Box 130 • Alexandria Bay, NY 13607 • (315) 482-9519

Alexandria Township Historical Society • Cornwall Brothers Store, Market St • Alexandria Bay, NY 13607 • (315) 482-4586

Boldt Castle Museum • Collins Landing, P.O. Box 428 • Alexandria Bay, NY 13607 • (315) 482-9724

Casa Blanca House Museum • Cherry Island, P.O. Box 217 • Alexandria Bay, NY 13607 • (315) 482-2279

Holland Library • 112 Walton St • Alexandria Bay, NY 13607 • (315) 482-2241 • http://www.macsherrylibrary.org

MacSherry Library • 112 Walton St • Alexandria Bay, NY 13607 • (315) 482-2241

Alfred

Alfred Historical Society • P.O. Box 1137 • Alfred, NY 14802 • (607) 587-8886

Jean B Lang Western New York Historical Collection • SUNY at Alfred, Hinkle Memorial Library, 10 Upper College Dr • Alfred, NY 14820 • (607) 587-4313 • http://web.alfredstate.edu/library/

Alfred Station

Alfred Historical Society • Terra Cotta Museum, 2080 Hemlock Hill Rd • Alfred Station, NY 14803 • (607) 587-8358 • http://www.alfredny.org

Baker's Bridge Historical Association of Alfred Station • 5971 Hamilton Hill Rd, P.O. Box 13 • Alfred Station, NY 14803 • (607) 587-9450 • http://www.bakersbridge.org

Allegany

Allegany Area Historical Association • United Methodist Church, 25 N 2nd St, P.O. Box 162 • Allegany, NY 14706 • (716) 372-2918 • http://aaha.bfn.org

Almond

20th Century Library Club • Main St, P.O. Box D • Almond, NY 14804-0504 • (607) 276-6311 • http://www.stls.org/almond

Almond Historical Society • 1830 Hagadorn House Museum, 7 N Main St, P.O. Box 36 • Almond, NY 14804 • (607) 276-6781 • http://www.rootsweb.com/~nyahs/almondhs.html

Altamont

Altamont Archives & Museum • 115 Main St • Altamont, NY 12009 • (518) 861-8554 • http://www.townofguilderland.org/Altamont.htm

Dutch Barn Preservation Society • P.O. Box 76 • Altamont, NY 12009 • (518) 827-5488 • http://www.schist.org/dbps.htm

Altmar

Albion Town Historian • 312 Bridge St, P.O. Box 394 • Altmar, NY 13302 • (315) 298-5723

Altmar Village Historian • 312 Bridge St, P.O. Box 394 • Altmar, NY 13302 • (315) 298-5723

Amagansett

Amagansett Historical Society • Montauk Hwy & Windmill Ln, P.O. Box 7077 • Amagansett, NY 11930 • (516) 267-3020

East Hampton Historical Society • Bluff Rd • Amagansett, NY 11930 • (631) 267-6544

East Hampton Town Marine Museum • 301 Bluff Rd • Amangansett, NY 11930 • (631) 267-6544 • http://www.easthamptonhistory.org

Amenia

Amenia Historical Society • Main St, P.O. Box 22 • Amenia, NY 12501 • (845) 373-9376

Wethersfield Estate and Gardens Museum • Pugsley Hill, P.O. Box 444 • Amenia, NY 12501 • (914) 373-8037

Amherst

Amherst Archives and Research Center • 5583 Main St • Amherst, NY 14221 • (716) 631-7010

Amherst Museum & Nederlander Research • 3755 Tonawanda Creek Rd • Amherst, NY 14228 • (716) 689-1440 • http://www.amherstmuseum.org

Amherst Public Library • 350 John James Audubon Pkwy • Amherst, NY 14228 • (716) 688-4919

Jewish Genealogical Society of Greater Buffalo • 100 Fruehauf Ave • Amherst, NY 14226 • (716) 833-0743 • http://www.jewishgen.org/jgs/jgs-buffalo

Amityville

Amityville Historical Society • Lauder Museum, 170 Broadway, P.O. Box 764 • Amityville, NY 11701-0764 • (631) 598-1486 • http://www.amityvillehistoricalsociety.org

Amsterdam

Amsterdam Free Library • 28 Church St • Amsterdam, NY 12010 • (518) 842-1080 • http://www.amsterdamfreelibrary.com

Guy Park State Historic Site Museum • Evelyn St • Amsterdam, NY 12010

Town of Perth Historical Society • Route 6 • Amsterdam, NY 12010 • (518) 842-9497 • http://www.perth-town.org/perth_mtngs.html

Walter Elwood Museum • 300 Guy Park Ave • Amsterdam, NY 12010 • (518) 843-5151 • http://www.walterelwoodmuseum.org

Andes

Andes Public Library • Main St, P.O. Box 116 • Andes, NY 13731 • (914) 676-3333 • http://www.rcls.org/webpages/members/Andes/Andes.html

Andes Society for History and Culture • 288 Main St, P.O. Box 455 • Andes, NY 13731 • (845) 676-3775 • http://www.andessociety.org

Andover

Andover Free Library • 40 Main St, P.O. Box 751 • Andover, NY 14806-0751 • (607) 478-8442 • http://www.stls.org/Andover

Andover Historic Preservation Corporation • 32 Rochambeau Ave • Andover, NY 14806 • (607) 478-8009

Andover Historical Society • P.O. Box 705 • Andover, NY 14806

Angelica

Angelica Free Library • Colonial Rooms, 55 W Main St, P.O. Box 128 • Angelica, NY 14709-0128 • (585) 466-7860 • http://www.stls.org/Angelica

Angola

Evans Historical Society • 8351 Erie Rd, P.O. Box 7 • Angola, NY 14006 • (716) 627-7878

Annandale-on-Hudson

Montgomery Place Museum • River Rd, P.O. Box 32 • Annandale-on-Hudson, NY 12504 • (914) 631-8200 • http://www.hudsonvalley.org/montgomeryplace/

Antwerp
Crosby Public Library • 59 Main St, P.O. Box 120 • Antwerp, NY 13608
• (315) 659-8564

Apalachin
Apalachin Reading Center • 719 Main St, P.O. Box 163 • Apalachin,
NY 13732 • (607) 625-3333

APO AE
Genealogical Association of English-Speaking Researchers in Europe
• CMR 420 Box 502 • APO AE, NY 90963 • (011) 49-6227-51942

Italian Genealogical and Heraldic Institute • P.O. Box 2815 • APO AE,
NY 09221

Appleton
Niagara County Genealogical Society • 2650 Hess Rd • Appleton, NY
14008

Apulia Station
Fabius Historical Society • P.O. Box 36 • Apulia Station, NY 13020 •
(315) 683-5674 • http://www.fabiusny.org/FabiusHistoricalSociety.html

Arcade
Arcade Historical Society • Gibby House Museum, 331 W Main St,
P.O. Box 237 • Arcade, NY 14009 • (585) 492-4466 • http://www.
arcadehistoricalsociety.org

Arden
Orange County Historical Society • Historical Museum, 21 Clove
Furnace Dr, P.O. Box 55 • Arden, NY 10910 • (845) 351-4696

Ardsley
Ardsley Historical Society • c/o Ardsley Public Library, 9 American
Legion Dr, P.O. Box 523 • Ardsley, NY 10502 • (914) 693-6027

Ardsley Public Library • 9 American Legion Dr • Ardsley, NY 10502 •
(914) 693-6636 • http://www.ardsleylibrary.org

Arkville
Catskill Regional Folklife and History Archives • Erpf House, Route
28, P.O. Box 504 • Arkville, NY 12406 • (845) 586-2611 • http://www.
catskillcenter.org

Armonk
North Castle Historical Society • Historical Museum, 440 Bedford Rd •
Armonk, NY 10504 • (914) 273-4510 • http://www.northcastleny.com

Ashville
Ashville Free Library • 2200 N Maple St, P.O. Box 379 • Ashville, NY
14710-0379 • (716) 763-9906

Harmony Historical Society • P.O. Box 127 • Ashville, NY 14710 • (716)
782-3074

Astoria
American Museum of the Moving Image • 35th Ave & 36th St • Astoria,
NY 11106 • (718) 777-6888 • http://www.movingimage.us

Greater Astoria Historical Society • 3520 Broadway • Astoria, NY
11106 • (718) 278-0700

Peoples Museum • 22-27 Crescent St • Astoria, NY 11105 • (718) 204-
7941 • http://www.thepeoplesmuseum.org

Athol
John Thurman Historical Society • P.O. Box 7 • Athol, NY 12810 •
http://www.thurman-ny.com/jths

Attica
Attica Historical Society • 130 Main St, P.O. Box 24 • Attica, NY 14011
• (585) 591-2161

Stevens Memorial Library • 146 Main St • Attica, NY 14011-1243 •
(585) 591-2733

Au Sable Forks
Au Sable Forks Free Library • 9 West Church St, P.O. Box 179 •
Au Sable Forks, NY 12912 • (518) 647-5596 • http://www.cefls.org/
ausable.htm

Black Brook Town Historian • 18 N Main St • Au Sable Forks, NY
12912 • (518) 647-5411

Auburn
Ancient Order of Hibernians in America • 31 Logan St • Auburn, NY
13021-3925 • (315) 252-4872 • http://www.aoh.com

Cayuga County Historian Library • Historic Old Post Office, 157
Genesee St • Auburn, NY 13021 • (315) 253-1300

Cayuga County Historical Society • Old Post Office Bldg, 157 Genesee
St • Auburn, NY 13021-3490 • (315) 253-1300

Cayuga-Owasco Lakes Historical Society • 14 West Cayuga St, P.O.
Box 247 • Auburn, NY 13021

Foundation Historical Association • Seward House Museum, 33 South
St • Auburn, NY 13021 • (315) 252-1283 • http://www.sewardhouse.org

Frontenac Historical Society • Historical Museum, 8 Cayuga St •
Auburn, NY 13021 • (315) 889-7273

Harriet Tubman House Museum • 180 S Street • Auburn, NY 13021 •
(315) 252-2081

Norman F Bourke Memorial Library • Cayuga Community College, 197
Franklin St • Auburn, NY 13021 • (315) 255-1743 • http://www.cayuga-
cc.edu/library

Owasco Teyetasta Indian Village, Cayuga Museum of History and Art
• 203 Genesee St • Auburn, NY 13021 • (315) 253-8051 • http://www.
cayuganet.org/cayugamuseum

Seymour Public Library • 176-178 Genesee St • Auburn, NY 13021 •
(315) 252-2571 • http://www.seymourlibrary.org

Ward W O'Hara Agricultural Museum • 6880 E Lake Rd, P.O. Box 309
• Auburn, NY 13021 • (315) 252-7644 • http://www.cauyganet.org/
agmuseum

Auriesville
Kateri Galleries-National Shring of the North American Martyrs •
Route 5 South • Auriesville, NY 12016 • (518) 853-3033 • http://www.
martyrshrine.org

Aurora
Louis Jefferson Long Library • Wells College, 170 Main St • Aurora, NY
13026 • (315) 364-3351 • http://www.wells.edu/library/li1.htm

Austerlitz
Austerlitz Historical Society • 9 Harvey Mountain Rd P.O. Box 104 •
Austerlitz, NY 12017 • (518) 392-0062 • http://www.oldausterlitz.org

Averill Park
Sand Lake Town Library • 8428 Miller Hill Rd • Averill Park, NY
12018 • (518) 674-5050 • http://www.timesunion.com/communities/
sandlakelibrary

Avoca
Avoca Free Library • 18 N Main St, P.O. Box S • Avoca, NY 14809 •
(607) 566-9279 • http://www.stls.org/Avoca

Avoca Historical Society • 4185 County Route 70 • Avoca, NY 14809 •
(607) 566-2884

Howard Historical Society • Mill Rd • Avoca, NY 14809 • (607) 566-
2412

Avon
Avon Preservation and Historical Society • 27 Genesee St • Avon, NY
14414 • (585) 226-3421 • http://www.avonhistorical.org

Babylon

Babylon Public Library • 24 S Carll Ave • Babylon, NY 11702 • (631) 669-1624 • http://www.suffolk.lib.ny.us/libraries/babl

Babylon Village Historical and Preservation Society • 117 W Main St, P.O. Box 484 • Babylon, NY 11702 • (631) 669-1756 • http://www.babylonvillagehistoricalsociety.org

Bainbridge

Bainbridge Free Library • 13 N Main St • Bainbridge, NY 13733-1210 • (607) 967-5305 • http://www.4cls.org/webpages/members/Bainbridge/Bainbridge.html

Bainbridge Historical Society • 38 S Main St, P.O. Box 146 • Bainbridge, NY 13733

Baldwin

Baldwin Historical Society • Historical Museum, 1980 Grand Ave, P.O. Box 762 • Baldwin, NY 11510 • (516) 223-6900 • http://www.baldwin.org

Baldwin Public Library • 2385 Grand Ave • Baldwin, NY 11510-3289 • (516) 223-6228 • http://www.nassau.library.org/baldwin

Baldwinsville

Baldwinsville Public Library • 33 E Genesee St • Baldwinsville, NY 13027-2575 • (315) 635-5631 • http://www.bville.lib.ny.us

Beauchamp Historical Club • 828 Fairway Cr • Baldwinsville, NY 13027 • (315) 635-9944

Ballston Lake

Charlton Historical Society • Charlton Historical Society • Ballston Lake, NY 12019 • (518) 399-4126

Ballston Spa

Ballston Spa Genealogy Club • c/o Ballston Spa Public Library, 21 Milton Ave • Ballston Spa, NY 12020 • (518) 885-5022

Ballston Spa Public Library • 21 Milton Ave • Ballston Spa, NY 12020 • (518) 885-5022

Saratoga County Historical Society • Saratoga County Museum, 6 Charlton St • Ballston Spa, NY 12020-1707 • (518) 885-4000 • http://www.brooksidemuseum.org

Saratoga Springs Library • 320 Broadway • Ballston Spa, NY 12020

Barker

Barker Free Library • 8706 Main St, P.O. Box 261 • Barker, NY 14012-0261 • (716) 795-3344 • http://www.nioga.org

Basom

Alabama Historical Society • 7079 Maple St • Basom, NY 14013-9770 • (716) 948-9886

Tonawanda Band of Seneca • 7027 Meadville Rd • Basom, NY 14013 • (716) 542-4244

Tonawanda Indian Reservation Historical Club • P.O. Box 516 • Basom, NY 14013

Batavia

Genesee Area Genealogists • c/o Richmond Memorial Library, 19 Ross St • Batavia, NY 14020 • (585) 343-9550 • http://www.batavialibrary.org

Genesee County Historical Department Library • Holland Land Office Museum, 131 W Main St • Batavia, NY 14020-2021 • (585) 344-2550 • http://www.hollandlandoffice.com

Holland Purchase Historical Society • Holland Land Office Museum, 131 W Main St • Batavia, NY 14020 • (585) 343-4727 • http://www.hollandlandoffice.com

Richmond Memorial Library • 19 Ross St • Batavia, NY 14020 • (585) 343-9550 • http://www.batavialibrary.org

Western New York Association of Historical Agencies • 131 W Main St • Batavia, NY 14020 • (585) 345-0023

Bath

Bath Historic Committee • Cameron St • Bath, NY 14810

Dormann Library • 101 W Morris St • Bath, NY 14810 • (607) 776-4613 • http://www.stls.org

Steuben County Historical Society • Magee House for Local History, Cameron Park, P.O. Box 349 • Bath, NY 14810-0349 • (607) 776-9930

Bay Shore

Bay Shore Historical Society • Gibson-Mack-Holt House Museum • Bay Shore, NY 11706 • (631) 665-1707 • http://www.bayshorehistorical.org

Sagtikos Manor Historical Society • Montauk Hwy & Gardiner Dr, P.O. Box 344 • Bay Shore, NY 11706 • (631) 661-8348 • http://www.satikosmanor.org

Bayport

Sachem Historical Society • 288 Gilette Ave • Bayport, NY 11705 • (631) 472-1559

Bayshore

Sagtikos Manor Museum • Route 27A, P.O. Box P-344 • Bayshore, NY 11706 • (516) 665-0093 • http://www.sagtikosmanor.com

Bayside

Bayside Historical Society • P.O. Box 133 • Bayside, NY 11361 • (718) 352-1548 • http://www.baysidehistorical.org

Bayville

Baysville Free Library & Museum • 34 School St • Bayville, NY 11709 • (516) 628-2765 • http://www.bayvillefreelibrary.org; http://www.bayvillevillagehall.com

Beacon

Beacon Historical Society • Historical Museum, 477 Main St, P.O. Box 89 • Beacon, NY 12508 • (845) 831-0514 • http://www.howlandculturalcenter.org

Howland Public Library • 313 Main St • Beacon, NY 12508 • (845) 831-1134 • http://howland.beacon.lib.ny.us

Madam Brett Homestead Museum • 50 Van Nydeck Ave • Beacon, NY 12508 • (845) 831-6533

Mount Gulian Historic Site • 145 Sterling St • Beacon, NY 12508 • (845) 831-8172 • http://www.mountgulian.org

Bear Mountain

Bear Mountain Trailside Museum • Bear Mtn State Park • Bear Mountain, NY 10911 • (845) 786-2301 • http://www.trailsidenewyork.com

Beaver Falls

Railway Historical Society of Northern NY • Main St • Beaver Falls, NY 13305 • (315) 346-6848

Bedford

Bedford Free Library • Village Green, Box 375 • Bedford, NY 10506 • (914) 234-3570 • http://www.westchesterlibraries.org

Bedford Historical Society • Historical Museum, 38 Village Green, P.O. Box 491 • Bedford, NY 10506 • (914) 234-9751 • http://www.bedfordhistoricalsociety.org

Belfast

Belfast Public Library • 75 S Main St, P.O. Box 455 • Belfast, NY 14711-0455 • (585) 365-2072 • http://www.stls.org/Belfast

Bellerose

Puerto Rican-Hispanic Genealogical Society • P.O. Box 260188 • Bellerose, NY 11426-0118 • (516) 834-2511 • http://www.rootsweb.com/~prhgs/

Belleville
Philomathean Free Library • 8086 County Route 75, P.O. Box 27 • Belleville, NY 13611 • (315) 846-5103

Bellmore
Grand Lodge of New York, Sons of Italy • 2101 Bellmore Ave • Bellmore, NY 11710 • (516) 785-4623 • http://www.nysosia.org

Bellport
Bellport-Brookhaven Historical Society • Post-Crowell House Museum, 31 Bellport Ln • Bellport, NY 11731 • (631) 776-7640 • http://bellportbrookhavenhistoricalsociety.org

South County Library • 22 Station Rd • Bellport, NY 11713 • (631) 286-0818 • http://sctylib.suffolk.lib.ny.us

Bellville
Philomathean Library • 8086 County Route 75, P.O. Box 27 • Bellville, NY 13611 • (315) 846-5103

Belmont
Allegany County Department of History • Alleghany County Museum, Courthouse, 11 Wells St • Belmont, NY 14813 • (585) 268-9293

Allegany County Historical Society • 20 Willets Ave • Belmont, NY 14813 • (585) 268-7428

Americana Manse Whitney-Halsey Home Museum • Whitney Pl & 39 South St • Belmont, NY 14813 • (585) 268-5130

Belmont Literary and Historical Society • 2 Willets Ave • Belmont, NY 14813-0058 • (585) 268-5308 • http://www.stls.org/Belmont

Bemus Point
Bemus Point Historical Society • Historical Museum, 13 Alburtus Dr, P.O. Box 105 • Bemus Point, NY 14712-0105

Bemus Point Public Library • 13 Main St • Bemus Point, NY 14712 • (716) 386-2274

Bergen
Bergen Historical Society • Bergen Museum of Local History, 7547 Lake Rd • Bergen, NY 14416 • (585) 494-1121

Byron-Bergen Public Library • 13 S Lake Ave, P.O. Box 430 • Bergen, NY 14416-0430 • (585) 494-1120

Berkshire
Berkshire Free Library • 12519-1 State Route 38 • Berkshire, NY 13736 • (607) 657-4418 • http://www.flls.org/memberpages/berkshir.htm

Berlin
Taconic Valley Historical Society • Hilltop Rd, P.O. Box 512 • Berlin, NY 12022 • (518) 658-2863

Berne
Town of Berne Historical Society • Historical Center, Main St, P.O. Box 34 • Berne, NY 12023 • (518) 872-0212 • http://Bernehistory.org

Bethpage
Central Park Historical Society • P.O. Box 178 • Bethpage, NY 11714 • (516) 933-1795 • http://www.nassaulibrary.org/bethpage/cphs/CPHS.html

Italian Genealogical Group • P.O. Box 626 • Bethpage, NY 11714-0626 • (516) 825-7988 • http://www.italiangen.org

Big Flats
Big Flats Historical Society • 258 Hibbard Rd, P.O. Box 232 • Big Flats, NY 14814-0232 • (607) 562-7460 • http://www.bigflatsny.gov

Binghampton
American Name Society • Binghampton Univ • Binghampton, NY 13902-6000 • http://www.wtsn.binghampton.edu/ANS

Binghampton Township Historical Society • 923 Hawleyton Rd • Binghampton, NY 13903-5811 • (607) 669-4363

Broome Community College Library • Upper Front St, P.O. Box 1017 • Binghampton, NY 13902 • (607) 778-5468

Broome County Historical Society • c/o Broome County Public Library, 185 Court St • Binghampton, NY 13865 • (607) 778-3572 • http://www.rootsweb.com/~nybroome/brcohis.htm

Broome County Public Library - Local History & Genealogy Center • 185 Court St • Binghampton, NY 13901-3503 • (607) 778-2076 • http://www.bclibrary.info

Conklin Historical Society • 82 Pierce Creek Rd • Binghampton, NY 13903 • (607) 723-1737

Glenn G Bartle Library • SUNY-Binghampton, Vestal Pkwy E, P.O. Box 6012 • Binghampton, NY 13902-6012 • (607) 777-2345 • http://library.lib.binghamton.edu

Phelps Mansion Museum • 191 Court St • Binghampton, NY 13901 • (607) 722-4872

Roberson Museum • 30 Front St • Binghampton, NY 13905 • (607) 772-0660 • http://www.kopernik.org; http://www.roberson.org

Broome County Public Library • 185 Court St • Binghamton, NY 13901 • (607) 778-3572 • http://www.bclibrary.info/

Black River
Black River Free Library • 102-104 Maple St, P.O. Box 253 • Black River, NY 13612 • (3150 773-5163

Blauvelt
Blauvelt Free Library • 541 Western Hwy • Blauvelt, NY 10913 • (845) 359-2811 • http://www.rcls.org/blv

Blockville
Harmony Historical Society • 1943 Open Meadows Rd • Blockville, NY 14710 • (716) 782-3074

Bloomfield
AWA Electronic-Communication Museum • 2 South Ave • Bloomfield, NY 14469 • (585) 392-3088 • http://www.antiquewireless.org

Bloomfield Academy Museum • 8 South Ave, P.O. Box 212 • Bloomfield, NY 14443 • (585) 657-7244

Blue Mountain Lake
Adirondack Historical Association • Adirondack Museum, Route 28N & 30, P.O. Box 99 • Blue Mountain Lake, NY 12812 • (518) 352-7311 • http://www.adirondackmuseum.org

Blue Point
Bayport-Blue Point Public Library • 203 Blue Point Ave • Blue Point, NY 11715 • (631) 363-6133 • http://www.suffolk.lib.ny.us/libraries/bprt/

Bohemia
Bartunef House Museum • Smithtown Ave, P.O. Box 67 • Bohemia, NY 11716-0067 • (61) 567-1095

Bohemia Historical Society • Historical Museum, 1519 Locust Ave, P.O. Box 67 • Bohemia, NY 11716-0067 • (631) 567-1095 • http://www.longisland.com/museums/museum.php

Bolivar
Bolivar Free Library • 390 Main St • Bolivar, NY 14715-0512 • (585) 928-2015

Bolivar, Richburg, Allentown and Genesee (BRAG) Historical Society • c/o Bolivar Free Library, 390 Main St • Bolivar, NY 14715 • (585) 928-2659

Bolton Landing
Bolton Free Library • 4922 Lakeshore Dr, P.O. Box 389 • Bolton Landing, NY 12814-0389 • (518) 644-2233

Historical Society of the Town of Bolton • Historical Museum, 4924 Main St • Bolton Landing, NY 12814 • (518) 644-9960 • http://www.boltonhistorical.org

New York

Boonville
Erwin Library and Institute • Post & Schuyler Sts • Boonville, NY 13309 • (315) 942-4834 • http://www.midyork.org/LibraryList/LibraryInfo/Boonville.html

Boston
Boston Historical Society • Old Pioneer Church Museum, 9410 Boston State Rd, P.O. Box 31 • Boston, NY 14025 • (716) 941-6525 • http://www.townofboston.com/historical_info.html

Bovina Center
Bovina Library Association • Maple Ave, P.O. Box 38 • Bovina Center, NY 13740 • (607) 832-4884 • http://www.4cls.org/webpages/members/BovinaCenter/BovinaCenter.html

Bramanville
Caverns Creek Grist Mill Museum • P.O. Box 21 • Bramanville, NY 12092 • (580) 296-8448 • http://www.cavernscreekgristmill.com

Branchport
Modeste Bedient Memorial Library • 3699 Route 54A • Branchport, NY 14418-0239 • (315) 595-2899 • http://www.branchportlibrary.org

Brant
Brant-Farnham Historical Society • 1294 Brant-North Collins Rd • Brant, NY 14027 • (716) 549-0282 • http://www.brantny.com

Brant Lake
Horicon Historical Society • Historical Museum, P.O. Box 51 • Brant Lake, NY 12815 • (518) 494-2804 • http://horiconhistoricalsociety.org

Brasher Falls
Brasher Town Historian • 234 Dullea Road, P.O. Box 132 • Brasher Falls, NY 13613 • (315) 389-5717

Brentwood
Brentwood Historical Society • P.O. Box 465 • Brentwood, NY 11717 • (631) 273-2949

Brentwood Public Library • 2nd Ave & 4th St • Brentwood, NY 11717 • (631) 273-7883 • http://brentwood.suffolk.lib.ny.us

Brewerton
Fort Brewerton Historical Society • 9 US Route 11, P.O. Box 392 • Brewerton, NY 13029-0392 • (315) 668-8801 • http://www.FortBrewerton.org

Northern Onondaga Public Library-Brewerton Branch • 5347 Library St, P.O. Box 624 • Brewerton, NY 13029-0624 • (315) 676-7484

Brewster
Brewster Public Library • 79 Main St • Brewster, NY 10509 • (845) 279-6421

Putnam County Archives • 68 Marvin Ave • Brewster, NY 10509-1515 • (845) 278-7209 • http://www.putnamcounty.ny.com/historican

Southeast Museum Association • 67 Main St • Brewster, NY 10509 • (845) 279-7500 • http://www.southeastmuseum.org

Briarcliff Manor
Briarcliff Manor-Scarborough Historical Society • 162 Macy Rd, P.O. Box 11 • Briarcliff Manor, NY 10510 • (914) 941-7016 • http://briarcliffmanor.americantowns.com

Bridgehampton
Bridgehampton Historical Society • Historical Museum, 2368 Main St, P.O. Box 977 • Bridgehampton, NY 11932 • (631) 537-1088 • http://www.hamptons.com/bhhs

Hampton Library • 2478 Main St, P.O. Box 3025 • Bridgehampton, NY 11932-3025 • (631) 537-0015 • http://www.hamptonlibrary.org

Bridgewater
Bridgewater Historical Society • P.O. Box 363 • Bridgewater, NY 13313

Brightwaters
Bay Shore-Brightwaters Public Library • 1 S County Rd • Brightwaters, NY 11718 • (516) 665-4360

Broad Channel
Broad Channel Historical Society • c/o Broad Channel Library, 1626 Crossbay Blvd • Broad Channel, NY 11693 • (718) 474-1127

Broad Channel Library • 1626 Crossbay Blvd • Broad Channel, NY 11693 • (718) 474-1127

Brockport
Drake Memorial Library & College Archives • SUNY-Brockport • Brockport, NY 14420 • (585) 395-5834 • http://cc.brockport.edu/~library1/archives.htm

Seymour Public Library • 161 East Ave • Brockport, NY 11420-1987 • (585) 637-1050

Western Monroe Historical Society • Morgan-Manning House, 151 Main St • Brockport, NY 14420 • (585) 637-3645 • http://www.frontier.net/morganmanninghouse

Bronx
Bartow-Pell Mansion Museum • 895 Shore Rd, Pelham Bay Park • Bronx, NY 10464 • (718) 885-1461 • http://www.bartowpellmansionmuseum.org

Bronx County Historical Society • c/o Theodore Kazimiroff Library & Museum, 3309 Bainbridge Ave • Bronx, NY 10467 • (718) 881-8900 • http://www.bronxhistoricalsociety.org

City Island Historical Society • Nautical Museum, 190 Fordham St, P.O. Box 82 • Bronx, NY 10464 • (718) 885-0008 • http://www.cityislandmuseum.org

Edgar Allan Poe Cottage Museum • Poe Park, E Kingsbridge Rd • Bronx, NY 10458 • (718) 881-8900 • http://www.bronxhistoricalsociety.org

Enrico Fermi Cultural Center • Belmont Regional Library, 610 E 186th St • Bronx, NY 10458 • (718) 933-6410 • http://www.nypl.org

Frisian Roundtable • 2885 Roosevelt Ave • Bronx, NY 10465

Hall of Fame for Great Americans Museum • Bronx Community College, Univ Ave & 181st St • Bronx, NY 10453 • (718) 289-5161 • http://www.bcc.cuny.edu/halloffame

Harlem Historical Society • 831 Bartholdi St • Bronx, NY 10467 • (718) 515-8947

Herbert H Lehman College Library & Bronx Institute Archives • City Univ of NY, 250 Bedford Park Blvd W • Bronx, NY 10468 • (718) 960-8577

Huntington Free Library and Reading Room • 9 Westchester Sq • Bronx, NY 10461 • (718) 829-7770

Judaica Museum at Riverdale • 5961 Palisade Ave • Bronx, NY 10471 • (718) 581-1787 • http://www.hebrewhome.org/museum/

Kingsbridge Historical Society • 426 W 259th St • Bronx, NY 10463 • (718) 796-1195

Maritime Industry Museum at Fort Schuyler • 6 Pennyfield Ave • Bronx, NY 10465 • (718) 409-7218

Museum of Bronx History • Valentine-Varian House, 3266 Bainbridge Ave • Bronx, NY 10467 • (718) 881-8900 • http://www.bronxhistoricalsociety.org

Museum of Migrating People • 750 Baychester Ave • Bronx, NY 10475 • (718) 904-5400

New York Public Library - Bronx • 310 E Kingsbridge Rd • Bronx, NY 10458 • (718) 579-4244 • http://www.nypl.org/branch/local/bx/blc.cfm

Pelham Masonic Historical Society of City Island • 241 City Island Ave • Bronx, NY 10464 • (718) 885-3233

United Baltic Appeal • 115 W 183rd St • Bronx, NY 10453-1103 • (212) 367-8802

Wave Hill Museum • 675 W 252nd St • Bronx, NY 14071 • (718) 549-2055 • http://www.wavehill.org

Bronxville

Bronxville Historical Conservancy • Village Hall, 200 Pondfield Rd • Bronxville, NY 10708 • (914) 793-2336 • http://www.villageofbronxville.com

Bronxville Public Library • 201 Pondfield Rd • Bronxville, NY 10708-4828 • (914) 337-7680 • http://www.bronxvillelibrary.org

Eastchester Historical Society • 1835 Marble Schoolhouse Museum, 388 California Rd • Bronxville, NY 10708-4402 • (914) 793-1900

Brookfield

Town of Brookfield Historical Society • Main St, P.O. Box 143 • Brookfield, NY 13314 • (315) 899-5893 • http://www.brookfieldnyhistory.org/

Brookhaven

Brookhaven Free Library • 273 Beaver Dam Rd • Brookhaven, NY 11719 • (631) 286-1923

Brooklyn

Afro-American Historical and Genealogical Society, Jean Sampson Scott-Greater New York Chapter • P.O. Box 022340 • Brooklyn, NY 11202-2340 • (212) 927-2551 • http://www.aahgsny.org

Brooklyn Genealogy Workshop • 125 Montague St • Brooklyn, NY 11201 • (908) 850-4323

Brooklyn Historical Society • Historical Museum, 128 Pierrepont St • Brooklyn, NY 11201-2711 • (718) 222-4111 • http://www.brooklynhistory.org

Brooklyn Museum and Archives • 200 Eastern Pkwy • Brooklyn, NY 11238-6052 • (718) 501-6307 • http://library.brooklynmuseum.org

Brooklyn Public Library • Grand Army Plaza • Brooklyn, NY 11238 • (718) 780-7794 • http://www.brooklynpubliclibrary.org

Center for Thanatology Research and Education • 391 Atlantic Ave • Brooklyn, NY 11217-1846 • (718) 858-3026

Coney Island Museum • 1208 Surf Ave • Brooklyn, NY 11224 • (718) 372-5159 • http://www.coneyisland.com/museum.shtml

Genealogical and Heraldic Institute of America • American Italian Congress, 111 Columbia Heights • Brooklyn, NY 11201

Harbor Defense Museum • Fort Hamilton Military Community, Bldg 230 • Brooklyn, NY 11252 • (718) 630-4349 • http://www.harbordefensemuseum.com

Historical Society of Jews from Egypt • P.O. Box 230445 • Brooklyn, NY 11223 • (718) 998-2497 • http://www.hsje.org

Holocaust Library & Research Center • 557 Bedford Ave • Brooklyn, NY 11211 • (718) 599-5833

Italian Historical Society of America • 111 Columbia Heights • Brooklyn, NY 11201 • (718) 852-2929 • http://www.italianhistorical.org

Kingsborough Community College Library • 2001 Oriental Blvd • Brooklyn, NY 11235 • (718) 358-5632

Kingsborough Historical Society • c/o Kingsborough Community College Library, 2001 Oriental Blvd • Brooklyn, NY 11235 • (718) 358-5632 • http://www.kbcc.cuny.edu

Kurdish Museum • 144 Underhill Ave • Brooklyn, NY 11238 • (718) 783-7930 • http://www.kurdishlibrarymuseum.com

Lefferts Historic House Museum • Flatbush Ave & Empire Blvd • Brooklyn, NY 11215 • (718) 789-2822 • http://www.prospectpark.org

McEntegart Hall Library • Saint Joseph's College, 222 Clinton Ave • Brooklyn, NY 11205-3697 • (718) 636-6858 • http://blib.sjcny.edu

Museum of the Borough of Brooklyn • Brooklyn College Archives, 2900 Bedford Ave • Brooklyn, NY 11210 • (718) 780-5152

Old Stone House Museum • 5th Ave & 3rd St, P.O. Box 150613 • Brooklyn, NY 11215 • (718) 768-3195 • http://www.theoldstonehouse.org

Pieter Cloesen Wyckoff House Museum • 5816 Clarendon Rd, P.O. Box 100-376 • Brooklyn, NY 11210 • (718) 629-5400 • http://www.wyckoffassociation.org

Society for the Preservation of Weeksville and Bedford-Stuyvestant History • 1698 Bergen St, P.O. Box 120, St Johns Sta • Brooklyn, NY 11213 • (718) 623-0600 • http://www.weeksvillesociety.org

Waterfront Museum • 290 Conover St, Pier 44 • Brooklyn, NY 11231 • (718) 624-4719 • http://www.waterfrontmuseum.org

World Jewish Genealogy Organization • Yochson Institute, 1605 48th St, P.O. Box 190420 • Brooklyn, NY 11219-0009 • (718) 435-4400

Brooklyn Heights

New York Transit Museum • Boerum Pl & Schermerhorn St • Brooklyn Heights, NY 11201 • (718) 694-1600 • http://www.mta.info

Brookville

B Davis Schwartz Memorial Library • Long Island Univ, 700 Northern Blvd • Brookville, NY 11548-1326 • (516) 299-2880 • http://www.cwpost.liunet.edu/cwis/cwp/library/sc/sc.htm

Brownville

Brownville-Glen Park Library • 216 Brown Blvd • Brownville, NY 13615 • (315) 788-7889

General Jacob Brown Historical Society • Brown Mansion Museum, 216 Brown Blvd • Brownville, NY 13615 • (315) 782-7650

Buffalo

Africana Research Museum • 3065 Bailey Ave • Buffalo, NY 14215-1618 • (716) 862-9260

Afro-American Historical Association of the Niagara Frontier • 322 E Utica, P.O. Box 63 • Buffalo, NY 14216 • (717) 886-1399 • http://www.aahanf.org

Andrew L Boushuis Library • Canisius College, 2001 Main St • Buffalo, NY 14208-1098 • (716) 888-2532 • http://library.canisius.edu/archives

Benjamin and Dr Edgar R Cofield Judaic Museum • Temple Beth Zion, 805 Delaware Ave • Buffalo, NY 14218 • (716) 831-6565 • http://www.tbz.org

Buffalo and Erie County Historical Society • Historical Museum, 25 Nottingham Ct • Buffalo, NY 14216-3199 • (716) 873-9612 • http://www.bechs.org

Buffalo and Erie County Military Park Museum • 1 Naval Park Cove • Buffalo, NY 14202 • (716) 847-1773 • http://www.buffalonavalpark.org

Buffalo and Erie County Public Library • 1 Lafayette Square • Buffalo, NY 14203-1887 • (716) 858-8900 • http://www.buffalolib.org

Buffalo Fire Historical Society • 1850 William St • Buffalo, NY 14206 • (716) 892-8400 • http://bfhsmuseum.bfn.org

Buffalo Genealogical Society of the African Diaspora • P.O. Box 2534 • Buffalo, NY 14240-2534 • (716) 878-8010

Buffalo Irish Genealogical Society • Irish Center, 245 Abbott Rd • Buffalo, NY 14220-1305 • (716) 662-1164 • http://www.buffaloirishcenter.com

Campaign for Buffalo History Architeture and Culture • 224 Elmwood Ave • Buffalo, NY 14222 • (716) 884-3138

Catholic Center • 795 Main St • Buffalo, NY 14203 • (716) 847-5561

E H Butler Library • SUNY, 1300 Elmwood Ave • Buffalo, NY 14222-1095 • (716) 878-6300 • http://www.buffalostate.edu/library

Buffalo, cont.

Lower Lakes Marine Historical Society • 66 Erie St • Buffalo, NY 14202 • (716) 849-0914

Medaille College Library • 18 Agassiz Cr • Buffalo, NY 14214 • (716) 884-3281 • http://eres.medaille.edu/library

Michigan Street Preservation Corporation • 36 Nash St • Buffalo, NY 14204 • (716) 856-4490

New York Office of Native American Services • 125 Main St, Rm 545 • Buffalo, NY 14203 • (716) 847-3123 • http://www.ocfs.state.ny.us

Polish Genealogical Society of Western New York • 299 Barnard St • Buffalo, NY 14206-3212 • (716) 826-9482 • http://feefhs.org/pol/fgpgswn.html

Rachel R Savarino Library • Trocaire College Archives, 110 Red Jacket Pkwy • Buffalo, NY 14220 • (716) 826-1200 • http://library.trocaire.edu/archives_3.htm

Theodore Roosevelt Inaugural Historic Site Museum • 641 Delaware Ave • Buffalo, NY 14202 • (716) 884-0095 • http://www.nps.gov/thri/

University at Buffalo Library - Special Collections • 420 Capen Hall • Buffalo, NY 14260 • (716) 645-2820 • http://ublib.buffalo.edu/libraries

Urhobo Historical Society • 125 Willow Green Dr • Buffalo, NY 14228 • (716) 691-5066 • http://www.waado.org

Western New York Documentary Heritage Program • 4455 Genesee St, P.O. Box 400 • Buffalo, NY 14225-0400 • (716) 633-0705 • http://www.wnylrc.org

Western New York Heritage Institute • P.O. Box 192 • Buffalo, NY 14205-0192

Burke

Almanzo and Laura Ingalls Wilder Association • 177 Stacy Rd • Burke, NY 12917 • (518) 483-1207

Burnt Hills

Burnt Hills-Ballston Lake Community Library • 2 Lawmar Ln • Burnt Hills, NY 12027 • (518) 399-8174 • http://burnthills.sals.edu

Burt

Newfane Historical Society • Van Horn Mansion Museum, 2165 Lockport-Alcott Rd, P.O. Box 155 • Burt, NY 14028 • (716) 778-7197 • http://www.niagaracounty.org/town_of_newfane_hs.htm

Byron

Byron Historical Museum • 6407 Town Line Rd • Byron, NY 14422 • (585) 548-9008

Byron Historical Society • 6148 Bird Rd, P.O. Box 201 • Byron, NY 14422 • (585) 548-2252

Cairo

Cairo Public Library • 512 Main St, P.O. Box 720 • Cairo, NY 12413-0720 • (518) 622-9864 • http://www.cairo.lib.ny.us

Mountain Top Historical Society • 5132 Route 23 #A • Cairo, NY 12413 • (518) 589-6657

Caledonia

Big Springs Historical Society • Historical Museum, 3095 Main St • Caledonia, NY 14423 • (585) 538-9880 • http://www.cal-mum.com/bsm/

Big Springs Museum • 3089 Main St • Caledonia, NY 14423 • (585) 538-9880

Callicoon

Delaware Free Library • 45 Lower Main St, P.O. Box 245 • Callicoon, NY 12723-0245 • (845) 887-4040 • http://www.rcls.org/wspl

Upper Delaware Heritage Alliance • P.O. Box 143 • Callicoon, NY 12723

Calverton

Baiting Hollow Free Library • 4 Warner Dr • Calverton, NY 11933 • (516) 727-8765

Grumman Memorial Park Museum • Route 25 & 25A, P.O. Box 147 • Calverton, NY 11933 • (631) 369-9488 • http://www.grummanpark.org

Cambridge

Cambridge Historical Society • Historical Museum, 21 Broad St • Cambridge, NY 12816 • (518) 677-5232 • http://CHS.gottry.com

Camden

Camden Public Library • 57 2nd St • Camden, NY 13316 • (315) 245-1980

Palatines to America, New York Chapter • 9666 Elpif Rd • Camden, NY 13316 • (315) 245-0990

Queen Village Historical Society • Carriage House Museum, 2 N Park St, P.O. Box 38 • Camden, NY 13316 • (315) 245-4652 • http://www.demdennychamber.com/camden.php

Cameron Mills

Middletown Historical Society of Steuben County • 5775 Learn Rd • Cameron Mills, NY 14820

Camillus

Camillus Historical Society • Sim's Store Museum, DeVoe Rd • Camillus, NY 13031 • (315) 487-2326

Wilcox Octagon House Museum • 5420 W Genesee St, P.O. Box 314 • Camillus, NY 13031 • (315) 488-7800

Campbell Hall

15th NY Cavalry Association • Hill-Hold Museum, Route 416, Box 299 • Campbell Hall, NY 10916 • (845) 294-7661 • http://www.15thnewyorkcavalry.org

Bull Stone House Museum • 183 County Rd 51 • Campbell Hall, NY 10916-9729 • (914) 496-3587

Canaan

Canaan Historical Society • Historical Museum, 12913 Route 22 • Canaan, NY 12029-9727 • (518) 781-4801 • http://www.canaannewyork.org/living/localorgs.shtml

Canajoharie

Canajoharie Library • 2 Erie Blvd • Canajoharie, NY 13317 • (518) 673-2314 • http://www.clag.org

Canandaigua

Granger Homestead Society • Historical Museum, 295 N Main St • Canandaigua, NY 14424 • (585) 394-1472 • http://www.grangerhomestead.org

Ontario County Archives • 3051 County Complex Dr • Canandaigua, NY 14424 • (585) 393-2910 • http://raims.com/historian/home.html

Ontario County Genealogical Society • Historical Museum, 55 N Main St • Canandaigua, NY 14424-1438 • (585) 394-4975 • http://www.ochs.org/Genealogy/Ocgs/

Ontario County Historical Society • Historical Museum, 55 N Main St • Canandaigua, NY 14424 • (585) 394-4975 • http://www.ochs.org

Sonnenberg Gardens & Mansion Museum • 151 Charlotte St • Canandaigua, NY 14424 • (585) 394-4922 • http://www.sonnenberg.org

Canaseraga

Essential Club Free Library • 11 Pratt St, P.O. Box 223 • Canaseraga, NY 14822 • (607) 545-6443

Candor

Candor Free Library • 2 Bank St, P.O. Box 104 • Candor, NY 13743 • (607) 659-7258 • http://www.flls.org/candor

Town of Candor Historical Society • P.O. Box 585 • Candor, NY 13743

Canisteo

Canisteo Historical Society • 23 Main St, P.O. Box 35 • Canisteo, NY 14823-0035 • (607) 698-9331

Canton

Canton Free Library • 8 Park St, P.O. Box 150 • Canton, NY 13617-0150 • (315) 386-3712 • http://www.cantonfreelibrary.org

Owen D Young Library - Special Collections • Saint Lawrence University, Park St • Canton, NY 13617 • (315) 229-5476 • http://www.stlawu.edu/library/odyinfo.html

Pierrepont Museum • 864 State Hwy 68 • Canton, NY 13617 • (315) 385-8311

Saint Lawrence County Historical Association • Silas Wright House Museum, 3 E Main St, P.O. Box 8 • Canton, NY 13617-1416 • (315) 386-8133 • http://www.sicha.org

Saint Lawrence Valley Genealogical Society • P.O. Box 205 • Canton, NY 13617-0205

Southworth Library & Archives • SUNY Canton, Cornell Dr • Canton, NY 13617 • (315) 386-7058 • http://www.canton.edu/library

Cape Vincent

Cape Vincent Community Library • 157 N Real • Cape Vincent, NY 13618 • (315) 654-2132

Cape Vincent Historical Museum • 175 N James St, P.O. Box 376 • Cape Vincent, NY 13618 • (315) 654-4400 • http://www.capevincent.org/history.asp

Carmel

Kent Historical Society • P.O. Box 123 • Carmel, NY 10512 • (845) 225-4882 • http://www.townofkentny.gov/historian.htm

Reed Memorial Library • 1733 Route 6 • Carmel, NY 10512 • (845) 225-2439 • http://reed.carmel.lib.ny.us

Carthage

Carthage Free Library • 412 Budd St • Carthage, NY 13619 • (315) 493-2620 • http://www.nc3r.org/carlibrary

Four River Valleys Historical Society • P.O. Box 504 • Carthage, NY 13619 • (315) 773-5133

Castile

Castile Historical Society • 17 Park Rd E, P.O. Box 49 • Castile, NY 14427 • (716) 493-5370 • http://www.glenirisinn.com

Cordelia A Greene Library • 11 S Main St, P.O. Box 208 • Castile, NY 14427-0208 • (585) 493-5466 • http://www.castile.pls-net.org

William Pryor Letchworth Museum • 1 Letchworth State Park • Castile, NY 14427 • (585) 493-3617 • http://www.letchworthparkhistory.org

Castleton-on-Hudson

Castleton Public Library • 85 S Main St • Castleton-on-Hudson, NY 12033 • (518) 732-2211

Esquatak Historical Society • P.O. Box 151 • Castleton-on-Hudson, NY 12033 • (518) 732-2626

Castorland

Croghan Town Historian • 9913 2nd Rd • Castorland, NY 13620 • (315) 346-6201

New Bremen Town Historian • 8794 Van Amber Rd • Castorland, NY 13620

Cato

Civic Heritage • P.O. Box 389 • Cato, NY 13033 • (315) 626-2378

Stewart B Lang Memorial Library • E Main St • Cato, NY 13033 • (315) 626-2101

Catskill

Catskill Public Library • 1 Franklin St • Catskill, NY 12414-1496 • (518) 943-4230 • http://catskill.lib.ny.us

Cattaraugus

Cattaraugus Area Historical Society • Historical Center, 23, Main St • Cattaraugus, NY 14719 • (716) 257-3429

Cazenovia

Cazenovia Historic Preservation • Lorenzo Carriage House • Cazenovia, NY 13035 • (315) 655-3044

Cazenovia Public Library Association • 100 Albany St • Cazenovia, NY 13035 • (315) 655-9322 • http://www.midyork.org/Cazenovia

Lorenzo State Historic Site Museum • 17 Rippleton Rd • Cazenovia, NY 13035 • (315) 655-3200 • http://www.lorenzo.org

Rothschild Peterson Patent Model Museum • 4796 W Lake Rd • Cazenovia, NY 13035 • http://www.patentmodel.org

Celeron

Celeron Historical Society • 22C Bradmar Ct • Celeron, NY 14720

Center Moriches

Center Moriches Free Public Library • 235 Main St • Center Moriches, NY 11934 • (631) 878-0940 • http://www.suffolk.lib.ny.us/libraries/cmor

Ketcham Inn Foundation • Havens-Terry-Ketcham Inn, 81 Main St, P.O. Box 626 • Center Moriches, NY 11934 • (631) 878-8862 • http://longislandgenealogy.com/inn/inn.html

Moriches Bay Historical Society • Haven's House Museum, Montauk Hwy & Chet Sweezy Rd, P.O. Box 31 • Center Moriches, NY 11934 • (631) 878-1776 • http://www.suffolk.lib.ny.us/libraries/cmor/illushis.htm

Centereach

Middle Country Public Library • 101 Eastwood Blvd • Centereach, NY 11720-2733 • (631) 585-9393 • http://www.mcpl.lib.ny.us

Centerport

Suffolk County Vanderbilt Museum • 180 Little Neck Rd, P.O. Box 0605 • Centerport, NY 17721 • (631) 854-5508 • http://www.vanderbuiltmuseum.org

Central Islip

Central Islip Historical Society • 490 Irving St • Central Islip, NY 11795

Central Islip Public Library • 33 Hawthorne Ave • Central Islip, NY 11722 • (631) 234-9333 • http://www.suffolk.lib.ny.us/libraries/cisp

Central Square

Central Square Library • 637 South Main St, P.O. Box 513 • Central Square, NY 13036 • (315) 668-6104

Central Square Village Historian • 196 County Route 33 • Central Square, NY 13036 • (315) 668-2178

Hastings Town Historian • 196 County Route 33 • Central Square, NY 13036 • (315) 668-2178

Champlain

Champlain Memorial Library • 148 Elm St, P.O. Box 279 • Champlain, NY 12919 • (518) 298-8620 • http://www.cefls.org/champlain.htm

Champlain Town Historian • P.O. Box 3144 • Champlain, NY 12919 • (518) 298-8160

Champlain Village Historian • 25 Moore St • Champlain, NY 12919 • (518) 298-4036

Chappaqua

New Castle Historical Society • Horace Greeley House, 100 King St, P.O. Box 55 • Chappaqua, NY 10514 • (914) 238-4666 • http://www.newdcastlehistoricalsociety.org

Charlotteville

Museum of the History of Charlotteville • 511 Charlotte Valley Rd • Charlotteville, NY 12036 • (607) 397-8606

Charlton

Charlton Historical Society • 2006 Maple Ave • Charlton, NY 12019 • (518) 882-6125 • http://www.townofcharlton.org

Chateaugay
Chatequgay Memorial Library • 191 E Main St, P.O. Box 10 • Chateaugay, NY 12920-0010 • (518) 497-0400 • http://www.cefls.org/chateaugay.htm

Chatham
Chatham Public Library • 11 Woodbridge Ave • Chatham, NY 12037-1399 • (518) 392-3666 • http://chatham.lib.ny.us

Chatham Village Historical Society • 32 Main St • Chatham, NY 12037 • (518) 392-9236 • http://www.bearsystems.com/chatham/chatham

Chaumont
Lyme Free Library • Main St, P.O. Box 369 • Chaumont, NY 13622 • (315) 649-5454 • http://www.lymefreelibrary.org

Chautauqua
Chautauqua Institution • c/o Smith Memorial Library & Archives, 21 Miller Ave, P.O. Box 1093 • Chautauqua, NY 14722 • (716) 357-6332 • http://www.chautauqua-inst.org

Smith Memorial Library • 21 Miller Ave, P.O. Box 1093 • Chautauqua, NY 14722 • (716) 357-6296

Chazy
Alice T Miner Colonial Collection Archives & Museum • 9818 Main St, P.O. Box 628 • Chazy, NY 12921 • (518) 846-7336 • http://www.minermuseum.org

Chazy Public Library • 9633 Rte 9, P.O. Box 88 • Chazy, NY 12921-0088 • (518) 846-7676

Chazy Town Historian • P.O. Box 177 • Chazy, NY 12921 • (518) 846-7544

Cheektowaga
Cheektowaga Historical Association • Historical Museum, 3329 Broadway • Cheektowaga, NY 14227 • (716) 683-5589 • http://www.tocny.org/museum.html

Julia Boyer-Reinstein Library • 1030 Losson Rd • Cheektowaga, NY 14227 • (716) 668-4991

Cherry Creek
Cherry Creek Town Museum • Village Hall, 6763 Main St • Cherry Creek, NY 14723 • (716) 296-5681

Cherry Valley
Cherry Valley Historical Association • Historical Museum, 49 Main St, P.O. Box 115 • Cherry Valley, NY 13320 • (607) 264-3303 • http://www.cherryvalleymuseum.org

Cherry Valley Memorial Library • 61 Main St, P.O. Box 25 • Cherry Valley, NY 13320-0025 • (607) 264-8214 • http://www.4cls.org

Cherry Valley Museum • 49 Main St, P.O. Box 115 • Cherry Valley, NY 13320 • (607) 264-3303 • http://www.cherryvalleymuseum.com

Chester
1915 Erie Rail Road Station Museum • 19 Winkler Pl • Chester, NY 10918 • (845) 469-2591 • http://homepage.mac.com/chester_historical/Welcome.html

Chester Historical Society • 47 Main St • Chester, NY 10918 • (845) 469-2388 • http://homepage.mac.com/chester_historical/Welcome.html

Chester Public Library • 1784 Kings Hwy • Chester, NY 10918 • (845) 469-4252 • http://www.rels.org/chs

Chestertown
Historical Society of the Town of Chester • Town Hall, Main St • Chestertown, NY 12817 • (518) 494-3758

Chittenango
Chittenango Landing Canal Boat Museum • 7010 Landing Rd • Chittenango, NY 13037 • (315) 687-3801 • http://www.chittenangolandingcanalboatmuseum.com

Cincinnatus
Cincinnatus Area Historical Society • P.O. Box 264 • Cincinnatus, NY 13040 • (607) 863-4251

Kellogg Free Library • 5681 Telephone Rd Ext, P.O. Box 150 • Cincinnatus, NY 13040 • http://www.flls.org/memberpages/cincin.htm

Taylor Historical Society • 3254 Chenango Solon Pond Rd • Cincinnatus, NY 13040

Clarence
Clarence Historical Society • Historical Museum, 10465 Main St, P.O. Box 86 • Clarence, NY 14031 • (781) 759-8575 • http://www.clarencehistory.org

Clarkson
Clarkson Historical Society • P.O. Box 600 • Clarkson, NY 14430 • http://clarksonny.org/History/historical_society.html

Clay
Clay Historical Association • 4894 Grange Rd • Clay, NY 13041 • (315) 652-3288 • http://www.townofclay.org

Clayton
Antique Boat Museum • 750 Mary St • Clayton, NY 13624 • (315) 686-4104 • http://www.abm.org

Clayton-Thousand Islands Area Historical Society • Historical Museum, 312 James St, P.O. box 27 • Clayton, NY 13624 • (315) 686-5794 • http://www.timuseum.org

Gilbart Mercier Memorial Library • 750 Mary St • Clayton, NY 13624 • (315) 686-4104 • http://www.abm.org

Grindstone Island Research • Heritage Center, 41591 Grindstone Island • Clayton, NY 13624 • (315) 686-3844

Hawn Memorial Library • 220 John St • Clayton, NY 13624-1107 • (315) 686-3762 • http://www.nc3r.org/clayton

Thousand Islands Museum • 312 James St, P.O. Box 27 • Clayton, NY 13624 • (315) 686-5794 • http://www.timuseum.org

Clayville
Paris Historical Society • P.O. Box 62 • Clayville, NY 13322

Clermont
Clermont State Historic Site Museum • 1 Clermont Ave • Clermont, NY 12526 • (518) 537-4240 • http://www.friendsofclermont.org

Cleveland
Cleveland Village Historian • 38 Bridge St, P.O. Box 154 • Cleveland, NY 13042 • (315) 675-8384

Constantia Town Historian • 32 Clay St • Cleveland, NY 13042 • (315) 675-8225

Clifton Park
Clifton Park-Half Moon Public Library • 475 Moe Rd • Clifton Park, NY 12065-3808 • (518) 371-8622 • http://www.shenpublib.org

Clifton Springs
Clifton Springs Historical Society • 8 E Main St • Clifton Springs, NY 14432 • (315) 462-7394

Clinton
Clinton Historical Society • 1832 Clinton Baptist Church, 1 Fountain St, P.O. Box 42 • Clinton, NY 11332 • (315) 859-1392 • http://clintonhistory.org

Hamilton College Library • 198 College Hill Rd • Clinton, NY 13323 • (315) 859-4479 • http://www.hamilton.edu/library/home.html

Kirkland Town Library • 55 1/2 College St • Clinton, NY 13323 • (315) 853-2038

Clintondale
Plattekill Historical Society • P.O. Box 250 • Clintondale, NY 12515 • (845) 883-6118 • http://plattekill.lib.ny.us/plattekill_historical_society.htm

Clintonville
Clintonville Town Historian • 1302 Route 9 N • Clintonville, NY 12924 • (518) 834-5267

Clyde
Galen Historical Society • Brick Church Museum, 31 N Park St, P.O. Box 43 • Clyde, NY 14433 • (315) 923-7150 • http://www.galenhistoricalsociety.org

Clymer
Clymer Area Historical Society • Clymer-Corry Rd, P.O. Box 114 • Clymer, NY 14724 • (716) 355-9950 • http://www.wnylrc.org/dhp/Archives/

French Creek Historical Society • Route 2 • Clymer, NY 14724 • (716) 355-4101

Clymer Center
Little Red Schoolhouse Museum • 7895 Clymer Center Rd • Clymer Center, NY 14724 • (716) 355-6450 • http://www.littleredschoolhouse.net

Cobleskill
Cobleskill Public Library • 110 Union St, P.O. Box 219 • Cobleskill, NY 12043-0219 • (518) 234-8997 • http://www2.telenet.net/community/mvla/cobl/

SUNY - Cobleskill Library • SUNY - Cobleskill • Cobleskill, NY 12043 • (518) 255-5841 • http://cobyweb.cobleskill.edu/library

Town of Cobleskill Historical Society • c/o Cobleskill Public Library, 110 Union St • Cobleskill, NY 12043 • (518) 234-8997 • http://www.schohariehistory.net

Coeymans Hollow
Little Red Schoolhouse Historical Society • P.O. Box 25 • Coeymans Hollow, NY 12046 • (518) 756-2562

Cohocton
Cohocton Historical Society • 14 Maple Ave, P.O. Box 177 • Cohocton, NY 14826 • (585) 534-5317 • http://www.cohocton.org

Cohoes
Cohoes Public Library • 169 Mohawk • Cohoes, NY 12047 • (518) 235-2570

Spindle City Historic Society • 58 Remsen St • Cohoes, NY 12047 • (518) 237-7999

Cold Spring
Julia L Butterfield Memorial Library • 10 Morris Ave • Cold Spring, NY 10516 • (845) 265-3040 • http://www.butterfieldlibrary.org

Putnam County Historical Society • Foundry School Museum, 63 Chestnut St • Cold Spring, NY 10516 • (845) 265-4010 • http://www.pchs-fsm.org

Cold Spring Harbor
Cold Spring Harbor Library • 75 Goose Hill Rd • Cold Spring Harbor, NY 11724-1315 • (631) 692-6820 • http://cshlibrary.suffolk.lib.ny.us

Cold Spring Harbor Whaling Museum • Main St, P.O. Box 25 • Cold Spring Harbor, NY 11724-0025 • (631) 367-3418 • http://www.cshwhalingmuseum.org

Society for the Preservation of Long Island Antiquities • Historical Museum, 161 Main St, P.O. Box 148 • Cold Spring Harbor, NY 11724 • (516) 692-4664 • http://www.splia.org

Colden
Colden Historical Society • Heath Rd • Colden, NY 14069 • http://members.tripod.com/~wnyroots/index-colden.html

College Point
Poppenhusen Institute • 114-04 14th Rd, P.O. Box 91 • College Point, NY 11356 • (718) 358-0067 • http://www.poppenhuseninstitute.org

Colton
Colton Historical Society • Colton Museum, Main St, P.O. Box 223 • Colton, NY 13625 • (315) 262-2524 • http://homepage.mac.com/clstph/coltonhist/

Saint Lawrence Valley Genealogical Society • P.O. Box 341 • Colton, NY 13625-0341

Commack
Long Island History Museum • Hoyt Farm Park, New Park • Commack, NY 11725 • (631) 929-8725

Conesus
Ga-ne-a-sos History Keepers - Conesus Historical Society • Town Hall • Conesus, NY 14435

Conklin
Conklin Historical Society • Town Hall, 1271 Conklin Rd • Conklin, NY 13748 • (607) 723-1737

Constable
Constable Town Historian • P.O. Box 43 • Constable, NY 12926 • (518) 483-1936

Westville Historical Organization • P.O. Box 157 • Constable, NY 12926 • (518) 358-2374

Westville Town Historian • 19 County Road 20 • Constable, NY 12926 • (518) 358-2374

Constableville
Constable Hall Association • Constable Hall, Box 36 • Constableville, NY 13325 • (315) 397-2323 • http://www.constablehall.org

Constable Hall Museum • John St & Summit Ave • Constableville, NY 13325 • (315) 397-2323

West Turin Town Historian • 3204 N Main St • Constableville, NY 13325 • (315) 397-2353

Cooperstown
Farmers' Museum • Route 80, Lake Rd, P.O. Box 30 • Cooperstown, NY 13326 • (607) 547-1450 • http://www.farmersmuseum.org

Farmer's Museum at Cooperstown • 5775 Hwy 80 • Cooperstown, NY 13326 • http://www.farmersmuseum.org

Historical Society of Early American Decoration • general delivery • Cooperstown, NY 13326 • (607) 547-5667

Hyde Hall House Museum • Glimmerglass State Park Rd, P.O. Box 721 • Cooperstown, NY 13326 • (607) 547-5098 • http://www.hydehall.org

International Genealogy and Heraldry Fellowship of Rotarians • 22 Delaware St, P.O. Box 62 • Cooperstown, NY 13326-0052 • (607) 547-9825 • http://www.rotaryfirst100.org/library/genealogy

New York State Historical Association • Fenimore House Museum, W Lake Rd, P.O. Box 800 • Cooperstown, NY 13326-0800 • (607) 547-1400 • http://www.nysha.org

Town of Middlefield Historical Association • Historical Museum, P.O. Box 348 • Cooperstown, NY 13326 • http://www.middlefieldmuseum.org

Village Library of Cooperstown • 22 Main St • Cooperstown, NY 13326 • (607) 547-8344

Copake Falls
Roeliff Jansen Historical Society • Old Copake Falls Church, Route 344, P.O. Box 172 • Copake Falls, NY 12517 • (518) 329-2376 • http://www.copake.org/roeliff_jansen_historical_society.htm

Copenhagen
Denmark Town Historian • P.O. Box 201 • Copenhagen, NY 13626 • (315) 688-2973

Corfu
Pembroke History Room • Town Hall, 1145 Main Rd • Corfu, NY 14036 • (716) 599-4892

Corinth
Corinth Free Library • 89 Main St • Corinth, NY 12822 • (518) 654-6913 • http://corinth.sals.edu/corinth.shtml

Corning
Arthur A Houghton Jr Library • Corning Community College, 1 Academic Dr • Corning, NY 14830 • (607) 962-9484 • http://www.corning-cc.edu/library/

Corning-Painted Post Historical Society • Patterson Inn Museum, 59 W Pulteney St • Corning, NY 14830 • (607) 937-5281 • http://www.pattersoninnmuseum.org

Southeast Steuben County Library • 300 Civic Center Plaza • Corning, NY 14830 • (607) 936-3713 • http://www.stls.org

Cornwall
Cornwall Public Library • 395 Hudson St • Cornwall, NY 12518-1552 • (845) 534-8282 • http://www.rcls.org/cor

Cornwall-on-Hudson
Cornwall Public Library • 24 Idlewild Ave • Cornwall-on-Hudson, NY 12520-1134 • (845) 534-8282

Corona
Louis Armstrong House Museum • 34-56 107th St • Corona, NY 11368 • (718) 997-3670

Cortland
1890 House Museum • 37 Tompkins St • Cortland, NY 13045 • (607) 756-7551

Cortland County Historical Society • Suggett House Museum, 25 Homer Ave • Cortland, NY 13045-2056 • (607) 756-6071 • http://www.rootsweb.com/~nycortla/chsfe.html

Cortland Free Library • 32 Church St • Cortland, NY 13045 • (607) 753-1042 • http://www.flls.org/memberpages/cortl.htm

Cortlandville Historical Society • 3577 Terrace Rd • Cortland, NY 13045 • (607) 756-7306

Dryden Historical Society • 36 W Main St • Cortland, NY 13045 • (607) 844-9209

SUNY Cortland Memorial Library • P.O. Box 2000 • Cortland, NY 13045 • (607) 753-2590 • http://library.cortland.edu

Virgil Historical Society • 1176 Church St • Cortland, NY 13045 • (607) 835-6321

Cortlandt Manor
Vancortlandtville Historical Society • 297 Locust Ave • Cortlandt Manor, NY 10567 • (914) 736-7868

Cowlesville
Bennington Historical Society • 211 Clinton St • Cowlesville, NY 14037 • (585) 937-9718 • http://www.benningtonny.com/history.htm

Coxsackie
Greene County Historical Society • Bronck House Museum, US Route 9 W • Coxsackie, NY 12051 • (518) 731-6490 • http://www.gchistory.org

Heermance Memorial Library • 1 Ely St • Coxsackie, NY 12051 • (518) 731-8084 • http://www.hml.lib.ny.us

Vededer Research Library • 90 County Route 42 • Coxsackie, NY 12051 • (518) 731-1033

Cragsmoor
Cragsmoor Free Library • 355 Cragsmoor Rd, P.O. Box 410 • Cragsmoor, NY 12420-0410 • (845) 647-4611 • http://www.rcls.org

Cranberry Lake
Clifton Community Library • 7171 State Road 3, P.O. Box 678 • Cranberry Lake, NY 12927-0678 • (315) 848-3256

Clifton Town Historian • P.O. Box 640 • Cranberry Lake, NY 12927 • (315) 848-2900

Croghan
American Maple Museum • 9756 Main St, P.O. Box 81 • Croghan, NY 13327 • (315) 346-1107 • http://www.lcida.org/maplemuseum.html

Croghan Free Library • Main St, P.O. Box 8 • Croghan, NY 13327 • (315) 346-6521

Cropseyville
Brunswick Historical Society • 1881 Schoolhouse, P.O. Box 1776 • Cropseyville, NY 12052 • (518) 279-4024 • http://www.brunswickhistory.cjb.net

Croton-on-Hudson
Croton-on-Hudson Historical Society • Municipal Bldg, 1 Van Wyck St • Croton-on-Hudson, NY 10520 • (914) 271-4574

Van Cortlandt House Museum • 525 S Riverside • Croton-on-Hudson, NY 10520 • (914) 271-8981 • http://www.vancourtlandhouse.org

Crown Point
Crown Point State Historic Site Museum • 739 Bridge Rd • Crown Point, NY 12928 • (518) 597-4666 • http://www.lakechamplainregion.com/cphistoricsite

Hammond Library • 2732 Main St, P.O. Box 245 • Crown Point, NY 12928 • (518) 597-3616 • http://www.hammondlibrary.com

Penfield Homestead Foundation • Historical Museum, 703 Creek Rd • Crown Point, NY 12928 • (518) 597-3804 • http://www.penfieldmuseum.org

Cuba
Cuba Circulating Library • 39 E Main St • Cuba, NY 14727 • (585) 968-1668 • http://www.stls.org/cuba

Cuba Historical Society • 16 Genesee St, P.O. Box 200 • Cuba, NY 14727 • (585) 968-2633

Cuddlebackville
Neversink Valley Area Museum • D&H Canal Park, P.O. Box 263 • Cuddlebackville, NY 12729 • (845) 754-8870 • http://www.neversinkmuseum.org

Cutchogue
Cutchogue Free Library • 27550 Main Rd, P.O. Box 935 • Cutchogue, NY 11935-0935 • (631) 734-6360 • http://www.cutchoguelibrary.org

Cutchogue-New Suffolk Historical Council • Village Green, Main Rd, P.O. Box 714 • Cutchogue, NY 11935 • (631) 734-7122

Old House Museum • Cutchogue Village Green, P.O. Box 714 • Cutchogue, NY 11935 • (516) 734-6977

Cuyler
Cuyler Historical Society • 4721 Bennett Rd • Cuyler, NY 13050

Dannemora
Village of Dannemora Historian • P.O. Box 411 • Dannemora, NY 12929 • (518) 492-7000

Dansville
Dansville Area Historical Society • Historical Museum, 14 Church St, P.O. Box 481 • Dansville, NY 14437-0481 • (585) 335-8090 • http://www.dansvillelibrary.org/historyo.html

Dansville Public Library • 200 Main St • Dansville, NY 14437 • (585) 335-6720 • http://www.dansvillelibrary.org

Livingston County Genealogical Society • 5 Elizabeth St • Dansville, NY 14437-1719 • http://www.rootsweb.com/~nylcgs

Dapauville
Depauville Free Library • Caroline St, P.O. Box 239 • Dapauville, NY 13632 • (315) 686-3299

Davenport
Davenport Historical Society • Town Hall, Davenport Center, RR 23 • Davenport, NY 13751 • (607) 278-5149

Davenport Center
Davenport Historical Society • Town Hall, Route 23, P.O. Box 88 • Davenport Center, NY 13751 • (607) 278-5600

Dayton
Town of Dayton Historical Society • 9561 Route 62, P.O. Box 15 • Dayton, NY 14041

De Kalb Junction
DeKalb Historical Association • 696 E DeKalb Rd, P.O. Box 111 • De Kalb Junction, NY 13630 • (315) 347-1900 • http://personalpages.tds.net/~hist1900

Deansboro
Marshall Historical Society • P.O. Box 232 • Deansboro, NY 13328 • (315) 841-4473

Delanson
Duanesburg Historical Society • P.O. Box 114 • Delanson, NY 12053 • (518) 895-2632 • http://www.duanesburghistorical.com

Delhi
Cannon Free Library • 40 Elm St • Delhi, NY 13753 • (607) 746-2662

Delaware County Historical Association • 46549 State Hwy 10 • Delhi, NY 13753 • (607) 746-3849 • http://www.rootsweb.com/~nydelaha

Louis and Mildred Resnik Library • SUNY-Delhi, Bush Hall • Delhi, NY 13753 • (607) 746-4635 • http://www.delhi.edu/library

Delmar
Bethelehem Public Library • 451 Delaware Ave • Delmar, NY 12054-3042 • (518) 439-9314 • http://www.bethlehempubliclibrary.org

Deposit
Deposit Free Library • 159 Front St • Deposit, NY 13754 • (607) 467-2577 • http://www.tds.net/depositchamber/Library.html

Deposit New York Community Historical Society • 145 2nd St • Deposit, NY 13754 • (607) 467-4422 • http://www.deposithistoricalsociety.org

Dewittville
Point Chautauqua Historical Society • c/o Doing Time Clocks Co, 5997 Diamond Ave • Dewittville, NY 14782 • (716) 753-2772

Dexter
Brownville Town Historian • 16431 Star School House Rd • Dexter, NY 13634-3066 • (315) 639-6266

Dexter Free Library • East Kirby St, P.O. Box 544 • Dexter, NY 13634 • (315) 639-6785 • http://www.nc34.org/dexterlib

Dexter Village Historian • 417 Liberty St, P.O. Box 145 • Dexter, NY 13634

Dix Hills
Deer Park Museum • 674 Deer Park Ave • Dix Hills, NY 11746 • (631) 667-8751

Italian Genealogical Group of New York • 7 Grayon Dr • Dix Hills, NY 11746

Jewish Genealogical Society of Long Island • 37 Westcliff Dr • Dix Hills, NY 11746 • (631) 549-9532 • http://www.jgsli.org

Dobbs Ferry
Dobbs Ferry Historical Society • c/o Dobbs Ferry Public Library, 153 Main St • Dobbs Ferry, NY 10522 • (914) 693-6614

Dobbs Ferry Historical Society • Mead House, 12 Elm St • Dobbs Ferry, NY 10522 • (914) 674-1007

Dobbs Ferry Public Library • 153 Main St • Dobbs Ferry, NY 10522 • (914) 693-6614

Dolgeville
Dolgeville Manheim Historical Society • Historical Museum, 74 S Main St • Dolgeville, NY 13329 • (315) 429-8835

Douglaston
Douglaston and Little Neck Historical Society • 328 Manor Rd • Douglaston, NY 11363 • (718) 225-4403 • http://www.queensbp.org

Downsville
Colchester Historical Society • Town Hall, 72 Tannery Rd, P.O. Box 112 • Downsville, NY 13755 • (607) 363-2212

Colchester Reading Center • Town Hall, 72 Tannery Rd, P.O. Box 321 • Downsville, NY 13755 • (607) 363-7169

Dresden
Robert Green Ingersoll Birthplace Museum • 57 Main St • Dresden, NY 14441 • http://www.secularhumanism.org/ingersoll

Dryden
Dryden Town Historical Society • History House, 36 W Main St, P.O. Box 97 • Dryden, NY 13053 • (607) 844-9209

Southworth Library Association • 24 W Main St, P.O. Box 45 • Dryden, NY 13053-0045 • (607) 84-4782 • http://home.twcny.rr.com/southworth

Tompkins-Cortland Community College Library • 170 N Main St, P.O. Box 139 • Dryden, NY 13053 • (607) 844-8222 • http://www.tc3.edu/library

Dundee
Dundee Area Historical Society • Schoolhouse Museum, 26 Seneca St, P.O. Box 153 • Dundee, NY 14837 • (607) 243-7047

Dundee Library • 32 Water St • Dundee, NY 14837 • (607) 243-5938 • http://www.stls.org

Dunkirk
Dunkirk Historical Museum • ALCO Brooks Railroad Display, 513 Washington Ave • Dunkirk, NY 14048 • (716) 366-3797

Eagle Mills
Brunswick Historical Society • 1881 Schoolhouse, 605 Brunswick Rd • Eagle Mills, NY 12180-6901 • (518) 279-4024

Earlville
Earlville Free Library • N Main St • Earlville, NY 13332 • (315) 691-5931

East Aurora
Aurora Historical Society • Historical Museum, 5 S Grove St, P.O. Box 472 • East Aurora, NY 14052 • (716) 652-4735 • http://www.aurorahistorical.org

Elbert Hubbard-Roycroft Historical Society • Historical Museum, 363 Oakwood Ave, P.O. Box 472 • East Aurora, NY 14052 • (716) 652-4735 • http://www.roycrofter.com/museum.htm

Millard Fillmore House Museum • 24 Shearer Ave, P.O. Box 472 • East Aurora, NY 14052 • (716) 652-8875 • http://www.millardfillmorehouse.org

Polish Genealogical Society of New York State • 12645 Route 78 • East Aurora, NY 14052-9511 • (716) 826-9482 • http://www.pgsnys.org

East Bloomfield
Historical Society of the Town of East Bloomfield • Academy Museum, 8 South Ave, P.O. Box 212 • East Bloomfield, NY 14443-0212 • (585) 657-7244 • http://www.rootsweb.com/~nyontari/ebhist.htm

New York

East Chatham
Canaan Historical Society • general delivery • East Chatham, NY 12060 • (518) 781-4605

Red Rock Historical Society • County Route 24, P.O. Box 50 • East Chatham, NY 12060 • (518) 392-2285 • http://www.canaannewyork.org/living/localorgs.shtml

East Concord
Concord Historical Society • 12102 Vaughn St • East Concord, NY 14055 • (716) 592-2097 • http://www.townofconcordnyhistoricalsociety.org

East Durham
Durham Center Museum & Genealogical Library • State Rte 145, P.O. Box 192 • East Durham, NY 12423 • (518) 239-8461 • http://www.rootsweb.com/~nygreen2/durham_center_museum.htm

Irish American Heritage Museum • 2267 Route 145 • East Durham, NY 12423 • (518) 634-7497 • http://www.irishamericanheritagemuseum.org/

East Greenbush
East Greenbush Community Library • 10 Community Way • East Greenbush, NY 12061 • (518) 477-7476 • http://www.eastgreenbushlibrary.org

Greenbush Historical Society • P.O. Box 66 • East Greenbush, NY 12061 • (518) 283-1923

East Hampton
Clinton Academy Museum • 151 Main St • East Hampton, NY 11937 • (631) 324-6850 • http://www.easthamptonhistory.org

East Hampton Free Library • 159 Main St • East Hampton, NY 11937 • (631) 324-0222 • http://www.peconic.net/easthampton/library/

East Hampton Historical Society • Osborn-Jackson House Museum, 101 Main St • East Hampton, NY 11937 • (631) 324-6850 • http://www.easthamptonhistory.org

Home Sweet Home Museum • 14 James Ln • East Hampton, NY 11937 • (631) 324-0713 • http://www.easthampton.com/homesweethome

Mulford House and Farm Museum • 10 James Ln • East Hampton, NY 11937 • (631) 324-6850 • http://www.easthamptononline.org

Pollack-Krasner House Museum • 830 Fireplace Rd • East Hampton, NY 11937 • (516) 324-4929 • http://www.pkhouse.org

Springs Historical Society • Parsons-Anderson House, Fireplace Rd & Old Stone Hwy, P.O. Box 1860 • East Hampton, NY 11937-1633 • http://www.springslibrary.org

East Islip
East Islip Public Library • 381 E Main St • East Islip, NY 11730-2896 • (631) 581-9200 • http://www.eipl.org

Heckscher State Park • Heckscher Pkwy • East Islip, NY 11730 • (631) 581-2100

East Meadow
East Meadow Public Library • 1886 Front St • East Meadow, NY 11554-1700 • (516) 794-2570

East Meredith
Hanford Mills Museum • 73 County Hwy 12, P.O. Box 99 • East Meredith, NY 13757 • (607) 278-5744 • http://www.hanfordmills.org

East Quogue
East Quogue Historical Group • 37 West Side Ave, P.O. Box 144 • East Quogue, NY 11942-0144

East Rockaway
East Rockaway Public Library • 477 Atlantic Ave • East Rockaway, NY 11518 • (516) 599-1664 • http://www.nassaulibrary.org/eastrock

Historical Society of East Rockaway and Lynbrook • P.O. Box 351 • East Rockaway, NY 11518-0351 • (516) 887-9094 • http://www.members.aol.com/hserl/

East Setauket
Three Village Historical Society • 93 North Country Rd, P.O. Box 76 • East Setauket, NY 11733-0076 • (631) 751-3730 • http://members.aol.com/tvhs

East Springfield
Boswell Museum • 5748 State Highway 20, P.O. Box 27 • East Springfield, NY 13333 • (607) 264-3321 • http://www.boswellmuseum.org

East Syracuse
East Syracuse Free Library • 4990 James St • East Syracuse, NY 13057 • (315) 437-4841

East Williston
East Williston Public Library • 2 Prospect St • East Williston, NY 11596 • (516) 741-1213 • http://www.nassaulibrary.org/eastwill/

Eastchester
Eastchester Historical Society • 40 Mill Rd, P.O. Box 37 • Eastchester, NY 10709 • (914) 337-7819 • http://www.ehs1835.org

Eden
Eden Historical Society • 8837 S Main St • Eden, NY 14057 • (716) 992-4165

Edinburg
Edinburg Historical Society • Nellie Tyrrell Museum, P.O. Box 801 • Edinburg, NY 12134 • (518) 863-2034 • http://www.edinburg-hist-soc.org

Edmeston
Edmeston Free Library • 6 West St, P.O. Box 167 • Edmeston, NY 13335-0167 • (607) 965-8208

Edmeston Museum • North St, P.O. Box 167 • Edmeston, NY 13335-0167 • (607) 965-8208

Edwards
Town of Edwards Historical Association • Edwards History Center • 161 Main St, P.O. Box 100 • Edwards, NY 13635 • (315) 562-3500 • http://www.edwardshistorycenter.org

Elba
Historical Society of Elba • Maple Avenue Ext • Elba, NY 14058 • (585) 757-9094

Elbridge
Elbridge Free Library • E Main St • Elbridge, NY 13060 • (315) 689-7111 • http://community.syracuse.com/cc/elbridgelibrary

Elizabethtown
Elizabethtown Library • River St, P.O. Box 7 • Elizabethtown, NY 12932 • (518) 873-2670

Essex County Historical Society • Adirondack History Center, 7590 Court St, P.O. Box 428 • Elizabethtown, NY 12932 • (518) 873-6466 • http://www.adkhistorycenter.org

Ellenville
Ellenville Public Library and Museum • 40 Center St • Ellenville, NY 12428-1396 • (845) 647-5530 • http://www.rcls.org/epl/

Ellicottville
Ellicottville Historical Society • Historical Museum, 2 W Washington St, P.O. Box 485 • Ellicottville, NY 14731 • (716) 699-2162

Ellisburg
Ellisburg Free Library • Eisenhower Rd, P.O. Box 115 • Ellisburg, NY 13636 • (315) 846-5087

Elma
Elma Historical Society • Elma Town Museum, 3011 Bowen Rd, P.O. Box 84 • Elma, NY 14059-0084 • (716) 652-0046 • http://www.elmanewyork.com

Marilla Historical Society • 1351 Jamison Rd • Elma, NY 14059 • (716) 652-5529

Elmira
Chemung County Historical Society • Chemung Valley History Museum, 415 E Water St • Elmira, NY 14901-3410 • (607) 734-4167 • http://www.chemungvalleymuseum.org

Chemung Valley History Museum • 415 E Water St • Elmira, NY 14901 • (607) 734-4167

Gannett-Tripp Library • Elmira College, 1 Park Pl • Elmira, NY 14901 • (607) 735-1864 • http://www.elmira.edu

John W Jones Museum • 1250 Davis St, P.O. Box 932 • Elmira, NY 14901 • (607) 733-6162

National Soaring Museum • Harris Hill, 51 Soaring Hill • Elmira, NY 14903 • (607) 734-3128 • http://www.soaringmuseum.org

Steele Memorial Library • 101 E Church St • Elmira, NY 14901-2799 • (607) 733-9175 • http://www.steele.lib.ny.us

Twin Tiers Genealogical Society • c/o Steele Memorial Library, 101 E Church St, P.O. Box 763 • Elmira, NY 14902 • (607) 733-9175

Elmira Heights
Elmira Heights Historical Society • 255 E 14th St, P.O. Box 2084 • Elmira Heights, NY 14903 • (607) 732-5167

Elmont
Elmont Public Library • 1735 Hempstead Tpk • Elmont, NY 11003-1896 • (516) 354-5280 • http://www.nassaulibrary.org/elmont

Elmsford
Greenburgh Public Library • 300 Tarrytown Rd • Elmsford, NY 10523 • (914) 993-1600 • http://www.greenburghlibrary.org

Lower Hudson Conference: Historical Agencies and Museums • 2199 Saw Mill River Rd • Elmsford, NY 10523 • (914) 592-6726 • http://www.lowerhudsonconference.org

Westchester County Historical Society • Historical Museum, 2199 Saw Mill River Rd • Elmsford, NY 10523 • (914) 592-4323 • http://www.westchesterhistory.com

Westchester County Records Center and Archives • 2199 Saw Mill River Rd • Elmsford, NY 10523 • (914) 285-3080 • http://www.co.westchester.ny.us/wcarchives

Endicott
Endicott Historical and Preservation Society • 928 Neal Rd, P.O. Box 52 • Endicott, NY 13760 • (607) 783-8373

George F Johnson Memorial Library • 1001 Park St • Endicott, NY 13760 • (607) 757-5350 • http://www.gfjlibrary.org

Old Village Union Historical Association • 407 E Main St • Endicott, NY 13760-4925 • (607) 754-6886

Endwell
Amos Patterson Museum • 3111 E Main St • Endwell, NY 13760 • (607) 786-5786

Erin
Erin Historical Society • Historical Museum, 53 Fairview Rd • Erin, NY 14838 • (607) 739-0242

Esperance
Charleston Historical Society • 1834 Church Museum, 741 Corbin Hill Rd • Esperance, NY 12066 • (518) 922-5867

Esperance Historical Society • Historical Museum, Church St, P.O. Box 55 • Esperance, NY 12066 • (518) 875-6854 • http://www.townofesperance.org

Essex
Belden Noble Memorial Library • Main St, P.O. Box 339 • Essex, NY 12936 • (518) 963-8079 • http://www.cefls.org/essex.htm

Essex Community Heritage Association • Historic Preservation Library, Station Rd, P.O. Box 250 • Essex, NY 12936-0250 • (518) 963-7088 • http://www.essexny.net

Evans Mills
Evans Mills Public Library • Noble St, P.O. Box 240 • Evans Mills, NY 13637 • (315) 629-4483

Fabius
Pioneer Museum • Highland Forest, P.O. Box 31 • Fabius, NY 13063 • (315) 683-5550

Fair Haven
Fair Haven Public Library • S Richmond Ave, P.O. Box 602 • Fair Haven, NY 13064 • (315) 947-5851 • http://www.fairhavenlibrary.org

Fairport
Documentary Heritage Program - Rochester Regional Library Council • 390 Packett's Landing, P.O. Box 66160 • Fairport, NY 14450 • (585) 223-7470 • http://www.rrlc.org

Perinton Historical Society • Historical Museum, 18 Perrin St • Fairport, NY 14450 • (585) 223-3989 • http://www.angelfire.com/ny5/fairporthistmuseum

Farmingdale
Farmingdale Public Library • 116 Merritts Rd • Farmingdale, NY 11735 • (516) 249-9090 • http://www.nassaulibrary.org/farmingd/

Farmingdale-Bethpage Historical Society • P.O. Box 500 • Farmingdale, NY 11735 • (516) 249-0976

Farmingville
Farmingville Historical Society • P.O. Box 311 • Farmingville, NY 11738 • (631) 698-0396

Fayetteville
Fayetteville Free Library • Historic Stickley Factory, 300 Orchard St • Fayetteville, NY 13066-1386 • (315) 637-6374 • http://www.fayettevillefreelibrary.org

Fillmore
Town of Hume Museum • P.O. Box 302 • Fillmore, NY 14735 • (585) 567-8399 • http://www.Humetown.org

Wide Awake Club Library • 46 W Main St, P.O. Box 199 • Fillmore, NY 14735-0199 • (585) 567-8301 • http://www.homestead.com/waclibrary

Findley Lake
Findley Lake and Mina Historical Society • P.O. Box 522 • Findley Lake, NY 14736

Fishers
Valentown Museum • Valentown Sq • Fishers, NY 14453 • (585) 924-4170

Fishkill
Blodgett Memorial Library • 37 Broad St • Fishkill, NY 12524-1836 • (845) 896-9215 • http://www.midhudson.org

Fishkill Historical Society • Van Wyck Homestead Museum, 605 Route 9, P.O. Box 133 • Fishkill, NY 12524 • (845) 896-9560 • http://www.pojonews.com

Fleischmanns
Greater Fleischmanns Museum of Memories • 1009 Main St, P.O. Box 914 • Fleischmanns, NY 12430 • (845) 254-5311

Skene Memorial Library • 1017 Main St, P.O. Box C3 • Fleischmanns, NY 12430 • (914) 254-4581 • http://www.skenelib.org

New York

Floral Park
Adriance Farmhouse Museum • 73-50 Little Neck Pkwy • Floral Park, NY 11004 • (718) 347-3276

Floral Park Public Library • 17 Caroline Pl • Floral Park, NY 11001 • (516) 326-6330 • http://www.nassaulibrary.org/fpark/

Queens County Farm Museum • 73-50 Little Neck Pkwy • Floral Park, NY 11004 • (718) 347-3276 • http://www.queensfarm.org

Flushing
Bowne House Historical Society • Historical Museum, 37-01 Bowne St • Flushing, NY 11354 • (718) 359-0528 • http://www.bownehouse.org

Greek Family Heritage Committee • 75-21 177th St • Flushing, NY 11366 • (718) 591-9342 • http://mediterraneangenweb.org/greece/

Queens Historical Society • Kingsland Homestead Museum, 143-35 37th Ave • Flushing, NY 11355 • (718) 939-0647 • http://www.queenshistoricalsociety.org

Fly Creek
Fly Creek Area Historical Society • 208 Cemetery Rd, P.O. Box 87 • Fly Creek, NY 13337 • (607) 547-2501

Fonda
Heritage and Genealogical Society of Montgomery County • Old Courthouse, Railroad St, P.O. Box 1500 • Fonda, NY 12068 • (518) 853-8187 • http://www.co-montgomery.ny.us/historian/ha_main.asp

Kanatsiohareke Mohawk Community • 4934 State Hwy 5 • Fonda, NY 12068 • (518) 673-5356 • http://www.mohawkcommunity.com

Montgomery County Department of History and Archives • Old Courthouse, Railroad St, P.O. Box 1500 • Fonda, NY 12068-1500 • (518) 853-8186 • http://www.co.montgomery.ny.us

National Kateri Shrine Museum • Route 5, P.O. Box 627 • Fonda, NY 12068 • (518) 853-3646 • http://www.katerishrine.com

Fort Covington
Fort Covington Reading Center and Museum • Route 37 • Fort Covington, NY 12937 • (518) 358-2025

Fort Edward
Fort Edward Historical Association • Old Fort House Museum, 29 Lower Broadway, P.O. Box 1066 • Fort Edward, NY 12828-0106 • (518) 747-9600 • http://www.ftedward.com

Washington County Historical Society • Heritage Research Library, 167 Broadway, P.O. Box 106 • Fort Edward, NY 12828 • (518) 747-9108 • http://www.wchs-ny.org

Fort Hamilton
Fort Hamilton Historical Society • Harbor Defense Museum • Fort Hamilton, NY 11252 • (607) 630-4349 • http://www.nad.usace.army.mil/fh.htm

Fort Hunter
Schoharie Crossing State Historic Site Museum • 129 Schoharie St, P.O. Box 140 • Fort Hunter, NY 12069 • (518) 829-7516

Fort Johnson
Montgomery County Historical Society • Old Ft Johnson, Route 5 • Fort Johnson, NY 12070 • (518) 843-0300

Old Fort Johnson Museum • Route 5, P.O. Box 196 • Fort Johnson, NY 12070 • (518) 843-0300 • http://www.oldfortjohnson.org

Fort Plain
Fort Plain Free Library • 19 Willert St • Fort Plain, NY 13339 • (518) 993-4646 • http://www2.telenet.net/community/mvla/ftpl.index.html

Fort Plain Museum • 389 Canal St, P.O. Box 324 • Fort Plain, NY 13339 • (518) 993-2527

Fort Ticonderoga
Fort Ticonderoga Museum • Fort Rd, P.O. Box 390 • Fort Ticonderoga, NY 12883-0390 • (518) 585-2821 • http://www.fort-ticonderoga.org

Fort Totten
Bayside Historical Society • 208 Totten Ave • Fort Totten, NY 11359 • (718) 352-1548 • http://www.baysidehistorical.org

Franklin
Franklin Free Library • 66 Main St, P.O. Box 947 • Franklin, NY 13775 • (607) 829-2941 • http://www.rcls.org/webpages/members/Franklin/Franklin.html

Ouleout Valley Historical Society • P.O. Box 942 • Franklin, NY 13775 • (607) 829-8293 • http://www.bearsystems.com/franklin/franklin.html

Franklin Square
Franklin Square Historical Society • Museum at John Street School, Nassau Blvd, P.O. Box 45 • Franklin Square, NY 11010 • (516) 481-2235 • http://iarchives.nysed.gov

Franklinville
Blount Library • 5 N Main St • Franklinville, NY 14737 • (716) 676-5715 • http://www.cclslib.org/fran/fran.html

Ischua Valley Historical Society • Miner's Cabin Museum, 9 Pine St • Franklinville, NY 14737 • (716) 676-5651

Fredonia
Chautauqua County Genealogical Society • D R Barker Museum, Route 20 & Day St, P.O. Box 404 • Fredonia, NY 14063-0404 • (716) 672-2114 • http://www.rootsweb.com/~nygenweb

Daniel A Reed Library • SUNY • Fredonia, NY 14063 • (716) 673-3184 • http://www.fredonia.edu/library

Darwin R Barker Library • Barker Historical Museum, 20 E Main St • Fredonia, NY 14063 • (716) 672-2114 • http://www.netsync.net/users/barkermu

Freeport
African-Atlantic Genealogical Society • P.O. Box 7385 • Freeport, NY 11520 • http://www.africantic.com

Freeport Historical Society • Historical Museum, 350 S Main St • Freeport, NY 11520 • (516) 623-9632

Freeport Memorial Library • 144 W Merrick Rd • Freeport, NY 11520 • (516) 379-3274 • http://www.nassaulibrary.org/freeport

Frewsburg
Carroll Historical Society • West Main St, P.O. Box 227 • Frewsburg, NY 14738 • http://www.carrollny.org/html/history.html

Myers Memorial Library • Ivory St P.O. Box 559 • Frewsburg, NY 14738 • (716) 569-5515

Friendship
Friendship Free Library • 40 W Main St, P.O. Box 37 • Friendship, NY 14739-0037 • (585) 973-7724 • http://www.stls.org/Friendship

Fulton
Friends of History in Fulton • John Wells Pratt House Museum, 117 S 1st St, P.O. Box 157 • Fulton, NY 13069 • (315) 598-4616

Fulton City Historian • 59 W 4th St • Fulton, NY 13069 • (315) 593-7766

Fulton Public Library • 160 S 1st St • Fulton, NY 13069 • (315) 592-5159 • http://www.fultonpubliclibrary.org

Granby Town Historian • 820 County Route 8 • Fulton, NY 13609 • (315) 598-6500

Volney Town Historian • 1445 County Route 6 • Fulton, NY 13069 • (315) 593-8288

Garden City
Cradle of Aviation Museum • 1 Davis Ave • Garden City, NY 11530 • (516) 572-4111 • http://www.cradleofaviation.org

Garden City Historical Society • Historical Museum, 109 11th St, P.O. Box 179 • Garden City, NY 11530-0179 • (516) 328-7534 • http://www.gardencityhistoricalsociety.org

Garden City Public Library • 60 7th St • Garden City, NY 11530 • (516) 742-8405 • http://www.naussaulibrary.org/gardenc/

Nassau County Historical Society • P.O. Box 207 • Garden City, NY 11530 • (516) 735-4783 • http://www.nassaucountyhistoricalsociety.org

Gardiner
Locust Lawn and Terwilliger House Museum • 400 Route 32 S • Gardiner, NY 12525 • (845) 255-1660 • http://www.huguenotstreet.org

Garnerville
North Rockland History Museum • 20 Oak St • Garnerville, NY 10923

Garrison
Mid-Atlantic Regional Archives Conference • Greymoor, Route 9, Box 300 • Garrison, NY 10524 • (914) 424-3671

Garrison-on-Hudson
Boscobel Restoration House Museum • 1601 Route 9D • Garrison-on-Hudson, NY 10524 • (845) 265-3638 • http://www.boscobel.org

Geneseo
Chinese Historians in the US • SUNY-Geneseo, Dept of History • Geneseo, NY 14454 • (585) 245-5375

Livingston County Historical Society • Cobblestone Museum, 30 Center St • Geneseo, NY 14454 • (585) 243-2281 • http://www.livingstoncountyhistoricalsociety.org

Geneva
Geneva Free Library • 244 Main St • Geneva, NY 14456-2370 • (315) 789-5303 • http://www.geneva.pls-net.org

Geneva Historical Society • Prouty-Chew House Museum, 543 S Main St • Geneva, NY 14456 • (315) 789-5151 • http://www.genevahistoricalsociety.com

John Johnston House Museum • Route 96A & E Lake Rd, P.O. Box 464 • Geneva, NY 14456 • (315) 789-3848

Rose Hill Mansion Museum • Route 96A, P.O. Box 464 • Geneva, NY 14456 • (315) 789-5151 • http://www.genevahistoricalsociety.com

Warren Hunting Smith Library • Hobart & William Smith College, 334 Pulteney St • Geneva, NY 14456 • (315) 781-3552 • http://www.hws.edu/aca/library/erc.html

Genoa
East Genoa Historical Society • P.O. Box 78 • Genoa, NY 13071 • (315) 497-0478

Smith's General Store Museum • Route 90 • Genoa, NY 13071 • (315) 497-1830

Germantown
Clermont State Historic Park Museum • 1 Clermont Ave • Germantown, NY 12526 • (518) 537-4240 • http://www.friendsofclermont.org

Germantown History Dept Archives • Old Reformed Church Parsonage, Maple Ave • Germantown, NY 12526 • (518) 537-6309

Germantown Library • 71 Palatine Park Rd • Germantown, NY 12526-5309 • (518) 537-5800 • http://www.germantownlibrary.org

Livingston History Barn • 490 County Route 10 • Germantown, NY 12526 • (518) 828-3442 • http://www.columbiacountyny.com/officers1.html

Ghent
Parker-O'Malley Air Museum • 1571 Route 66, P.O. Box 216 • Ghent, NY 12075 • (518) 392-7200

Gilbertsville
Gilbertsville Free Library • 19 Commercial St, P.O. Box 332 • Gilbertsville, NY 13776-0332 • (607) 783-2832 • http://www.gilbertsville.com/Library.htm

Gilbertsville Library Historical Committee • c/o Gilbertsville Library, 19 Commercial St • Gilbertsville, NY 13776 • (607) 783-2832

Historical Association of the Town of Butternuts • Commercial St & Marion Ave • Gilbertsville, NY 13776

Glen Cove
Glen Cove Public Library • 4 Glen Cove Ave • Glen Cove, NY 11542 • (516) 676-2130 • http://www.nassaulibrary.org/glencove/history.htm

Glen Head
Cedar Swamp Historical Society • Cedar Swamp Rd • Glen Head, NY 11545 • (516) 671-6156

Glens Falls
Chapman Historical Museum • 348 Glen St • Glens Falls, NY 12801 • (518) 793-2826 • http://www.chapmanmuseum.org

Crandall Public Library • City Park, 251 Glen St • Glens Falls, NY 12801-3593 • (518) 795-6508 • http://www.crandalllibrary.org

Glens Falls-Queensbury Historical Association • Chapman Historical Museum, 348 Glen St • Glens Falls, NY 12801 • (518) 793-2826

Queensbury Historical Association • 348 Glen St • Glens Falls, NY 12801 • (518) 793-2826

Warren County Historical Society • 71 Lawrence St • Glens Falls, NY 12801 • (518) 743-0734

Glenville
Empire State Aerosciences Museum • 250 Rudy Chase Dr • Glenville, NY 12302 • (518) 377-2191 • http://www.esam.org

Gloversville
Fulton County Historical Society • Historical Museum, 237 N Kingsboro Ave, P.O. Box 711 • Gloversville, NY 12078 • (518) 725-2203 • http://www.fultoncountymuseum.org

Gloversville Free Library • 58 E Fulton St • Gloversville, NY 12078 • (518) 725-2819 • http://www.gloversvillelibrary.org

Gorham
Town of Gorham Historical Society • P.O. Box 176 • Gorham, NY 14461 • (585) 554-6268

Goshen
Goshen Historical Society • c/o Goshen Public Library, 203 Main St • Goshen, NY 10924 • (845) 294-6606 • http://goshenpubliclibrary.org

Goshen Public Library • 203 Main St • Goshen, NY 10924 • (845) 294-6606 • http://goshenpubliclibrary.org

Orange County Genealogical Society • Historic 1841Courthouse, 101 Main St • Goshen, NY 10924 • http://www.ocgsny.org

Gouverneur
Gouverneur Historical Association • Historical Museum, 30 Church St • Gouverneur, NY 13642 • (315) 287-0570 • http://members.tripod.com/~gouvmuse/realpage.html

Village of Gouverneur Town Historian • 33 Clinton St • Gouverneur, NY 13642 • (315) 287-1720

Gowanda
Gowanda Area Historical Society • Persia Town Hall, 2 Chestnut St, P.O. Box 372 • Gowanda, NY 14070 • (716) 532-4064

Grafton
Grafton Historical Society • P.O. Box 244 • Grafton, NY 12082 • (518) 279-3051

New York

Grahamsville
Time and the Valleys Museum • Route 55 • Grahamsville, NY 12740 • (845) 985-2262 • http://www.timeandthevalleysmusuem.org

Grand Island
Grand Island Historical Society • Beaver Island State Park, P.O. Box 135 • Grand Island, NY 14072 • (716) 773-2436 • http://www.isledegrande.com/historicalsociety2006.htm

Western District Historic Preservation • general delivery • Grand Island, NY 14072 • (716) 773-9077

Granville
Pember Library and Museum • 33 W Main St • Granville, NY 12832 • (518) 642-2525

Slate Valley Museum • 17 Water St • Granville, NY 12832 • (518) 642-1417 • http://www.slatevalleymuseum.org

Gravesend
Gravesend Historical Society • P.O. Box 1643, Gravesend Sta • Gravesend, NY 11223 • (718) 375-6831

Great Neck
Great Neck Library • 159 Bayview Ave • Great Neck, NY 11023-1938 • (516) 466-8055 • http://www.nassaulibrary.org/gneck

Great River
East Islip Historical Society • P.O. Box 389 • Great River, NY 11739 • (516) 581-1384 • http://www.eastislip.org

Greene
Moore Memorial Library • 59 Genessee St • Greene, NY 13778 • (607) 656-9349 • http://www.4cls.org/Greene/Greene.html

Town of Greene Historical Society • 59 Genesee St, P.O. Box 412 • Greene, NY 13778 • (607) 656-8796

Greenfield Park
Western Mohegan Tribe and Nation • P.O. Box 309 • Greenfield Park, NY 12435 • (845) 647-2777

Greenlawn
Green-Centerport Historical Association • c/o Harborfields Public Library, 31 Broadway, P.O. Box 354 • Greenlawn, NY 11740 • (631) 754-1180 • http://gcha.suffolk.lib.ny.us

Harborfields Public Library • 31 Broadway • Greenlawn, NY 11740-1382 • (631) 757-4200 • http://harb.suffolk.lib.ny.us

Greenport
East End Seaport Museum • 3rd St & Ferry Dock, P.O. Box 624 • Greenport, NY 11944 • (631) 477-2100 • http://www.eastendseaport.org

Floyd Memorial Library • 539 1st St • Greenport, NY 11944-1399 • (631) 477-0660 • http://floydmemoriallibrary.org

Stirling Historical Society • 319 Main St, P.O. Box 590 • Greenport, NY 11944 • (631) 477-3026

Greenwich
Easton Library • 1074 State Route 40 • Greenwich, NY 12834 • (518) 692-2253 • http://easton.sals.edu

Greenwood
Greenwood Area Historical Society • 2662 Main St, P.O. Box 945 • Greenwood, NY 14839

Greenwood Lake
Hudson Valley Network • P.O. Box 67 • Greenwood Lake, NY 10925 • http://www.hvnet.com

Groton
Cortland County Genealogical Society • 113 S Parkway St • Groton, NY 13073 • (607) 898-3381

Groton Historical Association • Old Baptist Meeting House, 168 Main St, P.O. Box 142 • Groton, NY 13073 • (607) 898-5787 • http://www.historicgroton.com

Groton Public Library • 112 E Cortland St • Groton, NY 13073 • (607) 898-5055 • http://www.flls.org/memberpages/groton.htm

Groversville
Fulton County Museum • 237 N Kingsboro Ave, P.O. Box 711 • Groversville, NY 12078 • (518) 883-8646

Guilderland
Guilderland Public Library • 2228 Western Ave • Guilderland, NY 12084-9701 • (518) 456-2400

Guilderland Center
Guilderland Historical Society • 162 Main St, P.O. Box 282 • Guilderland Center, NY 12085 • (518) 861-8071 • http://www.guilderlandpublic.org

Guilford
Guilford Historical Society • Klee House, P.O. Box 201 • Guilford, NY 13780 • (607) 895-6532 • http://www.mkl.com/guilford/historical_society.htm

Haines Falls
Haines Falls Free Library • 52 N Lake Rd, P.O. Box 397 • Haines Falls, NY 12436-0397 • (518) 589-5707 • http://www.hainesfalls.lib.ny.us

Mountain Top Historical Society of Greene County • Twilight Park, Box 263 • Haines Falls, NY 12436 • (518) 589-5357 • http://www.mths.org

Halcottsville
Round Barn of Halcottsville • Route 30, P.O. Box 100 • Halcottsville, NY 12438 • (845) 586-3326

Hamburg
Hamburg Historical Society • Dunn House, S 5902 Gowanda State Rd, P.O. Box 400 • Hamburg, NY 14075 • (716) 648-6460

Western New York Genealogical Society • 5859 S Park Ave, P.O. Box 338 • Hamburg, NY 14075 • (716) 648-6320 • http://www.wnygs.org

Hamilton
Hamilton Public Library & Village Museum • 13 Broad St • Hamilton, NY 13346 • (315) 824-3060 • http://www.midyork.org/Hamilton

Hammond
Macomb Historical Association • 6726 State Hwy 58 • Hammond, NY 13646 • (315) 578-2349

Macomb Town Historian • 6726 State Hwy 58 • Hammond, NY 13646 • (315) 578-2247

R T Elethorp Historical Society • Historical Museum, Main St, P.O. Box 107 • Hammond, NY 13646 • (315) 324-5208 • http://www.blacklakeny.com/hammondmuseum

Hammondsport
Crooked Lake Historical Society • P.O. Box 154 • Hammondsport, NY 14840

Glenn H Curtiss Museum of Local History • 8419 Route 54 • Hammondsport, NY 14840-0326 • (607) 569-2160 • http://www.glennhcurtissmuseum.org

Hammondsport Public Library • 41 Lake St, P.O. Box 395 • Hammondsport, NY 14840-0395 • (607) 569-2045 • http://www.stls.org/hammondsport

Hampton
Hampton Bays Public Library • Ponquoque Ave • Hampton, NY 11946 • (516) 728-6241

Hancock
Hancock Chehocton Historical Association • 61 Wheeler St • Hancock, NY 13783

Louise Adelia Read Memorial Library & Museum • 104 Read St • Hancock, NY 13783-3377 • (607) 637-2519 • http://www.4cls.org/webpages/members/Hancock/Hancock.html

Hannibal
Hannibal Historical Society • 162 Oswego St, P.O. Box 150 • Hannibal, NY 13074 • (315) 564-5471 • http://www.rootsweb.com/~nyoswego/

Hannibal Town Historian • P.O. Box 325 • Hannibal, NY 13074 • (315) 564-5650 • http://www.rootsweb.com/~nyoswego/

Harpursville
Colesville & Windsor Museum • St Luke's Church, Maple St, P.O. Box 318 • Harpursville, NY 13787 • (607) 655-3174

Old Onanquaga Historical Society • Saint Luke's Museum, Maple Ave, P.O. Box 318 • Harpursville, NY 13787 • (607) 655-3174

Harrison
Harrison Public Library • Bruce Ave • Harrison, NY 10528 • (914) 835-0324

Harrisville
Diana Historical Museum • 14457 Wilder Dr, P.O. Box 216 • Harrisville, NY 13648 • (315) 543-2979

Harrisville-Bonaparte History Association • 8286 High St • Harrisville, NY 13648 • (315) 543-2987

Hartsdale
Ridge Historical Society • 40 Birchwood Ln • Hartsdale, NY 10530 • (914) 421-0075

Hartwick
Hartwick Historical Society • 3140 County Hwy 11, P.O. Box 1 • Hartwick, NY 13348

Hastings-on-Hudson
Hastings Historical Society • 407 Broadway • Hastings-on-Hudson, NY 10706 • (914) 478-2249 • http://hastingshistorical.org

Hastings-on-Hudson Historical Society • 41 Washington Ave • Hastings-on-Hudson, NY 10706-2204 • (914) 478-2249

Haverstraw
Haverstraw Kings Daughters Public Library • 85 Main St • Haverstraw, NY 10927 • (845) 429-3445 • http://www.hkdpl.org

Hempstead
African Atlantic Genealogical Society • 110 N Franklin St • Hempstead, NY 11550 • (516) 486-2210

Hempstead Public Library • 115 Nichols Ct • Hempstead, NY 11550 • (516) 481-6990 • http://www.naussaulibrary.org

Hempstead Village Historical Society • c/o Hempstead Public Library, 115 Nichols Ct • Hempstead, NY 11550 • (516) 481-6990 • http://www.nassaulibrary.org/hemstd

Hofstra University Library & Long Island Studies Institute • Hofstra Univ West Campus, 619 Fulton Ave • Hempstead, NY 11550-1090 • (516) 463-6409 • http://www.hofstra.edu

Henderson
Henderson Free Library • 8939 State Route 178, P.O. Box 302 • Henderson, NY 13650 • (315) 938-5032

Henderson Historical Society • Historical Museum, 12581 County Route 72, P.O. Box 322 • Henderson, NY 13650 • (315) 938-7163

Henrietta
Henrietta Historical Society • P.O. Box 435 • Henrietta, NY 14467 • (585) 334-2211 • http://ggw.org/~henhs

Herkimer
Frank J Basloe Library • 245 N Main St • Herkimer, NY 13350 • (315) 866-1733 • http://www.midyork.org/herkimer

Herkimer County Historical Society • Historical Museum, 400 N Main St • Herkimer, NY 13350 • (315) 866-6413 • http://www.rootsweb.com/~nyhchs

Hermon
Hermon Heritage Hall • 117 E Main St, P.O. Box 296 • Hermon, NY 13652-0296 • (315) 347-3221

Hermon Town Historian • 102 Germain St, P.O. Box 94 • Hermon, NY 13652 • (315) 347-2487

Hermon Village Historian • 138 Church St • Hermon, NY 13652-3189 • (315) 347-3221

Hicksville
Hicksville Historical Society • P.O. Box 443 • Hicksville, NY 11802 • (516) 931-1417

Hicksville Public Library • 169 Jerusalem Ave • Hicksville, NY 11801-4999 • (516) 931-1417 • http://www.nassaulibrary.org/hicksv/

High Falls
Delaware and Hudson Canal Historical Society • Historical Museum, 23 Mohonk Rd, P.O. Box 23 • High Falls, NY 12440 • (845) 687-9311 • http://www.canalmuseum.org

Highland
Lloyd Historical Society • 38-A Bellevue Rd • Highland, NY 12528 • (845) 691-2145

Vintage Village • Route 44 & Route 9W • Highland, NY 12528 • (845) 691-2145

Highland Falls
Highland Falls Library • 298 Main St • Highland Falls, NY 10928 • (845) 446-3113

Town of Highlands Historical Society • Village Hall, 303 Main St • Highland Falls, NY 10928 • (845) 446-0400 • http://highlandshistory.org

Highland Mills
Highland Mills Historical Society • HC 32 • Highland Mills, NY 10930 • (845) 928-6770

Woodbury Historical Society • 224 Smith Clove Rd • Highland Mills, NY 10930 • (845) 928-5227

Woodbury Public Library • County Route 105 • Highland Mills, NY 10930 • (845) 928-6162

Hilton
Hamlin Historical Society • 731 Walker-Lake Ontario Rd • Hilton, NY 14468 • (585) 964-2101

Parma Public Library • 7 West Ave, P.O. Box 785 • Hilton, NY 14468-0785 • (585) 392-8350

Parma-Hilton Historical Society • 1300 Hilton Parma Rd • Hilton, NY 14468 • (585) 392-9496 • http://www.parmany.org/History/historical-society.html

Hobart
Hobart Historical Society • 57 Cornell Ave, P.O. Box 11 • Hobart, NY 13788 • (607) 538-9279

Hoffmeister
Morehouse Historical Museum • Route 8, Box 1 • Hoffmeister, NY 13353 • http://www.rootsweb.com/~nyhamilt/MoreMus/museum.html

Morehouse Town Historian • P.O. Box 1 • Hoffmeister, NY 13353 • (315) 826-5764

Hogansburg
Akwesasne Library and Cultural Center • 321 State Route 37 • Hogansburg, NY 13655 • (518) 358-2240 • http://www.akwesapeculture.org

Hogansburg, cont.
Akwesasne Mohawk Tribe • Saint Regis Mohawk Reservation, 412 State Route 37 • Hogansburg, NY 13655 • (518) 358-2272 • http://www.cradleboard.org/sites/akwesasn.html

Holbrook
Sachem Historical Society • 59 Crescent Cr • Holbrook, NY 11741-4317 • (516) 588-3967

Sachem Public Library • 150 Holbrook Rd • Holbrook, NY 11741 • (631) 588-5024 • http://sachem.suffolk.lib.ny.us

Holland
Holland Historical Society • P.O. Box 95 • Holland, NY 14080 • (716) 537-2591

Holley
Community Free Library • 86 Public Sq • Holley, NY 14470 • (585) 638-6987 • http://www.nioga.org/holley/

Murray-Holley Historical Society • Historical Museum, Geddes Street Ext, P.O. Box 346 • Holley, NY 14470 • (585) 638-7566

Holliswood
Society for the History of Czechoslovak Jews • 87-08 Santiago St • Holliswood, NY 11423 • (718) 468-6844

Homer
Glen Haven Historical Society • 7325 Fairhaven Rd, P.O. Box 293 • Homer, NY 13077 • (607) 749-7907

Homerville Antique Fire Department Museum • 32 Center St • Homer, NY 13077 • (607) 749-4466 • http://members.aol.com/Mufire/home.htm

Homeville Museum • 49 Clinton St, Route 41 • Homer, NY 13077-1024 • (607) 749-3105

Phillips Free Library • 37 S Main St, P.O. Box 7 • Homer, NY 13077 • (607) 749-4616 • http://www.flls.org/memberpages/homer.htm

Hoosick Falls
Hoosick Township Historical Society • Louis Miller Museum, 166 Main St, P.O. Box 336 • Hoosick Falls, NY 12090 • (518) 686-4682 • http://www.hoosickhistory.com

Hopewell Junction
East Fishkill Historical Society • 68 Kensington Dr #N • Hopewell Junction, NY 12533 • (845) 227-4136

Hopkinton
Hopkinton Historical Group • 7 Church St • Hopkinton, NY 12965 • (315) 328-4684

Hornby
Hornby Historical Society • Historical Museum, County Rte 41 • Hornby, NY 14830 • (607) 962-4471 • http://homepages.rootsweb.com/~hornby/hornby.html

Hornell
Hornell Historical Society • general delivery • Hornell, NY 14843

Hornell Public Library • 64 Genesee St • Hornell, NY 14843-1651 • (607) 324-1210 • http://www.stls.org

Horseheads
Depot Museum • 312 W Broad St, P.O. Box 194 • Horseheads, NY 14845 • (607) 739-3938

Horseheads Cultural Center and Historical Society • Zim Center, 601 Pine St, P.O. Box 194 • Horseheads, NY 14845 • (607) 739-3938

National Warplane Museum • 17 Aviation Dr • Horseheads, NY 14845 • (607) 739-8200 • http://www.wingsofeagles.com

Houghton
Willard J Houghton Library & College Archives • Houghton College, 1 Willard Ave • Houghton, NY 14744 • (585) 567-2260 • http://houghton.edu/library

Howard
Howard Public Library • 3607 County Route 70A • Howard, NY 14843-9223 • (607) 566-2412 • http://www.howardpubliclibrary.com

Howes Cave
Caverns Creek Grist Mill Museum • 257 Caverns Rd • Howes Cave, NY 12092 • (580) 296-8448 • http://www.cavernscreekgristmill.com

Iroquois Indian Musuem • Caverns Rd, P.O. Box 7 • Howes Cave, NY 12092-0007 • (518) 296-8949 • http://www.IroquoisMuseum.rg

Hudson
FASNY Museum of Fire Fighting • 117 Harry Howard Ave • Hudson, NY 12534 • (518) 822-1875 • http://www.fasnyfiremuseum.org

Greenport Historical Society • Town Hall Dr • Hudson, NY 12534 • (518) 828-4656

Hudson Area Association Library • 400 State St • Hudson, NY 12534 • (518) 828-1792 • http://www.hudson.lib.ny.us

Olana State Historic Site Museum • 5720 Route 9G • Hudson, NY 12534 • (518) 828-0135 • http://www.olana.org

Robert Jenkins House Museum • 113 Warren St • Hudson, NY NY • (518) 851-9049

Hudson Falls
Hudson Falls Free Library • 220 Main St • Hudson Falls, NY 12839 • (518) 747-6406 • http://hudsonfalls.sals.edu

Seeley Genealogical Society • 314B Road 1, Vaughn Rd • Hudson Falls, NY 12839 • (518) 792-3867

Hume
Town of Hume Museum • 10842 Claybed Rd • Hume, NY 14745 • (585) 567-8399 • http://www.Humetown.org

Huntington
Arsenal House Museum • 425 Park Ave • Huntington, NY 11743 • (516) 351-3244

David Conklin Farmhouse Museum • 2 High St • Huntington, NY 11743 • (631) 427-7056 • http://www.huntingtonhistoricalsociety.org

Dr Daniel W Kissam House Museum • 434 Park Ave • Huntington, NY 11743 • (631) 427-7056 • http://www.huntingtonhistoricalsociety.org

Friends of Oheka • 135 W Gate Dr • Huntington, NY 11743 • (631) 367-2570

Huntington Historical Society and Genealogical Workshop • Huntington Trade School Museum, 209 Main St • Huntington, NY 11743 • (631) 427-7045 • http://www.huntingtonhistoricalsociety.org

Huntington Public Library • 338 Main St • Huntington, NY 11743 • (631) 427-5165 • http://www.suffolk.lib.ny.us/libraries/hunt

Joseph Lloyd Manor House Museum • Lloyd Ln • Huntington, NY 11743 • (516) 271-7760

Lloyd Harbor Historical Society • Lloyd Harbor Rd • Huntington, NY 11743 • (631) 424-6110

Soldiers & Sailors Memorial Bldg Museum • 228 Main St • Huntington, NY 11743 • (631) 427-7045 • http://www.huntingtonhistoricalsociety.org

Huntington Station
Walt Whitman Birthplace Historic Site Museum • 246 Old Walt Whitman Rd • Huntington Station, NY 11746 • (631) 427-5240 • http://www.waltwhitman.org

Hurley
Hurley Heritage Society • 52 Main St, P.O. Box 1661 • Hurley, NY 12443-0052 • (845) 338-1661 • http://www.HurleyHeritageSociety.org

Hurley Library • 44 Main St, P.O. Box 99 • Hurley, NY 12443-0099 • (845) 338-2092 • http://hurley.lib.ny.us

Hurley Patentee Manor Museum • 464 Old Route 209 • Hurley, NY 12443 • (845) 331-6515

Ulster County Genealogical Society • Hurley Reformed Church, 17 Main St, P.O. Box 536 • Hurley, NY 12443 • (845) 338-5496 • http://www.ucgsny.org

Hurleyville
Hurleyville Historian • 247 Main St • Hurleyville, NY 12747 • (845) 434-8044

Sullivan County Historical Society • Historical Museum, 265 Main St, P.O. Box 247 • Hurleyville, NY 12747-0247 • (914) 434-8044 • http://www.sullivancountyhistory.org

Hyde Park
Eleanor Roosevelt National Historic Site Museum • 4097 Albany Post Rd • Hyde Park, NY 12538 • (845) 229-9115 • http://www.nps.gov/elro

Franklin D Roosevelt Library • 511 Albany Post Rd • Hyde Park, NY 12538 • (845) 229-8114 • http://www.fdrlibrary.marist.edu

Home of Franklin D Roosevelt National Historic Site Museum • 519 Albany Post Rd • Hyde Park, NY 12538 • (845) 229-9115 • http://www.nps.gov/hofr

Hyde Park Historical Society • Historical Museum, 4389 Albany Post Rd, P.O. Box 182 • Hyde Park, NY 12538 • (845) 229-2559 • http://hydeparklibrary.org/h_s.html

Vanderbilt Mansion National Historic Site Museum • Route 9 • Hyde Park, NY 12538 • (845) 229-9115 • http://www.nps.gov/vama

Ilion
Ilion Free Public Library • 78 West St • Ilion, NY 13357-1797 • (315) 894-5028 • http://www.midyork.org/ilion

Remington Firearms Museum • 14 Hoeffler Ave • Ilion, NY 13357 • (315) 895-3200 • http://www.remington.com

Indian Lake
Indian Lake Museum • W Main St & Crow Hill Rd • Indian Lake, NY 12842 • (518) 648-5377 • http://indian-lake.com

Indian Lake Town Historian • 36 W Main St • Indian Lake, NY 12842-1503 • (518) 648-5377

Inlet
Inlet Town Historian • S Shore Rd, P.O. Box 355 • Inlet, NY 13360 • (315) 357-6635

Interlaken
Interlaken Historical Society • Historical Museum, 8391 Main St, P.O. Box 270 • Interlaken, NY 14847 • (607) 532-8505 • http://www.interlakenhistory.org

Interlaken Public Library • 8390 Main St, P.O. Box 317 • Interlaken, NY 14847-0317 • (607) 532-4341

Irving
Seneca Indian Historical Society • Cattaraugus Indian Reservation, 12199 Brant Reservation Rd • Irving, NY 14081 • (716) 549-3889

Seneca Nation Historical Society • 12199 Brant-Reservation Rd • Irving, NY 14081 • (716) 532-4900

Irvington
Irvington Historical Society • P.O. Box 23 • Irvington, NY 10533 • (914) 591-2564

Irvington Public Library • Town Hall, Main St • Irvington, NY 10533 • (914) 591-7840

Irvington Public Library • 12 S Astor St • Irvington, NY 10533 • (914) 591-7840 • http://www.irvingtonlibrary.org

Islip
Islip Public Library • 71 Monell Ave • Islip, NY 11751-3999 • (631) 581-5933 • http://www.suffolk.lib.ny.us/libraries/islip/

Ithaca
Africana Studies Research Center Library • Cornell Univ, 310 Triphammer Rd • Ithaca, NY 14850 • (607) 255-3822 • http://www.library.cornell.edu/africana/

Carl A Kroch Library - Manuscripts Collection • Cornell Univ • Ithaca, NY 14853-5302 • (607) 255-3530 • http://rmc.librar.cornell.edu/collections/HFL.html

Cornell Plantations Museum • 1 Plantations Rd • Ithaca, NY 14850 • (607) 256-3020 • http://www.plantations.cornell.edu

Hinckley Foundation Museum • 410 E Seneca St • Ithaca, NY 14850 • (607) 273-7053

Hinkley Foundation • Historical Museum, 410 E Seneca St • Ithaca, NY 14850 • (607) 273-7053

Historic Ithaca • 120 W State St • Ithaca, NY 14850 • (607) 273-6633 • http://www.historicithaca.com

History Center in Thompkins County • 401 E State St, Ste 100 • Ithaca, NY 14850 • (607) 273-8284 • http://www.thehistorycenter.net

John M Olin Library • Cornell Univ • Ithaca, NY 14853 • (607) 255-4144 • http://www.library.cornell.edu

Tomkins County Public Library • 101 E Green St • Ithaca, NY 14850-5613 • (607) 272-4556 • http://www.tcpl.org

Jamaica
Barnes Historical Society • P.O. Box 300049, JFK Sta • Jamaica, NY 11430-0049 • (718) 658-2515 • http://www.queensbp.org

King Manor Museum • 150-03 Jamaica Ave • Jamaica, NY 11432 • (718) 206-0545 • http://www.kingmanor.org

Queens Borough Public Library • 89-11 Merrick Blvd • Jamaica, NY 11432 • (718) 990-0770 • http://www.queenslibrary.org

Jamestown
Busti Historical Society • 3443 Lawson Rd • Jamestown, NY 14701 • (716) 483-3670 • http://www.cclslib.org/busti/community.htm

Chautauqua-Cattaraugus Library • 106 W 5th St • Jamestown, NY 14702-0730 • (716) 484-7135 • http://www.cclslib.org

Fenton Historical Society • History Center, 67 Washington St • Jamestown, NY 14701 • (716) 664-6256 • http://www.fentonhistorycenter.org

Fluvanna Free Library • 3532 Fluvanna Ave • Jamestown, NY 14701 • (716) 487-1773 • http://www.cclslib.org/fluvanna

James Predergast Library Association • 509 Cherry St • Jamestown, NY 14701 • (716) 484-7135 • http://www.prendergastlibrary.org

Kiantone Historical Society • 959 Prosser Hill • Jamestown, NY 14701

Painted Hills Genealogy Society • 333 Hazzard St • Jamestown, NY 14701 • http://www.paintedhills.org

Jamesville
Jamesville Historic Preservation • RR 173 • Jamesville, NY 13078 • (315) 492-6422

Town of Pompey Historical Society • 2944 Michael Ave • Jamesville, NY 13078 • (315) 682-4729 • http://www.pompeyhistory.org

Java Village
Java Historical Society • 4441 Route 78 • Java Village, NY 14083 • (585) 457-3898

Jay
Jay Town Historian • RR 1, Box 30 • Jay, NY 12941 • (518) 946-2597 • http://www.jaynewyork.com

Society of the Daughters of Holland Dames • P.O. Box 82 • Jay, NY 12941-0082 • http://www.hollanddames.org

Jefferson
Harpersfield Historical Society • County Route 29, P.O. Box 4044 • Jefferson, NY 12093 • (607) 652-9790

Jericho
Jericho Public Library • 1 Merry Ln • Jericho, NY 11753 • (516) 935-6790 • http://www.jericholibrary.org

Johnstown
Johnson Hall State Historic Site Museum • Hall Ave • Johnstown, NY 12095 • (518) 762-8712 • http://www.nysparks.com

Johnstown Historical Society • Historical Museum, 17 N William St • Johnstown, NY 12095 • (518) 762-7076 • http://www.cityofjohnstownny.com/historical_society1.htm

Johnstown Public Library • 38 S Market St • Johnstown, NY 12095 • (518) 762-8317 • http://www.johnstown.com/city/library.html

Jordan
Jordan Historical Society • Erie Canal Museum, Mechanic St, P.O. Box 622 • Jordan, NY 13080 • (315) 689-3296 • http://www.jordanny.com

Jordanville
Jordanville Public Library • 107 Main St, P.O. Box 44 • Jordanville, NY 13361 • (315) 858-2874 • http://www.midyork.org/joranville

Town of Warren Historical Society • Main St, P.O. Box 44 • Jordanville, NY 13407 • (315) 858-2874

Katonah
Caramoor Center Museum • 149 Girdle Ridge Rd, P.O. Box 816 • Katonah, NY 10536

John Jay Homestead State Historical Site Library • State Route 22, P.O. Box 832 • Katonah, NY 10536 • (914) 232-5651 • http://www.nysparks.com

Keene
Keene Public Library • P.O. Box 751 • Keene, NY 12942 • (518) 576-9550 • http://www.cefls.org/keene.htm

Keene Valley
Keene Valley Library • 1796 Rte 73, P.O. Box 86 • Keene Valley, NY 12943-0086 • (518) 576-4335 • http://www.kvvi.net/~library/

Keeseville
Anderson Falls Historical Society • Community Center, 1790 Main St, Ste 3-4 • Keeseville, NY 12944

Chesterfield Town Historian • 631 Highland Rd • Keeseville, NY 12944 • (518) 834-7364

Friends of the North Country • 1 Mill St, P.O. Box 446 • Keeseville, NY 12944 • (518) 834-9606

Keeseville Free Library • 1721 Front St • Keeseville, NY 12944 • (518) 834-9054 • http://www.cefls.org/keeseville.htm

Northern New York American Canadian Genealogical Society • Community Center, N Main • Keeseville, NY 12944 • (518) 834-5401 • http://www.rootsweb.com/~nnyacgs

Kenmore
Town of Tonawanda Public Library • 160 Delaware Rd • Kenmore, NY 14217 • (716) 873-2861

Keuka Park
Lightner Library • Keuka College, 141 Central Ave • Keuka Park, NY 14478-0038 • (315) 279-5224 • http://www.keuka.edu/library.html

Kinderhook
Columbia County Historical Society • Historical Museum, 5 Albany Ave, P.O. Box 311 • Kinderhook, NY 12106 • (518) 758-9265 • http://www.cchsny.org

James Vanderpoel House Museum • 16 Broad St, P.O. Box 311 • Kinderhook, NY 12106 • (518) 758-9265

Kinderhook Memorial Library • 18 Hudson St • Kinderhook, NY 12106 • (518) 758-6192

Martin Van Buren National Historic Site Museum • Route 9H, P.O. Box 545 • Kinderhook, NY 12106 • (518) 758-9689 • http://www.nps.gov/mava

Van Alen House Museum • Route 9, P.O. Box 311 • Kinderhook, NY 12106 • (518) 758-9265

King Ferry
Genoa Historical Association • Rural Life Museum, 920 Route 34B, P.O. Box 316 • King Ferry, NY 13081 • (315) 364-7550 • http://www.genoahistorical.com

Kings Park
German Genealogy Group • 24 Jonquill Ln, P.O. Box 1004 • Kings Park, NY 11754-3927 • (631) 567-4333 • http://www.germangenealogygroup.com

Kings Point
American Merchant Marine Museum • 300 Steamboat Rd • Kings Point, NY 11024 • (516) 773-5515 • http://www.usmma.edu/museum/

Kingston
Friends of Historic Kingston • Fred J Johnston House Museum, 63 Main St, P.O. Box 3763 • Kingston, NY 12402 • (845) 339-0720 • http://www.fohk.org

Hudson River Maritime Museum • 50 Rondout Landing • Kingston, NY 12401 • (845) 338-0071 • http://www.hrmm.org

Kingston Area Library • 55 Franklin St • Kingston, NY 12401 • (845) 331-0507 • http://www.kingstonlibrary.org

Senate House State Historic Site • Palisades Region, 296 Fair St • Kingston, NY 12401 • (845) 338-2786 • http://www.nysparks.com

Town of Ulster Public Library • 985 Morton Blvd • Kingston, NY 12401 • (845) 336-5767 • http://www.ulster.lib.ny.us

Trolley Museum of New York • 89 E Strand, P.O. Box 2291 • Kingston, NY 12401 • (845) 331-3399 • http://www.tmny.org

Ulster County Historical Society • P.O. Box 3752 • Kingston, NY 12402 • (845) 338-5614

Volunteer Firemen's Mall Museum • 265 Fair St • Kingston, NY 12401 • (845) 331-0866

Kirkwood
Kirkwood Historical Society • 303 Main St, P.O. Box 37 • Kirkwood, NY 13795 • (607) 775-4823

Knox
Knox Historical Society • Berne-Altamont Rd, P.O. Box 11 • Knox, NY 12107-0011 • (518) 872-2551 • http://www.helderweb.com/knoxhistorical

La Fargeville
Northern NY Agricultural Historical Society • Agricultural Museum, 30950 State Route 180, P.O. Box 108 • La Fargeville, NY 13656 • (315) 658-2353 • http://home.usadatanet.net/~agstonemills/

Orleans Public Library • Sunrise Ave, P.O. Box 139 • La Fargeville, NY 13656 • (315) 658-2271

La Grange
LaGrange Historical Society • P.O. Box 112 • La Grange, NY 12540 • (845) 227-0452 • http://www.lagrangeny.org/lagrange_clubs.cfm

La Grangeville
Union Vale Historical Society • 249 Duncan Rd • La Grangeville, NY 12540 • (845) 924-5600

Lackawanna
Buffalo & Erie County Public Library-Lackawanna • 560 Ridge Rd • Lackawanna, NY 14218 • (716) 823-0630 • http://www.buffalolib.org

Lackawanna Area Historical Association • P.O. Box 64 • Lackawanna, NY 14218 • (716) 822-5258

Lacona
Boylston Town Historian • 906 North Church Rd • Lacona, NY 13083 • (315) 387-5471

Lake George
Fort William Henry Museum • 48 Canada St • Lake George, NY 12845 • (518) 668-4926 • http://www.fwhmuseum.com

Lake George Historical Association • Old Warren County Courthouse, Canada & Amherst Sts, P.O. Box 472 • Lake George, NY 12845 • (518) 668-5044 • http://www.lakegeorgehistorical.org

Lake Luzerne
Hadley-Luzerne Historical Society • Kinnear Museum of Local History, 52 Main St, P.O. Box 275 • Lake Luzerne, NY 12846 • (518) 696-4520

Lake Placid
John Brown Farm State Historic Site Museum • 115 John Brown Rd • Lake Placid, NY 12946 • (518) 523-3900 • http://www.nysparks.com

Lake Placid Public Library • 67 Main St • Lake Placid, NY 12946 • (518) 523-3200 • http://www.lakeplacidlibrary.org

Lake Placid Winter Olympic Museum • Olympic Center, 2634 Main St • Lake Placid, NY 12946 • (518) 523-1655

Lake Placid-North Elba Historical Society • Historical Museum, 242 Station St, P.O. Box 189 • Lake Placid, NY 12946 • (518) 523-1608

Lake Pleasant
Lake Pleasant Town Historian • HC 1, Box 11 • Lake Pleasant, NY 12108-9701

Lake Ronkonkoma
Lake Ronkonkoma Historical Society • Fitz-Greene Hallock Homestead Museum, 328 Hawkins Ave, P.O. Box 2716 • Lake Ronkonkoma, NY 11779 • (631) 467-3152 • http://www.lakeronkonkomacivic.org

Lakeland
Solvay-Geddes Historical Society • State Fair Blvd & Stasko Dr • Lakeland, NY 13209 • http://www.rootsweb.com/~nysghs

Lakewood
Lakewood Memorial Library • 12 W Summit St • Lakewood, NY 14750 • (716) 763-6234

Lancaster
Hull Family Home and Farmstead Museum • 5976 Genesee Rd • Lancaster, NY 14086 • (716) 681-6451 • http://www.hullfamilyhome.org

Lancaster Historical Society • 40 Clark St • Lancaster, NY 14086 • (716) 681-7719 • http://intotem.buffnet.net/lancasterpast/society

Lansing
Lansing Historical Association • P.O. Box 100 • Lansing, NY 14882 • (607) 533-4514

Lansingburgh
Lansingburgh Historical Society • Herman Melville Park, 2 114th St, P.O. Box 219 • Lansingburgh, NY 12181 • (518) 235-3501

Larchmont
Larchmont Public Library • 121 Larchmont Ave • Larchmont, NY 10538 • (914) 834-2281 • http://www.larchmontlibrary.org

Lawrence
Rock Hall House Museum • 199 Broadway • Lawrence, NY 11010 • (516) 239-1157

Leroy
Leroy Historical Society • Leroy House Museum, 23 E Main St • Leroy, NY 14482 • (585) 768-7433 • http://www.jellomuseum.com

Stafford Historical Society • 6684 Randall Rd • Leroy, NY 14482-9316 • (585) 343-9424 • http://www.townofstafford.com/history.htm

Levittown
Levittown Historical Society • School Museum, Abbey Ln, P.O. Box 57 • Levittown, NY 11756 • (516) 735-9060 • http://www.levittownhistoricalsociety.org

Levittown
Levittown Public Library • 1 Bluegrass Ln • Levittown, NY 11756-1292 • (516) 731-5728 • http://www.nassaulibrary.org/levtown/

Lewis
Lewis Town Historian • HCR-1, Box 515 • Lewis, NY 12950 • (518) 873-6798

Lewiston
Historical Association and Society of Lewiston • Historical Museum, Plain & Niagara Sts, P.O. Box 43 • Lewiston, NY 14092 • (716) 754-4214 • http://www.townoflewiston.us/edu.htm

Lewiston Public Library • 305 S 8th St • Lewiston, NY 14092 • (716) 754-4720

Tuscarora Nation • 2006 Mt Hope Rd • Lewiston, NY 14092 • (716) 622-7061

Lexington
Town of Lexington Historical Society • P.O. Box 247 • Lexington, NY 12452

Liberty
Liberty Public Library • 189 N Main St • Liberty, NY 12754 • (845) 292-6070

Liberty Island
Ellis Island Immigration Museum • Statue of Liberty National Monument • Liberty Island, NY 10004 • (212) 363-3200 • http://www.ellisisland.org

Lima
Lima Historical Society • Tennie Burton Museum, 1850 Rochester St, P.O. Box 532 • Lima, NY 14485 • (585) 263-2700

Lima Public Library • 1872 Genesee St, P.O. Box 58A • Lima, NY 14485-0858 • (585) 582-1311

Lindenhurst
Lindenhurst Historical Society • Old Village Hall Museum, 215 S Wellwood Ave, P.O. Box 296 • Lindenhurst, NY 11757 • (631) 957-4385 • http://www.villageoflindenhurst.com/old_village_hall_museum.htm

Lindenhurst Historical Society • 215 S Wellwood Ave, P.O. Box 296 • Lindenhurst, NY 11757 • (631) 957-4385

Lindenhurst Memorial Library • 1 Lee Ave • Lindenhurst, NY 11757-5399 • (631) 957-7755 • http://ml.suffolk.lib.ny.us

Lisbon
Hepburn Library • 6899 County Rte 10, P.O. Box 86 • Lisbon, NY 13658-0086 • (315) 393-0111

Lisle
Lisle Free Library • 8998 Main St, P.O. Box 305 • Lisle, NY 13797 • (607) 692-3115

Little Falls
Herkimer Home State Historic Site Museum • 200 State Rte 169 • Little Falls, NY 13365 • (315) 923-0398

Little Falls Historical Society • Historical Museum, 319 S Ann St • Little Falls, NY 13365 • (315) 823-0643 • http://www.lfhistoricalsociety.org

Little Falls Public Library • 10 Waverly Pl • Little Falls, NY 13365 • (315) 823-1542 • http://www.midyork.org/LittleFalls

Little Genesee
Genesee Public Library • 8351 Main St, P.O. Box 10 • Little Genesee, NY 14754-0010 • (585) 928-1915

Little Valley
Cattaraugus County Historian Museum and Library • 302 Court St • Little Valley, NY 14755-1027 • (716) 938-9111 • http://www. co.cattaraugus.ny.us; http://www.rootsweb.com/~nycattar/society.htm

Memorial Library of Little Valley • 110 Rock City St • Little Valley, NY 14755 • (716) 938-6301

Liverpool
Historical Association of Greater Liverpool • Gleason Mansion Museum, 314 2nd St • Liverpool, NY 13088 • (315) 451-7091

Liverpool Public Library • 310 Tulip St • Liverpool, NY 13088-4997 • (315) 457-0310 • http://www.lpl.org

Sainte Marie Among the Iroquois Museum • 106 Lake Dr, P.O. Box 146 • Liverpool, NY 130388 • (315) 453-6767 • http://www. onondagacountyparks.com/parks/sainte_marie

Salt Museum • Onondaga Lake Park, 106 lake Dr • Liverpool, NY 13088 • (315) 453-6715 • http://www.onondagacountyparks.com

Livonia
Livonia Area Preservation and Historical Society • 10 Commercial St, P.O. Box 155 • Livonia, NY 14487-0155 • (585) 346-4579 • http://www. livoniahistory.org

Livonia Public Library • 2 Washington St, P.O. Box 107 • Livonia, NY 14487-0107 • (585) 346-3450 • http://www.livonia.pls-net.org

Lloyd Harbor
Lloyd Harbor Historical Society • Henry Lloyd House Museum, 41 Lloyd Harbor Rd • Lloyd Harbor, NY 11743 • (631) 424-6110 • http:// www.lloydharborhistoricalsociety.org

Locke
Locke History Explorers • Town Hall, 4941 Harris Hill Rd • Locke, NY 13092 • (315) 497-0537 • http://co.cayuga.ny.us/locke

Lockport
Cambria Historical Society • 4159 Lower Mountain Rd • Lockport, NY 14094 • (716) 434-8937 • http://www.niagaracounty.org/town_of_ cambria_historical_socie.htm

Colonel William M Bond House Museum • 143 Ontario St • Lockport, NY 14094 • (716) 434-7433

Lockport Public Library • 23 East Ave, P.O. Box 475 • Lockport, NY 14094 • (716) 433-6935 • http://www.lockportlibrary.org

Niagara County Genealogical Society • Historical Museum, 215 Niagara St • Lockport, NY 14094-2605 • (716) 433-1033 • http://www. niagaracounty.org/genealogical_society_home.htm

Niagara County Historical Society • Historical Museum, 215 Niagara St • Lockport, NY 14094 • (716) 433-1033 • http://www.niagaracounty.org

Locust Valley
Locust Valley Historical Society • c/o Locust Valley Library, 170 Buckram Rd • Locust Valley, NY 11560 • (516) 676-1837

Locust Valley Library • 170 Buckram Rd • Locust Valley, NY 11560-1999 • (516) 671-1837 • http://www.nassaulibrary.org/locustv

Lodi
Lodi Historical Society • S Main St, P.O. Box 279 • Lodi, NY 14860 • (607) 582-5077 • http://www.lodihistoricalsociety.com

Long Beach
Long Beach Historical and Preservation Society • Historical Museum, 226 W Penn St, P.O. Box 286 • Long Beach, NY 11561 • (516) 432-1192 • http://www.longbeachhistory.org

Long Beach Public Library • 111 W Park Ave • Long Beach, NY 11561 • (516) 432-7201 • http://www.nassaulibrary.org/longbeach

Long Eddy
Basket Historical Society of the Upper Delaware Valley • 36 Thyberg Rd, P.O. Box 198 • Long Eddy, NY 12760 • (845) 887-5417 • http:// www.rootsweb.com/~nysulliv/basket.htm

Long Island City
Fiorello H LaGuardia Museum • LaGuardia Community College, 31-10 Thomson Ave • Long Island City, NY 11101 • (718) 482-5421 • http:// www.laguardiawagnerarchive.lagcc.cuny.edu

Gantry Plaza State Park • 49 Avenue & East River • Long Island City, NY 11101 • (718) 786-6385

Greater Astoria Historical Society • 35-20 Broadway, 4th Fl • Long Island City, NY 11103-1193 • (718) 278-0700 • http://astorialic.org

Long Lake
Long Lake Town Historian • P.O. Box 187 • Long Lake, NY 12847 • (518) 624-3077

Longwood
Longwood Society For Historic Preservation, Genealogy Group • general delivery • Longwood, NY 10459

Loudonville
William K Sanford Town Library • 629 Albany-Shaker Rd • Loudonville, NY 12211-1196 • (518) 458-9274 • http://www.colonie.org/library

Lowville
Lewis County Historian • 7552 S State St, P.O. Box 446 • Lowville, NY 13367 • (315) 376-2825

Lewis County Historical Society • Historical Museum, 7552 S State St, P.O. Box 446 • Lowville, NY 13367 • (315) 376-8957 • http://www. frontiernet.net/~lchs

Lowville Free Library • 5387 Dayan St • Lowville, NY 13367 • (315) 376-2131 • http://www.nc3r.org/lowlibrary

Lowville Town Historian • 7641 Collins St • Lowville, NY 13367 • (315) 376-2437

Martinsburg Town Historian • 7024 West Rd • Lowville, NY 13367 • (315) 376-6805

Watson Town Historian • P.O. Box 2 • Lowville, NY 13367 • (315) 376-3920

Lycoming
Scriba Historical Society • P.O. Box 201 • Lycoming, NY 13093-0201 • http://scribany.org/Historical.htm

Lyndonville
Yates Community Library • 15 N Main St • Lyndonville, NY 14098 • (716) 765-9041

Lyons
Lyons Heritage Society • P.O. Box 150 • Lyons, NY 14489

Lyons School District Public Library • 67 Canal St • Lyons, NY 14489 • (315) 946-9262 • http://www.lyons.pls-net.org

New York State Grange Museum • 3033 Middle Sodus Rd • Lyons, NY 14489 • (607) 756-7553 • http://www.nysgrange.com/museum.htm

Wayne County Historical Society • Historical Museum, 21 Butternut St, P.O. Box 607 • Lyons, NY 14489 • (315) 946-4943 • http://www. waynehistory.org

Lyons Falls
Greig Town Historian • 6991 Fish Creek Rd • Lyons Falls, NY 13368 • (315) 348-8016

Lewis County Historical Society • High St, P.O. Box 277 • Lyons Falls, NY 13368 • (315) 348-8089

Lyons Falls Village Historian • 7338 McAlpine St • Lyons Falls, NY 13368 • (315) 348-8216

Macedon
Macedon Historical Society • Historical Museum, 1185 Macedon Center Rd, P.O. Box 303 • Macedon, NY 14502 • (315) 986-4845 • http://www.macedonhistoriclsociety.org

West Wayne Genealogical Society • 411 Canal Dr E • Macedon, NY 14502-9113

Machias
Cattaraugus County Historical Museum and Research Library • 9824 Route 16, P.O. Box 352 • Machias, NY 14101 • (716) 353-8200 • http://www.cattco.org/museum; http://www.co.cattaraugus.ny.us/museum

Madrid
Saint Lawrence Power and Equipment Museum • general delivery • Madrid, NY 13660 • http://www.slpowermuseum.com

Mahopac
Mahopac Library • 668 Route 6 • Mahopac, NY 10541 • (914) 628-1776

Town of Carmel Historical Society • 40 McAlpin Ave, P.O. Box 456 • Mahopac, NY 10541 • (845) 628-0500 • http://hometown.aol.com/carmelhistory

Maine
Nanticoke Valley Historical Society • 13 Nanticoke Rd, P.O. Box 75 • Maine, NY 13802 • (607) 862-3243

Malden Bridge
Riders Mills Historical Association • Riders Mills Schoolhouse, P.O. Box 1 • Malden Bridge, NY 12115 • (518) 794-7146

Malone
Bellmont Town Archives • 1251 County Route 24 • Malone, NY 12953 • (518) 483-2728

Duane Town Historian • 356 County Route 26 • Malone, NY 12953 • (518) 483-4369

Farmer Boy's Home Museum • Stacy Rd, P.O. Box 283 • Malone, NY 12953 • (518) 483-1207

Franklin County Historical Society • Historical Museum, 51 Milwaukee St, P.O. Box 388 • Malone, NY 12953 • (518) 483-2750 • http://www.franklinhistory.org

Wead Library • 64 Elm St • Malone, NY 12953-1594 • (518) 483-5251 • http://www.cefls.org/malone.htm

Malverne
Malverne Historical and Preservation Society • Historical Museum, 369 Ocean Ave, P.O. Box 393 • Malverne, NY 11565 • (516) 887-9727 • http://hometown.aol.com/lynhistory/malverne/malindex.htm

Mamaroneck
Larchmont Historical Society • Historical Museum, 740 W Boston Post Rd, P.O. Box 742 • Mamaroneck, NY 10543 • (914) 381-2239 • http://www.larchmonthistory.org

Mamaroneck Historical Society • c/o Mamaroneck Public Library District, 136 Prospect Ave, P.O. Box 776 • Mamaroneck, NY 10543 • (914) 777-2776

Mamaroneck Public Library District • 136 Prospect Ave • Mamaroneck, NY 10543 • (914) 698-1250 • http://www.mamaroncklibrary.org

Manhasset
Historical Society of the Town of North Hempstead • Historical Museum, 220 Plandome Rd, P.O. Box 3000 • Manhasset, NY 11030 • (516) 869-7757 • http://www.northhempstead.com

Manhasset Public Library • 30 Onderdonk Ave • Manhasset, NY 11030 • (516) 627-2300 • http://www.nassaulibrary.org/manhass

Manlius
Manlius Historical Society • Historical Museum, 101 Scoville Ave, P.O. Box 28 • Manlius, NY 13104 • (315) 682-6660 • http://www.manliushistory.org

Town of Pompey Historical Society • Pomeroy Museum and Research Center, 8347 Route 20 • Manlius, NY 13104 • (315) 677-9416 • http://www.pompeyhistory.org

Mannsville
Historical Society of Mannsville-Ellisburg • Historical Museum, 110 Lilac Park Dr, P.O. Box 121 • Mannsville, NY 13661 • (315) 465-4049

Mannsville Free Library • P.O. Box 156 • Mannsville, NY 13661 • (315) 465-4049 • http://www.nc3r.org/mannsvl_library

Manorville
Manorville Historical Society • 50 North St, P.O. Box 4 • Manorville, NY 11949-0004 • (631) 369-2250

Marathon
Peck Memorial Library • E Main St, P.O. Box 325 • Marathon, NY 13803 • (607) 849-6135 • http://www.flls.org/memberpages.mara.htm

Marbletown
Ulster County Historical Society • Historical Museum, 2682 Route 209 • Marbletown, NY 12401 • (845) 338-5614 • http://www.ulstercountyhistoricalsociety.org; http://bevierhousemuseum.org

Marcellus
Marcellus Free Library • 2 Slocombe St • Marcellus, NY 13108 • (315) 673-3221 • http://www.library.marcellusny.com

Marcellus Historical Society • Historical Museum, 6 Slocombe, P.O. Box 165 • Marcellus, NY 13108 • (315) 673-3112 • http://mhs.marcellusny.com

Margaretville
Fairview Public Library • 41 Walnut St, P.O. Box 609 • Margaretville, NY 12455-0609 • (845) 586-3791 • http://www.4cls.org/webpages/members/Margaretville/Margaretville.html

Marietta
Spafford Area Historical Society • Grange Building, P.O. Box 250 • Marietta, NY 13110 • (315) 636-8300 • http://www.borodinobullett.com/SAHS/

Marilla
Marilla Historical Society • Historical Museum, 1810 Two Rod Rd, P.O. Box 36 • Marilla, NY 14102 • (716) 652-5396

Marion
Marion Historical Society • Historical Museum, P.O. Box 22 • Marion, NY 14505-0022 • (315) 926-4436

Marlboro
Gomez Mill House Museum • 11 Mill House Rd • Marlboro, NY 12542 • (914) 236-3126 • http://www.gomez.org

Marlboro Free Library • 1251 Route 9 W, P.O. Box 780 • Marlboro, NY 12540-0780 • (845) 236-7272 • http://www.marlborolibrary.org

Martinsburg
William H Bush Memorial Library • Whitaker Rd, P.O. Box 141 • Martinsburg, NY 13404 • (315) 376-7490 • http://www.nc3r.org/whbml

Massapequa
Historical Society of the Massapequas • Old Grace Church, 4755 Merrick Rd, P.O. Box 211 • Massapequa, NY 11758 • (516) 799-2023

Massapequa Historical Society • 4755 Merrick Rd • Massapequa, NY 11758 • (516) 799-2023

Massena
Massena Historical Association • Historical Museum, 200 E Orvis St • Massena, NY 13662 • (315) 769-8571

New York

Massena, cont.
Nyando Roots Genealogical Society • 180 River Dr, P.O. Box 175 • Massena, NY 13662 • (315) 769-9914

Mastic
Unkechauge Indian Nation of Poospatuck Indians • P.O. Box 86 • Mastic, NY 11950 • (516) 281-6464

Mastic Beach
William Floyd Estate Museum • 245 Park Dr • Mastic Beach, NY 11951 • (516) 399-2030

Mattituck
Mattituck Historical Society • Jesse-Tuthill House, Main Rd, P.O. Box 766 • Mattituck, NY 11952 • (631) 298-8089

Maybrook
Montgomery Academy Museum • Village Hall, 133 Clinton St • Maybrook, NY 12543 • (845) 457-5135

Mayfield
Mayfield Historical Society • 33 W Main St • Mayfield, NY 12117 • (518) 661-5085

Mayville
Chautauqua Township Historical Society • Depot Museum, 15 Water St • Mayville, NY 14757-1326 • (716) 753-7535

McGraw
Lamont Memorial Free Library • 5 Main St, P.O. Box 559 • McGraw, NY 13101 • (607) 836-6767 • http://www.flls.org/memberpages/mcgraw.htm

McGraw Historical Society • History Room, P.O. Box 537 • McGraw, NY 13101 • (607) 836-6738

Mechanicville
Mechanicville District Public Library • 190 N Main • Mechanicville, NY 12118 • (518) 664-4646 • http://www.mechanicville.sals.edu

Medina
Medina Railroad Museum • 530 West Ave, P.O. Box 136 • Medina, NY 14103 • (585) 798-1829 • http://www.railroadmuseum.net

Menands
New York State Dept of Health - Vital Records • 800 N Pearl St • Menands, NY 12204 • (518) 474-3077 • http://www.health.state.ny.us/vital_records/genealogy.htm

Merrick
Historical Society of the Merricks • c/o Merrick Library, 2279 S Merrick Ave • Merrick, NY 11566 • (516) 379-3476 • http://www.merricklibrary.org

Merrick Library • 2279 S Merrick Ave • Merrick, NY 11566-4398 • (516) 379-3476 • http://www.nassaulibrary.org/merrick

Mexico
Mexico Historical Society • Historical Museum, S Jefferson St, P.O. Box 331 • Mexico, NY 13114 • (315) 963-8542 • http://www.easternlakeontario.com/mexico/history.htm

Mexico Town Historian • 3389 Main St, P.O. Box 357 • Mexico, NY 13114 • (315) 963-7034

Williamstown Historical Society • 625 County Route 64 • Mexico, NY 13114

Middle Island
Longwood Public Library & Local History Room • 800 Middle County Rd • Middle Island, NY 11953 • (516) 924-6400 • http://longwood.wuffolk.lib.ny.us/bayleslist.html

Middleburgh
Best House Museum & Dr Christopher Best Medical Exhibit • 34 Clauverwie, P.O. Box 232 • Middleburgh, NY 12122 • (518) 827-4239

Middleburgh Library • 7 Wells Ave • Middleburgh, NY 12122-9662 • (518) 827-5142

Palatines to America, New York Chapter • P.O. Box 449 • Middleburgh, NY 12122-0449 • (518) 827-5747

Middleport
Middleport Free Library • 9 Vernon St • Middleport, NY 14105 • (716) 735-3281

Middlesex
Middlesex Heritage Group • 1216 Main St, P.O. Box 147 • Middlesex, NY 14707 • (585) 554-3607

Middletown
Historical Society of Middletown and the Wallkill Precinct • Van Duzer Memorial House Museum, 25 East Ave, P.O. Box 34 • Middletown, NY 10940 • (845) 342-0941 • http://hwm-w.com

Middletown-Thrall Library • 11-19 Depot St • Middletown, NY 11940 • (845) 341-5454

Milford
Greater Milford Historical Association • David Sayre Store and House Museum, P.O. Box 130 • Milford, NY 13807 • (607) 286-7038 • http://www.cooperstownchamber.org/davidsayrehouse/GMHA.htm

Milford Free Library • S Main St, P.O. Box 118 • Milford, NY 13807 • (607) 286-9076 • http://www.4cls.org

Pike County Historical Society • 608 Broad • Milford, NY 13807 • (845) 296-8126

Millbrook
Town of Washington-Village of Millbrook Historical Society • P.O. Box 135 • Millbrook, NY 12544 • http://www.nhs.vh.net

Miller Place
Miller Place - Mount Sinai Historical Society • 1720 William Miller House Museum, 75 N Country Rd, P.O. Box 651 • Miller Place, NY 11764 • (631) 476-5742 • http://www.mpmshistoricalsociety.org

Mineola
Mineola Historical Society • 211 Westbury Ave, P.O. Box 423 • Mineola, NY 11501 • (516) 746-6722

Minerva
Minerva Historical Society • P.O. Box 906 • Minerva, NY 12851 • (518) 251-2229

Minerva Town Historian • P.O. Box 937 • Minerva, NY 12851 • (518) 251-2869

Minetto
Minetto Town Historian • P.O. Box 220 • Minetto, NY 13115 • (315) 343-2393

Moira
Moira Historical Association • State Route 776, P.O. Box 75 • Moira, NY 12957 • (518) 529-6522

Monroe
Monroe Free Library • 44 Millpond Pkwy • Monroe, NY 10950 • (845) 783-4411 • http://www.monroelibrary.org

Museum Village • 1010 Museum Village Rd • Monroe, NY 10950 • (845) 782-8248 • http://www.museumvillage.org

Montauk
Montauk Historical Society • Montauk Point Lighthouse Museum, 2000 Montauk Hwy, P.O. Box 943 • Montauk, NY 11954 • (631) 668-2544 • http://www.montauklighthouse.com/society.htm

Montauk Library • 871 Montauk Hwy, P.O. Box 700 • Montauk, NY 11954-0500 • (631) 668-3377

Pharoah Indian Museum • Theodore Roosevelt County Park, Montauk Hwy • Montauk, NY 11954 • (631) 852-7878

Montgomery
Brick House Museum • Route 17K • Montgomery, NY 12549 • (845) 457-4906

Hill-Hold House Museum • 211 Route 416 • Montgomery, NY 12549 • (845) 291-2404

Montour Falls
Montour Falls Memorial Library • 406 W Main St, P.O. Box 486 • Montour Falls, NY 14865-0486 • (607) 535-7489 • http://www.stls.org/MontourFalls

Schuyler County Historical Society • Gray Brick Tavern Museum, 108 N Catharine St, P.O. Box 651 • Montour Falls, NY 14865-0651 • (607) 535-9741 • http://www.rootsweb.com/~nyschs

Mooers
Mooers Town Historian • 2508 Route 11, P.O. Box 242 • Mooers, NY 12958 • (518) 236-7927

Moravia
Cayuga-Owasco Lakes Historical Society • Luther Museum and Archives, 14 W Cayuga St, P.O. Box 247 • Moravia, NY 13118 • (315) 497-3096 • http://www.rootsweb.com/~nycayuga/colhs:htm#LUTHER

Millard Fillmore Cabin Museum • RD3, Box 26 • Moravia, NY 13118 • (315) 497-0130

Morris
Morris Historical Society • c/o Village Library of Morris, 22 E Main St, P.O. Box 126 • Morris, NY 13808 • (607) 263-2080

Village Library of Morris • 152 Main St, P.O. Box 126 • Morris, NY 13808 • (607) 263-2080 • http://www.4cls.org/otsego.html

Morrisonville
Schuyler Falls Town Historian • 997 Mason St, P.O. Box 99 • Morrisonville, NY 12962 • (518) 563-1129

Morristown
Red Barn Museum • 518 River Rd E • Morristown, NY 13669 • (315) 375-6390

Mount Kisco
Mount Kisco Historical Society • P.O. Box 263 • Mount Kisco, NY 10549-0263 • (914) 666-4587

Mount Kisco Public Library • 100 Main St • Mount Kisco, NY 10549 • (914) 666-8041 • http://www.mountkiscolibrary.org

Westchester County Dept of Parks and Conservation • 25 Moore Ave • Mount Kisco, NY 10549 • (914) 864-7000 • http://www.westchestergov.com/parks

Mount Morris
Mount Morris Historical Society • Gen William Mills Mansion Museum, 14 Main St, P.O. Box 94 • Mount Morris, NY 14510 • (716) 658-3292

Mount Upton
Umadilla Valley Historical Society • 7-AA Main St • Mount Upton, NY 13908 • (607) 764-8492

Mount Vernon
Landmark and Historical Society of Mount Vernon • c/o Mount Vernon Library, 28 S 1st Ave • Mount Vernon, NY 10550 • (914) 668-1840

Mount Vernon Public Library • 28 S 1st Ave • Mount Vernon, NY 10550 • (914) 668-1840 • http://mountvernonpubliclibrary.org

Mumford
Genesee County Village Museum • 1410 Flint Hill Rd, P.O. Box 310 • Mumford, NY 14511-0310 • (585) 538-6822 • http://www.gcv.org

Munnsville
Fryer Memorial Museum • Williams St & Route 46, P.O. Box 177 • Munnsville, NY 13409 • (315) 495-5395 • http://www.rootsweb.com/~nymadiso/bit-of-past/borg/fryer.htm

Muttontown
Friends for Long Island's Heritage • Nassau County Museum, 1864 Muttontown Rd • Muttontown, NY 11791-9652 • (518) 571-7600 • http://www.garviespointmuseum.com

Naples
Naples Historical Society • P.O. Box 489 • Naples, NY 14512 • (585) 374-2560

Naples Library • 118 S Main St • Naples, NY 14512 • (716) 374-2757 • http://www.naples.pls-net.org

Narrowsburg
Fort Delaware Museum of Colonial History • 6615 Route 97, Sullivan County DPW, P.O. Box 5012 • Narrowsburg, NY 12764 • (845) 252-6660 • http://www.co.sullivan.ny.us

Tusten Historical Society • c/o Tusten-Cochecton Library, 198 Bridge St, P.O. Box 18 • Narrowsburg, NY 12764 • (845) 252-3360 • http://www.tusten-narrowsburg.org

Tusten-Cochecton Library • 198 Bridge St, P.O. Box 129 • Narrowsburg, NY 12764 • (845) 252-3360 • http://www.rcls.org/wspl

Nassau
Sons of the American Revolution, New York Society • 96 Old Mill Pond Rd • Nassau, NY 12123 • (518) 766-2142 • http://www.ess-sar.org

Nedrow
Onondaga Nation • 258C Route 11A • Nedrow, NY 13120 • (315) 492-4210 • http://www.onondaganation.org

New Berlin
New Berlin Library • 15 S Main St, P.O. Box J • New Berlin, NY 13411-0610 • (607) 847-8564 • http://www.rcls.org/chenango.html

New City
Genealogical Society of Rockland County • 20 Zukor Rd, P.O. Box 444 • New City, NY 10956-4302 • (845) 634-4962 • http://www.rocklandgenealogy.org

Historical Society of Rockland County • Historical Museum, 20 Zukor Rd • New City, NY 10956 • (845) 634-9629 • http://www.rocklandhistory.org

Jacob Blauvelt House Museum • 20 Zukor Rd • New City, NY 10956 • (914) 634-9645

New City Free Library • 220 N Main St • New City, NY 10956 • (845) 634-4997 • http://www.newcitylibrary.org

New Hartford
New Hartford Historical Society • Historical Museum, 2 Paris Rd, P.O. Box 238 • New Hartford, NY 13413 • (315) 724-7258 • http://www.newhartfordpubliclibrary.org/history.html

New Haven
New Haven Town Historian • P.O. Box 141 • New Haven, NY 13121 • (315) 963-8756

New Hyde Park
New Hyde Park Public Library • 1420 Jericho Tpk • New Hyde Park, NY 11040 • (516) 354-1413

New Lebanon
New Lebanon Historical Society • P.O. Box 627 • New Lebanon, NY 12125

New Lebanon Library • 550 Rte 20, P.O. Box 630 • New Lebanon, NY 12125-0630 • (518) 794-8844 • http://www.newlebanon.lib.ny.us

New Paltz
Elting Memorial Library • 93 Main St • New Paltz, NY 12561 • (845) 255-5030 • http://www.Elginlibrary.org

Huguenot Historical Society • Historical Museum, 18 Broadhead Ave • New Paltz, NY 12561 • (845) 255-1550 • http://www.huguenotstreet.org

New Paltz, cont.
Huguenot Historical Society of New Paltz New York • 18 Broadhead Ave • New Paltz, NY 12561 • (845) 255-1660

Huguenot Street National Historic Landmark District Museums • P.O. Box 339 • New Paltz, NY 12561 • (914) 255-1889

Mohonk Mountain House Museum • 1000 Mountain Rest Rd • New Paltz, NY 12561 • (914) 255-1000 • http://www.mohonk.com

New Rochelle
Columbia Genealogical Society • 168 Coligni Ave • New Rochelle, NY 10801-3516 • (914) 235-4080

Huguenot Historical Association • Thomas Paine Cottage, 20 Sicard Ave • New Rochelle, NY 10804 • (914) 633-1776 • http://www.thomaspainecottage.org

New Rochelle Public Library • 1 Library Plaza • New Rochelle, NY 10801 • (914) 632-7878 • http://www.nrpl.org

New Scotland
Town of New Scotland Historical Association • 7 Old New Salem Rd • New Scotland, NY 12127 • (518) 765-2071 • http://www.townofnewscotland.com

New Windsor
Edmonston House Museum • 1042 Route 94 • New Windsor, NY 12553

National Temple Hill Association • Historical Museum, 1042 Route 94 • New Windsor, NY 12553 • (845) 561-5073 • http://www.nationaltemplehill.org

Palatines to America, New York Chapter • 411 Philo St • New Windsor, NY 12553

New Woodstock
New Woodstock Historical Society • general delivery • New Woodstock, NY 13122

New York
369th Historical Society • 2366 5th Ave • New York, NY 10037 • (212) 281-9474

Abigail Adams Smith Museum • 421 E 61st St • New York, NY 10021 • (212) 838-6878

American Bible Society Library and Archives • 1865 Broadway • New York, NY 10023-9980 • (212) 408-1203 • http://www.bibles.com

American Friends of the Hermitage • Historical Museum, 26 Broadway • New York, NY 10004 • (212) 785-9445

American Hungarian Historical Society • Hungarian House, 215 E 82nd St • New York, NY 10028 • (212) 744-5298 • http://hungarianhouse.org

American Indian Community House • Historical Museum, 11 Broadway, 2nd Fl • New York, NY 10004-1303 • (212) 598-0100 • http://www.aich.org

American Irish Historical Society • Historical Museum, 991 5th Ave • New York, NY 10028 • (212) 288-2263 • http://www.aihs.org

American Jewish Committee • P.O. Box 705 • New York, NY 10150 • (212) 751-4000 • http://www.ajc.org

American Jewish Historical Society • Center for Jewish History, 15 W 16th St • New York, NY 10011 • (212) 294-6160 • http://www.ajhs.org

American Scottish Foundation • Scotland House, 575 Madison Ave, Ste 1006 • New York, NY 10022-2511 • (212) 605-0338 • http://www.americanscottishfoundation.com

American Society of Sephardic Studies • 500 W 185th St • New York, NY 10033-3201 • (212) 960-5236

American Society of the French Legion of Honor • 22 E 60th St, Rm 53 • New York, NY 10022-1077 • (212) 751-8537

American-Scandinavian Foundation • 58 Park Ave • New York, NY 10021 • (212) 879-9779 • http://www.amscan.org

Asia Society • 725 Park Ave • New York, NY 10021 • (212) 288-6400 • http://www.asiasociety.org

Association of Jewish Libraries • 330 7th Ave, 21st Fl • New York, NY 10001 • (212) 725-5359 • http://www.jewishlibraries.org

Belvedere Castle Museum • Mid-Central Park & 79th St • New York, NY 10021 • (212) 772-0210 • http://www.centralparknyc.org

Bernard Judaica Museum • Congregation Emanu-el, 1 E 65th St • New York, NY 10021 • (212) 744-1400 • http://www.emanuelnyc.org

Butler Library • Columbia Univ, 535 W 114th St • New York, NY 10027 • (212) 854-2247

Castle Clinton National Monument Museum • Battery Park, 26 Wall St • New York, NY 10005 • (212) 344-7220 • http://www.nps.gov

Cathedral of St John the Divine Museum • 1047 Amsterdam Ave • New York, NY 10025 • (212) 932-7325 • http://www.stjohndivine.org

Celtic League, American Branch • Dag Hammarskjold Center, P.O. Box 20153 • New York, NY 10017-0002

Center for Jewish History • Yeshiva Univ Museum, 15 W 16th St • New York, NY 10011 • (212) 744-6400 • http://www.yumuseum.org

Center for Migration Studies of New York • 27 Carmine St • New York, NY 10014-4423 • (212) 237-3080 • http://www.cmsny.org

Chancellor Robert R Livingston Masonic Library • 71 W 23rd St • New York, NY 10010 • (212) 337-6620 • http://www.livmalib.org

Chian Federation • 44-01 Broadway • New York, NY 11103 • (718) 204-2550 • http://www.chianfed.org

China Institute of America • 125 E 65th St • New York, NY 10021 • (212) 744-8181 • http://www.chinainstitute.org

Collectors Club Museum • 22 E 35th St • New York, NY 10016 • (212) 683-0559 • http://www.collectorsclub.org

Colonial Order of the Acorn • 122 E 58th St • New York, NY 10022-1939 • (212) 755-8532

Congregation Bina • 600 West End Ave #1C • New York, NY 10024-1643 • (212) 873-4261

Creole-American Genealogical Society • P.O. Box 2666, Church St Sta • New York, NY 10008

Daughters of the Cincinnati • 122 E 58th St • New York, NY 10022 • (212) 755-8532 • http://pasocietyofthecincinnati.org

Dyckman Farmhouse Museum • 4881 Broadway • New York, NY 10034 • (212) 304-9422 • http://www.dyckman.org

Eldridge Street Project Museum • 12 Eldridge St • New York, NY 10002 • (212) 219-0888 • http://www.eldridgestreet.org

Elisha Kent Kane Historical Society • 71 W 23rd St • New York, NY 10010 • (212) 242-5885

Episcopal Church Center Records Office • 815 2nd Ave • New York, NY 10017-4594 • (512) 472-6816 • http://www.episcopalchurch.org

Estonian American National Council • Estonian House, 243 E 34th St • New York, NY 10016 • (212) 685-0776 • http://www.estosite.org

Federal Hall National Memorial Museum • 26 Wall St • New York, NY 10005 • (212) 825-6888 • http://www.nps.gov/feha/

Fraunces Tavern Museum • 54 Pearl St • New York, NY 10004 • (212) 425-1778 • http://www.frauncestavernmuseum.org

French Institute-Alliance Francaise • 22 E 60th St • New York, NY 10022-1077 • (212) 355-6100 • http://www.fiaf.org

General Grant National Memorial Museum • Riverside Dr & W 122nd St • New York, NY 10027 • (212) 666-1640 • http://www.nps.gov/gegr/

General Society of Colonial Wars • 122 E 58th St • New York, NY 10022 • (212) 755-8532

German-Jewish Families Society • 129 E 73rd St • New York, NY 10021

Goethe-Institut New York • 1014 5th Ave • New York, NY 10028 • (212) 439-8700 • http://www.goethe.de/ins/us/ney/deindex.htm

Gotham Center for New York History • City Univ of New York, 365 5th Ave, Rm 6103 • New York, NY 10016-4309 • (212) 817-8460 • http://www.gothamcenter.org

Gracie Mansion Conservancy Museum • East End Ave & 88th St • New York, NY 10128 • (212) 570-4751 • http://www.nyc.gov

Grants and Historic Preservation Bureau • general delivery • New York, NY 10001 • (212) 866-2599

Greek Orthodox Archdiocese, North and South America Archives • 8 E 79th St • New York, NY 10021 • (212) 570-3565 • http://www.goarch.org/goa/departments/archives/

Greenwich Village Society for Historic Preservation • 232 E 11th St • New York, NY 10003 • (212) 475-9585

Hamilton Grange National Memorial Museum • 287 Convent Ave • New York, NY 10031 • (212) 283-5154 • http://www.hagr.nps.gov

Hidden Child Foundation • 823 United Nations Plaza • New York, NY 10017-3518 • (212) 885-7900

Hispanic Genealogical Society of New York • Puerto Rican Cultural Heritage House, 1230 5th Ave #458, P.O. Box 818, Murray Hill Sta • New York, NY 10156-0602 • (212) 532-3662 • http://www.hispanicgenealogy.com

Hispanic Institute of Columbia University • 612 W 116th St • New York, NY 10027 • (212) 954-5610 • http://www.columbia.edu/cu/spanish

Hispanic Society of America • Historical Museum, 613 W 155th St • New York, NY 10032 • (212) 926-2234 • http://www.hispanicsociety.org

Historic House Trust of New York City • The Arsenal, Rm 203, Central Park • New York, NY 10021 • (212) 360-8282 • http://www.historichousetrust.org

Holland Society of New York • 122 E 58th St • New York, NY 14304 • (212) 758-1675 • http://www.hollandsociety.com

Huguenot Heritage • 35 Sutton Pl, Ste 6E • New York, NY 10022-2464 • (212) 759-6222

Huguenot Society of America • 122 E 58th St • New York, NY 10022 • (212) 755-0592 • http://huguenotsocietyofamerica.org

Institute for Jewish Research • 1048 5th Ave • New York, NY 10028

Interchurch Center Museum • 475 Riverside Dr, Rm 253 • New York, NY 10015 • (212) 870-2200 • http://www.interchurch-center.org

International Association of Genocide Scholars • John Jay College of Criminal Justice, 899 10th Ave • New York, NY 10019 • (212) 237-8334 • http://www.isg-iags.org

International Center of Photography Museum • 1130 Avenue of the Americas • New York, NY 10036 • (212) 857-0000 • http://www.icp.org

Intrepid Sea-Air-Space Museum • W 46th St & 12th Ave • New York, NY 10036 • (212) 345-0072 • http://www.intrepidmuseum.org

Islamic Center of New York • Mosque of New York, 1711 3rd Ave • New York, NY 10029

Italian American Museum • 28 W 44th St, 17th Fl • New York, NY 10036 • (212) 642-2020 • http://www.italianamericanmuseum.org

Italian Historical Society of America • 410 Park Ave, Ste 1530 • New York, NY 10022 • (718) 852-2929 • http://www.italianhistorical.org

Jewish Genealogical Society • 15 W 16th St, P.O. Box 6398 • New York, NY 10128 • (212) 330-8257 • http://www.jgsny.org

Jewish Museum • 1109 5th St • New York, NY 10128 • (212) 423-3200 • http://www.thejewishmuseum.org

Jewish Theological Seminary Library • 3080 Broadway • New York, NY 10027 • (212) 678-8075

John D Calandra Italian American Institute • City Univ of New York, 25 W 43rd St • New York, NY 10036 • (212) 642-2094 • http://qcpages.qc.cuny.edu/calandra/

Jozef Pilsudski Institute of America • 180 2nd Ave • New York, NY 10003-5778 • (212) 505-9077

Judaica Museum of Central Synagogue • 123 E 55th St • New York, NY 10022 • (212) 838-5122 • http://www.censyn.org

Kielce-Radom Special Interest Group • Gracie Sta, P.O. Box 127 • New York, NY 10027 • http://www.jewishgen.org/KRSIG

League for Yiddish • 200 W 72nd St #40 • New York, NY 10023-2824 • (212) 787-6675

Legacy Project • 810 7th Ave, 31st Fl • New York, NY 10019 • (212) 843-0372 • http://www.legacy-project.org

Leo Baeck Institute • 129 E 73rd St • New York, NY 10021 • (212) 744-6400 • http://www.jewishgen.org; http://www.lbi.org

Lithuanian Alliance of America • 307 W 30th St • New York, NY 10001-2724 • (212) 563-2210

Living Memorial to the Holocaust • Museum of Jewish Heritage, 36 Battery Park Plaza • New York, NY 10004-1484 • (212) 968-1800 • http://www.njhnyc.org

Lower East Side Tenement Museum • 91 Orchard St • New York, NY 10002 • (212) 431-0233 • http://www.tenement.org

Masonic Grand Lodge of New York • Livingson Masonic Library, 71 W 23rd St, 14th Fl • New York, NY 11010 • (212) 337-6620 • http://nymasoniclibrary.org/library/genealogy.htm

Metropolitan Historic Structures Association • 5th Ave, Ste 1411 • New York, NY 10016 • (212_ 685-9723

Military Order of Foreign Wars of the United States 1894-1994 • 122 E 58th St • New York, NY 10022-1939 • http://foxfall.com/mofw.htm

Military Society of the War of 1812 • 7th Regiment Armory, 643 Park Ave • New York, NY 10021 • (212) 249-3919 • http://www.vca1790.org

Morris-Jumel Mansion Museum • 65 Jumel Terr • New York, NY 10032 • (212) 923-8008 • http://www.morrisjumel.org

Mount Vernon Hotel Museum • 421 E 61st St • New York, NY 10021 • (212) 838-6878 • http://www.myhm.org

Museum of Chinese in the Americas • 70 Mulberry St, 2nd Fl • New York, NY 10013 • (212) 619-4785 • http://www.moca-nyc.org

Museum of the City of New York • 1220 5th Ave • New York, NY 10029 • (212) 534-1672 • http://www.mcny.org

NARA-Northeast Region-New York • 201 Varick St, 12th Fl • New York, NY 10014-4811 • (212) 337-1300 • http://www.nara.gov/regional/newyork.html

National Foundation for Jewish Culture • 330 7th Ave, Fl 21 • New York, NY 10001-5010 • (212) 629-0500

National Museum of Catholic History • 443 E 115th St • New York, NY 10029 • (212) 828-5209

National Museum of the American Indian • George Gustav Heye Center, 1 Bowling Green • New York, NY 10004 • (212) 514-3700 • http://www.americanindian.si.edu

National Society of the Colonial Dames of America in the State of New York • 215 E 71st St • New York, NY 10021 • (212) 744-3572

Netherland Club of New York • 3 W 51st St • New York, NY 10019 • (212) 265-6160 • http://www.netherlandclub.com

New York

New York, cont.

New England Society in the City of New York • 635 Madison Ave, 11th Fl • New York, NY 10022 • (212) 752-1938 • http://www.nesnyc.org

New York Caledonian Club • P.O. Box 4542, Grand Central Sta • New York, NY 10163-4542 • (212) 662-1083 • http://www.nycaledonian.org

New York City Fire Museum • 278 Spring St • New York, NY 10013 • (212) 691-1303 • http://www.firemuseum.org

New York City Municipal Reference and Research Center • 31 Chambers St, Rm 112 • New York, NY 10007 • (212) 788-8590 • http://www.nyc.gov/html/doris

New York City Police Museum • 100 Old Slip • New York, NY 10005 • (212) 480-3100 • http://www.nycpolicemuseum.org

New York Conference of Patriotic and Historical Societies • P.O. Box 207 • New York, NY 10016-0207 • http://www.nycconference.org

New York Genealogical and Biographical Society • 122 E 58th St • New York, NY 10022-1939 • (212) 755-8532 • http://www.nygbs.org

New York Historical Society • Historical Museum, 170 Central Park W • New York, NY 10024-5194 • (212) 721-6905 • http://www.nyhistory.org

New York Irish History Roundtable • P.O. Box 2087, Church St Sta • New York, NY 10008

New York Public Library • 11 W 40th St • New York, NY 10018 • (212) 930-0828 • http://www.nypl.org/research/Chss/lhg/genea.html

New York Public Library • 188 Madison Ave • New York, NY 10016 • (212) 930-0800

New York Public Library-The Research Libraries • 5th Ave & 42nd St • New York, NY 10018 • (212) 930-0710 • http://www.nypl.org/researeh/ehss/lhg/genea.html

Old Merchants House of New York Museum • 29 E 4th St • New York, NY 10003 • (212) 777-1089 • http://www.merchyantshouse.com

Order of Lafayette • 243 W 70th St, #6F • New York, NY 10023 • (212) 873-9162 • http://phoenixmasonry.org/masonicmuseum/fraternalism/order_of_lafayette.htm

Orthodox Jewish Archives of Agudath Israel • 84 William St, Ste 1400 • New York, NY 10038 • (212) 979-9000

Pierpont Morgan Library • 29 E 36th St • New York, NY 10016 • (212) 685-0008 • http://www.morganlibrary.org

Ratner Center for the Study of Conservative Judaism • Jewish Theological Seminary of America, 3080 Broadway • New York, NY 10027 • (212) 280-6011 • http://www.jtsa.edu

Renaissance Society of America • Graduate School & Univ Ctr, 365 5th Ave • New York, NY 10016-4309 • (212) 998-3797

Romanian Cultural Institute • Romanian Library, 200 E 38th St • New York, NY 10016 • (212) 687-0180 • http://www.icrny.org

Russian Nobility Association • 971 1st Ave • New York, NY 10022 • (212) 755-7528 • http://www.russianobility.org

Saint Andrew's Society of New York • 150 E 55th St, Ste 3 • New York, NY 10022 • (212) 223-4248 • http://www.standrewsny.org

Saint George's Society of New York • 216 E 45 St, Suite 901 • New York, NY 10017 • (212) 682-6110

Saint Marks Historic Landmark Fund • 232 E 11th St • New York, NY 10003 • (212) 777-3359

Saint Nicholas Society of the City of New York • 20 W 44th St, 5th Fl • New York, NY 10036-6603 • (212) 991-9944 • http://www.saintnicholassociety.org

Schomburg Center for Research in Black Culture • New York Public Library, 515 Malcolm X Blvd • New York, NY 10037-1801 • (212) 491-2200 • http://www.schomburgcenter.org

Society of American Historians • Columbia Univ, 610 Fayerweather • New York, NY 10027 • (212) 854-2555 • http://wah.columbia.edu

Society of Colonial Wars • 122 E 58th St • New York, NY 10022-1940 • (212) 755-8532

Society of Mayflower Descendants • 122 E 58th St • New York, NY 10022-1939 • (212) 755-8532

South Street Seaport Museum • 12 Fulton St • New York, NY 10038 • (212) 748-8600 • http://www.southstreetseaportmuseum.org

Statue of Liberty-Ellis Island Foundation • American Family Immigration History Center, 292 Madison Ave • New York, NY 10017 • (212) 363-5804 • http://ellisislandrecords.org

Swiss Roots USA • Consulate General, 633 3rd Ave, 30th Fl • New York, NY 10017-6706 • http://www.swissroots.org

Theodore Roosevelt Birthplace National Historic Site Museum • 28 E 20th St • New York, NY 10003 • (212) 260-1616 • http://www.nps.gov/thrb/

Trinity Museum • Trinity Church, 74 Trinity Pl • New York, NY 10006 • (212) 602-0800 • http://www.trinitywallstreet.org

Ukrainian Museum • 222 E 6th St • New York, NY 10003 • (212) 228-0110 • http://www.ukrainianmuseum.org

Union for Reform Judaism • Historical Museum, 633 3rd Ave • New York, NY 10017-6778 • (212) 650-4000 • http://www.urj.org

Union of Orthodox Jewish Congregations of America • 11 Broadway • New York, NY 10004 • (212) 613-8124 • http://www.ou.org

United States Catholic Historical Society • 1011 1st Ave • New York, NY 10022 • (800) 225-7999 • http://www.catholic.org/uschs/

United Synagogues of Conservative Judaism • Rapaport House, 155 5th Ave • New York, NY 10010 • (212) 533-7800 • http://www.uscj.org

US-Japan Maritime Foundation • 420 Lexington Ave • New York, NY 10170 • (212) 867-7887

Veteran Corps of Artillery, State of New York • 7th Regiment Armory, 643 Park Ave • New York, NY 10021 • (212) 249-3919 • http://www.vca1790.org

Yeshiva University Archives • 500 W 185th St • New York, NY 10033 • (212) 960-5363 • http://www.yu.edu/libraries/archives/

Yivo Institute for Jewish Research • 15 W 16th St • New York, NY 10028 • (212) 294-6143 • http://www.yivoinstitute.org

Newark

Marbletown Schoolhouse Museum • 6631 Miller Rd • Newark, NY 14513 • (315) 331-6409

Newark Public Library • 121 High St • Newark, NY 14513-1492 • (315) 331-4370

Newark-Arcadia Historical Society • Historical Museum, 120 High St • Newark, NY 14513 • (315) 331-6409

Newark Valley

Newark Valley Depot Museum • Depot St, P.O. Box 222 • Newark Valley, NY 13811 • (607) 642-9516 • http://munex.arme.cornell.edu/nvhs

Newark Valley Historical Society • Bement-Billings Farmstead Museum, 9142 Route 38, P.O. Box 222 • Newark Valley, NY 13811 • (607) 642-9516 • http://www.nvhistory.org/societyhappenings.shtml

Tappan-Spaulding Memorial Library • 6 Rock St, P.O. Box 397 • Newark Valley, NY 13811 • (607) 642-9960

Newburgh

Historical Society of Newburgh Bay and the Highlands • Capt David Crawford House Museum, 189 Montgomery St • Newburgh, NY 12550 • (845) 561-2585 • http://www.newburghhistoricalsociety.com

Newburgh Free Library • 124 Grand St • Newburgh, NY 12550 • (845) 563-3600 • http://www.newburghlibrary.org

Washington's Headquarters State Historic Site Library • 84 Liberty St, P.O. Box 1783 • Newburgh, NY 12551-1476 • (845) 562-1195 • http://www.nysparks.state.ny.us

Newcomb
Newcomb Town Historian • P.O. Box 477 • Newcomb, NY 12852

Newfane
Town of Newfane Historical Society • P.O. Box 115 • Newfane, NY 14108-0015 • (716) 778-7197 • http://www.niagaracounty.org/town_of_newfane_hs.htm

Newfield
Newfield Historical Society • 541 Millard Hill Rd • Newfield, NY 14867 • (607) 564-3310

Newfield Public Library • 198 Main St, P.O. Box 154 • Newfield, NY 14867 • (607) 564-3594 • http://www.flls.org/newfield

Newport
Kuyahoora Valley Historical Society • Newport Historical Center, 7435 Main St • Newport, NY 13416 • (315) 845-8434

Newtonville
Historical Society of the Town of Colonie • Memorial Town Hall • Newtonville, NY 12128 • (518) 783-2713 • http://www.colonie.org/historian/historical

Pruyn House Museum • 207 Old Niskayuna Rd, P.O. Box 212 • Newtonville, NY 121128 • (518) 783-1435

Niagara Falls
Niagara Falls Historical Society • c/o Niagara Falls Public Library, 1425 Main St • Niagara Falls, NY 14305-2574 • (716) 286-4899

Niagara Falls Public Library • 1425 Main St • Niagara Falls, NY 14305-1574 • (716) 286-4881 • http://www.niagarafallspubliclib.org

Nichols
Platt Cady Library • 42 E River Rd, P.O. Box 70 • Nichols, NY 13812 • (607) 699-3835 • http://www.flls.org/memberpages/nichols.htm

Niskayuna
Association for the Protection of the Adirondacks • Adirondack Research Library, 897 St David's Ln • Niskayuna, NY 12309 • (518) 377-1452 • http://www.protectadks.org

Norfolk
Norfolk Historical Museum • 105 River Rd, P.O. Box 645 • Norfolk, NY 13667 • (315) 384-4575 • http://www.northnet.org/norfolkny/

North Babylon
North Babylon Public Library • 815 Deer Park Ave • North Babylon, NY 11703 • (631) 669-4020

North Bellmore
Historical Society of the Bellmores • 32 Stratford Ct, P.O. Box 912 • North Bellmore, NY 11710-0912 • (516) 785-2593 • http://www.bellmorechamber.com/community.mgi

North Blenheim
Blenheim Bridge Historical Association • Eastside Rd, P.O. Box 833 • North Blenheim, NY 12131

Lansing Manor House Museum • NY State Route 30, P.O. Box 898 • North Blenheim, NY 12131 • (800) 724-0309 • http://www.nps.gov/html/vcblenhe.html

Phillipsburg Manor Museum • NY SR 30, P.O. Box 898 • North Blenheim, NY 12131 • (518) 827-6121

North Chatham
North Chatham Free Library • P.O. Box 907 • North Chatham, NY 12131-0907 • (518) 766-3211 • http://northchatham.lib.ny.us

North Chatham Historical Society • P.O. Box 243 • North Chatham, NY 12132 • (518) 766-3058 • http://www.chathamnewyork.us/NorthChathamHistoricalSociety.htm

North Collins
North Collins Historical Society • 2093 Shirley, P.O. Box 32 • North Collins, NY 14111 • (716) 337-2702

North Collins Town Library • 2095 School St, P.O. Box 730 • North Collins, NY 14111-0730 • (716) 337-3211

North Hudson
North Hudson Town Historian • Town Hall, Route 9 • North Hudson, NY 12855-9702 • (518) 532-9273

North Lawrence
Lawrence Town Historian • 3444 State Hwy 11B • North Lawrence, NY 12967 • (315) 328-4566

North Merrick
North Merrick Public Library • 1691 Meadowbrook Rd • North Merrick, NY 11566 • (516) 378-7474 • http://www.nassaulibrary.org/nmerrick

North Rose
Bernard Farnsworth Museum • School St • North Rose, NY 14516 • (315) 587-4532 • http://www.rootsweb.com/~nywayne/townships/rose.html

Rose Historical Society • 10612 Salter Rd • North Rose, NY 14516-0502 • (315) 587-4532 • http://www.rootsweb.com/~nywayne/townships/rose.html

North Salem
North Salem Historical Society • 63 Keeler Ln, P.O. Box 31 • North Salem, NY 10560 • (914) 277-3200

North Tonawanda
Carrousel Society of the Niagara Frontier • Herschell Carrousel Factory Museum, 180 Thompson, P.O. Box 672 • North Tonawanda, NY 14120 • (716) 694-2859 • http://www.carrouselmuseum.org

North Tonawanda History Museum • 314 Oliver St • North Tonawanda, NY 14120 • (716) 213-0554 • http://www.nthistorymuseum.org

North Tonawanda Public Library • 505 Meadow Dr • North Tonawanda, NY 14120-2888 • (716) 693-4132 • http://www.ntonawanda.lib.ny.us

North White Plains
Washington's Headquarters Museum • 140 Virginia Rd • North White Plains, NY 10603 • (914) 949-1236

Northport
Northport Historical Society • Historical Museum, 215 Main St, P.O. Box 545 • Northport, NY 11768 • (631) 757-9859 • http://www.northporthistorical.org

Northport Public Library • 151 Laurel Ave • Northport, NY 11768 • (631) 261-6930

Northville
Hope Town Historian • Star Route HC01, Box 64 • Northville, NY 12134-9743

Northwood Narrows
Bryant Library Museum • 76 School St, P.O. Box 114 • Northwood Narrows, NY 03261 • (603) 942-8506

Norwich
Chenango County Historical Society • Historical Museum, 45 Rexford St • Norwich, NY 13815 • (607) 337-1845 • http://www.chenango.history.museum

Guernsey Memorial Library • 3 Court St • Norwich, NY 13815 • (607) 334-4034 • http://www.guernseylibrary.org

Northeast Classic Car Museum • 24 Rexford St • Norwich, NY 13815 • (607) 334-2886 • http://www.classicsmuseum.org

Norwood

Norwood Historical Association • Lyman Historical Museum, 39 N Main St, P.O. Box 163 • Norwood, NY 13668 • (315) 353-2751 • http://www.norwoodny.org/museum.html

Norwood Village Historian • 10 Morgan St • Norwood, NY 13668 • (315) 353-2537

Nunda

Nunda Historical Society • 24 Portage St, P.O. box 341 • Nunda, NY 14517-0341 • (585) 468-5420 • http://www.nundahistory.org

Nyack

Edward Hopper Landmark Preservation Foundation • Historical Museum, 82 N Broadway • Nyack, NY 10960 • (845) 358-0074 • http://www.edwardhopperhouseartcenter.org

Friends of the Nyacks • P.O. Box 120 • Nyack, NY 10960 • (845) 358-4973 • http://www.friendsofthenyacks.org

Nyack Public Library • 59 S Broadway • Nyack, NY 10960 • (845) 358-3370 • http://nyack.lib.ny.us

Winthrop Society • 11 Cresthill Dr #11A • Nyack, NY 10960-2723 • http://www.winthropsociety.org

Oakdale

William K Vanderbilt Historical Society at Dowling College • Burrstone Rd, P.O. Box 433 • Oakdale, NY 11769 • (516) 567-2277

Oakfield

Oakfield Historical Society • P.O. Box 74 • Oakfield, NY 14125

Ocean Beach

Ocean Beach Historical Society • Community House, P.O. Box 701 • Ocean Beach, NY 11770 • (631) 583-8972 • http://www.villageofoceanbeach.org/organizations.htm

Oceanside

Oceanside Library • 30 Davison Ave • Oceanside, NY 11572-2299 • (516) 766-2360

Ogdensburg

Catholic Diocese of Ogdensburg Archives • 622 Washington St, P.O. Box 369 • Ogdensburg, NY 13669 • (315) 292-2920

Frederic Remington Museum • 303 Washington St • Ogdensburg, NY 13669 • (315) 393-2425 • http://www.fredericremington.org

Ogdensburg Public Library • 312 Washington St • Ogdensburg, NY 13669-1599 • (315) 393-4325 • http://www.nc3r.org/ogdensburg

Old Bethpage

Old Bethpage Village Restoration Museum • 1303 Round Swamp Rd • Old Bethpage, NY 11804 • (516) 572-8401

Old Chatham

Shaker Museum • 88 Shaker Museum Rd • Old Chatham, NY 12136 • (518) 794-9100 • http://www.smandl.org

Old Forge

Old Force Library • Crosby Blvd, P.O. Box 128 • Old Forge, NY 13420 • (315) 369-6008

Town of Webb Historical Association • Gilbert & Main Sts, P.O. Box 513 • Old Forge, NY 13420 • (315) 369-3838 • http://www.webbhistory.org

Old Westbury

Old Westbury Historic Home and Gardens • 71 Old Westbury Rd • Old Westbury, NY 11568 • (516) 333-0048 • http://www.oldwestburygardens.org

Olean

Bartlett Historical House Museum • 302 Laurens St • Olean, NY 14760 • (716) 376-5642

Olean Historical and Preservation Society • 302 Laurens St • Olean, NY 14760-2514 • (716) 373-0285

Onchiota

Six Nations Indian Museum • 1462 County Route 60 • Onchiota, NY 12989 • (518) 891-2299 • http://www.thebeadsite.com/MUS-F4.htm

Oneida

Cottage Lawn Museum • 435 Main St, P.O. Box 415 • Oneida, NY 31421 • (315) 363-4136

Madison County Historical Society • Cottage Lawn Historic House Museum, 435 Main St, P.O. Box 415 • Oneida, NY 13421-2421 • (315) 363-4136 • http://www.dreamscape.com/mchs1900

Oneida Community Mansion Museum • 170 Kenwood Ave • Oneida, NY 13421 • (315) 363-0745 • http://www.oneidacommunity.org

Oneida Indian Nation of New York • 579A Main St • Oneida, NY 13421 • (315) 829-8801 • http://www.oneida-nation.net

Oneida Library • 220 Broad St • Oneida, NY 13421 • (315) 363-3050 • http://www.midyork.org/Oneida

Shakowi Cultural Center Museum • Oneida Indian Nation, 5 Territory Rd • Oneida, NY 13421 • (315) 829-8801 • http://www.oneida-nation.net

Oneonta

Greater Oneonta Historical Society • P.O. Box 814 • Oneonta, NY 13820 • (607) 432-0960 • http://www.OneontaHistory.org

Huntington Memorial Library • 62 Chestnut St • Oneonta, NY 13820-2498 • (607) 432-1980 • http://lib.4cty.org/oneonta/

James M Milne Library - Special Collections • SUNY - Oneonta • Oneonta, NY 13820 • (607) 436-2727 • http://www.oneonta.edu/library/scc/SCC.html

Stevens-German Library & Cooper Archives • Hartwock College • Oneonta, NY 13820 • (607) 431-4450 • http://www.hartwick.edu/archives.xml

Upstate History Alliance • 11 Ford Ave • Oneonta, NY 13820 • (800) 895-1648 • http://www.upstatehistory.org

Ontario

Ontario Historical Society • Heritage Square Museum, 7147 Ontario Center Rd, P.O. Box 462 • Ontario, NY 14519 • (315) 524-5356 • http://www.heritagesquaremuseum.org

Town of Ontario Historical and Landmark Preservation Society • Heritage Sq, P.O. Box 462 • Ontario, NY 14519 • (315) 524-8928

Orangeburg

Orangeburg Public Library • Old Greenbush Rd • Orangeburg, NY 10962-1311 • (845) 359-2244

Orchard Park

Orchard Park Historical Society • Johnson-Jolls House Museum, S4287 S Buffalo St • Orchard Park, NY 14127 • (716) 667-2301

Orient

Oysterponds Historical Society • Museum of Orient and East Marion History, Village Lane, P.O. Box 844 • Orient, NY 11957 • (631) 323-2480

Oriskany

Battle of Oriskany Historical Society • Oriskany Museum, 420 Utica St, P.O. Box 284 • Oriskany, NY 13424 • (315) 736-7529 • http://www.ussoriskany.com

Oriskany Battlefield State Historic Site Museum • 7801 State Rte 69 • Oriskany, NY 13424 • (315) 768-7224 • http://www.nysparks.com

USS Oriskany Reunion Association • 420 Uitca St, P.O. Box 284 • Oriskany, NY 13424 • (315) 736-7529 • http://www.ussoriskany.com

Oriskany Falls
Limestone Ridge Historical Society • 223 Main St • Oriskany Falls, NY 13425 • (315) 821-8103

Orwell
Orwell Town Historian • 1999 County Route 2, P.O. Box 355 • Orwell, NY 13426 • (315) 298-4347

Osceola
North American Fiddlers Hall of Fame & Museum • Comins Rd • Osceola, NY 13316 • (315) 599-7009

Ossining
Ossining Historical Society • Historical Museum, 196 Croton Ave • Ossining, NY 10562 • (914) 941-0001 • http://www.ossininghistorical.org

Oswego
Fort Ontario State Historic Site Library • 1 E 4th St • Oswego, NY 13126 • (315) 343-4711 • http://www.fortontario.com

H Lee White Marine Museum • 1 W 1st Street Pier, P.O. Box 101 • Oswego, NY 13126 • (315) 342-0480 • http://www.hleewhitemarinemuseum.com

Heritage Foundation of Oswego County • 161 W 1st St, P.O. Box 405 • Oswego, NY 13126 • (315) 342-3354

Oswego City Historian • 119 W 4th St • Oswego, NY 13126 • (315) 343-1748

Oswego County Archives • E Oneida St • Oswego, NY 13126 • (315) 349-3297

Oswego County Genealogy Society • P.O. Box 3025 • Oswego, NY 13126 • (315) 591-6778 • http://oswegocountygenealog.tripod.com

Oswego County Historical Society • Richardson-Bates House Museum, 135 E 3rd St • Oswego, NY 13126 • (315) 343-1342

Oswego County Records Center • 384 E River Rd • Oswego, NY 13126 • (315) 349-8460 • http://www.co.oswego.ny.us/clerk/inventory.html

Oswego School District Public Library • 120 E 2nd St • Oswego, NY 13126 • (315) 341-5867 • http://www.nc3r.org/oswegocitylibrary

Oswego Town Historian • 2320 County Route 7 • Oswego, NY 13126 • (315) 349-8460

Penfield Library • SUNY at Oswego • Oswego, NY 13126-3514 • (315) 312-4267 • http://www.oswego.edu/library/

Richardson-Bates House Museum • 135 E 3rd St • Oswego, NY 13126 • (315) 343-1342

Safe Haven Museum • 2 E 7th St, P.O. Box 846 • Oswego, NY 13126 • (315) 342-3003 • http://www.oswegohaven.org

Scriba Town Historical Association • 42 Creamery Rd • Oswego, NY 13126 • (315) 342-6420

Otego
Harris Memorial Library • 69 Main St, P.O. Box H • Otego, NY 13825-0552 • (607) 988-6661 • http://www.4cls.org/otsego.html

Otego Historical Society • 6 River St, P.O. Box 27 • Otego, NY 13825 • (607) 988-2225 • http://www.otegohistoricalsociety.org

Otisville
Eleazer Harding House Museum • 183 Old Mountain Rd • Otisville, NY 10932 • (914) 386-5945

Mount Hope Historical Society • Old Mountain Rd • Otisville, NY 10963 • (845) 386-5945

Ovid
Ovid Historical Society • Historical Museum, 7203 Main St, P.O. Box 373 • Ovid, NY 14521 • (607) 869-5222

Owego
Coburn Free Library • 275 Main St • Owego, NY 13827 • (607) 687-3520 • http://www.flls.org/memberpages/owego.htm

Tioga County Historical Society • Historical Museum, 110-112 Front St • Owego, NY 13827 • (607) 687-2460 • http://www.tiogahistory.org

Oxford
Oxford Historical Society • Historical Museum, 1 Depot St • Oxford, NY 13830 • (607) 843-9926 • http://www.oxfordny.com/community/groups/historical

Oxford Memorial Library • Fort Hill Park, P.O. Box 552 • Oxford, NY 13830-0552 • (607) 843-6146 • http://www.4cls.org/chenango.html

Oyster Bay
Coe Hall Museum • Planting Fields Rd, P.O. Box 58 • Oyster Bay, NY 11771-0058 • (516) 922-9210 • http://www.plantingfields.org

Oyster Bay Historical Society • Earle-Wightman House Museum • 20 Summit St, P.O. Box 297 • Oyster Bay, NY 11771 • (516) 922-5032 • http://www.oysterbayhistory.org

Oyster Bay-East Norwich Public Library • 89 E Main St • Oyster Bay, NY 11711 • (516) 922-1212 • http://www.nassaulibrary.org/oysterbay

Raynham Hall Museum • 20 W Main St • Oyster Bay, NY 11711-0297 • (516) 922-6808 • http://www.rayhamhallmuseum.org

Sagamore Hill National Historic Site Museum • 20 Sagamore Hill Rd • Oyster Bay, NY 11771 • (516) 922-4788 • http://www.nps.gov/sahi

Painted Post
Erwin-Painted Post Museum • Steuben & High St, P.O. Box 516 • Painted Post, NY 14870 • (607) 962-7021 • http://www.paintedpostny.com

Southern Tier Library System • 580 W Water St • Painted Post, NY 14870 • (607) 962-3141

Palisades
Palisades Free Library • 19 Closter Rd, P.O. Box 610 • Palisades, NY 10964 • (845) 359-0136 • http://www.rcls.org/pal/

Palmyra
Hill Cumorah Visitors Center Museum • 603 State Rte 21 • Palmyra, NY 14522 • (315) 597-5851 • http://www.hillcumorah.org

Historic Palmyra • Historical Museum, 132 Market St, P.O. Box 96 • Palmyra, NY 14522 • (315) 597-6981 • http://www.palmyrany.com

Palmyra King's Daughters' Free Library • 127 Cuyler St • Palmyra, NY 14522 • (315) 597-5276 • http://www.palmyra.pls-net.org

Pheps Store Museum • 140 Market St, P.O. Box 96 • Palmyra, NY 14522 • (315) 597-6981 • http://www.palmyrany.com

Parish
Parish Public Library • Main & Church Sts • Parish, NY 13131 • (315) 625-7130

Parish Town Historian • P.O. Box 195 • Parish, NY 13131 • (315) 625-7833

Parish Town Historical Society • E Main St, P.O. Box 145 • Parish, NY 13131 • (315) 625-4575 • http://pths.parish-ny.com

Parishville
Parishville Historical Association • Historical Museum, Main St, P.O. Box 534 • Parishville, NY 13672 • (315) 265-7619

Patchogue
Greater Patchogue Historical Society • P.O. Box 102 • Patchogue, NY 11772 • (631) 574-7871 • http://pnl.suffolk.lib.ny.us/pmllhis.htm

Patchogue-Medford Central Library • 54-60 E Main St • Patchogue, NY 11772 • (631) 654-4700 • http://pml.suffolk.lib.ny.us

Paul Smiths
Joan Weill Library & Historical Archives • Paul Smith's College, Route 86 & 30, P.O. Box 257 • Paul Smiths, NY 12970 • (518) 327-6313 • http://www.paulsmiths.edu

Pavilion
Covington Historical Society • 1088 Peoria Rd • Pavilion, NY 14524 • (585) 584-3254

Pavilion Historical Society • general delivery • Pavilion, NY 14525

Pawling
Akin Free Library • 397 Mizzentop Rd, P.O. Box 345 • Pawling, NY 12564-0345 • (914) 855-5099

Historical Society of Quaker Hill and Pawling • John Kane House, 126 E Main St, P.O. Box 99 • Pawling, NY 12564 • (845) 855-5891 • http://www.pawlinghistory.org

John Kane House Museum • E Main St, P.O. Box 99 • Pawling, NY 12564 • (914) 855-9316

Pearl River
Orangetown Historical Museum • 213 Blue Hill Rd • Pearl River, NY 10965 • (815) 735-0429 • http://www.orangetown.com/parks/

Peekskill
Field Library of Peekskill • 4 Nelson Ave • Peekskill, NY 10566-2138 • (914) 737-1212 • http://www.peekskill.org

National Maritime Historical Society • 5 John Walsh Blvd, P.O. Box 68 • Peekskill, NY 10566 • (914) 737-7878 • http://www.seahistory.org

Peekskill-Herrick House Museum • 124 Union Ave, P.O. Box 84 • Peekskill, NY 10566-0084 • (914) 736-0473 • http://www.peekskillmuseum.org

Van Cortlandtville Historical Society • 297 Locust Ave • Peekskill, NY 10566 • (914) 737-7785

Penfield
Genealogical Roundtable of Monroe County • 35 Country Ln • Penfield, NY 14526-1028 • (585) 586-4870

Penfield Public Library • 1985 Baird Rd • Penfield, NY 14526 • (585) 383-0500

Penn Yan
Agricultural Memories Museum • 1110 Townline Rd • Penn Yan, NY 14527 • (315) 536-1206 • http://www.agriculturalmemoriesmuseum.com

Penn Yan Public Library • 214 Main St • Penn Yan, NY 14527 • (315) 536-6114 • http://www.pypl.org

Yates County Genealogical and Historical Society • Oliver House Museum, 200 Main St • Penn Yan, NY 14527 • (315) 536-7318 • http://www.yatespast.com

Perry
Perry Public Library • 70 N Main St • Perry, NY 14530-1299 • (585) 237-2243 • http://www.perry.pls-net.org

Peru
Peru Free Library • 3024 N Main St, P.O. Box 96 • Peru, NY 12972 • (518) 643-8618 • http://www.cefls.org/pery.htm

Peru Town Historian • Town Hall, N Main St, P.O. Box 596 • Peru, NY 12972 • (518) 643-3745

Peterboro
Peterboro Area Historical Society • Historical Museum, Swamp Rd, P.O. Box 42 • Peterboro, NY 13134 • (315) 684-9022 • http://www.sca-peterboro.org

Phelps
Phelps Community Memorial Library • 15 Church St • Phelps, NY 14532 • (315) 548-3120

Phelps Historical Society • Historical Museum, 66 Main St, P.O. Box 200 • Phelps, NY 14532-1053 • (315) 548-4940

Philadelphia
Bodman Memorial Library and Museum • 8 Aldrich St • Philadelphia, NY 13673 • (315) 642-3323

Phoenix
Palermo Town Historian • 139 Island Rd • Phoenix, NY 13135 • (315) 593-6825

Phoenix Public Library • 34 Elm St • Phoenix, NY 13135 • (315) 695-4355

Schroeppel Historical Society • St John's Episcopal Church, Main & Voiney Sts • Phoenix, NY 13135 • (315) 695-2540

Schroeppel Town Historian • 69 County Route 57A • Phoenix, NY 13135 • (315) 695-6641

Piermont
Piermont Public Library • 153 Hudson Terr • Piermont, NY 10968 • (845) 359-4595 • http://www.rcls.org/pmt

Pine Bush
Cragsmoor Historical Society • Cragsmoor Rd • Pine Bush, NY 12566 • (845) 647-2362

Town of Crawford Historical Society • P.O. Box 109 • Pine Bush, NY 12566 • (845) 744-5418 • http://www.townofcrawford.us/TownofCrawfordHistoricalSociety.htm

Pine City
Southport Historical Society • Laurel St, P.O. Box 146 • Pine City, NY 14871

Pine Hill
Town of Shandaken Historical Museum • 26 Academy St, P.O. Box 678 • Pine Hill, NY 12465 • (845) 254-4460 • http://www.shandaken.us

Pine Island
Drowned Lands Historical Society • 140 Pulasky Hwy • Pine Island, NY 10969 • (914) 258-4528

Pine Plains
Little Nine Partners Historical Society • P.O. Box 243 • Pine Plains, NY 12567 • http://www.rootsweb.com/~nylnphs/_ancillaries/L9PHS.htm

Piseco
Piseco Lake Historical Society • Riley House & Tavern Museum, Old Piseco Rd • Piseco, NY 12139 • (518) 548-3892

Pittsford
Historic Pittsford • Historical Museum, 18 Monroe Ave, P.O. Box 38 • Pittsford, NY 14534 • (585) 381-2941 • http://www.historicpittsford.com

Tri-Town Genealogical Society • 323 Kreag Rd • Pittsford, NY 14534 • (585) 248-8964

Plainview
Irish Family History Forum • P.O. Box 67 • Plainview, NY 11803-0067 • (516) 616-3587 • http://www.ifhf.org

Plainview-Old Bethage Public Library • 999 Old Country Rd • Plainview, NY 11803 • (516) 938-0077 • http://www.nassaulibrary.org/plainv

Plattsburgh
Beekmantown Town Hall Archives • 29 North Point Rd • Plattsburgh, NY 12901 • (518) 563-7178

Clinton County Historian • Clinton County Gov Ctr, 137 Margaret St • Plattsburgh, NY 12901 • (518) 565-4749

Clinton County Historical Association • Historical Museum, 48 Court St, P.O. Box 332 • Plattsburgh, NY 12901 • (518) 561-0340 • http://www.clintoncountyhistorical.org

Clinton-Essex-Franklin Library System • 33 Oak St • Plattsburgh, NY 12901 • (518) 563-5190

Feinberg Library - Special Collections • Plattsburgh State University of New York, 2 Draper Ave • Plattsburgh, NY 12901 • (518) 564-5206 • http://research.plattsburgh.edu/specialcollections

Kent-Delord House Museum • 17 Cumberland Ave • Plattsburgh, NY 12901 • (518) 561-1035 • http://www.kentdelordhouse.org

Northern New York American-Canadian Genealogical Society • P.O. Box 1256 • Plattsburgh, NY 12901-1256 • (518) 846-7707 • http://www.rootsweb.com/~nnyacgs/

Plattsburgh City Historian • 62 Prospect Ave • Plattsburgh, NY 12901 • (518) 563-5794

Plattsburgh Public Library • 19 Oak St • Plattsburgh, NY 12901-2810 • (518) 563-0921 • http://www.plattsburghlib.org

Plattsburgh Town Historian • 151 Banker Rd • Plattsburgh, NY 12901 • (518) 562-6887

Pleasantville
American Veterans Historical Museum • P.O. Box 115 • Pleasantville, NY 10570 • (914) 769-5297

Mount Pleasant Public Library • 350 Bedford Rd • Pleasantville, NY 10570-3099 • (914) 769-0548 • http://www.mountpleasantlibrary.org

Plymouth
Town of Plymouth Historical Society • P.O. Box 41 • Plymouth, NY 13832 • (607) 334-9448

Pocantico Hills
Stone Barns Center Agricultural Museum • 630 Bedford Rd • Pocantico Hills, NY 10591 • (914) 366-6200 • http://www.stonebarnscenter.org

Poestenkill
Poestenkill Historical Society • P.O. Box 140 • Poestenkill, NY 12140

Poestenkill Library • 9 Plank Rd, P.O. Box 305 • Poestenkill, NY 12140 • (518) 283-3721 • http://www.poestenkilllibrary.org

Pomona
Rockland County Archives • Bldg S, Sanatorium Rd • Pomona, NY 10970 • (845) 364-3670 • http://www.rocklandcountyclerk.com

Poplar Ridge
Hazard Library Association • 2485 Route 34 B, P.O. Box 3 • Poplar Ridge, NY 13139-0003 • (315) 364-7975 • http://www.flls.org/poplar/

Port Byron
Lock 52 Historical Society of Port Byron • 73 Pine St, P.O. Box 289 • Port Byron, NY 13140 • (315) 776-4027 • http://www.rootsweb.com/~nycayuga/Lock52/

Port Chester
Port Chester Historical Society • Bush Homestead, 479 King St, P.O. Box 10573 • Port Chester, NY 10573 • (914) 939-8918

Port Chester Public Library • 1 Haseco Ave • Port Chester, NY 10573 • (914) 939-6710 • http://www.portchesterlibrary.org

Port Ewen
Port Ewen Library • 189 Broadway, P.O. Box 1167 • Port Ewen, NY 12466 • (845) 338-5580

Port Henry
Sherman Free Library • 20 Church St • Port Henry, NY 12974 • (518) 546-7461 • http://www.porthenry.com/phframes/library.htm

Town of Moriah Historical Society • Iron Center Museum, 34 Park Pl • Port Henry, NY 12974 • (518) 546-3587 • http://www.porthenry.com

Port Jefferson
Historical Society of Greater Port Jefferson • Mather House Museum, 115 Prospect, P.O. Box 586 • Port Jefferson, NY 11777 • (631) 473-2665 • http://www.portjeffhistorical.org

Port Jervis
Minisink Valley Historical Society • Historical Museum, 125-133 W Main St, P.O. Box 659 • Port Jervis, NY 12771 • (845) 856-2375 • http://www.minisink.org

Port Jervis Free Library • 138 Pike St • Port Jervis, NY 12771 • (845) 856-7313 • http://www.rcls.org/ptj

Port Leyden
Lyonsdale Town Historian • 2554 River Rd • Port Leyden, NY 13433 • (315) 942-4107

Port Leyden Community Library • 3145 Canal St, P.O. Box 97 • Port Leyden, NY 13433 • (315) 348-6077 • http://www.nc3r.org/portleydenlib

Port Washington
Cow Neck Peninsula Historical Society • Sands-Willets House, 336 Port Washington Blvd • Port Washington, NY 11050 • (516) 365-9074 • http://www.cowneck.org

Polish American Museum • 16 Belleview Ave • Port Washington, NY 11050 • (516) 883-6542 • http://www.liglobal.com/t_i/attractions/museums/polish/

Port Washington Public Library • 1 Library Dr • Port Washington, NY 11050-2794 • (516) 883-4400 • http://www.pwpl.org

Portland
Portland Historical Society • Depot Museum, E Main St • Portland, NY 14769

Portville
Portville Free Library • 2 N Main St, P.O. Box 768 • Portville, NY 14770-0768 • (716) 933-8441

Portville Historical and Preservation Society • P.O. Box 59 • Portville, NY 14770-0059 • http://www.portervillehistory.org

Potsdam
Clarkson University Archives • 8 Clarkson Ave, P.O. Box 5590 • Potsdam, NY 13699-5590 • (315) 268-2297 • http://www.clarkson.edu/library

North Country Reference and Research Resources Council • 6721 US Hwy 11 • Potsdam, NY 13676-3132

Potsdam Public Library • Civic Center, 2 Park St • Potsdam, NY 13676 • (315) 265-7230 • http://www.northnet.org/potsdamlib

Potsdam Public Museum • Civic Center, P.O. Box 5168 • Potsdam, NY 13676 • (315) 265-6910 • http://www.potsdam.ny.us/village/museumweb/

Potsdam Town Historian • 35 Market St • Potsdam, NY 13676 • (315) 265-3430

SUNY Potsdam College Library - Special Collections • 44 Pierrepont Ave • Potsdam, NY 13676 • (315) 267-3326

Poughkeepsie
Dutchess County Genealogical Society • 204 Spakenkill Rd, P.O. Box 708 • Poughkeepsie, NY 12602-0708 • (845) 462-4168 • http://www.kinshipny.com/membersh.htm; http://www.dcgs-gen.org

Dutchess County Historical Society • Clinton House Museum, 549 Main St, P.O. Box 88 • Poughkeepsie, NY 12602 • (845) 471-1630 • http://www.pojonews

Glebe House Museum • 635 Main St • Poughkeepsie, NY 12601 • (845) 454-0605

Hudson River Valley Institute • Marist College, 3399 North Rd • Poughkeepsie, NY 12601-1387 • (845) 575-3052 • http://www.hudsonrivervalley.net

Locust Grove-Samuel Morse Historic Site Museum • 2683 South Rd • Poughkeepsie, NY 12601 • (845) 454-4500 • http://www.morsehistoricsite.org

New York

Poughkeepsie, cont.
Mid-Hudson Library System • 103 Market St • Poughkeepsie, NY 12601 • (845) 471-6060

Poughkeepsie Public Library-Adriance Memorial • 93 Market St • Poughkeepsie, NY 12601 • (845) 485-3445 • http://www.poklib.org

Young-Morse Historic Site • 370 South Rd, P.O. Box 1649 • Poughkeepsie, NY 12601 • (914) 454-4500

Poughquag
Beekman Historical Society • P.O. Box 235 • Poughquag, NY 12533 • http://www.townofbeekman.com/historicalsociety.html

Beekman Library • Rte 55 & Dorn Rd, P.O. Box 697 • Poughquag, NY 12570-0697 • (845) 724-3414 • http://www.beekmanlibrary.org

Pound Ridge
Pound Ridge Historical Society • Historical Museum, 255 Westchester Ave, P.O. Box 51 • Pound Ridge, NY 10576 • (914) 764-4333 • http://www.prhsmuseum.org

Prattsburgh
Narcissa Prentiss House Museum • 7226 Mill Pond Rd, P.O. Box 384 • Prattsburgh, NY 14873 • (607) 522-4537

Prattsburgh Community Historical Society • Historical Museum, 19 N Main St, P.O. Box 384 • Prattsburgh, NY 14873 • (607) 522-5776

Prattsville
Lexington Historical Society • 18 Church St • Prattsville, NY 12468 • (518) 989-9570

Zadock Pratt Museum • Main St, P.O. Box 333 • Prattsville, NY 12468 • (518) 299-3395 • http://www.prattmuseum.com

Pulaski
Pulaski Historical Society • 3428 Maple Ave • Pulaski, NY 13142-4502 • (315) 298-4650

Pulaski Public Library • 4917 N Jefferson St • Pulaski, NY 13142 • (315) 298-2717

Pulaski Village Historian • 109 Lehigh Rd • Pulaski, NY 13142 • (315) 298-5235

Richland Town Historian • 85 Lake St • Pulaski, NY 13142 • (315) 298-3620

Pultneyville
Pultneyville Historical Society • Historical Museum, 4130 Mill St, P.O. Box 92 • Pultneyville, NY 14538-0092 • (315) 589-9892 • http://pultneyvillehistoricalsociety.org

Purchase
Purchase Free Library • 3093 Purchase St • Purchase, NY 10577 • (914) 948-0550 • http://www.purchasefreelibrary.org

Putnam Valley
Putnam Valley Historical Society • 301 Peekskill Hollow Rd, P.O. Box 297 • Putnam Valley, NY 10579 • (914) 528-1024 • http://www.lalobilla.com/pvhs

Queensbury
Adirondack Community College Library • 640 Bay Rd • Queensbury, NY 12804 • (518) 743-2200 • http://www.sunyacc.edu

Buck Hill Associates • P.O. Box 4736 • Queensbury, NY 12804-0736 • (518) 251-2349

Northeastern New York Genealogical Society • Robert Gardens South, P.O. Box 4264 • Queensbury, NY 12804 • (518) 793-9837 • http://www.rootsweb.com/~nywarren/community/nnygs.htm

Warren County Historical Society • 195 Sunnyside Rd • Queensbury, NY 12804-7762 • (518) 743-0734 • http://www.warrencountyhistoricalsociety.org

Quogue
Quogue Historical Society • P.O. Box 1207 • Quogue, NY 11969 • (631) 653-4111 • http://www.suffolk.lib.ny.us/libraries/quog/history.htm

Randolph
Randolph Free Library • 26 Jamestown St • Randolph, NY 14772 • (716) 358-3712 • http://www.cclslib.org/randolph

Raquette Lake
Raquette Lake Free Library • P.O. Box 129 • Raquette Lake, NY 13436 • (315) 354-4005

Raquette Lake Town Historian • Antlers Rd, P.O. Box 114 • Raquette Lake, NY 13436 • (315) 354-5122

Ravena
Ravena Coeymans Historical Society • Village Municipal Bldg, 15 Mountain Rd • Ravena, NY 12143 • http://www.coeymans.org/ravena_coeymans_historical_socie.htm

RCS Community Library • 15 Mountain Rd • Ravena, NY 12143 • (518) 756-2053

Red Creek
Red Creek Free Library • 6817 Main St, P.O. Box 360 • Red Creek, NY 13143 • (315) 754-5579

Red Creek Historical Society • P.O. Box 271 • Red Creek, NY 14143

Red Hook
Egbert Benson Historical Society of Red Hook • 58 Fraleigh St, P.O. Box 397 • Red Hook, NY 12571-0397 • (845) 758-5887

Historical Society of Red Hook • N Broadway • Red Hook, NY 12571 • (845) 758-1920

Redfield
Redfield Town Historian • 722 County Route 47 • Redfield, NY 13437 • (315) 599-7735

Redwood
Rossie Town Historian • 908 County Route 3 • Redwood, NY 13679 • (315) 324-5449

Remsen
Didymus Thompson Library • 9639 Main St, P.O. Box 410 • Remsen, NY 13438 • (315) 831-5651 • http://www.didymusthomaslibrary.cnynorthcountry.com

Remsen-Steuben Historical Society • 9793 Prospect Rd, P.O. Box 284 • Remsen, NY 13438 • (315) 831-8481 • http://villageofremsen.org

Steuben Memorial State Historic Site Museum • Starr Hill Rd • Remsen, NY 13438 • (315) 768-7224 • http://www.nysparks.com

Rensselaer
City of Rensselaer Historical Society • Agents House, 15 Forbes Ave • Rensselaer, NY 12144

Crailo State Historic Site Museum • 9 1/2 Riverside Ave • Rensselaer, NY 12144 • (518) 463-8738

Rensselaer Public Library • 810 Broadway • Rensselaer, NY 12144-2198 • (518) 462-1193 • http://www.uhls.org/rensselaer

Rensselaer Falls
Rensselaer Falls Library • 212 Rensselaer St, P.O. Box 237 • Rensselaer Falls, NY 13680 • (315) 344-7406 • http://www.nnyln.org/canlib/falls/

Rensselaer Falls Village Historian • 12 Heuvelton R • Rensselaer Falls, NY 13680 • (315) 344-6681

Rensselaerville
Rensselaerville Historical Society • P.O. Box 8 • Rensselaerville, NY 12147 • (518) 797-3194

Rhinebeck
Quitman House Library for Historic Preservation • Route 9, P.O. Box 624 • Rhinebeck, NY 12572 • (845) 871-1798 • http://www. quitmanpreservation.org

Rhinebeck Aerodrome Museum • Stone Church Rd & Norton Rd, P.O. Box 229 • Rhinebeck, NY 12572 • (845) 752-3200 • http://www. oldrhinebeck.org

Rhinebeck Historical Society • P.O. Box 291 • Rhinebeck, NY 12572 • (845) 876-7341 • http://www.rhinebeckhistory.org

Starr Library • 66 W Market St • Rhinebeck, NY 12572 • (845) 876-4030 • http://starr.rhinebeck.lib.ny.us

Wilderstein Preservation Museum • Morton Rd, P.O. Box 383 • Rhinebeck, NY 12572 • (914) 876-4818 • http://www.wilderstein.org

Riceville
Rice Homestead Museum • Riceville Rd • Riceville, NY 12117 • (518) 661-5085

Richburg
Colonial Library - Historical Room • 61 Main St, P.O. Box B • Richburg, NY 14774 • (585) 928-2694 • http://www.stls.org/Richburg

Richfield Springs
Richfield Springs Public Library • 102 Main St, P.O. Box 271 • Richfield Springs, NY 13439-0271 • (315) 858-0230

Richford
Richford Historical Society • Route 28 S, P.O. Box 28 • Richford, NY 13835-0028 • (607) 539-6283

Richland
Half-Shire Historical Society • 1100 County Route 48, P.O. Box 73 • Richland, NY 13144-0073 • (315) 298-3620 • http://halfshire.tripod. com/halfshirehistoricalsociety/

Richmond Hill
Richmond Hill Historical Society • 86-22 109th St • Richmond Hill, NY 11418 • (718) 847-7878 • http://www.richmondhillhistory.org

Richville
Richville Free Library • 87 Main St, P.O. Box 55 • Richville, NY 13681-0055 • (315) 287-1481

Richville Historical Association • 24 Depot St, P.O. Box 207 • Richville, NY 13681 • (315) 287-0182

Welsh Society of Richville • 214 Welch Rd • Richville, NY 13681 • (315) 287-3193

Ridgewood
Greater Ridgewood Historical Society • Vander Ende-Onderdonk House, 1820 Flushing Ave • Ridgewood, NY 11385-1041 • (718) 456-1776 • http://members.aol.com/ondrdnkhse/grhs.htm

Queens Genealogy Workshop • Vander Ende-Onderdonk House, 1820 Flushing Ave • Ridgewood, NY 11385-1041 • (718) 456-1776 • http://home.att.net/~CGohari/

Steuben Society of America • 6705 Fresh Pond Rd • Ridgewood, NY 11385-4505 • (718) 381-0900 • http://www.steubensociety.org

Riverhead
Hallockville Museum Farm • 6038 Sound Ave • Riverhead, NY 11901 • (631) 298-5292 • http://www.hallockville.com

National Society, Daughters of the Revolution of 1776 • Helen Raynor Hannah Memorial Library, 300 W Main St • Riverhead, NY 11901 • (631) 727-2881

Railroad Museum of Long Island • 416 Griffing Ave • Riverhead, NY 11901 • (631) 727-7920 • http://www.rmli.org

Riverhead Free Library • 330 Court St • Riverhead, NY 11901-2885 • (631) 727-3228 • http://river.suffolk.lib.ny.us

Suffolk County Historical Society • Helen Raynor Hannah Memorial Library, 300 W Main St • Riverhead, NY 11901-2894 • (631) 727-2881 • http://www.schs-museum.org

Rochester
American Baptist Historical Society • Samuel Colgate Historical Library, 1106 S Goodman St • Rochester, NY 14620-2532 • (585) 473-1740 • http://www.crds.edu/abhs/

Association of Asian Indians in America • 300 Clover St • Rochester, NY 14610-2225

Baker-Cederberg Museum • 1425 Portland Ave • Rochester, NY 14621 • (585) 922-3521 • http://www.viahealth.org/archives/

Beaman Museum • 2036 West Side Dr • Rochester, NY 14624 • (585) 594-2401

Brighton Historical Society • 52 Kimbark Rd • Rochester, NY 14610 • (585) 381-6202

Brighton Memorial Library • 2300 Elmwood Ave • Rochester, NY 14618 • (585) 784-5300 • http://www.brightonlibrary.org

Campbell-Whittlesey House Museum • 123 Fitzhugh St • Rochester, NY 14508 • (585) 546-7078

Charlotte-Genesee Lighthouse Historical Society • 70 Lighthouse St • Rochester, NY 14612 • (585) 621-6179

Chili Historical Society • Historic Streeter's Inn, 4145 Union St • Rochester, NY 14624

Chili Public Library • 3333 Chili Ave • Rochester, NY 14624-5494 • (585) 889-2200 • http://www.rochester.lib.ny.us/chili

Dar-Hervey Fly House Museum • 11 Livingston Park • Rochester, NY 14608 • (716) 232-4509

Episcopal Church Home Museum • 505 Mount Hope Ave • Rochester, NY 14620 • (716) 546-8400

Gates Historical Society • 634 Hinchey Rd • Rochester, NY 14624 • (585) 464-9740 • http://www.gateshistory.org

Gates Public Library • 1605 Buffalo Rd • Rochester, NY 14624 • (585) 247-6446 • http://www.gateslibrary.org

George Eastman House Museum • 900 East Ave • Rochester, NY 14607 • (585) 271-3361 • http://www.eastmanhouse.org

Greece Historical Society • Historical Museum, 595 Long Pond Rd, P.O. Box 16249 • Rochester, NY 14616 • (585) 225-7221 • http://historicalsociety.greeneny.org

Greece Public Library • 2 Vince Tofany Blvd • Rochester, NY 14612-5030 • (585) 225-8951

Henrietta Public Library • 455 Calkins Rd • Rochester, NY 14123 • (585) 359-7092 • http://www.hpl.org

Irondequoit Historical Office • 877 Helendale Rd • Rochester, NY 14609 • (585) 467-8840

Irondequoit Historical Society • Pioneer House, P.O. Box 67130 • Rochester, NY 14616 • (585) 266-5144 • http://www.ggw.org/~ihsociety

Irondequoit Public Library • 45 Cooper Rd • Rochester, NY 14617 • (585) 336-6062

Irondequoit Public Library - Helen McGraw Branch • 2180 E Ridge Rd • Rochester, NY 14622 • (585) 336-6060 • http://www.irondequoit.org

Jewish Genealogical Society of Rochester • 265 Viennawood Dr • Rochester, NY 14618 • (716) 261-2118 • http://jgsr.org

Jewish Genealogical Society of Rochester • 265 Viennawood Dr • Rochester, NY 14618 • (585) 271-2118 • http://jgsr.hq.net

Kodak Genealogical Club • Kodak Park Activities Association, Eastman Kodak Co, Bldg 28 • Rochester, NY 14652-3404 • (585) 377-3874

Rochester, cont.

Landmark Society of Western New York • Hoyt-Potter House Museum, 133 S Fitzhugh St • Rochester, NY 14608-2204 • (585) 546-7029 • http://www.landmarksociety.org

Margaret Woodbury Strong Museum • 1 Manhattan Square • Rochester, NY 14607 • (585) 263-2700

Monroe County Historian's Department Library • 115 South Ave • Rochester, NY 14604 • (585) 428-8352

National Railway Historical Society, Rochester Chapter • P.O. Box 23326 • Rochester, NY 14692 • (585) 533-1431

Rochester Genealogical Society • P.O. Box 10501 • Rochester, NY 14610-0501 • (585) 234-2584 • http://home.eznet.net/~halsey/rgs.html

Rochester Historical Society • Historical Museum, 485 East Ave • Rochester, NY 14607 • (585) 271-2705 • http://www.rochesterhistory.org

Rochester Municipal Archives and Records Center • 414 Andrews St • Rochester, NY 14604 • (585) 428-7331 • http://www.cityofrochester.gov

Rochester Museum & Science Center • Schuyler C Townson Research Library, 657 East Ave • Rochester, NY 14607 • (585) 271-4320 • http://www.rmsc.org

Rochester Public Library • 115 South Ave • Rochester, NY 14604-1896 • (585) 428-7300 • http://www.libraryweb.org

Rochester Public Library-Charlotte • 3615 Lake Ave • Rochester, NY 14612 • (585) 428-8216

Rush Rhees Library • University of Rochester, Wilson Blvd • Rochester, NY 14627 • (716) 275-4461 • http://www.lib.rochester.edu

Slovak Heritage and Folklore Society International • 151 Colebrook Dr • Rochester, NY 14617-2215 • (585) 342-9383 • http://feefhs.org/slovak/frgshfsi.html

South Wedge History Club • general delivery • Rochester, NY 14620 • (585) 244-4558 • http://www.swpc.org/history.htm

Stone-Tolan House Museum • 2370 East Ave • Rochester, NY 14610 • (585) 442-4606

Strong Museum • Gelser Library, 1 Manhattan Sq • Rochester, NY 14607 • (585) 263-2700 • http://www.strongmuseum.org

Susan B Anthony House Museum • 17 Madison St • Rochester, NY 14601 • (585) 235-6124 • http://www.susanbanthonyhouse.org

Woodside House Museum • 485 East Ave • Rochester, NY 14607 • (585) 271-2705

Rockville Center

Irish Family History Forum • P.O. Box 351 • Rockville Center, NY 11571-0351 • (631) 423-7135

Rockville Centre Historical Society • Phillips House, 28 Hempstead Ave, P.O. Box 605 • Rockville Centre, NY 11570 • (516) 678-9201 • http://www.nysed.gov

Rocky Point

Rocky Point Historical Society • P.O. Box 1720 • Rocky Point, NY 11778 • http://www.buoy.com/rphs/

Rome

Afro-American Heritage Association • P.O. Box 451 • Rome, NY 13440 • (315) 337-5018

Erie Canal Village Museum • 5789 New London Rd • Rome, NY 13440 • (315) 336-6000 x249 • http://www.eriecanalvillage.com

Fort Stanwix National Monument Museum • 112 E Park St • Rome, NY 13440 • (315) 336-2090 • http://www.nps.gov/fost

Jervis Public Library Association • 613 N Washington St • Rome, NY 13340-4296 • (315) 336-4570 • http://www.jervislibrary.org

Rome Historical Society • Historical Museum, 200 Church St • Rome, NY 13440 • (315) 336-5870 • http://www.dreamscape.com/romehist; http://when-in-rome.com/RomeHistorical

Rome-Delta Lake Historic Preservation • Westernville Rd • Rome, NY 13440 • (315) 337-4670

Roseboom

Town of Roseboom Historical Association • P.O. Box 46 • Roseboom, NY 13450 • (607) 264-8065

Rosedale

Civil War Round Table of NY • 13933 250th St • Rosedale, NY 11422 • (718) 341-9811

Rosendale

Century House Historical Society • A J Snyder Estate Museum, 688 Route 213, P.O. Box 150 • Rosendale, NY 12472-0150 • (845) 658-9900 • http://www.centuryhouse.org

Roslyn

Bryant Library & Local History Collection • 2 Paper Mill Rd • Roslyn, NY 11576-2193 • (516) 621-2240 • http://www.nassaulibrary.org/bryant

Roslyn Landmark Society • 36 Main St • Roslyn, NY 11576-2167 • (516) 625-4363

Van Nostrand-Starkins House Museum • 221 Main St • Roslyn, NY 11576 • (516) 625-4363

Rotterdam Junction

Mabee Farm Historic Site Museum • 1080 Main St • Rotterdam Junction, NY 12150 • (518) 887-5073 • http://www.mabeefarm.com

Round Lake

Round Lake Library • 31 Wesley Ave, P.O. Box 665 • Round Lake, NY 12151 • (518) 899-2285

Rouses Point

Dodge Memorial Library • 144 Lake St • Rouses Point, NY 12979 • (518) 297-6242 • http://www.cefls.org/rousespoint.htm

Rouses Point Village Historian • 139 Lake St, P.O. Box 185 • Rouses Point, NY 12979 • (518) 297-5502

Rouses Point-Champlain Historical Society • P.O. Box 144 • Rouses Point, NY 12979 • (518) 297-7913

Roxbury

John Burroughs State Historic Site Museum • Burroughs Memorial Rd • Roxbury, NY 12474 • http://www.nysparks.com

Roxbury Library • 53742 State Hwy 30, P.O. Box 186 • Roxbury, NY 12474 • (607) 326-7901 • http://www.4cls.org/webpages/members/Roxbury/Roxbury.html

Rushford

Rushford Free Library • 9012 Main St, P.O. Box 8 • Rushford, NY 14777-0008 • (585) 437-2533

Rushford Historical Society • Rushford Museum, Main St, P.O. Box 133 • Rushford, NY 14777-0133 • (585) 437-2340

Rushville

Southern Tier Library System-Mabel D Blodgett Memorial • 35 S Main St • Rushville, NY 14544-9648 • (716) 554-3939 • http://www.stls.org/Rushville

Russell

Clare Town Historian • 3495 County Route 27 • Russell, NY 13684 • (315) 386-3849

Russell Public Library • 9 Pestle St, P.O. Box 510 • Russell, NY 13684 • (315) 347-2115 • http://www.russellny.us/library.html

Rye

Rye Free Reading Room • 1061 Boston Post Rd • Rye, NY 10580 • (914) 967-0480 • http://www.ryelibrary.org

Rye Historical Society • Square House Museum, 1 Purchase St • Rye, NY 10580-3002 • (914) 967-7588 • http://www.ryehistoricalsociety.org

Sackets Harbor
Hay Memorial Library • 101 S Broad St, P.O. Box 288 • Sackets Harbor, NY 13685 • (315) 646-2228

Pickering-Beach Historical Society • Historical Museum, 501 W Main St, P.O. Box 204 • Sackets Harbor, NY 13685 • (315) 646-2321 • http://www.sacketsharborny.com/pbmuseum.html

Sackets Harbor Battlefield State Historic Site Museum • 504 W Main St P.O. Box 27 • Sackets Harbor, NY 13685 • (315) 646-3634 • http://www.nysparks.state.ny.us

Sackets Harbor Historical Society • 100 W Main St • Sackets Harbor, NY 13685 • (315) 646-3525

Sag Harbor
Customs House Museum • Garden & Main Sts • Sag Harbor, NY 11963 • (516) 725-0855

Eastville Community Historical Society • Sears Roebuck Mail Order House, 139 E Hampton St, P.O. Box 2036 • Sag Harbor, NY 11963 • (631) 725-3713

John Jermain Memorial Library • Sag Harbor History Room, Main St, P.O. Box 569 • Sag Harbor, NY 11963 • (631) 725-0049 • http://sagharbor.suffolk.lib.ny.us/libraries/jjer/

Old Sag Harbor Jain House • Division St, P.O. Box 1709 • Sag Harbor, NY 11963-1709 • http://www.sagharborhistoricalsociety.org

Sag Harbor Historical Society • Annie Cooper Boyd House, 174 Main St, P.O. Box 1709 • Sag Harbor, NY 11963 • (631) 725-5092 • http://www.sagharborhistoricalsociety.org/

Sag Harbor Whaling and Historical Museum • 200 Main St, P.O. Box 1327 • Sag Harbor, NY 11963 • (631) 725-0770 • http://www.sagharborwhalingmuseum.org

Shelter Island Historical Society • 16 Ferry Rd • Sag Harbor, NY 11963 • (631) 749-0025

Saint Johnsville
Fort Klock Historic Restoration • Historical Museum, 7214 State Hwy 5, P.O. Box 42 • Saint Johnsville, NY 13452 • (518) 568-7779

Margaret Reaney Memorial Library • 19 Kingsbury Ave • Saint Johnsville, NY 13452 • (518) 568-7822 • http://www2.telenet.net/community/mvla/stjo

Palatine Germans of the Mohawk Valley • c/o Margaret Reaney Memorial Library, 19 Kingsbury Ave • Saint Johnsville, NY 13452 • (518) 568-7822

Palatine Settlement Society • 10 W Main St, P.O. Box 183 • Saint Johnsville, NY 13452 • (518) 568-2346 • http://www.palatinesettlementsociety.org

Saint Regis Falls
Waverly Town Historian • P.O. Box 83 • Saint Regis Falls, NY 12980

Salamanca
Cattaraugus County Genealogical Society • P.O. Box 404 • Salamanca, NY 14779 • http://www.cattco.org/history/history_info.asp

Salamanca Public Library • 155 Wildwood Ave • Salamanca, NY 14779-1576 • (716) 945-1890

Salamanca Rail Museum • 170 Main St • Salamanca, NY 14779 • (716) 945-3133

Seneca Nation of Indians • P.O. Box 231 • Salamanca, NY 14779-0231 • (716) 945-1790 • http://www.sni.org

Seneca-Iroquois National Museum • 814 Broad St, P.O. Box 442 • Salamanca, NY 14779 • (716) 945-1738 • http://www.senecanation.org; http://www.senecamuseum.org

Salem
Dr Asa Fitch Historical Society • 342 Scotts Lake Rd • Salem, NY 12865 • (518) 854-3888 • http://www.salem-ny.com/histh13.html

Salisbury Center
Salisbury Historical Society • 1805 Frisbie House Museum, 109 State Route 29A • Salisbury Center, NY 13454 • (315) 429-3605

Sanborn
Niagara County Community College Library • 3111 Saunders Settlement Rd • Sanborn, NY 14132 • (716) 731-3271 x401 • http://www.niagaracc.suny.edu/library/special.html

Sanborn Area Historical Society • Historical Museum, 2822 Niagara St, P.O. Box 172 • Sanborn, NY 14132 • (716) 731-4708 • http://www.sanbornhistory.org

Sandy Creek
Annie Porter Ainsworth Memorial Library • 6064 S Main St, P.O. Box 69 • Sandy Creek, NY 13145 • (315) 387-3732

Lacona Village Historian • 1992 Harwood Dr, P.O. Box 52 • Sandy Creek, NY 13145 • (315) 387-5456 • http://sandycreekny.tripod.com

Sandy Creek Town Historian • 1992 Harwood Dr, P.O. Box 52 • Sandy Creek, NY 13145 • (315) 387-5456 • http://sandycreekny.tripod.com

Saranac Lake
Adirondack Genealogical-Historical Society • c/o Saranac Lake Free Library, 100 Main St • Saranac Lake, NY 12983 • (518) 891-2236 • http://freepages.genealogy.rootsweb.com/~adkghs

Harrietstown Town Historian • 39 Main St • Saranac Lake, NY 12983 • (518) 891-3471

Historic Saranac Lake • North Elba Town House, 89 Church St, P.O. Box 1030 • Saranac Lake, NY 12983 • (518) 891-0971 • http://www.historicsaranaclake.org

North Country Community College Library • 23 Santanoni Ave, P.O. Box 89 • Saranac Lake, NY 12983 • (518) 891-2915 • http://www.nccc.edu/library.html

Robert Louis Stevenson Memorial Cottage Museum • 44 Stevenson Ln • Saranac Lake, NY 12983 • (518) 891-1462 • http://www.pennypiper.com

Saint Armand Town Historian • RR 1, Box 4 • Saranac Lake, NY 12983 • (518) 891-3555

Saranac Lake Free Library • 109 Main St • Saranac Lake, NY 12983 • (518) 891-4190 • http://www.nc3r.org/slfl/white.htm

Saranac Lake Village Archives • 3 Main St, Ste 1 • Saranac Lake, NY 12983 • (518) 891-4150

Stevenson Society of America • Robert Louis Stevenson Memorial Cottage, 44 Stevenson Ln, P.O. Box 1212 • Saranac Lake, NY 12983 • (518) 891-1462 • http://www.pennypiper.org

Trudeau Institute • 154 Algonquin Ave, P.O. Box 59 • Saranac Lake, NY 12983 • (518) 891-3080 • http://www.trudeauinstitute.org

Saratoga Springs
Heritage Hunters • P.O. Box 1389 • Saratoga Springs, NY 12866-0884 • (518) 587-5852 • http://www.rootsweb.com/~nysarato/

Historical Society of Saratoga Springs • Historical Museum, Casino St & Congress Park, P.O. Box 216 • Saratoga Springs, NY 12866 • (518) 584-6920 • http://www.saratogasprings-historymuseum.org

New York State Military Museum • 61 Lake Ave • Saratoga Springs, NY 12866 • (518) 581-5111 • http://www.dmna.state.ny.us/historic/mil-hist.htm

Northeastern New York Genealogical Society • 222 Nelson Ave • Saratoga Springs, NY 12866-3419

Saratoga Springs, cont.

Saratoga Automobile Museum • 110 Avenue of the Pines • Saratoga Springs, NY 12866 • (518) 587-1935 • http://www. saratogaautomuseum.com

Saratoga Springs Public Library • 49 Henry St • Saratoga Springs, NY 12866 • (518) 584-7860 • http://www.library.saratoga.ny.us

Saratogian Library • 20 Lake Ave • Saratoga Springs, NY 12866 • (518) 584-4242 • http://www.saratogian.com

Sardinia

Sardinia Historical Society • Savage Rd • Sardinia, NY 14134 • (716) 496-8847

Saugerties

Opus 40 and the Quarryman's Museum • 50 Fite Rd • Saugerties, NY 12477 • (845) 246-3400 • http://www.opus40.org

Saugerties Historical Society • Kierstede House, 119 Main St, P.O. Box 194 • Saugerties, NY 12477 • (845) 246-9529

Saugerties Public Library • 91 Washington Ave • Saugerties, NY 12477 • (845) 246-4317 • http://saugertiespubliclibrary.org

Sayville

Sayville Historical Society • Edwards Homestead Museum, 39 Edwards St, P.O. Box 41 • Sayville, NY 11782 • (631) 563-0186 • http://www.sayville.com/history.html

Sayville Public Library • 11 Collins Ave • Sayville, NY 11782-3199 • (631) 589-4440 • http://www.sayville.suffolk.lib.ny.us

Scarsdale

Scarsdale Historical Society • Cudner-Hyatt House Museum, 937 Post Rd, P.O. Box 431 • Scarsdale, NY 10583 • (914) 723-1744 • http://www.scarsdalehistory.org

Scarsdale Public Library • 54 Olmstead Rd • Scarsdale, NY 10583 • (914) 722-1300 • http://www.scarsdalelibrary.org

Schaghticoke

Knickerbocker Historical Society • 166 Knickerbocker Rd, P.O. Box 29 • Schaghticoke, NY 12154 • (518) 677-3807

Schenectady

Efner History Center • City Hall, Rm A-1, 105 Jay St • Schenectady, NY 12305 • (518) 382-5088 • http://www.schist.org/cityhist.html

Niskayuna Historical Society • Town Hall, 1 Niskayuna Cr • Schenectady, NY 12309 • (518) 783-1190 • http://www. schenectadyhistory.org

Princetown Historical Society • 559 N Kelly Rd • Schenectady, NY 12306 • (518) 864-5218

Schaffer Library • Union College, 807 Union St • Schenectady, NY 12308 • (518) 388-6281 • http://www.union.edu/public/library/

Schenectady County Historical Society • Historical Museum, 32 Washington Ave • Schenectady, NY 12305 • (518) 374-0263 • http://www.schist.org

Schenectady County Public Library • 99 Clinton St • Schenectady, NY 12305-2083 • (518) 382-4500 • http://www.scpl.org

Schenectady Museum • 15 Nott Terrace Heights • Schenectady, NY 12308 • (518) 382-7890 • http://www.schenectadymuseum.org

Schoharie

Old Stone Fort Museum • 145 Fort Rd • Schoharie, NY 12157 • (518) 296-7192 • http://www.theoldstonefort.org

Schoharie Colonial Heritage Association • 1743 Palatine House Museum, Spring St, P.O. Box 554 • Schoharie, NY 12157 • (518) 295-7505 • http://www.midtel.net/~scha

Schoharie County Historical Society • 145 Fort Rd • Schoharie, NY 12157 • (518) 295-7192 • http://schohariehistory.net

Schoharie Free Library • Bridge St & Knower Ave, P.O. Box 519 • Schoharie, NY 12157-0519 • (518) 295-7127

Schroon Lake

Schroon Lake Public Library • South Ave, P.O. Box 398 • Schroon Lake, NY 12870 • (518) 532-7737 • http://www.cefls.org/schroonlake. htm

Schroon-North Hudson Historical Society • Main St, P.O. Box 444 • Schroon Lake, NY 12870 • (518) 532-9194 • http://www.schroon.net

Schuyler Lake

Exeter Historical Society • P.O. Box 153 • Schuyler Lake, NY 13457 • http://www.rootsweb.com/~nyotsego/exeterhistorical.htm

Schuylerville

General Philip Schuyler Home Museum • Rte 4 • Schuylerville, NY 12871 • (518) 664-9821

Schuylerville Public Library • 52 Ferry St • Schuylerville, NY 12871 • (518) 695-6641 • http://www.sals.edu/schuylerville.shtml

Scio

Scio Free Library • 4393 W Sciota St, P.O. Box 77 • Scio, NY 14880-0075 • (585) 593-4816 • http://www.stls.org/Scio

Scotia

Palatines to America, New York Chapter • 18 Droms Rd • Scotia, NY 13202-5304 • (518) 399-6187

Scotia History Center • Flint House, 4 N Ten Broeck St • Scotia, NY 12302 • (518) 377-8799 • http://www.flinthouse.org

Scottsville

Wheatland Historical Association • Sage-Marlow House & Local History Room, 69 Main St, P.O. Box 184 • Scottsville, NY 14546-0184 • (585) 889-4574 • http://www.townofwheatland.org/History/

Sea Cliff

Sea Cliff Village Museum • 95 10th Ave • Sea Cliff, NY 11579 • (516) 671-0090 • http://www.seacliffhistory.com

Seaford

Seaford Historical Society • Historical Museum, 3890 Waverly Ave • Seaford, NY 11783 • (516) 826-1150 • http://www.wantagh.lib.ny.us

Selkirk

Town of Bethelehem Historical Association • Old Cedar Hill Schoolhouse Museum, 1003 River Rd • Selkirk, NY 12158 • (518) 767-9432 • http://www.townofbethlehem.org

Seneca Falls

Becker 1880 House Museum • 55 Cayuga St • Seneca Falls, NY 13148 • (315) 568-8412

Elizabeth Cady Stanton House Museum • 32 Washington St • Seneca Falls, NY 13148

Finger Lakes Genealogical Society • P.O. Box 581 • Seneca Falls, NY 13148

Seneca Falls Historical Society • Historical Museum, 55 Cayuga St • Seneca Falls, NY 13148 • (315) 568-8412 • http://www. sfhistoricalsociety.org

Seneca Falls Library • 47 Cayuga St • Seneca Falls, NY 13148 • (315) 568-8265 • http://www.senecafallslibrary.org

Town and Village of Seneca Falls Heritage Area • 115 Fall St, P.O. Box 108 • Seneca Falls, NY 13148 • (315) 568-6894

Women's Rights National Historic Park • 136 Fall St • Seneca Falls, NY 13148 • (315) 568-2991

Setauket

Emma S Clark Memorial Library • 120 Main St • Setauket, NY 11733-2868 • (516) 941-4080 • http://emma.suffolk.lib.ny.us

Sherwood-Jayne House Museum • Old Post Rd • Setauket, NY 11733 • (516) 751-6610

Thompson House Museum • N Country Rd • Setauket, NY 11733 • (516) 971-9716

Three Village Historic Society • Historical Museum, 93 N Country Rd • Setauket, NY 11733-1347 • (631) 751-3730 • http://www.threevillagehistoricalsociety.org

Sharon Springs
Sharon Historical Society • Historical Museum, Main St, P.O. Box 176 • Sharon Springs, NY 13459 • (518) 284-2350 • http://sharonsprings.com/sharonhistoricalsociety.htm

Shelter Island
Shelter Island Historical Society • Old Havens House Museum, 16 S Ferry Rd, P.O. Box 847 • Shelter Island, NY 11964 • (631) 749-0025 • http://www.shelterislandhistsoc.org

Shelter Island Public Library • 37 N Ferry Rd, P.O. Box 2016 • Shelter Island, NY 11964-2016 • (631) 749-0042

Sherburne
Sherburne Public Library • 2 E State St, P.O. Box 702 • Sherburne, NY 13450-0702 • (607) 674-4242 • http://www.4cls.org/webpages/members/Sherburne/Sherburne.html

Sheridan
Sheridan Historical Society • Historical Center, Town Hall, 2702 Route 20, P.O. Box 95 • Sheridan, NY 14135 • (716) 672-2201 • http://www.townofsheridan.com/sheridan-ny-history.asp

Sherman
Yorker Museum • Park & Church Sts • Sherman, NY 14781 • (716) 761-6789

Shirley
DeVito Italian American Society • P.O. Box 538 • Shirley, NY 11967 • (631) 399-5408

Mastics-Moriches-Shirley Comm Library • 407 William Floyd Pkwy • Shirley, NY 11967-3492 • (631) 399-1511 • http://www.communitylibrary.org

Shokan
Town of Olive Historical Society • Historical Museum, P.O. Box 366 • Shokan, NY 12481 • (845) 657-2482 • http://olive.westshokan.lib.ny.us

Shortsville
Lehigh Valley Railroad Historical Society • 8 E High St • Shortsville, NY 14548 • (585) 289-9149

Sidney
Sidney Historical Association • Historical Museum, 21 Liberty St, P.O. Box 2217 • Sidney, NY 13838 • (607) 563-3916 • http://www.sidneyonline.com/sha.htm

Sidney Memorial Public Library • 8 River St • Sidney, NY 13838 • (607) 563-1200 • http://www.lib.4cty.org/sidney/smpl.htm

Sidney Center
Maywood Historical Group of Sidney Center • O&W Depot, P.O. Box 298 • Sidney Center, NY 13839 • (607) 369-7592 • http://www.nhgonline.org

Silver Creek
Anderson-Lee Library • 43 Main St • Silver Creek, NY 14136 • (716) 934-3468 • http://www.cclslib.org/silver~l/silver~/.htm

Hanover Historical Center • 68 Hanover St • Silver Creek, NY 14136 • (716) 934-0869 • http://www.co.chautauqua.ny.us/municipal/hanover_list.htm

Sinclairville
Sinclairville Free Library • 15 Main St, P.O. Box 609 • Sinclairville, NY 14782-0609 • (716) 962-5885 • http://www.cclslib.org/sinclairville

Valley Historical Society • Lester & Main St, P.O. Box 1045 • Sinclairville, NY 14782 • (716) 962-8520

Skaneateles
Skaneateles Historical Society • The Creamery, 28 Hannum St • Skaneateles, NY 13152 • (315) 685-1360 • http://www.skaneateles.com/history.html

Skaneateles Library Association • 49 E Genesee • Skaneateles, NY 13152 • (315) 685-5135 • http://www.skaneateleslibrary.com

Slaterville Springs
Town of Caroline History Room • Town Hall, 2670 Slaterville Rd, P.O. Box 36 • Slaterville Springs, NY 14881 • (607) 539-6400 • http://www.carolinehistorian.org

Sleepy Hollow
Friends of the Old Dutch Burying Ground • P.O. Box 832 • Sleepy Hollow, NY 10591 • http://www.olddutchburyingground.org

Kykuit-Rockefeller House Museum and Gardens • Route 9 • Sleepy Hollow, NY 10591 • (914) 631-8200

Old Dutch Church of Sleepy Hollow Museum • 430 N Broadway • Sleepy Hollow, NY 10591 • (914) 631-4497 • http://www.rctodc.org

Philipsburg Manor Museum • 381 N Broadway • Sleepy Hollow, NY 10591 • (914) 631-3992 • http://www.hudsonvalley.org

Rockefeller Archive Center • 15 Dayton Ave • Sleepy Hollow, NY 10591-1598 • (914) 631-4505 • http://rockefeller.edu/archive.ctr/

Sloatsburg
Sloatsburg Historical Society • P.O. Box 34 • Sloatsburg, NY 10974 • (845) 753-8248 • http://www.sloatsburgny.com/History.htm

Sloatsburg Public Library • 1 Liberty Rock Rd • Sloatsburg, NY 10974-2392 • (845) 753-2001 • http://www.bestweb.net/~slolib

Smithtown
Smithtown Historical Society • Caleb Smith House Museum, 5 N County Rd, P.O. Box 69 • Smithtown, NY 11787 • (631) 265-6768 • http://www.smithtownhistorical.org

Smithtown Library • 1 N Country Rd • Smithtown, NY 11787 • (631) 265-2072 x38 • http://www.smithlib.org

Straus Historical Society • 178 Oakside Dr • Smithtown, NY 11787 • (631) 265-0383

Smithville Flats
Smithville Historical Society • P.O. Box 176 • Smithville Flats, NY 13841 • (607) 656-8527

Smyrna
Smyrna Public Library • 7 E Main St, P.O. Box 202 • Smyrna, NY 13464-0202 • (607) 627-6271 • http://www.4cls.org/chenango.html

Sodus Point
Sodus Bay Historical Society • Historical Museum, 7606 N Ontario St, P.O. Box 94 • Sodus Point, NY 14551 • (315) 483-4936 • http://www.soduspointlighthouse.org

Solvay
Solvay Public Library • 615 Woods Rd • Solvay, NY 13209-1697 • (315) 468-2441 • http://www.ocpl.lib.ny.us

Somers
Somers Historical Society • Elephant Hotel Museum, 355 Route 202, P.O. Box 336 • Somers, NY 10589 • (914) 277-4977 • http://www.somersmuseum.org

Somers Public Library • Reis Park, Rte 139, P.O. Box 443 • Somers, NY 10589 • (914) 232-5717 • http://www.somerslibrary.org

South Butler
Butler Historical Preservation Society • Butler Center Church Museum, 4885 Butler Center Rd, P.O. Box 34 • South Butler, NY 13154 • (315) 594-2332

South Glens Falls
Historical Society of Moreau and South Glens Falls • Parks-Bentley House Museum, 53 Ferry Blvd • South Glens Falls, NY 12803 • (518) 745-7741 • http://www.townofmoreau.org/parks_bently_house.htm

Northeastern New York Genealogical Society • 9 Lydia St • South Glens Falls, NY 12803

South New Berlin
Nathan Taylor Yorkers Museum • N Main St • South New Berlin, NY 13843

South New Berlin Free Library • 8 Main St, P.O. Box 9 • South New Berlin, NY 13843-0009 • (607) 859-2420 • http://www.rcls.org/chenango.html

South Salem
Lewisboro Historical Society • 141 Spring St • South Salem, NY 10590 • (914) 763-3326

Southampton
Halsey Homestead Museum • S Main St, P.O. Box 303 • Southampton, NY 11969 • (516) 283-2494

Shinnecock Indian Nation • Historical Museum, P.O. Box 5006 • Southampton, NY 11969-5006 • (631) 283-6143 • http://www.shinnecocknation.com

Southampton Colonial Society • Historical Museum, 17 Meeting House Ln, P.O. Box 303 • Southampton, NY 11969 • (631) 283-1612 • http://www.southamptonhistorymuseum.com

Southold
Southold Free Library & Whitaker Historical Collection • 53705 Main Rd, P.O. Box 697 • Southold, NY 11971 • (516) 765-2077 • http://sohd.suffolk.lib.ny.us

Southold Historical Society • Historical Museum, 54235 Main St, P.O. Box 1 • Southold, NY 11971 • (631) 765-5500 • http://www.southholdhistoricalsociety.org

Southold Indian Museum • 1080 Bayview Rd, P.O. Box 268 • Southold, NY 11971 • (631) 765-5577 • http://southoldindianmuseum.org

Spencer
Spencer Historical Society • Historical Museum, Center St, P.O. Box 71 • Spencer, NY 14883 • (607) 589-4806

Spencer Library • 41 Main St, P.O. Box 305 • Spencer, NY 14883 • (607) 589-4496 • http://www.flls.org/memberpages/spencer.htm

Spencerport
Ogden Farmers' Library • 269 Ogden Center Rd • Spencerport, NY 14559-2076 • (585) 352-2141 • http://www.ogdenny.com/Library

Ogden Historical Society • Historical Museum, 568 Colby St • Spencerport, NY 14559 • (585) 352-0660

Western Monroe County Genealogical Society • c/o Ogden Farmers' Library, 269 Ogden Center Rd • Spencerport, NY 14559 • (585) 352-2141

Spring Valley
Finkelstein Memorial Library • 24 Chestnut St • Spring Valley, NY 10977-5594 • (845) 352-5700 • http://finkelsteinlibrary.org

Springfield Center
Springfield Historical Society • Community Center • Springfield Center, NY 13468 • (315) 858-2151

Springfield Library Association • County Route 29A, P.O. Box 142 • Springfield Center, NY 13468 • (315) 858-5802

Springville
Concord Historical Society • Warner Museum, 98 E Main St, P.O. Box 425 • Springville, NY 14141 • (716) 592-5546 • http://www.springvillechamber.com/historical_society

Springwater
East Springwater Historical Society • general delivery • Springwater, NY 14560 • (716) 383-1561

Springwater-Websters Crossing Historical Society • P.O. Box 68 • Springwater, NY 14560 • (585) 669-2740

Staatsburg
Mills Mansion State Historic Site • Old Post Rd, P.O. Box 308 • Staatsburg, NY 12580 • (914) 889-8851

Stamford
Stamford Historical Society • 64 Main St • Stamford, NY 12167-1141 • (607) 652-7299

Stamford Village Library • 117 Main St • Stamford, NY 12167 • (607) 652-5001 • http://www.4cls.org/webpages/members/Stamford/Stamford.html

Stanfordville
Stanford Historical Society • 1915 Bengall Post Office Museum, RR1, Box 461 • Stanfordville, NY 12581

Star Lake
Fine Town Historian • P.O. Box 238 • Star Lake, NY 13690 • (315) 848-3121

Staten Island
Alice Austen House Museum • Alice Austen Park, 2 Hylan Blvd • Staten Island, NY 10305 • (718) 816-4506 • http://www.aliceausten.org

Center for Migration Studies of New York Archives • 209 Flagg Pl • Staten Island, NY 10304 • (718) 351-8800 • http://www.cmsny.org

College of Staten Island - Special Collections • CUNY - Library 1L-216, 2800 Victory Blvd • Staten Island, NY 10314 • (718) 982-4128 • http://www.library.csu.cuny.edu/archives

Conference House Museum • 7455 Hylan Blvd, P.O. Box 171 • Staten Island, NY 10307 • (718) 984-6046

Friends of Abandoned Cemeteries of Staten Island • 315 Sharon Ave • Staten Island, NY 10301 • (917) 545-3309 • http://mystatenisland.com/facsi

Garibaldi and Meducci Museum • 420 Tompkins Ave • Staten Island, NY 10305 • (718) 442-1608 • http://www.garibaldimeuccimuseum.org

Historic Richmondtown Museum • 441 Clarke Ave • Staten Island, NY 10306 • (718) 351-1611 • http://www.historicrichmondtown.org

Horrmann Library • Wagner College, 1 Campus Rd • Staten Island, NY 10301 • (718) 390-3401 • http://www.wagner.edu

Noble Maritime Collection Museum • 1000 Richmond Terr • Staten Island, NY 10301 • (718) 447-6490 • http://www.noblemaritime.org

Sandy Ground Historical Society • 1538 Woodrow Rd • Staten Island, NY 10309 • (718) 317-5796 • http://www.statenislandusa.org/pages/sandy_ground.html

Seguine-Burke Plantation Museum • 440 Seguine Ave • Staten Island, NY 10307 • (718) 667-6042

Snug Harbor Cultural Center • 914 Richmond Terrace • Staten Island, NY 10301 • (718) 448-2500 • http://www.snug-harbor.org

Staten Island Historical Society • Historical Museum, 441 Clarke Ave • Staten Island, NY 10306-1125 • (718) 351-1611 • http://www.historicrichmondtown.org

Staten Island Museum • 75 Stuyvesant Pl • Staten Island, NY 10301-1912 • (718) 727-1135 • http://www.statenislandmuseum.org

Tottenville Historical Society • P.O. Box 70185 • Staten Island, NY 10307-0185 • (646) 291-7005 • http://tottenvillehistory.com

Stattsburg
Stattsburgh State Historic Site Museum • Old Post Rd • Stattsburg, NY 12580 • (845) 889-8851

Stephentown
Stephentown Historical Society • Staples & Garfield Rds, P.O. Box 11 • Stephentown, NY 12168 • (518) 733-6070 • http://www.cbsco.com/shs

Sterling
Sterling Historical Society • Little Red Schoolhouse Museum, 14352 Woods Rd • Sterling, NY 13156 • (315) 564-6189 • http://www.lakeontario.net/sterlinghistory

Stillwater
Satagoa National Historical Park • 648 Route 32 • Stillwater, NY 12170 • (518) 664-9821 • http://www.nps.gov/sara

Stockton
Mary E Seymour Memorial Free Library • 22 N Main St, P.O. Box 128 • Stockton, NY 14784-0128 • (716) 595-3323 • http://www.cclslib.org/cassadaga

Stone Ridge
Macdonald DeWitt Library • Ulster County Community College • Stone Ridge, NY 12484 • (845) 687-5208 • http://www.sunyulster.edu/resources/library.asp

Stone Ridge Library • Route 209, Box 188 • Stone Ridge, NY 12484 • (845) 687-7023

Stony Brook
Center for Italian Studies • Melville Library, Stony Brook Univ • Stony Brook, NY 11794 • (631) 632-7444 • http://www.italianstudies.org/center

Frank Melville Memorial Library - Special Collections • SUNY at Stony Brook • Stony Brook, NY 11794-3323 • (516) 632-7100 • http://www.sunysb.edu/libspecial/

Long Island Indian Culture Museum • Hoyt Farm Park, P.O Box 1542 • Stony Brook, NY 11790 • (516) 929-8725 • http://www.longisland.com/museums/

Long Island Museum of History • 1200 Route 25A • Stony Brook, NY 11790 • (631) 751-0066 • http://www.longislandmuseum.org

Long Islands Studies Council • P.O. Box 555 • Stony Brook, NY 11790 • http://www.sunysb.edu/libspecial/collections/manuscripts/liephemera.html

Museums at Stony Brook • Kate Strong Historical Library, 1208 Route 25-A • Stony Brook, NY 11790 • (631) 751-0066

Stony Brook Historical Society • P.O. Box 802 • Stony Brook, NY 11790

Stony Creek
Stony Creek Historical Association • 4 Murray Rd • Stony Creek, NY 12878 • (518) 696-3762 • http://www.stonycreekny.org

Stony Point
Rose Memorial Library Association • 79 E Main St • Stony Point, NY 10980-1699 • (845) 786-2100

Stony Point Battlefield Historic Site Museum • US Route 9W, P.O. Box 182 • Stony Point, NY 10980 • (845) 786-2521 • http://www.nysparks.com

Stony Ridge
Ulster County Historical Society • P.O. Box 279 • Stony Ridge, NY 12484 • (845) 338-5614 • http://www.bevierhousemuseum.org

Strykersville
Sheldon Historical Society • 3929 Main St • Strykersville, NY 14145 • (585) 457-3444 • http://freepages.genealogy.rootsweb.com/~evansandobertein/sheldonhistoricalsociety

Suffern
Suffern Free Library • 210 Lafayette Ave • Suffern, NY 10901 • (845) 357-1237 • http://www.rcls.org/sufpl

Sugar Loaf
Sugar Loaf Historical Society • P.O. Box 114 • Sugar Loaf, NY 10981-0114 • http://www.sugarloafhistoricalsociety.com

Syosset
Friends for Long Island's Heritage • 1864 Muttontown Rd • Syosset, NY 11791-9652 • (516) 571-7600

Orthodox Church in America • P.O. Box 675 • Syosset, NY 11791 • (516) 922-0550

Syosset Public Library • 225 S Oyster Bay Rd • Syosset, NY 11791-5897 • (516) 921-7161 • http://www.nassaulibrary.org/syosset

Syracuse
Canal Society of New York State • Historical Museum, 311 Montgomery St • Syracuse, NY 13202 • (315) 428-1862 • http://www.canalsyns.org

Central New York Genealogical Society • P.O. Box 104, Colvin Sta • Syracuse, NY 13205-0104 • http://www.rootsweb.com/~nycnygs

E S Bird Library • Syracuse Univ, 222 Waverly Ave • Syracuse, NY 13244-2010 • (315) 443-2573

Erie Canal Museum • Weighlock Bldg, 318 Erie Blvd E • Syracuse, NY 13202 • (315) 471-0593 • http://www.eriecanalmuseum.org

New York State Council of Genealogical Organizations • P.O. Box 2593 • Syracuse, NY 13220-2593 • (315) 262-2800 • http://www.rootsweb.com/~nyscogo/

Oneida Community Collection • Syracyse Univ Library, 222 Waverly Ave • Syracuse, NY 13244 • (315) 443-2093 • http://library.sry.edu

Onondaga County Public Library • 447 S Salina St • Syracuse, NY 13202-2494 • (315) 448-1800 • http://www.ocpl.lib.ny.us

Onondaga Free Library • 4840 W Seneca Tpk • Syracuse, NY 13215 • (315) 492-1727 • http://www.admass.com/library

Onondaga Historical Association • Historical Museum, 311 Montgomery St • Syracuse, NY 13202-2098 • (315) 428-1862 • http://www.cnyhistory.org

Parke S Avery Historical House Museum • 650 James St • Syracuse, NY 13203 • (315) 475-0119

Sidney B Coulter Library • Onondaga Community College, 4941 Onondaga Rd • Syracuse, NY 13215 • (315) 498-2622 • http://www.sunyocc.edu/library

Town of Camillus Historical Society • 4600 W Genesee St • Syracuse, NY 13019 • (315) 487-2326

Tappan
Tappan Library • 93 Main St • Tappan, NY 10983 • (845) 359-3877 • http://www.tappanlibrary.com

Tappantown Historical Society • Historical Museum, P.O. Box 71 • Tappan, NY 10983 • (845) 359-7790 • http://www.masonsamett.com/communitymain.htm

Tarrytown
Historical Society of Sleepy Hollow and Tarrytown • Historical Museum, 1 Grove St • Tarrytown, NY 10591 • (914) 631-8374 • http://www.sleepyhollowchamber.com/history.html

Lyndhurst House Museum • 635 S Broadway • Tarrytown, NY 10591 • (914) 631-4481 • http://www.lyndhurst.org

Tarrytown, cont.

Warner Library • 121 N Broadway • Tarrytown, NY 10591 • (914) 631-7734 • http://westchesterlibraries.org

Washington Irving's Sunnyside House Museum • 3 W Sunnyside Ln • Tarrytown, NY 10533 • (914) 591-8763 • http://www.hudsonvalley.org

Theresa

Antwerp Town Historian • 34542 County Route 22 • Theresa, NY 13691 • (315) 287-2293

Theresa Free Library • 301 Main St • Theresa, NY 13691 • (315) 628-5972 • http://www.northnet.org/theresalibrary

Thousand Island Park

Thousand Island Park Library • 42743 St Lawrence Ave, P.O. Box 1115 • Thousand Island Park, NY 13692 • (315) 482-9098

Three Mile Bay

Lyme Heritage Center • 28589 Empire Rd • Three Mile Bay, NY 13693 • (315) 649-5452

Ticonderoga

Black Watch Memorial Library • 99 Montcalm St • Ticonderoga, NY 12883 • (518) 585-7380 • http://www.cefls.org/ticonderoga.htm

Fort Ticonderoga Museum • 30 Fort Rd, P.O. Box 390 • Ticonderoga, NY 12883 • (518) 585-2821 • http://www.fort-ticonderoga.org

Fort Ticonderoga-Thompson-Pell Research Center • Fort Rd, P.O. Box 390 • Ticonderoga, NY 12883 • (518) 585-2821 • http://www.fort-ticonderoga.org

Ticonderoga Historical Society • Hancock House, 6 Moses Cr • Ticonderoga, NY 12883 • (518) 585-7868 • http://www.thehancockhouse.org

Tonawanda

Buffalo and Western New York Italian Genealogy Society • 238 Fairways Blvd • Tonawanda, NY 14510-3168 • (716) 632-6658

Historical Society of the Tonawandas • Historical Museum, 113 Main St • Tonawanda, NY 14150-2129 • (716) 694-7406 • http://www.tonawandahistory.org

Tonawanda-Kenmore Historical Society • Historical Museum, 100 Knoche Rd • Tonawanda, NY 14150 • (716) 873-5774 • http://www.tonawanda.ny.us/history

Troy

Brunswick Historical Society • RR 2 • Troy, NY 12180 • (518) 279-4024

Burden Iron Works Musuem • Polk St • Troy, NY 12180-5539 • (518) 274-5267 • http://www.rip.edu/~carroll/gateway1.html

Folsom Library • Rensselaer Univ, 110 8th St • Troy, NY 12180-3590 • (518) 276-8320 • http://www.lib.rpi.edu

Hudson Mohawk Industrial Gateway Society • Polk St • Troy, NY 12180

Rensselaer County Historical Society • Hart-Cluett Mansion Museum, 59 2nd St • Troy, NY 12180 • (518) 272-7232 • http://www.rchsonline.org

Troy Public Library • 100 2nd St • Troy, NY 12180-4005 • (518) 274-7071 • http://www.uhls.org/troy

Trumansburg

Enfield Historical Society • 398 Harvey Hill Rd • Trumansburg, NY 14886 • (607) 273-5369

Ulysses Historical Society • 39 South St, P.O. Box 445 • Trumansburg, NY 14886-0445 • (607) 387-6666 • http://www.rootsweb.com/~nytompki/ulysses/ulysses_hs.htm

Ulysses Philomathic Library • 74 E Main St, PO Box 705 • Trumansburg, NY 14886-0705 • (607) 387-5623 • http://www.flls.org

Tuckahoe

Tuckahoe Public Library • 71 Columbus Ave • Tuckahoe, NY 10707 • (914) 961-2121

Tully

Tully Area Historical Society • 22 State St, P.O. Box 22 • Tully, NY 13159-0022 • (315) 696-5219 • http://villageoftully.org/content/History

Tully Free Library • 12 State St, P.O. Box 250 • Tully, NY 13159-0250 • (315) 696-8606 • http://tullylibrary.org

Tupper Lake

Goff-Nelson Memorial Library • 41 Lake St • Tupper Lake, NY 12986 • (518) 359-9421 • http://www.cefls.org/tupperlake.htm

Turin

Turin Town Historian • 4116 State Route 26, P.O. Box 147 • Turin, NY 13473 • (315) 348-8507

Tuxedo Park

Hereditary Order of Descendants of Colonial Governors • 4 Stable Rd • Tuxedo Park, NY 10987-4025

Tuxedo Historical Society • 7 Hospital Rd, P.O. Box 188 • Tuxedo, NY 10987 • (845) 351-2926 • http://www.tuxedogov.org

Tuxedo Park Historic Preservation • 7 W Lake Dr • Tuxedo Park, NY 10987 • (845) 351-2568

Tuxedo Park Library • P.O. Box 776 • Tuxedo Park, NY 10987-0776 • (845) 351-2207 • http://www.rcls.org/tuxpl

Ulster Park

Klyne-Esopus Historical Society • Historical Museum, 764 Route 9W, P.O. Box 180 • Ulster Park, NY 12487 • (845) 338-8109 • http://www.klyneesopusmuseum.org

Unadilla

Unadilla Public Library • 193 Main St, P.O. Box 632 • Unadilla, NY 13849-0632 • (607) 369-3131

Union Springs

Frontenac Historical Society • 178 N Cayuga St, P.O. Box 338 • Union Springs, NY 13160 • (315) 889-7767 • http://www.members.aol.com/nhecht7725/FRONTENAC

Uniondale

Nassau Library System • 900 Jerusalem Ave • Uniondale, NY 11553-9998 • (516) 292-8920

Upper Jay

Wells Memorial Library • Route 9 N, P.O. Box 57 • Upper Jay, NY 12987-0057 • (518) 946-2644 • http://www.wellsmemoriallibrary.homestead.com

Utica

Children's Museum of History • 311 Main St • Utica, NY 13501 • (315) 724-6129 • http://www.museum4kids.net

Frank E Gannett Library • Uitca College, 1600 Burstone Rd • Utica, NY 13502 • (315) 792-3151 • http://www.utica.edu/academic/library

Oneida County Genealogical Club • 318 Genesee St • Utica, NY 13502

Oneida County Historical Society • Historical Museum, 1608 Genesee St • Utica, NY 13502-5425 • (315) 735-3642 • http://www.oneidacountyhistory.org

Utica Public Library • 303 Genesee St • Utica, NY 13501 • (315) 735-2279 • http://www.uticapubliclibrary.org

Vails Gate

Ellison House Museum • 289 Forge Hill Rd • Vails Gate, NY 12584 • (914) 561-5498

Knox Headquarters State Historic Site Museum • Forge Hill Rd & Route 94, P.O. Box 207 • Vails Gate, NY 12584 • (845) 561-5498 • http://www.friendsofpalisades.org

National Temple Hill Association • Edmonston House, 1042 Route 94, P.O. Box 315 • Vails Gate, NY 12584 • (845) 561-5073 • http://www.nationaltemplehill.org

New Windsor Catonment State Historic Site Museum • 374 Rte 300, Temple Hill Rd, P.O. Box 207 • Vails Gate, NY 12584 • (845) 561-1765 • http://www.friendsofpalisades.org

Valhalla
Mount Pleasant Historical Society • 1 Town Hall Plaza • Valhalla, NY 10595-1399 • (914) 769-4734

Westchester County Historical Society • Hartford House, 75 Grasslands Rd • Valhalla, NY 10595 • (914) 592-4323

Valley Cottage
Valley Cottage Free Library • 110 Route 303 • Valley Cottage, NY 10989 • (845) 268-7700 • http://www.vclib.org

Valley Falls
Pittstown Historical Society • P.O. Box 252 • Valley Falls, NY 12185

Valley Stream
Henry Waldinger Memorial Library • 60 Verona Pl • Valley Stream, NY 11582-3011 • (516) 825-6422 • http://www.nassaulibrary.org/valleyst/

Valley Stream Historical Society • 143 Hendrickson Ave, P.O. Box 22 • Valley Stream, NY 11582 • (516) 872-4159 • http://www.nassaulibrary.org/valleyst/ushist.html

Vernon
Vernon Historical Society • P.O. Box 786 • Vernon, NY 13476 • (315) 768-7091

Verplanck
Cortlandt Museum and Historical Society • Historical Museum, 137 7th St, P.O. Box 473 • Verplanck, NY 10596 • (914) 734-1110

Versailles
Cayuga Indian Nation • P.O. Box 11 • Versailles, NY 14168 • (716) 532-4847

Vestal
Southern Tier Genealogy Club of Broome County • P.O. Box 680 • Vestal, NY 13851-0680 • http://www.rootsweb.com/~nybroome/stgs/stgs.htm

Vestal Historical Society • Historical Museum, 328 Vestal Pkwy E • Vestal, NY 13850 • (607) 748-1432 • http://www.tier.net/vestalhistory

Vestal Public Library • 320 Vestal Pkwy E • Vestal, NY 13850-1682 • (607) 754-4243 • http://lib.4cty.org/vestal-r.html

Victor
Ganondagan State Historic Site Museum • 1488 Victor Bloomfield Rd, P.O. Box 113 • Victor, NY 14564 • (585) 924-5848 • http://www.ganondagan.org

Valentown Historical Society • Historical Museum, 7377 Valentown Sq, P.O. Box 472 • Victor, NY 14564 • (585) 924-4170 • http://www.valentown.org

Voorheesville
New Scotland Historical Association • P.O. Box 541 • Voorheesville, NY 12186 • (518) 756-7670 • http://www.townofnewscotland.com

Voorheesville Public Library • 51 School Rd • Voorheesville, NY 12186 • (518) 765-2791 • http://www.voorheesvillelibrary.org

Waddington
Moore Museum • 79 W Saint Lawrence Ave, P.O. Box 277 • Waddington, NY 13694 • (315) 388-5967

Waddington Historian • Moore Museum, P.O. Box 277 • Waddington, NY 13694 • (315) 388-5967

Wadhams
Wadhams Free Library • Route 22 • Wadhams, NY 12990 • (518) 962-8717 • http://www.cefls.org/wadhams.htm

Wading River
Wading River Historical Society • 300 N Country Rd, P.O. Box 263 • Wading River, NY 11792 • (631) 929-4082

Walden
Historical Society of Walden and Wallkill Valley • Walden House Museum, 34 N Montgomery St, P.O. Box 48 • Walden, NY 12586 • (845) 778-7428

Wallkill
Historical Society of Shawangunk and Gardiner • P.O. Box 570 • Wallkill, NY 12589 • http://www.shawangunk.org

Wallomsac
Bennington Battlefield State Historic Site Museum • Route 67 • Wallomsac, NY 12133 • (518) 279-1155 • http://www.nysparks.state.ny.us

Walton
Walton Historical Society • Eells House, 9 Townsend St, P.O. Box 165 • Walton, NY 13856 • (607) 865-5895 • http://www.waltonhistoricalsociety.org

William B Ogden Free Library • 42 Gardiner Pl • Walton, NY 13856 • (607) 865-5929 • http://www.4cls.org/webpages/members/Walton/Walton.html

Walworth
Walworth Historical Society • Historical Museum, 2257 Academy St, P.O. Box 142 • Walworth, NY 14568 • (315) 524-9528

Wantagh
Wantagh Historical and Preservation Society • Historical Museum, 1700 Wantaugh Ave, P.O. Box 132 • Wantagh, NY 11793 • (516) 926-8767

Wantagh Public Library • 3285 Park Ave • Wantagh, NY 11793 • (516) 221-1200 • http://www.nassaulibrary.org/wantagh

Wantagh Public Library • 3285 Park Ave • Wantagh, NY 11793 • (516) 221-1200

Wappingers Falls
Bowdoin Park Historical and Archeology Association • 85 Sheafe Rd • Wappingers Falls, NY 12590 • (845) 297-1224 • http://www.dutchessny.gov

Warrensburg
Richards Library • 35-38 Elm St • Warrensburg, NY 12885 • (518) 623-3011 • http://www.sals.edu/warrensburg.shtml

Warsaw
Warsaw Historical Society • Gates House Museum, 15 Perry Ave, P.O. Box 132 • Warsaw, NY 14569 • (585) 786-5240 • http://warsawhistory.org/society

Warwick
Albert Wisner Public Library • 2 Colonial Ave • Warwick, NY 10990-1191 • (845) 986-1047 • http://www.albertwisnerlibrary.org

Historical Society of the Town of Warwick • Shingle House Museum, Forester Ave, P.O. Box 353 • Warwick, NY 10990 • (845) 986-3236 • http://www.warwickhistoricalsociety.org

Pacem in Terris House Museum • 96 Covered Bridge Rd • Warwick, NY 10990 • (845) 986-4329

Water Mill
Water Mill Museum • 41 Old Mill Rd, P.O. Box 63 • Water Mill, NY 11976 • (631) 726-4358 • http://www.watermillmuseum.org

Waterford

New York State Bureau of Historic Sites • Peebles Island, P.O. Box 219 • Waterford, NY 12188 • (518) 237-8643 • http://www.nysparks.state.ny.us

Waterford Historical Museum • 2 Museum Ln, P.O. Box 175 • Waterford, NY 12188 • (518) 238-0809 • http://www.waterfordmuseum.com

Waterloo

Mary Ann and Thomas M'Clintock House Museum • general delivery • Waterloo, NY 13165

Memorial Day Museum • 35 E Main St • Waterloo, NY 13165 • (315) 539-0533 • http://www.waterloony.gov

Peter Whitmer Sr Home Museum • 1451 Aunkst Rd • Waterloo, NY 13165 • (315) 539-2552 • http://www.hillcumorah.org

Waterloo Historical Society • Terwiliger Museum, 31 E Williams St • Waterloo, NY 13165 • (315) 539-3313 • http://www.waterloony.gov

Watertown

East Hounsfield Free Library • 19438 State Route 3 • Watertown, NY 13601 • (315) 788-0637

Flower Memorial Library Genealogical Committee • 229 Washington St • Watertown, NY 13601

Jefferson County Genealogical Society • P.O. Box 6453 • Watertown, NY 13601-6453 • http://www.rootsweb.com/~nyjeffer/jeffsox.htm

Jefferson County Historical Society • Historical Museum, 228 Washington St • Watertown, NY 13601 • (315) 782-3491 • http://www.jeffcohistsoc.homstead.com

Melvil Dewey Library • Jefferson Community College, 1220 Coffeen St • Watertown, NY 13601-1897 • (315) 786-2225 • http://www.sunyjefferson.edu/library

Roswell P Flower Memorial Library • 229 Washington St • Watertown, NY 13601 • (315) 788-2352 • http://www.flowermemoriallibrary.org

Sackets Harbor Historical Society • Historical Museum, 100 W Main St • Watertown, NY 13601 • (315) 646-1708

Samaritan Medical Center Library Archives • 830 Washington St • Watertown, NY 13601 • (315) 785-4191 • http://www.samaritanhealth.com/library.html

Watertown City Historian • 245 Washington St, Rm 101 • Watertown, NY 13601 • (315) 785-7769

Watertown Daily Times Newspaper Archive • 260 Washington St • Watertown, NY 13601 • (315) 782-1000 • http://www.watertowndailytimes.com

Watertown Historical Society • 22867 County Route 67 • Watertown, NY 13601 • (315) 658-4774

Waterville

Limestone Ridge Historical Society • 223 E Main St • Waterville, NY 13480 • (315) 821-8103

Waterville Historical Society • 214 White St, P.O. Box 253 • Waterville, NY 13480 • http://www.watervilleny.com/WHS.htm

Waterville Public Library • 220 Main St • Waterville, NY 13480 • (315) 841-4651 • http://www.borg.com/~wpl

Watervliet

Dutch Settlers of Albany • 608 25th St • Watervliet, NY 12189 • (518) 456-7202 • http://www.timesunion.com/communities/dutchsettlers

Watervliet Arsenal Museum • Route 32, 1 Buffington St • Watervliet, NY 12189-4050 • (518) 266-5111 • http://www.wva.army.mil

Watervliet Historical Society • P.O. Box 123 • Watervliet, NY 12189 • (518) 235-6699

Watervliet Public Library • 1501 Broadway • Watervliet, NY 12189 • (518) 274-4471

Waverly

Waverly Free Library • Elizabeth Square, 18 Elizabeth St • Waverly, NY 14892 • (607) 565-9341 • http://www.flls.org/memberpages/waverly.htm

Wayland

Wayland Free Library • 101 W Naples St • Wayland, NY 14572 • (585) 728-5380 • http://www.gunlockelibrary.org

Wayland Historical Society • 100 S Main St, P.O. Box 494 • Wayland, NY 14572 • (716) 728-3610

Webster

Webster Historical Society • Historical Museum, 1000 Ridge Rd • Webster, NY 14580 • (585) 872-1000 • http://www.ci.webster.ny.us/about/history.php

Weedsport

Classic Car Museum • 1 Speedway Dr • Weedsport, NY 13166 • (315) 834-6606 • http://www.dirtmotorsports.com

Old Brutus Historical Society • Historical Museum, 8943 N Seneca St, P.O. Box 516 • Weedsport, NY 14895 • (315) 834-9342 • http://www.rootsweb.com/~nycayuga/obhs/

Weedsport Free Library • 2795 E Brutus St, P.O. Box 1165 • Weedsport, NY 13166 • (315) 834-6222 • http://www.flls.org/weedsport

Wells

Wells Town Historian • P.O. Box 97 • Wells, NY 12190 • (518) 924-2535

Wellsville

David A Howe Public Library • 155 N Main St • Wellsville, NY 14895 • (585) 593-3410 • http://www.davidahowelibrary.org

Mather Homestead Museum • 343 N Main St • Wellsville, NY 14895 • (585) 593-1630

Thelma Rogers Genealogical and Historical Society • 118 E Dyke St, P.O. Box 1331 • Wellsville, NY 14895 • (585) 593-1404

West Chazy

Dodge Library • 9 Rte 348, P.O. Box 226 • West Chazy, NY 12992-0226 • (518) 493-6131

West Harrison

Charles Dawson History Center • 2 E Madison St • West Harrison, NY 10604-1103 • (914) 948-2550

White Plains Historical Society • 60 Park Ave • West Harrison, NY 10604 • (914) 328-1776

West Hempstead

West Hempstead Historical and Preservation Society • P.O. Box 61 • West Hempstead, NY 11552 • (516) 538-6765

West Henrietta

New York Museum of Transportation • 6393 E River Rd, P.O. Box 136 • West Henrietta, NY 14586 • (585) 533-1113 • http://www.nymtmuseum.org

West Hurley

West Hurley Public Library • 42 Clover St • West Hurley, NY 12491 • (845) 679-6405 • http://westhurleylibrary.org

West Islip

West Islip Public Library • 3 Higbie Ln • West Islip, NY 11795-3999 • (631) 661-7080 • http://www.wipublib.org

West Monroe

West Monroe Historical Society • 2355 State Route 49, P.O. Box 53 • West Monroe, NY 13167 • (315) 676-7414 • http://westmonroehistory.org

West Monroe Town Historian • P.O. Box 25 • West Monroe, NY 13167 • (315) 668-2028

West Park
John Burroughs Association • House Museum, John Burroughs Dr • West Park, NY 12493 • (212) 769-5169 • http://www.research.amnh.org/burroughs/

West Point
Constitution Island Association • Warner House Museum, Constitution Island, P.O. Box 41 • West Point, NY 10996 • (914) 446-8676 • http://www.constitutionisland.org

West Point Museum • US Military Academy, Pershing Center, Bldg 2110 • West Point, NY 10996 • (845) 938-2203 • http://www.usma.edu

US Military Academy Library - Special Collections & Archives • 758 Cullum Rd • West Point, NY 10996 • (845) 938-8325 • http://www.usma.edu/library/SitePages/sca.aspx

West Sand Lake
Sand Lake Historical Society • P.O. Box 492 • West Sand Lake, NY 12196 • (518) 674-3127 • http://homeotwn.aol.com/sandlakehistory/

West Sayville
Friends for Long Island's Heritage • P.O. Box 144 • West Sayville, NY 11796 • (516) 571-7600 • http://www.garviewspointmuseum.com/friends-for-long-islands-heritage.php

Long Island Maritime Museum • 86 West Ave, P.O. Box 184 • West Sayville, NY 11796 • (631) 854-4974 • http://www.limaritime.org

West Seneca
West Seneca Historical Society • Historical Museum, 919 Mill Rd, P.O. Box 2 • West Seneca, NY 14224 • (716) 674-4283

West Shokan
Olive Free Library Association • Route 28 A • West Shokan, NY 12494 • (845) 657-2482 • http://olive.westshokan.lib.ny.us

Westbury
Historical Society of the Town of North Hempstead • 461 Newton St • Westbury, NY 11590 • (516) 333-3151

Historical Society of the Westburys • 445 Jefferson St • Westbury, NY 11590 • (516) 333-0176

Westernville
Town of Western Historical Society • P.O. Box 256 • Westernville, NY 13486

Westfield
Chautauqua County Historical Society • McClurg Museum, Village Park, E Main St, P.O. Box 7 • Westfield, NY 14787 • (716) 326-2977 • http://www.mcclurgmuseum.org

Patterson Library • 40 S Portage St • Westfield, NY 14787 • (716) 326-2154 • http://www.cclslib.org/westfield/index.html

Westford
Westford Historical Society • Town Hall, P.O. Box 184 • Westford, NY 13488 • (607) 638-9250

Westhampton Beach
Westhampton Beach Historical Society • Tuthill House Museum, 101 Mill Rd, P.O. Box 686 • Westhampton Beach, NY 11978 • (631) 288-1139 • http://www.shbhistorical.org

Westhampton Free Library • 7 Library Ave • Westhampton Beach, NY 11978-2697 • (631) 288-3335 • http://wham.suffolk.lib.ny.us

Westmoreland
Westmoreland Library Historical Society • Station Rd • Westmoreland, NY 13490 • (315) 853-8001

Westport
Westport Historical Society • Westport Train Station, Barksdale Rd • Westport, NY 12993 • (518) 962-4809

Westport Library Association • Washington St, P.O. Box 436 • Westport, NY 12993 • (518) 962-8219 • http://www.nc3r.org/wptlib

Westport Town Historian • 22 Champlain Ave, P.O. Box 465 • Westport, NY 12993 • (518) 962-8287

White Plains
City of White Plains Archives • 100 Martine Ave • White Plains, NY 10601-2409 • (914) 422-1450 • http://www.cityofwhiteplains.com

Westchester County Genealogical Society • P.O. Box 518, N White Plains Sta • White Plains, NY 10603-0518 • (914) 666-6165 • http://www.rootsweb.com/~nywcgs

White Plains Historical Society • Jacob Purdy House Museum, 60 Park Ave • White Plains, NY 10603-3528 • (914) 328-1776 • http://www.whiteplainshistory.org

White Plains Public Library • 100 Martine Ave • White Plains, NY 10601-2599 • (914) 422-1400 • http://www.whiteplainslibrary.org

Whitehall
Skemesborough Museum • Skenesborough Dr, P.O. Box 238 • Whitehall, NY 12887 • (518) 499-0225

Whitesville
Whitesville Public Library • 500 Main St, P.O. Box 158 • Whitesville, NY 14897-0158 • (607) 356-3645

Whitney Point
Mary L Wilcox Memorial Library • 2630 Main St • Whitney Point, NY 13862 • (607) 692-3159

Williamson
Pultneyville Historical Society • 4130 Mill St • Williamson, NY 14589 • (315) 589-9892

Williamstown
Amboy Town Historian • 2167 County Route 23 • Williamstown, NY 13493 • (315) 964-2415

Williamstown Town Historian • 2892 County Route 17, P.O. Box 54 • Williamstown, NY 13493 • (315) 964-2393

Williamsville
R R Dry Memorial Library • SUNY-Erie, 6205 Main St • Williamsville, NY 14221 • (716) 851-1273 • http://elinks.ecc.edu/library

Williamsville Historical Society • Village Meeting House, 5688 Main St • Williamsville, NY 14221 • (716) 626-4406

Willsboro
1812 Homestead Museum • Route 22 & Reber Rd, P.O. Box 507 • Willsboro, NY 12996 • (518) 963-4071

Paine Memorial Free Library • 1 School St • Willsboro, NY 12996 • (518) 963-4478 • http://www.willsborony.com/PaineMemorialLibrary/

Wilmington
Wilmington Town Historian • P.O. Box 148 • Wilmington, NY 12997 • (518) 946-7057

Wilson
Wilson Historical Society • Historical Museum, 645 Lake St, P.O. Box 830 • Wilson, NY 14172-0830 • (716) 751-9886 • http://www.wilsonnewyork.com/hist-society.html

Wilton
Ulysses S Grant Cottage Historic Site Museum • McGregor, P.O. Box 2284 • Wilton, NY 12831 • (518) 587-8277 • http://www.grantcottage.org

Windsor

Old Stone House Museum • 22 Chestnut St • Windsor, NY 13865 • (607) 655-1491

Winthrop

Stockholm Historical Organization • Municipal Bldg, Route 11 C • Winthrop, NY 13697 • (315) 384-4764

Wolcott

Wolcott Historical Society • Northrup Carriage House, 5994 Jefferson St, P.O. Box 51 • Wolcott, NY 14590 • (315) 594-9494 • http://www.wolcottny/history/

Woodgate

Woodgate Free Library • 11051 Woodgate Dr, P.O. Box 52 • Woodgate, NY 13494 • (315) 392-4814 • http://www.midyork.org/Woodgate

Woodhaven

Woodhaven Cultural and Historical Society • 93-34 91st Ave • Woodhaven, NY 11421 • (718) 846-1907 • http://www.queensbp.org

Woodside

Colonial Society of Americans of Colonial Descent • 4207 64th St • Woodside, NY 11377-5046

Woodstock

Center for Photography at Woodstock Museum • 59 Tinker Ln • Woodstock, NY 12498 • (845) 679-7747 • http://www.epw.org

Historical Society of Woodstock • Historical Museum, Comeau Dr, P.O. Box 841 • Woodstock, NY 12498 • (845) 679-2256 • http://www.woodstockhistory.org

Woodstock Museum • P.O. Box 73 • Woodstock, NY 12498-0073 • (845) 246-0600 • http://www.woodstockmuseum.com

Worcester

Worcester Free Library • 168 Main St, P.O. Box 461 • Worcester, NY 12197 • (607) 397-7309

Worcester Historical Society • 144 Main St P.O. Box 186 • Worcester, NY 12197 • (607) 397-1700 • http://worcesterhistoricalsociety.org

Wyoming

Middlebury Historical Society • Historical Museum, 22 S Academy St, P.O. Box 198 • Wyoming, NY 14591 • (585) 495-6582

Yaphank

Yaphank Historical Society • Hawkins House Museum, Yaphank Ave, P.O. Box 111 • Yaphank, NY 11980 • (631) 924-3401 • http://www.yaphank.org

Yonkers

Glenview Mansion Museum • 511 Warburton Ave • Yonkers, NY 10701 • (914) 963-4550 • http://www.hrm.org

Grinton I Will Library, 1500 Central Park Ave • Yonkers, NY 10708 • (914) 337-1500 • http://ypl.org/grinton

Hudson River Museum • 511 Warburton Ave • Yonkers, NY 10701 • (914) 963-4550 • http://www.hrm.org

Lemko (Slovakian) Society • 556 Yonkers Ave • Yonkers, NY 10704-2602 • (609) 758-1115

Philipse Manor Hall State Historic Site Museum • 29 Warburton Ave, P.O. Box 496 • Yonkers, NY 10702 • (914) 965-4027 • http://www.nystateparks.com

Yonkers Historical Society • c/o Grinton I Will Library, 1500 Central Park Ave, P.O. Box 190 • Yonkers, NY 10710 • (914) 961-8940 • http://www.yonkershistory.org

Yonkers Police Historical Society • George E Rutledge Museum, 104 S Broadway • Yonkers, NY 10701 • (914) 377-7900 • http://yonkerspd.com/historical.htm

Yonkers Public Library • 1 Larkin Plaza • Yonkers, NY 10701 • (914) 337-1500

York

Town of York Historical Society • 2431 Dow Rd, P.O. Box 464 • York, NY 14592 • (585) 243-2027 • http://www.yorkhistorical.org

Yorktown Heights

Yorktown Historical Society • P.O. Box 355 • Yorktown Heights, NY 10598 • (914) 962-5722 • http://www.yorktownhistory.org

Yorktown Museum • 1974 Commerce St • Yorktown Heights, NY 10598 • (914) 962-2970 • http://www.yorktownmuseum.org

Youngstown

Old Fort Niagara Museum • Fort Niagara State Park, 4 Scott Ave, P.O. Box 169 • Youngstown, NY 14174-0169 • (716) 745-7611 • http://www.oldfortniagara.org

Town of Porter Historical Society • Historical Museum, 240 Lockport St • Youngstown, NY 14174 • (716) 745-7203 • http://www.youngstownnewyork.us

Aberdeen

Malcolm Blue Historical Society • P.O. Box 603 • Aberdeen, NC 28315 • (910) 944-7558

Albemarle

Albemarle-Stanley County Historic Preservation Commission • Historical Museum, 112 N 3rd St • Albemarle, NC 28001 • (704) 986-3777

Freeman-Marks House Museum • 245 E Main St • Albemarle, NC 28001 • (704) 986-3777

Morrow Mountain State Park Museum • 49104 Morrow Mountain Rd • Albemarle, NC 28001 • (704) 982-4402

Snuggs House Museum • 112 N 3rd St • Albemarle, NC 28001 • (704) 986-3777

Stanley County Public Library • 133 E Main St • Albemarle, NC 28001 • (704) 986-3759 • http://www.stanlylib.org

Stanly County Genealogical Society • P.O. Box 31 • Albemarle, NC 28002-0031

Stanly County Historic Commission • Historical Museum, 245 E Main St • Albemarle, NC 28001 • (704) 986-3777 • http://www.stanlycountymuseum.com

Andrews

Valleytown Cultural Arts and Historical Society • Chestnut & 3rd Sts, P.O. Box 399 • Andrews, NC 27536 • (828) 360-5071 • http://www.andrewsvalleyarts.com

Apex

Apex Area Historical Society • Maynard Pearson House Museum, P.O. Box 506 • Apex, NC 27502 • (919) 362-8097 • http://www.apexhistoricalsociety.com

Arapahoe

Craven County Kinfolk Trackers • Route 65, Box 8A • Arapahoe, NC 28510

Asheboro

Randolph County Genealogical Society • c/o Randolph County Public Library, 201 Worth St, P.O. Box 4394 • Asheboro, NC 27204 • (336) 318-6800

Randolph County Public Library • 201 Worth St • Asheboro, NC 27203 • (336) 318-6800 • http://www.randolphlibrary.org

Asheville

Asheville-Bumcombe Library System • 67 Haywood St • Asheville, NC 28801 • (828) 225-5203 • http://www.librarybuncombe.org

Biltmore Estate Museum • 1 Lodge St • Asheville, NC 28803 • (800) 411-3812 • http://www.biltmore.com

D Hiden Ramsey Library • University of North Carolina at Asheville, 1 University Heights, CPO 1500 • Asheville, NC 28804-8504 • (828) 251-6111 • http://www.unca.edu/library/

Episcopal Diocese of Western North Carolina Library • 900B Centre Park Dr • Asheville, NC 28805 • (828) 225-6656 • http://www.diocesewnc.org

Estes-Winn Antique Automobile Museum • 111 Grovewood Rd • Asheville, NC 28804 • (828) 253-7651 • http://www.grovewood.com

North Carolina Homespun Museum • 111 Grovewood Rd • Asheville, NC 28804 • (877) 622-7238 • http://www.grovewood.com

Old Buncombe County Genealogical Society • 128 Bingham Rd, Ste 950, P.O. Box 2122 • Asheville, NC 28802-2122 • (828) 253-1894 • http://www.obcgs.com

Sons of the American Revolution, Blue Ridge Chapter • 337 Vanderbilt Rd • Asheville, NC 28803

Southern Highland Handicraft Guild Museum and Library • Blue Ridge Pkwy & Riceville Rd, P.O. Box 9545 • Asheville, NC 28815-0545 • (828) 298-7928 • http://www.southernhighlandguild.org

Thomas Wolfe Memorial Museum • 52 N Market St • Asheville, NC 28001 • (828) 253-8304 • http://www.wolfememorial.com

Western North Carolina Historical Association • Smith-Dowell House Museum, 283 Victoria Rd • Asheville, NC 28801 • (858) 253-9231 • http://www.wnchistory.org

Western Office, Division of Archives and History • 17 Riceville Rd • Asheville, NC 28803 • (828) 296-7230

Atkinson

Moores Creek Battleground Association • P.O. Box 1 • Atkinson, NC 28421-0001

Atlantic Beach

Fort Macon State Park • 2300 E Fort Macon Rd, P.O. Box 127 • Atlantic Beach, NC 28512 • (252) 726-3775 • http://www.clis.com/friends

Ayden

Mattamuskeet Foundation • 4377 Lewis Lane Rd • Ayden, NC 27513 • (252) 746-4221 • http://www.mattamuskeet.org

Bailey

Country Doctor Museum • 6642 Peele Rd, P.O. Box 34 • Bailey, NC 27807 • (252) 235-4165 • http://www.countrydoctormuseum.org

Bakersville

Mitchell Company Historical Society • Main St • Bakersville, NC 28705 • (828) 688-4371

Banner Elk

James H Carson Library • Lees-McRae College, P.O. Box 67 • Banner Elk, NC 28604-0067 • (828) 898-8727 • http://www.lmc.edu/lmclibrary

Barco

Currituck County Public Library • 4261 Caratoke Hwy • Barco, NC 27917 • (252) 453-8345 • http://www.earlibrary.org

Bath

Bonner House Museum • Front St, P.O. Box 148 • Bath, NC 27808 • (919) 923-3971

Historic Bath State Historic Site Museum • 207 Carteret St, P.O. Box 148 • Bath, NC 27808 • (252) 923-3971 • http://www.nchistoricsites.org

Palmer-Marsh House Museum • Main St, P.O. Box 148 • Bath, NC 27808 • (919) 923-3971

Bayboro

Pamlico County Genealogical Society • P.O. Box 175 • Bayboro, NC 28515

Pamlico County Library • 603 Main St • Bayboro, NC 28515 • (252) 745-3515 • http://www.pamlico.net/library

Beaufort

Beaufort Historical Association • Historic Site Museum, 138 Turner St, P.O. Box 1709 • Beaufort, NC 28516-0363 • (252) 728-5225 • http://www.beauforthistoricsite.org

Carteret County Public Library • 1702 Live Oak St, Ste 100 • Beaufort, NC 28516 • (252) 728-2050 • http://carteret.cpclib.org

North Carolina Maritime Museum • 315 Front St • Beaufort, NC 28516 • (252) 728-7317 • http://www.ncmaritimemuseum.org

Belhaven

Belhaven Memorial Museum • 211 E Main St, P.O. Box 220 • Belhaven, NC 27810 • (919) 943-6817 • http://www.beaufort-country.com/Belhaven/museu/Belhaven.htm

Belmont
Belmont Historical Society • R L Stowe House Museum, 40 Catawba St, P.O. Box 244 • Belmont, NC 28012 • (704) 825-4848 • http://www.belmontnc-hs.org/

Belvidere
Family Research Society of Northeastern North Carolina • Route 1, Box 159 • Belvidere, NC 27919 • (919) 297-2025

Bethania
Historic Bethania • 5393 Ham Horton Ln, P.O. Box 259 • Bethania, NC 27010 • (336) 0434 • http://www.townofbethania.org

Historic Bethania • Wolff-Moser House Museum, 5393 Ham Horton Ln, P.O. Box 259 • Bethania, NC 27010 • (336) 922-0434 • http://www.townofbethania.org

Black Mountain
Swannanoa Valley Museum • 223 W State St, P.O. Box 306 • Black Mountain, NC 28711 • (828) 669-9566 • http://www.swannanoavalleymuseum.org

Bladenboro
Bladenboro Historical Society • Town Museum, 818 S Main St • Bladenboro, NC 28320 • (910) 863-4707 • http://www.bladenborohistoricalsociety.org

Mother County Genealogical Society • 818 S Main St • Bladenboro, NC 28320

Blowing Rock
Appalachian Heritage Museum • 175 Mystery Hill Ln • Blowing Rock, NC 28605

Bolton
Waccamaw-Siouan Tribe • P.O. Box 221 • Bolton, NC 28423 • (910) 655-8778

Boone
Hickory Ridge Homestead Museum • Tatum Cabin, 591 Horn in the West Dr, P.O. Box 295 • Boone, NC 28607 • (704) 264-2120 • http://www.horninthewest.com/museum.htm

Appalachian Cultural Museum • 400 University Hall Dr • Boone, NC 28608 • (828) 262-3117

Carol Grotnes Belk Library • Appalachian State Univ, 325 College St • Boone, NC 28608 • (828) 262-2186 • http://www.library.appstate.edu

Center for Appalachian Studies • Berk Library, Appalachian State Univ, P.O. Box 32003 • Boone, NC 28608 • (828) 262-4072 • http://www.library.appstate.edu

Genealogical Society of Watauga County • 753 Forest Hill Dr, P.O. Box 126 • Boone, NC 28607-4461 • (828) 264-7813

Watauga County Public Library • 140 Queen St • Boone, NC 28607 • (828) 264-8784 • http://www.arlibrary.org

Boonville
Historic Richmond Hill Law School Commission • River Rd, P.O. Box 552 • Boonville, NC 27011 • http://www.shore-styers-mill.org

Brevard
McGaha Chapel Museum • P.O. Box 2061 • Brevard, NC 28712 • (828) 884-5137 • http://www.tchistoricalsociety.com/?page_id=13

Transylvania County Historical Society • P.O. Box 2061 • Brevard, NC 28712 • (828) 884-5137 • http://www.tchistoricalsociety.com

Transylvania County Library • 105 S Broad St • Brevard, NC 28712 • (828) 884-3151 • http://www.transylvania.lib.nc.us

Transylvania Genealogical Society • 189 W Main St, P.O. Box 2347 • Brevard, NC 28712 • http://www.transylvaniagenealogy.com

Bryson City
Marianna Black Library • 33 Fryemont Rd • Bryson City, NC 28713 • (828) 488-3030 • http://main.nc.us/libraries/fontana

Smoky Mountain Trains Museum • 100 Greenlee St, P.O. Box 2390 • Bryson City, NC 28713 • (828) 488-5200 • http://www.smokymountains.com

Swain County Genealogical and Historical Society • P.O. Box 267 • Bryson City, NC 28713 • http://www.rootsweb.ancestry.com/~ncscghs/

Buies Creek
Harnett County Genealogical Society • P.O. Box 247 • Buies Creek, NC 27506-0219 • (910) 893-3132 • http://ncgenweb.us/harnett/

North Carolina Society of Historians • Dept of Govt, Campbell Univ, P.O. Box 356 • Buies Creek, NC 27506 • (910) 997-6641 • http://ncassnhistorians.org

Burgaw
Pender County Historical Society • Historical Museum, 200 W Bridgers St, P.O. Box 1380 • Burgaw, NC 28425 • (910) 259-8543 • http://pendercountymuseum.webs.com

Pender County Museum • 200 W Bridgers ST, P.O. Box 1380 • Burgaw, NC 28425 • (910) 259-8543 • http://pendercountymuseum.webs.com

Pender County Public Library • 103 Cowan St, P.O. Box 879 • Burgaw, NC 28425-0879 • (910) 259-1234 • http://www.tlc.library.net/pender

Burlington
Alamance Battleground State Historic Site Museum • 5803 South NC 62 • Burlington, NC 27215 • (336) 227-4785 • http://www.alamancebattleground.nchistoricsites.org

Alamance County Genealogical Society • P.O. Box 3052 • Burlington, NC 27215-3052 • http://www.rootsweb.ancestry.com/~ncacgs/

Alamance County Historical Museum • 4777 S North Carolina 62 • Burlington, NC 27215 • (336) 226-8254

Central North Carolina Regional Library • 342 S Spring St • Burlington, NC 27215 • (336) 229-3588 • http://www.alamance-nc.com/library/

NCSSAR-Alamance Battleground Chapter • 804 W Davis St • Burlington, NC 27215

Burnsville
Avery-Mitchell-Yancey Regional Library • 289 Burnsville School Rd, P.O. Drawer 310 • Burnsville, NC 28714-0310 • (828) 682-4476 • http://www.avery.lib.nc.us

Mount Mitchell State Park Museum • 2388 State Hwy 128 • Burnsville, NC 28714 • (828) 674-4611

Yancey County Library • 18 Town Square • Burnsville, NC 28714 • (828) 682-2600 • http://www.amyregionallibrary.org

Camp Lejeune
Harriotte B Smith Library • USMC, Bldg 1220, 1401 West Rd • Camp Lejeune, NC 28547 • (910) 451-5724 • http://library.usmc-mccs.org

Candler
Sons of the American Revolution, Lt Col Felix Walker Chapter • 25 Monte Vista Cr • Candler, NC 28715

Carolina Beach
Federal Point Historic Preservation Society • History Center, 1121A N Lake Park Blvd, P.O. Box 623 • Carolina Beach, NC 28428 • (910) 458-0502 • http://www.federalpointhistory.org

Carthage
1760 McLendon Cabin & 1820 Bryant House Museums • 3361 Mount Carmel Rd • Carthage, NC 28388 • (910) 947-3995 • http://www.moorehistory.com/house_museums/mclendon_cabin.htm

Moore County Library • 101 Saunders St, P.O. Box 400 • Carthage, NC 28327-0400 • (910) 947-5335 • http://204.211.56.212

Cary

Cary Historical Society • P.O. Box 134 • Cary, NC 27512-0134 • (919) 467-6989

Friends of the Page-Walker Hotel • History Center, 119 Ambassador Loop, P.O. Box 4234 • Cary, NC 27519 • (919) 460-4963 • http://www.friendsofpagewalker.org

Cashiers

Cashiers Historical Society • Zachary-Tolbert House Museum, 1940 Highway 107 S, P.O. Box 104 • Cashiers, NC 28717 • (828) 743-7710 • http://www.cashiershistoricalsociety.org

Catawba

Murray's Mill Historic Site Museum • 1489 Murrays Mill Rd • Catawba, NC 28609 • (828) 241-4299

Chadbourn

Chadbourn Depot Museum • Colony St, P.O. Box 200 • Chadbourn, NC 28431 • (919) 942-7818

Chapel Hill

Chapel Hill Historical Society • 523 E Franklin St • Chapel Hill, NC 27514 • (919) 929-1793

Chapel Hill Public Library • 100 Library Dr • Chapel Hill, NC 27514 • (919) 968-2777 • http://www.chapelhillpubliclibrary.org

Dean E Smith Center Memorabilia Collection • Bowles Dr • Chapel Hill, NC 27515 • (919) 962-7777

Durham-Orange Genealogical Society • P.O. Box 4703 • Chapel Hill, NC 27515-4703 • (919) 967-4168 • http://www.rtpnet.org/dogs

North Carolina Collection • UNC at Chapel Hill, 201 South Rd • Chapel Hill, NC 27599 • (919) 962-1172 • http://www.lib.unc.edu/ncc/gallery.html

Preservation Chapel Hill • Horace Williams House Museum, 610 E Rosemary St • Chapel Hill, NC 27514 • (919) 942-7818 • http://www.preservationchapelhill.org

Southern Jewish Historical Society • 329 Burlage Cr • Chapel Hill, NC 27514-2703 • (919) 929-6054

Walter Royal Davis Library • University of North Carolina at Chapel Hill, 208 Raleigh St, Campus Box 3900 • Chapel Hill, NC 27514-8890 • (919) 962-1151 • http://www.lib.unc.edu

Wilson Library • Univ of North Carolina, P.O. Drawer 870 • Chapel Hill, NC 27514 • (919) 933-1172 • http://www.lib.unc.edu/mss/

Charlotte

Advent Christian Church Archives • 14601 Albermarle Rd, P.O. Box 23152 • Charlotte, NC 28227 • http://www.aedventchristian.org

African Methodist Episcopal Zion Church Library • P.O. Box 32843 • Charlotte, NC 28323 • http://www.amezion.org

Afro-American Cultural Center • 401 N Myers St • Charlotte, NC 28202 • (704) 374-1565 • http://www.aacc-charlotte.org

Carolinas Aviation Museum • 4108 Airport Dr • Charlotte, NC 28208 • (704) 359-8442 • http://www.chacweb.com

Carolinas Historic Aviation Commission • Historical Museum, 4672 First Flight Dr • Charlotte, NC 28208 • (704) 359-8442 • http://www.carolinasaviation.org

Charlotte Jewish Historical Society • P.O. Box 13574 • Charlotte, NC 28270 • (704) 366-5007 • http://users.vnet.net/lsstein/cjhs/cjhs.html

Charlotte Museum of History • Hezekiah Alexander Homesite, 3500 Shamrock Dr • Charlotte, NC 28215 • (704) 568-1774 • http://www.charlottemuseum.org

Charlotte-Mecklenburg Public Library • Spangler Carolina Room, 310 N Tryon St • Charlotte, NC 28202-2176 • (704) 336-2980 • http://cmstory.org/default.asp

Council of Scottish Clans and Associations • 3220 Frederick Pl • Charlotte, NC 28210 • http://www.maclachlans.org/games.html

Everett Library • Queens College, 1900 Selwyn Ave • Charlotte, NC 28274-0001 • (704) 337-2401 • http://www.queens.edu/library

Evrytanian Association • 121 Greenwich Rd • Charlotte, NC 28211 • (704) 366-6571

First Presbyterian Church Library • 200 W Trade St • Charlotte, NC 28202-1696 • (704) 332-5123 • http://www.firstpres.charlotte.org

Hezekiah Alexander Homesite Library • 3500 Shamrock Dr • Charlotte, NC 28215 • (704) 568-1774 • http://www.charlottemuseum.org

Historic Rosedale Foundation • Rosedale Plantation Museum, 3427 N Tryon St, P.O. Box 6212 • Charlotte, NC 28206 • (704) 335-0325 • http://www.historicrosedale.org

J Murrey Atkins Library • Univ of NC at Charlotte, 9201 University City Blvd • Charlotte, NC 28223 • (704) 687-2241 • http://www.uncc.edu/lis/collections/special

James B Duke Memorial Library • Johnson C Smith University, 100 Beatties Ford Rd • Charlotte, NC 28216 • (704) 371-6740 • http://www.jcsu.edu

Levine Museum of the New South • 200 E 7th St • Charlotte, NC 28202 • (704) 333-1887 • http://www.museumofthenewsouth.org

Mecklenburg Historical Association • 200 E 7th St, P.O. Box 35032 • Charlotte, NC 28202-2150 • (704) 333-6422 • http://www.meckdec.org

Metrolina Native American Association • 2601A E 7th St • Charlotte, NC 28204 • (704) 331-4818

Olde Mecklenburg Genealogical Society • P.O. Box 32453 • Charlotte, NC 28232-2453 • (704) 596-8639 • http://www.rootsweb.ancestry.com/~ncomgs/

Sons of the American Revolution, Mecklenburg Chapter • 9125B Fishers Pond Dr • Charlotte, NC 28277

Western North Carolina United Methodist Commission on Archives and History • 3400 Shamrock Dr, P.O. Box 18005 • Charlotte, NC 28218 • (704) 535-2260

Cherokee

Cherokee Heritage Museum • 35 Big Cove Rd, P.O. Box 607 • Cherokee, NC 28719 • (828) 497-3211 • http://www.cherokeeheritagemuseum-gallery.org

Cherokee Historical Association • US Hwy 441 N, P.O. Box 398 • Cherokee, NC 28719 • (828) 497-2111

Cherokee Welcome Center • 209 Tsali Blvd, P.O. Box 460 • Cherokee, NC 28719 • (800) 438-1601 • http://www.cherokee-nc.com

Eastern Band of Cherokee Indians • Hwy 441 N, P.O. Box 455 • Cherokee, NC 28719 • (828) 497-4072

Mountain Farm Museum and Mingus Mill • Great Smoky Mtns National Park, 1194 Newfound Gap Rd • Cherokee, NC 28719 • (828) 497-1900 • http://www.nps.gov/grsm

Museum of the Cherokee Indian • 589 Tsali Blvd, P.O. Box 1599 • Cherokee, NC 28719-1599 • (828) 497-3481 • http://www.cherokeemuseum.org

Qualla Boundary Public Library • Acquoni Rd, Cherokee Indian Reservation, P.O. Box 1839 • Cherokee, NC 28719-1839 • (828) 497-2771

Cherry Point

USMC Air Station Library • Bldg 298 E St, PSC Box 8009 • Cherry Point, NC 28533-0009 • (252) 466-3552 • http://library.usmc-mccs.org

Cherryville

C Grier Beam Truck Museum • 111 N Mountain St, P.O. Box 238 • Cherryville, NC 28021 • (704) 435-3072 • http://www.beamtruckmuseum.com

Cherryville, cont.

Cherryville Historical Association • Historical Museum, 109 E Main St, P.O. Box 307 • Cherryville, NC 28021-3406 • (704) 435-8011 • http://www.cityofcherryville.com/parksrecreation.htm

J Ralph Beam Heritage Park Museum • 102 S Jacob St • Cherryville, NC 28021

Claremont

Bunker Hill Covered Bridge Museum • Claremont Rd • Claremont, NC 28658 • (828) 465-0383 • http://www.catawbahistory.org/bunker_hill_covered_bridge.php

Clinton

Coharie Intra-Tribal Council • 7531 US Hwy 421 N • Clinton, NC 20328 • (910) 564-6909

J C Holliday Memorial Library • 217 Graham St • Clinton, NC 28328 • (910) 592-4153 • http://www.sampson.nc.us/publiclibrary/

Sampson County Historical Society • 2336 Honrine Rd, P.O. Box 1084 • Clinton, NC 28328 • (910) 564-6471 • http://www.ncgenweb.us/sampson/schs/SCGSHH.htm

Coinjock

Albemarle Genealogical Society • 142 Waterlily Rd • Coinjock, NC 27923

Colletsville

Collettsville Historical Society • P.O. Box 152 • Colletsville, NC 28611 • http://www.collettsvillehistoricalsociety.org

Columbia

Tyrrell County Genealogical and Historical Society • P.O. Box 686 • Columbia, NC 27825 • http://patriot.net/~cpbarnes/SOCIETY.HTM

Tyrrell County Public Library • P.O. Box 540 • Columbia, NC 27925 • (252) 796-3771

Columbus

Polk County Public Library • 51 Walker St • Columbus, NC 28722 • (828) 894-8721 • http://www.publib.polknc.org

Concord

Cabarrus County Public Library • 27 Union St N • Concord, NC 28025-4793 • (704) 920-2050 • http://www.cabarrus.lib.nc.us

Cabarrus Genealogy Society • P.O. Box 2981 • Concord, NC 28025-2981 • http://www.rootsweb.ancestry.com/~nccgs/

Cooleemee

Cooleemee Historical Association • Textile Heritage Center, 131 Church St, P.O. Box 667 • Cooleemee, NC 27014 • (704) 284-6040 • http://www.textileheritage.org/Cooleemee/cooleemee.htm

Mill Village Museum • 14 Church St • Cooleemee, NC 27014 • http://www.textileheritage.org/Cooleemee/cooleemee.htm

Corolla

Currituck Beach Lighthouse • 1101 Corolla Village Rd, P.O. Box 58 • Corolla, NC 27927 • (252) 453-8152 • http://www.currituckbeachlight.com

Historic Corolla Chapel • 1136 Corolla Village Rd • Corolla, NC 27927

Lewark-Gray House Museum • 1134 Corolla Village Rd • Corolla, NC 27927

Outer Banks Conservationists • Currituck Heritage Park, 1101 Corolla Village Rd, P.O. Box 58 • Corolla, NC 27927 • (252) 453-4939 • http://www.currituckbeachlight.com

Parker House Museum • 1129 Corolla Village Rd • Corolla, NC 27927

Whalehead Club at Currituck Heritage Park • 1100 Club Rd • Corolla, NC 27927

Creswell

Somerset Place State Historic Site Museum • 2572 Lake Shore Rd • Creswell, NC 27928 • (252) 797-4560 • http://www.nchistoricsites.org

Cullowhee

Hunter Library • Western Carolina Univ, 176 Central Dr • Cullowhee, NC 28723 • (828) 227-7129 • http://www.wcu.edu/mhc

Jackson County Genealogical Society • P.O. Box 2108 • Cullowhee, NC 28723 • http://www.jcncgs.com

Mountain Heritage Center Museum • Western Carolina Univ, 150 Robinson Blvd • Cullowhee, NC 28723 • (828) 227-7129 • http://www.wcu.edu/mhc

Currie

Moores Creek Battlefield Museum • 40 Patriots Hall Dr • Currie, NC 28435 • (910) 283-5591 • http://www.nps.gov/mocr

Currituck

Albemarle Genealogical Society • P.O. Box 87 • Currituck, NC 27929

Confederate War Memorial • 145 Courthouse Rd • Currituck, NC 27929

Currituck County Historic Jail & Courthouse • 145 Courthouse Rd • Currituck, NC 27929

Dallas

1890s Village • Gaston County Park • Dallas, NC 27120 • (704) 922-2160

Gaston County Museum of Art and History • 131 W Main St, P.O. Box 429 • Dallas, NC 28034-0429 • (704) 922-7681 • http://www.gastoncountymuseum.org

Morris Library • Gaston College, 201 Hwy 321 S • Dallas, NC 28034 • (704) 922-6357 • http://www.gaston.cc.nc.us

Danbury

Stokes County Historical Society • P.O. Box 304 • Danbury, NC 27016 • (336) 593-9407

Davidson

E H Little Library • Davidson College, 209 Ridge Rd, P.O. Box 7200 • Davidson, NC 28035-7200 • (704) 892-1837 • http://www.davidson.edu

Denton

Davidson County Public Library System-Denton Public • 310 W Salisbury St, PO Box 578 • Denton, NC 27239-0578 • (336) 859-2215

Dillsboro

Great Smoky Mountains Railway Train Museum • Front St, P.O. Box 397 • Dillsboro, NC 28725 • (800) 872-4681 • http://www.gsmr.com

Dobson

Surry Community College Library • 630 S Main St • Dobson, NC 27017-8432 • (336) 386-3260 • http://www.surry.edu/lrc/newlrc.htm

Surry County Genealogical Association • c/o Surry Community College Library, 630 S Main St, P.O. Box 997 • Dobson, NC 27017 • (336) 786-7449 • http://surrygenealogy.wordpress.com

Durham

American Society for Ethnohistory • Duke Univ, 6697 College Station, P.O. Box 906660 • Durham, NC 27708 • (919) 687-3602 • http://ethnohistory

Bennett Place State Historic Site Museum • 4409 Bennett Memorial Rd • Durham, NC 27705 • (919) 383-4345 • http://www.nchistoricsites.org

Duke Homestead State Historic Site Museum • 2828 Duke Homestead Rd • Durham, NC 27705 • (919) 477-5498 • http://www.dukehomestead.nchistoricsites.org

Duke University Special Collections Library • P.O. Box 90185 • Durham, NC 27708-0185 • (919) 660-5822 • http://www.lib.duke.edu

Durham County Library • 300 N Roxboro, P.O. Box 3809 • Durham, NC 27702-3809 • (919) 560-0100 • http://www.durhamcountylibrary.org

Forest History Society • Carl A Weyerhaeuser Library & Archives, 701 William Vickers Ave • Durham, NC 27701-3162 • (919) 682-9319 • http://www.foresthistory.org

Historic Stagville • Plantation Museum, 5825 Old Oxford Hwy • Durham, NC 27722-1217 • (919) 620-0120 • http://www.stagville.org

Historic Stagville Museum • 5828 Old Oxford Rd • Durham, NC 27712 • (919) 620-0120 • http://www.historicstagvillefoundation.org

History of Medicine Museum • Duke Univ Medical Ctr, DUMC 3702 • Durham, NC 27710 • (919) 660-1143 • http://www.nclibrary.duke.edu/hmc

James E Shepard Memorial Library • North Carolina Central University, 1801 Fayetteville St • Durham, NC 27707 • (919) 560-6475 • http://www.nccu.edu/library/shepard.html

Preservation Durham • 115 Market St, Ste 221, P.O. Box 25411 • Durham, NC 17702 • (919) 682-3036 • http://preservationdurham.org

Saint Joseph's Historic Foundation • 804 Old Fayetteville St • Durham, NC 27701 • http://hayti.org

Sons of the American Revolution, Gen Francis Nash Chapter • 13 Clearwater Dr • Durham, NC 27707

Triangle Jewish Genealogical Society • 6905 Fayetteville Rd, Ste 204 • Durham, NC 27713 • http://www.trianglejgs.org/

Eden
Rockingham County Public Library • 527 Boone Rd • Eden, NC 27288 • (336) 627-1106 • http://www.rcpl.org

Edenton
1767 Chowan County Courthouse • 117 E King St • Edenton, NC 27932 • (252) 482-2637 • http://www.nchistoricsites.org/iredell/

1886 Roanoke River Lighthouse Museum • Colonial Park on the Waterfront • Edenton, NC 27932 • http://www.edentonlighthouse.org

Barker House Museum • 505 S Broad • Edenton, NC 27932 • (252) 482-7800 • https://www.facebook.com/BarkerHouse

Cupola House Museum • 408 S Broad St • Edenton, NC 27932 • (252) 482-2637 • http://cupolahouse.org

Edenton Cotton Mill Museum of History • 420 Elliott St • Edenton, NC 27932 • (252) 482-7455 • http://edentoncottonmill.com

Edenton Historical Commission • 505 S Broad St • Edenton, NC 27932 • (252) 482-7800 • http://ehcnc.org

Historic 1736 St Paul's Episcopal Church • 101 W Gale St, P.O. Box 548 • Edenton, NC 27932 • (252) 482-3522 • http://stpauls-edenton.org

Historic Edenton State Historic Site Museum • 108 N Broad St, P.O. Box 474 • Edenton, NC 27932 • (252) 482-3400 • http://www.nchistoricsites.org

Iredell House Homesite Museum • 107 E Church St • Edenton, NC 27932 • (252) 482-2637

Shepard Pruden Memorial Library • 106 W Water St • Edenton, NC 27932 • (252) 482-4112

Elizabeth City
College of the Albemarle Library • Hwy 17 N, P.O. Box 2327 • Elizabeth City, NC 27909-2327 • (252) 335-0821 • http://www.albemarle.edu/acadaff/lrc/ec/rc/

East Albemarle Regional Library • 205 E Main St • Elizabeth City, NC 27909-0303 • (252) 335-2511 • http://www.earlibrary.org

Family Research Society • 410 E Main St • Elizabeth City, NC 27909 • (252) 333-1640

Family Research Society of Northeastern North Carolina • P.O. Box 1425 • Elizabeth City, NC 27906 • (252) 333-1640 • http://www.rootsweb.ancestry.com/~ncfrsnnc/

Museum of the Albemarle • 1116 US Hwy 17 S • Elizabeth City, NC 27909 • (252) 335-1453 • http://www.museumofthealbemarle.com

Pasquotank-Camden Regional Library • 100 E Colonial Ave • Elizabeth City, NC 27909 • (252) 335-2511

Elizabethtown
Bladen County Historical Society • P.O. Box 848 • Elizabethtown, NC 28337

Bladen County Public Library • 111 N Cypress St, P.O. Box 1419 • Elizabethtown, NC 28337-1419 • (910) 862-6990 • http://library.bladenco.org

Elkin
Elkin Public Library • 111 N Front St • Elkin, NC 28621 • (336) 835-5586 • http://www.nwrl.org

Ellerbe
Bostick Schoolhouse Museum • Clayton Carriker Rd • Ellerbe, NC 28379 • http://rchs-nc.net/bostick-schoolhouse/

Kemp Memorial Library • 279 2nd St • Ellerbe, NC 28338-9001 • (910) 652-6130

Rankin Museum • 131 Church St, P.O. Box 499 • Ellerbe, NC 28338 • (910) 652-6378 • http://www.rankinmuseum.com

Elon
Carol Grotnes Belk Library • Elon University, 308 N O'Kelly Ave, Campus Box 2550 • Elon, NC 27244 • (336) 278-6600 • http://www.elon.edu/library

Enfield
Lilly Pike Sullivan Municipal Library • 103 Railroad St • Enfield, NC 27823 • (252) 445-5203

Engelhard
Hyde County Historical and Genealogical Society • P.O. Box 517 • Engelhard, NC 27824 • (919) 926-4921 • http://www.ncgenweb.us/hyde/HCHGS.HTM

Erwin
Erwin Historical Society • P.O. Box 448 • Erwin, NC 28339

Fair Bluff
Greater Fair Bluff Historical Society • Depot Museum, 339 Railroad St, P.O. Box 234 • Fair Bluff, NC 28439 • (910) 649-7707

Faith
Faith Public Library • 100 N Main St, P.O. Box 37 • Faith, NC 28041-0037 • (704) 279-7500

Farmville
May Museum • Farmville Heritage Center, 213 S Main St, P.O. Box 86 • Farmville, NC 27828 • (252) 753-5814 • http://www.farmville-nc.com/departments_MayMuseum.htm

Fayetteville
Airborne and Special Operations Museum • 100 Bragg Blvd • Fayetteville, NC 28301 • (910) 483-3003 • http://www.asomf.org

Cumberland County Association for Indian People • 102 Indian Dr • Fayetteville, NC 28301 • (910) 483-8442

Cumberland County Genealogical Society • P.O. Box 53299 • Fayetteville, NC 28305-3299 • (919) 484-5217

Cumberland County Public Library • 300 Maiden Ln • Fayetteville, NC 28301-5000 • (919) 483-3745 • http://www.cumberland.lib.nc.us

Museum of the Cape Fear Historical Complex • Bradford & Arsenal Aves, P.O. Box 53693 • Fayetteville, NC 28305 • (910) 486-1330 • http://www.ncmuseumofhistory.org

North Carolina

Fayetteville, cont.

Sons of the American Revolution, Marquis de Lafayette Chapter • 5360 Amberhill Ct • Fayetteville, NC 28311

Sons of the American Revolution, North Carolina Society • 3812 Ithaca Pl • Fayetteville, NC 28311 • (910) 630-0875 • http://www.ncssar.com

Flat Rock

Carl Sandburg Home National Historic Site Museum • 81 Old Sandburg Ln • Flat Rock, NC 28731 • (828) 693-4178 • http://www.nps.gov/carl

Historic Flat Rock • P.O. Box 295 • Flat Rock, NC 28731 • (828) 693-1638 • http://www.historicflatrockinc.org

Forest City

Genealogical Society of Old Tryon County • Research Library, 319 Doggett Rd, P.O. Box 938 • Forest City, NC 28043 • (828) 247-8700 • http://www.visitnc.com/listing/genealogical-society-of-old-tryon-county-nc

Maimy Etta Global Black Fine Arts Museum and Historical Society • Historical Museum, 404 Hardin Rd • Forest City, NC 28043 • (828) 248-1525

Rutherford County Farm Museum • 240 Depot St • Forest City, NC 28043 • (828) 248-1248

Fort Bragg

82nd Airborne Division War Memorial Museum • Gela & Ardennes Sts, P.O. Box 70119 • Fort Bragg, NC 28307-0119 • (910) 432-5307 • http://www.bragg.army.mil/18abn/museums

JFK Special Warfare Museum • Ardennes & Marion Sts, Bldg D2502, AOHS-MU • Fort Bragg, NC 28307-5200 • (910) 432-1533

John L Throckmorton Library • Bldg 1-3346, Randolph St • Fort Bragg, NC 28310-5000 • (910) 396-3526

Fort Fisher

North Carolina Military History Museum at Fort Fisher • Fort Fisher, Riverfront Rd • Fort Fisher, NC 27607

Four Oaks

Bentonville Battleground State Historic Site Museum • Harper House Museum , 5466 Harper House Rd • Four Oaks, NC 27524 • (910) 594-0789 • http://www.nchistoricsites.org

Franklin

Macon County Historical and Genealogical Society • Historical Museum, 36 W Main St, P.O. Box 822 • Franklin, NC 28734 • (828) 524-9758 • http://www.maconnchistorical.org/gen/

Scottish Tartans Museum • 86 E Main St • Franklin, NC 29734 • (828) 524-7472 • http://www.scottishtartans.org

Fremont

Charles B Aycock Birthplace State Historic Site Museum • 264 Governor Aycock Rd, P.O. Box 207 • Fremont, NC 27830 • (919) 242-5581 • http://www.nchistoricsites.org/aycock/aycock.htm

Frisco

Frisco Native American Museum • 53536 Hwy 12, P.O. Box 399 • Frisco, NC 27936 • (252) 995-4440 • http://www.nativeamericanmuseum.org

Garner

Historic Depot Museum • 204 E Garner Rd • Garner, NC 27529 • (919) 773-8670

Gastonia

Gaston County Public Library • 1555 E Garrison Blvd • Gastonia, NC 28054 • (704) 868-2168 • http://www.glrl.lib.nc.us

Gaston-Lincoln Genealogical Society • 1734 Rhyne-Carter Rd • Gastonia, NC 28054

Schiele Museum of Southeastern Native American Studies • 1500 E Garrison Blvd • Gastonia, NC 28054 • (704) 866-6900

Gates

Gates County Historical Society • P.O. Box 98 • Gates, NC 27937

Gatesville

1836 Gates County Courthouse Museum • 115 Court St • Gatesville, NC 27937 • (252) 357-1420

Gates County Historical Society • Old Gates County Courthouse, P.O. Box 98 • Gatesville, NC 27937 • (919) 357-1733

Goldsboro

Old Dobbs County Genealogical Society • P.O. Box 617 • Goldsboro, NC 27530-0617 • (919) 242-4772

Wayne Community College Library • 3000 Wayne Memorial Dr, P.O. Box 8002 • Goldsboro, NC 27533-8002 • (919) 735-5151 • http://www.waynecc.edu

Wayne County Historical Association • Historical Museum, 116 N William St • Goldsboro, NC 27530 • (919) 734-5023 • http://www.waynemuseum.org

Wayne County Public Library • 1001 E Ash St • Goldsboro, NC 27530 • (919) 735-1824 • http://www.wcpl.org

Graham

Alamance County Historic Properties Commission • 124 W Elm St • Graham, NC 27253 • (336) 228-1312

Alamance County Historical Association • Historical Museum • Graham, NC 27253 • (336) 226-8254

Granite Quarry

Old Stone House Museum • Old Stone House Rd • Granite Quarry, NC 28072 • (704) 633-5946

Grantsboro

Pamlico County Historical Association • Historical Museum, 10642 NC 55 Hwy E, P.O. Box 33 • Grantsboro, NC 28529 • http://pamlicocountyhistorymuseum.com

Greensboro

Afro-American Family History Project • P.O. Box 6074 • Greensboro, NC 27405-6074

Afro-American Historical and Genealogical Society, Piedmont-Triad Chapter • P.O. Box 36254 • Greensboro, NC 27416 • http://onlinegreensboro.com/~aahgs

Greensboro Historical Museum • 130 Summit Ave • Greensboro, NC 27401-3004 • (336) 373-2043 • http://www.greensborohistory.org

Greensboro Masonic Museum • 425 W Market St, P.O. Box 466 • Greensboro, NC 27402-0466 • (336) 275-3579

Greensboro Public Library • 219 N Church St • Greensboro, NC 27401 • (336) 373-2471 • http://www.greensborolibrary.org

Guilford County Genealogical Society • P.O. Box 4713, Dept W • Greensboro, NC 27404-4713 • http://www.rootsweb.ancestry.com/~ncgcgs/

Guilford Courthouse National Military Park Library • 2332 New Garden Rd • Greensboro, NC 27410 • (336) 288-1776 • http://www.nps.gov/guco

Guilford Native American Association • P.O. Box 5623 • Greensboro, NC 27435 • (336) 273-8686 • http://www.guilfordnative.org

Hege Library • Guilford College, 5800 W Friendly Ave • Greensboro, NC 27410-4175 • (336) 316-2450 • http://www.guilford.edu/original/libraryart/

Mattye Reed African Heritage Center • NCA&T State Univ, 2711 McConnell Rd • Greensboro, NC 27411 • (336) 334-7874

North Carolina Friends Historical Society • Guilford College, 5800 W Friendly Ave, P.O. Box 8502 • Greensboro, NC 27410 • (336) 316-2264 • http://www.ncfhs.org

North Carolina Society of County and Local Historians • 1209 Hill St • Greensboro, NC 27408

Preservation Greensboro • Blandwood Mansion Museum, 447 W Washington St • Greensboro, NC 27401-2348 • (336) 272-5003

Sons of the American Revolution, Nathanael Greene Chapter • 1106 Gretchen Ln • Greensboro, NC 27410

Tannenbaum Historic Park • 2200 New Garden Rd • Greensboro, NC 27410 • (336) 545-5315 • http://www.greensboro-nc.gov/leisure/

Greenville
J Y Joyner Library • East Carolina Univ, E 5th St • Greenville, NC 27858-4353 • (252) 328-6514 • http://www.lib.ecu.edu

Pitt County Family Researchers • P.O. Box 2608 • Greenville, NC 27858-0608 • http://www.rootsweb.ancestry.com/~ncpcfr/

Pitt County Historical Society • Historic Red Banks Primitive Baptist Church, 14th & Fire Tower Rd, P.O. Box 1554 • Greenville, NC 27835 • (919) 355-5724 • http://www.pittcountyhistoricalsociety.com

Sheppard Memorial Library • 530 Evans St • Greenville, NC 27858 • (252) 329-4580 • http://www.sheppardlibrary.org

Halifax
Halifax County Genealogical Society • P.O. Box 447 • Halifax, NC 27839

Halifax County Historical Association • P.O. Box 12 • Halifax, NC 27839 • (919) 583-7821 • http://www.halifaxnc.com

Halifax County Library • 33 Granville St, P.O. Box 97 • Halifax, NC 27839-0097 • (252) 583-3631 • http://www.halifaxnc.com

Historic Halifax State Historic Site Museum • St David & Dobb Sts, P.O. Box 406 • Halifax, NC 27839 • (252) 583-7191 • http://www.nchistoricsites.org

Hamlet
Hamlet Public Library • 302 Main St • Hamlet, NC 28345-3304 • (910) 582-3477 • http://www.hamletnc.us/lib.htm

National Railroad Museum and Hall of Fame • 23 Hamlet Ave • Hamlet, NC 28345 • (910) 582-2383

Richmond Community College Library • Hwy 74, P.O. Box 1189 • Hamlet, NC 283459 • (910) 582-7000 • http://www.richmond.cc.nc.us

Hampstead
Pender County Public Library-Hampstead Branch • 17135 US Hwy 17 N • Hampstead, NC 28443 • (910) 270-4603

Harrisburg
Harrisburg Historical Society • 7676 Cotton St • Harrisburg, NC 28075 • http://www.harrisburghistoricalsociety.org

Haw River
Haw River Historical Association • general delivery • Haw River, NC 27258

Henderson
H Leslie Perry Memorial Library • 205 Breckenridge St • Henderson, NC 27356 • (252) 438-3316 • http://www.perrylibrary.org

Vance County Historical Society • P.O. Box 1533 • Henderson, NC 27536

Hendersonville
Henderson County Genealogical and Historical Society • Research Library, 400 N Main St, P.O. Box 1108 • Hendersonville, NC 28793-2616 • (828) 693-1531 • http://www.hcghs.com

Hendersonville
Henderson County Public Library • 301 N Washington St • Hendersonville, NC 28739 • (828) 697-4725 • http://www.henderson.lib.nc.us

Scottish District Families Association • 456 Beach Dr • Hendersonville, NC 28792

Hertford
Newbold-White House Museum • Harvey Point Rd, P.O. Box 103 • Hertford, NC 27944 • (252) 426-7567

Perquimans County Library • 110 W Academy St • Hertford, NC 27944 • (252) 426-5319 • http://www.pettigrew.lib.nc.us

Hickory
Catawba County Genealogical Society • P.O. Box 2406 • Hickory, NC 28603 • http://www.catawbacountygenealogicalsociety.org

Hickory Landmarks Society • Maple Grove House Museum, 542 5th Ave NE, P.O. Box 2341 • Hickory, NC 28603 • (828) 322-4731 • http://www.hickorylandmarks.com

Hickory Public Library • 375 3rd Ave NE • Hickory, NC 28601 • (828) 304-0500 • http://www.hickorygov.com/library/

Propst House Museum • 547 6th St • Hickory, NC 28603 • (704) 322-4731

Hiddenite
Alexander County Ancestry Association • P.O. Box 241 • Hiddenite, NC 28636-0241 • (828) 635-0064

Alexander County Genealogical Society • RR 2, Box 87-A • Hiddenite, NC 28636

Hiddenite Center Museum • 316 Church St, P.O. Box 311 • Hiddenite, NC 28636 • (828) 632-6966 • http://www.hiddenitecenter.com

High Point
High Point Historical Society • Historical Museum, 1805 E Lexington Ave • High Point, NC 27262 • (336) 885-6859 • http://highpointmuseum.org

High Point Museum and Historical Park • 1859 E Lexington Ave • High Point, NC 27262 • (336) 885-1859 • http://www.highpointmuseum.org

High Point Public Library • 901 N Main St, P.O. Box 2530 • High Point, NC 27261-2530 • (336) 883-3641 • http://www.hipopl.org

John Haley House Museum • 1859 E Lexington Ave • High Point, NC 27262 • (910) 885-6859

Smith Library • High Point University, 833 Montlieu Ave • High Point, NC 27262-4221 • (336) 841-9102 • http://www.library.highpoint.edu

Springfield Museum of Old Domestic Life • 555 E Springfield Rd • High Point, NC 27263 • (910) 889-4911

Highlands
Highlands Historical Society • 524 N 4th St, P.O. Box 670 • Highlands, NC 28741 • (828) 787-1050 • http://www.highlandshistory.com

Hillsborough
Alliance for Historic Hillsborough • 150 E King St • Hillsborough, NC 27278 • (919) 732-7741 • http://www.visithillsboroughnc.com/ahh

Ayr Mount Museum • 376 S Mary's Rd • Hillsborough, NC 27278 • (919) 732-6886

Moorefields House Museum • 2201 Moorfields Rd • Hillsborough, NC 27278 • (919) 732-4941

Orange County Historical Museum • 201 N Churton St • Hillsborough, NC 27278 • (919) 732-2201 • http://www.orangecountymuseum.org

Orange County Public Library • 300 W Tryon St, P.O. Box 8181 • Hillsborough, NC 27278 • (919) 732-8181 • http://www.co.orange.nc.us/library

Hollister
Haliwa-Saponi Tribe • 39021 NC Hwy 561, P.O. Box 99 • Hollister, NC 27844 • (919) 586-4017 • http://www.haliwa-saponi.com

Huntersville
Catawba Valley Scottish Society • P.O. Box 1009 • Huntersville, NC 28070-1009 • http://www.LochNorman.org

Center of Scottish Heritage Museum • Historic Rural Hill Farm, 4431 Neck Rd • Huntersville, NC 28078 • (704) 875-3113

Historic Latta Plantation Museum • 5225 Sample Rd • Huntersville, NC 27078 • (704) 875-2312 • http://www.lattaplantation.org

Hugh Torrance House and Store Museum • 8231 Gilead Rd • Huntersville, NC 28078 • (704) 875-3271

Jackson
Northampton Memorial Library • 207 W Jefferson St, P.O. Box 427 • Jackson, NC 27845-0427 • (252) 534-3571 • http://www.arlnc.org

Jacksonville
Onslow County Genealogical Society • P.O. Box 1739 • Jacksonville, NC 28541-1739 • (910) 347-5287

Onslow County Public Library • 58 Doris Ave E • Jacksonville, NC 28540 • (910) 455-7350 • http://www.co.onslow.nc.us/library

USMC MCAS Station Library • New River Air Sta, Bldg 213 • Jacksonville, NC 28545-5001 • (910) 449-6715 • http://library.usmc-mccs.org

Jamestown
Historic Jamestown Society • Mendenhall Plantation Museum, 603 W Main St, P.O. Box 512 • Jamestown, NC 27282 • (336) 454-3819 • http://www.mendenhallplantation.org

Jamestown Public Library • 200 W Main St, P.O. Box 1437 • Jamestown, NC 27282-1437 • (336) 454-4815

Jarvisburg
Historic Jarvisburg Colored School • 7300 Caratoke Hwy • Jarvisburg, NC 27947

Jonesville
Jonesville-Arlington Public Library • 150 W Main St • Jonesville, NC 28642 • (336) 835-7604 • http://www.nwrl.org/jonesville.htm

Kannapolis
Cannon Village Visitor Center Museum • 200 West Ave • Kannapolis, NC 28081 • (704) 938-3200 • http://www.cannonvillage.com

Kenansville
Dorothy Wightman Public Library • 107 Bowden Dr • Kenansville, NC 28349 • (910) 296-2117

Duplin County Historical Society • P.O. Box 775 • Kenansville, NC 28349 • http://www.duplinhistory.org

Duplin County Library • 107 Bowden Dr, P.O. Box 930 • Kenansville, NC 28349 • (910) 296-2117 • http://www2.youseemore.com/duplin/

James Sprunt Community College Library • P.O. Box 398 • Kenansville, NC 28349-0398 • (910) 296-2476 • http://www.jamessprunt.edu/library.html

Liberty Hall Museum • SR 11/24/50, P.O. Box 634 • Kenansville, NC 28349 • (910) 296-2175

Kenly
Tobacco Farm Life Museum • Hwy 301 N, 709 Church St, P.O. Box 88 • Kenly, NC 27542 • (919) 284-3431 • http://www.tobaccofarmlifemuseum.org

Kernersville
Kernersville Historical Preservation Society • P.O. Box 68 • Kernersville, NC 27285 • (336) 749-1222

Kernersville Historical Society • P.O. Box 2523 • Kernersville, NC 27285 • http://www.kernersvillenc.com

Korner's Folly Museum • 413 S Main St • Kernersville, NC 27284 • (336) 996-7922 • http://www.kornersfolly.org

Kill Devil Hills
Wright Brothers National Memorial Museum • Virginia Dare Trail, US 158 • Kill Devil Hills, NC 27948 • (252) 441-7430 • http://www.nps.gov/wrbr

Kings Mountain
Kings Mountain National Military Park Library • Hwy 216, Box 40 • Kings Mountain, NC 28086 • (864) 936-7921

Mauney Memorial Library • 100 S Piedmont Ave • Kings Mountain, NC 28086 • (704) 739-2371 • http://www.mauneylibrary.org

Kinston
CSS Neuse & Governor Richard Caswell Memorial • 2612 W Vernon Ave, P.O. Box 3043 • Kinston, NC 28502 • (252) 522-2091 • http://www.cssneuse.nchistoricsites.org

Harmony Hall Museum • 109 E King St • Kinston, NC 28501 • (252) 522-0421

Heritage Genealogical Society • c/o Heritage Place, Lenoir Community College Library, 231 Hwy 58 S, P.O. Box 6204 • Kinston, NC 28504 • (252) 427-6223 • http://www.historicalpreservationgroup.org

Heritage Place Archives • Lenoir Community College, 231 Hwy 58 S, P.O. Box 188 • Kinston, NC 28502 • (252) 427-6223 • http://www.lenoir.cc.nc.us

Historical Preservation Group of Lenoir County • 1603 West Rd • Kinston, NC 28501 • http://www.historicalpreservationgroup.org

Neuse Regional Library • 510 N Queen St • Kinston, NC 28501 • (252) 527-7066 • http://www.neuselibrary.org

Kure Beach
Fort Fisher State Historic Site Museum • 1610 Fort Fisher Blvd, P.O. Box 169 • Kure Beach, NC 28449 • (910) 458-5538 • http://www.nchistoricsites.org

Lake Junaluska
World Methodist Museum • 575 N Lakeshore Dr, P.O. Box 518 • Lake Junaluska, NC 28745 • (828) 456-9432 • http://www.worldmethodistcouncil.org

Lake Waccamaw
Lake Waccamaw Depot Museum • 201 Flemington Ave, P.O. Box 386 • Lake Waccamaw, NC 28450 • (910) 646-1992 • http://www.lakewaccamaw.com

Southeastern North Carolina Genealogical Society • P.O. Box 463 • Lake Waccamaw, NC 28450

Laurel Hill
Scotland County Genealogical Society • P.O. Box 496 • Laurel Hill, NC 28351 • http://ncgenweb.us/nc/scotland/

Laurinburg
Indian Museum of the Carolinas • 607 Turnpike Rd, P.O. Box 666 • Laurinburg, NC 28352 • (910) 276-5880

Scotland County Memorial Library • 312 W Church St, P.O. Box 369 • Laurinburg, NC 28353-0369 • (919) 276-0563

Lawndale
Lawndale Historical Society • Historical Museum, 119 Piedmont Dr, P.O. Box 733 • Lawndale, NC 28090 • (704) 538-7212 • http://www.lawndalenc.org

Lenoir
Caldwell County Genealogical Society • P.O. Box 2476 • Lenoir, NC 28645-2476 • (828) 757-1272

Caldwell County Public Library • 120 Hospital Ave • Lenoir, NC 28645 • (828) 757-1270 • http://www.ccpl.us/info/local_history_room.html

Caldwell Historical Society • Heritage Museum, 112 Vaiden St SW • Lenoir, NC 28645 • (828) 758-4004 • http://caldwellheritagemuseum.org

Fort Defiance Museum • 1792 Fort Defiance Dr • Lenoir, NC 28645 • (828) 758-1671

Lewisville

Lewisville Historical Society • P.O. Box 242 • Lewisville, NC 27023 • http://www.lewisvillehistory.com/

Lexington

Davidson County Historical Museum • Old Courthouse, 2 S Main St • Lexington, NC 27292 • (336) 242-2035 • http://www.co.davidson.nc.us/museum

Davidson County Public Library • 602 S Main St • Lexington, NC 27292 • (336) 242-2040 • http://www.co.davidson.nc.us/library

Genealogical Society of Davidson County • P.O. Box 1665 • Lexington, NC 27292-1665 • (910) 242-2040 • http://www.rootsweb.ancestry.com/~ncgsdc/

Grady E Love Library • Davidson County Community College, 297 DCCC Rd, P.O. Box 1287 • Lexington, NC 27293-1287 • (336) 475-7181 • http://www.davidson.cc.nc.us/lrc

Lillington

Harnett County Public Library • 601 N Main St, P.O. Box 1149 • Lillington, NC 27546 • (910) 893-3446 • http://www.harnett.org/library/

Lincolnton

African American Genealogical Association • 211 W Water St • Lincolnton, NC 28092 • (704) 736-8442

Lincoln County Historical Association • Historical Museum, 403 E Main St • Lincolnton, NC 28092 • (704) 748-9090 • http://www.lincolncountyhistory.com

Lincoln County Public Library • 306 W Main St • Lincolnton, NC 28092 • (704) 735-8044 • http://www.glrl.lib.nc.us

Louisburg

C W Robbins Library • Louisburg College, 501 N Main St • Louisburg, NC 27549-7704 • (919) 497-3269 • http://www.louisburg.edu

Franklin County Library • 906 N Main St • Louisburg, NC 27549-2199 • (919) 496-2111 • http://www.county.franklin.nc.com

Preservation North Carolina • 122 S Church St • Louisburg, NC 27549 • (252) 497-0434

Lumberton

Humphrey-Williams-Smith Plantation Museum • 5000 HC 211 W • Lumberton, NC 28358 • (910) 739-6670

Robeson County Historical and Genealogical Society • P.O. Box 2292 • Lumberton, NC 28359 • http://www.rootsweb.ancestry.com/~ncrcgs2/index.html

Robeson County Public Library • 101 N Chestnut St, P.O. Box 988 • Lumberton, NC 28359-0988 • (919) 738-4859 • http://robesoncountylibrary.libguides.com/content.php?pid=361138&sid=2953309

Madison

Rockingham County Public Library-Madison Branch • 140 E Murphy St • Madison, NC 27025 • (336) 548-6553

Manteo

Cape Hatteras National Seashore Library • Route 1, Box 675 • Manteo, NC 27954 • (252) 473-2111

Dare County Library • 700 N Hwy 64-264, P.O. Box 1000 • Manteo, NC 27954 • (252) 473-2372 • http://www.earlibrary.org

Fort Raleigh National Historic Site Museum • 1401 National Park Dr • Manteo, NC 27954 • (252) 473-2111 • http://www.nps.gov/for a

Outer Banks History Center • Roanoke Island Festival Park, P.O. Box 250 • Manteo, NC 27954-0250 • (252) 475-1500 • http://www.roanokeisland.com

Marion

Historic Carson House Museum • 1805 US Hwy, 70 W Marion • Marion, NC 28752 • (704) 724-4948 • http://www.mcdowellnc.org

McDowell County Public Library • 90 W Court St • Marion, NC 28752 • (828) 652-3858 • http://www.mcdowellpubliclibrary.org

Mars Hill

Madison County Genealogical Society • P.O. Box 155 • Mars Hill, NC 28754-0155 • https://www.facebook.com/pages/Madison-County-Genealogical-Society/205218599441

Renfro Library • Mars Hill College, 124 Cascade St, P.O. Box 220 • Mars Hill, NC 28754 • (828) 689-1468 • http://www.mhc.edu/library

Marshville

Union County Historical Society • P.O. Box 86 • Marshville, NC 28103

Matthews

Matthews Historical Foundation • Massey-Clark House Museum, 232 N Trade St, P.O. Box 1117 • Matthews, NC 28106 • (704) 849-7368 • http://www.matthewsheritagemuseum.org

Matthews Reid House Museum • 134 W John St • Matthews, NC 28105 • (704) 849-7368 • http://www.matthewsreidhouse.org

Maxton

Maxton Historical Society • 201 W Graham St, P.O. Box 55 • Maxton, NC 28364 • (910) 844-2377

Mayodan

Genealogical Society of Rockingham and Stokes Counties • P.O. Box 152 • Mayodan, NC 27027 • http://www.gsrsnc.com/

Mebane

Mebane Historical Society • Historical Museum, 209 W Jackson St, P.O. Box 1541 • Mebane, NC 27302 • (919) 563-5054 • http://www.mebanehistoricalsociety.org

Occaneechi Band of the Saponi Nation • 207 E Center St, P.O. Box 356 • Mebane, NC 27302 • (919) 304-3723 • http://www.occaneechi-saponi.org

Midland

Reed Gold Mine Museum • 9621 Reed Mine Rd • Midland, NC 28107 • (704) 721-4653 • http://www.reedmine.com

Mint Hill

Mint Hill Historical Society • 7601 Mathews-Mint Hill Rd • Mint Hill, NC 28227 • (704) 573-0726

Misenheimer

Gustavus Adolphus Pfeiffer Library • Pfeiffer Univ, 48380 US Hwy 52 N, P.O. Box 930 • Misenheimer, NC 28109-0930 • (704) 463-1360 • http://library.pfeiffer.edu

Mocksville

Davie County Historical & Genealogical Society • 371 N Main St • Mocksville, NC 27028 • http://www.rootsweb.ancestry.com/~ncdavhgs/

Davie County Public Library • 371 N Main St • Mocksville, NC 27028-2115 • (336) 751-2023 • http://www.daviecountync.gov/index.aspx?NID=400

Monroe

Carolinas Genealogical Society • 605 Craig St, P.O. Box 397 • Monroe, NC 28111-0397 • (704) 289-6737 • http://www.rootsweb.ancestry.com/~ncunion/Genealogical_society.htm

Monroe, cont.
Union County Heritage Room • Old Courthouse, 300 N Main St, P.O. Box 397 • Monroe, NC 28111 • (704) 289-6737

Union County Public Library • 316 E Windsor St • Monroe, NC 28110 • (704) 283-8184 • http://www.union.lib.nc.us

Montreat
Historic Foundation of the Presbyterian and Reformed Churches • 318 Georgia Terr, P.O. Box 849 • Montreat, NC 28757 • (828) 669-7061 • http://www.history.pcusa.org

Presbyterian Heritage Center • 318 Georgia Terr • Montreat, NC 28757 • (828) 669-6556 • http://www.phcmontreat.org

Mooresville
Mooresville Public Library-Special Collections • 413 N Main St • Mooresville, NC 28115 • (704) 664-2927 • http://ci.mooresville.nc.us/portal/library

Morehead City
Carteret County Historical Society • History Place Museum, 1008 Arendell St • Morehead City, NC 28557 • (252) 247-7533 • http://www.thehistoryplace.org

Morganton
Burke County Genealogical Society • c/o Burke County Public Library, 204 S King St, P.O. Box 661 • Morganton, NC 28655-0661 • (828) 437-5638 • http://www.ncgenweb.us/burke/burkegs.htm

Burke County Historical Society • c/o Burke County Public Library, 204 S King St, P.O. Box 151 • Morganton, NC 28655 • (828) 437-5638

Burke County Public Library • 204 S King St • Morganton, NC 28655-3535 • (828) 437-5638 • http://www.bcpls.org

Historic Burke Foundation • Old Burke Courthouse Museum, Courthouse Square, P.O. Box 915 • Morganton, NC 28655 • (704) 437-4104 • http://www.historicburke.org

Mount Airy
Edwards-Franklin House Museum • Haystack Rd • Mount Airy, NC 27030 • (336) 785-8359

Gertrude Smith House Museum • 708 N Main St • Mount Airy, NC 27030 • (336) 786-6856 • http://www.visitmountairy.com

Mount Airy Museum of Regional History • Research Library, 301 N Main St • Mount Airy, NC 27030 • (336) 786-4478 • http://www.northcarolinamuseum.org

Mount Gilead
Town Creek Indian Mound State Historic Site Museum • 509 Town Creek Mound Rd • Mount Gilead, NC 27306 • (910) 439-6802 • http://www.nchistoricsites.org

Mount Holly
Gaston County Historical Society • P.O. Box 986 • Mount Holly, NC 28120 • (704) 867-6712

Gaston-Lincoln Genealogical Society • P.O. Box 584 • Mount Holly, NC 28120-0584 • (704) 435-4725 • http://www.rootsweb.ancestry.com/~ncglgs/Index.htm

Mount Holly Historical Society • 131 S Main St, P.O. Box 12 • Mount Holly, NC 28120 • (704) 827-7552 • https://www.facebook.com/MHHSNC/info

Mount Olive
Moye Library • Mount Olive College, 634 Henderson St • Mount Olive, NC 28365-1699 • (919) 658-7168 • http://www.moc.edu

Mount Pleasant
Eastern Cabarrus Historical Society • Historic Museum, 1100 N Main St, P.O. Box 1299 • Mount Pleasant, NC 28124 • (704) 436-6570 • http://www.echsm.net

Murfreesboro
1810 John Wheeler House Museum • 4th & Broad Sts, P.O. Box 3 • Murfreesboro, NC 27855 • (252) 398-5922 • http://www.murfreesboronc.org/wheeler.htm

Brady C Jefcoat Museum of Americana • Old Murfreesboro High School, 201 W High St • Murfreesboro, NC 27855 • (252) 398-5922 • http://www.murfreesboronc.com

Hertford Academy Museum • Sycamore & Broad Sts, P.O. Box 3 • Murfreesboro, NC 27855 • (252) 398-6922 • http://www.murfreesboronc.org/hertford.htm

Murfreesboro Historical Association • Roberts-Vaughn House Museum, 116 E Main St, P.O. Box 3 • Murfreesboro, NC 27855 • (252) 398-5922 • http://www.murfreesboronc.com

Murfree-Smith Law Office Museum • P.O. Box 3 • Murfreesboro, NC 27855 • (252) 398-5922 • http://www.murfreesboronc.org/murfreesmith.htm

Whitaker Library • Chowan College, 200 Jones Dr • Murfreesboro, NC 27855 • (252) 398-6212 • http://library.chowan.edu

William Rea Office and Store Museum • 4th & Williams Sts, P.O. Box 3 • Murfreesboro, NC 27855 • (252) 398-5922 • http://www.murfreesboronc.org/rea.htm

Winborne Law Office and Country Store Museum • 4th & Broad Sts, P.O. Box 3 • Murfreesboro, NC 27855 • (252) 398-5922 • http://www.murfreesboronc.org/winbornlawstore.htm

Murphy
Cherokee County Historical Museum • 87 Peachtree St • Murphy, NC 28906 • (704) 837-6792 • http://www.tib.com/cchm

Cherokee County Historical Society • 205 Peachtree St • Murphy, NC 28906

Murphy Public Library • 9 Blumenthal St • Murphy, NC 28906-3095 • (828) 837-2417

Nantahala Regional Library • 11 Blumenthal St • Murphy, NC 28906-3095 • (828) 837-2025 • http://www.nantahalalibrary.org

Southwestern North Carolina Genealogical Society • 101 Blumenthal • Murphy, NC 28906 • (704) 837-2417

New Bern
Attmore-Oliver House Museum • 510 Pollock St, P.O. Box 119 • New Bern, NC 28563 • (252) 638-8558 • http://www.newbernhistorical.org

Bellair Plantation Museum • 1100 Washington Post Rd • New Bern, NC 28560 • (252) 637-3913

Craven County Genealogical Society • 1207 Forest Dr, P.O. Box 1344 • New Bern, NC 28563-1344 • http://www.cravengenealogy.org

Eastern North Carolina Genealogical Society • P.O. Box 395 • New Bern, NC 28560

Friends of Firemen's Museum • 408 Hancock St • New Bern, NC 28560 • (252) 636-4087 • http://www4.coastalnet.com/nerbern/psafepg6.htm

New Bern Historical Society • 511 Broad St, P.O. Box 119 • New Bern, NC 28563 • (252) 638-8558 • http://newbernhistorical.org

New Bern-Craven County Public Library • 400 Johnson St • New Bern, NC 28560-4098 • (252) 638-7800 • http://www.cpclib.org

Order of Descendants of Ancient Planters • 109 Southern Hills Dr • New Bern, NC 28562 • (252) 633-9069 • http://www.ancientplanters.org

Sons of the American Revolution, New Bern Chapter • 812 Plantation Dr • New Bern, NC 28562

Tryon Palace Historic Site & Gardens • 610 Pollock St, P.O. Box 1007 • New Bern, NC 28560 • (252) 514-4876 • http://www.tyronpalace.org

New Hill
North Carolina Railway Museum • 3900 Bonsal Rd, P.O. Box 40 • New Hill, NC 27562-0040 • (919) 362-5416 • http://www.triangletrain.com

Newland
Avery County Morrison Public Library • P.O. Box 250 • Newland, NC 28657 • (828) 733-9393 • http://www.amy.lib.nc.us

Avery County Museum • 1829 Schultz Cr, P.O. Box 266 • Newland, NC 28657 • (828) 733-7111 • http://www.averymuseum.com

Newton
Catawba County Historic Museum • 1 Courthouse Sq, P.O. Box 73 • Newton, NC 28658-0073 • (828) 465-0383 • http://www.catawbahistory.org

Catawba County Historical Association • Harper House-Hickory History Center, 310 N Center St, P.O. Box 73 • Newton, NC 28658-0073 • (828) 465-0383 • http://www.catawbahistory.org

Catawba County Library • 115 West C St • Newton, NC 28658 • (828) 465-8664 • http://www.catawbacountync.gov/library/

Old Catawba County Courthouse Museum • 15 N College Ave • Newton, NC 28658

Newton Grove
Bentonville Battlefield Historical Association • P.O. Box 432 • Newton Grove, NC 28366 • http://www.bbhainc.org

North Wilkesboro
Appalachian Regional Library • 215 10th St • North Wilkesboro, NC 28659 • (336) 838-2818 • http://www.arlibrary.org

Wilkes County Library • 215 10th St • North Wilkesboro, NC 28659 • (336) 838-2818

Wilkes Genealogical Society • c/o Wilkes County Library, 215 10th St, P.O. Box 1629 • North Wilkesboro, NC 28659-1629 • (336) 838-2818 • https://www.facebook.com/pages/Wilkes-Genealogical-Society/356882397738332

Ocracoke
Ocracoke Preservation Society • David Williams House Museum and Research Library, Hwy 12 at the Marina, P.O. Box 1240 • Ocracoke, NC 27960 • (252) 928-7375 • http://www.ocracokepreservation.org

Old Fort
1793 Col John Carson House Museum • Route 1, Box 182 • Old Fort, NC 28762 • (704) 724-4640

Daughters of the American Revolution • Old Fort, NC 28762 • (828) 668-1776

Mountain Gateway Museum • Water & Catawba Sts, P.O. Box 1286 • Old Fort, NC 28762 • (704) 668-9259 • http://www.medowellcounty.org

Oxford
Grandville County Library System • 210 Main St, P.O. Box 339 • Oxford, NC 27565 • (919) 693-1121 • http://www.granville.lib.nc.us

Granville County Genealogical Society • P.O. Box 1746 • Oxford, NC 27565 • http://www.gcgs.org

Granville County Historical Society • Historical Museum, 1 Museum Ln, P.O. Box 1433 • Oxford, NC 27565 • (919) 693-9706 • http://www.granvillemuseumnc.org

Granville County Historical Society Library • Historical Museum, 110 Court St, P.O. Box 1433 • Oxford, NC 27565 • (919) 693-9706

Pembroke
Founders of the New Haven Colony • P.O. Box 3636 • Pembroke, NC 28372 • (910) 844-2377 • http://www.bbtyner.com/NEWHAVEN.htm

Lumbee Tribe of North Carolina • P.O. Box 68 • Pembroke, NC 28372 • (910) 521-8602 • http://www.lumbeetribe.com

Native American Resource Center • Univ of NC at Pembroke, P.O. Box 1510 • Pembroke, NC 28372 • (910) 521-6282 • http://www.uncp.edu/nativemuseum/

Sampson-Livermore Library • Univ of North Carolina at Pembroke, Faculty Row, P.O. Box 1510 • Pembroke, NC 28372-1510 • (910) 521-6516 • http://www.uncp.edu/library

Pinehurst
Given Memorial Library • 150 Cherokee Rd, P.O. Box 159 • Pinehurst, NC 28370 • (910) 295-6022

Moore County Genealogical Society • P.O. Box 1183 • Pinehurst, NC 28374-1183 • http://www.rootsweb.ancestry.com/~ncmcgs/

Scottish Heritage USA • P.O. Box 457 • Pinehurst, NC 28374 • (919) 295-4448 • http://www.sandhills.org/shusa/

Pinetops
Edgecombe County Genealogical Society • P.O. Box 656 • Pinetops, NC 27864 • (252) 823-1411 • http://www.edgecombelibrary.org/genealogical%20society/edgecombe_county_genealogica.htm

Pineville
James E Polk Memorial State Historic Site Museum • 12031 Lancaster Hwy, P.O. Box 475 • Pineville, NC 28134 • (704) 889-7145 • http://www.nchistoricsites.org

Pinnacle
Horne Creek Farm Museum • 309 Horn Creek Farm Rd • Pinnacle, NC 27043 • (336) 325-2298 • http://www.nchistoricsites.org

Pisgah Forest
1815 Allison-Deaver House Museum • 2753 Asheville Hwy • Pisgah Forest, NC 28768 • (828) 884-5137 • http://www.tchistoricalsociety.com

Pittsboro
Chatham County Historical Association • Chatham County Courthouse Museum, P.O. Box 93 • Pittsboro, NC 27312 • (919) 542-3603 • http://www.chathamhistory.org

Plymouth
Pettigrew Regional Library • 201 E 3rd St, P.O. Box 906 • Plymouth, NC 27962-0906 • (252) 793-2875 • http://www.pettigrewlibraries.org

Washington County Genealogical Society • P.O. Box 567 • Plymouth, NC 27062-0567

Washington County Historical Society • 302 W Water St, P.O. Box 296 • Plymouth, NC 27962 • (252) 793-1377

Plymouth
Washington County Library • 3rd & Adams Sts, P.O. Box 786 • Plymouth, NC 27962 • (252) 793-2113

Polkton
South Piedmont Community College Library • Hwy 74 E, P.O. Box 126 • Polkton, NC 28135 • (704) 272-7635 • http://www.spcc.edu

Pollocksville
Neuse Regional Library-Pollocksville Public Library • 415 Greenhill St • Pollocksville, NC 28573 • (252) 224-5011 • http://www.neuselibrary.org

Pollocksville Public Library • Greenhill St, P.O. Box 6 • Pollocksville, NC 28573 • (252) 224-5011

Pope AFB
Pope Air Force Base Library FL4488 • 43 SVS/SVMG, 396 Sonic St Bldg 373 • Pope AFB, NC 28308-5225 • (910) 394-2195

Poplar Branch
Currituck County Historical Society • P.O. Box 115 • Poplar Branch, NC 27965

North Carolina

Raleigh

Afro-American Heritage Society of North Carolina • P.O. Box 26334 • Raleigh, NC 27611

Capital Area Preservation • P.O. Box 28072, Capitol Sta • Raleigh, NC 27611-8072 • (919) 833-6404 • http://capitalareapreservation.com

Descendants of the Knights of Bath - NC Society • 1404 Shadyside Dr • Raleigh, NC 27612

Federation of North Carolina Historical Societies • 109 E Jones St • Raleigh, NC 27601-2807 • (919) 807-7280 • http://www.fnchs.org

Friends of the Archives • 4614 Mail Service Center • Raleigh, NC 27699-4614 • (919) 733-3952 • http://www.history.ncdcr.gov

Haywood Hall and Gardens Museum • 211 New Bern Place • Raleigh, NC 27601 • (919) 832-8357 • http://www.haywoodhall.org

Historic Preservation Foundation of North Carolina • Raleigh City Museum, 220 Fayetteville St Mall, P.O. Box 27644 • Raleigh, NC 27611 • (919) 832-3652 • http://www.presnc.org

Hugenot Society of North Carolina • 4901 Deer Garden Ct • Raleigh, NC 27612 • http://www.huguenot.netnation.com/general/

Jewish Genealogy Society of Raleigh • 8701 Sleepy Creek Dr • Raleigh, NC 27612

Joel Lane House Museum • 728 W Hargett St, P.O. Box 10884 • Raleigh, NC 27605-0884 • (919) 833-3431 • http://www.joellane.org

Masonic Grand Lodge of North Carolina • 2921 Glenwood Ave, P.O. Box 6506 • Raleigh, NC 27628 • (919) 787-2021 • http://www.grandlodge-nc.org

Mordecai Square Historical Society • Historic Museum, 1 Mimosa St • Raleigh, NC 27604 • (919) 834-4844 • http://www.capitalareapreservation.org

North Carolina Division of Archives and History • State Library Bldg, 109 E Jones St • Raleigh, NC 27611 • (919) 733-3952 • http://www.history.ncdcr.gov

North Carolina Genealogical Society • P.O. Box 30815 • Raleigh, NC 27622-0815 • (919) 925-9281 • http://www.ncgenealogy.org

North Carolina Literary and Historical Association • 1104 Mordecai Dr • Raleigh, NC 27604 • (919) 807-7280 • http://www.history.ncdcr.gov/affiliates/lit-hist/lit-hist.htm

North Carolina Military Historical Society • 7410 Chapel Hill Rd • Raleigh, NC 27607-5096 • http://www.ncmhs.net

North Carolina Museum of History • 5 E Edenton St • Raleigh, NC 27601-1011 • (919) 807-7900 • http://www.ncmuseumofhistory.org

North Carolina Presbyterian Historical Society • P.O. Box 20804 • Raleigh, NC 27619-0804 • http://www.ncphsociety.org

North Carolina State Capitol Museum • 1 East Edenton St • Raleigh, NC 27699 • (919) 733-4994 • http://www.nchistoricsites.org

North Carolina State Library • 109 E Jones St • Raleigh, NC 27601-2807 • (919) 807-7400 • http://statelibrary.ncdcr.gov/ghl/resources/genealogy.html

North Carolina Supreme Court Historical Society • P.O. Box 26972 • Raleigh, NC 27511 • (919) 434-2603 • http://www.ncschs.net

Oak View House Museum • 4028 Carya Dr • Raleigh, NC 27610 • (919) 250-1013

PAF-Finders Club • 8501 Southampton Dr • Raleigh, NC 27615

Prezell R Robinson Library • Saint Augustine's College, 1315 Oakwood Ave • Raleigh, NC 27610-2298 • (919) 516-4145 • http://www.st-aug.edu

Raleigh City Cemeteries Preservation Inc • P.O. Box 829, Century Sta • Raleigh, NC 27602 • (919) 859-0348 • http://www.rccpreservation.org

Raleigh City Museum • 220 Fayetteville St • Raleigh, NC 27601 • (919) 832-3775 • http://www.raleighcitymuseum.org

Raleigh Historic Development Commission • 219 Fayetteville St Mall, P.O. Box 829, Century Sta • Raleigh, NC 27602 • (919) 832-7238 • http://www.rhdc.org

Society of North Carolina Archivists • P.O. Box 20448 • Raleigh, NC 27619 • (919) 787-6313 • http://www.ncarchivists.org

Sons of the American Revolution, Raleigh Chapter • 2108 Weybridge Dr • Raleigh, NC 27615

Ulster-Scots Society of America • P.O. Box 33772 • Raleigh, NC 27636 • http://www.ulsterscotssociety.com

Wake County Genealogical Society • c/o Olivia Raney Local History Library, 4016 Carya Dr, P.O. Box 17713 • Raleigh, NC 27619-7713 • (919) 851-2593 • http://www.rootsweb.ancestry.com/~ncwcgs/

Wake County Historical Society • P.O. Box 2 • Raleigh, NC 27602 • http://www.wakehistory.com

Wake County Public Library • 4020 Carya Dr • Raleigh, NC 27610-2900 • (919) 250-1200 • http://www.wakegov.com

Wake County Public Library System-Cameron Village Regional • 1930 Clark Ave • Raleigh, NC 27605 • (919) 856-6710

Wake County Public Libr-Olivia Raney Local History • 4016 Carya Dr • Raleigh, NC 27610 • (919) 250-1196 • http://www.wakegov.com/libraries/Research/collections/Pages/orl/default.aspx

Randleman

Saint Paul Museum • 411 High Point St • Randleman, NC 27317 • (336) 498-2447

Reidsville

Chinqua-Penn Plantation Museum • 2138 Wentworth St • Reidsville, NC 27320 • (336) 349-4576 • http://www.chinquapenn.com

Richlands

Onslow County Museum • 301 S Wilmington St, P.O. Box 384 • Richlands, NC 28574 • (910) 324-5008 • http://www.co.onslow.nc.us/museum

Roanoke Rapids

Roanoke Rapids Public Library • 319 Roanoke Ave • Roanoke Rapids, NC 27870 • (252) 533-2890 • http://www.roanokerapidsnc.com

Robersonville

Robersonville Public Library • 119 S Main St, P.O. Box 1060 • Robersonville, NC 27871-1060 • (252) 795-3591

Rockingham

Leak-Wall House Museum • P.O. Box 1763 • Rockingham, NC 28380

Richmond County Genealogical Society • P.O. Box 1763 • Rockingham, NC 28380

Richmond County Historical Society • 505 Rockingham Rd, P.O. Box 1763 • Rockingham, NC 28379 • (910) 895-9057 • http://rchs-nc.net

Rockingham Depot Museum • P.O. Box 1763 • Rockingham, NC 28380 • http://rchs-nc.net/railroad-museums/

Society of Loyalist Descendants of the American Revolution • P.O. Box 848 • Rockingham, NC 28379 • (910) 997-6641

Society of Richmond County (North Carolina) Descendants • P.O. Box 848 • Rockingham, NC 28379 • (910) 997-6641

Thomas H Leath Memorial Library • 412 E Franklin St • Rockingham, NC 28379-4995 • (910) 895-6337 • http://www.co.richmond.nc.us

Rockwell

Historic Rockwell Association • Historical Museum, 105 E Main St, P.O. Box 35 • Rockwell, NC 28138 • (704) 279-4979 • http://www.rockwellnc.gov/html/museum.html

Rocky Mount

Nash County Historical Association • Stonewall House Museum, 1331 Stonewall Ln • Rocky Mount, NC 27804 • (252) 443-4148

Pearsall Library • North Carolina Wesleyan College, 3400 N Wesleyan Blvd • Rocky Mount, NC 27804 • (252) 985-5350 • http://annex.ncwc.edu/library

Tar River Connections Genealogical Society • 101 Wildwood Ave, P.O. Box 8764 • Rocky Mount, NC 27804

Thomas Hackney Braswell Memorial Library • 727 N Grace St • Rocky Mount, NC 27804 • (252) 442-1951 • http://www.braswell-library.org

Rodanthe

Chicamacomico Historical Association • Life-Saving Station Historic Site, 23645 NC Hwy 12, P.O. Box 5 • Rodanthe, NC 27968 • (252) 987-1552 • http://www.chicamacomico.net

Rose Hill

Duplin County Historical Foundation • William Dallas Herring Memorial Library, 314 Main St, P.O. Box 237 • Rose Hill, NC 28458 • (910) 289-2654 • http://www.duplinhistory.org

Leora H McEachern Library of Local History • 306 E Main St, P.O. Box 130 • Rose Hill, NC 28458 • (910) 289-2430

Roxboro

Person County Historical Society • Historical Museum, 309 N Main St, P.O. Box 887 • Roxboro, NC 27573 • (336) 597-2884 • http://www.visitroxboronc.com/heritage.htm

Person County Public Library • 319 S Main St • Roxboro, NC 27573 • (336) 597-7881 • http://www2.person-net/person/library/

Sappony Tribe • P.O. Box 3265 • Roxboro, NC 27574 • http://www.sappony.org

Rutherfordton

Norris Public Library • 132 N Main • Rutherfordton, NC 28139 • (828) 287-4981

Salisbury

Carnegie Library • Livingstone College, 701 W Monroe St • Salisbury, NC 28144 • (704) 216-6030 • http://www.livingstonelibrary.org

Corriher-Linn-Black Library • Catawba College, 2300 W Innes St • Salisbury, NC 28144-2488 • (704) 637-4448 • http://www.catawba.edu

Genealogical Society of Rowan County • P.O. Box 4305 • Salisbury, NC 28144-4305 • https://www.lib.co.rowan.nc.us/HistoryRoom/html/gsrc.htm

Historic Salisbury Foundation • Depot, 215 Depot St, P.O. Box 4221 • Salisbury, NC 28144 • (704) 636-0103

Josephus Wells Hall House Museum • 226 S Jackson St, P.O. Box 4221 • Salisbury, NC 28145 • (704) 636-01016

Rowan Museum • 202 N Main St • Salisbury, NC 28146 • (704) 633-5946 • http://www.rowanmuseum.org

Rowan Public Library • 201 W Fisher St, P.O. Box 4039 • Salisbury, NC 28145-4039 • (704) 638-3010 • http://www.rowanpubliclibrary.org

Sons of the American Revolution, Salisbury Chapter • 114 Ridge Creek Rd • Salisbury, NC 28147

Utzman-Chambers House Museum • 114 S Jackson St • Salisbury, NC 28144 • (704) 633-5946

Sanford

House in the Horseshoe State Historic Site Museum • 288 Alston House Rd • Sanford, NC 27330-8713 • (910) 947-2051 • http://www.nchistoricsites.org

Lee County Genealogical Society • P.O. Box 3216 • Sanford, NC 27331-3216

Lee County Library • 107 Hawkins Ave • Sanford, NC 27330-4399 • (919) 774-6045 • http://www.leecountync.com/siteb.html#library

Railroad House Historical Association • Historical Museum, 110 Charlotte Ave, P.O. Box 1023 • Sanford, NC 27330 • (919) 776-7479 • http://www.leecountync.gov/History/RailroadHouseHistoricalAssociation.aspx

Scotland Neck

Halifax County Library-Scotland Neck Memorial • 1600 Main St, P.O. Box 126 • Scotland Neck, NC 27874-0126 • (252) 826-5578

Sedalia

Charlotte Hawkins Brown Museum • 6136 Burlington Rd, P.O. Box B • Sedalia, NC 27249 • (336) 449-4846 • http://www.nchistoricsites.org

Seven Springs

Cliffs of the Neuse State Park Museum • 345 A Park Entrance Rd • Seven Springs, NC 28578 • (919) 778-6234 • http://www.ncsparks.net

Shelby

Broad River Genealogical Society • 1145 County Home Rd, P.O. Box 2261 • Shelby, NC 28151-2261 • (704) 482-3016 • http://www.rootsweb.ancestry.com/~ncbrgs/index.htm

Cleveland Community College Library • 137 S Post Rd • Shelby, NC 28152 • (704) 484-4053 • http://www.cleveland.cc.nc.us/staff/mckibbin/

Cleveland County Historical Association • Historical Museum, Court Sq, P.O. Box 1333 • Shelby, NC 28150 • (704) 482-8186

Cleveland County Memorial Library • 104 Howie Dr, P.O. Box 1120 • Shelby, NC 28151-1120 • (704) 487-9069 • http://www.ccml.org

Sherrills Ford

North Carolina Society of Historians • P.O. Box 93 • Sherrills Ford, NC 28673 • http://www.ncsocietyofhistorians.org/NCSH/Welcome.html

Smithfield

Johnson County Heritage Center • 241 E Market St, P.O. Box 2709 • Smithfield, NC 27577 • (919) 934-2836 • http://www.johnstonnc.com/mainpage.cfm?category_level_id=436&CFID=4826071&CFTOKEN=83806505

Johnston County Genealogical and Historical Society • c/o Public Library of Johnston County and Smithfield, 305 Market St, P.O. Box 2373 • Smithfield, NC 27577-3919 • (919) 934-8146

Public Library of Johnston County & Smithfield • 305 E Market St • Smithfield, NC 27577-3919 • (919) 934-8146 • http://www.johnstonnc.com/pljcs/index.cfm

Snow Hill

Greene County Museum • 107 NW 3rd St, P.O. Box 266 • Snow Hill, NC 28580 • (252) 747-1999 • http://greenemuseum.embarqspace.com

South Nags Head

Bodie Island Museum • Bodie Island Lighthouse • South Nags Head, NC 27959 • (252) 473-2111 • http://www.nps.gov/caha

Southern Pines

Moore County Historical Association • Shaw House, Morgan & Broad Sts, P.O. Box 324 • Southern Pines, NC 28387 • (910) 692-2051 • http://www.moorehistory.com

Southern Pines Public Library • 170 W Connecticut Ave • Southern Pines, NC 28387-4819 • (910) 692-8235 • http://www.sppl.net

Weymouth Center Museum • 555 E Connecticut Ae, P.O. Box 939 • Southern Pines, NC 28388 • (910) 692-6261

Southport

Brunswick County Library • 109 W Moore St • Southport, NC 28461 • (910) 457-6237

Southport Historical Society • P.O. Box 10014 • Southport, NC 28461 • (910) 457-0575 • http://www.southporthistoricalsociety.org

Sparta
Alleghany County Public Library • 122 N Main St, P.O. Box 656 • Sparta, NC 28675-0656 • (336) 372-5573 • http://www.nwrl.org

Alleghany Historical and Genealogical Society • Historical Museum, 7 N Main St, P.O. Box 817 • Sparta, NC 28675 • (336) 372-2115 • http://www.ahgs.org/site/

Spencer
North Carolina Transportation Museum • 411 S Salisbury Ave, P.O. Box 165 • Spencer, NC 28159 • (704) 636-2889 • http://www.nctrans.org

Spindale
Isothermal Community College Library • 286 ICC Loop Rd, P.O. Box 804 • Spindale, NC 28160-0804 • (828) 286-3636 • http://www.isothermal.edu

Rutherford County Library • 205 Callahan Koone Rd • Spindale, NC 28160 • (828) 287-6115 • http://www.rutherfordcountylibrary.org

Spring Lake
Sandhills Family Heritage Association • P.O. Box 404 • Spring Lake, NC 28390

Spruce Pine
Mayland Community College Library • 200 Mayland Dr, P.O. Box 547 • Spruce Pine, NC 28777 • (828) 765-7351 • http://www.mayland.cc.nc.us

Spruce Pine Public Library • 142 Walnut Ave • Spruce Pine, NC 28777 • (828) 765-4673 • http://www.amy.lib.nc.us

Toe Valley Genealogical Society • 491 Beaver Creek Rd • Spruce Pine, NC 28777

Statesville
Fort Dobbs State Historic Site Museum • 438 Fort Dobbs Rd, P.O. Box 241 • Statesville, NC 28625 • (704) 873-5882 • http://www.fortdobbs.org

Genealogical Society of Iredell County • Old Courthouse, 200 S Center St, P.O. Box 946 • Statesville, NC 28687-0946 • (704) 878-5384

Historic Vance House Association • 501 W Sharpe St • Statesville, NC 28677 • (704) 878-0661

Iredell County Public Library • 201 N Tradd St, P.O. Box 1810 • Statesville, NC 28687-1810 • (704) 878-3090 • http://www.co.iredell.nc.us/library/icpl.html

Iredell Museum of Heritage • 1335 Museum Rd • Statesville, NC 28625 • (704) 873-8734 • http://www.iredellmuseum.com

Supply
Brunswick Community College Library • 50 College Rd, P.O. Box 30 • Supply, NC 28462-0030 • (910) 755-7331 • http://www.brunswick.cc.nc.us/library/library.htm

Surf City
Historical Society of Topsail Island • P.O. Box 2645 • Surf City, NC 28445 • (910) 328-8663

Swainsboro
Coastal Genealogical Society • P.O. Box 1421 • Swainsboro, NC 28584

Swan Quarter
Hyde County Historical and Genealogical Society • Mattamuskeet Library, 20418 US 264 • Swan Quarter, NC 27885 • (252) 926-1955

Swannanoa
Ellison Library • Warren Wilson College, 701 Warren Wilson Rd • Swannanoa, NC 28778 • (828) 771-3035 • http://www.warren-wilson.edu/~library/

Swansboro
Coastal Genealogical Society • P.O. Box 1421 • Swansboro, NC 28584 • (910) 347-5287

Swansboro Historical Association • P.O. Box 1574 • Swansboro, NC 28584 • (252) 726-1421 • http://swansborohistoricsite.org

Sylva
Jackson Company Genealogical Society • 42 Asheville Hwy • Sylva, NC 28779 • (828) 631-2646

Southwestern Community College Library • 447 College Dr • Sylva, NC 28779 • (828) 586-4091 • http://www.southwesterncc.edu

Tarboro
Blount-Bridgers House Museum • 130 Bridgers St • Tarboro, NC 27886 • (919) 823-4159

Edgecombe County Memorial Library • 909 Main St • Tarboro, NC 27586 • (252) 823-1141 • http://www.edgecombelibrary.org

Edgecome County Genealogical Society • c/o Edgecome County Memorial Library, 909 Main St • Tarboro, NC 27886 • (252) 823-1141

Historic Preservation Program • Edgecombe Community College, 2009 W Wilson St • Tarboro, NC 27886

Perry-Weston Educational & Cultural Institute • 200 E Baker St • Tarboro, NC 27886-3804 • http://www.perry-weston.org

Phoenix Society for African American Research • 200 E Baker St • Tarboro, NC 27886

Taylorsville
Alexander County Library • 115 1st Ave SW • Taylorsville, NC 28681 • (828) 632-4058 • http://www.co.alexander.nc.us

Sons of the American Revolution, Catawba Valley Chapter • 165 Lakeshore Ln • Taylorsville, NC 28681

Thomasville
Thomasville Public Library • 14 Randolf St, P.O. Box 519 • Thomasville, NC 27360 • (336) 474-2690 • http://www.co.davidson.nc.us/library/ThomasvilleLibrary.aspx

Trenton
Jones County Historical Society • P.O. Box 351 • Trenton, NC 28585 • (919) 448-3911 • http://www.linkpendium.com/genealogy/USA/NC/Jones/

Troy
Montgomery County Public Library • 215 W Main St • Troy, NC 27371 • (910) 572-1311 • http://www.204.211.56.212/

Tryon
Polk County Genealogical Society • 485 Hunting County Rd • Tryon, NC 28782

Polk County Historical Association • 22 Depot St • Tryon, NC 28782 • (828) 859-2287

Valdese
Waldensian Heritage Museum • 208 Rodoret St, P.O. Box 111 • Valdese, NC 28690 • (828) 874-2531 • http://www.waldensianpresbyterian.com

Wadesboro
Anson County Genealogical Society • 874 Moores Lake Rd • Wadesboro, NC 28170

Anson County Historical Society • Historical Museum, 209 E Wade St, P.O. Box 732 • Wadesboro, NC 28170 • (704) 694-6694 • http://www.ansonhistoricalsociety.org

Hampton B Allen Library • 120 S Greene St • Wadesboro, NC 28170 • (704) 694-5177

Wake Forest
Wake Forest College Birthplace Society • Historical Museum, 414 N Main St, P.O. Box 494 • Wake Forest, NC 27588 • (919) 556-2911

Walkertown
Walkertown Area Historical Society • 3058 Church St, P.O. Box 1183 • Walkertown, NC 27051-1183 • http://www.walkertownareahistoricalsociety.org

Walnut Cove
Stokes County Historical Society • 403 S Main St • Walnut Cove, NC 27052 • (336) 593-9407

Warrenton
Warren County Historical Association • 210 Plummer St • Warrenton, NC 27589

Washington
Beaufort County Genealogical Society • P.O. Box 1089 • Washington, NC 27889-1089 • (252) 946-4212 • http://www.ncroots.com/Beaufort/bcgs.htm

Beaufort, Hyde, Martin Regional Library • Old Court House, 158 N Market St • Washington, NC 27889 • (252) 946-6401 • http://bhmlib.org/website

George H and Laura E Brown Library • 122 Van Norden St • Washington, NC 27889 • (252) 946-4300 • http://washington-nc.com/library.aspx

Waxhaw
Museum of the Waxhaws and Andrew Jackson Memorial • 8215 Waxhaw Hwy, P.O. Box 7 • Waxhaw, NC 28173 • (704) 843-1832 • http://www.museumofthewaxhaws.com/

Waynesville
Haywood County Genealogical Society • P.O. Box 1331 • Waynesville, NC 28786-1331 • (828) 452-4306 • http://www.rootsweb.ancestry.com/~nchcgs/

Haywood County Public Library • 402 S Haywood St • Waynesville, NC 28786-4398 • (828) 452-5169 • http://www.haywoodlibrary.org

Weaverville
Dry Ridge Historical Museum • c/o Weaverville Public Library, 41 N Main St, P.O. Box 413 • Weaverville, NC 28390 • (828) 250-6482

Zebulon B Vance Birthplace State Historic Site Museum • 911 Reems Creek Rd • Weaverville, NC 28787 • (828) 645-6506 • http://www.nchistoricsites.org

Wendell
Wendell Historical Society • P.O. Box 426 • Wendell, NC 27591 • http://www.wendellhistoricalsociety.com/Pages/default.aspx

World War II Wilmington Home Front Heritage Coalition • P.O. Box 426 • Wendell, NC 28402 • http://wilburjones.com/world-war-two-wilmington-coalition/

Wentworth
Gerald B James Library • Rockingham Community College, P.O. Box 38 • Wentworth, NC 27375-0038 • (336) 342-4261 • http://www.rcc.cc.nc.us/lrc/index2.htm

Rockingham County Historical Society • Historical Museum & Archives, 1075 NC 65, P.O. Box 84 • Wentworth, NC 27375 • (336) 634-4949 • http://www.themarconline.org

West Jefferson
Ashe County Historical Society • 148 Library Dr, P.O. Box 1361 • West Jefferson, NC 28640 • http://www.ashehistoricalsociety.org

Ashe County Public Library • 148 Library Dr • West Jefferson, NC 28694 • (336) 246-2041 • http://www.arlibrary.org

Whiteville
Columbus County Historical Society • P.O. Box 339 • Whiteville, NC 28472-0339

Columbus County Public Library • 407 N Powell Blvd • Whiteville, NC 28472 • (910) 642-3116

North Carolina Museum of Forestry • 415 S Madison St • Whiteville, NC 28472 • (910) 914-4185

Southeastern Community College Library • 4564 Tavern Hwy, P.O. Box 151 • Whiteville, NC 28472-0151 • (910) 642-7141 • http://www.southeastern.cc.nc.us

Southeastern North Carolina Genealogical Society • Route 2, Box 291E • Whiteville, NC 28472

Wilkesboro
Wilkes Community College Library • 1328 Collegiate Dr, P.O. Box 120 • Wilkesboro, NC 28697-0120 • (336) 838-6114 • http://www.wilkes.cc.nc.us/library

Williamston
Asa Biggs House Museum • 100 E Church St, P.O. Box 468 • Williamston, NC 27892 • (252) 792-6605

Martin County Community College Library • 1161 Kehukee Park Rd • Williamston, NC 27892-9988 • (252) 792-1521 • http://www.martin.cc.nc.us

Martin County Genealogical Society • P.O. Box 121 • Williamston, NC 27892-0121

Martin County Historical Society • c/o Martin County Community College Library, 1161 Kehukee Park Rd, P.O. Box 468 • Williamston, NC 27892 • (919) 792-1521 x296

Wilmington
Battleship North Carolina Museum • Battleship Dr, P.O. Box 480 • Wilmington, NC 28402 • (910) 251-5797 • http://www.battleshipnc.com

Bellamy Mansion Museum • 503 Market St, P.O. Box 1176 • Wilmington, NC 28402 • (910) 251-3700 • http://www.bellamymansion.org

Burgwin-Wright House Museum • 224 Market St • Wilmington, NC 28401 • (910) 762-0570 • http://www.burgwinwrighthouse.com

Cape Fear Community College Library • 415 N 2nd St • Wilmington, NC 28401-3993 • (910) 362-7034 • http://cfcc.net

Cape Fear Museum • 914 Market St • Wilmington, NC 28401-4731 • (910) 341-4350 • http://www.capefearmuseum.com

Historic Saint Thomas Society • Preservation Hall, 208 Dock St • Wilmington, NC 28401-4435 • (910) 763-4054

Lower Cape Fear Historical Society • Latimer House Museum, 126 S 3rd St • Wilmington, NC 28401 • (910) 762-0492 • http://hslcf.org

National Society of the Colonial Dames of America, State of North Carolina • Burgwin-Wright House, 224 Market St • Wilmington, NC 28401 • (910) 762-0570

New Hanover County Public Library • 201 Chestnut St • Wilmington, NC 28401 • (919) 798-6300 • http://www.nhcgov.com/library/Pages/default.aspx

Old New Hanover County Genealogical Society • P.O. Box 2536 • Wilmington, NC 28402-2536 • (910) 452-9407 • http://www.onhgs.org

Poplar Grove Plantation Museum • 10200 US Hwy 17 • Wilmington, NC 28411 • (910) 686-9518 • http://www.poplargrove.com

Sons of the American Revolution, Lower Cape Fear Chapter • 900 Seven Oaks Dr • Wilmington, NC 28405

Sons of the American Revolution, North Carolina Society • 2221 Oleander Dr • Wilmington, NC 28403

Wilmington, cont.

Wilmington Railroad Museum • 501 Nutt St • Wilmington, NC 28401 • (910) 763-2634 • http://www.wrrm.org

Wilson

Barton Museum • Whitehead & Gold St, P.O. Box 5000 • Wilson, NC 27893 • (252) 399-6477 • http://www.barton.edu

Wilson County Genealogical Society • P.O. Box 802 • Wilson, NC 27894-0802 • http://www.wcgs.org

Wilson County Historical Association • P.O. Box 2046 • Wilson, NC 27894

Wilson County Public Library • 249 W Nash St, P.O. Box 400 • Wilson, NC 27894-0400 • (919) 237-5355

Windsor

1763 King-Bazemore House Museum • 132 Hope House Rd • Windsor, NC 27983 • (252) 794-3140 • http://www.hopeplantation.org

Historic Hope Foundation • 1803 Hope Mansion Museum, 132 Hope House Rd • Windsor, NC 27983 • (252) 794-3140 • http://www.hopeplantation.org

Lawrence Memorial Public Library • 204 E Dundee St • Windsor, NC 27983 • (252) 794-2244 • http://www.albemarle-regional.lib.nc.us

Winnabow

Brunswick Town State Historic Site Museum • Fort Anderson, 8884 St Philips Rd SE • Winnabow, NC 28479 • (910) 371-6613 • http://www.nchistoricsites.org

Winston-Salem

Archives of the Moravian Church in America, Southern Province • 457 S Church St, P.O. Box L • Winston-Salem, NC 27108-0377 • (336) 722-1742 • http://moravianarchives.org

Dale H Gramley Library • Salem College, 601 S Church St, P.O. Box 10548 • Winston-Salem, NC 27108-0548 • (336) 721-2649 • http://www.salem.edu

Forsyth County Genealogical Society • c/o Forsyth County Public Library, 660 W 5th St, P.O. Box 5715 • Winston-Salem, NC 27113 • (336) 727-2152 • http://www.rootsweb.ancestry.com/~ncfcgs/

Forsyth County Historical Association • 6025 Crestridge Ln • Winston-Salem, NC 27105 • http://www.forsythnchistory.com/forsythresearch.html

Forsyth County Public Library • 660 W 5th St • Winston-Salem, NC 27101 • (336) 727-2556 • http://www.forsythlibrary.org

Historic Bethabara Park Library • 2147 Bethabara Rd • Winston-Salem, NC 27106 • (336) 924-8191 • http://www.bethbarapark.org

Independent Order of Odd Fellows, Grand Lodge • 422 N Trade St • Winston-Salem, NC 27101-2830 • (336) 725-5955 • http://www.ioof.org/genealogy.html

International Association of Rebekah Assemblies • 422 N Trade St • Winston-Salem, NC 27101 • (336) 725-5955 • http://www.ioof.org

Krause-Butner Potter's House Museum • Bethabara Park, 2147 Bethabara Rd • Winston-Salem, NC 27106 • (336) 924-8191

Old Salem Museum and Gardens • 600 S Main St • Winston-Salem, NC 27101 • (336) 721-7300 • http://www.oldsalem.org

Old Salem Village Museum and Gardens • 600 S Main St, P.O. Box F, Salem Sta • Winston-Salem, NC 27983 • (336) 721-7300 • http://www.oldsalem.org

Piedmont Aviation Historical Society • 101 Candlewyck Dr • Winston-Salem, NC 27104 • (336) 765-4363

Wachovia Historical Society • 600 S Main St, P.O. Box 10667 • Winston-Salem, NC 27108 • (336) 721-7373 • http://www.wachoviahistoricalsociety.org

Z Smith Reynolds Library • Wake Forest Univ, Reynolda Sta, P.O. Box 7777 • Winston-Salem, NC 27109-7777 • (336) 758-5476 • http://www.wfu.edu/library/baptist

Winton

Albemarle Regional Library • 303 W Tryon St, P.O. Box 68 • Winton, NC 27986-0068 • (252) 358-7832 • http://www.arlnc.org

Hertford County Library • P.O. Box 68 • Winton, NC 27986-0068 • (252) 358-7855

Meherrin Indian Tribe • Hwy 11 • Winton, NC 27986 • (252) 398-3321 • http://groups.hamptonroads.com/MeherrinTribe/

Wrightsville Beach

Wrightsville Beach Museum of History • 303 W Salisbury St, P.O. Box 584 • Wrightsville Beach, NC 28480 • (910) 256-2569 • http://www.wbmuseum.com

Yadkinville

Charles Bruce Davis Museum • 127 Henlock St • Yadkinville, NC 27055 • (910) 679-2941

Yadkin County Historical and Genealogical Society • 216 S Van Buren St, P.O. Box 1250 • Yadkinville, NC 27055-1250 • (336) 679-2702

Yadkinville Public Library • 233 E Main St, P.O. Box 607 • Yadkinville, NC 27055-0607 • (336) 679-8792 • http://www.nwrl.org

Yanceyville

Caswell County Historical Association • Richmond-Miles History Museum, Main St, P.O. Box 278 • Yanceyville, NC 27379 • (919) 694-6426 • http://www.rootsweb.ancestry.com/~ncccha/

Gunn Memorial Public Library • 161 Main St E • Yanceyville, NC 27379 • (336) 694-6241

Abercrombie
Fort Abercrombie State Historic Site Museum • Hwy 22, P.O. Box 148 • Abercrombie, ND 58001 • (701) 328-2666 • http://history.nd.gov/historicsites/abercrombie/index.html

Adams
Knudt Salle Log Cabin Museum • Adams Park, P.O. Box 152 • Adams, ND 58210 • (701) 944-2425

Alexander
Lewis and Clark Trail Museum • Hwy 85 N • Alexander, ND 58331 • (701) 828-3595

Almont
Almont Heritage Park and Museum • Main St • Almont, ND 58520 • (701) 843-7927

Alsen
Alsen Museum • Main St • Alsen, ND 58311 • (701) 682-5301

Ashley
McIntosh County Heritage Center • 213 3rd Ave NE • Ashley, ND 58413 • (701) 288-3605

McIntosh County Historical Society • Historical Museum, 117 3rd Ave NE, P.O. Box 10 • Ashley, ND 58413 • (701) 288-3388

Battle View
Burke County Historical Museum • County Rd 16, Box 85 • Battle View, ND 58773-9241 • (701) 546-4491

Beach
Golden Valley County Museum • 180 1st Ave SE • Beach, ND 58621 • (701) 872-3908

Belcourt
Turtle Mountain Band of Chippewa • Hwy 5 W, P.O. Box 770 • Belcourt, ND 58316 • (701) 477-6451 • http://www.turtlemountainchippewa.com

Turtle Mountain Chippewa Historical Society • Heritage Center, Hwy 5, P.O. Box 257 • Belcourt, ND 58316 • (701) 447-2639 • http://www.chippewaheritage.com

Turtle Mountain Community College Library • 10145 BIA Rd 7, P.O. Box 340 • Belcourt, ND 58316-0340 • (701) 477-7862 • http://www.turtle-mountain.cc.nd.us

Beulah
Mercer County Historical Society • Historical Museum, 108 7th St NE • Beulah, ND 58523 • (701) 873-4733

Bismarck
Bismarck Public Library • 515 N 5th St • Bismarck, ND 58501 • (701) 222-6410 • http://www.bismarcklibrary.org

Bismarck State College Library • 1500 Edwards Ave, P.O. Box 5587 • Bismarck, ND 58506-5587 • (701) 224-5450 • http://www.bismarckstate.edu/library

Bismarck-Mandan Historical and Genealogical Society • 419 8th St, P.O. Box 485 • Bismarck, ND 58502-0485 • (701) 223-6273

Camp Hancock State Historic Site Museum • 101 E Main Ave • Bismarck, ND 58501 • (701) 328-2666 • http://www.history.nd.gov/historicsites/hancock/index.html

Former Governors' Mansion State Historic Site Museum • 320 Avenue B East • Bismarck, ND 58501 • (701) 328-9529 • http://www.history.nd.gov/historicsites/fgm/index.html

Germans from Russia Heritage Society • Historical Museum, 1125 W Turnpike Ave, P.O. Box 1671 • Bismarck, ND 58501 • (701) 223-6167 • http://www.grhs.com

North Dakota Heritage Center Museum • 612 East Boulevard Ave • Bismarck, ND 58505 • (701) 623-4355 • http://www.state.nd.us/hist/hcenter.htm

North Dakota State Genealogical Society • P.O. Box 485 • Bismarck, ND 58502

North Dakota State Library • Liberty Memorial Bldg, Capitol Grounds, 604 East Blvd Ave • Bismarck, ND 58505-0800 • (701) 328-2492 • http://www.ndsl.lib.state.nd.us

State Historical Society of North Dakota • Heritage Center, Capitol Grounds, 612 E Boulevard Ave • Bismarck, ND 58505-0660 • (701) 328-2799 • http://www.state.nd.us./hist/

Bottineau
Bottineau County Genealogical Society • 614 W Pine Cr • Bottineau, ND 58318

Bottineau Historical Society • Bottineau County Museum, N Main St • Bottineau, ND 58318 • (701) 228-2943

Bowman
Bowman County Genealogical Society • P.O. Box 1044 • Bowman, ND 58623

Pioneer Trails Museum • 12 1st St NE • Bowman, ND 58623 • (701) 523-3600 • http://www.ptrm.org

Cando
Cando Pioneer Foundation • Historical Museum, 502 Main St • Cando, ND 58324 • (701) 968-3943

Carrington
Foster County Museum • 2nd St & 16th Ave S • Carrington, ND 58421 • (701) 652-1313

James River Genealogy Club • 651 4th St N • Carrington, ND 58421 • http://www.rootsweb.com/~ndjrjc/

Carson
Grant County Historical Society • Historical Museum, Grant County Fairgrounds • Carson, ND 58529 • (701) 622-3541

Grant County Museum • 9260 56th Ave SW • Carson, ND 58529 • (701) 584-2900

Cavalier
Gunlogson Home Museum • Icelandic State Park, Hwy 5 • Cavalier, ND 58220 • (701) 265-4561

Pembina County Historical Museum • W Main • Cavalier, ND 58220 • (701) 265-4941

Pioneer Heritage Center - Icelandic State Park • 13571 Hwy 5 • Cavalier, ND 58220 • (701) 265-4561 • http://www.state.nd.us/ndparks

Center
Fort Clark Trading Post State Historic Site Museum • 1074 27th Ave SW • Center, ND 58530 • (701) 794-8832 • http://www.state.nd.us/hist

Oliver County Historical Exhibit • Main St • Center, ND 58530 • (701) 794-8721

Concord
Sons of the American Revolution, Lt Col John Phifer Chapter • 692 Williamsburg Ct • Concord, ND 28025

Cooperstown
Griggs County Genealogical Society • Griggs County Courthouse, P.O. Box 237 • Cooperstown, ND 58425

Griggs County Historical Society • Historical Museum, 12th St SE • Cooperstown, ND 58525 • (701) 797-2771 • http://www.griggscountyhistoricalsociety.com

Griggs County Public Library • 902 Burrell Ave, P.O. Box 546 • Cooperstown, ND 58425-0546 • (701) 797-2214

Crosby
Crosby Historical Society • Pioneer Village Museum, P.O. Box 130 • Crosby, ND 58730 • (701) 965-6705

Crosby, cont.
Divide County Public Library • 204 1st St NE, P.O. Box 90 • Crosby, ND 58730 • (701) 965-6305

Devils Lake
Carnegie Public Library • 623 4th Ave • Devils Lake, ND 58301-2421 • (701) 662-2220 • http://www.devilslakend.com

Pioneer Daughters Library & Lillian Wineman Collection • 4th St & 5th Ave • Devils Lake, ND 58301 • (701) 662-4537

Ramsey County Historical Society • Heritage House Museum, 416 6th St, P.O. Box 245 • Devils Lake, ND 58301 • (701) 662-3701

Dickinson
Dickinson Museum Center • 188 Museum Dr E • Dickinson, ND 58601 • (701) 456-6225 • http://www.dickinsonmuseumcenter.com

Dickinson Public Library • 130 3rd St W • Dickinson, ND 58601 • (701) 456-7700 • http://www.dickinsonnd.com

Joachim Regional Museum • 1226 Sims St, P.O. Box 1008 • Dickinson, ND 58602 • (701) 225-4409 • http://www.joachimmuseum.org

Prairie Outpost Park • I-94 • Dickinson, ND 58601 • (701) 225-4409 • http://dickinsonmuseumcenter.com/what-we-do/prairie-outpost-park/

Stoxen Library • Dickinson State University, 291 Campus Dr • Dickinson, ND 58601 • (701) 483-2135 • http://dickinsonstate.com/library.asp

Ukrainian Cultural Institute • DSU, Box 6 • Dickinson, ND 58601 • (701) 225-1286

Dresden
Cavalier County Museum • 10123 95th St • Dresden, ND 58249 • (701) 256-3342

Dunn Center
Dunn County Historical Society • Historical Museum, 153 Museum Tr, P.O. Box 86 • Dunn Center, ND 58626 • (701) 548-8111 • http://www.dunncountymuseum.org

Edgeley
South Central Area Library • 530 Main St, P.O. Box 218 • Edgeley, ND 58433-0218 • (701) 493-2769

Edmore
Edmore Historical Society • P.O. Box 111 • Edmore, ND 58330

Wheaton Manor Museum • P.O. Box 121 • Edmore, ND 58330 • (701) 644-2291

Egeland
Towner County Historical Museum • general delivery • Egeland, ND 58331 • (701) 656-3698

Elgin
Grant County Historical Society • Historical Museum, 119 Main St, P.O. Box 100 • Elgin, ND 58533 • (701) 584-2900

Ellendale
Coleman and Depot Museums • Main St & Railroad Ave • Ellendale, ND 58436 • (701) 349-2916 • http://www.ellendalend.com

Fred J Graham Library • Trinity Bible College, 50 6th Ave S • Ellendale, ND 58436-7150 • (701) 349-5407 • http://www.trinitybiblecollege.edu

Enderlin
Enderlin Historical Society • Historical Museum, 315 Railway St • Enderlin, ND 58027 • (701) 437-3205 • http://enderlinmuseum.org

Enderlin Municipal Library • 303 Railway St • Enderlin, ND 58027 • (701) 437-2953

Epping
Buffalo Trails Museum • Main St, P.O. Box 22 • Epping, ND 58843 • (701) 859-4361 • http://www.epping.govoffice.com

Fargo
Fargo Air Museum • 1609 19th Ave N • Fargo, ND 58102 • (701) 293-8043 • http://www.fargoairmuseum.org

Fargo Public Library • 4630 15th Ave N • Fargo, ND 58102 • (701) 241-1491 • http://www.fargolibrary.org

Germans from Russia Heritage Collection • ND State Univ Library, 1201 Albrecht Blvd • Fargo, ND 58105-5599 • (701) 231-8886 • http://www.lib.ndsu.nodak.edu

Landsmannschaft der Bessarabiendeutschen • c/o North Dakota State Univ Library, 12th & Albrecht Blvd, P.O. Box 6050 • Fargo, ND 58108 • (701) 237-8914 • http://feefhs.org/frghdblb.html

Landsmannschaft der Deutschen aus Russland • c/o North Dakota State Univ Library, 12th & Albrecht Blvd, P.O. Box 5599 • Fargo, ND 58105-5599 • (701) 237-8914 • http://feefhs.org/frgland.html

Masonic Grand Lodge of North Dakota • 201 14th Ave N • Fargo, ND 58102 • (701) 235-8321 • http://www.glnd.org

North Dakota Institute for Regional Studies Library • North Dakota State Univ, P.O. Box 5599 • Fargo, ND 58105-5599 • (701) 237-8914 • http://www.lib.ndsu.nodak.edu/ndirs/

North Dakota Jewish Historical Project • P.O. Box 2431 • Fargo, ND 58102

Red River Valley Genealogy Society • 112 N University Dr, Ste L116, P.O. Box 9284 • Fargo, ND 58106-9284 • (701) 239-4129

Roger Maris Museum • 3902 13th Ave S • Fargo, ND 58103 • (701) 282-2222 • http://www.rogermarismuseum.com

Stevens Hall Museum • ND State Univ, Stevens Hall • Fargo, ND 58102 • (701) 232-8421

Fessenden
Wells County Historical Exhibit • Fairgrounds • Fessenden, ND 58438 • (701) 547-3847

Wells County Historical Society • Historical Museum, P.O. Box 213 • Fessenden, ND 58438 • (701) 547-3100

Wells County Museum • 305 South One • Fessenden, ND 58438 • (701) 984-2688

Forbes
Shimmin Tveit Museum • Main St • Forbes, ND 58439

Forman
Sargent County Museum & Research Library • 8987 Hwy 32 • Forman, ND 58032 • (701) 724-3720

Fort Ransom
Fort Ransom State Park Visitor Center • 5981 Walter Hjelle Pkwy • Fort Ransom, ND 58033 • (701) 973-4331 • http://www.fortransomnd.com

Ransom County Historical Society • 101 Mill Rd SE • Fort Ransom, ND 58083 • (701) 678-2045 • http://www.ransomcountynd.com

T J Walker Historical Museum • general delivery • Fort Ransom, ND 58033 • (701) 973-2651

Fort Totten
Devils Lake Sioux - Mni Wakan Oyate Tribe • P.O. Box 359 • Fort Totten, ND 58335 • (701) 766-4221

Fort Totten State Historic Site Museum • Building 14, P.O. Box 224 • Fort Totten, ND 58335 • (701) 328-2666 • http://www.state.nd.us/hist/totten/totten.htm

Lake Region Pioneer Daughters Museum • Fort Totten State Historic Site • Fort Totten, ND 58335

Little Hoop Community College Museum • Main St • Fort Totten, ND 58335 • (701) 766-4415

Fort Yakes

Standing Rock Sioux • general delivery • Fort Yakes, ND 58538 • (701) 854-7201 • http://www.standingrock.org

Sitting Bull College Library • 1341 92nd St • Fort Yates, ND 58538 • (701) 854-3861 • http://www.sittingbull.edu

Standing Rock College and Historical Society • Historical Museum, HC1, Box 4 • Fort Yates, ND 58538 • (701) 854-3861

Garrison

Heritage Park and Museums • 1st St & 1st Ave NW • Garrison, ND 58540 • (701) 463-2546

McLean County Genealogical Society • P.O. Box 51 • Garrison, ND 58540 • (701) 463-2091

Glen Ullin

Glen Ullin Historical Society • P.O. Box 681 • Glen Ullin, ND 58631 • (701) 348-3149

Muggli Rock Shock and Museum • 701 Oak Ave E • Glen Ullin, ND 58631 • (701) 348-3897

Goodrich

Sheridan County Pioneer Exhibit • City Park • Goodrich, ND 58444 • (701) 885-2471

Grafton

Carnegie Regional Library • 49 W 7th St • Grafton, ND 58237 • (701) 352-2754

Heritage Village • Hwy 17 W • Grafton, ND 58237 • (701) 352-3280

Jugville Museum • Hwy 81 • Grafton, ND 58237 • (701) 732-0536

Grand Forks

Chester Fritz Library • Univ of North Dakota, Centennial & University Ave, P.O. Box 9000 • Grand Forks, ND 58202-9000 • (701) 777-4629 • http://www.und.edu/dept/library/

Grand Forks County Historical Society • Campbell House Museum, 2405 Belmont Rd • Grand Forks, ND 58201-7505 • (701) 775-2216 • http://www.grandforkshistory.com

Grand Forks County Historical Society Library • 2405 Belmont Rd • Grand Forks, ND 58201-7505 • (701) 775-2216

Grand Forks Historic Preservation • 1405 1st Ave N, P.O. Box 13876 • Grand Forks, ND 58208 • (701) 772-8756

Grand Forks Public Library • 2110 Library Cr • Grand Forks, ND 58201-6324 • (701) 772-8116 • http://www.grandforksgov.com/library

Minnkota Genealogical Society • P.O. Box 12744 • Grand Forks, ND 58208-2744 • http://www.rootsweb.com/~minnkota

Grand Rapids

LaMoure County Museum • Memorial Park • Grand Rapids, ND 58458 • (701) 778-7461

Grassy Butte

Old Sod Post Office Museum • 581 Hwy 85 S • Grassy Butte, ND 58624 • (701) 863-6604

Gwinner

Ransom County Historical Society • 12512 85th St SE • Gwinner, ND 58040-9743 • (701) 678-2045

Hanks

Pioneer Trails Museum • Hwy 85 & Hwy 50 • Hanks, ND 58856 • (701) 572-4759

Harvey

Central North Dakota Genealogical Society • c/o Harvey Public Library, 119 E 10th • Harvey, ND 58341 • (701) 324-2156

Harvey Public Library • 119 E 10th St • Harvey, ND 58341 • (701) 324-2156

Hatton

Hatton-Eielson Museum • 405 Eielson St, P.O. Box 278 • Hatton, ND 58240-0278 • (701) 543-3726 • http://www.eielson.org

Hebron

Hebron Historical and Arts Society • Historical Museum, Park & Lincoln Sts, P.O. Box 123 • Hebron, ND 58638 • (701) 878-4891

Hensler

River Peoples Visitors Center • Cross Ranch State Park • Hensler, ND 58530 • (701) 794-3731

Hettinger

Adams County Library • 103 N 6th St, P.O. Box 448 • Hettinger, ND 58639-0448 • (701) 567-2741 • http://www.adamscountylibrary.com

Dakota Buttes Museum • 400 11th St S • Hettinger, ND 58639 • (701) 567-4429

Hillsboro

Traill County Historical Society • Plummer House Museum, 306 Caledonia W Ave • Hillsboro, ND 58045 • (701) 436-5571

Hope

Steele County Historical Society • Steele County Museum, 301 Steele Ave, P.O. Box 144 • Hope, ND 58046-0144 • (701) 945-2394 • http://www.steelecomuseum.com

Jamestown

Fort Seward Interpretive Center • 605 10th Ave NW • Jamestown, ND 58401 • (701) 252-8421

Frontier Fort Museum • 1838 3rd Ave SE • Jamestown, ND 58401 • (701) 252-7492

Frontier Village Museum • 17th St SE, P.O. Box 324 • Jamestown, ND 58402 • (701) 252-6307

National Buffalo Museum • 500 17th St SE, P.O. Box 1712 • Jamestown, ND 58401 • (701) 252-8648 • http://www.buffalomuseum.com

Raugust Library • Jamestown College, 6070 College Lane • Jamestown, ND 58405-0001 • (701) 252-3467 • http://www.jc.edu/Raugust

Stutsman County Historical Society • Historical Museum, 321 3rd Ave SE, P.O. Box 1002 • Jamestown, ND 58402 • (701) 252-6741 • http://www.jamestownnd.com

Knox

Dale and Martha Hawk Museum • Hwy 30 • Knox, ND 58343

Kulm

Whitestone Hill Battlefield State Historic Site Museum • 23 mi SE of Kulm • Kulm, ND 58456 • (701) 396-7731 • http://history.nd.gov/historicsites/whitestone/index.html

Lakota

Finnish American Historical Society of North Dakota • HCR 2, Box 24 • Lakota, ND 58344 • (701) 259-2127

Tofthagen Library and Museum • 116 West B Ave, PO Box 307 • Lakota, ND 58344-0307 • (701) 247-2543

LaMoure

Toy Farmer Museum • 7496 106th Ave SE • LaMoure, ND 58458 • (701) 880-5206 • http://www.toyfarmer.com

Langdon

Cavalier County Historical Society • general delivery • Langdon, ND 58249

Lansford

Lansford Threshers and Historical Exhibit • general delivery • Lansford, ND 58750 • (701) 784-5831

North Dakota

Larimore
Larimore Community Museum • Towner Ave • Larimore, ND 58251 • (215) 482-6600

Lidgerwood
Lidgerwood Community Museum • 110 1st Ave NE • Lidgerwood, ND 58053 • (701) 538-4168

Linton
Emmons County Museum • NW 1st & Oak • Linton, ND 58552 • (701) 254-5393

Linton Public Library • 101 1st St NE, P.O. Box 416 • Linton, ND 58552-0416 • (701) 254-4737

Makoti
Makoti Threshers' Museum • general delivery • Makoti, ND 58756 • (701) 726-5656

Mandan
Fort Abraham Lincoln State Park • 4480 Ft Lincoln Rd • Mandan, ND 58554 • (701) 667-6340 • http://www.fortlincoln.com

Mandan Historical Society • 411 W Main St, P.O. Box 483 • Mandan, ND 58554 • (701) 667-1260

Mandan Public Library • 609 W Main St • Mandan, ND 58554 • (701) 667-5365 • http://www.infolynx.org

Morton County Library • 300 1st St NW • Mandan, ND 58554 • (701) 667-3327

North Dakota State Railroad Museum • 3102 37th St NW • Mandan, ND 58554 • (701) 663-9322 • http://www.ndrailroading.com/rrmuseum/index.html

Manvel
Manvel Museum • Main St • Manvel, ND 58256 • (701) 696-2279

Mayville
Byrnes-Quanbeck Library • Mayville State University, 330 3rd St NE • Mayville, ND 58257 • (701) 788-4815 • http://www.masu.nodak.edu/academics/library/

Goose River Heritage Center • Main St & 1st Ave SE • Mayville, ND 58257 • (701) 788-4115

Mayville Public Library • 52 Center Ave N • Mayville, ND 58257 • (701) 788-3388

Mothers Pioneer Park • general delivery • Mayville, ND 58257

McHenry
McHenry Railroad Loop and Depot Museum • general delivery • McHenry, ND 58464 • (701) 785-2333

Medora
Billings County Courthouse Museum • 301 5th St, P.O. Box 198 • Medora, ND 58645 • (701) 623-4829

Chateau de Mores State Historic Site Museum • 3448 Chateau de Mores Rd, P.O. Box 106 • Medora, ND 58645 • (701) 623-4355 • http://history.nd.gov/historicsites/chateau/index.html

Maltese Cross Cabin Museum • Theodore Roosevelt Natl Park, P.O. Box 7 • Medora, ND 58645 • (701) 623-4466

Medora Centennial Commission • P.O. Box 212 • Medora, ND 58645

Medora Doll House Museum • 485 Broadway • Medora, ND 58645 • (701) 623-4444

Museum of the Bad Lands • P.O. Box 198 • Medora, ND 58645 • (701) 623-4451

Theodore Roosevelt National Park Visitor Centers • P.O. Box 7 • Medora, ND 58645 • (701) 842-2333 • http://www.nps.gov/thro/

Theodore Roosevelt Nature and History Association • Historic Museum, 315 2nd Ave, P.O. Box 7 • Medora, ND 58645-0007 • (701) 623-4466 • http://www.nps.gov/thro

Minnewaukan
Minnewaukan Museum • 210 C Avenue S • Minnewaukan, ND 58351 • (701) 473-5488

Minot
Dakota Territory Air Museum • 100 34th Ave NE, P.O. Box 195 • Minot, ND 58702 • (701) 852-8500 • http://www.dakotaterritoryairmuseum.com

Minot Public Library • 516 2nd Ave SW • Minot, ND 58701-3792 • (701) 852-1045 • http://www.minotlibrary.org

Mouse River Loop Genealogical Society • P.O. Box 1391 • Minot, ND 58702-1391

Railroad Museum of Minot • 19 1st St NE • Minot, ND 58703 • (701) 852-7091

Scandinavian Heritage Association • 1412 Debbie Dr • Minot, ND 58701

Soo Depot Transportation Museum • 15 N Main St • Minot, ND 58701 • (701) 852-2234

Ward County Historical Society • Historical Museum, 2005 Burdick Exwy W, P.O. Box 994 • Minot, ND 58702 • (701) 839-0785 • http://www.co.ward.nd.us/historical/

Ward County Pioneer Village and Museum • State Fairgrounds • Minot, ND 58701 • (701) 839-0785

Minot AFB
Minot Air Force Base Library FL4528 • 5 SVS/SVMG, 210 Missile Ave Unit 1 Bldg 156 • Minot AFB, ND 58705-5026 • (701) 723-3344 • http://www.minotafblibrary.com

Minto
Walsh County Historical Society • 323 3rd St • Minto, ND 58261

Walsh County Museum • 323 3rd St • Minto, ND 58261 • (701) 248-3237

Mohall
Renville County Historical Society • Historical Museum, 504 1st St NE, P.O. Box 261 • Mohall, ND 58761 • (701) 756-6195

Renville County Museum • general delivery • Mohall, ND 58761 • (701) 756-6195

Mooreton
Bagg Bonanza Historical Farm Museum • I-29 S (45 mi S) • Mooreton, ND 58061 • (701) 274-8989 • http://www.wahpetonbreckenridgechamber.com/visitor_bagg.htm

Napoleon
Logan County Museum • 207 E Lake Ave • Napoleon, ND 58561 • (701) 754-2453

New Rockford
Eddy County Museum • 1113 1st Ave N • New Rockford, ND 58356 • (701) 947-2894

New Salem
Custer Trail Museum • I-94 • New Salem, ND 58563 • (701) 843-7384

New Town
Fort Berthold Reservation Public Library • Main St • New Town, ND 58763 • (701) 627-4635

Four Bears Museum • Hwy 23 • New Town, ND 58763 • (701) 627-4477

Three Affiliated Tribes Museum • P.O. Box 147 • New Town, ND 58763 • (701) 627-4477 • http://www.mhanation.com

Niagara
Niagara Community Historical Society • Historical Museum, Main St • Niagara, ND 58266 • (701) 397-5774

Noonan
Divide County Historical Society • Historical Museum, Pioneer Village, RR1, Box 80 • Noonan, ND 58765 • (701) 965-6297

Northwood
Northwood Pioneer Museum • Raymond St & Washington Ave • Northwood, ND 58267 • (701) 587-5421

Oakes
Dickey County Historical Park Museum • 5th & Main • Oakes, ND 58474 • (701) 783-4361 • http://www.oakesnd.com/dickey_county_historical_society.php

Pembina
Pembina City Library • P.O. Box 541 • Pembina, ND 58271 • (701) 825-6819

Pembina State Museum • 805 State Hwy 59, P.O. Box 456 • Pembina, ND 58271-0456 • (701) 825-6840 • http://www.state.nd.us/hist

Plaza
Plaza Museum • 5th Ave & Berthold St • Plaza, ND 58771

Powers Lake
Burke County Historical Society • Historical Museum, 9129 Powers Lake Rd, P.O. Box 213 • Powers Lake, ND 58773 • (701) 546-4491

Centennialville Museum • Old Hwy 50 • Powers Lake, ND 58773 • (701) 464-5771

Prairies
Griggs County Historical Museum • 12th St SE • Prairies, ND 58425 • (701) 797-2232

Shimmin Tveit Museum • Main St • Prairies, ND 58439 • (701) 759-8111

Ray
Ray Opera House Museum • 119 Main St • Ray, ND 58849 • (701) 568-3437

Regent
Hettinger County Historical Society • Hettinger County Museum, Main St, P.O Box 176 • Regent, ND 58650 • (701) 563-4547

Southwestern North Dakota Genealogical Society • HCR 01, Box 321 • Regent, ND 58650

Richardton
Assumption Abbey Library • 418 3rd Ave W, P.O. Box A • Richardton, ND 58652-0901 • (701) 0972-3315

Riverdale
McLean-Mercer Regional Library • 2nd St, P.O. Box 505 • Riverdale, ND 58656-0505 • (701) 654-7652

Rolla
Rolette County Historical Society • general delivery • Rolla, ND 58367 • (701) 477-5093

Rugby
Geographical Center Historical Society • Pioneer Village Museum, 102 Hwy 2 SE • Rugby, ND 58368-8801 • (701) 776-6414 • http://www.prairievillagemuseum.com

Heart of America Library • 201 3rd St SW • Rugby, ND 58368-1793 • (701) 776-6223

Victorian Dress Museum • 312 2nd St SW • Rugby, ND 58368 • (701) 776-2189

Ryder
Ryder Historical Society • Historical Museum, 184th St SW • Ryder, ND 58779 • (701) 758-2527

Saint John
Rolette County Museum • Main St • Saint John, ND 58369 • (701) 477-3026

Saint Michael
Bell Isle Indian Gallery and Museum • 120 Main St • Saint Michael, ND 58370 • (701) 766-4363

Shields
Weinhandl Museum • P.O. Box 867 • Shields, ND 58569 • (701) 442-3431

Stanley
Flickertail Village Museum • 5th St SE • Stanley, ND 58784 • (701) 628-2802

Mountrail County Historical Society • P.O. Box 582 • Stanley, ND 58784 • (701) 628-1909

Stanton
Knife River Indian Villages Historic Site Museum • 564 County Rd 37, P.O. Box 9 • Stanton, ND 58571 • (701) 745-3300 • http://www.nps.gov/knri

Marshall County Historical Society • general delivery • Stanton, ND 58571 • (701) 745-4803

Strasburg
Ludwig and Christina Welk Farmstead Museum • 619 Main St • Strasburg, ND 58573 • (701) 336-7519

Tioga
Norseman Museum • 17 2nd St NE • Tioga, ND 58852 • (701) 664-2702

Towner
McHenry County Historical Society • Historical Museum • Towner, ND 58788 • (815) 923-2257

Valley City
Allen Memorial Library • Valley City State University, 101 College St SW • Valley City, ND 58072 • (701) 845-7277 • http://library.vcsu.edu

Barnes County Historical Society • Historical Museum, 315 Central Ave N, P.O. Box 661 • Valley City, ND 58072 • (701) 845-0966 • http://www.hellovalley.com

Valley City-Barnes County Public Library • 410 N Central Ave • Valley City, ND 58072 • (701) 845-3821 • http://www.kleinonline.com/library.htm

Wahpeton
Genealogy Guild of Wilkin County, MN and Richland County, ND • c/o Leach Public Library, 417 2nd Ave N • Wahpeton, ND 58075 • (701) 642-5732

Leach Public Library • 417 2nd Ave N • Wahpeton, ND 58075 • (701) 642-5732 • http://www.wahpeton.com

Richland County Historical Society • Historical Museum, 11 7th Ave N, P.O. Box 1326 • Wahpeton, ND 58075 • (701) 642-3075 • http://www.wahpeton.com

Walhalla
Gingras Trading Post State Historic Site Museum • 10534 129th Ave NE • Walhalla, ND 58282 • (701) 328-1476 • history.nd.gov/historicsites/gringras/gtphistory3.html

Washburn
Fort Mandan and Heritage Park • general delivery • Washburn, ND 58577 • (701) 462-3411

McLean County Historical Society • Historical Museum, 605 Main Ave, P.O. Box 124 • Washburn, ND 58577 • (701) 462-3744 • http://www.wrtc.com/vmerkel/McLeanCountyMuseum

Watford City
McKenzie County Historical Society • Pioneer Museum, 104 Park Ave W, P.O. Box 126 • Watford City, ND 58854-0602 • (701) 842-2990 • http://econdev.mckenziecounty.net

West Fargo
Cass County Historical Society • Bonanzaville Pioneer Village Museum, 1351 W Main Ave, P.O. Box 719 • West Fargo, ND 58078 • (701) 282-2822 • http://www.bonanzaville.com

West Fargo Public Library • 401 7th St E • West Fargo, ND 58078 • (701) 282-0415

Williston
Fort Buford State Historic Site Museum • 15349 39th Ln • Williston, ND 58801 • (701) 572-9034 • http://history.nd.gov/historicsites/buford/index.html

Fort Union Trading Post National Historic Site Museum • 15550 Hwy 1804 • Williston, ND 58801 • (701) 572-8093 • http://www.nps.gov/fous

Frontier Museum • 6330 2nd Ave W, P.O. Box 285 • Williston, ND 58801 • (701) 572-9751

Williams County Genealogical Society • 703 W 7th St • Williston, ND 5801-4908

Williston Community Library • 1302 Davidson Dr • Williston, ND 58801 • (701) 774-8805 • http://www.willistonlibrary.org

Wolford
Dale and Martha Hawk Museum • SR 30, P.O. Box 19B • Wolford, ND 58385 • (701) 583-2381 • http://www.HawkMuseum.org

Woodworth
Melzer Museum • Main St • Woodworth, ND 58476 • (701) 752-4119

Ada
Ada Public Library • 320 N Main St • Ada, OH 45810 • (419) 634-5246

Akron
Akron-Summit County Public Library • 55 S Main St • Akron, OH 44326-0001 • (330) 643-9000 • http://www.ascpl.lib.oh.us

Bierce Library • Univ of Akron, Buchtel Ave • Akron, OH 44325-1702 • (330) 972-7670

Dr Bob's Home Museum • 855 Ardmore Ave • Akron, OH 44302 • (330) 864-1935

Hower House Museum • Univ of Akron, 60 Fir Hill • Akron, OH 44325 • (330) 972-6909 • http://www.uakron.edu/howerhse

Perkins Mansion Museum • Copley Rd & S Portage Path • Akron, OH 44320 • (330) 535-1120

Stan Hywet Hall Museum • 714 N Portage Path • Akron, OH 44303 • (330) 836-5533 • http://www.stanhywet.org

Summit County Genealogical Society • P.O. Box 2232 • Akron, OH 44309-2232 • (330) 699-4511

Summit County Historical Society • Historical Museum, 550 Copley Rd • Akron, OH 44320 • (330) 535-1120 • http://www.summithistory.org

Alexandria
Alexandria Public Library • 10 Maple Dr, P.O. Box 67 • Alexandria, OH 43001-0067 • (740) 924-3561 • http://www.alexandria.lib.oh.us

Alliance
Alliance Area Preservation Society • 1623 S Freedom Ave • Alliance, OH 44601 • (330) 821-6020

Alliance Genealogical Society • P.O. Box 3630 • Alliance, OH 44601-7630

Alliance Historical Society • Historical Museum, 840 N Park Ave, P.O. Box 2044 • Alliance, OH 44601 • (216) 823-1677 • http://alliancehistory.org

Alliance Rodman Public Library • 215 E Broadway St • Alliance, OH 44601 • (330) 821-2665 • http://www.rodman.lib.oh.us/rpl/

Mabel Hartzell Historical Home Museum • 840 N Park Ave, P.O. Box 2044 • Alliance, OH 44601 • (330) 823-4115 • http://www.rodman.lib.oh.us/nonprofit/hartzell

Amherst
Amherst Historical Society • Quigley Museum, 115 S Lake St, P.O. Box 272 • Amherst, OH 44001 • (440) 988-7255

Antwerp
Antwerp Preservation Society • Historical Museum, 2532 Rd 192 • Antwerp, OH 45813 • (419) 258-5511

Ehrhart Museum • 118 N Main St, P.O. Box 802 • Antwerp, OH 45813 • (419) 258-2665

Archbold
Archbold Community Library • 205 Stryker St • Archbold, OH 43502-1191 • (419) 446-2783 • http://www.archbold.lib.oh.us

Historic Sauder Village Museum • 22611 State Rte 2, P.O. Box 235 • Archbold, OH 43502 • (419) 445-5250 • http://www.saudervillage.org

Ashland
Ashland County Chapter, OGS • c/o Ashland School District Public Library, 224 Claremont Ave, P.O. Box 681 • Ashland, OH 44805-0681 • (419) 289-8188 • http://www.ashtabulagen.org

Ashland County Historical Society • Historical Museum, 420 Center St, P.O. Box 484 • Ashland, OH 44805 • (419) 289-3111 • http://ashlandhistory.org

Ashland Public Library • 224 Claremont Ave • Ashland, OH 44805 • (419) 289-8188 • http://www.ashland.lib.oh.us

Roger E Darling Memorial Library • Ashland Theological Seminary, 910 Center St • Ashland, OH 44805 • (419) 289-5168

Ashley
Wornstaff Memorial Public Library • 302 E High St • Ashley, OH 43003-9703 • (740) 747-2085

Ashtabula
Ashtabula County District Library • 335 W 44th St • Ashtabula, OH 44004-6897 • (440) 997-9341 • http://www.acdl.info/

Ashtabula Marine Museum • 1071 Walnut Blvd, P.O. Box 1546 • Ashtabula, OH 44005 • (440) 997-5370 • http://www.ashtabulamarinemuseum.org

Ashville
Ashville Area Heritage Society • Historical Museum, 34 Long St • Ashville, OH 43103 • (740) 983-9864 • http://ohiosmalltownmuseum.org

Slate Run Living Historical Farm Museum • 9130 Marcy Rd • Ashville, OH 43103 • (614) 833-1880 • http://www.metroparks.co.franklin.oh.us/slaterunfurnsched.htm

Athens
Athens County Chapter, OGS • Historical Museum, 65 N Court St • Athens, OH 45701 • (740) 592-2280 • http://www.athenshistory.org

Athens County Historical Society • Historical Museum, 65 N Court St • Athens, OH 45701 • (740) 592-2280 • http://www.athenshistory.org

Vernon R Alden Library • Ohio Univ, Park Pl • Athens, OH 45701-2978 • (740) 593-2710 • http://www.library.ohiou.edu/libinfo/depts/archives/archspeccoll.htm

Aurora
Aurora Historical Society • Historical Museum, 115 E Pioneer Tr, P.O. Box 241 • Aurora, OH 44202 • (330) 562-6502

Aurora Public Library • 115 E Pioneer Tr • Aurora, OH 44202 • (330) 562-6502

Avon Lake
Peter Miller House Museum • 33344 Lake Rd • Avon Lake, OH 44012 • (216) 933-6333

Bainbridge
Dr John Harris Dental Museum • 208 W Main St, P.O. Box 424 • Bainbridge, OH 45612 • (740) 634-2228

Barberton
Barberton Public Library • 602 W Park Ave • Barberton, OH 44203 • (330) 745-1194

Barnesville
Barnesville Hutton Memorial Library • 308 E Main St • Barnesville, OH 43713 • (740) 425-1651

Belmont County Chapter, OGS • 361 S Chestnut St, P.O. Box 285 • Barnesville, OH 43713-0285

Belmont County Victorian Mansion Museum • 532 N Chestnut St, P.O. Box 434 • Barnesville, OH 43713 • (740) 425-2926

Gay 90s Mansion Museum • 136 E Walnut • Barnesville, OH 43713 • (740) 425-2926

Batavia
Clermont County Genealogical Society • c/o Doris Wood Branch Library, 180 S 3rd St, P.O. Box 394 • Batavia, OH 45103-0394 • (513) 732-2128

Clermont County Public Library • 326 Broadway • Batavia, OH 45103 • (513) 732-2736 • http://www.clermont.lib.oh.us

Doris Wood Branch Library • 180 S 3rd St, P.O. Box 394 • Batavia, OH 45103-0394 • (513) 732-2128

Batavia, cont.
First Families of Clermont County, Ohio • c/o Doris Wood Branch Library, 180 S 3rd St, P.O. Box 394 • Batavia, OH 45103-3092 • (513) 723-3423

Bath
Hale Farm and Village Museum • 2686 Oak Hill Rd, P.O. Box 296 • Bath, OH 44210 • (330) 666-3711 • http://www.wrhs.org

Western Reserve Historical Society • 2686 Oak Hill Rd, P.O. Box 296 • Bath, OH 44210 • (330) 666-3711 • http://www.wrhs.org

Bay Village
Bay Village Historical Society • Rose Hill Museum, 27715 Lake Rd, P.O. Box 40187 • Bay Village, OH 44140 • (440) 871-7338 • http://www.bayhistorical.com

Rose Hill Museum • 27715 Lake Rd, P.O. Box 40187 • Bay Village, OH 44140 • (614) 871-7338

Beachwood
Jewish Genealogical Society of Cleveland • 27100 Cedar Rd • Beachwood, OH 44122 • (440) 449-2326 • http://www.clevelandjgs.org

Malz Museum of Jewish Heritage • 2929 Richmond Rd • Beachwood, OH 44122 • (216) 593-0575 • http://www.maltzmuseum.org

Beavercreek
American Aviation Historical Society • Historical Museum, 498 Carthage Dr • Beavercreek, OH 45434 • (937) 426-1289

French Ancestors • 2923 Tara Tr • Beavercreek, OH 45434-6252 • (937) 429-2979

Bedford
Bedford Historical Society • Historical Museum, 30 S Park Ave, P.O. Box 46282 • Bedford, OH 44146 • (440) 232-0796 • http://www.bedfordohiohistory.org

Bellaire
Bellaire Toy and Plastic Brick Museum • 4597 Noble St • Bellaire, OH 43906 • (740) 671-8890 • http://danstoymuseum.blogspot.com

National Imperial Glass Museum • 3200 Belmont St • Bellaire, OH 43906 • (740) 671-3971 • http://www.imperialglass.org/museum.htm

Bellbrook
Bellbrook Historical Museum • 42 N Main St • Bellbrook, OH 45305 • (937) 848-2415

Bellefontaine
Logan County District Library • 220 N Main St • Bellefontaine, OH 43311 • (937) 599-4189 • http://www.loganco.lib.oh.us

Logan County Genealogical Society • 521 E Columbus Ave, P.O. Box 36 • Bellefontaine, OH 43311-0036 • (937) 593-7557

Logan County Historical Society • Historical Museum, 521 E Columbus Ave, P.O. Box 296 • Bellefontaine, OH 43311-0036 • (937) 593-7557 • http://www.logancountymuseum.org

Shawnee-Woodland Native American Museum • 7092 State Rt 540 • Bellefontaine, OH 43311

Bellevue
Bellevue Heritage Museum • 200 E Main St, P.O. Box 304 • Bellevue, OH 44811 • (419) 483-7376

Bellevue Public Library • 224 E Main St • Bellevue, OH 44811-1409 • (419) 483-4769 • http://www.bellevue.lib.oh.us

Historic Lyme Village Association • Historical Museum, 5001 State Rte 4, P.O. Box 342 • Bellevue, OH 44811 • (419) 483-4949 • http://www.lymevillage.com

Mad River & NKP Railroad Museum • 233 York St • Bellevue, OH 44811 • (419) 483-2222 • http://www.madrivermuseum.org

Bellfontaine
Shawnee Nation United Remnant Band of Ohio • 7092 SR 540 • Bellfontaine, OH 43311 • (937) 591-9592

Belpre
Belpre Area Historical Society • 509 Ridge St, P.O. Box 731 • Belpre, OH 45714 • (740) 423-7588

Berea
Berea Area Historical Society • Mahler Museum & History Center, 118 E Bridge St, P.O. Box 173 • Berea, OH 44017 • (440) 243-2541 • http://www.bereahistoricalsociety.org

Bethel
Bethel Historical Association • P.O. Box 4 • Bethel, OH 45106

Beverly
Oliver Tucker Museum • 41 5th St, P.O. Box 122 • Beverly, OH 45715 • (740) 984-2489 • http://www.olivertuckermuseum.com

Bexley
Bexley Historical Society • Historical Museum, 2242 E Main St • Bexley, OH 43209 • (614) 235-8694

Bloomville
Bliss Memorial Public Library • 20 S Marion St, P.O. Box 39 • Bloomville, OH 44818-0038 • (419) 983-4675

Bluffton
Mennonite Historical Library • Bluffton College • Bluffton, OH 45817-1195 • (419) 358-3365 • http://mhlbluffton.mennonite.net

Musselman Library • Bluffton College, 280 W College Ave • Bluffton, OH 45817-1704 • (419) 358-3271

Swiss Community Historical Society • 9255 Lugabell Rd, P.O. Box 5 • Bluffton, OH 45817

Boardman
Mahoning County Chapter, OGS • P.O. Box 9333 • Boardman, OH 44513-9333

Bolivar
Fort Laurens State Memorial Museum • 11067 Fort Laurens Rd NW • Bolivar, OH 44612 • (330) 874-2059 • http://www.ohiohistory.org/places/ftlaurens

Botkins
Botkins Historical Society • Shelby House Hotel Museum, W State St, P.O. Box 256 • Botkins, OH 45306 • http://members.aol.com/BotkinsHS/history/bhshome.html

Bowerston
Bowerston Public Library • 200 Main St, P.O. Box 205 • Bowerston, OH 44695-0205 • (740) 269-8531 • http://www.bowerston.lib.oh.us

Bowling Green
Historical Construction Equipment Association • Historical Museum, 16623 Liberty Hi Rd • Bowling Green, OH 43402 • (419) 352-5616 • http://www.hcea.net

William T Jerome Library • Bowling Green State Univ • Bowling Green, OH 43403-0175 • (419) 372-6943 • http://www.bgsu.edu/colleges/library/cac/cac.html

Wood County District Public Library • 251 N Main St • Bowling Green, OH 43402 • (419) 352-5104 • http://www.wcnet.org/wcdpl

Wood County Genealogical Society • P.O. Box 722 • Bowling Green, OH 43402-0722 • (419) 352-4940

Wood County Historical Society • Historical Museum, 13660 County Home Rd • Bowling Green, OH 43402 • (419) 352-0967 • http://www.woodcountyhistory.org

Bradford
Bradford Ohio Railroad Museum • 501 E Main St, P.O. Box 107 • Bradford, OH 45308 • http://www.bradfordmuseum.org

Bradford Public Library • 138 E Main St • Bradford, OH 45308-1108 • (937) 448-2612

Brecksville
Cuyahoga Valley Chapter, OGS • P.O. Box 41414 • Brecksville, OH 44141-0414 • (330) 467-5483

Brewster
Brewster-Sugar Creek Township Historical Society • 45 Wabash Ave S • Brewster, OH 44613 • (330) 767-0045

Brimfield
German-American Family Society • 3871 Ranfield Rd • Brimfield, OH 44240 • (330) 678-8229

Broadview
Squire Rich Home & Museum • 6241 E Wallings Rd • Broadview, OH 44147 • (216) 526-6757

Brooklyn
Brooklyn Historical Society • Historical Museum, 4442 Ridge Rd, P.O. Box 44422 • Brooklyn, OH 44144 • (216) 749-2804

Brookville
Brookville Historical Society • 14 Market St, P.O. Box 82 • Brookville, OH 45309-0082 • (513) 833-3470

Clay Township Historical Society • 8991 Wellbaum Rd • Brookville, OH 45309 • (937) 884-7098

Brunswick
Brunswick Area Historical Society • 4613 Laurel Rd, P.O. Box 714 • Brunswick, OH 44212 • (330) 220-8352

Bryan
Williams County Genealogical Society • P.O. Box 293 • Bryan, OH 43506-0293 • (419) 636-4151

Williams County Public Library • 107 E High St • Bryan, OH 43506 • (419) 636-6734

Bucyrus
Bucyrus Historical Society • Historical Museum, 202 S Walnut St, P.O. Box 493 • Bucyrus, OH 44820 • (419) 562-6386 • http://www.bucyrusonline.com/bhs

Bucyrus Public Library • 200 E Mansfield St • Bucyrus, OH 44820-2381 • (419) 562-7327 • http://www.bucyrus.lib.oh.us

Burton
Burton Public Library • 14588 W Park St, P.O. Box 427 • Burton, OH 44021 • (440) 834-4466 • http://www.burton.lib.oh.us

Geauga County Historical Society • Century Village Museum, 14653 E Park St, P.O. Box 153 • Burton, OH 44021 • (440) 834-1492 • http://www.geaugahistorical.org

Butler
Butler-Clear Fork Valley Historical Society • Historical Museum, 43 Elm St, P.O. Box 186 • Butler, OH 44822 • (419) 989-1679

Cadiz
Harrison County Genealogical Society • 45507 Unionvale Rd • Cadiz, OH 43907-9703 • (740) 942-3900

Harrison County Historical Society • 168 E Market St • Cadiz, OH 43907 • (740) 942-3900

Harrison County History of Coal Museum • 200 E Market St • Cadiz, OH 43907 • (740) 942-2623 • http://www.harrisoncountyohio.org/coalmuseum/

Puskarich Public Library • 200 Market St • Cadiz, OH 43907 • (740) 942-2623

Caldwell
Caldwell Public Library • 517 Spruce St, P.O. Box 230 • Caldwell, OH 43724-0230 • (740) 732-4506

Coal Museum • P.O. Box 313 • Caldwell, OH 43724 • (740) 732-5616

Noble County Genealogical Society • 300 Cumberland St, P.O. Box 174 • Caldwell, OH 43724-0174 • (614) 732-2093

Noble County Historical Society • P.O. Box 128 • Caldwell, OH 43724

Cambridge
Cambridge Glass Company Museum • 136 S 9th St, P.O. Box 416 • Cambridge, OH 43725 • (740) 432-4245 • http://www.cambridgeglass.org/museum.php

First Families of Guernsey County • 65664 N 77th Dr • Cambridge, OH 43725

Guernsey County District Public Library • 800 Steubenville Ave • Cambridge, OH 43725-2385 • (740) 432-5946

Guernsey County Genealogical Society • 125 N 7th St, P.O. Box 661 • Cambridge, OH 43725-0661 • (740) 432-9249

Guernsey County Historical Society • Historical Museum, 218 N 8th St, P.O. Box 741 • Cambridge, OH 43725 • (740) 439-5884

Camp Dennison
Christian Waldschmidt Homestead and Camp Dennison Civil War Museum • 7567 Glendale-Milford Rd • Camp Dennison, OH 45111 • (513) 576-6327

Canal Fulton
Canal Fulton Heritage Society • Heritage House, 103 Tuscarawas St, P.O. Box 584 • Canal Fulton, OH 44614-1044 • (216) 854-3808 • http://www.ohioeriecanal.org

Canal Winchester
American War Museum • 4316 Winchester Southern Rd • Canal Winchester, OH 43110

Barber Museum • 2 1/2 S High St • Canal Winchester, OH 43110 • (614) 837-8400 • http://www.edjeffersbarbermuseum.com

Canal Winchester Historical Society • 10 W Oak St • Canal Winchester, OH 43110-1130 • (614) 833-1846

Mid-Ohio Historical Museum • 700 Winchester Pk • Canal Winchester, OH 43110 • (614) 837-5573

Canfield
Austintown Historical Society • Austin Log Cabin, 3797 S Raccoon Rd • Canfield, OH 44406 • (330) 799-8051

Canfield Historical Society • 44 W Main St • Canfield, OH 44406 • (330) 533-3458

Canfield War Veterans Museum • 23 E Main St • Canfield, OH 44406 • (330) 533-6311

Loghurst Farm Museum • 3967 Boardman-Canfield Rd • Canfield, OH 44046 • (330) 533-4330 • http://www.wrhs.org

Mahoning County Chapter, OGS • 3430 Rebecca Dr • Canfield, OH 44406-9218

Canton
Canton Classic Car Museum • 123 6th St SW • Canton, OH 44702 • (330) 455-3603 • http://www.cantonclassiccar.org

Everett L Cattell Library • Malone College, 515 25th St NW • Canton, OH 44709 • (330) 471-8317

Grand Lodge of Ohio, Sons of Italy • 22521 McDowell St NE • Canton, OH 44721 • (330) 493-9203 • http://www.ohiosonsofitaly.org

Heritage Information Center • 58 Park St, P.O. Box 8078 • Canton, OH 44711 • (828) 646-3412

Ohio

Canton, cont.

McKinley Presidential Library • 800 McKinley Monument Dr NW, P.O. Box 20070 • Canton, OH 44708 • (330) 455-7043 • http://www. mckinleymuseum.org

National First Ladies' Museum • 205 Market Ave S • Canton, OH 44702 • (330) 452-0876 • http://www.firstladies.org

North American Swiss Alliance • 2509 Lakeside Ave NW • Canton, OH 44708-2412 • (330) 456-1983

Pro Football Hall of Fame Museum • 2121 George Halas Dr NW • Canton, OH 44708 • (330) 456-8207 • http://www.profootballhof.com

Stark County District Library • 715 Market Ave N • Canton, OH 44702-1080 • (330) 452-0665 x252

Stark County Historical Society • McKinley Museum, 800 McKinley Monument Dr NW, P.O. Box 20070 • Canton, OH 44701 • (330) 455-7043 • http://www.mckinleymuseum.org

Steam Railroad Museum • P.O. Box 21175 • Canton, OH 44701 • (330) 868-8814

Carlisle

Carlisle Railway Museum • 760 E Central Ave • Carlisle, OH 45005

Carrollton

Carroll County District Library • 70 2nd St NE • Carrollton, OH 44615 • (330) 627-2613 • http://www.carroll.lib.oh.us

Carroll County Genealogical Society • 24 2nd St NE, P.O. Box 36 • Carrollton, OH 44615-1205 • (330) 627-9411

Carroll County Historical Society • McCook House Civil War Museum, Autumn Rd, P.O. Box 174 • Carrollton, OH 44615 • (330) 627-5910 • http://www.ohiohistory.org/places/mccookhse

McCook House State Memorial • 15 S Lisbon St, P.O. Box 174 • Carrollton, OH 44615 • (330) 627-3345 • http://ohsweb.ohiohistory.org/ places/ne03/

Cedarville

Centennial Library • Cedarville University, 251 N Main St • Cedarville, OH 45314-0601 • (937) 766-7850 • http://www.cedarville.edu/dept/ls/

Celina

Dwyer-Mercer County District Library • 303 N Main St • Celina, OH 45822 • (419) 586-4442

Mercer County Genealogical Society • P.O. Box 437 • Celina, OH 45822-0437 • (419) 942-1466

Mercer County Historical Society • Riley Home Museum, 130 E Market, P.O. Box 512 • Celina, OH 45822 • (419) 596-6065

Centerville

Centerville-Washington Township Historical Society • Historical Museum, 26 N Main St • Centerville, OH 45459 • (937) 291-2223 • http://www.mvcc.net/centerville/histsoc

Walton House Museum • 89 W Franklin St • Centerville, OH 45459 • (937) 433-0123 • http://www.nvcc.net/centerville/histsoc

Chagrin Falls

Chagrin Falls Historical Society • Historical Museum, 21 Walnut St, P.O. Box 15 • Chagrin Falls, OH 44022 • (440) 247-4695

Chardon

Chardon Library • 110 E Park St • Chardon, OH 44024 • (440) 285-7601

Geauga County Genealogical Society • c/o Chardon Library, 110 E Park St • Chardon, OH 44024-1213 • (440) 285-7601

Geauga County Public Library • 12701 Ravenwood Dr • Chardon, OH 44024 • (440) 286-6811

Chesterland

Chesterland Historical Foundation • Caves Rd • Chesterland, OH 44026 • (440) 729-1830

Geauga West Library • 13455 Chillicothe Road • Chesterland, OH 44026 • (440) 729-4250

Chesterville

Selover Public Library • P.O. Box 25 • Chesterville, OH 43317-0025 • (419) 768-3431

Chillicothe

Adena Mansion and Garden Museum • 846 Adena Rd, P.O. Box 831 • Chillicothe, OH 45601 • (740) 772-1500 • http://www.adenamansion. com

Chillicothe and Ross County Public Library • 140 S Paint St, P.O. Box 185 • Chillicothe, OH 45601-3214 • (740) 702-4145

Franklin House Museum • 80 S Paint St • Chillicothe, OH 45601 • (614) 772-1936

Hopewell Culture National Historic Park • 16062 State Route 104 • Chillicothe, OH 45601 • (740) 774-1126 • http://www.nps.gov/hocu

Lucy Hayes Heritage Center Museum • 90 W 6th St, P.O. Box 1790 • Chillicothe, OH 45601 • (740) 775-5829 • http://www.lucyhayes.org

Ross County Genealogical Society • 444 Douglas Ave, P.O. Box 6352 • Chillicothe, OH 45601-6352 • (740) 773-2715

Ross County Historical Society • Historical Museum, 45 W 5th St • Chillicothe, OH 45601 • (740) 772-1936 • http://www.countyhistorical. org

Scioto Historical Society • 215 W 2nd St, P.O. Box 73 • Chillicothe, OH 45601 • (614) 775-4100

Cincinnati

American Jewish Archives • Hebrew Union College, Skirball Museum, 3101 Clifton Ave • Cincinnati, OH 45220-2488 • (513) 221-7444 • http://www.hue.edu

Anderson Township Historical Society • 6550 Clough Pk, P.O. Box 30174 • Cincinnati, OH 45230 • (513) 231-2114

Betts House Research Center & Museum • 416 Clark St • Cincinnati, OH 45203 • (503) 651-0734 • http://www.bettshouse.org

Blegen Library • Univ of Cincinnati, P.O. Box 210113 • Cincinnati, OH 45221-0113 • (513) 556-1959

Caledonian Society of Cincinnati • 6910 Bridgetown Rd • Cincinnati, OH 45248 • (513) 574-2969 • http://orweb.com/caledonian

Cary Cottage Museum • 2000 Hamilton Ave • Cincinnati, OH 45231 • (513) 532-3860 • http://www.clovernook.org

Cincinnati Aviation Heritage Society • Historical Museum, 262 Wilmer Ave • Cincinnati, OH 45226 • (859) 442-7334 • http://www.cahslunken. org

Cincinnati Fire Museum • 315 W Court St • Cincinnati, OH 45202 • (513) 621-5553 • http://www.cincyfiremuseum.com

Cincinnati Historical Society • Cincinnati History Museum, 1301 Western Ave • Cincinnati, OH 45203-1129 • (513) 287-7080 • http://www.cincymuseum.org

Cincinnati Preservation Association • 342 W 4th St • Cincinnati, OH 45202 • (513) 721-4506

Delhi Historical Society • Historical Museum, 468 Anderson Ferry Rd • Cincinnati, OH 45238 • (513) 451-4313

Delhi Township Historical Society • 468 Anderson Ferry Rd • Cincinnati, OH 45238 • (513) 451-4313

Emsland Heritage Society • 4325 Saint Lawrence Ave • Cincinnati, OH 45205-1539 • (513) 921-0629

German Heritage Museum • 4764 W Fork Rd • Cincinnati, OH 45247 • (513) 256-0384 • http://www.gacl.org

Hamilton County Genealogical Society • P.O. Box 15851 • Cincinnati, OH 45215-0851 • (513) 956-7078 • http://members.aol.com/ogshc

Hamilton County Genealogical Society, African-American Interest Group • P.O. Box 15851 • Cincinnati, OH 45215-7078 • (513) 851-9549 • http://members.aol.com/ogshc

Hamilton County Genealogical Society, Computer Interest Group • P.O. Box 15851 • Cincinnati, OH 45215-7078 • (513) 851-9549 • http://members.aol.com/ogshc

Hamilton County Genealogical Society, German Interest Group • P.O. Box 15851 • Cincinnati, OH 45215 • (513) 851-9549 • http://members.aol.com/ogshc

Hamilton County Genealogical Society, Irish Interest Group • P.O. Box 15851 • Cincinnati, OH 45215-7078 • (513) 851-9549 • http://members.aol.com/ogshc

Harriet Beecher Stowe House Museum • 2950 Gilbert Ave • Cincinnati, OH 45214 • (513) 751-0651 • http://ohsweb.ohiohistory.org/places/sw18/index.shtml

Historic Southwest Ohio • John Hauck House Museum, 812 Dayton St • Cincinnati, OH 45214 • (513) 721-3570

Immigration History Society • Univ of Cincinnati, 3410 Bishop St • Cincinnati, OH 45220 • (513) 861-7462

Indian Hill Historical Society • 8100 Given Rd • Cincinnati, OH 45243 • (513) 794-1941 • http://www.indianhill.org

Jacob Rader Marcus Center of the American Jewish Archives • Hebrew Union College, 3101 Clifton Ave • Cincinnati, OH 45220-2488 • (513) 221-1875 • http://www.americanjewisharchives.org

Jewish Genealogical Society of Greater Cincinnati • Jacob Rader Marcus Ctr, 3101 Clifton Ave • Cincinnati, OH 45220-2488 • (513) 631-0233

National Underground Railroad Freedom Center Museum • 50 E Freedom Wy • Cincinnati, OH 45202 • (513) 333-7500 • http://www.freedomcenter.org

P Parker Historical Society • Historical Museum, 1014 Vine St #2520 • Cincinnati, OH 45202

Public Library of Cincinnati & Hamilton County • 800 Vine St • Cincinnati, OH 45202 • (513) 369-6900 • http://www.cincinnatilibrary.org

William Howard Taft National Historic Site Museum • 2038 Auburn Ave • Cincinnati, OH 45219 • (513) 684-3262 • http://www.nps.gov/wilho/

Wyoming Historical Society • 800 Oak Ave • Cincinnati, OH 45215 • (513) 842-1383

Circleville
Clarke May Museum • 162 W Union St • Circleville, OH 43113 • (740) 474-1495

Pickaway County Genealogical Society • 304 S Court St, P.O. Box 85 • Circleville, OH 43113-0085 • (740) 474-9144

Pickaway County Historical Society • 304 S Court St, P.O. Box 85 • Circleville, OH 43113 • (740) 474-9144

Sons of the American Revolution, Ohio Society • 1995 Ottowa Dr • Circleville, OH 43113 • (740) 474-6463 • http://www.ohssar.org

Ted Lewis Museum • 133 W Main St, P.O. Box 492 • Circleville, OH 43113 • (740) 477-3630

Clairesville
Cumberland Trail Genealogical Society • P.O. Box 576 • Clairesville, OH 43905

Clayton
Randolph Township Historical Society • P. O. Box 355 • Clayton, OH 45315

Cleveland
African American Museum • 1765 Crawford Rd • Cleveland, OH 44106 • (216) 791-1700 • http://www.aamcleveland.org

African-American Genealogical Society in Cleveland • 24500 S Woodland Rd, P.O. Box 200382 • Cleveland, OH 44122 • (216) 641-6489

Afro-American Cultural and Historical Society • Historical Museum, 1765 Crawford Rd • Cleveland, OH 44106 • (216) 791-1700

Alliance of Poles of America • 6966 Broadway Ave • Cleveland, OH 44105 • (216) 883-3131

Alliance of Transylvania Saxons • 5393 Pearl Rd • Cleveland, OH 44129-1547 • (440) 842-8442

American Hungarian Federation • 1450 Grace Ave • Cleveland, OH 44107

American Society for Croatian Migration • 1062 E 62nd St • Cleveland, OH 44103 • (216) 431-2770

American West Research Center and Historical Society • 8614 Euclid Ave • Cleveland, OH 44106 • (216) 721-9594

Association for Croatian Studies • John Carroll Univ, Dept of History • Cleveland, OH 44118 • (216) 397-4758

Byelorussian Autocephalic Orthodox Church Archives • 3517 W 25th St • Cleveland, OH 44109 • (216) 351-3730

Cleveland Grays • Armory Museum, 1234 Bolivar Rd • Cleveland, OH 44115 • (216) 621-5938 • http://graysarmorymuseum.org

Cleveland Police Historical Society • Historical Museum, 1300 Ontario St • Cleveland, OH 44113 • (216) 623-5055 • http://www.clevelandpolicemuseum.org

Cleveland Public Library • 325 Superior Ave • Cleveland, OH 44114-1271 • (216) 623-2800 • http://www.cpl.org

Crawford Auto-Aviation Museum • 10825 East Blvd • Cleveland, OH 44206 • (216) 720-5722 • http://www.wrhs.org

Cuyahoga County Archives Library • Robert Russell Rhodes House, 2905 Franklin Bovd NW • Cleveland, OH 44113 • (216) 443-3636

Cuyahoga County-Greater Cleveland Chapter, OGS • P.O. Box 40254 • Cleveland, OH 44140-0254 • (440) 333-1061 • http://www.rootsweb.com/~ohgcgg/

Department of Defense Finance and Accounting Service Records • Cleveland Center, DFAS-CL/RO, P.O. Box 99191 • Cleveland, OH 44199-1126

Dietrick Museum of Medical History • 11000 Euclid Ave • Cleveland, OH 44106 • (216) 368-3648

Dittrick Medical History Museum • 11000 Euclid Ave • Cleveland, OH 44106 • (216) 368-3648 • http://www.case.edu/artsci/dittrick/museum

Dunham Tavern Museum • 6709 Euclid Ave • Cleveland, OH 44107 • (216) 431-1060 • http://www.dunhamtavern.org

Garfield Heights Historical Society • Historical Museum, 9001 N Granger Rd • Cleveland, OH 44125 • (216) 587-3369

Hay-McKinney Mansion Museum • 10825 East Blvd • Cleveland, OH 44106 • (216) 721-5722

Historic Warehouse District Museum • 614 Superior Ave NW #100 • Cleveland, OH 44113 • (216) 344-3937 • http://www.warehousedistrict.org

Hungarian Jewish Special Interest Group • P.O. Box 34152 • Cleveland, OH 44134-0852 • (216) 661-3970 • http://feefhs.org/jsig/frg-hsig.html

Ohio

Cleveland, cont.

International Society for British Genealogy and Family History • P.O. Box 20425 • Cleveland, OH 44120 • (216) 991-7423

International Women's Air and Space Museum • 1600 N Marginal Rd • Cleveland, OH 44104 • (216) 625-1111 • http://www.iwaam.org

Lake View Cemetery Museum • 12316 Euclid Ave • Cleveland, OH 44106 • (216) 421-2665 • http://www.lakeviewcemetery.com

NASA Glenn Research Center • 21000 Brookpark Rd, MS 8-1 • Cleveland, OH 44138 • (216) 433-2646 • http://www.goc.nasa.gov

Nathan L Dauby Scout Museum • 2241 Woodland Ave • Cleveland, OH 44115 • (216) 861-6060

National Fort Daughters of '98 • 7101 Hope Ave • Cleveland, OH 44102

Polish Genealogical Society of Greater Cleveland • 906 College Ave • Cleveland, OH 44113 • (216) 459-0209 • http://feefhs.org/pol/frgpgsgc.html

Rock & Roll Hall of Fame Museum • 1100 Rock and Roll Blvd • Cleveland, OH 44114 • (216) 781-7625 • http://www.rockhall.com

Slavic Village Historical Society • Historical Museum, 12021 Woodward Blvd • Cleveland, OH 44125 • (216) 271-9300 • http://www.slavicvillagehistory.org

Slovak Institute • 10510 Buckeye Rd • Cleveland, OH 44104 • (216) 721-5300

Slovakia-Surname Locaiton Reference Project • P.O. Box 31831 • Cleveland, OH 44131-0831 • http://feefhs.org/frg-slrp.html

Steamship William G Mather Museum • 1001 E 9th St Pier • Cleveland, OH 44114 • (216) 574-9053 • http://www.wgmather.org

Ukrainian Museum & Archives • 1202 Kenilworth Ave • Cleveland, OH 44113 • (216) 781-4329 • http://www.umacleveland.org

Western Reserve Historical Society • Auto-Aviation Museum, 10825 East Blvd • Cleveland, OH 44106 • (216) 721-5722 • http://www.wrhs.org

Western Reserve Historical Society, Genealogy Club • 10825 East Blvd • Cleveland, OH 44106 • (216) 721-5722 • http://www.wrhs.org

Cleveland Heights

Cleveland Heights Heritage Center • 2745 Hampshire Rd • Cleveland Heights, OH 44106 • (216) 321-1268

Cleveland Heights-University Heights Public Library • 2345 Lee Rd • Cleveland Heights, OH 44118-3493 • (216) 932-3600 • http://www.heightslibrary.org

Coldwater

Coldwater Public Library • 305 W Main St • Coldwater, OH 45828-1604 • (419) 678-2431 • http://www.welcome.to/coldwater

Colerain Township

Coleraine Historical Society • 4200 Springdale Rd • Colerain Township, OH 45251 • (513) 385-7500 • http://www.rootsweb.com/~ohcths

Columbia Station

Columbia Historical Society • 51 Jefferson Ave, P.O. Box 983 • Columbia Station, OH 44028 • (614) 224-0822

Columbiana

Historical Society of Columbiana and Fairfield Township • 10 E Park Ave • Columbiana, OH 44408 • (330) 482-2983

Columbus

African American Historical & Educational Center • 1982 Velma Ave, P.O. Box 91132 • Columbus, OH 43209 • (614) 252-0678

Catholic Record Society • 197 E Gay St • Columbus, OH 43215 • (614) 241-2571

Central Ohio Fire Museum • 260 N 4th St • Columbus, OH 43215 • (614) 464-4099 • http://fire.ci.columbus.oh.us/Misc%20HTMLs/museum.htm

Columbus Historical Society • 699 S Front St • Columbus, OH 43206-1013 • (614) 445-8247

Columbus Jewish Historical Society • 1175 College Ave • Columbus, OH 43209-2890 • (614) 238-6977 • http://columbusjewishhistory.org

Columbus Jewish Historical Society, Genealogical Group • 1175 College Ave • Columbus, OH 43209 • (614) 238-6977 • http://columbusjewishhistory.org

Columbus Metropolitan Library • 96 S Grant Ave • Columbus, OH 43215-4781 • (614) 645-2275 • http://www.columbuslibrary.org

Franklin County Genealogical Society • 570 W Broad St, P.O. Box 44309 • Columbus, OH 43204-0309 • (614) 469-1300

Franklin County Historical Society • 580 E Broad St, P.O. Box 44309 • Columbus, OH 43216-4756 • (614) 469-1300

Gahanna Historical Society • 101 S High St • Columbus, OH 43230 • (614) 475-3342

German Village Society • Historical Museum, 588 S 3rd St • Columbus, OH 43215 • (614) 221-8888 • http://germanvillage.com

Grandview Heights Public Library • 1685 W 1st Ave • Columbus, OH 43212 • (614) 486-2951

Heritage Museum of Kappa Kappa Gamma • 530 E Town St, P.O. Box 2079 • Columbus, OH 43216 • (614) 228-6515 • http://www.kappakappagamma.org/voyage/museums/heritage/index.html

Hilltop Historical Society • 2300 W Broad St • Columbus, OH 43204 • (614) 276-0060

Historic Costume & Textiles Collection Museum • 1787 Neil Ave • Columbus, OH 43210 • (614) 292-3090 • http://www.hec.ohio-state.edu/cts/collect/buckel/

Jack Nicklaus Museum • 2355 Olentangy River Rd • Columbus, OH 43210 • (614) 247-5959 • http://www.nicklausmuseum.org

James Thurber House Museum • 77 Jefferson Ave • Columbus, OH 43215 • (614) 464-1032

Kelton House Museum & Gardens • 586 E Town St • Columbus, OH 43215-4888 • (614) 464-2717 • http://www.keltonhouse.com

Native American Indian Center of Central Ohio • 67 E Innis Ave, P.O. Box 07705 • Columbus, OH 43207 • (614) 443-6120

Ohio Association of Historical Societies and Museums • Ohio Village Museum, 1985 Velma Ave • Columbus, OH 43211 • (614) 297-2300 • http://ohsweb.ohiohistory.org/places/c11/index.shtml

Ohio Historical Society • Historical Museum, 1985 Velma Ave • Columbus, OH 43211 • (614) 297-2310 • http://www.ohiohistory.org

Ohio State Library • 274 E 1st Ave • Columbus, OH 43201 • (614) 644-7061 • http://winslo.ohio.gov/

Ohio Statehouse Museum • general delivery • Columbus, OH 43215 • (614) 728-2695

Ohioana Library • 274 E 1st Ave • Columbus, OH 43201 • (614) 466-3831

Orange Johnson House Museum • 956 High St • Columbus, OH 43085 • (614) 846-1676

Palatines to America, National Chapter • 611 E Weber Rd • Columbus, OH 43211-1097 • (614) 267-4700 • http://www.palam.org

Palatines to America, Ohio Chapter • 611 E Weber Rd • Columbus, OH 43211-1097 • (614) 267-4700 • http://oh-palam.org

Society of Ohio Archivists • 2700 Kenny Rd, P.O. Box 38 • Columbus, OH 43216-0038 • (614) 718-7599

Conneaut

Conneaut Area Historical Society • 235 Fifield Ave • Conneaut, OH 44030

Conneaut Carnegie Library • 304 Buffalo St • Conneaut, OH 44030-2658 • (440) 593-1608 • http://www.conneaut.lib.oh.us

Conneaut Railroad Museum • 363 Depot St, P.O. Box 643 • Conneaut, OH 44030 • (440) 599-7878 • http://www.pbase.com/vbcooke/conneaut

Conover

A B Graham Memorial Center • 8025 E US Hwy 36, P.O. Box 433 • Conover, OH 45317 • (937) 368-3700 • http://http://www.abgraham.org

Coshocton

Coshocton County Chapter, OGS • P.O. Box 128 • Coshocton, OH 43812-0128 • (740) 622-4706

Coshocton Public Library • 655 Main St • Coshocton, OH 43812-1697 • (740) 622-0956 • http://www.coshocton.lib.oh.us

Johnson-Humrick House Museum • Roscoe Village, 300 N Whitewoman St • Coshocton, OH 43812 • (740) 622-8710 • http://www.jhmuseum.org

Roscoe Village Foundation • Historical Museum, 381 Hill St • Coshocton, OH 43812 • (740) 623-6548 • http://www.roscoevillage.com

Roscoe Village Foundation Library • 381 Hill St • Coshocton, OH 43812 • (740) 622-9310 • http://www.roscoevillage.com

Crestline

Crestline Historical Society • Skunk Museum, 211 Thoman St, P.O. Box 456 • Crestline, OH 44827 • (419) 683-1703

Crestline Public Library • 324 N Thoman St • Crestline, OH 44827-1410 • (419) 683-3909

Crooksville

Ohio Ceramic Center Museum • 7327 Ceramic Rd NE, P.O. Box 200 • Crooksville, OH 43731 • (740) 697-7021

Cumberland

The Wilds Museum • 14000 International Rd • Cumberland, OH 43732 • (740) 638-5030 • http://www.thewilds.org

Cuyahoga Falls

Taylor Memorial Public Library • 2015 3rd St • Cuyahoga Falls, OH 44221 • (330) 928-2117

Dalton

Kidron Community Historical Society • 13153 Emerson Rd • Dalton, OH 44618 • (330) 857-9111

America's Packard Museum • 420 S Ludlow St • Dayton, OH 45402 • (937) 226-1710 • http://www.americaspackardmuseum.org

Arcade Museum Center • 33 W 1st St #600 • Dayton, OH 45402

Aullwood Audubon Center & Farm • 1000 Aullwood Dr • Dayton, OH 45414 • (937) 890-7360 • http://web4.audubon.org/local/sanctuary/aullwood/

Carillon Historical Park • 1000 Carillon Blvd • Dayton, OH 45409 • (937) 293-2841 • http://www.carillonpark.org

Centerville-Wash Township Historical Society • 26 N Main St • Dayton, OH 45459 • (937) 291-2223

Daniel Arnold House and Carriage Hill Metro Park Farm Museum • 7800 E Shull Rd • Dayton, OH 45424 • (937) 278-2609 • http://www.metroparks.org/Parks/CarriageHill/Home.aspx

Dayton Metro Library • 215 E 3rd St • Dayton, OH 45402-2103 • (937) 227-9500 • http://www.daytonmetrolirary.org

Dayton Power & Light County Museum • 3931 S Dixie Dr • Dayton, OH 45410 • (937) 643-5016

Jewish Genealogical Society of Dayton • P.O. Box 60338 • Dayton, OH 45406 • (937) 277-3995

Miami Valley County Genealogical Society • P.O. Box 1364 • Dayton, OH 45401-1364 • (513) 890-6883

Miami Valley Military History Museum • 120 Ohio Ave, Bldg 120 • Dayton, OH 45428 • (937) 267-7628 • http://www.mvmhm.com

Montgomery County Chapter, OGS • P.O. Box 1584 • Dayton, OH 45401-1584 • (937) 274-3502 • http://www.dayton.lib.oh.us/~ads_elli/newcom2.htm#TOC

Montgomery County Historical Society • Historical Museum, 224 N Saint Clair St • Dayton, OH 45402 • (937) 228-6271 • http://www.daytonhistory.org

National Aviation Hall of Fame • 1100 Spaatz St, P.O. Box 31096 • Dayton, OH 45437 • (888) 383-1903 • http://www.nationalaviation.org

Oakwood Historical Society • 1947 Far Hills Ave • Dayton, OH 45419 • (937) 299-3793

Patterson Homestead Museum • 1815 Brown St • Dayton, OH 45409 • (937) 293-2841 • http://www.pattersonhome.com

Paul Laurence Dunbar House Museum • 219 N Paul Laurence Dunbar St, P.O. Box 1872 • Dayton, OH 45401 • (937) 313-2010 • http://www.daytonhistory.org

Paul Laurence Dunbar Library • Wright State Univ, 219 N Paul Lawrence Dunbar St, P.O. Box 1872 • Dayton, OH 45435-0001 • (937) 873-2092 • http://www.ohiohistory.org/places/dunbar

Sun Watch Indian Village • 2301 West River St • Dayton, OH 45418 • (937) 268-8199 • http://www.sunwatch.org

United Theological Seminary Library • United Methodist Church, 1810 Harvard Blvd • Dayton, OH 45406-4599 • (513) 278-5817

West Carrollton Historical Society • 323 E Central Ave • Dayton, OH 45449 • (937) 859-5912

Defiance

Defiance County Chapter, OGS • P.O. Box 675 • Defiance, OH 43512 • (419) 782-1456 • http://www.rootsweb.com/~ohdcgs

Defiance County Historical Society • AuGlaize Village Museum, 12296 Krouse Rd, P.O. Box 801 • Defiance, OH 43512 • (419) 784-0107 • http://www.defiance-online.com/auglaize

Defiance Public Library • 320 Fort St • Defiance, OH 43512-2186 • (419) 782-1456 • http://www.defiancelibrary.org

Delaware

Beeghly Library • Ohio Wesleyan Univ, 43 Rowland • Delaware, OH 43015 • (740) 368-3246

Delaware County Chapter, OGS • 157 E William St, P.O. Box 1126 • Delaware, OH 43015-1126 • (740) 369-3831 • http://www.midohio.net/dchsdcgs

Delaware County District Library • 84 E Winter St • Delaware, OH 43015 • (740) 362-3861 • http://www.delawarelibrary.org

Delaware County Historical Society • Historical Museum, 157 E William St, P.O. Box 317 • Delaware, OH 43015 • (740) 369-3831 • http://www.midohio.net/dchsdcgs

Nash House Museum • 157 E Williams St, P.O. Box 317 • Delaware, OH 43015 • (740) 369-4900

Delphos

Delphos Public Library • 309 W 2nd St • Delphos, OH 45833-1695 • (419) 695-4015 • http://www.delphos.lib.oh.us

Museum of Postal History • 339 N Main St, P.O. Box 174 • Delphos, OH 45833 • (419) 303-5482 • http://www.postalhistorymuseum.org

Dennison
Dennison Railroad Depot Museum • 400 Center St, P.O. Box 11 • Dennison, OH 44621 • (740) 922-6776 • http://www.dennisondepot.org

Deshler
Desher Edwin Wood Memorial Library • 208 North East Ave • Deshler, OH 43516 • (419) 278-3616

Henry County Genealogical Society • c/o Desher Edwin Wood Memorial Library, 208 North East Ave, P.O. Box 231 • Deshler, OH 43516-1280 • (419) 278-3616

Dover
Dover Historical Society • J E Reeves Home Museum, 325 E Iron Ave • Dover, OH 44622 • (330) 343-7040 • http://web.tusco.net/reeves

Warther Museum • 331 Karl Ave • Dover, OH 44622 • (330) 343-7513 • http://www.warthers.com

Doylestown
Chippewa-Rogues' Hollow Historical Society • Historical Museum, 17500 Gale House Rd, P.O. Box 283 • Doylestown, OH 44230 • (330) 289-7252 • http://www.chippewarogueshollow.org

Dublin
Dublin Historical Society • 5300 Emerald Pkwy, P.O. Box 2 • Dublin, OH 43017-1024 • (614) 764-9906

East Liverpool
Carnegie Public Library • 219 E 4th St • East Liverpool, OH 43920-3143 • (330) 385-2048 • http://www.carnegie.lib.oh.us

Lou Holtz - Upper Ohio Valley Hall of Fame • 120 E 5th St, P.O. Box 60 • East Liverpool, OH 43920 • (330) 386-5443 • http://www.louholtzhalloffame.com

Museum of Ceramics • 400 E 5th St • East Liverpool, OH 43920 • (330) 386-6001 • http://www.themuseumofceramics.org

Tri-State Black Museum • 1102 Pennsylvania Ave • East Liverpool, OH 43920

Tri-State Genealogical Society • c/o Carnegie Public Library, 219 E 4th St, P.O. Box 5110 • East Liverpool, OH 43920 • (330) 385-2048

East Palestine
East Palestine Area Historical Society • 555 Bacon Ave • East Palestine, OH 44413 • (330) 426-9094

East Palestine Memorial Public Library • 309 N Market St • East Palestine, OH 44413 • (330) 426-3778 • http://www.east-palestine.lib.oh.us

Eastlake
Croatian Heritage Museum • 34900 Lakeshore Blvd • Eastlake, OH 44095 • (440) 946-2044 • http://www.croatiamuseum.com

Eaton
Fort St Clair State Memorial Museum • P.O. Box 27 • Eaton, OH 45320 • (513) 456-4125

Preble County Chapter, OGS • 301 N Barron St • Eaton, OH 45320-1705 • (937) 456-4331

Preble County District Library • 301 N Barron St • Eaton, OH 45320-1705 • (937) 456-4331

Preble County Historical Society • 7693 Swartsel Rd • Eaton, OH 45320 • (937) 787-4256

Elmore
Harris-Elmore Public Library • 300 Toledo St, P.O. Box 84 • Elmore, OH 43416 • (419) 862-2482

Elyria
Elyria Public Library • 320 Washington Ave • Elyria, OH 44035-5199 • (440) 323-5747 • http://www.elyria.lib.oh.us

Lorain County Genealogical Society • c/o Hicks Memorial Library, 509 Washington Ave, P.O. Box 865 • Elyria, OH 44036-0865 • (440) 322-3341

Lorain County Historical Society • Hickories Museum, 509 Washington Ave, P.O. Box 865 • Elyria, OH 44036-0865 • (440) 322-3341 • http://www.lchs.org

Enon
Enon Community Historical Society • 45 Indian Dr, P.O. Box 442 • Enon, OH 45323-1131 • (937) 864-7080

Euclid
Euclid Historical Society • Historical Museum, 21129 North St • Euclid, OH 44117 • (216) 738-0890 • http://www.ci.euclid.oh.us

Euclid Public Library • 631 E 222nd St • Euclid, OH 44123 • (216) 261-5300

Fairport Harbor
Fairport Harbor Historical Society • Historical Museum, 129 2nd St • Fairport Harbor, OH 44007 • (440) 354-4825 • http://www.fairportlighthouse.com

Montgomery Historical Society • Historical Museum, 419 Eagle St • Fairport Harbor, OH 44077

Fairview Park
Cuyahoga West Chapter, OGS • P.O. Box 26196 • Fairview Park, OH 44145-0196

Findlay
Findlay-Hancock County Public Library • 206 Broadway • Findlay, OH 45840 • (419) 422-1712

Hancock County Chapter, OGS • P.O. Box 672 • Findlay, OH 45840-0672 • (419) 299-3624 • http://www.bright.net/hanogs/

Hancock Historical Museum Association • Historical Museum, 422 W Sandusky St • Findlay, OH 45840 • (419) 423-4433 • http://www.hancockhistoricalmuseum.org

Historic Preservation Guild of Hancock County • 845 Liberty St, P.O. Box 621 • Findlay, OH 45839 • (419) 422-2826

Flushing
Underground Railroad Museum • P.O. Box 47 • Flushing, OH 43977 • (740) 968-2080 • http://www.ugrrf.org

Fort Recovery
Fort Recovery Museum • 1 Fort Site St • Fort Recovery, OH 45846 • (800) 283-8920

Fort Recovery State Memorial • 1741 Union City Rd • Fort Recovery, OH 45846 • (419) 375-4649

Fostoria
Fostoria Area Historical Society • Historical Museum, 123 W North St, P.O. Box 142 • Fostoria, OH 44830 • (419) 435-3588 • http://www.fostoria.org/Links/museum/museum.html

Fostoria Lineage Research Society • c/o Kaubisch Memorial Public Library, 205 Perry St • Fostoria, OH 44830 • (419) 435-2813

Kaubisch Memorial Public Library • 205 Perry St • Fostoria, OH 44830 • (419) 435-2813

Franklin
Franklin Area Historical Society • Historical Museum, 302 Park Ave, P.O. Box 345 • Franklin, OH 45005 • (937) 746-8295

Harding Museum • 302 Park Ave • Franklin, OH 45005 • (513) 746-8295

Fredericktown
Fredericktown Historical Society • 2 E Sandusky St • Fredericktown, OH 43019

Knox County Genealogical Society • 658 N Sandusky St • Fredericktown, OH 43019

Fremont
Birchard Public Library • 423 Croghan St • Fremont, OH 43420 • (419) 334-7101 • http://www.birchard.lib.oh.us

Rutherford B Hayes Presidential Center Library • Spiegel Grove, 1337 Hayes Ave • Fremont, OH 43420-2796 • (419) 332-2081 • http://www.rbhayes.org

Sandusky County Historical Society • 1337 Hayes Ave • Fremont, OH 43420-2796

Sandusky County Kin Hunter Society • 1337 Hayes Ave • Fremont, OH 43420-2796

Galion
Brownella Cottage Museum • 132 S Union St, Apt 19 • Galion, OH 44833 • (419) 468-9338

Crawford County Chapter, OGS • P.O. Box 92 • Galion, OH 44833-0092 • (419) 562-5420

Galion Historical Society • Historical Museum, 132 S Union St, P.O. Box 125 • Galion, OH 44833 • (419) 468-9938

Gallipolis
French Art Colony Historic Home Museum • 530 1st Ave, P.O. Box 472 • Gallipolis, OH 45631 • (740) 446-3834 • http://www.frenchartcolony.org

Gallia County Historical and Genealogical Society • 412 2nd Ave, P.O. Box 295 • Gallipolis, OH 45631-0295 • (740) 446-7200

Gallia County Historical Society • P.O. Box 295 • Gallipolis, OH 45631-0295 • (614) 446-1775

Our House State Memorial Museum • 432 1st Ave, P.O. Box 607 • Gallipolis, OH 45631 • (740) 446-0596 • http://www.ohiohistory.org/places/ourhouse

Garrettsville
Portage County District Library • 10482 South St • Garrettsville, OH 44231 • (330) 527-4378

Gates Mills
Gates Mills Historical Society • Historical Museum, 7580 Old Mill Rd, P.O. Box 249 • Gates Mills, OH 44040 • (440) 423-4808

Hungarian Genealogy Society of Greater Cleveland • 7830 Sugarbush Ln • Gates Mills, OH 44040-9317 • (440) 423-3469

Geneva
Ashtabula County Genealogical Society • c/o Geneva Library, 860 Sherman St • Geneva, OH 44041-9101 • (440) 466-4521

Platt R Spencer Memorial Museum • Special Collections, 860 Sherman St • Geneva, OH 44041 • (440) 466-4521 • http://www.acdl.info

Shandy Hall House Museum • 6333 S Ridge Rd • Geneva, OH 44041 • http://www.wrhs.org

Geneva-on-the-Lake
Ashtabula County Historical Society • Historical Museum, 5685 Lake Rd, P.O. Box 36 • Geneva-on-the-Lake, OH 44041 • (440) 466-7337 • http://www.ashtcohs.com

Georgetown
Brown County Chapter, OGS • Cherry & Apple Sts, P.O. Box 83 • Georgetown, OH 45121-0083 • (937) 444-3521

Brown County Public Library • 200 W Grant Ave • Georgetown, OH 45121-1299 • (937) 378-3197

Grant Homestead Association • Grant Boyhood Home, 318 W State St • Georgetown, OH 45121 • (937) 378-4222

U.S. Grant Homestead Museum • 219 Grant Ave • Georgetown, OH 45121 • (937) 378-4222

Germantown
Germantown Public Library • 51 N Plum St • Germantown, OH 45327 • (937) 855-4001

Glendale
Glendale Heritage Preservation Society • 30 Village Sq • Glendale, OH 45246 • (513) 771-7200 • http://www.glendaleohio.org

Glenford
Flint Ridge State Memorial Museum • 15300 Flint Ridge Rd • Glenford, OH 43739 • (740) 872-3143

Flint Ridge State Memorial Ohio Historical Society • 7091 Brownsville Rd • Glenford, OH 43739 • (740) 787-2476

Gnadenhutten
Gnadenhutten Historical Society • Historical Museum, 352 S Cherry St, P.O. Box 396 • Gnadenhutten, OH 44629-0396 • (614) 254-4143 • http://gnaden.tusco.net/history/museum.htm

Gnadenhutten Public Library • 160 N Walnut St, P.O. Box 216 • Gnadenhutten, OH 44629 • (740) 254-9224

Goshen
Goshen Historical Society • Goshen Township Museum, 1848 State Route 28, P.O. Box 671 • Goshen, OH 45122 • (513) 575-1027 • http://www.goshenhistory.org

Grafton
Belden Historical Society • general delivery • Grafton, OH 44044

Grafton-Midview Public Library • 983 Main St • Grafton, OH 44044 • (440) 926-3317

Grand Rapids
Seven Eagles Historical Earth and Education Center • 16486 Wapokoneta Rd • Grand Rapids, OH 43522 • (419) 509-0095 • http://www.aclew.org

Granville
Avery-Downer House Museum • 221 E Broadway, P.O. Box 183 • Granville, OH 43023 • (740) 587-0430

Denison Museum • 240 W Broadway, P.O. Box 810 • Granville, OH 43023 • (740) 587-5713 • http://www.denison.edu/museum

Granville Ohio Historical Society • Historical Museum, 115 E Broadway, P.O. Box 129 • Granville, OH 43023 • (740) 587-3951 • http://www.granvillehistory.org

Granville Public Library • 217 E Broadway • Granville, OH 43023 • (740) 587-0196

H D Robinson House Museum • 121 S Main St, P.O. Box 134 • Granville, OH 43023 • (740) 587-0373

Robbins Hunter Museum • P.O. Box 183 • Granville, OH 43023 • (740) 587-0430 • http://www.robbinshunter.org

Greenfield
Greenfield Historical Society • 103 S McArthur Way • Greenfield, OH 45123 • (937) 981-7890

Greenville
Darke County Chapter, OGS • P.O. Box 908 • Greenville, OH 45331

Darke County Historical Society • Garst Museum, 205 N Broadway • Greenville, OH 45331-222 • (937) 548-5250 • http://www.garstmuseum.org

Greenville Public Library • 520 Sycamore St • Greenville, OH 45220 • (937) 548-3915

Grove City
South Western Public Libraries • 3359 Park St • Grove City, OH 43123 • (614) 875-6716

Groveport
Motts Military Museum • 5075 S Hamilton Rd • Groveport, OH 43125 • (614) 836-1500 • http://www.mottsmilitarymuseum.org

Hamden
Vinton County Historical Society and Chapter, OGS • 20 W Railroad St, P.O. Box 306 • Hamden, OH 45634-0306 • (614) 384-6305

Hamilton
Butler County Historical Society • Benninghofen House Museum, 327 N 2nd St • Hamilton, OH 45011 • (513) 896-9930 • http://home.fuse. net/butlercountymuseum/

Historic Hamilton • Historical Museum, 319 N 3rd St • Hamilton, OH 45011 • (513) 863-1389

Lane Public Library • 300 N 3rd St • Hamilton, OH 45011-1629 • (513) 894-7156

Southwest Butler County Genealogical Society • 3 S Monument Ave, P.O. Box 243 • Hamilton, OH 45011

Hanoverton
Daughters of Union Veterans of the Civil War, Ohio Department • 31927 US Route 30 • Hanoverton, OH 44423

Harrison
Village Historical Society • Historical Museum, 10659 New Birklinger Rd • Harrison, OH 45030 • (513) 367-9379

Heath
Newark Earthworks State Memorial Museum • 455 Hebron Rd • Heath, OH 43056 • (800) 589-8224

Hicksville
Hicksville Historical Society • Historical Museum, P.O. Box 162 • Hicksville, OH 43526 • http://www.hicksvillehistoricalsociety.org

Hilliard
Northwest Franklin County Historical Society • 4162 Avery Rd, P.O. Box 413 • Hilliard, OH 43026-0413 • (614) 777-4852

Hillsboro
Fort Hill State Memorial Museum • 13614 Fort Hill Rd • Hillsboro, OH 45133 • (937) 588-3221

Highland County District Library • 10 Willettsville Pike • Hillsboro, OH 45133 • (937) 393-3114

Highland County Genealogy Society • Highland House Museum, 151 E Main St • Hillsboro, OH 45133 • (937) 393-3263

Highland County Historical Society • Highland House Museum, 151 E Main St • Hillsboro, OH 45133 • (937) 393-3392

Southern Ohio Genealogical Society • P.O. Box 414 • Hillsboro, OH 45133

Hinckley
Hinckley Historical Society • 1634 Center Rd, P.O. Box 471 • Hinckley, OH 44233 • (330) 278-3159

Holmesville
National Organization, Ladies of the Grand Army of the Republic • 9057 SR 83 N • Holmesville, OH 44633 • (330) 279-4393 • http://www. rootsweb.com/~nlgar/home.htm

Hudson
Council of Historic Institutions and Preservation Societies in Summit and Portage Counties • c/o Hudson Library, 22 Aurora St • Hudson, OH 44236 • (330) 230-5651

Hudson Chapter, OGS • c/o Hudson Library, 22 Aurora St • Hudson, OH 44236-2947 • (330) 230-5651

Hudson Heritage Association • 34 N Main St, P.O. Box 2218 • Hudson, OH 44236 • (330) 653-9817

Hudson Historical Society • c/o Hudson Library & Museum, 22 Aurora St • Hudson, OH 44236 • (330) 653-6658 • http://www.hudsonlibrary. org

Hudson Library • 22 Aurora St • Hudson, OH 44236-2947 • (330) 230-5651

Huron
Huron Historical Society • 401 Williams St • Huron, OH 44839

Ironton
Briggs-Lawrence County Public Library • 321 S 4th St • Ironton, OH 45638 • (740) 532-1124 • http://www.briggslibrary.com

Lawrence County Genealogy Society • 321 S 4th St, P.O. Box 945 • Ironton, OH 45638-0945 • (740) 532-1124 • http://www.wwd.net/user/ historical/

Lawrence County Historical Society • Gray House Museum, 506 S 6th St, P.O. Box 73 • Ironton, OH 45638 • (740) 532-1222

Jackson
Jackson City Library • 21 Broadway • Jackson, OH 45640 • (614) 286-2609

Jackson County Genealogical Society • 21 Broadway, P.O. Box 807 • Jackson, OH 45640-0807

Lillian E Jones Museum • 75 Broadway St • Jackson, OH 45640 • (740) 286-2556 • http://lillianjones.museum.com

Jefferson
Ashtabula County Historical Society • Historical Museum, P.O. Box 36 • Jefferson, OH 44047 • (440) 466-7337 • http://www.ashtocohs.com

Henderson Memorial Public Library • 54 E Jefferson St • Jefferson, OH 44047-1198 • (440) 576-3761

Joshua Giddings Law Office Museum • 102 E Jefferson ST • Jefferson, OH 44047 • http://www.ashtcohs.com

Johnstown
Johnstown Genealogy Society • P.O. Box 345 • Johnstown, OH 43031

Junction City
Perry County Chapter, OGS • P.O. Box 275 • Junction City, OH 43748-0275 • (614) 987-7646

Kalida
Putnam County Historical Society • Historical Museum, 201 E Main St, P.O. Box 264 • Kalida, OH 45853-0264 • (419) 532-3008 • http:// userpages.bright.net/~pchs/

Kelleys Island
Kelleys Island Historical Association • P.O. Box 328 • Kelleys Island, OH 43438

Kent
Kelso House Museum • 4158 State Rte 43, P.O. Box 1231 • Kent, OH 44240 • (330) 573-1058 • http://www.kelsohouse.org

Kent Free Library • 312 W Main St • Kent, OH 44240 • (330) 673-4414

Kent Historical Association • 152 Franklin Ave, P.O. Box 663 • Kent, OH 44240 • (330) 678-2712

Kent State University Museum • Rockwell Hall, 515 Hilltop Dr, P.O. Box 1590 • Kent, OH 44242 • (330) 672-3450 • http://www.kent.edu/ museum/

University Library • Kent State Univ • Kent, OH 44242 • (330) 672-2962 • http://www.library.kent.edu/speccoll/

Kenton
Dougherty House Museum • 215 N Detroit St, P.O. Box 521 • Kenton, OH 43326 • (419) 673-0275

Hardin County Genealogy Society • P.O. Box 520 • Kenton, OH 43326-0520 • (419) 675-1839

Hardin County Historical Museum • 233 N Main St, P.O. Box 521 • Kenton, OH 43326 • (419) 673-7147 • http://www.hardinmuseums.org

Mary Lou Johnson-Hardin County District Library • 325 E Columbus St • Kenton, OH 43326 • (419) 673-2278

Organette House Mechanical Music Museum • 15577 US Hwy 68 • Kenton, OH 43326 • (419) 673-0983 • http://www.organettehouse.com

Sullivan-Johnson Historic House Museum • 223 N Main St • Kenton, OH 43326 • http://www.graveaddiction.com/hardinmus.html

Kettering
Kettering-Morraine Museum and Historical Society • Historical Museum, 3600 Shroyer Rd • Kettering, OH 45439 • (937) 296-2400 • http://www.ketteringoh.org

Kingsville
Kingsville Public Library • 6006 Academy St • Kingsville, OH 44048-0057 • (440) 224-0239

Kirtland
Kirland Temple Historic Center Museum • 7809 Joseph St • Kirtland, OH 44094 • (440) 256-1830 • http://www.kirtlandtemple.org

Kirtland Public Library • 9267 Chillicothe Rd • Kirtland, OH 44094-9216 • (440) 256-7323

Kirtland Hill
Lake County Historical Society • Historical Museum, 8610 Mentor Rd • Kirtland Hill, OH 44060 • (440) 255-8979 • http://www.lakehistory.org

Lakeside Marblehead
Marblehead Light House Historical Society • 110 Lighthouse Dr • Lakeside Marblehead, OH 43440 • (419) 798-2094

Lakewood
Lakewood Historical Society • Oldest Stone House Museum, 14710 Lake Ave • Lakewood, OH 44107 • (216) 221-7343 • http://www.lakewoodhistory.org

Lakewood Public Library • 15425 Detroit Ave • Lakewood, OH 44107 • (216) 226-8275 • http://www.lkwdpl.org

Lancaster
Fairfield County Chapter, OGS • P.O. Box 1470 • Lancaster, OH 43130-0570 • http://www.greenapple.com/~ksmith/

Fairfield County District Library • 219 N Broad St • Lancaster, OH 43130 • (740) 653-2745

Fairfield Heritage Association • The Georgian Museum, 105 E Wheeling St • Lancaster, OH 43130-3706 • (740) 654-9923 • http://www.fairfieldheritage.org

Gen William T Sherman House Museum • 137 E Main St • Lancaster, OH 43130 • (740) 687-5891 • http://www.shermanhouse.org

Ohio Glass Museum • 126 W Main St • Lancaster, OH 43130 • (740) 687-0101 • http://www.ohioglassmuseum.org

Reese Peters House Museum & Decorative Arts Center • 145 E Main St • Lancaster, OH 43130 • (740) 681-1423 • http://www.decartsohio.org

Lebanon
Glendower Mansion Museum • 105 Cincinnati Ave • Lebanon, OH 45036 • (513) 932-1817 • http://www.wchsmuseum.com

Museum Post Office • 121 W Broadway • Lebanon, OH 45036 • (513) 932-1817 • http://www.wchsmuseum.org

Warren County Genealogical Society • Warren County Genealogical Rource Center, 406 Justice Dr, P.O. Box 296 • Lebanon, OH 45036-0296 • (513) 423-9799 • http://www.co.warren.oh.us/genealogy/

Warren County Historical Society • Local History & Genealogy Library, 105 S Broadway, P.O. Box 223 • Lebanon, OH 45063-1707 • (513) 932-1817 • http://wwww.wchsmuseum.com

Leetonia
Leetonia Community Public Library • 24 Walnut St • Leetonia, OH 44431 • (330) 427-6635

Leetonia Historical Society • c/o Leetonia Community Public Library, 24 Walnut St • Leetonia, OH 44431 • (330) 427-6635

Lewisburg
Preble County Historical Society • 9691 State Route 503 N • Lewisburg, OH 45338 • (937) 962-5561

Lexington
Richland County Museum • 51 Church St, P.O. Box 3154 • Lexington, OH 44904 • (419) 884-3260

Lima
Allen County Chapter, OGS • c/o Elizabeth M MacDonell Memorial Library, 620 W Market St • Lima, OH 45801-4665 • (419) 222-9426 • http://www.worcnet.gen.oh.us/acmuseum/

Allen County Historical Society • Allen County Museum, 620 W Market St • Lima, OH 45801-4604 • (419) 222-9426 • http://www.allencountymuseum.org

Fort Amanda Museum • 2355 Ada Road • Lima, OH 45801 • (800) 283-8713

Lima Public Library • 620 W Market St • Lima, OH 45801-4665 • (419) 228-5113

MacDonell House Museum • 632 W Market St • Lima, OH 45801 • (419) 224-1113

Lisbon
Erie Railroad Station Museum • 119 E Washington St • Lisbon, OH 44432 • (330) 242-0191 • http://www.lisbonhistory.org

Lepper Library • 303 E Lincoln Way • Lisbon, OH 44432 • (330) 424-3117

Lisbon Historical Society • Historical Museum, 119 E Washington St, P.O. Box 191 • Lisbon, OH 44432 • (330) 424-1861 • http://www.lisbonhistory.org

Litchfield
Litchfield Historical Society • 4700 Avon Lake Rd • Litchfield, OH 44253

Lithopolis
Wagnalls Memorial Museum • 150 E Columbus St, P.O. Box 217 • Lithopolis, OH 43136 • (614) 837-4765 • http://www.wagnalls.org

Lodi
Lodi Historical Society • 117 Wooster St • Lodi, OH 44254

Logan
Hocking County Historical Society • 92 N Culver St, P.O. Box 262 • Logan, OH 43140 • (740) 385-6026

Logan-Hocking County District Library • 230 E Main St • Logan, OH 43138 • (614) 385-2348

London
Madison County Genealogical Society • P.O. Box 102 • London, OH 43140-0102

Madison County Historical Society • 260 E High St, P.O. Box 124 • London, OH 43140 • (740) 852-2977

Lorain
Black River Genealogists • 351 6th St, P.O. Box 3131 • Lorain, OH 44052

Black River Historical Society • Historical Museum, 309 W 5th St • Lorain, OH 44052 • (440) 245-2563 • http://www.loraincityhistory.org

Lorain Public Library • 351 6th St • Lorain, OH 44052 • (440) 244-1192

Loudonville

Cleo Redd Fisher Museum • 203 E Main St • Loudonville, OH 44842 • (419) 994-4050 • http://www.loudonvillelibrary.org/cleo_redd.htm

Loudonville Public Library • 122 E Main St • Loudonville, OH 44842 • (419) 994-5531

Mohican Historical Society • Historical Museum, 203 E Main St • Loudonville, OH 44842 • (419) 994-4050

Louisville

Louisville Public Library • 700 Lincoln Ave • Louisville, OH 44641-1474 • (330) 875-1696

Loveland

Chateau Laroche Museum • 12025 Shore Dr, P.O. Box 135 • Loveland, OH 45140 • (513) 683-4686

Greater Loveland Historical Society • Historical Museum, 201 N Riverside Ave • Loveland, OH 45140 • (513) 683-5692 • http://www.lovelandmuseum.org

Lowellville

Poland Township Historical Society • 4515 Center Rd • Lowellville, OH 44436 • (330) 536-6877

Lucas

Malabar Farm State Park Museum • 4050 Bromfield Rd • Lucas, OH 44843 • (419) 892-2784 • http://www.malabarfarm.org

Lucasville

Lucasville Area Historical Society • P.O. Box 761 • Lucasville, OH 45648-0761 • (614) 259-4392

Lyndhurst

East Cuyahoga County Chapter, OGS • P.O. Box 24182 • Lyndhurst, OH 44124-0182

Ohio Cemetery Preservation Society • P.O. Box 24810 • Lyndhurst, OH 44124-0810

Madison

MacKenzie Memorial Public Library • 6111 Middle Range Rd • Madison, OH 44057 • (440) 428-2189

Madison Historical Society • Historical Museum, 13 W Main St, P.O. Box 91 • Madison, OH 44057 • (440) 428-6107

Manchester

Manchester Historical Society • 307 Pike St • Manchester, OH 45144-1232 • (937) 549-3888

Mansfield

Discovery Center at Richland Academy • 75 N Walnut St • Mansfield, OH 44902

Living Bible Museum • 500 Tingley Ave • Mansfield, OH 44905 • (800) 222-0139 • http://www.livingbiblemuseum.org

Mansfield Fire Museum • 1265 W 4th St • Mansfield, OH 44906 • (419) 529-2573 • http://www.mansfieldfiremuseum.com

Mansfield Memorial Museum • 34 Park Ave W • Mansfield, OH 44902 • (419) 524-9924 • http://www.themansfieldmuseum.com

Mansfield Reformatory Preservation Society • Historical Museum, 100 Reformatory Rd • Mansfield, OH 44905 • (419) 622-2644 • http://www.mrps.org

Mansfield-Richland County Public Library • 43 W 3rd St • Mansfield, OH 44902 • (419) 521-3115

North Central Ohio Industrial Museum • 2238 Breezeway Dr • Mansfield, OH 44904 • (419) 884-3884

Richland County Genealogical Society • P.O. Box 3823 • Mansfield, OH 44907-3823 • http://www.rootsweb.com/~ohrichgs

Richland County Historical Society • Historical Museum, 310 Springmill St • Mansfield, OH 44903

Women's Relief Corps, Ohio Dept • P.O. Box 2506 • Mansfield, OH 44906-2750

Marietta

Campus Martius Museum • 601 2nd St • Marietta, OH 45750 • (740) 373-3750 • http://www.ohiohistory.org/places/campus

Castle Museum • 418 4th St • Marietta, OH 45750 • (740) 373-4180 • http://www.mariettacastle.org

Children's Toy and Doll Museum • 206 Gilman St, P.O. Box 4034 • Marietta, OH 45750 • (740) 373-5900

Fearing House Museum • 131 Gilman St • Marietta, OH 45750 • (740) 373-9437

Harmar Station Museum • 220 Gilman St • Marietta, OH 45750 • (740) 374-9995

Ohio Historical Society • Martius Museum, 601 2nd St • Marietta, OH 45750 • (740) 373-3750

Ohio River Museum • 601 Front St • Marietta, OH 45750 • (740) 373-3750 • http://www.ohiohistory.org/places/ohriver

Sons and Daughters of Pioneer Rivermen • 126 Seneca Dr • Marietta, OH 45750 • http://s-and-d.jspsi.org

Washington County Chapter, OGS • c/o Washington County Public Library 615 5th St, P.O. Box 2174 • Marietta, OH 45750-2174 • (740) 373-1057 x230

Washington County Historical Society • 403 Harmar St • Marietta, OH 45740 • (740) 376-9823

Washington County Historical Society • 417 2nd St • Marietta, OH 45750 • (740) 373-1788

Washington County Public Library • 615 5th St • Marietta, OH 45750 • (740) 373-1057 x230

Marion

Charlie Sens Antique Auto Museum • State Rt 95 & Hwy 2 • Marion, OH 43302 • (740) 389-4686

Heber Museum • 185 N State St • Marion, OH 43302 • (740) 389-1098

Marion Area Chapter, OGS • 169 E Church St, P.O. Box 844 • Marion, OH 43302-0844 • (740) 382-4179 • http://www.genealogy.org/~smoore/marion/

Marion County Historical Society • Historical Museum, 169 E Church St, P.O. Box 169 • Marion, OH 43302 • (740) 387-4255 • http://www.historymarion.org

Marion Public Library • 445 E Church St • Marion, OH 43302 • (740) 387-0992

Ohio Academy of History • 1465 Mount Vernon Ave • Marion, OH 43302-5695 • (740) 389-2361

Ohio Preservation Alliance • 127 N Prospect St • Marion, OH 43302 • (740) 387-2577

President Warren G Harding Home and Museum • 380 Mount Vernon Ave • Marion, OH 43302 • (740) 387-9630 • http://www.ohiohistory.org

Stengel-True Museum • 504 S State St, P.O. Box 3 • Marion, OH 43302 • (740) 387-7150

Wyandot Popcorn Museum • 169 E Church St • Marion, OH 43302 • (740) 387-4255 • http://www.wyandotpopcornmus.com

Marshallville

Military Order of the Loyal Legion of the US, Ohio Commandery • 10096 Wadsworth Rd • Marshallville, OH 44645

Martins Ferry

Martins Ferry Public Library • 20 James Wright Pl, P.O. Box 130 • Martins Ferry, OH 43935-0130 • (740) 633-0314

Marysville

Marysville Public Library • 231 S Plum St • Marysville, OH 43040-1596 • (937) 642-1876

Union County Chapter, OGS • P.O. Box 438 • Marysville, OH 43040-0438 • (937) 642-4694

Union County Historical Society • Historical Museum, 246-254 W 6th St, P.O. Box 303 • Marysville, OH 43040 • (937) 644-0568

Mason

Mason Historical Society • Alverta Green Museum, 207 Church St, P.O. Box 82 • Mason, OH 45040 • (513) 398-6750 • http://ww2.eos.net/edsale/cities/Mason/museum.html

Mason Public Library • 200 Reading Rd • Mason, OH 45040 • (513) 398-2711

Massillon

Jackson Historical Society • 7756 Fulton Dr NW • Massillon, OH 44646 • (330) 830-8622

Masillon Museum • 121 Lincoln Way E • Massillon, OH 44646 • (330) 833-4061 • http://www.massillonmuseum.org

Massillon Public Library • 208 Lincoln Way E • Massillon, OH 44646 • (330) 832-9831

Ohio Society of Military History • Historical Museum, 316 Lincoln Wy E • Massillon, OH 44646 • (330) 832-5553

Spring Hill Historic Home Museum • 1401 Spring Hill Ln NE • Massillon, OH 44646 • (330) 833-6749

Maumee

Maumee Valley Historical Society • Wolcott House Museum, 1031 River Rd • Maumee, OH 43537-3460 • (419) 893-9602 • http://www.wolcotthouse.org

Mayfield Village

Mayfield Township Historical Society • 606 Som Center Rd • Mayfield Village, OH 44143 • (440) 461-0055

McArthur

Alice's House Museum • 207 S Sugar St • McArthur, OH 45651 • (740) 596-0253

Herbert Westcoat Memorial Library • 120 N Market St • McArthur, OH 45651 • (740) 596-5691

McComb

McComb Public Library • 113 S Todd St • McComb, OH 45858 • (419) 293-2425

McConnelsville

Kate Love Simpson Library • 358 E Main St • McConnelsville, OH 43756 • (740) 962-2533

Morgan County Genealogical Society • P.O. Box 418 • McConnelsville, OH 43756-0418 • (740) 962-3816

McCutchenville

McCutchen Overland Inn Museum • State Rte 53 N • McCutchenville, OH 44844 • (419) 981-2052

Medina

America's Ice Cream and Dairy Museum • 1050 Lafayette Rd • Medina, OH 44256 • (330) 722-3839 • http://www.elmfarm.com

Granger Historical Society • 1261 Granger Rd • Medina, OH 44256 • (330) 239-1523

Medina County District Library • 210 S Broadway • Medina, OH 44256-2699 • (330) 725-0588

Medina County Genealogical Society • 2862 Abbeyville Rd, P.O. Box 804 • Medina, OH 44256-0804

Medina County Historical Society • John Smart House Museum, 206 N Elmwood St, P.O. Box 306 • Medina, OH 44258 • (330) 722-1341 • http://www.medinahistory.com

Portholes into the Past Museum • 4450 Poe Rd • Medina, OH 44256 • (330) 725-0402

York Township Historical Society • 2862 Abbeyville Rd • Medina, OH 44256

Mentor

James A Garfield National Historic Site Museum • 8095 Mentor Ave • Mentor, OH 44060 • (440) 255-8722 • http://www.nps.gov/jaga

Lake County Historical Society • Historical Museum, 8610 King Memorial Rd • Mentor, OH 44060-8207 • (440) 255-8979

Mentor Public Library • 8215 Mentor Ave • Mentor, OH 44060 • (440) 255-8811

Miamisburg

Miamisburg Historical Society • 4 N Main St, P.O. Box 774 • Miamisburg, OH 45342-0774 • (937) 859-5000

Middlefield

Middlefield Historical Society • 14979 S State Ave • Middlefield, OH 44062 • (440) 632-0400

Middletown

Butler County Chapter, OGS • c/o Middletown Public Library, 125 S Broad St, P.O. Box 2011 • Middletown, OH 45042-2011 • (513) 424-1251 • http://da120757.tripod.com/bcogs/

Middletown African-American Historical Society • 4521 Poppy Dr • Middletown, OH 45044 • (513) 424-1791

Middletown Historical Society • 56 S Main St, P.O. Box 312 • Middletown, OH 45042 • (513) 424-5539

Midpointe Library System • 125 S Broad St • Middletown, OH 45044 • (513) 424-1251

Society for the Preservation of Ohio One Room Schools • Historical Museum, 4607 Roosevelt Ave • Middletown, OH 45044 • (513) 425-0154

Milan

Milan Historical Society • Historical Museum, 10 Edison Dr, P.O. Box 308 • Milan, OH 44846 • (419) 499-2944 • http://www.milanhistory.org

Milan Public Library • E Church St, P.O. Box 1550 • Milan, OH 44846 • (419) 499-4117

Thomas Edison Birthplace Museum • 9 Edison Dr, P.O. Box 451 • Milan, OH 44846 • (419) 499-2135 • http://www.tomedison.org

Milford

Brooking Society, American Chapter • 1007 Birdhaven Way • Milford, OH 45150

Milford Area Historical Society • Promont House Museum, 906 Main St • Milford, OH 45150 • (513) 831-4704 • http://www.promonthouse.org

Millersburg

Holmes County Chapter, OGS • Courthouse, P.O. Box 136 • Millersburg, OH 44654-0136

Holmes County District Public Library • 3102 Glen Dr, P.O. Box 111 • Millersburg, OH 44654 • (330) 674-5972

Holmes County Historical Society • Historical Museum, 484 Wooster Rd, P.O. Box 126 • Millersburg, OH 44654 • (330) 674-0022 • http://www.victorianhouse.org

Minerva

Minerva Public Library • 677 Lynnwood Dr • Minerva, OH 44657 • (330) 868-4101

Montpelier

Williams County Historical Society • Historical Museum, 611 E Main St, P.O. Box 415 • Montpelier, OH 43543 • (419) 485-8200 • http://www.williamscountyhistory.org

Mount Gilead

Morrow County Genealogical Society • P.O. Box 401 • Mount Gilead, OH 43338-0401 • http://www.rootsweb.com/ohmorrow

Mount Healthy

Mount Healthy Historical Society • 1546 McMakin Ave • Mount Healthy, OH 45231 • (513) 522-3939

Mount Pleasant

Friends Meeting House Museum • 298 Market St, P.O. Box 35 • Mount Pleasant, OH 43939 • (740) 769-2893

Mount Pleasant Historical Society • 342 Union St • Mount Pleasant, OH 43939 • (740) 769-2893 • http://users.1st.net/gudzent/

Mount Vernon

Knox County Agricultural Museum • Knox Cty Fairgrounds, P.O. Box 171 • Mount Vernon, OH 43050 • (740) 397-1423

Knox County Chapter, OGS • P.O. Box 1098 • Mount Vernon, OH 43050-1098 • (614) 392-7716

Knox County Historical Society • 997 Harcourt Rd • Mount Vernon, OH 43050

Mount Vernon and Knox County Public Library • 201 N Mulberry St • Mount Vernon, OH 43050 • (740) 392-8671 • http://www.knox.net/knox/library/welcome.htm

Utica Historical Society • Hufford Museum, 4 N Main St • Mount Vernon, OH 43050 • (740) 892-3218

Napoleon

Henry County Historical Society • P.O. Box 443 • Napoleon, OH 43545

Napoleon Public Library • 310 W Clinton St • Napoleon, OH 43545 • (419) 592-2531

Nelsonville

Hocking Valley Museum of Theatrical History • 46 Public Sq A, P.O. Box 217 • Nelsonville, OH 45764 • (740) 753-1924

Hocking Valley Scenic Railway Company Museum • 33 E Canal St • Nelsonville, OH 45764

Nelsonville Public Library • 95 W Washington St • Nelsonville, OH 45764 • (740) 753-2118

New Bremen

Auglaize County Historical Society • 23 S Main St • New Bremen, OH 45869 • (419) 394-7069

Bicycle Museum of America • 7 W Monroe St • New Bremen, OH 45869 • (419) 629-9249 • http://www.bicyclemuseum.com

New Knoxville

New Knoxville Historical Society • 09350 Bay Rd • New Knoxville, OH 45871

New Lexington

Perry County District Library • 117 S Jackson St • New Lexington, OH 43764-1368 • (740) 342-4194

New London

New London Public Library • 67 S Main St • New London, OH 44851 • (419) 929-3981

New Madison

New Madison Public Library • 142 S Main St, P.O. Box 32 • New Madison, OH 45346-0032 • (937) 996-1741

New Philadelphia

Schoenbrunn State Memorial Museum • 1984 E High Ave, P.O. Box 11 • New Philadelphia, OH 44621 • (330) 663-6610

Tuscarawas County Genealogy Society • 134 2nd St SW, P.O. Box 141 • New Philadelphia, OH 44663-0141 • (614) 269-2602

Tuscarawas County Public Library • 121 Fair NW • New Philadelphia, OH 44663-2600 • (330) 364-4474

New Richmond

Cardboard Boat Museum • 311 Front St • New Richmond, OH 45157 • (513) 910-9153 • http://www.newrichmond.org

Grant Birthplace Museum • P.O. Box 2 • New Richmond, OH 45157 • (513) 553-4911

Historic New Richmond • Historical Museum, 125 George St, P.O. Box 2 • New Richmond, OH 45157 • (513) 543-9149 • http://historicnr.org

Newark

First Families of Licking County Ohio • 101 W Main St, P.O. Box 4037 • Newark, OH 43055-4037 • (740) 927-9753

Heisey Collectors of America • Historical Museum, 169 W Church St • Newark, OH 43055 • (740) 345-2932

Historic Hudson Community Association • P.O. Box 5211 • Newark, OH 43058 • (740) 328-8054

Licking County Genealogical Society • 101 W Main St, P.O. Box 4037 • Newark, OH 43055-4037 • (740) 349-3310

Licking County Genealogical Society, Computer Interest Group • 101 W Main St, P.O. Box 4037 • Newark, OH 43055-4037 • (740) 349-3310

Licking County Historical Society • Sherwood-Davidson House Museum, Veterans Park, 6 N 6th St, P.O. Box 785 • Newark, OH 43058-0785 • (740) 345-4898 • http://www.lchsohio.org

Newark Public Library • 101 W Main St • Newark, OH 43055-5054

Webb House Museum • 303 Granville St • Newark, OH 43055 • (740) 345-8540 • http://www.lchsohio.org

WORKS Museum • 55 S 1st St, P.O. Box 721 • Newark, OH 43058 • (740) 349-9277

Newcomerstown

Newcomerstown Historical Society • Temperance Tavern Museum, 221 W Canal St, P.O. Box 443 • Newcomerstown, OH 43832 • (614) 498-7735

USS Radford National Naval Museum • 238 W Canal St • Newcomerstown, OH 43832 • (740) 498-4446 • http://www.ussradford446.org

Newton Falls

Newton Falls Public Library • 204 S Canal St • Newton Falls, OH 44444-1694 • (330) 872-1282

Newtown

Murray Military & Historical Museum • 6840 School St • Newtown, OH 45244

Niles

McKinley Birthplace Home Museum • 40 S Main St • Niles, OH 44446 • (530) 652-5788 • http://www.mckinley.lib.oh.us

McKinley Memorial Library • 40 N Main St • Niles, OH 44446 • (330) 652-1704 • http://www.mckinley.lib.oh.us

Niles Historical Society • 503 Brown St • Niles, OH 44446-1443 • (330) 544-2143

North Baltimore

North Baltimore Area Historical Society • 229 N Main St • North Baltimore, OH 45872 • (419) 257-2266

North Baltimore Public Library • 230 N Main St • North Baltimore, OH 45872-1195 • (419) 257-3621

North Bend
Three Rivers Historical Society • Historical Museum, 2655 Cliff Rd • North Bend, OH 45052 • (513) 941-4634

North Bloomfield
Association for Living History, Farm and Agricultural Museums • 8774 Route 45 NW • North Bloomfield, OH 44450 • (440) 685-4410 • http://www.alhfam.org

North Canton
Hoover Historical Center Museum • 1875 E Maple St • North Canton, OH 44720-3331 • (330) 499-0287 • http://www.walsh.edu

MAPS Air Museum • 2260 International Pkwy • North Canton, OH 44720 • (330) 896-6332 • http://www.mapsairmuseum.org

Stark County Chapter, OGS • 7300 Woodcrest NE • North Canton, OH 44721-1949 • (330) 494-9574

North Olmsted
Olmsted Historical Society • Frostville Museum, 24101 Cedar Point Rd • North Olmsted, OH 44070 • (216) 501-3345 • http://www.olmsteadhistoricalsociety.org

North Royalton
Slovenian Genealogical Society, Ohio Chapter • 12185 Pheasant Run Cr • North Royalton, OH 44133-5678 • http://sloveniangenealogy.org/chapters/Ohio.htm

Northfield
Historical Society of Old Northfield • Palmer House Museum, 9390 Olde Eight Rd, P.O. Box 99 • Northfield, OH 44067 • (440) 237-1813

Northfield Park Museum • 10705 Northfield Rd, P.O. Box 374 • Northfield, OH 44067 • (330) 467-4101 • http://www.northfieldpark.com

Norwalk
Firelands Historical Society • Historical Museum, 4 Case Ave, P.O. Box 572 • Norwalk, OH 44857-0572 • (419) 668-6038 • http://www.firelandsmuseum.org

Huron County Chapter, OGS • P.O. Box 923 • Norwalk, OH 44857-0923 • (519) 482-3866 • http://www.accnorwalk.com/~jkelble

Huron County Genealogical Society • P.O. Box 923 • Norwalk, OH 44857-0923 • (519) 482-3866

Norwalk Public Library • 46 W Main St • Norwalk, OH 44857 • (419) 668-6063

Norwich
National Road & Zane Grey Museum • 8850 East Pike • Norwich, OH 43767 • (740) 872-3143 • http://www.ohiohistory.org

Oak Hill
Welsh-American Heritage Musuem • 412 E Main St • Oak Hill, OH 45656 • (740) 682-7057 • http://www.jacksonohio.org/welshmuseum.htm

Oakwood
Wright Memorial Public Library • 1776 Far Hills Ave • Oakwood, OH 45419-2598 • (937) 294-7171

Oberlin
Oberlin College Library • 148 W College St • Oberlin, OH 44074 • (440) 775-8285 • http://www.oberlin.edu/archive/

Oberlin Historical and Improvement Organization • Historical Museum, 73 1/2 S Professor St, P.O. Box 0455 • Oberlin, OH 44074 • (440) 774-1700 • http://www.oberlinheritage.org

Oberlin Public Library • 65 S Main St • Oberlin, OH 44074 • (440) 775-4790

Olmsted Falls
Southwest Cuyahoga Chapter, OGS • 9991 Magnolia Dr • Olmsted Falls, OH 44138-2702

Oregon
Oregon Historic District Society • general delivery • Oregon, OH 43616 • (937) 223-6579

Oregon Jerusalem Historical Society • Historical Museum, 1133 Grasser St, P.O. Box 167532 • Oregon, OH 43616 • (419) 693-7052

Orient
Green's Heritage Museum • 10530 Thraikill Rd • Orient, OH 43146 • (614) 877-4254

Orrville
Orrville Historical Museum • 142 Depot St, P.O. Box 437 • Orrville, OH 44667 • (330) 930-0113 • http://www.orrvillehistory.org

Orrville Railroad Heritage Society • Historical Museum, 45 Depot St, P.O. Box 11 • Orrville, OH 44667 • (330) 683-2426 • http://www.orrvillerailroad.com

Toy & Hobby Museum • 531 Smith Ville Rd • Orrville, OH 44667

Orwell
Old Brick House Historical Society • Historical Museum, 7358 Route 45, P.O. Box 592 • Orwell, OH 44076 • (440) 437-5175

Ottawa
Heritage Hills Historical Farm Museum • 4546 Old State Rt 224 • Ottawa, OH 45875

Putnam County Chapter, OGS • P.O. Box 403 • Ottawa, OH 45875-0403 • (419) 523-3747

Putnam County District Library • 136 Putnam Pkwy • Ottawa, OH 45875 • (419) 523-3747

Otway
Otway Community Historical Landmarks Society • Historical Museum, P.O. Box 51 • Otway, OH 45667 • (740) 372-4851

Oxford
Delta Zeta National Historical Museum • 202 E Church St • Oxford, OH 45056 • (513) 523-7597 • http://www.deltazeta.org/gallery

DeWitt Log House Museum • East Campus, Miami Univ • Oxford, OH 45056 • (513) 523-8005

Doty Farm House Museum • Brown Rd • Oxford, OH 45056 • (513) 523-8005

Oxford Museum Association • P.O. Box 184 • Oxford, OH 45056 • (513) 523-8005

Smith Library of Regional History • 15 S College Ave • Oxford, OH 45056 • (513) 523-3035

William Holmes McGuffey Museum • Miami Univ, 410 E Spring St • Oxford, OH 45056 • (513) 529-2232 • http://www.units.muohio.edu/mcguffeymuseum

Painesville
Indian Museum of Lake County • Lake Erie College, 391 W Washington St, P.O. Box 883 • Painesville, OH 44007 • (440) 951-3813 • http://www.indianmuseumoflakecounty.org

Lake County Genealogical Society • c/o Morley Public Library, 184 Phelps St • Painesville, OH 44077-3927 • (440) 352-3383

Morley Library • 184 Phelps St • Painesville, OH 44077 • (440) 352-3383

Parma
Cuyahoga County Public Library • 2111 Snow Rd • Parma, OH 44134-2792 • (216) 398-1800 • http://www.cuyahogalibrary.org

Cuyahoga County-Parma Chapter, OGS • P.O. Box 29509 • Parma, OH 44129-0509

Parma Area Historical Society • 6975 Ridge Rd, P.O. Box 29002 • Parma, OH 44129 • (440) 845-9770

Parma, cont.
Parma Police Historical Society • Historical Museum, 5750 W 54th St • Parma, OH 44129 • (216) 888-3211

Parma Heights
Parma Cuyahoga Chapter, OGS • 6428 Nelwood Rd • Parma Heights, OH 44130-3211

Paulding
Paulding County Carnegie Public Library • 205 S Main St • Paulding, OH 45879-1492 • (419) 399-2032

Paulding County Chapter, OGS • c/o Paulding County Carnegie Public Library, 205 S Main St • Paulding, OH 45879-1492 • (419) 399-2032

Peebles
Adams County Museum on Native American History • State Route 781, P.O. Box 7226 • Peebles, OH 45660

Serpent Mound State Memorial • 3850 SR 73 • Peebles, OH 45660 • (937) 587-2796

Pemberville
Pemberville Public Library • 375 E Front St • Pemberville, OH 43450 • (419) 287-4012 • http://library.norweld.lib.oh.us/pemberville

Pemberville-Freedom Area Historical Society • P.O. Box 802 • Pemberville, OH 43450 • (419) 287-4305 • http://www.hcnet.org/organizations/p/pemhistsoc.html

Peninsula
Cuyahoga Valley Scenic Railroad Museum • 1664 W Main St, P.O. Box 158 • Peninsula, OH 44264 • (800) 468-4070 • http://www.cvsr.com

Peninsula Historical Society • 6105 Riverview Rd, P.O. Box 236 • Peninsula, OH 44264 • (330) 467-7323

Pepper Pike
Ursuline College Museum • 2550 Landor Rd • Pepper Pike, OH 44124 • (216) 646-8122

Perry
Perry Historical Society of Lake County • Historical Museum, 3885 Main St, P.O. Box 216 • Perry, OH 44081 • (440) 259-4541

Perry Public Library • 3753 Main St • Perry, OH 44081 • (440) 259-3300

Perrysburg
Fort Meigs State Memorial Museum • 29100 West River Rd, P.O. Box 3 • Perrysburg, OH 43552 • (419) 874-4121 • http://www.fortmeigs.org

Historic Perrysburg • Historical Museum, P.O. Box 703 • Perrysburg, OH 43551 • (419) 661-9241 • http://www.historicperrysburg.org

Hungarian Genealogy Society • 415 Bridgeview Dr • Perrysburg, OH 43551-1958

Willard V Way Public Library • 101 E Indiana Ave • Perrysburg, OH 43551 • (419) 874-3135

Pickerington
Motorcycle Hall of Fame Museum • 13515 Yarmouth Dr • Pickerington, OH 43147 • (800) 262-5646 • http://www.ama-cycle.org

Piqua
Flesh Public Library - Local History Collection • 124 W Greene St • Piqua, OH 45356 • (937) 773-6753 • http://www.piquaoh.org/library.htm

Johnson Farm & Indian Agency Museum • 9845 N Hardin Rd • Piqua, OH 45356 • (937) 773-2522 • http://www.johnsonfarmohio.com

Piqua Historical Area State Memorial • 9845 N Hardin St • Piqua, OH 45345-9707 • (937) 773-2522 • http://www.ohiohistory.org/places/piqua

Piqua Historical Society • c/o Flesh Public Library, 124 W Greene St • Piqua, OH 45356 • (937) 773-6753

Rossville Museum & Cultural Center • P.O. Box 627 • Piqua, OH 45356 • (937) 773-6789

Plain City
Plain City Public Library • 305 W Main St • Plain City, OH 43064-1148 • (614) 873-4912

Pleasant Hill
Oakes-Beitman Library & Museum • 12 N Main St • Pleasant Hill, OH 45359 • (513) 676-8651 • http://www.troypubliclibrary.org/content/oakes-beitman-memorial-library

Plymouth
Plymouth Area Historical Society • 7 E Main St • Plymouth, OH 44865 • (419) 687-5400

Point Pleasant
U.S. Grant's Birthplace State Memorial Museum • US 52 • Point Pleasant, OH 45153 • (513) 553-4911 • http://www.ohiohistory.org/places/grantbir

Pomeroy
Auxiliary to the Sons of Union Veterans of the Civil War, Ohio Department • 34465 Crew Rd • Pomeroy, OH 45769

Meigs County Genealogical Society • 34465 Crew Rd, P.O. Box 346 • Pomeroy, OH 45769-0346 • (740) 992-7874

Meigs County Pioneer and Historical Society • Historical Museum, 144 Butternut Ave, P.O. Box 145 • Pomeroy, OH 45769 • (740) 992-3810 • http://meigscohistorical.org

Ohio Society War of 1812 • 34465 Crew Rd • Pomeroy, OH 45769

Sons of the Union Veterans of the Civil War, Ohio Department (and Auxilliary) • 34465 Crew Rd • Pomeroy, OH 45769

Port Clinton
Ida Rupp Public Library • 310 Madison St • Port Clinton, OH 43452-1921 • (419) 732-3212 • http://library.norweld.lib.oh.us/idarupp/

Marine Historical Society of Detroit • 606 Laurel Ave • Port Clinton, OH 43452 • http://www.mhsd.org

Ottawa County Chapter, OGS • Historical Museum, P.O. Box 193 • Port Clinton, OH 43452-0193 • (419) 734-7396 • http://www.rootsweb.com/~ohoccgs/

Port Clinton Area Heritage Foundation • Historical Museum, 126 W 3rd St • Port Clinton, OH 43452 • (419) 732-2237

Portsmouth
Portsmouth Genealogy Society • 1220 Gallia St • Portsmouth, OH 45662

Portsmouth Public Library • 1220 Gallia St • Portsmouth, OH 45662 • (614) 354-5304

Scioto County Genealogy Society • P.O. Box 812 • Portsmouth, OH 45662-0812 • (614) 259-4649 • http://www.sccogs.com

Scioto County Historical Society • P.O. Box 1810 • Portsmouth, OH 45662

Southern Ohio Museum and Cultural Center • 825 Gallia St, P.O. Box 990 • Portsmouth, OH 45662 • (740) 354-5629

Powell
Powell-Liberty Historical Society • 103 E Olentangy St • Powell, OH 43065 • (614) 848-6210

Put-in-Bay
Lake Erie Islands Historical Society • Historical Museum, 441 Catawba Ave, P.O. Box 25441 • Put-in-Bay, OH 43456 • (419) 285-2804 • http://www.leihs.org

Perry's Victory and International Peace Memorial Museum • 93 Delaware St, P.O. Box 549 • Put-in-Bay, OH 43456 • (419) 285-2184 • http://www.nps.gov/pevi/

Ravenna
Portage County Genealogical Society • 6252 N Spring St, P.O. Box 821 • Ravenna, OH 44266-1338 • (216) 296-9873

Portage County Historical Society • Historical Museum, 6549 N Chestnut St • Ravenna, OH 44266-3907 • (330) 296-2886 • http://www.history.portage.oh.us

Reed Memorial Library • 167 E Main St • Ravenna, OH 44266 • (330) 296-2827

Reading
Reading Historical Society • Historical Museum, 22 W Benson St • Reading, OH 45215 • (513) 761-8535 • http://www.readingohio.org

Reynoldsburg
Livingston House Museum • 7627 Palmer Rd SW • Reynoldsburg, OH 43068 • (614) 861-8210

Richfield
Richfield Historical Society • 3907 Broadview Rd • Richfield, OH 44286 • (330) 659-0336

Richmond
Historic New Richmond • P.O. Box 2 • Richmond, OH 45157

Richwood
Richwood North Union Public Library • 4 E Ottawa • Richwood, OH 43344 • (740) 943-3054

Rio Grande
Esther Green Museum & Archives • Univ of Rio Grande, Box F-24 • Rio Grande, OH 45674 • (740) 671-1064

Ripley
Parker John Historical Society • Historical Museum, 330 N Front St, P.O. Box 246 • Ripley, OH 45167 • (606) 759-5336

Rankin House State Memorial Museum • Rankin Hill Rd, P.O. Box 176 • Ripley, OH 45167 • (937) 392-4188

Ripley Heritage • Rankin House, P.O. Box 176 • Ripley, OH 45167 • (937) 392-1627

Ripley Museum • 219 N 2nd St, P.O. Box 176 • Ripley, OH 45167-1002 • (937) 392-4660 • http://www.ripleyohio.net/htm/museums.htm

Union Township Public Library • 27 Main St • Ripley, OH 45167-1229 • (937) 392-4871

Rittman
Rittman Historical Society • Historical Museum, 393 W Sunset Dr, P.O. Box 583 • Rittman, OH 44270 • (330) 925-7572

Rockbridge
Hocking County Genealogical Society • c/o Logan-Hocking Public Library, E Main St, P.O. Box 115 • Rockbridge, OH 43149-0115 • (614) 385-6512

Rockford
Shanes Crossing Historical Society • Historical Museum, P.O. Box 92 • Rockford, OH 45882 • (419) 363-2998 • http://www.shanescrossinghistorical.org

Rocky River
Computer Assisted Genealogy Group of the Cleveland Area • P.O. Box 16794 • Rocky River, OH 44116

Cowan Pottery Museum • c/o Rocky River Public Library, 1600 Hampton Rd • Rocky River, OH 44116 • (440) 333-7610 • http://www.cowanpottery.org

Rocky River Public Library • 1600 Hamilton Rd • Rocky River, OH 44116-2699 • (440) 333-7610

Roseville
Roseville Historical Society • 91 Main St • Roseville, OH 43777

Saint Clairsville
Cumberland Trail Genealogical Society • P.O. Box 576 • Saint Clairsville, OH 43950 • (740) 695-2062

Saint Martin
Chatfield College Library • 20918 State Rte 251 • Saint Martin, OH 45118 • (513) 875-3344

Saint Marys
Auglaize County Historical Society • Historical Museum, 223 S Main • Saint Marys, OH 45885 • (419) 394-7069

Miami & Erie Canal Society • Historical Museum, 156 Watercrest Ave • Saint Marys, OH 45885 • (419) 394-5200

Saint Paris
Graham Museum • 122 E Main St • Saint Paris, OH 43072 • (513) 663-4725

Johnson-Saint Paris Library • 127 E Main St • Saint Paris, OH 43072 • (937) 663-4349

Pony Wagon Historical Museum • 315 S Springfield St, P.O. Box 602 • Saint Paris, OH 43072 • (937) 663-5454

Salem
Columbiana County Chapter, OGS • P.O. Box 861 • Salem, OH 44460-0861 • (330) 332-5263 • http://www.rootsweb.com/ohcccogs

Salem Historical Society • Historical Museum, 208 S Broadway Ave • Salem, OH 44460 • (330) 337-8514 • http://www.salemohio.com/historicalsociety/

Salem Public Library • 821 E State St • Salem, OH 44460 • (330) 332-0042 • http://www.salemohio.com/library

Sandusky
Eleutheros Cooke House Museum and Garden • 1415 Columbus Avenue, P.O. Box 1464 • Sandusky, OH 44870 • (419) 627-0640

Erie County Chapter, OGS • P.O. Box 1301 • Sandusky, OH 44871

Follett House Museum • 404 Wayne St • Sandusky, OH 44870 • (419) 625-3834 • http://www.sandusky.lib.oh.us

Museum of Carousel Art & History (Merry-Go-Round) • 301 Jackson St, P.O. Box 718301 • Sandusky, OH 44870 • (419) 626-6111 • http://www.merrygoroundmuseum.org

Sandusky Area Maritime Museum • 125 Meigs St • Sandusky, OH 44870 • (419) 624-0274 • http://www.sanduskymaritime.org

Sandusky Library • 114 W Adams St • Sandusky, OH 44870 • (419) 625-3834

Scio
Scio Historical Museum • 203 E Main St • Scio, OH 43988 • (740) 945-2172

Sebring
Sebring Railroad Museum & Historical Society • Railroad Museum, 216 E Pennsylvania Ave • Sebring, OH 44672 • (330) 938-6520

Seville
Seville Historical Society • 70 W Main St • Seville, OH 44273

Shaker Heights
Anglo-American Genealogical Society • 2686 Claybourne Rd • Shaker Heights, OH 44122

Dunham Tavern Museum • 20749 Almar Dr • Shaker Heights, OH 44122 • (216) 431-1060 • http://www.dunhamtavern.org

New York Central System Historical Society • 22360 Canterbury • Shaker Heights, OH 44122 • (216) 751-3672 • http://www.nycshs.org

Shaker Heights, cont.

Shaker Heights Public Library • 16500 Van Aken Rd • Shaker Heights, OH 44120-5318 • (216) 991-2030

Shaker Historical Society • Shaker Museum, 16740 S Park Blvd • Shaker Heights, OH 44120 • (216) 921-1201 • http://www.shakerhistory.org

Sharon Center

Akron, Canton & Youngstown Railroad Historical Society • Historical Museum, P.O. Box 196 • Sharon Center, OH 44276 • http://www.acyhs.org

Sharon Township Heritage Society • P.O. Box 57 • Sharon Center, OH 44274 • (330) 336-3932

Sharonville

Historic Southwest Ohio Museum • Sharon Woods Heritage Village, 11450 Lebanon Pike, P.O. Box 62475 • Sharonville, OH 45262 • (513) 563-9484 • http://www.heritagevillagecincinnati.org

Society of Historic Sharonville • general delivery • Sharonville, OH 45241

Sheffield Lake

103rd Ohio Volunteer Infantry Memorial Foundation • Civil War Museum, 5501 E Lake Rd • Sheffield Lake, OH 44054 • (440) 949-4790 • http://www.103ovi.org

One-Hundred Third Ohio Volunteer Infantry Memorial • 5501 E Lake Rd • Sheffield Lake, OH 44054

Shelby

Heuberger's Cabin Fever Village • 3075 Myers Rd • Shelby, OH 44875 • (419) 347-3762

Richland-Shelby Chapter, OGS • 6644 Baker Rd #47, P.O. Box 766 • Shelby, OH 44875-0766 • (419) 347-6943

Shelby Museum of History • 23 E Main St • Shelby, OH 44875 • (419) 347-2743 • http://www.rootsweb.ancestry.com/~ohsmh/

Sidney

Amos Memorial Public Library • 230 E North St • Sidney, OH 45365 • (937) 492-8354

Shelby County Genealogical Society • 17755 St Route 47 • Sidney, OH 45365-9242 • (937) 492-0071

Shelby County Historical Society • 201 N Main Ave, P.O. Box 376 • Sidney, OH 45365-0376 • (937) 498-1653 • http://www.bright.net/~richnsus/

Smithville

Smithville Community Historical Society • general delivery • Smithville, OH 44677

Somerset

Perry County Historical Society • 105 S Columbus St, P.O. Box 746 • Somerset, OH 43783-0746 • (740) 743-2591 • http://www.netpluscom.com/~pchs/

South Charleston

Heritage Commission Corporation • 147 W Mound Rd, P.O. Box 457 • South Charleston, OH 45368-9634 • (937) 462-7277

Spencer

Chatham Township Historical Society • 9610 Old Mill Rd • Spencer, OH 44275

Spencer Historical Society • 12221 Old Mill Rd • Spencer, OH 44275

Springboro

Springboro Historical Society • Historical Museum, 110 S Main St • Springboro, OH 45066 • (937) 748-0916

Springfield

Clark County Chapter, OGS • 102 E Main St, P.O. Box 2524 • Springfield, OH 45501-2524 • (937) 462-8430

Clark County Friends of the Library Genealogical Research Group • 1268 Kenwood Ave • Springfield, OH 45505 • (937) 323-2905

Clark County Historical Society • Heritage Center, 117 S Fountain Ave • Springfield, OH 45504 • (937) 324-0657 • http://www.heritagecenter.us

Clark County Public Library • 201 S Fountain Ave, P.O. Box 1080 • Springfield, OH 45501-1080 • (937) 328-6904

Daniel Hertzler House Museum • 930 S Tecumseh Rd • Springfield, OH 45506 • (937) 882-6000 • http://www.clarkcountyparkdistrict.org/HertzlerhouseMus/

Friends of the Library Genealogical Research Group • c/o Clark County Public Library, 201 S Fountain Ave, P.O. Box 1080 • Springfield, OH 45501-1080 • (937) 328-6904

George Rogers Clark Heritage Association • 936 S Tecumseh Rd • Springfield, OH 45506 • (937) 882-9216

Masonic Grand Lodge of Ohio • 1 Masonic Dr • Springfield, OH 45504 • (614) 885-5318 • http://www.freemason.com

Pennsylvania House Museum • 1311 W Main St • Springfield, OH 45504 • (937) 322-7668 • http://www.pennsylvaniahousemuseum.info

Sons of Union Veterans of the Civil War, Ohio Department • 4315 Cedar Hills Ave • Springfield, OH 45504

Warder Public Library • 137 E High St • Springfield, OH 45501-1080 • (937) 323-8617

Steubenville

Jefferson County Genealogical Society • P.O. Box 4712 • Steubenville, OH 43952-4712 • (614) 264-0410 • http://www.rootsweb.com/~ohjefogs

Jefferson County Historical Association • Historical Museum, 426 Franklin Ave, P.O. Box 4268 • Steubenville, OH 43952 • (740) 283-1133 • http://www.rootsweb.com/~ohjcha

Old Fort Steubenville Museum • 120 S 3rd St • Steubenville, OH 43952 • (740) 283-1787 • http://www.oldfortsteuben.com

Public Library of Steubenville and Jefferson County • 407 S 4th St • Steubenville, OH 43952 • (740) 282-9782

Stockport

Big Bottom Museum • 1685 Broadway St, P.O. Box 158 • Stockport, OH 43787 • (740) 559-2511

Stow

Stow Munroe Falls Public Library • 3512 Darrow Rd • Stow, OH 44224-4097 • (330) 688-3295

Strongsville

Saint Leo's Genealogy Group • 16253 Glendale Ave • Strongsville, OH 44136 • (440) 572-0139 • http://feefhs.org/slovak/frg-slgg.html

Southwest Cuyahoga Chapter, OGS • 13305 Pearl Rd • Strongsville, OH 44136-3403 • (440) 238-6370

Strongsville Historical Society • 13305 Pearl Rd • Strongsville, OH 44136 • (440) 572-0057

Sugar Grove

Ohio Historical Society • Wahkeena, 2200 Pump Station Rd • Sugar Grove, OH 43155-9709 • (740) 746-8695

Sugarcreek

Alpine Hills Historical Museum • 106 W Main St • Sugarcreek, OH 44681 • (216) 852-4113

Ragersville Historical Society • 8800 Crooked Run Rd SW • Sugarcreek, OH 44681-8019 • (330) 897-9204

Sunbury

Community Library on the Square • 44 Burrer Dr • Sunbury, OH 43074 • (740) 965-3901 • http://community.lib.oh.us

Swanton

Fulton County Chapter, OGS • P.O. Box 337 • Swanton, OH 43558-0037 • (419) 825-5437

Swanton Public Library • 305 Chestnut St • Swanton, OH 43558 • (419) 826-2760

Sycamore

Mohawk Historical Society • P.O. Box 336 • Sycamore, OH 44882 • (419) 927-2969

Tallmadge

Akron-Summit County Public Library-Tallmadge Branch • 90 Community Rd • Tallmadge, OH 44278 • (330) 633-4345

Tallmadge Church Museum • P.O. Box 483 • Tallmadge, OH 44278 • (330) 297-2630

Tallmadge Historical Society • 1 Tallmadge Cr, P.O. Box 25 • Tallmadge, OH 44278 • (330) 630-9750

Tecumseh

Tecumseh Historical Museum • 112 S Broadway • Tecumseh, OH 74873

Tiffin

Seneca County Genealogical Society • P.O. Box 157 • Tiffin, OH 44883-0157 • (419) 457-8082

Seneca County Historical Society • Seneca County Museum, 28 Clay St • Tiffin, OH 44883-2231 • (419) 447-5955 • http://www.senecacountymuseum.com

Tiffin-Seneca Public Library • 77 Jefferson St • Tiffin, OH 44883 • (419) 447-3751 • http://www.norweld.lib.oh.us/tiffinseneca/

Vallentine Village Museum • 6741 South St • Tiffin, OH 44883 • (419) 397-2236

Tipp City

Fellowship of Brethren Genealogists • 7690 S Peters Rd • Tipp City, OH 45371

Tippecanoe Historical Society • Historical Museum, 12 N 3rd St, P.O. Box 42 • Tipp City, OH 45371 • (937) 667-4092

Toledo

Alpha Sigma Phi Historical Society • Historical Museum, P.O. Box 352521 • Toledo, OH 43635

COSI Toledo • 1 Discovery Wy • Toledo, OH 43604 • (419) 244-2674

Historic Rosary Cathedral • 2535 Collingwood Blvd • Toledo, OH 43610 • (419) 244-9575

Historic Woodlawn Cemetery Museum • 1502 W Central Ave • Toledo, OH 43606 • (419) 472-2186

Hungarian Genealogical Society • 124 Esther St • Toledo, OH 43605-1435

Lucas County Chapter, OGS • c/o Toledo-Lucas County Public Library, 325 N Michigan St • Toledo, OH 43624-1614 • (419) 259-5233 • http://www.utoledo.edu/gried/lcogs.htm

Lucas County Genealogical Society • 1302 Corry Ave • Toledo, OH 43614-2730

Northwestern Ohio Genealogical Society • P.O. Box 17066 • Toledo, OH 43615

Oliver House Museum • 27 Broadway St • Toledo, OH 43602 • (419) 243-1302

S S Willis B Boyer Museum Ship • 26 Main St • Toledo, OH 43605 • (419) 936-3070

Toledo Area Genealogical Society • P.O. Box 352258 • Toledo, OH 43635-2258 • http://www.atoledo.edu/drostet/tags/

Toledo Firefighters Museum • 918 Sylvania Ave • Toledo, OH 43612 • (419) 478-3473 • http://www.toledofiremuseum.com

Toledo-Lucas County Public Library • 325 Michigan St • Toledo, OH 43624 • (419) 259-5233 • http://www.library.toledo.oh.us

Univ of Toledo History Museum • 2801 W Bancroft St • Toledo, OH 43606 • (419) 530-4540

Western Lake Erie Historical Society • 300 Phillips Ave, P.O. Box 5311 • Toledo, OH 43611-0311 • (419) 478-0008

Wildwood Manor House Museum • 5100 W Central Ave • Toledo, OH 43615 • (419) 535-3056

William S Carlson Library • Univ of Toledo, 2801 W Bancroft St • Toledo, OH 43606 • (419) 530-4488

Trenton

Chrisholm Historic Farmstead Museum • 2070 Woodsdale Rd • Trenton, OH 45067 • (513) 276-5265

Troy

Industrial Heritage Museum of Miami County • 405 SW Public Sq #255 • Troy, OH 45373 • (937) 339-9397

Miami County Historical and Genealogical Society • P.O. Box 305 • Troy, OH 45373-0305

Overfield Tavern Museum • 201 E Water St • Troy, OH 45373 • (937) 335-4019 • http://www.overfieldtavernmuseum.com

Troy Historical and Genealogical Society • Troy-Hayner Cultural Center, 301 W Main St • Troy, OH 45373 • (937) 339-0457 • http://www.troyhayner.org

WACO Air Museum • 1865 S Cty Rd 25A, P.O. Box 62 • Troy, OH 45373 • (937) 335-9226 • http://www.wacoairmuseum.org

Twinsburg

Twinsburg Historical Society • Historical Museum, 8996 Darrow Rd, P.O. Box 7 • Twinsburg, OH 44087 • (330) 487-5565 • http://www.twinsburg.com/historicalsociety/

Twinsburg Public Library • 9840 Ravenna Rd • Twinsburg, OH 44087 • (330) 425-4268

Upper Sandusky

Indian Mill Museum State Memorial • 616 N Sandusky Ave • Upper Sandusky, OH 43351 • (419) 294-3857 • http://www.ohiohistory.org/places/indian

Upper Sandusky Community Library • 301 N Sandusky St • Upper Sandusky, OH 43351-1139 • (419) 294-1345

Upper Sandusky Historical Society • 301 N Sandusky Ave • Upper Sandusky, OH 43351-1139

Wyandot County Historical Society • Historical Museum, 130 S 7th St, P.O. Box 372 • Upper Sandusky, OH 43351 • (419) 294-3857

Wyandot Tracers Genealogical Society • P.O. Box 414 • Upper Sandusky, OH 43351-0414

Urbana

Champaign County Chapter, OGS • P.O. Box 680 • Urbana, OH 43078-0680 • (937) 652-3673

Champaign County Historical Society • Historical Museum, 809 E Lawn Ave, P.O. Box 38202 • Urbana, OH 43078 • (937) 653-6721 • http://www.champaigncountyhistoricalmuseum.org

Champaign County Library • 1060 Scioto St • Urbana, OH 43078 • (937) 653-3811 • http://www.champaign.lib.oh.us

Johnny Appleseed Museum • Urbana Univ, 579 Colelge Wy • Urbana, OH 43078 • (937) 484-1303

Utica
Ye Olde Mill Museum • 11324 Mt Vernon Rd, P.O. Box 588 • Utica, OH 43080 • (740) 892-3921 • http://www.velveticecream.com

Valley City
Valley City Historical Society • 7060 Center Rd • Valley City, OH 44280

Van Wert
Brumback Library • 215 W Main St • Van Wert, OH 45891-1695 • (419) 238-2168 • http://www.brumbacklib.com

Central Insurance Fire Museum • 800 S Washington St • Van Wert, OH 45891 • (419) 238-1010

Van Wert County Genealogical Society • P.O. Box 485 • Van Wert, OH 45891-0485 • (419) 667-3153 • http://www.rootsweb.com/ohvanwer/

Van Wert County Historical Society • 602 N Washington St, P.O. Box 621 • Van Wert, OH 45891-0621 • (419) 238-5297

Vandalia
Historical Society of Vandalia • 336 E Alkaline Springs Rd • Vandalia, OH 45377-2602 • (937) 898-5300

Trapshooting Hall of Fame & Museum • 601 W National Rd • Vandalia, OH 45377 • (937) 898-4638 • http://www.traphof.org

Vermilion
Great Lakes Historical Society • Inland Seas Maritime Museum, 480 Main St, P.O. Box 435 • Vermilion, OH 44089-0435 • (440) 967-3467 • http://ww.inlandseas.org

Versailles
Worch Memorial Public Library • 161 E Main St • Versailles, OH 45380 • (937) 526-3416

Wadsworth
Ella M Everhard Public Library • 132 Broad St • Wadsworth, OH 44281 • (330) 334-5761

Walnut Creek
German Culture Museum • Olde Pump St, P.O. Box 51 • Walnut Creek, OH 44387 • (330) 893-2571 • http://www.germanculturemuseum.com

Wapakoneta
Anglaize County Public District Library • 203 S Perry St • Wapakoneta, OH 45895-1999 • (419) 738-2921 • http://ibrary.norweld.lib.oh.us/auglaizeco/

Armstrong Air & Space Museum • 500 Apollo Rd, P.O. Box 1978 • Wapakoneta, OH 45895 • (419) 738-8811 • http://www.armstrongmuseum.org

Auglaize County Genealogy Society • P.O. Box 2021 • Wapakoneta, OH 45895-0521 • http://www.rootsweb/~ohaugogs/

Auglaize County Historical Society • 206 W Main St • Wapakoneta, OH 45895 • (419) 738-9328

Warren
John Stark Edward House Museum • 303 Monroe St NW • Warren, OH 44483 • (330) 394-4653 • http://www.trumbullcountyhistory.org/museum.htm

National Packard Museum • 1899 Mahoning Ave NW • Warren, OH 44483 • (330) 394-1899 • http://www.packardmuseum.org

Trumbull County Genealogical Society • P.O. Box 309 • Warren, OH 44483-0309

Trumbull County Historical Society • John Stark Edwards House Museum, 303 Monroe St NW, P.O. Box 1907 • Warren, OH 44483 • (330) 394-4653 • http://www.trumbullcountyhistory.org

Warren-Trumbull County Public Library • 444 Mahoning Ave NW • Warren, OH 44483 • (330) 399-8807 x120 • http://www.wtcpl.lib.oh.us

Washington Court House
Carnegie Public Library • 127 S North St • Washington Court House, OH 43160 • (740) 335-2540 • http://www.cplwcho.org

Fayette County Chapter, OGS • P.O. Box 342 • Washington Court House, OH 43160-0342 • (614) 335-2540

Fayette County Historical Society • Historical Museum, 517 Columbus Ave • Washington Court House, OH 43160 • (740) 335-2953 • http://www.washingtonch.com/faytrav/museum.htm

Waterford
Lower Muskingum Historical Society • Oliver Tucker Museum, P.O. Box 191 • Waterford, OH 45786 • (740) 984-2489

Waterville
Rettig's Frontier Ohio Museum • 19 N 3rd St • Waterville, OH 43566 • (419) 787-5376

Wauseon
Fulton County Historical Society • Historical Museum, 229 Monroe St • Wauseon, OH 43567 • (419) 337-7922 • http://www.fultoncountyhs.org

Waverly
Pike County Genealogical Society • P.O. Box 224 • Waverly, OH 45690-0224

Waynesville
Caesar's Creek Pioneer Village Museum • 3999 Pioneer Village Rd, P.O. Box 652 • Waynesville, OH 45068 • (513) 897-1120 • http://www.caesarscreekpioneervillage.org

Mary L Cook Public Library • 380 Old Stage Rd • Waynesville, OH 45068 • (513) 897-4826

Waynesville Historical Society • general delivery • Waynesville, OH 45068

Wellington
Herrick Memorial Library • 101 Willard Memorial Sq • Wellington, OH 44090-1343 • (440) 647-2120

Southern Lorain County Historical Society • Spirit of '76 Museum, 201 N Main St, P.O. Box 76 • Wellington, OH 44090 • (440) 647-4367 • http://www.76museum.org

Wellington Genealogical Group • P.O. Box 265 • Wellington, OH 44090

Wellington Genealogical Workshop • 515 W Herrick Ave, P.O. Box 224 • Wellington, OH 44090

Wellston
Buckeye Furnace State Memorial Museum • 123 Buckeye Park Rd • Wellston, OH 45692 • (740) 384-3537

Wellsville
Scots Settlement Museum • 18970 Fife Coal Rd • Wellsville, OH 43968 • (330) 532-1339

Wellsville Carnegie Public Library • 115 9th St • Wellsville, OH 43968 • (330) 532-1526

Wellsville Historical Society • River Museum, 1003 Riverside, P.O. Box 13 • Wellsville, OH 43968 • (330) 532-1018

West Liberty
Castle Piatt-Mac-a-Cheek Museum • 10051 Township Rd 47, P.O. Box 497 • West Liberty, OH 43357 • (937) 465-2821 • http://www.piattcastles.org

West Milton
Milton-Union Public Library • 560 S Main St • West Milton, OH 45383 • (937) 698-5515

West Union
Adams County Genealogical Society • State Route 247 N, P.O. Box 231 • West Union, OH 45693 • (937) 544-8522

Adams County Historical Society • 507 N Cherry St, P.O. Box 306 • West Union, OH 45693 • (937) 544-8522

Westerville

American Ceramic Museum • 600 N Cleveland Ave • Westerville, OH 43081 • (240) 646-7054 • http://ceramics.org

Anti-Saloon League Museum • 126 S State St • Westerville, OH 43081 • (614) 882-7277 • http://www.wpl.lib.oh.us/antisaloon/

Westerville Historical Society •Hanby House State Memorial Museum • 160 W Main St, P.O. Box 1063 • Westerville, OH 43086 • (614) 891-6289

Westerville Public Library - Local History Resource Center • 126 S State St • Westerville, OH 43081-2095 • (614) 882-7277 • http://www.ohiohistory.org

Westfield Center

Westfield Historical Society • P.O. Box 158 • Westfield Center, OH 44251

Westlake

Ohio Postal History Society • Historical Museum, 1526 Marview Dr • Westlake, OH 44145 • (216) 871-8544

Plidco Pipeline Museum • 870 Canterbury Rd • Westlake, OH 44145 • (216) 871-5700

Westlake-Porter Public Library • 27333 Center Ridge Rd • Westlake, OH 44145 • (440) 871-2600

Weston

Weston Public Library • 13153 Main St, P.O. Box 345 • Weston, OH 43569 • (419) 669-3415

Whitehouse

Whitehouse Historical Society • Historical Museum, P.O. Box 2571 • Whitehouse, OH 43571 • (419) 877-5383 • http://whitehouseoh.gov

Wickliffe

Wickliffe Public Library • 1713 Lincoln Rd • Wickliffe, OH 44092 • (440) 944-6010

Wilberforce

National Afro-American Museum and Cultural Center • 1350 Brush Row Rd, P.O. Box 578 • Wilberforce, OH 45384 • (937) 376-4944 • http://winslo.ohio.gov/ohswww/places/afroam/

Willard

Huron County Historical Society • 705 Hettle Rd • Willard, OH 44890-9521

Plymouth Area Historical Society • 15 Sandusky St • Willard, OH 44890

Willard Memorial Library • 6 W Emerald St • Willard, OH 44890 • (419) 933-8564

Willoughby

Croatian Heritage Museum • 34900 Lake Shore Blvd • Willoughby, OH 44095-2043 • (440) 946-2044

Little Red School House & History Center • 5040 Shankland Rd • Willoughby, OH 44094 • (440) 975-3740

Morgan Library of Ohio Imprints • 4425 Glenbrook Rd • Willoughby, OH 44094-8219 • (440) 951-7316

Willowick

Willoughby Historical Society • c/o Willoughby-Eastlake Public Library, 30 Public Square • Willowick, OH 44095 • (440) 943-2203 • http://www.wept.lib.oh.us

Willoughby-Eastlake Public Library • 263 E 305th St • Willowick, OH 44095 • (440) 943-2203

Wilmington

Clinton County Chapter, OGS • 149 E Locust St, P.O. Box 529 • Wilmington, OH 45177-0529 • (937) 382-4684 • http://www.postcorn.com/ccgshs

Clinton County Historical Society • Historical Museum, 149 E Locust St, P.O. Box 529 • Wilmington, OH 45177-0529 • (937) 382-4684 • http://www.clintoncountyhistory.org

Sheppard Arthur Watson Library • Wilmington College, 251 Ludovic St • Wilmington, OH 45177 • (937) 382-6661

Wilmington Public Library • 268 N South St • Wilmington, OH 45177 • (937) 382-2417

Woodsfield

Monroe County Genealogical Society • P.O. Box 641 • Woodsfield, OH 43793-0641

Monroe County Historical Society • 118 Home Ave, P.O. Box 538 • Woodsfield, OH 43793-0538 • (740) 472-1933

Wooster

OMII Genealogical Project • Kidron Heritage Center, 1550 Spruce St • Wooster, OH 44691 • http://www.wgbc.org/hindex.htm

Wayne County Genealogical Society • Historical Museum, 546 E Bowman St, P.O. Box 856 • Wooster, OH 44691 • (330) 264-8856

Wayne County Historical Society • Historical Museum, 546 E Bowman St, P.O. Box 856 • Wooster, OH 44691-3110 • (330) 264-8856 • http://www.waynehistorical.org

Wayne County Public Library • 304 N Market St • Wooster, OH 44691 • (330) 262-0916 x225

Worthington

Ohio Railway Museum • 990 Proprietors Rd, P.O. Box 777 • Worthington, OH 43085 • (614) 885-7345 • http://www.ohiorailwaymuseum.org

Ohio Underground Railroad Society • P.O. Box 1080 • Worthington, OH 43085 • http://www.fofs-ours.org

Worthington Historical Society • Historical Museum, 50 W New England Ave, P.O. Box 355 • Worthington, OH 43085 • (614) 885-1247 • http://www.worthington.org

Worthington Public Library • 805 High St • Worthington, OH 43085-3112 • (614) 645-2646

Wright-Patterson AFB

US Air Force Museum • 1100 Spaatz St • Wright-Patterson AFB, OH 45433-7102 • (937) 255-3286 • http://www.nationalmuseum.af.mil

Xenia

Greene County Chapter, OGS • c/o Greene County District Library, 76 E Market St, P.O. Box 706 • Xenia, OH 45385-0706 • (937) 376-2995 • http://www.dsenter.com/ohio/greene/chapter.htm

Greene County District Library • 76 E Market St, P.O. Box 520 • Xenia, OH 45385 • (937) 376-4952

Greene County Historical Society • James Galloway Log House Museum, 74 W Church St • Xenia, OH 45385 • (937) 372-4606

Yellow Springs

Trailside Museum • Antioch College, 405 Corry St • Yellow Springs, OH 45387 • (937) 769-1902

Youngstown

Lanterman's Mill Museum • 980 Canfield Rd, P.O. Box 596 • Youngstown, OH 44511 • (330) 750-7115

Mahoning County Chapter, OGS • P.O. Box 9333 • Youngstown, OH 44513-9333 • (330) 757-1936

Youngstown, cont.

Mahoning County Chapter, OGS, Computer Interest Group • P.O. Box 9333 • Youngstown, OH 44513-9333 • (330) 757-1936

Mahoning Valley Historical Society • Arms Family Museum of Local History, 648 Wick Ave • Youngstown, OH 44502-1289 • (330) 743-2589 • http://www.mahoninghistory.org

Public Library of Youngstown & Mahoning Cty • 305 Wick Ave • Youngstown, OH 44503 • (330) 744-8636 x25

Saint Ephrem Educational Center • 1555 S Meridian Rd • Youngstown, OH 44511 • (330) 792-1532

Transylvania Saxon Genealogy and Heritage Society • Historical Museum, P.O. Box 3319 • Youngstown, OH 44513-3319 • (330) 783-1947 • http://www.feefhs.org/ah/hu/frgtsghs.html

William F Maag Library • Youngstown State Univ, 1 University Plaza • Youngstown, OH 44555 • (330) 742-3675

Youngstown Historical Center of Industry and Labor • 151 W Wood St, P.O. Box 533 • Youngstown, OH 44501 • (330) 743-5934 • http://winsio.ohio.gov/ohswww/youngst/arch_lib.html

Zanesville

Helen Purcell Home Museum • 1854 Norwood Blvd • Zanesville, OH 43701

Muskingum County District Library System • 220 N 5th St • Zanesville, OH 43701 • (740) 453-0391

Muskingum County Genealogical Library • John McIntire Library, 220 N 5 St, P.O. Box 3066 • Zanesville, OH 43702-3066 • (740) 453-0391

Muskingum County Genealogical Society • c/o Zanesville Campus Library, Ohio Univ, 1425 Newark Rd, P.O. Box 3066 • Zanesville, OH 43702-3066 • (740) 453-0762

Pioneer and Historical Society of Muskingum County • Dr Increase Matthews House Museum, 115 Jefferson St, P.O. Box 2201 • Zanesville, OH 43701 • (740) 454-9500

Schultz Mansion Museum • 411 Putnam Ave • Zanesville, OH 43701 • (740) 450-8425

Zanesville Campus Library • Ohio Univ, 1425 Newark Rd • Zanesville, OH 43701 • (740) 453-0762

Zoar

Schoenbrunn Village Museum • P.O. Box 404 • Zoar, OH 44697 • (330) 339-3636 • http://www.ohiohistory.org/places/schoenbr/

Zoar State Memorial Museum • 198 Main St, P.O. Box 404 • Zoar, OH 44697 • (330) 874-3011 • http://www.ohiohistory.org/places/zoar/

Zoar Village Museum • 198 W 3rd St, P.O. Box 508 • Zoar, OH 44697 • (330) 874-2646

Ada
Ada Public Library • 124 S Rennie • Ada, OK 74820-5189 • (580) 436-8123

Arbuckle Historical Society • 1201 S Ash St • Ada, OK 74820 • (580) 622-5593

Chickasaw Indian Nation Cultural Center • 124 S Broadway Ave, P.O. Box 1548 • Ada, OK 74820 • (580) 332-8685

Chickasaw Nation Tribal Government • Chickasaw Cultural Center, 520 E Arlington, P.O. Box 1548 • Ada, OK 74821-1548 • (580) 436-2603 • http://www.chickasaw.net

Pontotoc County Historical and Genealogical Society • Mattie Logsdon Memorial Library & Museum, 221 W 16th St • Ada, OK 74820-7603

Aline
Sod House Museum • State Hwy 48 • Aline, OK 73716 • (580) 463-2441 • http://www.ok-history.mus.ok.us

Altus
Altus Public Library • 421 N Hudson St • Altus, OK 73521 • (580) 477-2890 • http://www.spls.lib.ok.us

Jackson County Historical Society • Historical Museum, P.O. Box 546 • Altus, OK 73522

Oklahoma Historical Society • Museum of the Western Prairie, 1100 N Memorial Dr, P.O. Box 574 • Altus, OK 73521 • (580) 482-1044 • http://www.museumwesternprairie.org

Western Trail Genealogical Society • c/o Altus Public Library, 421 Hudson St, P.O. Box 70 • Altus, OK 73522 • (580) 266-3358

Western Trails Historical and Genealogical Society • 1100 N Hightower, P.O. Box 574 • Altus, OK 73521 • (580) 482-1044

Alva
Cherokee Strip Museum • 901 14th St, P.O. Drawer A • Alva, OK 73717 • (405) 327-2030

Woods County Genealogists • c/o Alva Public Library, 504 7th St, P.O. Box 234 • Alva, OK 73717 • (405) 327-1833

Anadarko
Anadarko Heritage Museum • 311 E Main St • Anadarko, OK 73005 • (405) 247-3240

Anadarko Philomathic Museum • 311 E Main St • Anadarko, OK 73005

Anadarko Public Library • 215 W Broadway • Anadarko, OK 73005 • (405) 247-7351 • http://www.anadarkopl.ok.pls.org

Apache Tribe of Oklahoma • P.O. Box 1220 • Anadarko, OK 73005-1220 • (405) 247-9493

Delaware Tribe of Western Oklahoma • P.O. Box 825 • Anadarko, OK 73005-0825 • (405) 247-2448

Indian City USA Museum • E 1363 Rd, P.O. Box 695 • Anadarko, OK 73005 • (405) 247-5661 • http://www.indiancityusa.com

National Hall of Fame for Famous American Indians • Hwy 62 E, P.O. Box 548 • Anadarko, OK 73005 • (405) 247-5555

Southern Plains Indian Museum • 715 E Central, P.O. Box 749 • Anadarko, OK 73005 • (405) 247-6221

Wichita and Affiliated Tribes • Wichita Tribal Cultural Center, P.O. Box 729 • Anadarko, OK 73005 • (405) 247-2425 • http://www.wichita.nsn.us

Antlers
Antlers Historical Museum • 800 NE 3rd St • Antlers, OK 74523

Pushmataha County Historical Society • Historical Museum, 125 W Main St, P.O. Box 285 • Antlers, OK 74523 • (580) 587-2304

Apache
Apache Historical Society • Apache State Bank Museum, 101 W Evans, P.O. Box 101 • Apache, OK 73006 • (580) 588-3392

Fort Sill Apache Tribe of Oklahoma • RR2, Box 121 • Apache, OK 73006 • (405) 588-2298 • http://fsat.tripod.com

Arcadia
Round Barn Museum • P.O. Box 134 • Arcadia, OK 73007

Ardmore
Ardmore Public Library • 320 E Street NW • Ardmore, OK 73401-4398 • (580) 223-8290 • http://www.ardmorepublic.lib.ok.us

Carter County Genealogical Society • P.O. Box 1014 • Ardmore, OK 73402

Chickasaw Regional Library System • 601 Railway Express • Ardmore, OK 73401 • (580) 223-3164 • http://www.regional-sys.lib.ok.us

Eliza Cruce Hall Doll Collection Museum • 320 E Street NW • Ardmore, OK 73401 • (580) 223-8290

Genealogical Society of Carter County Oklahoma • 35 Sunset Dr • Ardmore, OK 73401 • (580) 226-1247

Greater Southwest Historical Museum • 35 Sunset Dr • Ardmore, OK 73401 • (580) 226-3857 • http://www.gshm.org

Historical and Genealogical Society of Carter County • P.O. Box 1326 • Ardmore, OK 73402

Military Memorial Museum • 35 Sunset Dr, P.O. Box 225 • Ardmore, OK 73402 • (580) 226-3857

Arnett
Ellis County Historical Society • Historical Museum, RR2, Box 92 • Arnett, OK 73832

Log Cabin Museum • 211 E Barnes, P.O. Box 337 • Arnett, OK 73832 • (580) 885-7414

Atoka
Atoka County Genealogical Society • P.O. Box 245 • Atoka, OK 74525

Atoka County Historical Society • Historical Museum, Hwy 69 N, P.O. Box 245 • Atoka, OK 74525 • (580) 889-7192

Chickasaw Regional Library System-Atoka County Library • 215 East A Street • Atoka, OK 74525 • (580) 889-3555

Confederate Memorial Museum & Cemetery • 258 N Hwy 69, P.O. Box 245 • Atoka, OK 74525 • (580) 889-7192 • http://civilwarmuseum.com/atoka/

Barnsdall
Barnsdall Museum • 520 W Main St, P.O. Box 849 • Barnsdall, OK 74002 • (918) 847-2023

Barnsdall Public Library • 410 S 5th St, P.O. Box 706 • Barnsdall, OK 74002-0706 • (918) 847-2118

Bartlesville
Bartlesville Area History Museum • City Center, 401 S Johnsone Ave, 5th Fl • Bartlesville, OK 74005 • (918) 337-5336 • http://www.bartlesvillehistory.com

Bartlesville Genealogical Society • c/o Bartlesville Public Library, 600 SE Johnstone • Bartlesville, OK 74003 • (918) 337-5353 • http://netra.bartiesville.lib.ok.us:80801

Bartlesville Public Library • 600 S Johnstone • Bartlesville, OK 74003 • (918) 337-5353 • http://www.bartlesville.lib.ok.us

Delaware Tribe of Eastern Oklahoma • 108 S Seneca • Bartlesville, OK 74003 • (918) 336-5272 • http://www.delawaretribeofindians.nsn.us

Frank Phillips Home Museum • 1107 SE Cherokee Ave • Bartlesville, OK 74003 • (918) 336-2491 • http://www.frankphillipshome.org

Bartlesville, cont.
Phillips Corporate Archives • C20 Phillips Bldg • Bartlesville, OK 74004 • (918) 661-7326

Woolaroc Lodge Museum • 1925 Woolaroc Ranch Rd, P.O. Box 1647 • Bartlesville, OK 74005 • (918) 336-0307 • http://www.woolaroc.org

Beaver
Beaver County Historical Society • Historical Museum, Beaver County Fairgrounds, P.O. Box 457 • Beaver, OK 73932 • (580) 625-4439

Bernice
National Hot Rod & Custom Car Hall of Fame • Hwy 85A • Bernice, OK 74331 • (918) 257-4234 • http://www.darrylstarbird.com

Bethany
Bethany Historical Society • Historical Museum, 6700 NW 36th St • Bethany, OK 73008

Billings
Renfrow-Miller Museum • 201 W Broadway St, P.O. Box 102 • Billings, OK 74630 • (580) 725-3258

Binger
Caddo Nation of Oklahoma • P.O. Box 487 • Binger, OK 73009-0487 • (405) 656-2344 • http://www.rootsweb.com/~itwichit

Bixby
Bixby Historical Society • Historical Museum, 21 W Bixby, P.O. Box 1046 • Bixby, OK 74008 • (918) 366-1200 • http://www.rootsweb.ancestry.com/~okbhs/

Blackwell
Blackwell Public Library • 123 W Padon St • Blackwell, OK 74631-2805 • (580) 363-1809

Derailed Railroad Company Museum • 216 N Main • Blackwell, OK 74631

Top of Oklahoma Historical Society • Historical Museum, 303 S Main St, P.O. Box 108 • Blackwell, OK 74631 • (580) 363-0209

Boise City
Cimarron Heritage Center • 1300 N Cimarron, P.O. Box 214 • Boise City, OK 73933 • (580) 544-3479 • http://www.ptsi.net/user/museum

Bristow
Bristow Genealogical Society • 612 W 6th St • Bristow, OK 74010 • (918) 367-6633

Bristow Historical Society • Historical Museum, 1 Railroad Pl, P.O. Box 1224 • Bristow, OK 74010 • (918) 367-5151

Bristow Public Library • 111 W 7th Ave • Bristow, OK 74010-2401 • (918) 367-6562 • http://www.bristow.lib.ok.us

Broken Arrow
Broken Arrow Genealogical Society • 1800 S Main St, P.O. Box 1244 • Broken Arrow, OK 74013-1244 • (918) 455-8619

Broken Arrow Historical Society • Historical Museum, 400 S Main St • Broken Arrow, OK 74012 • (918) 258-2616 • http://www.brokenarrowok.gov

Broken Bow
Forest Heritage Center & Museum • Beavers Bend State Park, P.O. Box 157 • Broken Bow, OK 74728 • (580) 494-6497 • http://www.forestry.ok.gov/fhc

Gardner Mansion Museum • Hwy 70 • Broken Bow, OK 74728 • (405) 584-6588

Buffalo
Buffalo Museum • 108 S Hoy, P.O. Box 224 • Buffalo, OK 73834 • (405) 735-2008

Wacky Wacky Wilsons Museum • 108 N Hoy St • Buffalo, OK 73834 • http://www.wackywackywilsons.com

Cache
Quanah Parker Star House Museum • Eagle Park Ghost Town, Rt 2, Box 9 • Cache, OK 73527 • (405) 429-3238

Caddo
Caddo Indian Territory Museum and Library • 110 Buffalo St, P.O. Box 274 • Caddo, OK 74729 • (580) 367-2787 • http://www.indianterritoryinc.com

Calera
Bryant County Heritage Association • Main & McKinley Sts, P.O. Box 153 • Calera, OK 74730-0153 • (580) 434-5848

Canton
Canton Area Museum • P.O. Box 38 • Canton, OK 73724

Cheyenne-Arapahoe Museum & Archives • P.O. Box 488 • Canton, OK 73724

Canute
Canute Heritage Foundation • Historical Museum, 9th St & Route 66 • Canute, OK 73626

Carmen
Carmen Depot Museum • 111 N Grand, P.O. Box 243 • Carmen, OK 73726 • (405) 987-2321

Ralph Cain Jr Memorial Newspaper Museum • P.O. Box 243 • Carmen, OK 73726

Carnegie
Carnegie Public Library • 22 S Broadway • Carnegie, OK 73015 • (580) 654-1980

Kiowa Tribal Museum • SH 9 W, P.O. Box 369 • Carnegie, OK 73015 • (480) 654-2300

Kiowa Tribe • P.O. Box 369 • Carnegie, OK 73015 • (580) 654-2300

Catoosa
Arkansas River Historical Society • Historical Museum, 5350 Cimarron Rd • Catoosa, OK 74015 • (918) 266-2291 • http://www.tulsaweb.com/port/

Catoosa Historical Society • Historical Museum, 105 E Oak St, P.O. Box 738 • Catoosa, OK 74015 • (918) 266-1684

Cement
Cement Community Museum • P.O. Box 429 • Cement, OK 73017

Chandler
Chickamauga Cherokee Nation - White River Band • 615 Ponderson Dr • Chandler, OK 74834 • (918) 258-2073

Lincoln County Historical Society • Museum of Pioneer History, 717-719 Manvel, P.O. Box 458 • Chandler, OK 74834 • (405) 258-2425 • http://www.pioneermuseumok.org

Checotah
Honey Springs Battlefield Museum • 1863 Honey Springs Battlefield Rd • Checotah, OK 74426 • (918) 473-5572 • http://www.okhistory.org

Jim Lucas Checotah Public Library • 626 W Gentry • Checotah, OK 74426-2218 • (918) 473-6715 • http://www.eodls.lib.ok.us

Katy Depot Center Museum • Paul Carr Dr, P.O. Box 721 • Checotah, OK 74426 • (918) 473-6377

Chelsea
Hogue House Museum • 1001 S Olive St • Chelsea, OK 75016 • (918) 789-2220

Cherokee
Alfalfa County Historical Society • Historical Museum, 117 W Main St, P.O. Box 201 • Cherokee, OK 73728 • (580) 596-2513 • http://www.okgenweb.org/~okalfalf/

Cherokee City-County Public Library • 602 S Grand Ave • Cherokee, OK 73728 • (580) 596-2366

Cheyenne
Black Kettle Museum • US 283 & State Hwy 47, P.O. Box 252 • Cheyenne, OK 73628 • (580) 497-3929

Roger Mills County Genealogical Society • P.O. Box 205 • Cheyenne, OK 73628

Roll One Room School Museum • P.O. Box 34 • Cheyenne, OK 73628 • (580) 497-3882 • http://www.rogermills.org

Chichasha
Antique Automobile Museum • Chichasha Ave, P.O. Box 271 • Chichasha, OK 73023

Chickasha Public Library • 527 Iowa Ave • Chickasha, OK 73018 • (405) 222-6075

Grady County Genealogical Society • c/o Chickasha Public Library, 527 Iowa St, P.O. Box 792 • Chickasha, OK 73023 • (405) 224-7482 • http://www.telepath.com/dataman/okgrady.html

Grady County Historical Society • Historical Museum, 415 W Chickasha Ave • Chickasha, OK 73023 • (405) 224-6480

Muscle Car Ranch Museum • 3609 S 16th • Chickasha, OK 73108 • (405) 224-4910 • http://www.musclecarranch.com

Nash Library • University of Science & Arts of Oklahoma, 1901 S 17 St • Chickasha, OK 73018 • (405) 574-1343 • http://www.usao.edu/library

Verden Museum • Rt 1, Box 174 • Chickasha, OK 73018

Chouteau
Mayes County Genealogical Society • P.O. Box 924 • Chouteau, OK 74337

Mayes County Historical Society • Route 1, Box 231 • Chouteau, OK 74337

Claremore
Belvidere Mansion Museum • 121 N Chickasaw, P.O. Box 774 • Claremore, OK 74018 • (918) 342-1127

J M Davis Arms and Historical Museum • 333 N Lynn Riggs Blvd, P.O. Box 966 • Claremore, OK 74018 • (918) 341-5707 • http://www.thegunmuseum.com

Lynn Riggs Memorial Museum • 121 N Weenonah • Claremore, OK 74014 • (918) 342-1127 • http://members.cox.net/lynn.riggs/lrmem.htm

Oklahoma Military Academy Memorial Museum • Rogers State College, 1701 W Will Rogers Blvd • Claremore, OK 74017 • (918) 343-7777 • http://www.rsu.edu/oma/

Rogers County Genealogical and Historical Society • 4th & Chickasaw, P.O. Box 74 • Claremore, OK 74018 • (918) 342-1127

Totem Pole Park Museum • P.O. Box 774 • Claremore, OK 74018 • http://www.rchs1.org

Will Rogers Library • 1515 N Florence Ave • Claremore, OK 74017 • (918) 341-1564

Will Rogers Memorial Museum • 1720 W Will Rogers Blvd, P.O. Box 157 • Claremore, OK 74018-0157 • (918) 341-0719 • http://www.willrogers.org

Cleveland
Triangle Heritage Museum • 512 W Delaware • Cleveland, OK 74020 • (918) 519-6251

Clinton
Cheyenne Cultural Center Museum • 415 Gary Blvd, P.O. Box 1177 • Clinton, OK 73601 • (580) 323-0217

Oklahoma Route 66 Museum • 2229 Gray Blvd • Clinton, OK 73601 • (580) 323-7866 • http://www.route66.org

Coalgate
Coal Country Mining & Historical Museum • 212 S Broadway St • Coalgate, OK 74538

Coal County Historical and Genealogical Society • 111 W Ohio, P.O. Box 322 • Coalgate, OK 74538 • (405) 428-3237

Colbert
Colbert Historical Museum • 100 N Burney, P.O. Box 299 • Colbert, OK 74733 • (580) 296-2385

Colcord
Talbot Library and Museum • 500 S Colcord Ave, P.O. Box 349 • Colcord, OK 74338 • (918) 326-4532 • http://www.talbotlibrary.com

Collinsville
Collinsville Depot Museum • 115 S 10th St • Collinsville, OK 74021 • (918) 371-3540 • http://www.cvilleok.com/depot.html

Newspaper Museum in Collinsville • 1110 W Main • Collinsville, OK 74021 • (918) 371-1901 • http://www.cvilleok.com/museum.html

Commerce
Indian & Hardrock Mining Museum • P.O. Box 250 • Commerce, OK 74339

Mullen Rock Museum • Mickey Mantle Blvd • Commerce, OK 74339

Concho
Cheyenne-Arapahoe Tribes of Oklahoma • P.O Box 38 • Concho, OK 73022 • (405) 262-0345 • http://www.cheyenneandarapaho.org

Cordell
Washita County Museum • P.O. Box 153 • Cordell, OK 73632 • (580) 832-3681

Covington
Covington Historical Museum • 3rd & Main • Covington, OK 73730

Coweta
Mission Bell Historical Society • Historical Museum, 204 S Bristow Ave, P.O. Box 850 • Coweta, OK 74429 • (918) 486-2513

Coyle
Gerald Johnson's Museum • 216 E Main St • Coyle, OK 73027 • (405) 424-7757

Iowa Tribal Museum • P.O. Box 221 • Coyle, OK 73027 • (405) 547-2402

Cushing
Cimarron Valley Railroad Museum • S King Hwy, P.O. Box 844 • Cushing, OK 74023 • (918) 225-3936

Cushing Genealogical Society • c/o Cushing Public Library, 215 N Steele, P.O. Box 551 • Cushing, OK 74023 • (918) 225-4188

Cushing Public Library • 215 N Steele, P.O. Box 551 • Cushing, OK 74023-0551 • (918) 225-4188

Davis
American Heritage Library • 102 S 3rd, P.O. Box 176 • Davis, OK 73030

Arbuckle Historical Society • 201 S 4th St • Davis, OK 73030 • (580) 369-3721

Dewey
Dewey Hotel Museum • 801 N Delaware St • Dewey, OK 74029 • (918) 534-0215

Tom Mix Museum • 721 N Delaware, P.O. Box 190 • Dewey, OK 74029 • (918) 534-1555 • http://www.tommixmuseum.com

Washington County Historical Society • 900 N Shawnee • Dewey, OK 74029 • (918) 534-2040

Drummond
Drummond Historical Society • Historical Museum, 402 S Main • Drummond, OK 73735

Drumright

Drumright Community Historical Society • Historical Museum, 301 E Broadway, P.O. Box 668 • Drumright, OK 73030 • (918) 352-3002 • http://www.drumrighthistoricalsociety.org

Drumright Oil Field Museum • 409 W Broadway • Drumright, OK 74030

Duncan

Chisholm Trail Heritage Center Museum • 1000 Chisholm Trail Pkwy • Duncan, OK 73533 • (580) 252-6692 • http://www.onthechisholmtrail.com

Stephens County Genealogical Society • 301 N 8th St, P.O. Box 1850 • Duncan, OK 73534 • (580) 255-8718

Stephens County Historical Society • Historical Museum, Hwy 81 & Beach, P.O. Box 1294 • Duncan, OK 73534 • (580) 252-0717

Durant

Bryan County Heritage Society • 618 N 19th St • Durant, OK 74701

Choctaw Nation of Oklahoma • 16th & Locust, P.O. Drawer 1210 • Durant, OK 74702 • (580) 924-8280 • http://www.choctawnation.com

Fort Washita Historic Site Museum • 3348 State Road 199 • Durant, OK 74701 • (580) 924-6502 • http://www.texoma-ok.com/trooper/1842.htm

Three Valley Museum • 16th & Elm • Durant, OK 74701 • (405) 920-1907

Durham

Metcalf Museum • Rt1, Box 25 • Durham, OK 73642 • http://www.metcalfemuseum.org

Edmond

American Railway Museum • 106 W 3rd St • Edmond, OK 73083

Chambers Library • University of Central Oklahoma, 100 N University, P.O. Box 192 • Edmond, OK 73034-0192 • (405) 974-2878 • http://library.ucok.edu

Edmond Genealogical Society • P.O. Box 1984 • Edmond, OK 73083-1984 • (401) 348-4768 • http://www.rootsweb.com/~okegs

Edmond Historic Preservation Schoolhouse Project • 124 E 2nd St, P.O. Box 4101 • Edmond, OK 73083 • (405) 715-1889 • http://www.edmondhistoricpreservationtrust.com

Edmond Historical Society • Historical Museum, 431 South Blvd • Edmond, OK 73034 • (405) 340-0078 • http://www.edmondhistory.org

Holocaust Resource Center of Oklahoma • P.O. Box 774 • Edmond, OK 73073

El Reno

Canadian County Genealogical Society • P.O. Box 866 • El Reno, OK 73036 • (405) 262-2409 • http://www.rootsweb.com/~okcanadi/okcanad.htm

Canadian County Historical Museum • 300 S Grand • El Reno, OK 73036 • (405) 262-5121

El Reno Carnegie Library • 215 E Wade • El Reno, OK 73036-2753 • (405) 262-2409

El Reno Historic Hotel Museum • 300 S Grand • El Reno, OK 73036

Fort Reno Museum • 7107 W Cheyenne St, P.O. Box 1199 • El Reno, OK 73036 • (405) 262-3987 • http://www.fortreno.org

Eldorado

Eldorado Museum & Historical Society • Historical Museum, P.O. Box 234 • Eldorado, OK 73537 • (580) 633-2235

Elk City

Anadarko Basin Museum • 204 N Main St • Elk City, OK 73648 • (580) 243-0441

Elk City Carnegie Library • 221 W Broadway • Elk City, OK 73644 • (580) 225-0136

Elk City Genealogical Society of Western Oklahoma • 1119 Crestview Dr • Elk City, OK 73644

National Route 66 Museum • 2717 W Hwy 66, P.O. Box 5 • Elk City, OK 73648 • (405) 225-6266

Old Town Museum • US 66 & Pioneer Rd, P.O. Box 542 • Elk City, OK 73648 • (580) 225-6266

Western Oklahoma Historical Society • Historical Museum, P.O. Box 542 • Elk City, OK 73648 • (580) 225-2207 • http://wokhs.org

Enid

Dan Midgley Museum • 1001 Sequoyah Dr • Enid, OK 73703 • (405) 234-7265

Garfield County Genealogists • P.O. Box 1106 • Enid, OK 73702-1106 • (405) 234-6086 • http://www.harvestcomm.net/org/garfield_genealogy/

Garfield County Historical Society • c/o Public Library of Enid, 120 W Maine, P.O. Box 3337 • Enid, OK 73702-3337 • (405) 234-6313 • http://www.enid.org/library.htm

George's Antique Auto Museum • 508 S Grand • Enid, OK 73702

Museum of the Cherokee Strip • 507 S 4th St • Enid, OK 73701-5835 • (580) 237-1907 • http://www.ok-history.mus.ok.us

Public Library of Enid & Garfield County • 120 W Maine St, P.O. Box 8002 • Enid, OK 73702 • (405) 234-6313 • http://www.enid.lib.ok.us

Railroad Museum of Oklahoma • 702 N Washington • Enid, OK 73701 • (580) 233-3051 • http://www.railroadmuseumofoklahoma.org

Sons and Daughters of the Cherokee Strip Pioneers • P.O. Box 465 • Enid, OK 73702

Erick

100th Meridian Museum • Sheb Wooley Ave & Roger Miller Blvd, P.O. Box 564 • Erick, OK 73645

Eufala

McIntosh County Lake Eufaula Area Genealogical Society • P.O. Box 1035 • Eufala, OK 74432

Lake Eufaula Area Genealogical Society • P.O. Box 1035 • Eufaula, OK 74432

Fairfax

Fairfax Public Library • 158 E Elm St • Fairfax, OK 74637 • (918) 642-5535 • http://www.fairfax.lib.ok.us

Fairview

Fairview City Library • 115 S 6th Ave, P.O. Box 419 • Fairview, OK 73737-0419 • (580) 227-2190 • http://www.fairview.org

Major County Genealogical Research Library • P.O. Box 74 • Fairview, OK 73737

Major County Genealogical Society • c/o Fairview City Library, P.O. Box 419 • Fairview, OK 73737

Major County Historical Society • Historical Museum, P.O. Box 555 • Fairview, OK 73737 • (580) 227-2265 • http://www.mchsok.com

Fort Gibson

Fort Gibson Genealogical and Historical Society • P.O. Box 416 • Fort Gibson, OK 74434

Fort Gibson Historic Site Museum • 907 N Garrison Ave, P.O. Box 457 • Fort Gibson, OK 74434 • (918) 478-4088 • http://www.ok.history.mus.ok.us

Garrett Historic Home Museum • 504 E Coppinger Ave • Fort Gibson, OK 74434 • (918) 478-3732

Fort Sill
Fort Sill National Historic Landmark Museum • 437 Quanah Rd • Fort Sill, OK 73503 • (580) 442-5123 • http://www.sill.army.mil/museum

US Army Field Artillery Museum • 238 Randolph Rd • Fort Sill, OK 73503 • (580) 442-1819 • http://sill-www.army.mil/famuseum/

Fort Supply
Fort Supply Historic Site Museum • P.O. Box 247 • Fort Supply, OK 73841-0247 • (580) 766-3767

Fort Towson
Fort Towson Military Park Museum • HC 63, Box 1580 • Fort Towson, OK 74735 • (580) 873-2634 • http://www.ok-history.mus.ok.us

Frederick
Pioneer Heritage Townsite Center • 201 N 9th St, P.O. Box 921 • Frederick, OK 73542

Tillman County Historical Society • Historical Museum, P.O. Box 833 • Frederick, OK 73542 • (580) 335-5844 • http://tillmanokhistory.org/

Freedom
Freedom Museum • 505 Main St, P.O. Box 28 • Freedom, OK 73842 • (580) 621-3533

Gate
Gateway to the Panhandle Museum • Rt 1, Box 135 • Gate, OK 73844 • (580) 934-2004 • http://www.gatewaytothepanhandlemuseum.org

Geary
Canadian Rivers Historical Society • Historical Museum, 717 S Broadway • Geary, OK 73040 • (405) 884-2779

Geary Genealogical Society • 106 W Main • Geary, OK 73040

Gene Autry
Gene Autry Oklahoma Museum • Gene Autry Rd, P.O. Box 67 • Gene Autry, OK 73436 • (580) 294-3047 • http://www.geneautryokmuseum.com

Goodwell
No Man's Land Historical Society • Historical Museum, 207 WSewell St, P.O. Box 278 • Goodwell, OK 73939 • (580) 349-2670

Gore
Cherokee Courthouse Museum • Hwy 64, Route 2, Box 37-1 • Gore, OK 74435 • (918) 489-5663 • http://www.twinterritories.com

Granite
Oklahoma State Reformatory Museum • P.O. Box 514 • Granite, OK 73547

Grove
Delaware County Genealogical Society • c/o Grove Public Library, 206 S Elk St, P.O. Box 1269 • Grove, OK 74344 • (918) 786-2945

Delaware County Historical Society • Route 1, Box 467 • Grove, OK 74344

Grove Public Library • 1140 Neo Loop • Grove, OK 74344-8602 • (918) 786-2945 • http://www.eodls.lib.ok.us/grove.html

Har-Ber Village Museum • 4404 W 20th St • Grove, OK 74344 • (918) 786-3488 • http://www.har-bervillage.com

Seneca-Cayuga Tribe of Oklahoma • Historical Museum, 23701 S 655 Rd • Grove, OK 74344 • (918) 787-4452 • http://www.sctribe.com

Guthrie
Frontier Drugstore Museum • 214 W Oklahoma • Guthrie, OK 73044 • (405) 282-1895 • http://www.drugmuseum.org

Guthrie Museum Complex • 406 E Oklahoma • Guthrie, OK 73044 • (405) 282-1889

Guthrie Scottish Rite Masonic Temple • 900 E Oklahoma Ave, P.O. Box 70 • Guthrie, OK 73044 • (405) 282-1281 • http://www.guthriescottishrite.org

Logan County Genealogical Society • 406 E Oklahoma, P.O. Box 1419 • Guthrie, OK 73044 • (405) 282-2200 • http://www.rootsweb.com/~okicgs

Logan County Historical Society • Historical Museum, 521 E Columbus Ave, P.O. Box 1512 • Guthrie, OK 73044 • (405) 282-6000 • http://www.logancountyhistoricalsociety.com

Masonic Grand Lodge of Oklahoma • 102 South Broad, P.O. Box 1019 • Guthrie, OK 73044 • (405) 282-3212 • http://www.gloklahoma.com

National Lighter Museum • 107 S 2nd • Guthrie, OK 73044 • http://www.nationallightermuseum.com

Oklahoma Sports Museum • 315 W Oklahoma Ave, P.O. Box 1342 • Guthrie, OK 73044 • (405) 260-1342

Oklahoma Territorial Museum • 402 E Oklahoma Ave • Guthrie, OK 73044 • (405) 282-1889

State Capital Publishing Museum • 301 W Harrison Ave • Guthrie, OK 73044 • (408) 282-4123

Harrah
Harrah Historical Society • Historical Museum, 20881 E Main St, P.O. Box 846 • Harrah, OK 73045 • (405) 454-6911 • http://www.harrahhistorycenter.com

Haworth
Henry Harris Home Museum • HC 60, Box 2070 • Haworth, OK 74740 • (405) 245-1129

Healdton
Healdton Oil Museum • 315 E Main St • Healdton, OK 73438 • (580) 229-0900

Heavener
Heavener Area Historical Society • Historical Museum, E 1st St, P.O. Box 277 • Heavener, OK 74937 • (918) 653-4868

Heavener Runestone State Park • 18365 Runestone Rd • Heavener, OK 74937 • (918) 653-2241

Peter Conser House Museum • 47114 Conser Creek Rd • Heavener, OK 74937 • (918) 653-2493

Hennessey
Hennessey Public Library • 525 S Main • Hennessey, OK 73742 • (405) 853-2073 • http://www.hennessey.lib.ok.us

Henryetta
Alabama-Quassarte Tribal Town • 111 N 6th St • Henryetta, OK 74437 • (918) 652-8708

Henryetta Public Library • 518 W Main • Henryetta, OK 74437 • (918) 652-7377 • http://www.henryettalibrary.org

Henryetta Territorial Museum • 410 W Moore St, P.O. Box 459 • Henryetta, OK 74437 • (918) 653-7110 • http://www.territorialmuseum.org

Hinton
Hinton Historical Society • Historical Museum, 801 W Broadway, P.O. Box 2 • Hinton, OK 73047 • (405) 524-3181

Hobart
General Tommy Franks Leadership Institute & Museum • 501 S Main, P.O. Box 222 • Hobart, OK 73651 • (580) 726-5900 • http://www.tommyfranksmuseum.org

Hobart Public Library • 200 S Main St • Hobart, OK 73651 • (580) 726-2535 • http://www2.mmind.net/hobart.pl

Kiowa County Genealogical Society • P.O. Box 191 • Hobart, OK 73651-0191 • (508) 726-5476

Kiowa County Historical Society • c/o Hobart Public Library, 200 S Main St • Hobart, OK 73559 • (580) 726-2535

Oklahoma

Hobart, cont.
Kiowa County Museum • 518 S Main • Hobart, OK 73651 • (580) 726-6202

Holdenville
Grace M Pickens Public Library • 209 E 9th St • Holdenville, OK 74848 • (405) 379-3245

Hughes County Historical Society • 114 N Creek St • Holdenville, OK 74848 • (405) 379-6723

Hollis
Harmon County Historical Society • Historical Museum, 102 W Broadway • Hollis, OK 73550 • (580) 688-9545 • http://www.rootsweb. ancestry.com/~okhcgs/

Hominy
Drummond Home Museum • 305 N Price • Hominy, OK 74035 • (918) 885-2374

Hominy Heritage Association • Historical Museum, P.O. Box 672 • Hominy, OK 74035 • http://www.hominy.lib.ok.us/heritage/

Hooker
Beaver River Genealogical and Historical Society • Route 1, Box 79 • Hooker, OK 73945 • (405) 652-2716

Olive Warner Memorial Library • 111 S Broadway, P.O. Box 376 • Hooker, OK 73945-0376 • (580) 652-2835 • http://www.hookerok.com

Hugo
Caboose Museum • NE 23rd & Choctaw Rd • Hugo, OK 74743

Choctaw County Genealogical Society • P.O. Box 1056 • Hugo, OK 74743

Choctaw County Historical Society • Historical Museum, 502 W Duke • Hugo, OK 74743

Choctaw County Museum • 124 N Broadway • Hugo, OK 74743 • (205) 459-3383

Hugo Historical Society • Historical Museum, 208 E Jefferson St • Hugo, OK 74743

Hydro
Hydro Historical Society • Historical Museum, 2100 N Lincoln Blvd, P.O. Box 188 • Hydro, OK 73048 • (405) 521-2491

Idabel
Barnes-Stevenson House Museum • 302 SE Adams • Idabel, OK 74745

Idabel Public Library • 2 SE Avenue D, P.O. Box 778 • Idabel, OK 74745-0778 • (580) 286-6406 • http://www.idabel.lib.ok.us

Magnolia Mansion Museum • 6015 E Adams St • Idabel, OK 74745

McCurtain County Genealogy Society • 2 SE Avenue D, P.O. Box 1832 • Idabel, OK 74745 • (580) 286-4369 • http://members.tripod. com/~mccurtain_2/

McCurtain County Historical Society • Historical Museum, 302 SE Adams • Idabel, OK 74745 • (580) 212-3639

Museum of the Red River • 812 E Lincoln Rd • Idabel, OK 74745 • (508) 286-3616 • http://www.museumoftheredriver.org

Indiahoma
Quanah Parker Center • Rt 1, Box 448 • Indiahoma, OK 73552

Indianola
Choate House Museum • 403 Walnut, P.O. Box 239 • Indianola, OK 74442 • (918) 823-4421

Jay
Delaware County Historical Society • Mariee Wallace Museum, 538 Krause St, P.O. Box 855 • Jay, OK 74346 • (918) 253-4345

Jenks
Chickamauga Cherokee Nation - White River Band • 323 N 5th St • Jenks, OK 74037 • (918) 299-5207

Dr McLean Home and Office Museum • 123 East A Street • Jenks, OK 74037 • (918) 446-2745

Sunbelt Railroad Museum • P.O. Box 470331 • Jenks, OK 74147

Kaw City
Kanza Museum & Kaw Tribal Complex • 698 Grand View Dr, P.O. Box 50 • Kaw City, OK 74641 • (580) 269-2552 • http://www.kawnationa. com

Kaw City Museum • 910 Washungah Dr, P.O. Box 56 • Kaw City, OK 74641 • (580) 269-2366

Kaw City Public Library • 900 Morgan Square E, P.O. Box 30 • Kaw City, OK 74641-0030 • (580) 269-2525

Kaw Tribe of Oklahoma • 698 Grandview, P.O. Drawer 50 • Kaw City, OK 74641-0050 • (580) 269-2552 • http://www.kawnation.com

Keota
Overstreet-Kerr Historical Farm Museum • 29186 Kerr-Overstreet Rd • Keota, OK 74941 • (918) 966-3396 • http://www.kerrcenter.com/ overstreet/

Kingfisher
Chisholm Trail Museum • 605 Zellers Ave, P.O. Box 262 • Kingfisher, OK 73750 • (405) 375-5176 • http://www.ok-history.mus.ok.us

Governor A J Seay Mansion Museum • 605 Seay Ave • Kingfisher, OK 73750 • (408) 385-5176 • http://www.ok-history.mus.ok.us

Kingfisher Memorial Library • 505 W Will Rogers St • Kingfisher, OK 73750 • (405) 375-3384 • http://www.kingfisher.lib.ok.us

Krebs
Krebs Museum • 85 W Main St, P.O. Box 234 • Krebs, OK 74554 • (918) 423-7191

Langston
G Lamar Harrison Library • Langston University, P.O. Box 1600 • Langston, OK 73050-1600 • (405) 466-3293

Melvin B Tolson Black Heritage Center • Langston Univ • Langston, OK 73050 • (405) 466-3346

Laverne
Laverne Community Museum • P.O. Box 444 • Laverne, OK 73848

Lawton
Comanche National Museum • 710 NW Ferris Ave • Lawton, OK 73507 • (580) 353-0404 • http://www.comanche museum.com

Comanche Tribe of Oklahoma • P.O Box 908 • Lawton, OK 73502 • (580) 492-3775 • http://www.comanchenation.com

Fire, Transportation and Farm Museum • 816 SE 1st St • Lawton, OK 73501 • (580) 355-0692

Lawton Heritage Association • Historical Museum, P.O. Box 311 • Lawton, OK 73502

Lawton Public Library • 110 SW 4th St • Lawton, OK 73501-4034 • (580) 581-3450 • http://www.cityof.lawton.ok.us/library

Lawton Rangers Historical Society • 2102 SE 60th St • Lawton, OK 73501-9441 • (580) 357-8585

Lewis Museum • 3601 NW Arlington • Lawton, OK 73501 • (405) 355-0692

Mattie Beal Payne Mansion Museum • 1008 SW 5th, P.O. Box 311 • Lawton, OK 73502 • (580) 678-3156

Museum of the Great Plains Library • 601 NW Ferris Ave • Lawton, OK 73502 • (580) 581-3460 • http://www.museumgreatplains.org

Southwest Oklahoma Genealogical Society • 808 NW 48th St, P.O. Box 148 • Lawton, OK 73502-0148 • (580) 357-6095 • http://www.sirinet.net/~lgarris/swogs

US Army Air Defense Artillery Museum • 372 Gannahl Rd • Lawton, OK 73503 • (580) 442-0424 • http://sill-www.army.mil/adamuseum/

Leedey
Boswell Museum • P.O. Box 128 • Leedey, OK 73654

Lindsay
Lindsay Community Historical Society • Historical Museum, 410 W Creek • Lindsay, OK 73052 • (405) 745-3919

Murray-Lindsay Mansion Museum • P.O. Box 828 • Lindsay, OK 73052 • (405) 756-2121

Madill
Madill Genealogical and Historical Society • 403 E Main St • Madill, OK 73446 • (580) 795-5060

Museum of Southern Oklahoma • 400 W Overton • Madill, OK 73446 • (580) 795-5060 • http://www.museumofsouthernoklahoma.org

Mangum
Greer County Genealogical and Historical Society • 201 W Lincoln • Mangum, OK 73554 • (580) 782-3185 • http://www.rootsweb.com/~okgcghs/

Mangum Genealogical Society • 312 N Tittle • Mangum, OK 73554

Old Greer County Museum • 222 W Jefferson St, P.O. Box 2 • Mangum, OK 73554 • (580) 782-2851 • http://www.oldgreercountymuseum.com

Pocahontas Trails Genealogical Society • Route 2, Box 40 • Mangum, OK 73554 • (580) 679-3865

Mannford
Keystone Crossroads Historical Society • Historical Museum, Coonrod Ave & SH 51, P.O. Box 1661 • Mannford, OK 74044 • (918) 865-7206

Terri's Doll Museum • Rt 2, Box 70 • Mannford, OK 74044

Marietta
Love County Historical Society • Historical Museum, 409 W Chickasaw St, P.O. Box 134 • Marietta, OK 73448 • (405) 276-5888

Love County Military Museum • 408 1/2 W Chickasaw • Marietta, OK 73448

Marlow
Marlow Chamber of Commerce & Museum • 223 W Main St • Marlow, OK 73055

Maud
Maud Historical Museum • 130 E Main, P.O. Box A • Maud, OK 73854 • (405) 374-2880

McAlester
Garrard Ardeneum • 601 S 2nd • McAlester, OK 74501 • (918) 423-5482

McAlester Public Library • 401 N 2nd St • McAlester, OK 74501 • (918) 426-0930 • http://www.mcalester.lib.ok.us

McAlester Scottish Rite Masonic Center • P.O. Box 609 • McAlester, OK 74502 • (918) 423-6360

Oklahoma Trolley Museum • P.O. Box 145 • McAlester, OK 74501

Pittsburg County Genealogical and Historical Society • Historical Museum, 113 E Carl Albert Pkwy • McAlester, OK 74501 • (918) 426-0388

Tannehill Museum • 500 W Stonewall Ave • McAlester, OK 74502 • (918) 423-5953

McLoud
Kickapoo Tribe of Oklahoma • P.O. Box 70 • McLoud, OK 74851-0070 • (405) 964-2074

McLoud Museum • P.O. Box 235 • McLoud, OK 74851

Medford
Grant County Historical Society • Historical Museum, 124 N Main St, P.O. Box 127 • Medford, OK 73759 • (580) 395-2888

Grant County Museum • Main & Cherokee Sts, P.O. Box 31 • Medford, OK 73759 • (580) 395-2922

Meeker
Carl Hubbell Museum • 510 W Carl Hubbell Blvd, P.O. Box 186 • Meeker, OK 74855 • (405) 279-3813

Miami
Coleman Theatre Museum • 103 N Main, P.O. Box 2 • Miami, OK 74355 • (918) 540-2425 • http://www.colemantheatre.org

Inter-Tribal Council • Historical Museum, 114 S Eight Tribes Tr, P.O. Box 1308 • Miami, OK 74355 • (918) 542-3443

Miami Public Library • 200 N Main St • Miami, OK 74354 • (918) 541-2292 • http://www.miami.lib.ok.us

Miami Tribe of Oklahoma • Historical Museum, 202 S Eight Tribes Tr, P.O. Box 1326 • Miami, OK 74355 • (918) 542-1445 • http://www.miamination.com

Modoc Tribe of Oklahoma • 515 G Street SE, P.O. Box 939 • Miami, OK 74354-0939 • (918) 542-1190 • http://eighttribes.org/modoc

Northeast Oklahoma Native American Cultural Center • 200 I Street, P.O. Box 1308 • Miami, OK 74355 • (918) 542-8441

Ottawa County Genealogical Society • P.O. Box 1383 • Miami, OK 74355-1383

Ottawa County Historical Society • Dobson Museum, 110 A Street SW, P.O. Box 242 • Miami, OK 74355 • (918) 540-1404

Ottawa Tribe of Oklahoma • Historical Museum, 13 S 69 A, P.O. Box 110 • Miami, OK 74355 • (918) 540-1536 • http://www.ottawatribe.org

Peoria Tribe of Indians of Oklahoma • P.O. Box 1527 • Miami, OK 74354 • (918) 540-2535 • http://www.peoriatribe.com

Seneca-Cayuga Tribe of Oklahoma • P.O. Box 1283 • Miami, OK 74355 • (918) 542-6609 • http://eighttribes.org/seneca-cayuga

Shawnee Tribe • P.O. Box 189 • Miami, OK 74354 • (918) 542-2441

Moore
Hillsdale Free Will Baptist College Library • 3701 S I-35, P.O. Box 7208 • Moore, OK 73153 • (405) 912-9025 • http://www.library.hc.edu

Muldrow
Muldrow Genealogical Society • c/o Muldrow Public Library, 711 W Shanntel Smith Blvd, P.O. Box 1253 • Muldrow, OK 74948 • (918) 427-6703

Muldrow Public Library • 711 W Shanntel Smith Blvd, P.O. Box 449 • Muldrow, OK 74948-0449 • (918) 427-6703 • http://www.eodls.lib.ok.us

Muskogee
Ataloa Lodge Museum • Bacone College, 2299 Old Bacone Rd • Muskogee, OK 74403 • (918) 683-4581 x283 • http://ataloa.bacone.edu

Bacone College Library • 2299 Old Bacone Rd • Muskogee, OK 74403 • (918) 781-7263 • http://www.bacone.edu

Bureau of Indian Affairs-Tribal Operations • 101 N 5th St • Muskogee, OK 74401 • (918) 687-2313

Eastern Oklahoma District Library System • 814 W Okmulgee • Muskogee, OK 74401-6839 • (918) 683-2846 • http://www.eodls.lib.ok.us

Oklahoma

Muskogee, cont.

Five Civilized Tribes Museum • Agency Hill, Honor Heights Dr • Muskogee, OK 74401 • (918) 683-1701 • http://www.fivetribes.org

Muskogee County Genealogical Society • c/o Muskogee Public Library, 801 W Okmulgee • Muskogee, OK 74401-6800 • (918) 682-6657 • http://www.rootsweb.com/~okmuscgs/

Muskogee Public Library • 801 W Okmulgee • Muskogee, OK 74401 • (918) 682-6657 • http://www.eolds.lib.ok.us

Muskogee War Memorial Park and Military Museum • 3500 Batfish Rd, P.O. Box 253 • Muskogee, OK 74402 • (918) 682-6294 • http://www.ussbatfish.com

Thomas-Foreman Home Museum • 1419 W Okmulgee • Muskogee, OK 74401 • (918) 682-6938

Three Rivers Museum • 220 Elgin, P.O. Box 1813 • Muskogee, OK 74402 • (908) 686-6624 • http://www.3riversmuseum.com

Nardin

Nardin Heritage House Museum • 110 Memory Ln, P.O. Box 11 • Nardin, OK 74646 • (405) 363-4760

Newkirk

Newkirk Community Museum • 500 W 8th St • Newkirk, OK 74647 • (580) 362-2525

Noble

Timberlake Rose Rock Museum • 419 S Hwy 77, P.O. Box 663 • Noble, OK 73068 • (405) 872-9838 • http://www.roserockmuseum.com

Normal

Cleveland County Genealogical Society • P.O. Box 6176 • Normal, OK 73070

Norman

American Indian Institute • Univ of Oklahoma, 555 Constitution St, Ste 237 • Norman, OK 73037-0005

Cleveland County Genealogical Society • 1119 E Main St, P.O. Box 6176 • Norman, OK 73070-6176 • (405) 329-9180

History of Science Museum • 401 W Brooks • Norman, OK 73019

Moore-Lindsay Home Museum • 508 N Peters, P.O. Box 260 • Norman, OK 73069 • (405) 321-0156

Norman and Cleveland County Historical Museum • 508 N Peters, P.O. Box 260 • Norman, OK 73070 • (405) 321-0156 • http://www.normanhistorichouse.com

Norman Depot Museum • 200 S Jones Ave, P.O. Box 423 • Norman, OK 73069 • (405) 307-9320 • http://www.pasnorman.org

Pioneer Library System • 225 N Webster Ave • Norman, OK 73069-7133 • (405) 701-2600 • http://www.pioneer.lib.ok.us

University of Oklahoma Library • 401 W Brooks St • Norman, OK 73019 • (405) 325-2611 • http://libraries.ou.edu

Western History Collection • Univ of Oklahoma, Monnet Hall 452 • Norman, OK 73019 • (405) 325-3641

Western History Museum • Univ of Oklahoma, 630 Parrington Oval #452 • Norman, OK 73019 • (405) 325-3641

Nowata

Family Finders Genealogy Club • 432 S 5th St, P.O. Box 738 • Nowata, OK 74048

Glass Mansion Museum • 324 W Delaware, P.O. Box 51 • Nowata, OK 74048 • (918) 273-3514

Nowata County Historical Society • Historical Museum, 121 S Pine St, P.O. Box 87 • Nowata, OK 74048 • (918) 272-1191 • http://www.rootsweb.ancestry.com/~oknowata/

Okeene

Major County Genealogical Society • Route 2, Box 24 • Okeene, OK 73763

Okemah

Okfuskee County Genealogical Society • P.O. Box 507 • Okemah, OK 74859

Okfuskee County Historical Society • Historical Museum, 407 W Broadway St • Okemah, OK 74859 • (918) 623-2027

Territory Town Archives • Route 2, Box 297A • Okemah, OK 74859 • (918) 623-2599

Thlopthlocco Tribal Town • P.O. Box 188 • Okemah, OK 74859 • (918) 623-2620

Oklahoma City

1889'er Society • 313 NE 16th, P.O. Box 12300 • Oklahoma City, OK 73112-6359 • http://www.1889ers.org

45th Infantry Division Museum • 2145 NE 36th St • Oklahoma City, OK 73111 • (405) 424-5313 • http://www.45thdivisionmuseum.com

American Banjo Museum • 9 E Sheridan • Oklahoma City, OK 73104 • (405) 604-2793 • http://www.americanbanjomuseum.com

Central High School Museum • 800 N Harvey • Oklahoma City, OK 73102

Chickamauga Cherokee Nation - White River Band • 10001 Trafalgar • Oklahoma City, OK 73139 • (405) 232-3033

Daughers of the American Revolution • DAR State Library, Historical Bldg • Oklahoma City, OK 73105

Del City Historical Society • Historical Museum, 4609 SE 24th St • Oklahoma City, OK 73115

Dulaney-Browne Library • Oklahoma City University, 2501 N Blackwelder • Oklahoma City, OK 73106 • (405) 521-5065 • http://www.okcu.edu/library/libonlin.htm

Federation of Oklahoma Genealogical Societies • P.O. Box 26151 • Oklahoma City, OK 73126-0151 • (405) 672-2965

First Families of the Twin Territories • Oklahoma Genealogical Society, P.O. Box 12986 • Oklahoma City, OK 73157-2986 • http://www.rootsweb.com/~okgs/fftt.htm

Gaylord-Pickens Oklahoma Heritage Museum • 1400 Classen Dr • Oklahoma City, OK 73106 • (888) 501-2059 • http://www.oklahomaheritage.com

Genealogical Group of Oklahoma City LDS Stake • 3108 Windsor Terr • Oklahoma City, OK 73122

Genealogical Institute of Oklahoma • 3813 Cashion Pl • Oklahoma City, OK 73112-3325

German American Heritage Association of Oklahoma • Oklahoma City Univ, 2501 N Blackwelder • Oklahoma City, OK 73106

Harn Homestead and 1889er Museum • 313 NE 16th St • Oklahoma City, OK 73104 • (405) 235-4058 • http://www.harnhomestead.com

Henry Overnoiser House Museum • 405 1/2 NW 15th St • Oklahoma City, OK 73103 • (405) 525-5325

International Photography Hall of Fame • 2100 NE 52nd St • Oklahoma City, OK 73111 • (405) 424-4055

Judge R A Hefner Mansion Museum • 201 NW 14th St • Oklahoma City, OK 73103 • (405) 235-4458

Kirkpatrick Science and Air Space Museum • 2100 NE 52nd St • Oklahoma City, OK 73111 • (405) 602-6664 • http://www.omniplex.org

Lemuel Dorrance Museum • College of Pharmacy, OUHSC • Oklahoma City, OK 73190 • (405) 271-6484

Metropolitan Library System • 300 Park Ave • Oklahoma City, OK 73102 • (405) 231-8635 • http://www.metrolibrary.org

Metropolitan Library System-Downtown Libr • 300 Park Ave • Oklahoma City, OK 73102 • (405) 231-8650

National Cowboy Hall of Fame • 1700 NE 63rd St • Oklahoma City, OK 73111 • (405) 478-2250 • http://www.nationalcowboymuseum.org

National Guild of Saint Margaret of Scotland • 10717 Sunset Blvd • Oklahoma City, OK 73120-2427

National Softball Hall of Fame & Museum • 2801 NE 50th St • Oklahoma City, OK 73111 • (405) 424-5266 • http://www.asasoftball.com/hall_of_fame/index.asp

Native American Cultural Museum • P.O. Box 26980 • Oklahoma City, OK 73126 • (405) 815-5129

Oklahoma City National Memorial Museum • 620 N Harvey Ave • Oklahoma City, OK 73101 • (405) 235-2313 • http://www.oklahomacitynationalmemorial.org

Oklahoma Department of Libraries • 200 NE 18th St • Oklahoma City, OK 73105-3298 • (405) 521-2502 • http://www.odl.state.ok.us

Oklahoma Firefighters Museum • 2716 North East St • Oklahoma City, OK 73136 • (405) 424-3440 • http://www.osfa.info

Oklahoma Genealogical Society • P.O. Box 12986 • Oklahoma City, OK 73157 • http://www.rootsweb.com/~okgs/

Oklahoma Heritage Association • Heritage Museum, 1400 Classen Dr • Oklahoma City, OK 73106-6614 • (405) 235-4458 • http://www.oklahomaheritage.com

Oklahoma Historical Society • Oklahoma History Center, 2401 N Laird Ave • Oklahoma City, OK 73105 • (405) 522-5248 • http://www.okhistorycenter.org

Oklahoma Historical Society • Oklahoma Museum of History, 2100 N Lincoln Blvd • Oklahoma City, OK 73105-4997 • (405) 522-5243 • http://www.ok-history.mus.ok.us

Oklahoma Museums Association • 2100 NE 52nd • Oklahoma City, OK 73111 • (405) 424-7757 • http://www.okmuseums.org

Overholser Mansion Museum • 405 NW 15th • Oklahoma City, OK 73103 • (405) 528-8485

Ralph Ellison Library • 2000 NE 23rd St • Oklahoma City, OK 73111 • (405) 424-1437

Red Earth Museum • 2100 NE 52nd St • Oklahoma City, OK 73111 • (405) 427-5228 • http://www.redearth.org

Rodeo Historical Society • National Cowboy Hall of Fame, 1700 NE 63rd St • Oklahoma City, OK 73111 • (405) 478-6404

Tom & Ada Beam Library • Oklahoma Christian University, 2501 E Memorial Rd, P.O. Box 11000 • Oklahoma City, OK 73136-1100 • (405) 425-5312 • http://www.oc.edu/academics/library/

Westerners International • 1700 NE 63rd St • Oklahoma City, OK 73111 • (405) 478-8408

World of Wings Pigeon Center Museum • 2300 NE 63rd • Oklahoma City, OK 73111 • (405) 478-5155 • http://www.pigeoncenter.org

Okmulgee

Creek Indian Memorial Association • Creek Council House Museum, 106 W 6th St • Okmulgee, OK 74447 • (918) 756-2324 • http://www.creekcouncilhouse.com

Muscogee-Creek Nation • Historical Museum, Hwy 75 & Eufaula St, P.O. Box 580 • Okmulgee, OK 74447 • (918) 756-2911 • http://www.muscogeenation-nsn.gov

Okmulgee County Genealogical Society • 314 W 7th St, P.O. Box 904 • Okmulgee, OK 74447 • (918) 756-0788

Okmulgee Public Library • 218 S Okmulgee St • Okmulgee, OK 74447 • (918) 756-1448 • http://www.okmulgeelibrary.org

Yuchi-Euchee Tribe • P.O. Box 1990 • Okmulgee, OK 76067

Oologah

Dog Iron Ranch and Will Rogers Birthplace Museum • 9501 E 380 Rd, P.O. Box 157 • Oologah, OK 74018 • (918) 275-4201 • http://www.willrogers.com/birthplace

Oologah Historical Society • Historical Museum, 202 E Cooweescoowee Ave, P.O. Box 609 • Oologah, OK 74053 • (918) 443-2790 • http://www.oologah.com/oologah/ohmuseum.html

Owasso

Owasso Historical Museum • 26 S Main, P.O. Box 180 • Owasso, OK 74055 • (918) 272-4966

Paoli

Paoli Oklahoma Historical Society • Historical Museum, 29616 E Cty Rd 1520, P.O. Box 98 • Paoli, OK 73074 • (405) 484-7219

Park Hill

Cherokee National Museum • 21192 S Keeler Dr • Park Hill, OK 74451 • (918) 456-6007 • http://www.cherokeeheritage.org

Murrell Home Museum • 19479 E Murrell Home Rd • Park Hill, OK 74451 • (918) 456-2751 • http://www.ok-history.mus.ok.us

Pauls Valley

Beaty Historical Society • Historical Museum, RR1, Box 200AA • Pauls Valley, OK 73075

Pauls Valley Historical Society • Historical Museum, 204 S Santa Fe Ave • Pauls Valley, OK 73075 • http://www.paulsvalley.com/historical.html

Toy & Action Figure Museum • 111 S Chickasaw St, P.O. Box 314 • Pauls Valley, OK 73075 • (405) 238-6300 • http://www.actionfiguremuseum.com

Washinta Valley Museum • Wacker Park, P.O. Box 194 • Pauls Valley, OK 73075 • (405) 238-3048

Pawhuska

Osage County Historical Society • Historical Museum, 700 N Lynn Ave • Pawhuska, OK 74056 • (918) 287-9119 • http://www.osagecohistoricalmuseum.com

Osage Nation of Oklahoma • Tribal Museum, 627 Grandview, P.O. Box 779 • Pawhuska, OK 74056 • (918) 287-1060 • http://www.osagetribe.com

Osage Nation Tribal Museum, Library & Archives • 819 Grandview, P.O. Box 779 • Pawhuska, OK 74056 • (918) 287-5441 • http://www.osagetribe.com/museum/

Pawhuska Genealogical Society • 301 E 6th St, P.O. Box 807 • Pawhuska, OK 74056

Pawhuska Public Library • 1801 Lynn Ave • Pawhuska, OK 74056 • (918) 287-3989

Pawnee

Pawnee Bill Ranch Museum • 1141 Pawnee Bill Rd, P.O. Box 493 • Pawnee, OK 74058 • (918) 762-2513 • http://www.pawneebillswildwestshow.com

Pawnee County Historical Museum • 513 6th St • Pawnee, OK 74058 • (918) 762-4681 • http://www.pawneechs.org

Pawnee County Historical Society • Historical Museum, 513 6th St, P.O. Box 472 • Pawnee, OK 74058 • (918) 762-4681

Pawnee Historical and Cultural Museum • 657 Harrison St • Pawnee, OK 74058-2520 • (918) 762-3706

Pawnee Nation of Oklahoma • P.O. Box 470 • Pawnee, OK 74058-0470 • (918) 762-3624 • http://www.pawneenation.org

Pawnee Tribal Museum • Pawnee County Courthouse, P.O. Box 470 • Pawnee, OK 73058

Oklahoma

Perkins

Dave Sasser Memorial Museum & Old Church Center • 202 E Thomas • Perkins, OK 74059

Iowa Tribe of Oklahoma • RR1, Box 721 • Perkins, OK 74059 • (405) 547-2403 • http://www.cowboy.net/~iowa

Thomas Wilhite Memorial Library • 129 S Main St, P.O. Box 519 • Perkins, OK 74059 • (405) 547-5185 • http://www.t-w.lib.ok.us

Perry

Cherokee Strip Museum • 2617 W Fir St • Perry, OK 73077 • (405) 336-2405 • http://www.cherokee-strip-museum.org

Noble County Genealogical Society • 1409 Country Club Dr, P.O. Box 785 • Perry, OK 73077-0785 • http://www.rootsweb.com/~oknoble/histsoci.htm

Perry Carnegie Library • 302 N 7th St • Perry, OK 73077 • (580) 336-4721

Picher

Picher Mining Museum • 526 N Connel, P.O. Box 224 • Picher, OK 74360 • (918) 673-1192

Ponca City

101 Ranch Old Timers Association • Historical Museum, 1609 Donald Ave • Ponca City, OK 74602 • http://www.101ranchota.com

Marland Estate Museum • 901 Monument Rd • Ponca City, OK 74604 • (800) 422-8340 • http://www.marlandmansion.com

Marland's Grand Home Museum • 1000 E Grand • Ponca City, OK 74601 • (580) 767-0427

Merrick Historical Association • Historical Museum, 3107 Meadow Ln • Ponca City, OK 74604

Pioneer Genealogical Society • 515 E Grand, P.O. Box 1965 • Ponca City, OK 74602-1965 • http://www.brigadoon.com/~nipperb/pgs/piogenhp.htm

Pioneer Woman Museum • 701 Monument • Ponca City, OK 74601 • (580) 765-6108 • http://www.pioneerwomanmuseum.com

Ponca City Cultural Center and Indian Museum • 1000 E Grand • Ponca City, OK 74601 • (508) 767-0427

Ponca City Library • 515 E Grand Ave • Ponca City, OK 74601 • (580) 767-0345

Ponca Tribe of Oklahoma • 300 N 3rd St, P.O. Box 2, White Eagle • Ponca City, OK 74601 • (580) 765-3311 • http://www.poncacity.com/history/ponca_tribe.htm

Standing Bear Park Museum • P.O. Box 111 • Ponca City, OK 74602 • (580) 762-1514 • http://www.standingbearpark.com

Poteau

Buckley Public Library • 408 Dewey Ave • Poteau, OK 74953 • (918) 647-3833 • http://www.buckley.lib.ok.us

Eastern Oklahoma Historical Society • Historical Museum, Rt 1, Box 1060 • Poteau, OK 74953 • (918) 647-9579

Poteau Valley Genealogical Society • c/o Buckley Public Library, 408 Dewey Ave, P.O. Box 1031 • Poteau, OK 74953 • (918) 647-3833

Robert S Kerr Museum • 23009 Kerr Mansion Rd, Route 1, Box 1060 • Poteau, OK 74953 • (918) 647-9579

Prague

Prague Historical Society • Historical Museum, 1008 N Broadway • Prague, OK 74864

Pryor

Coo-Y-Yah County Museum • 847 Hwy 69 S & 8th St, P.O. Box 696 • Pryor, OK 74361

Pryor Public Library • 505 E Graham • Pryor, OK 74361 • (918) 825-0777

Purcell

McClain County Historical and Genealogical Society • Historical Museum, 203 W Washington St • Purcell, OK 73080 • (405) 527-5894 • http://www.mcclaincountymuseum.org

Quapaw

Quapaw Tribe of Oklahoma • P.O. Box 765 • Quapaw, OK 74363 • (918) 542-1853 • http://eighttribes.org/quapaw

Ralston

White Hair Memorial Museum • Hwy 20, P.O. Box 185 • Ralston, OK 74650 • (918) 538-2417

Ramona

Caney Valley Historical Society • Historical Museum, Main St • Ramona, OK 74061

Red Rock

Otoe-Missouri Tribe • P.O. Box 68 • Red Rock, OK 74651 • (405) 723-4466

Ripley

Kirk Auto Museum • 6404 S Ripley Rd • Ripley, OK 74062 • (918) 372-4537

Washington Irving Trail Museum • 3918 S Mehan Rd • Ripley, OK 74062 • (405) 624-9130

Rush Springs

Hampton House Museum • Blakely & Hampton • Rush Springs, OK 73082

Salina

Chouteau Memorial Museum • 420 E Ferry • Salina, OK 74365 • (918) 434-2224

Sallisaw

Dwight Presbyterian Mission Museum • Rt 2, Box 71 • Sallisaw, OK 74955

Fourteen Flags Museum • Rt 1, Box 103A • Sallisaw, OK 74955 • http://www.exploresouthernhistory.com/sallisawmuseum

Sequoyah Cabin Museum • Rt 1, Box 141 • Sallisaw, OK 74955 • (918) 775-2413

Sequoyah Genealogical Society • 101 E Cherokee • Sallisaw, OK 74955

Stanley Tubbs Memorial Library • 101 E Cherokee • Sallisaw, OK 74955 • (918) 775-4481

Sand Springs

Sand Springs Cultural and Historical Museum • 9 E Broadway • Sand Springs, OK 74063 • (918) 246-2509 • http://www.sandspringsmuseum.org

Sapulpa

Bartlett-Carnegie Sapulpa Public Library • 27 W Dewey • Sapulpa, OK 74066 • (918) 224-5624

Sapulpa Genealogical Association • P.O. Box 2244 • Sapulpa, OK 74066

Sapulpa Historical Society • Historical Museum, 100 E Lee, P.O. Box 278 • Sapulpa, OK 74067 • (918) 224-4871 • http://www.sapulpahistoricalsociety.com

Sayre

RS&K Railroad Museum • P.O. Box 321 • Sayre, OK 73662

Sayre Historical Society • Shortgrass Country Museum, 106 E Poplar Ave • Sayre, OK 73662 • (580) 928-5757

Sayre Public Library • 113 E Poplar • Sayre, OK 73662-2928 • (580) 928-2641 • http://www.sayre.lib.ok.us

Seminole

Hargis Tool Museum • 1717 SH 9 W • Seminole, OK 74868

Seminole Historical Society • Historical Museum, P.O. Box 202 • Seminole, OK 74818 • (405) 382-1500 • http://www.seminoleoklahoma.com/museum/

Seminole Public Library • 424 N Main St • Seminole, OK 74868 • (405) 382-4221 • http://www.ci.seminole.ok.us/splibrary/library.html

Shattuck

American Historical Society of Germans from Russia, Golden Spread Chapter • P.O. Box 307 • Shattuck, OK 73858 • (580) 938-2139 • http://www.ahsgr.org/Chapters/golden_spread_chapter.htm

Shattuck Public Library • 101 S Main St, P.O. Box 129 • Shattuck, OK 73858-0129 • (580) 938-5104

Shattuck Windmill Museum & Park • P.O. Box 227 • Shattuck, OK 73858 • (580) 938-5146

Shawnee

Absentee-Shawnee Tribe of Oklahoma • 2025 S Gordon Cooper, P.O. Box 1747 • Shawnee, OK 74802 • (405) 275-4030 • http://www.astribe.com

Citizen Band Potawatomi Indians • Tribal Museum, 1901 S Gordon Cooper Dr • Shawnee, OK 74801 • (405) 275-3119 • http://www.potawatomi.org

Classic & Antique Auto Museum • P.O. Box 456 • Shawnee, OK 74802

Mabee Library & University Library • Oklahoma Baptist University, 500 W University, OBU Box 61310 • Shawnee, OK 74804-2504 • (405) 878-2259 • http://www.okbu.edu/library/

Pottawatomi Tribal Museum • 1901 S Grodon Cooper Dr • Shawnee, OK 74801

Pottawatomie County Genealogical Society • 241 Masonic Bldg, 9th & Bell Sts, P.O. Box 3256 • Shawnee, OK 74801 • (405) 273-5695

Santa Fe Depot Museum • P.O. Box 114 • Shawnee, OK 74802 • http://www.santafedepotmuseum.org

Shawnee Mission Church Museum • Highland & Broadway • Shawnee, OK 74801 • http://www.rootsweb.ancestry.com/~okpcgc/towns/shawnee_mission.html

Skiatook

Shatook Museum • 115 S Broadway • Skiatook, OK 74017 • (918) 256-7558 • http://skiatook.com/skiatook/museum.html

Southard

US Gypsum Museum • P.O. Box 3 • Southard, OK 73770

Spencer

Spencer Historical Society • Historical Museum, 8622 NE 50th St, P.O. Box 394 • Spencer, OK 73084 • (405) 771-4576

Spencer Museum • 8622 NE 50th St, P.O. Box 394 • Spencer, OK 73084 • (405) 771-4576

Spiro

Spiro Historical Society • Historical Museum, 18154 1st St, P.O. Box 84 • Spiro, OK 74959 • (918) 962-2062 • http://www.okhistory.org/outreach/museums/spiromounds.html

Stigler

Haskell County Genealogy Society • 408 NE 6th St, P.O. Box 481 • Stigler, OK 74462 • (918) 967-8681 • http://www.rootsweb.com/~okhaskel/hasksoc.htm

Stillwater

Fred Pfeiffer Museum • Payne County Agr Ctr • Stillwater, OK 74074

National Wrestling Hall of Fame • 405 W Hall of Fame Ave • Stillwater, OK 74075

Oklahoma State University Library • general delivery • Stillwater, OK 74078 • (405) 744-9729 • http://www.library.okstate.edu/scuahp.htm

Payne County Genealogical Society • c/o Stillwater Public Library, 1107 S Duck, P.O. Box 2708 • Stillwater, OK 74076-2708 • (405) 372-3633 • http://www.pcgsok.org

Payne County Historical Society • P.O. Box 194 • Stillwater, OK 74074

Sheerar Museum • 702 S Duncan • Stillwater, OK 74074 • (405) 377-0359 • http://www.sheerarmuseum.org

Stillwater Airport Memorial Museum • 2020 W Airport Rd • Stillwater, OK 74075 • (405) 372-7881

Stillwater Public Library • 1107 S Duck • Stillwater, OK 74074 • (405) 372-3633 • http://www.stillwater.lib.ok.us

Stilwell

Adair County Historical and Genealogical Society • Historical Museum, Rt 2, Box 1710 • Stilwell, OK 74960

Stratford

Stratford Roots Genealogical Society • c/o Chandler-Watts Library, 321 N Oak, P.O. Box 696 • Stratford, OK 74872 • (405) 759-2684

Stroud

Sac and Fox Nation • Route 2, Box 246 • Stroud, OK 74079 • (918) 968-3526 • http://www.cowboy.net/native/sacnfox.html

Sac and Fox National Public Library • Route 2, Box 246 • Stroud, OK 74079 • (918) 968-3526

Stroud Public Library • 301 W 7th St, P.O. Box 599 • Stroud, OK 74079-0599 • (918) 968-2567

Sulphur

Arbuckle Historical Society • Murray County Museum, 402 W Muskogee • Sulphur, OK 73086 • (580) 622-5593 • http://www.ahsmc.org

Swink

Apuckshunubbee District Chief's House Museum • Heritage Rd, P.O. Box 165 • Swink, OK 74761 • (405) 873-2301

Choctaw Chief's House Museum • US 70 & Fort Towson, P.O. Box 165 • Swink, OK 74761 • (405) 873-2301

Choctaw County Genealogical Society • P.O. Box 55 • Swink, OK 74761 • (580) 873-2301

Tahlequah

Adams Corner Rural Village Museum • US 62, P.O. Box 515 • Tahlequah, OK 74465 • (918) 456-6007

Cherokee Heritage Museum • P.O. Box 948 • Tahlequah, OK 74465 • http://www.cherokee.org

Cherokee Nation of Oklahoma • P.O. Box 948 • Tahlequah, OK 74465-0948 • (918) 456-6485 • http://www.cherokee.org

Cherokee National Historical Society • Tsa-la-gi Museum, Hwy 62, P.O. Box 515 • Tahlequah, OK 74465-0515 • (918) 456-6007 • http://www.cherokeeheritage.org

Indian Territory Genealogical and Historical Society • Northeastern Oklahoma State Univ Library, 711 N Grand • Tahlequah, OK 74464 • (918) 456-5511

John Vaughan Library - Special Collections • Northeastern Oklahoma State Univ, 711 N Grand Ave • Tahlequah, OK 74464-2333 • (918) 456-5511 • http://library.nsuok.edu

Thompson House Museum • 300 S College Ave • Tahlequah, OK 74464 • (918) 456-1595

United Keetoowah Band of Cherokee Indians • 2450 S Muskogee Ave, P.O. Box 746 • Tahlequah, OK 74465-0746 • (918) 456-5491 • http://www.unitedkeetoowahband.org

Oklahoma

Taloga
Jail House Museum • P.O. Box 303 • Taloga, OK 73667 • (580) 328-5485

Terral
Terral Fleetwood Historical Society • P.O. Box 127 • Terral, OK 73569

Tishomingo
Bank of the Chickasaw National Museum • 100 S Capital Ave • Tishomingo, OK 73460

Chickasaw Council House Museum • Court House Sq, P.O. Box 717 • Tishomingo, OK 73460 • (405) 371-3351 • http://www.chickasaw.net

Johnston County Historical Society • Historical Museum, 413 W Main St, P.O. Box 804 • Tishomingo, OK 73460 • (580) 371-0254 • http://www.johnsoncounty.8m.com

Murray State College Library • 1 Murray Campus St LS 101 • Tishomingo, OK 73460 • (580) 371-2371

Tonkawa
Eleanor Hays Museum • Northern Oklahoma College, 1220 E Grand • Tonkawa, OK 74653

Tonkawa Historical Museum • P.O. Box 363 • Tonkawa, OK 74653

Tonkawa Public Library • 216 N 7th • Tonkawa, OK 74653 • (580) 628-3366

Tonkawa Tribal Museum • P.O. Box 70 • Tonkawa, OK 74653

Tonkawa Tribe of Oklahoma • P.O. Box 70 • Tonkawa, OK 74653-0070 • (405) 628-2561 • http://members.tripod.com/tonkawa/main.html

Vineyard Library • Northern Oklahoma College, 1220 E Grand Ave, P.O. Box 310 • Tonkawa, OK 74653-0310 • (580) 628-6250 • http://www.north-ok.edu

Tulsa
Dr B W McLean Home & Office Museum • 2623 W 68th Pl • Tulsa, OK 74132

Gilcrease Museum • 1400 Gilcrease Museum Rd • Tulsa, OK 74127-2100 • (918) 596-2700 • http://www.gilcrease.org

Ida Dennie Willis Museum of Miniatures, Dolls and Toys • 628 N Country Club Dr • Tulsa, OK 74127 • (918) 586-6654 • http://www.tulsaweb.com/doll.htm

International Linen Registry Museum • 4107 S Yale, P.O. Box 50516 • Tulsa, OK 74135 • (918) 622-5223

Jewish Genealogical Society of Tulsa • Sherwin Miller Museum of Jewish History, 2021 E 71st St • Tulsa, OK 74136 • (918) 492-1818 • http://jewishmuseum.net

Mac's Antique Car Museum • 1319 E 4th St, P.O. Box 3185 • Tulsa, OK 74101 • (918) 583-3108

McFarlin Library • Univ of Tulsa, 2933 E 6th St • Tulsa, OK 74104-3123 • (918) 631-2880 • http://www.lib.utulsa.edu

Oklahoma Confederate Archives • P.O. Box 691921 • Tulsa, OK 74153-0851

Oklahoma Jazz Hall of Fame • 111 E 1st St • Tulsa, OK 74103 • (918) 281-8600 • http://okjazz.org

Rudisill North Regional Library • 1520 N Hartford • Tulsa, OK 74106 • (918) 596-7280

Sons of the American Revolution, Oklahoma Society • 2832 E 87th St • Tulsa, OK 74137-2500 • http://okssar.comoj.com/home.htm

Southwest Tulsa Historical Society • Historical Museum, 4981 S Union Ave • Tulsa, OK 74107 • (918) 445-9260 • http://www.southwesttulsa.org

Tulsa Air and Space Museum • 3624 N 74th E Ave • Tulsa, OK 74115 • (918) 834-9900 • http://www.tulsaairandspacemuseum.com

Tulsa Central Library • 400 Civic Center • Tulsa, OK 74103 • (918) 596-7977 • http://www.tulsalibrary.org

Tulsa Genealogical Society • 9072 E 31st St, P.O. Box 585 • Tulsa, OK 74101-0585 • (918) 627-4224 • http://www.rootsweb.com/~oktgs/

Tulsa Historical Society • Historical Museum, P.O. Box 521145 • Tulsa, OK 74152 • (918) 712-9484 • http://www.tulsahistory.org

Tuskahoma
Choctaw Nation Museum • HC 64, Box 3270 • Tuskahoma, OK 74574 • (580) 931-6312 • http://www.choctawnationculture.com

Vinita
Craig County Oklahoma Genealogical Society • c/o Vinita Public Library, 215 W Illinois, P.O. Box 484 • Vinita, OK 74301 • (918) 256-2115

Daughters of the American Revolution, Abraham Coryelle Chapter • RR 3 • Vinita, OK 74301

Eastern Trails Museum • 215 W Illinois, P.O. Box 77 • Vinita, OK 74301 • (918) 256-2115

Northeast Oklahoma Genealogical Society • P.O. Box 484 • Vinita, OK 74301

Vinita Public Library • Maurice Haynes Memorial Bldg, 211 W Illinois • Vinita, OK 74301 • (918) 256-2115

Vinnie Ream Cultural Center • 1110 W Canadian, P.O. Box 594 • Vinita, OK 74301 • (918) 256-4911 • http://www.vinnieream.net

Wagoner
City of Wagoner Historical Museum • 231 Church St • Wagoner, OK 74467 • (918) 485-9111 • http://www.wagonercity.com/museum.html

Oklahoma Historic Fashions Museum • 810 N State • Wagoner, OK 74467

Original Historic Fashion Museum & Research Center • 1109 SE 7th St • Wagoner, OK 74467

Three Forks Genealogical Society • 102 1/2 S State St • Wagoner, OK 74467 • (918) 485-2370

Walters
Cotton County Museum • 116 N Broadway, P.O. Box 224 • Walters, OK 73572 • (580) 875-3335

Walters Depot Museum • P.O. Box 364 • Walters, OK 73572

Walters Public Library • 202 N Broadway St • Walters, OK 73572-1226 • (580) 875-2006

Warner
Wallis Museum • Connors State College, P.O. Box 571 • Warner, OK 74469 • (918) 463-2931 • http://www.connorstate.edu

Watonga
Cheyenne and Arapahoe Tribal Museum and Archives • Route 1, Box 138 • Watonga, OK 73772 • (580) 886-3479

T B Ferguson Home Museum • 519 N Weigel • Watonga, OK 73772 • (580) 623-5069 • http://www.watonga.com/ferguson.htm

Watonga Public Library • 301 N Prouty • Watonga, OK 73772 • (580) 623-7748 • http://www.watonga.lib.ok.us

Waurika
Chisholm Trail Historical Museum • US 81 & OK 70, P.O. Box 262 • Waurika, OK 73572 • (580) 228-2166

Rock Island Depot Museum • 98 Meridian • Waurika, OK 73573 • (580) 228-3274

Waurika Library • 98 Meridian St • Waurika, OK 73573 • (580) 228-3274

Waynoka

Waynoka Historical Society • 200 S Cleveland St, P.O. Box 193 • Waynoka, OK 73860 • (580) 824-1886 • http://www.waynoka.org/museum.php

Waynoka Public Library • 113 E Cecil St • Waynoka, OK 73860 • (580) 824-6181 • http://www.waynoka.pl.ok.pls.net

Weatherford

Stafford Air and Space Museum • 300 E Logan Rd, P.O. Box 569 • Weatherford, OK 73096 • (580) 772-5871 • http://www.staffordairandspacemuseum.com

Weatherford Public Library • 219 E Franklin • Weatherford, OK 73096-5134 • (580) 772-3591

Western Plains-Weatherford Genealogical Society • c/o Weatherford Public Library, 219 E Franklin, P.O. Box 1672 • Weatherford, OK 73096-1672 • (580) 772-3591

Webbers Falls

Cherokee Dixieland Historical Society • Historical Museum, P.O. Box 359 • Webbers Falls, OK 74470 • (918) 464-2728 • http://www.cherokeeheritage.org

Webbers Falls Historical Society • Historical Museum, P.O. Box 5 • Webbers Falls, OK 74470 • (918) 464-2728 • http://www.webbersfallsmuseum.org

Welling

Cherokee National Museum • Tsa-La-Gi • Welling, OK 74471 • (918) 456-6195

Westville

Goingsnake District Heritage Association • c/o John F Henderson Public Library, 116 N Williams, P.O. Box 180 • Westville, OK 74965 • (918) 723-5002

John F Henderson Public Library • 116 N Williams, P.O. Box 580 • Westville, OK 74965 • (918) 723-5002 • http://www.eodls.lib.ok.us

Wetumka

Kialegee Tribal Town • 108 N Main, P.O. Box 332 • Wetumka, OK 74883 • (405) 452-3262 • http://www.kialegee.org

Wewoka

Seminole Nation of Oklahoma • Seminole Nation Museum, 524 S Wewoka Ave, P.O. Box 1498 • Wewoka, OK 74884 • (405) 257-5580 • http://www.wewoka.com/seminole.htm

Seminole National Historical Society • Museum Library, 524 S Wewoka, P.O. Box 1532 • Wewoka, OK 74884-1532 • (405) 257-5580

Wilburton

Kiamichi Genealogical Society • Route 3, Box 53 • Wilburton, OK 74578

Latimer County Genealogical and Historical Society • 101 W Durant • Wilburton, OK 74578

Latimer County Public Library • 301 W Ada Ave, P.O. Box 126 • Wilburton, OK 74578 • (918) 465-3751 • http://www.latimer.lib.ok.us

Lutie Coal Miners Museum • 2307 E Main St • Wilburton, OK 74578 • (918) 465-2216

Wilson

Wilson Historical Museum • 1270 8th St • Wilson, OK 73463 • (580) 668-2505 • http://www.wilsonhistoricalmuseum.org

Woodward

Northwest Oklahoma Genealogical Society • c/o Woodward Public Library, 1508 Main Ave, P.O. Box 834 • Woodward, OK 73801-0834 • (580) 256-8916

Plains Indians and Pioneer Museum • 2009 Williams Ave • Woodward, OK 73801 • (580) 256-6136 • http://www.plainsindianandpioneermuseum.org

Woodward Public Library • 1500 Main St • Woodward, OK 73801 • (580) 254-8544

Wyandotte

Wyandotte of Oklahoma • P.O. Box 250 • Wyandotte, OK 74370 • (918) 678-2297 • http://eighttribes.org/wyandotte

Wynnewood

Eskridge Hotel Museum • 114 E Robert S Kerr Blvd • Wynnewood, OK 73098 • (405) 238-4567

Moore-Settle Historic Home Museum • 508 E Cherokee • Wynnewood, OK 73098

Wynnewood Historical Society • Historical Museum, P.O. Box 515 • Wynnewood, OK 73098 • (405) 238-4567

Yale

Jim Thorpe House Museum • 706 E Boston Ave • Yale, OK 74085 • (918) 387-2815

Yukon

Chisholm Trail Festival Museum • P.O. Box 850021 • Yukon, OK 73085

Oklahoma Czechs • 5th & Cedar, P.O. Box 850211 • Yukon, OK 73085 • (405) 354-7573

Yukon Historical Society • Historical Museum, 601 Oak • Yukon, OK 73099

Yukon's Best Railroad Museum • 3rd & Main • Yukon, OK 73099 • (405) 354-5079

OREGON

Agness
Agness Community Library • 03509 Cougar Lake, P.O. Box 33 • Agness, OR 978406-0033 • (541) 247-6323

Albany
Albany Public Library • 1390 Waverly Dr SE • Albany, OR 97322 • (541) 917-7581 • http://www.ci.albany.or.us

Albany Regional Museum • 136 Lyon St SW • Albany, OR 97321 • (541) 967-7122 • http://www.armuseum.com

Linn County Historical Society • Shedd Museum, 1132 30th Pl SW • Albany, OR 97321 • (541) 926-4680

Linn Genealogical Society • c/o Albany Public Library, 1390 Waverly Dr SE, P.O. Box 1222 • Albany, OR 97321 • (541) 917-7581

Linn Genealogical Society • 300 4th Ave SW • Albany, OR 97321 • (541) 791-1618

Linn-Benton Community College Library • 6500 SW Pacific Blvd • Albany, OR 97321-3799 • (541) 917-4638 • http://www.linnbenton.edu

Monteith House Museum • 518 2nd Ave, P.O. Box 965 • Albany, OR 97321 • (541) 928-0911 • http://albanyvisitors.com/historic-albany/museums/monteith-house/

Monteith Society • 518 2nd Ave SW • Albany, OR 97321-2239

Ashland
Southern Oregon University Library • 1250 Siskiyou Blvd • Ashland, OR 97520-5076 • (541) 552-6442 • http://www.sou.edu/library

Astoria
Astoria Heritage Association • Heritage Museum, 1618 Exchange St, P.O. Box 88 • Astoria, OR 97103-3615 • (503) 338-4849 • http://www.clatsophistoricalsociety.org

Astoria Public Library • 450 10th St • Astoria, OR 97103 • (503) 325-7323

Capt George Flavel House Museum • 441 8th St, P.O. Box 88 • Astoria, OR 97103 • (503) 325-2203 • http://www.cumtux.org

Clatsop Community College Library • 1680 Lexington • Astoria, OR 97103 • (503) 338-2462 • http://library.clatsop.cc.or.us

Clatsop County Genealogical Society • c/o Astoria Public Library, 450 10th St • Astoria, OR 97103 • (503) 325-7323

Clatsop County Historical Society • Heritage Museum, 1618 Exchange St • Astoria, OR 97103-3615 • (503) 325-2203

Columbia River Maritime Museum • 1792 Marine Dr • Astoria, OR 97103 • (503) 325-2323 • http://www.crmm.org

Fort Clatsop National Memorial Museum • 92343 Fort Clatsop Rd • Astoria, OR 97103 • (503) 861-2471 • http://www.nps.gov/focl

Uppertown Firefighters Museum • 2968 Marine Dr, P.O. Box 88 • Astoria, OR 97103 • (503) 325-0920 • http://www.cumtux.org

Aurora
Aurora Colony Historical Society • Old Aurora Colony Museum, 15008 2nd St, P.O. Box 202 • Aurora, OR 97002 • (503) 678-5754 • http://www.auroracolony.org

Baker City
Adler House Museum • 2305 Main St • Baker City, OR 97814 • (541) 523-9308 • http://www.bakerheritagemuseum.com/adler_house.htm

Baker County Genealogy Group • c/o Baker County Public Library, 2400 Resort St • Baker City, OR 97814 • (541) 523-6419

Baker County Public Library • 2400 Resort St • Baker City, OR 97814 • (541) 523-6419

National Historic Oregon Trail Museum • 22267 Hwy 86, P.O. Box 987 • Baker City, OR 97814 • (541) 523-1843 • http://oregontrail.blm.gov

Oregon Trail Regional Museum • 2480 Grove St • Baker City, OR 97814 • (541) 523-9308 • http://www.bakercounty.org

Bandon
Bandon Historical Society • Coquille River Museum, 270 Fillmore St, P.O. Box 737 • Bandon, OR 97411 • (541) 347-2164

Bandon Public Library • City Hall, P.O. Box 128 • Bandon, OR 97411-0128 • (541) 347-3221 • http://www.bandonbiblio.org

Beaverton
Beaverton City Library • 12375 SW 5th St • Beaverton, OR 97005-2883 • (503) 644-2197 • http://www.beavertonlibrary.org

Bend
Belgian American Heritage Association • 1008 NE Marion Pl • Bend, OR 97701-3727 • (541) 389-3678

Bend Genealogical Society • P.O. Box 8254 • Bend, OR 97708

Deschutes County Historical and Genealogical Society • Historical Museum, 129 NW Idaho St, P.O. Box 5252 • Bend, OR 97708 • (541) 389-1813 • http://www.deschuteshistory.org

Deschutes County Library • 507 NW Wall St • Bend, OR 97701-2698 • (541) 617-7045 • http://www.dpls.lib.or.us

High Desert Museum • 59800 S Hwy 97 • Bend, OR 97702-7963 • (541) 382-4754 • http://www.highdesertmuseum.org

Boardman
Oregon Trail Library • P.O. Box 107 • Boardman, OR 97818-0107 • (541) 481-2665

Boring
Oregon Historic Cemeteries Association • P.O. Box 802 • Boring, OR 97009-0802 • (503) 658-4255

Brandon
Brandon Historical Society • Historical Museum, 270 Fillmore, P.O. Box 737 • Brandon, OR 97411 • (541) 347-2164 • http://www.brandonhistoricalmuseum.org

Coquille River Lighthouse Museum • Hwy 101, P.O. Box 569 • Brandon, OR 97411 • (541) 347-2209 • http://www.brandonworld.com/thelight

Brookings
Blake House Museum • 15461 Museum Rd • Brookings, OR 97415 • (541) 469-6651

Chetco Community Public Library • 420 Alder St • Brookings, OR 97415 • (541) 469-7738 • http://www.chetcolibrary.org

Chetco Valley Historical Society • Chetco Valley Museum, 15461 Museum Rd • Brookings, OR 97415-9519 • (541) 469-2753 • http://www.curryhistory.com/curry-county-museums/26-chetco-valley-museum

Brooks
Antique Powerland Museum • 3995 Brooklake Rd NE • Brooks, OR 97303 • (503) 393-2424 • http://www.antiquepowerland.com

Brooks Depot Museum • 3995 Brooklake Rd, P.O. Box 9265 • Brooks, OR 97305 • (503) 390-0698

Pacific Northwest Truck Museum • 3995 Brooklake Rd NE, P.O. Box 9087 • Brooks, OR 97305 • (503) 312-0039 • http://www.pacificnwtruckmuseum.org

Brownsville
Brownsville Community Library • 146 Spalding, P.O. Box 68 • Brownsville, OR 97327-0068 • (541) 466-5454

Linn County Historical Museum • 101 Park Ave, P.O. Box 607 • Brownsville, OR 97327 • (541) 466-3390

Brownsville, cont.

Linn County Historical Society • Historical Museum, 101 Park Ave, P.O. Box 607 • Brownsville, OR 97327 • (541) 466-3070 • http://www.lchm-friends.peak.org

Moyer House Museum • 204 N Main St, P.O. Box 607 • Brownsville, OR 97327 • (541) 466-3390

Burns

Burns Paiute Tribe • 100 Pasigo St • Burns, OR 97720 • (503) 573-2088 • http://www.burnspaiute-nsn.gov

Harney County Genealogy Society • 426 E Jefferson • Burns, OR 97720

Harney County Historical Society • Historical Museum, 18 West D Street, P.O. Box 388 • Burns, OR 97720 • (541) 573-5618 • http://www.burnsmuseum.com

Harney County Library • 80 West D Street • Burns, OR 97720-1299 • (541) 573-6670 • http://www.co.harney.or.us

Butte Falls

Big Butte Historical Society • Bill Edmondson Memorial Museum, 432 Pine St, P.O. Box 379 • Butte Falls, OR 97522 • (541) 865-3332

Railroad Museum • P.O. Box 379 • Butte Falls, OR 97522

Canby

Canby Heritage Association • Canby Depot Museum, 888 NE 4th Ave, P.O. Box 160 • Canby, OR 97013-2300 • (503) 266-6712 • http://www.canbyhistoricalsociety.org

Cannon Beach

Cannon Beach Historical Society • 1387 S Spruce • Cannon Beach, OR 97110 • (503) 436-9301

Canyon City

Grant County Genealogical Society • 101 S Canyon Blvd, P.O. Box 416 • Canyon City, OR 97820 • (541) 575-0545

Grant County Historical Museum • 101 S Canyon City Blvd, P.O. Box 464 • Canyon City, OR 97820 • (541) 575-0362 • http://www.gchistoricalmuseum.com

Canyonville

South Umpqua Historical Society • 421 W 5th St • Canyonville, OR 97417

South Umpqua Pioneer-Indian Museum • 421 W 5th St, P.O. Box 1112 • Canyonville, OR 97417 • (541) 839-4845 • http://www.southumpquapioneers.org

Cascade Locks

Cascade Locks Historical Museum • 355 WaNaPa St, P.O. Box 307 • Cascade Locks, OR 97014 • (541) 374-8619 • http://www.portofcascadelocks.org/museum.htm

Cascade Locks Historical Society • 1 NW Portage Rd • Cascade Locks, OR 97014

Central Point

Crater Rock Museum • 2002 Scenic Ave, P.O. Box 3999 • Central Point, OR 97502 • (541) 664-6081 • http://www.craterrock.com

Phoenix Historical Society • 1200 Cherry St, Unit 18 • Central Point, OR 97502 • (541) 512-0614

Chiloquin

Collier Memorial State Park Logging Museum • 46000 Hwy 97 N • Chiloquin, OR 97624 • (541) 783-2471 • http://www.collierloggingmuseum.org

Klamath General Council • P.O. Box 436 • Chiloquin, OR 97624 • (503) 783-2219 • http://www.klamathtribes.org

Clackamas

Oregon Military Museum • Camp Withycombe, 10101 SE Clackamas Rd, Bldg 6232 • Clackamas, OR 97015 • (503) 557-5359 • http://www.swiftview.com/~ormilmuseum

Clatskanie

Clatskanie Library District • 11 Lillich St, P.O. Box 577 • Clatskanie, OR 97016-0577 • (503) 728-3732 • http://www.clatskanie.com

Flippin House Museum • 620 Tichenor St, P.O. Box 383 • Clatskanie, OR 97016 • (503) 728-3608 • http://www.twrps.com/ccor/castle.html

Columbia City

Charles Green Caples House Museum • 1915 1st St, P.O. Box 263 • Columbia City, OR 97018 • (503) 397-5390 • http://capleshouse.com

Condon

Gilliam County Historical Society • Depot Museum, 221 S Oregon St, P.O. Box 377 • Condon, OR 97823 • (541) 384-4233

Coos Bay

Confederated Tribes of Coos, Lower Umpqua and Siuslaw Indians • 455 S 4th St • Coos Bay, OR 97420-1570 • (503) 267-5454 • http://www.ctclusi.org

Coos Bay Public Library • 525 Anderson St • Coos Bay, OR 97420-1678 • (541) 269-1101 • http://www.cooslibraries.org

Marshfield Sun Printing Museum • P.O. Box 783 • Coos Bay, OR 97420

Southwestern Oregon Community College Library • 1988 Newmark • Coos Bay, OR 97420 • (541) 888-7448 • http://www.socc.edu/library/

Corvallis

Benton County Genealogical Society • P.O. Box 1511 • Corvallis, OR 97330 • (541) 757-2316 • http://www.rootsweb.com/~orbentgs

Corvallis-Benton County Public Library • 645 NW Monroe Ave • Corvallis, OR 97330 • (541) 757-6793 • http://www.ci.corvallis.or.us/library

Oregon State University Archives • 94 Kerr Administration Bldg • Corvallis, OR 97331-2103 • (541) 737-2165 • http://www.orst.edu/Dept/archives

Valley Library • Oregon State University, 121 The Valley Library • Corvallis, OR 97331-4501 • (541) 737-3411 • http://www.osulibrary.oregonstate.edu

Cottage Grove

Cottage Grove Genealogical Society • 207 North H Street, P.O. Box 388 • Cottage Grove, OR 97424 • (541) 942-2369 • http://www.rootsweb.com/~orlane/links/cggs.htm

Cottage Grove Museum • 147 H Street, P.O. Box 142 • Cottage Grove, OR 97424 • (541) 767-0600 • http://www.cottagegrove.net/history/museum/

Cottage Grove Public Library • 700 Gibbs Ave • Cottage Grove, OR 97424-1640 • (541) 942-3828 • http://library.cottagegrove.org

Oregon Aviation Historical Society • general delivery • Cottage Grove, OR 97424 • (541) 767-0244

Creswell

Creswell Historical Society • Historical Museum, 55 N 5th St, P.O. Box 414 • Creswell, OR 97426 • (541) 895-5464

Dallas

Dallas Public Library • 950 Main St • Dallas, OR 97338-2802 • (503) 623-2633 • http://www.ci.dallas.or.us/library/library.htm

Kutschurgan Village Project • 724 SW Hayter St • Dallas, OR 97338-1845 • (503) 623-5529

Polk County Genealogical Society • 535 SE Ash St • Dallas, OR 97338 • (503) 623-3467

Depoe Bay
Oregon Coast Sports Museum • 110 NE Hwy 101, P.O. Box 166 • Depoe Bay, OR 97341

Dufur
Dufur Historical Society • general delivery • Dufur, OR 97021 • (541) 467-2207

Living History Museum • 40 Main St, P.O. Box 462 • Dafur, OR 97021 • (541) 467-2205

Eagle Creek
Philip Foster Farm Museum • 229912 SE Hwy 211 • Eagle Creek, OR 97022 • (503) 637-6324 • http://philipfosterfarm.com

Eagle Point
Big Butte Historical Society • general delivery • Eagle Point, OR 97524 • (541) 865-3332

Eagle Point Historical Society • Historical Museum, 202 N Royal Ave, P.O. Box 201 • Eagle Point, OR 97524 • (541) 826-4212 • http://www.cityofeaglepoint.org

Lake Creek Historical Society • 1739 S Fork Little Butte Cr Rd • Eagle Point, OR 97524-9435 • (541) 826-1513

Echo
Chinese House Railroad Museum • 20 S Bonanza, P.O. Box 426 • Echo, OR 97826 • (541) 376-8411

Echo Historical Museum • P.O. Box 205 • Echo, OR 97826

Fort Henrietta Interpretive Park • 10 W Main, P.O. Box 9 • Echo, OR 97826 • (541) 376-8461 • http://www.echo-oregon.com

Saint Peter's Catholic Church Museum • 230 W Bridge, P.O. Box 426 • Echo, OR 97826 • (541) 376-8411 • http://www.echo-oregon.com

Elgin
Elgin Historical Society • Historical Museum, 360 Park St, P.O. Box 754 • Elgin, OR 97827

Elgin Public Library • 260 N 10th, P.O. Box 67 • Elgin, OR 97827-0067 • (541) 437-2860

Enterprise
Enterprise Public Library • 101 NE 1st St • Enterprise, OR 97828-1173 • (541) 426-3906

Wallowa County Library • 207 NW Logan • Enterprise, OR 97828-0186 • (541) 426-3969 • http://www.co.wallowa.or.us/library/

Estacada
Estacada Area Historical Museum • 585 SE 4th Ave, P.O. Box 887 • Estacada, OR 97023

Estacada Public Library • 475 SE Main, P.O. Box 609 • Estacada, OR 97023-0609 • (503) 630-8273 • http://www.estacada.lib.or.us

Eugene
Eugene Historical Society • 1574 Coburg Rd #545 • Eugene, OR 97401

Eugene Oregon Jewish Genealogy Study Group • 815 Park Terr • Eugene, OR 97404-3081 • (541) 345-8129 • http://www.mwfam.com/eugenegen.html

Eugene Public Library • 100 W 10th Ave • Eugene, OR 97401 • (541) 682-5450 • http://www.ci.eugene.or.us/library/

Historical Oregon Information Services • 2549 Cubit St • Eugene, OR 97402

Knight Library • Univ of Oregon, 1501 Kincaid St • Eugene, OR 97401-4540 • (541) 346-1818 • http://www.libweb.uoregon.edu

Lane County Historical Society • Historical Museum, 740 W 13th Ave, P.O. Box 11532 • Eugene, OR 97440-3732 • (541) 682-4242 • http://www.lanecountyhistoricalsociety.org

Oregon Air & Space Museum • 90377 Boeing Dr • Eugene, OR 97402 • (541) 461-1101 • http://www.oasm.org

Oregon Genealogical Society • 223 A Street, P.O. Box 10306 • Eugene, OR 97440-2306 • (541) 746-7924 • http://www.rootsweb.com/~genepool/ogsinfo.htm

Shelton-McMurphey-Johnson House Museum • 303 Williamette St • Eugene, OR 97401 • (541) 484-0808 • http://www.smjhouse.org

Wayne Morse Ranch Park Museum • 595 Crest Dr • Eugene, OR 97405

Fairview
Fairview-Rockwood-Wilkes Historical Society • P.O. Box 946 • Fairview, OR 97024

Florence
Dolly Wares Doll Museum • 3620 Hwy 101 • Florence, OR 97439

Siuslaw Genealogical Society • c/o Siuslaw Public Library, 1460 9th St, P.O. Box 1540 • Florence, OR 97439 • (541) 997-3132

Siuslaw Pioneer Museum • 278 Maple St, P.O. Box 2637 • Florence, OR 97439 • (541) 997-3037 • http://www.siuslawpioneermuseum.com

Siuslaw Public Library • 1460 9th St, P.O. Box A • Florence, OR 97439 • (541) 997-3132

Forest Grove
Harvey W Scott Memorial Library • Pacific University, 2043 College Wy • Forest Grove, OR 97116 • (503) 352-2892 • http://library.pacificu.edu

Masonic Grand Lodge of Oregon • 2150 Masonic Wy • Forest Grove, OR 97116 • (503) 357-3158 • http://www.masonic-oregon.com

Pacific University Museum • 2043 College Wy • Forest Grove, OR 97116 • (503) 352-2211 • http://www.pacific.edu

Fort Klamath
Fort Klamath Historical Society • general delivery • Fort Klamath, OR 97626

Fort Rock
Fort Rock Valley Historical Homestead Museum • 64608 Fort Rock Rd, P.O. Box 91 • Fort Rock, OR 97735 • (541) 576-2251 • http://fortrockoregon.com

Fossil
Fossil Museum • P.O. Box 465 • Fossil, OR 97830

Garibaldi
Garibaldi Museum • 112 Garibaldi Ave • Garibaldi, OR 97118 • (503) 322-8411 • http://garibaldimuseum.com

Gold Beach
Curry County Historical Society • Historical Museum, 29410 S Ellensburg, P.O> box 1598 • Gold Beach, OR 97444 • (541) 247-9396 • http://www.curryhistory.com

Gold Hill
Gold Hill Historical Society • Historical Museum, 504 1st Ave, P.O. Box 26 • Gold Hill, OR 97525 • (541) 855-1182 • http://www.ci.goldhill.or.us/historical.html

Grand Ronde
Confederated Tribes of the Grand Ronde • Historical Museum, 9615 Grand Ronde Rd, P.O. Box 38 • Grand Ronde, OR 97347-0338 • (503) 879-5211 • http://www.grandronde.org

Kwelth Tahlkie Cultural and Heritage Museum • 9615 Grand Ronde Rd • Grande Ronde, OR 97347 • (800) 422-0232

Grants Pass
Grants Pass Genealogical Society • P.O. Box 1834 • Grants Pass, OR 97528-0156

Grants Pass, cont.

Josephine County Historical Society • Historical Museum, 508 SW 5th St • Grants Pass, OR 97526 • (541) 479-7827 • http://www.webtrail.com/jchs/

Josephine County Library • 200 NW C Street • Grants Pass, OR 97526-2094 • (541) 474-5482

Schmidt House Museum • 508 SW 5th St • Grants Pass, OR 97526 • (541) 479-7827 • http://www.jocohistorical.org

Slavic Roots Genealogy Services • 6780 N Applegate Rd • Grants Pass, OR 97527 • http://www.slavicroots.com

Gresham

Gresham Historical Society • Gresham History Museum, 410 N Main Ave, P.O. Box 65 • Gresham, OR 97030 • (503) 661-0347 • http://community.gorge.net./ghs/

Gresham Pioneer Group • Pioneer Museum, 410 N Main Ave, P.O. Box 65 • Gresham, OR 97030 • (503) 661-0347

Historic Zimmerman House Museum • 17111 NE Sandy Blvd • Gresham, OR 97030 • (503) 261-8078

Haines

Eastern Oregon Museum on the Old Oregon Trail • 3rd & Wilcox, P.O. Box 182 • Haines, OR 97833 • (503) 856-3233 • http://www.hainesoregon.com/eomuseum

Halfway

Pine Valley Community Museum • 115 E Record St, P.O. Box 673 • Halfway, OR 97834

Hammond

Fort Stevens Historical Museum • Ridge Rd • Hammond, OR 97121

Helix

Helix Public Library • 119 Columbia St, P.O. Box 324 • Helix, OR 97835-0324 • (541) 457-6130

Heppner

Morrow County Historical Society • Historical Museum, 444 N Main St, P.O. Box 1153 • Heppner, OR 97856 • (541) 676-5524

Hillsboro

Washington County Family History Society • 32455 NW Padgett Rd • Hillsboro, OR 97124-8334 • (503) 648-9597

Hood River

Hood River County Historical Society • Historical Museum, 300 E Port Marina Dr, P.O. Box 781 • Hood River, OR 97031 • (541) 386-6772 • http://www.co.hood-river.or.us/museum

Hood River County Library • 502 State St • Hood River, OR 97031 • (541) 386-2535 • http://www.co.hood-river.or.us/library

Independence

Independence Heritage Association • Heritage Museum, 112 S 3rd St, P.O. Box 7 • Independence, OR 97351

Independence Public Library • 175 S Monumouth St • Independence, OR 97351-1998 • (503) 838-1811 • http://www.ccrls.org/independence

Jacksonville

Beekman House Museum • Laurewood & California Sts • Jacksonville, OR 97530 • (541) 773-6356

Jacksonville Museum • 206 N 5th St • Jacksonville, OR 97530 • (541) 899-8123 • http://www.sohs.org

Southern Oregon Historical Society • P.O. Box 1570 • Jacksonville, OR 97540 • (541) 899-8123 • http://www.sohs.org

Jefferson

Jefferson Public Library • 128 N Main St, P.O. Box 1068 • Jefferson, OR 97352-1068 • (541) 327-2826

John Day

Kam Wah Chung & Company Museum • Canton St, P.O. Box 663 • John Day, OR 97845 • (541) 575-0028

Joseph

Joseph City Library • 201 N Main, P.O. Box 15 • Joseph, OR 97846-0015 • (541) 432-0141

Manuel Museum • P.O. Box 905 • Joseph, OR 97846

Wallowa County Museum • Main St, P.O. Box 430 • Joseph, OR 97846 • (541) 432-1794

Junction City

Junction City Historical Society • Mary Pitney House Museum, 655 Holly St • Junction City, OR 97448 • (541) 952-0900 • http://www.junctioncity.com/history

Kerby

Illinois Valley Historical Society • Kerbyville Museum, 24195 Redwood Hwy, P.O. Box 3003 • Kerby, OR 97531 • (541) 592-5252 • http://www.kerbyvillemuseum.com

Klamath Falls

Baldwin Hotel Museum • 31 Main St • Klamath Falls, OR 97601 • (541) 883-4207

Favell Museum • 125 W Main St • Klamath Falls, OR 97601 • (541) 882-9996 • http://www.favellmuseum.org

Fort Klamath Museum • 1451 Main St • Klamath Falls, OR 97601 • (541) 883-4208

Klamath Basin Genealogical Society • 126 S 3rd St, P.O. Box 366 • Klamath Falls, OR 97601

Klamath County Library • 126 S 3rd St • Klamath Falls, OR 97601-6394 • (541) 882-8894 • http://www.lib.co.klamath.or.us

Klamath County Museum • 1451 Main St • Klamath Falls, OR 97601 • (541) 883-4208 • http://www.co.klamath.or.us

Shaw Historical Library • Oregon Institute of Technology, 3201 Campus Dr • Klamath Falls, OR 97601 • (541) 885-1773 • http://www.oit.edu

Shaw Historical Society • Shaw Historical Library, Oregon Institute of Technology, 3201 Campus Dr • Klamath Falls, OR 97601 • (541) 882-1276

La Grande

La Grande Public Library • 1006 Pennsylvania Ave • La Grande, OR 97850-2496 • (541) 962-1339 • http://www.ci.la-grande.or.us/dept_library.cfm

Walter M Pierce Library • East Oregon University, 1 University Blvd • La Grande, OR 97850 • (541) 962-3540 • http://pierce.eou.edu

La Pine

La Pine Genealogical Society • P.O. Box 1081 • La Pine, OR 97739

Lafayette

Yamhill County Historical Society • Historical Museum, 605 Market St, P.O. Box 484 • Lafayette, OR 97127 • (503) 864-2308 • http://yamhillcountyhistory.org

Lake Oswego

Lake Oswego Public Library • 706 4th St • Lake Oswego, OR 97034-2399 • (503) 636-7628 • http://www.ci.oswego.or.us/library

Lakeport

Lake County Museum • 255 N Main St, P.O. Box 1222 • Lakeport, OR 97453 • (707) 263-4555

Lakeview

Daughters of the American Revolution, Oregon Chapter • Schminck Museum, 128 South East St • Lakeview, OR 97630 • (541) 947-3134

Ed Garrett Memorial Museum • HC 60, Box 780 • Lakeview, OR 97630

Lake County Historical Society • 118 South E Street, P.O. Box 48 • Lakeview, OR 97630

Lake County Library • 513 Center St • Lakeview, OR 97630-1582 • (541) 947-6019

Lebanon
Lebanon Genealogical Society • c/o Lebanon Public Library, 626 2nd St • Lebanon, OR 97355 • (541) 451-7461 • http://www.usgennet.org/~or-lgs/

Lebanon Public Library • 626 2nd St • Lebanon, OR 97355-3320 • (541) 451-7461

Lincoln City
Driftwood Public Library • 801 SW Hwy 101, Suite 201 • Lincoln City, OR 97367-2720 • (541) 996-1257 • http://www.driftwoodlib.org

North Lincoln County Historical Museum • 4907 SW Hwy 101 • Lincoln City, OR 97367 • (541) 996-6614 • http://www.northlincolncountyhistoricalmuseum.org

Madras
Jefferson County Historical Museum • Historical Museum, 34 SE D Street, P.O. Box 647 • Madras, OR 97741 • (541) 408-2740 • http://jeffcohistorical.org

Jefferson County Library • 241 SE 7th St • Madras, OR 97741-1611 • (541) 475-3351 • http://www.jcld.lib.or.us

Juniper Branch of the Family Finders • P.O. Box 652 • Madras, OR 97741 • (541) 475-6918

Madras Genealogical Society • 671 SW Fairgrounds • Madras, OR 97741

Marylhurst
Shoen Library • Marylhurst University, 17600 Pacific Hwy, P.O. Box 261 • Marylhurst, OR 97036-0261 • (503) 699-6261 • http://www.marylhurst.edu/student/shoenlibrary.html

Maupin
Southern Wasco County Library-Maupin Library • 410 Deschutes Ave, P.O. Box 328 • Maupin, OR 97037-0328 • (541) 395-2208

McMinnville
Evergreen Aviation Museum • 500 NE Captain Michael King Smith Wy • McMinnville, OR 97128 • (503) 434-4185 • http://www.sprucegoose.org

McMinnville Public Library • 225 NW Adams St • McMinnville, OR 97128-5425 • (503) 435-5554 • http://www.ci.mcminnville.or.us

Nicholson Library • Linfield College, 900 S Baker St • McMinnville, OR 97128 • (503) 883-2518 • http://www.linfield.edu/library

Northup Library • Linfield College 900 SE Baker • McMinnville, OR 97128-9989 • (503) 434-2262

Yamhill County Genealogical Society • c/o McMinnville Public Library, 225 N Adams St, P.O. Box 568 • McMinnville, OR 97128 • (503) 472-5247

Medford
Beekman House Museum • 106 N Central Ave • Medford, OR 97501 • (541) 773-6536 • http://www.sohs.org

Hanley Farm Museum • 1053 Hanley Rd • Medford, OR 97501 • (541) 227-4601 • http://www.southernoregon.com/hanleyfarm/

International Military Order of the Southern Cross • 221 N Central #225 • Medford, OR 97501-2639 • (541) 773-1305

Rogue Valley Genealogical Society • c/o Jackson County Library System, 413 W Main St • Medford, OR 97501-7221 • (541) 776-7280 • http://www.grrtech.com/rvgs

Southern Oregon Historical Society • Southern Oregon History Center Museum, 106 N Central St • Medford, OR 97501-5926 • (541) 773-6536 • http://www.sohs.org

Talent Historical Society • 206 E Main St • Medford, OR 97501 • (541) 512-8838

Merlin
Rogue River Ranch Museum • 14335 Galice Rd • Merlin, OR 97532

Mill City
Canyon Life Museum • 143 Wall St, P.O. Box 574 • Mill City, OR 97346 • (503) 897-4088

North Santiam Historical Society • 143 NE Wall St • Mill City, OR 97360 • (503) 897-4088

Milton-Freewater
Frazier Farmstead Museum • 1403 Chestnut St • Milton-Freewater, OR 97862 • (541) 938-4636 • http://museum.bmi.net

Milton-Freewater Genealogical Club • 127 SE 6th St • Milton-Freewater, OR 97862

Milton-Freewater Public Library • 8 SW 8th Ave • Milton-Freewater, OR 97862-1501 • (541) 938-8244 • http://www.mfcity.com

Milwaukie
Ledding Library • 10660 SE 21st Ave • Milwaukie, OR 97222-7586 • (503) 786-7580 • http://www.milwaukie.lib.or.us

Milwaukie Museum • 3737 SE Adams • Milwaukie, OR 97222 • (503) 654-2292 • http://milwaukiemuseum.tripod.com

Molalla
Dibble House Museum • 616 S Molalla Ave, P.O. Box 838 • Molalla, OR 97013 • (503) 266-5571

Molalla Area Historical Society • Historical Museum, 620 S Molalla Ave, P.O. Box 828 • Molalla, OR 97038 • (503) 266-5571

Monmouth
Brunk Pioneer Homestead Museum • 5705 Salem-Dallas Hwy, P.O. Box 67 • Monmouth, OR 97361 • (503) 838-1807

Gentle House Museum • 345 N Monmouth Ave • Monmouth, OR 97361 • (503) 838-8000 • http://www.wou.edu

Monmouth Public Library • 168 S Ecols St, P.O. Box 10 • Monmouth, OR 97361-0010 • (503) 838-1932 • http://www.ccrls.org/monmouth/

Paul Jensen Arctic Museum • 590 W Church St • Monmouth, OR 97361 • (503) 838-8468

Moro
Sherman County Historical Society • Historical Museum, 200 Dewey St, P.O. Box 173 • Moro, OR 97039 • (541) 565-3232 • http://www.shermanmuseum.org

Myrtle Creek
South Umpqua Historical Society • Historical Museum • Myrtle Creek, OR 97457 • (541) 839-4845

Myrtle Point
Coos County Fairgrounds Museum • 733 4th South • Myrtle Point, OR 97458 • (541) 260-1457 • http://www.fairgroundsmuseum.coquillevalley.org

Coos County Logging Museum • 705 Maple St, P.O. Box 325 • Myrtle Point, OR 97701 • http://www.cooscountyloggingmuseum.4t.com

Newberg
Hoover-Minthorn House Museum • 115 S River St • Newberg, OR 97132 • (503) 539-6629 • http://www.thehoover-minthornhousemuseum.org

Murdock Library • George Fox University, 416 N Meridian St • Newberg, OR 97132 • (503) 554-2419 • http://library.georgefox.edu

Oregon

Newberg, cont.
Murdock Library • George Fox College, 416 N Meridian St • Newberg, OR 97132 • (503) 554-2410

Newport
Lincoln County Historical Society • Burroughs House Museum, 545 SW 9th St • Newport, OR 97365-4726 • (541) 265-7509 • http://www.newportnet.com/coasthistory/home

Oregon Coast History Center Museum • 545 SW 9th St • Newport, OR 97365 • (541) 265-7509 • http://www.oregoncoast.history.museum

Yaquina Bay Lighthouse Museum • Yaquina Bay State Park, P.O. Box 410 • Newport, OR 97365 • (541) 574-3116 • http://www.yaquinalights.org

Yaquina Head Interpretive Center • 740 NW Lighthouse Dr, P.O. Box 936 • Newport, OR 97365 • (541) 574-3100

North Bend
Coos Bay Genealogical Forum • P.O. Box 1067 • North Bend, OR 97459

Coos County Historical Society • Historical Museum, 1220 Sherman Ave • North Bend, OR 97459-3666 • (541) 756-6320 • http://www.cooshistory.org

Coquille Indian Tribe • 3201 Tremont • North Bend, OR 97459 • (503) 756-0663 • http://www.coquilletribe.org

North Bend Public Library • 1800 Sherman Ave • North Bend, OR 97459 • (541) 756-0400

Nyssa
Oregon Trail Agricultural Museum • 117 Good Ave, P.O. Box 2303 • Nyssa, OR 97913 • (541) 372-3574

Oakland
Oakland Museum • 130 Locust St • Oakland, OR 97462

Oakridge
Oakridge-Westfir Pioneer Museum • 76433 Pine St, P.O. Box 807 • Oakridge, OR 97463 • (541) 782-2402

Willamette Fish Hatchery Museum • 76389 Fish Hatchery Rd • Oakridge, OR 97463

Ontario
Four Rivers Cultural Center • 767 SW 5th Ave • Ontario, OR 97914 • (541) 889-8191 • http://www.4rcc.com

Malheur County Library • 388 SW 2nd Ave • Ontario, OR 97914-2788 • (541) 889-6371 • http://www.malheur.or.us/library.html

Oregon City
Baker Cabin Historical Society • general delivery • Oregon City, OR 97045 • (503) 631-8274

Clackamas County Family History Society • Historical Museum, 211 Tumwater Dr, P.O. Box 2211 • Oregon City, OR 97045 • (503) 655-5574 • http://www.clackamascountyhistoricalsociety.com

Clackamas County Historical Society • 211 Tumwater Dr, P.O. Box 294 • Oregon City, OR 97045 • (503) 655-5574

Historic Oregon City Museum • 1726 Washington St • Oregon City, OR 97045 • (503) 657-9336 • http://www.historicoregoncity.com

Marshall N Dana Memorial Library • Clackamas Community College, 19600 S Molalla Ave • Oregon City, OR 97045 • (503) 657-6958 • http://www.clackamas.edu

McLoughlin House National Historic Site • 713 Center St • Oregon City, OR 97045 • (503) 656-5146 • http://www.mcloughlinhouse.org

Mount Hood Genealogical Forum • 950 South End Rd, P.O. Box 744 • Oregon City, OR 97045 • (503) 656-6021

Oregon City Public Library & Carnegie Center • 606 John Adams St, P.O. Box 3040 • Oregon City, OR 97045 • (503) 496-1201 • http://www.orcity.org/library

Rose Farm Museum • 713 Center St • Oregon City, OR 97045 • (503) 656-5146 • http://www.mcloughlinhouse.org/rosefarm.html

Stevens Crawford Museum • 603 6th St • Oregon City, OR 97045 • (503) 655-2866

Parkdale
Hutson Museum • 4967 Baseline Dr, P.O. Box 501 • Parkdale, OR 97041 • (541) 352-6808

Pendleton
Blue Mountain Genealogical Society • P.O. Box 1801 • Pendleton, OR 97801

Confederated Tribes of the Umatilla Indian Reservation • P.O. Box 638 • Pendleton, OR 97801-0638 • (503) 276-3165 • http://www.umatilla.nsn.us

Pendleton Public Library • 502 SW Dorion • Pendleton, OR 97801-1698 • (541) 966-0380 • http://www.pendleton.or.us/library.htm

Pendleton Round-Up Hall Museum • 1114 SW Court Ave, P.O. Box 609 • Pendleton, OR 97801 • (541) 276-2553 • http://www.pendletonroundup.com

Tamastsklikt Cultural Center Museum • 47106 Wildhorse Blvd • Pendleton, OR 97801 • (541) 966-9748 • http://www.tcimuseum.com

Umatilla County Historical Society • Heritage Station Museum, 108 SW Frazer, P.O. Box 253 • Pendleton, OR 97801 • (541) 276-0012 • http://www.heritagestationmuseum.org

Philomath
Benton County Genealogical Society • P.O. Box 1646 • Philomath, OR 97370 • (541) 929-6079

Benton County Historical Society • Historical Museum, 1101 Main St, P.O. Box 35 • Philomath, OR 97370-0047 • (541) 929-6230 • http://www.bentoncountymuseum.org

Phoenix
Rogue Valley Genealogical Society • 95 Houston Rd • Phoenix, OR 97535 • (541) 512-2340

Port Orford
Historic Hughes House & Cape Blanco Lighthouse Museum • Cape Blanco Rd, P.O. Box 1345 • Port Orford, OR 97465 • (541) 332-0248

Port Orford District Library • 555 W 20th St, P.O. Box 130 • Port Orford, OR 97465 • (541) 332-5622 • http://www.portorfordlibrary.org

Port Orford Genealogical Society • c/o Port Orford District Library, 555 W 20th St, P.O. Box 130 • Port Orford, OR 97465 • (541) 332-5622

Port Orford Heritage Society • P.O. Box 1132 • Port Orford, OR 97465 • (541) 332-0521

Port Orford Lifeboat Station Museum • Hwy 101, P.O. Box 1132 • Port Orford, OR 97465 • (541) 332-0521 • http://www.portorfordlifeboatstation.org

Portland
American Advertising Museum • 211 NW 5th Ave • Portland, OR 97209

Aubrey R Watzek Library • Lewis & Clark College, 0615 SW Palatine Hill Rd • Portland, OR 97219 • (503) 768-7285 • http://library.lclark.edu

Bybee-Howell House Museum • Howell Territorial Park, 13901 NW Howell Rd • Portland, OR 97205 • (503) 621-3344

Cedar Mill Community Library • 12505 NW Cornell Rd • Portland, OR 97229 • (503) 644-0043 • http://www.cedarmill.org/library

Concordia University Library • 2811 NE Holman St • Portland, OR 97211-6099 • (503) 280-8507 • http://www.cu-portland.edu/library

Finnish-American Historical Society of the West • P.O. Box 5522 • Portland, OR 97228-5522 • (503) 654-0448 • http://www.teleport.com/~finamhsw

Friends of Timberline • 7310 SW Corbett Ave • Portland, OR 97219 • (503) 295-0827

Genealogical Forum of Oregon • 1505 SE Gideon St, P.O. Box 42567 • Portland, OR 97201-4934 • (503) 963-1932 • http://www.gfo.org

Germans from Russia - Oregon & SW Washington • 8618 SE 36th Ave • Portland, OR 97222-5522 • (503) 659-8248

Hat Museum • 1928 SE Ladd Ave • Portland, OR 97214 • (503) 232-0433 • http://www.thehatmuseum.com

Historic Preservation League of Oregon • 3534 SE Main St • Portland, OR 97214 • (503) 243-1923 • http://www.hplo.org

Irish Interest Group of Portland • P.O. Box 42567 • Portland, OR 97242-0567 • (503) 287-9672

Jewish Genealogical Society of Oregon • Mittleman Jewish Community Center, 6651 SW Capitol Hwy, P.O. Box 19736 • Portland, OR 97280 • (503) 246-9844 • http://www.rootsweb.ancestry.com/~orjgs/

Jewish Genealogical Society of Willamette Valley Oregon • Oregon Jewish Museum, 1953 NW Kearney St • Portland, OR 97209-1414 • (503) 226-3600 • http://www.nwfam.com/jgswvo.html

Multnomah County Public Library • 205 NE Russell St • Portland, OR 97212-3796 • (503) 248-5402 • http://www.multcolib.org

National Railway Historical Society • general delivery • Portland, OR 97201 • (503) 226-6747

Ninth Judicial Circuit Historical Society • 620 SW Main St • Portland, OR 97205 • (503) 326-3458

Old Church Society • Historical Museum, 1422 SW 11th Ave • Portland, OR 97201 • (503) 222-2031 • http://www.oldchurch.org

Oregon Historical Society • Historical Museum, 1200 SW Park Ave • Portland, OR 97205 • (503) 222-1741 • http://www.ohs.org

Oregon History Center • 1200 SW Park Ave • Portland, OR 97205-2441 • (503) 222-1741

Oregon Jewish Genealogical and Historical Society • Mittleman Jewish Community Ctr, 6651 SW Capitol Hwy • Portland, OR 97219 • (503) 245-5196

Oregon Jewish Museum and Archive • 1953 NW Kearney St • Portland, OR 97209 • (503) 226-3600 • http://www.ojm.org

Oregon Maritime Center & Museum • SW Naito Pkwy & Pine St • Portland, OR 97204 • (503) 224-7724 • http://www.oregonmaritimemuseum.org

Otto F Linn Library • Warner Pacific College, 2219 SE 68th Ave • Portland, OR 97215-4099 • (503) 517-1033 • http://www.warnerpacific.edu/library/

Pittock Mansion Museum • 3229 NW Pittock Dr • Portland, OR 97210 • (503) 823-3623 • http://www.pittockmansion.com

Portland Police Historical Museum • 1111 SW 2nd • Portland, OR 97208 • (503) 823-0019 • http://www.portlandpolicemuseum.com

Sons and Daughters of Oregon Pioneers • P.O. Box 6685 • Portland, OR 97228 • (503) 222-5014 • http://www.webtrail.com/sdop

State of Oregon Sports Museum • 321 SW Salmon • Portland, OR 97204

Washington County Historical Society • Historical Museum, 17677 NW Springville Rd • Portland, OR 97229-1743 • (503) 645-5353 • http://www.washingtoncountymuseum.org

Wells Fargo History Museum • 1300 SW 5th Ave • Portland, OR 97201 • (503) 886-1102 • http://www.wellsfargohistory.com

Western Seminary Cline-Tunnell Library • 5511 SE Hawthorne Blvd • Portland, OR 97215-3399 • (503) 517-1840 • http://www.westernseminary.edu

World Forestry Center Museum • 4033 SW Canyon Rd • Portland, OR 97221 • (503) 228-1367 • http://www.worldforestry.org

Powers
Hazel M Lewis Library • 511 3rd Ave, P.O. Box 559 • Powers, OR 97466-0559 • (541) 439-5311

Prairie City
Dewitt Museum • Depot Park, Main & Bridge Sts, P.O. Box 283 • Prairie City, OR 97869 • (541) 820-3603 • http://www.prairiecityoregon.com

Princeton
George M Benson Memorial Museum • HC 72, Box 245 • Princeton, OR 97721

Prineville
Crook County Genealogical Society • 246 N Main St, P.O. Box 906 • Prineville, OR 97754 • (541) 447-3715

Crook County Historical Society • A R Bowman Museum 246 N Main St • Prineville, OR 97754 • (541) 447-3715 • http://www.bowmanmuseum.org

Rainier
Rainier City Library • 106 B Street W, P.O. Box 100 • Rainier, OR 97048-0100 • (503) 556-7301

Redmond
Petersen Rock Garden & Museum • 7930 SW 77th St • Redmond, OR 97756 • (541) 382-5574

Reedsport
Umpqua Discovery Center Museum • 409 Riverfront Wy • Reedsport, OR 97467 • (541) 271-4816 • http://www.umpqadiscoverycenter.com

Umpqua River Lighthouse Museum • 1020 Lighthouse Rd • Reedsport, OR 97467 • http://www.winchesterbay.org/lighthouse.html

Rhododendron
Stage Stop Road Interpretive Center • P.O. Box 398 • Rhododendron, OR 97049 • (503) 622-4798 • http://cgs-mthood.tripod.com/

Rickreall
Historical Society Polk County • Historical Museum, 520 S Pacific Hwy W • Rickreall, OR 97371 • (503) 623-6251

Polk County Museum • 560 SW Pacific Hwy • Rickreall, OR 97371 • (503) 623-6251 • http://www.polkcountyhistoricalsociety.com

Rogue River
Woodville Museum • 1st & Oak St, P.O. Box 1288 • Rogue River, OR 97537 • (541) 582-3088

Roseburg
Cow Creek Band of Umpqua Indians • 2400 Stewart Pkwy, Ste 300 • Roseburg, OR 97470 • (503) 672-9405 • http://www.cowcreek.com

Douglas County Historical Society • Lane House Museum, 544 SE Douglas Ave • Roseburg, OR 97470-2807 • (541) 459-1393 • http://www.douglascountyhistoricalsociety.org/floed-lane-house/

Douglas County Library • 1409 NE Diamond Lake Blvd • Roseburg, OR 97470 • (541) 440-4305 • http://www.co.douglas.or.us/library

Douglas County Museum • 123 Museum Dr • Roseburg, OR 97470 • (541) 957-7007 • http://www.co.douglas.or.us/museum

Genealogical Society of Douglas County • Douglas County Courthouse, 1036 SE Douglas, P.O. Box 579 • Roseburg, OR 97420 • (541) 440-6178

Oregon

Saint Helens
Columbia County Historical Society • Old County Courthouse Museum, 2194 Columbia Blvd, P.O. Box 837 • Saint Helens, OR 97051 • (503) 366-3650

Saint Paul
Champoeg State Heritage Area Museum • 8329 Champoeg Rd NE • Saint Paul, OR 97137 • (503) 678-1649 • http://www.champoeg.org

Daughters of the American Revolution, Oregon Chapter • Robert Newell House Museum, 8089 Champoeg Rd • Saint Paul, OR 97137 • (503) 678-5537 • http://www.newellhouse.com

Friends of Champanoeg • 8239 Champoeg Rd NE • Saint Paul, OR 97437 • (503) 678-1251

Pioneer Mothers Memorial Cabin Museum • 8035 Champoeg Rd NE • Saint Paul, OR 97137-9709 • (503) 633-2237

Saint Paul Historical Society • 20310 Main St NE • Saint Paul, OR 97137

Salem
A C Gilbert's Discovery Village Museum • 116 Manon St NE • Salem, OR 97301 • (503) 371-3631 • http://www.acgilbert.org

Asahel Bush House Museum • 600 Mission St SE • Salem, OR 97302 • (503) 363-4714 • http://www.oregonlink.com/bush_house/

Brooks Historical Society • 3995 Brooklane Rd NE • Salem, OR 97303-9728 • (503) 390-0698

Brunk House Museum • 5705 Salem Dallas Hwy NW • Salem, OR 97304 • (503) 371-8586

Family History Finland • 545 Wildwind Dr SE • Salem, OR 97302 • (503) 315-8709 • http://www.open.org/~rumcd/genweb/finn.html

Genealogical Council of Oregon • P.O. Box 2639 • Salem, OR 97308-2639 • (800) 558-7589

Historic Deepwood Estate Museum • 1116 Mission St SE • Salem, OR 97302 • (503) 363-1825 • http://www.historicdeepwoodestate.org

Historic Deepwood Estate Museum • 1116 Mission St SE • Salem, OR 97301 • (503) 363-1825 • http://www.historicdeepwoodestate.org

Marion County Historical Society • Historical Museum, 260 12th St SE • Salem, OR 97301 • (503) 364-2128 • http://www.marionhistory.org

Mark O Hatfield Library • Willamette University, 900 State St • Salem, OR 97301 • (503) 370-6560 • http://library.willamette.edu

Mennonite Historical and Genealogical Society of Oregon • 675 Elma Ave • Salem, OR 97301

Mission Mill Museum • 1313 Mill St SE • Salem, OR 97301 • (503) 585-7012

Mission Mill Museum Association • John D Boon House Museum, 1313 Mill St SE • Salem, OR 97301 • (503) 585-7012 • http://www.missionmill.org

Oregon Archives Division • 1005 Broadway NE • Salem, OR 97310 • (503) 373-0701 • http://arcweb.sos.state.or.us

Oregon Electric Railway Historical Society • Historical Museum, 3395 Brooklake Rd NE • Salem, OR 97303 • (503) 88-4104 • http://www.oregonelectricrailway.org

Oregon State Library • State Library Bldg, 250 Winter St NE • Salem, OR 97301-3950 • (503) 378-4243 • http://www.osl.state.or.us/home/

Salem Public Library • 585 Liberty St SE, P.O. Box 14810 • Salem, OR 97309 • (503) 588-6052 • http://www.salemlibrary.org

Scandinavian Genealogical Society of Oregon • 8143 Olney St SE • Salem, OR 97304 • (503) 749-2874

Sons of the American Revolution, Oregon Society • P.O. Box 425 • Salem, OR 97308-0425 • (503) 269-7259 • http://www.saroregon.org

Willamette Valley Genealogical Society • c/o Oregon State Library Genealogy Rm, 250 Winter St NE, P.O. Box 2083 • Salem, OR 97308-2083 • (503) 378-4277 • http://www.osl.state.or.us/oslhome.html

Sandy
Sandy Historical Society • Historical Museum, 39065 Pioneer Blvd, P.O. Box 652 • Sandy, OR 97055 • (503) 668-3378 • http://www.sandyhistorical.org

Scappoose
Scappoose Public Library • 52469 SE 2nd St, P.O. Box 400 • Scappoose, OR 97056 • (503) 543-7123 • http://www.columbia-center.org/scappooselibrary

Scio
Scio Historical Society • Depot Museum, 39004 NE 1st Ave, P.O. Box 226 • Scio, OR 97374

Seaside
Clatsop-Nehalem Confederated Tribes • 783 First Ave, P.O. Box 190 • Seaside, OR 97138 • (503) 738-6738 • http://www.clatsop-nehalem.com

Seaside Historical Society • Historical Museum, 570 Necanicum Dr, P.O. Box 1024 • Seaside, OR 97138-1024 • (503) 738-7065 • http://www.seasidemuseum.org

Shedd
Linn County Historical Society • 29990 1st St • Shedd, OR 97377-9740 • (541) 491-3978

Sherwood
Sherwood Historical Society • Heritage Center, 90 NW Park St • Sherwood, OR 97140 • (503) 625-1236

Sherwood Public Library • 955 N Sherwood Blvd • Sherwood, OR 97140 • (503) 625-6688 • http://www.wilinet.wccls.lib.or.us

Siletz
Confederated Tribes of the Siletz Indians of Oregon • 201 SE Swan Ave, P.O. Box 549 • Siletz, OR 97380-0549 • (503) 444-2532 • http://ctsi.nsn.us

Silverton
Silver Falls Library District • 410 S Water St • Silverton, OR 97381-2198 • (503) 873-5173 • http://www.open.org/silverpl/

Silverton Country Historical Society • Historical Museum, 428 S Water St • Silverton, OR 97381 • (503) 873-7070 • http://www.silvertonmuseum.com

Spray
Spray Pioneer Museum • P.O. Box 234 • Spray, OR 97874

Springfield
Springfield Museum • 590 Main St • Springfield, OR 97477 • (541) 726-3677 • http://www.springfieldmuseum.com

Springfield Public Library • 225 N 5th St • Springfield, OR 97477-4697 • (541) 726-3766 • http://www.ci.springfield.or.us/library

Stanfield
Stanfield Public Library • 180 W Coe Ave, P.O. Box 489 • Stanfield, OR 97875-0489 • (541) 449-1254

Stayton
Santiam Historical Society • Historical Museum, 260 N 2nd Ave, P.O. Box 326 • Stayton, OR 97383 • (503) 769-0442

Stayton Public Library • 515 N 1st Ave • Stayton, OR 97383-1703 • (503) 769-3313 • http://www.open.org/~stayton/dept.library

Summer Lake
Fort Rock Valley Historical Society • 64696 Fort Rock Rd • Summer Lake, OR 97640 • (541) 576-2251

Sunny Valley
Applegate Trail Interpretive Center • 500 Sunny Valley Loop • Sunny Valley, OR 97497

Sweet Home
East Linn Historical Society • Historical Museum, 746 Long St • Sweet Home, OR 97368 • (541) 367-4580

Sweet Home Genealogical Society • 1223 Kalmia St, P.O. Box 279 • Sweet Home, OR 97386 • (541) 367-5034

Sweet Home Public Library • 1101 13th St • Sweet Home, OR 97386-2197 • (541) 367-5007 • http://www.sweet-home.or.us

Talent
Talent Historical Society • Historical Museum, P.O. Box 582 • Talent, OR 97540 • (541) 512-8838 • http://www.talenthistory.org

The Dalles
Columbia Gorge Genealogical Society • c/o Dalles City-Wasco County Public Library, 722 Court St • The Dalles, OR 97058 • (541) 296-2815 • http://community.oregonlive.com/cc/genealogy

Columbia Gorge-Wasco County Museum • 5000 Discovery Dr • The Dalles, OR 97058 • (541) 296-8600 • http://www.gorgediscovery.org

Dalles City-Wasco County Public Library • 722 Court St • The Dalles, OR 97058 • (541) 296-2815 • http://www.ci.the-dalles.or.us

Fort Dalles Museum • Anderson Homestead, 500 W 15th St, P.O. Box 806 • The Dalles, OR 97058 • (541) 296-4547 • http://www.fortdallesmuseum.org

Lewis Anderson Farmhouse and Granery Museum • 500 W 16th St • The Dalles, OR 97058 • (541) 296-4542

Linn Genealogical Society • c/o Dalles City-Wasco County Public Library, 722 Court St • The Dalles, OR 97058 • (541) 296-2815

Old St Peter's Landmark Museum • W 3rd & Lincoln Sts, P.O. Box 882 • The Dalles, OR 97058 • (541) 296-5686 • http://www.oldstpeterslandmark.org

Original Wasco County Courthouse Museum • 420 W 2nd Pl, P.O. Box 839 • The Dalles, OR 97058 • (541) 296-4798

Rorick House Museum • 300 W 13th St • The Dalles, OR 97058 • (541) 296-1867 • http://www.historicthedalles.org/history/rorick_house.htm

Wasco County Historical Museum • 5000 Discovery Pl, P.O. Box 998 • The Dalles, OR 97058 • (541) 296-8600

Wasco County Historical Society • 300 W 3rd St • The Dalles, OR 97058-2010 • (541) 296-1867

Tillamook
Latimer Quilt and Textile Center • 2105 Wilson River Loop • Tillamook, OR 97141 • (503) 842-8622 • http://latimerquiltandtextile.com

Tillamook County Historical Society • P.O. Box 123 • Tillamook, OR 97141

Tillamook County Library • 1716 3rd St • Tillamook, OR 97141 • (503) 842-4792 • http://tillabook.org

Tillamook County Pioneer Museum and Research Library • 2106 2nd St • Tillamook, OR 97141 • (503) 842-4553 • http://www.tcpm.org

Tillamook Genealogy Study Group • 6450 Curl Rd • Tillamook, OR 97141

Tillamook Naval Air Station Museum • 6030 Hanger Rd • Tillamook, OR 97141 • (503) 842-1130 • http://www.tillamookair.com

Toledo
Toledo Public Library • 173 NW 7th Ave • Toledo, OR 97391 • (541) 336-3132 • http://www.cityoftoledo.org/city_staff_library.html

Yaquina Genealogical Society • c/o Toledo Public Library, 173 NW 7th St • Toledo, OR 97391 • (541) 336-3132

Yaquina Pacific Railroad Historical Society • 100 NW A Street • Toledo, OR 97391 • (541) 336-5256

Trail
Trail Creek Tavern Museum • P.O. Box 245 • Trail, OR 97541

Troutdale
Barn Museum • 104 SE Kibling • Troutdale, OR 97060 • (503) 661-2164

Troutdale Historical Society • Harlow House Museum, 473 E Historic Columbia River Hwy • Troutdale, OR 97060 • (503) 661-2164

Troutdale Railroad Depot Museum • 473 E Historic Columbia River Hwy • Troutdale, OR 97060 • (503) 667-8268

Umatilla
Umatilla Historical Foundation • Historical Museum, 911 6th St, P.O. Box 975 • Umatilla, OR 97882 • (541) 922-0209

Union
Union County Historical Society • 333 S Main St • Union, OR 97883

Union County Museum • 311 S Main St, P.O. Box 190 • Union, OR 97883 • (541) 562-6003

Vale
Malheur Historical Project • Rinehart Stone House Museum, 225 Main St, P.O. Box 413 • Vale, OR 97918 • (541) 473-2070

Vernonia
Oregon Lewis and Clark Heritage Foundation • Pioneer Museum, 511 E Bridge St • Vernonia, OR 97064 • (503) 429-3713 • http://www.vernonia-or.gov

Waldport
Alsea Bay Bridge Interpretive Center • 620 NW Spring St, P.O. Box 693 • Waldport, OR 97394 • (541) 563-2002

ALSI Historical and Genealogical Society • 320 Grant, P.O. Box 822 • Waldport, OR 97394 • (541) 563-7092

Waldport Heritage Museum • 320 Grant St, P.O. Box 882 • Waldport, OR 97394 • (541) 563-7092

Wallowa
Wallowa Nez Perce Interpretive Center • P.O. Box 15 • Wallowa, OR 97885 • (541) 886-3101 • http://www.wallowanezperce.com

Warm Springs
Confederated Tribes of the Warm Springs Reservation • 1233 Veteran St, P.O. Box C • Warm Springs, OR 97761 • (503) 553-1161 • http://www.warmsprings.com

Museum at Warm Springs • 2189 Hwy 26, P.O. Box 909 • Warm Springs, OR 97761 • (503) 553-3331 • http://www.museumatwarmsprings.org

West Linn
American Historical Society of Germans from Russia, Oregon Chapter • 2280 Valley View Dr • West Linn, OR 97068 • (503) 635-6651 • http://www.ahsgroregon.com/

Williamette Falls Locks & Museum • Mill St • West Linn, OR 97068

White City
Camp White Military Museum • Hwy 62 & Avenue H • White City, OR 97503 • (541) 826-2111 • http://www.campwhite.org

Wilsonville
Wilsonville Public Library • 8200 SW Wilsonville Rd • Wilsonville, OR 97070 • (503) 682-2744 • http://www.wilsonville.lib.or.us

Wilsonville-Boones Ferry Historical Society • 8200 SW Wilsonville Rd • Wilsonville, OR 97070

Oregon

Woodburn

Settlemeier House Museum • 355 N Settlemeir Ave, P.O. Box 405 • Woodburn, OR 97071 • (503) 982-1897 • http://www.settlemierhouse.com

Woodburn World's Berry Center Museum • 455 N Front St • Woodburn, OR 97071

Yachats

Little Log Church & Museum • 328 W 3rd St, P.O. Box 712 • Yachats, OR 97498

Aaronsburg

Aaronsburg Historical Museum Association • Historical Museum, 114 W Plum St, P.O. Box 70 • Aaronsburg, PA 16820 • (814) 349-5328

Penns Valley Area Historical Museum • 244 W Aaron Sq, P.O. Box 80 • Aaronsburg, PA 16820 • (814) 349-5328 • http://www.pennsvalleymuseum.org

Abington

Abington Presbyterian Church Library • 1082 Old York Rd • Abington, PA 19001 • (215) 887-4530 • http://www.apcusa.org

Old York Road Genealogical Society • c/o Abington Free Library, 1030 Old York Rd • Abington, PA 19001-4530 • (215) 884-0593

Academia

Tuscarora Academy Museum • 498 Jefferson St • Academia, PA 17082 • (717) 436-5152

Addison

Old Petersburg-Addison Historical Society • Historical Museum, P.O. Box 82 • Addison, PA 15411 • (814) 395-5584

Albion

Valley School House Restoration Society • Historical Museum, 1 Harthan Wy • Albion, PA 16401

Alburtis

Alburtis-Lockridge Historical Society • Historical Museum, 407 Franklin St, P.O. Box 427 • Alburtis, PA 18011 • (484) 366-9987 • http://www.alhs18011.org

Alexandria

Hartslog Heritage Museum • Main St, P.O. Box 3 • Alexandria, PA 16611 • (814) 669-1968 • http://www.huntingdonhistory.org/hartslog.htm

Memorial Public Library of the Borough of Alexandria • Main St, P.O. Box 337 • Alexandria, PA 16611-0337 • (814) 669-4313

Aliquippa

Independence Township Historical Society • Historical Museum, RD1, P.O. Box 192 • Aliquippa, PA 15001

Allensville

Kishacoquillas Valley Historical Society • Historical Museum, 138 E Main St, P.O. Box 43 • Allensville, PA 17002 • (717) 483-6525

Allentown

Allentown Public Library • 1210 Hamilton St • Allentown, PA 18102-4371 • (610) 820-2400 • http://www.allentownpl.org

Allied Air Force Museum • 1730 Vultee St • Allentown, PA 18103 • (610) 683-8100 • http://www.visitpa.com/allied-air-force-museum

America on Wheels Museum • 5 N Front St, P.O. Box 1400 • Allentown, PA 18105 • (610) 432-4200 • http://www.americaonwheels.org

Frank Buchman House Museum • 117 N 11th St, P.O. Box 1548 • Allentown, PA 18105 • (610) 435-4664

Harry C Trexler Library • Muhlenberg College, 2400 Chew St • Allentown, PA 18104-5586 • (484) 664-3600 • http://www.muhlenberg.edu/library

Jewish Federation of the Lehigh Valley • Historical Museum, 702 N 22nd St • Allentown, PA 18104 • (610) 821-5500 • http://jflv.org

Lehigh County Historical Society • Historical Museum, 432 W Walnut St, P.O. Box 1548 • Allentown, PA 18102 • (610) 435-1074 • http://lchs.museum/

Lenni Lenape Historical Society • Museum of Indian Culture, 2825 Fish Hatchery Rd • Allentown, PA 18103-9801 • (610) 797-2121 • http://www.museumofindianculture.org

Liberty Bell Shrine of Allentown • 622 Hamilton Mall • Allentown, PA 18101 • (610) 435-4232 • http://www.libertybellmuseum.org

Lutheran Historical Society of Eastern Pennsylvania • Historical Museum, 1245 Hamilton St • Allentown, PA 18104

Old Allentown Preservation Association • 147 N 10th St, P.O. Box 1584 • Allentown, PA 18105

Parkland Community Library • 4422 Walbert Ave • Allentown, PA 18104-1619 • (610) 398-1333 • http://parkland.lib.pa.us

Pennsylvanian Cornish Society • 1835 Troxwell St • Allentown, PA 18103

Railway to Yesterday Library • 1060 Lehigh St, P.O. Box 1601 • Allentown, PA 18105-1601 • (610) 797-3242

Raymond E Holland Regional & Industrial History Collection • 2020 Hamilton • Allentown, PA 18104 • (610) 820-4930

Trout Hall Museum • 4th & Walnut Sts, P.O. Box 148 • Allentown, PA 18105 • (610) 435-4664

Allison Park

Depreciation Lands Museum • 4743 S Pioneer Rd, P.O. Box 174 • Allison Park, PA 15101 • (412) 486-0563

Altoona

Altoona Public Library • 1600 5th Ave • Altoona, PA 16602-3693 • (814) 946-0417 • http://www.altoonalibrary.org

Altoona Railroaders Memorial Museum • 1300 9th Ave • Altoona, PA 16602 • (814) 946-0834 • http://www.railroadcity.com

Blair County Genealogical Society • 431 Scotch Valley Rd • Altoona, PA 16648-9697 • (814) 696-3492

Blair County Historical Society • Baker Mansion Museum, 3419 Oak Ln, P.O. Box 1083 • Altoona, PA 16603-1083 • (814) 942-3916 • http://www.blairhistory.org

Fort Roberdeau Historic Site • 383 Fort Roberdeau Rd • Altoona, PA 16601 • (814) 946-0048 • http://www.fortroberdeau.org

Ambler

Conservancy of Montgomery County • P.O. Box 28 • Ambler, PA 19002-0028 • (215) 283-0383 • http://www.conservemontco.org

Wissahickon Valley Historical Society • Historical Museum, P.O. Box 96 • Ambler, PA 19002 • (215) 646-6541 • http://www.wvalleyhs.org

Ambridge

Harmonie Associates • Historical Museum, 14th & Church Sts • Ambridge, PA 15003 • (724) 843-7283

Laughlin Memorial Library • 99 11th St • Ambridge, PA 15003-2305 • (724) 266-3857

Pennsylvania Historical and Museum Commission • Old Economy Village, 270 16th St • Ambridge, PA 15003 • (724) 266-4500 • http://www.oldeconomyvillage.org

Andalusia

PenRyn Mansion Museum • 1601 State Rd • Andalusia, PA 19029 • (215) 633-9301

Annville

Bishop Library • Lebanon Valley College, 101 N College Ave • Annville, PA 17003-1404 • (717) 867-6970 • http://www.lvc.edu/library

Friends of Old Annville • Historical Museum, 155 N Moyer St • Annville, PA 17003 • (717) 867-0770

Apollo

Apollo Area Historical Society • Historical Museum, 2nd Ave, P.O. Box 343 • Apollo, PA 15613 • (724) 478-4214

Apollo Memorial Library • 219 N Pennsylvania Ave • Apollo, PA 15613-1397 • (724) 478-4214 • http://home.kiski.net/~alibrary

Drake Log Cabin Museum • Williams Alley, P.O. Box 434 • Apollo, PA 15613 • (724) 478-3037

Pennsylvania

Apollo, cont.
Roaring Run Watershed Association • Historical Museum, 116 Orchard St, P.O. Box 333 • Apollo, PA 15613 • (724) 295-2800 • http://www. roaringrun.org

Ardmore
Lower Merion Library System • 75 E Lancaster Ave • Ardmore, PA 19003-2388 • (610) 645-6110 • http://www.lmls.org

Scottish Historic and Research Society of the Delaware Valley • Historical Museum, 102 St Paul's Rd • Ardmore, PA 19003 • (610) 649-4144

Ashland
Ashland Anthracite Museum • 17th & Pine Sts • Ashland, PA 17911 • (717) 875-4708

Ashland Area Historic Preservation Society • Historical Museum, 316-318 Centre St • Ashland, PA 17921 • (570) 875-2632 • http://www. ashlandpahistory.com

Mahanoy Valley Historical Society • Historical Museum, P.O. Box 346 • Ashland, PA 17921

Pioneer Tunnel Coal Mine & Steam Train Museum • 19th & Oak Sts • Ashland, PA 17921 • (570) 875-3850 • http://www.pioneertunnel.com

Aston
Aston Historical Society • 3270 Concord Rd • Aston, PA 19014 • (610) 859-0651

Aston Township Historical Society • Historical Museum, 5021 Pennell Rd • Aston, PA 19014 • (610) 494-4707 • http://www.athsdelco.org

Athens
Spalding Memorial Library • 724 S Main St • Athens, PA 18810-1010 • (570) 888-7117 • http://www.athenspalibrary.org

Tioga Point Museum • 724 S Main St, P.O. Box 143 • Athens, PA 18840 • (570) 888-7225 • http://www.tiogapointmuseum.com

Atlasburg
Valenti Memorial Museum • P.O. Box 339 • Atlasburg, PA 15004 • (724) 947-5535

Audubon
Mill Grove Museum • P.O. Box 7125 • Audubon, PA 19407 • (610) 666-5593

Austin
Austin Dam Memorial Association • 133 Bittersweet Ln • Austin, PA 16720

Avella
Meadowcroft Foundation • Meadowcroft Village, 401 Meadowcroft Rd • Avella, PA 15312-2714 • (724) 587-3412 • http://www. heinzhistorycenter.org

Meadowcroft Museum of Rural Life • 410 Meadowcroft Rd • Avella, PA 15312 • (724) 587-3412 • http://www.visitpa.com/meadowcroft-rockshelter-and-museum-rural-life

Avonmore
Avonmore Area Historical Society • Historical Museum, P.O. Box 423 • Avonmore, PA 15618 • (724) 697-4123

Bakerstown
Historic Landmarks of Richland • P.O. Box 179 • Bakerstown, PA 15007 • (724) 443-2481

Bala Cynwyd
Afro-American Historical and Genealogical Society, Family Quest Chapter • P.O. Box 2272 • Bala Cynwyd, PA 19004 • http://www.aahgs. org

Lower Merion Historical Society • Historical Museum, 506 Bryn Mawr Ave, P.O. Box 2602 • Bala Cynwyd, PA 19004 • (610) 664-3216 • http://www.lowermerionhistory.org

Bala-Cynwyd Library • 131 Old Lancaster Rd • Bala-Cynwyd, PA 19004-3037 • (610) 664-1196 • http://mls.org

Bangor
Bangor Public Library • 39 S Main St • Bangor, PA 18013-2690 • (610) 588-4136 • http://www.bangorlibrary.org

Barto
Genealogical Computing Association of Pennsylvania • 51 Hillcrest Rd • Barto, PA 19504 • (610) 438-2858 • http://libertynet.org/~gencap

Bath
Governor Wolf Historical Society • Historical Museum, 6600 Jacksonville Rd, P.O. box 134 • Bath, PA 18014 • (610) 837-9015 • http://www.govwolf.org

Beach Lake
Zane Grey Museum • RR2, Box 2428 • Beach Lake, PA 18405 • (580) 729-8251

Bear Creek
Bear Creek Historical Society • Historical Museum, P.O. Box 315 • Bear Creek, PA 18602

Beaver
Beaver Area Heritage Foundation • Historical Museum, P.O. Box 147 • Beaver, PA 15009 • http://www.beaverheritage.org

Beaver County Genealogical Society • Historical Museum, 3225 Dutch Ridge Rd • Beaver, PA 15009 • http://www.rootsweb.com/~pabecgs

Brighton Township Historical Society • Historical Museum, 1300 Brighton Rd • Beaver, PA 15009 • (724) 774--4803 • http://www. brightontwp.org/residents_center/historical_society.html

Greek-Catholic Union of the USA • Historical Museum, 5400 Toscarawas Rd • Beaver, PA 15009 • (800) 722-4428 • http://www. gcuusa.com

H C Fry Glass Society of Beaver County • Historical Museum, P.O. Box 41 • Beaver, PA 15009 • http://thenostalgialeague.com/fryglass/society.htm

Richmond Little Red Schoolhouse Association • Historical Museum, 2145 Gypsy Glen Rd • Beaver, PA 15009 • http://www.brightontwp.org/residents_center/little_red_school_house.html

Seven Oaks Greek Church Museum • 132 Lisbon Rd • Beaver, PA 15009 • (724) 495-3400

Beaver Falls
Air Heritage Museum • 35 Piper St • Beaver Falls, PA 15010 • (724) 843-2820 • http://www.airheritage.org

Beaver County Genealogical Society • c/o Carnegie Free Library, 1301 7th Ave, P.O. Box 640 • Beaver Falls, PA 15010 • (724) 846-4340 x5

Beaver County, Pennsylvania Historical Research and Landmarks Foundation • c/o Carnegie Free Library, 1301 7th Ave • Beaver Falls, PA 15010 • (724) 846-4340 x5

Beaver Falls Historical Society • Historical Museum, 1301 7th Ave • Beaver Falls, PA 15010 • (724) 745-7713

Carnegie Free Library • 1301 7th Ave • Beaver Falls, PA 15010-4219 • (724) 846-4340 • http://www.co.beaver.pa.us/library/main.html

Research Center for Beaver County Local History • 1301 7th Ave, 2nd Fl • Beaver Falls, PA 15010 • (724) 847-9253 • http://www. bchistory.org/beavercounty/HistoricalSocieties/ResearchCenter/ResearchCenter.html

Sons of the American Revolution, General Anthony Wayne Chapter • Historical Museum, 1016 Highland Ave • Beaver Falls, PA 15010 • (724) 788-4222 • http://www.gawsar.org

Steele Museum • 3200 College Ave • Beaver Falls, PA 15010 • (724) 847-6632

Beaverdale
Beaverdale Community Library • 506 Jefferson Ave, P.O. Box 81 • Beaverdale, PA 15921-9998 • (814) 487-7742

Bedford
Fort Bedford Museum • Fort Bedford Dr, P.O. Box 1758 • Bedford, PA 15522 • (814) 623-2011 • http://www.nb.net/~fbm/

Old Bedford Village Museum • 220 Sawblade Rd, P.O. Box 1976 • Bedford, PA 15522 • (814) 623-1156 • http://www.oldbedfordvillage.com

Pioneer Historical Society of Bedford County • Pioneer Library, 242 E John St • Bedford, PA 15522-1750

Pioneer Historical Society of Bedford County • 6441 Lincoln Hwy • Bedford, PA 15522 • (814) 623-2011 • http://www.bedfordpahistory.com

Belle Vernon
Rostraver Township Historical Society • Historical Museum, 800 Fellsburg Rd • Belle Vernon, PA 15012 • (724) 823-0351

Bellefonte
Bellefonte Museum for Centre County • 133 N Allegheny St, P.O. Box 125 • Bellefonte, PA 16823 • (814) 355-4280 • http://www.bellefontemuseum.org

Centre County Library & Historical Museum • 203 N Allegheny St • Bellefonte, PA 16823-1691 • (814) 355-1516 • http://www.centrecountylibrary.org

Curtin Village Museum • P.O. Box 312 • Bellefonte, PA 16823 • (814) 355-1982 • http://www.curtinvillage.com

Belleville
Mifflin County Mennonite Historical Society • Historical Museum, 3922 W Main St, P.O. Box 5603 • Belleville, PA 17004 • (717) 935-2598 • http://mifflincomhs.mennonite.net

Bellevue
Andrew Bayne Memorial Library • 34 N Balph Ave • Bellevue, PA 15202-3297 • (412) 766-7447 • http://www.einpgh.org/ein/andbayne

Bensalem
Historical Society of Bensalem Township • Historical Museum, 3211 Knights Rd, P.O. Box 1101 • Bensalem, PA 19020 • (215) 639-6575 • http://www.thsbt.org

Berlin
Berlin Area Historical Society • Historical Museum, 400 Vine St, P.O. Box 35 • Berlin, PA 15530 • (814) 267-5987 • http://berlinpa.org

Berlin Historical Society • 400 Vine St • Berlin, PA 15530 • (814) 267-5987

Berwick
Berwick Historical Society • Historical Museum, 102 E 2nd St, P.O. Box 301 • Berwick, PA 18603 • (570) 759-8020 • http://www.berwickhistoricalsociety.org

Berwick Public Library • 205 Chestnut St • Berwick, PA 18603 • (570) 752-2241 • http://www.bplib.org

Berwyn
Easttown Township Library • 720 1st Ave • Berwyn, PA 19312-1769 • (610) 644-0138 • http://www.easttownlibrary.org

Bethayers
Frankfort Historical Society • Historical Museum, 1068 Huntington Pk • Bethayers, PA 19006

Bethel
Bethel-Tulpehocken Public Library • 8601 Lancaster Ave • Bethel, PA 19507 • (717) 933-4060 • http://www.berks.lib.pa.us/bethelpl

Bethel Park
Bethel Park Public Library • 5100 W Library Ave • Bethel Park, PA 15102-2790 • (412) 835-2207 • http://www.einetwork.net

Oliver Miller Homestead Museum • 1320 Stoltz Rd • Bethel Park, PA 15102 • (412) 835-1554 • http://olivermiller.org

Bethelehem
Johann Sebastian Goundie House Museum • 501 Main St, P.O. Box 1305 • Bethelehem, PA 18016 • (610) 691-0603

Archives of the Moravian Church • 41 W Locust St • Bethlehem, PA 18018 • (610) 866-3255

Banana Factory Museum • 25 W 3rd St • Bethlehem, PA 18015 • (610) 332-1300 • http://www.bananafactory.org

Bethelehem Area Public Library • 11 W Church St • Bethlehem, PA 18018 • (610) 867-3761 • http://www.bapl.org

Burnside Plantation Museum • 1461 Schoenersville Rd • Bethlehem, PA 18018 • (610) 868-5044 • http://www.historicbethlehem.org

Colonial Industrial Quarter Historic Site Museum • 459 Old York Rd • Bethlehem, PA 18018 • (610) 882-0450 • http://www.historicbethlehem.org

Fairchild-Martindale Library • Lehigh University, 8A E Packer Ave • Bethlehem, PA 18015-3170 • (610) 758-4357 • http://www.lehigh.edu/library/

Historic Bethlehem • 459 Old York Rd, P.O. Box 1305 • Bethlehem, PA 18016-1305 • (610) 691-5300 • http://www.historicbethlehem.org

Historical Arms Society • general delivery • Bethlehem, PA 18015 • (610) 997-8613

Moravian Museum • 66 W Church St • Bethlehem, PA 18018 • (610) 867-0173 • http://www.historicbethlehem.org

National Museum of Industrial History • 530 E 3rd St • Bethlehem, PA 18015 • (610) 694-6644 • http://www.nmih.org

South Bethlehem Historical Society • P.O. Box 5106 • Bethlehem, PA 18015 • (610) 758-8790

Sun Inn Preservation Association • Historical Museum, 556 Main St • Bethlehem, PA 18018 • (610) 866-1758 • http://www.suninnbethlehem.org

Biglerville
Biglerville Historical and Preservation Society • Historical Museum, P.O. box 656 • Biglerville, PA 17307 • (717) 677-4556

National Apple Museum • 154 W Hanover St, P.O. Box 656 • Biglerville, PA 17307 • (717) 677-4556 • http://www.nationalapplemuseum.com

National Vietnam War Museum • P.O. Box 496 • Biglerville, PA 17307 • (940) 325-4003 • http://www.nationalvnwarmuseum.org

Bird-in-Hand
Americana Museum of Bird-in-Hand • 2709 Old Philadelphia Pk, P.O. Box 401 • Bird-in-Hand, PA 17505 • (717) 391-9780 • http://bird-in-hand.com/americanamuseum/

Birdsboro
Daniel Boone Homestead Museum • 400 Daniel Boone Rd • Birdsboro, PA 19508 • (610) 582-4900 • http://www.danielboonehomestead.org

Roberson Township Historical Society • Historical Museum, 135 Quarry Rd • Birdsboro, PA 19506

Blairsville
Historical Society of the Blairsville Area • Historical Museum, 116 E Campbell St • Blairsville, PA 15717 • (724) 459-0580

Pennsylvania

Bloomsburg

Bloomsburg Public Library • 225 Market St • Bloomsburg, PA 17815 • (570) 784-0883 • http://www.bloomsburgpl.org

Columbia County Historical and Genealogical Society • c/o Bloomsburg Public Library, 225 Market St, P.O. Box 360 • Bloomsburg, PA 17815-0360 • (570) 784-1600 • http://www.colcohist-gensoc.org

Blue Ball

Wissahickon Valley Historical Society • School Rd • Blue Ball, PA 17506 • (215) 646-6541

Fred C Kuehner Memorial Library • Reform Episcopal Seminary, 826 2nd Ave • Blue Bell, PA 19422 • (610) 292-9852 • http://www.reseminary.edu

Historical Society of Whitpain • Franklinville School Museum, 1701 Morris Rd, P.O. Box 311 • Blue Bell, PA 19422 • (215) 646-7315 • http://www.histsocwhitpain.org

Wissahickon Valley Historic Society • 799 Shippack Pk, P.O. Box 2 • Blue Bell, PA 19422-1734

Boalsburg

Boalsburg Heritage Museum • 304 E Main St, P.O. Box 346 • Boalsburg, PA 16827 • (814) 466-3035 • http://www.boalsburgheritagemuseum.org

Boalsburg Village Conservancy • Historical Museum, Earlystown Rd • Boalsburg, PA 16827 • (814) 466-9266 • http://www.boalmuseum.com

Columbus Chapel & Boal Mansion Museum • 163 Boal Estate Dr, P.O. Box 116 • Boalsburg, PA 16827 • (814) 466-6210 • http://www.boalmuseum.com

Pennsylvania Military Museum and 28th Division Shrine • 602 Boalsburg Pk, P.O. Box 160A • Boalsburg, PA 16827 • (814) 466-6263 • http://pamilmuseum.org

Boothwyn

Bethel Township Historical Society • Historical Museum, 1369 Naaman's Creek Rd • Boothwyn, PA 19062 • (610) 459-4183 • http://betheltownshippreservationsociety.com

Bethel Township Preservation Society • Historical Museum, 1645 Bethel Rd • Boothwyn, PA 19061 • (610) 485-8341

Real World Computer Museum • 7 Creek Pkwy • Boothwyn, PA 19061

Upper Chichester Historical Society • Historical Museum, 1522 Rolling Glen Dr #A • Boothwyn, PA 19061 • (610) 497-5512 • http://www.chichesterhistory.org

Boston

Elizabeth Township Historical Society • Historical Museum, 5811 Smithfield St • Boston, PA 15135 • (412) 754-2030 • http://www.15122.com/ETHS/

Boswell

Boswell Historical Society • Historical Museum, 326 Main St • Boswell, PA 15531 • (814) 629-5945 • http//www.boswellpa.com

Boyertown

Boyertown Area Historical Society • Historical Museum, 43 S Chestnut St • Boyertown, PA 19512 • (610) 367-5255 • http://www.boyertownhistory.org

Boyertown Museum of Historic Vehicles • 85 S Walnut St • Boyertown, PA 19512 • (610) 367-2090 • http://www.boyertownmuseum.org

Braddock

Braddock's Field Historical Society • Historical Museum, 419 Library St • Braddock, PA 15104 • (412) 351-5356

Bradford

Bradford Area Public Library • 67 W Washington St • Bradford, PA 16701-1234 • (814) 362-6527 • http://www.bradfordlibrary.org

Bradford Landmark Society • Historical Museum, 45 E Corydon St • Bradford, PA 16701 • (814) 362-3906 • http://www.bradfordlandmark.org

Zippo-Case Museum • 1932 Zippo Dr • Bradford, PA 16701 • (814) 368-2864 • http://www.zippo.com

Bridgeville

Neville House Museum • 1375 Washington Pk • Bridgeville, PA 15017 • (412) 221-5797

Bristol

Bristol Cultural and Historical Foundation • Historical Museum, 321 Cedar St, P.O. Box 215 • Bristol, PA 19007 • (215) 781-9895 • http://www.bristolhistory.org

Grundy Museum • 610 Radcliffe St, P.O. Box 701 • Bristol, PA 19007 • (215) 788-7891 • http://www.grundymuseum.org

Margaret R Grundy Memorial Library • 680 Radcliffe • Bristol, PA 19007-5199 • (215) 788-7891 • http://www.buckslib.org/libraries/bristol

Brockway

Brockway Area Historical Society • Historical Museum, Taylor Park, 765 Park St, P.O. Box 73 • Brockway, PA 15824 • (814) 265-8519 • http://www.greatlite.com/bahs/

Brodheadsville

Western Pocono Community Library • 2000 Pilgrim Way, P.O. Box 318 • Brodheadsville, PA 18322-0318 • (570) 992-7934 • http://www.wpcl.lib.pa.us

Brooklyn

Brooklyn Historical Society • Historical Museum, P.O. Box 112 • Brooklyn, PA 18813 • (570) 434-2606

Brookville

Historic Brookville • 100 Franklin Ave • Brookville, PA 15825 • (814) 849-4695

Jefferson County Historical and Genealogical Society • 232 Jefferson St, P.O. Box 51 • Brookville, PA 15825 • (814) 849-0077

Jefferson County Historical Society • 176 Main St • Brookville, PA 15825 • (814) 849-0077

Jefferson County History Center • 172-176 Main St, P.O. Box 51 • Brookville, PA 15825 • (814) 849-0077 • http://www.jchonline.org

Rebecca M Arthurs Memorial Library • 223 Valley St • Brookville, PA 15825-0223 • (814) 849-5512 • http://home.alltel.net/rmarthur

Broomall

Church of Jesus Christ of Latter- Day Saints-Philadelphia Stake Family History Center • 721 Paxon Hollow Rd • Broomall, PA 19008 • (610) 356-8507 • http://www.familysearch.org

Delaware County Historical Society • Historical Museum, 85 N Malin Rd • Broomall, PA 19008 • (610) 359-1148 • http://www.delcohistory.org/dchs

Greek American Historical Society of Greater Philadelphia • Historical Museum, P.O. Box 103 • Broomall, PA 19008 • (215) 790-2213

Marple Newtown Historical Society • P.O. Box 755 • Broomall, PA 19008 • (610) 353-4967

Marple Public Library • 225 S Sproul Rd • Broomall, PA 19008-2399 • (610) 356-1510 • http://www.marplepubliclibrary.org

Brownsville

Brownsville Historical Society • Historical Museum, P.O. Box 24 • Brownsville, PA 15417 • (724) 785-6882 • http://www.nemacolincastle.org

Flatiron Building Heritage Center • 69 Market St • Brownsville, PA 15417 • (724) 785-9331 • http://www.flatironcenter.com

National Pike Steam, Gas & Horse Association • Historical Museum, 222 Spring Rd • Brownsville, PA 15417 • (724) 267-4780 • http://www.nationalpike.com

Nemacolin Castle Museum • 136 Front St, P.O. Box 24 • Brownsville, PA 15417 • (724) 785-6882 • http://www.nemacolincastle.org

Bryn Athyn
Cairnwood Estate Museum • 1005 Cathedral Rd, P.O. Box 691 • Bryn Athyn, PA 19009 • (215) 947-2004 • http://www.cairnwood.org

Glencairn Museum • Academy of the New Church, 1001 Cathedral Rd, P.O. Box 757 • Bryn Athyn, PA 19009 • (267) 502-2600 • http://www.glencairnmuseum.org

Bryn Mawr
Harriton House Museum • 500 Harriton Rd, P.O. Box 1364 • Bryn Mawr, PA 19010 • (610) 525-0201 • http://www.harritonhouse.org

King of Prussia Historical Society • Historical Museum, P.O. Box 767 • Bryn Mawr, PA 19010 • (610) 637-6508 • http://www.historicreeseville.com

Penickpacka Historical Society • Historical Museum, 2960 King Rd, P.O. Box 23 • Bryn Mawr, PA 19009

Scotch-Irish Society of the United States of America • P.O. Box 181 • Bryn Mawr, PA 19010 • (610) 429-5747 • http://www.rootsweb.com/~sisusa

Buck Hill Falls
Buck Hill Archives • P.O. Box 113 • Buck Hill Falls, PA 18323

Burgettstown
Fort Vance Historical Society • Historical Museum, 2 Kerr St • Burgettstown, PA 15021

Jefferson Township Historical Society • Historical Museum, 215 Eldersville Rd • Burgettstown, PA 15021 • (724) 947-4476 • http://jeffersontwp.angelfire.com/jths/

Bushkill
Pocono Indian Museum • Route 209, P.O. Box 261 • Bushkill, PA 18324 • (570) 588-9338 • http://www.poconoindianmuseumonline.com

Butler
Butler County Genealogical Society • P.O. Box 662 • Butler, PA 16002

Butler County Historical Society • Historical Museum, 123 W Diamond St, P.O. Box 414 • Butler, PA 16003 • (724) 283-8116 • http://www.butlerhistory.com

Cabot
Butler County Historical Society • RR1 • Cabot, PA 16023 • (724) 352-2120

Cairnbrook
Shade-Central City Historical Society • Historical Museum, 5251 Dark Shade Dr • Cairnbrook, PA 15924 • (814) 754-9997 • http://shadecentralcity.org

California
California Area Historical Society • Historical Museum, 429 Wood St, P.O. box 624 • California, PA 15419 • (724) 938-3250 • http://freepages.genealogy.rootsweb.ancestry.com/~pamonval/cityboro/files/californiahs.html

California Area Public Library • 100 Wood St • California, PA 15419 • (724) 938-2907 • http://calpublib.org

Monongahela River Bluffs Association • Historical Society, 847 Wood St • California, PA 15419 • (724) 938-7856

Cambridge Springs
Cambridge Springs Historical Society • Historical Museum, 26 Federal St • Cambridge Springs, PA 16403 • (814) 398-1827 • http://freepages.genealogy.rootsweb.ancestry.com/~fraber/cambridgehistsoc.htm

Woodcock Township Historical Society • Historical Museum, 25377 Gravel Run Rd • Cambridge Springs, PA 16403

Cammal
Jersey Shore Historical Society • Samuel Moss House • Cammal, PA 17723 • (570) 398-1973

Camp Hill
Peace Church Museum • St John & Trindle Rds • Camp Hill, PA 17011 • (717) 737-6492 • http://www.friendsofpeacechurch.tripod.com

Slovenian Genealogical Society • 52 Old Farm Rd • Camp Hill, PA 17011-2604 • (717) 731-8804 • http://fsloveniangenealogy.org

Welsh Society of Greater Harrisburg, PA • 1938 Walnut St • Camp Hill, PA 17011

Canadensis
Eastern Pennsylvania Conference Historical Society of the United Methodist Church • RD1, Box 127 • Canadensis, PA 18325 • (717) 595-7643

Canonsburg
Greater Canonsburg Public Library • 68 E Pike • Canonsburg, PA 15317 • (724) 745-1308

National Slovak Society of the USA • 333 Technology Dr, Ste 112 • Canonsburg, PA 15317 • (412) 488-1890

Canton
Canton Area Historical Society • Historical Museum, 20 Crooks Terr • Canton, PA 17724 • http://www.cantonhistoricalsociety.org

Carbondale
Carbondale Historical Society • Historical Museum, 1 N Main St, P.O. Box 151 • Carbondale, PA 18407 • (570) 282-0385

Carlisle
Bosler Free Library • 158 W High St • Carlisle, PA 17013-2988 • (717) 243-4642

Cumberland County Historical Society • Two Mile House Museum, 21 N Pitt St, P.O. Box 626 • Carlisle, PA 17013-0626 • (717) 249-7610 • http://www.historicalsociety.com

Oral History Association • Dickinson College, P.O. Box 1773 • Carlisle, PA 17013 • (717) 245-1036 • http://www.dickinson.edu/oha

Trout Gallery Museum • P.O. Box 1773 • Carlisle, PA 17013 • (717) 245-1344

US Army Heritage & Education Center • 950 Soldiers Dr • Carlisle, PA 17013-5008 • (717) 245-3157 • http://www.usahec.org

US Army Military History Institute Library • 22 Ashburn Dr • Carlisle, PA 17013-5008 • (717) 245-4139 • http://carlisle_www.army.mil/usarmhi

US Army War College Library • 122 Forbes Ave • Carlisle, PA 17013-5220 • (717) 245-3660 • http://www.carlisle.army.mil/library/

Waidner-Spahr Library • Dickinson College, 333 W High St • Carlisle, PA 17013-2896 • (717) 245-1397 • http://www.library.dickinson.edu

Carlisle Barracks
US Army Military History Institute • 22 Ashburn Dr, Carlisle Barracks Bldg • Carlisle Barracks, PA 17013-5008 • (717) 245-3971 • http://carlisle-www.army.mil/usamhi/

Carmichaels
Flenniken Memorial Library • 102 E George St • Carmichaels, PA 15320-1202 • (724) 966-5263 • http://www.greenepa.net/~flenniken

Carnegie
Andrew Carnegie Free Library • 300 Beechwood Ave • Carnegie, PA 15106-2699 • (412) 277-3456 • http://www.clpgh.org/ein/andrcarn

Historical Society of Carnegie Pennsylvania • Historical Museum, 1 W Main St, P.O. box 826 • Carnegie, PA 15106 • (412) 276-7447

Pennsylvania

Castanea
Clinton County Genealogical Society • P.O. Box 193 • Castanea, PA 17726

Castle Shannon
Castle Shannon Historical Society • Historical Museum, 1003 Castle Shannon Blvd • Castle Shannon, PA 15234 • (412) 561-7909

Catasauqua
George Taylor House Museum • Lehigh & Poplar Sts • Catasauqua, PA 18032 • (610) 435-4664

Catasauqua Public Library • 302 Bridge St, P.O. Box 127 • Catasauqua, PA 18032-0127 • (610) 264-4151 • http://www. catasauquapl.org

Historic Catasauqua Preservation Association • Historical Museum, 616 2nd St • Catasauqua, PA 18032 • http://www.hcpa.org

Lehigh County Historical Society • 432 Walnut St • Catasauqua, PA 18032 • (610) 435-1074

Catawissa
Catawissa Railroad Company Museum • 119 Pine St • Catawissa, PA 17020 • (570) 356-2675

Cecil
Daguerreian Society • Historical Museum, P.O. box 306 • Cecil, PA 15321 • (412) 221-0306 • http://daguerre.org

Chadds Ford
Brandywine Battlefield Park Museum • Baltimore Pike, P.O. Box 202 • Chadds Ford, PA 19317 • (610) 259-3342 • http://www.libertynet.org/iha/brandywine

Brandywine River Museum • 1 Hoffman's Mill Rd, P.O. Box 141 • Chadds Ford, PA 19317 • (610) 388-2700 • http://www. brandywinemuseum.org

Chadds Ford Historical Society • Historical Museum, 1736 N Creek Rd, P.O. Box 27 • Chadds Ford, PA 19317 • (610) 388-7376 • http://www.chaddsfordhistory.org

Christian C Sanderson Museum • 1755 Creek Rd, P.O. Box 153 • Chadds Ford, PA 19317 • (610) 388-6545 • http://www. sandersonmuseum.org

Chambersburg
Coyle Free Library • 102 N Main St • Chambersburg, PA 17201-1676 • (717) 263-1054 • http://www.fclspa.org

Franklin County Heritage • Historical Museum, E King & 2nd St • Chambersburg, PA 17201 • (717) 264-6364

Franklin County Library • 102 N Main St • Chambersburg, PA 17201 • (717) 263-1054

Kittochtinny Historical Society • Historical Museum, 175 E King St, P.O. Box 733 • Chambersburg, PA 17201-1806 • (717) 264-1667 • http://pafch.tripod.com

Ragged Edge Library • 35 Ragged Edge Rd • Chambersburg, PA 17201 • (717) 264-9663

State Historic Site of Fort Loudoun • 1720 Brooklyn Rd • Chambersburg, PA 17021 • (717) 787-3602 • http://www.fortloudoun-pa.com

Charleroi
Charleroi Area Historical Society • Historical Museum, 807 Fallowfield • Charleroi, PA 15022 • (724) 483-4961 • http://charleroi-historical.org

Charleroi Historic District • 638 Fallowfield Ave • Charleroi, PA 15022 • (724) 483-2030

Mon Valley Railroad Society • Historical Museum, 845 Rear Prospect Ave • Charleroi, PA 15022

Chester
Chester Historical Preservation Society • Historical Museum, 2320 Chestnut St • Chester, PA 19013 • (610) 876-5355 • http://www. delcohistory.org/chester/

J Lewis Crozer Library • 620 Engle St • Chester, PA 19013-2199 • (610) 494-3454

Wolfgram Memorial Library • Widener University, 1 University Ave • Chester, PA 19013-5792 • (610) 499-4087 • http://www.widener.edu/libraries.html

Chester Heights
Friends of Old St Thomas Church • Historical Museum, P.O. Box 19 • Chester Heights, PA 19017 • (610) 459-3151

Chester Springs
Chester Springs Library • 1685 A Art School Rd • Chester Springs, PA 19425-1402 • (610) 827-9212 • http://www.ccls.org

Historic Yellow Springs • Historical Museum, 1685 Art School Rd, P.O. Box 62 • Chester Springs, PA 19425 • (610) 827-7414 • http://www. yellowsprings.org

Cheyney
Thornbury Historical Society • Historical Museum, P.O. box 155 • Cheyney, PA 19319 • (610) 358-3397 • http://sites.google.com/site/thornburyhistoricalsociety/

Christiana
Christiana Historical Society • 315 Newport Pike • Christiana, PA 17509

Moores Memorial Library • 326 N Bridge St • Christiana, PA 17509-1202 • (610) 593-6683 • http://www.christianalibrary.org

Octorara Valley Historical Society • Historical Museum, general delivery • Christiana, PA 17509

Clairton
Clairton Public Library • 616 Miller Ave • Clairton, PA 15025-1497 • (412) 233-7966 • http://www.einpgh.org/ein/clairton/

Clarion
Clarion County Historical Society • Ralph J & Virginia A Fulton Library, 17 S 5th Ave • Clarion, PA 16214-1501 • (814) 226-4450 • http://www. csonline.net/cchs

Clarion Free Library • 644 Main St, P.O. Box 663 • Clarion, PA 16214-0663 • (814) 226-7172 • http://www.clarionfreelibrary.org

Sutton-Ditz House Museum • 18 Grant St • Clarion, PA 16214 • (814) 226-4450 • http://www.clarioncountyhistoricalsociety.org

Clarks Summit
Murphy Memorial Library • Baptist Bible College & Seminary, 538 Venard Rd • Clarks Summit, PA 18411-1250 • (570) 585-9280 • http://www.bbc.edu

Saint David's Society of Lackawanna County • 2 Gladiola Dr • Clarks Summit, PA 18411

Claussville
Claussville One-Room Schoolhouse Museum • 2917 Route 100 • Claussville, PA 18069 • (610) 435-4664

Clearfield
Clearfield County Historical Society • Historical Museum, 104 E Pine St • Clearfield, PA 16830 • (814) 765-6125

Joseph and Elizabeth Shaw Public Library • 1 S Front St • Clearfield, PA 16830 • (814) 765-3271 • http://www.clearfield.org/shaw/

Coaldale
Panther Valley Historical Society • 240 W Phillip • Coaldale, PA 18218

Coalport
Glendale Area Public Library • Community Bldg, 961 Forest St, P.O. Box 351 • Coalport, PA 16627-0351 • (814) 672-4378

Coatesville
Caln Township Historical Society • Historical Museum, 1115 Caln Meeting Rd • Coatesville, PA 19320

Coatesville Area Public Library • 501 E Lincoln Hwy • Coatesville, PA 19320 • (610) 384-4115 • http://www.ccls.org/othlibs/coats.htm

Fallowfield Historical Society • Historical Museum, 10 Boroline Rd • Coatesville, PA 19320 • (610) 857-1824

Graystone Society • Historical Museum, 76 S 1st Ave • Coatesville, PA 19320 • (610) 384-9282 • http://www.lukensnhd.org

Cogan Station
Blooming Grove Historical Society • Historical Museum, 297 Dunkard Church Rd, P.O. Box 105 • Cogan Station, PA 17728 • (570) 435-2997 • http://www.bloominggrovehistoricalsociety.org

Collegeville
Historical Society of Trappe, Collegeville and Perkiomen Valley • Historical Museum, 301 W Main St, P.O. Box 26708 • Collegeville, PA 19426 • (610) 489-8883 • http://www.trappehistoricalsociety.org

Myrin Library • Ursinus College, 601 Main St • Collegeville, PA 19426-1000 • (610) 409-3607

Pennsylvania Folklife Society • c/o Myrin Library, Ursinus College, P.O. Box 1000 • Collegeville, PA 19426 • (610) 409-3600 • http://www.pgs.org/dialect/Ursinus.asp

Pennsylvania Veterinary Historical Society • Historical Museum, 3344 Mill Rd • Collegeville, PA 19426 • (610) 489-1229

Columbia
Columbia Historic Preservation Society • Historical Museum, 19 N 2nd St, P.O. Box 578 • Columbia, PA 17512 • (717) 684-2894

Columbia Public Library • 24 S 6th St • Columbia, PA 17512-1599 • (717) 684-2255 • http://www.columbia.lib.pa.us

First National Bank Museum • 170 Locust St • Columbia, PA 17512 • (717) 684-8864 • http://www.bankmuseum.org

Louise Steinman von Hess Foundation • Wright's Ferry Mansion Museum, 2nd & Cherry Sts, P.O. Box 68 • Columbia, PA 17512 • (717) 684-4325

National Watch and Clock Museum • 512 Poplar St • Columbia, PA 17512 • (717) 684-8261 • http://www.museumoftime.org

Wrights Ferry Mansion Museum • 38 S 2nd St, P.O. Box 68 • Columbia, PA 17512 • (717) 684-4325 • http://www.paheritage.org/lawright.html

Columbus
Pioneer Steam & Gas Engine Society • Historical Museum, 26 East St • Columbus, PA 16403 • (814) 663-1291 • http://www.pioneersteamandgas.com

Concordville
Concord Township Historical Society • Historical Museum, P.O. Box 152 • Concordville, PA 19331 • (610) 459-8911 • http://www.delcohistory.org/concord/

Conestoga
Conestoga Area Historical Society • 49 Kendig Rd • Conestoga, PA 17616-9740 • (717) 782-1699

Connestoga Area Historical Society • Historical Museum, 51 Kendig Rd, P.O. Box 232 • Conestoga, PA 17516 • (717) 872-1699

Conneaut Lake
Conneaut Lake Area Historical Society • Historical Museum, 10498 US Hwy 6, P.O. Box 425 • Conneaut Lake, PA 16316 • (814) 382-6894 • http://www.conneautlakehistory.com

Lakeland Museum • P.O. Box 5072 • Conneaut Lake, PA 16316

Conneautville
Conneaut Valley Area Historical Society • 1625 Main St, P.O. Box 266 • Conneautville, PA 16406 • (814) 587-3782 • http://cvahs.org

Connellsville
Carnegie Free Library • 299 S Pittsburgh St • Connellsville, PA 15425-3580 • (724) 628-1380 • http://www.carnegiefreelib.org

Col William Crawford Log Cabin Museum • 275 S Pittsburgh St • Connellsville, PA 16425 • (412) 628-5640

Connellsville Area Historical Society • Historical Museum, 299 S Pittsburgh St • Connellsville, PA 15425-3580 • (724) 628-5640 • http://www.connellsvillehistoricalsociety.com

Conshohocken
Conshohocken Historical Society • Historical Museum, 120 E 5th Ave • Conshohocken, PA 19428 • (610) 828-7869 • http://conshohocken.pennsylvaniadata.com

Conshokochen Historical Society • 120 E 5th Ave • Conshokochen, PA 19428-1713 • (610) 828-7869

Coolspring
Coolspring Power Museum • 179 Coolspring Rd, P.O. Box 19 • Coolspring, PA 15730 • (814) 849-6883 • http://www.coolspringpowermuseum.com

Coopersburg
Coopersburg Historical Society • Historical Museum, State & Main Sts, P.O. Box 51 • Coopersburg, PA 18036 • (610) 282-3138 • http://www.coopersburg.org/HistoricalSociety.cfm

Coraopolis
Coraopolis Historical Society • Historical Museum, State Ave & School St • Coraopolis, PA 15108

Coraopolis Memorial Library • 601 School St • Coraopolis, PA 15108-1196 • (412) 264-3502 • http://www.einpgh.org/ein/coraopls/

Cornwall
Cornwall Iron Furnace Museum • 94 Rexmont Rd, P.O. Box 251 • Cornwall, PA 17016 • (717) 272-9711 • http://www.cornwallironfurnace.org

Corry
Corry Area Historical Society • Historical Museum, 937 Mead Ave, P.O. Box 107 • Corry, PA 16407 • (814) 664-4749 • http://www.corryareahistoricalsociety.org

Corry Public Library • 117 W Washington St • Corry, PA 16407 • (814) 664-7611 • http://www.corrylibrary.org

Coudersport
Potter County Historical Society • Historical Museum, 308 N Main St, P.O. Box 605 • Coudersport, PA 16915 • (814) 274-4410 • http://www.paintedhills.org

Cranberry Township
Cranberry Genealogy Club • P.O. Box 2491 • Cranberry Township, PA 16066

Cranberry Township Historical Society • Historical Museum, 2525 Rochester Rd, P.O. Box 1931 • Cranberry Township, PA 16066 • http://explorecranberry.org

Crescent
Crescent-Shousetown Area Historical Association • Historical Museum, Municipal Bldg, P.O. Box 253 • Crescent, PA 15046

Cresco
Cresco Township Historical Society • Cresco Station Museum, Rte 390 & Sand Spring Rd • Cresco, PA 18326 • (570) 595-6157 • http://www.barretthistory.org/museum.php

Pennsylvania

Cresson
Admiral Peary Monument Museum • 7468 Admiral Peary Hwy • Cresson, PA 16630 • (814) 886-5060

Allegheny Portage Railroad National Historic Site • 110 Federal Park Rd • Cresson, PA 16630 • (814) 885-6150 • http://www.nps.gov.alpo

Cresson Area Historical Association • Historical Museum, 3rd St, P.O. Box 352 • Cresson, PA 16630 • (814) 886-7082 • http://www.cahainc.org

Cressona
Cressona Historical Society • 76 Pottsville St • Cressona, PA 17929-1222

Curwensville
Clearfield County Public Library • 601 Beech St • Curwensville, PA 16833 • (814) 236-0589 • http://www.angelfire.com/pa2/curwensvillelibrary/

Custer City
Penn Brad Oil Museum • Rte 219 • Custer City, PA 16701 • (814) 362-1955 • http://www.visitpa.com/penn-brad-oil-museum

Dalmatia
Mahanoy and Mahantongo Historical Preservation Society • Historical Museum, P.O. Box 143 • Dalmatia, PA 17017 • (570) 758-8722 • http://www.mahantongo.org/mmhps/index.htm

Dalton
Dalton Community Library • 113 E Main St, P.O. Box 86 • Dalton, PA 18414-0086 • (570) 563-2014 • http://www.lackawannacountylibrarysystem.org/dalton

Overlook Estate Museum • Lily Lake Rd • Dalton, PA 18414 • http://www.overlook.org

Danville
Jankola Library and Slovak Archives • general delivery • Danville, PA 17821 • (570) 275-3581

Montour County Genealogical Society • Historical Museum, 205 Ferry St • Danville, PA 17821 • (570) 275-6177 • http://www.rootsweb.ancestry.com/~pamcgs/

Montour County Historical Society • Historical Museum, 205 Ferry St, P.O. Box 8 • Danville, PA 17821 • (570) 275-0830 • http://www.rootsweb.ancestry.com/~pamcgs/

Darby
Darby Borough Historical Preservation Society • Historical Museum, 16 Winthrop Rd, P.O. Box 108 • Darby, PA 19023 • (610) 583-4386 • http://www.delcohistory.org/darby

Darby Free Library • 1001 Main St, P.O. Box 164 • Darby, PA 19023-0164 • (610) 586-7310 • http://darbylibrary.org

Darlington
Little Beaver Historical Society • Historical Museum, 710 Market St, P.O. Box 304 • Darlington, PA 16115 • (724) 622-5342 • http://www.bchistory.org

Davidsville
Conemaugh Township Historical Society • Historical Museum, 100-104 S Main St, P.O. Box 307 • Davidsville, PA 15928 • (814) 479-2067

Dawson
Linden Hall Museum • Linden Hall Rd • Dawson, PA 15428 • (724) 529-0529

Dayton
Dayton Area Local History Society • Historical Museum, P.O. Box 15 • Dayton, PA 16222 • http://www.daytonpa.org

Marshall House Museum • N State St • Dayton, PA 16222 • (814) 257-8260

Delaware Water Gap
Antoine Dutot School & Museum • P.O. Box 484 • Delaware Water Gap, PA 18327 • (570) 476-4240 • http://www.dutotmuseum.com

Delta
Old Line Museum • 602 Main St, P.O. Box 35 • Delta, PA 17314 • (717) 456-7124 • http://www.oldlinemuseum.com

Derrick City
McKean County Genealogical Society • P.O. Box 207 A • Derrick City, PA 16727

Dillsburg
Northern York County Historical and Preservation Society • 35 Greenbrier Ln • Dillsburg, PA 17019 • (717) 502-1440 • http://www.northernyorkhistorical.org

Donora
Donora Historical Society • Historical Museum, 510 Meldon Ave • Donora, PA 15033 • (724) 379-7014 • http://www.westol.com/~shawley/dhs

Tri-State Historical Steam Engine Museum • 488 7th St • Donora, PA 15033 • (724) 483-5144

Downingtown
Downington Historical Society • Historical Museum, P.O. Box 9 • Downingtown, PA 19335 • (610) 269-1709 • http://www.downingtownareahistoricalsociety.org

Downingtown Library Company • 330 E Lancaster Ave • Downingtown, PA 19335-2946 • (610) 269-2741 • http://www.ccls.org

Doylestown
Bucks County Civil War Roundtable • Bucks County Civil War Library & Museum, 32 N Broad St • Doylestown, PA 18901 • (215) 348-8293 • http://www.buckscivilwar.com

Bucks County Free Library • 150 S Pine St • Doylestown, PA 18901-4932 • (215) 348-0332 • http://www.buckslib.org

Bucks County Genealogical Society • German Baptist Brethren Meeting House, Ferry Rd, P.O. Box 1092 • Doylestown, PA 18901-0020 • (215) 230-9410

Bucks County Historical Society • Mercer Castle Museum, 84 S Pine St • Doylestown, PA 18901-4999 • (215) 345-0210 • http://www.mercermuseum.org

Doylestown Borough Historical Society • Historical Museum, 57 W Court St • Doylestown, PA 18901 • http://www.doylestownborough.net

Fonthill Museum • E Court St & Rt 313 • Doylestown, PA 18901 • (215) 348-9461 • http://www.foothillmuseum.org

Heritage Conservancy • Aldie Mansion Museum, 85 Old Dublin Pk • Doylestown, PA 18901 • (215) 345-7020 • http://www.heritageconservancy.org

Dublin
Friendly Sons of Saint Patrick of Philadelphia • P.O. Box 969 • Dublin, PA 18917-0969 • (215) 249-9337 • http://www.friendlysons.com

DuBois
Dubois Area Historical Society • Historical Museum, 30 W Long Ave, P.O. Box 401 • DuBois, PA 15801-0401 • (814) 371-9006 • http://www.duboishs.com

Dushore
Sullivan County Library • 216 Center St, P.O. Box 309 • Dushore, PA 18614-0309 • (570) 928-9352

Eagles Mere
Eagles Mere Museum • Eagles Mere Ave • Eagles Mere, PA 17731 • (570) 525-3155 • http://www.eaglesmere.org/emmuseum.html

East Berlin
East Berlin Historical Preservation Society • Historical Museum, 332 W King St, P.O. Box 73 • East Berlin, PA 17316 • (717) 259-0822 • http://ebhpspa.org

East Brady
Bradys Bend Historical Society • Historical Museum, P.O. Box 451 • East Brady, PA 16028 • (724) 526-3363

East Freedom
Old Greenfield Township Society • Historical Museum, P.O. Box 59 • East Freedom, PA 16637

East Petersburg
East Petersburg Historical Society • Historical Museum, 6040 Main St, P.O. Box 176 • East Petersburg, PA 17520

Easton
American Friends of Lafayette • c/o Skillman Library, Lafayette College • Easton, PA 18042 • (610) 250-5200

David Bishop Skillman Library • Lafayette College • Easton, PA 18042 • (610) 330-5151 • http://www.library.lafayette.edu

Easton Area Public Library • 515 Church St • Easton, PA 18042-3587 • (610) 258-2917 • http://www.eastonpl.org

Easton Heritage Alliance • Historical Museum, 1753 Bachmann Publick House, 169 Northampton St • Easton, PA 18042 • (610) 258-1612 • http://www.eastonheritagealliance.com

Historic Easton • Historical Museum, 613 Paxinosa Ave • Easton, PA 18042

National Canal Museum and Hugh Moore Historic Park • 30 Centre Sq • Easton, PA 18042-7743 • (610) 559-6613 • http://www.canals.org

Northampton County Historical and Genealogical Society • c/o Mary Illick Memorial Library, 101 S 4th St • Easton, PA 18042 • (610) 253-1222 • http://www.northamptoncitymuseum.org

Parson-Taylor House Museum • 107 S 4th St • Easton, PA 18042 • (610) 253-1222

Ebensburg
Cambria County Historical Society • Historical Museum, 615 N Center St, P.O. Box 278 • Ebensburg, PA 15931-0278 • (814) 472-6674 • http://www.cambriacountyhistorical.com

Ebensburg Free Public Library • 225 W Highland Ave • Ebensburg, PA 15931-1507 • (814) 472-7957 • http://www.cclib.lib.pa.us/ebensburg

Eckley
Eckley Miners' Village Museum • Main St • Eckley, PA 18255 • (570) 636-2938 • http://www.phme.state.pa.us

Edinboro
Edinboro Area Historical Society • Historical Museum, 126 Water St, P.O. Box 18 • Edinboro, PA 16412 • (814) 734-6109 • http://www.edinborohistory.org

Edinboro University Museum • 219 Meadville St • Edinboro, PA 16444 • (814) 732-2000 • http://www.edinboro.edu

Egypt
Troxell-Steckel House and Farm Museum • 4229 Reliance St • Egypt, PA 18052 • (610) 435-1074

Eldred
Eldred World War II Museum • 210 Main St • Eldred, PA 16731 • (814) 225-2220 • http://www.eldredwwiimuseum.org

Elizabethtown
Donegal Society • Historical Museum, 540 E Willow St • Elizabethtown, PA 17022 • (717) 295-1711

Elizabethtown College Museum • 1 Alpha Dr • Elizabethtown, PA 17022 • (717) 361-1400 • http://www.etown.edu

Elizabethtown Historical Society • Historical Museum, 57 S Poplar St, P.O. Box 301 • Elizabethtown, PA 17022 • (717) 361-9382 • http://www.etownhistory.com

Elizabethtown Preservation Associates • Winters Heritage House Museum, 43 E High St, P.O. Box 14 • Elizabethtown, PA 17022 • (717) 367-4672 • http://www.elizabethtownhistory.org

High Library • Elizabethtown College, 1 Alpha Dr • Elizabethtown, PA 17022-2227 • (717) 361-1451 • http://www.etown.edu/library

Elkins Park
Temple Judea Museum • Reform Congregation Keneseth Israel, 8339 Old York Rd • Elkins Park, PA 19027 • (215) 887-2027 • http://www.kenesethisrael.org

Elkland
Elkland Area Community Library • 110 Parkway Dr • Elkland, PA 16920-1311 • (814) 258-7576 • http://www.elklandlibrary.com

Ellwood City
Ellwood City Area Historical Society • Elwood City Museum, 310 5th St, P.O. Box 611 • Ellwood City, PA 16117 • (724) 752-2021 • http://www.ellwoodhistory.com

Elverson
Hopewell Furnace Historic Site • 2 Mark Bird Ln • Elverson, PA 19520 • (610) 582-8773 • http://www.nps.gov/hofu/

Hopewell Village National Historic Site Library • 2 Mark Bird Ln • Elverson, PA 19520 • (610) 582-8773 • http://www.nps.gov/hofu/

Mennonite Family History Library • 10 W Main St • Elverson, PA 19520-0171 • (610) 286-0258 • http://feefhs.org/men/frg-mfh.html

Emmaus
1803 House Museum • 55 S Keystone Ave • Emmaus, PA 18049 • (610) 965-0152

Emmaus Historical Society • Historical Museum, 563 Chestnut St • Emmaus, PA 18049-2403 • (610) 966-6591 • http://www.emmaushistoric-pa.org/

Emmaus Public Library • 115 E Main St • Emmaus, PA 18049 • (610) 965-9284 • http://www.emmauspl.org

Lehigh County Historical Society • 100 North St • Emmaus, PA 18049 • (610) 391-1968

Lower Macungie Historical Society • Historical Museum, 5102 Kings Hwy N • Emmaus, PA 18049 • (610) 966-3979 • http://www.lmths.org

Shelter House Museum • 601 S 4th St, P.O. Box 254 • Emmaus, PA 18049 • (610) 965-9258

Emporium
Cameron County Historical Society • The Little Museum, 102 E 4th St, P.O. Box 433 • Emporium, PA 15834 • (814) 486-2621 • http://www.thelittlemuseum.org

Cameron County Public Library-Barbara Moscato Brown Memorial • 27 W 4th St, P.O. Box 430 • Emporium, PA 15834-0430 • (814) 486-8011 • http://users.adelphia.net/~brocampl/

Enola
Historical Society of East Pennsboro • 410 Cherry St, P.O. Box 195 • Enola, PA 17025-0195 • (717) 732-5801

Ephrata
Ephrata Cloister Museum • 632 W Main St • Ephrata, PA 17522 • (717) 733-6600 • http://www.ephratacloister.org

Historical Society of Cocalico Valley • Historical Museum, 249 W Main St, P.O. Box 193 • Ephrata, PA 17522 • (717) 733-1616 • http://www.cocalicovalleyhs.org

Moore-Connell Mansion Museum • 249 W Main St, P.O. Box 193 • Ephrata, PA 17522 • (717) 733-1616

Pennsylvania

Equinunk

Equinunk Historical Society • Historical Museum, P.O. Box 41 • Equinunk, PA 18417 • (717) 224-6722

Erie

Anshe Hesed Temple Library • 930 Liberty St • Erie, PA 16502 • (814) 454-2426

Cashier's House Museum • 417 State St • Erie, PA 16501 • (814) 454-1813

Erie County Historical Society • Erie History Center, 419 State St • Erie, PA 16501 • (814) 454-1813 • http://www.eriecountyhistory.org

Erie County Public Library • 160 E Front St • Erie, PA 16507 • (814) 451-6900 • http://www.erielibrary.org

Erie Historical Museum and Plantation • 356 W 6th St • Erie, PA 16507 • (814) 879-0988

Erie Maritime Museum • US Brig Niagara, Bayview Commons, 150 E Front St • Erie, PA 16507 • (814) 452-2744 • http://www.brigniagara.org

Erie Society for Genealogical Research • Erie History Center, 419 State St, P.O. Box 1403 • Erie, PA 16512-1403 • (814) 454-1813 • http://www.pa-roots.com/erie

Erie Yesterday Museum • 417 State St • Erie, PA 16501 • (814) 454-1813 • http://www.goerie.com/erieyesterday/

Firefighters Historical Museum • 428 Chestnut St • Erie, PA 16508 • (814) 864-2156 • http://firefightershistoricalmuseum.com

Hammermill Library • Mercyhurst College, 501 E 38th St • Erie, PA 16546 • (814) 824-2232 • http://merlin.mercyhurst.edu

Harborcreek Historical Society • Historical Museum, 5451 Mewin Ln • Erie, PA 16510 • (814) 899-4447 • http://www.harborcreekhistory.org

Lawrence Park Historical Society • 4230 Iroquois Ave • Erie, PA 16511 • (814) 899-7119

Museum of Erie GE History • 2901 E Lake Rd • Erie, PA 16531 • (814) 875-2494 • http://www.visitpa.com/pa-museums/museum-erie-ge-history

Steamship Niagara Museum • 100 State St • Erie, PA 16507

Watson-Curtze Mansion Museum • 356 W 6th St • Erie, PA 16507 • (814) 871-5790 • http://ww.eriecountyhistory.org

Erwinna

Isaac Stover House Museum • 845 River Rd • Erwinna, PA 18920 • (610) 294-8044

Essington

Governor Printz Park Museum • 2nd & Taylor Aves • Essington, PA 19029 • (610) 583-7221

Tinicum Township Historical Society • Historical Museum, P.O. Box 115 • Essington, PA 19029 • (610) 521-1698 • http://www.tinicumtownshipdelco.com

Evans City

Evans City Historical Society • Historical Museum, 220 Wahl Ave • Evans City, PA 16033 • (724) 538-3629

Everett

Everett Free Library • 137 E Main St • Everett, PA 15537-1259 • (814) 652-5922 • http://www.everettlibrary.org

Exton

Chester County Library System • 450 Exton Square Pkwy • Exton, PA 19341 • (610) 280-2600 • http://www.ccls.org

Thomas Newcomen Library & Museum • 412 Newcomen Rd • Exton, PA 19341 • (610) 363-6600 • http://www.newcomen.com

Fairless Hills

Historic Three Arches Museum • 335 Trenton Rd • Fairless Hills, PA 19030 • (215) 547-7823 • http://www.threearches.org

Fairview

Fairview Area Historical Society • 4302 Avonia Rd • Fairview, PA 16415 • (814) 474-5855 • http://www.fairviewhistoryeriecountypa.org

Fallsington

Fallsington Library Company • 139 Yardley Ave • Fallsington, PA 19054-1119 • (215) 295-4449

Historic Fallsington • Historic Museum, 4 Yardley Ave • Fallsington, PA 19054 • (215) 295-6567 • http://www.historicfallsington.org

Fort Necessity National Battlefield Museum • 1 Washington Pkwy • Farmington, PA 15437 • (724) 329-5512 • http://www.nps.gov/fone

Friendship Hill National Historic Site • RD 2, Box 528 • Farmington, PA 15437 • (724) 725-9190 • http://www.nps.gov/frhi/

Feasterville

Lower Southampton Historical Society • Historical Museum, 1500 Desire Ave • Feasterville, PA 19053

Fleetwood

Fleetwood Area Historical Society • Historical Museum, 110 W Arch St • Fleetwood, PA 19522 • (610) 698-2383 • http://www.fleetwoodpa.org

Ford City

Ford City Public Library • 1136 4th Ave • Ford City, PA 16226-1202 • (724) 763-3591

Forksville

Eastern Delaware Nations • Council House, RR1, Box 1148 • Forksville, PA 18616 • (570) 924-9082

Fort Loudon

Fort Loudon Historical Society • 1720 Brooklyn Rd • Fort Loudon, PA 17224 • (717) 369-3473

Fort Loudoun Museum • P.O. Box 181 • Fort Loudon, PA 17224 • (717) 369-3318 • http://www.fortloudoun-pa.com

Fort Washington

Highlands Historical Society • Historical Museum, 7001 Sheaff Ln • Fort Washington, PA 19034 • (215) 641-2687

Highlands House Museum • 7001 Sheaff Ln • Fort Washington, PA 19054 • (215) 641-2687 • http://www.highlandshistorical.org

Historical Society of Fort Washington • Clifton House Museum, 473 Bethlehem Pk • Fort Washington, PA 19034 • (215) 646-6065 • http://www.amblerhistory.com

Hope Lodge and Mather Hill Museum • 553 Bethlehem Pk • Fort Washington, PA 19034 • (215) 646-1595 • http://www.ushistory.org/hope/history/mill.htm

Upsala Foundation • Historical Museum, 1612 Conquest Wy • Fort Washington, PA 19034

Forty Fort

Nathan Denison House Museum • 35 Denison St • Forty Fort, PA 18704-4390 • (570) 288-5531

Frackville

Frackville Area Historical Society • Historical Museum, 104 Broad Mountain Ave • Frackville, PA 17931 • (717) 874-3219

Frackville Free Public Library • 56 N Lehigh Ave • Frackville, PA 17931-1424 • (570) 874-3382 • http://www.frackvillelibrary.com

Franklin

DeBence Antique Music World Museum • 1261 Liberty St • Franklin, PA 16323 • (814) 432-8350 • http://debencemusicworld.com

Franklin Public Library • 421 12th St • Franklin, PA 16323-0421 • (814) 432-5062 • http://www.franklinlibrary.org

Historic Franklin Preservation Association • Historical Museum, 430 13th St • Franklin, PA 16323 • http://www.franklinpa.gov/h_franklin_preservation_association/

Venango County Historical Society • Historical Museum, 301 S Park St, P.O. Box 101 • Franklin, PA 16323 • (814) 437-2275

Franklintown
Blair County Genealogical Society • Scotch Valley Rd • Franklintown, PA 17323 • (814) 696-3492

Fraxer
East Whiteland Historical Commission • Historical Museum, 209 Conestoga Rd • Fraxer, PA 19355 • (610) 648-0600 • http://www.eastwhiteland.org

Freedom
Beaver County Historical Research and Landmarks Foundation • Historical Museum, 1235 3rd Ave, P.O. Box 1 • Freedom, PA 15042 • (724) 775-1848 • http://www.bchrlf.org

Freeport
Freeport Area Historical Society • Historical Museum, P.O. Box 107 • Freeport, PA 16229

Friedens
Hooversville Historical Society • Historical Museum, 1264 Shoystown Rd • Friedens, PA 15541 • (814) 445-8264

Furlong
Doylestown Historical Society • Visitors Center, 3890 Robin Rd • Furlong, PA 18925 • (215) 345-9430

Galeton
Galeton Public Library • 3 W Main St • Galeton, PA 16922-1001 • (814) 435-2321 • http://www.ncldistrict.org/galeton/

Pennsylvania Lumber Museum • 5600 US 6 West, P.O. Box 239 • Galeton, PA 16922 • (814) 435-2652 • http://www.lumbermuseum.org

Gallitzin
Allegheny Portage Railroad and Johnstown Flood Memorial Museum • 110 Federal Park Rd • Gallitzin, PA 16641 • (814) 886-6116 • http://www.nps.gov/alpo

Geigertown
Hay Creek Historical Association • Historical Museum, 1250 Furnace Rd, P.O. Box 36 • Geigertown, PA 19523 • (610) 286-0388 • http://www.haycreek.org

Gettysburg
A R Wentz Library • Lutheran Theological Seminary • Gettysburg, PA 17325 • (717) 338-3014 • http://www.ltsg.edu

Adams County Historical Society • Historical Museum, 111 Seminary Ridge, P.O. Box 4325 • Gettysburg, PA 17325-4325 • (717) 334-4723 • http://www.achs-pa.org

Adams County Library System • 140 Baltimore St • Gettysburg, PA 17325-2311 • (717) 334-5716 • http://www.adamslibrary.org

Center for Civil War Photography Museum • 65 Steinwehr Ave • Gettysburg, PA 1325 • (813) 951-4962 • http://www.civilwarphotography.org

Dobbin House Museum • 89 Steinwehr Ave • Gettysburg, PA 17325 • (717) 334-2100 • http://www.dobbinhouse.com

Eisenhower National Historic Site • 1195 Baltimore Pk • Gettysburg, PA 17325 • (717) 338-9114 • http://www.nps.gov/eise/

General Lee's Headquarters Museum • 401 Burford Ave • Gettysburg, PA 17325 • (717) 334-3141

Gettysburg National Military Park • 1195 Baltimore Pike, P.O. Box 2804 • Gettysburg, PA 17325 • (717) 334-0909 • http://www.nps.gov/gett/

Great American Civil War Society • Historical Museum, 2449 Heidlersburg Rd • Gettysburg, PA 17325 • (717) 528-8761

Hall of Presidents and First Ladies Museum • 789 Baltimore St • Gettysburg, PA 17325 • (717) 334-5717 • http://www.gettysburgbattlefieldtours.com/hall-of-presidents.php

Historic Gettysburg-Adams County • Historical Museum, 12 Lincoln Sq, P.O. Box 4611 • Gettysburg, PA 17325 • (717) 334-7854 • http://www.hgaconline.org

Jennie Wade House Museum • 548 Baltimore St • Gettysburg, PA 17325 • (717) 334-6296 • http://www.gettysburgbattlefieldtours.com/jennie-wade-house.php

Lincoln Train Museum • 425 Steinwehr Ave • Gettysburg, PA 17325 • (717) 334-5678 • http://www.gettysburgbattlefieldtours.com/lincoln-train-museum.php

Lutheran Historical Society Gettysburg • 61 W Confederate Ave • Gettysburg, PA 17325

Musselman Library • Gettysburg College, 300 N Washington St, Box 420 • Gettysburg, PA 17325-1483 • (717) 337-6600 • http://www.gettysburg.edu

Seminary Ridge Historic Preservation Foundation • Historical Museum, 61 Seminary Ridge • Gettysburg, PA 17325 • (717) 338-3030 • http://seminaryridge.org

Shriver House Museum • 309 Baltimore St • Gettysburg, PA 17325 • (717) 337-2800 • http://www.shriverhouse.org

Soldiers National Museum • 777 Baltimore St • Gettysburg, PA 17325 • (717) 334-4890 • http://www.gettysburgbattlefieldtours.com/soldiers-national-museum.php

Gibsonia
Western Pennsylvania Model Railroad Museum • 5507 Lakeside Dr • Gibsonia, PA 15044 • (724) 444-6944 • http://www.wpmrm.org

Girard
Battles Museums of Rural Life • 436 Walnut St • Girard, PA 16501 • (814) 454-6890 • http://www.eriecountyhistory.org

Charlotte Elizabeth Battles Memorial Museum • 306 Walnut St • Girard, PA 16417

West Erie County Historical Society • Hazel Kibler Museum, 522 E Main St • Girard, PA 16417 • (814) 774-4168 • http://www.westcountyhistorical.com

Yellow House Museum • 436 Walnut St • Girard, PA 16417

Gladwyne
Gladwyne Free Library • 362 Righters Mill Rd • Gladwyne, PA 19035-1587 • (610) 642-3957 • http://www.lmls.org

Glen Mills
Millers House and Nathaniel Newlin Grist Mill Museums • 219 S Cheyney Rd • Glen Mills, PA 19342 • (610) 459-2359 • http://www.newlingristmill.org

Thornbury Historical Society • 130 Glen Mills Rd • Glen Mills, PA 19342-1748 • (610) 459-2307

Glen Rock
Arthur Hufnagel-Glen Rock Public Library • 32 Main St • Glen Rock, PA 17327 • (717) 235-1127 • http://www.yorklibraries.org/glenrock

Glenmore
Springton Manor Farm Museum • 860 Springton • Glenmore, PA 19343 • (610) 942-3285

Glenside
Cheltenham Township Library System • 215 S Keswick Ave • Glenside, PA 19038-4420 • (215) 885-0457 • http://www. cheltenhamtownshiplibraries.org

Gradyville
Edgemont Township Historical Commission • Historical Museum, 1000 Gradyville Rd • Gradyville, PA 19039 • (610) 459-1662 • http://www. edgmont.org/page14/page14.html

Ockehocking Historical Society • Historical Museum, P.O. Box 64 • Gradyville, PA 19039 • (610) 436-0378

Grantham
Archives of the Brethren in Christ Church • Messiah College • Grantham, PA 17027 • (717) 766-2511

Murray Library • Messiah College, 1 College Ave, P.O. Box 3002 • Grantham, PA 17027-9795 • (717) 691-6048 • http://www.messiah. edu/library/

Grantville
East Hanover Historical Society • 415 Manada Bottom Rd • Grantville, PA 17028

Gratz
Gratz Historical Society • Historical Museum, 8 W Market St, P.O. Box 507 • Gratz, PA 17030 • (717) 365-3342 • http://www.gratzpa.org

Green Lane
Goschenhoppen Historians • Folklife Library and Museum in Red Men's Hall, 116 Gravel Pike, P.O. Box 476 • Green Lane, PA 18054 • (610) 367-8286 • http://www.goschenhoppen.org

Greencastle
Allison-Antrim Museum • 365 S Ridge Ave • Greencastle, PA 17225 • (717) 597-9325 • http://www.greencastlemuseum.org

Lillian S Besore Memorial Library • 305 E Baltimore St • Greencastle, PA 17225-1004 • (717) 597-7920 • http://www.fclspa.org

Martin's Mill Covered Bridge Association • P.O. Box 175 • Greencastle, PA 17225 • (717) 762-9711

Greenfield
Greenfield Township Historical Society • 423 Hickory Ridge Rd • Greenfield, PA 18407 • (570) 282-2768 • http://www. greenfieldtownship.org

Greensburg
Baltzer Meyer Historical Society • Paul Miller Ruff Library and Museum, 642 Baltzer Meyer Pk • Greensburg, PA 15601 • (724) 836-6915 • http://baltzermeyer.pa-roots.com

Greensburg-Hempfield Area Library • 237 S Pennsylvania Ave • Greensburg, PA 15601-3086 • (724) 837-5620 • http://www.ghal.org

Reeves Memorial Library • 1 Seton Hill Dr • Greensburg, PA 15601 • (724) 838-4291 • http://maura.setonhill.edu/~library/

Westmoreland County Historical Society • Historic Hanna's Town Museum, 41 W Otterman St • Greensburg, PA 15601 • (724) 532-1935 • http://www.westmorelandhistory.org

Greentown
Greentown Historical Society • Historical Museum, P.O. Box 186 • Greentown, PA 18426-0186 • (570) 676-3509

Greenville
Canal Museum • 60 Alan Ave, P.O. Box 244 • Greenville, PA 16125 • (724) 588-7540 • http://www.greenvillecanalmuseum.org

Greenville Area Historical Society • Waugh House Museum, 23 W Main St, P.O. Box 25 • Greenville, PA 16125 • (724) 588-3230 • http:// www.greenvillehistoricalsociety.org

Greenville Railroad Park and Museum • 314 Main St • Greenville, PA 16125 • (724) 588-4009 • http://www.greenvillechamber-pa.com

Grove City
Grove City Area Historical Society • Historical Museum, 111 College Ave • Grove City, PA 16127 • (724) 458-1798 • http://www. grovecityhistoricalsociety.org

Guys Mills
John Brown Farm, Tannery & Museum • 17620 John Brown Rd • Guys Mills, PA 16327 • (814) 720-2873 • http://www.ftcgw.org/ johnbrownmuseum

Gwynedd
Lower Gwynedd Historical Association • Historical Museum, Meetinghouse Rd • Gwynedd, PA 19436

Halifax
Halifax Area Historical Society • Historical Museum, 228 Market St, P.O. Box 562 • Halifax, PA 17032 • (717) 896-8010

Hamburg
Hamburg Area Historical Society • 102 State St • Hamburg, PA 19526 • (610) 562-3664

Hamburg Public Library • 35 N Main St • Hamburg, PA 19526-1502 • (610) 562-2843 • http://www.berk.lib.pa.us/hamburgpl/

Hamlin
Salem Public Library • Wimmers Sta, Rte 191, Box 98 • Hamlin, PA 18427-0098 • (570) 689-0903

Hanover
Hanover Area Historical Society • Historical Museum, 105 High St, P.O. Box 305 • Hanover, PA 17331 • (717) 632-3207 • http://www. hanoverareahistoricalsociety.org

Hanover Public Library • 2 Library Pl • Hanover, PA 17331-2283 • (717) 632-5183 • http://www.hanoverlibrary.org

John Timon Reily Historical Society • 410 Irishtown Rd • Hanover, PA 17331

NEAS House Museum • 113 W Chestnut, P.O. Box 305 • Hanover, PA 17331

Harford
Harford Historical Society • Historical Museum, P.O. Box 236 • Harford, PA 18823

Harison City
Bushy Run Battlefield Museum • Route 993, P.O. Box 468 • Harison City, PA 15636 • (724) 527-5584

Harleysville
Heckler Plains Folklife Society • Historical Museum, 474 Main St • Harleysville, PA 19438 • (215) 538-0853 • http://www.hecklerplains.org

Mennonite Historians of Eastern Pennsylvania • Mennonite Heritage Center, 565 Yoder Rd, Box 82 • Harleysville, PA 19438 • (215) 256-3020 • http://www.mhep.org

Harmony
Historic Harmony • Historical Museum, 218 Mercer St, P.O. Box 524 • Harmony, PA 16037 • (724) 452-7341 • http://harmonymuseum.org

Harrisburg
African American Museum of Harrisburg • 300 North St, P.O. Box 5090 • Harrisburg, PA 17110

Camp Curtin Historical Society • Historical Museum, 2221 N 6th St, P.O. Box 5601 • Harrisburg, PA 17110 • (800) 732-0999 • http://www. campcurtin.org

Capital Area Genealogical Society • P.O. Box 4502 • Harrisburg, PA 17111-4502 • (717) 5435-2622

Capitol Preservation Committee • Main Capitol, Rm 627 • Harrisburg, PA 17120 • (717) 783-6484

Dauphin County Library • 101 Walnut St • Harrisburg, PA 17101 • (717) 234-4961 • http://www.dcls.org

Dorothea Dix Library & Museum • Harrisburg State Hospital, Cameron & Clay Sts • Harrisburg, PA 17105 • (717) 772-7461

Fort Hunter Mansion Museum • 5300 N Front St • Harrisburg, PA 17110 • (717) 599-5751 • http://www.forthunter.org

Harrisburg Chapter National Railway Historical Society • 637 Walnut St • Harrisburg, PA 17101 • (717) 232-6221

Historic Harrisburg Association • Historical Museum, 1230 N 3rd St • Harrisburg, PA 17102 • (717) 233-4646 • http://www.historicharrisburg.com

Historical Society of Dauphin County • John Harris-Simon Cameron Mansion, 219 S Front St • Harrisburg, PA 17104 • (717) 233-3462 • http://www.dauphincountyhistoricalsociety.org

Lower Paxton Historical Society • 429 Prince St • Harrisburg, PA 17109

National Civil War Museum • 1 Lincoln Cr at Reservoir Park, P.O. Box 1861 • Harrisburg, PA 17105 • (717) 260-1861 • http://www.nationalcivilwarmuseum.org

National Historical Society • 6405 Flank Dr • Harrisburg, PA 17112 • (717) 657-9555

Pennsylvania Federation of Museums and Historical Organizations • 234 N 3rd St, P.O. Box 1026 • Harrisburg, PA 17108-1026 • (717) 787-3253 • http://www.pamuseums.org

Pennsylvania Heritage Society • 300 North St • Harrisburg, PA 17120-0024 • (717) 787-2407 • http://www.paheritage.org

Pennsylvania Historical and Museum Commission • Historical Museum, 300 North St, P.O. Box 1026 • Harrisburg, PA 17120 • (717) 783-9898 • http://www.phmc.state.us

Pennsylvania National Fire Museum • 1820 N 4th St • Harrisburg, PA 17102 • (717) 232-8915 • http://www.pnfm.org

Sons of Union Veterans of the Civil War • P.O. Box 1865 • Harrisburg, PA 17105 • http://suvcw.org

State Museum of Pennsylvania • 300 North St • Harrisburg, PA 17120 • (717) 787-4980 • http://www.statemuseumpa.org

West Hanover Township Historical Society • Historical Museum, 1033 Piketown Rd • Harrisburg, PA 17112 • (717) 652-4841 • http://www.westhanover.com

Harrison City
Penn Area Library • 2001 Municipal Court, P.O. Box 499 • Harrison City, PA 15636-0499 • (724) 744-4414 • http://trfn.clpgh.org

Hartsville
Moland House Museum • 1641 Old York Rd • Hartsville, PA 18929 • (215) 918-1754 • http://www.moland.org

Hatboro
Delaware Valley Historical Aircraft Association • Historical Museum, Naval Air Sta • Hatboro, PA 19040 • (215) 675-4005

Hatboro Historical Society • Historical Museum, P.O. Box 1776 • Hatboro, PA 19040 • (215) 597-1877 • http://www.hatboro-pa.com/hathist.htm

Millbrook Society • Amy B Yerkes Museum, 32 N York Rd, P.O. Box 506 • Hatboro, PA 19040 • (215) 675-0119

Philadelphia Athletics Historical Society • Historical Museum, 6 N York Rd • Hatboro, PA 19040 • (215) 323-9901 • http://philadelphiaathletics.org

Union Library County of Hatborough • 243 S York Rd • Hatboro, PA 19040-3429 • (215) 672-1420 • http://www.hatborogov.com/library

Hatfield
Hatfield Historical Preservation Society • Historical Museum, 1950 School Rd • Hatfield, PA 19440 • (215) 822-7422

Haverford
Friends Historical Association • Haverford College Library, 370 Lancaster Ave • Haverford, PA 19041-1392 • (610) 896-1161

James P Magill Library - Quaker & Special Collections • Haverford College, 370 Lancaster Ave • Haverford, PA 19041-1392 • (610) 896-1356 • http://www.haverford.edu/library/special/

Havertown
Haverford Township Historical Society • Powder Mill Valley Park, Karakung Dr, P.O. Box 825 • Havertown, PA 19083 • (610) 446-7988 • http://www.haverfordhistoricalsociety.org

Historic Grange Estate Museum • Myrtle Ave & Warwick Rd, P.O. Box 853 • Havertown, PA 19083 • (610) 446-4958

Hazelton
Hazelton Area Public Library • 55 N Church St • Hazelton, PA 18201-5893 • (570) 454-2961 • http://www.hazletonlibrary.org

Hazelton Historical Society • Historical Museum, 55 N Wyoming St • Hazelton, PA 18201 • (717) 455-8576 • http://www.hazeltohistory.8m.com

Hellertown
Gilman Museum • 726 Durham St, P.O. Box M • Hellertown, PA 18055 • (610) 838-8767 • http://www.lostcave.com

Hellertown Historical Society • Historical Museum, 150 W Walnut St • Hellertown, PA 18055 • (610) 838-1770

Hermitage
Hermitage Historical Society • 5465 E State St • Hermitage, PA 16148 • (724) 346-0419 • http://www.rootsweb.ancestry.com/~pahhs/

Holy Cross Romanian Orthodox Church • 950 Maple St • Hermitage, PA 16146 • (412) 346-3151

Hershey
Derry Township Historical Society • Historical Museum, 40 Northeast Dr • Hershey, PA 17033 • (717) 520-0748 • http://www.hersheyhistory.com

Hershey Community Archives • 63 W Chocolate Ave, P.O. Box 64 • Hershey, PA 17033 • (717) 533-1777 • http://www.hersheyarchives.org

Hershey Museum • 63 W Chocolate Ave • Hershey, PA 17033 • (717) 520-5596 • http://www.hersheystory.org

Hershey Public Library • 701 Cocoa Ave • Hershey, PA 17033 • (717) 533-6555 • http://www.hersheylibrary.org

Museum of Bus Transportation • 161 Museum Dr • Hershey, PA 17033 • (717) 566-7100

Pennsylvania State Police Historical, Educational and Memorial Center • 1746 E Chocolate Ave • Hershey, PA 17033 • (717) 534-0565

Highspire
Highspire Historical Society • Historical Museum, 640 Eshelman St • Highspire, PA 17034 • (717) 939-3303 • http://www.highspire.org/historical-society.html

Hilltown
Historical Society of Hilltown Township • Historical Museum, 13 W Creamery Rd, P.O. Box 260 • Hilltown, PA 18927 • (215) 453-6000 • http://www.hilltown.org

Hollidaysburg
Armstrong-Kittanning Trail Society of Pennsylvania • Historical Museum, 514 Penn St • Hollidaysburg, PA 16648 • (814) 695-0777

Pennsylvania

Hollidaysburg, cont.

Blair County Genealogical Society • Research Library, 431 Scotch Valley Rd • Hollidaysburg, PA 16648 • (814) 696-3492 • http://www. bcgslibrary.org

Historic Holidaysburg • Historical Museum, 516 Walnut St • Hollidaysburg, PA 16648-1530 • (814) 696-0313

Hoenstine Rental Library • 414 Montgomery, P.O. Box 208 • Hollidaysburg, PA 16648 • (814) 695-0632

Hollidaysburg Area Public Library • 405 Clark St • Hollidaysburg, PA 16648-2101 • (814) 695-5961 • http://www.hollidaysburglibrary.org

Homestead

Homestead and Mifflin Township Historical Society • 510 10th Ave • Homestead, PA 15120 • (412) 461-7767

Homestead Pennsylvania Historical Society • 1110 Silvan Ave • Homestead, PA 15120

Honesdale

Bethany Public Library Historical Society • Historical Museum, RR 3, Box 650 • Honesdale, PA 18431 • http://bethanypubliclibrary.tripod. com/index.html

Mount Pleasant Township Historical Society • Historical Museum, RR 1, Box 560 • Honesdale, PA 18431

Southern Wayne & Machinery Historical Society • Historical Museum, RD 2, Box 1355 • Honesdale, PA 18431

Wayne County Historical Society • Historical Museum, 810 Main St, P.O. Box 446 • Honesdale, PA 18431 • (570) 253-3240 • http://www. waynehistorypa.com

Honey Brook

Honey Brook Community Library • 687 Compass Rd, P.O. Box 1082 • Honey Brook, PA 19344 • (610) 273-3303 • http://www.ccls.org

Hookstown

Mercer School and South Side Historical Village • Hookstown Grange Fairgrounds, P.O. Box 140 • Hookstown, PA 15050

Horsham

Graeme Park Museum • 859 County Line Rd • Horsham, PA 19044 • (215) 343-0965 • http://www.ushistory.org/graeme/

Horsham Preserveration and Historical Association • 212 Winchester Dr • Horsham, PA 19044

Howard

Milesburg Historical Society • Historical Museum, 2004 Old 220 Rd • Howard, PA 16841

Hughesville

East Lycoming Historical Society • Historical Museum, 304 S Main St, P.O. Box 97 • Hughesville, PA 17737 • (570) 368-1415 • http://www. lycoming.org/elhs/

Hummelstown

Hummelstown Area Historical Society • Historical Museum, 28 W Main St • Hummelstown, PA 17036 • (717) 566-6314 • http://www. hummelstownhistorical.org

Huntingdon

Huntingdon County Historical Society • Historical Museum, 106 4th St, P.O. Box 305 • Huntingdon, PA 16652 • (814) 643-5449 • http://www. huntingdonhistory.org

Huntingdon County Library • 330 Penn St • Huntingdon, PA 16652-1487 • (814) 643-0200 • http://www.huntingdon.net/library

Huntingdon County Transportation Society • Historical Museum, 2122 Cold Springs Rd • Huntingdon, PA 16652

L A Beeghly Library • Juniata College, 1815 Moore St • Huntingdon, PA 16652-2120 • (814) 641-3450 • http://www.juniata.edu

William E Swigart Automobile Museum • 12031 William Penn Hwy • Huntingdon, PA 16652 • (814) 643-2024 • http://www.swigartmuseum. com

Maen Hir Welsh Society • 3554 Cold Springs Rd • Huntington, PA 16652

Imperial

Slovene National Benevolent Society • 247 W Allegheny Rd • Imperial, PA 15126-9786 • (724) 695-1100

Indiana

Historical and Genealogical Society of Indiana County • Historical Museum, 200 S 6th St • Indiana, PA 15701 • (724) 463-9600 • http:// www.rootsweb.com/~paicgs/

Jimmy Stewart Museum • 835 Philadelphia St, P.O. Box 1 • Indiana, PA 15701 • (724) 349-6112 • http://www.jimmy.org

Stapleton Library • Indiana University of Pennsylvania, 431 S 11th St • Indiana, PA 15705-1096 • (724) 357-3006 • http://www.lib.iup.edu

University Museum • Sutton Hall, Indiana Univ of Pennsylvania, 1011 South Dr • Indiana, PA 15705 • (724) 357-2397 • http://www.arts.iup. edu/museum

Indianola

Indiana Township Historical Society • Historical Museum, P.O. Box 788 • Indianola, PA 15051 • (412) 767-5333

Industry

Ohioville One Room School Museum • 118 Eckles Dr • Industry, PA 15052 • (724) 495-7028

Ingomar

North Hills Genealogists • P.O. Box 304 • Ingomar, PA 15127

Irwin

Norwin Historical Society • Historical Museum, 321 Main St • Irwin, PA 15642 • http://www.norwinhistoricalsociety.org

Jamestown

Jamestown Area Historical Society • Historical Museum, 405 Summit St, P.O. Box 243 • Jamestown, PA 16134 • (724) 932-5717 • http:// www.jamestownpa.com/History/

Jamison

Warwick Township Historical Society • Historical Museum, P.O. Box 107 • Jamison, PA 18929 • (215) 345-6439

Jeannette

Busy Run Battlefield Heritage Society • Historical Museum, 1253 Bushy Run Rd • Jeannette, PA 15644 • (724) 527-5584 • http://www. bushyrunbattlefield.com

Jeannete Public Library Association • 500 Magee St • Jeannette, PA 15644-3416 • (724) 523-5702 • http://www.nb.net/~jntlib/

Jenkintown

Basileiad Library • Manor College, 700 Fox Chase Rd • Jenkintown, PA 19046-3399 • (215) 885-2360 • http://www.library.manor.edu

Bertolet Meeting House Museum and Burial Ground • 160 Woodpecker Rd • Jenkintown, PA 19045 • (717) 704-3000

Jenkintown Library • 460 Old York Rd • Jenkintown, PA 19046-2829 • (215) 884-0593 • http://jkl.mclinc.org

Jewish Reconstructionist Federation • 101 Greenwood Ave • Jenkintown, PA 19046 • (215) 885-5601 • http://www.jrf.org

Old York Road Historical Society • Historical Museum, 460 Old York Rd • Jenkintown, PA 19046 • (215) 886-8590 • http://www.oyrhs.org

Jermyn

Scott Township Historical Society • Historical Museum, 1127 Rushbrook Rd • Jermyn, PA 18433

Jersey Shore

Jersey Shore Historical Society • Historical Museum, 200 S Main St • Jersey Shore, PA 17740 • (570) 398-1973 • http://js-hs.tripod.com

Jim Thorpe

Asa Packer Mansion Museum • Packer Ave, P.O. Box 108 • Jim Thorpe, PA 18229 • (570) 325-3229 • http://www.asapackermansion.com

Dimmick Memorial Library • 54 Broadway • Jim Thorpe, PA 18229-2022 • (570) 325-2131 • http://www.dimmicklibrary.org

Josiah White Exhibition Center • 20 W Broadway • Jim Thorpe, PA 18229 • (570) 325-4856

Mauch Chunk Historical Society of Carbon County • Historical Museum, 14 W Broadway, P.O. Box 273 • Jim Thorpe, PA 18229 • (570) 325-4439 • http://www.mauchchunkhistory.com

Switchback Gravity Railroad Museum • P.O. Box 73 • Jim Thorpe, PA 18229 • (570) 325-8255 • http://www.switchbackgravityrr.org

Johnsonburg

Johnsonburg Public Library • 520 Market St • Johnsonburg, PA 15845-0240 • (814) 965-4110 • http://www.johnsonburglibrary.ncentral.com

Johnstown

Cambria County Area Community College Library • 727 Goucher St • Johnstown, PA 15905 • (814) 255-8219 • http://www.ccacc.cc.pa.us/library/libhome.htm

Cambria County Library System • 248 Main St • Johnstown, PA 15901 • (814) 536-5131 • http://ns.cclib.lib.pa.us

Conemaugh Township Area Historical Society • 100 Main St #106 • Johnstown, PA 15901-1507 • (814) 479-2067

Johnstown Area Genealogical and Historical Society • P.O. Box 5048 • Johnstown, PA 15905

Johnstown Area Heritage Association • Historical Museum, 201 6th Ave, P.O. Box 1889 • Johnstown, PA 15907 • (814) 539-1889 • http://www.jaha.org

Johnstown Flood Museum Association Library • 304 Washington St, P.O. Box 1889 • Johnstown, PA 19507 • (814) 539-1889 • http://www.ctnet.net/jaha

Windber-Johnstown Genealogical Society • 85 Colgate Ave, P.O. Box 5048 • Johnstown, PA 15904-5048 • (814) 536-5056

Jones Mills

Chestnut Ridge Historical Society • P.O. Box 62 • Jones Mills, PA 15646

Kane

Kane Community Depot & Museum • S Fraley St, P.O. box 525 • Kane, PA 16735 • (814) 837-6685

Kane Public Library • 300 Henlock Ave • Kane, PA 16735-1802 • (814) 837-9640

Thomas L Kane Memorial Chapel Museum • 30 Chestnut St • Kane, PA 16735 • (814) 837-9729

Kempton

Albany Township Historical Society • Historical Museum, P.O. Box 95 • Kempton, PA 19529 • http://www.albanyths.org

Kennett Square

Bayard Taylor Memorial Library • 216 E State St, P.O. Box 730 • Kennett Square, PA 19348-0730 • (610) 444-2988 • http://www.bayardtaylor.org

Kimberton Area Historical Society • Historical Museum, 26 Turkey Hollow Rd • Kennett Square, PA 19348

Southeastern Chester County Historical Society • Historical Museum, P.O. Box 394 • Kennett Square, PA 19348

King of Prussia

Upper Merion Township Library • 175 W Valley Forge Rd • King of Prussia, PA 19406-2399 • (610) 265-1196 • http://www.umtownship.org

Valley Forge National Historical Park Library • 1400 N Outer Line Dr • King of Prussia, PA 19406 • (610) 296-2593 • http://www.nps.gov/

Kingston

Hoyt Library • 284 Wyoming Ave • Kingston, PA 18704-3597 • (717) 287-2013 • http://www.hoytlibrary.org

Kirby Library • Wyoming Seminary, 201 N Sprague Ave • Kingston, PA 18704 • (570) 270-2168 • http://www.wyomingseminary.org/library

Kinzers

Rough and Tumble Engineers' Historical Association • Historical Museum, Route 30, P.O. Box 9 • Kinzers, PA 17535 • (717) 442-4249 • http://www.roughandtumble.org

Kittanning

Armstrong County Historical and Genealogical Society • Historical Museum, 300 N McKean St, P.O. Box 735 • Kittanning, PA 16201 • (724) 548-5707 • http://www.armstronghistory.org/armco/

Kittanning Public Library • 280 N Jefferson St • Kittanning, PA 16201 • (724) 543-1383 • http://www.ncdlc.org/kitt

Knoxville

Knoxville Public Library & Museum • 112 E Main St • Knoxville, PA 16928 • (814) 326-4448 • http://www.ncldistrict.org/knoxville

Kulpsville

Morgan Log House Museum • 850 Weikel Rd, P.O. Box 261 • Kulpsville, PA 19443 • (215) 368-2480

Welsh Valley Preservation Society • Historical Museum, 850 Weikel Rd, P.O. Box 261 • Kulpsville, PA 19443 • (215) 368-2480

Kutztown

Berks County Genealogical Society • 15197 Kutztown Rd, P.O. Box 305 • Kutztown, PA 19530-0305 • (610) 683-9420 • http://www.lebmato.com/berksgen

Kutztown Area Historical Society • Normal Ave & White Oak St, P.O. Box 307 • Kutztown, PA 19530 • (610) 683-7697 • http://www.kutztownhistory.org

Louisa Gonser Community Library • 70 Bieber Alley • Kutztown, PA 19530-1113 • (610) 683-5820 • http://www.berks.lib.pa.us/louisagonsercl/

Pennsylvania Dutch Folk Culture Society • P.O. Box 306 • Kutztown, PA 19530 • (610) 683-1589

Pennsylvania German Heritage Museum & Library • Kutztown Univ, 15197 Kutztown Rd, P.O. Box 306 • Kutztown, PA 19530-0306 • (610) 683-1589 • http://www.kutztown.edu/community/pgchc/lib.htm

Pennsylvania German Society • Historical Museum, 212 S White Oak St, P.O. Box 244 • Kutztown, PA 19530 • (717) 597-7940 • http://www.pgs.org

La Plume

Miller Library • Keystone College, 1 College Green • La Plume, PA 18440-0200 • (570) 945-6965 • http://www.keystone.edu

La Porte

Sullivan County Historical Society • Historical Museum, Courthouse Square, Meylert St P.O. Box 252 • La Porte, PA 18626 • (717) 946-5091 • http://www.rootsweb.ancestry.com/~pasulliv/SullivanCountyHistoricalSociety/SCHS.html

Laceyville

Tuscarora Township Historical Society • Historical Museum, RR 3, Box 3252 • Laceyville, PA 18623 • (570) 869-2184

Pennsylvania

Lackawaxen
Zane Grey Museum • Scenic Dr • Lackawaxen, PA 18435 • (570) 685-4871 • http://www.nps.gov/upde

Lafayette Hill
William Jeanes Memorial Library • 4051 Joshua Rd • Lafayette Hill, PA 19444-1430 • (610) 828-0441

Lake Ariel
Lacawac Sanctuary & Historic Home Museum • 94 Sanctuary Rd • Lake Ariel, PA 18436 • (570) 689-9494 • http://www.lacawac.org

Lancaster
Amish Farm and House Museum • 2395 Rte 30E • Lancaster, PA 17602 • (717) 394-6185

Archives of the United Church of Christ • Philip Schaff Library, 555 W James St • Lancaster, PA 17603 • (717) 397-0248

Edward Hand Medical Heritage Museum • 137 E Walnut St • Lancaster, PA 17602 • http://www.lancastermedicalsociety.com

Evangelical and Reformed Historical Society • c/o Philip Schaff Library, Lancaster Theological Seminary, 555 W James St • Lancaster, PA 17603-2803 • (717) 393-0654

Heritage Center of Lancaster County • 13 W King St • Lancaster, PA 17603-3813 • (717) 299-6440 • http://www.lancasterheritage.com

Historic Preservation Trust of Lancaster County • 123 N Prince St • Lancaster, PA 17603 • (717) 291-5861 • http://www.hptrust.org/

Historic Rock Ford Plantation Museum • 881 Rockford Rd, P.O. Box 264 • Lancaster, PA 17608 • (717) 392-7223 • http://www.rockfordplantation.org

James Buchanan Foundation for the Preservation of Wheatland Mansion • Wheatland Mansion Museum, 1120 Marietta Ave • Lancaster, PA 17603 • (717) 392-8721 • http://www.wheatland.org

Lancaster County Historical Society • 230 N President Ave • Lancaster, PA 17603-3125 • (717) 392-4633 • http://www.lancasterhistory.org

Lancaster County Library • 125 N Duke St • Lancaster, PA 17602-2883 • (717) 394-2651 • http://www.lancaster.lib.pa.us

Lancaster Mennonite Historical Society • Historical Museum, 2215 Millstream Road • Lancaster, PA 17602 • (717) 393-9745 • http://www.lmhs.org

Landis Valley Museum • 2451 Kissel Hill Rd • Lancaster, PA 17601 • (717) 569-0401 • http://www.landisvalleymuseum.org

Philip Schaff Library • Lancaster Theological Seminary, 555 W James St • Lancaster, PA 17603-9967 • (717) 290-8707 • http://www.lts.org

Shadek-Fackenthal Library • Franklin and Marshall College, 450 College Ave, P.O. Box 3003 • Lancaster, PA 17604-3003 • (717) 291-4217 • http://www.fandm.edu

Landisville
Amos Herr House Foundation and Historical Society • Historical Museum, 1756 Nissley Rd, P.O. Box 5 • Landisville, PA 17538 • (717) 898-8822

Langhorne
Historic Langhorne Association • Historical Museum, 160 W Maple Ave • Langhorne, PA 19047 • (215) 757-1888 • http://hla.buxcom.net

Lansdale
Association of the Belarusian Nobility • 2050 Spring Valley Rd • Lansdale, PA 19446-5114 • (215) 584-4742 • http://feefhs.org/by/frg-zbs.html

Lansdale Historical Society • Historical Museum, 137 Jenkins Ave, P.O. Box 293 • Lansdale, PA 19446 • (215) 855-1872 • http://www.lansdalehistory.org

Lansdale Public Library • 301 Vine St • Lansdale, PA 19446-3690 • (215) 855-3228 • http://www.lansdalelibrary.org

Lansford
No 9 Washanty Mine & Museum • 9 Dock St • Lansford, PA 18232 • (570) 645-7074

Latrobe
Center for Northern Appalachian Studies • Saint Vincent College, 300 Fraser Purchase Rd • Latrobe, PA 15650-2690 • (724) 805-2370 • http://www.stvincent.edu

Latrobe Area Historical Society • Historical Museum, 1501 Ligonier St, P.O. Box 266 • Latrobe, PA 15650 • (724) 539-8889 • http://www.greaterlatrobe.net/history/

Laughlintown
Heritage Society of Pennsylvania • P.O. Box 146 • Laughlintown, PA 15655

Ligonier Valley Historical Society • Compass Inn Museum, 1386 Route 30 E, P.O. Box 167 • Laughlintown, PA 15655 • (724) 238-4983 • http://www.compassinn.com

Laureldale
Berks County Genealogical Society • 3618 Kutztown Road • Laureldale, PA 19605

Muhlenberg Community Library • 3612 Kutztown Rd • Laureldale, PA 19605-1842 • (610) 929-0589 • http://www.berks.lib.pa.us/muhlenbergcl

Lebanon
Lebanon Community Library • 125 N 7th St • Lebanon, PA 17046-5000 • (717) 273-7624 • http://www.lebanoncountylibraries.org

Lebanon County Historical Society • c/o Hauck Memorial Library & Museum, 924 Cumberland St • Lebanon, PA 17042-1586 • (717) 272-1473 • http://lebanoncountyhistoricalsociety.org

United Christian Church Archives • 2080 White Oak St • Lebanon, PA 17042

Lederach
Lower Salford Historical Society • Historical Museum, P.O. Box 150 • Lederach, PA 19450

Leechburg
Allegheny Township Historical Society • Historical Museum, 136 Community Bldg Rd • Leechburg, PA 15656 • (724) 842-4641

Leechburg Area Historical Society • Historical Museum, 118 1st St, P.O. Box 156 • Leechburg, PA 15656 • (724) 845-8914 • http://home.alltel.net/lamahs/

Leesport
Leesport Lock House Library • 1105 Stinson Dr • Leesport, PA 19533

Reading Company Historical Society • Canal & Wall Sts • Leesport, PA 19533 • (610) 926-0253

Lemont
North American Society for Sports History • P.O. Box 1026 • Lemont, PA 16851 • (814) 238-1288

Lenhartsville
Pennsylvania Dutch Folk Culture Society • Folklife Museum, Main & Willow Sts, P.O. Box 306 • Lenhartsville, PA 19534 • (610) 683-1589

LeRoy
LeRoy Heritage Museum • Mill St • LeRoy, PA 17724 • http://www.leroyheritage.org

Levittown
Levittown Historical Society • P.O. Box 1641 • Levittown, PA 19058-1641

Lewisburg

Packwood House Museum • 15 N Water St • Lewisburg, PA 17837 • (570) 524-0323 • http://www.packwoodhousemuseum.com

Slifer House Museum • 80 Magnolia Dr • Lewisburg, PA 17837 • (570) 524-2245 • http://www.sliferhouse.org

Union County Historical Society • Courthouse Museum, 102 S 2nd St • Lewisburg, PA 17837 • (717) 524-8666 • http://www. unioncountyhistoricalsociety.org

Union County Public Library • 255 Reitz Blvd • Lewisburg, PA 17837 • (570) 523-1172 • http://www.publibuc.org

Lewistown

McCoy House Museum • 17 N Main St • Lewistown, PA 17044 • (717) 248-4711 • http://www.mccoyhouse.com

Mifflin County Historical Society • 1 W Market St #1 • Lewistown, PA 17044 • (717) 242-1022 • http://www.rootsweb.ancestry.com/~pamchs/MCHS/Home.html

Mifflin County Historical Society • 1 W Market St, Ste 1 • Lewistown, PA 17044-2128 • (717) 242-1022

Mifflin County Library • 123 N Wayne St • Lewistown, PA 17044-1794 • (717) 242-2391 • http://www.mifflincountylibrary.org

Liberty

Liberty Area Historical Society • Historical Museum, P.O. Box 22 • Liberty, PA 16930

Library

South Park Historical Society • Historical Museum, 6425 Pleasant St, P.O. Box 555 • Library, PA 15129 • (412) 835-8633 • http://www. southparkhistoricalsociety.com

Liegerville

Central Perkiomen Historical Society • Historical Museum, Little Rd • Liegerville, PA 19492 • (610) 287-9158

Ligonier

Fort Ligonier Association • Historical Museum, 200 S Market St • Ligonier, PA 15658-1242 • (724) 238-9701 • http://fortligonier.org

Fort Ligonier Association Library • 216 S Market St • Ligonier, PA 15658 • (724) 238-9701 • http://www.fortligonier.org

Ligonier Valley Historical Society • Star Route E, Box 115 • Ligonier, PA 15658 • (724) 238-6818

Ligonier Valley Library Association • 120 W Main St • Ligonier, PA 15658-1243 • (724) 238-6451 • http://www.ligonierlibrary.org

Lima

Middletown Township Historical Society • Historical Museum, P.O. Box 275 • Lima, PA 19037 • http://www.mthsdelco.org

Limerick

Limerick Township Historical Society • Historical Museum, 545 Ridge Pk • Limerick, PA 19468 • (610) 495-5229 • http://www. limerickpahistory.org

Linesville

Linesville Historical Society • Historical Museum, 102 W Erie St, P.O. Box 785 • Linesville, PA 16424 • (814) 683-4299

Linwood

Lower Chichester Historical Society • Historical Museum, 1683 Hughes Ave • Linwood, PA 19061 • (610) 485-1887

Lionville

Uwchlan Conservation Trust • Historical Museum, P.O. Box 212 • Lionville, PA 19353 • (610) 363-9726

Lititz

Johannes Mueller House Museum • 137 E Main St, P.O. Box 65 • Lititz, PA 17543 • (717) 627-4636

Lititz Historical Foundation • Historical Museum, 145 E Main St, P.O. Box 65 • Lititz, PA 17543 • (717) 627-4636

Lititz Moravian Archives & Museum • 8 Church Sq • Lititz, PA 17543 • (717) 626-8515

Lock Haven

Annie Halenbake Ross Library • 232 W Main St • Lock Haven, PA 17745-1298 • (570) 748-3321 • http://www.rosslibrary.org

Clinton County Historical Society • Heisey Museum, 362 E Water St • Lock Haven, PA 17745 • (570) 748-7254 • http://www. clintoncountyhistory.com

Piper Aviation Museum • 1 Piper Wy • Lock Haven, PA 17745 • (570) 748-8283 • http://www.pipermuseum.com

Loganton

Sugar Valley Historical Society • Historical Museum, State Rte 477, P.O. Box 62 • Loganton, PA 17747 • http://www.svhistory.org

Loretto

Italian Heritage Society • Historical Museum, 26 College Heights • Loretto, PA 15940

Pasquerilla Library • Saint Francis University, Franciscan Way, P.O. Box 600 • Loretto, PA 15940-0600 • (814) 472-3161 • http://library. francis.edu

Prince Gallitzin Historical Association • Historical Museum, St Mary's, P.O. Box 101 • Loretto, PA 15940 • (814) 472-6279

Loyalhanna

Derry Area Historical Society • Historical Museum, P.O. Box 176 • Loyalhanna, PA 15661 • (724) 694-8808 • http://www.derryhistory.org/pages/census.htm

MacUngie

Kalmbach Memorial Park Museum • 200 Cotton St • MacUngie, PA 18062 • (610) 965-1140 • http://www.kalmbackpark.com

MacUngie Historical Society • Historical Museum, 510 E Main St, P.O. Box 355 • MacUngie, PA 18062 • (610) 965-0372 • http://www. macungie.org

Mahanoy City

Mahanoy Area Historical Society • P.O. Box 127 • Mahanoy City, PA 17948

Malvern

Historic Sugartown • Historical Museum, 692 Sugartown Rd • Malvern, PA 19355 • (610) 640-2667 • http://historicsugartown.org

Swiss Pines Museum • Charlestown Rd • Malvern, PA 19355 • (610) 935-8795

Wharton Esherick Museum • 1520 Horseshoe Trail • Malvern, PA 19355 • (610) 644-5822

Manheim

Manheim Historical Society • Heritage Center, 88 S Grant St, P.O. Box 396 • Manheim, PA 17545 • (717) 665-7989

Manheim Historical Society • Railroad Station Museum, 210 S Charlotte St • Manheim, PA 17545 • (717) 665-4021

Maytown Historical Society • 4 E High St • Manheim, PA 17545 • (717) 426-1526

Mansfield

Mansfield Free Public Library • 71 N Main St • Mansfield, PA 16933 • (570) 662-3850 • http://www.ncldistrict.org/mansfield

Marcus Hook

Chichester-Marcus Hook Historical Society • Historical Museum, 7 W 2nd St • Marcus Hook, PA 19061 • (610) 485-3197 • http://www. chichesterhistory.org

Marietta
Marietta Restoration Associates • Old Town Hall Museum, P.O. Box 3 • Marietta, PA 17547 • (717) 426-4736 • http://www.mariettarestoration. org

Mars
Mars Area History & Landmarks Society • Historical Museum, P.O. Box 58 • Mars, PA 16046 • (724) 625-2455

Martinsburg
Martinsburg Community Library • 201 S Walnut St • Martinsburg, PA 16662-1129 • (814) 793-3335 • http://nbcsd.k12.pa.us/mar_lib.htm

Masontown
Fort Mason Historical Society • Historical Museum, 548 N Main St, P.O. Box 246 • Masontown, PA 15461 • (724) 583-8849

Masontown Historical Society • P.O. Box 769 • Masontown, PA 15461

Masontown Public Library • 9 S Washington St • Masontown, PA 15461-2025 • (724) 583-7030 • http://webpages.charter.net/germaslib

Maytown
Maytown Historical Society • Historical Museum, P.O. Box 293 • Maytown, PA 17550 • (717) 426-1526 • http://www.maytownhistory.org

McConnellsburg
Fulton County Historical Society • Historical Museum, 110 Lincoln Way E, P.O. Box 115 • McConnellsburg, PA 17233 • (717) 485-3172 • http:// www.fultonhistory.org

Fulton County Library • 227 N 1st St • McConnellsburg, PA 17233-1003 • (717) 485-5327 • http://www.fclspa.org/fulton/home.htm

McEwensville
Montgomery House-Warrior Run Area Public Library • 20 Church St, P.O. Box 5 • McEwensville, PA 17749-0005 • (570) 538-1381 • http:// www.ncldistrict.org/mcewensville

McKees Rocks
Robinson Township Historical Society • 1000 Church Ave • McKees Rocks, PA 15136 • (412) 788-6795

McKeesport
McKeesport Carnegie Free Library • 1507 Library Ave • McKeesport, PA 15132 • (412) 672-0625 • http://www.einetwork.net/ein/mckeespt

McKeesport Heritage Center • 1832 Arboretum Dr • McKeesport, PA 15132 • (412) 678-1832 • http://www.mckeesportheritage.org

McMurray
National Slovak Society of the USA • 351 Valley Brook Rd • McMurray, PA 15317 • (724) 731-0094

Peters Township Public Library • 610 E McMurray Rd • McMurray, PA 15317-3495 • (724) 941-9430 • http://www.ptlibrary.org

McSherrystown
John Timon Reily Historical Society • Historical Museum, 363 Main St • McSherrystown, PA 17344 • (717) 630-2454

Meadville
Baldwin-Reynolds House Museum • 639 Terrace St • Meadville, PA 16335 • (814) 333-9882 • http://ww.visitcrawford.org

Crawford County Federated Library • 848 N Main St • Meadville, PA 16335-2689 • (814) 336-1773 • http://www.meadvillelibrary.org

Crawford County Genealogical Society • 848 N Main St • Meadville, PA 16335

Crawford County Historical Society • Historical Museum, 411 Chestnut St, P.O. Box 411 • Meadville, PA 16335 • (814) 724-6080 • http://www. crawfordhistorical.org

John Brown Heritage Association • Historical Museum, 291 Park Ave • Meadville, PA 16335 • (814) 724-8625 • http://www.ftcgw.org/ johnbrownmuseum/

Lawrence Lee Pelletier Library • Allegheny College, 555 N Main St • Meadville, PA 16335 • (814) 332-3768 • http://allecat.alleg.edu

Mechanicsburg
Eastern Museum of Motor Racing • 1 Speedway Dr • Mechanicsburg, PA 17055

Keystone Model Railroad Historical Society • 833 W Trindle Rd • Mechanicsburg, PA 17055 • (717) 691-8033

Mechanicsburg Area Public Library • 16 N Walnut St • Mechanicsburg, PA 17055-3362 • (717) 766-0171 • http://www.ccpa.net/simpson

Mechanicsburg Museum • 2 Strawberry Alley • Mechanicsburg, PA 17055 • (717) 697-6088 • http://www.mechanicsburgmuseum.org

Media
Bishop's Mill Historical Institute • Ridley Creek State Park • Media, PA 19063 • (610) 566-1725

Colonial Pennsylvania Plantation Museum • Sol Feinstone Library, Ridley Creek State Park • Media, PA 19063 • (610) 566-1725 • http:// www.colonialplantation.org

Delaware County Historical Society • 991 Palmers Mill Rd • Media, PA 19063 • (610) 359-0824 • http://www.delcohistory.org/dchs

Media Historic Preservation • Historical Museum, 221 Brooke St, P.O. Box 683 • Media, PA 19063 • (610) 565-5755 • http://www. preservationproducts.com

Melrose Park
Jewish Genealogical Society of Greater Philadelphia • Tuttleman Jewish Public Library, Gratz College, 7605 Old York Rd • Melrose Park, PA 19027 • (215) 635-7300 • http://www.jgsgp.org

Tuttleman Library • Gratz College, 7605 Old York Rd • Melrose Park, PA 19027 • (215) 635-7300 • http://www.gratzcollege.edu

Mendenhall
General Society of the War of 1812 • P.O. Box 106 • Mendenhall, PA 19357 • (610) 388-6015 • http://www.societyofthewarof1812.org

Mercer
Mercer County Historical Society • Historical Museum, 119 S Pitt St • Mercer, PA 16137-1211 • (724) 662-3490 • http://www.mchspa.org

Mercersburg
Conococheague Institute for the Study of Cultural Heritage • Rock Hill Farm Museum, 12995 Bain Rd • Mercersburg, PA 17236 • (717) 328-3467

Mercersburg Historical Society • 5711 Oakwood Dr • Mercersburg, PA 17236

Merion
Barnes Foundation • Historical Museum, 300 N Latches Ln • Merion, PA 19066 • (610) 667-0290

Meyersdale
Meyersdale Area Historical Society • Historical Museum, 527 Main St, P.O. Box 134 • Meyersdale, PA 15552 • (814) 634-8654

Meyersdale Public Library • 210 Center St, P.O. Box 98 • Meyersdale, PA 15552-0098 • (814) 634-0512 • http://www.meyersdalelibrary.com

Middleburg
Snyder County Historical Society • Historical Museum, 30 E Market St, P.O. Box 276 • Middleburg, PA 17842 • (570) 837-6191 • http://www. snydercounty.org/Depts/Historical_Society/Pages/HistoricalSociety. aspx

Middletown
Middletown Area Historical Society • Historical Museum, 44 W Water St, P.O. Box 248 • Middletown, PA 17057 • (717) 350-8226 • http:// middletownareahistoricalsociety.org

Middletown Public Library • 20 N Catherine St • Middletown, PA 17057-1498 • (717) 944-6412 • http://www.middletownpubliclib.org

Slovak Museum and Archives • 1011 Rosedale Ave • Middletown, PA 17057 • (717) 944-2403 • http://www.visitpa.com/slovak-museum-and-archives

Midland
Midland Heritage Room • 936 9th St • Midland, PA 15059 • (724) 643-1917

Mifflinburg
Mifflinburg Buggy Museum • 598 Green St • Mifflinburg, PA 17844 • (570) 966-1355 • http://www.buggymuseum.org

Mifflintown
Juniata County Historical Society • Historical Museum, 498 Jefferson St, Ste B • Mifflintown, PA 17059-1424 • (717) 436-5152 • http://www.rootsweb.com/~pajchs

Juniata County Library • 498 Jefferson St • Mifflintown, PA 17059-1424 • (717) 436-6378 • http://www.juniatacountylibrary.org

Milford
Grey Tower National Historic Landmark • 151 Grey Towers Dr, P.O. Box 188 • Milford, PA 18337 • (570) 296-9630

Pike County Historical Society • Millford Community House Museum, 608 Broad St, P.O. Box 915 • Milford, PA 18337 • (717) 296-8126 • http://www.pikecountyhistoricalsociety.org

Upper Mill Museum • 150 Sawkill Ave • Milford, PA 18337 • (717) 296-3134

Mill Run
Fallingwater Historic Home Museum • 1491 Mill Run Rd, P.O. Box R • Mill Run, PA 15464 • (724) 329-8501 • http://www.fallingwater.org

Millersburg
Historical Society of Millersburg and Upper Paxton Township • Historical Museum, 330 Center St, P.O. Box 171 • Millersburg, PA 17061 • (717) 692-4084

Millersville
Helen A Ganser Library • Millersville University of Pennsylvania, 9 N George St, P.O. Box 1002 • Millersville, PA 17551-0302 • (717) 872-3611 • http://library.millersville.edu

Historic Schaefferstown • 406 Spring Dr • Millersville, PA 17551 • (717) 274-2297

Milton
Milton Historical Society • Historical Museum, P.O. Box 5 • Milton, PA 17847 • (570) 742-7057

Milton Public Library • 23 S Front St • Milton, PA 17847 • (717) 742-7111 • http://www.miltonlibrary.info/

North Central Pennsylvania Historical Association • Historical Museum, 311 N Front St • Milton, PA 17847 • (717) 742-9323

Minersville
Welsh Society of First Congregational Church • 479 Sunbury St #2 • Minersville, PA 17954

Monaca
Mill Creek Valley Historical Association • Baker-Dungan Museum, 100 University Dr • Monaca, PA 15061 • (724) 573-4895

Monessen
Greater Monessen Historical Society • Heritage Museum, 505 Donner Ave • Monessen, PA 15062 • (724) 684-8460

Monessen Public Library • 326 Donner Ave • Monessen, PA 15062-1182 • (724) 684-4750 • http://www.monpldc.org

Monongahela
Monongahela Area Historical Society • Historical Museum, 230 W Main St, P.O. Box 152 • Monongahela, PA 15063 • (724) 322-4247 • http://www.monongahelahistoricalsociety.com

Monongahela Area Library • 813 W Main St • Monongahela, PA 15063-2815 • (724) 258-5409 • http://www.monarealibrary.org

Monroeville
Monroeville Historical Society • Historical Museum, 2700 Monroeville Blvd • Monroeville, PA 15146 • (412) 856-1000 • http://monroevillehistorical.org

Monroeville Public Library • 4000 Gateway Campus Bldg • Monroeville, PA 15146-3381 • (412) 372-0500 • http://www.einetwork.net/ein/monroevl

Mont Clare
Schuylkill Canal Association • Historical Museum, Lock 60, 400 Towpath Rd • Mont Clare, PA 19453 • (610) 917-0021 • http://schuylkillcanal.org

Montgomery
Montgomery Area Historical Society • Historical Museum, 63 Penn St • Montgomery, PA 17752 • http://www.montgomeryareahistoricalsociety.org

Montgomery Area Public Library • 1 S Main St • Montgomery, PA 17752-1150 • (570) 547-6212

Montoursville
Dr W B Konkle Memorial Library • 384 Broad St • Montoursville, PA 17754-2206 • (570) 368-1840 • http://www.ncldistrict.org/montoursville

General John Burrows Historical Society • Historical Museum, 19 N Loyalsock Ave, P.O. Box 385 • Montoursville, PA 17754 • (570) 368-7455

Sons of the American Revolution, Pennsylvania Society • 213 Irion Dr • Montoursville, PA 17754-7922 • http://www.passar.org

Montrose
Center for Anti-Slavery Studies • 2 Maple St • Montrose, PA 18801 • http://www.antislaverystudies.org

Susquehanna County Free Library • 2 Monument Square • Montrose, PA 18801-1115 • (570) 278-1881 • http://www.susqcolibrary.org

Susquehanna County Historical Society • c/o Susquehanna County Free Library, 2 Monument Square • Montrose, PA 18801 • (717) 278-1881 • http://www.susqcohistsoc.org

Susquehanna Historical Society • Historical Museum, 18 Monument Sq • Montrose, PA 18801 • http://www.susqcohistsoc.org

Montville
Eastern Lanape Nation of Pennsylvania • 21 Cedar Ln • Montville, PA 17554

Moon Township
Old Moon Township Historical Society • Historical Museum, 900 Thorn Run Rd • Moon Township, PA 15108

Robert Morris University Library • 881 Narrows Run Rd • Moon Township, PA 15108-1189 • (412) 262-8367 • http://rmu.edu

Morgantown
Tri-County Heritage Society • Historical Museum, 8 Mill Rd, P.O. Box 352 • Morgantown, PA 19543 • (610) 286-7477

Morrisville
Historic Morrisville Society • Historical Museum, 613 Crowell St • Morrisville, PA 19067 • (215) 295-2194

Pennsbury Manor Museum • 400 Pennsbury Memorial Rd • Morrisville, PA 19067 • (215) 946-0400 • http://www.pennsburymanor.org

Morton
Morton Historical Society • general delivery • Morton, PA 19070 • (610) 328-3152

Mount Bethel
Slate Bett Historical Society • Historical Museum, P.O. Box 58 • Mount Bethel, PA 18343 • (570) 897-6181

Mount Carmel
Mount Carmel Public Library • 30 S Oak St • Mount Carmel, PA 17851-2185 • (570) 339-0703 • mountcarmelareapubliclibrary.com

Mount Holly Springs
Amelia S Givin Free Library • 114 N Baltimore Ave • Mount Holly Springs, PA 17065-1201 • (717) 486-3688 • http://ccpa.net

Mount Joy
Donegal Society • Museum & Archives, 1891 Donegal Springs Rd • Mount Joy, PA 17552

Mount Joy Area Historical Society • Historical Museum, 120 Fairview St, P.O. Box 152 • Mount Joy, PA 17552 • (717) 653-4718

Mount Pleasant
Commission on Archives and History-Western Pennsylvania Conference of the United Methodist Church • 714 Walnut St • Mount Pleasant, PA 15666 • (724) 547-2288

Mount Pleasant Area Historical Society • Historical Museum, 537 W Main St • Mount Pleasant, PA 15666 • (724) 547-9115

Mount Pleasant Free Public Library • 120 S Church St • Mount Pleasant, PA 15666-1879 • (724) 547-3850 • http://www. mountpleasantpalibrary.org

Mount Union
Mount Union Historical Society • Historical Museum, 8-22 W Water St, P.O. Box 1776 • Mount Union, PA 17066 • (814) 542-8888

Mount Wolf
South Central Pennsylvania Historic Lifestyles & Power Society • Historical Museum, P.O. Box 668 • Mount Wolf, PA 17347 • (717) 266-4884

Mountainhome
Barrett Township Historical Society • P.O. Box 358 • Mountainhome, PA 18325

Muncy
Muncy Historical Society • Historic School House, Church Rd • Muncy, PA 17756 • (570) 546-8962

Muncy Historical Society • Historical Museum, 40 N Main St, P.O. Box 11 • Muncy, PA 17756 • (570) 546-5917 • http://muncyhistoricalsociety. org

Muncy Public Library • 108 S Main St • Muncy, PA 17756-0119 • (570) 546-5014

Muncy Valley
Sullivan County Historical Society • Meyler St • Muncy Valley, PA 17758 • (570) 946-5020

Munhall
Ancient Order of Hibernians • McKeesport Heritage Center, 180 W Schwab Ave • Munhall, PA 15120

Carpatho-Rusyn Society • 915 Dickson St • Munhall, PA 15120 • (412) 749-9899

Homestead and Mifflin Township Historical Society • 510 10th Ave • Munhall, PA 15120

Murrysville
Murrysville Community Library • 4130 Sardis Rd • Murrysville, PA 15668-1120 • (724) 327-1102 • http://www.murrysville.library.org

Pennsylvania Labor History Society • Historical Museum, 5001 Nottingham Cr • Murrysville, PA 15568 • (724) 733-1026 • http:// palaborhistory.org

Myerstown
Isaac Meier Homestead Museum • Route 501 S, P.O. Box 461 • Myerstown, PA 17067 • (717) 866-2437

Myerstown Community Library • 199 N College St, P.O. Box 246 • Myerstown, PA 17067-0246 • (717) 866-2800 • http://www. lebanoncountylibraries.org

Rostad Library • Evangelical School of Theology, 121 S College St • Myerstown, PA 17067 • (717) 866-5775 • http://www.youseemore.com/ est

Nanticoke
Nanticoke Historical Society • 229 E Main St • Nanticoke, PA 18634 • (570) 258-1367

Natrona Heights
Burtner House Museum • Route 28, P.O. Box 292 • Natrona Heights, PA 15065 • (724) 224-7999 • http://www.akvalley.com/burtner/

Nazareth
Jacobsburg Historical Society • Pennsylvania Longrifle Museum, 441 Henry Rd, P.O. Box 345 • Nazareth, PA 18064-9247 • (610) 759-9029 • http://www.jacobsburg.org

Memorial Library of Nazareth • 295 E Center St • Nazareth, PA 18064-2298 • (610) 759-5932

Moravian Historical Society • Whitefield House Museum, 214 E Center St • Nazareth, PA 18064 • (610) 759-5070 • http://www. moravianhistoricalsociety.org

Osturna Descendants • 119 Belvedere St • Nazareth, PA 18064-2112 • (610) 759-2740 • http://feefhs.org/rusyn/frg-od.html

Pennsylvania Longrifle Museum • 402 Henry Rd, P.O. Box 345 • Nazareth, PA 18064 • (610) 759-9029 • http://www.jacobsburg.org

New Berlin
New Berlin Heritage Association • Historical Museum, Market & Vine Sts, P.O. Box 223 • New Berlin, PA 17855 • (570) 743-1676

New Bethlehem
New Bethlehem Area Free Public Library • 720 Broad St • New Bethlehem, PA 16242-1107 • (814) 275-2870 • http://users.adelphia. net/~newbiepl/

New Bloomfield
Perry Historians • Historical Museum, 763 Dix Hill Rd, P.O. Box 73 • New Bloomfield, PA 17074 • (717) 582-4896 • http://theperryhistorians. org

New Brighton
New Brighton Historical Society • Historical Museum, P.O. Box 408 • New Brighton, PA 15066

New Castle
First Christian Church Library • 23 W Washington St • New Castle, PA 16101 • (724) 652-6657

Harlansburg Station Museum • 424 Old Route 19 • New Castle, PA 16101 • (724) 652-9002 • http://www.harlansburgstation.com

Lawrence County Historical Society • Historical Museum, 408 N Jefferson St, P.O. Box 1745 • New Castle, PA 16103 • (724) 658-4022 • http://www.lawrencechs.com

New Castle Public Library • 207 E North St • New Castle, PA 16101-3691 • (724) 658-6659 • http://www.lawrencecountylibrary.org

New Cumberland
New Cumberland Public Library • 1 Benjamin Plaza • New Cumberland, PA 17070-1597 • (717) 774-7820 • http://www.ccpa.net

New Hope

Free Library of New Hope and Solebury • 93 W Ferry St • New Hope, PA 18938-1332 • (215) 862-2330 • http://www.buckslib.org/libraries/

Friends of the Delaware Canal • Historical Museum, 145 S Main St • New Hope, PA 18938 • (215) 862-2021 • http://www.fodc.org

New Hope Historical Society • Parry Mansion Museum, 45 S Main St, P.O. Box 41 • New Hope, PA 18938-0041 • (215) 862-5652 • http://www.parrymansion.org; www.newhopehs.org

New Kensington

Peoples Library • 880 Barnes St • New Kensington, PA 15068-6235 • (724) 339-1021 • http://www.peopleslink.org

New London

New London Area Historical Society • Historical Museum, Little Sunapee Rd, P.O. Box 132 • New London, PA 19360 • (603) 526-6564 • http://www.newlondonhistoricalsociety.org

New Milford

Old Mill Village Museum • Route 858, Harford Rd, P.O. Box 434 • New Milford, PA 18834 • (570) 434-2303 • http://www.oldmillvillage.org

New Richmond

John Brown Tannery Museum • 17620 John Brown Rd • New Richmond, PA 16327 • http://www.ftcgw.org/johnbrownmuseum/visit.htm

New Stanton

Apple Mills Historical Association • Historical Museum, Rd 1, Madison Heights • New Stanton, PA 15672

New Stanton Historical Society • Historical Museum, 440 N Center Ave • New Stanton, PA 15672 • (724) 925-2366

New Tripoli

Lynn Township Historical Society • 6751 Madison St • New Tripoli, PA 18066 • (610) 298-8722

Newmanstown

Fort Zeller Museum • 10 N Fort Zeller Rd • Newmanstown, PA 17073 • (717) 272-0662 • http://www.fortzeller.com

Newport

Historical Society of Perry County • Blue Ball Tavern Museum, P.O. Box 81 • Newport, PA 17074-0081 • (717) 567-9011 • http://hsofpc.org

Perry Historian Genealogical Society • P.O. Box 73 • Newport, PA 17074 • (717) 582-4896

Perry Historians • P.O. Box 73 • Newport, PA 17074 • (717) 582-4896

Newtown

Bucks County Community College Library • 275 Swamp Rd • Newtown, PA 18940-0999 • (215) 968-8013 • http://www.bucks.edu/library/

Newtown Historic Association • Historical Museum, E Centre Ave, P.O. Box 303 • Newtown, PA 18940 • (215) 968-4004 • http://www.newtownhistoric.org

Newtown Library Company • 114 E Centre St • Newtown, PA 18940 • (215) 968-7659

Newtown Square

Newtown Square Historical Preservation Society • Historical Museum, 2 Paper Mill Rd, P.O. Box 3 • Newtown Square, PA 19073 • (610) 975-0290 • http://www.historicnewtownsquare.org

Newville

John Graham Public Library • 9 Parsonage St • Newville, PA 17241-1399 • (717) 776-5900 • http://www.ccpa.net

Newville Historical Society • Historical Museum, 69 S High St • Newville, PA 17241 • (717) 776-6210

Norristown

Military Order of Foreign Wars of the United States 1894-1994 • 147 Jefferson Ct • Norristown, PA 19401 • (610) 275-7582 • http://foxfall.com/mofw.htm

Montgomery County Genealogical Club • 1654 DeKalb St • Norristown, PA 19401 • (215) 272-0297

Montgomery County Historical Society • Historical Museum, 1654 DeKalb St • Norristown, PA 190401 • (610) 272-0297

Montgomery County-Norristown Public Library • 1001 Powell St • Norristown, PA 19401-3817 • (610) 278-5100

Montgomery Township Historical Society • Historical Museum, 1654 DeKalb St • Norristown, PA 19401 • (610) 272-0297 • http://www.hsmpca.org

W S Hancock Society • Historical Museum, 1424 Sentry Ln • Norristown, PA 19403

North East

Hornby School Restoration Society • Historical Museum, 17 W Main St • North East, PA 16428 • (814) 725-9110

Lake Shore Railway Historical Society • Historical Museum, 31 Wall St, P.O. Box 571 • North East, PA 16428-0571 • (814) 725-1911 • http://www.grape-track.org

McCord Memorial Library • 32 W Main St • North East, PA 16428 • (814) 725-4057 • http://www.mccordlibrary.org

North East Historical Society • Historical Museum, 25 Vine St, P.O. Box 483 • North East, PA 16428 • (814) 725-2026

North Wales

Roth Farm Museum • Delaware Valley College, Rte 202 & Hancock Rd • North Wales, PA 19454 • (215) 699-3994 • http://www.delval.edu/roth/

North Warren

Warren County Genealogical Society • 6 Main St • North Warren, PA 16365-4616 • (814) 723-8026

Northampton

Northampton Area Public Library • 1615 Laubach Ave • Northampton, PA 18067-1597 • (610) 262-7537 • http://www.northamptonapl.org.htm/

Northumberland

Central Pennsylvania Genealogical Pioneers • 100 King St • Northumberland, PA 17857

Joseph Priestley House Museum • 472 Priestley Ave • Northumberland, PA 17857 • (570) 473-9474 • http://www.josephpriestleyhouse.org

Priestley-Forsyth Memorial Library • 100 King St • Northumberland, PA 17857-1670 • (570) 473-8201 • http://www.priestleyforsyth.org

Norwood

Norwood Historical Society • Historical Museum, 119 Mohawk Ave • Norwood, PA 19074 • http://www.norwoodpahistorical.org

Oakmont

Oakmont Carnegie Library • 700 Allegheny River Blvd • Oakmont, PA 15139 • (412) 828-9532 • http://www.einetwork.net/ein/oakmont

Oil City

Oil City Heritage Society • P.O. Box 692, Oil Creek Sta • Oil City, PA 16301

Oil City Library • 2 Central Ave • Oil City, PA 16301-2795 • (814) 678-3072 • http://www.csonline.net/oclibrary

Oil Creek Railway Historical Society • Historical Museum, P.O. Box 68 • Oil City, PA 16301 • (814) 676-1733

Venango County Genealogical Club • c/o Oil City Library, 2 Central Ave, P.O. Box 811 • Oil City, PA 16301 • (814) 677-4057

Pennsylvania

Oley
Oley Valley Historical Society • Historical Museum, P.O. Box 401 • Oley, PA 19547 • http://www.angelfire.com/pa/ovha/

Olyphant
Genealogical Research Society of Northeastern Pennsylvania • 113 Lackawanna Ave, P.O. Box 1 • Olyphant, PA 18447-0001 • (570) 383-7661 • http://www.clark.net/pub/mjloyd/grsnp/grsnp.html

Houdini Museum • 229 Willow Ave • Olyphant, PA 18447 • (570) 383-9297 • http://www.houdini.org

Orangeville
Central Susquehanna Valley Genealogy Society • P.O. Box 197 • Orangeville, PA 17859-0197

Orbisonia
Orbisonia-Rockhill Furnace Historical Society • Historical Museum, P.O. Box 382 • Orbisonia, PA 17243 • (814) 447-5668 • http://www.huntingdonhistory.org/orbisonia.htm

Oreland
Springfield Township Historical Society • 1610 Church Rd • Oreland, PA 19075

Orwigsburg
Orwigsburg Historical Society • 109 E Mifflin St • Orwigsburg, PA 17961 • (570) 366-8769

Oxford
Oxford Public Library • 48 S 2nd St • Oxford, PA 19363 • (610) 932-9625 • http://www.ccls.org

Palmerton
Lehigh Gap Historical & Preservation Society • Historical Museum, P.O. Box 267 • Palmerton, PA 18071 • (610) 824-6954

Palmerton Library Association • 402 Delaware Ave • Palmerton, PA 18071-1995 • (610) 826-3424 • http://www.palmertonpa.com/library

Palmyra
Palmyra Area Genealogical Society • P.O. Box 544 • Palmyra, PA 17078

Paoli
Historic Waynesborough Museum • 2049 Waynesborough Rd • Paoli, PA 19301 • (610) 647-1779

Tredyffrin Public Library-Paoli Branch • 18 Darby Rd • Paoli, PA 19301-1416 • (610) 296-7996 • http://www.ccls.org/orhlibs/paoli.htm

Paradise
National Christmas Center Museum • 3427 Lincoln Hwy • Paradise, PA 17562 • (717) 442-7950 • http://www.nationalchristmascenter.com

Paradise Valley
Paradise Township Historical Society • Historical Museum, Rte 940 • Paradise Valley, PA 18326 • (570) 595-9880 • http://www.paradisehistorical.org

Parkesburg
Greater Octorara Valley Historical Society • 440 Strasburg Ave • Parkesburg, PA 19365 • (610) 857-3830

Parkesburg Free Library • 105 West St • Parkesburg, PA 19365-1499 • (610) 857-5165 • http://www.ccls.org

Paupack
Players Card Museum • P.O. Box 491 • Paupack, PA 18451 • (717) 857-0658

Wallenpaupack Historical Society • Historical Museum, 103 Manor Woods Ct, P.O. Box 345 • Paupack, PA 18451 • (570) 226-8980 • http://www.wallenpaupackhistorical.org

Peckville
Interboro Public Library • 739 River St • Peckville, PA 18452 • (570) 489-1765 • http://www.lackawannacountylibrarysystem.org/interboro

Pen Argyl
Penkernewek: Pennsylvania Cornwall Association • 301 W Pennsylvania Ave • Pen Argyl, PA 18072 • (610) 588-3745 • http://www.pacornish.org

Penndel
Hulmeville Historical Society • Historical Museum, P.O. Box 7002 • Penndel, PA 19047 • (215) 752-8228 • http://hulmeville.org

Pennsburg
Schwenkfelder Historical Society • c/o Schwenkfelder Library, 1 Seminary Ave • Pennsburg, PA 18073 • (215) 679-3103

Schwenkfelder Library & Heritage Center • 105 Seminary St • Pennsburg, PA 18073 • (215) 679-3103 • http://www.schwenkfelder.com

Pennsylvania Furnace
Pasto Agricultural Museum • 2710 W Pine Grove Rd, Gate K • Pennsylvania Furnace, PA 16865 • (814) 863-1383 • http://agsci.psu.edu

Perkasie
Pearl S Buck House Museum • 520 Dublin Rd, P.O. Box 181 • Perkasie, PA 18944 • (215) 249-0100 • http://www.perryopolis.com/pahsmain.shtml

Perkasie Historical Society • Historical Museum, 513 W Walnut St • Perkasie, PA 18944 • (215) 257-4483

Perryopolis
Mary Fuller Frazier School Community Library • 142 Constitution St • Perryopolis, PA 15473-1390 • (724) 736-8480

Perryopolis Area Heritage Society • Historical Museum, 104 N Liberty St, P.O. Box 303 • Perryopolis, PA 15473 • (724) 736-8080

Philadelphia
103rd Engineers Museum • 32nd & Lancaster Sts • Philadelphia, PA 19104

1st Troop Philadelphia City Cavalry Museum • 22 S 23rd St • Philadelphia, PA 19103 • (215) 564-1488

African American Genealogy Group • African American Museum, 701 Arch St, P.O. Box 27356 • Philadelphia, PA 19118-0356 • (215) 572-6063 • http://www.aagg.org

African American Museum in Philadelphia • 701 Arch St • Philadelphia, PA 19106 • (215) 574-0380 • http://www.aampmuseum.org

American Catholic Historical Society • Historical Museum, 263 S 4th St, P.O. Box 84 • Philadelphia, PA 19105 • (215) 925-5752 • http://www.amchs.org

American Swedish Historical Foundation • Historical Museum, 1900 Pattison Ave • Philadelphia, PA 19145 • (215) 389-1776 • http://www.americanswedish.org

American Women's Heritage Society • Belmont Mansion Museum, 2000 Belmont Mansion Dr • Philadelphia, PA 19119 • (215) 878-8844

Annenberg Research Institute • 420 Walnut St • Philadelphia, PA 19106 • (215) 238-1290

Athenaeum of Philadelphia • 219 S 6th St • Philadelphia, PA 19106-3794 • (215) 925-2688 • http://www.philaathenaeum.org

Atwater Kent Museum • 15 S 7th St • Philadelphia, PA 19106 • (215) 685-4830 • http://www.phildelphiahistory.org

Balch Institute for Ethnic Studies • Center for Immigrant Research, 1300 Locust St • Philadelphia, PA 19106-3794 • (215) 732-6200 • http://www.hsp.org

Belfield Farm Museum • LaSalle Univ, 1900 W Olney Ave • Philadelphia, PA 19145 • (215) 951-1221

Bellaire Manor Museum • 2000 Pattison Ave • Philadelphia, PA 19145 • (215) 683-0211 • http://www.fairmountpark.org/BellaireManor.asp

Betsy Ross House and Flag Museum • 239 Arch St • Philadelphia, PA 19106 • (215) 686-1252 • http://www.betsyrosshouse.org

Bishop William White House Museum • Independence National Historic Park • Philadelphia, PA 19106 • (215) 597-8974

Blockson Afro-American Collection • Temple Univ, Sullivan Hall, 12th St & Berks Mall • Philadelphia, PA 19122 • (215) 204-6632 • http://www.temple.edu/blockson/

Blue Bell Tavern Museum • 7303 Woodland Ave • Philadelphia, PA 19143 • (215) 365-5914

Bridesburg Historical Society • 2801 Brill St • Philadelphia, PA 19137 • (215) 744-1674

Cambrian Society of the Delaware Valley • 96 Charlotte Drive • Philadelphia, PA 18966

Carpenter's Hall Museum • 320 Chestnut St • Philadelphia, PA 19106 • (215) 925-0167 • http://www.carpentershall.com/

Cedar Grove Museum • 45th & Parkside Ave, P.O. Box 7647 • Philadelphia, PA 19101 • (215) 763-8100

Center for Judaic Studies • Univ of Pennsylvania, 420 Walnut St • Philadelphia, PA 19106-3703 • (215) 238-1290 • http://www.library.upenn.edu/cjs

Chestnut Hill Historical Society • Historical Museum, 8708 Germantown Ave • Philadelphia, PA 19118 • (215) 247-0417 • http://chhist.org

Civil War and Underground Railroad Museum • 1805 Pine St • Philadelphia, PA 19103 • (215) 735-8196 • http://www.cwurmuseum.org

Cliveden House Museum • 6401 Germantown Ave • Philadelphia, PA 19144 • (215) 848-1777 • http://www.cliveden.org

Colonial Order of the Crown • P.O. Box 27023 • Philadelphia, PA 19118

Colonial Society of Pennsylvania • 215 S 16th St • Philadelphia, PA 19102

Congregation Rodeph Shalom Museum • 615 N Broad St • Philadelphia, PA 19123 • (215) 627-6747 • http://www.rodephshalom.org

Connelly Library • La Salle University, 1900 W Olney Ave • Philadelphia, PA 19141-1199 • (215) 951-1287 • http://www.lasalle.edu/library

Dames of the Loyal Legion of the United States • Civil War Library & Museum, 1805 Pine St • Philadelphia, PA 19103-6601 • (215) 546-2425 • http://suvcw.org/mollus.htm

Declaration House Museum • 7th & Market Sts • Philadelphia, PA 19106 • (215) 597-8974

Descendants of the Signers of the Declaration of Independence • 1300 Locust St • Philadelphia, PA 19107-5661 • (215) 545-0391 • http://libertynet.org/~gencap/gsp.html

Deshler-Morris House Museum • 5442 Germantown Ave • Philadelphia, PA 19144 • (215) 596-1748

Eastern Pennsylvania Conference of the United Methodist Church Historical Society • Methodist Historical Center, 326 New St • Philadelphia, PA 19118 • (215) 925-7788

Eastern State Penitentiary Historic Site Museum • 22nd St & Fairmount Ave • Philadelphia, PA 19130 • (215) 236-3300 • http://www.easternstate.org

Ebenezer Maxwell Mansion Museum • 200 W Tulpehocken St • Philadelphia, PA 19144 • (215) 438-1861 • http://www.maxwellmansion.org

Edgar Allan Poe National Historic Site Museum • 530-32 N 7th St • Philadelphia, PA 19123 • (215) 597-8780 • http://www.nps.gov/edal

Elfreth's Alley Association • Historical Museum, 126 Elfreths Alley • Philadelphia, PA 19106 • (215) 574-0560 • http://www.elfrethsalley.org

Fabric Workshop and Museum • 1214 Arch St • Philadelphia, PA 19107 • (215) 561-8888 • http://www.fabricworkshop.org

Fairmount Park Historic Preservation Trust • 4100 Chamounix Dr • Philadelphia, PA 19019 • (215) 877-8001

Fairmount Water Works Interpretative Center • 640 Waterworks Dr • Philadelphia, PA 19130 • (215) 685-0723 • http://www.fairmountwaterworks.org

Fireman's Hall Museum • 147 N 2nd St • Philadelphia, PA 19106 • (215) 923-1438 • http://www.firemanshallmuseum.org

Fort Mifflin on the Delaware Museum • 1 Fort Mifflin Rd • Philadelphia, PA 19153 • (215) 492-1881 • http://www.fortmifflin.org

Francis A Drexel Library • Saint Joseph's University, 5600 City Ave • Philadelphia, PA 19131-1395 • (610) 660-1904 • http://www.sju.edu/libraries/drexel

Free Library of Philadelphia • Logan Sq, 1901 Vine St • Philadelphia, PA 19103-1189 • (215) 686-5322 • http://www.library.phila.gov

Friends Free Library of Germantown • 5418 Germantown Ave • Philadelphia, PA 19144 • (215) 951-2355

Friends of Historic RittenhouseTown • Historical Museum, 206 Lincoln Dr • Philadelphia, PA 19144 • (215) 438-5711 • http://www.rittenhousetown.org

Genealogical Computing Association of Pennsylvania • 31 W Mount Pleasant St • Philadelphia, PA 19119 • (215) 848-0760 • http://www.libertynet.org/gspa/GenCAP

Genealogical Society of Pennsylvania • 2207 Chestnut St • Philadelphia, PA 19107 • (215) 545-0391 • http://www.genpa.org

German Society of Pennsylvania • Joseph Horner Memorial Library, 611 Spring Garden St • Philadelphia, PA 19123 • (215) 627-2332 • http://www.germansociety.org

Germantown Historical Society • Historical Museum, 5501 Germantown Ave • Philadelphia, PA 19144-2225 • (215) 844-0514 • http://www.germantownhistory.org

Germantown Mennonite Historic Trust • Historical Museum, 6133 Germantown Ave • Philadelphia, PA 19144 • (215) 843-0943 • http://www.meetinghouse.info

Grand Army of the Republic Museum • Ruan House, 4278 Griscom St • Philadelphia, PA 19124-3954 • (215) 289-6484 • http://www.garmuslib.org

Grand Lodge of Pennsylvania, Sons of Italy • Curtis Center, 601 Walnut St • Philadelphia, PA 19106-3737 • (215) 592-1713

Henry George Birthplace Museum • 413 S 10th St • Philadelphia, PA 19147 • (215) 922-4278

Historic Bartram's House and Garden Museum • 54th & Lindbergh Blvd • Philadelphia, PA 19143 • (215) 729-5281 • http://www.bartramsgarden.org

Historic Philadelphia • First Bank of the United States, 116 S 3rd St • Philadelphia, PA 19106 • (215) 629-4026 • http://historicphiladelphia.org

Historical Dental Museum • 3223 N Broad St • Philadelphia, PA 19140 • (215) 221-2889

Pennsylvania

Philadelphia, cont.

Historical Society of Frankford • Historical Museum, 1507 Orthodox St, P.O. Box 4888 • Philadelphia, PA 19124 • (215) 743-6030 • http://www.frankfordhistoricalsociety.org

Historical Society of Pennsylvania • Historical Museum, 1300 Locust St • Philadelphia, PA 19107 • (215) 732-6200 • http://www.hps.org

Historical Society of Tacony • 4817 Longshore Ave • Philadelphia, PA 19135 • (215) 338-8790

Holocaust Awareness Museum & Education Center • 10100 Jamison Ave • Philadelphia, PA 19116 • (215) 464-4701 • http://www.holocaustawarenessmuseum.org

Immigration History Society • Balch Institute for Ethnic Studies Library, 18 S 7th St • Philadelphia, PA 19106-2314 • (215) 925-8090 • http://www.libertynet.org:80/~balch/

Independence National Historic Park Library • 143 S 3rd St • Philadelphia, PA 19106 • (215) 597-8047 • http://www.nps.gov/inde

Independence Seaport Museum • 211 S Columbus Blvd • Philadelphia, PA 19106 • (215) 925-5439 • http://www.phillyseaport.org

Johnson House Historic Site Museum • 6306 Germantown Ave • Philadelphia, PA 19144 • (215) 438-1768 • http://www.johnsonhouse.org

Krauth Memorial Library • Lutheran Theological Seminary, 7301 Germantown Ave • Philadelphia, PA 19119-1794 • (215) 248-6329 • http://www.ltsp.edu/library

Laurel Hill Mansion Museum • 510 Walnut St • Philadelphia, PA 19106 • (215) 235-1776

Lemon Hill Mansion Museum • Lemon Hill & Sedgelay Drs • Philadelphia, PA 19130 • (215) 232-4337 • http://www.lemonhill.org

Library Company of Philadelphia • 1314 Locust St • Philadelphia, PA 19107 • (215) 546-3181 • http://www.librarycompany.org

Lutheran Historical Society of Eastern Pennsylvania • c/o Krauth Memorial Library, Lutheran Theological Seminary, 7301 Germantown Ave • Philadelphia, PA 19119-1794 • (215) 248-6383

Man Full of Trouble Tavern Museum • 1015 Haworth St • Philadelphia, PA 19124 • (215) 922-1759

Marion Lanza Institute and Museum • 712 Montrose St • Philadelphia, PA 19147 • (215) 238-9691 • http://www.mario-lanza-institute.org

Marvin Samson Center for Pharmacy History • 600 S 43rd St • Philadelphia, PA 19104 • (215) 895-1113 • http://www.usip.edu/museum

Masonic Grand Lodge of Pennsylvania • Library & Museum, 1 N Broad St • Philadelphia, PA 19107 • (215) 988-1900 • http://www.pagrandlodge.org

Military Order of the Loyal Legion of the United States • Civil War Library and Museum, 1805 Pine St • Philadelphia, PA 19103 • (215) 735-8196 • http://suvcw.org/mollus/molid.htm

Mount Pleasant Mansion Museum • Mount Pleasant Dr, E Fairmount Park, P.O. Box 7647 • Philadelphia, PA 19131 • (215) 763-8100

Moyamensing Historical Society • Historical Museum, 1234 S Sheridan St • Philadelphia, PA 19147 • (215) 334-6008

Museum of Nursing History • US Route 1, Roosevelt & Adams Aves • Philadelphia, PA 19107 • (215) 829-3971 • http://www.nursinghistory.org

Museum of the American Philosophical Society • 104 S 5th St • Philadelphia, PA 19106 • (215) 440-3442 • http://www.amphilsoc.org/exhibitions

Mutter Museum • College of Physicians of Philadelphia, 19 S 22nd St • Philadelphia, PA 19103 • (215) 563-3737 • http://www.collphyphil.org

National Archives & Records Administration-Philadelphia • 900 Market St, Rm 1350 • Philadelphia, PA 19144-4292 • (215) 606-0100 • http://www.archives.gov/philadelphia/

National Liberty Museum • 321 Chestnut St • Philadelphia, PA 19106 • (215) 925-2800 • http://www.libertymuseum.org

National Museum of American Jewish History • 55 N 5th St • Philadelphia, PA 19106-2197 • (215) 923-3812 • http://www.nmajh.org

National Railway Historical Society • 100 N 17th St, P.O. Box 58547 • Philadelphia, PA 19102-8547 • (215) 557-6606 • http://www.nrhs.com

National Society of Magna Charta Dames and Barons • P.O. Box 4222 • Philadelphia, PA 19144 • (215) 836-5022 • http://www.magnacharta.org

Netherlands Society of Philadelphia • P.O. Box 54017 • Philadelphia, PA 19105-4017 • (215) 875-2468

New Year's Shooters and Mummers • Philadelphia Mummers Museum, 1100 S 2nd St • Philadelphia, PA 19147 • (215) 336-3050 • http://www.mummers.com

Old First Reformed Church Museum • 151 4th St • Philadelphia, PA 19106 • (215) 922-4566 • http://www.oldfirstucc.org

Order of Washington • P.O. Box 27152 • Philadelphia, PA 19118

Ormiston Mansion Museum • Reservoir Dr • Philadelphia, PA 19102 • (215) 763-2222

Paley Design Center Textiles Museum • Philadelphia Univ, 4200 Henry Ave • Philadelphia, PA 19144 • (215) 951-2860

Paley Library • Temple University, 1210 W Berks St • Philadelphia, PA 19122-6088 • (215) 204-8212 • http://www.library.temple.edu

Philadelphia City Archives • 3101 Market St • Philadelphia, PA 19104 • (215) 695-9400 • http://www.phila.gov/phils

Philadelphia Doll Museum • 2253 N Broad St • Philadelphia, PA 19132 • (215) 787-0220 • http://philadollmuseum.com

Philadelphia Folkklore Project Museum • 735 S 50th St • Philadelphia, PA 19143 • (215) 726-1106 • http://www.folkloreproject.org

Philadelphia Historical Commission • 1515 Arch St, 13th fl • Philadelphia, PA 19107 • (215) 683-4594

Philadelphia Hospital Archives • 800 Spruce St, 3 Pine Bldg • Philadelphia, PA 19107 • (215) 829-5434

Philadelphia Jewish Archives Center • 125 N 8th St • Philadelphia, PA 19106 • (215) 925-8090 • http://www.jewisharchives.net

Philadelphia Marionette Theatre Museum • 5371 Belfield Ave • Philadelphia, PA 19144 • (215) 879-1213

Philadelphia Society for the Preservation of Landmarks • Historical Museum, 321 S 4th St • Philadelphia, PA 19106 • (215) 925-2251 • http://www.philalandmarks.org

Plantagenet Society • P.O. Box 27165 • Philadelphia, PA 19118

Polish American Cultural Center Museum • 308 Walnut St • Philadelphia, PA 19106 • (215) 922-1700 • http://www.polishamericancenter.org

Presbyterian Historical Society • Historical Museum, 425 Lombard St • Philadelphia, PA 19147 • (215) 627-1852 • http://www.history.pcusa.org

Preservation Alliance for Greater Philadelphia • 1616 Walnut St, Ste 2310 • Philadelphia, PA 19103 • (215) 546-1146 • http://www.preservationalliance.com

Prince Hall Masonic Grand Lodge of Pennsylvania • 4301 N Broad St • Philadelphia, PA 19140 • (215) 457-6110 • http://www.princehall-pa.org

Print Club Museum • 1614 Latimer St • Philadelphia, PA 19103 • (215) 735-6090

Robert W Ryerss Museum • Burholme Park, 7370 Central Ave • Philadelphia, PA 19111 • (215) 685-0599 • http://ryerssmuseum.org

Rosenbach Museum • 2010 Delancey Pl • Philadelphia, PA 19103 • (215) 732-1600 • http://www.rosenbach.org

Roxborough-Manayunk-Wissahickon Historical Society • Historical Museum, 3652 Ridge Ave • Philadelphia, PA 19128 • (215) 483-5022 • http://membrane.com/philanet/historical.html

Saint Andrew's Society of Philadelphia • 215 S 16th St • Philadelphia, PA 19102 • (215) 735-1525 • http://www.standrewsociety.org

Saint George's United Methodist Church Museum • 235 N 4th St • Philadelphia, PA 19106 • (215) 925-7788 • http://www.historicstgeorges.org

Samuel Powel House Museum • 244 S3rd St • Philadelphia, PA 19106 • (215) 627-0364

Society for Historians of the Early American Republic • 3355 Woodland Walk • Philadelphia, PA 19104-4531 • (215) 746-5393 • http://www.shear.org

Society of Descendants of Knights of the Most Noble Order of the Garter • P.O. Box 4944 • Philadelphia, PA 19119

Society of Descendants of the Signers of the Constitution • 325 Chestnut St • Philadelphia, PA 19106

Society of Friends • Philadelphia Yearly Meeting Library, 1515 Cherry St • Philadelphia, PA 19102 • (215) 241-7220

Sovereign Colonial Society, Americans of Royal Descent • P.O. Box 27112 • Philadelphia, PA 19118

Stenton Museum • 4601 N 18th St • Philadelphia, PA 19140 • (215) 329-7312 • http://www.stenton.org

Stephen Girard Museum • 2101 S College Ave • Philadelphia, PA 19121 • (215) 787-4404 • http://www.girardcollege.com

Swedish Colonial Society • 1300 Locust St • Philadelphia, PA 19107 • (215) 389-1513

Swedish Genealogy Club • American Swedish Historical Musuem, 2700 Pattison Ave • Philadelphia, PA 19145 • (215) 389-1776

Sweetbriar Mansion Museum • West Fairmount Park, 1 Sweetbriar Ln • Philadelphia, PA 19131 • (215) 222-1333 • http://www.sweetbriarmansion.org

Thaddeus Kosciuszko National Memorial Museum • 301 Pine St • Philadelphia, PA 19106 • (215) 597-8974

Thomas Eakins House Museum • 1729 Mt Vernon St • Philadelphia, PA 19130 • (215) 685-0750

Union League of Philadelphia Library • 140 S Broad St • Philadelphia, PA 19102 • (215) 587-5594 • http://www.unionleague.org

United American Indians of the Delaware Valley Museum • 225 Chestnut St • Philadelphia, PA 19106 • (215) 574-9020

United Ukranian American Relief Committee • 1206 Cootman Ave • Philadelphia, PA 19111 • (215) 728-1630

University City Historical Society • Historical Museum, P.O. Box 31927 • Philadelphia, PA 19104 • (215) 387-3019 • http://uchs.net

University of Pennsylvania Museum • 33rd & Spruce Sts • Philadelphia, PA 19104 • (215) 898-4050

US Mint Philadelphia Museum • 151 N Independence Mall East • Philadelphia, PA 19106 • (215) 408-0112 • http://www.usmint.gov

Van Pelt Library • University of Pennsylvania, 3420 Walnut • Philadelphia, PA 19104-6206 • (215) 898-7556 • http://www.library.upenn.edu

Victorian Society in America • Historical Museum, 205 S Camac St • Philadelphia, PA 19107 • (215) 627-4252 • http://www.victoriansociety.org

Welcome Society of Pennsylvania • 415 S Croskey St • Philadelphia, PA 19146 • (215) 732-2322 • http://www.welcomesociety.org

Welsh Guild of Arch Street Presbyterian Church • 1724 Arch St • Philadelphia, PA 19103

Women's Welsh Society of Philadelphia • 23rd & Race Sts, A1009 • Philadelphia, PA 19103

Woodford Mansion Museum • 33rd 7 Dauphin St E, Fairmount Park • Philadelphia, PA 19132 • (215) 229-6115

Woodlands Trust for Historic Preservation • Historical Museum, 4000 Woodland Ave • Philadelphia, PA 19104

Wyck House Museum • 6026 Germantown Ave • Philadelphia, PA 19144 • (215) 848-1690 • http://www.wyck.org

Philipsburg
Philipsburg Historical Foundation • Historical Museum, 203 N Front St • Philipsburg, PA 16866 • (814) 342-7115

Phoenixville
Historical Society of the Phoenixville Area • Historical Museum, 204 Church St • Phoenixville, PA 19460 • (610) 935-7646 • http://hspa-pa.org

Pennsylvania Postal History Society • Historical Museum, 750 S Main St, Ste 2 • Phoenixville, PA 19460 • http://www.paphs.org

Phoenixville Public Library • 183 2nd Ave • Phoenixville, PA 19460-3420 • (610) 933-3013 • http://web.pasd.k12.pa.us/ppl/

Pikeland Historical Society • Historical Museum, 1289 Evergreen Dr • Phoenixville, PA 19460 • (610) 933-2867

Sisterhood B'nai Jacob Library • Congregation B'Nai Jacob, Starr & Manavon Sts • Phoenixville, PA 19460 • (610) 933-5550 • http://www.uscj.org/epenn/phoenixville

Valley Forge Historical Society • 375 Morgan St, P.O. Box 122 • Phoenixville, PA 19460-3543 • (610) 917-3651

Picture Rocks
Williamsport and North Branch Railroad Historical Society • P.O. Box 392 • Picture Rocks, PA 17762-0392

Pine Grove
Pine Grove Historical Society • Historical Museum, 240 S Tulpehocken St, P.O. Box 65 • Pine Grove, PA 17963 • (717) 787-8517

Pitcairn
Pitcairn Historical Society • Historical Museum, 505 5th St • Pitcairn, PA 15140 • (412) 856-5414

Pittsburgh
Afro-American Historical and Genealogical Society, Western Pennsylvania Chapter • P.O. Box 5707 • Pittsburgh, PA 15208 • http://pittsburgh.aahgs.org

Allegheny Cemetery Historical Association • 4734 Butler St • Pittsburgh, PA 15201 • (412) 682-1624

Allegheny Foothills Historical Society • 675 Old Frankstown Rd • Pittsburgh, PA 15239 • (412) 327-0338

Associated American Jewish Museums • 4905 5th Ave • Pittsburgh, PA 15213 • (412) 621-6566

Bayernhof Museum • 225 St Charles Pl • Pittsburgh, PA 15215 • (412) 782-4231 • http://www.bayernhofmuseum.com

Bloomfield Preservation and Heritage Society • Historical Museum, 4727 Friendship Ave • Pittsburgh, PA 15224 • (412) 363-0222 • http://bloomfieldlive.com/bphs.html

Brentwood Borough Historical Society • 3501 Brownsville Rd • Pittsburgh, PA 15227 • (412) 882-5694

Byzantine Catholic Seminary Library • 3605 Perrysville Ave • Pittsburgh, PA 15214 • (412) 321-2036

Pennsylvania

Pittsburgh, cont.

Byzantine Catholic Seminary of Saints Cyril & Methodius Library • 3605 Perrysville Ave • Pittsburgh, PA 15214-2297 • (412) 321-8383

Carnegie Library of Pittsburgh • 4400 Forbes Ave • Pittsburgh, PA 15213-4080 • (412) 622-3175 • http://www.carnegielibrary.org

Carnegie Library of Pittsburgh-Squirrel Hill • 5801 Forbes Ave • Pittsburgh, PA 15217-1601 • (412) 422-9650 • http://www.carnegielibrary.org/locations/squirrelhill

Carpatho-Rusyn Society • 125 Westland Dr • Pittsburgh, PA 15217 • (412) 749-9899 • http://www.carpatho-rusyn.org

Clayton House Museum • 7227 Reynolds St • Pittsburgh, PA 15208 • (412) 371-0600

Crafton Historical Society • Historical Museum, 140 Bradford Ave • Pittsburgh, PA 15205 • (412) 922-6884 • http://www.craftonhistoricalsociety.org

Croatian Fraternal Union of America • 100 Delaney St • Pittsburgh, PA 15235 • (412) 351-3909 • http://www.croatianfraternalunion.org

Daughters of the American Revolution, Allegheny County • Fort Pitt Blockhouse, Point State Park, 101 Commonwealth Pl • Pittsburgh, PA 15222 • (412) 281-9284

Edgewood Historical Society • Historical Museum, 335 Locust St • Pittsburgh, PA 15218 • (412) 241-5418

Fort Pitt Block House Museum • Point State Park, 101 Commonwealth Pl • Pittsburgh, PA 15222 • (412) 471-1764 • http://www.fortpittmuseum.com

Frick Art and Historical Center • 7227 Reynolds St • Pittsburgh, PA 15208-2919 • (412) 371-0600 • http://www.frickart.org

Hillman Library • Univ of Pittsburgh • Pittsburgh, PA 15260 • (412) 648-7710

Historic Hartwood Mansion Museum • 200 Hartwood Acres • Pittsburgh, PA 15238 • (412) 767-9200

Historical Glass Club of Pittsburgh • Historical Museum, 516 Austin Ave • Pittsburgh, PA 15243 • http://www.hgcp.org

Historical Society of Greentree • Historical Museum, 10 W Manilla Ave • Pittsburgh, PA 15220 • (412) 921-9292 • http://www.greentreelibrary.org/histsoc.html

Historical Society of Mount Lebanon • P.O. Box 13423 • Pittsburgh, PA 15243

Historical Society of Upper Saint Clair • 1950 Washington Rd • Pittsburgh, PA 15241 • (412) 835-2050

Historical Society of Western Pennsylvania • Senator John Heinz Regional History Center, 1212 Smallman St • Pittsburgh, PA 15222-4208 • (412) 454-6000 • http://www.pghhistory.org

Holocaust Center of United Jewish Federation Pittsburgh • 5738 Darlington Rd • Pittsburgh, PA 15217 • (412) 421-1500 • http://www.ijfhc.net

Hunt Library • Carnegie Mellon University, 4909 Frew St • Pittsburgh, PA 15213-3890 • (412) 268-2446 • http://www.library.cmu.edu

Jewish Genealogical Society of Pittsburgh • 2131 5th Ave • Pittsburgh, PA 15219 • (412) 471-0772 • http://www.jewishgen.org/jgs-pittsburgh

Lawrenceville Historical Society • Historical Museum, P.O. Box 4015, Arsenal Sta • Pittsburgh, PA 15201-0015

Mount Lebanon Public Library • 16 Castle Shannon Blvd • Pittsburgh, PA 15228-2252 • (412) 531-1912 • http://www.mtlebanonlibrary.org

National Flag Foundation • Historical Museum, Flag Plaza • Pittsburgh, PA 15219 • (412) 261-1776 • http://www.americanflags.org

National Museum of Broadcasting • 407 Woodside Rd • Pittsburgh, PA 15221 • (412) 241-4508 • http://www.nmbpgh.org

National Slovak Society of the USA • 2325 E Carson • Pittsburgh, PA 15203 • (412) 281-5728

North Allegheny Historical Museum • 500 Cumberland Rd • Pittsburgh, PA 15237 • (412) 635-4141 • http://northallegheny.org

North Hills Genealogists • c/o Northland Public Library, 300 Cumberland Rd • Pittsburgh, PA 15237-5455 • (724) 366-8100

Northland Public Library • 300 Cumberland Rd • Pittsburgh, PA 15237-5455 • (412) 366-8100 • http://www.einetwork.net/ein/northland

Old Saint Luke's Church Museum • 217 Allenberry Cr • Pittsburgh, PA 15234 • (412) 851-9212

Order of Italian Sons and Daughters of America • 419 Wood St • Pittsburgh, PA 15222 • http://www.orderisda.org

Penn Hills Historical Commission • Historical Museum, 115 McKenzie Dr • Pittsburgh, PA 15235

Penn Hills Library • 240 Aster St • Pittsburgh, PA 15235-2099 • (412) 798-2189 • http://www.einetwork.net/ein/pennhills

Penn Hills Library-Lincoln Park Satellite • 7300 Ridgeview Ave • Pittsburgh, PA 15235 • (412) 362-7729

Pennsylvania Ethnic Heritage Studies Center • 1228 Cathedral of Learnin • Pittsburgh, PA 15260 • (412) 648-7420

Pioneer Heritage Association • Historical Museum, 309 Duff Rd • Pittsburgh, PA 15235 • (412) 242-3894

Pittsburgh History and Landmarks Foundation • James D Van Trump Library, 1 Station Sq Ste 450 • Pittsburgh, PA 15212 • (412) 471-5808

Polish Historical Commission, Central Council of Polish Organizations • 4291 Stanton Ave • Pittsburgh, PA 15201 • (412) 782-2166

Rauh Jewish Archives • Senator John Heinz History Center, 1212 Smallman St • Pittsburgh, PA 15222 • (412) 454-6406

Reformed Presbyterian Theological Seminary Library • 7418 Penn Ave • Pittsburgh, PA 15208-2594 • (412) 731-8690 • http://www.rpts.edu

Robinson Township Historical Society • Historical Museum, 1000 Churchill Rd • Pittsburgh, PA 15205 • (412) 788-6795 • http://www.rootsweb.ancestry.com/~parths/default.htm

Senator John Heinz Regional History Center • 1212 Smallman St • Pittsburgh, PA 15222 • (412) 454-6000 • http://www.pghhistory.com

Serb National Federation • 1 5th Ave, 7th Fl • Pittsburgh, PA 15222-3127 • (412) 263-2875

Society for the Preservation of Duquesne Heights Incline • 1197 W Carson St • Pittsburgh, PA 15219 • (412) 381-1665 • http://www.incline.cc

Soldiers and Sailors Memorial Hall • 4141 5th Ave • Pittsburgh, PA 15213 • (412) 621-4253 • http://www.soldiersandsailorshall.org

Swissvale Historical Society • Historical Museum, 1713 Hayes St • Pittsburgh, PA 15218 • http://swissvalelibrary.org

Transportation and Technology Museum • 616 Olive St • Pittsburgh, PA 15237 • (412) 281-0987

University of Pittsburgh Library • 3960 Forbes Ave • Pittsburgh, PA 15260 • (412) 648-7710 • http://www.library.pitt.edu

Western Pennsylvania Genealogical Society • c/o Carnegie Library of Pittsburgh, 4400 Forbes Ave • Pittsburgh, PA 15213-4007 • (412) 687-6811 • http://www.clpgh.org/clp/Pennsylvania/wpgs.html

Western Pennsylvania Genealogical Society, Computer Interest Group • 4400 Forbes Ave, P.O. Box 99518 • Pittsburgh, PA 15213-4080 • (412) 687-6811 • http://www.clpgh.org/clp/Pennsylvania/wpgs.html

Western Pennsylvania Genealogical Society, English-Welsh Interest Group • 4400 Forbes Ave, P.O. Box 99518 • Pittsburgh, PA 15213 • (412) 687-6811 • http://www.clpgh.org/clp/Pennsylvania/wpgs.html

Western Pennsylvania Genealogical Society, German Interest Group • 4400 Forbes Ave, P.O. Box 99518 • Pittsburgh, PA 15213-4080 • (412) 687-6811 • http://www.clpgh.org/clp/Pennsylvania/wpgs.html

Western Pennsylvania Genealogical Society, Irish Interest Group • 4400 Forbes Ave, P.O. Box 99518 • Pittsburgh, PA 15213-4080 • (412) 687-6811 • http://www.clpgh.org/clp/Pennsylvania/wpgs.html

Western Pennsylvania Research & Historical Society • Historical Museum, 1810 Funston Ave • Pittsburgh, PA 15235 • (412) 391-2444

Willkinsburg Historical Society • Historical Museum, 605 Ross Ave • Pittsburgh, PA 15221

Wilkinsburg Public Library • 605 Ross Ave • Pittsburgh, PA 15221-2195 • (412) 244-2940 • http://www.einetwork.net/ein/wlksbrg/

Women's Welsh Club of Pittsburgh • 1432 Orangewood Ave • Pittsburgh, PA 15216

Pleasant Mount
Pleasant Mount Historical Society • RR 1 Box 55 • Pleasant Mount, PA 18453 • (570) 448-2732

Pleasantville
Pithole Museum • 14118 Pithold Rd • Pleasantville, PA 16354 • (814) 827-2797

Plum
Allegheny Foothills Historical Society • Historical Museum, 445 Center-New Texas Rd • Plum, PA 15239 • (412) 832-0685 • http://www.plumhistory.org

Plymouth
Plymouth Historical Society • Historical Museum, 115 Gaylord • Plymouth, PA 18651 • (570) 779-5840

Plymouth Public Library • 107 W Main St • Plymouth, PA 18651-2919 • (570) 779-4775 • http://home.epix.net/~ppl/

Plymouth Meeting
Plymouth Meeting Historical Society • Historical Museum, 2130 Sierra Rd, P.O. Box 167 • Plymouth Meeting, PA 19462 • (610) 828-8111

Pocono Pines
Tobyhanna Township Historical Society • Historical Museum, P.O. Box 2084 • Pocono Pines, PA 18350 • http://www.tobyhannatwphistory.org

Point Marion
Friendship Hill National Historic Site Museum • RD1, Box 149A • Point Marion, PA 15474 • (412) 725-9190 • http://www.nps.gov

Port Carbon
Welsh Society • 211 Washington St • Port Carbon, PA 17965

Welsh Society of First United Methodist Church • 211 Washington St • Port Carbon, PA 17965

Portage
Portage Area Historical Society • Historical Museum, 400 Lee St, P.O. Box 45 • Portage, PA 15946 • (814) 736-9223

Pottstown
Lower Pottsgrove Historical Society • Historical Museum, 2341 E High St • Pottstown, PA 19464 • (610) 323-6033 • http://www.lowerpottsgrovehistoricalsociety.org

Pottsgrove Manor Museum • 100 W King St • Pottstown, PA 19464 • (610) 526-4014 • http://www.pottsgrove.org

Pottstown Historical Society • Historical Museum, P.O. Box 661 • Pottstown, PA 19464 • (610) 326-4650

Pottstown Public Library • 500 High St • Pottstown, PA 19464-5656 • (610) 970-6551 • http://www.ppl.mclinc.org

South Coventry Historical Society • Historical Museum, RD 2, Box 360 • Pottstown, PA 19464

Historical Society of Schuylkill County • Historical Museum, 305 N Centre St, P.O. Box 1356 • Pottsville, PA 17901 • (570) 622-7540 • http://www.schuylkillhistory.org

Jewish Museum of Eastern Pennsylvania • 2400 West End Ave • Pottsville, PA 17901 • (570) 622-5890 • http://www.synagogue-museum.org

Pottsville Free Public Library • 215 W Market St • Pottsville, PA 17901-2978 • (570) 622-8880 • http://www.pottsvillelibrary.org

Prospect Park
Governor Printz Park Museum • 100 Lincoln Ave • Prospect Park, PA 19076 • (610) 583-7221

Morton Homestead Museum • 100 Lincoln Ave • Prospect Park, PA 19076 • (610) 583-7221

Prosperity
Morris Township Historical Society • Historical Museum, RD 2 • Prosperity, PA 15329 • (724) 222-8855

Punxsutawney
Punxsutawney Area Historical and Genealogical Society • Historical Museum, 401 W Mahoning St, P.O. Box 286 • Punxsutawney, PA 15767 • (814) 938-2555 • http://www.punxsyhistory.org

Quakertown
Milford Township Historical Preservation Society • 1580 Sleepy Hollow Rd • Quakertown, PA 18951 • (215) 538-8101

Quakertown
Quakertown Historical Society • Historical Museum, P.O. Box 846 • Quakertown, PA 18951 • (215) 536-3298

Quakertown Train Station Historical Society • 15 Front St • Quakertown, PA 18951 • (215) 536-9155

Richland Historical Society • One Room School Museum, 303 S 9th St • Quakertown, PA 18951 • (215) 536-5505

Quarryville
Southern Lancaster County Historical Society • Robert Fulton Birthplace Museum, 1932 Robert Fulton Hwy, P.O. Box 33 • Quarryville, PA 17566 • (717) 548-2679 • http://www.rootsweb.com/~puslchs/

Radnor
Cabrini College Library • 610 King of Prussia Rd • Radnor, PA 19087-3698 • (610) 902-8538 • http://www.cabrini.edu/library/

Union League of Philadelphia Genealogy Affinity Club • 301 Tory Turn • Radnor, PA 19087-4629

Reading
Berks County Conservancy • 25 N 11th St • Reading, PA 19601

Berks County Genealogical Society • 201 Washington St, Rm 413 • Reading, PA 19601 • (610) 921-4970

Central Pennsylvania African American Museum • 119 N 10th St • Reading, PA 19601 • (610) 371-8713 • http://www.cpafricanamericanmuseum.org

City of Reading Historic Preservation • general delivery • Reading, PA 19601 • (610) 655-6414

Dr Frank A Franco Library • Alvernia College, 400 Saint Bernardine St • Reading, PA 19607-1799 • (610) 796-8223 • http://www.alvernia.edu/library/

F Wilbur Gingrich Library • Albright College, 13th & Exeter Sts, P.O. Box 15234 • Reading, PA 19612-5234 • (610) 921-7211 • http://www.albright.edu/library/

Historical Society of Berks County • Historical Museum, 940 Centre Ave • Reading, PA 19605 • (610) 375-4375 • http://www.berkshistory.org

Reading, cont.
Mid-Atlantic Air Museum • 11 Museum Dr • Reading, PA 19605 • (610) 372-7333 • http://www.maam.org

Reading Public Library • 100 S 5th St • Reading, PA 19602 • (610) 478-6355 • http://www.reading.lib.pa.us

Reading Public Museum • 500 Museum Rd • Reading, PA 19611-1425 • (610) 371-5850 • http://www.readingpublicmuseum.org

Reading Railroad Heritage Museum • 141 Tucker Ln, P.O. Box 15143 • Reading, PA 19605 • (610) 929-5661 • http://www.readingrailroad.org

Sinking Spring Historical Society • Heritage Park • Reading, PA 19608 • (610) 678-6255

Welsh Society of Berks County • 103 Goose Ln • Reading, PA 19608

Welsh Society of St Paul's Memorial Church • 123 N 6th St • Reading, PA 19601

Red Hill
Bahr's Mill Preservation Society • Historical Museum, 413 Main Sst • Red Hill, PA 18076 • (215) 679-5388

Red Lion
Red Lion Area Historical Society • Historical Museum, 10 E Broadway, P.O. Box 94 • Red Lion, PA 17356 • (717) 244-7717

Renovo
Greater Renovo Area Historical Society • Historical Museum, 237 5th St • Renovo, PA 17764 • (570) 923-0738

Richboro
Northhampton Township Historical Society • P.O. Box 732 • Richboro, PA 18954-0732

Richfield
Juniata Mennonite District Historical Society • Historical Museum, P.O. Box 81 • Richfield, PA 17086-0081 • (717) 694-3211

Ridgway
Elk County Historical Society • 109 Center St, P.O. Box 361 • Ridgway, PA 15853-0361 • (814) 776-1032 • http://www.elkcountyhistoricalsociety.org

Ridley Park
Ladies of the Grand Army of the Republic • 119 N Swarthmore Ave, Apt 1H • Ridley Park, PA 19078 • http://homepages.go.com/~aadar/nlgar.html

Tinicum Township Historical Society • general delivery • Ridley Park, PA 19078 • (610) 521-9002

Riegelsville
Durham Historical Society • 215 Old Furnace Rd • Riegelsville, PA 18077 • (610) 346-1672

Rimersburg
Eccles-Lesher Memorial Library • 673 Main St, P.O. Box 359 • Rimersburg, PA 16248-0359 • (814) 473-3800 • http://www.eccles-lesher.org

Roaring Branch
Union Township Historical Society • Historical Museum, RD 1, Box 143 • Roaring Branch, PA 17765 • (717) 673-5413

Roaring Spring
Roaring Spring Historical Society • Historical Museum, P.O. Box 174 • Roaring Spring, PA 16673

Robertsdale
Broad Top Area Coal Miners Historical Society • Historical Museum, Reality Theatre, Main St, P.O. Box 171 • Robertsdale, PA 16674 • (814) 635-3807 • http://www.angelfire.com/pa3/btcoal/

Robesonia
Robesonia Furnace Museum • 424 S Freeman St, P.O. Box 162 • Robesonia, PA 19551 • (484) 955-7381 • http://www.robesoniafurnace.org

Rochester
Rochester Area Historical Society • Historical Museum, 457 Adams St • Rochester, PA 15074

Rockhill Furnace
Railways to Yesterday Museum • State Rte 994 • Rockhill Furnace, PA 17249 • (610) 965-9028 • http://www.rockhilltrolley.org

Rockhill Trolley Museum • P.O. Box 203 • Rockhill Furnace, PA 17249 • (814) 447-9576

Rockwood
Rockwood Area Historical Society • Historical Museum, 610 W Main St • Rockwood, PA 15557 • (814) 926-1500

Rome
P P Bliss Gospel Songwriters Museum • Main St, P.O. Box 84 • Rome, PA 18837 • (570) 247-2228 • http://www.cableracer.com

Ronks
Ressler Mill Foundation • Historic Museum, 2880 Stumptown Rd • Ronks, PA 17557 • (717) 656-7616

Rosemont
Gertrude Kistler Memorial Library • Rosemont College, 1400 Montgomery Ave • Rosemont, PA 19010-1699 • (610) 527-0200 • http://trellis.rosemont.edu

Lower Merion Historical Society • 1301 Montgomery Ave • Rosemont, PA 19010

Rostraver
Rostraver Public Library • 800 Fellsburg Rd • Rostraver, PA 15012-9720 • (724) 379-5511 • http://users.sgi.net/~rospblib

Royersford
Limerick Township Historical Society • 545 W Ridge Pike • Royersford, PA 19468 • (610) 495-5229

Spring Ford Area Historical Society • 526 Main St • Royersford, PA 19468 • (610) 948-7127

Russell
Elk Township Historical Society • Historical Museum, RD 1, Box 1626 • Russell, PA 16345

Saegertown
Saegertown Historical Society • Historical Museum, 320 Broad St • Saegertown, PA 16433 • (814) 763-4101 • http://freepages.genealogy.rootsweb.ancestry.com/~fraber/saegertownhistsoc.htm

Saint Clair
Saint David's Society of Schuylkill and Carbon Counties • 139 S Mill St • Saint Clair, PA 17901

Saint Davids
Warner Memorial Library & Museum • Eastern University, 10 Fairview Ave • Saint Davids, PA 19087 • (610) 341-5958 • http://www.eastern.edu/library/

Saint Marys
Historical Society of Saint Marys and Benzinger Township • Historical Museum, 99 Erie Ave, P.O. Box 584 • Saint Marys, PA 15857 • (814) 834-6525 • http://smhistoricalsociety.com

Saint Marys Public Library • 127 Center St • Saint Marys, PA 15857 • (814) 834-6141 • http://www.stmaryslibrary.org

Saint Michael
1889 South Fork Fishing & Hunting Historic Preservation Society • Historical Museum, P.O. Box 210 • Saint Michael, PA 15951 • (814) 495-9273

Johnstown Flood National Memorial Museum • 723 Lake Rd, P.O. Box 355 • Saint Michael, PA 15951 • (814) 495-4643

Saint Thomas
Saint Thomas Historical Society • Historical Museum, 197 Pioneer Dr • Saint Thomas, PA 17252

Salfordville
Upper Salford Historical Society • Historical Museum, P.O. Box 7 • Salfordville, PA 18958

Salina
Bell Township Historic Preservation Society • Historical Museum, P.O. Box 286 • Salina, PA 15680 • (724) 349-3825

Salisbury
Salisbury-Elk Lick Historical Association • Historical Museum, 9102 Mason Dixon Hwy • Salisbury, PA 15558 • http://www.salisburypa.com

Saltsburg
Bell Township Historical Preservation Society • RR2 • Saltsburg, PA 15681 • (724) 697-4092

Historic Saltsburg • Historical Museum, P.O. Box 71 • Saltsburg, PA 15681

Saltsburg Area Branch Historical Society • Historical Museum, 521 High St • Saltsburg, PA 15681 • (724) 639-3983

Sandy Lake
Stoneboro Community Historical Society • 11 Railroad St • Sandy Lake, PA 16145 • (724) 376-4190

Saxonburg
Saxonburg Area Library • 240 W Main St, P.O. Box 454 • Saxonburg, PA 16056-0454 • (724) 352-4810

Saxton
Saxton Community Library • 315 Front St, P.O. Box 34 • Saxton, PA 16678-0034 • (814) 635-3533 • http://www.saxtonlibrary.org

Sayre
Sayre Historical Society • Historical Museum, 103 N Lehigh Ave • Sayre, PA 18840 • (570) 882-8221 • http://www.sayrehistoricalsociety.org

Sayre Public Library • 122 S Elmer Ave • Sayre, PA 18840 • (570) 888-2256 • http://www.sayrepl.org

Schaefferstown
Historic Schaefferstown • Thomas R Brendle Memorial Library, 106 N Market St, P.O. Box 307 • Schaefferstown, PA 17088 • (717) 949-2244 • http://www.hsimuseum.org

Schuylkill Haven
Ciletti Memorial Library • Pennsylvania State University, Schuylkill Campus, Capital College, 240 University Dr • Schuylkill Haven, PA 17972-2210 • (570) 385-6234 • http://www.hbg.psu.edu/library/ciletti/

Schuylkill Haven Free Public Library • 104 St John St • Schuylkill Haven, PA 17972-1614 • (570) 385-0542 • http://www.haven.k12.pa.us/havenpl/

Schwenksville
Pennypacker Mills Museum • 5 Haldeman Rd • Schwenksville, PA 19473 • (610) 287-9349 • http://www.montcopa.org

Scotland
Johannes Schwalm Historical Association • Historical Museum, P.O. Box 127 • Scotland, PA 17254-0127 • (610) 459-2380

Scottdale
Springhouse Museum • 84 Pennsylvania, P.O. Box 112 • Scottdale, PA 15300 • (724) 228-3339

West Overton Village Museum • Abraham Overhold Homestead, 109 W Overton Rd • Scottdale, PA 15683 • (724) 887-7910 • http://www.westovertonmuseum.org

Westmoreland-Fayette Historical Society • West Overton Museum • Scottdale, PA 15683-1168 • (724) 887-7910

Scranton
Electric City Trolley Museum • 300 Cliff St • Scranton, PA 18503 • (570) 963-6590 • http://www.ectma.org

Houdini Museum • 1433 N Main • Scranton, PA 18510 • (570) 342-5555 • http://www.houdini.org

Lackawanna & Wyoming Valley Railway Historical Society • Historical Museum, P.O. Box 3452 • Scranton, PA 18505 • (570) 343-6130 • http://www.nrhs.com/chapters/lackawanna-wyoming-valley

Lackawanna Coal Mine Museum • McDade Park • Scranton, PA 18504 • (717) 963-6463

Lackawanna County Historical Society • Catlin House Museum, 232 Monroe Ave • Scranton, PA 18510 • (570) 344-3841 • http://www.lackawannahistory.org

Lackawanna County Library • 520 Vine St • Scranton, PA 18509-3298 • (570) 348-3003 • http://www.lackawannacountylibrarysystem.org

Northeast Pennsylvania Professional Baseball Museum • 200 Adams Ave • Scranton, PA 18503

Pennsylvania Anthracite Heritage Museum • 22 Mountain Rd • Scranton, PA 18504 • (570) 963-4904 • http://www.anthracitemuseum.org

Scranton Public Library • 500 Vine St • Scranton, PA 18509-3298 • (570) 348-3000 • http://www.albright.org

Steamtown National Historic Site Museum • Lackawanna Ave & Cliff St • Scranton, PA 18503 • (570) 340-5200 • http://www.nps.gov/stea/

Tripp House Museum • 1011 N Main Ave • Scranton, PA 18508 • (570) 961-3317 • http://www.tripphouse.com

Ukrainian Fraternal Association • 1327 Wyoming Ave • Scranton, PA 18509 • (570) 342-0937

Sellersville
Lenape Nation • P.O. Box 322 • Sellersville, PA 18960 • (215) 257-0389 • http://www.lenapenation.org

Sellingsgrove
Snyder County Library • 1 N High St • Sellingsgrove, PA 17870 • (570) 374-7163

Sewickley
Daniel B Matthews Historical Society • Historical Museum, 861 Nevine Ave • Sewickley, PA 15143

Legion Ville Historical Society • Rd 4, 10 Pine Court • Sewickley, PA 15143 • (724) 266-1795 • http://www.legionville.com

Northwest Pennsylvania Steam & Antique Equipment Museum • 349 School St • Sewickley, PA 15143 • (412) 741-2447

Sewickley Public Library • 500 Thorn St • Sewickley, PA 15143-1333 • (412) 741-6920 • http://www.clpgh.org/ein/sewickley

Sewickley Valley Historical Society • 200 Broad St • Sewickley, PA 15143 • (412) 741-5315 • http://www.sewickleyhistory.org

Shamokin
Shamokin-Coal Township Public Library • 210 E Independence St • Shamokin, PA 17872 • (570) 658-3202 • http://www.sctpubliclibrary.lib.pa.us

Sharon
Mercer County Genealogical Society • 337 Jefferson Ave, P.O. Box 812 • Sharon, PA 16146-0812 • (724) 346-5117

Saint David's Society of Youngstown • 411 Tamplin St • Sharon, PA 16146 • (724) 981-3071

Shenango Valley Library • 11 N Sharpsville Ave • Sharon, PA 16146 • (724) 981-4360

Pennsylvania

Sharon Hill
Rose Valley Historical Society • Historical Museum, P.O. Box 1191 • Sharon Hill, PA 19079 • (610) 583-2757 • http://www.rosevalleymuseum.org

Sharpsville
Sharpsville Historical Society • Historical Museum, 203 Shenango Ave • Sharpsville, PA 16150 • (724) 962-2392 • http://www.sharpsvillehistorial.com

Shavertown
National Welsh-American Foundation • P.O. Box 1827 • Shavertown, PA 18708-0827 • (570) 696-NWAF • http://www.wales-usa.org

Northeast Pennsylvania Genealogical Society • P.O. Box 1776 • Shavertown, PA 18708-0776

Shinglehouse
Oswayo Valley Historical Society • Historical Museum, P.O. Box 639 • Shinglehouse, PA 16748 • (814) 697-6964

Shippensburg
Ezra Lehman Memorial Library • Shippensburg University, 1871 Old Main Dr • Shippensburg, PA 17257-2299 • (717) 477-1474 • http://www.ship.edu/~library

Fashion Archives & Museum • Shippensburg Univ, 1871 Old Main Dr • Shippensburg, PA 17257 • (717) 477-1239 • http://www.fashionarchives.org

Shippensburg Historical Society • Historical Museum, 52 W King St, P.O. Box 539 • Shippensburg, PA 17257 • (717) 532-6727 • http://www.shippensburghistory.org

Shiremanstown
Peace Church Museum • P.O. Box 3034 • Shiremanstown, PA 17011 • (717) 737-3692

Shirleysburg
Fort Shirley Heritage Association • Historical Museum, RD1 • Shirleysburg, PA 17260

Shrewsbury
Shrewsbury Area Preservation Society • Historical Museum, 35 W Railroad Ave • Shrewsbury, PA 17361

Sinking Spring
Governor Mifflin Historical Society • Historical Museum, 34 Evans Ave • Sinking Spring, PA 19608

Sinking Spring Historical Society • Historical Museum, 46 Montello Rd • Sinking Spring, PA 19608 • (610) 678-6255

Welsh Society of Berks County • Route 6, Box 53 • Sinking Spring, PA 19608 • (610) 777-7168

Skippack
Skippack Valley Historical Society • Historiccal Museum, P.O. Box 9 • Skippack, PA 19474 • (610) 584-1166 • http://www.skippack.org

Slippery Rock
Old Stone House Museum • Slippery Rock Univ, Rte 8 • Slippery Rock, PA 16057 • (724) 738-4964 • http://oldstonehousepa.org

Slippery Rock Heritage Association • Historical Museum, P.O. Box 511 • Slippery Rock, PA 16057 • (724) 794-3140

Smethport
Allegheny Arms & Armor Museum • 505 1/2 W Main St • Smethport, PA 16749 • (814) 558-6112 • http://armormuseum.com

Hamlin Memorial Library • 123 S Mechanic St, P.O. Box 422 • Smethport, PA 16749-0422 • (814) 887-9262 • http://hamlinlibrary.home.westpa.net

McKean County Historical Society • Historical Museum, 502 W King St, P.O. Box 202 • Smethport, PA 16749 • (814) 887-5142

Smicksburg
Smicksburg Area Heritage Society • 138 E Kittanning St • Smicksburg, PA 16256 • (724) 463-7505 • http://www.smicksburg.net

Somerset
Historical and Genealogical Society of Somerset County • Historical Center, 10649 Somerset Pk • Somerset, PA 15501-9805 • (814) 445-6077 • http://www.somersethistoricalcenter.org

Mary S Biesecker Public Library • 230 S Rosina Ave • Somerset, PA 15501 • (814) 445-4011 • http://www.maryslibrary.com

Somerset Historical Center Library • 10649 Somerset Pike • Somerset, PA 15501 • (814) 445-6077 • http://www.somersethistoricalcenter.org

Souderton
Anthracite Railroads Historical Society • Historical Museum, 126 W Summit St • Souderton, PA 18964

Zion Mennonite Church and Public Library • 149 Cherry Ln, P.O. Box 64495 • Souderton, PA 18964-0495 • (215) 723-3592 • http://www.zionmennonite.org

South Fork
Johnstown Flood National Memorial Museum • 733 Lake Rd • South Fork, PA 15956 • (814) 495-4643 • http:/www.nps.gov/jofl

South Mountain
Preserving Our Heritage Archives & Museum • 11191 South Mountain Rd, P.O. Box 128 • South Mountain, PA 17261 • (717) 762-2367 • http://preservingourheritage.intuitwebsites.com

Southampton
Descendants of the Signers the Declaration of Independence • 238 Street Road #B201 • Southampton, PA 18966-3116 • (252) 353-5200

Southeastern
Union League of Philadelphia Genealogy Affinity Club • P.O. Box 1772 • Southeastern, PA 19388-1772

Spraggs
Warrior Trail Association • Historical Museum, RD 1, Box 35 • Spraggs, PA 15362 • (724) 627-5030

Spring Grove
Spring Grove Area Historical Preservation Society • Historical Museum, 50 N East St, Ste 3 • Spring Grove, PA 17362 • (717) 225-0732 • http://www.springgroveboro.com/history.htm

Springboro
Springboro Historical Society • c/o Springboro Library, 110 S Main St • Springboro, PA 16435 • (814) 587-3901

Springboro Public Library • 110 S Main St, PO Box 51 • Springboro, PA 16435-0051 • (814) 587-3901

Springdale
Rachel Carson Homestead Museum • 613 Marion Ave • Springdale, PA 15144 • (724) 274-5459 • http://www.rachelcarson.org

Springfield
Museum of Nursing History • 761 Sproul Rd #299 • Springfield, PA 19064 • (215) 831-7819 • http://www.nursinghistory.org

Springfield Heritage Society • Historical Museum, 111 W Leamy Ave • Springfield, PA 19064 • (610) 938-6299

Springfield Historical Society • Historical Museum, P.O. Box 211 • Springfield, PA 19064 • (610) 544-6927

Springfield Township Library • 70 Powell Rd • Springfield, PA 19064-2495 • (610) 543-2113

Springs
Springs Historical Society • Springs Museum, 1317 Springs Rd, P.O. Box 62 • Springs, PA 15562 • (814) 662-4366 • http://www.springs.org

Stahlstown
Chestnut Ridge Historical Society • Historical Museum, 1698 Route 711 • Stahlstown, PA 15687 • (724) 593-3102

State College
Centre County Genealogical Society • Research Library, 1001 E College Ave, P.O. Box 1135 • State College, PA 16804-1135 • (814) 234-477 • http://www.centrecountygenealogy.org

Centre County Historical Society • Historical Museum, 1001 E College Ave • State College, PA 16801-6806 • (814) 234-4779 • http://www.centrecountyhistory.org

Centre Furnace Mansion Museum • E College & Porter Rd • State College, PA 16801 • (814) 234-4779

Pennsylvania Historical Association • 108 Weaver Bldg, Penn State Univ • State College, PA 16802 • (814) 865-1367

Schlow Memorial Library • 118 S Fraser St • State College, PA 16801-3852 • (814) 235-7816 • http://schlowlibrary.org

State Line
State Line Historica Society • Historical Museum, general delivery • State Line, PA 17263

Steelton
Slovenian Genealogical Society, Pennsylvania Chapter • 1350 Peiffers Ln • Steelton, PA 17113 • http://sloveniangenealogy.org/chapters/Pennsylvania.htm

Stewartstown
Stewartstown Historical Society • Historical Museum, 17 Mill St, P.O. Box 82 • Stewartstown, PA 17363 • (717) 993-5003 • http://www.stewartstown.org/historicalsociety.htm

Stoneboro
Stoneboro Community Historical Society • P.O. Box 132 • Stoneboro, PA 16163 • (724) 376-4190

Stonoboro Historical Society • Historical Museum, P.O. Box 382 • Stoneboro, PA 16153

Stoystown
Stoystown Historical Society • Historical Museum, P.O. Box 11 • Stoystown, PA 15563 • http://www.pottstownhistory.org/main/default.asp

Strasburg
National Toy Train Museum • 300 Paradise Ln, P.O. Box 248 • Strasburg, PA 17579 • (717) 687-8976 • http://www.traincollectors.org

Palatines to America, Pennsylvania Chapter • P.O. Box 280 • Strasburg, PA 17579-0280 • (717) 687-8234 • http://www.pa-palam.org

Railroad Museum of Pennsylvania • 300 Gap Rd, P.O. Box 15 • Strasburg, PA 17579 • (717) 687-8629 • http://www.rmuseumpa.org

Strasburg Heritage Society • Historical Museum, P.O. Box 81 • Strasburg, PA 17579 • (717) 687-3534 • http://www.strasburgheritagepa.org

Strongstown
Strongstown Historical Society • Historical Museum, 14895 Route 422 Hwy E, P.O. Box 75 • Strongstown, PA 15957 • (814) 749-8228

Stroudsburg
Eastern Monroe Public Library • 1002 N 9th St • Stroudsburg, PA 18360 • (570 421-0800 • http://www.monroepl.org

Monroe County Historical Association • Historical Museum, 900 Main St • Stroudsburg, PA 18360 • (717) 421-7703 • http://www.mcha-pa.org

Monroe County Historical Society • Historical Museum, 900 Main St, P.O. Box 488 • Stroudsburg, PA 18360 • (570) 421-7703 • http://www.monroehistorical.org

Pennsylvania Ski and Water Sports Museum • 529 Sarah St, P.O. Box 188 • Stroudsburg, PA 18360 • (570) 421-4727 • http://www.paskimuseum.org

Quiet Valley Living Historical Farm Museum • 1000 Turkey Hill Rd • Stroudsburg, PA 18360 • (570) 992-6161 • http://www.quietvalley.org

Stroud Mansion Museum • 900 Main St • Stroudsburg, PA 18360 • (717) 421-7703

Sugarloaf
Pennsylvania German Research Society • Route 1, Box 478 • Sugarloaf, PA 18249 • (570) 788-5133

Summerville
Summerville Public Library • W Penn St, P.O. Box 301 • Summerville, PA 15864-0301 • (814) 856-3169 • http://www.usachoice.net/cbreitz

Sunbury
Central Pennsylvania Genealogical Pioneers • 1150 N Front St • Sunbury, PA 17801

Degenstein Community Library • 40 S 5th St • Sunbury, PA 17801 • (570) 286-2461 • http://www.degensteinlibrary.org

John R Kauffman Jr Public Library • 228 Arch St • Sunbury, PA 17801 • (717) 286-2461

Northumberland County Historical Society • Hunter House Museum, 1150 N Front St • Sunbury, PA 17801 • (570) 286-4083 • http://www.northumberlandcountyhistoricalsociety.org

Susquehanna Trails Genealogy Club, Vallerchamp Council • 25 Royal Arch • Sunbury, PA 17801

Susquehanna
Susquehanna Depot Historical Society • Historical Museum, P.O. Box 161 • Susquehanna, PA 18847 • http://www.susqcohistsoc.org

Swarthmore
French Colonial Historical Society • Swarthmore College, Dept of History, 500 College Ave • Swarthmore, PA 19081-1397 • (610) 328-8131 • http://www.frenchcolonial.org

Friends Historical Library of Swarthmore College • 500 College Ave • Swarthmore, PA 19081-1399 • (610) 328-8496 • http://www.swarthmore.edu/library/friends

McCabe Library • Swarthmore College, 500 College Ave • Swarthmore, PA 19081-1399 • (610) 328-8477 • http://www.swarthmore.edu/library

National Episcopal Historians and Archivists • 509 Yale Ave • Swarthmore, PA 19081 • (610) 544-1886

Swarthmore Historical Society • Historical Museum, 114 Yale Ave • Swarthmore, PA 19081 • (610) 544-8558 • http://swarthmorehistoricalsociety.org

Swissvale
Swissvale Historical and Genealogical Society • 7326 Schley Ave • Swissvale, PA 15218-2440

Syncote
Baronial Order of Magna Carta • 109 Glenview Ave • Syncote, PA 19095 • (215) 887-8207 • http://www.magnacharta.com

Tamaqua
Tamaqua Historical Society • Historical Museum, 118 W Broad St • Tamaqua, PA 18252 • (717) 668-5722

Welsh Congregational Church Preservation Society • 547 Arlington St • Tamaqua, PA 18252

Tannersville
Millbrook Village Society • Fish Hill Rd • Tannersville, PA 18372 • (570) 629-0456 • http://www.millbrooknj.com

Pennsylvania

Tarentum
Allegheny-Kiski Valley Historical Society • Historical Museum, 224 E 7th Ave • Tarentum, PA 15084 • (724) 224-7666 • http://www.akvhs.org

Community Library of Allegheny Valley-Tarentum Branch • 315 E 6th Ave • Tarentum, PA 15084-1596 • (724) 226-0770

Tarentum Genealogical Society • c/o Community Library of Allegheny Valley, 315 E 6th Ave, P.O. Box 66 • Tarentum, PA 15084 • (724) 226-0770

Tarentum History & Landmarks Foundation • Historical Museum, 538 E 10th Ave • Tarentum, PA 15084 • (724) 224-8928

Tour-Ed Mine & Museum • RD 2 • Tarentum, PA 15084

Telford
Indian Valley Public Library • 100 E Church Ave • Telford, PA 18969 • (215) 723-9109 • http://www.ivpl.org

Thorndal
Old Caln Historical Society • Historical Museum, P.O. Box 72428 • Thorndal, PA 19372 • http://www.oldcaln.org

Three Springs
East Broad Top Railroad Museum • 421 Meadow St, P.O. Box 158 • Three Springs, PA 17264 • (814) 447-3011 • http://www.ebtrr.com

Three Springs Area Historical Society • general delivery • Three Springs, PA 17264 • (814) 448-3764 • http://www.huntingdonhistory.org/threeSpring.htm

Tionesta
Forest County Historical Society • Historical Museum, 688 Elm St, P.O. Box 546 • Tionesta, PA 16353 • (814) 755-8808 • http://www.frestcounty.com

Forest County Historical Society • Courthouse, P.O. Box 546 • Tionesta, PA 16353

Sarah Stewart Bovard Memorial Library • 156 Elm St, P.O. Box 127 • Tionesta, PA 16353-0127 • (814) 755-4454 • http://www.usachoice.net/bovard

Titusville
Benson Memorial Library • 213 N Franklin St • Titusville, PA 16354 • (814) 827-2913

Drake Well Museum • 202 Museum Lane • Titusville, PA 16354-8902 • (814) 827-2797 • http://www.drakewell.org

Titusville Historical Society • Historical Museum, 417 E Spruce St • Titusville, PA 16354 • (814) 827-8810 • http://www.oilregion.org

Tobyhanna
Coolbaugh Township Historical Association • Historical Museum, 5550 Memorial Blvd • Tobyhanna, PA 18466 • (717) 894-4207

National Railway Historical Society, Pocono Mountains Chapter • Railroad Station • Tobyhanna, PA 18466 • (570) 894-3338

Towanda
Bradford County Genealogical Society • Historical Museum, 21 Main St • Towanda, PA 18848 • (717) 265-2240

Bradford County Historical Society • Historical Museum, 109 Pine St • Towanda, PA 18848-1907 • (570) 265-2240 • http://www.bradfordhistory.com

French Azilum Historic Home Museum • 469 Queen's Wy • Towanda, PA 18842 • (570) 265-3376 • http://www.frenchazilum.org

Towanda Public Library • 104 Main St • Towanda, PA 18848-1895 • (570) 265-2470 • http://www.towandapubliclibrary.org

Trappe
Historical Society of Trappe • 301 W Main St • Trappe, PA 19426 • (610) 489-7560 • http://www.trappehistoricalsociety.org

Troy
Bradford County Heritage Association • Routes 6 & 14, P.O. Box 265 • Troy, PA 16947 • (570) 297-3410 • http://www.troyfarmmuseum.org

Bradford County Library • RD 3, Box 320 • Troy, PA 16947-9440 • (570) 297-2436 • http://www.bccpublb.org

Tunkhannock
Wyoming County Historical Society • Historical Museum, Bridge & Harrison Sts, P.O. Box 309 • Tunkhannock, PA 18657 • (570) 836-5303 • http://www.rootsweb.ancestry.com/~pawyomin/WCHS.html

Turbotville
Historic Warrior Run Church Museum • RR1, Box 415 • Turbotville, PA 17772-9628 • (717) 649-5363

Warrior Run-Fort Freeland Heritage Society • RD 1, Box 26 • Turbotville, PA 17772 • (717) 538-1417 • http://freelandfarm.com

Tyrone
Bellwood-Antis Historical Society • Historical Museum, RD 5, Box 204 • Tyrone, PA 16686

Tyrone Area Historical Society • 850 Pennsylvania Ave, P.O. Box 1850 • Tyrone, PA 16686 • (814) 684-2236 • http://www.tyronehistory.org

Tyrone-Snyder Township Public Library • 1019 Logan Ave • Tyrone, PA 16686-1521 • (814) 684-1133 • http://www.tyronelibrary.org

Union City
Union City Historical Society • Historical Museum, 11 S Main St, P.O. Box 321 • Union City, PA 16438 • (814) 438-7573 • http://www.unioncitypa.com/museum.htm

Union City Public Library • S Main & Stranahan • Union City, PA 16438-1322 • (814) 438-3209 • http://www.ucpl.org

Uniondale
Keltic Fringe • RD3, Box 3292 • Uniondale, PA 18470

Uniontown
Fayette County Genealogical Society • 24 Jefferson St • Uniontown, PA 15401-3699

Fayette County Historical Society • Historical Museum, P.O. Box 193 • Uniontown, PA 15401 • (724) 439-4422

George C Marshall Memorial Plaza • W Fayette & W Main Sts, P.O. Box 1464 • Uniontown, PA 15401 • (724) 415-2202

Uniontown Public Library • 24 Jefferson St • Uniontown, PA 15401 • (724) 437-1165 • http://www.uniontownlib.org

University Park
Eberly Family Special Collections • Pennsylvania State University, 104 Paterno Library • University Park, PA 16802-1808 • (814) 865-7931 • http://www.libraries.psu.edu/speccolls

North American Society for Sports History • Historical Museum, 101 White Bldg • University Park, PA 16802 • (814) 865-7931

Pattee & Paterno Library • Pennsylvania State Univ, 515 Paterno Library • University Park, PA 16802-1812 • (814) 865-0401 • http://www.libraries.psu.edu

Upland
1683 Caleb Pusey House Museum • 15 Race St, P.O. Box 1183 • Upland, PA 19015 • (610) 874-5665

Historic Upland • Historical Museum, 1200 Main St • Upland, PA 19014

Upper Darby
Upper Darby Free Public Library • 76 S State Rd • Upper Darby, PA 19082 • (610) 789-4440 • http://www.delco.lib.pa.us

Upper Darby Historical Society • Historical Museum, P.O. Box 731 • Upper Darby, PA 19026 • (610) 924-0222 • http://www.uchistory.org

Valencia
Center for the History of American Needlework • P.O. Box 359 • Valencia, PA 16059 • (724) 586-5325

Valley Forge
American Baptist Historical Society • Research Library, 588 N Gulph Rd, P.O. Box 851 • Valley Forge, PA 19482-0851 • (678) 547-6680 • http://www.abhsarchives.org

Society of the Descendants of Washington's Army at Valley Forge • P.O. Box 915 • Valley Forge, PA 19482 • (610) 666-5464 • http://www.valleyforgesociety.org

Valley Forge Historical Society • Historical Museum, P.O. Box 122 • Valley Forge, PA 19481-0122 • (610) 783-0535 • http://www.libertynet.org/lha/valleyforge

Valley Forge National Historical Park Museum • N Gulph Rd • Valley Forge, PA 18482 • (610) 783-1077 • http://www.nps.gov/vafo

Washington's Headquarters at Valley Forge • Isaac Potts House Museum, Rte 23 & N Gulph Rd, P.O. Box 953 • Valley Forge, PA 19482 • (610) 783-1000

World of Scouting Museum • Route 23 • Valley Forge, PA 19482 • (610) 783-5311 • http://www.worldofscoutingmuseum.org

Valley View
Tri-Valley Historical Society • Historical Museum, general delivery • Valley View, PA 17983

Vandergrift
Vandergrift Historical Society • Historical Museum, 184 Sherman Ave, P.O. Box 183 • Vandergrift, PA 15690 • (724) 568-1990 • http://www.laurelhighlands.org/members/victorian-vandergrift-museum-historical-society.asp

Venetia
Peters Creek Historical Society • Historical Museum, 815 Venetia Rd, P.O. Box 208 • Venetia, PA 15367 • (724) 941-5024

Villanova
Augustinian Historical Institute Library • Villanova University, 301 Old Falvey • Villanova, PA 19085 • (610) 519-7590 • http://www.ahi.villanova.edu

Falvey Memorial Library • Villanova University, 800 Lancaster Ave • Villanova, PA 19085 • (610) 519-4500 • http://www.library.villanova.edu

Wallingford
Marine Corps League Museum • P.O. Box 378 • Wallingford, PA 19086

Nether Providence Historical Society • Thomas Leiper House Museum, 521 Avondale Rd • Wallingford, PA 19086 • (610) 566-4501

Pendle Hill Library • 338 Plush Mill Rd • Wallingford, PA 19086 • (610) 566-4507

Walnutport
Walnutport Canal Association • Historical Museum, 309 Lehigh St • Walnutport, PA 18088 • (610) 767-5817

Wampum
Wampum Area Historical Society • Historical Museum, P.O. Box 763 • Wampum, PA 16157 • (724) 535-8866

Warminster
Craven Hall Historical Society • Craven Hall Museum, 599 Newtown Rd, P.O. Box 2042 • Warminster, PA 18974 • (215) 675-4698 • http://www.centennialsd.org/wth/sch/CravenHall/index.htm

Neshaminy-Warwick Presbyterian Church Library • 1401 Meetinghouse Rd • Warminster, PA 18974 • (215) 343-6060

Warren
Struthers-Wetmore-Schimmelfeng House Museum • 210 4th Ave, P.O. Box 427 • Warren, PA 16365 • (814) 728-3479

Warren County Historical Society • Historical Museum, 210 4th Ave, P.O. Box 427 • Warren, PA 16365 • (814) 723-1795 • http://www.warrenhistory.org

Warren Public Library • 205 Market St • Warren, PA 16365 • (814) 723-4650 • http://www.warrenlibrary.org

Warrington
Moland House Museum • 2066 Bristol Rd • Warrington, PA 18976 • (215) 343-6852

Warrington Township Historic Commission • 852 Easton Rd • Warrington, PA 18976 • (215) 343-9350

Washington
Citizens Library • 55 S College St • Washington, PA 15301 • (724) 222-2400 • http://www.citlib.org

David Bradford House Museum • 175 S Main St, P.O. Box 537 • Washington, PA 15301 • (724) 222-3604 • http://www.bradfordhouse.org

Duncan Miller Glass Museum • P.O. Box 965 • Washington, PA 15301 • (724) 225-6740

Genealogical Society of Southwestern Pennsylvania • c/o Citizens Library, 55 S College St, P.O. Box 894 • Washington, PA 15301-0894 • (724) 222-7022

Pennsylvania Trolley Museum • 1 Museum Rd • Washington, PA 15303 • (724) 228-9256 • http://www.pa-trolley.org

U Grant Miller Library • Washington & Jefferson College, 210 E Wheeling St • Washington, PA 15301-4802 • (724) 223-6070 • http://www.washjeff.edu/library/

Washington County Historical Society • LeMoyne House Museum, 49 E Maiden St • Washington, PA 15301-4941 • (724) 225-6740 • http://www.wchspa.org

Washington County History and Landmarks Foundation • Historical Museum, 1230 N 3rd St, P.O. Box 274 • Washington, PA 15301 • (724) 223-9598

Washington Crossing
David Library of the American Revolution • Route 32, 1201 River Rd, P.O. Box 748 • Washington Crossing, PA 18977-0748 • (215) 493-6776 • http://www.dlar.org

Upper Makefield Historical Society • P.O. Box 1737 • Washington Crossing, PA 18977

Washington Crossing Historic Park • 1112 River Hwy, P.O. Box 103 • Washington Crossing, PA 18977 • (214) 493-4076

Washington Crossing Historic Park Library • 1112 River Rd, P.O. Box 103 • Washington Crossing, PA 18977 • (215) 493-4076 • http://www.phmc.state.pa.us

Waterford
Fort Le Boeuf Historical Society • Historical Museum, 31 High St, P.O. Box 622 • Waterford, PA 16441 • (814) 796-6105 • http://www.fortleboeufhistoricalsociety.org

Watsontown
Historic Warrior Run Church Museum • Susquehanna Tr & 8th St • Watsontown, PA 17777 • (570) 742-3743 • http://www.wrffhs.org

Wattsburg
Wattsburg Area Historical Society • Historical Museum, 14438 Main St, P.O. Box 240 • Wattsburg, PA 16442-0240 • (814) 739-2952

Waymart
Waymart Area Historical Society • Historical Museum, 118 South ST, P.O. Box 255 • Waymart, PA 18472 • (570) 488-6750 • http://www.waymartpa.us/id38.html

Wayne

May H Baker Memorial Library • Valley Forge Military Academy & College, 1001 Eagle Rd • Wayne, PA 19087-3695 • (610) 989-1200 • http://www.vfmac.edu

Memorial Library of Radnor Township • 114 W Wayne Ave • Wayne, PA 19087-4098 • (610) 687-1124 • http://www.radnorlibrary.org

Natural Center for the American Revolution Museum • 435 Devon Park Dr, Bldg 800 • Wayne, PA 19087 • (610) 975-4939 • http://www.valleyforgemuseum.org

Radnor Historical Society • Finley House Museum, 113 W Beechtree Ln • Wayne, PA 19087 • (610) 688-2668 • http://www.radnorhistory.org

Tredyffrin Public Library • 582 Upper Gulph Rd • Wayne, PA 19087-2096 • (610) 688-7092 • http://www.ccls.org/libs/tredyffrin.htm

Upper Merion Park and Historic Foundation • Old Roberts Schoolhouse Museum, 889 Croton Rd • Wayne, PA 19087 • (484-550-9474 • http://www.enjoymckaig.org

Waynesboro

Alexander Hamilton Memorial Free Library • 45 E Main St • Waynesboro, PA 17263-1691 • (717) 762-3335 • http://fclspa.org/waynesboro/waynesboro.htm

Renfrew Museum and Park • 1010 E Main St • Waynesboro, PA 17268 • (717) 762-4723 • http://www.renfrewmuseum.org

Waynesboro Historical Society • Historical Museum, 138 W Main St • Waynesboro, PA 17268 • (717) 762-1747 • http://www.waynesborohistory.com

Waynesburg

Cornerstone Genealogical Society • 144 E Greene St, P.O. Box 547 • Waynesburg, PA 15370-0547 • (724) 627-5653

Eberly Library • Waynesburg College, 93 Locust Ave • Waynesburg, PA 15370-1242 • (724) 852-3278 • http://www.waynesburg.edu

Eva K Bowlby Public Library • 311 N West St • Waynesburg, PA 15370-1238 • (724) 627-9776 • http://www.alltel.net/bowlby

Greene County Historical Society • Historical Museum, 918 Rolling Meadows Rd, P.O. Box 127 • Waynesburg, PA 15370 • (724) 627-3204 • http://www.greenecountyhistory.com

Greene Hill Farms Museum • RR2, Old Rte 21, P.O. Box 127 • Waynesburg, PA 15370 • (724) 627-3204

Waynesburg College Museum • Waynesburg College, 51 W College St • Waynesburg, PA 15370 • (724) 627-8191

Weatherly

Eckley Miners' Village Museum • RR2, Box 236 • Weatherly, PA 18255 • (570) 636-2070

Red Dragon Welsh Society of Greater Hazelton • 431 6th St • Weatherly, PA 18201 • (717) 455-4518

Wellsboro

Green Free Library • 134 Main St • Wellsboro, PA 16901-1412 • (570) 724-4876 • http://epix.net/~greenlib/

Tioga County Historical Society • Historical Museum, 120 Main St, P.O. Box 724 • Wellsboro, PA 16901 • (570) 724-6116 • http://www.rootsweb.com/~patioga/tchs.htm

Wernersville

Heidelberg Heritage Society • Historical Museum, 182 W Penn Ave, P.O. Box 51 • Wernersville, PA 19565

Old Dry Road Farm Museum • 202 Highland Rd, P.O. Box 163 • Wernersville, PA 19565 • (610) 678-1226 • http://www.dryroadfarm.net

Wernersville Public Library • 100 N Reber St • Wernersville, PA 19565-1412 • (610) 678-8771 • http://www.berks.lib.pa.us/wernersvillepl/

Wescosville

Lower MacUngie Township Historical Society • Historical Museum, P.O. Box 3722 • Wescosville, PA 18106 • (610) 967-3653 • http://www.macungie.org/LMTHS

West Chester

American Helicopter Museum • 1220 American Blvd • West Chester, PA 19380 • (610) 436-9600 • http://www.helicoptermuseum.org

Chester County Archives and Records Service • 601 Westtown Rd, P.O. Box 2747 • West Chester, PA 19380-0990 • (610) 344-6760 • http://dsf.chesco.org/archives/site/default.asp

Chester County Historical Society • Historical Museum, 225 N High St • West Chester, PA 19380 • (610) 692-4800 • http://www.chestercohistorical.org

Pennsylvania Folklore Society • West Chester Univ, Dept of English • West Chester, PA 19383 • (570) 333-4007 • http://www.folkloresociety.org

Railways to Yesterday Museum • 1003 N Chester Rd • West Chester, PA 19380 • (610) 692-4107

Swedish Colonial Society • 371 Devon Way • West Chester, PA 19380 • http://www.colonialswedes.org

West Chester Public Library • 415 N Church St • West Chester, PA 19380-2401 • (610) 696-1721 • http://www.ccls.org/libs/wchester.htm

William Brinton 1704 House Museum • 21 Oakland Rd • West Chester, PA 19382 • (610) 399-0913

West Mifflin

Mifflin Township Historical Society • Historical Museum, 3000 Lebanon Church Rd, Ste 202 • West Mifflin, PA 15122 • (412) 600-0229 • http://www.mifflintownship.org

West Newton

West Newton Historical Society • Historical Museum, 303 Vernon Dr • West Newton, PA 15089

West Newton Public Library • 124 N Water St • West Newton, PA 15089 • (724) 872-8555

Westfield

Westfield Historical Society • Historical Museum, 417 Elm St • Westfield, PA 16950 • (814) 367-5424

Wheatland

Wheatland Historical Society • Historical Museum, P.O. Box 103 • Wheatland, PA 16161

White Deer

National Railway Historical Society • Depot Rd • White Deer, PA 17887 • (570) 538-5187

White Mills

Dorflinger Glass Museum • Elizabeth St, P.O. Box 356 • White Mills, PA 18473 • (570) 253-1185 • http://www.dorflinger.org/glass_museum.html

White Oak

Reburn's Station Museum and Angora Gardens • 3 Muse Ln • White Oak, PA 15131 • (412) 675-8556 • http://www.angoragardens.org

Whitehall

American Waldensian Society • P.O. Box 744 • Whitehall, PA 18052-0744 • (212) 870-2671

Whitehall Historical Preservation Society • Historical Museum, P.O. Box 39 • Whitehall, PA 18052 • (610) 776-7280 • http://www.whitehallhistoricalsociety.org

Whitehall Township Public Library • 3700 Mechanicsville Rd • Whitehall, PA 18052-3399 • (610) 432-4339 • http://whitehall.lib.pa.us

Whitsett
Whitsett Historical Society • Historical Museum, 110 A 2nd St • Whitsett, PA 15473 • (724) 736-0519

Wilcox
Jones Township Historical Society • Historical Museum, P.O. Box 360 • Wilcox, PA 15870 • (814) 929-5181 • http://www.jonestownship.com

Wilkes-Barre
Farley Library • Wilkes University, 187 S Franklin St • Wilkes-Barre, PA 18766-0998 • (570) 408-4250 • http://www.wilkes.edu/library

Heights Saint David's Society • 434 Academy St • Wilkes-Barre, PA 18702

Historical Preservation Society of Luzerne County • Historical Museum, 69 S Franklin St • Wilkes-Barre, PA 18701 • (570) 822-1727 • http://luzernehistory.org

HQ 1st Battalion 109th FA Museum • 280 Market St • Wilkes-Barre, PA 18704 • (717) 288-6641

Luzerne County Historical Society • Historical Museum, 49 S Franklin St • Wilkes-Barre, PA 18701-1290 • (570) 822-1727 • http://www.luzernecountyhistory.com

Osterhout Free Public Library • 71 S Franklin St • Wilkes-Barre, PA 18701-1287 • (570) 823-0156 • http://www.osterhout.lib.pa.us

Welsh Guild • 367 S River St • Wilkes-Barre, PA 18701

Williamsburg
Royer Mansion Museum • 3909 Piney Creek Rd • Williamsburg, PA 16693 • (814) 832-2479

Williamsburg Downtown Association • P.O. Box 12 • Williamsburg, PA 16693

Williamsburg Heritage & Historical Society • Williamsburg High School • Williamsburg, PA 16693 • (814) 832-2125

Williamsburg Public Library • 511 W 2nd St • Williamsburg, PA 16693 • (814) 832-3367 • http://www.williamspl.net

Williamsport
James V Brown Library • 19 E 4th St • Williamsport, PA 17701-6390 • (570) 327-2954 • http://www.jvbrown.edu

John G Snowden Memorial Library • Lycoming College, 700 College Pl • Williamsport, PA 17701-5192 • (570) 321-4053 • http://www.lycoming.edu/library

Little League Baseball Museum • Rte 15 S, P.O. Box 3485 • Williamsport, PA 17701 • (717) 326-3607 • http://www.littleleague.org

Lycoming County Genealogical Society • Taber Museum, 858 W 4th St, P.O. Box 3625 • Williamsport, PA 17701-8625 • (570) 326-3326 • http://www.tabermuseum.org

Lycoming County Historical Society • Taber Museum, 858 W 4th St • Williamsport, PA 17701-5824 • (717) 326-3326 • http://www.lycoming.org/lchsmuseum

Williamstown
Williamstown-Williamstown Township Historical Society • Historical Museum, 115 W Market St • Williamstown, PA 17098 • (717) 647-9220

Willow Grove
Upper Mooreland Free Public Library • 109 Park Ave • Willow Grove, PA 19090 • (215) 659-0741 • http://www.uppermorelandlibrary.org

Upper Moreland Historical Association • Park Ave • Willow Grove, PA 19090

Willow Street
1719 Hans Herr House Museum • 1849 Hans Herr Dr • Willow Street, PA 17584 • (717) 464-4438 • http://www.hansherr.org

1791 Boehm's Chapel Museum • 13 W Boehm's Rd, P.O. Box 272 • Willow Street, PA 17584 • (717) 872-4133 • http://www.boehmschapel.org

Wilmerding
George Westinghouse Museum • 325 Commerce St • Wilmerding, PA 15148 • (412) 825-3000 • http://www.georgewestinghouse.com

Wind Gap
Saint David's Welsh Society of the Slate Belt, Bangor, Pennsylvania • P.O. Box 174 • Wind Gap, PA 18091-0174 • http://www.yourpastconnections.com/sdws

Windber
Johnstown Genealogical Society • 26 Paint St • Windber, PA 15963

Windber Area Museum • 601 15th St • Windber, PA 15963 • (814) 467-8386

Windber Coal Heritage Center • 505 15th St • Windber, PA 15963

Womelsdorf
Conrad Weiser Homestead Museum • 28 Weiser Rd • Womelsdorf, PA 19567 • (610) 589-2934 • http://www.conradseiserhomestead.org

Tulpehocken Settlement Historical Society • Historical Museum, 116 N Front St, P.O. Box 53 • Womelsdorf, PA 19567 • (610) 589-2527 • http://www.tuopehockenroots.org

Wooddale
Bullskin Township Historical Society • Eutsey & Park Rds • Wooddale, PA 15666 • (724) 887-8514 • http://www.bulskintownshiphistoricalsociety.org

Worcester
Ironmaster's House and Museum • Skipack Pk • Worcester, PA 19490

Peter Wentz Farmstead Museum • 1100 Schultz Rd, P.O. Box 240 • Worcester, PA 19490 • (610) 584-5104 • http://peterwentzfarmsteadsociety.org

Worcester Historical Society • Historical Museum, 2011 Valley Forge Rd, P.O. Box 12 • Worcester, PA 19490 • (610) 584-5619 • http://www.worcesterhistorical.org

Wrightsville
Historic Wrightsville • Historical Museum, 309 Locust St, P.O. Box 125 • Wrightsville, PA 17368 • (717) 252-1169 • http://www.historicwrightsvillepa.org

Wyalusing
Council House Museum of the Eastern Delaware Nation • Route 6 • Wyalusing, PA 18853 • (570) 924-8092

Myalusing Valley Museum • 28 Homer Ln, P.O. Box 301 • Wyalusing, PA 18853 • (507) 746-3979 • http://www.wyalusingmuseum,com

Wyalusing Public Library • 202 Church St, P.O. Box 98 • Wyalusing, PA 18853-0098 • (570) 746-1711

Wyncote
Military Order of the Crusades • 109 Glenview Ave • Wyncote, PA 119095 • (215) 887-8207 • http://www.magnacharta.com

Wynnewood
Austen K deBlois Library • Eastern Baptist Theological Seminary, 6 Lancaster Ave • Wynnewood, PA 19096 • (610) 645-9318 • http://library.ebts.edu

Philadelphia Archdiocesan Historical Research Center • 100 E Wynnewood Rd • Wynnewood, PA 19096-3001 • (610) 667-2125 • http://www.rc.net/philadelphia/pahrc/

Wyoming
Swetland Homestead Museum • 885 Wyoming Ave • Wyoming, PA 18644 • (717) 693-2740

Pennsylvania

Wyomissing

Berks County Heritage Center • 2201 Tulpehocken Rd • Wyomissing, PA 19610 • (610) 374-8839

Yardley

Lower Makefield Township Historical Commission • Historical Museum, 1100 Edgewood Rd • Yardley, PA 19067 • (215) 493-3646 • http://www.lmt.org

Lower Makefield Township Historical Society • Historical Museum, P.O. Box 228 • Yardley, PA 19067 • http://www.lowermakefieldhistoricalsociety.com

Yardley Historical Association • 46 W Afton Ave, P.O. Box 212 • Yardley, PA 19067-1420 • (215) 493-9883

Yeadon

Yeadon Public Library • 809 Longacre Blvd • Yeadon, PA 19050-3398 • (610) 623-4090 • http://www.delco.lib.pa.us

York

Antique Motorcycle Museum • 1425 Eden Rd • York, PA 17402 • (717) 848-1177

Bonham House Museum • 152 E Market • York, PA 17403 • (717) 848-1587

Fire Museum • 757 W Market St • York, PA 17404 • (717) 848-1587 • http://www.yorkheritage.org

Gen Horatio Gates House Museum • 250 E Market St • York, PA 17403 • (717) 848-1587

Historical Society of York County • Barnett Bob Log House Museum & Archives, 250 E Market St • York, PA 17403 • (717) 812-1204 • http://www.yorkheritage.org

Industrial and Agricultural Museum • 217 W Princess St • York, PA 17403 • (717) 848-1587 • http://www.yorkheritage.org

Police Heritage Museum • 54 W Market St, P.O. Box 1941 • York, PA 17401 • http://www.policeheritagemuseum.com

South Central Pennsylvania Genealogical Society • P.O. Box 1824 • York, PA 17405-1824 • (717) 843-6169

Weightlighting Hall of Fame • 3300 Board Rd • York, PA 17406 • (717) 767-6481 • http://www.yorkbarbell.com

York County Heritage Trust • 250 E Market St • York, PA 17403 • (717) 848-1587 • http://www.yorkheritage.org

York County Library System • 118 Pleasant Acres Rd • York, PA 17402-9004 • (717) 840-7435 • http://www.yorklibraries.org

York Springs

Ye Old Sulpher Spa Historical Society • Historical Museum, 160 Latimore Valley Rd, P.O. Box 161 • York Springs, PA 17372

Youngwood

Youngwood Historical and Railroad Museum • 1 Depot St, P.O. Box 216 • Youngwood, PA 15697 • (724) 925-7355

Zelienople

Buhl House Museum • 221 S Main • Zelienople, PA 16063 • (724) 452-9457

Zelienople Historical Society • Passavant House Museum, 243 S Main St, P.O. Box 45 • Zelienople, PA 16063-0045 • (724) 452-9457 • http://www.zelienoplehistoricalsociety.com

Boulder County Commissioners

Boulder County Commissioners Journal, 1861-1871: An Annotated Transcription

ISBN 13 978-1-879579-77-4 $45.99 + $5.00 S&H

Boulder County was one of the original 17 counties established when Colorado became a territory on 14 February 1861. The Boulder County Commissioners Journal, 1861-1871, chronicles the building of the county and the people who helped build it. During that time, citizens in Boulder built new roads, a jail and a courthouse, paid for the care and keep of paupers, and maintained law and order. All the while, the County Commissioners hired and paid for work on behalf of the county, chose grand and petit jurors, appointed road viewers and overseers, and took applications for business licenses. Includes an *index to the original journal* as well as an index to this modern version.

Boulder County Commissioners Journal, 1871-1874: An Annotated Transcription

ISBN 978-1-879579-91-0 $39.95 + $5.00 S&H

The Boulder County Commissioner's Journal, 1871-1874, continues where the first Journal left off. Citizens in Boulder built new roads and fixed up old ones, paid for the care and keep of paupers, and maintained law and order. The County Commissioners hired and paid for work on behalf of the county, chose grand and petit jurors, appointed road viewers and overseers, and took applications for business licenses. This book includes an index to the original journal as well as an index to this modern version.

Masons

Colorado's Territorial Masons An Annotated Index of the Proceedings of the Grand Lodge of Colorado, 1861–1876

ISBN 978-1-879579-85-9 $29.95 + $5.00 S&H

The Masons have a history in Colorado longer than the state or territory itself. The first Masonic lodges formed in the area were done so under dispensation from the Grand Lodges of Kansas and Nebraska until Colorado became a Territory in 1861 and formed its own Grand Lodge. Between the time Colorado became a territory in 1861 and a state in 1876, thirty-one Masonic lodges were formed with the help of more than 4,000 local men whose names are included in this index. The Proceedings of the Grand Lodge of Colorado often included news from Masons in other states, as well as the names of officers of the other Grand Lodges around the county. Their names are also included.

Boulder's Masonic Pioneers, 1867-1886: Members of Columbia Lodge No. 14, Boulder County, Colorado Territory

ISBN 978-1-879579-57-6 $15.95 + $4.00 S&H

This title includes:
Index to Minute Book, Vol 1, Columbia Lodge No. 14, 1867-1873; Index to the Minute Book, Vol 2, Columbia Lodge, 1873-1879; Index to the Cash Book of the Columbia Lodge No. 14, Vol 1 1875-1884; Index to the Visitors Book of the Columbia Lodge, 1874-1886

Teachers

Boulder, Colorado Teachers, 1878-1900: An Annotated Index

ISBN 978-1-879579-93-4 $11.95 + $4.00 S&H

This index has been compiled from the *Annual Reports to the Superintendent of Public Instruction* for the years 1878-1900. Each listing shows the name of the teacher, the date the report was submitted (usually the first day of the school year), the archives location for the Annual Report from which the listing was taken, and the school district the teacher taught in. A few teachers taught in more than one school district in the same year. The introduction lists the 66 school districts in Boulder County prior to 1900, and gives details about what the *Annual Reports* include such as whether each school house was made of log, sod, adobe, frame or brick, what textbooks were used during the school year, and what kind of census of students was taken each year.

Court Records

Boulder County, Colorado District Court Execution Docket, 1875-1885: An Annotated Index

ISBN 978-1-879579-94-1 $11.95 + $4.00 S&H

This index has been compiled from the Boulder County, Colorado District Court Execution Docket for the years 1875-1885. An execution docket is used by the court to instruct the sheriff to settle a judgment of the court. The parties are listed as judgment against (the losing party in the lawsuit) and judgment for (the winning party), rather than by plaintiff or defendant. This index also lists the date the execution order was given and the county in which the order was served.

Other Titles Available

Arapahoe County, Colorado Territory Criminal Court Index, 1862-1879: An Annotated Index

ISBN 978-1-879579-70-5 $11.95 + $4.00 S&H
The Arapahoe County Criminal Court Index 1862-1879 contains an alphabetical list of criminal cases filed by the name of the first defendant listed on the case. It gives the date of filing, the case number, the charge, the book and page number of subsequent hearings, and a brief description of the findings of those hearings. Often, the dispensation of the case will be given in the notes. The very early cases, listed as occurring "before 1862," have no actual dates on the case but occur in the order of cases before others prosecuted in late 1862. These early cases being prosecuted as The People of the United States of America vs. the defendant, and were probably in the jurisdiction of the US Marshals. Most of these cases are listed as Treason, etc., most likely cases of Southern sympathizers as the Civil War was underway. It appears that the courts had their hands full with notorious saloon-owning brothers Edward and John Chase, not to mention forgers and miners passing off counterfeit gold dust.

Boulder County Probate Court Appraisement Record A, 1875-1888: An Annotated Index

ISBN 978-1-879579-72-9 $11.95 + $4.00 S&H
In the Boulder County Probate Court's Appraisement Record, you will find the name of the deceased, the Judge and Sheriff charged with administering the appraisement of personal property, the administrator or executor of the estate, the names of the appraisers of the estate, usually three. Occasionally, you will find the name of a Justice of the Peace before whom the Appraisers took their oath, if different from the Judge charged with administering the appraisement. The Appraisers estimate also includes the value of property allowed to the widow including: Beds, bedsteads and bedding, Wearing apparel, household furniture, family pictures, school books and library, stoves, cooking utensils, provisions and fuel necessary for six months, Working animals, one cow and calf, ten sheep, one horse, saddle and bridle, food necessary for animals for six months, one farm wagon, one plow, and one harrow. The second page(s) of the Appraisement includes all articles appraised and their value, including livestock, land, household goods, farm implements, and ownership in businesses or mines. Occasionally, you will find other people named if there are accounts owed or notes outstanding.

Vital Records

Boulder, Colorado Births 1892–1906: An Annotated Index

ISBN 978-1-879579-79-8 $11.95 + $4.00 S&H
This index has been compiled from the original birth records filled out by physicians after a birth and turned in to the County Clerk. They were then recorded in the Birth Records Book, Volume 2. Often the forms were not turned in until months after the birth. Based upon the form numbers recorded, there are many missing certificates for this time period. There are many different types of forms in the records so the information available for each individual can be quite different. The more complete forms include the following information: the record number, the child's name, the child's color, the child's sex, whether the child was born alive or not, the place where the child was born, the hour and date, the father's name and occupation, the mother's maiden name, where the parents lived at the time of the birth (often different than where the birth took place), the names of the other children (sometimes just the number of siblings), notes about any additional circumstances (including information about the death of the child or the death of one of the parents), the physician who attended the birth, where the physician resided, the date the form was filled out (or returned to the clerk) and the page and volume number where the birth was recorded.

Church Records

Boulder Valley Presbyterian Church Records, 1863-1900: An Annotated Index

ISBN 978-1-879579-58-3 $11.95 + $4.00 S&H
The Valmont Community Presbyterian Church, originally called the Boulder Valley Presbyterian Church, was one of the first churches organized in the Boulder Valley. The church was organized on 6 September 1863 in the community of Valmont near the confluence of the North Boulder and South Boulder Creeks. The early records of the church are privately held but were graciously opened to the Boulder Pioneers Project for extraction and indexing. This book is an annotated index of: The Minutes of the Session 6 Sept 1863-17 Feb 1900; Minutes of the Session, 19 May 1878 - 1 May 1886; Valmont Union Union Sabbath School Secretary's Book dated 1 Jan 1880, and the registers of Baptisms, Communicants, Deaths, Elders, Marriages and Trustees.

Denver Police Force

Denver, Colorado Police Force Record, 1879-1903: An Annotated Index

ISBN 13 978-1-879579-81-1 $11.95 + $4.00 S&H
This index has been compiled from a register of Denver Police Department hires beginning in 1879 and ending in 1903. Officers were hired as patrolmen and officers, detectives, turnkeys (keepers of the keys at the jail), clerks, doctors and surgeons, jailers, bailiffs, herders and hostlers (who took care of the department's horses), drivers (who drove the ambulance and paddy wagon), operators (who took emergency calls once the city had telephones), and license inspectors. The Denver Police Department first hired a police matron in the 1880s and used special police, sometimes unpaid citizens, other times paid temps to keep the streets safe during city-wide celebrations.

The register includes the following information: the officer's name, the rank hired, the star or badge number assigned, where the officer was born, the officer's age at hire, the officer's former occupation, whether married or single, the number of people in the officer's household, the officer's address at hire, dates of appointment and discharge (cause, if given), equipment assigned (fire key, police key, small buttons, large buttons, club, belt, nippers, regulation book, locker), and remarks.

Tax Records

Boulder County Assessor's Tax List, 1875: An Annotated Index

ISBN 978-1-879579-55-2 $11.95 + $4.00 S&H
In 1875, the tax records record either the residence (address) of the property in town lots and blocks or the legal description (section, township and range) and number of acres the property holds. It gives a valuation of the property and of the improvements. It makes an assessment of the capital investment in merchandise and manufacturing, how much is held in money and credits, shares and stocks. It notes household property, jewelry, gold and silver, the number and value of: clocks and watches, musical instruments, carriages and vehicles, horses, mules, cattle, sheep and other animals. It sums up by giving a valuation of all other property, and a total valuation. It lists how many polls (men able to vote), and remarks. Looking at the tax assessment role will give you a pretty good indication of how these people lived and worked.

Boulder County Assessor's Tax List, 1876: An Annotated Index

ISBN 978-1-879579-56-9 $11.95 + $4.00 S&H
In 1876, the tax records record either the residence (address) of the property in town lots and blocks or the legal description (section, township and range) and number of acres the property holds. It gives a valuation of the property and of the improvements. It makes an assessment of the capital investment in merchandise and manufacturing, how much is held in money and credits, shares and stocks. It notes household property, jewelry, gold and silver, the number and value of: clocks and watches, musical instruments, carriages and vehicles, horses, mules, cattle, sheep, swine and other animals. It shows improvements on homesteads and public lands, and the amount of other property. It sums up by giving a total valuation of city and county property. It lists how many polls (men able to vote), amount of increased or decreased valuation, and remarks. Looking at the tax assessment role will give you a pretty good indication of how these people lived and worked.

CPSIA information can be obtained at www.ICGtesting.com
Printed in the USA
LVOW02s2313080714

393491LV00009B/140/P

9 781879 579750